Use this handy reference for all your domestic relations law needs!

ILLINOIS DOMESTIC RELATIONS AND RELATED LAWS ANNOTATED

2005 EDITION

ILLINOIS DOMESTIC RELATIONS AND RELATED LAWS ANNOTATED

2005 EDITION

Reprinted from the Illinois Compiled Statutes Annotated
as amended through Public Act 93-1102

ILLINOIS STATE
BAR ASSOCIATION

QUESTIONS ABOUT THIS PUBLICATION?

For CUSTOMER SERVICE ASSISTANCE concerning replacement pages, shipments, billing, reprint permission, or other matters,

please call Customer Service Department at 800-833-9844
email *customer.support@lexisnexis.com*
or visit our interactive customer service website at *www.lexisnexis.com/printcdsc*

For EDITORIAL **content questions** concerning this publication,

please call 800-446-3410 ext. 7447
or email: *LLP.CLP@lexisnexis.com*

For **information on other LEXISNEXIS MATTHEW BENDER publications,**

please call us at 800-223-1940
or visit our online bookstore at *www.lexisnexis.com/bookstore*

ISBN: 0-8205-7792-8

LexisNexis®

Matthew Bender & Company, Inc.
Editorial Offices
P.O. Box 7587
Charlottesville, VA 22906-7587
800-446-3410
www.lexisnexis.com

Product Number 2393018

(Pub. 23930)

Foreword

As publishers of the *Illinois Compiled Statutes Annotated,* we are pleased to offer to the legal and domestic relations practice communities the 2005 edition of **Illinois Domestic Relations and Related Laws Annotated**. This compilation of selected laws is fully up to date with statutes enacted through Public Act 93-1102 of the 93rd General Assembly.

We are committed to providing attorneys and other professionals with the most comprehensive, current and useful publications available. We publish a host of publications covering various topics of Illinois law as well as publications in neighboring jurisdictions. Please refer to the pages at the front of this book for a partial list of available titles.

We actively solicit your comments and suggestions. Please write to us or call us toll-free at 1-800-833-9844; fax us toll-free at 1-800-643-1280; visit our website at http://www.lexisnexis.com; or E-mail us at llp.clp@lexisnexis.com. By providing us with your informed comments, you will be assured of having available a working tool which increases in value each year.

June 2005

LexisNexis®

Table of Contents

PAGE

Sections Affected by Public Acts 93-656 through 93-1102 xi

CHAPTER 750. FAMILIES

Illinois Marriage and Dissolution of Marriage Act.
- Part I. General Provisions, 750 ILCS 5/101 to 750 ILCS 5/107 7
- Part II. Marriage, 750 ILCS 5/201 to 750 ILCS 5/219 12
- Part III. Declaration of Invalidity of Marriage, 750 ILCS 5/301 to 750 ILCS 5/306 19
- Part IV. Dissolution and Legal Separation, 750 ILCS 5/401 to 750 ILCS 5/413 24
- Part IV-A. Joint Simplified Dissolution Procedure, 750 ILCS 5/451 to 750 ILCS 5/457 56
- Part V. Property, Support and Attorney Fees, 750 ILCS 5/501 to 750 ILCS 5/516 57
- Part VI. Custody, 750 ILCS 5/601 to 750 ILCS 5/611 306
- Part VII. Miscellaneous, 750 ILCS 5/701 to 750 ILCS 5/714 394
- Part VIII. Application and Severability, 750 ILCS 5/801, 750 ILCS 5/802 405

Illinois Uniform Premarital Agreement Act, 750 ILCS 10/1 to 750 ILCS 10/11 408

Non-Support of Spouse and Children Act [Repealed] 411

Non-Support Punishment Act, 750 ILCS 16/1 to 750 ILCS 16/999 411

Revised Uniform Reciprocal Enforcement of Support Act [Repealed] 421

Uniform Interstate Family Support Act.
- Article 1. General Provisions (Prior to Renumbering by P.A. 93-479), 750 ILCS 22/100 to 750 ILCS 22/103 421
- Article 1. General Provisions (As Amended and Renumbered by P.A. 93-479), 750 ILCS 22/101 to 750 ILCS 22/104 424
- Article 2. Jurisdiction, 750 ILCS 22/201 to 750 ILCS 22/211 427
- Article 3. Civil Provisions of General Application, 750 ILCS 22/301 to 750 ILCS 22/320 434
- Article 4. Establishment of Support Order, 750 ILCS 22/401 445
- Article 5. Enforcement of Order of Another State Without Registration, 750 ILCS 22/501 to 750 ILCS 22/507 445
- Article 6. Registration, Enforcement and Modification of Support Order, 750 ILCS 22/601 to 750 ILCS 22/615 448
- Article 7. Determination of Parentage, 750 ILCS 22/701 456
- Article 8. Interstate Rendition, 750 ILCS 22/801, 750 ILCS 22/802 456
- Article 9. Miscellaneous Provisions, 750 ILCS 22/901 to 750 ILCS 22/999 457

Unified Child Support Services Act, 750 ILCS 24/1 to 750 ILCS 24/920 459

Expedited Child Support Act of 1990, 750 ILCS 25/1 to 750 ILCS 25/13 462

Income Withholding for Support Act, 750 ILCS 28/1 to 750 ILCS 28/999 468

Emancipation of Mature Minors Act, 750 ILCS 30/1 to 750 ILCS 30/11 477

Uniform Child Custody Jurisdiction Act [Repealed] 480

Uniform Child-Custody Jurisdiction and Enforcement Act.
- Article 1. General Provisions, 750 ILCS 36/101 to 750 ILCS 36/112 481
- Article 2. Jurisdiction, 750 ILCS 36/201 to 750 ILCS 36/210 486
- Article 3. Enforcement, 750 ILCS 36/301 to 750 ILCS 36/317 498
- Article 4. Miscellaneous Provisions, 750 ILCS 36/401 to 750 ILCS 36/405 502

Illinois Parentage Act, 750 ILCS 40/1 to 750 ILCS 40/3 503

Illinois Parentage Act of 1984, 750 ILCS 45/1 to 750 ILCS 45/27 504

Gestational Surrogacy Act, 750 ILCS 47/1 to 750 ILCS 47/800 548

Adoption Act, 750 ILCS 50/0.01 to 750 ILCS 50/24 551

Contest of Adoptions Act, 750 ILCS 55/0.01, 750 ILCS 55/1 641

PAGE

Illinois Domestic Violence Act of 1986.
Article I. General Provisions, 750 ILCS 60/101 to 750 ILCS 60/103 642
Article II. Orders of Protection, 750 ILCS 60/201 to 750 ILCS 60/227.1 646
Article III. Law Enforcement Responsibility, 750 ILCS 60/301 to 750 ILCS 60/306 670
Article IV. Health Care Providers, 750 ILCS 60/401 673
Address Confidentiality for Victims of Domestic Violence Act, 750 ILCS 61/1 to 750 ILCS 61/45 673
Rights of Married Persons Act, 750 ILCS 65/0.01 to 750 ILCS 65/22 675
Parental Notice of Abortion Act of 1995, 750 ILCS 70/1 to 750 ILCS 70/99 687

RELATED LAWS

CHAPTER 20. EXECUTIVE BRANCH

Department of Children and Family Services

Children and Family Services Act, 20 ILCS 505/7 to 20 ILCS 505/7.7 692
Civil Administrative Code of Illinois.
Article 510. Department of Children and Family Services, 20 ILCS 510/510-1 to 20 ILCS 510/510-200 695

Department of Human Services

Domestic Violence Shelters Act, 20 ILCS 1310/0.01 to 20 ILCS 1310/3.2 697

CHAPTER 55. COUNTIES

Neutral Site Custody Exchange Funding Act, 55 ILCS 82/1 to 55 ILCS 82/99 699

CHAPTER 305. PUBLIC AID

Illinois Public Aid Code.
Article IV. Temporary Assistance for Needy Families, 305 ILCS 5/4-1.7 701
Article X. Determination and Enforcement of Support Responsibility of Relatives, 305 ILCS 5/10-1 to 305 ILCS 5/10-27 703

CHAPTER 320. AGING

Senior Citizens on State Boards and Commissions Act, 320 ILCS 5/0.01, 320 ILCS 5/1 743
Respite Program Act, 320 ILCS 10/1 to 320 ILCS 10/12 743
Elder Abuse Demonstration Project Act [Repealed] 746
Elder Abuse and Neglect Act, 320 ILCS 20/1 to 320 ILCS 20/13.5 746
Senior Citizens and Disabled Persons Property Tax Relief and Pharmaceutical Assistance Act, 320 ILCS 25/1 to 320 ILCS 25/13 755
Senior Citizens Real Estate Tax Deferral Act, 320 ILCS 30/1 to 320 ILCS 30/8 765
Partnership for Long-Term Care Act, 320 ILCS 35/1 to 320 ILCS 35/60 768
All-Inclusive Care for the Elderly Act, 320 ILCS 40/1 to 320 ILCS 40/30 773
Older Adult Services Act, 320 ILCS 42/1 to 320 ILCS 42/99 774
Senior Citizens Child Care Support Act, 320 ILCS 45/1 to 320 ILCS 45/25 781
Senior Pharmaceutical Assistance Act, 320 ILCS 50/1 to 320 ILCS 50/99 781
Senior Citizens and Disabled Persons Prescription Drug Discount Program Act, 320 ILCS 55/1 to 320 ILCS 55/990 784
Community Senior Services and Resources Act, 320 ILCS 60/1 to 320 ILCS 60/99 788
Family Caregiver Act, 320 ILCS 65/1 to 320 ILCS 65/99 790

CHAPTER 325. CHILDREN

Abandoned Newborn Infant Protection Act, 325 ILCS 2/1 to 325 ILCS 2/999 794
Abused and Neglected Child Reporting Act, 325 ILCS 5/1 to 325 ILCS 5/11.7 800

PAGE

Birth Control Services to Minors Act, 325 ILCS 10/0.01, 325 ILCS 10/1 826
Child Sexual Abuse Prevention Act, 325 ILCS 15/0.01 to 325 ILCS 15/7 827
Children's Privacy Protection and Parental Empowerment Act, 325 ILCS 17/1 to 325 ILCS 17/20 829
Early Intervention Services System Act, 325 ILCS 20/1 to 325 ILCS 20/20 830
High Risk Youth Career Development Act, 325 ILCS 25/0.01, 325 ILCS 25/1 843
Family Support Demonstration Project, 325 ILCS 30/1 to 325 ILCS 30/9 844
Interagency Board for Children who are Deaf or Hard-of-Hearing and have an Emotional or Behavioral Disorder Act, 325 ILCS 35/1 to 325 ILCS 35/12 846
Intergovernmental Missing Child Recovery Act of 1984, 325 ILCS 40/1 to 325 ILCS 40/8 ... 849
Minor Identification and Protection Act, 325 ILCS 45/1 to 325 ILCS 45/3 852
Missing Children Records Act, 325 ILCS 50/0.01 to 325 ILCS 50/5 853
Missing Children Registration Law, 325 ILCS 55/0.01 to 325 ILCS 55/7 854
Surgical Institute for Children Act, 325 ILCS 60/0.01 to 325 ILCS 60/12 856

CHAPTER 410. PUBLIC HEALTH

Health Information

Marriage, Dissolution, and Invalidity Records Act, 410 ILCS 530/0.01 to 410 ILCS 530/3.1 858

CHAPTER 720. CRIMINAL OFFENSES

Criminal Code

Criminal Code of 1961.
- Title III. Specific Offenses, 720 ILCS 5/10-1 to 720 ILCS 5/10-8, 720 ILCS 5/12-3.2, 720 ILCS 5/12-3.3, 720 ILCS 5/12-4.10, 720 ILCS 5/12-4.11 860

Offenses Against Persons

Neglected Children Offense Act, 720 ILCS 130/0.01 to 720 ILCS 130/3 892
Wrongs to Children Act, 720 ILCS 150/0.01 to 720 ILCS 150/5.1 895

Offenses Against the Public

Illinois Abortion Law of 1975, 720 ILCS 510/10 to 720 ILCS 510/15 897
Illinois Abortion Parental Consent Act of 1977 [Repealed] 900
Parental Notice of Abortion Act of 1983 [Repealed] 900
Adoption Compensation Prohibition Act, 720 ILCS 525/0.01 to 720 ILCS 525/5 900
Child Curfew Act, 720 ILCS 555/0.01 to 720 ILCS 555/2 903

CHAPTER 725. CRIMINAL PROCEDURE

Code of Criminal Procedure of 1963.
- Title IV. Proceedings to Commence Prosecution, 725 ILCS 5/112A-1 to 725 ILCS 5/112A-31 906

CHAPTER 735. CIVIL PROCEDURE

Code of Civil Procedure.
- Article VIII. Evidence, 735 ILCS 5/8-801, 735 ILCS 5/8-2601 923
- Article XI. Injunction, 735 ILCS 5/11-101 to 735 ILCS 5/11-110 925
- Article XXI. Change of Name, 735 ILCS 5/21-101 to 735 ILCS 5/21-104 959

CHAPTER 740. CIVIL LIABILITIES

Breach of Promise Act, 740 ILCS 15/0.01 to 740 ILCS 15/10 962

PAGE
Frauds Act, 740 ILCS 80/1 964
Parental Responsibility Law, 740 ILCS 115/1 to 740 ILCS 115/7 984
Parental Right of Recovery Act, 740 ILCS 120/1 to 740 ILCS 120/4 986
Right to Breastfeed Act, 740 ILCS 137/1 to 740 ILCS 137/99 987

CHAPTER 760. TRUSTS AND FIDUCIARIES

Instruments Regarding Adopted Children Act, 760 ILCS 30/0.01, 760 ILCS 30/1 988
Trusts and Dissolutions of Marriage Act, 760 ILCS 35/0.01, 760 ILCS 35/1 988

ILLINOIS SUPREME COURT RULES

Expedited Child Support Rules, Rules 100.1 to 100.13 990
Article II. Rules on Civil Proceedings in the Trial Court.
Part A. Process and Notice, Rule 101 997
Part J. Miscellaneous, Rule 296 1000
Article VI. Appeals in Criminal Cases, Post-Conviction Cases, and Juvenile Court Proceedings, Rules 660 to 663 1008

User's Guide to the Index 1013
Index 1015

Sections Affected by Public Acts 93-656 through 93-1102

Note: In addition to the sections listed below, users of this edition should be aware that additional section and case notes annotations have also been appropriately incorporated throughout this publication. The sections with new and/or revised annotations do *not* appear in this listing.

Section Affected	Effect	Public Act No.	Sec.
55 ILCS 82/15	Amended	93-746	5
305 ILCS 5/10-8.1	Amended	93-1061	5
305 ILCS 5/10-10	Amended	93-1061	5
305 ILCS 5/10-11	Amended	93-1061	5
305 ILCS 5/10-16.7	Added	93-736	30
320 ILCS 10/1.5	Amended	93-864	90
320 ILCS 10/2	Amended	93-864	90
320 ILCS 10/3	Amended	93-864	90
320 ILCS 10/4	Amended	93-864	90
320 ILCS 10/5	Amended	93-864	90
320 ILCS 10/6	Amended	93-864	90
320 ILCS 10/7	Repealed	93-864	91
320 ILCS 10/8	Amended	93-864	90
320 ILCS 10/9	Repealed	93-864	91
320 ILCS 10/10	Repealed	93-864	91
320 ILCS 10/11	Amended	93-864	90
320 ILCS 10/12	Amended	93-864	90
320 ILCS 25/6	Amended	93-841	35
320 ILCS 42/1	Added	93-1031	1
320 ILCS 42/5	Added	93-1031	5
320 ILCS 42/10	Added	93-1031	10
320 ILCS 42/15	Added	93-1031	15
320 ILCS 42/20	Added	93-1031	20
320 ILCS 42/25	Added	93-1031	25
320 ILCS 42/30	Added	93-1031	30
320 ILCS 42/35	Added	93-1031	35
320 ILCS 42/90	Added	93-1031	90
320 ILCS 42/99	Added	93-1031	99
320 ILCS 50/15	Amended	93-843	5
320 ILCS 60/32	Added	93-714	10
320 ILCS 65/1	Added	93-864	1
320 ILCS 65/5	Added	93-864	5
320 ILCS 65/10	Added	93-864	10
320 ILCS 65/15	Added	93-864	15
320 ILCS 65/16	Added	93-864	16
320 ILCS 65/20	Added	93-864	20
320 ILCS 65/25	Added	93-864	25
320 ILCS 65/30	Added	93-864	30
320 ILCS 65/35	Added	93-864	35
320 ILCS 65/40	Added	93-864	40
320 ILCS 65/90	Added	93-864	90
320 ILCS 65/99	Added	93-864	99
325 ILCS 2/10	Amended	93-820	5

Section Affected	Effect	Public Act No.	Sec.
325 ILCS 2/15	Amended	93-820	5
325 ILCS 2/20	Amended	93-820	5
325 ILCS 2/25	Amended	93-820	5
325 ILCS 2/27	Amended	93-820	5
325 ILCS 2/30	Amended	93-820	5
325 ILCS 2/35	Amended	93-820	5
325 ILCS 2/40	Amended	93-820	5
325 ILCS 2/50	Amended	93-820	5
325 ILCS 2/55	Amended	93-820	5
325 ILCS 2/65	Amended	93-820	5
325 ILCS 5/4	Amended	93-1041	905
720 ILCS 5/12-3.2	Amended	93-809	5
720 ILCS 525/4.1	Amended	93-1063	10
725 ILCS 5/112A-3	Amended	93-811	5
725 ILCS 5/112A-21	Amended	93-944	5
740 ILCS 137/1	Added	93-942	1
740 ILCS 137/5	Added	93-942	5
740 ILCS 137/10	Added	93-942	10
740 ILCS 137/15	Added	93-942	15
740 ILCS 137/99	Added	93-942	99
750 ILCS 5/505	Amended	93-1061	10
750 ILCS 5/601	Amended	93-1026	5
750 ILCS 5/607	Amended	93-911	5
750 ILCS 5/706.3	Amended	93-836	20
750 ILCS 16/20	Amended	93-1061	15
750 ILCS 28/32	Added	93-1061	20
750 ILCS 45/2.5	Added	93-921	800
750 ILCS 45/6	Amended	93-921	800
750 ILCS 45/13.1	Amended	93-1061	25
750 ILCS 45/14	Amended	93-1061	25
750 ILCS 47/	Added	93-921	1
750 ILCS 47/1	Added	93-921	1
750 ILCS 47/5	Added	93-921	5
750 ILCS 47/10	Added	93-921	10
750 ILCS 47/15	Added	93-921	15
750 ILCS 47/20	Added	93-921	20
750 ILCS 47/25	Added	93-921	25
750 ILCS 47/30	Added	93-921	30
750 ILCS 47/35	Added	93-921	35
750 ILCS 47/40	Added	93-921	40
750 ILCS 47/45	Added	93-921	45
750 ILCS 47/50	Added	93-921	50
750 ILCS 47/55	Added	93-921	55
750 ILCS 47/60	Added	93-921	60
750 ILCS 47/65	Added	93-921	65
750 ILCS 47/70	Added	93-921	70
750 ILCS 47/75	Added	93-921	75
750 ILCS 47/800	Added	93-921	800
750 ILCS 50/1	Amended	93-732	5
750 ILCS 50/9	Amended	93-732	5
750 ILCS 50/10	Amended	93-732	5
750 ILCS 50/13.1	Amended	93-732	5
750 ILCS 50/14	Amended	93-732	5

Section Affected	Effect	Public Act No.	Public Act Sec.
750 ILCS 60/103	Amended	93-811	10
750 ILCS 60/221	Amended	93-944	10

Illinois Domestic Relations and Related Laws Annotated

CHAPTER 750

FAMILIES

Illinois Marriage and Dissolution of Marriage Act

PART I.

GENERAL PROVISIONS

750 ILCS 5/101 Short Title
750 ILCS 5/102 Purposes; Rules of Construction
750 ILCS 5/103 Trial by Jury
750 ILCS 5/104 Venue
750 ILCS 5/105 Application of Civil Practice Law
750 ILCS 5/106 Employment of Administrative Aides
750 ILCS 5/107 Order of protection; status

PART II.

MARRIAGE

750 ILCS 5/201 Formalities
750 ILCS 5/202 Marriage License and Marriage Certificate
750 ILCS 5/203 License to Marry
750 ILCS 5/204 Medical information brochure
750 ILCS 5/205 Exceptions
750 ILCS 5/206 Records
750 ILCS 5/207 Effective Date of License
750 ILCS 5/208 Judicial Approval of Underage Marriages
750 ILCS 5/209 Solemnization and Registration
750 ILCS 5/210 Registration of Marriage Certificate
750 ILCS 5/211 Reporting
750 ILCS 5/212 Prohibited Marriages
750 ILCS 5/213 Validity
750 ILCS 5/213.1 Same-sex marriages; public policy
750 ILCS 5/214 Invalidity of Common Law Marriages
750 ILCS 5/215 Penalty
750 ILCS 5/216 Prohibited Marriages Void if Contracted in Another State
750 ILCS 5/217 Marriage by Non-residents — When Void
750 ILCS 5/218 Duty of Officer Issuing License
750 ILCS 5/219 Offenses

PART III.

DECLARATION OF INVALIDITY OF MARRIAGE

750 ILCS 5/301 Declaration of Invalidity — Grounds
750 ILCS 5/302 Time of Commencement
750 ILCS 5/303 Legitimacy of Children
750 ILCS 5/304 Retroactivity
750 ILCS 5/305 Putative Spouse
750 ILCS 5/306 Commencement of Action

PART IV.

DISSOLUTION AND LEGAL SEPARATION

750 ILCS 5/401 Dissolution of marriage
750 ILCS 5/402 Legal Separation
750 ILCS 5/403 Pleadings — Commencement — Abolition of Existing Defenses — Procedure
750 ILCS 5/404 Conciliation; mediation
750 ILCS 5/404.1 [Educational program concerning effects of dissolution on children]
750 ILCS 5/405 Hearing on Default — Notice
750 ILCS 5/406 Fault or Conduct of Petitioner
750 ILCS 5/407 Admission of Respondent
750 ILCS 5/408 Collusion — Assent or Consent of Petitioner
750 ILCS 5/409 Proof of Foreign Marriage
750 ILCS 5/410 Process — Practice — Proceedings — Publication
750 ILCS 5/411 Commencement of Action
750 ILCS 5/412 Filing of petition — Cases Requiring Service by Publication
750 ILCS 5/413 Judgment

PART IV-A.

JOINT SIMPLIFIED DISSOLUTION PROCEDURE

750 ILCS 5/451 Applicability
750 ILCS 5/452 Petition
750 ILCS 5/453 Procedure; Judgment
750 ILCS 5/454 Affidavit
750 ILCS 5/455 Copies of judgment
750 ILCS 5/456 Forms
750 ILCS 5/457 Brochure to describe proceedings

PART V.

PROPERTY, SUPPORT AND ATTORNEY FEES

750 ILCS 5/501 Temporary Relief
750 ILCS 5/501.1 Dissolution action stay
750 ILCS 5/502 Agreement
750 ILCS 5/503 Disposition of property
750 ILCS 5/504 Maintenance
750 ILCS 5/505 Child support; contempt; penalties
750 ILCS 5/505.1 [Unemployed obligor; powers of court]
750 ILCS 5/505.2 Health insurance
750 ILCS 5/505.3 Information to State Case Registry
750 ILCS 5/506 Representation of child
750 ILCS 5/507 Payment of maintenance or support to court
750 ILCS 5/507.1 Payment of Support to State Disbursement Unit
750 ILCS 5/508 Attorney's Fees; Client's Rights and Responsibilities Respecting Fees and Costs
750 ILCS 5/509 Independence of Provisions of Judgment or Temporary Order
750 ILCS 5/510 Modification and termination of provisions for maintenance, support, educational expenses, and property disposition
750 ILCS 5/511 Procedure
750 ILCS 5/512 Post-Judgment Venue
750 ILCS 5/513 Support for Non-minor Children and Educational Expenses
750 ILCS 5/514 Partition of Real Estate
750 ILCS 5/515 Partition to be Filed in Counties where Real Estate Located
750 ILCS 5/516 Public Aid collection fee

PART VI.

CUSTODY

750 ILCS 5/601 Jurisdiction; Commencement of Proceeding
750 ILCS 5/602 Best Interest of Child
750 ILCS 5/602.1 [Parental powers, rights and responsibilities; joint custody; access to child's records]
750 ILCS 5/603 Temporary Orders
750 ILCS 5/604 Interviews
750 ILCS 5/604.5 Evaluation of child's best interest
750 ILCS 5/605 Investigations and Reports
750 ILCS 5/606 Hearings

750 ILCS 5/607 Visitation
750 ILCS 5/607.1 Enforcement of visitation orders; visitation abuse
750 ILCS 5/608 Judicial Supervision
750 ILCS 5/609 Leave to Remove Children
750 ILCS 5/610 Modification
750 ILCS 5/611 Enforcement of custody order or order prohibiting removal of child from the jurisdiction of the court

PART VII.

MISCELLANEOUS

750 ILCS 5/701 Marital Residence — Order Granting Possession to Spouse
750 ILCS 5/702 Maintenance in Case of Bigamy
750 ILCS 5/703 Lien of judgment — Sales
750 ILCS 5/704 Public Aid Provisions
750 ILCS 5/705 Support payments; receiving and disbursing agents
750 ILCS 5/706.1 Withholding of Income to Secure Payment of Support
750 ILCS 5/706.2 Posting Security, Bond or Guarantee to Secure Payment
750 ILCS 5/706.3 Information concerning obligors
750 ILCS 5/707 Certificate of Dissolution or Invalidity of Marriage — Filing with Department of Public Health
750 ILCS 5/708 [Address disclosure]
750 ILCS 5/709 Mandatory child support payments to clerk
750 ILCS 5/710 Enforcement; Penalties
750 ILCS 5/711 Fees
750 ILCS 5/712 [Rules for certification; reimbursement; comparison report; supervision by the Child and Spouse Support Unit]
750 ILCS 5/713 Attachment of the Body
750 ILCS 5/714 Information to locate putative fathers and noncustodial parents

PART VIII.

APPLICATION AND SEVERABILITY

750 ILCS 5/801 Application
750 ILCS 5/802 Court Rules

ILLINOIS UNIFORM PREMARITAL AGREEMENT ACT

750 ILCS 10/1 [Short title]
750 ILCS 10/2 Definitions
750 ILCS 10/3 Formalities
750 ILCS 10/4 Content
750 ILCS 10/5 Effect of marriage
750 ILCS 10/6 Amendment, revocation
750 ILCS 10/7 Enforcement
750 ILCS 10/8 Enforcement: void marriage
750 ILCS 10/9 Limitation of actions
750 ILCS 10/10 Application and construction
750 ILCS 10/11 Time of taking effect

NON-SUPPORT OF SPOUSE AND CHILDREN ACT

750 ILCS 15/1 through 750 ILCS 15/12.2 [Repealed.]

NON-SUPPORT PUNISHMENT ACT

750 ILCS 16/1 Short title
750 ILCS 16/5 Prosecutions by State's Attorneys
750 ILCS 16/7 Prosecutions by Attorney General
750 ILCS 16/10 Proceedings
750 ILCS 16/15 Failure to support
750 ILCS 16/20 Entry of order for support; income withholding
750 ILCS 16/22 Withholding of income to secure payment of support
750 ILCS 16/23 Interest on support obligations
750 ILCS 16/25 Payment of support to State Disbursement Unit; clerk of the court
750 ILCS 16/30 Information to State Case Registry
750 ILCS 16/33 Information to locate putative fathers and noncustodial parents
750 ILCS 16/35 Fine; release of defendant on probation; violation of order for support; forfeiture of recognizance
750 ILCS 16/40 Evidence
750 ILCS 16/45 Husband or wife as competent witness
750 ILCS 16/50 Community service; work alternative program
750 ILCS 16/55 Offenses; how construed
750 ILCS 16/60 Unemployed persons owing duty of support
750 ILCS 16/65 Order of protection; status
750 ILCS 16/70 Severability.
750 ILCS 16/905 through 750 ILCS 16/992 [Not Set Out]
750 ILCS 16/995 Certain actions to be determined under prior law
750 ILCS 16/999 Effective date

REVISED UNIFORM RECIPROCAL ENFORCEMENT OF SUPPORT ACT

750 ILCS 20/1 through 750 ILCS 20/42 [Repealed]

UNIFORM INTERSTATE FAMILY SUPPORT ACT

ARTICLE 1.

GENERAL PROVISIONS

(PRIOR TO RENUMBERING BY P.A. 93-479; SEE NOTES UNDER 750 ILCS 22/100)

750 ILCS 22/100 (Prior to Renumbering by P.A. 93-479; see notes) Short title
750 ILCS 22/101 (Prior to Renumbering by P.A. 93-479; see notes) Definitions
750 ILCS 22/102 (Prior to Renumbering by P.A. 93-479; see notes under 750 ILCS 22/100) Tribunal of State
750 ILCS 22/103 (Prior to Renumbering by P.A. 93-479; see notes under 750 ILCS 22/100) Remedies cumulative

ARTICLE 1.

GENERAL PROVISIONS

(AS AMENDED AND RENUMBERED BY P.A. 93-479; SEE NOTES UNDER 750 ILCS 22/101)

750 ILCS 22/101 (As renumbered by P.A. 93-479; see notes) Short title
750 ILCS 22/102 (As amended and renumbered by P.A. 93-479; see notes under 750 ILCS 22/101) Definitions
750 ILCS 22/103 (As renumbered by P.A. 93-479; see notes under 750 ILCS 22/101) Tribunal of State
750 ILCS 22/104 (As amended and renumbered by P.A. 93-479; see notes under 750 ILCS 22/101) Remedies cumulative

ARTICLE 2.

JURISDICTION

Part 1.

Extended Personal Jurisdiction

750 ILCS 22/201 (Without amendments by P.A. 93-479; see notes for effective date) Bases for jurisdiction over nonresident
750 ILCS 22/201 (As amended by P.A. 93-479, see notes for effective date) Bases for jurisdiction over nonresident
750 ILCS 22/202 (Without amendments by P.A. 93-479; see notes for effective date) Procedure when exercising jurisdiction over nonresident
750 ILCS 22/202 (As amended by P.A. 93-479; see notes for effective date) Duration of personal jurisdiction

Part 2.

Proceedings Involving Two or More States

750 ILCS 22/203 Initiating and responding tribunal of State

750 ILCS 22/204 (Without amendments by P.A. 93-479; see notes for effective date) Simultaneous proceedings in another state
750 ILCS 22/204 (As amended by P.A. 93-479; see notes for effective date) Simultaneous proceedings
750 ILCS 22/205 (Without amendments by P.A. 93-479; see notes for effective date) Continuing, exclusive jurisdiction
750 ILCS 22/205 (As amended by P.A. 93-479; see notes for effective date) Continuing, exclusive jurisdiction to modify child-support order
750 ILCS 22/206 (Without amendments by P.A. 93-479; see notes for effective date) Enforcement and modification of support order by tribunal having continuing jurisdiction
750 ILCS 22/206 (As amended by P.A. 93-479; see notes for effective date) Continuing jurisdiction to enforce child-support order

Part 3.

Reconciliation of Multiple Orders

750 ILCS 22/207 (Without amendments by P.A. 93-479; see notes for effective date) Recognition of controlling child-support order
750 ILCS 22/207 (As amended by P.A. 93-479; see notes for effective date) Determination of controlling child-support order
750 ILCS 22/208 (Without amendments by P.A. 93-479; see notes for effective date) Multiple child-support orders for two or more obligees
750 ILCS 22/208 (As amended by P.A. 93-479; see notes for effective date) Child-support orders for two or more obligees
750 ILCS 22/209 (Without amendments by P.A. 93-479; see notes for effective date) Credit for payments
750 ILCS 22/209 (As amended by P.A. 93-479; see notes for effective date) Credit for payments
750 ILCS 22/210 (See notes for effective date) Application of Act to nonresident subject to personal jurisdiction
750 ILCS 22/211 (See notes for effective date) Continuing, exclusive jurisdiction to modify spousal-support order

ARTICLE 3.

CIVIL PROVISIONS OF GENERAL APPLICATION

750 ILCS 22/301 (Without amendments by P.A. 93-479; see notes for effective date) Proceedings under Act
750 ILCS 22/301 (As amended by P.A. 93-479; see notes for effective date) Proceedings under Act
750 ILCS 22/302 (As amended by P.A. 93-479; see notes for effective date) Proceeding by minor parent
750 ILCS 22/303 (Without amendments by P.A. 93-479; see notes for effective date) Application of law of State
750 ILCS 22/303 (As amended by P.A. 93-479; see notes for effective date) Application of law of State
750 ILCS 22/304 (Without amendments by PA 93-479) Duties of initiating tribunal
750 ILCS 22/304 (As amended by P.A. 93-479; see notes for effective date) Duties of initiating tribunal
750 ILCS 22/305 Duties and powers of responding tribunal
750 ILCS 22/306 (Without amendments by P.A. 93-479, see notes for effective date) Inappropriate tribunal
750 ILCS 22/306 (As amended by P.A. 93-479; see notes for effective date) Inappropriate tribunal
750 ILCS 22/307 (Without amendments by P.A. 93-479; see notes for effective date) Duties of support enforcement agency
750 ILCS 22/307 (As amended by P.A. 93-479; see notes for effective date) Duties of support enforcement agency
750 ILCS 22/308 Duty of Attorney General
750 ILCS 22/309 Private counsel
750 ILCS 22/310 Duties of the Illinois Department of Public Aid
750 ILCS 22/311 Pleadings and accompanying documents
750 ILCS 22/312 (Without amendments by P.A. 93-479; see notes for effective date) Nondisclosure of information in exceptional circumstances
750 ILCS 22/312 (As amended by P.A. 93-479; see notes for effective date) Nondisclosure of information in exceptional circumstances
750 ILCS 22/313 Costs and fees
750 ILCS 22/314 Limited immunity of petitioner
750 ILCS 22/315 Nonparentage as defense
750 ILCS 22/316 Special rules of evidence and procedure
750 ILCS 22/317 (Without amendments by P.A. 93-479; see notes for effective date) Communications between tribunals
750 ILCS 22/317 (As amended by P.A. 93-479; see notes for effective date) Communications between tribunals
750 ILCS 22/318 Assistance with discovery
750 ILCS 22/319 Receipt and disbursement of payments
750 ILCS 22/320 Payment of Support to State Disbursement Unit

ARTICLE 4.

ESTABLISHMENT OF SUPPORT ORDER

750 ILCS 22/401 Petition to establish support order

ARTICLE 5.

ENFORCEMENT OF ORDER OF ANOTHER STATE WITHOUT REGISTRATION

750 ILCS 22/501 Employer's receipt of income-withholding order of another state
750 ILCS 22/502 Employer's compliance with income-withholding order of another state
750 ILCS 22/503 Employer's compliance with two or more income-withholding orders
750 ILCS 22/504 Immunity from civil liability
750 ILCS 22/505 Penalties for noncompliance
750 ILCS 22/506 (Without amendments by P.A. 93-479) Contest by obligor
750 ILCS 22/506 (As amended by P.A. 93-479; see notes for effective date) Contest by obligor
750 ILCS 22/507 Administrative enforcement of orders

REGISTRATION, ENFORCEMENT, AND MODIFICATION OF SUPPORT ORDER

Part 1.

Registration and Enforcement of Support Order

750 ILCS 22/601 Registration of order for enforcement
750 ILCS 22/602 (Without amendments by P.A. 93-479) Procedure to register order for enforcement
750 ILCS 22/602 (As amended by P.A. 93-479; see notes for effective date) Procedure to register order for enforcement
750 ILCS 22/603 Effect of registration for enforcement
750 ILCS 22/604 (Without amendments by P.A. 93-479) Choice of law
750 ILCS 22/604 (As amended by P.A. 93-479; see notes for effective date) Choice of law

Part 2.

Contest of Validity or Enforcement

750 ILCS 22/605 (Without amendments by P.A. 93-479) Notice of registration of order
750 ILCS 22/605 (As amended by P.A. 93-479; see notes for effective date) Notice of registration of order
750 ILCS 22/606 Procedure to contest validity or enforcement of registered order
750 ILCS 22/607 Contest of registration or enforcement

750 ILCS 22/608 Confirmed order

Part 3.

Registration and Modification of Child Support Order

750 ILCS 22/609 Procedure to register child-support order of another state for modification
750 ILCS 22/610 (Without amendments by P.A. 93-479) Effect of registration for modification
750 ILCS 22/610 (As amended by P.A. 93-479; see notes for effective date) Effect of registration for modification
750 ILCS 22/611 (Without amendments by P.A. 93-479) Modification of Child-Support Order of Another State
750 ILCS 22/611 (As amended by P.A. 93-479; see notes for effective date) Modification of Child-Support Order of Another State
750 ILCS 22/612 (Without amendments by P.A. 93-479) Recognition of order modified in another state
750 ILCS 22/612 (As amended by P.A. 93-479; see notes for effective date) Recognition of order modified in another state
750 ILCS 22/613 Jurisdiction to modify child-support order of another state when individual parties reside in this State
750 ILCS 22/614 Notice to issuing tribunal of modification
750 ILCS 22/615 (See notes for effective date) Jurisdiction to modify child-support order of foreign country or political subdivision

ARTICLE 7.

DETERMINATION OF PARENTAGE

750 ILCS 22/701 (Without amendments by P.A. 93-479) Proceeding to determine parentage
750 ILCS 22/701 (As amended by P.A. 93-479; see notes for effective date) Proceeding to determine parentage

ARTICLE 8.

INTERSTATE RENDITION

750 ILCS 22/801 Grounds for rendition
750 ILCS 22/802 Conditions of rendition

ARTICLE 9.

MISCELLANEOUS PROVISIONS

750 ILCS 22/901 (Without amendments by P.A. 93-479) Uniformity of application and construction
750 ILCS 22/901 (As amended by P.A. 93-479; see notes for effective date) Uniformity of application and construction
750 ILCS 22/902 (Repealed by P.A. 93-479; see notes for effective date) Short title
750 ILCS 22/903 (Prior to renumbering by P.A. 93-479; see notes for effective date) Severability clause
750 ILCS 22/904 (Prior to renumbering by P.A. 93-479; see notes for effective date) Effective date
750 ILCS 22/905 (Prior to renumbering by P.A. 93-479; see notes for effective date) Repeal
750 ILCS 22/910 Conflict
750 ILCS 22/950 through 750 ILCS 22/975 [Not Set Out]
750 ILCS 22/999 Effective date

UNIFIED CHILD SUPPORT SERVICES ACT

750 ILCS 24/1 [Short title]
750 ILCS 24/5 Definitions
750 ILCS 24/10 Plan for Unified Child Support Services
750 ILCS 24/15 Components of a Unified Child Support Services Program
750 ILCS 24/20 Subcontracts
750 ILCS 24/25 Performance standards
750 ILCS 24/30 Annual report to General Assembly
750 ILCS 24/35 IV-D Child Support Program responsibilities
750 ILCS 24/905 through 750 ILCS 24/920 [Not Set Out]

EXPEDITED CHILD SUPPORT ACT OF 1990

750 ILCS 25/1 Short title
750 ILCS 25/2 Purpose
750 ILCS 25/3 Definitions
750 ILCS 25/4 Establishment of the Expedited Child Support System
750 ILCS 25/5 Actions Subject to Expedited Child Support Hearings
750 ILCS 25/6 Authority of hearing officers
750 ILCS 25/7 Expedited Child Support Hearings
750 ILCS 25/8 Authority retained by the court
750 ILCS 25/9 Judicial hearings
750 ILCS 25/10 Failure to Appear
750 ILCS 25/13 [Effective date]

INCOME WITHHOLDING FOR SUPPORT ACT

750 ILCS 28/1 Short title
750 ILCS 28/5 Purpose; intent
750 ILCS 28/15 Definitions
750 ILCS 28/20 Entry of order for support containing income withholding provisions; income withholding notice
750 ILCS 28/22 Use of National Medical Support Notice to enforce health insurance coverage
750 ILCS 28/25 Income withholding after accrual of delinquency
750 ILCS 28/30 Initiated withholding
750 ILCS 28/32 Unpaid arrearage or delinquency after current support obligation terminates
750 ILCS 28/35 Duties of payor
750 ILCS 28/40 Petitions to contest withholding or to modify, suspend, terminate, or correct income withholding notices
750 ILCS 28/45 Additional duties
750 ILCS 28/50 Penalties
750 ILCS 28/55 Alternative procedures for service of an income withholding notice
750 ILCS 28/60 Remedies in addition to other laws
750 ILCS 28/905 through 750 ILCS 28/930 [Not Set Out]
750 ILCS 28/999 Effective date

EMANCIPATION OF MATURE MINORS ACT

750 ILCS 30/1 Short title
750 ILCS 30/2 Purpose and policy
750 ILCS 30/3 Definitions
750 ILCS 30/3-1 Minor
750 ILCS 30/3-2 Mature minor
750 ILCS 30/3-2.5 Homeless minor
750 ILCS 30/3-2.10 Youth transitional housing program
750 ILCS 30/3-3 Parents
750 ILCS 30/3-4 Guardian
750 ILCS 30/3-5 Petition
750 ILCS 30/4 Jurisdiction
750 ILCS 30/5 Rights and responsibilities of an emancipated minor
750 ILCS 30/6 Duration of emancipation and discharge of proceedings
750 ILCS 30/7 Petition
750 ILCS 30/8 Notice
750 ILCS 30/9 Hearing on petition
750 ILCS 30/10 Joinder, Juvenile Court Proceedings
750 ILCS 30/11 Appeal

UNIFORM CHILD CUSTODY JURISDICTION ACT

750 ILCS 35/1 through 750 ILCS 35/26 [Repealed]

UNIFORM CHILD-CUSTODY JURISDICTION AND ENFORCEMENT ACT

ARTICLE 1.

GENERAL PROVISIONS

750 ILCS 36/101 Short Title
750 ILCS 36/102 Definitions

750 ILCS 36/103 Proceedings Governed By Other Law
750 ILCS 36/104 Application To Indian Tribes
750 ILCS 36/105 International Application Of Act
750 ILCS 36/106 Effect Of Child-Custody Determination
750 ILCS 36/107 Priority
750 ILCS 36/108 Notice To Persons Outside State
750 ILCS 36/109 Appearance And Limited Immunity
750 ILCS 36/110 Communication Between Courts
750 ILCS 36/111 Taking Testimony In Another State
750 ILCS 36/112 Cooperation Between Courts; Preservation Of Records

ARTICLE 2.

JURISDICTION

750 ILCS 36/201 Initial Child-Custody Jurisdiction
750 ILCS 36/202 Exclusive, Continuing Jurisdiction
750 ILCS 36/203 Jurisdiction To Modify Determination
750 ILCS 36/204 Temporary Emergency Jurisdiction
750 ILCS 36/205 Notice; Opportunity To Be Heard; Joinder
750 ILCS 36/206 Simultaneous Proceedings
750 ILCS 36/207 Inconvenient Forum
750 ILCS 36/208 Jurisdiction Declined By Reason Of Conduct
750 ILCS 36/209 Information To Be Submitted To Court
750 ILCS 36/210 Appearance Of Parties And Child

ARTICLE 3.

ENFORCEMENT

750 ILCS 36/301 Definitions
750 ILCS 36/302 Enforcement Under Hague Convention
750 ILCS 36/303 Duty To Enforce
750 ILCS 36/304 Temporary Visitation
750 ILCS 36/305 Registration Of Child-Custody Determination
750 ILCS 36/306 Enforcement Of Registered Determination
750 ILCS 36/307 Simultaneous Proceedings
750 ILCS 36/308 Expedited Enforcement Of Child-Custody Determination
750 ILCS 36/309 Service Of Petition And Order
750 ILCS 36/310 Hearing And Order
750 ILCS 36/311 Warrant To Take Physical Custody Of Child
750 ILCS 36/312 Costs, Fees, And Expenses
750 ILCS 36/313 Recognition And Enforcement
750 ILCS 36/314 Appeals
750 ILCS 36/315 Role Of State's Attorney
750 ILCS 36/316 Role Of Law Enforcement
750 ILCS 36/317 Costs And Expenses

ARTICLE 4.

MISCELLANEOUS PROVISIONS

750 ILCS 36/401 Application And Construction
750 ILCS 36/402 Severability Clause
750 ILCS 36/403 Effective Date
750 ILCS 36/405 Transitional Provision

ILLINOIS PARENTAGE ACT

750 ILCS 40/1 [Short title]
750 ILCS 40/2 [Status of child conceived by artificial insemination]
750 ILCS 40/3 [Status of husband of artificially inseminated wife; consent]

ILLINOIS PARENTAGE ACT OF 1984

750 ILCS 45/1 Short Title
750 ILCS 45/1.1 Public Policy
750 ILCS 45/2 Parent and Child Relationship Defined
750 ILCS 45/2.5 Definitions
750 ILCS 45/3 Relationship and Support Not Dependent on Marriage
750 ILCS 45/3.1 [Duty of minor parent to support]
750 ILCS 45/4 How Parent and Child Relationship Established
750 ILCS 45/4.1 Administrative paternity determinations
750 ILCS 45/5 Presumption of Paternity
750 ILCS 45/6 Establishment of Parent and Child Relationship by Consent of the Parties
750 ILCS 45/7 Determination of Father and Child Relationship; Who May Bring Action; Parties
750 ILCS 45/8 Statute of limitations
750 ILCS 45/9 Jurisdiction; Venue
750 ILCS 45/9.1 Notice to Presumed Father
750 ILCS 45/10 Pre-trial Proceedings
750 ILCS 45/11 Tests to determine inherited characteristics
750 ILCS 45/12 Pre-Trial Recommendations
750 ILCS 45/12.1 Settlement Orders
750 ILCS 45/13 Civil Action
750 ILCS 45/13.1 Temporary order for child support
750 ILCS 45/13.5 Injunctive relief
750 ILCS 45/14 Judgment
750 ILCS 45/14.1 Information to State Case Registry
750 ILCS 45/14.5 Information to locate putative fathers and noncustodial parents
750 ILCS 45/15 Enforcement of Judgment or Order
750 ILCS 45/15.1 [Unemployed obligor; court's powers]
750 ILCS 45/15.2 Order of protection; status
750 ILCS 45/16 Modification of Judgment
750 ILCS 45/17 Costs
750 ILCS 45/18 Right to Counsel; Free Transcript on Appeal
750 ILCS 45/19 Action to Declare Mother and Child Relationship
750 ILCS 45/20 Withholding of Income to Secure Payment of Support
750 ILCS 45/20.5 Information concerning obligors
750 ILCS 45/20.7 Interest on support obligations
750 ILCS 45/21 Support payments; receiving and disbursing agents
750 ILCS 45/21.1 Payment of Support to State Disbursement Unit
750 ILCS 45/22 [Collection fee]
750 ILCS 45/23 Notice to Clerk of Circuit Court of Payment Received by Illinois Department of Public Aid for Recording
750 ILCS 45/25 [Repeal of Paternity Act; effect]
750 ILCS 45/26 [Severability]
750 ILCS 45/27 Other states' establishments of paternity

GESTATIONAL SURROGACY ACT

750 ILCS 47/1 Short title
750 ILCS 47/5 Purpose
750 ILCS 47/10 Definitions
750 ILCS 47/15 Rights of parentage
750 ILCS 47/20 Eligibility
750 ILCS 47/25 Requirements for a gestational surrogacy contract
750 ILCS 47/30 Duty to support
750 ILCS 47/35 Establishment of the parent-child relationship
750 ILCS 47/40 Immunities
750 ILCS 47/45 Noncompliance
750 ILCS 47/50 Effect of Noncompliance
750 ILCS 47/55 Damages
750 ILCS 47/60 Rulemaking
750 ILCS 47/65 Severability
750 ILCS 47/70 Irrevocability
750 ILCS 47/75 Application
750 ILCS 47/800 [Not set out]

ADOPTION ACT

750 ILCS 50/0.01 Short title
750 ILCS 50/1 Definitions
750 ILCS 50/2 Who may adopt a child
750 ILCS 50/2.1 [Relation to other laws]
750 ILCS 50/3 Who may be adopted
750 ILCS 50/4 Jurisdiction and venue
750 ILCS 50/4.1 [Compliance with the Child Care Act of 1969 and the Interstate Compact on the Placement of Children]
750 ILCS 50/5 Petition, contents, verification, filing
750 ILCS 50/6 Investigation; all cases
750 ILCS 50/7 Process

750 ILCS 50/8 Consents to adoption and surrenders for purposes of adoption
750 ILCS 50/9 Time for taking a consent or surrender
750 ILCS 50/10 Forms of consent and surrender; execution and acknowledgment thereof
750 ILCS 50/11 Consents, surrenders, irrevocability
750 ILCS 50/12 Consent of child or adult
750 ILCS 50/12.1 Putative Father Registry
750 ILCS 50/12a Notice to putative father
750 ILCS 50/13 Interim order
750 ILCS 50/13.1 Order for standby adoption
750 ILCS 50/14 Judgment
750 ILCS 50/14a [Death of child during proceedings]
750 ILCS 50/14b Death of intended adoptive parent prior to entry of judgment
750 ILCS 50/15 [Prime consideration]
750 ILCS 50/15.1 [Foster parent; application for consent from guardian]
750 ILCS 50/16 Entry of Judgment
750 ILCS 50/17 Effect of order terminating parental rights or Judgment of Adoption
750 ILCS 50/18 Records confidential
750 ILCS 50/18.04 The Illinois Adoption Registry and Medical Information Exchange; legislative intent
750 ILCS 50/18.05 The Illinois Adoption Registry and Medical Information Exchange
750 ILCS 50/18.06 Definitions
750 ILCS 50/18.07 Adoption Registry Advisory Council
750 ILCS 50/18.1 Disclosure of identifying information
750 ILCS 50/18.1a Registry matches
750 ILCS 50/18.1b The Illinois Adoption Registry Application
750 ILCS 50/18.1c Effective date of registration
750 ILCS 50/18.2 Forms
750 ILCS 50/18.3 [Sharing of identifying information; written statement]
750 ILCS 50/18.3a Confidential intermediary
750 ILCS 50/18.4 [Information for adoptive parents]
750 ILCS 50/18.4a Medical and mental health histories
750 ILCS 50/18.5 Liability
750 ILCS 50/18.6 Registry fees
750 ILCS 50/18.7 Illinois Adoption Registry and Medical Information Exchange Fund
750 ILCS 50/18.8 Improper disclosure of identifying information
750 ILCS 50/19 Registration new birth certificate
750 ILCS 50/20 Practice
750 ILCS 50/20a Construction of Act
750 ILCS 50/20b Time limit for relief from final judgment or order
750 ILCS 50/21 Compensation for placing of children prohibited
750 ILCS 50/22 Partial invalidity
750 ILCS 50/23 Repeal — Saving
750 ILCS 50/24 Effective date

Contest of Adoptions Act

750 ILCS 55/0.01 Short title
750 ILCS 55/1 [Failure to give notice; attack]

Illinois Domestic Violence Act of 1986

ARTICLE I.

GENERAL PROVISIONS

750 ILCS 60/101 Short Title
750 ILCS 60/102 Purposes; rules of construction
750 ILCS 60/103 Definitions

ARTICLE II.

ORDERS OF PROTECTION

750 ILCS 60/201 Persons protected by this Act
750 ILCS 60/201.1 Access of high-risk adults
750 ILCS 60/202 Commencement of action; filing fees; dismissal
750 ILCS 60/203 Pleading; non-disclosure of address; non-disclosure of schools
750 ILCS 60/204 [Repealed]
750 ILCS 60/205 Application of rules of civil procedure; Domestic abuse advocates
750 ILCS 60/206 Trial by jury
750 ILCS 60/207 Subject matter jurisdiction
750 ILCS 60/208 Jurisdiction over persons
750 ILCS 60/209 Venue
750 ILCS 60/210 Process
750 ILCS 60/210.1 Service of notice in conjunction with a pending civil case
750 ILCS 60/211 Service of notice of hearings
750 ILCS 60/212 Hearings
750 ILCS 60/213 Continuances
750 ILCS 60/213.1 Hearsay exception
750 ILCS 60/213.2 Waiver of privilege
750 ILCS 60/213.3 Independent counsel; temporary substitute guardian
750 ILCS 60/214 Order of protection; remedies
750 ILCS 60/215 Mutual orders of protection; correlative separate orders
750 ILCS 60/216 Accountability for Actions of Others
750 ILCS 60/217 Emergency order of protection
750 ILCS 60/218 30-day interim order of protection
750 ILCS 60/219 Plenary Order of Protection
750 ILCS 60/220 Duration and extension of orders
750 ILCS 60/221 Contents of orders
750 ILCS 60/222 Notice of orders
750 ILCS 60/222.5 Filing of an order of protection issued in another state
750 ILCS 60/222.10 Short form notification
750 ILCS 60/223 Enforcement of orders of protection
750 ILCS 60/223.1 Order of protection status
750 ILCS 60/224 Modification and re-opening of orders
750 ILCS 60/225 Immunity from prosecution
750 ILCS 60/226 Untrue statements
750 ILCS 60/227 Privileged communications between domestic violence counselors and victims
750 ILCS 60/227.1 Other privileged information

ARTICLE III.

LAW ENFORCEMENT RESPONSIBILITY

750 ILCS 60/301 Arrest without warrant
750 ILCS 60/301.1 Law enforcement policies
750 ILCS 60/302 Data maintenance by law enforcement agencies
750 ILCS 60/303 Reports by law enforcement officers
750 ILCS 60/304 Assistance by law enforcement officers
750 ILCS 60/305 Limited law enforcement liability
750 ILCS 60/306 [Repealed]

ARTICLE IV.

HEALTH CARE PROVIDERS

750 ILCS 60/401 [Providing information on services; liability]

Address Confidentiality for Victims of Domestic Violence Act

750 ILCS 61/1 Short title
750 ILCS 61/5 Legislative findings
750 ILCS 61/10 Definitions
750 ILCS 61/11 Address confidentiality program; administration
750 ILCS 61/15 Address confidentiality program; application; certification
750 ILCS 61/20 Certification cancellation
750 ILCS 61/25 Agency use of designated address
750 ILCS 61/30 Voting by program participant; use of designated address by election authority
750 ILCS 61/35 Disclosure of address prohibited; exceptions
750 ILCS 61/40 Assistance for program applicants
750 ILCS 61/45 Rules

Rights of Married Persons Act

750 ILCS 65/0.01 Short title
750 ILCS 65/1 Rights to sue and be sued
750 ILCS 65/2 Defending in own right or for other
750 ILCS 65/3 [Defending in name of spouse]

750 ILCS 65/4 Recovery of damages
750 ILCS 65/5 [Responsibility for liabilities of spouse]
750 ILCS 65/6 Contracts
750 ILCS 65/7 Earnings
750 ILCS 65/9 Property
750 ILCS 65/10 [Unlawful possession of property by spouse]
750 ILCS 65/11 [Abandoned spouse; control over property]
750 ILCS 65/12 [Contracts, sales or incumbrances made by spouse]
750 ILCS 65/13 [Setting aside judgment]
750 ILCS 65/14 [Power of attorney]
750 ILCS 65/15 [Creditor's rights]
750 ILCS 65/16 [Removal of children from homestead]
750 ILCS 65/17 [Spouse under legal disability]
750 ILCS 65/18 [Petition to convey real estate; notice]
750 ILCS 65/19 [Granting petition to convey]
750 ILCS 65/20 [Security for petition]
750 ILCS 65/21 [Validity of deeds or mortgages]
750 ILCS 65/22 [Estate of tenancy by the entirety]

PARENTAL NOTICE OF ABORTION ACT OF 1995

750 ILCS 70/1 Short title
750 ILCS 70/5 Legislative findings and purpose
750 ILCS 70/10 Definitions
750 ILCS 70/15 Notice to adult family member
750 ILCS 70/20 Exceptions
750 ILCS 70/25 Procedure for judicial waiver of notice
750 ILCS 70/30 Minor's consent to abortion
750 ILCS 70/35 Reports
750 ILCS 70/40 Penalties
750 ILCS 70/45 Immunity
750 ILCS 70/50 Severability and inseverability
750 ILCS 70/85 through 750 ILCS 70/95 [Not Set Out]
750 ILCS 70/99 Effective date

ILLINOIS MARRIAGE AND DISSOLUTION OF MARRIAGE ACT

PART I. GENERAL PROVISIONS

750 ILCS 5/101 Short Title

Sec. 101. *Short Title.* This Act may be cited as the "Illinois Marriage and Dissolution of Marriage Act". (Source: P.A. 86-649.)

Derivation.

Title: An Act in relation to marriage and the dissolution of marriage and amending or repealing Acts and parts of Acts herein named.

Cite: 750 ILCS 5/101 et seq.
Source: P.A. 80-923.
Date: Approved September 22, 1977.

Note.

This section was Ill.Rev.Stat., Ch. 40, para. 101.

CASE NOTES

ANALYSIS

Constitutionality
In General
Applicability
Construction
—Habitual Drunkenness
—Pleadings
—Strict
Court Authority
—Equitable Powers
—Third Party Actions
Presumption
—Marital Property
Public Policy
Purpose
Statutory Jurisdiction

Constitutionality

This Act is not unconstitutional despite argument that it encompasses more than one subject, namely, that it includes both marriage and divorce. In re Thornqvist, 79 Ill. App. 3d 791, 35 Ill. Dec. 342, 399 N.E.2d 176 (1 Dist. 1979).

Argument that this Act violated equal protection by treating married persons differently than unmarried persons was without merit where it was not shown how a classification based upon marital status improperly discriminated against persons whose marriage had been dissolved or that the classification bore no rational relationship to an articulated legislative purpose. In re Thompson, 79 Ill. App. 3d 310, 34 Ill. Dec. 342, 398 N.E.2d 17 (1 Dist. 1979).

The former Domestic Relations Act of 1949, and its companion acts, Senate Bills Nos. 308 and 309 (see now 750 ILCS 5/101 et seq.), "concerning the interest of the state in the domestic relations of the people, and to provide for the establishment of agencies and instrumentalities to aid the courts in the protection of that interest in actions for divorce, separate maintenance and annulment of marriage, and to make appropriations therefor," were void on due process grounds. People ex rel. Bernat v. Bicek, 405 Ill. 510, 91 N.E.2d 588 (1950).

The former Domestic Relations Act (see now 750 ILCS 5/101 et seq.) was not unconstitutional in violation of § 22 of Article IV of the 1870 Constitution (see now Ill. Const. (1970), Art. IV, § 13) as a local or special law enacted for granting divorces, but was unconstitutional as a special law enacted where a general law could be made applicable, since the Domestic Relations Act applied only to one county. Hunt v. County of Cook, 398 Ill. 412, 76 N.E.2d 48 (1947).

In General

The requirements for the issuance of temporary restraining orders without notice are substantially the same under both 735 ILCS 5/11-101 and this Act. Bashwiner v. Bashwiner, 126 Ill. App. 3d 365, 81 Ill. Dec. 359, 466 N.E.2d 1161 (1 Dist. 1984).

This Act will be presumed to have been adopted with the construction placed upon it by states before its adoption by Illinois. Sexton v. Sexton, 82 Ill. App. 3d 482, 37 Ill. Dec. 887, 402 N.E.2d 889 (3 Dist. 1980), rev'd on other grounds, 84 Ill. 2d 312, 49 Ill. Dec. 709, 418 N.E.2d 729 (1981).

Applicability

Although parties were divorced in 1975, modification proceedings were governed by this Act because stipulation and modification order were filed October 10, 1978, which was after the effective date of the Act. Hartman v. Hartman, 89 Ill. App. 3d 969, 45 Ill. Dec. 360, 412 N.E.2d 711 (4 Dist. 1980).

This Act, effective October 1, 1977, applied to litigation involving a property settlement agreement where no judgment had been entered on the subject matter of the litigation at the time the new Act took effect. Claflin v. Claflin, 82 Ill. App. 3d 246, 37 Ill. Dec. 671, 402 N.E.2d 673 (1 Dist. 1980).

This Act applied to matters of substance pending on the effective date of the Act. Sexton v. Sexton, 82 Ill. App. 3d 482, 37 Ill. Dec. 887, 402 N.E.2d 889 (3 Dist. 1980), rev'd on other grounds, 84 Ill. 2d 312, 49 Ill. Dec. 709, 418 N.E.2d 729 (1981).

Where hearing on the issue of the petition to modify original child custody provisions of the divorce decree was not had until well after this Act became effective, the provisions of the Act were applicable. Sexton v. Sexton, 82 Ill. App. 3d 482, 37 Ill. Dec. 887, 402 N.E.2d 889 (3 Dist. 1980), rev'd on other grounds, 84 Ill. 2d 312, 49 Ill. Dec. 709, 418 N.E.2d 729 (1981).

Divorce action would not be reconsidered under this Act when the trial court had determined all the issues prior to the effective date of the Act, but the final written decree was filed after that date. In re LaSusa, 80 Ill. App. 3d 467, 35 Ill. Dec. 884, 400 N.E.2d 21 (1 Dist. 1979).

Applicability (Cont'd)

Where notice of cross-appeal in a divorce case was filed before effective date of this Act, the appeal was governed by the prior Divorce Act (see now 750 ILCS 5/101 et seq.). Belluomini v. Belluomini, 73 Ill. App. 3d 836, 30 Ill. Dec. 14, 392 N.E.2d 669 (1 Dist. 1979); Pettit v. Pettit, 85 Ill. App. 3d 280, 40 Ill. Dec. 696, 406 N.E.2d 899 (4 Dist. 1980).

Where judgment dissolving marriage and dividing property was entered five months after this Act became effective, the Act controlled the rights of the parties. In re Pieper, 79 Ill. App. 3d 835, 34 Ill. Dec. 877, 398 N.E.2d 868 (1 Dist. 1979).

Where this Act stated that it shall apply "to all pending actions commenced prior to its effective date" and the action was commenced prior to the effective date, and a hearing was held prior to that date but the final decree was entered subsequent to its effective date, the new Act applied. In re Franzetti, 77 Ill. App. 3d 1031, 33 Ill. Dec. 668, 397 N.E.2d 1 (3 Dist. 1979).

Construction

—Habitual Drunkenness

Habitual drunkenness had the same meaning in the former Divorce Act (see now 750 ILCS 5/101 et seq.) as in this Act and in determining whether a parent is unfit. People ex rel. Department of Children & Family Servs. v. Sanders, 77 Ill. App. 3d 78, 32 Ill. Dec. 847, 395 N.E.2d 1228 (4 Dist. 1979).

—Pleadings

Section 2-605 of the Code of Civil Procedure (735 ILCS 5/2-605) may not be used to require that pleadings governed by this Act be verified. Firkus v. Firkus, 200 Ill. App. 3d 982, 146 Ill. Dec. 591, 558 N.E.2d 554 (5 Dist. 1990).

—Strict

It is not the policy of the law to favor divorce, and the former divorce statute (see now 750 ILCS 5/101 et seq.), was given a strict rather than a liberal construction because the public had an interest in marriage status, its continuance, and its dissolution. Getz v. Getz, 332 Ill. App. 364, 75 N.E.2d 530 (3 Dist. 1947).

Court Authority

—Equitable Powers

A dissolution of marriage is an entirely statutory creation and, therefore, a trial court lacks authority to enter an order not in compliance with the statutory provisions of the Illinois Marriage and Dissolution of Marriage Act, 750 ILCS 5/101 et seq. Trial courts are not prohibited from exercising equitable powers consistent with the Illinois Marriage and Dissolution of Marriage Act, 750 ILCS 5/101 et seq.; indeed, where no prior remedy exists, courts are empowered to create equitable remedies. In re Marriage of Ramsey, 339 Ill. App. 3d 752, 275 Ill. Dec. 106, 792 N.E.2d 337, 2003 Ill. App. LEXIS 725 (5 Dist. 2003).

—Third Party Actions

Once a trial court obtains jurisdiction, its ability to grant relief under the Illinois Marriage and Dissolution of Marriage Act is controlled by the provisions of the Act; however, the trial court's equity power is not limited to merely effectuating compliance with the Act, but it extends, when necessary, to comply with the dictates of the Act over third party actions. In re Isaacs, 260 Ill. App. 3d 423, 198 Ill. Dec. 169, 632 N.E.2d 228 (1 Dist.), appeal denied, 157 Ill. 2d 502, 205 Ill. Dec. 164, 642 N.E.2d 1281 (1994).

Presumption

—Marital Property

The trial court found that petitioner-husband had overcome the presumption of marital property and that bank accounts in question were held in joint tenancy solely for purposes of convenience because he was blind and after a review of the record, characterization of the bank accounts as nonmarital property was sufficiently clear, convincing and unmistakable to rebut the presumption of gift. In re Rink, 136 Ill. App. 3d 252, 91 Ill. Dec. 34, 483 N.E.2d 316 (1 Dist. 1985).

Public Policy

There is no sufficiently mandated public policy in this state, as expressed in this Act, other statutes, case law or constitutional provisions, on which to base an action for retaliatory discharge. McCluskey v. Clark Oil & Ref. Corp., 147 Ill. App. 3d 822, 101 Ill. Dec. 235, 498 N.E.2d 559 (1 Dist. 1986).

Purpose

With the repeal of the former Divorce Act (see now 750 ILCS 5/101 et seq.) and enactment of this Act, Illinois joined the national trend toward adoption of the Uniform Marriage and Divorce Act, which was designed to reduce the adversary trappings of marital dissolution. In re Van Zuidam, 162 Ill. App. 3d 942, 114 Ill. Dec. 176, 516 N.E.2d 331 (1 Dist. 1987), appeal denied, 117 Ill. Dec. 232, 520 N.E.2d 393 (Ill. 1988).

Statutory Jurisdiction

In a proceeding brought pursuant to this Act, the circuit court is without jurisdiction to enter orders relating to adoption and the termination of parental rights. Rhodes v. Rhodes, 326 Ill. App. 3d 386, 260 Ill. Dec. 175, 760 N.E.2d 592, 2001 Ill. App. LEXIS 1468 (2 Dist. 2001).

Where a trial court is hearing matters relating to the dissolution of a marriage, it is not acting within the unlimited jurisdiction conferred on it by the Constitution, but rather is limited to that jurisdiction granted in this Act. In re Robinson, 225 Ill. App. 3d 1037, 167 Ill. Dec. 1113, 588 N.E.2d 1243 (3 Dist. 1992).

Where a circuit court is hearing matters relating to dissolution of a marriage, it is not acting within the unlimited jurisdiction conferred upon it by the Constitution of Illinois; it is necessarily acting in accordance with the authority vested in it by the applicable provisions of this Act. In re Rifkin, 114 Ill. App. 3d 555, 70 Ill. Dec. 299, 449 N.E.2d 173 (1 Dist. 1983).

LEGAL PERIODICALS

Student Note: Abandoned Equity and the Best Interests of the Child: Why Illinois Courts Must Recognize Same-Sex Parents Seeking Visitation, 76 Chi.-Kent. L. Rev. 1933 (2001).

For article, "The Real Estate Lawyer's Divorce Primer and the Divorce Lawyer's Guide to Real Estate", see 86 Ill. B.J. 488 (1998).

For article, "Marriage Contracts and the Family Economy", see 93 NW U.L. Rev. 65 (1998).

For note, "No Longer Following the Rule of Thumb — What To Do With Domestic Torts and Divorce Claims," see 1997 U. Ill. L. Rev. 923.

For article, "The Right of Access to Child Custody and Dependency Cases," see 62 U. Chi. L. Rev. 857 (1996).

For comment, "Civil Enforcement of Jewish Marriage and Divorce: Constitutional Accommodation of a Religious Mandate," see 45 De Paul L. Rev. 493 (1996).

For article, "Conflict of Laws Rules and the Interstate Recognition of Same-Sex Marriages," 1995 U. Ill. L. Rev. 911.

For article, "Survey of Illinois Law: Family Law," 19 S. Ill. U.L.J. 819 (1995).

For article, "Divorce Practice: Doing the Right Thing," see 9 CBA Rec. 48 (1995).

For essay, "The Criminal Courtroom: Is It Child Proof?," see 26 Loy. U. Chi. L.J. 681 (1995).

For article, "Illinois Moves Toward Reviewable (Maybe Permanent?) Maintenance," see 81 Ill. B.J. 630 (1993).

For article, "Survey of Illinois Law: Family Law," see 17 S. Ill. U.L.J. 903 (1993).

For article, "Divorce and the Displaced Homemaker: A Discourse on Playing with Dolls, Partnership Buyouts and Dissociation Under No-Fault," see 60 U. Chi. L. Rev. 67 (1993).

For article, "Divorce Illinois Style: Ten Years Under the Marriage and Dissolution of Marriage Act," see 75 Ill. B.J. 606 (1987).

For article, "Spafford v. Coats: An Alternative to Palimony," see 74 Ill. B.J. 286 (1986).

For article, "Irrationally Held Truths: A Mildly Iconoclastic Look at the Illinois Marriage and Dissolution of Marriage Act," see 70 Ill. B.J. 628 (1982).

For article, "Classification of Property Upon Dissolution of Marriage: Suggestions For Maintaining Our Dual System, In the Aftermath of Smith, 86 Ill.2d 518, 427 N.E.2d 1239 (1981)," see 71 Ill. B.J. 100 (1982).

For note, "Divorce and Marital Property — In re Marriage of Smith, 86 Ill.2d 518, 427 N.E.2d 1239 (1981)," see 71 Ill. B.J. 134 (1982).

For article, "Transmutation and Commingling: The Supreme Court's Rebuttable Presumption of Marital Property," see 71 Ill. B.J. 220 (1982).

For note, "Divorce Law and Property Division — In re Roger B., 118 N.E.2d 757 (1981)," see 70 Ill. B.J. 260 (1981).

For article, "Wisconsin, Illinois, Ontario — Three Roads to Marital Property Law Reform," see 12 Loy. U. Chi. L.J. 1 (1980-81).

For note, "Family Law, Property Rights — Hewitt v. Hewitt, 77 Ill.2d 49, 394 N.E.2d 1204 (1979)," see 69 Ill. B.J. 49 (1980).

For note, "Federal Income Tax Consequences of Appreciated Property Transfers Under the Illinois Marriage and Dissolution of Marriage Act," see 27 De Paul L. Rev. 815 (1978).

For note, "Best Interest of the Child in Custody Proceedings and Waiver of Jurisdictional Objection — Sommer v. Bororis," see 27 De Paul L. Rev. 853 (1978).

For article, "Marital Property, Top Ramification, and Maintenance Practice Under the Illinois Marriage and Dissolution of Marriage Act — A Comparative Study," see 66 Ill. B.J. 324 (1978).

For article, "Attorney Fees for Services Rendered in the Prosecution or Defense of Appeals from Post-Decree Divorce Proceeding," see 66 Ill. B.J. 568 (1978).

For article, "The Illinois Marriage and Dissolution Act: New Solutions to Old Problems," see 12 J. Marshall J. Prac. & Proc. 1 (1978).

For article, "Hewitt v. Hewitt: Middle America, Marvin and Common Law Marriage," see 60 Chi. B. Rec. 84 (1978).

For comments, "Federal Tax Law: Where Your Divorce Does Make a Difference," see 9 Loy. U. Chi. L.J. (1977-78).

750 ILCS 5/102 Purposes; Rules of Construction

Sec. 102. *Purposes; Rules of Construction.* This Act shall be liberally construed and applied to promote its underlying purposes, which are to:

(1) provide adequate procedures for the solemnization and registration of marriage;

(2) strengthen and preserve the integrity of marriage and safeguard family relationships;

(3) promote the amicable settlement of disputes that have arisen between parties to a marriage;

(4) mitigate the potential harm to the spouses and their children caused by the process of legal dissolution of marriage;

(5) make reasonable provision for spouses and minor children during and after litigation, including provision for timely awards of interim fees to achieve substantial parity in parties' access to funds for litigation costs;

(6) eliminate the consideration of marital misconduct in the adjudication of rights and duties incident to the legal dissolution of marriage, legal separation and declaration of invalidity of marriage;

(7) secure the maximum involvement and cooperation of both parents regarding the physical, mental, moral and emotional well-being of the children during and after the litigation; and

(8) make provision for the preservation and conservation of assets during the litigation.

(Source: P.A. 87-881; 89-712, § 5.)

Note.

This section was Ill.Rev.Stat., Ch. 40, para. 102.

Effect of Amendments.

The 1996 amendment by P.A. 89-712, effective June 1, 1997, in subsection (5) added at the end "including provision for timely awards of interim fees to achieve substantial parity in parties' access to funds for litigation costs".

CASE NOTES

Analysis

Dissolution of Marriage
Income History
Parent's Rights
Policy Conflicts
Purpose
Remand
Retaliatory Discharge
Unmarried Cohabitation
Use of Parties' Resources

Dissolution of Marriage

The legislature has recognized both the short term and long range effects of dissolution on the parties, and has expressly provided the means and methods to mitigate the potential harm to the spouses and children caused by the process of dissolution of marriage, and to make reasonable provision for the spouses and minor children during and after litigation. In re Thompson, 79 Ill. App. 3d 310, 34 Ill. Dec. 342, 398 N.E.2d 17 (1 Dist. 1979); In re Schroeder, 215 Ill. App. 3d 156, 158 Ill. Dec. 721, 574 N.E.2d 834 (4 Dist.), cert. denied, 141 Ill. 2d 560, 162 Ill. Dec. 508, 580 N.E.2d 134 (1991).

Income History

While it is appropriate to consider prior years' documentation to ascertain income trends when future income is uncertain, deviations from reliable current income data require a compelling showing of a definitive pattern of economic reversals. In re Schroeder, 215 Ill. App. 3d 156, 158 Ill. Dec. 721, 574 N.E.2d 834 (4 Dist.), cert. denied, 141 Ill. 2d 560, 162 Ill. Dec. 508, 580 N.E.2d 134 (1991).

Parent's Rights

Any common law rights parents may have had, which would have allowed them to recover for expenses incurred on behalf of their children, have been abrogated by 750 ILCS 65/15, and by this Act — the former applicable prior to divorce and the latter thereafter. In re Van Winkle, 107 Ill. App. 3d 73, 62 Ill. Dec. 831, 437 N.E.2d 358 (3 Dist. 1982).

Policy Conflicts

Judicial recognition of mutual property rights between unmarried cohabitants would clearly violate the policy of this Act. Hewitt v. Hewitt, 77 Ill. 2d 49, 31 Ill. Dec. 827, 394 N.E.2d 1204 (1979).

Purpose

A trial court's examination of a removal petition should be guided by the policies of the Illinois Marriage and Dissolution of Marriage Act, one of which is to secure the maximum involvement and cooperation of both parents regarding the physical, mental, moral, and emotional well-being of the children during and after the litigation. In re Marriage of Collingbourne, 204 Ill. 2d 498, 274 Ill. Dec. 440, 791 N.E.2d 532, 2003 Ill. LEXIS 780 (2003).

The purpose of this Act is to strengthen and preserve the integrity of marriage and safeguard family relationships. In re Davenport, 92 Ill. App. 3d 675, 48 Ill. Dec. 193, 416 N.E.2d 88 (4 Dist. 1981).

The intention of this Act is to foster and provide for the proper educational needs of adult children. Faust v. Faust, 100 Ill. App. 3d 232, 55 Ill. Dec. 669, 426 N.E.2d 994 (1 Dist. 1981).

Remand

The division of marital property is among those factors which must be considered in determining the amount of maintenance, child support, and attorney fees; therefore, all interrelated property and support issues were remanded where a marital asset was not properly considered at the time of the original disposition. In re Olsher, 78 Ill. App. 3d 627, 34 Ill. Dec. 32, 397 N.E.2d 488 (1 Dist. 1979).

Retaliatory Discharge

This Act is clearly intended to regulate parties to a marriage and

Retaliatory Discharge (Cont'd)
divorce, and not intended to regulate conduct of employers, and does not provide any basis for a claim of retaliatory discharge. McCluskey v. Clark Oil & Ref. Corp., 147 Ill. App. 3d 822, 101 Ill. Dec. 235, 498 N.E.2d 559 (1 Dist. 1986).

Unmarried Cohabitation
Claim for vehicles purchased during a period of cohabitation by unmarried parties is allowed where the claim is not founded simply on proof of cohabitation or plaintiff's performance of domestic services, and where permitting the defendant to retain vehicles would constitute an unjust enrichment. Spafford v. Coats, 118 Ill. App. 3d 566, 74 Ill. Dec. 211, 455 N.E.2d 241 (2 Dist. 1983).

Judicial recognition of claims of unmarried cohabitant which are substantially independent of the nonmarital relationship and not based on rights arising from cohabitation does not indicate court approval or legal recognition of the nonmarital relationship and does not violate public policy. Spafford v. Coats, 118 Ill. App. 3d 566, 74 Ill. Dec. 211, 455 N.E.2d 241 (2 Dist. 1983).

Use of Parties' Resources
This Act is to be liberally construed and any resources available to the parties are to be used to promote the underlying purposes of the Act, which include making reasonable provision for spouses and minor children during and after litigation. In re Brand, 123 Ill. App. 3d 1047, 79 Ill. Dec. 483, 463 N.E.2d 1037 (4 Dist. 1984).

LEGAL PERIODICALS

For article, "'Leveling the Playing Field' in Divorce: Questions and Answers About the New Law," see 85 Ill. B.J. 410 (1997).

For article, "Family Law: 1985-86 Survey," see 11 S. Ill. U.L.J. 741 (1987).

For article, "An Interpretation of Illinois New Joint Custody Amendments," see 75 Ill. B.J. 332 (1986).

For article, "Hewitt v. Hewitt: Non-Marital Cohabitation and the Doctrine of Immorality," see Ill. B.J. 368 (1981).

For article, "Caveat Amator: 'The State of Affairs' in Illinois After Hewitt v. Hewitt," see 29 De Paul L. Rev. 493 (1980).

For note, "Family Law, Property Rights — Hewitt v. Hewitt, 77 Ill.2d 49, 394 N.E.2d 1204 (1979)," see 69 Ill. B.J. 49 (1980).

750 ILCS 5/103 Trial by Jury

Sec. 103. *Trial by Jury.* There shall be no trial by jury under this Act.
(Source: P.A. 80-923.)

Note.
This section was Ill.Rev.Stat., Ch. 40, para. 103.

CASE NOTES

Chancery Action
Where plaintiff wife acknowledged the validity of a prior Arkansas divorce decree, and her complaint was concerned solely with alimony, property division and attorney fees under the former Divorce Act (see now 750 ILCS 5/101 et seq.), defendant husband had no common law right to a jury trial, as such actions were traditionally chancery actions, and the right arose only if it was expressly conferred by statute. Sidwell v. Sidwell, 28 Ill. App. 3d 580, 328 N.E.2d 595 (4 Dist. 1975).

LEGAL PERIODICALS

For note, "No Longer Following the Rule of Thumb — What To Do With Domestic Torts and Divorce Claims," see 1997 U. Ill. L. Rev. 923.

RESEARCH REFERENCES

Right to jury trial in state court divorce proceedings. 56 ALR4th 955.

750 ILCS 5/104 Venue

Sec. 104. *Venue.* The proceedings shall be had in the county where the plaintiff or defendant resides, except as otherwise provided herein, but process may be directed to any county in the State. Objection to venue is barred if not made within such time as the defendant's response is due. In no event shall venue be deemed jurisdictional.
(Source: P.A. 82-716.)

Note.
This section was Ill.Rev.Stat., Ch. 40, para. 104.

CASE NOTES

Analysis

In General
Appeal
—Pleadings
Dismissal
—Similar Action
Improper Venue
—Notice
Jurisdiction
—In General
—Fraudulent
—Presumption
Legislative Intent
Mandatory Requirement
Objection Barred
—Original Decree
Residence
—Adultery
—Effect of Decree
—Illustrative Cases
—Meaning
—Omission
Separate Maintenance Action
—Residence
—Statutory
Waiver

In General
The predecessor section did not relate solely to venue, but imposed jurisdictional requirements. People ex rel. Bradley v. McAuliffe, 24 Ill. 2d 75, 179 N.E.2d 616 (1962).

Appeal

—Pleadings
Under former section 6 of the Divorce Act (see now this section) and former sections 22, 23, and 23.2 of the Separate Maintenance Act (see now 750 ILCS 5/402, 750 ILCS 5/504, and 750 ILCS 5/410), former section 50(2) of the Civil Practice Act (see now 735 ILCS 5/2-1301), concerning appealability of claims, was held applicable, and an aggrieved party could appeal an order allowing temporary alimony without having the order state, in accordance with the statute, that there was not just reason for delaying enforcement or appeal. Micelli v. Micelli, 45 Ill. App. 2d 159, 195 N.E.2d 233 (1 Dist. 1963).

Dismissal

—Similar Action
Defendant's motion to dismiss a divorce action because of the pendency of a similar action between the same parties in the courts of Lebanon, which was instituted by plaintiff, was denied, since laws of foreign countries are not subject to judicial notice. Farah v. Farah, 25 Ill. App. 3d 481, 323 N.E.2d 361 (1 Dist. 1975).

Improper Venue

—Notice
It is incumbent upon parties to timely advise the court that the

Improper Venue (Cont'd)

—Notice (Cont'd)
forum selected is not one of proper venue and, having apprised the court of this, to attempt to secure an appropriate order from the court allowing a waiver of improper venue. In re Jones, 104 Ill. App. 3d 490, 60 Ill. Dec. 214, 432 N.E.2d 1113 (1 Dist. 1982).

Jurisdiction

—In General
Courts have no inherent equity power in divorce and separate maintenance actions; jurisdiction to hear and determine such cases and all related matters is conferred only by statute and the power of the court may be exercised only within the limits of the statutory grant of jurisdiction. Chrastka v. Chrastka, 2 Ill. App. 3d 722, 277 N.E.2d 729 (2 Dist. 1971).

—Fraudulent
A divorce decree will not be set aside upon the ground that it was obtained by false evidence, but only for fraud that gives the court colorable jurisdiction. Goldberg v. Goldberg, 288 Ill. App. 203, 5 N.E.2d 863 (2 Dist. 1937).

—Presumption
Jurisdictional challenge that was alleged in a complaint and admitted on motion, and subsequently collaterally attacked by way of an annulment proceeding in which plaintiff wife had testified she was married in Indiana to her first husband, did not defeat the presumption that the Indiana court had jurisdiction, which was not open to collateral attack, and thus the case in Illinois was dismissed. Cullen v. Stevens, 389 Ill. 35, 58 N.E.2d 456 (1944).

Legislative Intent
It is reasonable to assume that the legislature did not intend to confer upon parties to a dissolution proceeding the unfettered right to select any forum, and possibly an appellate district, and the meaning of the legislature is free from doubt and ambiguity; the only legitimate function of the court is to give it effect as written. In re Jones, 104 Ill. App. 3d 490, 60 Ill. Dec. 214, 432 N.E.2d 1113 (1 Dist. 1982).

Mandatory Requirement
This section is not an idle directive from the legislature which may be disregarded as the parties choose. In re Sales, 106 Ill. App. 3d 378, 62 Ill. Dec. 441, 436 N.E.2d 23 (1 Dist. 1982).

Objection Barred

—Original Decree
It was proper for a trial court to deny a motion for change of venue with reference to that portion of defendant's position which asked that the original decree of divorce be vacated. Kilbride v. Kilbride, 64 Ill. App. 2d 355, 212 N.E.2d 252 (1 Dist. 1965).

Residence

—Adultery
Where plaintiff committed adultery in county, plaintiff could properly invoke the jurisdiction of the court in her separate maintenance suit, without being a resident of that county, if her husband resided there, and even if he had only resided there for the last six months. Garrison v. Garrison, 107 Ill. App. 2d 311, 246 N.E.2d 9 (2 Dist. 1969).

—Effect of Decree
Where a divorce decree was proper on its face, it could not be declared null and void despite a plaintiff's contention that neither the plaintiff nor the defendant were ever residents of the county. LaSalle National Bank v. Strotz, 98 Ill. App. 2d 425, 240 N.E.2d 335 (1 Dist. 1968).

—Illustrative Cases
Plaintiff's mere presence within a county for the two months during which she was receiving treatment there could not make her a resident within the meaning of this section. Meyer v. Meyer, 333 Ill. App. 450, 77 N.E.2d 556 (1 Dist. 1948).

For purposes of filing a bill of divorce, two months' presence in a sanitarium was insufficient to constitute residence in the county in which the sanitarium was located, where such county was different from that of party's home. Meyer v. Meyer, 328 Ill. App. 408, 66 N.E.2d 457 (1 Dist. 1946).

—Meaning
The word "residence" may have a variety of meanings; it does not mean the same as "domicile", but denotes permanent abode. Garrison v. Garrison, 107 Ill. App. 2d 311, 246 N.E.2d 9 (2 Dist. 1969).

In order to establish a new residence, a person must abandon a former one and take up a new residence with an animus manendi; something more than a mere existence in the county is required. Meyer v. Meyer, 328 Ill. App. 408, 66 N.E.2d 457 (1 Dist. 1946).

—Omission
The omission of any mention of venue in an action for divorce and separate maintenance is not necessarily fatal, as it may be supplied by amendment before decree upon remand to the trial court. Chrastka v. Chrastka, 2 Ill. App. 3d 722, 277 N.E.2d 729 (2 Dist. 1971).

Separate Maintenance Action

—Residence
Where defendant in his answer admitted residence in the county alleged in the complaint, venue in that county was properly established for purposes of bringing the separate maintenance action by amendment to the divorce proceeding. Sidwell v. Sidwell, 75 Ill. App. 2d 133, 220 N.E.2d 479 (4 Dist. 1966).

—Statutory
Action for separate maintenance is a purely statutory action and was unknown to the common law. Micelli v. Micelli, 45 Ill. App. 2d 159, 195 N.E.2d 233 (1 Dist. 1963).

Waiver
Venue generally is not jurisdictional and can be waived; therefore, a divorce decree could not be overturned on the premise that it was entered in a county of which neither party was a resident. In re Heady, 115 Ill. App. 3d 126, 71 Ill. Dec. 27, 450 N.E.2d 462 (5 Dist. 1983).

The requirement of plaintiff's residence in the county in which suit is brought is not waived by failure to make objection in the trial court, but may be raised for the first time on appeal. People ex rel. Bradley v. McAuliffe, 24 Ill. 2d 75, 179 N.E.2d 616 (1962).

RESEARCH REFERENCES

Doctrine of forum non conveniens: Assumption or denial of jurisdiction of action involving matrimonial dispute. 55 ALR5th 647.

750 ILCS 5/105 Application of Civil Practice Law

Sec. 105. *Application of Civil Practice Law.* (a) The provisions of the Civil Practice Law [735 ILCS 5/2-101 et seq.] shall apply to all proceedings under this Act, except as otherwise provided in this Act.

(b) A proceeding for dissolution of marriage, legal separation or declaration of invalidity of marriage shall be entitled "In re the Marriage of .... and ....". A custody or support proceeding shall be entitled "In re the (Custody) (Support) of ....".

(c) The initial pleading in all proceedings under this Act shall be denominated a petition. A responsive pleading shall be denominated a response. All other pleadings under this Act shall be denominated as provided in the Civil Practice Law [735 ILCS 5/2-101 et seq.].

(Source: P.A. 82-783.)

Note.
This section was Ill.Rev.Stat., Ch. 40, para. 105.

CASE NOTES

ANALYSIS

Amendment
Failure to Comply
Summons
Timeliness

Amendment

Effective January 1, 1984, the Code of Civil Procedure was amended to permit pleadings to be verified by certification via the Civil Practice Law (735 ILCS 5/2-101 et seq.); the amendment was made applicable to this Act by this section and 750 ILCS 5/410 of the Act. In re Betts, 172 Ill. App. 3d 742, 122 Ill. Dec. 599, 526 N.E.2d 1138 (4 Dist. 1988).

Failure to Comply

Failure by appellee to comply with the rules of the appellate court made it unnecessary for the case to be discussed in full; the order vacating the decree of separate maintenance was reversed. Latronica v. Latronica, 97 Ill. App. 2d 332, 240 N.E.2d 458 (1 Dist. 1968).

Summons

The clerk of the circuit court had no authority under the former Divorce Act (see now 750 ILCS 5/101 et seq.) or the former Chancery Act (see now 735 ILCS 5/1-101 et seq.) to issue a summons on the day prior to the day the bill was filed, and the summons so issued was void. Landgraf v. Landgraf, 337 Ill. 451, 169 N.E. 175 (1929).

Timeliness

Where petitioner wife's motion to modify order of support was filed on the same date that judgment of dissolution was entered, it was timely filed pursuant to 750 ILCS 5/2-1203 and was properly addressed by the court. In re Pillot, 145 Ill. App. 3d 293, 99 Ill. Dec. 512, 495 N.E.2d 1247 (1 Dist. 1986).

750 ILCS 5/106 Employment of Administrative Aides

Sec. 106. *Employment of Administrative Aides.* The employment of qualified administrative aides to assist the court of any county in the administration of proceedings hereunder may be provided for by such county as the case may be. All such aides shall be appointed by the authority which provided for them, subject to the approval of a majority of the judges of each court involved, and shall serve for such terms and shall receive such compensation as provided by ordinance.

(a) The administrative aides shall perform such nonjudicial duties with respect to proceedings hereunder and matters ancillary thereto as the court shall direct.

(b) Any county may make such appropriations as may be necessary to provide for the expense and compensation of the administrative aides.

(Source: P.A. 80-923.)

Note.

This section was Ill.Rev.Stat., Ch. 40, para. 106.

LEGAL PERIODICALS

For article, "Child Custody: Evolution of Current Criteria," see 26 De Paul L. Rev. 241 (1977).

750 ILCS 5/107 Order of protection; status

Sec. 107. *Order of protection; status.* Whenever relief is sought under Part V, Part VI or Part VII of this Act, the court, before granting relief, shall determine whether any order of protection has previously been entered in the instant proceeding or any other proceeding in which any party, or a child of any party, or both, if relevant, has been designated as either a respondent or a protected person.

(Source: P.A. 87-743.)

Note.

This section was Ill.Rev.Stat., Ch. 40, para. 107.

PART II.
MARRIAGE

750 ILCS 5/201 Formalities

Sec. 201. *Formalities.* A marriage between a man and a woman licensed, solemnized and registered as provided in this Act is valid in this State.

(Source: P.A. 80-923.)

Note.

This section was Ill.Rev.Stat., Ch. 40, para. 201.

CASE NOTES

ANALYSIS

Ceremony
Consent
—Common Law
Same-Sex Marriage

Ceremony

Persons who had a marriage certificate from this state but never underwent a ceremony were not married under Illinois law. Farrell v. Peters, 951 F.2d 862 (7th Cir. 1992).

Consent

—Common Law

At common law the age of consent for marriage in the case of males was 14 years and in the case of females, 12 years; an attempt of an infant under seven years of age to contract in marriage was nugatory and without legal significance, but the marriage of an infant over seven years of age but below the legal consent was not absolutely void but was a voidable marriage. Long v. Long, 15 Ill. App. 2d 276, 145 N.E.2d 509 (2 Dist. 1957).

Same-Sex Marriage

Birth certificate changing petitioner's designation from female to male was insufficient basis to argue that surgical sexual transformation processes that had never been completed justified such a change in designation, where the registrar had not inquired beyond a doctor's affidavit that petitioner's doctor admitted having completed in order to help petitioner out; therefore, petitioner's marriage to a woman had never been valid, and the mere issuance of a new certificate did not remove the impediment to that marriage. In re Simmons, Ill. App. 3d , Ill. Dec. , N.E.2d , 2005 Ill. App. LEXIS 127 (1 Dist. Feb. 16, 2005).

The court did not have the authority to consider a relationship that at the time of its inception, did not carry with it the consequences of a legal marriage; as a result, petitioner could not be elevated to spousal status and was not entitled to a spousal share of same-sex partner's estate, and constitutional challenge to proscription of same-sex marriages was a moot issue. In re Estate of

Same-Sex Marriage (Cont'd)
Hall, 302 Ill. App. 3d 829, 236 Ill. Dec. 356, 707 N.E.2d 201 (1 Dist. 1998).

LEGAL PERIODICALS

For comment, "Civil Enforcement of Jewish Marriage and Divorce: Constitutional Accommodation of a Religious Mandate," see 45 De Paul L. Rev. 493 (1996).

For article, "Conflict of Laws Rules and the Interstate Recognition of Same-Sex Marriages," 1995 U. Ill. L. Rev. 911.

For case note, "Hewitt v. Hewitt — Property Rights of Unmarried Cohabitors upon Dissolution of Relationship," see 1980 U. Ill. L.J. 525.

For case note, "Hewitt v. Hewitt — Contract Cohabitation and 'Equitable Expectations' Relief for Meretricious Spouses," see 12 J. Marshall J. Prac. & Proc. 435 (1979).

RESEARCH REFERENCES

Validity of marriage as affected by lack of legal authority of person solemnizing it. 13 ALR4th 1323.

750 ILCS 5/202 Marriage License and Marriage Certificate

Sec. 202. *Marriage License and Marriage Certificate.* (a) The Director of Public Health shall prescribe the form for an application for a marriage license, which shall include the following information:

(1) name, sex, occupation, address, social security number, date and place of birth of each party to the proposed marriage;

(2) if either party was previously married, his name, and the date, place and court in which the marriage was dissolved or declared invalid or the date and place of death of the former spouse;

(3) name and address of the parents or guardian of each party; and

(4) whether the parties are related to each other and, if so, their relationship.

(b) The Director of Public Health shall prescribe the forms for the marriage license, the marriage certificate and, when necessary, the consent to marriage.
(Source: P.A. 80-923.)

Note.
This section was Ill.Rev.Stat., Ch. 40, para. 202.

750 ILCS 5/203 License to Marry

Sec. 203. *License to Marry.* When a marriage application has been completed and signed by both parties to a prospective marriage and both parties have appeared before the county clerk and the marriage license fee has been paid, the county clerk shall issue a license to marry and a marriage certificate form upon being furnished:

(1) satisfactory proof that each party to the marriage will have attained the age of 18 years at the time the marriage license is effective or will have attained the age of 16 years and has either the consent to the marriage of both parents or his guardian or judicial approval; provided, if one parent cannot be located in order to obtain such consent and diligent efforts have been made to locate that parent by the consenting parent, then the consent of one parent plus a signed affidavit by the consenting parent which (i) names the absent parent and states that he or she cannot be located, and (ii) states what diligent efforts have been made to locate the absent parent, shall have the effect of both parents' consent for purposes of this Section;

(2) satisfactory proof that the marriage is not prohibited; and

(3) an affidavit or record as prescribed in subparagraph (1) of Section 205 [750 ILCS 5/205] or a court order as prescribed in subparagraph (2) of Section 205 [750 ILCS 5/205], if applicable.

With each marriage license, the county clerk shall provide a pamphlet describing the causes and effects of fetal alcohol syndrome.
(Source: P.A. 86-832; 86-884; 86-1028.)

Note.
This section was Ill.Rev.Stat., Ch. 40, para. 203.

CASE NOTES

ANALYSIS

Consent
—Ratification or Repudiation
Obligation of Minor
—As Parent

Consent

—Ratification or Repudiation

One who marries before reaching the age of consent may avoid the marriage on reaching the age of consent, but such marriages are binding and valid until disaffirmed or until annulled by a judicial decree; when a party to such a voidable marriage reaches the age of consent, he may elect to ratify or repudiate the contract, and having elected to affirm, he may not thereafter disaffirm. Long v. Long, 15 Ill. App. 2d 276, 145 N.E.2d 509 (2 Dist. 1957).

Obligation of Minor

—As Parent

Where a minor contracts a voidable marriage, he assumes the same obligations which the law imposes on an adult so far as the issue of the marriage is concerned; if a marriage is voidable because of non-age of the husband, he may be relieved of his obligations as a husband, but his obligations as a father are enforceable. Long v. Long, 15 Ill. App. 2d 276, 145 N.E.2d 509 (2 Dist. 1957).

750 ILCS 5/204 Medical information brochure

Sec. 204. *Medical information brochure.* The county clerk shall distribute free of charge, to all persons applying for a marriage license, a brochure prepared by the Department of Public Health concerning sexually transmitted diseases and inherited metabolic diseases.
(Source: P.A. 86-884.)

Note.
This section was Ill.Rev.Stat., Ch. 40, para. 204.

CASE NOTES

Marriage License

Because the direction to the county clerk to issue a marriage license was directory only and not prohibitive, a marriage celebrated without complying with the license requirements of former Ill.Rev.Stat., ch. 89, para. 6a (see now this section and 750 ILCS 5/205) was not null and void. Boysen v. Boysen, 301 Ill. App. 573, 23 N.E.2d 231 (1 Dist. 1939).

750 ILCS 5/205 Exceptions

Sec. 205. *Exceptions.* (1) Irrespective of the results of laboratory tests and clinical examination relative to sexually transmitted diseases, the clerks of the respective counties shall issue a marriage license to parties to a proposed marriage (a) when a woman is pregnant at the time of such application, or (b) when a woman has, prior to the time of application, given birth to an illegitimate child which is living at the time of such application and the man making such application makes affidavit that he is the father of such illegitimate child. The county clerk shall, in lieu of the health certificate required hereunder, accept, as the case may be, either an affidavit on a form prescribed by the State Department of Public Health, signed by a physician duly licensed in this State, stating that the woman is pregnant, or a copy of the birth record of the illegitimate child, if one is available in this State, or if such birth record is not available, an affidavit signed by the woman that she is the mother of such child.

(2) Any judge of the circuit court within the county in which the license is to be issued is authorized and empowered on joint application by both applicants for a marriage license to waive the requirements as to medical examination, laboratory tests, and certificates, except the requirements of paragraph (4) of subsection (a) of Section 212 of this Act [750 ILCS 5/212] which shall not be waived; and to authorize the county clerk to issue the license if all other requirements of law have been complied with and the judge is satisfied, by affidavit, or other proof, that the examination or tests are contrary to the tenets or practices of the religious creed of which the applicant is an adherent, and that the public health and welfare will not be injuriously affected thereby.
(Source: P.A. 85-493; 89-187, § 70.)

Note.

This section was Ill.Rev.Stat., Ch. 40, para. 205.

Effect of Amendments.

The 1995 amendment by P.A. 89-187, effective July 19, 1995, in subsection (1), in the first sentence, substituted "sexually transmitted diseases" for "venereal diseases".

CASE NOTES

Marriage License

Because the direction to the county clerk to issue a marriage license was directory only and not prohibitive, a marriage celebrated without complying with the license requirements of former Ill.Rev.Stat., ch. 89, para. 6a (see now this section and 750 ILCS 5/204) was not null and void. Boysen v. Boysen, 301 Ill. App. 573, 23 N.E.2d 231 (1 Dist. 1939).

750 ILCS 5/206 Records

Sec. 206. *Records.* Any health certificate filed with the county clerk, or any certificate, affidavit, or record accepted in lieu thereof, shall be retained in the files of the office for one year after the license is issued and shall thereafter be destroyed by the county clerk.
(Source: P.A. 82-561.)

Note.

This section was Ill.Rev.Stat., Ch. 40, para. 206.

750 ILCS 5/207 Effective Date of License

Sec. 207. *Effective Date of License.* A license to marry becomes effective in the county where it was issued one day after the date of issuance, unless the court orders that the license is effective when issued, and expires 60 days after it becomes effective.
(Source: P.A. 81-397.)

Note.

This section was Ill.Rev.Stat., Ch. 40, para. 207.

CASE NOTES

Waiting Period

Failure to observe the one day waiting period of this section did not void the marriage. Pape v. Byre, 197 Ill. App. 3d 836, 144 Ill. Dec. 309, 555 N.E.2d 428 (4 Dist. 1990), rev'd on other grounds, 145 Ill. 2d 13, 163 Ill. Dec. 898, 582 N.E.2d 165 (1991).

750 ILCS 5/208 Judicial Approval of Underage Marriages

Sec. 208. *Judicial Approval of Underage Marriages.* (a) The court, after a reasonable effort has been made to notify the parents or guardian of each underaged party, may order the county clerk to issue a marriage license and a marriage certificate form to a party aged 16 or 17 years who has no parent capable of consenting to his marriage or whose parent or guardian has not consented to his marriage.

(b) A marriage license and a marriage certificate form may be issued under this Section only if the court finds that the underaged party is capable of assuming the responsibilities of marriage and the marriage will serve his best interest. Pregnancy alone does not establish that the best interest of the party will be served.
(Source: P.A. 80-923.)

Note.

This section was Ill.Rev.Stat., Ch. 40, para. 208.

CASE NOTES

ANALYSIS

Constitutionality
Annulment
Illustrative Case

Constitutionality

Former section 3(b) of the Marriage Act (see now this section) was held to be unconstitutional in that it discriminated in age requirements between males and females. Phelps v. Bing, 58 Ill. 2d 32, 316 N.E.2d 775 (1974).

Annulment

The purpose of an annulment proceeding is to have a marriage which is void or voidable judicially declared void; in such a proceeding, the marriage is not recognized, the theory being that no valid marriage ever came into existence. Long v. Long, 15 Ill. App. 2d 276, 145 N.E.2d 509 (2 Dist. 1957).

Illustrative Case

In a case decided under former law, the findings of a chancellor that the marriage of the parties, under the facts and the applicable law, was a valid marriage and not voidable was not error. Long v. Long, 15 Ill. App. 2d 276, 145 N.E.2d 509 (2 Dist. 1957).

750 ILCS 5/209 Solemnization and Registration

Sec. 209. *Solemnization and Registration.* (a) A marriage may be solemnized by a judge of a court of record, by a retired judge of a court of record, unless the retired judge was removed from office by the Judicial Inquiry Board, except that a retired judge shall not receive any compensation from the State, a county or any unit of local government in return for the solemnization of a marriage and there shall be no effect upon any pension benefits conferred by the Judges Retirement System of Illinois, by a judge of the Court of Claims, by a county clerk in counties having 2,000,000 or more inhabitants, by a public official whose powers include solemnization of marriages, or in accordance with the prescriptions of any religious denomination, Indian Nation or Tribe or Native Group, provided that when such prescriptions require an officiant, the officiant be in good standing with his religious denomination, Indian Nation or Tribe or Native Group. Either the person solemnizing the marriage, or, if no individual acting alone solemnized the marriage, both parties to the marriage, shall complete the marriage certificate form and forward it to the county clerk within 10 days after such marriage is solemnized.

(b) The solemnization of the marriage is not invalidated by the fact that the person solemnizing the marriage was not legally qualified to solemnize it, if either party to the marriage believed him to be so qualified.

(Source: P.A. 83-226; 87-1261, § 4.)

Note.

This section was Ill.Rev.Stat., Ch. 40, para. 209.

CASE NOTES

Analysis

Marriage by Proxy
Marriage License

Marriage by Proxy

Marriage by proxy is not recognized in Illinois. In re Estate of Crockett, 32 Ill. App. 3d 1167, 245 Ill. Dec. 683, 728 N.E.2d 765, 2000 Ill. App. LEXIS 251 (2000).

Marriage License

A duly ordained priest of the Catholic church has the authority to perform a marriage ceremony, and such marriage was valid notwithstanding there was no marriage license. Haderaski v. Haderaski, 415 Ill. 118, 112 N.E.2d 714 (1953).

RESEARCH REFERENCES

Validity of marriage as affected by lack of legal authority of person solemnizing it. 13 ALR4th 1323.

750 ILCS 5/210 Registration of Marriage Certificate

Sec. 210. *Registration of Marriage Certificate.* Upon receipt of the marriage certificate, the county clerk shall register the marriage. Within 45 days after the close of the month in which a marriage is registered, the county clerk shall make to the Department of Public Health a return of such marriage. Such return shall be made on a form furnished by the Department of Public Health and shall substantially consist of the following items:

(1) A copy of the marriage license application signed and attested to by the applicants, except that in any county in which the information provided in a marriage license application is entered into a computer, the county clerk may submit a computer copy of such information without the signatures and attestations of the applicants.

(2) The date and place of marriage.

(3) The marriage license number.

(Source: P.A. 85-1307.)

Note.

This section was Ill.Rev.Stat., Ch. 40, para. 210.

750 ILCS 5/211 Reporting

Sec. 211. *Reporting.* In transmitting the required returns, the county clerk shall make a report to the Department of Public Health stating the total number of marriage licenses issued during the month for which returns are made, and the number of marriage certificates registered during the month.

(Source: P.A. 80-923.)

Note.

This section was Ill.Rev.Stat., Ch. 40, para. 211.

750 ILCS 5/212 Prohibited Marriages

Sec. 212. *Prohibited Marriages.* (a) The following marriages are prohibited:

(1) a marriage entered into prior to the dissolution of an earlier marriage of one of the parties;

(2) a marriage between an ancestor and a descendant or between a brother and a sister, whether the relationship is by the half or the whole blood or by adoption;

(3) a marriage between an uncle and a niece or between an aunt and a nephew, whether the relationship is by the half or the whole blood;

(4) a marriage between cousins of the first degree; however, a marriage between first cousins is not prohibited if:

(i) both parties are 50 years of age or older; or

(ii) either party, at the time of application for a marriage license, presents for filing with the county clerk of the county in which the marriage is to be solemnized, a certificate signed by a licensed physician stating that the party to the proposed marriage is permanently and irreversibly sterile;

(5) a marriage between 2 individuals of the same sex.

(b) Parties to a marriage prohibited under subsection (a) of this Section who cohabit after removal of the impediment are lawfully married as of the date of the removal of the impediment.

(c) Children born or adopted of a prohibited or common law marriage are legitimate.

(Source: P.A. 85-493; 89-459, § 5.)

Note.

This section was Ill.Rev.Stat., Ch. 40, para. 212.

Effect of Amendments.

The 1996 amendment by P.A. 89-459, effective May 24, 1996, in subdivision (a)(4)(ii) substituted a semicolon for a period at the end; and added subdivision (a)(5).

CASE NOTES

ANALYSIS

Constitutionality
Applicability
Bigamous Marriage
—Impediment Removed
Cohabitation
Common Law Marriage
—Invalid
Consent Requirement
Cousins
—Construction
—Illustrative Cases
—Meaning
Legislative Intent
Legitimacy of Children
Putative Spouse
Same-Sex Marriage
Scienter
Validity
—Impediments Removed
—Presumed

Constitutionality

Subdivisions (a)(1) and (b) of this section are not unconstitutionally vague or indefinite. Long v. Schisler, 81 Ill. App. 3d 280, 36 Ill. Dec. 620, 401 N.E.2d 301 (3 Dist. 1980).

Applicability

Prior to decedent's 1977 divorce, his subsequent marriage was prohibited under subdivision (a)(1) of this section, an impediment which was removed by divorce decree, and since decedent's spouse from the subsequent marriage lived with decedent as his wife for a time after the dissolution of the prior marriage, the prohibited subsequent marriage became lawful as of the date of the divorce. Long v. Schisler, 81 Ill. App. 3d 280, 36 Ill. Dec. 620, 401 N.E.2d 301 (3 Dist. 1980).

Bigamous Marriage

—Impediment Removed

The court's decision that defendant was the legal wife of decedent at the time of his death, thereby qualifying her as an heir and as legal representative of decedent's estate, was not against the manifest weight of the evidence where the prohibited bigamous marriage became a valid marriage at the time the impediment to the marriage was removed under subsection (b); the first marriage was dissolved before the decedent's death. In re Estate of Banks, 258 Ill. App. 3d 529, 196 Ill. Dec. 379, 629 N.E.2d 1223 (5 Dist. 1994).

Cohabitation

Since common law marriages are not recognized in Illinois, cohabitation alone can never result in a valid marriage; because subsection (b) operates to create a valid marriage based solely upon cohabitation after the removal of an impediment, the legislature must ascribe some meaning to the wedding ceremony that created the bigamous marriage. May v. May, 286 Ill. App. 3d 1060, 222 Ill. Dec. 664, 678 N.E.2d 71 (3 Dist. 1997).

Where plaintiff was never divorced from first husband, and remarried, plaintiff's subsequent marriage became valid under this section when plaintiff continued to cohabit with subsequent husband after the impediment to their marriage was removed by first husband's death. McEvers v. Sullivan, 785 F. Supp. 1321 (C.D. Ill. 1992).

Even one night of cohabitation is sufficient to invoke subsection (b) of this section. Long v. Schisler, 81 Ill. App. 3d 280, 36 Ill. Dec. 620, 401 N.E.2d 301 (3 Dist. 1980).

Common Law Marriage

—Invalid

A couple was not considered married, even though the widow insisted they believed they were married under common law principles they thought the state recognized, where they were domiciled in state for their entire 38 years together, had three children, maintained a series of apartments together, introduced each other as husband and wife, signed various joint contracts, filed joint income tax returns, and widow was also the beneficiary of partner's life insurance policy; common law marriages cannot be established in this state, and the state will not recognize such a marriage contracted elsewhere by its own citizens. Lynch v. Bowen, 681 F. Supp. 506 (N.D. Ill. 1988).

Consent Requirement

Subsection (b) presupposes that the bigamous marriage is valid in every regard except for the fact that it took place prior to the dissolution of an earlier marriage of one of the parties; accordingly, a consent requirement need not be read into subsection (b) because a bigamous marriage does not necessarily lack the element of consent. May v. May, 286 Ill. App. 3d 1060, 222 Ill. Dec. 664, 678 N.E.2d 71 (3 Dist. 1997).

Cousins

—Construction

If the legislature had intended to embrace cousins of any other category than "cousins of the first degree," it would have so indicated; therefore it was its intention to exclude cousins of any other class. Merz v. Kathrein, 16 Ill. 2d 621, 158 N.E.2d 599 (1959).

—Illustrative Cases

Where trial court granted petition for dissolution of marriage and respondent asked the court to reconsider attaching birth certificates which showed that the mothers of petitioner and respondent were half-sisters, making the parties first cousins by one-half blood, and trial court declared the marriage between the parties void ab initio under this section, and petitioner asserted that she was the putative spouse of respondent and, therefore, entitled to the rights of a legal spouse, the marriage was properly declared invalid but the order denying the petitioner relief was reversed and remanded for an evidentiary hearing. In re Flores, 96 Ill. App. 3d 279, 51 Ill. Dec. 885, 421 N.E.2d 393 (1 Dist. 1981).

For a case discussing sufficiency of evidence to show incest, see People v. Wood, 318 Ill. 388, 149 N.E. 273 (1925).

—Meaning

First cousins are those who have the same grandfather or grandmother, while second cousins are those who have the same

Cousins (Cont'd)

—Meaning (Cont'd)
great-grandfather or great-grandmother. Merz v. Kathrein, 16 Ill. 2d 621, 158 N.E.2d 599 (1959).

Legislative Intent
The fact that the legislature has not expressly prohibited step-parent-stepchild marriages under this Act does not evince a legislative intent to exclude stepparents from an otherwise prohibited relationship. People v. Parker, 123 Ill. 2d 204, 121 Ill. Dec. 941, 526 N.E.2d 135 (1988).

Legitimacy of Children
A child born out of wedlock, whose parents subsequently enter into an invalid marriage, is thereby legitimized for the purpose of determining heirship. In re Estate of Bartolini, 285 Ill. App. 3d 613, 220 Ill. Dec. 803, 674 N.E.2d 74 (1 Dist. 1996).

Putative Spouse
Husband lost his status as wife's putative spouse under 750 ILCS 5/305 when his marriage was ratified by operation of subsection (b). May v. May, 286 Ill. App. 3d 1060, 222 Ill. Dec. 664, 678 N.E.2d 71 (3 Dist. 1997).

Same-Sex Marriage
Birth certificate changing petitioner's designation from female to male was insufficient basis to argue that surgical sexual transformation processes that had never been completed justified such a change in designation, where the registrar had not inquired beyond a doctor's affidavit that petitioner's doctor admitted having completed in order to help petitioner out; therefore, petitioner's marriage to a woman had never been valid, and the mere issuance of a new certificate did not remove the impediment to that marriage. In re Simmons, Ill. App. 3d , Ill. Dec. , N.E.2d , 2005 Ill. App. LEXIS 127 (1 Dist. Feb. 16, 2005).

The court did not have the authority to consider a relationship that at the time of its inception, did not carry with it the consequences of a legal marriage; as a result, petitioner could not be elevated to spousal status and was not entitled to a spousal share of same-sex partner's estate, and constitutional challenge to proscription of same-sex marriages was a moot issue. In re Estate of Hall, 302 Ill. App. 3d 829, 236 Ill. Dec. 356, 707 N.E.2d 201 (1 Dist. 1998).

Scienter
Subsection (b) operates to ratify a bigamous marriage regardless of whether the parties have knowledge that the impediment has been removed. May v. May, 286 Ill. App. 3d 1060, 222 Ill. Dec. 664, 678 N.E.2d 71 (3 Dist. 1997).

There is no scienter requirement in subsection (b). May v. May, 286 Ill. App. 3d 1060, 222 Ill. Dec. 664, 678 N.E.2d 71 (3 Dist. 1997).

Validity

—Impediments Removed
While bigamy is clearly grounds for annulment, once a bigamous marriage is legalized by operation of subsection (b), it can no longer be considered a prohibited marriage. May v. May, 286 Ill. App. 3d 1060, 222 Ill. Dec. 664, 678 N.E.2d 71 (3 Dist. 1997).

A second husband may not have his marriage declared void after his wife's prior marriage has been dissolved and he has lived in a conjugal relationship with his wife for almost four years thereafter. May v. May, 286 Ill. App. 3d 1060, 222 Ill. Dec. 664, 678 N.E.2d 71 (3 Dist. 1997).

Evidence was sufficient to find that a marriage ceremony occurred, that the impediment of previous marriage was removed, and that the couple cohabitated subsequent to prior divorce such that the requisites of subsection (b) were met. Estate of Whyte v. Whyte, 244 Ill. App. 3d 746, 185 Ill. Dec. 238, 614 N.E.2d 372 (1 Dist. 1993).

—Presumed
When a marriage is shown, the law raises a strong presumption in favor of its validity, and the burden is upon the party objecting to the validity to prove its invalidity. Whelan v. Whelan, 346 Ill. App. 445, 105 N.E.2d 314 (2 Dist. 1952).

LEGAL PERIODICALS

For article, "Warring with Wardle: Morality, Social Science, and Gay and Lesbian Parents", see 1998 U. Ill. L. Rev. 253 (1998).

For article, "Natural Law and Same Sex Marriages", see 48 DePaul L. Rev. 51 (1998).

For note, "Family Law, Property Rights — Hewitt v. Hewitt, 77 Ill.2d 49, 394 N.E.2d 1204 (1979)," see 69 Ill. B.J. 49 (1980).

RESEARCH REFERENCES

Child custody and visitation rights arising from same-sex relationship. 80 ALR5th 1.

Marriage between persons of the same sex. 81 ALR5th 1.

750 ILCS 5/213 Validity

Sec. 213. *Validity.* All marriages contracted within this State, prior to the effective date of this Act, or outside this State, that were valid at the time of the contract or subsequently validated by the laws of the place in which they were contracted or by the domicile of the parties, are valid in this State, except where contrary to the public policy of this State.
(Source: P.A. 80-923.)

Note.
This section was Ill.Rev.Stat., Ch. 40, para. 213.

CASE NOTES

ANALYSIS

Exceptions
—In General
Out-of-State

Exceptions

—In General
It is a general rule of law that a marriage valid where it is celebrated is valid everywhere, but there are two well recognized exceptions, namely, marriages which are contrary to the law of nature, and those which are declared by positive law to have no validity. Wilson v. Cook, 256 Ill. 460, 100 N.E. 222 (1912).

Out-of-State
Since the prohibitory terms of a prior provision were broad and sweeping, and declared that it would be unlawful for divorced persons to marry again within the year, and that any such marriage would be null and void, and there was no limitation as to the place of the pretended marriage in express terms, nor was language used from which a limitation could have been naturally implied, then the legislature intended to control the conduct of the residents of the state, whether they be within or outside of its boundaries. Wilson v. Cook, 256 Ill. 460, 100 N.E. 222 (1912).

750 ILCS 5/213.1 Same-sex marriages; public policy

Sec. 213.1. *Same-sex marriages; public policy.* A marriage between 2 individuals of the same sex is contrary to the public policy of this State.
(Source: P.A. 89-459, § 5.)

Effective Date.
Section 99 of P.A. 89-459 made this section effective upon becoming law. The Act was approved May 24, 1996.

CASE NOTES

Spouse Status
The court did not have the authority to consider a relationship that at the time of its inception, did not carry with it the consequences of a legal marriage; as a result, petitioner could not be elevated to spousal status and was not entitled to a spousal share of same-sex partner's estate, and constitutional challenge to proscription of same-sex marriages was a moot issue. In re Estate of Hall, 302 Ill. App. 3d 829, 236 Ill. Dec. 356, 707 N.E.2d 201 (1 Dist. 1998).

OPINIONS OF ATTORNEY GENERAL

In General
The State of Illinois is not required to extend to persons who have entered into a 'civil union" under the laws of Vermont the same benefits extended to married persons under the laws of Illinois. 2000 Op. Atty. Gen. 17.

RESEARCH REFERENCES

Child custody and visitation rights arising from same-sex relationship. 80 ALR5th 1.
Marriage between persons of the same sex. 81 ALR5th 1.

750 ILCS 5/214 Invalidity of Common Law Marriages

Sec. 214. *Invalidity of Common Law Marriages.* Common law marriages contracted in this State after June 30, 1905 are invalid.
(Source: P.A. 80-923.)

Note.
This section was Ill.Rev.Stat., Ch. 40, para. 214.

CASE NOTES

Analysis

In General
Absence of License
Evidence
Out-of-State
—Burden of Proof
—Domicile
—Marriage Valid
Public Policy
Reconciliation
Scope

In General
Illinois does not permit common law marriage. Farrell v. Peters, 951 F.2d 862 (7th Cir. 1992).
Illinois has not recognized the validity of common law marriages since the early part of this century. People v. McCarthy, 132 Ill. 2d 331, 138 Ill. Dec. 292, 547 N.E.2d 459 (1989).

Absence of License
A duly ordained priest of the Catholic church has the authority to perform a marriage ceremony and such marriage was valid notwithstanding there was no marriage license. Haderaski v. Haderaski, 415 Ill. 118, 112 N.E.2d 714 (1953).

Evidence
The true relation of a man and woman living together is always a matter of evidence. Herald v. Moker, 257 Ill. 27, 100 N.E. 277 (1912).

Out-of-State

—Burden of Proof
In an action for dissolution of marriage, where the parties agreed that the law of Iowa controlled the determination of whether a valid common-law marriage existed, the burden of proof was on the party asserting the common-law marriage, and such claim was regarded with suspicion, there being no public policy in Iowa favoring common-law marriage. In re Mosher, 243 Ill. App. 3d 97, 183 Ill. Dec. 911, 612 N.E.2d 838 (3 Dist.), appeal denied, 152 Ill. 2d 562, 190 Ill. Dec. 893, 622 N.E.2d 1210 (1993).

—Domicile
Under former Ill.Rev.Stat., ch. 3, para. 11(3) (see now 755 ILCS 5/2-1), a three day vacation trip to Texas, which recognizes common law marriage, and the consideration of that state as a future retirement site was insufficient to establish Texas as petitioner's domicile for the purposes of determining that she was decedent's common law widow and thus entitled to an intestate share of his estate. Stahl v. Chuhak, 13 Ill. App. 3d 680, 301 N.E.2d 82 (1 Dist. 1973).

—Marriage Valid
Although Illinois abolished common-law marriages, where the parties resided in another state at the time of contracting a common-law marriage that was valid in that state, such marriage would be considered valid upon their removal to Illinois. In re Mosher, 243 Ill. App. 3d 97, 183 Ill. Dec. 911, 612 N.E.2d 838 (3 Dist.), appeal denied, 152 Ill. 2d 562, 190 Ill. Dec. 893, 622 N.E.2d 1210 (1993).

Public Policy
The legislature has refused to confer a legal status on common law marriages because this would contravene Illinois' strong public policy in favor of strengthening and preserving the integrity of marriage. Mister v. A.R.K. Partnership, 197 Ill. App. 3d 105, 143 Ill. Dec. 166, 553 N.E.2d 1152 (2 Dist.), cert. denied, 133 Ill. 2d 559, 149 Ill. Dec. 324, 561 N.E.2d 694 (1990).

Reconciliation
Where parties had been married for 30 years and later divorced, and their friends desired to bring them together and arranged a meeting for the purpose, at which the two became reconciled, and after that lived together until one's death, then they intended to, and did, assume the marriage relation after reconciliation; the surviving husband was entitled to dower from wife's estate. Herald v. Moker, 257 Ill. 27, 100 N.E. 277 (1912).

Scope
This section prohibits only common law marriages contracted in this state, and Illinois cannot direct Ohio or any other state to declare invalid common law marriages. Allen v. Storer, 235 Ill. App. 3d 5, 175 Ill. Dec. 805, 600 N.E.2d 1263 (4 Dist. 1992).

LEGAL PERIODICALS

For article, "Hewitt v. Hewitt: Non-Marital Cohabitation and the Doctrine of Immorality," see Ill. B.J. 368 (1981).
For case note, "Hewitt v. Hewitt — Property Rights of Unmarried Cohabitors upon Dissolution of Relationship," see 1980 U. Ill. L.J. 525.
For article, "Caveat Amator: 'The State of Affairs' in Illinois After Hewitt v. Hewitt," see 29 De Paul L. Rev. 493 (1980).
For note, "Family Law, Property Rights — Hewitt v. Hewitt, 77 Ill.2d 49, 394 N.E.2d 1204 (1979)," see 69 Ill. B.J. 49 (1980).

RESEARCH REFERENCES

Property rights arising from relationship of couple cohabiting without marriage. 3 ALR4th 13.
Property rights arising from relationship of couple cohabiting without marriage. 69 ALR5th 219.

750 ILCS 5/215 Penalty

Sec. 215. *Penalty.* Unless otherwise provided by law, any person who violates any provision of Part II of this Act is guilty of a Class B misdemeanor.
(Source: P.A. 80-923.)

Note.
This section was Ill.Rev.Stat., Ch. 40, para. 215.

750 ILCS 5/216 Prohibited Marriages Void if Contracted in Another State

Sec. 216. *Prohibited Marriages Void if Contracted in Another State.* That if any person residing and intending to continue to reside in this state and who is disabled or prohibited from contracting marriage under the laws of this state, shall go into another state or country and there contract a marriage prohibited and declared void by the laws of this state, such marriage shall be null and void for all purposes in this state with the same effect as though such prohibited marriage had been entered into in this state.
(Source: P.A. 80-923.)

Note.
This section was Ill.Rev.Stat., Ch. 40, para. 216.

CASE NOTES

ANALYSIS

Cousins
—Illustrative Cases
Public Policy

Cousins

—Illustrative Cases
Where it was established that, at the time a marriage was celebrated, both parties were first cousins, were residents of this state, and they went to Kentucky for the sole purpose of evading the law of this state against marriages between first cousins, such marriage was incestuous and void. Whelan v. Whelan, 346 Ill. App. 445, 105 N.E.2d 314 (2 Dist. 1952).

Public Policy
To recognize the validity of marriage celebrated by crossing the state line to evade the laws of this state would render legislation to make and enforce public policy and govern the domestic relations of its citizens futile, and such a marriage was absolutely void under the former Divorce Act (see now this section). Stevens v. Stevens, 304 Ill. 297, 136 N.E. 785 (1922).

LEGAL PERIODICALS

For case note, "Hewitt v. Hewitt — Property Rights of Unmarried Cohabitors upon Dissolution of Relationship," see 1980 U. Ill. L.J. 525.

750 ILCS 5/217 Marriage by Non-residents — When Void

Sec. 217. *Marriage by Non-residents — When Void.* No marriage shall be contracted in this state by a party residing and intending to continue to reside in another state or jurisdiction if such marriage would be void if contracted in such other state or jurisdiction and every marriage celebrated in this state in violation of this provision shall be null and void.
(Source: P.A. 80-923.)

Note.
This section was Ill.Rev.Stat., Ch. 40, para. 217.

750 ILCS 5/218 Duty of Officer Issuing License

Sec. 218. *Duty of Officer Issuing License.* Before issuing a license to marry a person who resides and intends to continue to reside in another state, the officer having authority to issue the license shall satisfy himself by requiring affidavits or otherwise that such person is not prohibited from intermarrying by the laws of the jurisdiction where he or she resides.
(Source: P.A. 80-923.)

Note.
This section was Ill.Rev.Stat., Ch. 40, para. 218.

750 ILCS 5/219 Offenses

Sec. 219. *Offenses.* Any official issuing a license with knowledge that the parties are thus prohibited from intermarrying and any person authorized to celebrate marriage who shall knowingly celebrate such a marriage shall be guilty of a petty offense.
(Source: P.A. 80-923.)

Note.
This section was Ill.Rev.Stat., Ch. 40, para. 219.

PART III.
DECLARATION OF INVALIDITY OF MARRIAGE

750 ILCS 5/301 Declaration of Invalidity — Grounds

Sec. 301. *Declaration of Invalidity — Grounds.* The court shall enter its judgment declaring the invalidity of a marriage (formerly known as annulment) entered into under the following circumstances:

(1) a party lacked capacity to consent to the marriage at the time the marriage was solemnized, either because of mental incapacity or infirmity or because of the influence of alcohol, drugs or other incapacitating substances, or a party was induced to enter into a marriage by force or duress or by fraud involving the essentials of marriage;

(2) a party lacks the physical capacity to consummate the marriage by sexual intercourse and at the time the marriage was solemnized the other party did not know of the incapacity;

(3) a party was aged 16 or 17 years and did not have the consent of his parents or guardian or judicial approval; or

(4) the marriage is prohibited.

(Source: P.A. 80-923.)

Note.
This section was Ill.Rev.Stat., Ch. 40, para. 301.

CASE NOTES

ANALYSIS

In General
Action
—Choice of Law
—In Rem
Annulment
—Common Law Marriage
—Custody and Support
—Distinction
—Effect
Bigamy
Child
Duress
Exceptions
—Divorce Valid
Fraud
Fraudulent Misrepresentation
—Consummation
—Pregnancy
Habitual Drunkenness
Incapacity to Consummate
—Insufficient Grounds
Incompetency
—Illustrative Cases
Innocent Person
—Choice of Remedy
Legislative Intent
—Limitation of Actions
Non-Existent Marriage
Timeliness

In General

Under the former Divorce Act (see now 750 ILCS 5/101 et seq.), the law favored the preservation of the estate of marriage and would dissolve a marriage only upon sufficient proof of the grounds set forth under that section. Stanard v. Stanard, 108 Ill. App. 2d 240, 247 N.E.2d 438 (3 Dist. 1969).

Action

—Choice of Law

In an annulment action against a nonresident defendant, where the court had jurisdiction of the subject matter based upon the domicile of the plaintiff, the Illinois rule and interpretation, rather than the sister state rule, governed the question of jurisdiction. Newton v. Lehman, 67 Ill. App. 2d 302, 214 N.E.2d 142 (3 Dist. 1966).

—In Rem

An annulment action or an action to declare a purported marriage invalid should be considered an in rem action, since the state of plaintiff's domicile has an interest in the marital status of its resident, and since an annulment or similar action does in fact determine marital status. Newton v. Lehman, 67 Ill. App. 2d 302, 214 N.E.2d 142 (3 Dist. 1966).

Annulment

—Common Law Marriage

An action wherein a plaintiff sought to have declared invalid a purported common law marriage was in the nature of an annulment action rather than a traditional divorce action, since the plaintiff sought to show that no lawful marriage had ever been undertaken by the parties. Newton v. Lehman, 67 Ill. App. 2d 302, 214 N.E.2d 142 (3 Dist. 1966).

—Custody and Support

A court of equity has jurisdiction to provide for the care, support, and custody of children in annulment cases. Cardenas v. Cardenas, 12 Ill. App. 2d 497, 140 N.E.2d 377 (1 Dist. 1956).

—Distinction

An annulment proceeding differs from a divorce case in that the latter is instituted to sever a marriage relation admitted to exist, while an annulment proceeding is for the purpose of declaring, judicially, the marriage never to have taken place between the parties. Arndt v. Arndt, 399 Ill. 490, 78 N.E.2d 272 (1948).

—Effect

If parties are married, the law places upon the husband certain obligations of support and maintenance, and, in case of a divorce proceeding between them, the law authorizes the court to require the husband to pay legal expenses or support money as required by his order, but in annulment cases there is no marriage between the parties and therefore no matrimonial obligation, no requirement to pay support to the putative spouse, and no duty to pay support money or attorney fees exists, unless otherwise provided. Arndt v. Arndt, 399 Ill. 490, 78 N.E.2d 272 (1948).

There is no statute requiring the payment of legal fees or suit money in cases of annulment, and an order of the court for such payments was without authority. Arndt v. Arndt, 399 Ill. 490, 78 N.E.2d 272 (1948).

Bigamy

While a bigamous marriage was said to be void ab initio under the former Marriage Act (see now this section), it was nevertheless a ground for divorce, which presupposed a valid marriage. Cardenas v. Cardenas, 12 Ill. App. 2d 497, 140 N.E.2d 377 (1 Dist. 1956).

Child

Where defendant husband's religion prohibited marriage with a divorced person whose former spouse was still living and marriage between the defendant and plaintiff wife would not have occurred but for the fraud on wife's part for the purpose of inducing the plaintiff's consent, and since discovering the fraud, defendant was unable to continue marital cohabitation with plaintiff, fraud went to the essential elements of the marriage; the existence of a child from the marriage, although a factor, would not bar an annulment, inasmuch as the status of the child, under Illinois law, was unchanged. Wolfe v. Wolfe, 76 Ill. 2d 92, 27 Ill. Dec. 735, 389 N.E.2d 1143 (1979).

Duress

If a man under lawful arrest for seduction or bastardy, for which the complaint was based on probable cause, chooses to marry the woman as a means of terminating the proceedings against him, he cannot allege duress as a ground for annulling the marriage. Smith v. Saum, 324 Ill. App. 299, 58 N.E.2d 248 (1 Dist. 1944).

Exceptions

—Divorce Valid

Husband who remarried in reliance upon divorce decree, which was later declared invalid for want of jurisdiction, was not guilty of adultery and could later sue first wife for divorce. Meyer v. Meyer, 343 Ill. App. 554, 99 N.E.2d 706 (1 Dist. 1951).

Fraud

Where plaintiff admitted that she knew that her former husband was not dead, and the defendant's religion prohibited marriage with a divorced person whose former spouse was still living, the marriage would not have occurred but for the fraud, executed for the purpose of inducing defendant's consent; defendant was entitled to an annulment. Wolfe v. Wolfe, 76 Ill. 2d 92, 27 Ill. Dec. 735, 389 N.E.2d 1143 (1979).

Fraud that will warrant the annulment (now declaration of invalidity) of a marriage is such fraud that goes to the essence of the marriage contract and must be such as to vitiate consent, that is, it must be shown that, although there was actual consent, there was no reality of consent. The fraudulent representations for which a marriage may be annulled must be of something essential to the marriage relation, of something making impossible the performance of the duties and obligations of that relation, or rendering its assumption and continuance dangerous to health or life. Louis v. Louis, 124 Ill. App. 2d 325, 260 N.E.2d 469 (1 Dist. 1970).

Fraudulent Misrepresentation

—Consummation

Where one party fraudulently misrepresents a willingness to consummate the marriage, it will constitute ground for a declaration of invalidity. Naguit v. Scrivner, 104 Ill. App. 3d 709, 60 Ill. Dec. 499, 433 N.E.2d 296 (5 Dist. 1982).

Fraudulent Misrepresentation (Cont'd)

—Consummation (Cont'd)

Where respondent told petitioner the day before their marriage that she doubted whether she could fulfill his sexual desires, and petitioner nevertheless agreed to marry respondent upon the condition that she seek psychiatric help, alleged misrepresentation amounted, at most, to an agreement to consummate the marriage sometime in the future, which was insufficient to constitute a fraudulent representation which would warrant invalidating marriage. Naguit v. Scrivner, 104 Ill. App. 3d 709, 60 Ill. Dec. 499, 433 N.E.2d 296 (5 Dist. 1982).

—Pregnancy

Appellate court will not disturb the trial court's finding that wife induced husband to marry her by knowingly misrepresenting to him that she was pregnant with his child and that in reliance on this statement the husband married her, since this finding was not contrary to the manifest weight of the evidence. Hill v. Hill, 79 Ill. App. 3d 809, 35 Ill. Dec. 98, 398 N.E.2d 1048 (1 Dist. 1979).

False representations as to the paternity of a child which defendant was carrying were grounds for annulment of a marriage at the suit of the plaintiff, who had had illicit relations with defendant and accepted and believed her statement without investigating its truth or falsity. Arndt v. Arndt, 336 Ill. App. 65, 82 N.E.2d 908 (1 Dist. 1948).

Habitual Drunkenness

For a case granting a petition to vacate a default divorce decree, the grounds for which was habitual drunkenness for a period in excess of two years, see McDonnell v. McDonnell, 97 Ill. App. 2d 303, 240 N.E.2d 438 (1 Dist. 1968).

Incapacity to Consummate

While impotency, or physical inability to consummate a marriage, has been a ground for divorce in Illinois since 1827, it has never been held to be a ground for annulment (now declaration of invalidity), nor has any statute so provided, and therefore impotency is not ground for annulment in Illinois; a decree of a California court granting plaintiff an annulment from her second husband on this ground was of no force or effect in this state and was not binding on the defendant, her first ex-husband. Linneman v. Linneman, 1 Ill. App. 2d 48, 116 N.E.2d 182 (1 Dist. 1953).

—Insufficient Grounds

No fraud involving essentials of the marriage was shown to exist and any physical incapacity to consummate the marriage was not of a sufficient duration to warrant a declaration of invalidity. Naguit v. Scrivner, 104 Ill. App. 3d 709, 60 Ill. Dec. 499, 433 N.E.2d 296 (5 Dist. 1982).

Incompetency

—Illustrative Cases

For a case which determined that a disabled adult was incompetent at the time of her marriage, see Pape v. Byrd, 145 Ill. 2d 13, 163 Ill. Dec. 898, 582 N.E.2d 164 (1991).

Innocent Person

—Choice of Remedy

Judgment of annulment award was manifestly erroneous in that it denied a divorce to wife, the innocent party who married husband relying upon his misrepresentation that he had been granted a divorce from his previous wife, and granted annulment to the husband; the choice of remedy should have been reserved for wife as an innocent person. Belluomini v. Belluomini, 73 Ill. App. 3d 836, 30 Ill. Dec. 14, 392 N.E.2d 669 (1 Dist. 1979).

Legislative Intent

—Limitation of Actions

When seeking to annul a marriage for a ground stated in this section, the legislature intended for the limitations of 750 ILCS 5/302 to apply. Pape v. Byre, 197 Ill. App. 3d 836, 144 Ill. Dec. 309, 555 N.E.2d 428 (4 Dist. 1990), rev'd on other grounds, 145 Ill. 2d 13, 163 Ill. Dec. 898, 582 N.E.2d 165 (1991).

Non-Existent Marriage

Where a trial court found that no marriage ceremony was performed to unite the plaintiff and the defendant, by anyone authorized so to do, the court could not annul that which never existed; to annul the record in the county clerk's office, it would have been necessary to make the county clerk a party to the suit. O'Brien v. Eustice, 298 Ill. App. 510, 19 N.E.2d 137 (1 Dist. 1939).

Timeliness

Where petitioner was aware of his uncle's incompetence more than 90 days before filing an action, but petitioner was not then a proper party to seek a declaration and 42 days after uncle was appointed a conservator he filed a petition to have the marriage declared invalid, his petition was timely filed. Payton v. Payne, 90 Ill. App. 3d 892, 46 Ill. Dec. 311, 414 N.E.2d 33 (1 Dist. 1980).

RESEARCH REFERENCES

Homosexuality, transvestism, and similar sexual practices as grounds for annulment of marriage. 68 ALR4th 1069.

750 ILCS 5/302 Time of Commencement

Sec. 302. *Time of Commencement.* (a) A declaration of invalidity under paragraphs (1) through (3) of Section 301 [750 ILCS 5/301] may be sought by any of the following persons and must be commenced within the times specified:

(1) for any of the reasons set forth in paragraph (1) of Section 301 [750 ILCS 5/301], by either party or by the legal representative of the party who lacked capacity to consent, no later than 90 days after the petitioner obtained knowledge of the described condition;

(2) for the reason set forth in paragraph (2) of Section 301 [750 ILCS 5/301], by either party, no later than one year after the petitioner obtained knowledge of the described condition;

(3) for the reason set forth in paragraph (3) of Section 301 [750 ILCS 5/301], by the underaged party, his parent or guardian, prior to the time the underaged party reaches the age at which he could have married without needing to satisfy the omitted requirement.

(b) In no event may a declaration of invalidity of marriage be sought after the death of either party to the marriage under subsections (1), (2) and (3) of Section 301 [750 ILCS 5/301].

(c) A declaration of invalidity for the reason set forth in paragraph (4) of Section 301 [750 ILCS 5/301] may be sought by either party, the legal spouse in case of a bigamous marriage, the State's Attorney or a child of either party, at any time not to exceed 3 years following the death of the first party to die.

(Source: P.A. 80-923.)

Note.

This section was Ill.Rev.Stat., Ch. 40, para. 302.

CASE NOTES

Analysis

Annulment
Cause of Action
Guardianship
—Illustrative Cases

Marriage by Proxy
Statute of Limitations
—Second Marriage

Annulment

When seeking to annul a marriage for a ground stated in 750 ILCS 5/301, the legislature intended for the limitations of this section to apply. Pape v. Byre, 197 Ill. App. 3d 836, 144 Ill. Dec. 309, 555 N.E.2d 428 (4 Dist. 1990), rev'd on other grounds, 145 Ill. 2d 13, 163 Ill. Dec. 898, 582 N.E.2d 165 (1991).

Cause of Action

Where an injustice could occur by dismissal of an action if allegations made in plaintiff's complaint were true, and because the General Assembly may not have contemplated a situation where deceased spouse married only weeks before his death and where an action to invalidate the recent marriage was filed by his legal representative before his death, but an evidentiary hearing on the matter could not be held before the incompetent spouse died, and because it was logical under the circumstances to allow the invalidity action to survive the plaintiff's death, the word "sought" was construed to mean that if the invalidity action was initiated prior to the decedent's death, it would survive. Quick ex rel. Jones v. Quick, 213 Ill. App. 3d 97, 157 Ill. Dec. 187, 571 N.E.2d 1206 (5 Dist. 1991).

Guardianship

—Illustrative Cases

Where a guardian had been appointed for a disabled adult, the ward then married, and, after the time limit had expired, the guardian sought to invalidate the ward's marriage, the guardian lacked standing to pursue the action, although it was proven that the ward lacked capacity. Pape v. Byrd, 145 Ill. 2d 13, 163 Ill. Dec. 898, 582 N.E.2d 164 (1991).

Marriage by Proxy

Petitioners, the son and daughter of a decedent, had standing to challenge the validity of the decedent's marriage by proxy, which occurred shortly before his death while he suffered from an inoperable brain tumor and was mute and barely conscious. In re Estate of Crockett, 32 Ill. App. 3d 1167, 245 Ill. Dec. 683, 728 N.E.2d 765, 2000 Ill. App. LEXIS 251 (2000).

Statute of Limitations

—Second Marriage

The 90-day time limit did not begin to run on the date of the parties' second marriage, since the statute of limitations is tolled during those periods defendant is outside the state of Illinois unless he or she is subject to the jurisdiction of the court under a long-arm provision, and since the parties in this case did not reside in Illinois at any time after their second marriage. In re Davis, 217 Ill. App. 3d 273, 160 Ill. Dec. 18, 576 N.E.2d 972 (5 Dist. 1991).

LEGAL PERIODICALS

For article, "Divorce Illinois Style: Ten Years Under the Marriage and Dissolution of Marriage Act," see 75 Ill. B.J. 606 (1987).

750 ILCS 5/303 Legitimacy of Children

Sec. 303. *Legitimacy of Children.* Children born or adopted of a marriage declared invalid are legitimate. Children whose parents marry after their birth are legitimate.
(Source: P.A. 82-566.)

Note.

This section was Ill.Rev.Stat., Ch. 40, para. 303.

CASE NOTES

ANALYSIS

In General
Acknowledgment
Custody
Invalid Marriage
Presumption of Legitimacy
Presumption of Paternity
Probate Cases
—Parent's Inheritance
Purpose

In General

A similar section of the former Divorce Act (see now 750 ILCS 5/101 et seq.) pertained to children of the marriage and in effect provided that they be protected from any action or suit for divorce which would result in said children being illegitimatized; where a minor child was illegitimate, the former Divorce Act (see now 750 ILCS 5/101 et seq.) was barren of any provisions which could have been utilized to cloak the child with the status of legitimacy. In re Weller, 47 Ill. App. 3d 492, 5 Ill. Dec. 760, 362 N.E.2d 73 (3 Dist. 1977).

Acknowledgment

Where a trial court incorrectly believed that one of plaintiff's children was conclusively presumed to be the child of plaintiff's former husband, pursuant to the rules of illegitimacy of former Ill.Rev.Stat., ch. 3, p. 12 (see now this section), the ruling was reversed where plaintiff and defendant intermarried after the child's birth, and defendant acknowledged the child in accordance with the statutory requirements of the Probate Act (755 ILCS 5/1-1 et seq.), rendering the child the legitimate child of defendant. Collins v. Collins, 47 Ill. App. 3d 258, 5 Ill. Dec. 464, 361 N.E.2d 787 (1 Dist. 1977).

Despite decedent's concession that appellants were his children, and the fact that he held out their mother to be his wife, in order to bring them under the terms of the statute, a form of marriage ceremony must have been performed. Brainard v. Brainard, 373 Ill. 459, 26 N.E.2d 856 (1940).

Custody

The omission of mention of a child in a custody agreement did not have the effect of making the child illegitimate nor of depriving the child of support. Teich v. Teich, 132 Ill. App. 2d 348, 270 N.E.2d 525 (1 Dist. 1971).

Invalid Marriage

A child born out of wedlock, whose parents subsequently enter into an invalid marriage, is thereby legitimized for the purpose of determining heirship. In re Estate of Bartolini, 285 Ill. App. 3d 613, 220 Ill. Dec. 803, 674 N.E.2d 74 (1 Dist. 1996).

Presumption of Legitimacy

The birth of a child to a husband and wife creates a strong presumption that the child is legitimate and that husband is the father; this presumption of legitimacy prevails even if the marriage is subsequently voided. People ex rel. Valle v. Valle, 113 Ill. App. 3d 682, 69 Ill. Dec. 510, 447 N.E.2d 945 (1 Dist. 1983).

Presumption of Paternity

Like the presumption of legitimacy, the presumption of paternity should prevail despite the fact that a bigamous marriage is subsequently declared to be void; the right of children born into a valid marriage to be supported is protected by the strong presumption that the husband is the father. People ex rel. Valle v. Valle, 113 Ill. App. 3d 682, 69 Ill. Dec. 510, 447 N.E.2d 945 (1 Dist. 1983).

Probate Cases

—Parent's Inheritance

Under former Ill.Rev.Stat., ch. 89, para. 17a (see now this section), a father was entitled to be included as a lawful heir of his deceased son for purposes of a life insurance policy, even though the marriage of the father and mother, who had cohabited, was void. Stewart v. Jackson, 131 Ill. App. 2d 183, 268 N.E.2d 187 (1 Dist. 1971).

Purpose

Former Ill.Rev.Stat., ch. 89, para. 17a (see now this section) was not passed merely to give a child a name, although it did include that specific provision, but was founded in benevolence and charity, and its humanitarian principles required that it be liberally con-

Purpose (Cont'd)
strued to effectuate its benign purpose. Cardenas v. Cardenas, 12 Ill. App. 2d 497, 140 N.E.2d 377 (1 Dist. 1956).

750 ILCS 5/304 Retroactivity

Sec. 304. *Retroactivity.* Unless the court finds, after a consideration of all relevant circumstances, including the effect of a retroactive judgment on third parties, that the interests of justice would be served by making the judgment not retroactive, it shall declare the marriage invalid as of the date of the marriage. The provisions of this Act relating to property rights of the spouses, maintenance, support and custody of children on dissolution of marriage are applicable to non-retroactive judgments of invalidity of marriage only.
(Source: P.A. 80-923.)

Note.
This section was Ill.Rev.Stat., Ch. 40, para. 304.

CASE NOTES

Analysis

Applicability
Equities
Retroactive Application

Applicability
This section allows the court to make the judgment of invalidity of the marriage nonretroactive so that the provisions of this Act relating to property rights of spouses, maintenance, and support and custody of children may be applied. In re Plymale, 172 Ill. App. 3d 455, 122 Ill. Dec. 489, 526 N.E.2d 882 (2 Dist. 1988).

Equities
If the court decides not to invalidate a marriage retroactively based on equities of the case, then a determination as to maintenance, child support and property distribution is proper. In re Kolb, 99 Ill. App. 3d 895, 55 Ill. Dec. 128, 425 N.E.2d 1301 (1 Dist. 1981).

Retroactive Application
Where intent of judgment was to make the judgment nonretroactive, notwithstanding the one reference to the contrary in the judgment, and to adjudicate child custody and property issues between parties, the court properly exercised its jurisdiction over these matters pursuant to this section. In re Plymale, 172 Ill. App. 3d 455, 122 Ill. Dec. 489, 526 N.E.2d 882 (2 Dist. 1988).

750 ILCS 5/305 Putative Spouse

Sec. 305. *Putative Spouse.* Any person, having gone through a marriage ceremony, who has cohabited with another to whom he is not legally married in the good faith belief that he was married to that person is a putative spouse until knowledge of the fact that he is not legally married terminates his status and prevents acquisition of further rights. A putative spouse acquires the rights conferred upon a legal spouse, including the right to maintenance following termination of his status, whether or not the marriage is prohibited, under Section 212 [750 ILCS 5/212], or declared invalid, under Section 301 [750 ILCS 5/301]. If there is a legal spouse or other putative spouse, rights acquired by a putative spouse do not supersede the rights of the legal spouse or those acquired by other putative spouses, but the court shall apportion property, maintenance and support rights among the claimants as appropriate in the circumstances and in the interests of justice. This Section shall not apply to common law marriages contracted in the State after June 30, 1905.
(Source: P.A. 80-923.)

Note.
This section was Ill.Rev.Stat., Ch. 40, para. 305.

CASE NOTES

Analysis

Consortium
Engagement
Interests of First Spouse
Knowledge
Maintenance Award
—Rights Prior to Marriage
Putative Spouse
Ratification of Marriage
Same-Sex Marriage
Termination of Rights
Unmarried Cohabitation
Validity of Statute
Waiver

Consortium
A cause of action for loss of consortium did not extend in favor of a husband where injury to his wife occurred shortly before their marriage, notwithstanding that the couple was then engaged to be married. Sostock v. Reiss, 92 Ill. App. 3d 200, 47 Ill. Dec. 781, 415 N.E.2d 1094 (1 Dist. 1980).

Engagement
A mere engagement to marry does not entitle parties to the legal protection afforded to spouses. Sostock v. Reiss, 92 Ill. App. 3d 200, 47 Ill. Dec. 781, 415 N.E.2d 1094 (1 Dist. 1980).

Interests of First Spouse
In a situation where a man is obtaining his second divorce, the trial court should not enter an order which would be substantially inconsistent with interests of respondent's first wife and family. In re Belluomini, 104 Ill. App. 3d 301, 60 Ill. Dec. 59, 432 N.E.2d 958 (1 Dist. 1982).

Knowledge
Where plaintiff had knowledge that she was not legally married, she did not acquire putative spouse status under this section. Daniels v. Retirement Bd. of the Policeman's Annuity & Benefit Fund, 106 Ill. App. 3d 412, 62 Ill. Dec. 304, 435 N.E.2d 1276 (1 Dist. 1982).

Maintenance Award
In determining maintenance award upon dissolution of second marriage of a party whose first marriage had not yet been dissolved, it was not an abuse of discretion for the trial court to consider the current lifestyle of first wife and her family and to include the educational expenses of their non-minor child in its determination of maintenance. In re Belluomini, 104 Ill. App. 3d 301, 60 Ill. Dec. 59, 432 N.E.2d 958 (1 Dist. 1982).

—Rights Prior to Marriage
Because prior to a marriage ceremony, the status of husband and wife did not exist, upon engagement, plaintiff had no marital rights for the purpose of maintenance, marital property, inheritance, wrongful death, or workers' compensation. Sostock v. Reiss, 92 Ill. App. 3d 200, 47 Ill. Dec. 781, 415 N.E.2d 1094 (1 Dist. 1980).

Putative Spouse
Where a decedent was married to his third spouse at the time of his death and had been separated but not divorced from his first spouse for 30 years at the time of his death, under 750 ILCS 5/305 of the Illinois Marriage and Dissolution of Marriage Act both the

Putative Spouse (Cont'd)
first spouse and the third spouse had recognizable rights to the decedent's pension benefits; however, in the interests of justice the third spouse was deemed to be the entitled to the decedent's pension benefits under Illinois law. Where a putative marriage exists, a putative spouse acting in good faith has the same right in property acquired during the marital relationship as if she were a lawful spouse. Cent. States, S.E. & S.W. Areas Pension Fund v. Gray, F. Supp. 2d , 2003 U.S. Dist. LEXIS 18282 (N.D. Ill. Oct. 8, 2003).

Ratification of Marriage
Husband lost his status as wife's putative spouse when his marriage was ratified by operation of 750 ILCS 5/212(b). May v. May, 286 Ill. App. 3d 1060, 222 Ill. Dec. 664, 678 N.E.2d 71 (3 Dist. 1997).

Same-Sex Marriage
Where the petitioner knew that she was not lawfully married to her partner of the same-sex, she was precluded from obtaining spouse status through the provisions of this section. In re Estate of Hall, 302 Ill. App. 3d 829, 236 Ill. Dec. 356, 707 N.E.2d 201 (1 Dist. 1998).

Termination of Rights
Although any person, having gone through a marriage ceremony and cohabited with another to whom he is not legally married, in the good faith belief that he was married to that person, is a putative spouse, subsequent knowledge of the fact that he is not legally married terminates his status and prevents acquisition of further rights. Sostock v. Reiss, 92 Ill. App. 3d 200, 47 Ill. Dec. 781, 415 N.E.2d 1094 (1 Dist. 1980).

Unmarried Cohabitation
Judicial recognition of claims of unmarried cohabitants which are substantially independent of the nonmarital relationship and not based on rights arising from cohabitation does not indicate court approval or legal recognition of the nonmarital relationship and does not violate public policy. Spafford v. Coats, 118 Ill. App. 3d 566, 74 Ill. Dec. 211, 455 N.E.2d 241 (2 Dist. 1983).

Claim for vehicles purchased during a period of cohabitation by unmarried parties is allowed where the claim is not founded simply on proof of cohabitation or plaintiff's performance of domestic services, and where permitting the defendant to retain vehicles would constitute an unjust enrichment. Spafford v. Coats, 118 Ill. App. 3d 566, 74 Ill. Dec. 211, 455 N.E.2d 241 (2 Dist. 1983).

Validity of Statute
Where evidence was clear that decedent and his second wife were married ceremonially prior to the dissolution of decedent's prior marriage, to the extent that this section affected the parties, the statute was sufficiently definite, explicit, and consistent with public policy. Long v. Schisler, 81 Ill. App. 3d 280, 36 Ill. Dec. 620, 401 N.E.2d 301 (3 Dist. 1980).

Waiver
Where plaintiff contended that she was entitled to an annuity as the putative spouse of deceased, and the plaintiff first presented the claim on administrative review as a post-trial motion, since she did not raise it before the Retirement Board of the Policeman's Annuity and Benefit Fund of Chicago, she was foreclosed from asserting it on appeal. Daniels v. Retirement Bd. of the Policeman's Annuity & Benefit Fund, 106 Ill. App. 3d 412, 62 Ill. Dec. 304, 435 N.E.2d 1276 (1 Dist. 1982).

LEGAL PERIODICALS

For article, "Hewitt v. Hewitt: Non-Marital Cohabitation and the Doctrine of Immorality," see Ill. B.J. 368 (1981).

For article, "Caveat Amator: 'The State of Affairs' in Illinois After Hewitt v. Hewitt," see 29 De Paul L. Rev. 493 (1980).

For note, "Family Law, Property Rights — Hewitt v. Hewitt, 77 Ill.2d 49, 394 N.E.2d 1204 (1979)," see 69 Ill. B.J. 49 (1980).

For case note, "Hewitt v. Hewitt Contract — Cohabitation and 'Equitable Expectations' Relief for Meretricious Spouses," see 12 J. Marshall J. Prac. & Proc. 435 (1979).

For comment, "Right of the Putative Spouse Under Section 305 of the Illinois Marriage and Dissolution of Marriage Act," see 1978 S. Ill. U.L.J. 423.

RESEARCH REFERENCES

Property rights arising from relationship of couple cohabiting without marriage. 3 ALR4th 13.

Property rights arising from relationship of couple cohabiting without marriage. 69 ALR5th 219.

750 ILCS 5/306 Commencement of Action

Sec. 306. *Commencement of Action.* Actions for declaration of invalidity of marriage shall be commenced as in other civil cases.
(Source: P.A. 80-923.)

Note.
This section was Ill.Rev.Stat., Ch. 40, para. 306.

CASE NOTES

Fraud
Where plaintiff filed a suit for divorce in which defendant filed a motion to dismiss, but no action was taken on the motion, and later the plaintiff filed another suit for divorce and obtained a waiver of the former 60 day period in which the defendant made no appearance, and a decree was entered granting a divorce to plaintiff upon default, and where during this time there was no change in the representation of the parties by their respective attorneys, and approximately three and a half months after the entry of the decree, defendant's attorney filed an unverified motion to set aside, or in the alternative, to modify the decree and alleged that the waiver of the 60 day waiting period was obtained by a fraudulent and insufficient affidavit, the facts alleged were not sufficient to sustain a collateral attack on the final decree of divorce. The divorce decree was entered by a court that had jurisdiction of the subject matter and of the parties, and the failure of the defendant to assert an available defense did not make the plaintiff guilty of any fraud. Coolbaugh v. Coolbaugh, 33 Ill. App. 2d 444, 178 N.E.2d 702 (4 Dist. 1962).

PART IV.

DISSOLUTION AND LEGAL SEPARATION

750 ILCS 5/401 Dissolution of marriage

Sec. 401. *Dissolution of marriage.* (a) The court shall enter a judgment of dissolution of marriage if at the time the action was commenced one of the spouses was a resident of this State or was stationed in this State while a member of the armed services, and the residence or military presence had been maintained for 90 days next preceding the commencement of the action or the making of the finding; provided, however, that a finding of residence of a party in any judgment entered under this Act from January 1, 1982 through June 30, 1982 shall satisfy the former domicile requirements of this Act; and if one of the following grounds for dissolution has been proved:

(1) That, without cause or provocation by the petitioner: the respondent was at the time of such

marriage, and continues to be naturally impotent; the respondent had a wife or husband living at the time of the marriage; the respondent had committed adultery subsequent to the marriage; the respondent has wilfully deserted or absented himself or herself from the petitioner for the space of one year, including any period during which litigation may have pended between the spouses for dissolution of marriage or legal separation; the respondent has been guilty of habitual drunkenness for the space of 2 years; the respondent has been guilty of gross and confirmed habits caused by the excessive use of addictive drugs for the space of 2 years, or has attempted the life of the other by poison or other means showing malice, or has been guilty of extreme and repeated physical or mental cruelty, or has been convicted of a felony or other infamous crime; or the respondent has infected the other with a sexually transmitted disease. "Excessive use of addictive drugs", as used in this Section, refers to use of an addictive drug by a person when using the drug becomes a controlling or a dominant purpose of his life; or

(2) That the spouses have lived separate and apart for a continuous period in excess of 2 years and irreconcilable differences have caused the irretrievable breakdown of the marriage and the court determines that efforts at reconciliation have failed or that future attempts at reconciliation would be impracticable and not in the best interests of the family. If the spouses have lived separate and apart for a continuous period of not less than 6 months next preceding the entry of the judgment dissolving the marriage, as evidenced by testimony or affidavits of the spouses, the requirement of living separate and apart for a continuous period in excess of 2 years may be waived upon written stipulation of both spouses filed with the court. At any time after the parties cease to cohabit, the following periods shall be included in the period of separation:

(A) any period of cohabitation during which the parties attempted in good faith to reconcile and participated in marriage counseling under the guidance of any of the following: a psychiatrist, a clinical psychologist, a clinical social worker, a marriage and family therapist, a person authorized to provide counseling in accordance with the prescriptions of any religious denomination, or a person regularly engaged in providing family or marriage counseling; and

(B) any period of cohabitation under written agreement of the parties to attempt to reconcile.

In computing the period during which the spouses have lived separate and apart for purposes of this Section, periods during which the spouses were living separate and apart prior to July 1, 1984 are included.

(b) Judgment shall not be entered unless, to the extent it has jurisdiction to do so, the court has considered, approved, reserved or made provision for child custody, the support of any child of the marriage entitled to support, the maintenance of either spouse and the disposition of property. The court may enter a judgment for dissolution that reserves any of these issues either upon (i) agreement of the parties, or (ii) motion of either party and a finding by the court that appropriate circumstances exist.

The death of a party subsequent to entry of a judgment for dissolution but before judgment on reserved issues shall not abate the proceedings.

If any provision of this Section or its application shall be adjudged unconstitutional or invalid for any reason by any court of competent jurisdiction, that judgment shall not impair, affect or invalidate any other provision or application of this Section, which shall remain in full force and effect.

(Source: P.A. 86-790; 87-530; 89-187, § 70.)

Note.

This section was Ill.Rev.Stat., Ch. 40, para. 401.

Effect of Amendments.

The 1995 amendment by P.A. 89-187, effective July 19, 1995, in subdivision (a)(1), in the first sentence, substituted "sexually transmitted" for "communicable venereal".

CASE NOTES

Analysis

Constitutionality
In General
Abandonment
—Requirement
Action by Guardian
Adultery
—In General
—Evidence Held Insufficient
—Evidence Held Sufficient
—Proof
Appeal
—In General
—Estoppel
—Judgment
—Reserved Issues
—Waiver
Applicability
—Amendment During Appeal
Apportionment
—Upheld
Authority of Court
—In General
—Change of Decree
—Grounds for Divorce
—Limitations
—Order by Successor Judge
—Scope of Jurisdiction
—Scope of Review
—Sufficiency of Evidence
Bifurcated Judgment
—In General
—Appropriate Circumstances Found
—Appropriate Circumstances Not Found
—Live Testimony
—Public Policy
—Waiver of Objection
Bigamy
—Grounds
—Test
Blood Tests
Challenge to Decree
—In General

Condonation
Construction of Judgment
—Extrinsic Evidence
Conveyance of Property
—Court-Ordered
Conviction of Felony
Cruelty
—In General
—Burden of Proof
—Corroboration Not Required
—Defenses
—Evidence Held Insufficient
—Evidence Held Sufficient
—Extreme and Repeated
—Requirements
—Slight Acts of Violence
—Uncorroborated Testimony
Death of Spouse
—Abatement of Dissolution Judgement
—Abatement of Dissolution Judgment
—Judgment Prior to Death
—Property Issues
Decree
—Consent of Parties
—Default Decree
—Effect
—Finality
—Unconscionability
Defenses
—In General
—Adultery
Denial of Hearing
—Held Improper
Desertion
—Computation
—Constructive
—Defenses
—Defined
—Evidence Held Insufficient
—Evidence Held Sufficient
—Grounds
—Living Separate and Apart
—Not Shown
—Refusal of Sexual Relations
—Requirements
—Separation by Mutual Consent
Dismissal of Action
Disposal of All Issues
Distribution
—Factors
Domicile
Erroneous Entry of Judgment
Estoppel
—In General
—Reliance on Decree
—Subject Matter Jurisdiction
Evidence
—Admissibility
Fault
—Not Shown
Financial Losses
Foreign Decrees
Fraud
—Not Shown
—Standing
Grounds
—In General
—Burden of Proof
—Not Shown
Habitual Drunkenness
—Defined
—Evidence Held Insufficient
—Grounds
—Illustrative Case
—Not Shown
—Requirements
Impotency
—In General
—Requirements
Irreconcilable Differences
—Evidence Held Sufficient
—One Spouse
—Purpose of Provision
Joinder
Jurisdiction
—Adultery
—Appeal
—Basis
—Divestiture
—Equity
—Established
—Estoppel
—Foreign Decrees
—In Personam
—In Rem
—Nexus
—Notice
—Prima Facie Evidence
—Residency
—Subject Matter
—Temporary Relief
—Waiver Not Shown
Living Separate and Apart
—In General
—Not Required
—Reasonable Cause
—Shown
Marital Assets
—Law License
Mental Cruelty
—In General
—Burden of Proof
—Conduct Required
—Defined
—Effect on Complainant
—Evidence Held Insufficient
—Evidence Held Sufficient
—Humiliation Not Enough
—Inconsistent Findings
—Lack of Provocation
—Medical Evidence
—Offensive Conduct Found
—Particular Facts
—Physical Harm Unnecessary
—Preponderance of Evidence
—Requirements
—Single Episode
Motion for a Finding
No Fault Divorce
—Evidence Held Sufficient
—Retrospective Application
Physical Cruelty
—Burden of Proof
—Conduct Required
—Corroborating Witnesses
—Defined
—Evidence Held Insufficient
—Evidence Held Sufficient
—Extreme and Repeated
—Factors to Consider
—Physical Contact
—Proof
—Requirements
—Shown
Pleading
—Amendment of Petition
—Insufficiency of Petition
—Name on Petition
—Separate Grounds
Provocation
—Burden of Proof
—Effect

—Essential Element
—Evidence Held Insufficient
Public Policy
Reconciliation
—Time Period
Recrimination
Remarriage
—Defined
Reservation of Issues
—Appealability
—Held Improper
—Requirements
—Upheld
Residence
—In General
—Abandonment Not Shown
—Allegation
—Defined
—Established
—Evidence Held Insufficient
—Evidence Held Sufficient
—Multiple Residence
—Purpose of Requirement
Review
Separate Maintenance
Separation Period
—Failure to File Waiver
—Purpose
State as Party
Statute of Limitations and Laches
—Date of Accrual
—Lapse of Time

Constitutionality

Neither the state nor the federal Constitution's impairment of contract clauses (U.S. Const., Art. I, § 10; Ill. Const. (1970), Art. I, § 16) were applicable to the no fault divorce provisions of subdivision (a)(2) of this section. In re Semmler, 107 Ill. 2d 130, 89 Ill. Dec. 873, 481 N.E.2d 716 (1985).

Neither the ex post facto clause of U.S. Const., Art. I, § 10 nor Ill. Const. (1970), Art. I, § 16 were applicable to no-fault divorce provision of this section. In re Semmler, 107 Ill. 2d 130, 89 Ill. Dec. 873, 481 N.E.2d 716 (1985).

The statute concerning the former crime of wife abandonment did not authorize an imprisonment for debt; it provided as punishment for certain crimes that the person convicted might be fined or imprisoned, or might be fined and committed to jail until the fine was paid, and thus it was not in violation of former Ill. Const. (1870), Art. II, §§ 2, 5 and 12 (see now Ill. Const. (1970), Article I, § 14) or Ill. Const. (1870), Art. IV, § 20 (see now Ill. Const. (1970), Art. VIII, § 1). People v. Heise, 257 Ill. 443, 100 N.E. 1000 (1913).

In General

The facts of a particular case must be considered in light of the parties' pattern of conduct, their respective emotional make-up and the circumstances under which the conduct occurred, and the ultimate test is the effect of the conduct on the complaining spouse and the marriage itself; a plaintiff is not excused from proving the statutory grounds for dissolution of marriage by competent evidence, even though she might consider the marriage dead. A married person has no right to force a dissolution of marriage upon her spouse. In re Rittmeyer, 107 Ill. App. 3d 892, 63 Ill. Dec. 499, 438 N.E.2d 237 (5 Dist. 1982).

This Act contemplates entry of a judgment of dissolution and a reservation of questions of child custody, support, maintenance or property disposition only under appropriate circumstances. In re Cohn, 94 Ill. App. 3d 732, 50 Ill. Dec. 621, 419 N.E.2d 729 (2 Dist. 1981), aff'd, 93 Ill. 2d 190, 66 Ill. Dec. 615, 443 N.E.2d 541 (1982).

This section creates a cause of action or substantive right not theretofore existing, and, absent legislative provision to the contrary, should not have a retroactive effect. Honey v. Honey, 120 Ill. App. 2d 102, 256 N.E.2d 121 (4 Dist. 1970).

There is no common law governing divorce; resort to the courts for such purposes is a privilege existing solely by grant of the legislature. Morrow v. Morrow, 15 Ill. App. 2d 109, 145 N.E.2d 381 (2 Dist. 1957).

Abandonment

—Requirement

Former section 1 of the Divorce Act (see now this section), regarding divorce based upon desertion, contemplated more than the mere separation of husband and wife by mutual consent or acquiescence, in that it required an actual abandonment and abnegation of all marital relationships with an intent not to return and without legal justification or consent of the other spouse. Lemon v. Lemon, 14 Ill. 2d 15, 150 N.E.2d 608 (1958).

Action by Guardian

Neither the Probate Act (755 ILCS 5/1-1 et seq.) nor this Act specifically determines whether a guardian is permitted to or prohibited from instituting an action to dissolve a ward's marriage to another. In re Drews, 139 Ill. App. 3d 763, 94 Ill. Dec. 128, 487 N.E.2d 1005 (1 Dist. 1985), aff'd, 115 Ill. 2d 201, 104 Ill. Dec. 782, 503 N.E.2d 339 (1986), cert. denied, 483 U.S. 1001, 107 S. Ct. 3222, 97 L. Ed. 2d 729 (1987).

Adultery

—In General

A prior similar provision, which provided that the person decreed guilty of adultery should not marry for a term of two years, did not violate any constitutional property or liberty interest because by marriage, the parties did not enter into a contract so much as form a new relation or create a status or condition which was purely a matter of the state legislature's to control. Hobbs v. Hobbs, 279 Ill. 163, 116 N.E. 629 (1917).

—Evidence Held Insufficient

Evidence produced was not sufficient to furnish an adequate legal basis for a decree for divorce on the ground of adultery. Fowler v. Fowler, 315 Ill. App. 270, 42 N.E.2d 954 (4 Dist. 1942).

—Evidence Held Sufficient

The finding of the trial court that husband was guilty of adultery was not clearly and palpably erroneous. Overton v. Overton, 6 Ill. App. 3d 1086, 287 N.E.2d 47 (2 Dist. 1972).

Decree awarding husband divorce on the ground of adultery was sustained by the evidence which more than adequately established that wife and her gentleman friend were disposed to commit the offense charged and had ample opportunity to do so. Dubinka v. Dubinka, 126 Ill. App. 2d 436, 262 N.E.2d 133 (1 Dist. 1970).

Evidence was sufficient to find that wife was guilty of adultery. Wachowski v. Wachowski, 86 Ill. App. 2d 145, 229 N.E.2d 149 (2 Dist. 1967).

Evidence was sufficient to sustain finding that husband was guilty of adultery and, therefore, was not entitled to divorce, even though wife had deserted him. Kovac v. Kovac, 26 Ill. App. 2d 29, 167 N.E.2d 281 (2 Dist. 1960).

Testimony of witnesses including that of wife's father, stepmother and brother was sufficient proof of circumstances from which the trial judge could reasonably infer that wife was guilty of adultery. Wolfrum v. Wolfrum, 5 Ill. App. 2d 471, 126 N.E.2d 34 (3 Dist. 1955).

Where the evidence of a wife's adultery was established by proof of the specific charges alleged in the complaint, the evidence was held sufficient to sustain a decree of divorce for the husband. Marcy v. Marcy, 400 Ill. 152, 79 N.E.2d 207 (1947).

—Proof

Before a court will enter a decree based on adultery, the evidence and proof must convince the mind affirmatively that actual adultery was committed, since nothing but the carnal act can lay the foundation for a divorce on those grounds. Wachowski v. Wachowski, 86 Ill. App. 2d 145, 229 N.E.2d 149 (2 Dist. 1967).

To establish adultery there must be affirmative proof of the carnal act, and such proof is ordinarily established by circumstantial evidence. Wolfrum v. Wolfrum, 5 Ill. App. 2d 471, 126 N.E.2d 34 (3 Dist. 1955).

A divorce on the ground of adultery should be granted only upon proof of the clearest and most convincing character. Fowler v. Fowler, 315 Ill. App. 270, 42 N.E.2d 954 (4 Dist. 1942).

Appeal

—In General

A judgment of dissolution that disposes of all matters for which a

Appeal (Cont'd)

—In General (Cont'd)
claim is made is appealable as a matter of constitutional right, but those judgments which reserve pending claims for custody, maintenance or property are appealable only if a Supreme Court rule makes those judgments appealable. In re Lentz, 73 Ill. App. 3d 93, 29 Ill. Dec. 319, 391 N.E.2d 582 (4 Dist. 1979), aff'd, 79 Ill. 2d 400, 38 Ill. Dec. 582, 403 N.E.2d 1036 (1980).

—Estoppel
Where a party to a divorce has demonstrated an unqualified intention to be bound by the decree by contracting another marriage, that party is estopped from later prosecuting an appeal attacking the grounds upon which the divorce was granted; such a party is not estopped from attacking on appeal other elements of the divorce decree, such as awards of custody, alimony, property divisions, or any portion of the decree which upon a reversal and remand would not affect the validity of the marital dissolution. Royster v. Hammel, 51 Ill. App. 3d 710, 9 Ill. Dec. 278, 366 N.E.2d 535 (5 Dist. 1977).

—Judgment
A judgment which dissolved a marriage and which reserved other issues and claims between husband and wife was a final judgment, and since the judge included a finding that there was no just reason to delay an appeal, the judgment was appealable. In re Nilsson, 81 Ill. App. 3d 580, 37 Ill. Dec. 394, 402 N.E.2d 284 (3 Dist. 1980).

—Reserved Issues
Where, by an earlier court order, the issue of maintenance was reversed for consideration at a later date, because this issue was not determined by the order appealed from but rather was expressly reserved by the trial court, it was not properly before the appellate court. In re Ford, 91 Ill. App. 3d 1066, 47 Ill. Dec. 541, 415 N.E.2d 546 (1 Dist. 1980).

—Waiver
A wife did not waive her right to appeal by accepting the benefits of a divorce decree, even though she had taken $50 alimony and child support payments subsequent to the divorce, used the household furnishings granted to her by said decree, occupied the home premises without cost, accepted payment of her attorney fees in the amount specified by the court, and benefited from the transcript of proceedings purchased by the defendant. Lemon v. Lemon, 14 Ill. 2d 15, 150 N.E.2d 608 (1958).

Applicability

—Amendment During Appeal
The trial court on remand properly applied the law in effect at the time of the original dissolution of marriage judgment, rather than the amendment which became effective prior to remand. In re Smith, 162 Ill. App. 3d 792, 114 Ill. Dec. 622, 516 N.E.2d 777 (5 Dist. 1987).
Mere fact that a person could have had more than one residence and, therefore, could possibly secure a divorce in more than one jurisdiction under former Ill.Rev.Stat., ch. 40, para. 3 (see now this section) did not render action improper. Berlingieri v. Berlingieri, 372 Ill. 60, 22 N.E.2d 675 (1939).

Apportionment

—Upheld
Apportionment of marital interest in pension under the proportionality rule was upheld under which the marital interest in the pension was equal to the total pension benefit times the ratio of years of marriage in which there was participation in the plan to total years of participation in the plan. In re Wisniewski, 286 Ill. App. 3d 236, 221 Ill. Dec. 632, 675 N.E.2d 1362 (4 Dist. 1997), appeal denied, 173 Ill. 2d 549, 226 Ill. Dec. 140, 684 N.E.2d 1343 (1997).

Authority of Court

—In General
The court's authority to grant a dissolution of marriage is entirely statutory in origin and nature, and the court's authority is limited thereby. In re Cohn, 94 Ill. App. 3d 732, 50 Ill. Dec. 621, 419 N.E.2d 729 (2 Dist. 1981), aff'd, 93 Ill. 2d 190, 66 Ill. Dec. 615, 443 N.E.2d 541 (1982).
It was the duty of the court, as representative of the state, when a fact or circumstance appeared in evidence which might have affected the right to a divorce, to require a full and complete disclosure of all material matters if the parties themselves failed to take such steps. Mischler v. Mischler, 333 Ill. App. 214, 77 N.E.2d 209 (1 Dist. 1948).

—Change of Decree
A divorce decree is final as to the circumstances and conditions of the parties as of the date of its entry, and a court, therefore, can only consider such changes that have occurred subsequently. Waltrip v. Waltrip, 3 Ill. App. 3d 892, 279 N.E.2d 405 (2 Dist. 1972).

—Grounds for Divorce
The question of what shall constitute grounds for granting a divorce, or whether the marriage contract shall be dissolved under any circumstances, or for any cause, is one of public policy, and belongs to the legislature, and not to the judiciary. Mogged v. Mogged, 55 Ill. 2d 221, 302 N.E.2d 293 (1973).

—Limitations
The power of the court in determining matters incident to divorce is limited by statutory provisions. Morrow v. Morrow, 15 Ill. App. 2d 109, 145 N.E.2d 381 (2 Dist. 1957).

—Order by Successor Judge
Entry of order dissolving marriage, by a successor judge, based upon the factual findings of his predecessor, was not improper. In re Ayers, 82 Ill. App. 3d 164, 37 Ill. Dec. 511, 402 N.E.2d 401 (3 Dist. 1980).

—Scope of Jurisdiction
Where a written waiver of the required two year waiting period necessary to obtain a dissolution on grounds of irreconcilable differences was not filed, the court was without subject matter jurisdiction to enter an order of dissolution. In re Robinson, 225 Ill. App. 3d 1037, 167 Ill. Dec. 1113, 588 N.E.2d 1243 (3 Dist. 1992).
Where the parties were married in this state, the matrimonial domicile was established in this state as both became residents of state and remained when the cause of action arose, and acts of physical cruelty were committed by defendant at their home in this state, the trial court had jurisdiction over the person of defendant. Farah v. Farah, 25 Ill. App. 3d 481, 323 N.E.2d 361 (1 Dist. 1975).
The plaintiff's residence in a divorce case for the requisite period is necessary to confer on the court jurisdiction of his case. Davis v. Davis, 9 Ill. App. 3d 922, 293 N.E.2d 399 (1 Dist. 1973).
To give a court jurisdiction to entertain a petition to vacate based on cruelty filed nearly four years after a divorce decree was entered, it must allege specifically, as was formerly required in a bill of review, such facts as would establish that the court entering the decree of divorce was without jurisdiction. Neitzke v. Neitzke, 15 Ill. App. 2d 473, 146 N.E.2d 708 (1 Dist. 1957).
The court, having made provision for the custody of a minor child, had jurisdiction to enter necessary and proper orders with respect thereto, and to enforce its orders could invoke the inherent powers of a court of chancery. Solomon v. Solomon, 5 Ill. App. 2d 297, 125 N.E.2d 675 (1 Dist. 1955).
Where the matter of a change of name of a minor child of divorced parents was a matter incidental to the custody of the child, the court had the jurisdiction to entertain the motion and to enter the order involved in the appeal. Solomon v. Solomon, 5 Ill. App. 2d 297, 125 N.E.2d 675 (1 Dist. 1955).
Where wife was properly served by publication and submitted herself to the jurisdiction of the court through her own chosen attorneys, was given notice and had a right to present proofs upon that issue of fact, but she was not present at the hearing, though not because of any fraud on the part of appellee, and the court determined the evidence and entered a decree of divorce accordingly, she could not collaterally attack the decree with evidence that husband did not reside in the county where suit was filed, and thus that the court lacked jurisdiction to enter the decree. Steffens v. Steffens, 408 Ill. 150, 96 N.E.2d 458 (1951).
The jurisdiction of a court hearing divorce matters is based upon statute rather than upon general equity powers. Persico v. Persico, 409 Ill. 608, 100 N.E.2d 904 (1951).

Authority of Court (Cont'd)

—Scope of Jurisdiction (Cont'd)

A city court had jurisdiction of a divorce action for desertion where plaintiff was a state resident for over a year before filing a complaint. Conrad v. Conrad, 396 Ill. 101, 71 N.E.2d 54 (1947).

Where the bill for divorce properly alleged that wife had wilfully deserted and absented herself from husband for the space of one year and upwards, the court had jurisdiction of the subject matter. Friend v. Northern Trust Co., 314 Ill. App. 596, 42 N.E.2d 330 (1 Dist. 1942).

Superior Court had jurisdiction to hear a divorce case and to grant a decree on the ground of wilful desertion for a period of one year, even though the court erroneously counted the time. Friend v. Northern Trust Co., 314 Ill. App. 596, 42 N.E.2d 330 (1 Dist. 1942).

—Scope of Review

A judgment of divorce should not be disturbed unless it is against the manifest weight of the evidence; however, where grounds of mental cruelty are alleged, it is necessary that a judgment for plaintiff be supported by positive evidence establishing the statutory ground. McGowan v. McGowan, 15 Ill. App. 3d 913, 305 N.E.2d 261 (1 Dist. 1973).

Where the decree of the trial court is supported by credible evidence, the court will not disturb the decree unless the same is clearly and palpably against the preponderance of the evidence. Elston v. Elston, 344 Ill. App. 233, 100 N.E.2d 635 (2 Dist. 1951).

A chancellor should only be bound to exercise his discretion as to whether there is evidence which satisfies him that the cause for divorce has been proved by reliable witnesses in open court; in determining that controlling factor, the court may take into consideration the presence or absence of the plaintiff in open court at the time of the hearing. Kinsley v. Kinsley, 388 Ill. 194, 57 N.E.2d 449 (1944).

—Sufficiency of Evidence

It is within the province of the trial court to make the determination whether there has been sufficient evidence with which to establish either party's contentions. Hayes v. Hayes, 117 Ill. App. 2d 211, 254 N.E.2d 288 (5 Dist. 1969).

Bifurcated Judgment

—In General

Appropriate circumstances for bifurcation of judgment in a dissolution proceeding include, but are not limited to, situations where the court does not have in personam jurisdiction over the respondent; where a party is unable to pay child support or maintenance if so ordered; where the court has set aside an adequate fund for child support pursuant to 750 ILCS 5/503; or where the parties' child or children do not reside with either parent. In re Bogan, 116 Ill. 2d 72, 107 Ill. Dec. 188, 506 N.E.2d 1243 (1986); In re Kenik, 181 Ill. App. 3d 266, 129 Ill. Dec. 932, 536 N.E.2d 982 (1 Dist.), appeal denied, 136 Ill. Dec. 587, 545 N.E.2d 111 (1989).

—Appropriate Circumstances Found

Emotional status of elderly, very ill wife qualified as appropriate circumstance for entry of bifurcated judgment of divorce, which was entitled to considerable deference. Copeland v. McLean, 327 Ill. App. 3d 855, 261 Ill. Dec. 692, 763 N.E.2d 941, 2002 Ill. App. LEXIS 90 (4 Dist. 2002).

Husband's sworn statement and judicial admission that he had no income and no liquid assets, along with the entire court record showing wife's continual difficulty in obtaining any child support from husband, provided ample grounds for bifurcation. In re Schweihs, 272 Ill. App. 3d 653, 208 Ill. Dec. 875, 650 N.E.2d 569 (1 Dist. 1995), appeal denied, 163 Ill. 2d 588, 212 Ill. Dec. 437, 657 N.E.2d 638 (1995).

Benefits to the emotional status of petitioner wife, an elderly, very ill woman, were correctly determined by trial court to be appropriate circumstances to bifurcate a judgment. In re Blount, 197 Ill. App. 3d 816, 144 Ill. Dec. 217, 555 N.E.2d 114 (4 Dist. 1990).

Where marital property consisted of items all readily identifiable and easily divided between the parties, one spouse's objections to bifurcation manifested themselves late in the litigation chronology, few complications and entanglements arose from the bifurcation of judgment, and exigencies were created by the pregnancy of one spouse, the court did not abuse its discretion in bifurcating the judgment of dissolution of marriage. In re Kenik, 181 Ill. App. 3d 266, 129 Ill. Dec. 932, 536 N.E.2d 982 (1 Dist.), appeal denied, 136 Ill. Dec. 587, 545 N.E.2d 111 (1989).

—Appropriate Circumstances Not Found

A respondent's inability to perform the social functions expected by his employer in connection with his job does not constitute an appropriate circumstance for bifurcation. In re Bogan, 116 Ill. 2d 72, 107 Ill. Dec. 188, 506 N.E.2d 1243 (1986).

—Live Testimony

The trial court did not need to take live testimony concerning the undisputed statements in the affidavits prior to ordering bifurcation. In re Schweihs, 272 Ill. App. 3d 653, 208 Ill. Dec. 875, 650 N.E.2d 569 (1 Dist. 1995), appeal denied, 163 Ill. 2d 588, 212 Ill. Dec. 437, 657 N.E.2d 638 (1995).

—Public Policy

Sound policy reasons militate against an interpretation of this section that gives a trial judge unfettered discretion to bifurcate a judgment of dissolution; however, certain circumstances will justify bifurcation of a judgment. In re Blount, 197 Ill. App. 3d 816, 144 Ill. Dec. 217, 555 N.E.2d 114 (4 Dist. 1990).

—Waiver of Objection

Former wife waived her right to object to the bifurcated judgment of dissolution where after the judgment of dissolution she continued to appear in subsequent proceedings, thereby acquiescing and accepting the validity of the circuit court's prior judgment. In re Walters, 129 Ill. App. 3d 1040, 85 Ill. Dec. 212, 473 N.E.2d 580 (3 Dist. 1985).

Bigamy

—Grounds

While a bigamous marriage was said to be void ab initio under former Marriage Act (see now this section), it was nevertheless a ground for divorce under the former Marriage Act, which presupposed a valid marriage. Cardenas v. Cardenas, 12 Ill. App. 2d 497, 140 N.E.2d 377 (1 Dist. 1956).

—Test

In a divorce action, where wife married husband who was married to someone else, the trial court, pursuant to the former Divorce Act, (see now 750 ILCS 5/101 et seq.), erroneously applied the standard that wife "knew or should have known" that husband was previously married; the proper and only test to be applied was whether wife was "the injured party," defined as one who did not know that his or her intended spouse had a prior undissolved marriage. Belluomini v. Belluomini, 73 Ill. App. 3d 836, 30 Ill. Dec. 14, 392 N.E.2d 669 (1 Dist. 1979).

Blood Tests

A trial court in a divorce proceeding had the authority to order blood tests for mother and minor child of the parties to aid in determining the paternity of the minor child, and the mother was properly held in contempt for her failure to comply with the court's order. Zavaleta v. Zavaleta, 43 Ill. App. 3d 1017, 3 Ill. Dec. 13, 358 N.E.2d 13 (1 Dist. 1976).

Challenge to Decree

Where a husband attempted to attack a divorce decree, asserting matters within his knowledge at the time of the divorce proceedings, he was held to have deliberately committed a fraud upon the court by concealing them, and could not be permitted to raise a question of the court's jurisdiction of the subject matter in a collateral proceeding as to matters not appearing of record, where he had an opportunity to present the question in the divorce proceeding and which he raised for the first time eight years after the decree was entered. Antczak v. Antczak, 61 Ill. App. 2d 404, 209 N.E.2d 838 (1 Dist. 1965).

—In General

A party to a divorce decree cannot accept those portions of the decree which are beneficial to him and afterward prosecute an appeal to reverse those parts which are unfavorable to him, where to do so would place the opposing party at a distinct disadvantage

Challenge to Decree (Cont'd)

—In General (Cont'd)
upon a reversal of the decree. Royster v. Hammel, 51 Ill. App. 3d 710, 9 Ill. Dec. 278, 366 N.E.2d 535 (5 Dist. 1977).

Condonation

For a case discussing former application of the defense of condonation after the petition for divorce was filed, see Trapani v. Trapani, 109 Ill. App. 2d 202, 248 N.E.2d 294 (4 Dist. 1969).

Construction of Judgment

—Extrinsic Evidence

Phrase "verdict, settlement and recovery" was too ambiguous to state definitively when former husband would become the owner of half of the proceeds from litigation, and since language of judgment of dissolution contained this significant ambiguity, extrinsic evidence was to be considered to determine what was intended by the language in question. Listeman, Bandy & Hamilton Ass'n v. Wilson, 103 Ill. App. 3d 87, 58 Ill. Dec. 717, 430 N.E.2d 749 (5 Dist. 1982), aff'd, 94 Ill. 2d 60, 67 Ill. Dec. 843, 445 N.E.2d 323 (1983).

Conveyance of Property

—Court-Ordered

In determining the propriety or impropriety of divorce decree ordering conveyance of property under former section 17 of the Divorce Act (see now this section), the authority of the court was based upon powers conferred by statute rather than upon general equity powers. Debrey v. Debrey, 132 Ill. App. 2d 1072, 270 N.E.2d 43 (4 Dist. 1971).

Conviction of Felony

Conviction by court-martial for desertion from military service in time of war is not a "felony or other infamous crime" within the meaning of this section; therefore, spouse could not obtain a divorce under former law authorizing divorce where spouse was "convicted of a felony." Getz v. Getz, 332 Ill. App. 364, 75 N.E.2d 530 (3 Dist. 1947).

Cruelty

—In General

Historically, a divorce based on cruelty required acts of physical violence or acts or threats which might raise a reasonable apprehension of bodily hurt; neglect of wife and children and refusal to provide them with food, clothing and shelter did not constitute legal cruelty. Maddox v. Maddox, 189 Ill. 152, 59 N.E. 599 (1901).

—Burden of Proof

Plaintiff must allege and prove the lack of provocation for defendant's acts. Smith v. Smith, 47 Ill. App. 3d 583, 5 Ill. Dec. 810, 362 N.E.2d 123 (3 Dist. 1977).

To establish cruelty it was necessary to prove by a preponderance of the evidence that the guilty party had at least on two separate occasions committed acts of physical violence against his spouse resulting in pain and bodily harm. Riva v. Riva, 93 Ill. App. 2d 137, 235 N.E.2d 655 (3 Dist. 1968).

—Corroboration Not Required

There is no rule requiring corroboration in a case alleging cruelty; and if testimony is sufficiently credible in the light of opposing evidence to warrant acceptance by a reasonable person, the court may not direct a verdict or enter judgment notwithstanding the verdict. Surratt v. Surratt, 12 Ill. 2d 21, 145 N.E.2d 594 (1957).

—Defenses

The charge of adultery was formerly a good recriminatory defense to the charge of cruelty. Nesheim v. Nesheim, 293 Ill. App. 257, 12 N.E.2d 222 (1 Dist. 1938).

—Evidence Held Insufficient

Neither party met the quantum of proof necessary to support a decree of divorce under former Ill.Rev.Stat., ch. 40, para. 1 (see now this section) based upon mental cruelty where the plaintiff testified that at sporadic times during the marriage defendant's conduct embarrassed and humiliated him, but he failed to establish that the defendant's conduct was calculated or obviously of a nature to torture, discommode or render his life unendurable or miserable and actually affected his physical or mental health, and neither party established the lack of provocation. Gregory v. Gregory, 24 Ill. App. 3d 436, 321 N.E.2d 122 (2 Dist. 1974).

Trial court properly found that plaintiff had not proved her case by a preponderance of the evidence as to the acts of cruelty involved, and dismissed her complaint for want of equity. Balfour v. Balfour, 20 Ill. App. 2d 590, 156 N.E.2d 629 (2 Dist. 1959).

Evidence of violent acts was insufficient to sustain plaintiff's charges of extreme and repeated cruelty, and thus the court erred in entering a decree dissolving the marriage. Tesar v. Tesar, 13 Ill. App. 2d 478, 142 N.E.2d 504 (1 Dist. 1957).

There was not sufficient proof of cruelty to justify the plaintiff in abandoning the defendant, assuming that the defendant did the things charged by the plaintiff. Swan v. Swan, 331 Ill. App. 295, 73 N.E.2d 153 (4 Dist. 1947).

Where plaintiff, in a divorce suit, charged defendant with cruelty as a basis for divorce, and the appellate court determined that plaintiff had not made out such a case as would have entitled her to a divorce from her husband, the order of the circuit court granting plaintiff a divorce and allowing her alimony was reversed. Jackson v. Jackson, 294 Ill. App. 552, 14 N.E.2d 271 (2 Dist. 1938).

—Evidence Held Sufficient

Although the divorce decree did not contain a separate finding as to provocation, the general finding that plaintiff had proved mental and physical cruelty against defendant was sufficient as to all the elements of her cause of action. Smith v. Smith, 47 Ill. App. 3d 583, 5 Ill. Dec. 810, 362 N.E.2d 123 (3 Dist. 1977).

The concept of cruelty as a basis for divorce, whether mental or physical, contemplates that the propriety of the conduct be judged in light of all the circumstances including any precipitating conduct; whether defendant husband's conduct was appropriate under the circumstances presented a question of fact and the jury's resolution of this issue against him was supported by ample evidence. Woodshank v. Woodshank, 2 Ill. App. 3d 596, 274 N.E.2d 694 (3 Dist. 1971).

The trial court's finding that the defendant was guilty of cruelty was not against the manifest weight of the evidence. Stockman v. Stockman, 38 Ill. App. 2d 186, 186 N.E.2d 547 (4 Dist. 1962).

Evidence was insufficient to support charges of drunkenness, but findings and evidence with respect to cruelty justified the divorce decree. Jones v. Jones, 13 Ill. App. 2d 198, 141 N.E.2d 408 (1 Dist. 1957).

Evidence was sufficient to entitle husband to divorce on cruelty and adultery grounds. Jackson v. Jackson, 294 Ill. App. 552, 14 N.E.2d 271 (2 Dist. 1938).

Evidence was sufficient to warrant the finding of extreme cruelty and grant of divorce on the ground of extreme and repeated cruelty. Wesselhoeft v. Wesselhoeft, 369 Ill. 419, 17 N.E.2d 56 (1938).

Court properly ruled in favor of the wife where she sought a divorce on the grounds of cruelty and drunkenness, and so sought the cancellation of certain deeds and assignments from her grandmother and the cancellation of certain of her own deeds whereby she had placed her husband in joint tenancy with herself as to certain properties owned by her. Thomas v. Thomas, 361 Ill. 376, 198 N.E. 201 (1935).

—Extreme and Repeated

Plaintiff failed to prove extreme and repeated acts of cruelty to sustain the complaint for divorce. Sharer v. Sharer, 39 Ill. App. 3d 818, 350 N.E.2d 779 (5 Dist. 1976).

Under former Ill.Rev.Stat., ch. 40, para. 1 (see now this section), extreme and repeated mental cruelty was a cause for divorce, and whether certain acts constituted mental cruelty depended upon the total factual background of each case, the emotional and personal make-up of the parties, and the circumstances under which the incidents occurred. Gregory v. Gregory, 24 Ill. App. 3d 436, 321 N.E.2d 122 (2 Dist. 1974).

The standard to be applied by a trial court in evaluating evidence in passing upon a motion for a divorce based on extreme and repeated cruelty is whether the evidence, when viewed in its aspect most favorable to the opponent, so overwhelmingly favors the moving party that no contrary result based upon that evidence could ever stand. Bochenek v. Bochenek, 5 Ill. App. 3d 65, 283 N.E.2d 95 (1 Dist. 1972).

In a divorce proceeding based on extreme and repeated cruelty, a plaintiff had to prove two separate and distinct acts of cruelty in

Cruelty (Cont'd)

—Extreme and Repeated (Cont'd)

order to establish extreme and repeated cruelty. Lemanski v. Lemanski, 87 Ill. App. 2d 405, 231 N.E.2d 191 (2 Dist. 1967).

The evidence in a divorce proceeding was sufficient to sustain a finding of extreme and repeated cruelty where on one date the husband pulled the plaintiff out of bed, knocked her to the floor and knocked her into a dresser in the bedroom, and on another date the husband also knocked the plaintiff into a bedroom wall causing her to have a bruise on her arm, and when she attempted to call the police, he struck her. Lemanski v. Lemanski, 87 Ill. App. 2d 405, 231 N.E.2d 191 (2 Dist. 1967).

For a case discussing sufficiency of evidence to substantiate granting decree of divorce or grounds of extreme and repeated cruelty, see Coons v. Coons, 30 Ill. App. 2d 325, 174 N.E.2d 231 (2 Dist. 1961).

Plaintiff's evidence, viewed most favorably to her, set forth a prima facie case showing extreme and repeated cruelty on the part of the defendant. Collinet v. Collinet, 31 Ill. App. 2d 72, 175 N.E.2d 659 (1 Dist. 1961).

Extreme and repeated cruelty to warrant a divorce has been defined as physical acts of violence, bodily harm or suffering, or such acts as endanger life or limb or such as raise a reasonable apprehension of great bodily harm. Mason v. Mason, 342 Ill. App. 140, 95 N.E.2d 522 (1 Dist. 1950).

For a case discussing refusal of sexual intercourse as grounds for desertion and one act of violence preceded by insult and abuse as constituting extreme and repeated cruelty in a divorce action, see Fritz v. Fritz, 138 Ill. 436, 28 N.E. 1058 (1891).

—Requirements

Whether certain acts will constitute physical or mental cruelty depends upon the total factual background surrounding the conduct in question, including the particular emotional and personal makeup of the parties, and the varying circumstances under which any of the incidents occurred that may have given rise to the acts. Hayes v. Hayes, 117 Ill. App. 2d 211, 254 N.E.2d 288 (5 Dist. 1969).

To establish cruelty within the meaning of former Ill.Rev.Stat., ch. 40, para. 1 (see now this section), it was necessary to prove by a preponderance of the evidence that the guilty party had on at least two separate occasions committed acts of physical violence against his spouse resulting in pain and bodily harm. Tuyls v. Tuyls, 21 Ill. 2d 192, 171 N.E.2d 779 (1961).

—Slight Acts of Violence

Slight acts of violence by either spouse are not extreme cruelty within this section authorizing divorce on such grounds. Tesar v. Tesar, 13 Ill. App. 2d 478, 142 N.E.2d 504 (1 Dist. 1957).

—Uncorroborated Testimony

A divorce will not be granted upon uncorroborated testimony as to alleged acts of cruelty. Tesar v. Tesar, 13 Ill. App. 2d 478, 142 N.E.2d 504 (1 Dist. 1957).

Death of Spouse

—Abatement of Dissolution Judgement

Trial court erred by ordering an accounting of the parties' property and a division of marital property after the wife died because no judgment of dissolution had been entered, under 750 ILCS 5/401(b), so the trial court lost jurisdiction to rule on any matter regarding the parties' marital relationship. In re Marriage of Ignatius, 338 Ill. App. 3d 652, 273 Ill. Dec. 203, 788 N.E.2d 794, 2003 Ill. App. LEXIS 518 (2 Dist. 2003).

—Abatement of Dissolution Judgment

The trial court's decision to abate a divorce proceeding, after entry of an order dissolving the marriage but prior to deciding the issues of maintenance and attorney fees, because of the death of a party, was reversed. Stacke v. Bates, 163 Ill. App. 3d 893, 115 Ill. Dec. 58, 517 N.E.2d 23 (2 Dist. 1987), appeal denied, 119 Ill. 2d 575, 119 Ill. Dec. 398, 522 N.E.2d 1257 (1988).

Where a judgment of dissolution had not been entered before wife's death, the proceedings for dissolution abated. Brandon v. Caisse, 145 Ill. App. 3d 1070, 99 Ill. Dec. 894, 496 N.E.2d 755 (2 Dist. 1986); In re Black, 155 Ill. App. 3d 52, 107 Ill. Dec. 790, 507 N.E.2d 943 (3 Dist. 1987).

—Judgment Prior to Death

Where parties were separated by a final judgment prior to husband's death and prior to a property disposition ruling, the fact that the judgment was not immediately appealable did not alter the finality of the trial court's judgment of dissolution. In re Garlinski, 99 Ill. App. 3d 107, 54 Ill. Dec. 510, 425 N.E.2d 22 (2 Dist. 1981).

—Property Issues

Property issues survive the death of a party where the divorce decree is entered prior to his death. In re Garlinski, 99 Ill. App. 3d 107, 54 Ill. Dec. 510, 425 N.E.2d 22 (2 Dist. 1981).

Decree

—Consent of Parties

A decree for divorce may not be entered by the consent of the parties. Ullrich v. Ullrich, 299 Ill. App. 460, 20 N.E.2d 347 (1 Dist. 1939).

—Default Decree

Where in his testimony at a hearing on a motion to vacate a divorce decree, the defendant admitted that he had been personally served with the summons issued and that a copy of plaintiff's complaint was attached to the summons, he took the summons and complaint to consult with an attorney but did not engage the attorney to represent him, and at a subsequent date, but prior to the entry of the decree, the attorney wrote a letter to the defendant reminding him of the pendency of the case, but defendant still did not retain the attorney or any other attorney to represent him in the case, and the record indicated that the defendant was fully aware of the implications that could flow from the complaint, the trial court did not abuse its discretion in refusing to vacate the decree of divorce; defendant was guilty of unexcusable delay in retaining counsel and entering the case, and despite his delay and failure to appeal, the decree rendered by the trial court did not work an injustice upon the defendant. Morning v. Morning, 9 Ill. App. 3d 555, 291 N.E.2d 875 (5 Dist. 1973).

—Effect

A decree of divorce enables the parties to contract a new marriage; that it does not necessarily relieve them of all the obligations of the old is witnessed by the award of alimony upon, or even after, divorce. Pope v. Pope, 2 Ill. 2d 152, 117 N.E.2d 65 (1954).

—Finality

Where the record on appeal indicated that the issue of attorney fees remained unresolved, the last order in the record relating to fees indicated that the matter was continued, and the record contained no order granting, denying or dismissing the fee petitions, the order from which respondent appealed was not a final one. Tyler v. Tyler, 230 Ill. App. 3d 1009, 172 Ill. Dec. 840, 596 N.E.2d 119 (1 Dist. 1992).

A decree of divorce is final as to the circumstances and conditions of the parties as of the date of its entry; upon a subsequent application for a modification, only matters which have occurred subsequent to the entry of the decree may be considered by the court. Louthan v. Louthan, 130 Ill. App. 2d 281, 264 N.E.2d 797 (1 Dist. 1970).

—Unconscionability

In a divorce action where plaintiff wife had no counsel of record when the cause was called for trial, the trial court's ex parte decree of divorce entered upon defendant husband's counterclaim was totally one-sided and unconscionable in that it awarded the defendant husband virtually all of the parties' real and personal property besides granting him custody of the children who were then residing with the wife, and barred wife from receiving alimony; the decree was vacated. Eden v. Eden, 34 Ill. App. 3d 382, 340 N.E.2d 141 (1 Dist. 1975).

Defenses

—In General

A divorce on the ground of adultery was not barred by a defense of cruelty, habitual drunkenness, or other statutory grounds. Stanard v. Stanard, 108 Ill. App. 2d 240, 247 N.E.2d 438 (3 Dist. 1969).

—Adultery

Under former Ill.Rev.Stat., ch. 40, para. 1 (see now this section),

Defenses (Cont'd)

—Adultery (Cont'd)
adultery was a good defense to any statutory ground for divorce, including the charge of adultery. Stanard v. Stanard, 108 Ill. App. 2d 240, 247 N.E.2d 438 (3 Dist. 1969).

Denial of Hearing

—Held Improper
Where affidavit of wife for motion to set aside the decree for divorce alleged some specific facts which, if true, would have required setting aside of the decree, it was error for trial court to deny the motion without a hearing. Reynolds v. Reynolds, 11 Ill. App. 3d 149, 296 N.E.2d 42 (5 Dist. 1973).

Desertion

—Computation
A decree granted for wilful desertion which erroneously included in the period of one year of wilful desertion the time in which a bill of complaint for separate maintenance was pending was erroneous. Ullrich v. Ullrich, 299 Ill. App. 460, 20 N.E.2d 347 (1 Dist. 1939).

—Constructive
For a case discussing constructive desertion, see Nalepa v. Nalepa, 103 Ill. App. 2d 225, 243 N.E.2d 862 (1 Dist. 1969).

Evidence was sufficient to support the divorce decree granted on the grounds of constructive desertion where both sides testified to the fact that the parties had lived separate and apart for more than one year, and there was testimony that the husband was guilty of extreme and repeated cruelty and adultery. Dayan v. Dayan, 86 Ill. App. 2d 358, 229 N.E.2d 568 (5 Dist. 1967).

Where defendant refused to cohabit with husband after 33 years of marriage, refused to cook his meals, refused to talk to him and insisted on a support and property settlement, he could no longer be said to have a home; therefore, when he left what had been the marital home, he did only what he felt compelled to do, and thus, the rule of constructive desertion did not apply where the separation was without the consent of the plaintiff, as he was not the deserter but the deserted. Gillespie v. Gillespie, 70 Ill. App. 2d 38, 216 N.E.2d 462 (5 Dist. 1966).

Where it was clear that the husband made no serious objection to the marital circumstances but by his acts acquiesced in their continuance, his removal from the premises constituted a voluntary separation and not a constructive desertion, and therefore the trial court erred in granting a decree for divorce based upon desertion under former Ill.Rev.Stat., ch. 40, para. 1 (see now this section). Lemon v. Lemon, 14 Ill. 2d 15, 150 N.E.2d 608 (1958).

Evidence did not support granting wife a divorce based on ground of constructive desertion where she claimed to have been driven from family home by quarrels with husband over money, religion, and other matters. Coolidge v. Coolidge, 4 Ill. App. 2d 205, 124 N.E.2d 1 (1 Dist. 1955).

—Defenses
Where the complainant in a divorce proceeding has, either expressly or impliedly, consented to the original separation or its continuance, and has not revoked consent, he is not entitled to a divorce for desertion; if this consent appears in defense, it is a bar to the action. Larimore v. Larimore, 299 Ill. App. 547, 20 N.E.2d 902 (4 Dist. 1939).

A party charged with desertion may defeat the petition for divorce by showing that the plaintiff has been guilty of adultery after the alleged desertion, for the reason that the plaintiff in such a case does not come into court with clean hands, or at least is regarded as precluded, by his own guilty conduct which is itself a ground of divorce, from relying on the defendant's guilt with respect to the other cause of divorce. Nesheim v. Nesheim, 293 Ill. App. 257, 12 N.E.2d 222 (1 Dist. 1938).

—Defined
Desertion imports a cessation of cohabitation, a refusal to live together, which involves an abnegation of all the duties and obligations resulting from the marriage contract. Foster v. Foster, 110 Ill. App. 2d 128, 249 N.E.2d 114 (1 Dist. 1969).

Under former Ill.Rev.Stat., ch. 40, para. 1 (see now this section), a wife had a duty to follow her husband when he chose to change his residence, and her failure to do so in most circumstances, save for special circumstances, constituted desertion. Martin v. Martin, 62 Ill. App. 2d 105, 210 N.E.2d 590 (1 Dist. 1965).

—Evidence Held Insufficient
Plaintiff wife could not be guilty of desertion where trial court's decision that acts of extreme and repeated physical cruelty by husband were not condoned was not against the manifest weight of the evidence, so that there existed a reasonable cause for plaintiff wife's leaving the marital home. Jackson v. Jackson, 34 Ill. App. 3d 407, 339 N.E.2d 764 (1 Dist. 1975).

The finding of desertion was not against the manifest weight of the evidence and the divorce decree was sustained. Motykowski v. Motykowski, 4 Ill. App. 3d 957, 282 N.E.2d 458 (1 Dist. 1972).

Evidence did not support the finding that the defendant wilfully deserted the plaintiff where evidence was lacking as to actual abandonment and wife continued to live in home financially supported by husband. Williams v. Williams, 34 Ill. App. 2d 210, 181 N.E.2d 182 (4 Dist. 1962).

Evidence did not support granting of divorce to husband on ground of desertion. Bramson v. Bramson, 4 Ill. App. 2d 249, 124 N.E.2d 33 (1 Dist. 1955).

Neither a husband nor wife in this state was entitled to a divorce on the ground of desertion under the former Divorce Act (see now 750 ILCS 5/101 et seq.) where the alleged desertion took place with the consent of the other spouse. Maxwell v. Maxwell, 333 Ill. App. 625, 78 N.E.2d 140 (2 Dist. 1948).

Where a wife's brother testified only that he knew his sister was living separate and apart from her husband without her fault, and that she charged her husband with deserting and abandoning her since that date, this evidence did not sustain the charge of wilful desertion under the statute. Borin v. Borin, 335 Ill. App. 450, 82 N.E.2d 70 (1 Dist. 1948).

The court erred in granting a divorce to a husband on the ground of desertion where the wife was justified in such desertion because the proof absolutely showed that she was entitled to a divorce on the ground either of extreme and repeated cruelty or of habitual drunkenness; there was no evidence in the record of any wilful desertion on her part because his ill-treatment of her was the cause of their living separate and apart. Holmstedt v. Holmstedt, 383 Ill. 290, 49 N.E.2d 25 (1943).

—Evidence Held Sufficient
There was sufficient evidence to prove the grounds of constructive desertion. In re Yakin, 107 Ill. App. 3d 1103, 62 Ill. Dec. 547, 436 N.E.2d 573 (1 Dist. 1982).

Where the intention of the wife to abandon the marriage relationship, but not the marriage, as she testified that she did not believe in divorce, remained fixed and firm even during the trial, the evidence was more than ample to support the finding of the trial court that the defendant wife was guilty of wilful desertion for over a year without reasonable cause. Pohren v. Pohren, 13 Ill. App. 3d 380, 300 N.E.2d 288 (3 Dist. 1973).

A divorce decree was supported by the manifest weight of the evidence where the husband counterclaimed for divorce alleging mental cruelty and desertion, and the trial court held the wife in contempt of court and noted that, after the wife had taken the parties' child to another country, despite proceedings in that country's courts in which the care and control of the child was given to the husband, the wife still failed and refused to return him to the jurisdiction. Bejnarowicz v. Bejnarowicz, 8 Ill. App. 3d 835, 291 N.E.2d 345 (1 Dist. 1972).

There was no element of surprise presented to the defendant when, after more than one year had elapsed since the plaintiff justifiably abandoned him, the plaintiff sought to amend her complaint for divorce to include ground of desertion; therefore, the court's discretion was not abused in allowing the amendment for desertion. People v. Almanza, 76 Ill. App. 2d 395, 222 N.E.2d 74 (1 Dist. 1966).

Evidence supported an award of divorce on grounds of desertion where wife's teaching position in another state's school system, her home in that other state, her tenure as a teacher and her pension rights, and her pursuit of a master's degree in library science outweighed whatever desire she may have had to move to Illinois to be with her husband. Martin v. Martin, 62 Ill. App. 2d 105, 210 N.E.2d 590 (1 Dist. 1965).

Desertion (Cont'd)

—Evidence Held Sufficient (Cont'd)

When she refused to cohabit with her husband in a reasonable manner and ordered him to leave, the wife became the deserter, and the husband, by leaving, did not consent to the separation and could not be prevented from prosecuting a divorce action on the basis of desertion. Karman v. Karman, 24 Ill. App. 2d 123, 164 N.E.2d 521 (1 Dist. 1960).

Wife was properly granted a divorce on the ground of desertion where the evidence established that the husband, who had been found at fault in a separate maintenance action, wilfully continued to refuse normal cohabitation. Moyer v. Moyer, 17 Ill. App. 2d 404, 150 N.E.2d 394 (1 Dist. 1958).

Wife was shown to have deserted her husband without reasonable cause. Landrey v. Landrey, 13 Ill. App. 2d 202, 141 N.E.2d 405 (1 Dist. 1957).

In a wife's separate maintenance action in which there was a counterclaim by the husband for divorce, the trial court erred when it dismissed the wife's complaint but granted a divorce on the counterclaim since the evidence established that the husband was not justified in leaving his wife; therefore, as a matter of law, the wife could not have been guilty of desertion. Webber v. Webber, 349 Ill. App. 154, 110 N.E.2d 95 (1 Dist. 1953).

In a divorce action, where a wife wrongfully had her husband committed as mentally ill, the evidence was sufficient to find the wife guilty of wilful desertion. Snavely v. Snavely, 349 Ill. App. 369, 110 N.E.2d 685 (1 Dist. 1953).

Evidence sustained a finding of desertion under the former Divorce Act (see now 750 ILCS 5/101 et seq.) where it was undisputed that husband did not return to his residence to cohabit with wife as man and wife after the date of his hospital discharge and wife filed her complaint for divorce more than two years later. Nowogurski v. Nowogurski, 404 Ill. 276, 88 N.E.2d 831 (1949).

While the evidence was conflicting, the record contained ample testimony to support the finding that the defendant had wilfully deserted her husband for the space of one year without reasonable cause; therefore the decree for divorce was not contrary to the manifest weight of the evidence. Insoda v. Insoda, 400 Ill. 596, 81 N.E.2d 473 (1948).

Separation was with consent where plaintiff sent word to defendant that he had chosen to live with his mother instead of her, and had told that to others, and therefore defendant was justified in the belief that he did not desire her return. Larimore v. Larimore, 299 Ill. App. 547, 20 N.E.2d 902 (4 Dist. 1939).

—Grounds

For a case discussing desertion as grounds for divorce under a prior similar provision, see Edmond v. Edmond, 20 Ill. App. 3d 40, 312 N.E.2d 766 (5 Dist. 1974).

For a case discussing desertion and constructive desertion as grounds for divorce, see David v. David, 102 Ill. App. 2d 102, 243 N.E.2d 485 (1 Dist. 1968).

—Living Separate and Apart

Where the parties live separate and apart by mutual consent, it does not constitute desertion on the part of either and neither party is entitled to a divorce on the ground of desertion. Maxwell v. Maxwell, 333 Ill. App. 625, 78 N.E.2d 140 (2 Dist. 1948).

—Not Shown

Wife's conduct of leaving the husband three days after their marriage could not be evaluated as a desertion under 750 ILCS 5/401(a)(1), but the wife failed to explain how the statute precluded the use of such conduct as a factor in one of the other grounds for dissolution; the husband did not base his petition on the wife's alleged desertion but on her alleged mental cruelty which was based on the effects of her leaving the husband. In re Kirkpatrick, 329 Ill. App. 3d 202, 263 Ill. Dec. 727, 768 N.E.2d 808, 2002 Ill. App. LEXIS 301 (2 Dist. 2002).

After a decree for separate maintenance had been granted his wife, husband, who was guilty of desertion for more than one year and whose sincere attempts thereafter to effect a reconciliation were repulsed, could not obtain a divorce upon the theory that the refusal of his wife to resume marital relations constituted desertion. Hilliard v. Hilliard, 25 Ill. App. 2d 468, 167 N.E.2d 451 (1 Dist. 1960).

Where in wife's suit for separate maintenance the question of whether she was guilty of desertion was closely contested and wife was absent during part of trial due to illness, the court erred in denying wife's motion to set aside divorce decree. Nusser v. Nusser, 4 Ill. App. 2d 538, 124 N.E.2d 549 (1 Dist. 1955).

—Refusal of Sexual Relations

Refusal of sexual relations by one party does not constitute desertion, since such a refusal is a violation of only one aspect of marital life. Foster v. Foster, 110 Ill. App. 2d 128, 249 N.E.2d 114 (1 Dist. 1969).

—Requirements

The nature of a complaint for divorce based upon desertion requires that the parties be living separate and apart. Howison v. Howison, 128 Ill. App. 2d 377, 262 N.E.2d 1 (2 Dist. 1970).

Former Ill.Rev.Stat., ch. 40, para. 1 (see now this section) was applicable not only in cases where the complaining party was actually abandoned but also where she herself abandoned her spouse for causes which would have entitled her to a divorce. People v. Almanza, 76 Ill. App. 2d 395, 222 N.E.2d 74 (1 Dist. 1966).

The spouse alleging desertion must affirmatively prove, by a greater preponderance of the evidence, that the offending spouse has abnegated all of the marital obligations, wilfully and without the consent of the other. Williams v. Williams, 34 Ill. App. 2d 210, 181 N.E.2d 182 (4 Dist. 1962).

To constitute desertion, the living separate and apart must be against the will of the party claiming desertion. Maxwell v. Maxwell, 333 Ill. App. 625, 78 N.E.2d 140 (2 Dist. 1948).

Desertion, to constitute legal grounds for divorce, must be wilful and without reasonable cause and must exist for a period of more than one year. Insoda v. Insoda, 400 Ill. 596, 81 N.E.2d 473 (1948); Lutticke v. Lutticke, 406 Ill. 181, 92 N.E.2d 754 (1950).

Plaintiff, to establish the charge of desertion, was required to prove that defendant had absented herself and remained away from him without any reasonable cause and against his will. Larimore v. Larimore, 299 Ill. App. 547, 20 N.E.2d 902 (4 Dist. 1939).

Under a prior similar provision, before a complainant could obtain a divorce on the ground of desertion, he was required to prove that his wife wilfully deserted and absented herself from the complainant, without any reasonable cause, for the space of two years before the filing of the bill, and where the evidence showed that the complainant cohabited with the defendant on several occasions during the two years before the filing of the bill, this was a complete defense to the action. Phelan v. Phelan, 135 Ill. 445, 25 N.E. 751 (1890).

—Separation by Mutual Consent

Separation by mutual consent does not constitute desertion within the contemplation of this section. Lutticke v. Lutticke, 406 Ill. 181, 92 N.E.2d 754 (1950).

Dismissal of Action

It would have been improper for the trial court to refuse to vacate a divorce decree and dismiss the bill for attorney fees where both parties moved to have the case dismissed simply so court could order psychiatric counseling, particularly in light of the fact that no grave need for such testing was shown. In re Bauer, 82 Ill. App. 3d 294, 37 Ill. Dec. 715, 402 N.E.2d 717 (1 Dist. 1980).

Parties to a divorce action have a right to have it dismissed even after judgment if the parties seek dismissal within the 30 day period in which the trial court retains jurisdiction. In re Bauer, 82 Ill. App. 3d 294, 37 Ill. Dec. 715, 402 N.E.2d 717 (1 Dist. 1980).

Where the wife claimed by sworn statement that she was induced by her attorney to file her amended complaint for divorce upon the representation that she would be given exclusive custody of her child and that adequate provision for the support of herself and the child would be made, and this promise, at least as to the custody of the child, was not fulfilled, the complaint should have been dismissed on wife's motion. Borin v. Borin, 335 Ill. App. 450, 82 N.E.2d 70 (1 Dist. 1948).

Disposal of All Issues

The trial court cannot enter judgments of dissolution that fail to dispose of all issues raised by the petition for dissolution, except in appropriate circumstances. In re Walters, 129 Ill. App. 3d 1040, 85 Ill. Dec. 212, 473 N.E.2d 580 (3 Dist. 1985).

Distribution

—Factors

Where a marriage was of short duration, it was not unreasonable for the court to examine the financial condition of the parties for a period of time before the decree. Borowitz v. Borowitz, 19 Ill. App. 3d 176, 311 N.E.2d 292 (1 Dist. 1974).

Domicile

For cases construing former domicile requirements, see In re Weiss, 87 Ill. App. 3d 643, 42 Ill. Dec. 714, 409 N.E.2d 329 (1 Dist. 1980); In re Gryka, 90 Ill. App. 3d 443, 45 Ill. Dec. 820, 413 N.E.2d 153 (1 Dist. 1980); In re Goslin, 106 Ill. App. 3d 87, 62 Ill. Dec. 23, 435 N.E.2d 821 (4 Dist. 1982); In re Parks, 122 Ill. App. 3d 905, 78 Ill. Dec. 97, 461 N.E.2d 681 (2 Dist. 1984).

Where, according to the husband's testimony, in May or June of 1932 he determined to make his permanent domicile in Chicago and at that time stated the reasons for the change to the plaintiff and their son, several months after he voted in Chicago, and during the period covered by the income tax returns he had no business interest in Texas, but rather his business and general interests were in Chicago and all of the property involved was acquired in this state, the chancellor's finding that his domicile changed in 1932 was warranted by the evidence. Fry v. Fry, 332 Ill. App. 484, 76 N.E.2d 225 (1 Dist. 1947).

Erroneous Entry of Judgment

A judgment which may not reflect the circumstances of parties at time of its entry would not only be unreasonable as of the date of its entry, but also would be immune from modification, absent a change in the circumstances of the parties from those existing but not taken into account at the time of entry of the decree; thus where judgment on divorce action was entered nearly six years after last hearing on the circumstances of parties, and over objections of wife that circumstances had changed, entry of that judgment was error. Smith v. Smith, 73 Ill. App. 3d 423, 29 Ill. Dec. 735, 392 N.E.2d 292 (1 Dist. 1979).

Estoppel

—In General

A party accepting the benefits of a divorce decree may be estopped from later challenging validity of that decree. In re Paulius, 131 Ill. App. 3d 343, 86 Ill. Dec. 627, 475 N.E.2d 1006 (1 Dist. 1985).

—Reliance on Decree

Divorced spouse who not only remarried in reliance on the dissolution decree, but also enforced his child visitation rights thereunder, could not subsequently attempt to have that decree vacated. In re Paulius, 131 Ill. App. 3d 343, 86 Ill. Dec. 627, 475 N.E.2d 1006 (1 Dist. 1985).

Petitioner who filed a petition under 735 ILCS 5/2-1401 to vacate a divorce decree, and who was aware at all relevant times that his marriage had been terminated and whose subsequent marriage was consummated in reliance upon the validity of the instant decree of divorce, the benefits of which he had accepted, was estopped to vacate the same by collateral motion. Webb v. Webb, 130 Ill. App. 2d 618, 264 N.E.2d 594 (2 Dist. 1970).

—Subject Matter Jurisdiction

A party who remarried and had a child after a judgment for dissolution of marriage was entered was estopped from attacking that judgment by way of a petition to hold the judgment void for lack of subject matter jurisdiction on the grounds that neither party to that judgment had met the statutory requirement of domicile. In re Gryka, 90 Ill. App. 3d 443, 45 Ill. Dec. 820, 413 N.E.2d 153 (1 Dist. 1980).

Evidence

—Admissibility

Because the husband did not put his health in issue in a petition for dissolution of his marriage on the ground of mental cruelty, he did not waive his privilege under the AIDS Confidentiality Act. In re Bonneau, 294 Ill. App. 3d 720, 229 Ill. Dec. 187, 691 N.E.2d 123 (2 Dist. 1998), appeal denied, 178 Ill. 2d 574, 232 Ill. Dec. 845, 699 N.E.2d 1030 (1998).

Fault

—Not Shown

Where defendant admitted to openly consorting with another woman, and this was the main cause of the separation, plaintiff's steps to remove the defendant from the marital home were justified under the circumstances and did not constitute "fault" on the part of the plaintiff sufficient to justify a dismissal and denial of her suit for separate maintenance. Degeeter v. Degeeter, 16 Ill. App. 3d 262, 305 N.E.2d 727 (3 Dist. 1973).

Financial Losses

It was quite irrelevant as a ground for divorce that a spouse attempted two or three business ventures which were financially unsuccessful, where the complaining spouse was at all times aware of the details of the businesses and from time to time accepted certain receipts from businesses, as well as accepting the losses on the joint income tax returns. Voss v. Voss, 55 Ill. App. 3d 286, 13 Ill. Dec. 481, 371 N.E.2d 176 (2 Dist. 1977).

Evidence did not support granting wife a divorce based on ground that her husband mismanaged her estate inherited from her father. Coolidge v. Coolidge, 4 Ill. App. 2d 205, 124 N.E.2d 1 (1 Dist. 1955).

Foreign Decrees

A defendant spouse could not be permanently enjoined from prosecuting marital actions in other states or countries. Scott v. Scott, 131 Ill. App. 2d 863, 268 N.E.2d 458 (3 Dist. 1971).

Where wife alleged that husband committed fraud on a foreign court because he did not divulge that she had already commenced a divorce action in this state, foreign divorce decree could not be collaterally attacked in this state after the foreign court had acquired jurisdiction. Schwarz v. Schwarz, 27 Ill. 2d 140, 188 N.E.2d 673 (1963).

Where a bona fide domicile has been acquired in a state by either of the parties to a marriage and a suit is brought by the domiciled party in such state for divorce, the courts of that state, if they acquire personal jurisdiction also of the other party, have authority to enter a decree of divorce entitled to be enforced in every state under the full faith and credit clause. Jamieson v. Jamieson, 14 Ill. App. 2d 233, 144 N.E.2d 540 (2 Dist. 1957).

The introduction of an out-of-state divorce decree constitutes prima facie evidence of its validity; however, if the litigant who would escape the operation of the out-of-state decree sustains the burden of impeaching the jurisdictional prerequisite of bona fide domicile, then the decree will be deemed neither valid nor entitled to full faith and credit. Ludwig v. Ludwig, 413 Ill. 44, 107 N.E.2d 848 (1952).

The full faith and credit clause operates only with respect to judgments rendered by a court whose jurisdiction, either as to subject matter or the person, is not impeached. Ludwig v. Ludwig, 413 Ill. 44, 107 N.E.2d 848 (1952).

The court, in determining whether full faith and credit should be given to the out-of-state divorce decree, may properly inquire into the bona fide character of the domicile of the party who secured that divorce. Ludwig v. Ludwig, 413 Ill. 44, 107 N.E.2d 848 (1952).

A divorce decree that was valid in another state was also valid in the State of Illinois. Stephens v. Stephens, 319 Ill. App. 292, 49 N.E.2d 560 (2 Dist. 1943).

Fraud

—Not Shown

Where the evidence did not sustain former wife's allegations of former husband's insanity and the evidence did not establish that the actions of former husband in connection with the entry of the divorce decree constituted a fraud upon the court, the decree was not manifestly and palpably against the weight of the evidence. Friend v. Northern Trust Co., 314 Ill. App. 596, 42 N.E.2d 330 (1 Dist. 1942).

—Standing

An attack on the ground of fraud may not be made in another state unless by one who did not perpetrate the fraud or who was not in privity with such person; in other words, the attack may be made only by an innocent party. In re Estate of Owens, 7 Ill. App. 2d 428, 129 N.E.2d 573 (1 Dist. 1955).

Grounds

—In General

The question of what shall constitute grounds for granting a

Grounds (Cont'd)

—In General (Cont'd)

divorce, or whether the marriage contract shall be dissolved under any circumstances or for any cause, is one of public policy and belongs to the legislative and not the judicial department of our government. Friend v. Northern Trust Co., 314 Ill. App. 596, 42 N.E.2d 330 (1 Dist. 1942).

The issues in a suit for separate maintenance and a suit for divorce are not the same, and neither is the forum the same; in divorce proceedings the venue is in the county where the complainant resides, while in suits for separate maintenance it is in the county where the husband resides or where he has abandoned his wife. To entitle a wife to a decree for separate maintenance she must prove that she is living separate and apart from her husband without her fault; to warrant a decree for divorce on the ground of desertion complainant must show that defendant has wilfully deserted or absented himself or herself from the husband or wife, without any reasonable cause, for the space of two years. Hoffman v. Hoffman, 330 Ill. 413, 161 N.E. 723 (1928).

—Burden of Proof

The law in Illinois remains that a marriage should not be lightly terminated; a plaintiff is required to prove a statutory cause for divorce by competent evidence, even though the court might conclude the marriage to be dead. Sherman v. Sherman, 38 Ill. App. 3d 664, 30 Ill. Dec. 412, 348 N.E.2d 524 (2 Dist. 1976).

Grounds of divorce must be proved by more than one witness in cases where the complaint is taken as confessed. Farah v. Farah, 25 Ill. App. 3d 481, 323 N.E.2d 361 (1 Dist. 1975).

—Not Shown

Where the preponderance of evidence indicated that a marriage was stable, happy and relatively uneventful until just prior to the wife's leaving for another state, after all plans for the trip had been mutually agreed upon, the alleged grounds for divorce appeared to be both false in fact and irrelevant in law. Voss v. Voss, 55 Ill. App. 3d 286, 13 Ill. Dec. 481, 371 N.E.2d 176 (2 Dist. 1977).

Assuming that defendant did nag plaintiff and was disagreeable and quarrelsome, there was nothing in the statutes granting the courts the power to grant a divorce on those grounds. Swan v. Swan, 331 Ill. App. 295, 73 N.E.2d 153 (4 Dist. 1947).

Habitual Drunkenness

—Defined

Habitual drunkenness had the same meaning in former Ill.Rev.Stat., ch. 40, para. 1 et seq. (see now this section) and in determining whether a parent was unfit. People ex rel. Department of Children & Family Servs. v. Sanders, 77 Ill. App. 3d 78, 32 Ill. Dec. 847, 395 N.E.2d 1228 (4 Dist. 1979).

Habitual drunkenness is an irresistible habit of getting drunk, a fixed habit of drinking to excess, or an involuntary tendency to become intoxicated, which is acquired by frequent repetition, such a frequent indulgence to excess as to show a formed habit and inability to control the appetite. Murphy v. Murphy, 31 Ill. App. 3d 321, 334 N.E.2d 779 (1 Dist. 1975).

Habitual drunkenness does not mean constantly intoxicated, but merely that the party has acquired the habit of indulgence to excess, indicating inability to control the desire for intoxicating liquors. Grikietis v. Grikietis, 319 Ill. App. 216, 48 N.E.2d 775 (1 Dist. 1943).

—Evidence Held Insufficient

The finding of the trial court that wife was not an habitual drunkard was not against the manifest weight of the evidence. Murphy v. Murphy, 31 Ill. App. 3d 321, 334 N.E.2d 779 (1 Dist. 1975).

Where husband's period of habitual drunkenness could not possibly have existed for the period requisite to the entry of a decree of divorce, and where no other grounds of divorce were alleged, or found by the decree, the decree was in error for reasons apparent upon the face of the record and was in direct violation of the statutory provisions, and attack was therefore properly brought under 735 ILCS 5/2-1401. Collins v. Collins, 14 Ill. 2d 178, 151 N.E.2d 813 (1958).

—Grounds

For a case discussing the ground for divorce under habitual drunkenness, see Shorthose v. Shorthose, 319 Ill. App. 355, 49 N.E.2d 280 (3 Dist. 1943).

—Illustrative Case

Where wife complied with statutory requirements by filing her verified counter-petition to dismiss divorce suit, the grounds for which were clearly sufficient, and she alleged that husband was mentally incompetent; that knowledge of his incompetency came to her only after the hearing was had; that the misconduct of the husband which was alleged to furnish the basis of her claim for relief appeared to be the result of mental derangement rather than intemperance; and she proved by uncontroverted evidence that, subsequent to the hearing, she had spoken to her husband while he was a patient at a sanitarium and in the care of a private nurse, and had ascertained from him that he did not want a divorce and never had wanted one; upon the showing made by her verified counter-petition, supported by the foregoing evidence, the court was not justified in refusing to dismiss the case and in entering the decree for divorce. Norwood v. Norwood, 333 Ill. App. 469, 77 N.E.2d 552 (1 Dist. 1948).

—Not Shown

Where the complaint did not charge defendant with being guilty of "habitual drunkenness for the space of two years," which was the language of the statute and the only grounds relative to the use of intoxicating liquors contained in the divorce statute, but with "being guilty of continual and habitual use of intoxicating beverages for a period of at least two years prior to the time of the commencement of the cause," and where the same language found in the complaint was included among the findings in the decree and apparently was intended to serve as the sole ground for granting a decree of divorce, the finding did not and could not support the divorce decree. Morrow v. Morrow, 15 Ill. App. 2d 109, 145 N.E.2d 381 (2 Dist. 1957).

—Requirements

Evidence of intoxication without intermission is not necessary to prove habitual drunkenness in action for divorce. Vesolowski v. Vesolowski, 403 Ill. 284, 85 N.E.2d 695 (1949).

Impotency

—In General

Under similar prior law, it made no difference whether a husband's impotency existed at birth by some formation or nonformation of nature, or was caused by the party's own fault. Griffeth v. Griffeth, 162 Ill. 368, 44 N.E. 820 (1896).

—Requirements

Under prior similar law, to obtain a divorce upon the ground of impotency, it had to be shown that the defect existed at the time of the marriage, and that it was incurable; the burden of proof was upon the complainant to establish these facts. Griffeth v. Griffeth, 162 Ill. 368, 44 N.E. 820 (1896).

Irreconcilable Differences

—Evidence Held Sufficient

Where petitioner wife filed for dissolution for the third time and testimony showed that, though the parties were living together, petitioner began sleeping on the couch four years earlier when the parties first moved into their house, and that, although the parties usually took dinner together, it was done apparently for the sake of their son, and any dinner conversation was usually directed toward the son or about the son, it was apparent that irreconcilable differences existed and that an irretrievable breakdown of the marriage had occurred. In re Dowd, 214 Ill. App. 3d 156, 157 Ill. Dec. 894, 573 N.E.2d 312 (2 Dist.), cert. denied, 141 Ill. 2d 538, 162 Ill. Dec. 485, 580 N.E.2d 111 (1991).

—One Spouse

This section permits a finding of irreconcilable differences where only one of the parties desires to maintain the union, because where evidence shows that one spouse clearly desires to no longer continue to be married to the other, an irreconcilable difference necessarily arises between them, causing an irretrievable breakdown of the marriage. In re Smoller, 218 Ill. App. 3d 340, 161 Ill. Dec. 129, 578 N.E.2d 256 (1 Dist.), cert. denied, 142 Ill. 2d 665, 164 Ill. Dec. 928, 584 N.E.2d 140 (1991).

Irreconcilable Differences (Cont'd)

—Purpose of Provision
Adoption, in 1984, of subdivision (a)(2) of this section and its provision for dissolution based on irreconcilable differences indicated that the General Assembly recognized that the public policy to preserve marriages was no longer served when the state's interest in preserving a marriage was not also shared by the parties themselves. In re Smoller, 218 Ill. App. 3d 340, 161 Ill. Dec. 129, 578 N.E.2d 256 (1 Dist.), cert. denied, 142 Ill. 2d 665, 164 Ill. Dec. 928, 584 N.E.2d 140 (1991).

Joinder
Illinois law encourages resolution of all issues ancillary to dissolution, as well as dissolution itself, in a single proceeding for reasons of certainty and financial security. In re Kenik, 181 Ill. App. 3d 266, 129 Ill. Dec. 932, 536 N.E.2d 982 (1 Dist.), appeal denied, 136 Ill. Dec. 587, 545 N.E.2d 111 (1989).

Jurisdiction

—Adultery
Where plaintiff committed adultery in county, the plaintiff could properly invoke the jurisdiction of the court in her separate maintenance suit without being a resident of the county if her husband resided there, and even if he had only resided there for the last six months. Garrison v. Garrison, 107 Ill. App. 2d 311, 246 N.E.2d 9 (2 Dist. 1969).

—Appeal
Because the parties' adjudicated their rights before the court to a final judgment without objection to the court's right to hear the cause, the parties were bound on appeal so far as the question of jurisdiction over the particular case was concerned. Yelton v. Holtzman, 286 Ill. App. 3d 436, 222 Ill. Dec. 29, 676 N.E.2d 993 (1 Dist. 1997).

—Basis
The jurisdiction of the court in a divorce case, though including general equitable powers, is founded in statutes. Halloran v. Halloran, 39 Ill. App. 3d 528, 350 N.E.2d 318 (3 Dist. 1976).

—Divestiture
When dealing with such matters as grounds for divorce, payment of alimony and modification of divorce decrees, which are regulated by statute, a court exercises powers granted by the legislature and cannot, by incorporating a contractual provision in its decree, divest itself of the power to modify, contrary to the legislative will. Duvall v. Duvall, 8 Ill. App. 3d 53, 289 N.E.2d 59 (3 Dist. 1972).

—Equity
A trial judge in the domestic relations division of the circuit court constitutionally has jurisdiction to hear all justiciable matters but for the sake of administrative convenience entertains all issues related to dissolution of the marriage; once jurisdiction is obtained, the court's ability to act in granting relief available under this Act is governed by the provisions of the Act. However, this does not limit the court's equity power to effectuate compliance with the Act. In re Peshek, 89 Ill. App. 3d 959, 45 Ill. Dec. 347, 412 N.E.2d 698 (1 Dist. 1980).

—Established
The court possessed subject matter jurisdiction over a marriage dissolution case where wife resided in Illinois for more than 90 days prior to the judgment of dissolution, as this section requires either party to be domiciled in Illinois for 90 days prior to the court's final decision in order for the court to have jurisdiction. Hermann v. Hermann, 219 Ill. App. 3d 195, 161 Ill. Dec. 838, 579 N.E.2d 386 (3 Dist. 1991).

Petitioner wife established an appropriate ongoing connection with the state of Illinois and the trial court should have found it had jurisdiction when petitioner had resided in Illinois for more than 56 years, and the pleadings admitted that she was a domiciliary of Illinois at the time the action was commenced and for a durational period exceeding 90 days. In re Weiss, 87 Ill. App. 3d 643, 42 Ill. Dec. 714, 409 N.E.2d 329 (1 Dist. 1980).

—Estoppel
Petitioner was estopped from raising jurisdictional issue where the dissolution permitted her to avoid legal responsibility for respondent's ongoing medical expenses and therefore benefited from the dissolution and did not raise the jurisdictional issue until 2 years later. Yelton v. Holtzman, 286 Ill. App. 3d 436, 222 Ill. Dec. 29, 676 N.E.2d 993 (1 Dist. 1997).

—Foreign Decrees
The basic inequity against which courts in this state may afford relief is the effort by a party to fraudulently or colorably invoke the jurisdiction of some other state or country, and absent such inequity the courts in this state have no authority to interfere with the legitimate jurisdiction of other states. Scott v. Scott, 131 Ill. App. 2d 863, 268 N.E.2d 458 (3 Dist. 1971).

An attack on the method of restoring a divorce decree and a determination whether the signature on the duplicate original decree was genuine or forged could be made only in the state where the decree was procured. In re Estate of Owens, 7 Ill. App. 2d 428, 129 N.E.2d 573 (1 Dist. 1955).

—In Personam
Since personal jurisdiction is not required to dissolve a party's marriage, the validity of parties' divorce was unaffected by the issue of whether the court had personal jurisdiction over wife. In re Passiales, 144 Ill. App. 3d 629, 98 Ill. Dec. 419, 494 N.E.2d 541 (1 Dist. 1986).

Where divorce decree provided that marital residence be sold and from proceeds of the sale that certain obligations including mortgage be paid, and after payment of the obligations, balance of the proceeds be divided equally between parties, and in the event the parties could not agree upon those matters necessary to the sale of the marital residence, either party could apply to the court for modification of this decree in order to have the marital residence sold at a sheriff's sale, and it was apparent that the court emphasized the operative effect of divorce decree as an "in personam" decree, and further reserved jurisdiction to provide, in the event the parties, for good cause shown, could not complete the sale, that the parties should apply to the court for an in rem decree, case would be remanded for further proceedings. Halloran v. Halloran, 39 Ill. App. 3d 528, 350 N.E.2d 318 (3 Dist. 1976).

Where complaint alleged that "plaintiff is now and has been for more than one year a resident of the County of Champaign and State of Illinois," and defendant's answer admitted those allegations, the residency requirements for granting a decree of divorce were met. Jordan v. Jordan, 38 Ill. App. 3d 781, 349 N.E.2d 116 (4 Dist. 1976).

—In Rem
Petitioner who had been stationed in Illinois as a member of the armed forces for at least 90 days prior to commencing dissolution action, and who had respondent served personally in Virginia, had established at least in rem jurisdiction in order to obtain the dissolution of the marriage. In re Brown, 154 Ill. App. 3d 179, 106 Ill. Dec. 927, 506 N.E.2d 727 (4 Dist. 1987).

—Nexus
The requirement that one of the parties to a dissolution action reside in Illinois at the commencement of the action and for 90 days either preceding the commencement of the action or preceding the making of the finding is to ensure a sufficient nexus between the forum state and the action. In re Mates, 156 Ill. App. 3d 26, 108 Ill. Dec. 604, 508 N.E.2d 1181 (2 Dist. 1987).

—Notice
Where a husband filed an affidavit of nonresidence of the wife, constructive service was made on the wife by publication, and the husband obtained a decree of divorce by default, the trial court properly granted the wife's motion to vacate the decree of divorce since, during the period prior to the filing of the affidavit of nonresidency by the husband he had knowledge of the wife's whereabouts and that she resided in this state, and the court did not have jurisdiction to enter the divorce decree. Forest v. Forest, 9 Ill. App. 3d 111, 291 N.E.2d 880 (5 Dist. 1973).

—Prima Facie Evidence
Defendant wife's argument that the court lacked jurisdiction over the parties when it entered divorce decree was without merit because defendant's written entry of appearance was prima facie evidence of the court's jurisdiction, and there was nothing pre-

Jurisdiction (Cont'd)

—Prima Facie Evidence (Cont'd)

sented in the record to refute that showing. Semmens v. Semmens, 53 Ill. App. 3d 160, 11 Ill. Dec. 181, 368 N.E.2d 732 (4 Dist. 1977).

—Residency

In a divorce case plaintiff's residence is necessary to confer subject matter jurisdiction on the court. In re Passiales, 144 Ill. App. 3d 629, 98 Ill. Dec. 419, 494 N.E.2d 541 (1 Dist. 1986).

The term "residence" as used in this Act is not synonymous with domicile, but denotes a "permanent abode" or the place one considers as home. In re Passiales, 144 Ill. App. 3d 629, 98 Ill. Dec. 419, 494 N.E.2d 541 (1 Dist. 1986).

It was not against the manifest weight of evidence for the trial court to find that husband had not fulfilled the residency requirement when he filed for divorce, where he had been a life-long Illinois resident but moved to and from several places during the years prior to his filing for divorce and, most recently, had moved from Minnesota only three months before filing for divorce. In re Passiales, 144 Ill. App. 3d 629, 98 Ill. Dec. 419, 494 N.E.2d 541 (1 Dist. 1986).

—Subject Matter

There is no evidence that the legislature intended the written stipulation requirement of subdivision (a)(2) to be a limitation on the subject matter jurisdiction of the trial court. In re Fields, 288 Ill. App. 3d 1053, 224 Ill. Dec. 184, 681 N.E.2d 166 (4 Dist. 1997), appeal denied, 174 Ill. 2d 559, 227 Ill. Dec. 4, 686 N.E.2d 1160 (1997), overruled on other grounds, Belleville Toyota, Inc. v. Toyota Motor Sales, U.S.A., Inc., 199 Ill. 2d 325, 264 Ill. Dec. 283, 770 N.E.2d 177 (2002).

—Temporary Relief

An Illinois court has jurisdiction to grant temporary relief in a dissolution of marriage action if one of the spouses maintains a residence (or military presence) in Illinois at the commencement of the action. In re Mates, 156 Ill. App. 3d 26, 108 Ill. Dec. 604, 508 N.E.2d 1181 (2 Dist. 1987).

—Waiver Not Shown

Petitioner wife did not waive the right to contest the trial court's ruling that there was no jurisdiction simply because she failed to object to the ruling when it was announced by the court, because petitioner was under no duty to object or make an offer of proof concerning jurisdiction in order to preserve her right to appeal the adverse ruling. In re Weiss, 87 Ill. App. 3d 643, 42 Ill. Dec. 714, 409 N.E.2d 329 (1 Dist. 1980).

Living Separate and Apart

—In General

It is against public policy for parties to live together during the pendency of divorce action. Baumgartner v. Baumgartner, 16 Ill. App. 2d 286, 148 N.E.2d 327 (2 Dist. 1958).

Where a suit for divorce is brought and the same is pending between the parties to a marriage contract, the parties are not only justified in living apart but necessarily must do so; such living separate and apart does not constitute wilful desertion without reasonable cause. Borin v. Borin, 335 Ill. App. 450, 82 N.E.2d 70 (1 Dist. 1948).

—Not Required

The two year separation requirement can be satisfied even where the couple live in the same house because irreconcilable differences can be realized between the couple without living in separate residences. In re Gorman, 284 Ill. App. 3d 171, 219 Ill. Dec. 652, 671 N.E.2d 819 (1 Dist. 1996), appeal denied, 171 Ill. 2d 564, 222 Ill. Dec. 431, 677 N.E.2d 965 (1997).

—Reasonable Cause

Under former Ill.Rev.Stat., ch. 40, para. 1 (see now this section), wife had reasonable cause for living apart from husband where he had filed both divorce and annulment proceedings against her; it was not incumbent upon husband or wife to resume the marital relation and duties while a suit for divorce was in progress. Thornton v. Thornton, 298 Ill. App. 421, 19 N.E.2d 225 (3 Dist. 1939).

—Shown

Where couple not only ended all marital relations a year before petition for dissolution of marriage was filed, but also used separate bedrooms and had no meaningful communication with each other, and each party, further, was responsible for individual personal expenses, the couple was found to have satisfied the statutory requirement of living separate and apart for two years. In re Kenik, 181 Ill. App. 3d 266, 129 Ill. Dec. 932, 536 N.E.2d 982 (1 Dist.), appeal denied, 136 Ill. Dec. 587, 545 N.E.2d 111 (1989).

Marital Assets

—Law License

The trial court erred in ruling that respondent husband's law license was a marital asset and in retaining jurisdiction thereover for "future determination as to distribution or apportionment." In re Fahy, 208 Ill. App. 3d 677, 153 Ill. Dec. 594, 567 N.E.2d 552 (1 Dist. 1991).

Mental Cruelty

—In General

What constitutes mental cruelty depends upon the total circumstances of a given case. Bochenek v. Bochenek, 5 Ill. App. 3d 65, 283 N.E.2d 95 (1 Dist. 1972).

—Burden of Proof

To prove a case entitling a spouse to a dissolution of marriage on the grounds of mental cruelty, the evidence must show that the conduct of the offending spouse is unprovoked and constitutes a course of abusive and humiliating treatment that makes the life of the complaining spouse miserable. In re Burrows, 126 Ill. App. 3d 752, 81 Ill. Dec. 865, 467 N.E.2d 987 (1 Dist. 1984).

A complaining party has the burden of proving a course of abusive and humiliating treatment by his spouse calculated or obviously of a nature to render his life miserable and to affect his physical and mental health; whether the acts charged constitute mental cruelty depends on the total factual background and is determined primarily by the effect of the alleged misconduct upon the complaining party, and it is not sufficient to show that a reconciliation seems no longer possible and that the marriage appears dead. In re Semmler, 90 Ill. App. 3d 649, 46 Ill. Dec. 62, 413 N.E.2d 502 (2 Dist. 1980).

—Conduct Required

Generally, the elements of extreme and repeated mental cruelty have been recognized as a course of abusive and humiliating treatment, calculated or obviously of the nature to torture, discommode, or render miserable the life of the opposite spouse, which conduct actually affects the physical or mental health of the spouse. Sharer v. Sharer, 39 Ill. App. 3d 818, 350 N.E.2d 779 (5 Dist. 1976).

—Defined

Mental cruelty, as a ground for divorce, is commonly defined as a course of abusive and humiliating treatment that is of such nature as to trouble or render miserable the life of the other spouse or which causes the other spouse's life or personal health to be endangered. West v. West, 77 Ill. App. 3d 828, 33 Ill. Dec. 658, 396 N.E.2d 1382 (4 Dist. 1979).

To show mental cruelty as grounds for divorce the complaining party must prove that the alleged acts of mental cruelty caused embarrassment, humiliation, and anguish, so as to render life miserable and unendurable, or caused the complainant's life, person or health to be endangered, and that there was a lack of provocation for the alleged acts of the attacker. Murphy v. Murphy, 31 Ill. App. 3d 321, 334 N.E.2d 779 (1 Dist. 1975); Iverson v. Iverson, 38 Ill. App. 3d 308, 347 N.E.2d 6 (2 Dist. 1976); Sherman v. Sherman, 38 Ill. App. 3d 664, 30 Ill. Dec. 412, 348 N.E.2d 524 (2 Dist. 1976); Rosenbaum v. Rosenbaum, 38 Ill. App. 3d 1, 349 N.E.2d 73 (1 Dist. 1976); Graham v. Graham, 44 Ill. App. 3d 519, 3 Ill. Dec. 141, 358 N.E.2d 308 (5 Dist. 1976); McCarrel v. McCarrel, 48 Ill. App. 3d 666, 6 Ill. Dec. 669, 363 N.E.2d 198 (4 Dist. 1977); Christian v. Christian, 69 Ill. App. 3d 450, 26 Ill. Dec. 326, 387 N.E.2d 1254 (1 Dist. 1979); In re Rittmeyer, 107 Ill. App. 3d 892, 63 Ill. Dec. 499, 438 N.E.2d 237 (5 Dist. 1982); In re Burrows, 126 Ill. App. 3d 752, 81 Ill. Dec. 865, 467 N.E.2d 987 (1 Dist. 1984); In re Hanson, 170 Ill. App. 3d 298, 120 Ill. Dec. 665, 524 N.E.2d 695 (2 Dist. 1988); Reeder

Mental Cruelty (Cont'd)

—Defined (Cont'd)

v. Reeder, 212 Ill. App. 3d 56, 156 Ill. Dec. 400, 570 N.E.2d 876 (3 Dist.), cert. denied, 141 Ill. 2d 559, 162 Ill. Dec. 507, 580 N.E.2d 133 (1991).

The generally recognized elements of extreme and repeated mental cruelty are an unprovoked course of abusive and humiliating treatment, calculated or obviously of the nature to torture, discommode, or render miserable the life of the opposite spouse, which conduct actually affects the physical or mental health of the spouse. Gregory v. Gregory, 24 Ill. App. 3d 436, 321 N.E.2d 122 (2 Dist. 1974); Graham v. Graham, 44 Ill. App. 3d 519, 3 Ill. Dec. 141, 358 N.E.2d 308 (5 Dist. 1976).

Mental cruelty has been defined by courts in this state as conduct which causes embarrassment, humiliation and anguish so as to render life miserable and unendurable or to cause a spouse's life, person or health to become endangered. McGowan v. McGowan, 15 Ill. App. 3d 913, 305 N.E.2d 261 (1 Dist. 1973).

Abusive and humiliating treatment, calculated to or of such nature as to torture, discommode or render miserable the life of the opposite spouse, and which actually affects the physical or mental health of that spouse, is generally considered mental cruelty. Bochenek v. Bochenek, 5 Ill. App. 3d 65, 283 N.E.2d 95 (1 Dist. 1972).

The elements of mental cruelty consist of a course of abusive and humiliating treatment, calculated or obviously of a nature to torture, disturb, or render miserable the life of the opposite spouse, and which actually affects the physical or mental health of such spouse. Howison v. Howison, 128 Ill. App. 2d 377, 262 N.E.2d 1 (2 Dist. 1970).

—Effect on Complainant

In determining whether the acts charged amount to mental cruelty, the trial court is to primarily consider the effect on the complaining party. Reeder v. Reeder, 212 Ill. App. 3d 56, 156 Ill. Dec. 400, 570 N.E.2d 876 (3 Dist.), cert. denied, 141 Ill. 2d 559, 162 Ill. Dec. 507, 580 N.E.2d 133 (1991).

—Evidence Held Insufficient

Where respondent husband did not engage in a course of abusive treatment of his wife, but the conduct of which she complained appeared to be a result of his concern for the welfare of his wife rather than a course of mental cruelty, and there was no evidence to indicate that petitioner suffered from adverse physical or mental consequences due to respondent's conduct, the finding of the trial court that petitioner had failed to establish grounds for dissolution of marriage was not against the manifest weight of the evidence. In re Rittmeyer, 107 Ill. App. 3d 892, 63 Ill. Dec. 499, 438 N.E.2d 237 (5 Dist. 1982).

In husband's action for divorce on grounds of extreme and repeated mental cruelty, conclusion that the evidence as to the effect upon the husband's health was insufficient to constitute proof of mental cruelty did not appear to be against the manifest weight of the evidence. In re Semmler, 90 Ill. App. 3d 649, 46 Ill. Dec. 62, 413 N.E.2d 502 (2 Dist. 1980).

Where wife produced evidence of a continuing and repeated course of conduct on the part of husband, unprovoked by her, including verbal threats, vile language, rudeness, irrational behavior and fits of temper which caused her acute embarrassment and anguish in front of her children and their friends, her family, and her own friends, mental cruelty was proven. Graff v. Graff, 71 Ill. App. 3d 496, 27 Ill. Dec. 798, 389 N.E.2d 1206 (1 Dist. 1979).

Where a wife earned from outside employment much more than she lost from her business ventures and the business losses were offset against the parties' joint tax returns, the losses were not sufficiently serious to induce the emotional trauma the husband claimed as a basis of mental cruelty. Voss v. Voss, 55 Ill. App. 3d 286, 13 Ill. Dec. 481, 371 N.E.2d 176 (2 Dist. 1977).

Where in all the testimony relating the difficulties and differences of the parties, there was not any evidence that the wife was engaging in a course of abusive treatment of her husband or that the husband's life was thereby made miserable, his professing to be somewhat embarrassed over her departure being clearly insufficient, there was not sufficient evidence of extreme and repeated mental cruelty to support the decree of divorce entered in favor of the husband. Matthews v. Matthews, 36 Ill. App. 3d 508, 344 N.E.2d 21 (2 Dist. 1976).

Evidence did not prove mental cruelty as that concept is used in the law of divorce where plaintiff husband did not prove, in fact, did not allege, lack of provocation, where from his testimony, which was the only evidence on the subject, he left his family without a valid reason, and where there was no evidence that his health, physical or mental, was adversely affected by anything his wife did after he left the family home. Rosenbaum v. Rosenbaum, 38 Ill. App. 3d 1, 349 N.E.2d 73 (1 Dist. 1976).

A married person had no right to force a divorce upon his or her spouse, and the mere refusal of a wife, who had obtained a decree of separate maintenance, to avail herself of whatever grounds she may have for a divorce could not be deemed to constitute faulty conduct on her part amounting to extreme and repeated mental cruelty. Schneider v. Schneider, 43 Ill. App. 3d 1014, 3 Ill. Dec. 11, 358 N.E.2d 11 (1 Dist. 1976).

A finding only that wife's preoccupation with her job led to the breakdown of her marriage was not enough to fulfill the statutory ground of mental cruelty, which encompasses only that behavior calculated or obviously of a nature to torture, discommode or render spouse's life unendurable or miserable. Sherman v. Sherman, 38 Ill. App. 3d 664, 30 Ill. Dec. 412, 348 N.E.2d 524 (2 Dist. 1976).

The plaintiff failed to prove that she suffered such mental anguish or suffering or that the conduct of the defendant was such as to be injurious to the life or health of the plaintiff as to constitute "mental cruelty" within the meaning of this section. Sharpe v. Sharpe, 9 Ill. App. 3d 667, 292 N.E.2d 566 (2 Dist. 1973).

The court did not err in refusing to grant a divorce on the ground of mental cruelty where a doctor testified that defendant exhibited no mental disorders and also testified that his final diagnosis was tonsillitis. O'Donnell v. O'Donnell, 5 Ill. App. 3d 870, 284 N.E.2d 682 (4 Dist. 1972).

The fact that the wife was a poor housekeeper, that disorder resulted from pets in the house and that she did not prepare full meals regularly and was quarrelsome did not entitle the husband to a divorce on grounds of mental cruelty where the complained of conditions had existed for years, were in accord with the life style of the parties and the conduct under the circumstances was not necessarily unreasonable. Quilty v. Quilty, 5 Ill. App. 3d 801, 284 N.E.2d 690 (3 Dist. 1972).

—Evidence Held Sufficient

Where the court accepted wife's statements regarding husband's daily consumption of alcoholic beverages, his habit of becoming drunk once every three weeks and his attempts to force wife into involuntary sexual activity, and wife's testimony that she had become nervous, upset and physically ill as a result of husband's actions was uncontroverted, wife met her burden of proof in demonstrating that the husband had been guilty of extreme and repeated mental cruelty. Reeder v. Reeder, 212 Ill. App. 3d 56, 156 Ill. Dec. 400, 570 N.E.2d 876 (3 Dist.), cert. denied, 141 Ill. 2d 559, 162 Ill. Dec. 507, 580 N.E.2d 133 (1991).

Where petitioner wife's testimony indicated a long, continuing, and constant pattern of verbal abuse by respondent husband as well as a continuing pattern of respondent's alcohol abuse which was unprovoked by petitioner, unprovoked mental cruelty existed. In re Hanson, 170 Ill. App. 3d 298, 120 Ill. Dec. 665, 524 N.E.2d 695 (2 Dist. 1988).

Where evidence adduced at hearing indicated that the parties had not been living together since 1976; husband testified to the circumstances prior to and after separation, which included: wife's failure to cook for husband, wife's failure to do husband's laundry; wife's withholding sex as a punitive measure; wife's refusal to take any financial responsibility; and wife's refusal to allow husband visitation with the children; husband additionally stated that throughout the relationship, he was caused to suffer embarrassment, humiliation, stress, anxiety, loss of sleep, and loss of weight; husband claimed wife was not provoked; wife did not testify at the hearing and presented no evidence with respect to provocation; wife attempted to allege that husband had engaged in adulterous conduct, but testimony indicated that wife was not aware of this conduct prior to the initial hearing and had no evidence in support thereof; the record indicated that wife embarked upon an abusive course of conduct and as such, the judgment of the trial court was supported by the evidence. In re Wade, 158 Ill. App. 3d 255, 110 Ill. Dec. 321, 511 N.E.2d 156 (4 Dist. 1987).

Mental Cruelty (Cont'd)

—Evidence Held Sufficient (Cont'd)

Where wife's conduct was destructive to herself, her marriage and to her husband; she frequently stated that she wished she were dead; she also wished her husband dead; she refused to go to a doctor despite obvious signs of physical and/or emotional ill-being; she refused to participate in social functions important to husband's employment; and she frequently falsely accused him of marital infidelity, the evidence was sufficient to support trial court's finding of mental cruelty. In re Lawrence, 146 Ill. App. 3d 307, 99 Ill. Dec. 845, 496 N.E.2d 538 (3 Dist. 1986).

Petitioner husband's testimony that he suffered from headaches, nervousness, tenseness and depression was corroborated by respondent wife and supported the court's determination that petitioner proved his allegation of mental cruelty; accordingly, there was no error in the trial court's judgment granting petitioner a dissolution of marriage based upon mental cruelty. In re Burrows, 126 Ill. App. 3d 752, 81 Ill. Dec. 865, 467 N.E.2d 987 (1 Dist. 1984).

Evidence adduced at trial supported judgment dissolving the marriage on the grounds of respondent's mental cruelty. In re Nilsson, 81 Ill. App. 3d 580, 37 Ill. Dec. 394, 402 N.E.2d 284 (3 Dist. 1980); In re Yakin, 107 Ill. App. 3d 1103, 62 Ill. Dec. 547, 436 N.E.2d 573 (1 Dist. 1982).

Evidence amply supported judgment of the trial court and a finding of mental cruelty where plaintiff wife testified that defendant husband treated her as if she were "nobody," calling her names every time he came home, and daily accused plaintiff of infidelity, and where the name calling and accusations took place in front of their children and her testimony was corroborated by the parties' two oldest children. Christian v. Christian, 69 Ill. App. 3d 450, 26 Ill. Dec. 326, 387 N.E.2d 1254 (1 Dist. 1979).

Where defendant husband physically struck plaintiff wife without provocation, often shouted abusively at her, told her that he wished he were not married to her and did not love her, and related intimate details of their marriage on the telephone to an unidentified listener, evidence was sufficient to sustain divorce on mental cruelty grounds. Morris v. Morris, 70 Ill. App. 3d 125, 26 Ill. Dec. 505, 388 N.E.2d 129 (1 Dist. 1979).

Defendant's course of conduct obviously rendered life unbearable for plaintiff and adversely affected the lives of the children where the evidence showed that defendant spent most of his weekends hunting or fishing with friends; that he was frequently intoxicated; that many times he called plaintiff vulgar names, berated her housekeeping, ridiculed her efforts to obtain a nursing education, refused to help at home or to give her money for family necessities, accused her of infidelities, and frightened their two daughters, aged 10 and 15 years; that he struck plaintiff and injured her; that plaintiff suffered depression and anxiety and did not provoke any of defendant's abusive conduct; and defendant's evidence included flat denials of most of the events and conduct complained of by plaintiff. Smith v. Smith, 47 Ill. App. 3d 583, 5 Ill. Dec. 810, 362 N.E.2d 123 (3 Dist. 1977).

Where a husband committed several unprovoked physical acts of cruelty upon the wife, once breaking her jaw, evidence was presented of threats he made to her and of scurrilous remarks he made about her in the presence of others, at the times of many of these acts and remarks, he was said to be intoxicated, and some evidence was also presented of his failure to support her, such conduct would obviously cause her embarrassment, humiliation and anguish. Because of the repetition of this conduct, the trial court could have determined that, in toto, this conduct made the wife's life miserable and unendurable, and although not all of the acts of mental cruelty referred to were properly pleaded, those that were not could be considered to explain and give weight to those that were properly pleaded, and the finding that the husband had been guilty of mental cruelty was not contrary to the manifest weight of the evidence. McCarrel v. McCarrel, 48 Ill. App. 3d 666, 6 Ill. Dec. 669, 363 N.E.2d 198 (4 Dist. 1977).

Evidence presented by plaintiff husband made a prima facie case that defendant wife had been guilty of verbal abusive treatment without provocation of the plaintiff of such a nature that it rendered his life miserable, adversely affecting his health. Iverson v. Iverson, 38 Ill. App. 3d 308, 347 N.E.2d 6 (2 Dist. 1976).

The evidence was sufficient to grant a divorce in a plaintiff's favor on the issue of mental cruelty. Jackson v. Jackson, 24 Ill. App. 3d 810, 321 N.E.2d 506 (3 Dist. 1974).

Where there was abundant evidence which disclosed repeated attempts by defendant to humiliate and embarrass his wife, with the knowledge that she was seeking psychiatric help and that his conduct was contributing to her emotional despair, divorce on grounds of mental cruelty was appropriate. Deahl v. Deahl, 13 Ill. App. 3d 150, 300 N.E.2d 497 (1 Dist. 1973).

The ultimate test of mental cruelty is the effect defendant's conduct has upon plaintiff and the marriage; where the record showed, without contradiction, a lack of communication, frigidity in parties' intimate relationships, disparaging comments regarding husband's desire and ability to have children, and wife's jealousy of another woman, to the detriment of the husband's mental and physical health, the trial court's finding of mental cruelty was not disturbed. McGowan v. McGowan, 15 Ill. App. 3d 913, 305 N.E.2d 261 (1 Dist. 1973).

Evidence was sufficient to support the court's finding that the defendant husband was guilty of repeated acts of mental cruelty. Moynihan v. Moynihan, 9 Ill. App. 3d 520, 292 N.E.2d 105 (1 Dist. 1972).

—Humiliation Not Enough

Incidents of humiliation, by themselves, are not sufficient to cause mental cruelty. Gregory v. Gregory, 24 Ill. App. 3d 436, 321 N.E.2d 122 (2 Dist. 1974).

—Inconsistent Findings

The trial court's findings that wife was without fault and husband was guilty of extreme and repeated mental cruelty towards her, while simultaneously finding that husband was without fault and wife was guilty of extreme and repeated mental cruelty towards him, simply contradicted one another and could not stand together; remand for a new trial to allow consistent findings to be made by the trier of fact was required. In re Eltrevoog, 92 Ill. 2d 66, 64 Ill. Dec. 936, 440 N.E.2d 840 (1982).

—Lack of Provocation

In addition to proving mental cruelty, the complaining party must also plead and prove that such conduct was not provoked. In re Wade, 158 Ill. App. 3d 255, 110 Ill. Dec. 321, 511 N.E.2d 156 (4 Dist. 1987).

It is not necessary for a spouse seeking a divorce on grounds of mental cruelty to show that each separate instance complained of was unprovoked. Christian v. Christian, 69 Ill. App. 3d 450, 26 Ill. Dec. 326, 387 N.E.2d 1254 (1 Dist. 1979).

Proof of lack of provocation is an essential part of plaintiff's case; defendant is not required to plead or prove it as an affirmative defense. Morris v. Morris, 70 Ill. App. 3d 125, 26 Ill. Dec. 505, 388 N.E.2d 129 (1 Dist. 1979).

—Medical Evidence

Medical evidence of mental cruelty is not necessary in every case. Morris v. Morris, 70 Ill. App. 3d 125, 26 Ill. Dec. 505, 388 N.E.2d 129 (1 Dist. 1979).

—Offensive Conduct Found

Accusations that petitioner spouse was unfaithful, and that she had contracted and transmitted disease to respondent spouse, as well as respondent's refusal to remove his parents from the marital domicile, constituted offensive conduct toward petitioner and supported judgment granting petitioner a dissolution based upon mental cruelty. In re Jerome, 255 Ill. App. 3d 374, 193 Ill. Dec. 74, 625 N.E.2d 1195 (5 Dist. 1993).

—Particular Facts

A determination of whether given evidence constitutes proof of mental cruelty depends upon the particular circumstances present in each case. Hollo v. Hollo, 131 Ill. App. 3d 119, 85 Ill. Dec. 867, 474 N.E.2d 827 (5 Dist. 1985).

In determining whether grounds of mental cruelty are supported by evidence, the facts of the particular case must be considered in light of the parties' patterns of conduct, their respective emotional makeup, and the circumstances around which the complaint of conduct occurred; the alleged conduct must result in embarrassment, humiliation, and anguish. The ultimate test is whether the conduct complained of had the required adverse effects upon the physical or mental health of the complaining party. Christian v. Christian, 69 Ill. App. 3d 450, 26 Ill. Dec. 326, 387 N.E.2d 1254 (1

Mental Cruelty (Cont'd)

—Particular Facts (Cont'd)

Dist. 1979); In re Wade, 158 Ill. App. 3d 255, 110 Ill. Dec. 321, 511 N.E.2d 156 (4 Dist. 1987).

In determining effect of conduct alleged to be mental cruelty on the complaining party, consideration must be given to the particular emotional and personal makeup of the parties, and the varying circumstances under which any of the incidents occurred that may have given rise to the acts about which complaint is made. Rosenbaum v. Rosenbaum, 38 Ill. App. 3d 1, 349 N.E.2d 73 (1 Dist. 1976).

Whether the acts in question constitute mental cruelty depends upon the total factual background and is determined primarily by the effect of the alleged misconduct upon the complaining party. Rey v. Rey, 23 Ill. App. 3d 274, 319 N.E.2d 105 (2 Dist. 1974).

The emotional makeup of the plaintiff must be considered in determining the effect of the conduct of defendant in providing grounds for the mental cruelty allegation. Hayes v. Hayes, 117 Ill. App. 2d 211, 254 N.E.2d 288 (5 Dist. 1969).

—Physical Harm Unnecessary

Where respondent wife's conduct was of a nature to fall well within accepted definitions of mental cruelty, and circuit court was able to observe petitioner husband and gauge the effect of respondent's conduct upon him, it properly could have concluded that respondent's conduct had an adverse effect upon petitioner's mental health in spite of the absence of tangible physical harm. Hollo v. Hollo, 131 Ill. App. 3d 119, 85 Ill. Dec. 867, 474 N.E.2d 827 (5 Dist. 1985).

—Preponderance of Evidence

It is not error to award a divorce upon grounds of mental cruelty where defendant husband disputes the facts, and plaintiff wife's testimony is not corroborated; the test is the sufficiency of the evidence in behalf of plaintiff to establish a preponderance in the light of the opposing evidence. Harry v. Harry, 38 Ill. App. 3d 776, 349 N.E.2d 69 (4 Dist. 1976).

—Requirements

The ultimate test of whether an act constitutes mental cruelty is the effect the complained of conduct had upon the complaining party and the marriage. Gregory v. Gregory, 24 Ill. App. 3d 436, 321 N.E.2d 122 (2 Dist. 1974).

The conduct of defendant of which the plaintiff complained was of a nature to fall within accepted definitions of mental cruelty. Rey v. Rey, 23 Ill. App. 3d 274, 319 N.E.2d 105 (2 Dist. 1974).

To prove a case entitling a spouse to a divorce on the grounds of mental cruelty, the evidence must show that the conduct of the offending spouse is unprovoked and constitutes a course of abusive and humiliating treatment calculated or obviously of a nature to torture, discommode, or render miserable the life of the complaining spouse or to endanger his or her life, person or health. Rey v. Rey, 23 Ill. App. 3d 274, 319 N.E.2d 105 (2 Dist. 1974).

Conduct to be considered extreme and repeated mental cruelty must be such as to cause embarrassment, humiliation and anguish so as to render life miserable and unendurable or to cause the plaintiff's life, person, or health to be endangered. Akin v. Akin, 125 Ill. App. 2d 159, 260 N.E.2d 481 (4 Dist. 1970); Quilty v. Quilty, 5 Ill. App. 3d 801, 284 N.E.2d 690 (3 Dist. 1972).

Conduct by one spouse that would cause the other spouse to become nervous and upset under the circumstances here could not be held to be extreme mental cruelty; nor could the conduct be held to have made his living as the husband of the wife unendurable as he had already left the home without fault on the wife's part. Akin v. Akin, 125 Ill. App. 2d 159, 260 N.E.2d 481 (4 Dist. 1970).

—Single Episode

Because the conduct which was alleged to constitute extreme and repeated mental cruelty must be evidenced on at least two separate occasions, defendant husband failed to establish that plaintiff wife's unprovoked conduct met this standard when the conduct of which he complained occurred in a single episode. Collins v. Collins, 47 Ill. App. 3d 258, 5 Ill. Dec. 464, 361 N.E.2d 787 (1 Dist. 1977).

Motion for a Finding

Where there was evidence that defendant continuously entered plaintiff's apartment and turned down the heat, causing plaintiff physical discomfort, and that defendant's actions made plaintiff nervous and upset, defendant's motion for a finding should not have been allowed. Bochenek v. Bochenek, 5 Ill. App. 3d 65, 283 N.E.2d 95 (1 Dist. 1972).

No Fault Divorce

—Evidence Held Sufficient

Where the parties separated and lived apart since that time, the parties attempted reconciliation and obtained counseling, but the attempt failed, and there were irreconcilable differences between the parties and the parties no longer wished to live together, petitioner was entitled to a judgment of dissolution under the no fault provision. In re Bates, 141 Ill. App. 3d 566, 95 Ill. Dec. 922, 490 N.E.2d 1014 (2 Dist. 1986).

—Retrospective Application

Retrospective application of subsection (a)(2) of this section was not unconstitutional as applied to defendant wife because it would not divest her of any rights she acquired in the earlier judgment dismissing prior dissolution petition; judgment on the prior petition established only that prior to 1979, no grounds for dissolution of defendant's marriage existed. In re Semmler, 107 Ill. 2d 130, 89 Ill. Dec. 873, 481 N.E.2d 716 (1985).

Physical Cruelty

—Burden of Proof

To establish cruelty within the meaning of former Ill.Rev.Stat., ch. 40, para. 1 (see now this section), it was necessary to prove by a preponderance of the evidence that the guilty party had on at least two separate occasions committed acts of physical violence against his spouse resulting in pain and bodily harm, and if cause for divorce was so established and it appeared that either party held title to real estate equitably belonging to the other, the court could compel a conveyance to the party entitled thereto upon which terms as it deemed advisable under former Ill.Rev.Stat., ch. 40, para. 18 (see now 750 ILCS 5/502). Tuyls v. Tuyls, 21 Ill. 2d 192, 171 N.E.2d 779 (1961).

—Conduct Required

Two acts of physical violence resulting in pain and bodily harm, committed on separate occasions, are sufficient grounds for divorce. Kovack v. Kovack, 131 Ill. App. 2d 382, 268 N.E.2d 258 (1 Dist. 1971).

—Corroborating Witnesses

Where the testimony of a witness disclosed that on two occasions the complainant came to her house and exhibited bruises and marks, which the complainant told her had been inflicted by the defendant, the bruises and marks observed and sworn to were competent testimony in confirmation of the evidence given by the complainant. Muir v. Muir, 310 Ill. App. 443, 34 N.E.2d 873 (2 Dist. 1941).

—Defined

Cruelty constituting ground for divorce under this section means physical acts of violence, bodily harm or suffering, or such acts as endanger life or limb or such as raise a reasonable apprehension of great bodily harm. Wesselhoeft v. Wesselhoeft, 369 Ill. 419, 17 N.E.2d 56 (1938).

Cruelty constituting ground for divorce means physical acts of violence, bodily harm or suffering, or such acts as endanger life or limb or such as raise a reasonable apprehension of great bodily harm; bad temper, petulance, rude language, want of civil attentions, or angry and abusive words do not constitute extreme and repeated cruelty. Moore v. Moore, 362 Ill. 177, 199 N.E. 98 (1935).

—Evidence Held Insufficient

Evidence did not support granting wife a divorce on ground of physical cruelty. Coolidge v. Coolidge, 4 Ill. App. 2d 205, 124 N.E.2d 1 (1 Dist. 1955).

Where the evidence given by wife strongly contradicted that of doctor whom she claimed examined her for injuries she alleged were inflicted by drunken husband, divorce decree was against the manifest weight of the evidence and was reversed. Druce v. Druce, 313 Ill. App. 169, 39 N.E.2d 690 (2 Dist. 1942).

—Evidence Held Sufficient

The evidence was sufficient to prove the grounds of extreme and

Physical Cruelty (Cont'd)

—Evidence Held Sufficient (Cont'd)

repeated physical cruelty. In re Yakin, 107 Ill. App. 3d 1103, 62 Ill. Dec. 547, 436 N.E.2d 573 (1 Dist. 1982).

Evidence was sufficient to support the finding that the husband committed acts of violence against the wife which produced pain and bodily harm on at least two separate occasions and was thus guilty of extreme and repeated physical cruelty within the meaning of this section. Knox v. Knox, 31 Ill. App. 3d 816, 334 N.E.2d 891 (1 Dist. 1975).

The alleged acts of cruelty were sufficient to endanger plaintiff's life or limbs as to raise a reasonable apprehension of great bodily harm. Mills v. Mills, 13 Ill. App. 3d 288, 300 N.E.2d 842 (1 Dist. 1973).

The striking of the plaintiff by the defendant as set out in the plaintiff's testimony and that of the witnesses constituted extreme cruelty under the law; the finding of the trial court was not against the manifest weight of the evidence, and the evidence was sufficient to support the divorce decree. Pantle v. Pantle, 19 Ill. App. 2d 353, 153 N.E.2d 740 (1 Dist. 1958).

The evidence was held sufficient to support a divorce based upon acts of physical cruelty committed by the wife. Bogaerts v. Bogaerts, 344 Ill. App. 497, 101 N.E.2d 608 (1 Dist. 1951).

—Extreme and Repeated

This Act provides for dissolution of a marriage where either party had been guilty of extreme or repeated physical cruelty; violence resulting in pain and bodily harm on at least two separate occasions, if proved by a preponderance of the evidence, is sufficient within the meaning of the Act. Murphy v. Murphy, 31 Ill. App. 3d 321, 334 N.E.2d 779 (1 Dist. 1975); Knox v. Knox, 31 Ill. App. 3d 816, 334 N.E.2d 891 (1 Dist. 1975).

Where defendant held a knife to plaintiff's throat and threatened to kill her and a few months later pushed her across the room against a gas heater after she interceded as defendant was choking her son, these acts were illustrative of the defendant's obvious disregard for the safety and welfare of the plaintiff and sufficient to constitute extreme and repeated cruelty. Alanen v. Alanen, 84 Ill. App. 2d 53, 228 N.E.2d 492 (1 Dist. 1967).

Evidence held sufficient to establish that a husband was guilty of habitual drunkenness and extreme and repeated cruelty. Holmstedt v. Holmstedt, 383 Ill. 290, 49 N.E.2d 25 (1943).

—Factors to Consider

Although the sex of the plaintiff is one of the circumstances to be considered in determining whether acts of violence produced bodily harm, the fact that by exerting a superior strength the husband might have been able to avoid physical injury does not negate the existence of extreme cruelty if the acts in question caused physical pain. Surratt v. Surratt, 12 Ill. 2d 21, 145 N.E.2d 594 (1957).

—Physical Contact

While every act of physical contact is not an act of cruelty, when it produces pain and bodily harm it will support a decree for divorce. Stockman v. Stockman, 38 Ill. App. 2d 186, 186 N.E.2d 547 (4 Dist. 1962).

—Proof

If a husband's testimony by itself is sufficiently credible to establish two separate acts of physical violence resulting in pain and bodily harm, that testimony need not be corroborated by other evidence; however, the acts of physical cruelty must be clearly proved and the physical stature of the parties may be considered in weighing the sufficiency of the evidence. Kerbis v. Kerbis, 38 Ill. App. 3d 866, 350 N.E.2d 1 (1 Dist. 1976).

—Requirements

Physical cruelty may not be built upon trifling and insignificant incidents, but it need not be shown that the physical cruelty was so aggravated as to gravely endanger the life or limb of the spouse upon whom it has been inflicted. Farah v. Farah, 25 Ill. App. 3d 481, 323 N.E.2d 361 (1 Dist. 1975).

—Shown

Where plaintiff testified to an occasion upon which defendant kicked and struck her with his fists on the face, on the shoulders, arms and back and another occasion some three months later when defendant struck her with his fists on the arms and back, both of which were without reason or provocation and caused her pain and suffering and threatened her life, plaintiff was not impeached in any degree, and physical cruelty was found. Farah v. Farah, 25 Ill. App. 3d 481, 323 N.E.2d 361 (1 Dist. 1975).

Pleading

—Amendment of Petition

Where petitioner filed an amended petition for dissolution, but failed to obtain leave of court as required by section 46 of the former Civil Practice Act (see now 735 ILCS 5/2-616), amendment to the pleading filed without leave of court to do so constituted grounds for striking such amendment, and the amendment had to be disregarded on review. In re Peoples, 96 Ill. App. 3d 94, 51 Ill. Dec. 514, 420 N.E.2d 1072 (5 Dist. 1981).

—Insufficiency of Petition

A trial court properly refused to vacate a divorce decree upon a defendant's contention of an unconstitutional denial of due process of law by virtue of the failure of the court on its own motion to have continued the cause in order to permit defendant to get additional counsel, or denial of a constitutional right to be warned of rights that he had, including the right to a continuance, where defendant's petition in the trial court wholly omitted any mention of any constitutional provision. Davis v. Davis, 131 Ill. App. 2d 459, 268 N.E.2d 491 (1 Dist. 1971).

—Name on Petition

In the absence of evidence to the contrary, the general rule is that identity of name on a petition of divorce raises the presumption of identity of person. Anderson v. Anderson, 292 Ill. App. 421, 11 N.E.2d 216 (1 Dist. 1937).

—Separate Grounds

Amended complaint sufficiently stated one cause of action for divorce based upon two distinct and separate grounds: extreme and repeated mental cruelty and attempt to kill a spouse by means showing malice, arising out of the same set of facts. Iverson v. Iverson, 38 Ill. App. 3d 308, 347 N.E.2d 6 (2 Dist. 1976).

Provocation

—Burden of Proof

Although burden of proving lack of provocation remains with the complaining party, the burden of going forward shifts to the defending party once there has been a denial, explicit or implicit, that actions were provoked. In re Wade, 158 Ill. App. 3d 255, 110 Ill. Dec. 321, 511 N.E.2d 156 (4 Dist. 1987).

—Effect

Where the grounds for divorce are physical or mental cruelty, provocation is not an affirmative defense; indeed its presence is proof that an element of the plaintiff's prima facie case, namely cruelty, does not exist. Rosenbaum v. Rosenbaum, 38 Ill. App. 3d 1, 349 N.E.2d 73 (1 Dist. 1976).

—Essential Element

Lack of cause or provocation by petitioner for respondent's acts of mental or physical cruelty is a necessary element of proof under this section; the trial court erred in granting a dissolution to the petitioner in a case where the record was absolutely void as to cause or provocation. In re Ducey, 101 Ill. App. 3d 957, 57 Ill. Dec. 485, 428 N.E.2d 1165 (5 Dist. 1981).

Lack of provocation is an essential element of the case of one seeking a divorce who is alleging mental or physical cruelty. Sherman v. Sherman, 38 Ill. App. 3d 664, 30 Ill. Dec. 412, 348 N.E.2d 524 (2 Dist. 1976); Rosenbaum v. Rosenbaum, 38 Ill. App. 3d 1, 349 N.E.2d 73 (1 Dist. 1976).

Lack of provocation is a necessary element of an action for divorce based on mental cruelty. Sharer v. Sharer, 39 Ill. App. 3d 818, 350 N.E.2d 779 (5 Dist. 1976).

—Evidence Held Insufficient

Plaintiff's statement that he had been a good and considerate husband during the marriage was insufficient by itself to prove lack of provocation, especially in light of the nature of the testimony of plaintiff and defendant which established at least a basis for inquiry by defendant into plaintiff's habits and some duty on the

Provocation (Cont'd)

—Evidence Held Insufficient (Cont'd)

part of plaintiff to provide a reasonable explanation of his conduct. Sharer v. Sharer, 39 Ill. App. 3d 818, 350 N.E.2d 779 (5 Dist. 1976).

Public Policy

Where an appellant stated that she would pursue her remedy for separate maintenance if voluntary dismissal were granted, the public policy of protecting a continuing marriage relationship did not apply; since granting appellant's motion would have been destructive of appellee's rights in terms of costs and repetitious litigation, the trial court was not disregarding public policy in denying appellant's motion to dismiss. Juen v. Juen, 12 Ill. App. 3d 284, 297 N.E.2d 633 (5 Dist. 1973).

It is a basic interest of the state to preserve the integrity and continuity of marriages, and divorces will not be granted unless there is sufficient evidence of cause therefore as specified by statute. Woodshank v. Woodshank, 2 Ill. App. 3d 596, 274 N.E.2d 694 (3 Dist. 1971).

Because of the public policy involved in divorce actions, they are of a special character, since the state is considered to be a third party to every such action and has a definite interest in protecting the continuance of the marriage relation without destroying the rights of the parties, and the court in its position of protecting the interest of the state should favorably receive motions for the voluntary dismissal of a divorce case and grant them. Gonzalez v. Gonzalez, 6 Ill. App. 2d 310, 127 N.E.2d 673 (1 Dist. 1955).

Reconciliation

—Time Period

It would be incongruous to interpret the no-fault provision as requiring only two years in which to reconcile for spouses who separated subsequent to July 1, 1984, but to require a much longer period for spouses who separated prior to that date. In re Semmler, 107 Ill. 2d 130, 89 Ill. Dec. 873, 481 N.E.2d 716 (1985).

Recrimination

Evidence showed that the decree of divorce awarded by the trial court to the husband on his counterclaim was manifestly against the weight of the evidence and was barred by the former doctrine of recrimination. Elston v. Elston, 344 Ill. App. 233, 100 N.E.2d 635 (2 Dist. 1951).

Remarriage

Plaintiff wife's remarriage manifested an unqualified intention on her part to be bound by divorce decree. Royster v. Hammel, 51 Ill. App. 3d 710, 9 Ill. Dec. 278, 366 N.E.2d 535 (5 Dist. 1977).

Wife recognized the validity of the divorce decree and availed herself of its benefits by marrying another man and she accordingly was estopped to attempt to vacate the decree. Baker v. Baker, 2 Ill. App. 3d 795, 276 N.E.2d 792 (5 Dist. 1971).

—Defined

In construing a divorce decree, the clear meaning of the term "remarriage" was the occurrence of the event of the marriage ceremony. In re Kolb, 99 Ill. App. 3d 895, 55 Ill. Dec. 128, 425 N.E.2d 1301 (1 Dist. 1981).

Reservation of Issues

—Appealability

Judgment reserving maintenance was appealable. In re Lord, 125 Ill. App. 3d 1, 80 Ill. Dec. 360, 465 N.E.2d 151 (2 Dist. 1984).

—Held Improper

Even though the trial court improperly reserved jurisdiction to determine the method of distribution without following the appropriate procedures, the order was still not final until the method of distribution was established and therefore husband's appeal over ten years later was timely as it immediately followed the court's order of apportionment of marital interest in husband's pension. In re Wisniewski, 286 Ill. App. 3d 236, 221 Ill. Dec. 632, 675 N.E.2d 1362 (4 Dist. 1997), appeal denied, 173 Ill. 2d 549, 226 Ill. Dec. 140, 684 N.E.2d 1343 (1997).

The court abused its discretion in dividing military pension by failing to comply with subsection (b) to preserve jurisdiction for the distribution of military pension benefits. In re Burkhart, 267 Ill. App. 3d 761, 205 Ill. Dec. 317, 643 N.E.2d 268 (2 Dist. 1994).

Where there was no agreement of parties or motion of either party to reserve an issue, and a finding by the court that appropriate circumstances existed, the court improperly reserved the issue of pension benefits. In re Britton, 141 Ill. App. 3d 588, 96 Ill. Dec. 43, 490 N.E.2d 1079 (5 Dist. 1986).

—Requirements

Notwithstanding the plain language of subsection (b) of this section, a party is not required to make a formal motion to reserve an issue and a trial court is not required to make an express finding that appropriate circumstances exist therefor; rather, this section, similarly to 750 ILCS 5/504, is satisfied if the record reveals: (a) that one of the parties requested reservation of an issue; and (b) that appropriate circumstances existed therefor. In re Fahy, 208 Ill. App. 3d 677, 153 Ill. Dec. 594, 567 N.E.2d 552 (1 Dist. 1991).

—Upheld

In having reserved the issue of maintenance to petitioner wife as allowed under this section, the trial court did not reach or make the determinations required under 750 ILCS 5/504 for a maintenance award; as such, the trial court's reservation of that issue was not assailable on the ground that petitioner did not meet the statutory prerequisites to justify such an award. In re Fahy, 208 Ill. App. 3d 677, 153 Ill. Dec. 594, 567 N.E.2d 552 (1 Dist. 1991).

The trial court was justified in entering judgment of dissolution while reserving other questions until personal jurisdiction over the respondent husband had been obtained. In re Parks, 122 Ill. App. 3d 905, 78 Ill. Dec. 97, 461 N.E.2d 681 (2 Dist. 1984).

Where there was a finding that a party had organic symptoms which may or may not have manifested itself in a disabling disease, but that question was determinable, based on expert medical testimony, within a certain period of time, the trial court's finding that no maintenance was justified under the present circumstances, but that if the condition developed, distribution of property would be inadequate to protect wife, justified its decision to reserve maintenance. In re Lord, 125 Ill. App. 3d 1, 80 Ill. Dec. 360, 465 N.E.2d 151 (2 Dist. 1984).

Residence

—In General

For a case discussing the residence requirement under the former Divorce Act (see now 750 ILCS 5/101 et seq.), see Carbrey v. Carbrey, 108 Ill. App. 2d 363, 247 N.E.2d 818 (2 Dist. 1969).

—Abandonment Not Shown

Plaintiff did not abandon her residence in this state prior to the filing of her suit although plaintiff did leave the state for various reasons, and she did journey to another country with her lawyer in an attempt to assert her rights to visitation of her child; the mere fact, even of a lengthy absence, where her residence in this state had been established, did not constitute abandonment under former Ill.Rev.Stat., ch. 40, para. 3 (see now this section). Farah v. Farah, 25 Ill. App. 3d 481, 323 N.E.2d 361 (1 Dist. 1975).

—Allegation

Failure to allege the duration of residence was not fatal to plaintiff if the record disclosed that the necessary residence facts actually existed. Kijowski v. Kijowski, 36 Ill. App. 2d 94, 183 N.E.2d 583 (1 Dist. 1962).

—Defined

Residence does not consist simply of physical presence in any particular locality; it is primarily a matter of intent. Farah v. Farah, 25 Ill. App. 3d 481, 323 N.E.2d 361 (1 Dist. 1975).

—Established

Where judgment, which was part of the record, affirmatively showed that respondent husband was at the time of the filing and for one year (now 90 days) prior thereto a resident of the state of Illinois, indulging the presumptions in favor of the validity of the judgment in a collateral attack on the judgment, petitioner did not overcome those presumptions. Flynn v. Flynn, 45 Ill. App. 3d 865, 4 Ill. Dec. 465, 360 N.E.2d 401 (1 Dist. 1977).

—Evidence Held Insufficient

The trial court's finding that plaintiff was a resident of Illinois for

Residence (Cont'd)

—Evidence Held Insufficient (Cont'd)
one year (now 90 days) preceding the filing of her complaint was against the manifest weight of the evidence. Rosenshine v. Rosenshine, 60 Ill. App. 3d 514, 17 Ill. Dec. 942, 377 N.E.2d 132 (1 Dist. 1978).

—Evidence Held Sufficient
The record contained sufficient circumstances and evidence to support plaintiff's allegations in her complaint that she resided in Cook County and the State of Illinois for more than one year (now 90 days); thus, she satisfied residency requirements. Green v. Green, 41 Ill. App. 3d 154, 354 N.E.2d 661 (1 Dist. 1976).

Where parties contracted their marriage in this state, but left this state temporarily while defendant was employed in another country, and months later, they returned to Chicago where they leased an apartment, made an effort to purchase a home near Chicago, and where defendant was employed in Chicago, and plaintiff's home continued to be in Chicago until the next year, the parties were both residents of this state under former Ill.Rev.Stat., ch. 40, para. 3 (see now this section). Farah v. Farah, 25 Ill. App. 3d 481, 323 N.E.2d 361 (1 Dist. 1975).

Although there was considerable evidence of husband's ties with other states over his lifetime, there was also sufficient evidence of his intent to remain a citizen of this state to support the finding of continued residence in this state so as to enable the husband to institute a suit for divorce in this state. Davis v. Davis, 9 Ill. App. 3d 922, 293 N.E.2d 399 (1 Dist. 1973).

The defendant by his testimony, acts and conduct throughout the years evidenced an intent that a county was his residence where he was president of a company there and maintained a home which was ample for his entire family there, and the fact that the parties also owned a house in another state, where the plaintiff lived part of the year for health reasons, did not deprive the defendant of his residence in this state under a former version of this section. Garrison v. Garrison, 107 Ill. App. 2d 311, 246 N.E.2d 9 (2 Dist. 1969).

Plaintiff had resided in a county for more than one year prior to filing of her complaint, and this evidence was corroborated by facts appearing in defendant's sworn answer to the complaint. Kijowski v. Kijowski, 36 Ill. App. 2d 94, 183 N.E.2d 583 (1 Dist. 1962).

—Multiple Residence
Mere fact that a person could have had more than one residence and, therefore, could possibly secure a divorce in more than one jurisdiction under former Ill.Rev.Stat., ch. 40, para. 3 (see now this section) did not render action improper. Berlingieri v. Berlingieri, 372 Ill. 60, 22 N.E.2d 675 (1939).

—Purpose of Requirement
The apparent purpose of a 90 day requirement prior to the findings of dissolution of marriage rather than prior to commencement of the action is to allow a newly arrived litigant to obtain temporary relief even though the 90 day durational requirement has not yet vested. In re Weiss, 87 Ill. App. 3d 643, 42 Ill. Dec. 714, 409 N.E.2d 329 (1 Dist. 1980).

Review
The findings of the trial court as to the evidence of a material change in the circumstances of the parties since the original divorce decree should be reversed only if they are contrary to the manifest weight of the evidence. Gentile v. Gentile, 69 Ill. App. 3d 297, 26 Ill. Dec. 149, 387 N.E.2d 979 (3 Dist. 1979).

Separate Maintenance
A defendant in a prior separate maintenance proceeding, wherein plaintiff had obtained a decree of separate maintenance, may thereafter accrue a cause of action for a divorce. Schneider v. Schneider, 43 Ill. App. 3d 1014, 3 Ill. Dec. 11, 358 N.E.2d 11 (1 Dist. 1976).

Separation Period

—Failure to File Waiver
Motion to vacate the judgment of dissolution as being void because of a failure to file a written waiver of the two-year waiting period for a no-fault dissolution was denied. In re Monken, 255 Ill. App. 3d 1044, 194 Ill. Dec. 422, 627 N.E.2d 759 (5 Dist. 1994).

—Purpose
The legislative history of subdivision (a)(2) of this section makes it clear that the purpose of the separation period is to ensure that the family unit has already broken down and to preserve the possibility of a reconciliation; this aim is satisfied regardless of whether or not the separation period occurred before or after the effective date of the statute. In re Semmler, 107 Ill. 2d 130, 89 Ill. Dec. 873, 481 N.E.2d 716 (1985).

State as Party
The state has always been an interested third party in all divorce actions. Winning v. Winning, 366 Ill. 57, 7 N.E.2d 750 (1937).

Statute of Limitations and Laches

—Date of Accrual
The statutory period of divorce could not begin to run while the husband and wife were living in the same home although they were staying in separate rooms. Lindeman v. Lindeman, 337 Ill. App. 261, 85 N.E.2d 847 (1 Dist. 1949).

—Lapse of Time
The fact that another state decree was entered some ten years before plaintiff instituted divorce proceedings in this state did not operate to bar plaintiff's action, for lapse of time could not remedy the lack of jurisdiction of the court entering the void decree, nor constitute such laches as would estop plaintiff from proceeding with his action. Ludwig v. Ludwig, 413 Ill. 44, 107 N.E.2d 848 (1952).

LEGAL PERIODICALS

For article, "The Real Estate Lawyer's Divorce Primer and the Divorce Lawyer's Guide to Real Estate", see 86 Ill. B.J. 488 (1998).

For article, "Marriage as Contract, Opportunistic Violence, and Other Bad Arguments for Fault Divorce," see 1997 U. Ill. L. Rev. 719.

For article, "Divorce Practice: Doing the Right Thing," see 9 CBA Rec. 48 (1995).

For article, "Divorce and the Displaced Homemaker: A Discourse on Playing with Dolls, Partnership Buyouts and Dissociation Under No-Fault," see 60 U. Chi. L. Rev. 67 (1993).

For article, "Survey of Illinois Law, 1988-89 — Family Law," see 14 S. Ill. U.L.J. 1007 (1990).

For note, "Making Form Follow Function: Considerations in Creating and Applying a Statutory Parent-Child Privilege," see U. Ill. L. Rev. 879 (1990).

For article, "Family Law: 1988-89 Illinois Law Survey," see 21 Loy. U. Chi. L.J. 417 (1989-90).

For article, "Family Law: 1986-87 Illinois Law Survey," See 19 Loy. U. Chi. L.J. 489 (1987-88).

For article, "Divorce Illinois Style: Ten Years Under the Marriage and Dissolution of Marriage Act," see 75 Ill. B.J. 606 (1987).

For article, "Family Law: 1985-86 Survey," see 11 S. Ill. U.L.J. 741 (1987).

For article, "Family Law: 1985-86 Illinois Law Survey," see 18 Loy. U. Chi. L.J. 549 (1986-87).

For article, "Taming Transmutation: A Guide to Illinois' New Rules on Property Classification and Division upon Dissolution of Marriage," see 72 Ill. B.J. 336 (1984).

For case note, "In re Marriage of Conn, 443 N.E.2d 541 (1982): Bifurcation of Marriage Dissolution Judgments in Illinois," see 17 J. Marshall L. Rev. 217 (1984).

For article, "Caveat Amator: 'The State of Affairs' in Illinois After Hewitt v. Hewitt," see 29 De Paul L. Rev. 493 (1980).

For note, "Family Law, Property Rights — Hewitt v. Hewitt, 77 Ill.2d 49, 394 N.E.2d 1204 (1979)," see 69 Ill. B.J. 49 (1980).

For comment, "Civil Aspects of Intrafamily Eavesdropping in Illinois: Caveats to Comprehension Remedial Weaponry," see 12 J. Marshall J. Prac. & Proc. 537 (1979).

RESEARCH REFERENCES

Excessiveness or adequacy of amount of money awarded as separate maintenance, alimony, or support for spouse without absolute divorce. 26 ALR4th 1190.

Enforceability of agreement requiring spouse's cooperation in obtaining religious bill of divorce. 29 ALR4th 746.

Effect of death of party to divorce proceeding pending appeal or time allowed for appeal. 33 ALR4th 47.

Modern status of views as to validity of premarital agreements contemplating divorce or separation. 53 ALR4th 22.

Enforceability of premarital agreements governing support or property rights upon divorce or separation as affected by circumstances surrounding execution — modern status. 53 ALR4th 85.

Insanity as defense to divorce or separation suit — post-1950 cases. 67 ALR4th 277.

Divorced spouse's right to order that other spouse pay expert witness fees. 4 ALR5th 403.

Joinder of tort action between spouses with proceeding for dissolution of marriage. 4 ALR5th 972.

Power of incompetent spouse's guardian or representative to sue for granting or vacation of divorce or annulment of marriage, or to make compromise of settlement in such suit. 32 ALR5th 673.

Full faith and credit "last-in-time" rule as applicable to sister state divorce or custody judgment which is inconsistent with the forum state's earlier judgment. 36 ALR5th 527.

Doctrine of forum non conveniens: Assumption or denial of jurisdiction of action involving matrimonial dispute. 55 ALR5th 647.

Homosexuality as ground for divorce. 96 ALR5th 83.

750 ILCS 5/402 Legal Separation

Sec. 402. *Legal Separation.* (a) Any person living separate and apart from his or her spouse without fault may have a remedy for reasonable support and maintenance while they so live apart.

(b) Such action shall be brought in the circuit court of the county in which the respondent resides or in which the parties last resided together as husband and wife. In the event the respondent cannot be found within the State, the action may be brought in the circuit court of the county in which the petitioner resides. Commencement of the action, temporary relief and trials shall be the same as in actions for dissolution of marriage.

(c) A proceeding or judgment for legal separation shall not bar either party from instituting an action for dissolution of marriage, and if the party so moving has met the requirements of Section 401 [750 ILCS 5/401], a judgment for dissolution shall be granted.

(Source: P.A. 82-716.)

Note.

This section was Ill.Rev.Stat., Ch. 40, para. 402.

Cross References.

As to actions subject to expedited child support hearings, specifically actions for the establishment of child support and medical support orders involving parties who are married and living separately, see 750 ILCS 25/5.

CASE NOTES

Analysis

Accrued Divorce Action
Desertion
—Evidence Held Insufficient
—Evidence Held Sufficient
—Requirement
—Sufficient Allegations
Fault
—In General
—Burden of Proof
—Conduct
—Consent
—Illustrative Cases
Maintenance Denied
Mutual Consent
Party
Purpose
Separate Abodes
Separate Maintenance
—In General
—Amount Held Insufficient
—Attorney Fees
—Child Support
—Death of Wife
—Denial
—Failure to Pay
—Fault
—Grounds
—Jurisdiction
—Living Separate and Apart
—Modification
—Policies and Purposes
—Post-Nuptial Contract
—Principles
—Property Rights
—Purposes
—Standard of Proof
—Venue
Temporary Alimony
—Pendente Lite

Accrued Divorce Action

A defendant in a prior separate maintenance proceeding, wherein plaintiff had obtained a decree of separate maintenance, may thereafter accrue a cause of action for a divorce. Schneider v. Schneider, 43 Ill. App. 3d 1014, 3 Ill. Dec. 11, 358 N.E.2d 11 (1 Dist. 1976).

Desertion

—Evidence Held Insufficient

Alleged immodest conduct of wife on a single occasion where she removed bathing suit top at a party did not constitute grounds for constructive desertion, and even if it had, it would have been condoned by the parties having cohabited together for a considerable period of time afterwards. Slaight v. Slaight, 50 Ill. App. 2d 31, 199 N.E.2d 650 (2 Dist. 1964).

—Evidence Held Sufficient

There was sufficient evidence to show desertion on wife's part where she was the moving factor in the separation and in the securing of the settlement agreement, and where she refused to have marital relations or participate in any social activities with the plaintiff. Gillespie v. Gillespie, 70 Ill. App. 2d 38, 216 N.E.2d 462 (5 Dist. 1966).

—Requirement

If the separation between parties was by mutual consent or agreement there could be no desertion by either party; thus, mutual separation of husband and wife does not constitute wilful desertion. Gillespie v. Gillespie, 70 Ill. App. 2d 38, 216 N.E.2d 462 (5 Dist. 1966).

—Sufficient Allegations

In an action for legal separation, wife's allegation that husband, without cause or provocation by wife, wilfully deserted wife, which caused wife grievous mental anxiety and constituted extreme and repeated mental cruelty, was sufficient to allege the grounds of desertion. In re Jones, 90 Ill. App. 3d 95, 45 Ill. Dec. 540, 412 N.E.2d 1122 (5 Dist. 1980).

Fault

—In General

The concept of fault under this section does not require that wife be entirely blameless in order to be entitled to separate maintenance. Kerbis v. Kerbis, 38 Ill. App. 3d 866, 350 N.E.2d 1 (1 Dist. 1976).

Fault (Cont'd)

—In General (Cont'd)

In order to prevail in a separate maintenance action, it is essential that the plaintiff establish that the separation was without her fault; fault consists of either voluntary consent to a separation or failure of duty or misconduct materially contributing to a disruption of the marital relationship. Graham v. Graham, 44 Ill. App. 3d 519, 3 Ill. Dec. 141, 358 N.E.2d 308 (5 Dist. 1976).

—Burden of Proof

The complaining party need not be wholly blameless to prevail in a separate maintenance action, nor is it necessary that the conduct be itself a sufficient basis for a divorce by the other party, as the measure of proof and grounds of relief are not the same in cases for separate maintenance as in cases of divorce. Graham v. Graham, 44 Ill. App. 3d 519, 3 Ill. Dec. 141, 358 N.E.2d 308 (5 Dist. 1976).

—Conduct

The fault that would preclude relief for the complainant has been variously described as voluntary consent to the separation or a course of conduct that itself materially contributes to the destruction of the marital relation; it is not necessary that the conduct be itself a basis for a divorce by the other party for it to be fault in this sense. David v. David, 77 Ill. App. 2d 448, 222 N.E.2d 540 (2 Dist. 1966).

—Consent

If separation is with consent of plaintiff, she is not without fault within the meaning of this section. Graham v. Graham, 44 Ill. App. 3d 519, 3 Ill. Dec. 141, 358 N.E.2d 308 (5 Dist. 1976).

—Illustrative Cases

The manifest weight of competent evidence clearly indicated that plaintiff wife was without fault, even though defendant husband produced evidence that plaintiff threatened a divorce, where the record was uncontested that she never pursued this threat and that her sole attempt at judicial recourse was a separate maintenance action; thus, the trial court erred by denying separate maintenance. Kerbis v. Kerbis, 38 Ill. App. 3d 866, 350 N.E.2d 1 (1 Dist. 1976).

Where a husband had no practicable alternative but to live where his job existed and this required a separation from his wife, since his move nearer to his employment was with her consent, she did not meet her burden of proving that she was "without fault" within the terms of former Ill.Rev.Stat., ch. 68, para. 22 (see now this section and 750 ILCS 5/504). Graham v. Graham, 44 Ill. App. 3d 519, 3 Ill. Dec. 141, 358 N.E.2d 308 (5 Dist. 1976).

Where there was evidence that the wife cooked breakfast for her husband only "infrequently"; was seldom home at night; turned off the television set while her husband viewed it; interrupted and retained his mail; obtained an injunction to keep him out of the house when he sought to return following a prior separation; pushed him out of the kitchen when he attempted to prepare his meals; did not clean his room for "two or three years"; and rebutted his attempts to establish a reconciliation, the wife failed to establish the fact that the parties were living separate and apart without fault on her part. David v. David, 77 Ill. App. 2d 448, 222 N.E.2d 540 (2 Dist. 1966).

Maintenance Denied

Where trial court found that wife was not without fault, that husband had just provocation for leaving and wife engaged in a course of conduct which alienated her husband and culminated in his leaving the marital home, the trial court's judgment dismissing the wife's complaint for separate maintenance pursuant to former Ill.Rev.Stat., ch. 68, para. 22 (see now this section and 750 ILCS 5/504) was not against the manifest weight of the evidence. Heinz v. Heinz, 33 Ill. App. 3d 542, 338 N.E.2d 157 (2 Dist. 1975).

Mutual Consent

Mutual consent to a separation means that the separation was by agreement and at the request of both parties, and if the separation was against the will of one of the parties, there could be no separation by mutual consent. Gillespie v. Gillespie, 70 Ill. App. 2d 38, 216 N.E.2d 462 (5 Dist. 1966).

The evidence amply supported the findings of the trial judge that the property settlement and separation were not by mutual consent and that the proceedings were instituted and pushed by the wife, who not only wanted the property divided, but also insisted on discontinuing the marital relationship. Gillespie v. Gillespie, 70 Ill. App. 2d 38, 216 N.E.2d 462 (5 Dist. 1966).

Party

The word "party" can only mean one who, seeking a legal separation, is free from fault; this section does not enable a spouse at fault in a marriage to be able to prevent the other spouse from obtaining a dissolution. In re Eltrevoog, 92 Ill. 2d 66, 64 Ill. Dec. 936, 440 N.E.2d 840 (1982).

Purpose

This section is not intended to enable a spouse at fault in a marriage to be able to prevent the other spouse from obtaining a dissolution. In re Davenport, 92 Ill. App. 3d 675, 48 Ill. Dec. 193, 416 N.E.2d 88 (4 Dist. 1981).

The original purpose of the separate maintenance statute was to enable a married woman to sue in equity in her own name for her support. Graham v. Graham, 44 Ill. App. 3d 519, 3 Ill. Dec. 141, 358 N.E.2d 308 (5 Dist. 1976).

Separate Abodes

While this section is clear that parties must reside in separate abodes before the court grants judgment in form of legal separation, it is silent on the question as to whether the parties must reside in separate abodes at the time of filing, and thus such a requirement is not present. Smith v. Aaron, Aaron, Schimberg & Hess, 112 Ill. App. 3d 653, 67 Ill. Dec. 775, 445 N.E.2d 67 (2 Dist. 1983).

Separate Maintenance

—In General

Unless otherwise specifically provided, separate maintenance actions are governed by the same principles as are other civil cases. Shapiro v. Shapiro, 113 Ill. App. 2d 374, 252 N.E.2d 93 (1 Dist. 1969).

For a case discussing separate maintenance generally, see Barton v. Barton, 318 Ill. App. 68, 47 N.E.2d 496 (4 Dist. 1943).

For a case discussing the concept of separate maintenance, see American Woolen Co. v. Lesher, 267 Ill. 11, 107 N.E. 882 (1915).

—Amount Held Insufficient

The amount of support for the wife allowed by the court was insufficient where there was uncontroverted proof that she was in ill health and under a doctor's care, and she should have been allowed reasonable support and maintenance and reasonable counsel fees for the litigation in the trial court and for the appeal. Holmstedt v. Holmstedt, 383 Ill. 290, 49 N.E.2d 25 (1943).

—Attorney Fees

For a case discussing the allowance of attorney fees in a separate maintenance action, see Rasmussen v. Rasmussen, 334 Ill. App. 308, 79 N.E.2d 525 (1 Dist. 1948).

—Child Support

A woman may maintain a separate suit against her husband or former husband for the support and maintenance of their minor child. Loss v. Loss, 80 Ill. App. 2d 376, 224 N.E.2d 271 (2 Dist. 1967).

—Death of Wife

The death of wife prior to a final decree in separate maintenance action did not abate the action to the extent that the trial court had no jurisdiction to order additional attorney fees and expenses incurred during her lifetime under former Ill.Rev.Stat. ch. 68, para. 22 (see now this section and 750 ILCS 5/504). Spiro v. Spiro, 124 Ill. App. 2d 254, 260 N.E.2d 332 (1 Dist. 1970).

—Denial

For a case discussing the denial of separate maintenance, see Druce v. Druce, 313 Ill. App. 169, 39 N.E.2d 690 (2 Dist. 1942).

—Failure to Pay

For a case discussing remedies for failure of spouse to pay separate maintenance, see Sewell v. Sewell, 297 Ill. App. 283, 17 N.E.2d 593 (1 Dist. 1938).

—Fault

For a case discussing fault and amount of separate maintenance

Separate Maintenance (Cont'd)

—Fault (Cont'd)

awarded, see Glover v. Glover, 132 Ill. App. 2d 284, 268 N.E.2d 218 (4 Dist. 1971).

For a case discussing excessive award based on fault, see Amberson v. Amberson, 349 Ill. 249, 181 N.E. 825 (1932).

—Grounds

For cases discussing grounds for the award of separate maintenance, see Cooper v. Cooper, 160 Ill. App. 449 (2 Dist. 1911); Sewell v. Sewell, 297 Ill. App. 283, 17 N.E.2d 593 (1 Dist. 1938); Hellrung v. Hellrung, 321 Ill. App. 333, 53 N.E.2d 10 (4 Dist. 1943); Bertram v. Bertram, 346 Ill. App. 314, 105 N.E.2d 515 (3 Dist. 1952); Ribergaard v. Ribergaard, 349 Ill. App. 99, 110 N.E.2d 89 (2 Dist. 1952); Bramson v. Bramson, 4 Ill. App. 2d 249, 124 N.E.2d 33 (1 Dist. 1955); Bradshaw v. Bradshaw, 69 Ill. App. 2d 91, 216 N.E.2d 513 (1 Dist. 1966); Nalepa v. Nalepa, 103 Ill. App. 2d 225, 243 N.E.2d 862 (1 Dist. 1969).

—Jurisdiction

Regardless of the place of the plaintiff's residence, separate maintenance action was properly filed in county if the defendant resided there. Garrison v. Garrison, 107 Ill. App. 2d 311, 246 N.E.2d 9 (2 Dist. 1969).

For a case discussing jurisdiction over nonresident husband in a separate maintenance action, see Schneider v. Schneider, 312 Ill. App. 59, 37 N.E.2d 911 (1 Dist. 1941).

—Living Separate and Apart

The fact that the parties were living under one roof did not indicate that the complaint was filed in bad faith; however, in actions for separate maintenance and in actions for divorce based upon desertion, where the element of living apart is essential to establish probable cause or grounds on which to base the action, the fact that the parties live together under one roof may, under certain circumstances, indicate an absence of good faith in the filing of such action. Roback v. Roback, 59 Ill. App. 2d 222, 207 N.E.2d 130 (2 Dist. 1965).

Where the husband has left his wife, and she seeks to secure separate maintenance, the burden rests upon her to show that she is living separate and apart from him without her fault, and if she establishes that she reasonably performed her duties as a wife, then the burden is cast upon him to show that he had reasonable grounds for leaving her. Slaight v. Slaight, 50 Ill. App. 2d 31, 199 N.E.2d 650 (2 Dist. 1964).

—Modification

For a case discussing modification of a separate maintenance award, see Hoover v. Hoover, 307 Ill. App. 590, 30 N.E.2d 940 (1 Dist. 1940).

—Policies and Purposes

For cases discussing policies and purposes of separate maintenance, see Van Dolman v. Van Dolman, 378 Ill. 98, 37 N.E.2d 850 (1941); Schneider v. Schneider, 312 Ill. App. 59, 37 N.E.2d 911 (1 Dist. 1941).

—Post-Nuptial Contract

For a case discussing the illegality of a post-nuptial contract in a separate maintenance action, see Vock v. Vock, 365 Ill. 432, 6 N.E.2d 843 (1937).

—Principles

For cases discussing the principles of separate maintenance, see Brand v. Brand, 252 Ill. 134, 96 N.E. 918 (1911); Pamel v. Pamel, 292 Ill. App. 328, 11 N.E.2d 34 (1 Dist. 1937); Grossman v. Grossman, 315 Ill. App. 345, 43 N.E.2d 216 (1 Dist. 1942); Holmstedt v. Holmstedt, 383 Ill. 290, 49 N.E.2d 25 (1943); Young v. Young's Estate, 319 Ill. App. 527, 49 N.E.2d 743 (1 Dist. 1943); Levy v. Levy, 388 Ill. 179, 57 N.E.2d 366 (1944); Arndt v. Arndt, 399 Ill. 490, 78 N.E.2d 272 (1948); Abraham v. Abraham, 403 Ill. 312, 86 N.E.2d 224 (1949); Kohn v. Kohn, 337 Ill. App. 391, 86 N.E.2d 833 (2 Dist. 1949); Baumgartner v. Baumgartner, 16 Ill. App. 2d 286, 148 N.E.2d 327 (2 Dist. 1958); Strandquist v. Strandquist, 22 Ill. App. 2d 107, 159 N.E.2d 513 (2 Dist. 1959); Snyder v. Robert A. Black, Inc., 53 Ill. App. 2d 327, 203 N.E.2d 1 (1 Dist. 1964).

—Property Rights

For cases discussing property rights relative to separate maintenance, see Glennon v. Glennon, 299 Ill. App. 13, 19 N.E.2d 412 (1 Dist. 1939); Petta v. Petta, 321 Ill. App. 512, 53 N.E.2d 324 (1 Dist. 1944); Umshler v. Umshler, 332 Ill. App. 494, 76 N.E.2d 231 (1 Dist. 1947); Milewski v. Milewski, 351 Ill. App. 158, 114 N.E.2d 419 (1 Dist. 1953).

—Purposes

For cases discussing the policies and purposes of the former separate maintenance statute (see now this section and 750 ILCS 5/504), see Hoffman v. Hoffman, 330 Ill. 413, 161 N.E. 723 (1928); Crook v. Crook, 329 Ill. App. 588, 70 N.E.2d 209 (1 Dist. 1946); Strandquist v. Strandquist, 22 Ill. App. 2d 107, 159 N.E.2d 513 (2 Dist. 1959); Shapiro v. Shapiro, 113 Ill. App. 2d 374, 252 N.E.2d 93 (1 Dist. 1969); Reese v. Reese, 2 Ill. App. 3d 1054, 278 N.E.2d 122 (1 Dist. 1971); Zupancic v. Zupancic, 48 Ill. App. 3d 256, 6 Ill. Dec. 302, 362 N.E.2d 1124 (3 Dist. 1977); Hill v. Hill, 79 Ill. App. 3d 809, 35 Ill. Dec. 98, 398 N.E.2d 1048 (1 Dist. 1979).

—Standard of Proof

For a case discussing the standard of proof for separate maintenance, see Ryan v. Ryan, 321 Ill. App. 467, 53 N.E.2d 283 (1 Dist. 1944).

—Venue

For a case discussing venue in regard to separate maintenance, see Pamel v. Pamel, 292 Ill. App. 328, 11 N.E.2d 34 (1 Dist. 1937).

Temporary Alimony

—Pendente Lite

Wife having property in her own right, living separate and apart from her husband, could be awarded an allowance from husband pendente lite; the decision as to whether an allowance shall be made in the nature of temporary alimony rests in the judicial discretion of the court, to be exercised in view of the conditions and circumstances of each case, and an abuse of the discretion is necessarily subject to review. Harding v. Harding, 144 Ill. 588, 32 N.E. 206 (1892).

LEGAL PERIODICALS

For comment, "Civil Aspects of Intrafamily Eavesdropping in Illinois: Caveats to Comprehension Remedial Weaponry," see 12 J. Marshall J. Prac. & Proc. 537 (1979).

RESEARCH REFERENCES

Reconciliation as affecting decree for limited divorce, separation, alimony, separate maintenance, or spousal support. 36 ALR4th 502.

Separation agreements: enforceability of provision affecting property rights upon death of one party prior to final judgment of divorce. 67 ALR4th 237.

750 ILCS 5/403 Pleadings — Commencement — Abolition of Existing Defenses — Procedure

Sec. 403. *Pleadings — Commencement — Abolition of Existing Defenses — Procedure.* (a) The petition for dissolution of marriage or legal separation shall be verified and shall minimally set forth:

(1) the age, occupation and residence of each party and his length of residence in this State;

(2) the date of the marriage and the place at which it was registered;

(2.5) whether a petition for dissolution of marriage is pending in any other county or state;

(3) that the jurisdictional requirements of subsection (a) of Section 401 [750 ILCS 5/401] have been met and that there exist grounds for dissolution of marriage or legal separation. The petitioner need

only allege the name of the particular grounds relied upon, which shall constitute a legally sufficient allegation of the grounds; and the respondent shall be entitled to demand a bill of particulars prior to trial setting forth the facts constituting the grounds, if he so chooses. The petition must also contain:

(4) the names, ages and addresses of all living children of the marriage and whether the wife is pregnant;

(5) any arrangements as to support, custody and visitation of the children and maintenance of a spouse; and

(6) the relief sought.

(b) Either or both parties to the marriage may initiate the proceeding.

(c) The previously existing defense of recrimination is abolished. The defense of condonation is abolished only as to condonations occurring after a proceeding is filed under this Act and after the court has acquired jurisdiction over the respondent.

(d) The court may join additional parties necessary and proper for the exercise of its authority under this Act.

(e) Contested trials shall be on a bifurcated basis with the grounds being tried first. Upon the court determining that the grounds exist, the court may allow additional time for the parties to settle amicably the remaining issues before resuming the trial, or may proceed immediately to trial on the remaining issues. In cases where the grounds are uncontested and proved as in cases of default, the trial on all other remaining issues shall proceed immediately, if so ordered by the court or if the parties so stipulate, issue on the pleadings notwithstanding.

(f) Even if no bill of particulars shall have been filed demanding the specification of the particular facts underlying the allegation of the grounds, the court shall nonetheless require proper and sufficient proof of the existence of the grounds.

(Source: P.A. 85-754; 90-174, § 5.)

Note.

This section was Ill.Rev.Stat., Ch. 40, para. 403.

Effect of Amendments.

The 1997 amendment by P.A. 90-174, effective October 1, 1997, added subdivision (a)(2.5).

CASE NOTES

Analysis

Constitutionality
Alteration of Decree
Applicability
Bifurcation
Change of Venue
Condonation
—In General
—Defined
—Intent
—Requirement
Construction
Contested Trial
Default
Desertion
—Sufficiency of Petition
Judicial Economy
Jurisdiction
Paternity
Pleadings
—Certification
—Sufficiency
—Verification
Property
—Voluntarily Conveyed
Purpose
Recrimination
Residence
—Evidence Held Sufficient
—Failure to Object
—Unfair Advantage
Trifurcated Trial
Waiting Period

Constitutionality

Dissolution of marriage is a particular kind of action regulated in part by statute other than the former Civil Practice Act (see now the Code of Civil Procedure, 735 ILCS 5/1-101 et seq.) or the Supreme Court Rules; because of the nature of subsection (e) of this section, and because there is no conflict with a rule of court, the procedural requirements of subsection (e) of this section are not an unconstitutional legislative encroachment upon the rule making power of the judicial branch. Strukoff v. Strukoff, 76 Ill. 2d 53, 27 Ill. Dec. 762, 389 N.E.2d 1170 (1979).

Alteration of Decree

Where a decree of divorce was actually and correctly entered on January 28, 1938, as shown by the record in that case, even though the date of its entry was not correctly shown by the record, the correct procedure would have been to make application to the court entering the decree; since the date of entry of the decree of divorce, as incorporated in the record in the divorce proceeding, was admittedly correct, it was not vulnerable to attack even in a proper proceeding. Richmond v. Richmond, 326 Ill. App. 234, 61 N.E.2d 573 (1 Dist. 1945).

Applicability

The purpose of subsection (e) of this section is to encourage amicable settlement of peripheral issues between petitioner and respondent once grounds have been determined; it was inapplicable to the resolution of an intervenor's action for an equitable lien and the trial court properly proceeded on intervenor's claim following the determination of grounds. In re Pillot, 145 Ill. App. 3d 293, 99 Ill. Dec. 512, 495 N.E.2d 1247 (1 Dist. 1986).

Bifurcation

The trial court did not abuse its discretion in failing to bifurcate issues and granting former wife default judgment in a marriage dissolution proceeding because former husband's actions throughout litigation and his refusal to cooperate by appearing at hearing on grounds and property and custody issues made it unlikely that an amicable settlement of the issues was possible. In re Sheber, 121 Ill. App. 3d 328, 76 Ill. Dec. 921, 459 N.E.2d 1056 (1 Dist. 1984).

Where the trial court docket sheet indicated that on July 19, 1978, the court heard evidence, made a finding, granted the petition, and then set for hearing on August 31, 1978, the questions of custody, visitation, property settlement and child support, the first proceeding did not end with a final appealable order but rather postponed several issues for determination when the trial resumed later; the bifurcation was comparable to a recess in trial, and thus the record clearly supported the denial of defendant's motion for a change of venue. In re Hammel, 88 Ill. App. 3d 919, 44 Ill. Dec. 351, 411 N.E.2d 320 (3 Dist. 1980).

A bifurcated hearing was required in the trial court where respondent husband was challenging petitioner wife's proof on the issue of grounds as well as all other issues, as was evidenced by his cross-examination of petitioner and her mother; the fact that he ultimately informed the court that he no longer wished to challenge the grounds for dissolution or the entry of a judgment dissolving the marriage did not render his prior opposition to the matter a nullity, for he contested throughout the hearing the questions of child custody, child support, maintenance and division of the parties'

Bifurcation (Cont'd)
property. In re McCain, 75 Ill. App. 3d 875, 31 Ill. Dec. 639, 394 N.E.2d 841 (5 Dist. 1979).

Change of Venue
When a trial judge has ruled upon grounds for dissolution but has yet to conduct a hearing as to property distribution, the judge has ruled upon a substantial issue in the case and a litigant is not absolutely entitled to a change of venue. In re Pruitt, 101 Ill. App. 3d 755, 57 Ill. Dec. 182, 428 N.E.2d 732 (4 Dist. 1981).

Condonation

—In General
For cases discussing former application of the defense of condonation after petition for divorce was filed, see Moore v. Moore, 362 Ill. 177, 199 N.E. 98 (1935); Cohn v. Cohn, 327 Ill. App. 22, 63 N.E.2d 618 (4 Dist. 1945); McGaughy v. McGaughy, 410 Ill. 596, 102 N.E.2d 806 (1951); Rasgaitis v. Rasgaitis, 347 Ill. App. 477, 107 N.E.2d 273 (1 Dist. 1952); Schiff v. Schiff, 25 Ill. App. 2d 157, 165 N.E.2d 713 (1 Dist. 1960); Collinet v. Collinet, 31 Ill. App. 2d 72, 175 N.E.2d 659 (1 Dist. 1961); Rank v. Rank, 107 Ill. App. 2d 339, 246 N.E.2d 12 (2 Dist. 1969); Kovack v. Kovack, 131 Ill. App. 2d 382, 268 N.E.2d 258 (1 Dist. 1971); Deahl v. Deahl, 13 Ill. App. 3d 150, 300 N.E.2d 497 (1 Dist. 1973); Jackson v. Jackson, 24 Ill. App. 3d 810, 321 N.E.2d 506 (3 Dist. 1974); Farah v. Farah, 25 Ill. App. 3d 481, 323 N.E.2d 361 (1 Dist. 1975); Seniuta v. Seniuta, 31 Ill. App. 3d 408, 334 N.E.2d 261 (1 Dist. 1975); Jackson v. Jackson, 34 Ill. App. 3d 407, 339 N.E.2d 764 (1 Dist. 1975); Griner v. Griner, 34 Ill. App. 3d 792, 340 N.E.2d 304 (2 Dist. 1976); McCarrel v. McCarrel, 48 Ill. App. 3d 666, 6 Ill. Dec. 669, 363 N.E.2d 198 (4 Dist. 1977).

—Defined
Cohabitation is not necessarily equivalent to condonation. Farah v. Farah, 25 Ill. App. 3d 481, 323 N.E.2d 361 (1 Dist. 1975).

Condonation is an affirmative defense requiring a defendant to show by a preponderance of the evidence a plaintiff's intent to forgive defendant's prior acts which otherwise would constitute grounds for divorce; proof usually is shown by deeds and words of voluntary forgiveness, but continued cohabitation alone will not necessarily constitute condonation. Deahl v. Deahl, 13 Ill. App. 3d 150, 300 N.E.2d 497 (1 Dist. 1973).

Condonation, in the law of divorce, is the forgiveness of an antecedent matrimonial offense on the condition that it shall not be repeated and that the offender shall thereafter treat the forgiving party with conjugal kindness. Kovack v. Kovack, 131 Ill. App. 2d 382, 268 N.E.2d 258 (1 Dist. 1971).

For a case discussing the definition of condonation, see Simonson v. Simonson, 128 Ill. App. 2d 39, 262 N.E.2d 326 (1 Dist. 1970).

Condonation is defined as a full and free forgiveness of an offense upon condition that it will not be repeated. Rasgaitis v. Rasgaitis, 347 Ill. App. 477, 107 N.E.2d 273 (1 Dist. 1952).

—Intent
Even an act of intercourse does not necessarily constitute condonation when it is not accompanied by an intent to resume the marital relation in full. Rasgaitis v. Rasgaitis, 347 Ill. App. 477, 107 N.E.2d 273 (1 Dist. 1952).

—Requirement
Condonation is an affirmative defense which must be pleaded. Honey v. Honey, 120 Ill. App. 2d 102, 256 N.E.2d 121 (4 Dist. 1970).

Construction
Use of the word "resuming" indicates that the second hearing is a continuation of the first hearing and that both are parts of the same trial proceeding. In re Hammel, 88 Ill. App. 3d 919, 44 Ill. Dec. 351, 411 N.E.2d 320 (3 Dist. 1980).

Contested Trial
Although no cross-examination was conducted by either side during the first portion of the trial which established the necessary grounds, each party had petitioned for dissolution of marriage from the other and each presented evidence in support of his or her petition, much of it conflicting; furthermore, resolution of the remaining issues was strongly disputed, and the trial, therefore, was "contested" within the meaning of subsection (e) of this section. In re Aschwanden, 82 Ill. 2d 31, 44 Ill. Dec. 269, 411 N.E.2d 238 (1980).

Default
Subsection (e) of this section provides that bifurcation is unnecessary in a case of default. In re Sheber, 121 Ill. App. 3d 328, 76 Ill. Dec. 921, 459 N.E.2d 1056 (1 Dist. 1984).

Desertion

—Sufficiency of Petition
In an action for legal separation, wife's allegation that husband, without cause or provocation by wife, wilfully deserted wife, which caused wife grievous mental anxiety and constituted extreme and repeated mental cruelty, was sufficient to allege grounds of desertion. In re Jones, 90 Ill. App. 3d 95, 45 Ill. Dec. 540, 412 N.E.2d 1122 (5 Dist. 1980).

Judicial Economy
In causes where the parties have stipulated to grounds that there would be minimal opportunity for further provocation or rancor which could affect the decision on the other issues, it is difficult to see how a further 48 hour "cooling off" period would have any practical effect or how the chance of a settlement would be better after the 48 hour intermediate delay. In fact, the consideration of judicial economy would seem to operate the other way. The practical requirement of rescheduling a case to fit in with busy court calendars and requiring the parties and attorneys to undergo the time and expense involved in appearing again at a new date would appear to weigh in favor of permitting the parties to agree to go ahead when the grounds are not contested. In re Weidner, 75 Ill. App. 3d 1014, 31 Ill. Dec. 418, 394 N.E.2d 620 (2 Dist. 1979).

Jurisdiction
The out-of-state defendant in a divorce proceeding could not appear and participate in the grounds portion of the proceedings without waiving her special and limited appearance and being subjected to the personal jurisdiction of the court. In re Snider, 305 Ill. App. 3d 697, 238 Ill. Dec. 843, 712 N.E.2d 947 (2 Dist. 1999).

Where the parties adjudicated their rights, in proceeding for dissolution of marriage, before the circuit court to a final judgment without objection to the court's right to hear the cause, the parties were bound on appeal so far as the question subject matter jurisdiction over their particular case was concerned. In re Jerome, 255 Ill. App. 3d 374, 193 Ill. Dec. 74, 625 N.E.2d 1195 (5 Dist. 1993).

Where plaintiff filed his complaint for divorce in McHenry County on November 14, 1967, defendant filed her complaint for divorce in Cook County on November 15, 1967, on November 17, 1967, summons was purportedly served on plaintiff on the Cook County complaint, and defendant was purportedly served with summons in the McHenry County action on November 28, 1967, McHenry County acquired subject matter jurisdiction and personal jurisdiction over the wife. Mueller v. Mueller, 96 Ill. App. 2d 463, 239 N.E.2d 451 (2 Dist. 1968).

Paternity
Paternity was a proper issue to be considered in a divorce proceeding under former Ill.Rev.Stat., ch. 40, para. 7 (see now this section). Zavaleta v. Zavaleta, 43 Ill. App. 3d 1017, 3 Ill. Dec. 13, 358 N.E.2d 13 (1 Dist. 1976).

Pleadings

—Certification
Effective January 1, 1984, the Code of Civil Procedure was amended to permit pleadings to be verified by certification via the Civil Practice Law (735 ILCS 5/2-101 et seq.); the amendment was made applicable to this section by 750 ILCS 5/105(a) and 750 ILCS 5/410. In re Betts, 172 Ill. App. 3d 742, 122 Ill. Dec. 599, 526 N.E.2d 1138 (4 Dist. 1988).

—Sufficiency
There was no harm to husband in failure to mention pension fund or any other specific item of personal property in divorce pleadings where counsel for husband stipulated to the existence of the pension fund death benefits and the husband himself testified as to the amount, and thus he was not surprised when the pension fund became an issue. In re Stewart, 79 Ill. App. 3d 1125, 35 Ill. Dec. 249, 398 N.E.2d 1199 (1 Dist. 1979).

Pleadings (Cont'd)

—Sufficiency (Cont'd)

Property of parties need not be set out in pleadings. In re Stewart, 79 Ill. App. 3d 1125, 35 Ill. Dec. 249, 398 N.E.2d 1199 (1 Dist. 1979).

—Verification

This section may not be used to require that pleadings governed by this Act be verified. Firkus v. Firkus, 200 Ill. App. 3d 982, 146 Ill. Dec. 591, 558 N.E.2d 554 (5 Dist. 1990).

Property

—Voluntarily Conveyed

Under former Ill.Rev.Stat., ch. 40, para. 17 (see now this section), the mere circumstance that a husband purchased a joint interest in real estate as a gift for his wife did not, in the absence of anything more, make him the equitable owner of her interest and such property, voluntarily conveyed by a husband to his wife, without fraud or coercion, became the wife's separate property and, notwithstanding the husband purchased the property with his own money, the wife could hold the property against him. Lutticke v. Lutticke, 406 Ill. 181, 92 N.E.2d 754 (1950).

Purpose

Subsection (e) of this section was not designed to promote litigation, but to encourage amicable settlement of the remaining issues by eliminating marital misconduct and mutual grievances from consideration. In re Sheber, 121 Ill. App. 3d 328, 76 Ill. Dec. 921, 459 N.E.2d 1056 (1 Dist. 1984).

Recrimination

For cases discussing the former defense of recrimination see Lenning v. Lenning, 176 Ill. 180, 52 N.E. 46 (1898); Levy v. Levy, 388 Ill. 179, 57 N.E.2d 366 (1944); Hokin v. Hokin, 102 Ill. App. 2d 205, 243 N.E.2d 579 (1 Dist. 1968); Rank v. Rank, 107 Ill. App. 2d 339, 246 N.E.2d 12 (2 Dist. 1969); Haring v. Haring, 125 Ill. App. 2d 116, 260 N.E.2d 396 (5 Dist. 1970); Deahl v. Deahl, 13 Ill. App. 3d 150, 300 N.E.2d 497 (1 Dist. 1973).

Residence

—Evidence Held Sufficient

There was evidence to prove that defendant at the time of the filing of the complaint was an actual resident of the proper county where defendant made no attempt to obtain a room in another county until after his suit was filed, and then, presumably acting upon the advice of counsel, he obtained a room at the residence of a druggist in the other county and moved before his answer to the complaint was filed. It was a reasonable inference from the evidence that this move was intended to aid a defense of lack of jurisdiction. Blair v. Blair, 341 Ill. App. 93, 93 N.E.2d 95 (1 Dist. 1950).

—Failure to Object

Where there was a special finding of a jury that defendant was a resident of a county and defendant in his motion for a new trial failed to object to that special finding, defendant was conclusively bound by that finding if there was any evidence fairly tending to prove the allegation of the complaint that defendant at the time of the filing of the complaint was a resident of the county. Blair v. Blair, 341 Ill. App. 93, 93 N.E.2d 95 (1 Dist. 1950).

—Unfair Advantage

Plaintiff, in filing her complaint in one county, did not intend to take unfair advantage of defendant where defendant was certainly living in that county when he was served with summons, and his place of business was located there. Blair v. Blair, 341 Ill. App. 93, 93 N.E.2d 95 (1 Dist. 1950).

Trifurcated Trial

Where respondent contended on appeal that the trifurcated trial procedure used was improper after he expressly agreed to such procedure at trial, the argument was totally without merit and was not considered. In re Rizzo, 95 Ill. App. 3d 636, 51 Ill. Dec. 141, 420 N.E.2d 555 (1 Dist. 1981).

Waiting Period

The purpose of the specified waiting period between hearings in contested trials, obviously in aid of this Act's general purposes, is to encourage the amicable settlement of remaining issues; the objectives of legislation of this character are reasonable and within the province of legislative power. Strukoff v. Strukoff, 76 Ill. 2d 53, 27 Ill. Dec. 762, 389 N.E.2d 1170 (1979); In re Weidner, 75 Ill. App. 3d 1014, 31 Ill. Dec. 418, 394 N.E.2d 620 (2 Dist. 1979); In re Sheber, 121 Ill. App. 3d 328, 76 Ill. Dec. 921, 459 N.E.2d 1056 (1 Dist. 1984).

Parties could not waive the provision for an interval between hearings called for by subsection (e) of this section; the provision is mandatory and not discretionary, and the noncompliance in the trial court will require reversal of the judgment as it relates to the second hearing. Strukoff v. Strukoff, 76 Ill. 2d 53, 27 Ill. Dec. 762, 389 N.E.2d 1170 (1979).

750 ILCS 5/404 Conciliation; mediation

Sec. 404. *Conciliation; mediation.* (a) If the court concludes that there is a prospect of reconciliation, the court, at the request of either party, or on its own motion, may order a conciliation conference. The conciliation conference and counseling shall take place at the established court conciliation service of that judicial district or at any similar service or facility where no court conciliation service has been established.

(b) The facts adduced at any conciliation conference resulting from a referral hereunder, shall not be considered in the adjudication of a pending or subsequent action, nor shall any report resulting from such conference become part of the record of the case unless the parties have stipulated in writing to the contrary.

The court, upon good cause shown, may prohibit conciliation, mediation or other process that requires the parties to meet and confer without counsel.

(Source: P.A. 80-923; 87-1255, § 1.)

Note.

This section was Ill.Rev.Stat., Ch. 40, para. 404.

LEGAL PERIODICALS

For comment, "Wife Abuse: The Failure of Legal Remedies," see 11 J. Marshall J. Prac. & Proc. 549 (1978).

750 ILCS 5/404.1 [Educational program concerning effects of dissolution on children]

Sec. 404.1. (a) In an action for dissolution of marriage involving minor children, or in a post-judgment proceeding involving minor children, the court may on its own motion order the parties, excluding the minor children, to attend an educational program concerning the effects of dissolution of marriage on the children, if the court finds that it would be in the best interests of the minor children. The program may be divided into sessions, which in the aggregate shall not exceed 4 hours in duration. The program shall be educational in nature and not designed for individual therapy.

(b) The facts adduced at any educational session resulting from a referral under this Section shall not be considered in the adjudication of a pending or subsequent action, nor shall any report resulting from such educational session become part of the record of the case unless the parties have stipulated in writing to the contrary.

(c) The fees or costs of educational sessions under this Section shall be borne by the parties and may be assessed by the court as it deems equitable.
(Source: P.A. 86-288.)

Note.
This section was Ill.Rev.Stat., Ch. 40, para. 404.1.

750 ILCS 5/405 Hearing on Default — Notice

Sec. 405. *Hearing on Default — Notice.* If the respondent is in default, the court shall proceed to hear the cause upon testimony of petitioner taken in open court, and in no case of default shall the court grant a dissolution of marriage or legal separation or declaration of invalidity of marriage, unless the judge is satisfied that all proper means have been taken to notify the respondent of the pendency of the suit. Whenever the judge is satisfied that the interests of the respondent require it, the court may order such additional notice as may be required.
(Source: P.A. 80-923.)

Note.
This section was Ill.Rev.Stat., Ch. 40, para. 405.

CASE NOTES

ANALYSIS

In General
Abuse of Discretion
—Not Shown
Adequate Opportunity
Admission
Appearance
Confession of Judgment
Default Judgment
—Delay in Seeking Relief
—Vacation
Ex Parte Hearing
Notice
Proof

In General
Former Ill.Rev.Stat., ch. 40, para. 9 (see now this section) had no application to cases in which the defendant appeared in court and the grounds for divorce were contested; by its express terms it applied only to cases in which the complaint was taken as confessed. Farah v. Farah, 25 Ill. App. 3d 481, 323 N.E.2d 361 (1 Dist. 1975).

Abuse of Discretion

—Not Shown
Since former husband not only had notice of the pendency of dissolution action, but by his own admission had notice that the hearing thereon would take place but still failed to appear, the trial court did not abuse its discretion in proceeding without additional notice. In re Sheber, 121 Ill. App. 3d 328, 76 Ill. Dec. 921, 459 N.E.2d 1056 (1 Dist. 1984).

Adequate Opportunity
A party must receive notice that his interest in the marital home is involved in a divorce proceeding so that he may have an adequate opportunity to defend his interest in the property at the proceedings. In re Mierlak, 100 Ill. App. 3d 228, 55 Ill. Dec. 685, 426 N.E.2d 1010 (1 Dist. 1981).

Admission
Under this section and former Ill.Rev.Stat., ch. 110, para. 50(4) (see now 735 ILCS 5/2-1301), a defendant could admit to any part of a complaint without admitting all allegations in the complaint; on the other hand, a confession referred to a default by reason of the defendant's failure to appear or plead. Myers v. Myers, 51 Ill. App. 3d 830, 9 Ill. Dec. 603, 366 N.E.2d 1114 (3 Dist. 1977).

Appearance
There is no requirement in this section that the defendant in a divorce case must be present at the hearing. Kinsley v. Kinsley, 388 Ill. 194, 57 N.E.2d 449 (1944).

Confession of Judgment
To the extent confessions of judgment are valid in civil proceedings in this state, they are valid in proceedings to dissolve marriages. In re Lorenzi, 84 Ill. App. 3d 427, 39 Ill. Dec. 754, 405 N.E.2d 507 (3 Dist. 1980).

Default Judgment

—Delay in Seeking Relief
Although respondent could have obtained relief from the default judgment in dissolution of marriage proceeding had she diligently pursued a hearing on her motion to vacate; where she sat on her rights for 18 months before filing a notice of hearing, she simply waited too long to pursue relief and offered no satisfactory explanation for her delay nor any reason why the trial court erred in enforcing the rule against her. In re Jackson, 259 Ill. App. 3d 538, 197 Ill. Dec. 626, 631 N.E.2d 848 (4 Dist. 1994).

—Vacation
Where the attorney for plaintiff wife, without consultation with his client and in the exercise of his own judgment, determined to enter into an agreement for the entry of a default order against his client and stipulated to an uncontested hearing on a counter-complaint, under such circumstances, the trial court should have vacated the default divorce decree since such action was necessary to prevent injustice. Younkins v. Younkins, 121 Ill. App. 2d 416, 257 N.E.2d 521 (1 Dist. 1970).

Ex Parte Hearing
Where respondent husband was granted a hearing on October 10, 1980, and, thus had notice of pendency of the suit before entry of judgment for dissolution on October 23, 1980; respondent knew his attorney had withdrawn; and record showed that a notice of a July 31, 1980 hearing was mailed to him on July 23, 1980, the trial court did not abuse its discretion by proceeding with the ex parte hearing without additional notice to respondent. In re Kopec, 106 Ill. App. 3d 1060, 62 Ill. Dec. 658, 436 N.E.2d 684 (1 Dist. 1982).

Notice
Where the trial court was informed that the parties were living together and wife was unaware dissolution petition had been set for hearing, the court should have required notice to wife. In re Jackson, 259 Ill. App. 3d 538, 197 Ill. Dec. 626, 631 N.E.2d 848 (4 Dist. 1994).

Proof
It was necessary for petitioner to introduce proof of her grounds for divorce with practically the same formality as if no default order had been entered against her husband, the respondent. Venema v. Venema, 74 Ill. App. 3d 416, 30 Ill. Dec. 417, 393 N.E.2d 72 (2 Dist. 1979).

750 ILCS 5/406 Fault or Conduct of Petitioner

Sec. 406. *Fault or Conduct of Petitioner.* In every action for a dissolution of marriage or legal separation, or declaration of invalidity of marriage, the conduct of the petitioner, unless raised by the pleadings, is not a bar to the action nor a proper basis for the refusal of a judgment of dissolution of marriage or legal separation or declaration of invalidity of marriage. Defenses which may be raised by the

pleadings, however, shall not include the defenses abolished under Section 403(c) [750 ILCS 5/403].
(Source: P.A. 81-231.)

Note.
This section was Ill.Rev.Stat., Ch. 40, para. 406.

CASE NOTES

ANALYSIS

Affirmative Defenses
Amendment
—Permitted
Error
Pleadings
Provocation
Recrimination
Sufficiency of Pleadings

Affirmative Defenses
This section has been construed strictly, requiring that affirmative defenses be pleaded. In re Wade, 158 Ill. App. 3d 255, 110 Ill. Dec. 321, 511 N.E.2d 156 (4 Dist. 1987).

Fault or conduct of a spouse must be raised by the pleadings if such fault or conduct is to be relied upon as a bar to the granting of a divorce. Buzan v. Buzan, 45 Ill. App. 3d 181, 4 Ill. Dec. 1, 359 N.E.2d 834 (5 Dist. 1977).

Amendment

—Permitted
The court, in denying husband's motion to strike, specifically noted that it desired to hear all testimony from both sides prior to rendering a decision; although this Act provides for adherence to pleading requirements, the court's decision to allow wife to amend her pleadings and present testimony regarding husband's conduct was equitable and well within the discretion afforded the trial court. In re Wade, 158 Ill. App. 3d 255, 110 Ill. Dec. 321, 511 N.E.2d 156 (4 Dist. 1987).

Error
The trial court did not err in denying plaintiff's defense of condonation to an alleged act of cruelty. Still v. Still, 96 Ill. App. 2d 320, 238 N.E.2d 613 (4 Dist. 1968).

Pleadings
Where wife did not raise the fault or conduct of husband in her pleadings, such evidence was not a bar to action brought by husband for divorce on adultery grounds. La Roche v. La Roche, 32 Ill. App. 3d 475, 335 N.E.2d 518 (3 Dist. 1975).

Provocation
Where complaining party in a divorce has alleged that there was no provocation, defending party must specifically deny the allegations; otherwise, the allegation stands admitted, and since there has been no issue formed as to provocation and the issue has not been raised by the pleadings, the defending party cannot rely on any failure of the complaining party to produce evidence at the trial proving there was no provocation. Hecht v. Hecht, 49 Ill. App. 3d 334, 7 Ill. Dec. 169, 364 N.E.2d 330 (1 Dist. 1977).

A divorce suit plaintiff who charges either physical or mental cruelty must allege and prove that he did not provoke the acts and conduct about which he complains. Rosenbaum v. Rosenbaum, 38 Ill. App. 3d 1, 349 N.E.2d 73 (1 Dist. 1976).

Where grounds for divorce are physical or mental cruelty, provocation is not an affirmative defense; indeed, its presence is proof that an element of the plaintiff's prima facie case, namely cruelty, does not exist. Rosenbaum v. Rosenbaum, 38 Ill. App. 3d 1, 349 N.E.2d 73 (1 Dist. 1976).

To properly establish provocation as an issue in a divorce alleging cruelty by husband, husband should have followed the statutory requirement of former Ill.Rev.Stat., ch. 40, para. 9a (see now this section) and admitted the acts, but raised the fault of plaintiff as a defense. Del Rosario v. Del Rosario, 133 Ill. App. 2d 8, 270 N.E.2d 160 (1 Dist. 1970).

Recrimination
For a case discussing the former defense of recrimination, see Mogged v. Mogged, 55 Ill. 2d 221, 302 N.E.2d 293 (1973).

Sufficiency of Pleadings
Allegations of a complaint for separate maintenance could not serve to raise the issue of fault when no responsive pleadings were filed in answer to a counterclaim for divorce. Buzan v. Buzan, 45 Ill. App. 3d 181, 4 Ill. Dec. 1, 359 N.E.2d 834 (5 Dist. 1977).

750 ILCS 5/407 Admission of Respondent

Sec. 407. *Admission of Respondent.* **No admission of the respondent shall be taken as evidence unless the court shall be satisfied that such admission was made in sincerity and without fraud or collusion to enable the petitioner to obtain a dissolution of marriage or legal separation or declaration of invalidity of marriage.**
(Source: P.A. 84-551.)

Note.
This section was Ill.Rev.Stat., Ch. 40, para. 407.

CASE NOTES

Admission of Allegations
An admission of allegations of fault by answer to a complaint for a divorce does not alone create a necessary inference of collusive divorce or agreement not to defend. O'Connell v. O'Connell, 27 Ill. App. 3d 204, 326 N.E.2d 200 (4 Dist. 1975).

750 ILCS 5/408 Collusion — Assent or Consent of Petitioner

Sec. 408. *Collusion — Assent or Consent of Petitioner.* **If it appears, to the satisfaction of the court, that the injury complained of was occasioned by collusion of the parties, or done with the assent of the petitioner for the purpose of obtaining a dissolution of marriage or legal separation or declaration of invalidity of marriage, or that the petitioner was consenting thereto, then no dissolution of marriage or legal separation or declaration of invalidity of marriage may be adjudged.**
(Source: P.A. 80-923.)

Note.
This section was Ill.Rev.Stat., Ch. 40, para. 408.

CASE NOTES

ANALYSIS

Admission of Fault
Condonation
Credibility

Admission of Fault
An admission of allegations of fault by answer to a complaint for a divorce does not alone create a necessary inference of collusive divorce or agreement not to defend. O'Connell v. O'Connell, 27 Ill. App. 3d 204, 326 N.E.2d 200 (4 Dist. 1975).

Condonation
For a case discussing former application of the defense of condonation, see Still v. Still, 96 Ill. App. 2d 320, 238 N.E.2d 613 (4 Dist. 1968).

Credibility

Where petitioner expressly denied that he agreed to a marriage without sex, and respondent, on the other hand, testified that such an arrangement was agreed upon prior to the marriage, it was well within the trial court's discretion to choose to believe petitioner. Naguit v. Scrivner, 104 Ill. App. 3d 709, 60 Ill. Dec. 499, 433 N.E.2d 296 (5 Dist. 1982).

LEGAL PERIODICALS

For note, "Family Law, Property Rights — Hewitt v. Hewitt, 77 Ill.2d 49, 394 N.E.2d 1204 (1979)," see 69 Ill. B.J. 49 (1980).

750 ILCS 5/409 Proof of Foreign Marriage

Sec. 409. *Proof of Foreign Marriage.* A marriage which may have been celebrated or had in any foreign state or country, may be proved by the acknowledgment of the parties, their cohabitation, and other circumstantial testimony.
(Source: P.A. 80-923.)

Note.

This section was Ill.Rev.Stat., Ch. 40, para. 409.

CASE NOTES

ANALYSIS

Evidence Held Sufficient
Testimony

Evidence Held Sufficient

Evidence was held sufficient that petitioner had proven a ceremonial marriage to decedent and was entitled to be the administrator of decedent's estate. Bailey v. Bailey, 97 Ill. App. 3d 781, 53 Ill. Dec. 104, 423 N.E.2d 488 (5 Dist. 1981).

Where parties lived together and held themselves out to the community and to friends and relatives as being married, and real estate was conveyed to them as husband and wife in joint tenancy, and in all phases of day to day activity the parties acted in a manner fully consistent with a ceremonial marriage, the decision of the board of trustees of deceased's pension fund in denying wife's application for pension benefits as the surviving spouse of a union member was arbitrary and capricious, and the trial court was correct in overturning that decision. Patek v. Peick, 74 Ill. App. 3d 714, 30 Ill. Dec. 533, 393 N.E.2d 569 (1 Dist. 1979).

Testimony

Petitioner could prove her ceremonial marriage to decedent not only by her testimony but by the testimony of disinterested witnesses. Bailey v. Bailey, 97 Ill. App. 3d 781, 53 Ill. Dec. 104, 423 N.E.2d 488 (5 Dist. 1981).

Petitioner should have been allowed to testify as to her marriage to decedent where their marriage license had been lost during the course of moving. Bailey v. Bailey, 97 Ill. App. 3d 781, 53 Ill. Dec. 104, 423 N.E.2d 488 (5 Dist. 1981).

750 ILCS 5/410 Process — Practice — Proceedings — Publication

Sec. 410. *Process — Practice — Proceedings — Publication.* The process, practice and proceedings under this Act shall be the same as in other civil cases, except as otherwise provided by this Act, or by any law or rule of court, and except that when the parties resided in a municipality, in a county with a population under 2,000,000, at the time the cause of action arose, and if service by publication is necessary, publication shall be in a newspaper published in such municipality if there is one.
(Source: P.A. 80-923.)

Note.

This section was Ill.Rev.Stat., Ch. 40, para. 410.

CASE NOTES

ANALYSIS

Constitutionality
Authority of Court
—Decree in Equity
—Error of Law
—Scope of Jurisdiction
Certification
Confession of Judgment
Divorce Action
—Not Shown
Jurisdiction
Pending Suit
Polygraph Evidence

Constitutionality

In husband's action for divorce, wife waived her right to a jury trial under the provisions of former Ill.Rev.Stat., ch. 40, para. 7 (see now this section) and a former provision of the Civil Practice Act (see now 735 ILCS 5/2-1105) by her failure to demand a jury trial when she filed her appearance in the divorce action; such waiver provision did not violate constitutional guarantees of trial by jury. Fox v. Fox, 9 Ill. 2d 509, 138 N.E.2d 547 (1956).

Authority of Court

—Decree in Equity

Courts are reluctant to subject decrees in equity to review by bill of review for error of law. Ullrich v. Ullrich, 299 Ill. App. 460, 20 N.E.2d 347 (1 Dist. 1939).

—Error of Law

An error in a decree brought about by consent of the parties, or error existing because of the failure to present a defense where the opportunity was offered, or error which would require the examination of the evidence, or error which would amount to use of the bill of review as a substitute for an appeal or writ of error, or where the party has been guilty of laches, may not be corrected by a bill of review for error of law. Ullrich v. Ullrich, 299 Ill. App. 460, 20 N.E.2d 347 (1 Dist. 1939).

—Scope of Jurisdiction

Where a case was not a divorce action, but an application to enforce or modify a decree for custody or support of minor children, the case must have been made in the court where the decree was rendered. Kohler v. Kohler, 326 Ill. App. 105, 61 N.E.2d 687 (4 Dist. 1945).

Certification

Effective January 1, 1984, the Code of Civil Procedure was amended to permit pleadings to be verified by certification via the Civil Practice Law (735 ILCS 5/2-101 et seq.); the amendment was made applicable to 750 ILCS 5/410 by this section and 750 ILCS 5/105(a). In re Betts, 172 Ill. App. 3d 742, 122 Ill. Dec. 599, 526 N.E.2d 1138 (4 Dist. 1988).

Confession of Judgment

To the extent confessions of judgment are valid in civil proceedings in this state, they are valid in proceedings to dissolve marriages. In re Lorenzi, 84 Ill. App. 3d 427, 39 Ill. Dec. 754, 405 N.E.2d 507 (3 Dist. 1980).

Divorce Action

—Not Shown

Where a prayer of a complaint was that a separation agreement be declared null and void and that the court reopen all questions of property settlement between plaintiff and defendant and that defendant be required to make an adequate property settlement for the care, maintenance and education of the parties' minor children, and where there was no prayer for periodical payments to either of the children, the case was not a divorce action. Kohler v. Kohler, 326 Ill. App. 105, 61 N.E.2d 687 (4 Dist. 1945).

Jurisdiction

By publication and mailing of notice, the court acquired jurisdiction of the property, real and personal, of the former husband located in the county, with full power to render a decree binding upon such property and subjecting the same to the payment of whatever alimony, support money, attorney fees and costs as could be ordered or decreed. Ragen v. Ragen, 4 Ill. App. 2d 445, 124 N.E.2d 628 (1 Dist. 1954).

Pending Suit

Where a former suit to enforce a decree was pending in the same jurisdiction, in the same court of equity, and between the same parties respecting the same subject matter, the case could have been pleaded in abatement of the second suit. Kohler v. Kohler, 326 Ill. App. 105, 61 N.E.2d 687 (4 Dist. 1945).

Polygraph Evidence

The trial judge in a dissolution of marriage action could declare a mistrial where husband stated that he had been prejudiced by wife's offer of polygraph evidence which is not admissible even by stipulation. In re Turzitti, 161 Ill. App. 3d 822, 113 Ill. Dec. 507, 515 N.E.2d 316 (1 Dist. 1987).

OPINIONS OF ATTORNEY GENERAL

Applicability

The exception to the rules for service by publication contained in this section applies only in cases where the parties resided in a municipality within Illinois at the time the cause of action arose, and then only if they resided in a municipality in which a newspaper is published. 1977 Op. Atty. Gen. 82.

750 ILCS 5/411 Commencement of Action

Sec. 411. *Commencement of Action.* (a) Actions for dissolution of marriage or legal separation shall be commenced as in other civil cases or, at the option of petitioner, by filing a praecipe for summons with the clerk of the court and paying the regular filing fees, in which latter case, a petition shall be filed within 6 months thereafter.

(b) When a praecipe for summons is filed without the petition, the summons shall recite that petitioner has commenced suit for dissolution of marriage or legal separation and shall require the respondent to file his or her appearance not later than 30 days from the day the summons is served and to plead to the petitioner's petition within 30 days from the day the petition is filed.

Until a petition has been filed, the court, pursuant to subsections (c) and (d) herein, may dismiss the suit, order the filing of a petition, or grant leave to the respondent to file a petition in the nature of a counter petition.

After the filing of the petition, the party filing the same shall, within 2 days, serve a copy thereof upon the other party, in the manner provided by rule of the Supreme Court for service of notices in other civil cases.

(c) Unless a respondent voluntarily files an appearance, a praecipe for summons filed without the petition shall be served on the respondent not later than 30 days after its issuance, and upon failure to obtain service upon the respondent within the 30 day period, or any extension for good cause shown granted by the court, the court shall dismiss the suit.

(d) An action for dissolution of marriage or legal separation commenced by the filing a praecipe for summons without the petition shall be dismissed unless a petition for dissolution of marriage or legal separation has been filed within 6 months after the commencement of the action.

(Source: P.A. 86-630.)

Note.

This section was Ill.Rev.Stat., Ch. 40, para. 411.

CASE NOTES

ANALYSIS

In General
Jurisdiction
Rehearing
—Requirements

In General

This section provides immediate access to the courts by a procedural means applicable alike to all litigants, with no delay being interposed before jurisdiction is obtained. People ex rel. Doty v. Connell, 9 Ill. 2d 390, 137 N.E.2d 849 (1956).

Jurisdiction

Where court in divorce action filed by husband in one county had prior jurisdiction over parties, the circuit court of second county where wife subsequently filed for divorce upon being informed of prior action should have declined to proceed in the case filed by the wife and should have dismissed the same. Abbott v. Abbott, 52 Ill. App. 3d 728, 10 Ill. Dec. 464, 367 N.E.2d 1073 (3 Dist. 1977).

When defendant was served with process, jurisdiction over his person was acquired under former Ill.Rev.Stat., ch. 40, para. 7B (see now this section). Van Dam v. Van Dam, 21 Ill. 2d 212, 171 N.E.2d 594 (1961).

Rehearing

—Requirements

Where both plaintiff and defendant indicated that they would have liked to have had a hearing on all issues but that there was no opportunity to do so because they were limited by the trial court's declarations that the only point it was concerned with was whether or not it had jurisdiction to permit the filing of the petition and complaint under the "cooling off" provisions of a former similar provision, the case was remanded with directions to permit the plaintiff to plead over if he so desired to conduct a hearing on the issues formulated if he denied the defendant's allegations, or to enter an order based on those allegations if they were not denied or remained admitted. Haney v. Haney, 37 Ill. App. 2d 216, 185 N.E.2d 409 (1 Dist. 1962).

LEGAL PERIODICALS

For article, "The Demise of the Praecipe," see 11 S. Ill. U.L.J. 29 (1986).

750 ILCS 5/412 Filing of petition — Cases Requiring Service by Publication

Sec. 412. *Filing of petition — Cases Requiring Service by Publication.* In any case wherein the requisite affidavit for service by publication has been filed to obtain jurisdiction as to the party against whom a judgment of dissolution of marriage or of legal separation or of declaration of invalidity of marriage is sought, petitioner shall immediately, and without leave of court, file his or her petition.

(Source: P.A. 81-231.)

Note.
This section was Ill.Rev.Stat., Ch. 40, para. 412.

750 ILCS 5/413 Judgment

Sec. 413. *Judgment.* (a) A judgment of dissolution of marriage or of legal separation or of declaration of invalidity of marriage is final when entered, subject to the right of appeal. An appeal from the judgment of dissolution of marriage that does not challenge the finding as to grounds does not delay the finality of that provision of the judgment which dissolves the marriage, beyond the time for appealing from that provision, and either of the parties may remarry pending appeal. An order directing payment of money for support or maintenance of the spouse or the minor child or children shall not be suspended or the enforcement thereof stayed pending the appeal.

(b) The clerk of the court shall give notice of the entry of a judgment of dissolution of marriage or legal separation or a declaration of invalidity of marriage:

(1) if the marriage is registered in this State, to the county clerk of the county where the marriage is registered, who shall enter the fact of dissolution of marriage or legal separation or declaration of invalidity of marriage in the marriage registry; and within 45 days after the close of the month in which the judgment is entered, the clerk shall forward the certificate to the Department of Public Health on a form furnished by the Department; or

(2) if the marriage is registered in another jurisdiction, to the appropriate official of that jurisdiction, with the request that he enter the fact of dissolution of marriage or legal separation or declaration of invalidity of marriage in the appropriate record.

(c) Upon request by a wife whose marriage is dissolved or declared invalid, the court shall order her maiden name or a former name restored.

(d) A judgment of dissolution of marriage or legal separation, if made, shall be awarded to both of the parties, and shall provide that it affects the status previously existing between the parties in the manner adjudged.

(Source: P.A. 84-546.)

Note.
This section was Ill.Rev.Stat., Ch. 40, para. 413.

CASE NOTES

Analysis

Agreement
Appeal
—In General
—Subject to Right of Appeal
Attorney-Client Relationship
Competency of Party
Discretion of Court
—Use of Name
Enforcement
Estoppel
—Applicability to Lien
—Remarriage
Finality
Foreign Divorce Decree
Fraud
—Not Shown
Home Repairs
Increased Support
Interest
Jurisdiction
—Scope
—Shown
—Maintenance
Marital Agreement
—Not Modified
Modification of Decree
—Change in Tax Law
Multiple Claims for Relief
Release of Errors
Supplemental Judgment

Agreement

The restriction of terms of the judgment to the provisions of the agreement does not apply to terms affecting support, custody, or visitation of children. Bayuk v. Bayuk, 79 Ill. App. 3d 877, 35 Ill. Dec. 159, 398 N.E.2d 1109 (1 Dist. 1979).

Whether or not a military pension was marital property prior to the 1981 amendment to 10 USC § 1408, it should have been considered by the parties when they agreed to submit their property to the court's jurisdiction; therefore, the trial court was required to consider the property settlement which treated the pension as marital property, incorporated in the 1979 order, as barred from further consideration under the principles of res judicata. In re Lipkin, 163 Ill. App. 3d 1033, 115 Ill. Dec. 76, 517 N.E.2d 41 (4 Dist. 1987).

Appeal

—In General

Trial court did not err in denying a father's request to stay the payment of a judgment for arrearage of child support obligations pending the father's appeal of the judgment. Ackerley v. Ackerley, 333 Ill. App. 3d 382, 266 Ill. Dec. 973, 775 N.E.2d 1045, 2002 Ill. App. LEXIS 857 (2 Dist. 2002).

Direct appeal to the Supreme Court of a circuit court grant of divorce was improper where no constitutional issues or matters of state importance were involved. Huschen v. Huschen, 401 Ill. 518, 82 N.E.2d 337 (1948).

—Subject to Right of Appeal

The phrase "subject to the right of appeal" does not mean that judgment is appealable as a matter of right but means that the judgment is subject to whatever right of appeal is available for an order of that nature. In re Lentz, 73 Ill. App. 3d 93, 29 Ill. Dec. 319, 391 N.E.2d 582 (4 Dist. 1979), aff'd, 79 Ill. 2d 400, 38 Ill. Dec. 582, 403 N.E.2d 1036 (1980).

Attorney-Client Relationship

The attorney-client relationship terminates after the judgment of divorce is entered. In re Ponsart, 118 Ill. App. 3d 664, 74 Ill. Dec. 241, 455 N.E.2d 271 (1 Dist. 1983).

Competency of Party

Although the right of a guardian, conservator, or next friend to sue for divorce of his ward may be questionable, it is the rule in this state that a conservator or next friend may maintain an action on behalf of his ward to vacate and set aside a divorce decree. Newman v. Newman, 42 Ill. App. 2d 203, 191 N.E.2d 614 (1 Dist. 1963).

Discretion of Court

—Use of Name

The trial court has no discretion to deny wife's change of name request on dissolution of marriage on basis that where children were involved, their best interest required that the mother retain her married name. In re Dorks, 98 Ill. App. 3d 1046, 54 Ill. Dec. 537, 425 N.E.2d 49 (4 Dist. 1981).

The language of subsection (c) of this section is simple and direct; the word "shall" is mandatory and no qualifications to the request

Discretion of Court (Cont'd)

—Use of Name (Cont'd)
exist. In re Dorks, 98 Ill. App. 3d 1046, 54 Ill. Dec. 537, 425 N.E.2d 49 (4 Dist. 1981).

The trial court erred in summarily denying petitioner's request for restoration of her maiden name, as the name which the parent uses is not one of the relevant factors to the trial court in selecting the custodial parent. In re Thomas, 100 Ill. App. 3d 1080, 56 Ill. Dec. 604, 427 N.E.2d 1009 (1 Dist. 1981).

Enforcement
Where petitioner wife conveyed marital home to her father for health reasons, but she and her children continued to reside in the home uninterrupted during the period in question, and her father gave the property back to her prior to the filing of petition, petitioner could still enforce terms of the dissolution judgment. In re Aird, 175 Ill. App. 3d 870, 125 Ill. Dec. 398, 530 N.E.2d 556 (4 Dist. 1988).

Estoppel
In general, estoppel does not apply to void orders; however, in dissolution proceedings, a party who accepts the benefits of a divorce decree may be estopped from later challenging the order even if the challenge involves a claim that the order is void because the trial court lacked subject matter jurisdiction to enter it. In re Marriage of Chrobak, 349 Ill. App. 3d 894, 285 Ill. Dec. 369, 811 N.E.2d 1248, 2004 Ill. App. LEXIS 764 (2 Dist. 2004).

Where a wife had for five years accepted financial benefits from a separation judgment, which incorporated an agreement as to maintenance and the division of marital property, she was estopped from asserting that the judgment was void based on an argument that the circuit court lacked subject matter jurisdiction to enter the order because the wife had previously obtained a divorce in Canada. In re Marriage of Chrobak, 349 Ill. App. 3d 894, 285 Ill. Dec. 369, 811 N.E.2d 1248, 2004 Ill. App. LEXIS 764 (2 Dist. 2004).

—Applicability to Lien
Since the court in a divorce action adjudicated the extent of the wife's interest and she approved the divorce decree, she waived her right to assert an equitable lien against her husband's interest at a later date; she was thus estopped from asserting such a lien against the judgment creditor of her husband. Sterling Sav. & Loan Ass'n v. Schultz, 71 Ill. App. 2d 94, 218 N.E.2d 53 (1 Dist. 1966).

—Remarriage
Estoppel concept of "accepting benefits" is most often applied in divorce cases where a party remarries in reliance on a divorce decree and. in those instances, the rule is frequently called "estoppel by remarriage"; however, application of the estoppel rule is not limited to situations where at least one of the parties remarries. In re Marriage of Chrobak, 349 Ill. App. 3d 894, 285 Ill. Dec. 369, 811 N.E.2d 1248, 2004 Ill. App. LEXIS 764 (2 Dist. 2004).

Where it appeared from his answer that defendant recognized the validity of the divorce decree by marrying another woman, he was estopped to deny the validity of the divorce decree. Pierotti v. Pierotti, 343 Ill. App. 116, 98 N.E.2d 875 (1 Dist. 1951).

Finality
Although former wife's petition for attorney fees was filed after the trial court entered its judgment granting her petition for dissolution of marriage, the fact that a final judgment was entered prior to the former wife's request for attorney fees did not bar the trial court's award of attorney fees to her as the former husband did not object and the timing requirement was not jurisdictional even though 750 ILCS 5/503(j) stated that a petition for attorney fees had to be heard and decided before a final judgment was entered in a marriage dissolution case. In re Lindsey-Robinson, 331 Ill. App. 3d 261, 265 Ill. Dec. 17, 771 N.E.2d 976, 2002 Ill. App. LEXIS 365 (4 Dist. 2002).

Only an order which terminates litigation on the merits so that, if affirmed, the trial court has only to proceed with execution is a final order for appeal purposes; thus, a judgment of dissolution of marriage which terminated the dispute between the litigants with regard to the claim of the existence of sufficient statutory grounds for dissolution of a marriage was final and appealable. In re Nilsson, 81 Ill. App. 3d 580, 37 Ill. Dec. 394, 402 N.E.2d 284 (3 Dist. 1980).

A judgment of dissolution is final as to the claim that the marriage should be dissolved, but if other claims are left pending, the judgment is not final as to those claims and if the judgment does not contain the requisite finding that no just reason existed for delay of appeal, the judgment is not appealable. In re Lentz, 73 Ill. App. 3d 93, 29 Ill. Dec. 319, 391 N.E.2d 582 (4 Dist. 1979), aff'd, 79 Ill. 2d 400, 38 Ill. Dec. 582, 403 N.E.2d 1036 (1980).

Foreign Divorce Decree
A Nevada decree, which had been given full faith and credit, was declared void after the appellate court found that husband had failed to show that he had established a bona fide domicile there, and that the Nevada decree was void for lack of jurisdiction. Fink v. Fink, 37 Ill. App. 3d 604, 346 N.E.2d 415 (3 Dist. 1976).

The prima facie evidence of a prior valid divorce, afforded by the introduction of the out-of-state decree, was successfully impeached by the evidence that defendant did not establish a bona fide domicile in another state, and therefore, that court was without jurisdiction to enter the decree; consequently, the courts of this state were not bound to give it full faith and credit. Ludwig v. Ludwig, 413 Ill. 44, 107 N.E.2d 848 (1952).

Fraud

—Not Shown
Where defendant charged that plaintiff obtained divorce decree through fraud in that plaintiff's affidavit for publication asserted that defendant's place of residence could not be ascertained, the delay of 16 years between the date of the divorce and the filing of the petition to set aside the decree, particularly in view of the subsequent remarriage of the plaintiff, required strong and persuasive evidence to support the defendant's charge of fraud, lack of notice or of knowledge of facts sufficient to be put on notice, and the evidence in the case was not sufficiently clear and convincing to establish fraud on the part of the plaintiff. Sajich v. Sajich, 128 Ill. App. 2d 432, 262 N.E.2d 11 (2 Dist. 1970).

Home Repairs
Replacement of roof and gutters of marital home is a capital improvement of whose total cost the court may order each spouse to pay half under dissolution judgment. In re Aird, 175 Ill. App. 3d 870, 125 Ill. Dec. 398, 530 N.E.2d 556 (4 Dist. 1988).

Painting and carpeting of home are not capital improvements, and spouse in possession of the home alone is obligated to pay these maintenance repairs according to express terms of the judgment of dissolution. In re Aird, 175 Ill. App. 3d 870, 125 Ill. Dec. 398, 530 N.E.2d 556 (4 Dist. 1988).

Increased Support
Order directing that petitioner pay increased amount of support and that arrearage of $4,500 be paid to the clerk of the circuit court and retained by the clerk until further order of the court did not contravene this section. In re Raidbard, 87 Ill. App. 3d 158, 42 Ill. Dec. 312, 408 N.E.2d 1021 (1 Dist. 1980).

Interest
An award of interest on a supplemental judgment incorporating parties' property settlement agreement into their divorce decree is mandatory. In re Morris, 190 Ill. App. 3d 293, 137 Ill. Dec. 789, 546 N.E.2d 734 (1 Dist. 1989).

Jurisdiction

—Scope
Having entered a decree of divorce, final for some purposes, does not mean that a court of equity has thereby divested itself of jurisdiction to dispose of other matters necessarily incident to the divorce proceedings, especially when the court has by the express terms of its decree reserved jurisdiction to pass on the question of alimony (now maintenance), attorney fees and property rights. Bremer v. Bremer, 4 Ill. 2d 190, 122 N.E.2d 794 (1954).

—Shown
Where his answer showed that defendant had full knowledge of the entry of the divorce decree, acquiesced therein, and that upon the entry of the decree he arranged for "a permanent and comfortable home" for plaintiff and the child at the home of his mother, his claim that the decree of divorce was invalid because the court was without jurisdiction over the person of defendant, was false, as

Jurisdiction (Cont'd)

—Shown (Cont'd)
clearly appeared from the sworn statements he made in his answer. Pierotti v. Pierotti, 343 Ill. App. 116, 98 N.E.2d 875 (1 Dist. 1951).

—Maintenance
This section and 750 ILCS 5/504(c) do not create a substantive right to post-death maintenance pending appeal; they apply when a right to maintenance already exists, and therefore must be read in conjunction with the prohibition of 750 ILCS 5/510(c). Stacke v. Bates, 138 Ill. 2d 295, 149 Ill. Dec. 728, 562 N.E.2d 192 (1990).

Subsection (a) of this section creates a category of nonstayable orders whose purpose is to provide for the sustenance of dependent spouse and children during the appeal process and includes lump sum maintenance awards. In re Cleveland, 99 Ill. App. 3d 293, 54 Ill. Dec. 610, 425 N.E.2d 475 (1 Dist. 1981).

Marital Agreement

—Not Modified
Where there was little or nothing in the record to support an order requiring a former husband to pay $300 per month to his former wife for child support, nor any showing that she was unable to support the children herself, for the period designated and agreed upon in the original divorce decree, the order requiring defendant to pay support money in the amount of $300 per month was reversed. Leland v. Brower, 28 Ill. 2d 598, 192 N.E.2d 831 (1963).

Modification of Decree

—Change in Tax Law
Court could modify the terms of a divorce decree on the ground that the change in the federal income tax law in 1942 caused a material change in the financial status of wife; any decrease in her income, whether due to the payment of income taxes or to any other reason, which reduced her income beyond what was necessary for her station in life, could be considered. Jacobs v. Jacobs, 328 Ill. App. 133, 65 N.E.2d 588 (1 Dist. 1946).

Multiple Claims for Relief
Consistent with Rule 304(a), Supreme Court Rules, where there are multiple claims for relief in a particular dissolution case, an appeal may be taken from a final judgment as to one but fewer than all of the claims only if the trial court has made an express written finding that there is no just reason for delaying enforcement or appeal. In re Nilsson, 81 Ill. App. 3d 580, 37 Ill. Dec. 394, 402 N.E.2d 284 (3 Dist. 1980).

Release of Errors
In divorce proceeding, wife's conduct in accepting a quitclaim deed, $6,000, and the payment of the attorney fees to her amounted to an acceptance of the benefits of the decree and was a release of errors. Kissin v. Kissin, 29 Ill. App. 2d 126, 172 N.E.2d 635 (1 Dist. 1961).

Supplemental Judgment
This section applied with equal force to both a judgment of dissolution and a supplemental judgment containing a property settlement agreement between the parties; therefore, additional maintenance and an aggregate sum property settlement provided for in the supplemental judgment were "reduced to judgment" on the entry date of the supplemental judgment, and became immediately enforceable at that time. In re Morris, 190 Ill. App. 3d 293, 137 Ill. Dec. 789, 546 N.E.2d 734 (1 Dist. 1989).

LEGAL PERIODICALS

For article, "Divorce Illinois Style: Ten Years Under the Marriage and Dissolution of Marriage Act," see 75 Ill. B.J. 606 (1987).

RESEARCH REFERENCES

Full faith and credit "last-in-time" rule as applicable to sister state divorce or custody judgment which is inconsistent with the forum state's earlier judgment. 36 ALR5th 527.

Vacating or setting aside divorce decree after remarriage of party. 17 ALR4th 1153.

PART IV-A.

JOINT SIMPLIFIED DISSOLUTION PROCEDURE

750 ILCS 5/451 Applicability

Sec. 451. *Applicability.* In any proceeding under this Part IV-A, the provisions of this Part IV-A shall control where they conflict with other provisions of this Act.
(Source: P.A. 88-39, § 5.)

Effective Date.
This Part became effective January 1, 1994, pursuant to Ill. Const. (1970), Art. IV, § 10 and 5 ILCS 75/1.

750 ILCS 5/452 Petition

Sec. 452. *Petition.* The parties to a dissolution proceeding may file a joint petition for simplified dissolution if they certify that all of the following conditions exist when the proceeding is commenced:

(a) Neither party is dependent on the other party for support or each party is willing to waive the right to support; and the parties understand that consultation with attorneys may help them determine eligibility for spousal support.

(b) Either party has met the residency requirement of Section 401 of this Act [750 ILCS 5/401].

(c) Irreconcilable differences have caused the irretrievable breakdown of the marriage and the parties have been separated 6 months or more and efforts at reconciliation have failed or future attempts at reconciliation would be impracticable and not in the best interests of the family.

(d) No children were born of the relationship of the parties or adopted by the parties during the marriage, and the wife, to her knowledge, is not pregnant by the husband.

(e) The duration of the marriage does not exceed 8 years.

(f) Neither party has any interest in real property.

(g) The parties waive any rights to maintenance.

(h) The total fair market value of all marital property, after deducting all encumbrances, is less than $10,000 the combined gross annualized income from all sources is less than $35,000, and neither party has a gross annualized income from all sources in excess of $20,000.

(i) The parties have disclosed to each other all assets and their tax returns for all years of the marriage.

(j) The parties have executed a written agreement dividing all assets in excess of $100 in value and allocating responsibility for debts and liabilities between the parties.
(Source: P.A. 88-39, § 5; 90-731, § 10.)

Effect of Amendments.

The 1998 amendment by P.A. 90-731, effective July 1, 1999, in subsection (e) substituted "8 years" for "5 years"; in subsection (h) substituted "less than $10,000," for "less than $5,000 and" and "less than $35,000, and neither party has a gross annualized income from all sources in excess of $20,000" for "less than $25,000".

750 ILCS 5/453 Procedure; Judgment

Sec. 453. *Procedure; Judgment.* The parties shall use the forms provided by the circuit court clerk, and the clerk shall submit the petition to the court. The court shall expeditiously consider the cause. Both parties shall appear in person before the court and, if the court so directs, testify. The court, after examination of the petition and the parties and finding the agreement of the parties not unconscionable, shall enter a judgment granting the dissolution if the requirements of this Part IV-A have been met and the parties have submitted the affidavit required under Section 454 [750 ILCS 5/454]. No transcript of proceedings shall be required.
(Source: P.A. 88-39, § 5.)

750 ILCS 5/454 Affidavit

Sec. 454. *Affidavit.* At the time of the hearing, the parties shall submit to the court an affidavit executed by both parties stating that all property has been divided in accordance with the agreement of the parties and that they have executed all documents required to effectuate the agreement.
(Source: P.A. 88-39, § 5.)

750 ILCS 5/455 Copies of judgment

Sec. 455. *Copies of judgment.* Upon entry of the judgment and upon payment of the fee, the circuit court clerk shall furnish to each party a certified copy of the final judgment of dissolution.
(Source: P.A. 88-39, § 5.)

750 ILCS 5/456 Forms

Sec. 456. *Forms.* The contents of forms to be used in simplified dissolutions shall be provided for by court rule. The circuit court clerk shall supply forms upon request for use by parties seeking simplified dissolutions under this Part IV-A.
(Source: P.A. 88-39, § 5.)

750 ILCS 5/457 Brochure to describe proceedings

Sec. 457. *Brochure to describe proceedings.* The circuit court clerk may make available a brochure that describes the requirements, nature, and effect of a simplified dissolution. The brochure should state, in nontechnical language, the following:

(a) It is in the best interests of each of the parties to consult attorneys regarding the dissolution of their marriage, and that the services of attorneys may be obtained.

(b) The parties should not rely exclusively on the brochure, and the brochure is intended only as a guide for self-representation.

(c) A concise summary of the provisions and procedures of the simplified dissolution procedure.

(d) The nature and availability of counseling services.

(e) If the parties waive their rights to maintenance, neither party can in the future obtain maintenance from the other.

(f) A statement in boldface type that a judgment for dissolution of marriage permanently adjudicates all financial rights arising out of the marriage, including the right to property in the name of one's spouse and the right to support from one's spouse (maintenance or alimony), that a judgment is final, and the parties waive their right to appeal, except that neither party is barred from instituting an action to set aside a final judgment for fraud, duress, accident, mistake, or other grounds at law or in equity.

(g) The parties to the marriage remain married persons and cannot remarry until a judgment dissolving the marriage is entered.
(Source: P.A. 88-39, § 5.)

PART V.

PROPERTY, SUPPORT AND ATTORNEY FEES

750 ILCS 5/501 Temporary Relief

Sec. 501. *Temporary Relief.* In all proceedings under this Act, temporary relief shall be as follows:

(a) Either party may move for:

(1) temporary maintenance or temporary support of a child of the marriage entitled to support, accompanied by an affidavit as to the factual basis for the relief requested;

(2) a temporary restraining order or preliminary injunction, accompanied by affidavit showing a factual basis for any of the following relief:

(i) restraining any person from transferring, encumbering, concealing or otherwise disposing of any property except in the usual course of business or for the necessities of life, and, if so restrained, requiring him to notify the moving party and his attorney of any proposed extraordinary expenditures made after the order is issued;

(ii) enjoining a party from removing a child from the jurisdiction of the court;

(iii) enjoining a party from striking or interfering with the personal liberty of the other party or of any child; or

(iv) providing other injunctive relief proper in the circumstances; or

(3) other appropriate temporary relief.

(b) The court may issue a temporary restraining order without requiring notice to the other party only if it finds, on the basis of the moving affidavit or other evidence, that irreparable injury will result to the moving party if no order is issued until the time for responding has elapsed.

(c) A response hereunder may be filed within 21 days after service of notice of motion or at the time specified in the temporary restraining order.

(c-1) As used in this subsection (c-1), "interim attorney's fees and costs" means attorney's fees and costs assessed from time to time while a case is pending, in favor of the petitioning party's current counsel, for reasonable fees and costs either already incurred or to be incurred, and "interim award" means an award of interim attorney's fees and costs. Interim awards shall be governed by the following:

(1) Except for good cause shown, a proceeding for (or relating to) interim attorney's fees and costs shall be nonevidentiary, summary in nature, and expeditious. When a party files a petition for interim attorney's fees and costs supported by one or more affidavits that delineate relevant factors, the court (or a hearing officer) shall assess an interim award after affording the opposing party a reasonable opportunity to file a responsive pleading. A responsive pleading shall set out the amount of each retainer or other payment or payments, or both, previously paid to the responding party's counsel by or on behalf of the responding party. In assessing an interim award, the court shall consider all relevant factors, as presented, that appear reasonable and necessary, including:

(A) the income and property of each party, including alleged marital property within the sole control of one party and alleged non-marital property within access to a party;

(B) the needs of each party;

(C) the realistic earning capacity of each party;

(D) any impairment to present earning capacity of either party, including age and physical and emotional health;

(E) the standard of living established during the marriage;

(F) the degree of complexity of the issues, including custody, valuation or division (or both) of closely held businesses, and tax planning, as well as reasonable needs for expert investigations or expert witnesses, or both;

(G) each party's access to relevant information;

(H) the amount of the payment or payments made or reasonably expected to be made to the attorney for the other party; and

(I) any other factor that the court expressly finds to be just and equitable.

(2) Any assessment of an interim award (including one pursuant to an agreed order) shall be without prejudice to any final allocation and without prejudice as to any claim or right of either party or any counsel of record at the time of the award. Any such claim or right may be presented by the appropriate party or counsel at a hearing on contribution under subsection (j) of Section 503 [750 ILCS 5/503] or a hearing on counsel's fees under subsection (c) of Section 508 [750 ILCS 5/508]. Unless otherwise ordered by the court at the final hearing between the parties or in a hearing under subsection (j) of Section 503 [750 ILCS 5/503] or subsection (c) of Section 508 [750 ILCS 5/508], interim awards, as well as the aggregate of all other payments by each party to counsel and related payments to third parties, shall be deemed to have been advances from the parties' marital estate. Any portion of any interim award constituting an overpayment shall be remitted back to the appropriate party or parties, or, alternatively, to successor counsel, as the court determines and directs, after notice.

(3) In any proceeding under this subsection (c-1), the court (or hearing officer) shall assess an interim award against an opposing party in an amount necessary to enable the petitioning party to participate adequately in the litigation, upon findings that the party from whom attorney's fees and costs are sought has the financial ability to pay reasonable amounts and that the party seeking attorney's fees and costs lacks sufficient access to assets or income to pay reasonable amounts. In determining an award, the court shall consider whether adequate participation in the litigation requires expenditure of more fees and costs for a party that is not in control of assets or relevant information. Except for good cause shown, an interim award shall not be less than payments made or reasonably expected to be made to the counsel for the other party. If the court finds that both parties lack financial ability or access to assets or income for reasonable attorney's fees and costs, the court (or hearing officer) shall enter an order that allocates available funds for each party's counsel, including retainers or interim payments, or both, previously paid, in a manner that achieves substantial parity between the parties.

(4) The changes to this Section 501 made by this amendatory Act of 1996 apply to cases pending on or after June 1, 1997, except as otherwise provided in Section 508 [750 ILCS 5/508].

(d) A temporary order entered under this Section:

(1) does not prejudice the rights of the parties or the child which are to be adjudicated at subsequent hearings in the proceeding;

(2) may be revoked or modified before final judgment, on a showing by affidavit and upon hearing; and

(3) terminates when the final judgment is entered or when the petition for dissolution of marriage or legal separation or declaration of invalidity of marriage is dismissed.

(Source: P.A. 86-700; 89-712, § 5.)

Note.

This section was Ill.Rev.Stat., Ch. 40, para. 501.

Cross References.

As to "appropriate temporary relief", as stated in subdivision (a)(3) of this section, and its applicability to criminal orders of protection, see 725 ILCS 5/112A-14.

Concerning "appropriate temporary relief", as stated in subdivision (a)(3) of this section, specifically losses affecting family needs, and the reimbursement by respondent of such losses, see 750 ILCS 60/214.

Effect of Amendments.

The 1996 amendment by P.A. 89-712, effective June 1, 1997, added subsection (c-1).

CASE NOTES

ANALYSIS

Constitutionality
In General
Appealability
Applicability
Attorney Fees
Award
—Held Proper
—Not Punitive
Collateral Attack
Condonation
—In General
Construction with Other Laws
Contempt
—Relief Not Available
Death of Party
Discretion of Court
Dismissal of Action
—Erroneous
Disposition of Property
Estoppel
Evidentiary Hearing
Extension
—Change in Terms of Agreement
Factors
Findings of Court
Grounds for Relief
—Bodily Harm
—Good Faith Requirement
Household Expenses
—Award Proper
Injunction
—Business Assets
—Concurrent Jurisdiction
Interim Fees
Interior Fee
Irreparable Harm
—Shown
Jury Trial
Legislative Intent
—No Prejudice to Parties
—Res Judicata
Maintaining Status Quo
Maintenance
Notice
Operation of Business
Past Due Child Support
Pretrial Order
—Not Binding
Prospective Fees or Costs
Purpose
—Amicable Settlements
—Equality Between Spouses
Remand
Sale of Marital Home
Settlement
—Effect
Standard of Review
Temporary Custody
—Existing Custody Judgment
Temporary Maintenance
—In General
—Cohabitation
—Factors Considered
—Jurisdiction
—Upheld
Temporary Restraining Order
—In General
—Irreparable Injury
—Notice of Hearing
—Removal of Children from Jurisdiction
—Standard of Review
Travel Expenses
Visitation
Voluntary Dismissal
Waiver
—Vested Right

Constitutionality

The application of 750 ILCS 5/501(c-1) to both pre- and post-decree proceedings constitutes a violation of neither substantive nor procedural due process. Beyer v. Parkis, 324 Ill. App. 3d 305, 257 Ill. Dec. 406, 753 N.E.2d 1032, 2001 Ill. App. LEXIS 538 (1 Dist. 2001).

In General

Generally, injunctive relief is proper if petitioner establishes by a preponderance of the evidence: (1) a protectable right is threatened; (2) petitioner would otherwise be irreparably injured; (3) there is an adequate legal remedy, and (4) the petitioner will likely prevail on the merits. Joerger v. Joerger, 221 Ill. App. 3d 400, 163 Ill. Dec. 796, 581 N.E.2d 1219 (4 Dist. 1991).

Appealability

Trial court's interim award of attorney fees to the first attorney and the second attorney, payable by the law firm as directed in the trial court's disgorgement order, was not appealable since that award was one for temporary relied and did not constitute a final, appealable order. Johnson v. Johnson, 351 Ill. App. 3d 88, 285 Ill. Dec. 841, 812 N.E.2d 661, 2004 Ill. App. LEXIS 785 (1 Dist. 2004).

Trial court did not err in vacating the sheriff's sale of the owner's home where no valid lien on the home existed; the attempt to create a lien based on a prior order which was modified and thus, not a final judgment, was invalid. King v. King, 208 Ill. 2d 332, 280 Ill. Dec. 695, 802 N.E.2d 1216, 2003 Ill. LEXIS 2609 (2003).

The plain language of the statute does not authorize the appeal of interim orders. In re Tetzlaff, 304 Ill. App. 3d 1030, 238 Ill. Dec. 243, 711 N.E.2d 346 (1 Dist. 1999).

Orders reducing father's current payment of child support subject to accrual for later repayment of the amount of such reduction and providing for later review fully and finally disposed of his request for a permanent reduction in his support obligation, subject to accrual and later repayment and was appealable. In re Fink, 275 Ill. App. 3d 960, 212 Ill. Dec. 297, 656 N.E.2d 1131 (4 Dist. 1995).

There was no justification for precluding appellate review of the excessiveness or inadequacy of an award of maintenance for a three year period solely on technical ground that the trial court characterized the award as "temporary" instead of permanent; accordingly, the trial court's maintenance award was deemed "final," but subject to the trial court's later review. In re Lawrence, 146 Ill. App. 3d 307, 99 Ill. Dec. 845, 496 N.E.2d 538 (3 Dist. 1986).

Applicability

Trial court properly granted the husband's motion to dismiss the wife's request for preliminary injunctive relief as the wife's request for such relief did not show a factual basis for it as the wife's insufficiently pled that the parties had mutual wills or a binding contract not to revoke the mutual wills, a protectable interest, or that the husband had transferred any property that the husband did not have a right o transfer. Centioli v. Centioli, 335 Ill. App. 3d 650, 269 Ill. Dec. 814, 781 N.E.2d 611, 2002 Ill. App. LEXIS 1113 (1 Dist. 2002).

Subdivision (a)(2)(i) of this section does not preclude the enjoining of business assets; rather, if business property is restrained, the enjoined party may apply for modification of the injunctive order in the event that extraordinary expenditures are required. In re Grauer, 133 Ill. App. 3d 1019, 88 Ill. Dec. 962, 479 N.E.2d 982 (1 Dist. 1985).

Attorney Fees

Trial court erred in ruling that interim attorney's fees could not be recovered under the Illinois Parentage Act as 750 ILCS 45/17 allowed for attorney's fees based on the factors found in 750 ILCS 5/508, which allowed for interim attorney's fees based on the factors listed in 750 ILCS 5/501(c-1)(1),(2),(3). Stella v. Garcia (In re Stella), 353 Ill. App. 3d 415, 288 Ill. Dec. 889, 818 N.E.2d 824, 2004 Ill. App. LEXIS 1265 (1 Dist. 2004).

Interim attorney's fees can be awarded under the Illinois Parentage Act by using the methods, factors, and procedures set forth in § 501 of the Illinois Marriage Act, 750 ILCS 5/501(c-1)(1),(2),(3), and disgorgement cannot be considered or used in a Parentage Act proceeding. Stella v. Garcia (In re Stella), 353 Ill. App. 3d 415, 288 Ill. Dec. 889, 818 N.E.2d 824, 2004 Ill. App. LEXIS 1265 (1 Dist. 2004).

Appellate court did not have jurisdiction to hear law firm's appeal of the trial court's order directing the law firm to disgorge certain attorney fees paid by its client and to pay those fees to the first attorney and the second attorney as the order to disgorge was one for temporary relief and as it was not a final, appealable order. Johnson v. Johnson, 351 Ill. App. 3d 88, 285 Ill. Dec. 841, 812 N.E.2d 661, 2004 Ill. App. LEXIS 785 (1 Dist. 2004).

Because nothing in 750 ILCS 45/17, 750 ILCS 5/508, or 750 ILCS 5/501(c-1)(3) gave trial judges the power to order disgorgement of interim fees in parentage cases, the trial court improperly ordered the attorney to disgorge $20,000 to the opposing attorney. Stella v. Garcia (In re Stella), 339 Ill. App. 3d 610, 274 Ill. Dec. 391, 791 N.E.2d 187, 2003 Ill. App. LEXIS 650 (1 Dist. 2003).

The well established principle is that the amount of attorney fees rests in the sound discretion of the trial judge, which will not be interfered with unless abused, and the same rule applies to support awards. Collins v. Collins, 47 Ill. App. 3d 258, 5 Ill. Dec. 464, 361 N.E.2d 787 (1 Dist. 1977).

Granting plaintiff's petition for temporary alimony pending an appeal and for attorney fees to defend the appeal was not an abuse of discretion. People v. Almanza, 76 Ill. App. 2d 395, 222 N.E.2d 74 (1 Dist. 1966).

Award

—Held Proper

Where the trial court entered an order carefully designed to avoid harm to husband's business and personal finances while simultaneously protecting wife's interests, the trial court complied with subdivision (a)(2)(i) of this section. In re Grauer, 133 Ill. App. 3d 1019, 88 Ill. Dec. 962, 479 N.E.2d 982 (1 Dist. 1985).

Maintenance award was not an abuse of discretion although wife was neither destitute nor unemployed, as she was clearly living at a standard far below that which she enjoyed during her marriage and her earnings were far less than those of husband; generally, the manner in which the parties have been accustomed to live should be considered as regards to maintenance. In re Greenberg, 102 Ill. App. 3d 938, 58 Ill. Dec. 1, 429 N.E.2d 1334 (1 Dist. 1981).

Where ex-wife had greater need, and ex-husband was able to expend amounts ordered to support his family, order for husband to pay half of the monthly mortgage payment which was, in effect, a contribution to his own equity in the jointly owned property and to pay an additional $100 for monthly maintenance should his wife ever be dispossessed of the marital home by proceedings for partition or foreclosure was not an abuse of discretion. Kealey v. Kealey, 77 Ill. App. 3d 962, 33 Ill. Dec. 672, 397 N.E.2d 5 (5 Dist. 1979).

Under former Ill.Rev.Stat., ch. 68, para. 22 (see now this section), upon careful consideration of the discrepancy between plaintiff's income and expenses, the couple's station in life, and plaintiff's inability to obtain employment, plaintiff was unable to meet her own needs from her income alone despite her substantial securities holdings and other assets, such that the sums awarded as temporary alimony and attorney fees were just and equitable. Kenly v. Kenly, 47 Ill. App. 3d 694, 8 Ill. Dec. 141, 365 N.E.2d 379 (1 Dist. 1977).

Pursuant to former section 15 of the Divorce Act (see now this section), trial court did not abuse its discretion in awarding plaintiff $2,300 per month as alimony pending appeal. Green v. Green, 41 Ill. App. 3d 154, 354 N.E.2d 661 (1 Dist. 1976).

Where defendant testified that his estimated income tax would be about $15,000, and interest on $70,000 of indebtedness would be $4,000 to $5,000, and that he was also liable for $800 a month in child support plus college expenses for two children, alimony of $200 a month was not an abuse of discretion. Lamkin v. Lamkin, 43 Ill. App. 3d 422, 1 Ill. Dec. 932, 356 N.E.2d 1265 (4 Dist. 1976).

Husband plaintiff had the ability to pay the amount awarded wife; it was a reasonable award which conformed to standard of living which the wife and children enjoyed during her marriage to the plaintiff. McManus v. McManus, 37 Ill. App. 3d 658, 347 N.E.2d 109 (1 Dist. 1975).

—Not Punitive

Where the trial court indicated that a substantial disparity of income existed between parties, favoring defendant, and that plaintiff had not resumed living with her parents but was endeavoring to maintain an apartment and support herself, and it further went on to say that, considering the evidence and equities involved, it was of the opinion that the alimony ordered was not punitive, was measured upon reasonable needs of the wife and husband, and should not cause financial difficulties and personal embarrassment of the husband and should fairly allow defendant to resume a reasonable standard of living and enjoy a reasonable peace of mind, the trial court's reasoning was supported by evidence. Hepner v. Hepner, 42 Ill. App. 3d 491, 1 Ill. Dec. 146, 356 N.E.2d 146 (3 Dist. 1976).

Collateral Attack

The propriety of a temporary support order could be attacked within 30 days from rendition by an appropriate motion, and after 30 days from its entry, it could be attacked either by appeal or by a proper petition under former section 72 of the Civil Practice Act (see now 735 ILCS 5/2-1401), but such order could not be collaterally attacked unless it was void. Hirsh v. Hirsh, 81 Ill. App. 2d 354, 225 N.E.2d 42 (2 Dist. 1967).

Condonation

—In General

Condonation is not a defense to the allowance of temporary relief where the plaintiff need only establish good faith by showing probable grounds or cause for divorce. Roback v. Roback, 59 Ill. App. 2d 222, 207 N.E.2d 130 (2 Dist. 1965).

Construction with Other Laws

Because this section and 735 ILCS 5/11-101 relate to the same subject matter, they should be construed harmoniously where possible. In re Pick, 119 Ill. App. 3d 1061, 75 Ill. Dec. 865, 458 N.E.2d 33 (2 Dist. 1983).

Contempt

Mere absence of compliance is not a sufficient basis for a judgment of contempt; the evidence must show that failure to comply was a wilful and contumacious refusal to obey the court order. Henkel v. Morris, 155 Ill. App. 3d 816, 108 Ill. Dec. 469, 508 N.E.2d 780 (3 Dist. 1987).

An order for temporary support in either a divorce or separate maintenance proceeding may be enforced by contempt proceedings and is an appealable order. Hirsh v. Hirsh, 81 Ill. App. 2d 354, 225 N.E.2d 42 (2 Dist. 1967).

Order citing the defendant for wilful contempt and remanding him to jail for 30 days, unless he shall have purged himself of said contempt by payment of the arrearages in alimony and mortgage payments, was not a clear abuse of discretion. Janov v. Janov, 60 Ill. App. 2d 11, 207 N.E.2d 691 (3 Dist. 1965).

The order of contempt must find that the failure to comply with the decree was wilful. Janov v. Janov, 60 Ill. App. 2d 11, 207 N.E.2d 691 (3 Dist. 1965).

—Relief Not Available

Wife's petition for a rule to show cause why a securities company should not be held in contempt for allowing her husband to remove money from an individual retirement account (IRA), in violation of an order which the court issued under § 501(a)(2)(i) of the Illinois Marriage and Dissolution of Marriage Act, 750 ILCS 5/501(a)(2)(i) was dismissed, because the wife sought an order requiring the company to fund the husband's IRA at previous levels using its own money, and that relief was not available in a civil contempt proceeding. Blankshain v. Blankshain, 346 Ill. App. 3d 750, 282 Ill. Dec. 120, 805 N.E.2d 739, 2004 Ill. App. LEXIS 212 (1 Dist. 2004).

Death of Party

When a trial court modified its injunction prohibiting the transfer of marital assets to require that the parties' property be transferred into tenancy in common interests, due to the impending death of the wife, but this was not carried out before she died, the court's order was a temporary order which did not survive the dismissal of the proceedings due to her death, and could not be enforced after that dismissal. In re Marriage of Ignatius, 338 Ill. App. 3d 652, 273 Ill. Dec. 203, 788 N.E.2d 794, 2003 Ill. App. LEXIS 518 (2 Dist. 2003).

A preliminary injunction, which prohibited the husband from transferring property of the parties, terminated upon the death of the husband, but did not abate; thus, a transfer of property by the husband before his death was improper. New York Life Ins. Co. v. Sogol, 311 Ill. App. 3d 156, 243 Ill. Dec. 796, 724 N.E.2d 105, 1999 Ill. App. LEXIS 948 (1 Dist. 1999).

Discretion of Court

An award of temporary alimony and child support is dependent upon the financial ability and current circumstances of parties, but the trial court has considerable discretion in awarding temporary alimony and support, and a trial court's decision as to awards of temporary allowances will not be set aside unless it is contrary to the manifest weight of the evidence. In re Rogliano, 198 Ill. App. 3d 404, 144 Ill. Dec. 595, 555 N.E.2d 1114 (5 Dist. 1990).

Dismissal of Action

—Erroneous

Petitioner's right to increased support was not barred when trial court erroneously dismissed petitioner's prayer for dissolution. In re Weiss, 87 Ill. App. 3d 643, 42 Ill. Dec. 714, 409 N.E.2d 329 (1 Dist. 1980).

Disposition of Property

Award of possession of marital home to wife until the youngest child reached the age of 18 years was an award of child support for the benefit of the children, not a property settlement or award of alimony in gross; therefore, since the transfer of custody of the children to father was clearly a substantial change of circumstance, the marital home was no longer needed for their support. Lamp v. Lamp, 73 Ill. App. 3d 713, 29 Ill. Dec. 792, 392 N.E.2d 349 (5 Dist. 1979), aff'd, 81 Ill. 2d 364, 43 Ill. Dec. 31, 410 N.E.2d 31 (1980).

Estoppel

Husband was not estopped to prosecute appeal because he accepted benefits under a divorce decree, especially where husband actually received nothing under the decree which he did not already have. Pearson v. Pearson, 42 Ill. App. 3d 522, 1 Ill. Dec. 711, 356 N.E.2d 993 (2 Dist. 1976).

Evidentiary Hearing

There is no procedural due process violation in subdivision (c-1)(1) since an evidentiary hearing is still held if it is found to be necessary. Kaufman, Litwin & Feinstein v. Edgar, 301 Ill. App. 3d 826, 235 Ill. Dec. 183, 704 N.E.2d 756 (1 Dist. 1998), appeal denied, 182 Ill. 2d 551, 236 Ill. Dec. 670, 707 N.E.2d 1240 (1999).

Extension

—Change in Terms of Agreement

While trial court had statutory authority to allow child to remain with father after "experimental custody agreement," trial court was instructed to move modification hearing forward as seven month extension effectively changed terms of agreement and was not "appropriate temporary relief" under subsection (a)(3) of this section. In re Venner, 146 Ill. App. 3d 238, 100 Ill. Dec. 82, 496 N.E.2d 1147 (1 Dist. 1986).

Factors

Under former Ill.Rev.Stat., ch. 68, para. 22 (see now this section), the key factors in determining liability for temporary alimony or attorney fees were the wife's inability to pay, her needs within the context of the couple's prior standard of living, and the husband's ability to pay. Kenly v. Kenly, 47 Ill. App. 3d 694, 8 Ill. Dec. 141, 365 N.E.2d 379 (1 Dist. 1977).

Findings of Court

A trial court should make definite findings or in any event make clear from the record the relevant factors it considered in rendering a decision concerning support; however, reviewing courts have uniformly held that where the record is adequate to provide a basis upon which to review the propriety of the decision, and where that decision is supported by the evidence, the reviewing court will not reverse solely because special findings are lacking. Sostak v. Sostak, 113 Ill. App. 3d 954, 69 Ill. Dec. 658, 447 N.E.2d 1345 (2 Dist. 1983).

Grounds for Relief

—Bodily Harm

Temporary relief was authorized where the acts of cruelty described in complaint or enumerated by plaintiff in her deposition, including physical abuse, established good faith by reflecting probable cause or grounds for divorce. Roback v. Roback, 59 Ill. App. 2d 222, 207 N.E.2d 130 (2 Dist. 1965).

—Good Faith Requirement

In awarding temporary relief, the court may not inquire into the merits of the action and the likelihood of whether the plaintiff will prevail in determining whether temporary relief may be granted, but the court must satisfy itself that the complaint was filed in good faith, and that there is probable cause or grounds for divorce. Roback v. Roback, 59 Ill. App. 2d 222, 207 N.E.2d 130 (2 Dist. 1965).

Household Expenses

—Award Proper

Where the trial court awarded the plaintiff the sum of $75 per week as temporary alimony and support for herself and her two children, and further ordered the defendant to pay all of the expenses in connection with the operation and upkeep of the home, such award was ample, especially when consideration was given to the fact that the defendant was ordered to pay all expenses in connection with the operation and maintenance of the home, and the court did not abuse its discretion or ignore the elements to be considered. Roback v. Roback, 59 Ill. App. 2d 222, 207 N.E.2d 130 (2 Dist. 1965).

Injunction

—Business Assets

The statute does not preclude a court from enjoining business assets. In re Schmitt, 321 Ill. App. 3d 360, 254 Ill. Dec. 484, 747 N.E.2d 524, 2001 Ill. App. LEXIS 314 (2 Dist. 2001).

—Concurrent Jurisdiction

Extreme restraint should be exercised regarding the issuance of injunctions prohibiting a party from seeking relief in a court of concurrent jurisdiction in the same state. Bashwiner v. Bashwiner, 126 Ill. App. 3d 365, 81 Ill. Dec. 359, 466 N.E.2d 1161 (1 Dist. 1984).

Interim Fees

Trial court's order awarding a wife $ 4,000 in interim attorney's fees so she could defend a husband's action seeking modification of the court's order awarding the wife child support and custody of the parties' children was not appealable. Oleksy v. Oleksy, 337 Ill. App. 3d 946, 272 Ill. Dec. 497, 787 N.E.2d 312, 2003 Ill. App. LEXIS 317 (1 Dist. 2003).

Itemized billing statements and a copy of a retainer agreement are not necessary to establish the reasonableness of interim attorney fees. Beyer v. Parkis, 324 Ill. App. 3d 305, 257 Ill. Dec. 406, 753 N.E.2d 1032, 2001 Ill. App. LEXIS 538 (1 Dist. 2001).

Interim attorney fees were properly awarded in a post-decree proceeding where (1) a review of the wife's financial disclosure affidavit indicated that the balance between her income and expenses established that she was unable to pay her own fees; (2) she alleged that the husband had the ability to pay both her and his own attorney's fees because he had access to vast sources of income from the operation of one gas station, the proceeds from the sale of second gas station, and extensive lines of credit with financial institutions based on these assets and income; (3) she and her attorney further represented in affidavits that the husband had thwarted discovery in the past and retained control of the relevant information pertaining to these assets; and (4) the husband chose not to file a counter-affidavit or a financial disclosure statement, and did not deny having the ability to pay. Beyer v. Parkis, 324 Ill.

Interim Fees (Cont'd)
App. 3d 305, 257 Ill. Dec. 406, 753 N.E.2d 1032, 2001 Ill. App. LEXIS 538 (1 Dist. 2001).

The legislature intended 750 ILCS 5/501(c-1) to apply in both pre- and post-decree proceedings. Beyer v. Parkis, 324 Ill. App. 3d 305, 257 Ill. Dec. 406, 753 N.E.2d 1032, 2001 Ill. App. LEXIS 538 (1 Dist. 2001).

The legislature's goal is to level the playing field by equalizing the parties' litigation resources, to which interim fees and costs provisions bears a rational relationship, and that goal is not facially unconstitutional. Kaufman, Litwin & Feinstein v. Edgar, 301 Ill. App. 3d 826, 235 Ill. Dec. 183, 704 N.E.2d 756 (1 Dist. 1998), appeal denied, 182 Ill. 2d 551, 236 Ill. Dec. 670, 707 N.E.2d 1240 (1999).

Interior Fee

The "equalization" factor of subsection (c-1) applies only to attorney fees and costs awarded during the period while the litigation is pending; however, nothing in the subsection requires the trial court to equalize fees in a contribution fee hearing. In re Delarco, 313 Ill. App. 3d 107, 245 Ill. Dec. 921, 728 N.E.2d 1278, 2000 Ill. App. LEXIS 302 (2 Dist. 2000).

Irreparable Harm

—Shown

The circuit court did not abuse its discretion in issuing preliminary injunction which enjoined wife's participation in family-owned tavern business while divorce was pending where petitioner husband showed by a preponderance of the evidence that he had a protectable interest in the tavern, there was no adequate legal remedy, and absent injunctive relief he would suffer irreparable harm because customers would not patronize the business when both were working, and injunctive relief was proper because the financial detriment which the injunctive order posed for the wife could be remedied if she sought temporary maintenance as the court recommended. Joerger v. Joerger, 221 Ill. App. 3d 400, 163 Ill. Dec. 796, 581 N.E.2d 1219 (4 Dist. 1991).

Jury Trial

Where plaintiff wife acknowledged validity of a prior Arkansas divorce decree, and her complaint was concerned solely with alimony, property division and attorney fees under the former Divorce Act (see now 750 ILCS 5/101 et seq.), defendant husband had no common law right to a jury trial, as such actions were traditionally chancery actions, and the right arose only if it was expressly conferred by statute. Sidwell v. Sidwell, 28 Ill. App. 3d 580, 328 N.E.2d 595 (4 Dist. 1975).

Legislative Intent

—No Prejudice to Parties

The intent of subsection (d) of this section is to make clear that the amount established for temporary support will not prejudice the parties at later hearings held to determine the amount of permanent support. In re Bush, 209 Ill. App. 3d 671, 153 Ill. Dec. 851, 567 N.E.2d 1078 (1 Dist. 1991).

—Res Judicata

Subsection (d) of this section is intended to preclude the application of res judicata principles to grants of temporary relief vis-à-vis permanent relief. In re Bush, 209 Ill. App. 3d 671, 153 Ill. Dec. 851, 567 N.E.2d 1078 (1 Dist. 1991).

Maintaining Status Quo

Where an injunction is issued to maintain the status quo, a party need not show he or she is likely to succeed on the merits after full hearing. Joerger v. Joerger, 221 Ill. App. 3d 400, 163 Ill. Dec. 796, 581 N.E.2d 1219 (4 Dist. 1991).

Where the court made clear in its findings and order that its primary concern was to protect value of family-owned tavern as a marital asset from dissipating, the court did not abuse its discretion in determining that the status quo most appropriate to protect the marital estate was to allow petitioner husband to continue to manage the tavern, and to restrain his wife from participating in its operation. Joerger v. Joerger, 221 Ill. App. 3d 400, 163 Ill. Dec. 796, 581 N.E.2d 1219 (4 Dist. 1991).

Maintenance

Where an order providing for temporary alimony was entered on December 23, 1975, when the provision of former section 15 of the Divorce Act (see now this section) was in effect, and the court, in entering its order of May 23, 1977, was merely enforcing this prior, valid order and the parties' agreed modification thereof, the trial court had authority to enter the order notwithstanding the fact that a notice of appeal was filed because the matter of temporary alimony was collateral to the divorce decree and did not substantially affect the appeal, and the order of May 23, 1977, requiring defendant to pay temporary alimony was proper, even though the court lacked jurisdiction to enter other orders because the appellate court stayed the judgment pending appeal. Horzely v. Horzely, 71 Ill. App. 3d 542, 28 Ill. Dec. 46, 390 N.E.2d 28 (1 Dist. 1979).

Notice

Knowledge of marital discord is not the same as actual notice of a pending marriage dissolution proceeding, and thus defendant wife's reliance on a statement made by plaintiff husband that he knew the couple was having marital difficulties as a basis for assertion that he had actual knowledge of pending dissolution proceeding could not stand. Henkel v. Morris, 155 Ill. App. 3d 816, 108 Ill. Dec. 469, 508 N.E.2d 780 (3 Dist. 1987).

When a temporary restraining order is issued without notice in a dissolution case, the court may specify a time to respond to the order in the order itself. In re Pick, 119 Ill. App. 3d 1061, 75 Ill. Dec. 865, 458 N.E.2d 33 (2 Dist. 1983).

The plain meaning of the words "after service of notice of motion" in subsection (c) of this section requires that "notice of motion" be served in order for this response period to apply. In re Pick, 119 Ill. App. 3d 1061, 75 Ill. Dec. 865, 458 N.E.2d 33 (2 Dist. 1983).

Operation of Business

Allowing husband and wife, in the midst of divorce proceedings, to continue to operate their family-owned tavern and requiring husband petitioner to seek damages after the tavern's value plummeted due to loss of customers was not the most practical and efficient remedy where testimony showed the customers would not patronize the tavern if both parties continued to operate; this potential loss of future profits and of customers made injunctive relief proper. Joerger v. Joerger, 221 Ill. App. 3d 400, 163 Ill. Dec. 796, 581 N.E.2d 1219 (4 Dist. 1991).

Past Due Child Support

Past due installments of child support are a vested right which the trial court cannot terminate or modify as to the amount or time of payment absent a valid defense. Sostak v. Sostak, 113 Ill. App. 3d 954, 69 Ill. Dec. 658, 447 N.E.2d 1345 (2 Dist. 1983).

Pretrial Order

—Not Binding

The trial judge is not bound by the pretrial order in formulating the order for permanent child support. In re Bush, 209 Ill. App. 3d 671, 153 Ill. Dec. 851, 567 N.E.2d 1078 (1 Dist. 1991).

Prospective Fees or Costs

Subdivision (a)(3) of this section alone would not provide a basis for award of prospective attorney fees or costs. In re Justema, 95 Ill. App. 3d 483, 51 Ill. Dec. 382, 420 N.E.2d 796 (2 Dist. 1981).

Purpose

—Amicable Settlements

The purpose of this section is to encourage amicable temporary settlements without establishing precedent for later hearings as to need or ability to pay support. In re Schroeder, 215 Ill. App. 3d 156, 158 Ill. Dec. 721, 574 N.E.2d 834 (4 Dist.), cert. denied, 141 Ill. 2d 560, 162 Ill. Dec. 508, 580 N.E.2d 134 (1991).

—Equality Between Spouses

Under former Ill.Rev.Stat., ch. 68, para. 22 (see now this section), a principal purpose in granting temporary support and attorney fees was to create a semblance of equality between the spouses during the prosecution of the suit. Kenly v. Kenly, 47 Ill. App. 3d 694, 8 Ill. Dec. 141, 365 N.E.2d 379 (1 Dist. 1977).

The purpose of this section is to assist an impecunious spouse who might otherwise be precluded by lack of funds from filing and maintaining an action for divorce. Pearson v. Pearson, 42 Ill. App. 3d 522, 1 Ill. Dec. 711, 356 N.E.2d 993 (2 Dist. 1976).

Remand

Under the former Divorce Act (see now 750 ILCS 5/101 et seq.), the appellate court did not set an alimony award but rather remanded the cause to the circuit court for further proceedings so that it could determine an appropriate award of alimony, because circumstances of the parties might have significantly changed in the time which intervened since the original hearing, and because there was a serious question presented as to what alimony would be best suited to the facts, questions which could be resolved in the circuit court. Sullivan v. Sullivan, 68 Ill. App. 3d 242, 24 Ill. Dec. 719, 385 N.E.2d 860 (5 Dist. 1979).

Sale of Marital Home

There is no authority to order a sale of the marital home except as provided by this Act. Blazina v. Blazina, 42 Ill. App. 3d 159, 1 Ill. Dec. 164, 356 N.E.2d 164 (2 Dist. 1976).

Settlement

—Effect

Preliminary injunction enjoining husband from spending income from his law practice was terminated by dissolution proceeding; however, termination of the injunction did not remove all matters in controversy between parties. In re Grauer, 133 Ill. App. 3d 1019, 88 Ill. Dec. 962, 479 N.E.2d 982 (1 Dist. 1985).

Standard of Review

The statutory test in deciding whether to grant alimony is what the court in its discretion determines is “fit, reasonable and just” and “equitable”, and the determination of the amount of alimony to be awarded is a decision which rests within the sound discretion of the trial court; the award is not to be set aside unless it is contrary to the manifest weight of the evidence. Hepner v. Hepner, 42 Ill. App. 3d 491, 1 Ill. Dec. 146, 356 N.E.2d 146 (3 Dist. 1976).

Upon review, appellate court will refuse to set aside an order for temporary award and attorney fees, except for an abuse of discretion. Roback v. Roback, 59 Ill. App. 2d 222, 207 N.E.2d 130 (2 Dist. 1965).

Temporary Custody

Where parents of minor child entered into a temporary custody agreement allowing child to live with father for period of six months, trial court had authority under subsection (a)(3) of this section to allow father to retain custody until father’s modification petition was heard. In re Venner, 146 Ill. App. 3d 238, 100 Ill. Dec. 82, 496 N.E.2d 1147 (1 Dist. 1986).

—Existing Custody Judgment

Even though the custody relief requested by father was “temporary,” where such relief was a modification of an existing custody judgment which was not more than two years old, section 610(a) of the Act (750 ILCS 5/610) was the governing statute rather than section 5/501(a)(3) (750 ILCS 5/501). In re Oehm, 252 Ill. App. 3d 311, 192 Ill. Dec. 74, 625 N.E.2d 34 (1 Dist. 1993).

Temporary Maintenance

—In General

Temporary orders are not binding on the trial court and are terminated and superseded by provisions of the final decree, and are effective until resolution of prayers for dissolution. In re Schroeder, 215 Ill. App. 3d 156, 158 Ill. Dec. 721, 574 N.E.2d 834 (4 Dist.), cert. denied, 141 Ill. 2d 560, 162 Ill. Dec. 508, 580 N.E.2d 134 (1991).

—Cohabitation

Fact that the parties were living under one roof did not indicate that the complaint was filed in bad faith; however, in actions for separate maintenance and in actions for divorce based upon desertion, where the element of living apart is essential to establish probable cause or grounds on which to base the action, the fact that the parties live together under one roof may, under certain circumstances, indicate an absence of good faith in the filing of such action. Roback v. Roback, 59 Ill. App. 2d 222, 207 N.E.2d 130 (2 Dist. 1965).

—Factors Considered

The amount to be awarded as temporary support pending the suit should be controlled by the necessities of the wife as shown by the circumstances, and by the financial ability of the husband to make the necessary contributions to the end that in the prosecution of her suit she shall be placed upon an equality with him. Roback v. Roback, 59 Ill. App. 2d 222, 207 N.E.2d 130 (2 Dist. 1965).

The amount of temporary award is not limited solely by the husband’s income, but the amount of property possessed by him may also be taken into consideration. Roback v. Roback, 59 Ill. App. 2d 222, 207 N.E.2d 130 (2 Dist. 1965).

—Jurisdiction

Where plaintiff offered proof which was considered as conclusive by the trial court that the defendant was a resident of the forum county when divorce action was filed, and when he was served with process, and defendant offered no evidence on the issue of his domicile or otherwise, the court had jurisdiction over the person of the defendant and the subject matter of the suit, and temporary support order was valid and in full force and effect, and the judgment for the plaintiff and against the defendant in the sum of $2,600, based on the payments provided for in such order, was a valid judgment. Hirsh v. Hirsh, 81 Ill. App. 2d 354, 225 N.E.2d 42 (2 Dist. 1967).

—Upheld

Where plaintiff’s attorney did not request a hearing to advise the trial court that time spent by defendant’s counsel did not justify fee, the trial judge did not abuse his discretion in allowing said fee as part of temporary maintenance. McManus v. McManus, 37 Ill. App. 3d 658, 347 N.E.2d 109 (1 Dist. 1975).

Temporary Restraining Order

—In General

The term “temporary restraining order,” in section 11-101 of the Code of Civil Procedure (735 ILCS 5/11-101) and this section are describing the same type of relief. In re Pick, 119 Ill. App. 3d 1061, 75 Ill. Dec. 865, 458 N.E.2d 33 (2 Dist. 1983).

—Irreparable Injury

Although a trial court could have based its finding of irreparable injury upon the moving affidavit or other evidence, allegations and other unsworn testimony did not constitute evidence. Bashwiner v. Bashwiner, 126 Ill. App. 3d 365, 81 Ill. Dec. 359, 466 N.E.2d 1161 (1 Dist. 1984).

—Notice of Hearing

The granting of a temporary restraining order without notice is considered most drastic and is appropriate only under the most extreme and urgent circumstances. Bashwiner v. Bashwiner, 126 Ill. App. 3d 365, 81 Ill. Dec. 359, 466 N.E.2d 1161 (1 Dist. 1984).

Where a period of several days elapsed between respondent’s petition to remove the parties’ children from this state and petitioner’s motion for injunction to stop the removal, and between the motion and the date upon which court would set a hearing date, and where petitioner’s attorney was apparently readily accessible, it was error to issue the injunction without notice. Bashwiner v. Bashwiner, 126 Ill. App. 3d 365, 81 Ill. Dec. 359, 466 N.E.2d 1161 (1 Dist. 1984).

—Removal of Children from Jurisdiction

Where petitioner’s allegation that wife would remove their children from the state in violation of a prior court order prohibiting removal contained no factual basis for the allegation, and it was a mere conclusion, there were insufficient grounds for issuance of a temporary restraining order. Bashwiner v. Bashwiner, 126 Ill. App. 3d 365, 81 Ill. Dec. 359, 466 N.E.2d 1161 (1 Dist. 1984).

—Standard of Review

In reviewing the issuance of a temporary restraining order without notice, the critical inquiry is whether in the minutes or hours necessary to procure defendant’s appearance, defendant could and would take action as to obstruct the court from dealing justly and effectively with the issues in dispute. Bashwiner v. Bashwiner, 126 Ill. App. 3d 365, 81 Ill. Dec. 359, 466 N.E.2d 1161 (1 Dist. 1984).

Travel Expenses

Trial court did not abuse its discretion in denying husband’s request for temporary relief to pay his travel expenses from Sweden to Chicago so he could participate in proceedings where no information was provided by husband concerning the amount needed for

Travel Expenses (Cont'd)
his trip nor was any reason given why it could not be accumulated from his weekly income. In re Thornqvist, 79 Ill. App. 3d 791, 35 Ill. Dec. 342, 399 N.E.2d 176 (1 Dist. 1979).

Trial court exercised a proper discretion in ordering defendant to provide his wife and children with suitable transportation pending the appeal. Glassman v. Glassman, 133 Ill. App. 2d 609, 273 N.E.2d 177 (1 Dist. 1971).

Visitation

Trial court was empowered to award visitation of infant to grandparents despite the silence of this Act on the issue. Hawkins v. Hawkins, 102 Ill. App. 3d 1037, 58 Ill. Dec. 620, 430 N.E.2d 652 (3 Dist. 1981).

Voluntary Dismissal

Where hearing was on preliminary issues of temporary maintenance, support, and fees and did not relate to the issues of the dissolution action itself which petitioner sought to dismiss, no trial or hearing had begun for purposes of section 52 of the former Civil Practice Act (see now 735 ILCS 5/2-1009). In re Mostow, 95 Ill. App. 3d 915, 51 Ill. Dec. 317, 420 N.E.2d 731 (1 Dist. 1981).

The trial court properly refused to bar petitioner from seeking temporary maintenance in the future if she filed another dissolution action; such a penalty clearly contravened the express statutory language that the right to dismiss prior to trial is absolute. In re Mostow, 95 Ill. App. 3d 915, 51 Ill. Dec. 317, 420 N.E.2d 731 (1 Dist. 1981).

Waiver

—Vested Right

Under certain circumstances, such as where parties agree to reduce payments, vested right to past due installments of child support may be waived. Sostak v. Sostak, 113 Ill. App. 3d 954, 69 Ill. Dec. 658, 447 N.E.2d 1345 (2 Dist. 1983).

LEGAL PERIODICALS

For article, "'Leveling the Playing Field' in Divorce: Questions and Answers About the New Law," see 85 Ill. B.J. 410 (1997).

For article, "Hewitt v. Hewitt — A Dissent," see 70 Ill. B.J. 312 (1982).

For article, "Wisconsin, Illinois, Ontario — Three Roads to Marital Property Law Reform," see 12 Loy. U. Chi. L.J. 1 (1980-81).

For article, "Intent to Recovery May Destroy A Marital Settlement Agreement," see 66 Ill. B.J. 464 (1978).

RESEARCH REFERENCES

Court's authority to award temporary alimony or suit money in action for divorce, separate maintenance, or alimony where the existence of a valid marriage is contested. 34 ALR4th 814.

Order awarding temporary support or living expenses upon separation of unmarried partners pending contract action based on services relating to personal relationship. 35 ALR4th 409.

Reconciliation as affecting decree for limited divorce, separation, alimony, separate maintenance, or spousal support. 36 ALR4th 502.

Prejudgment interest awards in divorce cases. 62 ALR4th 156.

Death of obligor spouse as affecting alimony. 79 ALR4th 10.

750 ILCS 5/501.1 Dissolution action stay

Sec. 501.1. *Dissolution action stay.* (a) Upon service of a summons and petition or praecipe filed under the Illinois Marriage and Dissolution of Marriage Act [750 ILCS 5/101 et seq.] or upon the filing of the respondent's appearance in the proceeding, whichever first occurs, a dissolution action stay shall be in effect against both parties and their agents and employees, without bond or further notice, until a final judgement is entered, the proceeding is dismissed, or until further order of the court:

(1) restraining both parties from transferring, encumbering, concealing, destroying, spending, damaging, or in any way disposing of any property, without the consent of the other party or an order of the court, except in the usual course of business, for the necessities of life, or for reasonable costs, expenses, and attorney's fees arising from the proceeding, as well as requiring each party to provide written notice to the other party and his or her attorney of any proposed extraordinary expenditure or transaction;

(2) restraining both parties from physically abusing, harassing, intimidating, striking, or interfering with the personal liberty of the other party or the minor children of either party; and

(3) restraining both parties from removing any minor child of either party from the State of Illinois or from concealing any such child from the other party, without the consent of the other party or an order of the court.

The restraint provided in this subsection (a) does not operate to make unavailable any of the remedies provided in the Illinois Domestic Violence Act of 1986 [750 ILCS 60/101 et seq.].

A restraint of the parties' actions under this Section does not affect the rights of a bona fide purchaser or mortgagee whose interest in real property or whose beneficial interest in real property under an Illinois land trust was acquired before the filing of a lis pendens notice under Section 2-1901 of the Code of Civil Procedure [735 ILCS 5/2-1901].

(b) Notice of any proposed extraordinary expenditure or transaction, as required by subsection (a), shall be given as soon as practicable, but not less than 7 days before the proposed date for the carrying out or commencement of the carrying out of the extraordinary expenditure or transaction, except in an emergency, in which event notice shall be given as soon as practicable under the circumstances. If proper notice is given and if the party receiving the notice does not object by filing a petition for injunctive relief under the Code of Civil Procedure [735 ILCS 5/1-101 et seq.] within 7 days of receipt of the notice, the carrying out of the proposed extraordinary expenditure or transaction is not a violation of the dissolution action stay. The dissolution action stay shall remain in full force and effect against both parties for 14 days after the date of filing of a petition for injunctive relief by the objecting party (or a shorter period if the court so orders); and no extension beyond that 14 day period shall be granted by the court. For good cause shown, a party may file a petition for a reduction in time with respect to any 7 day notice requirement under this subsection.

(c) A party making any extraordinary expenditure or carrying out any extraordinary transaction after a dissolution action stay is in effect shall account promptly to the court and to the other party for all of those expenditures and transactions. This obligation to account applies throughout the pendency of the proceeding, irrespective of (i) any notice given by any party as to any proposed extraordinary expenditure or transaction, (ii) any filing of an objection and petition under this Section or the absence of any such filing, or (iii) any court ruling as to an issue presented to it by either party.

(d) If the party making an extraordinary expenditure or transaction fails to provide proper notice or if despite proper notice the other party filed a petition and prevailed on that petition, and the extraordinary expenditure or transaction results in a loss of income or reduction in the amount or in the value of property, there is a presumption of dissipation of property, equal to the amount of the loss or reduction, charged against the party for purposes of property distribution under Section 503 [750 ILCS 5/503].

(e) In a proceeding filed under this Act, the summons shall provide notice of the entry of the automatic dissolution action stay in a form as required by applicable rules.

(Source: P.A. 87-881; 88-24, § 5.)

Note.

This section was Ill.Rev.Stat., Ch. 40, para. 501.1.

CASE NOTES

Analysis

Constitutionality
Parentage Act
Standing
Violation Not Shown

Constitutionality

The excessively broad sweep of subdivision (a)(1) of this section to include a restraint affecting property that cannot be considered in any way a marital asset, was not a rational means of accomplishing the legislative purpose, to prevent the dissipation and concealment of marital assets once proceedings have begun to dissolve a marriage; therefore, the subsection exceeds constitutional bounds violation of the guarantee of substantive due process. Messenger v. Edgar, 157 Ill. 2d 162, 191 Ill. Dec. 65, 623 N.E.2d 310 (1993).

Parentage Act

References in the Parentage Act, 750 ILCS 45/1 et seq., to the Marriage and Dissolution of Marriage Act do not confer on the courts all of the powers conferred by the latter Act; in particular, in proceedings under the Parentage Act the court lacks the power to enjoin a party from removing the child from the state. Hall v. Melton, 314 Ill. App. 3d 476, 247 Ill. Dec. 295, 732 N.E.2d 11, 2000 Ill. App. LEXIS 584 (1 Dist. 2000).

Standing

By operation of the challenged portion of a section restraining parties to a marriage dissolution action from transferring or disposing of property, except under certain circumstances, plaintiff sustained a direct injury to a legally cognizable interest, the right to unfettered property, which injury could be redressed by the grant of declaratory judgment. Accordingly, plaintiff had standing to bring the action. Messenger v. Edgar, 157 Ill. 2d 162, 191 Ill. Dec. 65, 623 N.E.2d 310 (1993).

Violation Not Shown

Since deceased changed the beneficiary on his life insurance policy more than two months before he filed his petition for dissolution of marriage the trial court correctly found he did not violate the automatic stay provision. Schultz v. Schultz, 297 Ill. App. 3d 102, 231 Ill. Dec. 598, 696 N.E.2d 1169 (2 Dist. 1998).

750 ILCS 5/502 Agreement

Sec. 502. *Agreement.* (a) To promote amicable settlement of disputes between parties to a marriage attendant upon the dissolution of their marriage, the parties may enter into a written or oral agreement containing provisions for disposition of any property owned by either of them, maintenance of either of them and support, custody and visitation of their children.

(b) The terms of the agreement, except those providing for the support, custody and visitation of children, are binding upon the court unless it finds, after considering the economic circumstances of the parties and any other relevant evidence produced by the parties, on their own motion or on request of the court, that the agreement is unconscionable.

(c) If the court finds the agreement unconscionable, it may request the parties to submit a revised agreement or upon hearing, may make orders for the disposition of property, maintenance, child support and other matters.

(d) Unless the agreement provides to the contrary, its terms shall be set forth in the judgment, and the parties shall be ordered to perform under such terms, or if the agreement provides that its terms shall not be set forth in the judgment, the judgment shall identify the agreement and state that the court has approved its terms.

(e) Terms of the agreement set forth in the judgment are enforceable by all remedies available for enforcement of a judgment, including contempt, and are enforceable as contract terms.

(f) Except for terms concerning the support, custody or visitation of children, the judgment may expressly preclude or limit modification of terms set forth in the judgment if the agreement so provides. Otherwise, terms of an agreement set forth in the judgment are automatically modified by modification of the judgment.

(Source: P.A. 83-216.)

Note.

This section was Ill.Rev.Stat., Ch. 40, para. 502.

CASE NOTES

Analysis

Alteration
Ambiguity
—Not Shown
—Shown
Applicability
Attorney Fees
Authority of Court
—In General
—Discretion
—Duty of Court
Back Payments
Binding Agreement
Burden of Proof
Cancellation
Change in Circumstances
—Evidence
—Not Shown

—Shown
—Tax Status of Parties
Child Custody
Child Support
—In General
—College Expenses
—Modification
—Variable Amounts
Coercion
—Not Shown
—Proof
Consideration
Construction of Agreement
—In General
—Child Support
—Express Language
—Parol Evidence
—Parties' Intent
—Waiver of Rights
Contempt
Declaratory Judgment
Dissolution
Duress
—Burden of Proof
—Defined
—Not Shown
Duty to Disclose
Evidentiary Hearing
—Factors Considered
—Permitted
—Required
Fraud
—Evidence
—Sufficiency of Allegations
Future Modifiability
Garnishment
—Ambiguous Agreement Language
Household Expenses
Installment Contract
Insurance
Limitations
Maintenance
—Future Employment
—Modification
—Periodic Payments
—Public Policy
—Remarriage of Recipient
Merger of Settlement Agreement
Modification
—Agreement by Parties
—Approval
—Best Interest of Child
—Certain Conditions
—Change in Circumstances
—Child Support
—College Expenses
—Combination
—Discretion
—Education Expenses
—Enforceability
—Factors
—Grounds
—Jurisdiction
—Maintenance
—Medical Treatment
—Military Pension
—Not Permitted
—Permitted
—Petitioning the Court
—Precatory Language
—Preclusion
—Property
—Rights of Parties
—Unallocated Support
—Unconscionability
New Hearing
Oral Agreement
Order Vacating Decree
—Improper
Post-Judgment Procedure
Property Rights
—In General
—Adjudication
—Agreement Upheld
—Challenge
—Illustrative Cases
—Invalid Divorce Decree
—Transfers
—Vacating Settlement
Purpose
—Amicable Settlement
—Property Arrangements
Remarriage
—Modification of Support
—Restraint
Sale of Home
Separation Agreement
—In General
—Approval
—Binding
—Grounds to Set Aside
—Rejection
—Scope
—Uncontested
—Upheld
Settlement Negotiations
Standard of Review
Stipulation
—Ambiguous Term
—Not Valid
Tax Deduction
Termination of Agreement
—Reconciliation
Terms of Agreement
—Disposition of Property
—Educational Expenses
—Enforcement
—Merger into Foreign Judgment
—Merger into Judgment
—Oral Agreement Incorporated
—Religious Upbringing of Children
Unconscionability
—In General
—Considerations
—Contribution of Parties
—Defined
—Discretion
—Evidence
—Fear
—Full and Fair Disclosure
—Haste
—Inequities in Agreement
—Not Shown
—Opportunity to Investigate
—Parties' Economic Positions
—Shown
—Standard of Review
—Unfairness
Validity of Agreement
—In General
—Coercion, Duress and Fraud
—Conscionability
—Murder of Party
—Mutual Mistake
—Newly Discovered Evidence
—Presumptions
—Voluntariness
Waiver

Alteration

Where husband, with advice of counsel, signed a document which settled pending litigation, and the deletion of purported findings made by the court was not a material alteration in the circum-

Alteration (Cont'd)
stances, the order eventually entered by the court mirrored the operative provisions of that agreement; husband was properly bound to its terms. In re Maher, 95 Ill. App. 3d 1039, 51 Ill. Dec. 586, 420 N.E.2d 1144 (2 Dist. 1981).

Ambiguity

—Not Shown

Where agreement between parties was a transparent attempt to cloak the ordinary settlement and provision for child support in the garb of a lump sum settlement, and the details of the agreement immediately betrayed its actual identity and purpose, there was no ambiguity in the judgment of dissolution. Weber v. Weber, 77 Ill. App. 3d 383, 32 Ill. Dec. 930, 396 N.E.2d 43 (1 Dist. 1979).

—Shown

Provisions of an agreement regarding a contemplated increase in husband's income and recognition that the payments were much larger than usual based on the husband's income made the agreement ambiguous. In re Corkey, 269 Ill. App. 3d 392, 206 Ill. Dec. 862, 645 N.E.2d 1384 (2 Dist. 1995).

Applicability

Restriction of terms of judgment to the provisions of agreement does not apply to terms affecting support, custody, or visitation of children. Bayuk v. Bayuk, 79 Ill. App. 3d 877, 35 Ill. Dec. 159, 398 N.E.2d 1109 (1 Dist. 1979); In re Glickman, 211 Ill. App. 3d 792, 156 Ill. Dec. 162, 570 N.E.2d 638 (1 Dist. 1991).

Attorney Fees

This section does not indicate that the parties' agreement as to the division and allocation of liabilities is somehow binding upon third-party creditors, including prior counsel. Lee v. Lee, 302 Ill. App. 3d 607, 236 Ill. Dec. 222, 707 N.E.2d 67 (1 Dist. 1998).

A spouse's challenge to a supplemental judgment for dissolution which provided that the spouse was to pay her own attorney fees was defeated where the spouse could hardly complain she had insufficient funds to pay the fees when the separation agreement provided funds to her specifically for this purpose. In re Morris, 147 Ill. App. 3d 380, 100 Ill. Dec. 811, 497 N.E.2d 1173 (1 Dist. 1986).

Courts are not bound by this section to parties' settlement agreement relating to the amount to be paid by a client to her attorney, particularly where the trial court's authority to make the award is expressly provided for in 750 ILCS 5/508. In re Bennett, 131 Ill. App. 3d 1050, 87 Ill. Dec. 305, 476 N.E.2d 1297 (2 Dist. 1985).

Authority of Court

—In General

Where the trial court, in response to the former wife's motion to enforce the judgment of divorce, required the former husband to insure the daughter under the former husband's new wife's insurance plan, this was an improper modification of the divorce judgment, which did not specify how the former husband was to insure the daughter; while orders of support were modifiable under 750 ILCS 5/502(f), 510(a), orders of support were not modifiable unless a modification was requested, and the former wife had not requested a modification in the instant case. In re Marriage of Gowdy, 352 Ill. App. 3d 301, 287 Ill. Dec. 610, 816 N.E.2d 372, 2004 Ill. App. LEXIS 1118 (3 Dist. 2004).

Since this act provides that the parties' agreement binds the court, the terms of the marital agreement prevail over statutory directions and permit the court to enter judgment on agreed provisions for disposition of property and maintenance, even if the court could not have ordered such dispositions in the absence of the agreement. In re Sheetz, 254 Ill. App. 3d 695, 194 Ill. Dec. 38, 627 N.E.2d 154 (1 Dist. 1993).

The circuit court has the authority to modify a child support provision in a dissolution of marriage judgment that was entered in accordance with a settlement agreement. Falat v. Falat, 201 Ill. App. 3d 320, 147 Ill. Dec. 33, 559 N.E.2d 33 (1 Dist. 1990).

The courts of Illinois have long made a distinction between a property settlement in kind, sometimes referred to as alimony in gross, which requires no periodic payments, and a settlement which does require future payments of alimony (now maintenance) or of child support. In the former situation, the courts have viewed the matter as a contractual right and refused to interfere in the absence of fraud, duress or some other form of over-reaching; in the latter case, that of periodic payments, a court has the authority to intervene at any time. In re Bowman, 89 Ill. App. 3d 110, 44 Ill. Dec. 445, 411 N.E.2d 567 (4 Dist. 1980).

Circuit court had authority to alter child support provisions of settlement agreement. Powers v. Powers, 69 Ill. App. 3d 485, 26 Ill. Dec. 452, 388 N.E.2d 76 (1 Dist. 1979).

Earlier order of the circuit court, which stated that the child support provisions of the judgment of divorce could be modified, was not void. Powers v. Powers, 69 Ill. App. 3d 485, 26 Ill. Dec. 452, 388 N.E.2d 76 (1 Dist. 1979).

—Discretion

The circuit court can properly enforce provisions of a settlement agreement incorporated into a divorce judgment, for it possesses considerable discretion in modifying support judgments. In re Moriarty, 132 Ill. App. 3d 895, 88 Ill. Dec. 222, 478 N.E.2d 537 (1 Dist. 1985).

A trial court is not controlled by the terms of a proposed property settlement agreement, but may adopt or reject it as seems consistent and proper from the situations of the parties. Mayeur v. Mayeur, 42 Ill. App. 3d 7, 355 N.E.2d 358 (3 Dist. 1976).

—Duty of Court

Public policy did not require the trial court to make a full inquiry into all assets of the parties where both parties were represented by counsel and were in agreement as to all terms of the property agreement. Zeeb v. Zeeb, 76 Ill. App. 3d 894, 32 Ill. Dec. 430, 395 N.E.2d 660 (5 Dist. 1979).

In an action involving the welfare and support of minor children, the appellate district and the trial court not only have full and complete jurisdiction of the award and provision made for support of the children, but it is the duty of the court in which the action has been brought to ascertain all the pertinent facts and circumstances and to determine whether the award is fair and equitable or should be modified. Weber v. Weber, 77 Ill. App. 3d 383, 32 Ill. Dec. 930, 396 N.E.2d 43 (1 Dist. 1979).

Back Payments

Trial court was justified in ordering husband to pay back payments of child support, based on the public policy against non-court approved child support modification and in favor of the best interests of the child, where his argument for not paying was based on an alleged agreement between him and ex-wife stating that since one of the two children moved and lived with him in New York, he was relieved of his obligations with regard to the remaining child who still resided with ex-wife. Baker v. Baker, 193 Ill. App. 3d 294, 140 Ill. Dec. 303, 549 N.E.2d 954 (4 Dist. 1990).

Binding Agreement

A separation agreement, with regard to property, is binding upon the court unless the court finds, after considering the circumstances of the parties and any other relevant evidence, that the separation agreement is unconscionable. Reininger v. Reininger, 67 Ill. App. 3d 21, 23 Ill. Dec. 752, 384 N.E.2d 546 (4 Dist. 1978).

Burden of Proof

The rule that terms of a separation agreement are binding upon the court presumes there is a valid agreement, and it is the burden of the party asserting the agreement to establish its existence by clear and convincing evidence. In re Chaltin, 153 Ill. App. 3d 810, 106 Ill. Dec. 631, 506 N.E.2d 338 (2 Dist. 1987).

For a marital settlement agreement to be valid, the parties must have had the necessary mental capacity and understanding to enter into the agreement; the burden rests upon the party challenging the agreement to prove lack of capacity or understanding. In re Morris, 147 Ill. App. 3d 380, 100 Ill. Dec. 811, 497 N.E.2d 1173 (1 Dist. 1986).

Cancellation

Property settlements which have been assented to by parties may not be cancelled solely upon the withdrawal of one party's assent prior to entry of the judgment; agreements in settlement of pending litigation become effective when arrived at unless the parties have subjected their effectiveness to the occurrence of other contingencies. In re Maher, 95 Ill. App. 3d 1039, 51 Ill. Dec. 586, 420 N.E.2d 1144 (2 Dist. 1981).

Change in Circumstances

—Evidence

The court erred in striking petition, thereby precluding petitioner father from offering evidence of the changes in circumstances upon which he sought modification of divorce decree, where allegations, if established by evidence, would have constituted material changes in circumstances requiring modification of the child support responsibilities of the parties. Weinert v. Weinert, 105 Ill. App. 3d 56, 60 Ill. Dec. 920, 433 N.E.2d 1158 (2 Dist. 1982).

—Not Shown

Where parties freely negotiated that each should share their obligations and responsibilities in the manner specified by the terms of the settlement agreement, subsequent displeasure with the facts as they existed at the time of the agreement, and the actions taken to rectify these facts in the future, neither constituted a change in circumstances nor justified an increase in child support payments. In re Stadheim, 170 Ill. App. 3d 19, 120 Ill. Dec. 373, 523 N.E.2d 1284 (1 Dist. 1988).

—Shown

Where custodial parent has argued for an increase in child support because cost of living had increased, children had grown older, petitioner husband's income had substantially increased, and the expenses of the children had substantially increased since the entry of the judgment, a substantial change of circumstances had occurred. In re Glickman, 211 Ill. App. 3d 792, 156 Ill. Dec. 162, 570 N.E.2d 638 (1 Dist. 1991).

—Tax Status of Parties

Wife's actions in attempting to change parties' tax status should have been held to be a substantial change in circumstances requiring modification of the terms of the agreement. In re Mass, 102 Ill. App. 3d 984, 58 Ill. Dec. 941, 431 N.E.2d 1 (1 Dist. 1981).

Child Custody

The mediation provision of the parties' joint parenting agreement was a custody provision and, therefore, the trial court was not bound by the agreement, where the mediation provision addressed disagreements between the parties on major decisions affecting the education, health, or religion of their minor child. In re Duffy, 307 Ill. App. 3d 257, 240 Ill. Dec. 805, 718 N.E.2d 286 (2 Dist. 1999).

Child Support

—In General

Agreements for child support aid the trial court, but they do not relieve the trial court of the responsibility for ordering child support in accord with the best interest of the children. In re Sheetz, 254 Ill. App. 3d 695, 194 Ill. Dec. 38, 627 N.E.2d 154 (1 Dist. 1993).

The parties cannot by agreement waive the right to challenge child support provisions in settlement agreements or court orders. In re Sheetz, 254 Ill. App. 3d 695, 194 Ill. Dec. 38, 627 N.E.2d 154 (1 Dist. 1993).

—College Expenses

A provision for the payment of a child's college expenses is a matter pertaining to children and in the nature of child support. In re Loffredi, 232 Ill. App. 3d 709, 173 Ill. Dec. 933, 597 N.E.2d 907 (3 Dist. 1992).

—Modification

Trial court's ruling was erroneous where it denied increase in child support based on provision in separation agreement relating to child support payments which stated that there would be no consideration of change in circumstances until the husband's income increased to $53,000. Bayuk v. Bayuk, 79 Ill. App. 3d 877, 35 Ill. Dec. 159, 398 N.E.2d 1109 (1 Dist. 1979).

In matters regarding child support, the court has authority to award support where it is in the best interest of the child. Bayuk v. Bayuk, 79 Ill. App. 3d 877, 35 Ill. Dec. 159, 398 N.E.2d 1109 (1 Dist. 1979).

—Variable Amounts

Marital agreement between husband and wife could not, and as a matter of law, provide for a fixed and invariable amount to be paid for support of minor children and the award must necessarily be modified if required for the welfare of the minors. Weber v. Weber, 77 Ill. App. 3d 383, 32 Ill. Dec. 930, 396 N.E.2d 43 (1 Dist. 1979).

Coercion

—Not Shown

With the exception of respondent's immediate rejection of agreement, no event surrounding the finalization of settlement terms indicated any advantage taken of respondent or deprivation of her free will which supported her theory of coercion or duress. In re Smith, 164 Ill. App. 3d 1011, 115 Ill. Dec. 925, 518 N.E.2d 450 (1 Dist. 1987).

A wife's claim of coercion, based on allegations that she was upset, emotionally distraught, and under great pressure on the date of the prove-up, was unfounded where the wife had had three attorneys, took part in depositions, and had discussed settlement terms well in advance. In re Riedy, 130 Ill. App. 3d 311, 85 Ill. Dec. 614, 474 N.E.2d 28 (2 Dist. 1985).

Where a divorced wife failed to provide any support for her allegations that she was coerced into a property settlement agreement by four attorneys and that she did not have a choice as to whether to enter into the agreement, the allegation of coercion was insufficient to invalidate the settlement agreement. In re Black, 133 Ill. App. 3d 59, 87 Ill. Dec. 831, 477 N.E.2d 1359 (2 Dist. 1985).

—Proof

Coercion, fraud or duress must be proved by clear and convincing evidence. In re Smith, 164 Ill. App. 3d 1011, 115 Ill. Dec. 925, 518 N.E.2d 450 (1 Dist. 1987).

Consideration

Where respondent raises separation agreement as a defense and the agreement does not recite any consideration, respondent under these circumstances must show consideration for the agreement. In re Dodge, 150 Ill. App. 3d 486, 103 Ill. Dec. 816, 501 N.E.2d 1354 (2 Dist. 1986).

Construction of Agreement

—In General

A settlement agreement, rather than 750 ILCS 5/513, controlled the disposition of the case, because parties in a dissolution proceeding may voluntarily settle their property interests. In re Holderrieth, 181 Ill. App. 3d 199, 129 Ill. Dec. 896, 536 N.E.2d 946 (1 Dist. 1989).

As a general rule, provisions of settlement agreements will be interpreted by the normal rules in the construction of contracts. In re Hawkins, 160 Ill. App. 3d 71, 111 Ill. Dec. 897, 513 N.E.2d 143 (5 Dist. 1987).

For a case discussing applicability of rules of construction of contracts to divorce decree and property settlement agreement, see Kite v. Kite, 19 Ill. App. 3d 932, 312 N.E.2d 366 (1 Dist. 1974).

—Child Support

While all divorce judgments should be reasonably construed, those that seek to provide support to children receive special care and consideration of the courts. In re Moriarty, 132 Ill. App. 3d 895, 88 Ill. Dec. 222, 478 N.E.2d 537 (1 Dist. 1985).

—Express Language

If parties to a marital settlement agreement intend, on dissolution, to preclude judicial modification of maintenance as to amount, it may be better practice to do so in clear and express terms in a paragraph separate from that limiting termination of maintenance. In re Brent, 263 Ill. App. 3d 916, 200 Ill. Dec. 799, 635 N.E.2d 1382 (4 Dist. 1994).

If the language of agreement does not expressly preclude or limit modification of its terms, it is error to hold the maintenance nonmodifiable. In re Scott, 205 Ill. App. 3d 561, 150 Ill. Dec. 868, 563 N.E.2d 995 (4 Dist. 1990).

To take advantage of this section which except for terms concerning the support, custody, or visitation of children, allows judgment entered in a dissolution of marriage proceeding to expressly preclude or limit modification of the terms set forth therein if the separation agreement so provides, the parties must express an intent in clear language. In re Chalkley, 99 Ill. App. 3d 478, 55 Ill. Dec. 262, 426 N.E.2d 237 (1 Dist. 1981); In re Silber, 176 Ill. App. 3d 853, 126 Ill. Dec. 283, 531 N.E.2d 910 (1 Dist. 1988); In re Sutton,

Construction of Agreement (Cont'd)

—Express Language (Cont'd)
178 Ill. App. 3d 928, 128 Ill. Dec. 37, 533 N.E.2d 1125 (3 Dist. 1989); In re Scott, 205 Ill. App. 3d 561, 150 Ill. Dec. 868, 563 N.E.2d 995 (4 Dist. 1990).

Where settlement agreement and divorce decree stated in abundantly clear language that the respondent was to keep in force and unencumbered all of the insurance policies on his life, totalling $46,000, and that he was to pay the premiums thereon, and maintain the petitioner as "irrevocable beneficiary thereunder," such provisions were without ambiguity, and thus no question of construction arose. Brandel v. Brandel, 69 Ill. App. 2d 264, 216 N.E.2d 21 (2 Dist. 1966).

—Parol Evidence
Where the language of the agreement was ambiguous, parol evidence, including letters between the attorneys, would be admissible in determining the true intent and agreement of the parties as to whether a lump sum or periodic payment of maintenance was contemplated. Sudler v. Sudler, 6 Ill. App. 3d 546, 286 N.E.2d 113 (2 Dist. 1972).

—Parties' Intent
The interpretation of a property settlement agreement is a question of law, and a court should construe the agreement to give effect to the intent of the parties. Wilson v. Wilson, 225 Ill. App. 3d 115, 168 Ill. Dec. 214, 589 N.E.2d 614 (1 Dist. 1992).

The parties' intent must be ascertained from reading the language of a property settlement agreement as a whole, giving the words their plain and obvious meaning. Wilson v. Wilson, 225 Ill. App. 3d 115, 168 Ill. Dec. 214, 589 N.E.2d 614 (1 Dist. 1992).

A court should construe settlement agreements incorporated into divorce judgments to give effect to the intentions of the parties. In re Moriarty, 132 Ill. App. 3d 895, 88 Ill. Dec. 222, 478 N.E.2d 537 (1 Dist. 1985).

The settlement provisions incorporated within a decree of divorce should be construed so as to give effect to the intention of the parties. Schwartz v. Schwartz, 69 Ill. App. 2d 128, 216 N.E.2d 505 (1 Dist. 1966).

In interpreting the provisions of a divorce decree where the specific items constituting the quid pro quo for the agreement are recited therein, it is the intention of the parties as expressed in the agreement that the court seeks to ascertain. Brandel v. Brandel, 69 Ill. App. 2d 264, 216 N.E.2d 21 (2 Dist. 1966).

—Waiver of Rights
Although the consent order did waive "any and all other rights, including property rights," it did not go beyond general boilerplate language and without even a mention of beneficial interest in any property in the waiver, much less a specific waiver of any beneficial interest in the specific property at issue, the boilerplate language was not sufficient to waive ex-husband's beneficial interest in the proceeds from the certificates of deposit or the annuity. Deida v. Murphy, 271 Ill. App. 3d 296, 207 Ill. Dec. 616, 647 N.E.2d 1109 (5 Dist. 1995).

Contempt
Trial court's grant of a contempt petition with regard to maintenance and child support results in the issuance of a "rule to show cause." Berto v. Berto, 344 Ill. App. 3d 705, 279 Ill. Dec. 482, 800 N.E.2d 550, 2003 Ill. App. LEXIS 1383 (2 Dist. 2003).

Provisions regarding maintenance and child support contained in a marital settlement agreement and incorporated into a judgment of dissolution are enforced through contempt proceedings under 750 ILCS 5/502(e); the contempt petition is known as a "petition for rule to show cause." Berto v. Berto, 344 Ill. App. 3d 705, 279 Ill. Dec. 482, 800 N.E.2d 550, 2003 Ill. App. LEXIS 1383 (2 Dist. 2003).

Order finding that husband was guilty of contempt based not only upon the failure to pay money due under the settlement agreement, but also on his wilful failure to further comply with the decree, was improperly vague. Jones v. Jones, 336 Ill. App. 56, 82 N.E.2d 823 (1 Dist. 1948).

Declaratory Judgment
Inasmuch as complaint pled the existence of an agreement in settlement of pending litigation and requested that the court construe the agreement's terms and declare the rights of the parties, it constituted a request for the construction of a contract and was properly brought in a suit for a declaratory judgment. Stern v. Stern, 105 Ill. App. 3d 805, 61 Ill. Dec. 567, 434 N.E.2d 1164 (2 Dist. 1982).

To the extent that the trial court may have declined to adjudicate plaintiff's complaint for declaratory judgment because of possibility that dissolution of marriage proceedings might eventually have ensued, its dismissal of the complaint was error. Stern v. Stern, 105 Ill. App. 3d 805, 61 Ill. Dec. 567, 434 N.E.2d 1164 (2 Dist. 1982).

Dissolution
A property settlement agreement based upon this section must be attendant to a dissolution of marriage. Stern v. Stern, 105 Ill. App. 3d 805, 61 Ill. Dec. 567, 434 N.E.2d 1164 (2 Dist. 1982).

Duress

—Burden of Proof
Evidence of duress must be clear and convincing in order for a court to set aside the agreement on this basis, and the burden of proving duress is on the person asserting it. In re Morris, 147 Ill. App. 3d 380, 100 Ill. Dec. 811, 497 N.E.2d 1173 (1 Dist. 1986); In re Smith, 164 Ill. App. 3d 1011, 115 Ill. Dec. 925, 518 N.E.2d 450 (1 Dist. 1987).

—Defined
Stress is common in dissolution proceedings; the burden of proving duress, so as to set aside a settlement agreement by clear and convincing evidence, is on the person asserting it, and requires a showing of the imposition, oppression, undue influence, or the taking of undue advantage of the stress of the complaining spouse whereby she is deprived of the exercise of her free will. Flynn v. Flynn, 232 Ill. App. 3d 394, 173 Ill. Dec. 735, 597 N.E.2d 709 (1 Dist.), cert. denied, 146 Ill. 2d 626, 176 Ill. Dec. 813, 602 N.E.2d 451 (1992).

Duress is defined as including the imposition, oppression, undue influence or the taking of undue advantage of the stress of another whereby one is deprived of the exercise of his free will. In re Morris, 147 Ill. App. 3d 380, 100 Ill. Dec. 811, 497 N.E.2d 1173 (1 Dist. 1986); In re Smith, 164 Ill. App. 3d 1011, 115 Ill. Dec. 925, 518 N.E.2d 450 (1 Dist. 1987).

—Not Shown
Wife's belated assertions of confusion and compulsion were simply not supported by anything appearing in the record of the hearing on her motion to vacate where terms of settlement agreement were finally concluded after a lengthy conference at her attorney's office, and the final agreement was prepared by her attorney. In re Spomer, 123 Ill. App. 3d 31, 78 Ill. Dec. 605, 462 N.E.2d 724 (5 Dist. 1984); In re McCaskey, 167 Ill. App. 3d 860, 118 Ill. Dec. 845, 522 N.E.2d 300 (5 Dist. 1988).

Duty to Disclose
There was an affirmative duty upon a wife to speak or volunteer any information that was not asked of her during discovery or other court proceedings where the failure to disclose deprived the husband of a material fact necessary to intelligently arrive at a property settlement. In re Burch, 205 Ill. App. 3d 1082, 150 Ill. Dec. 922, 563 N.E.2d 1049 (1 Dist. 1990); Gurin v. Gurin, 212 Ill. App. 3d 806, 156 Ill. Dec. 877, 571 N.E.2d 857 (1 Dist. 1991).

Evidentiary Hearing

—Factors Considered
In determining whether and to what extent a maintenance award can be modified, a circuit court may consider the same factors which, under the statute, are to be assessed in making the initial award. In re Bryant, 206 Ill. App. 3d 167, 150 Ill. Dec. 707, 563 N.E.2d 834 (1 Dist. 1990).

—Permitted
The trial court erred when it refused to allow an evidentiary hearing for the purpose of determining whether there was a sufficient change of circumstances to allow modification of the divorce decree where the separation agreement did not expressly preclude or limit modification of its terms. In re Bowman, 89 Ill. App. 3d 110, 44 Ill. Dec. 445, 411 N.E.2d 567 (4 Dist. 1980).

—Required
Because proof was necessary to establish whether assets used to

Evidentiary Hearing (Cont'd)

—Required (Cont'd)
purchase contested property were nonmarital in nature, the trial court's failure to hold an evidentiary hearing was an abuse of discretion. In re Burch, 205 Ill. App. 3d 1082, 150 Ill. Dec. 922, 563 N.E.2d 1049 (1 Dist. 1990).

Fraud

—Evidence
Wife's amended petition stated that husband caused her to forego having her own lawyer and induced her to enter into an unfair marital settlement agreement by indicating that he would not pay the fees of two attorneys, by stating that his attorney would conclude a settlement that was fair to both sides, and by representing that any questions of property division, alimony, child custody and child support would not be treated by the court more beneficially than in the marital settlement agreement and that he had misrepresented the nature of his relationship with another woman and his intention to remarry after the divorce; therefore, there was enough evidence to allow defendant to present testimony and evidence in support of the amended petition so that questions of whether he was guilty of fraud and coercion which induced the defendant to enter into an inequitable marital settlement agreement could be resolved. Harris v. Harris, 45 Ill. App. 3d 820, 4 Ill. Dec. 366, 360 N.E.2d 113 (2 Dist. 1977).

—Sufficiency of Allegations
Where husband did not contend that signature on document setting out terms of agreement was not his, that he failed to understand its terms or that he failed to realize that his assent thereto would terminate the litigation, but instead, claimed that he signed the agreement because he was led to believe that the court would make certain findings consistent with those in the agreed order, this was an allegation insufficient to allege such fraud as would require the vacation of a settlement agreement. In re Maher, 95 Ill. App. 3d 1039, 51 Ill. Dec. 586, 420 N.E.2d 1144 (2 Dist. 1981).

Future Modifiability
By permitting parties to determine the future modifiability of their agreement, this section maximizes the advantages of careful future planning and eliminates uncertainties based on the fear of subsequent motions to increase or decrease the obligations of the parties. In re Chalkley, 99 Ill. App. 3d 478, 55 Ill. Dec. 262, 426 N.E.2d 237 (1 Dist. 1981).

Garnishment

—Ambiguous Agreement Language
Use of the word "forthwith" in dissolution agreement regarding payment of loan had more than one meaning and was, therefore, ambiguous; thus the trial court properly quashed the garnishment for both the home equity loan plus interest and the interest on sum paid overdue because the provision was contingent. In re Sloane, 255 Ill. App. 3d 653, 195 Ill. Dec. 734, 628 N.E.2d 1198 (2 Dist.), appeal denied, 156 Ill. 2d 566, 202 Ill. Dec. 931, 638 N.E.2d 1125 (1994); but see In re Marriage of Carrier, 332 Ill. App. 3d 654, 265 Ill. Dec. 893, 773 N.E.2d 657 (2 Dist. 2002).

Household Expenses
Payments voluntarily made by a wife for family expenses, during the time the husband and wife were living together, did not create an indebtedness from the husband to the wife in the absence of an agreement to that effect, even though plaintiff's contributions were substantial, but they did give her equity in the residence, especially since the divorce decree provided that she was to receive all the household furniture and furnishings. Everett v. Everett, 25 Ill. 2d 342, 185 N.E.2d 201 (1962).

Installment Contract
While it appears somewhat atypical to incorporate an installment contract in a dissolution order, there is no reason to forbid such a provision; by such incorporation it becomes part of the court's order, its subservient nature as a contract giving way to the dominant character of an adjudication. Davis v. Davis, 114 Ill. App. 3d 438, 71 Ill. Dec. 516, 451 N.E.2d 4 (4 Dist. 1983).

Insurance
Former wife waived her expectancy in her ex-husband's insurance proceeds at the time of the divorce by executing a release of those rights in property settlement agreement, even though ex-husband never changed the designation of the beneficiary on his policy after the divorce in the several years before his death. Principal Mut. Life Ins. Co. v. Juntunen, 189 Ill. App. 3d 224, 136 Ill. Dec. 700, 545 N.E.2d 224 (1 Dist. 1989).

Where it could not be determined exactly when husband's hospitalization insurance was actually dropped and if the husband was aware of any cancellation at the time of prove up, together with settlement agreement referring only to his obligation to retain health insurance for the children, evidence failed to support wife's claim of fraud and misrepresentation based on the husband's lapsed health policy. In re Riedy, 130 Ill. App. 3d 311, 85 Ill. Dec. 614, 474 N.E.2d 28 (2 Dist. 1985).

Limitations
The only limitations placed on parties' freedom to fashion their own property and maintenance agreements are that the end product to be incorporated into divorce decree may not be so unjust as to be unconscionable and the obligation to pay future maintenance is terminated upon the death of either party, or the remarriage of the party receiving maintenance, or if the party receiving maintenance cohabits with another person on a resident, continuing conjugal basis. Simmons v. Simmons, 77 Ill. App. 3d 740, 33 Ill. Dec. 242, 396 N.E.2d 631 (2 Dist. 1979).

Maintenance

—Future Employment
Where the divorce decree granted alimony to an ex-wife without regard to her future employment, the trial court was not compelled by the decree to terminate alimony in the event that the ex-wife should secure employment. In re Parks, 83 Ill. App. 3d 372, 38 Ill. Dec. 742, 403 N.E.2d 1346 (3 Dist. 1980).

—Modification
The settlement agreement as reflected in the supplemental judgment of dissolution did not expressly limit reduction of maintenance to the condition of wife's employment, and therefore did not preclude reduction of maintenance based upon a substantial change of circumstances. In re Brent, 263 Ill. App. 3d 916, 200 Ill. Dec. 799, 635 N.E.2d 1382 (4 Dist. 1994).

The legislature has set forth certain conditions upon which maintenance will be terminated or modified, however, parties to a dissolution action are permitted to enter into settlement agreements which alter the court's ability to terminate or modify maintenance and they take precedence over the statutory conditions. In re Brent, 263 Ill. App. 3d 916, 200 Ill. Dec. 799, 635 N.E.2d 1382 (4 Dist. 1994).

Where an agreed order provided for maintenance in gross which, by definition, is nonmodifiable, it was not necessary to insert additional language into the order that would have expressly precluded or limited modification of the terms set forth. In re Burgstrom, 135 Ill. App. 3d 854, 90 Ill. Dec. 564, 482 N.E.2d 383 (1 Dist. 1985).

Where record in proceeding in which former husband sought to modify periodic alimony payments did not permit a resolution of controversy because it was silent as to whether the trial court denied the petition for modification on the ground that defendant failed to prove a material change in circumstances or whether it concluded, as former wife argued, that the settlement agreement was not subject to modification under subsection (f) of this section, cause had to be remanded for further proceedings. Dull v. Dull, 73 Ill. App. 3d 1015, 29 Ill. Dec. 864, 392 N.E.2d 421 (5 Dist. 1979).

—Periodic Payments
Former section 18 of the Divorce Act (see now this section and 750 ILCS 5/503) meant that if the court ordered a party to make periodic payments of alimony to his or her ex-spouse, it could not also grant alimony in gross, such as requiring the conveyance of property from one to the other in lieu of alimony. Stotlar v. Stotlar, 50 Ill. App. 3d 790, 8 Ill. Dec. 711, 365 N.E.2d 1097 (5 Dist. 1977).

—Public Policy
While a husband and wife may make a valid agreement with respect to mutual property rights or for the settlement of claims for alimony or support, such agreement is against public policy where it attempts to relieve the husband from his legal obligation to

Maintenance (Cont'd)

—Public Policy (Cont'd)

support his wife. Rhodes v. Rhodes, 82 Ill. App. 2d 435, 225 N.E.2d 802 (2 Dist. 1967).

—Remarriage of Recipient

Marriage settlement agreements may extend maintenance payments beyond the recipient's remarriage. Broadway Bank v. Kakos, 160 Ill. App. 3d 6, 111 Ill. Dec. 851, 513 N.E.2d 97 (1 Dist. 1987).

Remarriage of the wife had no effect on continuing obligations created under a property settlement agreement made part of a divorce decree. Maybaum v. Maybaum, 349 Ill. App. 80, 110 N.E.2d 78 (1 Dist. 1952).

Merger of Settlement Agreement

When the provisions of a written or oral agreement are incorporated into a judgment, the agreement becomes merged in the judgment and is conclusive upon the parties in the same manner as if the court had made the determination. In re Morris, 147 Ill. App. 3d 380, 100 Ill. Dec. 811, 497 N.E.2d 1173 (1 Dist. 1986).

Modification

—Agreement by Parties

Where the parties agreed to a modification of an original agreement, which provided that the agreement was nonmodifiable, the modification was not inconsistent with subsection (f). In re Adamson, 308 Ill. App. 3d 759, 242 Ill. Dec. 198, 721 N.E.2d 166 (2 Dist. 1999).

Where an agreed modification of a decree of dissolution provided for $50 a month for rent payment so that former wife could move, such modification was consistent with public policy of state. In re Steel, 195 Ill. App. 3d 348, 142 Ill. Dec. 31, 552 N.E.2d 381 (4 Dist. 1990).

The parties' mutual adjustment of their marital rights so far as the education of their children was concerned was conclusive in the absence of unconscionability, fraud, coercion, duress or a violation of public policy or morals. In re Holderrieth, 181 Ill. App. 3d 199, 129 Ill. Dec. 896, 536 N.E.2d 946 (1 Dist. 1989).

—Approval

Allowing former spouses to modify a court ordered child support obligation by creating a new agreement between themselves without judicial approval would have circumvented the court's obligation in marital dissolution proceedings to protect the best interests of the children involved. Blisset v. Blisset, 123 Ill. 2d 161, 121 Ill. Dec. 931, 526 N.E.2d 125 (1988).

—Best Interest of Child

Parents may not bargain away their children's interests; it is for this reason that parents may create an enforceable agreement for modification of child support only by petitioning the court for support modification and then establishing, to the satisfaction of the court, that an agreement reached between the parents is in accord with the best interests of the children. Blisset v. Blisset, 123 Ill. 2d 161, 121 Ill. Dec. 931, 526 N.E.2d 125 (1988).

—Certain Conditions

A maintenance agreement incorporated in a judgment for dissolution of marriage which is modifiable only under certain express circumstances is nonmodifiable until the conditions are met. In re Mateja, 183 Ill. App. 3d 759, 132 Ill. Dec. 666, 540 N.E.2d 406 (1 Dist. 1989).

—Change in Circumstances

Any modification of child support is dependent upon a showing that there has been a material change in the circumstances of the parties since entry of the order sought to be altered. Weinert v. Weinert, 105 Ill. App. 3d 56, 60 Ill. Dec. 920, 433 N.E.2d 1158 (2 Dist. 1982); In re Glickman, 211 Ill. App. 3d 792, 156 Ill. Dec. 162, 570 N.E.2d 638 (1 Dist. 1991).

—Child Support

Parties to a dissolution proceeding are not at liberty to make agreements which affect the interests of their children without obtaining the approval of the court. In re Ingram, 259 Ill. App. 3d 685, 197 Ill. Dec. 383, 631 N.E.2d 386 (2 Dist. 1994).

This Act expressly prohibits parties to an agreement from limiting or precluding the modification of child support, and even where a settlement exists between the parents, no child is barred from seeking additional support. Department of Public Aid ex rel. Cox v. Miller, 146 Ill. 2d 399, 166 Ill. Dec. 922, 586 N.E.2d 1251 (1992).

Substantial economic reverses resulting from employment or investments are proper areas of inquiry in determining whether child support might be reduced or terminated. Weinert v. Weinert, 105 Ill. App. 3d 56, 60 Ill. Dec. 920, 433 N.E.2d 1158 (2 Dist. 1982).

Regardless of the presence or absence of any language limiting modification of contract terms, provisions relating to the support of minor children are always modifiable. Burks v. Burks, 100 Ill. App. 3d 700, 56 Ill. Dec. 273, 427 N.E.2d 353 (1 Dist. 1981); In re Glickman, 211 Ill. App. 3d 792, 156 Ill. Dec. 162, 570 N.E.2d 638 (1 Dist. 1991).

—College Expenses

The trial court erred in finding that a provision in a dissolution judgment which provided for the payment of children's college expenses was not modifiable when that provision was contained in a settlement agreement incorporated into the judgment and the agreement specifically precluded modification of its terms. In re Loffredi, 232 Ill. App. 3d 709, 173 Ill. Dec. 933, 597 N.E.2d 907 (3 Dist. 1992).

A provision in a dissolution judgment for the payment of a child's college expenses is a term in the nature of child support, and the circuit court therefore retains jurisdiction to modify such a provision at any time pursuant to this section and 750 ILCS 5/510, regardless of whether the provision was ordered by the court under 750 ILCS 5/513 or incorporated into the judgment as a result of a settlement agreement. In re Loffredi, 232 Ill. App. 3d 709, 173 Ill. Dec. 933, 597 N.E.2d 907 (3 Dist. 1992).

Modification of a separation agreement was not permitted where a father was not attempting to relieve himself of his obligation of support when he entered into the property settlement agreement, but on the contrary, he was contracting to do more than the law required when he promised to pay the costs of college tuition, books, incidental fees and board and room for the scholastic year, without contribution by the plaintiff and without a determination of his ability to pay having been made. Gaddis v. Gaddis, 20 Ill. App. 3d 267, 314 N.E.2d 627 (5 Dist. 1974).

—Combination

Parties cannot agree to make child support nonmodifiable; child support is modifiable even when combined with nonmodifiable alimony or maintenance. Burks v. Burks, 100 Ill. App. 3d 700, 56 Ill. Dec. 273, 427 N.E.2d 353 (1 Dist. 1981).

—Discretion

The modification of a child support obligation is a judicial function, administered exclusively by the court as a matter of discretion. Blisset v. Blisset, 123 Ill. 2d 161, 121 Ill. Dec. 931, 526 N.E.2d 125 (1988).

—Education Expenses

Provisions regarding a child's educational expenses contained in otherwise non-modifiable settlement agreements incorporated into dissolution judgments are modifiable; the purpose of subsection (f) is to permit the parties to preclude or limit modification of terms pertaining to maintenance, and other matters, excluding matters pertaining to children although a trial court cannot modify a spouse's child support obligations without a petition for modification first being filed. In re Sawyer, 264 Ill. App. 3d 839, 202 Ill. Dec. 20, 637 N.E.2d 559 (1 Dist. 1994).

—Enforceability

Where a separation agreement was not incorporated into a judgment, the trial court correctly ruled that the agreement was not modifiable upon a showing of changed circumstances, as the agreement remained a contract enforceable only by contract remedies. In re Dellitt, 213 Ill. App. 3d 155, 156 Ill. Dec. 739, 571 N.E.2d 523 (3 Dist. 1991).

—Factors

In determining whether and to what extent a maintenance award can be modified, a circuit court may consider the same factors which, under the statute, are to be assessed in making the initial

Modification (Cont'd)

—Factors (Cont'd)

award. In re Bryant, 206 Ill. App. 3d 167, 150 Ill. Dec. 707, 563 N.E.2d 834 (1 Dist. 1990).

—Grounds

Although the law looks with favor upon the amicable settlement of the rights of the parties to a dissolution of marriage, the terms of a marital separation agreement will not be given effect if procured by fraud or coercion or if contrary to any rule of law, public policy or morals. In re Pearson, 101 Ill. App. 3d 422, 57 Ill. Dec. 28, 428 N.E.2d 578 (1 Dist. 1981); In re Carlson, 101 Ill. App. 3d 924, 57 Ill. Dec. 325, 428 N.E.2d 1005 (1 Dist. 1981); In re Morris, 147 Ill. App. 3d 380, 100 Ill. Dec. 811, 497 N.E.2d 1173 (1 Dist. 1986); In re Cierny, 187 Ill. App. 3d 334, 134 Ill. Dec. 918, 543 N.E.2d 201 (1 Dist. 1989); In re Simard, 215 Ill. App. 3d 647, 159 Ill. Dec. 67, 575 N.E.2d 565 (3 Dist. 1991).

—Jurisdiction

Where modification of decree of dissolution involves an agreed order, not contrary to public policy and not shown to have resulted from fraud or coercion, respondent can challenge it on appeal only if the circuit court lacks jurisdiction to enter it. In re Steel, 195 Ill. App. 3d 348, 142 Ill. Dec. 31, 552 N.E.2d 381 (4 Dist. 1990).

—Maintenance

The marital settlement agreement showed an intent on the part of the parties to preclude modification of maintenance. In re Schweitzer, 289 Ill. App. 3d 425, 225 Ill. Dec. 15, 682 N.E.2d 759 (4 Dist. 1997).

Where parties' agreement clearly and unambiguously limited the duration of maintenance by stating that it would not extend beyond the earliest of three specific events, i.e., the expiration of 78 months, wife's death, or remarriage, the agreement precluded a modification extending wife's right to maintenance beyond that time; however, although the parties' agreement was sufficiently clear to make the duration of payments nonmodifiable, because the agreement incorporated into the judgment of dissolution did not clearly preclude modification of the amounts of maintenance and other benefits within the prescribed periods, the trial court could modify amounts payable with the time limitations prescribed by the parties' agreement. Tucker v. Tucker, 223 Ill. App. 3d 671, 166 Ill. Dec. 83, 585 N.E.2d 1105 (3 Dist. 1992).

Payments which the taxpayer became absolutely obligated to make in lieu of any further support as specified in the modification agreement and supplemental decree and not subject to any contingency were installment payments made by taxpayer in discharge of his principal sum obligation specified in the supplemental decree and amended agreement incident to the divorce. Ashcraft v. Commissioner, 252 F.2d 200 (7th Cir. 1958).

—Medical Treatment

Should any situation occur where failure to fulfill a condition precedent in a dissolution agreement would jeopardize availability of medical treatment due to financial inability of party who had not fulfilled the condition, the agreement could be modified as in the best interest of the children under subsection (b) of this section. In re Talmadge, 179 Ill. App. 3d 806, 128 Ill. Dec. 751, 534 N.E.2d 1356 (2 Dist. 1989).

—Military Pension

Evidence was insufficient to justify setting aside judgment incorporating and adopting agreement of the parties for nonmodification of terms pursuant to this section, although judgment granted entire interest in military pension to husband under law prevailing at that time, where wife was awarded substantial settlement, court considered pension in making determination regarding maintenance, and there was no evidence of fraud, overreaching or unconscionability; retroactive passage of Uniformed Services Former Spouses Protection Act (10 U.S.C., § 1408(c)(1)) authorized but did not mandate that military retirement pensions be shared by spouse and former wife. In re Habermehl, 135 Ill. App. 3d 105, 89 Ill. Dec. 939, 481 N.E.2d 782 (5 Dist. 1985).

—Not Permitted

Though "permanent alimony" was subject to modification since it referred to alimony awarded by a final decree of divorce as opposed to that awarded during the pendency of the action, the record failed to show a substantial change in circumstances required to justify a modification of alimony. Schoenhard v. Schoenhard, 74 Ill. App. 3d 296, 30 Ill. Dec. 109, 392 N.E.2d 764 (2 Dist. 1979).

—Permitted

Provisions pertaining to child support may not be made nonmodifiable, and a motion for modification that raises the issues of the failure of a condition precedent and legal impossibility, could be considered by the court. In re Corkey, 269 Ill. App. 3d 392, 206 Ill. Dec. 862, 645 N.E.2d 1384 (2 Dist. 1995).

Because terms of judgment did not incorporate terms of a settlement agreement pursuant to subsection (f) of this section, the court had power to modify the maintenance award. In re Bryant, 206 Ill. App. 3d 167, 150 Ill. Dec. 707, 563 N.E.2d 834 (1 Dist. 1990).

Where the agreement contained no provision which specifically precluded modification, the agreement was modifiable. In re Martino, 166 Ill. App. 3d 692, 117 Ill. Dec. 788, 520 N.E.2d 1139 (2 Dist. 1988).

—Petitioning the Court

Parents may create an enforceable agreement for modification of child support only by petitioning the court for support modification and then establishing, to the satisfaction of the court, that an agreement reached between the parents is in accord with the best interests of the children. Baker v. Baker, 193 Ill. App. 3d 294, 140 Ill. Dec. 303, 549 N.E.2d 954 (4 Dist. 1990).

—Precatory Language

Language in a settlement agreement purporting to settle the issue of alimony "now and forever" was in the preamble to the operative provisions of the agreement and, therefore, did not obligate the parties. In re Pearson, 101 Ill. App. 3d 422, 57 Ill. Dec. 28, 428 N.E.2d 578 (1 Dist. 1981).

Language employed in property settlement agreement was deemed to be precatory only and not the express preclusion of modification contemplated in subsection (f) of this section; therefore, trial court's award of periodic alimony was subject to modification. Dull v. Dull, 73 Ill. App. 3d 1015, 29 Ill. Dec. 864, 392 N.E.2d 421 (5 Dist. 1979).

—Preclusion

Post-dissolution modification of maintenance is judicially precluded only where a settlement agreement clearly and unambiguously expresses the parties' intent to make maintenance nonmodifiable. Tucker v. Tucker, 223 Ill. App. 3d 671, 166 Ill. Dec. 83, 585 N.E.2d 1105 (3 Dist. 1992).

Language purporting to prevent reductions in maintenance in the event payee's social security increased, or to preclude modification of the agreement without consent of the parties, did not evince an intent by the parties to preclude or limit any judicial modification of the maintenance agreement under this section. In re Sutton, 178 Ill. App. 3d 928, 128 Ill. Dec. 37, 533 N.E.2d 1125 (3 Dist. 1989).

Where agreement between parties in 1969 judgment and agreed order precluded termination of wife's maintenance payments based on her future income and reconsideration of maintenance payments was allowed upon unfavorable change in husband's economic circumstances alone, the trial court correctly denied husband's request to terminate maintenance payments where husband experienced a dramatic increase in income from 1969 to 1985 and the wife had rehabilitated herself. In re Silber, 176 Ill. App. 3d 853, 126 Ill. Dec. 283, 531 N.E.2d 910 (1 Dist. 1988).

The requirement in subsection (f) of this section that any agreement that would preclude modification of maintenance payments be expressed in settlement agreement had to be relaxed where an agreement was entered into prior to the effective date of this Act; therefore an inquiry into intent of parties when the agreement was entered into was necessary to determine whether such an agreement could be implied. Krug-Etheridge v. Krug, 111 Ill. App. 3d 780, 67 Ill. Dec. 454, 444 N.E.2d 690 (1 Dist. 1982).

—Property

Under subsection (f) of this section, the trial court may be precluded from modifying terms of incorporated property agreement, but this subsection was not applicable in a case where a property settlement agreement incorporated in the dissolution judgment failed to expressly preclude or limit modification of its

Modification (Cont'd)

—Property (Cont'd)
terms, and future revisions and modifications were foreseeable regarding sale of real estate, so that court orders leading to the sale of defendant's property interest to plaintiff were an implementation of the provisions of the dissolution judgment rather than a revision or modification of the terms of the judgment. Hubbard v. Hubbard, 84 Ill. App. 3d 761, 40 Ill. Dec. 270, 405 N.E.2d 1362 (1 Dist. 1980).

—Rights of Parties
Where a trial judge added a provision which parties had not agreed upon in their property settlement agreement, ordering wife to pay tax bill on real estate, he effectively modified the reference to a quit claim deed and the portion of the agreement mutually waiving and releasing claims and altered the substantive rights of the parties, and the court did not have discretion, even within the 30 day period before the decree became final, to apply general equitable principles which, in effect, modified the property agreement when no fraud or coercion or other proper basis for relief was alleged. Chodl v. Chodl, 37 Ill. App. 3d 52, 344 N.E.2d 711 (2 Dist. 1976).

—Unallocated Support
The unallocated combination of child support into a taxable maintenance amount necessarily carried with it the statutory right to modification of child support. In re Steadman, 283 Ill. App. 3d 703, 219 Ill. Dec. 258, 670 N.E.2d 1146 (3 Dist. 1996).

If unallocated support is treated as modifiable for the benefit of children, then it should be modifiable for the benefit of the payor. In re Gleason, 266 Ill. App. 3d 467, 203 Ill. Dec. 423, 639 N.E.2d 982 (4 Dist. 1994).

—Unconscionability
Modified dissolution judgment was not to be set aside where the terms of this judgment showed that petitioner wife was to receive $500 per month as support for three children, was awarded family home, and was relieved of bulk of marital debts, and considering that respondent husband earned on the average approximately $18,000 a year for the past three or four years in spite of experiencing periods of manic depression and received benefits under the modified dissolution judgment; agreement was not "unconscionable." In re Held, 73 Ill. App. 3d 561, 29 Ill. Dec. 612, 392 N.E.2d 169 (5 Dist. 1979).

Where the parties' intentions were clearly manifested and there was no claim of unconscionability, the trial court erred in modifying alimony. Simmons v. Simmons, 77 Ill. App. 3d 740, 33 Ill. Dec. 242, 396 N.E.2d 631 (2 Dist. 1979).

New Hearing
Where statements of the circuit court reflected that it did not give appropriate significance to the evidence and was laboring under the misconception of the law applicable to a petition for modification of support and attorney fees, this misconception deprived wife of fair hearing on her petition and entitled wife to new hearing. Powers v. Powers, 69 Ill. App. 3d 485, 26 Ill. Dec. 452, 388 N.E.2d 76 (1 Dist. 1979).

Oral Agreement
The fact that the parties expected that a formal agreement eventually would be executed does not invalidate the oral agreement where the terms of the agreement were set forth orally and in great detail before the court. In re Sarron, 247 Ill. App. 3d 819, 187 Ill. Dec. 526, 617 N.E.2d 1247 (3 Dist.), appeal denied, 153 Ill. 2d 569, 191 Ill. Dec. 629, 624 N.E.2d 817 (1993).

Where, before a judgment of dissolution was entered, husband alleged that parties had reached an oral settlement agreement, terms of which he alleged were set forth in a written agreement which bore only his signature, wife denied the existence of any agreement, oral or written, and stated she wished to proceed with a contested trial, and the parties continued the hearing of the case in order to reduce the agreement to writing and execute it, there was no binding oral settlement agreement. In re Chaltin, 153 Ill. App. 3d 810, 106 Ill. Dec. 631, 506 N.E.2d 338 (2 Dist. 1987).

The legislature chose to allow separation agreements, binding on the court, to be evidenced orally, despite the invitation to fraud that is thereby created in cases of uncontested marital dissolution. Although the better practice might be for a trial court to make some inquiry into the circumstances surrounding the execution of such oral "agreements" when one of the parties thereto waives notice and appearance, the failure to do so is not necessarily an abuse of discretion vested in the court by subsection (b) of this section. In re Lorenzi, 84 Ill. App. 3d 427, 39 Ill. Dec. 754, 405 N.E.2d 507 (3 Dist. 1980).

Order Vacating Decree

—Improper
The trial court was without authority to vacate decree granting marriage dissolution and incorporating terms of settlement agreement unless there was clear and convincing evidence that the agreement was entered as the result of fraud, coercion, duress or was contrary to public policy or morals; thus the trial court's order which vacated the decree was reversed and the decree was reinstated. In re Somes, 87 Ill. App. 3d 240, 42 Ill. Dec. 541, 409 N.E.2d 36 (1 Dist. 1980).

Post-Judgment Procedure
A petition under 735 ILCS 5/2-1401 was a proper method by which to attack validity and fairness of property settlement agreement which was incorporated into the judgment of dissolution. In re Reines, 184 Ill. App. 3d 392, 132 Ill. Dec. 654, 540 N.E.2d 394 (1 Dist. 1989).

Property Rights

—In General
Nonmarital property can be divided by agreement. Magna Mtg. Co. v. Donald Webber Mtg. Co., 166 Ill. App. 3d 992, 117 Ill. Dec. 861, 520 N.E.2d 1212 (4 Dist. 1988).

—Adjudication
Illinois does not authorize adjudication of property rights in legal separation proceedings. Stern v. Stern, 105 Ill. App. 3d 805, 61 Ill. Dec. 567, 434 N.E.2d 1164 (2 Dist. 1982).

—Agreement Upheld
Where property settlement agreement was not contingent upon reconciliation and provided for a detailed distribution of the property in the event of a divorce, husband's attorney drafted the agreement, and it was apparent that the parties anticipated that the reconciliation effort might fail since they incorporated a provision that the agreement would be submitted to the court for approval in the event a decree of divorce was entered between the parties, it was therefore evident that the husband was not fraudulently induced to sign the property settlement agreement, and the trial court properly denied the husband's motion to set aside that agreement. Reininger v. Reininger, 67 Ill. App. 3d 21, 23 Ill. Dec. 752, 384 N.E.2d 546 (4 Dist. 1978).

—Challenge
The settlement of property rights cannot be concluded by parties' oral consent when it is diligently challenged by one spouse before a decree has been entered. In re Chaltin, 153 Ill. App. 3d 810, 106 Ill. Dec. 631, 506 N.E.2d 338 (2 Dist. 1987).

—Illustrative Cases
Where a divorce settlement agreement stated that wife was entitled to one-half of stocks in husband's pension stock plan, the husband withdrew the stock prior to his retirement and after it split, and the wife subsequently died, her estate was entitled to one-half of the shares valued at the date of disbursement. In re Olsen, 124 Ill. 2d 19, 123 Ill. Dec. 980, 528 N.E.2d 684 (1988).

When salaries, contributions and other evidence were considered, it was clear that both parties contributed to bank accounts and both parties were entitled to divisional shares in them; therefore, the trial court abused its discretion in awarding wife the husband's joint tenancy interest in the bank accounts. Fuqua v. Fuqua, 60 Ill. App. 3d 819, 18 Ill. Dec. 200, 377 N.E.2d 353 (2 Dist. 1978).

Property disposition ordered by the trial court was equitable. La Roche v. La Roche, 32 Ill. App. 3d 475, 335 N.E.2d 518 (3 Dist. 1975).

—Invalid Divorce Decree
In the absence of a valid divorce decree, the court has no power to determine the interests of the parties in property; thus, a judgment

Property Rights (Cont'd)

—Invalid Divorce Decree (Cont'd)
was void and of no force or effect concerning the property interest of the parties. Sharer v. Sharer, 39 Ill. App. 3d 818, 350 N.E.2d 779 (5 Dist. 1976).

—Transfers
In absence of some governing statutory provision, a court may not interfere with property rights and interests of parties; however, the court may, where appropriate and where requested by one or both of the parties, order transfers of property or property interests from one party to another, according to the equities where special circumstances appear. Halloran v. Halloran, 39 Ill. App. 3d 528, 350 N.E.2d 318 (3 Dist. 1976).

The transfer of property from one spouse to another pursuant to a divorce decree is governed by statute. Gilmore v. Gilmore, 28 Ill. App. 3d 36, 328 N.E.2d 562 (1 Dist. 1975).

—Vacating Settlement
Property settlement must be set aside where there is misrepresentation, duress and coercion practiced upon a party to the settlement. In re Moran, 136 Ill. App. 3d 331, 91 Ill. Dec. 234, 483 N.E.2d 580 (1 Dist. 1985).

Purpose

—Amicable Settlement
This section is intended to encourage parties to reach an amenable settlement of their rights. Flynn v. Flynn, 232 Ill. App. 3d 394, 173 Ill. Dec. 735, 597 N.E.2d 709 (1 Dist.), cert. denied, 146 Ill. 2d 626, 176 Ill. Dec. 813, 602 N.E.2d 451 (1992).

The law favors the amicable settlement of property rights in marital dissolution cases. In re Morris, 147 Ill. App. 3d 380, 100 Ill. Dec. 811, 497 N.E.2d 1173 (1 Dist. 1986).

This section is generally intended to encourage parties to reach an amicable settlement of their rights. In re Black, 133 Ill. App. 3d 59, 87 Ill. Dec. 831, 477 N.E.2d 1359 (2 Dist. 1985); In re Brandt, 140 Ill. App. 3d 1019, 95 Ill. Dec. 340, 489 N.E.2d 902 (5 Dist. 1986).

—Property Arrangements
The provisions of subsection (f) of this section are intended to allow parties to agree that their future property and maintenance arrangements will not be altered except with their consent, and to eliminate uncertainties based on the fear that subsequent motions might increase or decrease their obligations. In re Sutton, 178 Ill. App. 3d 928, 128 Ill. Dec. 37, 533 N.E.2d 1125 (3 Dist. 1989).

Remarriage

—Modification of Support
Trial court properly found that wife's remarriage could not be considered by the court as grounds for modifying or terminating the support provisions of parties' agreement as of the date of husband's filing his petition for modification; though the provisions of this section would appear to require that parties must expressly agree in the separation agreement to extend maintenance terms beyond a wife's remarriage to effectively limit a court's power to modify or terminate the payments based on such remarriage, where the agreement was entered into before this Act was enacted, when agreements were not required to be so specific, the court did not require that the parties had to meet the strict standards of this Act when they entered into their agreement, especially since the parties clearly intended for the payments to extend beyond wife's remarriage. In re Mass, 102 Ill. App. 3d 984, 58 Ill. Dec. 941, 431 N.E.2d 1 (1 Dist. 1981).

—Restraint
Where parties' agreement was not a total restraint on remarriage, and only resulted in a forfeiture by wife if she remarried prior to the parties' youngest child reaching 18, when husband's obligation to pay real estate taxes would end, the restraint was not an unreasonable restraint on remarrying. In re Dodge, 150 Ill. App. 3d 486, 103 Ill. Dec. 816, 501 N.E.2d 1354 (2 Dist. 1986).

Sale of Home
Husband should not be allowed to deduct or receive credit for his share of payments made on behalf of wife and to satisfy his own proportionate share expenses upon sale of former marital home and division of proceeds under divorce decree. Gilmore v. Gilmore, 28 Ill. App. 3d 36, 328 N.E.2d 562 (1 Dist. 1975).

Separation Agreement

—In General
Where parties' settlement agreement was pursuant to a legal separation and not a dissolution of their marriage, this section was not applicable. In re Sutton, 136 Ill. 2d 441, 145 Ill. Dec. 890, 557 N.E.2d 869 (1990).

—Approval
Should a separation agreement be found unconscionable, or should the court find that no separation agreement had actually been entered into, the court would then be required to approve a conscionable agreement from the parties, if there is such an agreement, or to proceed under 750 ILCS 5/503, denominating parties' property as marital and nonmarital and dividing it in accordance with the requirements of that section. In re Lorenzi, 84 Ill. App. 3d 427, 39 Ill. Dec. 754, 405 N.E.2d 507 (3 Dist. 1980).

—Binding
The terms of a separation agreement are binding upon the court so long as the agreement is not unconscionable. In re Lorenzi, 84 Ill. App. 3d 427, 39 Ill. Dec. 754, 405 N.E.2d 507 (3 Dist. 1980).

—Grounds to Set Aside
Subsection (b) of this section does not eliminate many of the traditional grounds for setting aside settlement agreements, including grounds of fraud, duress, coercion and violation of any rule of law, public policy or morals. In re Lee, 135 Ill. App. 3d 509, 90 Ill. Dec. 245, 481 N.E.2d 1045 (1 Dist. 1985); In re Moran, 136 Ill. App. 3d 331, 91 Ill. Dec. 234, 483 N.E.2d 580 (1 Dist. 1985); In re Smith, 164 Ill. App. 3d 1011, 115 Ill. Dec. 925, 518 N.E.2d 450 (1 Dist. 1987).

—Rejection
Under subsection (b) of this section, the court may not reject a settlement agreement for unfairness, but only for unconscionability. In re Kloster, 127 Ill. App. 3d 583, 82 Ill. Dec. 847, 469 N.E.2d 381 (2 Dist. 1984); In re Stadheim, 170 Ill. App. 3d 19, 120 Ill. Dec. 373, 523 N.E.2d 1284 (1 Dist. 1988); In re Holderrieth, 181 Ill. App. 3d 199, 129 Ill. Dec. 896, 536 N.E.2d 946 (1 Dist. 1989).

—Scope
As of the effective date of this Act, parties were allowed to enter into written separation agreements in accordance with this section which extended maintenance beyond the terminating events of 750 ILCS 5/510(b). In re Mass, 102 Ill. App. 3d 984, 58 Ill. Dec. 941, 431 N.E.2d 1 (1 Dist. 1981).

—Uncontested
The trial court did not err in failing to denominate nonmarital and marital property and in declining to apportion the latter in light of uncontested evidence of a separation agreement between the parties purporting to dispose of all their property. In re Lorenzi, 84 Ill. App. 3d 427, 39 Ill. Dec. 754, 405 N.E.2d 507 (3 Dist. 1980).

—Upheld
Oral settlement agreement regarding distribution of marital assets was valid although husband claimed the parties intended to reduce their oral agreement to writing, he did not sign the written agreement presented to him by his attorney, and the agreement contained no provisions for credits for his payments on the mortgage, bank accounts, pensions, personal property, or the automobile where the record showed no intention by the parties to reduce the oral agreement to writing, only the intention of the parties to present a typed copy of the judgment, with the record, to the trial court. In re Carlson, 186 Ill. App. 3d 635, 134 Ill. Dec. 414, 542 N.E.2d 760 (1 Dist. 1989).

A settlement agreement was upheld as fair and equitable where it was shown that it was particularly advantageous to one spouse because it provided that spouse with many substantial benefits that could not be awarded from a trial court. In re Morris, 147 Ill. App. 3d 380, 100 Ill. Dec. 811, 497 N.E.2d 1173 (1 Dist. 1986).

Settlement Negotiations
The court refused to set aside a settlement agreement on grounds that it was hastily contrived where the settlement negotiations

Settlement Negotiations (Cont'd)
lasted about two hours, included discussions among both parties and their attorneys, and concluded with a conference between the parties and their attorneys. In re Cierny, 187 Ill. App. 3d 334, 134 Ill. Dec. 918, 543 N.E.2d 201 (1 Dist. 1989).

Standard of Review
Provisions of divorce judgments are construed by applying the same rules as those governing the construction of contracts. In re Blaine, 246 Ill. App. 3d 23, 186 Ill. Dec. 104, 615 N.E.2d 1161 (5 Dist.), cert. denied, 153 Ill. 2d 557, 191 Ill. Dec. 616, 624 N.E.2d 804 (1993).

When a party seeks to vacate or modify a property settlement incorporated into a dissolution judgment, the settlement is presumed valid; a reviewing court may not reverse the trial court's judgment merely because different conclusions could be drawn from the evidence. Flynn v. Flynn, 232 Ill. App. 3d 394, 173 Ill. Dec. 735, 597 N.E.2d 709 (1 Dist.), cert. denied, 146 Ill. 2d 626, 176 Ill. Dec. 813, 602 N.E.2d 451 (1992).

A reviewing court will set aside a settlement agreement only if it is shown that the agreement was procured through coercion, duress, or fraud, or if the reviewing court finds that the agreement is contrary to any rule of law, public policy, or morals, or is unconscionable. Flynn v. Flynn, 232 Ill. App. 3d 394, 173 Ill. Dec. 735, 597 N.E.2d 709 (1 Dist.), cert. denied, 146 Ill. 2d 626, 176 Ill. Dec. 813, 602 N.E.2d 451 (1992).

Given that the trial judge has the best opportunity to observe the witnesses and evaluate their credibility, his findings in this regard will not be disturbed unless they are palpably erroneous. In re Morris, 147 Ill. App. 3d 380, 100 Ill. Dec. 811, 497 N.E.2d 1173 (1 Dist. 1986).

A disposition of marital property under 750 ILCS 5/503 will be reviewed under a different standard than a trial court's determination of whether a separation agreement is unconscionable under this section; however, the same evidence can be relevant for both determinations. In re Miller, 98 Ill. App. 3d 1084, 54 Ill. Dec. 439, 424 N.E.2d 1342 (4 Dist. 1981).

Stipulation

—Ambiguous Term
Where the stipulation's use of the words "pension" or "pension plan," was ambiguous it was held to refer solely to an age-related pension and not a disability pension. In re Belk, 239 Ill. App. 3d 806, 178 Ill. Dec. 647, 605 N.E.2d 86 (2 Dist. 1992).

—Not Valid
Defendant's stipulation to separation agreement where plaintiff waived her right to automatic increases in child support had no merit where the court did not sign the stipulation as a separate judgment nor did defendant husband show that the court gave reasoned consideration to the stipulation. Marshall v. Marshall, 109 Ill. App. 3d 139, 64 Ill. Dec. 762, 440 N.E.2d 314 (5 Dist. 1982).

A written stipulation and a property settlement agreement in a divorce case cannot be enforced when not approved by the court, and a determination of property rights can be made after a divorce decree is entered. Johnson v. Johnson, 131 Ill. App. 2d 370, 266 N.E.2d 392 (1 Dist. 1970).

Tax Deduction
Where settlement agreement stated that a specified sum of money was to be paid to wife, subject to no contingency, in two installments, along with an assignment of an insurance policy, the husband making such payments could not deduct them as support from federal income taxes, since the payments were considered to be installment payments. Ashcraft v. Commissioner, 252 F.2d 200 (7th Cir. 1958).

Termination of Agreement

—Reconciliation
Where separation agreement expressed intention that husband and wife's separation would be permanent, and provided for wife's support by husband, clause allowing for termination of agreement in case of reconciliation did not invalidate agreement. Henderson v. Henderson, 290 Ill. App. 448, 8 N.E.2d 545 (1 Dist. 1937).

Terms of Agreement

—Disposition of Property
Husband's contention that property was held jointly because of an agreement between the parties that his property would be placed in joint tenancy, solely for purposes of avoiding probate, was insufficient to rebut the presumption that the property in joint tenancy was considered marital. Brongel v. Brongel, 48 Ill. App. 3d 27, 6 Ill. Dec. 115, 362 N.E.2d 750 (2 Dist. 1977).

—Educational Expenses
Where negotiated settlement agreement was incorporated into divorce decree, which agreement provided that the plaintiff would have the custody of the two minor sons of the parties, but that the defendant husband would pay all expenses of defendant children in preparatory school and college, but selection of the preparatory school and college to be attended by each child would be by joint agreement of the husband and the wife, the defendant did not violate the terms of the divorce decree by failing to pay expenses at private school to which child was sent without consent of the father. Nortwick v. Nortwick, 52 Ill. App. 2d 229, 201 N.E.2d 857 (2 Dist. 1964).

—Enforcement
Where a property settlement, made a part of the divorce decree, provided that each of the parties should have all real property belonging to him or her and now in his or her possession, and that each party should upon request execute to the other any instrument that the other party may reasonably require for the purpose of giving full force and effect to the provisions of the agreement, the master in chancery was empowered to execute an instrument of conveyance of the real estate in the event of the refusal of wife to execute and deliver an instrument conveying title to real estate to husband. Brevet v. Brevet, 316 Ill. App. 406, 45 N.E.2d 199 (1 Dist. 1942).

—Merger into Foreign Judgment
An agreement between a husband and wife which was made part of a California divorce was a property settlement agreement, not an agreement for alimony; therefore, the remarriage of wife did not affect or terminate the installment payments of the agreement falling due subsequent to remarriage. Maybaum v. Maybaum, 349 Ill. App. 80, 110 N.E.2d 78 (1 Dist. 1952).

—Merger into Judgment
The terms of a settlement agreement set forth in a divorce decree are enforceable as contract terms. In re Olsen, 156 Ill. App. 3d 540, 109 Ill. Dec. 105, 509 N.E.2d 766 (2 Dist. 1987), rev'd on other grounds, 124 Ill. 2d 19, 123 Ill. Dec. 980, 528 N.E.2d 684 (1988).

When a decree embodies an agreement constituting a settlement of property rights and interests between the parties, its terms will not thereafter be modified under any circumstances. Jamal v. Jamal, 98 Ill. App. 2d 180, 240 N.E.2d 246 (1 Dist. 1968).

Where plaintiff's petition alleged additional facts which indicated that her rights to enforce defendant's obligations under the property settlement portion of divorce decree had been compromised and settled by the terms of a second agreement, her claim under the decree thus became merged into the second agreement, and was no longer subject to the decretal enforcement procedures. Jamal v. Jamal, 98 Ill. App. 2d 180, 240 N.E.2d 246 (1 Dist. 1968).

Where a divorce decree did not of its volition attempt to transfer defendant's real estate to his former wife but did confirm the agreement of the parties and the voluntary act of the defendant in making the conveyance to his wife, upon entry of the divorce decree, the wife became vested with ownership of the property and was entitled to have the deed transferred to her. Cunningham v. Lawrence, 16 Ill. 2d 201, 157 N.E.2d 50 (1959).

After a decree is rendered, the rights of the parties rest upon the decree and not upon their prior agreement. Jacobs v. Jacobs, 328 Ill. App. 133, 65 N.E.2d 588 (1 Dist. 1946).

Where an agreement between the parties settling their property rights was made a part of the divorce decree, the agreement merged into the decree. Brevet v. Brevet, 316 Ill. App. 406, 45 N.E.2d 199 (1 Dist. 1942).

—Oral Agreement Incorporated
The judge being fully advised of husband's objection, as well as wife's contention that husband had agreed to her receiving 37% of his gross pension, concluded, in approving the judgment which included that provision, that husband had agreed to include the provision in the settlement agreement. In re Hartian, 172 Ill. App.

Terms of Agreement (Cont'd)

—Oral Agreement Incorporated (Cont'd)
3d 440, 122 Ill. Dec. 565, 526 N.E.2d 1104 (1 Dist.), appeal denied, 123 Ill. 2d 558, 128 Ill. Dec. 890, 535 N.E.2d 401 (1988).

—Religious Upbringing of Children
A premarital agreement relating to the religious upbringing of the children was not binding on the court in dissolution proceedings. In re Nuechterlien, 225 Ill. App. 3d 1, 167 Ill. Dec. 139, 587 N.E.2d 21 (4 Dist.), cert. denied, 145 Ill. 2d 636, 173 Ill. Dec. 6, 596 N.E.2d 630 (1992).

Unconscionability

—In General
An agreement is not unconscionable where it has been negotiated for several months, both parties were represented by counsel, there was no allegation of fraud, and it was not sufficiently one-sided. In re Van Zuidam, 162 Ill. App. 3d 942, 114 Ill. Dec. 176, 516 N.E.2d 331 (1 Dist. 1987), appeal denied, 117 Ill. Dec. 232, 520 N.E.2d 393 (Ill. 1988).

A settlement can be set aside by the court if it finds, after considering the economic circumstances of the parties and any other relevant evidence produced by the parties, on their own motion or on request of the court, that the separation agreement is unconscionable. In re Moran, 136 Ill. App. 3d 331, 91 Ill. Dec. 234, 483 N.E.2d 580 (1 Dist. 1985).

—Considerations
The inquiry into unconscionability involves at least two separate considerations: one, the conditions under which the agreement was made, and two, the economic circumstances of the parties resulting from the agreement. In re Foster, 115 Ill. App. 3d 969, 71 Ill. Dec. 761, 451 N.E.2d 915 (5 Dist. 1983); In re Riedy, 130 Ill. App. 3d 311, 85 Ill. Dec. 614, 474 N.E.2d 28 (2 Dist. 1985); In re Smith, 164 Ill. App. 3d 1011, 115 Ill. Dec. 925, 518 N.E.2d 450 (1 Dist. 1987).

—Contribution of Parties
The determination of unconscionability focuses on the parties' relative economic positions immediately following the making of the agreement; the contribution of the parties to the marriage before the entry of the agreement has no bearing on the question of unconscionability. In re Smith, 164 Ill. App. 3d 1011, 115 Ill. Dec. 925, 518 N.E.2d 450 (1 Dist. 1987).

—Defined
An agreement is unconscionable when it is improvident, totally one-sided, or oppressive. In re Morris, 147 Ill. App. 3d 380, 100 Ill. Dec. 811, 497 N.E.2d 1173 (1 Dist. 1986); In re Smith, 164 Ill. App. 3d 1011, 115 Ill. Dec. 925, 518 N.E.2d 450 (1 Dist. 1987).

An unconscionable bargain has been defined as one which no man in his right senses, not under delusion, would make, on the one hand, and which no fair and honest man would accept, on the other; the term "unconscionability" includes an absence of meaningful choice on the part of one of the parties together with contract terms which are unreasonably favorable to the other party, and a contract is unconscionable when it is improvident, totally one-sided or oppressive. In re Foster, 115 Ill. App. 3d 969, 71 Ill. Dec. 761, 451 N.E.2d 915 (5 Dist. 1983).

—Discretion
A party alleging unconscionability of a settlement agreement must be permitted to present evidence relevant to that agreement; however, the admission or exclusion of evidence is within the circuit court's discretion and will not be disturbed absent an abuse thereof. In re Smith, 164 Ill. App. 3d 1011, 115 Ill. Dec. 925, 518 N.E.2d 450 (1 Dist. 1987).

—Evidence
Evidence that a separation agreement is unconscionable may be produced by the parties, on their own motion or on the request of the court. In re Lorenzi, 84 Ill. App. 3d 427, 39 Ill. Dec. 754, 405 N.E.2d 507 (3 Dist. 1980).

—Fear
While wife's fear she may lose custody of children no doubt caused anxiety, her ability to exercise her free will and make meaningful choices was not impaired where record showed she took part in negotiations and presented substance of negotiations under oath to the trial court. In re Steadman, 283 Ill. App. 3d 703, 219 Ill. Dec. 258, 670 N.E.2d 1146 (3 Dist. 1996).

—Full and Fair Disclosure
Where both parties made a full and fair disclosure of their assets prior to execution of their agreement and a winning lottery ticket of $2.1 million was not among husband's contingent assets at the time the agreement was signed, the executed agreement was binding on the court since it was not unconscionable. In re Van Zuidam, 162 Ill. App. 3d 942, 114 Ill. Dec. 176, 516 N.E.2d 331 (1 Dist. 1987), appeal denied, 117 Ill. Dec. 232, 520 N.E.2d 393 (Ill. 1988).

—Haste
Wife's claims that hasty negotiations deprived her of the opportunity to make a meaningful choice were dismissed where the parties negotiated for two hours at arms length with the aid of counsel. In re Steadman, 283 Ill. App. 3d 703, 219 Ill. Dec. 258, 670 N.E.2d 1146 (3 Dist. 1996).

An agreement may be found unconscionable where it is hastily contrived and where movant objects immediately to the agreement. In re Smith, 164 Ill. App. 3d 1011, 115 Ill. Dec. 925, 518 N.E.2d 450 (1 Dist. 1987).

—Inequities in Agreement
Inequities in settlement agreement resulting from husband's failure to disclose fully his assets, as well as his retention of an attorney who counseled both spouses, rendered both the settlement agreement and the judgment of dissolution unconscionable. In re Reines, 184 Ill. App. 3d 392, 132 Ill. Dec. 654, 540 N.E.2d 394 (1 Dist. 1989).

—Not Shown
Former wife failed to show that settlement agreement into which she entered, after days of negotiation and with the assistance of counsel, that gave her a larger actual amount of her husband's pension benefits than she would have received if she had been awarded a property interest in the pension, was unconscionable so as to entitle her to relief from judgment. In re Bielawski, Ill. App. 3d , 262 Ill. Dec. 137, 764 N.E.2d 1254, 2002 Ill. App. LEXIS 116 (1 Dist. 2002), appeal denied, 199 Ill. 2d 551, 266 Ill. Dec. 439, 775 N.E.2d 1 (2002).

The economic circumstances resulting from property settlement did not require a finding of unconscionability where, due to husband's misrepresentations and omissions, court was unable to ascertain the actual value of the assets and liabilities allocated to the parties; additionally, although the agreement may favor wife, that an agreement merely favors one party over another does not make it unconscionable. In re Hamm-Smith, 261 Ill. App. 3d 209, 198 Ill. Dec. 763, 633 N.E.2d 225 (4 Dist. 1994).

Where settlement agreement on its face evinced no sign of unconscionability, it was binding upon the court absent any evidence of fraud, coercion or duress; therefore, trial court erred when it sua sponte vacated family support provision of the parties' settlement agreement and increased wife's award of maintenance. In re Stadheim, 170 Ill. App. 3d 19, 120 Ill. Dec. 373, 523 N.E.2d 1284 (1 Dist. 1988).

Mere allegation that husband purchased a lottery ticket and won, after execution of property settlement agreement and prove-up, did not rise to the standard of unconscionability required to relieve the trial court of the binding effect of the agreement mandated by this Act. In re Van Zuidam, 162 Ill. App. 3d 942, 114 Ill. Dec. 176, 516 N.E.2d 331 (1 Dist. 1987), appeal denied, 117 Ill. Dec. 232, 520 N.E.2d 393 (Ill. 1988).

Where respondent's claim of pain suffered at time of settlement negotiations, whether or not credible, did not appear to have clouded her cognitive abilities or capacity to recall and relate material facts, and the financial advantage enjoyed by petitioner as a result of the agreement was neither so one-sided nor so oppressive as to be unconscionable, the supplemental judgment of dissolution and denial of respondent's motion to vacate was against the manifest weight of the evidence. In re Smith, 164 Ill. App. 3d 1011, 115 Ill. Dec. 925, 518 N.E.2d 450 (1 Dist. 1987).

Where division of property may not have been perfect, and settlement agreement may have favored one party more than the other, decision that the agreement was not unconscionable was

Unconscionability (Cont'd)

—Not Shown (Cont'd)
supported by the manifest weight of the evidence. In re Kloster, 127 Ill. App. 3d 583, 82 Ill. Dec. 847, 469 N.E.2d 381 (2 Dist. 1984).

A separation agreement under which husband received less than half of parties' property, while wife received the rest, requiring husband to sell property in order to meet obligations imposed upon him, was held not unconscionable. In re Foster, 115 Ill. App. 3d 969, 71 Ill. Dec. 761, 451 N.E.2d 915 (5 Dist. 1983); In re Lee, 135 Ill. App. 3d 509, 90 Ill. Dec. 245, 481 N.E.2d 1045 (1 Dist. 1985).

The fact that anticipated sales from real estate in a separation agreement did not or would not yield the anticipated amounts did not render the separation agreement unconscionable. In re Miller, 98 Ill. App. 3d 1084, 54 Ill. Dec. 439, 424 N.E.2d 1342 (4 Dist. 1981).

—Opportunity to Investigate

Where wife had ample opportunity to protect her financial interests by disputing any portion of the separation agreement before, during or after the trial court granted the judgment yet affirmatively chose not to do so she could not claim herself a victim of a unconscionable bargain. In re Broday, 256 Ill. App. 3d 699, 195 Ill. Dec. 326, 628 N.E.2d 790 (1 Dist. 1993).

—Parties' Economic Positions

The fact that the parties agree to equally divide the tax deferred annuity account, after paying marital debt which necessarily lessened the amount to be shared, did not constitute economic unconscionability. In re Steadman, 283 Ill. App. 3d 703, 219 Ill. Dec. 258, 670 N.E.2d 1146 (3 Dist. 1996).

Wife had ample opportunity to discover error of omission of a second retirement benefit and to petition court to include omitted term in qualified domestic relations order; thus, and such omission did not support conclusion agreement was economically unconscionable. In re Steadman, 283 Ill. App. 3d 703, 219 Ill. Dec. 258, 670 N.E.2d 1146 (3 Dist. 1996).

In determining whether the parties' relative economic positions are unconscionable, courts employ commercial concepts of unconscionability: an absence of a meaningful choice on the part of one of the parties combined with terms unreasonably favorable to the other party. In re Smith, 164 Ill. App. 3d 1011, 115 Ill. Dec. 925, 518 N.E.2d 450 (1 Dist. 1987); In re Carlson, 186 Ill. App. 3d 635, 134 Ill. Dec. 414, 542 N.E.2d 760 (1 Dist. 1989).

—Shown

Where the former husband brought a 735 ILCS 5/2-1401 petition 20 months after the dissolution of marriage alleging that the separation agreement was unconscionable under 750 ILCS 5/502(b), the judgment was vacated despite the husband's failure to exercise due diligence in bringing the petition; justice and fairness required that the petition be granted, as the trial court that dissolved the marriage was unaware that the agreement required the husband, who was unrepresented by counsel, to make weekly payments of $ 450 for 15 years to the wife, who had waived maintenance, so that the husband could retain the husband's $ 100,000 pension, and the amount that the wife was to receive greatly exceeded the value of the marital estate. In re Marriage of Johnson, 339 Ill. App. 3d 237, 273 Ill. Dec. 949, 790 N.E.2d 91, 2003 Ill. App. LEXIS 636 (2 Dist. 2003).

Respondent shielded certain marital assets from the petitioner, and thus prevented petitioner from making an informed decision to enter into the property settlement or the trial court from making a fair and equitable distribution of the marital property in just proportion, post-nuptial agreement entered into between the parties fails as being both procedurally and substantively unconscionable. In re Richardson, 237 Ill. App. 3d 1067, 179 Ill. Dec. 224, 606 N.E.2d 56 (1 Dist. 1992), appeal denied, 149 Ill. 2d 660, 183 Ill. Dec. 871, 612 N.E.2d 523 (1993).

Spouse labored under an extraordinary amount of duress at the time post-nuptial agreement was executed, sufficient to warrant setting aside the agreement as unconscionable. In re Richardson, 237 Ill. App. 3d 1067, 179 Ill. Dec. 224, 606 N.E.2d 56 (1 Dist. 1992), appeal denied, 149 Ill. 2d 660, 183 Ill. Dec. 871, 612 N.E.2d 523 (1993).

Under an agreement that awarded petitioner custody of parties' two children, marital home and parties' automobile, and awarded respondent certain household items and $55 per week for 16 weeks, where circumstances surrounding the agreement's execution indicated that respondent did not make a meaningful choice, the trial court correctly found the agreement to be unconscionable and properly set aside that portion of the judgment for dissolution which incorporated the separation agreement. In re Carlson, 101 Ill. App. 3d 924, 57 Ill. Dec. 325, 428 N.E.2d 1005 (1 Dist. 1981).

—Standard of Review

On review, the circuit court's ruling regarding unconscionability will stand unless it is found to be against the manifest weight of the evidence. In re Smith, 164 Ill. App. 3d 1011, 115 Ill. Dec. 925, 518 N.E.2d 450 (1 Dist. 1987).

—Unfairness

Unfairness alone is not enough to render a settlement agreement unconscionable. In re Smith, 164 Ill. App. 3d 1011, 115 Ill. Dec. 925, 518 N.E.2d 450 (1 Dist. 1987).

Validity of Agreement

—In General

In determining whether a settlement agreement violates public policy, reviewing courts focus on whether such a contract is free from actual fraud or coercion and also whether it is reasonable, fair, and sufficient in light of the parties' circumstances and station in life. In re Frey, 258 Ill. App. 3d 442, 196 Ill. Dec. 531, 630 N.E.2d 466 (5 Dist. 1994).

The law favors the amicable settlement of property rights in marital dissolution cases and the validity of such property settlement agreements will be presumed absent a showing otherwise. In re Hawkins, 160 Ill. App. 3d 71, 111 Ill. Dec. 897, 513 N.E.2d 143 (5 Dist. 1987).

A court should not set aside a property settlement agreement merely because one party has second thoughts. In re Steichen, 163 Ill. App. 3d 1074, 115 Ill. Dec. 234, 517 N.E.2d 645 (2 Dist. 1987).

—Coercion, Duress and Fraud

A settlement agreement will be set aside if the agreement was procured by fraud or coercion or contrary to any rule of law, public policy, or morals. In re Frey, 258 Ill. App. 3d 442, 196 Ill. Dec. 531, 630 N.E.2d 466 (5 Dist. 1994).

The court will not vacate a property settlement on the basis of coercion where neither the court nor counsel subjected the party to extreme pressure to settle, and the party's statements affirming the agreement at the hearing clearly show that the party freely agreed to the settlement. In re Steichen, 163 Ill. App. 3d 1074, 115 Ill. Dec. 234, 517 N.E.2d 645 (2 Dist. 1987).

While property settlements are favored, a court will not effectuate the terms of an agreement if it is procured by fraud or coercion, or is otherwise contrary to the law, public policy, or morals. In re Steichen, 163 Ill. App. 3d 1074, 115 Ill. Dec. 234, 517 N.E.2d 645 (2 Dist. 1987).

In order for a court to vacate an agreement on the basis of coercion, the movant must demonstrate by clear and convincing evidence that such coercion took place. In re Steichen, 163 Ill. App. 3d 1074, 115 Ill. Dec. 234, 517 N.E.2d 645 (2 Dist. 1987).

Duress has been defined as including the imposition, oppression, undue influence or the taking of undue advantage of the stress of another whereby one is deprived of the exercise of his free will. In re Riedy, 130 Ill. App. 3d 311, 85 Ill. Dec. 614, 474 N.E.2d 28 (2 Dist. 1985).

Agreements to settle property rights, if fairly made and in good faith, will be enforced, but they will be set aside and vacated for fraud or coercion practiced by either party, or if contrary to any rule of law, public policy or morals. In re Beck, 83 Ill. App. 3d 976, 39 Ill. Dec. 381, 404 N.E.2d 972 (2 Dist. 1980).

For a case discussing sufficiency of divorced wife's petition for relief pursuant to former section 72 of the Civil Practice Act (see now 735 ILCS 5/2-1401) from divorce decree in which she alleged husband was guilty of fraud, inducing her to forego including settlement agreement in decree, and to waive claims for alimony, see Plavec v. Plavec, 30 Ill. App. 2d 345, 174 N.E.2d 578 (1 Dist. 1961).

—Conscionability

Prior to the determination of whether a post-nuptial agreement was contemplated to comport to this section or 750 ILCS 5/503(a)(4), the threshold question necessarily becomes whether

Validity of Agreement (Cont'd)

—Conscionability (Cont'd)

there was a conscionable, and, therefore, valid agreement. In re Richardson, 237 Ill. App. 3d 1067, 179 Ill. Dec. 224, 606 N.E.2d 56 (1 Dist. 1992), appeal denied, 149 Ill. 2d 660, 183 Ill. Dec. 871, 612 N.E.2d 523 (1993).

—Murder of Party

Although no provision in this Act excludes a person who intentionally and unjustifiably causes the death of a party to a marital settlement agreement from receiving the benefits of that agreement, the public policy set forth in 755 ILCS 5/2-6, which prevents a wrongdoer from receiving any property, benefit, or other interest from his intentionally committed wrongful act, must be regarded as incorporated in the dissolution legislation; therefore, a minor, as a result of his intentional and unjustifiable act of murdering decedent, was considered to have predeceased decedent and was not entitled to any benefits of a marital settlement agreement. First Nat'l Bank v. Braun, 222 Ill. App. 3d 178, 164 Ill. Dec. 717, 583 N.E.2d 633 (2 Dist. 1991).

—Mutual Mistake

A proper ground for relief from a divorce agreement would be a divorce decree which incorporates a written agreement which fails to express the real intention of the parties through mutual mistake, or through mistake of one side and fraud on the other, and where the proof clearly and convincingly shows that a mistake was made, and that it was mutual and common to both parties. Groak v. Groak, 64 Ill. App. 2d 439, 212 N.E.2d 139 (1 Dist. 1965).

—Newly Discovered Evidence

The existence of an additional fact, which became apparent after the cause proceeded to trial but prior to judgment, required the trial court to consider vacating the earlier judgment to make a determination as to whether such agreement was procured by fraud or at least to make a determination as to whether the additional factor rendered the agreement fair and conscionable under the circumstances. Gurin v. Gurin, 212 Ill. App. 3d 806, 156 Ill. Dec. 877, 571 N.E.2d 857 (1 Dist. 1991).

—Presumptions

When one party to the dissolution action seeks to vacate a property settlement incorporated into the dissolution judgment, all presumptions favor the validity of the settlement. In re Steichen, 163 Ill. App. 3d 1074, 115 Ill. Dec. 234, 517 N.E.2d 645 (2 Dist. 1987).

—Voluntariness

Determination of the trial court that a settlement agreement had been voluntarily entered into was against the manifest weight of the evidence where a letter which the husband's attorney prepared and which the wife signed was addressed to an attorney designated by her husband's attorney and whom she did not know, the letter did not clearly amount to a final property settlement agreement by its terms but purported to be an expression of terms the wife wanted to appear in any judgment to be entered, and the wife testified that she believed she was merely signing a preliminary agreement and that she would be contacted by her attorney before any papers were to be drawn up. In re Beck, 83 Ill. App. 3d 976, 39 Ill. Dec. 381, 404 N.E.2d 972 (2 Dist. 1980).

Waiver

Maintenance is a valuable right and unless there is an express and explicit waiver, a waiver will not be presumed. In re Popovich, 149 Ill. App. 3d 643, 103 Ill. Dec. 38, 500 N.E.2d 1109 (4 Dist. 1986).

LEGAL PERIODICALS

For article, "Family Law: 1987-88 Illinois Law Survey," see Loy. U. Chi. L.J. 461 (1988-89).

For article, "Secular Solutions to Obtaining a Jewish Divorce," see 76 Ill. B.J. 274 (1988).

For article, "Family Law: 1985-86 Survey," see 11 S. Ill. U. L.J. 741 (1987).

For article, "Caveat Amator: 'The State of Affairs' in Illinois After Hewitt v. Hewitt," see 29 De Paul L. Rev. 493 (1980).

RESEARCH REFERENCES

Modern status of views as to validity of premarital agreements contemplating divorce or separation. 53 ALR4th 22.

Enforceability of premarital agreements governing support or property rights upon divorce or separation as affected by circumstances surrounding execution — modern status. 53 ALR4th 85.

Divorce: propriety of using contempt proceeding to enforce property settlement award or order. 72 ALR4th 298.

750 ILCS 5/503 Disposition of property

Sec. 503. *Disposition of property.* (a) For purposes of this Act, "marital property" means all property acquired by either spouse subsequent to the marriage, except the following, which is known as "non-marital property":

(1) property acquired by gift, legacy or descent;

(2) property acquired in exchange for property acquired before the marriage or in exchange for property acquired by gift, legacy or descent;

(3) property acquired by a spouse after a judgment of legal separation;

(4) property excluded by valid agreement of the parties;

(5) any judgment or property obtained by judgment awarded to a spouse from the other spouse;

(6) property acquired before the marriage;

(7) the increase in value of property acquired by a method listed in paragraphs (1) through (6) of this subsection, irrespective of whether the increase results from a contribution of marital property, non-marital property, the personal effort of a spouse, or otherwise, subject to the right of reimbursement provided in subsection (c) of this Section; and

(8) income from property acquired by a method listed in paragraphs (1) through (7) of this subsection if the income is not attributable to the personal effort of a spouse.

(b)(1) For purposes of distribution of property pursuant to this Section, all property acquired by either spouse after the marriage and before a judgment of dissolution of marriage or declaration of invalidity of marriage, including non-marital property transferred into some form of co-ownership between the spouses, is presumed to be marital property, regardless of whether title is held individually or by the spouses in some form of co-ownership such as joint tenancy, tenancy in common, tenancy by the entirety, or community property. The presumption of marital property is overcome by a showing that the property was acquired by a method listed in subsection (a) of this Section.

(2) For purposes of distribution of property pursuant to this Section, all pension benefits (including pension benefits under the Illinois Pension Code [40 ILCS 5/1-101 et seq.]) acquired by either spouse after the marriage and before a judgment of dissolution of marriage or declaration of invalidity of the marriage are presumed to be marital property, regardless of which spouse participates in the pension plan. The presumption that these pension benefits are marital property is overcome by a showing that

the pension benefits were acquired by a method listed in subsection (a) of this Section. The right to a division of pension benefits in just proportions under this Section is enforceable under Section 1-119 of the Illinois Pension Code [40 ILCS 5/1-119].

The value of pension benefits in a retirement system subject to the Illinois Pension Code [40 ILCS 5/1-101 et seq.] shall be determined in accordance with the valuation procedures established by the retirement system.

The recognition of pension benefits as marital property and the division of those benefits pursuant to a Qualified Illinois Domestic Relations Order shall not be deemed to be a diminishment, alienation, or impairment of those benefits. The division of pension benefits is an allocation of property in which each spouse has a species of common ownership.

(3) For purposes of distribution of property under this Section, all stock options granted to either spouse after the marriage and before a judgment of dissolution of marriage or declaration of invalidity of marriage, whether vested or non-vested or whether their value is ascertainable, are presumed to be marital property. This presumption of marital property is overcome by a showing that the stock options were acquired by a method listed in subsection (a) of this Section. The court shall allocate stock options between the parties at the time of the judgment of dissolution of marriage or declaration of invalidity of marriage recognizing that the value of the stock options may not be then determinable and that the actual division of the options may not occur until a future date. In making the allocation between the parties, the court shall consider, in addition to the factors set forth in subsection (d) of this Section, the following:

(i) All circumstances underlying the grant of the stock option including but not limited to whether the grant was for past, present, or future efforts, or any combination thereof.

(ii) The length of time from the grant of the option to the time the option is exercisable.

(c) Commingled marital and non-marital property shall be treated in the following manner, unless otherwise agreed by the spouses:

(1) When marital and non-marital property are commingled by contributing one estate of property into another resulting in a loss of identity of the contributed property, the classification of the contributed property is transmuted to the estate receiving the contribution, subject to the provisions of paragraph (2) of this subsection; provided that if marital and non-marital property are commingled into newly acquired property resulting in a loss of identity of the contributing estates, the commingled property shall be deemed transmuted to marital property, subject to the provisions of paragraph (2) of this subsection.

(2) When one estate of property makes a contribution to another estate of property, or when a spouse contributes personal effort to non-marital property, the contributing estate shall be reimbursed from the estate receiving the contribution notwithstanding any transmutation; provided, that no such reimbursement shall be made with respect to a contribution which is not retraceable by clear and convincing evidence, or was a gift, or, in the case of a contribution of personal effort of a spouse to non-marital property, unless the effort is significant and results in substantial appreciation of the non-marital property. Personal effort of a spouse shall be deemed a contribution by the marital estate. The court may provide for reimbursement out of the marital property to be divided or by imposing a lien against the non-marital property which received the contribution.

(d) In a proceeding for dissolution of marriage or declaration of invalidity of marriage, or in a proceeding for disposition of property following dissolution of marriage by a court which lacked personal jurisdiction over the absent spouse or lacked jurisdiction to dispose of the property, the court shall assign each spouse's non-marital property to that spouse. It also shall divide the marital property without regard to marital misconduct in just proportions considering all relevant factors, including:

(1) the contribution of each party to the acquisition, preservation, or increase or decrease in value of the marital or non-marital property, including the contribution of a spouse as a homemaker or to the family unit;

(2) the dissipation by each party of the marital or non-marital property;

(3) the value of the property assigned to each spouse;

(4) the duration of the marriage;

(5) the relevant economic circumstances of each spouse when the division of property is to become effective, including the desirability of awarding the family home, or the right to live therein for reasonable periods, to the spouse having custody of the children;

(6) any obligations and rights arising from a prior marriage of either party;

(7) any antenuptial agreement of the parties;

(8) the age, health, station, occupation, amount and sources of income, vocational skills, employability, estate, liabilities, and needs of each of the parties;

(9) the custodial provisions for any children;

(10) whether the apportionment is in lieu of or in addition to maintenance;

(11) the reasonable opportunity of each spouse for future acquisition of capital assets and income; and

(12) the tax consequences of the property division upon the respective economic circumstances of the parties.

(e) Each spouse has a species of common ownership in the marital property which vests at the time dissolution proceedings are commenced and continues only during the pendency of the action. Any such interest in marital property shall not encumber that property so as to restrict its transfer, assignment or conveyance by the title holder unless such title holder is specifically enjoined from making such transfer, assignment or conveyance.

(f) In a proceeding for dissolution of marriage or declaration of invalidity of marriage or in a proceeding for disposition of property following dissolution of marriage by a court that lacked personal jurisdiction over the absent spouse or lacked jurisdiction to dispose of the property, the court, in determining the value of the marital and non-marital property for purposes of dividing the property, shall value the property as of the date of trial or some other date as close to the date of trial as is practicable.

(g) The court if necessary to protect and promote the best interests of the children may set aside a portion of the jointly or separately held estates of the parties in a separate fund or trust for the support, maintenance, education, and general welfare of any minor, dependent, or incompetent child of the parties. In making a determination under this subsection, the court may consider, among other things, the conviction of a party of any of the offenses set forth in Section 12-3.3, 12-4, 12-4.1, 12-4.2, 12-4.3, 12-13, 12-14, 12-14.1, 12-15, or 12-16 of the Criminal Code of 1961 [720 ILCS 5/12-3.3, 720 ILCS 5/12-4, 720 ILCS 5/12-4.1, 720 ILCS 5/12-4.2, 720 ILCS 5/12-4.3, 720 ILCS 5/12-13, 720 ILCS 5/12-14, 720 ILCS 5/12-14.1, 720 ILCS 5/12-15, or 720 ILCS 5/12-16] if the victim is a child of one or both of the parties, and there is a need for, and cost of, care, healing and counseling for the child who is the victim of the crime.

(h) Unless specifically directed by a reviewing court, or upon good cause shown, the court shall not on remand consider any increase or decrease in the value of any "marital" or "non-marital" property occurring since the assessment of such property at the original trial or hearing, but shall use only that assessment made at the original trial or hearing.

(i) The court may make such judgments affecting the marital property as may be just and may enforce such judgments by ordering a sale of marital property, with proceeds therefrom to be applied as determined by the court.

(j) After proofs have closed in the final hearing on all other issues between the parties (or in conjunction with the final hearing, if all parties so stipulate) and before judgment is entered, a party's petition for contribution to fees and costs incurred in the proceeding shall be heard and decided, in accordance with the following provisions:

(1) A petition for contribution, if not filed before the final hearing on other issues between the parties, shall be filed no later than 30 days after the closing of proofs in the final hearing or within such other period as the court orders.

(2) Any award of contribution to one party from the other party shall be based on the criteria for division of marital property under this Section 503 and, if maintenance has been awarded, on the criteria for an award of maintenance under Section 504 [750 ILCS 5/504].

(3) The filing of a petition for contribution shall not be deemed to constitute a waiver of the attorney-client privilege between the petitioning party and current or former counsel; and such a waiver shall not constitute a prerequisite to a hearing for contribution. If either party's presentation on contribution, however, includes evidence within the scope of the attorney-client privilege, the disclosure or disclosures shall be narrowly construed and shall not be deemed by the court to constitute a general waiver of the privilege as to matters beyond the scope of the presentation.

(4) No finding on which a contribution award is based or denied shall be asserted against counsel or former counsel for purposes of any hearing under subsection (c) or (e) of Section 508 [750 ILCS 5/508].

(5) A contribution award (payable to either the petitioning party or the party's counsel, or jointly, as the court determines) may be in the form of either a set dollar amount or a percentage of fees and costs (or a portion of fees and costs) to be subsequently agreed upon by the petitioning party and counsel or, alternatively, thereafter determined in a hearing pursuant to subsection (c) of Section 508 [750 ILCS 5/508] or previously or thereafter determined in an independent proceeding under subsection (e) of Section 508 [750 ILCS 5/508].

(6) The changes to this Section 503 made by this amendatory Act of 1996 apply to cases pending on or after June 1, 1997, except as otherwise provided in Section 508 [750 ILCS 5/508].

(Source: P.A. 87-881; 87-1115, § 1; 88-45, § 2-59; 89-428, § 298; 89-462, § 298; 89-712, § 5; 90-731, § 10; 91-445, § 20; 92-306, § 5.)

Note.

This section was Ill.Rev.Stat., Ch. 40, para. 503.

P.A. 91-445, § 95, contains a "no acceleration or delay" provision.

Effect of Amendments.

The 1995 amendment by P.A. 89-428, effective December 13, 1995 and the 1996 amendment by P.A. 89-462, effective May 29, 1996, made identical amendments: they each, in subsection (g), in the second sentence, inserted "12-14.1".

The 1996 amendment by P.A. 89-712, effective June 1, 1997, incorporated the amendments made by P.A. 89-462; and added subsection (j).

The 1998 amendment by P.A. 90-731, effective July 1, 1999, in subsection (b) added the subsection (b)(1) designation and added subsection (b)(2).

The 1999 amendment by P.A. 91-445, effective January 1, 2000, inserted "12-3.3" in subsection (g).

The 2001 amendment by P.A. 92-306, effective January 1, 2002, inserted subsection (b)(3).

CASE NOTES

ANALYSIS

Constitutionality
—Due Process
—Equal Protection
—Impairment of Contracts
—Vagueness

In General
Antenuptial Agreement
—Applicability
—Not Shown
—Real Property Contributions
—Upheld
—Writing Required
Attorney Fees
—Requirements
Award
—Attorney Fees
—Car
—Classification
—Corporate Stock
—Home
—Home Furnishings
—Improper
—Life Insurance Policy
—Ranch
—Upheld
Bank Accounts
—Evidence
Bias
—Not Shown
Children
—Award Improper
—Care of Minor
—Continuity in Environment
—Improperly Considered
—Life Insurance Policy
—Uncontested Needs
Choice of Law
—Original Judgment
Classification of Property
—In General
—Bank Accounts for Expenses
—Dental Practice
—Dual Status
—Exclusivity
—Presumption
—Professional Corporation
—Required
—Standard of Review
—Stock
—Stock Options
—Time of Acquisition
—Transmutation
—Workers' Compensation Award
Clean Hands Doctrine
Collateral Actions
—Diversion of Funds
—Personal Injury
Commingling
—Art Objects
—Business
—Cash Management Account
—Checking Accounts
—Gifts
—Home Construction
—Purchase of Real Property
—Reimbursement
—Repairs and Maintenance
—Savings Account
—Traceability
—Transformation of Property
Confidentiality
Consolidation of Action
Contingent Interests
—Fee Contracts
—Trusts
Contribution
—In General
—Both Spouses
—Burden
—Extent
—Fair Distribution
—Financial Contributions
—Improvement Not Shown
—Indebtedness Not Created
—Mortgage Debt
—Non-Marital Property
—Owner of Land Trust
—Reimbursement
—Specific Dollar Value
—Support of Children
Conveyance of Property
—In General
—Absolute Right
—Clear and Convincing Evidence
—Court Ordered
—Effect of Act
—Error
—Gift or Advancement
—Good Faith
—Illustrative Cases
—Special Circumstances and Equities
—Voidability
Credit
Criminal Contempt
De Minimus Claims
Debts
—Assignment
—Classification
—Contingent Liabilities
—Dischargeability in Bankruptcy
—Distribution Upheld
—Dual Responsibility
—Equal Division
—Excess of Assets
—Liability
—Non-Marital
—Reimbursement
—Tax Liability
Declaratory Relief
Deed
Desertion
Discretion of Court
—In General
—Apportionment
—Approximation of Income
—Authorization of Award
—Continuing Jurisdiction
—Contributions
—Equitable
—Income Tax Refund
—Just Proportions
—Non-Marital Assets
—Range of Reason
Dissipation
—Accountability
—Benefit of Children
—Burden of Proof
—Changing Species and Retiring Debts
—Charge Against Property Share
—Compensation
—Credibility of Spouse Charged
—Damage to Family Photographs
—Debt
—Defined
—Depletion of Pension Funds
—Determination
—Discretion of Court
—Factors
—Funds for Expenses
—Gambling
—General and Vague Statements
—Illustrative Cases
—Inclusion of Non-Marital Property
—Income
—In Contemplation of Dissolution
—Lack of Evidence
—Legitimate Family Expenses

—Living in Marital Residence
—Necessary Expenditures
—Not Shown
—Particular Facts of Case
—Personal Benefit
—Prior to Separation
—Proof
—Requirements
—Review
—Securing Housing
—Shown
—Specific Statement Not Required
—Timing and Nature of Act
—Vacation Trips
Dissolution
—Conduct in Accepting Terms
—Date
—Provisions of Decree
—Statute of Frauds
Distribution
—In General
—Abuse of Discretion
—After-Acquired Property
—Consideration of Factors
—Discretion
—Disproportionate Award
—Equal Proportions
—Evidence
—Evidentiary Hearing
—Factors
—Fairness
—Fund
—Future Earning Capacity
—Greater Financial Contributions
—Inventory
—Marital Home
—Mistaken Decisions
—Non-Monetary Contributions
—Not Upheld
—Objectives
—Professional Degree or License
—Reservation of Issues
—Statutory Authority
—Stock
—Tax Consequences
—Upheld
Divestment of Title
—Not Upheld
Due Process
Duration of Marriage
Duty to Disclose
Education of Children
—In General
—College Expenses
—Court's Discretion
—Disbursement of Proceeds
—Future Expenditures
—Necessary
—No Abuse of Discretion
—Religious Beliefs
Effect of Amendment
Effective Date
Election of Remedies
Equitable Distribution
—In General
—Attorney Fees
—Bankruptcy Proceedings
—Difference in Values
—Equitable Interest
—Evidence Held Insufficient
—Evidence Held Sufficient
—Homemaker's Contributions
—Illustrative Cases
—Income-Producing Property
—Not Shown
—Relevant Factors
—Shown
—Stock Proceeds
Equitable Interest
—Contribution Toward Acquisition
—Voluntary Payments
Estoppel
Evidence
—Accountant's Summary
—Affidavits
—Held Insufficient
—Relevance
Extension of Time
Factors
Fault
Fiduciary Relationship
—Burden of Proof
Findings
—Not Mandatory
—Specific
Foreign Decree
—Lack of Personal Jurisdiction
—Recourse in Illinois
Fraud
—Concealment of Property
—Evidence Held Insufficient
Fraudulent Conveyances
—In General
—Burden
—Marital Rights
—Motion to Vacate or Modify
—Not Shown
—Prima Facie Fraud
—Specific Intent Not Shown
—Third Party
—To Wife
Fund
—Not Warranted
Gift
—Burden of Proof
—Commingling Property
—Donative Intent
—Evidence
—Factors
—Intent
—Inter Vivos Gift
—Marital Asset
—Not Shown
—Pre-Marriage Funds
—Presumption
—In General
—Rebutted
—Reimbursement
—Requirements
—Shown
—Time of Acquisition
—To Children
—Upheld
Goodwill
—Business
—Corporate
—Professional
—Stock Valuation
Hearing
Homemaker's Contribution
—Abuse of Discretion
—Devalued
—Employed Outside the Home
—Entitled to Consideration
—Improvements to House
—Recognition
—Reimbursement
—Share of Assets
—Shown
—Sufficient Consideration
Improvements
—Credit

Indispensable Party
Inheritance
—Commingling
—Gift to Estate
—Joint Bank Account
—Potential
Injunction
—Preservation of Status Quo
—Proceeds
—Upheld
Interest
Joint Tenancy
—Bank Account
—Conveyance Voided
—Effect of Divorce Decree
—Intent to Create
—Non-Marital Property
—Partition
—Presumption of Gift
—Presumption of Marital Property
—Severance
Jurisdiction
—Disposition of Property
—Divorce
—Enforcement
—Equity
—Failure to Comply with Agreement
—Reimbursement of Fees
—Support Increase
—Third Parties
Just Proportions
—In General
—Abuse of Discretion
—Consideration of Contributions
—Economic Circumstances
—Equal Amount
—Equitable Distribution
—Evidence
—Larger Share
—Not Shown
—Objective
—Shown
—Unequal Amount
Lien
Life Insurance Policy
Loan Repayment
—Reimbursement to Marital Estate
Maintenance
—Award Considered
—Determination
—Effect of Award
—Future Life of Parties
—Guidelines
—Upheld
Marital Expenditures
Marital Home
—Award Upheld
—Children's Welfare
—Consideration
—Conveyance
—Date of Valuation
—Economic Circumstances
—Evidence Held Sufficient
—Evidence of Intent
—Expenses
—Factors
—Mortgage
—Non-Marital Funds
—Non-Marital Funds for Payment of Taxes
—Noncustodial Parent
—Partition Right Waived
—Possession
—Presumption
—Purchase
—Sale
—Taxes and Insurance Premiums
—Utilities
—Value
Marital Property
—In General
—Accounts Held in Joint Tenancy
—Acquired During Marriage
—Acquired in Contemplation of Marriage
—Annuity
—Award Not Proper
—Bank Accounts
—Bargain
—Business Assets
—Business Interests
—Change in Ownership
—Co-ownership
—Contribution
—Credit Union Savings Account
—Crops
—Damage
—Determination
—Disability Pension
—Division
—Effect of Amendment
—Effect of Decree
—Equitable Distribution
—Expended During Marriage
—Financial Contributions
—Future Book Royalties
—Future Income
—Gift
—Income
—Income Tax Refund
—Increased Value
—Individual Retirement Accounts
—Inflation
—Insurance
—Investment Accounts
—IRA Account
—Joint Business Ownership
—Joint Tenancy
—Line of Credit
—Loans
—Lottery Winnings
—Marital Credit
—Marital Misconduct Disregarded
—Materiality
—Military Pension
—Money From Parent
—Mutual Agreement
—Not Shown
—Operation of Property
—Partnership Interest
—Pensions
—Personal Injury Settlement
—Presumption
—Proper Designation
—Property Settlement Agreement
—Reasonable Division
—Rebuttal of Presumption
—Stock Bonus
Non-Marital Funds
—Not Shown
Non-Marital Property
—IRA Account
—Shown
Pension Benefits
—Application and Construction
—Division
—Offset
—Spouse's Interest
Post-dissolution Effect
Reimbursement
—Accounts Receivable
—Not Required
Residency Rights
—Scope

—Securities
—Separate Ownership
—Shown
—Sole Proprietorship
—Stock
—Unequal Distribution
—Upheld
—Waste
—Workers' Compensation Award
—Workers' Compensation Claim
Method of Distribution
Misconduct
—In General
—Apportionment
—Money Decree
—Murder
Modification of Decree
—Change in Tax Law
—Conditions
—Considerations
—Enforceability
—Properly Denied
Non-Marital Property
—Application and Construction
—Appreciated Value
—Bank Accounts
—Business Interests
—Cancelled Checks
—Commingling with Marital Property
—Corporation
—Debt
—Evidence
—Federal Employer's Liability Action
—Future Acquisition of Assets
—Future Earning Capacity
—Gift
—Home
—Improvement
—Individual Retirement Account
—Investment
—Joint Tenancy
—Keough Plan
—Legislative Intent
—Life Insurance
—Marital Contribution
—Personal Efforts
—Profit-Sharing Plan
—Reduction of Indebtedness
—Reimbursement
—Relationship
—Rental Business
—Repairs to Home
—S Corporation
—Savings Plan
—Scope
—Separate Ownership
—Shown
—Stock Ownership Plan
—Test
—Tracing of Funds
—Trust
—Value
—Workers' Compensation Claim
Option to Purchase
Oral Agreement
Partition
Partnership Interests
—Assets and Liabilities
—Award Modified
—Evidence
—Good Will
—Valuation
Pension Benefits
—Accrual
—Acquisition During Marriage
—Application and Construction
—Award Not Proper
—Award Proper
—Classification Held Improper
—Discretion
—Division
—Division Prior to Vesting
—Firemen's Retirement Fund
—Increase After Dissolution
—Intended Use
—Joinder
—Marital Property
—Merger with Profit-Sharing Plan
—Military Retirement Benefits
—Offset
—Ownership Interest
—Personal Entitlement
—Review
—Spouse's Interest
—Valuation
Pleading
—In General
—Maintenance
—Property Conveyance
—Property Interest
Premarital Property Rights
—Not Shown
Presumptions
—In General
—Evidence Held Insufficient
—Exceptions
—Gift
—Rebuttal
Proceeds
Property Rights
—Invalid Divorce Decree
—Powers of Court
—Special Circumstances and Equities Required
—Survival
—Transfers
—Voluntary Adjustment
Property Settlement
—Contract
—Discretion
—Mutual Consent
Purpose
Refinancing Provisions
—Exclusion Held Proper
Reimbursement
—In General
—Abuse of Discretion
—Contribution
—Equity
—Lack of Traceable Contributions
—Not Required
—Personal Efforts
—Prior Compensation
—Sale of Non-Marital Asset
—Transfers During Marriage
Remand
—Circumstances
—Issues
—Scope
Remarriage
—Estoppel
—Modification of Property Distribution
—Rights Restored
Rental Property
—Abuse of Discretion
—Award Upheld
—Transfer of Title
Representation
Requirements
—In General
—Compliance with Statute
—Specific Value Not Required
Reserved Jurisdiction

Residence for Business Purposes
—Evidence Held Insufficient
Retroactive Application
Sale of Chose in Action
Sale of Real Property
—Improper
—Tax Consequences
Security
Separate Property
—Inheritance
—Separate Funds
Separation Agreement
Settlement Agreements
Source of Law
Special Equities
—Allegations and Proof
—Business Holdings
—Contributions
—Conveyance Denied
—Court Discretion
—Jointly Held Property
—Maintenance
—Not Shown
—Pleading
—Proof
—Property Conveyance
—Value
Spousal Support
Standard of Review
—In General
—Abuse of Discretion
—Manifest Weight of the Evidence
—Questions of Law
—Reasonable Person View
—Substantial Injustice
Stipulation
—Absence of Fraud
—Effect
Stock
—Acquired After Marriage
—Award Not Proper
—Award Proper
—Characterization Held Proper
—No Interest Shown
—Non-Marital Property
—Reimbursement
—Split
—Valuation
Survivor Benefits
—Not Subject to Division
Tax Consequences
—Duty of Court
—Exemptions
—Immediate Consequences
—Income Taxes
—Individual Retirement Account
—Liability
—Not Considered
—Property Distribution
Tax Returns
—Ambiguity
—Use
Temporary Support
Tenancy in Common
Third Parties
—In General
—Action
—Rights of Spouses
Title
Transfer of Property
—In General
—By Titleholder
—Interspousal
—No Special Circumstances
—Not Warranted
—Statutory Authority
—Valuable Consideration
Transmutation
—In General
—Affirmative Acts
—Effect of Commingling
—Factors
—Improper Classification
—Methods
—Mortgage Note
—Motivation
—Not Shown
—Partnership Interest
—Presumption of Gift
—Rebuttal of Presumption
—Shown
—Significant Contribution
—Workers' Compensation Award
Trust
—Court Findings
—Factors
—Failure to Pay
—Interests of Children
—Not Proper
—Order Final and Appealable
—Ordered By Court
—Parent Trustee
—Procedures
—Responsibility of Parent
—Upheld
Trustees
—Impartial Third Party Required
Unconscionability
—Determination
—Shown
—Validity of Agreement
Unequal Distribution of Property
—Upheld
Use of Corpus
Valuation
—In General
—Accounts Receivable
—Appreciation of Assets
—Business
—Corporate Assets
—Corporate Stock
—Credibility
—Date of Dissolution
—Difficulties
—Discretion
—Error
—Evidence
—Evidence Held Insufficient
—Exactness
—Expert Testimony
—Failure of Proof
—Fraud
—Future Income
—Hearsay Evidence
—Home
—Home Furnishings
—Illustrative Cases
—Increase During Marriage
—Insurance Agency
—Inventions
—Just Apportionment
—Lack of Evidence
—Marital Assets
—Medical Practice
—Modification
—Offset Method
—Pension Plan
—Percentage Interest
—Professional Corporation
—Proper Value Required
—Question of Fact
—Record of Value

—Reserved Jurisdiction Method
—Right to Appeal
—Scope of Review
—Specific Value Not Required
—Stamp Collection
—Standard of Review
—Stipulation
—Tax Consequences
—Testimony
—Time and Specificity
—Total Offset Method
—Trust
—Upheld
—Vacated Order
—Veteran's Benefits
—Waiver
Vested Property Rights
Waiver
Ward of Court
Waste
—In General
Wilful Violation
—Not Shown
—Rights of Violator
Workers' Compensation Benefits
—In General
—Apportionment
—Marital Property
—Permanent Total Disability

Constitutionality

Public Act 89-428 was enacted in violation of the single subject rule of the state constitution and is therefore invalid in its entirety. Johnson v. Edgar, 176 Ill. 2d 499, 224 Ill. Dec. 1, 680 N.E.2d 1372 (1997).

—Due Process

The state interest to be promoted by applying this section retrospectively greatly outweighed asserted property interest, which was only slightly more impaired by such application, and therefore this section did not violate defendant's due process rights. In re Thornqvist, 79 Ill. App. 3d 791, 35 Ill. Dec. 342, 399 N.E.2d 176 (1 Dist. 1979).

—Equal Protection

This section and 750 ILCS 5/513 do not violate the equal protection guarantees of the federal and state Constitutions. Kujawinski v. Kujawinski, 71 Ill. 2d 563, 17 Ill. Dec. 801, 376 N.E.2d 1382 (1978); In re Thornqvist, 79 Ill. App. 3d 791, 35 Ill. Dec. 342, 399 N.E.2d 176 (1 Dist. 1979).

—Impairment of Contracts

Subsection (b) of this section does not impair preexisting contractual relationships; it merely classifies the aggregate property interests of the spouses for the purposes of equitably distributing the property. That which is classified as "marital property" is subject to distribution within those limitations set by laws governing transfers, assignments and conveyances of such property. Kujawinski v. Kujawinski, 71 Ill. 2d 563, 17 Ill. Dec. 801, 376 N.E.2d 1382 (1978).

—Vagueness

Subsection (c) of this section is not unconstitutionally vague. In re Thornqvist, 79 Ill. App. 3d 791, 35 Ill. Dec. 342, 399 N.E.2d 176 (1 Dist. 1979).

In General

While this Act does not mandate equal distribution of marital assets between spouses, the property must be divided in just proportion, taking into account listed factors. In re Rapacz, 135 Ill. App. 3d 1045, 90 Ill. Dec. 622, 482 N.E.2d 441 (2 Dist. 1985).

Non-marital property may be presumptively transmuted to marital property. In re Rink, 136 Ill. App. 3d 252, 91 Ill. Dec. 34, 483 N.E.2d 316 (1 Dist. 1985).

This section permits the court to allocate marital property, regardless of who holds title, to each spouse in just proportion after considering all relevant factors including, inter alia, the contributions of each spouse, their relative economic circumstances, their age, health, occupation, and other available income and whether the apportionment is in lieu of or in addition to maintenance. In re Lukas, 83 Ill. App. 3d 606, 39 Ill. Dec. 161, 404 N.E.2d 545 (1 Dist. 1980).

This Act does not purport to affect property interests during the marriage, but merely classifies the aggregate property interests of the spouses for the purposes of equitably distributing the property upon termination of the marriage. In re Nicks, 80 Ill. App. 3d 838, 36 Ill. Dec. 11, 400 N.E.2d 431 (5 Dist. 1979).

Under section 17 of the former Divorce Act (see now this section) courts in divorce actions could adjudicate property rights between parties regardless of fault or the grounds for divorce upon the basis of special circumstances, equitable ownership and other equities; particularly was this general rule to be followed where the property involved was acquired as the result of joint efforts by the parties to the marital contract. Furthermore, the circumstances and equities relied upon were required to be both alleged in the pleadings and supported by the evidence. Schouten v. Schouten, 129 Ill. App. 2d 418, 263 N.E.2d 715 (5 Dist. 1970).

Antenuptial Agreement

—Applicability

Antenuptial agreement stating that each party had certain property, interests, and assets, to which the agreement was meant to apply in the event that marriage was terminated by death or divorce, and that each party relinquished all rights in the other's property and assets resulting from the spousal relationship, and that both pre-marital property and earnings from that property should be kept separate, and that property acquired during the marriage should be kept separate, was properly found to be applicable in the event of death or divorce, and excluded all property from consideration as marital property. In re Byrne, 179 Ill. App. 3d 944, 128 Ill. Dec. 800, 535 N.E.2d 14 (1 Dist. 1989).

—Not Shown

Where parties admitted that no written antenuptial agreement was executed, the trial judge did not err in finding that no valid agreement as to non-marital property existed notwithstanding husband's allegation that couple's consistent course of conduct indicated an oral agreement was in effect. In re Jelinek, 244 Ill. App. 3d 496, 184 Ill. Dec. 692, 613 N.E.2d 1284 (1 Dist.), appeal denied, 152 Ill. 2d 560, 190 Ill. Dec. 890, 622 N.E.2d 1207 (1993).

—Real Property Contributions

Where clear language of the prenuptial agreement stated that husband's house remained his property, wife was not entitled to reimbursement for any contributions made to the house other than for specific contribution made to help pay off mortgage for which the agreement was modified to provide for reimbursement. In re Stufflebeam, 283 Ill. App. 3d 923, 219 Ill. Dec. 390, 671 N.E.2d 55 (3 Dist. 1996), appeal denied, 171 Ill. 2d 586, 222 Ill. Dec. 438, 677 N.E.2d 972 (1997).

—Upheld

Because wife suggested the antenuptial agreement, freely entered into it with knowledge and comprehension of the nature of the agreement, was represented by counsel, and there was neither misrepresentation of husband's assets, nor a gross disparity in the relative wealth of the parties, and there appeared to have been no fraud, coercion or unconscionability, the contract was properly executed, defenses to the contract were defeated, and the trial court correctly ruled that the antenuptial agreement was valid. In re Byrne, 179 Ill. App. 3d 944, 128 Ill. Dec. 800, 535 N.E.2d 14 (1 Dist. 1989).

—Writing Required

An antenuptial agreement is enforceable only if in writing. In re Jelinek, 244 Ill. App. 3d 496, 184 Ill. Dec. 692, 613 N.E.2d 1284 (1 Dist.), appeal denied, 152 Ill. 2d 560, 190 Ill. Dec. 890, 622 N.E.2d 1207 (1993).

Attorney Fees

Trial court did not err in awarding attorney fees to former wife in divorce even though the relevant statute, 750 ILCS 5/503(j), stated that a petition for attorney fees should be heard and decided before a final judgment was entered as the former husband did not object to the former wife's petition filed after the final judgment was

Attorney Fees (Cont'd)
entered and the timing requirement was not jurisdictional. In re Lindsey-Robinson, 331 Ill. App. 3d 261, 265 Ill. Dec. 17, 771 N.E.2d 976, 2002 Ill. App. LEXIS 365 (4 Dist. 2002).

A trial court must hear and decide a party's petition for contribution to attorney fees and costs after the close of proofs on all other issues; however, an additional hearing, which would further burden already overburdened trial courts, is not required, but, rather, a trial court must hear, through testimony or otherwise, additional proofs when a petition for contribution is filed in accordance with subsection (j) in the context of preexisting proceedings. Brackett v. Brackett, 309 Ill. App. 3d 329, 242 Ill. Dec. 798, 722 N.E.2d 287 (2 Dist. 1999).

An amendment to the statute which provided for the consideration of petitions for attorney fees in separate and distinct proceedings did not create a substantive change in the law. In re McGuire, 305 Ill. App. 3d 474, 712 N.E.2d 411 (5 Dist. 1999).

—Requirements
It was not an abuse of discretion to not require the husband to contribute to the wife's attorney fees as the wife failed to show an inability to pay her own attorney fees. Schneider v. Schneider, 343 Ill. App. 3d 628, 278 Ill. Dec. 485, 798 N.E.2d 1242, 2003 Ill. App. LEXIS 1295 (2 Dist. 2003).

750 ILCS 5/503(j) does not require an additional hearing, but, rather, requires a trial court to hear, through testimony or otherwise, additional proofs when a petition for contribution is filed in accordance with § 503(j) in the context of preexisting proceedings. Suriano v. Lafeber, 324 Ill. App. 3d 839, 258 Ill. Dec. 400, 756 N.E.2d 382, 2001 Ill. App. LEXIS 682 (1 Dist. 2001).

A party requesting attorney fees must do more than merely ask for attorney fees; the party requesting attorney fees must present the trial court with a detailed record containing the computations for fees, who performed the services for which fees are sought, the time spent representing the client, and the hourly rate charged. In re Konchar, 312 Ill. App. 3d 441, 245 Ill. Dec. 224, 727 N.E.2d 671, 2000 Ill. App. LEXIS 231 (2 Dist. 2000).

Award

—Attorney Fees
Under 750 ILCS 5/503(j), a contribution award may take the form of either a set dollar amount or a percentage of fees and costs and does not require allocation of attorney fees based on a percentage of fees ultimately paid rather than billed. Suriano v. Lafeber, 324 Ill. App. 3d 839, 258 Ill. Dec. 400, 756 N.E.2d 382, 2001 Ill. App. LEXIS 682 (1 Dist. 2001).

Trial court did not abuse its discretion when it ordered the husband to pay only half of the wife's attorney fees. In re Stufflebeam, 283 Ill. App. 3d 923, 219 Ill. Dec. 390, 671 N.E.2d 55 (3 Dist. 1996), appeal denied, 171 Ill. 2d 586, 222 Ill. Dec. 438, 677 N.E.2d 972 (1997).

Respondent's memorandum to the trial court only amounted to a general objection to an award of attorney fees and did not request a hearing on the fees; therefore, respondent waived his right for a hearing on the court's order to pay a portion of petitioner's attorney fees. In re Blazis, 261 Ill. App. 3d 855, 199 Ill. Dec. 941, 634 N.E.2d 1295 (4 Dist. 1994).

—Car
The award of a car was justified since the evidence was clear that the car was purchased for petitioner wife and she had driven it since that time. In re Zummo, 167 Ill. App. 3d 566, 118 Ill. Dec. 339, 521 N.E.2d 621 (4 Dist. 1988).

—Classification
It is not the label placed by decree upon payments which constitutes them either alimony or lump sum property settlements; it is the elements inherent in the case as a whole, the record of which the decree is a part, which determine to what category such payments belong. Warren v. Warren, 88 Ill. App. 3d 543, 43 Ill. Dec. 782, 410 N.E.2d 915 (3 Dist. 1980).

Assignment of defendant husband's military pension income was alimony and not a property settlement where the record disclosed that plaintiff wife received marital home, automobile, all of household goods, equipment, furniture and appliances, and all of her personal belongings consisting of jewelry and wearing apparel; defendant was ordered to pay $30 per week child support and all reasonable and necessary hospital, medical and dental care for the minor children; defendant was required to pay all outstanding bills for necessary expenses incurred by the parties during their marriage; and all that defendant was awarded under the decree was such of his personal belongings then in his possession. Warren v. Warren, 88 Ill. App. 3d 543, 43 Ill. Dec. 782, 410 N.E.2d 915 (3 Dist. 1980).

—Corporate Stock
Awarding corporate stock to respondent husband subject to an obligation to pay petitioner wife an appropriate sum constituted an equitable division, as unlike petitioner, respondent was directly involved in closely held corporations; this method of dividing the marital property served to disengage the parties' financial affairs as well as reduce the likelihood of interference with one another or with the operations of the companies. In re Hellwig, 100 Ill. App. 3d 452, 55 Ill. Dec. 762, 426 N.E.2d 1087 (1 Dist. 1981).

—Home
Award of marital residence, parties' major asset, to "homemaker," in poor health and with an overall limited opportunity for substantial income was not an abuse of discretion. In re Vernon, 253 Ill. App. 3d 783, 192 Ill. Dec. 668, 625 N.E.2d 823 (4 Dist. 1993).

Since petitioner was awarded custody of the two minor children, assignment of the house to her was justified. In re Tietz, 238 Ill. App. 3d 965, 178 Ill. Dec. 876, 605 N.E.2d 670 (4 Dist. 1992).

Where custodial parent had been the sole provider of support for the children, where non-custodial parent was not ordered to make any child support payments and where there was no indication in the record that the judge considered the desirability of awarding the right to reside in the marital home to the spouse having custody of the children, provision was made for the continued use of the marital residence by custodial parent and the children until the youngest child's 18th birthday; upon the youngest child's 18th birthday the house should be sold and the proceeds divided in accordance with the trial court's decision. In re Zirngibl, 237 Ill. App. 3d 1049, 179 Ill. Dec. 169, 606 N.E.2d 1 (1 Dist. 1991).

In a divorce proceeding, the award of equity in marital home to wife in lieu of her interest in husband's pension, without receiving evidence of value of the pension rights, was an abuse of the court's discretion. In re Donley, 83 Ill. App. 3d 367, 38 Ill. Dec. 733, 403 N.E.2d 1337 (3 Dist. 1980).

—Home Furnishings
Where respondent husband submitted a list of household property where he indicated what he believed was marital and non-marital property and who should receive specific pieces, and petitioner wife marked the list with yellow or red and gave her opinion concerning disposition, and where the court passed on the credibility of the parties and found petitioner's testimony more credible and awarded the property in conformity with her testimony, there was no abuse of discretion. In re Zummo, 167 Ill. App. 3d 566, 118 Ill. Dec. 339, 521 N.E.2d 621 (4 Dist. 1988).

—Improper
The trial court's 55 to 45% division of the marital estate in favor of the husband was improper based upon its failure to find that the husband had proved his right to reimbursement by clear and convincing evidence and its failure to follow a stipulation of the parties. In re Dunlap, 294 Ill. App. 3d 768, 228 Ill. Dec. 948, 690 N.E.2d 1023 (4 Dist. 1998).

The court's distribution of assets and debts represented an abuse of discretion. In re Winne, 239 Ill. App. 3d 273, 179 Ill. Dec. 945, 606 N.E.2d 777 (2 Dist. 1992).

There was no abuse of discretion in an award of one-third of marital property; however, where respondent wife received not the awarded third of the property, but a seven year old automobile that did not run and a stream of cash, and the record revealed ownership of no other assets, the court abused its discretion, and was required to order a lump sum distribution to respondent, reflecting the marital property she had already received. In re Rimmele, 102 Ill. App. 3d 88, 57 Ill. Dec. 762, 429 N.E.2d 879 (3 Dist. 1981).

The trial court abused its discretion in its award of property, maintenance and support where the parties invited the court to determine these matters on the pleadings, on the evidence it had heard throughout the proceedings, on the statements of counsel, and on the basis of extended discussions in chambers, even though

Award (Cont'd)

—Improper (Cont'd)

the record reflected that the court considered all the statutory factors set forth in this Act. In re Shedbalkar, 95 Ill. App. 3d 136, 50 Ill. Dec. 301, 419 N.E.2d 409 (1 Dist. 1981).

—Life Insurance Policy

A parent may be required to provide or maintain life insurance with his child as irrevocable beneficiary. In re Dulyn, 89 Ill. App. 3d 304, 44 Ill. Dec. 622, 411 N.E.2d 988 (1 Dist. 1980).

—Ranch

Where wife spent seven years working on and preserving the parties' only asset, an Arizona ranch, while husband had squandered millions of dollars on drugs, alcohol, women and poor business decisions, husband was the beneficiary of trust funds which paid him in excess of $200,000 per year and an additional $500,000 every five years, wife was 40 years old at the time of trial and her only marketable skill was working as a ranch hand, the trial court did not abuse its discretion in awarding petitioner the Arizona ranch. In re Norris, 252 Ill. App. 3d 230, 192 Ill. Dec. 46, 625 N.E.2d 6 (1 Dist. 1992).

—Upheld

Where marriage was of relatively short duration and the husband was retired, ill, and received only a modest monthly income, the trial court did not abuse its discretion when it awarded the wife one-half of the value of the marital property. In re Stufflebeam, 283 Ill. App. 3d 923, 219 Ill. Dec. 390, 671 N.E.2d 55 (3 Dist. 1996), appeal denied, 171 Ill. 2d 586, 222 Ill. Dec. 438, 677 N.E.2d 972 (1997).

Court properly exercised its discretion in assessing the credibility of witnesses, and made a just distribution of property in conformance with the mandates of this section. In re Marx, 281 Ill. App. 3d 897, 217 Ill. Dec. 645, 667 N.E.2d 734 (4 Dist. 1996).

Where the trial court found that respondent had income and assets sufficient to allow him to live in a comfortable lifestyle, even while assisting petitioner in meeting her needs, the trial court's award of $25,000 did not work a substantial injustice by virtually eliminating his 1993 income. In re Mohr, 260 Ill. App. 3d 98, 197 Ill. Dec. 563, 631 N.E.2d 785 (4 Dist. 1994).

Trial court's decision to divide marital property 60% to wife and 40% to husband was upheld where marital estate had approximate value of $2,000,000 even though husband had been terminated from job paying $135,000 plus bonus and wife had non-marital property of $223,529 plus the right to invade a lifetime income beneficiary trust. In re Benkendorf, 252 Ill. App. 3d 429, 191 Ill. Dec. 863, 624 N.E.2d 1241 (1 Dist. 1993).

There was nothing inequitable about the trial court's division of marital property. In re Thomas, 239 Ill. App. 3d 992, 181 Ill. Dec. 512, 608 N.E.2d 585 (3 Dist. 1993).

The court's property distribution order was affirmed. Schlosser v. Schlosser, 241 Ill. App. 3d 49, 181 Ill. Dec. 496, 608 N.E.2d 569 (3 Dist. 1993).

The court's apportionment of the marital assets was not an abuse of discretion considering the contribution of the parties, the value of the property awarded to each, the duration of the marriage, the disparity in income between the parties, the custodial provisions, the desire of awarding the family home to petitioner, and the health status and opportunity of the respective parties. In re Tietz, 238 Ill. App. 3d 965, 178 Ill. Dec. 876, 605 N.E.2d 670 (4 Dist. 1992).

A judgment ordering respondent husband to pay $53,000 to petitioner wife as her equitable portion of marital assets was upheld where, at the time the parties separated, they owned 5,000 bushels of stored corn, 10,000 bushels of stored soybeans, and 20 dairy cows valued at over $100,000. In re Schaufelberger, 120 Ill. App. 3d 114, 75 Ill. Dec. 551, 457 N.E.2d 993 (5 Dist. 1983).

Where the record indicated that sufficient marital assets, valued in excess of $600,000, existed to provide for parties' post-marital financial needs and showed husband's apparent unwillingness to comply with court orders, the court's award to wife of marital assets in lieu of maintenance was not error. In re Cook, 117 Ill. App. 3d 844, 73 Ill. Dec. 222, 453 N.E.2d 1357 (1 Dist. 1983).

Even though wife was arguably capable of obtaining employment and also possessed certain property, where she was unemployed and living outside the marital home during the pendency of proceedings while husband continued to earn income, and wife's monthly expenses were approximately $2,280, the order of temporary maintenance was not unreasonable. In re Cook, 117 Ill. App. 3d 844, 73 Ill. Dec. 222, 453 N.E.2d 1357 (1 Dist. 1983).

Where plaintiff specifically alleged in the complaint and testified at the hearing regarding her need and defendant's ability to pay for child support, expenses and attorney fees, and that defendant's drinking habits made periodic alimony payments unfeasible, although plaintiff was not questioned as to her exact earnings at the hearing, the omission was not grounds for a new hearing; the evidence offered, although succinct, was sufficient to sustain the divorce decree under former section 18 of the Divorce Act (see now this section) awarding plaintiff child support, attorney fees, and defendant's interest in the marital home in lieu of periodic alimony. Frank v. Frank, 34 Ill. App. 3d 957, 342 N.E.2d 404 (2 Dist. 1975).

Bank Accounts

—Evidence

There was no error in the trial court's failure to find the amount of value of bank accounts where there was testimonial and documentary evidence that parties had kept various accounts in four banks but that these accounts had been closed by husband and the husband also testified that he used these funds to pay marriage debts and that he distributed some of the money to the wife. In re Petramale, 102 Ill. App. 3d 1049, 58 Ill. Dec. 537, 430 N.E.2d 569 (2 Dist. 1981).

Bias

—Not Shown

Given the equitableness of property distribution, it could not be concluded that the trial court was prejudiced against husband where those portions of the record which the husband claimed demonstrated bias against him merely represented attempts by the trial court to either clarify testimony or further the progression of the trial. In re Randall, 157 Ill. App. 3d 892, 110 Ill. Dec. 122, 510 N.E.2d 1153 (1 Dist. 1987).

Children

—Award Improper

Where the father, who murdered the mother's boyfriend and attempted to murder the mother during the divorce proceedings, was sentenced to prison for the rest of the father's life, the trial court erred in refusing to set aside, pursuant to 750 ILCS 5/503(g), the father's nonmarital funds for child support purposes, as the father, due to incarceration, was unable to make child support payments. Hari v. Hari, 345 Ill. App. 3d 1116, 281 Ill. Dec. 518, 804 N.E.2d 144, 2004 Ill. App. LEXIS 91 (4 Dist. 2004).

It is improper to award the property in a divorce action to the children because this Act contemplates the division of marital property between the spouses; the duty of support normally continues only during the minority of the child and there is no provision in the Act authorizing an outright conveyance of marital property even in trust which is unrelated to a child's support or maintenance. In re Smith, 100 Ill. App. 3d 1126, 56 Ill. Dec. 716, 427 N.E.2d 1262 (2 Dist. 1981).

—Care of Minor

In a divorce case, where there was no reason to believe that the husband, or his estate, would not be able to provide the mandated child support, the trial court's decision not to require the husband to maintain a life insurance policy naming his children as the irrevocable beneficiaries was not against the manifest weight of the evidence. Schneider v. Schneider, 343 Ill. App. 3d 628, 278 Ill. Dec. 485, 798 N.E.2d 1242, 2003 Ill. App. LEXIS 1295 (2 Dist. 2003).

Under section 17 of the former Divorce Act (see now this section), there must have been a factual basis and equitable merit demonstrated of record to warrant the court to divest a spouse of particular personal property for the care of a child. Schouten v. Schouten, 129 Ill. App. 2d 418, 263 N.E.2d 715 (5 Dist. 1970).

—Continuity in Environment

Because the adverse effect which dissolution of a marriage has on children is self-evident, where possible, children should be afforded continuity in their environment in order to reduce the emotional disruption caused by the separation of their parents, and one of the

Children (Cont'd)

—Continuity in Environment (Cont'd)
ways this can be accomplished is by affording the children continued residence in the family home. In re Brenner, 95 Ill. App. 3d 100, 50 Ill. Dec. 292, 419 N.E.2d 400 (1 Dist. 1981).

—Improperly Considered
The trial court erred in considering the situation and needs of a non-minor physically disabled child when dividing the property between petitioner and respondent, since such a disposition could have resulted in one party never receiving a possessory interest during her lifetime, where the time for payment is not definite. In re Riech, 208 Ill. App. 3d 301, 152 Ill. Dec. 949, 566 N.E.2d 826 (4 Dist. 1991).

—Life Insurance Policy
The trial court did not abuse its discretion in awarding decedent's children one-third of $300,000 life insurance policy; even though under the terms of the dissolution judgment the decedent was to maintain a life insurance policy for the benefit of his children, at the time of the judgment decedent had two policies in the total amount of $55,000. Downey v. Downey, 293 Ill. App. 3d 234, 227 Ill. Dec. 265, 687 N.E.2d 339 (4 Dist. 1997).

—Uncontested Needs
The court, with jurisdiction of the parties and the subject matter, acted well within its powers in ordering, as part of the relief on wife's petition for sale of assets, that husband, who controlled the assets, had to meet the uncontested needs of the children. In re Schweihs, 272 Ill. App. 3d 653, 208 Ill. Dec. 875, 650 N.E.2d 569 (1 Dist. 1995), appeal denied, 163 Ill. 2d 588, 212 Ill. Dec. 437, 657 N.E.2d 638 (1995).

Choice of Law

—Original Judgment
The trial court on remand properly applied the law in effect at the time of the original judgment, rather than the amendment which became effective prior to remand. In re Smith, 162 Ill. App. 3d 792, 114 Ill. Dec. 622, 516 N.E.2d 777 (5 Dist. 1987).

Classification of Property

—In General
The gift principles applied for purposes of determining rights to reimbursement under subsection (c) of this section for contributions of non-marital property to property acquired jointly by spouses also apply for purposes of classifying jointly held property as marital or non-marital. In re Hagshenas, 234 Ill. App. 3d 178, 175 Ill. Dec. 506, 600 N.E.2d 437 (2 Dist. 1992), appeal denied, 148 Ill.2d 642, 183 Ill. Dec. 19, 610 N.E.2d 1263 (1993).

This section does not purport to affect property interests during marriage; the term "marital property" is a nomenclature devised to realize an equitable distribution of property upon termination of the marriage, and operation of the term is not triggered until the time of dissolution. Subdivision (a)(6) of this section does not prevent married persons from owning property separately during the marriage and disposing of it in any fashion that the property-owning spouse may choose. In re Olson, 96 Ill. 2d 432, 71 Ill. Dec. 671, 451 N.E.2d 825 (1983).

—Bank Accounts for Expenses
The deposit of certain funds in a joint account out of which the household expenses of parties were paid while retaining sole ownership of other funds tended to prove that it was respondent's intent that the jointly held funds be marital property. In re Emken, 86 Ill. 2d 164, 56 Ill. Dec. 45, 427 N.E.2d 125 (1981).

—Dental Practice
Where marital funds were spent on a dental practice, but there was no showing that these funds did any more than maintain the continued operation of this practice, plaintiff did not establish that marital funds significantly contributed to the dental practice; accordingly, plaintiff's assertion that the dental practice was marital property was rejected. In re Aud, 142 Ill. App. 3d 320, 96 Ill. Dec. 615, 491 N.E.2d 894 (5 Dist. 1986).

—Dual Status
Trial court's dual classification of a 59 acre tract of farm land and the marital home as 4/7 non-marital and 3/7 marital was erroneous because property may not have dual characteristics. In re Benefield, 131 Ill. App. 3d 648, 86 Ill. Dec. 831, 476 N.E.2d 7 (5 Dist. 1985).

By finding a business to be non-marital but inventory of the business to be marital property, a trial court did not improperly attribute dual characteristics to the same property. In re Pancner, 111 Ill. App. 3d 546, 67 Ill. Dec. 417, 444 N.E.2d 653 (1 Dist. 1982).

—Exclusivity
An asset cannot be both marital and non-marital. In re Brown, 110 Ill. App. 3d 782, 66 Ill. Dec. 488, 443 N.E.2d 11 (5 Dist. 1982).

—Presumption
As to newly acquired property, clear and convincing evidence is required to show that it has been acquired in exchange for non-marital property in order to classify it as non-marital property, and any doubts must be resolved in favor of finding that the property is marital. In re Eddy, 210 Ill. App. 3d 450, 155 Ill. Dec. 174, 569 N.E.2d 174 (1 Dist. 1991).

There is a legislative preference for classifying property as marital. In re Rink, 136 Ill. App. 3d 252, 91 Ill. Dec. 34, 483 N.E.2d 316 (1 Dist. 1985).

Where real property in question was placed jointly in the names of the parties before their first marriage was declared invalid, such was presumptively marital property. In re Flatow, 102 Ill. App. 3d 859, 58 Ill. Dec. 273, 430 N.E.2d 215 (1 Dist. 1981).

—Professional Corporation
A professional corporation may constitute marital property. In re White, 98 Ill. App. 3d 380, 53 Ill. Dec. 786, 424 N.E.2d 421 (5 Dist. 1981).

—Required
The court is to classify property as either marital or non-marital for the property division upon dissolution of marriage. In re Jones, 104 Ill. App. 3d 490, 60 Ill. Dec. 214, 432 N.E.2d 1113 (1 Dist. 1982); In re Voight, 111 Ill. App. 3d 623, 67 Ill. Dec. 458, 444 N.E.2d 694 (1 Dist. 1982); In re Durante, 201 Ill. App. 3d 376, 147 Ill. Dec. 56, 559 N.E.2d 56 (1 Dist. 1990); In re Eddy, 210 Ill. App. 3d 450, 155 Ill. Dec. 174, 569 N.E.2d 174 (1 Dist. 1991).

—Standard of Review
Before the court may dispose of property upon a dissolution of marriage, it must classify the property as either marital or non-marital and its classification will not be disturbed unless it is contrary to the manifest weight of the evidence. In re Hagshenas, 234 Ill. App. 3d 178, 175 Ill. Dec. 506, 600 N.E.2d 437 (2 Dist. 1992), appeal denied, 148 Ill.2d 642, 183 Ill. Dec. 19, 610 N.E.2d 1263 (1993).

A trial court's classification of property should not be disturbed unless contrary to the manifest weight of evidence. In re Marriage of Agazim, 147 Ill. App. 3d 646, 101 Ill. Dec. 418, 498 N.E.2d 742, 1986 Ill. App. LEXIS 2819 (2 Dist. 1986), cert. denied, 106 Ill. Dec. 44, 505 N.E.2d 350 (1987), appeal denied, 106 Ill. Dec. 44, 505 N.E.2d 350 (1987).

—Stock
The classification of stock as marital property terminated when the court entered its judgment dissolving marriage; from that time on, the terms of the judgment and the property settlement agreement, not this section, governed the classification of the stock. Davidson v. Belcor, Inc., 933 F.2d 603 (7th Cir. 1991).

The trial court's classification of stock as marital property was not against the manifest weight of the evidence. In re Rosen, 126 Ill. App. 3d 766, 81 Ill. Dec. 840, 467 N.E.2d 962 (1 Dist. 1984).

The error, if any, in classifying stock as non-marital property was harmless, and reversal on that issue was not required. In re Wilder, 122 Ill. App. 3d 338, 77 Ill. Dec. 824, 461 N.E.2d 447 (1 Dist. 1983).

For purposes of classification of property under this Act, both stock splits and stock dividends shall be treated as is economic appreciation; neither a stock split nor a stock dividend increases the shareholder's ownership rights in a corporation. In re Smith, 86 Ill. 2d 518, 56 Ill. Dec. 693, 427 N.E.2d 1239 (1981).

—Stock Options
Stock options do not constitute property under this section until such time as they are exercised. In re Moody, 119 Ill. App. 3d 1043,

Classification of Property (Cont'd)

—Stock Options (Cont'd)

75 Ill. Dec. 581, 457 N.E.2d 1023 (1 Dist. 1983); In re Frederick, 218 Ill. App. 3d 533, 161 Ill. Dec. 254, 578 N.E.2d 612 (2 Dist. 1991).

Where husband had an oral option to purchase stock in a seat on the commodities exchange prior to marriage, but he did not actually exercise this option and acquire the stock until several months following the marriage, and the acquisition was made possible through the financial assistance of the wife's brother, the seat was marital property. In re Wright, 180 Ill. App. 3d 911, 129 Ill. Dec. 650, 536 N.E.2d 700 (1 Dist. 1986).

—Time of Acquisition

If consideration were given to transfer of the title to a farm as indicative of when husband acquired legal ownership of the farm, then the date of acquisition was before the date of dissolution, and thus the farm would be considered in the circuit court's distribution of property, either as marital property or as non-marital property, as it was owned by respondent at the date of dissolution. In re Tatham, 173 Ill. App. 3d 1072, 123 Ill. Dec. 576, 527 N.E.2d 1351 (5 Dist. 1988).

Furniture brought to the marriage by one spouse was properly characterized as her non-marital property, despite the fact it had been used in the same rooms as furniture purchased during the marriage. In re Deem, 123 Ill. App. 3d 1019, 79 Ill. Dec. 542, 463 N.E.2d 1317 (4 Dist. 1984).

Marital home purchased during the marriage was properly characterized as marital property. In re Kopec, 106 Ill. App. 3d 1060, 62 Ill. Dec. 658, 436 N.E.2d 684 (1 Dist. 1982).

The shared enterprise or partnership notion underlies the presumption that all property acquired by either spouse after marriage is presumed to be marital property unless excepted under subsection (a) of this section; similarly, property which is acquired by gift or inheritance is deemed to be non-marital property because demonstrably it was not obtained through any joint enterprise but through an independent source. In re Komnick, 84 Ill. 2d 89, 49 Ill. Dec. 291, 417 N.E.2d 1305 (1981).

The trial court's finding that disputed art objects were acquired in former husband's business inventory prior to the marriage and hence acquired prior to the marriage was manifestly supported by the record, even though some small portion of the purchase price was paid out of the business after the marriage, and thus the court properly found the art objects to be non-marital property. In re Crouch, 88 Ill. App. 3d 426, 43 Ill. Dec. 580, 410 N.E.2d 580 (3 Dist. 1980).

—Transmutation

Real property purchased by the parties during their marriage was properly classified as marital property, notwithstanding that the funds used to purchase the property were traceable entirely to the husband's nonmarital assets, since the property was transmuted into marital property when it was placed in joint tenancy by the husband. In re Gattone, 317 Ill. App. 3d 346, 251 Ill. Dec. 65, 739 N.E.2d 998, 2000 Ill. App. LEXIS 900 (2 Dist. 2000).

Property designated as non-marital pursuant to exceptions in this Act may still be presumptively transmuted into marital property by the affirmative act of the contributing spouse. In re Hagshenas, 234 Ill. App. 3d 178, 175 Ill. Dec. 506, 600 N.E.2d 437 (2 Dist. 1992), appeal denied, 148 Ill.2d 642, 183 Ill. Dec. 19, 610 N.E.2d 1263 (1993).

—Workers' Compensation Award

When equitably apportioning the marital property of the parties, trial courts are to treat as marital property the workers' compensation award of an injured spouse, provided the award arose out of a claim accruing during the marriage. In re Thomas, 89 Ill. App. 3d 81, 44 Ill. Dec. 430, 411 N.E.2d 552 (3 Dist. 1980).

A workers' compensation award is marital property if the claim thereto accrues during the marriage, regardless of when received. In re Dettore, 86 Ill. App. 3d 540, 42 Ill. Dec. 51, 408 N.E.2d 429 (3 Dist. 1980); In re Thomas, 89 Ill. App. 3d 81, 44 Ill. Dec. 430, 411 N.E.2d 552 (3 Dist. 1980).

Clean Hands Doctrine

There was no authority for application of the "clean hands" doctrine in case where husband failed to pay temporary maintenance as ordered after alleging wife had dissipated marital assets. In re Sevon, 117 Ill. App. 3d 313, 73 Ill. Dec. 41, 453 N.E.2d 866 (1 Dist. 1983).

Collateral Actions

—Diversion of Funds

Trial judge denied wife's motion to stay a divorce action until separate actions the wife filed against her husband and others were resolved, even though the wife claimed in her separate actions that the husband had diverted funds from a corporation she owned and that the husband's actions affected the parties' marital property. Partipilo v. Partipilo, 331 Ill. App. 3d 394, 264 Ill. Dec. 440, 770 N.E.2d 1136, 2002 Ill. App. LEXIS 385 (1 Dist. 2002).

—Personal Injury

A separate trial within the dissolution proceeding to decide the issue of damages claimed for transmission of a sexually transmitted disease is not authorized by this Act; the proper method of obtaining such relief would be a separate personal injury action. Foran v. Foran, 225 Ill. App. 3d 756, 167 Ill. Dec. 301, 587 N.E.2d 570 (4 Dist. 1992).

Commingling

—Art Objects

Where alleged commingling was with clearly identifiable and traceable art objects which did not lose their individual identity upon remaining in husband's business inventory after marriage, the trial court properly held that the disputed personal property was originally non-marital property and retained that status even after the marriage. In re Crouch, 88 Ill. App. 3d 426, 43 Ill. Dec. 580, 410 N.E.2d 580 (3 Dist. 1980).

—Business

A business begun in 1960 by the parties was marital property because the parties' business was commingled and intertwined with father's business following his death, and the trial court erred in its finding that $193,571, which was the book value of the stock inherited by the husband and held in the husband's name alone, was non-marital property. In re Jones, 104 Ill. App. 3d 490, 60 Ill. Dec. 214, 432 N.E.2d 1113 (1 Dist. 1982).

—Cash Management Account

A cash management account, initially opened entirely with inherited assets, is considered a non-marital asset; however, the subsequent commingled marital and non-marital property resulted in a loss of identity of the initial contributed estate, therefore preventing the differentiation of marital and non-marital assets and the account was thus considered a marital asset. In re Davis, 215 Ill. App. 3d 763, 159 Ill. Dec. 375, 576 N.E.2d 44 (1 Dist.), appeal denied, 141 Ill. 2d 538, 162 Ill. Dec. 484, 580 N.E.2d 110 (1991).

—Checking Accounts

A checking account was marital property, notwithstanding that the account was opened in the name of the husband prior to the parties' marriage and contained nonmarital funds at the time of the marriage, where the parties were married for 16 years but never opened a joint account, the wife never opened any checking account in her name until the parties separated, and funds constituting marital property were regularly deposited into the checking account during the marriage. In re Henke, 313 Ill. App. 3d 159, 245 Ill. Dec. 780, 728 N.E.2d 1137, 2000 Ill. App. LEXIS 276 (2 Dist. 2000), appeal denied sub nom. Henke v. Henke, 191 Ill. 2d 530, 250 Ill. Dec. 457, 738 N.E.2d 926 (2000).

—Gifts

Trial court did not err in determining that the husband's transfer of a joint tenancy account to the wife was a gift that was presumed to be nonmarital property despite the fact that the property was presumed to be marital under 750 ILCS 5/503(b)(1); where the husband and wife presented conflicting testimony regarding the husband's donative intent, it was for the trial court to make the credibility determination.

Even if transfer gifts from husband's parents were considered to be non-marital property, i.e., gifts to husband individually and not to the marriage, the funds lost their identity when they were invested in the marital house; that commingling resulted in a transmutation of the funds into the classification of the estate

Commingling (Cont'd)

—Gifts (Cont'd)

receiving the contribution (the house), which was marital property. In re Schmidt, 242 Ill. App. 3d 961, 182 Ill. Dec. 804, 610 N.E.2d 673 (4 Dist. 1993).

—Home Construction

Trial court erred in ruling that the parties' home was non-marital property of husband where the husband claimed in his testimony that some $87,000 of his non-marital property went into the construction of a home which he testified cost some $145,000 to $150,000 to construct and, although the construction cost was disputed by the wife, it was clear that the balance of the funds were not shown to have come from non-marital sources and in addition, there was no evidence that even the funds which the husband sought to trace from property owned by him before the marriage were kept separate and distinct and solely used for the parties' residence. In re Amato, 80 Ill. App. 3d 395, 35 Ill. Dec. 729, 399 N.E.2d 1018 (2 Dist. 1980).

—Purchase of Real Property

While one residence was acquired in part with proceeds from the sale of another residence, which petitioner contended was non-marital property, marital funds were also used and so there was a commingling of funds; therefore, residence was deemed marital property. In re Van Ness, 136 Ill. App. 3d 185, 90 Ill. Dec. 766, 482 N.E.2d 1049 (4 Dist. 1985).

Although at the time of parties' marriage, home was husband's non-marital asset, payment of mortgage with marital assets consisting of husband's income during the marriage, caused a commingling of marital and non-marital assets and transmuted the entire property into marital property. In re Smith, 102 Ill. App. 3d 769, 58 Ill. Dec. 422, 430 N.E.2d 364 (1 Dist. 1981).

Where substantial marital property was diverted to enhancement of residence purchased prior to marriage, there had been a commingling of marital property and non-marital property which served to transmute the entire property into marital property. In re Lee, 88 Ill. App. 3d 1044, 44 Ill. Dec. 91, 410 N.E.2d 1183 (3 Dist. 1980), aff'd, 87 Ill. 2d 64, 58 Ill. Dec. 779 430 N.E.2d 1030 (1981).

Where respondent's non-marital funds were used in conjunction with parties' marital funds to purchase real property, the real property was marital property. In re Schriner, 88 Ill. App. 3d 380, 43 Ill. Dec. 572, 410 N.E.2d 572 (2 Dist. 1980).

—Reimbursement

Subsection (c)(1) of this section provides that when marital and non-marital property are commingled, the commingled property is transmuted into marital property, and, pursuant to subsection (c)(2) of this section, the party contributing the transmuted non-marital property is entitled to reimbursement of the value of such property provided (1) the contribution is traceable by clear and convincing evidence, and (2) the contributor did not make a gift of the non-marital property to the marital estate. In re Hagshenas, 234 Ill. App. 3d 178, 175 Ill. Dec. 506, 600 N.E.2d 437 (2 Dist. 1992), appeal denied, 148 Ill.2d 642, 183 Ill. Dec. 19, 610 N.E.2d 1263 (1993).

—Repairs and Maintenance

The commingling of marital and non-marital assets and the contribution of marital assets to non-marital property must be sufficiently significant to raise a presumption of a gift of the property to marital estate; thus, the making of or paying for repairs and maintenance on house that do not materially add to its value or payments that do not reduce the indebtedness of the mortgage should not raise the presumption of transmutation. In re Olson, 96 Ill. 2d 432, 71 Ill. Dec. 671, 451 N.E.2d 825 (1983).

—Savings Account

Respondent was not entitled to a credit on the parties' savings since his act of commingling his pre-marital savings with marital savings transmuted the funds into marital property. In re Schriner, 88 Ill. App. 3d 380, 43 Ill. Dec. 572, 410 N.E.2d 572 (2 Dist. 1980).

—Traceability

Wife was entitled to have her $9,000 reimbursed from husband's non-marital estate because such amount was retraceable by clear and convincing evidence and not intended to be a gift. In re Snow, 277 Ill. App. 3d 642, 214 Ill. Dec. 398, 660 N.E.2d 1347 (4 Dist. 1996).

Commingling non-marital property with newly acquired marital property did not transmute the non-marital property into marital property where the amount injected into the marital account was ascertainable and did not result in a loss of identity. In re Landfield, 209 Ill. App. 3d 678, 153 Ill. Dec. 834, 567 N.E.2d 1061 (1 Dist.), cert. denied, 139 Ill. 2d 597, 159 Ill. Dec. 109, 575 N.E.2d 916 (1991).

—Transformation of Property

Once marital and non-marital funds are commingled and lose their identity through the acquisition of a newly created asset during the marriage, the asset is marital. In re Eddy, 210 Ill. App. 3d 450, 155 Ill. Dec. 174, 569 N.E.2d 174 (1 Dist. 1991).

Where a tractor was acquired before the marriage but the loan on the tractor was paid during the marriage, the non-marital tractor was transmuted into marital property because of this commingling of marital and non-marital assets. In re Tatham, 173 Ill. App. 3d 1072, 123 Ill. Dec. 576, 527 N.E.2d 1351 (5 Dist. 1988).

Although property may be deemed to be non-marital property, its character may be transformed into marital property where non-marital property is commingled with marital property. In re Jones, 104 Ill. App. 3d 490, 60 Ill. Dec. 214, 432 N.E.2d 1113 (1 Dist. 1982).

The commingling of non-marital proprietorship assets with the later acquired marital proprietorship assets resulted in the characterization of all proprietorship assets as marital property. In re Westphal, 99 Ill. App. 3d 1042, 55 Ill. Dec. 328, 426 N.E.2d 303 (3 Dist. 1981).

Commingling property evidences an intent to treat the property as marital and, therefore, commingling of non-marital property with marital property transmutes the non-marital property into marital property. In re Amato, 80 Ill. App. 3d 395, 35 Ill. Dec. 729, 399 N.E.2d 1018 (2 Dist. 1980).

Confidentiality

Disallowing ex-wife's attorney's participation in an in camera hearing regarding ex-husband's claimed credits against trust property was not an abuse of discretion; where ex-wife had fled the jurisdiction with their child, ex-husband did not want to reveal progress of his search for his son to ex-wife's attorneys. In re Kriegsman, 218 Ill. App. 3d 909, 161 Ill. Dec. 540, 578 N.E.2d 1186 (1 Dist. 1991).

Consolidation of Action

Chancery court could have considered that, in the absence of any action seeking to reopen 1973 domestic relations case in 1983, nothing was pending in which transfer or consolidation to domestic relations division of divorce action would have been proper. In re Mercer, 117 Ill. App. 3d 377, 72 Ill. Dec. 869, 453 N.E.2d 744 (1 Dist. 1983).

Contingent Interests

—Fee Contracts

Even though expected contingent fees may not be considered a marital asset because of their speculative value, husband's expenses on behalf of contingent cases were comparable to an investment, and since husband received the value of the investment and its yield in the form of future income, wife had to receive the present value of the investment, which was an amount equal to the expenses attributable to the contingent cases prior to dissolution. In re Zells, 197 Ill. App. 3d 232, 143 Ill. Dec. 354, 554 N.E.2d 289 (1 Dist. 1990), rev'd on other grounds, 143 Ill. 2d 251, 157 Ill. Dec. 480, 572 N.E.2d 944 (1991).

Given the intangibility of a contingent fee, its unascertainable and speculative value, the aleatory nature of the right to receive it, and the uncertainty of collection, a contingent fee cannot be considered an asset of either the marital estate or of the law practice from which it is derived. In re Zells, 197 Ill. App. 3d 232, 143 Ill. Dec. 354, 554 N.E.2d 289 (1 Dist. 1990), rev'd on other grounds, 143 Ill. 2d 251, 157 Ill. Dec. 480, 572 N.E.2d 944 (1991).

A lawyer's contingent fee contracts are not subject to valuation, division and distribution as part of the marital estate, as such a division would comprise an impermissible ethical conflict. In re Zells, 143 Ill. 2d 251, 157 Ill. Dec. 480, 572 N.E.2d 944 (1991).

Contingent Interests (Cont'd)

—Trusts

Where the wife's eligibility to receive a portion of a trust was an expectancy contingent upon the discretion of the trustee or upon his intestate death and not a realization, the circuit court erred when it apportioned the interest to her as a current asset. In re Eddy, 210 Ill. App. 3d 450, 155 Ill. Dec. 174, 569 N.E.2d 174 (1 Dist. 1991).

Contribution

—In General

Pursuant to subsection (j)(2), the trial court may consider the relevant economic circumstances of the parties in ruling on a contribution petition. In re Delarco, 313 Ill. App. 3d 107, 245 Ill. Dec. 921, 728 N.E.2d 1278, 2000 Ill. App. LEXIS 302 (2 Dist. 2000).

This section incorporates a partnership theory of marriage, and thus an order disposing of the parties' property should recognize and compensate each party for his or her contribution to the marriage. In re Calisoff, 176 Ill. App. 3d 721, 126 Ill. Dec. 183, 531 N.E.2d 810 (1 Dist. 1988).

An order of distribution need not necessarily reflect the respective contributions of each party. In re Wentink, 132 Ill. App. 3d 71, 87 Ill. Dec. 117, 476 N.E.2d 1109 (1 Dist. 1984).

—Both Spouses

The court adequately considered the contribution of each of the parties to the acquisition of the marital estate where it found the wife's contribution to the marriage for 18½ years as a farm wife and homemaker, and eventually as a wage earner, to be equal to the husband's contribution as a farmer and wage earner for the same period in addition to his contribution as a homemaker for 18 months after the parties' separation. In re Moll, 232 Ill. App. 3d 746, 174 Ill. Dec. 18, 597 N.E.2d 1230 (2 Dist. 1992).

Where both parties have made more than nominal, though not equal, contributions toward acquisition of marital assets, absent countervailing factors, this tends to support the proposition that both parties should share, though not equally, the marital property. In re Clearman, 85 Ill. App. 3d 584, 40 Ill. Dec. 958, 407 N.E.2d 189 (3 Dist. 1980).

—Burden

The burden of proving a significant contribution is on the moving party, and even if a significant contribution were to be established, the presumption of transmutation created by the contribution may be rebutted with evidence that a gift of the non-marital property was not intended. In re Aud, 142 Ill. App. 3d 320, 96 Ill. Dec. 615, 491 N.E.2d 894 (5 Dist. 1986).

Under subsection (c) of this section, the burden rests on the spouse claiming contribution to the acquisition of marital property to trace that contribution. In re Van Ness, 136 Ill. App. 3d 185, 90 Ill. Dec. 766, 482 N.E.2d 1049 (4 Dist. 1985).

—Extent

The evidence of wife's contribution of $1,000 in savings, several months' outside employment over a period of 20 years, and assistance in answering the phone and making entries was too minimal to justify conveyance to her of one-half of all the property, including business assets and equipment, under former Ill.Rev.Stat., ch. 40, para. 18 (see now this section). Overton v. Overton, 6 Ill. App. 3d 1086, 287 N.E.2d 47 (2 Dist. 1972).

—Fair Distribution

The fact that one spouse contributed more financially than the other does not necessarily entitle one to a greater distribution of the marital property. In re Theeke, 105 Ill. App. 3d 119, 60 Ill. Dec. 944, 433 N.E.2d 1311 (1 Dist. 1981).

Though the non-marital property and its appreciated value remain the separate asset of the spouse who received it subsequent to marriage, a court, relying upon evidentiary proof, would have to distribute the marital property of the couple in a manner that would reflect the measure of contributions of the spouses. In re Komnick, 84 Ill. 2d 89, 49 Ill. Dec. 291, 417 N.E.2d 1305 (1981).

Where a wife by her own industry, earnings, labor, economy and frugality has added to the financial betterment of the parties or to the husband's acquisition of an estate, she has an equitable interest which must be recognized by a fair division of property. Gerhardt v. Gerhardt, 18 Ill. App. 3d 658, 310 N.E.2d 224 (3 Dist. 1974).

—Financial Contributions

Former section 18 of the Divorce Act (see now this section) vested the trial court with authority to award interest in the marital property to a spouse where she alleged and proved special equities by way of her financial contributions beyond her marital duties. Brongel v. Brongel, 48 Ill. App. 3d 27, 6 Ill. Dec. 115, 362 N.E.2d 750 (2 Dist. 1977).

—Improvement Not Shown

There was insufficient evidence presented to prove any increase in value in a business where no accountants, real estate appraisers or other experts testified regarding the value of the business before or after the marriage, and there was evidence that the improvements were the result of the parties' personal efforts, rather than some factor external to the marriage. In re Miller, 231 Ill. App. 3d 480, 172 Ill. Dec. 679, 595 N.E.2d 1349 (3 Dist. 1992).

—Indebtedness Not Created

Payments voluntarily made by a wife for family expenses during the time the husband and wife were living together did not create an indebtedness from the husband to the wife in the absence of an agreement to that effect even though plaintiff's contributions were substantial; they did give her equity in the residence, especially since the divorce decree provided that she was to receive all the household furniture and furnishings. Everett v. Everett, 25 Ill. 2d 342, 185 N.E.2d 201 (1962).

—Mortgage Debt

Under former Ill.Rev.Stat., ch. 40, paras, 18 and 19 (see now this section and 750 ILCS 5/504), where the wife was the sole beneficial owner of a farm and the husband did not know of the original mortgage thereon until after its execution, and it was only when the encumbrance was increased that he signed the mortgage, the wife was not entitled to contribution toward the payment of the mortgage debt and the divorce decree properly relieved the husband of any obligation to pay such debt. Olson v. Olson, 66 Ill. App. 2d 227, 213 N.E.2d 95 (2 Dist. 1965).

—Non-Marital Property

The trial court erred in failing to reimburse marital estate for its contributions to three non-marital life insurance policies of husband since subdivision (c)(2) of this section mandates reimbursement to the contributing estate for contributions retraceable by clear and convincing evidence. In re Ryman, 172 Ill. App. 3d 599, 122 Ill. Dec. 646, 527 N.E.2d 18 (2 Dist. 1988).

—Owner of Land Trust

As the owner of the entire beneficial interest in land trust prior to the marriage, husband was the "owner" of the property for purposes of determining contributions to the marital estate, and the trial court did not err in concluding that he made a greater contribution to the acquisition of the marital residence. In re Marriott, 264 Ill. App. 3d 23, 201 Ill. Dec. 709, 636 N.E.2d 1141 (2 Dist. 1994).

—Reimbursement

Where the respondent's non-marital rural property was enhanced in value by contribution of $19,333 from the marital property, i.e., $6,333 which was evidently paid by marital income on the principal owing on the trailer debt and $13,000 which was paid by marital income on the principal of the new home mortgage; the marital estate should be reimbursed from the respondent's non-marital property. In re Booth, 255 Ill. App. 3d 707, 194 Ill. Dec. 500, 627 N.E.2d 1142 (4 Dist. 1993).

Reimbursement for contributions made by the marital estate to enhance the value of an item of property classified as belonging to one of the parties alone is made to the contributing marital estate, not to the contributing spouse. McCoy v McCoy, 225 Ill. App. 3d 966, 168 Ill. Dec. 27, 589 N.E.2d 141 (3 Dist. 1992).

Reimbursement requires that a contribution be traceable by clear and convincing evidence. McCoy v McCoy, 225 Ill. App. 3d 966, 168 Ill. Dec. 27, 589 N.E.2d 141 (3 Dist. 1992).

In dividing property subsequent to dissolution proceedings, appreciation in value to the non-marital estate must be shown only if contribution is of personal effort. In re Adams, 183 Ill. App. 3d 296, 131 Ill. Dec. 730, 538 N.E.2d 1286 (4 Dist. 1989).

In valuing the right to reimbursement, if spouse's salary is found to be reasonable compensation for his efforts, the non-marital business need not reimburse marital estate because that salary

Contribution (Cont'd)

—Reimbursement (Cont'd)

during the marriage is marital property, and thus the marital estate has already been compensated. In re Morse, 143 Ill. App. 3d 849, 98 Ill. Dec. 67, 493 N.E.2d 1088 (5 Dist. 1986).

—Specific Dollar Value

Although the trial court did not place a dollar value on contributions of each party to acquisition of the marital estate, such specific finding was not required by the statute nor was it a prerequisite to the validity of property division orders. In re Lee, 78 Ill. App. 3d 1123, 34 Ill. Dec. 451, 398 N.E.2d 126 (1 Dist. 1979).

—Support of Children

Because wife generated all of marital assets and was the sole support of minor children, she would receive a significantly greater apportionment of the marital assets. In re Rai, 189 Ill. App. 3d 559, 136 Ill. Dec. 922, 545 N.E.2d 446 (1 Dist. 1989).

Conveyance of Property

—In General

As a general rule, Illinois courts require that special circumstances justifying a conveyance of property from one spouse to another must be alleged and proved. Leone v. Leone, 39 Ill. App. 3d 547, 350 N.E.2d 545 (3 Dist. 1976).

—Absolute Right

Generally, a spouse has an absolute right to dispose of his or her property in any manner and without the concurrence of the other spouse; such disposition of property is permissible even where its sole purpose is to minimize or defeat the statutory marital interest the other spouse may have in the property conveyed. In re Shehade, 137 Ill. App. 3d 692, 92 Ill. Dec. 398, 484 N.E.2d 1253 (1 Dist. 1985).

—Clear and Convincing Evidence

A conveyance of a marital residence from husband to his wife, where the husband continued to make mortgage, tax and improvement payments, was part of an estate tax planning scheme and constituted clear and convincing evidence necessary to rebut presumption of marital property. In re Davis, 215 Ill. App. 3d 763, 159 Ill. Dec. 375, 576 N.E.2d 44 (1 Dist.), appeal denied, 141 Ill. 2d 538, 162 Ill. Dec. 484, 580 N.E.2d 110 (1991).

Conveyance of the entire property to the wife upon divorce was justified where the wife testified that she made all mortgage payments, together with all taxes and insurance premiums, out of her own earnings from her employment. Dmitroca v. Dmitroca, 79 Ill. App. 2d 220, 223 N.E.2d 545 (2 Dist. 1967).

Decree compelling conveyance of property could not be rendered upon facts shown by the evidence which would warrant relief where those facts were not alleged in the complaint. Walsh v. Walsh, 372 Ill. 254, 23 N.E.2d 341 (1939).

—Court Ordered

A trial court in hearing divorce matters could only order property to be conveyed from one party to the other in two specific situations: under former section 17 of the Divorce Act (now repealed) where special equities must have been specifically alleged in the complaint and established by competent evidence adduced at trial; and in the second situation, the conveyance of property must have been in lieu of alimony under former section 18 of the Divorce Act (see now this section). Mueller v. Mueller, 49 Ill. App. 3d 666, 7 Ill. Dec. 513, 364 N.E.2d 674 (2 Dist. 1977).

This section makes it possible for the court to compel a conveyance in an appropriate case, vesting a large measure of discretion in the trial court to be applied on an equitable basis. Gottemoller v. Gottemoller, 37 Ill. App. 3d 689, 346 N.E.2d 393 (3 Dist. 1976).

The authority of courts to compel conveyance of realty in divorce actions is governed by statutory rather than general equity powers. Klaisner v. Klaisner, 28 Ill. App. 3d 110, 328 N.E.2d 341 (2 Dist. 1975).

A court could order a conveyance of realty in lieu of alimony under former section 18 of the Divorce Act (see now this section), provided the evidence revealed that the recipient spouse was entitled to alimony, the conveyance was equitable, and periodic payments of alimony would not have been feasible. Klaisner v. Klaisner, 28 Ill. App. 3d 110, 328 N.E.2d 341 (2 Dist. 1975); Seniuta v. Seniuta, 31 Ill. App. 3d 408, 334 N.E.2d 261 (1 Dist. 1975).

Where a property settlement, made a part of the divorce decree, provided that each of the parties should have all real property belonging to him or her and now in his or her possession, and that each party should upon request execute to the other any instrument that the other party may reasonably require for the purpose of giving full force and effect to the provisions of the agreement, the master in chancery was empowered to execute an instrument of conveyance of the real estate in the event of the refusal of wife to execute and deliver an instrument conveying title to real estate to husband. Brevet v. Brevet, 316 Ill. App. 406, 45 N.E.2d 199 (1 Dist. 1942).

Under former section 17 of the Divorce Act (see now this section), whenever a divorce was granted, if it appeared to the court that either party held the title to property equitably belonging to the other, the court could compel conveyance thereof to be made to the party entitled to the same, upon such terms as it deemed equitable. Bissett v. Bissett, 375 Ill. 551, 31 N.E.2d 955 (1941).

The court may compel a conveyance of property held by one party belonging to the other upon such terms as it shall deem equitable. Lewis v. Lewis, 316 Ill. 447, 147 N.E. 411 (1925).

—Effect of Act

The effect of subdivision (a)(2) of this section is to destroy the presumption heretofore existing that a transfer or conveyance of property from one spouse to another or into their joint names was presumptively a gift of the property or funds even though the property or funds were acquired before marriage. In re Dietz, 76 Ill. App. 3d 1029, 32 Ill. Dec. 532, 395 N.E.2d 762 (5 Dist. 1979).

—Error

Where the trial court refused to set aside the father's nonmarital funds, pursuant to 750 ILCS 5/503(g), for the payment of child support during the father's incarceration, the trial court's decision did not have support under 750 ILCS 5/505(a)(1), as § 505(a)(1) did not limit what assets the trial court could reach to assure that a child support award was satisfied. Hari v. Hari, 345 Ill. App. 3d 1116, 281 Ill. Dec. 518, 804 N.E.2d 144, 2004 Ill. App. LEXIS 91 (4 Dist. 2004).

Construction that trial court gave subsection (d) of this section as authorizing an outright conveyance of marital property in trust for a minor son, unrelated to his support or maintenance, was clearly in error. Raski v. Raski, 64 Ill. App. 3d 629, 21 Ill. Dec. 417, 381 N.E.2d 744 (5 Dist. 1978).

The court erred in requiring defendant to convey his one-half interest to plaintiff since she did not demonstrate special equities in the residence under former section 18 of the Divorce Act (see now this section). Hogan v. Hogan, 58 Ill. App. 3d 661, 16 Ill. Dec. 265, 374 N.E.2d 1040 (1 Dist. 1978).

Under former Ill.Rev.Stat., ch. 40, para. 18 (see now this section), where there were no allegations of special circumstances or allegations asking for relief with reference to a particular property which was owned in joint tenancy by a wife and husband, and there was no evidence as to any other value of the real estate except for a $3000 mortgage, nor was there evidence as to the value of the real estate at the time the decree was entered, that portion of a divorce decree which compelled the wife to convey her interest in the property upon the husband paying to her the sum of $3000 was erroneous. Marcy v. Marcy, 400 Ill. 152, 79 N.E.2d 207 (1947).

Where appellee did not file a brief and there was nothing in the record alleging any fact with respect to the real estate in question, or any ground whatsoever upon which appellee would be equitably entitled to have a conveyance made from appellant to him, the judgment of the court ordering the appellant to convey to appellee the real estate described in the decree pursuant to former section 17 of the Divorce Act (see now this section) was reversed. Skoronski v. Skoronski, 395 Ill. 301, 69 N.E.2d 690 (1946).

Where no special equities were present, it was error for the court to order a transfer of the one half interest of the husband's real and personal property to the wife, and error for the court to refuse to cause to be reconveyed to the husband the interest conveyed to the wife immediately before the marriage, and in not requiring the return of the automobile turned over to her as an inducement to resume marital relations. Bissett v. Bissett, 375 Ill. 551, 31 N.E.2d 955 (1941).

Conveyance of Property (Cont'd)

—Gift or Advancement

Where property is conveyed to the wife, even though the husband furnishes all of the purchase price, there is a presumption that the conveyance is a gift or advancement, and, unless this presumption is overcome, the husband is not in a position to claim a resulting trust by mere proof of the payment of the purchase money; moreover, the fact that the husband thereafter improved the property and paid taxes thereon was not inconsistent with the presumption that he intended it as a gift or advancement. Nickoloff v. Nickoloff, 384 Ill. 377, 51 N.E.2d 565 (1943).

—Good Faith

If a transaction is fair and honest and made in good faith, subsequent acts of misconduct do not warrant a court of equity in decreeing a cancellation of the conveyance. Peck v. Peck, 16 Ill. 2d 268, 157 N.E.2d 249 (1959).

—Illustrative Cases

Where husband repaid wife for down payment of a tract of land, he was entitled to the property upon dissolution, and entitlement was not contrary to the manifest weight of the evidence despite the parties' conflicting testimony. Marsh v. Marsh, 64 Ill. App. 3d 572, 21 Ill. Dec. 477, 381 N.E.2d 804 (4 Dist. 1978).

Where divorce decree under former provisions indicated that the court considered the equities of the parties in realty, yet there was no finding as to whether or not plaintiff was equitably entitled to any of the realty, but the decree simply ordered that defendant convey his interest to the domiciliary real estate to plaintiff as alimony in gross in lieu of periodical alimony, it was impossible to determine whether she had been awarded something to which she already had a right and thereby denied alimony where alimony would seem to be due. Yoselle v. Yoselle, 54 Ill. App. 2d 354, 204 N.E.2d 129 (1 Dist. 1964).

Where the husband neither claimed nor established any equity in the wife's property, the chancellor erred in depriving the wife of her freehold estate under former section 17 of the Divorce Act (see now this section). Stevens v. Stevens, 14 Ill. 2d 99, 150 N.E.2d 799 (1958).

For a case discussing conveyance of property under former section 17 of the Divorce Act (see now this section), see Czarnecki v. Czarnecki, 341 Ill. 629, 173 N.E. 752 (1930).

—Special Circumstances and Equities

To have justified a conveyance of property owned by one spouse to the other under former section 17 of the Divorce Act (see now this section), the party seeking the conveyance must have pleaded and proved special circumstances and equities which entitled that party to an interest in the property; the spouse claiming special equities in property had to show that he or she had contributed money or services other than those normally performed in the marriage relationship which directly or indirectly were used to acquire or enhance the value of the property. In re LaSusa, 80 Ill. App. 3d 467, 35 Ill. Dec. 884, 400 N.E.2d 21 (1 Dist. 1979).

Under former section 17 of the Divorce Act (see now this section), a court could compel a conveyance of property owned by one spouse to the other only where the party seeking such a conveyance proved special circumstances entitling that party to an equitable interest in the property. Hogan v. Hogan, 58 Ill. App. 3d 661, 16 Ill. Dec. 265, 374 N.E.2d 1040 (1 Dist. 1978).

Where a wife did not allege, nor did she adduce by proof, any equitable ownership, special circumstances, or existing equities relative to the household goods, under the authority of former section 17 of the former Divorce Act (see now this section), the court had no power to invest her with the property rights of her consort. Schouten v. Schouten, 129 Ill. App. 2d 418, 263 N.E.2d 715 (5 Dist. 1970).

In order to justify a conveyance of property under former Ill.Rev.Stat., ch. 40, para. 18 (see now this section) special circumstances and equities were required to be alleged and established by the evidence. Stevens v. Stevens, 14 Ill. 2d 99, 150 N.E.2d 799 (1958).

The general rule is that, in a divorce proceeding, the court will not transfer to the wife, who has prevailed in the suit, the fee-simple title to real estate of which the husband is seized unless the wife shows special circumstances and existing equities which justify it. Ylonen v. Ylonen, 2 Ill. 2d 111, 117 N.E.2d 98 (1954).

Where special circumstances exist, a court of equity may, in a divorce proceeding, divest the defendant husband of his interest in real estate and award it to the wife. Harwood v. Harwood, 412 Ill. 131, 105 N.E.2d 719 (1952).

While courts in divorce actions are empowered to determine the property rights of the parties solely upon the basis of equitable ownership and regardless of fault in the dissolution of the marriage, special circumstances and existing equities sufficient to justify the conveyance are required to be alleged in the complaint and established by the evidence. Persico v. Persico, 409 Ill. 608, 100 N.E.2d 904 (1951).

Under a similar prior provision, in order to warrant the court to direct a conveyance of property from one party to the other, there must have been special circumstances and existing equities to justify the conveyance, and such special circumstances and equities must have been alleged in the complaint. Skoronski v. Skoronski, 395 Ill. 301, 69 N.E.2d 690 (1946); Ward v. Sampson, 395 Ill. 353, 70 N.E.2d 324 (1961).

In a divorce action, under former section 18 of the Divorce Act (see now this section), the court could compel the conveyance of property held by one party which in equity belonged to the other, and could adjust the equities of the parties in any property owned by them jointly; in order to warrant directing the conveyance of property belonging to one to the other, there had to be special circumstances and existing equities justifying the conveyance, and such special circumstances and equities had to be alleged in the complaint and established by the proof. Podgornik v. Podgornik, 392 Ill. 124, 63 N.E.2d 715 (1945).

—Voidability

A trial court judge in the domestic relations division possesses the jurisdiction to hear all issues which are justiciable in nature and are related to the dissolution of marriage proceeding; thus a judge may declare a transfer void when it is demonstrated that the conveyance was colorable or illusory. In re Shehade, 137 Ill. App. 3d 692, 92 Ill. Dec. 398, 484 N.E.2d 1253 (1 Dist. 1985).

Credit

The trial court did not err in awarding defendant credit for one-half of expenses he was required to advance, since subsection (d) of this section prefers property distribution to maintenance awards in providing for the needs of parties to a divorce; the allocation of the net proceeds of this property after the payment of current expenses and expenses of sale was not unreasonable. In re Aud, 142 Ill. App. 3d 320, 96 Ill. Dec. 615, 491 N.E.2d 894 (5 Dist. 1986).

Criminal Contempt

In divorce proceeding where defendant husband personally appeared at hearing, but failed to produce passbook to savings account as earlier ordered by the trial court, this conduct constituted grounds for a finding of direct criminal contempt. Palacio v. Palacio, 33 Ill. App. 3d 1074, 339 N.E.2d 427 (1 Dist. 1975).

De Minimus Claims

The correct procedure to be applied under subdivision (c)(2) of this section is to determine whether either spouse contributed significant personal effort toward non-marital property which resulted in substantial appreciation of that property; the requirement that no reimbursement is to be made unless a spouse's personal efforts are significant and result in substantial appreciation of the non-marital property is designed to avoid de minimus claims. In re Morse, 143 Ill. App. 3d 849, 98 Ill. Dec. 67, 493 N.E.2d 1088 (5 Dist. 1986).

Debts

—Assignment

Where one party is substantially responsible for the creation of the debt and has a substantially greater capacity to earn money, it is not an abuse of discretion for the trial court to assign the overwhelming majority of debt to that party. In re Werries, 247 Ill. App. 3d 639, 186 Ill. Dec. 747, 616 N.E.2d 1379 (4 Dist. 1993).

—Classification

No showing of a wife's marital interest in an assignment was

Debts (Cont'd)

—Classification (Cont'd)

required where husband's interest was presumed to be marital property in which both the husband and the wife were presumed to have a species of common ownership, which vested upon the commencement of the dissolution action and continued during its pendency, and which was to be finally determined by the court at a later date. In re Shehade, 137 Ill. App. 3d 692, 92 Ill. Dec. 398, 484 N.E.2d 1253 (1 Dist. 1985).

Where a party to a divorce mortgages marital property during the pendency of the divorce proceedings, the appropriate relief would be a monetary judgment against the party executing the mortgage in an amount equal to one-half the amount of any overage generated when the mortgage value is compared to any marital debts it seeks to cover. In re Donovan, 122 Ill. App. 3d 803, 78 Ill. Dec. 293, 462 N.E.2d 9 (4 Dist. 1984).

The trial court did not abuse its discretion in ordering husband to pay the balance due on a charge account which was used entirely by wife for her clothing purchases; by ordering the husband to pay the $20,000 debt, the trial court in effect simply awarded the wife this sum as additional property in accordance with its division of marital property into just proportions. In re Block, 110 Ill. App. 3d 864, 65 Ill. Dec. 769, 441 N.E.2d 1283 (2 Dist. 1982).

Non-marital property is not transmuted into marital property merely as the result of the use of marital funds to reduce the indebtedness on the property. In re Resser, 97 Ill. App. 3d 838, 53 Ill. Dec. 632, 424 N.E.2d 45 (4 Dist. 1981).

—Contingent Liabilities

Contingent liabilities are not fairly treated as marital debt. Blackstone v. Blackstone, 288 Ill. App. 3d 905, 224 Ill. Dec. 90, 681 N.E.2d 72 (1 Dist. 1997).

—Dischargeability in Bankruptcy

Whether a debt is non-dischargeable as being in the nature of alimony, maintenance or support is a matter of federal, not state, law; the label placed on the decree and the language of the decree do not control the issue of dischargeability, but rather, the court must look to the substance of the decree to determine the essential character of the obligation. In re Rowden, 163 Ill. App. 3d 869, 114 Ill. Dec. 886, 516 N.E.2d 1041 (3 Dist. 1987).

—Distribution Upheld

The trial court did not abuse its discretion in assigning the debts to the wife where the wife had economic means to pay the debts because she had income from her employment and received liquid assets under the terms of the judgment. In re Stufflebeam, 283 Ill. App. 3d 923, 219 Ill. Dec. 390, 671 N.E.2d 55 (3 Dist. 1996), appeal denied, 171 Ill. 2d 586, 222 Ill. Dec. 438, 677 N.E.2d 972 (1997).

Apportionment of property and debts was proper where there was a disparity in net income between the parties, and respondent did not have to pay maintenance to petitioner. In re Ward, 282 Ill. App. 3d 423, 217 Ill. Dec. 964, 668 N.E.2d 149 (1 Dist. 1996).

The trial court did not abuse its discretion in allocating a $2,000 debt on the marital home to husband, even though wife received the home pursuant to the court's disposition of property, where husband failed to demonstrate how such assignment was unfair to him in light of the overall distribution of property and obligations. In re Klein, 231 Ill. App. 3d 901, 173 Ill. Dec. 335, 596 N.E.2d 1214 (4 Dist. 1992).

—Dual Responsibility

The trial court determination that wife should not be responsible for the parties' staggering debt, including the $300,000 debt to the Internal Revenue Service (IRS), which included $80,000 in penalties and interest, was an abuse of the trial court's discretion as both ineffective and unrealistic where the court specifically found wife was a party to the irresponsible, overindulgent, and lavish lifestyle established during the marriage. In re Dunseth, 260 Ill. App. 3d 816, 198 Ill. Dec. 620, 633 N.E.2d 82 (4 Dist. 1994).

—Equal Division

Where the partners to a marriage accumulate debts exceeding the value of their assets, then that debt must be distributed equitably, the same as marital assets. In re Simmons, 101 Ill. App. 3d 645, 57 Ill. Dec. 352, 428 N.E.2d 1032 (5 Dist. 1981).

—Excess of Assets

An award of $10,000 in marital property out of a marital estate in which the debts appeared to exceed the assets was upheld. In re DeGironemo, 206 Ill. App. 3d 1019, 151 Ill. Dec. 918, 565 N.E.2d 189 (1 Dist. 1990).

—Liability

Where the parties in a property settlement agreement provided that the wife would retain the marital residence "subject to the indebtedness" thereon, they did not indicate that the wife was to assume the obligation of paying this indebtedness. The language merely qualified the estate received by the wife and indicated that her interest in the marital residence was encumbered by the second mortgage so as to be susceptible to foreclosure in the event of nonpayment. Pollard v. Waggoner, 165 Ill. App. 3d 501, 116 Ill. Dec. 428, 519 N.E.2d 18 (5 Dist. 1988).

Where an examination of the trial court's property allocation revealed that petitioner wife received well over three times the net amount of property allocated to respondent husband, an allocation of $30,000 debt to respondent would raise a serious question as to the adequacy of respondent's property award; therefore, aside from the nature of the $30,000 debt, the trial court clearly did not abuse its discretion in allocating debt to petitioner. In re Hopkins, 106 Ill. App. 3d 135, 62 Ill. Dec. 99, 435 N.E.2d 897 (4 Dist. 1982).

Boilerplate language in a divorce decree concerning liability for personal debts was not intended to apply to debts between the parties; the customary interpretation of such a provision is that it applies as between the parties only to claims made by third persons to whom either of the individuals owes sums of money or other valuable consideration. Ringstrom v. Ringstrom, 101 Ill. App. 3d 677, 57 Ill. Dec. 193, 428 N.E.2d 743 (4 Dist. 1981).

The trial court erred in finding real property to be marital property, even though wife remained liable on the mortgage note which was jointly executed by the parties, because mere liability on the note itself was insufficient to determine whether the property was marital or non-marital. In re Drennan, 93 Ill. App. 3d 903, 49 Ill. Dec. 386, 418 N.E.2d 30 (4 Dist. 1981).

Where the authority exercised by the chancellor in a divorce proceeding where he ordered that creditors of the parties be paid from the proceeds of the sale of the wife's property, irrespective of when and by whom the debts were incurred, unwarrantably deprived the wife of her freehold estate and gave the husband a share which he did not even claim, and imposed upon the wife the additional penalty for the husband's extravagances, all of which was neither within the terms nor the purport of the former Divorce Act (see now 750 ILCS 5/101 et seq.), that portion of the divorce decree was reversed and the cause was remanded with directions to award the net proceeds of the sale remaining in the hands of the clerk to the wife. Stevens v. Stevens, 14 Ill. 2d 99, 150 N.E.2d 799 (1958).

—Non-Marital

The $20,000 defendant received from his father and used as down payment on home was a non-marital debt which defendant alone was required to pay. In re Marx, 281 Ill. App. 3d 897, 217 Ill. Dec. 645, 667 N.E.2d 734 (4 Dist. 1996).

Absent special circumstances, the spouse incurring non-marital debts should be required to pay them. In re Lees, 224 Ill. App. 3d 691, 167 Ill. Dec. 135, 587 N.E.2d 17 (1992).

The court was justified in requiring petitioner wife to pay respondent husband's non-marital debts where petitioner was gainfully employed and in relatively good health, respondent was confined to a nursing home, had no prospects for future employment and had his financial affairs handled by a guardian, and a cursory examination of each party's situation clearly showed petitioner was in a much better position, both physically and financially, to see to the liquidation of the necessary amount of property. In re Shields, 167 Ill. App. 3d 205, 118 Ill. Dec. 50, 521 N.E.2d 118 (4 Dist. 1988).

—Reimbursement

Because marital debts exceeded the value of the marital property when husband left the marital home, the court's refusal to order husband to reimburse wife for one-half of the marital debts which exceeded the value of marital property resulted in substantial injustice to wife and constituted an abuse of discretion. In re

Debts (Cont'd)

—Reimbursement (Cont'd)
Simmons, 101 Ill. App. 3d 645, 57 Ill. Dec. 352, 428 N.E.2d 1032 (5 Dist. 1981).

—Tax Liability
Portion of tax liability for spouse's income earned prior to dissolution was a marital liability; fact that parties were living separately did not change marital nature of their income, nor marital nature of income tax liability on that income, although the incurring of penalties and interest by one party may be deemed dissipation of assets. In re Charles, 284 Ill. App. 3d 339, 219 Ill. Dec. 742, 672 N.E.2d 57 (4 Dist. 1996).

Declaratory Relief
The mere possibility, always at least potentially present, that proceedings for dissolution of marriage might be commenced during the term of an agreement between spouses relating to their property or business dealings, should not preclude the availability of declaratory relief where an actual controversy has arisen with respect to the construction of the agreement. Stern v. Stern, 105 Ill. App. 3d 805, 61 Ill. Dec. 567, 434 N.E.2d 1164 (2 Dist. 1982).

Inasmuch as complaint pled the existence of an agreement in settlement of pending litigation and requested that the court construe the agreement's terms and declare the rights of the parties, it constituted a request for the construction of a contract and was properly brought in a suit for a declaratory judgment. Stern v. Stern, 105 Ill. App. 3d 805, 61 Ill. Dec. 567, 434 N.E.2d 1164 (2 Dist. 1982).

Deed
A deed showing that title to property in the name of one spouse was insufficient to show the transfer of the subject real estate was a gift. In re Deem, 123 Ill. App. 3d 1019, 79 Ill. Dec. 542, 463 N.E.2d 1317 (4 Dist. 1984).

Desertion
Where husband and wife purchased real estate for use as a home, and where the marriage was broken by wife without good cause as shown by the uncontested finding of her wilful desertion, the chancellor was justified in requiring the return to husband of the interest in the real estate standing in the name of wife. Shipman v. Shipman, 360 Ill. 635, 196 N.E. 797 (1935).

Discretion of Court

—In General
Trial courts have broad discretion in fashioning property dispositions and such decisions will not be set aside absent a clear abuse of discretion. Haas v. Haas, 215 Ill. App. 3d 959, 158 Ill. Dec. 983, 574 N.E.2d 1376 (3 Dist. 1991).

The distribution of marital property rests within the sound discretion of the trial court and will not be reversed absent an abuse of discretion; an abuse of discretion occurs where no reasonable person would take the view adopted by the trial court. In re Rink, 136 Ill. App. 3d 252, 91 Ill. Dec. 34, 483 N.E.2d 316 (1 Dist. 1985).

The trial court in its discretion may make whatever distribution it deems equitable under the circumstances, and review is limited to determining whether the trial court fairly considered the evidence in the context of the factors set forth in subsection (c) of this section. In re Rosen, 126 Ill. App. 3d 766, 81 Ill. Dec. 840, 467 N.E.2d 962 (1 Dist. 1984).

Distribution of marital property is a decision to be made in the sound discretion of the trial court, and a reviewing court will not reverse such a decision unless it reflects an abuse of discretion. In re Sevon, 117 Ill. App. 3d 313, 73 Ill. Dec. 41, 453 N.E.2d 866 (1 Dist. 1983).

The distribution of marital property rests within the sound discretion of the trial court and will not be disturbed absent an abuse of discretion. In re Ligas, 110 Ill. App. 3d 1, 65 Ill. Dec. 763, 441 N.E.2d 1277 (1 Dist. 1982).

Trial courts generally have a great amount of discretion in fashioning property dispositions in dissolution of marriage cases. In re Legge, 111 Ill. App. 3d 198, 66 Ill. Dec. 926, 443 N.E.2d 1089 (4 Dist. 1982); In re Westcott, 163 Ill. App. 3d 168, 114 Ill. Dec. 411, 516 N.E.2d 566 (1 Dist. 1987); In re Jacks, 200 Ill. App. 3d 112, 146 Ill. Dec. 143, 558 N.E.2d 106 (2 Dist. 1990); Haas v. Haas, 215 Ill. App. 3d 959, 158 Ill. Dec. 983, 574 N.E.2d 1376 (3 Dist. 1991).

The distribution of marital property rests within the sound discretion of the trial court. In re Fleming, 80 Ill. App. 3d 1006, 36 Ill. Dec. 205, 400 N.E.2d 625 (2 Dist. 1980).

—Apportionment
Apportionment of debts was held not to be an abuse of discretion. In re Nuechterlien, 225 Ill. App. 3d 1, 167 Ill. Dec. 139, 587 N.E.2d 21 (4 Dist.), cert. denied, 145 Ill. 2d 636, 173 Ill. Dec. 6, 596 N.E.2d 630 (1992).

The trial court has discretion in choosing the method to apportion the present value of the marital property interest in retirement benefits. In re Mantei, 222 Ill. App. 3d 933, 164 Ill. Dec. 870, 583 N.E.2d 1192 (4 Dist. 1991).

—Approximation of Income
The court only needs to make an approximation of the income available to both parties, and the decision to allow or exclude expert testimony is within the sound discretion of the trial court. In re Weinstein, 128 Ill. App. 3d 234, 83 Ill. Dec. 425, 470 N.E.2d 551 (1 Dist. 1984).

—Authorization of Award
The trial court has great discretion in applying the factors noted in this section and is authorized to award either property or maintenance, both property and maintenance, or property in lieu of maintenance. In re Rapacz, 135 Ill. App. 3d 1045, 90 Ill. Dec. 622, 482 N.E.2d 441 (2 Dist. 1985); In re Jones, 187 Ill. App. 3d 206, 134 Ill. Dec. 836, 543 N.E.2d 119 (1 Dist. 1989).

—Continuing Jurisdiction
The power over the subject matter of alimony is not exhausted by the entry of the original order, but is, under the statute, continuing for the purpose, at any time, of making such alterations thereof as shall appear to the chancellor, in the exercise of a judicial discretion, reasonable and proper. Cole v. Cole, 142 Ill. 19, 31 N.E. 109 (1892).

—Contributions
It was an abuse of discretion for the trial court to merely accept the amount of defendant's contributions as value of pension where the trial court indicated that the value was considerably more than defendant's contributions. In re Mantei, 222 Ill. App. 3d 933, 164 Ill. Dec. 870, 583 N.E.2d 1192 (4 Dist. 1991).

—Equitable
Trial court had broad discretion to make an equitable apportionment of marital property and that discretion was not abused even though the wife received about 84 percent of the total assets while the husband received 16 percent as the wife was not awarded maintenance, the wife had higher monthly expenses and a lower monthly income, and neither party could count on earning even a moderate income as the wife was 66 years old and the husband was 69 years old at the time they dissolved their 38-year marriage. In re Marriage of Gaumer, 336 Ill. App. 3d 1012, 271 Ill. Dec. 471, 785 N.E.2d 122, 2003 Ill. App. LEXIS 94 (5 Dist. 2003).

While the division of assets must be equitable, it need not be equal; trial court's decision will not be reversed on appeal absent an abuse of that discretion. In re Click, 169 Ill. App. 3d 48, 119 Ill. Dec. 701, 523 N.E.2d 169 (2 Dist.), appeal denied, 122 Ill. 2d 571, 125 Ill. Dec. 213, 530 N.E.2d 241 (1988).

It is true that the trial court in a divorce action is not clothed with equitable powers but is limited to the authority conferred on it by statute, but the court may adjust the equities of the parties in any property owned by them jointly. Gray v. Gray, 57 Ill. App. 3d 430, 15 Ill. Dec. 47, 373 N.E.2d 317 (2 Dist. 1978).

Where the appellate court on review of divorce case could see no legal or equitable basis for the award of certain lots to the wife, under Rule 366, Supreme Court Rules, the court would exercise its prerogative to reverse that part of the decree awarding the lots to the wife, and direct that such lots should be retained in joint tenancy, subject to such disposition as the parties themselves might wish. Gray v. Gray, 57 Ill. App. 3d 430, 15 Ill. Dec. 47, 373 N.E.2d 317 (2 Dist. 1978).

—Income Tax Refund
The respective interests of parties in federal income tax refund

Discretion of Court (Cont'd)

—Income Tax Refund (Cont'd)
could have been divided according to agreement of the parties, or could be determined by the court in the absence of agreement of the parties. In re Ormiston, 168 Ill. App. 3d 1016, 119 Ill. Dec. 680, 523 N.E.2d 148 (1 Dist. 1988).

—Just Proportions
Trial court's division of marital assets was not unjust under 750 ILCS 5/503(d), when considering the whole division, the award was in "just proportions;" the trail court's reliance on the husband's purported values was not erroneous. In re Marriage of Bowlby, 338 Ill. App. 3d 720, 273 Ill. Dec. 466, 789 N.E.2d 366, 2003 Ill. App. LEXIS 530 (5 Dist. 2003).

The trial court has broad discretion to apportion marital property in just proportions, and a court of review will not disturb that apportionment unless it can be clearly shown that the trial court abused its discretion. In re McNeeley, 117 Ill. App. 3d 320, 72 Ill. Dec. 873, 453 N.E.2d 748 (1 Dist. 1983); In re Callaway, 150 Ill. App. 3d 712, 104 Ill. Dec. 103, 502 N.E.2d 366 (1 Dist. 1986).

The trial court has discretion to divide marital property in what it considers to be "just proportions," taking into account the listed factors, along with any other factors that are deemed relevant in a particular case. In re Aschwanden, 82 Ill. 2d 31, 44 Ill. Dec. 269, 411 N.E.2d 238 (1980).

—Non-Marital Assets
Subsection (d) of this section vests the trial court with the discretion to dispose of non-marital assets as it determines, pursuant to its plan of resolution of the property issues. Eckert v. Eckert, 202 Ill. App. 3d 780, 147 Ill. Dec. 750, 559 N.E.2d 1090 (3 Dist. 1990).

—Range of Reason
A circuit court judge's resolution of property division is fettered only by the range of reason, and his judgment will not be disturbed in the absence of an abuse of discretion. In re Lee, 78 Ill. App. 3d 1123, 34 Ill. Dec. 451, 398 N.E.2d 126 (1 Dist. 1979).

Dissipation

—Accountability
A person charged with dissipation is obliged to establish by clear and convincing evidence how the funds were spent; general and vague statements that the funds were spent on marital expenses or to pay bills are inadequate to avoid a finding of dissipation. In re Meadow, 256 Ill. App. 3d 115, 195 Ill. Dec. 238, 628 N.E.2d 702 (1 Dist. 1993).

—Benefit of Children
A transfer of marital assets does not escape classification as dissipation merely because it is to, or for, the benefit of children of the marriage; expenditures for the children's immediate reasonable needs is a permissible use of marital funds, however, excessive expenditures, even if for a permissible purpose, may constitute a dissipation of marital assets. In re Yong Sun Lee, 246 Ill. App. 3d 628, 186 Ill. Dec. 257, 615 N.E.2d 1314 (4 Dist.), cert. denied, 153 Ill. 2d 560, 191 Ill. Dec. 620, 624 N.E.2d 808 (1993).

—Burden of Proof
Once petitioner spouse established that respondent spouse had obtained exclusive control over the martial savings, the burden shifted to respondent to show by clear and convincing evidence specifically how the funds were spent. In re Jerome, 255 Ill. App. 3d 374, 193 Ill. Dec. 74, 625 N.E.2d 1195 (5 Dist. 1993). In re Schmidt, 242 Ill. App. 3d 961, 182 Ill. Dec. 804, 610 N.E.2d 673 (4 Dist. 1993).

Testimony offered to explain or justify expenditures charged as dissipation must, at a minimum, be offered by the spouse charged with dissipation, and the explanation given then requires that the trial court determine the spouse's credibility as to whether these expenditures were for a purpose related to the marriage; the court's determination of credibility will not be disturbed unless it is manifestly against the weight of the evidence. In re Hagshenas, 234 Ill. App. 3d 178, 175 Ill. Dec. 506, 600 N.E.2d 437 (2 Dist. 1992), appeal denied, 148 Ill.2d 642, 183 Ill. Dec. 19, 610 N.E.2d 1263 (1993).

A party charged with dissipating marital assets is obliged to establish how those funds were spent by clear and specific evidence; general and vague statements that the funds were spent on marital expenses or to pay bills will not suffice to avoid a finding of dissipation. In re Hagshenas, 234 Ill. App. 3d 178, 175 Ill. Dec. 506, 600 N.E.2d 437 (2 Dist. 1992), appeal denied, 148 Ill.2d 642, 183 Ill. Dec. 19, 610 N.E.2d 1263 (1993).

A party charged with dissipating marital assets is obligated to establish by clear and convincing evidence how the funds were spent. In re Phillips, 229 Ill. App. 3d 809, 171 Ill. Dec. 501, 594 N.E.2d 353 (2 Dist. 1992).

A person charged with dissipation has the burden of establishing by clear and specific evidence how the funds in question were spent. In re Petrovich, 154 Ill. App. 3d 881, 107 Ill. Dec. 543, 507 N.E.2d 207 (2 Dist. 1987); In re Hazel, 219 Ill. App. 3d 920, 162 Ill. Dec. 451, 579 N.E.2d 1265 (5 Dist. 1991), cert. denied, 145 Ill. 2d 633, 173 Ill. Dec. 3, 596 N.E.2d 627 (1992).

Once it is established that one party has liquidated marital assets, the party charged with dissipation must establish by clear and specific evidence how the funds were spent; general and vague statements that they were spent on marital expenses or bills are inadequate to avoid a finding of dissipation. In re Smith, 128 Ill. App. 3d 1017, 84 Ill. Dec. 242, 471 N.E.2d 1008 (2 Dist. 1984); In re Osborn, 206 Ill. App. 3d 588, 151 Ill. Dec. 663, 564 N.E.2d 1325 (5 Dist. 1990), cert. denied, 137 Ill. 2d 666, 156 Ill. Dec. 563, 571 N.E.2d 150 (1991).

The spouse charged with dissipation of marital funds has the burden of showing, by clear and specific evidence, how the funds were spent and if expenditures are not documented adequately by the person charged with dissipation, courts will affirm a finding of dissipation; general and vague statements that funds were spent on marital expenses or to pay bills are inadequate to avoid a finding of dissipation. In re Rai, 189 Ill. App. 3d 559, 136 Ill. Dec. 922, 545 N.E.2d 446 (1 Dist. 1989).

—Changing Species and Retiring Debts
Merely changing the species of assets from stocks to cash or retiring debt is not, per se, dissipation. In re Hahin, 266 Ill. App. 3d 168, 205 Ill. Dec. 788, 644 N.E.2d 4 (2 Dist. 1994).

—Charge Against Property Share
Where the court was dividing up assets derived from a personal injury settlement worth $1.8 million, dissipation in the amount of $7,800 used in trips and gifts involving respondent's girlfriend and in unaccounted-for expenditures would not necessarily materially effect the division of property; there was no abuse of the trial court's discretion in failing to find respondent's dissipation of assets required a major charge against his share of marital property. In re Murphy, 259 Ill. App. 3d 336, 197 Ill. Dec. 671, 631 N.E.2d 893 (4 Dist.), appeal denied, 157 Ill. 2d 505, 205 Ill. Dec. 168, 642 N.E.2d 1285 (1994).

—Compensation
It is not an acceptable practice for one spouse, in contemplation of dissolution of marriage, to dissipate marital assets; the circuit court may consider such conduct and compensate the disadvantaged spouse when apportioning marital property, but an award of cash or property equal to half of the amount dissipated is not mandated. In re Hellwig, 100 Ill. App. 3d 452, 55 Ill. Dec. 762, 426 N.E.2d 1087 (1 Dist. 1981); In re Durante, 201 Ill. App. 3d 376, 147 Ill. Dec. 56, 559 N.E.2d 56 (1 Dist. 1990).

"Dissipation" is use of marital assets for one spouse's sole benefit or for a purpose unrelated to the marriage at a time when the marriage is undergoing an irreconcilable breakdown; where a party has dissipated marital assets, the trial court may charge the amount dissipated against the offending party's share of the marital property, so the other party is compensated. In re Jones, 187 Ill. App. 3d 206, 134 Ill. Dec. 836, 543 N.E.2d 119 (1 Dist. 1989).

Where the record was devoid of any proof that the compensation paid to the employees of defendant was inconsistent with the compensation generally paid to individuals with similar skills who performed similar jobs, the trial court correctly found that the compensation paid to these individuals was reasonable and was not dissipation. In re Aud, 142 Ill. App. 3d 320, 96 Ill. Dec. 615, 491 N.E.2d 894 (5 Dist. 1986).

Where a spouse uses marital property for his own benefit and for a purpose unrelated to the marriage at a time in which the

Dissipation (Cont'd)

—Compensation (Cont'd)

marriage is undergoing an irreconcilable breakdown, the court may consider that conduct and compensate the disadvantaged spouse when apportioning the marital property. In re Block, 110 Ill. App. 3d 864, 65 Ill. Dec. 769, 441 N.E.2d 1283 (2 Dist. 1982).

—Credibility of Spouse Charged

The explanation given by the spouse charged with dissipation as to how funds were spent requires the trial court to determine his or her credibility. In re Rai, 189 Ill. App. 3d 559, 136 Ill. Dec. 922, 545 N.E.2d 446 (1 Dist. 1989).

—Damage to Family Photographs

Where wife mutilated family pictures it was error for the trial court to grant husband no relief merely because it could place no economic value on the destroyed marital photographs; the destroyed marital property could be recovered if wife retained the negatives and made copies of the destroyed photographs or, if the marital property could not be restored, the trial court at a minimum should have determined damages and accordingly considered this issue in the distribution of the marital property. In re Ferkel, 260 Ill. App. 3d 33, 198 Ill. Dec. 522, 632 N.E.2d 1133 (5 Dist. 1994).

—Debt

Husband's purchase of a racing boat, shortly before parties physically separated, while he already owned a large yacht that he had leased out because he could not afford to maintain it, could properly be considered as a debt in dissipation of the marital estate, and the court could properly consider the dissipation in dividing marital property in just proportions. In re Block, 110 Ill. App. 3d 864, 65 Ill. Dec. 769, 441 N.E.2d 1283 (2 Dist. 1982).

—Defined

Dissipation is the use of marital property for the sole benefit of one of the spouses for a purpose unrelated to the marriage at a time when the marriage is undergoing an irreconcilable breakdown. In re Parker, 252 Ill. App. 3d 1015, 192 Ill. Dec. 277, 625 N.E.2d 237 (1 Dist. 1993); In re Frey, 258 Ill. App. 3d 442, 196 Ill. Dec. 531, 630 N.E.2d 466 (5 Dist. 1994).

In its legal sense, dissipation is defined as the use of marital property for the sole, but not necessarily personal, benefit of one of the spouses for a purpose unrelated to the marriage at a time when the marriage is undergoing an irreconcilable breakdown. In re Hagshenas, 234 Ill. App. 3d 178, 175 Ill. Dec. 506, 600 N.E.2d 437 (2 Dist. 1992), appeal denied, 148 Ill.2d 642, 183 Ill. Dec. 19, 610 N.E.2d 1263 (1993).

Dissipation is defined as the use of marital property for the sole benefit of one spouse for a purpose unrelated to the marriage at a time when the marriage is undergoing an irreconcilable breakdown. In re Phillips, 229 Ill. App. 3d 809, 171 Ill. Dec. 501, 594 N.E.2d 353 (2 Dist. 1992).

Dissipation refers to the use of marital property for the sole benefit of one of the spouses for a purpose unrelated to the marriage at a time that the marriage is undergoing irreconcilable breakdown. In re Hazel, 219 Ill. App. 3d 920, 162 Ill. Dec. 451, 579 N.E.2d 1265 (5 Dist. 1991), cert. denied, 145 Ill. 2d 633, 173 Ill. Dec. 3, 596 N.E.2d 627 (1992); In re Phillips, 229 Ill. App. 3d 809, 171 Ill. Dec. 501, 594 N.E.2d 353 (2 Dist. 1992).

By its very definition, dissipation occurs after the marriage is irreconcilably broken down. In re Getautas, 189 Ill. App. 3d 148, 136 Ill. Dec. 509, 544 N.E.2d 1284 (2 Dist. 1989).

Dissipation of marital assets by one spouse in contemplation of dissolution of marriage is an unacceptable practice, and may be found where a spouse uses marital property for his or her own benefit and for a purpose unrelated to the marriage at a time when the marriage relationship is in serious jeopardy. Head v. Head, 168 Ill. App. 3d 697, 119 Ill. Dec. 549, 523 N.E.2d 17 (1 Dist. 1988).

Dissipation may be found where spouse uses marital property for his own benefit and for a purpose unrelated to the marriage at a time at which the marriage is undergoing an irreconcilable breakdown. In re Hellwig, 100 Ill. App. 3d 452, 55 Ill. Dec. 762, 426 N.E.2d 1087 (1 Dist. 1981); In re Smith, 114 Ill. App. 3d 47, 69 Ill. Dec. 827, 448 N.E.2d 545 (1 Dist. 1983); In re Sevon, 117 Ill. App. 3d 313, 73 Ill. Dec. 41, 453 N.E.2d 866 (1 Dist. 1983); In re Malters, 133 Ill. App. 3d 168, 88 Ill. Dec. 460, 478 N.E.2d 1068 (1 Dist. 1985); In re Bauer, 138 Ill. App. 3d 379, 93 Ill. Dec. 108, 485 N.E.2d 1318 (1 Dist. 1985); In re Aud, 142 Ill. App. 3d 320, 96 Ill. Dec. 615, 491 N.E.2d 894 (5 Dist. 1986); In re Westcott, 163 Ill. App. 3d 168, 114 Ill. Dec. 411, 516 N.E.2d 566 (1 Dist. 1987); In re Wolf, 180 Ill. App. 3d 998, 129 Ill. Dec. 742, 536 N.E.2d 792 (1 Dist. 1989); In re Rai, 189 Ill. App. 3d 559, 136 Ill. Dec. 922, 545 N.E.2d 446 (1 Dist. 1989); In re Harding, 189 Ill. App. 3d 663, 136 Ill. Dec. 935, 545 N.E.2d 459 (1 Dist. 1989); In re O'Neill, 138 Ill. 2d 487, 150 Ill. Dec. 607, 563 N.E.2d 494 (1990); In re Osborn, 206 Ill. App. 3d 588, 151 Ill. Dec. 663, 564 N.E.2d 1325 (5 Dist. 1990), cert. denied, 137 Ill. 2d 666, 156 Ill. Dec. 563, 571 N.E.2d 150 (1991); Makar v. Makar, 211 Ill. App. 3d 692, 156 Ill. Dec. 154, 570 N.E.2d 630 (1 Dist. 1991).

—Depletion of Pension Funds

Trial court erred in its distribution of marital assets in failing to consider wife's partial responsibility for the depletion of pension funds. In re Malters, 133 Ill. App. 3d 168, 88 Ill. Dec. 460, 478 N.E.2d 1068 (1 Dist. 1985).

—Determination

Neither party accused the other of dissipation, but the trial court sua sponte found dissipation by the husband in maintaining his separate residence, thus the husband was never given the opportunity to present "clear and specific" evidence that his expenditures for the residence were legitimate, and the trial court abused its discretion in finding dissipation sua sponte because the trial produced no clear evidence that the husband spent more than reasonable sums to maintain his home. In re Hahin, 266 Ill. App. 3d 168, 205 Ill. Dec. 788, 644 N.E.2d 4 (2 Dist. 1994).

An irreconcilable breakdown period, for purposes of identifying dissipation, does not extend from the initial signs of trouble in a marriage. In re Hazel, 219 Ill. App. 3d 920, 162 Ill. Dec. 451, 579 N.E.2d 1265 (5 Dist. 1991), cert. denied, 145 Ill. 2d 633, 173 Ill. Dec. 3, 596 N.E.2d 627 (1992).

The issue in determining whether a dissipation is shown is whether the party used marital property for his own benefit for a purpose unrelated to the marriage during a period when only that party had access to the funds. In re Philips, 200 Ill. App. 3d 395, 146 Ill. Dec. 191, 558 N.E.2d 154 (1 Dist. 1990).

—Discretion of Court

Failure of trial court to address question of dissipation amounted to an abuse of discretion requiring reversal of judgment allocating marital assets, where there was dissipation of marital assets by husband who spent tens of thousands of dollars with respect to extramarital relationship, liquidated investments, and incurred interest and penalties by failing to satisfy tax debt. In re Charles, 284 Ill. App. 3d 339, 219 Ill. Dec. 742, 672 N.E.2d 57 (4 Dist. 1996).

If husband dissipated the sale proceeds of stock, the trial court was empowered to order that he reimburse the wife for such dissipation, and/or that the wife be awarded a greater portion of the marital estate to compensate her for the dissipation. In re Rayfield, 211 Ill. App. 3d 763, 164 Ill. Dec. 469, 583 N.E.2d 23 (1 Dist. 1991).

Whether there was dissipation is a matter for the trial court's discretion, and a finding concerning dissipation will not be disturbed unless it is against the manifest weight of the evidence. In re Rai, 189 Ill. App. 3d 559, 136 Ill. Dec. 922, 545 N.E.2d 446 (1 Dist. 1989).

—Factors

The court may consider the dissipation of marital assets when apportioning marital property. In re Wolf, 180 Ill. App. 3d 998, 129 Ill. Dec. 742, 536 N.E.2d 792 (1 Dist. 1989).

Subdivision (c)(1) of this section mandates that the trial court consider each party's contribution to or dissipation of marital properties. In re Rothbardt, 99 Ill. App. 3d 561, 54 Ill. Dec. 929, 425 N.E.2d 1146 (1 Dist. 1981).

—Funds for Expenses

Where the funds are spent for legitimate family expenses and necessary and appropriate purposes, there is no dissipation. In re Rai, 189 Ill. App. 3d 559, 136 Ill. Dec. 922, 545 N.E.2d 446 (1 Dist. 1989); In re Harding, 189 Ill. App. 3d 663, 136 Ill. Dec. 935, 545 N.E.2d 459 (1 Dist. 1989).

—Gambling

The trial court abused its discretion in not considering the husband's dissipation of marital assets in equitably distributing marital property in just proportions where: (1) the marriage was

Dissipation (Cont'd)

—Gambling (Cont'd)

irreconcilably broken as far back as 1992, when the parties separated and the wife filed the first dissolution petition; (2) they separated in 1992 because the husband incurred gambling-related debts; (3) the husband moved back into the marital residence in December, 1992 on the condition that he not incur more debts; (4) although the parties occasionally slept together, they lived separate lives for the most part; and (5) because the husband secretly continued to incur debts in spite of agreeing not to do so, the purported reconciliation in December, 1992 was pretextual. In re Carter, 317 Ill. App. 3d 546, 251 Ill. Dec. 252, 740 N.E.2d 82, 2000 Ill. App. LEXIS 953 (4 Dist. 2000).

The trial court in a marriage dissolution case did not err in holding that dissipation occurred with regard to the husband's gambling; however, in light of the husband's testimony which suggested that at least some of the gambling activity was related to the entertainment of business clients, there was no abuse of the court's discretion in not making any specific allotment for this in its property distribution. In re Hagshenas, 234 Ill. App. 3d 178, 175 Ill. Dec. 506, 600 N.E.2d 437 (2 Dist. 1992), appeal denied, 148 Ill.2d 642, 183 Ill. Dec. 19, 610 N.E.2d 1263 (1993).

—General and Vague Statements

General and vague statements that funds were spent on marital expenses or to pay bills are inadequate to avoid a finding of dissipation. In re Schmidt, 242 Ill. App. 3d 961, 182 Ill. Dec. 804, 610 N.E.2d 673 (4 Dist. 1993).

—Illustrative Cases

Evidence supported the determination that the husband dissipated marital funds where it was shown that, after the breakdown of the parties' marriage, he received over $340,000 in marital funds and invested such funds in a series of Illinois and Cayman corporations without informing his wife about such funds. Gurda v. Gurda, 304 Ill. App. 3d 1019, 238 Ill. Dec. 236, 711 N.E.2d 339 (1 Dist. 1999), appeal denied, 185 Ill. 2d 624, 242 Ill. Dec. 137, 720 N.E.2d 1092 (1999).

The court had ample evidence on which to base its finding of dissipation where husband took two expensive trips, ostensibly to maintain his continuing medical education credits, on which he spent nearly $5,000 and lost two weeks of employment; bought his girlfriend a $1,400 ring, spent $500 on music equipment and $1,500 on furniture, while refusing to pay the IRS and claiming insufficient funds to pay his wife's maintenance; continued to sign, and make payments on leases for thousands of dollars worth of medical equipment, even though his practice was declining; took a $5,000 cash advance; sold one of the Cadillacs for $2,800; and received $34,000 in cash from a lease and disposed of this money without accounting for it. In re Dunseth, 260 Ill. App. 3d 816, 198 Ill. Dec. 620, 633 N.E.2d 82 (4 Dist. 1994).

Payment of property taxes, a stock margin loan used to grow a stock portfolio, liquidation of a stock trading account when the market began to fall, maintenance on two marital properties, and loans obtained to cover family living expenses, were not dissipations of the marital estate by a husband and a trial court's findings to the contrary were erroneous. In re Marriage of Miller, 342 Ill. App. 3d 988, 277 Ill. Dec. 420, 796 N.E.2d 135, 2003 Ill. App. LEXIS 1032 (5 Dist. 2003).

—Inclusion of Non-Marital Property

Subdivision (d)(1) of this section by implication adds non-marital property to the definition of dissipation. In re Pittman, 212 Ill. App. 3d 99, 155 Ill. Dec. 667, 569 N.E.2d 1278 (5 Dist. 1991).

—Income

When husband's income was realized, it became marital property, and income used for his sole benefit, for purposes not related to the marriage, was dissipation. In re Zimmerman, 200 Ill. App. 3d 594, 146 Ill. Dec. 339, 558 N.E.2d 302 (1 Dist. 1990).

—In Contemplation of Dissolution

Dissipation of marital assets by one spouse in contemplation of dissolution of marriage is an unacceptable practice that will not be sanctioned. In re Smith, 114 Ill. App. 3d 47, 69 Ill. Dec. 827, 448 N.E.2d 545 (1 Dist. 1983); In re Harding, 189 Ill. App. 3d 663, 136 Ill. Dec. 935, 545 N.E.2d 459 (1 Dist. 1989).

—Lack of Evidence

The trial court's findings of dissipation were supported by the lack of adequate documentary evidence to substantiate the wife's claims that the marital estate was reimbursed for the expenditures in question. In re Blunda, 299 Ill. App. 3d 855, 234 Ill. Dec. 339, 702 N.E.2d 993 (2 Dist. 1998).

—Legitimate Family Expenses

When the funds are spent for legitimate family expenses and necessary and appropriate purposes, there is no dissipation. In re Schmidt, 242 Ill. App. 3d 961, 182 Ill. Dec. 804, 610 N.E.2d 673 (4 Dist. 1993).

—Living in Marital Residence

The action of husband in living in home without paying rent could not be considered use of marital property for a purpose unrelated to the marriage at a time when the marriage was undergoing an irreconcilable breakdown. Makar v. Makar, 211 Ill. App. 3d 692, 156 Ill. Dec. 154, 570 N.E.2d 630 (1 Dist. 1991).

—Necessary Expenditures

The expenditure of marital funds by one spouse for necessary, appropriate and legitimate living expenses at a time when the marriage is undergoing an irreconcilable breakdown will not be considered to be dissipation. In re Hagshenas, 234 Ill. App. 3d 178, 175 Ill. Dec. 506, 600 N.E.2d 437 (2 Dist. 1992), appeal denied, 148 Ill.2d 642, 183 Ill. Dec. 19, 610 N.E.2d 1263 (1993).

—Not Shown

The court erred in finding that the wife dissipated marital funds where the activity in question occurred well before the date the court believed the marriage suffered an irreconcilable breakdown. In re Blunda, 299 Ill. App. 3d 855, 234 Ill. Dec. 339, 702 N.E.2d 993 (2 Dist. 1998).

While it was true that the value of wife's firm probably dropped as a result of its debt equity ratio increasing due to the debt incurred in setting up the employee stock option plan, there was no error in the trial court's conclusion that wife acted in good faith, that the transaction was not a dissipation of marital assets or in the valuation of the firm. In re Isaacs, 260 Ill. App. 3d 423, 198 Ill. Dec. 169, 632 N.E.2d 228 (1 Dist.), appeal denied, 157 Ill. 2d 502, 205 Ill. Dec. 164, 642 N.E.2d 1281 (1994).

Where wife was not in a financial position to prevent the foreclosure of marital home the trial judge did not abuse her discretion when she did not find that wife dissipated marital assets. In re Parker, 252 Ill. App. 3d 1015, 192 Ill. Dec. 277, 625 N.E.2d 237 (1 Dist. 1993).

Where wife, who placed approximately $13,000 into a personal account, claimed that much of the money was spent on support for the parties' daughter, as she did not receive any child support for at least seven months after the separation and further claimed a portion was spent in securing housing for the daughter, herself, and her two sons from a previous marriage, while husband remained in the marital residence, the trial court's failure to find dissipation was not an abuse of discretion. In re Schmidt, 242 Ill. App. 3d 961, 182 Ill. Dec. 804, 610 N.E.2d 673 (4 Dist. 1993).

Where husband made his living by selling and reinvesting in real estate, and where his testimony sufficiently detailed the tracing of funds from the sale of investment properties, the trial court's decision that husband did not dissipate assets was not against the manifest weight of the evidence. In re Phillips, 229 Ill. App. 3d 809, 171 Ill. Dec. 501, 594 N.E.2d 353 (2 Dist. 1992).

At the point at which the marriage began undergoing irreconcilable breakdown, the court properly found no dissipation on the part of the respondent. In re Hazel, 219 Ill. App. 3d 920, 162 Ill. Dec. 451, 579 N.E.2d 1265 (5 Dist. 1991), cert. denied, 145 Ill. 2d 633, 173 Ill. Dec. 3, 596 N.E.2d 627 (1992).

It was clear from the record that a husband's trip to Aruba was a pleasure trip, and the trial court's findings that his excursions to Brazil and Minnesota were not business oriented were not an abuse of discretion such that these trips constituted a dissipation of marital assets. In re Osborn, 206 Ill. App. 3d 588, 151 Ill. Dec. 663, 564 N.E.2d 1325 (5 Dist. 1990), cert. denied, 137 Ill. 2d 666, 156 Ill. Dec. 563, 571 N.E.2d 150 (1991).

The $15,000 expenditure for attorney fees to defend husband on charge of attempted rape four years prior to dissolution of marriage did not constitute dissipation of marital assets, especially where

Dissipation (Cont'd)

—Not Shown (Cont'd)
wife did not claim that the expenditure occurred during the time that the marriage was undergoing an irreconcilable breakdown. In re O'Neill, 138 Ill. 2d 487, 150 Ill. Dec. 607, 563 N.E.2d 494 (1990).

Trial court did not abuse its discretion in not rendering a finding that dissipation had occurred where evidence in the record showed small amount of funds were alleged to have been dissipated over a period of at least 16 months. In re Adams, 183 Ill. App. 3d 296, 131 Ill. Dec. 730, 538 N.E.2d 1286 (4 Dist. 1989).

Where there was no evidence which suggested that petitioner used the funds for an inappropriate purpose, trial court was erroneous in ruling that wife dissipated cash receipts from husband's medical practice. In re Harding, 189 Ill. App. 3d 663, 136 Ill. Dec. 935, 545 N.E.2d 459 (1 Dist. 1989).

Where the court found that virtually all of alleged acts of dissipation occurred prior to irreconcilable breakdown of the marriage, and further, that spouse had not used any marital funds for purposes unrelated to the marriage, the trial court did not abuse its discretion in finding no dissipation. In re Getautas, 189 Ill. App. 3d 148, 136 Ill. Dec. 509, 544 N.E.2d 1284 (2 Dist. 1989).

Where wife admitted that subsequent to irreconcilable breakdown she took an early distribution of an IRA for a little over $200 and sold a piano to buy Christmas gifts, the wife sustained her burden and sufficiently established how the funds were spent. In re Getautas, 189 Ill. App. 3d 148, 136 Ill. Dec. 509, 544 N.E.2d 1284 (2 Dist. 1989).

In light of the fact that husband was an active participant in purchase of wife's car, the trial court's implicit finding that the wife dissipated marital assets was against the manifest weight of the evidence. In re Ryman, 172 Ill. App. 3d 599, 122 Ill. Dec. 646, 527 N.E.2d 18 (2 Dist. 1988).

The court improperly found that respondent had dissipated the amount of $225,000 where not all of respondent's spending was done at a time that the marriage was irreconcilably breaking down, nor was it done solely for her own benefit, and many of the checks with respondent's signature from early on in the parties' marriage were used to pay for household items or entertainment expenses for the mutual benefit of both parties and to support the lifestyle that both of them enjoyed. In re Westcott, 163 Ill. App. 3d 168, 114 Ill. Dec. 411, 516 N.E.2d 566 (1 Dist. 1987).

Wife's expenditures were necessary and appropriate legitimate family expenses, and there was no evidence in the record to indicate that she spent the money for purposes unrelated to the marriage. In re Sevon, 117 Ill. App. 3d 313, 73 Ill. Dec. 41, 453 N.E.2d 866 (1 Dist. 1983).

The evidence was insufficient to support a finding of dissipation of a brokerage account husband closed after dissolution proceedings had begun. In re Hellwig, 100 Ill. App. 3d 452, 55 Ill. Dec. 762, 426 N.E.2d 1087 (1 Dist. 1981).

Where there was no testimony at trial which indicated that wife disapproved of husband's racing hobby and there was no testimony to support the conclusion that the wife did not enjoy or otherwise participate in the husband's hobby, the trial court abused its discretion in considering the hobby to have dissipated the parties' marital estate. In re Resser, 97 Ill. App. 3d 838, 53 Ill. Dec. 632, 424 N.E.2d 45 (4 Dist. 1981).

Finding that the transfer of parcel of realty seven months before dissolution proceedings commenced, in the course of normal business activities, absent evidence suggesting the proceeds were used for respondent's benefit alone, was contrary to the manifest weight of the evidence. In re Hellwig, 100 Ill. App. 3d 452, 55 Ill. Dec. 762, 426 N.E.2d 1087 (1 Dist. 1981).

—Particular Facts of Case
Where the parties continued to engage in a sexual relationship until the finding for dissolution, the trial court's finding that the marriage of the parties was not undergoing irreconcilable breakdown, for the purpose of identifying dissipation, prior to the filing for dissolution was not an abuse of discretion. In re Hazel, 219 Ill. App. 3d 920, 162 Ill. Dec. 451, 579 N.E.2d 1265 (5 Dist. 1991), cert. denied, 145 Ill. 2d 633, 173 Ill. Dec. 3, 596 N.E.2d 627 (1992).

Whether a given course of conduct constitutes dissipation within the purview of subdivision (d)(1) of this section depends upon the facts of the particular case. In re Petrovich, 154 Ill. App. 3d 881, 107 Ill. Dec. 543, 507 N.E.2d 207 (2 Dist. 1987); In re Rai, 189 Ill. App. 3d 559, 136 Ill. Dec. 922, 545 N.E.2d 446 (1 Dist. 1989); In re Philips, 200 Ill. App. 3d 395, 146 Ill. Dec. 191, 558 N.E.2d 154 (1 Dist. 1990).

—Personal Benefit
A finding of dissipation is possible even though the dissipating party did not derive personal benefit from the dissipation of the asset. In re Frey, 258 Ill. App. 3d 442, 196 Ill. Dec. 531, 630 N.E.2d 466 (5 Dist. 1994).

The dissipating party need not derive a personal benefit from the dissipation in order to be held accountable; for example, a spouse's failure to make mortgage payments and prevent foreclosure on a family home, which results in a loss of equity therein, can constitute dissipation. In re Jones, 187 Ill. App. 3d 206, 134 Ill. Dec. 836, 543 N.E.2d 119 (1 Dist. 1989).

A finding of dissipation is possible even though the dissipating party did not derive personal benefit from the dissipation of the asset. In re Petrovich, 154 Ill. App. 3d 881, 107 Ill. Dec. 543, 507 N.E.2d 207 (2 Dist. 1987).

—Prior to Separation
A party can be found guilty of dissipation even though conduct occurred prior to separation or prior to the commencement of the dissolution proceedings. In re Rai, 189 Ill. App. 3d 559, 136 Ill. Dec. 922, 545 N.E.2d 446 (1 Dist. 1989).

—Proof
General and vague statements that the funds were spent on marital expenses or to pay bills are inadequate to avoid a finding of dissipation. In re Petrovich, 154 Ill. App. 3d 881, 107 Ill. Dec. 543, 507 N.E.2d 207 (2 Dist. 1987).

—Requirements
To show dissipation it is not necessary that marital property be sold or transferred at the time of separation or after dissolution proceedings are instituted; such a requirement would be overly restrictive. In re Harding, 189 Ill. App. 3d 663, 136 Ill. Dec. 935, 545 N.E.2d 459 (1 Dist. 1989).

—Review
The trial court's finding regarding allocation of marital property, including making allowances for dissipation, will not be reversed absent an abuse of discretion. In re Petrovich, 154 Ill. App. 3d 881, 107 Ill. Dec. 543, 507 N.E.2d 207 (2 Dist. 1987).

—Securing Housing
Use of marital property to secure housing after leaving the marital home is an expenditure for a purpose unrelated to the marriage. In re Harding, 189 Ill. App. 3d 663, 136 Ill. Dec. 935, 545 N.E.2d 459 (1 Dist. 1989).

—Shown
Where the wife failed to account for a $2,000 check she wrote to herself from the marital account, the trial court erred in failing to find that she had dissipated this amount. In re Blunda, 299 Ill. App. 3d 855, 234 Ill. Dec. 339, 702 N.E.2d 993 (2 Dist. 1998).

The trial court based on its evaluation of husband's credibility and his exhibits, and correctly found that the husband dissipated marital assets. In re Blunda, 299 Ill. App. 3d 855, 234 Ill. Dec. 339, 702 N.E.2d 993 (2 Dist. 1998).

The trial court's determination as to petitioner's dissipation of marital assets was proper and affirmed. In re Uehlein, 265 Ill. App. 3d 1080, 202 Ill. Dec. 838, 638 N.E.2d 706 (1 Dist. 1994).

The record reflected that both parties dissipated marital funds. In re Weiler, 258 Ill. App. 3d 454, 196 Ill. Dec. 372, 629 N.E.2d 1216 (5 Dist. 1994).

There was no abuse of discretion in the trial court's ruling that husband had dissipated marital property where he may not have gained a personal benefit from his acts against family business, but he did cause the corporation to become less profitable either through his inattention to the quality of service the corporation was supplying its clients or through his outright stealing from clients for his new business. In re Thomas, 239 Ill. App. 3d 992, 181 Ill. Dec. 512, 608 N.E.2d 585 (3 Dist. 1993).

The trial court did not abuse its discretion in finding that husband dissipated the marital assets when he failed to establish by clear and specific evidence how the funds were spent or that he used them for living expenses on a share-and-share-alike basis. In

Dissipation (Cont'd)

—Shown (Cont'd)
re Hensley, 210 Ill. App. 3d 1043, 155 Ill. Dec. 486, 569 N.E.2d 1097 (4 Dist.), cert. denied, 141 Ill. 2d 541, 162 Ill. Dec. 488, 580 N.E.2d 114 (1991).

Where husband incurred substantial debt following entry of trial court's restraining order prohibiting either party from utilizing marital assets without leave of court in order to satisfy his gambling debts, incurred without leave of court and without wife's consent, the trial court's factual finding that husband dissipated marital assets was upheld. In re Sobo, 205 Ill. App. 3d 357, 150 Ill. Dec. 280, 562 N.E.2d 1083 (4 Dist. 1990).

Respondent failed to establish by clear and specific evidence how funds were spent or that he used them for marital purposes since he gave vague and contradictory statements that the funds were spent on certain items, petitioner often established that respondent's testimony was false, and respondent admitted that he was unsure of where the money went or how the funds were spent. In re Rai, 189 Ill. App. 3d 559, 136 Ill. Dec. 922, 545 N.E.2d 446 (1 Dist. 1989).

The trial court correctly concluded that petitioner dissipated funds from her living trust account; this withdrawal was made during the pendency of the proceedings, and her bare assertion that the funds were used to pay necessary expenses was insufficient to allow the court to find that the funds were properly withdrawn. In re Harding, 189 Ill. App. 3d 663, 136 Ill. Dec. 935, 545 N.E.2d 459 (1 Dist. 1989).

Wife, who, while residing in residence and receiving funds from husband due to a court order which included an amount requested by her for payment of real estate taxes, failed to pay the real estate taxes, dissipated marital assets. In re Ryman, 172 Ill. App. 3d 599, 122 Ill. Dec. 646, 527 N.E.2d 18 (2 Dist. 1988).

The determinative issue was not the precise time at which the dissipation by the husband occurred, but the fact that he used marital property for his own benefit and for a purpose unrelated to the marriage during a period when only he had access to the fund; therefore, the trial court's apportionment of marital property was equitable. In re Kaplan, 149 Ill. App. 3d 23, 102 Ill. Dec. 719, 500 N.E.2d 612 (1 Dist. 1986).

The trial court's estimate that respondent had dissipated marital assets with a value between $50,000 and $80,000 was supported by the evidence. In re Smith, 128 Ill. App. 3d 1017, 84 Ill. Dec. 242, 471 N.E.2d 1008 (2 Dist. 1984).

Where the court in a dissolution proceeding did not specifically order the husband to pay the mortgage, but prescribed alternative payments to be made by him, and he had the financial ability to prevent a foreclosure on the marital home and failed so to do, the husband's actions constituted dissipation. In re Siegel, 123 Ill. App. 3d 710, 79 Ill. Dec. 219, 463 N.E.2d 773 (1 Dist. 1984).

Where respondent relinquished one-third interest in a business at one-tenth of the guaranteed price, at a very questionable time for reasons benefitting only himself, thereby willingly depriving marital estate of over $45,000 in assets, his action clearly qualified as a dissipation of marital assets for which respondent would be held accountable in the property division. In re Hilkovitch, 124 Ill. App. 3d 401, 79 Ill. Dec. 891, 464 N.E.2d 795 (1 Dist. 1984).

Record revealed ample support for finding that husband dissipated marital assets where husband failed to make monthly payments necessary to preserve and maintain property, resulting in mortgage foreclosure proceedings, resulting in the sale of the marital home, and failed to pay the taxes on Wisconsin property which accrued after the sale of the stocks ordered by the court. In re Cook, 117 Ill. App. 3d 844, 73 Ill. Dec. 222, 453 N.E.2d 1357 (1 Dist. 1983).

Where respondent never contributed financially to marriage in any way, yet she withdrew funds from a joint bank account and spent substantial sums of money during the brief course of the marriage, respondent dissipated marital resources. Naguit v. Scrivner, 104 Ill. App. 3d 709, 60 Ill. Dec. 499, 433 N.E.2d 296 (5 Dist. 1982).

Based upon the contradictions in respondent's testimony as to whether transfer of parcel of land to his son was a gift or for value and the transfer's proximity in time to the dissolution proceedings, the court did not err in finding that respondent dissipated this marital asset. In re Hellwig, 100 Ill. App. 3d 452, 55 Ill. Dec. 762, 426 N.E.2d 1087 (1 Dist. 1981).

Respondent acted contrary to the best interests of the marriage in his haste to reach the bank to withdraw $3,500 from joint account at about the time he left petitioner, and the evidence led to the conclusion that the money was taken to deprive the petitioner of it under circumstances which showed that the respondent was attempting to seize marital property before he left the petitioner, especially since he paid this money to his former wife for a questionable reason; the trial judge should have applied the relevant factors set forth in subsection (c) of this section to compensate the petitioner for the respondent's dissipation of funds. Klingberg v. Klingberg, 68 Ill. App. 3d 513, 25 Ill. Dec. 246, 386 N.E.2d 517 (1 Dist. 1979).

—Specific Statement Not Required
A trial court is not required to make a specific statement when finding dissipation. In re Dunseth, 260 Ill. App. 3d 816, 198 Ill. Dec. 620, 633 N.E.2d 82 (4 Dist. 1994).

—Timing and Nature of Act
A finding of dissipation is possible even though the act occurred prior to the commencement of the dissolution proceedings, and the dissipating party need not derive personal benefit from the dissipation of the asset to be held accountable. In re Smith, 128 Ill. App. 3d 1017, 84 Ill. Dec. 242, 471 N.E.2d 1008 (2 Dist. 1984).

—Vacation Trips
Taking vacation trips with someone other than the spouse has been held to constitute dissipation. In re Murphy, 259 Ill. App. 3d 336, 197 Ill. Dec. 671, 631 N.E.2d 893 (4 Dist.), appeal denied, 157 Ill. 2d 505, 205 Ill. Dec. 168, 642 N.E.2d 1285 (1994).

Dissolution

—Conduct in Accepting Terms
In divorce proceeding, wife's conduct in accepting a quitclaim deed, $6,000, and the payment of attorney fees to her amounted to an acceptance of the benefits of the decree and was a release of errors. Kissin v. Kissin, 29 Ill. App. 2d 126, 172 N.E.2d 635 (1 Dist. 1961).

—Date
It is the date of dissolution and not the date of the parties' separation that is determinative as to what property was acquired during a marriage. In re Tatham, 173 Ill. App. 3d 1072, 123 Ill. Dec. 576, 527 N.E.2d 1351 (5 Dist. 1988).

—Provisions of Decree
For the provisions of the divorce decree to be a bar to the husband's claim to co-ownership with wife of property, it would be necessary to establish that the matter was an issue in the divorce proceedings, since any adjudication, to constitute a bar, must have been on what was actually in issue. Szczurak v. Veitschegger, 59 Ill. App. 2d 411, 207 N.E.2d 494 (2 Dist. 1965).

—Statute of Frauds
Where the parties to a divorce proceeding contract in respect to alimony and property rights arising out of the marriage relationship, and the provisions agreed to are incorporated in the decree, the contract becomes merged in the decree, and the rights of the parties are thereafter based upon the decree, not the agreement, and the requirement of the Statute of Frauds that contracts concerning real estate be in writing has no application. Guyton v. Guyton, 17 Ill. 2d 439, 161 N.E.2d 832 (1959).

Distribution

—In General
After classification, each spouse's non-marital property is given to that spouse, and the marital property is divided in just proportions. Moore v. Moore, 251 Ill. App. 3d 41, 190 Ill. Dec. 370, 621 N.E.2d 239 (3 Dist. 1993).

The trial court is not required to award marital assets to a party in an amount equal to or in excess of the amount of marital liability assigned to that party. In re Werries, 247 Ill. App. 3d 639, 186 Ill. Dec. 747, 616 N.E.2d 1379 (4 Dist. 1993).

Subsection (a) of this section contains an exclusive list of non-marital property; once classified, the non-marital property of each spouse is assigned to that spouse and the marital property is

Distribution (Cont'd)

—In General (Cont'd)

equitably divided between them. In re Voight, 111 Ill. App. 3d 623, 67 Ill. Dec. 458, 444 N.E.2d 694 (1 Dist. 1982).

Property division is preferred to maintenance in the statutory scheme. In re Drennan, 93 Ill. App. 3d 903, 49 Ill. Dec. 386, 418 N.E.2d 30 (4 Dist. 1981).

For a case discussing disposition of property under former section 17 of the Divorce Act, see Lawyer v. Lawyer, 19 Ill. App. 3d 571, 312 N.E.2d 7 (2 Dist. 1974).

—Abuse of Discretion

Where there was evidence husband had substantial future earning ability, trial court committed an abuse of discretion by awarding him the bulk of marital assets, which included his medical practice, and should have awarded wife other marital property as an offset, or ordered husband to make payments to her. In re Charles, 284 Ill. App. 3d 339, 219 Ill. Dec. 742, 672 N.E.2d 57 (4 Dist. 1996).

Where the petitioner and the respondent were 54 years of age at the time the petition for distribution was filed, where both parties worked outside of the home during the marriage and contributed to the marital property, where the marriage lasted for almost 19 years and petitioner was awarded custody of child, and although child was 17 years old and would soon be going to college, she would stay at the marital residence with her mother when she came home from college and where the petitioner's income was approximately $18,000 per year, while respondent's annual income was approximately $44,000, the court's distribution of marital property was an abuse of discretion in light of the aforementioned factors and the fact that the respondent had significantly more earning power than petitioner and had sufficient resources to make the payments to petitioner as directed. In re Eidson, 235 Ill. App. 3d 907, 175 Ill. Dec. 901, 601 N.E.2d 298 (5 Dist. 1992).

The court found that a 55%-45% division of marital property in favor of petitioner wife was an abuse of discretion when respondent husband had the ability to generate significant future income from the value of property set apart to him and, in contrast, petitioner's total disability as the result of illness precluded her from returning to her former occupation as a court reporter, thereby limiting her employability and sources of income and, consequently, directed that petitioner's share be increased from 55% to 75% and respondent's share be decreased from 45% to 25%. In re Madoch, 212 Ill. App. 3d 1007, 157 Ill. Dec. 10, 571 N.E.2d 1029 (1 Dist. 1991).

The division of property in the light of the statutory factors in subsection (d) of this section was an abuse of discretion where the property allocated to the wife provided little income for her, where she was not capable, due to her vocational skills, of securing more than a minimum wage job, and where her health and child care responsibilities further limited her ability to acquire "capital assets and income" in the future. In re Emery, 179 Ill. App. 3d 744, 128 Ill. Dec. 569, 534 N.E.2d 1014 (4 Dist. 1989).

The trial court clearly abused its discretion in distributing the marital property and debts between parties where the trial court awarded petitioner wife assets worth $168,900, including marital home, while awarding respondent husband only $37,390 of assets and requiring him to assume virtually all of marital debts totalling nearly $63,000; respondent was required to pay under the dissolution order $57,500 in attorney fees, $832 per month maintenance, and college expenses for four years for the parties' two children; and, viewing these debts and expenses in light of respondent's current financial condition, respondent could not possibly meet his own personal obligations. In re Calisoff, 176 Ill. App. 3d 721, 126 Ill. Dec. 183, 531 N.E.2d 810 (1 Dist. 1988).

Where both husband and wife enjoyed a high standard of living, where the wife was well educated, earned a substantial salary when employed, worked during much of the marriage and contributed her earnings to it, but where she would be unable to work full time and might require a period of training to reenter the job market and where the husband had substantially greater earning power, the trial court abused its discretion in awarding 20% of the marital assets to the wife. In re Rapacz, 135 Ill. App. 3d 1045, 90 Ill. Dec. 622, 482 N.E.2d 441 (2 Dist. 1985).

Where the court merely withdrew its finding of transmutation and affirmed award of money as being based upon wife's share of marital property accumulated during marriage and as fair reimbursement of the wife's share of marital contributions, this was an abuse of discretion, in that subdivision (c)(2) unequivocally required that reimbursement for marital contributions must be traceable by clear and convincing evidence. In re Harmon, 133 Ill. App. 3d 673, 88 Ill. Dec. 809, 479 N.E.2d 422 (5 Dist. 1985).

Where petitioner's award was approximately 26% of the estate, under the specific circumstances of the case, the court's disposition was an abuse of discretion. In re Hobbs, 110 Ill. App. 3d 451, 66 Ill. Dec. 203, 442 N.E.2d 629 (3 Dist. 1982).

The court abused its discretion in failing to award all of the marital property. In re Hobbs, 110 Ill. App. 3d 451, 66 Ill. Dec. 203, 442 N.E.2d 629 (3 Dist. 1982).

The trial court abused its discretion in dividing the marital property as if obligations from daughters represented bona fide accounts receivable with values established with equal certainty to other marital assets. In re Smith, 105 Ill. App. 3d 980, 61 Ill. Dec. 554, 434 N.E.2d 1151 (3 Dist. 1982).

—After-Acquired Property

When property is acquired subsequent to marriage, the burden of proving that the property was acquired by gift, legacy or descent rests with the claimant spouse by clear, convincing and unmistakable evidence. In re Nicks, 177 Ill. App. 3d 76, 126 Ill. Dec. 442, 531 N.E.2d 1069 (4 Dist. 1988).

—Consideration of Factors

The evidence was sufficient to indicate that the trial court failed to take into consideration the relevant factors of dissipation of marital assets and relative earnings potential, thus warranting a reversal and remandment of the property division portion of the judgment of dissolution. In re Partyka, 158 Ill. App. 3d 545, 110 Ill. Dec. 499, 511 N.E.2d 676 (1 Dist. 1987).

Evidence showed that the trial court considered relevant factors in dividing marital property and in allocating debts of the marriage. In re Ryan, 138 Ill. App. 3d 1077, 93 Ill. Dec. 617, 487 N.E.2d 61 (1 Dist. 1985).

—Discretion

This section allows the court discretion to divide marital property in what it considers just proportions, considering listed factors and all other relevant matters. In re Hart, 194 Ill. App. 3d 839, 141 Ill. Dec. 550, 551 N.E.2d 737 (4 Dist. 1990).

The distribution of marital property rests within the sound discretion of the trial court and will not be disturbed absent an abuse of discretion. In re Hellwig, 100 Ill. App. 3d 452, 55 Ill. Dec. 762, 426 N.E.2d 1087 (1 Dist. 1981).

—Disproportionate Award

Both a wife's dissipation of marital assets and a consideration of her husband's pain, suffering, and disability as a quadriplegic were properly considered by a trial court in making a distribution of marital assets in the couple's divorce, and an award of 75 percent of the marital assets to the husband was not an abuse of discretion. In re Marriage of Zweig, 343 Ill. App. 3d 590, 278 Ill. Dec. 466, 798 N.E.2d 1223, 2003 Ill. App. LEXIS 1272 (5 Dist. 2003).

Where wife's salary, were she to return to teaching, would be approximately $18,000 per year and husband's gross income would be approximately 25 times this amount, an award of 55% of the marital assets to wife and 45% to husband was not an abuse of discretion. In re Scafuri, 203 Ill. App. 3d 385, 149 Ill. Dec. 124, 561 N.E.2d 402 (2 Dist. 1990).

In light of respondent's lower earning capacity, as evidenced by the fact that she remained out of the work force during most of the marriage and when she re-entered the work force she worked only low paying jobs, and the circumstances under which she lived during the year in which the petitioner had virtually full use of that year's lottery payment, division of marital property was not beyond the bounds of reason especially where each party would receive equal lottery payments thereby making any disparity insignificant, and where the overall percentages of marital property received would be approximately 51% for the respondent and 49% for the petitioner. In re Mahaffey, 206 Ill. App. 3d 859, 151 Ill. Dec. 638, 564 N.E.2d 1300 (1 Dist. 1990).

When one spouse makes a greater contribution to the marital assets, the court may be justified in awarding him or her a larger share of the marital property. In re Jones, 187 Ill. App. 3d 206, 134 Ill. Dec. 836, 543 N.E.2d 119 (1 Dist. 1989).

Distribution (Cont'd)

—Disproportionate Award (Cont'd)

Where, among other things, one spouse had little involvement with the other spouse's business and had contributed little to marital assets, and over the years, one spouse had advanced funds to the other for payment of bills, car repairs, and other expenses, in addition to temporary maintenance payments, the court's 60% apportionment of the business awarded to one spouse and 40% to the other was proper. In re Jones, 187 Ill. App. 3d 206, 134 Ill. Dec. 836, 543 N.E.2d 119 (1 Dist. 1989).

Where a wife was awarded a highly disproportionate amount, in view of her substantial contribution to the marital estate and the husband's dissipation thereof, there was no abuse of discretion in the trial court's award. In re Petrovich, 154 Ill. App. 3d 881, 107 Ill. Dec. 543, 507 N.E.2d 207 (2 Dist. 1987).

Where the trial court in its order pointed out that petitioner wife made large, traceable cash contributions toward property acquired during the marriage, where it further pointed out in its order that the respondent husband's contributions of material and labor were indefinite and in any event small relative to petitioner's large contributions, and where the trial court chose to disbelieve the respondent's testimony regarding his large expenditures on the marital property, there was no abuse of discretion on the part of the trial court in awarding a disproportionate award of marital property to the petitioner. In re Guntren, 141 Ill. App. 3d 1, 95 Ill. Dec. 392, 489 N.E.2d 1120 (4 Dist. 1986).

All marital property can be awarded to one spouse only where the totality of the evidence supports that result. In re Clearman, 85 Ill. App. 3d 584, 40 Ill. Dec. 958, 407 N.E.2d 189 (3 Dist. 1980).

Where the order of the court contained a detailed analysis of the economic status, backgrounds and anticipated future plans of the parties, there was ample evidence to support the court's unequal division of the marital property and award of maintenance so that the order of the trial court was not against the manifest weight of the evidence. In re Viehman, 91 Ill. App. 3d 315, 46 Ill. Dec. 800, 414 N.E.2d 853 (5 Dist. 1980).

Determining whether the totality of evidence supports the disparate division of marital property is within the discretion of the trial court and will not be disturbed on review absent an abuse of that discretion. In re Clearman, 85 Ill. App. 3d 584, 40 Ill. Dec. 958, 407 N.E.2d 189 (3 Dist. 1980).

The trial court's complete award of marital property to wife was not against the manifest weight of the evidence nor contrary to this section. In re Stallings, 75 Ill. App. 3d 96, 30 Ill. Dec. 718, 393 N.E.2d 1065 (5 Dist. 1979).

Where there was a clear discrepancy in the parties' abilities to earn income, especially in light of wife's age, lack of job skills and late entry into the job market, and her prospects of retiring at age 65 with sufficient income were unlikely, these factors considered in relation to the husband's relatively promising prospects of the future, highlighted the inequity and the portion of the trial court's order dealing with the equal division of the proceeds from the sale of the marital home was reversed and remanded for further consideration. In re Smith, 77 Ill. App. 3d 858, 33 Ill. Dec. 332, 396 N.E.2d 859 (2 Dist. 1979).

Trial court did not err in awarding to the wife in a divorce case her husband's interest in the jointly owned marital residence in addition to a monthly alimony award where the wife alleged and proved special equities to justify the trial court's order that the husband's interest in the jointly owned property be conveyed to her. Newhouse v. Newhouse, 17 Ill. App. 3d 1008, 309 N.E.2d 102 (2 Dist. 1974).

—Equal Proportions

The distribution need not be equal, as long as it is equitable. In re Werries, 247 Ill. App. 3d 639, 186 Ill. Dec. 747, 616 N.E.2d 1379 (4 Dist. 1993).

The trial court did not abuse its discretion in dividing marital property in approximately equal portions based upon the length of a 31-year marriage, the differences in the parties' income, the limited ability of the wife to acquire future income, the husband's better position to acquire capital assets and income in the future, and the liabilities of the parties. In re Cepek, 230 Ill. App. 3d 1045, 172 Ill. Dec. 852, 596 N.E.2d 131 (1 Dist. 1992).

Fair and equitable division of marital property does not require that the marital estate be split in equal proportions. In re Marthens, 215 Ill. App. 3d 590, 159 Ill. Dec. 3, 575 N.E.2d 3 (3 Dist. 1991).

This Act does not mandate an equal division of marital property. In re Smith, 105 Ill. App. 3d 980, 61 Ill. Dec. 554, 434 N.E.2d 1151 (3 Dist. 1982).

—Evidence

In the absence of evidence of stock's value, the trial court's division of the property was an abuse of discretion because without evidence of the respective values of the various items of marital property, it was impossible for the court to divide the marital property in just proportion as required by the statute. In re Olsher, 78 Ill. App. 3d 627, 34 Ill. Dec. 32, 397 N.E.2d 488 (1 Dist. 1979).

—Evidentiary Hearing

Because proof was necessary to establish whether the assets used to purchase contested property were non-marital in nature, the trial court's failure to hold an evidentiary hearing was an abuse of discretion. In re Burch, 205 Ill. App. 3d 1082, 150 Ill. Dec. 922, 563 N.E.2d 1049 (1 Dist. 1990).

—Factors

Two of the factors the trial court is to consider in dividing marital property are the contribution or dissipation of each party. In re O'Neill, 185 Ill. App. 3d 566, 133 Ill. Dec. 617, 541 N.E.2d 828 (4 Dist. 1989), rev'd on other grounds, 138 Ill. 2d 487, 150 Ill. Dec. 607, 563 N.E.2d 494 (1990).

In dividing marital assets, the trial court can consider the income and earning power of respective parties and the needs of the parties' children. In re Sobo, 205 Ill. App. 3d 357, 150 Ill. Dec. 280, 562 N.E.2d 1083 (4 Dist. 1990).

To divide marital property in just proportions, a court is to consider all relevant factors, which include: the duration of the marriage, the value of the property set apart to each spouse, the relevant economic circumstances of each spouse, the amounts and sources of each spouse's income, the age, occupation vocational skills, employability, and needs of each party, whether the apportionment is in lieu of or in addition to maintenance, and the reasonable opportunity for each spouse for future acquisition of assets and income. In re Heller, 153 Ill. App. 3d 224, 106 Ill. Dec. 503, 505 N.E.2d 1294 (1 Dist. 1987).

Where the trial court considered the contribution of the parties, the value of the parties' resources, the disparity of the parties' earning potentials subsequent to dissolution, the relevant economic circumstances including the health and employability of each of the parties, and the fact that the distribution was in lieu of maintenance, although the court did not list these factors serially with a separate finding for each, the record indicated facts noted by the court which showed that the court considered all relevant factors under subsection (c) of this section. In re Fuggiti, 130 Ill. App. 3d 190, 85 Ill. Dec. 658, 474 N.E.2d 386 (1 Dist. 1985).

The court must consider needs of each of parties in dividing the marital property and in awarding maintenance. In re De Bat, 127 Ill. App. 3d 463, 82 Ill. Dec. 568, 468 N.E.2d 1348 (1 Dist. 1984).

Value of non-marital assets is a factor to be considered in the division of marital property. In re Cuisance, 115 Ill. App. 3d 551, 71 Ill. Dec. 423, 450 N.E.2d 1302 (1 Dist. 1983).

Although long-term periodic maintenance would have been more appropriate and might be somewhat relevant to a judge's decision, other factors must necessarily figure into an award of property pursuant to this section. In re Jenkins, 107 Ill. App. 3d 387, 63 Ill. Dec. 39, 437 N.E.2d 688 (5 Dist. 1982).

A spouse's contributions to the appreciation in value of the other spouse's non-marital property is one of the factors to consider in the division of marital property. In re Pancner, 111 Ill. App. 3d 546, 67 Ill. Dec. 417, 444 N.E.2d 653 (1 Dist. 1982).

Because this section permits the court to consider relevant economic circumstances in disposing of the property and determining whether there is sufficient property to provide for a spouse's reasonable needs without awarding maintenance, it is thus contemplated that the court must make some approximation of the income available to a party in order to determine whether the marital home should be sold or maintenance should be awarded. In re Smith, 100 Ill. App. 3d 1126, 56 Ill. Dec. 716, 427 N.E.2d 1262 (2 Dist. 1981).

In a proceeding for the disposition of property following a dissolution of marriage, the court is directed to award each spouse

Distribution (Cont'd)

—Factors (Cont'd)
his own non-marital assets and to divide marital property without regard to marital misconduct in just proportions considering all relevant factors. In re Fleming, 80 Ill. App. 3d 1006, 36 Ill. Dec. 205, 400 N.E.2d 625 (2 Dist. 1980).

Value is only one factor to be considered by the court in disposing of the marital property. In re Sanborn, 78 Ill. App. 3d 146, 33 Ill. Dec. 468, 396 N.E.2d 1192 (1 Dist. 1979).

In determining whether the trial court abused its discretion in dividing property, the question is not whether the reviewing court agrees with the trial court but rather whether the trial court in the exercise of its discretion acted arbitrarily without the employment of conscientious judgment or, in view of all the circumstances, exceeded the bounds of reason and ignored recognized principles of law so that substantial injustice resulted. In re Lee, 78 Ill. App. 3d 1123, 34 Ill. Dec. 451, 398 N.E.2d 126 (1 Dist. 1979).

—Fairness
The fairness of the distribution of marital assets cannot be dealt with on a piecemeal basis, but the distribution as a whole must be considered to determine if the distribution of the assets was made in just proportions as required by the statute. In re Steele, 212 Ill. App. 3d 425, 156 Ill. Dec. 649, 571 N.E.2d 236 (5 Dist. 1991).

A disposition of property is not unfair merely because a party is unhappy with it. In re Borg, 96 Ill. App. 3d 282, 51 Ill. Dec. 706, 421 N.E.2d 214 (1 Dist. 1981).

—Fund
Unallocated maintenance and an award of attorney fees are proper distributions from a fund set up for child's benefit under this section. In re Gocal, 216 Ill. App. 3d 221, 159 Ill. Dec. 1023, 576 N.E.2d 946 (1 Dist. 1991).

—Future Earning Capacity
Greater future earning potential as an asset was taken into account when the maintenance-paying spouse had voluntarily retired during the dissolution proceedings in an attempt to avoid maintenance, and moreover, the parties had been married for 34 years and maintained an affluent standard of living. In re Goldstein, 97 Ill. App. 3d 1023, 53 Ill. Dec. 397, 423 N.E.2d 1201 (1 Dist. 1981).

Future earning capacity was considered a marital asset when the right to future income was not contingent on future events such as continuation of employment. In re Goldstein, 97 Ill. App. 3d 1023, 53 Ill. Dec. 397, 423 N.E.2d 1201 (1 Dist. 1981).

—Greater Financial Contributions
Greater financial contributions by one spouse alone will not automatically entitle that spouse to a greater distributive share of the marital assets. In re Cecil, 202 Ill. App. 3d 783, 148 Ill. Dec. 72, 560 N.E.2d 374 (3 Dist. 1990).

—Inventory
A trial court did not abuse its discretion in separating inventory from the business for the purpose of determining marital and non-marital property. In re Pancner, 111 Ill. App. 3d 546, 67 Ill. Dec. 417, 444 N.E.2d 653 (1 Dist. 1982).

—Marital Home
Where the spouse awarded possession became exclusively obligated to pay mortgage installments, real estate taxes, insurance, maintenance and upkeep, possession of the marital home should not have been considered as additional child support. In re Theeke, 105 Ill. App. 3d 119, 60 Ill. Dec. 944, 433 N.E.2d 1311 (1 Dist. 1981).

—Mistaken Decisions
A trial court should not penalize an individual in a dissolution of judgment order for mistaken decisions during a marriage; only conduct which amounts to dissipation, the use of property for one's sole benefit and for a purpose unrelated to the marriage, may be considered in awarding marital property. In re Dunseth, 260 Ill. App. 3d 816, 198 Ill. Dec. 620, 633 N.E.2d 82 (4 Dist. 1994).

—Non-Monetary Contributions
A larger property division, as opposed to maintenance, is the preferred method of reimbursing a spouse for such things as non-monetary contributions and contributions of capital. In re Durante, 201 Ill. App. 3d 376, 147 Ill. Dec. 56, 559 N.E.2d 56 (1 Dist. 1990).

—Not Upheld
Where the trial court did not make a specific finding of dissipation, but proceeded to distribute the marital properties as though a dissipation of funds had, in fact, occurred, an evaluation of the facts clearly indicated an abuse of discretion by the trial court in awarding the petitioner approximately 100% of the marital estate. In re Maczko, 263 Ill. App. 3d 991, 201 Ill. Dec. 127, 636 N.E.2d 559 (1 Dist. 1992).

Where distribution of property failed to recognize any of husband's contributions to marriage and did not put the parties in a position from which they could begin anew, but required the husband to shoulder the burdens of the marital finances, the court abused its discretion. Goforth v. Goforth, 121 Ill. App. 3d 673, 77 Ill. Dec. 125, 459 N.E.2d 1374 (5 Dist. 1984).

Where defendant's basic living expenses would require complete use of the maintenance award along with her present salary income, the trial court abused its discretion in awarding defendant only $120,000 worth of stock out of the couple's $543,000 net worth of marital property. In re Aschwanden, 82 Ill. 2d 31, 44 Ill. Dec. 269, 411 N.E.2d 238 (1980).

—Objectives
When distributing property, courts should seek a high degree of finality so that parties can plan their future with certainty and need not return repeatedly to the courts. In re Durante, 201 Ill. App. 3d 376, 147 Ill. Dec. 56, 559 N.E.2d 56 (1 Dist. 1990).

An important objective to be reached by the trial court in entering an order disposing of the parties' property is to place the parties in a position from which they can begin anew, in addition to providing adequate support for the children. In re Calisoff, 176 Ill. App. 3d 721, 126 Ill. Dec. 183, 531 N.E.2d 810 (1 Dist. 1988).

—Professional Degree or License
Increased earning potential obtained by earning a degree or professional license is a mere expectancy interest, not a divisible marital asset under Illinois law, although it is a factor to be considered in the distribution of property. In re Weinstein, 128 Ill. App. 3d 234, 83 Ill. Dec. 425, 470 N.E.2d 551 (1 Dist. 1984).

—Reservation of Issues
For a case discussing award of property with a reservation of the question of alimony, see David v. David, 102 Ill. App. 2d 102, 243 N.E.2d 485 (1 Dist. 1968).

—Statutory Authority
Subsection (d) of this section is the only statutory provision which authorizes the trial court to divide the assets of a marriage; it provides for disposition of property pursuant to a dissolution proceeding or an action to declare a marriage invalid. In re Lipkin, 163 Ill. App. 3d 1033, 115 Ill. Dec. 76, 517 N.E.2d 41 (4 Dist. 1987).

—Stock
Trial court's finding that stock was acquired in exchange for property acquired before marriage was not against the manifest weight of the evidence. In re Wilder, 122 Ill. App. 3d 338, 77 Ill. Dec. 824, 461 N.E.2d 447 (1 Dist. 1983).

—Tax Consequences
Requiring one party to bear the tax consequences of a division of property, where requirement may have resulted in an unequal division of property, did not constitute an abuse of discretion. In re Miller, 112 Ill. App. 3d 203, 68 Ill. Dec. 167, 445 N.E.2d 811 (1 Dist. 1983).

—Upheld
It was not against the manifest weight of the evidence for the trial court to award the wife approximately 75% of the marital estate, notwithstanding that the marriage lasted less than four years, where the husband had $800,000 in nonmarital assets and income of $40,000 to $50,000 per year, while the wife had no nonmarital assets. In re Gattone, 317 Ill. App. 3d 346, 251 Ill. Dec. 65, 739 N.E.2d 998, 2000 Ill. App. LEXIS 900 (2 Dist. 2000).

The court's determination of the property distribution award was not an abuse of discretion. In re Abma, 308 Ill. App. 3d 605, 242 Ill. Dec. 24, 720 N.E.2d 645 (1 Dist. 1999).

Distribution (Cont'd)

—Upheld (Cont'd)

No error occurred with respect to the court's consideration of the enumerated factors in subsection (d), including the parties' respective contributions to the marital estate, when making its property distribution. In re McHenry, 292 Ill. App. 3d 634, 226 Ill. Dec. 887, 686 N.E.2d 670 (1 Dist. 1997).

Court properly considered award of custody of son to father in distribution decision and properly awarded father the farm since he had custody. In re Koberlein, 281 Ill. App. 3d 880, 217 Ill. Dec. 599, 667 N.E.2d 695 (4 Dist. 1996).

Award of marital property to petitioner was fair and equitable where the trial court carefully considered and applied all of the factors enumerated in subsection (d) that were relevant to this case, and petitioner was awarded the assets most valuable and practical for her to retain. In re Puls, 268 Ill. App. 3d 882, 206 Ill. Dec. 520, 645 N.E.2d 525 (1 Dist. 1994).

The court's determination of the property distribution award was not an abuse of discretion. In re Zwart, 245 Ill. App. 3d 567, 185 Ill. Dec. 443, 614 N.E.2d 884 (2 Dist. 1993); In re Ackerman, 168 Ill. App. 3d 438, 118 Ill. Dec. 862, 522 N.E.2d 317 (2 Dist. 1988); In re Carini, 112 Ill. App. 3d 375, 67 Ill. Dec. 932, 445 N.E.2d 412 (1 Dist. 1983); In re Schriner, 88 Ill. App. 3d 380, 43 Ill. Dec. 572, 410 N.E.2d 572 (2 Dist. 1980); In re McCune, 86 Ill. App. 3d 311, 41 Ill. Dec. 897, 408 N.E.2d 319 (3 Dist. 1980).

Although some of the factors listed in this section, such as petitioner's custody of the child and the relative economic circumstances of the parties, weighed in favor of a larger property distribution to petitioner, other factors such as the length of the marriage and the contributions of each party in acquiring the property supported the trial court's decision, and there was no abuse of discretion in the property distribution. In re Miller, 231 Ill. App. 3d 480, 172 Ill. Dec. 679, 595 N.E.2d 1349 (3 Dist. 1992).

No abuse of discretion was found in awarding two-thirds of assets to the wife who had a limited education, had been a homemaker, had poor health, and had been married for 42 years. In re Orlando, 218 Ill. App. 3d 312, 160 Ill. Dec. 763, 577 N.E.2d 1334 (1 Dist. 1991).

The court's distribution of marital property was in just proportions. In re Drone, 217 Ill. App. 3d 758, 160 Ill. Dec. 601, 577 N.E.2d 926 (5 Dist. 1991).

In light of parties' long marriage, the disparity in their incomes, the fact that husband would reap the benefit of the home's appreciated value accrued during wife's possession, and the tax benefit to the husband for the payment of unallocated maintenance and support, the trial court did not abuse its discretion in awarding 70% of the proceeds from the sale of the marital home to the wife. In re Kennedy, 214 Ill. App. 3d 849, 158 Ill. Dec. 172, 573 N.E.2d 1357 (1 Dist. 1991).

Where respondent wife earned $1,500 prior to the judgment of dissolution and submitted no argument as to why the money should not be considered marital property or that it was improperly divided, there was no abuse of discretion to award appellant husband $750. In re Cesaretti, 203 Ill. App. 3d 347, 149 Ill. Dec. 28, 561 N.E.2d 306 (2 Dist. 1990).

The trial court did not abuse its discretion by awarding 60% of the marital property to the husband while awarding 40% to the wife; an equitable award does not require that the marital estate be divided equally. In re Harding, 189 Ill. App. 3d 663, 136 Ill. Dec. 935, 545 N.E.2d 459 (1 Dist. 1989).

If an examination of the record reveals that the trial court was aware of the requirements of subsection (d) of this section, and its disposition of marital property was consistent with subsection (d) of this section, then an abuse of discretion has not occurred. In re Wolf, 180 Ill. App. 3d 998, 129 Ill. Dec. 742, 536 N.E.2d 792 (1 Dist. 1989).

The trial court did not abuse its discretion when it divided marital property in approximately equal shares even though parties stood in unequal positions in terms of health, income, and the opportunity for future acquisition of assets and income. In re Swigers, 176 Ill. App. 3d 795, 126 Ill. Dec. 231, 531 N.E.2d 858 (1 Dist. 1988).

Where one spouse had earned $34,000 annually for the last 10 years with some exceptions and had saved and invested enough to own a large percentage of a limited partnership and to have half ownership of his own company, but the other's income was only $260 per month and she had no savings or business investments, there was no abuse of discretion in the trial court's maintenance or property award. In re Reimann, 178 Ill. App. 3d 288, 127 Ill. Dec. 486, 533 N.E.2d 104 (1 Dist. 1988).

The trial court did not erroneously consider the interests and motives of wife's father in awarding wife the entire marital interest in apartment complex; there was no evidence that the court placed any undue or even primary emphasis upon this factor, which was reasonably one of the concerns the court had to address in reaching its decision. In re Agazim, 176 Ill. App. 3d 225, 125 Ill. Dec. 701, 530 N.E.2d 1110 (2 Dist. 1988).

The trial court correctly found that husband had a greater ability to acquire assets from greater income-producing ability and a skill or talent to borrow money; because of this disparity in employment capacities, the court could reasonably fashion a disposition that awarded a majority of marital assets to wife. In re Agazim, 176 Ill. App. 3d 225, 125 Ill. Dec. 701, 530 N.E.2d 1110 (2 Dist. 1988).

Entering her early fifties with no job experience over two decades past, it was highly unlikely that petitioner's earning capacity would ever approach that of respondent's; therefore, respondent had a much greater opportunity for future acquisition of income and assets than petitioner, and the trial court properly relied on this disparity in earning capacity in dividing the marital property. In re Hanson, 170 Ill. App. 3d 298, 120 Ill. Dec. 665, 524 N.E.2d 695 (2 Dist. 1988).

The trial court did not abuse its discretion in apportioning the marital property on an approximately 50/50 basis where the wife contributed over 22 years as a homemaker, husband's income was much greater than the wife's and the husband's contention that he might have to liquidate assets to meet expenses was purely speculative. In re Heller, 153 Ill. App. 3d 224, 106 Ill. Dec. 503, 505 N.E.2d 1294 (1 Dist. 1987).

The trial court's division of property was equitable where wife was ordered to pay her husband $27,000 and award him an equal share in the net proceeds from the sale of the marital residence. In re Turzitti, 161 Ill. App. 3d 822, 113 Ill. Dec. 507, 515 N.E.2d 316 (1 Dist. 1987).

Division of marital assets was not an abuse of discretion where the husband received approximately 45% of the marital estate notwithstanding that certain assets awarded to the husband were uncollectible. In re Randall, 157 Ill. App. 3d 892, 110 Ill. Dec. 122, 510 N.E.2d 1153 (1 Dist. 1987).

Judgment entered by the trial court which awarded respondent 59% of the assets while awarding petitioner 41% of the marital assets was not an abuse of discretion, as the distribution was clearly within the statutory mandate of equitable apportionment. In re Callaway, 150 Ill. App. 3d 712, 104 Ill. Dec. 103, 502 N.E.2d 366 (1 Dist. 1986).

Where the court made a specific finding regarding the cash available at the time of the marital separation and did not make a specific finding regarding the amount available at the time of the judgment, this did not mean the court failed to consider the expenses incurred after the date of separation and the resulting change in the amount of cash available such that there was no abuse of discretion in the property distribution. Cooper v. Cooper, 146 Ill. App. 3d 943, 100 Ill. Dec. 627, 497 N.E.2d 805 (5 Dist. 1986).

Allocation of property in favor of wife was fair where she was 57 years old, with a history of strokes, no high school diploma, no demonstrated job skills and no job history in over 28 years, while husband had a doctorate in psychology, and was enjoying an income of approximately $51,000 a year as a college professor and had demonstrated the ability to earn over $5,000 more by working one of the three free months available to him in the summer. In re Mayzner, 144 Ill. App. 3d 645, 98 Ill. Dec. 493, 494 N.E.2d 615 (1 Dist. 1986).

Trial court did not err in its division of property favoring the husband where the evidence showed that wife was 61 years old, employed and earning slightly under $25,000 per year, husband was 68 years old and disabled, respondent's only income was a $446 monthly social security benefit and there was no evidence in the record indicating that wife was not in good health. In re Benefield, 131 Ill. App. 3d 648, 86 Ill. Dec. 831, 476 N.E.2d 7 (5 Dist. 1985).

Award of marital home to former wife in marriage dissolution action did not constitute a clear abuse of discretion because former wife had custody of three minor children. In re Sheber, 121 Ill. App. 3d 328, 76 Ill. Dec. 921, 459 N.E.2d 1056 (1 Dist. 1984).

Distribution (Cont'd)

—Upheld (Cont'd)

Where the trial court found that respondent husband's contribution to parties' asset accumulation was negated by his dissipation of these same assets, this fact justified an award of a larger percentage of the assets to petitioner wife even though courts have found it equitable to apportion property accumulated during longer marriages in equal proportions; thus, the trial court did not abuse its discretion. In re Smith, 128 Ill. App. 3d 1017, 84 Ill. Dec. 242, 471 N.E.2d 1008 (2 Dist. 1984).

While the trial court did not state relevant factors it considered in making division, after reviewing record and the factors found in subsection (c) of this section to be considered in the division of marital property, the apportionment of marital property did not constitute an abuse of discretion. In re Shafer, 122 Ill. App. 3d 991, 78 Ill. Dec. 323, 462 N.E.2d 39 (2 Dist. 1984).

Where petitioner received approximately 75% of the marital property, including two homes owned by the parties, respondent retained possession of non-marital real property totaling 60 acres and containing tillable land, a lake, and two dwellings, the court did not abuse its discretion in awarding petitioner a greater share of the marital assets; moreover, the distribution effectuated by the trial court was further justified by the vast difference in the future earning capacities of the parties because respondent needed only to complete a dissertation to obtain a doctorate in educational administration, while petitioner had only a high school education and thus, respondent had vastly greater opportunity for the future acquisition of assets and income, and the court properly relied on this fact in dividing the marital property. In re Stephenson, 121 Ill. App. 3d 698, 77 Ill. Dec. 142, 460 N.E.2d 1 (5 Dist. 1983).

Award to wife of a majority of marital assets plus exclusive possession of marital home for five years, with credit for all reduction in principal of the mortgage, was not an abuse of discretion even though award granted spouse exclusive possession of the marital residence when there were no minor children. In re McNeeley, 117 Ill. App. 3d 320, 72 Ill. Dec. 873, 453 N.E.2d 748 (1 Dist. 1983).

Award to wife of assets having twice the value of those awarded to husband was within the "range of reason" and not an abuse of discretion. In re Murphy, 117 Ill. App. 3d 649, 72 Ill. Dec. 808, 453 N.E.2d 113 (3 Dist. 1983).

Distribution of property was clearly not against the manifest weight of the evidence nor an abuse of judicial discretion where trial court considered all relevant factors in division of property and pointed out that the award to respondent of the business (valued at $600,000) and the land resulted in a "lopsided division of marital property" in favor of respondent but reasoned that the best interests of all concerned were served by such an award because the corporation had thrived under the direction of respondent over the years he had operated it and court attempted to equalize respondent's award by awarding petitioner the sum of $100,000. In re Rossi, 113 Ill. App. 3d 55, 68 Ill. Dec. 801, 446 N.E.2d 1198 (1 Dist. 1983).

There was no abuse of discretion in property division or award of maintenance where petitioner received 47% of net assets and respondent received 53%, and respondent was awarded $350 per month maintenance and $30,000 as her share of grain on hand with approximate value of $66,000, although petitioner's federal income tax returns showed losses from farming operations due to large amounts of depreciation and tax credits. In re McDonald, 113 Ill. App. 3d 116, 68 Ill. Dec. 653, 446 N.E.2d 559 (4 Dist. 1983).

Division of marital assets, totaling $189,000, by allocating to wife total assets valued at $112,400 and to husband total assets valued at $76,600, would be upheld, where the trial court considered the length of the marriage, wife's age and education, her employment background and absence from the labor market for more than 32 years, and fact that husband was a professional, earning a substantial income with a greater opportunity to acquire capital assets and additional income. In re McNeeley, 117 Ill. App. 3d 320, 72 Ill. Dec. 873, 453 N.E.2d 748 (1 Dist. 1983).

Division of property was supported by the evidence. In re Carini, 112 Ill. App. 3d 375, 67 Ill. Dec. 932, 445 N.E.2d 412 (1 Dist. 1983).

Where the parties were at an advanced age at the time they got married and the marital property substantially represented assets produced by the husband's business which he had established long before the marriage, the court may have reasoned that in view of these factors he was entitled to a greater share of the marital property, and its distribution of property was not an abuse of discretion. In re Pancner, 111 Ill. App. 3d 546, 67 Ill. Dec. 417, 444 N.E.2d 653 (1 Dist. 1982).

The award of marital home to wife was not erroneous where the marital home was valued at $140,000 with an outstanding mortgage of $55,000; wife's annual salary for her part-time work was $15,000; husband's annual income from his employment was $26,000; his annual income from his non-marital assets was about $27,800; and husband's economic circumstances, including his opportunity to acquire assets and income, were superior; moreover, the result was not inequitable under the circumstances, and the trial court acted within the scope of its discretion in awarding almost all of the marital property to wife. Atkinson v. Atkinson, 87 Ill. 2d 174, 57 Ill. Dec. 567, 429 N.E.2d 465 (1981), cert. denied, 456 U.S. 905, 102 S. Ct. 1751, 72 L. Ed. 2d 162 (1982).

The court order awarding one spouse 60% of the net proceeds from the sale of marital home, and 50% of the other spouse's profit and savings plan was a proper exercise of judicial discretion in light of the disparate future earning capacity of the respective parties. In re Theeke, 105 Ill. App. 3d 119, 60 Ill. Dec. 944, 433 N.E.2d 1311 (1 Dist. 1981).

If a property distribution resulted in substantially equal shares for both parties and it was apparent from the record that the court thoughtfully and carefully applied the rationale of the statute to the facts before it, then the court did not abuse its discretion and the award will not be disturbed on review. In re Reed, 100 Ill. App. 3d 873, 56 Ill. Dec. 202, 427 N.E.2d 282 (5 Dist. 1981).

Sufficient evidence existed to find that wife's just proportion of the marital estate was nearly one-half of the estate, even though husband had to support the five minor children, where husband retained possession of the marital residence, the 100 acre farm, the livestock, the farm equipment and the machinery, and taking into account his other assets, it was plain that he had sufficient resources to maintain a secure and productive style of life, while the wife had no marketable skills and was employed outside the home only once since she was married. In re Reed, 100 Ill. App. 3d 873, 56 Ill. Dec. 202, 427 N.E.2d 282 (5 Dist. 1981).

The evidence showed respondent's gross income was reflected in her 1979 income tax return as approximately $16,000; respondent was employed as a legal secretary; petitioner's gross income for 1979 was $41,870; the total amount of marital property involved was about $144,000; respondent received about 61 to 62% and petitioner about 38 to 39% plus the optometry business; the fact that the trial court awarded respondent more than half of the property did not make the division unfair; an equitable division of marital property is not necessarily an equal one. In re Greenberg, 102 Ill. App. 3d 938, 58 Ill. Dec. 1, 429 N.E.2d 1334 (1 Dist. 1981).

Residence was divided in just proportions considering all relevant factors. In re Davenport, 92 Ill. App. 3d 675, 48 Ill. Dec. 193, 416 N.E.2d 88 (4 Dist. 1981).

Where parties were married for 21 years, wife was a recovered alcoholic and at the time of the hearing she was attending beauty school, husband was awarded a $20,000 interest in marital home worth approximately $110,000 and he had an annual salary of $33,000 per year at the time of the hearing, the trial court's division of the marital property was equitable. In re Rogers, 86 Ill. App. 3d 904, 42 Ill. Dec. 70, 408 N.E.2d 448 (2 Dist. 1980), aff'd, 85 Ill. 2d 217, 52 Ill. Dec. 633, 422 N.E.2d 635 (1981).

A 60%-40% division of marital estate, omitting tax consequences, was not an abuse of the trial court's discretion where husband contributed more in the acquisition, preservation and appreciation in value of the marital estate. In re McMahon, 82 Ill. App. 3d 1126, 38 Ill. Dec. 499, 403 N.E.2d 730 (4 Dist. 1980).

The sex of a spouse should not be considered a factor in determining property disposition; however, the evidence amply supported the trial court's award of the marital residence to the petitioner when petitioner contributed to the parties' acquisition of marital assets through her various outside jobs and as a homemaker, she possessed no special skills, training, or education which at age 53 made it unlikely that she would be employed in the future, and an equitable property settlement had to reflect such facts. In re Parello, 87 Ill. App. 3d 926, 42 Ill. Dec. 846, 409 N.E.2d 461 (1 Dist. 1980).

Trial court's refusal to grant husband a larger portion of the equity in marital home was not an abuse of discretion where,

Distribution (Cont'd)

—Upheld (Cont'd)

although husband paid approximately $230 per month in expenses on the home, he occupied the premises for seven years without paying rent, and where, at the same time, wife assumed almost the entire responsibility of supporting their child. In re Fleming, 80 Ill. App. 3d 1006, 36 Ill. Dec. 205, 400 N.E.2d 625 (2 Dist. 1980).

Where in a marriage dissolution proceeding petitioner wife was awarded home of parties, household furnishings, joint bank account and was to remain beneficiary on respondent's life insurance policy until the last child reached majority, and respondent husband was awarded the pension fund, the stock in his employer, his bank account and other personal property he was to receive because of the stipulation, the value of property awarded to each spouse was substantially equivalent. In re Coram, 86 Ill. App. 3d 845, 42 Ill. Dec. 40, 408 N.E.2d 418 (5 Dist. 1980).

Where court had before it evidence tending to show that by far the larger part of the parties' assets represented wife's settlement for her serious personal injuries; that it was desirable to award family home to the wife because she had custody of the minor child; that her health was not good, she was unemployed, had relatively limited vocational skills, and was unemployable in the foreseeable future; that her needs would be greater than those of her ex-husband; and that she would have little opportunity for future acquisition of capital assets and income; each of these factors was properly considered by the court in apportioning property. In re Lloyd, 81 Ill. App. 3d 311, 36 Ill. Dec. 647, 401 N.E.2d 328 (5 Dist. 1980).

Where the court equalized the division by requiring wife, the recipient of cleaning plant valued at $60,000, to pay to the husband, the recipient of discount store valued at $30,000, $15,600, such was not an abuse of the trial court's discretion and was not against the manifest weight of the evidence. In re Lee, 78 Ill. App. 3d 1123, 34 Ill. Dec. 451, 398 N.E.2d 126 (1 Dist. 1979).

By ordering respondent husband to pay entire debt, the trial court was in effect awarding petitioner wife an amount to account for her non-marital and monetary estate, and therefore husband was not entitled to a 67% interest in the family home. In re Weidner, 75 Ill. App. 3d 1014, 31 Ill. Dec. 418, 394 N.E.2d 620 (2 Dist. 1979).

In divorce proceeding, the trial court's finding that former wife constructively deserted her husband, and was guilty of extreme and repeated mental cruelty over an extended period of time, along with order that former husband make child support payments of $125 per month for the two children of the marriage who were still minors and that the family home was to be sold and the former husband was to make mortgage payments until such sale, was not an abuse of discretion. Chattillion v. Chattillion, 52 Ill. App. 3d 390, 10 Ill. Dec. 52, 367 N.E.2d 440 (5 Dist. 1977).

Trial court did not err in awarding to the wife in a divorce case her husband's interest in the jointly owned marital residence in addition to a monthly alimony award where the wife alleged and proved special equities to justify the trial court's order that the husband's interest in the jointly owned property be conveyed to her. Newhouse v. Newhouse, 17 Ill. App. 3d 1008, 309 N.E.2d 102 (2 Dist. 1974).

In divorce action, trial court did not transcend its authority or abuse its discretion in ordering husband to pay wife $15,000 and order wife to convey her interest in farm jointly held by her and her husband. Rodely v. Rodely, 28 Ill. 2d 347, 192 N.E.2d 347 (1963).

The appellee's evidence amply supported the allegations of her complaint and it was more than sufficient to warrant the finding that she was entitled to the conveyance and division of property that was ordered. Ylonen v. Ylonen, 2 Ill. 2d 111, 117 N.E.2d 98 (1954).

Divestment of Title

—Not Upheld

The court erred in that part of its decree which divested appellant of her title, as joint tenant with appellee, in the two pieces of real estate, where the proof showed that appellant worked about nine hours a day as bookkeeper and office manager of the motor sales business two months after she and appellee were married until they separated, and that she received no pay for her labor, and that this property had been purchased out of the proceeds of the business, and that it was deeded to appellant and appellee as joint tenants. Arliskas v. Arliskas, 343 Ill. 112, 175 N.E. 6 (1931).

Due Process

Respondent's residence should not have been placed in trust to be sold for the children's support before respondent was allowed to offer evidence of his financial ability to support the children by other means. Milenkovic v. Milenkovic, 93 Ill. App. 3d 204, 48 Ill. Dec. 618, 416 N.E.2d 1140 (1 Dist. 1981).

Duration of Marriage

In a long term marriage, the source of the assets in acquiring marital property becomes less of a factor and a spouse's role as the homemaker becomes greater. In re Cecil, 202 Ill. App. 3d 783, 148 Ill. Dec. 72, 560 N.E.2d 374 (3 Dist. 1990).

Duty to Disclose

There was an affirmative duty upon a wife to speak or volunteer any information that was not asked of her during discovery or other court proceedings where the failure to disclose deprived the husband of a material fact necessary to intelligently arrive at a property settlement. In re Burch, 205 Ill. App. 3d 1082, 150 Ill. Dec. 922, 563 N.E.2d 1049 (1 Dist. 1990).

Education of Children

—In General

This section and 750 ILCS 5/513 do not mandate that divorced parents must provide their children of majority age with funds for education in all cases; however, it is certainly a legitimate legislative purpose for the legislature to furnish a means for providing that they do so after they have been divorced. Kujawinski v. Kujawinski, 71 Ill. 2d 563, 17 Ill. Dec. 801, 376 N.E.2d 1382 (1978).

—College Expenses

Where testimony at hearing established that room and board for daughter's first year of college was $1,170, a trial court in the exercise of its equitable powers was entitled to impart an ambulatory character to its decree, and because defendant was already aware of that obligation for the first year of college and during the remainder of daughter's college career, reference could be made to the room and board contract in effect for that particular year, and the trial court's failure to specify a dollar amount for the daughter's room and board while at college was not error. Flatley v. Flatley, 42 Ill. App. 3d 494, 1 Ill. Dec. 155, 356 N.E.2d 155 (3 Dist. 1976).

There is little merit in a rule which requires as a matter of law expenditure by a child of divorced parents of his or her own funds in obtaining a college education; such a decision is better left to the wisdom and discretion of the trial court after due consideration of respective net worth, income, and other responsibilities of the parents and of the child. Flatley v. Flatley, 42 Ill. App. 3d 494, 1 Ill. Dec. 155, 356 N.E.2d 155 (3 Dist. 1976).

—Court's Discretion

A court does have the discretion to order the establishment of a trust for a child's future educational expenses while he or she is of minority age if there is evidence showing a need to protect the interests of the child. In re Harsy, 193 Ill. App. 3d 415, 140 Ill. Dec. 344, 549 N.E.2d 995 (5 Dist. 1990).

—Disbursement of Proceeds

Provision in educational trust providing for disbursement of trust proceeds to respondent-husband's adult children upon termination of trusts was not allowed. In re Harsy, 193 Ill. App. 3d 415, 140 Ill. Dec. 344, 549 N.E.2d 995 (5 Dist. 1990).

—Future Expenditures

The trial court could impose a trust for future expenditures for the children's college educations even though there was no evidence that the children would even attend college upon becoming of age to do so. In re Harsy, 193 Ill. App. 3d 415, 140 Ill. Dec. 344, 549 N.E.2d 995 (5 Dist. 1990).

—Necessary

The establishment of the trust funds for respondent-father's children's future educational needs was necessary to promote and protect the minor children's interests, and the court did not abuse its discretion when it so ordered where the evidence revealed that the respondent was of the opinion that further education was not

Education of Children (Cont'd)

—Necessary (Cont'd)
something to be valued, and because of his opinion, it could be inferred that he would not take measures to assure that there would be funds available for that purpose. In re Harsy, 193 Ill. App. 3d 415, 140 Ill. Dec. 344, 549 N.E.2d 995 (5 Dist. 1990).

—No Abuse of Discretion
Where there was evidence in the record that respondent father had upon one occasion been held in contempt of court for failing to pay his child support as ordered by the court, which indicated that the respondent had either been unable or unwilling to pay, order that respondent establish educational trusts for his minor children for the purpose of paying their college expenses was not an abuse of discretion. In re Harsy, 193 Ill. App. 3d 415, 140 Ill. Dec. 344, 549 N.E.2d 995 (5 Dist. 1990).

—Religious Beliefs
It was proper to create a trust under this section for purposes of financing children's private education where the need for such education was prompted by sincere religious beliefs. In re Pickholtz, 178 Ill. App. 3d 512, 127 Ill. Dec. 657, 533 N.E.2d 529 (1 Dist. 1988).

Effect of Amendment
The 1983 amendment to this section did not change the fact that property acquired during a marriage is presumed to be marital property; nor did the amendment have any effect on the question of when a transfer of property is considered to be a gift so as to rebut the presumption of marital property. Hofmann v. Hofmann, 125 Ill. App. 3d 548, 81 Ill. Dec. 12, 466 N.E.2d 598 (3 Dist. 1984).

Effective Date
Divorce action would not be reconsidered under this Act when the trial court had determined all the issues prior to the effective date of the Act, but the final written decree was filed after that date. In re LaSusa, 80 Ill. App. 3d 467, 35 Ill. Dec. 884, 400 N.E.2d 21 (1 Dist. 1979).

Election of Remedies
The doctrine of election of remedies did not bar wife from seeking damages from her husband for his sale of her furniture, and from bringing a replevin action against buyer, where there was no threat of double recovery (wife's judgment for damages against her husband had not been collectible and appeared uncollectible), buyer was not misled and did not change his position by reason of wife's action for damages against her husband so that he would suffer some prejudice thereby, and there was nothing about the action for damages that would serve to bar the subsequent action by reason of res judicata or collateral estoppel. Altom v. Hawes, 63 Ill. App. 3d 659, 20 Ill. Dec. 330, 380 N.E.2d 7 (5 Dist. 1978).

Equitable Distribution

—In General
There is no requirement that marital property be divided in equal proportions. In re Atkinson, 82 Ill. App. 3d 617, 37 Ill. Dec. 829, 402 N.E.2d 831 (1 Dist. 1980), modified on other grounds, 87 Ill. 2d 174, 57 Ill. Dec. 567, 429 N.E.2d 465 (1981), cert. denied, 456 U.S. 905, 102 S. Ct. 1751, 72 L. Ed. 2d 162 (1982); In re McMahon, 82 Ill. App. 3d 1126, 38 Ill. Dec. 499, 403 N.E.2d 730 (4 Dist. 1980); In re Clearman, 85 Ill. App. 3d 584, 40 Ill. Dec. 958, 407 N.E.2d 189 (3 Dist. 1980); In re Coram, 86 Ill. App. 3d 845, 42 Ill. Dec. 40, 408 N.E.2d 418 (5 Dist. 1980); In re Thornton, 89 Ill. App. 3d 1078, 45 Ill. Dec. 612, 412 N.E.2d 1336 (1 Dist. 1980); In re Cihak, 92 Ill. App. 3d 1123, 48 Ill. Dec. 428, 416 N.E.2d 701 (4 Dist. 1981); In re Hyland, 95 Ill. App. 3d 31, 50 Ill. Dec. 554, 419 N.E.2d 662 (2 Dist. 1981); In re Pruitt, 101 Ill. App. 3d 755, 57 Ill. Dec. 182, 428 N.E.2d 732 (4 Dist. 1981); In re Rimmele, 102 Ill. App. 3d 88, 57 Ill. Dec. 762, 429 N.E.2d 879 (3 Dist. 1981); In re Theeke, 105 Ill. App. 3d 119, 60 Ill. Dec. 944, 433 N.E.2d 1311 (1 Dist. 1981); In re Ligas, 110 Ill. App. 3d 1, 65 Ill. Dec. 763, 441 N.E.2d 1277 (1 Dist. 1982); In re McNeeley, 117 Ill. App. 3d 320, 72 Ill. Dec. 873, 453 N.E.2d 748 (1 Dist. 1983); In re Carney, 122 Ill. App. 3d 705, 78 Ill. Dec. 477, 462 N.E.2d 596 (1 Dist. 1984); In re Fuggiti, 130 Ill. App. 3d 190, 85 Ill. Dec. 658, 474 N.E.2d 386 (1 Dist. 1985); In re Marriage of Roberts, 151 Ill. App. 3d 65, 104 Ill. Dec. 806, 503 N.E.2d 363, 1986 Ill. App. LEXIS 3290 (3 Dist. 1986), cert. denied, 106 Ill. Dec. 55, 505 N.E.2d 361 (1987), appeal denied, 106 Ill. Dec. 55, 505 N.E.2d 361 (1987) cert denied, 485 U.S. 963, 108 S. Ct. 1230, 99 L. Ed. 2d 430 (1988); In re Westcott, 163 Ill. App. 3d 168, 114 Ill. Dec. 411, 516 N.E.2d 566 (1 Dist. 1987); In re Ackerman, 168 Ill. App. 3d 438, 118 Ill. Dec. 862, 522 N.E.2d 317 (2 Dist. 1988); In re Wolf, 180 Ill. App. 3d 998, 129 Ill. Dec. 742, 536 N.E.2d 792 (1 Dist. 1989); In re Jones, 187 Ill. App. 3d 206, 134 Ill. Dec. 836, 543 N.E.2d 119 (1 Dist. 1989); In re Gentry, 188 Ill. App. 3d 372, 135 Ill. Dec. 939, 544 N.E.2d 435 (3 Dist. 1989); In re Hart, 194 Ill. App. 3d 839, 141 Ill. Dec. 550, 551 N.E.2d 737 (4 Dist. 1990); In re Jacks, 200 Ill. App. 3d 112, 146 Ill. Dec. 143, 558 N.E.2d 106 (2 Dist. 1990); In re Steele, 212 Ill. App. 3d 425, 156 Ill. Dec. 649, 571 N.E.2d 236 (5 Dist. 1991).

—Attorney Fees
With the creation of "marital property" and the adoption of this section, the allocation of attorney fees appears to have become a factor in the overall allocation of the financial resources of the parties. In re Carr, 211 Ill. App. 3d 609, 164 Ill. Dec. 189, 582 N.E.2d 752 (5 Dist. 1991).

—Bankruptcy Proceedings
While a discharge in bankruptcy might discharge a non-debtor spouse's claim for equitable distribution out of marital property, that is not so where the debtor neither lists the equitable distribution of marital property as a claim nor lists the divorce action as a pending legal proceeding, thus giving no notice to the non-debtor spouse that the bankruptcy court would exercise jurisdiction over equitable distribution of the marital property. In re Abma, 215 Bankr. 148 (Bankr. N.D. Ill. 1997).

—Difference in Values
No precise arithmetical equality was required under former section 18 of the Divorce Act (see now this section), and even though there may have been some difference in the values of the shares awarded to each party, the discrepancies were not of such magnitude that a different division was required as a matter of law. Hulslander v. Hulslander, 55 Ill. App. 3d 981, 13 Ill. Dec. 717, 371 N.E.2d 652 (3 Dist. 1977).

—Equitable Interest
Where a wife by her own industry, earnings, labor, economy and frugality has added to the financial settlement of the parties, she has an equitable interest which must be recognized by a fair division of property upon dissolution of marriage. Harambasic v. Harambasic, 55 Ill. App. 3d 648, 13 Ill. Dec. 224, 370 N.E.2d 1251 (1 Dist. 1977).

—Evidence Held Insufficient
The relief prayed in the complaint for an equitable division of property was not supported by the evidence introduced to support the decree entered. Carney v. Carney, 67 Ill. App. 3d 919, 24 Ill. Dec. 447, 385 N.E.2d 359 (4 Dist. 1979).

—Evidence Held Sufficient
The evidence before the trial court justified the findings and orders of that court as to the equitable ownership of the property, its value, and the ordered distribution and decree. Honey v. Honey, 3 Ill. App. 3d 948, 279 N.E.2d 751 (4 Dist. 1972).

—Homemaker's Contributions
Taking into account, inter alia, the 30 year marriage, petitioner's role in raising seven children and as homemaker to the family unit, and her limited opportunity for future acquisition of assets and income, an equal division of marital property was an appropriate exercise of discretion. In re Smith, 105 Ill. App. 3d 980, 61 Ill. Dec. 554, 434 N.E.2d 1151 (3 Dist. 1982).

The facts warranted an equal distribution of property where the wife made major contributions as a homemaker during the couple's 34 year marriage, including gardening, canning, and packaging of the meat, raising 14 children and managing the household. In re Reed, 100 Ill. App. 3d 873, 56 Ill. Dec. 202, 427 N.E.2d 282 (5 Dist. 1981).

—Illustrative Cases
Following her ex-husband's early retirement as a teacher, the ex-wife was ordered to pay her proportionate share of the contributions necessary for the ex-husband to qualify for early retirement

Equitable Distribution (Cont'd)

—Illustrative Cases (Cont'd)

benefit enhancements, and in return, the ex-wife received her awarded share of the benefits. In re Marriage of Ramsey, 339 Ill. App. 3d 752, 275 Ill. Dec. 106, 792 N.E.2d 337, 2003 Ill. App. LEXIS 725 (5 Dist. 2003).

Where wife had substantial non-marital property, earned more income, and had a greater opportunity to acquire assets and income in the future than husband, the application of the statutory factors to the facts of the present case mandated a finding that award of only $62,070 of the net marital estate of $274,006 to husband did not constitute an equitable award of property. In re Forbes, 251 Ill. App. 3d 133, 190 Ill. Dec. 543, 621 N.E.2d 996 (4 Dist. 1993).

An award of the marital residence and furnishings to a plaintiff was justified under former section 18 of the Divorce Act (see now this section) where the residence, home furnishings and the business were all jointly owned assets, and an approximately equal division of the assets in common best satisfied the interest of both parties. The award of the business to the defendant and the award of the equity in the residence and household furniture to plaintiff resulted in an approximately equal division of the assets. Hulslander v. Hulslander, 55 Ill. App. 3d 981, 13 Ill. Dec. 717, 371 N.E.2d 652 (3 Dist. 1977).

—Income-Producing Property

Even though the wife was awarded the more fruitful income-producing of two businesses, distribution was equitable, where husband was awarded a larger share of marital assets to offset the business award. In re McHenry, 292 Ill. App. 3d 634, 226 Ill. Dec. 887, 686 N.E.2d 670 (1 Dist. 1997).

When awarding income-producing assets to one spouse becomes necessary, the trial court may achieve an equitable distribution by authorizing off-setting payments to the other spouse or by awarding a greater share of total marital assets to the spouse who does not receive the income-producing assets. In re Swanson, 275 Ill. App. 3d 519, 212 Ill. Dec. 62, 656 N.E.2d 215 (4 Dist. 1995), appeal denied, 165 Ill. 2d 566, 214 Ill. Dec. 866, 662 N.E.2d 432 (1996).

An equitable distribution may be attained by awarding the spouse who does not receive the income-producing assets a greater share of the total net marital assets. In re Jarvis, 245 Ill. App. 3d 1007, 185 Ill. Dec. 609, 614 N.E.2d 1294 (4 Dist. 1993).

—Not Shown

Based upon the ages of the parties, the disparity in the incomes of the parties, husband's disability and needs, and wife's disposable income and much greater opportunity for future acquisition of capital assets and income, no reasonable person would take the view adopted by the trial court in distributing the marital property equally. In re Ferkel, 260 Ill. App. 3d 33, 198 Ill. Dec. 522, 632 N.E.2d 1133 (5 Dist. 1994).

—Relevant Factors

Appellate court erred in holding that the trial court should have considered the husband's expected Social Security benefits in dividing the wife's pension benefits in their divorce case as the Social Security Act expressly barred use of a Social Security benefits to divide or offset other benefits in state divorce proceedings. In re Marriage of Crook, 211 Ill. 2d 437, 286 Ill. Dec. 141, 813 N.E.2d 198, 2004 Ill. LEXIS 991 (2004).

Under this section, the legislature provided for an equitable division of property after consideration is given to certain relevant factors, and Illinois courts have held that an equitable division need not be an equal one. In re Woodward, 83 Ill. App. 3d 253, 39 Ill. Dec. 191, 404 N.E.2d 575 (3 Dist. 1980).

—Shown

Where the trial court conscientiously evaluated all of the relevant circumstances of the parties prior to distributing marital property, the marital property was divided by the court in approximately equal portions, each party was awarded a car, wife was awarded all of the household furnishings and 50% of the stipulated value of husband's pension, and each party was awarded bank accounts in their names, the division of property was equitable; it adequately provided for wife's financial needs, and consequently, there was no abuse of discretion. In re Wade, 158 Ill. App. 3d 255, 110 Ill. Dec. 321, 511 N.E.2d 156 (4 Dist. 1987).

—Stock Proceeds

An additional distribution of stock proceeds to wife was consistent with the intent of subsection (d), as husband received a much greater share of the marital assets and possessed a greater ability to earn and acquire assets in the future. In re Parker, 245 Ill. App. 3d 870, 185 Ill. Dec. 802, 615 N.E.2d 361 (2 Dist. 1993).

Equitable Interest

—Contribution Toward Acquisition

Where plaintiff and defendant had nominally contracted to purchase property jointly from plaintiff's father, but had invested nothing in the property at any time, where plaintiff was bequeathed the vendor's interest in the land by her father when he died, and her interest, if any, as a purchaser, merged with the acquisition of the interest in the real estate as a result of her father's will, at a very minimum plaintiff had all the right her father had, which meant the right to receive all the balance of the proceeds from the sale of the remaining one-half, which might have been vested in the defendant, and the right to forfeit the contract for non-performance; thus, the trial court properly decreed that the equities were with the plaintiff, and ordered that all interest, if any, which still remained in the husband-defendant should be conveyed to plaintiff as being equitably and fairly her property. Fowler v. Fowler, 26 Ill. App. 3d 313, 325 N.E.2d 98 (3 Dist. 1975).

Where, in the counterclaim upon which appellant was granted a divorce, she alleged that the residence property occupied by the parties, title to which was in the husband, had been paid for in part by money she had earned and prayed for a finding that she was entitled to a one-half interest therein, although the husband's answer to the counterclaim put at issue the question of the parties' equity in the property, the court made no ruling thereon but reserved it and continued the cause of that purpose, and where, in the supplemental counterclaim which appellant was permitted to file after the death of her husband and after making the sole devisee and executrix of his estate parties defendant, appellant alleged facts tending to establish an equitable interest in the property by reason of the fact that her earnings and savings had aided her husband in acquiring the residence and that the residence represented their joint earnings and work, the appellant was entitled to a full hearing on the issue raised and the court erred in refusing proof of the equities alleged under former Ill.Rev.Stat., ch. 40, para. 18 (see now this section). Cross v. Cross, 2 Ill. 2d 104, 116 N.E.2d 892 (1954).

—Voluntary Payments

Bearing children or residing in the marital home do not operate to increase a wife's equitable interest in property, and voluntary payments by a wife for family expenses during the time the husband and the wife are living together do not create an indebtedness from the husband to the wife in the absence of an agreement. Crenshaw v. Crenshaw, 45 Ill. App. 3d 880, 4 Ill. Dec. 640, 360 N.E.2d 576 (1 Dist. 1977).

Estoppel

Wife's acceptance of benefits under the decree did not estop her from attacking the decree in action for marital dissolution on appeal although wife accepted other benefits under the decree which were not in the nature of support or maintenance, such as attorney fees, and had collected rental proceeds on the property awarded to her under the decree for disposition of property, which virtually left the parties in a status quo position. In re Parr, 103 Ill. App. 3d 199, 58 Ill. Dec. 624, 430 N.E.2d 656 (2 Dist. 1981).

Wife was barred from attacking a divorce decree by accepting benefits of divorce decree to the distinct disadvantage of husband where wife had been awarded marital home and all personal property therein, and subsequent to the divorce decree, she sold two pieces of personal property out of the marital home and she sold the marital residence and purchased another residence. Adams v. Adams, 44 Ill. App. 3d 656, 3 Ill. Dec. 336, 358 N.E.2d 734 (3 Dist. 1976).

The doctrine of equitable estoppel did not apply where plaintiff never communicated with defendant either verbally or in writing during the intervening years which followed the entry of decretal order, although plaintiff was silent during a long period when arrearages persisted because she sought legal advice during that

Estoppel (Cont'd)
time. Ellingwood v. Ellingwood, 25 Ill. App. 3d 587, 323 N.E.2d 571 (1 Dist. 1975).

Evidence

—Accountant's Summary
It was not improper for the court to rely on petitioner husband's exhibits which were an accountant's summary of various documents; where original documents were voluminous and could not conveniently be examined to extract the fact to be proved, then any competent witness who had seen the originals, such as an accountant, could testify to the fact, provided it was capable of being determined by calculation. In addition, the documents summarized had to be available in court or made available to the opponent. In re Westcott, 163 Ill. App. 3d 168, 114 Ill. Dec. 411, 516 N.E.2d 566 (1 Dist. 1987).

—Affidavits
The use of affidavits to aid a court in determining property settlement and maintenance awards is not improper. In re Johnson, 106 Ill. App. 3d 502, 62 Ill. Dec. 478, 436 N.E.2d 228 (1 Dist. 1982).

—Held Insufficient
Where, considering the totality of the circumstances, the record in the case lacked evidence as to the marital nature of property, this issue was to be further determined on the basis of competent evidence on remand. In re Olbrecht, 232 Ill. App. 3d 358, 173 Ill. Dec. 661, 597 N.E.2d 635 (1 Dist. 1992).

—Relevance
By seeking an equal division of the marital assets without maintenance, the husband's pleadings did not specifically or affirmatively place his health in issue. In re Bonneau, 294 Ill. App. 3d 720, 229 Ill. Dec. 187, 691 N.E.2d 123 (2 Dist. 1998), appeal denied, 178 Ill. 2d 574, 232 Ill. Dec. 845, 699 N.E.2d 1030 (1998).

Extension of Time
Under subsection (j), a petition for attorney fees must be heard and decided before the final judgment is entered, and the phrase "before judgment is entered" in (j) limits subsection (1) of subsection (j) so that the 30-day extension only applies to situations where a final judgment has not been entered. In re Konchar, 312 Ill. App. 3d 441, 245 Ill. Dec. 224, 727 N.E.2d 671, 2000 Ill. App. LEXIS 231 (2 Dist. 2000).

Factors
There is no requirement that the trial court set forth a finding as to all of the factors under this subsection; it need merely consider them. In re Kennedy, 214 Ill. App. 3d 849, 158 Ill. Dec. 172, 573 N.E.2d 1357 (1 Dist. 1991).

Subsection (d) of this section sets out the factors to be considered by the trial court in dividing marital property. These factors include: the contribution of each party in acquiring and preserving the property, the value of the property set apart to each spouse, the duration of the marriage, the relative economic circumstances of the parties, and the age, health and income of each party. In re Kristie, 156 Ill. App. 3d 821, 109 Ill. Dec. 393, 510 N.E.2d 14 (1 Dist. 1987).

The trial court need not make specific findings with reference to each of the 11 statutory factors set out in this section. In re Guntren, 141 Ill. App. 3d 1, 95 Ill. Dec. 392, 489 N.E.2d 1120 (4 Dist. 1986).

Under subdivision (c)(1) of this section, a court may consider conduct where a spouse uses marital property for his or her own benefit and for a purpose unrelated to the marriage at a time when the marriage relationship is in serious jeopardy and compensate the disadvantaged spouse when apportioning the marital property. In re Los, 136 Ill. App. 3d 26, 90 Ill. Dec. 739, 482 N.E.2d 1022 (2 Dist. 1985).

While each party's contribution in acquiring marital property is one factor to be considered in dividing the marital property, it is only one of many factors. In re Los, 136 Ill. App. 3d 26, 90 Ill. Dec. 739, 482 N.E.2d 1022 (2 Dist. 1985).

In making a property division a trial court must take into consideration the value of non-marital property set apart to each spouse. In re Mullins, 121 Ill. App. 3d 86, 76 Ill. Dec. 560, 458 N.E.2d 1360 (4 Dist. 1984).

In disposing of marital property the court may consider the desirability of awarding the family home, or the right to live therein for reasonable periods, to the spouse having custody of the children and may set aside a portion of the parties' property for the support, maintenance, education and general welfare of any minor, dependent, or incompetent child of the parties, but such provisions create no property right per se for children of broken marriages. In re Mercer, 117 Ill. App. 3d 377, 72 Ill. Dec. 869, 453 N.E.2d 744 (1 Dist. 1983).

Where the marriage was short-lived, as the parties resided together as husband and wife for four years, the trial court could properly accord greater weight to the parties' respective contributions to the acquisition, preservation and appreciation of the subject property; the law is clear that an equal distribution was not mandated. In re Wojcicki, 109 Ill. App. 3d 569, 65 Ill. Dec. 173, 440 N.E.2d 1028 (1 Dist. 1982).

Among the factors a court is to consider in dividing the marital property under subsection (c) of this section are the relevant economic circumstances of the parties, their occupations, income and skill, and the reasonable opportunity of each for the future acquisition of capital assets and income. In re Woolsey, 85 Ill. App. 3d 636, 40 Ill. Dec. 775, 406 N.E.2d 1142 (4 Dist. 1980).

Fault
This Act provides for the division of marital property without regard to marital fault. In re Rogers, 85 Ill. 2d 217, 52 Ill. Dec. 633, 422 N.E.2d 635 (1981).

Fiduciary Relationship

—Burden of Proof
Because the parties stood in a relation of trust and confidence, appellant had the burden of showing the justness and fairness of his dealings with wife's stocks. Wesselhoeft v. Wesselhoeft, 369 Ill. 419, 17 N.E.2d 56 (1938).

Findings

—Not Mandatory
While a trial court must consider all relevant factors before exercising its discretion in distributing marital property, it need not make specific findings as to each of the factors set forth in subsection (d) of this section. In re Benz, 165 Ill. App. 3d 273, 116 Ill. Dec. 336, 518 N.E.2d 1316 (4 Dist. 1988).

The trial court was not required to make specific findings as to the reasons for its award where the evidence presented at the hearings justified the award and provided an adequate basis for the appellate court to review the property division. In re Caldwell, 124 Ill. App. 3d 898, 80 Ill. Dec. 411, 465 N.E.2d 523 (4 Dist. 1984).

This section requires that the trial court consider the value of the property set apart to each spouse; while it need not make specific findings of fact as to the value of each item in dispute, there must be before the court proper evidence of the value of the marital property. In re Petramale, 102 Ill. App. 3d 1049, 58 Ill. Dec. 537, 430 N.E.2d 569 (2 Dist. 1981).

Findings regarding factors the court considered under this section are not required unless there is not a valid separation agreement. In re Miller, 98 Ill. App. 3d 1084, 54 Ill. Dec. 439, 424 N.E.2d 1342 (4 Dist. 1981).

—Specific
A trial court should make specific findings regarding the factors it considered under subsection (d) of this section in rendering its decision; however, where the record adequately provides a basis for a reviewing court to determine the propriety of the decision and the decision is supported by the evidence, the trial court will not be reversed solely because the record does not contain specific findings. In re Wolf, 180 Ill. App. 3d 998, 129 Ill. Dec. 742, 536 N.E.2d 792 (1 Dist. 1989).

Foreign Decree

—Lack of Personal Jurisdiction
Wife could bring an action under a prior similar provision for the determination of equities in property and of alimony and attorney fees where the marital status had been determined by a valid ex parte foreign decree, but such latter court was without personal

Foreign Decree (Cont'd)

—Lack of Personal Jurisdiction (Cont'd)

jurisdiction to determine equities in property or alimony. Sidwell v. Sidwell, 132 Ill. App. 2d 1055, 271 N.E.2d 115 (4 Dist. 1971).

—Recourse in Illinois

Former wife, whose marriage had been dissolved by German court, had no recourse under this Act for determination of allocation of former husband's military pension or other marital property. In re Brown, 225 Ill. App. 3d 733, 167 Ill. Dec. 379, 587 N.E.2d 648 (4 Dist. 1992).

Fraud

—Concealment of Property

Where the evidence established concealment assets and a meritorious claim for fraud, and the petitioner met the due diligence requirement, the trial court did not abuse its discretion in granting the petition to vacate judgment of dissolution based upon a settlement agreement. In re Armstrong, 255 Ill. App. 3d 844, 192 Ill. Dec. 953, 625 N.E.2d 1108 (3 Dist. 1993).

The plaintiff alleging fraudulent concealment of property in a settlement agreement covered by the former Divorce Act (see now 750 ILCS 5/101 et seq.) had the burden of showing by clear and convincing evidence that the defendant knowingly concealed a fact at the time of the settlement agreement, that neither plaintiff nor her attorney were aware of that fact, and that the concealment injured plaintiff. Lagen v. Lagen, 14 Ill. App. 3d 74, 302 N.E.2d 201 (1 Dist. 1973).

—Evidence Held Insufficient

There was no fraud where evidence did not support claim that husband told wife he wanted her to work for the "family business" and promised to convert corporate assets to both their names. In re Weaver, 133 Ill. App. 3d 825, 88 Ill. Dec. 839, 479 N.E.2d 452 (4 Dist. 1985).

Fraudulent Conveyances

—In General

A sham transfer of property is one which is either colorable or illusory, such that the transferor had no intent to convey any present interest in the property, but, in fact, intended to retain complete ownership. In re Shehade, 137 Ill. App. 3d 692, 92 Ill. Dec. 398, 484 N.E.2d 1253 (1 Dist. 1985).

—Burden

In order to establish that a transfer of property amounted to a fraud subject to defeasance, the complaining spouse must prove such allegations by clear and convincing evidence; the determination of whether a conveyance was fraudulent depends upon all of the circumstances surrounding the transfer. In re Shehade, 137 Ill. App. 3d 692, 92 Ill. Dec. 398, 484 N.E.2d 1253 (1 Dist. 1985).

—Marital Rights

With respect to her marital rights, the law affords the same protection to a wife as it does to a creditor, and it is generally held that a disposition of property made with specific intent to defeat such rights may be set aside. Robertson v. Robertson, 123 Ill. App. 3d 323, 78 Ill. Dec. 593, 462 N.E.2d 712 (5 Dist. 1984).

—Motion to Vacate or Modify

A decree disposing of property upon divorce, based upon a separation agreement procured by fraud or coercion, may be modified via a motion under 735 ILCS 5/2-1401, if the injured party acts with reasonable diligence. In re Beck, 83 Ill. App. 3d 976, 39 Ill. Dec. 381, 404 N.E.2d 972 (2 Dist. 1980).

—Not Shown

Conveyance by husband of his real estate, two months after the death of his first wife and a year prior to his marriage to plaintiff, was neither a fraud in law nor in fact upon plaintiff. Ellet v. Farmer, 384 Ill. 343, 51 N.E.2d 570 (1943).

—Prima Facie Fraud

A voluntary conveyance by either party to a marriage contract of his or her real estate, made without the knowledge of the other and on the eve of or in contemplation of marriage, is prima facie a fraud upon the other's marital rights, and the burden is upon the grantee to establish its validity. Ellet v. Farmer, 384 Ill. 343, 51 N.E.2d 570 (1943).

—Specific Intent Not Shown

Conveyance of land from husband to mother was established as fraudulent in law as to wife's marital rights, but the evidence failed to sustain fraud in fact, that husband maintained a specific intent to deprive wife of her marital rights. Robertson v. Robertson, 123 Ill. App. 3d 323, 78 Ill. Dec. 593, 462 N.E.2d 712 (5 Dist. 1984).

—Third Party

Where a conveyance from a spouse to a third party is essentially nothing more than a sham transaction, it is tantamount to a fraud and subject to defeasance by the other spouse. In re Shehade, 137 Ill. App. 3d 692, 92 Ill. Dec. 398, 484 N.E.2d 1253 (1 Dist. 1985).

—To Wife

Under former Ill.Rev.Stat., ch. 59, para. 4 (see now 740 ILCS 160/5), where transfers were made by a debtor-husband to his creditor-wife before and after they were divorced, such transfers being ordered or approved by the decree divorcing them, the transfers were made by debtor to respondent with intent to defraud creditor; reconveyance was ordered for purposes of sale to satisfy judgment. Wilkey v. Wax, 82 Ill. App. 2d 67, 225 N.E.2d 813 (4 Dist. 1967).

Former section 18 of the Divorce Act (see now this section), which permitted transfers to a wife in lieu of alimony if such transfers could be effected without fraud, was never intended to be a vehicle to effect a fraudulent end, or to transmute that which would otherwise be fraudulent into something lawful. Wilkey v. Wax, 82 Ill. App. 2d 67, 225 N.E.2d 813 (4 Dist. 1967).

Fund

—Not Warranted

No special circumstances existed which would have warranted the establishment of a trust or fund, and there was no evidence that the respondent was unlikely to provide for the support of the child; while there was an interruption of support during these proceedings and the instigation of contempt procedures, the record clearly indicated that respondent supported both petitioner and his child from the time the parties were separated until the filing of this action. In re Dulyn, 89 Ill. App. 3d 304, 44 Ill. Dec. 622, 411 N.E.2d 988 (1 Dist. 1980).

Although respondent was 55 at the time of the hearing, and in allegedly poor health, this was not a sufficient reason to require the establishment of a fund to insure the continuation of child's support. In re Dulyn, 89 Ill. App. 3d 304, 44 Ill. Dec. 622, 411 N.E.2d 988 (1 Dist. 1980).

Gift

—Burden of Proof

The burden of proof rests on those seeking to establish that a transaction was intended as a gift. Hofmann v. Hofmann, 94 Ill. 2d 205, 68 Ill. Dec. 593, 446 N.E.2d 499 (1983).

—Commingling Property

Where non-marital funds are commingled with marital property or placed in joint tenancy, a presumption of gift arises which can only be rebutted by clear, convincing, and unmistakable evidence that no gift was intended. In re Caldwell, 124 Ill. App. 3d 898, 80 Ill. Dec. 411, 465 N.E.2d 523 (4 Dist. 1984); In re Flemming, 143 Ill. App. 3d 592, 97 Ill. Dec. 859, 493 N.E.2d 666 (3 Dist. 1986).

—Donative Intent

Donative intent was presumed because the transfer was from parent to child. In re Brown, 110 Ill. App. 3d 782, 66 Ill. Dec. 488, 443 N.E.2d 11 (5 Dist. 1982).

—Evidence

The bankruptcy court's refusal to order depositions of the debtor's former husband's siblings regarding a post-divorce gift to the debtor's husband, pursuant to 750 ILCS 5/503(d), was harmless error because the debtor could have obtained equivalent information through other discovery means. Mungo v. Taylor (In re Mungo), F. Supp. 2d , 2003 U.S. Dist. LEXIS 3412 (N.D. Ill. Mar. 6, 2003), aff'd, 355 F.3d 969 (7th Cir. 2004).

Gift (Cont'd)

—Evidence (Cont'd)

Where petitioner testified that she made no promises in exchange for the purchase of residence, since the credibility of witnesses and the weight to be given their testimony was a question of fact for the trial court or jury, it was within the province of the trial court to accept the petitioner's version of the events and conclude that no promises were made to the respondent in exchange for the parties' decision to purchase the home in joint tenancy, and the presumption that a gift was intended was not overcome by clear, convincing and unmistakable evidence. In re Wingader, 95 Ill. App. 3d 9, 50 Ill. Dec. 503, 419 N.E.2d 611 (1 Dist. 1981).

—Factors

Some of the factors considered significant in determining whether the presumption of a gift to the marital estate had been rebutted or shown to be unreasonable are (1) the size of the gift relative to the entire estate; (2) who paid the purchase price, made improvements, and paid taxes for the property with solely acquired funds and exercised control and management over the property; (3) when the asset was purchased; and (4) how the parties handled their prior financial dealings with each other. In re Hagshenas, 234 Ill. App. 3d 178, 175 Ill. Dec. 506, 600 N.E.2d 437 (2 Dist. 1992), appeal denied, 148 Ill.2d 642, 183 Ill. Dec. 19, 610 N.E.2d 1263 (1993).

The factors used to determine whether the presumption of gift to the marital estate has been overcome include the making of improvements, the payment of taxes and mortgages, the occupancy of the premises as a home or business and the extent of control and management of the property. In re Hunter, 223 Ill. App. 3d 947, 166 Ill. Dec. 242, 585 N.E.2d 1264 (2 Dist.), appeal denied, 145 Ill. 2d 634, 173 Ill. Dec. 4, 596 N.E.2d 628 (1992).

—Intent

Where father testified that he wanted his son to share in business, "to have half the income" and to give him "the opportunity to buy the rest in case something happened to me," the testimony was indicative of a gift. In re Brown, 110 Ill. App. 3d 782, 66 Ill. Dec. 488, 443 N.E.2d 11 (5 Dist. 1982).

Despite husband's denial of donative intent and his continued control of property he purchased, he failed to rebut the presumption that the conveyance to his wife was a gift and plaintiff's intent at the time that he deeded the property to defendant was the controlling factor; consequently, the circumstances at time of the conveyance and his own testimony established that he intended a present, irrevocable transfer of the property to wife. West v. West, 77 Ill. App. 3d 828, 33 Ill. Dec. 658, 396 N.E.2d 1382 (4 Dist. 1979).

—Inter Vivos Gift

Where, at any time prior to his death, decedent had the ability to withdraw the contents of safe deposit box by virtue of duplicate key and therefore a sufficient delivery was negated, and where he did not have the government bonds in the box reissued in the name of petitioner and she did not enter the box until after his death, 15 months after she became a co-renter, nor did she otherwise attempt to exercise any control over the contents of the box prior to his death, petitioner failed to establish by clear and convincing evidence the alleged gift and the decedent did not effectuate a valid inter vivos gift. Stahl v. Chuhak, 13 Ill. App. 3d 680, 301 N.E.2d 82 (1 Dist. 1973).

—Marital Asset

One spouse is not empowered to make the unilateral determination regarding ownership of property purchased with marital funds; by conditioning the gift of his interest in the ring to wife upon the continuation of the marriage, husband prevented her from, upon dissolution, claiming the ring as her non-marital property. However, since the ring was purchased with marital funds, it was a marital asset and the condition did not prevent the trial court from awarding wife the ring as part of her share of the marital assets. In re Yong Sun Lee, 246 Ill. App. 3d 628, 186 Ill. Dec. 257, 615 N.E.2d 1314 (4 Dist.), cert. denied, 153 Ill. 2d 560, 191 Ill. Dec. 620, 624 N.E.2d 808 (1993).

—Not Shown

The wife failed to establish that a residence was a gift to her from her father and her separate property where (1) the record contained her own testimony that she purchased the lot from her father, a closing statement indicating a purchase price of $29,870, and Illinois and county real estate transfer declarations to that effect, and (2) she failed to establish that she paid for the construction of the residence with nonmarital funds. In re Didier, 318 Ill. App. 3d 253, 252 Ill. Dec. 270, 742 N.E.2d 808, 2000 Ill. App. LEXIS 988 (1 Dist. 2000).

Trial court's determination that husband's purchase of farm from his parents was not a gift was supported by credible evidence. Hofmann v. Hofmann, 94 Ill. 2d 205, 68 Ill. Dec. 593, 446 N.E.2d 499 (1983).

—Pre-Marriage Funds

Property acquired with pre-marriage funds should not be considered a gift to the husband even though the property on which the home was built was in the former husband's name alone. In re Dietz, 76 Ill. App. 3d 1029, 32 Ill. Dec. 532, 395 N.E.2d 762 (5 Dist. 1979).

—Presumption

Where property owned by the wife prior to the marriage was later placed in some form of co-ownership during the marriage and there was no evidence offered to rebut the presumption of gift, the trial court was not free to ignore the presumption that the property was a gift to the marital estate. In re Johns, 311 Ill. App. 3d 699, 244 Ill. Dec. 157, 724 N.E.2d 1045, 2000 Ill. App. LEXIS 81 (2 Dist. 2000).

—In General

Where the husband offered no evidence to overcome the presumption of a gift to the marital estate or to suggest the deposit of his legacy into the parties' joint account was anything other than a gift to the marital estate, the court erred in awarding the full legacy to the husband. McCoy v McCoy, 225 Ill. App. 3d 966, 168 Ill. Dec. 27, 589 N.E.2d 141 (3 Dist. 1992).

This section has been interpreted to permit both inter-spousal gifts as well as gifts from third parties; however, where the property is acquired during the marriage, a presumption in favor of recognition as marital property is controlling and the "donee" spouse must rebut this presumption with clear and convincing evidence. In re Weinstein, 128 Ill. App. 3d 234, 83 Ill. Dec. 425, 470 N.E.2d 551 (1 Dist. 1984).

Property voluntarily conveyed by a husband to his wife, without fraud or coercion, is presumed to be a gift even though the husband may have purchased the property with his own money and in that case, the wife may hold the property against him. West v. West, 77 Ill. App. 3d 828, 33 Ill. Dec. 658, 396 N.E.2d 1382 (4 Dist. 1979).

Property voluntarily conveyed by a husband to a wife is presumed to be a gift. James v. James, 14 Ill. 2d 295, 152 N.E.2d 582 (1958).

Property voluntarily conveyed by a husband to his wife, without fraud or coercion, is presumed to be a gift, notwithstanding the fact the husband purchased the property with his own money, and the wife may hold the property against him; this presumption is not conclusive but may be rebutted by proof, but can only be overcome by clear, convincing, and unmistakable evidence that no gift was intended. Baker v. Baker, 412 Ill. 511, 107 N.E.2d 711 (1952).

—Rebutted

Where the husband presented clear and convincing evidence that property which was acquired after the marriage was in exchange for property acquired before the marriage, the evidence was sufficient to rebut the presumption of gift. In re Guerra, 153 Ill. App. 3d 550, 106 Ill. Dec. 201, 505 N.E.2d 748 (2 Dist. 1987).

Where there was no evidence whatsoever that a gift was not intended when the title to property was placed in the names of plaintiff and defendant as joint tenants, the trial court erred when it directed the plaintiff wife to quitclaim her interest in the marital home to the defendant husband. Larocco v. Larocco, 10 Ill. App. 3d 366, 293 N.E.2d 756 (5 Dist. 1973).

Absent fraud or coercion, a voluntary conveyance by a husband to his wife will be presumed to be a gift; however, where the conveyance is made upon the promise of the wife to return to the home, or to act as a good and kind wife and such promise has not been kept, equity will hold the conveyance a nullity. Sullivan v. Sullivan, 79 Ill. App. 2d 194, 223 N.E.2d 461 (4 Dist. 1967).

The rebuttable presumption of a gift to the wife of a portion of the real property was overcome by the evidence of the intention of the

Gift (Cont'd)

—Rebutted (Cont'd)

parties where the property was purchased and improved with plaintiff's own funds acquired before marriage, and at the time title was taken it was explained by an attorney and understood by defendant that the title was placed in joint tenancy only to avoid the expense of probate in case either party died, and to insure defendant survivorship rights if her husband died during marriage; defendant at no time regarded herself as having any interest in the property, as evidenced by her conduct and her refusal to believe that she had any such interest when husband's attorney requested her to sign a quitclaim deed to clear the record. Ludwig v. Ludwig, 413 Ill. 44, 107 N.E.2d 848 (1952).

—Reimbursement

There is a rebuttable presumption that a contribution of non-marital funds to a marital home held in joint tenancy constitutes a nonreimbursable gift. In re Mayzner, 144 Ill. App. 3d 645, 98 Ill. Dec. 493, 494 N.E.2d 615 (1 Dist. 1986).

Husband's $30,000 non-marital contribution to the parties' condominium, which was held in joint tenancy, was presumed to be a gift and since husband presented no evidence to rebut this presumption, he was not entitled to any reimbursement. In re Mayzner, 144 Ill. App. 3d 645, 98 Ill. Dec. 493, 494 N.E.2d 615 (1 Dist. 1986).

Subdivision (c)(2) of this section does not mandate reimbursement for property which was gifted to the marital estate. In re Flemming, 143 Ill. App. 3d 592, 97 Ill. Dec. 859, 493 N.E.2d 666 (3 Dist. 1986).

—Requirements

A valid gift requires proof of donative intent and delivery of the subject matter. In re Brown, 110 Ill. App. 3d 782, 66 Ill. Dec. 488, 443 N.E.2d 11 (5 Dist. 1982).

—Shown

Money loaned by the wife to her husband's corporation was a gift rather than a loan since the wife testified that she considered the transfer of funds a loan, but there was conflicting testimony as to whether she had ever discussed with the husband the matter of repayment, and she requested no security whatsoever for the transfer. In re Didier, 318 Ill. App. 3d 253, 252 Ill. Dec. 270, 742 N.E.2d 808, 2000 Ill. App. LEXIS 988 (1 Dist. 2000).

Petitioner did sustain her burden in proving that ex-husband's deposits into I.R.A. account were gifts, as he testified at length to his intent and knowledge that the money would go into petitioner's I.R.A. account and would be in her sole control and the fact that the respondent made the gift for tax purposes was of no consequence. In re Weiler, 258 Ill. App. 3d 454, 196 Ill. Dec. 372, 629 N.E.2d 1216 (5 Dist. 1994).

The finding of the trial court that real property held by the respondent subject to his obligation to care for the grantor was a gift to respondent and was non-marital property had ample support in the record and was not against the manifest weight of the evidence. In re Bentley, 82 Ill. App. 3d 25, 36 Ill. Dec. 947, 401 N.E.2d 1085 (1 Dist. 1980), vacated on other grounds, 84 Ill. 2d 97, 49 Ill. Dec. 295, 417 N.E.2d 1309 (1981).

—Time of Acquisition

In lieu of the common law presumption of gift, the statute substitutes a new presumption under this section, namely, that all property acquired after the marriage is marital property, and the presumption can be overcome by showing that it was a gift. In re Severns, 93 Ill. App. 3d 122, 48 Ill. Dec. 713, 416 N.E.2d 1235 (4 Dist. 1981).

—To Children

Under 750 ILCS 5/503(b)(1), the presumption that the funds which were transferred into a trust for the children by the former husband were marital property was rebutted by proof that the funds were a gift to the children and were acquired from the grandfather. Mungo v. Taylor, 355 F.3d 969, 2004 U.S. App. LEXIS 762 (7th Cir. 2004).

—Upheld

The fact that husband and wife paid monthly payments on both original and refinanced mortgages from marital funds, and that their separately filed tax returns showed that they each claimed ½ of the mortgage interest and real estate taxes as deductions, strengthened the presumption of gift to the marital estate where husband's name was added to title of house. Zito v. Zito, 196 Ill. App. 3d 1031, 143 Ill. Dec. 606, 554 N.E.2d 541 (1 Dist. 1990).

Where there was no evidence whatsoever that a gift was not intended when the title to property was placed in the names of plaintiff and defendant as joint tenants, the trial court erred when it directed the plaintiff wife to quitclaim her interest in the marital home to the defendant husband. Larocco v. Larocco, 10 Ill. App. 3d 366, 293 N.E.2d 756 (5 Dist. 1973).

Plaintiff did not meet his burden of rebutting the presumption of a gift of a joint-tenancy interest in the property by testimony of a convincing character. Baker v. Baker, 412 Ill. 511, 107 N.E.2d 711 (1952).

Goodwill

—Business

The trial judge considered the various circumstances listed in subsection (d) in dividing the couple's marital estate and therefore overlapped to some degree the elements that underlie the valuation of the personal goodwill of the car dealership in which the husband was a co-partner. In re Talty, 166 Ill. 2d 232, 209 Ill. Dec. 790, 652 N.E.2d 330 (1995).

To the extent that goodwill inheres in the business, existing independently of husband's personal efforts, and will outlast his involvement with the enterprise, it should be considered an asset of the business, and hence of the marriage; in contrast, to the extent that goodwill of the business is personal to husband, depends on his efforts, and will cease when his involvement with the dealership ends, it should not be considered property. In re Talty, 166 Ill. 2d 232, 209 Ill. Dec. 790, 652 N.E.2d 330 (1995).

The trial court's calculation was speculative, arbitrary and without basis in the record where the trial court did not choose between two opposing values, both supported by proper evidence, but the trial court rejected expert's valuation because it included consideration of husband's earning potential but somehow, the trial court concluded that wife had established that medical practices have some unproved intangible value and determined that the excess cash value of husband's practice was fifty (50%) percent of his 1983 income, being $153,840.00 divided by 2 equals $76,920.00 and subtracting the $58,000 in stipulated tangible assets from this figure left the $18,920 in dispute. In re Head, 273 Ill. App. 3d 404, 210 Ill. Dec. 270, 652 N.E.2d 1246 (1 Dist. 1995).

—Corporate

A fair and just disposition of marital property requires considering goodwill in valuing professional corporations; to ignore the intangible asset of goodwill could result in undervaluing the practice and the corporation's stock, and thereby lead to an inequitable distribution of the property. In re Rubinstein, 145 Ill. App. 3d 31, 99 Ill. Dec. 212, 495 N.E.2d 659 (2 Dist. 1986).

—Professional

Professional goodwill is not subject to valuation, division, or distribution as a marital asset, but should instead be reflected in maintenance and support awards. In re Phillips, 244 Ill. App. 3d 577, 186 Ill. Dec. 108, 615 N.E.2d 1165 (4 Dist. 1993).

As professional goodwill value is reflected in maintenance and support awards, it is not a divisible marital asset. In re Zells, 143 Ill. 2d 251, 157 Ill. Dec. 480, 572 N.E.2d 944 (1991).

Illinois courts have differed on whether the goodwill developed in a professional practice deserves separate consideration and specification as an asset of the practice or whether it is a factor already given consideration in the statutory distribution of property. In re Courtright, 155 Ill. App. 3d 55, 107 Ill. Dec. 738, 507 N.E.2d 891 (3 Dist. 1987).

—Stock Valuation

Since the trial court considered respondent's earning potential, i.e., "good will," it did not abuse its discretion in failing to set a fixed monetary value for good will in valuing the stock. In re Wilder, 122 Ill. App. 3d 338, 77 Ill. Dec. 824, 461 N.E.2d 447 (1 Dist. 1983).

Hearing

Considering petitioner's attorney's stipulation that a fee hearing was unnecessary, the attorneys' readiness to have the trial court

Hearing (Cont'd)
rule on the issue, and the fact that the court heard a great deal of evidence on the subject, no error occurred with respect to the award of attorney fees. In re McHenry, 292 Ill. App. 3d 634, 226 Ill. Dec. 887, 686 N.E.2d 670 (1 Dist. 1997).

Homemaker's Contribution

—Abuse of Discretion
While the value of the property is but one element to consider in ascertaining an equitable distribution, that element considered with other relevant factors demonstrated that the trial court abused its discretion where the wife contributed substantial services as a homemaker over the duration of the 22-year marriage. In re Scoville, 233 Ill. App. 3d 746, 174 Ill. Dec. 394, 598 N.E.2d 1026 (5 Dist. 1992).

The trial judge abused his discretion in making award of marital property when he expressly stated that he was not interested in wife's contribution as a homemaker. In re Rothbardt, 99 Ill. App. 3d 561, 54 Ill. Dec. 929, 425 N.E.2d 1146 (1 Dist. 1981).

—Devalued
Where the evidence established that the marriage lasted three years, and respondent moved out of the home at least six times, her contribution as a homemaker was appropriately devalued. In re Cecil, 202 Ill. App. 3d 783, 148 Ill. Dec. 72, 560 N.E.2d 374 (3 Dist. 1990).

—Employed Outside the Home
The circuit court erred when it ordered husband to pay wife for her homemaker contribution where wife worked outside the home and failed to show that her contribution as homemaker was greater than husband's contribution to the home. In re Tatham, 173 Ill. App. 3d 1072, 123 Ill. Dec. 576, 527 N.E.2d 1351 (5 Dist. 1988).

—Entitled to Consideration
A spouse's contribution as a homemaker should be considered by the court in making an award of marital property. In re Cecil, 202 Ill. App. 3d 783, 148 Ill. Dec. 72, 560 N.E.2d 374 (3 Dist. 1990).

A spouse who has no income and contributes no money to a marital residence is nonetheless entitled to consideration of her homemaking contributions under this section. In re Cullman, 185 Ill. App. 3d 1029, 133 Ill. Dec. 836, 541 N.E.2d 1274 (1 Dist.), appeal denied, 136 Ill. Dec. 583, 545 N.E.2d 107 (Ill. 1989).

—Improvements to House
Where wife helped to increase or at least maintain the value of the home by landscaping the property, painting the interior, and seeing to needed repairs and cleaning, such was considered relevant to the division of marital property under this section. In re Cullman, 185 Ill. App. 3d 1029, 133 Ill. Dec. 836, 541 N.E.2d 1274 (1 Dist.), appeal denied, 136 Ill. Dec. 583, 545 N.E.2d 107 (Ill. 1989).

—Recognition
This section was intended to recognize and to compensate the homemaker as an equal partner to marriage whose domestic contributions have assisted in giving economic value to marital assets. In re Kennedy, 214 Ill. App. 3d 849, 158 Ill. Dec. 172, 573 N.E.2d 1357 (1 Dist. 1991).

—Reimbursement
A spouse's homemaking services were held not to be a contribution to the other spouse's non-marital business venture and therefore not reimbursable where the homemaking services were unrelated to the non-marital property. In re Marthens, 215 Ill. App. 3d 590, 159 Ill. Dec. 3, 575 N.E.2d 3 (3 Dist. 1991).

—Share of Assets
Because of respondent's contribution as a homemaker, he was entitled to a significant share of the marital assets. In re Rai, 189 Ill. App. 3d 559, 136 Ill. Dec. 922, 545 N.E.2d 446 (1 Dist. 1989).

—Shown
The court is to consider contributions of a spouse as a homemaker or to the family in making the award of marital property; where evidence revealed that, although at times the couple employed domestic help, wife contributed substantial services as a homemaker over the long duration of the couple's marriage and, moreover, she also helped to entertain executives and customers, an award to wife of just 22% of marital property was an abuse of discretion. In re Aschwanden, 82 Ill. 2d 31, 44 Ill. Dec. 269, 411 N.E.2d 238 (1980).

—Sufficient Consideration
The trial court did not fail to give sufficient consideration to wife's services as a homemaker in making the award of marital property. In re Caldwell, 124 Ill. App. 3d 898, 80 Ill. Dec. 411, 465 N.E.2d 523 (4 Dist. 1984).

Improvements

—Credit
Where the marriage lasted only six years and petitioner presented evidence in the form of receipts for at least some of the improvements she claimed were made, the trial court must determine based on the evidence already presented whether those contributions to the marital estate made to respondent's non-marital residence were clearly proved, and whether the marital estate had already been compensated; the amounts proved as contributed to respondent's house and uncompensated should be credited to the marital estate and divided according to the provisions of this section. In re Albrecht, 266 Ill. App. 3d 399, 203 Ill. Dec. 394, 639 N.E.2d 953 (4 Dist. 1994).

Indispensable Party
The fact that a retirement plan holds an asset which becomes, upon dissolution of a marriage, subject to allocation of property rights between the spouses does not qualify it as an indispensable party to a suit between the spouses. In re Degener, 119 Ill. App. 3d 1079, 75 Ill. Dec. 878, 458 N.E.2d 46 (2 Dist. 1983).

Inheritance

—Commingling
By commingling her non-marital inheritance with the marital residence seven years before the parties separated and ten years before their marriage was dissolved, petitioner showed an intent to benefit both herself and respondent by converting the non-marital property into marital property; therefore it was error for the trial court to award petitioner a credit for the property as non-marital property. In re Johnson, 106 Ill. App. 3d 502, 62 Ill. Dec. 478, 436 N.E.2d 228 (1 Dist. 1982).

—Gift to Estate
The trial court did not err in awarding wife property that was inherited by husband after the marriage where the evidence demonstrated husband's intent to make the property a gift to the marital estate. In re Nicks, 177 Ill. App. 3d 76, 126 Ill. Dec. 442, 531 N.E.2d 1069 (4 Dist. 1988).

—Joint Bank Account
Wife's non-marital funds, acquired by inheritance but deposited into a joint bank account by husband, and the interest on the funds, put into a marital account for expenses before the separation, were marital property. In re Orlando, 218 Ill. App. 3d 312, 160 Ill. Dec. 763, 577 N.E.2d 1334 (1 Dist. 1991).

—Potential
Potential inheritances, just as expected degrees or licenses, are not property which can be valued and awarded to a spouse, although they can be given some consideration in determining property distribution. In re Eddy, 210 Ill. App. 3d 450, 155 Ill. Dec. 174, 569 N.E.2d 174 (1 Dist. 1991).

Injunction

—Preservation of Status Quo
A trial court abused its discretion in granting injunctive relief where that relief did not preserve the status quo of the parties for purposes of equitable distribution of property. In re Schwartz, 131 Ill. App. 3d 351, 86 Ill. Dec. 698, 475 N.E.2d 1077 (1 Dist. 1985).

A mandatory injunction was not necessary to preserve the status quo in terms of the condition of the apartment which had served as the marital domicile prior to the wife's unilateral removal of the furnishings; disruption to the status quo by itself does not mandate the issuance of injunctive relief, and husband must also establish the existence of a certain and ascertainable legal right, irreparable

Injunction (Cont'd)

—Preservation of Status Quo (Cont'd)

injury and an inadequate remedy at law. In re Sherwin, 123 Ill. App. 3d 748, 79 Ill. Dec. 201, 463 N.E.2d 755 (1 Dist. 1984).

—Proceeds

Where the major part of the sum enjoined was the proceeds from the sale of defendant's home, the appropriate disposition of the money enjoined was an issue to be determined by the court in the dissolution proceedings, and court's injunction against returning the money to defendant was properly issued to preserve the disputed property pendente lite. People v. Dorsey, 109 Ill. App. 3d 218, 64 Ill. Dec. 842, 440 N.E.2d 394 (1 Dist. 1982), cert. denied, 460 U.S. 1053, 103 S. Ct. 1503, 75 L. Ed. 2d 933 (1983).

—Upheld

Wife in a divorce action was properly granted an injunction preventing husband from disposing of his assets where he faced large expenses with respect to defending the divorce action and pending criminal charges, and such dissipation would have been to the children's detriment because husband would no longer be able to contribute to their support. In re Stamberg, 218 Ill. App. 3d 333, 161 Ill. Dec. 134, 578 N.E.2d 261 (1 Dist. 1991).

Interest

It was error to award the appellee a money judgment bearing interest at the statutory rate as a means of equalizing the property division and awarding judgment interest payable to the appellee by the appellant during the children's minority; no basis in statute or case law existed for such an award of interest. In re Fairchild, 110 Ill. App. 3d 470, 66 Ill. Dec. 131, 442 N.E.2d 557 (3 Dist. 1982).

Joint Tenancy

—Bank Account

When salaries, contributions and other evidence were considered, it was clear that both parties contributed to bank accounts and both parties were entitled to divisional shares in them; therefore the trial court abused its discretion in awarding wife-plaintiff the husband-defendant's joint tenancy interest in the bank accounts. Fuqua v. Fuqua, 60 Ill. App. 3d 819, 18 Ill. Dec. 200, 377 N.E.2d 353 (2 Dist. 1978).

Trial court did not err in finding that the defendant overcame the presumption of a gift of one-half of the $21,000 balance in the account and that the account was jointly held for convenience. Anagnostopoulos v. Anagnostopoulos, 22 Ill. App. 3d 479, 317 N.E.2d 681 (1 Dist. 1974).

—Conveyance Voided

Husband's conveyance of land to joint tenancy was void where the wife admitted that she went to her mother's home town within several days after the deed was returned from the recorder, and there was evidence that within a month following she entered into an adulterous relationship. Sullivan v. Sullivan, 79 Ill. App. 2d 194, 223 N.E.2d 461 (4 Dist. 1967).

—Effect of Divorce Decree

When property is found to be non-marital and held in joint tenancy, the parties' joint interest should not be affected by the dissolution and property distribution order. In re Voight, 111 Ill. App. 3d 623, 67 Ill. Dec. 458, 444 N.E.2d 694 (1 Dist. 1982).

The decree for divorce and property settlement agreement was given effect where the property continued to be held by the parties in joint tenancy until one spouse's death; a severance of the joint tenancy was intended by the property settlement which provided for the former wife to convey to the former husband her interest in the property on the stated terms. Coleman v. Coleman, 77 Ill. App. 3d 397, 32 Ill. Dec. 828, 395 N.E.2d 1209 (2 Dist. 1979).

A divorce decree alone does not effect a severance of joint tenancy real estate. Sebben v. Woodshank, 27 Ill. App. 3d 444, 325 N.E.2d 686 (3 Dist. 1975).

A divorce decree taken with the judgment for attorney fees and liens impressed on decedent's one-half interest in real estate were insufficient to terminate a joint tenancy. Sebben v. Woodshank, 27 Ill. App. 3d 444, 325 N.E.2d 686 (3 Dist. 1975).

A divorce alone is insufficient to effect a severance of joint tenancy to real estate. Thomas v. Johnson, 12 Ill. App. 3d 302, 297 N.E.2d 712 (2 Dist. 1973).

—Intent to Create

When, knowing the meaning of joint tenancy, appellant took deed to real estate held in joint name with appellee and continued to purchase securities in their joint names without placing a restricted meaning on the term, she could not say she did not intend to create a joint tenancy. Walker v. Walker, 369 Ill. 627, 17 N.E.2d 567 (1938).

—Non-Marital Property

Trial judge erred in awarding wife half of the one-half interest husband would receive if the probate court found that he succeeded to co-joint tenants interest in the property as the surviving joint tenant; the undivided one-half interest that husband would receive as the survivor of the joint tenancy, therefore, was non-marital property which had to be awarded to him. In re Parker, 252 Ill. App. 3d 1015, 192 Ill. Dec. 277, 625 N.E.2d 237 (1 Dist. 1993).

Generally, the placing of title to non-marital property in joint tenancy raises the presumption of a gift to the marital estate; the presumption can only be overcome by clear and convincing evidence. In re Hunter, 223 Ill. App. 3d 947, 166 Ill. Dec. 242, 585 N.E.2d 1264 (2 Dist.), appeal denied, 145 Ill. 2d 634, 173 Ill. Dec. 4, 596 N.E.2d 628 (1992).

Placing non-marital property in joint tenancy with a spouse creates a presumption that a gift has been made to the marital estate; the donor spouse may rebut the presumption of gift only by clear, convincing and unmistakable evidence. McCoy v McCoy, 225 Ill. App. 3d 966, 168 Ill. Dec. 27, 589 N.E.2d 141 (3 Dist. 1992).

—Partition

Where a decree of divorce ordered that all real estate owned by the parties be sold and the net proceeds divided equally, and the decree embodied the terms of a settlement agreement, since the plaintiff was specifically asked whether she had entered into a property settlement which she wanted the judge to approve and answered "Yes," the parties intended a division of the property, in the absence of clear language to the contrary or any evidence inconsistent with the settlement provisions, and the parties sought to partition their jointly held property in the context of a divorce proceeding. Thomas v. Johnson, 12 Ill. App. 3d 302, 297 N.E.2d 712 (2 Dist. 1973).

—Presumption of Gift

The creation of marital joint tenancy property using non-marital funds results in a gift to the marital estate absent clear and convincing evidence. In re Flemming, 143 Ill. App. 3d 592, 97 Ill. Dec. 859, 493 N.E.2d 666 (3 Dist. 1986).

Where the parties held certain property in joint tenancy, a rebuttable presumption arose that defendant made a gift of an undivided one half interest in such property. Brongel v. Brongel, 48 Ill. App. 3d 27, 6 Ill. Dec. 115, 362 N.E.2d 750 (2 Dist. 1977).

When property is taken in joint tenancy by husband and wife, there is a presumption of gift from the one furnishing the consideration to the other, and while this is the general rule, it is subject to the provisions governing the division and transfer of marital property and the award of property in lieu of alimony. Benson v. Benson, 26 Ill. App. 3d 50, 324 N.E.2d 469 (2 Dist. 1975).

—Presumption of Marital Property

Husband's contention that property was held jointly because of an agreement between the parties that his property would be placed in joint tenancy solely for purposes of avoiding probate was insufficient to rebut the presumption that the property in joint tenancy was considered marital where the evidence indicated that the parties had established a pattern of ownership of individual and joint property prior to that time in which each party held title to their individual property in their own names and title to their joint property in joint tenancy. Brongel v. Brongel, 48 Ill. App. 3d 27, 6 Ill. Dec. 115, 362 N.E.2d 750 (2 Dist. 1977).

—Severance

An agreement between joint tenants to hold as tenants in common will sever an existing joint tenancy, and such an agreement may be inferred from the manner in which the parties deal with the property. Sebben v. Woodshank, 27 Ill. App. 3d 444, 325 N.E.2d 686 (3 Dist. 1975).

Jurisdiction

—Disposition of Property

Under normal circumstances, a court does not have jurisdiction

Jurisdiction (Cont'd)

—Disposition of Property (Cont'd)
to dispose of property in a proceeding for legal separation except where property is submitted for disposition by agreement of the parties. In re Lipkin, 163 Ill. App. 3d 1033, 115 Ill. Dec. 76, 517 N.E.2d 41 (4 Dist. 1987).

Circuit court had jurisdiction to adjudicate property interests of parties to a proceeding for legal separation under this Act. In re Leff, 148 Ill. App. 3d 792, 101 Ill. Dec. 262, 499 N.E.2d 1042 (2 Dist. 1986).

This Act does not give the court authority to distribute property until after the dissolution of marriage has been granted. In re Pahlke, 120 Ill. App. 3d 1009, 76 Ill. Dec. 487, 458 N.E.2d 1141 (1 Dist. 1983).

The circuit court had full and complete jurisdiction of the subject matter of the petition filed by the respondent that petitioner had abandoned the marital home and that he might be required to provide a home for their three children; therefore, trial court's granting of interest in home to petitioner was proper. English v. English, 72 Ill. App. 3d 736, 30 Ill. Dec. 363, 393 N.E.2d 18 (1 Dist. 1979).

If the trial court had not ordered the property sold and the debts paid, it would have been impossible for the defendant to make the child support payments ordered by the court; under these circumstances, the trial court had implied or ancillary jurisdiction to order the sale of the real and personal property in question. Fields v. Fields, 54 Ill. App. 3d 400, 12 Ill. Dec. 89, 369 N.E.2d 586 (5 Dist. 1977).

In determining the propriety or impropriety of a divorce decree ordering conveyance of property under former section 17 of the Divorce Act (see now this section), the authority of the court was based upon powers conferred by statute rather than upon general equity powers. Debrey v. Debrey, 132 Ill. App. 2d 1072, 270 N.E.2d 43 (4 Dist. 1971).

Under former section 17 of the Divorce Act (see now this section), absent specific legislated authority, a chancery court was devoid of jurisdiction to adjudicate, allot, dispense or otherwise dabble with the separate property of the parties to a divorce. Schouten v. Schouten, 129 Ill. App. 2d 418, 263 N.E.2d 715 (5 Dist. 1970).

A court's power to determine property rights can be based only upon a valid divorce decree. Lemon v. Lemon, 14 Ill. 2d 15, 150 N.E.2d 608 (1958).

The court had no power to finally determine the interest defendant had in plaintiff's property until a divorce had been granted. Klajbor v. Klajbor, 398 Ill. 152, 75 N.E.2d 353 (1947).

A court cannot, in the absence of a decree of divorce, determine property rights, award alimony, or dispose of the custody of the child. Ollman v. Ollman, 396 Ill. 176, 71 N.E.2d 50 (1947).

—Divorce
Where the court had jurisdiction of the parties and the subject matter, it had jurisdiction to grant a divorce. Ward v. Sampson, 395 Ill. 353, 70 N.E.2d 324 (1961).

—Enforcement
A court does retain jurisdiction to enforce terms of its original divorce decree. Brickey v. Brickey, 44 Ill. App. 3d 563, 3 Ill. Dec. 239, 358 N.E.2d 406 (5 Dist. 1976).

—Equity
This Act does not enlarge the general equity powers of the court in divorce cases, but it does confer a limited power to make orders touching alimony and maintenance of the parties and the custody, care and support of children. Being a power specially conferred by statute, it cannot be extended beyond its terms to permit an alteration of the provisions of the decree relating to property rights. Brickey v. Brickey, 44 Ill. App. 3d 563, 3 Ill. Dec. 239, 358 N.E.2d 406 (5 Dist. 1976).

—Failure to Comply with Agreement
The circuit court is the proper forum in which to seek redress for a spouse's failure to comply with the terms of the parties' settlement agreement. Jamal v. Jamal, 98 Ill. App. 2d 180, 240 N.E.2d 246 (1 Dist. 1968).

—Reimbursement of Fees
Trial court had subject matter jurisdiction over wife's petition under the Illinois Marriage and Dissolution Act; wife was not seeking modification of the property provisions of the supplemental order to the dissolution judgment in filing a petition (1) to have former husband held in contempt for failure to pay debt assigned to him and (2) to be reimbursed for legal fees incurred defending herself from a lawsuit on that debt. In re Davis, 292 Ill. App. 3d 802, 226 Ill. Dec. 765, 686 N.E.2d 395 (4 Dist. 1997).

—Support Increase
It was unnecessary, in order to vest the court with jurisdiction to hear and determine an application for increase of support for the child or plaintiff, that either the property settlement agreement or the decree make any such reservation of jurisdiction. Glick v. Glick, 338 Ill. App. 637, 88 N.E.2d 509 (1 Dist. 1949).

—Third Parties
The trial court was authorized to enjoin a mortgagee of marital property threatening foreclosure as a party to the mortgagor's dissolution proceeding, and to enjoin the mortgagee from initiating a foreclosure proceeding in a different division of the circuit court of the county, in aid of its own jurisdiction so that the interests of all parties in the property could be adjudicated in one proceeding. Schweihs v. Schweihs, 222 Ill. App. 3d 887, 165 Ill. Dec. 293, 584 N.E.2d 472 (1 Dist. 1991).

Just Proportions

—In General
This section does not require a showing of extraordinary circumstances to justify an unequal distribution of marital property; it requires only that the court divide marital property in just proportions considering all relevant factors. In re Ryan, 138 Ill. App. 3d 1077, 93 Ill. Dec. 617, 487 N.E.2d 61 (1 Dist. 1985).

—Abuse of Discretion
Merely because the trial court has awarded a larger share of the marital estate to one party does not necessarily demonstrate an abuse of discretion. In re Caldwell, 124 Ill. App. 3d 898, 80 Ill. Dec. 411, 465 N.E.2d 523 (4 Dist. 1984).

—Consideration of Contributions
The fact that one party's contributions to the marital estate can be readily quantified in dollars in no way maximizes that party's interest over another's and it does not automatically entitle him or her to a greater share of the marital property. In re Wentink, 132 Ill. App. 3d 71, 87 Ill. Dec. 117, 476 N.E.2d 1109 (1 Dist. 1984).

—Economic Circumstances
Property award to defendant wife which represented only about 22% of the couple's net worth failed to meet the "just proportions" requirement of this section where plaintiff husband's occupation and his long standing employment afforded him both a very high and steady income and the prospect of continued high income in the future; he was also assured of a generous pension upon retirement; his opportunity for future acquisition of capital assets was excellent; and by contrast, defendant's station and health left her with little opportunity to regain and maintain the standard of living to which the couple had become accustomed or acquire significant amounts of assets or income in the future. In re Aschwanden, 82 Ill. 2d 31, 44 Ill. Dec. 269, 411 N.E.2d 238 (1980).

—Equal Amount
Court's division of marital assets equally between the parties was not an abuse of discretion; wife's contribution was considerable as she completed necessary household chores so husband could continue work on the farm, she worked and cared for three children and paid for many of the family's day to day expenses. In re Nelson, 297 Ill. App. 3d 651, 232 Ill. Dec. 654, 698 N.E.2d 1084 (3 Dist. 1998).

The division of marital property in "just proportions," does not mean that the property must be divided with mathematical equality; an unequal division may be made where the court has properly applied this section. In re Eidson, 235 Ill. App. 3d 907, 175 Ill. Dec. 901, 601 N.E.2d 298 (5 Dist. 1992).

The requirement that division be just does not mean that division must be equal. In re Sevon, 117 Ill. App. 3d 313, 73 Ill. Dec. 41, 453 N.E.2d 866 (1 Dist. 1983).

Just Proportions (Cont'd)

—Equal Amount (Cont'd)

A just proportion is not synonymous with an equal proportion of marital property. In re Clearman, 85 Ill. App. 3d 584, 40 Ill. Dec. 958, 407 N.E.2d 189 (3 Dist. 1980); In re Legge, 111 Ill. App. 3d 198, 66 Ill. Dec. 926, 443 N.E.2d 1089 (4 Dist. 1982); In re Sevon, 117 Ill. App. 3d 313, 73 Ill. Dec. 41, 453 N.E.2d 866 (1 Dist. 1983); In re Caldwell, 124 Ill. App. 3d 898, 80 Ill. Dec. 411, 465 N.E.2d 523 (4 Dist. 1984); In re Benz, 165 Ill. App. 3d 273, 116 Ill. Dec. 336, 518 N.E.2d 1316 (4 Dist. 1988); In re Cecil, 202 Ill. App. 3d 783, 148 Ill. Dec. 72, 560 N.E.2d 374 (3 Dist. 1990).

The legislature could have provided for a 50-50 split of marital assets, but instead required the trier of fact to weigh the specified factors. In re Woodward, 83 Ill. App. 3d 253, 39 Ill. Dec. 191, 404 N.E.2d 575 (3 Dist. 1980).

—Equitable Distribution

The court is required to make an equitable distribution, not necessarily an equal one. In re Schriner, 88 Ill. App. 3d 380, 43 Ill. Dec. 572, 410 N.E.2d 572 (2 Dist. 1980).

—Evidence

The touchstone of proper and just apportionment is whether it is equitable in nature with each case to rest on its own facts. In re Benz, 165 Ill. App. 3d 273, 116 Ill. Dec. 336, 518 N.E.2d 1316 (4 Dist. 1988).

—Larger Share

While the award of a larger share of marital property to one spouse may be justified in proper circumstances because of that spouse's greater contribution to the marital estate, caution is required to avoid placing too much emphasis on that factor. In re Rapacz, 135 Ill. App. 3d 1045, 90 Ill. Dec. 622, 482 N.E.2d 441 (2 Dist. 1985).

—Not Shown

The trial court clearly failed to divide the property in "just proportions" where it split the value of the house equally between husband and wife, as most of the mortgage and real estate tax payments were tax deductible, and to equate husband's payment of them with wife's capital investment was error. In re Carney, 122 Ill. App. 3d 705, 78 Ill. Dec. 477, 462 N.E.2d 596 (1 Dist. 1984).

Under certain circumstances, it is proper to award the marital home to one spouse even though the home is virtually all of the marital property; however, the award of the marital home to the wife was not in "just proportion" where both parties contributed toward the financial obligations of the marriage and occupied similar financial positions. In re Miller, 84 Ill. App. 3d 931, 40 Ill. Dec. 7, 405 N.E.2d 1099 (1 Dist. 1980).

—Objective

The objective of this section is to achieve a division of property which is in just proportions. In re Cabaj, 118 Ill. App. 3d 789, 74 Ill. Dec. 393, 455 N.E.2d 822 (1 Dist. 1983).

—Shown

Respondent's greater amounts of non-marital assets, her capability of employment, and petitioner's total disability and lack of significant non-marital funds supported the trial court's disproportional award of marital property. In re Caldwell, 124 Ill. App. 3d 898, 80 Ill. Dec. 411, 465 N.E.2d 523 (4 Dist. 1984).

Given the nature of marital assets and income needs of parties, award of marital property was in just proportions. In re Holman, 122 Ill. App. 3d 1001, 78 Ill. Dec. 314, 462 N.E.2d 30 (2 Dist. 1984).

The apportionment of the marital property by the trial court was in just proportions and was supported by the manifest weight of the evidence. In re Crouch, 88 Ill. App. 3d 426, 43 Ill. Dec. 580, 410 N.E.2d 580 (3 Dist. 1980).

—Unequal Amount

The division of marital property in "just proportions" does not necessitate mathematical equality; an unequal division may be made where the court has properly applied the statute. In re Adan, 263 Ill. App. 3d 566, 200 Ill. Dec. 439, 635 N.E.2d 778 (1 Dist. 1994).

Lien

Award to respondent husband of part of the marital property by granting him a lien was within the broad powers of the trial court under this section and did not deprive husband respondent of his due process. In re Panozzo, 93 Ill. App. 3d 1085, 49 Ill. Dec. 372, 418 N.E.2d 16 (1 Dist. 1981).

Life Insurance Policy

A life insurance policy could be required under the proper circumstances to secure the support, education, maintenance, and general welfare of a party's children; such a "fund" may not be required, however, absent a finding that it was required to protect and promote the best interests of the children. In re Dulyn, 89 Ill. App. 3d 304, 44 Ill. Dec. 622, 411 N.E.2d 988 (1 Dist. 1980).

Loan Repayment

—Reimbursement to Marital Estate

Where a loan to purchase 50% interest in a farm operation was taken out several years prior to the marriage and only a portion, albeit a significant portion, was paid back after the marriage, the clear result was that the partnership interest was non-marital; an order of reimbursement to the marital estate would have been appropriate if there was clear and convincing evidence to establish the right to reimbursement; but the burden of proof was on the party requesting reimbursement and petitioner never established how much the marital estate contributed to the repayment of the loan. In re Werries, 247 Ill. App. 3d 639, 186 Ill. Dec. 747, 616 N.E.2d 1379 (4 Dist. 1993).

Maintenance

—Award Considered

Where the trial court heard proposals and arguments only on the division of property and then divided the property without reference to maintenance, and prior to its ruling on the division of marital property, the trial court was advised that in addition to the property division petitioner would seek maintenance, the trial court's procedure fully complied with the requirements of this section. In re Swigers, 176 Ill. App. 3d 795, 126 Ill. Dec. 231, 531 N.E.2d 858 (1 Dist. 1988).

Plaintiff's argument that the appellate court failed to consider the maintenance award was without merit because the appellate court's statement that "the trial court's maintenance award and award of attorney's fees do not make the marital property award equitable" demonstrated that the court did consider the maintenance award in determining that the marital property awarded defendant was insufficient. In re Aschwanden, 82 Ill. 2d 31, 44 Ill. Dec. 269, 411 N.E.2d 238 (1980).

—Determination

The issue of maintenance relates directly to the final property disposition, which must be considered first. In re Weiss, 129 Ill. App. 3d 166, 84 Ill. Dec. 378, 472 N.E.2d 128 (1 Dist. 1984).

—Effect of Award

An award of maintenance in lieu of property is improper. Brackett v. Brackett, 309 Ill. App. 3d 329, 242 Ill. Dec. 798, 722 N.E.2d 287 (2 Dist. 1999).

Where a husband had sufficient income to meet his needs while meeting the wife's, the award of maintenance to the wife had no effect on the amount of marital property apportioned to her. In re Heller, 153 Ill. App. 3d 224, 106 Ill. Dec. 503, 505 N.E.2d 1294 (1 Dist. 1987).

Findings of the chancellor that an order for regular periodic payments for the support and maintenance of defendant would be both unworkable and unsatisfactory and that continued common ownership of property would lead to endless bickering and possible future litigation were fully supported by the evidence. Persico v. Persico, 409 Ill. 608, 100 N.E.2d 904 (1951).

—Future Life of Parties

It is not unfair or an abuse of discretion for the trial court to tie the duration of petitioner's maintenance to the date of her former husband's retirement. In re Puls, 268 Ill. App. 3d 882, 206 Ill. Dec. 520, 645 N.E.2d 525 (1 Dist. 1994).

It does not appear wise to review the matters of maintenance and child support without also giving careful consideration to the ownership of the marital home and to its function in assisting the future life of the parties and their children. In re Cabaj, 118 Ill. App. 3d 789, 74 Ill. Dec. 393, 455 N.E.2d 822 (1 Dist. 1983).

Maintenance (Cont'd)

—Guidelines

At all times, the court is to keep in mind that the ultimate objective is to achieve a division of property which is in "just proportions," and where the property available to the defendant spouse is sufficient to satisfy that spouse's needs and entitlements, the use of maintenance should be limited; thus, if sufficient marital property is found, an award of maintenance may be unnecessary, but if there is not sufficient marital property, maintenance should be considered. In re Aschwanden, 82 Ill. 2d 31, 44 Ill. Dec. 269, 411 N.E.2d 238 (1980).

—Upheld

Where the only marital property awarded respondent was three notes, two of which were delinquent at the time of dissolution and of questionable value and because of his debilitating stroke, respondent could not work and his only sources of income outside of maintenance were from social security and an annuity which barely paid for his nursing home care and other expenses, the trial court did not abuse its discretion in awarding maintenance to respondent. In re Shields, 167 Ill. App. 3d 205, 118 Ill. Dec. 50, 521 N.E.2d 118 (4 Dist. 1988).

The trial court did not abuse its discretion in ordering husband to make monthly maintenance payments in an amount equal to 20% of his net income for five years, terminable upon wife becoming employed full time, where wife was 56 years old, had been married for nearly 25 years, had not been employed for over a year, and had limited employment potential in that she walked with a cane and suffered from leg and hand injuries arising out of an accident involving her husband. In re Randall, 157 Ill. App. 3d 892, 110 Ill. Dec. 122, 510 N.E.2d 1153 (1 Dist. 1987).

Marital Expenditures

Given the income of the family, the family's style of living could not be financed through any means other than the depletion of the family's savings, and the husband could not help but have noticed the questioned expenditures from a close corporation of which husband was the sole stockholder; thus, the trial court's finding that the expenditures were made for marital purposes was not an abuse of discretion. In re Getautas, 189 Ill. App. 3d 148, 136 Ill. Dec. 509, 544 N.E.2d 1284 (2 Dist. 1989).

The expense of a final payment due upon a note which had financed the purchase of a lot could not be included within those ordinary household expenses the parties agreed the husband should pay during the pendency of litigation. In re Rapacz, 135 Ill. App. 3d 1045, 90 Ill. Dec. 622, 482 N.E.2d 441 (2 Dist. 1985).

The circuit court did not err in refusing to consider certain money credits to which husband may have been entitled before entering the instant judgment, namely, reimbursement for one-half the taxes, mortgage payments, and maintenance costs he was required to pay since the divorce, as well as a sum of money the order directed wife to pay him, which was never done, because the foregoing items merely related to setoffs against the amount of her portion of the proceeds of the sale; such matters could be presented and considered after the property had been sold since they did not affect the right to partition the property. In re Mercer, 117 Ill. App. 3d 377, 72 Ill. Dec. 869, 453 N.E.2d 744 (1 Dist. 1983).

Marital Home

—Award Upheld

Court properly awarded the marital home to the wife, considering that she was awarded custody of the couple's child and that she operated a day care facility, licensed by the Department of Children and Family Services, from the home, garnering necessary familial income. Craig v. Craig, 326 Ill. App. 3d 1127, 261 Ill. Dec. 274, 762 N.E.2d 1201, 2002 Ill. App. LEXIS 54 (4 Dist. 2002).

Where petitioner wife had custody of the children, assignment of marital house to her was justified. In re Zummo, 167 Ill. App. 3d 566, 118 Ill. Dec. 339, 521 N.E.2d 621 (4 Dist. 1988).

Where the court properly considered not only the factors outlined in this section, but also other relevant factors including petitioner wife's contribution as a homemaker, her vocational skills and employability and custodial provisions for the minor child, the court did not abuse its discretion by awarding marital home to petitioner. In re De Bat, 127 Ill. App. 3d 463, 82 Ill. Dec. 568, 468 N.E.2d 1348 (1 Dist. 1984).

Where financial positions of parties were not equal, and wife had experienced medical problems that increased her expenses and curtailed her ability to work in the future, the trial judge properly found that wife's low income compared to the standard of living she had experienced during the marriage made an award of maintenance appropriate, and that husband's past behavior made the award of the marital residence to wife in lieu of periodic maintenance payments appropriate. In re Sevon, 117 Ill. App. 3d 313, 73 Ill. Dec. 41, 453 N.E.2d 866 (1 Dist. 1983).

Award of the marital home to wife, evaluated on the circumstances of the parties, balancing husband's superior earning capacity and retirement benefits with providing wife with the marital home, considering that wife was the custodial parent, that the children were quite small, and that she contributed to the acquisition of the marital assets with her savings and earnings when first married, and later as homemaker, was proper. In re Murphy, 117 Ill. App. 3d 649, 72 Ill. Dec. 808, 453 N.E.2d 113 (3 Dist. 1983).

Despite the considerable amount of physical labor which the husband devoted to the construction and planning of the home, and his use of the money which his father gave him for the acquisition of the land on which the home was located and the construction and landscaping of the home, the husband did not overcome the presumption that he did not intend to retain any portion of the amount which he contributed toward acquisition and construction of the parties' marital home as his non-marital property; therefore, the trial court did not abuse its discretion by awarding the entire marital residence to the wife. In re Legge, 111 Ill. App. 3d 198, 66 Ill. Dec. 926, 443 N.E.2d 1089 (4 Dist. 1982).

A husband had no absolute right to a partition of the marital residence and the court did not err in awarding the wife possession of the marital home until the youngest child became emancipated, and even though this event may not have occurred for nine years, the period of possession awarded the wife was not unreasonable. In re Woolsey, 85 Ill. App. 3d 636, 40 Ill. Dec. 775, 406 N.E.2d 1142 (4 Dist. 1980).

Where the marital residence was purchased shortly after the marriage with proceeds from an account to which wife had contributed over $13,000 and husband had contributed over $8,000 and in view of the short duration of the marriage, the trial court did not abuse its discretion in awarding wife a share of the proceeds of the sale of the marital home which reflected the amount by which her contribution to its purchase exceeded husband's. In re Pedersen, 77 Ill. App. 3d 716, 33 Ill. Dec. 270, 396 N.E.2d 659 (2 Dist. 1979).

Notwithstanding the fact that the marital home was owned by the parties as joint tenants, there was no abuse of discretion by the court in awarding the real estate equally to the parties without requiring husband to reimburse wife for homeowner expenses, such as real estate taxes, mortgage installments, insurance and maintenance, incurred by the wife; the disposition of the real estate was properly based upon the factors mandated in subsection (c) of this section, not on the legal form of ownership of the property. Junge v. Junge, 73 Ill. App. 3d 767, 29 Ill. Dec. 756, 392 N.E.2d 313 (5 Dist. 1979).

—Children's Welfare

Keeping the children in the marital home was clearly outweighed by the need to give husband sufficient funds so that he could pay child support, provide for his new family's needs, and pay off his outstanding debts. In re Agazim, 176 Ill. App. 3d 225, 125 Ill. Dec. 701, 530 N.E.2d 1110 (2 Dist. 1988).

Where the primary consideration inducing the trial court to award the marital home to the petitioner was the desire to provide an adequate, stable and relatively inexpensive dwelling place for the minor children, and to allow the petitioner to retain the house while the minor children were very young, thus avoiding the uncertainties, both in costs and environmental qualities, that might arise in connection with rented living quarters, and where the equity in the house was so small that the sale of the house would provide only a very reduced sum to each party, awarding the house to the petitioner, who would thereafter be liable for maintenance and mortgage payments, was not an abuse of discretion. In re Piktel, 81 Ill. App. 3d 567, 36 Ill. Dec. 743, 401 N.E.2d 584 (2 Dist. 1980).

Where it was clear that the welfare of the children was the motive for the award of the house to the petitioner rather than being an attempt to award her maintenance under another name,

Marital Home (Cont'd)

—Children's Welfare (Cont'd)
the award was within the court's discretion. In re Piktel, 81 Ill. App. 3d 567, 36 Ill. Dec. 743, 401 N.E.2d 584 (2 Dist. 1980).

Where a trial court ordered a marital home sold in 1979 because the couple's remaining minor child would be changing schools at that time, and it seemed in the best interest of the child to effect a move at that time, then the trial court acted within its sound discretion. Laing v. Laing, 55 Ill. App. 3d 231, 13 Ill. Dec. 462, 371 N.E.2d 157 (2 Dist. 1977).

—Consideration
A marital residence owned by both spouses, even if one spouse has furnished all of the consideration for it out of non-marital funds, is presumed in fact as marital property, absent convincing rebutting evidence. In re Rogers, 85 Ill. 2d 217, 52 Ill. Dec. 633, 422 N.E.2d 635 (1981).

—Conveyance
The court could reasonably deem the conveyance of the jointly owned marital home an equitable one, as a settlement in lieu of alimony. Smothers v. Smothers, 25 Ill. 2d 86, 182 N.E.2d 758 (1962).

—Date of Valuation
In light of a husband's greater opportunity to acquire additional assets in the future, a trial court did not err in fixing the husband's interest in the marital home as of the date of the dissolution of the marriage instead of giving him a continuing interest so that he might benefit from any increase in the value of the home between the date of dissolution and eventual sale of the premises. In re Woolsey, 85 Ill. App. 3d 636, 40 Ill. Dec. 775, 406 N.E.2d 1142 (4 Dist. 1980).

—Economic Circumstances
The court did not abuse its discretion in awarding the entire interest in the marital home to petitioner where the trial judge considered petitioner's contribution to the marriage as a home-maker, the desirability of awarding the marital home to petitioner, who had custody of the parties' children, petitioner's inferior earning capacity, and the fact that petitioner was not awarded maintenance. In re Legge, 111 Ill. App. 3d 198, 66 Ill. Dec. 926, 443 N.E.2d 1089 (4 Dist. 1982).

Where the marital home was the major asset of the parties, and respondent was without funds, assets, income, or employment and not likely to secure any of them in the near future, the court did not err in awarding the marital home to respondent, a non-custodial parent. In re Peoples, 96 Ill. App. 3d 94, 51 Ill. Dec. 514, 420 N.E.2d 1072 (5 Dist. 1981).

—Evidence Held Sufficient
Where plaintiff used his equity in first residence to purchase a new home titled in both parties' names, thereby commingling the properties so as to transmute his equity into marital property, the residence was properly classified as marital. In re Thacker, 185 Ill. App. 3d 465, 133 Ill. Dec. 573, 541 N.E.2d 784 (5 Dist. 1989).

A family residence was properly deemed marital property where the husband purchased the house approximately two months before the parties were married by borrowing $3,000 for the down payment and mortgaging the remaining purchase price, as he never spent any money from personal funds accumulated prior to the marriage, and the mortgage payments were made with marital funds. In re Ohrt, 154 Ill. App. 3d 738, 107 Ill. Dec. 496, 507 N.E.2d 160 (3 Dist. 1987).

Where house was purchased by the parties prior to, but "in contemplation of" their marriage; the parties were living together at the time of the purchase and had discussed acquiring a marital home; they both accompanied the real estate agent to view the property for the first time; they both signed the offer to purchase the property; former wife's parents provided a loan of $5,000 towards the down payment; and additional $5,000 came from the parties joint funds; they used joint funds in addition to the rental income from the property to make the mortgage payments prior to moving into the home; and during the marriage all mortgage payments were made from marital funds, the house was considered a marital asset. In re Malters, 133 Ill. App. 3d 168, 88 Ill. Dec. 460, 478 N.E.2d 1068 (1 Dist. 1985).

—Evidence of Intent
Where a husband testified that he and his wife, prior to the purchase of their house, had conversations regarding the method of holding title to it in which they discussed the house being an investment of his inheritance money, and they segregated a portion of their inheritances, these actions tended to indicate that the portion invested in the marital home, used for the parties' mutual benefit, and treated, during the marriage, as joint property, was intended to be marital property. In re Rogers, 85 Ill. 2d 217, 52 Ill. Dec. 633, 422 N.E.2d 635 (1981).

—Expenses
Since petitioner was awarded sole possession of the marital estate as well as the household furniture and furnishings, it was not inequitable to require her to pay those expenses relating to maintaining the home's value, such as mortgage, taxes and insurance. In re Hellwig, 100 Ill. App. 3d 452, 55 Ill. Dec. 762, 426 N.E.2d 1087 (1 Dist. 1981).

—Factors
Where marital home was awarded to former wife with the requirement that she pay former husband one-half of the home's present equity within four years, but she did not have to sell the home or otherwise disrupt the children in order to fulfill this obligation, the trial court properly balanced the needs of the former wife and the children with the right of the former husband to share in the home's equity. In re Keller, 108 Ill. App. 3d 556, 64 Ill. Dec. 115, 439 N.E.2d 44 (1 Dist. 1982).

The court affirmed the holding of the trial court that the marital home was marital property where, although defendant could trace some non-marital funds to the purchase of the home, the home was purchased after the marriage, title was held in joint tenancy, and marital funds were used to pay mortgage payments. In re Smith, 86 Ill. 2d 518, 56 Ill. Dec. 693, 427 N.E.2d 1239 (1981).

A trial court's award to a husband of a share of the marital house less than his contribution to its purchase was reasonable when balanced against the facts that the marriage lasted a long time, his economic circumstances, including his occupation and employability and his opportunity to acquire assets and income, were superior to the wife's, and although the parties' daughter was working full time as a secretary and their son was working part time at a restaurant, both were living at home, and custody was awarded to petitioner. In re Rogers, 85 Ill. 2d 217, 52 Ill. Dec. 633, 422 N.E.2d 635 (1981).

—Mortgage
The statute authorizes a court to order that the marital residence be mortgaged in order to pay marital debts. In re Carter, 317 Ill. App. 3d 546, 251 Ill. Dec. 252, 740 N.E.2d 82, 2000 Ill. App. LEXIS 953 (4 Dist. 2000).

—Non-Marital Funds
Under subsection (c)(1) of this section, there is a rebuttable presumption that a contribution of non-marital funds to a marital home held in joint tenancy constitutes a gift; this presumption of transmutation may be rebutted by clear and convincing evidence that a gift to the marital estate was not intended, but the fact that the commingling occurs after marital difficulties have arisen will support a finding that no gift to the marital estate was intended. In re Sokolowski, 232 Ill. App. 3d 535, 173 Ill. Dec. 701, 597 N.E.2d 675 (1 Dist. 1992).

Home of the parties was marital property where, although the down payment of the parties' first home came from a non-marital source, the mortgage payments were made with marital funds which were commingled in a joint account and further, the money which was used to pay the mortgage on both the first and second houses came from the husband's earnings as an insurance broker which were deposited in a joint account. In re Leon, 80 Ill. App. 3d 383, 35 Ill. Dec. 717, 399 N.E.2d 1006 (2 Dist. 1980).

—Non-Marital Funds for Payment of Taxes
To the extent husband earmarked non-marital funds for the payment of taxes on marital residence and the funds were actually used for that purpose, husband contributed to the preservation of property notwithstanding the temporary intermediate character of the funds as marital property; the trial court's conclusion that husband contributed to the preservation of the marital residence

Marital Home (Cont'd)

—Non-Marital Funds for Payment of Taxes (Cont'd)
was supported by the record. In re Marriott, 264 Ill. App. 3d 23, 201 Ill. Dec. 709, 636 N.E.2d 1141 (2 Dist. 1994).

—Noncustodial Parent
Although award of marital residence to custodial parent is normally preferred, where trial court awarded custodial parent the service station which was the main income producing asset of the marriage, award of home to noncustodial parent was upheld. In re Minear, 287 Ill. App. 3d 1073, 223 Ill. Dec. 405, 679 N.E.2d 856 (4 Dist. 1997), aff'd, 181 Ill. 2d 552, 230 Ill. Dec. 250, 693 N.E.2d 379 (1998).

—Partition Right Waived
Even though either of the parties to a divorce may have initially had the right to partition premises upon which the marital residence was situated, the right was waived when the parties sought a resolution of their conflicting claims irrespective of any remedy of partition; the court's failure to partition the premises was not in error under former § 18 of the Divorce Act (see now this section). Hulslander v. Hulslander, 55 Ill. App. 3d 981, 13 Ill. Dec. 717, 371 N.E.2d 652 (3 Dist. 1977).

—Possession
Where the court's payment plan left petitioner without a home and under the decree left her without a substantial share of the marital estate for many years, this was error and on remand the court was to revise the marital division and reconsider the disposition of the house; unless respondent was to have the major portion of the physical custody of the children, an award whereby he received the house for an extended period was not likely to be proper unless substantial sums from the marital estate were awarded to petitioner. In re Hacker, 239 Ill. App. 3d 658, 179 Ill. Dec. 816, 606 N.E.2d 648 (4 Dist. 1992), appeal denied, 151 Ill. 2d 563, 186 Ill. Dec. 380, 616 N.E.2d 333 (1993).

Where third party and husband may have acted in collusion to deprive wife and children of marital home and violated the domestic relations court's preliminary injunction, the trial court did not err in granting possession of the marital home to the wife pending the dissolution of marriage. In re Pahlke, 120 Ill. App. 3d 1009, 76 Ill. Dec. 487, 458 N.E.2d 1141 (1 Dist. 1983).

—Presumption
Respondent failed to offer evidence sufficient to rebut the presumption that the marital residence was a gift to the marital estate, and therefore he was not entitled to be reimbursed for his contribution to the marital residence. In re Hacker, 239 Ill. App. 3d 658, 179 Ill. Dec. 816, 606 N.E.2d 648 (4 Dist. 1992), appeal denied, 151 Ill. 2d 563, 186 Ill. Dec. 380, 616 N.E.2d 333 (1993).

In marriage dissolution proceeding, husband failed to overcome presumption that family residence was marital property where the wife never directly refuted husband's contention that he expressed an oral intention that his inheritance, a portion of which was used to pay for the residence, remain non-marital property, but she stated in rebuttal that she and her husband had never agreed that their respective inheritances would remain separate, non-marital property. In re Rogers, 86 Ill. App. 3d 904, 42 Ill. Dec. 70, 408 N.E.2d 448 (2 Dist. 1980), aff'd, 85 Ill. 2d 217, 52 Ill. Dec. 633, 422 N.E.2d 635 (1981).

—Purchase
Where the marital residence was purchased in contemplation of marriage, and all the equity in the home, other than the down payment, was accumulated with marital funds, even though the marital residence was purchased prior to the marriage, it was part of the marital estate and pursuant to subdivision (c)(1) the non-marital funds contributed by respondent to purchase the marital home commingled the properties and transmuted his contribution into marital property. In re Hacker, 239 Ill. App. 3d 658, 179 Ill. Dec. 816, 606 N.E.2d 648 (4 Dist. 1992), appeal denied, 151 Ill. 2d 563, 186 Ill. Dec. 380, 616 N.E.2d 333 (1993).

A home purchased prior to but in contemplation of marriage is treated as a marital asset. In re Leisner, 219 Ill. App. 3d 752, 162 Ill. Dec. 277, 579 N.E.2d 1091 (1 Dist. 1991).

Where the marital home was bought with funds from a joint tenancy checking account, the home was considered marital property. In re Drone, 217 Ill. App. 3d 758, 160 Ill. Dec. 601, 577 N.E.2d 926 (5 Dist. 1991).

Where it was the uncontroverted testimony of plaintiff that all the money used to purchase property came from her personal funds, the wisdom and fairness of the finding and determination that plaintiff had special equities in the marital home which entitled her to receive defendant's interest in the property was readily apparent especially when plaintiff waived all claims for future alimony. Johnston v. Johnston, 130 Ill. App. 2d 1042, 266 N.E.2d 685 (1 Dist. 1971).

—Sale
The trial court did not abuse its discretion in ordering the sale of the marital residence. In re Clabault, 249 Ill. App. 3d 641, 188 Ill. Dec. 799, 619 N.E.2d 163 (2 Dist. 1993), cert. denied, 154 Ill. 2d 558, 197 Ill. Dec. 484, 631 N.E.2d 706 (1994).

It is within the discretion and authority of a trial court to order the sale of the marital home without a prayer for partition where it would be equitable to do so. In re Wade, 158 Ill. App. 3d 255, 110 Ill. Dec. 321, 511 N.E.2d 156 (4 Dist. 1987).

—Taxes and Insurance Premiums
The trial court did not err in dismissing petitioner's request for directions regarding the payment of real estate taxes and insurance premiums on the marital home. In re Legge, 111 Ill. App. 3d 198, 66 Ill. Dec. 926, 443 N.E.2d 1089 (4 Dist. 1982).

—Utilities
Trial court did not err in ordering respondent to reimburse petitioner for utilities supplied to the marital residence following their separation. In re Skahn, 149 Ill. App. 3d 764, 103 Ill. Dec. 208, 501 N.E.2d 229 (1 Dist. 1986).

—Value
Although it is preferable for a trial court to make a specific finding as to the value of the marital residence, such finding is not mandatory. In re Woolsey, 85 Ill. App. 3d 636, 40 Ill. Dec. 775, 406 N.E.2d 1142 (4 Dist. 1980).

Marital Property
Pension benefits earned by a husband while he was married were property acquired during the marriage pursuant to § 503 of the Illinois Marriage and Dissolution of Marriage Act, 750 ILCS 5/503, and were subject to division upon dissolution of the marriage, and the appellate court held that the Employee Retirement Income Security Act of 1974, 29 U.S.C.S. § 1001 et seq., did not prohibit the trial court from issuing a qualified domestic relations order that transferred the value of the husband's pension and retirement accounts to his ex-wife to satisfy support arrearages as long as the assignment was limited to the value of the accounts at the time of the marriage dissolution. In re Marriage of Thomas, 339 Ill. App. 3d 214, 273 Ill. Dec. 647, 789 N.E.2d 821, 2003 Ill. App. LEXIS 568 (2 Dist. 2003).

—In General
This Act directs the court to divide marital property, taking into account certain specified factors, and empowers the court to reimburse a spouse for his or her contribution by imposing a lien on non-marital property. In re Richardson, 75 Bankr. 601 (Bankr. C.D. Ill. 1987).

—Accounts Held in Joint Tenancy
Joint tenancy bank accounts bearing respondent's and his son's name, acquired after the respondent's marriage, were presumed to be marital property instead of separate accounts not reachable by his spouse, and based upon the evidence of the timing and circumstances of respondent's withdrawals, the court properly concluded that these funds were marital property transferred by respondent for no apparent marital purpose. In re Hellwig, 100 Ill. App. 3d 452, 55 Ill. Dec. 762, 426 N.E.2d 1087 (1 Dist. 1981).

—Acquired During Marriage
Farm equipment acquired by the husband during the parties' marriage was marital property, notwithstanding his contention that he acquired such equipment in exchange for old farm equipment that he owned prior to marriage, where he did not testify concerning which specific pieces of equipment were traded in, what equipment he purchased in exchange for the old equipment, or

Marital Property (Cont'd)

—Acquired During Marriage (Cont'd)

what amount he received for trading in his old equipment. In re Henke, 313 Ill. App. 3d 159, 245 Ill. Dec. 780, 728 N.E.2d 1137, 2000 Ill. App. LEXIS 276 (2 Dist. 2000), appeal denied sub nom. Henke v. Henke, 191 Ill. 2d 530, 250 Ill. Dec. 457, 738 N.E.2d 926 (2000).

This Act creates a presumption that all property acquired during the marriage is marital property regardless of the manner in which title is held. In re Hunter, 223 Ill. App. 3d 947, 166 Ill. Dec. 242, 585 N.E.2d 1264 (2 Dist.), appeal denied, 145 Ill. 2d 634, 173 Ill. Dec. 4, 596 N.E.2d 628 (1992).

Where equipment was bought during the marriage and paid for by parties, the items were marital property. In re Dietz, 76 Ill. App. 3d 1029, 32 Ill. Dec. 532, 395 N.E.2d 762 (5 Dist. 1979).

—Acquired in Contemplation of Marriage

Property acquired "in contemplation of marriage," is marital property, even if purchased prior to the marriage. In such cases, to determine whether property was acquired in contemplation of marriage, courts will look to the totality of the circumstances, finding relevant the following factors: the proximity in time between acquisition of the property and the marriage, whether equity in the property was acquired with marital funds, evidence that the parties intended the property to serve as the marital home, whether the parties' names appear on the offer sheet, and the manner in which title is held. In re Olbrecht, 232 Ill. App. 3d 358, 173 Ill. Dec. 661, 597 N.E.2d 635 (1 Dist. 1992).

Property acquired prior to marriage, but in contemplation of marriage, should be classified as marital property. In re Jacks, 200 Ill. App. 3d 112, 146 Ill. Dec. 143, 558 N.E.2d 106 (2 Dist. 1990).

—Annuity

Even though it is of a contingent nature, a survivor's benefit has a determinable value, computed by using life-expectancy tables, and it is properly considered a marital asset. Moore v. Moore, 251 Ill. App. 3d 41, 190 Ill. Dec. 370, 621 N.E.2d 239 (3 Dist. 1993).

—Award Not Proper

In an action brought by administrator of surviving wife against her late husband's brother, in which administrator sought recovery of funds which husband had allegedly given to his brother prior to the time wife filed for marriage dissolution, it was error to award administrator half of the funds in joint savings account and trust account as marital property under this section when a judgment of dissolution was never entered. Chandler v. Chandler, 90 Ill. App. 3d 674, 46 Ill. Dec. 46, 413 N.E.2d 486 (2 Dist. 1980).

—Bank Accounts

Husband failed to adequately establish that credit union funds were acquired before marriage and thus were not subject to distribution as marital property. In re Romashko, 212 Ill. App. 3d 1018, 156 Ill. Dec. 1015, 571 N.E.2d 995 (1 Dist. 1991).

A joint checking account, even if one spouse has furnished all of the consideration for it out of non-marital funds, will be presumed "in fact" as marital property, absent convincing rebutting evidence. In re Emken, 86 Ill. 2d 164, 56 Ill. Dec. 45, 427 N.E.2d 125 (1981).

Where plaintiff was employed during most all of her married life, and where she endorsed each of her paychecks to defendant, since her earnings were traceable into the joint bank accounts of the parties, then an even division of the accounts was equitable. Kijowski v. Kijowski, 36 Ill. App. 2d 94, 183 N.E.2d 583 (1 Dist. 1962).

—Bargain

Where the evidence showed that the husband reimbursed his father for at least part of the interest he acquired in the company from his father during the marriage, and the evidence also indicated that the transaction involved a "bargain" distribution of property that would rarely occur in a transaction among strangers, the trial court correctly held the entirety of the husband's interest in the company marital in nature. Wesselhoft v. Wesselhoft, 228 Ill. App. 3d 269, 169 Ill. Dec. 424, 591 N.E.2d 928 (3 Dist. 1992).

The court concluded that transfer of 235 shares of stock in a closely held corporation was not a gift but was a sale for less than adequate consideration and could be characterized as a "bargain" qualifying it as marital property; the court noted that there was no gift tax return filed and that there was a contract for the sale of stock signed between respondent and his father. In re Walker, 203 Ill. App. 3d 632, 149 Ill. Dec. 112, 561 N.E.2d 390 (4 Dist. 1990).

—Business Assets

Business assets, acquired after the parties' marriage and not shown to be among the non-marital exceptions, were held properly classified by the trial court as marital property. In re Perlmutter, 225 Ill. App. 3d 362, 167 Ill. Dec. 340, 587 N.E.2d 609 (2 Dist.), appeal denied, 146 Ill. 2d 650, 176 Ill. Dec. 820, 602 N.E.2d 474 (1992), cert. denied, 507 U.S. 1006, 113 S. Ct. 1648, 123 L. Ed. 2d 269 (1993).

Machinery which was business property acquired in the course of the marriage was subject to division as part of the marital estate. In re Perino, 224 Ill. App. 3d 605, 167 Ill. Dec. 172, 587 N.E.2d 54 (1992).

—Business Interests

Respondent's business was never used together with marital property to obtain new property; thus, it retained the status of respondent's non-marital property. In re Booth, 255 Ill. App. 3d 707, 194 Ill. Dec. 500, 627 N.E.2d 1142 (4 Dist. 1993).

The business interest of a spouse acquired subsequent to marriage constitutes "marital property" subject to equitable distribution upon dissolution. In re Stone, 155 Ill. App. 3d 62, 107 Ill. Dec. 747, 507 N.E.2d 900 (4 Dist. 1987).

Where the trial court found that the success of two uniform businesses was due to the joint efforts of the parties, its findings would not be disturbed where no other evidence existed except the husband's testimony to overcome the presumption created by the statute. In re Rowe, 130 Ill. App. 3d 689, 85 Ill. Dec. 894, 474 N.E.2d 854 (3 Dist. 1985).

Business interests can be classified as marital property. In re Brown, 110 Ill. App. 3d 782, 66 Ill. Dec. 488, 443 N.E.2d 11 (5 Dist. 1982).

Plaintiff clearly and convincingly established her equitable right to an interest in defendant's assets commensurate with her contributions in business services and funds to the property he acquired during the marriage where the evidence in the record indicated that plaintiff made contributions to the common marital funds totaling $110,800, including her savings, gifts, outside earnings, work for the business, her salary as corporate secretary, her one-half rent from the elevator property and her one-half of the proceeds from a 1972 sale of stock. Leone v. Leone, 39 Ill. App. 3d 547, 350 N.E.2d 545 (3 Dist. 1976).

—Change in Ownership

Spouse correctly asserted that mere change in form of ownership of property should not alter its marital/non-marital character, but the uncontroverted facts suggested that when proprietorship assets were incorporated, the assets were marital in character because of commingling; it followed that the resulting interest of spouse in company was marital in character and subject to equitable apportionment by the circuit court. In re Westphal, 99 Ill. App. 3d 1042, 55 Ill. Dec. 328, 426 N.E.2d 303 (3 Dist. 1981).

—Co-ownership

Claims asserted under subdivision (a)(1) of this section are subject to the general presumption in subsection (b) that all property acquired by either spouse during the marriage shall be marital property, including property transferred into some form of co-ownership between the spouses. McCoy v McCoy, 225 Ill. App. 3d 966, 168 Ill. Dec. 27, 589 N.E.2d 141 (3 Dist. 1992).

—Contribution

If non-marital property is transmuted into marital property, the party contributing the non-marital property is entitled to reimbursement of the value of such property provided: (1) the contribution is traceable by clear and convincing evidence; and (2) the contributor did not make a gift of the non-marital property to the marital estate. In re Guntren, 141 Ill. App. 3d 1, 95 Ill. Dec. 392, 489 N.E.2d 1120 (4 Dist. 1986).

Where petitioner claimed to have contributed rent money and prior savings to the marriage, the court did not err in awarding $18,000 to petitioner before the proceeds from the sale of the house were to be equally divided. In re Gustke, 78 Ill. App. 3d 274, 33 Ill. Dec. 813, 397 N.E.2d 146 (1 Dist. 1979).

Marital Property (Cont'd)

—Credit Union Savings Account

Where a credit union savings account was in respondent's name, the court properly considered it to be among marital property awarded to respondent. In re Pickell, 76 Ill. App. 3d 855, 32 Ill. Dec. 443, 395 N.E.2d 673 (5 Dist. 1979).

—Crops

Crops grown on non-marital property can be considered in determining marital income and marital property. In re Mohr, 260 Ill. App. 3d 98, 197 Ill. Dec. 563, 631 N.E.2d 785 (4 Dist. 1994).

The trial court could consider that growing crops may have a value when determining marital property division. In re Mohr, 260 Ill. App. 3d 98, 197 Ill. Dec. 563, 631 N.E.2d 785 (4 Dist. 1994).

—Damage

Where property damaged was purchased during defendant's marriage with marital funds, and where defendant signed the bill of sale, and paid for the muffler system and a portion of the fire repair bill, the car was marital property in which the defendant had an interest. People v. Jones, 145 Ill. App. 3d 835, 99 Ill. Dec. 636, 495 N.E.2d 1371 (3 Dist. 1986).

—Determination

This section sets forth a procedure in which the court is to determine what property is marital property, as defined, and then divide the marital property in just proportions considering all relevant factors, including the contribution or dissipation of each party in the acquisition, preservation, or depreciation or appreciation in value of the property. In re Nicks, 80 Ill. App. 3d 838, 36 Ill. Dec. 11, 400 N.E.2d 431 (5 Dist. 1979).

—Disability Pension

Husband's disability pension constituted marital property. In re Smith, 84 Ill. App. 3d 446, 39 Ill. Dec. 905, 405 N.E.2d 884 (3 Dist. 1980).

—Division

In a dissolution proceeding, the trial court divides marital property considering all relevant factors and an abuse of discretion occurs only where no reasonable person would adopt the trial court's decision. In re Ward, 267 Ill. App. 3d 35, 204 Ill. Dec. 449, 641 N.E.2d 879 (2 Dist. 1994), appeal denied, 161 Ill. 2d 542, 208 Ill. Dec. 370, 649 N.E.2d 426 (1995).

Marital property will be distributed pursuant to subsection (b) of this section so as to avoid the impairment of any contractual obligations owed to third parties who are not parties to the dissolution proceedings. Schweihs v. Schweihs, 222 Ill. App. 3d 887, 165 Ill. Dec. 293, 584 N.E.2d 472 (1 Dist. 1991).

This Act does not require that the marital property be divided into equal shares. In re Frazier, 164 Ill. App. 3d 207, 115 Ill. Dec. 364, 517 N.E.2d 775 (5 Dist. 1988).

Based upon subsection (c) of this section, the trial court's division of marital property was not so unreasonable as to constitute an abuse of the court's discretion. In re Burrows, 126 Ill. App. 3d 752, 81 Ill. Dec. 865, 467 N.E.2d 987 (1 Dist. 1984).

Evidence was sufficient regarding the distribution of marital property. In re Clearman, 97 Ill. App. 3d 641, 53 Ill. Dec. 91, 423 N.E.2d 283 (3 Dist. 1981).

In a divorce proceeding where the trial court divided the real and personal property of the parties essentially along the lines of what each had owned prior to the marriage and what each had purchased since, such division of property was correct. Norris v. Norris, 16 Ill. App. 3d 879, 307 N.E.2d 181 (5 Dist. 1974).

—Effect of Amendment

A legislative change in the law during the pendency of multiple appeals has the same effect as a contrary law announced by the Supreme Court; the determination of a question on a former appeal is not the law of the case when a higher court during the interval between appeals has announced a contrary law. Therefore, issues concerning whether disputed property was marital property, on appeal at the time of amendment of this section, were to be re-evaluated in light of the 1983 amendment to this section. Hofmann v. Hofmann, 125 Ill. App. 3d 548, 81 Ill. Dec. 12, 466 N.E.2d 598 (3 Dist. 1984).

—Effect of Decree

After a decree is rendered, the rights of the parties rest upon the decree and not upon their prior agreement. Jacobs v. Jacobs, 328 Ill. App. 133, 65 N.E.2d 588 (1 Dist. 1946).

—Equitable Distribution

Where the major asset of the marital estate, the marital residence, was awarded to husband as custodial parent, wife received the majority of the money in the bank accounts, and the retirement accounts, the insurance policies and the personal property were divided almost equally, the vehicles were divided by agreement and husband was required to pay almost $60,000 of marital debt, which included wife's attorney fees, the trial court did not abuse its discretion in dividing the marital assets. In re Phillips, 244 Ill. App. 3d 577, 186 Ill. Dec. 108, 615 N.E.2d 1165 (4 Dist. 1993).

An equitable division of marital property is not necessarily an equal one. In re Borg, 96 Ill. App. 3d 282, 51 Ill. Dec. 706, 421 N.E.2d 214 (1 Dist. 1981).

The rights or interests that one spouse has in the property of the other by virtue of the marriage relation alone will not justify a conveyance of an undivided one half interest but it must be alleged and proved by the spouse seeking a part or all of the property in the name of the other that he or she has furnished valuable consideration such as money or services other than those normally performed in the marriage relation which has directly or indirectly been used to acquire or enhance the value of the property; thus, the signing of the mortgage, plaintiff's residence in the home, and the birth of the children there did not give her an equity in the property. Everett v. Everett, 25 Ill. 2d 342, 185 N.E.2d 201 (1962).

—Expended During Marriage

While settlement proceeds from an insurance company following a burglary received by a spouse were in fact marital assets, where such proceeds were expended by the spouse on living expenses, they no longer existed as a marital asset and thus could not be apportioned as marital property under this section. In re Bauer, 138 Ill. App. 3d 379, 93 Ill. Dec. 108, 485 N.E.2d 1318 (1 Dist. 1985).

—Financial Contributions

Former section 18 of the Divorce Act (see now this section and 750 ILCS 5/502) vested the trial court with authority to award interest in the marital property to a spouse where she alleged and proved special equities by way of her financial contributions beyond her marital duties. Brongel v. Brongel, 48 Ill. App. 3d 27, 6 Ill. Dec. 115, 362 N.E.2d 750 (2 Dist. 1977).

—Future Book Royalties

Where petitioner received substantial book royalties from books written during the marriage, the prospect of future book royalties was neither unproven or speculative; future book royalties should have been classified as marital property and allocated between the parties. In re Heinze, 257 Ill. App. 3d 782, 197 Ill. Dec. 506, 631 N.E.2d 728 (3 Dist. 1994).

—Future Income

Although a jointly owned fruit orchard was properly valued as of the date of dissolution, the orchard and the income derived from it continued to be marital property until the court awarded the property to the petitioner as his separate property. In re Hawkins, 160 Ill. App. 3d 71, 111 Ill. Dec. 897, 513 N.E.2d 143 (5 Dist. 1987).

Considering the relevant factors listed in subsection (c) of this section, the division of marital assets and liabilities was not an abuse of discretion; however, to maintain equity the award was modified in the event of a sale of the property. In re Weinberg, 125 Ill. App. 3d 904, 81 Ill. Dec. 123, 466 N.E.2d 925 (1 Dist. 1984).

—Gift

In evaluating an attorney's proof of claim against a Chapter 11 debtor related to the attorney's representation of the debtor during a divorce proceeding, the bankruptcy court did not clearly err in excluding gifts to the debtor's children under 750 ILCS 5/503(b)(5) in determining the couple's marital estates, where the attorney testified that the source of the funds in the couple's marital account was a gift from the husband's grandfather. Mungo v. Taylor (In re Mungo), F. Supp. 2d , 2003 U.S. Dist. LEXIS 3413 (N.D. Ill. Mar. 6, 2003).

There is a presumption all property acquired during the marriage is marital property; however, the presumption may be rebut-

Marital Property (Cont'd)

—Gift (Cont'd)

ted by showing it was a gift. In re Yong Sun Lee, 246 Ill. App. 3d 628, 186 Ill. Dec. 257, 615 N.E.2d 1314 (4 Dist.), cert. denied, 153 Ill. 2d 560, 191 Ill. Dec. 620, 624 N.E.2d 808 (1993).

The court's conclusion that silver was non-marital property of the wife was against the manifest weight of the evidence where the husband testified that the silver was a gift to the family and the wife did not rebut that contention nor did she claim at trial that the property was non-marital. In re Smith, 100 Ill. App. 3d 1126, 56 Ill. Dec. 716, 427 N.E.2d 1262 (2 Dist. 1981).

Oil producing property was not marital property where there was no evidence of any intent on the part of petitioner to make a gift of any part of his property to respondent. In re Cihak, 92 Ill. App. 3d 1123, 48 Ill. Dec. 428, 416 N.E.2d 701 (4 Dist. 1981).

—Income

Although property acquired before marriage is non-marital and its increase in value is likewise non-marital, any income derived from such property during marriage is deemed marital; the legislature intended this to apply to premarital accounts drawing interest during marriage. In re Reed, 100 Ill. App. 3d 873, 56 Ill. Dec. 202, 427 N.E.2d 282 (5 Dist. 1981).

Husband's income during marriage is not considered non-marital property. In re Fleming, 80 Ill. App. 3d 1006, 36 Ill. Dec. 205, 400 N.E.2d 625 (2 Dist. 1980).

—Income Tax Refund

Federal income tax refund, based upon income earned during the time parties were married, and all property, including income, acquired by either spouse after marriage was marital property, irrespective of how title was held. In re Ormiston, 168 Ill. App. 3d 1016, 119 Ill. Dec. 680, 523 N.E.2d 148 (1 Dist. 1988).

—Increased Value

If the increase in the value of a pension and an IRA (profit sharing account) resulted from a contribution of the marital estate, then the marital estate was entitled to reimbursement; moreover, if that contribution from the marital estate was in the form of the personal effort of petitioner, the marital estate would still be entitled to reimbursement if that personal effort was significant and resulted in substantial appreciation of the pension and IRA (profit sharing account). In re Di Angelo, 159 Ill. App. 3d 293, 111 Ill. Dec. 394, 512 N.E.2d 783 (2 Dist. 1987).

—Individual Retirement Accounts

A consent of spouse to the designation of the beneficiary of an individual retirement account (IRA), which waived rights to the IRA under community property laws, did not operate to exclude the IRA from designation as marital property. Gurda v. Gurda, 304 Ill. App. 3d 1019, 238 Ill. Dec. 236, 711 N.E.2d 339 (1 Dist. 1999), appeal denied, 185 Ill. 2d 624, 242 Ill. Dec. 137, 720 N.E.2d 1092 (1999).

—Inflation

Farm was marital property from the beginning; just as inflation cannot create marital property where none existed before, neither can it spontaneously generate non-marital property from property which was marital when acquired. Hofmann v. Hofmann, 94 Ill. 2d 205, 68 Ill. Dec. 593, 446 N.E.2d 499 (1983).

—Insurance

Health and life insurance benefits which were a right to current payments by reason of current employment were not "property" within the contemplation of this section. In re Fairchild, 110 Ill. App. 3d 470, 66 Ill. Dec. 131, 442 N.E.2d 557 (3 Dist. 1982).

Insurance which provided husband with a series of monthly payments to compensate him for the loss of his pilot's license was marital property. In re Smith, 84 Ill. App. 3d 446, 39 Ill. Dec. 905, 405 N.E.2d 884 (3 Dist. 1980).

—Investment Accounts

An investment account was properly classified as marital property, notwithstanding that the husband's nonmarital assets funded most of the account, where he made no effort to segregate his funds or limit the wife's access to them and the parties used the account to fund their joint checking account. In re Gattone, 317 Ill. App. 3d 346, 251 Ill. Dec. 65, 739 N.E.2d 998, 2000 Ill. App. LEXIS 900 (2 Dist. 2000).

—IRA Account

The money in the wife's IRA account on the date she married was non-marital property, as well as any increase in value attributable to that amount. In re Raad, 301 Ill. App. 3d 683, 235 Ill. Dec. 391, 704 N.E.2d 964 (2 Dist. 1998), cert. denied, 526 U.S. 1051, 119 S. Ct. 1358, 143 L. Ed. 2d 519 (1999).

—Joint Business Ownership

The trial court did not err in its judgment that the parties' business was marital property where, except for the litigation, the manifest weight of the evidence showed that the parties gave no particular thought to a division of ownership in the business at the time it was formed and the parties intended to own it as a marital asset. In re Hagshenas, 234 Ill. App. 3d 178, 175 Ill. Dec. 506, 600 N.E.2d 437 (2 Dist. 1992), appeal denied, 148 Ill.2d 642, 183 Ill. Dec. 19, 610 N.E.2d 1263 (1993).

—Joint Tenancy

Where property is taken in joint tenancy by a husband and wife, that property is marital property even where the purchase money is supplied by one spouse, unless the presumption that a gift was intended is overcome. In re Wingader, 95 Ill. App. 3d 9, 50 Ill. Dec. 503, 419 N.E.2d 611 (1 Dist. 1981).

—Line of Credit

A line of credit is not recognized as a marital asset. In re Phillips, 229 Ill. App. 3d 809, 171 Ill. Dec. 501, 594 N.E.2d 353 (2 Dist. 1992).

—Loans

The trial court erred in failing to classify a loan made by respondent to a non-marital asset as marital property where respondent held a ⅓ interest in the non-marital asset, a balance sheet listing its assets and liabilities showed a note payable to respondent in the amount of $6,200, respondent admitted loaning the money to it, but he stated that another person paid almost all of it for him and he owed the money to that person, respondent later admitted making payments of $800 and $350, and petitioner identified three withdrawals made from the parties' joint savings account as funds given to the non-marital asset. In re Miller, 231 Ill. App. 3d 480, 172 Ill. Dec. 679, 595 N.E.2d 1349 (3 Dist. 1992).

The evidence did not support the conclusion that loans to the respondent were income; accordingly, the distribution of marital property was against the manifest weight of the evidence. In re Smith, 132 Ill. App. 3d 694, 88 Ill. Dec. 909, 479 N.E.2d 929 (1 Dist. 1985).

—Lottery Winnings

Lottery proceeds acquired during marriage are marital property. In re Palacios, 275 Ill. App. 3d 561, 211 Ill. Dec. 915, 656 N.E.2d 107 (1 Dist. 1995), appeal denied, 165 Ill. 2d 554, 214 Ill. Dec. 861, 662 N.E.2d 427 (1996).

Since it was uncontroverted that the money for the lottery ticket came from petitioner at a time when he was still married and the irrevocable right to receive the lottery payments was established during the marriage, the winnings were presumed to be marital property; the fact that the payments were made solely in petitioner's name and that the majority of the lottery payments would not be received until after entry of the judgment of dissolution of marriage did not change the fact that the winnings were marital property. In re Morris, 266 Ill. App. 3d 277, 203 Ill. Dec. 685, 640 N.E.2d 344 (2 Dist. 1994).

Where lottery jackpot, including the right to future payments, was acquired during the marriage through the efforts of one spouse who wagered marital funds, the jackpot would be treated as marital property, especially where the parties themselves treated the jackpot as marital property, depositing the installments in the parties' joint marital accounts and then using the funds to acquire items some of which were placed in their joint names, or to jointly open accounts. In re Mahaffey, 206 Ill. App. 3d 859, 151 Ill. Dec. 638, 564 N.E.2d 1300 (1 Dist. 1990).

Where the money used to purchase a winning lottery ticket came from either petitioner's or respondent's earnings, the purchase of the ticket occurred during their marriage, and the irrevocable right to receive the lottery payments was established during the marriage, the winnings would be presumed to be marital property. In re

Marital Property (Cont'd)

—Lottery Winnings (Cont'd)
Mahaffey, 206 Ill. App. 3d 859, 151 Ill. Dec. 638, 564 N.E.2d 1300 (1 Dist. 1990).

—Marital Credit
Property bought with money raised substantially on marital credit was marital property. In re Kennedy, 94 Ill. App. 3d 537, 49 Ill. Dec. 927, 418 N.E.2d 947 (1 Dist. 1981).

—Marital Misconduct Disregarded
The court must divide the marital property in just proportions without regard to marital misconduct. In re Parker, 252 Ill. App. 3d 1015, 192 Ill. Dec. 277, 625 N.E.2d 237 (1 Dist. 1993).

—Materiality
Absent any evidence of value, a court has no way of determining whether assets are substantial enough to be relevant. In re Wilder, 122 Ill. App. 3d 338, 77 Ill. Dec. 824, 461 N.E.2d 447 (1 Dist. 1983).

—Military Pension
The court abused its discretion in dividing military pension by failing to comply with § 401(b) of the Marriage Act (750 ILCS 5/401(b)) to preserve jurisdiction for the distribution of military pension benefits. In re Burkhart, 267 Ill. App. 3d 761, 205 Ill. Dec. 317, 643 N.E.2d 268 (2 Dist. 1994).

Military pensions may be treated as marital property under Illinois law and are subject to the division provisions of this section. In re Brown, 225 Ill. App. 3d 733, 167 Ill. Dec. 379, 587 N.E.2d 648 (4 Dist. 1992).

Even had the husband's military pension not been considered marital property and subject to apportionment, it would certainly have been considered as a relevant factor in a "fair and equitable" division of marital property. In re Lipkin, 163 Ill. App. 3d 1033, 115 Ill. Dec. 76, 517 N.E.2d 41 (4 Dist. 1987).

A marital property interest may be recognized in retirement benefits from a military pension. In re Dooley, 137 Ill. App. 3d 401, 92 Ill. Dec. 163, 484 N.E.2d 894 (2 Dist. 1985).

Where no evidence was presented in trial of the present value of the husband's military retirement pension, and the accommodation made with maintenance awarded to the wife to balance the award of all the retirement pay to the husband was difficult to evaluate, the matter was not fully presented to the trial court and the judgment distributing the marital property of the parties and awarding maintenance in the amount and for the term ordered had to be reconsidered by the trial court. In re Dooley, 137 Ill. App. 3d 401, 92 Ill. Dec. 163, 484 N.E.2d 894 (2 Dist. 1985).

Military retirement pension is "marital property" under this Act. Musser v. Musser, 70 Ill. App. 3d 706, 27 Ill. Dec. 240, 388 N.E.2d 1289 (4 Dist. 1979).

—Money From Parent
The trial court did not abuse its discretion by disregarding money transfers between respondent's mother and respondent when it divided the parties' marital estate, because the evidence supported the court's conclusion that these transfers were not loans. In re Blazis, 261 Ill. App. 3d 855, 199 Ill. Dec. 941, 634 N.E.2d 1295 (4 Dist. 1994).

—Mutual Agreement
Where property was acquired with a down payment of partially non-marital funds, the property was considered a marital asset. In re Malters, 133 Ill. App. 3d 168, 88 Ill. Dec. 460, 478 N.E.2d 1068 (1 Dist. 1985).

Where husband and wife entered a mutual agreement adjusting their marital property rights, no evidence was necessary to show that the order was fair and equitable, as the question of fairness was determined by the parties themselves. Guyton v. Guyton, 17 Ill. 2d 439, 161 N.E.2d 832 (1959).

—Not Shown
Respondent's own testimony corroborated that of petitioner and supported the trial court's conclusion that, except for the payment made from the parties' joint checking account, the property was non-marital property owned by petitioner. In re Uehlein, 265 Ill. App. 3d 1080, 202 Ill. Dec. 838, 638 N.E.2d 706 (1 Dist. 1994).

Although the evidence established that petitioner had held an ownership interest in a parcel of real property located in Germany, there was no evidence that this property should have been included as a marital asset in the court's decree. In re Uehlein, 265 Ill. App. 3d 1080, 202 Ill. Dec. 838, 638 N.E.2d 706 (1 Dist. 1994).

All property acquired by either spouse after the marriage, including non-marital property transferred into some form of co-ownership between the spouses, is presumed to be marital property, regardless of title; however, this presumption was rebutted where the designation of ownership on tax returns in and of itself was too ambiguous to establish that a spouse intended to convey a gift to the marriage, wife was to receive 20 shares of stock on the advice of the parties' accountant to keep the business in operation should husband die but wife never received 20 shares of stock, and more importantly, husband never intended to give her any stock; thus, under such circumstances, a company was not marital property. In re Thacker, 185 Ill. App. 3d 465, 133 Ill. Dec. 573, 541 N.E.2d 784 (5 Dist. 1989).

The wife in a dissolution proceeding failed to sustain her burden of establishing that the parties' residence, purchased before the marriage and held only in the husband's name, was purchased in contemplation of the parties' future marriage. In re Resser, 97 Ill. App. 3d 838, 53 Ill. Dec. 632, 424 N.E.2d 45 (4 Dist. 1981).

Finding of the chancellor that plaintiff had no equity or any special interest in the property of defendant was not contrary to the manifest weight of the evidence. Persico v. Persico, 409 Ill. 608, 100 N.E.2d 904 (1951).

—Operation of Property
The fact that only one spouse operated most of the disputed property was not dispositive; the statute is clear on its face that so long as it was acquired during the marriage and did not fall within the enumerated exceptions, it was marital property. In re Dietz, 76 Ill. App. 3d 1029, 32 Ill. Dec. 532, 395 N.E.2d 762 (5 Dist. 1979).

—Partnership Interest
The trial court abused its discretion in equitably dividing marital assets where it neglected to consider husband's partnership interest as a valuable marital asset, failed to consider assets used to retire business debts as dissipated assets, and allowed the husband to deduct amounts used to repay marital debts from his personal income for purposes of calculating his child support obligation. In re Hart, 194 Ill. App. 3d 839, 141 Ill. Dec. 550, 551 N.E.2d 737 (4 Dist. 1990).

—Pensions
When an early retirement incentive enhances pension benefits, to the extent that such enhancements are derivative of the right to receive the pension as deferred compensation, the proportion of the enhancement that is marital property is exactly the same as the proportion of the pension as a whole that is marital; in the unusual case where the entitlement to such enhancements is not purely derivative, however, that portion of the enhancement not derived from the right to receive the pension itself is the pensioner's sole property. Because early retirement incentives come in a multitude of forms, the decision concerning the most equitable method of apportionment in the circumstances present in a case may not be the most equitable or logical method in all cases where this problem arises; therefore, trial courts must not always apportion partially derivative pension enhancements through requiring reimbursements. In re Marriage of Ramsey, 339 Ill. App. 3d 752, 275 Ill. Dec. 106, 792 N.E.2d 337, 2003 Ill. App. LEXIS 725 (5 Dist. 2003).

Marital property includes pensions that accrue during a marriage. Brackett v. Brackett, 309 Ill. App. 3d 329, 242 Ill. Dec. 798, 722 N.E.2d 287 (2 Dist. 1999).

—Personal Injury Settlement
Trial court's inclusion of husband's personal injury settlement as part of marital estate was proper. In re Pace, 278 Ill. App. 3d 932, 215 Ill. Dec. 923, 664 N.E.2d 320 (1 Dist. 1996), appeal denied, 169 Ill. 2d 570, 221 Ill. Dec. 439, 675 N.E.2d 634 (1996).

There was no abuse of discretion in the award to wife of $220,000 of $1.8 million personal injury settlement received by husband for injuries which resulted in total paralysis from the chest down; as a spouse she did suffer but husband would live with the paralysis for the remainder of his life while she leaves the marriage the same way she entered it: an employed, healthy, able-bodied person. In re

Marital Property (Cont'd)

—Personal Injury Settlement (Cont'd)

Murphy, 259 Ill. App. 3d 336, 197 Ill. Dec. 671, 631 N.E.2d 893 (4 Dist.), appeal denied, 157 Ill. 2d 505, 205 Ill. Dec. 168, 642 N.E.2d 1285 (1994).

Where petitioner accrued cause of action for personal injuries after filing his petition for dissolution of marriage but prior to the final order dividing the marital property, the trial court properly classified the proceeds of the cause of action as marital property. In re Burt, 144 Ill. App. 3d 177, 98 Ill. Dec. 746, 494 N.E.2d 868 (4 Dist. 1986).

Damages incurred for pain and suffering arising from a cause of action which accrued during the marriage are marital property and the court should consider the division of the damages under subsection (d) of this section, which allows the court to consider the disability of an injured spouse and, if appropriate, award a larger portion of the marital property to the injured spouse. In re Burt, 144 Ill. App. 3d 177, 98 Ill. Dec. 746, 494 N.E.2d 868 (4 Dist. 1986).

The entirety of a cause of action for personal injuries, including potential damages for pain, suffering and disability, is marital property. In re Burt, 144 Ill. App. 3d 177, 98 Ill. Dec. 746, 494 N.E.2d 868 (4 Dist. 1986).

Since a personal injury settlement does not fit within any of the exceptions to marital property enumerated in this Act, the presumption that a personal injury settlement was marital property as provided in subsection (b) of this section applied, and the settlement proceeds were properly deemed marital property. In re Gan, 83 Ill. App. 3d 265, 38 Ill. Dec. 882, 404 N.E.2d 306 (5 Dist. 1980).

The proceeds of a personal injury settlement, properly declared to be marital property, were subject to disposition along with other marital property, pursuant to the provisions of subdivisions (c) and (d) of this section. In re Gan, 83 Ill. App. 3d 265, 38 Ill. Dec. 882, 404 N.E.2d 306 (5 Dist. 1980).

—Presumption

The presumption of marital property can be overcome only by clear, convincing, and unmistakable evidence. In re Weiler, 258 Ill. App. 3d 454, 196 Ill. Dec. 372, 629 N.E.2d 1216 (5 Dist. 1994).

All property acquired by either spouse during the marriage is presumed to be marital property, including property transferred into some form of co-ownership between the spouses. McCoy v McCoy, 225 Ill. App. 3d 966, 168 Ill. Dec. 27, 589 N.E.2d 141 (3 Dist. 1992).

As a general rule, under this section all property acquired by either spouse after the marriage, but prior to a judgment of dissolution, is presumed to be marital property. Kew v. Kew, 198 Ill. App. 3d 61, 144 Ill. Dec. 372, 555 N.E.2d 731 (3 Dist. 1990).

Once non-marital property is transferred to a husband and wife in joint tenancy, a presumption of transmutation and of gift to the marital estate arises. In re Durante, 201 Ill. App. 3d 376, 147 Ill. Dec. 56, 559 N.E.2d 56 (1 Dist. 1990).

The party asserting the existence of an agreement to exclude certain property from marital property pool has the burden of proving its existence by clear and convincing evidence. In re Harris, 178 Ill. App. 3d 282, 127 Ill. Dec. 489, 533 N.E.2d 107 (1 Dist. 1988).

In Illinois, all property acquired during the marriage is presumed marital unless excepted by statute; the burden is on the party seeking to rebut this presumption to prove by clear evidence that the property is statutorily excepted. In re Brooks, 138 Ill. App. 3d 252, 93 Ill. Dec. 166, 486 N.E.2d 267 (1 Dist. 1985).

Where evidence essentially raised two separate presumptions with respect to the marital residence, including first the fact that the residence was acquired after the marriage raised a presumption of marital property, and, secondly, the fact that the property was taken in joint tenancy, presumption of a gift to the marital estate was raised and was not overcome. In re Nagel, 133 Ill. App. 3d 498, 88 Ill. Dec. 584, 478 N.E.2d 1192 (4 Dist. 1985).

Presumption of marital property applied to farm that husband acquired from his parents where wife's uncontradicted testimony was that she worked to support the family during the years during which husband owned and attempted to make payments on farm. Hofmann v. Hofmann, 94 Ill. 2d 205, 68 Ill. Dec. 593, 446 N.E.2d 499 (1983).

A party claiming that property is non-marital by virtue of this section has the burden of proof to establish that it is non-marital. In re Scott, 85 Ill. App. 3d 773, 41 Ill. Dec. 547, 407 N.E.2d 1045 (2 Dist. 1980).

—Proper Designation

Respondent's contention that court failed to designate which property was marital or non-marital was not supported by the record where the court specifically found utility stock purchased from a gift from petitioner's parents was non-marital property, and where it also found the bank account solely in petitioner's name to be marital property, and where all other property was held either in joint tenancy or was acquired during the marriage and was presumed to be marital property pursuant to subsection (b) of this section. In re Hyland, 95 Ill. App. 3d 31, 50 Ill. Dec. 554, 419 N.E.2d 662 (2 Dist. 1981).

—Property Settlement Agreement

Where a divorce decree incorporated the property settlement agreement, which the parties had created of their own volition, and each of them had been entitled to its enforcement at all times since the entry of the decree, the property settlement agreement defined the nature and extent of the rights and liabilities of the parties with respect to the marital real estate, and the trial court was required to direct performance of those obligations under the decree so as to fully execute its terms. Coleman v. Coleman, 77 Ill. App. 3d 397, 32 Ill. Dec. 828, 395 N.E.2d 1209 (2 Dist. 1979).

—Reasonable Division

A reviewing court will find an abuse of discretion in the division of marital property only where no reasonable person would have so allocated the property. In re Frazier, 164 Ill. App. 3d 207, 115 Ill. Dec. 364, 517 N.E.2d 775 (5 Dist. 1988).

—Rebuttal of Presumption

The rebuttable presumption that all property acquired by either spouse after marriage and before dissolution is marital property regardless of how title is held is rebutted by a showing that the property was acquired by a method listed in subsection (a) of this section. In re Hagshenas, 234 Ill. App. 3d 178, 175 Ill. Dec. 506, 600 N.E.2d 437 (2 Dist. 1992), appeal denied, 148 Ill.2d 642, 183 Ill. Dec. 19, 610 N.E.2d 1263 (1993).

The presumption of marital property can be overcome only by clear, convincing, and unmistakable evidence, and mere proof that title to a tract was placed in one party's name does not rebut the presumption created by this section; there must be a donative intent to pass title and relinquish all present and future dominion over the property. In re Davis, 215 Ill. App. 3d 763, 159 Ill. Dec. 375, 576 N.E.2d 44 (1 Dist.), appeal denied, 141 Ill. 2d 538, 162 Ill. Dec. 484, 580 N.E.2d 110 (1991).

This section creates a rebuttable presumption that property acquired after the marriage is marital; the party seeking the benefit of an exception, including the exception of property acquired by gift, bears the burden of proof. In re Landfield, 209 Ill. App. 3d 678, 153 Ill. Dec. 834, 567 N.E.2d 1061 (1 Dist.), cert. denied, 139 Ill. 2d 597, 159 Ill. Dec. 109, 575 N.E.2d 916 (1991).

This section creates a presumption that property acquired after marriage and before a judgment of dissolution, including non-marital property transferred into a form of co-ownership, is marital property; however, that presumption is rebutted where it is shown that the property was acquired before the marriage. In re Philips, 200 Ill. App. 3d 395, 146 Ill. Dec. 191, 558 N.E.2d 154 (1 Dist. 1990).

The marital property presumption can be rebutted only by clear and convincing evidence. In re Durante, 201 Ill. App. 3d 376, 147 Ill. Dec. 56, 559 N.E.2d 56 (1 Dist. 1990); In re Landfield, 209 Ill. App. 3d 678, 153 Ill. Dec. 834, 567 N.E.2d 1061 (1 Dist.), cert. denied, 139 Ill. 2d 597, 159 Ill. Dec. 109, 575 N.E.2d 916 (1991).

Where the evidence showed part of the purchase price of property came from petitioner's employee savings plan, which accumulated prior to the marriage, and the proceeds of the sale of other property which petitioner owned prior to the marriage, unless some intervening act occurred, the property at issue was acquired in exchange for property acquired before marriage, and the statutory presumption was overcome. In re Cecil, 202 Ill. App. 3d 783, 148 Ill. Dec. 72, 560 N.E.2d 374 (3 Dist. 1990).

Factors to be considered in determining whether a party has rebutted the presumption of gift under such circumstances include the size of the gift relative to the entire estate, when the property was purchased, and who paid the purchase price, made improve-

Marital Property (Cont'd)

—Rebuttal of Presumption (Cont'd)
ments, paid the taxes, and exercised control and management over the property. In re Thacker, 185 Ill. App. 3d 465, 133 Ill. Dec. 573, 541 N.E.2d 784 (5 Dist. 1989).

This Act creates a rebuttable presumption that all property acquired after marriage is "marital property." In re Stone, 155 Ill. App. 3d 62, 107 Ill. Dec. 747, 507 N.E.2d 900 (4 Dist. 1987).

Respondent failed to rebut presumption that respondent's interest in the real property was marital property. In re Moody, 119 Ill. App. 3d 1043, 75 Ill. Dec. 581, 457 N.E.2d 1023 (1 Dist. 1983).

Wife's refusal to place the house in joint tenancy with her husband, her insistence that the house belonged to her parents, and the continuation of the title to her beneficial interest in her name completely rebutted any presumption that she intended to make a gift of the house or her interest in it to the marital estate. In re Olson, 96 Ill. 2d 432, 71 Ill. Dec. 671, 451 N.E.2d 825 (1983).

The presumption of marital property was rebutted where petitioner purchased his new residence with his own non-marital funds. Naguit v. Scrivner, 104 Ill. App. 3d 709, 60 Ill. Dec. 499, 433 N.E.2d 296 (5 Dist. 1982).

This section defines marital property as all property acquired by either spouse subsequent to the marriage, but the marital property presumption can be overcome by showing that the source of the property was an exclusion set forth in this section. In re Cleveland, 99 Ill. App. 3d 293, 54 Ill. Dec. 610, 425 N.E.2d 475 (1 Dist. 1981); In re Cuisance, 115 Ill. App. 3d 551, 71 Ill. Dec. 423, 450 N.E.2d 1302 (1 Dist. 1983); In re Tatham, 173 Ill. App. 3d 1072, 123 Ill. Dec. 576, 527 N.E.2d 1351 (5 Dist. 1988).

—Stock Bonus
Husband's stock bonus was similar to nonvested pension benefits and nonvested stock option, and, therefore, was considered marital property subject to reserved-jurisdiction distribution upon dissolution of marriage. Peters v. Peters, 326 Ill. App. 3d 364, 260 Ill. Dec. 169, 760 N.E.2d 586, 2001 Ill. App. LEXIS 1473 (2 Dist. 2001).

Non-Marital Funds

—Not Shown
The trial court's classification of various accounts as the wife's nonmarital property was against the manifest weight of the evidence since balance statements provided the trial court with a recent balance for each of the accounts but clearly failed to satisfy the tracing requirement of affirmatively identifying the source of the funds. In re Didier, 318 Ill. App. 3d 253, 252 Ill. Dec. 270, 742 N.E.2d 808, 2000 Ill. App. LEXIS 988 (1 Dist. 2000).

Non-Marital Property

—IRA Account
The money the wife contributed to her IRA account during the fifteen months she was married was marital property, as well as any increase in value attributable to that amount. In re Raad, 301 Ill. App. 3d 683, 235 Ill. Dec. 391, 704 N.E.2d 964 (2 Dist. 1998), cert. denied, 526 U.S. 1051, 119 S. Ct. 1358, 143 L. Ed. 2d 519 (1999).

—Shown
Debtor's argument that his current wife, who was not in title to the residential real property owned by debtor, had contributed funds for the benefit of the real property, did not create an interest in the real property such that the wife could claim a homestead exemption in the property; instead, any contribution was transmuted to non-marital property. In re Carver, Bankr. , 2003 Bankr. LEXIS 70 (Bankr. S.D. Ill. Jan. 24, 2003).

A life insurance policy purchased by the husband prior to the parties' marriage was non-marital property, and marital funds contributed to the life insurance policy when used to pay policy premiums were transmuted into nonmarital property, subject to reimbursement to the marital estate. In re Henke, 313 Ill. App. 3d 159, 245 Ill. Dec. 780, 728 N.E.2d 1137, 2000 Ill. App. LEXIS 276 (2 Dist. 2000), appeal denied sub nom. Henke v. Henke, 191 Ill. 2d 530, 250 Ill. Dec. 457, 738 N.E.2d 926 (2000).

The court did not abuse its discretion in finding that the stocks given to the wife by her father were a gift and therefore nonmarital property; the father filed a gift tax return and the fact that the stock was not given to other siblings who were not employees of family company did not rebut the presumption that stock was a gift and not compensation. In re Blunda, 299 Ill. App. 3d 855, 234 Ill. Dec. 339, 702 N.E.2d 993 (2 Dist. 1998).

Where the wife's father executed a corporate resolution gifting shares of stock to the wife it was nonmarital property. In re Blunda, 299 Ill. App. 3d 855, 234 Ill. Dec. 339, 702 N.E.2d 993 (2 Dist. 1998).

Pension Benefits

—Application and Construction
Property division section of the Illinois Marriage and Dissolution of Marriage Act, 750 ILCS 5/503(a), 504(a), was preempted by 42 U.S.C.S. § 407(a) of the Social Security Act, 42 U.S.C.S. § 301 et seq., which barred the transfer of social security benefits. In re Marriage of Hulstrom, 342 Ill. App. 3d 262, 276 Ill. Dec. 730, 794 N.E.2d 980, 2003 Ill. App. LEXIS 978 (2 Dist. 2003).

—Division
Trial court did not err in dividing the husband's disability pension equally between himself and the wife in their divorce case, as application of the relevant factors and the fact that the disability pension was marital property warranted an equal division of that marital asset between the parties. Sawicki v. Sawicki, 346 Ill. App. 3d 1107, 282 Ill. Dec. 404, 806 N.E.2d 701, 2004 Ill. App. LEXIS 269 (3 Dist. 2004).

—Offset
Trial court erred by not reducing the portion of the husband's disability awarded to the wife by the cost of a joint and survivor annuity he obtained for her, as that annuity reduced the amount of the amount of the pension, thus, it was just to reduce the amount awarded to her by that cost. Sawicki v. Sawicki, 346 Ill. App. 3d 1107, 282 Ill. Dec. 404, 806 N.E.2d 701, 2004 Ill. App. LEXIS 269 (3 Dist. 2004).

—Spouse's Interest
Trial court did not err in not reducing any portion of the husband's disability pension awarded to the wife for when his supplementary pension terminates, as the trial court indicated that it would consider a reduction in the payment amount if the marital portion of the pension were reduced at some point in the future, but it properly refused to make a prospective reduction of the amount awarded to her. Sawicki v. Sawicki, 346 Ill. App. 3d 1107, 282 Ill. Dec. 404, 806 N.E.2d 701, 2004 Ill. App. LEXIS 269 (3 Dist. 2004).

Post-dissolution Effect
The procedural requirements of 750 ILCS 5/503(j) have no effect in post-dissolution proceedings. Macaluso v. Macaluso, 334 Ill. App. 3d 1043, 268 Ill. Dec. 636, 779 N.E.2d 250, 2002 Ill. App. LEXIS 387 (3 Dist. 2002).

Reimbursement

—Accounts Receivable
The accounts receivable of the husband's medical corporation were not subject to reimbursement where they indisputably existed due to the personal efforts of the husband, a sole practitioner, and where the amount of the accounts receivable more than doubled over the course of the marriage, the husband's compensation during the marriage adequately compensated the marital estate. In re Steinberg, 299 Ill. App. 3d 603, 233 Ill. Dec. 611, 701 N.E.2d 254 (1 Dist. 1998).

Accounts receivable are subject to reimbursement under this statute. In re Steinberg, 299 Ill. App. 3d 603, 233 Ill. Dec. 611, 701 N.E.2d 254 (1 Dist. 1998).

—Not Required
A husband was not entitled to reimbursement on a five year loan financing the purchase of shares; the loan was almost completely repaid at time of judgment of dissolution thus no personal assets of the estate were expended, therefore there was nothing to reimburse and there was no proof of a contribution from the martial estate. In re Blunda, 299 Ill. App. 3d 855, 234 Ill. Dec. 339, 702 N.E.2d 993 (2 Dist. 1998).

Residency Rights
The residency rights of the custodial parent in the former marital home were not equated as marital property, and did not support

Residency Rights (Cont'd)
offsetting other marital property, nor offsetting the noncustodial spouse's pension and stock assets to the custodial spouse's detriment. In re Lovell, 98 Ill. App. 3d 865, 54 Ill. Dec. 245, 424 N.E.2d 995 (3 Dist. 1981).

—Scope

Marital property means all property acquired by either spouse subsequent to the marriage with the exception of certain property which is statutorily considered to be non-marital property. In re Waeckerle, 219 Ill. App. 3d 937, 162 Ill. Dec. 461, 579 N.E.2d 1275 (5 Dist. 1991).

Subsection (b) of this section does not purport to affect property interests during marriage; the term "marital property" is a nomenclature devised to realize an equitable distribution of property upon termination of the marriage, and operation of the term "marital property" is not triggered until the time of dissolution. Kujawinski v. Kujawinski, 71 Ill. 2d 563, 17 Ill. Dec. 801, 376 N.E.2d 1382 (1978).

—Securities

In action brought by ex-wife against her ex-husband alleging violations of section 10(b) of the Securities Exchange Act of 1934 (15 U.S.C. § 78j(b)) where she claimed that during their settlement negotiations defendant concealed the value of certain marital property, corporate stock, thereby causing plaintiff to relinquish her share of the stock in exchange for other less valuable assets, plaintiff's marital property interest in ex-husband's corporate stock was inchoate, measurable only in state court, and it was not sufficiently identifiable to make plaintiff a seller of securities for purposes of federal securities laws by virtue of her negotiations in connection with division of marital assets. McHugh v. McHugh, 676 F. Supp. 856 (N.D. Ill. 1988).

—Separate Ownership

Where some items of husband's were exchanged for other property during the course of the marriage, but these "new acquisitions" were also separately titled, such assets remained separate property regardless of the number or type of postmarital exchanges as long as there has been no evidence of an intent to transmute. In re Siddens, 225 Ill. App. 3d 496, 167 Ill. Dec. 680, 588 N.E.2d 321 (5 Dist.), appeal denied, 145 Ill. 2d 644, 173 Ill. Dec. 13, 596 N.E.2d 637 (1992).

It is only property owned at the time of the judgment of dissolution that the court may classify as "marital property"; property owned separately by the spouse before dissolution may be disposed of as he/she deems fit, absent any contrary order of the court. In re Schwartz, 131 Ill. App. 3d 351, 86 Ill. Dec. 698, 475 N.E.2d 1077 (1 Dist. 1985).

Subsection (b) of this section does not prevent married persons from owning property separately during the marriage and disposing of it in any fashion that the property owning spouse may choose. Kujawinski v. Kujawinski, 71 Ill. 2d 563, 17 Ill. Dec. 801, 376 N.E.2d 1382 (1978).

—Shown

Half interest in farm was acquired during marriage and held in joint tenancy, therefore the farm was presumed to be marital property and husband failed to rebut presumption that money used to pay for the property was a gift to the marital estate. In re Nelson, 297 Ill. App. 3d 651, 232 Ill. Dec. 654, 698 N.E.2d 1084 (3 Dist. 1998).

Wife failed to demonstrate by clear and convincing evidence that property should be considered nonmarital property; the property was acquired with funds from undisputed nonmarital property in part but both husband and wife were listed as mortgagors, mortgage was paid out of a joint checking account and from husband's own funds. In re Hegge, 285 Ill. App. 3d 138, 220 Ill. Dec. 853, 674 N.E.2d 124 (2 Dist. 1996), appeal denied, 172 Ill. 2d 551, 223 Ill. Dec. 195, 679 N.E.2d 380 (1997).

Because the funds received by petitioner for the sale of the non-marital property were commingled with the marital funds when deposited in the parties' joint checking account and used to acquire other property, the check drawn on this account for the purchase of the other property was properly considered a marital asset by the trial court. In re Uehlein, 265 Ill. App. 3d 1080, 202 Ill. Dec. 838, 638 N.E.2d 706 (1 Dist. 1994).

Where respondent withdrew $15,000 in marital funds and belatedly tried to justify the withdrawal as the repayment of an $8,000 "loan" from his mother plus $7,000 "interest," the trial court did not believe his explanation; the record supported the court's conclusion that the respondent was evasive and untruthful during his testimony and that the $15,000 was marital property. In re Heinze, 257 Ill. App. 3d 782, 197 Ill. Dec. 506, 631 N.E.2d 728 (3 Dist. 1994).

Trial court did not err in holding that funds deposited in a joint bank account were marital property. In re Ackerman, 168 Ill. App. 3d 438, 118 Ill. Dec. 862, 522 N.E.2d 317 (2 Dist. 1988).

Where wife's father transferred apartment buildings to wife, such was considered a sale, thus making apartments marital property and not a non-marital gift, even though father stated to wife that she was not required to make payments and that the apartments were intended as gifts, for the articles of agreement transferring the buildings constituted a contract for sale of property and the wife paid for the property out of rental proceeds, no gift tax was filed by father, and a certified public accountant represented that the transaction would be treated by Internal Revenue Service as a sale for income tax purposes. In re Marriage of Agazim, 147 Ill. App. 3d 646, 101 Ill. Dec. 418, 498 N.E.2d 742, 1986 Ill. App. LEXIS 2819 (2 Dist. 1986), cert. denied, 106 Ill. Dec. 44, 505 N.E.2d 350 (1987), appeal denied, 106 Ill. Dec. 44, 505 N.E.2d 350 (1987).

While tools and equipment purchased with spouse's $1,600 investment prior to remarriage were non-marital assets, those items purchased after remarriage were marital in character. In re Westphal, 99 Ill. App. 3d 1042, 55 Ill. Dec. 328, 426 N.E.2d 303 (3 Dist. 1981).

Where parties agreed that the marital home was built and paid for during the marriage and that they lived in the home as husband and wife, the house was built on farmland that they acquired, and each party made material contributions to its construction, although the greater portion of the construction cost came from the former wife's funds acquired prior to the marriage, the husband expended considerable labor and used some of his farm revenue for building expenses, and title to the home was in the husband's name only, the property was marital property. In re Dietz, 76 Ill. App. 3d 1029, 32 Ill. Dec. 532, 395 N.E.2d 762 (5 Dist. 1979).

That portion of the parties' property which was attributable to their salaries during the marriage and the individual labors which they contributed were undeniably marital property not within any of the exceptions identified in the statute. In re Key, 71 Ill. App. 3d 722, 27 Ill. Dec. 732, 389 N.E.2d 963 (4 Dist. 1979).

—Sole Proprietorship

Business interests, such as a sole proprietorship or stock in a closed corporation, which are acquired subsequent to the marriage are regarded as marital property under this section. In re White, 98 Ill. App. 3d 380, 53 Ill. Dec. 786, 424 N.E.2d 421 (5 Dist. 1981).

—Stock

As stock options granted to wife were contingent upon the passage of time and retention of employment, they only become marital property if and when they were exercised; it would have been necessary on remand for the trial court to retain jurisdiction for the purpose of allocating the proceeds from the exercise of the options if and when they were exercised. In re Isaacs, 260 Ill. App. 3d 423, 198 Ill. Dec. 169, 632 N.E.2d 228 (1 Dist.), appeal denied, 157 Ill. 2d 502, 205 Ill. Dec. 164, 642 N.E.2d 1281 (1994).

Testimony was insufficient to establish that respondent received corporation by bequest, devise or descent so as to make it a non-marital asset; furthermore, purchase of the stock took place during the marriage and was presumed marital property and therefore subject to apportionment. In re Rossi, 113 Ill. App. 3d 55, 68 Ill. Dec. 801, 446 N.E.2d 1198 (1 Dist. 1983).

—Unequal Distribution

The court can properly award one spouse a greater share of the marital property if it decides that the relative contribution of that spouse and other relevant factors warrant such a result. In re Gustke, 78 Ill. App. 3d 274, 33 Ill. Dec. 813, 397 N.E.2d 146 (1 Dist. 1979).

—Upheld

Wife's failure to object to contract for purchase of farm by husband from his parents, which excluded wife from acquiring interest in farm, failed to establish there was ever a "valid agree-

Residency Rights (Cont'd)

—Upheld (Cont'd)
ment" by wife to give up a marital right, and trial court's finding farm was marital property was well-founded. Hofmann v. Hofmann, 94 Ill. 2d 205, 68 Ill. Dec. 593, 446 N.E.2d 499 (1983).

—Waste
It is entirely within the realm of possibility that one spouse's use of marital funds for his or her own living expenses at a time when the marriage is undergoing an irreconcilable breakdown could be shown to be so selfish and excessive and improper as to constitute an outright waste of marital funds. In re Hagshenas, 234 Ill. App. 3d 178, 175 Ill. Dec. 506, 600 N.E.2d 437 (2 Dist. 1992), appeal denied, 148 Ill.2d 642, 183 Ill. Dec. 19, 610 N.E.2d 1263 (1993).

—Workers' Compensation Award
Where a claim for a workers' compensation award accrues during marriage, the award is marital property, regardless of when it is received. In re Hall, 278 Ill. App. 3d 782, 215 Ill. Dec. 419, 663 N.E.2d 430 (3 Dist. 1996).

Where respondent's workers' compensation settlement was determined to be non-marital property, but respondent placed it in a joint tenancy checking account, it was transmuted into marital property. In re Drone, 217 Ill. App. 3d 758, 160 Ill. Dec. 601, 577 N.E.2d 926 (5 Dist. 1991).

A pending workers' compensation award, arising out of a claim accrued during the marriage, is to be classified as marital property. In re Thomas, 89 Ill. App. 3d 81, 44 Ill. Dec. 430, 411 N.E.2d 552 (3 Dist. 1980).

A workers' compensation award paid to an injured employee during his marriage is marital property subject to allocation by the court in a dissolution of marriage proceeding. In re Lukas, 83 Ill. App. 3d 606, 39 Ill. Dec. 161, 404 N.E.2d 545 (1 Dist. 1980).

A workers' compensation award paid out to and received by an injured employee during his marriage is not property acquired by gift, bequest, devise or descent or property acquired in exchange for property, and thus does not fall into the category of non-marital property which cannot be allocated between the spouses; nor can it be considered non-marital property under the definitions set forth in subdivisions (a)(3) through (a)(6) of this section. In re Lukas, 83 Ill. App. 3d 606, 39 Ill. Dec. 161, 404 N.E.2d 545 (1 Dist. 1980).

Workers' compensation, to the extent that it accrued and was actually paid over to the injured employee during the marriage, is marital property that is allocable in accordance with the standards set forth in this Act. In re Lukas, 83 Ill. App. 3d 606, 39 Ill. Dec. 161, 404 N.E.2d 545 (1 Dist. 1980).

—Workers' Compensation Claim
The use of the time of the accrual of the workers' compensation claim as the sole basis of classification of marital property has been described as the mechanical approach, as opposed to the analytical approach which separates the awards into at least two potential elements of damages; (1) those compensating the injured spouse for pain and suffering, disability, and disfigurement or lost limbs, and (2) those compensating the injured spouse for lost wages or lost earning capacity, and medical and hospital expenses. In re Waggoner, 261 Ill. App. 3d 787, 199 Ill. Dec. 844, 634 N.E.2d 1198 (5 Dist. 1994).

Method of Distribution
There was no abuse of discretion in the distribution of property but method of distribution was to be reexamined where the trial court ordered the $23,000 to be paid in monthly installments of $350 which did not constitute income producing property for petitioner nor provide the finality sought when a relationship is severed. In re Albrecht, 266 Ill. App. 3d 399, 203 Ill. Dec. 394, 639 N.E.2d 953 (4 Dist. 1994).

Misconduct

—In General
The misconduct referred to is that which occurred in the course of the marriage leading to its dissolution. In re Cihak, 92 Ill. App. 3d 1123, 48 Ill. Dec. 428, 416 N.E.2d 701 (4 Dist. 1981).

If the transaction is fair and honest and made in good faith, subsequent acts of misconduct of the wife not in contemplation at the time of the conveyance would probably not warrant a court of equity in decreeing a cancellation of the conveyance. If, however, the transfer is procured by the wife and is attended with circumstances from which it can be reasonably inferred that she contemplated an abandonment of her marital duties after securing such conveyance, a court of equity will grant relief and restore the property to the husband. Baker v. Baker, 412 Ill. 511, 107 N.E.2d 711 (1952).

—Apportionment
In an action under this section, the court should not have considered the earlier court's impression of one party's alleged misconduct in apportioning the property between the parties. In re Parker, 216 Ill. App. 3d 672, 159 Ill. Dec. 131, 575 N.E.2d 938 (2 Dist. 1991).

—Money Decree
Even though there was evidence which would justify a finding that appellant had misappropriated funds belonging to appellee, this would not have justified the court in directing the conveyance of properties; all the court would have been authorized to do would be to enter a money decree for the payment of the money, which would have been a lien on appellant's real estate under former Ill.Rev.Stat., ch. 40, para. 18 (see now this section) and former Ill.Rev.Stat., ch. 22, para. 44 (see now 735 ILCS 5/2-101). Podgornik v. Podgornik, 392 Ill. 124, 63 N.E.2d 715 (1945).

—Murder
The fact that respondent murdered petitioner should not have been a factor in the division of property under this section. In re Cihak, 92 Ill. App. 3d 1123, 48 Ill. Dec. 428, 416 N.E.2d 701 (4 Dist. 1981).

Modification of Decree

—Change in Tax Law
Court could modify the terms of a divorce decree on the ground that the change in the federal income tax law in 1942 caused a material change in the financial status of wife; any decrease in her income, whether due to the payment of income taxes or to any other reason which reduced her income beyond what was necessary for her station in life, could be considered. Jacobs v. Jacobs, 328 Ill. App. 133, 65 N.E.2d 588 (1 Dist. 1946).

—Conditions
The provisions of a dissolution judgment governing property disposition may not be revoked or modified unless the court finds the existence of conditions that satisfy the reopening of a judgment under the laws of this state. Meyer v. Meyer, 222 Ill. App. 3d 357, 164 Ill. Dec. 800, 583 N.E.2d 716 (5 Dist. 1991).

—Considerations
When making a change in alimony (now maintenance), the court should take into consideration the property and income of the parties, their ages, health, and social conditions, and whether there are children dependent upon them for support. Jacobs v. Jacobs, 328 Ill. App. 133, 65 N.E.2d 588 (1 Dist. 1946).

—Enforceability
A court may enforce a post-decree, contractual modification of a property settlement agreement that had been incorporated into the divorce decree. Semmens v. Semmens, 77 Ill. App. 3d 936, 33 Ill. Dec. 558, 396 N.E.2d 1282 (4 Dist. 1979).

—Properly Denied
In connection with the value of real estate, in a property settlement suit incident to a divorce, where the trial judge observed that both parties had been represented by counsel, and that both had ample opportunity to ascertain its value prior to the entry of the divorce decree, the trial court exercised sound discretion in denying defendant's petition to modify the property settlement agreement where there was no suggestion that plaintiff committed any fraudulent act or attempted to conceal its value. Kolar v. Kolar, 47 Ill. App. 3d 37, 5 Ill. Dec. 428, 361 N.E.2d 751 (1 Dist. 1977).

Non-Marital Property

—Application and Construction
In order to preserve a property's non-marital status one must prove that the entire property was acquired exclusively by one of

Non-Marital Property (Cont'd)

—Application and Construction (Cont'd)

the methods listed in subsection (a), and that its character was not subsequently altered by action of the owner; the interpretation of the effect of subsection (b) upon subsection (a) of this section is consistent with the Act's expressed preference for the classification of property as marital and the shifting of the burden of proof to the party seeking control of the property. In re Smith, 86 Ill. 2d 518, 56 Ill. Dec. 693, 427 N.E.2d 1239 (1981).

—Appreciated Value

Under this Act, the increase in the value of a spouse's non-marital funds in an account, irrespective of whether the increase results from a contribution of marital property, is non-marital subject only to the right of reimbursement provided in subsection (c) of this section. In re Hagshenas, 234 Ill. App. 3d 178, 175 Ill. Dec. 506, 600 N.E.2d 437 (2 Dist. 1992), appeal denied, 148 Ill.2d 642, 183 Ill. Dec. 19, 610 N.E.2d 1263 (1993).

An appreciation in value of non-marital property acquired by devise does not take on the character of marital property notwithstanding the fact that the property has not been improved or changed and has increased in value without any action of the marital parties. In re Komnick, 84 Ill. 2d 89, 49 Ill. Dec. 291, 417 N.E.2d 1305 (1981).

The General Assembly did not intend that the appreciated value of non-marital property become marital property. Bentley v. Bentley, 84 Ill. 2d 97, 49 Ill. Dec. 295, 417 N.E.2d 1309 (1981).

Subsection (c) of this section provides that upon dissolution the court shall "assign" the non-marital property and "divide" the marital property; division of the increased value would frequently necessitate division of the entire parcel or item of non-marital property, and to subject the non-marital property to division between the parties would contravene legislative intent. The enhanced value of non-marital property is to be considered in dividing the marital property and in determining whether maintenance is appropriate and in what amount. Bentley v. Bentley, 84 Ill. 2d 97, 49 Ill. Dec. 295, 417 N.E.2d 1309 (1981).

The Illinois Supreme Court has established that the increase in value of non-marital property acquired before and during the marriage is also non-marital property. In re Westphal, 99 Ill. App. 3d 1042, 55 Ill. Dec. 328, 426 N.E.2d 303 (3 Dist. 1981).

—Bank Accounts

Where the trial court erred in classifying wife's savings plan as marital property, on remand, the trial court was to include the savings in wife's non-marital estate, and the marital estate was to be reimbursed for the contributions made to the savings plan after the date of marriage. In re Phillips, 229 Ill. App. 3d 809, 171 Ill. Dec. 501, 594 N.E.2d 353 (2 Dist. 1992).

—Business Interests

Non-marital, closely-held corporations, partnerships, or individually owned businesses, including farm operations, can accumulate income and assets in a variety of ways resulting in a substantial increase to the non-marital estate which should continue to be treated as non-marital property; if this fact can be demonstrated by competent evidence, such as accurate bookkeeping and a segregation of business funds, a court is justified in finding that some or all of the increased value of the business is non-marital. In re Werries, 247 Ill. App. 3d 639, 186 Ill. Dec. 747, 616 N.E.2d 1379 (4 Dist. 1993).

Trial court's conclusions that business qualified as marital property were held to be against the manifest weight of the evidence. In re Perlmutter, 225 Ill. App. 3d 362, 167 Ill. Dec. 340, 587 N.E.2d 609 (2 Dist.), appeal denied, 146 Ill. 2d 650, 176 Ill. Dec. 820, 602 N.E.2d 474 (1992), cert. denied, 507 U.S. 1006, 113 S. Ct. 1648, 123 L. Ed. 2d 269 (1993).

Where the collateral for the loans of money and the funds used to purchase the restaurants that were the genesis of a corporation were derived from the properties the husband received through inheritance and as gifts, the husband proved by clear and convincing evidence that the property which formed the corporation was non-marital property; therefore, the husband's interest in the corporation was properly classified as non-marital property. In re Eddy, 210 Ill. App. 3d 450, 155 Ill. Dec. 174, 569 N.E.2d 174 (1 Dist. 1991).

Even though there was inconsistent testimony from respondent's father and brother with respect to income derived from the bakeries and actual ownership, the court found that sufficient evidence existed to show that respondent's interest in these business entities constituted non-marital property acquired by gift where it was undisputed that respondent's father initially purchased his interest in one bakery in 1972 and the remaining interest in that enterprise in 1976, and the brothers and respondent all testified consistently that another bakery was purchased with funds from a bank account funded by their father and that none of them invested any of their personal funds towards its purchase. In re Madoch, 212 Ill. App. 3d 1007, 157 Ill. Dec. 10, 571 N.E.2d 1029 (1 Dist. 1991).

The trial court did not err in failing to award wife an equitable interest in the business operated by husband. Scruggs v. Scruggs, 23 Ill. App. 3d 1004, 320 N.E.2d 406 (5 Dist. 1974).

Where a husband and his brothers started operating a restaurant in 1946 approximately 15 months before his marriage to the wife, he acquired his brothers' interests and became the sole proprietor, and thereafter, during the period of his marriage to appellant, the operation of the business was generally in his name alone, no personal funds of hers went into the acquisition or establishment of the business and there was no proof that she was ever held out as a partner or part owner, it appearing that her duties were much the same as they were prior to the marriage, there was no evidence that a business increase was the result of any unusual services performed by her, the wife failed to show by competent testimony that a business partnership existed or that she had proved special equities which would justify a court of equity to order that any share of the business be transferred to her. Peck v. Peck, 16 Ill. 2d 268, 157 N.E.2d 249 (1959).

Business assets of cleaner business operated by husband and wife were properly awarded to wife pursuant to former Ill.Rev.Stat., ch. 40, para. 18 (see now this section) where all of the real estate was carried in her name, all money was handled by her and all checks signed by her, she operated as the sole and exclusive owner, and there was no proof that she ever recognized or held out her husband to be a partner in the business or to have any other interest save as an employee. Sykes v. Sykes, 404 Ill. 152, 88 N.E.2d 484 (1949).

—Cancelled Checks

Where husband's cancelled checks for items established they were purchased prior to the parties' marriage, the items constituted non-marital property. In re Thacker, 185 Ill. App. 3d 465, 133 Ill. Dec. 573, 541 N.E.2d 784 (5 Dist. 1989).

—Commingling with Marital Property

Where a spouse commingles non-marital property with marital property by investing non-marital funds in the marital home, a court may refuse to trace the investment and refund it to the paying spouse. In re Cleveland, 99 Ill. App. 3d 293, 54 Ill. Dec. 610, 425 N.E.2d 475 (1 Dist. 1981).

—Corporation

Corporation was classified as non-marital property where the stock issued to husband was merely an exchange of assets for his non-marital interests in the business; wife had authority to sign checks for the business, paid some of the corporate bills, attended various business meetings with husband and performed some bookkeeping services for the corporation but these contributions were insufficient to convert the business into a marital asset. In re Phillips, 244 Ill. App. 3d 577, 186 Ill. Dec. 108, 615 N.E.2d 1165 (4 Dist. 1993).

—Debt

Where there was evidence to support a finding that a debt was too uncertain to be included in the marital estate, the decision was not against the manifest weight of the evidence nor an abuse of discretion. In re Pickell, 76 Ill. App. 3d 855, 32 Ill. Dec. 443, 395 N.E.2d 673 (5 Dist. 1979).

—Evidence

Where wife testified she told husband prior to the marriage that she wanted to continue paying the mortgage, insurance premiums and real estate taxes, she expressed an intention to maintain the residence as her separate property, and placed in trust the title to the residence with her daughters as beneficiaries, testimony rebut-

Non-Marital Property (Cont'd)

—Evidence (Cont'd)
ted the presumption of marital property raised. In re Holman, 122 Ill. App. 3d 1001, 78 Ill. Dec. 314, 462 N.E.2d 30 (2 Dist. 1984).

—Federal Employer's Liability Action
The cause of action set forth in count II of the husband's Federal Employer's Liability Action complaint was a separate property right and non-marital in nature where it arose following the entry of the judgment of dissolution; it could not properly have been considered part of the property settlement agreement. In re Waeckerle, 219 Ill. App. 3d 937, 162 Ill. Dec. 461, 579 N.E.2d 1275 (5 Dist. 1991).

—Future Acquisition of Assets
The court must consider non-marital property, even where the non-marital property will be received in the future, when it determines the relevant economic circumstances of each spouse and the amount and sources of income of the parties, as well as the reasonable opportunity of each spouse for future acquisition of capital assets and income. In re Smith, 100 Ill. App. 3d 1126, 56 Ill. Dec. 716, 427 N.E.2d 1262 (2 Dist. 1981).

—Future Earning Capacity
Future earning capacity flowing from an education was not considered a marital asset and, thus, not divided by the court in a dissolution of marriage proceeding. In re Goldstein, 97 Ill. App. 3d 1023, 53 Ill. Dec. 397, 423 N.E.2d 1201 (1 Dist. 1981).

—Gift
The circuit court's conclusion that the bracelet given to petitioner by respondent's mother, who carried insurance on it, belonged to the petitioner was contrary to the manifest weight of the evidence; therefore, bracelet was not included in marital property. In re Simmons, 87 Ill. App. 3d 651, 42 Ill. Dec. 706, 409 N.E.2d 321 (1 Dist. 1980).

The trial court erred in awarding gold cross to petitioner wife as her separate non-marital property where the evidence established that it was given to husband by his uncle many years prior to the marriage and there was no affirmative proof of an intention to make a gift to the wife. In re Uluhogian, 86 Ill. App. 3d 654, 41 Ill. Dec. 761, 408 N.E.2d 107 (5 Dist. 1980).

—Home
The fact that non-marital trust income was placed in a marital account which was then used to pay the mortgage on wife's non-marital home did not transmute the residence into marital property. In re Holman, 122 Ill. App. 3d 1001, 78 Ill. Dec. 314, 462 N.E.2d 30 (2 Dist. 1984).

Since the funds used to reduce mortgage obligation were non-marital and the account from which the mortgage was paid also was non-marital, the trial court properly characterized the residence as wife's non-marital property. In re Holman, 122 Ill. App. 3d 1001, 78 Ill. Dec. 314, 462 N.E.2d 30 (2 Dist. 1984).

Where the subject property was the marital home of respondent's parents and respondent's mother received all the income from the property and, although the deed which conveyed an interest in the property to respondent and his brothers showed consideration of $100,000, there was testimony that such consideration was never paid, respondent's interest in the property was non-marital property. In re Carini, 112 Ill. App. 3d 375, 67 Ill. Dec. 932, 445 N.E.2d 412 (1 Dist. 1983).

Where a husband purchased a house as an investment prior to his decision to marry his wife, he transferred title into joint ownership to end her badgering and in reliance upon her promise to name him as a beneficiary in her will, the down payment was furnished by the husband as well as a majority of the funds used for the mortgage payments, the trial court's finding that the property was non-marital was proper. In re Voight, 111 Ill. App. 3d 623, 67 Ill. Dec. 458, 444 N.E.2d 694 (1 Dist. 1982).

One-half interest in residence which was given to wife by husband of a previous marriage and was acquired by her before subsequent valid marriage was non-marital property and as such, upon dissolution of the marriage, should have been assigned to her. In re Flatow, 102 Ill. App. 3d 859, 58 Ill. Dec. 273, 430 N.E.2d 215 (1 Dist. 1981).

—Improvement
The stores owned by a husband prior to the marriage remained non-marital despite their absorption of some marital resources because it was permissible for one spouse to improve the other spouse's non-marital property without making that property marital. In re Kennedy, 94 Ill. App. 3d 537, 49 Ill. Dec. 927, 418 N.E.2d 947 (1 Dist. 1981).

—Individual Retirement Account
Where an Individual Retirement Account was treated as the exclusive property of husband since he used the account as an adjustment to income on his separate tax return, this was property acquired solely by husband during the marriage and fell within the exclusion of the prenuptial agreement. In re Burgess, 123 Ill. App. 3d 487, 78 Ill. Dec. 345, 462 N.E.2d 203 (3 Dist. 1984).

—Investment
The interest earned during the marriage on one spouse's investment account was her non-marital property, as an increase in the value of property acquired before marriage remained non-marital property. In re Deem, 123 Ill. App. 3d 1019, 79 Ill. Dec. 542, 463 N.E.2d 1317 (4 Dist. 1984).

—Joint Tenancy
The trial court's finding was not against the manifest weight of the evidence in determining that property deeded to the parties in joint tenancy from the wife's parents was the wife's non-marital property where the evidence established that the wife alone, or in conjunction with various family members, made improvements on the property and on the one occasion that the husband assisted, he was paid for his efforts, the wife paid the taxes on the property from accounts held in her name, and although she never occupied the property, but used it as a source of rental income, which was deposited in accounts solely in her name, the wife solely managed the property, which included finding renters and collecting the rent. In re Hunter, 223 Ill. App. 3d 947, 166 Ill. Dec. 242, 585 N.E.2d 1264 (2 Dist.), appeal denied, 145 Ill. 2d 634, 173 Ill. Dec. 4, 596 N.E.2d 628 (1992).

Where husband brought non-marital property into the marriage and his sole motivation for transferring title to the properties into joint tenancy with wife was to avoid the type of difficulties in succeeding to title in the event of one of their deaths which he had encountered after the death of his first wife, the real estate in question was solely respondent's non-marital property and wife could be ordered to convey over her interests. In re Wojcicki, 135 Ill. App. 3d 248, 90 Ill. Dec. 139, 481 N.E.2d 939 (1 Dist. 1985).

The placing of title to non-marital property in joint tenancy with a spouse raises a presumption that a gift was made to the marital estate and the property becomes marital property. In re Rink, 136 Ill. App. 3d 252, 91 Ill. Dec. 34, 483 N.E.2d 316 (1 Dist. 1985).

—Keough Plan
Where a Keough plan started out as husband's non-marital property which he augmented with additional non-marital cash borrowed from his wife, and husband then repaid the loan with interest after selling non-marital property of his own, the fact that the loan transactions produced tax benefits for both parties did not permit the court to redesignate the plan as marital property and ignore a valid prenuptial agreement. In re Burgess, 123 Ill. App. 3d 487, 78 Ill. Dec. 345, 462 N.E.2d 203 (3 Dist. 1984).

Although by loaning her non-marital cash to husband, wife freed up his earned income so as to facilitate a better standard of living, this did not change the Keough plan into marital property. In re Burgess, 123 Ill. App. 3d 487, 78 Ill. Dec. 345, 462 N.E.2d 203 (3 Dist. 1984).

—Legislative Intent
The intent of this section as a whole was designed to eliminate disparity between the marriage partners; however, the exceptions (1) through (6) of subsection (a) of this section manifest the legislative purpose to preserve the character of non-marital property in those situations where the actions of the parties have not created ambiguity. In re Smith, 86 Ill. 2d 518, 56 Ill. Dec. 693, 427 N.E.2d 1239 (1981).

—Life Insurance
Where two life insurance policies were purchased long before the parties were married and the policies were listed in the separate

Non-Marital Property (Cont'd)

—Life Insurance (Cont'd)

schedule attached to the prenuptial agreement, the agreement controlled, making them non-marital property. In re Burgess, 123 Ill. App. 3d 487, 78 Ill. Dec. 345, 462 N.E.2d 203 (3 Dist. 1984).

—Marital Contribution

Where the evidence established that both parties contributed personal effort in the remodeling of husband's non-marital residence, and there was no clear evidence of the value of the appreciation, if any, due to wife's personal efforts, the trial court properly denied reimbursement to the marital estate from husband's non-marital estate for wife's personal efforts in remodeling husband's non-marital residence. In re Snow, 277 Ill. App. 3d 642, 214 Ill. Dec. 398, 660 N.E.2d 1347 (4 Dist. 1996).

Court's failure to reimburse the marital estate for marital contributions made to husband's non-marital residence, such as respondent's efforts in remodeling, any alleged appreciation and payment of $25,000 mortgage payment was not an abuse of discretion. In re Snow, 277 Ill. App. 3d 642, 214 Ill. Dec. 398, 660 N.E.2d 1347 (4 Dist. 1996).

—Personal Efforts

In the case of personal efforts, no reimbursement is to be made unless the effort is significant and results in substantial appreciation of non-marital property. In re Jelinek, 244 Ill. App. 3d 496, 184 Ill. Dec. 692, 613 N.E.2d 1284 (1 Dist.), appeal denied, 152 Ill. 2d 560, 190 Ill. Dec. 890, 622 N.E.2d 1207 (1993).

—Profit-Sharing Plan

The increase during the marriage in the value of the now-consolidated non-marital profit-sharing plan, regardless of its source, was husband's non-marital property, subject to the right of reimbursement. In re Leisner, 219 Ill. App. 3d 752, 162 Ill. Dec. 277, 579 N.E.2d 1091 (1 Dist. 1991).

—Reduction of Indebtedness

Non-marital property is not transmuted into marital property merely as the result of the use of marital funds to reduce the indebtedness. In re Perlmutter, 225 Ill. App. 3d 362, 167 Ill. Dec. 340, 587 N.E.2d 609 (2 Dist.), appeal denied, 146 Ill. 2d 650, 176 Ill. Dec. 820, 602 N.E.2d 474 (1992), cert. denied, 507 U.S. 1006, 113 S. Ct. 1648, 123 L. Ed. 2d 269 (1993).

—Reimbursement

Court did not abuse its discretion in ordering husband to reimburse marital estate the value of the cash payment for non-marital farm machinery. In re Nelson, 297 Ill. App. 3d 651, 232 Ill. Dec. 654, 698 N.E.2d 1084 (3 Dist. 1998).

While the residence was a nonmarital asset, wife's contributions to the marital residence were significant as she worked full time, provided health care benefits and completed household chores; thus reimbursement of the payments from husband was not against the weight of the evidence. In re Nelson, 297 Ill. App. 3d 651, 232 Ill. Dec. 654, 698 N.E.2d 1084 (3 Dist. 1998).

The trial court correctly determined that respondent was entitled to reimbursement for her contribution to the value of the property, which included answering the telephones, dealing with tenants, and cleaning the buildings and it was not an abuse of discretion for the court to include an amount for that contribution into the marital estate. In re Uehlein, 265 Ill. App. 3d 1080, 202 Ill. Dec. 838, 638 N.E.2d 706 (1 Dist. 1994).

Where the husband was awarded his non-marital residence as non-marital property, the court was also required to order the husband to reimburse the marital estate for marital funds contributed to the residence for improvements and mortgage reduction. McCoy v McCoy, 225 Ill. App. 3d 966, 168 Ill. Dec. 27, 589 N.E.2d 141 (3 Dist. 1992).

Because husband's contribution of personal efforts were both significant and resulted in substantial appreciation of non-marital land, the marital estate was entitled to reimbursement for that contribution and wife was properly awarded one-half of that reimbursement. In re Tatham, 173 Ill. App. 3d 1072, 123 Ill. Dec. 576, 527 N.E.2d 1351 (5 Dist. 1988).

Where identifiable, non-marital assets, whether in the form of cash or tangible property, have been exchanged for jointly held property, the parties, upon dissolution of marriage are entitled to a refund of their original contribution. In re Key, 71 Ill. App. 3d 722, 27 Ill. Dec. 732, 389 N.E.2d 963 (4 Dist. 1979).

—Relationship

There is no inverse relationship between the amount of non-marital property that should be awarded to a spouse. In re Wentink, 132 Ill. App. 3d 71, 87 Ill. Dec. 117, 476 N.E.2d 1109 (1 Dist. 1984).

—Rental Business

Husband's rental business did not become marital property simply because new properties were added and older ones were maintained when all of the funds came from husband's separate accounts; mere marital use of the rental income certainly did not transmute the properties themselves into marital assets. In re Siddens, 225 Ill. App. 3d 496, 167 Ill. Dec. 680, 588 N.E.2d 321 (5 Dist.), appeal denied, 145 Ill. 2d 644, 173 Ill. Dec. 13, 596 N.E.2d 637 (1992).

—Repairs to Home

Where husband did not establish that his repairs materially added to the value of the house, his evidence of repairs was insufficient to raise the rebuttable marital property presumption. In re Holman, 122 Ill. App. 3d 1001, 78 Ill. Dec. 314, 462 N.E.2d 30 (2 Dist. 1984).

—S Corporation

The mere fact that husband's primary business enterprise was incorporated into an "S" corporation during the marriage did not automatically transfer it into marital assets. In re Siddens, 225 Ill. App. 3d 496, 167 Ill. Dec. 680, 588 N.E.2d 321 (5 Dist.), appeal denied, 145 Ill. 2d 644, 173 Ill. Dec. 13, 596 N.E.2d 637 (1992).

—Savings Plan

Where wife's savings plan was funded through salary contributions and matching company funds, the cash contributions into the savings plan during the marriage lost their identity and became part of the non-marital savings plan; thus, her savings plan should have been classified as non-marital because the savings plan was the property receiving the contributions. In re Phillips, 229 Ill. App. 3d 809, 171 Ill. Dec. 501, 594 N.E.2d 353 (2 Dist. 1992).

—Scope

This Act does not authorize the trial court to consider non-owned property as non-marital property under this section. In re Weaver, 133 Ill. App. 3d 825, 88 Ill. Dec. 839, 479 N.E.2d 452 (4 Dist. 1985).

—Separate Ownership

Subsection (b) of this section does not prevent married persons from owning property separately during the marriage and disposing of it in any fashion that the property-owning spouse may choose. In re Cleveland, 99 Ill. App. 3d 293, 54 Ill. Dec. 610, 425 N.E.2d 475 (1 Dist. 1981).

—Shown

The property given to the husband by gift and the property distributed to him upon the death of his father were properly classified as non-marital. In re Eddy, 210 Ill. App. 3d 450, 155 Ill. Dec. 174, 569 N.E.2d 174 (1 Dist. 1991).

Trial court did not err in setting off to the respondent as his non-marital property the value of grain and farm equipment which he owned at the time of the marriage where there was nothing in the record which showed that it was the intent of the parties that the property in question be marital property. In re Emken, 86 Ill. 2d 164, 56 Ill. Dec. 45, 427 N.E.2d 125 (1981).

Wife's isolated statement that "we bought a ring" was insufficient to indicate that husband contributed toward its purchase, and the quoted words imported at most that husband was present when the ring was purchased and assisted in its selection and the ring was properly classified as non-marital property. In re Pedersen, 77 Ill. App. 3d 716, 33 Ill. Dec. 270, 396 N.E.2d 659 (2 Dist. 1979).

—Stock Ownership Plan

Under subdivision (c)(1) of this section, wife's stock ownership plan was a non-marital asset that increased after marriage through contributions based on wife's salary, a marital asset; as such, the entire stock plan would be classified as non-marital property subject to reimbursement to the marital estate for contributions

Non-Marital Property (Cont'd)

—Stock Ownership Plan (Cont'd)
made to the plan during the marriage. In re Phillips, 229 Ill. App. 3d 809, 171 Ill. Dec. 501, 594 N.E.2d 353 (2 Dist. 1992).

—Test
Where property was acquired before marriage, title is a relevant indicator to determine at the time of dissolution whether the property has remained non-marital. In re Drennan, 93 Ill. App. 3d 903, 49 Ill. Dec. 386, 418 N.E.2d 30 (4 Dist. 1981).

—Tracing of Funds
Tracing of funds is a procedure which allows the court to find that property which would otherwise fall within the definition of marital property is actually non-marital property under one of the statutory exceptions. In re Jelinek, 244 Ill. App. 3d 496, 184 Ill. Dec. 692, 613 N.E.2d 1284 (1 Dist.), appeal denied, 152 Ill. 2d 560, 190 Ill. Dec. 890, 622 N.E.2d 1207 (1993).

—Trust
Where the evidence demonstrated that husband's father's will directed that the residue of his estate be distributed in accordance with the provisions of trust, and since the trust provided that husband was to receive the legal ownership of the farm as part of his distributive share of the trust assets, husband met the burden of overcoming the presumption that the farm was marital property; however, even though farm was non-marital property, husband's personal efforts towards the non-marital property were a contribution by the marital estate. In re Tatham, 173 Ill. App. 3d 1072, 123 Ill. Dec. 576, 527 N.E.2d 1351 (5 Dist. 1988).

Where a respondent testified that no money acquired since his marriage to the petitioner was invested in a trust which was non-marital property, the respondent had not commingled marital funds with his original investment. In re Frazier, 125 Ill. App. 3d 473, 80 Ill. Dec. 838, 466 N.E.2d 290 (5 Dist. 1984).

A respondent's equitable interest in a land trust which held legal title to an apartment building was not a marital asset where the respondent made no capital improvements to the apartment building, and his services as manager were not shown to have added to the value of the building; those services, including the payment of insurance premiums, were primarily conservative in nature, and did not transform the interest in the land trust into marital property. In re Frazier, 125 Ill. App. 3d 473, 80 Ill. Dec. 838, 466 N.E.2d 290 (5 Dist. 1984).

Husband's payment of the parties' income tax liability was insufficient to effect a transmutation on wife's non-marital trust. In re Holman, 122 Ill. App. 3d 1001, 78 Ill. Dec. 314, 462 N.E.2d 30 (2 Dist. 1984).

Where condominium was purchased in part with funds from a trust established by gift from the husband to three of the parties' children, and the balance from a loan to husband, although the condominium was held in trust for the children, it remained non-marital property. In re Glessner, 119 Ill. App. 3d 306, 74 Ill. Dec. 809, 456 N.E.2d 311 (1 Dist. 1983).

Beneficial interest in farmland should have been classified as wife's non-marital property where prior to the parties' marriage the husband transferred farmland into a land trust with beneficial interest in this land running to the wife for her life, and a legal agreement between the parties specifically stated that the beneficial interest in the property would remain with the wife in the event of divorce. In re Redden, 89 Ill. App. 3d 1073, 45 Ill. Dec. 86, 412 N.E.2d 219 (4 Dist. 1980).

—Value
The value of the non-marital assets is an important consideration in the apportionment of marital property, and the failure of a trial court to determine the value of substantial assets can justify reversal. In re Rosen, 126 Ill. App. 3d 766, 81 Ill. Dec. 840, 467 N.E.2d 962 (1 Dist. 1984).

—Workers' Compensation Claim
Where respondent's workers' compensation claim accrued at the time of his injury, which was prior to his marriage, his settlement check, which he received after he was married, was non-marital property as it was acquired at the time the claim accrued, prior to the marriage. In re Drone, 217 Ill. App. 3d 758, 160 Ill. Dec. 601, 577 N.E.2d 926 (5 Dist. 1991).

Option to Purchase
Trial judge, who placed land in a tenancy in common between the husband and wife in divorce proceedings, should have determined the value of that property and then given the respondent the option to purchase the petitioner's interest at the price determined. In re Simmons, 87 Ill. App. 3d 651, 42 Ill. Dec. 706, 409 N.E.2d 321 (1 Dist. 1980).

Oral Agreement
Oral property settlement should not have been reduced to written judgment, where petitioner, before entry of judgment, raised significant concerns regarding tax consequences that could impact the economic circumstances of the parties, respondent raised concerns regarding her tax liability and the payment of credit card debts, and there was a significant likelihood of protracted postjudgment litigation over the disputed provisions of settlement agreement. In re Lakin, 278 Ill. App. 3d 135, 214 Ill. Dec. 1051, 662 N.E.2d 617 (5 Dist. 1996), appeal denied, 167 Ill. 2d 554, 217 Ill. Dec. 665, 667 N.E.2d 1058 (1996).

Respondent shielded certain marital assets from the petitioner, thus preventing petitioner from making an informed decision to enter into the property settlement, or the trial court from making a fair and equitable distribution of the marital property in just proportion, such that the orally agreed-to settlement was unconscionable. In re Burch, 205 Ill. App. 3d 1082, 150 Ill. Dec. 922, 563 N.E.2d 1049 (1 Dist. 1990).

Partition
A party's right to partition is not affected by the fact that the property in question is the family home in which minor children presently reside. In re Mercer, 117 Ill. App. 3d 377, 72 Ill. Dec. 869, 453 N.E.2d 744 (1 Dist. 1983).

In a divorce action the trial court erred in denying defendant husband his right to partition the marital home which was held with wife in joint tenancy. Renwick v. Renwick, 52 Ill. App. 3d 701, 10 Ill. Dec. 400, 367 N.E.2d 1009 (2 Dist. 1977).

Where a husband established no special or superior equities in business property, under former section 17 of the Divorce Act (see now this section), and the decree referred to none, which would serve as an equitable basis for denying the wife her right to partition, but instead the decree referred only to inconvenience and possible hardship that may have resulted to the husband from the change in the relations of the parties to the estate, in the absence of statutory provision to the contrary, the absolute right to partition yielded to no consideration of hardship, inconvenience or difficulty, and the decree denying partition was improper. Peck v. Peck, 16 Ill. 2d 268, 157 N.E.2d 249 (1959).

For a case discussing partition of real property see Adams v. Adams, 398 Ill. 581, 76 N.E.2d 495 (1947).

Partnership Interests

—Assets and Liabilities
A partner's share of the firm's profits and surplus is his personal property, and a partner may assign his right to receive those profits without dissolving the firm. Sahs v. Sahs, 48 Ill. App. 3d 610, 6 Ill. Dec. 627, 363 N.E.2d 156 (2 Dist. 1977).

In determining the value of partnership interest for purposes of the division of marital property, consideration should be given to both the assets and liabilities of the partnership. In re Wilson, 110 Ill. App. 3d 809, 66 Ill. Dec. 508, 443 N.E.2d 31 (5 Dist. 1982).

—Award Modified
Where there was sufficient other property from which to award petitioner an equitable share without dividing respondent's interest in a partnership, that portion of the judgment awarding petitioner a 20% interest in respondent's partnership was modified. In re Sales, 106 Ill. App. 3d 378, 62 Ill. Dec. 441, 436 N.E.2d 23 (1 Dist. 1982).

—Evidence
There was sufficient evidence introduced at trial to support husband's contention that the real estate purchased by him and his brother belonged to the partnership and did not constitute a separate marital asset where both husband and wife testified that the ten acres was purchased by the partnership and constituted a business asset, and where husband's testimony that the $20,000 purchase price was carried on the books of the partnership as the

Partnership Interests (Cont'd)

—Evidence (Cont'd)

value of the real estate was borne out by the business records introduced by wife. In re Wilson, 110 Ill. App. 3d 809, 66 Ill. Dec. 508, 443 N.E.2d 31 (5 Dist. 1982).

—Good Will

The existence and value of good will as an asset of a partnership should be considered. In re Wilson, 110 Ill. App. 3d 809, 66 Ill. Dec. 508, 443 N.E.2d 31 (5 Dist. 1982).

—Valuation

The trial court's valuation of husband's partnership interest was arbitrary and unsupported by the evidence presented. In re Wilson, 110 Ill. App. 3d 809, 66 Ill. Dec. 508, 443 N.E.2d 31 (5 Dist. 1982).

Valuation of a partnership interest for purposes of the disposition of marital property is generally approached in the same manner as valuation of a withdrawing partner's interest upon dissolution of the partnership in accordance with applicable statutory provisions. In re Wilson, 110 Ill. App. 3d 809, 66 Ill. Dec. 508, 443 N.E.2d 31 (5 Dist. 1982).

Pension Benefits

—Accrual

Where a portion of the respondent's employment benefits accrued after the parties' separation and prior to the dissolution of the marriage, the portion was marital property and the trial court properly awarded the petitioner a portion of this asset. In re Steele, 212 Ill. App. 3d 425, 156 Ill. Dec. 649, 571 N.E.2d 236 (5 Dist. 1991).

In valuing employee pension/savings benefits, the benefits that have accrued should be considered marital property regardless of whether the benefit is vested or nonvested. In re Fairchild, 110 Ill. App. 3d 470, 66 Ill. Dec. 131, 442 N.E.2d 557 (3 Dist. 1982).

—Acquisition During Marriage

It is clear that an interest in a pension plan, if a portion accrues during the marriage, is marital property regardless of whether the interest is matured, unmatured, vested, non-vested, contributory, or non-contributory so long as the employee spouse acquired the interest in the plan during the marriage. Robinson v. Robinson, 146 Ill. App. 3d 474, 100 Ill. Dec. 260, 497 N.E.2d 140 (3 Dist. 1986).

—Application and Construction

The mere existence of 40 ILCS 5/15-120 is unpersuasive as evidence of legislative intent to absolutely exclude the pension benefits as marital property; rather, it is more readily inferred that such provision is merely a statutory safeguard of the pensioner's interest by automatically doing what the legislature presumed he would desire, i.e., dropping his divorced spouse as beneficiary. Thus petitioner's pension was properly classified as marital property. In re Wisniewski, 107 Ill. App. 3d 711, 63 Ill. Dec. 378, 437 N.E.2d 1300 (4 Dist. 1982).

—Award Not Proper

There was error in the division of marital property where the pension was allocated (one-third, two-thirds) to obtain an approximate even division of marital assets and then an immediate payout of this pension was ordered and characterized as "property in lieu of maintenance"; the court considered the pension twice: first in dividing the marital property, and second, when considering an award of maintenance. In re Emery, 179 Ill. App. 3d 744, 128 Ill. Dec. 569, 534 N.E.2d 1014 (4 Dist. 1989).

—Award Proper

Where the parties made a contribution of marital property in order to purchase a marital asset, namely, a pension, the trial court did not abuse its discretion by awarding the wife appropriate share at dissolution. Kew v. Kew, 198 Ill. App. 3d 61, 144 Ill. Dec. 372, 555 N.E.2d 731 (3 Dist. 1990).

An employee's widower was entitled to an annuity where it was admitted that the employee and beneficiary were married at the time of her death, regardless of separation, for former Ill.Rev.Stat., ch. 68, para. 22 (see now 750 ILCS 5/101 et seq.) had been repealed, and when its provisions were reenacted under this Act, the provision that persons who live separate from their spouses "without their fault" were entitled to support was deleted. Stuart v. Niemann, 100 Ill. App. 3d 242, 55 Ill. Dec. 683, 426 N.E.2d 1008 (1 Dist. 1981).

—Classification Held Improper

Trial court erred in designating the military pension earned prior to the divorce between the parties as non-marital, and under the reserved jurisdiction approach, the matter of valuing and distributing the marital asset should be resolved at the time parties reconvene according to the trial court's order. In re Lawrence, 146 Ill. App. 3d 307, 99 Ill. Dec. 845, 496 N.E.2d 538 (3 Dist. 1986).

—Discretion

The choice of the method of apportioning the present value of the marital property interest in the retirement benefits to which a spouse is entitled is a matter left to the discretion of the trial court. In re Korper, 131 Ill. App. 3d 753, 86 Ill. Dec. 766, 475 N.E.2d 1333 (5 Dist. 1985).

—Division

Illinois courts have developed two methods to apportion pension benefits upon dissolution: the first method is known as the "immediate offset" approach under which a trial court may, upon the determination of the present value of the pension benefits, award the value of the benefit to the employee spouse and offset that award with other marital property of similar value, the second method is known as the "reserved jurisdiction" approach. Under this approach, the court orders the employee spouse to pay an allocated portion of the pension fund to the former spouse, as it is disbursed, while retaining jurisdiction to enforce the decree. In re Clabault, 249 Ill. App. 3d 641, 188 Ill. Dec. 799, 619 N.E.2d 163 (2 Dist. 1993), cert. denied, 154 Ill. 2d 558, 197 Ill. Dec. 484, 631 N.E.2d 706 (1994).

Two basic methods in dividing interests in pensions are: first, the "reserved jurisdiction" approach, in which the division of the pension is delayed until it is actually paid out and the court retains jurisdiction to enforce the decree, a method best employed where it is difficult to place a present value on a pension due to uncertainties regarding vesting or maturation; and second, the "total offset" approach, in which the trial court determines the value of the pension based on actuarial evidence, discounts this amount to a present value, and then determines the marital amount of this pension, an approach frequently utilized where retirement is imminent and there are sufficient other assets to allow an offset to the nonpensioner spouse. In re Emery, 179 Ill. App. 3d 744, 128 Ill. Dec. 569, 534 N.E.2d 1014 (4 Dist. 1989); In re Wiley, 199 Ill. App. 3d 169, 145 Ill. Dec. 191, 556 N.E.2d 809 (4 Dist. 1990).

Using the immediate offset approach, the court, using actuarial evidence, determines the present value of the pension rights, and then determines what portion of that value represents marital property. To determine what portion of the pension rights represents marital property, the present value of the pension rights is multiplied by a fraction whose numerator is the number of years or months of marriage during which benefits were accumulated, and whose denominator is the total number of years or months during which benefits accumulated. The court may then award the pension rights to the employee spouse and give the nonemployee spouse other marital property to offset her marital share in the pension rights. Helber v. Helber, 180 Ill. App. 3d 507, 129 Ill. Dec. 426, 536 N.E.2d 110 (5 Dist. 1989).

—Division Prior to Vesting

The trial court's choice of immediate offset of retirement benefits vested but not yet received was not only clearly within its discretion, but was preferable to a deferred distribution approach. In re Korper, 131 Ill. App. 3d 753, 86 Ill. Dec. 766, 475 N.E.2d 1333 (5 Dist. 1985).

If a trial court deems it best to divide the pension interest prior to vesting, it must take the value of the pension as determined by actuarial evidence, discount this amount to an extent in consideration of the probability it will not vest, discount to present value, and then determine the marital portion of that amount; in some cases the trial court may be able to evaluate this risk in determining the value, but this method is best only where the pensioner is close to mandatory retirement age or retirement is otherwise imminent, and there are sufficient other marital assets to allow an offset to the nonpensioner spouse. In re Wisniewski, 107 Ill. App. 3d 711, 63 Ill. Dec. 378, 437 N.E.2d 1300 (4 Dist. 1982).

Pension Benefits (Cont'd)

—Firemen's Retirement Fund

The circuit court, in distributing property pursuant to a marriage dissolution, did not have the power to order the firemen's retirement fund to refund money paid into it by a non-employee spouse; the claim itself was barred under the Firemen's Annuity and Benefit Fund Act (see 40 ILCS 5/6-213). In re Papeck, 95 Ill. App. 3d 624, 51 Ill. Dec. 114, 420 N.E.2d 528 (1 Dist. 1981).

Where the source of money in husband's firemen's retirement fund was proceeds from the sale of real estate petitioner owned prior to the marriage, the court did not abuse its discretion in classifying the money as non-marital property. In re Papeck, 95 Ill. App. 3d 624, 51 Ill. Dec. 114, 420 N.E.2d 528 (1 Dist. 1981).

—Increase After Dissolution

Trial court erred in granting former wife benefits based upon increases in former husband's pension after the dissolution. In re Blackston, 258 Ill. App. 3d 401, 196 Ill. Dec. 606, 630 N.E.2d 541 (5 Dist. 1994).

—Intended Use

A pension is specifically intended for living expenses. In re Mullins, 121 Ill. App. 3d 86, 76 Ill. Dec. 560, 458 N.E.2d 1360 (4 Dist. 1984).

—Joinder

Where retirement plan had no interest or title which a judgment in dissolution proceedings could affect, where judgment in these proceedings dealt with division of property rights between spouses, where the husband who was bound by the decree could be required under court's continuing jurisdiction to pay out as directed to the wife, and where the plan was not concerned with what percentage of the proceeds would be due by the husband to the wife, the retirement plan was not subject to joinder. In re Degener, 119 Ill. App. 3d 1079, 75 Ill. Dec. 878, 458 N.E.2d 46 (2 Dist. 1983).

—Marital Property

The vested right to a pension was correctly held to be marital property. In re Hackett, 113 Ill. 2d 286, 100 Ill. Dec. 790, 497 N.E.2d 1152 (1986).

Pension rights, whether matured, vested or not vested, contributory or noncontributory, are property under this section. In re Hobbs, 110 Ill. App. 3d 451, 66 Ill. Dec. 203, 442 N.E.2d 629 (3 Dist. 1982); In re Campise, 115 Ill. App. 3d 610, 71 Ill. Dec. 454, 450 N.E.2d 1333 (1 Dist. 1983); In re Hughes, 160 Ill. App. 3d 680, 112 Ill. Dec. 594, 513 N.E.2d 1203 (5 Dist. 1987); In re Benz, 165 Ill. App. 3d 273, 116 Ill. Dec. 336, 518 N.E.2d 1316 (4 Dist. 1988); In re Mahaffey, 206 Ill. App. 3d 859, 151 Ill. Dec. 638, 564 N.E.2d 1300 (1 Dist. 1990).

The Illinois Pension Code (40 ILCS 5/14-147) does not prohibit consideration of husband's public pension fund as marital property. In re Uluhogian, 86 Ill. App. 3d 654, 41 Ill. Dec. 761, 408 N.E.2d 107 (5 Dist. 1980).

—Merger with Profit-Sharing Plan

Where the pension and the profit-sharing plan at the time of husband's marriage were his non-marital properties, the merger of the pension plan into the profit-sharing plan during the fiscal year 1985 did not change either plan's status. In re Leisner, 219 Ill. App. 3d 752, 162 Ill. Dec. 277, 579 N.E.2d 1091 (1 Dist. 1991).

—Military Retirement Benefits

Where parties and the trial court gave full recognition to payments generated by a military retirement pension in making the division of the marital property in a dissolution action, the trial court erred in awarding petitioner one-half of respondent's pension. In re Vest, 208 Ill. App. 3d 325, 153 Ill. Dec. 332, 567 N.E.2d 47 (5 Dist.), cert. denied, 141 Ill. 2d 562, 162 Ill. Dec. 510, 580 N.E.2d 136 (1991).

—Offset

Trial judge did not abuse her discretion because she did not award husband the non-marital portion of his pension for the approximately three years the pension accumulated before he was married; the judge specifically found that the pension would be divided equally because husband alone received benefits from the pension for approximately two years which offset the years that the pension accumulated before he was married. In re Parker, 252 Ill. App. 3d 1015, 192 Ill. Dec. 277, 625 N.E.2d 237 (1 Dist. 1993).

—Ownership Interest

The employee spouse's pension/savings benefits were marital property, and the non-employee spouse had an apportionable ownership interest in those benefits; the nature and extent of that apportionable interest was a matter reserved for subsequent judgment by that court and subject to its continuing jurisdiction. In re Fairchild, 110 Ill. App. 3d 470, 66 Ill. Dec. 131, 442 N.E.2d 557 (3 Dist. 1982).

—Personal Entitlement

Ex-wife had an interest in ex-husband's net retirement benefits as a part of property settlement; however, since the pay was a personal entitlement payable to the retired member himself as long as he lived, no part of the pay would pass to the former wife's estate should she predecease him. Musser v. Musser, 70 Ill. App. 3d 706, 27 Ill. Dec. 240, 388 N.E.2d 1289 (4 Dist. 1979).

—Review

Trial court's failure to evaluate husband's pension precluded appropriate review by appellate court of the overall property apportionment, and, therefore, case was remanded so trial court could determine the value of the pension plan to assure an equitable apportionment of the marital estate. In re Davis, 131 Ill. App. 3d 1065, 87 Ill. Dec. 145, 476 N.E.2d 1137 (1 Dist. 1985).

—Spouse's Interest

A former spouse's interest in a debtor's pension becomes the sole and separate property of the nondebtor spouse upon entry of a final judgment of divorce; the divorce decree does not create a debtor/creditor relationship between the debtor spouse and the nondebtor spouse, instead, each becomes an owner of a portion of the pension. Bigelow v. Brown, 168 Bankr. 331 (Bankr. N.D. Ill. 1994).

—Valuation

The decision of whether to use the total offset on the reserved jurisdiction method for disposing of pension rights and the decision whether to use the formula or actuarial method for valuing the pension rights under the Illinois Teachers' Retirement System during a dissolution proceeding should be made by the trial court based upon the relevant circumstances of each case, and no specific combination of these approaches and method is improper. In re Blazis, 261 Ill. App. 3d 855, 199 Ill. Dec. 941, 634 N.E.2d 1295 (4 Dist. 1994).

The value of appellee's pension rights is the amount of benefits appellee will be expected to receive upon retirement. Helber v. Helber, 180 Ill. App. 3d 507, 129 Ill. Dec. 426, 536 N.E.2d 110 (5 Dist. 1989).

Although marital assets must be valued as of the date of the judgment of dissolution, in the case of pension rights, which may not be actualized until some years in the future, the value as of the date of dissolution is the present value at the time of dissolution of the benefits expected to be received upon retirement. Helber v. Helber, 180 Ill. App. 3d 507, 129 Ill. Dec. 426, 536 N.E.2d 110 (5 Dist. 1989).

Pension rights whether matured, vested, contributory or noncontributory, are property under this section, and this value should be determined as of the time of the divorce. In re Rubinstein, 145 Ill. App. 3d 31, 99 Ill. Dec. 212, 495 N.E.2d 659 (2 Dist. 1986).

Having provided, and stipulated to, the amounts of his contribution in the pension plan and of his expected monthly benefits based thereon, and having thereafter failed to present any data which would contradict those figures or establish the present actuarial value of the plan, respondent's contention that the trial court somehow erred in failing to place a specific value on it was without merit. In re Skahn, 149 Ill. App. 3d 764, 103 Ill. Dec. 208, 501 N.E.2d 229 (1 Dist. 1986).

Trial court abused its discretion in evaluating and apportioning certain marital assets where in valuing the pension plans the court did not take into consideration husband's unrebutted testimony that the title to property, which had already been included within the estate, had been placed in his pension plans; thus, the trial court duplicated the value of the property thereby overstating the parties' assets. In re Malters, 133 Ill. App. 3d 168, 88 Ill. Dec. 460, 478 N.E.2d 1068 (1 Dist. 1985).

Pension Benefits (Cont'd)

—Valuation (Cont'd)

Absent sufficient evidence of the present value of future pension fund benefits, an award to an interest in such benefits is inappropriate under this section. In re Kundit, 107 Ill. App. 3d 310, 63 Ill. Dec. 128, 437 N.E.2d 777 (1 Dist. 1982).

Any part of a pension plan which is earned during the marriage is marital property; the amount included as marital property is the present value of the pension interest, taking into account the total time during which the benefits were accumulated prior to the divorce, as against the total time span of the marriage during which benefits were being accumulated. In re Bodford, 94 Ill. App. 3d 91, 49 Ill. Dec. 633, 418 N.E.2d 487 (2 Dist. 1981).

Pleading

—In General

In order to be entitled to a finding of special equities, they must be specially pleaded and proved by plaintiff. Pettit v. Pettit, 60 Ill. App. 3d 375, 17 Ill. Dec. 636, 376 N.E.2d 782 (4 Dist. 1978).

—Maintenance

If special equities are not pleaded and proved, it will be error for the court to order a property conveyance in addition to an award of alimony. Pettit v. Pettit, 60 Ill. App. 3d 375, 17 Ill. Dec. 636, 376 N.E.2d 782 (4 Dist. 1978).

—Property Conveyance

Where plaintiff's complaint did not pray for partition of the parties' jointly held real estate and personal property, and since special equities in the defendant's property were neither pleaded nor proved by the plaintiff, the circuit court exceeded its jurisdiction in ordering the partition of parties' jointly held property and in ordering the transfer of personal property from the defendant to the plaintiff. Pettit v. Pettit, 60 Ill. App. 3d 375, 17 Ill. Dec. 636, 376 N.E.2d 782 (4 Dist. 1978).

To justify the conveyance of one spouse's interest in property to the other spouse, special equities or circumstances were required to be specifically alleged in the complaint or counterclaim for divorce and established by the evidence. Crenshaw v. Crenshaw, 45 Ill. App. 3d 880, 4 Ill. Dec. 640, 360 N.E.2d 576 (1 Dist. 1977).

—Property Interest

Where all of property placed in trust by husband was considered his, being property which he either acquired through inheritance or his employment, and wife could have been awarded an interest in this property only if she had alleged and proved special equities in it or if the trial court had chosen to award her an interest as alimony in gross in lieu of the more customary periodic alimony, since she did not allege or prove any special equities in this property, and the trial court ordered husband to make periodic payments of alimony, thus precluding any award of alimony in gross, the appellate court could not reverse the trial court's disposition with respect to this property. Staub v. Staub, 67 Ill. App. 3d 1004, 24 Ill. Dec. 630, 385 N.E.2d 771 (5 Dist. 1978).

Where wife who got a divorce was never intended to be a party to written contract to purchase farm, or to oral arrangement, and where she did not plead that she had any special equities in the farm and husband testified that wife did not work on the farm or make any contributions toward the purchase of the farm, the trial court properly found that the wife had neither a legal nor an equitable interest of any kind in the farm. Andrews v. Andrews, 54 Ill. App. 3d 1017, 12 Ill. Dec. 683, 370 N.E.2d 306 (3 Dist. 1977).

Premarital Property Rights

—Not Shown

Where defendant aided growing business by purchasing its first ladder and contributing secretarial work, but never exerted any control over the operation of the business, never claimed any income from the business on her individual tax returns prior to the parties' marriage, and never claimed to be a joint owner or partner prior to incorporation, she was not entitled to any premarital property rights in the business. In re Thacker, 185 Ill. App. 3d 465, 133 Ill. Dec. 573, 541 N.E.2d 784 (5 Dist. 1989).

Presumptions

—In General

This Act creates a presumption that property acquired during the marriage is marital property, and the party seeking to rebut the presumption bears the burden of showing the property was acquired in a manner that makes it non-marital, such as a gift. Wesselhoft v. Wesselhoft, 228 Ill. App. 3d 269, 169 Ill. Dec. 424, 591 N.E.2d 928 (3 Dist. 1992).

This Act presumes that all property acquired during the marriage is marital property; this is true regardless whether the property is also taxable as income. In re Mahaffey, 206 Ill. App. 3d 859, 151 Ill. Dec. 638, 564 N.E.2d 1300 (1 Dist. 1990).

Property acquired after the marriage is presumed to be marital property. In re Van Ness, 136 Ill. App. 3d 185, 90 Ill. Dec. 766, 482 N.E.2d 1049 (4 Dist. 1985).

This statute creates a rebuttable presumption that all property acquired after marriage is marital property. Hofmann v. Hofmann, 94 Ill. 2d 205, 68 Ill. Dec. 593, 446 N.E.2d 499 (1983).

—Evidence Held Insufficient

Wife's testimony was not clear and convincing and, therefore, was insufficient to rebut the presumption that property acquired during marriage was presumed to be marital property where husband testified he transferred the property to wife only to protect the property from a possible malpractice action against him, and that he did not intend the property to be a gift. In re Leff, 148 Ill. App. 3d 792, 101 Ill. Dec. 262, 499 N.E.2d 1042 (2 Dist. 1986).

—Exceptions

All property acquired during the marriage is presumed to be marital property unless the presumption is overcome by a showing that it falls within one of the statutory exceptions, including property acquired before marriage, and property acquired in exchange for property acquired before marriage; the party claiming that the property is non-marital has the burden of proof. In re Schriner, 88 Ill. App. 3d 380, 43 Ill. Dec. 572, 410 N.E.2d 572 (2 Dist. 1980).

—Gift

Although wife testified that she expected home received on death of her father and subsequently transferred to husband and herself in joint tenancy to stay in the family and never intended it to be a gift, similar testimony has been considered insufficient to rebut the presumption of transmutation; thus, the circuit court's decision that wife had not rebutted the presumption of gift to the marital estate did not constitute an abuse of discretion nor was it against the manifest weight of the evidence. In re Durante, 201 Ill. App. 3d 376, 147 Ill. Dec. 56, 559 N.E.2d 56 (1 Dist. 1990).

Factors to consider in determining whether a party has rebutted the presumption of gift or has shown that presumption to be unreasonable are: the size of the gift relative to the entire estate; who paid the purchase price, made improvements, and paid taxes for the property with solely acquired funds and exercised control and management over the property; when the assets were purchased; and how the parties handled their prior financial dealings with each other. In re Guerra, 153 Ill. App. 3d 550, 106 Ill. Dec. 201, 505 N.E.2d 748 (2 Dist. 1987).

The presumption of marital property is overcome upon a showing by clear, convincing, and unmistakable evidence that the property was a gift. In re Deem, 123 Ill. App. 3d 1019, 79 Ill. Dec. 542, 463 N.E.2d 1317 (4 Dist. 1984).

Evidence was insufficient in finding that a presumption of gift arose where defendant husband who held title to real property prior to his marriage to plaintiff wife and who caused the title to be transferred to plaintiff and defendant in joint tenancy where there was absence of an intention to make a gift to wife by such transfer so as to permit the trial court directing conveyance of the interest of wife to husband as the equitable owner of the property concluding wife's joint interest. Comstock v. Comstock, 55 Ill. App. 3d 140, 12 Ill. Dec. 841, 370 N.E.2d 645 (3 Dist. 1977).

—Rebuttal

Petitioner's self-serving assertion of his intent was not clear and convincing evidence sufficient to rebut the presumption that property placed in joint tenancy was marital property. In re Smith, 265 Ill. App. 3d 249, 202 Ill. Dec. 738, 638 N.E.2d 384 (4 Dist. 1994).

Proceeds

Funds in an escrow account acquired in exchange for non-marital and marital property must be divided into their marital and non-marital components, with the marital components subject to

Proceeds (Cont'd)
equitable distribution. In re Humphrey, 101 Ill. App. 3d 1134, 57 Ill. Dec. 436, 428 N.E.2d 1116 (3 Dist. 1981).

Because parties were not able to divide household goods between themselves and because husband-defendant did not establish a special equity in all or part of the contents, the trial court did not abuse its discretion by ordering the sale and equal distribution of the proceeds and therefore, value placed on the goods by the trial court was irrelevant because of the equal distribution order. West v. West, 77 Ill. App. 3d 828, 33 Ill. Dec. 658, 396 N.E.2d 1382 (4 Dist. 1979).

Husband could not be allowed to deduct or receive credit for his share of payments made on behalf of wife and to satisfy his own proportionate share of the expenses upon sale of former marital home and division of proceeds under divorce decree. Gilmore v. Gilmore, 28 Ill. App. 3d 36, 328 N.E.2d 562 (1 Dist. 1975).

Where the court was unable to determine from the record and from the vague and incomplete testimony of the witness for the bank exactly how the bank came into possession of the note and mortgage on the marital estate, the evidence was insufficient to support award of proceeds of sale to bank instead of wife. Kitzer v. Kitzer, 1 Ill. App. 3d 1016, 274 N.E.2d 610 (2 Dist. 1971).

Property Rights

—Invalid Divorce Decree
In the absence of a valid divorce decree, the court has no power to determine the interests of the parties in property, and a court judgment would be void and of no force or effect concerning the property interest of the parties. Sharer v. Sharer, 39 Ill. App. 3d 818, 350 N.E.2d 779 (5 Dist. 1976).

—Powers of Court
The court has power to adjust equities and determine rights of one party in property of other party where a divorce has been granted. In re Pahlke, 120 Ill. App. 3d 1009, 76 Ill. Dec. 487, 458 N.E.2d 1141 (1 Dist. 1983).

—Special Circumstances and Equities Required
The rights and interest a wife had in the property of her husband by virtue of the marriage relation alone would not support a conveyance of property under former Ill.Rev.Stat., ch. 40, para. 18 (see now this section); special circumstances and equities had to be alleged and proven, such as the contribution of money or services other than those normally performed in the marriage relationship which had directly or indirectly been used to acquire or enhance the value of the property. Overton v. Overton, 6 Ill. App. 3d 1086, 287 N.E.2d 47 (2 Dist. 1972).

—Survival
Property rights of a husband and wife which exist independently of the marriage survive the divorce decree. Sebben v. Woodshank, 27 Ill. App. 3d 444, 325 N.E.2d 686 (3 Dist. 1975).

—Transfers
In absence of some governing statutory provision, a court may not interfere with property rights and interests of parties; however, the court may, where appropriate, and where requested by one or both of the parties, order transfers of property or property interests from one party to another, according to the equities where special circumstances appear. Halloran v. Halloran, 39 Ill. App. 3d 528, 350 N.E.2d 318 (3 Dist. 1976).

—Voluntary Adjustment
Parties to a divorce suit may voluntarily adjust their property interests and the amount, if any, to be paid as alimony; when such agreements are made a part of the decree, the parties are concluded thereby. Garmisa v. Garmisa, 4 Ill. App. 3d 411, 280 N.E.2d 444 (1 Dist. 1972).

Property Settlement

—Contract
A property settlement agreement incorporated into a divorce decree constitutes a contract and is to be construed according to the ordinary rules for the construction of contracts. Pollard v. Waggoner, 165 Ill. App. 3d 501, 116 Ill. Dec. 428, 519 N.E.2d 18 (5 Dist. 1988).

—Discretion
A trial court is not controlled by the terms of a proposed property settlement agreement but may adopt or reject it, as seems consistent and proper from the situations of the parties. Mayeur v. Mayeur, 42 Ill. App. 3d 7, 355 N.E.2d 358 (3 Dist. 1976).

—Mutual Consent
The evidence amply supported the findings of the trial judge that the property settlement and separation were not by mutual consent, and that the proceedings were instituted and pushed by the wife who not only wanted the property divided but also insisted on discontinuing the marital relationship. Gillespie v. Gillespie, 70 Ill. App. 2d 38, 216 N.E.2d 462 (5 Dist. 1966).

Purpose
By enacting subsection (d) of this section, the legislature did not intend to cause the courts to become auditing agencies for every marriage that falters; allowing lawyers, or possibly requiring them under a threat of malpractice, to question all expenses and economic decisions of a marriage in the hope of uncovering something that could be called dissipation adds an unnecessary and wasteful burden of time and expense especially when no initial triggering event or threshold had been crossed. In re Getautas, 189 Ill. App. 3d 148, 136 Ill. Dec. 509, 544 N.E.2d 1284 (2 Dist. 1989).

The objective of this section is to achieve a division of property which is in just proportions. Hofmann v. Hofmann, 125 Ill. App. 3d 548, 81 Ill. Dec. 12, 466 N.E.2d 598 (3 Dist. 1984).

The purpose of this Act is to make the division of property the primary means of providing for the future financial needs of the spouses. In re Cook, 117 Ill. App. 3d 844, 73 Ill. Dec. 222, 453 N.E.2d 1357 (1 Dist. 1983).

The statutory directive of subdivision (c)(4) of this section is intended to minimize disruption in the lives of children whose parents have dissolved their marriage. In re Keller, 108 Ill. App. 3d 556, 64 Ill. Dec. 115, 439 N.E.2d 44 (1 Dist. 1982).

When subsection (c) of this section and 750 ILCS 5/504 are considered together, it is apparent that the legislature intended to enlarge greatly the discretion of courts in providing for just and equitable property settlements and maintenance awards. If the court gives proper regard to the factors the legislature has provided the court may award either property or maintenance, or may award both property and maintenance, and also may award property in lieu of maintenance. In re Gan, 83 Ill. App. 3d 265, 38 Ill. Dec. 882, 404 N.E.2d 306 (5 Dist. 1980).

Rather than recognizing equity in the non-marital property, this section contemplates a scheme by which the contributing spouse is compensated by the allocation to him of a disproportionate share of the marital property. In re Glidden, 71 Ill. App. 3d 376, 27 Ill. Dec. 593, 389 N.E.2d 657 (2 Dist. 1979).

The purpose of subsection (c) of this section is to divide the marital property without regard to marital misconduct in just proportions considering all relevant factors, including those set forth in order to promote the amicable settlement of disputes between the parties to a marriage, and mitigate the potential harm to the spouses and children caused by the process of legal dissolution of marriage. In re Thompson, 79 Ill. App. 3d 310, 34 Ill. Dec. 342, 398 N.E.2d 17 (1 Dist. 1979).

The plain and unmistakable purpose of the 1949 amendment to former section 18 of the Divorce Act (see now this section) was to authorize a court in a divorce action to compel the conveyance of property from one spouse to the other as a settlement in lieu of alimony. Persico v. Persico, 409 Ill. 608, 100 N.E.2d 904 (1951).

Refinancing Provisions

—Exclusion Held Proper
Trial court properly excluded the projected cost of refinancing marital home in its determination of husband's income after expenses in determining support and distribution provisions because defendant assumed that expense in the agreement between the parties of his own volition. Gauger v. Gauger, 70 Ill. App. 3d 378, 26 Ill. Dec. 499, 388 N.E.2d 123 (1 Dist. 1979).

Reimbursement

—In General
While there is no right to reimbursement when a gift has been made, there is a right to reimbursement when assets have changed

Reimbursement (Cont'd)

—In General (Cont'd)

character by reason of commingling as long as the contributions between estates can be traced by clear and convincing evidence. In re Werries, 247 Ill. App. 3d 639, 186 Ill. Dec. 747, 616 N.E.2d 1379 (4 Dist. 1993).

—Abuse of Discretion

Where the parties did not have a legally recognized marriage until July 21, 1980, the trial court abused its discretion when it granted a right of reimbursement for the time prior to the parties' legally recognized marriage. In re Hughes, 160 Ill. App. 3d 680, 112 Ill. Dec. 594, 513 N.E.2d 1203 (5 Dist. 1987).

—Contribution

No contribution which is not traceable by clear and convincing evidence is reimbursable. In re Werries, 247 Ill. App. 3d 639, 186 Ill. Dec. 747, 616 N.E.2d 1379 (4 Dist. 1993).

Trial court erred when it failed to reimburse the marital estate for the contributions made from the marital estate to husband's non-marital residence. McCoy v McCoy, 225 Ill. App. 3d 966, 168 Ill. Dec. 27, 589 N.E.2d 141 (3 Dist. 1992).

Reimbursement for contributions is not mandated when property is given as a gift to the marital estate. In re Durante, 201 Ill. App. 3d 376, 147 Ill. Dec. 56, 559 N.E.2d 56 (1 Dist. 1990).

If non-marital property is transmuted into marital property, the party contributing the non-marital property is entitled to reimbursement of the value of such property provided: (1) the contribution is traceable by clear and convincing evidence; and (2) the contributor did not make a gift of the non-marital property to the marital estate. In re Guerra, 153 Ill. App. 3d 550, 106 Ill. Dec. 201, 505 N.E.2d 748 (2 Dist. 1987).

Because personal effort of a spouse is deemed a contribution by the marital estate, one spouse's contribution of personal effort toward the non-marital property may entitle the marital estate, not the other spouse, to reimbursement from the non-marital estate receiving the contribution. In re Morse, 143 Ill. App. 3d 849, 98 Ill. Dec. 67, 493 N.E.2d 1088 (5 Dist. 1986).

—Equity

Since wife was deprived of her equity in house in divorce proceeding, the trial court properly found that it was equitable for husband to reimburse the wife for her contribution toward the "purchase" of the house, less interest. Andrews v. Andrews, 54 Ill. App. 3d 1017, 12 Ill. Dec. 683, 370 N.E.2d 306 (3 Dist. 1977).

—Lack of Traceable Contributions

The absence of clear and convincing evidence of traceable contributions from the marital estate to the non-marital partnership interest precludes any reasonable attempt to order reimbursement to the marital estate. In re Werries, 247 Ill. App. 3d 639, 186 Ill. Dec. 747, 616 N.E.2d 1379 (4 Dist. 1993).

—Not Required

Although the husband's limited partnership interest appreciated substantially, the evidence was not clear and convincing that this increase was due to the significant efforts of the husband and therefore reimbursement to the marital estate was not required. In re Eddy, 210 Ill. App. 3d 450, 155 Ill. Dec. 174, 569 N.E.2d 174 (1 Dist. 1991).

—Personal Efforts

No reimbursement is to be made for personal efforts unless the effort was significant and resulted in substantial appreciation of the non-marital property. In re Werries, 247 Ill. App. 3d 639, 186 Ill. Dec. 747, 616 N.E.2d 1379 (4 Dist. 1993).

In valuing the right to reimbursement, if husband's salary is found to be reasonable compensation for his efforts, the non-marital business need not reimburse the marital estate because husband's salary during the marriage is marital property and, thus, the marital estate has already been compensated. In re Landfield, 209 Ill. App. 3d 678, 153 Ill. Dec. 834, 567 N.E.2d 1061 (1 Dist.), cert. denied, 139 Ill. 2d 597, 159 Ill. Dec. 109, 575 N.E.2d 916 (1991).

It is the appreciation resulting from significant personal effort, not inflation or other factors external to the marriage, which entitles the marital estate to reimbursement. In re Morse, 143 Ill. App. 3d 849, 98 Ill. Dec. 67, 493 N.E.2d 1088 (5 Dist. 1986); In re Landfield, 209 Ill. App. 3d 678, 153 Ill. Dec. 834, 567 N.E.2d 1061 (1 Dist.), cert. denied, 139 Ill. 2d 597, 159 Ill. Dec. 109, 575 N.E.2d 916 (1991).

—Prior Compensation

In determining whether the marital estate is entitled to reimbursement from a non-marital business for the contribution of personal efforts of a spouse, the court may inquire as to whether the spouse was reasonably compensated by the business for those efforts; if the spouse has already been reasonably compensated for the personal effort, no reimbursement is necessary. In re Werries, 247 Ill. App. 3d 639, 186 Ill. Dec. 747, 616 N.E.2d 1379 (4 Dist. 1993).

—Sale of Non-Marital Asset

Where the source of the payment of a mortgage was the sale of a non-marital asset, respondent was entitled to reimbursement from the marital estate under subdivision (c)(2) of this section. In re Miller, 231 Ill. App. 3d 480, 172 Ill. Dec. 679, 595 N.E.2d 1349 (3 Dist. 1992).

—Transfers During Marriage

This section contemplates the transfer of property of the various estates during the pendency of a valid marriage. In re Hughes, 160 Ill. App. 3d 680, 112 Ill. Dec. 594, 513 N.E.2d 1203 (5 Dist. 1987).

Remand

—Circumstances

Where the trial court, upon remandment, heard additional evidence and made its distribution based on the extraordinary circumstances of the wife's ill health which had arisen after the appellate court had filed its order under Rule 23, Supreme Court Rules, its actions were proper because the court could not have made an equitable disposition of marital property or determined the need for maintenance without having considered the current health and economic circumstances of the parties. In re Fuggiti, 130 Ill. App. 3d 190, 85 Ill. Dec. 658, 474 N.E.2d 386 (1 Dist. 1985).

—Issues

Where neither party has claimed on appeal that the trial court erred in determining the value of the marital property, the trial court's finding as to the value of the marital property is the law of the case, and the only issue to be decided on remand is the proper distribution of the marital property. In re Parker, 216 Ill. App. 3d 672, 159 Ill. Dec. 131, 575 N.E.2d 938 (2 Dist. 1991).

Where it has been determined that the trial court erred in failing to consider or to evaluate a significant marital asset, the trial court upon remand must review all property and support awards in order to determine if any reallocation of assets is necessary. In re Rothbardt, 99 Ill. App. 3d 561, 54 Ill. Dec. 929, 425 N.E.2d 1146 (1 Dist. 1981).

—Scope

Where the related issues of maintenance to petitioner and the minor child and the payment of educational expenses were directly affected by the final property disposition, since these awards were substantially dependent upon the financial resources of the parties, including marital property, the maintenance and support awards would have to be re-evaluated by the trial court on remand so that it could properly consider any changes required in the disposition of such property. In re Walsh, 109 Ill. App. 3d 171, 64 Ill. Dec. 758, 440 N.E.2d 310 (1 Dist. 1982).

Remarriage

—Estoppel

The rule of estoppel, founded upon the public policy of protecting the marital status and good character of innocent third persons, the legitimacy of children, and the rights and positions of persons whose status has been finalized by decree of divorce, will not permit parties to assert inconsistent legal rights; petitioner could not seek additional property from her former husband's estate after her own remarriage. McDonald v. Neale, 35 Ill. App. 2d 140, 182 N.E.2d 366 (1 Dist. 1962).

—Modification of Property Distribution

Where the phrase "maintenance in gross" was simply another name for the petitioner's award of marital property and was

Remarriage (Cont'd)

—Modification of Property Distribution (Cont'd)
employed solely for tax purposes, and periodic maintenance was denied, the petitioner's remarriage did not constitute grounds for a modification of the property distribution. Hofmann v. Hofmann, 125 Ill. App. 3d 548, 81 Ill. Dec. 12, 466 N.E.2d 598 (3 Dist. 1984).

—Rights Restored
Once the parties to a dissolution remarry each other, they are restored to their respective rights as husband and wife and parents as if they had never been divorced, and if they again divorce, the original support and custody agreements are unenforceable. Ringstrom v. Ringstrom, 101 Ill. App. 3d 677, 57 Ill. Dec. 193, 428 N.E.2d 743 (4 Dist. 1981).

Rental Property

—Abuse of Discretion
The trial court did not abuse its discretion in treating rental property as part of the marital estate. In re Agazim, 176 Ill. App. 3d 225, 125 Ill. Dec. 701, 530 N.E.2d 1110 (2 Dist. 1988).

—Award Upheld
Where there was no evidence to support husband's contention that he made a substantial contribution to owned rental property and wife obviously made the sole contribution to the property's acquisition, the trial court did not abuse its discretion in awarding wife the complete interest in the property. In re Agazim, 176 Ill. App. 3d 225, 125 Ill. Dec. 701, 530 N.E.2d 1110 (2 Dist. 1988).

—Transfer of Title
While a divorce decree, of itself, could not formally vest title to a rental property subject to a lease/option in the wife, it could divest plaintiff of his interest in the contract, award that interest to defendant, and authorize her to complete the purchase; title would be vested in her by the deed she procured from the owner of the property and not by the decree. Harwood v. Harwood, 412 Ill. 131, 105 N.E.2d 719 (1952).

Representation
Where petitioner wife was well represented by able and experienced counsel and the record showed that there had been pretrial conferences on a number of occasions, depositions had been taken in behalf of petitioner wife so that she was ostensibly fully informed, and she has been the sole operator of a good-sized business enterprise, there was no evidence of misrepresentation, coercion or overreaching; therefore, the property settlement agreement was not set aside. Nitzkin v. Nitzkin, 66 Ill. App. 3d 495, 23 Ill. Dec. 435, 384 N.E.2d 71 (1 Dist. 1978).

Requirements

—In General
This section requires the court to consider the relevant statutory factors and divide the marital property in just proportions. In re Jacks, 200 Ill. App. 3d 112, 146 Ill. Dec. 143, 558 N.E.2d 106 (2 Dist. 1990).

If an examination of the entire record reveals that the trial court was aware of the requirements of this section, and if further examination of the entire record reveals that the trial court arrived at an ultimate disposition in harmony with the rationale of this section, no abuse of discretion has occurred. In re Fryer, 88 Ill. App. 3d 454, 43 Ill. Dec. 596, 410 N.E.2d 596 (4 Dist. 1980).

—Compliance with Statute
In making its division of marital property and in providing for child support the circuit court did not abuse its discretion and made its decisions in compliance with the rationale of the statute. In re Fryer, 88 Ill. App. 3d 454, 43 Ill. Dec. 596, 410 N.E.2d 596 (4 Dist. 1980).

—Specific Value Not Required
Although subdivision (c)(2) of this section requires a court to consider the value of the property set apart to each spouse, the court is not required in its judgment to place a specific value on each item of property. In re Hyland, 95 Ill. App. 3d 31, 50 Ill. Dec. 554, 419 N.E.2d 662 (2 Dist. 1981).

Reserved Jurisdiction
Where determination of the value of a pension plan under present actuarial methods would have been difficult, if not impossible, the reserved jurisdiction approach should have been used such that the trial court would reserve jurisdiction in order to make an allocation of spouse's interest in the pension when, as and if the retirement or pension benefits became payable; the formula that should be employed at that time would be a "just proportion" of the benefits determined by dividing the years of marriage by the total years of employment. Robinson v. Robinson, 146 Ill. App. 3d 474, 100 Ill. Dec. 260, 497 N.E.2d 140 (3 Dist. 1986).

The trial court was directed to reserve jurisdiction over the future pension benefits; whether it would make a present percentage allocation of those benefits, or would reserve the decision for the future, was left to the court's sound discretion. In re Hobbs, 110 Ill. App. 3d 451, 66 Ill. Dec. 203, 442 N.E.2d 629 (3 Dist. 1982).

As maintenance is subject to the continuing jurisdiction of the court, reserved jurisdiction over pension/savings benefits allows the court to apportion to the non-employee spouse an interest in pension benefits accrued during the marriage, yet at a time in future when the value of those benefits is no longer speculative. In re Fairchild, 110 Ill. App. 3d 470, 66 Ill. Dec. 131, 442 N.E.2d 557 (3 Dist. 1982).

Appropriate circumstances to enter a judgment of dissolution and reservation of questions for child custody, support and maintenance would be where the court does not have in personam jurisdiction over the respondent, or inability of a party to pay child support or maintenance if so ordered, or where the court has set aside an adequate fund for child support pursuant to subsection (d) of this section, or where the child or children of the parties do not reside with either parent. In re Cohn, 94 Ill. App. 3d 732, 50 Ill. Dec. 621, 419 N.E.2d 729 (2 Dist. 1981), aff'd, 93 Ill. 2d 190, 66 Ill. Dec. 615, 443 N.E.2d 541 (1982).

Residence for Business Purposes

—Evidence Held Insufficient
Husband's claim that he needed marital home for business purposes was not supported by the evidence where he testified at trial that he received his business mail at a post office box, and that he stored his tools, equipment and materials in a rented garage and at a lot in another town. In re Randall, 157 Ill. App. 3d 892, 110 Ill. Dec. 122, 510 N.E.2d 1153 (1 Dist. 1987).

Retroactive Application
Amended statute was not applied on remand of marriage dissolution where, even though amendment affected a significant change in Illinois marriage law, application of 750 ILCS 5/801(d), which governs whether an amendment should be applied to new hearings, was both reasonable and appropriate. In re Brown, 127 Ill. App. 3d 831, 83 Ill. Dec. 5, 469 N.E.2d 612 (5 Dist. 1984).

The retrospective application of subsection (b) of this section to property which was already subject to divestment in a divorce proceeding could not be said to impair an absolute property interest; it merely enhanced a remedy already available to the non-property-owning spouse. Kujawinski v. Kujawinski, 71 Ill. 2d 563, 17 Ill. Dec. 801, 376 N.E.2d 1382 (1978).

Sale of Chose in Action
Where a chose in action was the only asset of the parties from which they could meet support obligations, the power granted in subsection (i) was sufficiently broad to permit the divorce court, within its discretion, to order the sale of interest in litigation. In re Schweihs, 272 Ill. App. 3d 653, 208 Ill. Dec. 875, 650 N.E.2d 569 (1 Dist. 1995), appeal denied, 163 Ill. 2d 588, 212 Ill. Dec. 437, 657 N.E.2d 638 (1995).

Sale of Real Property

—Improper
Trial court erred in ordering the sale of the real property with the proceeds to be divided between the parties; such was in the nature of a partition and neither party requested a partition. In re Pieper, 79 Ill. App. 3d 835, 34 Ill. Dec. 877, 398 N.E.2d 868 (1 Dist. 1979).

Where the authority exercised by the chancellor in a divorce proceeding ordered that creditors of the parties be paid from the proceeds of the sale of the wife's property, irrespective of when and by whom the debts were incurred, unwarrantably deprived the wife

Sale of Real Property (Cont'd)

—Improper (Cont'd)

of her freehold estate and gave the husband a share which he did not even claim, and imposed upon the wife the additional penalty for the husband's extravagances, all of which was neither within the terms nor the purport of the former Divorce Act (see now 750 ILCS 5/101 et seq.), that portion of the divorce decree was reversed and the cause was remanded with directions to award the net proceeds of the sale remaining in the hands of the clerk, to the wife. Stevens v. Stevens, 14 Ill. 2d 99, 150 N.E.2d 799 (1958).

—Tax Consequences

While the trial court in its judgment did not specifically discuss the tax consequences of the sale of the farm and the office and rental property, where both parties would be equally affected by the sale the trial court, did not err with regard to the determination of tax consequences. In re Smith, 162 Ill. App. 3d 792, 114 Ill. Dec. 622, 516 N.E.2d 777 (5 Dist. 1987).

Security

A lien by one spouse on the stock of a closely held corporation owned by the other spouse, which was held in escrow upon court order, was sufficient to secure a spouse's property interest until the property judgment awarded to that spouse was satisfied. In re Jones, 187 Ill. App. 3d 206, 134 Ill. Dec. 836, 543 N.E.2d 119 (1 Dist. 1989).

Where respondent had provided for the needs of his children since the separation, and there was no indication that he would not continue to do so in the future, respondent's estate would be liable for future support "to the extent just and appropriate under the circumstances," and should he otherwise fail to provide for them, there was no reason to believe that respondent, or his estate would not have been able to provide the support mandated, and respondent had ample assets apart from the pension and profit sharing plan to provide all the necessary support, the trial court did not abuse its discretion in failing to require that respondent furnish security for his support obligations. In re Wilder, 122 Ill. App. 3d 338, 77 Ill. Dec. 824, 461 N.E.2d 447 (1 Dist. 1983).

Separate Property

—Inheritance

Where petitioner used his inheritance to purchase a boat, then invested sale proceeds from the boat in securities, subsequently liquidated the securities, and finally used their proceeds toward purchase of the marital home, he could assert separate ownership in a corresponding portion of the value of the house as long as there was no evidence that he intended any of the intermediate purchases to be marital property. In re Preston, 81 Ill. App. 3d 672, 37 Ill. Dec. 442, 402 N.E.2d 332 (5 Dist. 1980).

—Separate Funds

Assets purchased with separate funds remain separate property, regardless of the manner of holding title and regardless of the number of post-marital exchanges. In re Preston, 81 Ill. App. 3d 672, 37 Ill. Dec. 442, 402 N.E.2d 332 (5 Dist. 1980).

The entire increase in the value of a marital home should be considered marital property, even though husband was entitled to assert separate ownership of that portion of the home which was paid for by separate funds belonging to him. In re Preston, 81 Ill. App. 3d 672, 37 Ill. Dec. 442, 402 N.E.2d 332 (5 Dist. 1980).

Separation Agreement

The terms of a separation agreement are binding upon the court so long as the agreement is not unconscionable. In re Lorenzi, 84 Ill. App. 3d 427, 39 Ill. Dec. 754, 405 N.E.2d 507 (3 Dist. 1980).

In order to give effect to both 750 ILCS 5/502 and this section, this section must mandate the court to denominate property as marital and non-marital and to justly apportion the marital property of the parties, considering the factors therein enumerated, only in the absence of a conscionable settlement agreement entered into by the parties, as discussed in section 502. In re Lorenzi, 84 Ill. App. 3d 427, 39 Ill. Dec. 754, 405 N.E.2d 507 (3 Dist. 1980).

The trial court did not err in failing to denominate non-marital and marital property and in declining to apportion the latter in light of the uncontested evidence of a separation agreement between the parties purporting to dispose of all their property. In re Lorenzi, 84 Ill. App. 3d 427, 39 Ill. Dec. 754, 405 N.E.2d 507 (3 Dist. 1980).

Should a separation agreement be found unconscionable, or should the court find that no separation agreement had actually been entered into, the court would then be required to approve a conscionable agreement from the parties, if there is such an agreement, or to proceed under this section denominating the parties' property as marital and non-marital and dividing it in accordance with the requirements of this section. In re Lorenzi, 84 Ill. App. 3d 427, 39 Ill. Dec. 754, 405 N.E.2d 507 (3 Dist. 1980).

Where a separation is imminent or has already occurred, an agreement making a fair and equitable provision for the separate support and maintenance of the wife and for a settlement of property rights is not against public policy. Rooks v. Plavec, 40 Ill. App. 2d 298, 188 N.E.2d 251 (1 Dist. 1963).

Settlement Agreements

Where two parties enter into a marital settlement agreement, and where performance of the agreement is carried out, notwithstanding the dismissal of the divorce proceedings, the agreement is a valid allocation of marital and non-marital property rights. In re Vella, 237 Ill. App. 3d 194, 177 Ill. Dec. 328, 603 N.E.2d 109 (2 Dist. 1992).

The husband's assumption of car loan payments was in the nature of a property settlement in lieu of maintenance and did not terminate when the wife remarried, because the judgment provided that the husband would pay the loan according to its current schedule, the loan was for a specific sum to be paid over a specific period of time, except for the husband's payment of the marital debts, each party would surrender all claims to maintenance and all claims to the property of the other spouse, the marital property was divided by the court giving consideration to whether the appointment was in lieu of maintenance, and neither the label attached nor the method of payment prescribed in the judgment conclusively determined the nature of the award. In re Rowden, 163 Ill. App. 3d 869, 114 Ill. Dec. 886, 516 N.E.2d 1041 (3 Dist. 1987).

Where the parties to a divorce have voluntarily adjusted their property rights and their agreement is then incorporated into a judgment, the parties are bound by the settlement; however, such an agreement of the parties will be vacated for fraud, coercion or if the settlement is unfair, inequitable and unjust. Nitzkin v. Nitzkin, 66 Ill. App. 3d 495, 23 Ill. Dec. 435, 384 N.E.2d 71 (1 Dist. 1978).

Unless plaintiff established special equities in defendant's property, she was not entitled to both a lump sum settlement and periodic support payments. Mayeur v. Mayeur, 42 Ill. App. 3d 7, 355 N.E.2d 358 (3 Dist. 1976).

Source of Law

Public Act 83-129 constituted a legislative rejection of the rationale of the Supreme Court's holding in In re Marriage of Smith (1981), 86 Ill.2d 518, 56 Ill.Dec. 693, 427 N.E.2d 1239. In re Smith, 162 Ill. App. 3d 792, 114 Ill. Dec. 622, 516 N.E.2d 777 (5 Dist. 1987).

Special Equities

—Allegations and Proof

It must be alleged and proved by the spouse seeking a part or all of the property in the name of the other that he or she has furnished valuable consideration such as money or services other than those normally performed in the marriage relation which has directly or indirectly been used to acquire or enhance the value of the property. Alvarado v. Alvarado, 22 Ill. App. 3d 10, 316 N.E.2d 561 (3 Dist. 1974).

Under former section 17 of the Divorce Act (see now this section), special equities in property were to be pleaded and proved by the party claiming them. Katz v. Katz, 10 Ill. App. 3d 39, 293 N.E.2d 904 (1 Dist. 1973).

Where special equities are claimed, justifying the conveyance of the husband's property to the wife, the special circumstances must be alleged in the complaint and established by the proof. Ylonen v. Ylonen, 2 Ill. 2d 111, 117 N.E.2d 98 (1954).

—Business Holdings

Each party was entitled to property held in his or her own name, except to the extent of plaintiff's special equities in defendant's business holdings. Leone v. Leone, 39 Ill. App. 3d 547, 350 N.E.2d 545 (3 Dist. 1976).

Special Equities (Cont'd)

—Contributions

Alimony is conditional upon one spouse's present and future need for support and the other's ability to pay, and is separate from the right to special equities which arises from past contributions to the marital estate. Leone v. Leone, 39 Ill. App. 3d 547, 350 N.E.2d 545 (3 Dist. 1976).

—Conveyance Denied

Under former section 17 of the Divorce Act (see now this section), the trial court erred in granting plaintiff special equities in all real estate owned by defendant because the conveyance of property held by defendant was bought with funds from the joint family checking account, comprised entirely of defendant's earnings. Hogan v. Hogan, 58 Ill. App. 3d 661, 16 Ill. Dec. 265, 374 N.E.2d 1040 (1 Dist. 1978).

—Court Discretion

One spouse may have a special equitable interest in property held in the other's name, which interest may arise in many ways, and the court may award a share of the property representing such special interest in it. Gerhardt v. Gerhardt, 18 Ill. App. 3d 658, 310 N.E.2d 224 (3 Dist. 1974).

—Jointly Held Property

Under former sections 18 and 19 of the Divorce Act (see now this section), the court could order a conveyance from one spouse to another, either on account of special equities or in lieu of alimony, where title to property was held by the parties in joint tenancy; the court could have, if requested, ordered partition. Pettit v. Pettit, 60 Ill. App. 3d 375, 17 Ill. Dec. 636, 376 N.E.2d 782 (4 Dist. 1978).

In a divorce proceeding, based upon the meager support which the husband was able to contribute to the support of his children, the arrearage on the mortgage, the need to provide a home for the minor children, and the past performances of each party, the trial court was justified in finding that sufficient equities existed to award a jointly owned home to the plaintiff. Lemanski v. Lemanski, 87 Ill. App. 2d 405, 231 N.E.2d 191 (2 Dist. 1967).

—Maintenance

A monthly alimony award in lieu of plaintiff's special equity in property owned by defendant was an improper exercise of the equitable powers of the court. Leone v. Leone, 39 Ill. App. 3d 547, 350 N.E.2d 545 (3 Dist. 1976).

—Not Shown

The court erred in requiring defendant to convey his one-half interest to plaintiff since she did not demonstrate special equities in the residence under former section 18 of the Divorce Act (see now this section). Hogan v. Hogan, 58 Ill. App. 3d 661, 16 Ill. Dec. 265, 374 N.E.2d 1040 (1 Dist. 1978).

The contributions described by the plaintiff: the raising of chickens, daily trips to fill stock feeders, the hauling of grain and fertilizer, and keeping the farm accounts, fell into the category of services normally performed in the marriage relation and could not serve to establish "special equities." Musgrave v. Musgrave, 38 Ill. App. 3d 532, 347 N.E.2d 831 (5 Dist. 1976).

—Pleading

Special equities or circumstances were required to be alleged and proven, to justify a transfer of property from one spouse to another. Fowler v. Fowler, 26 Ill. App. 3d 313, 325 N.E.2d 98 (3 Dist. 1975).

The court could have compelled a conveyance of marital property upon equitable terms, but such relief could have been obtained only in accordance with the allegations of special equities in the complaint and when sustained by the proof. Benson v. Benson, 26 Ill. App. 3d 50, 324 N.E.2d 469 (2 Dist. 1975).

—Proof

The spouse claiming special equities in order to receive an interest in the property must allege and prove that he or she contributed money or services, other than those normally performed in the marriage relationship, which were used directly or indirectly to acquire or enhance the value of the property in question. Hogan v. Hogan, 58 Ill. App. 3d 661, 16 Ill. Dec. 265, 374 N.E.2d 1040 (1 Dist. 1978).

—Property Conveyance

A conveyance of property may be ordered in lieu of alimony, separate and apart from any special equities. Leone v. Leone, 39 Ill. App. 3d 547, 350 N.E.2d 545 (3 Dist. 1976).

—Value

To obtain a transfer of property, aside from alimony or property settlement, where it appears that one party holds title to property which belongs equitably in whole or in part to the other, a party must show that he or she has furnished valuable consideration, such as money or services, over and above the usual contributions arising out of the marital relationship, which was directly or indirectly used to acquire or enhance the value of the property held in the name of the other. Gottemoller v. Gottemoller, 37 Ill. App. 3d 689, 346 N.E.2d 393 (3 Dist. 1976).

Spousal Support

A spouse is not required to sell her assets or impair her capital in order to generate income from which she can support herself in the manner enjoyed during the marriage. Head v. Head, 168 Ill. App. 3d 697, 119 Ill. Dec. 549, 523 N.E.2d 17 (1 Dist. 1988).

Standard of Review

—In General

A disposition of marital property will be reviewed under a different standard than a trial court's determination of whether a separation agreement is unconscionable; however, the same evidence can be relevant for both determinations. In re Miller, 98 Ill. App. 3d 1084, 54 Ill. Dec. 439, 424 N.E.2d 1342 (4 Dist. 1981).

A final determination must be made with regard to the division of property before a conclusive appellate review of the issues of child support and attorney fees. In re Clearman, 85 Ill. App. 3d 584, 40 Ill. Dec. 958, 407 N.E.2d 189 (3 Dist. 1980).

In determining the propriety of the divorce decree's property disposition, the trial court's authority in this regard was based upon the powers conferred by the former Divorce Act (see now 750 ILCS 5/101 et seq.) rather than upon general equity powers. Stotlar v. Stotlar, 50 Ill. App. 3d 790, 8 Ill. Dec. 711, 365 N.E.2d 1097 (5 Dist. 1977).

—Abuse of Discretion

The trial court has broad discretion under subsection (d) of this section to make an equitable apportionment of marital property, and abuse of discretion occurs only when no reasonable man could take the view adopted by the trial court. In re Eidson, 235 Ill. App. 3d 907, 175 Ill. Dec. 901, 601 N.E.2d 298 (5 Dist. 1992).

The test for abuse of discretion in property distribution is whether the trial court acted arbitrarily without the employment of conscientious judgment or exceeded the bounds of reason and ignored recognized principles of law so that substantial injustice resulted. In re Schroeder, 215 Ill. App. 3d 156, 158 Ill. Dec. 721, 574 N.E.2d 834 (4 Dist.), cert. denied, 141 Ill. 2d 560, 162 Ill. Dec. 508, 580 N.E.2d 134 (1991).

Upon review, a trial court's division of marital property will not be reversed absent a showing that the court acted arbitrarily and beyond the bounds of reason. In re Mahaffey, 206 Ill. App. 3d 859, 151 Ill. Dec. 638, 564 N.E.2d 1300 (1 Dist. 1990).

The proper division of marital property rests within the sound discretion of the trial court, and a court of appeals cannot reverse a trial court's division of property absent an abuse of discretion. In re Koral, 194 Ill. App. 3d 933, 141 Ill. Dec. 249, 551 N.E.2d 242 (1 Dist. 1989).

A reviewing court will not disturb a division of marital property unless an abuse of discretion is shown. In re Wolf, 180 Ill. App. 3d 998, 129 Ill. Dec. 742, 536 N.E.2d 792 (1 Dist. 1989); In re Jones, 187 Ill. App. 3d 206, 134 Ill. Dec. 836, 543 N.E.2d 119 (1 Dist. 1989).

The trial court's division of marital property will not be disturbed on appeal absent a showing of abuse or discretion; abuse of discretion will be found when the trial court acts arbitrarily without conscientious judgment or when it exceeds the bound of reason and ignores recognized principles of law so that substantial injustice results. In re Einhorn, 178 Ill. App. 3d 212, 127 Ill. Dec. 411, 533 N.E.2d 29 (1 Dist. 1988).

The trial court's decision will not be disturbed absent an abuse of discretion. In re Calisoff, 176 Ill. App. 3d 721, 126 Ill. Dec. 183, 531 N.E.2d 810 (1 Dist. 1988).

Standard of Review (Cont'd)

—Abuse of Discretion (Cont'd)

Upon review, the trial court's determination regarding the dissipation of assets lies within the sole discretion of the trial court and will not be reversed absent an abuse of discretion. Head v. Head, 168 Ill. App. 3d 697, 119 Ill. Dec. 549, 523 N.E.2d 17 (1 Dist. 1988).

It is the task of the trial court to distribute marital property in an equitable manner taking into account all relevant factors, and its decision in this regard will not be reversed absent an abuse of discretion. In re Benefield, 131 Ill. App. 3d 648, 86 Ill. Dec. 831, 476 N.E.2d 7 (5 Dist. 1985).

When a dispositional order is entered upon dissolution of a marriage, it must be equitable, and in reviewing such an order, this court should consider the sum of its provisions, because the distribution of marital property both affects and is affected by the amount of maintenance and child support . Goforth v. Goforth, 121 Ill. App. 3d 673, 77 Ill. Dec. 125, 459 N.E.2d 1374 (5 Dist. 1984).

The basic premise underlying review of a trial judge's decisions regarding property division is that his judgment will not be disturbed in the absence of an abuse of discretion. In re Hilkovitch, 124 Ill. App. 3d 401, 79 Ill. Dec. 891, 464 N.E.2d 795 (1 Dist. 1984).

The trial court has broad discretion to apportion marital property in just proportions; an abuse of discretion occurs only when no reasonable man would take the view adopted by the trial court. In re Bentivenga, 109 Ill. App. 3d 967, 65 Ill. Dec. 423, 441 N.E.2d 336 (2 Dist. 1982).

Where the trial court considers factors listed in this section, its decision will not be reversed absent an abuse of discretion. In re Sales, 106 Ill. App. 3d 378, 62 Ill. Dec. 441, 436 N.E.2d 23 (1 Dist. 1982).

The appropriate standard of review is whether, after considering the factors enumerated in subsection (c) of this section, the trial court abused its discretion when dividing the marital property. In re McMahon, 82 Ill. App. 3d 1126, 38 Ill. Dec. 499, 403 N.E.2d 730 (4 Dist. 1980).

A reviewing court in reviewing a trial court's division of property in a dissolution of marriage case is not justified in substituting its discretion for that of the trial court. In re Lee, 78 Ill. App. 3d 1123, 34 Ill. Dec. 451, 398 N.E.2d 126 (1 Dist. 1979).

—Manifest Weight of the Evidence

A trial court's classification of property as marital or non-marital will not be disturbed unless contrary to the manifest weight of the evidence. In re Perlmutter, 225 Ill. App. 3d 362, 167 Ill. Dec. 340, 587 N.E.2d 609 (2 Dist.), appeal denied, 146 Ill. 2d 650, 176 Ill. Dec. 820, 602 N.E.2d 474 (1992), cert. denied, 507 U.S. 1006, 113 S. Ct. 1648, 123 L. Ed. 2d 269 (1993).

—Questions of Law

Although a reviewing court will not disturb the circuit court's equitable distribution of property without a showing of an abuse of discretion, when there is an error of law, the distribution is reviewable de novo. In re Eddy, 210 Ill. App. 3d 450, 155 Ill. Dec. 174, 569 N.E.2d 174 (1 Dist. 1991).

—Reasonable Person View

The trial court has broad discretion in justly apportioning the marital assets and its decision will not be disturbed absent a showing of abuse of discretion, which is established if no reasonable person would reach a similar result. In re Kennedy, 214 Ill. App. 3d 849, 158 Ill. Dec. 172, 573 N.E.2d 1357 (1 Dist. 1991).

Absent an abuse of discretion whereby no reasonable man could adopt the trial court's position, a reviewing court will not substitute its judgment for the lower court's disposition in marital property matters. In re Benz, 165 Ill. App. 3d 273, 116 Ill. Dec. 336, 518 N.E.2d 1316 (4 Dist. 1988).

The appellate court should reverse division of marital property by the trial court only where no reasonable person would take the view adopted by the trial court. In re Cabaj, 118 Ill. App. 3d 789, 74 Ill. Dec. 393, 455 N.E.2d 822 (1 Dist. 1983); In re Korper, 131 Ill. App. 3d 753, 86 Ill. Dec. 766, 475 N.E.2d 1333 (5 Dist. 1985); In re Bauer, 138 Ill. App. 3d 379, 93 Ill. Dec. 108, 485 N.E.2d 1318 (1 Dist. 1985); In re Flemming, 143 Ill. App. 3d 592, 97 Ill. Dec. 859, 493 N.E.2d 666 (3 Dist. 1986); In re Heller, 153 Ill. App. 3d 224, 106 Ill. Dec. 503, 505 N.E.2d 1294 (1 Dist. 1987); In re Kristie, 156 Ill. App. 3d 821, 109 Ill. Dec. 393, 510 N.E.2d 14 (1 Dist. 1987); In re Turzitti, 161 Ill. App. 3d 822, 113 Ill. Dec. 507, 515 N.E.2d 316 (1 Dist. 1987); In re Swigers, 176 Ill. App. 3d 795, 126 Ill. Dec. 231, 531 N.E.2d 858 (1 Dist. 1988); In re Wolf, 180 Ill. App. 3d 998, 129 Ill. Dec. 742, 536 N.E.2d 792 (1 Dist. 1989); In re Jones, 187 Ill. App. 3d 206, 134 Ill. Dec. 836, 543 N.E.2d 119 (1 Dist. 1989); In re Harding, 189 Ill. App. 3d 663, 136 Ill. Dec. 935, 545 N.E.2d 459 (1 Dist. 1989); In re Hart, 194 Ill. App. 3d 839, 141 Ill. Dec. 550, 551 N.E.2d 737 (4 Dist. 1990); In re Kennedy, 214 Ill. App. 3d 849, 158 Ill. Dec. 172, 573 N.E.2d 1357 (1 Dist. 1991); In re Kerber, 215 Ill. App. 3d 248, 158 Ill. Dec. 717, 574 N.E.2d 830 (4 Dist. 1991); In re Davis, 215 Ill. App. 3d 763, 159 Ill. Dec. 375, 576 N.E.2d 44 (1 Dist.), appeal denied, 141 Ill. 2d 538, 162 Ill. Dec. 484, 580 N.E.2d 110 (1991).

—Substantial Injustice

In nearly every dissolution-related appeal, the applicable standard of review is whether the trial court abused its discretion in rendering its decision; such an abuse of discretion will be found where a court acts arbitrarily and without employing its conscientious judgment or where it exceeds the bounds of reason and ignores the recognized principals of law so that substantial injustice arises. In re Gentry, 188 Ill. App. 3d 372, 135 Ill. Dec. 939, 544 N.E.2d 435 (3 Dist. 1989).

Stipulation

—Absence of Fraud

A trial court's findings will be affirmed on appeal if they are supported by any evidence, especially evidence as strong as a stipulation to property values, which is binding on the parties in the absence of a showing of fraud. In re Hilkovitch, 124 Ill. App. 3d 401, 79 Ill. Dec. 891, 464 N.E.2d 795 (1 Dist. 1984).

—Effect

A wife who stipulated as to the value of disputed marital property cannot avoid the effect of her stipulation where she has not alleged that fraud or duress tainted that stipulation. In re Jones, 187 Ill. App. 3d 206, 134 Ill. Dec. 836, 543 N.E.2d 119 (1 Dist. 1989).

Stock

—Acquired After Marriage

Where classification of stock as marital or non-marital is at issue, a spouse, in order to overcome the presumption, must prove not only that the stock acquired after marriage was obtained by him in one of the ways for which the legislature created an exception, but also that the entire stock acquired after his marriage was acquired exclusively by one of the listed methods. In re Landfield, 209 Ill. App. 3d 678, 153 Ill. Dec. 834, 567 N.E.2d 1061 (1 Dist.), cert. denied, 139 Ill. 2d 597, 159 Ill. Dec. 109, 575 N.E.2d 916 (1991).

—Award Not Proper

The trial court erred in awarding the wife a 50% interest in stock solely owned by the husband where he did not contend or show that the stock was exempt under subdivision (a) of this section. Schuppe v. Schuppe, 69 Ill. App. 3d 200, 25 Ill. Dec. 690, 387 N.E.2d 346 (2 Dist. 1979).

—Award Proper

Although some of the husband's shares in a business representing his interest in the new stores were marital property, it was proper to award all the stock to the husband so as to avoid future friction over the conduct of the business. In re Kennedy, 94 Ill. App. 3d 537, 49 Ill. Dec. 927, 418 N.E.2d 947 (1 Dist. 1981).

The trial court's order that respondent transfer 20% of his stock to petitioner as her share of marital property or to pay her $6,000, the value of the stock, was not against the manifest weight of the evidence even if, as respondent suggested, the stock was worth nothing. In re Simmons, 87 Ill. App. 3d 651, 42 Ill. Dec. 706, 409 N.E.2d 321 (1 Dist. 1980).

Trial court did not abuse its discretion in awarding to wife husband's corporate shares of stock where she contributed $450 from the sale of her automobile to the corporation, she sold her own stock in another company for $3,000 and invested the proceeds in the corporation, and she personally borrowed $20,000, which she loaned to the corporation. In re Thornqvist, 79 Ill. App. 3d 791, 35 Ill. Dec. 342, 399 N.E.2d 176 (1 Dist. 1979).

—Characterization Held Proper

There was insufficient evidence introduced by the parties to

Stock (Cont'd)

—Characterization Held Proper (Cont'd)

establish a value for the "nonvested" shares of stock and for the retirement benefits, and the trial court accordingly did not err in failing to characterize these items as marital property and to award a marital share in them. In re Evans, 85 Ill. 2d 523, 55 Ill. Dec. 529, 426 N.E.2d 854 (1981).

—No Interest Shown

Where plaintiff's complaint failed to allege any special circumstances or equities with respect to the 500 shares of stock in defendant's name, nor did she pray for a transfer of any of the shares to her, and there was no evidence that any of her savings, earnings, or services were contributed in acquiring the shares of stock, the trial court erred in ordering defendant to transfer one half of the shares of stock to plaintiff. Everett v. Everett, 25 Ill. 2d 342, 185 N.E.2d 201 (1962).

—Non-Marital Property

Shares of stock which were acquired by husband more than four years prior to the marriage, and were titled in the names of husband and his mother were non-marital property. In re Kerman, 253 Ill. App. 3d 492, 191 Ill. Dec. 682, 624 N.E.2d 870 (2 Dist. 1993).

Where husband's premarital 40,000 common shares were undeniably non-marital property, and where husband received an additional 40,000 Class B shares during the marriage in order to preserve his proportionate share of ownership in the company, husband's acquisition of the Class B stock was analogous to a stock split or stock dividend which would be considered an appreciation in value to the premarital holding and would remain non-marital property subject to a right of contribution. In re Jelinek, 244 Ill. App. 3d 496, 184 Ill. Dec. 692, 613 N.E.2d 1284 (1 Dist.), appeal denied, 152 Ill. 2d 560, 190 Ill. Dec. 890, 622 N.E.2d 1207 (1993).

—Reimbursement

Where wife contended simply that because stock appreciated considerably in value between the years 1965 and 1982, the marital estate was entitled to reimbursement for those increases in value, but she failed to show that these increases were extraordinary or that they resulted from the husband's personal efforts, the appreciation of stock was not considered a marital asset. In re Thornton, 138 Ill. App. 3d 906, 93 Ill. Dec. 453, 486 N.E.2d 1288 (1 Dist. 1985).

—Split

Shares of stock owned prior to the marriage, or received as an inheritance during the marriage, are undeniably non-marital property; additional shares received through stock splits of such shares are not an increase in the value of an ownership interest, but merely an increase in the number of shares held, and all these new shares clearly retain the same non-martial character as the originals. In re Scott, 85 Ill. App. 3d 773, 41 Ill. Dec. 547, 407 N.E.2d 1045 (2 Dist. 1980).

—Valuation

Given the evidence that the stock declined in value because of the generally unprofitable nature of the company operations, the bankruptcy judge's decision to base his damages calculation on the subsequent valuation was not clearly erroneous, because the relevant time for the valuation of stock was as close as practicable to the date of the trial under 750 ILCS 5/503(f). Mungo v. Taylor, 355 F.3d 969, 2004 U.S. App. LEXIS 762 (7th Cir. 2004).

Bankruptcy court's finding regarding the value of a stock held in the marital estate during a Chapter 11 debtor's divorce proceeding was not clearly erroneous where the court based the valuation on a report prepared by an accounting firm closer to the date of the trial pursuant to 750 ILCS 5/503(f), rather than accepting the valuation prepared earlier. Mungo v. Taylor (In re Mungo), F. Supp. 2d , 2003 U.S. Dist. LEXIS 3413 (N.D. Ill. Mar. 6, 2003).

Stock in a corporation is usually valued at its market value, that price which a willing purchaser will pay to a willing seller in a voluntary transaction. In re Reib, 114 Ill. App. 3d 993, 70 Ill. Dec. 572, 449 N.E.2d 919 (1 Dist. 1983).

Survivor Benefits

—Not Subject to Division

Unlike other pension rights, survivor benefits have no possibility of becoming available for the employee's direct enjoyment; rather, they are statutorily designated for survivors and not for the control of the employee and are not subject to division as marital property. In re Hannon, 207 Ill. App. 3d 329, 152 Ill. Dec. 334, 565 N.E.2d 1016 (2 Dist.), cert. denied, 137 Ill. 2d 664, 156 Ill. Dec. 561, 571 N.E.2d 148 (1991).

Tax Consequences

—Duty of Court

Trial court, by refusing to grant petitioner opportunity to present evidence as to necessity of inserting specific language in judgment to address tax concerns prior to entry of written judgment order based on oral property settlement, failed to meet its statutory mandate under subdivision (d)(12) to consider tax implications of division of marital property. In re Lakin, 278 Ill. App. 3d 135, 214 Ill. Dec. 1051, 662 N.E.2d 617 (5 Dist. 1996), appeal denied, 167 Ill. 2d 554, 217 Ill. Dec. 665, 667 N.E.2d 1058 (1996).

—Exemptions

The trial court did not abuse its discretion in concluding petitioner contributed more than 51% toward son's support and awarding the tax exemption to petitioner. In re Clabault, 249 Ill. App. 3d 641, 188 Ill. Dec. 799, 619 N.E.2d 163 (2 Dist. 1993), cert. denied, 154 Ill. 2d 558, 197 Ill. Dec. 484, 631 N.E.2d 706 (1994).

The trial court has within its discretion the power to allocate the tax dependency exemption by ordering the custodial parent to sign a declaration he will not claim the exemption. Such an order must provide that the execution of the declaration is contingent upon the custodial parent's receipt of child support payments, if the noncustodial parent is ordered to make them. In re Einhorn, 178 Ill. App. 3d 212, 127 Ill. Dec. 411, 533 N.E.2d 29 (1 Dist. 1988).

—Immediate Consequences

Tax consequences that must be considered are those that immediately flow from the court's decision; remote consequences or the result of voluntary actions should not be considered. In re Perino, 224 Ill. App. 3d 605, 167 Ill. Dec. 172, 587 N.E.2d 54 (1992).

—Income Taxes

Trial court could order either each party to pay his or her own income tax liability after separation in light of the disparity in income to each, or have the liabilities paid from the marital estate to the extent the incomes of each party were substantially equivalent; however, when income and tax liability of one party far exceed income and tax liability of other party, it may be an abuse of discretion to order payment of both parties' income taxes out of marital funds which inadvertently penalizes the party with lower income. In re Charles, 284 Ill. App. 3d 339, 219 Ill. Dec. 742, 672 N.E.2d 57 (4 Dist. 1996).

—Individual Retirement Account

In disposition of marital property, husband's possible future tax consequences from use of his individual retirement account (IRA) were speculative, and the trial court was not required to consider such potential liabilities. In re Olson, 223 Ill. App. 3d 636, 166 Ill. Dec. 60, 585 N.E.2d 1082 (2 Dist.), appeal denied, 145 Ill. 2d 636, 173 Ill. Dec. 6, 596 N.E.2d 630 (1992).

—Liability

The court did not abuse its discretion in refusing to reduce the value of the spouse's pension by a speculative future tax liability. In re Kapusta, 141 Ill. App. 3d 1010, 96 Ill. Dec. 234, 491 N.E.2d 48 (1 Dist. 1986).

—Not Considered

Although a judge must consider the tax consequences when dividing the marital property, the judge cannot consider the tax consequences of actions which are not necessary as a result of the judgment entered. In re Parker, 252 Ill. App. 3d 1015, 192 Ill. Dec. 277, 625 N.E.2d 237 (1 Dist. 1993).

—Property Distribution

Tax consequences of a property distribution are one of the factors to be considered by the court in making a property distribution upon dissolution of marriage; however, speculative tax consequences are inappropriate for the court's consideration. In re Olson, 223 Ill. App. 3d 636, 166 Ill. Dec. 60, 585 N.E.2d 1082 (2 Dist.),

Tax Consequences (Cont'd)

—Property Distribution (Cont'd)

appeal denied, 145 Ill. 2d 636, 173 Ill. Dec. 6, 596 N.E.2d 630 (1992).

Tax Returns

—Ambiguity

The designation of ownership on the parties' tax returns is too ambiguous in and of itself to evidence an intention to convey a gift to the marriage. In re Pancner, 111 Ill. App. 3d 546, 67 Ill. Dec. 417, 444 N.E.2d 653 (1 Dist. 1982).

—Use

Although federal income tax returns are admissible, given the proper foundation proof, it is incumbent on the trier of fact to determine as best he can what disposition is being made of the funds generated through depreciation or other sheltered income and this requires a balancing test: viz., the disposition of the current cash flow versus the ability to pay in a dissolution proceeding. In re McDonald, 113 Ill. App. 3d 116, 68 Ill. Dec. 653, 446 N.E.2d 559 (4 Dist. 1983).

Temporary Support

In dividing marital property, one spouse was not given a credit for temporary support payments paid to the other spouse. In re Wright, 180 Ill. App. 3d 911, 129 Ill. Dec. 650, 536 N.E.2d 700 (1 Dist. 1986).

Tenancy in Common

The aim of this Act is to end the discord and animosity which led to the dissolution of the marriage; a tenancy in common only encourages friction, and for that reason is discouraged. In re Simmons, 87 Ill. App. 3d 651, 42 Ill. Dec. 706, 409 N.E.2d 321 (1 Dist. 1980).

Third Parties

—In General

The marital property provisions cannot affect the rights of persons other than the parties to the marriage because deviation from this rule denies the third party a day in court. In re Simmons, 87 Ill. App. 3d 651, 42 Ill. Dec. 706, 409 N.E.2d 321 (1 Dist. 1980).

—Action

Although this Act makes no provision for the filing of a third-party action in a dissolution proceeding to determine the parties' rights in alleged marital property action held by the third party, the right to file a third-party action has been recognized where the alleged marital asset is held in trust. In re Pahlke, 120 Ill. App. 3d 1009, 76 Ill. Dec. 487, 458 N.E.2d 1141 (1 Dist. 1983).

—Rights of Spouses

In a dissolution proceeding, trial court had the authority, pursuant to former section 25 of the Civil Practice Act (see now 735 ILCS 5/2-406), to entertain the third-party action to determine rights of husband and wife in alleged marital property deeded to wife's parents in trust and the court was authorized to bring in wife's parents and bank, as trustee, as third-party defendants to probe the validity of the trust during the dissolution proceeding. In re Peshek, 89 Ill. App. 3d 959, 45 Ill. Dec. 347, 412 N.E.2d 698 (1 Dist. 1980).

Title

The trial court erred in assuming that, simply because title to certain items acquired by husband during the marriage was in husband's name individually, that they did not require distribution by the court. Schubert v. Schubert, 66 Ill. App. 3d 29, 22 Ill. Dec. 790, 383 N.E.2d 266 (3 Dist. 1978).

Transfer of Property

—In General

The transfer of property from one spouse to another pursuant to a divorce decree is governed by statute. Gilmore v. Gilmore, 28 Ill. App. 3d 36, 328 N.E.2d 562 (1 Dist. 1975).

—By Titleholder

Where property titled in name of one spouse might be considered marital property, titleholder has complete power to dispose of property during marriage as he or she sees fit; transfer for inadequate consideration may constitute dissipation, but where an attempted dissipation of assets is not an issue, it is irrelevant whether spouse's motives were improper so long as he actually intended to make a transfer and did not intend the transfer to be one in form only. Wood v. Wood, 284 Ill. App. 3d 718, 219 Ill. Dec. 877, 672 N.E.2d 385 (4 Dist. 1996).

—Interspousal

Where an engagement ring was acquired prior to a marriage and was purchased by the husband's parents and given to the couple as a gift, the facts did not present an inter-spousal transfer of property acquired prior to marriage to which the common-law presumption of a gift to the wife would apply; rather, the record reflected that the property was a gift to the couple and consequently part of the marital estate, and the trial court did not err in including the ring as part of the marital estate. In re Weinstein, 128 Ill. App. 3d 234, 83 Ill. Dec. 425, 470 N.E.2d 551 (1 Dist. 1984).

While the trial court exceeded its authority in calling transfer of former husband's one half interest in 160 acre farm to his wife a "taxable event," it was within the court's discretion to characterize it as an exchange rather than a division of property, with the tax consequences to be borne by former husband. In re McCune, 86 Ill. App. 3d 311, 41 Ill. Dec. 897, 408 N.E.2d 319 (3 Dist. 1980).

—No Special Circumstances

Where was no allegation of fraud in connection with the conveyance of the one-half interest in the properties to appellant by appellee, there were no special circumstances alleged which would justify or warrant the court in decreeing that appellant's one-half interest in two of the properties be conveyed to appellee, or that appellee's one-half interest in the remaining property be conveyed to appellant under former Ill.Rev.Stat., ch. 40, para. 18 (see now this section). Podgornik v. Podgornik, 392 Ill. 124, 63 N.E.2d 715 (1945).

—Not Warranted

Transfer of the legal title to the residential property in the husband's name alone, totally acquired by inheritance from his parents, was not warranted under former section 18 of the Divorce Act (see now this section). Debrey v. Debrey, 132 Ill. App. 2d 1072, 270 N.E.2d 43 (4 Dist. 1971).

—Statutory Authority

The transfer of property from one spouse to another pursuant to a divorce decree is governed by statute. Gilmore v. Gilmore, 28 Ill. App. 3d 36, 328 N.E.2d 562 (1 Dist. 1975).

—Valuable Consideration

To obtain a transfer of property, a party had to show that he or she had furnished valuable consideration, such as money or services, over and above the usual contributions arising out of the marital relationship, which directly or indirectly was used to acquire or enhance the value of the property held in the same name of the other. Valdez v. Valdez, 57 Ill. App. 3d 81, 14 Ill. Dec. 808, 372 N.E.2d 1087 (1 Dist. 1978).

Transmutation

—In General

A transmutation occurs when the contributing spouse evidences his intent to make a gift of the non-marital property to the marriage by significantly changing the character of the property to marital. In re Nicks, 177 Ill. App. 3d 76, 126 Ill. Dec. 442, 531 N.E.2d 1069 (4 Dist. 1988).

The principle of transmutation is based on the presumption that the owner of the non-marital property intended to make a gift of that property to the marital estate. In re Benz, 165 Ill. App. 3d 273, 116 Ill. Dec. 336, 518 N.E.2d 1316 (4 Dist. 1988); In re Aud, 142 Ill. App. 3d 320, 96 Ill. Dec. 615, 491 N.E.2d 894 (5 Dist. 1986).

—Affirmative Acts

Property designated as non-marital pursuant to the exceptions of subsection (a) of this section may be presumptively transmuted into marital property by an affirmative act of the contributing spouse. McCoy v McCoy, 225 Ill. App. 3d 966, 168 Ill. Dec. 27, 589 N.E.2d 141 (3 Dist. 1992).

Transmutation (Cont'd)

—Affirmative Acts (Cont'd)

Property designated as non-marital pursuant to the exceptions in subsection (a) of this section may still be presumptively transmuted into marital property by the affirmative act of the contributing spouse, based on the presumption that the contributing spouse intended to make a gift of the property to the marital estate. In re Riech, 208 Ill. App. 3d 301, 152 Ill. Dec. 949, 566 N.E.2d 826 (4 Dist. 1991).

That which is designated non-marital property under the exceptions to subsection (a) of this section may still be presumptively transmuted to marital property by affirmative act of the contributing spouse. In re Benz, 165 Ill. App. 3d 273, 116 Ill. Dec. 336, 518 N.E.2d 1316 (4 Dist. 1988).

—Effect of Commingling

Every act of commingling or every use of marital funds for the maintenance of non-marital property should not work a transmutation. In re Aud, 142 Ill. App. 3d 320, 96 Ill. Dec. 615, 491 N.E.2d 894 (5 Dist. 1986).

—Factors

Husband's dental practice, established prior to the marriage, did not become marital property through transmutation by virtue of wife's contributions as a homemaker because contribution as a homemaker is a factor to be considered when marital property is distributed, not to the determination of whether the dental practice was transmuted from non-marital to marital property. In re Aud, 142 Ill. App. 3d 320, 96 Ill. Dec. 615, 491 N.E.2d 894 (5 Dist. 1986).

—Improper Classification

Trial court erred in ruling that farm acquired by husband prior to marriage was non-marital where principal payments and interest payments were made on the farm during the marriage, wife worked to support the family throughout marriage, and she worked for some time on the farm itself, operating the tractor, working in the fields and at one point keeping the farm books as well. Hofmann v. Hofmann, 94 Ill. 2d 205, 68 Ill. Dec. 593, 446 N.E.2d 499 (1983).

—Methods

Transmutation of non-marital property to marital property can take place in two ways: one involves converting the separate ownership of non-marital property into a form of common ownership, and the second involves commingling of non-marital property with marital property, thereby converting the entire non-marital property interest into marital property. In re Brown, 110 Ill. App. 3d 782, 66 Ill. Dec. 488, 443 N.E.2d 11 (5 Dist. 1982).

—Mortgage Note

The mere execution of a mortgage note is insufficient to constitute a transmutation of non-marital property into marital property. In re Drennan, 93 Ill. App. 3d 903, 49 Ill. Dec. 386, 418 N.E.2d 30 (4 Dist. 1981).

—Motivation

Where respondent's motivation at the time of transferring property title was to insulate himself and petitioner from difficulties in the event of the death of one or the other, the court's decision to accept respondent's testimony over that of petitioner was not an abuse of discretion. In re Wojcicki, 109 Ill. App. 3d 569, 65 Ill. Dec. 173, 440 N.E.2d 1028 (1 Dist. 1982).

—Not Shown

Where the petitioner deposited money from a retirement fund into the parties' joint checking account prior to a rollover of funds into her IRA, there was no transmutation of nonmarital property to marital property. In re Raad, 301 Ill. App. 3d 683, 235 Ill. Dec. 391, 704 N.E.2d 964 (2 Dist. 1998), cert. denied, 526 U.S. 1051, 119 S. Ct. 1358, 143 L. Ed. 2d 519 (1999).

—Partnership Interest

Partnership interest was non-marital property transmuted to marital property. In re Brown, 110 Ill. App. 3d 782, 66 Ill. Dec. 488, 443 N.E.2d 11 (5 Dist. 1982).

—Presumption of Gift

Petitioner's evidence was not so clear and convincing so as to rebut the presumption that she intended to make a gift to the marital estate where she was never asked questions about her intent at the time her husband's name was added to title of house and where the husband provided consideration to place his name on the title. Zito v. Zito, 196 Ill. App. 3d 1031, 143 Ill. Dec. 606, 554 N.E.2d 541 (1 Dist. 1990).

Where money was transferred to a joint trust, a presumption of transmutation and of gift to the marital estate arose which was rebutted by clear and convincing evidence because of the respondent's control over petitioner's financial matters, his insistence the money be transferred, and petitioner's attempts to appease her husband while at the same time giving her son the money to alleviate his represented financial difficulties. In re Benz, 165 Ill. App. 3d 273, 116 Ill. Dec. 336, 518 N.E.2d 1316 (4 Dist. 1988).

The affirmative act of placing title to non-marital property in joint tenancy or some other form of co-ownership with a spouse will support a presumption of gift to the marital estate. In re Nicks, 177 Ill. App. 3d 76, 126 Ill. Dec. 442, 531 N.E.2d 1069 (4 Dist. 1988).

Where respondent paid the purchase price for the properties in question, and his contributions, both in money and physical labor, to the preservation and improvement of the properties far outweighed the contributions to be credited to petitioner during the parties' brief marriage, the gift presumption was overcome. In re Wojcicki, 109 Ill. App. 3d 569, 65 Ill. Dec. 173, 440 N.E.2d 1028 (1 Dist. 1982).

—Rebuttal of Presumption

The presumption of transmutation of separate property to marital property may be rebutted by clear and convincing evidence that no gift to the marital estate was intended. Zito v. Zito, 196 Ill. App. 3d 1031, 143 Ill. Dec. 606, 554 N.E.2d 541 (1 Dist. 1990).

The failure of a non-marital property holder to segregate that property will give rise to the rebuttable presumption that the non-marital property has been transmuted, regardless of the status of title. In re Nicks, 177 Ill. App. 3d 76, 126 Ill. Dec. 442, 531 N.E.2d 1069 (4 Dist. 1988).

Presumption of a gift to the marital estate may be rebutted by clear, convincing and unmistakable evidence presented by the donor spouse. In re Nicks, 177 Ill. App. 3d 76, 126 Ill. Dec. 442, 531 N.E.2d 1069 (4 Dist. 1988).

—Shown

Farm equipment constituted newly acquired, transmuted marital property, which was derived from commingled marital and non-marital property, resulting in a loss of identity of the contributing estates, where spouse's non-marital estate contributed the trade-in value of the old equipment, while the marital estate contributed funds that he earned from his work on the farm; the commingled property from both estates lost its identity because the purchase resulted in a new piece of property: the newly acquired equipment. In re Patrick, 233 Ill. App. 3d 561, 174 Ill. Dec. 571, 599 N.E.2d 117 (4 Dist.), cert. denied, 147 Ill. 2d 629, 180 Ill. Dec. 151, 606 N.E.2d 1228 (1992).

Bedroom set, which was purchased by husband three to four days prior to marriage, although paid for entirely before the marriage, was marital property because it was not purchased for the husband's sole use, and the unrestricted use of the property by both parties for their mutual benefit resulted in a transmutation of it as a non-marital asset into a marital asset. In re Schriner, 88 Ill. App. 3d 380, 43 Ill. Dec. 572, 410 N.E.2d 572 (2 Dist. 1980).

—Significant Contribution

Transmutation occurs only where the contribution of marital assets to non-marital property is significant. In re Siddens, 225 Ill. App. 3d 496, 167 Ill. Dec. 680, 588 N.E.2d 321 (5 Dist.), appeal denied, 145 Ill. 2d 644, 173 Ill. Dec. 13, 596 N.E.2d 637 (1992).

Transmutation occurs only in cases in which the contribution of marital assets to the non-marital property is significant; a contribution is not significant if it merely maintains the non-marital asset. In re Aud, 142 Ill. App. 3d 320, 96 Ill. Dec. 615, 491 N.E.2d 894 (5 Dist. 1986).

—Workers' Compensation Award

Where, long after the last deposit of a worker's compensation award was made, the funds were still being used to pay marital debts and expenses, even if the worker's compensation awards were originally of a non-marital composition, through the process of transmutation, they were rendered into marital property allocable

Transmutation (Cont'd)

—Workers' Compensation Award (Cont'd)
by the court under the provisions of the Dissolution Act. In re Lukas, 83 Ill. App. 3d 606, 39 Ill. Dec. 161, 404 N.E.2d 545 (1 Dist. 1980).

Trust

—Court Findings
Trial court failed to make the necessary findings regarding the creation of the trust under subsection (g) so cause was remanded for court to describe the terms of the trust with sufficient particularity. In re Wolfe, 298 Ill. App. 3d 510, 232 Ill. Dec. 743, 699 N.E.2d 190 (2 Dist. 1998), appeal denied, 181 Ill. 2d 590, 235 Ill. Dec. 949, 706 N.E.2d 504 (1998).

—Factors
This section does not require, as a prerequisite to establishing a trust, a finding that the party has been in wilful contempt of a court order; the lack of a wilful contempt order is a factor among other factors that the court may consider in determining whether a trust should be established. In re Gocal, 216 Ill. App. 3d 221, 159 Ill. Dec. 1023, 576 N.E.2d 946 (1 Dist. 1991).

—Failure to Pay
A trust may be appropriate where a parent has shown unwillingness to pay support as ordered by the court. In re Bush, 191 Ill. App. 3d 249, 138 Ill. Dec. 423, 547 N.E.2d 590 (4 Dist. 1989).

Establishing a discreet trust pursuant to this section was proper where the evidence illustrated the ex-husband's inability to render direct child support payments to his first family. In re Pickholtz, 178 Ill. App. 3d 512, 127 Ill. Dec. 657, 533 N.E.2d 529 (1 Dist. 1988).

—Interests of Children
Absent funds from the estate of non-custodial parents aunt and because he was, by his own admission, unable or unwilling to work or make support payments, the circuit court did not abuse its discretion in finding the establishment of a trust was in the best interest of respondent's children. In re Steffen, 253 Ill. App. 3d 966, 192 Ill. Dec. 709, 625 N.E.2d 864 (4 Dist. 1993), appeal denied, 155 Ill. 2d 576, 198 Ill. Dec. 553, 633 N.E.2d 15 (1994).

Trial court was held not to have created a child support trust in division of assets from marriage dissolution. In re Schuster, 224 Ill. App. 3d 958, 167 Ill. Dec. 73, 586 N.E.2d 1345 (1992).

Trial court was not required to make a finding of special circumstances that a trust was necessary to protect and promote the best interests of the parties' children before requiring husband to name wife as trustee for the benefit of their sons on husband's life insurance policies for the benefit of the parties' two sons until the completion of their college education or emancipation. In re Olson, 223 Ill. App. 3d 636, 166 Ill. Dec. 60, 585 N.E.2d 1082 (2 Dist.), appeal denied, 145 Ill. 2d 636, 173 Ill. Dec. 6, 596 N.E.2d 630 (1992).

A court could find it necessary to place funds in trust in order to protect the best interests of a child where the record was replete with pleadings indicating that the father was not complying with the support order, and where it was uncontroverted that the father had settled one child support arrearage with the mother and was at the time of the trial again in arrears. In re Gocal, 216 Ill. App. 3d 221, 159 Ill. Dec. 1023, 576 N.E.2d 946 (1 Dist. 1991).

The imposition of a trust is inappropriate in the absence of evidence showing some need to protect the interests of the children. Atkinson v. Atkinson, 87 Ill. 2d 174, 57 Ill. Dec. 567, 429 N.E.2d 465 (1981), cert. denied, 456 U.S. 905, 102 S. Ct. 1751, 72 L. Ed. 2d 162 (1982).

The court may establish a trust or separate "fund" from a portion of the jointly or separately held estates of the parties to protect and promote the best interests of the children and to provide for their support, maintenance, education, and general welfare; a trust is not established merely because of the relative financial positions of the parties, but rather only where it is clear that it is necessary to protect and promote the best interests of the child. In re Dulyn, 89 Ill. App. 3d 304, 44 Ill. Dec. 622, 411 N.E.2d 988 (1 Dist. 1980).

The establishment of a trust fund may not be proper for minor children where there is financial ability and willingness to support a minor child through direct payments. In re Preston, 81 Ill. App. 3d 672, 37 Ill. Dec. 442, 402 N.E.2d 332 (5 Dist. 1980).

—Not Proper
A court's order requiring respondent to establish a trust fund with the child support arrearages was not legally justified under this Act and deprived petitioner of a vested right. In re Bush, 191 Ill. App. 3d 249, 138 Ill. Dec. 423, 547 N.E.2d 590 (4 Dist. 1989).

—Order Final and Appealable
That part of an order appealed from which disposed of the merits of a case on a separate and distinct branch thereof, namely the controversy as to whether, as between the husband and wife, part of the legal title to a trust should equitably be in the appellee wife, was final and appealable. Ylonen v. Ylonen, 2 Ill. 2d 111, 117 N.E.2d 98 (1954).

—Ordered By Court
Trust was created by appellee for his own benefit and was therefore invalid as a spendthrift trust; therefore prohibition of this section in reaching the trust for future child support payments did not apply so the trust was converted into a trust under 750 ILCS 5/503(g). In re Chapman, 297 Ill. App. 3d 611, 231 Ill. Dec. 811, 697 N.E.2d 365 (1 Dist. 1998), (decided under former 750 ILCS 15/4.1).

—Parent Trustee
General rule that an interested party should not be appointed trustee of a trust established from marital property, for minor child's education and support, did not apply where adequate safeguards were instituted to ensure proper distribution of trust funds. In re Andrew, 258 Ill. App. 3d 924, 194 Ill. Dec. 724, 628 N.E.2d 221 (1 Dist. 1993).

—Procedures
The circuit court has authority to order the creation of trust under subsection (g) in proceedings after the original decree. In re Steffen, 253 Ill. App. 3d 966, 192 Ill. Dec. 709, 625 N.E.2d 864 (4 Dist. 1993), appeal denied, 155 Ill. 2d 576, 198 Ill. Dec. 553, 633 N.E.2d 15 (1994).

—Responsibility of Parent
The imposition of a trust under subsection (g) of this section is inappropriate, absent evidence of a need to protect the interests of the children, and therefore is inappropriately applied to a responsible parent. In re Bates, 141 Ill. App. 3d 566, 95 Ill. Dec. 922, 490 N.E.2d 1014 (2 Dist. 1986).

—Upheld
The circuit court did not abuse its discretion in establishing a trust under subsection (g) since there was a substantial arrearage in child support at the time of the dissolution judgment, and the evidence demonstrated that the husband-obligor elected to pay attorney's fees and discretionary employee bonuses and bought computers and digital cameras without having paid his child support obligation. In re Petersen, 319 Ill. App. 3d 325, 253 Ill. Dec. 144, 744 N.E.2d 877, 2001 Ill. App. LEXIS 46 (1 Dist. 2001), appeal denied sub nom. Petersen v. Petersen, 195 Ill. 2d 597, 258 Ill. Dec. 100, 755 N.E.2d 483 (2001).

Evidence of necessity for a support trust was sufficient where respondent made only two payments during the nine month period between the supplemental decree approving the settlement and the hearing on the petition to modify, which was in conformity to the decree for child support, but was totally inadequate to support the children; the $20,000 fund was the only reasonably certain source of support payments where the respondent's financial picture was partially contingent upon settlement by him of a worker's compensation claim and a possible claim for retaliatory discharge, and opportunities for employment were clearly impaired and also contingent upon his diligence in seeking work. In re Hobson, 220 Ill. App. 3d 1006, 163 Ill. Dec. 437, 581 N.E.2d 388 (4 Dist. 1991), cert. denied, 143 Ill. 2d 638, 167 Ill. Dec. 400, 587 N.E.2d 1015 (1992).

Court did not abuse its discretion in providing for the creation of a trust for the benefit of the minor children pursuant to subsection (d) of this section; although it was possible that the trust would be imposed at a time when the older child had reached majority, the language of the judgment clearly limited the beneficiaries of the trust to "the minor child or children," and as such the trust did not require a gift to an adult child. In re Miller, 112 Ill. App. 3d 203, 68 Ill. Dec. 167, 445 N.E.2d 811 (1 Dist. 1983).

Trustees

—Impartial Third Party Required
Trial court's choice of the divorced mother to be trustee for a

Trustees (Cont'd)

—Impartial Third Party Required (Cont'd)
trust, to be used to insure child support payments, the corpus of which was to be returned to the divorced father upon the trust's termination, was an abuse of discretion; a neutral and impartial third party should have been appointed by the trial court as trustee. In re Vucic, 216 Ill. App. 3d 692, 159 Ill. Dec. 737, 576 N.E.2d 406 (2 Dist. 1991), appeal denied, 164 Ill. 2d 584, 214 Ill. Dec. 332, 660 N.E.2d 1281 (1995).

Unconscionability

—Determination
Terms of a marital property settlement agreement are binding on the court unless the agreement is found to be unconscionable; the determination of unconscionability in a divorce agreement requires consideration of the conditions under which the agreement was made and the economic circumstances of the parties resulting from the agreement. In re Chapman, 162 Ill. App. 3d 308, 113 Ill. Dec. 615, 515 N.E.2d 424 (2 Dist. 1987).

—Shown
Husband failed to establish either duress or economic inequality to render marital property settlement agreement unconscionable. In re Chapman, 162 Ill. App. 3d 308, 113 Ill. Dec. 615, 515 N.E.2d 424 (2 Dist. 1987).

In a divorce action where the plaintiff wife had no counsel of record when the cause was called for trial, the trial court's ex parte decree of divorce entered upon defendant husband's counterclaim was totally one-sided and unconscionable in that it awarded the defendant husband virtually all of the parties' real and personal property besides granting him custody of the children who were then residing with the wife, and barred plaintiff wife from receiving alimony, such decree was vacated. Eden v. Eden, 34 Ill. App. 3d 382, 340 N.E.2d 141 (1 Dist. 1975).

—Validity of Agreement
Prior to the determination of whether a post-nuptial agreement was contemplated to comport to 750 ILCS 5/502 or subdivision (a)(4) of this section the threshold question necessarily becomes whether there was a conscionable, and therefore, valid agreement. In re Richardson, 237 Ill. App. 3d 1067, 179 Ill. Dec. 224, 606 N.E.2d 56 (1 Dist. 1992), appeal denied, 149 Ill. 2d 660, 183 Ill. Dec. 871, 612 N.E.2d 523 (1993).

Unequal Distribution of Property

—Upheld
A distribution of more than half the marital property to the wife was upheld where (1) the husband had significant nonmarital assets, including a farm which was appraised at $600,000, (2) a majority of the debt assigned to the husband consisted of the operating expenses of the farm, (3) the husband had a superior earning capacity, had more sources of income, and had a greater opportunity for future acquisition of capital assets and income, and (4) trial court awarded the wife sole custody of the children, but did not award her maintenance. In re Henke, 313 Ill. App. 3d 159, 245 Ill. Dec. 780, 728 N.E.2d 1137, 2000 Ill. App. LEXIS 276 (2 Dist. 2000), appeal denied sub nom. Henke v. Henke, 191 Ill. 2d 530, 250 Ill. Dec. 457, 738 N.E.2d 926 (2000).

Award of less than one-half of the marital property to wife, while not generous, was justified in view of the husband's greater contribution to the marital estate, the wife's greater share of property immediately capable of producing income, and the substantial value of the property awarded to the wife. In re Bentivenga, 109 Ill. App. 3d 967, 65 Ill. Dec. 423, 441 N.E.2d 336 (2 Dist. 1982).

Use of Corpus
Where trust did not allow the use of corpus during minority, it was not in compliance with provisions of subsection (g) of this section, and appeared to be an unlawful court-ordered inheritance. In re Bush, 191 Ill. App. 3d 249, 138 Ill. Dec. 423, 547 N.E.2d 590 (4 Dist. 1989).

Valuation
In a divorce case, the trial court erred in valuing the husband's dental practice where personal goodwill, cash on hand, cash surrender value in insurance policies, and loans to officers should have been included in determining the fair market value of the practice. Schneider v. Schneider, 343 Ill. App. 3d 628, 278 Ill. Dec. 485, 798 N.E.2d 1242, 2003 Ill. App. LEXIS 1295 (2 Dist. 2003).

—In General
The analysis of subsection (c) of this section can be used to determine value of contributions for purposes of subsection (d) of this section. In re Van Ness, 136 Ill. App. 3d 185, 90 Ill. Dec. 766, 482 N.E.2d 1049 (4 Dist. 1985).

For a trial court to apportion marital assets, the proper value of such assets must be established. In re Wilson, 110 Ill. App. 3d 809, 66 Ill. Dec. 508, 443 N.E.2d 31 (5 Dist. 1982); In re Weiss, 129 Ill. App. 3d 166, 84 Ill. Dec. 378, 472 N.E.2d 128 (1 Dist. 1984); In re Melnick, 127 Ill. App. 3d 102, 82 Ill. Dec. 228, 468 N.E.2d 490 (1 Dist. 1984); In re Brooks, 138 Ill. App. 3d 252, 93 Ill. Dec. 166, 486 N.E.2d 267 (1 Dist. 1985).

—Accounts Receivable
Accounts receivable are business assets and must be included in the valuation of a medical practice. In re Feldman, 199 Ill. App. 3d 1002, 146 Ill. Dec. 62, 557 N.E.2d 1004 (2 Dist. 1990).

Accounts receivable and unbilled accounts are assets and should be properly considered in the valuation of a business; where the husband incorporated his medical practice, these corporate assets were to be taken into consideration in determining the value of his stock. In re Rubinstein, 145 Ill. App. 3d 31, 99 Ill. Dec. 212, 495 N.E.2d 659 (2 Dist. 1986).

—Appreciation of Assets
Subdivision (c)(2) of this section limits required evidence of appreciation of non-marital property to contributions of personal effort. In re Adams, 183 Ill. App. 3d 296, 131 Ill. Dec. 730, 538 N.E.2d 1286 (4 Dist. 1989).

Fairness required both parties to share equally in appreciation or depreciation of marital residence, subject to a credit to wife for mortgage payments and improvements. In re Fairchild, 110 Ill. App. 3d 470, 66 Ill. Dec. 131, 442 N.E.2d 557 (3 Dist. 1982).

Where appreciation in value of a stock trust was not due to an addition of marital funds, but was due to economic factors, the appreciation was non-marital property. In re Jones, 104 Ill. App. 3d 490, 60 Ill. Dec. 214, 432 N.E.2d 1113 (1 Dist. 1982).

Evidence which monetized the value of husband's contribution to the appreciation of farmstead devised to wife during marriage did not warrant his award of 30% of the appreciation in value of 51 acre portion of farmstead, and remand was thus proper. In re Humphrey, 101 Ill. App. 3d 1134, 57 Ill. Dec. 436, 428 N.E.2d 1116 (3 Dist. 1981).

The appreciation on stocks acquired during the marriage is marital property. In re Scott, 85 Ill. App. 3d 773, 41 Ill. Dec. 547, 407 N.E.2d 1045 (2 Dist. 1980).

—Business
Since the personal goodwill of a dental practice had already been taken into account as an income-generating factor in awarding a disproportionate share of marital assets to a non-dentist spouse who had waived alimony and in setting child support amounts, it should not have been considered a second time in valuing the practice for property division purposes; since accounts receivable of the practice were ascertainable assets already owned by the practice, however, they should have been taken into account in valuing the practice. In re Marriage of Schneider, Ill. 2d , 291 Ill. Dec. 601, 824 N.E.2d 177, 2005 Ill. LEXIS 7 (2005).

To determine the value of a business which is marital property, the court must consider (1) fixed assets, (2) other assets, including accounts receivable, (3) the good will in the business, and (4) business-related liabilities. In re Hagshenas, 234 Ill. App. 3d 178, 175 Ill. Dec. 506, 600 N.E.2d 437 (2 Dist. 1992), appeal denied, 148 Ill.2d 642, 183 Ill. Dec. 19, 610 N.E.2d 1263 (1993).

To determine the value of a business which is marital property, the court must consider: fixed assets, other assets, including accounts receivable, the goodwill in the business, and business related liabilities. In re Feldman, 199 Ill. App. 3d 1002, 146 Ill. Dec. 62, 557 N.E.2d 1004 (2 Dist. 1990).

The court had before it sufficient evidence upon which to value the assets in dispute where wife, based on her six years experience in the ceramics field, was able to attest to the value of each asset

Valuation (Cont'd)

—Business (Cont'd)

used in the parties ceramics business. In re Randall, 157 Ill. App. 3d 892, 110 Ill. Dec. 122, 510 N.E.2d 1153 (1 Dist. 1987).

Where the businesses were not service oriented businesses which relied solely upon the continuous "personally produced" services of husband, but were well established ongoing businesses to which wife, too, had contributed her time and efforts, where the businesses had inventory and equipment and would not disappear as an entity if the husband was forced to leave, the businesses were marketable and had a present value if they were offered for sale, future earnings of the corporation were properly taken into account for a valuation under this section. Creditors Disct. & Audit, Inc. v. Zook, 130 Ill. App. 3d 402, 85 Ill. Dec. 689, 474 N.E.2d 417 (4 Dist. 1985).

There was competent evidence as to the fair market value of the business from which the court could make an informed decision and which was sufficient to support the trial court's valuation. In re Shafer, 122 Ill. App. 3d 991, 78 Ill. Dec. 323, 462 N.E.2d 39 (2 Dist. 1984).

A trial court did not err in failing to assign a value to business since it had determined that the business was non-marital property. In re Pancner, 111 Ill. App. 3d 546, 67 Ill. Dec. 417, 444 N.E.2d 653 (1 Dist. 1982).

—Corporate Assets

While the valuation of a closely held corporation is not an exact science, this does not mean that such entities are incapable of being appropriately evaluated. In re Davis, 131 Ill. App. 3d 1065, 87 Ill. Dec. 145, 476 N.E.2d 1137 (1 Dist. 1985).

Although the value of a subsidiary corporation properly may have been discounted, the trial court lacked a proper foundation on which to base a determination that there was no value to its holding company; without consideration of the remaining values to the parent company, it was inappropriate to ascribe no value to it in determining an apportionment of marital property. In re Reib, 114 Ill. App. 3d 993, 70 Ill. Dec. 572, 449 N.E.2d 919 (1 Dist. 1983).

—Corporate Stock

Trial court did not abuse its discretion by valuing respondent's share in the corporation in accordance with appraisal of said assets by following the capitalization of excess earnings method outlined in Revenue Rules 59-60 and 68-609. In re Puls, 268 Ill. App. 3d 882, 206 Ill. Dec. 520, 645 N.E.2d 525 (1 Dist. 1994).

Evidence as to value of the stock awarded to respondent as non-marital property could do nothing other than show that respondent's financial worth was greater than that shown by the record and such a showing could not work to respondent's benefit insofar as the division of marital property was concerned. In re Schaufelberger, 120 Ill. App. 3d 114, 75 Ill. Dec. 551, 457 N.E.2d 993 (5 Dist. 1983).

In light of the fact that respondent's certified public accountant placed the corporation's net worth at slightly over one-half of petitioner's valuation, cause was remanded for reconsideration of value of the stock of husband's closely held corporation, and modification of the previously ordered distribution of marital property was authorized if, upon remand, such modification was dictated by the evidence elicited on the revaluation of stock. In re Rossi, 113 Ill. App. 3d 55, 68 Ill. Dec. 801, 446 N.E.2d 1198 (1 Dist. 1983).

In the absence of evidence of the stock's value, the reviewing court could not readily determine the reasonableness of the trial court's action in awarding the stock and the car to husband, supposedly offset by the award of furniture to wife. There was no basis in the record on which to determine whether the trial court's award was a distribution in "just proportions," and accordingly, the trial court erred in failing to value the stocks prior to allocating the marital property. In re Rothbardt, 99 Ill. App. 3d 561, 54 Ill. Dec. 929, 425 N.E.2d 1146 (1 Dist. 1981).

—Credibility

Where plaintiff "puffed" her valuation based upon defendant's alleged "puffed" valuation, the trial court was at liberty to accept the valuation of the property to be as plaintiff had represented it to the court even if defendant was more financially able to develop the real estate. In re Aud, 142 Ill. App. 3d 320, 96 Ill. Dec. 615, 491 N.E.2d 894 (5 Dist. 1986).

—Date of Dissolution

It is well established in Illinois that assets are to be valued at the time of the dissolution of marriage. In re Weiler, 258 Ill. App. 3d 454, 196 Ill. Dec. 372, 629 N.E.2d 1216 (5 Dist. 1994).

The date of valuing marital assets is the date the judgment of dissolution was entered, unless the cause is a remanded case, and the reviewing court has directed otherwise. In re Jones, 187 Ill. App. 3d 206, 134 Ill. Dec. 836, 543 N.E.2d 119 (1 Dist. 1989).

The value of the marital property should be based upon the value as of the date of dissolution and not at time of physical separation, and properties acquired before and after separation should not be considered differently. Hollensbe v. Hollensbe, 165 Ill. App. 3d 522, 116 Ill. Dec. 450, 519 N.E.2d 40 (5 Dist. 1988).

The proper valuation date for marital property was date on which court entered both its judgment dissolving the marriage and settling the matters of custody, child support, maintenance and property division. In re Suarez, 148 Ill. App. 3d 849, 102 Ill. Dec. 85, 499 N.E.2d 642 (2 Dist. 1986).

The date of valuing marital assets is the date the judgment of dissolution was entered. In re Brooks, 138 Ill. App. 3d 252, 93 Ill. Dec. 166, 486 N.E.2d 267 (1 Dist. 1985); In re Rubinstein, 145 Ill. App. 3d 31, 99 Ill. Dec. 212, 495 N.E.2d 659 (2 Dist. 1986).

Proper valuation date for corporation owned by husband was date of dissolution of marriage; to hold otherwise would have the effect of treating appreciation of the corporation subsequent to the dissolution as marital property contrary to subdivision (c)(3) of this section. In re Rossi, 113 Ill. App. 3d 55, 68 Ill. Dec. 801, 446 N.E.2d 1198 (1 Dist. 1983).

—Difficulties

Placing a present value on a pension or on a profit sharing interest may be difficult, particularly if they have not matured; however, difficulties in valuation are not an insurmountable barrier to including a pension or profit sharing interest, whether matured, vested or nonvested, as marital property. In re Hunt, 78 Ill. App. 3d 653, 34 Ill. Dec. 55, 397 N.E.2d 511 (1 Dist. 1979).

—Discretion

Establishing valuations of marital property is properly a matter for the trial court to determine. In re Boone, 86 Ill. App. 3d 250, 41 Ill. Dec. 750, 408 N.E.2d 96 (3 Dist. 1980).

—Error

Trial judge abused his discretion in valuing husband's medical practice nine months prior to the date of dissolution, failing to consider any evidence offered valuing the corporate assets of accounts receivable and unbilled but completed services, and failing to consider any evidence offered toward the value of the corporation's goodwill. In re Rubinstein, 145 Ill. App. 3d 31, 99 Ill. Dec. 212, 495 N.E.2d 659 (2 Dist. 1986).

—Evidence

It is the parties' obligation to provide the trial court with sufficient evidence of the value of the property, including pension rights, and the trial court will base its division of property upon the evidence presented. In re Wolf, 180 Ill. App. 3d 998, 129 Ill. Dec. 742, 536 N.E.2d 792 (1 Dist. 1989).

It is the obligation of the parties in a dissolution proceeding to present the court with sufficient evidence of the value of the property. In re Courtright, 155 Ill. App. 3d 55, 107 Ill. Dec. 738, 507 N.E.2d 891 (3 Dist. 1987).

This section requires division of marital property in just proportions considering all relevant factors and does not require that the court place a specific value on each item of property, but does require that there be competent evidence of value, that the court's property division be supported by the evidence, and that the record provide a basis upon which a reviewing court can determine the propriety of the property award. In re Ales, 148 Ill. App. 3d 305, 101 Ill. Dec. 801, 102 Ill. Dec. 801, 499 N.E.2d 168 (3 Dist. 1986).

Although there is no requirement that the court place a specific value on each item of property, there must be competent evidence of value to support the court's division of property. In re Aud, 142 Ill. App. 3d 320, 96 Ill. Dec. 615, 491 N.E.2d 894 (5 Dist. 1986).

Where a party in a marriage dissolution action did not offer evidence of an asset's value, the party could not complain as to

Valuation (Cont'd)

—Evidence (Cont'd)
disposition of that asset by the court because parties are not allowed to benefit on review from their failure to introduce evidence at trial. In re Tyrrell, 132 Ill. App. 3d 348, 87 Ill. Dec. 546, 477 N.E.2d 523 (3 Dist. 1985).

There is no requirement that a court place a specific value on each item of property, but only that there be competent evidence of value and that the trial court's division of property be supported by the evidence. In re Deem, 123 Ill. App. 3d 1019, 79 Ill. Dec. 542, 463 N.E.2d 1317 (4 Dist. 1984).

There must be competent evidence of value of both non-marital and marital assets in the record. In re Caldwell, 124 Ill. App. 3d 898, 80 Ill. Dec. 411, 465 N.E.2d 523 (4 Dist. 1984).

Where the parties have stipulated to the admission of evidence of valuation, providing some evidence to review the trial court's exercise of discretion, further proceedings on remand are unnecessary. In re Caldwell, 124 Ill. App. 3d 898, 80 Ill. Dec. 411, 465 N.E.2d 523 (4 Dist. 1984).

Although the trial court did conduct hearings and made findings that should have been conclusive, the absence of sufficient credible evidence to establish the valuation of several major assets mandated reversal of the cause since without such evidence, there was no support for the court's finding that the parties' debts and obligations far exceeded their assets. In re Reib, 114 Ill. App. 3d 993, 70 Ill. Dec. 572, 449 N.E.2d 919 (1 Dist. 1983).

This Act only requires that there be competent evidence of value of property and that the court's division of the property be supported by the evidence. In re Hyland, 95 Ill. App. 3d 31, 50 Ill. Dec. 554, 419 N.E.2d 662 (2 Dist. 1981).

—Evidence Held Insufficient
Evidence was insufficient for the determination of the value of husband's law firm where the only evidence introduced was that of four corporate assets, two vehicles, the accounts receivable, and the husband's interest in the office building which he had assigned to the firm. In re Davis, 131 Ill. App. 3d 1065, 87 Ill. Dec. 145, 476 N.E.2d 1137 (1 Dist. 1985).

—Exactness
While specific findings of value may be required if they are necessary to provide a basis for the trial and reviewing courts to determine the propriety of the property division, an apportionment in kind need not be accompanied by an exact evaluation. In re Viehman, 91 Ill. App. 3d 315, 46 Ill. Dec. 800, 414 N.E.2d 853 (5 Dist. 1980).

—Expert Testimony
Where in action for dissolution of marriage and for allocation of the marital property, expert witness was a certified public accountant with 15 years of auditing and accounting experience, had both formal academic training and practical experience in the area of accounting, and had on several occasions valued medical practices for purposes of dissolution of marriage proceedings, although he had not testified in those proceedings at the time of the trial, argument that specific experience or training in valuation was necessary was without merit because valuation is merely a small part of the larger discipline of accounting, and trial court's determination that witness was qualified as an expert and that his limited experience in valuation proceedings went only to the weight of his testimony was not an abuse of discretion. In re Olson, 223 Ill. App. 3d 636, 166 Ill. Dec. 60, 585 N.E.2d 1082 (2 Dist.), appeal denied, 145 Ill. 2d 636, 173 Ill. Dec. 6, 596 N.E.2d 630 (1992).

—Failure of Proof
Once the court made a specific finding that the only witness to offer evidence on the valuation issue was not credible, there was a necessary failure of the proof, and any valuation made by the court without a financial analysis of the health of the corporations was necessarily arbitrary. Blackstone v. Blackstone, 288 Ill. App. 3d 905, 224 Ill. Dec. 90, 681 N.E.2d 72 (1 Dist. 1997).

—Fraud
Where a wife alleged that her husband was guilty of fraud and that he had secretly started new companies after the date of the judgment of dissolution to hide marital assets from her, the court was not required to admit evidence on the value of any assets of the new company, which was formed subsequent to the date of the judgment of dissolution, absent a specific order from the reviewing court pursuant to subsection (h) of this section or a showing of fraud or a sham transaction. In re Jones, 187 Ill. App. 3d 206, 134 Ill. Dec. 836, 543 N.E.2d 119 (1 Dist. 1989).

—Future Income
Adding a sum to the value of the professional corporation awarded to the husband based upon a stream of future income was error because it resulted in a "double count" of potential future income by considering such income in both the valuation of the asset and considering it in apportioning the total marital assets and awarding maintenance. Head v. Head, 168 Ill. App. 3d 697, 119 Ill. Dec. 549, 523 N.E.2d 17 (1 Dist. 1988).

—Hearsay Evidence
Husband's testimony as to the value of the home not only was of a self-serving nature but also constituted rank hearsay, and such testimony was inherently lacking in credibility. In re Carney, 122 Ill. App. 3d 705, 78 Ill. Dec. 477, 462 N.E.2d 596 (1 Dist. 1984).

—Home
Due to the uncertainty of the valuation of the home, it could not be determined whether the trial court distributed the marital assets in favor of the husband. In re Rai, 189 Ill. App. 3d 559, 136 Ill. Dec. 922, 545 N.E.2d 446 (1 Dist. 1989).

Where respondent failed to show due diligence in that he did not secure a more recent appraisal of his home until after the hearing on the dissolution of marriage, where he attempted to avoid his lack of diligence by arguing that the actual value of the residence was not an important issue until the trial court awarded the residence to petitioner as maintenance in gross, and stated that such an award afforded petitioner $71,000 in value, the argument lacked merit because value became important prior to trial when both parties sought ownership of the home, and especially when petitioner by her interrogatories sought to learn the value of the home. In re Sanborn, 78 Ill. App. 3d 146, 33 Ill. Dec. 468, 396 N.E.2d 1192 (1 Dist. 1979).

—Home Furnishings
Where furniture was divided sensibly so that each party had an adequately furnished residence, a monetary evaluation was not essential to an appropriate division, and the decision of the trial court was clearly within its discretion. In re Hilkovitch, 124 Ill. App. 3d 401, 79 Ill. Dec. 891, 464 N.E.2d 795 (1 Dist. 1984).

—Illustrative Cases
Pursuant to Fed. R. Bankr. P. 8013, the bankruptcy court's calculation of the value of the marital estate, pursuant to 750 ILCS 5/503(f), was not clearly erroneous, the bankruptcy court's measure of the date regarding the debtor's dissipation claim and the specific calculation of the value of the dissipation claim was not clearly erroneous, and the debtor's collateral estoppel argument failed. Mungo v. Taylor (In re Mungo), F. Supp. 2d , 2003 U.S. Dist. LEXIS 3412 (N.D. Ill. Mar. 6, 2003), aff'd, 355 F.3d 969 (7th Cir. 2004).

The trial court's valuation of a corporation was against the manifest weight of the evidence because it was below the valuation the respondent paid to shareholder's widow four years earlier and evidence showed the corporation's financial health had greatly improved since the earlier transaction. Grunsten v. Grunsten, 304 Ill. App. 3d 12, 237 Ill. Dec. 342, 709 N.E.2d 597 (1 Dist. 1999), appeal denied, 185 Ill. 2d 624, 242 Ill. Dec. 137, 720 N.E.2d 1092 (1999).

Returning petitioner's share of couple's initial investment to her six years later, as if nothing had happened in the intervening period of time, was necessarily arbitrary, particularly when only testimony on financial health of company suggested it had financial problems. Blackstone v. Blackstone, 288 Ill. App. 3d 905, 224 Ill. Dec. 90, 681 N.E.2d 72 (1 Dist. 1997).

For a case discussing valuation methodology used in assessing business assets, see In re Perlmutter, 225 Ill. App. 3d 362, 167 Ill. Dec. 340, 587 N.E.2d 609 (2 Dist.), appeal denied, 146 Ill. 2d 650, 176 Ill. Dec. 820, 602 N.E.2d 474 (1992), cert. denied, 507 U.S. 1006, 113 S. Ct. 1648, 123 L. Ed. 2d 269 (1993).

—Increase During Marriage
A business property interest owned by one spouse prior to the

Valuation (Cont'd)

—Increase During Marriage (Cont'd)
parties' marriage is non-marital property and retains its non-marital classification despite even a significant increase in its value during the marriage. In re Landfield, 209 Ill. App. 3d 678, 153 Ill. Dec. 834, 567 N.E.2d 1061 (1 Dist.), cert. denied, 139 Ill. 2d 597, 159 Ill. Dec. 109, 575 N.E.2d 916 (1991).

—Insurance Agency
Trial court's decision valuing the husband's insurance agency business in marriage dissolution proceeding was against the manifest weight of the evidence where the trial court used an approach in valuing the insurance agency that improperly took into account post-dissolution labor rather than the asset approach method that was supported by the expert testimony of the husband's valuation expert and which subtracted liabilities from assets to properly arrive at a value as of the date of the dissolution. Cutler v. Cutler, 334 Ill. App. 3d 731, 268 Ill. Dec. 496, 778 N.E.2d 762, 2002 Ill. App. LEXIS 973 (5 Dist. 2002).

Where the capitalization of earnings method used by an expert to determine the worth of an insurance agency produced an unrealistically high figure for interest in the agency, these shortcomings produced a grossly excessive valuation of the agency as a marital asset, and the cause was remanded for revaluation and redistribution of the value of the agency. In re Frazier, 125 Ill. App. 3d 473, 80 Ill. Dec. 838, 466 N.E.2d 290 (5 Dist. 1984).

—Inventions
There was sufficient evidence in the record to support the trial court's finding as to the value of "inventions." In re Aud, 142 Ill. App. 3d 320, 96 Ill. Dec. 615, 491 N.E.2d 894 (5 Dist. 1986).

—Just Apportionment
Valuation of marital property is necessary in order to reach a just apportionment except where the parties are awarded percentage interests in a particular item. In re Boone, 86 Ill. App. 3d 250, 41 Ill. Dec. 750, 408 N.E.2d 96 (3 Dist. 1980).

—Lack of Evidence
Where evidence on marital property valuation is totally lacking, there is no basis upon which an appeals court can review the propriety of the trial court's determination. In re Wilder, 122 Ill. App. 3d 338, 77 Ill. Dec. 824, 461 N.E.2d 447 (1 Dist. 1983).

—Marital Assets
Where the trial court did not have evidence of the valuation of the exclusive possession of the marital home for five years, the current values of the pension plans and Individual Retirement Account, the values of the automobiles, and the value of furniture and furnishings, the case had to be remanded for the purpose of receiving evidence concerning these marital assets and then to apportion them in equitable proportions. In re Walsh, 109 Ill. App. 3d 171, 64 Ill. Dec. 758, 440 N.E.2d 310 (1 Dist. 1982).

—Medical Practice
The trial court abused its discretion by failing to take into account the entire value of the medical practice when the trial court failed to include all of the elements of the purchase agreement and consultation agreement between the husband and a third party. In re Harding, 189 Ill. App. 3d 663, 136 Ill. Dec. 935, 545 N.E.2d 459 (1 Dist. 1989).

Where court should have considered the effort that the spouse expended on his surgical practice in determining the excess earnings of his practice, because he worked from 50 to 70 hours a week, he may have had a significantly greater income than a hypothetical employee who regularly worked a 40 hour week, but that increased income may have been due solely to longer hours and greater productivity, the court's failure to take these factors into account resulted in an artificially inflated valuation of the spouse's medical corporation and constituted an abuse of discretion, and the court's valuation was reversed and remanded for a reconsideration of the value of the spouse's practice. In re Kapusta, 141 Ill. App. 3d 1010, 96 Ill. Dec. 234, 491 N.E.2d 48 (1 Dist. 1986).

—Modification
Where the related issues of maintenance to petitioner and the minor child and the payment of educational expenses were directly affected by the final property disposition, since these awards were substantially dependent upon the financial resources of the parties, including marital property, the maintenance and support awards would have to be re-evaluated by the trial court on remand so that it could properly consider any changes required in the disposition of such property. In re Walsh, 109 Ill. App. 3d 171, 64 Ill. Dec. 758, 440 N.E.2d 310 (1 Dist. 1982).

—Offset Method
Under the approach for valuing a pension, the trial court may, upon determination of the present value of the pension benefits, award the value of the benefit to the employee spouse and offset that award with other marital property of similar value. Robinson v. Robinson, 146 Ill. App. 3d 474, 100 Ill. Dec. 260, 497 N.E.2d 140 (3 Dist. 1986).

The immediate offset approach is best used when there is sufficient actuarial evidence to determine the present value of the pension, when the employee spouse is close to retirement age, and when there is sufficient marital property to allow an offset. Robinson v. Robinson, 146 Ill. App. 3d 474, 100 Ill. Dec. 260, 497 N.E.2d 140 (3 Dist. 1986).

—Pension Plan
The "reserved jurisdiction" approach alleviates the inequities inherent in being unable to determine the present value of the plan benefits. Robinson v. Robinson, 146 Ill. App. 3d 474, 100 Ill. Dec. 260, 497 N.E.2d 140 (3 Dist. 1986).

—Percentage Interest
In a divorce proceeding, valuation of marital property is necessary in order to reach a just apportionment except where the parties are awarded percentage interests in a particular item. In re Donley, 83 Ill. App. 3d 367, 38 Ill. Dec. 733, 403 N.E.2d 1337 (3 Dist. 1980).

Where it is difficult to place a present value on the pension or profit sharing interest due to uncertainties or it is impractical or impossible to award sufficient offsetting marital property to the nonemployee spouse, then the trial court in its discretion may award each spouse an appropriate percentage of the pension to be paid if, as, and when the pension becomes payable. In re Hunt, 78 Ill. App. 3d 653, 34 Ill. Dec. 55, 397 N.E.2d 511 (1 Dist. 1979).

—Professional Corporation
Placing a fair market value on a professional corporation is an art, not a science, and the court must rely on expert witnesses to assist it in this difficult task; there is no exact formula that can be applied, so the trial court must rely on experts who may differ significantly in both methodology and valuation. The trial court must consider the relevant evidence before it; determine the credibility of the experts, the reasonableness of their testimony, the weight given to each of them, and their expertise in the particular area of valuation; and then determine fair market value. In re Gunn, 233 Ill. App. 3d 165, 174 Ill. Dec. 381, 598 N.E.2d 1013 (5 Dist. 1992).

—Proper Value Required
In order to apportion marital assets under this section, the proper value of such assets must be established, and where the record lacks proper evidence of valuation, there is no basis upon which an appellate court can review the propriety of a trial court's apportionment of marital property. In re Kundit, 107 Ill. App. 3d 310, 63 Ill. Dec. 128, 437 N.E.2d 777 (1 Dist. 1982).

—Question of Fact
Valuation of assets in a divorce matter is a question of fact for the trial court to determine. In re Ayers, 82 Ill. App. 3d 164, 37 Ill. Dec. 511, 402 N.E.2d 401 (3 Dist. 1980).

—Record of Value
Evidence of the value of both marital and non-marital assets must be shown on the record in order for a reviewing court to determine the propriety of the division of marital property. In re Deem, 123 Ill. App. 3d 1019, 79 Ill. Dec. 542, 463 N.E.2d 1317 (4 Dist. 1984).

—Reserved Jurisdiction Method
Under the reserved jurisdiction method, the court orders the employee spouse to pay an allocated portion of the pension fund to

Valuation (Cont'd)

—Reserved Jurisdiction Method (Cont'd)
the former spouse, as it is disbursed, while retaining jurisdiction to enforce the decree; the payments are made by the employee spouse "if, as and when" the benefits become payable. Robinson v. Robinson, 146 Ill. App. 3d 474, 100 Ill. Dec. 260, 497 N.E.2d 140 (3 Dist. 1986); In re Mantei, 222 Ill. App. 3d 933, 164 Ill. Dec. 870, 583 N.E.2d 1192 (4 Dist. 1991).

—Right to Appeal
The failure to offer evidence of the value of assets subject to division upon the dissolution of a marriage does not necessarily waive the right to appeal on this issue. In re Deem, 123 Ill. App. 3d 1019, 79 Ill. Dec. 542, 463 N.E.2d 1317 (4 Dist. 1984).

—Scope of Review
When the trial court renders a valuation that is outside the expert testimony presented at trial, the reviewing court must carefully scrutinize the trial court's determination. Blackstone v. Blackstone, 288 Ill. App. 3d 905, 224 Ill. Dec. 90, 681 N.E.2d 72 (1 Dist. 1997).

A reviewing court will not reverse the trial court where the parties have failed to produce evidence of the valuation of assets in dissolution cases when there was an adequate opportunity to do so. In re Wolf, 180 Ill. App. 3d 998, 129 Ill. Dec. 742, 536 N.E.2d 792 (1 Dist. 1989).

—Specific Value Not Required
This Act does not require the court to place a specific value on each item of property in considering the value of the property to be set aside to each spouse; it requires only that there be sufficient evidence of value in the record to permit review of the court's distribution. In re Hagshenas, 234 Ill. App. 3d 178, 175 Ill. Dec. 506, 600 N.E.2d 437 (2 Dist. 1992), appeal denied, 148 Ill.2d 642, 183 Ill. Dec. 19, 610 N.E.2d 1263 (1993).

There is no requirement that the court place a specific value on each item of property in dividing it between married parties, but only that there be competent evidence of value and that the court's division of property be supported by the evidence. In re Randall, 157 Ill. App. 3d 892, 110 Ill. Dec. 122, 510 N.E.2d 1153 (1 Dist. 1987).

Although more evidence of the value of husband's interest in his business could have been received, appellate court declined to reverse and remand for a new hearing when to do so would have, in effect, allowed wife to benefit from her failure to introduce at trial evidence which she apparently had available to her, and where it was clear the court equated the value of husband's interest in the business with its income potential to him, and considered that value in apportioning the parties, assets, and in determining maintenance and child support. In re Leff, 148 Ill. App. 3d 792, 101 Ill. Dec. 262, 499 N.E.2d 1042 (2 Dist. 1986).

The trial court did not commit reversible error in failing to make a specific finding of fact as to the fair market value of the marital residence. In re Thompson, 79 Ill. App. 3d 310, 34 Ill. Dec. 342, 398 N.E.2d 17 (1 Dist. 1979).

—Stamp Collection
The trial court did not abuse its discretion in determining that the value of petitioner's stamp collection was $150,000 where both parties testified that petitioner spent in excess of that amount on the collection; the trial court was entitled to utilize purchase price as a valuation tool and to disregard the testimony of the expert, particularly in view of the fact that the trial court specifically noted that it did not believe the expert had seen the entire collection amassed during the marriage. In re Harding, 189 Ill. App. 3d 663, 136 Ill. Dec. 935, 545 N.E.2d 459 (1 Dist. 1989).

—Standard of Review
The valuation of the marital property of the parties, which is to be valued as of the date of the judgment dissolving the marriage of the parties and on the basis of what a willing purchaser will pay to a willing seller in a voluntary transaction, is a matter within the discretion of the trial court which will not be overturned absent an abuse of that discretion, that is, where no reasonable person would take the view adopted by the trial court. In re Hagshenas, 234 Ill. App. 3d 178, 175 Ill. Dec. 506, 600 N.E.2d 437 (2 Dist. 1992), appeal denied, 148 Ill.2d 642, 183 Ill. Dec. 19, 610 N.E.2d 1263 (1993).

A trial court's allocation of marital property, including making allowances for dissipation, will not be reversed absent an abuse of discretion; such discretion will be considered abused only when no reasonable man would agree with the decision reached by the trial court. In re Hagshenas, 234 Ill. App. 3d 178, 175 Ill. Dec. 506, 600 N.E.2d 437 (2 Dist. 1992), appeal denied, 148 Ill.2d 642, 183 Ill. Dec. 19, 610 N.E.2d 1263 (1993).

—Stipulation
The trial court properly divided a Keogh plan where it valued according to the parties' stipulation. In re Keller, 108 Ill. App. 3d 556, 64 Ill. Dec. 115, 439 N.E.2d 44 (1 Dist. 1982).

—Tax Consequences
A trial court, when valuing an asset, is not required to deduct from that value the amount of taxes which were paid on it; rather, it is to consider the tax consequences of the property division. In re Leisner, 219 Ill. App. 3d 752, 162 Ill. Dec. 277, 579 N.E.2d 1091 (1 Dist. 1991).

Trial court's apparent failure to consider the tax consequences of the transfer of property was contrary to this section and therefore error. In re Malters, 133 Ill. App. 3d 168, 88 Ill. Dec. 460, 478 N.E.2d 1068 (1 Dist. 1985).

—Testimony
Testimony concerning the valuation of assets in an action for dissolution of marriage are matters to be resolved by the trier of fact, and as long as the court's valuation is within the range testified to by the expert witnesses, it ordinarily will not be disturbed on appeal. In re Brooks, 138 Ill. App. 3d 252, 93 Ill. Dec. 166, 486 N.E.2d 267 (1 Dist. 1985).

—Time and Specificity
The trial court should value the marital property of the parties as of the date of the judgment of dissolution of marriage; however, the court is not required to place a specific value on each item of property, but rather, only competent evidence of the value supported by evidence of that valuation is required for a property division. In re Courtright, 155 Ill. App. 3d 55, 107 Ill. Dec. 738, 507 N.E.2d 891 (3 Dist. 1987).

—Total Offset Method
Under the total offset method, the trial court must determine the actual value of the pension according to actuarial evidence, discounting an amount in light of the risk that the pension will not vest, discounting also to present value, and then determining the marital portion of that amount; usually expert testimony will be required. In re Mantei, 222 Ill. App. 3d 933, 164 Ill. Dec. 870, 583 N.E.2d 1192 (4 Dist. 1991).

—Trust
The complete dearth of evidence or findings concerning the terms and value of the respondent's trust, the nature of the proceeds therefrom, and the effects of these determinations upon other interests related to the dissolution rendered the property division arbitrary. In re Rosen, 126 Ill. App. 3d 766, 81 Ill. Dec. 840, 467 N.E.2d 962 (1 Dist. 1984).

—Upheld
Where respondent valued the household furnishings at $10,000, petitioner's jewelry at $15,000 and her furs at $5,000, respondent's claim that these assets were of substantial but unknown value was without merit. In re Skahn, 149 Ill. App. 3d 764, 103 Ill. Dec. 208, 501 N.E.2d 229 (1 Dist. 1986).

The trial court, in determining the value of husband's business, did not abuse its discretion where it took into consideration the nature of the business, the history of the enterprise from its inception, the economic outlook in general and the earnings of the business, the unique nature and valuation of a personal services business, and rejected the testimony as to valuation and the valuation method used by respondent's expert as unreasonable in light of the salaries earned by respondent, the expense accounts and entertainment costs, and other expenses absorbed by the corporation. In re Bauer, 138 Ill. App. 3d 379, 93 Ill. Dec. 108, 485 N.E.2d 1318 (1 Dist. 1985).

—Vacated Order
When a trial court vacates the property division of a dissolution

Valuation (Cont'd)

—Vacated Order (Cont'd)

judgment pursuant to 735 ILCS 5/2-1401, the court may in its discretion value marital property as of the date of the post-vacation hearing on property issues. In re Hale, 278 Ill. App. 3d 53, 214 Ill. Dec. 826, 662 N.E.2d 180 (3 Dist. 1996).

—Veteran's Benefits

The respondent's receipt of veteran's benefits, as non-marital property set aside to him, was a factor to be considered in the division of marital property, but error was committed when the trial court did not determine a value for the respondent's non-marital property; the value of the respondent's veterans' benefits would depend upon such factors as the respondent's life expectancy and the present value of future increased benefits and absent such a valuation, the marital property of the parties could not have been equitably divided without an evidentiary determination of the value of the respondent's non-marital assets. In re Hapaniewski, 107 Ill. App. 3d 848, 63 Ill. Dec. 535, 438 N.E.2d 466 (1 Dist. 1982).

—Waiver

A party cannot argue for the first time on appeal regarding the value of a pension when he has failed to object to the value before the trial court and failed to introduce to the trial court evidence to the contrary. In re Wolf, 180 Ill. App. 3d 998, 129 Ill. Dec. 742, 536 N.E.2d 792 (1 Dist. 1989).

Vested Property Rights

Property rights created in a divorce decree become vested and after 30 days the court is without jurisdiction to modify them. Brickey v. Brickey, 44 Ill. App. 3d 563, 3 Ill. Dec. 239, 358 N.E.2d 406 (5 Dist. 1976).

Where an original divorce decree was entirely silent with regard to apportionment of any income tax refund, wife could not by her petition requesting the award of income taxes withheld from her salary, which had been included in a joint income tax return, invoke the court's jurisdiction to adjudicate property rights upon which the final word had already been spoken in the decree. Brickey v. Brickey, 44 Ill. App. 3d 563, 3 Ill. Dec. 239, 358 N.E.2d 406 (5 Dist. 1976).

Waiver

Respondent cannot claim error in division of property to which he acquiesced in the trial court. In re Cheger, 213 Ill. App. 3d 371, 157 Ill. Dec. 116, 571 N.E.2d 1135 (4 Dist. 1991).

Although wife had no separate income in 1984, she retained a property right in refund check and did not waive her interest in the refund in property settlement agreement. In re Ormiston, 168 Ill. App. 3d 1016, 119 Ill. Dec. 680, 523 N.E.2d 148 (1 Dist. 1988).

Where the record clearly refuted respondent's assertions regarding the absence of evidence of the value of foreclosed real estate, the trial court properly found respondent had waived any interest in the property's redemption. In re Skahn, 149 Ill. App. 3d 764, 103 Ill. Dec. 208, 501 N.E.2d 229 (1 Dist. 1986).

Respondent, who failed to assert her homestead claim to the trial court, could not rely on the fact that such claim was not considered in order to reverse the trial court's judgment on appeal. Naguit v. Scrivner, 104 Ill. App. 3d 709, 60 Ill. Dec. 499, 433 N.E.2d 296 (5 Dist. 1982).

Ward of Court

The decision of the trial court making three children wards of the court but leaving them in their mother's home and making a fourth child a ward of the court but allowing her to reside with her natural father were not against the manifest weight of the evidence. People v. Craig, 131 Ill. App. 3d 401, 86 Ill. Dec. 737, 475 N.E.2d 1116 (4 Dist. 1985).

Waste

—In General

It is entirely with the realm of possibility that one spouse's use of marital funds for his or her own living expenses at a time when the marriage is undergoing an irreconcilable breakdown could be shown to be so selfish and excessive and improper as to constitute an outright waste of marital funds. In re Hagshenas, 234 Ill. App. 3d 178, 175 Ill. Dec. 506, 600 N.E.2d 437 (2 Dist. 1992), appeal denied, 148 Ill.2d 642, 183 Ill. Dec. 19, 610 N.E.2d 1263 (1993).

Wilful Violation

—Not Shown

Where settlement agreement required that the house be put on the market but neither party was exclusively responsible for performance, where the house was placed on the market within the time provided in the agreement, and where the husband rejected third party's offer, although he offered to buy out the wife's interest for as much or more than she would have received under the rejected offer, his reason for rejecting the offer was not valid, the wife's rejection of his offer seemed equally improper, and the court's finding that the husband wilfully violated the agreement was against the manifest weight of the evidence. In re Anthony, 94 Ill. App. 3d 827, 50 Ill. Dec. 227, 419 N.E.2d 94 (2 Dist. 1981).

—Rights of Violator

A party who was adjudged to be in contempt of the trial court for failure to abide by its orders, who removed himself beyond its process and concealed himself outside the State of Illinois, and sought to attack the final decree of the court ordering maintenance in gross and marital property division which he was defying, was not entitled to appellate relief. In re Timke, 219 Ill. App. 3d 423, 162 Ill. Dec. 114, 579 N.E.2d 928 (1 Dist. 1991).

Workers' Compensation Benefits

—In General

Awards paid to the injured spouse for wage loss and medical and hospital expenses incurred during the marriage are deemed marital property. In re Waggoner, 261 Ill. App. 3d 787, 199 Ill. Dec. 844, 634 N.E.2d 1198 (5 Dist. 1994).

—Apportionment

In apportioning petitioner's workers' compensation award the court must consider the petitioner's diminished earning capacity due to the injury. In re DeRossett, 173 Ill. 2d 416, 219 Ill. Dec. 487, 671 N.E.2d 654 (1996).

—Marital Property

Petitioner's workers' compensation award constituted marital property because the claim accrued during the marriage of the parties. In re DeRossett, 173 Ill. 2d 416, 219 Ill. Dec. 487, 671 N.E.2d 654 (1996).

—Permanent Total Disability

The analytical approach was used when disposing of workers' compensation permanent total disability benefits under this section. In re Waggoner, 261 Ill. App. 3d 787, 199 Ill. Dec. 844, 634 N.E.2d 1198 (5 Dist. 1994).

LEGAL PERIODICALS

For Note, "A Practical Guide to Illinois' New QILDRO Law", see 87 Ill. B.J. 354 (1999).

For article, "The Real Estate Lawyer's Divorce Primer and the Divorce Lawyer's Guide to Real Estate", see 86 Ill. B.J. 488 (1998).

For article, "Survey of Illinois Law: Workers' Compensation," see 21 S. Ill. U.L.J. 931 (1997).

For article, "'Leveling the Playing Field' in Divorce: Questions and Answers About the New Law," see 85 Ill. B.J. 410 (1997).

For article, "Survey of Illinois Law: Family Law," 19 S. Ill. U.L.J. 819 (1995).

For article, "The Pension Trip: Trading Pension Rights in Divorce Settlements," see 83 Ill. B.J. 302 (1995).

For note, "Til Success Do Us Part: How Illinois Promotes Inequities in Property Distribution Pursuant to Divorce by Excluding Professional Goodwill", see 26 J. Marshall L. Rev. 147 (1992).

For article, "Professional Goodwill in Divorce After Zells (572 N.E.2d 944 (1991))," see 79 Ill. B. J. 624 (1991).

For note on domestic relations and dissipation of marital assets in light of In re Marriage of O'Neill (563 N.E.2d 494 (1990)), see 79 Ill. B. J. 639 (1991).

For article, "Dissipation of Marital Assets: A Review and Criticism," see 79 Ill. B. J. 186 (1991).

For article, "The Session of Reform: Illinois Statutory Tenancy by the Entirety," see 78 Ill. B. J. 198 (1990).

For article, "Personal Injury, Workers' Compensation, and Disability Awards in Illinois Divorce Cases," see 78 Ill. B. J. 506 (1990).

For article, "Survey of Illinois Law [1988-89]—Family Law," see 14 S. Ill. U. L. J. 1007 (1990).

For article, "Family Law: 1988-89 Illinois Law Survey," see 21 Loy. U. Chi. L. J. 417 (1989-90).

For article, "Family Law: 1985-86 Survey," see 11 S. Ill. U. L. J. 741 (1987).

For article, "Divorce Illinois Style: Ten Years Under the Marriage and Dissolution of Marriage Act," see 75 Ill. B. J. 606 (1987).

For note, "Uniform Marital Property Act: Suggested Revisions for Equality Between Spouses," see U. Ill. L. Rev. 471 (1987).

For article, "Family Law: 1986-87 Illinois Law Survey," See 19 Loy. U. Chi. L. J. 489 (1987-88).

For article, "Distribution of Property: Compensation for Marital Energies Applied to Non-marital Property," see 76 Ill. B. J. 904 (1987).

For article, "Family Law: 1985-86 Illinois Law Survey," see 18 Loy. U. Chi. L. J. 549 (1986-87).

For article, "Has the Illinois Equitable Distribution Statute Advanced the Course of the Home Maker?," see 74 Ill. B. J. 492 (1986).

For article, "Valuation of Professional Practices in Dissolution Cases," see 74 Ill. B. J. 14 (1985).

For article, "Taming Transmutation: A Guide to Illinois' New Rules on Property Classification and Division upon Dissolution of Marriage," see 72 Ill. B. J. 336 (1984).

For article, "The Marital Home: Equal or Equitable Distribution?," see 50 U. Chi. L. Rev. 1089 (1983).

For article, "Marital Property in Illinois: The Complexities Wrought by the Presumption of Gift, Transmutation, and Commingling," see 1982 S. Ill. U. L. J. 159.

For case note, "In re Marriage of Komnick 417 N.E. 2d 1305 (1981): The Appreciation of Nonmaterial Property in the Illinois Marital Property Distribution Scheme," see 15 J. Marshall L. Rev. 531 (1982).

For article, "Classification of Property Upon Dissolution of Marriage: Suggestions For Maintaining Our Dual System," "In the Aftermath of Smith," 86 Ill. 2d 518, 427 N.E.2d 1239 (1981), see 71 Ill. B. J. 100 (1982).

For note, "Divorce and Marital Property discussing In re Marriage of Smith, 86 Ill. 2d 518, 427 N.E.2d 1239 (1981)," see 71 Ill. B. J. 134 (1982).

For article, "Transmutation and Commingling: The Supreme Court's Rebuttable Presumption of Marital Property," see 71 Ill. B. J. 220 (1982).

For note on Marital Property and Future Employment Benefits discussing In re Marriage of Evans, 85 Ill. 2d 523, 426 N.E.2d 854 (1981), see 70 Ill. B. J. 582 (1982).

For article, "The Sequestrator—The Court's Enforcer," see 70 Ill. B. J. 494 (1982).

For note, "McCarty v. McCarty: A Former Spouse's Claim to a Service Member's Military Retired Pay is Shot Down," see Loy. U. Chi. L. J. 555 (1981-82).

For note, "Divorce Law and Property Division—In re Roger B. 118 N.E.2d 757 (1981)," see 70 Ill. B. J. 260 (1981).

For article, "Wisconsin, Illinois, Ontario—Three Roads to Marital Property Law Reform," see 12 Loy. U. Chi. L. J. 1 (1980-81).

For article, "Caveat Amator: The State of Affairs in Illinois After Hewitt v. Hewitt," see 29 De Paul L. Rev. 493 (1980).

For article, "Developments in Marital Property Law," see 68 Ill. B. J. 698 (1980).

For article, "Intention Controls: The Theory of Transmutation—The Effect of Placing Property Which was Initially Non-Marital into Joint Tenancy; The Theory of Commingling—The Effect of Intermingling Marital and Non-Marital Funds," see 68 Ill. B. J. 320 (1980).

For article, "Allocation of Private Pension Benefits as Property in Illinois Divorce Proceedings," see 29 De Paul L. Rev. 1 (1979).

For case note, "Hewitt v. Hewitt—Contract Cohabitation" and "Equitable Expectations Relief for Meretricious Spouses," see 12 J. Marshall J. Prac. & Proc. 435 (1979).

For article, "The Federal Tax Treatment of Transfers of 'Marital Property' Under the New Illinois Marriage and Dissolution of Marriage Act," see 59 Chi. B. Rec. 286 (1978).

For article, "Marital Property, Top Ramification, and Maintenance Practice Under the Illinois Marriage and Dissolution of Marriage Act—A Comparative Study," see 66 Ill. B. J. 324 (1978).

For note, "Federal Income Tax Consequences of Appreciated Property Transfers Under the Illinois Marriage and Dissolution of Marriage Act," see 27 De Paul L. Rev. 815 (1978).

RESEARCH REFERENCES

Spouse's professional degree or license as marital property for purposes of alimony, support, or property settlement. 4 ALR4th 1294.

Appointment or discharge of receiver for marital or community property necessitated by suit for divorce or separation. 15 ALR4th 224.

Divorce and separation: Effect of trial court giving consideration to needs of children in making property division—modern status. 19 ALR4th 239.

Divorce and separation: appreciation in value of separate property during marriage without contribution by either spouse as separate or community property. 24 ALR4th 453.

Property settlement agreement as affecting divorced spouse's right to recover as named beneficiary under former spouse's life insurance policy. 31 ALR4th 59.

Proper date for valuation of property being distributed pursuant to divorce. 34 ALR4th 63.

Spouse's right to discovery of closely held corporation records during divorce proceeding. 38 ALR4th 145.

Spouse's dissipation of marital assets prior to divorce as factor in divorce court's determination of property division. 41 ALR4th 416.

Divorce and separation: Treatment of stock options for purposes of dividing marital property. 46 ALR4th 640.

Valuation of stock options for purposes of divorce court's property distribution. 46 ALR4th 689.

Necessity that divorce court value property before distributing it. 51 ALR4th 11.

Enforceability of premarital agreements governing support or property rights upon divorce or separation as affected by fairness or adequacy of those terms—modern status. 53 ALR4th 161.

Divorce and separation: method of valuation of life insurance policies in connection with trial court's division of property. 54 ALR4th 1203.

Divorce: excessiveness or adequacy of combined property division and spousal support awards—modern cases. 55 ALR4th 14.

Divorce: excessiveness or adequacy of trial court's property award—modern cases. 56 ALR4th 12.

Divorce: propriety of property distribution leaving both parties with substantial ownership interest in same business. 56 ALR4th 862.

Antenuptial contracts: parties' behavior during marriage as abandonment, estoppel, or waiver regarding contractual rights. 56 ALR4th 998.

Divorce: order requiring that party not complete with former marital business. 59 ALR4th 1075.

Divorce property distribution: real estate or trust property in which interest vested before marriage and was realized during marriage. 60 ALR4th 217.

Divorce property distribution: treatment and method of valuation of future interest in real estate or trust property not realized during marriage. 62 ALR4th 107.

Divorce and separation: effect of court order prohibiting sale or transfer of property on party's right to change beneficiary of insurance policy. 68 ALR4th 929.

Divorce and separation: attributing undisclosed income to parent or spouse for purposes of making child or spousal support award. 70 ALR4th 173.

Divorce and separation: goodwill in medical or dental practice as property subject to distribution on dissolution of marriage. 76 ALR4th 1025.

Valuation of goodwill in accounting practice for purposes of divorce court's property distribution. 77 ALR4th 609.

Divorce and separation: goodwill in accounting practice for purposes of divorce court's property distribution. 77 ALR4th 645.

Valuation of goodwill in law practice for purposes of divorce court's property distribution. 77 ALR4th 683.

Valuation of goodwill in medical or dental practice for purposes of divorce court's property distribution. 78 ALR4th 853.

Accrued vacation, holiday time, and sick leave as marital or separate property. 78 ALR4th 1107.

Divorce and separation: goodwill in law practice as property subject to distribution on dissolution of marriage. 79 ALR4th 171.

What constitutes order made pursuant to state domestic relations law for purposes of qualified domestic relations order exception to antialienation provision of Employee Retirement Income Security Act of 1974 (29 U.S.C § 1056(d)). 79 ALR4th 1081.

Divorce and separation: Consideration of tax consequences in distribution of marital property. 9 ALR5th 568.

Divorce and separation: attorney's contingent fee contracts as marital property subject to distribution. 44 ALR5th 671.

Admissibility of expert testimony regarding questions of domestic law. 66 ALR5th 135.

Copyright, patent, or other intellectual property as marital property for purposes of alimony, support, or divorce settlement. 80 ALR5th 487.

Divorce decree or settlement agreement as affecting divorced spouse's right to recover as named beneficiary on former spouse's individual retirement account. 99 ALR5th 637.

Divorce and separation: Determination of whether proceeds from personal injury settlement or recovery constitute marital property. 109 ALR5th 1.

Division of lottery proceeds in divorce proceedings. 124 ALR5th 537.

750 ILCS 5/504 Maintenance

Sec. 504. *Maintenance.* (a) In a proceeding for dissolution of marriage or legal separation or declaration of invalidity of marriage, or a proceeding for maintenance following dissolution of the marriage by a court which lacked personal jurisdiction over the absent spouse, the court may grant a temporary or permanent maintenance award for either spouse in amounts and for periods of time as the court deems just, without regard to marital misconduct, in gross or for fixed or indefinite periods of time, and the maintenance may be paid from the income or property of the other spouse after consideration of all relevant factors, including:

(1) the income and property of each party, including marital property apportioned and non-marital property assigned to the party seeking maintenance;

(2) the needs of each party;

(3) the present and future earning capacity of each party;

(4) any impairment of the present and future earning capacity of the party seeking maintenance due to that party devoting time to domestic duties or having forgone or delayed education, training, employment, or career opportunities due to the marriage;

(5) the time necessary to enable the party seeking maintenance to acquire appropriate education, training, and employment, and whether that party is able to support himself or herself through appropriate employment or is the custodian of a child making it appropriate that the custodian not seek employment;

(6) the standard of living established during the marriage;

(7) the duration of the marriage;

(8) the age and the physical and emotional condition of both parties;

(9) the tax consequences of the property division upon the respective economic circumstances of the parties;

(10) contributions and services by the party seeking maintenance to the education, training, career or career potential, or license of the other spouse;

(11) any valid agreement of the parties; and

(12) any other factor that the court expressly finds to be just and equitable.

(b) (Blank).

(c) The court may grant and enforce the payment of maintenance during the pendency of an appeal as the court shall deem reasonable and proper.

(d) No maintenance shall accrue during the period in which a party is imprisoned for failure to comply with the court's order for the payment of such maintenance.

(e) When maintenance is to be paid through the clerk of the court in a county of 1,000,000 inhabitants or less, the order shall direct the obligor to pay to the clerk, in addition to the maintenance payments, all fees imposed by the county board under paragraph (3) of subsection (u) of Section 27.1 of the Clerks of Courts Act [705 ILCS 105/27.1]. Unless paid in cash or pursuant to an order for withholding, the payment of the fee shall be by a separate instrument from the support payment and shall be made to the order of the Clerk.

(Source: P.A. 86-969; 87-881; 91-357, § 256.)

Note.

This section was Ill.Rev.Stat., Ch. 40, para. 504.

705 ILCS 105/27.1, referred to above, was repealed.

Effect of Amendments.

The 1999 amendment by P.A. 91-357, effective July 29, 1999, substituted "forgone" for "foregone" in subsection (a)(4); and deleted subsection (b).

CASE NOTES

Analysis

In General
Amendment of Order
Appellate Review
—Factors Considered
—Jurisdiction
—Standard of Review
Applicability of Amendments
Application
Attorney Fees
—In General
—Allowed
—Criteria
—Disparity in Incomes
Award
—In General
—Abuse of Discretion
—Amount
—Denied
—Determination
—Discretion of Court
—Duration
—Evidence in Support
—Factors Considered
—Health Insurance
—Held Inadequate
—Indefinite Award

—Lien on Land
—Limitations
—Necessary
—Of Property
—Reduction
—Relation to Property Disposition
—Specific Findings Not Required
—Unjustified
—Upheld
Balancing Test
—Economic Circumstances
Bankruptcy
Barring of Maintenance
Burden of Proof
Change in Circumstances
Conditions
Contempt
Conveyance of Realty
—In General
—Court-Ordered
—Statutory Authority
Cost of Living
Dependent Spouse
—Duty
Disability Benefits
Discretion of Court
—In General
—Amount of Award
—Review and Modification
Dissipation
—Shown
Duration of Award
—Factors Considered
—Future Conditions
—Indefinite
—Limited
—Permanent
Educational Expenses
Effective Date
Employment
—In General
—Capacity
—Duty to Seek
—Effect
—Full Time
—Inadequate Income
Enforcement
Equal Living Standard
Equitable Contribution
—Change in Circumstances
Evidence
—Hearing Required
—Held Insufficient
—Held Sufficient
—Use of Affidavits
—Valuation
Excess Payment
Expenses
Factors Considered
Failure to Pay
Fault
Federal Income Tax
Financial Independence
—In General
—Defined
—Discretion of Court
—Duty to Seek
—Not Required
Financial Resources
Foreign Divorce
Fraud
Fringe Benefits
Future Security Investment
Good Faith
Grounds
—Alimony
Homemaker's Contribution
Housekeeping Services
Illegal Agreement
Illustrative Cases
Impairment of Capital
Income
—In General
—Averaging Method
—Definition
—Disparity
In Gross
—In General
—Cash Value
—Defined
—Held Inequitable
—Lump Sum
—Not Modifiable
—Proper
Insurance
Joint and Several Obligations
Jurisdiction
—In General
—Death of Wife
—Respondent Failure to Plead
Jury Trial
Legislative Intent
Length of Marriage
Liens
Life Insurance Policy
—Wife as Beneficiary
Life Insurance Proceeds
—Constructive Trust
Lifestyle
Limit on Duration
Liquidation of Assets
Maintenance Determination
Marital Misconduct
Modification
—In General
—Agreement
—Burden of Proof
—Considered on Remand
—Denied
—Education or Training
—Factors Considered
—Failure to Rehabilitate
—Improper
—Maintenance in Gross
—Not Precluded
—Reduction in Income
—Review
—Spouse's Needs
—Sufficient Cause
—Unrelated Factors
—Unwarranted
Mortgage Payments
Needs of Parties
New Trial
—Denied
Oral Promise
Original Decree
—Effect of Collateral Matter
Partnership Property
Pensions and Stocks
Periodic Payments
Permanent Maintenance
Physical Condition of Parties
Primary Means of Support
Prior Maintenance
Property Disposition
—In General
—Agreement of Parties
—Court Authority
—Factors Considered
—Maintenance Distinguished
—Preferred

—Remand
—Upheld
—When Considered
Property Rights
—Separate Action
Property Settlement
—Distinguished
Property Value
Purpose
Realty Conveyance
—In General
—In Lieu of Maintenance
Reasonable Needs
Reciprocal Spousal Support
Reconsideration
Rehabilitative Maintenance
—In General
—Abuse of Discretion
Remarriage
Reservation of Issues
Reservation of Maintenance
—Upheld
Retirement Benefits
Sale of Assets
Savings
Scope
Security
Self-Imposed Poverty
Settlement Agreements
—Language in Preamble
—Public Policy
—Remarriage
Share of Marital Property
Special Equities
Spendable Income
Spouse's Contribution
Spouse's Needs
Spouse's Net Income
Standard of Living
Standard of Review
Statutory Construction
Statutory Foundation
—Not Required
Subsequent Divorces
Subsequent Review
Substitution
Sufficient Assets Lacking
Surplus of Income
Tax Consequences
—Consideration
—Exemptions
—Returns
Temporary Awards
Tender Age of Children
Termination of Payments
—Cohabitation
—Upheld
Terminology Held Irrelevant
Three Year Review of Award
—Proper
Time Period
—Just
—Sufficient Evidence
Tools
Types of Maintenance
—In General
—Prior Law
Unconscionability
—Not Shown
—Shown
Unreported Income
Valuation
—Business
—Law Practice
—Professional Corporation
—Property Disposition
Voluntary Retirement
Waiver
Wilful Contempt
—Appellate Relief
Work Outside the Home

In General

Property division section of the Illinois Marriage and Dissolution of Marriage Act, 750 ILCS 5/503(a), 504(a), was preempted by 42 U.S.C.S. § 407(a) of the Social Security Act, 42 U.S.C.S. § 301 et seq., which barred the transfer of social security benefits. In re Marriage of Hulstrom, 342 Ill. App. 3d 262, 276 Ill. Dec. 730, 794 N.E.2d 980, 2003 Ill. App. LEXIS 978 (2 Dist. 2003).

The effect of dividing one household into two is especially severe when there has been but one wage earner, and where there is insufficient income-producing property, maintenance is both a valid and a necessary consideration. In re Gunn, 233 Ill. App. 3d 165, 174 Ill. Dec. 381, 598 N.E.2d 1013 (5 Dist. 1992).

An award of maintenance is warranted when the court finds the spouse seeking maintenance lacks sufficient property, including marital property, to provide for her reasonable needs and is unable to support herself; the spouse need not be reduced to poverty before maintenance is appropriate and a spouse is not required to sell off his or her assets or capital in order to maintain the standard of living established by the marriage. In re Martin, 223 Ill. App. 3d 855, 166 Ill. Dec. 136, 585 N.E.2d 1158 (4 Dist.), appeal denied, 145 Ill. 2d 635, 173 Ill. Dec. 6, 596 N.E.2d 630 (1992).

The award of maintenance to a spouse capable of improving her income can be an abuse of discretion. In re Seymour, 206 Ill. App. 3d 506, 152 Ill. Dec. 27, 565 N.E.2d 269 (2 Dist. 1990).

Maintenance for a limited period is appropriate where the spouse is employable at an income not overly disproportionate to the standard of living established during the marriage; conversely, where the spouse is not employable or is employable only at a lower income, as compared to her previous standard of living, permanent maintenance would be appropriate. In re Heller, 153 Ill. App. 3d 224, 106 Ill. Dec. 503, 505 N.E.2d 1294 (1 Dist. 1987).

Maintenance is inappropriate where a spouse has sufficient property or a combination of property and income to satisfy his or her reasonable needs. In re Hughes, 160 Ill. App. 3d 680, 112 Ill. Dec. 594, 513 N.E.2d 1203 (5 Dist. 1987).

Maintenance may be awarded where the spouse lacks sufficient property or employment to provide for his or her reasonable needs and be self-supportive. In re Los, 136 Ill. App. 3d 26, 90 Ill. Dec. 739, 482 N.E.2d 1022 (2 Dist. 1985).

An award of maintenance is a matter within the sound discretion of the trial court and will not be reversed on appeal unless it amounts to an abuse of discretion. In re Los, 136 Ill. App. 3d 26, 90 Ill. Dec. 739, 482 N.E.2d 1022 (2 Dist. 1985).

Maintenance may be awarded in such amounts and for such periods of time as the court deems just after consideration of all relevant factors in this section. In re De Bat, 127 Ill. App. 3d 463, 82 Ill. Dec. 568, 468 N.E.2d 1348 (1 Dist. 1984).

An order disposing of the parties' property and awarding maintenance or child support should recognize and compensate each party for his or her contribution to the marriage; an important objective to be reached by the trial court in entering such an order is to place the parties in a position from which they can begin anew, in addition to providing adequate support for the children. Goforth v. Goforth, 121 Ill. App. 3d 673, 77 Ill. Dec. 125, 459 N.E.2d 1374 (5 Dist. 1984).

This section provides that the court may award maintenance to either spouse if the spouse seeking maintenance is unable to support himself through appropriate employment or is otherwise without sufficient income. In re Cleveland, 99 Ill. App. 3d 293, 54 Ill. Dec. 610, 425 N.E.2d 475 (1 Dist. 1981).

Maintenance may be awarded where a spouse lacks sufficient property to provide for reasonable needs and is unable to be self-supporting through appropriate employment. In re Brenner, 95 Ill. App. 3d 100, 50 Ill. Dec. 292, 419 N.E.2d 400 (1 Dist. 1981).

The criteria in this section are not absolute because maintenance may be awarded even though the marital property of the spouse has not been consumed or where a spouse's salary is insufficient to maintain the standard of living established during the marriage. In re Brenner, 95 Ill. App. 3d 100, 50 Ill. Dec. 292, 419 N.E.2d 400 (1 Dist. 1981).

In General (Cont'd)

This section allows for maintenance only where a party's needs cannot otherwise be provided. In re Hyland, 95 Ill. App. 3d 31, 50 Ill. Dec. 554, 419 N.E.2d 662 (2 Dist. 1981).

Maintenance is a term equivalent to periodic alimony. Ihle v. Ihle, 92 Ill. App. 3d 893, 48 Ill. Dec. 335, 416 N.E.2d 366 (3 Dist. 1981).

Maintenance, child support, and attorney fees are directly related to a final property disposition since these awards are dependent upon the financial resources of the party, including marital property, for whom the award is made. In re White, 98 Ill. App. 3d 380, 53 Ill. Dec. 786, 424 N.E.2d 421 (5 Dist. 1981).

Where the division of marital property by the trial court was improper, remand of the entire cause for a new trial was warranted so that the maintenance and child support awards and the decision to allow or deny attorney fees could be determined in view of the resources available to the wife after an equitable division of marital property is effected. In re White, 98 Ill. App. 3d 380, 53 Ill. Dec. 786, 424 N.E.2d 421 (5 Dist. 1981).

That known as alimony under prior law is labeled "maintenance" in this Act. Berkheimer v. Berkheimer, 63 Ill. App. 3d 19, 20 Ill. Dec. 496, 380 N.E.2d 474 (4 Dist. 1978).

Amendment of Order

Where a maintenance order did not contain an automatic termination date, and where the trial court specifically amended its original order to provide that the termination of payments not be automatic but instead last for three years, the trial court fashioned its order to allow for changes in the conditions of the parties, and thus the method adopted appeared to be in the best interests of all concerned and was not an abuse of discretion. In re Asch, 100 Ill. App. 3d 293, 55 Ill. Dec. 741, 426 N.E.2d 1066 (1 Dist. 1981).

Appellate Review

—Factors Considered

The trial court did not abuse its discretion when determining the ex-wife's maintenance where, considering the marital and nonmarital award, maintenance, and the ex-wife's marketable skills, the ex-wife could achieve financial independence, and if problems developed in the future, the maintenance award was modifiable under the provisions of the Illinois Marriage and Dissolution of Marriage Act. Reynard v. Reynard, 344 Ill. App. 3d 785, 279 Ill. Dec. 917, 801 N.E.2d 591, 2003 Ill. App. LEXIS 1560 (4 Dist. 2003).

In determining whether monetary award was proper, the appellate court must review the award in light of the statutory factors set out in this section. In re Hughes, 160 Ill. App. 3d 680, 112 Ill. Dec. 594, 513 N.E.2d 1203 (5 Dist. 1987).

—Jurisdiction

Where two appeals were taken from a judgment of the circuit court which reserved inter alia the question of maintenance and which did not contain a finding that no just reason existed for delay of enforcement or appeal, the appellate court did not have jurisdiction to hear the appeals. In re Peterson, 85 Ill. App. 3d 520, 40 Ill. Dec. 731, 406 N.E.2d 934 (3 Dist. 1980).

—Standard of Review

An award of maintenance is within the court's discretion and will not be disturbed on appeal unless it is an abuse of discretion or against the manifest weight of the evidence. In re Calisoff, 176 Ill. App. 3d 721, 126 Ill. Dec. 183, 531 N.E.2d 810 (1 Dist. 1988); In re Swigers, 176 Ill. App. 3d 795, 126 Ill. Dec. 231, 531 N.E.2d 858 (1 Dist. 1988); In re Jacks, 200 Ill. App. 3d 112, 146 Ill. Dec. 143, 558 N.E.2d 106 (2 Dist. 1990).

The standard for determining whether the trial court abused its discretion in awarding maintenance is whether no reasonable person would take the view of the trial court. In re Swigers, 176 Ill. App. 3d 795, 126 Ill. Dec. 231, 531 N.E.2d 858 (1 Dist. 1988).

In reviewing a maintenance award, the appellate court must consider the marital property awarded. In re Swigers, 176 Ill. App. 3d 795, 126 Ill. Dec. 231, 531 N.E.2d 858 (1 Dist. 1988).

The modification of a maintenance award will not be set aside on review unless the trial court abused its discretion. In re Lasota, 125 Ill. App. 3d 37, 80 Ill. Dec. 537, 465 N.E.2d 649 (1 Dist. 1984).

Applicability of Amendments

The 1982 amendments to this section and 750 ILCS 5/510 were fully applicable to proceedings conducted prior to the effective dates of the amendments. In re Davis, 124 Ill. App. 3d 1088, 80 Ill. Dec. 364, 465 N.E.2d 155 (3 Dist. 1984), modified on other grounds, 106 Ill. 2d 290, 88 Ill. Dec. 11, 478 N.E.2d 326 (1985).

Application

The trial court's denial of petitioner's request for maintenance was not an abuse of its discretion where the trial court heard testimony regarding the factors set forth in this statute and the assets awarded to petitioner generated income sufficient to meet her needs. In re Harding, 189 Ill. App. 3d 663, 136 Ill. Dec. 935, 545 N.E.2d 459 (1 Dist. 1989).

Attorney Fees

—In General

For cases discussing the attorney fees for the purposes of alimony (now maintenance), see Wright v. Wright, 317 Ill. App. 607, 47 N.E.2d 347 (1 Dist. 1943); Barton v. Barton, 323 Ill. App. 357, 55 N.E.2d 542 (4 Dist. 1944).

—Allowed

Because wife was an unemployed travel agent whose sole income was a temporary maintenance award, to require her to sell the marital home and deplete her reserves to pay attorney fees would have defeated the trial court's efforts at equitable distribution; therefore, husband's payment of 75% of wife's attorney fees was proper. In re Kaplan, 149 Ill. App. 3d 23, 102 Ill. Dec. 719, 500 N.E.2d 612 (1 Dist. 1986).

Where petitioner was financially unable to pay her counsel and respondent had the ability to do so, and where petitioner was represented by two attorneys from different law firms and the attorneys were both highly qualified in their field, the issues involved were fairly complex, their rates were not unusually high, and some duplication of work between petitioner's attorneys was disallowed by reducing the total fee request, the award of attorney fees was not an abuse of discretion. In re Weinberg, 125 Ill. App. 3d 904, 81 Ill. Dec. 123, 466 N.E.2d 925 (1 Dist. 1984).

Where the evidence indicated that the petitioner spouse was able to pay reasonable attorney fees incurred by the respondent, the trial court abused its discretion in denying respondent spouse reasonable attorney fees. Courson v. Courson, 47 Ill. App. 3d 318, 5 Ill. Dec. 645, 361 N.E.2d 1173 (3 Dist. 1977).

—Criteria

The criteria for determining whose obligations the attorney fees will be in a divorce action is similar to the criteria for determining whether a spouse is entitled to maintenance; the court must consider the financial resources of the parties. Richards v. Loncar, 14 Bankr. 276 (N.D. Ill. 1981).

—Disparity in Incomes

Where there was a gross disparity in income, with husband making much more than wife, trial court abused its discretion in failing to find that wife was unable to pay her attorney fees and in failing to make an award. In re Carpenter, 286 Ill. App. 3d 969, 222 Ill. Dec. 260, 677 N.E.2d 463 (5 Dist. 1997).

Award

—In General

The trial court, when determining the amount of the maintenance, should consider on remand both (1) the parties' incomes at the time of the dissolution of their marriage, and (2) their potential incomes, as well as that can be determined; by doing so, a court is better able to put both parties in positions of equity regarding their present and future financial circumstances. In re Harlow, 251 Ill. App. 3d 152, 190 Ill. Dec. 476, 621 N.E.2d 929 (4 Dist. 1993), appeal denied, 154 Ill. 2d 559, 197 Ill. Dec. 486, 631 N.E.2d 708 (1994).

That the appellate court might have reached a decision different from that reached by the trial court did not constitute adequate grounds for reversal. In re Ribordy, 128 Ill. App. 3d 1073, 84 Ill. Dec. 263, 471 N.E.2d 1029 (3 Dist. 1984).

Where respondent conceded that petitioner was entitled to some maintenance and he had the ability to pay, the award of permanent maintenance was not excessive where trial court reduced maintenance to slightly above the amount respondent suggested; the support award was unallocated and thus deductible from respondent's adjusted gross income and taxable to petitioner, and peti-

Award (Cont'd)

—In General (Cont'd)

tioner would not be required to sell her assets or impair her capital in order to generate income from which she could support herself in the manner enjoyed during the marriage. In re Weinberg, 125 Ill. App. 3d 904, 81 Ill. Dec. 123, 466 N.E.2d 925 (1 Dist. 1984).

—Abuse of Discretion

Monthly maintenance awarded by the court of $5,000 a month for three years was an abuse of discretion. In re Norris, 252 Ill. App. 3d 230, 192 Ill. Dec. 46, 625 N.E.2d 6 (1 Dist. 1992).

—Amount

Order awarding the wife $900 per month, in addition to the award of one-half of the husband's pension, was upheld as the trial court did consider the wife's inability to work when making the award, specifically finding that any employment that could have been gained by the wife would have been nominal and that, therefore, the total amount of the award conformed with the goal of helping the wife meet her needs. In re Marriage of Rogers, 352 Ill. App. 3d 896, 288 Ill. Dec. 204, 817 N.E.2d 562, 2004 Ill. App. LEXIS 1257 (4 Dist. 2004).

Husband had the financial resources to meet his needs and those of wife and their children to the extent of $1,500 per month in temporary maintenance and support. In re Elies, 248 Ill. App. 3d 1052, 188 Ill. Dec. 364, 618 N.E.2d 934 (1 Dist. 1993).

The proper basis on which to determine alimony (now maintenance) would have been net earnings with further consideration as to the income tax consequences, both federal and state, which would have resulted as to each of the parties from the court's award of alimony. Crosby v. Crosby, 48 Ill. App. 3d 759, 6 Ill. Dec. 682, 363 N.E.2d 211 (3 Dist. 1977).

For cases discussing factors affecting the amount of an award of alimony (now maintenance), see Campbell v. Leonard, 132 Ill. 232, 24 N.E. 65 (1890); Bobowski v. Bobowski, 242 Ill. 524, 90 N.E. 361 (1909); Meyer v. Meyer, 255 Ill. 436, 99 N.E. 591 (1912); Smith v. Smith, 334 Ill. 370, 166 N.E. 85 (1929); Buehler v. Buehler, 373 Ill. 626, 27 N.E.2d 466 (1940); McVeigh v. McConnell, 313 Ill. App. 75, 38 N.E.2d 962 (1 Dist. 1942); Joslyn v. Joslyn, 315 Ill. App. 160, 42 N.E.2d 875 (1 Dist. 1942); Cahill v. Cahill, 316 Ill. App. 324, 45 N.E.2d 69 (1 Dist. 1942); Franceschi v. Franceschi, 326 Ill. App. 494, 62 N.E.2d 1 (2 Dist. 1945); Felton v. Felton, 326 Ill. App. 444, 62 N.E.2d 39 (1 Dist. 1945); Recklein v. Recklein, 327 Ill. App. 641, 64 N.E.2d 787 (4 Dist. 1946); Condy v. Condy, 328 Ill. App. 8, 65 N.E.2d 219 (1946); Kohl v. Kohl, 330 Ill. App. 284, 71 N.E.2d 358 (1 Dist. 1947); Rardin v. Rardin, 339 Ill. App. 68, 89 N.E.2d 67 (1 Dist. 1949); Coleman v. Coleman, 341 Ill. App. 462, 94 N.E.2d 507 (4 Dist. 1950); Walters v. Walters, 341 Ill. App. 561, 94 N.E.2d 726 (1 Dist. 1950), aff'd, 408 Ill. 298, 99 N.E.2d 342 (1951); Walters v. Walters, 409 Ill. 298, 99 N.E.2d 342 (1951); Persico v. Persico, 409 Ill. 608, 100 N.E.2d 904 (1951); Bertram v. Bertram, 346 Ill. App. 314, 105 N.E.2d 515 (3 Dist. 1952); Kuchenbecker v. Estate of Kuchenbecker, 4 Ill. App. 2d 314, 124 N.E.2d 52 (1 Dist. 1955); Fox v. Fox, 9 Ill. 2d 509, 138 N.E.2d 547 (1956); Balasa v. Balasa, 11 Ill. App. 2d 103, 136 N.E.2d 594 (1 Dist. 1956); Coolidge v. Coolidge, 13 Ill. App. 2d 170, 141 N.E.2d 636 (1 Dist. 1957); Whitney v. Whitney, 15 Ill. App. 2d 425, 146 N.E.2d 800 (1 Dist. 1957); James v. James, 14 Ill. 2d 295, 152 N.E.2d 582 (1958); Curran v. Curran, 19 Ill. 2d 164, 166 N.E.2d 13 (1960); Plavec v. Plavec, 30 Ill. App. 2d 345, 174 N.E.2d 578 (1 Dist. 1961); Page v. Page, 32 Ill. App. 2d 422, 178 N.E.2d 129 (1 Dist. 1961); Smothers v. Smothers, 25 Ill. 2d 86, 182 N.E.2d 758 (1962); Snip v. Snip, 35 Ill. App. 2d 427, 183 N.E.2d 175 (1 Dist. 1962); Warren v. Warren, 40 Ill. App. 2d 286, 189 N.E.2d 401 (1 Dist. 1963); Newman v. Newman, 42 Ill. App. 2d 203, 191 N.E.2d 614 (1 Dist. 1963); Canady v. Canady, 30 Ill. 2d 440, 197 N.E.2d 42 (1964); Jacobson v. Jacobson, 50 Ill. App. 2d 244, 200 N.E.2d 379 (1 Dist. 1964); Rabin v. Rabin, 57 Ill. App. 2d 193, 206 N.E.2d 850 (1 Dist. 1965); Boyd v. Boyd, 58 Ill. App. 2d 1, 207 N.E.2d 350 (5 Dist. 1965); Richheimer v. Richheimer, 59 Ill. App. 2d 354, 208 N.E.2d 346 (1 Dist. 1965); Central Nat'l Bank v. Schwarz, 76 Ill. App. 2d 114, 220 N.E.2d 889 (4 Dist. 1966); Blowitz v. Blowitz, 75 Ill. App. 2d 386, 221 N.E.2d 160 (1 Dist. 1966); Dmitroca v. Dmitroca, 79 Ill. App. 2d 220, 223 N.E.2d 545 (2 Dist. 1967); Vokaty v. Vokaty, 91 Ill. App. 2d 104, 234 N.E.2d 150 (1 Dist. 1968); Imbrie v. Imbrie, 94 Ill. App. 2d 60, 236 N.E.2d 381 (1 Dist. 1968); Still v. Still, 96 Ill. App. 2d 320, 238 N.E.2d 613 (4 Dist. 1968); Turns v. Turns, 96 Ill. App. 2d 347, 239 N.E.2d 144 (5 Dist. 1968); Hoffman v. Hoffman, 40 Ill. 2d 344, 239 N.E.2d 792 (1968); David v. David, 102 Ill. App. 2d 102, 243 N.E.2d 485 (1 Dist. 1968); Klebba v. Klebba, 108 Ill. App. 2d 32, 246 N.E.2d 681 (5 Dist. 1969); Barbara v. Barbara, 110 Ill. App. 2d 189, 249 N.E.2d 269 (1 Dist. 1969); Honey v. Honey, 120 Ill. App. 2d 102, 256 N.E.2d 121 (4 Dist. 1970); Scott v. Scott, 129 Ill. App. 2d 176, 262 N.E.2d 728 (3 Dist. 1970); Bernardini v. Bernardini, 130 Ill. App. 2d 692, 264 N.E.2d 295 (4 Dist. 1970); Webb v. Webb, 130 Ill. App. 2d 618, 264 N.E.2d 594 (2 Dist. 1970); Ulm v. Ulm, 132 Ill. App. 2d 726, 270 N.E.2d 581 (1 Dist. 1971); Turner v. Turner, 133 Ill. App. 2d 710, 271 N.E.2d 377 (3 Dist. 1971); Garmisa v. Garmisa, 4 Ill. App. 3d 411, 280 N.E.2d 444 (1 Dist. 1972); Furth v. Furth, 5 Ill. App. 3d 73, 283 N.E.2d 102 (1 Dist. 1972); Overton v. Overton, 6 Ill. App. 3d 1086, 287 N.E.2d 47 (2 Dist. 1972); Fulwider v. Fulwider, 8 Ill. App. 3d 581, 290 N.E.2d 264 (4 Dist. 1972); Demos v. Demos, 8 Ill. App. 3d 906, 290 N.E.2d 304 (2 Dist. 1972); Sandberg v. Sandberg, 11 Ill. App. 3d 495, 297 N.E.2d 654 (1 Dist. 1973); Mills v. Mills, 13 Ill. App. 3d 288, 300 N.E.2d 842 (1 Dist. 1973); Atwater v. Atwater, 18 Ill. App. 3d 202, 309 N.E.2d 632 (1 Dist. 1974); Scruggs v. Scruggs, 23 Ill. App. 3d 1004, 320 N.E.2d 406 (5 Dist. 1974); Rich v. Rich, 24 Ill. App. 3d 1083, 322 N.E.2d 610 (5 Dist. 1975); Lieberman v. Lieberman, 25 Ill. App. 3d 654, 323 N.E.2d 785 (1 Dist. 1975); Baker v. Baker, 28 Ill. App. 3d 680, 329 N.E.2d 408 (1 Dist. 1975); McClure v. McClure, 29 Ill. App. 3d 930, 331 N.E.2d 829 (4 Dist. 1975); Pierson v. Pierson, 31 Ill. App. 3d 106, 334 N.E.2d 838 (2 Dist. 1975); Knox v. Knox, 31 Ill. App. 3d 816, 334 N.E.2d 891 (1 Dist. 1975); Palacio v. Palacio, 33 Ill. App. 3d 1074, 339 N.E.2d 427 (1 Dist. 1975); Schwartz v. Schwartz, 38 Ill. App. 3d 959, 349 N.E.2d 567 (1 Dist. 1976); Shellene v. Shellene, 52 Ill. App. 3d 889, 10 Ill. Dec. 667, 368 N.E.2d 153 (2 Dist. 1977); Smith v. Smith, 47 Ill. App. 3d 583, 5 Ill. Dec. 810, 362 N.E.2d 123 (3 Dist. 1977); Comstock v. Comstock, 55 Ill. App. 3d 140, 12 Ill. Dec. 841, 370 N.E.2d 645 (3 Dist. 1977).

—Denied

The court's award of maintenance was unauthorized. Schlosser v. Schlosser, 241 Ill. App. 3d 49, 181 Ill. Dec. 496, 608 N.E.2d 569 (3 Dist. 1993).

The court did not abuse its discretion in rejecting husband's position that maintenance should not be awarded based on his inability to pay. Schlosser v. Schlosser, 241 Ill. App. 3d 49, 181 Ill. Dec. 496, 608 N.E.2d 569 (3 Dist. 1993).

The decision not to award a wife rehabilitative maintenance was upheld where she did not support her request for rehabilitation with any evidence of the amount of education, expense, or time she needed to be rehabilitated and the husband remained in a highly leveraged position. In re DeGironemo, 206 Ill. App. 3d 1019, 151 Ill. Dec. 918, 565 N.E.2d 189 (1 Dist. 1990).

The denial of maintenance was not an abuse of discretion in the light of the wife's fairly substantial anticipated annual gross income of $24,000. In re Bentivenga, 109 Ill. App. 3d 967, 65 Ill. Dec. 423, 441 N.E.2d 336 (2 Dist. 1982).

Where the record established that the wife was gainfully employed and able to support herself by appropriate employment, the trial court was correct in denying maintenance. Robinson v. Robinson, 100 Ill. App. 3d 437, 57 Ill. Dec. 532, 429 N.E.2d 183 (2 Dist. 1981).

Where a trial court heard testimony from both parties regarding their needs and their earning capacities, there was a reasonable basis in the record to support the court's decision to deny petitioner maintenance, although the monthly displacement allowance was too uncertain for the court to fully include in its calculation of respondent's ability to pay. In re Pickell, 76 Ill. App. 3d 855, 32 Ill. Dec. 443, 395 N.E.2d 673 (5 Dist. 1979).

—Determination

In determining a maintenance award, if the wife is employable at an income not overly disproportionate to the standard of living she enjoyed during marriage, then generally speaking, if support is appropriate it should be for a limited period; conversely, if the wife is not employable or only employable at a low income compared to her standard of living during marriage, then generally speaking, permanent support is appropriate. In re Pieper, 79 Ill. App. 3d 835, 34 Ill. Dec. 877, 398 N.E.2d 868 (1 Dist. 1979); In re Wade, 158 Ill. App. 3d 255, 110 Ill. Dec. 321, 511 N.E.2d 156 (4 Dist. 1987).

—Discretion of Court

Where a former husband and a former wife had been married for

Award (Cont'd)

—Discretion of Court (Cont'd)
24 years before their divorce, the husband's present and future income was much greater than the wife's, the wife's standard of living after the divorce was substantially lower than what she enjoyed during the marriage, and she had not been required to work full-time during the marriage but held two jobs after the divorce in order to make ends meet, the trial court did not abuse its discretion under 750 ILCS § 5/504(a) by awarding permanent maintenance to the wife. In re Marriage of Culp, 341 Ill. App. 3d 390, 275 Ill. Dec. 221, 792 N.E.2d 452, 2003 Ill. App. LEXIS 861 (4 Dist. 2003).

Maintenance may be awarded in any amount and for any time period which the court deems just after considering all relevant factors. In re Marcello, 247 Ill. App. 3d 304, 187 Ill. Dec. 81, 617 N.E.2d 289 (1 Dist. 1993).

The propriety and amount of any award of maintenance are matters within the sound discretion of the trial court and will not be overturned on appeal absent an abuse of discretion by that court. In re Siddens, 225 Ill. App. 3d 496, 167 Ill. Dec. 680, 588 N.E.2d 321 (5 Dist.), appeal denied, 145 Ill. 2d 644, 173 Ill. Dec. 13, 596 N.E.2d 637 (1992).

An award of maintenance is within the sound discretion of the trial court and will not be disturbed on appeal unless it is an abuse of discretion or is against the manifest weight of the evidence. In re Lees, 224 Ill. App. 3d 691, 167 Ill. Dec. 135, 587 N.E.2d 17 (1992); In re Asch, 100 Ill. App. 3d 293, 55 Ill. Dec. 741, 426 N.E.2d 1066 (1 Dist. 1981); In re Bramson, 100 Ill. App. 3d 657, 56 Ill. Dec. 205, 427 N.E.2d 285 (1 Dist. 1981); Schuppe v. Schuppe, 69 Ill. App. 3d 200, 25 Ill. Dec. 690, 387 N.E.2d 346 (2 Dist. 1979); Stotlar v. Stotlar, 50 Ill. App. 3d 790, 8 Ill. Dec. 711, 365 N.E.2d 1097 (5 Dist. 1977).

An abuse of discretion will occur where no reasonable man would take the view of the trial court. In re Wolf, 180 Ill. App. 3d 998, 129 Ill. Dec. 742, 536 N.E.2d 792 (1 Dist. 1989).

This section has been interpreted by reviewing courts as requiring less than an express finding by the trial court, and thus reviewing courts have accepted the trial court's determination if the record establishes a manifest basis for determining that maintenance should be awarded. In re Jones, 187 Ill. App. 3d 206, 134 Ill. Dec. 836, 543 N.E.2d 119 (1 Dist. 1989).

Where a property disposition was altered somewhat upon subsequent appeal and remanded to the trial court, the plaintiff's final property disposition did not differ greatly from that considered by the trial court in denying maintenance in its original judgment; although the plaintiff was employed at the time of the hearing on the remand, she was unable to pay her living expenses and otherwise provide for herself, so, in the absence of evidence to otherwise sustain the trial court's later award of maintenance, the award of maintenance constituted an abuse of discretion. In re Smith, 162 Ill. App. 3d 792, 114 Ill. Dec. 622, 516 N.E.2d 777 (5 Dist. 1987).

The amount and duration of a maintenance award lies within the discretion of the trial court, whose judgment will not be substituted absent an abuse of discretion, which occurs only where no reasonable man would take the view adopted by the trial court. In re Brooks, 138 Ill. App. 3d 252, 93 Ill. Dec. 166, 486 N.E.2d 267 (1 Dist. 1985).

It was an abuse of discretion to award wife additional money annually since she had demonstrated an ability to provide for herself and her children through suitable employment and had no lack of sufficient income. In re Donovan, 122 Ill. App. 3d 803, 78 Ill. Dec. 293, 462 N.E.2d 9 (4 Dist. 1984).

The mere fact that the appellate court might have reached a different result from the trial court's decision not to award maintenance to wife did not amount to an abuse of discretion. In re Ribordy, 128 Ill. App. 3d 1073, 84 Ill. Dec. 263, 471 N.E.2d 1029 (3 Dist. 1984).

Trial court's award of maintenance will not be overturned unless against the manifest weight of the evidence, thus showing an abuse of discretion by that court. In re Mittra, 114 Ill. App. 3d 627, 71 Ill. Dec. 350, 450 N.E.2d 1229 (4 Dist. 1983).

The necessity for and the amount of an award, both as to maintenance and child support, are decisions within the sound discretion of the trial court in each individual case, and those decisions will not be set aside unless found to be contrary to the manifest weight of the evidence, thus showing an abuse of discretion. In re Lovejoy, 84 Ill. App. 3d 53, 39 Ill. Dec. 501, 404 N.E.2d 1092 (3 Dist. 1980); In re Reyna, 78 Ill. App. 3d 1010, 34 Ill. Dec. 818, 398 N.E.2d 641 (3 Dist. 1979).

Both the form for an award of alimony (now maintenance), whether it be periodic or in gross, and its amount rest primarily in the sound discretion of the court. Harambasic v. Harambasic, 55 Ill. App. 3d 648, 13 Ill. Dec. 224, 370 N.E.2d 1251 (1 Dist. 1977).

Whether alimony in gross (now maintenance) was justified was a matter reserved to the discretion of the trial court, to be exercised after due consideration of all facts and circumstances which were in evidence; whether the award of alimony was periodic or in gross, the decision of the trial court would not be disturbed on review unless found to be against the manifest weight of the evidence. McArdle v. McArdle, 55 Ill. App. 3d 829, 13 Ill. Dec. 282, 370 N.E.2d 1309 (3 Dist. 1977).

The trial court has a discretion as to whether maintenance is to be awarded and the exercise of which depends on all facts in the particular case and should not be exercised arbitrarily. Comstock v. Comstock, 55 Ill. App. 3d 140, 12 Ill. Dec. 841, 370 N.E.2d 645 (3 Dist. 1977).

The form of an award of alimony (now maintenance) and its amount rest primarily in the discretion of the trial court. Schasker v. Schasker, 34 Ill. App. 3d 980, 341 N.E.2d 717 (2 Dist. 1975).

An award of temporary alimony (now maintenance) rests within the sound discretion of the trial court, to be reversed only upon evidence of an abuse of discretion. Eule v. Eule, 24 Ill. App. 3d 83, 320 N.E.2d 506 (1 Dist. 1974).

For a case discussing court's discretion to award alimony (now maintenance), see Popeil v. Popeil, 21 Ill. App. 3d 571, 315 N.E.2d 629 (1 Dist. 1974).

—Duration
Where the court found a disparity between the parties' relative earning powers and assets, it found that a better approach would have been to make the maintenance award reviewable at the end of five years instead of after only one. In re Marthens, 215 Ill. App. 3d 590, 159 Ill. Dec. 3, 575 N.E.2d 3 (3 Dist. 1991).

Trial court has the power to order maintenance for an indefinite period. In re Mittra, 114 Ill. App. 3d 627, 71 Ill. Dec. 350, 450 N.E.2d 1229 (4 Dist. 1983).

One of the appropriate considerations which should govern the duration of the maintenance award is the extent to which the receiving spouse is shown to have either the present ability to become self-sufficient or the future ability to acquire skills which would allow entry into the job market. In re Mittra, 114 Ill. App. 3d 627, 71 Ill. Dec. 350, 450 N.E.2d 1229 (4 Dist. 1983).

—Evidence in Support
Maintenance award was not an abuse of discretion where spouse awarded support lacked sufficient property and income to support herself and would have difficulty in securing appropriate employment. In re Vernon, 253 Ill. App. 3d 783, 192 Ill. Dec. 668, 625 N.E.2d 823 (4 Dist. 1993).

An award not supported by the evidence must be set aside. In re Hilkovitch, 124 Ill. App. 3d 401, 79 Ill. Dec. 891, 464 N.E.2d 795 (1 Dist. 1984).

—Factors Considered
Maintenance award was upheld after the court considered the following factors; (1) wife's financial resources, including marital property apportioned and her ability to meet her needs independently; (2) the time necessary to acquire sufficient education or training to enable wife to find appropriate employment; (3) the standard of living established during the marriage; (4) the duration of the marriage; (5) the ages and physical and emotional conditions of both parties; and (6) the ability of husband to meet his needs while meeting those of wife. In re Waggoner, 261 Ill. App. 3d 787, 199 Ill. Dec. 844, 634 N.E.2d 1198 (5 Dist. 1994).

The factors to be considered in determining the amount of maintenance, whether temporary or permanent, include the reasonable needs of the spouse seeking maintenance in view of the standard of living established during the marriage, the duration of the marriage, the ability to become self-supporting, the income-producing property of the spouse, and the value of the non-marital property. In re Elies, 248 Ill. App. 3d 1052, 188 Ill. Dec. 364, 618 N.E.2d 934 (1 Dist. 1993).

Award (Cont'd)

—Factors Considered (Cont'd)

Although an award may be for a definite time period, it should not be based on speculation as to the future conditions, but on circumstances disclosed by the evidence. In re Werries, 247 Ill. App. 3d 639, 186 Ill. Dec. 747, 616 N.E.2d 1379 (4 Dist. 1993).

Only if it finds that the spouse seeking maintenance lacks sufficient property to provide for her reasonable needs and is either unable to support herself through appropriate employment or is otherwise without sufficient income may the trial court issue a maintenance order. In re Werries, 247 Ill. App. 3d 639, 186 Ill. Dec. 747, 616 N.E.2d 1379 (4 Dist. 1993).

Of the seven relevant factors for the trial court to consider when making a determination of the amount and duration of a maintenance award, no one factor is determinative of the issue concerning the propriety of the maintenance award once it has been determined that an award is appropriate. In re Martin, 223 Ill. App. 3d 855, 166 Ill. Dec. 136, 585 N.E.2d 1158 (4 Dist.), appeal denied, 145 Ill. 2d 635, 173 Ill. Dec. 6, 596 N.E.2d 630 (1992).

Under subsection (b) of this section, no one factor is determinative; courts have wide latitude in considering what factors should be used in determining reasonable needs and a trial court is not limited to the factors listed in the statute. In re Krupp, 207 Ill. App. 3d 779, 152 Ill. Dec. 742, 566 N.E.2d 429 (1 Dist. 1990), cert. denied, 137 Ill. 2d 665, 156 Ill. Dec. 562, 571 N.E.2d 149 (1991).

An award of maintenance may be made in such amounts as the court deems just after consideration of all relevant factors, including the financial resources of the party seeking maintenance, including marital property apportioned to him. In re De Bat, 127 Ill. App. 3d 463, 82 Ill. Dec. 568, 468 N.E.2d 1348 (1 Dist. 1984).

Although the division of marital property is among the factors which must be considered in the award of maintenance, it is not the only factor. In re Carini, 112 Ill. App. 3d 375, 67 Ill. Dec. 932, 445 N.E.2d 412 (1 Dist. 1983).

Under this Act, maintenance and child support are directly related to the final property disposition since these awards are substantially dependent upon the financial resources of the parties, including marital property. In re Kundit, 107 Ill. App. 3d 310, 63 Ill. Dec. 128, 437 N.E.2d 777 (1 Dist. 1982).

Subsection (a) of this section allows for the awarding of maintenance only where the spouse seeking maintenance: (1) lacks sufficient property, including marital property apportioned to him, to provide for his reasonable needs, and (2) is unable to support himself through appropriate employment, or (3) is otherwise without sufficient income. In re Asch, 100 Ill. App. 3d 293, 55 Ill. Dec. 741, 426 N.E.2d 1066 (1 Dist. 1981).

The court is permitted to consider factors not listed in this Act in determining the amount of alimony awarded. In re Bramson, 100 Ill. App. 3d 657, 56 Ill. Dec. 205, 427 N.E.2d 285 (1 Dist. 1981).

—Health Insurance

When petitioner convinced the court that she was unable to obtain adequate health insurance for herself, and respondent admitted that he could obtain coverage for her under his policy, and the trial court ordered him to obtain that insurance, said order was a legitimate exercise of the court's power to award maintenance. In re Flory, 171 Ill. App. 3d 822, 121 Ill. Dec. 701, 525 N.E.2d 1008 (1 Dist. 1988).

—Held Inadequate

An award of maintenance was inadequate where (1) the wife, who suffered from multiple sclerosis, had a shortfall of over $650 after taking into account the award, a child support award, and her expenses, (2) the husband had a surplus of about $1,200, which would jump to $2,200 after his child support obligation ceased, after taking into account his income and expenses, and (3) it was likely that the husband's income would continue to increase. Brackett v. Brackett, 309 Ill. App. 3d 329, 242 Ill. Dec. 798, 722 N.E.2d 287 (2 Dist. 1999).

The paucity of the court's maintenance award was evident 1) in light of the fact that the petitioner's monthly maintenance award was set at less than half the amount the respondent claimed he needed for clothing and entertainment, 2) the court failed to take into account several of the petitioner's long term expenses such as real estate taxes, health insurance and home repairs, 3) the court unreasonably discounted petitioner's long term health care expenses, and 4) the court overestimated her ability to earn salary income. Grunsten v. Grunsten, 304 Ill. App. 3d 12, 237 Ill. Dec. 342, 709 N.E.2d 597 (1 Dist. 1999), appeal denied, 185 Ill. 2d 624, 242 Ill. Dec. 137, 720 N.E.2d 1092 (1999).

Where a maintenance award together with petitioner's gross earnings was insufficient to meet her monthly mortgage and utility expenses alone, petitioner could be required to dispose of the asset intended by the parties as a permanent residence for petitioner and the children; therefore, considering respondent's substantial income and future earning ability, sufficient to meet not only his needs but those of petitioner, the trial court's maintenance award was an abuse of discretion. In re Schroeder, 215 Ill. App. 3d 156, 158 Ill. Dec. 721, 574 N.E.2d 834 (4 Dist.), cert. denied, 141 Ill. 2d 560, 162 Ill. Dec. 508, 580 N.E.2d 134 (1991).

An award of permanent maintenance in a dissolution proceeding containing no provision for modification review was deemed an abuse of discretion by the trial judge. In re Girrulat, 219 Ill. App. 3d 164, 161 Ill. Dec. 734, 578 N.E.2d 1380 (5 Dist. 1991).

Given the state of the record and the alternatives available, the awarding of maintenance in gross was an abuse of discretion. Smith v. Smith, 150 Ill. App. 3d 34, 103 Ill. Dec. 785, 501 N.E.2d 1323 (3 Dist. 1986).

Where respondent's net monthly income, after paying, pursuant to the order, his allocated debts, child support, insurance premiums, children's medical and dental expenses, and maintenance, totaled $79.35, and petitioner's net income, after paying her allocated debts and receiving from respondent the ordered child support and maintenance, totaled $880.80, the award of $150 per month to the petitioner was an abuse of discretion by the trial court. In re Chambers, 125 Ill. App. 3d 507, 80 Ill. Dec. 810, 466 N.E.2d 262 (5 Dist. 1984).

The factors listed in subsection (b) of this section to be considered in awarding maintenance were not considered where the trial court incorrectly found no maintenance had been requested, and maintenance had only been waived under circumstances which had not occurred. In re Shafer, 122 Ill. App. 3d 991, 78 Ill. Dec. 323, 462 N.E.2d 39 (2 Dist. 1984).

Where after adjusting their earned incomes for the amount of maintenance and support, respondent wife was being asked to support two children and herself with less than half the funds available to husband, the award of maintenance and support was inadequate. In re Fairchild, 110 Ill. App. 3d 470, 66 Ill. Dec. 131, 442 N.E.2d 557 (3 Dist. 1982).

Where the parties enjoyed a modest but comfortable standard of living, they lived in a series of homes which they owned and accumulated significant assets, considering their income, at the time of hearing, respondent had no earnings and no individual assets, income producing or otherwise, and her ability to support herself through appropriate employment was dubious for lack of skills and good health, the court abused its discretion in denying respondent maintenance. In re Rimmele, 102 Ill. App. 3d 88, 57 Ill. Dec. 762, 429 N.E.2d 879 (3 Dist. 1981).

Because the reasonable needs of the parties were so nearly equal, petitioner's $1,556 and respondent's $1,667, the simplest "just" disposition was for them to share equally the cost of the failure of the marriage; therefore, the total award of maintenance should have been $248.50 per month and trial court's award of maintenance of $530 per month was an abuse of discretion. In re Simmons, 87 Ill. App. 3d 651, 42 Ill. Dec. 706, 409 N.E.2d 321 (1 Dist. 1980).

Award of $200 per month maintenance to wife was contrary to the manifest weight of the evidence and therefore an abuse of discretion because record disclosed that wife did not require maintenance from husband to support herself in a manner commensurate with that established during the marriage. In re McGrew, 90 Ill. App. 3d 27, 45 Ill. Dec. 414, 412 N.E.2d 996 (5 Dist. 1980).

Award of maintenance was insufficient when viewed in conjunction with the trial court's distribution of the marital property. In re Thornton, 89 Ill. App. 3d 1078, 45 Ill. Dec. 612, 412 N.E.2d 1336 (1 Dist. 1980).

—Indefinite Award

Where it was reasonable to expect respondent spouse to adjust her situation so that she could support herself within a definite time period, the award of maintenance for an indefinite period of time was an abuse of discretion. In re Wisniewski, 107 Ill. App. 3d 711, 63 Ill. Dec. 378, 437 N.E.2d 1300 (4 Dist. 1982).

Award (Cont'd)

—Lien on Land

The court may compel the conveyance of property equitably belonging to the other; therefore, where the wife had property equitably belonging to the husband, the court, instead of ordering the conveyance of land from appellant, was justified in giving the wife a lien on land to secure its payment. Killebrew v. Killebrew, 398 Ill. 432, 75 N.E.2d 855 (1947).

—Limitations

The award of maintenance should be limited where there is sufficient property available to satisfy a spouse's needs and entitlements. In re Rapacz, 135 Ill. App. 3d 1045, 90 Ill. Dec. 622, 482 N.E.2d 441 (2 Dist. 1985).

Trial court erred in limiting maintenance award to a period of five years to wife due to wife's age, lengthy marriage, poor health, educational background, lack of special skills, and long absence from the labor market which indicated that she was not employable now or in the foreseeable future. In re Campise, 115 Ill. App. 3d 610, 71 Ill. Dec. 454, 450 N.E.2d 1333 (1 Dist. 1983).

—Necessary

Where a judgment made apportionment of property "in lieu of any maintenance entitlement by respondent," and a stay of the judgment pending appeal was entered so that respondent did not have the use of the assets awarded to her during appeal, an award of equitable maintenance was particularly appropriate. In re Di Angelo, 159 Ill. App. 3d 293, 111 Ill. Dec. 394, 512 N.E.2d 783 (2 Dist. 1987).

—Of Property

Where the spouse who would be required to make periodic maintenance payments, were it not for the award of property in lieu thereof, was dilatory in the extreme as to the payment of his bills, an award of property in lieu of maintenance was equitable under the circumstances. In re Gan, 83 Ill. App. 3d 265, 38 Ill. Dec. 882, 404 N.E.2d 306 (5 Dist. 1980).

—Reduction

Reduction in monthly maintenance from $1,400 to $400 was affirmed. In re Breuer, 259 Ill. App. 3d 94, 197 Ill. Dec. 121, 630 N.E.2d 1245 (1 Dist. 1994).

Where the parties were married for 34 years, the wife was 52 years old and had little prospect of earning an adequate salary, where she was being forced to work full-time in order to maintain a standard of living much lower than what she enjoyed during the marriage, where she had little security for the future in terms of retirement or illness, especially in the event that her husband predeceased her, the facts did not justify a reduced maintenance award because of the husband's resignation from company. In re Smith, 77 Ill. App. 3d 858, 33 Ill. Dec. 332, 396 N.E.2d 859 (2 Dist. 1979).

—Relation to Property Disposition

Under this Act, maintenance and child support are directly related to the final property disposition since these awards are substantially dependent upon the financial resources of the parties, including marital property. In re Kundit, 107 Ill. App. 3d 310, 63 Ill. Dec. 128, 437 N.E.2d 777 (1 Dist. 1982).

—Specific Findings Not Required

Trial court was not required to make explicit findings when entering its order of support. In re Reyna, 78 Ill. App. 3d 1010, 34 Ill. Dec. 818, 398 N.E.2d 641 (3 Dist. 1979).

—Unjustified

Injunctive decree preventing husband from withdrawing money in jointly held safety deposit box was insufficient to justify an award of one-half of the amount of the moneys contained in the safety deposit box. Olmsted v. Olmsted, 332 Ill. App. 454, 75 N.E.2d 774 (1 Dist. 1947).

—Upheld

The husband was properly ordered to pay maintenance to the wife where (1) the wife had an earning capacity of $35-36,000 per year as a full-time nurse and was not awarded any income producing property to assist her, and (2) the husband's gross income was over $200,000 plus an additional $75,000 in loans and gifts from family members, and his future earning capacity was high as he was awarded his surgical practice. In re Petersen, 319 Ill. App. 3d 325, 253 Ill. Dec. 144, 744 N.E.2d 877, 2001 Ill. App. LEXIS 46 (1 Dist. 2001), appeal denied sub nom. Petersen v. Petersen, 195 Ill. 2d 597, 258 Ill. Dec. 100, 755 N.E.2d 483 (2001).

The court properly ordered the husband to pay $1,000 per month in maintenance for 6 years and to maintain medical insurance for her until she was covered by Medicare or was able to obtain insurance through employment, notwithstanding that the marriage lasted less than four years, where: (1) the wife left her employment in Wisconsin to move to Illinois with the husband and, at his insistence, did not work during the marriage; (2) after they separated, the wife worked as a bartender; and (3) the wife testified that she was not aware of any reason why she could not find a job, although she thought her age might make it somewhat difficult, and that she had both physical and emotional problems, including a heart problem and depression that required inpatient treatment. In re Gattone, 317 Ill. App. 3d 346, 251 Ill. Dec. 65, 739 N.E.2d 998, 2000 Ill. App. LEXIS 900 (2 Dist. 2000).

An award of maintenance to the husband was proper, notwithstanding the wife's assertion that he was in a substantially different financial position from when the parties were married and that they were in similar financial situations, where the wife had a significantly higher salary than did the husband, the wife was the majority shareholder in a company from which she was entitled to substantial distributions as the majority shareholder, and the husband lacked sufficient property and income to meet his reasonable needs. In re Shinn, 313 Ill. App. 3d 317, 246 Ill. Dec. 173, 729 N.E.2d 546, 2000 Ill. App. LEXIS 368 (4 Dist. 2000), appeal denied sub nom. Shinn v. Shinn, 191 Ill. 2d 560, 250 Ill. Dec. 467, 738 N.E.2d 936 (2000).

The trial court set forth its findings in considerable detail and it was not an abuse of discretion to award petitioner maintenance in the amount of $6,500 per month based on length of marriage, each parties' ability to earn and wife's depression. In re Severino, 298 Ill. App. 3d 224, 232 Ill. Dec. 355, 698 N.E.2d 193 (2 Dist. 1998).

Plaintiff was not prejudiced by judge's wrong application of incorrect law as she was still awarded temporary maintenance even though the judge applied the older law, which arguably made it more difficult to obtain maintenance. In re Koberlein, 281 Ill. App. 3d 880, 217 Ill. Dec. 599, 667 N.E.2d 695 (4 Dist. 1996).

Based upon the amount of respondent's income, living expenses, and the debt she was forced to incur after petitioner moved out of the marital home, the trial court did not abuse its discretion in awarding her maintenance. In re Uehlein, 265 Ill. App. 3d 1080, 202 Ill. Dec. 838, 638 N.E.2d 706 (1 Dist. 1994).

In light of the trial court's findings that husband's salary was voluntarily decreased in anticipation of the instant litigation, that husband continued to maintain his level of lifestyle, that wife was ordered to maintain the family home for the children until their college education was completed, that wife was responsible for the payment of the $60,000 mortgage and the $7,200 loan on the car and that wife was currently unemployed, the trial court did not abuse its discretion in awarding wife maintenance of $1,500 a month for five years. In re Brown v. Brown, 241 Ill. App. 3d 305, 181 Ill. Dec. 716, 608 N.E.2d 967 (3 Dist. 1993).

Where wife had a high school education, four minor children, was permanently disabled, and had received no formal training in job skills and where husband's unemployment was not involuntary, award of $1,000 per month maintenance was not an abuse of discretion. In re Morse, 240 Ill. App. 3d 296, 180 Ill. Dec. 563, 607 N.E.2d 632 (2 Dist. 1993).

Where wife was employed as a secretary for a real estate firm, earned approximately $18,000 per year, had been employed in this capacity for approximately two years and had not expressed any intentions of changing her position or furthering her education, order of the trial court, which did not provide for automatic termination at the end of three-year period, was not an abuse of discretion by the trial court. In re Maczko, 263 Ill. App. 3d 991, 201 Ill. Dec. 127, 636 N.E.2d 559 (1 Dist. 1992).

Where, based on petitioner's medical condition and her monthly income from the trusts, petitioner needed maintenance to support herself in the manner commensurate with that established during the marriage, the award of maintenance was not an abuse of discretion or against the manifest weight of the evidence. In re

Award (Cont'd)

—Upheld (Cont'd)

Tietz, 238 Ill. App. 3d 965, 178 Ill. Dec. 876, 605 N.E.2d 670 (4 Dist. 1992).

The trial court did not abuse its discretion by ordering a $600 per month maintenance award. In re Pearson, 236 Ill. App. 3d 337, 177 Ill. Dec. 650, 603 N.E.2d 720 (1 Dist. 1992).

The trial court correctly considered the applicable statutory factors, and did not abuse her discretion in setting the duration and amount of the maintenance award, where the court considered: petitioner's lack of sufficient property to provide for her reasonable needs; her lack of sufficient income in light of the limited job skills and education and training that she had currently; her inability to meet her needs independently in light of her minimal skills, and her very limited and sporadic work history; the very high standard of living established during the marriage; the length of the marriage (28 years); the limited job opportunities available to her given her age, educational background and work history; the respondent's financial and employment security, and his ability to meet his own as well as petitioner's needs; and the tax consequences of a maintenance award. In re Vendredi, 230 Ill. App. 3d 1061, 174 Ill. Dec. 329, 598 N.E.2d 961 (1 Dist. 1992).

Considering the length of the marriage, the wife's financial resources including the property apportioned to her, her inability to meet her needs independently, her loss of job skills, her age, physical and emotional condition, her lack of higher education, her station in life and standard of living established during the marriage, the economic circumstances of the parties, and the ability for the defendant to meet his own needs while meeting those of petitioner, the wife met her burden of proof, and the trial court did not abuse its discretion in the award of long-term maintenance. In re Gunn, 233 Ill. App. 3d 165, 174 Ill. Dec. 381, 598 N.E.2d 1013 (5 Dist. 1992).

Considering the age and condition of the parties, the standard of living achieved during the marriage, and all relevant facts determined by the record, the trial court did not abuse its discretion in fixing the amount and duration of maintenance nor were its findings against the manifest weight of the evidence. In re Gunn, 233 Ill. App. 3d 165, 174 Ill. Dec. 381, 598 N.E.2d 1013 (5 Dist. 1992).

Trial court did not abuse its discretion in awarding wife maintenance of $350 per month where record revealed that she was 61 years of age at the time and was earning $29,182.63 a year, was a year away from retirement, and suffered from chronic health problems, thus having few prospects to increase her income or acquire capital assets in the future. In re Toth, 224 Ill. App. 3d 43, 166 Ill. Dec. 478, 586 N.E.2d 436 (1 Dist. 1991).

The trial court did not abuse its discretion in awarding two-year maintenance payments to the wife when the maintenance payments constituted less than 10% of husband's monthly net income and which would be reviewed on a specific future date. In re Orlando, 218 Ill. App. 3d 312, 160 Ill. Dec. 763, 577 N.E.2d 1334 (1 Dist. 1991).

Where petitioner testified that her monthly expenses totalled $2,000 and that she received $1,500 per month as disability income, an award of $500 as monthly maintenance was adequate considering also that after three years from entry of the award, it was subject to review by the court. In re Madoch, 212 Ill. App. 3d 1007, 157 Ill. Dec. 10, 571 N.E.2d 1029 (1 Dist. 1991).

A recently divorced woman who, though talented, had been absent from the workaday world and was having trouble reestablishing herself after 20-plus years of homemaking, was properly awarded maintenance for a period of five years. In re Hanson, 170 Ill. App. 3d 298, 120 Ill. Dec. 665, 524 N.E.2d 695 (2 Dist. 1988).

Maintenance award was held to be equitable under the circumstances and well within the trial court's discretion in light of the earning potential, the ages of the parties, and the consideration by the court of the appropriate factors under this section. Head v. Head, 168 Ill. App. 3d 697, 119 Ill. Dec. 549, 523 N.E.2d 17 (1 Dist. 1988).

An award of $269 a month to wife at her retirement at 60 was not an abuse of discretion where her income would be $800—$900 a month and her expenses would be $2,000 a month, and her husband had income of $1,420 a month with expenses of about $1,100 a month. In re Flory, 171 Ill. App. 3d 822, 121 Ill. Dec. 701, 525 N.E.2d 1008 (1 Dist. 1988).

Where one spouse had earned $34,000 annually for the last 10 years with some exceptions and had saved and invested enough to own a large percentage of a limited partnership and to have half ownership of his own company, but the other's income was only $260 per month and she had no savings or business investments, there was no abuse of discretion in the trial court's maintenance or property award. In re Reimann, 178 Ill. App. 3d 288, 127 Ill. Dec. 486, 533 N.E.2d 104 (1 Dist. 1988).

Absent the trial court's abuse of discretion, where wife received a greater share of marital assets than husband, and she had a college education and was qualified to teach, and where the maintenance awarded was subject to review in 24 months, the trial court's award of $750 per month maintenance would not be reversed. In re Albiani, 159 Ill. App. 3d 519, 111 Ill. Dec. 126, 512 N.E.2d 30 (1 Dist. 1987).

Awarding $800 per month held not to constitute an abuse of discretion, particularly in view of respondent's modest salary, about $16,000 per year, out of which she was also required to support a son from a previous marriage. In re Di Angelo, 159 Ill. App. 3d 293, 111 Ill. Dec. 394, 512 N.E.2d 783 (2 Dist. 1987).

A trial court properly awarded maintenance to the wife where she did not have sufficient income with which to provide for her reasonable needs or to maintain the standard of living established during the marriage, the husband did have sufficient income from his salary alone to meet his own expenses while meeting hers, and the award of maintenance to the wife plus the husband's responsibility for the college tuition of the parties' daughters constituted only 50% of his net income; also, the husband had been able to pay these expenses, with the exception of the wife's monthly psychologist's fee during the marriage and during the two years the parties were separated preceding the dissolution of their marriage, and there was no indication in the record that payment of these expenses derived from any source other than his salary. In re Heller, 153 Ill. App. 3d 224, 106 Ill. Dec. 503, 505 N.E.2d 1294 (1 Dist. 1987).

Maintenance award of $400 per month was justified even though the wife had been employed as a receptionist for ten years, had a net income of $227 per week, received free hospitalization coverage from her employer, and even though her mortgage would be paid off in two years, and her total monthly expenses were only $1000 per month. In re Kristie, 156 Ill. App. 3d 821, 109 Ill. Dec. 393, 510 N.E.2d 14 (1 Dist. 1987).

The award of maintenance was proper because the wife seeking maintenance lacked sufficient property including marital property to provide for her reasonable needs; had husband not dissipated all the marital assets, an award of maintenance might not have been proper. In re Aslaksen, 148 Ill. App. 3d 784, 102 Ill. Dec. 469, 500 N.E.2d 91 (2 Dist. 1986).

Evidence introduced through husband was adequate to support the amount of maintenance determined by the trial court; therefore, the amount per month of taxable maintenance awarded to wife was not contrary to the manifest weight of the evidence or an abuse of the court's discretion. In re Lawrence, 146 Ill. App. 3d 307, 99 Ill. Dec. 845, 496 N.E.2d 538 (3 Dist. 1986).

Where the parties enjoyed a comfortable standard of living during the marriage, the wife was entitled to a reasonable period of adjustment and her maintenance award was not reduced. In re Wright, 180 Ill. App. 3d 911, 129 Ill. Dec. 650, 536 N.E.2d 700 (1 Dist. 1986).

The court's award of $225 per week maintenance, reviewable every 36 months, was not an abuse of discretion. In re Brooks, 138 Ill. App. 3d 252, 93 Ill. Dec. 166, 486 N.E.2d 267 (1 Dist. 1985).

In light of petitioner's age, history of alcoholism, and insufficient training for particular employment, and considering the comfortable standard of living to which she had grown accustomed and the 33-year duration of the marriage, a 10-year rehabilitative maintenance period was not an abuse of discretion. In re Bauer, 138 Ill. App. 3d 379, 93 Ill. Dec. 108, 485 N.E.2d 1318 (1 Dist. 1985).

Trial court did not abuse its discretion in awarding wife $500 per month for child support though she contended the award was not sufficient. In re Rink, 136 Ill. App. 3d 252, 91 Ill. Dec. 34, 483 N.E.2d 316 (1 Dist. 1985).

Where all of respondent's arguments pertaining to the award of maintenance and child support were based on a single assumption, that no evidence refuted his assertion, based on his income tax returns, that his net income was any more than $25,000, it was not

Award (Cont'd)

—Upheld (Cont'd)

an abuse of discretion for the trial court to consider the ample evidence introduced at trial showing respondent's income was far higher than he alleged. In re Hilkovitch, 124 Ill. App. 3d 401, 79 Ill. Dec. 891, 464 N.E.2d 795 (1 Dist. 1984).

Where petitioner did not possess sufficient liquid assets or marketable skills to provide for her and the children's needs, the amount of which respondent did not challenge, and where petitioner's deteriorating health, her child-rearing responsibilities, limited education and long absence from the job market were all factors which militated against her being able to support herself, future, at a level consistent with or even a reasonable approximation of the standard of living established during the marriage, then permanent maintenance was proper. In re Weinberg, 125 Ill. App. 3d 904, 81 Ill. Dec. 123, 466 N.E.2d 925 (1 Dist. 1984).

Where wife worked only for a brief period as a clerk in husband's business, had no employment skills, and both her 92-year-old mother and disabled daughter lived with her, an order granting maintenance was proper. In re Holman, 122 Ill. App. 3d 1001, 78 Ill. Dec. 314, 462 N.E.2d 30 (2 Dist. 1984).

No abuse of discretion in the property division or award of maintenance was found where petitioner received 47% of the net assets and respondent received 53%, respondent was awarded $350 per month maintenance and $30,000 as her share of grain on hand with an approximate value of $66,000, although petitioner's federal income tax returns showed losses from farming operations due to large amounts of depreciation and tax credits. In re McDonald, 113 Ill. App. 3d 116, 68 Ill. Dec. 653, 446 N.E.2d 559 (4 Dist. 1983).

Where joint tax returns showed gross receipts of approximately $81,670 and discounting this figure by petitioner's yearly earnings of $6,720 left respondent with well over $70,000 gross per year, an award of maintenance based on husband's future earning potential was not improper. In re Mittra, 114 Ill. App. 3d 627, 71 Ill. Dec. 350, 450 N.E.2d 1229 (4 Dist. 1983).

The fact that trial court did not determine the mathematical certainty of a reasonable rate of return for wife's assets did not indicate trial court failed to consider such assets, among several, in fixing the award. In re Mittra, 114 Ill. App. 3d 627, 71 Ill. Dec. 350, 450 N.E.2d 1229 (4 Dist. 1983).

After subtracting wife's monthly income of $226 from her monthly needs of $2,325, she had a monthly deficit of $2,099, and although certainly some income could be expected from the income-producing assets, she would also be required to pay income taxes on the monthly maintenance payment, and thus award of $1800 per month in maintenance to wife was not an abuse of discretion. In re Mittra, 114 Ill. App. 3d 627, 71 Ill. Dec. 350, 450 N.E.2d 1229 (4 Dist. 1983).

Where wife had never been employed in her field of study during the marriage and the evidence did not show that she had embarked upon a planned course of study to develop marketable skills, awarding wife maintenance was not erroneous. In re Mittra, 114 Ill. App. 3d 627, 71 Ill. Dec. 350, 450 N.E.2d 1229 (4 Dist. 1983).

Trial court did not err in not awarding permanent maintenance to wife where there was evidence that wife suffered from health problems which prevented her from working, though there appeared to be no evidence that these problems were permanent. In re Campise, 115 Ill. App. 3d 610, 71 Ill. Dec. 454, 450 N.E.2d 1333 (1 Dist. 1983).

Maintenance award was upheld in consideration of the short duration of the marriage, the relatively small contribution, if any, that respondent made to the marriage, and the fact that respondent was capable of supporting herself. Naguit v. Scrivner, 104 Ill. App. 3d 709, 60 Ill. Dec. 499, 433 N.E.2d 296 (5 Dist. 1982).

It was not an abuse of discretion to award maintenance in lieu of an adequate share of the marital property, even though because of the wife's age and her few skills for employment it was unlikely that she would become self-sustaining before the maintenance payments terminated either at the husband's death or at the expiration of 60 months, and it was arguably doubtful that the husband would survive the 60 month period of maintenance payments. In re Pancner, 111 Ill. App. 3d 546, 67 Ill. Dec. 417, 444 N.E.2d 653 (1 Dist. 1982).

Where respondent was employed, owned businesses, and retained his full interest in them, petitioner was unable to meet her expenses regardless of the allocation of marital assets, and the property awarded to her was not income-producing property nor was it readily convertible to cash; petitioner had been employed only six of the 27 years of marriage and testified that the few skills she had were difficult to perform because of arthritis; the only source of income other than support from respondent was from house-sitting and occasionally caring for others' children; and petitioner was to pay the mortgage, taxes, and maintenance expenses for the residence, the evidence supported the $1,000 per month award of maintenance. In re Sales, 106 Ill. App. 3d 378, 62 Ill. Dec. 441, 436 N.E.2d 23 (1 Dist. 1982).

Where the parties had enjoyed a fairly comfortable life style during their marriage and there was evidence that petitioner would experience some difficulty in finding employment capable of keeping her in that life style, the trial court did not abuse its discretion in awarding maintenance to petitioner. In re Johnson, 106 Ill. App. 3d 502, 62 Ill. Dec. 478, 436 N.E.2d 228 (1 Dist. 1982).

Denial of permanent maintenance was not against the manifest weight of the evidence where a reasonable return on investment coupled with wife's potential ability to have some employment earnings and receive child support appeared to adequately provide for the needs of the wife and minor children. In re Smith, 100 Ill. App. 3d 1126, 56 Ill. Dec. 716, 427 N.E.2d 1262 (2 Dist. 1981).

In addition to the $150 per week in maintenance, respondent could generate income from the property apportioned her in the settlement; included in this property was $1,000 of stock and a condominium unit with $13,000 equity; if these assets were liquidated and added to the $34,000 in cash allotted to respondent, she could have $48,000 available to generate income, and thus a review of the record did not reveal an abuse of discretion by the trial court, nor did it show that the maintenance award was against the manifest weight of the evidence. In re Asch, 100 Ill. App. 3d 293, 55 Ill. Dec. 741, 426 N.E.2d 1066 (1 Dist. 1981).

Where petitioner's 1979 tax return showed gross income of $41,870 from his business, payment of the $100 per week maintenance ($5,200 per year) left a significant sum available to petitioner, and this maintenance award was for only two years, the award of maintenance was not against the manifest weight of the evidence and did not demonstrate an abuse of discretion by the trial court. In re Greenberg, 102 Ill. App. 3d 938, 58 Ill. Dec. 1, 429 N.E.2d 1334 (1 Dist. 1981).

The trial court did not abuse its discretion in awarding the wife $65 per month in maintenance. In re Schriner, 88 Ill. App. 3d 380, 43 Ill. Dec. 572, 410 N.E.2d 572 (2 Dist. 1980).

Where the former wife was without work or qualifications for work, and where the considerable property which she was awarded was nevertheless nonliquid, an award of maintenance for two years was consistent with the purposes of this Act and was neither contrary to the weight of the evidence, nor was it an abuse of discretion by the trial court. In re McCune, 86 Ill. App. 3d 311, 41 Ill. Dec. 897, 408 N.E.2d 319 (3 Dist. 1980).

Where former husband would continue to enjoy income he derived from the operation of one 500 acre farm while former wife was without income, the order that former husband pay the $30,000 mortgage balance on the 160 acre farm awarded to former wife was consistent with the weight of the evidence, and not an abuse of discretion. In re McCune, 86 Ill. App. 3d 311, 41 Ill. Dec. 897, 408 N.E.2d 319 (3 Dist. 1980).

Even while holding a responsible position in a large bank earning a decent salary, former wife could not match the earning power of former husband; maintenance was appropriate because even petitioner's substantial earning power was not adequate to make her self-sufficient when measured against her reasonable needs. In re Simmons, 87 Ill. App. 3d 651, 42 Ill. Dec. 706, 409 N.E.2d 321 (1 Dist. 1980).

The award of maintenance to petitioner was not inconsistent with the evidence concerning petitioner's poor health or employment picture; therefore, petitioner's award of a percentage of respondent's income was not an abuse of the trial court's discretion. In re Parello, 87 Ill. App. 3d 926, 42 Ill. Dec. 846, 409 N.E.2d 461 (1 Dist. 1980).

Where the wife lacked sufficient property, including marital property apportioned to her, to provide for her reasonable needs and was unable to support herself through appropriate employment, the trial court did not err in awarding maintenance to her. In re Lloyd, 81 Ill. App. 3d 311, 36 Ill. Dec. 647, 401 N.E.2d 328 (5 Dist. 1980).

Award (Cont'd)

—Upheld (Cont'd)

The trial court's award of maintenance to former wife was not an abuse of discretion where wife was awarded no income-producing assets, needed income to pay monthly expenses, and husband was able to contribute. In re Coram, 86 Ill. App. 3d 845, 42 Ill. Dec. 40, 408 N.E.2d 418 (5 Dist. 1980).

Award of $1,200 per month as maintenance was not against the manifest weight of the evidence where a marriage had been of fairly long duration, and where the wife was 49 years of age and had no real prospect of finding "appropriate" employment, and where the record revealed that the court considered the relevant factors in detail. In re Scott, 85 Ill. App. 3d 773, 41 Ill. Dec. 547, 407 N.E.2d 1045 (2 Dist. 1980).

Trial court did not abuse its discretion when it reserved for six years the wife's right to seek maintenance from the husband due to wife's lesser potential of earnings ability. In re Lee, 78 Ill. App. 3d 1123, 34 Ill. Dec. 451, 398 N.E.2d 126 (1 Dist. 1979).

Trial court's award of maintenance of $30 per week to wife was not an abuse of discretion where wife received all the marital assets except an automobile and husband was paying all the outstanding bills except a small mortgage on the house and husband took home approximately $60 a week from his paycheck. In re Gammons, 78 Ill. App. 3d 1001, 34 Ill. Dec. 655, 398 N.E.2d 330 (3 Dist. 1979).

There was no abuse of discretion in the circuit court's award of maintenance of $700 to wife from husband when husband earned between $21,000 and $24,000 a year. In re Reyna, 78 Ill. App. 3d 1010, 34 Ill. Dec. 818, 398 N.E.2d 641 (3 Dist. 1979).

Considering the husband's monthly income, with both the required and optional deductions plus the tax benefits he received, the monthly family support awarded was neither against the manifest weight of the evidence nor an abuse of discretion on the part of the trial court where the husband testified that he earned a base salary of $60,000 per year; in 1976 he also received a bonus of $600 in addition to his base salary; the wife was a registered nurse prior to their marriage but terminated such employment shortly after the marriage; the parties had been married for approximately 20 years, during which time the husband advanced himself in business while the wife devoted herself to maintaining a home and raising the couple's children; and her maximum expected salary was $11,000 per year. Schuppe v. Schuppe, 69 Ill. App. 3d 200, 25 Ill. Dec. 690, 387 N.E.2d 346 (2 Dist. 1979).

Where the husband's monthly income was sufficient to meet his own needs while meeting the needs of the wife and his minor children, and in addition, the maintenance award would aid the wife in maintaining the standard of living established during the marriage and would enable her to obtain the necessary training to resume her career, trial court did not abuse its discretion in awarding the wife maintenance of $200 per month. Reininger v. Reininger, 67 Ill. App. 3d 21, 23 Ill. Dec. 752, 384 N.E.2d 546 (4 Dist. 1978).

Where husband, who was granted an uncontested divorce after wife's claim was dismissed, contributed monetarily and otherwise to wife's beauty shop operation, trial court did not abuse its discretion by denying wife's request for alimony (now maintenance). Comstock v. Comstock, 55 Ill. App. 3d 140, 12 Ill. Dec. 841, 370 N.E.2d 645 (3 Dist. 1977).

In divorce proceeding, the trial court's finding that former wife constructively deserted her husband, was guilty of extreme and repeated mental cruelty over an extended period of time, along with order that the former husband make child support payments of $125 per month for the two children of the marriage who were still minors and that the family home was to be sold and the former husband was to make mortgage payments until such sale, was not an abuse of discretion. Chattillion v. Chattillion, 52 Ill. App. 3d 390, 10 Ill. Dec. 52, 367 N.E.2d 440 (5 Dist. 1977).

Where the evidence supporting any allegation of wife's misconduct was scant and minimal and where, upon the stipulation of the parties, the cause was heard as a default matter on husband's counterclaim for divorce on basis of desertion, there was not an abuse of discretion in determining that wife would be entitled to alimony (now maintenance). Harambasic v. Harambasic, 55 Ill. App. 3d 648, 13 Ill. Dec. 224, 370 N.E.2d 1251 (1 Dist. 1977).

In view of evidence of husband's arrearages in his child support payments and his apparent frequent intoxication, the settlement of alimony (now maintenance) to the wife was a proper exercise of the court's discretion. Harambasic v. Harambasic, 55 Ill. App. 3d 648, 13 Ill. Dec. 224, 370 N.E.2d 1251 (1 Dist. 1977).

Where husband had substantial net worth in comparison to a relatively low annual income, the trial court was within its discretion in granting alimony (now maintenance) in gross in lieu of periodic alimony. McArdle v. McArdle, 55 Ill. App. 3d 829, 13 Ill. Dec. 282, 370 N.E.2d 1309 (3 Dist. 1977).

Where plaintiff specifically alleged in the complaint and testified at the hearing regarding her need and defendant's ability to pay for child support, expenses and attorney fees, defendant's drinking habits made periodic alimony (now maintenance) payments unfeasible, and although plaintiff was not questioned as to her exact earnings at the hearing, the omission was not grounds for a new hearing; the evidence offered, although succinct, was sufficient to sustain the divorce decree awarding plaintiff child support, attorney fees, and defendant's interest in the marital home in lieu of periodic alimony. Frank v. Frank, 34 Ill. App. 3d 957, 342 N.E.2d 404 (2 Dist. 1975).

Award to defendant was not excessive where defendant was awarded $32,000 from interest in the marital domicile, one-half of the joint checking account, alimony (now maintenance) in gross from plaintiff, and personal savings, plaintiff received one-half the joint checking account and at retirement would be entitled to the full amount in his retirement fund totaling approximately $31,978.64, and he was awarded defendant's interest in a second house. Schasker v. Schasker, 34 Ill. App. 3d 980, 341 N.E.2d 717 (2 Dist. 1975).

Circumstances justified the award of alimony (now maintenance) in gross where testimony indicated the relationship between the parties was characterized by rancor and suspicion culminating in plaintiff's physical abuse of defendant, plaintiff lied at trial regarding his possession of the proceeds in the joint bank account, and plaintiff's testimony that he spent $8,500 of the proceeds from the joint checking account and his weekly salary drinking and gambling supported the trial court's holding that an award of alimony in gross was the appropriate means of assuring defendant's financial security. Schasker v. Schasker, 34 Ill. App. 3d 980, 341 N.E.2d 717 (2 Dist. 1975).

Balancing Test

—Economic Circumstances

Wife was entitled to a share of the marital property and/or an award of maintenance/child support such as to provide her with income sufficient to maintain herself and four children in the same style as was enjoyed during the marriage, and this had to be balanced against husband's similar entitlement to enjoy that same standard of living; to achieve this balance the court had to look at the statutory factors. In re Thornton, 89 Ill. App. 3d 1078, 45 Ill. Dec. 612, 412 N.E.2d 1336 (1 Dist. 1980).

Bankruptcy

The trial court impermissibly characterized a property distribution as maintenance when it awarded maintenance to the wife in an amount equal to half of the marital debts on the basis that husband intended to file for bankruptcy and that the wife would, therefore, become liable for the entire marital debt; the court properly allocated marital liabilities and awarded maintenance on the basis, in part, that the husband increased his ability to pay maintenance by discharging his debts in bankruptcy. In re Underwood, 314 Ill. App. 3d 325, 247 Ill. Dec. 230, 731 N.E.2d 1003, 2000 Ill. App. LEXIS 495 (4 Dist. 2000).

The fact that Illinois law terminated the obligation to pay maintenance after the marriage of the party receiving maintenance, and the fact that an award stated that the obligation would not terminate upon remarriage of the debtor's wife, did not dictate that the award was not maintenance with regard to determining the dischargeability of the debtor's obligation. Renzulli v. Renzulli, 28 Bankr. 41 (Bankr. N.D. Ill. 1982).

For a case discussing effect of characterization of alimony (now maintenance) in settlement agreement for purposes of dischargeability in bankruptcy, see Tilmon v. Tilmon, 9 Bankr. 979 (Bankr. N.D. Ill. 1981).

Barring of Maintenance

Where there was no question concerning when wife would become self-sufficient because, based on property distribution and

Barring of Maintenance (Cont'd)
her inherited estate, she was already self-sufficient, judgment that parties were forever barred from seeking maintenance was not an abuse of discretion, as it enabled the parties to plan their futures with certainty and to maintain themselves in the style established during the marriage without selling assets or impairing capital. In re Durante, 201 Ill. App. 3d 376, 147 Ill. Dec. 56, 559 N.E.2d 56 (1 Dist. 1990).

Burden of Proof
In light of the provision of this section, which directs the court to consider the time necessary for the spouse seeking maintenance to acquire a sufficient education or training to obtain appropriate employment, the burden is on the spouse seeking permanent or long-term maintenance to show the necessity for such maintenance. In re Gunn, 233 Ill. App. 3d 165, 174 Ill. Dec. 381, 598 N.E.2d 1013 (5 Dist. 1992).

Change in Circumstances
Trial court's reduction of child support payments was not an abuse of discretion where husband showed reduction in income. In re Carpenter, 286 Ill. App. 3d 969, 222 Ill. Dec. 260, 677 N.E.2d 463 (5 Dist. 1997).

The evidence from appellant's affidavits of income and expenses indicate that, other than his alleged increase in expenses, did not show any change in circumstances since the last order that would justify a further modification of maintenance. In re Pedersen, 237 Ill. App. 3d 952, 178 Ill. Dec. 835, 605 N.E.2d 629 (4 Dist. 1992).

Although appellee had become employed, the record supported the trial court's determination that she remained unable to adequately support herself through her employment and that no substantial change of circumstances had occurred for her financially since the maintenance amount was last reduced. In re Pedersen, 237 Ill. App. 3d 952, 178 Ill. Dec. 835, 605 N.E.2d 629 (4 Dist. 1992).

In light of divorced wife's increase in salary and her former husband's decrease in salary due to health problems, there was a sufficient showing of a change in circumstances whereby the divorce decree could be modified to suspend alimony (now maintenance) and reduce child support. Broday v. Broday, 43 Ill. App. 3d 628, 2 Ill. Dec. 151, 357 N.E.2d 128 (1 Dist. 1976).

Conditions
Subdivision (a)(8) is designed to call the court's attention to the needs of a party based upon age and physical and emotional condition; it does not authorize the trial court to "punish" a party because that party's behavior regarding her physical and emotional condition meets with the court's disapproval. In re Offer, 275 Ill. App. 3d 986, 212 Ill. Dec. 493, 657 N.E.2d 694 (4 Dist. 1995).

It is implicit in the trial court's granting of maintenance that it take into account the conditions outlined in subsection (a) of this section. In re Hanson, 170 Ill. App. 3d 298, 120 Ill. Dec. 665, 524 N.E.2d 695 (2 Dist. 1988).

Contempt
Where the respondent earned a regular net income of $255 a week while he was under the order to pay maintenance, but he failed to pay any maintenance, the trial judge did not abuse his discretion in finding the respondent to be in contempt. In re Scordo, 176 Ill. App. 3d 269, 125 Ill. Dec. 761, 530 N.E.2d 1170 (3 Dist. 1988).

Where a sanction was imposed in order to compel compliance with a court order to pay a specified amount of money as part of a settlement to the dissolution of a marriage, the respondent's right to purge himself of charges of contempt had to be based on his ability to pay. In re Ramos, 126 Ill. App. 3d 391, 81 Ill. Dec. 214, 466 N.E.2d 1016 (1 Dist. 1984), cert. denied, 471 U.S. 1017, 105 S. Ct. 2023, 85 L. Ed. 2d 305 (1985).

For a case discussing contempt for failure to pay alimony (now maintenance) or support payments pursuant to a decree, see Mattioda v. Mattioda, 101 Ill. App. 2d 475, 243 N.E.2d 495 (1 Dist. 1968); Shapiro v. Shapiro, 113 Ill. App. 2d 374, 252 N.E.2d 93 (1 Dist. 1969).

Conveyance of Realty

—In General
While it was true once the marital house was sold, the wife would have some capital, she was not required to consume her share of the marital property in order to maintain herself such that a court's reduction of husband's maintenance payments to wife upon the sale of the marital residence was improper. In re Gable, 205 Ill. App. 3d 696, 151 Ill. Dec. 109, 563 N.E.2d 1215 (5 Dist. 1990).

Special equities or circumstances need not be pled in order to justify conveyance of property in lieu of alimony (now maintenance); what is required is that the recipient spouse be entitled to alimony and that the conveyance be equitable. Schade v. Schade, 45 Ill. App. 3d 455, 4 Ill. Dec. 232, 359 N.E.2d 1184 (4 Dist. 1977).

—Court-Ordered
A trial court in hearing divorce matters could only order property to be conveyed from one party to the other in two specific situations: in one situation, special equities must have been specifically alleged in the complaint and established by competent evidence adduced at trial; in the second situation, the conveyance of property must have been in lieu of alimony (now maintenance) under former Section 18 of the Divorce Act (see now this section). Mueller v. Mueller, 49 Ill. App. 3d 666, 7 Ill. Dec. 513, 364 N.E.2d 674 (2 Dist. 1977).

—Statutory Authority
The authority of courts to compel conveyance of realty in divorce actions is governed by statutory rather than general equity powers. Klaisner v. Klaisner, 28 Ill. App. 3d 110, 328 N.E.2d 341 (2 Dist. 1975).

Cost of Living
The trial court can take judicial notice of the increase in the cost of living in awarding maintenance. Baker v. Baker, 53 Ill. App. 3d 186, 10 Ill. Dec. 784, 368 N.E.2d 379 (1 Dist. 1977).

Dependent Spouse

—Duty
Where the circumstances of the dependent former spouse indicate education or training is likely to successfully enable the dependent former spouse to obtain more lucrative employment, it is reasonable to place an obligation on the spouse to obtain such training or education, however, where the dependent former spouse's circumstances indicate mandatory education or training would be little more than an exercise in futility, it is appropriate to charge the dependent former spouse with the obligation to seek and accept appropriate employment. In re Lenkner, 241 Ill. App. 3d 15, 181 Ill. Dec. 646, 608 N.E.2d 897 (4 Dist. 1993).

Due to wife's age, lack of formal education experience, lack of guarantees of success, and the improbability she could greatly enhance her earning potential by embarking upon an educational or training program, it was inappropriate to place an obligation upon wife to seek training or education. In re Lenkner, 241 Ill. App. 3d 15, 181 Ill. Dec. 646, 608 N.E.2d 897 (4 Dist. 1993).

Disability Benefits
Because petitioner's proposed interpretation of settlement agreement led to an unfair and unreasonable result, the court would not conclude that the parties intended that petitioner receive a portion of respondent's disability benefits. Davis v. Davis, 286 Ill. App. 3d 1065, 222 Ill. Dec. 661, 678 N.E.2d 68 (3 Dist. 1997).

Discretion of Court

—In General
A circuit court's denial of a petition to terminate maintenance will not be reversed unless such denial was an abuse of discretion. In re Bryant, 206 Ill. App. 3d 167, 150 Ill. Dec. 707, 563 N.E.2d 834 (1 Dist. 1990).

The trial court need not provide its reasoning behind the maintenance award, but there must be a basis for the award in the record, and the record must indicate to some extent the trial court's reasoning when it exercised its discretion to award maintenance. In re Nicks, 177 Ill. App. 3d 76, 126 Ill. Dec. 442, 531 N.E.2d 1069 (4 Dist. 1988).

The trial courts have wide latitude in determining what needs are reasonable and must decide on a case by case basis, taking into consideration such factors as the circumstances of the parties, the standard of living during the marriage, the duration of the marriage and the social position of the spouse seeking maintenance. In

Discretion of Court (Cont'd)

—In General (Cont'd)

re Kristie, 156 Ill. App. 3d 821, 109 Ill. Dec. 393, 510 N.E.2d 14 (1 Dist. 1987).

The trial court must exercise its discretion in awarding or denying maintenance, and its determination is presumed to be correct. In re Kristie, 156 Ill. App. 3d 821, 109 Ill. Dec. 393, 510 N.E.2d 14 (1 Dist. 1987).

The propriety of a maintenance award, as well as the granting of such an award, are matters within the sound discretion of the trial court, and the award will not be disturbed on appeal unless it amounts to an abuse of discretion or is against the manifest weight of the evidence; however, the basis for the award must be established in the record. In re Aslaksen, 148 Ill. App. 3d 784, 102 Ill. Dec. 469, 500 N.E.2d 91 (2 Dist. 1986); In re Bentivenga, 109 Ill. App. 3d 967, 65 Ill. Dec. 423, 441 N.E.2d 336 (2 Dist. 1982); In re Lord, 125 Ill. App. 3d 1, 80 Ill. Dec. 360, 465 N.E.2d 151 (2 Dist. 1984); In re Lasota, 125 Ill. App. 3d 37, 80 Ill. Dec. 537, 465 N.E.2d 649 (1 Dist. 1984); In re Wilder, 122 Ill. App. 3d 338, 77 Ill. Dec. 824, 461 N.E.2d 447 (1 Dist 1983); In re Johnson, 106 Ill. App. 3d 502, 62 Ill. Dec. 478, 436 N.E.2d 228 (1 Dist. 1982).

An award of maintenance is within the discretion of the trial court. In re Sales, 106 Ill. App. 3d 378, 62 Ill. Dec. 441, 436 N.E.2d 23 (1 Dist. 1982); In re Belluomini, 104 Ill. App. 3d 301, 60 Ill. Dec. 59, 432 N.E.2d 958 (1 Dist. 1982).

Where petitioner had limited income, but respondent had no income and poor prospects for employment, the court was justified in not accepting petitioner's estimate as to the amount of his own expenses, and did not abuse its discretion in awarding respondent maintenance. In re Peoples, 96 Ill. App. 3d 94, 51 Ill. Dec. 514, 420 N.E.2d 1072 (5 Dist. 1981).

The parties enjoyed a modest but comfortable standard of living; they lived in a series of homes which they owned and accumulated significant assets, considering their income; at the time of hearing, respondent had no earnings and no individual assets, income producing or otherwise; and her ability to support herself through appropriate employment was dubious for lack of skills and good health; the court abused its discretion in denying respondent maintenance. In re Rimmele, 102 Ill. App. 3d 88, 57 Ill. Dec. 762, 429 N.E.2d 879 (3 Dist. 1981).

Modification of alimony provisions in a divorce decree rests in the sound judicial discretion of the trial court, and unless the record shows an abuse of discretion, the modification will not be reversed on appeal. Baker v. Baker, 53 Ill. App. 3d 186, 10 Ill. Dec. 784, 368 N.E.2d 379 (1 Dist. 1977).

A trial court could refuse to grant defendant a hearing on the resolution of all property interests after the court had refused to adopt a property settlement agreement in its entirety and after the hearing has been concluded; the trial court could consider the proposed property settlement agreement along with all other evidence in formulating its decree. Mayeur v. Mayeur, 42 Ill. App. 3d 7, 355 N.E.2d 358 (3 Dist. 1976).

—Amount of Award

Where the maintenance award together with petitioner's gross earnings was insufficient to meet her monthly mortgage and utility expenses alone, petitioner could be required to dispose of the asset intended by the parties as a permanent residence for petitioner and the children; therefore, considering respondent's substantial income and future earning ability, sufficient to meet not only his needs but those of petitioner, the trial court's maintenance award was an abuse of discretion. In re Schroeder, 215 Ill. App. 3d 156, 158 Ill. Dec. 721, 574 N.E.2d 834 (4 Dist.), cert. denied, 141 Ill. 2d 560, 162 Ill. Dec. 508, 580 N.E.2d 134 (1991).

—Review and Modification

An award of permanent maintenance in a dissolution proceeding containing no provision for modification review was deemed an abuse of discretion by the trial judge. In re Girrulat, 219 Ill. App. 3d 164, 161 Ill. Dec. 734, 578 N.E.2d 1380 (5 Dist. 1991).

Modification of alimony provisions in a divorce decree rests in the sound judicial discretion of the trial court, and unless the record shows an abuse of discretion, the modification will not be reversed on appeal. Baker v. Baker, 53 Ill. App. 3d 186, 10 Ill. Dec. 784, 368 N.E.2d 379 (1 Dist. 1977).

Dissipation

—Shown

Where husband set up trust for education of children where corpus reverted back to him in 10 years, paid attorney fees, and loaned his brother $6,000 from marital estate, it was not an abuse of discretion for trial court to hold husband was dissipating marital assets. Head v. Head, 168 Ill. App. 3d 697, 119 Ill. Dec. 549, 523 N.E.2d 17 (1 Dist. 1988).

By seeking an equal division of the marital assets without maintenance, the husband's pleadings did not specifically or affirmatively place his health in issue. In re Bonneau, 294 Ill. App. 3d 720, 229 Ill. Dec. 187, 691 N.E.2d 123 (2 Dist. 1998), appeal denied, 178 Ill. 2d 574, 232 Ill. Dec. 845, 699 N.E.2d 1030 (1998).

Duration of Award

—Factors Considered

Trial court failed to take into account that the wife had been the primary caretaker for the parties' four children over a 21-year span and thus abused its discretion in requiring that the maintenance terminate after only one year. Keip v. Keip, 332 Ill. App. 3d 876, 266 Ill. Dec. 157, 773 N.E.2d 1227, 2002 Ill. App. LEXIS 613 (5 Dist. 2002).

Wife's emotional problems, her long absence from the labor market, her educational background, and her age required a maintenance award which was reviewable at the end of four years rather than automatically terminating at that time. In re Teauseau, 185 Ill. App. 3d 22, 132 Ill. Dec. 898, 540 N.E.2d 820 (3 Dist. 1989).

—Future Conditions

Notwithstanding that the parties were married for five years but only lived together for two and one-half of those years where, at the time of dissolution action, wife had contracted multiple sclerosis and was unable to work and the trial court ordered husband to pay maintenance of $621 per month for three years, at which time the award was to be reviewed; the trial court reviewed the maintenance award and subsequently found that the award should be extended to four more years, and made it reviewable at that time, the trial court did not abuse its discretion in reserving jurisdiction to review the maintenance award. In re Stam, 260 Ill. App. 3d 754, 198 Ill. Dec. 467, 632 N.E.2d 1078 (3 Dist. 1994).

In marital dissolution proceedings, maintenance awards of limited duration should not be based on speculation as to the future conditions of the parties. In re Pieper, 79 Ill. App. 3d 835, 34 Ill. Dec. 877, 398 N.E.2d 868 (1 Dist. 1979); In re Rothbardt, 99 Ill. App. 3d 561, 54 Ill. Dec. 929, 425 N.E.2d 1146 (1 Dist. 1981); In re Wilder, 122 Ill. App. 3d 338, 77 Ill. Dec. 824, 461 N.E.2d 447 (1 Dist. 1983); In re Hart, 181 Ill. App. 3d 1066, 130 Ill. Dec. 500, 537 N.E.2d 829 (3 Dist. 1989).

—Indefinite

The court did not err in awarding biweekly maintenance to a 32-year-old wife, following a 13-year marriage, without ordering that the award be time-limited/reviewable and without ordering that the wife seek employment, where the wife had a high school education and no further training or education; further, notwithstanding the absence of such conditions, the award was reviewable and the wife was required to seek employment as 750 ILCS 5/510 allows modification upon a showing of a substantial change of circumstances, and the failure to make a good faith effort to achieve financial independence can be the basis for a petition for modification. In re Mayhall, 311 Ill. App. 3d 765, 244 Ill. Dec. 227, 725 N.E.2d 22, 2000 Ill. App. LEXIS 72 (4 Dist. 2000).

Where the spouse is not employable or is employable only at a low income as compared to the previous standard of living, maintenance for an indefinite period would be appropriate. In re Werries, 247 Ill. App. 3d 639, 186 Ill. Dec. 747, 616 N.E.2d 1379 (4 Dist. 1993).

—Limited

In the event the spouse is employable at an income not overly disproportionate relative to the standard of living established during the marriage, maintenance for a limited period is appropriate. In re Werries, 247 Ill. App. 3d 639, 186 Ill. Dec. 747, 616 N.E.2d 1379 (4 Dist. 1993).

Duration of Award (Cont'd)

—Limited (Cont'd)

The trial court may award limited maintenance and such decision will not be reversed on appeal unless it is an abuse of discretion or is against the manifest weight of the evidence. In re Malinowski, 211 Ill. App. 3d 536, 156 Ill. Dec. 3, 570 N.E.2d 479 (1 Dist. 1991).

Once the trial court determines that maintenance is appropriate, the court can exercise its discretion in making an award of a limited duration. In re Hart, 181 Ill. App. 3d 1066, 130 Ill. Dec. 500, 537 N.E.2d 829 (3 Dist. 1989).

The court did not abuse its discretion in limiting a maintenance award to a period of 36 months where spouse conceded that income from her rental properties, together with her salary, would meet her living expenses. In re Hackett, 113 Ill. 2d 286, 100 Ill. Dec. 790, 497 N.E.2d 1152 (1986).

In determining maintenance award upon dissolution of second marriage of a party whose first marriage had not yet been dissolved, it was not an abuse of discretion for the trial court to consider the current life style of the first wife and her family and to include the educational expenses of their non-minor child in its determination of maintenance. In re Belluomini, 104 Ill. App. 3d 301, 60 Ill. Dec. 59, 432 N.E.2d 958 (1 Dist. 1982).

Limitation of maintenance for the second "wife" where the first marriage had not been dissolved was justified because of the short duration of the marriage and the fact that the parties had not established a marital standard of living, but should have had no bearing upon the proper support of the child of the husband and the second "wife." In re Belluomini, 104 Ill. App. 3d 301, 60 Ill. Dec. 59, 432 N.E.2d 958 (1 Dist. 1982).

Limiting awards to specific time periods has been upheld in cases in which the award was intended to maintain a party for a period during which such party's income producing potential might be fully realized. In re Rothbardt, 99 Ill. App. 3d 561, 54 Ill. Dec. 929, 425 N.E.2d 1146 (1 Dist. 1981).

The maintenance award was limited to exclude not only extraordinary income, such as that from a winning lottery ticket, but also income for all sources other than employment. In re Parello, 87 Ill. App. 3d 926, 42 Ill. Dec. 846, 409 N.E.2d 461 (1 Dist. 1980).

—Permanent

Wife was entitled to permanent maintenance where, inter alia, wife, even under the best circumstances, was only capable of earning half of what the husband earned and the husband had the means to provide for the wife to continue in her prior lifestyle without compromising his own needs. In re Marriage of Selinger, 351 Ill. App. 3d 611, 286 Ill. Dec. 502, 814 N.E.2d 152, 2004 Ill. App. LEXIS 904 (4 Dist. 2004).

Permanent maintenance is appropriate where it is evident that the recipient spouse is either unemployable or employable only at an income substantially lower than the previous standard of living. Haas v. Haas, 215 Ill. App. 3d 959, 158 Ill. Dec. 983, 574 N.E.2d 1376 (3 Dist. 1991).

Permanent maintenance is not justified where petitioner has been employed throughout the marriage and seemingly has the potential to become self-sufficient. Haas v. Haas, 215 Ill. App. 3d 959, 158 Ill. Dec. 983, 574 N.E.2d 1376 (3 Dist. 1991).

Propriety of maintenance awards must be assessed in relation to evidence adduced at trial concerning the parties' circumstances to determine what is just, rather than in relation to the amount of temporary maintenance ordered in preliminary proceedings. In re Dodge, 184 Ill. App. 3d 495, 132 Ill. Dec. 700, 540 N.E.2d 440 (1 Dist. 1989).

Illinois courts give consideration to a more permanent award of maintenance to wives who have undertaken to have children, raise and support the family, and who have lost or been substantially impaired in maintaining their skills for continued employment during the years when the husband was getting his education and becoming established. In re Rubinstein, 145 Ill. App. 3d 31, 99 Ill. Dec. 212, 495 N.E.2d 659 (2 Dist. 1986).

The evidence failed to support an award of time-limited maintenance where wife's medical history and lack of a college education or any skills or training rendered highly uncertain, if not doubtful, her ability to support herself in five years on a level approximating the above average standard of living enjoyed by the parties during their marriage; action remanded for consideration of permanent maintenance. In re Carney, 122 Ill. App. 3d 705, 78 Ill. Dec. 477, 462 N.E.2d 596 (1 Dist. 1984).

Educational Expenses

Although the trial court did not order respondent to pay for child's education, it was not error for the court to consider this expense when it determined the amount of the maintenance award. In re Swigers, 176 Ill. App. 3d 795, 126 Ill. Dec. 231, 531 N.E.2d 858 (1 Dist. 1988).

Where the parties' marital settlement agreement provided that defendant first pay unallocated maintenance and child support, and then, as he was financially able, to pay educational expenses, even though the trial court did not proportionately reduce defendant's support payment by the $34,000 in educational expenses incurred by defendant, the $3,900 reduction did reflect an accurate interpretation of the settlement agreement that maintenance and child support took priority over educational expenses. In re Geis, 159 Ill. App. 3d 975, 111 Ill. Dec. 717, 512 N.E.2d 1354 (1 Dist. 1987).

Effective Date

Divorce action would not be reconsidered under this Act when the trial court had determined all the issues prior to the effective date of the Act, but the final written decree was filed after that date. In re LaSusa, 80 Ill. App. 3d 467, 35 Ill. Dec. 884, 400 N.E.2d 21 (1 Dist. 1979).

Employment

—In General

The recipient of maintenance has an affirmative obligation to seek gainful employment. In re Einhorn, 178 Ill. App. 3d 212, 127 Ill. Dec. 411, 533 N.E.2d 29 (1 Dist. 1988).

That the wife had been employed for 10 years was only one factor to be considered in determining whether maintenance should have been awarded. In re Kristie, 156 Ill. App. 3d 821, 109 Ill. Dec. 393, 510 N.E.2d 14 (1 Dist. 1987).

An alimony (now maintenance) award is an incentive to assist one in reclaiming employment skills outside the home, which have atrophied during the marriage relationship, and enable a formerly dependent spouse to acquire financial independence for the future. In re Bramson, 100 Ill. App. 3d 657, 56 Ill. Dec. 205, 427 N.E.2d 285 (1 Dist. 1981).

—Capacity

Where wife had been away from the labor force for a substantial period of time, she was 53 years old, and it appeared from the record that she had made no attempt to find suitable employment, this Act created an affirmative obligation on the part of the spouse seeking maintenance to seek appropriate employment. Thus, while wife's educational and employment backgrounds were limited, these limitations alone were insufficient to support a conclusion that she was unemployable and award of $3,200 monthly was an abuse of discretion. In re McNeeley, 117 Ill. App. 3d 320, 72 Ill. Dec. 873, 453 N.E.2d 748 (1 Dist. 1983).

—Duty to Seek

There is an affirmative obligation on the party requesting maintenance to seek appropriate employment and to make a good faith effort to become financially independent. In re Werries, 247 Ill. App. 3d 639, 186 Ill. Dec. 747, 616 N.E.2d 1379 (4 Dist. 1993).

A spouse cannot use self-imposed poverty as a basis for claiming maintenance when he has the means to earn more income; this Act creates an affirmative duty on a spouse requesting maintenance to seek and accept appropriate employment. In re Schuster, 224 Ill. App. 3d 958, 167 Ill. Dec. 73, 586 N.E.2d 1345 (1992).

This Act creates an affirmative duty on a spouse requesting maintenance to seek and accept appropriate employment. In re Seymour, 206 Ill. App. 3d 506, 152 Ill. Dec. 27, 565 N.E.2d 269 (2 Dist. 1990).

A spouse has an affirmative obligation pursuant to law to acquire gainful employment which should enable her to live with independent means, apart from any contribution from her ex-spouse. In re Gentry, 188 Ill. App. 3d 372, 135 Ill. Dec. 939, 544 N.E.2d 435 (3 Dist. 1989).

Where respondent had only an eighth grade education and had not previously worked outside the home, these limitations alone were not sufficient to support contention that she was entitled to

Employment (Cont'd)

—Duty to Seek (Cont'd)

permanent maintenance as respondent was only 47 years old, in good health, and had turned down several job offers. In re Callaway, 150 Ill. App. 3d 712, 104 Ill. Dec. 103, 502 N.E.2d 366 (1 Dist. 1986).

A spouse applying for maintenance has an affirmative duty to seek gainful employment. In re Kaplan, 149 Ill. App. 3d 23, 102 Ill. Dec. 719, 500 N.E.2d 612 (1 Dist. 1986); In re Callaway, 150 Ill. App. 3d 712, 104 Ill. Dec. 103, 502 N.E.2d 366 (1 Dist. 1986); In re Heller, 153 Ill. App. 3d 224, 106 Ill. Dec. 503, 505 N.E.2d 1294 (1 Dist. 1987); In re Einhorn, 178 Ill. App. 3d 212, 127 Ill. Dec. 411, 533 N.E.2d 29 (1 Dist. 1988); In re Wolf, 180 Ill. App. 3d 998, 129 Ill. Dec. 742, 536 N.E.2d 792 (1 Dist. 1989); In re Philips, 200 Ill. App. 3d 395, 146 Ill. Dec. 191, 558 N.E.2d 154 (1 Dist. 1990); In re Marthens, 215 Ill. App. 3d 590, 159 Ill. Dec. 3, 575 N.E.2d 3 (3 Dist. 1991).

There is no authority for the proposition that the wife is obliged to seek employment, if able to work, to relieve the husband of the obligation of support when he has the ability to support; even assistance obtained from other sources does not relieve the husband of his obligation. Marriott v. Marriott, 347 Ill. App. 372, 106 N.E.2d 876 (1 Dist. 1952).

—Effect

Maintenance may be appropriate where a spouse is employed but has little prospect of earning a salary commensurate with her needs. In re Kennedy, 214 Ill. App. 3d 849, 158 Ill. Dec. 172, 573 N.E.2d 1357 (1 Dist. 1991).

—Full Time

It is proper to award maintenance in order to permit the custodial ex-spouse, if he or she elects to do so, to be employed full time or part time as a homemaker, because part-time employment plus acting as a homemaker is fully equivalent to obtaining full-time employment outside the home and placing the children in day care. In re Hensley, 210 Ill. App. 3d 1043, 155 Ill. Dec. 486, 569 N.E.2d 1097 (4 Dist.), cert. denied, 141 Ill. 2d 541, 162 Ill. Dec. 488, 580 N.E.2d 114 (1991).

—Inadequate Income

Maintenance may be appropriate where a spouse has little prospect of earning sufficient income to meet her needs, even if she is employed. In re Marcello, 247 Ill. App. 3d 304, 187 Ill. Dec. 81, 617 N.E.2d 289 (1 Dist. 1993).

Maintenance may be appropriate where a spouse is employed but has little prospect of earning a salary commensurate with her needs or where she has insufficient property to provide an adequate income. In re Kristie, 156 Ill. App. 3d 821, 109 Ill. Dec. 393, 510 N.E.2d 14 (1 Dist. 1987).

Enforcement

For a case discussing enforcement of an award of alimony (now maintenance), see Wilson v. Smart, 324 Ill. 276, 155 N.E. 288 (1927); White v. Adolph, 305 Ill. App. 76, 26 N.E.2d 993 (3 Dist. 1940); Shuff v. Fulte, 344 Ill. App. 157, 100 N.E.2d 502 (3 Dist. 1951); Kazubowski v. Ray, 48 Ill. 2d 413, 272 N.E.2d 225 (1971).

Equal Living Standard

An award of maintenance was required where the wife had an income deficit, and the husband had a surplus, in order to obtain a more equal standard of living, though it would not be the same as that enjoyed during their marriage. In re Emery, 179 Ill. App. 3d 744, 128 Ill. Dec. 569, 534 N.E.2d 1014 (4 Dist. 1989).

Equitable Contribution

—Change in Circumstances

The trial court abused its discretion in denying a father's request to require a non-custodial mother to contribute an equitable amount in the support of their minor child where its decision failed to consider the circumstances of all the parties as required by 750 ILCS 5/510 and this section, particularly that the mother was earning more than the father and there had been a custody change from the home of the mother to the home of the father. Hursh v. Hursh, 26 Ill. App. 3d 947, 326 N.E.2d 95 (1 Dist. 1975).

Evidence

—Hearing Required

It was error for the trial court to fail to obtain knowledge of petitioner's needs by means of hearing evidence of her living expenses prior to denying her request for maintenance. In re Rundle, 107 Ill. App. 3d 880, 63 Ill. Dec. 491, 438 N.E.2d 229 (5 Dist. 1982).

A trial court could refuse to grant defendant a hearing on the resolution of all property interests after the court had refused to adopt a property settlement agreement in its entirety and after the hearing has been concluded; the trial court could consider the proposed property settlement agreement along with all other evidence in formulating its decree. Mayeur v. Mayeur, 42 Ill. App. 3d 7, 355 N.E.2d 358 (3 Dist. 1976).

—Held Insufficient

Where the marriage was of short duration, the marital lifestyle was not lavish and the petitioner was employable, health problems notwithstanding, petitioner did not meet her burden of showing an abuse of discretion in the ruling of the trial court against maintenance. In re Albrecht, 266 Ill. App. 3d 399, 203 Ill. Dec. 394, 639 N.E.2d 953 (4 Dist. 1994).

To the extent there was no evidence in the record to justify the limited nature of the wife's maintenance award, the trial court abused its discretion in granting maintenance that was nonmodifiable and was to terminate at the end of two years. In re Ryman, 172 Ill. App. 3d 599, 122 Ill. Dec. 646, 527 N.E.2d 18 (2 Dist. 1988).

There was no evidence to support the trial court's assumption that petitioner would be able, at the end of five years, to support herself in some reasonable approximation of the standard of living established during the marriage; however, this fact did not entitle her to permanent maintenance. In re Wilder, 122 Ill. App. 3d 338, 77 Ill. Dec. 824, 461 N.E.2d 447 (1 Dist. 1983).

The evidence did not sustain the trial court's award of $450 a month to petitioner as maintenance. In re Coram, 86 Ill. App. 3d 845, 42 Ill. Dec. 40, 408 N.E.2d 418 (5 Dist. 1980).

There was insufficient proof that respondent was unable to support himself or was without sufficient income; therefore, maintenance was not proper. In re Stallings, 75 Ill. App. 3d 96, 30 Ill. Dec. 718, 393 N.E.2d 1065 (5 Dist. 1979).

—Held Sufficient

Maintenance award was supported by the evidence where, prior to the initiation of the proceedings, petitioner worked 30 to 32 hours per week in a very successful family business in a management and bookkeeping position at a salary less than $5,000 per year; petitioner had primary responsibility for her son; after the petition for dissolution was filed, petitioner returned to school to continue her education, which she stated was needed for her to gain appropriate employment; and respondent presented no evidence to the contrary. In re Cheger, 213 Ill. App. 3d 371, 157 Ill. Dec. 116, 571 N.E.2d 1135 (4 Dist. 1991).

Where the court has specific evidence regarding educational background, present educational pursuits, and income at the time of dissolution, there is sufficient evidence to set a specific period of time for maintenance. In re Cheger, 213 Ill. App. 3d 371, 157 Ill. Dec. 116, 571 N.E.2d 1135 (4 Dist. 1991).

Where the trial court noted that the husband had a degree in electrical engineering, had operated his own business for a number of years, was found to be in good health and had demonstrated throughout the years an ability to generate an income more than adequate to support himself, but wife had a more minimal opportunity for the acquisition and accumulation of capital assets, this constituted a sufficient basis for the trial court's award of maintenance. In re Getautas, 189 Ill. App. 3d 148, 136 Ill. Dec. 509, 544 N.E.2d 1284 (2 Dist. 1989).

Where the court found that since the time of the first judgment five years earlier, the four children, two of whom were now 18, were no longer living at home but were enrolled in boarding schools paid by the husband; that the wife's non-marital assets had more than doubled since the time of the first judgment; that the parties were married for less than 13 years and were now divorced for six years; that the wife had received more than five years of unallocated maintenance of $48,000 per year; and that the husband no longer voted a majority of outstanding shares of stock as he did at the time of the first judgment, the trial court in awarding maintenance properly considered the increased award of marital property and the changed circumstances since the entry of the first judgment. In re Thornton, 138 Ill. App. 3d 906, 93 Ill. Dec. 453, 486 N.E.2d 1288 (1 Dist. 1985).

Evidence (Cont'd)

—Held Sufficient (Cont'd)

Evidence was held sufficient to sustain the trial court's denial of husband's motion to vacate judgment of distribution of marital property and maintenance award in a marriage dissolution action where husband had notice of hearing and the judgment was not fundamentally unfair to the parties. In re Garde, 118 Ill. App. 3d 303, 73 Ill. Dec. 816, 454 N.E.2d 1065 (5 Dist. 1983).

Where the order of the court contained a detailed analysis of the economic status backgrounds and anticipated future plans of the parties, there was ample evidence to support the court's unequal division of the marital property and award of maintenance so that the order of the trial court was not against the manifest weight of the evidence. In re Viehman, 91 Ill. App. 3d 315, 46 Ill. Dec. 800, 414 N.E.2d 853 (5 Dist. 1980).

—Use of Affidavits

The use of affidavits to aid a court in determining property settlement and maintenance awards is not improper. In re Johnson, 106 Ill. App. 3d 502, 62 Ill. Dec. 478, 436 N.E.2d 228 (1 Dist. 1982).

—Valuation

Where evaluating defendant's net worth was a matter of resolving conflicting testimony, it was a matter for the trial court to determine. Sandberg v. Sandberg, 11 Ill. App. 3d 495, 297 N.E.2d 654 (1 Dist. 1973).

Excess Payment

Former husband who paid in excess of specific sum set forth in settlement agreement and, at the time of the agreement, had a retarded child, and who made payments equal to 50% of his then income, did not have to pay 50% of his income to ex-wife for alimony (now maintenance) and support years later. In re Whetstone, 87 Ill. App. 3d 164, 42 Ill. Dec. 546, 409 N.E.2d 41 (1 Dist. 1980).

Expenses

Respondent's expenses, particularly for housing and clothing, were not overstated where respondent explained that housing costs in Los Angeles were approximately 50% higher than in Chicago and his clothing costs were expensive because he was "hard to fit"; accordingly, petitioner's claim that respondent's expenses were overstated was not supported by the evidence. In re Swigers, 176 Ill. App. 3d 795, 126 Ill. Dec. 231, 531 N.E.2d 858 (1 Dist. 1988).

Factors Considered

Where petitioner proved respondent had the ability to pay, denial of maintenance did not amount to an abuse of discretion, given the considerable assets of petitioner. In re Homann, 276 Ill. App. 3d 236, 213 Ill. Dec. 22, 658 N.E.2d 492 (4 Dist. 1995).

It is not only just and equitable to consider the factors listed in 750 ILCS 5/510(c), but also it is statutorily required when awarding maintenance pursuant to this section. In re Toole, 273 Ill. App. 3d 607, 210 Ill. Dec. 551, 653 N.E.2d 456 (2 Dist. 1995).

In awarding maintenance, courts have wide latitude in considering what factors should be used in determining reasonable needs, and the trial court is not limited to the factors listed in the governing statute. In re Mohr, 260 Ill. App. 3d 98, 197 Ill. Dec. 563, 631 N.E.2d 785 (4 Dist. 1994).

Where the trial court's order stated that it considered all the factors contained in this section, but it appeared that the court was heavily influenced by two factors, petitioner's potential ability to support herself and the short duration of the marriage, while this section requires a court to consider all relevant factors, there is no requirement that the factors be given equal weight, so long as the balance struck by the court is reasonable under the circumstances, and there was no abuse of discretion. In re Miller, 231 Ill. App. 3d 480, 172 Ill. Dec. 679, 595 N.E.2d 1349 (3 Dist. 1992).

The same factors considered under this section in making an initial award of maintenance are used in determining whether and to what degree a maintenance award shall be modified. Rice v. Rice, 173 Ill. App. 3d 1098, 123 Ill. Dec. 630, 528 N.E.2d 14 (5 Dist. 1988).

The wife's refusal to file a joint tax return should not have been considered in awarding maintenance. In re Ryman, 172 Ill. App. 3d 599, 122 Ill. Dec. 646, 527 N.E.2d 18 (2 Dist. 1988).

The trial court should have estimated a reasonable rate of return to approximate the income producing ability of wife's investment funds, and if the parties failed to introduce evidence as to the income producing ability of these funds, the trial court should have determined a reasonable rate of return on the investment of these funds in order to make some determination of their effect on the wife's income. In re Ryman, 172 Ill. App. 3d 599, 122 Ill. Dec. 646, 527 N.E.2d 18 (2 Dist. 1988).

In deciding whether to modify maintenance or child support, the trial court must consider the same factors it weighs under this section and 750 ILCS 5/505 when it formulates an original support order. In re Lyons, 155 Ill. App. 3d 300, 108 Ill. Dec. 297, 508 N.E.2d 458 (2 Dist. 1987).

In view of the total circumstances including the age of the wife, her long absence from the labor market, the condition of her physical and emotional health, the standard of living of the parties, and the husband's ability to pay maintenance, a 48 month limitation on the maintenance award to the wife was speculative. In re Magnuson, 156 Ill. App. 3d 691, 109 Ill. Dec. 569, 510 N.E.2d 437 (2 Dist. 1987).

While an award may be for a definite time frame, it should not be based on speculation as to future conditions, but on circumstances disclosed by the evidence; where the court has specific evidence regarding educational background, present educational pursuits, and income at the time of dissolution, there is sufficient evidence to set a specific period of time for maintenance. In re Wade, 158 Ill. App. 3d 255, 110 Ill. Dec. 321, 511 N.E.2d 156 (4 Dist. 1987).

The maintenance awarded to wife of $8,400 per year for at most six years was unreasonable given wife's evident unemployability and the fact that her income would be about $8,000 less than her yearly requirements. In re Mayzner, 144 Ill. App. 3d 645, 98 Ill. Dec. 493, 494 N.E.2d 615 (1 Dist. 1986).

The court must consider the needs of each of the parties in dividing the marital property and in awarding maintenance. In re De Bat, 127 Ill. App. 3d 463, 82 Ill. Dec. 568, 468 N.E.2d 1348 (1 Dist. 1984).

An award of maintenance is warranted where the court finds that the party seeking maintenance lacks sufficient property, including marital property apportioned to her, to provide for her reasonable needs and is unable to support herself through appropriate employment or is otherwise without sufficient income. In re McNeeley, 117 Ill. App. 3d 320, 72 Ill. Dec. 873, 453 N.E.2d 748 (1 Dist. 1983).

Standard of living before and during the marriage, duration of the marriage and the social position of the spouse seeking maintenance can all be relevant, as would be special needs such as medical expenses; however, the trial judge may take into account many other considerations, including but not limited to the factors listed in subsection (b) of this section. In re Simmons, 87 Ill. App. 3d 651, 42 Ill. Dec. 706, 409 N.E.2d 321 (1 Dist. 1980).

In determining whether wife had sufficient income with which to support herself, consideration should have been given to the income level which she was able to attain and not merely that which she set for herself through arrangements which clearly were unfavorable to her. In re McGrew, 90 Ill. App. 3d 27, 45 Ill. Dec. 414, 412 N.E.2d 996 (5 Dist. 1980).

Trial court did not abuse its discretion in the denial of maintenance to husband where there was nothing factual in his affidavit or elsewhere in the record to establish, as required by this section, that he lacked sufficient assets or property to provide for his reasonable needs or that he was unable to support himself through appropriate employment or otherwise without sufficient income. In re Thornqvist, 79 Ill. App. 3d 791, 35 Ill. Dec. 342, 399 N.E.2d 176 (1 Dist. 1979).

For cases discussing age, health and physical condition of the parties in determining whether to award alimony (now maintenance) to a wife against whom a decree for divorce has been entered, see Comstock v. Comstock, 55 Ill. App. 3d 140, 12 Ill. Dec. 841, 370 N.E.2d 645 (3 Dist. 1977); In re Gammons, 78 Ill. App. 3d 1001, 34 Ill. Dec. 655, 398 N.E.2d 330 (3 Dist. 1979); In re Parello, 87 Ill. App. 3d 926, 42 Ill. Dec. 846, 409 N.E.2d 461 (1 Dist. 1980); In re Asch, 100 Ill. App. 3d 293, 55 Ill. Dec. 741, 426 N.E.2d 1066 (1 Dist. 1981); In re Reed, 100 Ill. App. 3d 873, 56 Ill. Dec. 202, 427 N.E.2d 282 (5 Dist. 1981); In re Lord, 125 Ill. App. 3d 1, 80 Ill. Dec. 360, 465 N.E.2d 151 (2 Dist. 1984); In re De Bat, 127 Ill. App. 3d 463, 82 Ill. Dec. 568, 468 N.E.2d 1348 (1 Dist. 1984); In re Rink, 136 Ill. App. 3d 252, 91 Ill. Dec. 34, 483 N.E.2d 316 (1 Dist. 1985); In re Kristie, 156 Ill. App. 3d 821, 109 Ill. Dec. 393, 510 N.E.2d 14 (1 Dist. 1987); In re Albiani, 159 Ill. App. 3d 519, 111 Ill. Dec. 126, 512 N.E.2d 30 (1 Dist. 1987); In re Jones, 187 Ill. App. 3d 206, 134 Ill.

Factors Considered (Cont'd)
Dec. 836, 543 N.E.2d 119 (1 Dist. 1989); In re Gentry, 188 Ill. App. 3d 372, 135 Ill. Dec. 939, 544 N.E.2d 435 (3 Dist. 1989).

The proper measure of alimony (now maintenance) is the need of the wife considered in connection with the husband's ability to pay; no single criterion is controlling and each case depends on the individual facts of that case. Stotlar v. Stotlar, 50 Ill. App. 3d 790, 8 Ill. Dec. 711, 365 N.E.2d 1097 (5 Dist. 1977).

Failure to Pay

Wilful failure to pay allowances for child support and maintenance as ordered by the court may be declared contemptuous misconduct and may be sanctioned accordingly. In re Hilkovitch, 124 Ill. App. 3d 401, 79 Ill. Dec. 891, 464 N.E.2d 795 (1 Dist. 1984).

The failure to make the payments directed to be made pursuant to a court order or judgment is prima facie evidence of contempt. In re Hilkovitch, 124 Ill. App. 3d 401, 79 Ill. Dec. 891, 464 N.E.2d 795 (1 Dist. 1984).

A party who fails to pay the allowances ordered has the burden of proving that his failure to comply was not wilful or contumacious and that he has a valid excuse for his failure to pay. In re Hilkovitch, 124 Ill. App. 3d 401, 79 Ill. Dec. 891, 464 N.E.2d 795 (1 Dist. 1984).

Whether the person charged for failure to pay child support and maintenance is in wilful contempt and whether a sanction is to be imposed are factual matters to be determined by the trial court from the evidence presented to it. In re Hilkovitch, 124 Ill. App. 3d 401, 79 Ill. Dec. 891, 464 N.E.2d 795 (1 Dist. 1984).

A reviewing court will not upset the trial court's finding of wilful or contumacious misconduct on the part of the person obligated to make the payment of allowances unless the trial court's factual conclusions are contrary to the manifest weight of the evidence. In re Hilkovitch, 124 Ill. App. 3d 401, 79 Ill. Dec. 891, 464 N.E.2d 795 (1 Dist. 1984).

Fault

Since the statute does not refer to nor make an award dependent upon the question of fault, the court is empowered to award alimony (now maintenance) to a wife against whom a divorce is granted. Harambasic v. Harambasic, 55 Ill. App. 3d 648, 13 Ill. Dec. 224, 370 N.E.2d 1251 (1 Dist. 1977).

An award of alimony (now maintenance) does not depend on the question of fault. When a divorce is granted to a husband because of the fault or misconduct of the wife, she is not entitled to, nor will she be awarded, permanent alimony unless the circumstances and the equities of the case justify it. Carterfield v. Carterfield, 39 Ill. App. 3d 525, 350 N.E.2d 491 (3 Dist. 1976).

Federal Income Tax

For case discussing husband's entitlement to a deduction for alimony (now maintenance) payments made by him to wife and wife's obligation to include such payments in her gross income, see Joslyn v. Commissioner, 230 F.2d 871 (7th Cir. 1956).

Financial Independence

—In General

Financial independence does not mean the ability to merely meet one's minimum requirements, but entails the ability to earn an income which will provide a standard of living similar to that enjoyed during the marriage. In re Courtright, 185 Ill. App. 3d 74, 133 Ill. Dec. 161, 540 N.E.2d 1027 (3 Dist. 1989).

Where the wife was almost 50 years old and had not been in the work force for approximately 15 years, although she indicated a desire to return to school to obtain her nursing degree, she had no cognizable income to achieve this goal, much less support herself; wife's employability, should she obtain her degree, would have been greatly enhanced, but until this goal was achieved, wife's financial status required maintenance. The wife had an affirmative obligation to seek appropriate employment and to make a good faith effort to become financially independent. In re Wade, 158 Ill. App. 3d 255, 110 Ill. Dec. 321, 511 N.E.2d 156 (4 Dist. 1987).

Trial court's finding that respondent possessed marketable skills and was able to work and contribute toward support of the minor child was consistent with evidence at trial including that respondent supported herself for nine years prior to her marriage to the petitioner. In re Rink, 136 Ill. App. 3d 252, 91 Ill. Dec. 34, 483 N.E.2d 316 (1 Dist. 1985).

The objective of this Act in authorizing rehabilitative maintenance is to enable a formerly dependent spouse to become financially independent in the future. In re Wilder, 122 Ill. App. 3d 338, 77 Ill. Dec. 824, 461 N.E.2d 447 (1 Dist. 1983).

Petitioner was under an affirmative obligation to seek appropriate training and skills to become financially independent in the future although she was awarded maintenance. In re Mittra, 114 Ill. App. 3d 627, 71 Ill. Dec. 350, 450 N.E.2d 1229 (4 Dist. 1983).

—Defined

Financial independence does not mean the ability to merely meet one's minimum requirements, but entails the ability to earn an income which will provide a standard of living similar to that enjoyed during the marriage. In re Sisul, 234 Ill. App. 3d 1038, 175 Ill. Dec. 463, 600 N.E.2d 86 (3 Dist. 1992).

—Discretion of Court

Although there is a mandated duty to acquire financial independence, and rehabilitative maintenance is an incentive to assist a spouse in achieving that goal, it is the trial judge who is better able to determine if such an incentive is necessary, and that determination will not be overturned absent a clear abuse of discretion. In re Gunn, 233 Ill. App. 3d 165, 174 Ill. Dec. 381, 598 N.E.2d 1013 (5 Dist. 1992).

—Duty to Seek

The recipient of the maintenance award is under an affirmative obligation to seek appropriate training and skills to become financially independent in the future; the failure to make good faith efforts to achieve this goal, following a reasonable time frame during which the objective should be accomplished, might form the basis for a petition for modification. In re Martin, 223 Ill. App. 3d 855, 166 Ill. Dec. 136, 585 N.E.2d 1158 (4 Dist.), appeal denied, 145 Ill. 2d 635, 173 Ill. Dec. 6, 596 N.E.2d 630 (1992).

—Not Required

The goal of establishing the spouse's financial independence must be balanced against a realistic appraisal of the likelihood that the spouse will be able to support herself in some reasonable approximation of the standard of living established during the marriage, and is thus not required in all cases; the dependent former spouse is entitled to continue to live in some approximation to the standard of living established during the marriage, unless the payor spouse's financial situation indicates otherwise. In re Dunseth, 260 Ill. App. 3d 816, 198 Ill. Dec. 620, 633 N.E.2d 82 (4 Dist. 1994).

Financial Resources

In considering the financial resources of the parties, the trial court was required to consider the age of the respondent and his testimony concerning retirement in the near future since when retirement occurred, income from the 300 rented acres ended and while farm equipment would be sold, it was apparent the overall income would decrease. In re Mohr, 260 Ill. App. 3d 98, 197 Ill. Dec. 563, 631 N.E.2d 785 (4 Dist. 1994).

While respondent's adjusted gross income in the year prior to trial was approximately $40,000, his earnings four years prior to trial preceding the couple's separation were $96,000; thus, the trial court could reasonably infer that respondent's decline in earnings was only a temporary situation which would improve following the divorce proceedings. In re Calisoff, 176 Ill. App. 3d 721, 126 Ill. Dec. 183, 531 N.E.2d 810 (1 Dist. 1988).

In making a maintenance award, the trial court must also consider the financial resources of the party seeking maintenance, including marital property apportioned to her. In re Mittra, 114 Ill. App. 3d 627, 71 Ill. Dec. 350, 450 N.E.2d 1229 (4 Dist. 1983).

Foreign Divorce

For a case discussing the grant of alimony (now maintenance) after an ex parte divorce in a foreign jurisdiction, see Schwarz v. Schwarz, 27 Ill. 2d 140, 188 N.E.2d 673 (1963).

Fraud

In the absence of any claim by petitioner that stocks were fraudulently acquired from her, or that the funds provided by the loan were not used in the manner contemplated by the parties, petitioner was not entitled to reimbursement for any portion of the stock sale proceeds used to retire the loan. In re Brenner, 95 Ill. App. 3d 100, 50 Ill. Dec. 292, 419 N.E.2d 400 (1 Dist. 1981).

Fringe Benefits

The finding of respondent's net monthly income was not against the manifest weight of the evidence even though the trial court did not "value" respondent's fringe benefits, such as an annual bonus and a company car. In re Swigers, 176 Ill. App. 3d 795, 126 Ill. Dec. 231, 531 N.E.2d 858 (1 Dist. 1988).

Future Security Investment

Inasmuch as the standard of living during the marriage is to be considered when the court makes an award of maintenance, investing in future security can be considered an element of the marital lifestyle. Kusper v. Kusper, 195 Ill. App. 3d 494, 142 Ill. Dec. 282, 552 N.E.2d 1023 (1 Dist. 1990).

Good Faith

Wife with teaching degree who failed to obtain a current teaching certificate, after not working outside the home for 28 years, who put forth substantial effort to find other suitable employment, made good faith effort to become self-sufficient. In re Courtright, 185 Ill. App. 3d 74, 133 Ill. Dec. 161, 540 N.E.2d 1027 (3 Dist. 1989).

Grounds

—Alimony

For cases discussing grounds for awarding alimony (now maintenance), see Spitler v. Spitler, 108 Ill. 120 (1883); Harding v. Harding, 144 Ill. 588, 32 N.E. 206 (1892); Harding v. Harding, 180 Ill. 481, 54 N.E. 587 (1899); Lehmann v. Lehmann, 225 Ill. App. 513 (1 Dist. 1922); Maginnis v. Maginnis, 323 Ill. 113, 153 N.E. 654 (1926); Bandy v. Bandy, 326 Ill. App. 55, 61 N.E.2d 586 (3 Dist. 1945); Bateman v. Bateman, 337 Ill. App. 7, 85 N.E.2d 196 (4 Dist. 1949); Ylonen v. Ylonen, 2 Ill. 2d 111, 117 N.E.2d 98 (1954); Larson v. Larson, 2 Ill. 2d 451, 118 N.E.2d 433 (1954); Cross v. Cross, 5 Ill. 2d 456, 125 N.E.2d 488 (1955); Savich v. Savich, 12 Ill. 2d 454, 147 N.E.2d 85 (1957); Goldstine v. Goldstine, 25 Ill. App. 2d 319, 167 N.E.2d 30 (1 Dist. 1960); Loeb v. Gendel, 29 Ill. App. 2d 155, 172 N.E.2d 408 (1 Dist.), rev'd on other grounds, 23 Ill. 2d 502, 179 N.E.2d 7 (1961); Newman v. Newman, 42 Ill. App. 2d 203, 191 N.E.2d 614 (1 Dist. 1963); Simpson v. Simpson, 29 Ill. 2d 49, 193 N.E.2d 10 (1963); Yoselle v. Yoselle, 54 Ill. App. 2d 354, 204 N.E.2d 129 (1 Dist. 1964); Kilbride v. Kilbride, 64 Ill. App. 2d 355, 212 N.E.2d 252 (1 Dist. 1965); Blowitz v. Blowitz, 75 Ill. App. 2d 386, 221 N.E.2d 160 (1 Dist. 1966); Grabowski v. Grabowski, 95 Ill. App. 2d 311, 237 N.E.2d 766 (1 Dist. 1968); Hoffman v. Hoffman, 40 Ill. 2d 344, 239 N.E.2d 792 (1968); Mancou v. Mancou, 95 Ill. App. 2d 142, 237 N.E.2d 801 (1 Dist. 1968); Ganzer v. Ganzer, 110 Ill. App. 2d 394, 249 N.E.2d 660 (1 Dist. 1969); Springfield Marine Bank v. Property Tax Appeal Bd., 44 Ill. 2d 428, 256 N.E.2d 334 (1970); Dubinka v. Dubinka, 126 Ill. App. 2d 436, 262 N.E.2d 133 (1 Dist. 1970); Fox v. Fox, 129 Ill. App. 2d 209, 262 N.E.2d 607 (4 Dist. 1970); Bernardini v. Bernardini, 130 Ill. App. 2d 692, 264 N.E.2d 295 (4 Dist. 1970); Loucks v. Loucks, 130 Ill. App. 2d 961, 266 N.E.2d 924 (5 Dist. 1971); Demos v. Demos, 8 Ill. App. 3d 906, 290 N.E.2d 304 (2 Dist. 1972); Busby v. Busby, 11 Ill. App. 3d 426, 296 N.E.2d 585 (3 Dist. 1973); Pohren v. Pohren, 13 Ill. App. 3d 380, 300 N.E.2d 288 (3 Dist. 1973); Norris v. Norris, 16 Ill. App. 3d 879, 307 N.E.2d 181 (5 Dist. 1974); Gold v. Gold, 17 Ill. App. 3d 11, 308 N.E.2d 75 (1 Dist. 1974); Newhouse v. Newhouse, 17 Ill. App. 3d 1008, 309 N.E.2d 102 (2 Dist. 1974); Gross v. Gross, 23 Ill. App. 3d 228, 318 N.E.2d 659 (3 Dist. 1974); Eule v. Eule, 24 Ill. App. 3d 83, 320 N.E.2d 506 (1 Dist. 1974); Benson v. Benson, 26 Ill. App. 3d 50, 324 N.E.2d 469 (2 Dist. 1975); Jackson v. Jackson, 34 Ill. App. 3d 407, 339 N.E.2d 764 (1 Dist. 1975); Crawford v. Crawford, 39 Ill. App. 3d 457, 350 N.E.2d 103 (1 Dist. 1976); Harry v. Harry, 38 Ill. App. 3d 776, 349 N.E.2d 69 (4 Dist. 1976); Smith v. Smith, 47 Ill. App. 3d 583, 5 Ill. Dec. 810, 362 N.E.2d 123 (3 Dist. 1977); Shive v. Shive, 57 Ill. App. 3d 754, 15 Ill. Dec. 211, 373 N.E.2d 557 (5 Dist. 1978); Halford v. Halford, 70 Ill. App. 3d 609, 27 Ill. Dec. 168, 388 N.E.2d 1131 (5 Dist. 1979).

Homemaker's Contribution

The value of a party's contribution as a homemaker is irrelevant in considering an issue of maintenance. In re Caldwell, 124 Ill. App. 3d 898, 80 Ill. Dec. 411, 465 N.E.2d 523 (4 Dist. 1984).

Housekeeping Services

Trial court properly considered the fact that ex-wife resided with her sister in exchange for housekeeping services in determining ex-wife's income for purposes of reaching equitable maintenance award. In re Simmons, 101 Ill. App. 3d 645, 57 Ill. Dec. 352, 428 N.E.2d 1032 (5 Dist. 1981).

Illegal Agreement

In a wife's action for separate maintenance where the husband counterclaimed for divorce, the trial court did not err in excluding an agreement between the parties not to prosecute for aggravated assault because the agreement not to prosecute was void, not only because it was against the policy of the law, but because the agreement itself was a crime. Griner v. Griner, 34 Ill. App. 3d 792, 340 N.E.2d 304 (2 Dist. 1976).

Illustrative Cases

Award of maintenance was inadequate, where parties had grossly disparate earning potentials, and wife's realistic ability to support herself in some approximation of the standard of living enjoyed during the marriage was minimal. In re Charles, 284 Ill. App. 3d 339, 219 Ill. Dec. 742, 672 N.E.2d 57 (4 Dist. 1996).

In reserving the issue of maintenance to the petitioner as allowed under 750 ILCS 5/401(b), the trial court did not reach or make the determinations required under this section for a maintenance award; as such, the trial court's reservation of that issue was not assailable on the ground that petitioner did not meet the statutory prerequisites to justify such an award. In re Fahy, 208 Ill. App. 3d 677, 153 Ill. Dec. 594, 567 N.E.2d 552 (1 Dist. 1991).

Based on an examination of the factors listed in this section, the award of maintenance was not an abuse of discretion. In re Mantei, 222 Ill. App. 3d 933, 164 Ill. Dec. 870, 583 N.E.2d 1192 (4 Dist. 1991).

A maintenance award and its reviewability were deemed reasonable where the trial court considered the factors set forth in this section and balanced husband's ability to pay against wife's reasonable monthly expenses. In re Zells, 197 Ill. App. 3d 232, 143 Ill. Dec. 354, 554 N.E.2d 289 (1 Dist. 1990), rev'd on other grounds, 143 Ill. 2d 251, 157 Ill. Dec. 480, 572 N.E.2d 944 (1991).

The propriety and amount of a maintenance award are matters within the sound discretion of the trial court and the award will not be disturbed on appeal unless it is against the manifest weight of the evidence or amounts to an abuse of discretion. In re Nicks, 177 Ill. App. 3d 76, 126 Ill. Dec. 442, 531 N.E.2d 1069 (4 Dist. 1988); In re Jones, 187 Ill. App. 3d 206, 134 Ill. Dec. 836, 543 N.E.2d 119 (1 Dist. 1989); In re Seymour, 206 Ill. App. 3d 506, 152 Ill. Dec. 27, 565 N.E.2d 269 (2 Dist. 1990).

The trial court did not abuse its discretion under former subsection (b) of this section by awarding to the wife maintenance to terminate once any appeal was concluded, or when she accepted $80,000 if no appeal was taken. In re Flosman, 160 Ill. App. 3d 832, 513 N.E.2d 879 (1 Dist. 1987).

Given the state of the record and the alternatives available, the awarding of maintenance in gross was an abuse of discretion. Smith v. Smith, 150 Ill. App. 3d 34, 103 Ill. Dec. 785, 501 N.E.2d 1323 (3 Dist. 1986).

Where respondent's net monthly income, after paying, pursuant to the order, his allocated debts, child support, insurance premiums, children's medical and dental expenses, and maintenance, totaled $79.35, and petitioner's net income, after paying her allocated debts and receiving from respondent the ordered child support and maintenance, totaled $880.80, the award of $150 per month to the petitioner was an abuse of discretion by the trial court. In re Chambers, 125 Ill. App. 3d 507, 80 Ill. Dec. 810, 466 N.E.2d 262 (5 Dist. 1984).

Where husband's monthly expenses were $1150 and his monthly maintenance payment was $900, husband would spend $24,000 per year, which was $2,900 less than his net income; the order of the trial court awarding $900 per month unallocated maintenance was not contrary to the manifest weight of the evidence. In re Murphy, 117 Ill. App. 3d 649, 72 Ill. Dec. 808, 453 N.E.2d 113 (3 Dist. 1983).

Where the amount of the maintenance and support awarded was approximately 20% of the husband's receipts for one year, the trial court did not abuse its discretion. In re Dwan, 108 Ill. App. 3d 808, 64 Ill. Dec. 340, 439 N.E.2d 1005 (1 Dist. 1982).

Where petitioner's greatest gross hourly wage was $3.25, she was granted custody of her ten-year-old daughter, who had emotional problems requiring professional assistance, and petitioner would have to manage a rental property and serve in an elected office, an award of maintenance to supplement the income from two part-

Illustrative Cases (Cont'd)
time jobs was appropriate. In re Smith, 105 Ill. App. 3d 980, 61 Ill. Dec. 554, 434 N.E.2d 1151 (3 Dist. 1982).

Where the trial court, in determining the amount and duration of maintenance in a marital dissolution case, did not consider such factors as the financial resources of both parties, the duration of the marriage, the age of the parties, and the standard of living established during the marriage, remand for reconsideration was necessary. In re Pieper, 79 Ill. App. 3d 835, 34 Ill. Dec. 877, 398 N.E.2d 868 (1 Dist. 1979).

Record fully supported the judgment of the circuit court on the issue of fault, and the decree dismissing plaintiff's complaint and granting defendant's petition for divorce was correct. Carterfield v. Carterfield, 39 Ill. App. 3d 525, 350 N.E.2d 491 (3 Dist. 1976).

Record supported the circuit court's determination that plaintiff established no special equities in any property vested in defendant's sole name, all of which he inherited from his ancestors. Carterfield v. Carterfield, 39 Ill. App. 3d 525, 350 N.E.2d 491 (3 Dist. 1976).

Considering the nature of the misconduct, the length of time the parties lived together, their present ages, and relative conditions of health and wealth, the award of alimony (now maintenance) to plaintiff in the amount of $150 per month, with the assessment of plaintiff's attorney fees against defendant, was justified and within the range of what the proof equitably supported. Carterfield v. Carterfield, 39 Ill. App. 3d 525, 350 N.E.2d 491 (3 Dist. 1976).

Monthly alimony (now maintenance) payments of $1,000 were sufficient for plaintiff's needs. Leone v. Leone, 39 Ill. App. 3d 547, 350 N.E.2d 545 (3 Dist. 1976).

Impairment of Capital

The spouse seeking maintenance is not required to sell assets or impair her capital in order to generate income from which she can support herself in the manner enjoyed during the marriage. In re Landfield, 209 Ill. App. 3d 678, 153 Ill. Dec. 834, 567 N.E.2d 1061 (1 Dist.), cert. denied, 139 Ill. 2d 597, 159 Ill. Dec. 109, 575 N.E.2d 916 (1991).

Income

—In General

It is the income producible by the property, rather than its value, which is to be considered regarding an award of maintenance. In re Gentry, 188 Ill. App. 3d 372, 135 Ill. Dec. 939, 544 N.E.2d 435 (3 Dist. 1989).

—Averaging Method

Maintenance payments based on a single year's income or an average of several year's income present problems and inherent inequities where the payor spouse's income fluctuates from year to year. In re Carpenter, 286 Ill. App. 3d 969, 222 Ill. Dec. 260, 677 N.E.2d 463 (5 Dist. 1997).

Where the data used by the trial court to determine husband's 1991 income extended back only three years, and there was no dispute as to the reliability of the income data for those years and, in addition, his income fluctuated from year to year depending upon the profitability of the family business, the averaging method was a reasonable means of determining his current income. In re Elies, 248 Ill. App. 3d 1052, 188 Ill. Dec. 364, 618 N.E.2d 934 (1 Dist. 1993).

—Definition

It was not error for the trial court to define "income" as all income from any source in the form of money or property that became available to the respondent for his support, including, but not limited to, salary, wages, interest, distributions of corporate income, capital gains and income tax refunds, state and federal, or to define "net income" as income less taxes. In re Stegbauer, 84 Ill. App. 3d 83, 39 Ill. Dec. 549, 404 N.E.2d 1140 (4 Dist. 1980).

—Disparity

Petitioner was entitled to maintenance where there was a great disparity in the incomes of the parties and petitioner was clearly unable to support herself at a level consistent with the standard of living established during the marriage. In re Brenner, 95 Ill. App. 3d 100, 50 Ill. Dec. 292, 419 N.E.2d 400 (1 Dist. 1981).

In Gross

—In General

The effect of subsection (b) of this section is merely to authorize the trial judge to award maintenance in gross if he finds it to be appropriate in a particular case. In re Freeman, 106 Ill. 2d 290, 88 Ill. Dec. 11, 478 N.E.2d 326 (1985).

To sustain an award of alimony (now maintenance) in gross, the recipient spouse must be entitled to alimony and the award must be equitable; whether the award is equitable is resolved by a determination that special circumstances exist which require a departure from the usual and preferred practice of awarding a deserving spouse periodic alimony. McArdle v. McArdle, 55 Ill. App. 3d 829, 13 Ill. Dec. 282, 370 N.E.2d 1309 (3 Dist. 1977).

An award of alimony (now maintenance) in gross is proper where circumstances indicate that periodic alimony would not be feasible, such as where an award of alimony in gross will lead to a final settlement between the parties and eliminate financial bickering and ill-will. Harambasic v. Harambasic, 55 Ill. App. 3d 648, 13 Ill. Dec. 224, 370 N.E.2d 1251 (1 Dist. 1977).

—Cash Value

Former Ill.Rev.Stat., ch. 40, para. 19 (see now this section) stated that the court should enter an order concerning alimony (now maintenance) which fit the circumstances and which the court deemed equitable; the statute did not require that alimony in gross be reduced to its present cash value. Hall v. Hall, 43 Ill. App. 3d 97, 1 Ill. Dec. 874, 356 N.E.2d 1156 (4 Dist. 1976).

—Defined

The phrase "maintenance in gross" is defined as a non-modifiable sum certain to be received by the former spouse regardless of changes in circumstances. In re Freeman, 106 Ill. 2d 290, 88 Ill. Dec. 11, 478 N.E.2d 326 (1985).

—Held Inequitable

Under former section 18 of the Divorce Act (see now this section), trial court's award of alimony (now maintenance) in gross was inequitable and periodic alimony should have been awarded. Green v. Green, 41 Ill. App. 3d 154, 354 N.E.2d 661 (1 Dist. 1976).

—Lump Sum

The record did not support a finding of abuse of discretion on the part of the court in ordering periodic payments rather than alimony (now maintenance) in gross. Musgrave v. Musgrave, 38 Ill. App. 3d 532, 347 N.E.2d 831 (5 Dist. 1976).

—Not Modifiable

"Maintenance in gross" could not be changed by a court due to a change in circumstance. In re Davis, 124 Ill. App. 3d 1088, 80 Ill. Dec. 364, 465 N.E.2d 155 (3 Dist. 1984), modified on other grounds, 106 Ill. 2d 290, 88 Ill. Dec. 11, 478 N.E.2d 326 (1985).

Petitioner was correct in her assertion that maintenance in gross awarded under this section was equivalent to an award of non-modifiable alimony in gross. In re Davis, 124 Ill. App. 3d 1088, 80 Ill. Dec. 364, 465 N.E.2d 155 (3 Dist. 1984), modified on other grounds, 106 Ill. 2d 290, 88 Ill. Dec. 11, 478 N.E.2d 326 (1985).

Maintenance payments characterized as alimony in gross, as opposed to periodic maintenance, cannot be judicially modified. Pacione v. Pacione, 81 Ill. App. 3d 600, 37 Ill. Dec. 426, 402 N.E.2d 316 (3 Dist. 1980).

—Proper

There was no error in the court's decision to award wife "maintenance in gross" payable periodically and in the amount as specified. Schlosser v. Schlosser, 241 Ill. App. 3d 49, 181 Ill. Dec. 496, 608 N.E.2d 569 (3 Dist. 1993).

Insurance

Trial court abused its discretion when it ordered husband to provide health insurance for only two years for wife diagnosed with myotonic dystrophy; since it is possible that wife will be unable to obtain any health insurance coverage at the end of the two years, the court must review the cost and the parties' ability to obtain health insurance prior to the end of the two year period. Chapman v. Chapman, 285 Ill. App. 3d 377, 220 Ill. Dec. 889, 674 N.E.2d 432 (3 Dist. 1996).

Joint and Several Obligations

The financial responsibility for the support of the children of divorced parents is the joint and several obligation of each parent, and the amount to be assessed against each parent shall be

Joint and Several Obligations (Cont'd)
determined by the facts and circumstances of each case. Hursh v. Hursh, 26 Ill. App. 3d 947, 326 N.E.2d 95 (1 Dist. 1975).

Jurisdiction

—In General
Where no real provision was made to monitor spouse's efforts to find suitable employment, it was necessary and appropriate that the trial court retain jurisdiction of the maintenance award. In re Gentry, 188 Ill. App. 3d 372, 135 Ill. Dec. 939, 544 N.E.2d 435 (3 Dist. 1989).

In general, once either party has filed a notice of appeal from the judgment of the trial court, the trial court loses jurisdiction over the case, but subsection (c) of this section provides a limited exception to that rule: the trial court may order maintenance after the filing of the notice of appeal in a proceeding for dissolution of marriage, but in that case it may award maintenance only to a party against whom the appeal is prosecuted. In re Flosman, 160 Ill. App. 3d 832, 513 N.E.2d 879 (1 Dist. 1987).

Where the trial court ordered maintenance when it clearly had jurisdiction to make the award before the notice of appeal was filed, subsection (c) of this section was irrelevant to the proceedings, and the award of maintenance was proper under this section. In re Flosman, 160 Ill. App. 3d 832, 513 N.E.2d 879 (1 Dist. 1987).

The trial court did not lack jurisdiction to award equitable maintenance because respondent did not file a petition and an affidavit requesting it. In re Di Angelo, 159 Ill. App. 3d 293, 111 Ill. Dec. 394, 512 N.E.2d 783 (2 Dist. 1987).

The filing of a written petition and an affidavit are not necessary to the trial court's jurisdiction to award equitable maintenance pending appeal. In re Di Angelo, 159 Ill. App. 3d 293, 111 Ill. Dec. 394, 512 N.E.2d 783 (2 Dist. 1987).

Because of maintenance and because there was no basis for reserved jurisdiction, the question of maintenance was properly before the trial court which was vested with subject matter jurisdiction. In re Popovich, 149 Ill. App. 3d 643, 103 Ill. Dec. 38, 500 N.E.2d 1109 (4 Dist. 1986).

Even though there was no subject matter jurisdiction based on divorce decree entered in Cuba for child support by grant of statute, jurisdiction existed in the common law under the plenary jurisdiction of courts of equity over the persons and estates of minors and under the provisions of the Illinois Constitution of 1870, in effect at the commencement of the original action in 1970. Zalduendo v. Zalduendo, 45 Ill. App. 3d 849, 4 Ill. Dec. 450, 360 N.E.2d 386 (1 Dist. 1977).

For a case discussing jurisdiction to award alimony (now maintenance) over nonresident plaintiff, see Killebrew v. Killebrew, 398 Ill. 432, 75 N.E.2d 855 (1947).

—Death of Wife
The death of wife prior to a final decree in a separate maintenance action did not abate the action to the extent that the trial court had no jurisdiction to order additional attorney fees and expenses incurred during her lifetime under former Ill.Rev.Stat., ch. 68, para. 22, (see now this section). Spiro v. Spiro, 124 Ill. App. 2d 254, 260 N.E.2d 332 (1 Dist. 1970).

—Respondent Failure to Plead
The failure of respondent to plead did not divest the trial court of its statutory jurisdiction to award maintenance where the issue was raised in the petition for dissolution, the parties were properly before the court, and an evidentiary hearing was conducted on the matter. In re Hochleutner, 260 Ill. App. 3d 684, 198 Ill. Dec. 702, 633 N.E.2d 164 (2 Dist. 1994).

Jury Trial
Where plaintiff wife acknowledged the validity of a prior Arkansas divorce decree, and her complaint was concerned solely with alimony (now maintenance), property division, and attorney fees, defendant husband had no common-law right to a jury trial; such actions were traditionally chancery actions, and the right arose only if it was expressly conferred by statute. Sidwell v. Sidwell, 28 Ill. App. 3d 580, 328 N.E.2d 595 (4 Dist. 1975).

Legislative Intent
This Act intends that postmarital support be accomplished through a just distribution of marital assets wherever possible, rather than maintenance. Flynn v. Flynn, 232 Ill. App. 3d 394, 173 Ill. Dec. 735, 597 N.E.2d 709 (1 Dist.), cert. denied, 146 Ill. 2d 626, 176 Ill. Dec. 813, 602 N.E.2d 451 (1992).

Maintenance is designed to be rehabilitative in nature and to allow a dependent spouse to become financially independent. Haas v. Haas, 215 Ill. App. 3d 959, 158 Ill. Dec. 983, 574 N.E.2d 1376 (3 Dist. 1991).

The legislature intended to encourage the courts to provide for the financial needs of the spouses by property distribution rather than by an award of maintenance. In re Aud, 142 Ill. App. 3d 320, 96 Ill. Dec. 615, 491 N.E.2d 894 (5 Dist. 1986).

The statute read as a whole indicates the desire of the legislature that awards of maintenance be based solely upon the perceived need of the spouse and not in lieu of marital property. In re Donovan, 122 Ill. App. 3d 803, 78 Ill. Dec. 293, 462 N.E.2d 9 (4 Dist. 1984).

When subsection (c) of 750 ILCS 5/503 and this section are considered together, it is apparent that the legislature intended to enlarge greatly the discretion of courts in providing for just and equitable property settlements and maintenance awards; if the court gives proper regard to the factors the legislature has provided, the court may award either property or maintenance, or may award both property and maintenance, and also may award property in lieu of maintenance. In re Gan, 83 Ill. App. 3d 265, 38 Ill. Dec. 882, 404 N.E.2d 306 (5 Dist. 1980).

Length of Marriage
Trial court's order barring wife from receiving maintenance was an abuse of discretion; court placed too much emphasis on the short duration of the marriage and did not adequately consider wife's physical condition (diagnosed with myotonic dystrophy) and her present and future earning capacity. Chapman v. Chapman, 285 Ill. App. 3d 377, 220 Ill. Dec. 889, 674 N.E.2d 432 (3 Dist. 1996).

Liens
For a case discussing the payment of alimony (now maintenance) becoming a lien on the realty of the person against whom it is entered, see Enoch v. Walter, 209 Ill. App. 619 (1 Dist. 1918); Masters v. Masters, 249 Ill. App. 252 (3 Dist. 1928).

Life Insurance Policy

—Wife as Beneficiary
Trial court's requirement that husband keep wife as a beneficiary on his life insurance policy was not prohibited by the Marriage and Dissolution of Marriage Act. In re Vernon, 253 Ill. App. 3d 783, 192 Ill. Dec. 668, 625 N.E.2d 823 (4 Dist. 1993).

Life Insurance Proceeds

—Constructive Trust
Divorce decree requiring the former husband to retain his former wife as the beneficiary of his life insurance policy for the benefit of their children gave rise to a constructive trust on the proceeds of a second, subsequently executed, life insurance policy when the former husband allowed the first insurance policy to lapse and named a different beneficiary to the second policy, although obligation to maintain the former wife as beneficiary for the children arose as a part of a divorce decree and not a marital settlement agreement. Perkins v. Stuemke, 223 Ill. App. 3d 839, 166 Ill. Dec. 103, 585 N.E.2d 1125 (4 Dist. 1992).

Lifestyle
The resources of the parties dictate whether they can maintain their lifestyle after dissolution. In re Mantei, 222 Ill. App. 3d 933, 164 Ill. Dec. 870, 583 N.E.2d 1192 (4 Dist. 1991).

Limit on Duration
The limitations on maintenance awards serve the purpose of encouraging the recipient spouse to use diligence in procuring self-sufficiency. Kusper v. Kusper, 195 Ill. App. 3d 494, 142 Ill. Dec. 282, 552 N.E.2d 1023 (1 Dist. 1990).

The purpose of granting the trial court the discretion to authorize rehabilitative or time limited maintenance is to provide incentive for the spouse receiving support to use diligence in procuring training or skills necessary to attain self-sufficiency. In re Albiani, 159 Ill. App. 3d 519, 111 Ill. Dec. 126, 512 N.E.2d 30 (1 Dist. 1987); In re Wolf, 180 Ill. App. 3d 998, 129 Ill. Dec. 742, 536 N.E.2d 792 (1

Limit on Duration (Cont'd)
Dist. 1989); In re Jones, 187 Ill. App. 3d 206, 134 Ill. Dec. 836, 543 N.E.2d 119 (1 Dist. 1989).

A limit on the duration of the alimony (now maintenance) period was inappropriate where it appeared that the limit was based on speculation as to the future condition of the parties, specifically, that wife's employment income would be sufficient to support her needs. In re Bramson, 100 Ill. App. 3d 657, 56 Ill. Dec. 205, 427 N.E.2d 285 (1 Dist. 1981).

Liquidation of Assets
It is not necessary that a person sell assets or impair capital when the other spouse has sufficient income to meet his needs and make a contribution to hers. In re Gentry, 188 Ill. App. 3d 372, 135 Ill. Dec. 939, 544 N.E.2d 435 (3 Dist. 1989).

Maintenance Determination
To deny petitioner maintenance while allotting her in excess of one million dollars was not an abuse of discretion. In re Andrew, 258 Ill. App. 3d 924, 194 Ill. Dec. 724, 628 N.E.2d 221 (1 Dist. 1993).

Where petitioner had limited income, but respondent had no income and poor prospects for employment, the court was justified in not accepting petitioner's estimate as to the amount of his own expenses, and did not abuse its discretion in awarding respondent maintenance. In re Peoples, 96 Ill. App. 3d 94, 51 Ill. Dec. 514, 420 N.E.2d 1072 (5 Dist. 1981).

The parties enjoyed a modest but comfortable standard of living; they lived in a series of homes which they owned and accumulated significant assets, considering their income; at the time of hearing, respondent had no earnings and no individual assets, income producing or otherwise; and her ability to support herself through appropriate employment was dubious for lack of skills and good health; the court abused its discretion in denying respondent maintenance. In re Rimmele, 102 Ill. App. 3d 88, 57 Ill. Dec. 762, 429 N.E.2d 879 (3 Dist. 1981).

Marital Misconduct
An award of maintenance based upon marital misconduct would be improper. In re Drennan, 93 Ill. App. 3d 903, 49 Ill. Dec. 386, 418 N.E.2d 30 (4 Dist. 1981).

Issues concerning the final property disposition must be determined prior to the maintenance issues because the issues of maintenance relate directly to the results of the property disposition; once the property issues are determined, the maintenance award must then be reviewed on the whole record. In re Thornton, 89 Ill. App. 3d 1078, 45 Ill. Dec. 612, 412 N.E.2d 1336 (1 Dist. 1980).

Modification

—In General
As with an initial award, a modification of support or maintenance rests within the sound discretion of the trial court, whose decisions in these matters will not be reversed in the absence of an abuse of discretion. In re Lyons, 155 Ill. App. 3d 300, 108 Ill. Dec. 297, 508 N.E.2d 458 (2 Dist. 1987).

For cases discussing modification of an alimony (now maintenance) award, see Cole v. Cole, 142 Ill. 19, 31 N.E. 109 (1892); Craig v. Craig, 163 Ill. 176, 45 N.E. 153 (1896); Smith v. Johnson, 236 Ill. App. 339 (1 Dist. 1925), aff'd, 321 Ill. 134, 151 N.E. 550 (1926); Herrick v. Herrick, 319 Ill. 146, 149 N.E. 820 (1925); McGrath v. Dunne, 363 Ill. 549, 2 N.E.2d 895 (1936); De la Cour v. De la Cour, 363 Ill. 545, 2 N.E.2d 896 (1936); Wiseman v. Wiseman, 290 Ill. App. 535, 8 N.E.2d 960 (4 Dist. 1937); Igney v. Igney, 303 Ill. App. 563, 25 N.E.2d 608 (1 Dist. 1940); Arnold v. Arnold, 332 Ill. App. 586, 76 N.E.2d 335 (1 Dist. 1947); San Fillippo v. San Fillippo, 340 Ill. App. 353, 92 N.E.2d 201 (1 Dist. 1950); Marriott v. Marriott, 347 Ill. App. 372, 106 N.E.2d 876 (1 Dist. 1952); Pokorney v. Pokorney, 348 Ill. App. 364, 109 N.E.2d 254 (1 Dist. 1952); Pearlman v. Pearlman, 131 Ill. App. 2d 388, 266 N.E.2d 388 (1 Dist. 1970); Glassmeyer v. Glassmeyer, 131 Ill. App. 2d 419, 268 N.E.2d 251 (1 Dist. 1971); Booth v. Booth, 6 Ill. App. 3d 62, 284 N.E.2d 506 (1 Dist. 1972); Bowman v. Bowman, 11 Ill. App. 3d 719, 298 N.E.2d 339 (1 Dist. 1973); Borowitz v. Borowitz, 19 Ill. App. 3d 176, 311 N.E.2d 292 (1 Dist. 1974); Tuey v. Tuey, 20 Ill. App. 3d 445, 314 N.E.2d 371 (1 Dist. 1974); Lane v. Lane, 35 Ill. App. 3d 276, 340 N.E.2d 705 (1 Dist. 1976); Gorman v. Gorman, 72 Ill. App. 3d 658, 28 Ill. Dec. 871, 391 N.E.2d 70 (1 Dist. 1979).

—Agreement
Where parties' agreement awarded wife a lump sum payment representing her interest in marital property, and provided for monthly payments of $400 for five years, which was designated as maintenance, and the parties agreed to prohibit any increase in the payments, yet were silent as to a possible decrease, the agreement created a periodic maintenance payment subject to modification. Olson v. Olson, 114 Ill. App. 3d 28, 69 Ill. Dec. 769, 448 N.E.2d 229 (3 Dist. 1983).

—Burden of Proof
The burden of showing changed circumstances is on the party seeking the modification; where there was no showing at all on the part of petitioner as to his disposable income after taxes, either at the time of the original judgment or at the hearing on modification, he failed to meet his burden of proof in the matter. Thomas v. Thomas, 18 Ill. App. 3d 673, 310 N.E.2d 432 (3 Dist. 1974).

—Considered on Remand
Any change in the distribution of marital property necessarily requires a re-examination of the award of maintenance, and where appellate court remanded case for a division of property, trial court was also ordered to consider whether the new division of property required any change in its prior finding regarding the maintenance allowance. Schubert v. Schubert, 66 Ill. App. 3d 29, 22 Ill. Dec. 790, 383 N.E.2d 266 (3 Dist. 1978).

—Denied
Circuit court abused its discretion in denying former wife's petition to review and extend temporary maintenance award where, although she may not have begun her efforts toward financial independence as soon as she might have and the marriage was of short duration, she did not have sufficient resources to meet her financial obligations; the standard of living during the marriage was lavish, wife was in her late forties when the parties were divorced, she had worked only two years and eight months in her life, and had not, at former husband's request, worked during the marriage. Former wife also had physical and emotional problems which may have prevented her from seeking full time employment and husband had ability to pay maintenance. In re Martin, 223 Ill. App. 3d 855, 166 Ill. Dec. 136, 585 N.E.2d 1158 (4 Dist.), appeal denied, 145 Ill. 2d 635, 173 Ill. Dec. 6, 596 N.E.2d 630 (1992).

Where the parties' marriage lasted 12 years, during which time petitioner was employed as a teacher, where with only three years of college, she could not obtain a teaching position and where as of the date the petition was filed, respondent had supported her for seven years, the trial court was correct in refusing to modify or terminate maintenance. In re Ingrassia, 140 Ill. App. 3d 826, 95 Ill. Dec. 165, 489 N.E.2d 386 (2 Dist. 1986).

Although former husband's income increased since the original maintenance order, former wife had not established that she had "absolutely no income" or that her expenses had "greatly increased"; therefore, the trial court did not abuse its discretion in denying former wife's petition for an increase in maintenance. In re Lasota, 125 Ill. App. 3d 37, 80 Ill. Dec. 537, 465 N.E.2d 649 (1 Dist. 1984).

—Education or Training
Upon remand, petitioner may seek to have the court modify the automatic termination date, but she must first present the issue before the trial court and she must show that she has met the affirmative duty to acquire sufficient education or training to find employment. In re Robinson, 184 Ill. App. 3d 235, 132 Ill. Dec. 559, 539 N.E.2d 1365 (5 Dist. 1989).

—Factors Considered
The factors to be considered in making an award of maintenance under subsection (b) of this section are applicable to modification proceedings under subsection (a) of 750 ILCS 5/510. In re Martin, 223 Ill. App. 3d 855, 166 Ill. Dec. 136, 585 N.E.2d 1158 (4 Dist.), appeal denied, 145 Ill. 2d 635, 173 Ill. Dec. 6, 596 N.E.2d 630 (1992).

In determining whether and to what degree a maintenance award shall be modified, the circuit court should consider the same factors which, under the statute, are to be assessed in making the initial award. In re Lasota, 125 Ill. App. 3d 37, 80 Ill. Dec. 537, 465 N.E.2d 649 (1 Dist. 1984); Faris v. Faris, 142 Ill. App. 3d 987, 97 Ill.

Modification (Cont'd)

—Factors Considered (Cont'd)
Dec. 209, 492 N.E.2d 645 (2 Dist. 1986), appeal denied, 100 Ill. Dec. 603, 497 N.E.2d 781 (Ill. 1986).

For increased alimony (now maintenance) and child support to be warranted, the law requires only that there has been an increase in the needs of the children and the custodial parent since the time of the prior award of alimony and support, and an increase in the other parent's ability to pay. Sullivan v. Sullivan, 57 Ill. App. 3d 958, 15 Ill. Dec. 483, 373 N.E.2d 829 (3 Dist. 1978).

When making a change in alimony (now maintenance), the court would take into consideration the property and income of the parties, their ages, health, and social conditions, and whether there were children dependent upon them for support. Jacobs v. Jacobs, 328 Ill. App. 133, 65 N.E.2d 588 (1 Dist. 1946).

—Failure to Rehabilitate
Although the recipient of maintenance had an affirmative duty to rehabilitate herself pursuant to this section, where agreement entered into between the parties precluded petitioner from seeking modification of maintenance on grounds of rehabilitation, petitioner was not entitled to modification or termination of maintenance payments on the grounds that respondent had failed to rehabilitate and support herself. In re McFarlane, 160 Ill. App. 3d 721, 112 Ill. Dec. 537, 513 N.E.2d 1146 (2 Dist. 1987).

—Improper
Where wife's testimony concerning her assets, liabilities, investments, expenses, job search, and educational plans included many vague and unclear, contradictory answers; she invested in a rental home but had collected no rent; she purchased carpet costing more than $7,000 and a ring costing $17,000, but was delinquent in such important expenses as real estate taxes and health insurance; she began her unsuccessful job search in 1987 but did not enroll in college until 1990, and then attended on a part-time basis for three out of four terms, the trial court did not abuse its discretion in concluding that she had managed her income and assets in an improvident manner and that she was not diligent in seeking employment or further education, therefore, the reduction in maintenance was not error. Clark v. Clark, 237 Ill. App. 3d 492, 178 Ill. Dec. 483, 604 N.E.2d 1006 (3 Dist. 1992).

—Maintenance in Gross
750 ILCS 5/510 makes a maintenance award subject to divestment or modification upon a showing of a substantial change in circumstances, taking into consideration the enumerated factors in this section; however, such provisions do not contemplate the court being deprived of the authority to award maintenance in gross when special circumstances dictate the propriety of such an award. In re Preston, 81 Ill. App. 3d 672, 37 Ill. Dec. 442, 402 N.E.2d 332 (5 Dist. 1980).

—Not Precluded
The specific reasons for termination set forth in an ancillary order did render the maintenance award nonmodifiable. In re Scott, 205 Ill. App. 3d 561, 150 Ill. Dec. 868, 563 N.E.2d 995 (4 Dist. 1990).

—Reduction in Income
Trial court did not abuse its discretion in terminating the maintenance payments where obligor spouse presented an adequate amount of evidence to show that his income was reduced to approximately one-tenth of what it was at the time of the initial award of maintenance. In re Gallagher, 256 Ill. App. 3d 439, 194 Ill. Dec. 892, 628 N.E.2d 389 (1 Dist. 1993).

—Review
An award of permanent maintenance in a dissolution proceeding containing no provision for modification review was deemed an abuse of discretion by the trial judge. In re Girrulat, 219 Ill. App. 3d 164, 161 Ill. Dec. 734, 578 N.E.2d 1380 (5 Dist. 1991).

—Spouse's Needs
A maintenance award can be modified either when the needs of the spouse receiving it change or the ability of the other spouse to pay changes. In re Lasota, 125 Ill. App. 3d 37, 80 Ill. Dec. 537, 465 N.E.2d 649 (1 Dist. 1984).

—Sufficient Cause
In an application for modification or termination of support, the only inquiry should be whether sufficient cause has intervened since the entry of the decree to authorize the court to change the allowance. Borowitz v. Borowitz, 19 Ill. App. 3d 176, 311 N.E.2d 292 (1 Dist. 1974).

—Unrelated Factors
Nothing in this section or 755 ILCS 5/510 authorizes or permits the consideration of the fact that ex-wife was overweight and continued to smoke in the consideration of modification of maintenance; the existence of these "factors" was none of the trial court's business. In re Offer, 275 Ill. App. 3d 986, 212 Ill. Dec. 493, 657 N.E.2d 694 (4 Dist. 1995).

Items which should not have been considered in determining whether husband's expenses justified a reduction in spousal maintenance included: entire cost of maintenance of condominium occupied by husband and his financially independent second wife, his voluntary undertaking of mortgage payments on his father's home, and debt owed to his second wife for payment of his own income tax obligations. In re Rushing, 258 Ill. App. 3d 1057, 194 Ill. Dec. 748, 628 N.E.2d 245 (1 Dist. 1993), appeal denied, 155 Ill. 2d 576, 198 Ill. Dec. 552, 633 N.E.2d 14 (1994).

—Unwarranted
Where plaintiff failed to establish an increase in the needs of her children, no material change in circumstances existed which warranted an increase in defendant's child support obligation. Liss v. Liss, 62 Ill. App. 3d 170, 19 Ill. Dec. 545, 379 N.E.2d 60 (1 Dist. 1978).

Mortgage Payments
Where upon sale petitioner would receive a credit for all mortgage payments she had made following the dissolution judgment, the credit for mortgage payments did not amount to maintenance. In re Rizzo, 95 Ill. App. 3d 636, 51 Ill. Dec. 141, 420 N.E.2d 555 (1 Dist. 1981).

Needs of Parties
When the Act refers to needs of the spouse seeking maintenance, it does not necessarily mean minimum needs. In re Fields, 288 Ill. App. 3d 1053, 224 Ill. Dec. 184, 681 N.E.2d 166 (4 Dist. 1997), appeal denied, 174 Ill. 2d 559, 227 Ill. Dec. 4, 686 N.E.2d 1160 (1997), overruled on other grounds, Belleville Toyota, Inc. v. Toyota Motor Sales, U.S.A., Inc., 199 Ill. 2d 325, 264 Ill. Dec. 283, 770 N.E.2d 177 (2002).

Without the testimony of petitioner or other evidence presented to show specifically the resources and needs of petitioner in addition to the needs of the children, the trial court was unable to make a proper determination regarding whether maintenance should be awarded and what a reasonable award of maintenance would be; thus, the trial court abused its discretion by failing adequately to consider all relevant factors. Stern v. Stern, 179 Ill. App. 3d 313, 128 Ill. Dec. 351, 534 N.E.2d 533 (1 Dist. 1989).

The trial court's failure to make any finding as to financial needs required remand for the taking of the additional evidence and a new determination of the award of maintenance. In re Ryman, 172 Ill. App. 3d 599, 122 Ill. Dec. 646, 527 N.E.2d 18 (2 Dist. 1988).

It was error for the trial court to fail to obtain knowledge of petitioner's needs by hearing evidence of her living expenses prior to denying her request for maintenance. In re Rundle, 107 Ill. App. 3d 880, 63 Ill. Dec. 491, 438 N.E.2d 229 (5 Dist. 1982).

New Trial

—Denied
Given that this Act is geared towards a party's present ability to pay, and not future financial resources, a wife was unable to demonstrate that the trial court's disposition could be any different if the case were retried where the wife did not propose any evidence to show that her husband's financial condition was different than the evidence at trial indicated. In re DeGironemo, 206 Ill. App. 3d 1019, 151 Ill. Dec. 918, 565 N.E.2d 189 (1 Dist. 1990).

Oral Promise
Where petitioner argued that she was entitled to additional support from the respondent to enable her to complete the requirements for a Ph.D. in sociology because of an oral promise made by

Oral Promise (Cont'd)
the respondent prior to the marriage and reaffirmed during the marriage, as the petitioner had a satisfactory income from her present job and a substantial property settlement, the trial court's denial of maintenance was not contrary to the manifest weight of the evidence. In re Key, 71 Ill. App. 3d 722, 27 Ill. Dec. 732, 389 N.E.2d 963 (4 Dist. 1979).

Original Decree

—Effect of Collateral Matter
In suit by former wife to compel former husband to make support payments pursuant to agreement embodied in original divorce decree, trial court erred in directing husband to pay money to clerk of court to hold until wife released possessions of husband; original decree could not be impaired by collateral matter. King v. King, 290 Ill. App. 160, 8 N.E.2d 375 (1 Dist. 1937).

Partnership Property
Where a husband's share of his partnership's profits was slightly more than $27,000, this was his personal property; he paid taxes on it, he could have assigned his right to receive it, and therefore, it was proper to base an alimony (now maintenance) award upon it. Sahs v. Sahs, 48 Ill. App. 3d 610, 6 Ill. Dec. 627, 363 N.E.2d 156 (2 Dist. 1977).

Pensions and Stocks
The plain language of subsection (b) of this section made clear that the circuit court properly considered respondent's pension and stock dividend income, even though they were awarded as part of a property award, in ruling on his petition to modify because this income bore directly on respondent's ability to meet his needs while also meeting the needs of petitioner. In re Bryant, 206 Ill. App. 3d 167, 150 Ill. Dec. 707, 563 N.E.2d 834 (1 Dist. 1990).

Periodic Payments
Where in a divorce proceeding the former husband was a professional man who worked hard and payed his bills, there was no showing that defendant was regularly intoxicated or that his occupation was so hazardous that his income was jeopardized or that his future income was speculative, bitterness between the parties was not significant, former wife had already received $13,000 as her part of the equity in the house, and former husband had made a good faith effort to assume the financial responsibilities of the failed marriage, provisions for alimony (now maintenance) should have been in periodic form. Brandis v. Brandis, 51 Ill. App. 3d 467, 9 Ill. Dec. 728, 367 N.E.2d 162 (4 Dist. 1977).

Where former wife agreed to forego receiving periodic alimony (now maintenance) for an indefinite period of time and agreed to a certain lump sum settlement paid in installments, these was no reason to rescind this aspect of the stipulation or decree where no fraud had been pleaded or proven by former husband. Koivun v. Koivun, 45 Ill. App. 3d 39, 3 Ill. Dec. 805, 359 N.E.2d 215 (3 Dist. 1977).

It was well settled that if the court ordered a party to make periodic payments of alimony (now maintenance) to his or her ex-spouse, it could not also grant alimony in gross, such as requiring the conveyance of property from one to the other in lieu of alimony. Stotlar v. Stotlar, 50 Ill. App. 3d 790, 8 Ill. Dec. 711, 365 N.E.2d 1097 (5 Dist. 1977).

Periodic payments of alimony (now maintenance) were preferable to awards in gross. Seniuta v. Seniuta, 31 Ill. App. 3d 408, 334 N.E.2d 261 (1 Dist. 1975).

Under former Ill.Rev.Stat., ch. 40, para. 19 (see now this section), the court was authorized to order the husband or wife to pay to the other such sum of money or convey such real or personal property as the court may have deemed to be equitable; the authority granted in this section was not based upon special equities in the sense of ownership but rather was based upon the existence of special circumstances which led to the conclusion that periodic alimony, although judicially preferred, was inappropriate under the facts. Hall v. Hall, 18 Ill. App. 3d 583, 310 N.E.2d 186 (4 Dist. 1974).

Findings of the chancellor that an order for regular periodic payments for the support and maintenance of defendant would be both unworkable and unsatisfactory and that continued common ownership of property would lead to endless bickering and possible future litigation were fully supported by the evidence. Persico v. Persico, 409 Ill. 608, 100 N.E.2d 904 (1951).

Permanent Maintenance
The trial court should have awarded permanent, rather than rehabilitative, maintenance where the wife suffered from multiple sclerosis and was not employable and the husband was clearly able to pay permanent maintenance. Brackett v. Brackett, 309 Ill. App. 3d 329, 242 Ill. Dec. 798, 722 N.E.2d 287 (2 Dist. 1999).

Where it was unlikely that wife would be able to support herself in any reasonable approximation of the standard of living established during the marriage because of emotional problems and lack of education, the trial court abused its discretion in failing to order a permanent maintenance award. In re Carpenter, 286 Ill. App. 3d 969, 222 Ill. Dec. 260, 677 N.E.2d 463 (5 Dist. 1997).

While wife showed some need for permanent maintenance, court could reasonably conclude that husband simply did not have the financial resources to justify an award of permanent maintenance. In re Koberlein, 281 Ill. App. 3d 880, 217 Ill. Dec. 599, 667 N.E.2d 695 (4 Dist. 1996).

Permanent maintenance may be more appropriate than rehabilitative maintenance when the receiving spouse is not employable or is employable only at a low income when compared to the standard of living enjoyed during the marriage. In re Harlow, 251 Ill. App. 3d 152, 190 Ill. Dec. 476, 621 N.E.2d 929 (4 Dist. 1993), appeal denied, 154 Ill. 2d 559, 197 Ill. Dec. 486, 631 N.E.2d 708 (1994).

A request for permanent maintenance cannot be made for the first time on appeal. In re Harlow, 251 Ill. App. 3d 152, 190 Ill. Dec. 476, 621 N.E.2d 929 (4 Dist. 1993), appeal denied, 154 Ill. 2d 559, 197 Ill. Dec. 486, 631 N.E.2d 708 (1994).

Physical Condition of Parties
By seeking an equal division of the marital assets without maintenance, the husband's pleadings did not specifically or affirmatively place his health in issue. In re Bonneau, 294 Ill. App. 3d 720, 229 Ill. Dec. 187, 691 N.E.2d 123 (2 Dist. 1998), appeal denied, 178 Ill. 2d 574, 232 Ill. Dec. 845, 699 N.E.2d 1030 (1998).

It is incumbent upon a trial judge to take a spouse's physical condition into account as a significant factor in determining whether an award of maintenance is proper. Chapman v. Chapman, 285 Ill. App. 3d 377, 220 Ill. Dec. 889, 674 N.E.2d 432 (3 Dist. 1996).

The physical condition of the parties is but one of several factors under this section for the trial court to consider in establishing the amount and duration of maintenance and only after the trial court makes a finding that the spouse seeking maintenance is entitled to it. In re Pruitt, 101 Ill. App. 3d 755, 57 Ill. Dec. 182, 428 N.E.2d 732 (4 Dist. 1981).

Primary Means of Support
This Act contemplates that the property division will be the primary means of support and that maintenance will be awarded only if the property division is inadequate to provide for a spouse's need. In re Leon, 80 Ill. App. 3d 383, 35 Ill. Dec. 717, 399 N.E.2d 1006 (2 Dist. 1980); Hollensbe v. Hollensbe, 165 Ill. App. 3d 522, 116 Ill. Dec. 450, 519 N.E.2d 40 (5 Dist. 1988).

Prior Maintenance
Great weight should not be given to prior maintenance; the income of the former spouse could have been well above that of respondent. In re Mohr, 260 Ill. App. 3d 98, 197 Ill. Dec. 563, 631 N.E.2d 785 (4 Dist. 1994).

Property Disposition

—In General
The statutory scheme of this section requires that the issues concerning the final property disposition must be determined prior to the maintenance issues, because the issues of maintenance relate directly to the results of the property disposition. In re Douglas, 195 Ill. App. 3d 1053, 142 Ill. Dec. 605, 552 N.E.2d 1346 (5 Dist. 1990).

—Agreement of Parties
Under normal circumstances, a court does not have jurisdiction to dispose of property in a proceeding for legal separation except where property is submitted for disposition by agreement of the parties. In re Lipkin, 163 Ill. App. 3d 1033, 115 Ill. Dec. 76, 517 N.E.2d 41 (4 Dist. 1987).

Property Disposition (Cont'd)

—Agreement of Parties (Cont'd)

Where in a separate maintenance action both parties asked for adjudication of property rights, and introduced evidence in regard thereto, the court was held to have acted within its power in adjudicating these rights. Shapiro v. Shapiro, 113 Ill. App. 2d 374, 252 N.E.2d 93 (1 Dist. 1969).

—Court Authority

Generally, courts have no power to adjudicate property rights in a separate maintenance action. Shapiro v. Shapiro, 113 Ill. App. 2d 374, 252 N.E.2d 93 (1 Dist. 1969).

Ordinarily a trial court could not adjudicate the property rights of the parties in a separate maintenance action; however where both parties sought adjudication of their rights and the husband introduced evidence in regard to the rights of the parties to the property, the trial court properly adjudicated the rights of the parties as set forth in the decree. Ribergaard v. Ribergaard, 349 Ill. App. 99, 110 N.E.2d 89 (2 Dist. 1952).

—Factors Considered

Due consideration to all of the requisite factors, including petitioner's potential for employment, respondent's potential for employment, the division of property, and respondent's financial situation, was given. In re Kaplan, 149 Ill. App. 3d 23, 102 Ill. Dec. 719, 500 N.E.2d 612 (1 Dist. 1986).

—Maintenance Distinguished

While it may have been appropriate for the trial court to order former husband to pay a portion of the marital debt in dissolution proceeding, it was not appropriate to use maintenance as a vehicle to accomplish it; maintenance and property distribution are two separate concepts which cannot be interchanged. In re Lees, 224 Ill. App. 3d 691, 167 Ill. Dec. 135, 587 N.E.2d 17 (1992).

—Preferred

A larger property division, as opposed to maintenance, is the preferred method of reimbursing a spouse for such things as nonmonetary contributions and contributions of capital. In re Durante, 201 Ill. App. 3d 376, 147 Ill. Dec. 56, 559 N.E.2d 56 (1 Dist. 1990).

—Remand

Where the court made no express findings of fact in awarding maintenance, the property distribution was inequitable and the trial court had to reapportion the marital assets, and because the issue of maintenance is related to and dependent upon the distribution of marital property, it was to be reconsidered by the trial court. In re Scoville, 233 Ill. App. 3d 746, 174 Ill. Dec. 394, 598 N.E.2d 1026 (5 Dist. 1992).

Because issues of maintenance and child support relate directly to the final property disposition, which must be reached first, where a cause is remanded with specific instructions to take evidence establishing valuation and division of the parties' various assets, it follows that the award of maintenance must too be reversed. In re Cuisance, 115 Ill. App. 3d 551, 71 Ill. Dec. 423, 450 N.E.2d 1302 (1 Dist. 1983).

—Upheld

Where trial court divided property, giving husband property that couple bought for $30,000 and wife property that couple bought for $88,000 instead of alimony (now maintenance), and husband had to make one-quarter of payments on the mortgage and wife three-quarters, and wife had to repay amounts her father contributed, this was an equitable and fair adjustment of the property rights of the parties. Harambasic v. Harambasic, 55 Ill. App. 3d 648, 13 Ill. Dec. 224, 370 N.E.2d 1251 (1 Dist. 1977).

—When Considered

The trial court erred where it did not make a determination as to the distribution of assets and allocation of a one million dollar marital debt, because issues involving final property disposition must be determined before maintenance issues are settled. In re Douglas, 195 Ill. App. 3d 1053, 142 Ill. Dec. 605, 552 N.E.2d 1346 (5 Dist. 1990).

The issue of maintenance relates directly to the final property disposition, which must be considered first. In re Weiss, 129 Ill. App. 3d 166, 84 Ill. Dec. 378, 472 N.E.2d 128 (1 Dist. 1984).

Issues concerning the final property disposition must be determined prior to the maintenance issues because the issues of maintenance relate directly to the results of the property disposition; once the property issues are determined, the maintenance award must then be reviewed on the whole record. In re Thornton, 89 Ill. App. 3d 1078, 45 Ill. Dec. 612, 412 N.E.2d 1336 (1 Dist. 1980).

Property Rights

—Separate Action

Since a wife has the right to her separate property and may not be precluded from asserting this right in an appropriate action, she might properly join an action at law for her property as a separate count in a separate maintenance suit. Shapiro v. Shapiro, 113 Ill. App. 2d 374, 252 N.E.2d 93 (1 Dist. 1969).

Property Settlement

—Distinguished

Assignment of defendant's military pension income was alimony (now maintenance) and not a property settlement where the record disclosed that plaintiff received the marital home, the automobile, all of the household goods, equipment, furniture and appliances, and all of her personal belongings consisting of jewelry and wearing apparel; defendant was ordered to pay $30 per week child support and all reasonable and necessary hospital, medical and dental care for the minor children; defendant was required to pay all outstanding bills for necessary expenses incurred by the parties during their marriage; and all that defendant was awarded under the decree was such of his personal belongings then in his possession. Warren v. Warren, 88 Ill. App. 3d 543, 43 Ill. Dec. 782, 410 N.E.2d 915 (3 Dist. 1980).

It is not the label placed by decree upon payments which constitutes them either alimony (now maintenance) or lump sum property settlements; the elements inherent in the case as a whole, the record of which the decree is a part, determine to what category such payments belong. Warren v. Warren, 88 Ill. App. 3d 543, 43 Ill. Dec. 782, 410 N.E.2d 915 (3 Dist. 1980).

Property Value

Even if residential property were valued as proposed by wife, the amount of the maintenance award would not be affected since given husband's substantial assets and income, his ability to pay maintenance would not be substantially affected by increasing the assigned value of his non-marital assets by $75,000; therefore request that the value of this property be redetermined was rejected. In re Thornton, 89 Ill. App. 3d 1078, 45 Ill. Dec. 612, 412 N.E.2d 1336 (1 Dist. 1980).

Purpose

One objective of this Act is to encourage a formerly dependent spouse to become financially independent in the future, if possible. In re Sisul, 234 Ill. App. 3d 1038, 175 Ill. Dec. 463, 600 N.E.2d 86 (3 Dist. 1992).

The purpose of maintenance is to assist spouses in becoming financially independent by placing an affirmative duty on them to rehabilitate themselves. In re Silber, 176 Ill. App. 3d 853, 126 Ill. Dec. 283, 531 N.E.2d 910 (1 Dist. 1988).

This Act, whenever possible, seeks to cut off all entanglements between the parties so that they may each go their separate ways in life. At the same time, the Act was not meant to change the test for the propriety of maintenance by eliminating consideration of the style of living to which a spouse has become accustomed; reasonable needs are still to be measured by the standard of living the party seeking maintenance previously enjoyed. In re Simmons, 87 Ill. App. 3d 651, 42 Ill. Dec. 706, 409 N.E.2d 321 (1 Dist. 1980).

For cases discussing the policies and purposes of alimony, see Supp v. Wightman, 103 Ill. 150 (1882); Welty v. Welty, 195 Ill. 335, 63 N.E. 161 (1902); Gercke v. Gerke, 331 Ill. 413, 163 N.E. 323 (1928); Boylan v. Boylan, 349 Ill. 471, 182 N.E. 614 (1932); Byerly v. Byerly, 363 Ill. 517, 2 N.E.2d 898 (1936); Kohl v. Montgomery, 373 Ill. 200, 25 N.E.2d 826 (1940); Bush v. Bush, 316 Ill. App. 295, 44 N.E.2d 767 (3 Dist. 1942); Wadler v. Wadler, 325 Ill. App. 83, 59 N.E.2d 505 (1 Dist. 1945); Farris v. Kiriazis, 329 Ill. App. 225, 67 N.E.2d 701 (1 Dist. 1946); Hotzfield v. Hotzfield, 336 Ill. App. 238, 83 N.E.2d 605 (1 Dist. 1948); Rardin v. Rardin, 339 Ill. App. 68, 89 N.E.2d 67 (1 Dist. 1949); Walters v. Walters, 341 Ill. App. 561, 94 N.E.2d 726 (1 Dist. 1950), aff'd, 408 Ill. 298, 99 N.E.2d 342 (1951);

Purpose (Cont'd)
Bertram v. Bertram, 346 Ill. App. 314, 105 N.E.2d 515 (3 Dist. 1952); Stewart v. Stewart, 1 Ill. App. 2d 283, 117 N.E.2d 579 (4 Dist. 1954); Bramson v. Bramson, 17 Ill. App. 2d 87, 149 N.E.2d 399 (1 Dist. 1958); In re Fisher, 15 Ill. 2d 139, 153 N.E.2d 832 (1958); Fox v. Coyne, 25 Ill. App. 2d 352, 166 N.E.2d 474 (2 Dist. 1960); Blowitz v. Blowitz, 75 Ill. App. 2d 386, 221 N.E.2d 160 (1 Dist. 1966); Roberts v. Roberts, 90 Ill. App. 2d 184, 234 N.E.2d 372 (1 Dist. 1967); Fox v. Fox, 129 Ill. App. 2d 209, 262 N.E.2d 607 (4 Dist. 1970); Hager v. Hager, 1 Ill. App. 3d 1047, 274 N.E.2d 157 (4 Dist. 1971); Volid v. Volid, 6 Ill. App. 3d 386, 286 N.E.2d 42 (1 Dist. 1972); Duvall v. Duvall, 8 Ill. App. 3d 53, 289 N.E.2d 59 (3 Dist. 1972); Rattray v. Rattray, 43 Ill. App. 3d 853, 2 Ill. Dec. 534, 357 N.E.2d 701 (2 Dist. 1976); Stotlar v. Stotlar, 50 Ill. App. 3d 790, 8 Ill. Dec. 711, 365 N.E.2d 1097 (5 Dist. 1977); Olson v. Olson, 58 Ill. App. 3d 276, 15 Ill. Dec. 812, 374 N.E.2d 247 (3 Dist. 1978); Bellow v. Bellow, 94 Ill. App. 3d 361, 50 Ill. Dec. 656, 419 N.E.2d 924 (1 Dist. 1981); In re Hellwig, 100 Ill. App. 3d 452, 55 Ill. Dec. 762, 426 N.E.2d 1087 (1 Dist. 1981).

Realty Conveyance

—In General

A court could not award petitioner a restaurant and adjoining marital residence in lieu of maintenance where the record showed that petitioner had the ability to support herself and, therefore, was not entitled to maintenance. In re Banach, 140 Ill. App. 3d 327, 95 Ill. Dec. 142, 489 N.E.2d 363 (2 Dist. 1986).

For a case discussing alimony (now maintenance) and disposition of real estate under former Ill.Rev.Stat., ch. 40, paras. 18, 19 and 21, see Anderson v. Anderson, 380 Ill. 435, 44 N.E.2d 54 (1942).

—In Lieu of Maintenance

The trial court had ample basis for its division of the property where the former spouse was awarded an apartment building in lieu of permanent maintenance, and the order barred her from seeking maintenance in the future. In re Ligas, 110 Ill. App. 3d 1, 65 Ill. Dec. 763, 441 N.E.2d 1277 (1 Dist. 1982).

Trial court's actions were warranted in authorizing the conveyance of interests in real property in lieu of alimony (now maintenance) payments. Schade v. Schade, 45 Ill. App. 3d 455, 4 Ill. Dec. 232, 359 N.E.2d 1184 (4 Dist. 1977).

Reasonable Needs

Although reasonable needs are equated with the items that comprised the parties' lifestyles during the marriage, those needs are limited where the marriage was of a very short duration. In re Hughes, 160 Ill. App. 3d 680, 112 Ill. Dec. 594, 513 N.E.2d 1203 (5 Dist. 1987).

One benchmark of reasonable needs is whether an award is sufficient to maintain the spouse seeking maintenance in the standard of living established during the marriage. In re Rimmele, 102 Ill. App. 3d 88, 57 Ill. Dec. 762, 429 N.E.2d 879 (3 Dist. 1981).

Except where the financial situation of the paying spouse, the duration of the marriage, or the health of the parties otherwise indicates, this section requires that the amount of maintenance be sufficient to provide the spouse seeking maintenance with the standard of living established during the marriage; amount of maintenance is reduced by the amount the party seeking maintenance has available to provide herself with this standard of living. In re Thornton, 89 Ill. App. 3d 1078, 45 Ill. Dec. 612, 412 N.E.2d 1336 (1 Dist. 1980).

Maintenance is appropriate only if the income from petitioner's property (including marital property apportioned to her) is insufficient to provide for her reasonable needs and the petitioner is unable to support herself through appropriate employment or is otherwise without sufficient income. In re Simmons, 87 Ill. App. 3d 651, 42 Ill. Dec. 706, 409 N.E.2d 321 (1 Dist. 1980).

Reciprocal Spousal Support

Common law doctrines which impose a duty of support solely on the husband are inconsistent with the constitutional mandate and the statutory scheme recognizing equal rights and responsibilities, and are no longer valid. McGloon v. Zmigrocki, 191 Ill. App. 3d 968, 139 Ill. Dec. 53, 548 N.E.2d 438 (1 Dist. 1989).

Reconsideration

Where the trial court, in determining the amount and duration of maintenance in a marital dissolution case, did not consider such factors as the financial resources of both parties, the duration of the marriage, the age of the parties, and the standard of living established during the marriage, remand for reconsideration was necessary. In re Pieper, 79 Ill. App. 3d 835, 34 Ill. Dec. 877, 398 N.E.2d 868 (1 Dist. 1979).

Rehabilitative Maintenance

—In General

As used in connection with former subsection (b)(2) of this section (see now subsection (a)(5)), rehabilitative maintenance may be appropriate when the spouse's future employability would provide an approximately similar standard of living as enjoyed during the marriage; under the doctrine of rehabilitative maintenance, the court should consider the receiving spouse's present or future ability to become self-sufficient and should only consider the evidence presented, not mere speculation. In re Harlow, 251 Ill. App. 3d 152, 190 Ill. Dec. 476, 621 N.E.2d 929 (4 Dist. 1993), appeal denied, 154 Ill. 2d 559, 197 Ill. Dec. 486, 631 N.E.2d 708 (1994).

Trial court abused its discretion in ordering a 36-month limitation on rehabilitative maintenance where, although the receiving spouse did not have systematic lupus, she had a medical condition for which she was under a doctor's care, and where the record was speculative as to her future ability to support herself at the standard of living established during the marriage. In re Pearson, 236 Ill. App. 3d 337, 177 Ill. Dec. 650, 603 N.E.2d 720 (1 Dist. 1992).

The doctrine of rehabilitative maintenance requires the court to consider the extent to which the receiving spouse has either: (1) the present ability; or (2) the future ability to become self-sufficient; or (3) the future ability to acquire skills that would allow entry into the job market. In re Jones, 187 Ill. App. 3d 206, 134 Ill. Dec. 836, 543 N.E.2d 119 (1 Dist. 1989).

It is inherent in the concept of rehabilitative maintenance under this Act that the ex-spouse awarded maintenance is under an affirmative obligation to seek appropriate training and skills to become financially independent in the future. In re Henzler, 134 Ill. App. 3d 318, 89 Ill. Dec. 261, 480 N.E.2d 147, 480 N.E.2d 198 (4 Dist. 1985); In re Garelick, 168 Ill. App. 3d 321, 119 Ill. Dec. 76, 522 N.E.2d 738 (1 Dist. 1988); In re Jones, 187 Ill. App. 3d 206, 134 Ill. Dec. 836, 543 N.E.2d 119 (1 Dist. 1989).

Where the petitioner had come from being unemployed with no outside income at the time of the dissolution, to having completed her college education in accounting, and employment with earnings of $20,000 per year, respondent's petition for termination of maintenance payments should have been granted because the statutory goal of rehabilitative maintenance had been achieved. In re Henzler, 134 Ill. App. 3d 318, 89 Ill. Dec. 261, 480 N.E.2d 147, 480 N.E.2d 198 (4 Dist. 1985).

—Abuse of Discretion

A trial court abuses its discretion by awarding only rehabilitative maintenance when the facts clearly demonstrate that a spouse is unable to support herself in a manner similar to that established during the marriage. In re Harlow, 251 Ill. App. 3d 152, 190 Ill. Dec. 476, 621 N.E.2d 929 (4 Dist. 1993), appeal denied, 154 Ill. 2d 559, 197 Ill. Dec. 486, 631 N.E.2d 708 (1994).

Remarriage

An award of maintenance in gross is nonmodifiable, even if the recipient spouse remarries. Smith v. Smith, 150 Ill. App. 3d 34, 103 Ill. Dec. 785, 501 N.E.2d 1323 (3 Dist. 1986).

Maintenance in gross awarded the petitioner under this section was not subject to termination upon remarriage pursuant to 750 ILCS 5/510. In re Davis, 124 Ill. App. 3d 1088, 80 Ill. Dec. 364, 465 N.E.2d 155 (3 Dist. 1984), modified on other grounds, 106 Ill. 2d 290, 88 Ill. Dec. 11, 478 N.E.2d 326 (1985).

For cases discussing the effect of remarriage on alimony (now maintenance), see Banck v. Banck, 322 Ill. App. 369, 54 N.E.2d 577 (3 Dist. 1944); Drangle v. Lindauer, 323 Ill. App. 23, 54 N.E.2d 751 (1 Dist. 1944).

Reservation of Issues

The record need not reflect a formal motion by a party to reserve an issue nor a formal finding by the trial court that appropriate circumstances for reservation exist. In re Fahy, 208 Ill. App. 3d 677, 153 Ill. Dec. 594, 567 N.E.2d 552 (1 Dist. 1991).

Reservation of Issues (Cont'd)

A trial court is not required to make express findings consistent with the plain language of this section; rather, this section is satisfied as long as the record reveals a basis for the award. In re Fahy, 208 Ill. App. 3d 677, 153 Ill. Dec. 594, 567 N.E.2d 552 (1 Dist. 1991).

Where there was no question about the husband's ability to pay maintenance, the court was not seeking to monitor wife's future circumstances, and the wife had control over future consequences that would entitle her to maintenance, it was an abuse of discretion or a failure to exercise discretion to reserve the issue of maintenance for a five year period. In re Scafuri, 203 Ill. App. 3d 385, 149 Ill. Dec. 124, 561 N.E.2d 402 (2 Dist. 1990).

Although petitioner had recently secured a teaching position, where the trial court decided to reserve maintenance to allow her time to begin working and to become self-supporting after her long absence from the teaching profession, there was no error in the trial court's reservation of maintenance. In re Smith, 132 Ill. App. 3d 694, 88 Ill. Dec. 909, 479 N.E.2d 929 (1 Dist. 1985).

Where the court gave due consideration to all the relevant factors regarding the situations of the parties, including present and future potential for employment and further income, its reservation of maintenance upon entering a judgment of dissolution of marriage was permissible. In re Carini, 112 Ill. App. 3d 375, 67 Ill. Dec. 932, 445 N.E.2d 412 (1 Dist. 1983).

Reservation of Maintenance

—Upheld

The trial court did not abuse its discretion in reserving maintenance for wife for a limited time period in light of her tenuous employment situation, lack of insurance in the event of disability, restrictive medical insurance, and unsuccessful efforts to secure a better paying job. In re Cepek, 230 Ill. App. 3d 1045, 172 Ill. Dec. 852, 596 N.E.2d 131 (1 Dist. 1992).

Retirement Benefits

Petitioner was entitled to receive only a fractional share of respondent's retirement benefits based on settlement agreement but only when respondent began to receive his normal age related retirement benefits. Davis v. Davis, 286 Ill. App. 3d 1065, 222 Ill. Dec. 661, 678 N.E.2d 68 (3 Dist. 1997).

Sale of Assets

A spouse is not required to sell her assets or impair her capital in order to generate income from which she can support herself in the manner enjoyed during the marriage. Head v. Head, 168 Ill. App. 3d 697, 119 Ill. Dec. 549, 523 N.E.2d 17 (1 Dist. 1988); In re Emery, 179 Ill. App. 3d 744, 128 Ill. Dec. 569, 534 N.E.2d 1014 (4 Dist. 1989); In re Kerber, 215 Ill. App. 3d 248, 158 Ill. Dec. 717, 574 N.E.2d 830 (4 Dist. 1991).

Savings

Where maintenance recipient had approximately $6,000 in a savings account and had made practically no effort to find employment, she was not entitled to additional maintenance in order to reserve her savings. In re Einhorn, 178 Ill. App. 3d 212, 127 Ill. Dec. 411, 533 N.E.2d 29 (1 Dist. 1988).

Scope

This Act was not applicable in setting aside a property settlement on public policy grounds where the decree was entered prior to the effective date of the Act. Pierce v. Pierce, 69 Ill. App. 3d 42, 25 Ill. Dec. 511, 386 N.E.2d 1175 (5 Dist. 1979).

Security

Court can require defendant to give reasonable security when it enters a modification order. Robin v. Robin, 45 Ill. App. 3d 365, 3 Ill. Dec. 950, 359 N.E.2d 809 (1 Dist. 1977).

Self-Imposed Poverty

A spouse cannot use self-imposed poverty as a basis for claiming maintenance when she has the means of earning more income. In re Seymour, 206 Ill. App. 3d 506, 152 Ill. Dec. 27, 565 N.E.2d 269 (2 Dist. 1990).

Settlement Agreements

—Language in Preamble

Language in a settlement agreement purporting to settle the issue of alimony (now maintenance) "now and forever" was in the preamble to the operative provisions of the agreement, and therefore, did not obligate the parties. In re Pearson, 101 Ill. App. 3d 422, 57 Ill. Dec. 28, 428 N.E.2d 578 (1 Dist. 1981).

—Public Policy

Where a separation is imminent or has already occurred, an agreement making a fair and equitable provision for the separate support and maintenance of the wife and for a settlement of property rights is not against public policy. Rooks v. Plavec, 40 Ill. App. 2d 298, 188 N.E.2d 251 (1 Dist. 1963).

—Remarriage

An agreement between a husband and wife, made part of a California divorce, was a property settlement agreement, not an agreement for alimony (now maintenance); therefore, the remarriage of wife did not affect or terminate the installment payments of the agreement falling due subsequent to remarriage. Maybaum v. Maybaum, 349 Ill. App. 80, 110 N.E.2d 78 (1 Dist. 1952).

Share of Marital Property

It is not necessary for a spouse to consume his or her share of marital property before being entitled to maintenance. In re Coram, 86 Ill. App. 3d 845, 42 Ill. Dec. 40, 408 N.E.2d 418 (5 Dist. 1980).

Special Equities

Unless plaintiff established special equities in defendant's property, she was not entitled to both a lump sum settlement and periodic support payments. Mayeur v. Mayeur, 42 Ill. App. 3d 7, 355 N.E.2d 358 (3 Dist. 1976).

Spendable Income

Where the former husband derived income of approximately $150,000 from his medical practice and deducted approximately $87,000 in business expenses, including portions of the cost of 11 business trips, depreciation on his car, depreciation on that part of his dwelling which he used as an office, various "one-time-only" deductions, and a woman, with whom he lived, for some bookkeeping work, the trial court could reasonably have concluded that he had more spendable income than the $40,000 he claimed. In re Dwan, 108 Ill. App. 3d 808, 64 Ill. Dec. 340, 439 N.E.2d 1005 (1 Dist. 1982).

Spouse's Contribution

Where the spouse seeking maintenance can in part provide for herself, the amount of the maintenance award shall be determined by subtracting from the standard of living that amount which the spouse can contribute to her own support. In re Magnuson, 156 Ill. App. 3d 691, 109 Ill. Dec. 569, 510 N.E.2d 437 (2 Dist. 1987).

Spouse's Needs

Where property available to each spouse is sufficient to satisfy that spouse's needs and entitlements, the use of maintenance should be limited; however, if there is not sufficient marital property, maintenance should be considered. In re Flory, 171 Ill. App. 3d 822, 121 Ill. Dec. 701, 525 N.E.2d 1008 (1 Dist. 1988).

Spouse's Net Income

The spouse's net income is a factor to be considered in determining whether to grant maintenance. In re Kristie, 156 Ill. App. 3d 821, 109 Ill. Dec. 393, 510 N.E.2d 14 (1 Dist. 1987).

Standard of Living

The standard of living established during marriage does affect what constitutes "reasonable needs" under subdivision (a)(1); the trial court must balance the realistic ability of the spouse to support herself in some approximation of the standard of living enjoyed during their marriage against a goal of financial independence. In re Harlow, 251 Ill. App. 3d 152, 190 Ill. Dec. 476, 621 N.E.2d 929 (4 Dist. 1993), appeal denied, 154 Ill. 2d 559, 197 Ill. Dec. 486, 631 N.E.2d 708 (1994).

While this act may seek to terminate the financial entanglement of the parties, it does not eliminate the parties' standard of living established during their marriage as a factor in determining whether maintenance is appropriate. In re Harlow, 251 Ill. App. 3d 152, 190 Ill. Dec. 476, 621 N.E.2d 929 (4 Dist. 1993), appeal denied, 154 Ill. 2d 559, 197 Ill. Dec. 486, 631 N.E.2d 708 (1994).

The trial court can assess whether the spouse receiving maintenance will realistically be able to fully or partially support him or

Standard of Living (Cont'd)
herself through employment with the standard of living established during the marriage; the longer one is married without employment the more difficult it will be to obtain a marketable skill and assimilate back into the work force. In re Gunn, 233 Ill. App. 3d 165, 174 Ill. Dec. 381, 598 N.E.2d 1013 (5 Dist. 1992).

This section primarily concerns the standard of living established during the marriage in relation to the recipient spouse's ability to maintain that standard of living without maintenance. Haas v. Haas, 215 Ill. App. 3d 959, 158 Ill. Dec. 983, 574 N.E.2d 1376 (3 Dist. 1991).

Subsection (b) of this section requires that the amount of maintenance be sufficient to provide the spouse seeking maintenance with the standard of living established during the marriage. In re Magnuson, 156 Ill. App. 3d 691, 109 Ill. Dec. 569, 510 N.E.2d 437 (2 Dist. 1987).

Where the former spouse's standard of living was $28,000 per year and her assets were valued at $180,000, a permanent maintenance award of $1,200 per month was not against the manifest weight of the evidence. In re Magnuson, 156 Ill. App. 3d 691, 109 Ill. Dec. 569, 510 N.E.2d 437 (2 Dist. 1987).

Maintenance for a limited period is appropriate only where the spouse is employable at an income which would provide approximately the standard of living enjoyed during the marriage. In re Wilder, 122 Ill. App. 3d 338, 77 Ill. Dec. 824, 461 N.E.2d 447 (1 Dist. 1983).

A former spouse should not have been required to provide maintenance to permit his former wife to eat in restaurants instead of taking her meals in her own apartment simply because she preferred to do that when accommodating that preference substantially increased her food budget; she ate at home during the marriage and that she must now do so alone was but a necessary concomitant to the dissolution of her marriage. In re Simmons, 87 Ill. App. 3d 651, 42 Ill. Dec. 706, 409 N.E.2d 321 (1 Dist. 1980).

Standard of Review
A circuit court's decision on the matter of maintenance awards of limited duration will not be overturned on appeal unless the court's findings and conclusions were against the manifest weight of the evidence, thus showing an abuse of discretion. In re Sisul, 234 Ill. App. 3d 1038, 175 Ill. Dec. 463, 600 N.E.2d 86 (3 Dist. 1992).

The trial court has the discretion to set maintenance as it sees appropriate, and reviewing courts will not disturb its judgment absent an abuse of discretion. In re Patrick, 233 Ill. App. 3d 561, 174 Ill. Dec. 571, 599 N.E.2d 117 (4 Dist.), cert. denied, 147 Ill. 2d 629, 180 Ill. Dec. 151, 606 N.E.2d 1228 (1992).

To insist that every award of long-term maintenance be automatically reviewed does not take into account judicial economy or whether, under the unique circumstances of the parties, the facts of the case, and the standard of living achieved during the marriage, the spouse receiving maintenance could ever obtain the training or skills necessary to provide partial or full independence. In re Gunn, 233 Ill. App. 3d 165, 174 Ill. Dec. 381, 598 N.E.2d 1013 (5 Dist. 1992).

The award of maintenance resides within the sound discretion of the trial court and will not be disturbed on review unless it constitutes an abuse of discretion or is against the manifest weight of the evidence. In re De Bat, 127 Ill. App. 3d 463, 82 Ill. Dec. 568, 468 N.E.2d 1348 (1 Dist. 1984); In re Wright, 180 Ill. App. 3d 911, 129 Ill. Dec. 650, 536 N.E.2d 700 (1 Dist. 1986); In re Heller, 153 Ill. App. 3d 224, 106 Ill. Dec. 503, 505 N.E.2d 1294 (1 Dist. 1987); In re Einhorn, 178 Ill. App. 3d 212, 127 Ill. Dec. 411, 533 N.E.2d 29 (1 Dist. 1988); In re Wolf, 180 Ill. App. 3d 998, 129 Ill. Dec. 742, 536 N.E.2d 792 (1 Dist. 1989); In re Jones, 187 Ill. App. 3d 206, 134 Ill. Dec. 836, 543 N.E.2d 119 (1 Dist. 1989); In re Gentry, 188 Ill. App. 3d 372, 135 Ill. Dec. 939, 544 N.E.2d 435 (3 Dist. 1989).

Where, if wife became employed, husband could pursue any relevant remedies for modification of the maintenance award available under this Act, it would have been appropriate for the trial court to reserve for review the maintenance award after a certain time period, giving wife an opportunity to seek appropriate employment. In re McNeeley, 117 Ill. App. 3d 320, 72 Ill. Dec. 873, 453 N.E.2d 748 (1 Dist. 1983).

A modification of a maintenance award will not be set aside on review unless the circuit court clearly abused its discretion. In re Chalkley, 99 Ill. App. 3d 478, 55 Ill. Dec. 262, 426 N.E.2d 237 (1 Dist. 1981).

Statutory Construction
750 ILCS 5/413 and this section do not create a substantive right to post-death maintenance pending appeal; they apply when a right to maintenance already exists and therefore must be read in conjunction with the prohibition of 750 ILCS 5/510. Stacke v. Bates, 138 Ill. 2d 295, 149 Ill. Dec. 728, 562 N.E.2d 192 (1990).

The statutory provisions in this section are mandates to the trial court, not merely guidelines. In re Hilkovitch, 124 Ill. App. 3d 401, 79 Ill. Dec. 891, 464 N.E.2d 795 (1 Dist. 1984).

Statutory Foundation

—Not Required
It was not necessary for the trial court to specifically designate that portion upon which it founded the award of maintenance where the basis for the award of maintenance was established in the record. In re Coram, 86 Ill. App. 3d 845, 42 Ill. Dec. 40, 408 N.E.2d 418 (5 Dist. 1980).

Subsequent Divorces
In a situation where a man is obtaining his second divorce, the trial court should not enter an order which would be substantially inconsistent with the interests of his first wife and family. In re Belluomini, 104 Ill. App. 3d 301, 60 Ill. Dec. 59, 432 N.E.2d 958 (1 Dist. 1982).

Subsequent Review
Where the duration and amount of the maintenance payments were subject to review after two years in order for the court to assess the development of petitioner's income, the trial court did not abuse its discretion in granting petitioner maintenance. In re Calisoff, 176 Ill. App. 3d 721, 126 Ill. Dec. 183, 531 N.E.2d 810 (1 Dist. 1988).

Substitution
The recent trend of authority is to attempt to substitute an adequate property settlement in lieu of maintenance, because a property settlement sends each of the parties on their respective ways while maintenance keeps a continuing relationship between them and generally leads to additional litigation; however, if there is to be property settlement in lieu of maintenance, the judgment order must be clear and unequivocal on the issue. In re Popovich, 149 Ill. App. 3d 643, 103 Ill. Dec. 38, 500 N.E.2d 1109 (4 Dist. 1986).

For a case discussing factors affecting the awarding of substitute alimony (now maintenance), see Fuqua v. Fuqua, 60 Ill. App. 3d 819, 18 Ill. Dec. 200, 377 N.E.2d 353 (2 Dist. 1978).

Sufficient Assets Lacking
Maintenance should be awarded only when the spouse requesting it lacks sufficient assets and income to provide for his or her needs. In re Smith, 122 Ill. App. 3d 213, 77 Ill. Dec. 637, 460 N.E.2d 1201 (4 Dist. 1984).

Surplus of Income
A spouse who lived frugally during the marriage is not required to live frugally following dissolution where the other spouse's superior earning power justifies additional maintenance and a resulting surplus of income. In re Fields, 288 Ill. App. 3d 1053, 224 Ill. Dec. 184, 681 N.E.2d 166 (4 Dist. 1997), appeal denied, 174 Ill. 2d 559, 227 Ill. Dec. 4, 686 N.E.2d 1160 (1997), overruled on other grounds, Belleville Toyota, Inc. v. Toyota Motor Sales, U.S.A., Inc., 199 Ill. 2d 325, 264 Ill. Dec. 283, 770 N.E.2d 177 (2002).

Simply because a trial court's award of maintenance results in one spouse having a surplus of income does not automatically mean the court abused its discretion. In re Fields, 288 Ill. App. 3d 1053, 224 Ill. Dec. 184, 681 N.E.2d 166 (4 Dist. 1997), appeal denied, 174 Ill. 2d 559, 227 Ill. Dec. 4, 686 N.E.2d 1160 (1997), overruled on other grounds, Belleville Toyota, Inc. v. Toyota Motor Sales, U.S.A., Inc., 199 Ill. 2d 325, 264 Ill. Dec. 283, 770 N.E.2d 177 (2002).

Tax Consequences

—Consideration
Concerning the allocation of the award between maintenance and child support, the trial court is allowed, even encouraged, to consider tax consequences in making its determination. In re Belluomini, 104 Ill. App. 3d 301, 60 Ill. Dec. 59, 432 N.E.2d 958 (1 Dist. 1982).

Tax Consequences (Cont'd)

—Exemptions

Where there was no indication in the record that a waiver was executed by the custodial parent of her entitlement to a dependent tax exemption, nor was it alleged on appeal that a waiver was signed, the trial court was without authority to award the exemption to the noncustodial parent in direct contravention of federal law (26 U.S.C. § 152(e)). In re Emery, 179 Ill. App. 3d 744, 128 Ill. Dec. 569, 534 N.E.2d 1014 (4 Dist. 1989).

—Returns

Although federal income tax returns are admissible, given the proper foundation proof, it is incumbent on the trier of fact to determine as best he can what disposition is being made of the funds generated through depreciation or other sheltered income and this requires a balancing test: viz., the disposition of the current cash flow versus the ability to pay in a dissolution proceeding. In re McDonald, 113 Ill. App. 3d 116, 68 Ill. Dec. 653, 446 N.E.2d 559 (4 Dist. 1983).

If a spouse pleads an inability to pay in proceedings to determine maintenance and distribution of marital property, something more than a copy of a tax return is necessary to establish a preponderance of such evidence; expert testimony would be one available method. In re McDonald, 113 Ill. App. 3d 116, 68 Ill. Dec. 653, 446 N.E.2d 559 (4 Dist. 1983).

Temporary Awards

For a case discussing an award of temporary alimony (now maintenance) and attorney fees see Rich v. Rich, 24 Ill. App. 3d 1083, 322 N.E.2d 610 (5 Dist. 1975).

Trial court abused its discretion in basing its order of temporary alimony (now maintenance) on prior assets of defendant rather than on his ability to pay at the time of the hearing; therefore, the order of the trial court was reversed and remanded with instructions to determine the current assets and earnings of the defendant and to base any future order on those current assets and earnings. Dejoie v. Dejoie, 6 Ill. App. 3d 381, 286 N.E.2d 38 (1 Dist. 1972).

Granting plaintiff's petition for temporary alimony (now maintenance) pending an appeal was not an abuse of discretion under a prior similar provision. Varap v. Varap, 76 Ill. App. 2d 402, 222 N.E.2d 77 (1 Dist. 1966).

Tender Age of Children

Although it appeared that the respondent was required to pay out more than half of his net income for support, insurance premiums and accrued debts, the monthly sum the respondent was to pay for support was hardly sufficient for the wife and two children to live on where the poor health and tender age of the children required the wife to be at home most of the time, making it difficult for her to engage in gainful employment. In re Piktel, 81 Ill. App. 3d 567, 36 Ill. Dec. 743, 401 N.E.2d 584 (2 Dist. 1980).

Termination of Payments

—Cohabitation

The termination of maintenance based upon a party cohabiting with another person on a resident, continuing, conjugal basis is a factual situation, and a trial court's finding that the recipient spouse is not living with another person under circumstances amounting to a de facto husband-wife relationship will not be reversed unless it is contrary to the manifest weight of the evidence. In re Leming, 227 Ill. App. 3d 154, 169 Ill. Dec. 108, 590 N.E.2d 1027 (5 Dist.), cert. denied, 146 Ill. 2d 630, 176 Ill. Dec. 802, 602 N.E.2d 456 (1992).

—Upheld

Where the wife performed a less than diligent attempt to earn a degree that properly should have taken two years, and further failed in the meantime to diligently seek employment, the court did not abuse its discretion in terminating maintenance payments. In re McGory, 185 Ill. App. 3d 517, 133 Ill. Dec. 590, 541 N.E.2d 801 (3 Dist. 1989).

The evidence supported the trial court's conclusion that former wife failed to meet her affirmative obligation to seek appropriate training or education in order to become financially independent; therefore, the trial court's termination of maintenance was not an abuse of discretion. In re Lasota, 125 Ill. App. 3d 37, 80 Ill. Dec. 537, 465 N.E.2d 649 (1 Dist. 1984).

Terminology Held Irrelevant

Where the record indicated that the approximately $400 former wife would receive from former husband would barely cover the difference between her income and the family's reasonable needs, whether it was termed "child support" or "unallocated support and maintenance," the award was neither an abuse of discretion nor contrary to the manifest weight of the evidence. In re Sheber, 121 Ill. App. 3d 328, 76 Ill. Dec. 921, 459 N.E.2d 1056 (1 Dist. 1984).

Three Year Review of Award

—Proper

There was no abuse of discretion in a court's determination that it would review a maintenance award once every three years, in light of uncertainty about the parties' financial futures and the statutory provisions for modification in the case of substantially changed circumstances. In re Feldman, 199 Ill. App. 3d 1002, 146 Ill. Dec. 62, 557 N.E.2d 1004 (2 Dist. 1990).

Time Period

—Just

Where wife and husband were married approximately 12 years, most of which wife spent as a homemaker and mother, and just prior to the dissolution, she obtained her college degree in accounting and full-time employment as a CPA, and at the time of the hearing, wife was earning approximately $23,000 gross as a CPA and husband had a salary of approximately $105,000 per year, the standard of living was quite high during the marriage and wife's standard of living drastically changed after the dissolution, and both parties were in good physical and emotional condition, the trial court did not abuse its discretion in awarding maintenance for a specific period of time. In re Phillips, 244 Ill. App. 3d 577, 186 Ill. Dec. 108, 615 N.E.2d 1165 (4 Dist. 1993).

What constitutes a "just" time period for the award is made on the consideration of all relevant factors, including the financial resources of the party seeking maintenance, including his or her marital property; the time necessary to acquire sufficient education or training to enable the party seeking maintenance to find appropriate employment; the standard of living established during the marriage; the duration of the marriage; the age and the physical and emotional condition of each of the parties; the ability of the spouse paying maintenance to meet his or her needs while meeting those of the spouse seeking maintenance; and the tax consequences of the property division of the parties. In re Kerber, 215 Ill. App. 3d 248, 158 Ill. Dec. 717, 574 N.E.2d 830 (4 Dist. 1991).

—Sufficient Evidence

Where there is specific evidence regarding educational background, present educational pursuits, and income at the time of dissolution, there is sufficient evidence to set a specific period of time for maintenance. In re Werries, 247 Ill. App. 3d 639, 186 Ill. Dec. 747, 616 N.E.2d 1379 (4 Dist. 1993).

Tools

While the award of the tools, camera equipment and other items used by the husband in his business and hobbies at values established by the wife's testimony was an ingenuous and simple way of apportioning marital property in relatively equal shares, once the decision was made to award the marital home to the husband, it was an abuse of discretion to award the wife, as her share of the marital property, tools which were only useful to the husband. In re Meyer, 140 Ill. App. 3d 1031, 95 Ill. Dec. 344, 489 N.E.2d 906 (5 Dist. 1986).

Types of Maintenance

—In General

Payments for a fixed period of time are not synonymous with maintenance in gross since this section expressly permits a maintenance award for a fixed period of time which is not maintenance in gross. In re Harris, 284 Ill. App. 3d 389, 219 Ill. Dec. 875, 672 N.E.2d 383 (4 Dist. 1996).

—Prior Law

For a case discussing distinct types of alimony, see Roberts v. Roberts, 90 Ill. App. 2d 184, 234 N.E.2d 372 (1 Dist. 1967).

Unconscionability

—Not Shown

The absence of maintenance, by itself, did not render a settlement agreement unconscionable where the property distribution provided ex-wife with a cash payment, proceeds from the sale of the real estate, several bank accounts, several certificates of deposit, an Individual Retirement Account, and half of her ex-husband's pension. Flynn v. Flynn, 232 Ill. App. 3d 394, 173 Ill. Dec. 735, 597 N.E.2d 709 (1 Dist.), cert. denied, 146 Ill. 2d 626, 176 Ill. Dec. 813, 602 N.E.2d 451 (1992).

Where petitioner asserted that she was only given twenty minutes to read and sign the marital agreement, it appeared that this was all the time that petitioner chose to devote to the matter, and where the terms of the agreement were relatively simple to comprehend and petitioner was given every opportunity to question any terms she did not understand, the conditions surrounding the formation of the marital settlement agreement did not support a finding of unconscionability. In re Brandt, 140 Ill. App. 3d 1019, 95 Ill. Dec. 340, 489 N.E.2d 902 (5 Dist. 1986).

—Shown

In a divorce action where the plaintiff wife had no counsel of record when the cause was called for trial, the trial court's ex parte decree of divorce entered upon defendant husband's counterclaim was totally one-sided and unconscionable in that it awarded the defendant husband virtually all of the parties' real and personal property, besides granting him custody of the children who were then residing with the wife, and barred plaintiff wife from receiving alimony (now maintenance), and such decree was vacated. Eden v. Eden, 34 Ill. App. 3d 382, 340 N.E.2d 141 (1 Dist. 1975).

Unreported Income

Where there was a wide discrepancy between respondent's supposed income and his actual spending, there was only one explanation: the parties' pre-separation lifestyle was supported by at least $35,000 yearly in unreported income, which provided the basis for the trial judge's award to petitioner of $3,000 per month in unallocated maintenance and child support. In re Hilkovitch, 124 Ill. App. 3d 401, 79 Ill. Dec. 891, 464 N.E.2d 795 (1 Dist. 1984).

Valuation

—Business

The trial court's failure to consider the income tax ramifications of a theoretical sale of respondent's two business did not lead to an excessive value assigned to the businesses. In re Johnson, 106 Ill. App. 3d 502, 62 Ill. Dec. 478, 436 N.E.2d 228 (1 Dist. 1982).

The trial court overstated the value of respondent's two corporations by $17,249; therefore, one half of this amount was subtracted from the equalization note which the court used to balance the amount of property apportioned the parties in the property settlement. In re Johnson, 106 Ill. App. 3d 502, 62 Ill. Dec. 478, 436 N.E.2d 228 (1 Dist. 1982).

—Law Practice

The trial court did not err in including accounts receivable in valuing the respondent's law practice, and as there was sufficient evidence to support its valuation of the practice, it was not an abuse of discretion or against the manifest weight of the evidence. In re Tietz, 238 Ill. App. 3d 965, 178 Ill. Dec. 876, 605 N.E.2d 670 (4 Dist. 1992).

—Professional Corporation

Adding sum to the value of the professional corporation awarded to the husband based upon a stream of future income was error because it resulted in a "double count" of potential future income by considering such income in both the valuation of the asset and considering it in apportioning the total marital assets and awarding maintenance. Head v. Head, 168 Ill. App. 3d 697, 119 Ill. Dec. 549, 523 N.E.2d 17 (1 Dist. 1988).

—Property Disposition

Where the related issues of maintenance to petitioner and the minor child and the payment of educational expenses were directly affected by the final property disposition, since these awards were substantially dependent upon the financial resources of the parties, including marital property, the maintenance and support awards would have to be re-evaluated by the trial court on remand so that it could properly consider any changes required in the disposition of such property. In re Walsh, 109 Ill. App. 3d 171, 64 Ill. Dec. 758, 440 N.E.2d 310 (1 Dist. 1982).

Voluntary Retirement

Husband's use of the word "retirement" to describe his voluntary leaving of his job and subsequent reduction of his income did not automatically confer some preferred status upon his actions. In re Smith, 77 Ill. App. 3d 858, 33 Ill. Dec. 332, 396 N.E.2d 859 (2 Dist. 1979).

Waiver

Where an original decree stated that maintenance for wife and child would cease when child reached age of majority, wife did not waive her right to maintenance because neither the decree nor the transcript disclosed an express waiver of maintenance, and because the transcript of the divorce proceeding did not reveal that this right to maintenance was explained to wife or that she knew she would be forever barred from maintenance after her daughter's 18th birthday. Faris v. Faris, 142 Ill. App. 3d 987, 97 Ill. Dec. 209, 492 N.E.2d 645 (2 Dist. 1986), appeal denied, 100 Ill. Dec. 603, 497 N.E.2d 781 (Ill. 1986).

Wilful Contempt

—Appellate Relief

A party who was adjudged to be in contempt of the trial court for failure to abide by its orders, and who removed himself beyond its process and concealed himself outside the State of Illinois and sought to attack the final decree of the court ordering maintenance in gross and marital property division which he was defying, was not entitled to appellate relief. In re Timke, 219 Ill. App. 3d 423, 162 Ill. Dec. 114, 579 N.E.2d 928 (1 Dist. 1991).

Work Outside the Home

Where wife's work outside the home did not provide her the means to obtain employment after dissolution of marriage at a salary level that would allow her to meet her reasonable needs or to maintain the standard of living she enjoyed during the marriage, she was entitled to maintenance. In re Harlow, 251 Ill. App. 3d 152, 190 Ill. Dec. 476, 621 N.E.2d 929 (4 Dist. 1993), appeal denied, 154 Ill. 2d 559, 197 Ill. Dec. 486, 631 N.E.2d 708 (1994).

LEGAL PERIODICALS

For comment, "Out with the Old and In with the New: An Analysis of Illinois Maintenance Law under the Uniform Marriage and Divorce Act and a Proposal for Its Replacement," see 23 N. Ill. U. L. Rev. 581 (2003).

For article, "All Principles of Family Dissolution: Some Comments," see 1997 U. Ill. L. Rev. 801.

For article, "Survey of Illinois Law: Family Law," 19 S. Ill. U.L.J. 819 (1995).

For article, "Illinois Moves Toward Reviewable (Maybe Permanent?) Maintenance," see 81 Ill. B.J. 630 (1993).

For article, "Equalizing the Cost of Divorce Under the Uniform Marriage and Divorce Act: Maintenance Awards in Illinois," see 23 Loy. U. Chi. L.J. 459 (1991-92).

For article, "Survey of Illinois Law [1988-89] — Family Law," see 14 S. Ill. U. L. J. 1007 (1990).

For article, "Family Law: 1988-89 Illinois Law Survey," see 21 Loy. U. Chi. L. J. 417 (1989-90).

For article, "Family Law: 1986-87 Illinois Law Survey," see 19 Loy. U. Chi. L. J. 489 (1987-88).

For article, "Divorce Illinois Style: Ten Years Under the Marriage and Dissolution of Marriage Act," see 75 Ill. B. J. 606 (1987).

For article, "Rehabilitation Maintenance in Illinois," see 75 Ill. B. J. 658 (1987).

For article, "Family Law: 1985-86 Survey," see 11 S. Ill. U. L. J. 741 (1987).

For article, "Family Law: 1985-86 Illinois Law Survey," see 18 Loy. U. Chi. L. J. 549 (1986-87).

For recent developments, "Recent Amendments to Illinois Child Support Status: Income Percentage Guidelines," see 19 J. Marshall L. Rev. 207 (1985-86).

For article, "The Use (and Abuse) of Child Support Schedules in Illinois," see 71 Ill. B. J. 314 (1983).

For article, "Classification of Property Upon Dissolution of Marriage: Suggestions For Maintaining Our Dual System, In the Aftermath of Smith, 86 Ill. 2d 518, 427 N.E.2d 1239 (1981)," see 71 Ill. B. J. 100 (1982).

For article, "Caveat Amator: 'The State of Affairs' in Illinois After Hewitt v. Hewitt," see 29 De Paul L. Rev. 493 (1980).

For article, "Marital Property, Tax Ramification, and Maintenance: Practice Under the Illinois Marriage and Dissolution of Marriage Act — A Comparative Study," see 66 Ill. B. J. 388 (1978).

RESEARCH REFERENCES

Validity and enforceability of escalation clause in divorce decree relating to alimony and child support. 19 ALR4th 830.

Excessiveness or adequacy of amount of money awarded as separate maintenance, alimony, or support for spouse without absolute divorce. 26 ALR4th 1190.

Excessiveness or adequacy of money awarded as temporary alimony. 26 ALR4th 1218.

Excessiveness or adequacy of amount of money awarded as permanent alimony following divorce. 28 ALR4th 786.

Order awarding temporary support or living expenses upon separation of unmarried partners pending contract action based on services relating to personal relationship. 35 ALR4th 409.

Reconciliation as affecting decree for limited divorce, separation, alimony, separate maintenance, or spousal support. 36 ALR4th 502.

Divorced or separated spouse's living with member of opposite sex as affecting other spouse's obligation of alimony or support under separation agreement. 47 ALR4th 38.

Divorce: excessiveness or adequacy of combined property division and spousal support awards—modern cases. 55 ALR4th 14.

Enforceability of premarital agreements governing support or property rights upon divorce or separation as affected by fairness or adequacy of those terms — modern status. 53 ALR4th 161.

Power to modify spousal support award for a limited term, issued in conjunction with divorce, so as to extend the term or make the award permanent. 62 ALR4th 180.

Withholding visitation rights for failure to make alimony or support payments. 65 ALR4th 1155.

Divorce and separation: attributing undisclosed income to parent or spouse for purposes of making child or spousal support award. 70 ALR4th 173.

Death of obligor spouse as affecting alimony. 79 ALR4th 10.

Consideration of obligated spouse's earnings from overtime or "second job" held in addition to regular full-time employment in fixing alimony or child support awards. 17 ALR5th 143.

Divorce and separation: Workers' compensation benefits as marital property subject to distribution. 30 ALR5th 139.

Enforcement of claim for alimony or support, or for attorneys' fees and costs incurred in connection therewith, against exemption. 52 ALR5th 221.

Consideration of obligor spouse's or parent's personal-injury recovery or settlement in fixing alimony or child-support award. 59 ALR5th 489.

Effect of same-sex relationship on right to spousal support. 73 ALR5th 599.

Propriety of equalizing income of spouses through alimony awards. 102 ALR5th 395.

750 ILCS 5/505 Child support; contempt; penalties

Sec. 505. *Child support; contempt; penalties.* (a) In a proceeding for dissolution of marriage, legal separation, declaration of invalidity of marriage, a proceeding for child support following dissolution of the marriage by a court which lacked personal jurisdiction over the absent spouse, a proceeding for modification of a previous order for child support under Section 510 of this Act [750 ILCS 5/510], or any proceeding authorized under Section 501 or 601 of this Act [750 ILCS 5/501 or 750 ILCS 5/601], the court may order either or both parents owing a duty of support to a child of the marriage to pay an amount reasonable and necessary for his support, without regard to marital misconduct. The duty of support owed to a child includes the obligation to provide for the reasonable and necessary physical, mental and emotional health needs of the child. For purposes of this Section, the term "child" shall include any child under age 18 and any child under age 19 who is still attending high school.

(1) The Court shall determine the minimum amount of support by using the following guidelines:

Number of Children	Percent of Supporting Party's Net Income
1	20%
2	28%
3	32%
4	40%
5	45%
6 or more	50%

(2) The above guidelines shall be applied in each case unless the court makes a finding that application of the guidelines would be inappropriate, after considering the best interests of the child in light of evidence including but not limited to one or more of the following relevant factors:

(a) the financial resources and needs of the child;

(b) the financial resources and needs of the custodial parent;

(c) the standard of living the child would have enjoyed had the marriage not been dissolved;

(d) the physical and emotional condition of the child, and his educational needs; and

(e) the financial resources and needs of the non-custodial parent.

If the court deviates from the guidelines, the court's finding shall state the amount of support that would have been required under the guidelines, if determinable. The court shall include the reason or reasons for the variance from the guidelines.

(3) "Net income" is defined as the total of all income from all sources, minus the following deductions:

(a) Federal income tax (properly calculated withholding or estimated payments);

(b) State income tax (properly calculated withholding or estimated payments);

(c) Social Security (FICA payments);

(d) Mandatory retirement contributions required by law or as a condition of employment;

(e) Union dues;

(f) Dependent and individual health/hospitalization insurance premiums;

(g) Prior obligations of support or maintenance actually paid pursuant to a court order;

(h) Expenditures for repayment of debts that represent reasonable and necessary expenses for the production of income, medical expenditures necessary to preserve life or health, reasonable expenditures for the benefit of the child and the other parent, exclusive of gifts. The court shall reduce net income in determining the minimum amount of support to be ordered only for the period that such payments are due and shall enter an order containing provisions for its self-executing modification upon termination of such payment period.

(4) In cases where the court order provides for health/hospitalization insurance coverage pursuant to Section 505.2 of this Act [750 ILCS 5/505.2], the premiums for that insurance, or that portion of the premiums for which the supporting party is responsible in the case of insurance provided through an employer's health insurance plan where the employer pays a portion of the premiums, shall be subtracted from net income in determining the minimum amount of support to be ordered.

(4.5) In a proceeding for child support following dissolution of the marriage by a court that lacked personal jurisdiction over the absent spouse, and in which the court is requiring payment of support for the period before the date an order for current support is entered, there is a rebuttable presumption that the supporting party's net income for the prior period was the same as his or her net income at the time the order for current support is entered.

(5) If the net income cannot be determined because of default or any other reason, the court shall order support in an amount considered reasonable in the particular case. The final order in all cases shall state the support level in dollar amounts. However, if the court finds that the child support amount cannot be expressed exclusively as a dollar amount because all or a portion of the payor's net income is uncertain as to source, time of payment, or amount, the court may order a percentage amount of support in addition to a specific dollar amount and enter such other orders as may be necessary to determine and enforce, on a timely basis, the applicable support ordered.

(6) If (i) the non-custodial parent was properly served with a request for discovery of financial information relating to the non-custodial parent's ability to provide child support, (ii) the non-custodial parent failed to comply with the request, despite having been ordered to do so by the court, and (iii) the non-custodial parent is not present at the hearing to determine support despite having received proper notice, then any relevant financial information concerning the non-custodial parent's ability to provide child support that was obtained pursuant to subpoena and proper notice shall be admitted into evidence without the need to establish any further foundation for its admission.

(a-5) In an action to enforce an order for support based on the respondent's failure to make support payments as required by the order, notice of proceedings to hold the respondent in contempt for that failure may be served on the respondent by personal service or by regular mail addressed to the respondent's last known address. The respondent's last known address may be determined from records of the clerk of the court, from the Federal Case Registry of Child Support Orders, or by any other reasonable means.

(b) Failure of either parent to comply with an order to pay support shall be punishable as in other cases of contempt. In addition to other penalties provided by law the Court may, after finding the parent guilty of contempt, order that the parent be:

(1) placed on probation with such conditions of probation as the Court deems advisable;

(2) sentenced to periodic imprisonment for a period not to exceed 6 months; provided, however, that the Court may permit the parent to be released for periods of time during the day or night to:

(A) work; or

(B) conduct a business or other self-employed occupation.

The Court may further order any part or all of the earnings of a parent during a sentence of periodic imprisonment paid to the Clerk of the Circuit Court or to the parent having custody or to the guardian having custody of the children of the sentenced parent for the support of said children until further order of the Court.

If there is a unity of interest and ownership sufficient to render no financial separation between a non-custodial parent and another person or persons or business entity, the court may pierce the ownership veil of the person, persons, or business entity to discover assets of the non-custodial parent held in the name of that person, those persons, or that business entity. The following circumstances are sufficient to authorize a court to order discovery of the assets of a person, persons, or business entity and to compel the application of any discovered assets toward payment on the judgment for support:

(1) the non-custodial parent and the person, persons, or business entity maintain records together.

(2) the non-custodial parent and the person, persons, or business entity fail to maintain an arms length relationship between themselves with regard to any assets.

(3) the non-custodial parent transfers assets to the person, persons, or business entity with the intent to perpetrate a fraud on the custodial parent. With respect to assets which are real property, no order entered under this paragraph shall affect the rights of bona fide purchasers, mortgagees, judgment creditors, or other lien holders who acquire their interests in the property prior to the time a notice of lis pendens pursuant to the Code of Civil Procedure [735 ILCS 5/1-101 et seq.] or a copy of the order is placed of record in the office of the recorder of deeds for the county in which the real property is located.

The court may also order in cases where the parent is 90 days or more delinquent in payment of support or has been adjudicated in arrears in an amount equal to 90 days obligation or more, that the parent's Illinois driving privileges be suspended until the court determines that the parent is in compliance with the order of support. The court may also order that the parent be issued a family financial responsibility driving permit that would allow limited driving privileges for employment and medical purposes in accordance with Section 7-702.1 of the Illinois Vehicle Code [625 ILCS 5/7-702.1]. The clerk of the circuit court shall certify the order suspending the driving privileges of the parent or granting the issuance of a family financial responsibility driving permit to the Secretary of State on forms prescribed by the Secretary. Upon receipt of the authenticated documents, the Secretary of State shall suspend the parent's driving privileges until further order of the court and shall, if ordered by the court, subject to the provisions of Section 7-702.1 of the Illinois Vehicle Code [625 ILCS 5/7-702.1], issue a family financial responsibility driving permit to the parent.

In addition to the penalties or punishment that may be imposed under this Section, any person whose conduct constitutes a violation of Section 15 of the Non-Support Punishment Act [750 ILCS 16/15] may be prosecuted under that Act, and a person convicted under that Act may be sentenced in accordance with that Act. The sentence may include but need not be limited to a requirement that the person perform community service under Section 50 of that Act [750 ILCS 16/50] or participate in a work alternative program under Section 50 of that Act [750 ILCS 16/50]. A person may not be required to participate in a work alternative program under Section 50 of that Act [750 ILCS 16/50] if the person is currently participating in a work program pursuant to Section 505.1 of this Act [750 ILCS 5/505.1].

A support obligation, or any portion of a support obligation, which becomes due and remains unpaid for 30 days or more shall accrue simple interest at the rate of 9% per annum. An order for support entered or modified on or after January 1, 2002 shall contain a statement that a support obligation required under the order, or any portion of a support obligation required under the order, that becomes due and remains unpaid for 30 days or more shall accrue simple interest at the rate of 9% per annum. Failure to include the statement in the order for support does not affect the validity of the order or the accrual of interest as provided in this Section.

(c) A one-time charge of 20% is imposable upon the amount of past-due child support owed on July 1, 1988 which has accrued under a support order entered by the court. The charge shall be imposed in accordance with the provisions of Section 10-21 of the Illinois Public Aid Code [305 ILCS 5/10-21] and shall be enforced by the court upon petition.

(d) Any new or existing support order entered by the court under this Section shall be deemed to be a series of judgments against the person obligated to pay support thereunder, each such judgment to be in the amount of each payment or installment of support and each such judgment to be deemed entered as of the date the corresponding payment or installment becomes due under the terms of the support order. Each such judgment shall have the full force, effect and attributes of any other judgment of this State, including the ability to be enforced. A lien arises by operation of law against the real and personal property of the noncustodial parent for each installment of overdue support owed by the noncustodial parent.

(e) When child support is to be paid through the clerk of the court in a county of 1,000,000 inhabitants or less, the order shall direct the obligor to pay to the clerk, in addition to the child support payments, all fees imposed by the county board under paragraph (3) of subsection (u) of Section 27.1 of the Clerks of Courts Act [705 ILCS 105/27.1]. Unless paid in cash or pursuant to an order for withholding, the payment of the fee shall be by a separate instrument from the support payment and shall be made to the order of the Clerk.

(f) All orders for support, when entered or modified, shall include a provision requiring the obligor to notify the court and, in cases in which a party is receiving child and spouse services under Article X of the Illinois Public Aid Code [305 ILCS 5/10-1 et seq.], the Illinois Department of Public Aid, within 7 days, (i) of the name and address of any new employer of the obligor, (ii) whether the obligor has access to health insurance coverage through the employer or other group coverage and, if so, the policy name and number and the names of persons covered under the policy, and (iii) of any new residential or mailing address or telephone number of the non-custodial parent. In any subsequent action to enforce a support order, upon a sufficient showing that a diligent effort has been made to ascertain the location of the non-custodial parent, service of process or provision of notice necessary in the case may be made at the last known address of the non-custodial parent in any manner expressly provided by the Code of Civil Procedure [735 ILCS 5/1-101 et seq.] or this Act, which service shall be sufficient for purposes of due process.

(g) An order for support shall include a date on which the current support obligation terminates. The termination date shall be no earlier than the date on which the child covered by the order will attain the age of 18. However, if the child will not graduate from high school until after attaining the age of 18, then the termination date shall be no earlier than the earlier of the date on which the child's high school graduation will occur or the date on which the child will attain the age of 19. The order for support shall state that the termination date does not apply to any arrearage that may remain unpaid on that date. Nothing in this subsection shall be construed to prevent the court from modifying the order or terminating the order in the event the child is otherwise emancipated.

(g-5) If there is an unpaid arrearage or delinquency (as those terms are defined in the Income Withholding for Support Act [750 ILCS 28/1 et seq.]) equal to at least one month's support obligation on the termination date stated in the order for support or, if there is no termination date stated in the order, on the date the child attains the age of majority or is otherwise emancipated, the periodic amount required to be paid for current support of that child immediately prior to that date shall automatically continue to be an obligation, not as current support but as periodic payment toward satisfaction of the unpaid arrearage or delinquency. That periodic payment shall be in addition to any periodic payment previously required for satisfaction of the arrearage or delinquency. The total periodic amount to be paid toward satisfaction of the arrearage or delinquency may be enforced and collected by any method provided by law for enforcement and collection of child support, including but not limited to income withholding under the Income Withholding for Support Act [750 ILCS 28/1 et seq.]. Each order for support entered or modified on or after the effective date of this amendatory Act of the 93rd General Assembly [P.A. 93-1061] must contain a statement notifying the parties of the requirements of this subsection. Failure to include the statement in the order for support does not affect the validity of the order or the operation of the provisions of this subsection with regard to the order. This subsection shall not be construed to prevent or affect the establishment or modification of an order for support of a minor child or the establishment or modification of an order for support of a non-minor child or educational expenses under Section 513 of this Act [750 ILCS 5/513].

(h) An order entered under this Section shall include a provision requiring the obligor to report to the obligee and to the clerk of court within 10 days each time the obligor obtains new employment, and each time the obligor's employment is terminated for any reason. The report shall be in writing and shall, in the case of new employment, include the name and address of the new employer. Failure to report new employment or the termination of current employment, if coupled with nonpayment of support for a period in excess of 60 days, is indirect criminal contempt. For any obligor arrested for failure to report new employment bond shall be set in the amount of the child support that should have been paid during the period of unreported employment. An order entered under this Section shall also include a provision requiring the obligor and obligee parents to advise each other of a change in residence within 5 days of the change except when the court finds that the physical, mental, or emotional health of a party or that of a child, or both, would be seriously endangered by disclosure of the party's address.

(i) The court does not lose the powers of contempt, driver's license suspension, or other child support enforcement mechanisms, including, but not limited to, criminal prosecution as set forth in this Act, upon the emancipation of the minor child or children.

(Source: P.A. 86-649; 86-700; 86-969; 86-1028; 86-1184; 88-307, § 10; 88-687, § 13; 89-88, § 5; 89-92, § 20; 89-626, § 2-78; 90-18, § 100; 90-476, § 10; 90-539, § 10; 90-655, § 170; 90-733, § 25; 91-113, § 5; 91-397, § 10; 91-655, § 5; 91-767, § 10; 92-16, § 96; 92-203, § 5; 92-374, § 10; 92-651, § 87; 92-876, § 910; 93-148, § 5; 93-1061, § 10.)

Note.

This section was Ill.Rev.Stat., Ch. 40, para. 505.

705 ILCS 105/27.1, referred to above, was repealed.

Section 996 of P.A. 92-16 contains a "no acceleration or delay" provision, and Section 997 contains a "no revival or extension" provision.

Section 997 of P.A. 92-651 is a no acceleration or delay provision, and Section 998 is a no revival or extension provision.

Cross References.

As to revival of judgments, see 735 ILCS 5/13-218.

Concerning a judgment for child support, specifically the determination of the amount of any child support award, see 750 ILCS 45/14.

Illinois Administrative Code.

See 89 Illinois Administrative Code, § 160.60.

Effect of Amendments.

The 1994 amendment by P.A. 88-687, effective January 24, 1995, added subdivision (a)(4.5); and in subsection (e), in the first sentence, substituted "the Clerks of Courts Act" for "'An Act in relation to clerks of courts', approved July 1, 1874, as now or hereafter amended".

The 1995 amendment by P.A. 89-88, effective June 30, 1995, in subdivision (a)(2)(a) inserted "and needs".

The 1995 amendment by P.A. 89-92, effective July 1, 1996, in subsection (b) added the third paragraph.

The 1996 amendment by P.A. 89-626, effective August 9, 1996, combined the amendments by P.A. 89-88 and P.A. 89-92.

The 1997 amendment by P.A. 90-18, effective July 1, 1997, in subsection (d) added the third sentence; and in subsection (f), in the first sentence, substituted "All orders" for "An order", inserted "when", deleted "in a case in which a party is receiving child and spouse support services under article X of the Illinois Public Aid Code" preceding "shall include", inserted "the court and, in cases in which a party is receiving child and spouse services under Article X of the Illinois Public Aid Code" and added at the end "and (iii) of any new residential or mailing address or telephone number of the non-custodial parent" and added the fourth sentence.

The 1997 amendment by P.A. 90-476, effective January 1, 1998, in subsection (b) added the third and fourth paragraphs.

The 1997 amendment by P.A. 90-539, effective June 1, 1998, added subsection (h).

The 1998 amendment by P.A. 90-655, effective July 30, 1998, incorporated the amendments by P.A. 90-18, P.A. 90-476 and P.A. 90-539.

The 1998 amendment by P.A. 90-733, effective August 11, 1998, added the last paragraph under subsection (b).

The 1999 amendment by P.A. 91-113, effective July 15, 1999, incorporated the amendments by P.A. 90-655 and P.A. 90-733, and inserted subsection (a-5).

The 1999 amendment by P.A. 91-397, effective January 1, 2000, incorporated the amendments by P.A. 90-655 and P.A. 90-733, and added the last paragraph in subsection (b).

The 1999 amendment by P.A. 91-655, effective June 1, 2000, incorporated the amendments by P.A. 90-655 and P.A. 90-733, and added the third sentence in subsection (a)(5).

The 2000 amendment by P.A. 91-767, effective June 9, 2000, combined the amendments by P.A. 91-113 and P.A. 91-397; inserted subsection (a)(6); and in the next-to-last paragraph of subsection (b) substituted "Section 15 of the Non-Support Punishment Act" for "Section 1 of the Non-Support of Spouse and Children Act" in the first sentence, and substituted "Act" for "Section" and "Section 50" for "subsection (c)" throughout the paragraph.

The 2001 amendment by P.A. 92-16, effective June 28, 2001, combined the amendments by P.A. 91-113, P.A. 91-397, P.A. 91-655 and P.A. 91-767.

The 2001 amendment by P.A. 92-203, effective August 1, 2001, added subsection (i).

The 2001 amendment by P.A. 92-374, effective August 15, 2001, in the last paragraph of subsection (b) inserted "simple" preceding "interest" in the first sentence and added the second and third sentences.

The 2002 amendment by P.A. 92-651, effective July 11, 2002, combined the amendments by P.A. 92-16, P.A. 92-203 and P.A. 92-374.

The 2002 amendment by P.A. 92-876, effective June 1, 2003, in subsection (a) deleted "minor" before "child" in the second sentence and added the last sentence; and in subsection (g) substituted "age of 18. However, if the child will not graduate from high school until after attaining the age of 18, then the termination date shall be no earlier than the earlier of the date on which the child's high school graduation will occur or the date on which the child will attain the age of 19" for "age of majority or is otherwise emancipated", and added "or terminating the order in the event the child is otherwise emancipated" at the end.

The 2003 amendment by P.A. 93-148, effective July 10, 2003, substituted "28%" for "25%" in subsection (a)(1).

The 2004 amendment by P.A. 93-1061, effective January 1, 2005, inserted subsection (g-5).

CASE NOTES

Analysis

Constitutionality
In General
Abatement
Ability to Pay
—In General
—Preemption
—Temporary Abatement
—Unemployed Custodial Parent
—Valuation of Business Assets
Additional Support
—Required
Age of Majority
Agreement Between Parties
—In General
—Best Interests of Child
—Improper
—Percentage of Income as Support
Ambiguous Language
Appeal
Applicability
Arrearages
—In General
—Burden of Proof
—Enforcing Payment
—Equitable Estoppel
—Improper Order
—Insufficient Evidence
—Interest
—No Valid Claim
—Setoffs
—Vested Rights
Attorney Fees
—Allowed
—Denied
—Financial Resources
Automatic Increases
Award
—Ability to Pay
—Adequacy
—Certain and Definite
—Change of Circumstances
—Collection
—Denied
—Determination
—Evidence
—Exceeding Guidelines
—Excess of Needs
—Explicit Findings Not Required
—Factors
—Improper
—Increase Proper
—Insufficient
—Intent of Parties
—Retroactive Allowance
—Specificity
—Upheld
Best Interests of Children
—Child Support Settlement Agreements
—Custody Agreement
—Stable Environment
Burden of Proof
Calculation
—Improper
Change in Circumstances
—Court Involvement
—Employment Status
—Evidence
—Factors Considered
—Health Condition
—Held Sufficient
—Increased Need
—Justification for Modification
—Lacking
Child Support
—In General
—Characterization of Payments
—Dollar Amounts
—Extended Care
—Future
—Improper Designation
—Military Allowance
—Mortgage Payments
—Not Affected by Visitation Schedule
—Petitioner's Inability to Pay
—Separate Suit
—Severability
—Shown Needs
—Statutory Minimum
—Therapy Bills
—Upheld
—Vested Right
Child's Estate
Collateral Attack
Conditions for Support
Construction
Contempt
—In General
—Applicability
—Appropriate
—Burden of Proof
—Discretion of Court
—Found
—Not Found
—Power to Enforce
—Purging
—Remedy
—Willful Conduct
Contracts
Credit
—Limitation
—Not Proper
—State Subsidy
Credit Card Debt
Day Care Expense
Debt Repayment
Denial of Hearing
—Improper

Depreciation
Discretion of Court
—In General
—Abuse of Discretion
—No Abuse of Discretion
Dissolution of Judgment
—Affected Obligations
Duty to Support
—In General
—Agreement
—Financial Status of Spouse
—Found
—Laches
—Noncustodial Parent
—Not Destroyed by Divorce
—Not Dischargeable
—Termination
Educational Expenses
Employment Order
Entry of Order
Equitable Credit
Equitable Estoppel
Equity
Evidence
—In General
—Burden to Dispute
—Held Insufficient
—Held Sufficient
Expenses
—Considered
—Equality
—Increase
Factors
—Child by Another
—Express Findings
—Improper for Net Income
—Insufficient Consideration
Failure to Pay
Final Judgment
Foster Children
Good Faith
Guidelines
—In General
—Amount
—Derivation
—Deviation
—Effect of Amendment
—Factors for Modification
—Findings
—Improper Considerations
—Minimum Support
—Noncompliance
—Split Custody
—Use Upheld
—Variance
Health Insurance
Illegitimate Children
Income
—Above Average
—Averaging
—Business Expenses
—Data
—Deduction
—Deferred Compensation
—Depreciation
—Determination
—Federal Employer's Liability Act Settlement
—Fluctuating
—Gifts
—Gratuities
—History
—Investment Income
—Lost Earnings
—New Spouse
—Nonrecurring
—Passive
—Percentage
—Ratio
—Stock Distributions
—Unreported
—Unreported Cash Income
Insurance Premiums
Interest
Intervention
—Not Allowed
Judgment Liens
Jurisdiction
—In General
—Continuing
—Duty of Father
—Foreign Divorce Decree
—In Personam
—Non-Minor Children
Jury Trial
Laches
Lien of Trust
Life Insurance
Maintenance
Medical Expenses
—In General
—Extraordinary
—Not Allowed
—Reimbursement
—Unusual
—Upheld
Minor Children
—Defined
Modification
—Discretion of Court
—Dollar Amounts
—Effects
—Factors
—Incarceration
—Incorporated Settlement Agreement
—Increase
—Not warranted
—Percentage-Based Child Support Order
—Tax Gimmicks
—Upheld
Needs of Child
Net Income
—In General
—Averaging Income
—Averaging of Income
—Definition in Other Sections
—Disability Pension Income
—IRA income
—Nonreimbursed Business Expenses
—Not Able to Ascertain
—Payments on Principal
—Personal Bank Loan
—Personal Injury Claims
—Prior Obligation
—Repayment of Debts
—Tax Refund
—Tax Withholdings
Net Worth
—Determination
Nonpayment
—Burden of Proof
—Contempt
—Defense of Poverty
—Laches
—Unwarranted
Notice
Overpayments
Partnership Income
Past Earnings
Payments
—Child as Recipient
—Method
—Monthly

—Past Due
—Third Parties
—Type of Currency
Percentage of Household Costs
Percentage of Income
—Void as Child Support
Previous Marriage
Prior Obligations
Public Aid Requirement
Public Policy
Real Estate Investment
Rebuttable Presumption
Receipts
—Not Required
Rehearing
Relation with Supreme Court Rules
Relative Financial Positions
—Illustrative Cases
Remand
Remarriage
Repayment of Debts
—Depreciation
—Payment of Mortgage
—Present Mortgage
—Qualification for Deduction
Res Judicata
Reservation of Decision
Retroactivity
Review
Scope
Source of Support
Specific Findings
Spendable Income
Split Custody
Standard of Living
Standard of Review
Statement
—Not Improper
Student Loan
Suit by Child
Tax Considerations
Tax Exemption
Tax Overpayment
Tender Years Doctrine
Two Households
Unilateral Reduction of Support
—Death of Child
—Emancipation of Child
—Termination
Vested Right
Violation of Decree
Voluntary Contributions
Waiver

Constitutionality

The amendment to subsection (a) of this section which established certain support guidelines was constitutional. In re Cook, 147 Ill. App. 3d 134, 100 Ill. Dec. 760, 497 N.E.2d 1029 (3 Dist. 1986).

Subsection (a) of this section does not violate the separation of powers requirement of Ill. Const. (1970), Art. II, § 1. Blaisdell v. Blaisdell, 142 Ill. App. 3d 1034, 97 Ill. Dec. 186, 492 N.E.2d 622 (1 Dist. 1986).

Subsection (a) of this section is not special legislation prohibited by Ill. Const. (1970), Art. IV, § 13. Blaisdell v. Blaisdell, 142 Ill. App. 3d 1034, 97 Ill. Dec. 186, 492 N.E.2d 622 (1 Dist. 1986).

Subsection (a) of this section does not violate the substantive or procedural due process requirements of Ill. Const. (1970), Art. I, § 2. Blaisdell v. Blaisdell, 142 Ill. App. 3d 1034, 97 Ill. Dec. 186, 492 N.E.2d 622 (1 Dist. 1986).

Subsection (a) of this section does not violate the equal protection clause of Ill. Const. (1970), Art. I, § 2. Blaisdell v. Blaisdell, 142 Ill. App. 3d 1034, 97 Ill. Dec. 186, 492 N.E.2d 622 (1 Dist. 1986).

In General

This section creates a rebuttable presumption that a specified percentage of a noncustodial parent's income constitutes an appropriate child support award. Parks ex rel. Parks v. Romans, 187 Ill. App. 3d 445, 135 Ill. Dec. 42, 543 N.E.2d 277 (1 Dist. 1989).

Consideration of the statutory provisions of this section is mandatory rather than directory. Parks ex rel. Parks v. Romans, 187 Ill. App. 3d 445, 135 Ill. Dec. 42, 543 N.E.2d 277 (1 Dist. 1989).

The circuit court has authority to modify child support provisions in a judgment of divorce entered pursuant to a settlement agreement. In re Winters, 160 Ill. App. 3d 277, 111 Ill. Dec. 734, 512 N.E.2d 1371 (2 Dist. 1987).

The trial court has jurisdiction to consider future child support in a dissolution proceeding and need not expressly retain jurisdiction. In re Winters, 160 Ill. App. 3d 277, 111 Ill. Dec. 734, 512 N.E.2d 1371 (2 Dist. 1987).

The original divorce decree awarding child support payments is res judicata only so long as there is no change in the circumstances underlying the decree. In re Winters, 160 Ill. App. 3d 277, 111 Ill. Dec. 734, 512 N.E.2d 1371 (2 Dist. 1987).

The statutory provisions in this section are mandates to the trial court, not merely guidelines. In re Hilkovitch, 124 Ill. App. 3d 401, 79 Ill. Dec. 891, 464 N.E.2d 795 (1 Dist. 1984).

An order disposing of the parties' property and awarding maintenance or child support should recognize and compensate each party for his or her contribution to the marriage; an important objective to be reached by the trial court in entering such an order is to place the parties in a position from which they can begin anew, in addition to providing adequate support for the children. Goforth v. Goforth, 121 Ill. App. 3d 673, 77 Ill. Dec. 125, 459 N.E.2d 1374 (5 Dist. 1984).

Child support awards were determined by accommodating the needs of the child with the available means of the parents. Sullivan v. Sullivan, 68 Ill. App. 3d 242, 24 Ill. Dec. 719, 385 N.E.2d 860 (5 Dist. 1979).

The paramount concern in child support litigation is support of minor children. Gentile v. Gentile, 69 Ill. App. 3d 297, 26 Ill. Dec. 149, 387 N.E.2d 979 (3 Dist. 1979).

The necessity for and the amount of an award, both as to maintenance and child support, are decisions within the sound discretion of the trial court in each individual case, and those decisions will not be set aside unless found to be contrary to the manifest weight of the evidence, thus showing an abuse of discretion. In re Reyna, 78 Ill. App. 3d 1010, 34 Ill. Dec. 818, 398 N.E.2d 641 (3 Dist. 1979).

Abatement

Trial court could not temporarily abate that portion of a support order which supporting parent was without means to presently pay. Coons v. Wilder, 93 Ill. App. 3d 127, 48 Ill. Dec. 512, 416 N.E.2d 785 (2 Dist. 1981).

Ability to Pay

—In General

This Act is geared towards a present ability to pay support and does not suggest in its terms that possible future financial resources of a party may also be taken into account. Coons v. Wilder, 93 Ill. App. 3d 127, 48 Ill. Dec. 512, 416 N.E.2d 785 (2 Dist. 1981).

Child support payments must necessarily reflect a balance of the intensity of the child's needs with the ability of the parents to provide for that need. Gentile v. Gentile, 69 Ill. App. 3d 297, 26 Ill. Dec. 149, 387 N.E.2d 979 (3 Dist. 1979).

Where the trial court ordered that the jointly owned property be sold and the proceeds applied to the unpaid obligations on the jointly owned property, assuming that the proceeds will be at least equal to the amount of existing joint indebtedness, defendant would have sufficient ability to meet the child support payments. Fields v. Fields, 54 Ill. App. 3d 400, 12 Ill. Dec. 89, 369 N.E.2d 586 (5 Dist. 1977).

It is not error for the trial court to consider necessities which are attributable to the need of the children, however one of the considerations which must be taken into account is the ability of the husband to pay. Gray v. Gray, 39 Ill. App. 3d 675, 349 N.E.2d 926 (4 Dist. 1976).

—Preemption

42 U.S.C.S. § 407 bars state courts from burdening Supplemental Security Income (SSI) payments with child support obligations when SSI is the recipient's sole source of income. Department of

Ability to Pay (Cont'd)

—Preemption (Cont'd)
Pub. Aid ex rel. Lozada v. Rivera, 324 Ill. App. 3d 476, 258 Ill. Dec. 165, 755 N.E.2d 548, 2001 Ill. App. LEXIS 687 (2 Dist. 2001).

—Temporary Abatement
Although the general rule is there is no statutory or case authority to temporarily abate a portion of a support order that the supporting parent is without present means to pay, there are limits to that general rule; if a payor of child support sacrifices $10,000 of income this year in exchange for receiving $20,000 of income in future years, the court should not allow him to impose the burden of child support on the custodian based on his current sacrifice and ignore his future benefit (which may not be reachable for child support at the time it is received). The rejection of abatement is no longer applicable to situations which, by their very nature, are inherently temporary. In re Horn, 272 Ill. App. 3d 472, 209 Ill. Dec. 130, 650 N.E.2d 1103 (4 Dist. 1995).

—Unemployed Custodial Parent
The fact that the child's custodial parent received public assistance was no reason to deprive the child of support from the noncustodial parent who certainly had the financial ability to meet the payments. People ex rel. Stokely v. Goodenow, 211 Ill. App. 3d 802, 164 Ill. Dec. 548, 583 N.E.2d 102 (4 Dist. 1991).

—Valuation of Business Assets
For a case discussing valuation methodology used in assessing business assets to determine a parent's ability to make court ordered child support payments, see In re Perlmutter, 225 Ill. App. 3d 362, 167 Ill. Dec. 340, 587 N.E.2d 609 (2 Dist.), appeal denied, 146 Ill. 2d 650, 176 Ill. Dec. 820, 602 N.E.2d 474 (1992), cert. denied, 507 U.S. 1006, 113 S. Ct. 1648, 123 L. Ed. 2d 269 (1993).

Additional Support

—Required
Wife had monthly expenses of $875 a month and an assured income of $527 a month which evinced an inability by her to properly care for the children without additional support while the children were in her custody. In re Pitts, 169 Ill. App. 3d 200, 119 Ill. Dec. 908, 523 N.E.2d 664 (5 Dist. 1988).

Age of Majority
The trial court did not abuse its discretion in ordering respondent to pay retroactive child support; he should not be allowed to benefit from his children reaching the age of majority because of the delay in the child support proceedings. In re Toole, 273 Ill. App. 3d 607, 210 Ill. Dec. 551, 653 N.E.2d 456 (2 Dist. 1995).

The trial court's award of child support extending beyond the age of majority if the child reached majority before leaving school was not erroneous. In re Coram, 86 Ill. App. 3d 845, 42 Ill. Dec. 40, 408 N.E.2d 418 (5 Dist. 1980).

The "duty of support" in this section clearly does not modify the existing common law and statutory rules regarding the age at which child support terminates. Raski v. Raski, 64 Ill. App. 3d 629, 21 Ill. Dec. 417, 381 N.E.2d 744 (5 Dist. 1978).

Where, under former Ill.Rev.Stat., ch. 40, para. 19 (see now this section), the situation as it existed at the rendition of the divorce decree included a statutory provision that the age of majority for males was 21 years, that was the reference point at that time for determining what was meant by "minor" children and the trial court was correct in ordering that the child support payments be continued until the subject children reached 21 years of age even though subsequent legislation, former Ill.Rev.Stat., ch. 3, para. 131 (see now 755 ILCS 5/11-1), lowered the age of majority for males from 21 years of age to 18;a statutory change of the age of majority did not affect the pre-existing rights of a person, and child support payments were a matter of vested right. Waldron v. Waldron, 13 Ill. App. 3d 964, 301 N.E.2d 167 (5 Dist. 1973).

Agreement Between Parties

—In General
The general rule is that child support payments may be modified only by court order; however, an exception to that rule exists where the parties agree between themselves to alter the obligation. In re Runge, 102 Ill. App. 3d 356, 58 Ill. Dec. 116, 430 N.E.2d 58 (1 Dist. 1981).

—Best Interests of Child
As a matter of public policy, it would be imprudent to conclude that all orders for child support not set in dollar amounts are void; child support is for the benefit of the child, and the parties cannot deprive the child of such support by agreement. In re Florence, 260 Ill. App. 3d 116, 198 Ill. Dec. 351, 632 N.E.2d 681 (4 Dist.), appeal denied, 157 Ill. 2d 498, 205 Ill. Dec. 160, 642 N.E.2d 1277 (1994).

This statute was intended to protect the rights of children to be supported by their parents in an amount commensurate with their income; agreements between the parties which ignore the statute's mandate cannot be condoned. In re Perry, 260 Ill. App. 3d 374, 198 Ill. Dec. 227, 632 N.E.2d 286 (1 Dist. 1994).

If a child support agreement between parties is not in the best interests of the children's welfare, or if by reason of changed circumstances it becomes contrary to their best interests, the court is not bound by that agreement. Page v. Page, 30 Ill. App. 3d 514, 334 N.E.2d 212 (3 Dist. 1975).

—Improper
Where demands were placed upon defendant from other jurisdictions for other children and for debts other than the standard debts of his personal household, an order for child support in an amount less than the guidelines prescribed by this section was not appropriate. People ex rel. Browning v. Melton, 180 Ill. App. 3d 519, 129 Ill. Dec. 449, 536 N.E.2d 133 (5 Dist. 1989).

—Percentage of Income as Support
Where the agreement states a percentage of income as support, the trial court should apply subdivision (a)(3) to determine the net income, and then state the child support as a dollar amount. In re Sheetz, 254 Ill. App. 3d 695, 194 Ill. Dec. 38, 627 N.E.2d 154 (1 Dist. 1993).

Ambiguous Language
Former husband who paid in excess of specific sum set forth in settlement agreement who, at the time of the agreement, had a retarded child, and who made payments equal to 50% of his income, did not have to pay 50% of his income to ex-wife for alimony and support years later. In re Whetstone, 87 Ill. App. 3d 164, 42 Ill. Dec. 546, 409 N.E.2d 41 (1 Dist. 1980).

Appeal
Order setting a mother's child support at a certain percentage of her income was not final and appealable, and therefore related orders on the issues of custody and visitation were not final and appealable, where the child support order did not set a particular dollar amount. Shermach v. Brunory, 333 Ill. App. 3d 313, 266 Ill. Dec. 611, 775 N.E.2d 173, 2002 Ill. App. LEXIS 691 (1 Dist. 2002).

Although each judgment of support order arrearages has the full force, effect, and attributes of any judgment of this state, including the ability to be enforced, this fact alone will not confer appellate jurisdiction; if such judgments for arrearages were deemed final for the purposes of appeal, then an appeal conceivably could be taken with every monthly installment, thereby creating piecemeal appeals. In re Ryan, 188 Ill. App. 3d 679, 136 Ill. Dec. 1, 544 N.E.2d 454 (2 Dist. 1989).

Applicability
In accordance with the Illinois Parentage Act of 1984, 750 ILCS 45/1 through 27, trial courts "shall" use the guidelines and standards set forth in 750 ILCS 5/505 in determining whether to modify an order for child support in accordance with 750 ILCS 5/510. Anderson v. Heckman, 343 Ill. App. 3d 449, 278 Ill. Dec. 190, 797 N.E.2d 1108, 2003 Ill. App. LEXIS 1242 (4 Dist. 2003).

The standards contained in this section regarding child support are applicable to the determination of temporary child support. In re Rogliano, 198 Ill. App. 3d 404, 144 Ill. Dec. 595, 555 N.E.2d 1114 (5 Dist. 1990).

The guidelines in this section for awarding minimum child support are to be applied unless the court, after considering evidence presented on certain relevant factors, finds a reason for deviating from them. In re Steichen, 163 Ill. App. 3d 1074, 115 Ill. Dec. 234, 517 N.E.2d 645 (2 Dist. 1987).

Arrearages

—In General
With respect to a trail court's calculation of a father's child-

Arrearages (Cont'd)

—In General (Cont'd)

support arrearage, the trial court (1) did not err either in finding that the father's unreported bonuses were to be included in the father's income for determining arrears of the father's child support obligations, failing to deduct FICA and dependent health care insurance costs from the father's bonuses in determining arrears, or deviating from the statutory guidelines in determining the father's future child support obligations, but (2) did err in adding the father's tax refunds back into his bonuses for purposes of determining the arrears. Therefore, the appellate court modified the amount of the father's arrears. Ackerley v. Ackerley, 333 Ill. App. 3d 382, 266 Ill. Dec. 973, 775 N.E.2d 1045, 2002 Ill. App. LEXIS 857 (2 Dist. 2002).

Neither estoppel nor laches barred a parent from petitioning the court for back child support from her husband, where the husband had agreed to forbear visitation in return for cancelling support arrearages. Blisset v. Blisset, 144 Ill. App. 3d 1088, 99 Ill. Dec. 161, 495 N.E.2d 608 (4 Dist. 1986), rev'd on other grounds, 123 Ill. 2d 161, 121 Ill. Dec. 931, 526 N.E.2d 125 (1988).

A minor child, by his grandmother as next friend, could not compel his father to pay him arrearages in child support. Kelleher v. Kelleher, 21 Ill. App. 3d 601, 316 N.E.2d 212 (1 Dist. 1974).

Insofar as the question of payment for a child taken from the jurisdiction without permission of the court was concerned, residence in another state was not to be considered as to past-due support payments. Voss v. Voss, 23 Ill. App. 3d 312, 319 N.E.2d 72 (3 Dist. 1974).

The court may not cancel or deny past due child support payments granted pursuant to a decree of divorce, because past due installments of support money are a vested right and are not subject to modification either as to amount or time of payment. Baldwin v. Baldwin, 21 Ill. App. 3d 380, 315 N.E.2d 649 (3 Dist. 1974); Ellingwood v. Ellingwood, 25 Ill. App. 3d 587, 323 N.E.2d 571 (1 Dist. 1975).

The trial court did not err in ruling that the assignment to the former husband's attorney of funds owed the former husband from a corporation was void on the basis of fraud and was of no effect and that the funds due to the former husband from said corporation were properly ordered delivered to appellee as partial payment of child support arrearages. Till v. Till, 87 Ill. App. 2d 358, 231 N.E.2d 641 (1 Dist. 1967).

Past due installments of alimony and support money are a vested right, and the court has no authority to modify them in any particular, either as to amount or time of payment. Shuff v. Fulte, 344 Ill. App. 157, 100 N.E.2d 502 (3 Dist. 1951).

—Burden of Proof

Subsection (d) operates to define the person entitled to support as a judgment debtor and, therefore, such a person need only establish the existence of the obligation itself, i.e., the dissolution judgment and underlying agreement, and the obligor has the burden of proof with regard to a claim that he or she has satisfied the obligation in whole or in part. In re Jorczak, 315 Ill. App. 3d 954, 248 Ill. Dec. 862, 735 N.E.2d 182, 2000 Ill. App. LEXIS 714 (4 Dist. 2000).

—Enforcing Payment

Contempt is not a proper means of enforcing payment of child support arrearages where the children being supported have reached their majority. Fox v. Fox, 56 Ill. App. 3d 446, 14 Ill. Dec. 201, 371 N.E.2d 1254 (5 Dist. 1978).

—Equitable Estoppel

Equitable estoppel did not bar a judgment for the full amount of the arrearages where the noncustodial parent unilaterally reduced child support payments to custodial parent, but continued to make direct payments to the adult children. In re Bjorklund, 88 Ill. App. 3d 576, 43 Ill. Dec. 757, 410 N.E.2d 890 (1 Dist. 1980).

—Improper Order

The trial court erred in relying on an order in determining the amount of arrearage where while entitled an "Agreed Order," it did not contain the signature of either husband or his attorney. In re Getautas, 189 Ill. App. 3d 148, 136 Ill. Dec. 509, 544 N.E.2d 1284 (2 Dist. 1989).

—Insufficient Evidence

Where there was insufficient testimony concerning the purpose of the disputed checks, the trial court could not possibly determine whether there was an arrearage in child support. Jamal v. Jamal, 98 Ill. App. 2d 180, 240 N.E.2d 246 (1 Dist. 1968).

—Interest

Where the respondent did not reduce his payments in order to relinquish his support of his adult children and did not enjoy the use of the additional money during the interim between the reduction of the support payments and the outcome of the action for arrearages, the trial court could have determined that the respondent acted in good faith and that interest was not appropriate. In re Bjorklund, 88 Ill. App. 3d 576, 43 Ill. Dec. 757, 410 N.E.2d 890 (1 Dist. 1980).

—No Valid Claim

Where the record contained the requisite clear and unequivocal evidence that husband and wife agreed to modify husband's child support obligations, the terms being reflected in the manner in which husband made the payments, the wife had no basis for claiming child support arrearages. In re Runge, 102 Ill. App. 3d 356, 58 Ill. Dec. 116, 430 N.E.2d 58 (1 Dist. 1981).

—Setoffs

It was error for the trial court to allow a set off against arrearages owed for child support of the amount paid directly by respondent to his adult children, as respondent never petitioned the court for modification of the child support award. In re Bjorklund, 88 Ill. App. 3d 576, 43 Ill. Dec. 757, 410 N.E.2d 890 (1 Dist. 1980).

—Vested Rights

The trial court properly dismissed that portion of a father's petition that requested relief from his arrearage for child support payments that had accumulated since his incarceration, since children have a vested right to past-due child support and an obligated parent may have support payments modified only as to installments accruing subsequent to the due notice of the petition for modification. In re Burbridge, 317 Ill. App. 3d 190, 250 Ill. Dec. 510, 738 N.E.2d 979, 2000 Ill. App. LEXIS 831 (3 Dist. 2000).

Past due installments of child support are vested rights and cannot be modified by a court. Escott v. Escott, 26 Ill. App. 3d 417, 325 N.E.2d 395 (4 Dist. 1975).

Attorney Fees

The trial court in its discretion, had the right to award attorney's fees to a plaintiff to enforce her rights under the divorce decree, particularly where the rights affected the welfare of the parties' children. Neeland v. Neeland, 17 Ill. App. 3d 803, 308 N.E.2d 651 (3 Dist. 1974).

—Allowed

Court's finding that appellant was willfully in violation of a court order was supported by the evidence and thus the statute required that appellant pay his former spouse's reasonable attorney fees. In re Scott, 286 Ill. App. 3d 1056, 222 Ill. Dec. 594, 678 N.E.2d 1 (3 Dist. 1996).

—Denied

The trial court did not abuse its discretion in denying wife a hearing to determine whether husband should pay any or all of her attorney fees, as husband's failure to make support payments during the time the boys lived with him was not without justification. In re Duerr, 250 Ill. App. 3d 232, 190 Ill. Dec. 251, 621 N.E.2d 120 (1 Dist.), appeal denied, 152 Ill. 2d 557, 190 Ill. Dec. 886, 622 N.E.2d 1203 (1993).

—Financial Resources

The Marriage and Dissolution Act merely requires the court to consider the financial resources of the parties in coming to a conclusion about attorney fees. In re Duerr, 250 Ill. App. 3d 232, 190 Ill. Dec. 251, 621 N.E.2d 120 (1 Dist.), appeal denied, 152 Ill. 2d 557, 190 Ill. Dec. 886, 622 N.E.2d 1203 (1993).

Automatic Increases

Because changes in the factors relevant to a child support award cannot be anticipated with accuracy, a circuit court should ordinarily not try to anticipate such changes by making its award of child support to increase automatically with the child's age; thus a self-adjusting aspect of the award of child support must, therefore, be reversed. McManus v. McManus, 38 Ill. App. 3d 645, 348 N.E.2d

Automatic Increases (Cont'd)
507 (5 Dist. 1976); In re Moore, 117 Ill. App. 3d 206, 72 Ill. Dec. 797, 453 N.E.2d 102 (5 Dist. 1983).

Award

—Ability to Pay

Children are not expected to have to live at a minimal level of comfort while the noncustodial parent is living a life of luxury; thus, where a noncustodial parent has the ability to pay support in excess of the stated needs of a child, a court may order child support in excess of that which would enable the child to enjoy the standard of living he would have had if a marriage had not been dissolved. Hall v. Clark (In re Keon C.), 344 Ill. App. 3d 1137, 279 Ill. Dec. 674, 800 N.E.2d 1257, 2003 Ill. App. LEXIS 1498 (4 Dist. 2003), appeal denied sub nom. In re Keon C., 208 Ill. 2d 538, 284 Ill. Dec. 340, 809 N.E.2d 1286 (2004).

Whether sums of money withdrawn from husband's corporate interests were dividends and therefore income for federal income tax purposes or loans and not income was relevant only as it affected one of the crucial factors in determining the amount of alimony and child support, namely, defendant's ability to pay. If the sums withdrawn were loans, plaintiff's estimation of defendant's income was less than if they were labeled dividends, and therefore income, which would have increased his annual income but reduced his equity and subjected him to income tax would have materially reduced his purported income. Sandberg v. Sandberg, 11 Ill. App. 3d 495, 297 N.E.2d 654 (1 Dist. 1973).

—Adequacy

For a case discussing factors affecting the adequacy of an award of child support, see Sandberg v. Sandberg, 11 Ill. App. 3d 495, 297 N.E.2d 654 (1 Dist. 1973).

—Certain and Definite

The provision for the payment of alimony by husband as "one-half of his salary earned and received as a teacher or employee of the public schools of the City of Chicago, Illinois, as long as he is so employed" was held reasonably definite and certain while husband was employed as a school teacher. Condy v. Condy, 328 Ill. App. 8, 65 N.E.2d 219 (1946).

—Change of Circumstances

Defendant did not sustain his burden in showing a change of circumstances that would justify a court in changing child support provisions of a divorce decree. Chamberlin v. Chamberlin, 119 Ill. App. 2d 295, 256 N.E.2d 159 (1 Dist. 1969).

—Collection

Under former Ill.Rev.Stat., ch. 40, para. 19 of the Divorce Act, (see now this section), where a divorced father's cessation of child support payments were made against the will of the divorced mother, the divorced father's child support payments were not made uncollectable just because the child reached the age of majority. Wilson v. Wilson, 122 Ill. App. 2d 142, 257 N.E.2d 810 (2 Dist. 1970).

—Denied

Given the great disparity in the parties' incomes and future earning capacities, the parties' standard of living and the wife's reasonable needs, the trial court's denial of the husband's request for child support was a proper exercise of discretion. In re Vendredi, 230 Ill. App. 3d 1061, 174 Ill. Dec. 329, 598 N.E.2d 961 (1 Dist. 1992).

—Determination

Wife's military allowances were required to be included in her income for the computation of child support. In re Baylor, 324 Ill. App. 3d 213, 257 Ill. Dec. 638, 753 N.E.2d 1264, 2001 Ill. App. LEXIS 625 (4 Dist. 2001).

Trial court's decision to award child support, based upon financial information from the marriage dissolution proceedings six months earlier rather than compelling production of current information on income, asset holdings and liabilities and expenses for former spouse and children, was held proper. In re Schuster, 224 Ill. App. 3d 958, 167 Ill. Dec. 73, 586 N.E.2d 1345 (1992).

It is the court's responsibility and not the parties' to determine the adequacy of child support and the amount of child support. Blisset v. Blisset, 144 Ill. App. 3d 1088, 99 Ill. Dec. 161, 495 N.E.2d 608 (4 Dist. 1986), rev'd on other grounds, 123 Ill. 2d 161, 121 Ill. Dec. 931, 526 N.E.2d 125 (1988).

An award for child support must necessarily reflect a balance of the intensity of the child's need with the ability of the parents to provide for that need. Harding v. Harding, 59 Ill. App. 3d 25, 16 Ill. Dec. 426, 374 N.E.2d 1304 (4 Dist. 1978).

The court properly considered the subsequent employment and earnings of the defendant-mother, which also was a proper consideration in determining a reasonable and proper support amount to be ordered. Edwards v. Edwards, 125 Ill. App. 2d 91, 259 N.E.2d 820 (4 Dist. 1970).

—Evidence

An award not supported by the evidence must be set aside. In re Hilkovitch, 124 Ill. App. 3d 401, 79 Ill. Dec. 891, 464 N.E.2d 795 (1 Dist. 1984).

—Exceeding Guidelines

Award of child support for one child was generally a minimum of 20 percent of a supporting net parent's income and the trial court erred in awarding an amount in excess of that by miscalculating the husband's income. Sawicki v. Sawicki, 346 Ill. App. 3d 1107, 282 Ill. Dec. 404, 806 N.E.2d 701, 2004 Ill. App. LEXIS 269 (3 Dist. 2004).

It was not error for the court to order support in excess of the minimum provided for in the guidelines; it was agreed upon between the parties as allowed by subdivision (a)(2) of this section, and even though it was not required to do so, the trial court did enter findings which concerned the agreement and the basis for the child support amount. In re Steichen, 163 Ill. App. 3d 1074, 115 Ill. Dec. 234, 517 N.E.2d 645 (2 Dist. 1987).

—Excess of Needs

Child support award was not an abuse of discretion because 750 ILCS 5/503(g) trust proceeds took care of the minor child's other needs, and award was in excess of the amount indicated on custodial parent's affidavit listing expenses for minor. In re Andrew, 258 Ill. App. 3d 924, 194 Ill. Dec. 724, 628 N.E.2d 221 (1 Dist. 1993).

Where a noncustodial parent has the ability to pay support in excess of the stated needs of the child, a court may order child support in excess of the needs to enable the child to enjoy the standard of living he would have had if the marriage had not been dissolved. In re Rogliano, 198 Ill. App. 3d 404, 144 Ill. Dec. 595, 555 N.E.2d 1114 (5 Dist. 1990).

—Explicit Findings Not Required

Trial court was not required to make explicit findings when entering its order of support. In re Reyna, 78 Ill. App. 3d 1010, 34 Ill. Dec. 818, 398 N.E.2d 641 (3 Dist. 1979).

—Factors

Among the factors to be considered in determining the amount of child support are the ages of the parties, their condition of health, the property and income of the husband, any separate property and income of the wife, and the station in life of the parties. Fields v. Fields, 54 Ill. App. 3d 400, 12 Ill. Dec. 89, 369 N.E.2d 586 (5 Dist. 1977); Sullivan v. Sullivan, 68 Ill. App. 3d 242, 24 Ill. Dec. 719, 385 N.E.2d 860 (5 Dist. 1979); In re Preston, 81 Ill. App. 3d 672, 37 Ill. Dec. 442, 402 N.E.2d 332 (5 Dist. 1980); In re Edelstein, 82 Ill. App. 3d 574, 38 Ill. Dec. 235, 403 N.E.2d 323 (1 Dist. 1980); In re Dulyn, 89 Ill. App. 3d 304, 44 Ill. Dec. 622, 411 N.E.2d 988 (1 Dist. 1980); In re Roth, 99 Ill. App. 3d 679, 55 Ill. Dec. 271, 426 N.E.2d 246 (1 Dist. 1981); In re Butler, 106 Ill. App. 3d 831, 62 Ill. Dec. 535, 436 N.E.2d 561 (1 Dist. 1982); In re Rundle, 107 Ill. App. 3d 880, 63 Ill. Dec. 491, 438 N.E.2d 229 (5 Dist. 1982); In re Moriarty, 132 Ill. App. 3d 895, 88 Ill. Dec. 222, 478 N.E.2d 537 (1 Dist. 1985); Blisset v. Blisset, 123 Ill. 2d 161, 121 Ill. Dec. 931, 526 N.E.2d 125 (1988); In re McBride, 166 Ill. App. 3d 504, 116 Ill. Dec. 880, 519 N.E.2d 1095 (1 Dist. 1988); Rawles v. Hartman, 172 Ill. App. 3d 931, 123 Ill. Dec. 217, 527 N.E.2d 680 (2 Dist. 1988).

Maintenance, child support, and attorney fees are directly related to a final property disposition since these awards are dependent upon the financial resources of the party, including marital property, for whom the award is made. In re White, 98 Ill. App. 3d 380, 53 Ill. Dec. 786, 424 N.E.2d 421 (5 Dist. 1981).

—Improper

The trial judge's deviation from the statutory guidelines in

Award (Cont'd)

—Improper (Cont'd)

establishing child support constituted error which necessitated reversal. In re Jelinek, 244 Ill. App. 3d 496, 184 Ill. Dec. 692, 613 N.E.2d 1284 (1 Dist.), appeal denied, 152 Ill. 2d 560, 190 Ill. Dec. 890, 622 N.E.2d 1207 (1993).

The trial court abused its discretion by basing the award of child support on the assumption, unsupported by the evidence, that respondent earned more than the record indicated and by requiring respondent to pay a disproportionate portion of the children's expenses. In re Smith, 132 Ill. App. 3d 694, 88 Ill. Dec. 909, 479 N.E.2d 929 (1 Dist. 1985).

Where the names of the children were mentioned in the complaint but the only relief sought was a divorce, plaintiff could not be required to pay $40 per week to the clerk for the support of his minor children. Weldon v. Weldon, 3 Ill. App. 3d 947, 279 N.E.2d 537 (3 Dist. 1972).

—Increase Proper

Husband's increase in child support was proper where he admitted that his income had increased and, in fact, the record reflected a substantial increase. In re Mitteer, 241 Ill. App. 3d 217, 181 Ill. Dec. 534, 608 N.E.2d 607 (4 Dist. 1993).

—Insufficient

Where the trial court refused to set aside the father's nonmarital funds, pursuant to 750 ILCS 5/503(g), for the payment of child support during the father's incarceration, the trial court's decision did not have support under 750 ILCS 5/505(a)(1), as § 505(a)(1) did not limit what assets the trial court could reach to assure that a child support award was satisfied. Hari v. Hari, 345 Ill. App. 3d 1116, 281 Ill. Dec. 518, 804 N.E.2d 144, 2004 Ill. App. LEXIS 91 (4 Dist. 2004).

Where, after adjusting their earned incomes for the amount of maintenance and support, the mother was being asked to support two children and herself with less than half the funds available to the father, the award of maintenance and support was inadequate. In re Fairchild, 110 Ill. App. 3d 470, 66 Ill. Dec. 131, 442 N.E.2d 557 (3 Dist. 1982).

Where divorced wife received an increase in child support from $60 a week to 34% of divorced husband's monthly income of $1600, a new hearing was required since such increase was not supported by evidence, trial court overemphasized percentage of income formula and the financial situation of the divorced couple was not suitably determined. In re Cooper, 102 Ill. App. 3d 872, 58 Ill. Dec. 437, 430 N.E.2d 379 (1 Dist. 1981).

Evidence clearly showed needs of the child exceeding the amount awarded for support. Carney v. Carney, 67 Ill. App. 3d 919, 24 Ill. Dec. 447, 385 N.E.2d 359 (4 Dist. 1979).

—Intent of Parties

The evidence adduced by the plaintiff clearly showed that it was the intention of the parties at the time of the entry of the decree that defendant was to pay child support in the amount of $145 per month or 25% of his net income after taxes, whichever was greater. Schwartz v. Schwartz, 69 Ill. App. 2d 128, 216 N.E.2d 505 (1 Dist. 1966).

—Retroactive Allowance

For a case discussing the court's ability to make a retroactive allowance for child support in divorce or separate maintenance proceeding, see Plant v. Plant, 20 Ill. App. 3d 5, 312 N.E.2d 847 (5 Dist. 1974).

—Specificity

A judgement awarding child support to be paid as a percentage of net income with fixed dollar limitations was voidable, not void, and was not subject to collateral attack. In re Mitchell, 181 Ill. 2d 169, 229 Ill. Dec. 508, 692 N.E.2d 281 (1998).

Subdivision (a)(5) requires that the final order state the support level solely in dollar amounts. In re Mitchell, 181 Ill. 2d 169, 229 Ill. Dec. 508, 692 N.E.2d 281 (1998).

Increases in support that corresponded with the periodic increases in strike benefits that the father would receive were not speculative, and did not violate the dollar amount requirement under subdivision (a)(5). In re Burris, 263 Ill. App. 3d 495, 200 Ill. Dec. 880, 636 N.E.2d 71 (5 Dist. 1994).

Where the circuit court ordered the husband to pay 20 percent of his net income for child support, it erred in failing to state the child support obligation in a specific dollar amount. In re Campbell, 261 Ill. App. 3d 483, 199 Ill. Dec. 1, 633 N.E.2d 797 (1 Dist. 1993), appeal denied, 156 Ill. 2d 556, 202 Ill. Dec. 919, 638 N.E.2d 1113 (1994).

—Upheld

In awarding child support, the trial court did not erroneously fail to consider assistance the husband received from his parents, the husband's standard of living, or the husband's earning potential where the husband has supported his family by farming during the marriage and there was no evidence that he acted in bad faith in continuing to farm, the husband's father expected repayment for the assistance he provided, and the award was for more than 25 percent of the father's net income. In re Marriage of Bowlby, 338 Ill. App. 3d 720, 273 Ill. Dec. 466, 789 N.E.2d 366, 2003 Ill. App. LEXIS 530 (5 Dist. 2003).

Trial court properly weighed the relevant factors and did not abuse its discretion in awarding $2,000 per month for child support, which was less than 20% of payor's net income. In re Singleteary, 293 Ill. App. 3d 25, 227 Ill. Dec. 598, 687 N.E.2d 1080 (1 Dist. 1997).

The trial court did not err in setting child support at $1,500 per month, notwithstanding the father's claim in his affidavit that he only had a net monthly income of $8,216; the trial court found the father's affidavit to be untrustworthy, and instead found his annual income to be in excess of $205,000. Janssen ex rel. Janssen v. Turner, 292 Ill. App. 3d 219, 226 Ill. Dec. 202, 685 N.E.2d 16 (4 Dist. 1997).

It was apparent the court took into consideration the statutory factors, and in light of these factors, it was not an abuse of discretion to award petitioner $1,700 per month in child support because it was consistent with the standard of living these children would have enjoyed had the marriage not been dissolved, and the financial resources and needs of the parties. In re Tietz, 238 Ill. App. 3d 965, 178 Ill. Dec. 876, 605 N.E.2d 670 (4 Dist. 1992).

The trial court did not abuse its discretion by ordering supporting parent to pay 20% of his net income although his pay only increased 8% over the years. People ex rel. Stokely v. Goodenow, 211 Ill. App. 3d 802, 164 Ill. Dec. 548, 583 N.E.2d 102 (4 Dist. 1991).

Where it was clear that the trial court took into consideration the transportation costs the husband would incur and the cost of term life insurance the husband was ordered to acquire, and credited the husband with an amount equal to four weeks" support to compensate for the time the husband would exercise visitation, the court did not agree that the trial court's award of child support was contrary to the facts or the law, and affirmed the trial court's judgment ordering the husband to pay $3,300 per month child support based on an average net monthly income of approximately $9,800. In re Osborn, 206 Ill. App. 3d 588, 151 Ill. Dec. 663, 564 N.E.2d 1325 (5 Dist. 1990), cert. denied, 137 Ill. 2d 666, 156 Ill. Dec. 563, 571 N.E.2d 150 (1991).

Where support payments per month constituted less than one-seventh of petitioner husband's net income, there was no breach of discretion in the trial court's determination. In re Bussey, 128 Ill. App. 3d 730, 84 Ill. Dec. 34, 471 N.E.2d 563 (4 Dist. 1984).

An award of $250 monthly was not unreasonable support for a 15 month old child, considering that support awards may be changed from time to time as circumstances dictate. In re Spomer, 123 Ill. App. 3d 31, 78 Ill. Dec. 605, 462 N.E.2d 724 (5 Dist. 1984).

Child support award to former wife was adequate, based upon her relatively good income, the upcoming ability of the twins to commence part-time work, former husband's needs for his second family, and the fact that the present award takes over 21% of his income. In re Runge, 102 Ill. App. 3d 356, 58 Ill. Dec. 116, 430 N.E.2d 58 (1 Dist. 1981).

Based on the financial position of the parties and the needs of their two minor children, the evidence held sufficient to award child support in the amount of $50 weekly for each child. In re Clearman, 97 Ill. App. 3d 641, 53 Ill. Dec. 91, 423 N.E.2d 283 (3 Dist. 1981).

Court's award of child support in the amount of $100 per month per child was not excessive. In re Coram, 86 Ill. App. 3d 845, 42 Ill. Dec. 40, 408 N.E.2d 418 (5 Dist. 1980).

Child support award was not against the manifest weight of the evidence. In re Sipich, 80 Ill. App. 3d 883, 36 Ill. Dec. 276, 400 N.E.2d 696 (1 Dist. 1980).

Award (Cont'd)

—Upheld (Cont'd)

An award of $300 per month was adequate considering the income of the appellee, the maintenance and property award to the appellant, and the fact that appellee would have custody of the child for three months of the year. In re Preston, 81 Ill. App. 3d 672, 37 Ill. Dec. 442, 402 N.E.2d 332 (5 Dist. 1980).

An award of $1,000 per month for child support was proper where in addition to the father's increased ability to pay, other factors, such as the financial resources and needs of the mother as custodial parent and the standard of living the child would have enjoyed had the marriage not been dissolved, supported the award. In re Edelstein, 82 Ill. App. 3d 574, 38 Ill. Dec. 235, 403 N.E.2d 323 (1 Dist. 1980).

Amounts of maintenance and child support awarded by the circuit court in this case were based upon consideration of all relevant factors where court considered the husband as a police officer had regular salary and that he had previously earned income from overtime although this income was not certain to continue. In re Reyna, 78 Ill. App. 3d 1010, 34 Ill. Dec. 818, 398 N.E.2d 641 (3 Dist. 1979).

Court-ordered child support sum of $35 a week, which was approximately ⅙th of wife's gross income before taxes, was not so manifestly unfair or unjust as to be disturbed by appellate court. Schaperkoetter v. Schaperkoetter, 13 Ill. App. 3d 120, 299 N.E.2d 780 (5 Dist. 1973).

Child support of $200 per month for a 16 year old child was not grossly inadequate despite father's income of $41,000. Saxon v. Saxon, 24 Ill. App. 2d 116, 164 N.E.2d 248 (1 Dist. 1960).

Best Interests of Children

—Child Support Settlement Agreements

Requiring courts to comply with subsection (a) before entering settlement agreements concerning child support is an assurance toward the end that the best interests of children will be protected; courts may approve of and enter agreed orders for child support, however, when the agreed upon support is less than that provided for in the guidelines, the court must hear evidence on the relevant factors set forth in subdivision (a)(2) and make express findings for allowing the deviation. In re Perry, 260 Ill. App. 3d 374, 198 Ill. Dec. 227, 632 N.E.2d 286 (1 Dist. 1994).

—Custody Agreement

The agreement of petitioner and respondent that the court enter an order granting custody of their children to the respondent was in the best interests of the children where petitioner herself testified that she was in fact unable to care for the children at the time the order was entered, in that she was at the time pregnant and about to be married, she and her husband-to-be were planning to move into a small apartment where young children were not permitted to live, and she was afraid of leaving the children with her parents because of their poor relationship. Kminek v. Kminek, 27 Ill. App. 3d 78, 325 N.E.2d 741 (1 Dist. 1975).

Child custody agreements between parties to a divorce do not deprive the court of its jurisdiction to determine questions regarding the welfare of children and do not provide a "strait jacket" for the court in its obligation to make a determination as to what is for the best interest of the children. Kminek v. Kminek, 27 Ill. App. 3d 78, 325 N.E.2d 741 (1 Dist. 1975).

—Stable Environment

Stability of environment is an important factor in determining the best interests and welfare of children. Kminek v. Kminek, 27 Ill. App. 3d 78, 325 N.E.2d 741 (1 Dist. 1975).

Where the welfare of children is at stake, care must be taken so that their best interests are not impaired by being shuttled between contesting parents. Kminek v. Kminek, 27 Ill. App. 3d 78, 325 N.E.2d 741 (1 Dist. 1975).

Where the record indicated that children were making a good adjustment to their present environment, and the court specifically found that it would be an unfair and improvident act to uproot them and change them back, this finding was not against the manifest weight of the evidence. Kminek v. Kminek, 27 Ill. App. 3d 78, 325 N.E.2d 741 (1 Dist. 1975).

Burden of Proof

This section shifted the burden of presenting evidence in a child support hearing to the parent who wishes to shift the noncustodial parent's contribution below or above the specified percentages. Blaisdell v. Blaisdell, 142 Ill. App. 3d 1034, 97 Ill. Dec. 186, 492 N.E.2d 622 (1 Dist. 1986); In re Rogliano, 198 Ill. App. 3d 404, 144 Ill. Dec. 595, 555 N.E.2d 1114 (5 Dist. 1990).

Calculation

—Improper

Trial court abused its discretion in calculating the amount of child support that the husband should be paying, as it did not deduct the child's health insurance premiums before determining the husband's net income for the purpose of determining the proper amount of child support. Sawicki v. Sawicki, 346 Ill. App. 3d 1107, 282 Ill. Dec. 404, 806 N.E.2d 701, 2004 Ill. App. LEXIS 269 (3 Dist. 2004).

By excluding the husband's full pro form a allocation from child support calculation, the trial court abused its discretion. In re Winne, 239 Ill. App. 3d 273, 179 Ill. Dec. 945, 606 N.E.2d 777 (2 Dist. 1992).

Trial court erred where its determination of a child support order of less than the guidelines call for was due to the court's miscalculation of husband's net income and was not due to any intent of the trial court to impose a child support order under the guidelines because husband was self-employed; the trial court was to start with his reported gross income from all sources from the years 1989-1991, not his claimed income after he had deducted therefrom sums permitted under the Federal tax code, and deduct from that figure what it deemed appropriate under subdivision (a)(3)(h) of this section as reasonable and necessary expenses for producing income in determining his net income under the Act. In re Carpel, 232 Ill. App. 3d 806, 173 Ill. Dec. 873, 597 N.E.2d 847 (4 Dist.), cert. denied, 147 Ill. 2d 625, 180 Ill. Dec. 148, 606 N.E.2d 1225 (1992).

Change in Circumstances

—Court Involvement

If the change in a parent's income is sufficiently substantial to merit a change in that parent's child support obligations, the court should have the opportunity to evaluate the parties' circumstances in light of the best interests of the children before the change in child support takes effect. In re Ingram, 259 Ill. App. 3d 685, 197 Ill. Dec. 383, 631 N.E.2d 386 (2 Dist. 1994).

—Employment Status

Father's change in employment status, which yielded a 130 percent increase in the father's weekly income, was sufficient to support a petition for modification of the father's support obligation under 750 ILCS 5/510(a) and required application of the support guidelines found in 750 ILCS 5/505. Anderson v. Heckman, 343 Ill. App. 3d 449, 278 Ill. Dec. 190, 797 N.E.2d 1108, 2003 Ill. App. LEXIS 1242 (4 Dist. 2003).

A divorced parent should not see the fact that his child support obligation has been limited to a fixed payment based on his income as an opportunity to change careers; this is especially true where the noncustodian continues to enjoy his previous life style due to the income of a current spouse. In re Kern, 245 Ill. App. 3d 575, 185 Ill. Dec. 843, 615 N.E.2d 402 (4 Dist. 1993).

In determining whether a parent's change in employment status was made in good faith, the crucial consideration is whether the change was prompted by a desire to evade financial responsibility for supporting his her children or to otherwise jeopardize their interests. In re Schuster, 224 Ill. App. 3d 958, 167 Ill. Dec. 73, 586 N.E.2d 1345 (1992).

—Evidence

Where there has been a substantial change in circumstances, such as a change of custody, the factors set forth in this section should be applied and it is the responsibility of the parties to present the evidence with respect to the factors set forth therein. White v. White, 204 Ill. App. 3d 579, 149 Ill. Dec. 691, 561 N.E.2d 1387 (4 Dist. 1990).

If the court determines that a substantial change in circumstances has occurred, then the court should determine the amount of child support to be paid and in doing so, the court should follow the statutory guidelines set forth in this section. In re Stone, 191 Ill. App. 3d 172, 138 Ill. Dec. 547, 547 N.E.2d 714 (4 Dist. 1989).

Change in Circumstances (Cont'd)

—Factors Considered

Trial court erred in granting summary judgment to former husband on former wife's petition to increase child support because, even though the husband's salary had not increased, an important component for the purpose of calculating child support had increased because the court had miscalculated his net income by not including the realized distributions from certain marital property in the net income figure for the purpose of calculating child support. In re Marriage of Colangelo, Ill. App. 3d , 290 Ill. Dec. 986, 822 N.E.2d 571, 2005 Ill. App. LEXIS 39 (2 Dist. 2005).

In considering modification of child support based on an increase in the children's needs and the ability of the father to pay, it was not appropriate for the trial court to focus on the fact that the mother was living with a man to whom she was not married, and to limit child support without any evidence or argument as to the effect of the living arrangement on the children or her resources. Department of Pub. Aid ex rel. Nale v. Nale, 294 Ill. App. 3d 747, 229 Ill. Dec. 5, 690 N.E.2d 1052 (4 Dist. 1998).

—Health Condition

When a voluntary job change is precipitated by health reasons and the change results in substantial reduction of income, a corresponding modification of support responsibilities may be justified. In re Maczko, 263 Ill. App. 3d 991, 201 Ill. Dec. 127, 636 N.E.2d 559 (1 Dist. 1992).

—Held Sufficient

In light of divorced wife's increase in salary and her former husband's decrease in salary due to health problems, there was a sufficient showing of a change in circumstances whereby the divorce decree could be modified to suspend alimony and reduce child support. Broday v. Broday, 43 Ill. App. 3d 628, 2 Ill. Dec. 151, 357 N.E.2d 128 (1 Dist. 1976).

—Increased Need

Once the court found a change in circumstances had occurred, and the child support was increased from $200 per month, with a six week abatement during the summer visitation, to $325 per month with no such abatement, this increase was excessive where defendant presented a schedule which showed his expenses required by a previous order totaling approximately $3,025 where these expenses included child support, medical insurance premiums for son, medicine and dentist expenses for son, and premiums for life and disability insurance policies on himself which have plaintiff as the beneficiary for son's benefit. Fedun v. Kuczek, 155 Ill. App. 3d 798, 108 Ill. Dec. 370, 508 N.E.2d 531 (4 Dist. 1987).

Increasing the noncustodial parent's support payments from $45 per week to $640 per month, although a significant increase from the original order, was not an abuse of discretion where the evidence indicated both increased needs of the children and an increased ability of respondent to pay. Gibson v. Barton, 118 Ill. App. 3d 576, 74 Ill. Dec. 252, 455 N.E.2d 282 (4 Dist. 1983).

Where a plaintiff had demonstrated to some extent a change of circumstances reflecting increased need, it was an abuse of discretion for the trial court to deny her petition for increased child support without a proper determination of that increased need. Addington v. Addington, 48 Ill. App. 3d 859, 6 Ill. Dec. 622, 363 N.E.2d 151 (1 Dist. 1977).

Sufficient change in circumstances existed to warrant an increase in child support where the needs of the children had increased since the entry of the divorce decree, where the mother's employment necessitated the additional expense of a full-time baby sitter, where costs for the children's clothing doubled, where entertainment expenses tripled due to the frequency of having to go out for dinner, and where defendant's financial capabilities increased. Killinger v. Killinger, 40 Ill. App. 3d 962, 353 N.E.2d 284 (1 Dist. 1976).

—Justification for Modification

In modifying support payments, the court must inquire whether sufficient cause has intervened since the entry of the judgment to authorize the court to modify the allowance; new or changed circumstances must be material or substantial and courts must consider both the circumstances of the parents and the children. In re Raidbard, 87 Ill. App. 3d 158, 42 Ill. Dec. 312, 408 N.E.2d 1021 (1 Dist. 1980).

In all cases where petitions to modify payments under a divorce decree are involved, the primary question is whether changes in circumstances of the parties justify the modification. Bulmer v. Bulmer, 28 Ill. App. 3d 406, 328 N.E.2d 622 (5 Dist. 1975).

—Lacking

Custodial parent's support modification request where noncustodial parent was ordered to pay custodial parent $35 per week toward child support was reversed as it failed to meet the clear rule that the custodial parent prove a material change in circumstances by clearly establishing an increased need for the support of the children and a corresponding increased ability to pay on the part of the noncustodial parent since the time of entry of the divorce decree. Gauger v. Gauger, 70 Ill. App. 3d 378, 26 Ill. Dec. 499, 388 N.E.2d 123 (1 Dist. 1979).

Child Support

—In General

Where a divorce has been granted with custody of the children to the mother and a gross sum had been allowed her as alimony, such a situation does not release the father from his legal liability to provide the necessary support for his minor children. Kemp v. Kemp, 332 Ill. App. 432, 75 N.E.2d 385 (1 Dist. 1947).

—Characterization of Payments

The trial court did not err in characterizing former husband's monthly payments to former spouse as child support and not alimony, where the original divorce judgment provided and further set forth that these payments would decrease by 60% from $1,500 to $600 a month upon former spouse's remarriage. In re Kessler, 110 Ill. App. 3d 61, 65 Ill. Dec. 707, 441 N.E.2d 1221 (1 Dist. 1982).

—Dollar Amounts

An order of dissolution must express child support obligations in dollar amounts. In re Ingram, 259 Ill. App. 3d 685, 197 Ill. Dec. 383, 631 N.E.2d 386 (2 Dist. 1994).

—Extended Care

There should not be an automatic deduction in child support because a noncustodial parent has the opportunity to spend substantial time with children and to fulfill the parental responsibility of caring for children. In re Demattia, 302 Ill. App. 3d 390, 235 Ill. Dec. 807, 706 N.E.2d 67 (4 Dist. 1999).

—Future

Future child support should be based on reliable evidence of respondent's current income and either party will be able to request a change in child support if respondent's income changes, or if there is any other substantial change in circumstances. In re Sheetz, 254 Ill. App. 3d 695, 194 Ill. Dec. 38, 627 N.E.2d 154 (1 Dist. 1993).

—Improper Designation

Where original dissolution of marriage order improperly designated child support as a percentage of father's income rather than listing a dollar amount as required by statute, case was remanded for proper designation. In re Baggett, 281 Ill. App. 3d 34, 217 Ill. Dec. 181, 666 N.E.2d 850 (5 Dist. 1996).

—Military Allowance

The Act's reference to "all sources" must be given effect to include military allowances in the computation of child support. In re McGowan, 265 Ill. App. 3d 976, 202 Ill. Dec. 827, 638 N.E.2d 695 (1 Dist. 1994).

—Mortgage Payments

Where petitioner owned a one-half interest in the marital residence and would, upon the sale of the house, receive one-half of the proceeds, while payments technically supported the children, they, in effect, amounted to a compulsory savings program for petitioner and given that petitioner would recoup these payments upon the residence's sale, they did not qualify as child support. In re Pihaly, 258 Ill. App. 3d 851, 194 Ill. Dec. 655, 627 N.E.2d 1297 (2 Dist. 1994).

—Not Affected by Visitation Schedule

Where visitation order provided wife had visitation with the children every other weekend, one-half of the summer vacation, for 312 hours on Tuesdays and Thursdays and alternate holidays in

Child Support (Cont'd)

—Not Affected by Visitation Schedule (Cont'd)
the year, there was no authority to support her contention that she should not have to pay child support because of the visitation schedule. In re Phillips, 244 Ill. App. 3d 577, 186 Ill. Dec. 108, 615 N.E.2d 1165 (4 Dist. 1993).

—Petitioner's Inability to Pay
The trial court did not err in refusing to make petitioner pay child support but rather ordered a review of the matter in one year where petitioner lacked sufficient financial resources, experience, or vocational training to provide for her needs in the same standard of living as that established during the marriage and she could not support herself and provide support for the children. In re Frey, 258 Ill. App. 3d 442, 196 Ill. Dec. 531, 630 N.E.2d 466 (5 Dist. 1994).

—Separate Suit
A woman may maintain a separate suit against her husband or former husband for the support and maintenance of their minor child. Loss v. Loss, 80 Ill. App. 2d 376, 224 N.E.2d 271 (2 Dist. 1967).

—Severability
The portion of the agreement which provided for percentage-based child support payments was clearly separable from the portion which provided for payments in the amount of $660 per month. In re Ingram, 259 Ill. App. 3d 685, 197 Ill. Dec. 383, 631 N.E.2d 386 (2 Dist. 1994).

—Shown Needs
Child's entitlement to a level of support is not limited to his or her "shown needs." Hall v. Clark (In re Keon C.), 344 Ill. App. 3d 1137, 279 Ill. Dec. 674, 800 N.E.2d 1257, 2003 Ill. App. LEXIS 1498 (4 Dist. 2003), appeal denied sub nom. In re Keon C., 208 Ill. 2d 538, 284 Ill. Dec. 340, 809 N.E.2d 1286 (2004).

Child support is not limited to the "shown needs" of the child; the trial court may award support in excess of the needs of the child. Department of Pub. Aid ex rel. Temple v. Van Kampen, 243 Ill. App. 3d 767, 184 Ill. Dec. 6, 612 N.E.2d 882 (3 Dist. 1993).

—Statutory Minimum
Where without comment or explanation court awarded child support for 25 years of future net income rather than the 12 years that would have taken daughter to majority, the court deviated from statutory minimum and abused its discretion. In re Wolfe, 298 Ill. App. 3d 510, 232 Ill. Dec. 743, 699 N.E.2d 190 (2 Dist. 1998), appeal denied, 181 Ill. 2d 590, 235 Ill. Dec. 949, 706 N.E.2d 504 (1998).

—Therapy Bills
Requiring respondent to pay the therapy bills most certainly required a finding that he was responsible for such medical expenses in the future, although a future court may be called upon to ensure that subsequent medical expenses are within the ambit of the judgment of dissolution. In re McGowan, 265 Ill. App. 3d 976, 202 Ill. Dec. 827, 638 N.E.2d 695 (1 Dist. 1994).

—Upheld
Where both of the parties earned substantially the same income, the mother had assumed the mortgage on the marital residence compensating the father for his interest in the property, and the mother was solely responsible for maintaining the children's standard of living, the father was not entitled to a downward deviation from the guidelines based on the fact that the father kept the children four days a week. In re Demattia, 302 Ill. App. 3d 390, 235 Ill. Dec. 807, 706 N.E.2d 67 (4 Dist. 1999).

—Vested Right
Past-due child support payments which accrue prior to the filing of a petition for modification constitute a vested and unmodifiable right. In re Ingram, 259 Ill. App. 3d 685, 197 Ill. Dec. 383, 631 N.E.2d 386 (2 Dist. 1994).

Child's Estate
The resources of the children are relevant under this section, however, this factor justifies a reduction in child support only when a child has significant financial resources relative to his parents. Department of Pub. Aid ex rel. Nale v. Nale, 294 Ill. App. 3d 747, 229 Ill. Dec. 5, 690 N.E.2d 1052 (4 Dist. 1998).

Where a child's parents are unable to provide for his needs, his estate may be invaded to pay for his necessities. In re Frazier, 205 Ill. App. 3d 621, 151 Ill. Dec. 130, 563 N.E.2d 1236 (3 Dist. 1990).

Collateral Attack
Even though the trial court erred in 1989 in ordering child support to be paid as a percentage of income, the respondent failed to challenge the agreement in a timely manner; therefore, he could not collaterally attack the judgment five years later. In re Steinberg, 302 Ill. App. 3d 845, 236 Ill. Dec. 21, 706 N.E.2d 895 (1 Dist. 1998), appeal denied, 184 Ill. 2d 557, 239 Ill. Dec. 608, 714 N.E.2d 527 (1999).

Conditions for Support
Where the trial court awarded husband temporary custody of child, but specifically stated that child should spend approximately equal time with each parent as indicated by a schedule set forth in the decision, it was not error to order husband to pay wife child support, particularly in light of a large disparity in the financial conditions of the parties. In re Cesaretti, 203 Ill. App. 3d 347, 149 Ill. Dec. 28, 561 N.E.2d 306 (2 Dist. 1990).

Construction
A court cannot read into a statute words which are not within the plain intention of the legislature as determined from the statute itself; the court can neither restrict nor enlarge the plain meaning of an unambiguous statute. Ferguson v. Hoferle, 207 Ill. App. 3d 649, 152 Ill. Dec. 648, 566 N.E.2d 335 (1 Dist. 1990).

Contempt

—In General
The policy behind subsection (b) of this section is to make a noncustodial parent accountable for the costs of his or her contemptuous refusal to pay child support. In re Betts, 172 Ill. App. 3d 742, 122 Ill. Dec. 599, 526 N.E.2d 1138 (4 Dist. 1988).

Contempt proceedings have long been an appropriate method of enforcing the terms of divorce decrees. Taapken v. Taapken, 39 Ill. App. 3d 785, 350 N.E.2d 794 (4 Dist. 1976).

—Applicability
This section has no application to cases where a spouse is found in arrears but not in contempt. Boyd v. Sussenbach, 108 Ill. 2d 489, 92 Ill. Dec. 556, 485 N.E.2d 367 (1985).

—Appropriate
The court acted properly in holding the husband in contempt of court for failing to make the child support payments for the two summer months during which he had custody, in denying the husband's request for an equitable credit toward his child support obligation during those months, in denying the husband's motion for a modification of the child support provision of the divorce decree since there were no changed circumstances, and in refusing to allow the husband's attorney to testify that he did not recall that the subject of child support payments during the summer had been discussed by the parties during their negotiations. Escott v. Escott, 26 Ill. App. 3d 417, 325 N.E.2d 395 (4 Dist. 1975).

—Burden of Proof
The failure of a husband to comply with a decree directing the payment of support money for children was prima facie evidence of contempt and the burden was on the husband to show that he had a valid excuse for nonpayment. Cole v. Cole, 85 Ill. App. 2d 105, 229 N.E.2d 293 (1 Dist. 1967).

—Discretion of Court
Where respondent was found to be in wilful contempt, under subsection (e) of this section, the trial court would have abused its discretion if it refused to enforce the judgment through appropriate sanctions. In re Ramos, 126 Ill. App. 3d 391, 81 Ill. Dec. 214, 466 N.E.2d 1016 (1 Dist. 1984), cert. denied, 471 U.S. 1017, 105 S. Ct. 2023, 85 L. Ed. 2d 305 (1985).

—Found
The trial court's finding of contempt was not against the manifest weight of the evidence as record showed that the respondent wilfully failed to comply. In re Steinberg, 302 Ill. App. 3d 845, 236

Contempt (Cont'd)

—Found (Cont'd)
Ill. Dec. 21, 706 N.E.2d 895 (1 Dist. 1998), appeal denied, 184 Ill. 2d 557, 239 Ill. Dec. 608, 714 N.E.2d 527 (1999).

Where respondent's last minute payment of the past-due support was a mockery of the trial court causing needless inconvenience and cost to all, and that respondent, while a litigant, was also an officer of the court and should have conducted himself accordingly, the finding of contempt, and the purge order demanding that respondent bear the cost of the reasonable attorney fees of the contempt proceeding, was approved. In re Betts, 172 Ill. App. 3d 742, 122 Ill. Dec. 599, 526 N.E.2d 1138 (4 Dist. 1988).

Where respondent had assets valued at as much as $20 million, and $790,900 passed through his hands within a 19 month period, respondent's failure to pay maintenance pursuant to a court order was wilful, and a contempt order under subsection (b) of this section was proper. In re Ramos, 126 Ill. App. 3d 391, 81 Ill. Dec. 214, 466 N.E.2d 1016 (1 Dist. 1984), cert. denied, 471 U.S. 1017, 105 S. Ct. 2023, 85 L. Ed. 2d 305 (1985).

Defendant was in contempt of court for failure to pay court-ordered child support where the court found the defendant was behind in the support payments, that the defendant had a housekeeper whom he subsequently married, that the defendant had income from wages and also farming, that he was physically able to work, and that he made no attempt to modify the decree until such time as the plaintiff obtained the show cause order. Daum v. Daum, 11 Ill. App. 3d 245, 296 N.E.2d 614 (5 Dist. 1973).

—Not Found
The failure to pay child support as required by court order was not wilful and contumacious and, therefore, not in contempt of court where respondent testified that extra money was used to pay his attorney's fees and loans which were currently due before he was advised that his wages would be reduced, and even after his wages were reduced $300 per month, he made child support payments of $200 from each bimonthly paycheck. Gibson v. Barton, 118 Ill. App. 3d 576, 74 Ill. Dec. 252, 455 N.E.2d 282 (4 Dist. 1983).

Husband's counsel was improperly refused permission to cross-examine wife or to present evidence in an attempt to purge husband of contempt, where it was evident from the record that the arrearages for support of the children commenced after wife voluntarily relinquished custody of two children and stated in a letter to the defendant that she would retain custody of the two younger children "including their support which you may cease to pay"; therefore, the finding by the court holding the husband to be in contempt of court was premature. Cole v. Cole, 85 Ill. App. 2d 105, 229 N.E.2d 293 (1 Dist. 1967).

Mere absence of compliance with the provisions of the decree was not a sufficient basis for a judgment of contempt of court where the evidence did not show the failure to comply was a wilful and contumacious refusal to obey the court order. Cole v. Cole, 85 Ill. App. 2d 105, 229 N.E.2d 293 (1 Dist. 1967).

This Act provides a wide range of remedies and one may choose to seek the simpler, more expeditious remedy of contempt proceedings rather than resorting to civil execution. In re Ramos, 126 Ill. App. 3d 391, 81 Ill. Dec. 214, 466 N.E.2d 1016 (1 Dist. 1984), cert. denied, 471 U.S. 1017, 105 S. Ct. 2023, 85 L. Ed. 2d 305 (1985).

Where the defendant had been led to believe that his daughter had been adopted by his ex-wife's current husband, and that his own obligation of support had ceased, as neither the plaintiff nor her husband informed defendant that the adoption had not been effected, there was no basis for a finding that defendant's conduct during that period was wilful and contumacious, therefore a finding of contempt was not supported. Anderson v. Anderson, 48 Ill. App. 2d 140, 198 N.E.2d 342 (2 Dist. 1964).

Where under alleged oral agreement former wife accepted without protest for five years an amount of child support less than what was provided for in divorce decree, former husband would not be held in contempt for failure to pay the amount provided for in the decree. Wolfe v. Wolfe, 303 Ill. App. 188, 24 N.E.2d 871 (1 Dist. 1940).

—Power to Enforce
The power to enforce payment of child support money by contempt is limited to cases of wilful and continuous refusal to obey the order of the court. Cole v. Cole, 85 Ill. App. 2d 105, 229 N.E.2d 293 (1 Dist. 1967).

Extraordinary power is vested in the court to commit a person for contempt, to compel obedience to decrees for payment of child support money, where it appears the defendant had pecuniary ability to comply and his disobedience was wilful. Cole v. Cole, 85 Ill. App. 2d 105, 229 N.E.2d 293 (1 Dist. 1967).

—Purging
In civil contempt proceedings, the court must allow the contemner to purge his contempt. In re Harvey, 136 Ill. App. 3d 116, 91 Ill. Dec. 115, 483 N.E.2d 397 (3 Dist. 1985).

The purging provision in a civil contempt sanction for nonpayment of child support must be based upon the contemner's ability to pay. In re Harvey, 136 Ill. App. 3d 116, 91 Ill. Dec. 115, 483 N.E.2d 397 (3 Dist. 1985).

Purging provision was unrealistic in a civil contempt sanction against father for disobeying court order to make child support payments which provided that the father could protect himself from imminent imprisonment by paying his $2,860 in child support arrears where the father was unpropertied, unemployed, and apparently unemployable. In re Harvey, 136 Ill. App. 3d 116, 91 Ill. Dec. 115, 483 N.E.2d 397 (3 Dist. 1985).

Where contempt proceedings were employed to compel compliance with a court order to pay child support, made for the benefit of the petitioning party, the sanction imposed is remedial or coercive in nature, and the trial court therefore must specify how the respondent may purge himself of contempt. In re Ramos, 126 Ill. App. 3d 391, 81 Ill. Dec. 214, 466 N.E.2d 1016 (1 Dist. 1984), cert. denied, 471 U.S. 1017, 105 S. Ct. 2023, 85 L. Ed. 2d 305 (1985).

—Remedy
The order requiring respondent's payment of attorney fees to purge was an appropriate remedy for his contemptuous conduct. In re Betts, 172 Ill. App. 3d 742, 122 Ill. Dec. 599, 526 N.E.2d 1138 (4 Dist. 1988).

An order denying the petition of former wife for allowance of suit money and attorney's fees was erroneous where defendant refused to pay alimony or support money under an order of court and it was necessary in order to enforce such order for the plaintiff to petition the court to compel the payment of the money. Simpson v. Simpson, 4 Ill. App. 2d 526, 124 N.E.2d 573 (1 Dist. 1955).

—Willful Conduct
The court did not err by holding defendant in contempt for his failure to pay $1,400 in child support, where his conduct was both wilful and contumacious. Cooper v. Cooper, 59 Ill. App. 3d 457, 16 Ill. Dec. 818, 375 N.E.2d 925 (1 Dist. 1978).

Contracts
Parties to divorce or dissolution of marriage matters are not allowed to contract away their responsibilities with regard to child support. Blisset v. Blisset, 144 Ill. App. 3d 1088, 99 Ill. Dec. 161, 495 N.E.2d 608 (4 Dist. 1986), rev'd on other grounds, 123 Ill. 2d 161, 121 Ill. Dec. 931, 526 N.E.2d 125 (1988).

An alleged agreement purporting to absolve defendant from liability for child support was void as being contrary to public policy, the claim for support of children being one which transcends any contractual obligations. Nelson v. Nelson, 340 Ill. App. 463, 92 N.E.2d 534 (1 Dist. 1950).

Credit

—Limitation
Order to credit petitioner's social security dependent disability benefit's against respondent's child support obligation based on recent Supreme Court ruling was properly limited to payments made after the Supreme Court's decision and not those payments made before. In re Rogers, 283 Ill. App. 3d 719, 219 Ill. Dec. 266, 670 N.E.2d 1154 (3 Dist. 1996), appeal denied, 169 Ill. 2d 588, 221 Ill. Dec. 445, 675 N.E.2d 640 (1996).

—Not Proper
Respondent should not have receipted a credit against the nonagreed to arrearage in child support payments for the time the divorced parties resumed living together and pooled their resources to pay for expenses and support of the child; merely because the parties were living together is no evidence that the respondent

Credit (Cont'd)

—Not Proper (Cont'd)

supported the child. Childers v. Childers, 50 Ill. App. 3d 177, 8 Ill. Dec. 755, 365 N.E.2d 1141 (3 Dist. 1977).

—State Subsidy

Adopted children's Iowa state subsidy was properly credited against a father's Illinois support obligation where the subsidy was meant to supplement the children's support, the amount of the subsidy was greater than the father's obligation would have been under Illinois child support guidelines, and the parents' incomes were approximately equal. Newberry v. Newberry, 346 Ill. App. 3d 526, 282 Ill. Dec. 21, 805 N.E.2d 640, 2004 Ill. App. LEXIS 186 (3 Dist. 2004).

Credit Card Debt

Credit card payments did not meet the parameters of subsection (h),therefore, defendant's net income should not be reduced by the amount of such payments. In re Benish, 273 Ill. App. 3d 955, 210 Ill. Dec. 468, 653 N.E.2d 55 (1 Dist. 1995).

Defendant's credit card payments represented current obligations owed in conjunction with the same marital dissolution in which modification of support payments was being sought; they were not "prior" within the meaning of subdivision (a)(3)(g), and therefore not deductible, as they were not obligations to a "family that is first in time in relation to another family." In re Benish, 273 Ill. App. 3d 955, 210 Ill. Dec. 468, 653 N.E.2d 55 (1 Dist. 1995).

Day Care Expense

The trial court did not abuse its discretion in dividing the day care costs evenly between parents in addition to awarding child support. In re Serna, 172 Ill. App. 3d 1051, 123 Ill. Dec. 164, 527 N.E.2d 627 (4 Dist. 1988).

Debt Repayment

Nothing in the record demonstrated that the depreciation expenses claimed on taxpayer's forms were utilized to repay an outstanding debt, nor was any specific repayment schedule provided as a result of the expense, thus the expense did not fall into the category of debt repayment. In re Nelson, 297 Ill. App. 3d 651, 232 Ill. Dec. 654, 698 N.E.2d 1084 (3 Dist. 1998).

The word "necessary" as used in subdivision (a)(3)(h) was intended to describe those expenses outlaid by a parent with a good faith belief his or her income would increase as a result, and which actually did act to increase income, or would have done so absent some extenuating circumstances. In re Davis, 287 Ill. App. 3d 846, 223 Ill. Dec. 166, 679 N.E.2d 110 (5 Dist. 1997).

Simply because an expense falls into the category of a debt repayment does not mean that it is necessarily deductible from gross income for child support payments; merely qualifying as a repayment of a debt is a necessary but not sufficient condition for deductibility under subdivision (a)(3)(h). In re Davis, 287 Ill. App. 3d 846, 223 Ill. Dec. 166, 679 N.E.2d 110 (5 Dist. 1997).

Denial of Hearing

—Improper

A father was denied his right to a full hearing on the issue whether he had a valid excuse for not complying with the court's order to pay child support and medical bills where his counsel requested an opportunity to present evidence which would demonstrate that he was telling the truth when he stated that he had no funds and the court refused to permit him to adduce such evidence. In re Mayer, 97 Ill. App. 3d 313, 52 Ill. Dec. 945, 422 N.E.2d 1154 (1 Dist. 1981).

Depreciation

A depreciation expense is not an expenditure for repayment of debts within the meaning of the statute; however, a court may nevertheless consider depreciation expense, in the appropriate case, in examining the financial resources and needs of the noncustodial parent. In re Boland, 308 Ill. App. 3d 1063, 242 Ill. Dec. 536, 721 N.E.2d 815 (4 Dist. 1999).

Since respondent's depreciation deduction represented a reasonable and necessary expense for the production of income, the circuit court abused its discretion by not allowing it as a deduction. In re Davis, 287 Ill. App. 3d 846, 223 Ill. Dec. 166, 679 N.E.2d 110 (5 Dist. 1997).

Discretion of Court

—In General

In order to avoid an unexplained difference between a supporting parent's large income and an order for child support payments that reflects a smaller income, trial courts ought to expressly state their findings and calculations. In re Carpel, 232 Ill. App. 3d 806, 173 Ill. Dec. 873, 597 N.E.2d 847 (4 Dist.), cert. denied, 147 Ill. 2d 625, 180 Ill. Dec. 148, 606 N.E.2d 1225 (1992).

The trial court's discretion will not be interfered with in the absence of an abuse of that discretion or unless a manifest injustice has been done. In re Ingrassia, 140 Ill. App. 3d 826, 95 Ill. Dec. 165, 489 N.E.2d 386 (2 Dist. 1986).

The determination of the amount of child support payments lies within the sound discretion of the trial court, and its decision will not be set aside unless it is contrary to the manifest weight of the evidence. Riordan v. Riordan, 47 Ill. App. 3d 1019, 8 Ill. Dec. 254, 365 N.E.2d 492 (1 Dist. 1977); Raski v. Raski, 64 Ill. App. 3d 629, 21 Ill. Dec. 417, 381 N.E.2d 744 (5 Dist. 1978); Smith v. Smith, 78 Ill. App. 3d 80, 33 Ill. Dec. 717, 397 N.E.2d 50 (1 Dist. 1979); In re Sipich, 80 Ill. App. 3d 883, 36 Ill. Dec. 276, 400 N.E.2d 696 (1 Dist. 1980); In re Mitchell, 103 Ill. App. 3d 242, 58 Ill. Dec. 684, 430 N.E.2d 716 (2 Dist. 1981); In re Butler, 106 Ill. App. 3d 831, 62 Ill. Dec. 535, 436 N.E.2d 561 (1 Dist. 1982); In re Moriarty, 132 Ill. App. 3d 895, 88 Ill. Dec. 222, 478 N.E.2d 537 (1 Dist. 1985); In re Pitts, 169 Ill. App. 3d 200, 119 Ill. Dec. 908, 523 N.E.2d 664 (5 Dist. 1988); In re Harding, 189 Ill. App. 3d 663, 136 Ill. Dec. 935, 545 N.E.2d 459 (1 Dist. 1989); In re Bush, 191 Ill. App. 3d 249, 138 Ill. Dec. 423, 547 N.E.2d 590 (4 Dist. 1989).

The trial court has broad power to provide for and secure support for minor children. Gentile v. Gentile, 69 Ill. App. 3d 297, 26 Ill. Dec. 149, 387 N.E.2d 979 (3 Dist. 1979).

—Abuse of Discretion

Trial court abused its discretion when it ruled that it was not required to apply statutory child support guidelines to a petition to modify a father's child support obligation and that it did not have to make any written findings of fact as to why it was refusing to apply the guidelines. Anderson v. Heckman, 343 Ill. App. 3d 449, 278 Ill. Dec. 190, 797 N.E.2d 1108, 2003 Ill. App. LEXIS 1242 (4 Dist. 2003).

Where the evidence established that payor's net weekly income was $267, since 20% of that amount is $53.40, and the trial court's only reason for setting the award at $80 per week was that the court felt that amount was "fair," the court abused its discretion. In re Metz, 233 Ill. App. 3d 50, 174 Ill. Dec. 172, 598 N.E.2d 369 (2 Dist. 1992).

The trial court's overall award of 20% of respondent's net income was excessive for one four year old boy and, as such, constituted an abuse of discretion. In re Bush, 191 Ill. App. 3d 249, 138 Ill. Dec. 423, 547 N.E.2d 590 (4 Dist. 1989).

A child support award is a matter within the sound discretion of the trial court and will not be disturbed on appeal absent an abuse of discretion; such abuse occurs only where no reasonable man would take the view adopted by the trial court. Ivanyi v. Granoff, 171 Ill. App. 3d 411, 122 Ill. Dec. 49, 526 N.E.2d 189 (2 Dist. 1988).

Where one spouse was earning approximately 60% more than the other noncustodial spouse, where each was ordered to provide the same amount of child support, and where just prior to the custody change the trial court ordered the spouse with a higher income to pay less per week child support, there was an abuse of discretion. In re Cook, 147 Ill. App. 3d 134, 100 Ill. Dec. 760, 497 N.E.2d 1029 (3 Dist. 1986).

Trial court abused its discretion in modifying divorce decree by eliminating a provision in the decree allowing the amount of support to increase proportionately with the father's gross income which was a reasonable attempt to ensure that the support of the children be continually interrelated with the ability of the father to contribute to their support. Swanson v. Swanson, 51 Ill. App. 3d 999, 10 Ill. Dec. 124, 367 N.E.2d 512 (3 Dist. 1977).

—No Abuse of Discretion

Where the trial court found that petitioner had adequate resources to support his children on his income, and also considered respondent's health problems, alcoholism and employability, the

Discretion of Court (Cont'd)

—No Abuse of Discretion (Cont'd)

trial court did not abuse its discretion in ordering respondent to pay less than 32% of her net income for child support. In re Harmon, 210 Ill. App. 3d 92, 154 Ill. Dec. 727, 568 N.E.2d 948 (2 Dist. 1991).

Where the court specifically discussed and provided its reasoning for rejecting the three items of indebtedness that husband claims should have been deducted to arrive at net income as expenditures for repayment of debts that represent reasonable and necessary expenses for the production of income, the court did not abuse its discretion in determining net income. In re Scafuri, 203 Ill. App. 3d 385, 149 Ill. Dec. 124, 561 N.E.2d 402 (2 Dist. 1990).

There was no abuse of discretion in the trial court's determination of the proper amount of child support. In re Dodge, 150 Ill. App. 3d 486, 103 Ill. Dec. 816, 501 N.E.2d 1354 (2 Dist. 1986).

Court did not abuse discretion by not following child support guidelines where it stated at hearing that the statute was not being followed because husband was solely responsible for daughter's college expenses and solely responsible for all of son's expenses. Faris v. Faris, 142 Ill. App. 3d 987, 97 Ill. Dec. 209, 492 N.E.2d 645 (2 Dist. 1986), appeal denied, 100 Ill. Dec. 603, 497 N.E.2d 781 (Ill. 1986).

The trial court did not abuse its discretion in increasing child support from $275 per month to $400 per month because petitioner failed to introduce any evidence of the increased needs for a minor child. Blaisdell v. Blaisdell, 142 Ill. App. 3d 1034, 97 Ill. Dec. 186, 492 N.E.2d 622 (1 Dist. 1986).

The trial court did not abuse its discretion by increasing father's support payments to $900 per month, per child, due to "needed expenses," mother's income, father's income and other factors specified in this section. In re Bussey, 108 Ill. 2d 286, 91 Ill. Dec. 594, 483 N.E.2d 1229 (1985).

Where all of respondent's arguments pertaining to the award of maintenance and child support were based on a single assumption: that no evidence refuted his assertion, based on his income tax returns, that his net income was not any more than $25,000, it was not an abuse of discretion for the trial court to consider the ample evidence introduced at trial showing respondent's income was far higher than he alleged. In re Hilkovitch, 124 Ill. App. 3d 401, 79 Ill. Dec. 891, 464 N.E.2d 795 (1 Dist. 1984).

Where the amount of the maintenance and support awarded was approximately 20% of the husband's receipts for one year, the trial court did not abuse its discretion. In re Dwan, 108 Ill. App. 3d 808, 64 Ill. Dec. 340, 439 N.E.2d 1005 (1 Dist. 1982).

Trial court did not abuse its discretion in denying child support payments to the husband, where the trial court required the wife to pay for child's medical insurance and clothing and all of expenses during visitation. In re Mitchell, 103 Ill. App. 3d 242, 58 Ill. Dec. 684, 430 N.E.2d 716 (2 Dist. 1981).

An order requiring a father to pay two-thirds of minor's support was not an abuse of discretion, where the court determined that since the father enjoyed a greater income, he should pay a greater percentage of the support. In re McMahon, 82 Ill. App. 3d 1126, 38 Ill. Dec. 499, 403 N.E.2d 730 (4 Dist. 1980).

There was no abuse of discretion in the circuit court's award of maintenance of $700 to wife from husband when husband earned between $21,000 and $24,000 a year. In re Reyna, 78 Ill. App. 3d 1010, 34 Ill. Dec. 818, 398 N.E.2d 641 (3 Dist. 1979).

The trial court's award to plaintiff of $150 a week for alimony and child support was not contrary to the manifest weight of the evidence or an abuse of the court's discretion. Lewanski v. Lewanski, 59 Ill. App. 3d 805, 16 Ill. Dec. 854, 375 N.E.2d 961 (1 Dist. 1978).

Trial court did not abuse its discretion when, in addition to periodic alimony, it awarded to plaintiff all of the furniture in the marital apartment, and one-half of the coin collection, but did abuse its discretion when awarding a 1973 Pontiac automobile. Lewanski v. Lewanski, 59 Ill. App. 3d 805, 16 Ill. Dec. 854, 375 N.E.2d 961 (1 Dist. 1978).

Trial court did not abuse its discretion in awarding mother child support payments of $165 per month where wife, in addition to supporting her son, had to maintain herself and the home, and further, she testified that even with the $150 per month support payments she was still having trouble meeting the child's financial needs. Raski v. Raski, 64 Ill. App. 3d 629, 21 Ill. Dec. 417, 381 N.E.2d 744 (5 Dist. 1978).

In view of the relative incomes of the parties and the amount required to provide necessaries for the children, modification of monthly child support payments from $250 to $400 was neither excessive nor an abuse of discretion. Huffman v. Huffman, 50 Ill. App. 3d 217, 8 Ill. Dec. 32, 365 N.E.2d 270 (5 Dist. 1977).

The trial court did not abuse its discretion where it modified a divorce decree to require father to pay the educational expenses of a child, but only if the child went away to college. Imes v. Imes, 52 Ill. App. 3d 792, 10 Ill. Dec. 466, 367 N.E.2d 1075 (3 Dist. 1977).

The trial court did not abuse its discretion by requiring father to pay the medical expenses of children to the extent those expenses were covered by his insurance. Imes v. Imes, 52 Ill. App. 3d 792, 10 Ill. Dec. 466, 367 N.E.2d 1075 (3 Dist. 1977).

The trial court did not abuse its discretion by setting the child support payments of father at $25 per week for daughter. Imes v. Imes, 52 Ill. App. 3d 792, 10 Ill. Dec. 466, 367 N.E.2d 1075 (3 Dist. 1977).

Dissolution of Judgment

—Affected Obligations

Where respondent husband did not object to the terms of the dissolution judgment imposing support obligations solely on him, and where he never appealed the dissolution judgment, the trial court properly ordered that the noncustodial wife was not required to pay child support. In re Kraft, 217 Ill. App. 3d 502, 160 Ill. Dec. 392, 577 N.E.2d 522 (2 Dist. 1991).

Duty to Support

—In General

The support of a child is the joint and several obligation of both the husband and the wife. In re Butler, 106 Ill. App. 3d 831, 62 Ill. Dec. 535, 436 N.E.2d 561 (1 Dist. 1982); In re Schuster, 224 Ill. App. 3d 958, 167 Ill. Dec. 73, 586 N.E.2d 1345 (1992).

The financial responsibility for the support of the child is a joint and several obligation of each parent, and it is proper for the court to consider the income and assets of the wife and husband in setting the amount awarded. Riordan v. Riordan, 47 Ill. App. 3d 1019, 8 Ill. Dec. 254, 365 N.E.2d 492 (1 Dist. 1977); In re Reed, 100 Ill. App. 3d 873, 56 Ill. Dec. 202, 427 N.E.2d 282 (5 Dist. 1981); In re Butler, 106 Ill. App. 3d 831, 62 Ill. Dec. 535, 436 N.E.2d 561 (1 Dist. 1982); In re Rink, 136 Ill. App. 3d 252, 91 Ill. Dec. 34, 483 N.E.2d 316 (1 Dist. 1985); In re Stone, 155 Ill. App. 3d 62, 107 Ill. Dec. 747, 507 N.E.2d 900 (4 Dist. 1987).

The obligation of the father to support his children begins when the child is born and continues during the minority of the child. This obligation of the father to support his minor child is not affected by a decree granting a divorce, nor by a decree granting the care and custody of his child to his wife or some other suitable person. Nelson v. Nelson, 340 Ill. App. 463, 92 N.E.2d 534 (1 Dist. 1950); Sturdy v. Sturdy, 67 Ill. App. 2d 469, 214 N.E.2d 607 (4 Dist. 1966); Elble v. Elble, 100 Ill. App. 2d 221, 241 N.E.2d 328 (5 Dist. 1968).

When the parents of a child are divorced and no mention is made in the decree for the care and custody of minor child, under the law, the father is still bound to provide a reasonable and proper support for a minor child. People ex rel. Hartshorn v. Hartshorn, 21 Ill. App. 2d 91, 157 N.E.2d 563 (2 Dist. 1959); Sturdy v. Sturdy, 67 Ill. App. 2d 469, 214 N.E.2d 607 (4 Dist. 1966).

The duty of a parent to support his minor child arises out of a natural relationship. Nelson v. Nelson, 340 Ill. App. 463, 92 N.E.2d 534 (1 Dist. 1950).

—Agreement

A father cannot be relieved of his obligation to support his minor child by agreement with the mother. Martin v. Comer, 25 Ill. App. 3d 1038, 324 N.E.2d 240 (3 Dist. 1975).

—Financial Status of Spouse

The financial status of plaintiff's wife had no bearing upon the obligation of plaintiff to support his minor child. Edwards v. Edwards, 125 Ill. App. 2d 91, 259 N.E.2d 820 (4 Dist. 1970).

—Found

Former wife is not relieved of obligation to pay support for children in custody of former husband merely because she is not

Duty to Support (Cont'd)

—Found (Cont'd)
currently employed and has no income. Keown v. Wright, 225 Ill. App. 3d 808, 167 Ill. Dec. 375, 587 N.E.2d 644 (4 Dist. 1992).

The fact that former wife had two young children at home, one from her current marriage, did not relieve her from the obligation to pay support for the two living with her former husband. Keown v. Wright, 225 Ill. App. 3d 808, 167 Ill. Dec. 375, 587 N.E.2d 644 (4 Dist. 1992).

—Laches

Laches is not available as a defense unless the party pleading it was prejudiced by the opposite party's delay. Martin v. Comer, 25 Ill. App. 3d 1038, 324 N.E.2d 240 (3 Dist. 1975).

—Noncustodial Parent

Although both parents should generally exercise responsibility for their children's support, this obligation is not mandatory in all situations, and the courts will not impose support payments on the noncustodial parent regardless of the needs of the children. In re Reed, 100 Ill. App. 3d 873, 56 Ill. Dec. 202, 427 N.E.2d 282 (5 Dist. 1981).

—Not Destroyed by Divorce

A father's duty to support his child is not destroyed by a divorce decree, nor a decree granting the care and custody of his child to his wife or some other person. Martin v. Comer, 25 Ill. App. 3d 1038, 324 N.E.2d 240 (3 Dist. 1975).

—Not Dischargeable

Where the trial court determined that the husband's obligation to pay the second mortgage on the marital home was part of an order for support rather than part of a property distribution, the obligation was not dischargeable in bankruptcy proceedings. In re LaShelle, 213 Ill. App. 3d 730, 157 Ill. Dec. 726, 572 N.E.2d 1190 (2 Dist. 1991).

—Termination

As a general rule, liability of a spouse in a divorce action for support of a child continues during the child's minority and is terminated by the child's coming of age. Crane v. Crane, 45 Ill. App. 2d 316, 196 N.E.2d 27 (1 Dist. 1964).

When a child who is physically and mentally able to take care of himself, voluntarily abandons the parental roof and leaves its protection and influence, and goes out into the world to fight the battle of life on his own account, the parent is no longer under legal obligation to support him. Shuff v. Fulte, 344 Ill. App. 157, 100 N.E.2d 502 (3 Dist. 1951).

Educational Expenses

This section authorized the trial court to include in its modified child support order son's parochial school tuition, in light of the legislature's apparent intention to provide for such expenses, and the fact that the child had attended parochial school, without objection from the paying spouse, for about five years prior to the modification order. In re Alexander, 231 Ill. App. 3d 950, 173 Ill. Dec. 456, 596 N.E.2d 1335 (4 Dist. 1992).

Where parties' marital settlement agreement provided that defendant first pay unallocated maintenance and child support, and then, as he was financially able, to pay educational expenses; even though the trial court did not proportionately reduce defendant's support payment by the $34,000 in educational expenses incurred by defendant, the $3,900 reduction does reflect an accurate interpretation of the settlement agreement that maintenance and child support took priority over educational expenses. In re Geis, 159 Ill. App. 3d 975, 111 Ill. Dec. 717, 512 N.E.2d 1354 (1 Dist. 1987).

Court did not abuse discretion by not following child support guidelines where it stated at hearing that the statute was not being followed because husband was solely responsible for daughter's college expenses and solely responsible for all of son's expenses. Faris v. Faris, 142 Ill. App. 3d 987, 97 Ill. Dec. 209, 492 N.E.2d 645 (2 Dist. 1986), appeal denied, 100 Ill. Dec. 603, 497 N.E.2d 781 (Ill. 1986).

The trial court did not abuse its discretion in ordering husband to pay for the parochial high school tuition of his children. In re Moriarty, 132 Ill. App. 3d 895, 88 Ill. Dec. 222, 478 N.E.2d 537 (1 Dist. 1985).

The trial court's allowance of high school tuition for husband's children was neither excessive nor an abuse of discretion. In re Moriarty, 132 Ill. App. 3d 895, 88 Ill. Dec. 222, 478 N.E.2d 537 (1 Dist. 1985).

Where petitioner husband was required to pay substantial additional sums for private schooling and counseling for children, if such schooling and counseling were necessary and actually took place, no error resulted. In re Bussey, 128 Ill. App. 3d 730, 84 Ill. Dec. 34, 471 N.E.2d 563 (4 Dist. 1984).

Considering the great disparities in incomes between the parties, child's tuition and books, along with the cost of his college and professional education, should be paid by the father and not be included as part of the $1,000per month child support. In re Edelstein, 82 Ill. App. 3d 574, 38 Ill. Dec. 235, 403 N.E.2d 323 (1 Dist. 1980).

Where the father's financial ability is ample to provide a college education for his child and the child shows an aptitude that would indicate he would benefit from such college education, the court may in the exercise of its discretion require that the father provide such college education; provision for college education may be required even though the child may be an adult. Sovey v. Sovey, 30 Ill. App. 3d 690, 333 N.E.2d 299 (3 Dist. 1975).

Trial court had jurisdiction to enter an order for payments of educational expenses for children who have reached their majority. Strum v. Strum, 22 Ill. App. 3d 147, 317 N.E.2d 59 (4 Dist. 1974).

Where the father entered into a written agreement to pay for the college education of his child which was then evidenced by an order of the court or by the divorce decree, the court could then order the divorced father to carry out the terms of his agreement even though the child had reached the age of majority. Crane v. Crane, 45 Ill. App. 2d 316, 196 N.E.2d 27 (1 Dist. 1964).

Where the father had not made any formal agreement of record to pay for his majority aged daughter's college education, the court had no jurisdiction to consider requiring the father to provide that support. Crane v. Crane, 45 Ill. App. 2d 316, 196 N.E.2d 27 (1 Dist. 1964).

Employment Order

The trial court lacked authority to fashion an employment order that required former husband to seek or find suitable employment to enforce a child support award where the order was not entered following a rule to show cause nor a finding of contempt as set forth in subdivision (b)(1) of this section. In re Page, 162 Ill. App. 3d 515, 113 Ill. Dec. 902, 515 N.E.2d 1061 (2 Dist. 1987).

Entry of Order

This Act provides a statutory remedy for the entry of an original order of child support, but that remedy is limited in that such order can only be entered in conjunction with a dissolution proceeding, a legal separation proceeding, a proceeding for the declaration of invalidity of a marriage, or a proceeding following dissolution of the marriage by a court which lacked personal jurisdiction over the absent spouse. Skilling v. Skilling, 104 Ill. App. 3d 213, 59 Ill. Dec. 937, 432 N.E.2d 881 (1 Dist. 1982).

Equitable Credit

Where the parties agreed that the children would reside with the husband for two months during the summers, and the husband was to make monthly child support payments, the husband was not entitled to an equitable credit because the agreement of the parties provided to the contrary; furthermore, the wife's expenses for the children did not decline in their temporary absence from her home because she still had expenses such as payments on the mortgage, other loans, maintenance of the house, and summer clothing for the children. Escott v. Escott, 26 Ill. App. 3d 417, 325 N.E.2d 395 (4 Dist. 1975).

Equitable Estoppel

A claim of equitable estoppel exists whereby one's own statements or conduct induces a second person to rely, to his or her detriment, on the statements or conduct of the first person; the party asserting a claim of estoppel must have relied upon the acts or representations of the other and have had no knowledge or convenient means of knowing the true facts and such reliance should be reasonable. Blisset v. Blisset, 123 Ill. 2d 161, 121 Ill. Dec. 931, 526 N.E.2d 125 (1988).

Equitable Estoppel (Cont'd)

Forfeiting visitation rights and failing to anticipate unpaid support payments does not constitute the detriment required to establish an equitable estoppel claim, because to allow these reasons to suffice as a detriment, sufficient to establish estoppel, would allow parents to look past the best interests of their children and, by their own agreement, frustrate the intent of child support and visitation orders; such a result is untenable because it would circumvent and undermine a court's role in the establishment and modification of a child support obligation. Blisset v. Blisset, 123 Ill. 2d 161, 121 Ill. Dec. 931, 526 N.E.2d 125 (1988).

The doctrine of equitable estoppel is an exception to the otherwise rigid rule that child support payments become vested when and as they accrue. Ruster v. Ruster, 91 Ill. App. 3d 355, 46 Ill. Dec. 874, 414 N.E.2d 927 (2 Dist. 1980).

The right to past due installments of child support payments is a vested right which may not be reduced or eliminated by courts. The exception to this rule is when the doctrine of equitable estoppel is applied and then the doctrine may be applied to all or part of the past installments in an appropriate case. Lewis v. Lewis, 48 Ill. App. 3d 281, 6 Ill. Dec. 577, 363 N.E.2d 106 (5 Dist. 1977).

The doctrine of equitable estoppel was not applicable where it did not appear that defendant did anything that he otherwise would not have done assuming that plaintiff had agreed to a reduction; the defendant had remedies available to which he did not avail himself, and plaintiff had not by her statements or conduct led defendant into his current situation. Lewis v. Lewis, 48 Ill. App. 3d 281, 6 Ill. Dec. 577, 363 N.E.2d 106 (5 Dist. 1977).

Where, in a suit for child support arrearages brought by wife 16 years after decree of divorce was entered, wife's claim was estopped, where from the evidence it could have been inferred that plaintiff did not expect child support from the defendant, but instead expected that such support would come from her second husband, and her conduct over the years was consistent with this position and there could have been little doubt but that she intended defendant to rely on these circumstances and that the defendant did so rely on such circumstances believing the necessity of modifying the decree of divorce unnecessary. Martin v. Comer, 25 Ill. App. 3d 1038, 324 N.E.2d 240 (3 Dist. 1975).

The doctrine of equitable estoppel can be applied as to all or part of past installments in an appropriate case. Johnson v. Johnson, 26 Ill. App. 3d 64, 324 N.E.2d 450 (2 Dist. 1975).

The mere passage of time does not bring into effect the principle of equitable estoppel. Martin v. Comer, 25 Ill. App. 3d 1038, 324 N.E.2d 240 (3 Dist. 1975).

A mother was estopped from asserting any claim to support payment from her children's father for the period of time that their daughter lived with him. Strum v. Strum, 22 Ill. App. 3d 147, 317 N.E.2d 59 (4 Dist. 1974).

Equity

Nothing in subsection (a) of this section or this entire Act indicates that the legislature intended to abolish all actions in equity that existed for child support before the statute was enacted and the provisions of the Act did not preclude the court from entertaining a child custody and support action notwithstanding that the parties were divorced in England. Skilling v. Skilling, 104 Ill. App. 3d 213, 59 Ill. Dec. 937, 432 N.E.2d 881 (1 Dist. 1982).

Evidence

—In General

The trial court correctly relied on evidence outside the record when it noted that father noncustodial parent had some benefits available to him through his self-employment status as a farmer. In re Kern, 245 Ill. App. 3d 575, 185 Ill. Dec. 843, 615 N.E.2d 402 (4 Dist. 1993).

—Burden to Dispute

Sufficient evidence was presented that son had some physical and mental difficulties for which he was being treated and if father truly disputed the existence of the condition, or the fact that the condition was a matter of substantial expense to wife, then it was his burden to introduce evidence supporting his position; it was not enough for father to criticize the evidence presented by wife, or to criticize the trial court for doing its best on the evidence presented to it. In re Kern, 245 Ill. App. 3d 575, 185 Ill. Dec. 843, 615 N.E.2d 402 (4 Dist. 1993).

—Held Insufficient

The trial court abused its discretion in determining the award of child support where it did not have before it sufficient evidence regarding respondent's income, the crucial factor relied upon in determining the child support award, where the only evidence it considered regarding the circumstances of petitioner was that given through the testimony of respondent, and where the testimony of respondent regarding the financial resources and needs of the children was very limited. Stern v. Stern, 179 Ill. App. 3d 313, 128 Ill. Dec. 351, 534 N.E.2d 533 (1 Dist. 1989).

While the expectation of a substantial income for husband was present, it was not certain; therefore, child support in the amount of $24,000 per year was not warranted by the evidence, and the trial court committed a breach of discretion in fixing it in that amount. In re Moore, 117 Ill. App. 3d 206, 72 Ill. Dec. 797, 453 N.E.2d 102 (5 Dist. 1983).

—Held Sufficient

The trial court was able to make a sufficiently accurate determination of the financial status of both parties and thereby set an appropriate allowance for support. In re Rizzo, 95 Ill. App. 3d 636, 51 Ill. Dec. 141, 420 N.E.2d 555 (1 Dist. 1981).

Increase of child support payments to $650 per month was equitable to both parties and required by the evidence. In re Raidbard, 87 Ill. App. 3d 158, 42 Ill. Dec. 312, 408 N.E.2d 1021 (1 Dist. 1980).

Where ex-husband's income which was considerably greater than wife's, and fluctuated a great deal, the modification of child support payments to be self-modifying as a percentage of his income was neither an abuse of the trial court's discretion nor against the manifest weight of the evidence. Smith v. Smith, 78 Ill. App. 3d 80, 33 Ill. Dec. 717, 397 N.E.2d 50 (1 Dist. 1979).

Where the record indicated that the trial court heard evidence on the needs of the child and of the parties and on the parties' means and concluded that the noncustodial mother should not make an added contribution to the support of their daughter, the trial court's order was not an abuse of its discretion. Mitchell v. Mitchell, 54 Ill. App. 3d 18, 11 Ill. Dec. 822, 369 N.E.2d 276 (1 Dist. 1977).

Expenses

—Considered

While husband had not married the woman with whom he resided at the time of the hearing, his testimony indicated that he was supporting both her and her children; consequently, the trial court's refusal to consider the aspects of husband's expenses relating to his companion and her children was not error, and in no way supported husband's contention that the trial court did not consider his expenses in determining the child support award. In re Earhart, 149 Ill. App. 3d 469, 102 Ill. Dec. 667, 500 N.E.2d 560 (1 Dist. 1986).

—Equality

Where a husband's gross annual income was $30,600, he owned his own car and home, he owed $6,000 to his credit union on which he paid $200 monthly installments, various monthly living expenses of his household totaled approximately $500, and he had no savings, and the wife's gross income was $15,578, she had $84 in liquid assets, she owed $500 for a housing repair, and her monthly living expenses, including mortgage and automobile payments, totaled approximately $1,090, the trial court could reasonably have believed that the wife was not financially able to contribute to the parties' children's support, and did not abuse its discretion in denying the husband's cross-petition for child support. In re Janetzke, 97 Ill. App. 3d 418, 52 Ill. Dec. 705, 422 N.E.2d 914 (1 Dist. 1981).

—Increase

As children grow older and inflation continues, a court may presume that the expenses connected with raising the children are increasing each year. In re Loomis, 153 Ill. App. 3d 404, 106 Ill. Dec. 219, 505 N.E.2d 766 (3 Dist. 1987).

Factors

—Child by Another

To allow a reduction in child support below the statutory mini-

Factors (Cont'd)

—Child by Another (Cont'd)
mum based solely on the fact that the custodial parent supports other persons not entitled to support by the noncustodial parent would penalize the child for living arrangements over which the child had no control; the statutory guidelines should be applied unless the trial court finds reason for deviating therefrom based on its consideration of the applicable statutory factors and pertinent case law. Department of Pub. Aid ex rel. Temple v. Van Kampen, 243 Ill. App. 3d 767, 184 Ill. Dec. 6, 612 N.E.2d 882 (3 Dist. 1993).

Where wife had children other than respondent's child to support, a child support payment decision could be decided on only a "needs" basis, the child's need was a relevant factor in determining support under subdivision (a)(2), other relevant factors must be considered, and those include the social problems surrounding one sibling having more than others, the visitation (or relationship) with noncustodial parent, and the extent payments by the noncustodial parent actually benefit those who are not directly entitled to the support benefit. People ex rel. Graham v. Adams, 239 Ill. App. 3d 643, 181 Ill. Dec. 541, 608 N.E.2d 614 (4 Dist. 1993).

—Express Findings
Where the court made general statements about the factors listed in subdivision (a)(2), they were ruled sufficient to satisfy the statutory requirement for express findings under subdivision (a)(2)(e). In re Burns, 25 Ill. 2d 56, 182 N.E.2d 740 (1962).

—Improper for Net Income
Expenses which would be improper to deduct under subdivision (a)(3)can still play a role in a trial court's decision regarding departure from statutory guidelines. Gay ex rel. Gay v. Dunlap, 279 Ill. App. 3d 140, 215 Ill. Dec. 691, 664 N.E.2d 88 (4 Dist. 1996), appeal denied, 168 Ill. 2d 589, 219 Ill. Dec. 563, 671 N.E.2d 730 (1996).

—Insufficient Consideration
The trial court did not meet the express requirements of this section where it stated that its main concern was petitioner's medical needs but did not take into consideration any of the other factors listed within this section. In re DeBow, 236 Ill. App. 3d 1038, 177 Ill. Dec. 89, 602 N.E.2d 984 (5 Dist. 1992), cert. denied, 148 Ill. 2d 640, 183 Ill. Dec. 17, 610 N.E.2d 1261 (1993).

Where the court only heard evidence as to defendant's reduced income and the fact he had another minor child to support, but heard no evidence regarding any of the other factors enumerated in subsection (a) of the Act, the court abused its discretion in failing to consider all relevant factors before reducing support. People v. Hines, 236 Ill. App. 3d 739, 177 Ill. Dec. 7, 602 N.E.2d 902 (4 Dist. 1992).

Failure to Pay
Wilful failure to pay allowances for child support and maintenance as ordered by the court may be declared contemptuous misconduct and may be sanctioned accordingly. In re Hilkovitch, 124 Ill. App. 3d 401, 79 Ill. Dec. 891, 464 N.E.2d 795 (1 Dist. 1984).

The failure to make the payments directed to be made pursuant to a court order or judgment is prima facie evidence of contempt. In re Hilkovitch, 124 Ill. App. 3d 401, 79 Ill. Dec. 891, 464 N.E.2d 795 (1 Dist. 1984).

A party who fails to pay the allowances ordered has the burden of proving that his failure to comply was not wilful or contumacious and that he has a valid excuse for his failure to pay. In re Hilkovitch, 124 Ill. App. 3d 401, 79 Ill. Dec. 891, 464 N.E.2d 795 (1 Dist. 1984).

Whether the person charged for failure to pay child support and maintenance is in wilful contempt and whether a sanction is to be imposed are factual matters to be determined by the trial court from the evidence presented to it. In re Hilkovitch, 124 Ill. App. 3d 401, 79 Ill. Dec. 891, 464 N.E.2d 795 (1 Dist. 1984).

A reviewing court will not upset the trial court's finding of wilful or contumacious misconduct on the part of the person obligated to make the payment of allowances unless the trial court's factual conclusions are contrary to the manifest weight of the evidence. In re Hilkovitch, 124 Ill. App. 3d 401, 79 Ill. Dec. 891, 464 N.E.2d 795 (1 Dist. 1984).

For a case discussing contempt for failure to pay alimony, child support and mortgage payments in a separate maintenance action, Mattioda v. Mattioda, 101 Ill. App. 2d 475, 243 N.E.2d 495 (1 Dist. 1968).

Final Judgment
Where the trial court set retroactive support at 20% of defendant's net income, but had not yet determined what the amount would be, where there were potential disputes about the materials submitted, the inferences drawn from any material, and where the method of payment was not addressed by the trial court, but was delayed until defendant submitted proof of income, a mere affirmation of the lower court would not constitute a final judgment. Department of Pub. Aid ex rel. Chiapelli v. Viviano, 195 Ill. App. 3d 1033, 142 Ill. Dec. 747, 553 N.E.2d 97 (5 Dist. 1990).

Foster Children
Where there was no support in the record for the belief that the trial court's decision on child support payments should be affected by defendant's foster children, as he had no financial responsibility for them because they were provided for by the state, defendant's foster children should not have been a consideration in the court's child support payment decision. People v. Hines, 236 Ill. App. 3d 739, 177 Ill. Dec. 7, 602 N.E.2d 902 (4 Dist. 1992).

Good Faith
Evidence of defendant's emotional problems after being involuntarily discharged in 1975, his attempts to find work both in Chicago and California, and his current financial and employment situation supported the trial court's conclusion that defendant was acting in good faith in seeking an abatement of his child support obligations. Glass v. Peitchel, 63 Ill. App. 3d 57, 20 Ill. Dec. 442, 380 N.E.2d 420 (1 Dist. 1978).

Guidelines

—In General
A construction of the act that does not enforce provisions which rely solely upon a percentage, but does enforce provisions with a minimum or "final" dollar figure carries out the statutory goals of the legislative enactment. In re Liss, 268 Ill. App. 3d 919, 206 Ill. Dec. 336, 645 N.E.2d 341 (1 Dist. 1994).

The standards contained in this section regarding child support are applicable to the determination of temporary child support. In re Rogliano, 198 Ill. App. 3d 404, 144 Ill. Dec. 595, 555 N.E.2d 1114 (5 Dist. 1990).

The guidelines for determining child support contained in this section must be followed when a court determines support in cases brought under the Public Aid Code (305 ILCS 5/10-10). People ex rel. Browning v. Melton, 180 Ill. App. 3d 519, 129 Ill. Dec. 449, 536 N.E.2d 133 (5 Dist. 1989).

The percentage guidelines set forth in subsection (a) of this section establish a "minimum" amount of supporting party's net income, not a "maximum." In re McBride, 166 Ill. App. 3d 504, 116 Ill. Dec. 880, 519 N.E.2d 1095 (1 Dist. 1988).

The substantive factors of subsection (a) of this section have been adopted by the courts as a point of reference for determining motions filed pursuant to subsection (a) of this section; however, it does not require the trial court to either adhere to the minimum percentage guidelines or to make specific findings to explain its departure therefrom. Deardeuff v. Deardeuff, 149 Ill. App. 3d 406, 102 Ill. Dec. 891, 500 N.E.2d 992 (5 Dist. 1986).

—Amount
Where trial court ordered respondent to pay $700 or 45% of his net income, whichever would be greater, and as for child support, the trial court's judgment may be affirmed to the extent that it stated respondent's support obligation in a specific dollar amount if that determination is otherwise valid. In re Fahy, 208 Ill. App. 3d 677, 153 Ill. Dec. 594, 567 N.E.2d 552 (1 Dist. 1991).

Where the individual incomes of both parents are more than sufficient to provide the reasonable needs of the parties' children, taking into account the lifestyle the children would have absent the dissolution, the court is justified in setting a figure below the guideline amount. In re Bush, 191 Ill. App. 3d 249, 138 Ill. Dec. 423, 547 N.E.2d 590 (4 Dist. 1989).

A reasonable basis for setting a figure below the guidelines existed where both parties had more than enough income to provide for a child, and an award of 20% of the noncustodial parent's income exceeded the bounds of anything the child could reasonably need or

Guidelines (Cont'd)

—Amount (Cont'd)
desire. In re Bush, 191 Ill. App. 3d 249, 138 Ill. Dec. 423, 547 N.E.2d 590 (4 Dist. 1989).

A large income does not necessarily trigger an extravagant lifestyle or the accumulation of a trust fund. In re Bush, 191 Ill. App. 3d 249, 138 Ill. Dec. 423, 547 N.E.2d 590 (4 Dist. 1989).

Where the incomes for both the mother and father are far above average, there is no rule of law requiring excessive child support so that the child or the custodial parent can diminish the accumulation of an estate by the noncustodial parent. In re Bush, 191 Ill. App. 3d 249, 138 Ill. Dec. 423, 547 N.E.2d 590 (4 Dist. 1989).

The court has the leeway to set an award below the guideline figure. In re Bush, 191 Ill. App. 3d 249, 138 Ill. Dec. 423, 547 N.E.2d 590 (4 Dist. 1989).

This Act was not intended to create windfalls but, rather, adequate support payments for the upbringing of the children. In re Bush, 191 Ill. App. 3d 249, 138 Ill. Dec. 423, 547 N.E.2d 590 (4 Dist. 1989).

—Derivation
The court may deviate from the established child support guidelines, after considering all of the relevant factors set forth in subdivision (a)(2);the trial court's award of $25-per-month child support was not an abuse of discretion. In re Burris, 263 Ill. App. 3d 495, 200 Ill. Dec. 880, 636 N.E.2d 71 (5 Dist. 1994).

—Deviation
Although the noncustodial parent was entitled to a credit for the dissipation of marital property and for the overpayment of child support, the trial court erred in reducing the child support award based solely on its findings that the custodial parent dissipated marital assets and that noncustodial parent overpaid child support. In re DiFatta, 306 Ill. App. 3d 656, 239 Ill. Dec. 795, 714 N.E.2d 1092 (2 Dist. 1999).

Trial court's failure to give any reason for its downward deviation from the statutory guidelines where it specifically found parent financially able to pay child support warranted reversal. In re Charles, 284 Ill. App. 3d 339, 219 Ill. Dec. 742, 672 N.E.2d 57 (4 Dist. 1996).

Court abuses its discretion when it deviates from the statutory child support guidelines solely because the noncustodial parent has a prior child support obligation pursuant to a court order. In re Stanley, 279 Ill. App. 3d 1083, 216 Ill. Dec. 890, 666 N.E.2d 340 (4 Dist. 1996).

Where the trial court found "it was appropriate on the basis of the distribution of the marital and nonmarital assets and the relative financial position of each of the parties, including marital and nonmarital assets assigned, current income and potential future income," that wife pay child support of16% of her net income, although, in accordance with the statutory guidelines, she would be ordered to pay 32% of her net income to husband in child support for their three children, the trial court deviated from the guidelines and properly stated its reasons for doing so. In re Phillips, 244 Ill. App. 3d 577, 186 Ill. Dec. 108, 615 N.E.2d 1165 (4 Dist. 1993).

Petitioner was allowed to contend for the first time on appeal that the trial court erred in failing to set forth in its order the reasons for deviating from the child support guidelines. In re Wright, 212 Ill. App. 3d 392, 156 Ill. Dec. 610, 571 N.E.2d 197 (5 Dist. 1991).

Although the guidelines are in the nature of a mandate to the court, an abuse of discretion can be found in awarding the guideline amount where it exceeds the child's reasonable needs and where both parents have a large income. In re Partney, 212 Ill. App. 3d 586, 156 Ill. Dec. 679, 571 N.E.2d 266 (5 Dist. 1991).

The custodial parent's ability to contribute to the child's welfare as well as the child's actual needs are important factors to be considered in determining a child support award, and when the individual incomes of both parents are more than sufficient to provide for the reasonable needs of the minor child, the court is justified in setting a figure below the statutory guidelines. In re Cornale, 199 Ill. App. 3d 134, 145 Ill. Dec. 188, 556 N.E.2d 806 (4 Dist. 1990).

The trial court erred in denying the petition to increase child support without making provisions to adjust the amount of support to meet the guidelines of this section. In re Fowler, 197 Ill. App. 3d 95, 143 Ill. Dec. 305, 554 N.E.2d 240 (3 Dist. 1989).

The court was within its discretion in considering the actual costs of supporting a minor child and the expenses of a college education for an adult child as factors supporting its determination to set child support below the statutory guidelines. In re Stockton, 169 Ill. App. 3d 318, 119 Ill. Dec. 817, 523 N.E.2d 573 (4 Dist. 1988).

Only if the circuit court were going to impose more or less than the minimum standard required under the statutory guidelines is a circuit court required to consider the relevant factors of this section. In re Tatham, 173 Ill. App. 3d 1072, 123 Ill. Dec. 576, 527 N.E.2d 1351 (5 Dist. 1988); People ex rel. Browning v. Melton, 180 Ill. App. 3d 519, 129 Ill. Dec. 449, 536 N.E.2d 133 (5 Dist. 1989); Parks ex rel. Parks v. Romans, 187 Ill. App. 3d 445, 135 Ill. Dec. 42, 543 N.E.2d 277 (1 Dist. 1989); In re Harding, 189 Ill. App. 3d 663, 136 Ill. Dec. 935, 545 N.E.2d 459 (1 Dist. 1989).

The trial court did not abuse its discretion in ordering husband to pay wife only 1212% of his net income in child support where it felt that its award would enable the child to maintain the standard of living the child would have enjoyed had the marriage not been dissolved. In re Fleming, 80 Ill. App. 3d 1006, 36 Ill. Dec. 205, 400 N.E.2d 625 (2 Dist. 1980).

—Effect of Amendment
Since the enactment of the 1985 amendment to the act, courts have refused to enforce the court-approved terms of agreements which set forth the parent's responsibility for child support only as a percentage of his or her income because the precise reason for the enactment of the 1985 amendment was to avoid confusion in collecting and processing for distribution moneys owing for child support. In re Liss, 268 Ill. App. 3d 919, 206 Ill. Dec. 336, 645 N.E.2d 341 (1 Dist. 1994).

—Factors for Modification
Courts must consider the statutory guidelines in this section as part of a modification analysis; this approach comports with the principle that courts consider the same factors they considered in formulating the original support order. In re Stockton, 169 Ill. App. 3d 318, 119 Ill. Dec. 817, 523 N.E.2d 573 (4 Dist. 1988).

—Findings
The trial court must make express findings when it orders an award lower than the one set forth in the guidelines. In re Wright, 212 Ill. App. 3d 392, 156 Ill. Dec. 610, 571 N.E.2d 197 (5 Dist. 1991).

—Improper Considerations
Where the trial court did not meet the statutory guidelines of this section in that it failed to award the appropriate 25% of petitioner's net income without giving an adequate explanation in the order as to why a deviation from the statutory percentage was justified, that portion of the order awarding respondent $1,500 per month in child support was reversed. In re DeBow, 236 Ill. App. 3d 1038, 177 Ill. Dec. 89, 602 N.E.2d 984 (5 Dist. 1992), cert. denied, 148 Ill. 2d 640, 183 Ill. Dec. 17, 610 N.E.2d 1261 (1993).

To consider only the "shown needs" of a minor child is in effect to eliminate the consideration of the "standard of living the child would have enjoyed had the marriage not been dissolved." In re Osborn, 206 Ill. App. 3d 588, 151 Ill. Dec. 663, 564 N.E.2d 1325 (5 Dist. 1990), cert. denied, 137 Ill. 2d 666, 156 Ill. Dec. 563, 571 N.E.2d 150 (1991).

It was error for the trial court to substitute a pre-determined schedule for evidence of the needs of the child and the circumstances of the parents. In re Rundle, 107 Ill. App. 3d 880, 63 Ill. Dec. 491, 438 N.E.2d 229 (5 Dist. 1982).

—Minimum Support
The guidelines in subsection (a) of this section establish a minimum level of support, not a maximum. Rawles v. Hartman, 172 Ill. App. 3d 931, 123 Ill. Dec. 217, 527 N.E.2d 680 (2 Dist. 1988).

Subdivision (a)(1) of this section sets forth guidelines for the court to use in determining the minimum amount of child support that could be awarded. In re Steichen, 163 Ill. App. 3d 1074, 115 Ill. Dec. 234, 517 N.E.2d 645 (2 Dist. 1987).

—Noncompliance
The trial court was not in compliance with subdivision (a)(2) of this section where the judge failed to give specific reasons for his deviation from the child support guidelines, stating only that there were some circumstances that warranted lower payment and

Guidelines (Cont'd)

—Noncompliance (Cont'd)

remand was necessary. In re Morgan, 219 Ill. App. 3d 973, 162 Ill. Dec. 400, 579 N.E.2d 1214 (5 Dist. 1991).

—Split Custody

A strict mathematical application of child support guidelines where there is split custody of the children is not contemplated by the statute. Keown v. Wright, 225 Ill. App. 3d 808, 167 Ill. Dec. 375, 587 N.E.2d 644 (4 Dist. 1992).

—Use Upheld

Where it appeared that the husband had an aptitude for shifting money around on paper, but it is not at all clear that he actually had any and the only evidence of a definite and regular income for the husband was the evidence of his salaried employment with a communications company, the trial court properly rejected the wife's argument that the best evidence of her husband's income was neither the salary he received from the communications company nor the income indicated on his personal tax returns but the amount he was actually able to spend. In re DeGironemo, 206 Ill. App. 3d 1019, 151 Ill. Dec. 918, 565 N.E.2d 189 (1 Dist. 1990).

—Variance

Where the relevant factors call for variance from the support guidelines, variances should be made. Carnes v. Dressen, 215 Ill. App. 3d 166, 158 Ill. Dec. 732, 574 N.E.2d 845 (4 Dist. 1991).

Health Insurance

Trial court has discretion to order payment of a health insurance premium, and the trial court's ruling will not be disturbed on review absent an abuse of discretion. Hall v. Clark (In re Keon C.), 344 Ill. App. 3d 1137, 279 Ill. Dec. 674, 800 N.E.2d 1257, 2003 Ill. App. LEXIS 1498 (4 Dist. 2003), appeal denied sub nom. In re Keon C., 208 Ill. 2d 538, 284 Ill. Dec. 340, 809 N.E.2d 1286 (2004).

Where father's pay records were not current and did not show any amount which was currently being paid by respondent for dependent and individual health and hospitalization insurance, the trial court was not obligated to accept respondent's figure for such a deduction presented in the motion for reconsideration or to allow respondent to present evidence at the time of hearing the motion for reconsideration since this was not newly discovered evidence. In re Florence, 260 Ill. App. 3d 116, 198 Ill. Dec. 351, 632 N.E.2d 681 (4 Dist.), appeal denied, 157 Ill. 2d 498, 205 Ill. Dec. 160, 642 N.E.2d 1277 (1994).

It is within the sound discretion of the trial court to order payment of a health insurance premium, and there are few discernible guidelines regarding contingent medical expenses not covered by such insurance. In re Schroeder, 215 Ill. App. 3d 156, 158 Ill. Dec. 721, 574 N.E.2d 834 (4 Dist.), cert. denied, 141 Ill. 2d 560, 162 Ill. Dec. 508, 580 N.E.2d 134 (1991).

Illegitimate Children

When read together, the Parentage Act (750 ILCS 45/1 et seq.) and this Act establish that the court has broad discretion to determine any award of child support, including support for educational expenses beyond the age of majority despite the absence of a specific provision for the education of , illegitimate children. Rawles v. Hartman, 172 Ill. App. 3d 931, 123 Ill. Dec. 217, 527 N.E.2d 680 (2 Dist. 1988).

Income

—Above Average

Support of a child is the joint obligation of the parents; however, when one parent earns a disproportionately greater income than the other, that parent clearly should bear a larger share of the support. Hall v. Clark (In re Keon C.), 344 Ill. App. 3d 1137, 279 Ill. Dec. 674, 800 N.E.2d 1257, 2003 Ill. App. LEXIS 1498 (4 Dist. 2003), appeal denied sub nom. In re Keon C., 208 Ill. 2d 538, 284 Ill. Dec. 340, 809 N.E.2d 1286 (2004).

Where the individual incomes of both parents are more than sufficient to provide for the reasonable needs of the parties' children, taking into account the life style the children would have absent the dissolution, the court is justified in setting a figure below the guideline amount. In re Yong Sun Lee, 246 Ill. App. 3d 628, 186 Ill. Dec. 257, 615 N.E.2d 1314 (4 Dist.), cert. denied, 153 Ill. 2d 560, 191 Ill. Dec. 620, 624 N.E.2d 808 (1993).

Nonreimbursed business expenses are deductible to determine net income; however, the business expenses must be shown to be reasonable and necessary. Rimkus v. Rimkus, 199 Ill. App. 3d 903, 145 Ill. Dec. 868, 557 N.E.2d 638 (1 Dist. 1990).

It was an abuse of discretion to adhere strictly to statutory guidelines in setting child support payments at $10,000 per month; when dealing with above-average incomes, the specific of facts of each case become more critical in determining whether the guidelines should be adhered to. In re Scafuri, 203 Ill. App. 3d 385, 149 Ill. Dec. 124, 561 N.E.2d 402 (2 Dist. 1990).

Although the calculation of respondent's net income was not sufficiently precise to make a determination of child support based on percentage of net income, petitioner was not prejudiced by the inaccuracy, as it is within the discretion of the trial court to rely on other evidence as well. In re Stockton, 169 Ill. App. 3d 318, 119 Ill. Dec. 817, 523 N.E.2d 573 (4 Dist. 1988).

To determine husband's net income in order to set child support amount, the trial court properly allowed a 40% overhead figure for his self-owned business. In re Lefler, 185 Ill. App. 3d 677, 134 Ill. Dec. 1, 542 N.E.2d 1 (1 Dist. 1988).

The proper method of computing net income is to calculate the amount of federal and state income tax which the noncustodial parent would actually pay, rather than the amount of tax withheld, as reflected on a W2 form. In re Werner, 144 Ill. App. 3d 263, 98 Ill. Dec. 178, 493 N.E.2d 1199 (5 Dist. 1986).

—Averaging

Income averaging is not to be confined solely to self-employment cases and where respondent was not self-employed but his income varied through the years, by reason of the presence or absence of large bonuses from contractor employer income, averaging was appropriate. In re Freesen, 275 Ill. App. 3d 97, 211 Ill. Dec. 761, 655 N.E.2d 1144 (4 Dist. 1995), appeal denied, 165 Ill. 2d 550, 214 Ill. Dec. 858, 662 N.E.2d 424 (1996).

—Business Expenses

Where respondent's business paid for his car expenses, country club dues and golf expenses, and groceries, it was apparent that the trial court found that some of these items represented income to respondent, although which items and to what extent was unclear; the court could have found that some of these items represented reasonable business expenses rather than income, and there was no abuse of discretion. In re Miller, 231 Ill. App. 3d 480, 172 Ill. Dec. 679, 595 N.E.2d 1349 (3 Dist. 1992).

—Data

Data six years old cannot reflect the current circumstances of the parties so as to enable the court to comport with or deviate from the guidelines under subsection (a) of this section. In re Schroeder, 215 Ill. App. 3d 156, 158 Ill. Dec. 721, 574 N.E.2d 834 (4 Dist.), cert. denied, 141 Ill. 2d 560, 162 Ill. Dec. 508, 580 N.E.2d 134 (1991).

—Deduction

A tax deductible per diem paid to an over-the-road truck driver constituted income within the statute and was not deductible from his current wages. In re Crossland, 307 Ill. App. 3d 292, 240 Ill. Dec. 456, 717 N.E.2d 549 (3 Dist. 1999).

Respondent was not entitled to a deduction for a loan that he secured through investment corporation in order for him to be able to pay his 1992 income taxes. In re Davis, 287 Ill. App. 3d 846, 223 Ill. Dec. 166, 679 N.E.2d 110 (5 Dist. 1997).

If respondent did spend $1,200 on daughter, exclusive of gifts, he was entitled to a deduction for that amount. In re Davis, 287 Ill. App. 3d 846, 223 Ill. Dec. 166, 679 N.E.2d 110 (5 Dist. 1997).

Although, in calculating net income, federal and state income taxes are deducted, penalties and interest incurred for late payment and nonpayment of taxes are not deductible in arriving at supporting parent's net income under this section. In re Charles, 284 Ill. App. 3d 339, 219 Ill. Dec. 742, 672 N.E.2d 57 (4 Dist. 1996).

The deduction of straight line depreciation expense from net income by defendant, a taxpayer who was obligated to pay child support, was fair and proper, where he had shown such a deduction to be a "reasonable and necessary expense for the production of income," and that it was subject to a specified repayment schedule,

Income (Cont'd)

—Deduction (Cont'd)

as contemplated by subdivision (a)(3)(h). Posey v. Tate, 275 Ill. App. 3d 822, 212 Ill. Dec. 69, 656 N.E.2d 222 (1 Dist. 1995).

Noncustodial parent's payments of country club fees and premium for life insurance policy for benefit of minor child were court ordered payments and noncustodial parent could not deduct these payments from gross income pursuant to subdivision (a)(3)(h) of this section. In re Baptist, 232 Ill. App. 3d 906, 174 Ill. Dec. 81, 598 N.E.2d 278 (4 Dist. 1992).

Principal and income payments on the loan husband incurred, in order to comply with parties' property settlement did not qualify as a deduction from his net income for child support purposes. In re Partney, 212 Ill. App. 3d 586, 156 Ill. Dec. 679, 571 N.E.2d 266 (5 Dist. 1991).

—Deferred Compensation

Because deferred compensation falls under none of the allowable deductions specified under subdivision (a)(3), it should be included in a defendant's gross income. Posey v. Tate, 275 Ill. App. 3d 822, 212 Ill. Dec. 69, 656 N.E.2d 222 (1 Dist. 1995).

—Depreciation

Trial court did not abuse its discretion by adding husband's claimed depreciation expense back to his income for purposes of determining child support and maintenance. In re Minear, 287 Ill. App. 3d 1073, 223 Ill. Dec. 405, 679 N.E.2d 856 (4 Dist. 1997), aff'd, 181 Ill. 2d 552, 230 Ill. Dec. 250, 693 N.E.2d 379 (1998).

Depreciation expenses cannot be reasonably construed as payments subject to payment periods as required by the Act. In re Minear, 287 Ill. App. 3d 1073, 223 Ill. Dec. 405, 679 N.E.2d 856 (4 Dist. 1997), aff'd, 181 Ill. 2d 552, 230 Ill. Dec. 250, 693 N.E.2d 379 (1998).

—Determination

Even though it was difficult to ascertain the exact amount of husband's income because his financial statements appeared to misstate his earnings and there was conflicting testimony regarding income derived from his businesses, the trial court did not abuse its discretion in finding his income was at least $40,000. In re Karonis, 296 Ill. App. 3d 86, 230 Ill. Dec. 531, 693 N.E.2d 1282 (2 Dist. 1998).

The court has sole responsibility for calculating the net income of the parties. In re Sheetz, 254 Ill. App. 3d 695, 194 Ill. Dec. 38, 627 N.E.2d 154 (1 Dist. 1993).

Tax-reported income did not provide conclusive evidence of either husband's gross or net income under the Act, which provides its own guidelines on deductions from business income that reflect different policies and purposes than the Federal tax code. In re Carpel, 232 Ill. App. 3d 806, 173 Ill. Dec. 873, 597 N.E.2d 847 (4 Dist.), cert. denied, 147 Ill. 2d 625, 180 Ill. Dec. 148, 606 N.E.2d 1225 (1992).

Trial court had ample evidence that husband enjoyed substantially more than the $5,500 in gross income to which he testified where there was evidence that husband earned more than what was reflected on his payroll receipts, which did not reflect his election to forego bonuses of expenses paid by his company and the trial court did not abuse its discretion in finding that husband earned net income of at least $6,000 monthly for purposes of determining the proper amount of child support. In re Olson, 223 Ill. App. 3d 636, 166 Ill. Dec. 60, 585 N.E.2d 1082 (2 Dist.), appeal denied, 145 Ill. 2d 636, 173 Ill. Dec. 6, 596 N.E.2d 630 (1992).

Where it appeared that the husband had an aptitude for shifting money around on paper, but it was not at all clear that he actually had any and the only evidence of a definite and regular income was his salaried employment, the trial court properly rejected the wife's argument that the best evidence of her husband's income was neither the salary he received nor the income indicated on his personal tax returns, but the amount he was actually able to spend. In re DeGironemo, 206 Ill. App. 3d 1019, 151 Ill. Dec. 918, 565 N.E.2d 189 (1 Dist. 1990).

This Act dictates that the courts look not to gross income, but rather to net income of the supporting spouse in determining increased ability to pay, however, it may be helpful for the courts to look to gross income as a starting point in determining the spouse's net income. In re Geis, 159 Ill. App. 3d 975, 111 Ill. Dec. 717, 512 N.E.2d 1354 (1 Dist. 1987).

Under this section, maintenance and child support are directly related to the final property disposition in a dissolution of marriage proceeding, since these awards are substantially dependent upon the financial resources of the parties, including marital property. In re Kundit, 107 Ill. App. 3d 310, 63 Ill. Dec. 128, 437 N.E.2d 777 (1 Dist. 1982).

—Federal Employer's Liability Act Settlement

Where defendant failed to present requested information regarding settlement, there was no abuse of discretion in trial court's determination that the Federal Employer's Liability Act Settlement was entirely for lost wages and as such income for the purposes of child support. Illinois Dep't of Public Aid ex rel. Jennings v. White, 286 Ill. App. 3d 213, 221 Ill. Dec. 561, 675 N.E.2d 985 (2 Dist. 1997).

—Fluctuating

There is no iron-clad rule requiring a trial court to consider only the last three years of income in arriving at net income for child support purposes; at least the three prior years should be used to obtain an accurate income picture, beyond that, however, it must be left to the discretion of the trial court, as facts will vary in each case. In re Freesen, 275 Ill. App. 3d 97, 211 Ill. Dec. 761, 655 N.E.2d 1144 (4 Dist. 1995), appeal denied, 165 Ill. 2d 550, 214 Ill. Dec. 858, 662 N.E.2d 424 (1996).

Where the data used by the trial court to determine husband's 1991income extended back only three years, and there was no dispute as to the reliability of the income data for those years and, in addition, his income fluctuated from year to year depending upon the profitability of the family business or the averaging method was a reasonable means of determining his current income. In re Elies, 248 Ill. App. 3d 1052, 188 Ill. Dec. 364, 618 N.E.2d 934 (1 Dist. 1993).

Although husband's self-employment in his own law firm — specializing in personal injury litigation — complicated matters, and both his self-employment and the nature of personal injury practice could make his income fluctuate unpredictably, despite these complications, the trial court was required to evaluate the evidence presented to determine his net income, thereby complying with subsection (a) of this section. In re Carpel, 232 Ill. App. 3d 806, 173 Ill. Dec. 873, 597 N.E.2d 847 (4 Dist.), cert. denied, 147 Ill. 2d 625, 180 Ill. Dec. 148, 606 N.E.2d 1225 (1992).

Although it was within the trial court's discretion due to fluctuations in husband's income, to order respondent to submit a quarterly accounting of his net income to petitioner, order was modified to require an annual accounting. Smith v. Smith, 78 Ill. App. 3d 80, 33 Ill. Dec. 717, 397 N.E.2d 50 (1 Dist. 1979).

—Gifts

Gifts are properly includable in net income for purposes of calculating child support obligations; to the extent that In re Marriage of Bowlby 338 Ill. App. 3d 720, 273 Ill. Dec. 466 (2003) and In re Marriage of Harmon, 210 Ill. App. 3d 92, 154 Ill. Dec. 727 (1991) are inconsistent with this view, they are both overruled. In re Marriage of Rogers, 213 Ill. 2d 129, 289 Ill. Dec. 610, 820 N.E.2d 386, 2004 Ill. LEXIS 1676 (2004).

Circuit court properly modified a child support obligation to include gifts and loans made to a father by his family because they were a source of income, despite the fact that the amount of such was not certain; moreover, loans were also properly included in net income because they were merely disguised gifts since there was no obligation to repay. In re Marriage of Rogers, 213 Ill. 2d 129, 289 Ill. Dec. 610, 820 N.E.2d 386, 2004 Ill. LEXIS 1676 (2004).

Loans and gifts were to be considered in calculating an ex-husband's child support payments, and the circuit court did not commit error by failing to deduct the gifts and loans from his annual income in calculating an increase to his child support obligation. Rogers v. Rogers, 345 Ill. App. 3d 77, 280 Ill. Dec. 726, 802 N.E.2d 1247, 2003 Ill. App. LEXIS 1584 (1 Dist. 2003).

Money respondent received as a gift cannot be considered income, nor can the monthly interest payments which comprise her share of the marital assets. In re Harmon, 210 Ill. App. 3d 92, 154 Ill. Dec. 727, 568 N.E.2d 948 (2 Dist. 1991).

—Gratuities

It was inappropriate to consider factor of gratuities in setting

Income (Cont'd)

—Gratuities (Cont'd)
child support awards as by their very nature, gratuities may be given or withheld by father at any time at his unfettered discretion; any consideration of such gratuities in setting the child support award was improper. In re Freesen, 275 Ill. App. 3d 97, 211 Ill. Dec. 761, 655 N.E.2d 1144 (4 Dist. 1995), appeal denied, 165 Ill. 2d 550, 214 Ill. Dec. 858, 662 N.E.2d 424 (1996).

—History
The court may use historical income data to determine the appropriate amount of retroactive support. In re Sheetz, 254 Ill. App. 3d 695, 194 Ill. Dec. 38, 627 N.E.2d 154 (1 Dist. 1993).

—Investment Income
In determining a parent's income for purposes of the statute, the trial court acted within its discretion in allocating investment income from life insurance proceeds arising from the death of the parent's first husband three-fourths to the three children born of that marriage and one-fourth to the parent. Slagel v. Wessels, 314 Ill. App. 3d 330, 247 Ill. Dec. 665, 732 N.E.2d 720, 2000 Ill. App. LEXIS 525 (4 Dist. 2000).

—Lost Earnings
Reimbursement for lost earnings may be considered income for purposes of setting a support award. Villanueva v. O'Gara, 282 Ill. App. 3d 147, 218 Ill. Dec. 105, 668 N.E.2d 589 (2 Dist 1996).

—New Spouse
Income and net worth of ex-husband's new wife was properly admitted in child support modification hearing where new wife sought, and was granted, permission to intervene in the modification proceedings to protect her own financial interests, which she conceded were commingled with her husband's and where without testimony about the new wife's income and net worth, the trial judge could not have determined whether husband's transfers of business interests to the new wife were proper and what interests were the new wife's, and therefore not subject to consideration in determining husband's child support obligation. In re Baptist, 232 Ill. App. 3d 906, 174 Ill. Dec. 81, 598 N.E.2d 278 (4 Dist. 1992).

—Nonrecurring
This section does not provide for a deduction of nonrecurring income in calculating net income for purposes of child support. In re Hart, 194 Ill. App. 3d 839, 141 Ill. Dec. 550, 551 N.E.2d 737 (4 Dist. 1990).

—Passive
Where there was unrefuted testimony party did not actually receive the passive income, even if it was reported on income tax returns, it was not error to refuse to consider such amounts in calculating net income for child support purposes. In re Freesen, 275 Ill. App. 3d 97, 211 Ill. Dec. 761, 655 N.E.2d 1144 (4 Dist. 1995), appeal denied, 165 Ill. 2d 550, 214 Ill. Dec. 858, 662 N.E.2d 424 (1996).

—Percentage
A child support provision is not rendered void when the amount of support is listed as a percentage of income. In re Scott, 286 Ill. App. 3d 1056, 222 Ill. Dec. 594, 678 N.E.2d 1 (3 Dist. 1996).

—Ratio
The court was without justification for apportioning final child support figure based on a ratio of the parties' gross incomes. In re Stockton, 169 Ill. App. 3d 318, 119 Ill. Dec. 817, 523 N.E.2d 573 (4 Dist. 1988).

—Stock Distributions
Even though unvested stock options awarded to former husband were characterized as marital property, they could still be characterized as income for child support purposes once they vested and were transformed into a realized distribution; thus, the trial court erred in denying former wife's petition for a rule to show cause claiming that husband was required to pay 20 percent of the realized distribution as child support pursuant to the judgment of dissolution after he refused to do so on the ground that marital property could not be "income" for child support purposes. In re Marriage of Colangelo, Ill. App. 3d , 290 Ill. Dec. 986, 822 N.E.2d 571, 2005 Ill. App. LEXIS 39 (2 Dist. 2005).

—Unreported
Where there was a wide discrepancy between respondent's supposed income and his actual spending there was only one explanation: the parties' pre-separation lifestyle was supported by at least $35,000 yearly in unreported income, which provided the basis for the trial judge's award to petitioner of $3,000 per month in unallocated maintenance and child support. In re Hilkovitch, 124 Ill. App. 3d 401, 79 Ill. Dec. 891, 464 N.E.2d 795 (1 Dist. 1984).

Where the trial court's estimation of respondent's income was based on his admitted expenditures rather than on his tax returns, the trial court did not abuse its discretion in awarding petitioner $3,000 per month in unallocated support and maintenance, since the documentary evidence provided by a respondent was not only inherently unbelievable but also was revealed to have no independent basis of reliability. In re Hilkovitch, 124 Ill. App. 3d 401, 79 Ill. Dec. 891, 464 N.E.2d 795 (1 Dist. 1984).

—Unreported Cash Income
There was no error by the trial court in failing to consider alleged unreported cash income received by respondent where petitioner's testimony regarding these sums largely concerned events prior to the parties' marriage and respondent denied receiving any such payments for several years. In re Miller, 231 Ill. App. 3d 480, 172 Ill. Dec. 679, 595 N.E.2d 1349 (3 Dist. 1992).

Insurance Premiums
Considering the financial position of both parties, the court did not abuse its discretion in ordering father to provide insurance coverage for children through mother's place of employment. In re Nelson, 297 Ill. App. 3d 651, 232 Ill. Dec. 654, 698 N.E.2d 1084 (3 Dist. 1998).

Circuit court abused its discretion in failing to deduct respondent's health hospitalization insurance premiums when it determined his net income. In re Davis, 287 Ill. App. 3d 846, 223 Ill. Dec. 166, 679 N.E.2d 110 (5 Dist. 1997).

Interest
Child support obligation that becomes due and remains unpaid for 30 days or more shall accrue simple interest at the rate of nine percent per annum, but the decision to award interest on any dissolution judgment, other than a judgment for child support, is a discretionary matter for the trial court; a trial court did not abuse its discretion in refusing to award interest where the support payments a husband failed to pay were for unallocated support. Berto v. Berto, 344 Ill. App. 3d 705, 279 Ill. Dec. 482, 800 N.E.2d 550, 2003 Ill. App. LEXIS 1383 (2 Dist. 2003).

The trial court erred in ruling that it had no discretion to decide whether to award interest. In re Steinberg, 302 Ill. App. 3d 845, 236 Ill. Dec. 21, 706 N.E.2d 895 (1 Dist. 1998), appeal denied, 184 Ill. 2d 557, 239 Ill. Dec. 608, 714 N.E.2d 527 (1999).

Subsection (d) does not relate to the issue of interest on dissolution judgments and does not make an award of interest mandatory. In re Kaufman, 299 Ill. App. 3d 508, 233 Ill. Dec. 543, 701 N.E.2d 186 (1 Dist. 1998), appeal denied, 181 Ill. 2d 573, 235 Ill. Dec. 942, 706 N.E.2d 497 (1998); but see In re Marriage of Carrier, 332 Ill. App. 3d 654, 265 Ill. Dec. 893, 773 N.E.2d 657 (2 Dist. 2002).

An award of interest on past due child support payments was justified where for approximately 20 years petitioner was deprived of child support money that was rightfully hers, for the same length of time respondent enjoyed the use of the money, and respondent had maintained a fairly steady employment record at fairly well-paying jobs. People ex rel. Jones v. Cartledge, 125 Ill. App. 3d 510, 80 Ill. Dec. 837, 466 N.E.2d 289 (5 Dist. 1984).

Where the trial court properly found the amount of arrearages in child support payments owed to plaintiff by defendant, since a decree of divorce providing for periodic support payments is a money decree, interest was recoverable thereon from the due date until satisfied. Neeland v. Neeland, 17 Ill. App. 3d 803, 308 N.E.2d 651 (3 Dist. 1974).

A trial court, in entering judgment for the principal amount, erred in failing to include in its order interest on past-due child support payments. Simpson v. Simpson, 4 Ill. App. 2d 526, 124 N.E.2d 573 (1 Dist. 1955).

Interest (Cont'd)

A decree of divorce that provides for weekly payments for support and maintenance for the children of the marriage is a money decree and subject to an annual interest rate until satisfied. Shuff v. Fulte, 344 Ill. App. 157, 100 N.E.2d 502 (3 Dist. 1951).

Intervention

—Not Allowed

In a child support and paternity action, the father of another child born to female petitioner could not intervene in the action as a matter of right, although he was indirectly affected by the amount of support that respondent must pay. People ex rel. Collins v. Burton, 282 Ill. App. 3d 649, 218 Ill. Dec. 353, 668 N.E.2d 1185 (4 Dist. 1996).

Judgment Liens

The legislature has made no provision for the creation of a judgment lien on past due payments for the "settlement of property." Saldeen v. Hamelberg, 198 Ill. App. 3d 146, 144 Ill. Dec. 384, 555 N.E.2d 743 (4 Dist. 1990).

Jurisdiction

—In General

Where the trial court had personal jurisdiction over both parties at the time of their divorce, subsection (a) of this section was not applicable to plaintiff's petition seeking past-due child support. Nerini v. Nerini, 140 Ill. App. 3d 848, 95 Ill. Dec. 36, 488 N.E.2d 1379 (2 Dist. 1986).

—Continuing

Where the wife and the parties' child continued to reside in Illinois and there was no evidence that the parties entered into a written agreement consenting to the transfer of jurisdiction over the case to another state, the trial court retained continuing, exclusive jurisdiction over the child support order it entered and had the authority to exercise its contempt powers to require the husband to comply with the original order for support. In re Hartman, 305 Ill. App. 3d 338, 238 Ill. Dec. 645, 712 N.E.2d 367 (2 Dist. 1999).

—Duty of Father

Circuit courts have jurisdiction to hear and determine matters concerning the welfare of a child including the enforcement of the duty of the father to provide reasonable support for the child. Skilling v. Skilling, 104 Ill. App. 3d 213, 59 Ill. Dec. 937, 432 N.E.2d 881 (1 Dist. 1982).

—Foreign Divorce Decree

Judgment purporting to register Scottish decree of divorce was void because the circuit court lacked subject matter jurisdiction to register the judgment; registration and enforcement of a judgment of a foreign country in a matrimonial matter is not a justiciable matter and there was no cause of action to do so at common law and no statute has created one. In re Mullins, 135 Ill. App. 3d 279, 89 Ill. Dec. 771, 481 N.E.2d 322 (4 Dist. 1985).

This Act provides a statutory remedy for the entry of original orders of child support, but that remedy is limited in that such orders can only be entered in conjunction with a dissolution proceeding, a legal separation proceeding, a proceeding for the declaration of the invalidity of a marriage, or a proceeding following dissolution of the marriage by a court which lacked personal jurisdiction over the absent spouse, and the Act also provides for modification procedures of the decrees of other states, but is silent on possible modification of the decrees of foreign nations. Skilling v. Skilling, 104 Ill. App. 3d 213, 59 Ill. Dec. 937, 432 N.E.2d 881 (1 Dist. 1982).

A minor, whose parents were divorced in another state in a proceeding where no support order could be entered because the defendant father was outside the jurisdiction of the court and served only by publication, was permitted to maintain a petition for support in Illinois, where the father had an established residence. Parker v. Parker, 335 Ill. App. 293, 81 N.E.2d 745 (2 Dist. 1948).

—In Personam

The execution of a judgment ordering payment of child support requires in personam jurisdiction. In re Weishaupt, 160 Ill. App. 3d 563, 113 Ill. Dec. 6, 514 N.E.2d 788 (4 Dist. 1987).

—Non-Minor Children

Under former sections 13 and 18 of the Divorce Act (see now this section), the jurisdiction of a court of chancery to provide for the care and education of a child did not end the moment that child attained majority; where such care and education were necessary to equip the child for adult life and where the financial circumstances of the father were entirely adequate to meet such requirements, equity could and should continue its jurisdiction. Strom v. Strom, 13 Ill. App. 2d 354, 142 N.E.2d 172 (1 Dist. 1957).

Jury Trial

Where plaintiff wife acknowledged the validity of a prior Arkansas divorce decree, and her complaint was concerned solely with alimony, property division and attorneys fees, defendant husband had no common law right to a jury trial, as such actions were traditionally chancery actions, and the right arose only if it was expressly conferred by statute. Sidwell v. Sidwell, 28 Ill. App. 3d 580, 328 N.E.2d 595 (4 Dist. 1975).

Laches

Laches is not available as a defense for delinquent child support payments, if the spouse seeking relief delayed instituting a lawsuit for almost seven years, unless the party asserting the doctrine has suffered injury or prejudice as a result of the other party's delay in instituting an action, therefore, a spouse is not injured if he is forced to pay the accumulated support in one lump sum, as opposed to weekly payments. Blisset v. Blisset, 123 Ill. 2d 161, 121 Ill. Dec. 931, 526 N.E.2d 125 (1988).

Lien of Trust

The trial court has the power to impose a lien of trust upon the property of the noncustodial parent to secure and guarantee the enforcement of court ordered child support. Gentile v. Gentile, 69 Ill. App. 3d 297, 26 Ill. Dec. 149, 387 N.E.2d 979 (3 Dist. 1979).

Life Insurance

A trial court is vested with the authority to order a parent to provide life insurance for the benefit of his children. In re Osborn, 206 Ill. App. 3d 588, 151 Ill. Dec. 663, 564 N.E.2d 1325 (5 Dist. 1990), cert. denied, 137 Ill. 2d 666, 156 Ill. Dec. 563, 571 N.E.2d 150 (1991).

Where specific evidence as to the cost of term life insurance policies that the trial court ordered the husband to provide was not presented, where the trial court stated that it gave credit for the appropriate expense of the insurance in determining the child support obligation, and where the husband did not show that he was unable to obtain term life insurance, the trial court did not err in ordering the husband to provide insurance to insure that the minor children would be provided for in the event of the husband's death. In re Osborn, 206 Ill. App. 3d 588, 151 Ill. Dec. 663, 564 N.E.2d 1325 (5 Dist. 1990), cert. denied, 137 Ill. 2d 666, 156 Ill. Dec. 563, 571 N.E.2d 150 (1991).

Maintenance

Court's finding that petitioner was a candidate for maintenance was based upon the proper factors including the emotional condition of petitioner, noting that petitioner's frail and fragile condition was the result of abuse from respondent did not mean that court considered the conduct of respondent in an effort to punish him. In re Severino, 298 Ill. App. 3d 224, 232 Ill. Dec. 355, 698 N.E.2d 193 (2 Dist. 1998).

Court's finding was express and sufficient to order maintenance based on disparity in income. In re Minear, 287 Ill. App. 3d 1073, 223 Ill. Dec. 405, 679 N.E.2d 856 (4 Dist. 1997), aff'd, 181 Ill. 2d 552, 230 Ill. Dec. 250, 693 N.E.2d 379 (1998).

Medical Expenses

—In General

In addition to monthly support payments for all children, a parent may be ordered to pay the medical, dental and hospital expenses of all children, inclusive of orthodontic treatment which may be recommended for each child, with a cost of $2,100 per child, with $600 to be paid initially for each child, followed by payments of $60 per month per child for 25 months. Additionally, to pay $1,000 for a noncustodial child's college expenses, spread over 12 months averages over $83 per month, and the parent may be required to contribute to the college expenses of the parties'

Medical Expenses (Cont'd)

—In General (Cont'd)

younger child or children. Blisset v. Blisset, 123 Ill. 2d 161, 121 Ill. Dec. 931, 526 N.E.2d 125 (1988).

—Extraordinary

Despite discernable guidelines on contingent medical expenses not covered by insurance, a trial court also has discretion to order the payment of uncovered and extraordinary medical expenses. Hall v. Clark (In re Keon C.), 344 Ill. App. 3d 1137, 279 Ill. Dec. 674, 800 N.E.2d 1257, 2003 Ill. App. LEXIS 1498 (4 Dist. 2003), appeal denied sub nom. In re Keon C., 208 Ill. 2d 538, 284 Ill. Dec. 340, 809 N.E.2d 1286 (2004).

Considering that wife received $35 per week child support, a medical expense that amounted to more than one-third of the support funds could hardly be considered "small" or "ordinary." In re Arnold, 122 Ill. App. 3d 776, 78 Ill. Dec. 335, 462 N.E.2d 51 (3 Dist. 1984).

—Not Allowed

Requirement in judgment that husband pay for the children's medical and dental expenses past the age of their attainment of majority was error. In re Moore, 117 Ill. App. 3d 206, 72 Ill. Dec. 797, 453 N.E.2d 102 (5 Dist. 1983).

—Reimbursement

A wife's failure to notify her husband of a lawsuit which awarded their son money damages, including amounts to pay the son's medical expenses, after father paid some of the medical bills did not entitle the husband to reimbursement from the wife. In re Frazier, 205 Ill. App. 3d 621, 151 Ill. Dec. 130, 563 N.E.2d 1236 (3 Dist. 1990).

—Unusual

Under former Ill. Rev. Stat., ch. 40, para. 19 (see now this section), payments made monthly to an institution for the full care of the parties' twins were not unusual expenses for medical care, drugs or hospitalization for the minor children within the meaning of the parties' property settlement agreement, and defendant was entitled to a set-off for these payments which he made to the institution against his alimony obligation. Needler v. Needler, 131 Ill. App. 2d 11, 268 N.E.2d 517 (1 Dist. 1971).

—Upheld

Where the court's order only required petitioner to pay for the medical expenses of the children after their majority if they were attending school, there was no error. In re Bates, 141 Ill. App. 3d 566, 95 Ill. Dec. 922, 490 N.E.2d 1014 (2 Dist. 1986).

Minor Children

—Defined

When the court used the words "minor children" it meant minor children as defined under the statute existing at the time of the decree. Strum v. Strum, 22 Ill. App. 3d 147, 317 N.E.2d 59 (4 Dist. 1974).

Modification

—Discretion of Court

The trial court has considerable discretion in the modification of child support and the court's decision should not be disturbed by a reviewing court absent an abuse of discretion. In re Fowler, 197 Ill. App. 3d 95, 143 Ill. Dec. 305, 554 N.E.2d 240 (3 Dist. 1989).

Modification of child support lies within the sound discretion of the trial court and will not be disturbed on appeal absent an abuse of discretion. In re Cook, 147 Ill. App. 3d 134, 100 Ill. Dec. 760, 497 N.E.2d 1029 (3 Dist. 1986); In re Lyons, 155 Ill. App. 3d 300, 108 Ill. Dec. 297, 508 N.E.2d 458 (2 Dist. 1987); In re Winters, 160 Ill. App. 3d 277, 111 Ill. Dec. 734, 512 N.E.2d 1371 (2 Dist. 1987); In re Frazier, 205 Ill. App. 3d 621, 151 Ill. Dec. 130, 563 N.E.2d 1236 (3 Dist. 1990); In re Partney, 212 Ill. App. 3d 586, 156 Ill. Dec. 679, 571 N.E.2d 266 (5 Dist. 1991).

—Dollar Amounts

The trial court erred in refusing to modify the child support amount to a dollar figure because, although the amount of the figure remained discretionary with the trial court, subdivision (a)(5) of this section clearly requires a final order to state the support level in dollar amounts. In re Wassom, 165 Ill. App. 3d 1076, 116 Ill. Dec. 932, 519 N.E.2d 1147 (4 Dist. 1988).

—Effects

Where an adjustment was made in the child support payments, the case will not be remanded in is entirety for reconsideration of the disposition of the marital property, as to do so would constitute a suggestion to the trial court to tilt its disposition of marital property in such a manner as to compensate for the reduction in child support payments that has now been made. In re Moore, 117 Ill. App. 3d 206, 72 Ill. Dec. 797, 453 N.E.2d 102 (5 Dist. 1983).

—Factors

Even if respondent's income had not increased, that is merely one factor which the court must consider and it does not preclude a modification of child support. In re Johnson, 206 Ill. App. 3d 992, 151 Ill. Dec. 891, 565 N.E.2d 162 (1 Dist. 1990).

Trial court is to consider the same factors in considering modifying the amount of child support as it considers in formulating an original support order. In re Erickson, 136 Ill. App. 3d 907, 91 Ill. Dec. 346, 483 N.E.2d 692 (2 Dist. 1985).

—Incarceration

Incarceration is not a form of voluntary unemployment and, therefore, does not automatically fail to justify a reduction in child support as a matter of law; in determining whether to reduce or suspend child support payments due to the incarceration of the obligor, a trial court must consider all relevant factors, including: (1) the assets of the incarcerated person; (2) the length of the incarceration; (3) the reason of the obligated parent entered prison; (4) the potential for work release. In re Burbridge, 317 Ill. App. 3d 190, 250 Ill. Dec. 510, 738 N.E.2d 979, 2000 Ill. App. LEXIS 831 (3 Dist. 2000).

—Incorporated Settlement Agreement

A settlement agreement provision that husband would not advance as a reason for modification of the child support payments any future employment of wife did not divest the court of its power to modify the divorce decree into which the agreement was incorporated. Wohl v. Wohl, 28 Ill. App. 3d 298, 328 N.E.2d 138 (1 Dist. 1975).

—Increase

Where the evidence indicates that the standard of living of the mother and the two children residing with her had decreased substantially since the original child support and maintenance award, this was one of the factors which the court must consider along with the financial needs and resources of all the parties, and where there was a great disparity between the income of the mother, even with child support, and that of the father, the trial court did not abuse its discretion by increasing the father's monthly child support payments. In re Loomis, 153 Ill. App. 3d 404, 106 Ill. Dec. 219, 505 N.E.2d 766 (3 Dist. 1987).

—Not warranted

Determination that an obligor parent had failed to show changed circumstances warranting a reduced child support obligation was not against the manifest weight of the evidence; trial court had properly compared the obligor's circumstances with circumstances at the time of a previous order at which its denial of a modification request had not been appealed, not with the obligor's circumstances at the time of the original divorce. Armstrong v. Armstrong, 346 Ill. App. 3d 818, 282 Ill. Dec. 124, 805 N.E.2d 743, 2004 Ill. App. LEXIS 271 (4 Dist. 2004).

—Percentage-Based Child Support Order

Where agreement was entered into after the enactment of subdivision(a)(5) and was therefore improper from the outset, the portion of the agreement which set father's support obligations at a percentage of his income was void and unenforceable; subdivision (a)(5) cut off the authority of the trial court to enter a percentage-based child support order which allowed the parties to modify their support obligations without the approval of the trial court. In re Ingram, 259 Ill. App. 3d 685, 197 Ill. Dec. 383, 631 N.E.2d 386 (2 Dist. 1994).

—Tax Gimmicks

The use of federal tax gimmicks will not be allowed to avoid child

Modification (Cont'd)

—Tax Gimmicks (Cont'd)
support modification provisions. In re Gleason, 266 Ill. App. 3d 467, 203 Ill. Dec. 423, 639 N.E.2d 982 (4 Dist. 1994).

—Upheld
Petitioner's expenses as the custodial parent totaled about $2,600per month on an income of $1,400 per month plus $300 in maintenance, leaving a deficit of $900 per month and respondent's net earnings were about $4,700 per month and he has not remarried and has no other dependents; under the trial court's child support order or $700 per month, petitioner would have $2,400 to support herself and the children, or a deficit of $200 per month and respondent, on the other hand, would have substantial discretionary income remaining which would have enhanced the children's standard of living had the marriage not been dissolved, and under these circumstances, respondent should bear a greater portion of the support obligation for the children so as to compensate for the deficit incurred by petitioner. In re Leva, 125 Ill. App. 3d 55, 77 Ill. Dec. 615, 460 N.E.2d 1179 (1 Dist. 1983).

After a review of the factors set forth in subsection (a) of this section and considering the reasonable and necessary needs for support and the ability of the parties to pay, the support was modified to an amount which was sufficient to furnish the children a high, though not lavish, standard of living and permit some payment for household expenses. In re Moore, 117 Ill. App. 3d 206, 72 Ill. Dec. 797, 453 N.E.2d 102 (5 Dist. 1983).

Order of the trial court modifying defendant's child support payments was proper where defendant, at the time of divorce, failed to inform the court about his year-end commission and plaintiff introduced evidence at the hearing on her petition to modify the child support payments that her expenses for maintaining a home and the care, feeding and clothing of the two children was approximately $172.80 per week while the defendant's original child support payments supplied $80 per week. Robbins v. Robbins, 40 Ill. App. 3d 653, 353 N.E.2d 110 (2 Dist. 1976).

Under the language of the divorce decree it was proper for the support payment sums to be modified as of the date the governmental allotment payments terminated where such modification was not only equitable, but was well within the purport of the original order. Edwards v. Edwards, 125 Ill. App. 2d 91, 259 N.E.2d 820 (4 Dist. 1970).

Needs of Child
Trial court in this case incorrectly considered only the reasonable needs of the children in setting the child support award. In re Freesen, 275 Ill. App. 3d 97, 211 Ill. Dec. 761, 655 N.E.2d 1144 (4 Dist. 1995), appeal denied, 165 Ill. 2d 550, 214 Ill. Dec. 858, 662 N.E.2d 424 (1996).

A child's support needs are determined in reference to the financial resources of the parties to the dissolution of the marriage and the child individually, the standard of living the child would have enjoyed had the marriage not dissolved and the physical, emotional and educational needs of the child. In re Winters, 160 Ill. App. 3d 277, 111 Ill. Dec. 734, 512 N.E.2d 1371 (2 Dist. 1987).

Net Income

—In General
The definition of net income contained in the statute, rather than the Internal Revenue Code, controls the determination of income for child support purposes. In re Sweet, 316 Ill. App. 3d 101, 249 Ill. Dec. 212, 735 N.E.2d 1037, 2000 Ill. App. LEXIS 727 (2 Dist. 2000).

—Averaging Income
It was clear father's income fluctuated from year to year depending on the profitability of the farming industry, therefore the method of income averaging employed by the court was a reasonable means of determining father's net income for purposes of child support. In re Nelson, 297 Ill. App. 3d 651, 232 Ill. Dec. 654, 698 N.E.2d 1084 (3 Dist. 1998).

—Averaging of Income
The trial court properly set child support at a level substantially greater than the reasonable needs of the child by averaging an ex-husband's income for the previous three years to establish his obligation. In re Marriage of Garrett, 336 Ill. App. 3d 1018, 271 Ill. Dec. 521, 785 N.E.2d 172, 2003 Ill. App. LEXIS 107 (5 Dist. 2003), appeal denied sub nom. Garrett v. Garrett, 204 Ill. 2d 658, 275 Ill. Dec. 75, 792 N.E.2d 306 (2003).

—Definition in Other Sections
The definition of net income found in 750 ILCS 570/6.1 does not limit the definition of net income in this section. Illinois Dep't of Public Aid ex rel. Jennings v. White, 286 Ill. App. 3d 213, 221 Ill. Dec. 561, 675 N.E.2d 985 (2 Dist. 1997).

—Disability Pension Income
A firefighter's disability pension income was properly included in his net income for purposes of 750 ILCS 5/505(a)(3), notwithstanding the language of 40 ILCS 5/4-135. People ex rel. Myers v. Kidd, 308 Ill. App. 3d 593, 242 Ill. Dec. 170, 720 N.E.2d 1125 (5 Dist. 1999).

—IRA income
Father did not show that he was entitled to have IRA disbursements deducted from the calculation of his net income for the purpose of determining whether his child support obligation should be modified based on his claim of financial hardship; although statutory law allowed a deduction from "net income" for reasonable expenditures for the benefit of the child and the other parent, that law only applied to situations where the noncustodial parent voluntarily contributed to necessary expenses for which he or she is not already obligated to contribute or pay, which did not include the child support obligation that the father, the noncustodial parent, was required to pay based on the terms of his divorce. In re Marriage of Lindman, Ill. App. 3d , Ill. Dec. , N.E.2d , 2004 Ill. App. LEXIS 1619 (2 Dist. Dec. 16, 2004).

Trial court did not err in concluding that disbursements from father's IRA were "income" for the purpose of calculating "net income" pursuant to this section, and in denying his petition to modify his child support obligation, as the substantial disbursements from his IRA to him after he divorced his wife undercut his argument that modification was warranted due to financial hardship. In re Marriage of Lindman, Ill. App. 3d , Ill. Dec. , N.E.2d , 2004 Ill. App. LEXIS 1619 (2 Dist. Dec. 16, 2004).

—Nonreimbursed Business Expenses
Only such expenses as constitute "repayment of debts" may be deducted from net income under the first clause of subdivision (a)(3)(h) and nonreimbursed business expenses do not fit into this category. Gay ex rel. Gay v. Dunlap, 279 Ill. App. 3d 140, 215 Ill. Dec. 691, 664 N.E.2d 88 (4 Dist. 1996), appeal denied, 168 Ill. 2d 589, 219 Ill. Dec. 563, 671 N.E.2d 730 (1996).

—Not Able to Ascertain
Where the judge determined the respondent's net income was too difficult to determine, he properly ordered support in an amount considered reasonable. In re Takata, 304 Ill. App. 3d 85, 237 Ill. Dec. 460, 709 N.E.2d 715 (2 Dist. 1999).

Without credible evidence of respondent's net income, trial court's determination of $650 per week as necessary to allow the minor child to enjoy the standard of living she would have enjoyed had the marriage not been dissolved, was reasonable. In re Severino, 298 Ill. App. 3d 224, 232 Ill. Dec. 355, 698 N.E.2d 193 (2 Dist. 1998).

—Payments on Principal
Court correctly refused to deduct payments of principal on farm operating loans from father's net income; court used Schedule F to determine father's farming income for purposes of computing his total net income thus allowing father another deduction for the repayment of farm operating loans would permit him to take the same deduction twice. In re Nelson, 297 Ill. App. 3d 651, 232 Ill. Dec. 654, 698 N.E.2d 1084 (3 Dist. 1998).

—Personal Bank Loan
Where trial court found Federal Employer's Liability Act Settlement was entirely for lost wages and as such income for purposes of child support, the court correctly found a personal loan defendant secured against his anticipated settlement to use for living expenses was not deductible under this section. Illinois Dep't of Public Aid ex rel. Jennings v. White, 286 Ill. App. 3d 213, 221 Ill. Dec. 561, 675 N.E.2d 985 (2 Dist. 1997).

Net Income (Cont'd)

—Personal Injury Claims

The trial court failed to correctly determine net income prior to the allocation for child support where court failed to deduct personal injury awards of husband apportioned to wife. In re Wolfe, 298 Ill. App. 3d 510, 232 Ill. Dec. 743, 699 N.E.2d 190 (2 Dist. 1998), appeal denied, 181 Ill. 2d 590, 235 Ill. Dec. 949, 706 N.E.2d 504 (1998).

Entire settlements from personal injury claims are not included in the definition of net income for the purposes of determining the amount of child support. Villanueva v. O'Gara, 282 Ill. App. 3d 147, 218 Ill. Dec. 105, 668 N.E.2d 589 (2 Dist 1996).

—Prior Obligation

A temporary support order entered in Michigan was not included in determination of the father's net income because it was not a prior obligation for support even though it was dated before the order awarding college expenses was entered in Illinois action; the word "prior" in subdivision (a)(3)(g) means obligations to a family that is "first in time" in relation to another family. In re Zukausky, 244 Ill. App. 3d 614, 184 Ill. Dec. 367, 613 N.E.2d 394 (2 Dist. 1993).

—Repayment of Debts

Reasonable, as used in subdivision (a)(3)(h), applies to the relationship between the amount of the expense and the amount by which income is in good faith expected to increase as a result. Gay ex rel. Gay v. Dunlap, 279 Ill. App. 3d 140, 215 Ill. Dec. 691, 664 N.E.2d 88 (4 Dist. 1996), appeal denied, 168 Ill. 2d 589, 219 Ill. Dec. 563, 671 N.E.2d 730 (1996).

By the word "necessary" found in subdivision (a)(3)(h), the legislature did not intend only to describe those expenses without which no income could be generated but intended to describe those expenses outlaid by a parent with a good-faith belief his or her income would increase as a result, and which actually did act to increase income, or would have done so absent some extenuating circumstance. Gay ex rel. Gay v. Dunlap, 279 Ill. App. 3d 140, 215 Ill. Dec. 691, 664 N.E.2d 88 (4 Dist. 1996), appeal denied, 168 Ill. 2d 589, 219 Ill. Dec. 563, 671 N.E.2d 730 (1996).

—Tax Refund

A tax refund should be included to determine net income. Pylawka v. Pylawka, 277 Ill. App. 3d 728, 214 Ill. Dec. 651, 661 N.E.2d 505 (2 Dist. 1996).

—Tax Withholdings

Where a father actually was filing his tax return as a married person with five withholding exemptions, the tax withheld there was the correct amount to use for the purpose of calculating child support not that based on his filing status as a single individual following his divorce. Dep't of Pub. Aid ex rel. Schmid v. Williams, 336 Ill. App. 3d 553, 271 Ill. Dec. 198, 784 N.E.2d 416, 2003 Ill. App. LEXIS 114 (4 Dist. 2003).

Net Worth

—Determination

In a hearing to award child support, evaluating defendant's net worth was a matter of resolving conflicting testimony, and was a matter for the trial court to determine. Sandberg v. Sandberg, 11 Ill. App. 3d 495, 297 N.E.2d 654 (1 Dist. 1973).

Nonpayment

—Burden of Proof

Following a showing of a failure to make payment of support, the burden is then on the defendant to prove that his failure to comply with the judgment order was not wilful and contumacious and that he had a valid excuse for his failure to pay. People v. Stanley, 60 Ill. App. 3d 909, 17 Ill. Dec. 766, 376 N.E.2d 1095 (3 Dist. 1978).

—Contempt

Striking of respondent husband's petition seeking to be allowed to make periodic payments of the child support for which he had been adjudged liable did not bar a defense upon the question of contempt for refusal to pay the judgment or make unnecessary a hearing upon the issue of wilful and contumacious failure to pay the judgment. Archer v. Archer, 71 Ill. App. 3d 938, 28 Ill. Dec. 462, 390 N.E.2d 629 (4 Dist. 1979).

In this state, failure to pay support as ordered by the court is prima facie evidence of contempt. People v. Stanley, 60 Ill. App. 3d 909, 17 Ill. Dec. 766, 376 N.E.2d 1095 (3 Dist. 1978).

—Defense of Poverty

The defense of poverty and misfortune for failure to make support payments has been found applicable only in the most extreme cases, notably those in which a defendant has no money and no way of getting money to meet support obligations. People v. Stanley, 60 Ill. App. 3d 909, 17 Ill. Dec. 766, 376 N.E.2d 1095 (3 Dist. 1978).

—Laches

An ex-wife who filed suit against the ex-husband's estate for unpaid child support, five years after the last child turned 18, and who had not sought the support while the ex-husband was alive was not barred by laches from recovering the unpaid support, but was barred under the circumstances from receiving interest. Ierulli v. Rosier, 174 Ill. App. 3d 134, 124 Ill. Dec. 117, 528 N.E.2d 1008 (3 Dist. 1988).

—Unwarranted

Where it was apparent that the small amount of the child support award with respect to defendant's four minor children was apparently based on the trial court's awareness of the limited financial resources and strained circumstances of defendant and, also, where the record showed that defendant received substantially the same amount of money as when the award was set, the defense of poverty or misfortune normally would not prevail, unless there had been a showing of other extraordinary circumstances justifying nonpayment of support, which defendant failed to present to the court. People v. Stanley, 60 Ill. App. 3d 909, 17 Ill. Dec. 766, 376 N.E.2d 1095 (3 Dist. 1978).

Where the amount of workers' compensation award which defendant received was based upon his obligations toward all of his children, the fact that the defendant was disabled and not able to work or that he did not "earn" any income did not make sufficient difference to justify defendant's failure to make payments for the support of the four minor children by his prior marriage. People v. Stanley, 60 Ill. App. 3d 909, 17 Ill. Dec. 766, 376 N.E.2d 1095 (3 Dist. 1978).

Notice

Where at the time the agreement was signed and the order entered by the court, there was no factual dispute between the parties that it was in the children's best interests that respondent father take care of the children in view of the inability of the petitioner to do so, and having agreed upon the disposition of the custody issue in the order, there was no requirement of notice as to entry of the agreed order. Kminek v. Kminek, 27 Ill. App. 3d 78, 325 N.E.2d 741 (1 Dist. 1975).

Overpayments

The general rule is that no credit is given for voluntary overpayments of child support, even if they are made under mistaken belief that are legally required. In re Rogers, 283 Ill. App. 3d 719, 219 Ill. Dec. 266, 670 N.E.2d 1154 (3 Dist. 1996), appeal denied, 169 Ill. 2d 588, 221 Ill. Dec. 445, 675 N.E.2d 640 (1996).

Partnership Income

Where ex-husband and his new wife provided services for the businesses, the new wife provided credit for the initial operations of the business, and ex-husband contributed assets to the business; also, all the money earned by the business was put into their joint account and used for reinvestment in the businesses or for their personal needs; accordingly, the trial court did not err by finding that ex-husband sustained his burden of proving that his businesses were partnerships with his new wife; consequently, the trial court did not err in according ex-husband only half of the income from the two businesses. In re Hassiepen, 269 Ill. App. 3d 559, 207 Ill. Dec. 261, 646 N.E.2d 1348 (4 Dist. 1994).

Past Earnings

The award of $250 per week child support was not an abuse of discretion even though the court considered noncustodial parent's past earnings. In re Butler, 106 Ill. App. 3d 831, 62 Ill. Dec. 535, 436 N.E.2d 561 (1 Dist. 1982).

Payments

—Child as Recipient

Where a defendant was paying in excess of the amount required by the divorce decree in that he made "voluntary payments" or "required allowance payments" to the children, such payment, whether considered gratuity or required allowance, was not to be computed into the amount of support defendant was required to pay to plaintiff according to the children's need. Addington v. Addington, 48 Ill. App. 3d 859, 6 Ill. Dec. 622, 363 N.E.2d 151 (1 Dist. 1977).

—Method

Where the court determined that a payor in arrears and entered judgment for a fixed amount without finding payor in contempt, this section had no application and there was no requirement that the court make any provision for the payment of the judgment. Boyd v. Sussenbach, 108 Ill. 2d 489, 92 Ill. Dec. 556, 485 N.E.2d 367 (1985).

—Monthly

Where no prejudice was alleged by the respondent because of a monthly payment schedule for child support payments rather than a weekly payment schedule, the court found no abuse of discretion. In re Osborn, 206 Ill. App. 3d 588, 151 Ill. Dec. 663, 564 N.E.2d 1325 (5 Dist. 1990), cert. denied, 137 Ill. 2d 666, 156 Ill. Dec. 563, 571 N.E.2d 150 (1991).

—Past Due

Past-due child support installments were vested rights and appellee was not entitled to equitable credit if appellee felt that he should not have to provide child support payments during the summer months in which he had custody of their child; his remedy was to have sought modification by the court of the support order prior to the due date of the opposed installments. McAdams v. Scullin, 53 Ill. App. 3d 374, 11 Ill. Dec. 428, 368 N.E.2d 1036 (5 Dist. 1977).

—Third Parties

Where the temporary maintenance and child support orders directed the former husband to make payments to his former wife, the payments made to third parties on the wife's behalf were not credited against his arrearage for payments. In re Dwan, 108 Ill. App. 3d 808, 64 Ill. Dec. 340, 439 N.E.2d 1005 (1 Dist. 1982).

The circuit court's ordering defendant to pay $859.16 to plaintiff's parents for reimbursement of medical payments was improper; the plaintiff's parents were not parties to the divorce proceeding, and, consequently, no relief could be awarded them against the defendant. McManus v. McManus, 38 Ill. App. 3d 645, 348 N.E.2d 507 (5 Dist. 1976).

—Type of Currency

Because this section does not provide an adjusted scale to compensate for differences in exchange rates, the court properly utilized this section in determining the percentage of the husband's income to be allocated to child support based on United States currency. In re Osborn, 206 Ill. App. 3d 588, 151 Ill. Dec. 663, 564 N.E.2d 1325 (5 Dist. 1990), cert. denied, 137 Ill. 2d 666, 156 Ill. Dec. 563, 571 N.E.2d 150 (1991).

Percentage of Household Costs

Assigning a straight percentage of household costs to a boy 12 years of age results in an exaggerated figure of support; the benefits to such a child are not equivalent to the benefits to adults for such things as house payments, real estate taxes, homeowners insurance, home improvements, heat, electricity, water, gasoline, and auto insurance. In re Stockton, 169 Ill. App. 3d 318, 119 Ill. Dec. 817, 523 N.E.2d 573 (4 Dist. 1988).

Percentage of Income

—Void as Child Support

Neither this Act nor the trial court's inherent powers authorize the court to order child support as a percentage of income; an order which states child support as a percentage of income, therefore, exceeds the court's jurisdiction, so it is void. In re Sheetz, 254 Ill. App. 3d 695, 194 Ill. Dec. 38, 627 N.E.2d 154 (1 Dist. 1993).

Previous Marriage

Undertaking new family obligations does not lessen the duty of a divorced husband to provide for his family by previous marriage. In re Vucic, 216 Ill. App. 3d 692, 159 Ill. Dec. 737, 576 N.E.2d 406 (2 Dist. 1991), appeal denied, 164 Ill. 2d 584, 214 Ill. Dec. 332, 660 N.E.2d 1281 (1995).

Prior Obligations

Court incorrectly concluded that court order for support of second family was a prior order to be deducted from father's net income before determining award of support for first child. In re Potts, 297 Ill. App. 3d 110, 231 Ill. Dec. 692, 696 N.E.2d 1263 (2 Dist. 1998).

Subdivision (a)(3)(g) of this section applies only when the obligation arose from a previous, unrelated marital action, and it does not allow payor to deduct current obligations owed in conjunction with the same marital dissolution in which modification of child support payments is being sought. In re Baptist, 232 Ill. App. 3d 906, 174 Ill. Dec. 81, 598 N.E.2d 278 (4 Dist. 1992).

Public Aid Requirement

Trial court's award of a penalty on the amount of past-due child support payments was in error where would-be recipient was not a public aid recipient. Baker v. Baker, 193 Ill. App. 3d 294, 140 Ill. Dec. 303, 549 N.E.2d 954 (4 Dist. 1990).

Public Policy

The inclusion of percentages in the guidelines for determination of child support shows that public policy supports the use of percentages as a basis for a court's calculation of child support. In re Sheetz, 254 Ill. App. 3d 695, 194 Ill. Dec. 38, 627 N.E.2d 154 (1 Dist. 1993).

Waiver of child support was not contrary to public policy, where the supporting parent changed his position for the worse in reliance upon the agreement. Bartlett v. Bartlett, 70 Ill. App. 3d 661, 27 Ill. Dec. 329, 389 N.E.2d 15 (3 Dist. 1979).

Real Estate Investment

The circuit court did not err when it declined to deduct wife's monthly payments for a real estate investment in calculating her net income when there was no indication that these payments were reasonable and necessary for the production of her income. In re Cornale, 199 Ill. App. 3d 134, 145 Ill. Dec. 188, 556 N.E.2d 806 (4 Dist. 1990).

Rebuttable Presumption

This section creates a rebuttable presumption that all income, unless specifically excluded by the statute, is income for child support purposes. Illinois Dep't of Public Aid ex rel. Jennings v. White, 286 Ill. App. 3d 213, 221 Ill. Dec. 561, 675 N.E.2d 985 (2 Dist. 1997).

Receipts

—Not Required

This section imposes no requirement to make verified itemized reports of payments received or to produce receipts for the expenditure of funds paid as child support. Williams v. Williams, 316 Ill. App. 6, 44 N.E.2d 63 (3 Dist. 1942).

Rehearing

To justify granting a rehearing on the basis of newly discovered evidence, a party must demonstrate that the evidence is of a conclusive or decisive nature, making it probable that a different judgment would have been entered, and that the evidence could not have been discovered prior to trial in the exercise of due diligence. Gibson v. Barton, 118 Ill. App. 3d 576, 74 Ill. Dec. 252, 455 N.E.2d 282 (4 Dist. 1983).

Relation with Supreme Court Rules

Rule 296, Supreme Court Rules, does not authorize the court to ignore this section or 750 ILCS 5/510, but merely provides an additional tool for the court to use in fairly resolving child-support disputes. In re Fink, 275 Ill. App. 3d 960, 212 Ill. Dec. 297, 656 N.E.2d 1131 (4 Dist. 1995).

Relative Financial Positions

Where the judge explained his reasons for granting custody to the husband noting the strength of his financial position and the weakness of the wife's stating that her living expenses exceeded her income, the award of child support from the wife to the husband

Relative Financial Positions (Cont'd)

was against the manifest weight of the evidence. Makar v. Makar, 211 Ill. App. 3d 692, 156 Ill. Dec. 154, 570 N.E.2d 630 (1 Dist. 1991).

While both divorced parents are responsible for the care and well-being of their children, it does not follow that their burden is equal and it is only equitable that the parent with the disproportionately greater income bear a greater share of the costs of support, especially if it is the noncustodial parent who is earning the greater income. In re Rogliano, 198 Ill. App. 3d 404, 144 Ill. Dec. 595, 555 N.E.2d 1114 (5 Dist. 1990).

It was reasonable to expect mother to assume remaining portion of the support obligation where her personal assets yielded an income of nearly $100,000, in contrast to father's earnings of approximately one half that amount. In re Wentink, 132 Ill. App. 3d 71, 87 Ill. Dec. 117, 476 N.E.2d 1109 (1 Dist. 1984).

—Illustrative Cases

Child support of $2300 per month was justified where evidence was presented that former husband provided his second family with a sizable annual income averaging well above $200,000, a second home in Michigan, two boats and other luxuries, while at the same time former wife had few financial resources of her own, working low-paying jobs to earn money for day to day living expenses; at$2,300 per month, after deducting school expenses, former wife received approximately $633 per month with which to maintain a home for child, buy him clothes, pay for his travel and provide him money for his personal needs. In re Campbell, 252 Ill. App. 3d 653, 191 Ill. Dec. 852, 624 N.E.2d 1230 (1 Dist. 1993), appeal denied, 155 Ill. 2d 562, 198 Ill. Dec. 540, 633 N.E.2d 2 (1994).

Remand

Where the division of marital property by the trial court was improper, remand of the entire cause for a new trial was warranted so that the maintenance and child support awards and the decision to allow or deny attorney fees could be determined in view of the resources available to the wife after an equitable division of marital property is effected. In re White, 98 Ill. App. 3d 380, 53 Ill. Dec. 786, 424 N.E.2d 421 (5 Dist. 1981).

Remarriage

A reduction of $1,000 per month for unallocated maintenance and child support to $430 a month in child support due to wife's remarriage was not abuse of discretion where child's monthly expenses of $856 included the child's one-quarter share of the new husband's real estate taxes owed on his home and one-quarter portion of new husband's monthly mortgage payment. In re Erickson, 136 Ill. App. 3d 907, 91 Ill. Dec. 346, 483 N.E.2d 692 (2 Dist. 1985).

Mother's remarriage, of itself, should not affect natural father's obligation to make adequate child support payments; the stepfather usually has no duty to support his stepchildren, at least so long as the natural father has that obligation. Page v. Page, 30 Ill. App. 3d 514, 334 N.E.2d 212 (3 Dist. 1975).

Repayment of Debts

—Depreciation

While in some circumstances depreciation may be a reasonable and necessary expense for the production of the income, it is not an expenditure for repayment of debts as those terms are defined. In re Minear, 287 Ill. App. 3d 1073, 223 Ill. Dec. 405, 679 N.E.2d 856 (4 Dist. 1997), aff'd, 181 Ill. 2d 552, 230 Ill. Dec. 250, 693 N.E.2d 379 (1998).

—Payment of Mortgage

The husband's payment of the mortgage on the marital domicile was a reasonable expenditure for the benefit of the parties' child and the wife, and in accordance with subdivision (a)(3)(h), the circuit court properly reduced husband's net income in determining the child support payable directly to wife. In re Avery, 251 Ill. App. 3d 648, 190 Ill. Dec. 914, 622 N.E.2d 1231 (5 Dist. 1993).

—Present Mortgage

The trial court premised the self-executing modification of child support, which included a mortgage payment, upon termination of the "present mortgage" but, in order to comply with subdivision (a)(3)(h), "present mortgage" could not be construed as including any extension or modification of the mortgage payment. In re Avery, 251 Ill. App. 3d 648, 190 Ill. Dec. 914, 622 N.E.2d 1231 (5 Dist. 1993).

—Qualification for Deduction

Simply because an expense falls into the category of a debt repayment does not mean it is deductible; once this hurdle is overcome, the proponent of the deduction must also show the debts being repayed represent reasonable and necessary expenses for the production of income. Gay ex rel. Gay v. Dunlap, 279 Ill. App. 3d 140, 215 Ill. Dec. 691, 664 N.E.2d 88 (4 Dist. 1996), appeal denied, 168 Ill. 2d 589, 219 Ill. Dec. 563, 671 N.E.2d 730 (1996).

Res Judicata

Husband's failure to raise the issue of possible prior overpayments in the proceedings relating to wife's previous petition therefore barred him from asserting the matter in subsequent proceedings. In re Stanley, 133 Ill. App. 3d 963, 89 Ill. Dec. 146, 479 N.E.2d 1152 (4 Dist. 1985).

The original decree awarding child support payments is res judicata so long as there is no change in the circumstances underlying the decree. Gentile v. Gentile, 69 Ill. App. 3d 297, 26 Ill. Dec. 149, 387 N.E.2d 979 (3 Dist. 1979).

Reservation of Decision

Even though the trial court did enter written findings as to why it felt that noncustodial parent's obligation to pay child support should be reserved, the trial court abused its discretion in failing to compel noncustodial parent to pay child support at a time when she could barely support herself; at the time of oral arguments, custodial parent had never gone in to the trial court on a petition for child support, however, nothing precluded him from petitioning the trial court for child support based upon a change in circumstances of the parties at a future date. In re Zirngibl, 237 Ill. App. 3d 1049, 179 Ill. Dec. 169, 606 N.E.2d 1 (1 Dist. 1991).

Where the record indicated that the husband, throughout the dissolution proceedings, frequently attempted to hide or divert his assets and there was evidence that he deliberately understated his income presumably so the court would not find out that he was in a financial situation superior to that of the wife, the trial court properly denied his request for child support and reserved the right to reconsider its decision at a later date should a change in circumstances warrant reconsideration. In re Gruer, 153 Ill. App. 3d 125, 106 Ill. Dec. 340, 505 N.E.2d 1131 (1 Dist. 1987).

Retroactivity

Retroactive allowance of support in a dissolution proceeding is within the discretionary power of the trial court if such allowance is deemed fit, reasonable and just. In re Rogliano, 198 Ill. App. 3d 404, 144 Ill. Dec. 595, 555 N.E.2d 1114 (5 Dist. 1990).

Even though more than two years had elapsed between the time when the plaintiff filed her petition for support modification, and the entry of the order granting a support increase, the trial court acted within its discretion in ordering the increase in support retroactive to the date of the filing of the petition where the extended delay was attributed to the routine judicial process. In re Geis, 159 Ill. App. 3d 975, 111 Ill. Dec. 717, 512 N.E.2d 1354 (1 Dist. 1987).

A circuit court is not statutorily barred from imposing a retroactive child support obligation upon a respondent in an ongoing child support proceeding who, contrary to the court's directive, has failed to inform the court of his having resumed employment. People ex rel. Williams v. Williams, 191 Ill. App. 3d 311, 138 Ill. Dec. 560, 547 N.E.2d 727 (4 Dist. 1989).

Review

When a dispositional order is entered upon dissolution of a marriage, it must be equitable and in reviewing such an order, this court should consider the sum of its provisions, because the distribution of marital property both affects and is affected by the amount of maintenance and child support. Goforth v. Goforth, 121 Ill. App. 3d 673, 77 Ill. Dec. 125, 459 N.E.2d 1374 (5 Dist. 1984).

Considerable discretion is placed in the trial court and its order of modification will not be disturbed on review, absent an abuse of discretion. In re Roth, 99 Ill. App. 3d 679, 55 Ill. Dec. 271, 426 N.E.2d 246 (1 Dist. 1981).

A final determination must be made with regard to the division of property before a conclusive appellate review of the issues of child

Review (Cont'd)
support and attorney fees. In re Clearman, 85 Ill. App. 3d 584, 40 Ill. Dec. 958, 407 N.E.2d 189 (3 Dist. 1980).

Where the order of the trial court found that defendant was the father of the child but the order specifying that defendant should make the payments of $25 per week and the further sum of $210.64, did not appear to be clearly supported by the evidence, the cause was remanded for the limited purpose of conducting a hearing on the financial resources of defendant to determine a reasonable amount to be specified as payment for child support by defendant. People ex rel. Gerard v. Wilson, 22 Ill. App. 3d 331, 317 N.E.2d 170 (3 Dist. 1974).

Scope
Although subsection (b) of this section provides for the use of contempt proceedings, because of the complexities of dissolution matters, the Court of Appeals is reluctant to change a fact finder's determination as to the use of this power. In re Bush, 191 Ill. App. 3d 249, 138 Ill. Dec. 423, 547 N.E.2d 590 (4 Dist. 1989).

Subsection (a) of this section prescribes that a court may enter orders for child support in certain proceedings but it does not expressly preclude a court from entering child support orders in other proceedings not covered by the statute. Skilling v. Skilling, 104 Ill. App. 3d 213, 59 Ill. Dec. 937, 432 N.E.2d 881 (1 Dist. 1982).

The power to enforce payment of support money by contempt is limited to cases of wilful and contumacious refusal to obey the order of the court; however, that does not preclude the trial court from making a finding of liability as to the amount of arrearages even though defendant's conduct was not wilful and contumacious. Bartlett v. Bartlett, 70 Ill. App. 3d 661, 27 Ill. Dec. 329, 389 N.E.2d 15 (3 Dist. 1979).

It does not necessarily follow that the noncustodial parent must make support payments to the custodial parent for a child's support in addition to the amounts which the noncustodial parent expends for a child's support while the child is being cared for by the noncustodial parent. Mitchell v. Mitchell, 54 Ill. App. 3d 18, 11 Ill. Dec. 822, 369 N.E.2d 276 (1 Dist. 1977).

Source of Support
Payments to defendant's minor child from defendant's social security and defendant's providing health insurance coverage on behalf of the minor satisfied defendant's support obligations where defendant had no other income than his social security or pension and there was no indication that his retirement was an effort to avoid child support payments. Childerson v. Hess, 198 Ill. App. 3d 395, 144 Ill. Dec. 551, 555 N.E.2d 1070 (5 Dist. 1990).

Specific Findings
The statements made by the court in announcing its decision from the bench — that: (1) son had special needs, (2) it was difficult to determine the net income of a self-employed farmer, especially one sharing expenses with a new family, and (3) suggesting that wife had additional expenses with a college student living in her home — were sufficient to satisfy the statutory requirement for express findings. In re Kern, 245 Ill. App. 3d 575, 185 Ill. Dec. 843, 615 N.E.2d 402 (4 Dist. 1993).

The requirement that the court make express findings under subdivision (a)(2) is not a requirement that the findings be written or incorporated into the court's order. In re Kern, 245 Ill. App. 3d 575, 185 Ill. Dec. 843, 615 N.E.2d 402 (4 Dist. 1993).

A trial court is not required to enter specific findings of fact regarding the factors the court considered in making its support determination; nonetheless, there must be some indication in the record that the trial court considered the factors listed. In re Fahy, 208 Ill. App. 3d 677, 153 Ill. Dec. 594, 567 N.E.2d 552 (1 Dist. 1991).

Spendable Income
Where former husband derived income of approximately $150,000 from his medical practice and deducted approximately $87,000 in business expenses, including portions of the cost of 11 business trips, depreciation on his car, depreciation on that part of his dwelling which he used as an office, various "one-time-only" deductions, and a woman, with whom he lived for some bookkeeping work, the trial court could reasonably have concluded that he had more spendable income than the $40,000 he claimed. In re Dwan, 108 Ill. App. 3d 808, 64 Ill. Dec. 340, 439 N.E.2d 1005 (1 Dist. 1982).

Split Custody
Where the parties agreed to share in the legal and physical custody of their three children, the court was not obligated to rely on the statutory guidelines and, therefore, an order that the father pay $75 per week in child support was not an abuse of discretion, especially where he paid the children's health insurance and 75 percent of their extraordinary medical expenses. In re Reppen-Sonneson, 299 Ill. App. 3d 691, 233 Ill. Dec. 885, 701 N.E.1159 (2 Dist. 1998).

When parties to a dissolution of marriage settlement agreement agree to divide the custody of their children there are no specific guidelines to follow in awarding support. In re Steadman, 283 Ill. App. 3d 703, 219 Ill. Dec. 258, 670 N.E.2d 1146 (3 Dist. 1996).

Standard of Living
In an action for child support brought pursuant to the Parentage Act (750 ILCS 45/1 et seq.), the trial court does not have to consider the standard of living a child would have enjoyed if the child were living with the noncustodial parent even though it is a relevant factor in determining child support. Ivanyi v. Granoff, 171 Ill. App. 3d 411, 122 Ill. Dec. 49, 526 N.E.2d 189 (2 Dist. 1988).

Standard of Review
The trial court has wide discretion in awarding or modifying child support, and its decision will not be reversed by a court of review absent an abuse of discretion. In re Alexander, 231 Ill. App. 3d 950, 173 Ill. Dec. 456, 596 N.E.2d 1335 (4 Dist. 1992).

The amount of an award of child support is within the discretion of the trial court and will not be reversed absent a showing that the trial court abused such discretion. In re Olson, 223 Ill. App. 3d 636, 166 Ill. Dec. 60, 585 N.E.2d 1082 (2 Dist.), appeal denied, 145 Ill. 2d 636, 173 Ill. Dec. 6, 596 N.E.2d 630 (1992).

Statement

—Not Improper
Trial judge's comment at the start of the modification hearing that he was "pretty rigid about applying the 20% figure" did not demonstrate an improper "rigid adherence" to the statutory guidelines where the court stated, just prior to finding that the guidelines applied, that it had carefully listened to the testimony presented and had reviewed all the affidavits, tax returns, and pleadings in the case, there was no error. In re Johnson, 209 Ill. App. 3d 1025, 154 Ill. Dec. 706, 568 N.E.2d 927 (3 Dist. 1991).

Student Loan
Trial court, in a child support modification proceeding, properly exercised its discretion in determining what portion of a father's student loan payments, for university and graduate degrees, could be deducted in determining a child support award for the child that he had while in high school, but the trial court's calculations failed to account for the interest on the father's student loans so that the case was remanded for a recalculation of the proper child support amount. Roper v. Johns, 345 Ill. App. 3d 1127, 281 Ill. Dec. 655, 804 N.E.2d 620, 2004 Ill. App. LEXIS 65 (5 Dist. 2004).

A student loan represents an expenditure for repayment of debts that represent reasonable and necessary expenses for the production of income and the circuit court abused its discretion in failing to deduct those payments when it determined net income. In re Davis, 287 Ill. App. 3d 846, 223 Ill. Dec. 166, 679 N.E.2d 110 (5 Dist. 1997).

Suit by Child
Since a child is furnished support by other persons, an equitable result would not be obtained if the child had a right to sue his father for past-due support. Kelleher v. Kelleher, 21 Ill. App. 3d 601, 316 N.E.2d 212 (1 Dist. 1974).

Tax Considerations
Where real estate investment losses were not shown to be reasonable or necessary to the production of any income to the supporting parent and because, as such, the losses could not be presented in a specified repayment schedule, the trial court erred in allowing a deduction for the losses from appellee's gross income reported on his income taxes when it calculated the child support obligation. In re Partney, 212 Ill. App. 3d 586, 156 Ill. Dec. 679, 571 N.E.2d 266 (5 Dist. 1991).

Tax Considerations (Cont'd)

Trial court erred in awarding dependency tax exemption to wife where noncustodial husband contributed majority of support for the child. In re Rogliano, 198 Ill. App. 3d 404, 144 Ill. Dec. 595, 555 N.E.2d 1114 (5 Dist. 1990).

Trial judge did not err in transferring to mother the claim of the youngest child as a dependent for income tax purposes where trial court found a sufficient change in circumstances. Killinger v. Killinger, 40 Ill. App. 3d 962, 353 N.E.2d 284 (1 Dist. 1976).

Tax Exemption

It was not an abuse of discretion for the court to allow each parent to take child as an exemption for federal and state income tax purposes in alternate years, notwithstanding the father's assertion that the amount of child support he was ordered to pay covered more than half of the child's expenses as enumerated by the mother, where the mother also listed other expenses that benefited the child, such as utilities, food, cleaning and laundry supplies, automobile expenses, mortgage and property taxes. Stockton v. Oldenburg, 305 Ill. App. 3d 897, 238 Ill. Dec. 1013, 713 N.E.2d 259 (4 Dist. 1999).

Tax Overpayment

If a noncustodial parent over withholds, thereby overpaying income tax, that amount should be added back to his net income for the purpose of determining his support obligation pursuant to subsection (a). In re Davis, 287 Ill. App. 3d 846, 223 Ill. Dec. 166, 679 N.E.2d 110 (5 Dist. 1997).

Tender Years Doctrine

Although Illinois is an advocate of the "tender years," doctrine where interests of children of tender years was best served if their custody is entrusted to their mother, this does not preclude the propriety of awarding custody of children to their father under some circumstances. Kminek v. Kminek, 27 Ill. App. 3d 78, 325 N.E.2d 741 (1 Dist. 1975).

Two Households

The argument that provisions of this section should be interpreted as providing a maximum amount of 25% for two children, regardless of whether the children reside in different households is inconsistent with the statutory provision requiring net income to be determined by deducting previously ordered and paid child support. Carnes v. Dressen, 215 Ill. App. 3d 166, 158 Ill. Dec. 732, 574 N.E.2d 845 (4 Dist. 1991).

Unilateral Reduction of Support

—Death of Child

The death of a minor child does not give the parent obligor the right to unilaterally reduce child support payments. Lewis v. Staub, 95 Ill. App. 3d 243, 50 Ill. Dec. 774, 419 N.E.2d 1223 (4 Dist. 1981).

—Emancipation of Child

Absent an express or implied court-ordered provision, a parent who pays collective or lump-sum child support payments for the support of two or more children may not unilaterally reduce the amount of that payment pro rata as each child becomes emancipated. Clay v. Clay, 210 Ill. App. 3d 778, 155 Ill. Dec. 280, 569 N.E.2d 280 (4 Dist. 1991).

—Termination

Under former Ill. Rev. Stat., ch. 40, para. 19 of the Divorce Act (see now this section), a divorced father could not terminate child support payments unilaterally as the decree was a continuing order, and it was not for the divorced father to decide when and for what reasons he should stop support payments. Wilson v. Wilson, 122 Ill. App. 2d 142, 257 N.E.2d 810 (2 Dist. 1970).

Vested Right

It is well settled that past-due child support payments constitute a vested and unmodifiable right. In re Frazier, 205 Ill. App. 3d 621, 151 Ill. Dec. 130, 563 N.E.2d 1236 (3 Dist. 1990).

The right to past-due installments of child support constitutes a vested right which may not be reduced or eliminated by the court. Ellingwood v. Ellingwood, 25 Ill. App. 3d 587, 323 N.E.2d 571 (1 Dist. 1975).

Payments of alimony or child support, when properly directed by a court, become a vested right of the designated recipient as and when they accrue. Ellingwood v. Ellingwood, 25 Ill. App. 3d 587, 323 N.E.2d 571 (1 Dist. 1975).

Any child support payments which accrued prior to the filing of a petition to reconsider the amount of support payments were vested in the parent who had custody of the child or children, and, normally, could not be divested retroactively by order of court; payments, however, which accrue after the date of the filing of the petition to reconsider are not vested. Voss v. Voss, 23 Ill. App. 3d 312, 319 N.E.2d 72 (3 Dist. 1974).

Violation of Decree

A violation of the visitation terms of a divorce decree by the mother will not excuse the father's failure to comply with the alimony and child support terms. Slavis v. Slavis, 12 Ill. App. 3d 467, 299 N.E.2d 413 (1 Dist. 1973).

A wife was still entitled to child support and alimony despite the fact that she violated terms of her divorce decree by taking child to Jamaica. Slavis v. Slavis, 12 Ill. App. 3d 467, 299 N.E.2d 413 (1 Dist. 1973).

Voluntary Contributions

Subdivision (a)(3)(h) of this section applies when the noncustodial parent voluntarily contributes to necessary expenses which they are not already obligated to contribute to or pay for. In re Baptist, 232 Ill. App. 3d 906, 174 Ill. Dec. 81, 598 N.E.2d 278 (4 Dist. 1992).

Waiver

Where defendant stopped visiting his children and stopped making his support payments, it was clear that plaintiff expressly agreed to waive her right to support and that defendant relied upon that agreement to his detriment when he relinquished his right to maintain a parental relationship with his children; plaintiff was estopped from claiming back and future child support. Bartlett v. Bartlett, 70 Ill. App. 3d 661, 27 Ill. Dec. 329, 389 N.E.2d 15 (3 Dist. 1979).

LEGAL PERIODICALS

For article, "Illinois Supreme Court Civil '98: Back to the Nuts and Bolts", see 87 Ill. B.J. 250 (1998).

For article, "Child Custody in a Changing World: A Study of Post divorce Arrangements," see 1997 U. Ill. L. Rev. 773.

For article, "Survey of Illinois Law: Family Law," 19 S. Ill. U.L.J. 819 (1995).

For article, "What's Good for the Goose is Good for the Gander: Toward Recognition of Men's Reproductive Rights," see 15 N. Ill. U.L. Rev. 141 (1994).

For article, "Survey of Illinois Law [1988-89] — Family Law," see 14 S. Ill. U.L.J. 1007 (1990).

For note, "Making Form Follow Function: Considerations in Creating and Applying a Statutory Parent-Child Privilege," see U. Ill. L. Rev. 879 (1990).

For article, "Family Law: 1985-86 Survey," see 11 S. Ill. U.L.J. 741 (1987).

For article, "Family Law: 1986-87 Illinois Law Survey," see 19 Loy. U. Chi. L.J. 489 (1987-88).

For article, "Family Law: 1985-86 Illinois Law Survey," see 18 Loy. U. Chi. L. J. 549 (1986-87).

For article, "The Use (and Abuse) of Child Support Schedules in Illinois," see 71 Ill. B. J. 314 (1983).

For article, "Marital Property, Tax Ramification, and Maintenance: Practice Under the Illinois Marriage and Dissolution of Marriage Act — A Comparative Study," see 66 Ill. B. J. 388 (1978).

RESEARCH REFERENCES

Effect of remarriage of spouses to each other on child custody and support provisions of prior divorce decree. 26 ALR4th 325.

Excessiveness or adequacy of money awarded as child support. 27 ALR4th 864.

Stepparent's post-divorce duty to support stepchild. 44 ALR4th 520.

Postmajority disability as reviving parental duty to support child. 48 ALR4th 919.

Divorce and separation: attributing undisclosed income to parent or spouse for purposes of making child or spousal support award. 70 ALR4th 173.

State court's authority, in marital or child custody proceeding, to allocate federal income tax dependency exemption for child to noncustodial parent under § 152(e) of the Internal Revenue Code (26 USCS § 152(e)). 77 ALR4th 786.

Authority of court, upon entering default judgment, to make orders for child custody or support which were not specifically requested in pleadings of prevailing party. 5 ALR5th 863.

Consideration of obligated spouse's earnings from overtime or "second job" held in addition to regular full-time employment in fixing alimony or child support awards 17 ALR5th 143.

Treatment of depreciation expenses claimed for tax or accounting purposes in determining ability to pay child or spousal support. 28 ALR5th 46.

Support provisions of Judicial Decree or Order as Limit of Parent's Liability for Expenses of Child. 35 ALR5th 757.

Application of child-support guidelines to cases of joint-, split-,or similar shared-custody arrangements. 57 ALR5th 389.

Consideration of obligor spouse's or parent's personal-injury recovery or settlement in fixing alimony or child-support award. 59 ALR5th 489.

Basis for imputing income for purpose of determining child support where obligor spouse is voluntarily unemployed or underemployed. 76 ALR5th 191.

Right to credit against child support arrearages for time child lived in custody of noncustodial parent, other than for visitation, where custodial parent's approval was not in issue or disputed by parties. 112 ALR5th 185.

Right to credit against child support arrearages for time children spent in custody of noncustodial parent pursuant to visitation or court order. 118 ALR5th 385.

Right to credit on child-support arrearages for money given directly to child. 119 ALR5th 445.

Right to credit against child support arrearages for time child lived with noncustodial parent, other than for visitation or by court order, with approval of custodial parent. 120 ALR5th 229.

Right to credit on child support for contributions to housing costs, utility bills, and other alleged household necessities made for child's benefit while child is not living with obligor parent. 123 ALR5th 565.

Right to credit on child support arrearages for gifts to child. 124 ALR5th 441.

750 ILCS 5/505.1 [Unemployed obligor; powers of court]

Sec. 505.1. (a) Whenever it is determined in a proceeding to establish or enforce a child support or maintenance obligation that the person owing a duty of support is unemployed, the court may order the person to seek employment and report periodically to the court with a diary, listing or other memorandum of his or her efforts in accordance with such order. Additionally, the court may order the unemployed person to report to the Department of Employment Security for job search services or to make application with the local Job Training Partnership Act [29 U.S.C. § 1501 et seq.] provider for participation in job search, training or work programs and where the duty of support is owed to a child receiving child support enforcement services under Article X of The Illinois Public Aid Code, as amended [305 ILCS 5/10-1 et seq.], the court may order the unemployed person to report to the Illinois Department of Public Aid for participation in job search, training or work programs established under Section 9-6 and Article IXA of that Code [305 ILCS 5/9-6 and 305 ILCS 5/9A-1 et seq.].

(b) Whenever it is determined that a person owes past-due support for a child or for a child and the parent with whom the child is living, and the child is receiving assistance under the Illinois Public Aid Code [305 ILCS 5/1-1 et seq.], the court shall order at the request of the Illinois Department of Public Aid [305 ILCS 5/1-1 et seq.]:

(1) that the person pay the past-due support in accordance with a plan approved by the court; or

(2) if the person owing past-due support is unemployed, is subject to such a plan, and is not incapacitated, that the person participate in such job search, training, or work programs established under Section 9-6 and Article IXA of the Illinois Public Aid Code [305 ILCS 5/9-6 and 305 ILCS 5/9A-1 et seq.] as the court deems appropriate.

(Source: P.A. 85-1155; 90-18, § 100; 91-357, § 256; 92-590, § 10.)

Note.

This section was Ill.Rev.Stat., Ch. 40, para. 505.1.

Effect of Amendments.

The 1997 amendment by P.A. 90-18, effective July 1, 1997, added the subsection (a) designation; in subsection (a), in the second sentence, inserted "and Article IXA"; and added subsection (b).

The 1999 amendment by P.A. 91-357, effective July 29, 1999, substituted "Job" for "Jobs" in the second sentence of subsection (a).

The 2002 amendment by P.A. 92-590, effective July 1, 2002, substituted "child support enforcement services" for "support services" in subsection (a).

RESEARCH REFERENCES

Basis for imputing income for purpose of determining child support where obligor spouse is voluntarily unemployed or underemployed. 76 ALR5th 191.

750 ILCS 5/505.2 Health insurance

Sec. 505.2. *Health insurance.* (a) Definitions. As used in this Section:

(1) "Obligee" means the individual to whom the duty of support is owed or the individual's legal representative.

(2) "Obligor" means the individual who owes a duty of support pursuant to an order for support.

(3) "Public office" means any elected official or any State or local agency which is or may become responsible by law for enforcement of, or which is or may become authorized to enforce, an order for support, including, but not limited to: the Attorney General, the Illinois Department of Public Aid, the Illinois Department of Human Services, the Illinois Department of Children and Family Services, and the various State's Attorneys, Clerks of the Circuit Court and supervisors of general assistance.

(4) "Child" shall have the meaning ascribed to it in Section 505 [750 ILCS 5/505].

(b) Order.

(1) Whenever the court establishes, modifies or enforces an order for child support or for child support and maintenance the court shall include in the order a provision for the health care coverage of

the child which shall, upon request of the obligee or Public Office, require that any child covered by the order be named as a beneficiary of any health insurance plan that is available to the obligor through an employer or labor union or trade union. If the court finds that such a plan is not available to the obligor, or that the plan is not accessible to the obligee, the court may, upon request of the obligee or Public Office, order the obligor to name the child covered by the order as a beneficiary of any health insurance plan that is available to the obligor on a group basis, or as a beneficiary of an independent health insurance plan to be obtained by the obligor, after considering the following factors:

(A) the medical needs of the child;

(B) the availability of a plan to meet those needs; and

(C) the cost of such a plan to the obligor.

(2) If the employer or labor union or trade union offers more than one plan, the order shall require the obligor to name the child as a beneficiary of the plan in which the obligor is enrolled.

(3) Nothing in this Section shall be construed to limit the authority of the court to establish or modify a support order to provide for payment of expenses, including deductibles, copayments and any other health expenses, which are in addition to expenses covered by an insurance plan of which a child is ordered to be named a beneficiary pursuant to this Section.

(c) Implementation and enforcement.

(1) When the court order requires that a minor child be named as a beneficiary of a health insurance plan, other than a health insurance plan available through an employer or labor union or trade union, the obligor shall provide written proof to the obligee or Public Office that the required insurance has been obtained, or that application for insurability has been made, within 30 days of receiving notice of the court order. Unless the obligor was present in court when the order was issued, notice of the order shall be given pursuant to Illinois Supreme Court Rules. If an obligor fails to provide the required proof, he may be held in contempt of court.

(2) When the court requires that a child be named as a beneficiary of a health insurance plan available through an employer or labor union or trade union, the court's order shall be implemented in accordance with the Income Withholding for Support Act [750 ILCS 28/1 et seq.].

(d) Failure to maintain insurance. The dollar amount of the premiums for court-ordered health insurance, or that portion of the premiums for which the obligor is responsible in the case of insurance provided under a group health insurance plan through an employer or labor union or trade union where the employer or labor union or trade union pays a portion of the premiums, shall be considered an additional child support obligation owed by the obligor. Whenever the obligor fails to provide or maintain health insurance pursuant to an order for support, the obligor shall be liable to the obligee for the dollar amount of the premiums which were not paid, and shall also be liable for all medical expenses incurred by the child which would have been paid or reimbursed by the health insurance which the obligor was ordered to provide or maintain. In addition, the obligee may petition the court to modify the order based solely on the obligor's failure to pay the premiums for court-ordered health insurance.

(e) Authorization for payment. The signature of the obligee is a valid authorization to the insurer to process a claim for payment under the insurance plan to the provider of the health care services or to the obligee.

(f) Disclosure of information. The obligor's employer or labor union or trade union shall disclose to the obligee or Public Office, upon request, information concerning any dependent coverage plans which would be made available to a new employee or labor union member or trade union member. The employer or labor union or trade union shall disclose such information whether or not a court order for medical support has been entered.

(g) Employer obligations. If a parent is required by an order for support to provide coverage for a child's health care expenses and if that coverage is available to the parent through an employer who does business in this State, the employer must do all of the following upon receipt of a copy of the order of support or order for withholding:

(1) The employer shall, upon the parent's request, permit the parent to include in that coverage a child who is otherwise eligible for that coverage, without regard to any enrollment season restrictions that might otherwise be applicable as to the time period within which the child may be added to that coverage.

(2) If the parent has health care coverage through the employer but fails to apply for coverage of the child, the employer shall include the child in the parent's coverage upon application by the child's other parent or the Illinois Department of Public Aid.

(3) The employer may not eliminate any child from the parent's health care coverage unless the employee is no longer employed by the employer and no longer covered under the employer's group health plan or unless the employer is provided with satisfactory written evidence of either of the following:

(A) The order for support is no longer in effect.

(B) The child is or will be included in a comparable health care plan obtained by the parent under such order that is currently in effect or will take effect no later than the date the prior coverage is terminated.

The employer may eliminate a child from a parent's health care plan obtained by the parent under such order if the employer has eliminated dependent health care coverage for all of its employees.

(Source: P.A. 86-649; 87-988, § 2; 89-183, § 40; 89-507, § 90D-93; 89-626, § 3-40; 90-18, § 100; 92-16, § 96; 92-876, § 910.)

Note.

This section was Ill.Rev.Stat., Ch. 40, para. 505.2.

Section 996 of P.A. 92-16 contains a "no acceleration or delay" provision, and Section 997 contains a "no revival or extension" provision.

Effect of Amendments.

The 1996 amendment by P.A. 89-507, effective July 1, 1997, in subdivision (a)(3) substituted "Human Services" for "Mental Health and Developmental Disabilities"; and added the subdivision (b)(1) designation.

The 1996 amendment by P.A. 89-626, effective August 9, 1996, added the subdivision (b)(1) designation.

The 1997 amendment by P.A. 90-18, effective July 1, 1997, combined the amendments by P.A. 89-507 and P.A. 89-626; in subdivision (b)(1), in the introductory language, in the first sentence, inserted "shall include in the order a provision for the health care coverage of the child which" and substituted "require" for "order".

The 2001 amendment by P.A. 92-16, effective June 28, 2001, substituted "the Income Withholding for Support Act" for "Section 706.1, as now or hereafter amended" at the end of subsection (c)(2).

The 2002 amendment by P.A. 92-876, effective June 1, 2003, inserted subsection (a)(4).

CASE NOTES

ANALYSIS

Discretion of Court
—Mandatory
—Upheld
Health Insurance Coverage
Public Aid Insurance

Discretion of Court

—Mandatory

The first sentence of subsection (b) of the Act is clear and leaves no room for discretion. In re Self, 265 Ill. App. 3d 804, 202 Ill. Dec. 831, 638 N.E.2d 699 (4 Dist. 1994).

—Upheld

It was not an abuse of discretion for the trial court to order the father to pay the mother health insurance premiums for the health insurance policy she carried on their child, notwithstanding that he provided health insurance coverage for the child. Janssen ex rel. Janssen v. Turner, 292 Ill. App. 3d 219, 226 Ill. Dec. 202, 685 N.E.2d 16 (4 Dist. 1997).

Health Insurance Coverage

Pursuant to 750 ILCS 5/505.2(b), the trial court should have ordered the husband to contribute half the cost of health insurance for his daughter as part of its judgment awarding child custody. Seitzinger v. Seitzinger, 333 Ill. App. 3d 103, 266 Ill. Dec. 720, 775 N.E.2d 282, 2002 Ill. App. LEXIS 763 (4 Dist. 2002).

Where health insurance coverage is requested, question of support cannot be regarded as fully resolved until court has ruled on issue of health insurance; duty to provide health insurance is an integral part of parent's current and future support obligations. Franson ex rel. Franson v. Micelli, 172 Ill. 2d 352, 217 Ill. Dec. 250, 666 N.E.2d 1188 (1996).

Public Aid Insurance

Under subsection (d) a parent who insures her child through public aid, at no cost, has the right to collect the dollar value of the unpaid insurance premiums from a parent who was under a court order to provide health insurance. In re Takata, 304 Ill. App. 3d 85, 237 Ill. Dec. 460, 709 N.E.2d 715 (2 Dist. 1999).

750 ILCS 5/505.3 Information to State Case Registry

Sec. 505.3. *Information to State Case Registry.* (a) In this Section:

"Order for support", "obligor", "obligee", and "business day" are defined as set forth in the Income Withholding for Support Act [750 ILCS 28/1 et seq.].

"State Case Registry" means the State Case Registry established under Section 10-27 of the Illinois Public Aid Code [305 ILCS 5/10-27].

(b) Each order for support entered or modified by the circuit court under this Act shall require that the obligor and obligee (i) file with the clerk of the circuit court the information required by this Section (and any other information required under Title IV, Part D of the Social Security Act [42 U.S.C. § 601 et seq.] or by the federal Department of Health and Human Services) at the time of entry or modification of the order for support and (ii) file updated information with the clerk within 5 business days of any change. Failure of the obligor or obligee to file or update the required information shall be punishable as in cases of contempt. The failure shall not prevent the court from entering or modifying the order for support, however.

(c) The obligor shall file the following information: the obligor's name, date of birth, social security number, and mailing address.

If either the obligor or the obligee receives child support enforcement services from the Illinois Department of Public Aid under Article X of the Illinois Public Aid Code [305 ILCS 5/10-1 et seq.], the obligor shall also file the following information: the obligor's telephone number, driver's license number, and residential address (if different from the obligor's mailing address), and the name, address, and telephone number of the obligor's employer or employers.

(d) The obligee shall file the following information:

(1) The names of the obligee and the child or children covered by the order for support.

(2) The dates of birth of the obligee and the child or children covered by the order for support.

(3) The social security numbers of the obligee and the child or children covered by the order for support.

(4) The obligee's mailing address.

(e) In cases in which the obligee receives child support enforcement services from the Illinois Department of Public Aid under Article X of the Illinois Public Aid Code [305 ILCS 5/10-1 et seq.], the order for support shall (i) require that the obligee file the information required under subsection (d) with the Illinois Department of Public Aid for inclusion in the State Case Registry, rather than file the information with the clerk, and (ii) require that the obligee include the following additional information:

(1) The obligee's telephone and driver's license numbers.

(2) The obligee's residential address, if different from the obligee's mailing address.

(3) The name, address, and telephone number of the obligee's employer or employers.

The order for support shall also require that the obligee update the information filed with the Illinois Department of Public Aid within 5 business days of any change.

(f) The clerk shall provide the information filed under this Section, together with the court docket number and county in which the order for support was entered, to the State Case Registry within 5 business days after receipt of the information.

(g) In a case in which a party is receiving child support enforcement services under Article X of the Illinois Public Aid Code [305 ILCS 5/10-1 et seq.], the clerk shall provide the following additional information to the State Case Registry within 5 business days after entry or modification of an order for support or request from the Illinois Department of Public Aid:

(1) The amount of monthly or other periodic support owed under the order for support and other amounts, including arrearage, interest, or late payment penalties and fees, due or overdue under the order.

(2) Any such amounts that have been received by the clerk, and the distribution of those amounts by the clerk.

(h) Information filed by the obligor and obligee under this Section that is not specifically required to be included in the body of an order for support under other laws is not a public record and shall be treated as confidential and subject to disclosure only in accordance with the provisions of this Section, Section 10-27 of the Illinois Public Aid Code [305 ILCS 5/10-27], and Title IV, Part D of the Social Security Act [42 U.S.C. § 601 et seq.].

(Source: P.A. 91-212, § 25; 92-16, § 96; 92-463, § 10; 92-651, § 87.)

Note.

Section 996 of P.A. 92-16 contains a "no acceleration or delay" provision, and Section 997 contains a "no revival or extension" provision.

Section 997 of P.A. 92-651 is a no acceleration or delay provision, and Section 998 is a no revival or extension provision.

Effect of Amendments.

The 2001 amendment by P.A. 92-16, effective June 28, 2001, substituted "required to be" for "required to the" in subsection (c).

The 2001 amendment by P.A. 92-463, effective August 22, 2001, rewrote the section to the extent that a detailed comparison would be impracticable.

The 2002 amendment by P.A. 92-651, effective July 11, 2002, combined the amendments by P.A. 92-16 and P.A. 92-463.

750 ILCS 5/506 Representation of child

Sec. 506. *Representation of child.* (a) Duties. In any proceedings involving the support, custody, visitation, education, parentage, property interest, or general welfare of a minor or dependent child, the court may, on its own motion or that of any party, and subject to the terms or specifications the court determines, appoint an attorney to serve in one of the following capacities:

(1) as an attorney to represent the child;

(2) as a guardian ad litem to address issues the court delineates;

(3) as a child's representative whose duty shall be to advocate what the representative finds to be in the best interests of the child after reviewing the facts and circumstances of the case. The child's representative shall have the same power and authority to take part in the conduct of the litigation as does an attorney for a party and shall possess all the powers of investigation and recommendation as does a guardian ad litem. The child's representative shall consider, but not be bound by, the expressed wishes of the child. A child's representative shall have received training in child advocacy or shall possess such experience as determined to be equivalent to such training by the chief judge of the circuit where the child's representative has been appointed. The child's representative shall not disclose confidential communications made by the child, except as required by law or by the Rules of Professional Conduct. The child's representative shall not be called as a witness regarding the issues set forth in this subsection.

During the proceedings the court may appoint an additional attorney to serve in another of the capacities described in subdivisions (a)(1), (a)(2), or (a)(3) on its own motion or that of a party only for good cause shown and when the reasons for the additional appointment are set forth in specific findings.

(b) Fees and costs. The court shall enter an order as appropriate for costs, fees, and disbursements, including a retainer, when the attorney, guardian ad litem, or child's representative is appointed, and thereafter as necessary. Such orders shall require payment by either or both parents, by any other party or source, or from the marital estate or the child's separate estate. The court may not order payment by the Illinois Department of Public Aid in cases in which the Department is providing child support enforcement services under Article X of the Illinois Public Aid Code [305 ILCS 5/10-1 et seq.]. Unless otherwise ordered by the court at the time fees and costs are approved, all fees and costs payable to an attorney, guardian ad litem, or child's representative under this Section are by implication deemed to be in the nature of support of the child and are within the exceptions to discharge in bankruptcy under 11 U.S.C.A. 523. The provisions of Sections 501 and 508 of this Act [750 ILCS 5/501 and 750 ILCS 5/508] shall apply to fees and costs for attorneys appointed under this Section.

(Source: P.A. 85-357; 89-364, § 70; 90-309, § 5; 91-410, § 5; 92-590, § 10.)

Note.

This section was Ill.Rev.Stat., Ch. 40, para. 506.

Effect of Amendments.

The 1995 amendment by P.A. 89-364, effective August 18, 1995, in the fourth sentence inserted "or any adult party".

The 1997 amendment by P.A. 90-309, effective January 1, 1998, in the first sentence, inserted "best", substituted a comma for "and" preceding "visitation" and added "and property" at the end.

The 1999 amendment by P.A. 91-410, effective January 1, 2000, inserted the subsection (a) and (b) designations and rewrote the section to the extent that a detailed comparison would be impracticable.

The 2002 amendment by P.A. 92-590, effective July 1, 2002, substituted "child support enforcement services" for "child and spouse support services" in the third sentence of subsection (b).

CASE NOTES

ANALYSIS

Constitutionality
Attorney Fees
—Abuse of Discretion
—Appeal
—Award Against State
—Child's Attorney
—Improper
—Necessary Services
—Proper
Discretion of Court
—In General
—Abuse of Discretion
—Guardian Ad Litem Not Appointed
Enforcement of Divorce Decree
—College Expenses
—Standing
Evidence Held Sufficient
Factors Considered
—Improper
—Sufficient Showing
Guardian Ad Litem
—In General
—Child's Interests
—College Expenses
—Evidence Considered
—Fees
—Not Mandatory
—Paternity Proceedings
Improper Actions
Independent Action
Parentage Petition Barred
Petition for Dissolution
—Not Final Judgment
Quality of Representation

Constitutionality

Section 506(a)(3) of the Illinois Marriage and Dissolution of Marriage Act, 750 ILCS 5/506(a)(3) was unconstitutional as applied in this case because the child's representative's report was adverse to the mother and she was deprived of her due process under U.S. Const. Amend IV, and Ill. Const. 1970, Art. I, § 2 to cross-examine the representative. One of the fundamental rights protected under the fourteenth amendment is the right of parents to make decisions concerning the care, custody, and control of their children without unwarranted state intrusion. In re Marriage of De Bates, 212 Ill. 2d 489, 289 Ill. Dec. 218, 819 N.E.2d 714, 2004 Ill. LEXIS 1619 (2004).

Attorney Fees

—Abuse of Discretion

Where the trial court awarded fees of $2,500 to the attorney appointed by the court to represent the interests of the children, the award was an abuse of the trial court's discretion. In re Olsher, 78 Ill. App. 3d 627, 34 Ill. Dec. 32, 397 N.E.2d 488 (1 Dist. 1979).

—Appeal

Where order for attorney fees from which appeal was taken arose from a contempt proceeding, it was final and appealable. Spizzo v. Langman, 168 Ill. App. 3d 487, 119 Ill. Dec. 146, 522 N.E.2d 808 (2 Dist. 1988).

Although this section does allow for an award of attorney fees in favor of the child's attorney, it does not specifically authorize the award of such fees during the pendency of an appeal. In re Macaluso, 110 Ill. App. 3d 838, 66 Ill. Dec. 478, 443 N.E.2d 1 (2 Dist. 1982).

—Award Against State

This section does not allow an award of attorney fees against the state. Williams ex rel. Williams v. Davenport, 306 Ill. App. 3d 465, 239 Ill. Dec. 374, 713 N.E.2d 1224 (1 Dist. 1999).

—Child's Attorney

While 750 ILCS 5/508 provides that a court may order either spouse to pay attorney's fees, and this section permits the court to award fees to an attorney who has been appointed by the court to represent the interest of a minor or dependent child, neither provides for the award of attorney fees to an adult child of the marriage. In re Garrison, 99 Ill. App. 3d 717, 54 Ill. Dec. 653, 425 N.E.2d 518 (2 Dist. 1981).

Court properly assessed an appointed child guardian's fees to the parents under the Marriage Act, because the guardian's representation of the child was related to issues concerning the father's parentage and sibling visitation, all of which were related to issues of custody, visitation, and parentage as required under his section. In re Marriage of Nienhouse, Ill. App. 3d , 290 Ill. Dec. 654, 821 N.E.2d 1228, 2004 Ill. App. LEXIS 1551 (1 Dist. 2004).

—Improper

Where the trial court assessed attorney fees against wife and her attorney in custody action without considering the financial resources of the parents and the relevant circumstantial factors, the court-ordered fees were improper. Spizzo v. Langman, 168 Ill. App. 3d 487, 119 Ill. Dec. 146, 522 N.E.2d 808 (2 Dist. 1988).

—Necessary Services

The amount of attorney fees awarded should be only in such an amount as will compensate for services rendered, and those services must have been reasonably required and necessary to the case. In re Zannis, 114 Ill. App. 3d 1034, 70 Ill. Dec. 545, 449 N.E.2d 892 (1 Dist. 1983).

—Proper

Language of this section does not limit its application to proceedings brought under the Marriage Act; indeed, 750 ILCS 5/508 specifically authorizes the payment of attorney fees in litigation reasonably connected with a proceeding under the Act. In re Marriage of Nienhouse, Ill. App. 3d , 290 Ill. Dec. 654, 821 N.E.2d 1228, 2004 Ill. App. LEXIS 1551 (1 Dist. 2004).

Trial court apportioning attorney fees between former spouses for guardian ad litem appointed for child, whom mother claimed was sexually abused by father, was not abuse of discretion where mother brought charges of sexual abuse and satanic cult practices against father without presenting evidence to substantiate the charges and, as a result of mother's actions and pleadings, father had to incur significant attorneys' fees and costs to defend himself and the child's attorney likewise expended a great amount of time in defending the child's welfare. McClelland v. McClelland, 231 Ill. App. 3d 214, 172 Ill. Dec. 461, 595 N.E.2d 1131 (1 Dist. 1992).

Discretion of Court

—In General

An appointment under this section is subject to the sound discretion of the trial court and where a child's interests are vigorously asserted, appointment of separate counsel is not required. In re Stuckert, 138 Ill. App. 3d 788, 93 Ill. Dec. 294, 486 N.E.2d 395 (2 Dist. 1985).

—Abuse of Discretion

The trial court did not abuse its discretion in failing to appoint a guardian ad litem, sua sponte, or in ordering an investigation and report by the Department of Children and Family Services in an action modifying the custody provisions of a divorce decree. De Franco v. De Franco, 67 Ill. App. 3d 760, 24 Ill. Dec. 130, 384 N.E.2d 997 (1 Dist. 1978).

—Guardian Ad Litem Not Appointed

The trial court did not err in not appointing a guardian ad litem to the children in determining custody, as both children's best interests were adequately considered by the trial court and numerous witnesses, including psychologists and therapists, testified concerning the children's best interests. In re Doty, 255 Ill. App. 3d 1087, 196 Ill. Dec. 134, 629 N.E.2d 679 (5 Dist. 1994).

Enforcement of Divorce Decree

—College Expenses

A custodial parent could not waive child's claim to college expenses in a property settlement agreement with noncustodial parent; parents cannot bargain away the child's right under the agreement without benefit to the child, without judicial approval, and without means available to the child to judicially contest the

Enforcement of Divorce Decree (Cont'd)

—College Expenses (Cont'd)

parents' agreement in violation of the Illinois law. Miller v. Miller, 163 Ill. App. 3d 602, 114 Ill. Dec. 682, 516 N.E.2d 837 (1 Dist. 1987).

—Standing

Evidence held sufficient that child of divorced parents had standing in the trial court divorce proceedings to enforce the terms of the divorce decree which obligated the non-custodial parent to pay his college expenses. Miller v. Miller, 163 Ill. App. 3d 602, 114 Ill. Dec. 682, 516 N.E.2d 837 (1 Dist. 1987).

Evidence Held Sufficient

Where, despite the court's expressed uncertainties, the court ultimately decided in favor of the maternal grandparents over uncle in custody dispute, there was sufficient evidence to support the court's decision. In re Russell, 169 Ill. App. 3d 97, 119 Ill. Dec. 725, 523 N.E.2d 193 (2 Dist. 1988).

Factors Considered

The trial court correctly considered the relevant factors in deciding whether the amount of attorney fees was reasonable where at the hearing on fees for petitioner's attorneys, the expertise of the attorneys was testified to; each attorney testified as to the hourly rate he charged and that each had in fact rendered the services specified; the motion judge stated that he was acquainted with the case and that the parties were "litigious people" requiring their attorney's frequent presence in court; respondent's gross income for two years was established; and petitioner was found not to be employed but was dependent upon the moneys which respondent was ordered to pay as temporary maintenance. In re Zannis, 114 Ill. App. 3d 1034, 70 Ill. Dec. 545, 449 N.E.2d 892 (1 Dist. 1983).

—Improper

The granting of an award is improper where no evidence is presented concerning the services performed, the basis of the award, or the reasonableness of the fees charged for the services performed. Soraparu v. Soraparu, 147 Ill. App. 3d 857, 101 Ill. Dec. 241, 498 N.E.2d 565 (1 Dist. 1986).

—Sufficient Showing

It is sufficient to support an award of fees if the party seeking the fees would be stripped of financial resources if required to pay. In re Zannis, 114 Ill. App. 3d 1034, 70 Ill. Dec. 545, 449 N.E.2d 892 (1 Dist. 1983).

Guardian Ad Litem

—In General

Child representative appointment did not violate a custodial parent's due process rights, since the parent had opportunity to question the basis for the representative's recommendations; if the representative were ultimately required to testify in court, another attorney would be appointed to represent the child, so that no ethical violation would occur. Bates v. Bates, 342 Ill. App. 3d 207, 276 Ill. Dec. 618, 794 N.E.2d 868, 2003 Ill. App. LEXIS 879 (2 Dist. 2003), aff'd sub nom. In re Marriage of De Bates, 212 Ill. 2d 489, 289 Ill. Dec. 218, 819 N.E.2d 714 (2004).

This section governs the appointment of an attorney or guardian ad litem for the minor children. Gibson v. Barton, 118 Ill. App. 3d 576, 74 Ill. Dec. 252, 455 N.E.2d 282 (4 Dist. 1983).

—Child's Interests

Where child's custodial parent asked the court to appoint an attorney to act in the child's best interests, where he filed an appearance, attended some hearings, but never joined or intervened in the mother's petition to declare paternity, the child's interests were adequately protected so as not to necessitate the additional appointment of a guardian ad litem. Koenig ex rel. Koenig v. Koenig, 211 Ill. App. 3d 1045, 156 Ill. Dec. 385, 570 N.E.2d 861 (1 Dist. 1991).

—College Expenses

Although this section does not provide for the appointment of an attorney to represent the interest of a child with respect to payment of the child's college expenses, this section does recognize that circumstances may exist in which a child's interest may need protection by an attorney "with respect to his support, custody and visitation" from the conflicting interest of the child's parents. Miller v. Miller, 163 Ill. App. 3d 602, 114 Ill. Dec. 682, 516 N.E.2d 837 (1 Dist. 1987).

—Evidence Considered

Trial court did not err in allowing guardians ad litem to listen to tapes that were inadmissible at trial where review of the tapes materially advanced their ability to determine and defend the child's interests. In re Karonis, 296 Ill. App. 3d 86, 230 Ill. Dec. 531, 693 N.E.2d 1282 (2 Dist. 1998).

—Fees

This section does not allow an award of fees against the state. Williams ex rel. Williams v. Davenport, 306 Ill. App. 3d 465, 239 Ill. Dec. 374, 713 N.E.2d 1224 (1 Dist. 1999).

The decision regarding the allowance and amount of fees to be awarded a guardian ad litem rests within the sound discretion of the trial court, and will not be disrupted on review unless the discretion is clearly abused; the amount to be awarded depends upon the factors and circumstances of each case, and the court in determining the amount must consider the total circumstances involved, including the circumstances of the mother and father; the importance, novelty, and difficulty of the questions raised, especially from a family law standpoint; the degree of responsibility involved from a management perspective; the time and labor required; the usual and customary charge in the community; and the benefits of the client. Soraparu v. Soraparu, 147 Ill. App. 3d 857, 101 Ill. Dec. 241, 498 N.E.2d 565 (1 Dist. 1986).

Award of a $500 fee to guardian ad litem was an abuse of discretion where the guardian testified that he spent "25 hours or more" on the case, and no showing was made concerning what particular services were included in these "25 hours or more," nor was there any indication of their necessity. Soraparu v. Soraparu, 147 Ill. App. 3d 857, 101 Ill. Dec. 241, 498 N.E.2d 565 (1 Dist. 1986).

—Not Mandatory

Under certain circumstances, the circuit court has an obligation to appoint a guardian ad litem, particularly when a minor is without proper representation; however, a guardian ad litem need not be appointed in every case and is not mandatory. Koenig ex rel. Koenig v. Koenig, 211 Ill. App. 3d 1045, 156 Ill. Dec. 385, 570 N.E.2d 861 (1 Dist. 1991).

—Paternity Proceedings

A trial court has the inherent power and statutory authority to appoint a guardian ad litem for a child subject to paternity proceedings. Denofrio v. Kuc, 201 Ill. App. 3d 810, 146 Ill. Dec. 1021, 558 N.E.2d 1355 (1 Dist. 1990).

Improper Actions

An attorney who serves in the dual capacity of guardian ad litem and legal representative for the children pursuant to this section cannot base his custody recommendation on independent interviews with persons who did not testify at the trial. In re Pool, 118 Ill. App. 3d 1035, 74 Ill. Dec. 458, 455 N.E.2d 887 (3 Dist. 1983), overruled on other grounds, In re Wycoff, 266 Ill. App. 3d 408 203 Ill. Dec. 338, 639 N.E.2d 897 (4 Dist. 1994).

Independent Action

Because petitioner's filing of a request for temporary attorney fees in a divorce proceeding did not constitute a new action, respondent did not have an absolute right to a substitution of judges, and absent specific allegations of prejudice, the trial court correctly denied the motion. In re Zannis, 114 Ill. App. 3d 1034, 70 Ill. Dec. 545, 449 N.E.2d 892 (1 Dist. 1983).

Parentage Petition Barred

A parentage petition is barred by a prior, uncontested judgment of dissolution, where a court-appointed guardian ad litem represented the minor during the dissolution proceedings. In re Griesmeyer, 302 Ill. App. 3d 905, 236 Ill. Dec. 227, 707 N.E.2d 72 (1 Dist. 1998).

Petition for Dissolution

—Not Final Judgment

A petition for dissolution of marriage advances only a single claim and the numerous other issues involved, such as custody, property distribution, and support are merely questions which are

Petition for Dissolution (Cont'd)

—Not Final Judgment (Cont'd)
ancillary to the cause of action; therefore a petition for dissolution is not a final judgment until the remaining issues are resolved. In re Derning, 117 Ill. App. 3d 620, 72 Ill. Dec. 785, 453 N.E.2d 90 (2 Dist. 1983).

Quality of Representation
A minor child could not challenge the quality of the guardian ad litem's representation for the first time after the child custody judgment was rendered. In re Apperson, 215 Ill. App. 3d 378, 158 Ill. Dec. 864, 574 N.E.2d 1257 (4 Dist. 1991).

LEGAL PERIODICALS

For Note, "A Lawyer's Guide to Eavesdropping in Illinois," see 87 Ill. B.J. 362 (1999).

For note, "Guardians Ad Litem: The Guardian Angels of Our Children in Domestic Violence Courts", see 30 Loy. U. Chi. L.J. 281 (1999).

For article, "Family Law: 1987-88 Illinois Law Survey," see Loy. U. Chi. L. J. 461 (1988-89).

For article, "The Ambiguous Role of the Lawyer Representing the Minor In Domestic Relations Litigation," see 70 Ill. B. J. 510 (1982).

750 ILCS 5/507 Payment of maintenance or support to court

Sec. 507. *Payment of maintenance or support to court.* (a) In actions instituted under this Act, the court shall order that maintenance and support payments be made to the clerk of court as trustee for remittance to the person entitled to receive the payments. However, the court in its discretion may direct otherwise where circumstances so warrant.

Upon notification in writing or by electronic transmission from the Illinois Department of Public Aid to the clerk of the court that a person who is receiving support payments under this Section is receiving services under the Child Support Enforcement Program established by Title IV-D of the Social Security Act [42 U.S.C. § 651 et seq.], any support payments subsequently received by the clerk of the court shall be transmitted in accordance with the instructions of the Illinois Department of Public Aid until the Department gives notice to the clerk of the court to cease the transmittal. After providing the notification authorized under this paragraph, the Illinois Department of Public Aid shall be entitled as a party to notice of any further proceedings in the case. The clerk of the court shall file a copy of the Illinois Department of Public Aid's notification in the court file. The failure of the clerk to file a copy of the notification in the court file shall not, however, affect the Illinois Department of Public Aid's right to receive notice of further proceedings.

(b) The clerk of court shall maintain records listing the amount of payments, the date payments are required to be made and the names and addresses of the parties affected by the order. For those cases in which support is payable to the clerk of the circuit court for transmittal to the Illinois Department of Public Aid by order of the court or upon notification of the Illinois Department of Public Aid, and the Illinois Department of Public Aid collects support by assignment, offset, withholding, deduction or other process permitted by law, the Illinois Department shall notify the clerk of the date and amount of such collection. Upon notification, the clerk shall record the collection on the payment record for the case.

(c) The parties affected by the order shall inform the clerk of court of any change of address or of other condition that may affect the administration of the order.

(d) The provisions of this Section shall not apply to cases that come under the provisions of Sections 709 through 712 [750 ILCS 5/709 through 750 ILCS 5/712].

(e) To the extent the provisions of this Section are inconsistent with the requirements pertaining to the State Disbursement Unit under Section 507.1 of this Act [750 ILCS 5/507.1] and Section 10-26 of the Illinois Public Aid Code [305 ILCS 5/10-26], the requirements pertaining to the State Disbursement Unit shall apply.

(Source: P.A. 82-988; 88-307, § 10; 88-687, § 13; 90-18, § 100; 90-673, § 915; 90-790, § 10; 91-212, § 25; 91-357, § 256.)

Note.
This section was Ill.Rev.Stat., Ch. 40, para. 507.

Effect of Amendments.
The 1994 amendment by P.A. 88-687, effective January 24, 1995, added the second paragraph in subsection (a); in subsection (b), in the second sentence, substituted "the court or upon notification of the Illinois Department of Public Aid" for "court".

The 1997 amendment by P.A. 90-18, effective July 1, 1997, in subsection (a) added the second paragraph.

The 1998 amendment by P.A. 90-673, effective January 1, 1999, incorporated the amendment by P.A. 90-18; and substituted "in accordance with the Income Withholding for Support Act" for "under Section 10-16.2 of this Act" in the second paragraph in subsection (a).

The 1998 amendment by P.A. 90-790, effective August 14, 1998, deleted the former second paragraph in subsection (a), relating to support orders pursuant to Article X of the Illinois Public Aid Code.

The 1999 amendment by P.A. 91-212, effective July 20, 1999, incorporated the amendments by P.A. 90-673 and P.A. 90-790, deleted "in accordance with the Income Withholding for Support" from the end of the second sentence in subsection (a); and added subsection (e).

The 1999 amendment by P.A. 91-357, effective July 29, 1999, incorporated the amendments by P.A. 90-673 and P.A. 90-790, and deleted "in accordance with the Income Witholding for Support" from the end of the second sentence in subsection (a).

Although the amendments made to this section by P.A. 91-212, § 25 and P.A. 91-357, § 256 did not take into account the amendments made by the other, the amendments have been combined into a single version by the publisher.

750 ILCS 5/507.1 Payment of Support to State Disbursement Unit

Sec. 507.1. *Payment of Support to State Disbursement Unit.* (a) As used in this Section:

"Order for support", "obligor", "obligee", and "payor" mean those terms as defined in the Income Withholding for Support Act [750 ILCS 28/1 et seq.], except that "order for support" shall not mean orders providing for spousal maintenance under which there is no child support obligation.

(b) Notwithstanding any other provision of this Act to the contrary, each order for support entered or modified on or after October 1, 1999 shall require that support payments be made to the State Disbursement Unit established under Section 10-26 of the Illinois Public Aid Code [305 ILCS 5/10-26] if:

(1) a party to the order is receiving child support enforcement services under Article X of the Illinois Public Aid Code [305 ILCS 5/10-1 et seq.]; or

(2) no party to the order is receiving child support enforcement services, but the support payments are made through income withholding.

(c) Support payments shall be made to the State Disbursement Unit if:

(1) the order for support was entered before October 1, 1999, and a party to the order is receiving child support enforcement services under Article X of the Illinois Public Aid Code [305 ILCS 5/10-1 et seq.]; or

(2) no party to the order is receiving child support enforcement services, and the support payments are being made through income withholding.

(c-5) If no party to the order is receiving child support enforcement services under Article X of the Illinois Public Aid Code [305 ILCS 5/10-1 et seq.], and the support payments are not made through income withholding, then support payments shall be made as directed by the order for support.

(c-10) At any time, and notwithstanding the existence of an order directing payments to be made elsewhere, the Department of Public Aid may provide notice to the obligor and, where applicable, to the obligor's payor:

(1) to make support payments to the State Disbursement Unit if:

(A) a party to the order for support is receiving child support enforcement services under Article X of the Illinois Public Aid Code [305 ILCS 5/10-1 et seq.]; or

(B) no party to the order for support is receiving child support enforcement services under Article X of the Illinois Public Aid Code [305 ILCS 5/10-1 et seq.], but the support payments are made through income withholding; or

(2) to make support payments to the State Disbursement Unit of another state upon request of another state's Title IV-D child support enforcement agency, in accordance with the requirements of Title IV, Part D of the Social Security Act [42 U.S.C. § 601 et seq.] and regulations promulgated under that Part D.

The Department of Public Aid shall provide a copy of the notice to the obligee and to the clerk of the circuit court.

(c-15) Within 15 days after the effective date of this amendatory Act of the 91st General Assembly [P.A. 91-677], the clerk of the circuit court shall provide written notice to the obligor to make payments directly to the clerk of the circuit court if no party to the order is receiving child support enforcement services under Article X of the Illinois Public Aid Code [305 ILCS 5/10-1 et seq.], the support payments are not made through income withholding, and the order for support requires support payments to be made directly to the clerk of the circuit court. The clerk shall provide a copy of the notice to the obligee.

(c-20) If the State Disbursement Unit receives a support payment that was not appropriately made to the Unit under this Section, the Unit shall immediately return the payment to the sender, including, if possible, instructions detailing where to send the support payment.

(d) The notices under subsections (c-10) and (c-15) may be sent by ordinary mail, certified mail, return receipt requested, facsimile transmission, or other electronic process, or may be served upon the obligor or payor using any method provided by law for service of a summons.

(Source: P.A. 91-212, § 25; 91-677, § 15; 92-590, § 10.)

Illinois Administrative Code.

See 89 Illinois Administrative Code, § 160.60.

Effective Date.

Section 999 of P.A. 91-212 made this section effective upon becoming law. The Act was approved July 20, 1999.

Effect of Amendments.

The 1999 amendment by P.A. 91-677, effective January 5, 2000, in subsection (a) inserted "except that 'order for support' shall not mean orders providing for spousal maintenance under which there is no child support obligation"; in subsection (c) deleted "The Illinois Department of Public Aid shall provide notice to the obligor and, where applicable, to the obligor's payor to make" at the beginning and inserted "shall be made"; in subsection (c)(2) deleted "the order for support was entered after January 1, 1994" at the beginning; added subsections (c-5), (c-10), (c-15) and (c-20); in subsection (d) substituted "subsections (c-10) and (c-15)" for "subsection (c)" and made stylistic changes.

The 2002 amendment by P.A. 92-590, effective July 1, 2002, substituted references to "support enforcement services" for references to "spouse support services" throughout the section; rewrote subsection (c-10); added the last sentence in subsection (c-15); and deleted the former last sentence from subsection (d), which read: "The Illinois Department of Public Aid shall provide a copy of the notice to the obligee and to the clerk of the court."

750 ILCS 5/508 Attorney's Fees; Client's Rights and Responsibilities Respecting Fees and Costs

Sec. 508. *Attorney's Fees; Client's Rights and Responsibilities Respecting Fees and Costs.* (a) The court from time to time, after due notice and hearing, and after considering the financial resources of the parties, may order any party to pay a reasonable amount for his own or the other party's costs and attorney's fees. Interim attorney's fees and costs may be awarded from the opposing party, in accordance with subsection (c-1) of Section 501 [750 ILCS 5/501]. At the conclusion of the case, contribution to attorney's fees and costs may be awarded from the opposing party in accordance with subsection (j) of Section 503 [750 ILCS 5/503]. Fees and costs may be awarded to counsel from a former client in accordance with subsection (c) of this Section. Awards may be made in connection with the following:

(1) The maintenance or defense of any proceeding under this Act.

(2) The enforcement or modification of any order or judgment under this Act.

(3) The defense of an appeal of any order or judgment under this Act, including the defense of appeals of post-judgment orders.

(3.1) The prosecution of any claim on appeal (if the prosecuting party has substantially prevailed).

(4) The maintenance or defense of a petition brought under Section 2-1401 of the Code of Civil Procedure [735 ILCS 5/2-1401] seeking relief from a final order or judgment under this Act.

(5) The costs and legal services of an attorney rendered in preparation of the commencement of the proceeding brought under this Act.

(6) Ancillary litigation incident to, or reasonably connected with, a proceeding under this Act.

The court may order that the award of attorney's fees and costs (including an interim or contribution award) shall be paid directly to the attorney, who may enforce the order in his or her name, or that it shall be paid to the appropriate party. Judgment may be entered and enforcement had accordingly. Except as otherwise provided in subdivision (e)(1) of this Section, subsection (c) of this Section is exclusive as to the right of any counsel (or former counsel) of record to petition a court for an award and judgment for final fees and costs during the pendency of a proceeding under this Act.

(b) In every proceeding for the enforcement of an order or judgment when the court finds that the failure to comply with the order or judgment was without compelling cause or justification, the court shall order the party against whom the proceeding is brought to pay promptly the costs and reasonable attorney's fees of the prevailing party. If non-compliance is with respect to a discovery order, the non-compliance is presumptively without compelling cause or justification, and the presumption may only be rebutted by clear and convincing evidence. If at any time a court finds that a hearing under this Section was precipitated or conducted for any improper purpose, the court shall allocate fees and costs of all parties for the hearing to the party or counsel found to have acted improperly. Improper purposes include, but are not limited to, harassment, unnecessary delay, or other acts needlessly increasing the cost of litigation.

(c) Final hearings for attorney's fees and costs against an attorney's own client, pursuant to a Petition for Setting Final Fees and Costs of either a counsel or a client, shall be governed by the following:

(1) No petition of a counsel of record may be filed against a client unless the filing counsel previously has been granted leave to withdraw as counsel of record or has filed a motion for leave to withdraw as counsel. On receipt of a petition of a client under this subsection (c), the counsel of record shall promptly file a motion for leave to withdraw as counsel. If the client and the counsel of record agree, however, a hearing on the motion for leave to withdraw as counsel filed pursuant to this subdivision (c)(1) may be deferred until completion of any alternative dispute resolution procedure under subdivision (c)(4). As to any Petition for Setting Final Fees and Costs against a client or counsel over whom the court has not obtained jurisdiction, a separate summons shall issue. Whenever a separate summons is not required, original notice as to a Petition for Setting Final Fees and Costs may be given, and documents served, in accordance with Illinois Supreme Court Rules 11 and 12.

(2) No final hearing under this subsection (c) is permitted unless: (i) the counsel and the client had entered into a written engagement agreement at the time the client retained the counsel (or reasonably soon thereafter) and the agreement meets the requirements of subsection (f); (ii) the written engagement agreement is attached to an affidavit of counsel that is filed with the petition or with the counsel's response to a client's petition; (iii) judgment in any contribution hearing on behalf of the client has been entered or the right to a contribution hearing under subsection (j) of Section 503 [750 ILCS 5/503] has been waived; (iv) the counsel has withdrawn as counsel of record; and (v) the petition seeks adjudication of all unresolved claims for fees and costs between the counsel and the client. Irrespective of a Petition for Setting Final Fees and Costs being heard in conjunction with an original proceeding under this Act, the relief requested under a Petition for Setting Final Fees and Costs constitutes a distinct cause of action. A pending but undetermined Petition for Setting Final Fees and Costs shall not affect appealability of any judgment or other adjudication in the original proceeding.

(3) The determination of reasonable attorney's fees and costs either under this subsection (c), whether initiated by a counsel or a client, or in an independent proceeding for services within the scope of subdivisions (1) through (5) of subsection (a), is within the sound discretion of the trial court. The court shall first consider the written engagement agreement and, if the court finds that the former client and the filing counsel, pursuant to their written engagement agreement, entered into a contract which meets applicable requirements of court rules and addresses all material terms, then the contract shall be enforceable in accordance with its terms, subject to the further requirements of this subdivision (c)(3). Before ordering enforcement, however, the court shall consider the performance pursuant to the contract. Any amount awarded by the court must be found to be fair compensation for the services, pursuant to the contract, that the court finds were reasonable and necessary. Quantum meruit principles shall govern any award for legal services performed that is not based on the terms of

the written engagement agreement (except that, if a court expressly finds in a particular case that aggregate billings to a client were unconscionably excessive, the court in its discretion may reduce the award otherwise determined appropriate or deny fees altogether).

(4) No final hearing under this subsection (c) is permitted unless any controversy over fees and costs (that is not otherwise subject to some form of alternative dispute resolution) has first been submitted to mediation, arbitration, or any other court approved alternative dispute resolution procedure, except as follows:

(A) In any circuit court for a single county with a population in excess of 1,000,000, the requirement of the controversy being submitted to an alternative dispute resolution procedure is mandatory unless the client and the counsel both affirmatively opt out of such procedures; or

(B) In any other circuit court, the requirement of the controversy being submitted to an alternative dispute resolution procedure is mandatory only if neither the client nor the counsel affirmatively opts out of such procedures.

After completion of any such procedure (or after one or both sides has opted out of such procedures), if the dispute is unresolved, any pending motion for leave to withdraw as counsel shall be promptly granted and a final hearing under this subsection (c) shall be expeditiously set and completed.

(5) A petition (or a praecipe for fee hearing without the petition) shall be filed no later than the end of the period in which it is permissible to file a motion pursuant to Section 2-1203 of the Code of Civil Procedure [735 ILCS 5/2-1203]. A praecipe for fee hearing shall be dismissed if a Petition for Setting Final Fees and Costs is not filed within 60 days after the filing of the praecipe. A counsel who becomes a party by filing a Petition for Setting Final Fees and Costs, or as a result of the client filing a Petition for Setting Final Fees and Costs, shall not be entitled to exercise the right to a substitution of a judge without cause under subdivision (a)(2) of Section 2-1001 of the Code of Civil Procedure [735 ILCS 5/2-1001].

(d) A consent judgment, in favor of a current counsel of record against his or her own client for a specific amount in a marital settlement agreement, dissolution judgment, or any other instrument involving the other litigant, is prohibited. A consent judgment between client and counsel, however, is permissible if it is entered pursuant to a verified petition for entry of consent judgment, supported by an affidavit of the counsel of record that incorporates an itemization of the billing or billings to the client, detailing hourly costs, time spent, and tasks performed, and by an affidavit of the client acknowledging receipt of that documentation, awareness of the right to a hearing, the right to be represented by counsel (other than counsel to whom the consent judgment is in favor), and the right to be present at the time of presentation of the petition, and agreement to the terms of the judgment. The petition may be filed at any time during which it is permissible for counsel of record to file a petition (or a praecipe) for a final fee hearing, except that no such petition for entry of consent judgment may be filed before adjudication (or waiver) of the client's right to contribution under subsection (j) of Section 503 [750 ILCS 5/503] or filed after the filing of a petition (or a praecipe) by counsel of record for a fee hearing under subsection (c) if the petition (or praecipe) remains pending. No consent security arrangement between a client and a counsel of record, pursuant to which assets of a client are collateralized to secure payment of legal fees or costs, is permissible unless approved in advance by the court as being reasonable under the circumstances.

(e) Counsel may pursue an award and judgment against a former client for legal fees and costs in an independent proceeding in the following circumstances:

(1) While a case under this Act still pends, a former counsel may pursue such an award and judgment at any time subsequent to 90 days after the entry of an order granting counsel leave to withdraw; and

(2) After the close of the period during which a petition (or praecipe) may be filed under subdivision (c)(5), if no such petition (or praecipe) for the counsel remains pending, any counsel or former counsel may pursue such an award and judgment, provided the complaint in the independent proceeding is filed within one year after the close of the foregoing period.

In an independent proceeding, the prior applicability of this Section shall in no way be deemed to have diminished any other right of any counsel (or former counsel) to pursue an award and judgment for legal fees and costs on the basis of remedies that may otherwise exist under applicable law. In an independent proceeding under subdivision (e)(1) in which the former counsel had represented a former client in a dissolution case that still pends, the former client may bring in his or her spouse as a third-party defendant, provided on or before the final date for filing a petition (or praecipe) under subsection (c), the party files an appropriate third-party complaint under Section 2-406 of the Code of Civil Procedure [735 ILCS 5/2-406]. In any such case, any judgment later obtained by the former counsel shall be against both spouses or ex-spouses, jointly and severally (except that, if a hearing under subsection (j) of Section 503 [750 ILCS 5/503] has already been concluded and the court hearing the contribution issue has imposed a percentage allocation between the parties as to fees and costs otherwise being adjudicated in the independent proceeding, the allocation shall be applied without deviation by the court in the independent proceeding and a separate judgment shall be entered against each spouse for the appropriate amount). After the period for the commencement of a proceeding under subsection (c), the provisions of this Section (other than the standard set forth in subdivision (c)(3) and the terms respecting consent security arrangements in subsection (d) of this Section 508) shall be inapplicable.

(f) Unless the Supreme Court by rule addresses the matters set out in this subsection (f), a written engagement agreement within the scope of subdivision (c)(2) shall have appended to it verbatim the following Statement:

"STATEMENT OF CLIENT'S RIGHTS AND RESPONSIBILITIES

(1) WRITTEN ENGAGEMENT AGREEMENT. The written engagement agreement, prepared by the counsel, shall clearly address the objectives of representation and detail the fee arrangement, including all material terms. If fees are to be based on criteria apart from, or in addition to, hourly rates, such criteria (e.g., unique time demands and/or utilization of unique expertise) shall be delineated. The client shall receive a copy of the written engagement agreement and any additional clarification requested and is advised not to sign any such agreement which the client finds to be unsatisfactory or does not understand.

(2) REPRESENTATION. Representation will commence upon the signing of the written engagement agreement. The counsel will provide competent representation, which requires legal knowledge, skill, thoroughness and preparation to handle those matters set forth in the written engagement agreement. Once employed, the counsel will act with reasonable diligence and promptness, as well as use his best efforts on behalf of the client, but he cannot guarantee results. The counsel will abide by the client's decision concerning the objectives of representation, including whether or not to accept an offer of settlement, and will endeavor to explain any matter to the extent reasonably necessary to permit the client to make informed decisions regarding representation. During the course of representation and afterwards, the counsel may not use or reveal a client's confidence or secrets, except as required or permitted by law.

(3) COMMUNICATION. The counsel will keep the client reasonably informed about the status of representation and will promptly respond to reasonable requests for information, including any reasonable request for an estimate respecting future costs of the representation or an appropriate portion of it. The client shall be truthful in all discussions with the counsel and provide all information or documentation required to enable the counsel to provide competent representation. During representation, the client is entitled to receive all pleadings and substantive documents prepared on behalf of the client and every document received from any other counsel of record. At the end of the representation and on written request from the client, the counsel will return to the client all original documents and exhibits. In the event that the counsel withdraws from representation, or is discharged by the client, the counsel will turn over to the substituting counsel (or, if no substitutions, to the client) all original documents and exhibits together with complete copies of all pleadings and discovery within thirty (30) days of the counsel's withdrawal or discharge.

(4) ETHICAL CONDUCT. The counsel cannot be required to engage in conduct which is illegal, unethical, or fraudulent. In matters involving minor children, the counsel may refuse to engage in conduct which, in the counsel's professional judgment, would be contrary to the best interest of the client's minor child or children. A counsel who cannot ethically abide by his client's directions shall be allowed to withdraw from representation.

(5) FEES. The counsel's fee for services may not be contingent upon the securing of a dissolution of marriage, upon obtaining custody, or be based upon the amount of maintenance, child support, or property settlement received, except as specifically permitted under Supreme Court rules. The counsel may not require a non-refundable retainer fee, but must remit back any overpayment at the end of the representation. The counsel may enter into a consensual security arrangement with the client whereby assets of the client are pledged to secure payment of legal fees or costs, but only if the counsel first obtains approval of the Court. The counsel will prepare and provide the client with an itemized billing statement detailing hourly rates (and/or other criteria), time spent, tasks performed, and costs incurred on a regular basis, at least quarterly. The client should review each billing statement promptly and address any objection or error in a timely manner. The client will not be billed for time spent to explain or correct a billing statement. If an appropriately detailed written estimate is submitted to a client as to future costs for a counsel's representation or a portion of the contemplated services (i.e., relative to specific steps recommended by the counsel in the estimate) and, without objection from the client, the counsel then performs the contemplated services, all such services are presumptively reasonable and necessary, as well as to be deemed pursuant to the client's direction. In an appropriate case, the client may pursue contribution to his or her fees and costs from the other party.

(6) DISPUTES. The counsel-client relationship is regulated by the Illinois Rules of Professional Conduct (Article VIII of the Illinois Supreme Court Rules), and any dispute shall be reviewed under the terms of such Rules."

(g) The changes to this Section 508 made by this amendatory Act of 1996 apply to cases pending on or after June 1, 1997, except as follows:

(1) Subdivisions (c)(1) and (c)(2) of this Section 508, as well as provisions of subdivision (c)(3) of this Section 508 pertaining to written engagement agreements, apply only to cases filed on or after June 1, 1997.

(2) The following do not apply in the case of a hearing under this Section that began before June 1, 1997:

(A) Subsection (c-1) of Section 501 [750 ILCS 5/501].

(B) Subsection (j) of Section 503 [750 ILCS 5/503].

(C) The changes to this Section 508 made by this amendatory Act of 1996 pertaining to the final setting of fees.

(Source: P.A. 85-357; 86-1452; 89-712, § 5.)

Note.

This section was Ill.Rev.Stat., Ch. 40, para. 508.

Cross References.

As to costs for reasonable fees of counsel under the Parentage Act of 1984, which are paid by the parties in accordance with the relevant factors specified in this section, see 750 ILCS 45/17.

Effect of Amendments.

The 1996 amendment by P.A. 89-712, effective June 1, 1997, in the section catchline added "Client's Rights and Responsibilities Respecting Fees and Costs"; in subsection (a), in the first paragraph, in the first sentence, inserted "or the other party's" and deleted from the end "and for the costs and attorney's fees necessarily incurred or, for the purpose of enabling a party lacking sufficient financial resources to obtain or retain legal representation expected to be incurred by any party, which award shall be made in connection with the following" and added the second through fifth sentences; added subdivisions (a)(3.1) and (a)(6); added the second paragraph of subsection (a); in subsection (b), in the first sentence, inserted "compelling" and "promptly" and added the second through fourth sentences; substituted the present subsection (c) for the former regarding recipient of payment; and added subsections (d) through (g).

CASE NOTES

ANALYSIS

Constitutionality
In General
Ability to Pay
—In General
—Burden of Proof
—Custodial Parents
—Destitution
—Determination
—Disparity in Income
—Enforcement of Rights
—Financial Resources
—Former Law
—Hearing
—Installment Order
—Not Shown
—Resources
—Shown
Abuse of Discretion
—In General
—Ability to Pay
—Assessment of Fee in Advance
—Not Shown
—Shown
Adult Child
Amendment
Amount of Award
—Determinative Factors
—Discretion of Court
—Excessive Attorney's Fees
—Financial Ability
—Illustrative Cases
—Impeding Progress
—Not Excessive
—Not Inadequate
—Quantum Meruit
—Illustrative Cases
—Reasonableness
—Separate Maintenance Action
—Time Spent by Attorney
Appeals
Applicability
Apportionment
Arbitration
Attorney Collection Action
Attorney's Lien
—Abuse of Discretion
Authority of Court
—Either Spouse
—Prior Law
Award of Fees
—Ability to Pay
—Additional Services
—Award Denied
—Award Upheld
—Bad Faith
—Bankruptcy Proceeding
—Custody Proceedings
—Discretion of Court
—Dismissal of Action
—Disobedience of Court Order
—Held Improper
—Per Issue
Award to Former Attorney
Burden of Proof
Contractual Limitation
Discretion of Court
Enforcement
Enforcement of Court Order
—Evidentiary Basis
—Fee Petition Preparation Time
—Former Law
—Good Faith Shown
—Harassment of Ex-Spouse
—Held Improper
—Held Proper
—History
—Insufficient Evidence
—Legislative Intent
—Life-Style and Standard of Living
—Misuse of Trust Funds
—Petition After Satisfaction
—Post-Decretal Proceedings
—Reasonableness
—Retroactive Allowance
—Statement by Attorney
—Supplemental Fees
Bankruptcy
—Discharge of Debt
—Effect of Award
—Nondischargeable Debt
Billing
Burden of Proof
Calculation
Child Custody Proceedings
Child Support Proceedings
Contempt
Contingent Fees
Contractual Limitation
Default
Destitution
Enforcement
Evidence
Factors
Foreclosure Proceeding
Former Law
From Time to Time
Guardian Ad Litem
Hearing
Incurred

Itemization of Expenses
Jurisdiction
—In General
—Abatement of Action
—Ancillary
—Appeals
—Court Error
—Dismissal
—New Proceeding
—No Enforcement Authority
—Party in Interest
—Post-Judgment Petitions
—Pre-Judgment Award
—Supplementary Proceeding
—Waiver
Legislative Purpose
Maintenance
Mandatory Provisions
Method
—Monthly Installments
Modification Proceeding
Motion to Vacate
—Denial Held Proper
—Due Diligence
—Fees Allowed
Notice
Paralegals
Paternity Proceeding
Payment of Fees
—Attorney Fees
—Determination
—Dismissal of Action
—Either Party
—In Other Proceedings
—No Basis
—Responsibility
—Sale of Residence
Pleadings
Prospective Award
Public Policy
Purpose
Purpose of Amendment
Reasonableness of Fees
—In General
—Contract
—Illustrative Cases
—Relevance of Judge's Knowledge and Experience
—Sanctions Against Attorney
Reduction
Related Provision
Res Judicata
Retroactive Application
Review
Sequestration Proceeding
Settlement Agreement
Spousal Guardian
Spouse
Standing
Substitution of Judges
Tax Exemptions
Temporary Attorney Fees
Testimony
Time and Labor
—Independent Proof Required
Undue Influence
Voluntary Dismissal
Waiver
Wilful Violation

Constitutionality

It is not special legislation to provide clients with safeguards against the potential for exploitation created by the unique power this section has given to divorce attorneys. Kaufman, Litwin & Feinstein v. Edgar, 301 Ill. App. 3d 826, 235 Ill. Dec. 183, 704 N.E.2d 756 (1 Dist. 1998), appeal denied, 182 Ill. 2d 551, 236 Ill. Dec. 670, 707 N.E.2d 1240 (1999).

Subdivision (j)(3) protects the interests of both the attorney and the client by allowing the attorney to have a hearing for fees without the concern that the other party will use the hearing as an opportunity to discover otherwise privileged information and does not violate the separation of powers. Kaufman, Litwin & Feinstein v. Edgar, 301 Ill. App. 3d 826, 235 Ill. Dec. 183, 704 N.E.2d 756 (1 Dist. 1998), appeal denied, 182 Ill. 2d 551, 236 Ill. Dec. 670, 707 N.E.2d 1240 (1999).

An attorney must follow the requirements of subsection (f) if he wishes to seek fees from his client in a dissolution case; however, because an attorney who does not wish to maintain time records may still seek fees through an independent law suit, this section does not conflict with common law. Kaufman, Litwin & Feinstein v. Edgar, 301 Ill. App. 3d 826, 235 Ill. Dec. 183, 704 N.E.2d 756 (1 Dist. 1998), appeal denied, 182 Ill. 2d 551, 236 Ill. Dec. 670, 707 N.E.2d 1240 (1999).

Subsection (d) requires the parties to provide the court with more information than the Supreme Court Rules, enabling the court to exercise its discretion fairly and reasonably, and does not conflict with any supreme court rule nor does it create a separation of powers problem. Kaufman, Litwin & Feinstein v. Edgar, 301 Ill. App. 3d 826, 235 Ill. Dec. 183, 704 N.E.2d 756 (1 Dist. 1998), appeal denied, 182 Ill. 2d 551, 236 Ill. Dec. 670, 707 N.E.2d 1240 (1999).

Subdivision (c)(3) does not mandate how a court should rule in a particular case, rather, it leaves the matter up to the discretion of the court the manner in which attorney-client fee contracts should be enforced in each individual case, and therefore does not violate the separation of powers clause. Kaufman, Litwin & Feinstein v. Edgar, 301 Ill. App. 3d 826, 235 Ill. Dec. 183, 704 N.E.2d 756 (1 Dist. 1998), appeal denied, 182 Ill. 2d 551, 236 Ill. Dec. 670, 707 N.E.2d 1240 (1999).

Subdivision (c)(2), providing that relief requested under a petition for setting final fees and costs brought against an attorney's own client constitutes a distinct cause of action that does not affect the appealability of any judgment or other adjudication in original proceeding, does not violate the separation of powers clause. Kaufman, Litwin & Feinstein v. Edgar, 301 Ill. App. 3d 826, 235 Ill. Dec. 183, 704 N.E.2d 756 (1 Dist. 1998), appeal denied, 182 Ill. 2d 551, 236 Ill. Dec. 670, 707 N.E.2d 1240 (1999).

Subdivision (c)(1) does not violate the separation of powers clause. Kaufman, Litwin & Feinstein v. Edgar, 301 Ill. App. 3d 826, 235 Ill. Dec. 183, 704 N.E.2d 756 (1 Dist. 1998), appeal denied, 182 Ill. 2d 551, 236 Ill. Dec. 670, 707 N.E.2d 1240 (1999).

This section does not violate the separation of powers clause of the Illinois Constitution (Ill. Const. (1970), Art. II, § 1) in that the trial court loses jurisdiction to award attorney fees under the Supreme Court Rules upon the filing of the notice of appeal; a trial court retains jurisdiction to award fees for defending an appeal even after the filing of the notice of appeal, on the rationale that the award of attorney's fees is subsequent in time and merely collateral to the appeal and involves a matter independent of any question raised by the appeal. In re Pahlke, 154 Ill. App. 3d 256, 107 Ill. Dec. 407, 507 N.E.2d 71 (1 Dist.), appeal denied, 113 Ill. Dec. 304, 515 N.E.2d 113 (Ill. 1987).

Subsection (a) of this section is not prohibited special legislation. In re Galvin, 94 Ill. App. 3d 1032, 50 Ill. Dec. 309, 419 N.E.2d 417 (1 Dist. 1981).

The allowance of attorney fees under former Ill.Rev.Stat., ch. 40, para. 16 (see now this section), for the prosecution of an appeal and post-judgment petitions does not conflict with the provisions of the Illinois Constitution prohibiting special and discriminatory legislation. Gilmore v. Gilmore, 74 Ill. App. 3d 831, 30 Ill. Dec. 378, 393 N.E.2d 33 (1 Dist. 1979).

In General

Competent representation of a client in support or maintenance collection proceedings requires the attorney to seek the relief afforded by subsection (b) of this section. Fletcher v. Fletcher, 227 Ill. App. 3d 194, 169 Ill. Dec. 211, 591 N.E.2d 91 (4 Dist. 1992).

In marriage and dissolution of marriage cases, attorney fees can be by agreement between the attorney and client or set by the court under subsection (a) of this section, and if determined under subsection (a), the fee must be reasonable in amount an necessarily incurred. Fletcher v. Fletcher, 227 Ill. App. 3d 194, 169 Ill. Dec. 211, 591 N.E.2d 91 (4 Dist. 1992).

The court will not award attorney fees under this section where the record discloses that the parties were equally responsible for

In General (Cont'd)
causing exhaustive and protracted litigation. In re Landfield, 209 Ill. App. 3d 678, 153 Ill. Dec. 834, 567 N.E.2d 1061 (1 Dist.), cert. denied, 139 Ill. 2d 597, 159 Ill. Dec. 109, 575 N.E.2d 916 (1991).

The court's authority to order attorney fees under subsection (a) of this section is strictly limited to what is statutorily permissible; thus, an award under the former version of this section was not permitted unless the party seeking the award was the legally married "spouse" of the other. Ziemann v. Ziemann, 214 Ill. App. 3d 988, 158 Ill. Dec. 654, 574 N.E.2d 767 (1 Dist. 1991).

A consideration in awarding attorney fees, in addition to the financial resources of the parties, is the identity of the party who precipitated the need for the legal proceedings. In re Parker, 216 Ill. App. 3d 672, 159 Ill. Dec. 131, 575 N.E.2d 938 (2 Dist. 1991).

The standard prescribed by subsection (b) of this section is not one of wilful and contemptuous failure to pay support, but failure to pay without cause or justification. In re Young, 200 Ill. App. 3d 226, 147 Ill. Dec. 178, 559 N.E.2d 178 (4 Dist. 1990).

An award of attorney fees in a dissolution proceeding rests in the sound discretion of the trial court, and a court of review will reverse only for an abuse of discretion. In re Osborn, 206 Ill. App. 3d 588, 151 Ill. Dec. 663, 564 N.E.2d 1325 (5 Dist. 1990), cert. denied, 137 Ill. 2d 666, 156 Ill. Dec. 563, 571 N.E.2d 150 (1991).

The payment of attorney fees is the primary obligation of the party on whose behalf the services are rendered. In re Wolf, 180 Ill. App. 3d 998, 129 Ill. Dec. 742, 536 N.E.2d 792 (1 Dist. 1989).

Whether an award of attorney fees is proper depends upon a showing of the spouse seeking them of an inability to pay and the ability of the other spouse to pay fees. In re Wolf, 180 Ill. App. 3d 998, 129 Ill. Dec. 742, 536 N.E.2d 792 (1 Dist. 1989).

Trial court abused its discretion in ordering petitioner to contribute toward respondent's attorney fees and costs where respondent would receive funds which would be adequate to pay those fees and where it was respondent's actions in dissipating marital assets and his concealment of that dissipation which largely contributed to the necessity of those fees. In re Rai, 189 Ill. App. 3d 559, 136 Ill. Dec. 922, 545 N.E.2d 446 (1 Dist. 1989).

Attorney fees are the primary responsibility of the person for whom the services are rendered. In re Ziemer, 189 Ill. App. 3d 966, 137 Ill. Dec. 475, 546 N.E.2d 229 (4 Dist. 1989).

In determining a request for attorney fees, it is proper for the court to give consideration to who precipitated the need for the legal fees. In re Ziemer, 189 Ill. App. 3d 966, 137 Ill. Dec. 475, 546 N.E.2d 229 (4 Dist. 1989).

Courts generally interpret this section to mean that the party seeking relief must show financial inability to pay with the corresponding ability of the other party to pay. In re McGory, 185 Ill. App. 3d 517, 133 Ill. Dec. 590, 541 N.E.2d 801 (3 Dist. 1989).

Financial inability exists where payment would undermine economic instability of the spouse incurring the debt. In re McGory, 185 Ill. App. 3d 517, 133 Ill. Dec. 590, 541 N.E.2d 801 (3 Dist. 1989).

Where wife's move required her to use part of her savings account to provide for her living expenses, where she had no job, and where she had just lost her maintenance payments, the court granted her request for her husband to pay attorney fees. In re McGory, 185 Ill. App. 3d 517, 133 Ill. Dec. 590, 541 N.E.2d 801 (3 Dist. 1989).

The payment of attorney fees is the primary obligation of the party on whose behalf the services are rendered. In re Jones, 187 Ill. App. 3d 206, 134 Ill. Dec. 836, 543 N.E.2d 119 (1 Dist. 1989).

The trial court has the authority to order one spouse to pay the other spouse's attorney fees and costs. In re Jones, 187 Ill. App. 3d 206, 134 Ill. Dec. 836, 543 N.E.2d 119 (1 Dist. 1989).

Under subsection (b) of this section, a trial court has no discretion as to whether to award attorney fees and costs, as its only discretion is to decide whether the failure to pay was without cause or justification. If the trial court so finds, the award of reasonable attorney fees and costs is mandatory, but if the trial court finds that the failure to pay was justified, or that the failure was not willful and wanton, it may deny attorney fees and costs. In re Garelick, 168 Ill. App. 3d 321, 119 Ill. Dec. 76, 522 N.E.2d 738 (1 Dist. 1988).

A spouse who is seeking an award of attorney fees and costs must show financial inability to pay the fees as well as the financial ability of the other spouse to pay them. In re Einhorn, 178 Ill. App. 3d 212, 127 Ill. Dec. 411, 533 N.E.2d 29 (1 Dist. 1988).

An attorney's gratuitous statement to respondent that he would not charge respondent for fees incurred during appeal did not preclude the attorney from recovering fees from petitioner, considering that subsection (a) of this section provides that one spouse can be ordered to pay attorney fees necessarily incurred by the other spouse, that the statement did not mean the fees were unnecessarily incurred, and that no such statement was made to petitioner. In re Pick, 167 Ill. App. 3d 294, 118 Ill. Dec. 53, 521 N.E.2d 121 (2 Dist. 1988).

The trial court's decision will not be disturbed absent a clear abuse of discretion. In re Calisoff, 176 Ill. App. 3d 721, 126 Ill. Dec. 183, 531 N.E.2d 810 (1 Dist. 1988).

The award of attorney fees is mandatory upon a court's finding of a failure to pay without cause or justification. In re Kennedy, 170 Ill. App. 3d 726, 121 Ill. Dec. 362, 525 N.E.2d 168 (5 Dist. 1988).

Once the trial court determines that an award of attorney fees is appropriate, the court must then determine the reasonableness of the request. In re Felson, 171 Ill. App. 3d 923, 121 Ill. Dec. 796, 525 N.E.2d 1103 (1 Dist. 1988).

The award of attorney fees and the amount to be paid by the parties is within the discretion of the trial court and will not be disturbed absent a clear showing of an abuse of discretion. Head v. Head, 168 Ill. App. 3d 697, 119 Ill. Dec. 549, 523 N.E.2d 17 (1 Dist. 1988).

An award of attorney fees in an Illinois divorce proceeding is ordinarily in the nature of support. Doss, Puchalski, Keenan & Bargiel, Ltd. v. Cockhill, 72 Bankr. 339 (Bankr. N.D. Ill. 1987).

Attorney fees may be awarded to a litigant only when they are expressly authorized by statute or by agreement of the parties, and a trial court is bound by the statutory grant. In re Magnuson, 156 Ill. App. 3d 691, 109 Ill. Dec. 569, 510 N.E.2d 437 (2 Dist. 1987).

The allowance of attorney fees is within the sound discretion of the court. In re Gibbons, 158 Ill. App. 3d 998, 111 Ill. Dec. 148, 512 N.E.2d 52 (4 Dist. 1987).

Under this section the legislature has provided the circuit court with the authority to award attorney fees incurred by either spouse in connection with proceedings under this Act. Didzerekis v. Birt, 159 Ill. App. 3d 281, 111 Ill. Dec. 274, 512 N.E.2d 390 (2 Dist. 1987).

A court may order the other spouse to pay a reasonable amount for attorney fees for services rendered in a proceeding under this Act, including the defense of appeals from post-judgment orders or petitions seeking relief from final judgments under the Act. In re Bashwiner, 155 Ill. App. 3d 531, 108 Ill. Dec. 258, 508 N.E.2d 419 (1 Dist. 1987).

This section authorizes an attorney in a pending dissolution proceeding to recover his earned fees from either his own client or the other party. In re Baltzer, 150 Ill. App. 3d 890, 104 Ill. Dec. 196, 502 N.E.2d 459 (2 Dist. 1986).

The general rule is that a party seeking an award of attorney fees must show his own financial inability to pay and the financial ability of the other spouse; however, a party who must use judicial process to obtain compliance with the terms of a decree of dissolution is entitled to reasonable attorney fees, even absent a showing of his own ability to pay. In re Wardell, 149 Ill. App. 3d 537, 102 Ill. Dec. 859, 500 N.E.2d 960 (2 Dist. 1986).

The Act contains no language limiting the trial court's authority to award attorney fees when presented with a proper fee petition. In re Hirsch, 135 Ill. App. 3d 945, 90 Ill. Dec. 646, 482 N.E.2d 625 (1 Dist. 1985).

To justify an award of attorney fees, the party seeking relief must demonstrate financial inability to pay and the ability of the other spouse to do so. In re Moriarty, 132 Ill. App. 3d 895, 88 Ill. Dec. 222, 478 N.E.2d 537 (1 Dist. 1985).

An award of attorney fees is justified where the spouse seeking relief demonstrates: (1) financial inability to pay, and (2) the ability of the other spouse to pay. In re Ryan, 138 Ill. App. 3d 1077, 93 Ill. Dec. 617, 487 N.E.2d 61 (1 Dist. 1985).

Financial inability exists where payment would strip the person of the means of support and undermine her economic stability. In re Ryan, 138 Ill. App. 3d 1077, 93 Ill. Dec. 617, 487 N.E.2d 61 (1 Dist. 1985).

While the trial court should consider the property received by each party and their overall economic status before allocating responsibility for payment of attorney's fees, there is nothing in this section to prohibit the trial court from requiring the petition on fees to be filed and the hearing to be held prior to the disposition of the property and maintenance/child support issues. In re Thornton, 138 Ill. App. 3d 906, 93 Ill. Dec. 453, 486 N.E.2d 1288 (1 Dist. 1985).

In General (Cont'd)

This section has been construed to authorize prospective fee awards in appropriate circumstances, but such awards should be made cautiously. In re Savas, 139 Ill. App. 3d 68, 93 Ill. Dec. 483, 486 N.E.2d 1318 (1 Dist. 1985).

The allowance of attorney fees and costs in divorce proceedings is not a matter of right but rests with the sound discretion of the trial court and, in exercising its discretion, the court may consider, in addition to the abilities of the parties to pay, the questions at issue, the significance or importance of the subject matter, the degree of responsibility involved, the standing and skill of the person employed, and the time and labor involved. In re Bennett, 131 Ill. App. 3d 1050, 87 Ill. Dec. 305, 476 N.E.2d 1297 (2 Dist. 1985).

An award of attorney fees is not mandatory, but discretionary. Jones v. Meade, 126 Ill. App. 3d 897, 81 Ill. Dec. 786, 467 N.E.2d 657 (4 Dist. 1984).

Under Illinois divorce law, the responsibility to pay attorney fees is generally determined by the relative income of the parties. Schroeder v. Schroeder, 25 Bankr. 190 (Bankr. N.D. Ill. 1982).

Although subsection (a) of this section allows for an award of attorney fees made in connection with the defense of an appeal, it has no specific provision to negate the general rule that the filing of a notice of appeal deprives the trial court of further jurisdiction. In re Pease, 106 Ill. App. 3d 617, 62 Ill. Dec. 389, 435 N.E.2d 1361 (2 Dist. 1982).

It is clear that the trial court has general power to award attorney fees pursuant to subsection (a) of this section and also pursuant to the plenary equitable powers of the trial court; however, regardless of the source, the power must be exercised while the trial court retains general jurisdiction over the cause. In re Pease, 106 Ill. App. 3d 617, 62 Ill. Dec. 389, 435 N.E.2d 1361 (2 Dist. 1982).

Where the court had evidence before it of the financial resources of both parties when ruling on the issue of attorney fees and where no hearing had been requested, the trial court's failure to conduct a hearing on the propriety of the award of attorney fees was not error. In re Hellwig, 100 Ill. App. 3d 452, 55 Ill. Dec. 762, 426 N.E.2d 1087 (1 Dist. 1981).

The award of attorney fees is based on a showing of the inability of one spouse to pay and the ability of the other spouse to do so. In re Bramson, 100 Ill. App. 3d 657, 56 Ill. Dec. 205, 427 N.E.2d 285 (1 Dist. 1981).

The court may order either spouse to pay a reasonable amount for the costs and attorney fees necessarily incurred by the other spouse. Burks v. Burks, 100 Ill. App. 3d 700, 56 Ill. Dec. 273, 427 N.E.2d 353 (1 Dist. 1981).

The granting of attorney fees is improper where no evidence is heard as to the items of service which were performed, the basis of the amount requested, or the reasonableness of such fees. In re Janetzke, 97 Ill. App. 3d 418, 52 Ill. Dec. 705, 422 N.E.2d 914 (1 Dist. 1981).

Where petition for fees was submitted prior to entry of a judgment dispositive of the merits of the action, and where the clear import of the language of subsection (a) of this section was that the court may order attorney fees to be paid by either party to either attorney, the provision was given its clear meaning and the trial court properly entered judgment in favor of a firm against its own client. In re Galvin, 94 Ill. App. 3d 1032, 50 Ill. Dec. 309, 419 N.E.2d 417 (1 Dist. 1981).

The general rule concerning awards of attorney fees in a divorce suit is that the party seeking such relief must show financial inability to pay and the ability of the other spouse to do so. Greiman v. Friedman, 90 Ill. App. 3d 941, 46 Ill. Dec. 355, 414 N.E.2d 77 (1 Dist. 1980).

The fees allowed in a dissolution proceeding should be fair to all the parties involved: the attorney to be compensated, the client, and the person required to make the payment. In re Kruse, 92 Ill. App. 3d 335, 48 Ill. Dec. 145, 416 N.E.2d 40 (1 Dist. 1980).

The amount awarded should be fair compensation for those services which were reasonable and necessary to the action. In re Kruse, 92 Ill. App. 3d 335, 48 Ill. Dec. 145, 416 N.E.2d 40 (1 Dist. 1980).

The propriety of an award of attorney fees depends on the particular facts of each case; in determining whether a party is unable to pay attorney fees the assets of that party must be weighed in light of the parties' standard of living. Donnelley v. Donnelley, 80 Ill. App. 3d 597, 35 Ill. Dec. 919, 400 N.E.2d 56 (1 Dist. 1980).

To justify the allowance of attorney fees, the party seeking relief must show financial inability to pay and the ability of the other spouse to do so. In re Pedersen, 77 Ill. App. 3d 716, 33 Ill. Dec. 270, 396 N.E.2d 659 (2 Dist. 1979).

The party seeking to recover attorney fees must show financial inability to pay and the ability of the other spouse to do so; the decision in regard to fees then rests within the sound discretion of the trial court. Scott v. Scott, 75 Ill. App. 3d 710, 31 Ill. Dec. 577, 394 N.E.2d 779 (2 Dist. 1979).

Attorney fees in a dissolution of marriage proceeding are the primary obligation of the party for whom the services are rendered. In re Sanborn, 78 Ill. App. 3d 146, 33 Ill. Dec. 468, 396 N.E.2d 1192 (1 Dist. 1979).

The allowance of attorney fees to an opposing party is justified where the party seeking relief demonstrates financial inability to pay and the ability of the other spouse to do so. In re Sanborn, 78 Ill. App. 3d 146, 33 Ill. Dec. 468, 396 N.E.2d 1192 (1 Dist. 1979).

Although the trial court is permitted wide discretion in awarding attorney fees, that discretion is not unbounded. In re Uphoff, 80 Ill. App. 3d 145, 35 Ill. Dec. 293, 398 N.E.2d 1243 (3 Dist. 1980).

The allowance of attorney fees for appeal rests within the sound discretion of the trial court, which allowance will not be disturbed on review in the absence of a clear showing of abuse; fees may be allowed only upon findings of inability to pay by the petitioning spouse, and that the other spouse is able to pay. Gasperini v. Gasperini, 57 Ill. App. 3d 578, 15 Ill. Dec. 230, 373 N.E.2d 576 (1 Dist. 1978).

The well-established principle that the amount of attorney fees rests in the sound discretion of the trial judge, and will not be interfered with unless abused, applies to support awards. Collins v. Collins, 47 Ill. App. 3d 258, 5 Ill. Dec. 464, 361 N.E.2d 787 (1 Dist. 1977).

The allowance of attorney fees in a divorce proceeding is not automatic, but depends on a showing that one spouse is financially unable to pay the fees, while the other is able to do so. Karaskiewicz v. Karaskiewicz, 38 Ill. App. 3d 509, 348 N.E.2d 184 (1 Dist. 1976).

The decisions whether to grant periodic alimony, attorney fees, and suit money rest in the sound discretion of the circuit court. McManus v. McManus, 38 Ill. App. 3d 645, 348 N.E.2d 507 (5 Dist. 1976).

The matter of fixing attorney fees is one of the few areas in which a trial judge may rely on the pleadings, affidavits on file and on his own experience. Welsh v. Welsh, 38 Ill. App. 3d 35, 347 N.E.2d 512 (1 Dist. 1976).

Former section 15 of the Divorce Act (see now this section), authorized the trial court to order the payment of such attorney fees as may seem equitable, regardless of the disposition of the case. Gold v. Gold, 17 Ill. App. 3d 11, 308 N.E.2d 75 (1 Dist. 1974).

The awarding of attorney fees rests in the sound discretion of the trial court and will not be interfered with unless such discretion is clearly abused. Ylonen v. Ylonen, 2 Ill. 2d 111, 117 N.E.2d 98 (1954); Kijowski v. Kijowski, 36 Ill. App. 2d 94, 183 N.E.2d 583 (1 Dist. 1962); Roback v. Roback, 59 Ill. App. 2d 222, 207 N.E.2d 130 (2 Dist. 1965); Brandel v. Brandel, 69 Ill. App. 2d 264, 216 N.E.2d 21 (2 Dist. 1966); Lauzen v. Lauzen, 81 Ill. App. 2d 472, 225 N.E.2d 427 (2 Dist. 1967); Riordan v. Riordan, 47 Ill. App. 3d 1019, 8 Ill. Dec. 254, 365 N.E.2d 492 (1 Dist. 1977); Moore v. Moore, 53 Ill. App. 3d 228, 10 Ill. Dec. 950, 368 N.E.2d 545 (1 Dist. 1977); In re Sanborn, 78 Ill. App. 3d 146, 33 Ill. Dec. 468, 396 N.E.2d 1192 (1 Dist. 1979); Donnelley v. Donnelley, 80 Ill. App. 3d 597, 35 Ill. Dec. 919, 400 N.E.2d 56 (1 Dist. 1980); In re Sipich, 80 Ill. App. 3d 883, 36 Ill. Dec. 276, 400 N.E.2d 696 (1 Dist. 1980); In re Bramson, 100 Ill. App. 3d 657, 56 Ill. Dec. 205, 427 N.E.2d 285 (1 Dist. 1981); Bellow v. Bellow, 94 Ill. App. 3d 361, 50 Ill. Dec. 656, 419 N.E.2d 924 (1 Dist. 1981); In re Donahoe, 114 Ill. App. 3d 470, 70 Ill. Dec. 152, 448 N.E.2d 1030 (2 Dist. 1983); In re Siegel, 123 Ill. App. 3d 710, 79 Ill. Dec. 219, 463 N.E.2d 773 (1 Dist. 1984); In re Smith, 128 Ill. App. 3d 1017, 84 Ill. Dec. 242, 471 N.E.2d 1008 (2 Dist. 1984); In re Angiuli, 134 Ill. App. 3d 417, 89 Ill. Dec. 328, 480 N.E.2d 513 (2 Dist. 1985); In re Savas, 139 Ill. App. 3d 68, 93 Ill. Dec. 483, 486 N.E.2d 1318 (1 Dist. 1985); In re Wright, 180 Ill. App. 3d 911, 129 Ill. Dec. 650, 536 N.E.2d 700 (1 Dist. 1986); In re Wettstein, 160 Ill. App. 3d 554, 113 Ill. Dec. 1, 514 N.E.2d 783 (4 Dist. 1987); In re Wolf, 180 Ill. App. 3d 998, 129 Ill. Dec. 742, 536 N.E.2d 792 (1 Dist. 1989); In re Jones, 187 Ill. App.

In General (Cont'd)
3d 206, 134 Ill. Dec. 836, 543 N.E.2d 119 (1 Dist. 1989); In re Cierny, 187 Ill. App. 3d 334, 134 Ill. Dec. 918, 543 N.E.2d 201 (1 Dist. 1989); In re Ziemer, 189 Ill. App. 3d 966, 137 Ill. Dec. 475, 546 N.E.2d 229 (4 Dist. 1989); Jiles v. Spratt, 195 Ill. App. 3d 354, 142 Ill. Dec. 21, 552 N.E.2d 371 (4 Dist. 1990); In re Mantei, 222 Ill. App. 3d 933, 164 Ill. Dec. 870, 583 N.E.2d 1192 (4 Dist. 1991).

Ability to Pay

—In General

The trial court did not err in requiring ex-wife to pay a majority of her attorney fees. In re Pearson, 236 Ill. App. 3d 337, 177 Ill. Dec. 650, 603 N.E.2d 720 (1 Dist. 1992).

For purposes of determining an award of attorney fees, financial inability exists where the forced payment of available funds would strip a person of his or her means of support and undermine his or her economic stability. In re Kennedy, 214 Ill. App. 3d 849, 158 Ill. Dec. 172, 573 N.E.2d 1357 (1 Dist. 1991).

The party seeking attorney fees must show an inability to pay, and the ability of the other spouse to pay fees. In re Jones, 187 Ill. App. 3d 206, 134 Ill. Dec. 836, 543 N.E.2d 119 (1 Dist. 1989).

Before one spouse may recover attorney fees from the other, the spouse seeking fees must demonstrate that he or she is financially unable to pay and that the other spouse has the ability to pay; a mere showing that the other spouse has a greater ability to pay attorney fees is not sufficient to justify an award of fees under this section. In re Bean, 181 Ill. App. 3d 671, 130 Ill. Dec. 275, 537 N.E.2d 342 (5 Dist. 1989).

Under subdivision (a)(5) of this section, a court need not determine the ability or inability of a party to pay the requested fees. Davis v. Sprague, 186 Ill. App. 3d 249, 133 Ill. Dec. 620, 541 N.E.2d 831 (4 Dist. 1989).

Favorable financial status of a client to pay $150 per hour was not significant, as no client of an attorney may properly be required to pay more than the reasonable value of the legal services rendered simply because he has the ability to do so. In re Angiuli, 134 Ill. App. 3d 417, 89 Ill. Dec. 328, 480 N.E.2d 513 (2 Dist. 1985).

Financial inability is a relative term and is not to be equated with destitution. In re Smith, 128 Ill. App. 3d 1017, 84 Ill. Dec. 242, 471 N.E.2d 1008 (2 Dist. 1984).

It is sufficient to support an award of fees if the party seeking the fees would be stripped of financial resources if required to pay. In re Zannis, 114 Ill. App. 3d 1034, 70 Ill. Dec. 545, 449 N.E.2d 892 (1 Dist. 1983).

Where the only evidence presented by plaintiff concerning attorney fees was that he owed his counsel about $400, and where there was no evidence that he was unable to pay the fees, the trial court's order denying plaintiff's request for attorney fees would not be disturbed. Mitchell v. Mitchell, 54 Ill. App. 3d 18, 11 Ill. Dec. 822, 369 N.E.2d 276 (1 Dist. 1977).

Under former Ill.Rev.Stat., ch. 40, para. 16 (see now this section), in order to justify allowance of attorney's fees in a divorce action, the party seeking such relief was required to show financial inability to pay the fees and the ability of the other spouse to do so. Stotlar v. Stotlar, 50 Ill. App. 3d 790, 8 Ill. Dec. 711, 365 N.E.2d 1097 (5 Dist. 1977).

It is well settled that the granting of attorney fees in a divorce action is discretionary with the trial court, but depends, nonetheless, on the relative ability to pay. Rosenbaum v. Rosenbaum, 38 Ill. App. 3d 1, 349 N.E.2d 73 (1 Dist. 1976).

The allowance of attorney fees in divorce matters is a discretionary matter; however, the allowance is justified only when the court finds that one spouse is financially unable to pay the fees and the other spouse is able to do so. Cimino v. Cimino, 93 Ill. App. 2d 412, 236 N.E.2d 299 (1 Dist. 1968).

Granting of fees in a divorce case is proper when there is a showing of the financial inability of one party to pay the fees and the ability of the other to do so. Patterson v. Patterson, 28 Ill. App. 2d 76, 170 N.E.2d 11 (4 Dist. 1960); Lauzen v. Lauzen, 81 Ill. App. 2d 472, 225 N.E.2d 427 (2 Dist. 1967); Breuer v. Breuer, 4 Ill. App. 3d 179, 280 N.E.2d 518 (1 Dist. 1972); Gold v. Gold, 17 Ill. App. 3d 11, 308 N.E.2d 75 (1 Dist. 1974); Kinzora v. Kinzora, 37 Ill. App. 3d 290, 345 N.E.2d 499 (4 Dist. 1976); In re Fleming, 80 Ill. App. 3d 1006, 36 Ill. Dec. 205, 400 N.E.2d 625 (2 Dist. 1980); In re Dulyn, 89 Ill. App. 3d 304, 44 Ill. Dec. 622, 411 N.E.2d 988 (1 Dist. 1980); In re Thornton, 89 Ill. App. 3d 1078, 45 Ill. Dec. 612, 412 N.E.2d 1336 (1 Dist. 1980); Bellow v. Bellow, 94 Ill. App. 3d 361, 50 Ill. Dec. 656, 419 N.E.2d 924 (1 Dist. 1981); In re Roth, 99 Ill. App. 3d 679, 55 Ill. Dec. 271, 426 N.E.2d 246 (1 Dist. 1981); In re Donahoe, 114 Ill. App. 3d 470, 70 Ill. Dec. 152, 448 N.E.2d 1030 (2 Dist. 1983); Goforth v. Goforth, 121 Ill. App. 3d 673, 77 Ill. Dec. 125, 459 N.E.2d 1374 (5 Dist. 1984); In re Bussey, 108 Ill. 2d 286, 91 Ill. Dec. 594, 483 N.E.2d 1229 (1985); In re Holder, 137 Ill. App. 3d 596, 91 Ill. Dec. 926, 484 N.E.2d 485 (5 Dist. 1985); In re Wettstein, 160 Ill. App. 3d 554, 113 Ill. Dec. 1, 514 N.E.2d 783 (4 Dist. 1987); In re Hazard, 167 Ill. App. 3d 61, 117 Ill. Dec. 770, 520 N.E.2d 1121 (1 Dist. 1988); In re Ziemer, 189 Ill. App. 3d 966, 137 Ill. Dec. 475, 546 N.E.2d 229 (4 Dist. 1989); In re Gable, 205 Ill. App. 3d 696, 151 Ill. Dec. 109, 563 N.E.2d 1215 (5 Dist. 1990); In re Jaster, 222 Ill. App. 3d 122, 164 Ill. Dec. 743, 583 N.E.2d 659 (2 Dist. 1991); In re Kennedy, 214 Ill. App. 3d 849, 158 Ill. Dec. 172, 573 N.E.2d 1357 (1 Dist. 1991); In re Marthens, 215 Ill. App. 3d 590, 159 Ill. Dec. 3, 575 N.E.2d 3 (3 Dist. 1991); In re Parker, 216 Ill. App. 3d 672, 159 Ill. Dec. 131, 575 N.E.2d 938 (2 Dist. 1991).

—Burden of Proof

Respondent/husband could not contest petitioner/wife's alleged failure to prove his financial ability to pay her fees where his own conduct contributed to any deficiencies in her proof. In re Blinderman, 283 Ill. App. 3d 26, 218 Ill. Dec. 544, 669 N.E.2d 687 (1 Dist. 1996).

Assuming that the payment of attorney fees rests primarily with the party for whom the services were rendered, the spouse seeking attorney fees must show she is financially unable to pay the fees while the other spouse is able to do so. In re Siddens, 225 Ill. App. 3d 496, 167 Ill. Dec. 680, 588 N.E.2d 321 (5 Dist.), appeal denied, 145 Ill. 2d 644, 173 Ill. Dec. 13, 596 N.E.2d 637 (1992).

A party who received a cash award of approximately $70,000 and was not without the capacity to eventually acquire the training that could enable her to earn future income failed to carry her burden of proving either her financial inability to pay her own attorney fees or her husband's ability to pay them for her. In re Bauer, 138 Ill. App. 3d 379, 93 Ill. Dec. 108, 485 N.E.2d 1318 (1 Dist. 1985).

In order to justify an allowance to a wife in a divorce action of attorney fees from the husband, it is necessary that the complainant make a proper demand for such fees, show that she is financially unable to pay them herself and that her husband is able to do so. Jones v. Jones, 48 Ill. App. 2d 232, 198 N.E.2d 195 (1 Dist. 1964).

—Custodial Parents

A court shall award reasonable attorney fees incurred by custodial parents during child support enforcement proceedings if the court finds that noncustodial parent's failure to pay was without cause or justification. Davis v. Sprague, 186 Ill. App. 3d 249, 133 Ill. Dec. 620, 541 N.E.2d 831 (4 Dist. 1989).

—Destitution

Where regardless of the portion petitioner received from the marital estate, she would be basically destitute, the entire attorney fee award, which certainly appeared reasonable, should have been paid by respondent. In re Booth, 255 Ill. App. 3d 707, 194 Ill. Dec. 500, 627 N.E.2d 1142 (4 Dist. 1993).

—Determination

Trial court erred in awarding attorney fees to mother in child support modification case, as the mother did not show that she had a financial inability to pay the fees; the mother's financial disclosure statement indicated that she had a savings account with a large balance, as well as other financial assets, and, thus, was well able to pay her own attorney fees. In re Marriage of Adams, 348 Ill. App. 3d 340, 284 Ill. Dec. 124, 809 N.E.2d 246, 2004 Ill. App. LEXIS 435 (3 Dist. 2004).

The trial court must consider the financial circumstances of the parties to ascertain if one ex-spouse has an inability to pay and the other ex-spouse has the ability to pay attorney fees incurred by the opposing party. In re Mantei, 222 Ill. App. 3d 933, 164 Ill. Dec. 870, 583 N.E.2d 1192 (4 Dist. 1991).

A party seeking an award of attorney fees must show a financial inability to pay the fees and a corresponding ability of the ex-spouse to do so; financial inability to pay does not require a showing of destitution and the party seeking fees should not be required to liquidate assets to pay their own fees before there can be a finding of inability. In re Vest, 208 Ill. App. 3d 325, 153 Ill. Dec. 332, 567

Ability to Pay (Cont'd)

—Determination (Cont'd)

N.E.2d 47 (5 Dist.), cert. denied, 141 Ill. 2d 562, 162 Ill. Dec. 510, 580 N.E.2d 136 (1991).

Neither the trial judge's inability to determine what respondent's income would be, nor the determination that respondent had not shown her inability to pay fees by a failure to show why she was incapable of gaining full-time employment, was a sufficient basis upon which to deny attorney fees. Edsey v. Edsey, 199 Ill. App. 3d 39, 144 Ill. Dec. 874, 556 N.E.2d 552 (1 Dist. 1990).

Attorney's fees in a dissolution of marriage proceeding are the primary obligation of the party for whom the services are rendered; the allowance of attorney's fees to the opposing party is justified, however, where the party seeking relief shows financial inability to pay and the ability of the other spouse to do so; financial inability exists where to enforce payment of available funds would strip the person of the means of her support and undermine her economic stability. In re Garelick, 168 Ill. App. 3d 321, 119 Ill. Dec. 76, 522 N.E.2d 738 (1 Dist. 1988).

A party seeking an award of attorney fees must show a financial inability to pay the fees and a corresponding ability of the ex-spouse to do so; financial inability to pay does not require a showing of destitution. In re Stadheim, 170 Ill. App. 3d 19, 120 Ill. Dec. 373, 523 N.E.2d 1284 (1 Dist. 1988).

It is not necessary for a party to be destitute in order for the trial court to award attorney fees, as an award is justified if disbursement of the party's funds would exhaust her own estate or strip her of her means of support and undermine her economic stability. In re Zummo, 167 Ill. App. 3d 566, 118 Ill. Dec. 339, 521 N.E.2d 621 (4 Dist. 1988).

A party seeking an award of attorney fees must show a financial inability to pay and a corresponding ability of the other spouse to do so; financial inability to pay does not require a showing of destitution, nor is it necessary for a spouse seeking such fees to divest herself of capital assets or deplete her means of support and thereby undermine her economic stability. In re Felson, 171 Ill. App. 3d 923, 121 Ill. Dec. 796, 525 N.E.2d 1103 (1 Dist. 1988).

The controlling consideration in determining whether to grant attorney fees is the relative financial resources of the parties and the awarding of attorney fees under this statute is based on a showing of the inability of one spouse to pay and the ability of the other spouse to do so. Doss, Puchalski, Keenan & Bargiel, Ltd. v. Cockhill, 72 Bankr. 339 (Bankr. N.D. Ill. 1987).

In awarding fees, the court looks to the relative financial position of the parties, and the party seeking attorney fees must show an inability to pay and the ability of the other spouse to do so. In re Gibbons, 158 Ill. App. 3d 998, 111 Ill. Dec. 148, 512 N.E.2d 52 (4 Dist. 1987).

When the financial and other circumstances of both parties are substantially similar and where the wife's inability and the husband's ability to pay has not been shown, an award of attorney fees is an abuse of discretion. In re Moriarty, 132 Ill. App. 3d 895, 88 Ill. Dec. 222, 478 N.E.2d 537 (1 Dist. 1985).

The court may order an ex-spouse to pay attorney fees where the party seeking payment of fees demonstrates her own financial inability to pay them and the ability of her ex-spouse to pay the fees. In re Erickson, 136 Ill. App. 3d 907, 91 Ill. Dec. 346, 483 N.E.2d 692 (2 Dist. 1985).

Although the award of fees is within the sound discretion of the trial court, the party seeking an award must show financial inability to pay the fees, as well as the ability of the other spouse to pay them. In re Savas, 139 Ill. App. 3d 68, 93 Ill. Dec. 483, 486 N.E.2d 1318 (1 Dist. 1985).

An award of attorney fees requires a consideration of the financial resources of the parties and is justified when the party seeking relief demonstrates financial inability to pay coupled with the ability of the other spouse to do so; however, financial inability is not to be equated with destitution, and it exists where payment of fees would strip the individual of his or her means of support and undermine his or her economic stability. In re Siegel, 123 Ill. App. 3d 710, 79 Ill. Dec. 219, 463 N.E.2d 773 (1 Dist. 1984).

An allowance of attorney fees is never automatic and is not mandated simply by a showing that one spouse has a slightly greater ability to pay the fees; however, financial inability for purposes of awarding attorney fees in a divorce proceeding exists where payment of fees would strip the individual of his or her means of support and undermine his or her economic stability. In re Macaluso, 110 Ill. App. 3d 838, 66 Ill. Dec. 478, 443 N.E.2d 1 (2 Dist. 1982).

Financial inability does not necessarily mean that the party would be destitute as a result of paying his or her own fees. In re Macaluso, 110 Ill. App. 3d 838, 66 Ill. Dec. 478, 443 N.E.2d 1 (2 Dist. 1982).

Where the court's finding that petitioner was well employed and financially solvent was supportive of its decision to deny her attorney fees, but where it was also possible that the trial court's decision on attorney fees was based in part on its holding that the petitioner was not entitled to succeed on her petition, the question of attorney fees was remanded. Luthy v. Luthy, 95 Ill. App. 3d 987, 51 Ill. Dec. 350, 420 N.E.2d 764 (3 Dist. 1981).

It is not necessary that the spouse seeking fees be destitute; it is sufficient that disbursement of his funds would exhaust his estate, or strip him of his means of support and undermine his economic stability. In re Roth, 99 Ill. App. 3d 679, 55 Ill. Dec. 271, 426 N.E.2d 246 (1 Dist. 1981).

Although allowance of fees rests largely in the trial court's discretion, such an award will be reversed when the financial circumstances of both parties are substantially similar and where the party seeking fees has not shown his inability to pay. In re Roth, 99 Ill. App. 3d 679, 55 Ill. Dec. 271, 426 N.E.2d 246 (1 Dist. 1981).

Where plaintiff did not show an inability to pay her own attorney fees in that the requirement that she pay her own fees would neither exhaust her estate nor undermine her economic stability, an order which provided that defendant must contribute toward plaintiff's attorney fees was reversed. In re Roth, 99 Ill. App. 3d 679, 55 Ill. Dec. 271, 426 N.E.2d 246 (1 Dist. 1981).

In order to justify the allowance of attorney fees, one must show a financial inability to pay; however, inability to pay does not suggest an absolute lack of funds, but rather a situation where payment would undermine the party's economic stability. In re Westphal, 99 Ill. App. 3d 1042, 55 Ill. Dec. 328, 426 N.E.2d 303 (3 Dist. 1981).

Financial inability to pay exists where payment of the fees and costs would strip the means of support and undermine the economic stability of a party. In re Brenner, 95 Ill. App. 3d 100, 50 Ill. Dec. 292, 419 N.E.2d 400 (1 Dist. 1981); In re Smith, 128 Ill. App. 3d 1017, 84 Ill. Dec. 242, 471 N.E.2d 1008 (2 Dist. 1984); In re Wright, 180 Ill. App. 3d 911, 129 Ill. Dec. 650, 536 N.E.2d 700 (1 Dist. 1986); In re Wettstein, 160 Ill. App. 3d 554, 113 Ill. Dec. 1, 514 N.E.2d 783 (4 Dist. 1987); In re Hazard, 167 Ill. App. 3d 61, 117 Ill. Dec. 770, 520 N.E.2d 1121 (1 Dist. 1988); In re Calisoff, 176 Ill. App. 3d 721, 126 Ill. Dec. 183, 531 N.E.2d 810 (1 Dist. 1988); In re Gable, 205 Ill. App. 3d 696, 151 Ill. Dec. 109, 563 N.E.2d 1215 (5 Dist. 1990).

Where no evidentiary hearing took place on the issue of fees, where evidence had earlier been presented by the parties as to petitioner's assets and potential for employment, and where petitioner testified that, apart from the marital property, she owned no assets, that she was a housewife and was unemployed, the trial court's finding that the petitioner's ability to pay was remote constituted sufficient compliance with this Act. In re Shedbalkar, 95 Ill. App. 3d 136, 50 Ill. Dec. 301, 419 N.E.2d 409 (1 Dist. 1981).

Where the division of marital property by the trial court was improper, remand of the entire cause for a new trial was warranted so that the maintenance and child support awards and the decision to allow or deny attorney fees could be determined in view of the resources available to the wife after an equitable division of marital property was effected. In re White, 98 Ill. App. 3d 380, 53 Ill. Dec. 786, 424 N.E.2d 421 (5 Dist. 1981).

Financial inability to pay does not necessarily mean that a party would be destitute as a result of paying his own fees, as inability to pay in these circumstances implies a relative inability to pay; financial inability exists when a disbursement of the party's available funds would undermine that person's economic stability. In re Scott, 85 Ill. App. 3d 773, 41 Ill. Dec. 547, 407 N.E.2d 1045 (2 Dist. 1980).

The allowance of attorney fees in a divorce proceeding is not automatic but depends upon the showing that one of the parties is financially unable to pay the fees and that the opposing party does have such ability. Carr v. Borowczyk, 78 Ill. App. 3d 425, 33 Ill. Dec. 738, 397 N.E.2d 71 (1 Dist. 1979).

Trial court improperly denied petitioner's motion for attorney fees arising out of an action brought pursuant to former section 72

Ability to Pay (Cont'd)

—Determination (Cont'd)

of the Civil Practice Act (see now 735 ILCS 5/2-1401), where it failed to consider the respective financial resources of the parties. In re Held, 73 Ill. App. 3d 561, 29 Ill. Dec. 612, 392 N.E.2d 169 (5 Dist. 1979).

The allowance of attorney fees in a divorce proceeding is not automatic but depends upon the showing that one of the parties is financially unable to pay the fees and that the opposing party does have such ability. Carr v. Borowczyk, 78 Ill. App. 3d 425, 33 Ill. Dec. 738, 397 N.E.2d 71 (1 Dist. 1979).

Under former Ill.Rev.Stat., ch. 40, para. 16 (see now this section), where the evidence at trial adequately established plaintiff's inability to pay her attorney fees, and defendant's ability to do so, the circuit court was directed to conduct further proceedings to determine just and equitable attorneys fees and to enter an appropriate order making defendant liable for them. Sullivan v. Sullivan, 68 Ill. App. 3d 242, 24 Ill. Dec. 719, 385 N.E.2d 860 (5 Dist. 1979).

Attorney fees may be awarded in post-decree proceedings in the trial court to modify the provisions of the decree; the allowance of attorney fees falls within the discretion of the trial court, and, in order to justify such an allowance, the moving party must show a financial inability to pay and the ability of the other party to do so. Winter v. Winter, 69 Ill. App. 3d 359, 25 Ill. Dec. 819, 387 N.E.2d 695 (1 Dist. 1978).

The granting of fees in a divorce case is proper when there is a showing of the financial inability of one party to pay the fees and the ability of the other to do so; however, financial disability is not equated with destitution, and to support an award of fees it is sufficient that the party seeking the fees would be stripped of his or her financial resources if required to pay. Christian v. Christian, 69 Ill. App. 3d 450, 26 Ill. Dec. 326, 387 N.E.2d 1254 (1 Dist. 1979).

Award of attorney's fees was reversed and remanded to the trial court for a proper hearing concerning the ability of plaintiff and defendant to pay all or part of the attorney fees. Lewanski v. Lewanski, 59 Ill. App. 3d 805, 16 Ill. Dec. 854, 375 N.E.2d 961 (1 Dist. 1978).

Allowance of attorney fees under the former Divorce Act (see now this Act) depended upon a showing that one of the parties was financially unable to pay his own fees and that the opposing party did have such ability; if the spouse requesting attorneys fees was unable to pay those fees out of her own funds or out of any award of alimony, whether periodic or in gross, reasonable attorneys fees and costs could be allowed. McArdle v. McArdle, 55 Ill. App. 3d 829, 13 Ill. Dec. 282, 370 N.E.2d 1309 (3 Dist. 1977).

Although the allowance of attorney fees rests in the discretion of the trial court, in order to justify such allowance, the complainant must show financial inability to pay and the ability of the spouse to do so. Woodshank v. Woodshank, 13 Ill. App. 3d 692, 300 N.E.2d 494 (3 Dist. 1973); Scott v. Scott, 75 Ill. App. 3d 710, 31 Ill. Dec. 577, 394 N.E.2d 779 (2 Dist. 1979).

Where the plaintiff did not have sufficient financial ability to pay her attorney fees and costs, and defendant did have capacity to pay the additional attorney fees and costs, the defendant was properly assessed the attorney fees. Woodshank v. Woodshank, 13 Ill. App. 3d 692, 300 N.E.2d 494 (3 Dist. 1973).

—Disparity in Income

A trial court abuses its discretion in not awarding attorney fees under this section when the evidence reveals a great disparity in actual earnings and earning capacity. In re Carpel, 232 Ill. App. 3d 806, 173 Ill. Dec. 873, 597 N.E.2d 847 (4 Dist.), cert. denied, 147 Ill. 2d 625, 180 Ill. Dec. 148, 606 N.E.2d 1225 (1992).

Where, although the trial court found that both parties had sufficient assets or income to pay their own attorney fees, the evidence established a gross disparity in their actual income and income potential, which would warrant the trial court to award such fees, because the case was being returned to the trial court for further proceedings on other matters, the attorney fees could be considered on remand. In re Carpel, 232 Ill. App. 3d 806, 173 Ill. Dec. 873, 597 N.E.2d 847 (4 Dist.), cert. denied, 147 Ill. 2d 625, 180 Ill. Dec. 148, 606 N.E.2d 1225 (1992).

—Enforcement of Rights

A party who has been forced to resort to the judicial process to secure compliance with the terms of an order or judgment is entitled to her reasonable attorney fees even absent a showing of inability to pay. In re Irvine, 215 Ill. App. 3d 629, 160 Ill. Dec. 332, 577 N.E.2d 462 (4 Dist. 1991).

The trial court has no discretion as to whether to award reasonable attorney fees and costs incurred in enforcement of its orders, for if the failure to pay was without cause of justification, the award of reasonable attorney fees is mandatory. In re Irvine, 215 Ill. App. 3d 629, 160 Ill. Dec. 332, 577 N.E.2d 462 (4 Dist. 1991).

Where defendant's net income was higher than plaintiff's, where plaintiff had the custodial expense of her son, and where defendant's actions required plaintiff to be involved in substantial judicial processes to enforce her rights, the trial court's ruling denying plaintiff's request for fees and costs was against the manifest weight of the evidence. Carnes v. Dressen, 215 Ill. App. 3d 166, 158 Ill. Dec. 732, 574 N.E.2d 845 (4 Dist. 1991).

An order for attorney fees under subsection (b) of this section does not permit the balancing tests normally applicable to the question of attorney fees; instead, under this subsection, the court is simply to decide what the costs and reasonable attorney fees of the prevailing party are and to order them paid by the party found to have failed to comply with the order or judgment without cause or justification. The legislature intended this result to serve as a sanction against parties in marital cases who wilfully disobey court orders. In re Young, 200 Ill. App. 3d 226, 147 Ill. Dec. 178, 559 N.E.2d 178 (4 Dist. 1990).

Where husband was found in contempt for failing to comply with a dissolution order, the trial court correctly found that wife was entitled to an award for attorney fees incurred in connection with the enforcement of that order, regardless of husband's ability to pay. In re Wiley, 199 Ill. App. 3d 223, 145 Ill. Dec. 170, 556 N.E.2d 788 (4 Dist. 1990).

Given that the instant action was brought to enforce the agreement which was made a part of the order of dissolution and that subsection (b) of this section does not require the court to determine the financial abilities of the parties prior to awarding attorney fees in such actions, the trial court was not required to consider the financial ability of petitioner to pay her attorney fees. In re Talmadge, 179 Ill. App. 3d 806, 128 Ill. Dec. 751, 534 N.E.2d 1356 (2 Dist. 1989).

A party who must seek court enforcement of the terms of a judgment of dissolution is entitled to reasonable attorney fees, even absent a showing of that party's inability to pay the fees and the other party's ability to pay, where the failure to comply with the terms of the judgment is without cause or justification. In re Cierny, 187 Ill. App. 3d 334, 134 Ill. Dec. 918, 543 N.E.2d 201 (1 Dist. 1989).

Subsection (b) of this section is a mandatory provision by which the trial court must, in a child support enforcement proceeding, order the noncustodial parent to pay the custodial parent's costs and reasonable attorney fees. In re Wassom, 165 Ill. App. 3d 1076, 116 Ill. Dec. 932, 519 N.E.2d 1147 (4 Dist. 1988).

Where an ex-husband received a cash disbursement of his pension plan, he should have honored his divorce settlement agreement and divorce decree and paid to his deceased ex-wife's estate the portion due her under the agreement; since the estate was obligated to bring suit and appeal to enforce the decree and agreement, the estate of the deceased was entitled to recover attorney fees. In re Olsen, 124 Ill. 2d 19, 123 Ill. Dec. 980, 528 N.E.2d 684 (1988).

While respondent may not have wilfully and contemptuously miscalculated when he multiplied $50 per week by four weeks to arrive at his payment of $200 per month, the respondent failed to pay without cause or justification and therefore was obligated to reimburse petitioner for reasonable attorney fees. In re Kennedy, 170 Ill. App. 3d 726, 121 Ill. Dec. 362, 525 N.E.2d 168 (5 Dist. 1988).

Where the trial court explicitly found that husband's failure to pay child support was without cause or justification, no finding of wife's financial circumstances was necessary by the court in order to award her attorney fees pursuant to this section. In re Robertson, 151 Ill. App. 3d 214, 104 Ill. Dec. 619, 502 N.E.2d 1279 (1 Dist. 1986).

A party who must use judicial process to enforce rights under, and to secure compliance with, the terms of a divorce judgment is entitled to reasonable attorney fees, even absent a showing of the party's inability to pay. In re Moriarty, 132 Ill. App. 3d 895, 88 Ill. Dec. 222, 478 N.E.2d 537 (1 Dist. 1985).

Ability to Pay (Cont'd)

—Enforcement of Rights (Cont'd)

Where a guardian ad litem was specifically authorized to defend the interests of a ward in court, and where a defense in court necessarily entailed legal representation, it was proper to award attorney fees to the guardian ad litem. In re Hirsch, 135 Ill. App. 3d 945, 90 Ill. Dec. 646, 482 N.E.2d 625 (1 Dist. 1985).

Subsection (b) of this section is a mandatory provision which required the trial court to order the parent against whom a child support enforcement action was brought to pay the costs and reasonable attorney fees incurred by the custodial parent in bringing the action when the delinquent parent failed to pay support without cause or justification. In re Chenoweth, 134 Ill. App. 3d 1015, 89 Ill. Dec. 922, 481 N.E.2d 765 (5 Dist. 1985).

When it becomes necessary for a party to go into court in order to enforce rights under a judgment of dissolution, the party who is thus forced to resort to judicial process to secure compliance with the judgment is entitled to her reasonable attorney fees even absent a showing of inability to pay those fees. In re Donahoe, 114 Ill. App. 3d 470, 70 Ill. Dec. 152, 448 N.E.2d 1030 (2 Dist. 1983).

When it becomes necessary for one to retain an attorney for the purpose of enforcing a previously entered child support order, she is entitled to reasonable attorney fees, provided the financial standards of the Act are met. Coons v. Wilder, 93 Ill. App. 3d 127, 48 Ill. Dec. 512, 416 N.E.2d 785 (2 Dist. 1981).

—Financial Resources

Requiring petitioner to pay her own attorney and expert witness fees would neither undermine her financial stability nor strip her of her means of support. In re Puls, 268 Ill. App. 3d 882, 206 Ill. Dec. 520, 645 N.E.2d 525 (1 Dist. 1994).

Under subsection (b), it is not necessary for the petitioning party to show an inability to pay, or the relative financial position of the parties. In re Sanda, 245 Ill. App. 3d 314, 184 Ill. Dec. 186, 612 N.E.2d 1346 (2 Dist. 1993).

Where petitioner would be unable to pay her attorney fees and costs without depleting part of the marital assets awarded to her and respondent would be able to pay his fees as well as petitioner's fees without depleting assets, based on his income and additional bonuses, it was appropriate that respondent pay all of the fees. Haas v. Haas, 215 Ill. App. 3d 959, 158 Ill. Dec. 983, 574 N.E.2d 1376 (3 Dist. 1991).

A spouse need not sell her assets in order to pay attorney fees. Kusper v. Kusper, 195 Ill. App. 3d 494, 142 Ill. Dec. 282, 552 N.E.2d 1023 (1 Dist. 1990).

The court did not abuse its discretion in requiring husband to pay $3,500 of wife's attorney fees, where the court could have found from the evidence presented that wife was financially unable to pay the fees and doing so would have undermined her economic stability, and, that with husband's income, he had the ability to pay. In re Jacks, 200 Ill. App. 3d 112, 146 Ill. Dec. 143, 558 N.E.2d 106 (2 Dist. 1990).

Where the lack of evidence of respondent's ability to pay was the direct result of his refusal to present evidence of his financial condition, respondent waived the issue of his ability or inability to pay the attorney fees. In re Cierny, 187 Ill. App. 3d 334, 134 Ill. Dec. 918, 543 N.E.2d 201 (1 Dist. 1989).

Where the trial court determined that wife was financially unable to pay her attorney fees while husband had the ability to do so, the court was well within its discretion in requiring husband to pay the wife's attorney fees. In re Stadheim, 170 Ill. App. 3d 19, 120 Ill. Dec. 373, 523 N.E.2d 1284 (1 Dist. 1988).

Trial court did not err in finding that neither husband nor wife was in a financial position to pay their own attorney fees or that the husband did not have the financial ability to pay the wife's fees and costs where the record established that the husband's monthly expenses exceeded his income by approximately $120. In re Einhorn, 178 Ill. App. 3d 212, 127 Ill. Dec. 411, 533 N.E.2d 29 (1 Dist. 1988).

Trial court properly exercised its discretion in requiring husband to pay a portion of wife's attorney fees where it carefully considered the financial position of each party. In re Felson, 171 Ill. App. 3d 923, 121 Ill. Dec. 796, 525 N.E.2d 1103 (1 Dist. 1988).

Where wife's income was held to be insufficient to cover costs and fees incurred during lengthy litigation and as the husband had superior earning power and potential for acquiring additional assets, he was better able to bear costs. Head v. Head, 168 Ill. App. 3d 697, 119 Ill. Dec. 549, 523 N.E.2d 17 (1 Dist. 1988).

Wife was not required to convert substantial marital assets into cash to pay her own attorney fees, as a party need not deplete savings or divest herself of assets awarded to her to enable her to pay attorney fees. Head v. Head, 168 Ill. App. 3d 697, 119 Ill. Dec. 549, 523 N.E.2d 17 (1 Dist. 1988).

Although respondent was not without financial resources, she was not required by law to deplete her capital assets or strip her means of support or undermine her economic stability in order to pay her own fees; accordingly, the court did not abuse its discretion in holding that while respondent had the ability to pay, to do so would substantially deplete her source of income and therefore, petitioner should contribute $7,500 toward payment of $20,015 fee. In re McFarlane, 160 Ill. App. 3d 721, 112 Ill. Dec. 537, 513 N.E.2d 1146 (2 Dist. 1987).

Former wife was not entitled to an award of attorney fees where the financial resources of the parties were not considered by the trial court. Padgett v. Padgett, 157 Ill. App. 3d 492, 109 Ill. Dec. 567, 510 N.E.2d 435 (5 Dist. 1987).

Evidence was sufficient to conclude one spouse showed an inability to pay attorney fees and other spouse's ability to do so. In re Wettstein, 160 Ill. App. 3d 554, 113 Ill. Dec. 1, 514 N.E.2d 783 (4 Dist. 1987).

Petitioner's income was insufficient to cover the costs and fees incurred during divorce litigation and because of his superior earning power and potential for acquiring additional assets, respondent was better able to bear those expenses. In re Skahn, 149 Ill. App. 3d 764, 103 Ill. Dec. 208, 501 N.E.2d 229 (1 Dist. 1986).

Although petitioner was awarded substantial marital and nonmarital assets, she was not capable of assuming responsibility for her own attorney fees. In re Skahn, 149 Ill. App. 3d 764, 103 Ill. Dec. 208, 501 N.E.2d 229 (1 Dist. 1986).

The trial judge exercised sound discretion in awarding wife $7,500 in attorney fees, even though she asked for a significantly greater amount, where the parties' financial abilities were substantially similar and where the husband had fallen on economic hard times; however, the court also did not abuse its discretion in awarding some fees to the wife in view of the fact that she had to call upon the legal system to attack a divorce secured by her husband. In re Passiales, 144 Ill. App. 3d 629, 98 Ill. Dec. 419, 494 N.E.2d 541 (1 Dist. 1986).

Even assuming an incidental benefit to the children under a clause requiring payment of taxes on marital estate, this was not a provision for child support, and the trial court could properly award attorney fees in its discretion upon a finding of inability to pay on the part of petitioner and respondent's ability to pay. In re Dodge, 150 Ill. App. 3d 486, 103 Ill. Dec. 816, 501 N.E.2d 1354 (2 Dist. 1986).

A denial of fees for wife's defense of post-decree motions brought by the husband was proper where the evidence showed that the parties continued to have the financial means to pay their own attorney fees. In re Wardell, 149 Ill. App. 3d 537, 102 Ill. Dec. 859, 500 N.E.2d 960 (2 Dist. 1986).

Where it did not appear that requiring plaintiff to pay her own attorney fees would strip her of her means of support or undermine her economic stability, fees were not awarded. In re Ryan, 138 Ill. App. 3d 1077, 93 Ill. Dec. 617, 487 N.E.2d 61 (1 Dist. 1985).

Where the record supported a finding that petitioner was financially unable to pay the fees, the evidence failed to sustain the finding that the income of respondent was then equal to his expenses; thus, the record failed to sufficiently show respondent's financial ability to pay the fees and, the award of $2,800 against respondent on account of prospective fees to defend an appeal was reversed. In re Savas, 139 Ill. App. 3d 68, 93 Ill. Dec. 483, 486 N.E.2d 1318 (1 Dist. 1985).

Since the ability to pay by either spouse was based largely upon the valuation and just distribution of the parties' assets, in the absence of evidence of valuation of such assets, award of attorney fees would be reversed. In re Cuisance, 115 Ill. App. 3d 551, 71 Ill. Dec. 423, 450 N.E.2d 1302 (1 Dist. 1983).

A review of the financial positions of the parties supported the conclusion that husband was in a superior position to acquire income and additional capital assets which would enable him to contribute to the payment of wife's attorney fees. In re McNeeley, 117 Ill. App. 3d 320, 72 Ill. Dec. 873, 453 N.E.2d 748 (1 Dist. 1983).

Ability to Pay (Cont'd)

—Financial Resources (Cont'd)

Husband should not have been ordered to pay attorney fees incurred by wife in defending appeal because there was no evidence in the record to indicate he had the financial ability to pay these fees. In re Sevon, 117 Ill. App. 3d 313, 73 Ill. Dec. 41, 453 N.E.2d 866 (1 Dist. 1983).

In assessing the relative financial resources of the parties, the trial court found that respondent had substantially greater resources and a greater potential and capacity for future earnings, and therefore the court did not err in requiring respondent to pay attorney fees incurred by petitioner. In re Carini, 112 Ill. App. 3d 375, 67 Ill. Dec. 932, 445 N.E.2d 412 (1 Dist. 1983).

The granting of fees in a divorce case is proper when there is a showing of the financial inability of one party to pay the fees and the ability of the other to do so; however, financial inability is not equated with destitution, and the fact that the party seeking the fees would be stripped of his or her financial resources if required to pay is sufficient to support the award of fees. In re Ligas, 110 Ill. App. 3d 1, 65 Ill. Dec. 763, 441 N.E.2d 1277 (1 Dist. 1982).

An award of attorney fees requires consideration of the financial resources of the parties, and is left to the sound discretion of the trial court, reversible only for an abuse of discretion. In re Macaluso, 110 Ill. App. 3d 838, 66 Ill. Dec. 478, 443 N.E.2d 1 (2 Dist. 1982).

An award of attorney fees is justified when the party seeking relief demonstrates financial inability to pay coupled with the ability of the former spouse to do so. In re Macaluso, 110 Ill. App. 3d 838, 66 Ill. Dec. 478, 443 N.E.2d 1 (2 Dist. 1982).

Evidence was sufficient to establish wife's financial inability to pay the full amount expended in attorney fees, as well as husband's ability to do so. In re Macaluso, 110 Ill. App. 3d 838, 66 Ill. Dec. 478, 443 N.E.2d 1 (2 Dist. 1982).

Where parties' earnings were substantially equal, and where petitioner received a substantial cash award while respondent was left with relatively no liquid assets, petitioner had not shown an inability to pay her own attorney fees. In re Wojcicki, 109 Ill. App. 3d 569, 65 Ill. Dec. 173, 440 N.E.2d 1028 (1 Dist. 1982).

The criteria for determining whose obligations the attorney fees will be in a divorce action is similar to the criteria for determining whether a spouse is entitled to alimony; the court must consider the financial resources of the parties. Richards v. Loncar, 14 Bankr. 276 (N.D. Ill. 1981).

The circuit court's order requiring defendant to pay a portion of the attorney fees incurred by plaintiff was in error where plaintiff could pay for her own attorney without undermining her economic stability. In re Westphal, 99 Ill. App. 3d 1042, 55 Ill. Dec. 328, 426 N.E.2d 303 (3 Dist. 1981).

Considering the relative financial resources of the parties, it was not against the manifest weight of the evidence that respondent had to pay petitioner attorney's fees for defense of the cross appeal where petitioner owned stock worth $1,500, had funds in bank accounts totaling $220, had no regular income from employment, was receiving $900 per month from respondent, and had to borrow money for her living expenses. In re Hellwig, 100 Ill. App. 3d 452, 55 Ill. Dec. 762, 426 N.E.2d 1087 (1 Dist. 1981).

Where an attorney seeks fees from his own client pursuant to subsection (a) of this section, the purpose of the proceeding is not to enable the less affluent spouse to maintain or defend the action but is directed to promoting judicial economy by eliminating the former requirement that an attorney bring a separate suit for such fees against his own client; regardless of the respective financial circumstances of the spouses, an attorney is still entitled to seek payment for his services from his own client and the legislature in providing this procedure did not intend that it be conditioned upon the financial abilities of the parties. In re Ransom, 102 Ill. App. 3d 38, 57 Ill. Dec. 696, 429 N.E.2d 594 (2 Dist. 1981).

The lack of evidence concerning the relative financial position of parties required remand for a hearing to determine the financial ability of the parties and the determination of the question of attorney fees. In re Kolb, 99 Ill. App. 3d 895, 55 Ill. Dec. 128, 425 N.E.2d 1301 (1 Dist. 1981).

Although respondent's income was rather inadequate to his obligations, the petitioner was not able to pay attorney fees since she was unable to work consistently because of the demands of the minor children; the resources of the husband were limited, but the court's order requiring respondent to pay attorney fees was the only practical disposition possible. In re Piktel, 81 Ill. App. 3d 567, 36 Ill. Dec. 743, 401 N.E.2d 584 (2 Dist. 1980).

The court may order either spouse to pay the costs and fees incurred by the other party in any proceeding after considering the financial resources of the parties; no other considerations are mandated. In re Hammel, 88 Ill. App. 3d 919, 44 Ill. Dec. 351, 411 N.E.2d 320 (3 Dist. 1980).

Before one spouse may recover attorney fees from the other, the former must prove that he or she is unable to pay the fees and that the opposing party does have such ability. In re Jacobson, 89 Ill. App. 3d 273, 44 Ill. Dec. 581, 411 N.E.2d 947 (1 Dist. 1980).

After considering the financial resources of the parties, the court properly ordered that petitioner and respondent would be responsible for their own attorney fees. In re Gustke, 78 Ill. App. 3d 274, 33 Ill. Dec. 813, 397 N.E.2d 146 (1 Dist. 1979).

Although attorney fees may be awarded in connection with the defense of a proceeding under this Act, the criterion for assessing fees is the relative financial resources of the parties. In re Stewart, 79 Ill. App. 3d 1125, 35 Ill. Dec. 249, 398 N.E.2d 1199 (1 Dist. 1979).

Where husband was a pipe fitter, considered a skilled laborer earning $1,385 net per month and wife plaintiff was an unskilled clerical worker earning $173.65 net per week, the disparity between the earning capacities of the parties as well as their respective incomes was clear, and constituted a sufficient evidentiary basis for partial award of attorneys' fees. Gauger v. Gauger, 70 Ill. App. 3d 378, 26 Ill. Dec. 499, 388 N.E.2d 123 (1 Dist. 1979).

Where there was no evidence presented of the relative financial resources of the parties, the award of attorney fees was set aside. Blankenship v. Blankenship, 63 Ill. App. 3d 803, 20 Ill. Dec. 956, 380 N.E.2d 1165 (4 Dist. 1978).

Attorneys' fees in a divorce proceeding are the primary obligation of the party for whom the services are rendered, but where the plaintiff shows that he or she is financially unable to pay them and that the other spouse is able to do so, justification exists for an award of fees in favor of plaintiff. Moore v. Moore, 53 Ill. App. 3d 228, 10 Ill. Dec. 950, 368 N.E.2d 545 (1 Dist. 1977).

The assets wife received by the terms of the rulings of the trial court were worth approximately $95,000 and the value of the assets husband retained was of comparable magnitude, and thus each party was to bear the cost of his or her own attorney fees. McArdle v. McArdle, 55 Ill. App. 3d 829, 13 Ill. Dec. 282, 370 N.E.2d 1309 (3 Dist. 1977).

Where defendant in a divorce proceeding had an annual income of $16,000 and, outside of the receipt of alimony of $105 per week, the plaintiff's only income was $35 per week for the rental of a flat in her home, an award of attorney's fees to plaintiff was justified. Karaskiewicz v. Karaskiewicz, 38 Ill. App. 3d 509, 348 N.E.2d 184 (1 Dist. 1976).

Allowance of attorney fees is not automatic but depends upon a showing that one of the parties is financially unable to pay their own fees and that the opposing party does have such ability. Welsh v. Welsh, 38 Ill. App. 3d 35, 347 N.E.2d 512 (1 Dist. 1976).

Appellate court found no error in the trial court's decision that husband was obligated to pay wife's attorney fees for services rendered at the trial court level where husband had a greater financial ability to pay while the wife had a limited ability to pay. Goldberg v. Goldberg, 30 Ill. App. 3d 769, 332 N.E.2d 710 (1 Dist. 1975).

Where a trial court found no inability on plaintiff's part to pay her attorney fees, and there was nothing in this record which would indicate to the contrary, the trial court did not abuse its discretion in denying the allowance of attorney fees to plaintiff. Tuey v. Tuey, 20 Ill. App. 3d 445, 314 N.E.2d 371 (1 Dist. 1974).

A wife who is more financially able than her husband to pay her attorney's fees and expenses should not be allowed to recover from him. Lauzen v. Lauzen, 81 Ill. App. 2d 472, 225 N.E.2d 427 (2 Dist. 1967).

—Former Law

Under former Ill.Rev.Stat., ch. 40, para. 16 (see now this section), in order to justify allowance of attorney's fees in a divorce case, the party seeking the relief needed to show financial inability to pay and the ability of the other spouse to do so; however, financial inability was not synonymous with destitution for the income and assets of both parties were considered, and if use of the available funds of the party seeking the attorney's fees would strip the person

Ability to Pay (Cont'd)

—Former Law (Cont'd)

of the means of his support and undermine his economic stability, financial inability to pay such fees was shown. Sullivan v. Sullivan, 68 Ill. App. 3d 242, 24 Ill. Dec. 719, 385 N.E.2d 860 (5 Dist. 1979).

—Hearing

To justify the award of attorney fees, it must be shown that the party seeking this relief is financially unable to pay and that the other party is able to do so; however, when a party does not request a hearing on his ability to pay or his opponent's inability to pay, the right to such a hearing is waived and the court may base its decision on the financial conditions of the parties as shown by the record. In re Cierny, 187 Ill. App. 3d 334, 134 Ill. Dec. 918, 543 N.E.2d 201 (1 Dist. 1989).

—Installment Order

Few can afford the expense of divorce without incurring debt, which must be paid by someone; a party who does not have the present ability to pay his own attorney fees can nevertheless be ordered to pay his own attorney, although enforcement might have to be accomplished by an installment order. In re McCoy, 272 Ill. App. 3d 125, 208 Ill. Dec. 732, 650 N.E.2d 3 (4 Dist. 1995).

—Not Shown

Even though respondent had greater earning capacity he could not pay the bulk of petitioner's attorney's fees and continue to pay his own monthly expenses and attorney fees. In re Krivi, 283 Ill. App. 3d 772, 219 Ill. Dec. 274, 670 N.E.2d 1162 (5 Dist. 1996).

—Resources

The evidence did not demonstrate that petitioner was financially unable to pay her own attorney fees where she was earning approximately $16,000 per year, had savings of $1,500 and stock worth $2,842, and where the court awarded her ownership of the marital residence which had a market value of at least $142,000. In re Sanborn, 78 Ill. App. 3d 146, 33 Ill. Dec. 468, 396 N.E.2d 1192 (1 Dist. 1979).

—Shown

Petitioner failed to show that she was financially unable to pay her attorney fees where, according to the record of the hearing on her petition to modify child support, she had a gross income of $21,511 per year, she had received annual cost-of-living increases, and was likely to qualify for a 5% merit increase in 1991; she further testified that her home was worth approximately $45,000 and that her equity in the home was approximately $18,000, she owned a new automobile, and at the close of the hearing, the trial court increased her child support payments from $150 to $170 per week. In re Sparagowski, 232 Ill. App. 3d 257, 172 Ill. Dec. 931, 596 N.E.2d 210 (3 Dist. 1992).

Abuse of Discretion

—In General

It was error for the trial court to have reopened the proofs for determining attorney fees over defendant's objection in order to allow evidence tending to establish an obligation which was not considered by the parties in their agreed settlement, nor claimed at the prove-up. Pearson v. Pearson, 42 Ill. App. 3d 522, 1 Ill. Dec. 711, 356 N.E.2d 993 (2 Dist. 1976).

Where, in a court order without any further evidentiary hearings, the court allowed defendant leave to bring appeal as a poor person, while at the same time finding defendant financially able to pay plaintiff's attorney fees for an appeal, the findings of the trial court were sufficiently inconsistent to motivate the appellate court to conclude that the trial court abused its discretion in entering such order. Matthews v. Matthews, 42 Ill. App. 3d 1049, 1 Ill. Dec. 801, 356 N.E.2d 1083 (1 Dist. 1976).

The awarding of attorney fees lies within the sound discretion of the court, but if the opposite party has requested a hearing on the question of attorney fees, the court must hear some evidence on that point. Jones v. Jones, 48 Ill. App. 2d 232, 198 N.E.2d 195 (1 Dist. 1964).

In the absence of a request for the hearing of evidence, the chancellor could base an award of attorney fees on the financial circumstances of the parties as shown by the record, statements of counsel as to necessary services, and the chancellor's own experience. Kijowski v. Kijowski, 36 Ill. App. 2d 94, 183 N.E.2d 583 (1 Dist. 1962).

—Ability to Pay

Where wife was gainfully employed and enjoyed disposable income of approximately $379 per month, while husband was disabled on a fixed income of social security and was unable to maintain the modest lifestyle that the parties enjoyed during the course of the marriage, the trial court abused its discretion in ordering husband to pay any of wife's attorney fees. In re Ferkel, 260 Ill. App. 3d 33, 198 Ill. Dec. 522, 632 N.E.2d 1133 (5 Dist. 1994).

Where a court allowed an additional sum to defendant's attorney to defend the first appeal, this allowance was error, inasmuch as the defendant had assets with which to defend the appeal and could pay her attorney from her share of the proceeds of the sale of the parties' house. Altman v. Altman, 131 Ill. App. 2d 427, 268 N.E.2d 211 (1 Dist. 1971).

—Assessment of Fee in Advance

Where it was obvious the defendant had a one-half interest in the real estate and was not without assets with which to pay her attorney, it was an abuse of discretion and error for the trial judge to assess an advance attorney fee against plaintiff. Altman v. Altman, 131 Ill. App. 2d 427, 268 N.E.2d 211 (1 Dist. 1971).

—Not Shown

Based on an ex-wife's assets of $129,215.53, exclusive of the children's custodial accounts, her IRA, and her home equity, plus the substantial maintenance payments of $7,000 a month she was to receive for five years after the parties' divorce, a trial court did not abuse its discretion in ordering her to pay $4,000 of the $10,000 it determined to be a reasonable fee for post-dissolution attorney fees, notwithstanding the wife's law school expenses, which she was not required to pay in a lump sum and would not have to begin repaying until six months after her graduation. In re Marriage of Beeler, Ill. App. 3d , Ill. Dec. , N.E.2d , 2004 Ill. App. LEXIS 1400 (2 Dist. Nov. 19, 2004).

Trial court did not abuse its discretion in determining that $10,000, not the requested $70,000+, was a reasonable amount for the wife's attorneys fees in post-dissolution proceedings concerning the children's summer camp expenses and vacations. The issues were not complex, the disputed issues were minor, the drawn-out litigation was due to both parties' litigiousness and were not solely the fault of the husband, neither party "won" the majority of the claims, and the wife's attorneys did not submit any evidence that its firm's fees of $375 and $425 an hour were customary or that the wife needed their most experienced counsel for over 100 hours of the work that he billed. In re Marriage of Beeler, Ill. App. 3d , Ill. Dec. , N.E.2d , 2004 Ill. App. LEXIS 1400 (2 Dist. Nov. 19, 2004).

It was not an abuse of discretion to not require the husband to contribute to the wife's attorney fees as the wife failed to show an inability to pay her own attorney fees. Schneider v. Schneider, 343 Ill. App. 3d 628, 278 Ill. Dec. 485, 798 N.E.2d 1242, 2003 Ill. App. LEXIS 1295 (2 Dist. 2003).

Trial court did not abuse its discretion in declining to award the wife payment for her attorney fees, despite allegations that the vast majority of her expenses were caused by the husband's lack of cooperation, where the wife's earned income was greater than the husband's, the husband's financial circumstances were not so much better than the wife's that he should have been required to pay the wife's attorneys fees, and the expenses were unreasonable considering the nature of the proceedings and the limited monetary resources of the parties. In re Marriage of Bowlby, 338 Ill. App. 3d 720, 273 Ill. Dec. 466, 789 N.E.2d 366, 2003 Ill. App. LEXIS 530 (5 Dist. 2003).

Where the trial court properly considered all of the attendant facts and acted reasonably under the circumstances, the award of attorney fees was not erroneous. In re Alshouse, 255 Ill. App. 3d 960, 194 Ill. Dec. 394, 627 N.E.2d 731 (3 Dist.), appeal denied, 156 Ill. 2d 555, 202 Ill. Dec. 918, 638 N.E.2d 1112 (1994).

The trial court did not abuse its discretion by requiring each party to pay its own attorney fees, based on the parties' financial circumstances and the parties' unwillingness to compromise. In re Mantei, 222 Ill. App. 3d 933, 164 Ill. Dec. 870, 583 N.E.2d 1192 (4 Dist. 1991).

Abuse of Discretion (Cont'd)

—Not Shown (Cont'd)

Where petitioner's job paid only $14,000 a year with no benefits, she estimated that it would cost $1,700 a month to care for herself and her child, and conversely, respondent earned $47,000 a year and in addition had his own business which had generated as much as $15,000 a year, it was not an abuse of discretion to order respondent to pay petitioner's attorney fees. In re Radae, 208 Ill. App. 3d 1027, 153 Ill. Dec. 802, 567 N.E.2d 760 (5 Dist. 1991).

Trial court did not abuse its discretion in ruling that attorney fees for matters unrelated to the dissolution proceedings were recoverable under subsection (a) of this section; it would be an extreme waste of judicial time to require an attorney seeking the payment of fees to file a separate action requesting payment for those services, especially given his testimony that some of his time reflected conferences involving the marital, partially marital, and nonmarital property. In re Waltrip, 216 Ill. App. 3d 776, 159 Ill. Dec. 730, 576 N.E.2d 399 (2 Dist. 1991).

Where the evidence presented showed that wife's attorney fees were in excess of $20,000 and that husband had the ability to absorb the fees in view of the significant disparity in incomes between the parties led to a holding that the trial court's award of attorney fees to the wife was not an abuse of discretion. In re Osborn, 206 Ill. App. 3d 588, 151 Ill. Dec. 663, 564 N.E.2d 1325 (5 Dist. 1990), cert. denied, 137 Ill. 2d 666, 156 Ill. Dec. 563, 571 N.E.2d 150 (1991).

The trial court did not abuse its discretion in ordering wife to pay $2,000 out of $4,082 of husband's attorney fees where husband's expenses exceeded his income, where his present liquid assets were likely to be used to offset the difference, and where the record clearly demonstrated that the wife possessed the ability to pay the $2,000 attorney fee award. In re Westerlund, 193 Ill. App. 3d 56, 140 Ill. Dec. 169, 549 N.E.2d 820 (1 Dist. 1989).

Trial court's order directing husband to pay attorney fees was not an abuse of discretion where the evidence indicated that requiring the wife to pay the attorney fees would undermine her economic stability and where the record indicated that the husband was able to pay the fees. In re Hazard, 167 Ill. App. 3d 61, 117 Ill. Dec. 770, 520 N.E.2d 1121 (1 Dist. 1988).

The court did not abuse its discretion where it awarded attorney fees to wife, even though the cause of action was unsuccessful. In re McCaskey, 167 Ill. App. 3d 860, 118 Ill. Dec. 845, 522 N.E.2d 300 (5 Dist. 1988).

Where, prior to hearing on fees, wife and other persons in her behalf paid attorney $5,725, of which $2,000 apparently was for post-judgment matters relating to the case but not a part of the billings reflected by the evidence, there was evidence that she had the ability to pay her fees, and therefore the trial court did not abuse its discretion in denying attorney fees. Faris v. Faris, 142 Ill. App. 3d 987, 97 Ill. Dec. 209, 492 N.E.2d 645 (2 Dist. 1986), appeal denied, 100 Ill. Dec. 603, 497 N.E.2d 781 (Ill. 1986).

Where the record lacked any evidentiary support for a final award of fees, and where neither the amount of attorney fees nor the reasonableness of charges was submitted for the trial court's consideration, there was no abuse of the trial court's denial of fees. In re Lawrence, 146 Ill. App. 3d 307, 99 Ill. Dec. 845, 496 N.E.2d 538 (3 Dist. 1986).

Where the record showed that husband not only refused to pay his children's high school tuition, but that he did not attempt to resolve the matter at any step in the proceedings, the trial court did not abuse its discretion in awarding attorney fees to wife. In re Moriarty, 132 Ill. App. 3d 895, 88 Ill. Dec. 222, 478 N.E.2d 537 (1 Dist. 1985).

Trial court did not abuse its discretion in determining that reasonable fees for representation in post-dissolution proceedings were $445 where petitioner admitted that the nature of the controversy was relatively simple, that the case presented no novel or difficult question, and that there was no important family law issue involved. In re Erickson, 136 Ill. App. 3d 907, 91 Ill. Dec. 346, 483 N.E.2d 692 (2 Dist. 1985).

Considering the respective financial resources of the parties, the trial court did not abuse its discretion in requiring respondent to pay $10,000 for petitioner's attorney fees. In re Bailey, 130 Ill. App. 3d 158, 85 Ill. Dec. 666, 474 N.E.2d 394 (1 Dist. 1985).

Where a wife's $9,000 in attorney fees amounted to approximately double her annual gross earnings, where she did not own any income-producing assets, and where her husband's ability to pay attorney fees was considerably greater than that of the wife's, the award of attorney fees to the wife was not an abuse of discretion. Goforth v. Goforth, 121 Ill. App. 3d 673, 77 Ill. Dec. 125, 459 N.E.2d 1374 (5 Dist. 1984).

There was no abuse of discretion in requiring that respondent pay $1,200 towards petitioner's reasonable attorney fees where petitioner's income and assets were minimal while those of respondent were substantial. Jones v. Meade, 126 Ill. App. 3d 897, 81 Ill. Dec. 786, 467 N.E.2d 657 (4 Dist. 1984).

Where petitioner was unable on a relative basis to pay all of her own attorney fees without depleting her capital assets, the trial court's conclusion that respondent should pay $3,500 of petitioner's attorney fees was not an abuse of discretion. In re Smith, 128 Ill. App. 3d 1017, 84 Ill. Dec. 242, 471 N.E.2d 1008 (2 Dist. 1984).

After considering the financial resources of the parties, the court did not abuse its discretion in denying their motion to award attorney fees. Robertson v. Robertson, 123 Ill. App. 3d 323, 78 Ill. Dec. 593, 462 N.E.2d 712 (5 Dist. 1984).

Trial court did not abuse its discretion in denying attorney fees to wife on the basis that there was no evidence of husband's assets, his past income, or his current income, other than his testimony that while recovering from an operation he was only receiving income of $475 per month from a partnership. In re Donahoe, 114 Ill. App. 3d 470, 70 Ill. Dec. 152, 448 N.E.2d 1030 (2 Dist. 1983).

Where the parties' incomes were substantially unequal, but the wife received more marital property capable of producing income in the near future, and the husband was required to pay a substantial part of the wife's fees, the trial court did not abuse its discretion in failing to award wife attorney fees. In re Bentivenga, 109 Ill. App. 3d 967, 65 Ill. Dec. 423, 441 N.E.2d 336 (2 Dist. 1982).

One spouse's earlier part-time employment and probationary employment at the time of hearing did not provide a sufficient basis upon which to find equality in earning power with that of her husband, a college graduate employed by the same company since 1967 with steady increases in compensation, such that the trial court's award of attorney fees was not an abuse of discretion. In re Theeke, 105 Ill. App. 3d 119, 60 Ill. Dec. 944, 433 N.E.2d 1311 (1 Dist. 1981).

Trial court did not abuse its discretion by requiring husband to pay a portion of wife's attorney fees where it could have reasonably concluded that the husband had the ability to pay and that the respondent wife did not have the ability to pay that portion of the fees. Burks v. Burks, 100 Ill. App. 3d 700, 56 Ill. Dec. 273, 427 N.E.2d 353 (1 Dist. 1981).

Award of attorney fees to former wife was consistent with the weight of the evidence and not an abuse of the court's discretion. In re McCune, 86 Ill. App. 3d 311, 41 Ill. Dec. 897, 408 N.E.2d 319 (3 Dist. 1980).

In view of respondent's income and his obligations under the property division, the trial court's award of $500 in attorney fees was not an abuse of discretion. In re Bentley, 82 Ill. App. 3d 25, 36 Ill. Dec. 947, 401 N.E.2d 1085 (1 Dist. 1980), vacated on other grounds, 84 Ill. 2d 97, 49 Ill. Dec. 295, 417 N.E.2d 1309 (1981).

The circuit court's order that respondent pay two-thirds of petitioner's attorney fees was not an abuse of discretion, even though petitioner had the ability to pay the entire amount of her fees out of her bank accounts and stock. In re Simmons, 87 Ill. App. 3d 651, 42 Ill. Dec. 706, 409 N.E.2d 321 (1 Dist. 1980).

Trial court's determination that the plaintiff was unable to pay all of her attorneys' fees was not palpably erroneous or an abuse of discretion. Donnelley v. Donnelley, 80 Ill. App. 3d 597, 35 Ill. Dec. 919, 400 N.E.2d 56 (1 Dist. 1980).

Where each party had approximately $100 left after the payment of its monthly expenses, and where petitioner's obligations were comparably greater and included, in addition to his own attorney fees, payment of the child's attorney fees, the trial court's denial of attorney fees to respondent was not an abuse of discretion. Scott v. Scott, 75 Ill. App. 3d 710, 31 Ill. Dec. 577, 394 N.E.2d 779 (2 Dist. 1979).

Where petitioner had sufficient resources for which to pay her attorney and there was no indication that such payment would strip the petitioner of her means of support or undermine her financial stability, the trial court did not abuse its discretion by requiring each party to pay its own attorney's fees. Scott v. Scott, 72 Ill. App. 3d 117, 27 Ill. Dec. 863, 389 N.E.2d 1271 (1 Dist. 1979).

Abuse of Discretion (Cont'd)

—Not Shown (Cont'd)

The trial court did not abuse its discretion in requiring defendant to pay a portion of plaintiff's attorney fees incurred in connection with several post-decree proceedings. Winter v. Winter, 69 Ill. App. 3d 359, 25 Ill. Dec. 819, 387 N.E.2d 695 (1 Dist. 1978).

The trial court did not abuse its discretion in awarding attorney fees to plaintiff, since plaintiff was not required to exhaust her estate to protect her rights in the marital litigation, and where she was financially unable to pay the fees but defendant was able to do so. Hogan v. Hogan, 58 Ill. App. 3d 661, 16 Ill. Dec. 265, 374 N.E.2d 1040 (1 Dist. 1978).

A plaintiff's contention that the court abused its discretion by ordering him to pay the defendant's attorney's fees of $5,000 within 90 days of the entry of the supplemental judgment for divorce was without merit since additional time was not required to make the payment. Laing v. Laing, 55 Ill. App. 3d 231, 13 Ill. Dec. 462, 371 N.E.2d 157 (2 Dist. 1977).

In light of former husband's ability to absorb some of the legal costs of divorce, the trial court did not abuse its discretion in awarding former wife $2,000 in attorney fees. Brandis v. Brandis, 51 Ill. App. 3d 467, 9 Ill. Dec. 728, 367 N.E.2d 162 (4 Dist. 1977).

Where custodial modification appeared to have been sought primarily for the convenience of the parties rather than as a means of properly presenting the needs of the children to the court, the court did not abuse its discretion in denying plaintiff's petition for attorney fees. Roth v. Roth, 52 Ill. App. 3d 220, 10 Ill. Dec. 54, 367 N.E.2d 442 (1 Dist. 1977).

Trial court did not abuse its discretion in ordering defendant to pay the attorney fees and costs to plaintiff's attorney pursuant to former section 15 of the Divorce Act (see now this section); however, the aggregate amount of attorneys fees allowed in the trial court was excessive and unreasonably high. Green v. Green, 41 Ill. App. 3d 154, 354 N.E.2d 661 (1 Dist. 1976).

Where defendant did not establish any abuse of discretion by the trial court in awarding her $800 toward her trial attorney fees, defendant's request for a reversal of that award and a remand of the matter for a new hearing was rejected. Rosenbaum v. Rosenbaum, 38 Ill. App. 3d 1, 349 N.E.2d 73 (1 Dist. 1976).

The trial court did not abuse its discretion in requiring defendant to make payment of attorney fees, where in the property settlement agreement defendant expressly assumed liability to pay attorney fees in such amount as might be agreed upon between the parties or as should be determined by the court. Welsh v. Welsh, 38 Ill. App. 3d 35, 347 N.E.2d 512 (1 Dist. 1976).

Since an award for attorney's fees is a matter within the sound discretion of the trial court, and since defendant was the party at fault in the divorce proceeding, the trial court did not abuse its discretion in ordering husband to pay wife's attorney fees. Leone v. Leone, 39 Ill. App. 3d 547, 350 N.E.2d 545 (3 Dist. 1976).

In an action under the former Divorce Act (see now this section), there was no abuse of discretion in allowing an award of attorney fees to wife where the trial judge was well informed about the relative financial positions of the parties. Borg v. Borg, 32 Ill. App. 3d 1075, 337 N.E.2d 391 (1 Dist. 1975).

The court did not err in directing that $3,000 be paid to the plaintiff's attorney because the court has the discretion to award attorney fees to either party regardless of which party was awarded the divorce. Anagnostopoulos v. Anagnostopoulos, 22 Ill. App. 3d 479, 317 N.E.2d 681 (1 Dist. 1974).

Where the trial court inquired deeply into the evidence and arguments of counsel and felt that the wife should not automatically be awarded attorney fees, the court acted within its discretion. Finn v. Finn, 11 Ill. App. 3d 385, 297 N.E.2d 1 (2 Dist. 1973).

With respect to the award of $50 as plaintiff's attorney fees, the court did not abuse its discretion in that regard, and the order was affirmed. Grabowski v. Grabowski, 95 Ill. App. 2d 311, 237 N.E.2d 766 (1 Dist. 1968).

The trial court was well within its discretion in awarding temporary award of attorney fees in the amount of $500 in divorce action. Roback v. Roback, 59 Ill. App. 2d 222, 207 N.E.2d 130 (2 Dist. 1965).

The allowance of attorney fees was not an abuse of the chancellor's discretion. Page v. Page, 32 Ill. App. 2d 422, 178 N.E.2d 129 (1 Dist. 1961).

—Shown

Evidence did not support finding that petitioner was unable to meet her living expenses; although she may not have had a lot of extra money left over after paying her living expenses she did not demonstrate an inability to pay her own attorney's fees nor would her economic stability be undermined if she had to pay. In re Krivi, 283 Ill. App. 3d 772, 219 Ill. Dec. 274, 670 N.E.2d 1162 (5 Dist. 1996).

Where a former husband unilaterally reduced his unallocated maintenance payments, the trial court abused its discretion by expressly refusing to find him in contempt and by not making the necessary finding of lack of cause or justification. In re Garelick, 168 Ill. App. 3d 321, 119 Ill. Dec. 76, 522 N.E.2d 738 (1 Dist. 1988).

Assessing 75% of petitioner's attorney fees against respondent was improper where the assessment would strip respondent of his means of support and undermine his economic stability. In re Calisoff, 176 Ill. App. 3d 721, 126 Ill. Dec. 183, 531 N.E.2d 810 (1 Dist. 1988).

Trial court abused its discretion by refusing to award the respondent attorney fees where the record indicated a significant disparity between the ability of the petitioner and the ability of the respondent to pay respondent's fees; specifically, the petitioner earned $2,000 a month and respondent was totally disabled within nine months after the divorce, earning $527 per month from disability payments and receiving $300 per month as voluntary payments from her parents. In re Pitts, 169 Ill. App. 3d 200, 119 Ill. Dec. 908, 523 N.E.2d 664 (5 Dist. 1988).

The trial court abused its discretion in ordering respondent to pay petitioner's fees where the record failed to show that respondent had the ability to pay those fees and that petitioner did not. In re Westcott, 163 Ill. App. 3d 168, 114 Ill. Dec. 411, 516 N.E.2d 566 (1 Dist. 1987).

The circuit court had no statutory authority to order the execution of a note and mortgage on a marital residence to secure the payment of attorney fees and arrearages in owelty, maintenance, and child support. In re Stanley, 133 Ill. App. 3d 963, 89 Ill. Dec. 146, 479 N.E.2d 1152 (4 Dist. 1985).

The order to pay attorney fees in the amount of $25,000 was an abuse of discretion, where the trial court had no information upon which to base a finding of reasonableness and necessity as required by this section. In re Bennett, 131 Ill. App. 3d 1050, 87 Ill. Dec. 305, 476 N.E.2d 1297 (2 Dist. 1985).

Based on the clear disparity in the circumstances of the parties and the health problems and fragile financial status of the wife, the failure of the trial court to order the husband to pay all of the wife's attorney fees incurred during dissolution proceedings. In re Ribordy, 128 Ill. App. 3d 1073, 84 Ill. Dec. 263, 471 N.E.2d 1029 (3 Dist. 1984).

Trial court's denial of petitioner's request for attorney fees without hearing evidence of her needs as well as of her income constituted an abuse of discretion. In re Rundle, 107 Ill. App. 3d 880, 63 Ill. Dec. 491, 438 N.E.2d 229 (5 Dist. 1982).

The court abused its discretion in ordering the sale of marital stock for payment of attorney fees; subsection (c) of this section does not empower the court to order an asset sold for the direct payment of fees. In re Walsh, 109 Ill. App. 3d 171, 64 Ill. Dec. 758, 440 N.E.2d 310 (1 Dist. 1982).

Evidence was held to be sufficient to show that the trial court abused its discretion in denying respondent attorney fees. In re Rimmele, 102 Ill. App. 3d 88, 57 Ill. Dec. 762, 429 N.E.2d 879 (3 Dist. 1981).

A court's denial of petitioner's request for attorney fees, without first establishing some basis for such a denial, constituted a clear abuse of discretion. In re Gardner, 85 Ill. App. 3d 1004, 41 Ill. Dec. 304, 407 N.E.2d 802 (1 Dist. 1980).

Where respondent was employed as a butcher, had a salary of at least $12,000, his present wife was also employed, he never made any showing to the trial court of his inability to pay attorney fees, and he never submitted any pleadings or affidavits setting forth his income or expenses, nor did he deny any of petitioner's statements regarding his earnings, and where respondent was in a superior position financially, the trial court abused its discretion in denying the petitioner's petition for fees and in ordering petitioner to pay fees to respondent's attorney. Carr v. Borowczyk, 78 Ill. App. 3d 425, 33 Ill. Dec. 738, 397 N.E.2d 71 (1 Dist. 1979).

Abuse of Discretion (Cont'd)

—Shown (Cont'd)

The trial court abused its discretion by ordering husband to pay $750 to wife as attorney fees where the facts established that the husband had a greater ability to pay attorney fees but did not establish that the wife was unable to pay her fees. Imes v. Imes, 52 Ill. App. 3d 792, 10 Ill. Dec. 466, 367 N.E.2d 1075 (3 Dist. 1977).

The trial court abused its discretion in awarding plaintiff temporary alimony and attorney fees without first admitting and considering exhibits which tended to impeach plaintiff's testimony that she lacked any assets. Eule v. Eule, 24 Ill. App. 3d 83, 320 N.E.2d 506 (1 Dist. 1974).

Where the court found the defendant husband to be at fault and granted the divorce to his wife, and his motions to strike contained the untrue allegation that the parties were living together as husband and wife, and his counterclaim for divorce was not pursued in good faith and contained untrue allegations concerning his wife's fitness as a mother in order to extend litigation, it was an abuse of discretion for the trial court not to grant the plaintiff wife the full amount of her attorney fees. Albert v. Albert, 10 Ill. App. 3d 539, 294 N.E.2d 695 (1 Dist. 1972).

An attorney fee award under the former Divorce Act (see now this section), which represented compensation in the sum of $14 per hour, was inadequate and represented an abuse of discretion. Greenbaum v. Greenbaum, 14 Ill. App. 3d 217, 302 N.E.2d 165 (1 Dist. 1973).

Where plaintiff, by her own misconduct, precipitated post-decree proceedings and, when apprehended in company with a fugitive from justice, relinquished the custody of her children to defendant, her voluntary transfer of the children to defendant not only justified defendant's subsequent actions in seeking modification of custody order, but in fact compelled him to seek the assistance of the court in order to protect the welfare of the children; therefore, his request for a change of custody, immediately filed, was proper and advisable in order to give judicial protection to the acts which plaintiff had made necessary and it was unreasonable and an abuse of discretion to assess attorney fees against defendant. Kuhns v. Kuhns, 7 Ill. App. 3d 884, 288 N.E.2d 884 (1 Dist. 1972).

Trial court order requiring payment by defendant to plaintiff's counsel of $1,000,000 for temporary fees pending appeal was an abuse of discretion. McLeod v. McLeod, 133 Ill. App. 2d 111, 272 N.E.2d 834 (1 Dist. 1971).

Adult Child

While this section provides that a court may order either spouse to pay attorney fees, and 750 ILCS 5/506 permits the court to award fees to an attorney who has been appointed by the court to represent the interest of a minor or dependent child, neither section provides for the award of attorney fees to an adult child of the marriage. In re Garrison, 99 Ill. App. 3d 717, 54 Ill. Dec. 653, 425 N.E.2d 518 (2 Dist. 1981).

Amendment

The trial court properly denied the plaintiff's request for attorney fees to defend an appeal, which was filed subsequent to the effective date of the amendment to former section 15 of the Divorce Act, (see now this section), since that amendment operated to deprive the trial court of authority to enter an award of attorney fees pending appeal (see now this section). Winter v. Winter, 69 Ill. App. 3d 359, 25 Ill. Dec. 819, 387 N.E.2d 695 (1 Dist. 1978).

Amount of Award

—Determinative Factors

The factors to be considered in determining what are reasonable fees include the attorney's skill and standing, the nature of the controversy, the novelty and difficulty of the questions at issue, the significance or importance of the subject matter, the degree of responsibility involved in the management of the case, the standing and skill of the person employed, the time and labor required, the usual and customary charge in the community and the benefits to the client; in applying these factors the trial court quite properly may rely on its own knowledge and experience in determining the value of the legal services rendered. Roback v. Roback, 59 Ill. App. 2d 222, 207 N.E.2d 130 (2 Dist. 1965); Lauzen v. Lauzen, 81 Ill. App. 2d 472, 225 N.E.2d 427 (2 Dist. 1967); In re Siddens, 225 Ill. App. 3d 496, 167 Ill. Dec. 680, 588 N.E.2d 321 (5 Dist.), appeal denied, 145 Ill. 2d 644, 173 Ill. Dec. 13, 596 N.E.2d 637 (1992).

In making the award of fees, the trial court should consider the attorney's skill and standing, the nature of the controversy and the novelty and difficulty of the issues the case presents, the importance of the subject matter from the perspective of family law, the degree of responsibility involved in the management of the case, the time required and labor expended, the customary charge in the community, and the benefits the client derived from the representation. In re McFarlane, 160 Ill. App. 3d 721, 112 Ill. Dec. 537, 513 N.E.2d 1146 (2 Dist. 1987).

—Discretion of Court

Finding that petitioner should pay some, but not all, of respondent's attorney fee was not an abuse of discretion. In re Pihaly, 258 Ill. App. 3d 851, 194 Ill. Dec. 655, 627 N.E.2d 1297 (2 Dist. 1994).

If no hearing is requested on the question of attorney fees the court may grant fees in an amount based on its own experience; this rule is usable only where there is no contest as to the fees and no request for a hearing on them, but where a party specifically asked to be heard on the question of the fees the court should hear evidence as to what work was done and the value of the services rendered. Jones v. Jones, 48 Ill. App. 2d 232, 198 N.E.2d 195 (1 Dist. 1964).

—Excessive Attorney's Fees

Where attorney fees had gone "amuck" and the amount of money in controversy was dwarfed by the overall attorney fees, the economic situation of both parties justified determination that both parties should determine the costs of their own fees; allowing $4,000 attorney fees to wife and denying attorney fees to husband was not an abuse of discretion. In re Rushing, 258 Ill. App. 3d 1057, 194 Ill. Dec. 748, 628 N.E.2d 245 (1 Dist. 1993), appeal denied, 155 Ill. 2d 576, 198 Ill. Dec. 552, 633 N.E.2d 14 (1994).

—Financial Ability

The financial ability of the spouse required to pay attorney fees may limit the amount awarded regardless of the expenditure of time and labor by the attorney; by the same token, however, financial ability to pay does not warrant an award beyond what is fair and reasonable. In re Siddens, 225 Ill. App. 3d 496, 167 Ill. Dec. 680, 588 N.E.2d 321 (5 Dist.), appeal denied, 145 Ill. 2d 644, 173 Ill. Dec. 13, 596 N.E.2d 637 (1992).

—Illustrative Cases

The trial court erred when it ordered the husband to contribute $19,000 toward the wife's attorney's fees where it appeared that the trial court only awarded a contribution in an amount equivalent to what the trial court believed the husband paid his own attorney, but the husband actually only paid about $11,000 to his own attorney. In re Delarco, 313 Ill. App. 3d 107, 245 Ill. Dec. 921, 728 N.E.2d 1278, 2000 Ill. App. LEXIS 302 (2 Dist. 2000).

—Impeding Progress

In a divorce action, if a party deliberately impedes the progress of the trial or files a complaint which is not abandoned until trial thus necessitating extensive preparation by the opposing party, under such circumstances courts generally uphold the amount of attorney fees. Albert v. Albert, 10 Ill. App. 3d 539, 294 N.E.2d 695 (1 Dist. 1972).

—Not Excessive

Where plaintiff presented evidence of the reasonableness of attorney fees for the prior appeal, remand, and the subsequent appeal, but defendant presented none and the evidence indicated that many hours were spent on the prior appeal and remand, that more would have to be spent on the appeal, that it was an important case from the family law standpoint, and that it involved a great deal of responsibility because of the amount of money involved, the trial court's award of $32,000 for the previous appeal and remand, and $7,500 for the subsequent appeal was not excessive. Hall v. Hall, 43 Ill. App. 3d 97, 1 Ill. Dec. 874, 356 N.E.2d 1156 (4 Dist. 1976).

—Not Inadequate

An award of $3,000 toward the wife's attorney fees of $8,000 was not an abuse of discretion in light of the parties' economic circumstances and the significant amount of debt which the husband was

Amount of Award (Cont'd)

—Not Inadequate (Cont'd)
ordered to assume. In re Reppen-Sonneson, 299 Ill. App. 3d 691, 233 Ill. Dec. 885, 701 N.E.1159 (2 Dist. 1998).

—Quantum Meruit
A discharged attorney is not necessarily entitled to the full amount of a retainer agreement, but is entitled only to reasonable fees on a quantum meruit basis. In re Savas, 139 Ill. App. 3d 68, 93 Ill. Dec. 483, 486 N.E.2d 1318 (1 Dist. 1985).

—Illustrative Cases
Where the court order allowed first attorney only $200 and the court indicated that the $2,500 that husband was required to pay was to be distributed among all three of wife's attorneys, and where the first attorney's verified motion showed that he had spent over 80 hours on the matter, the order of the trial court was reversed and remanded for a rehearing as to what portion of the $2,500 paid by husband was to be paid to first attorney for the reasonable value of his services. Serio v. Serio, 85 Ill. App. 2d 102, 229 N.E.2d 281 (1 Dist. 1967).

—Reasonableness
In making an award of attorney fees pursuant to a petition for contribution to attorney fees, the trial court must also consider whether the attorney fees charged by the petitioning party's attorney are reasonable. In re Delarco, 313 Ill. App. 3d 107, 245 Ill. Dec. 921, 728 N.E.2d 1278, 2000 Ill. App. LEXIS 302 (2 Dist. 2000).

—Separate Maintenance Action
In a separate maintenance action, the trial court erred in allowing the plaintiff $1,000 for attorney fees where the attorney was engaged five days in the trial of the case and also attended a hearing taking depositions for the trial, but there was no evidence offered in regard to the value of these services. Ribergaard v. Ribergaard, 349 Ill. App. 99, 110 N.E.2d 89 (2 Dist. 1952).

—Time Spent by Attorney
Where defendant asserted that there was no evidence of how much time his attorney spent on a case, and since the defendant failed to request an evidentiary hearing on the matter, he could not complain that one was not held, and therefore a decision on fees could be reached. Anagnostopoulos v. Anagnostopoulos, 22 Ill. App. 3d 479, 317 N.E.2d 681 (1 Dist. 1974).

Appeals
Fact that former wife's former attorney had a fee petition pending against did not affect the finality of the dissolution of marriage judgment, and since the wife's fee petition against a third party had been filed in the dissolution of marriage proceeding, its appealability was not affected by the attorney's filing of a petition, which meant that the wife had 30 days from the date her petition was denied to file a notice of appeal challenging that decision and her failure to do so meant the appellate court had no appellate jurisdiction to review the denial of her fee petition against the third party. Devick v. Devick, 335 Ill. App. 3d 734, 269 Ill. Dec. 687, 781 N.E.2d 484, 2002 Ill. App. LEXIS 1074 (2 Dist. 2002), appeal denied, 204 Ill. 2d 657, 275 Ill. Dec. 75, 792 N.E.2d 306 (2003).

To substantially prevail suggested that one had to obtain at least 50 percent of the relief she sought; where wife prevailed on one of four issues raised on appeal, she had not substantially prevailed, and trial court erred in ordering her husband to pay a portion of her appellate fees. Murphy v. Murphy, 327 Ill. App. 3d 845, 261 Ill. Dec. 684, 763 N.E.2d 933, 2002 Ill. App. LEXIS 91 (4 Dist. 2002).

A trial court may determine prospective attorney fees for conducting an appeal after appellate court jurisdiction has attached. In re McBride, 102 Ill. App. 3d 84, 57 Ill. Dec. 750, 429 N.E.2d 867 (3 Dist. 1981).

The appellate court's order that defendant pay plaintiff's attorney fees for the defense of an appeal was not appropriate. Finley v. Finley, 81 Ill. 2d 317, 43 Ill. Dec. 12, 410 N.E.2d 12 (1980).

In the absence of specific statutory authority to award attorney fees in divorce proceedings pending appeal, the general rule is that such fees may not be allowed. McArdle v. McArdle, 55 Ill. App. 3d 829, 13 Ill. Dec. 282, 370 N.E.2d 1309 (3 Dist. 1977).

Trial court erred when it ordered husband to pay $1,500 in attorney fees for wife to defend appeal brought by him, as it is error for a trial court to award attorney fees in an appeal from a post-decretal order. Goldberg v. Goldberg, 30 Ill. App. 3d 769, 332 N.E.2d 710 (1 Dist. 1975).

Applicability
Language of 750 ILCS 5/506 does not limit its application proceedings brought under the Marriage Act; indeed, this section specifically authorizes the payment attorney fees in litigation reasonably connected with a proceeding under the Act. In re Marriage of Nienhouse, Ill. App. 3d , 290 Ill. Dec. 654, 821 N.E.2d 1228, 2004 Ill. App. LEXIS 1551 (1 Dist. 2004).

Trial court erred in ruling that interim attorney's fees could not be recovered under the Illinois Parentage Act, as 750 ILCS 45/17 allowed for attorney's fees based on the factors found in 750 ILCS 5/508, which allowed for interim attorney's fees based on the factors listed in 750 ILCS 5/501(c-1)(1),(2),(3). Stella v. Garcia (In re Stella), 353 Ill. App. 3d 415, 288 Ill. Dec. 889, 818 N.E.2d 824, 2004 Ill. App. LEXIS 1265 (1 Dist. 2004).

Because nothing in 750 ILCS 45/17, 750 ILCS 5/508, or 750 ILCS 5/501(c-1)(3) gave trial judges the power to order disgorgement of interim fees in parentage cases, the trial court improperly ordered the attorney to disgorge $ 20,000 to the opposing attorney. Stella v. Garcia (In re Stella), 339 Ill. App. 3d 610, 274 Ill. Dec. 391, 791 N.E.2d 187, 2003 Ill. App. LEXIS 650 (1 Dist. 2003).

This section is not mandatory, and only applies if an attorney seeks to utilize this section to obtain fees, Kaufman, Litwin & Feinstein v. Edgar, 301 Ill. App. 3d 826, 235 Ill. Dec. 183, 704 N.E.2d 756 (1 Dist. 1998), appeal denied, 182 Ill. 2d 551, 236 Ill. Dec. 670, 707 N.E.2d 1240 (1999).

Former section 52 of the Illinois Civil Practice Act (see now 735 ILCS 5/2-1009) does not provide for the taxation of attorney fees and expenses as costs; thus it is subsection (a) of this section which governs the issue of the allowance of attorney fees, expenses and costs. In re Adams, 92 Ill. App. 3d 797, 48 Ill. Dec. 285, 416 N.E.2d 316 (1 Dist. 1981).

Subdivision (a)(3) of this section did not allow an award for attorney fees assessed for appeal where the appeal was from a judgment for divorce entered before the effective date of this Act. Christian v. Christian, 69 Ill. App. 3d 450, 26 Ill. Dec. 326, 387 N.E.2d 1254 (1 Dist. 1979).

Where proceeding was not a case of divorce but merely an attempt by plaintiff to vacate a property settlement contract she had entered into with the defendant, plaintiff was not entitled to attorney fees to defend against defendant's cross appeal or equitable alimony during the pendency of the appeal. Garmisa v. Garmisa, 4 Ill. App. 3d 134, 280 N.E.2d 458 (1 Dist. 1972).

Apportionment
Where respondent was in no better position than petitioner to pay attorney's fees, petitioner benefited from reopening of the case and subsequent property division in that she was given more property, yet respondent's misconduct led to the proceedings under 735 ILCS 5/2-1401, it was not an abuse of discretion to assess only a portion of the attorney fees against the respondent. In re Hale, 278 Ill. App. 3d 53, 214 Ill. Dec. 826, 662 N.E.2d 180 (3 Dist. 1996).

Where a trial court finds that both parties have failed to comply with an order or judgment, it is appropriate under subsection (b) for the court to apportion attorney fees in a manner that reflects the parties' relative culpability. In re Aleshire, 273 Ill. App. 3d 81, 209 Ill. Dec. 843, 652 N.E.2d 383 (3 Dist. 1995).

Since petitioner was not guilty of visitation abuse, respondent was accountable under subsection (b) for all of the fees petitioner incurred in bringing her petition to enforce visitation. In re Aleshire, 273 Ill. App. 3d 81, 209 Ill. Dec. 843, 652 N.E.2d 383 (3 Dist. 1995).

In apportioning the obligation between the parents to pay attorney appointed to represent the interests of the children in a divorce action, the court must consider the parents' financial resources. In re Kennedy, 94 Ill. App. 3d 537, 49 Ill. Dec. 927, 418 N.E.2d 947 (1 Dist. 1981).

Arbitration
Subdivision (c)(4) does not conflict with Rule 86, Supreme Court Rules; Rule 86 specifies the conditions under which a court can institute arbitration programs, but does not preclude the legislature from enacting new causes of action that would contain arbitration provisions. Kaufman, Litwin & Feinstein v. Edgar, 301 Ill.

Arbitration (Cont'd)
App. 3d 826, 235 Ill. Dec. 183, 704 N.E.2d 756 (1 Dist. 1998), appeal denied, 182 Ill. 2d 551, 236 Ill. Dec. 670, 707 N.E.2d 1240 (1999).

Attorney Collection Action

A claim for fees, whether made under this section or in a separate common law action must satisfy the professional standards of Rules of Professional Conduct, Rule 1.5, and that rule is not relevant to whether attorneys may file a claim under this section or in a separate common law action. Nottage v. Jeka, 172 Ill. 2d 386, 217 Ill. Dec. 298, 667 N.E.2d 91 (1996).

This section is not the sole means by which an attorney may recover a fee from a client in a domestic relations matter, and nothing in this section suggests that the legislature intended to eliminate common law actions for fees by attorney's against their clients. Nottage v. Jeka, 172 Ill. 2d 386, 217 Ill. Dec. 298, 667 N.E.2d 91 (1996).

While dissolution or Parentage Act (750 ILCS 45/1 et seq.) proceedings are ongoing, no separate action may be instituted; however, nothing precludes an attorney, whether discharged or not, from bringing a separate suit against his or her own client for fees earned in a dissolution or Parentage Act proceeding after the circuit court has lost jurisdiction of those statutory proceedings, nor will an attorney be barred from bringing such a separate action at that time because that issue was not raised in the underlying proceedings. Myers v. Brantley, 204 Ill. App. 3d 832, 149 Ill. Dec. 891, 562 N.E.2d 355 (4 Dist. 1990).

An attorney who performed numerous hours of in-court and out-of-court service which furthered the completion of divorce litigation and who performed services counseling wife when she was confused by the divorce process had standing to pursue a collection action against the wife. In re Kosterka, 174 Ill. App. 3d 954, 124 Ill. Dec. 295, 529 N.E.2d 12 (2 Dist. 1988).

An attorney has the right to bring an action for fees in his own name. In re Conway, 139 Ill. App. 3d 1062, 94 Ill. Dec. 363, 487 N.E.2d 1240 (5 Dist. 1986).

Under subsection (c) of this section, the court may order that attorney fees be paid directly to the attorney, who may enforce the order in his own name so as to promote judicial economy by eliminating the need for an attorney to bring a separate suit to collect fees from his client. In re Baltzer, 150 Ill. App. 3d 890, 104 Ill. Dec. 196, 502 N.E.2d 459 (2 Dist. 1986).

As subsection (a) of this section permits an attorney to proceed against his client for fees, it would not be considered to be in violation of the canons of ethics to do so. In re Ransom, 102 Ill. App. 3d 38, 57 Ill. Dec. 696, 429 N.E.2d 594 (2 Dist. 1981).

After a dissolution action has been dismissed, an attorney's proper remedy lies in a separate action at law, not in an adjunct hearing to the matrimonial action; thus, an order of a trial court awarding attorney's fees to an attorney was void in that it was issued after the petition for dissolution was dismissed. In re Erby, 84 Ill. App. 3d 672, 40 Ill. Dec. 378, 406 N.E.2d 79 (1 Dist. 1980).

Attorney's Lien

—Abuse of Discretion

Where an attorney had properly obtained a judgment for fees against his client in a marriage dissolution action which was still pending and had taken all steps necessary to perfect its judgment lien against his client's interest in the marital home, the trial court did not possess the discretionary authority to deny his petition. In re Mostow, 126 Ill. App. 3d 67, 81 Ill. Dec. 490, 466 N.E.2d 1292 (1 Dist. 1984).

Where an attorney had a valid judgment and lien for fees, the trial court's suggestion that because it had awarded the marital residence to client's opponent that property could not be the subject of a turnover order lacked authority since any transfer of the client's interest in that home was subject to the lien previously established by the attorney. In re Mostow, 126 Ill. App. 3d 67, 81 Ill. Dec. 490, 466 N.E.2d 1292 (1 Dist. 1984).

Authority of Court

—Either Spouse

The trial court in dissolution cases has the authority, after considering the financial resources of the parties, to order either spouse to pay a reasonable amount of the costs and attorney fees incurred by the other spouse. In re Schmidt, 242 Ill. App. 3d 961, 182 Ill. Dec. 804, 610 N.E.2d 673 (4 Dist. 1993).

—Prior Law

Under a prior similar provision (see now this section), there was no authority given the courts to require either party to a divorce action to pay his or her own attorney, and there was no authority to require both parties to pay the wife's attorney. Hefner v. Hefner, 338 Ill. App. 179, 86 N.E.2d 885 (1 Dist. 1949).

Award of Fees

—Ability to Pay

The propriety of an award of attorney fees is dependent upon (1) a showing by the party seeking them of an inability to pay, and (2) a demonstration of the ability of the other to do so. In re Schmidt, 242 Ill. App. 3d 961, 182 Ill. Dec. 804, 610 N.E.2d 673 (4 Dist. 1993).

—Additional Services

Where the allowance for attorney fees in the original decree did not include services to be rendered after the entry of the decree, plaintiff was entitled to additional fees for services to enforce the decree. Riddlesbarger v. Riddlesbarger, 341 Ill. App. 107, 93 N.E.2d 380 (1 Dist. 1950).

—Award Denied

Trial court's denial of a spouse's request for an award of fees and costs was proper where it was shown that both spouses' contentiousness led to inflated fee amounts and that the spouse who requested an award failed to establish an inability to pay because she had been awarded a disproportionate share of the marital assets. In re Marriage of Schneider, Ill. 2d , 291 Ill. Dec. 601, 824 N.E.2d 177, 2005 Ill. LEXIS 7 (2005).

Denial of the wife's request for attorney fees was upheld because the trial court properly concluded that, after the equal distribution of the marital estate, the award of child support, the award of maintenance, and the order that the husband pay the costs of the child's school tuition, the resources available to each party were sufficiently similar to require that each party pay his or her own attorney fees. In re Marriage of Selinger, 351 Ill. App. 3d 611, 286 Ill. Dec. 502, 814 N.E.2d 152, 2004 Ill. App. LEXIS 904 (4 Dist. 2004).

Where the petitioner's conduct was held to be contumacious, there was no error in the trial court's denial of the request for attorney fees. Ingwerson v. Woeckener, 141 Ill. App. 3d 647, 95 Ill. Dec. 916, 490 N.E.2d 1008 (3 Dist. 1986).

When the court found that husband's failure to pay the full amount was not without cause or justification, there was no basis to award fees. In re Peterson, 139 Ill. App. 3d 391, 93 Ill. Dec. 854, 487 N.E.2d 679 (3 Dist. 1985).

—Award Upheld

Trial court did not err in ordering the father to pay the mother's attorney's fees where the trial court found the father to be in indirect contempt for failure to provide the mother with the father's W-2 forms, and the father did not pay all the amounts of child support that the father was ordered to pay by a divorce decree and a settlement agreement. Ackerley v. Ackerley, 333 Ill. App. 3d 382, 266 Ill. Dec. 973, 775 N.E.2d 1045, 2002 Ill. App. LEXIS 857 (2 Dist. 2002).

The trial court properly awarded attorney fees to the wife for time spent filing motions to remove liens against the marital residence since such fees were related to the central issue of the petition for relief and, as such, were reasonable and necessary. In re Letsinger, 321 Ill. App. 3d 961, 255 Ill. Dec. 108, 748 N.E.2d 812, 2001 Ill. App. LEXIS 328 (2 Dist. 2001).

The trial court did not abuse its discretion by ordering the husband to pay the wife's attorney fees where: (1) the wife's fees were approximately $4,500, the payment of which would compel her to invade her financial assets, further exhaust her estate, and clearly undermine her economic stability; and (2) the husband's salary, approximately $270,000 per year, established his financial ability to pay the attorney fees. In re Cantrell, 314 Ill. App. 3d 623, 247 Ill. Dec. 742, 732 N.E.2d 797, 2000 Ill. App. LEXIS 586 (2 Dist. 2000).

Wife was entitled to reimbursement of attorney fees where she incurred the fees in an effort to enforce the property provisions of a

Award of Fees (Cont'd)

—Award Upheld (Cont'd)
supplemental dissolution order. In re Davis, 292 Ill. App. 3d 802, 226 Ill. Dec. 765, 686 N.E.2d 395 (4 Dist. 1997).

The award of attorney fees from respondent was proper where the record showed that a significant portion of the attorney fees run up in this case were due to numerous breaches of restraining orders by respondent and respondent was in a better position to pay the fees given respondent's sizable income and petitioner's unemployment. In re Auriemma, 271 Ill. App. 3d 68, 207 Ill. Dec. 662, 648 N.E.2d 118 (1 Dist. 1994).

Where it was clear petitioner lacked the financial ability to pay the attorney fees incurred in defending the petition and respondent had considerable income and assets from which to do so the award of attorney fees to petitioner was not an abuse of discretion. In re Frasco, 265 Ill. App. 3d 171, 202 Ill. Dec. 787, 638 N.E.2d 655 (4 Dist.), appeal denied, 158 Ill. 2d 551, 206 Ill. Dec. 835, 645 N.E.2d 1357 (1994).

Where there was evidence that respondent earned more money than petitioner, there was no evidence of petitioner's inability to pay her attorney fees and respondent's ability to pay all or a portion of those fees and the petitioner testified that prior to the dissolution of the parties' marriage, she withdrew $2,500 in marital funds to pay a portion of her attorney fees, the court did not abuse its discretion in ordering each party to pay his or her own attorney fees. In re Hacker, 239 Ill. App. 3d 658, 179 Ill. Dec. 816, 606 N.E.2d 648 (4 Dist. 1992), appeal denied, 151 Ill. 2d 563, 186 Ill. Dec. 380, 616 N.E.2d 333 (1993).

The trial court's award of a portion of attorney fees to respondent, which was grounded in a significant disparity in income between the parties, was not an abuse of discretion. In re Klein, 231 Ill. App. 3d 901, 173 Ill. Dec. 335, 596 N.E.2d 1214 (4 Dist. 1992).

There was no abuse in the award of attorney fees, despite allegations that the fees were unreasonable and that the rates charged were improper because the issues were not novel or complex, where the parties reached an agreement as to the division of marital property, but only after the prerequisite evaluation of property values and employee benefit plans, such as employee stock options and profit sharing, the marital assets were sizable and indicated a more complex case, and the matter involved a long marriage, and contested issues of maintenance, child support, and the value of the marital home. In re Vendredi, 230 Ill. App. 3d 1061, 174 Ill. Dec. 329, 598 N.E.2d 961 (1 Dist. 1992).

—Bad Faith
A party in a divorce action may make use of whatever procedures are open to him under the law, but if there is a lack of good faith he is under an obligation to pay for the resulting litigation. Albert v. Albert, 10 Ill. App. 3d 539, 294 N.E.2d 695 (1 Dist. 1972).

—Bankruptcy Proceeding
Court found no authority to indicate that attorney fees incurred in the bankruptcy proceeding automatically do not fall under the statutory scheme of this section; the mere fact that the fees were incurred in a Federal court does not remove said fees from the purview of the statute. In re Kent, 267 Ill. App. 3d 142, 203 Ill. Dec. 823, 640 N.E.2d 973 (2 Dist. 1994).

—Custody Proceedings
Allowance of attorney fees was proper where petition for modification of custody was in the best interests of children and not for the convenience of the parties. Williams v. Williams, 320 Ill. App. 354, 51 N.E.2d 284 (3 Dist. 1943).

—Discretion of Court
750 ILCS 5/508(b) is a mandatory provision by which the trial court must, in an enforcement proceeding, order the delinquent parent to pay the other parent's costs and reasonable attorney fees; since the trial court found that the father violated order relating to child support, statute required court to enter award for reasonable attorney fees and trial court improperly considered ability to pay as factor in awarding fees. Jennifer B. v. King, 324 Ill. App. 3d 1, 257 Ill. Dec. 822, 754 N.E.2d 480, 2001 Ill. App. LEXIS 663 (2 Dist. 2001).

The award of attorney fees is within the discretion of the trial court and will not be disturbed absent an abuse of discretion. In re Agostinelli, 250 Ill. App. 3d 492, 189 Ill. Dec. 898, 620 N.E.2d 1215 (1 Dist. 1993).

The awarding of attorney fees and the proportion to be paid are within the sound discretion of the trial court and will not be disturbed on appeal, absent an abuse of discretion. In re Schmidt, 242 Ill. App. 3d 961, 182 Ill. Dec. 804, 610 N.E.2d 673 (4 Dist. 1993).

—Dismissal of Action
An attorney may not file a petition for attorney fees in a divorce action after the case has been voluntarily dismissed, even where the petition is filed within 30 days of the dismissal. In re Lucht, 299 Ill. App. 3d 541, 233 Ill. Dec. 624, 701 N.E.2d 267 (1 Dist. 1998), appeal denied, 182 Ill. 2d 552, 236 Ill. Dec. 670, 707 N.E.2d 1240 (1999).

A former version of this statute contemplated the allowance to the wife of expenses to be incurred in maintaining or defending her suit, or, if already incurred, where payment thereof was essential to the further prosecution of her rights, but when the suit had been dismissed, or should have been, the conditions contemplated by the statute did not obtain. Watson v. Watson, 335 Ill. App. 637, 82 N.E.2d 671 (1 Dist. 1948).

—Disobedience of Court Order
A party who has been forced to resort to the judicial process to secure compliance with the terms of an order or judgment is entitled to his or her reasonable attorney fees even absent a showing of inability to pay. In re Schmidt, 242 Ill. App. 3d 961, 182 Ill. Dec. 804, 610 N.E.2d 673 (4 Dist. 1993).

The trial court should have entered an order allowing solicitor's fees for the work made necessary by the wilful failure of defendant to pay court-ordered alimony. Slezak v. Slezak, 293 Ill. App. 489, 13 N.E.2d 91 (1 Dist. 1938).

—Held Improper
In a child support modification case, the trial court erred in awarding the former wife attorney fees of $250 because she had the ability to pay her own fees where her financial disclosure statement indicated that she had a savings account with a balance of $74,000, as well as other financial assets. In re Marriage of Adams, 348 Ill. App. 3d 340, 284 Ill. Dec. 124, 809 N.E.2d 246, 2004 Ill. App. LEXIS 690 (3 Dist. 2004).

An award of attorney's fees to the wife under subsection (b) was improper where: (1) the evidence did not support a finding that the husband violated a court order; (2) the trial court did not state that the alleged violation was without cause or justification; (3) the record seemed to indicate that the trial court did not limit the award of attorney fees to the wife's efforts to enforce an order, but instead ordered the husband to contribute toward the wife's attorney fees for the dissolution proceeding as a whole; and (4) the trial court did not determine the basis for the amount of fees the wife requested or whether that amount was reasonable. In re Gattone, 317 Ill. App. 3d 346, 251 Ill. Dec. 65, 739 N.E.2d 998, 2000 Ill. App. LEXIS 900 (2 Dist. 2000).

—Per Issue
Where a wife substantially prevailed on one issue on appeal but not others, an appellate court erred in denying attorney's fees on that one issue pursuant to 750 ILCS 5/508(a)(3.1). In re Marriage of Murphy, Ill. App. 3d , 271 Ill. Dec. 874, 786 N.E.2d 132, 2003 Ill. LEXIS 8 (1 Dist. 2003).

Award to Former Attorney
Former wife was not obligated that portion of the former attorney's request for attorney fees and cost that involved a sanction imposed solely against the former attorney since an award of attorney fees under 750 ILCS 5/508(c) had to be related to work done on behalf of the client in connection with the specific provisions of 750 ILCS 5/508(a) and the work involved in incurring the sanction was not performed on behalf of the former wife. Devick v. Devick, 335 Ill. App. 3d 734, 269 Ill. Dec. 687, 781 N.E.2d 484, 2002 Ill. App. LEXIS 1074 (2 Dist. 2002), appeal denied, 204 Ill. 2d 657, 275 Ill. Dec. 75, 792 N.E.2d 306 (2003).

Burden of Proof
Party that fails to comply with an order for maintenance or child support bears the burden of proving that compelling cause or justification for the noncompliance exists; an award of attorney fees is mandatory upon a court's finding of a failure to pay without cause

Burden of Proof (Cont'd)

or justification. Berto v. Berto, 344 Ill. App. 3d 705, 279 Ill. Dec. 482, 800 N.E.2d 550, 2003 Ill. App. LEXIS 1383 (2 Dist. 2003).

Contractual Limitation

A marital settlement agreement which purports to allocate attorney fees will not, as a general rule, extinguish the statutory right of a spouse's prior attorney to pursue an award of fees from the other spouse. Lee v. Lee, 302 Ill. App. 3d 607, 236 Ill. Dec. 222, 707 N.E.2d 67 (1 Dist. 1998).

Discretion of Court

In awarding attorney fees under 750 ILCS 5/508(b), a trial court exercises its discretion in deciding whether the delinquent respondent's failure to abide by the terms of the marital settlement agreement and timely pay the proper amount of support to the petitioner is without cause or justification. Berto v. Berto, 344 Ill. App. 3d 705, 279 Ill. Dec. 482, 800 N.E.2d 550, 2003 Ill. App. LEXIS 1383 (2 Dist. 2003).

Enforcement

There are two separate provisions under 750 ILCS 5/508 that apply to enforcement; under § 508(a), the award of attorney fees is discretionary with the trial court and is made after considering the relative financial resources of the parties, but § 508(b) is a mandatory provision by which the trial court must, in a support enforcement proceeding, order the delinquent respondent to pay the petitioner's costs and reasonable attorney fees. Berto v. Berto, 344 Ill. App. 3d 705, 279 Ill. Dec. 482, 800 N.E.2d 550, 2003 Ill. App. LEXIS 1383 (2 Dist. 2003).

Law firm had an enforceable order that did not require a hearing because the dissolution of marriage judgment incorporated by reference the marital settlement agreement, and the marital settlement agreement contained specific language identifying the party sought to be charged, the client, and the sum certain. James T. Haddon, Ltd. v. Weiss, 342 Ill. App. 3d 144, 277 Ill. Dec. 394, 796 N.E.2d 109, 2003 Ill. App. LEXIS 712 (1 Dist. 2003).

Based on the existence of the marital settlement agreement containing express language indicating that the law firm was owed its fees and that partial payment had been made, the law firm's actions to collect fees from the client operated as a revival of the original judgment because the proceedings were commenced within 20 years from the date of the underlying judgment for dissolution of marriage. James T. Haddon, Ltd. v. Weiss, 342 Ill. App. 3d 144, 277 Ill. Dec. 394, 796 N.E.2d 109, 2003 Ill. App. LEXIS 712 (1 Dist. 2003).

Enforcement of Court Order

There is no conflict between subsection (b) and Rules 137 and 219, Supreme Court Rules, since this section simply delineates more specific standards for sanctioning violations of court orders in the specific context of dissolution of marriage cases. It is not a separation of powers violation for the legislature to remedy abuses of a statutory cause of action by enacting procedural rules more specific than those general remedies set forth in the Supreme Court Rules. Kaufman, Litwin & Feinstein v. Edgar, 301 Ill. App. 3d 826, 235 Ill. Dec. 183, 704 N.E.2d 756 (1 Dist. 1998), appeal denied, 182 Ill. 2d 551, 236 Ill. Dec. 670, 707 N.E.2d 1240 (1999).

—Evidentiary Basis

Where petitioner asked the trial court for a specific amount of fees and presented evidence concerning the cost to defend this appeal and petitioner's attorney testified about his experience and how these factors led him to the figure requested, the trial court did not abuse its discretion in awarding petitioner a prospective award for attorney fees. In re Norris, 252 Ill. App. 3d 230, 192 Ill. Dec. 46, 625 N.E.2d 6 (1 Dist. 1992).

—Fee Petition Preparation Time

The trial court properly awarded attorney fees to wife's attorney for time spent preparing the petition requesting attorney fees. In re Powers, 252 Ill. App. 3d 506, 191 Ill. Dec. 541, 624 N.E.2d 390 (2 Dist. 1993).

—Former Law

For a case discussing the award of attorney fees under similar prior provisions, see Harding v. Harding, 180 Ill. 481, 54 N.E. 587 (1899).

—Good Faith Shown

A party seeking to vacate a divorce settlement agreement may receive attorney fees if she proceeds in good faith, even if she is unsuccessful. In re Broday, 256 Ill. App. 3d 699, 195 Ill. Dec. 326, 628 N.E.2d 790 (1 Dist. 1993).

The evidence was held sufficient to justify an award of attorney fees to the mother, where she exercised good faith in seeking to defend the right of visitation which the court had ordered, especially in light of the many petitions filed and the relief sought and particularly when the father conceded, and the court found, that the mother did not interfere or influence the children in their refusal to visit with their father. Lauzen v. Lauzen, 81 Ill. App. 2d 472, 225 N.E.2d 427 (2 Dist. 1967).

—Harassment of Ex-Spouse

Attorney fees can be assessed against a husband who has been guilty of repeated harassment of a wife who has obtained a valid divorce decree. Jones v. Jones, 48 Ill. App. 2d 232, 198 N.E.2d 195 (1 Dist. 1964).

—Held Improper

Where husband's business went bankrupt through no fault of his own, the husband was justified in not making child support payments, and, therefore, the trial court erred in awarding attorney fees to the wife pursuant to subsection (b) of this section. In re Lavelle, 206 Ill. App. 3d 607, 152 Ill. Dec. 49, 565 N.E.2d 291 (5 Dist. 1990).

Where wife was unemployed and virtually unemployable and where husband, on the other hand, not only had full-time employment with the state, but also ran a farming business, the disparate economic circumstances of the parties dictated a greater award of attorney fees to the wife. In re Gable, 205 Ill. App. 3d 696, 151 Ill. Dec. 109, 563 N.E.2d 1215 (5 Dist. 1990).

Where an award of attorney fees in mother's favor was predicated upon her success in persuading the circuit court to modify father's visitation rights, and where the appellate court reversed the circuit court's decision and remanded the case for further proceedings, the attorney fee award could not stand; however, after completion of the proceedings on remand, the parties were free to seek such fees again. In re L. R., 202 Ill. App. 3d 69, 147 Ill. Dec. 439, 559 N.E.2d 779 (1 Dist. 1990).

Where the trial court assessed attorney fees against wife and her attorney in custody action without considering the financial resources of the parents and the relevant circumstantial factors, the court-ordered fees were improper. Spizzo v. Langman, 168 Ill. App. 3d 487, 119 Ill. Dec. 146, 522 N.E.2d 808 (2 Dist. 1988).

Trial court's order directing husband to pay $1,500 to wife's former attorney, as husband's contribution to attorney fees, was not entered upon a consideration of this section but, instead, was entered upon an independent compromise agreement between the husband and his attorney and, as a result, the court's order constituted a modification of its previous final order more than 30 days after rendition, which the court was without authority to effect; the trial court's order directing husband to pay a portion of attorney fees and permitting attorney to dismiss his petition voluntarily as against wife was therefore erroneous. In re Reidy, 134 Ill. App. 3d 534, 89 Ill. Dec. 454, 480 N.E.2d 1197 (1 Dist. 1985).

Where the evidence demonstrated that a wife might not have been able to pay attorney fees, but did not establish that her former husband was able to do so, an award of attorney fees was held improper. In re Stanley, 133 Ill. App. 3d 963, 89 Ill. Dec. 146, 479 N.E.2d 1152 (4 Dist. 1985).

Attorney fees should not have been awarded to husband respondent where, although he was defending the court's order, he at the same time attacked the order in his cross-appeal. In re Wentink, 132 Ill. App. 3d 71, 87 Ill. Dec. 117, 476 N.E.2d 1109 (1 Dist. 1984).

Where the only major item of marital property, the home, was awarded to wife, leaving husband without assets with which to pay attorney fees as ordered, the trial court's order that husband pay for wife's attorney's defense of appeal was error. In re Sevon, 117 Ill. App. 3d 313, 73 Ill. Dec. 41, 453 N.E.2d 866 (1 Dist. 1983).

In a dissolution case which was not complex or unusual, where the trial took one afternoon and where there was no dispute over the value or nature of the parties' assets, an award of $16,000 in attorney fees was held excessive. In re McNeeley, 117 Ill. App. 3d 320, 72 Ill. Dec. 873, 453 N.E.2d 748 (1 Dist. 1983).

Enforcement of Court Order (Cont'd)

—Held Improper (Cont'd)

An award of attorney fees is improper where there is no evidence presented as to the reasonableness of the fees for such services. Naguit v. Scrivner, 104 Ill. App. 3d 709, 60 Ill. Dec. 499, 433 N.E.2d 296 (5 Dist. 1982).

It was error for the court to award fees to respondent's attorney, who did not file a petition for fees in accordance with subsection (a) of this section, requesting that the court award him fees for services. In re Walsh, 109 Ill. App. 3d 171, 64 Ill. Dec. 758, 440 N.E.2d 310 (1 Dist. 1982).

Although the record amply supported an eighty percent-twenty percent allocation for the responsibility for attorney fees, the amount of attorney fees awarded was excessive where the issues involved were not complex and where counsel shared in the responsibility for unnecessary prolongation of the proceedings. In re Rizzo, 95 Ill. App. 3d 636, 51 Ill. Dec. 141, 420 N.E.2d 555 (1 Dist. 1981).

Where one of wife's attorneys sought $75 per hour for office time and $150 per hour for court time in accordance with his retainer agreement, the trial court's reduction to $90 per court hour and $65 per office hour, in explicit recognition of the financial resources of the parties, rendered the order excessive, particularly when considering the attorney's experience on domestic relations matters. In re Theeke, 105 Ill. App. 3d 119, 60 Ill. Dec. 944, 433 N.E.2d 1311 (1 Dist. 1981).

Where no evidence was presented as to the nature of legal services performed or concerning the number of hours incurred necessary to the resolution of the case, and where the costs advanced were not itemized in any way, then the attorney fee award was to be set aside and the matter remanded for further hearing at which the requisite factors relating to fees were to be considered by the trial court. In re Ransom, 102 Ill. App. 3d 38, 57 Ill. Dec. 696, 429 N.E.2d 594 (2 Dist. 1981).

Where, after respondent had been awarded temporary maintenance, counsel for respondent orally requested an order for temporary attorney's fees, and no petition for fees had been filed, but counsel for respondent stated he had performed approximately 20 hours of work and had been paid only costs, but counsel for petitioner argued such request was premature, and the trial court awarded counsel for respondent $1,000 as temporary fees, this allowance was an abuse of discretion by the trial court; although the award was made after the trial court had heard evidence as to the financial status of the parties, no petition stating the detailed services performed and the amount of fees claimed was ever presented to the trial court by counsel for respondent. The granting of attorney's fees is improper where no evidence is heard as to the items of service performed, or as to the basis of the amount requested or as to the reasonableness of the fees for such services. In re Greenberg, 102 Ill. App. 3d 938, 58 Ill. Dec. 1, 429 N.E.2d 1334 (1 Dist. 1981).

Eighteen thousand dollar award of attorney fees for 100 hours work was excessive even considering the great disparity in income between the parties, the excellent credentials of the wife's attorney and the fact that the case involved an early test of the provisions of the then new Illinois Marriage Act. In re Leon, 80 Ill. App. 3d 383, 35 Ill. Dec. 717, 399 N.E.2d 1006 (2 Dist. 1980).

Where the case was not complex or unusual, the issues were relatively uncomplicated, and the case did not present any novel or significant questions which would justify the fee awarded, the fee was reduced. In re Kruse, 92 Ill. App. 3d 335, 48 Ill. Dec. 145, 416 N.E.2d 40 (1 Dist. 1980).

The evidence indicated that an award of attorney fees was excessive where, although a variety of motions was filed as to custody and visitation, the issues presented were neither novel nor relatively complex from a family law viewpoint. In re Dulyn, 89 Ill. App. 3d 304, 44 Ill. Dec. 622, 411 N.E.2d 988 (1 Dist. 1980).

There was no evidence, given wife's additional income from maintenance, that she was unable to pay her own attorney fees; accordingly, the trial court's award of attorney fees was reversed. In re Schriner, 88 Ill. App. 3d 380, 43 Ill. Dec. 572, 410 N.E.2d 572 (2 Dist. 1980).

An award of $65,000 in attorney fees was improper where the issues were routine and uncomplicated, where vigorous advocacy was not required, and where child support and custody issues were minimized. Donnelley v. Donnelley, 80 Ill. App. 3d 597, 35 Ill. Dec. 919, 400 N.E.2d 56 (1 Dist. 1980).

Where respondent's financial inability to pay his own attorney fees was not established, where there was nothing in the record stating the amount of the attorney fees, and where it appeared that respondent had assets from which to pay such fees, the trial court's order that each party pay his own fees was affirmed. In re Ford, 91 Ill. App. 3d 1066, 47 Ill. Dec. 541, 415 N.E.2d 546 (1 Dist. 1980).

The party seeking an award of attorney fees in a dissolution of marriage action must show his or her financial inability to pay and the ability of the other party to do so; therefore, where both parties conceded that petitioner was financially unable to pay her attorney fees, but where petitioner failed to demonstrate that respondent had the financial ability to pay attorney fees and costs, an order directing respondent to pay those fees was reversed. In re De Frates, 91 Ill. App. 3d 607, 47 Ill. Dec. 72, 414 N.E.2d 1188 (1 Dist. 1980).

Attorney fees allowed should be fair and just to all of the parties involved, namely, the attorney to be compensated, the client, and the person who is required to pay. Christian v. Christian, 69 Ill. App. 3d 450, 26 Ill. Dec. 326, 387 N.E.2d 1254 (1 Dist. 1979); In re Jacobson, 89 Ill. App. 3d 273, 44 Ill. Dec. 581, 411 N.E.2d 947 (1 Dist. 1980).

An award for attorney fees on appeal was set aside where it was made without any supporting evidence as to the financial resources of either party or as to the services rendered; furthermore, there was no evidence that such expenses were necessarily incurred, that is, that under the plaintiff's agreement with her attorney she would have been obligated to pay any appeal fee if the defendant did not do so. In re Jacobson, 89 Ill. App. 3d 273, 44 Ill. Dec. 581, 411 N.E.2d 947 (1 Dist. 1980).

The amount of attorney fees awarded was excessive where the issues involved were uncomplicated. Christian v. Christian, 69 Ill. App. 3d 450, 26 Ill. Dec. 326, 387 N.E.2d 1254 (1 Dist. 1979).

Trial court erred in the award of attorney fees to wife because the court based its award not on the relative financial abilities of the parties, but on the husband's decision to present live witnesses on the property distribution issue instead of agreeing to stipulated facts. In re Stewart, 79 Ill. App. 3d 1125, 35 Ill. Dec. 249, 398 N.E.2d 1199 (1 Dist. 1979).

Where petitioner demonstrated her inability to pay fees and costs, showed that respondent was financially able, and proved she acted in the best interest of the children in instituting the post-decree proceedings, the trial court erred in denying her petition for fees and in granting respondent's attorney's petition for fees under this section. Carr v. Borowczyk, 78 Ill. App. 3d 425, 33 Ill. Dec. 738, 397 N.E.2d 71 (1 Dist. 1979).

A trial court's order awarding attorney fees under former § 16 (see now this section) for the appellee pending the appeal was set aside. Fox v. Fox, 56 Ill. App. 3d 446, 14 Ill. Dec. 201, 371 N.E.2d 1254 (5 Dist. 1978).

In order to justify an allowance of attorney fees in a divorce proceeding, the party seeking relief must show financial inability to pay and the ability of the other spouse to do so. Kolar v. Kolar, 47 Ill. App. 3d 37, 5 Ill. Dec. 428, 361 N.E.2d 751 (1 Dist. 1977).

Where defendant's statements, accepted as true by the trial court, revealed that he was in debt, was unable to borrow money, and was without resources of any kind to pay any part of plaintiff's attorney fees, and where he even expressed a willingness to abandon his appeal from the order denying his petition to modify their divorce decree if he could be excused from paying any fees, which was rejected by plaintiff's counsel, the trial court erred in ordering defendant to pay plaintiff attorney fees to defend the appeal. Kolar v. Kolar, 47 Ill. App. 3d 37, 5 Ill. Dec. 428, 361 N.E.2d 751 (1 Dist. 1977).

Trial court erred in awarding attorney fees to ex-wife when she prevailed in suit against a city to garnish wages of her ex-husband, a city employee, due to her for back alimony and child support payments under a prior statutory provision (see now 750 ILCS 5/706.1). Fair v. City of Chicago, 45 Ill. App. 3d 240, 3 Ill. Dec. 914, 359 N.E.2d 773 (1 Dist. 1977).

In an ordinary divorce case, where a prior attorney had filed the complaint and obtained the grant of temporary alimony, and where plaintiff's petition for attorney's fees itemized 49 hours of work allegedly performed and 100 hours which was merely characterized as miscellaneous telephone calls and conferences with parties and

Enforcement of Court Order (Cont'd)

—Held Improper (Cont'd)

attorneys not dictated, research and other conferences, the record did not support the $8,000 attorney's fees award. Schwartz v. Schwartz, 38 Ill. App. 3d 959, 349 N.E.2d 567 (1 Dist. 1976).

Where the evidence was insufficient to support the award of attorney fees to the wife, the trial court abused its discretion in allowing the attorney fees to her. Gold v. Gold, 17 Ill. App. 3d 11, 308 N.E.2d 75 (1 Dist. 1974).

The trial court erred in awarding temporary attorney fees of $2,500 without a hearing in light of defendant's denial of his ability to pay such fees and in the absence of evidence in regard to the value of the services plaintiff's attorney performed. Dejoie v. Dejoie, 6 Ill. App. 3d 381, 286 N.E.2d 38 (1 Dist. 1972).

Order for wife allowing attorney fees and costs for defending an appeal was in error where although the order found wife was unemployed and had no income of her own, the record disclosed that she held with her second husband two joint bank accounts with funds totalling $2,700 and owned a home in joint tenancy, and, further, the order made no finding as to the husband's ability to pay. Berg v. Berg, 85 Ill. App. 2d 98, 229 N.E.2d 282 (1 Dist. 1967).

The court did not reach the question of excessiveness of an award of attorney fees to plaintiff because, in view of the plaintiff's conduct and the lack of merit to her petition, she should not have been awarded fees at all. Nortwick v. Nortwick, 52 Ill. App. 2d 229, 201 N.E.2d 857 (2 Dist. 1964).

Where a plaintiff filed a petition which she had no action to maintain or defend as all the controversies between herself and her husband as to alimony and support money had been theretofore terminated, which her entire petition should have been stricken on motion, and where in her proceeding in the Supreme Court, she filed a petition for leave to appeal, and she was not defending any decree or order in her favor, there was no duty to allow her any expense money or attorney fees under a prior similar provision (see now this section). Barnett v. Barnett, 341 Ill. App. 26, 93 N.E.2d 93 (3 Dist. 1950).

Under prior similar provision (see now this section), the trial court erred in vacating an order of dismissal and in ordering the payment of attorney fees; it was against the policy of the state to interfere with a reconciliation of married persons in order to provide, after dismissal of the suit, fees for an unpaid attorney. Hefner v. Hefner, 338 Ill. App. 179, 86 N.E.2d 885 (1 Dist. 1949).

—Held Proper

Trial court's award of attorney fees based upon the disparate income of the parties was upheld. In re Minear, 287 Ill. App. 3d 1073, 223 Ill. Dec. 405, 679 N.E.2d 856 (4 Dist. 1997), aff'd, 181 Ill. 2d 552, 230 Ill. Dec. 250, 693 N.E.2d 379 (1998).

Where in presenting wife's request for an award of prospective fees, wife's attorney distinguished the time he would spend in responding to husband's appeal from the time he would spend in prosecuting wife's cross-appeal and in granting wife's request for the prospective award and in later denying husband's motion to vacate the order, the judge emphasized that the fee was being awarded only for counsel's work in the defense of the appeal and not for counsel's separate efforts challenging the circuit court judgment, there was no error in the trial court's award. In re Talty, 166 Ill. 2d 232, 209 Ill. Dec. 790, 652 N.E.2d 330 (1995).

The court's order specifically stated that the petitioner's hiding of assets and providing false accountings to the court caused substantially greater work for respondent's counsel to find assets and to prove his case, and based upon this record, the trial court's award of fees incurred on behalf of respondent was not an abuse of discretion. In re Uehlein, 265 Ill. App. 3d 1080, 202 Ill. Dec. 838, 638 N.E.2d 706 (1 Dist. 1994).

Award of attorney's fees was authorized even though the trial court did not find respondent in contempt for failure to pay child support. In re Florence, 260 Ill. App. 3d 116, 198 Ill. Dec. 351, 632 N.E.2d 681 (4 Dist.), appeal denied, 157 Ill. 2d 498, 205 Ill. Dec. 160, 642 N.E.2d 1277 (1994).

Trial judge did not abuse her discretion when she found that husband was financially able to pay the fees and wife was financially unable to pay them; wife was earning half of husband's income. Husband had the discretion to work more to earn a higher income and the property division was essentially equal. In re Parker, 252 Ill. App. 3d 1015, 192 Ill. Dec. 277, 625 N.E.2d 237 (1 Dist. 1993).

Award of attorney fees in the amount of $27,000 and $2,416 to wife was not an abuse of discretion given the financial positions of the parties and the voluntary actions of the husband in selling his business and becoming unemployed. In re Morse, 240 Ill. App. 3d 296, 180 Ill. Dec. 563, 607 N.E.2d 632 (2 Dist. 1993).

Where the record was replete with inordinate delays and orders finding defendant in contempt for his failure to remain current in his child support payments and clearly supported an implicit finding by the court that defendant's repeated failures to comply with the court's order were "without cause or justification," the court did not err in ordering defendant to pay plaintiff's attorney fees. Davis v. Sprague, 186 Ill. App. 3d 249, 133 Ill. Dec. 620, 541 N.E.2d 831 (4 Dist. 1989).

Where the trial court reviewed the fee petition, heard testimony, and considered arguments of counsel, the court properly exercised its broad discretion in setting an attorney fee award; however, the cost of two depositions used at trial should have been included in wife's recoverable costs. In re Lefler, 185 Ill. App. 3d 677, 134 Ill. Dec. 1, 542 N.E.2d 1 (1 Dist. 1988).

Respondent's wilful and contumacious refusal to pay child support when he had sufficient funds to pay was self-evident of conduct without cause or justification so as to allow attorney fees under subsection (b) of this section. In re Betts, 172 Ill. App. 3d 742, 122 Ill. Dec. 599, 526 N.E.2d 1138 (4 Dist. 1988).

An award of attorney fees is justified where the spouse seeking relief demonstrates financial inability to pay, and the ability of the other spouse to pay. In re Calisoff, 176 Ill. App. 3d 721, 126 Ill. Dec. 183, 531 N.E.2d 810 (1 Dist. 1988).

Where trial court explicitly found that former husband's failure to pay support was without cause or justification, subsection (b) of this section mandated an award of attorney fees. In re Robertson, 151 Ill. App. 3d 214, 104 Ill. Dec. 619, 502 N.E.2d 1279 (1 Dist. 1986).

A review of the record led to the conclusion that the trial court did not abuse its discretion in awarding attorney fees to wife. In re Weaver, 133 Ill. App. 3d 825, 88 Ill. Dec. 839, 479 N.E.2d 452 (4 Dist. 1985).

Where court ordered petitioner to pay $10,092.33 to respondent's attorney as petitioner's 90% share of the fees and expense reimbursements to which the attorney was entitled, the fee award was not excessive. In re Bussey, 128 Ill. App. 3d 730, 84 Ill. Dec. 34, 471 N.E.2d 563 (4 Dist. 1984).

There was no abuse of discretion in ordering husband to pay wife's attorney fees in support modification proceedings where the record indicated that she was unemployed and had no income other than the child support paid by husband and where he did have income. In re Arnold, 122 Ill. App. 3d 776, 78 Ill. Dec. 335, 462 N.E.2d 51 (3 Dist. 1984).

An award of attorney fees in dissolution proceedings rests within the sound discretion of the trial court, and the exercise thereof will not be disturbed on review unless such discretion is clearly abused. In re Cook, 117 Ill. App. 3d 844, 73 Ill. Dec. 222, 453 N.E.2d 1357 (1 Dist. 1983).

Where husband's conduct made necessary an unusual amount of legal services, a trial court order directing him to pay $30,000 of the $50,000 awarded to wife's attorneys was upheld, in view of husband's failure or inability to comply with court order and procedures and in view of his failure to document his finances and to demonstrate his inability to pay the prescribed fees. In re Cook, 117 Ill. App. 3d 844, 73 Ill. Dec. 222, 453 N.E.2d 1357 (1 Dist. 1983).

The award of petitioner's attorney fees and costs was well within the court's discretion. In re Hobbs, 110 Ill. App. 3d 451, 66 Ill. Dec. 203, 442 N.E.2d 629 (3 Dist. 1982).

Where virtually all of the facts presented to the court were in the form of stipulations, and where the issues involved were neither complex nor difficult, the limited amount of attorney fees awarded by the trial court was well within the scope of its discretion. In re Keller, 108 Ill. App. 3d 556, 64 Ill. Dec. 115, 439 N.E.2d 44 (1 Dist. 1982).

In a marriage dissolution proceeding, the allowance of a total fee to petitioner-wife's attorney in the amount of $5,500 was fair and reasonable, and respondent-husband was to pay one-half of this allowance and petitioner wife was to pay the other half. In re

Enforcement of Court Order (Cont'd)

—Held Proper (Cont'd)
Panozzo, 93 Ill. App. 3d 1085, 49 Ill. Dec. 372, 418 N.E.2d 16 (1 Dist. 1981).

The record amply supported the 80%-20% allocation for the responsibility of attorney fees. In re Rizzo, 95 Ill. App. 3d 636, 51 Ill. Dec. 141, 420 N.E.2d 555 (1 Dist. 1981).

Husband's financial resources were sufficiently greater than those of the wife so as to warrant an award of attorney fees. In re Sipich, 80 Ill. App. 3d 883, 36 Ill. Dec. 276, 400 N.E.2d 696 (1 Dist. 1980).

The evidence in the record fully supported an award of $771.20 in attorney fees to former wife where she was financially unable to pay. In re Coram, 86 Ill. App. 3d 845, 42 Ill. Dec. 40, 408 N.E.2d 418 (5 Dist. 1980).

Where husband's net monthly take-home pay was $1,535, where wife's weekly earnings were approximately $59, and where the marital home was not a liquid asset, the trial court did not abuse its discretion in requiring the husband to pay $3,500 of the attorney fees. In re Rogers, 86 Ill. App. 3d 904, 42 Ill. Dec. 70, 408 N.E.2d 448 (2 Dist. 1980), aff'd, 85 Ill. 2d 217, 52 Ill. Dec. 633, 422 N.E.2d 635 (1981).

Where the trial judge had before him sufficient evidence to make a determination on the relative financial ability of each party to pay his own fees and concluded on the basis of that evidence that an award of attorney fees was proper, that determination would not be disturbed absent an abuse of discretion. In re Preston, 81 Ill. App. 3d 672, 37 Ill. Dec. 442, 402 N.E.2d 332 (5 Dist. 1980).

The trial court was justified in requiring petitioner to pay fees to respondent's attorneys. In re Raidbard, 87 Ill. App. 3d 158, 42 Ill. Dec. 312, 408 N.E.2d 1021 (1 Dist. 1980).

For costs and expenses, the award of $1,851 was proper, where it included a $1,300 fee paid to an accountant who was retained by petitioner to analyze petitioner's financial status. In re Kruse, 92 Ill. App. 3d 335, 48 Ill. Dec. 145, 416 N.E.2d 40 (1 Dist. 1980).

Under former Ill.Rev.Stat., ch. 40, para. 16 (see now this section), the trial court properly awarded attorney fees for services to plaintiff in prosecuting an appeal and several post-judgment petitions in her behalf. Gilmore v. Gilmore, 74 Ill. App. 3d 831, 30 Ill. Dec. 378, 393 N.E.2d 33 (1 Dist. 1979).

Evidence was sufficient to support an award of fees where the disbursement of the wife's funds would exhaust her own estate, strip her of her means of support, and undetermine her economic stability; the trial court's decision that the plaintiff was unable to pay her fees while defendant was able to do so was correct, but the amount of fees awarded was unjustified and excessive. Gasperini v. Gasperini, 57 Ill. App. 3d 578, 15 Ill. Dec. 230, 373 N.E.2d 576 (1 Dist. 1978).

Trial court did not err in awarding appellee attorney fees where it became necessary for a party to employ counsel to come into court to enforce his rights under a decree of the court; such party was entitled to an allowance of reasonable attorney fees, and attorney fees could have been awarded in post-decree proceedings in the trial court to modify the provisions of the decree. Doggett v. Doggett, 51 Ill. App. 3d 868, 9 Ill. Dec. 474, 366 N.E.2d 985 (5 Dist. 1977).

Because wife was receiving public assistance and was without means to pay for an attorney and thus unable to properly protect the rights of her child, the services provided by counsel on appeal were for the child's benefit and support in the same way that the action itself was for the support and benefit of the child; therefore, the trial court could award attorney fees under the same plenary equitable powers authorizing it to make such orders as were necessary for the support of the child, and this should have included fees for the defense of an appeal involving the rights of the child. Zalduendo v. Zalduendo, 45 Ill. App. 3d 849, 4 Ill. Dec. 450, 360 N.E.2d 386 (1 Dist. 1977).

In a modification proceeding, where it was clear that wife was without sufficient assets of her own to pay her attorney fees, trial court did not abuse its discretion in awarding attorney's fees to her. Robin v. Robin, 45 Ill. App. 3d 365, 3 Ill. Dec. 950, 359 N.E.2d 809 (1 Dist. 1977).

Where the trial court was familiar with the skill and reputation of counsel, given the nature of the controversy, the amount involved, the time spent, and the results achieved, an award of $1,250 attorneys' fees was well within the discretion of the trial court. Hickey v. Hickey, 31 Ill. App. 3d 257, 333 N.E.2d 271 (1 Dist. 1975).

Where the record revealed both that the plaintiff, who merely speculated as to her potential earnings upon receipt of her doctorate, was unable to pay her attorney and that the defendant was able to pay the fees, the amount of the attorney fees awarded was held proper. Anagnostopoulos v. Anagnostopoulos, 22 Ill. App. 3d 479, 317 N.E.2d 681 (1 Dist. 1974).

Although former wife had $13,000 from which she purchased a new automobile, where the pleadings contained a decree finding that, without her fault, she was living apart from the plaintiff with custody of a growing boy on a monthly temporary alimony of $650 and she alleged, and plaintiff did not reply, that she was unable to pay her attorney fees, it was equitable and proper for the trial judge to consider plaintiff's greater financial ability and allow defendant's motion for additional temporary attorneys fees. Kaufman v. Kaufman, 22 Ill. App. 3d 1045, 318 N.E.2d 282 (1 Dist. 1974).

The trial court was justified in awarding fees to plaintiff's attorney where it heard evidence on the financial status of the parties and considered the extent and character of legal services rendered. Mills v. Mills, 13 Ill. App. 3d 288, 300 N.E.2d 842 (1 Dist. 1973).

Ordering a husband to pay an ex-wife's attorney an allowance for her defense on the husband's initial appeal from a post-decretal order was not error. Waltrip v. Waltrip, 3 Ill. App. 3d 892, 279 N.E.2d 405 (2 Dist. 1972).

The allowance of $750 to plaintiff's attorney for his services relating to a support order was not excessive. Saxon v. Saxon, 24 Ill. App. 2d 116, 164 N.E.2d 248 (1 Dist. 1960).

—History
When the legislature amended the former Divorce Act by deleting the 1975 provision of former section 16 (see now this section), the trial court was stripped of its authority to allow attorney fees for the appellee pending the appeal. Fox v. Fox, 56 Ill. App. 3d 446, 14 Ill. Dec. 201, 371 N.E.2d 1254 (5 Dist. 1978).

—Insufficient Evidence
Where no evidence was heard by the court on the question of the inability of plaintiff to pay her own attorney's fees and the only evidence offered was the testimony of plaintiff's counsel regarding extent and value of his services, the refusal of counsel for defendant to cross-examine opposing counsel could not be construed as a waiver of the necessary evidence regarding ability of the parties to pay; consequently, the issue was reversed and remanded with directions to hear the evidence and determine if attorney's fees were properly allowable against defendant. Breuer v. Breuer, 4 Ill. App. 3d 179, 280 N.E.2d 518 (1 Dist. 1972).

—Legislative Intent
The language "decree or order" in former section 16 of the Divorce Act (see now 750 ILCS 5/501 and this section) indicated the legislature contemplated that fees could be awarded in situations other than an appeal from the decree itself. Booth v. Booth, 132 Ill. App. 2d 758, 270 N.E.2d 171 (1 Dist. 1971).

—Life-Style and Standard of Living
Where wife had made sacrifices by working three jobs while caring for her children and husband worked one job and was apparently living at the same standard of living he enjoyed prior to the dissolution, the trial court was entitled to give weight to his life-style and the fact he litigated case to the fullest, without any apparent regard to cost; trial court did not abuse its discretion when it found that husband should pay one-half of wife's fees. In re McCoy, 272 Ill. App. 3d 125, 208 Ill. Dec. 732, 650 N.E.2d 3 (4 Dist. 1995).

—Misuse of Trust Funds
Father who used son's trust fund money to pay for father's share of son's college expenses was required to pay costs and reasonable attorney's fees of former wife in her action against former husband as husband's action was without cause or justification. In re Kaplan, 244 Ill. App. 3d 401, 184 Ill. Dec. 225, 612 N.E.2d 1385 (4 Dist. 1993).

—Petition After Satisfaction
A court could have allowed attorney fees after entry of a decree in defense of an appeal where the enforcement of the decree was divested by the circumstance that the petition for the allowance of fees was filed after the payment and satisfaction of the money

Enforcement of Court Order (Cont'd)

—Petition After Satisfaction (Cont'd)
judgment contained in the divorce decree. Riddlesbarger v. Riddlesbarger, 341 Ill. App. 107, 93 N.E.2d 380 (1 Dist. 1950).

—Post-Decretal Proceedings
Attorney fees may be awarded in post-decree proceedings in the trial court to modify the provisions of the decree. Horwitz v. Horwitz, 130 Ill. App. 2d 424, 264 N.E.2d 723 (1 Dist. 1970).

Where post-decree proceedings are brought to modify the custodial provisions of a decree, the husband is liable for legal services rendered necessary to properly present the needs of the children to the court; however, where the custodial modification is sought primarily for the convenience of the parties and not the welfare of the children, the attorney's allowance will be disallowed. Horwitz v. Horwitz, 130 Ill. App. 2d 424, 264 N.E.2d 723 (1 Dist. 1970).

Attorney fees are not awarded in advance of a post-decree proceeding but only after a full adjudication on the merits of the petition. Horwitz v. Horwitz, 130 Ill. App. 2d 424, 264 N.E.2d 723 (1 Dist. 1970).

—Reasonableness
Without evidence of the reasonableness of attorney fees, attorney fees cannot be awarded in marriage dissolution proceeding. In re Uphoff, 110 Ill. App. 3d 608, 66 Ill. Dec. 404, 442 N.E.2d 965 (4 Dist. 1982), modified on other grounds, 99 Ill. 2d 90, 75 Ill. Dec. 432, 457 N.E.2d 426 (1983).

—Retroactive Allowance
Where a plaintiff found means to finance various steps of her litigation, including an appeal to the Supreme Court, a retroactive allowance for attorney fees was not made. Barnett v. Barnett, 341 Ill. App. 26, 93 N.E.2d 93 (3 Dist. 1950).

—Statement by Attorney
Where the amount of time the former wife's lawyer devoted to the case did not appear unreasonable, the compensation sought was within reasonable limits, and there was no showing that discovery proceedings would have revealed anything that would have helped former husband defend the motion for fees, the trial court did not err in determining the amount of additional temporary attorney fees to be paid by former husband by relying on the statement of former wife's attorney concerning the hours he said had been spent in defending the suit filed by the husband. Kaufman v. Kaufman, 22 Ill. App. 3d 1045, 318 N.E.2d 282 (1 Dist. 1974).

—Supplemental Fees
Where the order for supplemental attorney fees was supported by the law and the evidence, and it was not obtained in violation of defendant's constitutional rights, such award was affirmed. Kazubowski v. Kazubowski, 45 Ill. 2d 405, 259 N.E.2d 282, cert. denied, 400 U.S. 926, 91 S. Ct. 188, 27 L. Ed. 2d 186 (1970).

Bankruptcy

—Discharge of Debt
An award of attorney fees pursuant to this section is based on the financial resources of the parties, which ordinarily indicates that the award is in the nature of maintenance or support; however, certain factors may demonstrate that the award of fees is in the nature of a property settlement, and the considerations include whether the provision creating the obligation to pay the attorney fees is located within the property settlement provisions or within the support provisions, or whether the obligation relates to the support of the children and/or whether the obligation was intended to balance the income of the parties. Skryd v. Kijewski, 91 Bankr. 48 (Bankr. N.D. Ill. 1988).

Where the only support awarded to the debtor's ex-wife was minimal child support, and where the debtor and his ex-wife expressly waived all rights to receive maintenance or support, and where the waiver specified that both parties were employed and neither party was dependent upon the other for support or maintenance, all factors indicated that the award of fees was not based on the financial resources of the parties; therefore, the award of attorney's fees was in the nature of a property settlement and was subject to discharge under § 727(a) of the Bankruptcy Code (11 U.S.C. § 727(a)). Skryd v. Kijewski, 91 Bankr. 48 (Bankr. N.D. Ill. 1988).

—Effect of Award
Where husband was gainfully employed as an attorney and owned a practice which had been very lucrative, and where the wife was not employed outside the home during the marriage, the state court's award of attorney fees was interpreted as an attempt to balance the income of the parties and was in the nature of maintenance and support. Berks v. Doss (In re Calisoff), 92 Bankr. 346 (Bankr. N.D. Ill. 1988).

The award of attorney fees to be paid for wife by debtor in bankruptcy in Illinois divorce proceedings were viewed as a form of maintenance or support, and were not dischargeable in bankruptcy. Abitua v. Abitua, 18 Bankr. 674 (Bankr. N.D. Ill. 1982).

—Nondischargeable Debt
Where attorney fees were incurred to collect a past due child support payment, and where the divorce court ordered the debtor to pay those fees pursuant to this section, the debtor's obligation to pay attorney fees in the amount of $2,500.00, incurred to secure post-decree enforcement of child support payments, were in the nature of maintenance and support and were therefore nondischargeable under § 523(a)(5) of the Bankruptcy Code (11 U.S.C.A. § 523(a)(5)). Jacobs v. Zimberoff, 91 Bankr. 839 (Bankr. N.D. Ill. 1988).

Debtor's obligation to pay attorney fees incurred by spouse as mandated by the divorce court's order was in the nature of maintenance and support and, therefore, nondischargeable in bankruptcy. Doss, Puchalski, Keenan & Bargiel, Ltd. v. Cockhill, 72 Bankr. 339 (Bankr. N.D. Ill. 1987).

Since an award of attorney fees under this section is based upon the husband's duty to support his wife, such an award falls within the definition of alimony for purposes of dischargeability in bankruptcy, regardless whether the fees are payable to the wife or her attorney; attorney fees of this nature are not dischargeable in bankruptcy. Richter v. Pelikant, 5 Bankr. 404 (Bankr. N.D. Ill. 1980).

Attorney fees awarded to the wife in an Illinois divorce action but which were ordered paid directly to her attorney constituted a nondischargeable debt in a voluntary bankruptcy proceeding filed by the husband. In re Cornish, 529 F.2d 1363 (7th Cir. 1976).

Attorney fees awarded in a divorce decree are in the nature of alimony and are not dischargeable in bankruptcy; the fact that the claim for attorney fees has been merged into a decree does not render it dischargeable in bankruptcy. Morrey ex rel. Beaver v. Morrey, 24 Ill. App. 3d 77, 320 N.E.2d 503 (1 Dist. 1974).

Award of solicitors' fees to the wife in a divorce suit pursuant to former paragraph 16 of this chapter (see now this section), constituted alimony within the meaning of the Bankruptcy Act, which prevented discharge of liabilities for alimony due or to become due, or for maintenance or support of wife or child. Merriman v. Hawbaker, 5 F. Supp. 432 (E.D. Ill. 1934).

Billing
The client's right to an itemized statement is not waived because the client failed to object to the amount of the attorney's fee or failed to request a hearing under this section prior to the entry of the judgment. In re Pitulla, 141 Ill. App. 3d 956, 96 Ill. Dec. 276, 491 N.E.2d 90 (1 Dist. 1986).

Burden of Proof
Wife bore the burden of showing her financial inability to pay attorney's fees as well as husband's financial ability to pay them; thus, the circuit court did not abuse its discretion in denying petition for attorney's fees and costs under subsection (a). In re Goldberg, 282 Ill. App. 3d 997, 218 Ill. Dec. 272, 668 N.E.2d 1104 (1 Dist. 1996).

A spouse seeking an award of attorneys' fees and costs must show financial inability to pay the fees as well as the financial ability of the other spouse to pay them. In re Goldberg, 282 Ill. App. 3d 997, 218 Ill. Dec. 272, 668 N.E.2d 1104 (1 Dist. 1996).

A party who has failed to comply with a court order should be required to bear the burden of both presenting evidence upon and proving justification for the lack of compliance, or at least that the lack of compliance was not without cause or justification. In re

Burden of Proof (Cont'd)
Young, 200 Ill. App. 3d 226, 147 Ill. Dec. 178, 559 N.E.2d 178 (4 Dist. 1990).

A party seeking attorney fees has the burden in the trial court to present sufficiently specific evidence of his entitlement. In re Ahmad, 198 Ill. App. 3d 15, 144 Ill. Dec. 320, 555 N.E.2d 439 (2 Dist. 1990).

A party seeking attorney fees must show a financial inability to pay and must show the financial ability of the opposing spouse to pay. In re Osborn, 206 Ill. App. 3d 588, 151 Ill. Dec. 663, 564 N.E.2d 1325 (5 Dist. 1990), cert. denied, 137 Ill. 2d 666, 156 Ill. Dec. 563, 571 N.E.2d 150 (1991).

Financial inability does not mean destitution, but rather that the required payment would strip the petitioner of her means of support and undermine her financial stability. In re Osborn, 206 Ill. App. 3d 588, 151 Ill. Dec. 663, 564 N.E.2d 1325 (5 Dist. 1990), cert. denied, 137 Ill. 2d 666, 156 Ill. Dec. 563, 571 N.E.2d 150 (1991).

A party seeking attorney fees must show financial inability to pay, financial needs within the context of the prior couple's standard of living, and the ability of the other spouse to pay. In re Ackerman, 168 Ill. App. 3d 438, 118 Ill. Dec. 862, 522 N.E.2d 317 (2 Dist. 1988).

To justify allowance of attorney fees, the party seeking the relief must show financial inability to pay and the ability of the other spouse to do so. Faris v. Faris, 142 Ill. App. 3d 987, 97 Ill. Dec. 209, 492 N.E.2d 645 (2 Dist. 1986), appeal denied, 100 Ill. Dec. 603, 497 N.E.2d 781 (Ill. 1986).

Calculation
Nothing in subsection (a) directs a court to use the net income formula contained in 750 ILCS 505(a)(3). In re Krivi, 283 Ill. App. 3d 772, 219 Ill. Dec. 274, 670 N.E.2d 1162 (5 Dist. 1996).

Child Custody Proceedings
In an action to modify a child custody order, it was inequitable to require a father to pay his wife's attorney fees where the father rescued the child from a dangerous environment and acted in her best interest. In re Cotton, 103 Ill. 2d 346, 83 Ill. Dec. 143, 469 N.E.2d 1077 (1984).

An award of attorney fees in a child custody proceeding is not authorized by subsection (a) of this section where the parties were never married to each other. Mac Harg v. Bremer, 120 Ill. App. 3d 753, 76 Ill. Dec. 500, 458 N.E.2d 1154 (1 Dist. 1983).

Where, at the time the original decree was entered, the mother was a patient in a hospital for the mentally ill and the decree provided that in the event of her recovery she would have the right to apply to the court for custody of her son, the evidence was sufficient to sustain the order granting an allowance to the mother for her attorney fees, and stenographic and printing costs in defending the appeal challenging her right to custody of her son. Gerst v. Gerst, 349 Ill. App. 201, 110 N.E.2d 470 (1 Dist. 1953).

Child Support Proceedings
Once a noncustodial parent withholds child support without cause or justification, that party will be ordered to pay costs and reasonable fees to the prevailing party for the services rendered both in the trial and the appellate court proceedings, regardless of who initiates the appeal. Clay v. Clay, 210 Ill. App. 3d 778, 155 Ill. Dec. 280, 569 N.E.2d 280 (4 Dist. 1991).

Attorney fees were properly awarded by the trial court to wife where husband's failure to comply with child support order was unjustified. Baker v. Baker, 193 Ill. App. 3d 294, 140 Ill. Dec. 303, 549 N.E.2d 954 (4 Dist. 1990).

While petitioner's motion for child support arrearages was based on the provision in the original judgment that support be adjusted automatically, upward or downward, each year based on the consumer price index, petitioner's motion was more properly characterized as requesting a determination of support rather than enforcement of the prior judgment; therefore, the trial court could properly award fees in its discretion based on the parties' ability to pay such fees. In re Dodge, 150 Ill. App. 3d 486, 103 Ill. Dec. 816, 501 N.E.2d 1354 (2 Dist. 1986).

A petition for attorney fees filed by petitioner in connection with her defense of respondent's petition to suspend child support payments did not come within the provisions of subsection (b) of this section and was governed by the general rule that the allowance of attorney fees is within the sound discretion of the trial court, and its determination would not be overturned unless the trial court had clearly abused its discretion. In re Chenoweth, 134 Ill. App. 3d 1015, 89 Ill. Dec. 922, 481 N.E.2d 765 (5 Dist. 1985).

An order finding husband in contempt carried with it an implicit finding that his failure to make child support payments was without cause or justification, thus providing the basis for a mandatory award of attorney fees to wife pursuant to subsection (b) of this section. In re Stanley, 133 Ill. App. 3d 963, 89 Ill. Dec. 146, 479 N.E.2d 1152 (4 Dist. 1985).

A trial court in the matter of enforcement of child support orders has no discretion as to whether to award costs and fees, as its only discretion is to decide whether the failure to pay was without cause or justification; if the court so finds, the payment of fees and costs in a reasonable amount is mandatory; if it finds that there was justification or, to state it another way, the failure was not wilful and wanton, it may deny fees and costs. Elliott v. Elliott, 137 Ill. App. 3d 277, 91 Ill. Dec. 923, 484 N.E.2d 482 (4 Dist. 1985).

Where a father apparently relied upon what he thought was an agreement to reduce child support payments and the amount owed to the mother was paid to his daughter, which was evidence that he acted in good faith, and where his decision to unilaterally reduce child support payments as each child attained the age of majority was made in reliance on the incorrect and improper legal advice of the circuit clerk, his unilateral reduction of child support payments was not without cause or justification and the trial court's denial of attorney fees was proper. Elliott v. Elliott, 137 Ill. App. 3d 277, 91 Ill. Dec. 923, 484 N.E.2d 482 (4 Dist. 1985).

Subsection (b) of this section is a mandatory provision which required the trial court to order the parent against whom a child support enforcement action was brought to pay the costs and reasonable attorney fees incurred by the custodial parent in bringing the action. Fogliano v. Fogliano, 113 Ill. App. 3d 1018, 69 Ill. Dec. 785, 448 N.E.2d 245 (3 Dist. 1983).

Attorney fees are recoverable under this Act when child support is sought. Skilling v. Skilling, 104 Ill. App. 3d 213, 59 Ill. Dec. 937, 432 N.E.2d 881 (1 Dist. 1982).

Where defendant husband failed to make child support payments, and where it was necessary for plaintiff wife to retain an attorney for the purpose of enforcing the child support decree, she was entitled to reasonable attorney fees. Hurt v. Hurt, 351 Ill. App. 427, 115 N.E.2d 638 (1 Dist. 1953).

Contempt
Although respondent characterized attorney fees award as "punishment" and that original order found criminal contempt, a subsequent order clearly stated that the $1,000 in attorney fees were awarded to petitioner pursuant to this section and not as a remedy requested by petitioner in the petition for rule to show cause or as a sanction imposed by the court; therefore, the trial court failed to impose any sanction and there was no vehicle for determining whether the finding of contempt was civil or criminal. In re Depew, 246 Ill. App. 3d 960, 186 Ill. Dec. 482, 616 N.E.2d 672 (5 Dist. 1993).

After assessing attorney fees, the trial court is not mandated to require their payment in order to purge a contempt finding; however, the trial court may do so. In re Betts, 172 Ill. App. 3d 742, 122 Ill. Dec. 599, 526 N.E.2d 1138 (4 Dist. 1988).

Contingent Fees
A contingent fee contract is not invalid if it relates to the collection of unpaid child support and maintenance. Fletcher v. Fletcher, 227 Ill. App. 3d 194, 169 Ill. Dec. 211, 591 N.E.2d 91 (4 Dist. 1992).

Contractual Limitation
Where a former spouse's liability for attorney fees was limited by a contract entered into between herself and her attorney, an award for attorney fees could not be based on any amount which exceeded the amount for which she herself could be held liable under the contract. In re Magnuson, 156 Ill. App. 3d 691, 109 Ill. Dec. 569, 510 N.E.2d 437 (2 Dist. 1987).

Default
Each support or maintenance payment is vested on the date it becomes due, and this date becomes the default/vesting date, which is important for (1) calculating the total arrearage; (2) calculating the interest owed, if any; (3) an indicator or factor in determining whether the conduct was wilful or contumacious; and (4) calculat-

Default (Cont'd)
ing attorney fees under this section. In re Hardy, 191 Ill. App. 3d 685, 138 Ill. Dec. 909, 548 N.E.2d 139 (5 Dist. 1989).

Destitution
Just as a party does not have to be destitute to receive an award of fees, neither does the opposing party have to be destitute to avoid paying attorney fees. In re Werries, 247 Ill. App. 3d 639, 186 Ill. Dec. 747, 616 N.E.2d 1379 (4 Dist. 1993).

Enforcement
An award of attorney fees may be made for expenses incurred in connection with a proceeding to enforce the provisions of a dissolution order, even if that proceeding occurs in another court. In re Davis, 292 Ill. App. 3d 802, 226 Ill. Dec. 765, 686 N.E.2d 395 (4 Dist. 1997).

Evidence
Husband was entitled to an award of attorney's fees, notwithstanding the absence of actual contemporaneous time records of the attorney, where: (1) the attorney testified that 90% of the time she wrote down her hours the same day, (2) the attorney presented the court with two sets of computer-generated documents which detailed the work performed, and (3) each exhibit listed the time and billing records for the husband's case, but each was recorded in a slightly different format. In re Shinn, 313 Ill. App. 3d 317, 246 Ill. Dec. 173, 729 N.E.2d 546, 2000 Ill. App. LEXIS 368 (4 Dist. 2000), appeal denied sub nom. Shinn v. Shinn, 191 Ill. 2d 560, 250 Ill. Dec. 467, 738 N.E.2d 936 (2000).

While typically it is a spouse who requests a hearing, there is no reason why an attorney, when faced with opposition to his fee petition by the other spouse, should be precluded from presenting evidence in support of the petition. Lee v. Lee, 302 Ill. App. 3d 607, 236 Ill. Dec. 222, 707 N.E.2d 67 (1 Dist. 1998).

A summary of fees charged and an attorney's testimony at a hearing on the petition for fees was sufficient evidence to substantiate the amount of attorney fees awarded. In re Orlando, 218 Ill. App. 3d 312, 160 Ill. Dec. 763, 577 N.E.2d 1334 (1 Dist. 1991).

The trial court should have permitted the attorney to introduce the fee agreement with the client into evidence, as the agreement and the fact that the client executed it are relevant in determining the reasonableness of the attorney's fee request. In re Gorsich, 208 Ill. App. 3d 852, 153 Ill. Dec. 643, 567 N.E.2d 601 (2 Dist. 1991).

Where, six days following the trial, the wife's attorney submitted a supplemental statement showing the time spent on each task performed six days following the trial, the court concluded that there was sufficient evidence of the relevant factors used to consider the award of attorney fees to the wife and that the amount awarded was supported by the evidence. In re Osborn, 206 Ill. App. 3d 588, 151 Ill. Dec. 663, 564 N.E.2d 1325 (5 Dist. 1990), cert. denied, 137 Ill. 2d 666, 156 Ill. Dec. 563, 571 N.E.2d 150 (1991).

It must be apparent that attorney fees sought were necessarily incurred, and more must be shown to justify a fee request than a mere compilation of hours and an hourly rate. In re Angiuli, 134 Ill. App. 3d 417, 89 Ill. Dec. 328, 480 N.E.2d 513 (2 Dist. 1985).

To justify the reasonableness of an award of attorney fees, something more must be shown than merely a compilation of an hourly rate. In re Hirsch, 135 Ill. App. 3d 945, 90 Ill. Dec. 646, 482 N.E.2d 625 (1 Dist. 1985).

An attorney's general statement as to the time spent is an insufficient basis for a fee award and detailed time records are usually required. In re Pease, 106 Ill. App. 3d 617, 62 Ill. Dec. 389, 435 N.E.2d 1361 (2 Dist. 1982).

An attorney's general statement as to time spent on a matter is an insufficient basis for a fee award and detailed time records are usually required; he must itemize both the time expended and the work performed. In re Ransom, 102 Ill. App. 3d 38, 57 Ill. Dec. 696, 429 N.E.2d 594 (2 Dist. 1981).

The time charged must have been necessary for the proper handling of the matters involved, the fees must be fair and just to all parties involved, and the time expended and the work done must be itemized. In re Janetzke, 97 Ill. App. 3d 418, 52 Ill. Dec. 705, 422 N.E.2d 914 (1 Dist. 1981).

The time expended by an attorney as shown by detailed records is a factor of great importance in ascertaining a reasonable fee; however, it is not sufficient to merely multiply the number of hours expended by counsel, even as shown by detailed records, by whatever hourly rate is determined to be reasonable without consideration of the other factors. In re Janetzke, 97 Ill. App. 3d 418, 52 Ill. Dec. 705, 422 N.E.2d 914 (1 Dist. 1981).

Where there was no petition filed for attorney fees, where no time records or other supporting documents were presented, and where the record showed that the only contested proceeding was of limited duration and difficulty, an award of attorney fees was not supported. In re Janetzke, 97 Ill. App. 3d 418, 52 Ill. Dec. 705, 422 N.E.2d 914 (1 Dist. 1981).

Where the record reflected no attorney time records of any kind, but only a statement of the approximate number of hours contained in unverified petitions without itemization, an award of $5,000 for attorney fees was unjustified. In re Raidbard, 87 Ill. App. 3d 158, 42 Ill. Dec. 312, 408 N.E.2d 1021 (1 Dist. 1980).

Hours which were billed as court time but which were spent on uncontested matters, such as agreed orders and continuances, should not be fully compensable as court time since the work done did not require courtroom skills. In re Kruse, 92 Ill. App. 3d 335, 48 Ill. Dec. 145, 416 N.E.2d 40 (1 Dist. 1980).

The granting of attorney fees is improper where no evidence is heard as to the items of service which were performed, or as to the basis of the amount requested or as to the reasonableness of the fees for such services. In re Jacobson, 89 Ill. App. 3d 273, 44 Ill. Dec. 581, 411 N.E.2d 947 (1 Dist. 1980).

Factors
The amount of fees to be allowed in a divorce proceeding depends on a consideration of the skill and standing of the attorneys employed, the nature of the controversy, the novelty and difficulty of the questions at issue, the amount and importance of the subject matter, especially from a family law standpoint, the degree of responsibility involved in the management of the case, the time and labor required, the usual and customary charge in the community, and the benefits resulting to the client. In re Drone, 217 Ill. App. 3d 758, 160 Ill. Dec. 601, 577 N.E.2d 926 (5 Dist. 1991).

The allocation of assets, liabilities, the award of any maintenance, and the relative earning abilities of the parties should be considered when determining an allocation of attorney fees pursuant to this section. In re Carr, 211 Ill. App. 3d 609, 164 Ill. Dec. 189, 582 N.E.2d 752 (5 Dist. 1991).

The factors to consider in determining the amount of attorney fees are the skill and standing of the attorney, the nature of the case, the novelty and difficulty of the questions at issue, the amount and importance of the subject matter, the degree of responsibility, the usual and customary charges, and the benefits resulting to the client. In re Osborn, 206 Ill. App. 3d 588, 151 Ill. Dec. 663, 564 N.E.2d 1325 (5 Dist. 1990), cert. denied, 137 Ill. 2d 666, 156 Ill. Dec. 563, 571 N.E.2d 150 (1991).

In determining the fee award, the trial court is to consider the following factors: the importance, novelty and difficulty of the questions raised, the degree of responsibility of the attorney, the time and labor required, the benefits resulting to the client, the skill and standing of the attorneys employed, the usual and customary charge in the community and the financial position of the parties. In re Wardell, 149 Ill. App. 3d 537, 102 Ill. Dec. 859, 500 N.E.2d 960 (2 Dist. 1986).

In making an award of attorney fees, the trial court should consider the attorney's skill and standing; the nature of the controversy and the novelty and difficulty of the issues the case presents; the importance of the subject matter from the perspective of family law; the degree of responsibility involved in the management of the case; the time required and labor expended; the customary charge in the community; and the benefits the client derived from the representation. In re Erickson, 136 Ill. App. 3d 907, 91 Ill. Dec. 346, 483 N.E.2d 692 (2 Dist. 1985).

Factors to be considered by the court in determining what are reasonable fees are the attorney's skill and standing, the nature of the controversy, the novelty and difficulty of the questions at issue, the importance of the subject matter, the degree of responsibility involved in the management of the case, the time and labor required, the usual and customary charge in the community and the benefits to the client; in applying these factors the court may rely on its own knowledge and experience in determining the value of legal services. In re Angiuli, 134 Ill. App. 3d 417, 89 Ill. Dec. 328, 480 N.E.2d 513 (2 Dist. 1985).

Factors (Cont'd)

The awarding of attorney fees under this section is dependent upon the ultimate division of property. In re Thornton, 138 Ill. App. 3d 906, 93 Ill. Dec. 453, 486 N.E.2d 1288 (1 Dist. 1985).

In determining the reasonableness of an attorney fees award, the trial court is to consider the importance, novelty and difficulty of the questions raised, the degree of responsibility of the attorney, the time and labor required, the benefits resulting to the client, the skill and standing of the attorneys employed, the usual and customary charge in the community, and the financial position of the parties. In re Hirsch, 135 Ill. App. 3d 945, 90 Ill. Dec. 646, 482 N.E.2d 625 (1 Dist. 1985).

In determining whether the amount of fees awarded is reasonable, the factors to be considered are: (1) the skill and standing of the attorneys employed, (2) the nature of the controversy, and the novelty and difficulty of the questions at issue, (3) the amount and importance of the subject matter, especially from a family law standpoint, (4) the degree of responsibility involved in the management of the case, (5) the time and labor required, (6) the usual and customary charge in the community, and (7) the benefits resulting to the client. In re Siegel, 123 Ill. App. 3d 710, 79 Ill. Dec. 219, 463 N.E.2d 773 (1 Dist. 1984).

In determining whether the amount of fees awarded is reasonable, the factors to be considered are: the skill and standing of the attorneys employed; the nature of the controversy, and the novelty and difficulty of the questions at issue; the amount and importance of the subject matter, especially from a family law standpoint; the degree of responsibility involved in the management of the case; the time and labor required; the usual and customary charge in the community; and the benefits resulting to the client. In re Ligas, 110 Ill. App. 3d 1, 65 Ill. Dec. 763, 441 N.E.2d 1277 (1 Dist. 1982).

To justify the allowance of attorney's fees, the party seeking relief must show financial inability to pay and the ability of the other spouse to do so; among the factors to be considered are the nature of the controversy, the question at issue, the significance or importance of the subject matter, the degree of responsibility involved, the standing or skill of the attorney employed and the time and labor involved. Robinson v. Robinson, 100 Ill. App. 3d 437, 57 Ill. Dec. 532, 429 N.E.2d 183 (2 Dist. 1981).

In awarding fees, the trial court must look to the attorney's skill and standing, the nature of the controversy, the novelty and difficulty of the questions at issue, the importance of the subject matter, the degree of responsibility involved in the management of the case, the time and labor required, the usual and customary charge in the community, and the benefits resulting to the client. In re Ransom, 102 Ill. App. 3d 38, 57 Ill. Dec. 696, 429 N.E.2d 594 (2 Dist. 1981).

Factors to be considered in a fee determination are the nature of the controversy, the questions at issue, the significance or importance of the subject matter, the degree of the responsibility involved, the standing or skill of the person employed, the time and labor involved and the relative financial positions of the parties. In re Janetzke, 97 Ill. App. 3d 418, 52 Ill. Dec. 705, 422 N.E.2d 914 (1 Dist. 1981).

Some factors to be considered in making the award of attorney fees are the skill and expertise of the attorneys employed, the nature of the controversy, the novelty or difficulty of the questions raised, the degree of responsibility involved, the time and labor required, the usual and customary charge in the community, and the benefit or result provided. In re Kruse, 92 Ill. App. 3d 335, 48 Ill. Dec. 145, 416 N.E.2d 40 (1 Dist. 1980).

The court should consider each parties' total financial resources in making an award for attorney's fees. Greiman v. Friedman, 90 Ill. App. 3d 941, 46 Ill. Dec. 355, 414 N.E.2d 77 (1 Dist. 1980).

In awarding fees, consideration is given to a variety of factors including: the skill and expertise of the attorneys employed; the financial positions of the parties; the nature of the controversy; the novelty or difficulty of the questions raised; the importance of the question from a family law viewpoint; the degree of responsibility involved from a management perspective; the time and labor involved; the usual and customary charge for the same or similar services; and the benefit or result provided; of these the time factor is probably given the same or greater weight than any other factor. In re Dulyn, 89 Ill. App. 3d 304, 44 Ill. Dec. 622, 411 N.E.2d 988 (1 Dist. 1980).

To justify an allowance of attorney fees, the party seeking this relief must show financial inability to pay, financial needs within the context of the couple's prior standard of living, and the ability of the other spouse to pay the attorneys' fees. Donnelley v. Donnelley, 80 Ill. App. 3d 597, 35 Ill. Dec. 919, 400 N.E.2d 56 (1 Dist. 1980).

In addition to the relative financial positions of the parties, the amount of fees to be allowed in a divorce proceeding depends on a consideration of the skill and standing of the attorneys employed, the nature of the controversy, and the novelty and difficulty of the question at issue; the amount and importance of the subject matter, especially from a family law standpoint; the degree of responsibility involved in the management of the case; the time and labor required; the usual and customary charge in the community; and the benefits resulting to the client. Christian v. Christian, 69 Ill. App. 3d 450, 26 Ill. Dec. 326, 387 N.E.2d 1254 (1 Dist. 1979); In re Jacobson, 89 Ill. App. 3d 273, 44 Ill. Dec. 581, 411 N.E.2d 947 (1 Dist. 1980).

In connection with the allowance of fees (in addition to the financial ability of the parties), the court should consider the nature of the controversy, the question at issue, the significance or importance of the subject matter, the degree of responsibility involved, the standing or skill of the person employed, and the time and labor involved; the attorney's fees allowed by the court were higher than they should reasonably have been. Welsh v. Welsh, 38 Ill. App. 3d 35, 347 N.E.2d 512 (1 Dist. 1976).

In case of appeal by the husband or wife, the court in which the divorce decree or order is rendered may grant and enforce the payment of such attorney fees for her or his defense and such equitable alimony during the pendency of the appeal as to such court should seem reasonable and proper. Quagliano v. Quagliano, 94 Ill. App. 2d 233, 236 N.E.2d 748 (3 Dist. 1968).

Foreclosure Proceeding

Where husband was charged with a responsibility for payment of the mortgage indebtedness and upon the foreclosure action, wife became a necessary party and could well have been held liable for any deficiency judgment, then she was justified in seeking legal assistance regarding the foreclosure, the default was the fault of husband, not wife; the evidence regarding the foreclosure and wife incurring fees in relation thereto was sufficient to transfer the burden of proof regarding "without cause or justification" to husband. In re Young, 200 Ill. App. 3d 226, 147 Ill. Dec. 178, 559 N.E.2d 178 (4 Dist. 1990).

Former Law

Under former law and prior to Seniuta v. Seniuta (1977), 49 Ill. App. 3d 329, 7 Ill. Dec. 166, 364 N.E.2d 327, an attorney could not seek fees from his or her own client in a divorce proceeding; Seniuta changed that rule and subsection (a) of this section codified that change. Myers v. Brantley, 204 Ill. App. 3d 832, 149 Ill. Dec. 891, 562 N.E.2d 355 (4 Dist. 1990).

Under former similar provisions (see now this section), the allowance of attorney fees in a divorce proceeding rested in the sound discretion of the trial court, and exercise thereof would not be interfered with unless such discretion was clearly abused. Sullivan v. Sullivan, 68 Ill. App. 3d 242, 24 Ill. Dec. 719, 385 N.E.2d 860 (5 Dist. 1979).

Former section 16 of the Divorce Act (see now this section) permitted an award of attorney fees by the trial court after an appeal had been completed and the case remanded. McCarrel v. McCarrel, 48 Ill. App. 3d 666, 6 Ill. Dec. 669, 363 N.E.2d 198 (4 Dist. 1977).

Under former section 16 of the Divorce Act (see now this section), the allowance of attorney fees in a divorce proceeding was within the sound discretion of the trial court, and unless such discretion was clearly abused its exercise would not be interfered with by the reviewing court. Stotlar v. Stotlar, 50 Ill. App. 3d 790, 8 Ill. Dec. 711, 365 N.E.2d 1097 (5 Dist. 1977).

From Time to Time

Since subsection (a) of this section encompasses attorney fees for prefiling and post-decree activities, the language "from time to time" only refers to the recurring need for such orders. In re Pease, 106 Ill. App. 3d 617, 62 Ill. Dec. 389, 435 N.E.2d 1361 (2 Dist. 1982).

Guardian Ad Litem

Trial court apportioning attorney fees between former spouses for

Guardian Ad Litem (Cont'd)
guardian ad litem appointed for child, whom mother claimed was sexually abused by father, was not abuse of discretion where mother brought charges of sexual abuse and satanic cult practices against father without presenting evidence to substantiate the charges and, as a result of mother's actions and pleadings, father had to incur significant attorney fees and costs to defend himself and the child's attorney likewise expended a great amount of time in defending the child's welfare. McClelland v. McClelland, 231 Ill. App. 3d 214, 172 Ill. Dec. 461, 595 N.E.2d 1131 (1 Dist. 1992).

Hearing
Where attorney fees are contested, the court must conduct a hearing on the issue. Lee v. Lee, 302 Ill. App. 3d 607, 236 Ill. Dec. 222, 707 N.E.2d 67 (1 Dist. 1998).

A party can request a hearing on attorney fees and is entitled to an opportunity to present evidence in support of his request. In re Wolf, 180 Ill. App. 3d 998, 129 Ill. Dec. 742, 536 N.E.2d 792 (1 Dist. 1989).

A party can waive her right to a hearing under this section where there is evidence of the reasonableness and necessity of the fees. In re Pagano, 181 Ill. App. 3d 547, 130 Ill. Dec. 331, 537 N.E.2d 398 (2 Dist. 1989).

This section requires a hearing upon a party's request where the amount of a client's own attorney fees is incorporated in the parties' settlement agreement and judgment of dissolution. In re Bennett, 131 Ill. App. 3d 1050, 87 Ill. Dec. 305, 476 N.E.2d 1297 (2 Dist. 1985).

A full and separate hearing on the issue of attorney fees may be held under this Act. In re Shedbalkar, 95 Ill. App. 3d 136, 50 Ill. Dec. 301, 419 N.E.2d 409 (1 Dist. 1981).

Where petitioner's counsel discussed the parties' assets and petitioner's needs in light of evidence introduced at earlier proceedings, where the trial court stated that it had considered all the exhibits, the statements of counsel and the maintenance provisions under this Act, and where the parties invited the court to make a ruling on support and maintenance issues and the court made highly detailed findings, petitioner was not denied an evidentiary hearing on these issues even though she did not request a hearing. In re Shedbalkar, 95 Ill. App. 3d 136, 50 Ill. Dec. 301, 419 N.E.2d 409 (1 Dist. 1981).

When the court order was entered, the trial court had before it evidence of the financial status of both parties, and as no hearing was requested by either party, it was not error for the trial court not to conduct a hearing at that time on the propriety of an award of attorney's fees. Scott v. Scott, 72 Ill. App. 3d 117, 27 Ill. Dec. 863, 389 N.E.2d 1271 (1 Dist. 1979).

Where petitioner requested attorney fees, and where respondent denied the propriety of such an award, petitioner's request for a hearing on her petition should have been allowed. Scott v. Scott, 72 Ill. App. 3d 117, 27 Ill. Dec. 863, 389 N.E.2d 1271 (1 Dist. 1979).

While a hearing on the reasonable nature of attorney fees is not necessary in every case, especially where the trial judge is familiar with the procedural history of the case, the party contesting the award was entitled to a hearing upon request. Hogan v. Hogan, 58 Ill. App. 3d 661, 16 Ill. Dec. 265, 374 N.E.2d 1040 (1 Dist. 1978).

Under the former Divorce Act (see now 750 ILCS 5/401 et seq.), when the question of attorney fees was contested, the trial court had to conduct a hearing on the question, and if the court found the requesting party lacked the financial ability to pay the fees and the other party had such an ability, it could award the fees, and attorney fees were improperly awarded where the trial court held no such hearing and made no such findings. Sahs v. Sahs, 48 Ill. App. 3d 610, 6 Ill. Dec. 627, 363 N.E.2d 156 (2 Dist. 1977).

Incurred
The word "incurred" as used in the statute is not meant to exclude those represented by legal service agencies from awards of attorney fees. In re Brockett, 130 Ill. App. 3d 499, 85 Ill. Dec. 794, 474 N.E.2d 754 (5 Dist. 1984).

Itemization of Expenses
Prior to entering an award of attorney fees on behalf of an attorney against his client, the trial court must be presented with a petition for attorney fees and an itemization of the billing including the hourly cost, the time spent on the case, and an itemization of the tasks performed, so that the trial court will have a basis for ensuring that the fees awarded are fair. In re Pagano, 181 Ill. App. 3d 547, 130 Ill. Dec. 331, 537 N.E.2d 398 (2 Dist. 1989).

Jurisdiction

—In General
The awarding of attorney fees within a dissolution proceeding is a justiciable matter over which a trial court has subject matter jurisdiction. In re Pagano, 181 Ill. App. 3d 547, 130 Ill. Dec. 331, 537 N.E.2d 398 (2 Dist. 1989).

—Abatement of Action
The cause of action for dissolution of the marriage of the parties had abated upon the death of the wife prior to the judgment in the circuit court, thus removing from the trial court its jurisdiction over all aspects of the marriage relationship, including post-appeal petitions for attorney fees. Brandon v. Caisse, 172 Ill. App. 3d 841, 122 Ill. Dec. 746, 527 N.E.2d 118 (2 Dist. 1988).

A circuit court retains jurisdiction to hear issues of attorney fees and to enter allowance for them in spite of the fact that the death or remarriage of one of the parties resulted in an abatement of the dissolution proceedings. In re Conway, 139 Ill. App. 3d 1062, 94 Ill. Dec. 363, 487 N.E.2d 1240 (5 Dist. 1986).

While it is true that a dissolution proceeding abates with the death of one of the parties, the trial court retains jurisdiction to hear the issue of attorney fees and to enter an allowance for them even after the death. Schiff, Hardin & Waite v. Dague, 136 Ill. App. 3d 297, 91 Ill. Dec. 40, 483 N.E.2d 322 (1 Dist. 1985).

—Ancillary
In a dissolution of marriage proceeding, the trial court retains ancillary jurisdiction under this section to adjudicate attorney fee petitions during the pendency of an appeal; therefore, the trial court did not lose jurisdiction 30 days after its dismissal of the petition, but retained jurisdiction to entertain the wife's attorney fee petition while the appeal involving the dissolution action was pending before the Illinois Supreme Court. In re Drews, 179 Ill. App. 3d 110, 128 Ill. Dec. 229, 534 N.E.2d 411 (1 Dist. 1989).

—Appeals
The court in which a dissolution proceeding is pending has jurisdiction over the matter of attorney's fees and continues to do so for a period of 30 days after entry of its final judgment. In re Baltzer, 150 Ill. App. 3d 890, 104 Ill. Dec. 196, 502 N.E.2d 459 (2 Dist. 1986).

The trial court has jurisdiction to award attorney fees for the defense of pending appeals. In re Hellwig, 100 Ill. App. 3d 452, 55 Ill. Dec. 762, 426 N.E.2d 1087 (1 Dist. 1981).

After notice of appeal has been filed, the trial court retains jurisdiction to award attorney fees for the defense of an appeal. In re McBride, 102 Ill. App. 3d 84, 57 Ill. Dec. 750, 429 N.E.2d 867 (3 Dist. 1981).

To hold that the trial court is deprived of jurisdiction to award attorney fees under the Act because a notice of appeal has been filed would be to apply a general principle to a specific situation where it is inapposite; the filing of a notice of appeal does not deprive the trial court of jurisdiction in all instances. Giammerino v. Giammerino, 94 Ill. App. 3d 1058, 50 Ill. Dec. 490, 419 N.E.2d 598 (1 Dist. 1981).

The trial court had jurisdiction to award attorney fees for the defense of the appeal. Woodshank v. Woodshank, 13 Ill. App. 3d 692, 300 N.E.2d 494 (3 Dist. 1973).

Under a prior similar provision (see now this section), the trial court did not lose jurisdiction of the subject matter or of the person upon the appeal from a divorce proceeding, the appeal only restrained the trial court from entering any order which would change or modify the judgment or decree appealed from or the scope thereof and from entering any order which would have the effect of interfering with the review of the judgment or decree. Holmes v. Kammerman, 10 Ill. App. 2d 450, 135 N.E.2d 162 (1 Dist. 1956).

The phrase "during the pendency of the appeal" in former section 16 of the Divorce Act (see now this section), did not limit the court's authority to grant payments to the period prior to final disposition of the appeal, and thus an order allowing additional attorney fees, entered on a petition filed after the appeal was no longer pending, did not exceed the jurisdiction of the court. Riddlesbarger v. Riddlesbarger, 410 Ill. 329, 102 N.E.2d 319 (1951).

Jurisdiction (Cont'd)

—Court Error

If a court has jurisdiction to enter an order for attorney fees, that order must be obeyed even if erroneously entered until it is reversed or set aside in a direct proceeding for that purpose. Holmes v. Kammerman, 10 Ill. App. 2d 450, 135 N.E.2d 162 (1 Dist. 1956).

—Dismissal

Under both the former Divorce Act and under subsection (a) of this section of the present Act, a trial court lacks jurisdiction to award attorney's fees once the action has been dismissed; nor does jurisdiction continue beyond 30 days after the entry of a final order in an action. Didzerekis v. Birt, 159 Ill. App. 3d 281, 111 Ill. Dec. 274, 512 N.E.2d 390 (2 Dist. 1987).

Where an attorney's petition for fees earned in a previously dismissed dissolution proceeding was filed in a subsequent dissolution proceeding to which he was a stranger, some 19 months after he ceased to represent the client in the first proceeding, the circuit court lacked jurisdiction to consider the petition for attorney's fees incurred in the dismissed proceeding, and filed more than 30 days after entry of the final order dismissing that action, and the trial court correctly dismissed the attorney's petition filed in this case. Didzerekis v. Birt, 159 Ill. App. 3d 281, 111 Ill. Dec. 274, 512 N.E.2d 390 (2 Dist. 1987).

Orders for the payment of fees in a divorce case cannot be made after a motion to dismiss the case has been or should have been granted the plaintiff. Richheimer v. Richheimer, 59 Ill. App. 2d 354, 208 N.E.2d 346 (1 Dist. 1965).

—New Proceeding

Trial court had subject matter jurisdiction over wife's petition under the Illinois Marriage and Dissolution Act; wife was not seeking modification of the property provisions of the supplemental order to the dissolution judgment in filing a petition (1) to have former husband held in contempt for failure to pay debt assigned to him and (2) to be reimbursed for legal fees incurred defending herself from a lawsuit on that debt. In re Davis, 292 Ill. App. 3d 802, 226 Ill. Dec. 765, 686 N.E.2d 395 (4 Dist. 1997).

Plaintiff's application for attorney fees and costs had to be made in the pending visitation proceeding and could not, during the period of the proceeding, be brought as a new action in another court. Gitlin v. Hartmann, 175 Ill. App. 3d 805, 125 Ill. Dec. 426, 530 N.E.2d 584 (2 Dist. 1988).

An application for attorney's fees and costs must be made in a pending dissolution proceeding and may not, during that period, be brought as a new action in another court. In re Baltzer, 150 Ill. App. 3d 890, 104 Ill. Dec. 196, 502 N.E.2d 459 (2 Dist. 1986).

In dissolution proceedings, a most important function of the trial court is to make divisions and allocations of property, enter orders of support, and determine whether one spouse should pay the other spouse's attorney's fees; these matters are unique in dissolution proceedings, and it is reasonable for the legislature to have provided that the same court determine fee disputes between attorney and client. In re Galvin, 94 Ill. App. 3d 1032, 50 Ill. Dec. 309, 419 N.E.2d 417 (1 Dist. 1981).

—No Enforcement Authority

Under prior law, where there was no statutory provision for the enforcement in a divorce suit of an attorney's claim against his client for services rendered in the suit, the court of equity lacked jurisdiction to adjudicate the question of claimants' fees, and want of jurisdiction could not be cured by agreement of the parties. Pressney v. Pressney, 339 Ill. App. 371, 90 N.E.2d 119 (1 Dist. 1950).

—Party in Interest

The trial court had jurisdiction to entertain a petition for fees when signed only by the attorneys, because the attorneys were the party in interest to the extent that while fees were generally awarded to the litigant, they properly "belonged" to counsel under former Ill.Rev.Stat., ch. 40, para. 16 (see now this section). Gilmore v. Gilmore, 74 Ill. App. 3d 831, 30 Ill. Dec. 378, 393 N.E.2d 33 (1 Dist. 1979).

—Post-Judgment Petitions

In a petition for post-judgment attorney fees, there is nothing in this section that would cause a petition for fees to have to be filed within thirty days of the time the services were rendered, and it is likewise clear that the court has subject matter jurisdiction to allow post-judgment fees; hence, the question is whether the court has subject matter jurisdiction over the post-judgment fees. Burger, Frombelle, Baxter, Zachry & Rathburn v. Burton, 203 Ill. App. 3d 890, 148 Ill. Dec. 874, 561 N.E.2d 180 (5 Dist. 1990).

A prior statutory provision did not authorize the allowance of attorney's fees to either side in an appeal from a post-decretal order. Matthews v. Matthews, 42 Ill. App. 3d 1049, 1 Ill. Dec. 801, 356 N.E.2d 1083 (1 Dist. 1976).

—Pre-Judgment Award

Pursuant to 750 ILCS 5/508, so long as the trial court otherwise has jurisdiction over the case, either party may petition for contribution toward attorney fees at the conclusion of the case. Macaluso v. Macaluso, 334 Ill. App. 3d 1043, 268 Ill. Dec. 636, 779 N.E.2d 250, 2002 Ill. App. LEXIS 387 (3 Dist. 2002).

The trial court was without jurisdiction to entertain petitioner's request for pre-judgment attorney fees where the petition for pre-judgment attorney fees was filed more than 30 days after the final order. Burger, Frombelle, Baxter, Zachry & Rathburn v. Burton, 203 Ill. App. 3d 890, 148 Ill. Dec. 874, 561 N.E.2d 180 (5 Dist. 1990).

—Supplementary Proceeding

Plaintiff's petition for attorney fees for services made necessary by defendant's failure to comply with the original decree was a supplementary proceeding; thus, the court had jurisdiction to act with or without a prior express reservation of jurisdiction since plaintiff's petition did not seek to avoid or impeach the decree. Riddlesbarger v. Riddlesbarger, 341 Ill. App. 107, 93 N.E.2d 380 (1 Dist. 1950).

—Waiver

Where the trial court asserted it had jurisdiction to decide whether to award attorney fees and that to raise jurisdiction would be a waste of time, and both parties stipulated to jurisdiction, the jurisdictional issue was waived. Facchini & Minton v. Reczek, 95 Ill. App. 3d 220, 50 Ill. Dec. 844, 420 N.E.2d 161 (2 Dist. 1981).

Legislative Purpose

The principal purpose of subsection (a) of this section is to shift liability for attorney fees from one party to the other. Lee v. Lee, 302 Ill. App. 3d 607, 236 Ill. Dec. 222, 707 N.E.2d 67 (1 Dist. 1998).

Maintenance

The trial court erred when it awarded attorney fees as maintenance in that this section does not provide for the payment of an award of attorney fees as maintenance. In re Aslaksen, 148 Ill. App. 3d 784, 102 Ill. Dec. 469, 500 N.E.2d 91 (2 Dist. 1986).

Assigning maintenance payments to satisfy a judgment for attorney fees is not authorized under this section and violates public policy. Armstrong v. Marovitz, 107 Ill. App. 3d 217, 63 Ill. Dec. 112, 437 N.E.2d 761 (1 Dist. 1982).

Mandatory Provisions

Under subsection (b), a trial court has no discretion as to whether to award fees and costs, if it finds that the underlying failure to comply with an order was without cause or justification; its only discretion in this regard extends to its determination of the amount of reasonable fees. In re Sanda, 245 Ill. App. 3d 314, 184 Ill. Dec. 186, 612 N.E.2d 1346 (2 Dist. 1993).

Provisions of subsection (b) of this section are mandatory and, while allowing a determination of reasonableness, do not allow for discretion as to payment if the defaulting party's conduct was without cause or justification. Clay v. Clay, 210 Ill. App. 3d 778, 155 Ill. Dec. 280, 569 N.E.2d 280 (4 Dist. 1991).

Normally, an award of attorney fees is mandatory in a child support enforcement proceeding in which the custodial parent is granted relief and the court finds that the failure to pay child support was without cause or justification. In re Betts, 200 Ill. App. 3d 26, 146 Ill. Dec. 441, 558 N.E.2d 404 (4 Dist. 1990), appeal denied, 136 Ill. 2d 541, 153 Ill. Dec. 370, 567 N.E.2d 328 (1991).

An award of attorney fees is mandatory upon a court's finding of a failure to pay without cause or justification. In re Fowler, 197 Ill. App. 3d 95, 143 Ill. Dec. 305, 554 N.E.2d 240 (3 Dist. 1989).

Subsection (b) of this section is the mandatory provision by which the trial court, in a proceeding to enforce an order for child support,

Mandatory Provisions (Cont'd)
must order the noncustodial parent to pay the custodial parent's costs and reasonable attorney fees if the failure to pay was without cause or justification. In re Betts, 172 Ill. App. 3d 742, 122 Ill. Dec. 599, 526 N.E.2d 1138 (4 Dist. 1988).

In an action for the enforcement of a provision for child support, an award of attorney fees is mandatory upon the court finding that the failure to pay child support was without cause or justification. In re Dodge, 150 Ill. App. 3d 486, 103 Ill. Dec. 816, 501 N.E.2d 1354 (2 Dist. 1986).

The language in subsection (b) of this section is mandatory. Elliott v. Elliott, 137 Ill. App. 3d 277, 91 Ill. Dec. 923, 484 N.E.2d 482 (4 Dist. 1985).

The word "shall" in the 1982 amendment to this section evidenced that the legislature intended a mandatory construction. Sostak v. Sostak, 113 Ill. App. 3d 954, 69 Ill. Dec. 658, 447 N.E.2d 1345 (2 Dist. 1983).

In view of the mandatory nature of this section, the trial court was required to determine whether or not respondent's failure to pay support was without cause or justification, and if so, to award petitioner the full amount of attorney fees which the court determined to be reasonable. Sostak v. Sostak, 113 Ill. App. 3d 954, 69 Ill. Dec. 658, 447 N.E.2d 1345 (2 Dist. 1983).

Method

—Monthly Installments
Trial court properly ordered former husband to reimburse wife for attorney fees by means of monthly installments; even though the court found the husband was insolvent, the wife had been required to pay fees from monies from her mother's estate, and husband's payment in monthly installments of approximately one percent of his gross income over five years would enable wife to rebuild the capital depleted by the judgment against her for these fees. In re Davis, 292 Ill. App. 3d 802, 226 Ill. Dec. 765, 686 N.E.2d 395 (4 Dist. 1997).

Modification Proceeding
In a proceeding to modify a dissolution judgment, the court may in its discretion order one spouse to pay some or all of the attorney fees and costs necessarily incurred by the other. In re Bean, 181 Ill. App. 3d 671, 130 Ill. Dec. 275, 537 N.E.2d 342 (5 Dist. 1989).

Allowance of attorney's fees under this section is not based on the outcome of the proceedings; therefore, where an unsuccessful custodial modification is sought for the welfare of the children and not for the convenience of the parties, attorney's fees will be allowed. Carr v. Borowczyk, 78 Ill. App. 3d 425, 33 Ill. Dec. 738, 397 N.E.2d 71 (1 Dist. 1979).

The legislature made vexation and harassment relevant considerations in the award of attorney fees for the cost of a proceeding to modify a dissolution order under 750 ILCS 5/610(c), but it did not do so in the award of fees under this Act for the defense of an action to distribute marital property. In re Stewart, 79 Ill. App. 3d 1125, 35 Ill. Dec. 249, 398 N.E.2d 1199 (1 Dist. 1979).

Wife was not entitled to an award of attorney fees incurred in defending against ex-husband's petition to modify a judgment of dissolution where the record disclosed transfers of property valued in excess of $200,000, and thus the trial judge erred in concluding that the appellee wife was unable to pay the cost of her attorney's representation. In re Uphoff, 80 Ill. App. 3d 145, 35 Ill. Dec. 293, 398 N.E.2d 1243 (3 Dist. 1980).

Attorney fees can be awarded to a divorced wife in subsequent proceedings to modify the decree under proper circumstances; the allowance of the aforesaid attorney fees depends not upon who initiates the proceeding but rather upon the circumstances peculiar to the individual case. Mabbatt v. Mabbatt, 78 Ill. App. 2d 455, 223 N.E.2d 191 (1 Dist. 1967).

Motion to Vacate

—Denial Held Proper
Where the trial court denied motion to vacate award of attorney fees to former husband, giving as grounds the findings made when the court allowed the fees, and plaintiff's failure to call the motion for hearing within 90 days as required by a court rule, such ruling was correct. Kaufman v. Kaufman, 22 Ill. App. 3d 1045, 318 N.E.2d 282 (1 Dist. 1974).

—Due Diligence
Petitioner acted with due diligence as required by 735 ILCS 5/2-1401 in a petition to vacate an order of fees awarded to her attorney where she did not take action until after the attorney/client relationship ended. In re Pagano, 181 Ill. App. 3d 547, 130 Ill. Dec. 331, 537 N.E.2d 398 (2 Dist. 1989).

—Fees Allowed
The court could find no reason to expand subsection (b) of this section to cover proceedings to vacate a judgment rather than proceedings to enforce a judgment, as the ability to receive fees in connection with the bringing of a petition under 735 ILCS 5/2-1401 is expressly provided for in subdivision (a)(4) of this section. In re Parker, 216 Ill. App. 3d 672, 159 Ill. Dec. 131, 575 N.E.2d 938 (2 Dist. 1991).

Notice
Receipt of the petition for attorney fees a few hours before the latest time the court was willing to hear it was not "due notice." Ingrassia v. Ingrassia, 156 Ill. App. 3d 483, 109 Ill. Dec. 68, 509 N.E.2d 729 (2 Dist. 1987).

Wife's failure to object to the quoted fee and her failure to request a special hearing did not constitute a waiver where her counsel did not give wife notice, as required by subsection (a), of his intention to seek the entry of an order in the decree that she pay him $25,000 as his fee. In re Bennett, 131 Ill. App. 3d 1050, 87 Ill. Dec. 305, 476 N.E.2d 1297 (2 Dist. 1985).

Paralegals
This section allows a party to recover paralegal fees. In re Ahmad, 198 Ill. App. 3d 15, 144 Ill. Dec. 320, 555 N.E.2d 439 (2 Dist. 1990).

Paternity Proceeding
In awarding attorney fees in paternity cases, factors such as the relative financial abilities of the parties, the nature of the controversy, and the skill of the attorney become evident during the proceedings, and no independent proofs need be made concerning such factors; however, factors such as the amount of time and labor involved in a case require independent proof. Jiles v. Spratt, 195 Ill. App. 3d 354, 142 Ill. Dec. 21, 552 N.E.2d 371 (4 Dist. 1990).

Payment of Fees

—Attorney Fees
Finding of contempt is sufficient to require an award of fees under 750 ILCS 5/508(b), but such a finding is not necessary. Berto v. Berto, 344 Ill. App. 3d 705, 279 Ill. Dec. 482, 800 N.E.2d 550, 2003 Ill. App. LEXIS 1383 (2 Dist. 2003).

—Determination
Trial court's interim award of attorney fees to the first attorney and the second attorney, payable pursuant to a disgorgement order directed against the law firm, was not a final, appealable order since the award was one of temporary relief in the nature of an interlocutory order and the law firm still had pending in the trial court a petition against its client to recover fees from him as a result of the disgorgement order. Johnson v. Johnson, 351 Ill. App. 3d 88, 285 Ill. Dec. 841, 812 N.E.2d 661, 2004 Ill. App. LEXIS 785 (1 Dist. 2004).

Subsection (a) of this Act makes no distinction between the party's own fees and those of a spouse, but puts both on an equal footing; in determining which party is better able to assume the debt, the trial court may consider the prospective income of the parties. In re McCoy, 272 Ill. App. 3d 125, 208 Ill. Dec. 732, 650 N.E.2d 3 (4 Dist. 1995).

—Dismissal of Action
There is no justification in practice for keeping a suit alive to require the payment of solicitor's fees for which no order had been entered prior to a motion to dismiss the bill; an order for defendant's solicitor's fees contemplates the necessity of future service. Watson v. Watson, 335 Ill. App. 637, 82 N.E.2d 671 (1 Dist. 1948).

—Either Party
The trial court, after considering the financial resources of the parties, may order either spouse to pay the attorney fees necessarily incurred by the other spouse. In re Werries, 247 Ill. App. 3d 639, 186 Ill. Dec. 747, 616 N.E.2d 1379 (4 Dist. 1993).

Payment of Fees (Cont'd)

—In Other Proceedings

The court had no jurisdiction in a dissolution case to award attorney fees for work performed in husband's criminal case, which was proceeding in a different court totally independent of the dissolution case. In re Campbell, 261 Ill. App. 3d 483, 199 Ill. Dec. 1, 633 N.E.2d 797 (1 Dist. 1993), appeal denied, 156 Ill. 2d 556, 202 Ill. Dec. 919, 638 N.E.2d 1113 (1994).

—No Basis

Where plaintiff wife filed suit for divorce from plaintiff husband and in her complaint joined defendant savings and loan association, as a party defendant, and plaintiffs were later reconciled, and an order was entered dismissing the suit for divorce and dissolving the injunction, and where without notice to, or authorization from plaintiffs, defendant debited plaintiffs' account to reimburse itself for attorney fees, there was no basis, statutory or contractual, for the payment of defendant's attorney fees. Barth v. West Highland Sav. & Loan Ass'n, 99 Ill. App. 2d 303, 240 N.E.2d 446 (1 Dist. 1968).

—Responsibility

Law firm had petition remaining in the trial court against the client to determine whether the client would be responsible to pay fees that the trial court ordered the law firm to disgorge to the first attorney and the second attorney in order to "level the playing field" in divorce proceedings involving the client and the woman, his wife, and, thus, since there was no final, appealable order involved in the case and issues remained pending in the appellate court, the appellate court lacked jurisdiction over the law firm's appeal of the interim award order. Johnson v. Johnson, 351 Ill. App. 3d 88, 285 Ill. Dec. 841, 812 N.E.2d 661, 2004 Ill. App. LEXIS 785 (1 Dist. 2004).

It is upon the party for whom services are rendered that the primary obligation for the payment of attorney fees must fall, although under certain circumstances the court may order another party to pay them. Jones v. Jones, 48 Ill. App. 2d 232, 198 N.E.2d 195 (1 Dist. 1964).

—Sale of Residence

The court did not order the residence to be sold in order to satisfy the payment of attorney fees; however, the husband voluntarily sold his residence and once it was determined that the funds from the sale belonged solely to the husband, the court directed that the funds be disbursed to the attorneys directly. In re Campbell, 261 Ill. App. 3d 483, 199 Ill. Dec. 1, 633 N.E.2d 797 (1 Dist. 1993), appeal denied, 156 Ill. 2d 556, 202 Ill. Dec. 919, 638 N.E.2d 1113 (1994).

Pleadings

Where respondent filed a false pleading, did not withdraw the false pleading for five months and the evidence established that petitioner had no ability to pay the fees, but that respondent did, the award was proper under the Act as a sanction against respondent for his false pleading. In re Cheger, 213 Ill. App. 3d 371, 157 Ill. Dec. 116, 571 N.E.2d 1135 (4 Dist. 1991).

Wife's failure to add a prayer of relief for attorney fees in her answer to husband's counterpetition for dissolution of marriage did not deprive the trial court of its jurisdictional power to order the husband to make such payment in the judgment order. In re Gruer, 153 Ill. App. 3d 125, 106 Ill. Dec. 340, 505 N.E.2d 1131 (1 Dist. 1987).

A deficiency in the pleadings does not adversely affect the authority vested in the trial court to include an attorney fees provision in its final judgment, since subdivision (a)(1) of this section grants the court the authority to order the payment of said fees; the only concerns are whether the petition for fees was properly filed, whether due notice was given, and whether a hearing on the matter was conducted. In re Gruer, 153 Ill. App. 3d 125, 106 Ill. Dec. 340, 505 N.E.2d 1131 (1 Dist. 1987).

Prospective Award

With the 1988 amendment to subsection (a), the legislature has now made clear that prospective fees may be awarded under the Act. In re Talty, 166 Ill. 2d 232, 209 Ill. Dec. 790, 652 N.E.2d 330 (1995).

The legislation has, in subdivision (a)(3), expressly provided for the prospective attorney fee award in conjunction with an appeal. In re Brent, 263 Ill. App. 3d 916, 200 Ill. Dec. 799, 635 N.E.2d 1382 (4 Dist. 1994).

A prospective award of attorney fees for defense of a dissolution appeal can be awarded during the pendency of the appeal, although prospective awards should be made cautiously and are to be based upon some viable evidentiary basis; as with any award for attorney fees and costs in a dissolution proceeding, the party seeking such an award must show not only his or her own financial inability to pay, but also the ability of the other spouse to do so. In re Pittman, 213 Ill. App. 3d 60, 157 Ill. Dec. 177, 571 N.E.2d 1196 (5 Dist. 1991).

Although other districts of the Illinois Appellate Court have held to the contrary, the First District has expressly approved the awarding of prospective attorney fees to defend an appeal where the award is made cautiously and with a basis in the record. In re Pahlke, 154 Ill. App. 3d 256, 107 Ill. Dec. 407, 507 N.E.2d 71 (1 Dist.), appeal denied, 113 Ill. Dec. 304, 515 N.E.2d 113 (Ill. 1987).

Where the services for which one spouse sought advance payment had already been rendered, the appeal of the court order directing the other spouse to pay prospective attorney fees became moot. In re Landfield, 118 Ill. 2d 229, 113 Ill. Dec. 93, 514 N.E.2d 1005 (1987).

The court looks to the benefits resulting to the client as a basis for a prospective fee award. In re Pease, 106 Ill. App. 3d 617, 62 Ill. Dec. 389, 435 N.E.2d 1361 (2 Dist. 1982).

This section and the case law rejects the idea of prospective fees. In re Pease, 106 Ill. App. 3d 617, 62 Ill. Dec. 389, 435 N.E.2d 1361 (2 Dist. 1982).

Although there is nothing inherently improper in awarding prospective attorney fees, such awards should be made cautiously; therefore, the trial court did not err nor abuse its discretion in awarding petitioner prospective attorney fees. In re Ligas, 110 Ill. App. 3d 1, 65 Ill. Dec. 763, 441 N.E.2d 1277 (1 Dist. 1982).

A court may not award prospective attorney's fees for the defense of an appeal. In re Pease, 106 Ill. App. 3d 617, 62 Ill. Dec. 389, 435 N.E.2d 1361 (2 Dist. 1982).

A court having jurisdiction may award prospective fees in anticipation of time to be spent in pursuance of pending litigation. In re Edelberg, 105 Ill. App. 3d 407, 61 Ill. Dec. 287, 434 N.E.2d 440 (1 Dist. 1982).

Prospective temporary attorney's fees may not be awarded under this Act. In re Justema, 95 Ill. App. 3d 483, 51 Ill. Dec. 382, 420 N.E.2d 796 (2 Dist. 1981).

Defendant wife, as the party prosecuting the appeal from the denial of her request for temporary support and maintenance, was not entitled to a prospective award of maintenance pending appeal. Sherman v. Sherman, 74 Ill. App. 3d 451, 30 Ill. Dec. 412, 393 N.E.2d 67 (2 Dist. 1979).

Public Policy

Public policy is best served by allowing the court hearing the domestic relations matter to have, as set forth in this section, the "final word" in determining the reasonableness of an attorney's fees. Gitlin v. Hartmann, 175 Ill. App. 3d 805, 125 Ill. Dec. 426, 530 N.E.2d 584 (2 Dist. 1988).

Purpose

Policy behind 750 ILCS 5/508(b) is to eliminate the financial burden on a custodial parent that is the consequence of an enforcement action. Berto v. Berto, 344 Ill. App. 3d 705, 279 Ill. Dec. 482, 800 N.E.2d 550, 2003 Ill. App. LEXIS 1383 (2 Dist. 2003).

The policy behind subsection (b) of this section is to eliminate or lessen the financial burden on a party to a marital matter that is the consequence of an enforcement action. In re Young, 200 Ill. App. 3d 226, 147 Ill. Dec. 178, 559 N.E.2d 178 (4 Dist. 1990).

This section derives from former section 313 of the Uniform Marriage and Divorce Act, with certain modifications, and has the objective of diminishing any advantage one spouse may have over the other in the presentation of a case due to a disparity in their respective financial resources. Didzerekis v. Birt, 159 Ill. App. 3d 281, 111 Ill. Dec. 274, 512 N.E.2d 390 (2 Dist. 1987).

This section was modeled in part after former section 313 of the Uniform Marriage and Divorce Act and was designed to equalize the status of the parties in a divorce proceeding. In re Pahlke, 154 Ill. App. 3d 256, 107 Ill. Dec. 407, 507 N.E.2d 71 (1 Dist.), appeal denied, 113 Ill. Dec. 304, 515 N.E.2d 113 (Ill. 1987).

Subsection (a) of this section is intended to promote judicial economy by obviating the need for an attorney to sue his own client.

Purpose (Cont'd)
In re Bennett, 131 Ill. App. 3d 1050, 87 Ill. Dec. 305, 476 N.E.2d 1297 (2 Dist. 1985).

Under this section, a court in a dissolution proceeding is authorized to adjudicate the liability of either spouse for the costs and attorney's fees necessarily incurred by the other spouse, as well as for his or her own costs and attorney's fees; this procedure was obviously designed to allow the spouse with depleted financial resources to turn to the more affluent spouse to pay his or her attorney's fees and costs incurred in the proceeding. In re Erby, 84 Ill. App. 3d 672, 40 Ill. Dec. 378, 406 N.E.2d 79 (1 Dist. 1980).

The intent of the legislature in enacting this section was to ensure that disparate financial resources of the spouses would not result in an undue advantage for the more affluent party to the suit. In re Erby, 84 Ill. App. 3d 672, 40 Ill. Dec. 378, 406 N.E.2d 79 (1 Dist. 1980).

The purpose of this section is to assist an impecunious spouse (usually the wife) who might otherwise be precluded by lack of funds from filing and maintaining an action for divorce. Pearson v. Pearson, 42 Ill. App. 3d 522, 1 Ill. Dec. 711, 356 N.E.2d 993 (2 Dist. 1976).

The purpose of this section was to protect the spouse in whose favor a decree had been rendered from being subjected to the hardship of an appeal during which payments were suspended and expenses would be incurred for defending the litigation. Riddlesbarger v. Riddlesbarger, 348 Ill. App. 31, 107 N.E.2d 770 (1 Dist. 1952).

Purpose of Amendment
The 1997 amendment to subdivision (c)(1) seeks to eliminate the problems created by the 1976 amendment and to prevent the attorney and client from being placed in an adversarial position. Kaufman, Litwin & Feinstein v. Edgar, 301 Ill. App. 3d 826, 235 Ill. Dec. 183, 704 N.E.2d 756 (1 Dist. 1998), appeal denied, 182 Ill. 2d 551, 236 Ill. Dec. 670, 707 N.E.2d 1240 (1999).

Reasonableness of Fees

—In General
A court considering a fee petition under this section is to weigh the reasonableness of the fee sought, even if it is sought pursuant to a definite contract. Ziemann v. Ziemann, 214 Ill. App. 3d 988, 158 Ill. Dec. 654, 574 N.E.2d 767 (1 Dist. 1991).

In order to recover expert fees as necessary costs under this section, the reasonableness of the fees must be established. In re Winton, 216 Ill. App. 3d 1084, 159 Ill. Dec. 933, 576 N.E.2d 856 (2 Dist. 1991).

In light of the lack of benefits resulting to the husband, the trial court should have considered the question of whether the amounts charged by his attorney for routine motions, agreed orders, and office telephone calls were excessive in light of the results achieved. In re Heller, 153 Ill. App. 3d 224, 106 Ill. Dec. 503, 505 N.E.2d 1294 (1 Dist. 1987).

The trial court in a dissolution of marriage proceeding may properly evaluate the reasonableness of all fees sought by an attorney in that proceeding notwithstanding the fact that the client may have advanced a retainer or paid earlier billings; to hold otherwise would work an unauthorized diminution of the court's power to determine the reasonableness of claimed fees. In re Angiuli, 134 Ill. App. 3d 417, 89 Ill. Dec. 328, 480 N.E.2d 513 (2 Dist. 1985).

Chicago attorney who was engaged in Chicago to perform services in another county was not entitled to recover fees in accordance with the usual, customary and established fees of Chicago lawyers; the inquiry should have been what is usually and customarily charged and paid for like services in the court where said services are rendered. In re Angiuli, 134 Ill. App. 3d 417, 89 Ill. Dec. 328, 480 N.E.2d 513 (2 Dist. 1985).

The amount of attorney fees awarded should be only in such an amount as will compensate for services rendered, and those services must have been reasonably required and necessary to the case. In re Zannis, 114 Ill. App. 3d 1034, 70 Ill. Dec. 545, 449 N.E.2d 892 (1 Dist. 1983).

The court is not bound by the attorney's opinion as to what constitutes a reasonable fee, and it must inquire into all of the necessary factors; the time spent on the case is the factor of greatest importance. In re Ransom, 102 Ill. App. 3d 38, 57 Ill. Dec. 696, 429 N.E.2d 594 (2 Dist. 1981).

The trial court, after considering the financial resources of the parties, may order either party to pay the other's reasonable attorney's fees. In re Fleming, 80 Ill. App. 3d 1006, 36 Ill. Dec. 205, 400 N.E.2d 625 (2 Dist. 1980).

The work for which the compensation is sought must be shown to be reasonably required and necessary for the proper performance of legal services under the circumstances. Christian v. Christian, 69 Ill. App. 3d 450, 26 Ill. Dec. 326, 387 N.E.2d 1254 (1 Dist. 1979); In re Jacobson, 89 Ill. App. 3d 273, 44 Ill. Dec. 581, 411 N.E.2d 947 (1 Dist. 1980).

Where counterdefendant's conduct necessitated a hearing and expenses of counsel, but there was no opportunity to consider the reasonableness of attorney fees, order of attorney fees was remanded for further consideration. Newton v. Newton, 38 Ill. App. 3d 626, 347 N.E.2d 839 (3 Dist. 1976).

Attorney fees should be reasonable for services rendered. Altman v. Altman, 131 Ill. App. 2d 427, 268 N.E.2d 211 (1 Dist. 1971).

—Contract
Retention agreements stating hourly rates are commonplace in divorce cases, and such agreements have never precluded the courts of this state from reducing attorney fees where a court deems such fees were not reasonable for the services rendered or necessary. Gitlin v. Hartmann, 175 Ill. App. 3d 805, 125 Ill. Dec. 426, 530 N.E.2d 584 (2 Dist. 1988).

A client is permitted to prove that his or her attorney's fee is excessive or otherwise unreasonable, even though he or she assented to a fixed attorney's fee. In re Pitulla, 141 Ill. App. 3d 956, 96 Ill. Dec. 276, 491 N.E.2d 90 (1 Dist. 1986).

Although attorneys should be free to adjust their fees to whatever the legal marketplace will bear, the public is entitled to protection to the extent that an attorney's fee must be reasonable, irrespective of whether the fee is determined per diem or by a fixed contractual provision. In re Pitulla, 141 Ill. App. 3d 956, 96 Ill. Dec. 276, 491 N.E.2d 90 (1 Dist. 1986).

—Illustrative Cases
Rates of attorneys for petitioner and respondent were reasonable, even though too much time was spent on all matters due to the parties' failure to compromise, and some of petitioner's attorney fees were not sufficiently defined. In re Walters, 238 Ill. App. 3d 1086, 178 Ill. Dec. 176, 604 N.E.2d 432 (2 Dist. 1992).

The trial court accurately and adequately considered the time necessarily applied by an attorney and his associates on a client's behalf in awarding fees; a fee reduction from $62,202 to $36,000 appeared to be reasonable for the services rendered. In re Angiuli, 134 Ill. App. 3d 417, 89 Ill. Dec. 328, 480 N.E.2d 513 (2 Dist. 1985).

Where it was clear from the statements of the trial judge that he was only concerned with enforcing the retainer, in spite of the fact that the only authority he possessed for providing fees was this section which requires reasonableness, failure to find that the retainer amount was reasonable precluded award of retainer amount without further proceedings. Facchini & Minton v. Reczek, 95 Ill. App. 3d 220, 50 Ill. Dec. 844, 420 N.E.2d 161 (2 Dist. 1981).

Where the court order allowed first attorney only $200 and the court indicated that the $2,500 that husband was required to pay was to be distributed among all three of wife's attorneys, and where the first attorney's verified motion showed that he had spent over 80 hours on the matter, the order of the trial court was reversed and remanded for a rehearing as to what portion of the $2,500 paid by husband was to be paid to first attorney for the reasonable value of his services. Serio v. Serio, 85 Ill. App. 2d 102, 229 N.E.2d 281 (1 Dist. 1967).

—Relevance of Judge's Knowledge and Experience
The trial judge may rely on his or her own knowledge and experience when deciding the value of the services provided as the award of attorney fees is within the discretion of the trial judge, whose decision will not be reversed absent an abuse of that discretion. In re Powers, 252 Ill. App. 3d 506, 191 Ill. Dec. 541, 624 N.E.2d 390 (2 Dist. 1993).

—Sanctions Against Attorney
Although the determination of reasonable attorney fees and costs was within the sound discretion of the trial court, the trial court

Reasonableness of Fees (Cont'd)

—Sanctions Against Attorney (Cont'd)
abused its discretion in ordering the former wife to pay the former attorney fees that included an amount for a sanction that was entered against the attorney and the time the attorney spent defending against the sanction as the sanction was imposed solely against the attorney. Devick v. Devick, 335 Ill. App. 3d 734, 269 Ill. Dec. 687, 781 N.E.2d 484, 2002 Ill. App. LEXIS 1074 (2 Dist. 2002), appeal denied, 204 Ill. 2d 657, 275 Ill. Dec. 75, 792 N.E.2d 306 (2003).

Reduction
Respondent's child support payments could not be applied to reduce the amount of attorney fees owed by petitioner to respondent. In re Tatham, 293 Ill. App. 3d 471, 228 Ill. Dec. 166, 688 N.E.2d 864 (5 Dist. 1997).

Related Provision
Although section 17 of the Illinois Parentage Act of 1984 (750 ILCS 45/17) contains no express provision linking the award of attorney fees incurred in enforcing support orders to similar provisions of subsection (b) of this section, because of the close relationship between the two provisions, it is appropriate to hold that the attorney fees awarded under section 17 of the former Divorce Act are awarded under the same standard as those awarded under subsection (b) of this section. Davis v. Sprague, 186 Ill. App. 3d 249, 133 Ill. Dec. 620, 541 N.E.2d 831 (4 Dist. 1989).

Res Judicata
Nothing within this section limits the rights of a client injured by her attorney's malpractice to seek redress, and there is no reason for exempting issues raised in proceedings under this section from the doctrine of res judicata. Bennett v. Gordon, 282 Ill. App. 3d 378, 217 Ill. Dec. 924, 668 N.E.2d 109 (1 Dist. 1996).

Trial court was held to have been barred from considering attorney fees petitions filed by attorneys following a marriage dissolution suit by the doctrine of res judicata. Stacke v. Bates, 225 Ill. App. 3d 1050, 168 Ill. Dec. 81, 589 N.E.2d 195 (2 Dist. 1992).

Where the matter of responsibility for attorney fees in a divorce action had been fully litigated under this section, the trial court was barred from considering the petition of the attorneys themselves under 735 ILCS 5/2-1401 by the doctrine of res judicata; attorneys' petition for fees was properly struck down. Stacke v. Bates, 225 Ill. App. 3d 1050, 168 Ill. Dec. 81, 589 N.E.2d 195 (2 Dist. 1992).

Where plaintiff sought to recover fees and expenses under a prior similar provision (see now this section) for which the trial court, after hearing testimony, had disposed of the matter, the issue presented was res judicata and therefore properly rejected. Barnett v. Barnett, 341 Ill. App. 26, 93 N.E.2d 93 (3 Dist. 1950).

Retroactive Application
Since the provisions of this section, both before and after the 1982 amendment, are remedial in nature, the trial court correctly applied the amendment retroactively. Sostak v. Sostak, 113 Ill. App. 3d 954, 69 Ill. Dec. 658, 447 N.E.2d 1345 (2 Dist. 1983).

Review
Absent an abuse of discretion, the trial court's decision to award attorney fees in a dissolution proceeding should not be overturned. In re Klein, 231 Ill. App. 3d 901, 173 Ill. Dec. 335, 596 N.E.2d 1214 (4 Dist. 1992).

A trial court's distribution should not be disturbed absent an abuse of discretion, which occurs only when the trial court exceeds the bounds of reason and ignores judicial principles so that substantial injustice results. In re Klein, 231 Ill. App. 3d 901, 173 Ill. Dec. 335, 596 N.E.2d 1214 (4 Dist. 1992).

Where an attorney was entitled to be notified of and participate in any appeal where his fees were in issue, he had a right to intervene in an appeal subsequent to the rendering of the court's decision. In re Hartian, 172 Ill. App. 3d 440, 122 Ill. Dec. 565, 526 N.E.2d 1104 (1 Dist.), appeal denied, 123 Ill. 2d 558, 128 Ill. Dec. 890, 535 N.E.2d 401 (1988).

Where the record reflected that husband never served a notice of appeal on wife's former attorney, the appellate court was unable to address husband's argument concerning the award of attorney fees to wife's attorney. In re Gluszek, 168 Ill. App. 3d 987, 119 Ill. Dec. 658, 523 N.E.2d 126 (1 Dist. 1988).

Although subdivision (a)(3) of this section provides for payment of attorney fees for the defense of an appeal, the Supreme Court has not provided the appellate court with the authority to make an initial award of attorney fees. In re Stockton, 169 Ill. App. 3d 318, 119 Ill. Dec. 817, 523 N.E.2d 573 (4 Dist. 1988).

Where order for attorney fees from which appeal was taken arose from a contempt proceeding, it was final and appealable. Spizzo v. Langman, 168 Ill. App. 3d 487, 119 Ill. Dec. 146, 522 N.E.2d 808 (2 Dist. 1988).

After notice of appeal has been filed, a trial court retains jurisdiction to award attorney fees for the defense of an appeal. In re Magnuson, 128 Ill. App. 3d 130, 83 Ill. Dec. 254, 470 N.E.2d 9 (3 Dist. 1984).

Allowance of attorney fees is a matter of discretion and will not be lightly changed on appeal. In re Cabaj, 118 Ill. App. 3d 789, 74 Ill. Dec. 393, 455 N.E.2d 822 (1 Dist. 1983).

Appellate Court had no authority to fix the amount of an award of fees for an attorney's services on appeal. In re Estates of Azevedo, 115 Ill. App. 3d 260, 70 Ill. Dec. 950, 450 N.E.2d 423 (5 Dist. 1983).

A trial court does not have jurisdiction to make a prospective award of attorney fees for defense of an appeal in a dissolution of marriage proceeding while the appeal is pending. In re Legge, 111 Ill. App. 3d 198, 66 Ill. Dec. 926, 443 N.E.2d 1089 (4 Dist. 1982).

A request for attorney fees in matrimonial cases is a claim as that term is used in Rule 304, Supreme Court Rules. In re Janetzke, 97 Ill. App. 3d 418, 52 Ill. Dec. 705, 422 N.E.2d 914 (1 Dist. 1981).

Order entered awarding temporary attorney's fees was not final and, therefore, was not appealable. In re Justema, 95 Ill. App. 3d 483, 51 Ill. Dec. 382, 420 N.E.2d 796 (2 Dist. 1981).

Where order reserved the issues of attorneys' fees to the jurisdiction of the trial court, the filing of the first notice of appeal did not operate to divest the trial court of the power to allow attorneys' fees. In re Raidbard, 87 Ill. App. 3d 158, 42 Ill. Dec. 312, 408 N.E.2d 1021 (1 Dist. 1980).

A final determination must be made with regard to the division of property before a conclusive appellate review of the issues of child support and attorney fees. In re Clearman, 85 Ill. App. 3d 584, 40 Ill. Dec. 958, 407 N.E.2d 189 (3 Dist. 1980).

A court review will not hesitate to reduce attorney fees awarded if they are unreasonably high. Donnelley v. Donnelley, 80 Ill. App. 3d 597, 35 Ill. Dec. 919, 400 N.E.2d 56 (1 Dist. 1980).

Where defendant husband did not request a hearing on the issue of attorney fees, the issue could not be raised for the first time on appeal. Renwick v. Renwick, 52 Ill. App. 3d 701, 10 Ill. Dec. 400, 367 N.E.2d 1009 (2 Dist. 1977).

Upon review, an appellate court will refuse to set aside an order for temporary award of attorney fees, except for an abuse of discretion. Roback v. Roback, 59 Ill. App. 2d 222, 207 N.E.2d 130 (2 Dist. 1965).

Any fair construction of the statute authorizes an allowance of fees after the proceedings on appeal have ended and after the decree has been satisfied. Riddlesbarger v. Riddlesbarger, 348 Ill. App. 31, 107 N.E.2d 770 (1 Dist. 1952).

Where no evidence was heard on the petition for allowance of attorney's fees, the court on appeal would not consider such matter. Swan v. Swan, 331 Ill. App. 295, 73 N.E.2d 153 (4 Dist. 1947).

Sequestration Proceeding
Where sequestration proceeding was brought to enforce compliance with an earlier judgment, one condition of which was the payment of attorney fees, it was not necessary for petitioner or her attorneys to resort to a suit at law for recovery of the fees. In re Rochford, 91 Ill. App. 3d 769, 46 Ill. Dec. 943, 414 N.E.2d 1096 (1 Dist. 1980).

Settlement Agreement
Settlement agreement which obligated husband to pay wife's attorney fees did not relieve her of the responsibility of paying any additional portion of fees; it is presumed that a wife shall bear the expense of her own attorney fees, absent a showing of financial inability to do so. In re Reidy, 134 Ill. App. 3d 534, 89 Ill. Dec. 454, 480 N.E.2d 1197 (1 Dist. 1985).

Courts are not bound by 750 ILCS 5/502 to the parties' settlement agreement relating to the amount to be paid by a client to her attorney, particularly where the trial court's authority to make the award is expressly provided for in this section. In re Bennett, 131 Ill. App. 3d 1050, 87 Ill. Dec. 305, 476 N.E.2d 1297 (2 Dist. 1985).

Spousal Guardian

This section permits a wife to seek from her husband through his guardian, reasonable attorney fees incurred by her to defend appeals from the trial court's dismissal of the petition of her husband's guardian to dissolve their marriage. In re Drews, 179 Ill. App. 3d 110, 128 Ill. Dec. 229, 534 N.E.2d 411 (1 Dist. 1989).

Spouse

The term "spouse" refers to a legal wife or husband. Mac Harg v. Bremer, 120 Ill. App. 3d 753, 76 Ill. Dec. 500, 458 N.E.2d 1154 (1 Dist. 1983).

Standing

Although fees are generally awarded to the client, they belong to the attorney, who has standing to pursue an action for fees as the party in interest, without the participation of the client or former client. Lee v. Lee, 302 Ill. App. 3d 607, 236 Ill. Dec. 222, 707 N.E.2d 67 (1 Dist. 1998).

Strict application of the judge-made doctrine of standing was relaxed, permitting a divorce attorney acting as a creditor to challenge the division and distribution of his client's assets; even though the client was the proper party to contact or challenge the substantive rulings of the court, the fact that she had fled the jurisdiction, thus violating the court's orders, influenced the court's ruling. In re Kriegsman, 218 Ill. App. 3d 909, 161 Ill. Dec. 540, 578 N.E.2d 1186 (1 Dist. 1991).

Attorneys for litigants in a dissolution proceeding are considered as parties in interest in an action for attorney fees, and the attorney has standing in such cases to pursue an action himself for fees. In re Pagano, 181 Ill. App. 3d 547, 130 Ill. Dec. 331, 537 N.E.2d 398 (2 Dist. 1989).

Subsection (c) promotes judicial economy by eliminating the need for an attorney to bring a separate suit to collect fees from his client. Didzerekis v. Birt, 159 Ill. App. 3d 281, 111 Ill. Dec. 274, 512 N.E.2d 390 (2 Dist. 1987).

Plaintiff lacked standing to request of the trial court a denial of a request for an award of attorney fees and alimony pending appeal since the purpose of a prior similar provision (see this section) was to protect the spouse in whose favor a decree had been entered from being subjected to the hardship of an appeal during which payments were suspended and expenses would be incurred for defending the litigation. Dendrinos v. Dendrinos, 58 Ill. App. 3d 639, 16 Ill. Dec. 241, 374 N.E.2d 1016 (1 Dist. 1978).

Where defendant-appellant filed a motion to dismiss the cross-appeals of attorneys on the ground that plaintiff did not cross-appeal from award of attorneys' fees, but only from alimony and child support provisions of the separate maintenance decree, although the cross-appellants were not parties to the suit below, they had standing to seek personal relief on appeal. Richheimer v. Richheimer, 59 Ill. App. 2d 354, 208 N.E.2d 346 (1 Dist. 1965).

Substitution of Judges

One of the primary purposes of subdivision (c)(5) is to have the judge, who is familiar with the litigation, determine what is a reasonable fee, therefore there is a rational basis for limiting substitution of judges and due process is not violated. Kaufman, Litwin & Feinstein v. Edgar, 301 Ill. App. 3d 826, 235 Ill. Dec. 183, 704 N.E.2d 756 (1 Dist. 1998), appeal denied, 182 Ill. 2d 551, 236 Ill. Dec. 670, 707 N.E.2d 1240 (1999).

Because petitioner's filing of a request for temporary attorney fees in a divorce proceeding did not constitute a new action, respondent did not have an absolute right to a substitution of judges, and absent specific allegations of prejudice, the trial court correctly denied the motion. In re Zannis, 114 Ill. App. 3d 1034, 70 Ill. Dec. 545, 449 N.E.2d 892 (1 Dist. 1983).

Tax Exemptions

A trial court can order a custodial parent to sign a written declaration that he will not claim dependency exemptions under section 152(e)(2) of the Internal Revenue Code, effectively allocating the exemptions to the noncustodial parent. In re Einhorn, 178 Ill. App. 3d 212, 127 Ill. Dec. 411, 533 N.E.2d 29 (1 Dist. 1988).

Temporary Attorney Fees

While a temporary attorney may be allowed where necessary to maintain a divorce action, it is not allowable as a supplement to the property settlement after a default divorce and a property settlement based thereon has been approved by the court without reference to such fee, because this would amount to writing a new contract for the parties after the stipulated contract had been submitted and approved by the court. Pearson v. Pearson, 42 Ill. App. 3d 522, 1 Ill. Dec. 711, 356 N.E.2d 993 (2 Dist. 1976).

Testimony

Where husband defendant correctly stated his monthly net income to be $950 at time of hearing, and there was no denial of his testimony of monthly expenses exceeding $1,400 (of which about $600 was an obligation in divorce decree of his prior marriage) or of his testimony of liabilities in excess of assets, those facts, considered with testimony of his wife that she had a net worth of $20,000, show that an award of $700 per month temporary alimony was not supported by the record and was an abuse of the court's discretion. Moore v. Moore, 53 Ill. App. 3d 228, 10 Ill. Dec. 950, 368 N.E.2d 545 (1 Dist. 1977).

Time and Labor

—Independent Proof Required

Such factors as the amount of time and labor involved in a case do not come out in the ordinary course of proceedings; thus, such factors require independent proof. In re Sanda, 245 Ill. App. 3d 314, 184 Ill. Dec. 186, 612 N.E.2d 1346 (2 Dist. 1993).

Undue Influence

The court properly concluded that an attorney did not exert undue influence upon a client in obtaining an agreement to pay fees which the client then contested; the client was aware of the fees as they were incurred, the fees resulted from services which benefited the client, the client received an explanation of her rights in conformance with this section, the client was an intelligent, capable adult and the client approved the settlement agreement and fees provision on several occasions during the negotiation process. Malkin v. Malkin, 301 Ill. App. 3d 303, 234 Ill. Dec. 599, 703 N.E.2d 460 (1 Dist. 1998), appeal denied, 182 Ill. 2d 552, 236 Ill. Dec. 670, 707 N.E.2d 1240 (1999).

Voluntary Dismissal

Where the hearing was on the preliminary issues of temporary maintenance, support, and fees, and did not relate to the issues of the dissolution action itself which petitioner sought to dismiss, no trial or hearing had begun for purposes of former section 52 of the former Civil Practice Act (see now 735 ILCS 5/2-1009). In re Mostow, 95 Ill. App. 3d 915, 51 Ill. Dec. 317, 420 N.E.2d 731 (1 Dist. 1981).

The petitioner was not required to exhaust her estate to pay her own attorney fees to maintain a dissolution action, and the trial court properly denied respondent's request that petitioner's right to voluntary dismissal (see 735 ILCS 5/2-1009) be subject to reimbursement of her attorney's fees and costs and payment of his accountant's fees. In re Mostow, 95 Ill. App. 3d 915, 51 Ill. Dec. 317, 420 N.E.2d 731 (1 Dist. 1981).

Waiver

It makes little sense to say that the court in a 735 ILCS 5/2-1401 proceeding can or should allow inquiry and testimony to ascertain whether a mere conclusory allegation of excessive fee can be proven after the client has knowingly and deliberately waived the opportunity provided by this section to reach that issue before judgment and where the client has not shown that the waiver of the hearing was obtained by fraud, undue influence, coercion, or other breach of fiduciary duties by the attorney. Malkin v. Malkin, 301 Ill. App. 3d 303, 234 Ill. Dec. 599, 703 N.E.2d 460 (1 Dist. 1998), appeal denied, 182 Ill. 2d 552, 236 Ill. Dec. 670, 707 N.E.2d 1240 (1999).

When a client has waived the right to a hearing under this section, that client's ability to seek vacatur of a judgment for fees is not patently apparent and when there is nothing more than a request for an investigatory hearing on that question, a hearing which was already waived, a second opportunity for a hearing should not become available unless the waiver of the first hearing was obtained through undue influence, fraud, or other manipulative conduct in breach of the attorney's fiduciary duties. Malkin v. Malkin, 301 Ill. App. 3d 303, 234 Ill. Dec. 599, 703 N.E.2d 460 (1 Dist. 1998), appeal denied, 182 Ill. 2d 552, 236 Ill. Dec. 670, 707 N.E.2d 1240 (1999).

Plaintiff attorney was precluded from bringing an action to recover attorney fees against client wife on the grounds of res

Waiver (Cont'd)
judicata, when a judgment order existed on this issue in a prior action brought by wife against husband; at that hearing, plaintiff presented evidence as to all the work done by him and associate counsel in the course of the dissolution proceedings. Plaintiff had the opportunity to have his "day in court," and based upon some misplaced loyalty to a client who directed him to proceed in a different direction, he waived his "day in court." Cantwell v. Reinhart, 244 Ill. App. 3d 199, 185 Ill. Dec. 40, 614 N.E.2d 174 (1 Dist.), appeal denied, 152 Ill. 2d 555, 190 Ill. Dec. 884, 622 N.E.2d 1201 (1993).

While the waiver of important rights such as those granted by this section cannot be made unless the client acts deliberately and understands the rights that he or she is waiving, the question of whether a proper waiver is made must turn on the particular factual situations that surround the parties. In re Pagano, 154 Ill. 2d 174, 180 Ill. Dec. 729, 607 N.E.2d 1242 (1992).

A party waives his right to a hearing on attorney fees where he did not request a hearing before the trial court and was thereby left with the judge's ruling on the basis of the fee petition and affidavits alone. In re Jones, 187 Ill. App. 3d 206, 134 Ill. Dec. 836, 543 N.E.2d 119 (1 Dist. 1989).

Because attorney did not object in the trial court to the trial court order delaying determination of his fees, he waived the issue. In re Coltman, 148 Ill. App. 3d 1001, 102 Ill. Dec. 613, 500 N.E.2d 506 (1 Dist. 1986).

Where three attorneys submitted detailed petitions for fees and discussed with the trial court the issue of fees based on evidence already presented in the proceedings, where no evidentiary hearing was sought nor was any other request made by either party, and where respondent did not attempt to assert a counterclaim, demand a jury trial, seek discovery, or attempt to raise any affirmative matter, respondent waived any alleged rights and could not be deemed to have suffered any deprivation under the statute. In re Shedbalkar, 95 Ill. App. 3d 136, 50 Ill. Dec. 301, 419 N.E.2d 409 (1 Dist. 1981).

This section does not authorize a court to grant fees to prosecute an appeal. Hall v. Hall, 25 Ill. App. 3d 524, 323 N.E.2d 541 (1 Dist. 1975).

Wilful Violation
Even though court's initial finding of contempt was erroneous, petitioner was required to follow the dictates of the trial court until such time as the trial court's order was set aside by either the issuing court of the reviewing court. In re Tatham, 293 Ill. App. 3d 471, 228 Ill. Dec. 166, 688 N.E.2d 864 (5 Dist. 1997).

Although respondent contended that the trial court erred in finding that he was in wilful violation of his obligation to pay for his child's education expenses because his employment was terminated and he could not afford to pay for those education expenses, the record revealed that, in addition to owning assets in excess of $200,000, respondent was paid a salary of $82,000 per year by his employer through November 1990 and that he did not pay all of the education expenses that his child incurred at that time and those that he did pay, he claimed were paid by mistake; thus, despite being both able and aware of his obligation to pay his child's present and future education expenses, respondent did not fulfill his obligation in accordance with the marital settlement agreement, therefore the trial court did not abuse its discretion in awarding petitioner attorney fees and holding respondent in contempt because it could properly find that respondent's failure to pay his child's education expenses in accordance with marital settlement agreement was wilful and thus without justification. In re Dieter, 271 Ill. App. 3d 181, 207 Ill. Dec. 848, 648 N.E.2d 304 (1 Dist. 1995).

LEGAL PERIODICALS

For note, "Guardians Ad Litem: The Guardian Angels of Our Children in Domestic Violence Courts", see 30 Loy. U. Chi. L.J. 281 (1999).

For article, "'Leveling the Playing Field' in Divorce: Questions and Answers About the New Law," see 85 Ill. B.J. 410 (1997).

For article, "Survey of Illinois Law [1988-89] — Family Law," see 14 S. Ill. U. L. J. 1007 (1990).

For article, "A Practical Guide to the Recovery of Attorneys' Fees," see 74 Ill. B. J. 124 (1985).

For article, "Award of Attorneys Fees in Court Cases Where Provided by Statute or Circuit Court Rule," see 67 Ill. B. J. 720 (1979).

RESEARCH REFERENCES

Authority of divorce court to award prospective or anticipated attorneys' fees to enable parties to maintain or defend divorce suit. 22 ALR4th 407.

Right to attorneys' fees in proceeding, after absolute divorce, for modification of child custody or support order 57 ALR4th 710.

Excessiveness or adequacy of attorneys' fees in domestic relations cases. 17 ALR5th 366.

Validity, construction, and application of provision in separation agreement affecting distribution or payment of attorneys' fees. 47 ALR5th 207.

750 ILCS 5/509 Independence of Provisions of Judgment or Temporary Order

Sec. 509. *Independence of Provisions of Judgment or Temporary Order.* If a party fails to comply with a provision of a judgment, order or injunction, the obligation of the other party to make payments for support or maintenance or to permit visitation is not suspended; but he may move the court to grant an appropriate order.
(Source: P.A. 80-923.)

Note.
This section was Ill.Rev.Stat., Ch. 40, para. 509.

CASE NOTES

Analysis

Appropriate Order
Contempt Found

Appropriate Order
Parents who wilfully disregard appropriate court orders may properly have their fitness to be custodial parents questioned. Huckaby v. Huckaby, 75 Ill. App. 3d 195, 30 Ill. Dec. 909, 393 N.E.2d 1256 (5 Dist. 1979).

Contempt Found
Father was held in contempt for his wilful refusal to pay support to his ex-wife and instead placing the money in a bank account. Cooper v. Cooper, 59 Ill. App. 3d 457, 16 Ill. Dec. 818, 375 N.E.2d 925 (1 Dist. 1978).

750 ILCS 5/510 Modification and termination of provisions for maintenance, support, educational expenses, and property disposition

Sec. 510. *Modification and termination of provisions for maintenance, support, educational expenses, and property disposition.* (a) Except as otherwise provided in paragraph (f) of Section 502 [750 ILCS 5/502] and in subsection (b), clause (3) of Section 505.2 [750 ILCS 5/505.2], the provisions of any judgment respecting maintenance or support may be modified only as to installments accruing subsequent to due notice by the moving party of the filing of the motion for modification. An order for child support may be modified as follows:

(1) upon a showing of a substantial change in circumstances; and

(2) without the necessity of showing a substantial change in circumstances, as follows:

(A) upon a showing of an inconsistency of at least 20%, but no less than $10 per month, between the amount of the existing order and the amount of child support that results from application of the guidelines specified in Section 505 of this Act [750 ILCS 5/505] unless the inconsistency is due to the fact that the amount of the existing order resulted from a deviation from the guideline amount and there has not been a change in the circumstances that resulted in that deviation; or

(B) Upon a showing of a need to provide for the health care needs of the child under the order through health insurance or other means. In no event shall the eligibility for or receipt of medical assistance be considered to meet the need to provide for the child's health care needs.

The provisions of subparagraph (a)(2)(A) shall apply only in cases in which a party is receiving child support enforcement services from the Illinois Department of Public Aid under Article X of the Illinois Public Aid Code [305 ILCS 5/10-1 et seq.], and only when at least 36 months have elapsed since the order for child support was entered or last modified.

(a-5) An order for maintenance may be modified or terminated only upon a showing of a substantial change in circumstances. In all such proceedings, as well as in proceedings in which maintenance is being reviewed, the court shall consider the applicable factors set forth in subsection (a) of Section 504 [750 ILCS 5/504] and the following factors:

(1) any change in the employment status of either party and whether the change has been made in good faith;

(2) the efforts, if any, made by the party receiving maintenance to become self-supporting, and the reasonableness of the efforts where they are appropriate;

(3) any impairment of the present and future earning capacity of either party;

(4) the tax consequences of the maintenance payments upon the respective economic circumstances of the parties;

(5) the duration of the maintenance payments previously paid (and remaining to be paid) relative to the length of the marriage;

(6) the property, including retirement benefits, awarded to each party under the judgment of dissolution of marriage, judgment of legal separation, or judgment of declaration of invalidity of marriage and the present status of the property;

(7) the increase or decrease in each party's income since the prior judgment or order from which a review, modification, or termination is being sought;

(8) the property acquired and currently owned by each party after the entry of the judgment of dissolution of marriage, judgment of legal separation, or judgment of declaration of invalidity of marriage; and

(9) any other factor that the court expressly finds to be just and equitable.

(b) The provisions as to property disposition may not be revoked or modified, unless the court finds the existence of conditions that justify the reopening of a judgment under the laws of this State.

(c) Unless otherwise agreed by the parties in a written agreement set forth in the judgment or otherwise approved by the court, the obligation to pay future maintenance is terminated upon the death of either party, or the remarriage of the party receiving maintenance, or if the party receiving maintenance cohabits with another person on a resident, continuing conjugal basis.

(d) Unless otherwise provided in this Act, or as agreed in writing or expressly provided in the judgment, provisions for the support of a child are terminated by emancipation of the child, or if the child has attained the age of 18 and is still attending high school, provisions for the support of the child are terminated upon the date that the child graduates from high school or the date the child attains the age of 19, whichever is earlier, but not by the death of a parent obligated to support or educate the child. An existing obligation to pay for support or educational expenses, or both, is not terminated by the death of a parent. When a parent obligated to pay support or educational expenses, or both, dies, the amount of support or educational expenses, or both, may be enforced, modified, revoked or commuted to a lump sum payment, as equity may require, and that determination may be provided for at the time of the dissolution of the marriage or thereafter.

(e) The right to petition for support or educational expenses, or both, under Sections 505 and 513 [750 ILCS 5/505 and 750 ILCS 5/513] is not extinguished by the death of a parent. Upon a petition filed before or after a parent's death, the court may award sums of money out of the decedent's estate for the child's support or educational expenses, or both, as equity may require. The time within which a claim may be filed against the estate of a decedent under Sections 505 and 513 [750 ILCS 5/505 and 750 ILCS 5/513] and subsection (d) and this subsection shall be governed by the provisions of the Probate Act of 1975 [755 ILCS 5/1-1 et seq.], as a barrable, noncontingent claim.

(f) A petition to modify or terminate child support, custody, or visitation shall not delay any child support enforcement litigation or supplementary proceeding on behalf of the obligee, including, but not limited to, a petition for a rule to show cause, for non-wage garnishment, or for a restraining order.

(Source: P.A. 86-649; 87-714; 88-42, § 5; 88-307, § 10; 88-670, § 2-68; 92-289, § 5; 92-590, § 10; 92-651, § 87; 92-876, § 910; 93-353, § 5.)

Note.

This section was Ill.Rev.Stat., Ch. 40, para. 510.

Section 997 of P.A. 92-651 is a no acceleration or delay provision, and Section 998 is a no revival or extension provision.

Cross References.

As to revival of judgments, see 735 ILCS 5/13-218.

As to the modification of judgments under the Parentage Act of 1984, and its applicability to this section, see 750 ILCS 45/16.

Illinois Administrative Code.

See 89 Illinois Administrative Code, §§ 160.65, 160.60.

Effect of Amendments.

The 1994 amendment by P.A. 88-670, effective December 2, 1994, combined the amendments by P.A. 88-42 and P.A. 88-307.

The 2001 amendment by P.A. 92-289, effective August 9, 2001, added subsection (f).

The 2002 amendment by P.A. 92-590, effective July 1, 2002, substituted "subsection (b)" for "subsection (d)" in the first paragraph of subsection (a), and in the last paragraph of subsection (a) substituted "child support enforcement services" for "child and spouse support service".

The 2002 amendment by P.A. 92-651, effective July 11, 2002, substituted "subsection (b)" for "subsection (d)" in the introductory paragraph of subsection (a).

The 2002 amendment by P.A. 92-876, effective June 1, 2003, in subsection (a) substituted "(b)" for "(d)"; and rewrote the first sentence in subsection (d), which formerly read: "Unless otherwise agreed in writing or expressly provided in a judgment, provisions for the support of a child are terminated by emancipation of the child, except as otherwise provided herein, but not by the death of a parent obligated to support or educate the child."

The 2003 amendment by P.A. 93-353, effective January 1, 2004, deleted "and, with respect to maintenance, only upon a showing of a substantial change in circumstance" following "the motion for modification" in the introductory language of subsection (a); and added subsection (a-5).

CASE NOTES

Analysis

Constitutionality
In General
Alimony
—Binding
—Cost of Living
—In Gross
—Modification
—Separation Agreements
—Termination
Applicability
—Alimony
—Effective Date
—Reimbursement of Fees
Arrearages
—In General
—Computation
—Emancipation
—Waiver
Attorney Fees
—In General
—Allocation
—Factors
—Malpractice
—Modification
—Time of Award
Award
—Certain and Definite
—Retroactive
Back Payments
Burden of Proof
Change in Circumstances
—In General
—Ability to Pay
—Application
—Authority of Old Case Law
—Burden of Proof
—Consent Decree
—Cost of Living
—Death of Child
—Discharge from Military Service
—Effect on Child
—Employment
—Evidence
—Evidentiary Hearing
—Factors Considered
—Failure to Make Effort to Achieve Financial Independence
—Failure to Seek Employment
—Illustrative Cases
—Increase in Income
—Insufficient
—Loss of Job
—Needs of Recipient
—Net Worth
—Not Shown
—Offsetting Changes
—Proceedings on Remand
—Review
—Settlement Agreement
—Shown
—Special Finding
—Standard of Living
—Suspension from Employment
—Time Period Considered
—Transfer of Custody
—Undisclosed Assets
—Worker's Compensation Settlement
Cohabitation
—Another Person
—Burden of Proof
——Not Met
—Conjugal
——Belief
——Burden of Proof
——Defined
——Sexual Conduct
——Termination of Maintenance
—Continuing Basis
——Not Shown
—Effect
—Evidence Insufficient
—Factors
——Not Shown
——Shown
—Finding
——Review
—Husband/Wife Relationship
—Purpose
—Settlement Agreement
——Basis for Termination
—Termination of Maintenance
Collateral Estoppel
Consent Decree
—Continuing Jurisdiction
—Contractual
—Divestiture of Jurisdiction
—Effect
—Effect of Amendment
—Fraud or Coercion
—Modification Allowed
—Trial of Issues
Construction
—Mandatory Provision
—With Supreme Court Rules
Default/Vesting Date
Educational Expenses
—Age of Majority
—Burden of Proof
—College
—Consent Decree
—Death of Obligor
—Death of Parent
—Emancipation
—Modification in Error
—Termination
Employment

—Reasonable Diligence
Equitable Estoppel
—Applicability
Evidence
—Parol Evidence
Extraordinary Circumstances
—Not Shown
Failure to Pay
Failure to Reserve Right to Modification
Filing
Final Order
Foreign Court's Modification
Guardian ad Litem
—Abuse of Discretion
Illustrative Cases
Indefinite Maintenance
Jurisdiction
Law of the Case
Legislative Intent
Life Insurance
—Child As Beneficiary
—Illustrative Cases
Limitations
—Death
Maintenance
—In General
—Ability to Pay
—Appeal
—Bankruptcy
—Characterization
—Credit
—Defined
—Employment Secured
—Equitable
—Factors Considered
—Failure to Pay
—Failure to Seek Independence
—Financial Independence
—Grant Held Erroneous
—In Gross
—Job Search
—Modification
——Allowed
——Burden of Proof
——Factors Considered
——Not Allowed
——Standard
—Need of Support
—Paramour
—Party Agreement
—Past Due Installments
—Permanent
—Post Death
—Reduction
—Reduction for Property Charge
—Rehabilitative
—Reinstatement
—Retroactive Modification
—Review
——Allowed
——Change in Circumstances
——Discretion
—Standard
—Settlement Agreement
—Termination
——In General
——Allowed
——Effective Date
——Factors Considered
——Indefinite Time
——Not Allowed
——Settlement Agreement
——Significant Misfortune
—Upheld
Medical Expenses
Modification
—In General
—Allowed
—Burden of Proof
—Cohabitation
—Cost of Raising Children
—Cross-Petition Necessary
—Discharge in Bankruptcy
—Disparity in Income
—Estoppel
—Factors Considered
—Fraudulent Misrepresentation
—Jurisdiction
—Lifestyle During Marriage
—Movant's Burden
—Not Allowed
—Oral Modification
—Post-Judgment Relief
—Remarriage of Supporting Parent
—Retroactivity
—Review
—Settlement Agreement
—Typographical Error
—Upheld
Property Disposition
—In General
—Between Spouses
—Changed Circumstances
—Civil Procedure
—Consent Decree
—Credit
—Fraud or Coercion
—In Lieu of Maintenance
—Maintenance Distinguished
—Marital Home
—Modification of Agreement
—Modification Improper
—Modification Proper
—Power of Court
—Property Settlement Agreement
—Rent for Marital Home
—Revestment
—Settlement
—Trust
Remarriage
Res Judicata
Retirement
Revestment
Review
—Abuse of Discretion
—Discretion of Court
—Insufficient Record
—New Hearing Required
—Standard
Settlement Agreement
Standing
Support
—In General
—Accounting
—Arrearages
—Burden of Proof
—Calculation
—Change in Circumstances
—Child Support
——Life Insurance
—Consent Decrees
—Continuing Jurisdiction
—Contract
—Cost of Living Increase
—Death of Obligor
—Delayed Modification
—Determination
—Discretion of Court
—Dissolution Judgment
—Effect of Agreement or Consent Decree
—Emancipation
—Equitable Estoppel

—Estate Liability
—Factors Considered
—Failure to Pay
—Failure to Reinstate Obligation
—Held Sufficient
—Incarceration of Obligor
—Increase Denied
—Increase in Child Support
—Involuntary Unemployment
—Joint Decision
—Jurisdiction
—Laches
—Minimum Support Guidelines
—Modification
——In General
——Allowed
——Burden of Proof
——Court's Power
——Factors Considered
——Not Allowed
——Retroactivity
—Need
——In General
——Ability to Pay
——Evidence
——In Excess
——Increase
—Notice
——In General
——Pleadings
——Retroactivity
——Review
——Settlement Agreement
—Obligation
—Oral Agreement
—Past Due
——In General
——Estoppel
—Payments
—Private Agreements
—Punitive Abatement Improper
—Reduction
——Agreement
——Death of Child
——Emancipation
——Employment
——Repayment
——Temporary
——Upheld
—Res Judicata
—Retroactivity
—Same Day Modifications
—Security
—Social Security Benefits
—Standing
—Temporary Cessation of Income
—Termination
——In General
——Discretion of Court
——Mandatory Termination
——Not Allowed
—Timeliness
—Trust Fund
—Trust Taxes
—Unenforceable Adoption Agreement
—Unilateral Reduction
Termination
—Cohabitation Requirement
—Not Justified
—Same-Sex Relationship
—Settlement Agreement
—Upheld
Unallocated Award

Constitutionality

A trial court erred in holding that the amendment to this section which became effective January 1, 1982, was unconstitutional to the extent that the law precludes the court from doing what it should have done in justice and equity. Krug-Etheridge v. Krug, 111 Ill. App. 3d 780, 67 Ill. Dec. 454, 444 N.E.2d 690 (1 Dist. 1982).

Subsection (c) of this section does not invidiously discriminate against divorced parents in defiance of equal protection. Kujawinski v. Kujawinski, 71 Ill. 2d 563, 17 Ill. Dec. 801, 376 N.E.2d 1382 (1978).

In General

At any time, either party may seek modification of the maintenance award, and the judgment does not, in any way, restrict that right under the Act. In re Gunn, 233 Ill. App. 3d 165, 174 Ill. Dec. 381, 598 N.E.2d 1013 (5 Dist. 1992).

This section, while allowing termination upon death, remarriage, or cohabitation under subsection (c) of this section, also allows modification upon a showing of substantial change of circumstances under subsection (a) of this section. In re Scott, 205 Ill. App. 3d 561, 150 Ill. Dec. 868, 563 N.E.2d 995 (4 Dist. 1990).

Prior to the Marriage and Dissolution of Marriage Act (750 ILCS 5/101 et seq.), there was no specific statutory provision in Illinois that the morality of a wife's post-dissolution behavior affected her right to alimony. Under this standard, a wife's cohabitation, while perhaps immoral under section 19 of the Divorce Act (see now this section), did not provide a legal basis for termination of maintenance or alimony; had any portion of her conduct occurred on or after the effective date of this Marriage Act, the court could have terminated her maintenance from the date of the petition for modification or termination. Kowalski v. Kowalski, 96 Ill. App. 3d 830, 52 Ill. Dec. 402, 422 N.E.2d 83 (1 Dist. 1981).

The court has power to modify child support orders of a divorce decree if subsequent changes in the conditions and circumstances of the parties render such modification necessary. Edwards v. Edwards, 125 Ill. App. 2d 91, 259 N.E.2d 820 (4 Dist. 1970).

Alimony

—Binding

Alimony provisions in a divorce decree are of a vested and binding character upon a defendant. Hallett v. Hallett, 10 Ill. App. 2d 513, 135 N.E.2d 224 (2 Dist. 1956).

—Cost of Living

An increase in the cost of living, standing alone, has been repeatedly rejected as a sufficient reason to increase or augment alimony awards, because inflation affects both parties rather than merely one spouse or the other. Bellow v. Bellow, 94 Ill. App. 3d 361, 50 Ill. Dec. 656, 419 N.E.2d 924 (1 Dist. 1981).

—In Gross

Where defendant offered little evidence to show in what manner an award of alimony in gross (made under prior law) was so excessive as to constitute an abuse of discretion and plaintiff's claim that the award was inadequate was equally unpersuasive, the trial court's estimate of plaintiff's actual needs was correct and not contrary to the manifest weight of the evidence presented. Lieberman v. Lieberman, 25 Ill. App. 3d 654, 323 N.E.2d 785 (1 Dist. 1975).

—Modification

A court was required to consider the conduct or condition in issue affecting modification of alimony only if it still occurred at the time of the petition or on or after the effective date of the Marriage Act. Kowalski v. Kowalski, 96 Ill. App. 3d 830, 52 Ill. Dec. 402, 422 N.E.2d 83 (1 Dist. 1981).

For cases discussing modification of alimony, see Hickey v. Hickey, 31 Ill. App. 3d 257, 333 N.E.2d 271 (1 Dist. 1975); Barrow v. Barrow, 33 Ill. App. 3d 654, 342 N.E.2d 237 (5 Dist. 1975); Pierce v. Pierce, 69 Ill. App. 3d 42, 25 Ill. Dec. 511, 386 N.E.2d 1175 (5 Dist. 1979); Schuppe v. Schuppe, 69 Ill. App. 3d 200, 25 Ill. Dec. 690, 387 N.E.2d 346 (2 Dist. 1979); Pacione v. Pacione, 81 Ill. App. 3d 600, 37 Ill. Dec. 426, 402 N.E.2d 316 (3 Dist. 1980); In re Parks, 83 Ill. App. 3d 372, 38 Ill. Dec. 742, 403 N.E.2d 1346 (3 Dist. 1980); Kowalski v. Kowalski, 96 Ill. App. 3d 830, 52 Ill. Dec. 402, 422 N.E.2d 83 (1 Dist. 1981); National Tea Co. v. Industrial Comm'n, 97 Ill. 2d 424, 73 Ill. Dec. 575, 454 N.E.2d 672 (1983); In re Wettstein, 160 Ill. App. 3d 554, 113 Ill. Dec. 1, 514 N.E.2d 783 (4 Dist. 1987); In re Garelick, 168 Ill. App. 3d 321, 119 Ill. Dec. 76, 522 N.E.2d 738 (1 Dist. 1988).

Alimony (Cont'd)

—Modification (Cont'd)

Where practically all of the living expenses of a paramour of a defendant's spouse were provided by defendant, who received almost all of her income from the alimony, and defendant paid all of the taxes, utility bills, insurance and provided almost all of the food for the paramour, then alimony was modified. Hall v. Hall, 25 Ill. App. 3d 524, 323 N.E.2d 541 (1 Dist. 1975).

—Separation Agreements

When a trial court entered its decree for divorce and expressly approved the parties' settlement agreement, it thereby incorporated into its decree the provisions of the agreement as to alimony. The rights of the parties thereafter rested upon the decree and it was subject to modification by the court pursuant to former Ill.Rev.Stat., ch. 40, para. 19 (see now this section). Larson v. Larson, 21 Ill. App. 2d 264, 157 N.E.2d 689 (2 Dist. 1959).

—Termination

For cases discussing termination of alimony, see Pierce v. Pierce, 69 Ill. App. 3d 42, 25 Ill. Dec. 511, 386 N.E.2d 1175 (5 Dist. 1979); Halford v. Halford, 70 Ill. App. 3d 609, 27 Ill. Dec. 168, 388 N.E.2d 1131 (5 Dist. 1979); Schoenhard v. Schoenhard, 74 Ill. App. 3d 296, 30 Ill. Dec. 109, 392 N.E.2d 764 (2 Dist. 1979); In re Parks, 83 Ill. App. 3d 372, 38 Ill. Dec. 742, 403 N.E.2d 1346 (3 Dist. 1980).

Although a complete termination of alimony to the plaintiff was an abuse of the trial court's discretion, the continued payment of $16,000 a year to a woman of the plaintiff's means, after her brief marriage to the defendant, was not justified. Borowitz v. Borowitz, 19 Ill. App. 3d 176, 311 N.E.2d 292 (1 Dist. 1974).

The trial court did not err in its judgment that plaintiff, by using the $1,000 in additional payments awarded to her as a condition to termination of alimony, could make herself employable either by undergoing surgery on her feet or by obtaining additional education, and that defendant's remarriage, and the birth of a child from the new marriage, constituted substantial change of circumstances justifying termination of alimony. Tan v. Tan, 3 Ill. App. 3d 671, 279 N.E.2d 486 (1 Dist. 1972).

Similar prior provision allowing the court to make reasonable and proper alterations in its alimony requirement also vested the court with ample power to declare the termination of all alimony upon the occurrence of facts reasonably justifying such a declaration. Lennahan v. O'Keefe, 107 Ill. 620 (1883).

Absent unequivocal language that the court intended a spouse's heirs to be bound by its alimony decree, the alimony obligation terminated at paying spouse's death. Lennahan v. O'Keefe, 107 Ill. 620 (1883).

Applicability

—Alimony

This section required that the court look to the former Divorce Act to determine whether a decree entered in 1975 which incorporated a property settlement agreement waiving alimony could be modified to add an alimony provision, under which the trial judge had no authority to modify the decree by adding an alimony provision. Hartman v. Hartman, 89 Ill. App. 3d 969, 45 Ill. Dec. 360, 412 N.E.2d 711 (4 Dist. 1980).

—Effective Date

Any proceedings commenced subsequent to the effective date of subsection (b) of this section to modify alimony or maintenance are governed by its provisions. Kowalski v. Kowalski, 96 Ill. App. 3d 830, 52 Ill. Dec. 402, 422 N.E.2d 83 (1 Dist. 1981).

—Reimbursement of Fees

Trial court had subject matter jurisdiction over wife's petition under the Illinois Marriage and Dissolution Act; wife was not seeking modification of the property provisions of the supplemental order to the dissolution judgment in filing a petition (1) to have former husband held in contempt for failure to pay debt assigned to him and (2) to be reimbursed for legal fees incurred defending herself from a lawsuit on that debt. In re Davis, 292 Ill. App. 3d 802, 226 Ill. Dec. 765, 686 N.E.2d 395 (4 Dist. 1997).

Arrearages

—In General

750 ILCS 5/510 evidences the legislature's intent to allow a court to adjust a marital settlement agreement by entering a qualified domestic relations order that ensures the equitable distribution of money in a retirement account which belongs to a spouse who has not met his or her support obligations under the settlement agreement to a spouse who has not been paid. In re Marriage of Thomas, 339 Ill. App. 3d 214, 273 Ill. Dec. 647, 789 N.E.2d 821, 2003 Ill. App. LEXIS 568 (2 Dist. 2003).

—Computation

The trial court's reliance on a retroactive application when computing support arrearage created error because trial court could not provide for reduction in father's support payments. In re Jobe, 151 Ill. App. 3d 998, 105 Ill. Dec. 140, 503 N.E.2d 1146 (4 Dist. 1987).

—Emancipation

Although this section provides that the obligation to pay child support generally terminates upon emancipation, this does not mean that after emancipation the custodial parent is not entitled to child support arrearages. In re Homan, 126 Ill. App. 3d 133, 81 Ill. Dec. 487, 466 N.E.2d 1289 (1 Dist. 1984).

—Waiver

Although a court cannot reduce the amount owing on past-due installments of child support, in a proper case the court can give effect to an agreement by a party to waive the payments or accept a lesser amount. Anderson v. Anderson, 48 Ill. App. 2d 140, 198 N.E.2d 342 (2 Dist. 1964).

Attorney Fees

—In General

Attorney fees may be awarded by the trial court in post-decree proceedings to modify the provisions of a decree. Horwitz v. Horwitz, 130 Ill. App. 2d 424, 264 N.E.2d 723 (1 Dist. 1970).

—Allocation

Where husband had additional income each year, in excess of his own living expenses and the maintenance payment he must make, trial court's order of husband's financial responsibility for wife's attorney fees was not an abuse of discretion as her ability to pay was limited. In re Murphy, 117 Ill. App. 3d 649, 72 Ill. Dec. 808, 453 N.E.2d 113 (3 Dist. 1983).

—Factors

Attorney fees can be awarded to a divorced wife in subsequent proceedings to modify the decree under proper circumstances; the allowance of the aforesaid attorney fees depends not upon who initiates the proceeding but rather upon the circumstances peculiar to the individual case. Mabbatt v. Mabbatt, 78 Ill. App. 2d 455, 223 N.E.2d 191 (1 Dist. 1967).

—Malpractice

Because subsection (b) of this section, before 1982 amendments, permitted parties to agree to maintenance that would be payable following the remarriage of the recipient, a settlement agreement that included a provision that maintenance payments were not modifiable did not warrant imposition of liability on an attorney based on a breach of the standard of care owed to his client. Boyer v. Rudman, 161 Ill. App. 3d 237, 112 Ill. Dec. 734, 514 N.E.2d 200 (3 Dist. 1987).

—Modification

Where a petition for attorney fees was not filed until after 30 days had elapsed from entry of a marital dissolution judgment, the provision of the judgment relating to attorney fees had become final and could be modified only in accordance with the provisions of (a) of this section, which in turn required the filing of a petition under former section 72 of the Civil Practice Act (now 735 ILCS 5/2-1401) showing not only a meritorious cause of action but also the exercise of due diligence by the moving party. In re Rifkin, 114 Ill. App. 3d 555, 70 Ill. Dec. 299, 449 N.E.2d 173 (1 Dist. 1983).

—Time of Award

Attorney's fees are not awarded in advance of a post-decree proceeding, but only after a full adjudication on the merits of the petition. Horwitz v. Horwitz, 130 Ill. App. 2d 424, 264 N.E.2d 723 (1 Dist. 1970).

Award

—Certain and Definite

The provision for the payment of alimony by husband as "one-half of his salary earned and received as a teacher or employee of the public schools of the City of Chicago, Illinois, as long as he is so employed" was held reasonably definite and certain. Condy v. Condy, 328 Ill. App. 8, 65 N.E.2d 219 (1946).

—Retroactive

The trial court did not err in refusing to make the child support award retroactive to September, the date when petitioner's maintenance payments ceased, as there was no indication in the record that notice of hearing on petitioner's petition for modification was served in September. In re Freesen, 275 Ill. App. 3d 97, 211 Ill. Dec. 761, 655 N.E.2d 1144 (4 Dist. 1995), appeal denied, 165 Ill. 2d 550, 214 Ill. Dec. 858, 662 N.E.2d 424 (1996).

Back Payments

Modifications of support are only applicable to payments made after the filing of the modification petition, therefore the trial court's imposition of back payments was beyond the power granted to it by statute. In re Boyden, 164 Ill. App. 3d 385, 115 Ill. Dec. 458, 517 N.E.2d 1144 (2 Dist. 1987).

Burden of Proof

The burden of demonstrating the alleged substantial change in circumstances is on the party seeking relief. In re Lasota, 125 Ill. App. 3d 37, 80 Ill. Dec. 537, 465 N.E.2d 649 (1 Dist. 1984).

The burden of proving fraud or concealment is on the party asserting it, and that burden is more onerous when a party seeks to vacate or modify a property settlement incorporated in a divorce decree, all presumptions being in favor of the validity of the settlement; fraud may consist in the concealment of what is true as in the assertion of what is false, and the concealment must be shown to have been done with the intention to deceive under circumstances creating an opportunity and a duty to speak. Dendrinos v. Dendrinos, 58 Ill. App. 3d 639, 16 Ill. Dec. 241, 374 N.E.2d 1016 (1 Dist. 1978).

The burden of proof is upon the party seeking relief to show that material changes in circumstances exist as would justify modification. Elizer v. Elizer, 36 Ill. App. 3d 552, 344 N.E.2d 493 (5 Dist. 1976); In re Potter, 88 Ill. App. 3d 606, 43 Ill. Dec. 866, 410 N.E.2d 999 (1 Dist. 1980); In re Chalkley, 99 Ill. App. 3d 478, 55 Ill. Dec. 262, 426 N.E.2d 237 (1 Dist. 1981); In re Garelick, 168 Ill. App. 3d 321, 119 Ill. Dec. 76, 522 N.E.2d 738 (1 Dist. 1988); Rice v. Rice, 173 Ill. App. 3d 1098, 123 Ill. Dec. 630, 528 N.E.2d 14 (5 Dist. 1988); In re Bean, 181 Ill. App. 3d 671, 130 Ill. Dec. 275, 537 N.E.2d 342 (5 Dist. 1989).

The burden of demonstrating circumstances warranting modification is on the party seeking the modification. Graham v. Graham, 21 Ill. App. 3d 1032, 316 N.E.2d 143 (4 Dist. 1974).

The burden of proof is on the petitioner in an action to increase support payments to prove the increased needs to support the child, and also to prove that the defendant has the ability to pay the increased amount needed. Grinton v. Grinton, 131 Ill. App. 2d 684, 264 N.E.2d 845 (3 Dist. 1970).

In a proceeding to modify child support the burden of proof is on the petitioner to clearly establish the increased need and corresponding increased ability to pay and the findings, and order of the trial court, on matters of this nature, will not be reversed unless contrary to the manifest weight of the evidence. Kelleher v. Kelleher, 67 Ill. App. 2d 410, 214 N.E.2d 139 (3 Dist. 1966).

Where the plaintiff's petition seeking modification of a divorce decree's property settlement was based upon the alleged fraud of the respondents, it was incumbent upon plaintiff to establish this charge by clear and convincing evidence. Wilson v. Wilson, 56 Ill. App. 2d 187, 205 N.E.2d 636 (2 Dist. 1965).

Although custody provisions can be modified, the party seeking to modify such provisions has the burden of proving altered conditions. Hirth v. Hirth, 59 Ill. App. 2d 240, 207 N.E.2d 114 (2 Dist. 1965).

The burden of proof is upon the applicant to show such material changes in circumstances as would justify modification, and where no evidence of a change in the financial condition of the parties is offered in evidence, the petition must be denied. Patterson v. Patterson, 28 Ill. App. 2d 76, 170 N.E.2d 11 (4 Dist. 1960).

Change in Circumstances

—In General

A "substantial change in circumstances" may not be founded on changes in financial conditions contemplated by the judgment for dissolution of marriage. In re Hughes, 322 Ill. App. 3d 815, 255 Ill. Dec. 929, 751 N.E.2d 23, 2001 Ill. App. LEXIS 310 (2 Dist. 2001).

Changed conditions are necessary to warrant a change in support payments. In re Wettstein, 160 Ill. App. 3d 554, 113 Ill. Dec. 1, 514 N.E.2d 783 (4 Dist. 1987).

When a material change has occurred, creating an imbalance between the child's needs and the parent's support capabilities, the act requires modification. Ingwerson v. Woeckener, 141 Ill. App. 3d 647, 95 Ill. Dec. 916, 490 N.E.2d 1008 (3 Dist. 1986).

Maintenance and child support are continuing obligations subject to change as the conditions and circumstances of the parties warrant. In re Kessler, 110 Ill. App. 3d 61, 65 Ill. Dec. 707, 441 N.E.2d 1221 (1 Dist. 1982).

Although the law looks with favor upon amicable settlement of property rights between parties to a divorce and is reluctant to disturb judgments based upon such settlements, whenever a request for modification is sought, it is the duty of the court in which the action has been brought to ascertain all of the pertinent facts and circumstances and then apply the statutory standard of "substantial change of circumstances" to determine if a modification should be made. In re Helfrich, 101 Ill. App. 3d 1070, 57 Ill. Dec. 469, 428 N.E.2d 1149 (1 Dist. 1981).

Maintenance provisions are modifiable upon a showing of a substantial change in circumstances, while property settlement provisions are not. In re Christianson, 89 Ill. App. 3d 167, 44 Ill. Dec. 397, 411 N.E.2d 519 (3 Dist. 1980).

Upon application for a modification of support, the court's paramount consideration is whether a substantial and material change in circumstances has occurred since entry of the decree which would authorize the court to change the allowance. Roqueplot v. Roqueplot, 88 Ill. App. 3d 59, 43 Ill. Dec. 441, 410 N.E.2d 441 (2 Dist. 1980).

Subsection (a) of this section allows the provisions of a judgment respecting support to be modified only upon a showing of substantial change in circumstances. What "change in circumstances" is required is left to the interpretation of the courts. That interpretation should be guided by the basic premise that the court should act in such manner as to serve the best interests of the children while giving due consideration to the rights and interests of the parents. Legan v. Legan, 69 Ill. App. 3d 304, 25 Ill. Dec. 757, 387 N.E.2d 413 (3 Dist. 1979).

A party may not unilaterally terminate child support payments when there is a change in circumstances. Jozwick v. Jozwick, 72 Ill. App. 3d 17, 28 Ill. Dec. 321, 390 N.E.2d 488 (1 Dist. 1979); Claflin v. Claflin, 82 Ill. App. 3d 246, 37 Ill. Dec. 671, 402 N.E.2d 673 (1 Dist. 1980); In re Erickson, 136 Ill. App. 3d 907, 91 Ill. Dec. 346, 483 N.E.2d 692 (2 Dist. 1985).

Under former Ill.Rev.Stat., ch. 40, para. 19 (see now this section), reasonable and proper alterations in support were those necessitated when the conditions and circumstances of the parties had materially changed subsequent to the entry of the divorce decree. Liss v. Liss, 62 Ill. App. 3d 170, 19 Ill. Dec. 545, 379 N.E.2d 60 (1 Dist. 1978).

Although this Act does not specify the conditions on which alimony may be terminated or modified, it has been construed to allow modification of an award upon a showing of substantial change in the circumstances of the parties. Baker v. Baker, 53 Ill. App. 3d 186, 10 Ill. Dec. 784, 368 N.E.2d 379 (1 Dist. 1977).

In all cases where petitions to modify payments under a divorce decree are involved, the primary question is whether or not changes in circumstances of the parties justify the modification. Bulmer v. Bulmer, 28 Ill. App. 3d 406, 328 N.E.2d 622 (5 Dist. 1975).

The issue on a petition for modification of child support payments is whether there has been a material change of circumstances since the entry of the original decree. Thomas v. Thomas, 23 Ill. App. 3d 936, 321 N.E.2d 159 (1 Dist. 1974).

Before an order for support payments can be modified there must be a finding of changed circumstances which relate either to the needs of the children or the financial condition of the parents. Metcoff v. Metcoff, 4 Ill. App. 3d 160, 280 N.E.2d 572 (1 Dist. 1972).

The court may not arbitrarily or capriciously modify the provisions for alimony or child support but can do so after a substantial

Change in Circumstances (Cont'd)

—In General (Cont'd)

change is shown to have occurred and the burden of proof is upon the applicant to show such material changes in circumstances as would justify modification. Loucks v. Loucks, 130 Ill. App. 2d 961, 266 N.E.2d 924 (5 Dist. 1971).

The issue on a petition for modification of child support payments is whether there has been a material change of circumstances of the parties since the entry of the decree. Lewis v. Lewis, 120 Ill. App. 2d 263, 256 N.E.2d 660 (3 Dist. 1970).

Under former section 19 of the Divorce Act (see now this section), the issue in a hearing on a petition to modify a divorce decree to require the former husband to pay an increased amount for support of the children of the parties, is whether there have been material changes in the circumstances of the parties since the entry of the divorce decree; an increase in monthly support payments is warranted when the evidence establishes that the needs of the children have increased, and the means of the supporting parent have also increased so as to enable him to contribute additional sums to his children's support. Kelleher v. Kelleher, 67 Ill. App. 2d 410, 214 N.E.2d 139 (3 Dist. 1966).

On a petition for modification the inquiry is necessarily directed to the question whether there have been material changes in the circumstances of the parties since the entry of the original decree; if petitioner's wants and necessities have increased and the means of the defendant is shown to have grown so as to enable him to contribute to such increased needs, then an additional allowance is proper. Patterson v. Patterson, 28 Ill. App. 2d 76, 170 N.E.2d 11 (4 Dist. 1960).

—Ability to Pay

In a child support modification case, the trial court did not abuse its discretion in determining that there was a substantial change of circumstances justifying an increase in child support because the child's needs increased as the child grew older and the cost of living rose, and the husband had the ability to pay the increased amount as his monthly income exceeded his expenses by more than $700; in addition, the trial court did not exceed its authority in setting child support based on the husband's prior income because he was voluntarily unemployed and his prior income reflected his earning potential. In re Marriage of Adams, 348 Ill. App. 3d 340, 284 Ill. Dec. 124, 809 N.E.2d 246, 2004 Ill. App. LEXIS 690 (3 Dist. 2004).

The increased ability of the obligor parent alone can justify an increase in child support. In re Heil, 233 Ill. App. 3d 888, 174 Ill. Dec. 622, 599 N.E.2d 168 (5 Dist. 1992).

—Application

Subsection (a) of this section governed cases in which the trial court was making an initial determination of child support or an initial award of child support and maintenance, not, as occurred in the case at bar, the termination of maintenance and the modification of child support; therefore, plaintiff, who met her burden of establishing a substantial change in circumstances, was entitled to some increase in support payments. Deardeuff v. Deardeuff, 149 Ill. App. 3d 406, 102 Ill. Dec. 891, 500 N.E.2d 992 (5 Dist. 1986).

—Authority of Old Case Law

Since subsection (a) of this section codifies previous case law by requiring a showing of a substantial change in circumstances before a support order can be modified, cases determined prior to the new Act are relevant in determining what disposition should be made with respect to child support cases. Spencer v. Spencer, 73 Ill. App. 3d 735, 29 Ill. Dec. 845, 392 N.E.2d 402 (3 Dist. 1979).

—Burden of Proof

In a case arising out of the construction and application of an agreement incorporated into the parties' divorce decree, the appellate court determined that further proceedings were required to determine whether the former wife had established changed circumstances warranting an increase in child support; the former husband had carried his burden of showing that changed circumstances warranted an adjustment in procedures regarding the son's medical expenses, but further proceedings were required to determine how the procedures should be implemented. Turrell v. Turrell, 335 Ill. App. 3d 297, 269 Ill. Dec. 633, 781 N.E.2d 430, 2002 Ill. App. LEXIS 1065 (2 Dist. 2002), appeal denied, 203 Ill. 2d 571, 273 Ill. Dec. 144, 788 N.E.2d 735 (2003).

The payor spouse is not relieved of demonstrating changed circumstances; rather, the lack of good-faith effort to achieve financial independence may, if proved, constitute the changed circumstances necessary for modification; this distinction is important due to the burden of proof. In re Lenkner, 241 Ill. App. 3d 15, 181 Ill. Dec. 646, 608 N.E.2d 897 (4 Dist. 1993).

A modification may only be had upon the showing of a "substantial change" in circumstances. In re Olsen, 229 Ill. App. 3d 107, 171 Ill. Dec. 39, 593 N.E.2d 859 (1 Dist. 1992).

After the threshold question of whether a substantial change in circumstances has occurred is answered, then and only then may the court determine the amount of the increase in child support. In re Heil, 233 Ill. App. 3d 888, 174 Ill. Dec. 622, 599 N.E.2d 168 (5 Dist. 1992).

The burden of demonstrating a substantial change in circumstances is on the party seeking modification. In re Lyons, 155 Ill. App. 3d 300, 108 Ill. Dec. 297, 508 N.E.2d 458 (2 Dist. 1987).

In order to obtain relief under either this section or 750 ILCS 5/610, a petitioner must show a change in circumstances from the situation which existed at the time the original order was entered; in both cases, relief may be necessary while an appeal is pending but the appellate court cannot grant such relief because its only power to change the effect of the judgment on appeal is that to stay the enforcement of the judgment. In re Spangler, 124 Ill. App. 3d 1023, 80 Ill. Dec. 137, 464 N.E.2d 1120 (4 Dist. 1984).

To receive increased support pursuant to a modification of settlement agreement, a moving party must show that the children have grown older and the cost of living has risen if, at the same time, the moving party can also demonstrate an increased ability on the part of the defendant to pay. In re Helfrich, 101 Ill. App. 3d 1070, 57 Ill. Dec. 469, 428 N.E.2d 1149 (1 Dist. 1981).

Modification of child support may be made only upon a showing of substantial change in circumstances. In re Schmerold, 88 Ill. App. 3d 348, 43 Ill. Dec. 629, 410 N.E.2d 629 (2 Dist. 1980).

In order to establish a substantial change in circumstances the petitioning party must show an increased ability of the supporting spouse to pay and increased needs of the children since the previous order. In re Schmerold, 88 Ill. App. 3d 348, 43 Ill. Dec. 629, 410 N.E.2d 629 (2 Dist. 1980); In re Roth, 99 Ill. App. 3d 679, 55 Ill. Dec. 271, 426 N.E.2d 246 (1 Dist. 1981); In re Bean, 181 Ill. App. 3d 671, 130 Ill. Dec. 275, 537 N.E.2d 342 (5 Dist. 1989).

A trial court may terminate or alter child support provisions previously ordered; however, only a material change in circumstances will justify any such modification and the burden of demonstrating circumstances warranting modification is on the person seeking it. Glass v. Peitchel, 42 Ill. App. 3d 240, 355 N.E.2d 750 (1 Dist. 1976).

The burden is on plaintiff to show that the circumstances of the parties have materially changed, and where no evidence of a change in the financial condition of the parties is offered, the petition must be denied. Nordstrom v. Nordstrom, 36 Ill. App. 3d 181, 343 N.E.2d 640 (1 Dist. 1976).

Under former section 18 of the Divorce Act (see now this section), the burden was on the plaintiff to prove a material change in circumstances by clearly establishing an increased need for the support of the children and a corresponding increased ability to pay on the part of the defendant since the time of entry of the divorce decree. Goldberg v. Goldberg, 36 Ill. App. 3d 778, 344 N.E.2d 721 (1 Dist. 1976).

—Consent Decree

When an agreement of the parties with respect to alimony and property rights is adopted by the court and incorporated into the final decree, the agreement becomes merged in the decree, and the rights of the parties thereafter rest upon the decree; however, the incorporation of the settlement agreement into the decree by agreement of the parties does not affect the power of the court to alter that provision of the decree when a change of circumstances warrants a modification. Brandel v. Brandel, 69 Ill. App. 2d 264, 216 N.E.2d 21 (2 Dist. 1966).

—Cost of Living

An increase in the child's needs can be presumed on the basis that the child has grown older and the cost of living has risen. People ex rel. Stokely v. Goodenow, 211 Ill. App. 3d 802, 164 Ill. Dec. 548, 583 N.E.2d 102 (4 Dist. 1991).

Change in Circumstances (Cont'd)

—Cost of Living (Cont'd)

If a former spouse's increased ability to pay is shown, the fact that the child receiving support has grown older and the cost of living has risen are proper bases for establishing increased need under this section. In re Boyden, 164 Ill. App. 3d 385, 115 Ill. Dec. 458, 517 N.E.2d 1144 (2 Dist. 1987).

—Death of Child

The circumstances were clearly changed from the time when an original divorce decree was entered and both children were alive and living at home, to when, after the death of one child, the only expenses for the care and support of the other child were monthly payments to the institution in which he lived until his death. Needler v. Needler, 131 Ill. App. 2d 11, 268 N.E.2d 517 (1 Dist. 1971).

—Discharge from Military Service

The trial court determining that the discharge of plaintiff from military service was a material change in the husband's circumstances necessitating further consideration of support for the minor child, when this discharge and discontinuance of the government allotment for child support were viewed in connection with the subsequent financial condition and amount of earnings of plaintiff. Edwards v. Edwards, 125 Ill. App. 2d 91, 259 N.E.2d 820 (4 Dist. 1970).

—Effect on Child

Mere fact that there has been a change in conditions is not sufficient in itself to warrant modification of provisions of divorce decree dealing with custody of a child unless those changed conditions affect the welfare of the child. Stark v. Stark, 13 Ill. App. 3d 35, 299 N.E.2d 605 (3 Dist. 1973).

—Employment

Father's change in employment status, which yielded a 130 percent increase in the father's weekly income, was sufficient to support a petition for modification of the father's support obligation under 750 ILCS 5/510(a) and required application of the support guidelines found in 750 ILCS 5/505. Anderson v. Heckman, 343 Ill. App. 3d 449, 278 Ill. Dec. 190, 797 N.E.2d 1108, 2003 Ill. App. LEXIS 1242 (4 Dist. 2003).

Where a trial court's decision reducing child support is based on a finding of an obligor's good-faith voluntary change of employment, on appeal the party opposing the motion may attack either the finding the obligor acted in good faith in changing employment or that such a change justified a reduction in child support. In re Barnard, 283 Ill. App. 3d 366, 218 Ill. Dec. 583, 669 N.E.2d 726 (4 Dist. 1996).

Whether respondent's conduct leading to the loss of his employment constituted acts of commission or omission, the evidence was sufficient to allow the trial court to conclude that his conduct was deliberate and his discharge was not merely a fortuitous occurrence; under these circumstances, the trial court could properly view his change of employment as "voluntary" and the record supported the trial court's exercise of its discretion in denying respondent's petition to modify his support obligation. In re Imlay, 251 Ill. App. 3d 138, 190 Ill. Dec. 539, 621 N.E.2d 992 (4 Dist. 1993).

If the trial court, upon allowing a petition for modification under this section, finds that a spouse receiving maintenance is appropriately employed, it may reduce maintenance commensurate with her ability to gain financial independence; on the other hand, if the spouse receiving maintenance is able to work but unwilling to obtain appropriate employment and is not making a good faith effort to gain financial independence, it may reduce or discontinue maintenance. Conversely, if the court finds that there is a good reason for her inability to achieve full or partial financial independence, it may continue such maintenance and extend its duration. In re Gunn, 233 Ill. App. 3d 165, 174 Ill. Dec. 381, 598 N.E.2d 1013 (5 Dist. 1992).

If the employment change is voluntary, the change in employment must be made in good faith and not prompted by a desire to avoid one's child support obligation for modification to be allowed. In re Lavelle, 206 Ill. App. 3d 607, 152 Ill. Dec. 49, 565 N.E.2d 291 (5 Dist. 1990).

Child support payments should be reduced where substantial economic reversals result from an involuntary change or loss of employment. In re Lavelle, 206 Ill. App. 3d 607, 152 Ill. Dec. 49, 565 N.E.2d 291 (5 Dist. 1990).

A good faith, voluntary change in employment which results in reduced financial ability can constitute a substantial change in circumstances justifying a reduction in a child support obligation by the court; the test for determining if a decision was made in good faith is whether the change was prompted by a desire to evade financial responsibility for supporting the children or to otherwise jeopardize their interests. In re Webber, 191 Ill. App. 3d 327, 138 Ill. Dec. 582, 547 N.E.2d 749 (4 Dist. 1989).

Where the record supported a determination that respondent's decision to return to college and reduce the hours of his employment was made in good faith and not out of a desire to evade his financial responsibilities, the court did not abuse its discretion in ordering a reduction in his child support payments. In re Webber, 191 Ill. App. 3d 327, 138 Ill. Dec. 582, 547 N.E.2d 749 (4 Dist. 1989).

Good faith in a spouse's voluntary change of employment is not shown where it can be determined that the change has been prompted by a desire to evade financial responsibilities to the supported spouse. In re Kowski, 123 Ill. App. 3d 811, 79 Ill. Dec. 286, 463 N.E.2d 840 (1 Dist. 1984).

A voluntary, good faith change in employment need not equal or increase the spouse's income; indeed, substantial reductions may be permissible and do not per se constitute lack of good faith. In re Kowski, 123 Ill. App. 3d 811, 79 Ill. Dec. 286, 463 N.E.2d 840 (1 Dist. 1984).

Unless good faith is shown, a voluntary termination of employment by a supporting spouse is not considered a material change in circumstances sufficient to warrant abatement or modification of support obligations. In re Ebert, 81 Ill. App. 3d 44, 36 Ill. Dec. 415, 400 N.E.2d 995 (5 Dist. 1980).

The crucial consideration in determining whether or not voluntary termination of employment by a supporting spouse is sufficient to warrant abatement or modification of support obligations is whether the change in status was prompted by a desire to evade responsibility. In re Ebert, 81 Ill. App. 3d 44, 36 Ill. Dec. 415, 400 N.E.2d 995 (5 Dist. 1980).

It was within the discretion of the trial court to abate the child support payments on the uncontradicted testimony of the father that he was discharged from his employment and had no other income. Glass v. Peitchel, 42 Ill. App. 3d 240, 355 N.E.2d 750 (1 Dist. 1976).

—Evidence

Where a defendant filed a judicial admission of his ability to pay, but never attempted to put his financial condition in issue until after a judgment was rendered, the defendant could not assert as a substantial change in circumstances any change in his financial condition which occurred before the judgment, because the defendant never asserted before that date that the admission did not represent his then current financial condition. Giamanco v. Giamanco, 111 Ill. App. 3d 1017, 67 Ill. Dec. 606, 444 N.E.2d 1090 (5 Dist. 1982).

A trial court was in error in decreeing that plaintiff's right to receive support payments from the defendant was strictly limited to the net rentals from their business property, and limiting a testimony at a hearing on the petition for increase of payments for support and maintenance to the question of net rentals from the business property, in refusing to hear any evidence as to any change in circumstances and conditions since the entry of the original divorce decree, and in limiting and restricting the payment of a certain amount per month which was ordered to the net rentals received from the business property and ordering that payments terminate on the sale of property. Larson v. Larson, 21 Ill. App. 2d 264, 157 N.E.2d 689 (2 Dist. 1959).

—Evidentiary Hearing

The trial court erred when it refused to allow an evidentiary hearing for the purpose of determining whether there was a sufficient change of circumstances to allow modification of the divorce decree where the separation agreement did not expressly preclude or limit modification of its terms. In re Bowman, 89 Ill. App. 3d 110, 44 Ill. Dec. 445, 411 N.E.2d 567 (4 Dist. 1980).

—Factors Considered

Trial courts have wide latitude in determining whether a substantial change in circumstances has occurred and should consider

Change in Circumstances (Cont'd)

—Factors Considered (Cont'd)

not only the needs of the child and the financial status of the noncustodial parent, but also the needs and financial status of the custodial parent, the financial resources of the child, the standard of living the child would have enjoyed had the marriage not been dissolved, and the physical, emotional, and educational needs of the child. In re Riegel, 242 Ill. App. 3d 496, 183 Ill. Dec. 168, 611 N.E.2d 21 (3 Dist. 1993).

Subsection (a) of this section allows for modification of a child support order upon a showing of a substantial change in circumstances, in deciding whether to modify a support order, the court must consider the same factors it weighs under section 505 of the Act (750 ILCS 5/505) when it formulates an original support order. In re Dodds, 222 Ill. App. 3d 99, 164 Ill. Dec. 692, 583 N.E.2d 608 (2 Dist. 1991), cert. denied, 144 Ill. 2d 632, 169 Ill. Dec. 140, 591 N.E.2d 20 (1992).

Whether a spouse may rely on his retirement as a change in circumstances justifying a modification of maintenance depends on the circumstances of the individual case; relevant factors include his age, his health, his motives and timing for the retirement, his ability to pay maintenance after retirement, and the other spouse's ability to provide for himself. In re Colombo, 197 Ill. App. 3d 767, 144 Ill. Dec. 159, 555 N.E.2d 56 (2 Dist. 1990).

Economic reversals as a result of changes in employment or bad investments, if made in good faith, may constitute a material change in circumstances sufficient to warrant a modification of a child support order. In re Hardy, 191 Ill. App. 3d 685, 138 Ill. Dec. 909, 548 N.E.2d 139 (5 Dist. 1989).

In determining whether a change in status was made in good faith, the crucial consideration is whether the change was prompted by a desire to evade financial responsibility for supporting the children or otherwise jeopardize their interests. In re Hardy, 191 Ill. App. 3d 685, 138 Ill. Dec. 909, 548 N.E.2d 139 (5 Dist. 1989).

If the threshold question of substantial change is met, the court, in determining the modification, considers the same factors it considered in formulating the original amount. In re Wettstein, 160 Ill. App. 3d 554, 113 Ill. Dec. 1, 514 N.E.2d 783 (4 Dist. 1987).

In determining whether there is a substantial change in circumstances, factors to be considered include the needs of the child, the financial status of the noncustodial parent, the financial status and needs of the custodial parent, and the physical, emotional and educational needs of the child. Ingwerson v. Woeckener, 141 Ill. App. 3d 647, 95 Ill. Dec. 916, 490 N.E.2d 1008 (3 Dist. 1986).

In making a determination as to whether a substantial change has occurred, the court must take into consideration the circumstances of the parents, the circumstances of the children, the ability of the mother as well as that of the father to provide support, their ages, health, property and income, and stations in life, and the court may also consider whether the supporting spouse has remarried. Roqueplot v. Roqueplot, 88 Ill. App. 3d 59, 43 Ill. Dec. 441, 410 N.E.2d 441 (2 Dist. 1980).

Where a former spouse's ability to pay is shown, the fact that children have grown older and the cost of living has risen are proper bases for establishing increased need, considering the best interests of the children. In re Schmerold, 88 Ill. App. 3d 348, 43 Ill. Dec. 629, 410 N.E.2d 629 (2 Dist. 1980).

The increase in the children's needs must be balanced against the relative ability of the parents to provide for them, and where a change has occurred which creates a substantial imbalance between the child's needs and the parent's support capabilities modification is required. In re Schmerold, 88 Ill. App. 3d 348, 43 Ill. Dec. 629, 410 N.E.2d 629 (2 Dist. 1980).

Assets derived from the divorce settlement itself cannot be considered in measuring the alleged improvement in spouse's financial circumstances, for to do so would constitute an attack on the divorce decree itself. In re McGowan, 84 Ill. App. 3d 609, 40 Ill. Dec. 64, 405 N.E.2d 1156 (1 Dist. 1980).

A change of circumstances which will permit a modification of the child support provisions contained in a divorce decree may relate either to the needs of the child, the financial condition of the parents, or both. Harding v. Harding, 59 Ill. App. 3d 25, 16 Ill. Dec. 426, 374 N.E.2d 1304 (4 Dist. 1978).

Changed circumstances which permit modification of child support payment provisions relate to the needs of the minor child and the financial circumstances of the parties. Lewis v. Lewis, 120 Ill. App. 2d 263, 256 N.E.2d 660 (3 Dist. 1970).

An increase in monthly support payments is warranted when the evidence establishes that the needs of the children have increased, and the means of the father have also increased so as to enable him to contribute additional sums to his children's support. Grinton v. Grinton, 131 Ill. App. 2d 684, 264 N.E.2d 845 (3 Dist. 1970).

—Failure to Make Effort to Achieve Financial Independence

The court did not err in awarding biweekly maintenance to a 32-year-old wife, following a 13-year marriage, without ordering that the award be time-limited/reviewable and without ordering that the wife seek employment, where the wife had a high school education and no further training or education; further, notwithstanding the absence of such conditions, the award was reviewable and the wife was required to seek employment as this section allows modification upon a showing of a substantial change of circumstances, and the failure to make a good faith effort to achieve financial independence can be the basis for a petition for modification. In re Mayhall, 311 Ill. App. 3d 765, 244 Ill. Dec. 227, 725 N.E.2d 22, 2000 Ill. App. LEXIS 72 (4 Dist. 2000).

—Failure to Seek Employment

The wife achieved the statutory goal of rehabilitative maintenance, and the trial court abused its discretion when it failed to grant the husband's motion to terminate maintenance where: (1) the wife obtained a bachelor's degree in fine arts with honors, paid for by the husband pursuant to the trial court's order; (2) the wife was employable, her children were emancipated, she had received a substantial amount of the marital assets, and she had no apparent health impairments that might restrict her from working; (3) the trial court's maintenance review decision clearly reflects that the wife was under an affirmative obligation to seek appropriate employment to become self-sufficient; and (4) the record reflected that, in the four years since she graduated from college, the wife had done little toward finding gainful employment or advancing her efforts at becoming self-sufficient. In re Cantrell, 314 Ill. App. 3d 623, 247 Ill. Dec. 742, 732 N.E.2d 797, 2000 Ill. App. LEXIS 586 (2 Dist. 2000).

—Illustrative Cases

The circuit court did not abuse its discretion when it declined to terminate maintenance but extended it at a reduced level in light of each party's change of circumstances. Hupe v. Hupe, 305 Ill. App. 3d 118, 238 Ill. Dec. 402, 711 N.E.2d 789 (3 Dist. 1999).

The uncontroverted evidence presented clearly showed that the average monthly cost of raising the children had risen dramatically where, even after removing the items that husband considered luxuries, i.e., allowing the children to attend summer camp, son's involvement in band and daughter's involvement in gymnastics, the increase was shown to be about $450 a month; since this was a substantial change, the trial court erred in determining that no change of circumstances had occurred. In re Riegel, 242 Ill. App. 3d 496, 183 Ill. Dec. 168, 611 N.E.2d 21 (3 Dist. 1993).

—Increase in Income

Trial court erred in granting summary judgment to former husband on former wife's petition to increase child support, where the wife alleged miscalculation of his net income and changes in the federal tax laws which increased his net income; these claims were potentially meritorious grounds for increasing child support. In re Marriage of Colangelo, Ill. App. 3d , 290 Ill. Dec. 986, 822 N.E.2d 571, 2005 Ill. App. LEXIS 39 (2 Dist. 2005).

Husband was not entitled to modification of support award where his nondisclosure of income prior to the circuit court's adoption of the marital settlement agreement precluded the husband was proving that the there had been a substantial change in income necessitating modification. In re Sassano, 337 Ill. App. 3d 186, 271 Ill. Dec. 864, 785 N.E.2d 1058, 2003 Ill. App. LEXIS 306 (2 Dist. 2003).

Where the trial court applied a type of "sliding scale" approach to modification of child support, it erred; every time a paying parent's income increases it does not mean that child support payments increase in a like percentage, but rather, the petitioning party must show that there has been a material change in circumstances. In re Plotz, 229 Ill. App. 3d 389, 171 Ill. Dec. 514, 594 N.E.2d 366 (3

Change in Circumstances (Cont'd)

—Increase in Income (Cont'd)

Dist.), cert. denied, 146 Ill. 2d 651, 176 Ill. Dec. 821, 602 N.E.2d 475 (1992).

A modification of a judgment respecting child support may be made only upon a showing of a substantial change in circumstances. In re Bean, 181 Ill. App. 3d 671, 130 Ill. Dec. 275, 537 N.E.2d 342 (5 Dist. 1989).

Subsection (a) of this section provides that a support judgment can only be modified after showing a substantial change in circumstances, which requires the petitioning party to show that the support spouse has an increased ability to pay and the child receiving support has increased needs. In re Boyden, 164 Ill. App. 3d 385, 115 Ill. Dec. 458, 517 N.E.2d 1144 (2 Dist. 1987).

When a supporting spouse's financial condition improves, notably where there is a discussion suggesting that increases should be made, child support payments may be required to be increased, even though there is no showing that the child's or children's needs have increased specifically where the original support payments did not adequately meet the children's needs. Legan v. Legan, 69 Ill. App. 3d 304, 25 Ill. Dec. 757, 387 N.E.2d 413 (3 Dist. 1979).

—Insufficient

Where defendant lost his job, was adjudicated a bankrupt, then chose to revive a debt to the potential harm of his child, there was insufficient change of circumstance. Gaines v. Gaines, 106 Ill. App. 2d 9, 245 N.E.2d 574 (1 Dist. 1969).

Having an income of $490.36 a month, and debts including a judgment against him for $143.65, an internal revenue assessment of $141.49, a doctor bill of $145, and attorney's fees for his defense in another lawsuit did not constitute sufficient basis for reducing the child support payments from $56 twice a month to $20 per week. Gaines v. Gaines, 106 Ill. App. 2d 9, 245 N.E.2d 574 (1 Dist. 1969).

—Loss of Job

Where the valid, enforceable portion of the agreement required father to pay $660 per month in child support, this obligation continued until father petitioned for and was granted a modification regardless of his loss of job. In re Ingram, 259 Ill. App. 3d 685, 197 Ill. Dec. 383, 631 N.E.2d 386 (2 Dist. 1994).

—Needs of Recipient

A termination or modification of alimony must reflect a substantial change in the needs of the parties and cannot be used to punish the moral transgressions of the wife. Hall v. Hall, 25 Ill. App. 3d 524, 323 N.E.2d 541 (1 Dist. 1975).

—Net Worth

Where petitioner claimed that the focus of the court should have been the change in his income and not his net worth because the parties did not contemplate that petitioner would have to liquidate assets to meet his maintenance and child support obligations under the separation agreement, then the court had discretion to consider evidence of his net worth. In re Eisenstein, 172 Ill. App. 3d 264, 122 Ill. Dec. 237, 526 N.E.2d 496 (1 Dist. 1988).

—Not Shown

Mother's move to Indiana, where she took a lower paying job and ostensibly intended to pursue further education, did not constitute a good-faith voluntary change in employment that would support a reduction in her child support obligation; her educational plans were vague at best and the evidence supported a finding that the move was made simply as a device by the mother to evade her financial responsibilities. In re Ross, Ill. App. 3d , Ill. Dec. , N.E.2d , 2005 Ill. App. LEXIS 128 (5 Dist. Feb. 16, 2005).

The trial court erred in determining the existence of a "substantial change in circumstances" based on the termination of alimony and automobile payments as contemplated by the divorce judgment. In re Hughes, 322 Ill. App. 3d 815, 255 Ill. Dec. 929, 751 N.E.2d 23, 2001 Ill. App. LEXIS 310 (2 Dist. 2001).

There was no substantial change in circumstances so as to justify a downward modification of a father's child support obligation, notwithstanding the father's argument that his payment of college expenses created such a substantial change in circumstances, where the parties' agreement provided for this very occurrence and, in addition, the father's income had actually increased since the last modification of judgment. Mulry v. Mulry, 314 Ill. App. 3d 756, 247 Ill. Dec. 612, 732 N.E.2d 667, 2000 Ill. App. LEXIS 510 (4 Dist. 2000).

An increase in father's net income due to his ability to deduct maintenance payments does not constitute a substantial change in circumstances. Pylawka v. Pylawka, 277 Ill. App. 3d 728, 214 Ill. Dec. 651, 661 N.E.2d 505 (2 Dist. 1996).

While it is true that a change in the ability of a recipient of maintenance to support herself could constitute a substantial change in circumstances under subsection (a), the record indicated that husband failed to present evidence of a change in wife's ability to support herself and the court found that husband failed to meet his burden of showing a substantial change in circumstances. In re Waggoner, 261 Ill. App. 3d 787, 199 Ill. Dec. 844, 634 N.E.2d 1198 (5 Dist. 1994).

Although appellee had become employed, the record supported the trial court's determination that she remained unable to adequately support herself through her employment and that no substantial change of circumstances had occurred for her financially since the maintenance amount was last reduced. In re Pedersen, 237 Ill. App. 3d 952, 178 Ill. Dec. 835, 605 N.E.2d 629 (4 Dist. 1992).

The evidence from appellant's affidavits of income and expenses indicate that, other than his alleged increase in expenses, did not show any change in circumstances since the last order that would justify a further modification of maintenance. In re Pedersen, 237 Ill. App. 3d 952, 178 Ill. Dec. 835, 605 N.E.2d 629 (4 Dist. 1992).

Where neither husband nor wife demonstrated a material or substantial change in their relative positions, the trial court did not abuse its discretion in refusing to modify the original maintenance award. In re Plotz, 229 Ill. App. 3d 389, 171 Ill. Dec. 514, 594 N.E.2d 366 (3 Dist.), cert. denied, 146 Ill. 2d 651, 176 Ill. Dec. 821, 602 N.E.2d 475 (1992).

There was sufficient evidence to determine that there was no substantial change in circumstances of the petitioner since petitioner did not change employment other than to vary interests he owned, and even though he indicated some losses, his overall employment and investment scheme continued. In re Eisenstein, 172 Ill. App. 3d 264, 122 Ill. Dec. 237, 526 N.E.2d 496 (1 Dist. 1988).

Where subsequent to an initial maintenance award the former husband's salary decreased from $61,000 to $50,000, his wife was found to be completely rehabilitated and her salary had increased from $12,949 to $23,580, the trial court did not abuse its discretion by requiring continued maintenance payments by the former husband. In re Garelick, 168 Ill. App. 3d 321, 119 Ill. Dec. 76, 522 N.E.2d 738 (1 Dist. 1988).

Where court did make specific findings regarding petitioner's income for 1982, the year in which his marriage was dissolved, and used these findings for comparison to determine petitioner's change in circumstances, testimony regarding the nature of his business practices and the current status of his business affairs, as well as testimony at the prove up in 1982 regarding his income in 1981 and 1982, and thus the decline in income from 1981 to 1982, it was correctly determined that overall he had not undergone a substantial change in circumstances; hence, the use of 1982 income figures in addition to all the other evidence heard and considered was not error or an abuse of the court's discretion. In re Eisenstein, 172 Ill. App. 3d 264, 122 Ill. Dec. 237, 526 N.E.2d 496 (1 Dist. 1988).

Evidence presented was wholly inadequate to prove a substantial change in circumstances necessary for the termination of monthly maintenance payment. In re Logston, 103 Ill. 2d 266, 82 Ill. Dec. 633, 469 N.E.2d 167 (1984).

The trial court did not abuse its discretion in finding there had been no change in circumstances which would permit the modification sought by plaintiff where father did not show a change in financial resources of child, mother or father or in physical, emotional and educational needs of child. In re Emerson, 115 Ill. App. 3d 712, 71 Ill. Dec. 299, 450 N.E.2d 987 (2 Dist. 1983).

The trial court could properly have determined that the small increase in custodial parent's salary did not constitute a substantial change in circumstances sufficient to warrant a modification of the child support order. In re Butler, 106 Ill. App. 3d 831, 62 Ill. Dec. 535, 436 N.E.2d 561 (1 Dist. 1982).

Where an ex-husband's financial position appeared to have improved since the divorce, it appeared that the wife had never earned more than $3,500 in any given year, and that her monthly

Change in Circumstances (Cont'd)

—Not Shown (Cont'd)

expenses exceeded her maintenance, and her testimony concerning her health and as to her ability to maintain limited employment was uncontroverted, there was nothing in the record of a substantial change in circumstances which would have warranted a reduction in maintenance and the trial court erred in so ordering. Goldberg v. Goldberg, 84 Ill. App. 3d 728, 40 Ill. Dec. 459, 406 N.E.2d 160 (1 Dist. 1980).

The record did not demonstrate that the former husband sustained his burden of showing that a substantial change in circumstances had occurred which would have justified a downward modification of support payment. Roqueplot v. Roqueplot, 88 Ill. App. 3d 59, 43 Ill. Dec. 441, 410 N.E.2d 441 (2 Dist. 1980).

Defendant did not establish a substantial change of his circumstances to justify suspension or termination of payments. In re Potter, 88 Ill. App. 3d 606, 43 Ill. Dec. 866, 410 N.E.2d 999 (1 Dist. 1980).

Under section 19 of the former Divorce Act, (see now this section), where a court's order of March 22, 1977, clearly stated that plaintiff had failed to show a material change in circumstances since entry of the order entered on or about November 26, 1975, the court's modification of the decree was error since there was no finding of a material change in the circumstances of the parties, and assuming arguendo that the court found a material change in plaintiff's circumstances only, a modification of the decree still could not stand since a careful examination of the record revealed no evidence that defendant was able to pay additional alimony. Dunn v. Dunn, 71 Ill. App. 3d 649, 28 Ill. Dec. 154, 390 N.E.2d 136 (1 Dist. 1979).

Husband's increased expenses, largely the result of the purchase of a house pursuant to his remarriage, were of only secondary consideration vis-à-vis the obligation owed to his former wife on the question of support and were not a change in circumstances warranting a reduction in maintenance. Berkheimer v. Berkheimer, 63 Ill. App. 3d 19, 20 Ill. Dec. 496, 380 N.E.2d 474 (4 Dist. 1978).

Where the trial court considered the provisions at issue and the various arguments of counsel and concluded that the decree contemplated a monthly child support payment of $550, without contingencies or abatements and, therefore, the sale of the former marital residence was not a material change in circumstances so as to warrant a reduction in child support payments, this construction was reasonable and not clearly erroneous so as to require the reviewing court to disturb the trial court's ruling. Winter v. Winter, 69 Ill. App. 3d 359, 25 Ill. Dec. 819, 387 N.E.2d 695 (1 Dist. 1978).

A judgment terminating the respondent's child support obligation, setting aside a lien of trust from respondent's interest in a trust and removing the obligations of injunction prohibiting him from conveying, transferring or assigning his interest in that property was reversed where no change in circumstances existed and where the original reason for ordering the respondent's chief asset, his fractional interest in the trust, to be placed in trust as security for the future payment of the court ordered child support was because of the respondent's demonstrated untrustworthiness and to insure continued payment of child support from the respondent's assets in the event of the respondent's refusal to do so. Gentile v. Gentile, 69 Ill. App. 3d 297, 26 Ill. Dec. 149, 387 N.E.2d 979 (3 Dist. 1979).

While there was a statement in the record by wife's counsel that husband was making the payments on the second mortgage, there was no indication that he ceased making those payments and thus, there simply was no evidence in the record to support the wife's allegation that circumstances had changed since the entry of the decree and thus modification of child support was not warranted. Waggoner v. Waggoner, 78 Ill. 2d 50, 34 Ill. Dec. 330, 398 N.E.2d 5 (1979).

There was insufficient evidence to support the trial court's finding that intervening circumstances had substantially changed to justify a modification of support payment under this section. Westerberg v. Stephens, 76 Ill. App. 3d 119, 31 Ill. Dec. 673, 394 N.E.2d 875 (2 Dist. 1979).

Even had defendant lost overtime earnings, this would not have been a permanent change in circumstances and thus could not have been a valid basis for permanent reduction of child support payments. Dixon v. Dixon, 45 Ill. App. 3d 934, 4 Ill. Dec. 550, 360 N.E.2d 486 (1 Dist. 1977).

The evidence did not reveal a change of circumstances warranting an increase in child support. Nordstrom v. Nordstrom, 36 Ill. App. 3d 181, 343 N.E.2d 640 (1 Dist. 1976).

As to the children's increased needs, plaintiff's testimony consisted almost entirely of general statements and was often concerned with the rise in prices due to inflation; increased expenditures due to inflation apply to defendant as well as to plaintiff; consequently, this factor, in and of itself, is not sufficient to establish a material change in circumstances. Nordstrom v. Nordstrom, 36 Ill. App. 3d 181, 343 N.E.2d 640 (1 Dist. 1976).

Under former section 18 of the Divorce Act (see now this section), where a plaintiff did not offer any evidence demonstrating a change which necessarily increased the support needs of the children, and failed to show that defendant's income had changed substantially since the divorce, she was not entitled to an increase in child support. Goldberg v. Goldberg, 36 Ill. App. 3d 778, 344 N.E.2d 721 (1 Dist. 1976).

Under former section 18 of the Divorce Act (see now this section), the mere fact that defendant received a higher base salary rather than income from stock options or bonuses did not necessitate a finding that his financial condition had increased substantially where the record reflected that his overall financial picture has changed little since the divorce. Goldberg v. Goldberg, 36 Ill. App. 3d 778, 344 N.E.2d 721 (1 Dist. 1976).

Wife was not entitled to increase in alimony where there was no evidence that her circumstances had materially changed since the entry of the divorce decree. Goldberg v. Goldberg, 30 Ill. App. 3d 769, 332 N.E.2d 710 (1 Dist. 1975).

Where it was clear from defendant's own brief that the matter he attempted to raise before the trial court on the hearing to modify or terminate and on appeal did not occur for the first time during the period after the decree was entered, nor was there any substantial change in circumstances that would have justified modification or termination of payments, defendant's motion to modify was denied. Dubin v. Dubin, 25 Ill. App. 3d 323, 323 N.E.2d 152 (1 Dist. 1974).

Where husband's take-home pay was reduced from $750 to $730 a month due to a change in his withholding for Federal income tax as a result of the divorce, his asserted financial difficulties allegedly stemming from his obligation on prior family indebtedness could not be considered a change in condition subsequent to the divorce decree, and the order of the trial court that modified the decree was reversed. Green v. Green, 86 Ill. App. 2d 362, 229 N.E.2d 565 (2 Dist. 1967).

No change in circumstances were held to support a change in the decree. Nortwick v. Nortwick, 52 Ill. App. 2d 229, 201 N.E.2d 857 (2 Dist. 1964).

Provision in divorce decree giving plaintiff the right "to determine the religion in which each child shall be raised" and defendant the right "to determine the education which each child is to have and the schools which each child shall attend" should not have been modified by chancellor since there was no change in circumstances. Taylor v. Taylor, 32 Ill. App. 2d 45, 176 N.E.2d 640 (1 Dist. 1961).

A petition for modification of divorce decree, which alleged no fact indicating an increased ability on the part of the defendant to pay, nor stated any facts relative to the needs of the plaintiff other than their increased ages, should not have been granted by the circuit court. Patterson v. Patterson, 28 Ill. App. 2d 76, 170 N.E.2d 11 (4 Dist. 1960).

—Offsetting Changes

Where any change in non-custodial parent's physical ability to work which would indicate reduction or elimination of support payments was offset by the present potential for him to receive money from his aunt's estate, the circuit court did not abuse its discretion in refusing to modify the support order. In re Steffen, 253 Ill. App. 3d 966, 192 Ill. Dec. 709, 625 N.E.2d 864 (4 Dist. 1993), appeal denied, 155 Ill. 2d 576, 198 Ill. Dec. 553, 633 N.E.2d 15 (1994).

—Proceedings on Remand

Where a change in the economic circumstances of one or both of the parties occurred between the remand and the new hearing, the wife's proper recourse was to file a motion for modification pursuant to subsection (a) of this section, in which she could have presented any evidence of a substantial change in circumstances. In re Jones, 187 Ill. App. 3d 206, 134 Ill. Dec. 836, 543 N.E.2d 119 (1 Dist. 1989).

Change in Circumstances (Cont'd)

—Review

The findings of the trial court as to the evidence of a material change in the circumstances of the parties since the original divorce decree should be reversed only if they are contrary to the manifest weight of the evidence. Gentile v. Gentile, 69 Ill. App. 3d 297, 26 Ill. Dec. 149, 387 N.E.2d 979 (3 Dist. 1979).

—Settlement Agreement

A property settlement agreement which stated that "it is agreed that the payment as heretofore provided of alimony in the amount, of $550 per month will in no way be effected or amended because of an increase in income to either party," did not divest the court of its power to modify its decree under former section 18 of the Divorce Act (see now this section), but simply precluded consideration of income in determining whether a change in circumstances had occurred and, such a limiting provision could not be against public policy, because by agreeing on a waiver of alimony or a property settlement in lieu of alimony, the parties could have eliminated alimony completely and permanently from the court's consideration. Pollard v. Pollard, 41 Ill. App. 3d 907, 355 N.E.2d 41 (2 Dist. 1976).

—Shown

Trial court did not err in granting the mother's petition to increase child support, as the mother showed both that the father had an increased ability to pay and that the child's needs had increased since the original support order was entered three years earlier. In re Marriage of Adams, 348 Ill. App. 3d 340, 284 Ill. Dec. 124, 809 N.E.2d 246, 2004 Ill. App. LEXIS 435 (3 Dist. 2004).

A substantial change in circumstances was shown, and the case reversed and remanded with directions to enter an order to abate maintenance retroactive to filing of the petition to modify. In re Johnson, 245 Ill. App. 3d 816, 185 Ill. Dec. 861, 615 N.E.2d 420 (4 Dist. 1993).

Father's obligation to pay a portion of one son's college expenses had ended and thus he no longer had any financial obligation to this son; this change in circumstances was sufficient to justify the trial court's order providing for a pro rata reduction in the life insurance obligation. In re Tieman, 237 Ill. App. 3d 847, 178 Ill. Dec. 575, 604 N.E.2d 1098 (3 Dist. 1992).

Generally, evidence that a child has attained the age of majority constitutes a substantial change in circumstances which necessitates the modification of child support unless: (1) the parties agree on a different terminating event; (2) the court orders support payments to continue based on the non-minor child's physical or mental disability or when educational expenses are sought; or (3) the child becomes emancipated at an earlier age. In re Ferraro, 211 Ill. App. 3d 797, 156 Ill. Dec. 160, 570 N.E.2d 636 (1 Dist. 1991).

Where the husband's business entered bankruptcy and there was no evidence that he voluntarily chose to have his business fail, there was a substantial change in his circumstances that would warrant a reduction or modification of his support obligations. In re Lavelle, 206 Ill. App. 3d 607, 152 Ill. Dec. 49, 565 N.E.2d 291 (5 Dist. 1990).

Inheritances received by wife constituted a substantial change in her circumstances, and the court failed to make any determination of the amount of income which could be generated therefrom, and some approximation of the income-producing ability of the inheritances was required, explicit findings by the trial court are not required so long as a sufficiently detailed basis exists in the record to support a modification of the award. In re Zeman, 198 Ill. App. 3d 722, 145 Ill. Dec. 149, 556 N.E.2d 767 (2 Dist. 1990).

The trial court appropriately balanced the needs of the child with the significant increase in petitioner's income and did not abuse its discretion in awarding child support where it determined that the child's expenses increased after he entered high school, and that the father's income grew substantially after winning the lottery. In re Boyden, 164 Ill. App. 3d 385, 115 Ill. Dec. 458, 517 N.E.2d 1144 (2 Dist. 1987).

Where three of the four children had attained the age of majority, the remaining minor child was older and expenses of her maintenance had increased, a substantial change of circumstances occurred thereby justifying a modification of child support payments. In re Wettstein, 160 Ill. App. 3d 554, 113 Ill. Dec. 1, 514 N.E.2d 783 (4 Dist. 1987).

Where at the time of the divorce, defendant's gross income was approximately $12,800 and then became around $21,000, where the total increase was about 64% and where the increased needs of the child could be presumed from the fact that he had grown older and the cost of living had risen the trial court was correct in finding a substantial change of circumstances had occurred. Fedun v. Kuczek, 155 Ill. App. 3d 798, 108 Ill. Dec. 370, 508 N.E.2d 531 (4 Dist. 1987).

If the parties cannot agree upon child support after cessation of the unallocated support provided in the decree, such cessation would present a substantial change in circumstances which would permit modification of the judgment for dissolution upon petition of a party and support for the minor child will then be determined by the court. In re Rapacz, 135 Ill. App. 3d 1045, 90 Ill. Dec. 622, 482 N.E.2d 441 (2 Dist. 1985).

There was a substantial change in circumstances since the entry of the previous judgment because the children's needs increased and the defendant's ability to support his children had increased significantly. In re Roth, 99 Ill. App. 3d 679, 55 Ill. Dec. 271, 426 N.E.2d 246 (1 Dist. 1981).

Plaintiff's real needs had increased and also the defendant's real income and ability to pay where defendant's annual income had risen by more than $12,000, and he had gained interest in an inheritance and a residential building and such a substantial change in circumstances warranted modification. In re Helfrich, 101 Ill. App. 3d 1070, 57 Ill. Dec. 469, 428 N.E.2d 1149 (1 Dist. 1981).

Substantial changes in circumstances including the emancipation of the couple's only child and the sufficiency of former wife's own assets and income to meet her needs, considered in light of former wife's request that former husband now contribute toward meeting the cost of the son's college education, warranted a modification of a maintenance award ordered by the court. Potocki v. Potocki, 98 Ill. App. 3d 501, 53 Ill. Dec. 923, 424 N.E.2d 714 (1 Dist. 1981).

A reduction in child support is proper only if based on a substantial change in circumstances; the fact that three of the six children had attained the age of majority at the time of the modification order was such a substantial change in circumstances; as a result, the court did not abuse its discretion in reducing the amount of weekly child support payments from $125 to $100. In re Christianson, 89 Ill. App. 3d 167, 44 Ill. Dec. 397, 411 N.E.2d 519 (3 Dist. 1980).

In light of divorced wife's increase in salary and her former husband's decrease in salary due to health problems, there was a sufficient showing of a change in circumstances whereby the divorce decree could be modified to suspend alimony and reduce child support. Broday v. Broday, 43 Ill. App. 3d 628, 2 Ill. Dec. 151, 357 N.E.2d 128 (1 Dist. 1976).

An order of a trial court continuing the liability of the father for support for educational purposes was against the manifest weight of the evidence and was reversed where the trial court found that he had suffered substantial economic reverses, there was no evidence that his circumstances had improved since the suspension of payments following a hearing, while the father may have had prospects for future employment, that could not be translated into a present ability to pay, he clearly had no present resources from which to pay educational expenses, and his liability to pay $40 per week for his minor, physically afflicted son would preclude his ability to make any payments for education for his older son. Elizer v. Elizer, 36 Ill. App. 3d 552, 344 N.E.2d 493 (5 Dist. 1976).

The trial court abused its discretion in denying a father's request to require a non-custodian mother to contribute an equitable amount in the support of their minor child where its decision failed to consider the circumstances of all the parties as required by former Ill.Rev.Stat., ch. 40, para. 19 (see now this section), particularly that the mother was earning more than the father and, there had been a custody change from the home of the mother to the home of the father. Hursh v. Hursh, 26 Ill. App. 3d 947, 326 N.E.2d 95 (1 Dist. 1975).

There was a sufficient showing of change of circumstances to warrant a modification of the amount of payments. Juen v. Juen, 24 Ill. App. 3d 140, 320 N.E.2d 431 (5 Dist. 1974).

The trial court, which conducted a long hearing, had ample justification to conclude from the evidence, that there was a change in circumstances such as would justify a modification of the divorce

Change in Circumstances (Cont'd)

—Shown (Cont'd)

decree reducing the weekly child support payments. Lewis v. Lewis, 120 Ill. App. 2d 263, 256 N.E.2d 660 (3 Dist. 1970).

There was no abuse of discretion by the trial court in its modification order when it determined that the financial condition of the defendant had sufficiently changed since the entry of the divorce decree so as to warrant its modification. Scalfaro v. Scalfaro, 123 Ill. App. 2d 23, 259 N.E.2d 644 (1 Dist. 1970).

—Special Finding

A previous special finding made in a support order which varies from the guideline and which is no longer found to be a factor is a proper consideration in determining a substantial change in circumstances. People ex rel. Stokely v. Goodenow, 211 Ill. App. 3d 802, 164 Ill. Dec. 548, 583 N.E.2d 102 (4 Dist. 1991).

—Standard of Living

Where the original amount of child support was below the 25% statutory guideline and the court found that children would have enjoyed a different standard of living had the marriage not been dissolved, constituting a substantial change in circumstances, the circuit court did not abuse its discretion in modifying the child support, especially considering that the modified amount was raised to conform to the statutory guidelines. In re Koenigsknecht, 302 Ill. App. 3d 474, 236 Ill. Dec. 267, 707 N.E.2d 112 (1 Dist. 1998).

—Suspension from Employment

Suspension from the police force for five days was not a permanent change of circumstances thus would not be a valid basis for permanent reduction in support payments. Gaines v. Gaines, 106 Ill. App. 2d 9, 245 N.E.2d 574 (1 Dist. 1969).

—Time Period Considered

Outstanding obligations incurred during the marriage previous to the entry of the decree placed financial demands upon defendant; however, this was not a change in circumstances during the relevant period because the change in circumstances must have occurred after the date of the decree. Dixon v. Dixon, 45 Ill. App. 3d 934, 4 Ill. Dec. 550, 360 N.E.2d 486 (1 Dist. 1977).

—Transfer of Custody

It is well settled that a substantial change in circumstances will warrant modification of child support, and the transfer of custody of a child has been determined to be such a change in circumstances. In re Van Winkle, 107 Ill. App. 3d 73, 62 Ill. Dec. 831, 437 N.E.2d 358 (3 Dist. 1982).

—Undisclosed Assets

There was a change of circumstances after the divorce decree was entered where the husband received an additional $13,230 of income for a year prior to the divorce; the court had the authority to enter an order compelling him to pay an additional amount for child support despite the fact that if the books had been examined at the time of the decree, a bookkeeping entry as to the bonus would have been found. Waltrip v. Waltrip, 3 Ill. App. 3d 892, 279 N.E.2d 405 (2 Dist. 1972).

—Worker's Compensation Settlement

The one time receipt of money from a lump-sum payment of worker's compensation settlement comes within the parameters of net income as defined in 750 ILCS 5/505(a)(3), and was available for allocation as child support pursuant to this section. In re Dodds, 222 Ill. App. 3d 99, 164 Ill. Dec. 692, 583 N.E.2d 608 (2 Dist. 1991), cert. denied, 144 Ill. 2d 632, 169 Ill. Dec. 140, 591 N.E.2d 20 (1992).

Cohabitation

Evidence that ex-wife and her boyfriend did not intermingle any funds, and neither paid any money towards the other's household expenses supported a finding that they were not engaged in a conjugal relationship; the boyfriend testified that he would occasionally buy food for the ex-wife as a recompense for that which he had consumed as leftovers and that he would replenish gas in her car on those occasions that he would use it. In re Marriage of Sunday, 354 Ill. App. 3d 184, 289 Ill. Dec. 860, 820 N.E.2d 636, 2004 Ill. App. LEXIS 1518 (2 Dist. 2004).

—Another Person

As a matter of law, cohabitation with "another person" referred to cohabitation with someone other than a party to the dissolution. In re Antonich, 148 Ill. App. 3d 575, 102 Ill. Dec. 97, 499 N.E.2d 654 (2 Dist. 1986).

—Burden of Proof

——Not Met

The standard for modification due to cohabitation was not met where former spouse's roommate made only one contribution toward household expenses, the couple did not have a joint checking account and did not commingle funds in any manner, wife's cohabitation with roommate did not affect her need for support, maintenance payments were not used to support roommate, couple seldom ate together, wife never did his laundry, they only occasionally slept in the same bedroom, and wife's cohabitation with roommate was not on a resident, continuing conjugal basis. In re Arvin, 184 Ill. App. 3d 644, 133 Ill. Dec. 53, 540 N.E.2d 919 (2 Dist. 1989).

—Conjugal

——Belief

Courts have generally looked to those facts which would lead a reasonable observer to believe a man and woman who were cohabiting were husband and wife. Rosche v. Rosche, 163 Ill. App. 3d 308, 114 Ill. Dec. 846, 516 N.E.2d 1001 (5 Dist. 1987).

——Burden of Proof

Whether a conjugal relationship exists between two people so as to justify termination of maintenance is a factual determination which the spouse seeking to terminate such maintenance has the burden of proving. In re Nolen, 200 Ill. App. 3d 1072, 146 Ill. Dec. 818, 558 N.E.2d 781 (5 Dist. 1990).

The burden of proving a conjugal relationship rests with the spouse seeking to terminate maintenance. In re Reeder, 145 Ill. App. 3d 1013, 99 Ill. Dec. 648, 495 N.E.2d 1383 (5 Dist. 1986); In re Johnson, 215 Ill. App. 3d 174, 158 Ill. Dec. 742, 574 N.E.2d 855 (4 Dist. 1991).

Once an ex-spouse paying maintenance has demonstrated that a conjugal relationship does exist, it should be incumbent upon the maintenance recipient to demonstrate that the relationship in which he or she is engaged is not the type of relationship which was intended by the legislature to justify the termination of the obligation to pay maintenance. In re Sappington, 106 Ill. 2d 456, 88 Ill. Dec. 61, 478 N.E.2d 376 (1985).

——Defined

The term "conjugal" as used in subsection (c) of this section does not necessarily require that the parties engage in sexual intercourse or sexual conduct. In re Sappington, 106 Ill. 2d 456, 88 Ill. Dec. 61, 478 N.E.2d 376 (1985).

The legislature did not intend the term "conjugal" to be defined as familial rather than marital. In re McGowan, 84 Ill. App. 3d 609, 40 Ill. Dec. 64, 405 N.E.2d 1156 (1 Dist. 1980).

By "conjugal" the legislature meant a relationship of a husband and wife nature, including its sexual aspects. In re McGowan, 84 Ill. App. 3d 609, 40 Ill. Dec. 64, 405 N.E.2d 1156 (1 Dist. 1980).

——Sexual Conduct

While proof of sexual conduct between spouse receiving maintenance and the person with whom the spouse is living is no longer necessary to establish cohabitation on a conjugal basis, something more than merely living with another person of the opposite sex is required. In re Nolen, 200 Ill. App. 3d 1072, 146 Ill. Dec. 818, 558 N.E.2d 781 (5 Dist. 1990).

A conjugal relationship does not require sexual conduct; an impotent male is capable of a conjugal relationship. In re Sappington, 106 Ill. 2d 456, 88 Ill. Dec. 61, 478 N.E.2d 376 (1985).

While the term "cohabitation" means living together as husband and wife, but does not necessarily imply sexual intercourse, "conjugal basis" implies the assertion of the right of sexual intercourse between husband and wife; thus continuing sexual intercourse must occur between parties one of whom is receiving maintenance payments from an ex-spouse before the pertinent provision of subsection (b) of this section is triggered. In re Cohenour, 101 Ill. App. 3d 362, 56 Ill. Dec. 876, 428 N.E.2d 195 (3 Dist. 1981).

Out-of-wedlock intercourse can be proved by circumstantial evidence, but the law requires either direct or circumstantial evidence of sexual conduct before maintenance payments can be terminated.

Cohabitation (Cont'd)

—Conjugal (Cont'd)

——Sexual Conduct (Cont'd)

In re Cohenour, 101 Ill. App. 3d 362, 56 Ill. Dec. 876, 428 N.E.2d 195 (3 Dist. 1981).

Requiring evidence of sexual conduct does not pose a public policy problem as to the standard of proof. In re McGowan, 84 Ill. App. 3d 609, 40 Ill. Dec. 64, 405 N.E.2d 1156 (1 Dist. 1980).

This statute contemplates acts of sexual intercourse as part of the conjugal husband-wife relationship which it seeks to describe. Halford v. Halford, 70 Ill. App. 3d 609, 27 Ill. Dec. 168, 388 N.E.2d 1131 (5 Dist. 1979).

——Termination of Maintenance

This section, which authorizes termination of a spouse's maintenance award on grounds of cohabitation, similarly requires a court to deny the cohabiting spouse's original request for maintenance if cohabitation is proven. In re Klein, 231 Ill. App. 3d 901, 173 Ill. Dec. 335, 596 N.E.2d 1214 (4 Dist. 1992).

Where respondent's counsel conceded respondent was cohabiting, neither the trial court or the appellate court had to evaluate changes in recipient spouse's need for support in order to determine whether respondent's relationship amounted to cohabiting which justified denying her maintenance. In re Klein, 231 Ill. App. 3d 901, 173 Ill. Dec. 335, 596 N.E.2d 1214 (4 Dist. 1992).

A former spouse's obligation to pay maintenance can be terminated by order of court whenever the recipient spouse has entered into a conjugal relationship with another person, whether by legal or other means. In re Nolen, 200 Ill. App. 3d 1072, 146 Ill. Dec. 818, 558 N.E.2d 781 (5 Dist. 1990).

—Continuing Basis

——Not Shown

Where the wife's paramour bought groceries for her and her children and bought some clothing for her, he took his meals with her and her children, he worked with her to clean and maintain their residence, she did his laundry and cooked his meals, he moved into her residence in October and left in January, and after moving out, phoned weekly, Christmas gifts to her children were signed "Larry and Mom," and she spent the holidays at his parents' home, the evidence was insufficient to establish cohabitation on a continuing basis. In re Clark, 111 Ill. App. 3d 960, 67 Ill. Dec. 686, 444 N.E.2d 1369 (3 Dist. 1983).

—Effect

The trial court's assertion that "[o]nce you live with a man, you have voided your chance to get alimony," was an overbroad and erroneous interpretation of legislative intent. In re Bramson, 83 Ill. App. 3d 657, 39 Ill. Dec. 85, 404 N.E.2d 469 (1 Dist. 1980).

—Evidence Insufficient

In determining whether an ex-wife was engaged in a resident, continuing, conjugal relationship with a third party, thereby providing grounds to terminate her maintenance, a trial court should have found the "nature of activities" they engaged in to favor only slightly a finding of a conjugal relationship because the evidence showed only limited domesticity; she did his laundry only sometimes and he would merely help out with the chores, such as taking out trash and cutting the lawn, on occasion. In re Marriage of Sunday, 354 Ill. App. 3d 184, 289 Ill. Dec. 860, 820 N.E.2d 636, 2004 Ill. App. LEXIS 1518 (2 Dist. 2004).

Trial court miscalculated the weight to accord the "amount-of-time" together factor, which it used when considering whether a new relationship was grounds to terminate alimony. Because the ex-wife showed that the frequency of her boyfriend's overnight visits was due in part to her ex-husband's harassing behavior, the trial court should have accorded relatively little weight to the "amount-of-time" factor in determining the existence of a conjugal and cohabiting relationship. In re Marriage of Sunday, 354 Ill. App. 3d 184, 289 Ill. Dec. 860, 820 N.E.2d 636, 2004 Ill. App. LEXIS 1518 (2 Dist. 2004).

Four month relationship between ex-wife and boyfriend was too brief to support a trial court's finding of conjugal cohabitation, which it used as a basis to terminate alimony; the length of the relationship is a proxy to help determine whether the new relationship is in fact a substitute for the marital relationship. In re Marriage of Sunday, 354 Ill. App. 3d 184, 289 Ill. Dec. 860, 820 N.E.2d 636, 2004 Ill. App. LEXIS 1518 (2 Dist. 2004).

The trial court's decision not to terminate maintenance was not against the manifest weight of the evidence where trial court considered the short period of cohabitation, the continuing need for support, the lack of commingling of funds, the petitioner's payment of all her bills with the exception of rent and utilities, and the termination of the relationship, and ruled that there was no de facto relationship. In re Leming, 227 Ill. App. 3d 154, 169 Ill. Dec. 108, 590 N.E.2d 1027 (5 Dist.), cert. denied, 146 Ill. 2d 630, 176 Ill. Dec. 802, 602 N.E.2d 456 (1992).

The trial court's finding that the relationship implied more of a dating relationship and not a de facto marriage was not against the manifest weight of the evidence, where the former wife and her friend dated other people as well as each other, took trips separately as well as together, maintained separate residences, and did not commingle assets. Rosche v. Rosche, 163 Ill. App. 3d 308, 114 Ill. Dec. 846, 516 N.E.2d 1001 (5 Dist. 1987).

The evidence fell short of establishing a husband-wife relationship where both the wife and her boyfriend dated other people, her boyfriend considered her arrangement as rooming with a friend on a temporary basis until she rejoined her children, she moved in, in part, to provide more room for visitation with her children, she retained her name, received mail at more than one address and had identification cards listing several addresses, and additionally, there was no evidence that the two commingled their funds, as might be expected in a husband-wife relationship. In re Bramson, 83 Ill. App. 3d 657, 39 Ill. Dec. 85, 404 N.E.2d 469 (1 Dist. 1980).

—Factors

——Not Shown

Where there was no evidence of a sexual relationship, no evidence of sharing expenses, no evidence of the alleged cohabitant paying any of respondent's expenses the evidence was insufficient evidence to warrant a termination of maintenance. In re Johnson, 215 Ill. App. 3d 174, 158 Ill. Dec. 742, 574 N.E.2d 855 (4 Dist. 1991).

The fact that wife's relationship was terminated before hearing and lasted only approximately six months weighed against finding a conjugal relationship. In re Caradonna, 197 Ill. App. 3d 155, 143 Ill. Dec. 175, 553 N.E.2d 1161 (2 Dist. 1990).

Where the nature of an ex-wife's employment as a full-time housekeeper and nurse required she live in her employer's house, and there was no indication that either she or her employer considered themselves to have a husband-wife relationship, the ex-wife's relationship with the employer did not justify termination of all support on the basis of cohabitation. In re Nolen, 200 Ill. App. 3d 1072, 146 Ill. Dec. 818, 558 N.E.2d 781 (5 Dist. 1990).

There was ample support for the view that plaintiff's need for support had not been materially affected and that defendant has failed to sustain his burden of establishing that plaintiff was involved in a de facto husband-wife relationship with her landlord; accordingly, the trial court's finding that plaintiff was not cohabiting with another person on a resident, continuing and conjugal basis was not against the manifest weight of the evidence. In re Reeder, 145 Ill. App. 3d 1013, 99 Ill. Dec. 648, 495 N.E.2d 1383 (5 Dist. 1986).

——Shown

In hearing to determine whether to terminate an ex-wife's alimony, a trial court properly interpreted evidence that ex-wife and her boyfriend spent all of the holidays together as a factor in favor of a finding of a conjugal relationship. In re Marriage of Sunday, 354 Ill. App. 3d 184, 289 Ill. Dec. 860, 820 N.E.2d 636, 2004 Ill. App. LEXIS 1518 (2 Dist. 2004).

The trial court's finding that petitioner cohabitated with another man on a "resident, continuing conjugal basis" was not against the manifest weight of the evidence where the record revealed they shared meals, bank accounts, household chores, and credit accounts, as well as exchanged holiday and birthday gifts and the two also took vacations together and maintained a sexual relationship. In re Toole, 273 Ill. App. 3d 607, 210 Ill. Dec. 551, 653 N.E.2d 456 (2 Dist. 1995).

—Finding

——Review

A trial court's finding that the recipient spouse is not living with

Cohabitation (Cont'd)

—Finding (Cont'd)

——Review (Cont'd)

another person under circumstances amounting to a de facto husband-wife relationship will not be reversed unless it is contrary to the manifest weight of the evidence. In re Caradonna, 197 Ill. App. 3d 155, 143 Ill. Dec. 175, 553 N.E.2d 1161 (2 Dist. 1990).

—Husband/Wife Relationship

The evidence established that petitioner had entered into a relationship which amounted to that of husband and wife and fell within the provisions of subsection (c). In re Frasco, 265 Ill. App. 3d 171, 202 Ill. Dec. 787, 638 N.E.2d 655 (4 Dist.), appeal denied, 158 Ill. 2d 551, 206 Ill. Dec. 835, 645 N.E.2d 1357 (1994).

—Purpose

The termination of maintenance upon the recipient's resident, continuing and conjugal cohabitation with another person was most likely added to subsection (b) of this section to end the inequities caused when a former spouse had in fact entered into a husband-wife relationship, although not formalized legally, and was still entitled to maintenance merely because Illinois does not recognize common law marriages. In re McGowan, 84 Ill. App. 3d 609, 40 Ill. Dec. 64, 405 N.E.2d 1156 (1 Dist. 1980); In re Olson, 98 Ill. App. 3d 316, 53 Ill. Dec. 751, 424 N.E.2d 386 (3 Dist. 1981).

The requirement that maintenance terminate upon the recipient's residing with another person on a resident, continuing conjugal basis presumably was added to this Act to avoid the injustice of cases in which the payor spouse is unable to prove the marriage of the recipient spouse. In re Bramson, 83 Ill. App. 3d 657, 39 Ill. Dec. 85, 404 N.E.2d 469 (1 Dist. 1980).

—Settlement Agreement

——Basis for Termination

Where parties expressly provided in clear and unequivocal language for maintenance and for its termination upon the occurrence of either of two conditions, the death or the remarriage of the respondent, the execution of this agreement, voluntarily signed by both parties who were each represented by counsel, constituted a clear, unequivocal, and decisive act from which it may be inferred that petitioner waived conjugal cohabitation as a condition for the termination of maintenance. In re Giles, 197 Ill. App. 3d 421, 143 Ill. Dec. 779, 554 N.E.2d 714 (5 Dist. 1990).

The omission of conjugal cohabitation as a condition for termination in a maintenance agreement indicates that the parties did not intend to have this statutory condition apply. In re Arvin, 184 Ill. App. 3d 644, 133 Ill. Dec. 53, 540 N.E.2d 919 (2 Dist. 1989).

—Termination of Maintenance

The trial court erred in terminating maintenance from the date of the former husband's petition, rather than the date his former wife began conjugal cohabitation with another man. Snow v. Snow, 322 Ill. App. 3d 953, 255 Ill. Dec. 883, 750 N.E.2d 1268, 2001 Ill. App. LEXIS 438 (3 Dist. 2001).

Cohabitation automatically terminates a maintenance obligation; thus, the payor spouse is not required to file a petition before a maintenance obligation terminates. Gray v. Gray, 314 Ill. App. 3d 249, 247 Ill. Dec. 169, 731 N.E.2d 942, 2000 Ill. App. LEXIS 467 (2 Dist. 2000).

When termination of maintenance was sought based on cohabitation under subsection (c) the trial court appropriately considered various factors defining the relationship, such as (1) its length; (2) the amount of time spent together; (3) the nature of the activities they engaged in; (4) the interrelation of their personal affairs; (5) their vacationing together; and (6) their spending holidays together; the test the court employed was the totality of the circumstances. In re Herrin, 262 Ill. App. 3d 573, 199 Ill. Dec. 814, 634 N.E.2d 1168 (4 Dist.), appeal denied, 157 Ill. 2d 501, 205 Ill. Dec. 162, 642 N.E.2d 1279 (1994).

Collateral Estoppel

Since the facts considered by the trial court at the modification hearing were different from the facts in the prior hearings on maintenance award, the doctrine of collateral estoppel was not applicable. In re Connors, 303 Ill. App. 3d 219, 236 Ill. Dec. 430, 707 N.E.2d 275 (2 Dist. 1999).

Consent Decree

—Continuing Jurisdiction

When parties incorporated a property settlement agreement in a decree it became merged therein, and the alimony provided in the agreement became subject to modification from time to time as appeared reasonable and proper. Page v. Page, 32 Ill. App. 2d 422, 178 N.E.2d 129 (1 Dist. 1961).

—Contractual

A property settlement, standing alone, is merely a contract between the parties. One who seeks to vacate only the property settlement provisions in a divorce decree is in the same position as a person seeking to set aside an ordinary contract. Garmisa v. Garmisa, 4 Ill. App. 3d 134, 280 N.E.2d 458 (1 Dist. 1972).

—Divestiture of Jurisdiction

When dealing with such matters as grounds for divorce, payment of alimony, and modification of divorce decrees, which are regulated by statute, a court is exercising powers granted by the legislature and cannot by incorporating a contractual provision in its decree divest itself of the power to modify, contrary to the legislative will. Duvall v. Duvall, 8 Ill. App. 3d 53, 289 N.E.2d 59 (3 Dist. 1972).

—Effect

The court has the power to modify a decree or order as to child support and educational payments and there are no exceptions in regard to prior agreements or "consent decrees;" the trial court is not deprived of the power to modify a consent decree. Duvall v. Duvall, 8 Ill. App. 3d 53, 289 N.E.2d 59 (3 Dist. 1972).

—Effect of Amendment

The 1981 amendment to subdivision (b), adding the language, "Unless otherwise agreed by the parties in a written agreement set forth in the judgment or otherwise approved by the court", was not intended to change the law but was instead intended to clarify the law. In re Arvin, 184 Ill. App. 3d 644, 133 Ill. Dec. 53, 540 N.E.2d 919 (2 Dist. 1989).

A marital settlement agreement which predated the 1981 amendment to subsection (c) of this section did not include provision for termination of maintenance on basis of conjugal cohabitation, and therefore there could be no termination on this basis. In re Arvin, 184 Ill. App. 3d 644, 133 Ill. Dec. 53, 540 N.E.2d 919 (2 Dist. 1989).

The 1982 amendment to subsection (b) of this section, is fully applicable to proceedings conducted prior to the effective dates of the amendments. In re Davis, 124 Ill. App. 3d 1088, 80 Ill. Dec. 364, 465 N.E.2d 155 (3 Dist. 1984), modified on other grounds, 106 Ill. 2d 290, 88 Ill. Dec. 11, 478 N.E.2d 326 (1985).

The amendment to subsection (b) of this section, which became effective January 1, 1982, was the applicable law on the appeal of a pending case because of the general rule that when the legislature changes the law while an appeal is pending, the reviewing court will apply the law as it exists at the time of its decision, rather than the law as it was at the time of the trial court's judgment. Krug-Etheridge v. Krug, 111 Ill. App. 3d 780, 67 Ill. Dec. 454, 444 N.E.2d 690 (1 Dist. 1982).

—Fraud or Coercion

A consent decree will be set aside and vacated where it has resulted from fraud or coercion by either party, or from inequity and unfairness in the terms of the settlement, at least where its execution has been accompanied by some element of coercion or misrepresentation. Garmisa v. Garmisa, 4 Ill. App. 3d 411, 280 N.E.2d 444 (1 Dist. 1972).

—Modification Allowed

The trial court properly concluded that a husband and wife could, under the terms of the property settlement agreement approved by a divorce decree, agree to a modification and that the court could ratify such agreement. Armstrong v. Ingram, 7 Ill. App. 3d 370, 287 N.E.2d 532 (4 Dist. 1972).

—Trial of Issues

Where the respondent's answer to plaintiff's petition seeking modification of a divorce decree's property settlement squarely put in issue the basic allegations of the petition, and contained aver-

Consent Decree (Cont'd)

—Trial of Issues (Cont'd)
ments which, if supported by the evidence, strongly suggested the absence of any fraudulent concealment, such pleadings raised issues of fact which had to be tried and the trial court's order granting relief was reversed and remanded. Wilson v. Wilson, 56 Ill. App. 2d 187, 205 N.E.2d 636 (2 Dist. 1965).

Construction

—Mandatory Provision
Subsection (a) of this section is permissive and allows the trial court to exercise its discretion in modifying maintenance or support, while subsection (b) of this section is mandatory and flatly states that the obligation to pay maintenance is terminated by the resident, continuing conjugal cohabitation of the recipient with another person. In re McGowan, 84 Ill. App. 3d 609, 40 Ill. Dec. 64, 405 N.E.2d 1156 (1 Dist. 1980).

—With Supreme Court Rules
Rule 296, Supreme Court Rules, does not authorize the court to ignore 750 ILCS 5/505 or this section, but merely provides an additional tool for the court to use in fairly resolving child-support disputes. In re Fink, 275 Ill. App. 3d 960, 212 Ill. Dec. 297, 656 N.E.2d 1131 (4 Dist. 1995).

Default/Vesting Date
Each support or maintenance payment is vested on the date it becomes due, this date becoming the default/vesting date, which is important for: (1) calculating the total arrearage, (2) calculating the interest owed, if any (3) an indicator or factor in determining whether the conduct was wilful or contumacious, and (4) calculating attorney fees under section 508 of the Illinois Marriage and Dissolution of Marriage Act (750 ILCS 5/508). In re Hardy, 191 Ill. App. 3d 685, 138 Ill. Dec. 909, 548 N.E.2d 139 (5 Dist. 1989).

Educational Expenses

—Age of Majority
Where marital settlement agreement contained definition for when emancipation occurred, since the agreement did not specifically limit the provision to the husband only, wife was ordered to pay child support until youngest child in husband's custody reached emancipation under terms of the agreement. In re Sweders, 296 Ill. App. 3d 919, 231 Ill. Dec. 9, 695 N.E.2d 526 (2 Dist. 1998), appeal denied, 179 Ill. 2d 620, 235 Ill. Dec. 577, 705 N.E.2d 450 (1998).

The respondent was not obligated for additional postmajority expenses unless by virtue of the marital settlement agreement. In re Leming, 227 Ill. App. 3d 154, 169 Ill. Dec. 108, 590 N.E.2d 1027 (5 Dist.), cert. denied, 146 Ill. 2d 630, 176 Ill. Dec. 802, 602 N.E.2d 456 (1992).

The court could properly require the continuation of support payments for educational purposes after the child attained the age of majority. Harding v. Harding, 59 Ill. App. 3d 25, 16 Ill. Dec. 426, 374 N.E.2d 1304 (4 Dist. 1978).

—Burden of Proof
Where no information other than that elicited by husband's counsel was presented regarding the daughter's financial resources and her financial dependency on her mother, and the little information received on cross-examination did not support the mother's request that the father contributed to the daughter's education and maintenance, wife failed to meet her burden of supporting request for educational support. In re McGory, 185 Ill. App. 3d 517, 133 Ill. Dec. 590, 541 N.E.2d 801 (3 Dist. 1989).

—College
A provision in a dissolution judgment for the payment of a child's college expenses is a term in the nature of child support, and the circuit court therefore retains jurisdiction to modify such a provision at any time pursuant to 750 ILCS 5/502 and this section, regardless of whether the provision was ordered by the court under 750 ILCS 5/513 or incorporated into the judgment as a result of a settlement agreement. In re Loffredi, 232 Ill. App. 3d 709, 173 Ill. Dec. 933, 597 N.E.2d 907 (3 Dist. 1992).

Where an institution was not a "college" as that term was contemplated under the marital settlement agreement, the trial court's award of four months' additional postmajority child support pursuant to the marital settlement agreement was against the manifest weight of the evidence and was contrary to the express language of the marital settlement agreement. In re Leming, 227 Ill. App. 3d 154, 169 Ill. Dec. 108, 590 N.E.2d 1027 (5 Dist.), cert. denied, 146 Ill. 2d 630, 176 Ill. Dec. 802, 602 N.E.2d 456 (1992).

Although defendant no longer practiced medicine, evidence concerning his financial condition reflected that he retained a substantial income from his investments and did not demonstrate that defendant had experienced a substantial economic reversal which would have prohibited the trial court from ordering that defendant provide additional educational support for his child; thus, the manifest weight of the evidence did not reflect that the college expenditures were excessive or otherwise unreasonable. Harding v. Harding, 59 Ill. App. 3d 25, 16 Ill. Dec. 426, 374 N.E.2d 1304 (4 Dist. 1978).

Defendant's contention that an obligation for the payment of educational expenses should only be imposed on him after it was demonstrated that his daughter would satisfactorily complete her studies was without merit. Harding v. Harding, 59 Ill. App. 3d 25, 16 Ill. Dec. 426, 374 N.E.2d 1304 (4 Dist. 1978).

—Consent Decree
The court has power to modify a decree or order as to child support and educational payments and there are no exceptions in regard to prior agreements or "consent decrees;" the trial court is not deprived of the power to modify a consent decree. Duvall v. Duvall, 8 Ill. App. 3d 53, 289 N.E.2d 59 (3 Dist. 1972).

—Death of Obligor
Where a stipulation and agreed order did not contain any language limiting the obligation to pay a nonminor child's college education expense to the decedent's lifetime, the order did not terminate upon the decedent's death, and his estate was responsible for these expenses. DeFrancesca v. Estate of Champagne, 153 Ill. App. 3d 560, 106 Ill. Dec. 561, 505 N.E.2d 1352 (2 Dist. 1987).

—Death of Parent
Where the settlement agreement established the father's obligation to pay for the children's college expenses even where they attained their majority, subject only to his financial ability to pay and the children's aptitude for higher education, the fact that he died before his ability to pay was adjudicated did not mitigate that responsibility. In re Oldham, 222 Ill. App. 3d 744, 165 Ill. Dec. 206, 584 N.E.2d 385 (1 Dist. 1991).

Under subsection (d) of this section and section 513 of the Illinois Marriage and Dissolution of Marriage Act (750 ILCS 5/513), the circuit court may not enter an order against the estate of a noncustodial deceased parent for the payment of college expenses of a non-minor child when no such previous obligation was imposed upon the parent to be charged prior to his death. Treacy v. Treacy, 204 Ill. App. 3d 282, 149 Ill. Dec. 802, 562 N.E.2d 266 (1 Dist. 1990).

—Emancipation
A parent's obligation to pay for the educational expenses of a child terminated upon the marriage of that child, an emancipating event. In re Daniels, 296 Ill. App. 3d 446, 231 Ill. Dec. 257, 695 N.E.2d 1376 (4 Dist. 1998).

—Modification in Error
Trial court abused its discretion in modifying respondent's obligation to provide that respondent did not have any obligation to pay for the college expenses of his son, which obligation was conditioned on his son being college material and on respondent's financial ability to provide for the expenses, because in order to make an intelligent and useful decision, there would have to be facts to indicate whether respondent's son was college material, what his expenses would be, and respondent's financial ability at that time to provide for the expenses; at the time respondent brought his petition, none of these things could be ascertained. In re Walters, 238 Ill. App. 3d 1086, 178 Ill. Dec. 176, 604 N.E.2d 432 (2 Dist. 1992).

—Termination
Where a divorce decree did not provide support for the educational expenses of the parties' non-minor children and stated that the question of educational expenses was to be reserved for future consideration, and the support awarded in the decree was support for the three minor children, this type of support terminated when

Educational Expenses (Cont'd)

—Termination (Cont'd)
the children were emancipated and the divorce decree did not obligate the father to continue paying child support after the youngest child attained majority. In re Pauley, 104 Ill. App. 3d 100, 59 Ill. Dec. 875, 432 N.E.2d 661 (4 Dist. 1982).

Employment

—Reasonable Diligence
The trial court properly determined respondent had used reasonable diligence in seeking employment where, since the last hearing, she had been substitute teaching and had gained certification and had taken the only full-time position offered. In re Connors, 303 Ill. App. 3d 219, 236 Ill. Dec. 430, 707 N.E.2d 275 (2 Dist. 1999).

Equitable Estoppel

—Applicability
Even in the absence of an enforceable agreement, there was no reason why the doctrine of equitable estoppel could not be applied as to all or part of past installments in an appropriate case. Anderson v. Anderson, 48 Ill. App. 2d 140, 198 N.E.2d 342 (2 Dist. 1964).

Evidence

—Parol Evidence
Where the evidence established a mutual mistake of fact contained within a property settlement agreement, the court properly considered parol evidence of the settlement negotiations. In re Johnson, 237 Ill. App. 3d 381, 178 Ill. Dec. 122, 604 N.E.2d 378 (4 Dist. 1992).

Extraordinary Circumstances

—Not Shown
It was unnecessary for the court to make any findings as to matters on the economic circumstances of the parties since the date the judgment of dissolution was entered where the record reflected that following the remand order no extraordinary circumstances had arisen. In re Jones, 187 Ill. App. 3d 206, 134 Ill. Dec. 836, 543 N.E.2d 119 (1 Dist. 1989).

Failure to Pay
Where the court found husband was able to make payment to wife but had chosen to spend his money in other ways, the trial court's determination that husband's failure to pay was wilful certainly was not against the manifest weight of the evidence; the trial court did not abuse its discretion in finding husband in contempt and sentencing him to 30 days in jail. In re Dunseth, 260 Ill. App. 3d 816, 198 Ill. Dec. 620, 633 N.E.2d 82 (4 Dist. 1994).

The power of a court to enforce payment for child support by contempt is limited to cases of wilful and contumacious refusal to obey the order of the court. In re Lavelle, 206 Ill. App. 3d 607, 152 Ill. Dec. 49, 565 N.E.2d 291 (5 Dist. 1990).

Where the record supported the husband's contention that his non-payment was due to a lack of sufficient income respondent's failure to maintain health insurance or his failure to pay medical expenses not covered by insurance was wilful and contumacious. In re Lavelle, 206 Ill. App. 3d 607, 152 Ill. Dec. 49, 565 N.E.2d 291 (5 Dist. 1990).

While it was true that the husband did not make his payments through the clerk's office, the court found that the parties had a mutual agreement whereby respondent would make the payments directly to petitioner, the husband's failure to make payments through the clerk's office did not constitute contempt when petitioner at the least acquiesced in such method of payment if not encouraged payment directly to her. In re Lavelle, 206 Ill. App. 3d 607, 152 Ill. Dec. 49, 565 N.E.2d 291 (5 Dist. 1990).

Where petitioner reduced his maintenance and support payments without authorization from the court, and failed to satisfactorily establish that his failure to pay was due to his financial inability to pay, the judgment finding petitioner in contempt of court was affirmed. In re Eisenstein, 172 Ill. App. 3d 264, 122 Ill. Dec. 237, 526 N.E.2d 496 (1 Dist. 1988).

Mere absence of compliance with the provisions of the decree is not sufficient basis for a judgment of contempt of court unless the evidence shows the failure to comply was a willful and contumacious refusal to obey the court order. Giamanco v. Giamanco, 111 Ill. App. 3d 1017, 67 Ill. Dec. 606, 444 N.E.2d 1090 (5 Dist. 1982).

A court should have considered the defendant's financial condition at the time of the contempt hearing to determine whether his failure to pay was willful and contumacious. Giamanco v. Giamanco, 111 Ill. App. 3d 1017, 67 Ill. Dec. 606, 444 N.E.2d 1090 (5 Dist. 1982).

Failure to Reserve Right to Modification
A court can modify a maintenance order when the order sought to be modified does not expressly reserve the right of the court to review that order at some future time. In re Carpel, 232 Ill. App. 3d 806, 173 Ill. Dec. 873, 597 N.E.2d 847 (4 Dist.), cert. denied, 147 Ill. 2d 625, 180 Ill. Dec. 148, 606 N.E.2d 1225 (1992).

Filing
The Illinois General Assembly, in moving the "due notice" phrase from one location to another, changed the law as it had been previously interpreted by this state's judiciary, the filing date of the modification petition is no longer the earliest point to which a retroactive modification of maintenance or support payments may be ordered; rather, consistent with the Federal mandate, the earliest point to which retroactive modification of maintenance or support payments may be ordered is the date on which the nonmoving party receives "due notice" from the moving party of the filing of the modification petition. In re Hawking, 240 Ill. App. 3d 419, 181 Ill. Dec. 254, 608 N.E.2d 327 (1 Dist. 1992), appeal denied, 149 Ill. 2d 649, 183 Ill. Dec. 861, 612 N.E.2d 513 (1993).

Final Order
Circuit court's order, which ordered the payment each month of maintenance in a fixed amount but, because of circumstances shown by the evidence, reserved review of the decision for modification two years or less after the order was entered, was final and appealable. In re Cannon, 112 Ill. 2d 552, 98 Ill. Dec. 368, 494 N.E.2d 490 (1986).

The legislative pronouncement contained in subsection (a) of this section requires that judgments in dissolution proceedings be accorded the same degree or status of finality that is accorded to judgments in other proceedings; otherwise, the integrity of judgments in dissolution proceedings would be subject to erosion. King v. King, 130 Ill. App. 3d 642, 85 Ill. Dec. 874, 474 N.E.2d 834 (5 Dist. 1985).

A decree of divorce is final as to the circumstances and conditions of the parties on the date of its entry; upon a subsequent application for a modification, only matters which have occurred subsequent to the entry of the decree may be considered by the court. Louthan v. Louthan, 130 Ill. App. 2d 281, 264 N.E.2d 797 (1 Dist. 1970).

It has long been recognized that a decree in the divorce case is final as to conditions then existing. Maupin v. Maupin, 339 Ill. App. 484, 90 N.E.2d 234 (4 Dist. 1950).

Foreign Court's Modification
One state must recognize a sister state's judgment to the degree that it is nonmodifiable, and the second forum must apply the first forum's law to determine the extent of modification; thus, to determine the degree to which an Illinois decree is modifiable, the foreign court should refer to this section. Sullivan v. Sullivan, 98 Ill. App. 3d 928, 54 Ill. Dec. 207, 424 N.E.2d 957 (3 Dist. 1981).

Guardian ad Litem

—Abuse of Discretion
An appointment of a guardian ad litem for a child who was not a party to modification of child support action and without an evidentiary showing of the need for a guardian was an abuse of the trial court's discretionary power. Robin v. Robin, 45 Ill. App. 3d 365, 3 Ill. Dec. 950, 359 N.E.2d 809 (1 Dist. 1977).

Illustrative Cases
The court would not reduce or terminate the respondent's support obligations simply because his children had resisted visitation with him where there was sufficient evidence that this resistance was due to his own behavior and not attributable to any interference by the petitioner. In re Heldebrandt, 301 Ill. App. 3d 265, 234 Ill. Dec. 839, 703 N.E.2d 939 (4 Dist. 1998), appeal denied, 183 Ill. 2d 568, 238 Ill. Dec. 713, 712 N.E.2d 817 (1999).

Illustrative Cases (Cont'd)

The circuit court abused its discretion in denying wife's petition to review and extend a temporary maintenance award where, although the former wife may not have begun her efforts toward financial independence as soon as she might have and the marriage was of short duration, she did not have sufficient resources to meet her financial obligations, where the standard of living during the marriage was lavish, where she was in her late forties when the parties were divorced, and where she had worked only two years and eight months in her life, had not, at former husband's request, worked during the marriage, and had physical and emotional problems which may have prevented her from seeking full-time employment, and where husband had ability to pay maintenance. In re Martin, 223 Ill. App. 3d 855, 166 Ill. Dec. 136, 585 N.E.2d 1158 (4 Dist.), appeal denied, 145 Ill. 2d 635, 173 Ill. Dec. 6, 596 N.E.2d 630 (1992).

Indefinite Maintenance

Court did not abuse its discretion in awarding indefinite maintenance where trial court concluded that it was unlikely wife would be able to increase her income to a level approaching her husband's. In re Minear, 287 Ill. App. 3d 1073, 223 Ill. Dec. 405, 679 N.E.2d 856 (4 Dist. 1997), aff'd, 181 Ill. 2d 552, 230 Ill. Dec. 250, 693 N.E.2d 379 (1998).

Jurisdiction

Property rights created by a judgment of dissolution become vested when the judgment is final, and a trial court lacks general jurisdiction to modify an order affecting these rights. In re Hubbard, 215 Ill. App. 3d 113, 158 Ill. Dec. 747, 574 N.E.2d 860 (2 Dist. 1991).

Where modification of decree of dissolution is an agreed order, not contrary to public policy and not shown to have resulted from fraud or coercion, respondent can challenge it on appeal only if the circuit court lacks jurisdiction to enter it. In re Steel, 195 Ill. App. 3d 348, 142 Ill. Dec. 31, 552 N.E.2d 381 (4 Dist. 1990).

Where the trial court has not expressly reserved jurisdiction to extend the term of rehabilitative maintenance, the court retains authority to extend the maintenance beyond the original term in view of subsection (a) of this section when the petition for modification is filed during the period set for rehabilitative maintenance. Rice v. Rice, 173 Ill. App. 3d 1098, 123 Ill. Dec. 630, 528 N.E.2d 14 (5 Dist. 1988).

The trial court lacks jurisdiction to extend the duration of the maintenance award once the original time period for maintenance has expired. Rice v. Rice, 173 Ill. App. 3d 1098, 123 Ill. Dec. 630, 528 N.E.2d 14 (5 Dist. 1988).

A trial court lacked jurisdiction to consider a respondent's petition seeking modification of a fixed, limited award of rehabilitative maintenance which was filed after the maintenance obligation had been satisfied, and where the court did not reserve jurisdiction to review such an award. Rice v. Rice, 173 Ill. App. 3d 1098, 123 Ill. Dec. 630, 528 N.E.2d 14 (5 Dist. 1988).

The trial court lacked jurisdiction to grant defendant's petition to modify as to the marital residence when in the interim between the entry of the judgment and the filing of defendant's petition to modify, the trial court terminated the maintenance provision, leaving nothing further to modify with respect to maintenance. In re Clark, 149 Ill. App. 3d 613, 103 Ill. Dec. 21, 500 N.E.2d 1092 (3 Dist. 1986).

While the court had jurisdiction to modify the distribution of the proceeds, it was not necessary to reverse and remand the portion of the order which did so. In re Demond, 142 Ill. App. 3d 134, 96 Ill. Dec. 455, 491 N.E.2d 501 (5 Dist. 1986).

Trial court has inherent jurisdiction to consider future child support in a dissolution proceeding and need not expressly retain jurisdiction. In re Petramale, 102 Ill. App. 3d 1049, 58 Ill. Dec. 537, 430 N.E.2d 569 (2 Dist. 1981).

Where there were no facts of record that demonstrated whose circumstances had changed, or in what manner, or who accepted what benefits from whom, there could be no estoppel to prevent wife from asserting that the court did not have jurisdiction to modify a divorce decree. Hartman v. Hartman, 89 Ill. App. 3d 969, 45 Ill. Dec. 360, 412 N.E.2d 711 (4 Dist. 1980).

A trial court's order purportedly clarifying the supplemental judgment disposing of the property of the parties pursuant to the dissolution of their marriage, which actually modified the property rights of the husband, and which was entered more than 17 months after the supplemental judgment, was not effective, as the trial court lacked subject matter jurisdiction to enter such a modification. In re Kekstadt, 85 Ill. App. 3d 952, 41 Ill. Dec. 248, 407 N.E.2d 746 (1 Dist. 1980).

Where the petition for modification did not request that any increase be retroactive, and petitioner first requested this relief in a later petition for rehearing which was abandoned, this issue was not properly before the court. Scott v. Scott, 72 Ill. App. 3d 117, 27 Ill. Dec. 863, 389 N.E.2d 1271 (1 Dist. 1979).

Where an original divorce decree was entirely silent with regard to apportionment of any income tax refund, wife could not by her petition, requesting the award of income taxes withheld from her salary which had been included in a joint income tax return, invoke the court's jurisdiction to adjudicate property rights upon which the final word had already been spoken in the decree. Brickey v. Brickey, 44 Ill. App. 3d 563, 3 Ill. Dec. 239, 358 N.E.2d 406 (5 Dist. 1976).

The property rights created in a divorce decree become vested and after 30 days the court is without jurisdiction to modify them. Brickey v. Brickey, 44 Ill. App. 3d 563, 3 Ill. Dec. 239, 358 N.E.2d 406 (5 Dist. 1976).

Law of the Case

The law of the case doctrine was inapplicable to preclude the court from modifying a maintenance award upon a showing of a substantial change in circumstances. In re Connors, 303 Ill. App. 3d 219, 236 Ill. Dec. 430, 707 N.E.2d 275 (2 Dist. 1999).

Legislative Intent

The legislative purpose behind the adoption of subsection (c) of this section is to allow the parties to a dissolution proceeding to remain liable for the support of children beyond emancipation. Falat v. Falat, 201 Ill. App. 3d 320, 147 Ill. Dec. 33, 559 N.E.2d 33 (1 Dist. 1990).

Subsection (b) of this section does not represent an attempt by the legislature to control public morals. In re Reeder, 145 Ill. App. 3d 1013, 99 Ill. Dec. 648, 495 N.E.2d 1383 (5 Dist. 1986).

The legislature intended to allow future maintenance to survive the remarriage of the receiving party if the judge approves. In re Freeman, 106 Ill. 2d 290, 88 Ill. Dec. 11, 478 N.E.2d 326 (1985).

The legislative purpose behind subsection (c) of this section is to permit the parties to agree to remain liable for the support of the child beyond emancipation. In re Donahoe, 114 Ill. App. 3d 470, 70 Ill. Dec. 152, 448 N.E.2d 1030 (2 Dist. 1983).

Prior to the enactment of subsection (c) of this section, support orders were of no legal effect after the death of the obligor and, for various reasons, children of a previous marriage often were not included in the obligor's will; subsection (c) of this section was designed to correct this problem and eliminate the hardship imposed upon children through loss of support by disinheritance. Halas v. Executor of Estate of Halas, 112 Ill. App. 3d 940, 68 Ill. Dec. 411, 445 N.E.2d 1264 (1 Dist. 1983).

The purpose of a modification proceeding is to show that a substantial change in circumstances has occurred since the prior judgment. Giamanco v. Giamanco, 111 Ill. App. 3d 1017, 67 Ill. Dec. 606, 444 N.E.2d 1090 (5 Dist. 1982).

The legislative purpose behind subsection (c) of this section is to permit the parties to agree to remain liable for the support of the child beyond emancipation. Finley v. Finley, 81 Ill. 2d 317, 43 Ill. Dec. 12, 410 N.E.2d 12 (1980); In re Donahoe, 114 Ill. App. 3d 470, 70 Ill. Dec. 152, 448 N.E.2d 1030 (2 Dist. 1983).

Reading subsections (a) and (b) of this section together would disregard the clearly expressed intention of the legislature to establish a new and distinct standard for termination of maintenance. In re McGowan, 84 Ill. App. 3d 609, 40 Ill. Dec. 64, 405 N.E.2d 1156 (1 Dist. 1980).

It was the intention of the legislature to provide for the termination of an ex-spouse's obligation to pay future maintenance whenever the spouse receiving the maintenance has entered into a husband-wife relationship with another, whether this be by legal or other means. Halford v. Halford, 70 Ill. App. 3d 609, 27 Ill. Dec. 168, 388 N.E.2d 1131 (5 Dist. 1979); In re Reeder, 145 Ill. App. 3d 1013, 99 Ill. Dec. 648, 495 N.E.2d 1383 (5 Dist. 1986).

Life Insurance

—Child As Beneficiary

A parent may be required to provide or maintain life insurance

Life Insurance (Cont'd)

—Child As Beneficiary (Cont'd)

with his child as irrevocable beneficiary to ensure the fulfillment of his support obligation if he should die within the child's minority. In re Dulyn, 89 Ill. App. 3d 304, 44 Ill. Dec. 622, 411 N.E.2d 988 (1 Dist. 1980).

—Illustrative Cases

The trial court did not abuse its discretion in awarding decedent's children one-third of $300,000 life insurance policy; even though under the terms of the dissolution judgment the decedent was to maintain a life insurance policy for the benefit of his children, at the time of the judgment decedent had two policies in the total amount of $55,000. Downey v. Downey, 293 Ill. App. 3d 234, 227 Ill. Dec. 265, 687 N.E.2d 339 (4 Dist. 1997).

Limitations

—Death

A court does not have authority either: (1) to order a spouse or the estate of that spouse to make maintenance payments for a period extending beyond the death of that spouse, or (2) to require that spouse to secure income in lieu of maintenance to the other spouse after death of the first spouse by making the other spouse or a trustee for the other spouse the beneficiary of insurance policies on the life of the first spouse, or other contracts payable at the death of the first spouse. In re Clarke, 125 Ill. App. 3d 432, 80 Ill. Dec. 629, 465 N.E.2d 975 (4 Dist. 1984).

Maintenance

—In General

Maintenance has been defined as follows: it is for an indefinite period of time and usually for an indefinite total sum; it is based upon the payor's income and the needs of the recipient determined from the standpoint of the manner in which they have been accustomed to live; it is modifiable after decree when the recipient's needs increase or decrease, or when the payor's ability to pay increases or decreases; it usually terminates upon the death of the payor, although by agreement payments may be made a charge upon the payor's estate after they become due; it is never a charge on an estate in advance of the due date because it is not, prior to that time, vested; payments are not based upon any consideration but are based upon the common-law duty of support. In re Marquardt, 110 Ill. App. 3d 271, 65 Ill. Dec. 956, 442 N.E.2d 267 (2 Dist. 1982).

—Ability to Pay

Where respondent presented evidence of outstanding debts, neither the tax liability nor the debt owed to a hospital was responsible for respondent's failure to pay maintenance since he had made no payments towards those debts by the time of the hearing, thus, the record supported the trial court's finding that the respondent had the ability to pay maintenance during the period in question. In re Ingram, 185 Ill. App. 3d 395, 133 Ill. Dec. 520, 541 N.E.2d 731 (5 Dist. 1989).

—Appeal

The appeal of an award of maintenance is barred where the defendant's acceptance of the benefits of the divorce decree which would distinctly disadvantage the plaintiff upon any redetermination of those rights. In re Lawver, 82 Ill. App. 3d 198, 37 Ill. Dec. 540, 402 N.E.2d 430 (3 Dist. 1980).

—Bankruptcy

Although this section terminates the obligation to pay maintenance upon the marriage of the party receiving maintenance, the fact that an award stated that the obligation would not terminate upon remarriage of the debtor's wife, did not dictate that the award was not maintenance with regard to determining the dischargeability in bankruptcy of the debtor's obligation. Renzulli v. Renzulli, 28 Bankr. 41 (Bankr. N.D. Ill. 1982).

—Characterization

Maintenance agreement was an award of periodic maintenance for a fixed period rather than maintenance in gross and subject to modification or termination, where it was denominated as "transitional maintenance" and for a fixed rather than indefinite duration. In re Harris, 284 Ill. App. 3d 389, 219 Ill. Dec. 875, 672 N.E.2d 383 (4 Dist. 1996).

An award of maintenance may be modified regardless of whether it is characterized as permanent or temporary as long as it does not explicitly preclude such modification; this also applies to situations in which a party seeks to terminate (or abate) an award of maintenance. In re Krupp, 207 Ill. App. 3d 779, 152 Ill. Dec. 742, 566 N.E.2d 429 (1 Dist. 1990), cert. denied, 137 Ill. 2d 665, 156 Ill. Dec. 562, 571 N.E.2d 149 (1991).

Under prior law, the fact that payments were for a sum certain to be paid over a specified time (five years) would have resulted in the characterization of the payments as in the nature of a property settlement, but this section allows maintenance for a limited time and sum, and the factors of definiteness in amount and time are not conclusive. In re Marquardt, 110 Ill. App. 3d 271, 65 Ill. Dec. 956, 442 N.E.2d 267 (2 Dist. 1982).

—Credit

Former husband was not entitled to a credit toward his maintenance obligation for social security benefits received by his former wife by virtue of contributions made by the husband. In re Schrimpf, 293 Ill. App. 3d 246, 227 Ill. Dec. 248, 687 N.E.2d 171 (5 Dist. 1997).

—Defined

The word "alimony" in former section 18 of the Divorce Act (see now this section), is synonymous with the word "maintenance" used in subsection (a) of this section. Pierce v. Pierce, 69 Ill. App. 3d 42, 25 Ill. Dec. 511, 386 N.E.2d 1175 (5 Dist. 1979).

—Employment Secured

Even though respondent had obtained employment, the court properly continued maintenance, since she did not have her own pension and would never earn as much as petitioner. In re Connors, 303 Ill. App. 3d 219, 236 Ill. Dec. 430, 707 N.E.2d 275 (2 Dist. 1999).

—Equitable

Just as the court is without authority, after a husband's death, to award maintenance to the wife, it is without authority, after the husband's death, to award equitable maintenance pending appeal. Stacke v. Bates, 200 Ill. App. 3d 85, 146 Ill. Dec. 118, 557 N.E.2d 1305 (2 Dist. 1990).

—Factors Considered

In determining whether maintenance should be modified, the court properly considered that respondent no longer owned a home and had been awarded only 15% of petitioner's pension. In re Connors, 303 Ill. App. 3d 219, 236 Ill. Dec. 430, 707 N.E.2d 275 (2 Dist. 1999).

It is not only just and equitable to consider the factors listed in subsection (c), but also it is statutorily required when awarding maintenance pursuant to 750 ILCS 5/504. In re Toole, 273 Ill. App. 3d 607, 210 Ill. Dec. 551, 653 N.E.2d 456 (2 Dist. 1995).

The factors to be considered in making an award of maintenance under subsection (b) of 750 ILCS 5/504 are applicable to modification proceedings under subsection (a) of this section. In re Martin, 223 Ill. App. 3d 855, 166 Ill. Dec. 136, 585 N.E.2d 1158 (4 Dist.), appeal denied, 145 Ill. 2d 635, 173 Ill. Dec. 6, 596 N.E.2d 630 (1992).

In determining whether to modify maintenance and to what degree, the trial court is to consider the same factors as those for making the initial award: the financial resources of the party seeking maintenance, including marital property apportioned to her; the standard of living established during the marriage; the duration of the marriage; the age and the physical and emotional condition of both parties; the ability of the spouse seeking maintenance to meet her needs independently; and the ability of the other spouse to pay. In re Zeman, 198 Ill. App. 3d 722, 145 Ill. Dec. 149, 556 N.E.2d 767 (2 Dist. 1990).

—Failure to Pay

The noncompliance with an order to pay maintenance constitutes prima facie evidence of contempt of court, and once the prima facie showing is made, the burden of proof shifts to the defendant to show by definite and explicit evidence that he is unable to pay. In re Dall, 212 Ill. App. 3d 85, 155 Ill. Dec. 520, 569 N.E.2d 1131 (5 Dist. 1991).

A defense to contempt, applicable only in the most extreme cases, exists where the failure of a person to obey an order to pay

Maintenance (Cont'd)

—Failure to Pay (Cont'd)

maintenance is due to poverty, insolvency, or other misfortune, unless that inability to pay is the result of a wrongful or illegal act, or where a defendant can show that he neither has money now with which he can pay nor has disposed wrongfully of money or assets with which he might have paid. In re Dall, 212 Ill. App. 3d 85, 155 Ill. Dec. 520, 569 N.E.2d 1131 (5 Dist. 1991).

If it is established that a party has failed to comply with a divorce decree in paying maintenance, prima facie evidence of contempt is established and the burden shifts to the alleged contemnor to show the conduct was not wilful. Taapken v. Taapken, 39 Ill. App. 3d 785, 350 N.E.2d 794 (4 Dist. 1976).

If the husband establishes that he is unable to pay the maintenance, he should not be found guilty of contempt. Taapken v. Taapken, 39 Ill. App. 3d 785, 350 N.E.2d 794 (4 Dist. 1976).

—Failure to Seek Independence

The recipient of maintenance is under an affirmative obligation to seek appropriate training and skills to become financially independent in the future; the failure to make good faith efforts to achieve this goal, following a reasonable time frame during which the objective should be accomplished, might form the basis for a petition for modification pursuant to subsection (a) of this section. In re Martin, 223 Ill. App. 3d 855, 166 Ill. Dec. 136, 585 N.E.2d 1158 (4 Dist.), appeal denied, 145 Ill. 2d 635, 173 Ill. Dec. 6, 596 N.E.2d 630 (1992).

—Financial Independence

Where former wife had completed the necessary training and received certification as a respiratory therapist and had begun making inquiries into available employment opportunities when she was involved in an automobile accident, injuring her back, the trial court was not required to compel her to actively seek employment when she would be unable to fulfill the job requirements. In re Hucker, 259 Ill. App. 3d 551, 197 Ill. Dec. 296, 631 N.E.2d 299 (4 Dist. 1994).

A spouse who receives maintenance is under an affirmative obligation to seek appropriate training and skills in order to reach the goal of becoming financially independent; a failure to make good faith efforts toward this goal, following a reasonable time frame during which this objective should have been accomplished, may be grounds for modification of maintenance. In re Hucker, 259 Ill. App. 3d 551, 197 Ill. Dec. 296, 631 N.E.2d 299 (4 Dist. 1994).

Where one spouse was found to be in good health at the time the judgment of dissolution was entered, and the record five years later did not reflect a substantial or extraordinary change in that spouse's circumstances, but revealed that the other spouse had suffered a heart attack and remained hospitalized in a coma for a period of time, and nothing indicated that the spouse seeking maintenance was completely handicapped or suffered from any terminal illness or other physical impairment absent a showing of extraordinary circumstances, that spouse still had a continuing duty to become financially independent. In re Jones, 187 Ill. App. 3d 206, 134 Ill. Dec. 836, 543 N.E.2d 119 (1 Dist. 1989).

Where the record showed that wife had the ability to support herself and that her financial transactions had increased her difficulties in meeting her expenses, there was no abuse of discretion in the trial court's decision not to increase maintenance. Faris v. Faris, 142 Ill. App. 3d 987, 97 Ill. Dec. 209, 492 N.E.2d 645 (2 Dist. 1986), appeal denied, 100 Ill. Dec. 603, 497 N.E.2d 781 (Ill. 1986).

The failure of the spouse that was awarded maintenance to make good-faith efforts to achieve goal of financial independence following a reasonable time frame during which the objective should be accomplished, might form the basis for a petition for modification. In re Mittra, 114 Ill. App. 3d 627, 71 Ill. Dec. 350, 450 N.E.2d 1229 (4 Dist. 1983).

—Grant Held Erroneous

Grant of permanent alimony to wife in addition to husband's interest in the marital residence was held erroneous. Demos v. Demos, 8 Ill. App. 3d 906, 290 N.E.2d 304 (2 Dist. 1972).

—In Gross

Subsection (c) of this section does not authorize the court to award maintenance in gross after the death of the payor spouse. Stacke v. Bates, 200 Ill. App. 3d 85, 146 Ill. Dec. 118, 557 N.E.2d 1305 (2 Dist. 1990).

Maintenance in gross is a nonmodifiable sum certain to be received by the former spouse regardless of any change of circumstances; where indefinite period was fixed and monthly payments were not a sum certain, such an award could not be considered maintenance in gross. In re Arvin, 184 Ill. App. 3d 644, 133 Ill. Dec. 53, 540 N.E.2d 919 (2 Dist. 1989).

Where the marital separation agreement executed by petitioner and respondent prescribed that the respondent pay a lump sum over a definite number of installments, the intent of the parties, as determined from the written marital separation agreement, was to create an award of maintenance in gross in a lump sum payable over a definite number of installments. In re Hildebrand, 166 Ill. App. 3d 795, 117 Ill. Dec. 644, 520 N.E.2d 995 (5 Dist. 1988).

Maintenance in gross awarded the petitioner under 750 ILCS 5/504(b) was not subject to termination upon remarriage pursuant to subsection (b) of this section. In re Davis, 124 Ill. App. 3d 1088, 80 Ill. Dec. 364, 465 N.E.2d 155 (3 Dist. 1984), modified on other grounds, 106 Ill. 2d 290, 88 Ill. Dec. 11, 478 N.E.2d 326 (1985).

—Job Search

Extension of maintenance constituted an abuse of discretion in light of the court's finding that respondent's job searching efforts were insufficient. In re Koenigsknecht, 302 Ill. App. 3d 474, 236 Ill. Dec. 267, 707 N.E.2d 112 (1 Dist. 1998).

—Modification

——Allowed

Reduction of income was the type of substantial change in circumstances contemplated by subsection (a) and thus it was error for the trial court to decline to modify the maintenance award. In re Izzo, 264 Ill. App. 3d 790, 202 Ill. Dec. 184, 637 N.E.2d 723 (1 Dist. 1994).

Because the terms of the judgment did not incorporate the terms of a settlement agreement pursuant to 75 ILCS 5/502(f), the court had power to modify the maintenance award. In re Bryant, 206 Ill. App. 3d 167, 150 Ill. Dec. 707, 563 N.E.2d 834 (1 Dist. 1990).

Modification of maintenance was appropriate where the husband presented evidence that he had chosen to cease working upon the advice of his physician and following heart pains significant enough to cause his hospitalization and his business required work seven days a week. In re Colombo, 197 Ill. App. 3d 767, 144 Ill. Dec. 159, 555 N.E.2d 56 (2 Dist. 1990).

Although the ancillary order limited termination of maintenance to the conditions therefor in this section, it made no express reference to any conditions precluding modification as to the amount of maintenance and, therefore, did not preclude modification. In re Scott, 205 Ill. App. 3d 561, 150 Ill. Dec. 868, 563 N.E.2d 995 (4 Dist. 1990).

Modification of maintenance provisions of a 1975 settlement agreement was allowed using the standards of this section, even though enacted after 1975. Ingrassia v. Ingrassia, 156 Ill. App. 3d 483, 109 Ill. Dec. 68, 509 N.E.2d 729 (2 Dist. 1987).

Where an option concerning disposition of a home required respondent to pay monthly rent to petitioner, the award was a form of maintenance which the court could not allow where petitioner was cohabiting with another. In re Combs, 78 Ill. App. 3d 533, 33 Ill. Dec. 922, 397 N.E.2d 255 (5 Dist. 1979).

——Burden of Proof

The party seeking modification of maintenance has the burden of demonstrating that a substantial change of circumstances has occurred. In re Krupp, 207 Ill. App. 3d 779, 152 Ill. Dec. 742, 566 N.E.2d 429 (1 Dist. 1990), cert. denied, 137 Ill. 2d 665, 156 Ill. Dec. 562, 571 N.E.2d 149 (1991).

In an action for the modification of maintenance, proof of need and proof of a change in circumstances are not separate and distinct issues; the need of the recipient spouse is one of the circumstances the court is to consider in determining the original award of maintenance. Similarly, a change in the need of the recipient spouse would be a circumstance to be considered in determining whether an award should be modified, and the burden of establishing such a change in the need rests with the movant. In re Krupp, 207 Ill. App. 3d 779, 152 Ill. Dec. 742, 566 N.E.2d 429 (1

Maintenance (Cont'd)

—Modification (Cont'd)

——Burden of Proof (Cont'd)
Dist. 1990), cert. denied, 137 Ill. 2d 665, 156 Ill. Dec. 562, 571 N.E.2d 149 (1991).

——Factors Considered
The same factors considered under 750 ILCS 5/504(b)(2) in making an initial award of maintenance are used in determining whether and to what degree a maintenance award shall be modified under subsection (a) of this section. Rice v. Rice, 173 Ill. App. 3d 1098, 123 Ill. Dec. 630, 528 N.E.2d 14 (5 Dist. 1988).

If a source of income, no matter how certain the probability it will continue, should cease, this matter then becomes an appropriate fact to support a petition to modify an order of maintenance. In re Mittra, 114 Ill. App. 3d 627, 71 Ill. Dec. 350, 450 N.E.2d 1229 (4 Dist. 1983).

In determining whether and to what degree a maintenance award shall be modified, the circuit court is to consider the same factors to be assessed in making the initial award. In re Chalkley, 99 Ill. App. 3d 478, 55 Ill. Dec. 262, 426 N.E.2d 237 (1 Dist. 1981); In re Garelick, 168 Ill. App. 3d 321, 119 Ill. Dec. 76, 522 N.E.2d 738 (1 Dist. 1988); In re Bryant, 206 Ill. App. 3d 167, 150 Ill. Dec. 707, 563 N.E.2d 834 (1 Dist. 1990).

——Not Allowed
Trial court's denial of a reduction or termination of former husband's maintenance was not an abuse of discretion, notwithstanding husband's retirement and increased medical costs because of his present wife's ill health; evidence established that the former husband had substantial assets from which to pay his present wife's medical bills and the maintenance award. In re Schrimpf, 293 Ill. App. 3d 246, 227 Ill. Dec. 248, 687 N.E.2d 171 (5 Dist. 1997).

The evidence was clear that the parties intended monthly payments to be something more than simple maintenance: where respondent conveyed away substantive marital property interests, in return for conveying her interest in farmland and farm equipment, she received only interest income from the trust and the monthly payments, and the payments were nonmodifiable monthly payments until her death, rather than maintenance terminable by the provisions of this section. In re Sherrick, 214 Ill. App. 3d 92, 157 Ill. Dec. 917, 573 N.E.2d 335 (4 Dist. 1991).

Petitioner was earning $4 per hour, a sum only slightly above the minimum wage, while respondent had a career position with the State of Illinois, petitioner had no medical insurance and was afflicted with serious medical problems and housing difficulties; therefore, there was not basis to disturb the trial court's order awarding periodic permanent maintenance to petitioner. In re Popovich, 149 Ill. App. 3d 643, 103 Ill. Dec. 38, 500 N.E.2d 1109 (4 Dist. 1986).

The court did not abuse its discretion in failing to reduce the amount of maintenance ordered, there was conflicting evidence regarding petitioners' ability to pay the amount awarded, and the court chose to believe there was no substantial change in circumstances, because the petitioner had lied at trial about certain assets, and the court clearly could question petitioners' credibility, therefore, petitioner's request for a modification of support was denied. In re Demond, 142 Ill. App. 3d 134, 96 Ill. Dec. 455, 491 N.E.2d 501 (5 Dist. 1986).

Where, due to illness, respondent's need for maintenance had increased substantially since the entry of the divorce decree, and where petitioner's inability to pay maintenance was largely the result of indebtedness incurred by him, denial of modification of award was proper. Geittmann v. Geittmann, 126 Ill. App. 3d 470, 81 Ill. Dec. 597, 467 N.E.2d 297 (5 Dist. 1984).

——Standard
The discretionary standard for modification of maintenance found in subsection (a) of this section is essentially unchanged from its applications under the former Divorce Act. In re McGowan, 84 Ill. App. 3d 609, 40 Ill. Dec. 64, 405 N.E.2d 1156 (1 Dist. 1980).

—Need of Support
A shown need for support cannot be controlling and in itself sufficient to defeat a petition to terminate maintenance when all other factors demonstrate an ongoing, conjugal relationship to exist. In re Frasco, 265 Ill. App. 3d 171, 202 Ill. Dec. 787, 638 N.E.2d 655 (4 Dist.), appeal denied, 158 Ill. 2d 551, 206 Ill. Dec. 835, 645 N.E.2d 1357 (1994).

—Paramour
A divorced spouse should not be required to support the other spouse's paramour. Hall v. Hall, 25 Ill. App. 3d 524, 323 N.E.2d 541 (1 Dist. 1975).

—Party Agreement
Maintenance agreements may be modified or terminated under circumstances stated in statutory provisions, unless the parties' intent is clearly manifested in such agreement to limit or preclude such judicial modification or termination. In re Scott, 205 Ill. App. 3d 561, 150 Ill. Dec. 868, 563 N.E.2d 995 (4 Dist. 1990).

If the language of the agreement does not expressly preclude or limit modification of its terms, it is error to hold the maintenance nonmodifiable. In re Scott, 205 Ill. App. 3d 561, 150 Ill. Dec. 868, 563 N.E.2d 995 (4 Dist. 1990).

The parties may agree that reductions or termination of maintenance can only occur under specific circumstances, regardless of "good faith," and that their agreement controls. In re Mateja, 183 Ill. App. 3d 759, 132 Ill. Dec. 666, 540 N.E.2d 406 (1 Dist. 1989).

The mandate of this section, as it applies to future maintenance, cannot be avoided by agreement between the parties. Ihle v. Ihle, 92 Ill. App. 3d 893, 48 Ill. Dec. 335, 416 N.E.2d 366 (3 Dist. 1981).

The only limitations placed on the parties' freedom to fashion their own property and maintenance agreements are that the end product to be incorporated into the divorce decree may not be so unjust as to be unconscionable and the obligation to pay future maintenance is terminated upon the death of either party, or the remarriage of the party receiving maintenance, or if the party receiving maintenance cohabits with another person on a resident, continuing conjugal basis. Simmons v. Simmons, 77 Ill. App. 3d 740, 33 Ill. Dec. 242, 396 N.E.2d 631 (2 Dist. 1979).

—Past Due Installments
Since a court has no power to modify past due installments of maintenance a petition for modification or termination would only apply to payments owed subsequent to the date of the filing of the petition. In re Kessler, 110 Ill. App. 3d 61, 65 Ill. Dec. 707, 441 N.E.2d 1221 (1 Dist. 1982).

—Permanent
An award of permanent maintenance in a dissolution proceeding containing no provision for modification review was deemed an abuse of discretion by the trial judge. In re Girrulat, 219 Ill. App. 3d 164, 161 Ill. Dec. 734, 578 N.E.2d 1380 (5 Dist. 1991).

Where an agreement characterized the maintenance as "permanent," this term may also be used simply to distinguish permanent maintenance from temporary maintenance awarded during the pendency of a dissolution action; such as when the agreement was too vague to establish that the parties intended to contravene the general policy of Illinois and provide for continuing maintenance payments after the former wife's remarriage. In re Jensen, 212 Ill. App. 3d 60, 156 Ill. Dec. 405, 570 N.E.2d 881 (3 Dist. 1991).

There is no language in this section which prohibits modification of a permanent maintenance award, and such awards are therefore modifiable. In re Arvin, 184 Ill. App. 3d 644, 133 Ill. Dec. 53, 540 N.E.2d 919 (2 Dist. 1989).

—Post Death
750 ILCS 5/413(a) and 750 ILCS 5/504(c) do not create a substantive right to post-death maintenance pending appeal; they apply when a right to maintenance already exists and therefore, must be read in conjunction with the prohibition of subsection (c) of this section. Stacke v. Bates, 138 Ill. 2d 295, 149 Ill. Dec. 728, 562 N.E.2d 192 (1990).

—Reduction
Where respondent presented evidence that his income had decreased by 70%, the trial court did not abuse its discretion in reducing petitioner's temporary maintenance by approximately 66%. In re Borg, 96 Ill. App. 3d 282, 51 Ill. Dec. 706, 421 N.E.2d 214 (1 Dist. 1981).

—Reduction for Property Charge
The trial court did not exceed its authority where it reduced a

Maintenance (Cont'd)

—Reduction for Property Charge (Cont'd)

husband's monthly maintenance obligation and placed a charge of $300 per month against the husband's real property which was to be satisfied from the sale of the property because the "charge" against the property was more in the nature of a deferred obligation and not a lien. Biondolino v. Biondolino, 94 Ill. App. 3d 184, 49 Ill. Dec. 946, 418 N.E.2d 966 (5 Dist. 1981).

—Rehabilitative

Because petitioner cohabited on a resident, continuing conjugal basis with another party and did not subsequently reconcile, respondents obligation to pay all forms of maintenance, including rehabilitative maintenance, had been terminated. In re Toole, 273 Ill. App. 3d 607, 210 Ill. Dec. 551, 653 N.E.2d 456 (2 Dist. 1995).

—Reinstatement

The reinstatement of maintenance obligations where a party has cohabited on a conjugal basis, but is no longer cohabiting on a conjugal basis, is not provided for by statute. In re Toole, 273 Ill. App. 3d 607, 210 Ill. Dec. 551, 653 N.E.2d 456 (2 Dist. 1995).

—Retroactive Modification

Where a decree of separate maintenance between the parties in a case decided prior to the adoption of the Marriage and Dissolution of Marriage Act (see now this section), provided that the defendant pay his wife $15,500 per year for alimony and support, and where on appeal the cause was remanded with directions to reduce the alimony to $11,500 a year, the reduction was made effective as of the date of the separate maintenance decree such that from the date of the original award to the date of the reviewing court's mandate, the defendant paid a larger amount of alimony than he rightfully should have paid, the increment to the plaintiff was an advantage which could not justly be retained and the trial court corrected the overpayment by retroactively adjusting the alimony to the date of the erroneous decree. Richheimer v. Richheimer, 81 Ill. App. 2d 328, 225 N.E.2d 451 (1 Dist. 1967).

—Review

——Allowed

An award of maintenance is always reviewable and modifiable, if the requisite requirements are met, under subsection (a). In re Jones, 187 Ill. App. 3d 206, 134 Ill. Dec. 836, 543 N.E.2d 119 (1 Dist. 1989).

——Change in Circumstances

While receiving maintenance, petitioner has an affirmative obligation to seek appropriate employment and to make a good-faith effort to become financially independent and should petitioner not fulfill her obligations, subsection (a) of this section directs that the maintenance award may be modified upon respondent's showing of substantial change in circumstances; thus, while the order did not provide for review of the maintenance award, respondent is not precluded from seeking a review during the 10-year period if there is a substantial change in circumstances. In re Cheger, 213 Ill. App. 3d 371, 157 Ill. Dec. 116, 571 N.E.2d 1135 (4 Dist. 1991).

——Discretion

Whether the terms of a dissolution judgment providing for maintenance should be modified or terminated rests within the sound discretion of the trial court, and its determination will not be disturbed on review unless the record shows an abuse of that discretion. In re Whiting, 179 Ill. App. 3d 187, 128 Ill. Dec. 286, 534 N.E.2d 468 (5 Dist. 1989).

—Standard

The trial court's decision to terminate maintenance will not be disturbed on review unless it is contrary to the manifest weight of the evidence. In re Johnson, 215 Ill. App. 3d 174, 158 Ill. Dec. 742, 574 N.E.2d 855 (4 Dist. 1991).

—Settlement Agreement

Where parties' agreement clearly and unambiguously limited the duration of maintenance by stating that it would not extend beyond the earliest of three specific events, the expiration of 78 months, and the wife's death or remarriage, and the agreement precluded a modification extending wife's right to maintenance beyond that time, although the parties' agreement was sufficiently clear to make the duration of payments non-modifiable, because the agreement incorporated into the judgment of dissolution did not clearly preclude modification of the amounts of maintenance and other benefits within the prescribed periods, the trial court could modify amounts payable with the time limitations prescribed by the parties' agreement. Tucker v. Tucker, 223 Ill. App. 3d 671, 166 Ill. Dec. 83, 585 N.E.2d 1105 (3 Dist. 1992).

Post-dissolution modification of maintenance is judicially precluded only where a settlement agreement clearly and unambiguously expresses the parties' intent to make maintenance non-modifiable. Tucker v. Tucker, 223 Ill. App. 3d 671, 166 Ill. Dec. 83, 585 N.E.2d 1105 (3 Dist. 1992).

—Termination

——In General

Each case for termination of maintenance must rest on its own facts, given the unique nature of personal relationships. In re Johnson, 215 Ill. App. 3d 174, 158 Ill. Dec. 742, 574 N.E.2d 855 (4 Dist. 1991).

——Allowed

Where the petitioner had come from being unemployed with no outside income at the time of the dissolution, to having completed her college education in accounting, and employment with earnings of $20,000 per year, respondent's petition for termination of maintenance payments should have been granted because the statutory goal of rehabilitative maintenance had been achieved. In re Henzler, 134 Ill. App. 3d 318, 89 Ill. Dec. 261, 480 N.E.2d 147, 480 N.E.2d 198 (4 Dist. 1985).

——Effective Date

Termination of maintenance may not be effected prior to the date a petitioner received notice a petition had been filed. In re Frasco, 265 Ill. App. 3d 171, 202 Ill. Dec. 787, 638 N.E.2d 655 (4 Dist.), appeal denied, 158 Ill. 2d 551, 206 Ill. Dec. 835, 645 N.E.2d 1357 (1994).

A determination of the effective date of termination is a matter within the court's discretionary authority. In re Frasco, 265 Ill. App. 3d 171, 202 Ill. Dec. 787, 638 N.E.2d 655 (4 Dist.), appeal denied, 158 Ill. 2d 551, 206 Ill. Dec. 835, 645 N.E.2d 1357 (1994).

The termination of maintenance on the basis of the payee's cohabitation with another on a resident, continuing conjugal basis became effective when the petition for termination was filed. In re Stanley, 133 Ill. App. 3d 963, 89 Ill. Dec. 146, 479 N.E.2d 1152 (4 Dist. 1985).

——Factors Considered

While the trial court can consider the financial interaction between the interested parties in a petition for termination of maintenance, that factor is not controlling; if the court finds the required cohabitating relationship exists based on its assessment of the totality of the circumstances, it need not make any specific finding as to the maintenance recipient's financial need. In re Herrin, 262 Ill. App. 3d 573, 199 Ill. Dec. 814, 634 N.E.2d 1168 (4 Dist.), appeal denied, 157 Ill. 2d 501, 205 Ill. Dec. 162, 642 N.E.2d 1279 (1994).

An important consideration in evaluating payment of maintenance to an ex-spouse cohabiting with another individual, divorced from the morality of the conduct, is whether the cohabitation has materially affected the recipient spouse's need for support because she either received support from her co-resident or used maintenance moneys to support him. In re Olson, 98 Ill. App. 3d 316, 53 Ill. Dec. 751, 424 N.E.2d 386 (3 Dist. 1981); In re Caradonna, 197 Ill. App. 3d 155, 143 Ill. Dec. 175, 553 N.E.2d 1161 (2 Dist. 1990).

——Indefinite Time

Since this section of the Marriage and Dissolution of Marriage Act permits either spouse to modify or terminate the maintenance award, should circumstances change, an award for an indefinite period of time is not necessarily an interminable award. In re Stegbauer, 84 Ill. App. 3d 83, 39 Ill. Dec. 549, 404 N.E.2d 1140 (4 Dist. 1980).

——Not Allowed

The trial court properly abated, rather than terminated, maintenance to the wife, where she received $3.7 million in a medical

Maintenance (Cont'd)

—Termination (Cont'd)

——Not Allowed (Cont'd)

malpractice action, given the uncertainty of her future medical expenses and insurability. In re Bothe, 309 Ill. App. 3d 352, 242 Ill. Dec. 812, 722 N.E.2d 301 (2 Dist. 1999).

Where the relationship between ex-wife and male friend was of a relatively short duration, although they did have sexual relations, she would see him usually only every other month, they had not taken vacations together, owned no real estate or personal property together, and they had no joint bank accounts, the evidence showed she did not do his laundry and did not use maintenance to buy anything for him, he did not discipline the children and his principal involvement was playing chess with them, although there was sufficient evidence presented to grant the petition to terminate, there also was sufficient evidence to deny the petition; in such circumstances, that ex-wife and male friend were not engaged in a resident, continuing, conjugal relationship was not against the manifest weight of the evidence. In re Lambdin, 245 Ill. App. 3d 797, 184 Ill. Dec. 789, 613 N.E.2d 1381 (4 Dist. 1993).

The trial court did not abuse its discretion in denying husband's petition to terminate maintenance based on ex-wife's failure to seek appropriate training or education to become financially independent; ex-wife only had a general equivalency diploma and was custodian of two minor children. Moreover, she had a hearing problem which required her to read lips and caused a speech impediment and finally, only three years had passed since the dissolution of the marriage. In re Lambdin, 245 Ill. App. 3d 797, 184 Ill. Dec. 789, 613 N.E.2d 1381 (4 Dist. 1993).

Where the wife was able to secure employment but there was evidence in the record indicating that she had held her new job for only two years and that even with this new source of income, her resources were insufficient to provide for her reasonable needs, where the prospects of this situation improving were speculative at best, especially considering that the wife suffered from a physical condition which apparently rendered her incontinent, and where by contrast, the record indicated that the husband continued to prosper and that he could still comfortably provide the maintenance payments specified in the dissolution judgment, there was no basis for disturbing the circuit court's determination that the maintenance payments should not be terminated. In re Whiting, 179 Ill. App. 3d 187, 128 Ill. Dec. 286, 534 N.E.2d 468 (5 Dist. 1989).

There was no abuse of discretion in refusing to terminate maintenance payments where the record indicated that the respondent suffered some significant financial misfortune, but respondent failed to present sufficient evidence of a substantial change in circumstances to warrant a termination of maintenance payments. In re Ingram, 185 Ill. App. 3d 395, 133 Ill. Dec. 520, 541 N.E.2d 731 (5 Dist. 1989).

Where respondent received custody of the children at the same time he was ordered to pay $100 a week in maintenance to allow the petitioner to rehabilitate herself through schooling, and he did not show a substantial change in his circumstances following the maintenance order, the trial judge did not abuse his discretion in denying termination of maintenance. In re Scordo, 176 Ill. App. 3d 269, 125 Ill. Dec. 761, 530 N.E.2d 1170 (3 Dist. 1988).

Husband's obligation to pay wife a maintenance sum of $500 per month under the couple's settlement agreement survived his death. Bartlett v. Illinois Nat'l Bank, 138 Ill. App. 3d 102, 92 Ill. Dec. 755, 485 N.E.2d 566 (4 Dist. 1985).

——Settlement Agreement

Where the parties to a settlement agreement intend to limit the automatic termination of certain terms, they must do so in clear language. In re Jensen, 212 Ill. App. 3d 60, 156 Ill. Dec. 405, 570 N.E.2d 881 (3 Dist. 1991).

Where the parties entered an agreement which provided for the termination of maintenance payments only upon wife's death or remarriage or at the end of ten years, the parties did not intend to conclude that cohabitation was a condition for termination of maintenance under the settlement agreement. In re Tucker, 148 Ill. App. 3d 1097, 102 Ill. Dec. 685, 500 N.E.2d 578 (4 Dist. 1986).

As of the effective date of this Act, parties were allowed to enter into written separation agreements in accordance with 750 ILCS 5/502 which extended maintenance beyond the terminating events of subsection (b) of this section. In re Mass, 102 Ill. App. 3d 984, 58 Ill. Dec. 941, 431 N.E.2d 1 (1 Dist. 1981).

The trial court did not abuse its discretion by failing to terminate maintenance by former husband to former wife completely where the parties had agreed to the amount in a contractual agreement prior to the divorce. Biondolino v. Biondolino, 94 Ill. App. 3d 184, 49 Ill. Dec. 946, 418 N.E.2d 966 (5 Dist. 1981).

——Significant Misfortune

A showing that some significant misfortune has taken place does not always mean maintenance will be terminated. In re Dunseth, 260 Ill. App. 3d 816, 198 Ill. Dec. 620, 633 N.E.2d 82 (4 Dist. 1994).

—Upheld

Where wife had a high school education, four minor children, was permanently disabled, and had received no formal training in job skills and where husband's unemployment was not involuntary, award of $1,000 per month maintenance was not an abuse of discretion. In re Morse, 240 Ill. App. 3d 296, 180 Ill. Dec. 563, 607 N.E.2d 632 (2 Dist. 1993).

Medical Expenses

Where petitioner testified at length as to the manifestations of his son's emotional problems, treatment by various doctors and counselors, and the remedial educational program in which he had been placed, where the petitioner also testified as to the medical expenses incurred when another son suffered an ankle injury, and where respondent did not call any witnesses to dispute the nature of these expenses, nor did cross-examination of the petitioner establish any serious dispute as to the nature of the expenses, the petitioner established that the medical expenses were extraordinary in nature and therefore modification of respondent's obligation to pay child support was granted. In re Morrisroe, 155 Ill. App. 3d 765, 108 Ill. Dec. 303, 508 N.E.2d 464 (2 Dist. 1987).

Modification of child support that required the defendant pay medical and dental but not optical expenses for the children was not a breach of discretion. Blisset v. Blisset, 144 Ill. App. 3d 1088, 99 Ill. Dec. 161, 495 N.E.2d 608 (4 Dist. 1986), rev'd on other grounds, 123 Ill. 2d 161, 121 Ill. Dec. 931, 526 N.E.2d 125 (1988).

Trial court properly ordered husband to pay $5,094.35 in medical expenses where it was provided in the original divorce decree that husband was to pay extraordinary medical expenses. Goldberg v. Goldberg, 30 Ill. App. 3d 769, 332 N.E.2d 710 (1 Dist. 1975).

Order allowing wife attorney's fees and costs for defending the appeal was in error where although the order found that wife was unemployed and had no income of her own, the record disclosed that she held, with her second husband, two joint bank accounts with funds totalling $2,700, and owned a home in joint tenancy, and the order made no finding as to the husband's ability to pay. Berg v. Berg, 85 Ill. App. 2d 98, 229 N.E.2d 282 (1 Dist. 1967).

Modification

—In General

The legislature has set forth certain conditions upon which maintenance will be terminated or modified, however, parties to a dissolution action are permitted to enter into settlement agreements which alter the court's ability to terminate or modify maintenance and they take precedence over the statutory conditions. In re Brent, 263 Ill. App. 3d 916, 200 Ill. Dec. 799, 635 N.E.2d 1382 (4 Dist. 1994).

In determining whether there is sufficient cause to modify, the court may consider both the circumstances of the parents and the circumstances of the child. In re Stone, 191 Ill. App. 3d 172, 138 Ill. Dec. 547, 547 N.E.2d 714 (4 Dist. 1989).

For a case discussing modification of alimony award, see Osborn v. Osborn, 20 Ill. App. 3d 397, 313 N.E.2d 610 (5 Dist. 1974).

—Allowed

Denial of the husband's motion to reduce the child support order was reversed because the trial court committed impermissible "double counting" of the husband's workers' compensation settlement proceeds when it awarded half of the settlement to wife and children but did not adjust the husband's child support obligation. In re Marriage of Schacht, 343 Ill. App. 3d 348, 277 Ill. Dec. 889, 797 N.E.2d 236, 2003 Ill. App. LEXIS 1179 (2 Dist. 2003).

Where an order awarded a former wife rehabilitative maintenance and provided for review of the award some months later with

Modification (Cont'd)

—Allowed (Cont'd)
no further pleadings to be filed by the parties, the review did not constitute a modification of the maintenance award; hence, § 510 of the Illinois Marriage and Dissolution of Marriage Act, 750 ILCS 5/510, did not apply. In re Marriage of Culp, 341 Ill. App. 3d 390, 275 Ill. Dec. 221, 792 N.E.2d 452, 2003 Ill. App. LEXIS 861 (4 Dist. 2003).

Trial court did not abuse its discretion by finding a substantial change in circumstances by a substantial reduction in wife's income and ordering a $250 per month increase in maintenance even though, in the original judgment, the court did provide for the diminution of payments when the husband's salary as a reserve officer terminated; the court made no effort to prophesy or even speculate about the consequence of such reduction and certainly made no finding that the cessation of such payment would be reasonable for both parties. Thurston v. Thurston, 260 Ill. App. 3d 731, 198 Ill. Dec. 656, 633 N.E.2d 118 (3 Dist. 1994).

A trial court did not abuse its discretion in increasing maintenance and child support where evidence showed that the fact that the parties' daughter had asthma could have necessitated the wife's decision to become self-employed, the wife had health problems, and the husband filed a written judicial admission of his ability to pay. Giamanco v. Giamanco, 111 Ill. App. 3d 1017, 67 Ill. Dec. 606, 444 N.E.2d 1090 (5 Dist. 1982).

—Burden of Proof
On a petition to modify under this section, the burden is on the moving party to present to the court sufficient evidence upon which a decision can be made. In re McGory, 185 Ill. App. 3d 517, 133 Ill. Dec. 590, 541 N.E.2d 801 (3 Dist. 1989).

—Cohabitation
One change in conditions which justifies the modification of maintenance is if the party receiving maintenance cohabits with another person on a resident, continuing conjugal basis. In re Lowe, 101 Ill. App. 3d 317, 56 Ill. Dec. 821, 427 N.E.2d 1367 (2 Dist. 1981).

—Cost of Raising Children
A court may presume that the cost of raising children increases as the children grow older. In re Riegel, 242 Ill. App. 3d 496, 183 Ill. Dec. 168, 611 N.E.2d 21 (3 Dist. 1993).

—Cross-Petition Necessary
Respondents in child support modification actions must file a cross-petition if the relief they seek is different from the relief sought by the petitioner. In re Zukausky, 244 Ill. App. 3d 614, 184 Ill. Dec. 367, 613 N.E.2d 394 (2 Dist. 1993).

—Discharge in Bankruptcy
The trial court did not err in considering that the discharge of marital debt in bankruptcy constituted a substantial change in circumstances justifying an increase in support since (1) the discharge in bankruptcy relieved the father of the legal obligation of paying certain debts, thereby affecting a significant change in his financial condition, and (2) the wife became responsible for a substantial debt due to the father's discharge of that debt. In re Letsinger, 321 Ill. App. 3d 961, 255 Ill. Dec. 108, 748 N.E.2d 812, 2001 Ill. App. LEXIS 328 (2 Dist. 2001).

—Disparity in Income
Where husband may not have been able to develop his career as successfully as he did without wife's support in her role as the family's designated homemaker, viewed in legal terms, their marriage, because of its duration and circumstances, constituted a "moral and financial" partnership in which the interest of each partner could be neither easily ascertained nor easily terminated because of the substantial and continuing effect that partnership had and would likely continue to have on their lives. Thus, where the trial court viewed the matter as if wife bore an obligation to find a full-time job to support herself, which at best would have provided her with but a fraction of husband's income or the income they enjoyed while married, and her failure to do so precluded her from receiving any extension or increase in her maintenance, in punishing wife for what the court perceived as her lack of diligence, the court unduly encroached upon her reasonable expectations to be able to live in the future in a fashion remotely resembling how she had been able to live in the past, and her expectations in this regard were particularly reasonable in view of husband's six-figure income; thus the gross disparity in potential incomes and the apparently drastic change in wife's lifestyle supported her claim that her maintenance should have been extended and increased. In re Carpel, 232 Ill. App. 3d 806, 173 Ill. Dec. 873, 597 N.E.2d 847 (4 Dist.), cert. denied, 147 Ill. 2d 625, 180 Ill. Dec. 148, 606 N.E.2d 1225 (1992).

—Estoppel
Wife was barred from attacking a divorce decree by accepting the benefits of the divorce decree to the distinct disadvantage of the husband where wife had been awarded the marital home and all the personal property therein, and subsequent to the divorce decree, she sold two pieces of personal property out of the marital home, she sold the marital residence and purchased another residence. Adams v. Adams, 44 Ill. App. 3d 656, 3 Ill. Dec. 336, 358 N.E.2d 734 (3 Dist. 1976).

—Factors Considered
Trial court abused its discretion when it ruled that it was not required to apply statutory child support guidelines to a petition to modify a father's child support obligation and that it did not have to make any written findings of fact as to why it was refusing to apply the guidelines. Anderson v. Heckman, 343 Ill. App. 3d 449, 278 Ill. Dec. 190, 797 N.E.2d 1108, 2003 Ill. App. LEXIS 1242 (4 Dist. 2003).

In accordance with the Illinois Parentage Act of 1984, 750 ILCS 45/1 through 27 (2000), trial courts "shall" use the guidelines and standards set forth in 750 ILCS 5/505 (2000) in determining whether to modify an order for child support in accordance with 750 ILCS 5/510 (2000). Anderson v. Heckman, 343 Ill. App. 3d 449, 278 Ill. Dec. 190, 797 N.E.2d 1108, 2003 Ill. App. LEXIS 1242 (4 Dist. 2003).

Nothing in 755 ILCS 5/504 or this section authorizes or permits the consideration of the fact that ex-wife was overweight and continued to smoke in the consideration of modification of maintenance; the existence of these "factors" was none of the trial court's business. In re Offer, 275 Ill. App. 3d 986, 212 Ill. Dec. 493, 657 N.E.2d 694 (4 Dist. 1995).

Deviation from the guidelines may be had upon the consideration of relevant factors, and the factors to be considered in a modification proceeding are the same factors which may be considered when formulating an original support award. In re Olsen, 229 Ill. App. 3d 107, 171 Ill. Dec. 39, 593 N.E.2d 859 (1 Dist. 1992).

—Fraudulent Misrepresentation
Orders rendered in the context of a dissolution of marriage case may be vacated or modified if procured through fraud; in order to show fraudulent misrepresentation, plaintiff must show (1) a false statement of material fact; (2) the party making the statement knew or believed in to be untrue; (3) the recipient of the statement had a right to rely on it and did so; (4) the statement was made for the purpose of inducing the recipient to act; and (5) injury from the recipient's reliance on the statement. In re Ealy, 269 Ill. App. 3d 971, 207 Ill. Dec. 345, 647 N.E.2d 307 (4 Dist. 1995).

—Jurisdiction
The trial court had jurisdiction to modify custody support, notwithstanding the argument that the trial court was divested of jurisdiction by the failure to file a petition for modification of child support within 30 days of the final judgment of dissolution, since a trial court has inherent jurisdiction to modify child support in a dissolution proceeding upon a showing of a substantial change in circumstances, and the trial court need not expressly retain jurisdiction. In re Letsinger, 321 Ill. App. 3d 961, 255 Ill. Dec. 108, 748 N.E.2d 812, 2001 Ill. App. LEXIS 328 (2 Dist. 2001).

—Lifestyle During Marriage
The trial court had to admit testimony on how the parties lived during their marriage; such testimony would bear directly on the propriety of any extended and increased maintenance. In re Carpel, 232 Ill. App. 3d 806, 173 Ill. Dec. 873, 597 N.E.2d 847 (4 Dist.), cert. denied, 147 Ill. 2d 625, 180 Ill. Dec. 148, 606 N.E.2d 1225 (1992).

—Movant's Burden
The burden of demonstrating circumstances warranting modification is on the party seeking the modification. Graham v. Graham, 21 Ill. App. 3d 1032, 316 N.E.2d 143 (4 Dist. 1974).

Modification (Cont'd)

—Not Allowed

Where the trial court, in response to the former wife's motion to enforce the judgment of divorce, required the former husband to insure the daughter under the former husband's new wife's insurance plan, this was an improper modification of the divorce judgment, which did not specify how the former husband was to insure the daughter; while orders of support were modifiable under 750 ILCS 5/502(f), 510(a), orders of support were not modifiable unless a modification was requested, and the former wife had not requested a modification in the instant case. In re Marriage of Gowdy, 352 Ill. App. 3d 301, 287 Ill. Dec. 610, 816 N.E.2d 372, 2004 Ill. App. LEXIS 1118 (3 Dist. 2004).

A party cannot stop or reduce his child support payments unless the trial court has approved the modification. In re Ingram, 259 Ill. App. 3d 685, 197 Ill. Dec. 383, 631 N.E.2d 386 (2 Dist. 1994).

Although the father's income had drastically diminished, his standard of living had not and the court was apprehensive about reducing the father's $550-per-month support obligation where he had not seen fit to reduce his discretionary expenses. In re Burris, 263 Ill. App. 3d 495, 200 Ill. Dec. 880, 636 N.E.2d 71 (5 Dist. 1994).

Where original dissolution agreement stated husband (petitioner) was to pay mortgage until date of sale of home, trial court's modification of the petitioner's obligation to pay the entire sum of the mortgage payments until the date of the sale of the home was thus clearly in violation of subsection (a) of this section. In re Pitts, 169 Ill. App. 3d 200, 119 Ill. Dec. 908, 523 N.E.2d 664 (5 Dist. 1988).

Past-due installments of child support are the vested right of the designated recipient; thus, the court lacks the authority to modify those amounts that have already accrued. In re Erickson, 136 Ill. App. 3d 907, 91 Ill. Dec. 346, 483 N.E.2d 692 (2 Dist. 1985).

The trial court would not reverse a concededly adequate award of maintenance and child support based on a hypothetical and highly speculative argument regarding the possible future increase in the reasonable needs of petitioner or the minor children; should those needs in fact increase, petitioner could simply seek modification of the judgment by direct motion to the trial court. In re Wilder, 122 Ill. App. 3d 338, 77 Ill. Dec. 824, 461 N.E.2d 447 (1 Dist. 1983).

The portions of the circuit court's orders which modified the provision of the judgment of divorce concerning Bar Mitzvah expenses was reversed, because the settlement unambiguously stated that defendant would pay for the party. In re Roth, 99 Ill. App. 3d 679, 55 Ill. Dec. 271, 426 N.E.2d 246 (1 Dist. 1981).

While the appeal of a prior order was still pending, and the trial court changed the order by specifically adding the following: (1) "that the only material change it could consider would be the termination of plaintiff's social security benefits, and (2) that there was no substantial change in defendant's income since November 26, 1975 order," the trial court did not have authority to modify its order after a notice of appeal from such order had been filed. Dunn v. Dunn, 71 Ill. App. 3d 649, 28 Ill. Dec. 154, 390 N.E.2d 136 (1 Dist. 1979).

Modification of a separation agreement was not permitted where a father was not attempting to relieve himself of his obligation of support when he entered into a property settlement agreement, but on the contrary, when he promised to pay the costs of his daughter's college tuition, and expenses for a scholastic year, without contribution by the plaintiff and without a determination of his ability to pay he was contracting to do more than the law required of him; the property settlement agreement was founded upon sufficient consideration; and the father sought a reduction of his obligation with no reciprocal offer on his part to restore the property rights which the mother released to him. The court could not release one of the contracting parties from terms actually agreed upon but later found disadvantageous when that party had already enjoyed the benefits of the agreement. Gaddis v. Gaddis, 20 Ill. App. 3d 267, 314 N.E.2d 627 (5 Dist. 1974).

—Oral Modification

Where an oral modification between ex-husband and ex-wife was alleged, although the conduct of the parties was not in total accord with the divorce decree, this did not establish that a modification occurred. Gordon v. Joseph, 51 Ill. App. 3d 401, 9 Ill. Dec. 251, 366 N.E.2d 508 (1 Dist. 1977).

—Post-Judgment Relief

A petition under 735 ILCS 5/2-1401 is a proper ground for relief from a divorce decree which incorporates a written agreement which fails to express the real intention of the parties through mutual mistake, or through mistake of one side and fraud on the other, where the proof clearly and convincingly shows that a mistake was made and that it was mutual and common to both parties. In re Johnson, 237 Ill. App. 3d 381, 178 Ill. Dec. 122, 604 N.E.2d 378 (4 Dist. 1992).

—Remarriage of Supporting Parent

A factor the court may consider in an action to modify child support is whether the supporting parent has remarried; this fact is relevant because couples are likely to pool their resources, thereby possibly increasing the resources available to the supporting parent. In re Riegel, 242 Ill. App. 3d 496, 183 Ill. Dec. 168, 611 N.E.2d 21 (3 Dist. 1993).

—Retroactivity

The court did not abuse its discretion in making an increase in child support retroactive to the date the petition was filed, notwithstanding the assertion that the petitioner's delay in responding to discovery slowed the proceedings, where the respondent did not explain how this prejudiced him and did not contend that he did not receive notice of the petition within a short time after it was filed. In re Sweet, 316 Ill. App. 3d 101, 249 Ill. Dec. 212, 735 N.E.2d 1037, 2000 Ill. App. LEXIS 727 (2 Dist. 2000).

With regard to the notice date for purposes of calculating the support amount subject to retroactive abatement, the husband's voluntary dismissal of his first motion to modify was not properly vacated and, therefore, the date of the husband's second motion to modify was the date to which his support obligation could be retroactively abated. In re Semonchik, 315 Ill. App. 3d 395, 248 Ill. Dec. 136, 733 N.E.2d 811, 2000 Ill. App. LEXIS 553 (1 Dist. 2000).

The circuit court erred in requiring the respondent to pay retroactive child support and interest between the date of the judgment of dissolution and when the petition for modification was filed. In re Pettifer, 304 Ill. App. 3d 326, 237 Ill. Dec. 525, 709 N.E.2d 994 (3 Dist. 1999).

Under the Illinois Marriage and Dissolution of Marriage Act, retroactive modification of child support orders is not permitted. In re Smak, 267 Ill. App. 3d 231, 204 Ill. Dec. 551, 641 N.E.2d 981 (2 Dist. 1994).

Although subsection (a) prohibits retroactive modification of an existing order of support, where the trial court determined that no order directing any payment was in existence at the time of the court's finding because the original agreement had expired, no order was in existence to be modified by the trial court and no violation of subsection (a) occurred upon the court's order for retroactive child support. In re Campbell, 252 Ill. App. 3d 653, 191 Ill. Dec. 852, 624 N.E.2d 1230 (1 Dist. 1993), appeal denied, 155 Ill. 2d 562, 198 Ill. Dec. 540, 633 N.E.2d 2 (1994).

Any modification allowed by the court of a child support agreement will only act prospectively. In re Macino, 236 Ill. App. 3d 886, 177 Ill. Dec. 324, 603 N.E.2d 105 (2 Dist. 1992).

The question of whether modification should be retroactive is within the sound discretion of the trial court. In re Heil, 233 Ill. App. 3d 888, 174 Ill. Dec. 622, 599 N.E.2d 168 (5 Dist. 1992).

There was no basis on which to conclude the trial court abused its discretion when it denied retroactive support where husband caused no delay in the court's hearing wife's petition to modify child support, and the court did hear that petition in a timely fashion, and where wife had petitioned the court in 1987 and 1988 for an increase in support based on the same allegations in her 1989 petition, but failed to pursue those claims. In re Carpel, 232 Ill. App. 3d 806, 173 Ill. Dec. 873, 597 N.E.2d 847 (4 Dist.), cert. denied, 147 Ill. 2d 625, 180 Ill. Dec. 148, 606 N.E.2d 1225 (1992).

There was no breach of discretion in the order of the trial court refusing to make a modification order retroactive. Blisset v. Blisset, 144 Ill. App. 3d 1088, 99 Ill. Dec. 161, 495 N.E.2d 608 (4 Dist. 1986), rev'd on other grounds, 123 Ill. 2d 161, 121 Ill. Dec. 931, 526 N.E.2d 125 (1988).

Whether a modification is to be retroactive to the date of the filing of the petition, or any time after, is a matter within the trial court's discretion. Brandt v. Brandt, 99 Ill. App. 3d 1089, 55 Ill. Dec. 78, 425 N.E.2d 1251 (1 Dist. 1981).

Where under the original divorce decree wife was responsible for all medical expenses, and a 1964 modification of the divorce decree requiring the husband to pay medical bills applied only to medical

Modification (Cont'd)

—Retroactivity (Cont'd)

expenses which would be incurred in the future, the trial court erred in assessing husband for one-half of a 1963 medical bill. Berg v. Berg, 85 Ill. App. 2d 98, 229 N.E.2d 282 (1 Dist. 1967).

—Review

When a petition or petitions are filed which seek modification of issues determined in dissolution proceedings, all matters which are interrelated, that is, where the resolution of one affects the outcome of the other, must be determined before an appeal may be filed. In re Stockton, 169 Ill. App. 3d 318, 119 Ill. Dec. 817, 523 N.E.2d 573 (4 Dist. 1988).

—Settlement Agreement

Modification of a maintenance order based on the former wife's receipt of social security disability benefits was not required where the settlement agreement referred to her impending receipt of such benefits. In re Neuman, 295 Ill. App. 3d 212, 230 Ill. Dec. 398, 693 N.E.2d 876 (4 Dist. 1998), appeal denied, 179 Ill. 2d 588, 235 Ill. Dec. 566, 705 N.E.2d 439 (1998).

The marital settlement agreement showed an intent on the part of the parties to preclude modification of maintenance. In re Schweitzer, 289 Ill. App. 3d 425, 225 Ill. Dec. 15, 682 N.E.2d 759 (4 Dist. 1997).

The settlement agreement as reflected in the supplemental judgment of dissolution did not expressly limit reduction of maintenance to the condition of wife's employment, and therefore did not preclude reduction of maintenance based upon a substantial change of circumstances. In re Brent, 263 Ill. App. 3d 916, 200 Ill. Dec. 799, 635 N.E.2d 1382 (4 Dist. 1994).

Where a separation agreement was not incorporated into the judgment, the trial court correctly ruled that the agreement was not modifiable upon a showing of changed circumstances, as the agreement remained a contract enforceable only by contract remedies. In re Dellitt, 213 Ill. App. 3d 155, 156 Ill. Dec. 739, 571 N.E.2d 523 (3 Dist. 1991).

A clause in a settlement agreement prohibiting its modification is effective and not violative of public policy. In re Kozloff, 101 Ill. 2d 526, 79 Ill. Dec. 165, 463 N.E.2d 719 (1984).

—Typographical Error

A petition brought under 735 ILCS 5/2-1401 by former wife was not a property settlement modification which would have violated this section where she brought the petition to merely correct a typographical error and reform the agreement to accurately reflect the intent of all the parties involved. In re Johnson, 237 Ill. App. 3d 381, 178 Ill. Dec. 122, 604 N.E.2d 378 (4 Dist. 1992).

—Upheld

Where an agreed modification of a decree of dissolution provided for a $50 a month rent payment so that former wife could have moved, such modification was consistent with public policy of state. In re Steel, 195 Ill. App. 3d 348, 142 Ill. Dec. 31, 552 N.E.2d 381 (4 Dist. 1990).

Property Disposition

—In General

The award of their interests in the home to the parties in the original dissolution of marriage judgment was a property disposition and not subject to modification as a form of child support. In re Redmer, 111 Ill. App. 3d 317, 66 Ill. Dec. 912, 443 N.E.2d 1075 (2 Dist. 1982).

Provisions of what is construed as a property settlement are not modifiable or revocable unless the court finds the existence of conditions that justify the reopening of a judgment under the laws of this state. In re Lowe, 101 Ill. App. 3d 317, 56 Ill. Dec. 821, 427 N.E.2d 1367 (2 Dist. 1981).

—Between Spouses

It is improper to award the property in a divorce action to the children because the Act contemplates the division of marital property between the spouses. The duty of support normally continues only during the minority of the child and there is no provision in the Act authorizing an outright conveyance of marital property, even in trust, which is unrelated to a child's support or maintenance. In re Smith, 100 Ill. App. 3d 1126, 56 Ill. Dec. 716, 427 N.E.2d 1262 (2 Dist. 1981).

—Changed Circumstances

Where the award to wife of use of the marital residence was not a part of the court's property disposition, but was instead intended to be in the nature of an award of additional maintenance and child support, the duration of her occupancy was modifiable upon a showing of substantially changed circumstances. In re Stanley, 133 Ill. App. 3d 963, 89 Ill. Dec. 146, 479 N.E.2d 1152 (4 Dist. 1985).

—Civil Procedure

Under this Act, conditions that justify the reopening of a judgment under the laws permit the revocation or modification of provisions as to property disposition. In re Beck, 83 Ill. App. 3d 976, 39 Ill. Dec. 381, 404 N.E.2d 972 (2 Dist. 1980).

—Consent Decree

A consent decree regarding a property settlement did not affect the question of divorce, which was beyond the power of the parties to adjust by agreement or collusion, and as a contract, it was binding on the parties unless induced by fraud. Garmisa v. Garmisa, 4 Ill. App. 3d 134, 280 N.E.2d 458 (1 Dist. 1972).

—Credit

Since the right to receive a past-due alimony payment and the right to be relieved of paying taxes on a marital home were similar in that both were economic benefits, a supplemental judgment for divorce was modified to give the plaintiff full credit for having paid the taxes when the marital home was sold. Laing v. Laing, 55 Ill. App. 3d 231, 13 Ill. Dec. 462, 371 N.E.2d 157 (2 Dist. 1977).

—Fraud or Coercion

Generally, provisions as to property dispositions may not be modified, however, a settlement agreement will be set aside and vacated if procured by fraud, coercion, or if contrary to any rule of law, public policy, or morals. In re Lipkin, 163 Ill. App. 3d 1033, 115 Ill. Dec. 76, 517 N.E.2d 41 (4 Dist. 1987).

A decree disposing of property upon divorce, based upon a separation agreement procured by fraud or coercion, may be modified via a motion under 735 ILCS 5/2-1401 if the injured party acts with reasonable diligence. In re Beck, 83 Ill. App. 3d 976, 39 Ill. Dec. 381, 404 N.E.2d 972 (2 Dist. 1980).

—In Lieu of Maintenance

The husband's assumption of car loan payments was in the nature of a property settlement in lieu of maintenance and did not terminate when the wife remarried, because the judgment provided that: the husband would pay the loan according to its current schedule; the loan was for a specific sum to be paid over a specific period of time; except for the husband's payment of the marital debts, each party would surrender all claims to maintenance and all claims to the property of the other spouse; marital property was divided by a court giving consideration to whether the appointment was in lieu of maintenance; and neither the label attached nor the method of payment prescribed in the judgment conclusively determined the nature of the award. In re Rowden, 163 Ill. App. 3d 869, 114 Ill. Dec. 886, 516 N.E.2d 1041 (3 Dist. 1987).

—Maintenance Distinguished

Monthly payments former husband made towards payoff of a loan on a car, which was awarded to his former wife under the parties marital settlement agreement, were part of the parties property settlement and did not constitute maintenance, even though the settlement agreement referred to them as maintenance; thus, the payments could not be terminated under 750 ILCS 5/510(c) regardless of the wife's living arrangement with a new boyfriend. In re Dundas, Ill. App. 3d , 291 Ill. Dec. 229, 823 N.E.2d 239, 2005 Ill. App. LEXIS 85 (2 Dist. 2005).

The parties to a divorce intended that their agreement constitute a property settlement, where the agreement plainly provided that the payments were for and in consideration of the wife quitclaiming her interest in various pieces of marital property, both parties expressly waived all claims to alimony, and the agreement's provision for a definite total sum was to be paid at the end of a definite period of time rather than on a periodic basis for an indefinite period of time which is characteristic of maintenance. In re Lowe, 101 Ill. App. 3d 317, 56 Ill. Dec. 821, 427 N.E.2d 1367 (2 Dist. 1981).

Property Disposition (Cont'd)

—Marital Home

Award of exclusive possession of the marital home to wife unambiguously constituted a property disposition which could not be modified and not an award of nonmonetary child support or other modifiable subsidy. Taber v. Taber, 248 Ill. App. 3d 435, 187 Ill. Dec. 931, 618 N.E.2d 522 (1 Dist. 1993).

—Modification of Agreement

The awarding of exclusive possession of the residence to petitioner was in the nature of a property settlement where this award was part of the paragraph awarding two parcels of real property, both previously owned in joint tenancy, to the respondent, in return for quitclaiming to respondent all her interests in the property, petitioner was allowed to remain in the premises unless she remarried; this conclusion is buttressed by the fact that a different paragraph of the decree provided for monetary payments to petitioner of up to $1,000 each year depending on respondent's level of income, therefore, the trial court improperly modified a property settlement provision of the original divorce decree. In re Christianson, 89 Ill. App. 3d 167, 44 Ill. Dec. 397, 411 N.E.2d 519 (3 Dist. 1980).

—Modification Improper

Husband's obligation to pay the outstanding indebtedness on a house owed to bank amounted to a nonmodifiable property settlement in lieu of maintenance, and was not periodic maintenance terminable on the wife's remarriage. In re Gallentine, 216 Ill. App. 3d 1067, 159 Ill. Dec. 906, 576 N.E.2d 575 (3 Dist. 1991).

Provisions in a judgment of dissolution which constitute a disposition of property or property settlement are generally not modifiable or revocable as property rights created by such judgment become vested when judgment is final, therefore court lacks general jurisdiction to modify. In re Hubbard, 215 Ill. App. 3d 113, 158 Ill. Dec. 747, 574 N.E.2d 860 (2 Dist. 1991).

Circuit court's determination to modify the property settlement agreement requiring petitioner to pay the entire sum of the monthly mortgage payments as they came due was in error as a matter of law because the award was a property disposition and nonmodifiable under subsection (a) of this section. In re Pitts, 169 Ill. App. 3d 200, 119 Ill. Dec. 908, 523 N.E.2d 664 (5 Dist. 1988).

Subsection (a) of this section did not grant the trial court the broad authority upon which it relied to vary the terms of the initial marriage dissolution judgment. In re Redmer, 111 Ill. App. 3d 317, 66 Ill. Dec. 912, 443 N.E.2d 1075 (2 Dist. 1982).

Pursuant to section 18 of the former Divorce Act (see now this section), provisions respecting the disposition of the parties' property incorporated in a divorce decree are not subject to modification, whether labeled a property settlement or an award of alimony in gross payable in installments. Lamp v. Lamp, 73 Ill. App. 3d 713, 29 Ill. Dec. 792, 392 N.E.2d 349 (5 Dist. 1979), aff'd, 81 Ill. 2d 364, 43 Ill. Dec. 31, 410 N.E.2d 31 (1980).

—Modification Proper

Where petitioner did not contend that the trial court's order was, in fact, a modification of maintenance or support, the order at issue could only affect the property disposition contained in the judgment; thus, the trial court had jurisdiction to enter an order modifying the property disposition only if conditions existed which would justify the reopening of a judgment as in other civil cases. In re Hubbard, 215 Ill. App. 3d 113, 158 Ill. Dec. 747, 574 N.E.2d 860 (2 Dist. 1991).

—Power of Court

In determining the propriety or impropriety of divorce decree ordering conveyance of property under former section 17 of the Divorce Act, the authority of the court was based upon powers conferred by statute rather than upon general equity powers. Debrey v. Debrey, 132 Ill. App. 2d 1072, 270 N.E.2d 43 (4 Dist. 1971).

—Property Settlement Agreement

When a party seeks to vacate or modify a property settlement incorporated in a divorce decree, all presumptions are in favor of the validity of the settlement. Garmisa v. Garmisa, 4 Ill. App. 3d 411, 280 N.E.2d 444 (1 Dist. 1972).

—Rent for Marital Home

Where under the terms of a dissolution judgment, defendant had "the right to the exclusive possession of the marital home for a period of six years or until his remarriage," and plaintiff moved to have defendant's girl friend ousted from the marital residence to have the house sold pursuant to conditions set forth in the dissolution judgment to collect certain rental payments for the period during which the girl friend lived with defendant in the house, the award of rental payments to plaintiff was plainly improper and would be set aside since the circuit court made no finding that the judgment should be reopened, and plaintiff never claimed that conditions existed which would have justified its being reopened. Meyer v. Meyer, 222 Ill. App. 3d 357, 164 Ill. Dec. 800, 583 N.E.2d 716 (5 Dist. 1991).

—Revestment

The trial court, under the doctrine of revestment, had jurisdiction to modify a property disposition more than 30 days after entry of the original judgment without satisfying the requirements of this section. Elmore v. Elmore, 219 Ill. App. 3d 61, 162 Ill. Dec. 656, 580 N.E.2d 619 (3 Dist. 1991).

—Settlement

A property settlement is a sum certain, often payable in installments, passing between the parties as consideration for their release of marital rights. In re Lowe, 101 Ill. App. 3d 317, 56 Ill. Dec. 821, 427 N.E.2d 1367 (2 Dist. 1981).

—Trust

Trial court was not required to make a finding of special circumstances that a trust was necessary to protect and promote the best interests of the parties' children before requiring husband to name wife as trustee for the benefit of their sons on husband's life insurance policies for the benefit of the parties' two sons until the completion of their college education or emancipation. In re Olson, 223 Ill. App. 3d 636, 166 Ill. Dec. 60, 585 N.E.2d 1082 (2 Dist.), appeal denied, 145 Ill. 2d 636, 173 Ill. Dec. 6, 596 N.E.2d 630 (1992).

Remarriage

Where the petitioner agreed to a modified judgment after the respondent had remarried, implicit in the agreement was a waiver of the remarriage provision. In re Adamson, 308 Ill. App. 3d 759, 242 Ill. Dec. 198, 721 N.E.2d 166 (2 Dist. 1999).

Remarriage of the parties does render the prior divorce decree unenforceable. In re Parks, 258 Ill. App. 3d 479, 196 Ill. Dec. 574, 630 N.E.2d 509 (5 Dist. 1994).

The first Illinois case to discuss the effect of a remarriage upon a prior divorce decree is In re Marriage of Leon (1980), 84 Ill. App. 3d 50, 39 Ill. Dec. 480, 404 N.E.2d 1071, where the court held that the trial court in a first divorce action is divested of further jurisdiction with regard to the division of property upon the subsequent remarriage and redivorce of the parties. In re Parks, 258 Ill. App. 3d 479, 196 Ill. Dec. 574, 630 N.E.2d 509 (5 Dist. 1994).

The term "remarriage" as it appears in this section means the ceremony of marriage and not the status of marriage, and the declaration of the invalidity of petitioner's remarriage did not act to reinstate the maintenance obligation. In re Harris, 203 Ill. App. 3d 241, 148 Ill. Dec. 541, 560 N.E.2d 1138 (1 Dist. 1990).

Marriage settlement agreements may extend maintenance payments beyond the recipient's remarriage. Broadway Bank v. Kakos, 160 Ill. App. 3d 6, 111 Ill. Dec. 851, 513 N.E.2d 97 (1 Dist. 1987).

Remarriage of the recipient spouse does not automatically reduce an unallocated award of maintenance and child support; rather, as is required in other cases where a modification is sought, the party desiring the reduction must petition the court to modify its prior decree. In re Erickson, 136 Ill. App. 3d 907, 91 Ill. Dec. 346, 483 N.E.2d 692 (2 Dist. 1985).

Where ex-husband ceased his alimony payments on the remarriage of his ex-wife but voluntarily resumed his alimony payments upon the judicial declaration of invalidity of his ex-wife's remarriage, the actions of the parties evidenced an intent that the term remarriage, as used in the parties' decree of divorce, referred to a status of marriage rather than a ceremony of marriage. Thomas v. Thomas, 111 Ill. App. 3d 1032, 67 Ill. Dec. 590, 444 N.E.2d 826 (4 Dist. 1983).

Remarriage (Cont'd)

The trial court properly denied former husband retroactive recovery of a portion of the monthly payments made to former spouse during the period she resided with her present husband before her marriage, where the payments were characterized as child support. In re Kessler, 110 Ill. App. 3d 61, 65 Ill. Dec. 707, 441 N.E.2d 1221 (1 Dist. 1982).

The provisions of a consent decree that the husband pay each year for two plastic eyes required by the wife violated the public policy against payment of alimony and maintenance after remarriage and was therefore a nullity. Balasa v. Balasa, 11 Ill. App. 2d 103, 136 N.E.2d 594 (1 Dist. 1956).

Res Judicata

The trial court was not barred by res judicata from considering facts that were new since the last hearing in relation to the propriety of the maintenance award. In re Connors, 303 Ill. App. 3d 219, 236 Ill. Dec. 430, 707 N.E.2d 275 (2 Dist. 1999).

Res judicata and collateral estoppel did not bar husband's action for arrearage in wife's contributions to children's educational expenses. Wife's action seeking an increase in child support had no effect on husband's action seeking reimbursement from wife for her alleged failure to contribute to children's college expenses. In re Potts, 186 Ill. App. 3d 273, 134 Ill. Dec. 179, 542 N.E.2d 179 (3 Dist. 1989).

While the decree is conclusive and res judicata as to all facts and circumstances existing prior to its entry, the court has the continuing power, for causes accruing subsequent to its entry, to modify the provisions of the decree to meet the changed conditions of the parties. Scalfaro v. Scalfaro, 123 Ill. App. 2d 23, 259 N.E.2d 644 (1 Dist. 1970).

Retirement

Whether a spouse may rely on his retirement as a change in circumstances to justify the modification of maintenance depends upon the circumstances of each individual case; relevant factors include his age, health, motives and timing of retirement, ability to pay maintenance after retirement, and the former spouse's ability to provide for herself. In re Waller, 253 Ill. App. 3d 360, 192 Ill. Dec. 403, 625 N.E.2d 363 (1 Dist. 1993).

Revestment

The court had authority to modify the distribution of proceeds under the doctrine of revestment; under this doctrine, litigants may revest a court which has general jurisdiction over the matter, with both personal and subject matter jurisdiction, over the particular cause after the 30 day period following final judgment during which post-judgment motions must ordinarily be filed. In re Demond, 142 Ill. App. 3d 134, 96 Ill. Dec. 455, 491 N.E.2d 501 (5 Dist. 1986); Elmore v. Elmore, 219 Ill. App. 3d 61, 162 Ill. Dec. 656, 580 N.E.2d 619 (3 Dist. 1991).

In order for the revestment rule to apply, the parties must actively participate without objection in proceedings which are inconsistent with the merits of the prior judgment. In re Demond, 142 Ill. App. 3d 134, 96 Ill. Dec. 455, 491 N.E.2d 501 (5 Dist. 1986).

Review

—Abuse of Discretion

Defendant failed to demonstrate that the court abused its discretion in modifying a divorce decree. Harding v. Harding, 59 Ill. App. 3d 25, 16 Ill. Dec. 426, 374 N.E.2d 1304 (4 Dist. 1978).

—Discretion of Court

The modification of child support provisions rests in the sound discretion of the trial court and will not be interfered with in the absence of an abuse of that discretion or unless a manifest injustice has been done. In re Runge, 102 Ill. App. 3d 356, 58 Ill. Dec. 116, 430 N.E.2d 58 (1 Dist. 1981).

Although the modification or termination of alimony provisions in a divorce decree rests in the sound judicial discretion of the trial court, such a modification or termination must not be made arbitrarily or capriciously, but rather must be equitable and must be based upon a showing of a substantial change in the circumstances of the parties. Gorman v. Gorman, 72 Ill. App. 3d 658, 28 Ill. Dec. 871, 391 N.E.2d 70 (1 Dist. 1979).

Modification of a divorce decree rests in the sound discretion of the trial court, and courts of review will not disturb its findings unless the evidence clearly so requires. Dendrinos v. Dendrinos, 58 Ill. App. 3d 639, 16 Ill. Dec. 241, 374 N.E.2d 1016 (1 Dist. 1978).

Whether the alimony to be paid by the defendant should have been terminated rested in the sound discretion of the court. Tan v. Tan, 3 Ill. App. 3d 671, 279 N.E.2d 486 (1 Dist. 1972).

Alteration of an order respecting support payments rests in the sound judicial discretion of the trial court, and unless the record shows an abuse of that discretion such an order will generally not be disturbed on review. Edwards v. Edwards, 125 Ill. App. 2d 91, 259 N.E.2d 820 (4 Dist. 1970).

The modification of provisions for the payment of alimony and child support rests in the sound discretion of the court and a reviewing court will not interfere with the exercise of such discretion in the absence of its abuse. Scalfaro v. Scalfaro, 123 Ill. App. 2d 23, 259 N.E.2d 644 (1 Dist. 1970).

—Insufficient Record

Where there was no indication of the court's judgment concerning the evidence on husband's allegedly greater income, wife's allegedly greater need, and the causes underlying such but the record merely consisted of the testimony of the parties, the argument of their counsel, and general "findings" in the order, then the appellate court was unable to assess the validity of the circuit court's decision and remanded the case to give the circuit court the opportunity to indicate on the record its rationale underlying the exercise of discretion which it undertook. In re Chalkley, 99 Ill. App. 3d 478, 55 Ill. Dec. 262, 426 N.E.2d 237 (1 Dist. 1981).

—New Hearing Required

Where the statements of the circuit court reflected that it did not give appropriate significance to the evidence and was laboring under the misconception of the law applicable to a petition for modification of support and attorney's fees, that misconception deprived the wife of fair hearing on her petition and entitled wife to new hearing. Powers v. Powers, 69 Ill. App. 3d 485, 26 Ill. Dec. 452, 388 N.E.2d 76 (1 Dist. 1979).

—Standard

The findings of the trial court in an action to increase support payments will not be reversed unless contrary to the manifest weight of the evidence. Grinton v. Grinton, 131 Ill. App. 2d 684, 264 N.E.2d 845 (3 Dist. 1970).

Settlement Agreement

If parties to a marital settlement agreement intend, on dissolution, to preclude judicial modification of maintenance as to amount, it may be better practice to do so in clear and express terms in a paragraph separate from that limiting termination of maintenance. In re Brent, 263 Ill. App. 3d 916, 200 Ill. Dec. 799, 635 N.E.2d 1382 (4 Dist. 1994).

While maintenance provisions are modifiable upon a showing of a substantial change in circumstances, property settlement provisions are not, unless a court finds the execution of the settlement agreement was accompanied by some element of fraud, coercion or misrepresentation. In re Munford, 173 Ill. App. 3d 576, 123 Ill. Dec. 254, 527 N.E.2d 892 (1 Dist. 1988).

Where the agreement contained no provision which specifically precluded modification, the agreement was modifiable. In re Martino, 166 Ill. App. 3d 692, 117 Ill. Dec. 788, 520 N.E.2d 1139 (2 Dist. 1988).

Once an agreement is embodied in a divorce decree, its terms will not be modified absent fraud, coercion or contrariness to public policy. In re Roth, 99 Ill. App. 3d 679, 55 Ill. Dec. 271, 426 N.E.2d 246 (1 Dist. 1981).

The power of the court to modify periodic payments of maintenance and child support is not diminished because the amount of payments was fixed by a settlement agreement agreed to by the parties and incorporated in the decree. Potocki v. Potocki, 98 Ill. App. 3d 501, 53 Ill. Dec. 923, 424 N.E.2d 714 (1 Dist. 1981).

Standing

The Department of Public Aid had standing to bring a petition to modify a child support obligation on behalf of a public aid recipients without regard to any assignment of an arrearage to the Department. Illinois Dep't of Pub. Aid ex rel. Marshall v. Ringo, 303 Ill. App. 3d 250, 236 Ill. Dec. 173, 706 N.E.2d 1047 (3 Dist. 1999).

The filing of a petition to modify a child support obligation is a support service contemplated under the Public Aid Code (305 ILCS

Standing (Cont'd)
5/10-1 et seq.) providing the department with standing to file a petition. Illinois Dep't of Pub. Aid ex rel. Marshall v. Ringo, 303 Ill. App. 3d 250, 236 Ill. Dec. 173, 706 N.E.2d 1047 (3 Dist. 1999).

Support

—In General

Bankruptcy court determined that the Illinois state court ordered child support debt was nondischargeable; the court found that the debtor waited too long after his divorce and after he assumed the responsibility of support payments to challenge paternity of the child and get retroactive relief, pursuant to 750 ILCS 45/5(a)(1). Alter v. Ill. Dep't of Pub. Aid (In re Alter), 301 Bankr. 300, 2003 Bankr. LEXIS 1485 (Bankr. C.D. Ill. 2003).

"Support" is simply a general term that can include educational expenses for a child who has turned 18 but is still in high school, and educational expenses may include room and board, just as the more generic term, support, may include shelter and food; a trial court can award support to disabled unemancipated children, minor or nonminor under 750 ILCS 5/513(a)(1), and a particular kind of support, educational expenses, to nonminor children in school under 750 ILCS 5/513(a)(2). In short, if the child has attained majority, the trial court must turn to § 513 of the Illinois Marriage and Dissolution of Marriage Act, 750 ILCS 5/513, when deciding whether to award support for that nonminor child. Waller v. Waller, 339 Ill. App. 3d 743, 274 Ill. Dec. 582, 791 N.E.2d 674, 2003 Ill. App. LEXIS 766 (4 Dist. 2003).

Subsection (a) of this section allows for modification of child support orders only upon a showing of substantial change in circumstances, and the burden of proof is on the party who seeks the modification. In re Fuesting, 228 Ill. App. 3d 339, 169 Ill. Dec. 456, 591 N.E.2d 960 (5 Dist. 1992).

Where no benefit accrued to the custodial parent by the noncustodial parent's action of reducing the received child support, and it could not be concluded that the payor's actions were the result of apparent or implied authority or that there was a principal and agent relationship between the parties, consequently, the legal concept of ratification was misapplied. In re Jackson, 179 Ill. App. 3d 479, 128 Ill. Dec. 505, 534 N.E.2d 687 (5 Dist. 1989).

This section guarantees the dependent minor child of divorced parents from loss of support through disinheritance; while a divorced parent is free to disinherit a child of his divorced marriage, he may do so only subject to the limited obligation of support. In re Dulyn, 89 Ill. App. 3d 304, 44 Ill. Dec. 622, 411 N.E.2d 988 (1 Dist. 1980).

The paramount concern in child support litigation is the support of the minor children. Gentile v. Gentile, 69 Ill. App. 3d 297, 26 Ill. Dec. 149, 387 N.E.2d 979 (3 Dist. 1979).

In a modification proceeding, the fact that at least a part of a trial court's reasoning consisted of the assumption that the parties knew what they were getting into was not a valid basis for affirming a divorce agreement which provided for no child support. Cross v. Cross, 48 Ill. App. 3d 1055, 7 Ill. Dec. 12, 363 N.E.2d 933 (3 Dist. 1977).

—Accounting

Since it was within the trial court's discretion, due to fluctuations in husband's income, to order respondent husband to submit a quarterly accounting of his net income to petitioner wife, the child support order was modified to require an annual accounting. Smith v. Smith, 78 Ill. App. 3d 80, 33 Ill. Dec. 717, 397 N.E.2d 50 (1 Dist. 1979).

—Arrearages

Where the testimony of the plaintiff and defendant was directly in conflict with respect to the extent with which defendant had met his child support obligation to spend an additional $15 per month per child, the trial court had the responsibility of resolving this conflict and to determine the credibility of witnesses; the finding of the trial court under such conditions should be approved unless it is found to be contrary to the manifest weight of the evidence. Neeland v. Neeland, 17 Ill. App. 3d 803, 308 N.E.2d 651 (3 Dist. 1974).

Past-due installments of child support are a vested right, and the court has no authority to modify them, either as to amount or time of payment. Gregory v. Gregory, 52 Ill. App. 2d 262, 202 N.E.2d 139 (5 Dist. 1964).

—Burden of Proof

A trial court may, on application, terminate or make such alterations in the allowance of child support, as shall appear reasonable and proper and the burden of proof is on the person seeking modification to show such material change in circumstances as would warrant modification. In re McDavid, 97 Ill. App. 3d 1044, 54 Ill. Dec. 577, 425 N.E.2d 442 (1 Dist. 1981).

—Calculation

Per diem payments made to the husband, an over-the-road truck driver, constituted income for the purpose of calculating child support but could be deducted from income to the extent the husband proved he used those payments for actual travel expenses, but the husband had the burden of proving his actual expenses and of establishing a lawful basis for deducting them. Worrall v. Worrall, 334 Ill. App. 3d 550, 268 Ill. Dec. 411, 778 N.E.2d 397, 2002 Ill. App. LEXIS 972 (2 Dist. 2002).

Because the language "$30.00 child support" was susceptible of being understood as ordering respondent to make either a lump sum payment in the amount of $30 or periodic payments in $30 increments, and the record did not justify an interpretation of $30 per week child support, the award calculated on the basis of that interpretation was improper. In re Szczotka, 87 Ill. App. 3d 314, 42 Ill. Dec. 559, 409 N.E.2d 54 (1 Dist. 1980).

—Change in Circumstances

The uncontroverted evidence was such that the child support order should have been reduced or modified to reflect respondent's financial resources which at best could have been described as limited. In re Donovan, 122 Ill. App. 3d 803, 78 Ill. Dec. 293, 462 N.E.2d 9 (4 Dist. 1984).

In order to justify a decrease in child support payments, the moving party is required to show a significant material change in the circumstances and conditions of the divorced parents since the entry of the original divorce decree. Gentile v. Gentile, 69 Ill. App. 3d 297, 26 Ill. Dec. 149, 387 N.E.2d 979 (3 Dist. 1979).

The issue before the trial court on a motion to modify child support payments was whether the circumstances of the parties and the children had materially changed since the divorce decree, and only if that were so would a modification of the child support be proper. Gentile v. Gentile, 69 Ill. App. 3d 297, 26 Ill. Dec. 149, 387 N.E.2d 979 (3 Dist. 1979).

In all cases where petitions to modify payments under a divorce decree are involved, the primary question is whether or not changes in circumstances of the parties justify the modification. Bulmer v. Bulmer, 28 Ill. App. 3d 406, 328 N.E.2d 622 (5 Dist. 1975).

In an application for modification or termination of support, the only inquiry should be whether sufficient cause has intervened since the entry of the decree to authorize the court to change the allowance. Borowitz v. Borowitz, 19 Ill. App. 3d 176, 311 N.E.2d 292 (1 Dist. 1974).

—Child Support

Child support provisions in a dissolution agreement adopted by the trial court are void, in excess of the court's jurisdiction, if the trial court could not order those provisions in the absence of the agreement. In re Sheetz, 254 Ill. App. 3d 695, 194 Ill. Dec. 38, 627 N.E.2d 154 (1 Dist. 1993).

——Life Insurance

In a divorce case, where there was no reason to believe that the husband, or his estate, would not be able to provide the mandated child support, the trial court's decision not to require the husband to maintain a life insurance policy naming his children as the irrevocable beneficiaries was not against the manifest weight of the evidence. Schneider v. Schneider, 343 Ill. App. 3d 628, 278 Ill. Dec. 485, 798 N.E.2d 1242, 2003 Ill. App. LEXIS 1295 (2 Dist. 2003).

—Consent Decrees

The statutory power of a court to reduce the amount of periodic payments, whether by way of alimony or child support, is not defeated by the fixing of the amount of the payments in a settlement agreement which was incorporated in the decree. Lamp v. Lamp, 81 Ill. 2d 364, 43 Ill. Dec. 31, 410 N.E.2d 31 (1980).

Support (Cont'd)

—Continuing Jurisdiction

Regardless of the presence or absence of any language limiting modification of contract terms, provisions relating to the support of minor children are always modifiable. Burks v. Burks, 100 Ill. App. 3d 700, 56 Ill. Dec. 273, 427 N.E.2d 353 (1 Dist. 1981).

A court is concerned with the adequacy of a child support award when made; the wife can always petition for an increase in the future. In re Smith, 100 Ill. App. 3d 1126, 56 Ill. Dec. 716, 427 N.E.2d 1262 (2 Dist. 1981).

—Contract

While defendant was under no legal obligation to leave his estate or any part of it to the children and his obligation to do so was created by contract and only by the contract, the contract could not be altered without his consent and the court was without authority to modify it or to enter a decree contrary to it. Herhold v. Herhold, 123 Ill. App. 2d 293, 260 N.E.2d 86 (1970).

—Cost of Living Increase

Evidence presented to the trial court indicated that the cost of supporting a child had substantially increased and that defendant's income had substantially increased so as to enable him to pay this additional amount; in light of this evidence it was error for the trial court not to order the defendant to pay modified amount plaintiff sought for child support. Grinton v. Grinton, 131 Ill. App. 2d 684, 264 N.E.2d 845 (3 Dist. 1970).

—Death of Obligor

Subsection (c) of this section provides that the obligation to support, unless otherwise agreed in writing or provided in the judgment, will survive the death of the parent obliged to provide child support and seeks to protect the dependent child of divorced parents from loss of support through disinheritance, a loss from which a child of nondivorced parents is indirectly insulated. DeFrancesca v. Estate of Champagne, 153 Ill. App. 3d 560, 106 Ill. Dec. 561, 505 N.E.2d 1352 (2 Dist. 1987).

An order under 750 ILCS 5/513 for education and maintenance of a child, whether of minor or majority age, is intended to be included within subsection (c) of this section the same as a support order and is not terminated by the death of a parent obligated to pay for these expenses. DeFrancesca v. Estate of Champagne, 153 Ill. App. 3d 560, 106 Ill. Dec. 561, 505 N.E.2d 1352 (2 Dist. 1987).

An order of support for a non-minor child, although only to be granted under special circumstances under 750 ILCS 5/513 is the same as any other order of support and does not terminate upon the death of the parent obligated to pay the support unless otherwise agreed in writing or expressly provided in the judgment. DeFrancesca v. Estate of Champagne, 153 Ill. App. 3d 560, 106 Ill. Dec. 561, 505 N.E.2d 1352 (2 Dist. 1987).

Subsection (c) of this section authorizes modification of child support, when a parent obligated to pay support dies, "to the extent just and appropriate in the circumstances"; however, no modification of a support order is warranted where the decedent has adequately provided for the children. Halas v. McCaskey, 104 Ill. 2d 83, 83 Ill. Dec. 540, 470 N.E.2d 960 (1984).

No modification of a support order is warranted where the person obligated to pay support has adequately provided for the children in a testamentary device. Halas v. Executor of Estate of Halas, 112 Ill. App. 3d 940, 68 Ill. Dec. 411, 445 N.E.2d 1264 (1 Dist. 1983).

Subsection (c) of this section seeks to protect the dependent child of divorced parents from loss of support through disinheritance, a loss from which a child of nondivorced parents is indirectly insulated; a divorced parent is still free to disinherit a child of his divorced marriage, subject only to the limited obligation of support. Kujawinski v. Kujawinski, 71 Ill. 2d 563, 17 Ill. Dec. 801, 376 N.E.2d 1382 (1978).

Since an original decree made no provision for support of the minor children by the father, the former wife's petition filed after the father's death constituted in effect an effort to enforce a claim against plaintiff's estate for child support unrelated to the divorce decree, and, since the death of the plaintiff rendered it impossible for the trial court to enter any personal decree against him, there could be no basis for granting relief provided by an amended decree under former Ill.Rev.Stat., ch. 40, para. 19 (see now this section). Kramp v. Kramp, 2 Ill. App. 2d 17, 117 N.E.2d 859 (3 Dist. 1954).

—Delayed Modification

Where at the time the petition for modification was filed, the defendant was receiving his full salary, he had incurred additional expenses because of a heart attack, but he had also recently received an inheritance, the trial court properly found that reduction of his alimony and support payments was not justified at the time of the filing of the petition, but that a modification was justified effective six months later. Vail v. Vail, 98 Ill. App. 234, 240 N.E.2d 519 (1968).

—Determination

Support should be determined by accommodating the needs of the children with the available means of the parties. In re Riegel, 242 Ill. App. 3d 496, 183 Ill. Dec. 168, 611 N.E.2d 21 (3 Dist. 1993).

—Discretion of Court

Modification of child support payments rests within the sound discretion of the trial court. Legan v. Legan, 69 Ill. App. 3d 304, 25 Ill. Dec. 757, 387 N.E.2d 413 (3 Dist. 1979).

—Dissolution Judgment

Where respondent husband did not object to the terms of the dissolution judgment imposing support obligations solely on him, and where he never appealed the dissolution judgment, the trial court properly ordered that the noncustodial wife was not required to pay child support. In re Kraft, 217 Ill. App. 3d 502, 160 Ill. Dec. 392, 577 N.E.2d 522 (2 Dist. 1991).

Trial court erred in striking husband's petition to modify dissolution judgment granting child support that was filed after notice of appeal and cross appeal. In re Petramale, 102 Ill. App. 3d 1049, 58 Ill. Dec. 537, 430 N.E.2d 569 (2 Dist. 1981).

—Effect of Agreement or Consent Decree

The court has power to modify a decree or order as to child support and educational payments and there are no exceptions in regard to prior agreements or "consent decrees;" the trial court is not deprived of the power to modify a consent decree. Duvall v. Duvall, 8 Ill. App. 3d 53, 289 N.E.2d 59 (3 Dist. 1972).

—Emancipation

Section 510(a) of the Illinois Marriage and Dissolution of Marriage Act, 750 ILCS 5/510(a), imposes conditions for modifying an order of support and, on its face, makes no exception for extending the period during which the parent must pay support; there was no change in circumstances within the meaning of 750 ILCS 5/510(a)(1) in a child's eighteenth birthday coming before his graduation from high school where the parties must have know, from the child's birth date, that he would reach the age of majority before graduating from high school. Waller v. Waller, 339 Ill. App. 3d 743, 274 Ill. Dec. 582, 791 N.E.2d 674, 2003 Ill. App. LEXIS 766 (4 Dist. 2003).

Minor child was not emancipated prior to her reaching age 18 where she earned approximately $41 per week from her part-time job, she did not seek to be financially independent and she had not abandoned her mother's home despite the fact that she quit school against her father's wishes. In re Donahoe, 114 Ill. App. 3d 470, 70 Ill. Dec. 152, 448 N.E.2d 1030 (2 Dist. 1983).

The modification of a divorce decree was not arbitrary or capricious where the reduction of child support payments was justified by the substantial change in circumstances consisting of the fact that two of the plaintiff's children had reached majority and ceased to be under plaintiff's care and custody. Thomas v. Thomas, 23 Ill. App. 3d 936, 321 N.E.2d 159 (1 Dist. 1974).

Where by stipulation at the time of divorce, a former husband agreed to pay child support only during the minority of his children, appellant's legal obligation to support his daughter ceased on her eighteenth birthday. Stecher v. Stecher, 16 Ill. App. 3d 297, 306 N.E.2d 86 (5 Dist. 1973).

—Equitable Estoppel

The doctrine of equitable estoppel is an exception to the otherwise inflexible rule that alimony and child support payments become vested when and as they accrue. Jozwick v. Jozwick, 72 Ill. App. 3d 17, 28 Ill. Dec. 321, 390 N.E.2d 488 (1 Dist. 1979).

—Estate Liability

This section cannot be construed as providing that the support obligation is to be considered a priority claim against an estate.

Support (Cont'd)

—Estate Liability (Cont'd)

Meyers v. Meyers, 113 Ill. App. 3d 886, 68 Ill. Dec. 721, 446 N.E.2d 892 (2 Dist. 1983).

A parent's estate is liable for that parent's support obligation to the extent just and appropriate in the circumstances, and the court may determine at the time of the dissolution of the marriage the amount of support for which a deceased parent's estate will be held liable. In re Dulyn, 89 Ill. App. 3d 304, 44 Ill. Dec. 622, 411 N.E.2d 988 (1 Dist. 1980).

—Factors Considered

When setting an amount for modification of child support, the court may consider the same factors used when formulating an original support order; these factors include the standard of living the child would have enjoyed if the marriage had not been dissolved, and the financial resources of the noncustodial parent. In re Boyden, 164 Ill. App. 3d 385, 115 Ill. Dec. 458, 517 N.E.2d 1144 (2 Dist. 1987).

The factors to be considered for modification or termination as to each party are: (1) their ages, social conditions, health, and whether there are any children dependent upon them for support, (2) the duration of the marriage, since the longer the marriage the greater a woman's claim for support becomes, and (3) their agreement as to the property settlement adopted in the divorce decree. Gorman v. Gorman, 72 Ill. App. 3d 658, 28 Ill. Dec. 871, 391 N.E.2d 70 (1 Dist. 1979).

—Failure to Pay

Noncompliance with a court order to make support payments is prima facie evidence of contempt. In re Dunseth, 260 Ill. App. 3d 816, 198 Ill. Dec. 620, 633 N.E.2d 82 (4 Dist. 1994).

Where defendant's inability to pay child support was because of economic circumstances, the court was correct to find that an employment layoff and an attempt to become self-employed were not attempts to evade financial responsibility. In re Hardy, 191 Ill. App. 3d 685, 138 Ill. Dec. 909, 548 N.E.2d 139 (5 Dist. 1989).

Father, who did not make child support payments because of reliance on a late 1967 order which relieved him of the obligation to make such payments, and who did not wilfully and contumaciously refuse to obey the child support provision of the divorce decree warranted the refusal by the trial court to issue a rule to show cause against father. Gentile v. Gentile, 87 Ill. App. 3d 311, 42 Ill. Dec. 557, 409 N.E.2d 52 (1 Dist. 1980).

—Failure to Reinstate Obligation

The trial court, after entering an order suspending a husband's child support payments during a period when the husband was disabled, could not subsequently hold the husband responsible for payments accruing after the disability had ended, when the court failed to reinstate the obligation according to the terms of its own order. Rodgers v. Rodgers, 118 Ill. App. 3d 334, 73 Ill. Dec. 904, 454 N.E.2d 1153 (5 Dist. 1983).

—Held Sufficient

Trial court's finding that children were adequately provided for was supported by the evidence when $604,000, in addition to a portion of the annual alimony payments, had become available to provide for the two children's support upon decedent's death. Halas v. McCaskey, 104 Ill. 2d 83, 83 Ill. Dec. 540, 470 N.E.2d 960 (1984).

Child support of $200 per month for a 16 year old was not grossly inadequate despite father's income of $41,000. Saxon v. Saxon, 24 Ill. App. 2d 116, 164 N.E.2d 248 (1 Dist. 1960).

—Incarceration of Obligor

Incarceration is comparable to an involuntary loss of employment, however, incarceration, as a foreseeable result of criminal activity, does not ipso facto relieve one of the obligation to pay child support. People ex rel. Meyer v. Nein, 209 Ill. App. 3d 1087, 154 Ill. Dec. 436, 568 N.E.2d 436 (4 Dist. 1991).

—Increase Denied

Trial court properly denied petitioner's request for increased child support. Halas v. Executor of Estate of Halas, 112 Ill. App. 3d 940, 68 Ill. Dec. 411, 445 N.E.2d 1264 (1 Dist. 1983).

Modification of support is required where there is a substantial imbalance between the supporting parent's capabilities and the child's needs. In re Boyden, 164 Ill. App. 3d 385, 115 Ill. Dec. 458, 517 N.E.2d 1144 (2 Dist. 1987).

Where there was sufficient evidence to justify the finding that, since the entry of the original divorce decree, the needs of the defendant's children had increased materially, and the evidence also sustained a finding that defendant was able to pay an increased amount of child support, trial court findings that defendant should pay increased child support was not contrary to the manifest weight of the evidence. Neeland v. Neeland, 17 Ill. App. 3d 803, 308 N.E.2d 651 (3 Dist. 1974).

—Increase in Child Support

Trial court abused its discretion in failing to comply with 750 ILCS 5/510(a) and 750 ILCS 5/513 of the Illinois Marriage and Dissolution of Marriage Act, 750 ILCS 5/510(a) and 750 ILCS 5/513, before extending the termination date of a support order to provide child support for an 18-year-old until his graduation from high school. Waller v. Waller, 339 Ill. App. 3d 743, 274 Ill. Dec. 582, 791 N.E.2d 674, 2003 Ill. App. LEXIS 766 (4 Dist. 2003).

The trial court did not abuse its discretion in increasing the amount of child support where the children had grown older and, thus, the court could presume their needs increased, ex-wife testified that as the children were older, they became more involved in school activities, thereby increasing their expenses, husband's financial affidavits indicated he was making a higher salary than he did at the time of dissolution and this was not contradicted, and ex-wife was not making much more money and testified she needed the child support in order to make ends meet. In re Lambdin, 245 Ill. App. 3d 797, 184 Ill. Dec. 789, 613 N.E.2d 1381 (4 Dist. 1993).

Petitioner clearly established both increased expenses for her daughters and respondent's increased ability to support them; hence, the appellate court found an abuse of discretion in the circuit court's dismissal of petitioner's petition for modification and found that the record supported an increase in child support in an amount calculated pursuant to 750 ILCS 5/505(a). In re Heil, 233 Ill. App. 3d 888, 174 Ill. Dec. 622, 599 N.E.2d 168 (5 Dist. 1992).

—Involuntary Unemployment

Child support payments may properly be abated or reduced where an inability to pay results from involuntary loss of employment, but such relief should be temporary in nature in the sense that the petitioning party should be required within a reasonable time to establish that continued unemployment was in good faith; i.e., was the result of mental or physical disability or unsuccessful attempts to obtain other employment. Glass v. Peitchel, 42 Ill. App. 3d 240, 355 N.E.2d 750 (1 Dist. 1976).

—Joint Decision

Where divorce decree required a joint decision of the parents, it did not contemplate that one parent could select a school, enroll the child, pay the tuition, and then present the other parent with a fait accompli and a request to impose the financial burden on the one who was not consulted. Van Nortwick v. Van Nortwick, 87 Ill. App. 2d 55, 230 N.E.2d 391 (2 Dist. 1967).

—Jurisdiction

The court's jurisdiction to alter custody and support of the children is exclusive and continuing until the child or children attain their majority, and the decree or order fixing the custody of the child or children is final only as to the conditions then existing. Eggemeyer v. Eggemeyer, 86 Ill. App. 2d 224, 229 N.E.2d 144 (2 Dist. 1967).

—Laches

The doctrine of laches would not be applied where there was no injury or prejudice to the adverse party and where there was no change in the situation of the parties due to the delay to the detriment of the adverse party, and the defendant would not be prejudiced or injured by merely requiring him to pay child support that he had owed for a number of years. Jozwick v. Jozwick, 72 Ill. App. 3d 17, 28 Ill. Dec. 321, 390 N.E.2d 488 (1 Dist. 1979).

—Minimum Support Guidelines

The guidelines for minimum support in 750 ILCS 5/505 are to be used when considering the modification of a support judgment. In re Boyden, 164 Ill. App. 3d 385, 115 Ill. Dec. 458, 517 N.E.2d 1144 (2 Dist. 1987).

Support (Cont'd)

—Modification

——In General

Parties cannot agree to make child support nonmodifiable; child support is modifiable even when combined with nonmodifiable alimony or maintenance. Burks v. Burks, 100 Ill. App. 3d 700, 56 Ill. Dec. 273, 427 N.E.2d 353 (1 Dist. 1981).

Unlike other final orders, a decree of child support is always modifiable. In re Petramale, 102 Ill. App. 3d 1049, 58 Ill. Dec. 537, 430 N.E.2d 569 (2 Dist. 1981).

When a supporting spouse's financial condition improves notably, where there is a discussion suggesting that increases should be made, child support payments may be required to be increased, even though there is no showing that the child's or children's needs have increased specifically where the original support payments did not adequately meet the children's needs. Legan v. Legan, 69 Ill. App. 3d 304, 25 Ill. Dec. 757, 387 N.E.2d 413 (3 Dist. 1979).

The proper issue before the trial court on a motion to modify child support payments was whether the circumstances of the parties and the children had materially changed since the divorce decree and only if these circumstances have changed since the time of the original decree would a modification of the child support be proper. Gentile v. Gentile, 69 Ill. App. 3d 297, 26 Ill. Dec. 149, 387 N.E.2d 979 (3 Dist. 1979).

The modification of child support payments is a judicial function which is to be administered solely by the court and at its discretion. Jozwick v. Jozwick, 72 Ill. App. 3d 17, 28 Ill. Dec. 321, 390 N.E.2d 488 (1 Dist. 1979).

For a case discussing modification of payments for children's education, see Booth v. Booth, 122 Ill. App. 2d 1, 258 N.E.2d 834 (1 Dist 1970).

——Allowed

Where respondent expressly agreed to remain obligated to pay child support if the children were enrolled as full-time students in high school or college, trial court did not err in entering order increasing child support for adult children 19 and 20 years of age who were attending college, due to inflation and the increased expenses of the children in general, including utilities and food. Falat v. Falat, 201 Ill. App. 3d 320, 147 Ill. Dec. 33, 559 N.E.2d 33 (1 Dist. 1990).

Where ex-spouse changed occupations to improve his prospects for the future he was allowed a reduction in child support until the new occupation became lucrative. In re Lavelle, 206 Ill. App. 3d 607, 152 Ill. Dec. 49, 565 N.E.2d 291 (5 Dist. 1990).

Evidence presented regarding a child's increased food, clothing, baby-sitting, and preschool expenses provided sufficient grounds for the trial court's modification of father's child support obligation. In re Stone, 191 Ill. App. 3d 172, 138 Ill. Dec. 547, 547 N.E.2d 714 (4 Dist. 1989).

Where there was no evidence to support the conclusion that respondent's participation in a strike was motivated by a desire to jeopardize his children's interests or to evade financial responsibility for their support, respondent participated in the strike in "good faith" and was therefore entitled to a reduction in child support reflective of his present ability to pay. Cohn v. Cohn, 122 Ill. App. 3d 763, 78 Ill. Dec. 194, 461 N.E.2d 1028 (2 Dist. 1984).

The court's order increasing support by $85 per month was not an abuse of discretion, where the record was devoid of any evidence of the lifestyle of the child and testimony concerning expenses admittedly involved only guesses. Harner v. Harner, 105 Ill. App. 3d 430, 61 Ill. Dec. 312, 434 N.E.2d 465 (1 Dist. 1982).

Where the financial situation of the mother required her to contribute to the children's support, it was not equitable to require her to bear 82% of the amount of the increase in the cost of raising the children, therefore, since the father's income and net worth had also increased substantially the child support payment for the father was increased. In re Roth, 99 Ill. App. 3d 679, 55 Ill. Dec. 271, 426 N.E.2d 246 (1 Dist. 1981).

The provision of the decree awarding possession of the marital home to the defendant was characterized as a provision for child support, and, therefore, subject to modification, based upon the fact that the children were now residing with the plaintiff, and that their use of the marital home of the parties as a residence was no longer required. Lamp v. Lamp, 81 Ill. 2d 364, 43 Ill. Dec. 31, 410 N.E.2d 31 (1980).

The record did not clearly support the amount of the increase which was awarded. In re Schmerold, 88 Ill. App. 3d 348, 43 Ill. Dec. 629, 410 N.E.2d 629 (2 Dist. 1980).

A petition for an increase in child support is allowed if there has been a substantial change in circumstances and the petitioner has provided the opposing party with notice. Bayuk v. Bayuk, 79 Ill. App. 3d 877, 35 Ill. Dec. 159, 398 N.E.2d 1109 (1 Dist. 1979).

Where ex-husband's income was considerably greater than wife's and fluctuated a great deal, the modification of child support payments to be self-modifying as a percentage of his income was neither an abuse of the trial court's discretion nor against the manifest weight of the evidence. Smith v. Smith, 78 Ill. App. 3d 80, 33 Ill. Dec. 717, 397 N.E.2d 50 (1 Dist. 1979).

In a modification action, the increased needs of the children required that the father be ordered to increase his child support payments, consistent with his increased earnings; it was clearly apparent that the father could readily afford more than the amount which was ordered by the trial court and that in light of his salary increase, the husband had not been carrying his share of the cost of supporting his own children. Spencer v. Spencer, 73 Ill. App. 3d 735, 29 Ill. Dec. 845, 392 N.E.2d 402 (3 Dist. 1979).

Although some of the costs to which petitioner testified were excessive, the trial court did not abuse its discretion by awarding an increase in child support. Scott v. Scott, 72 Ill. App. 3d 117, 27 Ill. Dec. 863, 389 N.E.2d 1271 (1 Dist. 1979).

A decree which modified support upon the plaintiff/wife's remarriage was upheld where there was a substantial basis in this record for the findings of the chancellor, where plaintiff, the adult daughter of the parties, and several other witnesses, corroborated the basis for the findings, and where an attorney who was friendly with both parties testified that defendant admitted the basis for the chancellor's findings. Loeb v. Gendel, 42 Ill. App. 2d 111, 191 N.E.2d 642 (1 Dist. 1963).

——Burden of Proof

The trial court is only justified in increasing child support upon a showing that the needs of the children and the earnings of the supporting parent have increased since the judgment granting child support was entered. Falat v. Falat, 201 Ill. App. 3d 320, 147 Ill. Dec. 33, 559 N.E.2d 33 (1 Dist. 1990).

In order to obtain a modification of child support, the moving party must allege and sustain facts demonstrating a substantial change in circumstances. In re McBride, 166 Ill. App. 3d 504, 116 Ill. Dec. 880, 519 N.E.2d 1095 (1 Dist. 1988).

Child support directed to be paid by a party is subject to modification upon showing of a substantial change in circumstances. In re Redmer, 111 Ill. App. 3d 317, 66 Ill. Dec. 912, 443 N.E.2d 1075 (2 Dist. 1982).

An award of child support may be modified only upon a showing of a substantial change in circumstances; the evidence must establish that both the needs of the child and the supporting parent's ability to pay have increased. Harner v. Harner, 105 Ill. App. 3d 430, 61 Ill. Dec. 312, 434 N.E.2d 465 (1 Dist. 1982).

A party seeking modification of a provision for child support must show that there has been a substantial change in circumstances since the entry of the previous judgment. In re Roth, 99 Ill. App. 3d 679, 55 Ill. Dec. 271, 426 N.E.2d 246 (1 Dist. 1981).

Once a petition has been filed, upon a showing of material change of circumstances, support payments can be modified as of the date the petition was filed. In re Roth, 99 Ill. App. 3d 679, 55 Ill. Dec. 271, 426 N.E.2d 246 (1 Dist. 1981).

Under this Act, child support may be modified only upon the showing of a substantial change of circumstances; to establish such change as would warrant an increase in support, petitioner must show that the children's needs and the noncustodial spouse's ability to pay have increased. In re Cooper, 102 Ill. App. 3d 872, 58 Ill. Dec. 437, 430 N.E.2d 379 (1 Dist. 1981).

The court possesses jurisdiction to modify a decree as to child support payments but, it may only do so when conditions and circumstances of the parties have materially changed since the entry of the divorce decree. Waggoner v. Waggoner, 78 Ill. 2d 50, 34 Ill. Dec. 330, 398 N.E.2d 5 (1979).

In order to justify a decrease in child support payments the moving party is required to show a significant material change in circumstances and conditions of the divorced parents since the

Support (Cont'd)

—Modification (Cont'd)

——Burden of Proof (Cont'd)

entry of the original divorce decree. Gentile v. Gentile, 69 Ill. App. 3d 297, 26 Ill. Dec. 149, 387 N.E.2d 979 (3 Dist. 1979).

To warrant an increase in child support payments the petitioner has the burden of proving a change in circumstances which could warrant the increase, and also that the income of the defendant has increased. Heady v. Simmons, 25 Ill. App. 3d 978, 324 N.E.2d 100 (5 Dist. 1975).

——Court's Power

The circuit court does have the authority to modify a child support provision in a dissolution of marriage judgment that was entered in accordance with a settlement agreement. Falat v. Falat, 201 Ill. App. 3d 320, 147 Ill. Dec. 33, 559 N.E.2d 33 (1 Dist. 1990).

The trial court has the power to modify child support provisions of a divorce judgment if a modification has been shown to be necessitated by changes in the conditions and circumstances of the parties occurring subsequent to entry of the divorce judgment. In re Kessler, 110 Ill. App. 3d 61, 65 Ill. Dec. 707, 441 N.E.2d 1221 (1 Dist. 1982).

Circuit court had authority to alter child support provisions of settlement agreement. Powers v. Powers, 69 Ill. App. 3d 485, 26 Ill. Dec. 452, 388 N.E.2d 76 (1 Dist. 1979).

The trial court has the power to modify child support provisions of a divorce decree if the modification has been shown to be necessitated by changes in the conditions and circumstances of the parties occurring subsequent to entry of the divorce decree. Winter v. Winter, 69 Ill. App. 3d 359, 25 Ill. Dec. 819, 387 N.E.2d 695 (1 Dist. 1978).

There is no question that a trial court has the authority to order a modification in a divorce decree regarding child support payments. Heady v. Simmons, 25 Ill. App. 3d 978, 324 N.E.2d 100 (5 Dist. 1975).

——Factors Considered

Courts must consider the statutory guidelines in 750 ILCS 5/505 as part of a modification analysis. This approach comports with the principle that courts consider the same factors they considered in formulating the original support order. In re Stockton, 169 Ill. App. 3d 318, 119 Ill. Dec. 817, 523 N.E.2d 573 (4 Dist. 1988).

When setting an amount for modification of child support, the court may consider the same factors used when formulating an original support order, including the standard of living the child would have enjoyed if the marriage had not been dissolved and the financial resources of the noncustodial parent. In re Boyden, 164 Ill. App. 3d 385, 115 Ill. Dec. 458, 517 N.E.2d 1144 (2 Dist. 1987).

When determining whether there is sufficient cause to modify an award of child support, courts consider both the circumstances of the parents and the circumstances of the child. In re Wettstein, 160 Ill. App. 3d 554, 113 Ill. Dec. 1, 514 N.E.2d 783 (4 Dist. 1987).

Upon application for a modification of support, the court's paramount consideration is whether a substantial and material change in circumstances has occurred since the entry of the decree which would authorize the court to change the allowance. In re Morrisroe, 155 Ill. App. 3d 765, 108 Ill. Dec. 303, 508 N.E.2d 464 (2 Dist. 1987).

In determining whether to modify child support, the increase in the children's needs must be balanced against the relative ability of the parents to provide for them, and where a change has occurred which creates a substantial imbalance between the child's needs and the parent's support capabilities, modification is required. Fedun v. Kuczek, 155 Ill. App. 3d 798, 108 Ill. Dec. 370, 508 N.E.2d 531 (4 Dist. 1987).

If the threshold question of substantial change is met when determining whether to modify child support, the court, in determining the amount of increase in child support, considers the same factors it considered in formulating the original amount. Fedun v. Kuczek, 155 Ill. App. 3d 798, 108 Ill. Dec. 370, 508 N.E.2d 531 (4 Dist. 1987).

Trial court is to consider the same factors in considering modifying the amount of child support as it considers in formulating an original support order. In re Erickson, 136 Ill. App. 3d 907, 91 Ill. Dec. 346, 483 N.E.2d 692 (2 Dist. 1985).

Modification of support obligation is appropriate where the supporting spouse terminates his employment to further his education, has suffered substantial economic setbacks resulting from investments, or has encountered a reduction in income because of a change in employment or occupation. In re Kowski, 123 Ill. App. 3d 811, 79 Ill. Dec. 286, 463 N.E.2d 840 (1 Dist. 1984).

Under this Act, the paramount consideration of the court in determining whether to modify a child support order is to determine whether a substantial and material change has intervened since the original support allowance was made; while the needs of the child and the financial status of the noncustodial parent are important factors in making the decision, the court must also consider the financial resources of the child, the financial status and needs of the custodial parent, the standard of living the child was accustomed to prior to dissolution, and the physical and emotional needs and educational needs of the child. In re Daniels, 115 Ill. App. 3d 173, 70 Ill. Dec. 888, 450 N.E.2d 361 (5 Dist. 1983).

Factors to be considered by the trial court in exercising its discretion regarding modification of child support provisions include financial resources of children, financial status of custodial parent, financial resources of noncustodial parent, standard of living the children would have enjoyed in absence of divorce, and physical, emotional and educational needs of the children. In re Emerson, 115 Ill. App. 3d 712, 71 Ill. Dec. 299, 450 N.E.2d 987 (2 Dist. 1983).

The factors to be considered in making an award of child support are applicable to modification proceedings. In re Butler, 106 Ill. App. 3d 831, 62 Ill. Dec. 535, 436 N.E.2d 561 (1 Dist. 1982).

The needs of the children should be considered with the available means of both parents to contribute to or satisfy those needs; the accommodation or balance between the needs of the children and means of providing support is not dependent alone upon the existence or nonexistence of an increase in the income of the supporting parties. Luthy v. Luthy, 95 Ill. App. 3d 987, 51 Ill. Dec. 350, 420 N.E.2d 764 (3 Dist. 1981).

The trial court erred in holding that modification of child support is allowable only upon a showing that the noncustodial parent's ability to pay has increased; on remandment, the court was ordered to consider all relevant factors in making its determination, including the income and other assets of both the parents, and the income and assets of the children. Luthy v. Luthy, 95 Ill. App. 3d 987, 51 Ill. Dec. 350, 420 N.E.2d 764 (3 Dist. 1981).

Whenever a request for modification of child support is sought, it is the duty of the court in which the action has been brought to ascertain all the pertinent facts and circumstances and to determine whether the award is fair and equitable or should be modified. Bayuk v. Bayuk, 79 Ill. App. 3d 877, 35 Ill. Dec. 159, 398 N.E.2d 1109 (1 Dist. 1979).

Just as in initially determining the amount of support, the facts to be considered by the trial court in modifying the support provisions of the divorce decree includes the ages of the parties, their condition of health, the property and income of the mother, the property and income of the father, and the station in life of the parties. Winter v. Winter, 69 Ill. App. 3d 359, 25 Ill. Dec. 819, 387 N.E.2d 695 (1 Dist. 1978).

——Not Allowed

Trial court did not err in declining to modify father's child support obligation because, in determining whether modification should occur, the court was charged with first looking to see whether there had been a change in the father's net income and, in so doing, the court properly counted IRA disbursements father received after the divorce as "net income" and determined that those substantial disbursements undercut his argument that he was suffering from financial hardship. In re Marriage of Lindman, Ill. App. 3d , Ill. Dec. , N.E.2d , 2004 Ill. App. LEXIS 1619 (2 Dist. Dec. 16, 2004).

Although various household expenses were expenses that could have been partly attributable to the children, wife had not shown any specific increased needs of the children for which husband was not already voluntarily paying; to the extent that wife demonstrated that some of the children's needs for which husband was already providing increased, the trial court modified the judgment and ordered husband to pay these expenses; although it was clear that the husband's income and net worth had increased over the years, his responsibilities had also increased; further, wife also had an obligation to financially contribute to the support of the family; there was nothing in the record to suggest that she was unable to

Support (Cont'd)

—Modification (Cont'd)

——Not Allowed (Cont'd)

do so; the trial court increased the husband's payments by the amount it felt the children's needs had increased; on this record, the trial court did not abuse its discretion in refusing wife's request for additional sums. In re Fazioli, 202 Ill. App. 3d 245, 147 Ill. Dec. 495, 559 N.E.2d 835 (1 Dist. 1990).

Arguments advanced by wife that the cost of living had increased and that the children had grown older were previously contemplated by the parties and subsequently provided for in the settlement agreement therefore, record supported the conclusion that the findings of the trial court increasing child support per wife's modification request were against the manifest weight of the evidence. In re Stadheim, 170 Ill. App. 3d 19, 120 Ill. Dec. 373, 523 N.E.2d 1284 (1 Dist. 1988).

The duty of the respondent to pay support was not enlarged, nor was the petitioner's need for support diminished in any way during or after post-dissolution, cohabitational relationship, therefore respondent's petition for modification was dismissed. In re Antonich, 148 Ill. App. 3d 575, 102 Ill. Dec. 97, 499 N.E.2d 654 (2 Dist. 1986).

Father's petition for modification of child support was properly denied where the original judgment of divorce indicated that both parties intended that their son would receive support if he attended college, both parties acknowledged that it was contemplated that their son would be attending college in the near future and any decrease in the financial needs of the mother or increase in the father's financial need generated by a prior change in custody was minimal. In re Milburn, 144 Ill. App. 3d 76, 98 Ill. Dec. 234, 494 N.E.2d 161 (5 Dist. 1986).

Where son's college attendance would require mother to spend substantial sums of money, and since there was evidence that petitioner's child care costs for her daughter, who resided with mother, had increased at the same time mother's income had increased, a finding that the pro rata decrease in child support requested by the father would result in a decrease in the daughter's standard of living was not an abuse of discretion and such modification was not allowed. In re Milburn, 144 Ill. App. 3d 76, 98 Ill. Dec. 234, 494 N.E.2d 161 (5 Dist. 1986).

Reducing child support payments to wife as a method of repayment for transportation expenses owed to husband was an abuse of discretion under the circumstances. Faris v. Faris, 142 Ill. App. 3d 987, 97 Ill. Dec. 209, 492 N.E.2d 645 (2 Dist. 1986), appeal denied, 100 Ill. Dec. 603, 497 N.E.2d 781 (Ill. 1986).

The circuit court correctly denied an increase in support where the record was devoid of evidence of the mother's expenses for the child at the time of the original decree, and where she did not even attempt to itemize the individual factors underlying her determination of the amount she spent per month. Harner v. Harner, 105 Ill. App. 3d 430, 61 Ill. Dec. 312, 434 N.E.2d 465 (1 Dist. 1982).

The summer camp provision unambiguously required defendant to pay the entire amount of the expenses, therefore, that portion of the trial court order which required defendant to pay only 60% of future summer camp tuition was reversed. In re Roth, 99 Ill. App. 3d 679, 55 Ill. Dec. 271, 426 N.E.2d 246 (1 Dist. 1981).

Where divorced wife received an increase in child support from $60.00 a week to 34% of divorced husband's monthly income of $1,600, a new hearing was required since such an increase was not supported by the evidence as the trial court overemphasized percentage of income formula and the financial situation of the divorced spouses was not suitably determined. In re Cooper, 102 Ill. App. 3d 872, 58 Ill. Dec. 437, 430 N.E.2d 379 (1 Dist. 1981).

Considering the husband's monthly income, with both the required and optional deductions plus the tax benefits he received, the monthly family support awarded was neither against the manifest weight of the evidence nor an abuse of discretion on the part of the trial court, where the husband testified that he earned a base salary of $60,000 per year; in 1976 he also received a bonus of $600 in addition to his base salary; the wife was a registered nurse prior to their marriage but terminated such employment shortly after the marriage; the parties had been married for approximately 20 years, during which time the husband advanced himself in business while the wife devoted herself to maintaining a home and raising the couple's children and her maximum expected salary was $11,000 per year. Schuppe v. Schuppe, 69 Ill. App. 3d 200, 25 Ill. Dec. 690, 387 N.E.2d 346 (2 Dist. 1979).

An award of $550 per month in child support payments was not unjustified where it was adduced that since entry of the decree plaintiff had remarried and shared a home with her spouse and child; plaintiff retained a live-in housekeeper at a salary of $80 per week; the plaintiff's itemized monthly expenses for the child were as follows: food: $111; medical: $17.77; clothes: $85; allowance: $4.25; entertainment: $6.40; gifts for friends: $6; vacations: $58; tutoring: $46; haircuts: $5; summer camp expenses were $425 and tennis and art lessons totaled $335 per year; plaintiff was a licensed real estate salesperson and prior to the date of the hearing had earned $11,800 from that endeavor, and plaintiff also realized approximately $30,000 from the sale of the marital home. Winter v. Winter, 69 Ill. App. 3d 359, 25 Ill. Dec. 819, 387 N.E.2d 695 (1 Dist. 1978).

Because the trial court erred in modifying child support and because defendant failed to prove a substantial change of circumstances, it also erred when it arbitrarily reduced the arrearage from $890 to $400. Dixon v. Dixon, 45 Ill. App. 3d 934, 4 Ill. Dec. 550, 360 N.E.2d 486 (1 Dist. 1977).

A father's alleged inability to pay any child support, with no showing of good faith, resulted in not only manifest injustice to plaintiff, but perhaps also to the children, in view of the fact that there was no evidence in the record concerning plaintiff's ability to support them; therefore, the portion of an order which abated the child support payments was reversed and remanded with directions. Glass v. Peitchel, 42 Ill. App. 3d 240, 355 N.E.2d 750 (1 Dist. 1976).

——Retroactivity

A trial court has no authority to retroactively modify a child support order. In re Henry, 156 Ill. 2d 541, 190 Ill. Dec. 773, 622 N.E.2d 803 (1993).

—Need

——In General

The trial court may presume that the expenses associated with the raising of children are increased each year. Falat v. Falat, 201 Ill. App. 3d 320, 147 Ill. Dec. 33, 559 N.E.2d 33 (1 Dist. 1990).

Child support is to be determined by accommodating the needs of the children with the available means of the parties. It is incumbent upon the trial court to consider both the needs of the children and the ability of the former spouses to pay. Gentile v. Gentile, 69 Ill. App. 3d 297, 26 Ill. Dec. 149, 387 N.E.2d 979 (3 Dist. 1979).

——Ability to Pay

Child support obligations may be increased pursuant to this section based upon the supporting parent's increased ability to pay, regardless of whether the child's needs have also increased. Wilson v. Wilson, 166 Ill. App. 3d 1035, 117 Ill. Dec. 879, 520 N.E.2d 1230 (4 Dist. 1988); In re Bean, 181 Ill. App. 3d 671, 130 Ill. Dec. 275, 537 N.E.2d 342 (5 Dist. 1989).

The financial status of a divorced parent's current spouse should not be considered in determining the ability of that spouse to fulfill his or her duty to support. In re Kessler, 110 Ill. App. 3d 61, 65 Ill. Dec. 707, 441 N.E.2d 1221 (1 Dist. 1982).

In assessing the children's increased needs, it is proper to consider that they have grown older and that the cost of living has risen, but this must be balanced against the relative ability of the parents to provide for the children. In re Cooper, 102 Ill. App. 3d 872, 58 Ill. Dec. 437, 430 N.E.2d 379 (1 Dist. 1981).

Child support payments must necessarily reflect a balance of the intensity of the child's needs with the ability of the parents to provide for that need. Gentile v. Gentile, 69 Ill. App. 3d 297, 26 Ill. Dec. 149, 387 N.E.2d 979 (3 Dist. 1979).

Trial court abused its discretion in strictly adhering to the formula set out in the property settlement regarding child support payments based upon ex-husband's income where his income increased significantly, so as to double the amount of child support, and that a hearing should be held to determine the child's actual needs compared with the ex-husband's ability to pay an increased amount and ex-wife's increased ability to support the child. Dull v. Dull, 73 Ill. App. 3d 1015, 29 Ill. Dec. 864, 392 N.E.2d 421 (5 Dist. 1979).

Support (Cont'd)

—Need (Cont'd)

——Evidence

Once the respondent's increased ability to pay has been demonstrated, the petitioner may establish increased needs of the children based on the fact that the children have grown older and the cost of living has risen. Falat v. Falat, 201 Ill. App. 3d 320, 147 Ill. Dec. 33, 559 N.E.2d 33 (1 Dist. 1990).

Where the supporting parent's ability to pay is shown, the fact that the child has grown older and the fact that the cost of living has risen are proper bases for establishing increased need. In re Roth, 99 Ill. App. 3d 679, 55 Ill. Dec. 271, 426 N.E.2d 246 (1 Dist. 1981).

——In Excess

Where the noncustodial parent has ability to pay support in excess of the stated needs of the child, the court may order child support in excess of the needs to enable the child to enjoy the standard of living he would have had if the marriage had not been dissolved. In re Bean, 181 Ill. App. 3d 671, 130 Ill. Dec. 275, 537 N.E.2d 342 (5 Dist. 1989).

——Increase

The trial court is justified in increasing child support if the needs of the children and the earnings of the supporting parent have increased since the judgment granting child support was entered. In re Heil, 233 Ill. App. 3d 888, 174 Ill. Dec. 622, 599 N.E.2d 168 (5 Dist. 1992).

Where a former spouse's ability to pay child support is shown, the fact that the children have grown older and the cost of living has risen are proper bases for establishing increased need. In re Fazioli, 202 Ill. App. 3d 245, 147 Ill. Dec. 495, 559 N.E.2d 835 (1 Dist. 1990).

The increase in the children's needs must be balanced against the relative ability of the parents to provide for them, and where a change has occurred which creates a substantial imbalance between the child's needs and the parent's support capabilities, modification is required. In re Fazioli, 202 Ill. App. 3d 245, 147 Ill. Dec. 495, 559 N.E.2d 835 (1 Dist. 1990).

The increased needs of the child may be established by the child's growing older and the increase in the cost of living established by the expert testimony. Giamanco v. Giamanco, 111 Ill. App. 3d 1017, 67 Ill. Dec. 606, 444 N.E.2d 1090 (5 Dist. 1982).

New or changed conditions are necessary to warrant a change in support payments, and increased needs of children may be presumed from the fact that children have grown older and the cost of living has risen. In re Kessler, 110 Ill. App. 3d 61, 65 Ill. Dec. 707, 441 N.E.2d 1221 (1 Dist. 1982).

An increase in support payments is warranted when the evidence establishes that the needs of the children have increased, and the means of the father have also increased so as to enable him to contribute additional sums to his children's support. Nordstrom v. Nordstrom, 36 Ill. App. 3d 181, 343 N.E.2d 640 (1 Dist. 1976).

—Notice

——In General

Modification of child support payments can be had only as to those installments accruing subsequent to due notice by the moving party of the motion for modification. People ex rel. Stokely v. Goodenow, 211 Ill. App. 3d 802, 164 Ill. Dec. 548, 583 N.E.2d 102 (4 Dist. 1991).

Support payments may be modified only as to installments accruing after the party moving for modification has given due notice. In re Frazier, 205 Ill. App. 3d 621, 151 Ill. Dec. 130, 563 N.E.2d 1236 (3 Dist. 1990).

——Pleadings

Where petitioner sought modification of divorce decree to compel ex-spouse to support the parties' mentally disabled child after she attained majority; the petition adequately asserted a "change in circumstances" based on the child's continuing handicap after attaining majority; however, it may not have been necessary to plead a "change in circumstances" under this section since there may be a substantive obligation to support a mentally disabled child in 750 ILCS 5/513, unrelated to the terms of any prior divorce decree. In re Winters, 160 Ill. App. 3d 277, 111 Ill. Dec. 734, 512 N.E.2d 1371 (2 Dist. 1987).

——Retroactivity

Child support payments may be modified only as to installments accruing after the party moving for modification has given due notice. In re Macino, 236 Ill. App. 3d 886, 177 Ill. Dec. 324, 603 N.E.2d 105 (2 Dist. 1992).

A modification for child support 20 years after the divorce could not be applied retroactively. Nerini v. Nerini, 140 Ill. App. 3d 848, 95 Ill. Dec. 36, 488 N.E.2d 1379 (2 Dist. 1986).

The question of whether modification of child support should be retroactive is within the discretion of the trial court. In re Ingrassia, 140 Ill. App. 3d 826, 95 Ill. Dec. 165, 489 N.E.2d 386 (2 Dist. 1986); Fedun v. Kuczek, 155 Ill. App. 3d 798, 108 Ill. Dec. 370, 508 N.E.2d 531 (4 Dist. 1987).

The question whether modification of child support should be retroactive is within the discretion of the trial court. Where there was an interim of over one year between the filing of the petition and the entry of the order but at least five months of that delay was attributable to respondent's wilful failure to comply with petitioner's discovery requests, it was inequitable to allow respondent to benefit due to his dilatory behavior; the support order was made effective retroactive five additional months. In re Leva, 125 Ill. App. 3d 55, 77 Ill. Dec. 615, 460 N.E.2d 1179 (1 Dist. 1983).

A court may, within its discretion, modify a support order retroactively to the date that the petition for modification was filed and, thus, child support payments in arrears which accrue thereafter do not become vested. In re McDavid, 97 Ill. App. 3d 1044, 54 Ill. Dec. 577, 425 N.E.2d 442 (1 Dist. 1981).

——Review

A petition to modify child support must be decided on the facts of each case, and the decision rests within the sound discretion of the trial court. People ex rel. Meyer v. Nein, 209 Ill. App. 3d 1087, 154 Ill. Dec. 436, 568 N.E.2d 436 (4 Dist. 1991).

A determination of the proper amount of child support, and modification thereof, lies within the sound discretion of the trial court and will not be set aside absent an abuse of that discretion, which occurs only where no reasonable man would take the view adopted by the trial court. In re Partney, 212 Ill. App. 3d 586, 156 Ill. Dec. 679, 571 N.E.2d 266 (5 Dist. 1991).

The decision of the trial court to modify or not to modify child support payments will only be disturbed if such decision is clearly against the manifest weight of the evidence. In re Lavelle, 206 Ill. App. 3d 607, 152 Ill. Dec. 49, 565 N.E.2d 291 (5 Dist. 1990).

The modification of child support payments is a judicial function; the court's decision to modify the payment of child support is discretionary in nature and only takes effect prospectively. In re Erickson, 136 Ill. App. 3d 907, 91 Ill. Dec. 346, 483 N.E.2d 692 (2 Dist. 1985).

Modification of child support payment rests within the sound discretion of the trial court and it will not be set aside unless the finding is clearly contrary to the manifest weight of the evidence. Legan v. Legan, 69 Ill. App. 3d 304, 25 Ill. Dec. 757, 387 N.E.2d 413 (3 Dist. 1979); Smith v. Smith, 78 Ill. App. 3d 80, 33 Ill. Dec. 717, 397 N.E.2d 50 (1 Dist. 1979); In re Schmerold, 88 Ill. App. 3d 348, 43 Ill. Dec. 629, 410 N.E.2d 629 (2 Dist. 1980); In re Butler, 106 Ill. App. 3d 831, 62 Ill. Dec. 535, 436 N.E.2d 561 (1 Dist. 1982); In re Emerson, 115 Ill. App. 3d 712, 71 Ill. Dec. 299, 450 N.E.2d 987 (2 Dist. 1983); In re Wettstein, 160 Ill. App. 3d 554, 113 Ill. Dec. 1, 514 N.E.2d 783 (4 Dist. 1987); In re Bean, 181 Ill. App. 3d 671, 130 Ill. Dec. 275, 537 N.E.2d 342 (5 Dist. 1989); In re Stone, 191 Ill. App. 3d 172, 138 Ill. Dec. 547, 547 N.E.2d 714 (4 Dist. 1989); In re Hardy, 191 Ill. App. 3d 685, 138 Ill. Dec. 909, 548 N.E.2d 139 (5 Dist. 1989).

Considerable discretion is placed in the trial court and an order of modification of child support will not be disturbed on review, absent an abuse of discretion. Winter v. Winter, 69 Ill. App. 3d 359, 25 Ill. Dec. 819, 387 N.E.2d 695 (1 Dist. 1978).

The court erred in its order modifying the decree of divorce which in effect provided that the defendant father need pay no more for the support of the minor children except when he requested that they be brought to his home and then he was required to pay plaintiff $30 on each and every occasion, where he was financially able to support the children. Kemp v. Kemp, 332 Ill. App. 432, 75 N.E.2d 385 (1 Dist. 1947).

Support (Cont'd)

—Notice (Cont'd)

——Settlement Agreement

A settlement agreement provision that husband would not advance as a reason for modification of the child support payments any future employment of wife did not divest the court of its power to modify the divorce decree into which the agreement was incorporated. Wohl v. Wohl, 28 Ill. App. 3d 298, 328 N.E.2d 138 (1 Dist. 1975).

—Obligation

Where the trial court determined that the husband's obligation to pay the second mortgage on the marital home was part of an order for support rather than part of a property distribution, the obligation was not dischargeable in bankruptcy proceedings. In re LaShelle, 213 Ill. App. 3d 730, 157 Ill. Dec. 726, 572 N.E.2d 1190 (2 Dist. 1991).

The general rule is that the obligation of a parent to support his children terminates when the child reaches majority. Falat v. Falat, 201 Ill. App. 3d 320, 147 Ill. Dec. 33, 559 N.E.2d 33 (1 Dist. 1990).

Once legal and physical custody is placed in one parent, that custodial parent has no obligation to pay child support to the noncustodial parent. Shoff v. Shoff, 179 Ill. App. 3d 178, 128 Ill. Dec. 280, 534 N.E.2d 462 (5 Dist. 1989).

The parental duty of support extends until a child's emancipation, unless otherwise agreed in writing by the parties or expressly provided in the judgment. In re Rapacz, 135 Ill. App. 3d 1045, 90 Ill. Dec. 622, 482 N.E.2d 441 (2 Dist. 1985).

—Oral Agreement

An oral agreement between former spouses (defendant husband was an attorney) that after plaintiff's remarriage defendant would increase child support payments and create a trust into which defendant would pay from the date of plaintiff's remarriage until a set time, approximately nine years later, at which time the principal of the trust would be paid to plaintiff, was binding based on plaintiff's testimony, corroborating testimony actions of defendant, and the rule that no person shall be permitted to utilize the Statute of Frauds to work an injustice or fraud. Loeb v. Gendel, 42 Ill. App. 2d 111, 191 N.E.2d 642 (1 Dist. 1963).

—Past Due

——In General

Past-due installments are a vested right and the court has no authority to modify them. In re Hardy, 191 Ill. App. 3d 685, 138 Ill. Dec. 909, 548 N.E.2d 139 (5 Dist. 1989).

The circuit court's procedure for discharging vested support and maintenance payments which are in arrears lies within the sound discretion of the trial judge and will not be set aside absent an abuse of that discretion. In re Hardy, 191 Ill. App. 3d 685, 138 Ill. Dec. 909, 548 N.E.2d 139 (5 Dist. 1989).

Past-due child support payments are a vested right, and reduction relating to a period of time prior to filing of the petition or motion for modification is error. In re Jobe, 151 Ill. App. 3d 998, 105 Ill. Dec. 140, 503 N.E.2d 1146 (4 Dist. 1987).

Past-due child support installments were vested rights and appellee was not entitled to equitable credit, if appellee felt that he should not have to provide child support payments during the summer months in which he had custody of their child, his remedy was to have sought modification by the court of the support order prior to the due date of the opposed installments. McAdams v. Scullin, 53 Ill. App. 3d 374, 11 Ill. Dec. 428, 368 N.E.2d 1036 (5 Dist. 1977).

Past-due installments of child support are a vested right and usually are not subject to modification by the court as to amount. Johnson v. Johnson, 26 Ill. App. 3d 64, 324 N.E.2d 450 (2 Dist. 1975).

——Estoppel

The doctrine of equitable estoppel did not bar the custodial parent's petition for arrearages where there was no act or omission of the custodial parent upon which he relied; rather, he did not comply with the provisions of the divorce decree because of his reliance on the advice of his attorney and because he believed he was no longer liable for the amount specified in the decree and that he could unilaterally reduce his payment. In re Jackson, 179 Ill. App. 3d 479, 128 Ill. Dec. 505, 534 N.E.2d 687 (5 Dist. 1989).

Where respondent took custody of his son with the understanding he would not have to continue to pay child support so long as the son remained with him, and in becoming the custodial parent of his son and providing for his son's needs while he lived with him, respondent suffered a detriment, his reliance on an agreement was not unreasonable for he and petitioner had entered into similar agreements in the past without incident; thus, the trial court's determination to deny petitioner support arrearages was supported on a theory of equitable estoppel. In re Webber, 191 Ill. App. 3d 327, 138 Ill. Dec. 582, 547 N.E.2d 749 (4 Dist. 1989).

Where the only act or omission on the part of the wife that could have been considered in estoppel was the statement by the wife that she would not pursue the support if the husband would not visit the children, there was no showing of any detriment to the husband, and equitable estoppel was neither appropriate nor applicable. Blisset v. Blisset, 144 Ill. App. 3d 1088, 99 Ill. Dec. 161, 495 N.E.2d 608 (4 Dist. 1986), rev'd on other grounds, 123 Ill. 2d 161, 121 Ill. Dec. 931, 526 N.E.2d 125 (1988).

Where father testified that his wife agreed to the reduction in child support on the condition that he help his son find a place to live and that he support him financially, where father testified further that he paid his son more than $4,000 over a two-year period for housing, food and clothing, and where according to father, mother did not at any time during the almost five-year period between the first reduced payment and the filing of her petition for arrearages object to the reduction in child support payments, father's payments to his son were made in reliance upon the statements and conduct of mother and, therefore, mother was barred from recovering child support arrearages by the doctrine of equitable estoppel. In re Strand, 86 Ill. App. 3d 827, 42 Ill. Dec. 37, 408 N.E.2d 415 (1 Dist. 1980).

Child support payments become a vested right as they accrue and cannot be unilaterally terminated by the defendant, and neither can they be modified as to amount or time of payment. In the proper case, however, courts will give effect to an agreement between the parties to waive or reduce payments, or courts will apply the doctrine of equitable estoppel. Matzen v. Matzen, 69 Ill. App. 3d 69, 25 Ill. Dec. 557, 387 N.E.2d 14 (3 Dist. 1979).

Where the mother, who was the custodial parent under the divorce decree, either consented to or acquiesced in a child living with the father and the father supported the child, the doctrine of equitable estoppel may be applied to allow the father an equitable credit against his support arrearages for the time he had actual custody. The test has also been stated more broadly to be whether the conduct of the plaintiff mother, as shown by all the circumstances of the case, was sufficient to justify the conclusion that the enforcement of the decree as to unpaid support would be unjust and inequitable to the defendant father. Matzen v. Matzen, 69 Ill. App. 3d 69, 25 Ill. Dec. 557, 387 N.E.2d 14 (3 Dist. 1979).

In cases allowing an equitable credit against support arrearages, the essential element of detrimental reliance has been present; that is, the court has found that the defendant father relied upon the plaintiff mother's conduct indicating her willingness to give up or modify her right to custody or support. Matzen v. Matzen, 69 Ill. App. 3d 69, 25 Ill. Dec. 557, 387 N.E.2d 14 (3 Dist. 1979).

It is well-established that past-due installments for child support are the vested rights of the designated recipients and the court lacks the authority to modify those amounts which have already accrued; therefore, any modification in child support payments will only act prospectively. Jozwick v. Jozwick, 72 Ill. App. 3d 17, 28 Ill. Dec. 321, 390 N.E.2d 488 (1 Dist. 1979).

The required elements for equitable estoppel were not presented where the plaintiff had not by her conduct caused the defendant to suffer any irreparable harm, the failure on the plaintiff's part to make any demand on the defendant until five years after the defendant reduced payment did not create an equitable estoppel, and the record did not reveal that there was an agreement between the parties to reduce the amount due for child support nor did it indicate that the defendant relied upon any conduct by the plaintiff. Jozwick v. Jozwick, 72 Ill. App. 3d 17, 28 Ill. Dec. 321, 390 N.E.2d 488 (1 Dist. 1979).

—Payments

Even though ex-husband was paid bimonthly, he could be ordered to make weekly payments, and the trial court was within its

Support (Cont'd)

—Payments (Cont'd)

discretion to order an increase in child support to $90 per week. In re Fuesting, 228 Ill. App. 3d 339, 169 Ill. Dec. 456, 591 N.E.2d 960 (5 Dist. 1992).

Trial court did not err in refusing to abate child support payments for the time during which husband claimed that he did not know the whereabouts of the wife and child and this section precluded any modification of child support payments which had accrued. In re Feliciano, 103 Ill. App. 3d 666, 59 Ill. Dec. 363, 431 N.E.2d 1120 (1 Dist. 1981).

—Private Agreements

The determination of child support is the court's responsibility and not the parties; to allow or condone a private agreement between the parties, even if made to be binding upon them and upon the court would promote such agreements and the resulting effects would be burdensome upon the custodians as well as this state. Blisset v. Blisset, 144 Ill. App. 3d 1088, 99 Ill. Dec. 161, 495 N.E.2d 608 (4 Dist. 1986), rev'd on other grounds, 123 Ill. 2d 161, 121 Ill. Dec. 931, 526 N.E.2d 125 (1988).

Parties to divorce or dissolution matters should not be allowed to contract away their responsibilities for child support in return for an agreement not to visit the children. Blisset v. Blisset, 144 Ill. App. 3d 1088, 99 Ill. Dec. 161, 495 N.E.2d 608 (4 Dist. 1986), rev'd on other grounds, 123 Ill. 2d 161, 121 Ill. Dec. 931, 526 N.E.2d 125 (1988).

Even though plaintiff, under separation agreement, had waived her right under court order to automatic increases in child support, this had no merit and defendant's estoppel argument was rejected. Marshall v. Marshall, 109 Ill. App. 3d 139, 64 Ill. Dec. 762, 440 N.E.2d 314 (5 Dist. 1982).

The test for determining the validity of an agreement between the parties to reduce child support payments is whether that agreement meets the test of validity applicable to all releases. In re Strand, 86 Ill. App. 3d 827, 42 Ill. Dec. 37, 408 N.E.2d 415 (1 Dist. 1980).

Trial court's ruling was erroneous where it denied increase in child support based on provision in the separation agreement relating to child support payments which stated that there shall be no consideration of change in circumstances until the husband's income increased to $53,000. Bayuk v. Bayuk, 79 Ill. App. 3d 877, 35 Ill. Dec. 159, 398 N.E.2d 1109 (1 Dist. 1979).

In a proper case, the court can give effect to an agreement by a party to waive child support payments, or accept a lesser amount. Johnson v. Johnson, 26 Ill. App. 3d 64, 324 N.E.2d 450 (2 Dist. 1975).

In determining the validity and effect, as between divorced spouses, of an agreement by which one party released the other party from an obligation under the provisions of the divorce decree to pay child support, the first question to be considered is whether the agreement meets the tests of validity applicable to all releases, and in particular, the agreement must be supported by a valid consideration. Johnson v. Johnson, 26 Ill. App. 3d 64, 324 N.E.2d 450 (2 Dist. 1975).

—Punitive Abatement Improper

Where abatement of support payments was solely for the purpose of forcing compliance with the order that the children be sent to visit their father, the order punished the recalcitrant plaintiff at the children's expense and was improvidently entered. Metcoff v. Metcoff, 4 Ill. App. 3d 160, 280 N.E.2d 572 (1 Dist. 1972).

—Reduction

——Agreement

In an action to enforce child support provisions, the parties did not have an agreement to reduce support payments, and even if the parties did enter into such an agreement, it was unenforceable as to installments accruing prior to due notice of the filing of a motion to modify and a showing that an agreement reached between the parties was in accord with the children's best interests. In re Michael, 226 Ill. App. 3d 1088, 169 Ill. Dec. 79, 590 N.E.2d 998 (3 Dist. 1992).

——Death of Child

The death of one child does not give the obligor/parent the right to reduce unilaterally such unallocated child support payments. In re Erickson, 136 Ill. App. 3d 907, 91 Ill. Dec. 346, 483 N.E.2d 692 (2 Dist. 1985).

——Emancipation

Modification of child support payments is solely a judicial function and it is the circuit court who must determine whether upon emancipation of a child, a reduction should be made pro rata or whether other equitable considerations require a different amount be paid. In re Jackson, 179 Ill. App. 3d 479, 128 Ill. Dec. 505, 534 N.E.2d 687 (5 Dist. 1989).

Even though a parent's obligation to support a child terminates upon emancipation, the parent responsible for tendering the payments may not make a unilateral pro rata reduction in the amount of unallocated child support payments upon one child's emancipation absent an agreement to the contrary. In re Erickson, 136 Ill. App. 3d 907, 91 Ill. Dec. 346, 483 N.E.2d 692 (2 Dist. 1985).

A noncustodial parent may not unilaterally reduce unallocated child support as each child is emancipated by reaching the age of majority, even if he continues to provide for the support of his adult children by making direct payments to them. In re Bjorklund, 88 Ill. App. 3d 576, 43 Ill. Dec. 757, 410 N.E.2d 890 (1 Dist. 1980).

Where an order is entered for the support of more than one child but the order does not specify the amount of support for each child, the unilateral pro rata reduction of the support payments upon the emancipation of one child is not permissible; rather, the entire amount of support ordered must be paid until the youngest child has reached majority or until the order of support is modified. In re Strand, 86 Ill. App. 3d 827, 42 Ill. Dec. 37, 408 N.E.2d 415 (1 Dist. 1980).

It was improper for husband unilaterally to reduce his child support payments pro rata after children each attained majority, where he never petitioned the court for modification of the support award. In re Rosenbaum, 85 Ill. App. 3d 931, 41 Ill. Dec. 213, 407 N.E.2d 711 (1 Dist. 1980).

Amounts due for child support cannot be reduced pro rata automatically as each child reaches majority; a party directed to pay child support must obtain a court order to modify such payments. Jozwick v. Jozwick, 72 Ill. App. 3d 17, 28 Ill. Dec. 321, 390 N.E.2d 488 (1 Dist. 1979).

A parent who has been ordered by a divorce decree to pay a collective or lump sum weekly for the support of four minor children may not unilaterally reduce the amount of such payments pro rata as each child is emancipated. Finley v. Finley, 81 Ill. 2d 317, 43 Ill. Dec. 12, 410 N.E.2d 12 (1980).

——Employment

Father was not required to wait until his change of employment became an involuntary one to justify a reduction in child support. In re Barnard, 283 Ill. App. 3d 366, 218 Ill. Dec. 583, 669 N.E.2d 726 (4 Dist. 1996).

——Repayment

If a trial court reduces child support payments because of financial changes caused by participation in a strike, the trial court may require that the amount of any reduction in child support payments be accrued and repaid at a later date. In re Fink, 275 Ill. App. 3d 960, 212 Ill. Dec. 297, 656 N.E.2d 1131 (4 Dist. 1995).

——Temporary

Where the record amply demonstrated that defendant's request for reduction of child support payments was not prompted by a desire to evade his responsibility, and the order of the trial judge did not relieve defendant of all responsibility for child support for the period in question; the defendant's temporary cessation of income, although incurred voluntarily, but in good faith, prompted the trial judge, in the exercise of judgment and discretion to enter the order reducing his child support payments, thus, there was no abuse of discretion. Graham v. Graham, 21 Ill. App. 3d 1032, 316 N.E.2d 143 (4 Dist. 1974).

——Upheld

Considering the income of defendant, the fact that one child was no longer in need of support, and in view of the subsequent remarriage of plaintiff, the reduction of defendant's future support payments was not in error or not against the manifest weight of the evidence under former section 19 of this chapter (see now this

Support (Cont'd)

—Reduction (Cont'd)

——Upheld (Cont'd)
section). Voss v. Voss, 23 Ill. App. 3d 312, 319 N.E.2d 72 (3 Dist. 1974).

—Res Judicata
The original decree awarding child support payments is res judicata so long as there is no change in the circumstances underlying the decree. Gentile v. Gentile, 69 Ill. App. 3d 297, 26 Ill. Dec. 149, 387 N.E.2d 979 (3 Dist. 1979).

—Retroactivity
A circuit court is not statutorily barred from imposing a retroactive child support obligation upon a respondent in an ongoing child support proceeding who, contrary to the court's directive, has failed to inform the court of his having resumed employment. People ex rel. Williams v. Williams, 191 Ill. App. 3d 311, 138 Ill. Dec. 560, 547 N.E.2d 727 (4 Dist. 1989).

In this case no award of support was made in the original judgment, therefore, any subsequent award of support would constitute a modification of the previous judgment, thereby bringing the case within the purview of subsection (a) of this section, which prohibits the award of retroactive support, hence, the trial court properly denied plaintiff's request for retroactive child support. Conner v. Watkins, 158 Ill. App. 3d 759, 110 Ill. Dec. 365, 511 N.E.2d 200 (4 Dist. 1987).

It was proper under former section 18 of the Divorce Act (see now this section), for the trial court to direct the father of a child to reimburse the mother for moneys expended after their divorce for their child's support during his infancy even though in the original proceeding there was no order made relative to the obligation to provide child support. Gill v. Gill, 56 Ill. 2d 139, 306 N.E.2d 281 (1973).

Where notification of alimony and support payments was proper, the trial court did not err in refusing to make the modification order retroactive to the date on which the petition to modify was filed rather than to the date on which the defendant's monthly income was decreased. Vail v. Vail, 98 Ill. App. 234, 240 N.E.2d 519 (1968).

—Same Day Modifications
The trial court had discretionary power to insert an amendment in a child support agreement incorporated in the divorce decree, on the same day as the decree was issued, that deemed the support order temporary for a six-month term, even though the court inserted the amendment without prior notice to the parties and contrary to their express wishes. Conces v. Conces, 16 Ill. App. 3d 835, 306 N.E.2d 890 (3 Dist. 1974).

—Security
Where respondent had provided for the needs of his children since the separation, and there was no indication that he would not continue to do so in the future, respondent's estate would be liable for future support "to the extent just and appropriate under the circumstances" should he otherwise fail to provide for them, there was no reason to believe that respondent, or his estate, would not be able to provide the support mandated, and respondent had ample assets apart from the pension and profit-sharing plan which provided all the necessary support, the trial court did not abuse its discretion in failing to require that respondent furnish security for his support obligations. In re Wilder, 122 Ill. App. 3d 338, 77 Ill. Dec. 824, 461 N.E.2d 447 (1 Dist. 1983).

—Social Security Benefits
Because social security dependent disability benefits are earned by the noncustodial parent, made on behalf of such parent, and, in fact, paid at least in part with contributions from the noncustodial parent's own earnings, payment of social security dependent disability benefits satisfies a noncustodial parent's child support obligation. In re Henry, 156 Ill. 2d 541, 190 Ill. Dec. 773, 622 N.E.2d 803 (1993).

—Standing
A child may not bring suit against his father to recover arrearages in child support payments. Kelleher v. Kelleher, 21 Ill. App. 3d 601, 316 N.E.2d 212 (1 Dist. 1974).

A minor child, by his grandmother as next friend, cannot compel the father to pay to the child arrearages in child support. Kelleher v. Kelleher, 21 Ill. App. 3d 601, 316 N.E.2d 212 (1 Dist. 1974).

—Temporary Cessation of Income
Where the record amply demonstrated that defendant's request for reduction of child support payments was not prompted by a desire to evade his responsibility, and the order of the trial judge did not relieve defendant of all responsibility for child support for the period in question; the defendant's temporary cessation of income, incurred voluntarily, but in good faith, prompted the trial judge, in the exercise of judgment and discretion, to enter the questioned order; there was no abuse of that discretion. Graham v. Graham, 21 Ill. App. 3d 1032, 316 N.E.2d 143 (4 Dist. 1974).

—Termination
Term in martial settlement agreement providing that child support ended when the child graduated from high school was interpreted to mean that child support also ended when the child earned general education development certificate before high school graduation. In re Hahn, 324 Ill. App. 3d 44, 257 Ill. Dec. 803, 754 N.E.2d 461, 2001 Ill. App. LEXIS 635 (2 Dist. 2001).

——In General
The general rule is that child support terminates when the child reaches majority. In re Pauley, 104 Ill. App. 3d 100, 59 Ill. Dec. 875, 432 N.E.2d 661 (4 Dist. 1982).

A father may not decide when and for what reason he will discontinue child support; that decision is within the sole province of the court. Cooper v. Cooper, 59 Ill. App. 3d 457, 16 Ill. Dec. 818, 375 N.E.2d 925 (1 Dist. 1978).

The court has clear statutory authority, in the proper case, to terminate child support. Cooper v. Cooper, 59 Ill. App. 3d 457, 16 Ill. Dec. 818, 375 N.E.2d 925 (1 Dist. 1978).

A mere violation of visitation terms by the mother will not excuse the father's obligation to support his children. Cooper v. Cooper, 59 Ill. App. 3d 457, 16 Ill. Dec. 818, 375 N.E.2d 925 (1 Dist. 1978).

——Discretion of Court
A court cannot order termination of support for a child before the legal duty of support ends. In re Smith, 100 Ill. App. 3d 1126, 56 Ill. Dec. 716, 427 N.E.2d 1262 (2 Dist. 1981).

——Mandatory Termination
The terminating events contained in subsection (b) of this section are mandatory. Warren v. Warren, 88 Ill. App. 3d 543, 43 Ill. Dec. 782, 410 N.E.2d 915 (3 Dist. 1980).

——Not Allowed
The circumstances of the case could not be considered so extraordinary as to permit defendant's support of his son to have been terminated before the son reached majority. In re Wilde, 141 Ill. App. 3d 464, 95 Ill. Dec. 622, 490 N.E.2d 95 (2 Dist. 1986).

Where the trial court employed the statutory definition of majority (formerly Ill.Rev.Stat., ch. 3, para. 131 (see now this section)), which became effective subsequent to the entry of the divorce decree in arriving at its conclusion that a male child ceases to be a minor at age 18, but the statute in effect on the date of the entry of the decree provided that males attained majority at age 21; the trial court's determination that plaintiff's son, upon reaching 18 years of age on June 14, 1973, was no longer entitled to support under the terms of the divorce decree was erroneous. Venegas v. Venegas, 46 Ill. App. 3d 998, 5 Ill. Dec. 335, 361 N.E.2d 658 (1 Dist. 1977).

—Timeliness
Guardian's claims against the guardian's ex-husband's estate on behalf of the guardian's disabled daughter pursuant to 750 ILCS 5/510 and 750 ILCS 5/513 were properly found to be time-barred under 755 ILCS 5/18-12, as the guardian filed the claims more than two years after the ex-husband's death, and neither a similar timely claim filed in California, nor the daughter's mental disability, pursuant to 735 ILCS 5/13-208 through 735 ILCS 5/13-211, tolled the statute of limitations. Epsteen v. Epsteen, 339 Ill. App. 3d 586, 274 Ill. Dec. 379, 791 N.E.2d 175, 2003 Ill. App. LEXIS 652 (1 Dist. 2003).

—Trust Fund
The court's order, requiring respondent to establish a trust fund

Support (Cont'd)

—Trust Fund (Cont'd)
with the child support arrearages, was not legally justified under this Act, and deprived petitioner of a vested right. In re Bush, 191 Ill. App. 3d 249, 138 Ill. Dec. 423, 547 N.E.2d 590 (4 Dist. 1989).

—Trust Taxes
Where child support payments were left for children through testamentary and insurance trusts, a court should not require a result different from the decedent's wishes in order to secure the most favorable tax consequences involving discretionary assets. Halas v. McCaskey, 104 Ill. 2d 83, 83 Ill. Dec. 540, 470 N.E.2d 960 (1984).

—Unenforceable Adoption Agreement
An adoptive father's unenforceable contractual adoption agreement did not give rise to either a legal or a moral obligation sufficient to constitute a dependency relationship with the child at the time of the child's birth. Peeters v. Chicago Dist. Council, 97 Ill. App. 3d 594, 53 Ill. Dec. 101, 423 N.E.2d 485 (1 Dist. 1980).

—Unilateral Reduction
Where husband's payment of the mortgage was part of his child support obligation, when he unilaterally reduced his payments to the bank on the mortgage, he was reducing the amount of child support in violation of subsection (a). In re Avery, 251 Ill. App. 3d 648, 190 Ill. Dec. 914, 622 N.E.2d 1231 (5 Dist. 1993).

Termination

—Cohabitation Requirement
Termination requires a showing that the recipient spouse is involved in a de facto husband-wife relationship; while proof of sexual conduct between the spouse receiving maintenance and the person with whom the spouse is living is no longer necessary to establish cohabitation on a conjugal basis, something more than merely living with another person of the opposite sex is required. A lesser involvement by the recipient spouse does not require termination of maintenance. In re Lambdin, 245 Ill. App. 3d 797, 184 Ill. Dec. 789, 613 N.E.2d 1381 (4 Dist. 1993).

—Not Justified
Balancing the goal of financial independence against the dependent former spouse's entitlement to maintain a standard of living similar to that established during the marriage, the circuit court properly determined wife's maintenance should not be terminated based on public policy grounds. In re Lenkner, 241 Ill. App. 3d 15, 181 Ill. Dec. 646, 608 N.E.2d 897 (4 Dist. 1993).

Where defendant was nearly 50 years old, with no career training or significant work experience, where parties were married for 24 years, during which time plaintiff built a successful dentistry practice, defendant's efforts contributed to that success, assets transferred to defendant at the time of the divorce, were acquired through the joint efforts of both parties, and subsequent to divorce, defendant agreed to a thirty percent reduction in alimony, despite the fact that plaintiff's income had increased substantially, the trial court erred in totally terminating alimony but alimony was modified. Hall v. Hall, 25 Ill. App. 3d 524, 323 N.E.2d 541 (1 Dist. 1975).

—Same-Sex Relationship
A same-sex relationship may be the basis for terminating maintenance, even though such a relationship cannot be formalized as a marriage. In re Weisbruch, 304 Ill. App. 3d 99, 710 N.E.2d 439 (2 Dist. 1999).

—Settlement Agreement
The provision in a settlement agreement that "Thirty days after Wife's remarriage, the parties shall agree to an amount for child support and if the parties can not agree, then the matter shall be submitted to the Circuit Court" did not mean that, by implication, the wife's remarriage was the only event that could trigger the termination of maintenance. In re Weisbruch, 304 Ill. App. 3d 99, 710 N.E.2d 439 (2 Dist. 1999).

Obligation, as part and parcel of the parties' marital property settlement, could not be revoked by a court according to this section absent a finding of extrinsic fraud or want of jurisdiction. Ihle v. Ihle, 92 Ill. App. 3d 893, 48 Ill. Dec. 335, 416 N.E.2d 366 (3 Dist. 1981).

—Upheld
Evidence supported the termination of maintenance on the basis of the former wife's same-sex conjugal relationship where the evidence showed far more than a casual friendship; the former wife's partner was the primary beneficiary of the former wife's will, deferred income plan, retirement plan, and life insurance policy, and the former wife had disinherited her two sons. In re Weisbruch, 304 Ill. App. 3d 99, 710 N.E.2d 439 (2 Dist. 1999).

Even though the trial court could have made it clearer that it had considered all statutory factors in reaching its decision, on the record it did not appear the trial court abused its discretion in terminating permanent maintenance based on change in circumstances. In re Kocher, 282 Ill. App. 3d 655, 218 Ill. Dec. 167, 668 N.E.2d 651 (4 Dist. 1996).

Unallocated Award
Dividing the previously unallocated award into separate awards for child support and maintenance effective retroactively to date of former wife's remarriage instead of date the former husband filed petition to stop maintenance was appropriate. In re Erickson, 136 Ill. App. 3d 907, 91 Ill. Dec. 346, 483 N.E.2d 692 (2 Dist. 1985).

LEGAL PERIODICALS

For article, "Survey of Illinois Law: Family Law," 19 S. Ill. U.L.J. 819 (1995).

For article, "Survey of Illinois Law [1988-89] — Family Law," see 14 S. Ill. U. L. J. 1007 (1990).

For article, "Family Law: 1988-89 Illinois Law Survey," see 21 Loy. U. Chi. L. J. 417 (1989-90).

For article, "Family Law: 1986-87 Illinois Law Survey," see 19 Loy. U. Chi. L. J. 489 (1987-88).

For article, "Family Law: 1985-86 Survey," see 11 S. Ill. U. L. J. 741 (1987).

For article, "Family Law: 1985-86 Survey," see 11 S. Ill. U. L. J. 741 (1987).

For article, "Family Law: 1985-86 Illinois Law Survey," see 18 Loy. U. Chi. L. J. 549 (1986-87).

RESEARCH REFERENCES

Removal by custodial parents of child from jurisdiction in violation of court order as justifying termination, suspension, or reduction of child support payments. 8 ALR4th 1231.

Excessiveness or adequacy of money awarded as child support. 27 ALR4th 864.

Postmajority disability as reviving parental duty to support child. 48 ALR4th 919.

Divorce: voluntary contributions to child's education expenses as factor justifying modification of spousal support award. 63 ALR4th 436.

Withholding visitation rights for failure to make alimony or support payments. 65 ALR4th 1155.

Divorce: court's authority to institute or increase spousal support award after discharge of prior property award in bankruptcy. 87 ALR4th 353.

Death of obligor parent as affecting decree for support of child. 14 ALR5th 557.

Loss of income due to incarceration as affecting child support obligation. 27 ALR5th 540.

Treatment of depreciation expenses claimed for tax or accounting purposes in determining ability to pay child or spousal support. 28 ALR5th 46.

Right to credit on child support payments for social security or other government dependency payments made for the benefit of child. 34 ALR5th 447.

Decrease in income of obligor spouse following voluntary termination of employment as basis for modification of child support award. 39 ALR5th 1.

Alimony as affected by recipient spouse's remarriage in absence of controlling specific statute. 47 ALR5th 129.

What voluntary acts of child, other than marriage or entry into military service, terminate parent's obligation to support. 55 ALR5th 557.

Consideration of obligor spouse's or parent's personal-injury recovery or settlement in fixing alimony or child-support award. 59 ALR5th 489.

750 ILCS 5/511 Procedure

Sec. 511. *Procedure.* A judgment of dissolution or of legal separation or of declaration of invalidity of marriage may be enforced or modified by order of court pursuant to petition.

(a) Any judgment entered within this State may be enforced or modified in the judicial circuit wherein such judgment was entered or last modified by the filing of a petition with notice mailed to the respondent at his last known address, or by the issuance of summons to the respondent. If neither party continues to reside in the county wherein such judgment was entered or last modified, the court on the motion of either party or on its own motion may transfer a post-judgment proceeding, including a proceeding under the Income Withholding for Support Act [750 ILCS 28/1 et seq.], to another county or judicial circuit, as appropriate, where either party resides. If the post-judgment proceeding is with respect to maintenance or support, any such transfer shall be to the county or judicial circuit wherein the recipient or proposed recipient of such maintenance or support resides.

(b) In any post-judgment proceeding to enforce or modify in one judicial circuit the judgment of another judicial circuit of this State, the moving party shall commence the proceeding by filing a petition establishing the judgment and attaching a copy of the judgment as a part of the petition. The parties shall continue to be designated as in the original proceeding. Notice of the filing of the petition shall be mailed to the clerk of the court wherein the judgment was entered and last modified in the same manner as notice is mailed when registering a foreign judgment. Summons shall be served as provided by law.

(c) In any post-judgment proceeding to enforce or modify the judgment of another state, the moving party shall commence the proceeding by filing a petition to enroll that judgment, attaching a copy thereof as a part of the petition and proceed as provided for in paragraph (b) hereof.

(d) In any post-judgment proceeding to enforce a judgment or order for payment of maintenance or support, including a proceeding under the Income Withholding for Support Act [750 ILCS 28/1 et seq.], where the terms of such judgment or order provide that payments of such maintenance or support are to be made to the clerk of the court and where neither party continues to reside in the county wherein such judgment or order was entered or last modified, the court on the motion of either party or on its own motion may transfer the collection of the maintenance or support to the clerk of the court in another county or judicial circuit, as appropriate, wherein the recipient of the maintenance or support payments resides.

(Source: P.A. 85-2; 90-673, § 915.)

Note.
This section was Ill.Rev.Stat., Ch. 40, para. 511.

Cross References.
As to revival of judgments, see 735 ILCS 5/13-218.

Effect of Amendments.
The 1998 amendment by P.A. 90-673, effective January 1, 1999, substituted "the Income Withholding for Support Act" for "Section 706.1 of this Act" in subsections (a) and (d).

CASE NOTES

Analysis

Appeal
—Prior Petition Not Filed
Enforcement
—Foreign Decree
—Forum
—Standing
Filing of Petition
—Failure to File
Foreign Judgment
—Failure to Follow Procedure
—Modification
—Registration in Illinois
Hearing
Jurisdiction
Maintenance
—Modification Not Necessary
—Modification Proper
—Timely Appeal
Notice
—By Mail
—Insufficient
Nunc Pro Tunc Order
Pleadings
—Verification
Support
—Modification
—Voluntary Unemployment

Appeal

—Prior Petition Not Filed
Where the appellant was not requesting a modification of the divorce decree but, rather, a termination of support payments in accord with his interpretation of the divorce decree, his appeal was not barred by a failure to file a petition to modify the decree under former Ill.Rev.Stat., ch. 40, para. 19 (see now this section). Waldron v. Waldron, 13 Ill. App. 3d 964, 301 N.E.2d 167 (5 Dist. 1973).

Enforcement

—Foreign Decree
A court can enforce the existing terms of a foreign court decree without re-opening the judgment. Osborne ex rel. Osborne v. Sprowls, 83 Ill. App. 3d 968, 39 Ill. Dec. 474, 404 N.E.2d 1065 (3 Dist. 1980), aff'd, 84 Ill. 2d 390, 50 Ill. Dec. 645, 419 N.E.2d 913 (1981).

—Forum
The proper forum in which to apply for the enforcement of the divorce decree is the court which entered it. Stewart v. Stewart, 1 Ill. App. 2d 283, 117 N.E.2d 579 (4 Dist. 1954).

—Standing
Child of wife who failed to establish a trust for his benefit as ordered in the divorce decree lacked standing to seek enforcement of the provisions of the judgment for divorce to which he was not a party. In re Garrison, 99 Ill. App. 3d 717, 54 Ill. Dec. 653, 425 N.E.2d 518 (2 Dist. 1981).

A child may not bring suit against his father to recover arrearages in child support payments. Kelleher v. Kelleher, 21 Ill. App. 3d 601, 316 N.E.2d 212 (1 Dist. 1974).

Since a child is furnished support by other persons, an equitable result would not be obtained if the child had a right to sue his father

Enforcement (Cont'd)

—Standing (Cont'd)
for past-due support. Kelleher v. Kelleher, 21 Ill. App. 3d 601, 316 N.E.2d 212 (1 Dist. 1974).

Filing of Petition
A party is not required to file a petition to "enroll" the judgment and another separate petition to "modify" the judgment. In re Bussey, 108 Ill. 2d 286, 91 Ill. Dec. 594, 483 N.E.2d 1229 (1985).

—Failure to File
Where father failed to file an appropriate petition his obligations for college expenses continued to accrue and became rights vested in mother, and she was entitled to a judgment for the sum shown to be due. In re Sawyer, 264 Ill. App. 3d 839, 202 Ill. Dec. 20, 637 N.E.2d 559 (1 Dist. 1994).

Foreign Judgment

—Failure to Follow Procedure
Police officers were not entitled to absolute immunity in a civil rights action by a mother following the officers' seizure of her daughter where they were acting pursuant to an unenforceable out-of-state order which had not been filed with a state court as required by 735 ILCS 5/12-652 and 750 ILCS 5/511(c). Dunn v. City of Elgin, 347 F.3d 641, 2003 U.S. App. LEXIS 21186 (7th Cir. 2003).
Where father simply refused to follow the appropriate statutory procedures for enforcing an out-of-state custody judgment, the trial court properly refused to consider his claim to temporary custody. Gasaway v. Gasaway, 246 Ill. App. 3d 531, 186 Ill. Dec. 420, 616 N.E.2d 610 (3 Dist. 1993).

—Modification
Although an Illinois court cannot act contrary to a foreign judgment as regards disposition of property, unless the trial court finds the existence of conditions that justify the re-opening of the judgment; a court can enforce the existing terms of a foreign court decree without re-opening the judgment. Osborne ex rel. Osborne v. Sprowls, 83 Ill. App. 3d 968, 39 Ill. Dec. 474, 404 N.E.2d 1065 (3 Dist. 1980), aff'd, 84 Ill. 2d 390, 50 Ill. Dec. 645, 419 N.E.2d 913 (1981).

—Registration in Illinois
Orders registering out-of-state dissolution judgments under subsection (c) are not in and of themselves causes of action and do not adjudicate the rights of parties; rather, they are merely procedural devices by which a party may seek enforcement or modification in Illinois of a judgment entered in another state, and are not necessary to confer jurisdiction on the court. In re Buchanio, 262 Ill. App. 3d 910, 200 Ill. Dec. 641, 635 N.E.2d 980 (1 Dist.), appeal denied, 157 Ill. 2d 496, 205 Ill. Dec. 157, 642 N.E.2d 1274 (1994).

Hearing
Defendant was entitled to a full hearing on his petition for a reduction in support payments, including the right to have witnesses appear and be cross-examined. Regan v. Regan, 38 Ill. App. 2d 383, 187 N.E.2d 286 (1 Dist. 1962).

Jurisdiction
Without a petition to modify child support on file, the circuit court's subject matter jurisdiction was not invoked, and the orders entered with regard to petitioner's rights to child support were void. Ottwell v. Ottwell, 167 Ill. App. 3d 901, 118 Ill. Dec. 873, 522 N.E.2d 328 (5 Dist. 1988).
In order for a circuit court to have jurisdiction of the subject matter and of the parties, it is necessary that a petition for modification of a divorce decree regarding child support be filed to invoke subject matter jurisdiction, and that notice be mailed to the respondent of the petition. Ottwell v. Ottwell, 167 Ill. App. 3d 901, 118 Ill. Dec. 873, 522 N.E.2d 328 (5 Dist. 1988).
The circuit court had subject matter jurisdiction to modify an out-of-state divorce decree because the change-in-custody petition filed by the petitioner was sufficient to enroll the decree in Illinois. In re Bussey, 108 Ill. 2d 286, 91 Ill. Dec. 594, 483 N.E.2d 1229 (1985).
Strict compliance with the statutory requirements of subsection (c) of this section was not necessary for the court to have subject matter jurisdiction over a proceeding to modify custody and child support because a trial court's jurisdiction arises from the constitution rather than from the statutes; the inquiry must be whether there exists a justiciable controversy, and if so, are there any statutory conditions precedent to judicial intervention. In re Bussey, 128 Ill. App. 3d 730, 84 Ill. Dec. 34, 471 N.E.2d 563 (4 Dist. 1984).
The trial court acquired subject matter jurisdiction over petition to modify custody and child support upon the filing of the original petition accompanied by a copy of the foreign order. In re Bussey, 128 Ill. App. 3d 730, 84 Ill. Dec. 34, 471 N.E.2d 563 (4 Dist. 1984).
Illinois circuit courts have jurisdiction in all justiciable matters and may exercise jurisdiction in cases involving enforcement or modification of out-of-state divorce decrees when they are registered as statutorily provided. Coons v. Wilder, 93 Ill. App. 3d 127, 48 Ill. Dec. 512, 416 N.E.2d 785 (2 Dist. 1981).
When dealing with such matters as grounds for divorce, payment of alimony and modification of divorce decrees, which are regulated by statute, a court is exercising powers granted by the legislature and cannot by incorporating a contractual provision in its decree divest itself of the power to modify, contrary to the legislative will. Duvall v. Duvall, 8 Ill. App. 3d 53, 289 N.E.2d 59 (3 Dist. 1972).
In determining the propriety or impropriety of divorce decree ordering conveyance of property under the former Divorce Act, the authority of the court was based upon powers conferred by statute rather than upon general equity powers. Debrey v. Debrey, 132 Ill. App. 2d 1072, 270 N.E.2d 43 (4 Dist. 1971).

Maintenance

—Modification Not Necessary
The provision for the payment of alimony by husband as one-half of his salary earned and received as a teacher or employee of the public schools of the City of Chicago, Illinois, as long as he is so employed was held reasonably definite and certain while the husband was employed as a school teacher. Condy v. Condy, 328 Ill. App. 8, 65 N.E.2d 219 (1946).

—Modification Proper
The court's order directing respondent to provide for reinstatement of the contingent survivorship benefit or, in the alternative, to adequately fund an equivalent benefit, was proper since respondent's action in destroying this benefit was interference with a provision of the separate maintenance settlement agreement which, like the respondent's right to his pension benefits, was adopted by the dissolution judgment. In re Lipkin, 208 Ill. App. 3d 214, 153 Ill. Dec. 122, 566 N.E.2d 972 (4 Dist. 1991).

—Timely Appeal
A proceeding resulting in a final judgment order which dismissed the plaintiff's petition for alimony and maintenance with prejudice and in bar of action was a "trial" or adjudication upon the merits; where the plaintiff filed a motion for rehearing and to vacate the final judgment order within 30 days of the order, and a notice of appeal was given within 30 days of the order denying the motion to vacate, the appeal was timely filed. Fulwider v. Fulwider, 8 Ill. App. 3d 581, 290 N.E.2d 264 (4 Dist. 1972).

Notice

—By Mail
Service by mail of a petition was proper despite respondent's objections thereto where the court already had personal jurisdiction over him and such service was all that was required for modification by post-judgment proceedings. Wait v. Wait, 158 Ill. App. 3d 271, 109 Ill. Dec. 732, 510 N.E.2d 600 (4 Dist. 1987).

—Insufficient
Order which purportedly modified former husband's support obligation was in error, if not void, where only notice given was to respondent's then attorney of record; since only appearance made by respondent was special and limited, the impropriety of the notice was not waived. In re Mullins, 135 Ill. App. 3d 279, 89 Ill. Dec. 771, 481 N.E.2d 322 (4 Dist. 1985).

Nunc Pro Tunc Order
Where the court entered its order nunc pro tunc modifying the decree and reducing the alimony to be paid, the route by which the trial court reached its destination was out of line with all recog-

Nunc Pro Tunc Order (Cont'd)
nized procedure under former Ill.Rev.Stat., ch. 40, para. 19 (see now this section). Briggs v. Briggs, 299 Ill. App. 577, 20 N.E.2d 908 (4 Dist. 1939).

Pleadings

—Verification
Since the appellant has the burden of presenting the record on appeal to support his theory of the case, his failure to include any prior verified pleadings required the court to reject his contention that the wife's post-decree petition should have been verified. In re Sreenan, 81 Ill. App. 3d 1025, 37 Ill. Dec. 458, 402 N.E.2d 348 (2 Dist. 1980).

Support

—Modification
Although it is the rule that modification of child support provisions generally rests in the sound discretion of the trial court, such an order may be reversed when manifest injustice has been done. Glass v. Peitchel, 42 Ill. App. 3d 240, 355 N.E.2d 750 (1 Dist. 1976).
The court has the power to modify a decree or order as to child support and educational payments, with no exceptions for prior agreements or "consent decrees." Duvall v. Duvall, 8 Ill. App. 3d 53, 289 N.E.2d 59 (3 Dist. 1972).

—Voluntary Unemployment
A parent should not be permitted to avoid responsibility for support payments by the bad faith refusal to earn income or in the case of a voluntary loss of employment. Glass v. Peitchel, 42 Ill. App. 3d 240, 355 N.E.2d 750 (1 Dist. 1976).

LEGAL PERIODICALS

For article, "The Sequestrator — The Court's Enforcer," see 70 Ill. B. J. 494 (1982).

750 ILCS 5/512 Post-Judgment Venue

Sec. 512. *Post-Judgment Venue.* After 30 days from the entry of a judgment of dissolution of marriage or the last modification thereof, any further proceedings to enforce or modify the judgment shall be as follows:

(a) If the respondent does not then reside within this State, further proceedings shall be had either in the judicial circuit wherein the moving party resides or where the judgment was entered or last modified.

(b) If one or both of the parties then resides in the judicial circuit wherein the judgment was entered or last modified, further proceedings shall be had in the judicial circuit that last exercised jurisdiction in the matter; provided, however, that the court may in its discretion, transfer matters involving a change in child custody to the judicial circuit where the minor or dependent child resides.

(c) If neither party then resides in the judicial circuit wherein the judgment was entered or last modified, further proceedings shall be had in that circuit or in the judicial circuit wherein either party resides or where the respondent is actively employed; provided, however, that the court may, in its discretion, transfer matters involving a change in child custody to the judicial circuit where the minor or dependent child resides.

(d) Objection to venue is waived if not made within such time as the respondent's answer is due. Counter relief shall be heard and determined by the court hearing any matter already pending.
(Source: P.A. 80-923.)

Note.
This section was Ill.Rev.Stat., Ch. 40, para. 512.

CASE NOTES

ANALYSIS

Construction
Enforcement of Decree
Registration Obsolete
Transferred Action
—Jurisdiction
Venue
—Mandatory
—Waiver

Construction
This section is clear and unambiguous; inasmuch as the court enrolled a 30 day old custody order prior to 30 day time span elapsed from final dissolution of marriage, this was error. In re Skinner, 149 Ill. App. 3d 788, 103 Ill. Dec. 290, 501 N.E.2d 311 (4 Dist. 1986).

Enforcement of Decree
The adoption of subsection (a) of this section, rendered obsolete the former procedure for enforcing a divorce decree entered in another county. In re Hostetler, 124 Ill. App. 3d 31, 79 Ill. Dec. 401, 463 N.E.2d 955 (1 Dist. 1984).

Registration Obsolete
The former practice of registering a divorce decree has been rendered obsolete by the adoption of this section which provides that post-judgment venue of proceedings to enforce or modify a judgment "shall" be as provided in the statute. In re Nelson, 128 Ill. App. 3d 635, 83 Ill. Dec. 501, 470 N.E.2d 627 (2 Dist. 1984).

Transferred Action

—Jurisdiction
There was no "transfer" of a McLean County dissolution action to Cook County where no order seeking a transfer was entered and where wife failed to comply with the procedure for enforcing a divorce decree entered in another county, as the latter court lacked personal jurisdiction over husband. In re Hostetler, 124 Ill. App. 3d 31, 79 Ill. Dec. 401, 463 N.E.2d 955 (1 Dist. 1984).

Venue

—Mandatory
The word "shall" in subsection (b) of this section is mandatory; the legislature granted discretion to a court only to "transfer matters involving a change in child custody" and since this statute permits the exercise of discretion only in the one specified matter, its provision that other post-judgment proceedings shall be in the judicial circuit which last exercised jurisdiction in the matter must be viewed as mandatory. In re Nelson, 128 Ill. App. 3d 635, 83 Ill. Dec. 501, 470 N.E.2d 627 (2 Dist. 1984).

—Waiver
Venue of the county court to grant visitation privileges to the maternal grandparents issue was waived under subsection (d) of this section where no timely objection was made. Hawkins v. Hawkins, 102 Ill. App. 3d 1037, 58 Ill. Dec. 620, 430 N.E.2d 652 (3 Dist. 1981).

750 ILCS 5/513 Support for Non-minor Children and Educational Expenses

Sec. 513. *Support for Non-minor Children and Educational Expenses.* (a) The court may award sums of money out of the property and income of either or both parties or the estate of a deceased parent, as equity may require, for the support of the child or children of the parties who have attained majority in the following instances:

(1) When the child is mentally or physically disabled and not otherwise emancipated, an application for support may be made before or after the child has attained majority.

(2) The court may also make provision for the educational expenses of the child or children of the parties, whether of minor or majority age, and an application for educational expenses may be made before or after the child has attained majority, or after the death of either parent. The authority under this Section to make provision for educational expenses extends not only to periods of college education or professional or other training after graduation from high school, but also to any period during which the child of the parties is still attending high school, even though he or she attained the age of 19. The educational expenses may include, but shall not be limited to, room, board, dues, tuition, transportation, books, fees, registration and application costs, medical expenses including medical insurance, dental expenses, and living expenses during the school year and periods of recess, which sums may be ordered payable to the child, to either parent, or to the educational institution, directly or through a special account or trust created for that purpose, as the court sees fit.

If educational expenses are ordered payable, each parent and the child shall sign any consents necessary for the educational institution to provide the supporting parent with access to the child's academic transcripts, records, and grade reports. The consents shall not apply to any non-academic records. Failure to execute the required consent may be a basis for a modification or termination of any order entered under this Section.

The authority under this Section to make provision for educational expenses, except where the child is mentally or physically disabled and not otherwise emancipated, terminates when the child receives a baccalaureate degree.

(b) In making awards under paragraph (1) or (2) of subsection (a), or pursuant to a petition or motion to decrease, modify, or terminate any such award, the court shall consider all relevant factors that appear reasonable and necessary, including:

(1) The financial resources of both parents.

(2) The standard of living the child would have enjoyed had the marriage not been dissolved.

(3) The financial resources of the child.

(4) The child's academic performance.

(Source: P.A. 86-637; 87-910, § 1; 91-204, § 5; 92-876, § 910.)

Note.

This section was Ill.Rev.Stat., Ch. 40, para. 513.

Effect of Amendments.

The 1999 amendment by P.A. 91-204, effective January 1, 2000, inserted the last two paragraphs in subsection (a); and in subsection (b) inserted "or pursuant to a petition or motion to decrease, modify, or terminate any such award" in the introductory paragraph and added item (4).

The 2002 amendment by P.A. 92-876, effective June 1, 2003, in subsection (a)(2) substituted "age of 19" for "age of 18" in the second sentence.

CASE NOTES

Analysis

Constitutionality
In General
Attorney Fees
Bankruptcy Proceedings
Change in Circumstances
—In General
Child Support
—Award Upheld
—Duration
—Obligation
—Parent's Liability
Disability
—In General
—Not Shown
—Shown
Educational Expenses
—In General
—Ability to Pay
—Application
—Award Denied
—Award Upheld
—Burden of Proof
—Child's Resources
—College or University
—Contempt
—Disability Not Required
—Duty to Pay
—Emancipation
—Factors Considered
—Financial Resources
—Illegitimate Children
—Illustrative Cases
—Living Expenses Included
—Modification
—Noncustodial Deceased Parent
—Pending Marriage Dissolution
—Relationship of Parent and Child
—Settlement Agreement
—Shortages
—Standing
—Trust
—Unaccredited Religious School
—Waiver
Effect of Amendment
—Educational Expense Guidelines
Emancipation
—By Marriage
—Not Shown
Enforcement of Decree
—Adult Child
Jurisdiction
Legislative Intent
Matters Pertaining to Children
—College Expenses
Medical and Dental Expenses
Modification of Orders
Modification of Payments
Out of Property
—Defined
Purpose
Review
Settlement Agreement
—Held Modifiable
Unilateral Reduction
Valuation

Constitutionality

This section does not violate the equal protection guarantees of the U.S. or Illinois Constitution. Kujawinski v. Kujawinski, 71 Ill. 2d 563, 17 Ill. Dec. 801, 376 N.E.2d 1382 (1978).

In General

The general rule is that child support terminates when a child reaches the age of 18 when the child has attained majority and becomes emancipated. In re Ferraro, 211 Ill. App. 3d 797, 156 Ill. Dec. 160, 570 N.E.2d 636 (1 Dist. 1991).

This section authorizes the trial court to make provisions for the education and maintenance of children after they have attained the age of majority. Falat v. Falat, 201 Ill. App. 3d 320, 147 Ill. Dec. 33, 559 N.E.2d 33 (1 Dist. 1990).

The trial court has the authority to make an equitable contingency provision for the education of a child during and beyond her minority. In re Block, 110 Ill. App. 3d 864, 65 Ill. Dec. 769, 441 N.E.2d 1283 (2 Dist. 1982).

The fact that a child may be emancipated does not preclude the court from ordering the payment of educational expenses. In re Greenberg, 102 Ill. App. 3d 938, 58 Ill. Dec. 1, 429 N.E.2d 1334 (1 Dist. 1981).

The trial court is empowered to provide for the education and maintenance of non-minor children as equity may require after considering, among other things, the financial resources of both parents and the financial resources of the child. In re Fleming, 80 Ill. App. 3d 1006, 36 Ill. Dec. 205, 400 N.E.2d 625 (2 Dist. 1980).

Attorney Fees

Respondent was ordered to pay petitioner's attorney's fees, necessitated by respondent's noncompliance with an agreement to pay for his child's college education. In re Houston, 150 Ill. App. 3d 608, 103 Ill. Dec. 698, 501 N.E.2d 1015 (5 Dist. 1986).

Bankruptcy Proceedings

Attorney's fee award in paternity action was a support debt under 11 U.S.C. § 522(f)(1)(A). In re Allen, 217 Bankr. 247 (Bankr. S.D. Ill. 1998).

Change in Circumstances

—In General

The factors set out in this section are irrelevant in enforcement proceedings, and are likewise irrelevant in a modification proceeding; the pertinent question in determining whether to grant a petition for modification of a provision for payment of college expenses is the same as that on a petition to modify any other support term, that is, whether the petitioner has shown a substantial change in circumstances. In re Loffredi, 232 Ill. App. 3d 709, 173 Ill. Dec. 933, 597 N.E.2d 907 (3 Dist. 1992).

Child Support

—Award Upheld

The trial court's award of child support extending beyond the majority of each child, if the child reached majority before leaving school, was not erroneous. In re Coram, 86 Ill. App. 3d 845, 42 Ill. Dec. 40, 408 N.E.2d 418 (5 Dist. 1980).

—Duration

An order under this section for education and maintenance of a child, whether of minor or majority age, is intended to be included within 750 ILCS 5/510(c) as a support order and is not terminated by the death of a parent obligated to pay for these expenses. DeFrancesca v. Estate of Champagne, 153 Ill. App. 3d 560, 106 Ill. Dec. 561, 505 N.E.2d 1352 (2 Dist. 1987).

Where a stipulation and agreed order did not contain any language limiting the obligation to pay a non-minor child's college education expense to the decedent's lifetime, the order did not terminate upon the decedent's death, and his estate was responsible for these expenses. DeFrancesca v. Estate of Champagne, 153 Ill. App. 3d 560, 106 Ill. Dec. 561, 505 N.E.2d 1352 (2 Dist. 1987).

—Obligation

The obligation of a parent to support his or her minor child begins when the child is born and continues until the child attains majority. In re Holderrieth, 181 Ill. App. 3d 199, 129 Ill. Dec. 896, 536 N.E.2d 946 (1 Dist. 1989).

A parent cannot bargain away his or her obligation of child support. In re Holderrieth, 181 Ill. App. 3d 199, 129 Ill. Dec. 896, 536 N.E.2d 946 (1 Dist. 1989).

Even if the change of name was granted to the child, who resided with her mother and her mother's new husband, her father must continue to support and educate her, extending through college. In re Omelson, 112 Ill. App. 3d 725, 68 Ill. Dec. 307, 445 N.E.2d 951 (5 Dist. 1983).

This section has been interpreted as obligating the parents to extend support only during a child's minority or other dependency. In re Stribling, 96 Ill. App. 3d 317, 51 Ill. Dec. 895, 421 N.E.2d 403 (3 Dist. 1981).

—Parent's Liability

A parent's liability for child support continues during the minority of a child, which ends at age 18. Prenzler v. Prenzler, 55 Ill. App. 3d 244, 12 Ill. Dec. 838, 370 N.E.2d 642 (3 Dist. 1977).

Disability

—In General

Guardian's claims against the guardian's ex-husband's estate on behalf of the guardian's disabled daughter pursuant to 750 ILCS 5/510 and 750 ILCS 5/513 were properly found to be time-barred under 755 ILCS 5/18-12, as the guardian filed the claims more than two years after the ex-husband's death, and neither a similar timely claim filed in California, nor the daughter's mental disability, pursuant to 735 ILCS 5/13-208, -211, tolled the statute of limitations. Epsteen v. Epsteen, 339 Ill. App. 3d 586, 274 Ill. Dec. 379, 791 N.E.2d 175, 2003 Ill. App. LEXIS 652 (1 Dist. 2003).

An allegedly disabled adult child is not a necessary party to a proceeding by the child's custodial parent for child support. Lerner v. Lerner, 316 Ill. App. 3d 1072, 250 Ill. Dec. 219, 738 N.E.2d 183, 2000 Ill. App. LEXIS 800 (1 Dist. 2000).

A probate court's determination of disability is not required by the statute, and a domestic relations judge has the power to make a determination of disability pursuant to a petition under the statute. Lerner v. Lerner, 316 Ill. App. 3d 1072, 250 Ill. Dec. 219, 738 N.E.2d 183, 2000 Ill. App. LEXIS 800 (1 Dist. 2000).

—Not Shown

It was an abuse of discretion to award nonminor child support on the basis that the parties' 20-year-old son was mentally disabled, notwithstanding testimony that he was a slow learner and had an IQ bordering on below average, where he graduated from high school in four years, received relatively high grades, tested in the nineteenth percentile on the ACT, was accepted in junior college, and was able to obtain employment to earn money to assist in his postsecondary education. In re Thurmond, 306 Ill. App. 3d 828, 240 Ill. Dec. 127, 715 N.E.2d 814 (2 Dist. 1999).

—Shown

The trial court's refusal to continue respondent's child support payments past child's eighteenth birthday was error where the child had a severe learning disability and had a behavioral disorder. In re Kennedy, 170 Ill. App. 3d 726, 121 Ill. Dec. 362, 525 N.E.2d 168 (5 Dist. 1988).

Child who had learning disability and behavior disorder was mentally disabled pursuant to statute for payment of child support after reaching majority. In re Kennedy, 170 Ill. App. 3d 726, 121 Ill. Dec. 362, 525 N.E.2d 168 (5 Dist. 1988).

Educational Expenses

—In General

"Support" is simply a general term that can include educational expenses for a child who has turned 18 but is still in high school, and educational expenses may include room and board, just as the more generic term, support, may include shelter and food; a trial court can award support to disabled unemancipated children, minor or nonminor under 750 ILCS 5/513(a)(1), and a particular kind of support, educational expenses, to nonminor children in school under 750 ILCS 5/513(a)(2). In short, if the child has attained majority, the trial court must turn to § 513 of the Illinois Marriage and Dissolution of Marriage Act, 750 ILCS 5/513, when deciding whether to award support for that nonminor child. Waller v. Waller, 339 Ill. App. 3d 743, 274 Ill. Dec. 582, 791 N.E.2d 674, 2003 Ill. App. LEXIS 766 (4 Dist. 2003).

Educational Expenses (Cont'd)

—In General (Cont'd)

Dissolution agreement that provided husband would pay one-half of child's college expenses, but was silent as to a specific price or method by which a specific price would be determined, implied that the price for college expenses would be reasonable. In re Schmidt, 292 Ill. App. 3d 229, 226 Ill. Dec. 152, 684 N.E.2d 1355 (4 Dist. 1997), appeal denied, 176 Ill. 2d 592, 229 Ill. Dec. 60, 690 N.E.2d 1387 (1998).

The determination of educational expenses is in the trial court's discretion. In re Zukausky, 244 Ill. App. 3d 614, 184 Ill. Dec. 367, 613 N.E.2d 394 (2 Dist. 1993).

Trial court is authorized to require either or both parents to contribute to the college education expenses of their children. Blisset v. Blisset, 123 Ill. 2d 161, 121 Ill. Dec. 931, 526 N.E.2d 125 (1988).

A divorce decree may require a parent to provide for a child's education expenses beyond the age of majority. Prenzler v. Prenzler, 55 Ill. App. 3d 244, 12 Ill. Dec. 838, 370 N.E.2d 642 (3 Dist. 1977).

—Ability to Pay

An order that a father pay for half of his two daughters' college expenses was upheld on appeal as not being an abuse of discretion; even though the father submitted evidence supporting his position that it would be difficult for him to fit the financial burden into his budget and that the mother was likely in a better financial position than he was, the evidence also showed that the father had previously been able to handle a similar financial burden in child support payments and payments for private high school for the daughters and that those responsibilities were terminated when the daughters became enrolled in college. In re Marriage of Cianchetti, 351 Ill. App. 3d 832, 286 Ill. Dec. 807, 815 N.E.2d 17, 2004 Ill. App. LEXIS 976 (3 Dist. 2004).

Where the court properly considered the necessary factors, its determination that the husband would assume responsibility for 75% of the parties' sons' college education was not an abuse of discretion. In re Olson, 223 Ill. App. 3d 636, 166 Ill. Dec. 60, 585 N.E.2d 1082 (2 Dist.), appeal denied, 145 Ill. 2d 636, 173 Ill. Dec. 6, 596 N.E.2d 630 (1992).

A party's ability to pay must be evaluated with regard to the party's resources at the time of the hearing. In re Calisoff, 176 Ill. App. 3d 721, 126 Ill. Dec. 183, 531 N.E.2d 810 (1 Dist. 1988); In re Fahy, 208 Ill. App. 3d 677, 153 Ill. Dec. 594, 567 N.E.2d 552 (1 Dist. 1991).

The trial court abused its discretion in making respondent solely responsible for his children's college expenses for four years, excluding grants or scholarships, considering respondent's adverse financial position after the disposition of marital property and petitioner's ability to contribute to such education. In re Calisoff, 176 Ill. App. 3d 721, 126 Ill. Dec. 183, 531 N.E.2d 810 (1 Dist. 1988).

Where wife had the training and rehabilitative capacity to earn a sum of money which, when combined with $9,000 unallocated maintenance, was substantially similar to husband's income; the trial court's equal division of responsibility for 21-year-old son's pharmacy school costs was not an abuse of discretion. In re Albiani, 159 Ill. App. 3d 519, 111 Ill. Dec. 126, 512 N.E.2d 30 (1 Dist. 1987).

The court should not order a party to pay more for educational expenses than he or she can afford. In re Pearson, 111 Ill. 2d 545, 96 Ill. Dec. 69, 490 N.E.2d 1274 (1986); In re Calisoff, 176 Ill. App. 3d 721, 126 Ill. Dec. 183, 531 N.E.2d 810 (1 Dist. 1988); In re Fahy, 208 Ill. App. 3d 677, 153 Ill. Dec. 594, 567 N.E.2d 552 (1 Dist. 1991).

The trial court's refusal to allocate the college expenses of the minor child between the parties was not erroneous because rather than allocating amounts between the parties, both parties would be held responsible in accordance with their financial abilities at the time the child enrolled at a college. In re Kaplan, 149 Ill. App. 3d 23, 102 Ill. Dec. 719, 500 N.E.2d 612 (1 Dist. 1986).

It was an abuse of discretion for the trial court to refuse to hear defendant's relevant testimony concerning his financial obligations to his second family. Greiman v. Friedman, 90 Ill. App. 3d 941, 46 Ill. Dec. 355, 414 N.E.2d 77 (1 Dist. 1980).

Considering the great disparities in incomes between the parties, child's tuition and books, along with the cost of his college and professional education, should be paid by the father and not be included as part of the $1,000 per month child support. In re Edelstein, 82 Ill. App. 3d 574, 38 Ill. Dec. 235, 403 N.E.2d 323 (1 Dist. 1980).

—Application

There is no indication in this section that the child himself must make the application for educational expenses but one of the parties could make it on his behalf providing the court considers the resources of both parties in ordering payment. Wait v. Wait, 158 Ill. App. 3d 271, 109 Ill. Dec. 732, 510 N.E.2d 600 (4 Dist. 1987).

An application for educational expenses pursuant to this section is considered a modification of a divorce decree even if the decree contained no provision requiring either party to contribute to their children's college education. Wait v. Wait, 158 Ill. App. 3d 271, 109 Ill. Dec. 732, 510 N.E.2d 600 (4 Dist. 1987).

—Award Denied

Where a divorce decree did not provide support for the educational expenses of the parties' non-minor children and stated that the question of educational expenses was to be reserved for future consideration, and the support awarded in the decree was support for the three minor children, this type of support terminated when the children were emancipated and the divorce decree did not obligate the father to continue paying child support after the youngest child attained majority. In re Pauley, 104 Ill. App. 3d 100, 59 Ill. Dec. 875, 432 N.E.2d 661 (4 Dist. 1982).

Denial of the petition that divorced husband pay college expenses of the children was not an abuse of discretion where respondent's testimony indicated that his expenses were in excess of his take-home pay was unrebutted and there was no contention that the deductions used in arriving at his net income or the amounts claimed as living expenses were improperly considered. Singer v. Singer, 70 Ill. App. 3d 472, 27 Ill. Dec. 88, 388 N.E.2d 1051 (1 Dist. 1979).

Where the decree did not mention college education, but rather required husband to make support payments for his minor children, and husband asserting that obligation ended at age 18 was entitled to a hearing on the merits for substantial justice was not done between the parties when the default judgment was entered for the wife. Prenzler v. Prenzler, 55 Ill. App. 3d 244, 12 Ill. Dec. 838, 370 N.E.2d 642 (3 Dist. 1977).

Where although a child had chosen to leave her father and live with her mother, the evidence failed to show a change of circumstances which would have warranted a modification of the provision of the decree awarding her custody to the father and the court could not, and would not, "force a 17 year old girl to live with her father if she did not desire"; the order to have the father pay the mother for the child's support during her minority, and an attorney's fee, but not to provide for the child's college education was affirmed. Elble v. Elble, 100 Ill. App. 2d 221, 241 N.E.2d 328 (5 Dist. 1968).

—Award Upheld

The circuit court order, which ordered the respondent to pay the parties' daughter's book costs, tuition, and fees, did not constitute an abuse of discretion where the court followed the order relied upon by the parties and gave their daughter the funds she needed to repay school loans and deliver her from the burden of substantial debt as a consequence of having pursued her college education. Hupe v. Hupe, 305 Ill. App. 3d 118, 238 Ill. Dec. 402, 711 N.E.2d 789 (3 Dist. 1999).

The trial court did not abuse its discretion by ordering ex-husband to pay only his daughter's future college tuition, books, and supplies, without reimbursing his ex-wife for their daughter's first-year college expenses or any of their son's college expenses. In re Pearson, 236 Ill. App. 3d 337, 177 Ill. Dec. 650, 603 N.E.2d 720 (1 Dist. 1992).

Where child did not abandon his education but merely suspended it, testified that he planned to resume his college education in the near future, saved money he was earning, along with other money paid to him by his father and where father had the ability to pay child's educational expenses, mother also contributed to child's education by supporting him while he lived with her and the court ordered the money to be put in a separate account to protect child's best interests, the trial court did not abuse its discretion in ordering father to pay arrearages and continue educational support to child. Alltop v. Alltop, 203 Ill. App. 3d 606, 149 Ill. Dec. 116, 561 N.E.2d 394 (4 Dist. 1990).

Educational Expenses (Cont'd)

—Award Upheld (Cont'd)

The circuit court was well within its discretion in ordering plaintiff to make payments for college expenses which would not require his son to go into substantial debt to procure a college education. Gibb v. Triezenberg, 188 Ill. App. 3d 695, 135 Ill. Dec. 948, 544 N.E.2d 444 (4 Dist. 1989).

Where husband and wife owned a house and property valued at approximately $200,000, of which husband was awarded 50% and husband and his present wife owned real estate with a net equity of about $40,000; where he had stock in a restaurant in which he invested $20,000 and owned a construction company; and where husband had outstanding loans, it was not against the manifest weight of the evidence for a trial court to conclude that husband had sufficient property and income to contribute $6,000 toward his daughter's first year of college. Larsen v. Larsen, 126 Ill. App. 3d 1072, 82 Ill. Dec. 103, 468 N.E.2d 165 (3 Dist. 1984).

Where agreements incorporated into the original decree of divorce authorized defendant to direct the secular and religious education of the children, but also provided that defendant's responsibility for his children's college and post-graduate education was to be consistent with the abilities and wishes of the children, defendant was required to pay his son's future college expenses even at a school not of defendant's choice. Willcutts v. Willcutts, 88 Ill. App. 3d 813, 43 Ill. Dec. 924, 410 N.E.2d 1057 (3 Dist. 1980).

The court properly ordered that divorce decree be modified to require defendant to pay plaintiff $100 per month over a four year period while his daughter, age 17, was pursuing an education, and that he pay in installments to plaintiff $400 out of $631 incurred for medical expenses. O'Berry v. O'Berry, 36 Ill. App. 2d 163, 183 N.E.2d 539 (1 Dist. 1962).

—Burden of Proof

Husband did not need to present his own evidence to meet his burden of proof in challenging the reasonableness of the price of a college where the party's child did not provide meaningful reasons for her choice of a private school over state schools; husband needed only to show the costs of the state schools and his finances. In re Schmidt, 292 Ill. App. 3d 229, 226 Ill. Dec. 152, 684 N.E.2d 1355 (4 Dist. 1997), appeal denied, 176 Ill. 2d 592, 229 Ill. Dec. 60, 690 N.E.2d 1387 (1998).

The trial court did not err in ruling that the husband failed to sustain his burden of proof under this section where no evidence was introduced regarding the financial resources of the parents at the time the children were in college, the standard of living either child would have enjoyed had the marriage not been dissolved, or the children's financial resources other than the son's current income and expenses, and the evidence that was introduced indicated that most of the son's educational expenses were paid by his grandfather without contribution by the wife. Rosche v. Rosche, 163 Ill. App. 3d 308, 114 Ill. Dec. 846, 516 N.E.2d 1001 (5 Dist. 1987).

Ex-wife had the burden of proving that ex-husband should contribute toward the college expenses of the two children and of proving how much his share should be; the financial resources of the parties and the children must be considered by the trial court in deciding this issue; ex-wife established a prima facie case by introducing evidence that the children's incomes were nominal, that ex-husband earned $24,526 net annually and that she had no income but had previously earned $8,112 net annually; ex-husband therefore had the burden of going forward with evidence that would at least equally balance ex-wife's evidence. In re Taylor, 89 Ill. App. 3d 278, 44 Ill. Dec. 584, 411 N.E.2d 950 (1 Dist. 1980).

—Child's Resources

In view of the equitable considerations mandated by this section and the fact that the child lived with petitioner and was employed, court should have considered the contribution that the child was able to make toward financing the first year of his education, particularly since the chosen institution was not an educational facility supported by the state, where as a state resident he could have availed himself of the in-state tuition fee. In re Brust, 145 Ill. App. 3d 257, 99 Ill. Dec. 68, 495 N.E.2d 133 (5 Dist. 1986).

—College or University

Where flight instruction, as well as the resulting "flight costs," was an integral part of the curriculum, for all majors, at the college of airway sciences at the University of North Dakota and even though child elected to pursue a degree in airway sciences and incurred costs in connection with flight instruction required by that program, the program leads to a bachelor's degree and incorporates traditional liberal arts courses into its requirements; accordingly, the school at issue was a "college or university" as contemplated by the marital settlement agreement and respondent was required to pay for flight costs in connection with his child's education. In re Dieter, 271 Ill. App. 3d 181, 207 Ill. Dec. 848, 648 N.E.2d 304 (1 Dist. 1995).

An institute of technology offering a baccalaureate degree in four academic areas and requiring students to take traditional liberal arts courses such as English composition, speech, and writing was a college or university for the purposes of fulfilling a settlement agreement. In re Oldham, 222 Ill. App. 3d 744, 165 Ill. Dec. 206, 584 N.E.2d 385 (1 Dist. 1991).

—Contempt

Respondent's noncompliance with the provision of the dissolution judgment requiring him to pay his daughter's college expenses constituted prima facie evidence of contempt. In re Houston, 150 Ill. App. 3d 608, 103 Ill. Dec. 698, 501 N.E.2d 1015 (5 Dist. 1986).

—Disability Not Required

There is no requirement that an emancipated child be mentally or physically disabled where the support ordered is for education and maintenance expenses. In re Taylor, 89 Ill. App. 3d 278, 44 Ill. Dec. 584, 411 N.E.2d 950 (1 Dist. 1980).

—Duty to Pay

This section does not mandate divorced parents to provide funds for their children's post-secondary education; a determination as to whether a parent shall contribute is left to the sound discretion of the trial court and even then, a child cannot force his parents to provide funds if both parents agree that such funds will not be provided. In re Kuhn, 221 Ill. App. 3d 1, 163 Ill. Dec. 429, 581 N.E.2d 380 (2 Dist. 1991), appeal denied, 143 Ill. 2d 639, 167 Ill. Dec. 401, 587 N.E.2d 1016, cert. denied, 506 U.S. 818, 113 S. Ct. 62, 121 L. Ed. 2d 30 (1992).

Under this section, it is clear that a court, acting upon the petition of one former spouse, may order the other former spouse to assume all or a portion of the college expenses incurred by the couple's child. Miller v. Miller, 160 Ill. App. 3d 354, 112 Ill. Dec. 191, 513 N.E.2d 605 (3 Dist. 1987).

The expense of providing a college education for a child who is no longer a minor is not a burden that every parent is required to assume, but rather it is a matter for discretion of the trial court in each case. In re Stribling, 96 Ill. App. 3d 317, 51 Ill. Dec. 895, 421 N.E.2d 403 (3 Dist. 1981).

There is no absolute duty for a father to pay college expenses; such a duty is created only by a trial court's order, after a hearing, either to enforce an agreement between the parties or to create a post-divorce decree duty, upon proper petition of a party. Greiman v. Friedman, 90 Ill. App. 3d 941, 46 Ill. Dec. 355, 414 N.E.2d 77 (1 Dist. 1980).

This section and 750 ILCS 5/503 do not mandate that divorced parents must provide their children of majority age with funds for education in all cases, however, it is certainly a legitimate legislative purpose for the legislature to furnish a means for providing that they do so after they have been divorced. Kujawinski v. Kujawinski, 71 Ill. 2d 563, 17 Ill. Dec. 801, 376 N.E.2d 1382 (1978); In re Pearson, 111 Ill. 2d 545, 96 Ill. Dec. 69, 490 N.E.2d 1274 (1986); In re Calisoff, 176 Ill. App. 3d 721, 126 Ill. Dec. 183, 531 N.E.2d 810 (1 Dist. 1988); Treacy v. Treacy, 204 Ill. App. 3d 282, 149 Ill. Dec. 802, 562 N.E.2d 266 (1 Dist. 1990).

—Emancipation

Trial court abused its discretion in failing to comply with §§ 510(a) and 513 of the Illinois Marriage and Dissolution of Marriage Act, 750 ILCS 5/510(a) and 513, before extending the termination date of a support order to provide child support for an 18-year-old until his graduation from high school. Waller v. Waller, 339 Ill. App. 3d 743, 274 Ill. Dec. 582, 791 N.E.2d 674, 2003 Ill. App. LEXIS 766 (4 Dist. 2003).

—Factors Considered

In determining a reasonable price for college expenses where the obligation to pay these expenses have been provided for in a

Educational Expenses (Cont'd)

—Factors Considered (Cont'd)

settlement agreement, the court may use the factors in subsection (b). In re Schmidt, 292 Ill. App. 3d 229, 226 Ill. Dec. 152, 684 N.E.2d 1355 (4 Dist. 1997), appeal denied, 176 Ill. 2d 592, 229 Ill. Dec. 60, 690 N.E.2d 1387 (1998).

In deciding whether to increase husband's payments for child's education the trial court could consider that when the child came home, she would bring the dirty laundry to petitioner, not respondent, and if she brought home friends, they would stay with petitioner, not respondent. In re Korte, 193 Ill. App. 3d 243, 140 Ill. Dec. 255, 549 N.E.2d 906 (4 Dist. 1990).

While the lack of a parent-child relationship would not, of itself, terminate the parent's obligation to pay college expenses; the circuit court could, and perhaps should, have considered that factor in addition to the factors enumerated in this section. Gibb v. Triezenberg, 188 Ill. App. 3d 695, 135 Ill. Dec. 948, 544 N.E.2d 444 (4 Dist. 1989).

In determining the respective responsibility of each party, the trial court should consider the children's access to less expensive academic institutions. In re Calisoff, 176 Ill. App. 3d 721, 126 Ill. Dec. 183, 531 N.E.2d 810 (1 Dist. 1988).

The trial court properly considered the parties' educational expenditures on their other children prior to the dissolution. In re Pearson, 111 Ill. 2d 545, 96 Ill. Dec. 69, 490 N.E.2d 1274 (1986).

While in some instances it may be proper for the court to provide for a child's attendance at a private school, the child's access to a less expensive public institution is a factor to be considered. In re Pearson, 111 Ill. 2d 545, 96 Ill. Dec. 69, 490 N.E.2d 1274 (1986).

In making awards of education and maintenance the court shall consider all relevant factors, including: the financial resources of both parents, the standard of living the child would have enjoyed had the marriage not been dissolved, and the financial resources of the child. Larsen v. Larsen, 126 Ill. App. 3d 1072, 82 Ill. Dec. 103, 468 N.E.2d 165 (3 Dist. 1984); Rawles v. Hartman, 172 Ill. App. 3d 931, 123 Ill. Dec. 217, 527 N.E.2d 680 (2 Dist. 1988).

In determining maintenance award, it was not an abuse of discretion for the trial court to consider the current lifestyle of the first wife, and her family and to include the educational expenses of their non-minor child, in its determination of maintenance. In re Belluomini, 104 Ill. App. 3d 301, 60 Ill. Dec. 59, 432 N.E.2d 958 (1 Dist. 1982).

A student's academic record is merely one relevant factor, under this section for the court to consider in assessing educational expenses. Greiman v. Friedman, 90 Ill. App. 3d 941, 46 Ill. Dec. 355, 414 N.E.2d 77 (1 Dist. 1980).

Where one daughters' performance extended her schooling needs by an extra semester, yet she maintained a "B" average, her overall performance was not so poor that the lower court abused its discretion in requiring her father to contribute to one final semester, nor did the court abuse its discretion by requiring a second daughter to maintain at least a "C" average. Greiman v. Friedman, 90 Ill. App. 3d 941, 46 Ill. Dec. 355, 414 N.E.2d 77 (1 Dist. 1980).

A court may consider the private/public school issue as a relevant factor under this section. Greiman v. Friedman, 90 Ill. App. 3d 941, 46 Ill. Dec. 355, 414 N.E.2d 77 (1 Dist. 1980).

Remarriage and subsequent birth of a child are factors to be taken into account together with all other circumstances. Greiman v. Friedman, 90 Ill. App. 3d 941, 46 Ill. Dec. 355, 414 N.E.2d 77 (1 Dist. 1980).

Because it is likely that both parties pool their resources with those of their second spouses, so that their assets and liabilities are substantially intertwined, the parties should be allowed to submit detailed information of their finances so the court may reach a more principled, and more equitable determination of the share that each party should contribute. Greiman v. Friedman, 90 Ill. App. 3d 941, 46 Ill. Dec. 355, 414 N.E.2d 77 (1 Dist. 1980).

—Financial Resources

Income and assets of mother's new husband were not relevant to father's contribution to son's college educational expenses, but should have been considered in determining how they were or could have been used to contribute to mother's living expenses. Street v. Street, 325 Ill. App. 3d 108, 258 Ill. Dec. 613, 756 N.E.2d 887, 2001 Ill. App. LEXIS 711 (3 Dist. 2001).

In determining the financial resources available to a custodial mother, the court properly considered her new husband's income where she testified that she and new current husband pooled their income and money to pay their family expenses. In re Drysch, 314 Ill. App. 3d 640, 247 Ill. Dec. 409, 732 N.E.2d 125, 2000 Ill. App. LEXIS 509 (2 Dist. 2000).

In determining the financial resources available to a parent, the trial court should consider all the money or property to which a parent has access, including the parent's income, his or her property and investment holdings, and money or property that could be available to him or her through a new spouse. In re Drysch, 314 Ill. App. 3d 640, 247 Ill. Dec. 409, 732 N.E.2d 125, 2000 Ill. App. LEXIS 509 (2 Dist. 2000).

—Illegitimate Children

In a parentage proceeding, it is proper to apply this section so as to provide for the education of a non-minor, illegitimate child as equity requires, effectuating the legislative intent to treat all children equally in matters of support, such intent being manifested in section 3 of the Parentage Act (750 ILCS 45/3). Rawles v. Hartman, 172 Ill. App. 3d 931, 123 Ill. Dec. 217, 527 N.E.2d 680 (2 Dist. 1988).

—Illustrative Cases

It was an abuse of discretion to order the father to pay 70 percent of the college expenses of son where the father had insufficient income to meet his monthly obligations. In re Thurmond, 306 Ill. App. 3d 828, 240 Ill. Dec. 127, 715 N.E.2d 814 (2 Dist. 1999).

The trial court correctly determined that respondent was under a legal duty to provide for the maximum amount of his child's future education expenses in accordance with the marital settlement agreement. In re Dieter, 271 Ill. App. 3d 181, 207 Ill. Dec. 848, 648 N.E.2d 304 (1 Dist. 1995).

When the court determines parental responsibility for educational expenses, it is not mandatory that the trial court order that child's expenses be shouldered by father; the trial court ordered father to pay for child's entire cost of schooling, plus an additional amount as maintenance and medical and dental insurance including all deductibles but not mother's calculations which included her mortgage payment, homeowner's insurance, and other costs which she would have to pay whether child lived at home or not. In re Hillebrand, 258 Ill. App. 3d 835, 196 Ill. Dec. 583, 630 N.E.2d 518 (5 Dist. 1994).

—Living Expenses Included

Educational expenses entitle a mother to receive reasonable living expenses in addition to the cost of tuition and books when the children are residing at home while attending college. Falat v. Falat, 201 Ill. App. 3d 320, 147 Ill. Dec. 33, 559 N.E.2d 33 (1 Dist. 1990).

—Modification

A court order providing for the education of the child even after he reaches the age of majority is modifiable at all times, as changing circumstances warrant. In re Holderrieth, 181 Ill. App. 3d 199, 129 Ill. Dec. 896, 536 N.E.2d 946 (1 Dist. 1989).

Denial of the petition that a divorced husband pay college the expenses of the children was not an abuse of discretion where the respondent's testimony indicating that his expenses were in excess of his take-home pay was unrebutted and there was no contention that the deductions used in arriving at his net income or the amounts claimed as living expenses were improperly considered. Singer v. Singer, 70 Ill. App. 3d 472, 27 Ill. Dec. 88, 388 N.E.2d 1051 (1 Dist. 1979).

Where the trial court ordered both parties to contribute one-half of the college expenses of their daughter, but limited plaintiff's expenditures to $1,000, and the financial circumstances of the parties did not differ so greatly as to justify a limitation on the support obligation of one party and not the other, the judgment had to be modified to remove the limitation placed upon plaintiff's educational support obligation. Harnois v. Harnois, 10 Ill. App. 3d 1062, 295 N.E.2d 511 (1 Dist. 1973).

A court properly exercised its discretion under former section 19 of the Divorce Act to increase the amount of child support to provide for an adult child's educational expenses where the father was financially capable of providing for such expenses (see now 750

Educational Expenses (Cont'd)

—Modification (Cont'd)
ILCS 5/510 and this section). Maitzen v. Maitzen, 24 Ill. App. 2d 32, 163 N.E.2d 840 (1 Dist. 1959).

—Noncustodial Deceased Parent
Under 750 ILCS 5/510(d) and this section, the circuit court may not enter an order against the estate of a noncustodial deceased parent for the payment of college expenses of a non-minor child when there no such previous obligation was imposed upon the parent to be charged prior to his death. Treacy v. Treacy, 204 Ill. App. 3d 282, 149 Ill. Dec. 802, 562 N.E.2d 266 (1 Dist. 1990).

—Pending Marriage Dissolution
The trial court properly denied ordering ex-husband to reimburse ex-wife for the children's high school expenses while the dissolution of marriage was pending in court. In re Pearson, 236 Ill. App. 3d 337, 177 Ill. Dec. 650, 603 N.E.2d 720 (1 Dist. 1992).

—Relationship of Parent and Child
A child's relationship to his or her parent is not relevant in determining to what extent the parent should pay the child's educational expenses. In re Drysch, 314 Ill. App. 3d 640, 247 Ill. Dec. 409, 732 N.E.2d 125, 2000 Ill. App. LEXIS 509 (2 Dist. 2000).

—Settlement Agreement
A settlement agreement which made provisions for the college expenses of the son, rather than this section, controlled the disposition of the case because the parties in a dissolution proceeding may voluntarily settle their property interest. In re Holderrieth, 181 Ill. App. 3d 199, 129 Ill. Dec. 896, 536 N.E.2d 946 (1 Dist. 1989).

The parties' mutual adjustment of their marital rights so far as the education of their children was concerned was conclusive in the absence of unconscionability, fraud, coercion, duress or a violation of public policy or morals. In re Holderrieth, 181 Ill. App. 3d 199, 129 Ill. Dec. 896, 536 N.E.2d 946 (1 Dist. 1989).

Where under the settlement agreement, father's obligation to pay for daughter's college education was limited to a reasonable price, the order which set his obligation at a price which was not unreasonably low was upheld on a contract theory; moreover, under this section, the trial court's order was not against the manifest weight of the evidence. Ingrassia v. Ingrassia, 156 Ill. App. 3d 483, 109 Ill. Dec. 68, 509 N.E.2d 729 (2 Dist. 1987).

The "educational expenses" clause in a property distribution settlement was not an express agreement obligating either party to pay specific expenses; the clause did no more than to reserve until a later date the question of educational expenses under this section. In re Pearson, 111 Ill. 2d 545, 96 Ill. Dec. 69, 490 N.E.2d 1274 (1986).

The trial court did not abuse its discretion in ordering husband to pay toward his daughter's first year of college without directly receiving testimony regarding wife's finances where the clear intent of a divorce decree which incorporated a property settlement agreement was that the husband would bear the burden of his daughter's college expenses if he was financially able to do so. Larsen v. Larsen, 126 Ill. App. 3d 1072, 82 Ill. Dec. 103, 468 N.E.2d 165 (3 Dist. 1984).

Where the obligation to provide for a child's college expenses is included in a property settlement agreement which is later incorporated in a divorce decree, the obligation to provide for a child's education embodied in this section is said to be even more definite and obligatory. Larsen v. Larsen, 126 Ill. App. 3d 1072, 82 Ill. Dec. 103, 468 N.E.2d 165 (3 Dist. 1984).

—Shortages
Trial court did not abuse its discretion in finding a $3,500 shortage of child's education fund where she needed $7,000 and the grants she received provided only $3,648.90 and raising father's payments to cover this shortage. In re Korte, 193 Ill. App. 3d 243, 140 Ill. Dec. 255, 549 N.E.2d 906 (4 Dist. 1990).

—Standing
A child of divorced parents does not have standing to bring a separate action in his own name to enforce the provisions of his parents' divorce decree with regard to payment of college expenses. Miller v. Miller, 160 Ill. App. 3d 354, 112 Ill. Dec. 191, 513 N.E.2d 605 (3 Dist. 1987).

Only parties to the divorce may petition the court for relief under the support provisions of the Act; a court may provide for the education of a child of divorced parents under this paragraph only upon petition of one of the child's parents. Miller v. Miller, 160 Ill. App. 3d 354, 112 Ill. Dec. 191, 513 N.E.2d 605 (3 Dist. 1987).

—Trust
The trial court could impose a trust for future expenditures for the children's college educations even though there was no evidence that the children would even attend college upon becoming of age to do so. In re Harsy, 193 Ill. App. 3d 415, 140 Ill. Dec. 344, 549 N.E.2d 995 (5 Dist. 1990).

A court does have the discretion to order the establishment of a trust for a child's future educational expenses while he or she is of minority age if there is evidence showing a need to protect the interests of the child. In re Harsy, 193 Ill. App. 3d 415, 140 Ill. Dec. 344, 549 N.E.2d 995 (5 Dist. 1990).

The establishment of trust funds for children's future educational needs was necessary to promote and protect the minor children's interests, and the court did not abuse its discretion when it so ordered where the evidence revealed that the father was of the opinion that further education was not something to be valued, and because of his opinion, it could be inferred that he would not take measures to assure that there would be funds available for that purpose. In re Harsy, 193 Ill. App. 3d 415, 140 Ill. Dec. 344, 549 N.E.2d 995 (5 Dist. 1990).

Father was ordered to establish an educational trust where there was evidence in the record that the respondent had upon one occasion been held in contempt of court for failing to pay his child support as ordered by the court, which indicated that the respondent had either been unable or unwilling to pay. In re Harsy, 193 Ill. App. 3d 415, 140 Ill. Dec. 344, 549 N.E.2d 995 (5 Dist. 1990).

—Unaccredited Religious School
Divorced father was not required to pay college expenses for emancipated child where she enrolled in an unaccredited religious school whose credits were nontransferable and where she expressed no desire to pursue a religious vocation but testimony indicated that she would probably go to a secular school after bible college even though there were questions whether any of her credits would transfer. In re Spear, 244 Ill. App. 3d 626, 184 Ill. Dec. 331, 613 N.E.2d 358 (4 Dist.), appeal denied, 152 Ill. 2d 581, 190 Ill. Dec. 911, 622 N.E.2d 1228 (1993).

—Waiver
A custodial parent could not waive a child's claim to college expenses in a property settlement agreement with the noncustodial parent; parents cannot bargain away the child's right under the agreement without benefit to the child, without judicial approval, and without means available to the child to judicially contest the parents' agreement in violation of the Illinois law. Miller v. Miller, 163 Ill. App. 3d 602, 114 Ill. Dec. 682, 516 N.E.2d 837 (1 Dist. 1987).

Effect of Amendment

—Educational Expense Guidelines
When the legislature amended this section, effective January 1, 1993, it did not adopt the guidelines of section 505 (750 ILCS 5/505) but rather continued to require courts to consider the relevant factors as were previously used in the statute. In re Hillebrand, 258 Ill. App. 3d 835, 196 Ill. Dec. 583, 630 N.E.2d 518 (5 Dist. 1994).

Emancipation

—By Marriage
A parent's obligation to pay for the educational expenses of a child terminated upon the marriage of that child, an emancipating event. In re Daniels, 296 Ill. App. 3d 446, 231 Ill. Dec. 257, 695 N.E.2d 1376 (4 Dist. 1998).

This section does not allow for provision for college expenses and maintenance of a child to be made even if the child is emancipated other than by age. In re Walters, 238 Ill. App. 3d 1086, 178 Ill. Dec. 176, 604 N.E.2d 432 (2 Dist. 1992).

—Not Shown
Respondent's obligation to provide maintenance and to pay for college expenses of his daughters terminated when the children became emancipated through marriage; however, as to one of

Emancipation (Cont'd)

—Not Shown (Cont'd)
respondent's daughters, she was not emancipated by her marriage because she continued to live at home and be supported by her mother and because her marriage was eventually declared invalid. In re Walters, 238 Ill. App. 3d 1086, 178 Ill. Dec. 176, 604 N.E.2d 432 (2 Dist. 1992).

Enforcement of Decree

—Adult Child
An adult child of divorced parents has standing to enforce the educational provision of a divorce decree on the basis that he or she is a third-party beneficiary. Orr v. Orr, 228 Ill. App. 3d 234, 170 Ill. Dec. 117, 592 N.E.2d 553 (1 Dist. 1992).

Jurisdiction
A provision in a dissolution judgment for the payment of a child's college expenses is a term in the nature of child support, and the circuit court therefore retains jurisdiction to modify such a provision at any time pursuant to 750 ILCS 5/502 and 750 ILCS 5/510, regardless of whether the provision was ordered by the court under this section or incorporated into the judgment as a result of a settlement agreement. In re Loffredi, 232 Ill. App. 3d 709, 173 Ill. Dec. 933, 597 N.E.2d 907 (3 Dist. 1992).

The court had continuing personal jurisdiction over the respondent for purposes of former wife's petition to require the respondent to contribute to son's college expenses due to his continuing support obligation for the minor daughter of the parties. Wait v. Wait, 158 Ill. App. 3d 271, 109 Ill. Dec. 732, 510 N.E.2d 600 (4 Dist. 1987).

The courts have jurisdiction to order support payments for the education of children, regardless of whether the children are minors or adults and regardless of whether the petition is filed before or after the attainment of majority. Stecher v. Stecher, 16 Ill. App. 3d 297, 306 N.E.2d 86 (5 Dist. 1973).

Legislative Intent
The legislative intent of this section was to furnish a means to provide for the education of children of divorced parents. Treacy v. Treacy, 204 Ill. App. 3d 282, 149 Ill. Dec. 802, 562 N.E.2d 266 (1 Dist. 1990).

Matters Pertaining to Children

—College Expenses
A provision for the payment of a child's college expenses is a matter pertaining to children and in the nature of child support. In re Loffredi, 232 Ill. App. 3d 709, 173 Ill. Dec. 933, 597 N.E.2d 907 (3 Dist. 1992).

Medical and Dental Expenses
The court abused its discretion in ordering the husband to pay child's medical and dental expenses until she reached the age of emancipation or graduated from college, whichever occurred last, as the court's order was not limited to the period in which a duty of support existed under this section and would require the husband to pay all medical and dental expenses of his adult daughter even if she was not disabled or then attending school, but self-supporting out of her income producing assets. In re Block, 110 Ill. App. 3d 864, 65 Ill. Dec. 769, 441 N.E.2d 1283 (2 Dist. 1982).

Modification of Orders
Orders entered pursuant to this section are always modifiable. In re Loffredi, 232 Ill. App. 3d 709, 173 Ill. Dec. 933, 597 N.E.2d 907 (3 Dist. 1992).

Modification of Payments
In all cases where petitions to modify payments under a divorce decree are involved, the primary question is whether or not changes in circumstances of the parties justify the modification. Bulmer v. Bulmer, 28 Ill. App. 3d 406, 328 N.E.2d 622 (5 Dist. 1975).

Out of Property

—Defined
The words "out of property" as used in this section is sufficiently broad and encompassing so as to include income from wages, profit from investments, property holdings and the ownership of other assets and resources of value. Faust v. Faust, 100 Ill. App. 3d 232, 55 Ill. Dec. 669, 426 N.E.2d 994 (1 Dist. 1981).

Purpose
The purpose of this section is to furnish a means to provide for the education of children of divorced parents. In re Kuhn, 221 Ill. App. 3d 1, 163 Ill. Dec. 429, 581 N.E.2d 380 (2 Dist. 1991), appeal denied, 143 Ill. 2d 639, 167 Ill. Dec. 401, 587 N.E.2d 1016, cert. denied, 506 U.S. 818, 113 S. Ct. 62, 121 L. Ed. 2d 30 (1992).

Review
Since respondent had not provided the court with a record to determine what factors the trial court considered when it made the petitioner contribute to daughter's education expenses, the court could not determine if there was an abuse of discretion. In re Betts, 172 Ill. App. 3d 742, 122 Ill. Dec. 599, 526 N.E.2d 1138 (4 Dist. 1988).

The trial court's discretion will not be interfered with in the absence of an abuse of that discretion or unless a manifest injustice has been done. In re Ingrassia, 140 Ill. App. 3d 826, 95 Ill. Dec. 165, 489 N.E.2d 386 (2 Dist. 1986).

Where the trial court had the discretionary power, based upon the law and the evidence presented, to decide the issue of the respondent's responsibility to contribute to the technical school expenses of his adult child, the evidence indicated that the trial court exercised its discretion properly and that its determination was not at all contrary to the manifest weight of the evidence. Faust v. Faust, 100 Ill. App. 3d 232, 55 Ill. Dec. 669, 426 N.E.2d 994 (1 Dist. 1981).

An abuse of discretion in not awarding money for maintenance and educational expenses will not be found unless the record demonstrates that the financial resources of both parents, the standard of living during the marriage and the financial resources of the child were such as to require a party to provide for the education and maintenance of his non-minor children. In re Gardner, 85 Ill. App. 3d 1004, 41 Ill. Dec. 304, 407 N.E.2d 802 (1 Dist. 1980).

Settlement Agreement

—Held Modifiable
The trial court erred in finding that a provision in a dissolution judgment which provided for the payment of children's college expenses was not modifiable when that provision was contained in a settlement agreement incorporated into the judgment and the agreement specifically precluded modification of its terms. In re Loffredi, 232 Ill. App. 3d 709, 173 Ill. Dec. 933, 597 N.E.2d 907 (3 Dist. 1992).

Unilateral Reduction
Absent an express or implied court-ordered provision, a parent who pays collective or lump-sum child support payments for the support of two or more children may not unilaterally reduce the amount of that payment pro rata as each child becomes emancipated. Clay v. Clay, 210 Ill. App. 3d 778, 155 Ill. Dec. 280, 569 N.E.2d 280 (4 Dist. 1991).

Valuation
Where the related issues of maintenance to petitioner and the minor child and the payment of educational expenses were directly affected by the final property disposition since these awards were substantially dependent upon the financial resources of the parties, including marital property (750 ILCS 5/504(b)(1), 750 ILCS 5/505(a)(2), 750 ILCS 5/508(a) and this section), the maintenance and support awards would have to be re-evaluated by the trial court on remand so that it may properly consider any changes required in the disposition of such property. In re Walsh, 109 Ill. App. 3d 171, 64 Ill. Dec. 758, 440 N.E.2d 310 (1 Dist. 1982).

LEGAL PERIODICALS

For article, "Survey of Illinois Law: Family Law," 19 S. Ill. U.L.J. 819 (1995).

For article, "Support for Disabled Children Past Majority," see 78 Ill. B. J. 138 (1990).

For article, "Support for a Child's Post-Majority Education," see 22 Loy. U. Chi. L. J. 695 (1990-91).

For article, "Trusts and Estates: 1986-87 Survey," see 12 S. Ill. U. L. J. 1143 (1988).

For article, "Family Law: 1985-86 Survey," see 11 S. Ill. U. L. J. 741 (1987).

For article, "Family Law: 1986-87 Illinois Law Survey," see 19 Loy. U. Chi. L. J. 489 (1987-88).

For article, "Family Law: 1985-86 Illinois Law Survey," see 18 Loy. U. Chi. L. J. 549 (1986-87).

RESEARCH REFERENCES

Postsecondary education as within nondivorced parent's child support obligation. 42 ALR4th 819.

750 ILCS 5/514 Partition of Real Estate

Sec. 514. *Partition of Real Estate.* A court having jurisdiction in an action for dissolution of marriage may, upon petition of one of the parties, hear and decide an action for partition subject to the provisions of Article XVII of the Code of Civil Procedure, as now or hereafter amended [735 ILCS 5/17-101 et seq.], except as otherwise provided in this Act.
(Source: P.A. 82-783.)

Note.
This section was Ill.Rev.Stat., Ch. 40, para. 514.

CASE NOTES

ANALYSIS

Admission in Error
Award
—Upheld
Jurisdiction
Nonmarital Property

Admission in Error
In marital dissolution action, it was error to admit the postnuptial agreement providing for partition of marital property into evidence for want of compliance with former section 36 of the Civil Practice Act (see now 735 ILCS 5/2-606). Carney v. Carney, 67 Ill. App. 3d 919, 24 Ill. Dec. 447, 385 N.E.2d 359 (4 Dist. 1979).

Award

—Upheld
A husband had no absolute right to partition of the marital residence and the court did not err in awarding the wife possession of the marital home until the youngest child became emancipated, and even though this event may not have occurred for nine years, the period of possession awarded the wife was not unreasonable. In re Woolsey, 85 Ill. App. 3d 636, 40 Ill. Dec. 775, 406 N.E.2d 1142 (4 Dist. 1980).

The trial court did not err in ordering the associate judge in the Land Title Division to execute a deed for husband's one-half interest in the marital home. Graff v. Graff, 71 Ill. App. 3d 496, 27 Ill. Dec. 798, 389 N.E.2d 1206 (1 Dist. 1979).

Jurisdiction
Wife's prayer for use of the marital home and other equitable relief, and husband's request for a division of the marital property and other equitable relief was sufficient to place the issue of the disposition of the marital home, including its sale, before the trial court, even though neither party specifically requested partition. In re Glessner, 119 Ill. App. 3d 306, 74 Ill. Dec. 809, 456 N.E.2d 311 (1 Dist. 1983).

Nonmarital Property
The right to partition of nonmarital property interests is an appropriate action under this section. In re Voight, 111 Ill. App. 3d 623, 67 Ill. Dec. 458, 444 N.E.2d 694 (1 Dist. 1982).

750 ILCS 5/515 Partition to be Filed in Counties where Real Estate Located

Sec. 515. *Partition to be Filed in Counties where Real Estate Located.* A court hearing an action for partition pursuant to Section 514 of this Act [750 ILCS 5/514] may determine and declare the rights, titles and interests of all parties to that action without regard to the location within this State of the land in question. However, if the land in question is located in a county other than that in which the dissolution of marriage action is commenced, notice of the action for partition and a certified copy of the judgment of dissolution of marriage must be filed, by the party filing the petition for partition, in the office of the recorder or registrar of titles in each county, other than that where the action is brought, where any part of the land in question is located.
(Source: P.A. 83-358.)

Note.
This section was Ill.Rev.Stat., Ch. 40, para. 515.

750 ILCS 5/516 Public Aid collection fee

Sec. 516. *Public Aid collection fee.* In all cases instituted by the Illinois Department of Public Aid on behalf of a child or spouse, other than one receiving a grant of financial aid under Article IV of The Illinois Public Aid Code [305 ILCS 5/4-1 et seq.], on whose behalf an application has been made and approved for child support enforcement services as provided by Section 10-1 of that Code [305 ILCS 5/10-1], the court shall impose a collection fee on the individual who owes a child or spouse support obligation in an amount equal to 10% of the amount so owed as long as such collection is required by federal law, which fee shall be in addition to the support obligation. The imposition of such fee shall be in accordance with provisions of Title IV, Part D, of the Social Security Act [42 U.S.C. § 651 et seq.] and regulations duly promulgated thereunder. The fee shall be payable to the clerk of the circuit court for transmittal to the Illinois Department of Public Aid and shall continue until child support enforcement services are terminated by that Department.
(Source: P.A. 82-979; 92-590, § 10.)

Note.
This section was Ill.Rev.Stat., Ch. 40, para. 516.

Effect of Amendments.
The 2002 amendment by P.A. 92-590, effective July 1, 2002, substituted "child support enforcement services" for "support services" twice.

PART VI.
CUSTODY

750 ILCS 5/601 Jurisdiction; Commencement of Proceeding

Sec. 601. *Jurisdiction; Commencement of Proceeding.* (a) A court of this State competent to decide child custody matters has jurisdiction to make a child custody determination in original or modification proceedings as provided in Section 201 of the Uniform Child-Custody Jurisdiction and Enforcement Act [750 ILCS 35/201] as adopted by this State.

(b) A child custody proceeding is commenced in the court:

(1) by a parent, by filing a petition:

(i) for dissolution of marriage or legal separation or declaration of invalidity of marriage; or

(ii) for custody of the child, in the county in which he is permanently resident or found; or

(2) by a person other than a parent, by filing a petition for custody of the child in the county in which he is permanently resident or found, but only if he is not in the physical custody of one of his parents; or

(3) by a stepparent, by filing a petition, if all of the following circumstances are met:

(A) the child is at least 12 years old;

(B) the custodial parent and stepparent were married for at least 5 years during which the child resided with the parent and stepparent;

(C) the custodial parent is deceased or is disabled and cannot perform the duties of a parent to the child;

(D) the stepparent provided for the care, control, and welfare to the child prior to the initiation of custody proceedings;

(E) the child wishes to live with the stepparent; and

(F) it is alleged to be in the best interests and welfare of the child to live with the stepparent as provided in Section 602 of this Act [750 ILCS 5/602].

(4) When one of the parents is deceased, by a grandparent who is a parent or stepparent of a deceased parent, by filing a petition, if one or more of the following existed at the time of the parent's death:

(A) the surviving parent had been absent from the marital abode for more than one month without the deceased spouse knowing his or her whereabouts;

(B) the surviving parent was in State or federal custody; or

(C) the surviving parent had: (i) received supervision for or been convicted of any violation of Article 12 of the Criminal Code of 1961 [720 ILCS 5/12-1 et seq.] directed towards the deceased parent or the child; or (ii) received supervision or been convicted of violating an order of protection entered under Section 217, 218, or 219 of the Illinois Domestic Violence Act of 1986 [750 ILCS 60/217, 750 ILCS 60/218, or 750 ILCS 60/219] for the protection of the deceased parent or the child.

(c) Notice of a child custody proceeding, including an action for modification of a previous custody order, shall be given to the child's parents, guardian and custodian, who may appear, be heard, and file a responsive pleading. The court, upon showing of good cause, may permit intervention of other interested parties.

(d) Proceedings for modification of a previous custody order commenced more than 30 days following the entry of a previous custody order must be initiated by serving a written notice and a copy of the petition for modification upon the child's parent, guardian and custodian at least 30 days prior to hearing on the petition. Nothing in this Section shall preclude a party in custody modification proceedings from moving for a temporary order under Section 603 of this Act [750 ILCS 5/603].

(e) (Blank).

(f) The court shall, at the court's discretion or upon the request of any party entitled to petition for custody of the child, appoint a guardian ad litem to represent the best interest of the child for the duration of the custody proceeding or for any modifications of any custody orders entered. Nothing in this Section shall be construed to prevent the court from appointing the same guardian ad litem for 2 or more children that are siblings or half-siblings.

(Source: P.A. 83-1396; 87-1255, § 1; 90-782, § 5; 93-108, § 402.5; 93-1026, § 5.)

Note.

This section was Ill.Rev.Stat., Ch. 40, para. 601.

Cross References.

As to the requirement of a court, prior to granting a custody judgment, to inquire with LEADS and the National Crime Information Center to ascertain whether the child or children in question have been reported missing or have been involved in or are the victims of a parental or noncustodial abduction, see 325 ILCS 40/7.1.

Effect of Amendments.

The 1998 amendment by P.A. 90-782, effective August 14, 1998, added subdivision (b)(3), making related stylistic changes in subdivisions (b)(1) and (b)(2).

The 2003 amendment by P.A. 93-108, effective January 1, 2004, substituted "Section 201 of the Uniform Child-Custody Jurisdiction and Enforcement Act" for "Section 4 of the Uniform Child Custody Jurisdiction Act" in subsection (a) and deleted the text from subsection (e).

The 2004 amendment by P.A. 93-1026, effective January 1, 2005, added subsections (b)(4) and (f).

CASE NOTES

Analysis

Adoption Distinguished
Appeal
—Appealable Order
—Findings of Trial Court
Applicability
Best Interests of Child
—In General
—Agreement
—Comments by Court
—Connection with Foreign State
—Custody to Mother
—Custody to Non-Parent
—Discretion of Court
—Evidence Held Insufficient
—Modification
—Presumption
Change in Circumstances
Changing Custody

—Burden of Proof
—Desire of Parent
—Proper
—Remarriage
—Standard of Proof
Child's Preference
Child's Testimony
Compliance
Custody Agreement
Custody Hearing
—Improper
Custody Order
—Violation
Death of Custodial Parent
Discretion of Trial Court
Equitable Action
Finality
Foreign Custody Decrees
Habeas Corpus
Hearsay
Home State
Incorporated Settlement Agreement
—Modification
Injunction
Interlocutory Order
Interrelation
Jurisdiction
—In General
—Challenge
—Conceding
—Continuing and Exclusive
—Decree Necessary
—Held Improper
—Held Proper
—Juvenile Court
—Non-Party
—Requirements
—Standards
—Sufficient Contacts
Jury Trial
Liability of Parent
Misconduct
Natural Parent's Right
—Not Absolute
—Presumption
Non-Parent
—Custody Requirement
—Lack of Standing
—Seeking Custody
—Standing Required
Notice of Hearing
Particular Facts
Physical Custody
Possession of Child
Procedures
—Exclusivity
Purpose
Putative Father
Relinquishment of Parental Custody
Res Judicata
Right to Hearing
Standing
—In General
—Abduction of Child
—Applicability
—Aunt and Uncle
—Child with In-Laws
—Conditions to Appeal
—Death of Custodial Parent
—Determination
—Established
—Failure to Satisfy Requirement
—Father's Unfitness
—Grandparents
—Limited
—Minor Child
—Non-Natural Parent
—Non-Parent
—Not Shown
—Physical Custody
—Preservation of Defense
—Purpose
—Shown
—Step Parent
—Superior Rights Doctrine
—Unilateral Relinquishment
—Waiver
Temporary Care
Unconscionable Decree
Unfitness Finding
—Not Required
—Required
Unlawful Transportation of Child
Unwed Father
—Due Process Rights
—Procedural Safeguards
Venue
—Change of Venue
—Location of Relevant Evidence
Visitation
Wards of Court

Adoption Distinguished

Custody and adoption proceedings are distinguishable in that adoption severs the rights and interests of the natural parents; it permanently terminates the relation between parent and child. Wittig v. Atherton, 107 Ill. App. 3d 1006, 63 Ill. Dec. 582, 438 N.E.2d 513 (1 Dist. 1982).

Appeal

—Appealable Order

An order for the custody of a child, even though partial and temporary, is an appealable order. Schneeman v. Schneeman, 317 Ill. App. 286, 45 N.E.2d 1016 (1 Dist. 1942).

—Findings of Trial Court

The findings of the trial court ordinarily are entitled to considerable weight in custody cases since the court is most intimately familiar with the facts and persons involved. In re Ross, 29 Ill. App. 3d 157, 329 N.E.2d 333 (3 Dist. 1975).

Applicability

Though the question of what statute applies to proceedings for custody of a child of unmarried parents is not clearly agreed in Illinois law, the best interest of the child guides the decision, no matter what form the proceedings may take. Giagnoni v. Bourey, 127 Ill. App. 3d 530, 82 Ill. Dec. 852, 469 N.E.2d 386 (2 Dist. 1984).

Subsection (b) of this section and 750 ILCS 5/610, regarding custody modifications are not mutually exclusive since subsection (b) applies to both initial determinations of custody and modification of judgments. People ex rel. Bukovic v. Smith, 98 Ill. App. 3d 144, 53 Ill. Dec. 498, 423 N.E.2d 1302 (1 Dist. 1981).

Best Interests of Child

—In General

When a child's custody is brought before the court, the key to the resolution of that issue should in all cases be the best interests of the child. In re Ross, 29 Ill. App. 3d 157, 329 N.E.2d 333 (3 Dist. 1975).

Where the custody of a child is concerned, the question of primary importance is the preservation of the best interests of the minor. Lucado v. Lucado, 1 Ill. App. 2d 548, 118 N.E.2d 40 (1 Dist. 1954).

—Agreement

Where order provided that custody would be changed to father when it was determined to be in the best interest of daughter to do so, father expressly agreed to have custody determined on the basis of the best interest of the child standard. Gonzalez ex rel. Gonzalez v. Donnelly, 204 Ill. App. 3d 28, 149 Ill. Dec. 580, 561 N.E.2d 1276 (3 Dist. 1990).

—Comments by Court

Isolated statement, made by trial judge in a custody action,

Best Interests of Child (Cont'd)

—Comments by Court (Cont'd)

concerning the dangerous environment, where he termed the care a horrible episode of child abuse yet said that he did not want to term it a dangerous environment, did not alter the general verdict on the question of custody; there was sufficient evidence to justify the trial court's view that the child had been the victim of serious child abuse and that it was in the best interests of the child to modify the custody decree. In re Cotton, 103 Ill. 2d 346, 83 Ill. Dec. 143, 469 N.E.2d 1077 (1984).

—Connection with Foreign State

Where Illinois, which was once the "home state" of children involved in custody determination, had been superseded in that capacity by California, information concerning the children's mental and physical well-being, their education and training, their personal relationships with friends and some family members, all of which is vital to intelligent custody judgments was much more readily available to the California courts; this section was designed to provide that custody disputes be resolved in the forum where the facts necessary to a determination of the children's best interests are most readily accessible and it superseded the "continuing jurisdiction" principle wherever that principle conflicted with the statutory provisions and thus it vitiated the circuit court's order limiting the rights of the parties to petition other courts for modification, and also indicated the continuing jurisdiction of the circuit court over the subject matter of the custody of the children should not have been exercised. Siegel v. Siegel, 84 Ill. 2d 212, 49 Ill. Dec. 298, 417 N.E.2d 1312 (1981).

Where the facts indicated that the children developed a significant connection with another state, where they enrolled in and attended local schools, established relationships with medical care professions, and adjusted to life in that state, and no equivalent connection with Illinois existed upon commencement of the proceedings, and where Illinois was at one time an appropriate venue in which to exercise subject matter jurisdiction, this Act requires "custody disputes to be resolved in the forum where the facts necessary to a determination of the children's best interests are most readily accessible," the circuit court of Cook County no longer retained subject matter jurisdiction over the custody dispute. In re Wass, 94 Ill. App. 3d 436, 50 Ill. Dec. 165, 419 N.E.2d 32 (1 Dist. 1981).

—Custody to Mother

Where the prior misconduct of defendant gave no evidence of adverse effect on the future welfare of the children, where the evidence showed defendant to be an affectionate, caring and dutiful mother who is devoted to her children, where the trial court had before it letters of the children to their mother, heard and saw the witnesses and conferred with the children and presumably exercised his discretion with the best interest of the children in mind, there was no showing that custody award to the mother was contrary to the best interests of the children. Bergan v. Bergan, 42 Ill. App. 3d 740, 1 Ill. Dec. 485, 356 N.E.2d 673 (5 Dist. 1976).

—Custody to Non-Parent

The argument of petitioners (grandparents seeking custody) that they had standing based upon the best interests of the child was misplaced because it is only after a non-parent has established standing that the court determines custody or guardianship using the best interests of the child standard. Starr v. Barnhart, 232 Ill. App. 3d 317, 174 Ill. Dec. 26, 597 N.E.2d 1238 (2 Dist. 1992).

The trial court need not find that the natural parent is unfit or has forfeited her custodial rights before awarding custody to a non-parent if the best interests of the child will be served. Rose v. Potts, 217 Ill. App. 3d 661, 160 Ill. Dec. 486, 577 N.E.2d 811 (5 Dist. 1991).

Where evidence showed that the grandparents have provided stable, positive, and supportive relationships for child and that father was lacking in parenting skills and in stability, the trial court's award of custody to the grandparents was not contrary to the manifest weight of the evidence. Gonzalez ex rel. Gonzalez v. Donnelly, 204 Ill. App. 3d 28, 149 Ill. Dec. 580, 561 N.E.2d 1276 (3 Dist. 1990).

A non-parent must show that the child is "not in the physical custody of one of his parents"; when this requirement has been met, the non-parents will be considered for legal custody of the child under "a best interest of the child" standard. Butler v. Butler, 192 Ill. App. 3d 135, 139 Ill. Dec. 197, 548 N.E.2d 582 (1 Dist. 1989).

—Discretion of Court

Where an order awarding custody to the wife did not conform to the prayer for relief of either party, and the order was more favorable to the wife than she requested, the contention that the award was in error was without merit, as the principal duty of the chancellor was to consider the best interests of the child, as it might appear from the evidence, and to enter a proper order based on the relevant testimony. Handrich v. Handrich, 339 Ill. App. 151, 89 N.E.2d 191 (4 Dist. 1949).

—Evidence Held Insufficient

The evidence presented by the grandparents fell far short of the proof required by the "good of the child test" to take away custody of a child from his natural parent where, at best, the evidence showed a single act of physical discipline administered by the father for disciplinary reasons. Butler v. Butler, 192 Ill. App. 3d 135, 139 Ill. Dec. 197, 548 N.E.2d 582 (1 Dist. 1989).

—Modification

Where there was an agreement between the parties to terminate a joint-custody arrangement, together with a stipulation that a motion to modify could be presented without evidence of serious endangerment, it was obvious that the parties had agreed to terminate the joint-custody arrangement provided for in the judgment; subsection (b) of this section clearly provides that the trial court shall make any modification which is in the child's best interest as opposed to applying the more stringent serious endangerment standard. In re Oertel, 216 Ill. App. 3d 806, 159 Ill. Dec. 766, 576 N.E.2d 435 (2 Dist. 1991).

—Presumption

Mother was entitled to the presumption that awarding her custody would serve the best interests of the child. Rose v. Potts, 217 Ill. App. 3d 661, 160 Ill. Dec. 486, 577 N.E.2d 811 (5 Dist. 1991).

The limitation on non-parent standing contained in this section has been construed as evincing a policy favoring parental custody rights by permitting third-party standing and the consequent application of the less stringent best interests standard only in those cases where the parent does not have physical custody. Menconi v. Menconi, 117 Ill. App. 3d 394, 73 Ill. Dec. 10, 453 N.E.2d 835 (1 Dist. 1983).

Change in Circumstances

Where subsequent to their divorce, the father remarried, the mother did not, the father was well employed while the mother became unemployed, the mother acquired a boyfriend and embarked upon a course of immoral conduct, and the conduct of the mother after her divorce clearly resulted in the neglect of the five minor children and most certainly did not provide them with a proper moral atmosphere such as is desired when children are at an impressionable age, the record disclosed a large number of changed circumstances, which supported the order of the trial court which changed the custody of the children. Gehn v. Gehn, 51 Ill. App. 3d 946, 10 Ill. Dec. 120, 367 N.E.2d 508 (3 Dist. 1977).

If a divorce decree, or an order subsequent thereto, grants custody of the children to one of the parties, that order is binding on other courts; it cannot be subject to collateral attack, although, another court may subsequently decide on a change of the custody of the children based upon a subsequent change of circumstances. People ex rel. Brown v. Walls, 38 Ill. App. 2d 385, 187 N.E.2d 288 (1 Dist. 1962).

Whether there has been a sufficient presentation of a change in circumstances so as to justify a change in custody, is a question of fact and the overriding consideration must be the welfare of the children. People ex rel. Brown v. Walls, 38 Ill. App. 2d 385, 187 N.E.2d 288 (1 Dist. 1962).

Changing Custody

—Burden of Proof

Every presumption is indulged in the validity of a custody decree and if its provisions are to be changed, the burden of proof is on the moving party to show why the change should be made. King v. Vancil, 34 Ill. App. 3d 831, 341 N.E.2d 65 (5 Dist. 1975).

Changing Custody (Cont'd)

—Burden of Proof (Cont'd)

One who seeks to modify the custody provisions of a divorce decree, whether those provisions are based upon stipulation or are the results of a trial court determination after a contested hearing, must carry the burden of showing a material change of circumstances adversely affecting the best interests of the children occurring after the entry of the original decree. Golden v. Braunfeld, 22 Ill. App. 3d 344, 317 N.E.2d 336 (4 Dist. 1974).

—Desire of Parent

Where there has been no change in the conditions attending the child's custody, he is healthy and happy and properly cared for by the parent having custody, the desire of the other parent to have custody is not a sufficient, positive reason for the court to order such change. McWilliams v. McWilliams, 43 Ill. App. 3d 65, 1 Ill. Dec. 842, 356 N.E.2d 1124 (2 Dist. 1976).

—Proper

Where father had voluntarily relinquished physical custody of child in favor of the grandparents, the child lived in the virtually uninterrupted care and custody of her grandparents for 6½ years, and the report of the court-appointed psychologist indicated that child was firmly integrated into the grandparents' household, the voluntary nature of the initial transfer of the child, coupled with the lengthy period of care by the grandparents and the corresponding integration of the child into the home of her grandparents was sufficient to divest the father of physical custody of the child. Menconi v. Menconi, 117 Ill. App. 3d 394, 73 Ill. Dec. 10, 453 N.E.2d 835 (1 Dist. 1983).

Where former wife became deeply involved in an affair with her boyfriend, who was separated but still married to his wife, such involvement resulted in the former wife becoming pregnant which pregnancy was terminated by a miscarriage, the plaintiff had no qualms in exposing the exhibiting to her children her illicit relationship with her boyfriend, she continuously left the home at night and imposed the responsibility of babysitting on a 12½ year old daughter, and once left on a lengthy trip when one child was dangerously ill in the hospital, the trial court's grant of a change of custody of the children to the former husband was not manifestly unjust. Gehn v. Gehn, 51 Ill. App. 3d 946, 10 Ill. Dec. 120, 367 N.E.2d 508 (3 Dist. 1977).

Where the plaintiff, by her own misconduct, precipitated post-decree proceedings when she was apprehended in the company of a fugitive from justice and relinquished the custody of her children to defendant, her voluntary transfer of the children to defendant not only justified the defendant's subsequent actions in seeking modification of custody order, but in fact compelled him to seek the assistance of the court in order to protect the welfare of the children; his request for a change of custody, immediately filed, was proper and advisable. Kuhns v. Kuhns, 7 Ill. App. 3d 884, 288 N.E.2d 884 (1 Dist. 1972).

—Remarriage

Remarriage of the mother had no bearing on the immediate environment of the child since she did not have custody especially where it did not appear from the testimony that there had been any disadvantageous change whatsoever in his environment since the decree because the evidence indicated he was healthy and happy and doing reasonably well in school, the trial court was correct in finding both parties good and proper persons to have custody and in not changing the existing arrangement. McWilliams v. McWilliams, 43 Ill. App. 3d 65, 1 Ill. Dec. 842, 356 N.E.2d 1124 (2 Dist. 1976).

—Standard of Proof

Any petition for a change of custody must be supported by clear and convincing evidence, but a determination that a party has failed to prove a case by a preponderance of the evidence is, a fortiori, a determination that a claim was not proved by clear and convincing evidence. In re Gordon, 233 Ill. App. 3d 617, 175 Ill. Dec. 137, 599 N.E.2d 1151 (1 Dist.), appeal denied, 147 Ill. 2d 626, 180 Ill. Dec. 149, 606 N.E.2d 1226 (1992).

Child's Preference

A child's custodial preference may be an appropriate factor for the court's consideration where the child is of more mature age. Rathke v. Peebles, 31 Ill. App. 3d 711, 334 N.E.2d 362 (5 Dist. 1975).

Child's Testimony

It had been held to be improper for the court to conduct an interview with a child out of the presence of the attorneys and off the record to receive testimony bearing on issues at trial; however, the welfare of the child is paramount in custody decisions and, in that regard, interviews with the children by the court are permissible. Seniuta v. Seniuta, 31 Ill. App. 3d 408, 334 N.E.2d 261 (1 Dist. 1975).

A private interview with children involved in a divorce proceeding is permitted to assist the court in determining custody, but to protect the right to appeal, the court upon motion should state for the record, if that becomes necessary, the substantive parts of the child's statement to him; however, a child's testimony as to other issues should be given in the presence of the parties and their counsel, unless there is a waiver thereof. Seniuta v. Seniuta, 31 Ill. App. 3d 408, 334 N.E.2d 261 (1 Dist. 1975).

Compliance

Petitioner's failure to comply with a court order compelled dismissal of an appeal until such time that she returned the children to the jurisdiction and conformed with the legal process. Kramer v. Kramer, 150 Ill. App. 3d 264, 103 Ill. Dec. 615, 501 N.E.2d 932 (1 Dist. 1986).

Custody Agreement

Where divorced wife freely and voluntarily entered into a child custody agreement awarding physical possession of minor child to paternal grandparents, upon agreement of the parties to such a custody arrangement, the divorced wife had no basis to question the propriety of the custody award. In re Black, 133 Ill. App. 3d 59, 87 Ill. Dec. 831, 477 N.E.2d 1359 (2 Dist. 1985).

Custody Hearing

—Improper

Adoptive parents cannot, once an invalid adoption is vacated, attempt to circumvent the rights afforded fathers under the Adoption Act (750 ILCS 50/0.01 et seq.) by seeking a custody hearing under this section which, unlike the Adoption Act, could result in a father's being divested of his right to the care, custody and control of his child without being found unfit by clear and convincing evidence. In re Kirchner, 164 Ill. 2d 468, 208 Ill. Dec. 268, 649 N.E.2d 324 (1995), cert. denied, 515 U.S. 1152, 115 S. Ct. 2599, 132 L. Ed. 2d 846 (1995).

Custody Order

—Violation

Where trial court originally awarded custody to the mother and had continued subject matter jurisdiction over the matters affecting the child of the divorced parents, the order on its face indicated that all parties were notified and that the court retained jurisdiction over the parties, and the court apparently had jurisdiction to enter the order, defendant violated a valid custody order when she took child away from custodial parent. People v. Rodriguez, 169 Ill. App. 3d 131, 119 Ill. Dec. 717, 523 N.E.2d 185 (2 Dist. 1988).

Where judge found that both parents were fit and proper persons to have custody of the children, but made a statement that he was modifying prior custody award and awarding custody to the mother because of the age of the two boys, six and three, the court's reasoning was not supported by the law, and violated equal protection provision. King v. Vancil, 34 Ill. App. 3d 831, 341 N.E.2d 65 (5 Dist. 1975).

Death of Custodial Parent

The natural mother did not have the right to unilaterally retake physical custody of her son since the legal custody of him upon his father's death did not automatically revert to her; the proper procedure was to petition the court for a modification of custody pursuant to this section. In re Carey, 188 Ill. App. 3d 1040, 136 Ill. Dec. 518, 544 N.E.2d 1293 (2 Dist. 1989), appeal denied, 129 Ill. 2d 561, 140 Ill. Dec. 669, 550 N.E.2d 554 (1990).

Upon the death of the custodial parent, the non-custodial parent is not immediately vested with custody. In re Nicholas, 170 Ill. App. 3d 171, 120 Ill. Dec. 698, 524 N.E.2d 728 (3 Dist. 1988).

Child custody proceedings are not jurisdictionally precluded by the absence or termination of dissolution proceedings, hence, the general principle that death of a party abates the divorce action

Death of Custodial Parent (Cont'd)
should not be too hastily applied to child custody matters. Milenkovic v. Milenkovic, 93 Ill. App. 3d 204, 48 Ill. Dec. 618, 416 N.E.2d 1140 (1 Dist. 1981).

The circuit court did not lack jurisdiction in amending custody provisions upon a party's death. Jarrett v. Jarrett, 415 Ill. 126, 112 N.E.2d 694 (1953).

Discretion of Trial Court
Great discretion is vested in the trial court on issues of custody due to the judge's superior opportunity to evaluate the evidence and determine the best interests of the child. In re Simmons, 221 Ill. App. 3d 89, 163 Ill. Dec. 562, 581 N.E.2d 716 (5 Dist. 1991).

In cases regarding custody issues, there is a strong and compelling presumption in favor of the result reached by the trial court; the result will be reversed only if it is contrary to the manifest weight of the evidence. In re Simmons, 221 Ill. App. 3d 89, 163 Ill. Dec. 562, 581 N.E.2d 716 (5 Dist. 1991).

Where respondent never alleged that neighbor was unfit to care for the children, there was nothing in the record to support any inference that she should not retain custody; thus, in awarding temporary custody to her, the court did not abuse its discretion. Milenkovic v. Milenkovic, 93 Ill. App. 3d 204, 48 Ill. Dec. 618, 416 N.E.2d 1140 (1 Dist. 1981).

Where no harm to the child was to be apprehended from allowing him to go with his father, the trial court did not abuse its broad discretion in awarding custody to father. Blazina v. Blazina, 42 Ill. App. 3d 159, 1 Ill. Dec. 164, 356 N.E.2d 164 (2 Dist. 1976).

In post-decree proceedings for the modification of child custody provisions of divorce decree, the discretion of the trial court is a judicial discretion limited to the pleadings and proof pertaining to a change in circumstances which affect the welfare of the child, sufficient to warrant the modification of the decree. King v. Vancil, 34 Ill. App. 3d 831, 341 N.E.2d 65 (5 Dist. 1975).

Where the court has stated that the welfare and best interests of the children require that the children remain in the custody of the respondent, it must be presumed that the court heard sufficient evidence of a change of circumstances upon which to base its finding and that it was for the best interests of the children that the respondent should be granted custody. People ex rel. Brown v. Walls, 38 Ill. App. 2d 385, 187 N.E.2d 288 (1 Dist. 1962).

The trial court in divorce proceedings is vested with a broad discretion in determining the custody of minor children. Wolfrum v. Wolfrum, 5 Ill. App. 2d 471, 126 N.E.2d 34 (3 Dist. 1955).

Equitable Action
Where mother had been informed by father prior to his filing for divorce in Illinois that he intended to bring suit there, where she filed her special appearance in the Illinois action prior to entry of a Montana dissolution decree, and neither that decree nor any prior pleadings in the Montana action of record indicated that court's knowledge of a pending Illinois suit, the mother did not inform the Montana court of the Illinois action, as required under former 750 ILCS 35/10, even after her knowledge of it was irrefutably shown by her active participation and, therefore, invocation of equitable principles on her behalf was inappropriate, particularly since the father did not violate any court order by removing the children to Illinois. In re Weinstein, 87 Ill. App. 3d 101, 42 Ill. Dec. 243, 408 N.E.2d 952 (1 Dist. 1980).

Finality
Where trial judge incorporated in the custody modification order a provision which continued the case to a subsequent date and time so that the court can further evaluate the results of the modification order, this Act should have been followed as the children and parents are entitled to a certain degree of finality and conclusiveness when an order of custody is entered. King v. Vancil, 34 Ill. App. 3d 831, 341 N.E.2d 65 (5 Dist. 1975).

Foreign Custody Decrees
In matters involving divorce decrees of other states, where new circumstances have arisen since the divorce decree, the courts in this state are not prevented from re-examining custody questions even with full faith and credit to the original divorce decree; however, there must be a change in circumstances since the entry of the decree in the foreign state. Wilner v. Wilner, 131 Ill. App. 2d 891, 266 N.E.2d 918 (3 Dist. 1971).

Habeas Corpus
The fiction of habeas corpus is no longer a proper vehicle to enforce a putative father's rights, but at least the right of visitation is encompassed by this section. In re Myer, 100 Ill. App. 3d 27, 55 Ill. Dec. 358, 426 N.E.2d 333 (4 Dist. 1981).

In a divorce proceeding, where the parties induced the court to decide the issue of child custody, since the court had general jurisdiction of the subject matter and the parties induced the court to act, the court could disregard the informality of the proceedings and consider the record as though the plaintiff had filed a petition for a writ of habeas corpus. Szewczyk v. Szewczyk, 320 Ill. App. 562, 51 N.E.2d 801 (1 Dist. 1943).

Hearsay
In an action by a father to obtain custody of his two children, testimony given by maternal grandmother as to what the children supposedly told her about the father's conduct and living conditions was inadmissible; such evidence was from a party who attempted to obtain legal custody and was rebuffed. In re Gustafson, 187 Ill. App. 3d 551, 135 Ill. Dec. 192, 543 N.E.2d 575 (4 Dist. 1989).

Home State
Where upon commencement of the proceedings under this section, the state was neither the children's "home state" nor had it been within the previous six months, where pursuant to agreement of the parties the circuit court granted mother permission to remove the children to another state, where the children have lived in the other state, where father filed his petition for a preliminary injunction more than a year later, Illinois could not be considered the children's "home state" in any ordinary sense of those words. In re Wass, 94 Ill. App. 3d 436, 50 Ill. Dec. 165, 419 N.E.2d 32 (1 Dist. 1981).

Incorporated Settlement Agreement

—Modification
A settlement agreement provision that husband would not advance as a reason for modification of the child support payments any future employment of wife did not divest the court of its power to modify the divorce decree into which the agreement was incorporated. Wohl v. Wohl, 28 Ill. App. 3d 298, 328 N.E.2d 138 (1 Dist. 1975).

Injunction
Persons subject to an injunctive order issued by a court with jurisdiction are expected to obey that decree until it is modified or reversed even if they have proper grounds to object to this order. People v. Rodriguez, 169 Ill. App. 3d 131, 119 Ill. Dec. 717, 523 N.E.2d 185 (2 Dist. 1988).

An injunctive order entered by a court having jurisdiction over the person and the subject matter is not void, and although it may be declared erroneous, it, again, as a general rule, must be obeyed and will support a contempt order. People v. Rodriguez, 169 Ill. App. 3d 131, 119 Ill. Dec. 717, 523 N.E.2d 185 (2 Dist. 1988).

Interlocutory Order
Order awarding custody of a child is, by its nature, an interlocutory order and not a final one. Sommer v. Borovic, 69 Ill. 2d 220, 13 Ill. Dec. 1, 370 N.E.2d 1028 (1977).

Interrelation
Subdivision (b)(2) and subsection (c) of this section interrelate in that subdivision (b)(2) of this section applies to those persons initiating custody proceedings and subsection (c) of this section applies to those persons seeking to intervene in previously initiated proceedings; the standing requirements for non-parents necessarily applies to both sections to read them harmoniously. In re Nicholas, 170 Ill. App. 3d 171, 120 Ill. Dec. 698, 524 N.E.2d 728 (3 Dist. 1988).

Jurisdiction

—In General
In distinguishing "jurisdiction" under this section from traditional jurisdiction, the supreme court has found the General Assembly used "jurisdiction" in this section to limit the circuit court's exercise of existing jurisdiction. In re Schlam, 271 Ill. App. 3d 788, 207 Ill. Dec. 889, 648 N.E.2d 345 (2 Dist. 1995).

"Jurisdiction," as the term is used in this section, refers to a standing requirement for persons petitioning for child custody. In re

Jurisdiction (Cont'd)

—In General (Cont'd)
Schlam, 271 Ill. App. 3d 788, 207 Ill. Dec. 889, 648 N.E.2d 345 (2 Dist. 1995).

Although a trial court ordinarily loses jurisdiction to vacate or modify a final and appealable judgment more than 30 days after it is entered, a circuit court has continuing jurisdiction in cases involving child custody judgments under subsection (a) of this section, which states that trial courts have jurisdiction to make child custody determinations in original or modification proceedings. In re Oertel, 216 Ill. App. 3d 806, 159 Ill. Dec. 766, 576 N.E.2d 435 (2 Dist. 1991).

Where both prospective custodians are present in a state and there is an opportunity for a full hearing on the custody issue, the jurisdictional requirements of this Act may be satisfied. In re Weinstein, 87 Ill. App. 3d 101, 42 Ill. Dec. 243, 408 N.E.2d 952 (1 Dist. 1980).

Subsection (a) of this section is virtually identical to the Uniform Child Custody Jurisdiction Act (750 ILCS 35/1 et seq.) provisions on jurisdiction. Ehr v. Ehr, 77 Ill. App. 3d 540, 33 Ill. Dec. 11, 396 N.E.2d 87 (2 Dist. 1979).

—Challenge
Parties must bring a motion to dismiss within the time for pleading if they wish to challenge the standing of petitioners acting pursuant to subdivision (b)(1) which must allege that the petitioner is not a "parent" within the meaning of the Act. In re Schlam, 271 Ill. App. 3d 788, 207 Ill. Dec. 889, 648 N.E.2d 345 (2 Dist. 1995).

—Conceding
Trial court did not abuse its discretion in conceding jurisdiction to another state where other state was child's home, had a closer connection with the child and with respondent than did Illinois and there was substantial evidence there, as settlement agreement provided that post decree proceedings would be construed under Illinois law not filed only in Illinois. In re Walker, 287 Ill. App. 3d 634, 222 Ill. Dec. 833, 678 N.E.2d 705 (1 Dist. 1997).

—Continuing and Exclusive
Where respondent was twice made subject to rules to show cause for violating the court's injunction, and for violating the visitation order, the children told the trial judge that they had seen their father strike and threaten their mother, and the record indicates that there was at least a possibility that the daughter's physical safety had also been threatened by respondent, on these facts, the trial court's continued jurisdiction over the children's welfare following their mother's death rested on a firm foundation. Milenkovic v. Milenkovic, 93 Ill. App. 3d 204, 48 Ill. Dec. 618, 416 N.E.2d 1140 (1 Dist. 1981).

Jurisdiction acquired by a court in a divorce proceeding over the custody and maintenance of children of parties to the suit is not only continuing but is also exclusive and precludes any other court in the state where the custody proceedings were held from later acquiring or exercising jurisdiction over the same subject. Sommer v. Borovic, 69 Ill. 2d 220, 13 Ill. Dec. 1, 370 N.E.2d 1028 (1977).

Because the circuit court that rendered divorce decree which awarded custody of children had continuing and exclusive jurisdiction over the question of custody, former husband's filing of a complaint in the circuit court of another county to register the divorce decree was inappropriate and could not operate to confer jurisdiction upon the circuit court of that county. Sommer v. Borovic, 69 Ill. 2d 220, 13 Ill. Dec. 1, 370 N.E.2d 1028 (1977).

The court's jurisdiction to alter the custody and support of children is exclusive and continuing until the child or children attain their majority; a decree or order fixing the custody of a child or children is final only as to the conditions then existing. Eggemeyer v. Eggemeyer, 86 Ill. App. 2d 224, 229 N.E.2d 144 (2 Dist. 1967).

—Decree Necessary
Court cannot, in the absence of a decree of divorce, determine property rights, award alimony, or dispose of the custody of a child. Ollman v. Ollman, 396 Ill. 176, 71 N.E.2d 50 (1947).

—Held Improper
Illinois court was without jurisdiction to entertain plaintiff's complaint to modify the child custody provisions of a divorce decree where the child's home state was New Mexico, where contacts with Illinois were limited, and where there was no substantial evidence available in Illinois concerning the child's present or future personal relationships, care and training. Tanner v. Smith, 61 Ill. App. 3d 456, 18 Ill. Dec. 702, 378 N.E.2d 166 (5 Dist. 1978).

—Held Proper
Where children were present in Illinois, where parties had been raised, married, lived several years and borne their older child in Illinois, where both maternal and paternal grandparents resided here, where father intended to do so for an indefinite period in the future, and where the mother presented testimony of witnesses from both Montana and Illinois, the absence of immediate past connections with this state directly by the parties did not preclude its jurisdiction over the custody issue. In re Weinstein, 87 Ill. App. 3d 101, 42 Ill. Dec. 243, 408 N.E.2d 952 (1 Dist. 1980).

—Juvenile Court
The juvenile court did not usurp jurisdiction over the action pending in the divorce division because it possessed jurisdiction to decide whether two girls for whom a guardian had been appointed by the divorce division were in a condition of neglect. People v. Anast, 22 Ill. App. 3d 750, 318 N.E.2d 18 (1 Dist. 1974).

—Non-Party
Where the former wife petitioned to cite the sister of her former husband for contempt for her refusal to relinquish the custody of child, which was awarded to wife in a prior divorce decree, the court could not order the transfer of custody because it never acquired personal jurisdiction over the defendant and the defendant was not party to original proceeding. Hale v. Hale, 5 Ill. App. 2d 90, 124 N.E.2d 596 (3 Dist. 1955).

—Requirements
Subdivision (b)(1), like subdivision (b)(2), contains a standing requirement; parties petitioning for child custody pursuant to subdivision (b)(1) have standing only if they are "parents" within the meaning of the Act. In re Schlam, 271 Ill. App. 3d 788, 207 Ill. Dec. 889, 648 N.E.2d 345 (2 Dist. 1995).

There are two requirements for the exercise of jurisdiction over a custody determination which emerge from the provisions of this Act and this section: a significant connection with the state by the children and one of both custodial contestants and substantial evidence bearing upon their future environment. In re Weinstein, 87 Ill. App. 3d 101, 42 Ill. Dec. 243, 408 N.E.2d 952 (1 Dist. 1980).

—Standards
This section establishes the jurisdictional standards which must be present before an Illinois court, competent to decide child custody matters, may make a child custody determination by initial or modification judgment. Tanner v. Smith, 61 Ill. App. 3d 456, 18 Ill. Dec. 702, 378 N.E.2d 166 (5 Dist. 1978).

—Sufficient Contacts
Where both minor child and petitioner had a significant connection with Illinois where the child was born in Illinois in March, 1974 and resided here until April, 1978 when he was removed to Florida without leave of court where he was returned to Illinois in October, 1978 and resided with petitioner until his second removal without leave of court in November, 1978 where petitioner resided and worked in Illinois and had done so since at least August, 1973 where the only contact with another state occurred as a result of two unsanctioned removals of the child from Illinois, the trial court properly exercised jurisdiction in modifying the judgment of dissolution of marriage. Hawkins v. Colson, 77 Ill. App. 3d 873, 33 Ill. Dec. 279, 396 N.E.2d 668 (3 Dist. 1979).

Jury Trial
Where plaintiff wife acknowledged the validity of a prior Arkansas divorce decree, and her complaint was concerned solely with alimony, property division and attorney fees, defendant husband had no common-law right to a jury trial, as such actions were traditionally chancery actions, and the right arose only if it was expressly conferred by statute. Sidwell v. Sidwell, 28 Ill. App. 3d 580, 328 N.E.2d 595 (4 Dist. 1975).

Liability of Parent
Imposition of an "absolute responsibility" on a parent to keep a

Liability of Parent (Cont'd)
child out of harm's way is tantamount to making a parent an insurer of a child's safety; that the sanction to be imposed on a defaulting insurer parent, regardless of the diligence of the parent, may be loss of custody of the child is not, and obviously cannot be, the law. In re Gordon, 233 Ill. App. 3d 617, 175 Ill. Dec. 137, 599 N.E.2d 1151 (1 Dist.), appeal denied, 147 Ill. 2d 626, 180 Ill. Dec. 149, 606 N.E.2d 1226 (1992).

Misconduct
Where alleged promiscuity and marijuana use all took place between one and two years prior to child custody hearing with no evidence that it continued, where sexual activity and marijuana use alone were not determinative of a mother's right to continued custody, where there was no proof of the likelihood of future misconduct, trial court's granting of father's petition to modify was against manifest weight of evidence. Ehr v. Ehr, 77 Ill. App. 3d 540, 33 Ill. Dec. 11, 396 N.E.2d 87 (2 Dist. 1979).

Natural Parent's Right

—Not Absolute
While a natural parent has a superior right to the custody of his child, that right is not absolute and does not require a rigid and unthinking construction of this section. Menconi v. Menconi, 117 Ill. App. 3d 394, 73 Ill. Dec. 10, 453 N.E.2d 835 (1 Dist. 1983); In re Nicholas, 170 Ill. App. 3d 171, 120 Ill. Dec. 698, 524 N.E.2d 728 (3 Dist. 1988).

—Presumption
In child-custody disputes it is an accepted presumption that the right or interest of a natural parent in the care, custody and control of a child is superior to the claim of a third person; but the presumption is not absolute and serves only as one of several factors used by courts in resolving the ultimately controlling question of where the best interests of the child lie. In re Peterson, 112 Ill. 2d 48, 96 Ill. Dec. 690, 491 N.E.2d 1150 (1986).

Non-Parent

—Custody Requirement
Before non-parents are allowed to petition for custody of a child, they must satisfy a standing requirement, i.e., that the child is not in the physical custody of one of his parents. In re Haslett, 257 Ill. App. 3d 999, 195 Ill. Dec. 874, 629 N.E.2d 182 (5 Dist. 1994).

—Lack of Standing
Once non-parents are held to lack standing under the Dissolution Act or the Probate Act, the non-parents must be dismissed from the case. In re Haslett, 257 Ill. App. 3d 999, 195 Ill. Dec. 874, 629 N.E.2d 182 (5 Dist. 1994).

—Seeking Custody
When seeking custody of a child under the Illinois Marriage and Dissolution of Marriage Act, 750 ILCS 5/102 et seq. or the Probate Act, a nonparent must meet a threshold standing requirement; to have standing, the party must allege and prove that the child was not in the physical custody of one parent at the time the petition was filed. In re Estate of K.E.S., 347 Ill. App. 3d 452, 283 Ill. Dec. 76, 807 N.E.2d 681, 2004 Ill. App. LEXIS 346 (4 Dist. 2004).

To acquire standing to petition for custody of a minor child under subdivision (b)(2), a non-parent must show that the child is not in the physical possession of one of his or her parents and a non-parent failing to satisfy the standing requirement of subdivision (b)(2) must proceed under the stricter requirements imposed by the Adoption or Juvenile Court Acts. In re Cannon, 268 Ill. App. 3d 937, 206 Ill. Dec. 343, 645 N.E.2d 348 (1 Dist. 1994).

Illinois courts appear reluctant to find the child has been with the non-parent for a "substantial" period of time if the non-parent had physical custody only for several months. In re Cannon, 268 Ill. App. 3d 937, 206 Ill. Dec. 343, 645 N.E.2d 348 (1 Dist. 1994).

Aunt and uncle had to show that child was not in the physical custody of a parent at the time they sought custody under subdivision (b)(2) and subsection (c) of this section. In re Nicholas, 170 Ill. App. 3d 171, 120 Ill. Dec. 698, 524 N.E.2d 728 (3 Dist. 1988).

Where the petitioner was a nurse's aide at a state foundling home in Riga, Latvia, where the child was taken shortly after her birth, and as an employee of this institution took care of the minor, left the home with the child as a result of an evacuation of refugees and became her godmother, however laudable as a work of mercy, it did not vest her with any legal rights to the child's custody; the petitioner was not one in loco parentis and did not have to be made a party defendant in adoption proceedings or be given notice thereof. Klabis v. Hoyer, 345 Ill. App. 365, 103 N.E.2d 378 (1 Dist. 1952).

—Standing Required
Before a non-parent can demand a custody hearing to determine the best interests of a child, the non-parent must first show that he or she has standing to invoke this extraordinary provision. In re Kirchner, 164 Ill. 2d 468, 208 Ill. Dec. 268, 649 N.E.2d 324 (1995), cert. denied, 515 U.S. 1152, 115 S. Ct. 2599, 132 L. Ed. 2d 846 (1995).

Notice of Hearing
A custody petition, filed by a neighbor, pursuant to this section was not a "new" proceeding that would require additional service of summons upon the respondent. Milenkovic v. Milenkovic, 93 Ill. App. 3d 204, 48 Ill. Dec. 618, 416 N.E.2d 1140 (1 Dist. 1981).

Particular Facts
Since no one factor is controlling in the determination of whether or not a child is in the physical custody of one of his parents under subdivision (b)(2) of this section, such a determination in a given case will depend heavily on the particular facts of the individual case. In re Carey, 188 Ill. App. 3d 1040, 136 Ill. Dec. 518, 544 N.E.2d 1293 (2 Dist. 1989), appeal denied, 129 Ill. 2d 561, 140 Ill. Dec. 669, 550 N.E.2d 554 (1990).

Physical Custody
The determination that a parent does not have physical custody of a child turns not on possession but rather, it requires that that parent somehow has voluntarily and indefinitely relinquished custody of the child; whether the relinquishment results from a calculated decision on the parent's part or is the product of abandonment, the relinquishment must be voluntary for subdivision (b)(2) to apply. In re Kirchner, 164 Ill. 2d 468, 208 Ill. Dec. 268, 649 N.E.2d 324 (1995), cert. denied, 515 U.S. 1152, 115 S. Ct. 2599, 132 L. Ed. 2d 846 (1995).

Physical custody does not depend on who has physical possession of the child; factors to be considered in this regard include how the child came into the non-parent's physical possession and the duration of the possession. Hanson v. McGowan, 197 Ill. App. 3d 708, 144 Ill. Dec. 183, 555 N.E.2d 80 (2 Dist. 1990); Gonzalez ex rel. Gonzalez v. Donnelly, 204 Ill. App. 3d 28, 149 Ill. Dec. 580, 561 N.E.2d 1276 (3 Dist. 1990).

Natural mother, although exercising her visitation rights, had not provided for the care, custody and welfare of the son in such a manner that, when natural father died, the trial court was required to find that physical custody as used in subdivision (b)(2) of this section was in the natural mother, who had voluntarily relinquished permanent legal custody. In re Carey, 188 Ill. App. 3d 1040, 136 Ill. Dec. 518, 544 N.E.2d 1293 (2 Dist. 1989), appeal denied, 129 Ill. 2d 561, 140 Ill. Dec. 669, 550 N.E.2d 554 (1990).

Physical custody, as defined in subdivision (b)(2) of this section, requires a determination of who was providing for the care, custody and welfare of the child prior to the initiation of custody proceedings. In re Nicholas, 170 Ill. App. 3d 171, 120 Ill. Dec. 698, 524 N.E.2d 728 (3 Dist. 1988).

Although the custodian had chosen not to retain physical custody of her children, she did not change the finality of the judgment upon which she relied. People ex rel. Bukovic v. Smith, 98 Ill. App. 3d 144, 53 Ill. Dec. 498, 423 N.E.2d 1302 (1 Dist. 1981).

Possession of Child
Father and natural guardian neither voluntarily placed baby with the non-parents whose adoption of the child had been vacated nor had he consented to their continued possession; non-parents did not have "custody" rather, they had mere possession. In re Kirchner, 164 Ill. 2d 468, 208 Ill. Dec. 268, 649 N.E.2d 324 (1995), cert. denied, 515 U.S. 1152, 115 S. Ct. 2599, 132 L. Ed. 2d 846 (1995).

Possession of the child at the time a petition is filed is not sufficient to equate the standing required under this section to invade a natural parent's right. Butler v. Butler, 192 Ill. App. 3d 135, 139 Ill. Dec. 197, 548 N.E.2d 582 (1 Dist. 1989).

Procedures

—Exclusivity

Custodial father who argued that the court erred in awarding custody of infant to custodian without any petition on file by custodian for custody of infant and without an adjudication as to him, the custodial father, failed to realize that procedures under this Act are not the exclusive means by which the trial court acquires jurisdiction in child custody cases; child custody proceedings may also be initiated under the Juvenile Court Act of 1987 (705 ILCS 405/1-1 et seq.). People v. Baker, 213 Ill. App. 3d 274, 157 Ill. Dec. 101, 571 N.E.2d 1120 (4 Dist. 1991).

Purpose

The only purpose of this Act is the determination of the proper forum for the trial of a custody dispute. Schomer v. Scheidt, 89 Ill. App. 3d 92, 44 Ill. Dec. 432, 411 N.E.2d 554 (3 Dist. 1980).

The Illinois Supreme Court has concluded that this Act reflects an underlying policy favoring the finality of child custody judgments, and making their modification more difficult. Ehr v. Ehr, 77 Ill. App. 3d 540, 33 Ill. Dec. 11, 396 N.E.2d 87 (2 Dist. 1979).

Putative Father

The rights of a putative father who acknowledges an illegitimate child are recognized under the law and he thereby assumes burdens along with benefits. In re Myer, 100 Ill. App. 3d 27, 55 Ill. Dec. 358, 426 N.E.2d 333 (4 Dist. 1981).

Relinquishment of Parental Custody

The trial court's finding that neither parent had voluntarily relinquished custody of the child was not contrary to the manifest weight of the evidence because the parents visited the child, provided financial resources to the child, and all parties believed that the custody arrangement was only temporary. Franklin v. DeVriendt, 288 Ill. App. 3d 651, 224 Ill. Dec. 263, 681 N.E.2d 578 (1 Dist. 1997).

Res Judicata

A divorce decree, including custody provisions, is normally res judicata as to facts existing at the time of its entry, but the decree in respect to custody is temporary in nature and may be changed from time to time as the best interests of the child require. Randolph v. Dean, 27 Ill. App. 3d 913, 327 N.E.2d 473 (3 Dist. 1975).

Right to Hearing

Aunt and uncle were entitled to an evidentiary hearing to determine who had physical custody of child at the time of his mother's death to determine if they had standing to proceed with motion for custody. In re Nicholas, 170 Ill. App. 3d 171, 120 Ill. Dec. 698, 524 N.E.2d 728 (3 Dist. 1988).

Standing

—In General

There is no discernible legitimate benefit from granting a minor standing to bring a petition on behalf of non-parental parties. If the non-parents wish to obtain custody of the child and believe that they can show that the child is not in the physical custody of a parent, they may file a petition themselves; if the non-parents do not desire custody, it would be untenable to allow the minor to bring an action to force the court (and the natural parent) to give the non-parents what they do not want. In re Thompson, 272 Ill. App. 3d 257, 209 Ill. Dec. 294, 651 N.E.2d 222 (2 Dist. 1995).

—Abduction of Child

The abduction of a minor in order to satisfy the literal terms of the standing requirement will not be tolerated. In re Rudsell, 291 Ill. App. 3d 626, 225 Ill. Dec. 736, 684 N.E.2d 421 (4 Dist. 1997).

Where grandparents would have had standing under subdivision (b)(2) of this section prior to the time of the abduction of the child by the father, the lapse of four days between the time of the abduction and the filing of the custody petition was insufficient to reinvest the father with physical custody so as to deprive grandparents of standing. Menconi v. Menconi, 117 Ill. App. 3d 394, 73 Ill. Dec. 10, 453 N.E.2d 835 (1 Dist. 1983).

—Applicability

The requirement of subdivision (b)(2) of this section that the minor not be in the custody of a parent does not apply to a petition for guardianship under the Probate Act; the requirement of 755 ILCS 5/11-7 that the parent be found unfit or, if the parents lived apart, that good cause exists to award custody to some other person, provides sufficient protection for parents' superior right to the custody and control of their children within the context of proceedings pursuant to the Probate Act. Timmons v. Ronald L.S. (In re R.L.S.), 354 Ill. App. 3d 462, 290 Ill. Dec. 134, 820 N.E.2d 1201, 2004 Ill. App. LEXIS 1529 (3 Dist. 2004).

The standing provisions embodied in subdivision (b)(2) apply to those seeking custody under the Parentage Act (750 ILCS 45/1 et seq.) regardless of whether they are intervenors or interested parties. Brumfield v. Yard, 284 Ill. App. 3d 950, 220 Ill. Dec. 549, 673 N.E.2d 461 (4 Dist. 1996), appeal denied, 172 Ill. 2d 548, 223 Ill. Dec. 193, 679 N.E.2d 378 (1997).

The standing requirement of this Act applies equally to the guardianship proceedings of the Probate Act (755 ILCS 5/11-5). Lewis v. Newsome, 173 Ill. App. 3d 376, 123 Ill. Dec. 61, 527 N.E.2d 524 (4 Dist. 1988).

—Aunt and Uncle

The trial court reversibly erred in failing to follow its own ruling, that the aunt and uncle of child lacked standing to ask for custody, when it effectively awarded them custody. In re Haslett, 257 Ill. App. 3d 999, 195 Ill. Dec. 874, 629 N.E.2d 182 (5 Dist. 1994).

—Child with In-Laws

A mother does not relinquish custody for purposes of subdivision (b)(2) of this section merely because she leaves a child with her in-laws for the weekend. In re McCuan, 176 Ill. App. 3d 421, 125 Ill. Dec. 923, 531 N.E.2d 102 (5 Dist. 1988).

—Conditions to Appeal

A litigant may not disobey a decree of the court with reference to the custody of a child, take the child to a place unknown, defy the orderly legal processes of the courts, and then seek the aid of appellate court in determining whether or not his rights were adequately protected by the trial court; however, instead of dismissing the appeal, appellate court entered an order that the appeal would be dismissed 30 days after the date of filing of opinion unless within that period the defendant filed in appellate court a supplementary record showing that he had appeared in his own proper person in the trial court and had returned the custody of the minor to his mother. Burns v. Burns, 35 Ill. App. 2d 34, 181 N.E.2d 605 (1 Dist. 1962).

—Death of Custodial Parent

The death of a custodial parent after a final divorce judgment has been entered does not automatically revert custody to the surviving parent. In re McCarthy, 157 Ill. App. 3d 377, 109 Ill. Dec. 687, 510 N.E.2d 555 (2 Dist. 1987).

—Determination

The facts of obvious importance in determining standing concern the legal incidents of custody: (1) who has immediate physical possession of the minor child; (2) how that person took over control; and (3) the nature, manner, and duration of possession. Brown v. Brown, 207 Ill. App. 3d 139, 152 Ill. Dec. 70, 565 N.E.2d 312 (4 Dist. 1990), appeal denied, 139 Ill. 2d 596, 159 Ill. Dec. 108, 575 N.E.2d 915, cert. denied, 502 U.S. 939, 112 S. Ct. 374, 116 L. Ed. 2d 325 (1991).

—Established

"Standing" has been found in custody cases when a parent does not have custody of the child, thereby allowing a non-parent to petition for custody; once standing is established, the court will apply the "best interest of the child" standard to determine custody. Gonzalez ex rel. Gonzalez v. Donnelly, 204 Ill. App. 3d 28, 149 Ill. Dec. 580, 561 N.E.2d 1276 (3 Dist. 1990).

—Failure to Satisfy Requirement

A non-parent failing to satisfy the standing requirement under this Act must proceed under stricter requirements imposed by the Adoption Act (750 ILCS 50/0.01 et seq.), or the Juvenile Court Act (705 ILCS 405/1-1 et seq.), which basically require a showing that the parents are unfit. In re Nicholas, 170 Ill. App. 3d 171, 120 Ill. Dec. 698, 524 N.E.2d 728 (3 Dist. 1988).

—Father's Unfitness

Maternal aunt and uncle, who sought custody of children in

Standing (Cont'd)

—Father's Unfitness (Cont'd)

custody of natural father since mother's death, could be considered for custody only by alleging and proving the unfitness of the father in an appropriate proceeding under either the Juvenile Court Act (705 ILCS 405/1-1 et seq.) or the Adoption Act (750 ILCS 50/0.01 et seq.). O'Rourke v. O'Rourke, 160 Ill. App. 3d 584, 112 Ill. Dec. 610, 514 N.E.2d 6 (3 Dist. 1987).

—Grandparents

Grandparents did not have standing to seek custody of child since the fact that the mother signed a consent to guardianship, which was either done under a misapprehension as to the consent's meaning or was simply recanted within a week of its execution, without a change in the minor child's physical custody, was not enough to effect a waiver, and the grandparents did not have physical possession of the child when they filed their petition. Groff v. Groff, 332 Ill. App. 3d 1108, 266 Ill. Dec. 387, 774 N.E.2d 826, 2002 Ill. App. LEXIS 701 (5 Dist. 2002).

Maternal grandparents did not waive their right to intervene in proceedings on father's petition to modify child custody based on their failure to intervene in prior custody litigation. In re Feig, 296 Ill. App. 3d 405, 230 Ill. Dec. 685, 694 N.E.2d 654 (3 Dist. 1998), appeal denied, 179 Ill. 2d 581, 235 Ill. Dec. 563, 705 N.E.2d 436 (1998).

Maternal grandparents standing to intervene in proceedings on father's petition to modify child custody was supported by sufficient evidence. In re Feig, 296 Ill. App. 3d 405, 230 Ill. Dec. 685, 694 N.E.2d 654 (3 Dist. 1998), appeal denied, 179 Ill. 2d 581, 235 Ill. Dec. 563, 705 N.E.2d 436 (1998).

Where custodial parent surrendered her custodial possession by delivering the child to her parents, the child's maternal grandparents, the grandparents did not have standing to seek custody under subdivision (b)(2) of this section in a custody determination against the noncustodial parent. In re Gustafson, 181 Ill. App. 3d 472, 130 Ill. Dec. 148, 536 N.E.2d 1359 (4 Dist. 1989).

The child's grandparents failed to demonstrate standing where the evidence disclosed only that the father and the child lived with the grandparents before the father was awarded custody, that subsequently, the child lived with his natural father, and the petition for custody was filed while the child was visiting his grandparents. Butler v. Butler, 192 Ill. App. 3d 135, 139 Ill. Dec. 197, 548 N.E.2d 582 (1 Dist. 1989).

Petitioner, the child's parental grandmother, had standing to file her custody petition because child's natural father voluntarily surrendered her care and custody to the petitioner while the child was still an infant, and the petitioner's care and custody continued uninterrupted for approximately three years, the child was not in the physical custody of her natural father, additionally, the record clearly established that child's natural mother abandoned the child while she was an infant. McKerr v. Bozarth, 182 Ill. App. 3d 345, 131 Ill. Dec. 410, 538 N.E.2d 785 (2 Dist. 1989).

If boyfriend proves to be the actual father of child, and he had physical custody of the boy at time of mother's death, grandparents are without standing to file custody petition. Lewis v. Newsome, 173 Ill. App. 3d 376, 123 Ill. Dec. 61, 527 N.E.2d 524 (4 Dist. 1988).

Grandparents have been held to have standing under subdivision (b)(2) of this section. In re Black, 133 Ill. App. 3d 59, 87 Ill. Dec. 831, 477 N.E.2d 1359 (2 Dist. 1985).

—Limited

The limited standing requirement protects both the custody rights of the natural parent and the environmental stability of the minor child. Brown v. Brown, 207 Ill. App. 3d 139, 152 Ill. Dec. 70, 565 N.E.2d 312 (4 Dist. 1990), appeal denied, 139 Ill. 2d 596, 159 Ill. Dec. 108, 575 N.E.2d 915, cert. denied, 502 U.S. 939, 112 S. Ct. 374, 116 L. Ed. 2d 325 (1991).

As a jurisdictional matter, the petitioners had to satisfy a limited standing requirement to file their petition for guardianship over the minor child. Brown v. Brown, 207 Ill. App. 3d 139, 152 Ill. Dec. 70, 565 N.E.2d 312 (4 Dist. 1990), appeal denied, 139 Ill. 2d 596, 159 Ill. Dec. 108, 575 N.E.2d 915, cert. denied, 502 U.S. 939, 112 S. Ct. 374, 116 L. Ed. 2d 325 (1991).

—Minor Child

Subdivision (b)(2) does not give a minor child standing to petition for a change in his own custody. In re Thompson, 272 Ill. App. 3d 257, 209 Ill. Dec. 294, 651 N.E.2d 222 (2 Dist. 1995).

—Non-Natural Parent

An interpretation of subdivision (b)(1) that makes the date of seeking relief the date that determines whether a person has standing as a "parent" is sensible even though respondent challenged father's paternity with her first pleading. The concerns of those who advocate an estoppel theory or a doctrine of "equitable parent" are real; by rejecting those latter theories but giving persons who are not natural parents a standing to seek relief, the court is answering those concerns while still upholding the superior rights of natural parents. In re Roberts, 271 Ill. App. 3d 972, 208 Ill. Dec. 683, 649 N.E.2d 1344 (4 Dist. 1995), appeal denied, 163 Ill. 2d 586, 212 Ill. Dec. 437, 657 N.E.2d 638 (1995).

—Non-Parent

Any error the court may have committed in finding the maternal grandmother to have standing for her custody petition, based on the father's pretrial incarceration for killing the mother, did not result in a jurisdictional defect and did not affect the proceedings as the father subsequently died. Tawrel v. Patterson, 197 Ill. 2d 492, 259 Ill. Dec. 392, 758 N.E.2d 800, 2001 Ill. LEXIS 1432 (2001).

A non-parent seeking standing under this section must establish that the child is in the physical custody of a non-parent, which necessarily requires that both of the child's parents must have voluntarily relinquished custody of the child. Franklin v. DeVriendt, 288 Ill. App. 3d 651, 224 Ill. Dec. 263, 681 N.E.2d 578 (1 Dist. 1997).

To satisfy the standing requirement under subdivision (b)(2), the non-parent must show that the child is "not in the physical custody of one of his parents"; when the non-parent meets this requirement, the court may then consider the non-parent's claim for the legal custody of the child under the "best interests of the child" standard. In re Dile, 248 Ill. App. 3d 683, 188 Ill. Dec. 595, 618 N.E.2d 1165 (5 Dist. 1993).

Non-parents must show that the parent has relinquished "legal custody" of the child, rather than merely physical possession, before satisfying the standing requirement of subdivision (b)(2). In re Dile, 248 Ill. App. 3d 683, 188 Ill. Dec. 595, 618 N.E.2d 1165 (5 Dist. 1993).

The natural parent's right to the custody of the child is presumptively superior to claims by non-parents; to have standing to seek custody under subdivision (b)(2), non-parents must overcome the presumption by demonstrating that the natural parent does not have physical custody of his or her child. In re Thompson, 272 Ill. App. 3d 257, 209 Ill. Dec. 294, 651 N.E.2d 222 (2 Dist. 1995).

Non-parents must first satisfy a standing requirement in order to be considered for legal custody of a child. In re Peterson, 112 Ill. 2d 48, 96 Ill. Dec. 690, 491 N.E.2d 1150 (1986); In re Nicholas, 170 Ill. App. 3d 171, 120 Ill. Dec. 698, 524 N.E.2d 728 (3 Dist. 1988); In re McCuan, 176 Ill. App. 3d 421, 125 Ill. Dec. 923, 531 N.E.2d 102 (5 Dist. 1988); In re Sechrest, 202 Ill. App. 3d 865, 148 Ill. Dec. 615, 560 N.E.2d 1212 (4 Dist. 1990).

The non-parent must show more than merely weekend, or even daily care of the children to support standing. In re McCuan, 176 Ill. App. 3d 421, 125 Ill. Dec. 923, 531 N.E.2d 102 (5 Dist. 1988).

The non-parent must show that the parent has relinquished "legal custody" of the child, rather than merely physical possession, before satisfying the standing requirement of subdivision (b)(2) of this section. In re McCuan, 176 Ill. App. 3d 421, 125 Ill. Dec. 923, 531 N.E.2d 102 (5 Dist. 1988).

The non-parent bears the burden of demonstrating that he or she has standing to commence the custody action. In re Santa Cruz, 172 Ill. App. 3d 775, 122 Ill. Dec. 759, 527 N.E.2d 131 (2 Dist. 1988).

—Not Shown

The maternal grandmother did not have standing under subdivision (b)(2) to seek custody after the mother's death, because the evidence did not show father that the ever voluntarily relinquished custody of the child. In re Houghton, 301 Ill. App. 3d 775, 235 Ill. Dec. 60, 704 N.E.2d 409 (4 Dist. 1998), appeal denied, 184 Ill. 2d 557, 239 Ill. Dec. 608, 714 N.E.2d 527 (1999).

The petitioner's amended complaint was devoid of any factual allegation from which it could be inferred that the father relinquished custody; the mere fact of physical possession of the children by the petitioner for a short time following the mother's death, be it

Standing (Cont'd)

—Not Shown (Cont'd)

voluntary or involuntary, was wholly inadequate to establish standing. In re Siegel, 271 Ill. App. 3d 540, 207 Ill. Dec. 907, 648 N.E.2d 607 (2 Dist. 1995).

Where petitioner made clear her intention to cease living with her parents but she did not indicate any desire to relinquish physical custody of her child and two to six days after leaving, the petitioner returned to her parent's household to retrieve her child, but her mother refused to allow the child to leave, the trial court did not err in ruling that parents did not have standing under this Act. Hanson v. McGowan, 197 Ill. App. 3d 708, 144 Ill. Dec. 183, 555 N.E.2d 80 (2 Dist. 1990).

Mother did not voluntarily relinquish custody of her child when she left the child with the baby-sitter for five days; therefore, third party respondents lacked standing to seek custody of the child as she was in the physical custody of one of her parents at the time they intervened in the custody portion of the dissolution proceeding. In re Sechrest, 202 Ill. App. 3d 865, 148 Ill. Dec. 615, 560 N.E.2d 1212 (4 Dist. 1990).

Father's unilateral decision to relinquish custody to the third-party respondents did not confer standing on them. In re Sechrest, 202 Ill. App. 3d 865, 148 Ill. Dec. 615, 560 N.E.2d 1212 (4 Dist. 1990).

Mother did not voluntarily relinquish physical custody of child when she relinquished residence in the home of grandmother and announced her intention to return for the child later, thus, grandmother did not have standing under subdivision (b)(2) of this section to commence a custody proceeding. In re Santa Cruz, 172 Ill. App. 3d 775, 122 Ill. Dec. 759, 527 N.E.2d 131 (2 Dist. 1988).

Maternal aunt and uncle, who sought custody of children in custody of natural father since mother's death, lacked standing to seek custody because legal custody was with the mother, not the aunt and uncle, up to the time of the mother's death. O'Rourke v. O'Rourke, 160 Ill. App. 3d 584, 112 Ill. Dec. 610, 514 N.E.2d 6 (3 Dist. 1987).

The appellate court erred in its holding that the grandparents had standing under subdivision (b)(2) of this section simply because they were, in a sense, in physical possession of the child at the time the petition was filed. In re Peterson, 112 Ill. 2d 48, 96 Ill. Dec. 690, 491 N.E.2d 1150 (1986).

—Physical Custody

Child was in the "physical custody" of father at time non-parents seeking adoption filed petition to intervene, thus denying non-parents standing to seek child's custody, where father acted to protect his interest and establish his relationship with child, father had not been declared father of child when child was placed with persons seeking adoption, father brought suit for declaration of paternity before child was born, and non-parents who took possession of child had no contact with father to determine his desires. Brumfield v. Yard, 284 Ill. App. 3d 950, 220 Ill. Dec. 549, 673 N.E.2d 461 (4 Dist. 1996), appeal denied, 172 Ill. 2d 548, 223 Ill. Dec. 193, 679 N.E.2d 378 (1997).

Where mother of the child and her parents, the child's grandparents who legally adopted the child, all lived in the physical presence of the child and contributed to the child's care and welfare, mother was entitled to an evidentiary hearing on the standing issue of whether the child was in the physical custody of mother when the household arrangement was unilaterally terminated by grandparents. In re Kulawiak, 256 Ill. App. 3d 956, 194 Ill. Dec. 934, 628 N.E.2d 431 (1 Dist. 1993), appeal denied, 155 Ill. 2d 564, 198 Ill. Dec. 543, 633 N.E.2d 5 (1994).

To satisfy standing under subdivision (b)(2) of this section, a non-parent must show that the child is not in the physical custody of one of his parents. In re McCuan, 176 Ill. App. 3d 421, 125 Ill. Dec. 923, 531 N.E.2d 102 (5 Dist. 1988).

The standing requirement under subdivision (b)(2) of this section should not turn on who is in physical possession, so to speak, of the child at the moment of filing the petition for custody; to hold differently would be to encourage abductions of minors in order to satisfy the literal terms of the standing requirement and would, in reality, defeat the statutory intendment. In re McCuan, 176 Ill. App. 3d 421, 125 Ill. Dec. 923, 531 N.E.2d 102 (5 Dist. 1988).

The fact that defendant parent did not have physical possession of the child on the day the non-parent plaintiffs filed their petition was not dispositive of whether the plaintiffs met the requirements for standing under subdivision (b)(2) of this section. In re McCuan, 176 Ill. App. 3d 421, 125 Ill. Dec. 923, 531 N.E.2d 102 (5 Dist. 1988).

To have standing under this section, the petitioners must prove that, upon the death of the custodial parent, the children were not in the physical custody of the noncustodial parent. In re McCarthy, 157 Ill. App. 3d 377, 109 Ill. Dec. 687, 510 N.E.2d 555 (2 Dist. 1987).

—Preservation of Defense

Defendant's answer affirmatively stated that the child resided with the defendant for her entire life, and that plaintiffs gained custody because they had refused to return the child to the defendant after visitation; therefore, no further pleading was required of the defendant to preserve her defense of lack of standing. In re McCuan, 176 Ill. App. 3d 421, 125 Ill. Dec. 923, 531 N.E.2d 102 (5 Dist. 1988).

—Purpose

The purpose of the standing requirement imposed on non-parents is to preserve the presumed superior rights of natural parents to custody of their children. In re Nicholas, 170 Ill. App. 3d 171, 120 Ill. Dec. 698, 524 N.E.2d 728 (3 Dist. 1988).

—Shown

The trial court correctly determined that the natural mother voluntarily relinquished physical custody of the child to nonparents so as to satisfy the standing requirement. In re Rudsell, 291 Ill. App. 3d 626, 225 Ill. Dec. 736, 684 N.E.2d 421 (4 Dist. 1997).

The standing requirement was satisfied when the petitioners depended on the voluntary, not fortuitous, relinquishment of child custody by the respondent. Brown v. Brown, 207 Ill. App. 3d 139, 152 Ill. Dec. 70, 565 N.E.2d 312 (4 Dist. 1990), appeal denied, 139 Ill. 2d 596, 159 Ill. Dec. 108, 575 N.E.2d 915, cert. denied, 502 U.S. 939, 112 S. Ct. 374, 116 L. Ed. 2d 325 (1991).

Where the respondent voluntarily relinquished some degree of control of the minor child to petitioners by entering a rehabilitation program for substance abuse following the birth of the minor child, arranging for the petitioners to assume care, control, and custody of the minor child in that interim time period, moving into the residence of the petitioners upon her release from the rehabilitation program, then leaving alone from that residence without explanation, remaining incommunicado, and signing a notarized document designed to grant petitioners permission to care for the child and to obtain medical or other care for him, the respondent defaulted on her parental responsibilities, leaving an integrated familial relationship between the minor child and the petitioners and therefore the petitioners had standing to initiate a guardianship proceeding. Brown v. Brown, 207 Ill. App. 3d 139, 152 Ill. Dec. 70, 565 N.E.2d 312 (4 Dist. 1990), appeal denied, 139 Ill. 2d 596, 159 Ill. Dec. 108, 575 N.E.2d 915, cert. denied, 502 U.S. 939, 112 S. Ct. 374, 116 L. Ed. 2d 325 (1991).

Maternal aunt and uncle and maternal grandparents had proper standing to petition for custody of minor children where the petitioners proved that the children were not in the custody of the respondent father at the time of their mother's death. In re McCarthy, 157 Ill. App. 3d 377, 109 Ill. Dec. 687, 510 N.E.2d 555 (2 Dist. 1987).

—Step Parent

Record was clear step mother and natural father were responsible for welfare and care of his children prior to custody proceeding, were responsible for the financial support of the children, they had physical possession of the children and the nature of the relationship between the step mother and children had been one of mother and child and had been on going; thus, step mother had standing to bring custody proceeding following father's death. In re Brownfield, 283 Ill. App. 3d 728, 219 Ill. Dec. 310, 670 N.E.2d 1198 (4 Dist. 1996).

—Superior Rights Doctrine

Limitation of the application of the superior rights doctrine to the standing requirement of 750 ILCS 5/601(b)(2) is improper and the doctrine is also to be considered as a factor in determining a child's best interests under 750 ILCS 5/602. Mary F. v. Seth O. (In re Alexander O.), 336 Ill. App. 3d 325, 270 Ill. Dec. 711, 783 N.E.2d 673, 2003 Ill. App. LEXIS 66 (2 Dist. 2003).

Standing (Cont'd)

—Unilateral Relinquishment

A unilateral relinquishment by one parent cannot serve as the basis for establishing standing under subdivision (b)(2) as against the other parent. In re Kirchner, 164 Ill. 2d 468, 208 Ill. Dec. 268, 649 N.E.2d 324 (1995), cert. denied, 515 U.S. 1152, 115 S. Ct. 2599, 132 L. Ed. 2d 846 (1995).

—Waiver

The natural father of a child waived his right to challenge the standing of nonparents in a custody proceeding where he failed to properly raise the issue below. In re K.P.L., 304 Ill. App. 3d 481, 238 Ill. Dec. 78, 710 N.E.2d 875 (3 Dist. 1999).

Mother waived the issue of standing by failing to raise it at the temporary custody hearing and throughout the subsequent three year permanent custody proceeding. In re Sechrest, 202 Ill. App. 3d 865, 148 Ill. Dec. 615, 560 N.E.2d 1212 (4 Dist. 1990).

Where father agreed to continue temporary custody of daughter with grandparents during the pendency of their petition for permanent custody at a time when he had no way to care for daughter, he waived any objection to the grandparent's standing to petition for custody. Gonzalez ex rel. Gonzalez v. Donnelly, 204 Ill. App. 3d 28, 149 Ill. Dec. 580, 561 N.E.2d 1276 (3 Dist. 1990).

Respondent father waived all objections to petitioners' standing by his failure to make a more timely motion to dismiss on the basis of petitioners' lack of standing where he failed to file a motion to dismiss for lack of standing for more than 11 months after custody proceeding began. In re McCarthy, 157 Ill. App. 3d 377, 109 Ill. Dec. 687, 510 N.E.2d 555 (2 Dist. 1987).

Temporary Care

The mere fact that a child has been in the temporary care of relatives in no way proves that he is not in the "physical custody" of a natural parent. In re Thompson, 272 Ill. App. 3d 257, 209 Ill. Dec. 294, 651 N.E.2d 222 (2 Dist. 1995).

Father who left child with maternal grandparents after mother's suicide did so because of the trauma of mother's death in a "temporary care" situation; father consistently made it known that he wanted physical custody of child and temporary agreement did not confer custody with grandparents. In re Dile, 248 Ill. App. 3d 683, 188 Ill. Dec. 595, 618 N.E.2d 1165 (5 Dist. 1993).

Unconscionable Decree

In a divorce action where plaintiff wife had no counsel of record when the cause was called for trial, the trial court's ex parte decree of divorce entered upon defendant husband's counterclaim was totally one-sided and unconscionable in that it awarded the defendant husband virtually all of the parties' real and personal property besides granting him custody of the children who were then residing with the wife, and barred plaintiff wife from receiving alimony, such decree was vacated. Eden v. Eden, 34 Ill. App. 3d 382, 340 N.E.2d 141 (1 Dist. 1975).

Unfitness Finding

—Not Required

A finding of unfitness on natural mother's part was not necessary to award great aunt custody of the child; a finding of unfitness is not required in either a habeas corpus proceeding or in a cause of action brought pursuant to this section, rather, the standard to be applied in guardianship and custody cases is the best interest of the child. Montgomery v. Roudez, 156 Ill. App. 3d 262, 108 Ill. Dec. 803, 509 N.E.2d 499 (1 Dist. 1987).

—Required

The holding of Giacopelli v. Florence Crittenton Home, 16 Ill. 2d 556, 158 N.E.2d 613, (1959) that a married father could be denied his rights to the care, custody and control of his child without a finding of unfitness if this is in the child's best interests is clearly unconstitutional; married parents cannot be deprived of the care, custody and control of their child without a prior showing of unfitness for the sole reason that doing so is thought to be in the child's best interests, rather, unfitness must first be found. In re Kirchner, 164 Ill. 2d 468, 208 Ill. Dec. 268, 649 N.E.2d 324 (1995), cert. denied, 515 U.S. 1152, 115 S. Ct. 2599, 132 L. Ed. 2d 846 (1995).

Unlawful Transportation of Child

Trial court acted properly in refusing to hear a petition to modify an Ohio custody decree where petitioner admitted that she had brought the child to Illinois unlawfully and in violation of the foreign decree and that she secreted herself and the child in Illinois. Weimer v. Weimer, 82 Ill. App. 3d 290, 37 Ill. Dec. 704, 402 N.E.2d 706 (1 Dist. 1980).

Court, and not the custodian, is the lawful judge of what shall best serve the interest of the children; the custodian is not free to carry children from the jurisdiction and thus deprive the noncustodial parent of visitorial rights. Trimble v. Trimble, 16 Ill. App. 2d 408, 148 N.E.2d 612 (1 Dist. 1958).

Unwed Father

—Due Process Rights

Unwed fathers whose parental rights are not properly terminated and who, through deceit, are kept from assuming responsibility for and developing a relationship with their children, are entitled to the same due process rights as fathers who actually are given an opportunity and do develop this relationship. In re Kirchner, 164 Ill. 2d 468, 208 Ill. Dec. 268, 649 N.E.2d 324 (1995), cert. denied, 515 U.S. 1152, 115 S. Ct. 2599, 132 L. Ed. 2d 846 (1995).

—Procedural Safeguards

Where an unwed father is fit and willing to develop a relationship with and raise his child, but is prevented from doing so through deceit and an invalid adoption proceeding, that father is entitled to the care, custody and control of his child upon the subsequent vacatur of the invalid adoption; a hearing under subdivision (b)(2) would be improper because it would contravene the safeguards afforded unwed fathers in the Adoption Act. In re Kirchner, 164 Ill. 2d 468, 208 Ill. Dec. 268, 649 N.E.2d 324 (1995), cert. denied, 515 U.S. 1152, 115 S. Ct. 2599, 132 L. Ed. 2d 846 (1995).

Venue

—Change of Venue

Where petitions for modification of a divorce decree and for change of venue were filed on the same day and the venue petition was timely and notice thereof was served on the plaintiff who filed an answer thereto, the defendant had the right to have the custody issue, presented by her petition, heard and determined by a judge who was not, according to her belief, prejudiced against her. Smith v. Smith, 87 Ill. App. 2d 21, 230 N.E.2d 474 (2 Dist. 1967).

—Location of Relevant Evidence

Where the relief requested is a change or modification of prior determinations, this section reflects a policy requiring the action to be brought in the state where the relevant evidence regarding the child's welfare is located. Siegel v. Siegel, 80 Ill. App. 3d 583, 35 Ill. Dec. 869, 400 N.E.2d 6 (1 Dist. 1979), modified on other grounds, 84 Ill. 2d 212, 49 Ill. Dec. 298, 417 N.E.2d 1312 (1981).

Visitation

Where plaintiff claims he was deceived into believing he was child's father and consequently developed a mutually loving and nurturing relationship with child, trial court erred in ruling that because this Act and Illinois Parentage Act (750 ILCS 45/1 et seq.) do not authorize visitation privileges for a nonparent, plaintiff was not entitled to such privileges. Koelle v. Zwiren, 284 Ill. App. 3d 778, 220 Ill. Dec. 51, 672 N.E.2d 868 (1 Dist. 1996).

Statutory provisions relating to custody may be employed to adjudicate only a question of visitation, as visitation is a form of custody and subject to the custody rules as set forth in this Act. In re Myer, 100 Ill. App. 3d 27, 55 Ill. Dec. 358, 426 N.E.2d 333 (4 Dist. 1981); Padin v. Padin, 193 Ill. App. 3d 554, 140 Ill. Dec. 640, 550 N.E.2d 276 (3 Dist.), cert. denied, 132 Ill. 2d 547, 144 Ill. Dec. 259, 555 N.E.2d 378 (1990).

Where the wife was awarded the right to the sole custody of the child, the action of the trial court in ordering that the husband's parents had the right to the custody of the child for a certain period of time on the first Sunday and third Sunday of each month was a material abridgment of wife's right and would be reversed. Lucchesi v. Lucchesi, 330 Ill. App. 506, 71 N.E.2d 920 (1 Dist. 1947).

Wards of Court

Children of divorced parents traditionally have been considered

Wards of Court (Cont'd)
wards of the divorce granting court, which has continuing jurisdiction over matters affecting them. In re Noble, 192 Ill. App. 3d 501, 139 Ill. Dec. 133, 548 N.E.2d 518 (2 Dist. 1989).

LEGAL PERIODICALS

Schlam, Children "Not in the Physical Custody of One of [Their] Parents:" the Superior Rights Doctrine and Third-party Standing under the Uniform Marriage and Dissolution of Marriage Act, 24 S. Ill. U. L. J. 405 (Spring, 2000).

For article, "Baby Richard and Beyond: The Future for Adopted Children", see 18 N. Ill. U.L. Rev. 445 (1999).

For article, "Conference on Ethical Issues in the Legal Representation of Children in Illinois: Reconsidering the Need for Counsel for Children in Custody, Visitation and Child Protection Proceedings", see 29 Loy. U. Chi. L.J. 299 (1998).

For comment, "Paternity Actions in Illinois: Why Not Consider What is in the Best Interest of the Child?," see 21 S. Ill. U.L.J. 613 (1997).

For note, "Born to Lose: The Illinois 'Baby Richard' Case — How Examining His Father's Pre-Birth Conduct Might Have Led to a Different Ending for Richard," see 16 N. Ill. U.L. Rev. 543 (1996).

For article, "Survey of Illinois Law: Family Law," 19 S. Ill. U.L.J. 819 (1995).

For note, "Baby Richard: The Case That Won't Go Away," see 9 CBA Rec. 8 (1995).

For article, "Defining the Best Interest of Children: Parents v. Others in Custody Proceedings," see 79 Ill. B. J. 566 (1991).

For article, "Survey of Illinois Law [1988-89] — Family Law," see 14 S. Ill. U. L. J. 1007 (1990).

For article, "Family Law: 1985-86 Survey," see 11 S. Ill. U. L. J. 741 (1987).

For article, "Illinois Child Custody Law: An Overview," see 76 Ill. B. J. 732 (1987).

For article, "Family Law: 1985-86 Illinois Law Survey," see 18 Loy. U. Chi. L. J. 549 (1986-87).

For article, "The Continuing Jurisdiction Dilemma in Interstate Child Custody Disputes," see 70 Ill. B. J. 304 (1982).

For note, "Best Interest of the Child in Custody Proceedings and Waiver of Jurisdictional Objection — Sommer v. Bororis," see 27 De Paul L. Rev. 853 (1978).

For article, "Child Custody: Evolution of Current Criteria," see 26 De Paul L. Rev. 241 (1977).

RESEARCH REFERENCES

Admissibility of social worker's expert testimony on child custody issues. 1 ALR4th 837.

Initial award or denial of child custody to homosexual or lesbian parent. 6 ALR4th 1297.

Award of custody of child where contest is between natural parent and stepparent. 10 ALR4th 767.

Race as factor in custody award or proceedings. 10 ALR4th 796.

Desire of child as to geographical location of residence or domicile as factor in awarding custody or terminating parental rights. 10 ALR4th 827.

Right of incarcerated mother to retain custody of infant in penal institution. 14 ALR4th 748.

Religion as factor in child custody and visitation cases. 22 ALR4th 971.

Court-authorized permanent or temporary removal of child by parent to foreign county. 30 ALR4th 548.

Right of parent to regain custody of child after temporary conditional relinquishment of custody. 35 ALR4th 61.

Parent's transsexuality as factor in award of custody of children, visitation rights, or termination of parental rights. 59 ALR4th 1170.

Mother's status as "working mother" as factor in awarding child custody. 62 ALR4th 259.

Significant connection jurisdiction of court under section 3(a)(2) of the Uniform Child Custody Jurisdiction Act (UCCJA) and the Parental Kidnapping Prevention Act (PKPA), 28 USCS § 1738A(c)(2)(B). 5 ALR5th 550.

Abandonment and emergency jurisdiction of court under section 3(a)(3) of the Uniform Child Custody Jurisdiction Act (UCCJA) and the Parental Kidnapping Prevention Act (PKPA), 28 USCS § 1738A(c)(2)(C). 5 ALR5th 788.

Authority of court, open entering default judgment, to make orders for child custody or support which were not specifically requested in pleadings of prevailing party. 5 ALR5th 863.

Full faith and credit "last-in-time" rule as applicable to sister state divorce or custody judgment which is inconsistent with the forum state's earlier judgment. 36 ALR5th 527.

Recognition and enforcement of out-of-state custody decree under § 13 of the Uniform Child Custody Jurisdiction Act (UCCJA) or the Parental Kidnapping Prevention Act (PKPA), 28 USCS § 1738A(a). 40 ALR5th 227.

Initial award or denial of child custody to homosexual or lesbian parent. 62 ALR5th 591.

Custodial parent's homosexual or lesbian relationship with third person as justifying modification of child custody order. 65 ALR5th 591.

Admissibility of expert testimony regarding questions of domestic law. 66 ALR5th 135.

Significant connection jurisdiction of court to modify foreign child custody decree under §§ 3(a)(2) and 14(b) of the Uniform Child Custody Jurisdiction Act (UCCJA) and the Parental Kidnapping Prevention Act (PICPA), 28 U.S.C.A. §§ 1738A(c)(2)(b) and 1738A(f)(1). 67 ALR5th 1.

Custodial parent's relocation as grounds for change of custody. 70 ALR5th 377.

Home state jurisdiction of court to modify foreign child custody decree under §§ 3(a)(1) and 14(a)(2) of Uniform Child Custody Jurisdiction Act (UCCJA) and Parental Kidnapping Prevention Act (PKPA), §§ 28 U.S.C.A. 1738A(c)(2)(A) and 1738A(f)(1). 72 ALR5th 249.

Declining jurisdiction to modify prior child custody decree under § 14(a)(1) of Uniform Child Custody Jurisdiction Act (UCCJA) and Parental Kidnapping Prevention Act (PKPA), 28 U.S.C.A. § 1738A(f)(2). 73 ALR5th 185.

750 ILCS 5/602 Best Interest of Child

Sec. 602. *Best Interest of Child.* (a) The court shall determine custody in accordance with the best interest of the child. The court shall consider all relevant factors including:

(1) the wishes of the child's parent or parents as to his custody;

(2) the wishes of the child as to his custodian;

(3) the interaction and interrelationship of the child with his parent or parents, his siblings and any other person who may significantly affect the child's best interest;

(4) the child's adjustment to his home, school and community;

(5) the mental and physical health of all individuals involved;

(6) the physical violence or threat of physical violence by the child's potential custodian, whether directed against the child or directed against another person;

(7) the occurrence of ongoing abuse as defined in Section 103 of the Illinois Domestic Violence Act of 1986 [750 ILCS 60/103], whether directed against the child or directed against another person; and

(8) the willingness and ability of each parent to facilitate and encourage a close and continuing relationship between the other parent and the child.

In the case of a custody proceeding in which a stepparent has standing under Section 601 [750 ILCS 5/601], it is presumed to be in the best interest of the minor child that the natural parent have the custody of the minor child unless the presumption is rebutted by the stepparent.

(b) The court shall not consider conduct of a present or proposed custodian that does not affect his relationship to the child.

(c) Unless the court finds the occurrence of ongoing abuse as defined in Section 103 of the Illinois Domestic Violence Act of 1986 [750 ILCS 60/103], the court shall presume that the maximum involvement and cooperation of both parents regarding the physical, mental, moral, and emotional well-being of their child is in the best interest of the child. There shall be no presumption in favor of or against joint custody.

(Source: P.A. 86-612; 87-1186, § 2; 88-409, § 1; 90-782, § 5.)

Note.

This section was Ill.Rev.Stat., Ch. 40, para. 602.

Effect of Amendments.

The 1998 amendment by P.A. 90-782, effective August 14, 1998, added the undesignated paragraph at the end of subsection (a).

CASE NOTES

ANALYSIS

Constitutionality
—Due Process
—Equal Protection
In General
Abortion
Abuse of Discretion
—Not Shown
—Shown
Actual Harm
—Not Required
Adultery
Age
Applicability
Attorney Fees
—Awarded
—Denied
Balancing Test
Bond
Burden of Proof
—In General
—Change of Custody
—Natural Parent
—Not Met
Change in Circumstances
—In General
—Marital Status
—Modification Not Warranted
—Modification Warranted
—Standard
Change of Name
Child Abuse
Child Support
Cohabitation
Continuity
Criminal Convictions
Custodial Parent
—Duties and Responsibilities
Custody
—In General
—Ability to Cooperate
—Award Improper
—Award Upheld
—Changes
—Failure to Deliver
—Grounds
—Nature of Judgment
—Parentage Proceedings
—Parental Cohabitation
—Separation of Children
—Superior Rights Doctrine
—Surviving Parent
—Unfounded Allegations
Custody Decree
—Temporary Nature
Custody Hearing
Discretion of Court
Distance
Division of Custody
Economic Considerations
Evidence
—In General
—Expert Witnesses
—Hearsay
—Improperly Excluded
—Interview
—Prior Hearing
—Properly Excluded
Factors
—In General
—Considered
—Statutory
—Unspecified
Failure to Pay Support
Fitness of Parent
Guardian Ad Litem
Guardianship
Health of Parents
Homestead
—Effect of Custody
Homosexual Parent
Illustrative Cases
Initial Custody Order
Integration of the Child
Joint Custody
—Termination
Judge's Statement
Knowledge of Child
Legislative Intent
Living Arrangements
Mature Children
Modification
—In General
—Agreement Between Parties
—Burden of Proof
—Custody Order
—Denial Upheld
—Illustrative Cases
—Petition Required
Mother
—Presumption of Better Custodian
Murder of Parent
Name Change
Natural Parents
—Animosity Between
—Claim of Third Party
—Presumption
—Superior Right
Non-Parent
—In General
—Awarded Custody
—Grandparents
Notice of Appeal
Past Conduct
Physical Custody
Physical Violence
Preference of Child
Presumption of Harm
Previous Orders
Prior Hearing

—Transcript
Psychologist's Testimony
Putative Father
Relationship with Child
Religious Beliefs
Remarriage
Removal of Child
Rotating Custody
Separation
Stability of Environment
Standard of Review
Stipulated Awards
Substance Abuse
Temporary Custody
—Prejudicial Effect
Tender Years Doctrine
—Applied
—Not Applied
—Not Inflexible
—Presumption
—Validity
Unmarried Parents
Visitation
Witnesses
—Children
—Cross-Examination
—Experts
—Testimony of Doctor

Constitutionality

—Due Process

Due process does not require a showing of fault on the part of a natural mother before she can be deprived of the custody of her son. Montgomery v. Roudez, 156 Ill. App. 3d 262, 108 Ill. Dec. 803, 509 N.E.2d 499 (1 Dist. 1987).

—Equal Protection

With respect to custody, the equal protection clause provides an avenue for challenging governmental classifications that treat one group of persons as inferior or superior to others and for contending that general rules are being applied in an arbitrary or discriminatory way. In re Diehl, 221 Ill. App. 3d 410, 164 Ill. Dec. 73, 582 N.E.2d 281 (2 Dist. 1991), cert. denied, 144 Ill. 2d 632, 169 Ill. Dec. 140, 591 N.E.2d 20 (1992).

Natural mother who voluntarily relinquished custody of her son placed herself within the class of natural parents subject to having custody of their child determined pursuant to subdivision (b)(2) of this section, and since the best interest of the child standard was rationally related to the goals the provisions of this section seeks to promote and the interests it strives to protect; therefore, natural mother's equal protection rights were not violated. Montgomery v. Roudez, 156 Ill. App. 3d 262, 108 Ill. Dec. 803, 509 N.E.2d 499 (1 Dist. 1987).

In General

There is a strong and compelling presumption in favor of the trial court's determination of custody because the trial court is in a better position to evaluate the credibility, temperaments, personalities and capabilities of both parents through the several days of the proceedings. Cooper v. Cooper, 146 Ill. App. 3d 943, 100 Ill. Dec. 627, 497 N.E.2d 805 (5 Dist. 1986).

A custody determination does not require a showing that one parent is a "better" or "worse" person than the other; it is the children's best interest that is paramount. In re Milovich, 105 Ill. App. 3d 596, 61 Ill. Dec. 456, 434 N.E.2d 811 (1 Dist. 1982).

The law presumes that it is in the best interest of a child to be raised by his natural parent. Lloyd v. Lloyd, 92 Ill. App. 3d 124, 47 Ill. Dec. 792, 415 N.E.2d 1105 (1 Dist. 1980).

It is not necessary that the natural parent be found unfit or be found to have legally forfeited his right to custody if it is in the best interest of the child that he be placed in the custody of someone other than the natural parent. Lloyd v. Lloyd, 92 Ill. App. 3d 124, 47 Ill. Dec. 792, 415 N.E.2d 1105 (1 Dist. 1980).

In determining the best interest of the child, the court must consider the particular facts and circumstances of each case. Lloyd v. Lloyd, 92 Ill. App. 3d 124, 47 Ill. Dec. 792, 415 N.E.2d 1105 (1 Dist. 1980); In re Krause, 111 Ill. App. 3d 604, 67 Ill. Dec. 408, 444 N.E.2d 644 (1 Dist. 1982).

The commands of this section and 750 ILCS 5/610 to consider only whether the child's environment endangers his physical, mental, moral and emotional health and to disregard any conduct of the custodian that does not affect his relationship with the child reemphasize the principle that the focus of custody determinations must be the welfare of the child. Jarrett v. Jarrett, 78 Ill. 2d 337, 36 Ill. Dec. 1, 400 N.E.2d 421 (1979), cert. denied, 449 U.S. 927, 101 S. Ct. 329, 66 L. Ed. 2d 155 (1980).

Although the best interest of the child is the standard against which all actions must be measured in all cases in an effort to achieve a situation which is beneficial to the children, a trial court cannot avoid the possible consequences of an order by making all orders temporary "experiments" to see which set of circumstances will result in the best living conditions for the children. Carroll v. Carroll, 64 Ill. App. 3d 925, 21 Ill. Dec. 713, 382 N.E.2d 7 (1 Dist. 1978).

Regardless of the nature of the proceedings, the rights of the parents must be subservient to the well-being and interest of the children. Hinton v. Searles, 53 Ill. App. 3d 433, 11 Ill. Dec. 329, 368 N.E.2d 937 (5 Dist. 1977).

In proceedings affecting the custody of a child, the primary consideration is the present and prospective welfare of the child. Each case must be determined according to its own circumstances and the question rests largely in the sound discretion of the trial court. Look v. Look, 21 Ill. App. 3d 454, 315 N.E.2d 623 (3 Dist. 1974).

The best interest of the child is the standard; it is not necessary that the natural parent be found unfit, or be found to have legally forfeited his rights to custody, if it is in the best interest of the child that he be placed in the custody of someone other than the natural parent. People ex rel. Edwards v. Livingston, 42 Ill. 2d 201, 247 N.E.2d 417 (1969).

Where both principals to a divorce proceeding are fit persons, they have equal right to custody of their minor children; the paramount consideration in settling the issue of child custody is the welfare and best interests of the children themselves, without any purpose of penalizing the parent upon whom the blame for the dissolution of the marital union may be fixed. Kline v. Kline, 57 Ill. App. 2d 244, 205 N.E.2d 775 (3 Dist. 1965).

In awarding the custody of a minor child, the best interests of such child must be the primary consideration. Buehler v. Buehler, 373 Ill. 626, 27 N.E.2d 466 (1940); Kent v. Kent, 315 Ill. App. 284, 42 N.E.2d 958 (4 Dist. 1942); Martinec v. Sharapata, 328 Ill. App. 339, 66 N.E.2d 103 (1 Dist. 1946); Serotzke v. Serotzke, 335 Ill. App. 485, 82 N.E.2d 375 (1 Dist. 1948); Dunning v. Dunning, 14 Ill. App. 2d 242, 144 N.E.2d 535 (2 Dist. 1957); Arden v. Arden, 25 Ill. App. 2d 181, 166 N.E.2d 111 (3 Dist. 1960); Strouse v. Strouse, 75 Ill. App. 2d 362, 220 N.E.2d 485 (4 Dist. 1966); Marcus v. Marcus, 109 Ill. App. 2d 423, 248 N.E.2d 800 (1 Dist. 1969); Akin v. Akin, 109 Ill. App. 2d 150, 248 N.E.2d 829 (5 Dist. 1969); People ex rel. Morris v. Morris, 44 Ill. 2d 66, 254 N.E.2d 478 (1969); Mathey v. Mathey, 1 Ill. App. 3d 1008, 274 N.E.2d 501 (2 Dist. 1971); Jacobs v. Jacobs, 25 Ill. App. 3d 175, 323 N.E.2d 21 (1 Dist. 1974); Huey v. Huey, 25 Ill. App. 3d 20, 322 N.E.2d 560 (5 Dist. 1975); Drake v. Hohimer, 35 Ill. App. 3d 529, 341 N.E.2d 399 (4 Dist. 1976); In re Kennedy, 94 Ill. App. 3d 537, 49 Ill. Dec. 927, 418 N.E.2d 947 (1 Dist. 1981); In re Diehl, 221 Ill. App. 3d 410, 164 Ill. Dec. 73, 582 N.E.2d 281 (2 Dist. 1991), cert. denied, 144 Ill. 2d 632, 169 Ill. Dec. 140, 591 N.E.2d 20 (1992); In re Quindry, 223 Ill. App. 3d 735, 166 Ill. Dec. 290, 585 N.E.2d 1312 (5 Dist. 1992).

Abortion

Although the trial court erroneously considered evidence of a mother's previous abortion but such consideration was not reversible error where the trial court reached a proper decision. Thompson v. Thompson, 83 Ill. App. 3d 97, 38 Ill. Dec. 485, 403 N.E.2d 716 (3 Dist. 1980).

Abuse of Discretion

—Not Shown

Where a child, during her in camera testimony, stated that she loved both her parents and did not want to hurt either of them by choosing the other; nevertheless, she felt more comfortable living with her mother, with whom she could talk more freely, the trial

Abuse of Discretion (Cont'd)

—Not Shown (Cont'd)

court did not abuse its discretion in granting custody of the child to her mother. In re Seymour, 206 Ill. App. 3d 506, 152 Ill. Dec. 27, 565 N.E.2d 269 (2 Dist. 1990).

It was not an abuse of discretion to award custody of 15 year old daughter to husband, where he testified that daughter told him she does not want to make a decision "because she feels guilty leaving her mother," and where doctor's report observed that daughter was "the most conflicted and anxious emotionally" of the three children because she felt she might be happier with her dad, but would feel too guilty about leaving her mother, and her stated preference to the court that she live with her mother was based on guilt and fear that something would happen to her mother if she was not there; the court was not precluded from finding that the child's preference was not in the child's best interest. In re Leff, 148 Ill. App. 3d 792, 101 Ill. Dec. 262, 499 N.E.2d 1042 (2 Dist. 1986).

Where a trial court considered all the relevant factors and found that an award of custody to the natural father was in the best interests of the child, this finding was supported by the evidence and was not an abuse of discretion. In re Krause, 111 Ill. App. 3d 604, 67 Ill. Dec. 408, 444 N.E.2d 644 (1 Dist. 1982).

The court did not abuse its discretion in awarding custody of the minor children to the petitioner. In re Yakin, 107 Ill. App. 3d 1103, 62 Ill. Dec. 547, 436 N.E.2d 573 (1 Dist. 1982).

The court did not abuse its discretion in awarding custody of child to grandparents, instead of to natural father, following the death of the custodial parent, the child's mother. In re Piccirilli, 88 Ill. App. 3d 621, 43 Ill. Dec. 953, 410 N.E.2d 1086 (1 Dist. 1980).

It was a proper exercise of judicial discretion for the trial court to award temporary custody to husband and to delay a final determination of custody for eight months where husband's health and economic circumstances were uncertain, as was wife's marriage to her boyfriend; the court may have properly believed that these matters might be more settled after eight months and that the court could make a more sound determination for the child's welfare at that time. Junge v. Junge, 73 Ill. App. 3d 767, 29 Ill. Dec. 756, 392 N.E.2d 313 (5 Dist. 1979).

Where the evidence revealed plaintiff was living with her husband, and his three children and a child of plaintiff and her new husband, plaintiff worked two days every two weeks, while her sister-in-law watched the children, and plaintiff had temporary custody of the girl and the right of visitation with the boy when both children initially had difficulty adjusting, there was jealousy between the children of the two families, and defendant had a full-time job and the boy attended kindergarten in the afternoon and went to a babysitter before and after school, plaintiff argued that although the defendant was at work all day, and plaintiff was not, the trial court did not abuse its discretion in awarding custody to the father, even though he will not be at home during the day. Drake v. Hohimer, 35 Ill. App. 3d 529, 341 N.E.2d 399 (4 Dist. 1976).

Where the chancellor had the opportunity to observe the interested parties to the proceeding, the several witnesses who testified and their conduct and demeanor while testifying, his findings and conclusions, under all the authorities, would not be disturbed. People ex rel. Hermann v. Jenkins, 34 Ill. App. 2d 255, 180 N.E.2d 359 (2 Dist. 1962).

—Shown

The trial court abused its discretion in awarding custody to the father because the evidence demonstrated that the mother had a close, full-time daily involvement with the child and that she took an active interest in his life, whereas the father had only a passive interest in the child, knew little about the day-to-day details of his life, was rarely at home, and showed interest in the child primarily by giving him toys and candy. In re Leopando, 106 Ill. App. 3d 444, 62 Ill. Dec. 340, 435 N.E.2d 1312 (1 Dist. 1982), aff'd, 96 Ill. 2d 114, 70 Ill. Dec. 263, 449 N.E.2d 137 (1983).

Actual Harm

—Not Required

Subdivision (b)(3) of this section does not require that there must be actual harm to the physical, mental, moral or emotional health of the child before a change in custody can be awarded; rather, the statute in expressly prescribing that the child's present environment endangers seriously his physical, mental, moral or emotional health, contemplates potential harm as well as present harm as a result of the child's present environment. In re Padiak, 101 Ill. App. 3d 306, 56 Ill. Dec. 826, 427 N.E.2d 1372 (2 Dist. 1981).

Adultery

Where the adulterous relationship of petitioners was practically the only factor considered in making an award of custody, and that adulterous relationship had terminated, a more meaningful inquiry would be made into the best interests of the minor child with regard to placement of her custody. In re Combs, 78 Ill. App. 3d 533, 33 Ill. Dec. 922, 397 N.E.2d 255 (5 Dist. 1979).

Where the flagrant adulterous relationship between the custodial mother and a married man did affect the relationship of mother and children and negatively affected the moral health of children, the trial court did not err or abuse its discretion in transferring custody of the minor children to their father, despite the mother's remorse over her actions. De Franco v. De Franco, 67 Ill. App. 3d 760, 24 Ill. Dec. 130, 384 N.E.2d 997 (1 Dist. 1978).

Where the trial court found against defendant on his counterclaim which alleged plaintiff's adultery as ground for divorce, the court did not err in awarding custody to plaintiff. Fields v. Fields, 54 Ill. App. 3d 400, 12 Ill. Dec. 89, 369 N.E.2d 586 (5 Dist. 1977).

Fact that a divorce has been awarded to a husband on the grounds that the wife was guilty of adultery does not prevent the trial court from exercising its discretion and awarding custody of the children to the wife. Huey v. Huey, 25 Ill. App. 3d 20, 322 N.E.2d 560 (5 Dist. 1975).

Plaintiff's adultery was a reflection on her moral values; the moral climate in which children are to be raised is a valid consideration for the court to evaluate. Mulvihill v. Mulvihill, 20 Ill. App. 3d 440, 314 N.E.2d 342 (1 Dist. 1974).

Where a mother had exposed her children to immoral behavior by living with one married man in the home occupied by herself and children, by residing with another married man in a home visited by the children, and had pleaded guilty to a crime involving moral turpitude, the court's decision that the children should remain with the father could have been sustained either on the basis of her unfitness or on the basis of her failure to prove a change in circumstances. Filipello v. Filipello, 130 Ill. App. 2d 1089, 268 N.E.2d 478 (1 Dist. 1971).

Age

Fact that child was in college did not mean that she should be considered a minor for custody purposes. In re Smith, 114 Ill. App. 3d 47, 69 Ill. Dec. 827, 448 N.E.2d 545 (1 Dist. 1983).

Child's impending puberty was a relevant but not conclusive reason to award custody to the mother. In re Milovich, 105 Ill. App. 3d 596, 61 Ill. Dec. 456, 434 N.E.2d 811 (1 Dist. 1982).

In deciding custody of the minor children, the ages of all of the parties interested was an influencing factor. Scott v. Ashcraft, 342 Ill. App. 33, 95 N.E.2d 122 (3 Dist. 1950).

Applicability

Though the question of what statute applies to proceedings for custody of a child of unmarried parents is not clearly agreed in Illinois law, the best interest of the child guides the decision, no matter what form the proceedings may take. Giagnoni v. Bourey, 127 Ill. App. 3d 530, 82 Ill. Dec. 852, 469 N.E.2d 386 (2 Dist. 1984).

Where the parties have previously agreed inter se to a custody provision, the standard to be applied in such situations is that of this section with consideration of the child's best interests under subsection (a) of this section only after the former showing. Smart v. Smart, 94 Ill. App. 3d 791, 50 Ill. Dec. 587, 419 N.E.2d 695 (3 Dist. 1981).

The language of subsection (b) of this section is applicable to evidentiary matters at trial rather than a limitation on the court's power of review. In re Marks, 96 Ill. App. 3d 360, 51 Ill. Dec. 626, 420 N.E.2d 1184 (2 Dist. 1981).

Attorney Fees

—Awarded

Attorney fees were properly ordered to be paid to the attorney who was appointed to represent the interest of the child. Giagnoni v. Bourey, 127 Ill. App. 3d 530, 82 Ill. Dec. 852, 469 N.E.2d 386 (2 Dist. 1984).

Attorney Fees (Cont'd)

—Denied

Where the custodial modification appeared to have been sought primarily for the convenience of the parties rather than as a means of properly presenting the needs of the children to the court, the court did not abuse its discretion in denying plaintiff's petition for attorney's fees. Roth v. Roth, 52 Ill. App. 3d 220, 10 Ill. Dec. 54, 367 N.E.2d 442 (1 Dist. 1977).

Balancing Test

By applying the "best interest" factors as if in a trial de novo, the circuit court fashioned a judicious integration of two seemingly competing policies by balancing the policy favoring custodial continuity with the policy disfavoring the bounty of fraud, when the trial court decided the issue of custody for the first time on a motion to vacate. Mayes v. Mayes, 86 Ill. App. 3d 644, 42 Ill. Dec. 517, 409 N.E.2d 12 (3 Dist. 1980).

Bond

Where the custody decree provided that the husband would have the care and custody of his two children until the further order of the trial court, and that they would live at the home of their paternal grandparents in Massachusetts while the husband was in the Naval Service, the husband was required to furnish a bond in an amount to be determined by the trial court on remand, signed by himself, his father and mother, stating that they will return said children to county in Illinois, at such time as the court shall direct, and will abide the further order of the court. Wolfrum v. Wolfrum, 5 Ill. App. 2d 471, 126 N.E.2d 34 (3 Dist. 1955).

Burden of Proof

—In General

Every presumption is indulged in the validity of a custody decree and if its provisions are to be changed, the burden of proof is on the moving party to show why the change should be made. King v. Vancil, 34 Ill. App. 3d 831, 341 N.E.2d 65 (5 Dist. 1975).

—Change of Custody

In order to justify a change in child custody, a material change of circumstance which affects the welfare of the child must be shown, and the party seeking the change in custody has the burden of proving that the child's best interests warrants the change. Sorenson v. Sorenson, 10 Ill. App. 3d 980, 295 N.E.2d 347 (4 Dist. 1973).

To justify a change in custody, the evidence must establish that the parent to whom the children were last awarded is unfit to retain custody or that a change of circumstances makes a change of custody in the children's best interest. Filipello v. Filipello, 130 Ill. App. 2d 1089, 268 N.E.2d 478 (1 Dist. 1971).

It is not necessary for the validity of an order changing custody to another parent that the evidence of new facts establish the present unfitness of the parent to whom custody has been previously entrusted if other circumstances are clearly shown which require a modification for the welfare of the children. Kline v. Kline, 57 Ill. App. 2d 244, 205 N.E.2d 775 (3 Dist. 1965).

If provisions of a custody disposition are to be changed, the burden of proof is on the party so moving to show why it should be done. Martinec v. Sharapata, 328 Ill. App. 339, 66 N.E.2d 103 (1 Dist. 1946).

—Natural Parent

Court was not required to find that the natural parent was unfit, or that she had forfeited her custodial rights, before awarding custody to another person if the best interests of the child would be served; the burden was on the great aunt to establish good cause or reason to overcome the presumption that the natural mother had the first and superior right to the custody of her son; as applied, the superior right doctrine was subservient to the best interests of the child. Montgomery v. Roudez, 156 Ill. App. 3d 262, 108 Ill. Dec. 803, 509 N.E.2d 499 (1 Dist. 1987).

—Not Met

Where no question was raised by mother as to the fitness of the father to care for the children, no effort was made to show any change or deterioration in the conditions of the father's home since he was originally awarded custody, the judge did not make any adverse findings concerning the present care of the children, mother did not meet the burden of proof to show a change was in the best interests of the children. King v. Vancil, 34 Ill. App. 3d 831, 341 N.E.2d 65 (5 Dist. 1975).

Change in Circumstances

—In General

A change in circumstances justifying a modification of a child custody award need not relate solely to the custodial parent, nor is it necessary for the court to find that the custodial parent is an unfit person if other circumstances warrant modification. Kjellesvik v. Shannon, 41 Ill. App. 3d 674, 355 N.E.2d 120 (3 Dist. 1976).

In all cases where petitions to modify payments under a divorce decree are involved, the primary question is whether or not changes in circumstances of the parties justify the modification. Bulmer v. Bulmer, 28 Ill. App. 3d 406, 328 N.E.2d 622 (5 Dist. 1975).

—Marital Status

A change in marital status is not sufficient cause to change the custody of children unless it proves that the children's welfare could be affected thereby. King v. Vancil, 34 Ill. App. 3d 831, 341 N.E.2d 65 (5 Dist. 1975).

—Modification Not Warranted

The trial court's decision that there had been a change of circumstances which required a modification of an earlier custody order was against the manifest weight of the evidence where a mother's actions seriously endangered the mental or emotional health of the child and that the harm if any which might be caused by a change of environment to the custody of the father was outweighed by the advantages of that change to the child. Thompson v. Thompson, 83 Ill. App. 3d 97, 38 Ill. Dec. 485, 403 N.E.2d 716 (3 Dist. 1980).

Where the mother was not an unfit person to have custody of two minor children, nor was there any change of circumstances that would warrant a change in custody from the mother to the father, and the father was the instigator of the divorce of the parties, had remarried and was able to furnish a home and material possessions to a better degree than the divorced wife who was not remarried, there was not a change in circumstance within the meaning of the terms in Illinois. Finn v. Finn, 11 Ill. App. 3d 385, 297 N.E.2d 1 (2 Dist. 1973).

A mother's remarriage, and acquisition of a larger house than the father, were factors to be considered by the court, but were not sufficient reasons for a change of custody. Filipello v. Filipello, 130 Ill. App. 2d 1089, 268 N.E.2d 478 (1 Dist. 1971).

Where the child had been in the legal custody of the father since it was a baby, its physical custody had been with the father's cousins for the last two or three years, the mother during all this time had shown no interest whatever in her child, and the child was being reared properly in a fine home, the fact that the mother now had a good home and was a good woman did not give her the right to have custody of her daughter. Wade v. Wade, 345 Ill. App. 170, 102 N.E.2d 356 (2 Dist. 1951).

—Modification Warranted

Mother's frequent changes in residence, the instability of her second marriage, and the uncertainty of her vocational and child care plans were facts that arose since the prior initial judgment awarding her custody judgment which constituted a change in circumstances warranting modification of custody. Russell v. Kellum, 80 Ill. App. 3d 41, 35 Ill. Dec. 378, 399 N.E.2d 212 (5 Dist. 1979).

—Standard

The fact of changed conditions, in itself, is not sufficient to warrant modification of the custody provisions of the decree, unless such changed conditions affect the welfare of the child or children. Jacobs v. Jacobs, 25 Ill. App. 3d 175, 323 N.E.2d 21 (1 Dist. 1974).

Change of Name

Where there was no evidence in the record that the trial court considered any relevant factors in adjudicating whether a parent may change a child's name but merely articulated its conclusion that the child's name should be changed, the court erred in ordering the name change. Sullivan v. McGaw, 134 Ill. App. 3d 455, 89 Ill. Dec. 540, 480 N.E.2d 1283 (2 Dist. 1985).

Child Abuse

The trial court had a right and duty to consider the child abuse question in deciding the proper award of custody. Hinton v. Searles, 53 Ill. App. 3d 433, 11 Ill. Dec. 329, 368 N.E.2d 937 (5 Dist. 1977).

In light of the evidence produced by respondent and petitioner on the question of child abuse, the allegations of child abuse were verified to the extent that the petitioner should have been awarded custody of the children under all the facts presented to the trial court. Hinton v. Searles, 53 Ill. App. 3d 433, 11 Ill. Dec. 329, 368 N.E.2d 937 (5 Dist. 1977).

Questions of fitness to be entrusted with the care and custody of children are left to the sound discretion of the chancellor, subject of course to review where abuse is shown. Williams v. Williams, 320 Ill. App. 354, 51 N.E.2d 284 (3 Dist. 1943).

Child Support

In matters regarding child support, the court has authority to award support where it is in the best interest of the child. Bayuk v. Bayuk, 79 Ill. App. 3d 877, 35 Ill. Dec. 159, 398 N.E.2d 1109 (1 Dist. 1979).

Cohabitation

An intimate cohabitation relationship of a parent, be it heterosexual, homosexual or lesbian in nature, is a proper factor to be considered by the trial court in making a custody determination. In re Diehl, 221 Ill. App. 3d 410, 164 Ill. Dec. 73, 582 N.E.2d 281 (2 Dist. 1991), cert. denied, 144 Ill. 2d 632, 169 Ill. Dec. 140, 591 N.E.2d 20 (1992).

Where no open and notorious cohabitation existed, petitioner's encounters with men did not provide sufficient evidence that her moral standards were low. In re Smith, 132 Ill. App. 3d 694, 88 Ill. Dec. 909, 479 N.E.2d 929 (1 Dist. 1985).

There is no conclusive presumption that, because a custodial parent cohabits with a member of the opposite sex, the child is harmed. In re Thompson, 96 Ill. 2d 67, 70 Ill. Dec. 214, 449 N.E.2d 88 (1983).

A per se rule requiring a change in custody of minor children where the custodial parent cohabits, in the children's presence, with a member of the opposite sex openly and on a continuing conjugal basis, has not been established, although the trial court should give due consideration to the custodial parent's living arrangement and its effect on the well-being of the children in determining whether a change in custody is warranted. Brandt v. Brandt, 99 Ill. App. 3d 1089, 55 Ill. Dec. 78, 425 N.E.2d 1251 (1 Dist. 1981).

The resident presence of the custodial mother's paramour must be considered in light of the moral values which the parent is actually demonstrating to the children. In re Olson, 98 Ill. App. 3d 316, 53 Ill. Dec. 751, 424 N.E.2d 386 (3 Dist. 1981).

Trial court's transfer of custody to father, based on mother's cohabitation with boyfriend, was not contrary to the manifest weight of the evidence, and tangible manifestations of damage to the children's character were not required to effectuate the custody modification. Jarrett v. Jarrett, 78 Ill. 2d 337, 36 Ill. Dec. 1, 400 N.E.2d 421 (1979), cert. denied, 449 U.S. 927, 101 S. Ct. 329, 66 L. Ed. 2d 155 (1980).

Where the only evidence of unfitness on the part of the father was that contained in the stipulation of his having lived with a woman out of wedlock for eight years, such conduct amounted to past misbehavior, which had been discontinued; thus, the evidence failed to establish unfitness of the father as of the time of the hearing on the petition. Scott v. Ashcraft, 342 Ill. App. 33, 95 N.E.2d 122 (3 Dist. 1950).

Continuity

Where parties seeking custody of children were natural father and aunt and uncle of the natural father who have raised the children for 10 years, and both children desire to remain with aunt and uncle although father was not adjudged an unfit person, the best interests of the children were served by continuing the familial environment they knew for over 10 years. Markham v. Markham, 91 Ill. App. 3d 1122, 47 Ill. Dec. 235, 414 N.E.2d 1351 (3 Dist. 1981).

Nothing is more injurious to the welfare of a child than to have the child shuttled between contesting parents. Pratt v. Pratt, 29 Ill. App. 3d 214, 330 N.E.2d 244 (4 Dist. 1975).

Criminal Convictions

A single criminal conviction, without more, will not support a finding of unfitness based upon depravity. Tranel v. Lutgen, 177 Ill. App. 3d 954, 127 Ill. Dec. 147, 532 N.E.2d 976 (2 Dist. 1988).

Custodial Parent

—Duties and Responsibilities

The custodial parent has the duty to strengthen and nurture in every way possible the relationship between the children and their noncustodial parent; this requires, at a minimum, that the custodial parent refrain from speaking ill of the noncustodial parent to the children, and keep others from doing so as well. In re Dobey, 258 Ill. App. 3d 874, 196 Ill. Dec. 267, 629 N.E.2d 812 (4 Dist. 1994).

Custody

—In General

Trial court erred when it required wife who was given joint custody and primary physical custody of her daughter to remain in one of two counties as a condition for retaining joint custody and primary physical custody. Seitzinger v. Seitzinger, 333 Ill. App. 3d 103, 266 Ill. Dec. 720, 775 N.E.2d 282, 2002 Ill. App. LEXIS 763 (4 Dist. 2002).

This Act requires the trial judge to determine custody in accordance with the best interest of the child; that is the court's paramount consideration in child custody cases. In re Petraitis, 263 Ill. App. 3d 1022, 201 Ill. Dec. 259, 636 N.E.2d 691 (1 Dist. 1993).

For a case discussing the award of custody of minor children under similar prior provisions, see Harding v. Harding, 180 Ill. 481, 54 N.E. 587 (1899).

—Ability to Cooperate

Mother's constant efforts to destroy the father's relationship with the parties' child was such an egregious instance of failure to cooperate that the trial court's determination that the father had rebutted the presumption that the current custody arrangement was in the child's best interests was not against the weight of the evidence. In re Ricketts, 329 Ill. App. 3d 173, 263 Ill. Dec. 753, 768 N.E.2d 834, 2002 Ill. App. LEXIS 321 (2 Dist. 2002).

Where ample evidence existed that the parents had not shown an ability to cooperate, the trial court did not abuse its discretion in awarding mother sole custody. In re Dobey, 258 Ill. App. 3d 874, 196 Ill. Dec. 267, 629 N.E.2d 812 (4 Dist. 1994).

Problem areas including health issues and the children's activities, and the likelihood of an endless battleground with respect to any joint custody arrangement, with the children being the casualties of the arrangement, supported trial court's award of sole custody. In re Jerome, 255 Ill. App. 3d 374, 193 Ill. Dec. 74, 625 N.E.2d 1195 (5 Dist. 1993).

—Award Improper

Where the trial court found that a child's natural father and prospective adoptive parents were on approximately equal footing in terms of fitness and the child's best interests and notwithstanding that the prospective adoptive parents made an invaluable contribution to the child's life and well-being following her traumatic separation from her mother, the trial court's award of joint custody was against the manifest weight of the evidence and the natural father was entitled to both legal and physical custody in light of the presumption that it is in the best interests of a child to be raised by the natural parent. In re E.L., 315 Ill. App. 3d 137, 248 Ill. Dec. 171, 733 N.E.2d 846, 2000 Ill. App. LEXIS 557 (1 Dist. 2000).

Ruling that the consideration of the best interest of the child dictated that custody be given to the putative father was against the manifest weight of the evidence. Giagnoni v. Bourey, 127 Ill. App. 3d 530, 82 Ill. Dec. 852, 469 N.E.2d 386 (2 Dist. 1984).

The evidence was held to be insufficient to demonstrate "serious endangerment"; modification of physical custody was unnecessarily disruptive of the lives of the children and accordingly was improper. In re Gargus, 97 Ill. App. 3d 598, 53 Ill. Dec. 1, 423 N.E.2d 193 (1 Dist. 1981).

Where both parents had demonstrated instances of erratic and immature behavior, mother had been diligent in attending to child's needs and her nurture of child could not be characterized as substandard, father had had minimal contact with the child, and had not willingly provided her with substantial support, paternal grandfather did not see child at all until dissolution proceedings began, and paternal grandmother visited her only twice immedi-

Custody (Cont'd)

—Award Improper (Cont'd)

ately after her birth, trial court erred in awarding custody of child to paternal grandparents, and it was in the best interests of the child that custody remain with her mother, subject to reasonable visitation of father. Braden v. Braden, 70 Ill. App. 3d 535, 26 Ill. Dec. 938, 388 N.E.2d 939 (5 Dist. 1979).

Where judge found that both parents were fit and proper persons to have custody of the children, but made a statement that he was modifying prior custody award and awarding custody to the mother because of the age of the two boys, six and three, the court's reasoning was not supported by the law, and violated equal protection provision. King v. Vancil, 34 Ill. App. 3d 831, 341 N.E.2d 65 (5 Dist. 1975).

The finding that the wife was a fit and proper person to have the care, custody and education of the child and that it was for the best interest and welfare of the child that he remain with her, was clearly against the manifest weight of the evidence. Landrey v. Landrey, 13 Ill. App. 2d 202, 141 N.E.2d 405 (1 Dist. 1957).

—Award Upheld

Trial court did not abuse it discretion in awarding husband custody of the parties' children based upon its finding that wife's pretrial and trial claims that she did not intend to sell the marital house and move to another town were a prevarication. In re Wolff, Ill. App. 3d , 290 Ill. Dec. 1011, 822 N.E.2d 596, 2005 Ill. App. LEXIS 59 (2 Dist. 2005).

Where the court awarded custody of the parties' two sons to the mother, there was no abuse of discretion, as it considered all of the evidence and all of the relevant factors, including those under 750 ILCS 5/602, the trial court did not ignore applicable principles of law, and its judgment did not exceed the bounds of reason. Marsh v. Marsh, 343 Ill. App. 3d 1235, 279 Ill. Dec. 234, 799 N.E.2d 1037, 2003 Ill. App. LEXIS 1389 (4 Dist. 2003).

Trial court did not err in rejecting custody evaluator's advice and granting custody to a mother with an I.Q. of 67; she was child's primary caregiver, and the record showed she could protect him from harm and, with help, assist in his intellectual development. In re Stopher, 328 Ill. App. 3d 1037, 263 Ill. Dec. 199, 767 N.E.2d 925, 2002 Ill. App. LEXIS 261 (4 Dist. 2002).

Award of custody to the father was not against the manifest weight of the evidence. In re D.R., 295 Ill. App. 3d 115, 229 Ill. Dec. 583, 692 N.E.2d 356 (2 Dist. 1998).

The trial court's decision that it was in the best interest of the child to award custody to nonparents was not against the manifest weight of evidence; the nonparents had cared for the child for two and one-half years, the mother failed to maintain any significant degree of parental involvement with the child during this time, and there was some evidence that the mother's husband was not a good person to have around young children. In re Rudsell, 291 Ill. App. 3d 626, 225 Ill. Dec. 736, 684 N.E.2d 421 (4 Dist. 1997).

Where the trial court had the opportunity to evaluate the credibility, temperaments, personalities, and capabilities of both parties to determine what weight to place on the testimony of the witnesses and where it had an opportunity to observe and evaluate the child, the trial court's decision regarding custody was not against the manifest weight of the evidence. Prince v. Herrera, 261 Ill. App. 3d 606, 199 Ill. Dec. 174, 633 N.E.2d 970 (1 Dist. 1994).

The judge, having considered the statutory factors in light of the evidence presented and having possessed a superior vantage point for evaluating the temperaments, personalities, and capabilities of the parents and the child decided that, while both parents were fit and proper to have custody, it was in child's best interest that custody be awarded to his mother; the trial court's decision to award custody of child to his mother was not against the manifest weight of the evidence. In re Petraitis, 263 Ill. App. 3d 1022, 201 Ill. Dec. 259, 636 N.E.2d 691 (1 Dist. 1993).

In light of the proper application of subsection (a) factors to the facts, and the trial court's discretion in resolving conflicts in testimony and determining the best interests of the child, the trial court's award of custody to wife was not an abuse of discretion. In re Yong Sun Lee, 246 Ill. App. 3d 628, 186 Ill. Dec. 257, 615 N.E.2d 1314 (4 Dist.), cert. denied, 153 Ill. 2d 560, 191 Ill. Dec. 620, 624 N.E.2d 808 (1993).

Trial court did not abuse its discretion in awarding custody of minor child to father with drinking problem where the trial court found that he had rehabilitated himself, that he functioned well and that alcohol had no adverse impact on his life or on his parenting skills. In re Mangan, 182 Ill. App. 3d 140, 130 Ill. Dec. 631, 537 N.E.2d 960 (1 Dist. 1989).

Trial court's award of custody to mother was not against the manifest weight of the evidence, where report indicated that while both parties were competent to care for child, neither parent were without problems and where, while report indicated that mother may have been more stern than father, the report implied that father often had his parents' help in caring for child. In re Felson, 171 Ill. App. 3d 923, 121 Ill. Dec. 796, 525 N.E.2d 1103 (1 Dist. 1988).

The trial court's custody determination that the father should retain full custody was not against the manifest weight of the evidence where there was evidence the mother left the marital home with the children and without notice to her husband, as well as evidence of her living in quarters in Florida and the fact that she moved three times. In re Stone, 164 Ill. App. 3d 1046, 115 Ill. Dec. 877, 518 N.E.2d 402 (1 Dist. 1987).

The mother's living arrangements, the three moves she made in a year, and her relationship with another man were not totally irrelevant evidence bearing on the stability of the child's environment. In re Stone, 164 Ill. App. 3d 1046, 115 Ill. Dec. 877, 518 N.E.2d 402 (1 Dist. 1987).

The trial court acted properly in awarding wife custody of one child who expressed a preference based upon sound reasoning, but awarding husband custody of the other children who either had no preference, or could not express any reasons for wishing to live with their mother, when the evidence supported award to the husband as being in the children's best interests. In re Werner, 144 Ill. App. 3d 263, 98 Ill. Dec. 178, 493 N.E.2d 1199 (5 Dist. 1986).

Where the trial court had ample evidence before it to which the relevant factors could be applied in making its custody determination, the father had a close relationship with the children and described their relationship as very good whereas the mother's relationship was described as fairly good, the father was described as an excellent father who spent quality time with his children, and the mother incurred problems dealing with the children when they were younger and babysitters were frequently employed to help care for the children and consulted a psychiatrist for what she described as marital problems and was prescribed tranquilizers and antidepressants, the award of custody to the father was not contrary to the manifest weight of the evidence nor an abuse of discretion. In re Holder, 137 Ill. App. 3d 596, 91 Ill. Dec. 926, 484 N.E.2d 485 (5 Dist. 1985).

Where the circuit court heard testimony from the petitioner and the respondent, from petitioner's supervisor and from parties' friends, neighbors and relatives, including information concerning each of the factors listed in the section there was sufficient basis for the circuit court's custody decision. Hollo v. Hollo, 131 Ill. App. 3d 119, 85 Ill. Dec. 867, 474 N.E.2d 827 (5 Dist. 1985).

There was sufficient evidence to support the trial court's decision to split custody between the parties where the two children frequently fought, and where they would be spending every weekend together. In re Slavenas, 139 Ill. App. 3d 581, 93 Ill. Dec. 914, 487 N.E.2d 739 (2 Dist. 1985).

A trial court did not abuse its discretion in awarding custody of minor son to the wife in dissolution proceeding, where disputed testimony was presented that the father had told the boy that the boy need not obey the law, and the father's attitude in court was such that the judge could have concluded the father had a disdain for the law; although the son expressed a strong desire to live with his father, that was only one factor to be considered. In re Brand, 123 Ill. App. 3d 1047, 79 Ill. Dec. 483, 463 N.E.2d 1037 (4 Dist. 1984).

There was no abuse of discretion in awarding custody to the father where a considerable number of witnesses testified on his behalf indicating that the child was sickly, undisciplined and overweight prior to coming into his custody, and that thereafter, the child improved, and a warm, loving relationship developed between the father and the son. In re Thompson, 96 Ill. 2d 67, 70 Ill. Dec. 214, 449 N.E.2d 88 (1983).

Evidence was held to be sufficient to uphold the custody award to the child's mother, as this would be in the best interests of the child. In re Olson, 96 Ill. 2d 432, 71 Ill. Dec. 671, 451 N.E.2d 825 (1983).

Custody (Cont'd)

—Award Upheld (Cont'd)

Evidence was held sufficient to sustain trial court's granting of custody of a 3½ year old daughter to her father in a marriage dissolution based partially on the threat to the child from mother's autistic son from another marriage, where the trial court had the opportunity to observe the parties and other witnesses and thus had a superior vantage point to assess and evaluate their temperaments and personalities. In re Benevento, 118 Ill. App. 3d 16, 73 Ill. Dec. 669, 454 N.E.2d 766 (1 Dist. 1983).

The order of the trial court granting custody to father was not against the manifest weight of the evidence. In re Macaluso, 110 Ill. App. 3d 838, 66 Ill. Dec. 478, 443 N.E.2d 1 (2 Dist. 1982).

The trial court, after carefully considering all of the evidence presented, properly concluded that no traumatic or harmful consequence would befall the children were the petitioner to resume residing with them in the marital home, and that, in fact, it would be in the children's best interest to place them in petitioner's custody. In re Rizzo, 95 Ill. App. 3d 636, 51 Ill. Dec. 141, 420 N.E.2d 555 (1 Dist. 1981).

Where a psychiatrist testified that he could not say either party was unfit to have custody of the children, where other witnesses similarly testified regarding the virtue of each parent's ability to raise the children, the trial court was in a better position than the reviewing court to evaluate the credibility of the witnesses and the needs of the children in custody cases, and the trial court's decision to award custody of the children to petitioner was not erroneous. In re Shedbalkar, 95 Ill. App. 3d 136, 50 Ill. Dec. 301, 419 N.E.2d 409 (1 Dist. 1981).

The trial court did not err in awarding custody of minor children to the father in a divorce where the trial judge was well advised of the circumstances of both the parents from personal friends of the parties and from experts who rendered impersonal opinions; therefore, the award was not against the manifest weight of the evidence. In re Kennedy, 94 Ill. App. 3d 537, 49 Ill. Dec. 927, 418 N.E.2d 947 (1 Dist. 1981).

The determination of the trial court that former husband should be granted custody of two minor children was not contrary to the manifest weight of the evidence where the children were mature and showed a preference for their father. In re McCune, 86 Ill. App. 3d 311, 41 Ill. Dec. 897, 408 N.E.2d 319 (3 Dist. 1980).

Court's findings of fact regarding parental fitness and the children's best interests were not contrary to the manifest weight of the evidence. Wurm v. Howard, 82 Ill. App. 3d 116, 37 Ill. Dec. 517, 402 N.E.2d 407 (3 Dist. 1980).

In a custody proceeding where the court found that the mother had had primary responsibility over the children's school work, speech therapy, cultural development, and medical treatment and the father took the children on outings, played sports with them, took them to church, and was very active in community affairs which indirectly benefited the children, these findings supported the conclusion of the court that the mother could continue to perform her valuable services toward the children only if she had their custody on a continuous basis, whereas the father could contribute to their development, as he had so far, through liberal visitation; thus, the findings and conclusions of the court were not contrary to the manifest weight of the evidence. Switalla v. Switalla, 87 Ill. App. 3d 168, 42 Ill. Dec. 430, 408 N.E.2d 1139 (3 Dist. 1980).

That it was in the child's best interest that he be placed in the custody of his father was supported by the evidence. Lloyd v. Lloyd, 92 Ill. App. 3d 124, 47 Ill. Dec. 792, 415 N.E.2d 1105 (1 Dist. 1980).

The trial court properly awarded custody of a five year old boy to his father where there was an extremely close relationship between father and son; the father had a regular, full-time job, with which to provide security without significantly keeping father and son apart, while mother's employment plans were uncertain; the father spent more time with his son than did the mother, who led an active social life which frequently excluded the child and required a variety of babysitters for him; the father would retain and live in the house owned by the couple, while the mother admitted she would soon have to find a new place to live; the child attended church functions regularly with the father, which would continue if the father received custody, and a strong system of support was promised by neighbors and relatives. In re Ramer, 84 Ill. App. 3d 213, 39 Ill. Dec. 648, 405 N.E.2d 401 (5 Dist. 1980).

Where the trial court heard considerable evidence relating to the factors listed in this section, including the wishes of the parents, the wishes of the child, the interrelationship of the child with his parents, his sister, and others who could significantly affect his best interest, his adjustment to his home, school and community, the mental and physical health of all persons involved, and the stability of the environments available to him, and concluded that the father's care would be less to the child's best interest than that which was being provided by his mother, such a conclusion was not palpably erroneous or contrary to the manifest weight of the evidence. Allen v. Allen, 81 Ill. App. 3d 517, 36 Ill. Dec. 767, 401 N.E.2d 608 (3 Dist. 1980).

Evidence was sufficient to support the decision of the trial court that it was in the best interest of the child to leave custody with the father. Melear v. Melear, 76 Ill. App. 3d 706, 32 Ill. Dec. 261, 395 N.E.2d 208 (3 Dist. 1979).

Based on all the evidence, the appellate court could not say that the trial court's award of permanent custody of child to the father was contrary to the manifest weight of the evidence. Katzer v. Katzer, 61 Ill. App. 3d 299, 18 Ill. Dec. 852, 378 N.E.2d 316 (1 Dist. 1978).

The order of the trial court was not beyond the manifest weight of the evidence in that it found that a substantial change of circumstances existed and that, based upon their best interests, the permanent care and custody of the children should be transferred to the father. Gren v. Gren, 59 Ill. App. 3d 624, 16 Ill. Dec. 892, 375 N.E.2d 999 (2 Dist. 1978).

The trial court did not err in its custody determination where the trial court intentionally allowed the introduction of a wide variety of evidence relating to the fitness of the parents and to the proper award of custody, conducted extensive in camera proceedings with each of the minor children and asked numerous questions relative to the preference of the children and the allegations of the parties. Huffman v. Huffman, 50 Ill. App. 3d 217, 8 Ill. Dec. 32, 365 N.E.2d 270 (5 Dist. 1977).

Where trial court stated the mother's past attitude and conduct toward her children was detrimental to them, this did not require reversal because there was some evidence that at times subsequent to the divorce the children were not too clean when they came from their mother's house, and even if the trial court considered improper evidence, reversal will result only if the ultimate decision was contrary to the manifest weight of the evidence; therefore the trial court's award of custody to the father was not against the manifest weight of the evidence. Drake v. Hohimer, 35 Ill. App. 3d 529, 341 N.E.2d 399 (4 Dist. 1976).

Where there were no facts to indicate that defendant was not a proper person to have custody of her children, and the children indicated a preference for her, awarding custody to her was proper in the absence of anything to indicate that the best interests of the girls would not be served by giving defendant custody. Rosenberger v. Rosenberger, 21 Ill. App. 3d 550, 316 N.E.2d 1 (1 Dist. 1974).

Where a mother was frequently absent from the home and her children during the evening hours, was somewhat untidy in the upkeep of her household, had hit her child with a wooden ladle, and the father had made preparations in the event he received custody which included the fact that his mother would move in to assist him, the court found that the best interests of the children would be served by giving custody to defendant. Mulvihill v. Mulvihill, 20 Ill. App. 3d 440, 314 N.E.2d 342 (1 Dist. 1974).

The trial judge did not abuse his discretion in determining that the best interests of the child warranted the modification. Cave v. Cave, 2 Ill. App. 3d 782, 276 N.E.2d 793 (5 Dist. 1971).

Where there was a preponderance and adequate evidence to establish that a divorced father was not a fit person to have custody of his minor children, the trial judge did not abuse his discretion in awarding the custody of the minor children to their uncle after their mother had been killed in an automobile accident. Shores v. Shores, 119 Ill. App. 2d 85, 255 N.E.2d 214 (2 Dist. 1970).

—Changes

The trial court erred in not finding by clear and convincing evidence that the changes in circumstances indicated that it would be in the best interests of the minor children to modify the custody arrangement where most of the statutory factors weighed heavily in favor of finding that the best interests of the minor children would be served by transferring residential custody of the children to the father. In re Martins, 269 Ill. App. 3d 380, 206 Ill. Dec. 562,

Custody (Cont'd)

—Changes (Cont'd)
645 N.E.2d 567 (2 Dist.), appeal denied, 161 Ill. 2d 528, 208 Ill. Dec. 362, 649 N.E.2d 418 (1995).

Determination that a change in custody to father would not have served the welfare of the children was not erroneous where the evidence showed that father resided in a three-bedroom home with his new wife and their four children, that he has become disabled and has lost income. Therefore, an award of custody to him would have resulted in a family of eight residing in a three-bedroom home, on approximately $550 income per month. Burris v. Burris, 70 Ill. App. 3d 503, 26 Ill. Dec. 810, 388 N.E.2d 811 (5 Dist. 1979).

Evidence was insufficient to order change of custody to establish the present environment did not endanger the physical, mental, moral, or emotional health of the children and that the conduct of the mother did not affect her relationship with them. Holt v. Holt, 71 Ill. App. 3d 87, 27 Ill. Dec. 304, 388 N.E.2d 1353 (4 Dist. 1979).

The trial court erred when it changed child's custody from that of his mother to that of his father simply because the child preferred such a change. Garner v. Garner, 46 Ill. App. 3d 56, 4 Ill. Dec. 437, 360 N.E.2d 373 (2 Dist. 1977).

Even though a decree granting custody is regarded as temporary, changes in custody should not be varied constantly, fluctuating with the health, employment or residence of the party not in custody. Rayburn v. Rayburn, 45 Ill. App. 3d 712, 4 Ill. Dec. 395, 360 N.E.2d 142 (3 Dist. 1977).

Where a wife had custody of the child for about three months following the separation of the parties, at the time of the entry of the divorce decree, the husband had had the temporary custody of the child for nearly eight months, the trial court's finding that the best interests of the child would be served by preservation of the status quo, i.e., that the husband should retain the custody of the child, was not against the manifest weight of the evidence. Pratt v. Pratt, 29 Ill. App. 3d 214, 330 N.E.2d 244 (4 Dist. 1975).

—Failure to Deliver
Where the trial court entered a temporary restraining order and later a preliminary injunction against respondent from proceeding with any matrimonial action in any other jurisdiction and awarding temporary custody of the child, who was still in West Germany, to the petitioner, respondent's appeal would be dismissed without further consideration of the issues raised on appeal unless, within 30 days after the date of filing the court opinion, the respondent filed an additional record showing she, in her own proper person, appeared in the trial court and turned over custody of the minor child to the petitioner. In re Marks, 96 Ill. App. 3d 360, 51 Ill. Dec. 626, 420 N.E.2d 1184 (2 Dist. 1981).

—Grounds
For a case discussing custody, see Davison v. Davison, 111 Ill. App. 2d 186, 249 N.E.2d 298 (4 Dist. 1969).

—Nature of Judgment
A decree respecting the custody of the child is exceptional in its character and is always regarded as temporary. In re Bartha, 107 Ill. App. 2d 214, 245 N.E.2d 779 (2 Dist. 1969).

—Parentage Proceedings
As custody is obviously an aspect of the legal relationship between a father and child, the legislature has provided the procedural course for a putative father to file an action seeking custody within the framework of the Parentage Act (750 ILCS 40/1 et seq.); courts in parentage proceedings are thus bound to consider custody determinations upon the proper filing of an action and in accordance with the best interests of the child. Ligon ex rel. Williams v. Williams, 264 Ill. App. 3d 701, 202 Ill. Dec. 94, 637 N.E.2d 633 (1 Dist. 1994).

—Parental Cohabitation
In a custody proceeding, where the court stated that petitioner's decision to allow a man to move in with her was an example of poor judgment; however, this conduct had no affect on child who was between 16 months and three and one-half years old at the time the conduct occurred and petitioner was now married to the man in question who was a well adjusted adult who had established a relationship with the child, the trial court's decision to award custody to petitioner was not against the manifest weight of the evidence. In re Arcaute, 261 Ill. App. 3d 263, 198 Ill. Dec. 471, 632 N.E.2d 1082 (3 Dist. 1994).

—Separation of Children
Where the children were initially awarded one to the mother, and the other to the father, trial court did not abuse its discretion in finding a change of condition necessitating a modification which would award both children to the mother where the evidence showed that it was in the best interests of each of the boys that they be raised together. McDonald v. McDonald, 13 Ill. App. 3d 87, 299 N.E.2d 787 (4 Dist. 1973).

—Superior Rights Doctrine
Custody of a child was properly granted to the child's parent as opposed to the child's grandparent, and it was not error to consider the superior right of the parent to custody as a factor, albeit not controlling, in determining the child's best interests under the statute. Mary F. v. Seth O. (In re Alexander O.), 336 Ill. App. 3d 325, 270 Ill. Dec. 711, 783 N.E.2d 673, 2003 Ill. App. LEXIS 66 (2 Dist. 2003).

In determining custody, superior rights of natural parents doctrine would not be absolute in Dissolution Act proceedings but would only be a factor to consider. In re Roberts, 271 Ill. App. 3d 972, 208 Ill. Dec. 683, 649 N.E.2d 1344 (4 Dist. 1995), appeal denied, 163 Ill. 2d 586, 212 Ill. Dec. 437, 657 N.E.2d 638 (1995).

—Surviving Parent
Where mother was awarded legal custody and father was given rights of visitation, and the mother and child lived with the mother's parents' and the father regularly exercised his visitation rights with the child, the child must be considered to have been, upon her mother's death, in the physical custody of her father. In re Peterson, 112 Ill. 2d 48, 96 Ill. Dec. 690, 491 N.E.2d 1150 (1986).

—Unfounded Allegations
Unfounded allegations of sexual abuse made by one parent can be grounds for granting custody to the other parent. Hartman v. Hartman, 252 Ill. App. 3d 481, 190 Ill. Dec. 464, 621 N.E.2d 917 (3 Dist. 1993), appeal denied, 154 Ill. 2d 559, 197 Ill. Dec. 486, 631 N.E.2d 708 (1994).

Custody Decree

—Temporary Nature
A divorce decree, including custody provisions, is normally res judicata as to facts existing at the time of its entry, but the decree in respect to custody is temporary in nature and may be changed from time to time as the best interests of the child require. Randolph v. Dean, 27 Ill. App. 3d 913, 327 N.E.2d 473 (3 Dist. 1975).

Custody Hearing
Where the custody of a minor child is in dispute between a mother and father, a hearing should be had, whereby evidence on the question is adduced after the parties have had the opportunity to present testimony and each party as well as other witnesses are available for cross-examination. Henrikson v. Henrikson, 26 Ill. App. 3d 37, 324 N.E.2d 473 (3 Dist. 1975).

A custody determination by a trial court is subject to an appeal by a reviewing court, and as the result of failing to have a separate hearing pertaining to custody, the appeals court is placed in the position of being unable to consider the evidence and examine the factors which led to the trial court's decision. Henrikson v. Henrikson, 26 Ill. App. 3d 37, 324 N.E.2d 473 (3 Dist. 1975).

Evidence of father's unfitness was sufficient to require a hearing on the issue of child custody. Szewczyk v. Szewczyk, 320 Ill. App. 562, 51 N.E.2d 801 (1 Dist. 1943).

Discretion of Court
The statutory law does not require that the trial court make explicit findings with regard to the "best interest of the children." Lyons v. Lyons, 228 Ill. App. 3d 407, 169 Ill. Dec. 502, 591 N.E.2d 1006 (5 Dist. 1992).

There is a strong and compelling presumption that the trial court, the entity closest to the litigation, has made the proper custody decision. In re Diehl, 221 Ill. App. 3d 410, 164 Ill. Dec. 73, 582 N.E.2d 281 (2 Dist. 1991), cert. denied, 144 Ill. 2d 632, 169 Ill. Dec. 140, 591 N.E.2d 20 (1992).

Discretion of Court (Cont'd)

The trial court's determination of custody will not be reversed unless there has been a clear abuse of discretion or the decision was contrary to the manifest weight of the evidence. In re Seymour, 206 Ill. App. 3d 506, 152 Ill. Dec. 27, 565 N.E.2d 269 (2 Dist. 1990).

The presumption favoring the result reached by the trial court is strong and compelling in custody cases because it, rather than the reviewing court, is in a better position to evaluate the credibility of the witnesses and the needs of the children. In re Williams, 205 Ill. App. 3d 613, 151 Ill. Dec. 89, 563 N.E.2d 1195 (3 Dist. 1990).

A judge has not abused his discretion unless his judgment is palpably erroneous, contrary to the manifest weight of the evidence or manifestly unjust. In re Yakin, 107 Ill. App. 3d 1103, 62 Ill. Dec. 547, 436 N.E.2d 573 (1 Dist. 1982).

Although the issue presented by the pleadings was strictly limited to father's alleged fraud to get custody of his two children, the practical effect of the decision of the trial court on the petition to vacate the father's custody was to determine the custodial arrangement for the children; the trial court, clothed with the duty to protect the welfare of the minor children was not powerless under those limited circumstances to raise the custody issue by its own motion. Mayes v. Mayes, 86 Ill. App. 3d 644, 42 Ill. Dec. 517, 409 N.E.2d 12 (3 Dist. 1980).

In a child custody matter, the trial court is vested with broad discretion, subject to review, in determining where the best interests of the child lie. Kjellesvik v. Shannon, 41 Ill. App. 3d 674, 355 N.E.2d 120 (3 Dist. 1976); In re Piccirilli, 88 Ill. App. 3d 621, 43 Ill. Dec. 953, 410 N.E.2d 1086 (1 Dist. 1980); In re Yakin, 107 Ill. App. 3d 1103, 62 Ill. Dec. 547, 436 N.E.2d 573 (1 Dist. 1982); In re Macaluso, 110 Ill. App. 3d 838, 66 Ill. Dec. 478, 443 N.E.2d 1 (2 Dist. 1982); In re Seymour, 206 Ill. App. 3d 506, 152 Ill. Dec. 27, 565 N.E.2d 269 (2 Dist. 1990).

The trial court has authority to modify or alter the decree provisions relating to custody plus the broad discretion to make alterations in the decree concerning visitation; however, the discretion that is vested in the court, whether it be to modify provisions of the decree concerning custody or to alter visitation rights, must be exercised for the best interest of the children involved, and the parents' natural rights must give way to the welfare and best interest of the children. Chodzko v. Chodzko, 66 Ill. 2d 28, 4 Ill. Dec. 313, 360 N.E.2d 60 (1976).

The trial court must always have uppermost in mind the welfare and best interests of the child, but it has wide discretion in determining questions of custody and the right and terms of visitation; and the exercise of this discretion will not be interfered with unless it appears that the discretion has been abused. Smith v. Smith, 36 Ill. App. 2d 55, 183 N.E.2d 559 (1 Dist. 1962).

In determining to which parent the custody of the children will be awarded the court has wide discretion. Serotzke v. Serotzke, 335 Ill. App. 485, 82 N.E.2d 375 (1 Dist. 1948).

Distance

Trial court determination that joint custody would not be in the best interests of the children, in large part, because the husband resided far from his children, was not against the manifest weight of the evidence or an abuse of discretion. In re Hahin, 266 Ill. App. 3d 168, 205 Ill. Dec. 788, 644 N.E.2d 4 (2 Dist. 1994).

Division of Custody

Where the best method of ensuring continued contact between the children and both parents was through the division of custody, and the court determined custody in accordance to the individual preferences of the children and in accordance with his determination of the best interests of each child, the determinations of the trial court were not contrary to the manifest weight of the evidence and would not result in a manifest injustice. In re Bailey, 130 Ill. App. 3d 158, 85 Ill. Dec. 666, 474 N.E.2d 394 (1 Dist. 1985).

Economic Considerations

Given that respondent was not working at the time of the custody award to petitioner and had not worked for ten years preceding and thus could not make any monetary contributions to the support of the children, the trial court did not err in considering the parties' financial circumstances. In re Fahy, 208 Ill. App. 3d 677, 153 Ill. Dec. 594, 567 N.E.2d 552 (1 Dist. 1991).

Mere financial disparity is insufficient to deprive a natural parent of the custody of his child; however, the right of a parent to care for his child is associated with concomitant responsibilities, e.g., to support the child, at least in part. As such, the relative economic positions of the parties are a factor that must be considered in determining the best interests of the child. In re Fahy, 208 Ill. App. 3d 677, 153 Ill. Dec. 594, 567 N.E.2d 552 (1 Dist. 1991).

The economic positions of the parties are a factor that must be considered in determining the best interests of the child, especially where one party has no visible means of support. Montgomery v. Roudez, 156 Ill. App. 3d 262, 108 Ill. Dec. 803, 509 N.E.2d 499 (1 Dist. 1987).

The trial court did not err in refusing to hear evidence of the financial circumstances of the parties prior to ruling on the issue of child custody. In re Theeke, 105 Ill. App. 3d 119, 60 Ill. Dec. 944, 433 N.E.2d 1311 (1 Dist. 1981).

Evidence

—In General

The evidentiary ingredients in a custody dispute, by the very nature of the contest and the individuality of the disputants are, indeed, numerous, varied, and interrelated and thus each factor must be weighed and considered in its relationship to all of the others shown to exist. Brandt v. Brandt, 99 Ill. App. 3d 1089, 55 Ill. Dec. 78, 425 N.E.2d 1251 (1 Dist. 1981).

—Expert Witnesses

When considering the issue of custody of a child, the court was not obliged to follow the advice of an expert. In re Seymour, 206 Ill. App. 3d 506, 152 Ill. Dec. 27, 565 N.E.2d 269 (2 Dist. 1990); In re Petraitis, 263 Ill. App. 3d 1022, 201 Ill. Dec. 259, 636 N.E.2d 691 (1 Dist. 1993).

Recommendation of expert that the parties continue splitting physical custody of child was not binding on the court. In re Felson, 171 Ill. App. 3d 923, 121 Ill. Dec. 796, 525 N.E.2d 1103 (1 Dist. 1988).

In a case involving custody of a child, receiving the opinion of a psychiatrist would not usurp the decisionmaking function of the court. Marcus v. Marcus, 24 Ill. App. 3d 401, 320 N.E.2d 581 (1 Dist. 1974).

—Hearsay

Statements concerning custody preference of the children made to a third party shortly before trial expressing their then existing state of mind, though hearsay, were admissible if made under conditions assuring trustworthiness; though it was error to exclude the statements, the error did not result in any prejudice to respondent. In re Rizzo, 95 Ill. App. 3d 636, 51 Ill. Dec. 141, 420 N.E.2d 555 (1 Dist. 1981).

Where a probation office's report was entirely hearsay, as the person who made the report was not under oath or subject to cross-examination, and the probation reports were not in the record on appeal, the appellate court could not determine the propriety of the trial court's custody award and remanded for further evidence. Walter v. Walter, 61 Ill. App. 2d 476, 209 N.E.2d 691 (2 Dist. 1965).

—Improperly Excluded

Where there was no hearing on the merits of the mother's petition to change the custody of the child and the custodial father was not permitted to introduce testimony bearing on the dispute as to the proper person to have the care and custody of the child, as the child was treated as a ward of the court, it was the duty of the court to hear testimony in order to ascertain whether a change in the custody should be made; therefore, the trial court committed reversible error in declining to hear the witnesses tendered by the custodial father on the issue of custody. Gerst v. Gerst, 349 Ill. App. 201, 110 N.E.2d 470 (1 Dist. 1953).

—Interview

The scope of questioning in a child custody interview is largely a matter of the judge's discretion; he is not limited to asking what the children expressly prefer but may determine this from their answers to other questions, their personality, and other circumstances. In re Milovich, 105 Ill. App. 3d 596, 61 Ill. Dec. 456, 434 N.E.2d 811 (1 Dist. 1982).

—Prior Hearing

The trial court erred in considering evidence obtained from a previous hearing held before a different judge in determining

Evidence (Cont'd)

—Prior Hearing (Cont'd)

custody of the children; where evidence is contradictory on matters crucial to a determination of comparative parental fitness, the court does not serve the best interests of the child unless it has the ability to discern the truth by personally observing the demeanor of the conflicting witnesses. In re Akins, 188 Ill. App. 3d 951, 136 Ill. Dec. 356, 544 N.E.2d 1131 (5 Dist. 1989).

—Properly Excluded

Evidence, offered by a former husband, to show that prior to the order awarding his former wife custody, evidence that wife had temporarily worked in a tavern, at hours which precluded her giving proper care to the child was properly excluded where this was not a continuing condition. Handrich v. Handrich, 339 Ill. App. 151, 89 N.E.2d 191 (4 Dist. 1949).

Factors

—In General

This Act does not mandate a recital of the specified factors in the judgment order or require written findings in any other form. Allen v. Allen, 81 Ill. App. 3d 517, 36 Ill. Dec. 767, 401 N.E.2d 608 (3 Dist. 1980); In re Ramer, 84 Ill. App. 3d 213, 39 Ill. Dec. 648, 405 N.E.2d 401 (5 Dist. 1980); In re Auer, 86 Ill. App. 3d 84, 41 Ill. Dec. 536, 407 N.E.2d 1034 (1 Dist. 1980); In re Kennedy, 94 Ill. App. 3d 537, 49 Ill. Dec. 927, 418 N.E.2d 947 (1 Dist. 1981); In re Shedbalkar, 95 Ill. App. 3d 136, 50 Ill. Dec. 301, 419 N.E.2d 409 (1 Dist. 1981); In re Carlson, 101 Ill. App. 3d 924, 57 Ill. Dec. 325, 428 N.E.2d 1005 (1 Dist. 1981); In re Siegel, 123 Ill. App. 3d 710, 79 Ill. Dec. 219, 463 N.E.2d 773 (1 Dist. 1984); In re Stuckert, 138 Ill. App. 3d 788, 93 Ill. Dec. 294, 486 N.E.2d 395 (2 Dist. 1985); In re Slavenas, 139 Ill. App. 3d 581, 93 Ill. Dec. 914, 487 N.E.2d 739 (2 Dist. 1985); Cooper v. Cooper, 146 Ill. App. 3d 943, 100 Ill. Dec. 627, 497 N.E.2d 805 (5 Dist. 1986); In re Lovejoy, 158 Ill. App. 3d 1, 109 Ill. Dec. 768, 510 N.E.2d 636 (3 Dist. 1987); In re Felson, 171 Ill. App. 3d 923, 121 Ill. Dec. 796, 525 N.E.2d 1103 (1 Dist. 1988); In re Lombaer, 200 Ill. App. 3d 712, 146 Ill. Dec. 425, 558 N.E.2d 388 (1 Dist. 1990); In re Seymour, 206 Ill. App. 3d 506, 152 Ill. Dec. 27, 565 N.E.2d 269 (2 Dist. 1990); In re Stribling, 219 Ill. App. 3d 105, 161 Ill. Dec. 749, 579 N.E.2d 6 (5 Dist. 1991).

—Considered

Trial court's temporary order was not contrary to the manifest weight of the evidence where the record showed that the trial court heard evidence that touched on various factors, including those listed in this section. Levy v. Skilling, 136 Ill. App. 3d 727, 91 Ill. Dec. 431, 483 N.E.2d 917 (1 Dist. 1985).

The judgment below could not be affirmed as consistent with the best interests of the children when the judgment was silent as to those factors which this section required that the court consider. Wurm v. Wurm, 68 Ill. App. 3d 168, 24 Ill. Dec. 753, 385 N.E.2d 894 (3 Dist. 1979).

The determining factor in a custody case is the best interests of the child and the decision whether or not to modify the child's custody rests upon the court's determination as to where that interest lies. McWilliams v. McWilliams, 43 Ill. App. 3d 65, 1 Ill. Dec. 842, 356 N.E.2d 1124 (2 Dist. 1976).

—Statutory

In determining the best interest of the child in a custody proceeding, the factors enumerated in subsection (a) of this section are not an exclusive list of factors; the trial court is not required to make specific findings for each factor so long as the record reflects that evidence of the factors was considered by the trial court before making its decisions. In re Diehl, 221 Ill. App. 3d 410, 164 Ill. Dec. 73, 582 N.E.2d 281 (2 Dist. 1991), cert. denied, 144 Ill. 2d 632, 169 Ill. Dec. 140, 591 N.E.2d 20 (1992).

The record adequately reflected that the trial court considered the factors listed in this section in awarding custody. In re Slavenas, 139 Ill. App. 3d 581, 93 Ill. Dec. 914, 487 N.E.2d 739 (2 Dist. 1985).

Where a trial court heard considerable evidence relating to the factors listed in this section, including the wishes of parents, the inter-relationship of the child with her parents and others who may significantly affect her best interest, her adjustment to her home, the mental and physical health of all persons involved, and the stability of the environment available to her, the trial court did not err. Melear v. Melear, 76 Ill. App. 3d 706, 32 Ill. Dec. 261, 395 N.E.2d 208 (3 Dist. 1979).

This section clearly does require some indication in the record that the trial court considered the factors listed. Melear v. Melear, 76 Ill. App. 3d 706, 32 Ill. Dec. 261, 395 N.E.2d 208 (3 Dist. 1979).

—Unspecified

The statutory list of factors to be considered is not exclusive, nor must trial judge recite each factor upon which the court's determination is made; but where non-statutory factors are considered determinative of the custody decision, such factors should not remain obscure, and must be supported by the record. Hall v. Hall, 226 Ill. App. 3d 686, 168 Ill. Dec. 153, 589 N.E.2d 553 (3 Dist. 1991), cert. denied, 146 Ill. 2d 627, 176 Ill. Dec. 797, 602 N.E.2d 451 (1992).

This section does not require that any specific findings or recitals be made; there is compliance with this Act where the record contains sufficient evidence concerning the specified factors. Hollo v. Hollo, 131 Ill. App. 3d 119, 85 Ill. Dec. 867, 474 N.E.2d 827 (5 Dist. 1985).

Failure to Pay Support

Father's failure to pay child support was both a relevant and proper factor in determining the best interest of the child. Soraparu v. Soraparu, 147 Ill. App. 3d 857, 101 Ill. Dec. 241, 498 N.E.2d 565 (1 Dist. 1986).

Fitness of Parent

Exhibitionism and sexual conduct of child's mother did not preclude an award of child custody to her where the conduct did not affect the mother's relationship to the child. Craig v. Craig, 326 Ill. App. 3d 1127, 261 Ill. Dec. 274, 762 N.E.2d 1201, 2002 Ill. App. LEXIS 54 (4 Dist. 2002).

The way a mother chooses to spend her free time with child is a proper factor to be considered in weighing the child's best interests. In re Quindry, 223 Ill. App. 3d 735, 166 Ill. Dec. 290, 585 N.E.2d 1312 (5 Dist. 1992).

Unfitness under the Adoption Act (750 ILCS 50/1 et seq.) is different than unfitness for the purpose of child custody under this Act. Tranel v. Lutgen, 177 Ill. App. 3d 954, 127 Ill. Dec. 147, 532 N.E.2d 976 (2 Dist. 1988).

Fitness of the parent is only one element to be considered in determining what is in a child's best interest. Lyons v. Bute, 124 Ill. App. 3d 198, 79 Ill. Dec. 539, 463 N.E.2d 1314 (3 Dist. 1984), rev'd on other grounds, 107 Ill. 2d 169, 90 Ill. Dec. 892, 483 N.E.2d 210 (1985).

It is not necessary to find one parent "unfit" to justify an award to the other parent. In re Milovich, 105 Ill. App. 3d 596, 61 Ill. Dec. 456, 434 N.E.2d 811 (1 Dist. 1982); In re Macaluso, 110 Ill. App. 3d 838, 66 Ill. Dec. 478, 443 N.E.2d 1 (2 Dist. 1982); In re Mangan, 182 Ill. App. 3d 140, 130 Ill. Dec. 631, 537 N.E.2d 960 (1 Dist. 1989).

The fact that the mother is fit is only one factor to be considered by the trial court and the court cannot recognize a presumption in favor of the mother in a contest for custody of children of tender years. Drake v. Hohimer, 35 Ill. App. 3d 529, 341 N.E.2d 399 (4 Dist. 1976).

Although ex-wife was shown to have a drinking problem, and that she had been dating other men prior to her divorce, it does not follow that the wife was therefore unfit to have custody of the children. Kauffman v. Kauffman, 30 Ill. App. 3d 159, 333 N.E.2d 695 (4 Dist. 1975).

Although allegations of misuse of alcohol and acts of adultery, were relevant to the court's determination of the fitness of a particular parent to the custody of a minor child, trial court's determination that the mother was a fit and proper parent was not against the manifest weight of the evidence. Huey v. Huey, 25 Ill. App. 3d 20, 322 N.E.2d 560 (5 Dist. 1975).

Father was bound by a determination that the mother was a fit and proper person unless he could affirmatively show a material change of circumstances adversely affecting the best interests of the children occurring after the original decree. Golden v. Braunfeld, 22 Ill. App. 3d 344, 317 N.E.2d 336 (4 Dist. 1974).

Proof was insufficient to sustain the conclusion that the defendant was an unfit mother where she was remarried, established a home for her children, had a good relationship between herself, her second husband and her children, as shown by an impartial report

Fitness of Parent (Cont'd)

of the Cook County Department of Public Aid, and her older daughter expressed a preference to remain with her mother. Laughlin v. Laughlin, 97 Ill. App. 2d 480, 240 N.E.2d 323 (1 Dist. 1968).

Where it was established that the children's mother was committed to state hospital from December of 1963 to May, 1965, during which time the father had sole custody of the children; the children were in good health and doing well in school, the father was a fit and proper person to have custody of the children, it was within the discretion and power of the chancellor to award the custody of the children to the father. Carlson v. Carlson, 80 Ill. App. 2d 251, 225 N.E.2d 130 (1 Dist. 1967).

The evidence established that the father was a fit and proper person to have the care, custody and education of the child. Landrey v. Landrey, 13 Ill. App. 2d 202, 141 N.E.2d 405 (1 Dist. 1957).

Where a divorced husband seeking to deprive the mother of custody of a small child upon the ground the mother was no longer a fit and proper person to have such custody, the petition was denied as unjustified and husband was given the right to take the child for weekends, every other week during school, and for two separate periods of two weeks each during the summer. Handrich v. Handrich, 339 Ill. App. 151, 89 N.E.2d 191 (4 Dist. 1949).

The burden of proving unfitness is on the party asserting it; unless such unfitness be established by clear evidence, fitness will be presumed. Szewczyk v. Szewczyk, 320 Ill. App. 562, 51 N.E.2d 801 (1 Dist. 1943).

Guardian Ad Litem

A guardian ad litem may make a recommendation as to custody. In re Wycoff, 266 Ill. App. 3d 408, 203 Ill. Dec. 338, 639 N.E.2d 897 (4 Dist.), appeal denied, 158 Ill. 2d 566, 206 Ill. Dec. 847, 645 N.E.2d 1369 (1994).

Guardianship

A guardianship determination will not be disturbed unless the trial court has clearly abused its discretion or its decision is against the manifest weight of the evidence. In re Russell, 169 Ill. App. 3d 97, 119 Ill. Dec. 725, 523 N.E.2d 193 (2 Dist. 1988).

Health of Parents

Where husband argued that the court did not consider wife's poor health in awarding her custody, appellate court held that the trial court adequately considered petitioner's poor health in deciding the custody issue where the court recognized that despite her health problems, wife had been able to adequately care for the children during the 2½ years the parties had been separated and respondent testified as to his own severe health problems, and in his brief he stated that his health "may not be appreciably better than petitioner's." In re Smith, 114 Ill. App. 3d 47, 69 Ill. Dec. 827, 448 N.E.2d 545 (1 Dist. 1983).

The physical health of the father is just one of many factors to be weighed by the trial court in determining the best interest and welfare of the child in determining custody in a marriage dissolution. In re Benevento, 118 Ill. App. 3d 16, 73 Ill. Dec. 669, 454 N.E.2d 766 (1 Dist. 1983).

Homestead

—Effect of Custody

Where the deceased was living with his recent wife and their child, and a child of the deceased's previous marriage, the homestead exemption went to the second wife and all of the deceased's children, jointly, although custody of his children from the previous marriage had been awarded to his second wife. Walker v. Walker, 181 Ill. 260, 54 N.E. 956 (1899).

Homosexual Parent

A lesbian parent's arguments of unconstitutional discrimination in a child custody proceeding, based on sexual orientation, was without merit because the cohabitation relationship of the parent was a relevant factor to be considered by the court in making a custody determination; contrary to the claimed discrimination, such an approach was sexual orientation neutral, in that any sexual relationship having impact on the child would be examined. In re Diehl, 221 Ill. App. 3d 410, 164 Ill. Dec. 73, 582 N.E.2d 281 (2 Dist. 1991), cert. denied, 144 Ill. 2d 632, 169 Ill. Dec. 140, 591 N.E.2d 20 (1992).

Because a parent's associations were relevant to her ability to care for a child, the parent's freedom of association was not violated by the trial court's consideration of her sexual orientation. In re Diehl, 221 Ill. App. 3d 410, 164 Ill. Dec. 73, 582 N.E.2d 281 (2 Dist. 1991), cert. denied, 144 Ill. 2d 632, 169 Ill. Dec. 140, 591 N.E.2d 20 (1992).

Where the evidence revealed that mother, a nurse, exhibited gross character defects by actively recruiting a patient who was a minor, to engage in an illicit and criminal sexual relationship and in so doing, showed her propensity to feed her sexual appetite without regard to morals, ethics or law, the decision that father was better able to provide for the child's mental, moral and emotional needs was correct. In re Williams, 205 Ill. App. 3d 613, 151 Ill. Dec. 89, 563 N.E.2d 1195 (3 Dist. 1990).

The trial court was correct in taking into consideration mother's homosexual relationship in determining original custody. In re Williams, 205 Ill. App. 3d 613, 151 Ill. Dec. 89, 563 N.E.2d 1195 (3 Dist. 1990).

Eighteen year old drug abuser, living in the same household with mother, who considered herself to be an authoritative adult with the ability to discipline and correct daughter was properly considered by the court with its determination to award custody of the child to the father. In re Williams, 205 Ill. App. 3d 613, 151 Ill. Dec. 89, 563 N.E.2d 1195 (3 Dist. 1990).

Illustrative Cases

Decision to award custody to father was against manifest weight of the evidence where: 1) children expressed a preference to live with father; 2) children had adjusted to living with father over period of the appeal; 3) mother was sole custodian during four years temporary custody order was in effect and two preceding years which were during initial separation; 4) mother was primary custodian during marriage; 5) there were no serious objections to children's care while in mother's custody; 6) father had moved to a new city; and 7) father had interfered with mother's visitation during pending appeal. In re Hefer, 282 Ill. App. 3d 73, 217 Ill. Dec. 701, 667 N.E.2d 1094 (4 Dist. 1996).

The trial court considered whether respondent was a good role model for the parties' four minor male children in light of his failures to work for 10 years and to assist the petitioner in maintaining a livable family environment during that time. In re Fahy, 208 Ill. App. 3d 677, 153 Ill. Dec. 594, 567 N.E.2d 552 (1 Dist. 1991).

Trial court decision that the father could provide a more stable environment for the children was not "manifestly unjust" or against the manifest weight of the evidence. In re Milovich, 105 Ill. App. 3d 596, 61 Ill. Dec. 456, 434 N.E.2d 811 (1 Dist. 1982).

References to the record and to alleged errors were not sufficient to constitute grounds for reversal of custody award. In re Ford, 91 Ill. App. 3d 1066, 47 Ill. Dec. 541, 415 N.E.2d 546 (1 Dist. 1980).

For a case discussing factors affecting the award of custody, see Barbara v. Barbara, 110 Ill. App. 2d 189, 249 N.E.2d 269 (1 Dist. 1969).

Initial Custody Order

This section is used when the court is required to make an initial custody decision. In re Gibbons, 158 Ill. App. 3d 998, 111 Ill. Dec. 148, 512 N.E.2d 52 (4 Dist. 1987).

Where there was not a full hearing by the trial court at the time of the original placement of the child but custody was achieved by the stipulation of the parties upon their divorce, the trial court may use initial discretion in deciding what custody provisions provide for the children's best interests. De Franco v. De Franco, 67 Ill. App. 3d 760, 24 Ill. Dec. 130, 384 N.E.2d 997 (1 Dist. 1978).

Integration of the Child

The trial court did not err in considering a child's integration into his father's home without his mother's consent, where the child's integration would not have occurred except for the mother's actions, and the integration was not considered separately but as a part of the home environment. Thompson v. Thompson, 83 Ill. App. 3d 97, 38 Ill. Dec. 485, 403 N.E.2d 716 (3 Dist. 1980).

Joint Custody

—Termination

Even where the joint custody arrangement is terminated by agreement there is no justification for ignoring the bond which has

Joint Custody (Cont'd)

—Termination (Cont'd)
developed between the child and the primary physical custodian, whether the case is decided under the presumption favoring the present custodian of 750 ILCS 5/610 or as an initial award of custody based on the best interest of the child under this section. In re Wycoff, 266 Ill. App. 3d 408, 203 Ill. Dec. 338, 639 N.E.2d 897 (4 Dist.), appeal denied, 158 Ill. 2d 566, 206 Ill. Dec. 847, 645 N.E.2d 1369 (1994).

Judge's Statement
It was not reversible error for the trial court to state her belief that it was desirable to keep the children together as a reason for granting custody of both children to petitioner. In re Ford, 91 Ill. App. 3d 1066, 47 Ill. Dec. 541, 415 N.E.2d 546 (1 Dist. 1980).

Knowledge of Child
The best interests of the child may necessitate removing the child from a potentially harmful environment irrespective of the child's state of knowledge; a trial court need not refrain from modifying custody until children have suffered actual tangible harm. In re Williams, 104 Ill. App. 3d 16, 59 Ill. Dec. 791, 432 N.E.2d 375 (3 Dist. 1982).

Legislative Intent
The intent of the legislature to prefer custodial arrangements which maximize the involvement of both parents in the welfare of the child is manifested in subsection (c) of this section. In re Burke, 185 Ill. App. 3d 253, 133 Ill. Dec. 408, 541 N.E.2d 245 (2 Dist. 1989).

Although there is a legislative presumption in favor of the present custodian and against modification, the purpose of the presumption is to promote the stability and continuity of the child's custodial and environmental relationships. Shoff v. Shoff, 179 Ill. App. 3d 178, 128 Ill. Dec. 280, 534 N.E.2d 462 (5 Dist. 1989).

Living Arrangements
Father's living arrangement, where he lived with an unmarried adult female, was one factor among many in the court's custody decision. In re Hanson, 112 Ill. App. 3d 564, 68 Ill. Dec. 268, 445 N.E.2d 912 (5 Dist. 1983).

Where the plaintiff had no adequate accommodations for the child, and the defendant, who was the mother of the minor lived with her second husband, had satisfactory accommodations for the minor, there could be no question but that the child's interests would be better served if she was cared for by her mother. Lucado v. Lucado, 1 Ill. App. 2d 548, 118 N.E.2d 40 (1 Dist. 1954).

Mature Children
Preferences of mature children should be given considerable weight, when they are based on sound reasoning. In re McCune, 86 Ill. App. 3d 311, 41 Ill. Dec. 897, 408 N.E.2d 319 (3 Dist. 1980).

Modification

—In General
In a hearing to modify child custody provision the paramount concern is the best interests of the child; after a divorce decree custody may be changed as the best interests of the child dictate, based on new conditions which have arisen since the decree and which affect the welfare of the child. Kjellesvik v. Shannon, 41 Ill. App. 3d 674, 355 N.E.2d 120 (3 Dist. 1976).

—Agreement Between Parties
Parents may not bargain away their children's interests; it is for this reason that parents may create an enforceable agreement for modification of child support only by petitioning the court for support modification and then establishing, to the satisfaction of the court, that an agreement reached between the parents is in accord with the best interests of the children. Blisset v. Blisset, 123 Ill. 2d 161, 121 Ill. Dec. 931, 526 N.E.2d 125 (1988).

—Burden of Proof
The party seeking a change in custody has the burden of demonstrating that the child's best interests warrant the change and that circumstances have changed sufficiently to permit the modification. Katzer v. Katzer, 61 Ill. App. 3d 299, 18 Ill. Dec. 852, 378 N.E.2d 316 (1 Dist. 1978).

—Custody Order
The policy favoring finality and stability in children's lives would be endangered if the custody standards in this section were used to modify custody judgments; it is clear that in order to modify an existing custody judgment, 750 ILCS 5/610 should be used. In re Gibbons, 158 Ill. App. 3d 998, 111 Ill. Dec. 148, 512 N.E.2d 52 (4 Dist. 1987).

Litigation that is neither a motion for temporary custody nor an initial custody determination, but rather a modification of the original custody order, is governed by the dictates of 750 ILCS 5/610 and not this section. In re Strader, 101 Ill. App. 3d 779, 57 Ill. Dec. 232, 428 N.E.2d 912 (5 Dist. 1981).

—Denial Upheld
A petition to modify a custody judgment under this section was properly denied since section applies to initial determinations of custody; modification of custody should be sought pursuant to 750 ILCS 5/610. In re Gibbons, 158 Ill. App. 3d 998, 111 Ill. Dec. 148, 512 N.E.2d 52 (4 Dist. 1987).

The trial court did not abuse its discretion in denying father's petition for a modification of custody where it was determined that it was in the best interest of the child that she remain with her mother despite the fact that the mother had been living with a man who was not her husband. Boyer v. Boyer, 83 Ill. App. 3d 52, 38 Ill. Dec. 565, 403 N.E.2d 796 (3 Dist. 1980).

—Illustrative Cases
Where support obligation and visitation rights were established in the respondent, along with a prior judgment of parentage, when respondent filed petition to transfer custody it should have been treated as a motion to modify custody under 750 ILCS 5/610 rather than treated as if it were an initial custody determination under this section. In re M.M.W., 296 Ill. App. 3d 877, 231 Ill. Dec. 238, 695 N.E.2d 1357 (2 Dist. 1998).

—Petition Required
The court cannot modify custody under 750 ILCS 5/607.1 absent a petition to modify pursuant to this section or 750 ILCS 5/610. In re M.M.W., 296 Ill. App. 3d 877, 231 Ill. Dec. 238, 695 N.E.2d 1357 (2 Dist. 1998).

Mother

—Presumption of Better Custodian
Illinois courts no longer presume that the mother is necessarily the better custodian for young children. In re Milovich, 105 Ill. App. 3d 596, 61 Ill. Dec. 456, 434 N.E.2d 811 (1 Dist. 1982).

A presumption in favor of granting custody of a child to the mother solely on the basis of gender under such conditions should be condemned. Kauffman v. Kauffman, 30 Ill. App. 3d 159, 333 N.E.2d 695 (4 Dist. 1975).

Murder of Parent
Where the father was convicted of voluntary manslaughter, not murder, of the mother of the children he sought custody of, and the trial court determined that the father was a fit and proper person for the custody of the children and that it was in the best interests of the children that they be placed with the father, the factors cited by the Supreme Court in In re Abdullah, 85 Ill. 2d 306, 423 N.E.2d 915 (1983) support the finding that unfitness based upon depravity was not present in this case. Tranel v. Lutgen, 177 Ill. App. 3d 954, 127 Ill. Dec. 147, 532 N.E.2d 976 (2 Dist. 1988).

Neither the legislature nor case law in Illinois has seen fit to set forth a rule of law that the killing of one parent by the other in the presence of the children, no matter what the circumstances, standing alone, is sufficient to deprive that parent of his or her children on the basis of unfitness. Tranel v. Lutgen, 177 Ill. App. 3d 954, 127 Ill. Dec. 147, 532 N.E.2d 976 (2 Dist. 1988).

Name Change
In determining whether or not any restraint should have been put upon the plaintiff's action in aiding a minor child to change his name, the first and most important consideration before the trial court should be the welfare of the child. Solomon v. Solomon, 5 Ill. App. 2d 297, 125 N.E.2d 675 (1 Dist. 1955).

Natural Parents

—Animosity Between
A mother's covert departure with her child from the marital home

Natural Parents (Cont'd)

—Animosity Between (Cont'd)

without telling the father where his daughter could be reached, and her failure to inform the father of her new address and phone number when she and her child moved out of her parents' house, reflected negatively upon mother's willingness to facilitate and encourage a close and continuing relationship between the father and the child; this information was necessarily factored into the custody resolution. In re Quindry, 223 Ill. App. 3d 735, 166 Ill. Dec. 290, 585 N.E.2d 1312 (5 Dist. 1992).

—Claim of Third Party

Where testimony indicated that the child frequently arrived at the baby sitter in the morning wearing the same diaper she had on when she left the baby sitter the night before, the baby's formula was almost always spoiled, and prescription medication intended for the baby was not used to control the infant's asthma, the circuit court was correct in concluding it was in the baby's best interests for the third-party respondent to have custody rather than the natural parent. In re Sechrest, 202 Ill. App. 3d 865, 148 Ill. Dec. 615, 560 N.E.2d 1212 (4 Dist. 1990).

Ordinarily the right of a natural parent will prevail over the claim of a third party where both parties are equally fit. In re Krause, 111 Ill. App. 3d 604, 67 Ill. Dec. 408, 444 N.E.2d 644 (1 Dist. 1982).

In a habeas corpus proceeding in which petitioners, non-parents, sought custody of a child, although the mother's conduct in allowing her child to remain in the petitioner's home was unusual, the trial court's conclusion that it fell short of abandonment or desertion was fully supported by the evidence; therefore, the petitioner was not entitled to custody of the child. People ex rel. Bryant v. Williams, 35 Ill. 2d 372, 220 N.E.2d 177 (1966).

—Presumption

The law presumes that it is in the best interest of a child to be raised by the natural parent. In re Krause, 111 Ill. App. 3d 604, 67 Ill. Dec. 408, 444 N.E.2d 644 (1 Dist. 1982).

The court could not deny the natural mother her right to have custody of her child, on a record which did not support the trial court's finding of parental unfitness and dependency. In re Bartha, 107 Ill. App. 2d 214, 245 N.E.2d 779 (2 Dist. 1969).

Parents are entitled to custody of their child unless they are unfit or if the welfare of the child would be best served by denying the parents custody of their child. McAdams v. McAdams, 46 Ill. App. 2d 294, 197 N.E.2d 93 (4 Dist. 1964).

—Superior Right

A third party seeking to obtain or retain custody of a child over the natural parent must demonstrate good cause to overcome the presumption that a parent has a superior right to custody and further must show that it is in the child's best interest that the third party be awarded the care, custody, and control of the minor. In re Rudsell, 291 Ill. App. 3d 626, 225 Ill. Dec. 736, 684 N.E.2d 421 (4 Dist. 1997).

The superior right doctrine, or presumption in favor of the natural parent, need not always be applied automatically in conjunction with the best interests of the child standard; in a dissolution of marriage proceeding, the superior right doctrine will not be applied where both the natural parents are seeking custody of their children, as each starts out on equal footing, with the court ultimately determining custody in accordance with the best interest of the child. In re Townsend, 86 Ill. 2d 502, 56 Ill. Dec. 685, 427 N.E.2d 1231 (1981).

Divorced spouses who lose custody of their children may still retain visitation rights and the legal status of parents; they retain rights to their child, subservient to the custodial spouse, but greater than those of the rest of the world. People v. Abdullah, 85 Ill. 2d 300, 53 Ill. Dec. 246, 423 N.E.2d 915 (1981).

Although parents are the natural guardians and custodians of their children, the rights of parents are not absolute; the state may intervene to terminate the parents' right to the child's continued custody and place it in a more suitable environment, if the circumstances warrant such action. People ex rel. Dep't of Children & Family Servs. v. Robertson, 45 Ill. App. 3d 148, 3 Ill. Dec. 852, 359 N.E.2d 491 (3 Dist. 1977).

A natural parent has a superior right to custody of the child so long as it is in accord with the best interest of the child. People ex rel. Lutz v. Lutz, 24 Ill. App. 3d 948, 322 N.E.2d 62 (2 Dist. 1975); In re Piccirilli, 88 Ill. App. 3d 621, 43 Ill. Dec. 953, 410 N.E.2d 1086 (1 Dist. 1980); Lloyd v. Lloyd, 92 Ill. App. 3d 124, 47 Ill. Dec. 792, 415 N.E.2d 1105 (1 Dist. 1980); Markham v. Markham, 91 Ill. App. 3d 1122, 47 Ill. Dec. 235, 414 N.E.2d 1351 (3 Dist. 1981); In re Krause, 111 Ill. App. 3d 604, 67 Ill. Dec. 408, 444 N.E.2d 644 (1 Dist. 1982).

The paramount issue in determining custody of a child is the determination of what will be the best interest of the minor involved; the superior right of the natural parent to custody of his child can only be determined in the context of the best interest of that child, and may be limited by the conduct of such parent, or other circumstances. Sholty v. Sholty, 67 Ill. App. 2d 60, 214 N.E.2d 15 (3 Dist. 1966).

The right of the parent surpasses that of the stepmother who is in law a stranger; thus, the court erred in awarding the custody of the children to the stepmother. McAdams v. McAdams, 46 Ill. App. 2d 294, 197 N.E.2d 93 (4 Dist. 1964).

As a party to the original proceeding, the mother had a right to petition for modification of the custody provisions of the decree, and as the mother of the child she had a natural right to custody, subject only to the like natural right of the father, and to the best interests and welfare of the child. Horn v. Horn, 5 Ill. App. 2d 346, 125 N.E.2d 539 (3 Dist. 1955).

A court is only warranted in depriving a father of the custody of his child where the evidence discloses that the child is destitute, abandoned or dependent; that the father is living an immoral life or in vicious or disreputable circumstances; that he has neglected or treated the child cruelly or unkindly or that he may so treat the child; that he is wanting in good principles or that he is illy adapted to the care of the child on account of defects in his mental or physical qualities which prevent him from being a kind and affectionate father. Jarrett v. Jarrett, 348 Ill. App. 1, 107 N.E.2d 622 (3 Dist. 1952), aff'd, 415 Ill. 126, 112 N.E.2d 694 (1953).

Where the child's mother is dead, the right of the father to custody is paramount, unless one or more of the following conditions is present: (a) the father is unfit or (b) by his conduct he has forfeited his right to custody. Jarrett v. Jarrett, 348 Ill. App. 1, 107 N.E.2d 622 (3 Dist. 1952), aff'd, 415 Ill. 126, 112 N.E.2d 694 (1953).

Where the mother is dead, the law presumes the interest and welfare of the child to be best served in the custody of its father, and that the right of a parent to the custody of his child is superior to that of any other person when he is fit, can provide the necessities of life and where both contestants are equally proper persons, the father will be awarded the preference. Jarrett v. Jarrett, 348 Ill. App. 1, 107 N.E.2d 622 (3 Dist. 1952), aff'd, 415 Ill. 126, 112 N.E.2d 694 (1953).

The rule that a parent has the right to the custody of his child against all the world, unless he has forfeited that right, was born of the natural desire of mankind to create and maintain a home; to deprive worthy parents of their natural right to the custody of their children, where they have not forfeited that right, would undermine the home. Jarrett v. Jarrett, 348 Ill. App. 1, 107 N.E.2d 622 (3 Dist. 1952), aff'd, 415 Ill. 126, 112 N.E.2d 694 (1953).

Legal precedent has always recognized the inherent right of a father to the custody of his motherless children and will even presume the father to be capable of caring for them until the contrary is clearly established; however, these rights of the father to the custody of such children are certainly not absolute, but are subject to being lost as a result of his misconduct, if the same might cause him to be unfit for such duties or if he has been found to have abandoned the children. Scott v. Ashcraft, 342 Ill. App. 33, 95 N.E.2d 122 (3 Dist. 1950).

The rights of the parent are superior to those of any other person, when that parent is a fit person to have the custody of children and is so circumstanced that he can provide the necessaries of life and administer to the requirements of such a charge; the mere fact that some other person may have more money or property, in any form, is not a proper basis for depriving an otherwise fit parent of custody. Szewczyk v. Szewczyk, 320 Ill. App. 562, 51 N.E.2d 801 (1 Dist. 1943).

Non-Parent

—In General

In a custody dispute, a court should give great weight to the claim

Non-Parent (Cont'd)

—In General (Cont'd)

of a third person who has had actual or legal custody of the child for a substantial period of time, especially if the evidence shows that the child has become an integral member of a true family unit. In re Krause, 111 Ill. App. 3d 604, 67 Ill. Dec. 408, 444 N.E.2d 644 (1 Dist. 1982).

Prior long term actual or legal custody is not controlling and does not transfer the superior right from the natural parent to the third person; it remains simply a factor to consider in ascertaining what will best serve the interests of the child. In re Krause, 111 Ill. App. 3d 604, 67 Ill. Dec. 408, 444 N.E.2d 644 (1 Dist. 1982).

—Awarded Custody

Under a similar prior provision, the custody of a 15-year-old girl was given to her aunt, rather than her father. People ex rel. Kuhn v. Weeks, 228 Ill. App. 262 (1 Dist. 1923).

—Grandparents

Where petitioner grandparents did not plead any compelling reasons that would justify placing custody with them, natural father's slight instability referred to in the petitioners' brief was not of the type that would compel a court to deny him custody. In re Strocher, 95 Ill. App. 3d 339, 50 Ill. Dec. 908, 420 N.E.2d 225 (4 Dist. 1981).

The law presumes that it is in the child's best interest to be raised by the natural parent, and ordinarily the natural right of the father will prevail in a contest between him and the grandparents where both parties are equally fit to care for the child. In re Piccirilli, 88 Ill. App. 3d 621, 43 Ill. Dec. 953, 410 N.E.2d 1086 (1 Dist. 1980).

Where the mother was found unfit, there was a presumption that custody by the father, who was found to be fit, would be in the best interest of the child; ordinarily the natural right of the father will prevail in a contest between him and the grandparents where both parties are equally fit to care for the child but not where the father had left the child with the other party for five years. Look v. Look, 21 Ill. App. 3d 454, 315 N.E.2d 623 (3 Dist. 1974).

Where appellee, child's father, made no effort to visit his child after leaving the appellant's home until his wife died, even though he never lived a greater distance than 30 miles from the boy, it was not conducive to the child's best interest to remove him from the stable and adequately wholesome environment of his maternal grandparent for the apparently primary purpose of placing him with his natural father, who was for practical purposes a stranger. People ex rel. Edwards v. Livingston, 42 Ill. 2d 201, 247 N.E.2d 417 (1969).

Placement of a minor with grandparents instead of to parents who were willing and fit was in contradiction to the rule that recognizes the superior right of the parent and, therefore, was reversed. Stingley v. Wesch, 77 Ill. App. 2d 472, 222 N.E.2d 505 (4 Dist. 1966).

Where both the child's natural father and maternal grandparents were fit and proper persons, well able and qualified to undertake the duties incident to the custody of the minor involved, and the father by his conduct had not forfeited his rights or abandoned his interest in his minor son, there was sufficient evidence to justify the order of the trial court awarding custody of the child to the father. Sholty v. Sholty, 67 Ill. App. 2d 60, 214 N.E.2d 15 (3 Dist. 1966).

Where the record disclosed that from the date of the ten-year-old child's birth the defendants, the child's maternal grandparents had his exclusive control and custody, and that this arrangement was entirely satisfactory and agreeable with the child's father for more than eight years and three months before appellant sought to change it, the best interests of the child required that it be not discontinued. People ex rel. Hermann v. Jenkins, 34 Ill. App. 2d 255, 180 N.E.2d 359 (2 Dist. 1962).

Where a father petitioned to modify the divorce decree so as to award custody of his daughter to him, the finding of the chancellor that it was in the best interests of the child to remain with her grandmother was not against the manifest weight of the evidence. Kokotekian v. Kokotekian, 23 Ill. App. 2d 171, 161 N.E.2d 712 (1 Dist. 1959).

Where the child will be well cared for in either home, that of his maternal grandmother or that of his father, the best interest of the child will be served if the custody is granted to the father. Jarrett v. Jarrett, 348 Ill. App. 1, 107 N.E.2d 622 (3 Dist. 1952), aff'd, 415 Ill. 126, 112 N.E.2d 694 (1953).

Where the father of a child had been drafted into military service and desired that his parents have visitation rights, the mother was entitled to be heard and to offer evidence in opposition to his application for the right of visitation in the paternal grandparents. Solomon v. Solomon, 319 Ill. App. 618, 49 N.E.2d 807 (1 Dist. 1943).

The maternal grandmother was not entitled to obtain custody of her grandchild as against the father, whose claim of fitness as a parent was unchallenged. Schneeman v. Schneeman, 317 Ill. App. 286, 45 N.E.2d 1016 (1 Dist. 1942).

Notice of Appeal

Absence of notice to the representative of the minor child in a custody proceeding did not affect the appellate court's jurisdiction to consider the appeal, although the better procedure here would have been to have notified said minor through his duly court-appointed representative, and since the representative sought no leave to intervene in the appeal or to file a brief, the court would proceed to the merits of the appeal. In re Leopando, 106 Ill. App. 3d 444, 62 Ill. Dec. 340, 435 N.E.2d 1312 (1 Dist. 1982), aff'd, 96 Ill. 2d 114, 70 Ill. Dec. 263, 449 N.E.2d 137 (1983).

Past Conduct

Past immoral conduct which has been terminated will not render a parent unfit unless it can be shown that a child would be adversely affected by such conduct. In re Combs, 78 Ill. App. 3d 533, 33 Ill. Dec. 922, 397 N.E.2d 255 (5 Dist. 1979).

Past misconduct, where the evidence indicates no probable future misconduct, should not be the basis for denying custody to the mother. Drake v. Hohimer, 35 Ill. App. 3d 529, 341 N.E.2d 399 (4 Dist. 1976).

Where evidence of past indiscretions by the mother which occurred before her remarriage and where no claim was made by the father, during that period of time, that she was unfit to have custody of the children, although he had knowledge of the facts, the incidents complained of since her remarriage were palpably insufficient to prove that she was unfit to care for her children. Laughlin v. Laughlin, 97 Ill. App. 2d 480, 240 N.E.2d 323 (1 Dist. 1968).

At a hearing on the father's petition for modification of a divorce decree to give him custody of his children, evidence of facts pre-dating that decree could not be heard for the purpose of impeaching the mother's fitness, but such evidence was competent where it related to other new circumstances having bearing on the question of the children's welfare. Kline v. Kline, 57 Ill. App. 2d 244, 205 N.E.2d 775 (3 Dist. 1965).

Past misconduct, where the evidence indicates no probable future misconduct, should not be a basis for denying custody to the mother. Wolfrum v. Wolfrum, 5 Ill. App. 2d 471, 126 N.E.2d 34 (3 Dist. 1955).

Where prior misconduct of the mother gave no evidence of adverse effect on the future welfare of the child, the mother was able to care for her minor daughter and was not shown to lack the proper attributes of good motherhood, past misconduct, with no evidence indicating probable future misconduct, should not be a basis for denying custody to the mother. Nye v. Nye, 411 Ill. 408, 105 N.E.2d 300 (1952).

Physical Custody

While the fact that the nonparent has had physical custody of the child for a substantial length of time does not neutralize the superior-right doctrine, it may, in a given case, be the determining factor in the custody decision. Rose v. Potts, 217 Ill. App. 3d 661, 160 Ill. Dec. 486, 577 N.E.2d 811 (5 Dist. 1991).

Physical Violence

Allegations of father's abusive conduct towards mother were relevant, and could properly be a decisive factor in the court's determination as to custody. In re Wiley, 199 Ill. App. 3d 169, 145 Ill. Dec. 191, 556 N.E.2d 809 (4 Dist. 1990).

The physical violence to the custodial parent witnessed by the children, is but one of the factors the legislature has set forth for determining custody in the best interest of the children, and had the legislature wished to make this factor all controlling, it could have done so by the appropriate legislation. Tranel v. Lutgen, 177 Ill. App. 3d 954, 127 Ill. Dec. 147, 532 N.E.2d 976 (2 Dist. 1988).

Physical Violence (Cont'd)

It was not error for the trial court to consider evidence pertaining to a brutal beating received by the wife at the hands of the husband in deciding the question of the custody of the parties' infant child, where she was struck from behind on the head with such force as to propel her across the room, the husband then sat on her chest and began hitting her in the face with his fists, stripped off her clothes and forced her to engage in sexual relations, during which he continued to say, "I will kill you." In re Williams, 104 Ill. App. 3d 16, 59 Ill. Dec. 791, 432 N.E.2d 375 (3 Dist. 1982).

Subsection (b) of this section does not relegate a wanton and brutal physical beating by the father of a child's mother to be an act of no significance when determining which parent shall be granted custody. In re Williams, 104 Ill. App. 3d 16, 59 Ill. Dec. 791, 432 N.E.2d 375 (3 Dist. 1982).

Preference of Child

A better way than in camera hearing to get the child's preferences before the court may be through admission of the child's hearsay statements, through the testimony of the guardian ad litem, or through professional personnel. In re Hefer, 282 Ill. App. 3d 73, 217 Ill. Dec. 701, 667 N.E.2d 1094 (4 Dist. 1996).

There are problems with making the decision of the child the determinant: such an approach places a tremendous amount of pressure on the child and such reliance provides an incentive for parental manipulation and intimidation of the child, and an opportunity for a child's manipulation of the parents. In re Hefer, 282 Ill. App. 3d 73, 217 Ill. Dec. 701, 667 N.E.2d 1094 (4 Dist. 1996).

While it has been said that a child's preference as to custody should only be given weight when it is based on sound reasoning, the statute does not require the child to give a good reason for his preference. In re Wycoff, 266 Ill. App. 3d 408, 203 Ill. Dec. 338, 639 N.E.2d 897 (4 Dist.), appeal denied, 158 Ill. 2d 566, 206 Ill. Dec. 847, 645 N.E.2d 1369 (1994).

In a custody proceeding the trial court is in a good position to evaluate the credibility, temperaments, personalities, and capabilities of both parents along with an inference from the totality of the child's statements and under these circumstances, therefore, the trial court did not err in failing to specifically ask the child whether she preferred to live with her father or her mother. In re Balzell, 207 Ill. App. 3d 310, 152 Ill. Dec. 492, 566 N.E.2d 20 (3 Dist. 1991).

Where the father, as the sole surviving parent, wished to have custody of the children, and they wished to live with him and did not wish to be separated from each other, there was sufficient evidence to support the trial court's decision to award custody to father. Tranel v. Lutgen, 177 Ill. App. 3d 954, 127 Ill. Dec. 147, 532 N.E.2d 976 (2 Dist. 1988).

Even had the five year old child unequivocally indicated a preference for living with his father, this preference, while entitled to consideration, is not binding on the court in determining custody. Cooper v. Cooper, 146 Ill. App. 3d 943, 100 Ill. Dec. 627, 497 N.E.2d 805 (5 Dist. 1986).

The preferences of a child, especially one who is mature, are to be given serious weight in custody decisions, especially where the child's desire is based upon reasons related to his best interests such as a desire to remain with friends, to continue attending the same school and to remain in the same environment. In re Siegel, 123 Ill. App. 3d 710, 79 Ill. Dec. 219, 463 N.E.2d 773 (1 Dist. 1984).

Record demonstrated that the court was adequately apprised of the children's wishes and gave them due consideration in determining custody where guardian ad litem stated that the children felt that they could communicate better with their mother, and they were upset with their father for swearing at mother and degrading her in front of them. In re Smith, 114 Ill. App. 3d 47, 69 Ill. Dec. 827, 448 N.E.2d 545 (1 Dist. 1983).

Although the act requires that the court consider the wishes of the children, when these wishes conflict, the court does not abuse its discretion in giving greater weight to the desires of the older and more mature child. In re Lovejoy, 84 Ill. App. 3d 53, 39 Ill. Dec. 501, 404 N.E.2d 1092 (3 Dist. 1980).

Although weight should be given to a child's preference as to his custodian, such a preference may not always accord with the child's best interest. Allen v. Allen, 81 Ill. App. 3d 517, 36 Ill. Dec. 767, 401 N.E.2d 608 (3 Dist. 1980).

The wishes of children alone do not warrant a change in custody. Hinton v. Searles, 53 Ill. App. 3d 433, 11 Ill. Dec. 329, 368 N.E.2d 937 (5 Dist. 1977).

Where the children told the court that they were happy and preferred to live with their mother, the children mentioned that they liked school where they were living and had made some friends there, and respondent testified that the younger boy was receiving special help for a speech problem, and that the school in which the children were enrolled had special classes for just such problems, it was against the manifest weight of the evidence for the trial court to transfer custody to the father. Hinton v. Searles, 53 Ill. App. 3d 433, 11 Ill. Dec. 329, 368 N.E.2d 937 (5 Dist. 1977).

Preference of a child in a custody case may often be an important element for consideration by the courts but such preference, necessarily, is not controlling. Crownover v. Crownover, 33 Ill. App. 3d 327, 337 N.E.2d 56 (3 Dist. 1975); In re Milovich, 105 Ill. App. 3d 596, 61 Ill. Dec. 456, 434 N.E.2d 811 (1 Dist. 1982); In re Lovejoy, 158 Ill. App. 3d 1, 109 Ill. Dec. 768, 510 N.E.2d 636 (3 Dist. 1987).

The child's preferences are normally entitled to receive some consideration depending upon the circumstances in each case. Crownover v. Crownover, 33 Ill. App. 3d 327, 337 N.E.2d 56 (3 Dist. 1975).

Standing alone, wishes and preferences of a child do not warrant or justify a change in custodial preferences. Rosenberger v. Rosenberger, 21 Ill. App. 3d 550, 316 N.E.2d 1 (1 Dist. 1974).

In determining the custody of children of divorced parents, the children's feeling are an element to be given most serious consideration. Rosenberger v. Rosenberger, 21 Ill. App. 3d 550, 316 N.E.2d 1 (1 Dist. 1974).

The trial court's determination that it was in the best interests of the children to award their custody to the defendant was not against the manifest weight of the evidence; furthermore, the children's preference was properly considered by the court as a factor in determining their best interests. Rosenberger v. Rosenberger, 21 Ill. App. 3d 550, 316 N.E.2d 1 (1 Dist. 1974).

Where the oldest child indicated a preference for his father, and his reasons for making the preference, this was a factor to be considered. Mulvihill v. Mulvihill, 20 Ill. App. 3d 440, 314 N.E.2d 342 (1 Dist. 1974).

The order of the trial court in Illinois in changing custody from the mother as ordered in the trial court of California, to the father, was against the manifest weight of the evidence where the sole reason for the change was the preference of the two parties' children. Finn v. Finn, 11 Ill. App. 3d 385, 297 N.E.2d 1 (2 Dist. 1973).

The children's desire to live with their mother was not controlling. Filipello v. Filipello, 130 Ill. App. 2d 1089, 268 N.E.2d 478 (1 Dist. 1971).

Children nine and 12 years of age were not old enough, or capable enough, to choose the parent with whom they should live; their preference had to yield to their welfare as determined by the court. Filipello v. Filipello, 130 Ill. App. 2d 1089, 268 N.E.2d 478 (1 Dist. 1971).

Preferences of children alone, when the children are under 14 years of age, should not warrant a change in custody. Wilner v. Wilner, 131 Ill. App. 2d 891, 266 N.E.2d 918 (3 Dist. 1971).

If children are of sufficient maturity, their choice is an important element to be taken into account; but even the desire of older children to live with a particular parent is not binding on the court. Filipello v. Filipello, 130 Ill. App. 2d 1089, 268 N.E.2d 478 (1 Dist. 1971).

The fact that a 17 year old child preferred to live with her mother was not sufficient to warrant a transfer of custody from father to mother. Elble v. Elble, 100 Ill. App. 2d 221, 241 N.E.2d 328 (5 Dist. 1968).

Where a child had chosen to leave her father and live with her mother, and the evidence failed to show a change of circumstances which would have warranted a modification of the provision of the decree awarding her custody to the father, the court could not, and would not, force a 17 year old girl to live with her father if she did not desire; the order to have the father pay the mother for the child's support during her minority, and an attorney's fee, but not to provide for the child's college education, was affirmed. Elble v. Elble, 100 Ill. App. 2d 221, 241 N.E.2d 328 (5 Dist. 1968).

The child's preference is a proper factor to be considered by the court but per se is not sufficient standing alone to warrant a change of custody once adjudicated. Strouse v. Strouse, 75 Ill. App. 2d 362, 220 N.E.2d 485 (4 Dist. 1966).

Preference of Child (Cont'd)

Where the court allowed a 16 year old girl to remain with her 19 year old sister instead of giving custody to the father, the court did not intend to infer that the request of a minor child, standing alone, was necessarily either decisive or controlling on the question of custody; it was just one factor for consideration. Nichols v. Nichols, 70 Ill. App. 2d 376, 216 N.E.2d 690 (4 Dist. 1966).

Where the chancellor found both parties fit to be awarded custody of the children, and ruled that the two older girls and the boy should remain with defendant, while the two younger girls were to remain with plaintiff, thus leaving undisturbed the children's residence, the arrangement appeared to be preferred by the children and seemed to be the most satisfactory solution. Coolidge v. Coolidge, 13 Ill. App. 2d 170, 141 N.E.2d 636 (1 Dist. 1957).

In a situation involving a change of custody the interest of the child is preeminently the thing to be considered. Martinec v. Sharapata, 328 Ill. App. 339, 66 N.E.2d 103 (1 Dist. 1946).

Presumption of Harm

There would be no presumption of any kind that the child has been harmed in the case of covert sexual encounters not amounting to cohabitation of which the child was unaware. Cooper v. Cooper, 146 Ill. App. 3d 943, 100 Ill. Dec. 627, 497 N.E.2d 805 (5 Dist. 1986).

Previous Orders

Where the court entertained evidence of child abuse by the father previous to a foreign modification, but stated that it was prevented from considering the evidence because it occurred prior to the modification, this was error, for the court had the duty to consider all facts and circumstances which related to the well-being of the children. Hinton v. Searles, 53 Ill. App. 3d 433, 11 Ill. Dec. 329, 368 N.E.2d 937 (5 Dist. 1977).

The trial court in its consideration of the best interest of the children can make a just determination without being hindered by a previous order in another court. Hinton v. Searles, 53 Ill. App. 3d 433, 11 Ill. Dec. 329, 368 N.E.2d 937 (5 Dist. 1977).

Prior Hearing

—Transcript

The parties' stipulation to the court's consideration of a transcript of a prior hearing, insofar as it relates to a determination of child custody, is inconsistent with the declared policy of our state and, as such, was inoperative. In re Akins, 188 Ill. App. 3d 951, 136 Ill. Dec. 356, 544 N.E.2d 1131 (5 Dist. 1989).

Where the record was adequate for purposes of this section, the judgment was not disturbed merely because written findings of facts were not made in statutory form. Melear v. Melear, 76 Ill. App. 3d 706, 32 Ill. Dec. 261, 395 N.E.2d 208 (3 Dist. 1979).

Psychologist's Testimony

Although it was found that the submission of a child's representative's report without the mother being allowed to cross-examine in a custody hearing denied the mother due process, the error was harmless because the mother received the report prior to the modification hearing under § 610 of the Illinois Marriage and Dissolution of Marriage Act, 750 ILCS 5/610, and presented no evidence to rebut the report as required by Ill. Sup. Ct. R. 341(e)(7), and there was substantial expert testimony that supported the conclusion that the mother had consistently failed to facilitate and encourage a close and continuing relationship between the child and the father under 750 ILCS 5/602. In re Marriage of De Bates, 212 Ill. 2d 489, 289 Ill. Dec. 218, 819 N.E.2d 714, 2004 Ill. LEXIS 1619 (2004).

In considering the mental health of individuals involved in a child custody dispute, the testimony of a psychologist, although providing the court with relevant evidence to aid in its considerations, is not determinative. In re Siegel, 123 Ill. App. 3d 710, 79 Ill. Dec. 219, 463 N.E.2d 773 (1 Dist. 1984).

While the testimony of psychologists is permissible in custody cases, such testimony is not determinative of the custody issue. In re Milovich, 105 Ill. App. 3d 596, 61 Ill. Dec. 456, 434 N.E.2d 811 (1 Dist. 1982).

Putative Father

The rights of a putative father who acknowledges an illegitimate child are recognized under the law and he thereby assumes burdens along with benefits. In re Myer, 100 Ill. App. 3d 27, 55 Ill. Dec. 358, 426 N.E.2d 333 (4 Dist. 1981).

Relationship with Child

In a child custody case, where father spent time with his son, regularly bathed and read to his son, frequently communicated with his son and performed many responsibilities associated with parenthood, while mother had trouble in disciplining son and had little time to devote to her son, the best interests of the son were best served by awarding custody to father. In re Bush, 170 Ill. App. 3d 523, 121 Ill. Dec. 357, 525 N.E.2d 163 (2 Dist. 1988).

Religious Beliefs

It was improper for the trial court's decision concerning the awarding of child custody to be premised on the belief that active participation in an organized religion should be given preference over a more passive form of religious faith. In re Zucco, 150 Ill. App. 3d 146, 103 Ill. Dec. 558, 501 N.E.2d 875 (5 Dist. 1986).

Where evidence of the parents' religious beliefs was admitted only as a means to gain insight into the entire family picture, and nowhere in the statements of the trial judge or in any action involved in the trial did it appear that the judge's decision was influenced or determined by the question of religion, the inquiry into respondent's religious beliefs was not grounds for reversal of the trial court's custody award. In re Ford, 91 Ill. App. 3d 1066, 47 Ill. Dec. 541, 415 N.E.2d 546 (1 Dist. 1980).

Remarriage

The trial court did not err in drawing adverse inferences from the mother's failure to call her new husband to appear on her behalf in a child custody action; as the mother's new husband played an important part in the child's life, the trial court should have been given the opportunity to evaluate the mother's new husband on its own. In re Quindry, 223 Ill. App. 3d 735, 166 Ill. Dec. 290, 585 N.E.2d 1312 (5 Dist. 1992).

A subsequent marriage of a parent and stability of environment are important considerations in child custody modification proceedings. Kjellesvik v. Shannon, 41 Ill. App. 3d 674, 355 N.E.2d 120 (3 Dist. 1976).

Although the mother was a fit parent, her remarriage constituted a change in circumstances necessitating a change in custody for the best interests of the child where the court found the second husband demonstrated weakness of character and instability and that his mental illness and separations from the family created an unstable environment for the child. Kjellesvik v. Shannon, 41 Ill. App. 3d 674, 355 N.E.2d 120 (3 Dist. 1976).

Subsequent marriages are a factor to consider as a change in circumstances; it is not necessary for the court to find that the person having custody is an unfit person if other circumstances warrant modification. Cave v. Cave, 2 Ill. App. 3d 782, 276 N.E.2d 793 (5 Dist. 1971).

Where the evidence established that the character and conduct of the person to whom the mother subsequently married was unsatisfactory, that the children's interests were adversely affected by the earlier divorce decree awarding custody to their mother, and that the children's father was of good moral character, the evidence was sufficient to support the decree of modification granting custody to the father. Kline v. Kline, 57 Ill. App. 2d 244, 205 N.E.2d 775 (3 Dist. 1965).

Removal of Child

Petitioner did not carry her burden of proving that moving child to Georgia would be in child's best interest, but instead the evidence demonstrated that child's visitation with respondent would decrease by at least 50% and her interaction with her relatives would also be significantly diminished; though the quality of child's life in Georgia might possibly be better in a material sense, it would be diminished in many important ways, and because child's best interest was not reflected in trial court's determination to permit removal of child from Illinois, it was found to be against the manifest weight of the evidence. Tysl v. Levine, 278 Ill. App. 3d 431, 215 Ill. Dec. 14, 662 N.E.2d 915 (2 Dist. 1996).

In cases where the parties were never married, the custodial parent is not required to file a petition for removal, thus, the court will not yet have engaged in a best interest of the child analysis to determine whether the custodial parent should be allowed to remove the minor child from the state, therefore, where the parties

Removal of Child (Cont'd)
were never married, the fact that a custodial parent wishes to move out of the state with the minor child is sufficient to show a change of circumstances which would satisfy the first prong of 750 ILCS 5/610 and the court would then be required to engage in a best interests of the child analysis, utilizing the factors enumerated in this section. In re R.M.F., 275 Ill. App. 3d 43, 211 Ill. Dec. 754, 655 N.E.2d 1137 (2 Dist. 1995).

It is the province of the trial court to determine whether removal of child from Illinois to Colorado would permit a degree of involvement and cooperation between parents and child that would foster their son's physical, mental, moral and emotional well-being. In re Bednar, 146 Ill. App. 3d 704, 100 Ill. Dec. 84, 496 N.E.2d 1149 (1 Dist. 1986).

Where the father having custody of the minor child had moved to Mississippi with the child since the hearing, any modification of the custody order because of changes in circumstances arising since the hearing should have been initiated in the trial court pursuant to 750 ILCS 5/610. Melear v. Melear, 76 Ill. App. 3d 706, 32 Ill. Dec. 261, 395 N.E.2d 208 (3 Dist. 1979).

For a case discussing custodial's parent removal of children to another state, see Garland v. Garland, 19 Ill. App. 3d 951, 312 N.E.2d 811 (1 Dist. 1974).

Subsequent to a divorce decree, the court granting such decree retains continuing jurisdiction of the parties with regard to children of the marriage, custody and support; a party may not avoid this continuing jurisdiction of the trial court which entered the original divorce decree by moving outside the court's geographical jurisdiction. Crawley v. Bauchens, 13 Ill. App. 3d 791, 300 N.E.2d 603 (5 Dist. 1973), aff'd, 57 Ill. 2d 360, 312 N.E.2d 236 (1974).

The best interests of the child required her expatriation with her mother in Germany for a period of 11 months and her return to the United States for one month in the summer, rather than living with the father in the United States because the mother had sufficient financial resources and was otherwise able to care for said child. Radivojevic v. Radivojevic, 11 Ill. App. 3d 116, 295 N.E.2d 570 (4 Dist. 1973).

Under former Ill.Rev.Stat., ch. 40, para. 19 (1967) (see now this section), the removal of a child from the jurisdiction was not alone sufficient grounds for a change of custody. Norris v. Norris, 121 Ill. App. 2d 226, 257 N.E.2d 545 (1 Dist. 1970).

The removal of the parties' child to Ohio when the mother moved there with her second husband was not grounds for revoking her custody. Jingling v. Trtanj, 99 Ill. App. 2d 64, 241 N.E.2d 39 (5 Dist. 1968).

The court should grant permission to take the children out of the jurisdiction if it is deemed to be for the best interests of the children; the court should make such provisions as are reasonably necessary to protect the rights given the father as the noncustodial parent in the divorce. Trimble v. Trimble, 16 Ill. App. 2d 408, 148 N.E.2d 612 (1 Dist. 1958).

Custody of children may be awarded to a non-resident on a showing of circumstances which would better promote the welfare and interests of the children; all other considerations will be subordinate to the children's welfare. Trimble v. Trimble, 16 Ill. App. 2d 408, 148 N.E.2d 612 (1 Dist. 1958).

Rotating Custody

The trial court did not err in finding that the father met his burden of proof by clear and convincing evidence on the basis of new circumstances or previously unknown facts, and properly instituted a rotating custody arrangement and ongoing therapy in an attempt to break the cycle of parental alienation and to assist the parties' child in her adjustment. In re Divelbiss, 308 Ill. App. 3d 198, 241 Ill. Dec. 514, 719 N.E.2d 375 (2 Dist. 1999).

Separation

Keeping a family together is not an overriding factor when there is a substantial disparity in the ages of the siblings and other important factors are in the best interests of a young child. In re Seymour, 206 Ill. App. 3d 506, 152 Ill. Dec. 27, 565 N.E.2d 269 (2 Dist. 1990).

It is usually in the best interests of the children that they not be separated; however, separation of the children may occasionally be in the children's best interest. In re Slavenas, 139 Ill. App. 3d 581, 93 Ill. Dec. 914, 487 N.E.2d 739 (2 Dist. 1985).

Stability of Environment

Stability of the home environment is a judicial gloss added to the factors specifically enumerated in this section. In re Pool, 118 Ill. App. 3d 1035, 74 Ill. Dec. 458, 455 N.E.2d 887 (3 Dist. 1983), overruled on other grounds, In re Wycoff, 266 Ill. App. 3d 408 203 Ill. Dec. 338, 639 N.E.2d 897 (4 Dist. 1994).

The trial court's judgment modifying a minor's custody from mother to father would not be overturned where it weighed the instability of the environment provided by the mother, her frequent changes in residence, her unsuccessful remarriage, her poor choice of male companions who associated with her in the presence of the child, and the fact that the mother was unemployed. In re Padiak, 101 Ill. App. 3d 306, 56 Ill. Dec. 826, 427 N.E.2d 1372 (2 Dist. 1981).

In a custody modification, the court can consider the stability of the children's environment in judging their best interests. De Franco v. De Franco, 67 Ill. App. 3d 760, 24 Ill. Dec. 130, 384 N.E.2d 997 (1 Dist. 1978); Russell v. Kellum, 80 Ill. App. 3d 41, 35 Ill. Dec. 378, 399 N.E.2d 212 (5 Dist. 1979).

Where the effect of the trial court's order was to remove the child from an unstable home into a two-parent, stable atmosphere and to eliminate exposure to conditions which were not conducive to physical and moral well-being, the trial court did not abuse its discretion, nor was its judgment against the manifest weight of the evidence. Sorenson v. Sorenson, 10 Ill. App. 3d 980, 295 N.E.2d 347 (4 Dist. 1973).

It was not an abuse of discretion to award custody of minor children to the husband where the award of custody placed the children in a stable home, and in circumstances conducive to their emotional well-being. O'Donnell v. O'Donnell, 5 Ill. App. 3d 870, 284 N.E.2d 682 (4 Dist. 1972).

Stability of environment is an important factor in determining the best interests and welfare of children; removal of a child to another state as a result of a modification of the decree, if it is in the best interest of the child, does not prohibit modification. Cave v. Cave, 2 Ill. App. 3d 782, 276 N.E.2d 793 (5 Dist. 1971).

The law should not and does not demand that each individual shall attain the same level of achievement; rather, recognizing the physical, emotional, and mental differences in individuals, the law requires only that individuals shall attain a reasonable standard of decency, opportunity and respect so that his children may partake of that which society has to offer, subject only to his own individual limitations. McAdams v. McAdams, 46 Ill. App. 2d 294, 197 N.E.2d 93 (4 Dist. 1964).

Standard of Review

Where the evidence before the trial court did not clearly favor either party, the reviewing court could not say that the trial court's decision to place permanent custody of the child with one of the parents was against the manifest weight of the evidence. Prince v. Herrera, 261 Ill. App. 3d 606, 199 Ill. Dec. 174, 633 N.E.2d 970 (1 Dist. 1994).

Where, in prior order, the court clearly stated its position that custody of the minor child was yet to be determined, it was futile to argue that that order should be deemed a custody determination in favor of the mother; accordingly an order granting permanent custody of minor to his father was the initial custody determination, and did not involve the standards and requirements for modification, as contended by mother; being an initial determination of custody, the trial court correctly relied on the "best interest" standard as provided by law. In re Koca, 264 Ill. App. 3d 291, 201 Ill. Dec. 240, 636 N.E.2d 672 (1 Dist. 1993).

A trial court's custody decision will not be reversed unless there has been a clear abuse of discretion or the decision was contrary to the manifest weight of the evidence. In re Willis, 234 Ill. App. 3d 156, 174 Ill. Dec. 633, 599 N.E.2d 179 (3 Dist. 1992).

In cases regarding custody, there is a strong and compelling presumption in favor of the result reached by the trial court. In re Willis, 234 Ill. App. 3d 156, 174 Ill. Dec. 633, 599 N.E.2d 179 (3 Dist. 1992).

A reviewing court will not overturn a determination of custody unless the trial court's decision is contrary to the manifest weight of the evidence or exhibits a clear abuse of discretion since the trial court, having had a superior opportunity to observe the witnesses, evaluate the evidence and consider the needs of the child, is in a better position than a reviewing court to determine just what that best interest is. In re Quindry, 223 Ill. App. 3d 735, 166 Ill. Dec. 290, 585 N.E.2d 1312 (5 Dist. 1992).

Standard of Review (Cont'd)

A reviewing court will not disturb the trial court's determination of credibility because the trial court has a superior vantage point, which cannot be reproduced from the old record, to observe and judge the witnesses' demeanor and credibility; the trial court is therefore in a better position to evaluate the credibility, temperaments, personalities, and capabilities of both parents. In re Diehl, 221 Ill. App. 3d 410, 164 Ill. Dec. 73, 582 N.E.2d 281 (2 Dist. 1991), cert. denied, 144 Ill. 2d 632, 169 Ill. Dec. 140, 591 N.E.2d 20 (1992).

The trial court's determination of custody will not be disturbed upon review unless it is against the manifest weight of the evidence, manifestly unjust or there has been a clear abuse of discretion. In re Diehl, 221 Ill. App. 3d 410, 164 Ill. Dec. 73, 582 N.E.2d 281 (2 Dist. 1991), cert. denied, 144 Ill. 2d 632, 169 Ill. Dec. 140, 591 N.E.2d 20 (1992).

The trial court has broad discretion in making a custody determination; however, its discretion is not unlimited, and when the award is contrary to the manifest weight of the evidence, it is the duty of the reviewing court to reverse that decision. In re Bush, 170 Ill. App. 3d 523, 121 Ill. Dec. 357, 525 N.E.2d 163 (2 Dist. 1988).

In cases involving custody, a strong and compelling presumption exists in favor of the result reached by the trial court. Hollo v. Hollo, 131 Ill. App. 3d 119, 85 Ill. Dec. 867, 474 N.E.2d 827 (5 Dist. 1985).

Only where the custody award is contrary to the manifest weight of the evidence will it be reversed. In re Yakin, 107 Ill. App. 3d 1103, 62 Ill. Dec. 547, 436 N.E.2d 573 (1 Dist. 1982).

Although the original custody judgment had resulted from an agreement of the parties and the trial court had not heard evidence concerning the child's best interest, the reviewing court would not hear all the evidence de novo when one party subsequently petitioned for modification. In re Gargus, 97 Ill. App. 3d 598, 53 Ill. Dec. 1, 423 N.E.2d 193 (1 Dist. 1981).

As the trial court is in a superior position to determine the best interests, that determination will not be disturbed on review unless it is clearly against the manifest weight of the evidence or represents an abuse of discretion. Kjellesvik v. Shannon, 41 Ill. App. 3d 674, 355 N.E.2d 120 (3 Dist. 1976); In re Piccirilli, 88 Ill. App. 3d 621, 43 Ill. Dec. 953, 410 N.E.2d 1086 (1 Dist. 1980); Lloyd v. Lloyd, 92 Ill. App. 3d 124, 47 Ill. Dec. 792, 415 N.E.2d 1105 (1 Dist. 1980); In re Milovich, 105 Ill. App. 3d 596, 61 Ill. Dec. 456, 434 N.E.2d 811 (1 Dist. 1982); In re Krause, 111 Ill. App. 3d 604, 67 Ill. Dec. 408, 444 N.E.2d 644 (1 Dist. 1982); Cooper v. Cooper, 146 Ill. App. 3d 943, 100 Ill. Dec. 627, 497 N.E.2d 805 (5 Dist. 1986); In re Williams, 205 Ill. App. 3d 613, 151 Ill. Dec. 89, 563 N.E.2d 1195 (3 Dist. 1990).

Stipulated Awards

Child custody awards stipulated by the parents may be granted by the court under this section. In re Ayers, 82 Ill. App. 3d 164, 37 Ill. Dec. 511, 402 N.E.2d 401 (3 Dist. 1980).

Substance Abuse

Where the custodial parent's involvement with alcohol resulted in numerous incidents which were viewed by third parties, was serious enough to impair her ability to function as a physician and endangered the life of her son, the trial court's decision to transfer custody to the father was not contrary to the manifest weight of the evidence. In re Neeld, 96 Ill. App. 3d 40, 51 Ill. Dec. 522, 420 N.E.2d 1080 (5 Dist. 1981).

It would be error for the trial court to exclude evidence of petitioner's alleged alcohol and drug abuse, particularly with regard to the impact such activity would have upon the children, if the custodial parent's consumption of alcohol and drugs can be shown to affect that parent's mental or physical health and that parent's relationship with the children. In re Rizzo, 95 Ill. App. 3d 636, 51 Ill. Dec. 141, 420 N.E.2d 555 (1 Dist. 1981).

Temporary Custody

—Prejudicial Effect

A court may consider the period of time that a child has spent with a parent by virtue of a temporary custody order but there is no presumption in favor of the existing custodian under this section as there is in modification cases under 750 ILCS 5/610. In re Hefer, 282 Ill. App. 3d 73, 217 Ill. Dec. 701, 667 N.E.2d 1094 (4 Dist. 1996).

Tender Years Doctrine

—Applied

Implicit in the court's decision was the fact that the two children of the parties were of tender years, (10 years old, and 8 years and 9 months, at the time of the hearing), and that the maternal affection was better adapted to the care of the children. People ex rel. Morris v. Morris, 44 Ill. 2d 66, 254 N.E.2d 478 (1969).

While there will undoubtedly be unusual situations when the best interests of a young child dictate that custody be awarded to the father, under the facts award of custody of six-year-old boy to mother would be upheld. People ex rel. Bukovich v. Bukovich, 39 Ill. 2d 76, 233 N.E.2d 382 (1968).

Custody in the mother is preferred where small children, particularly daughters, are concerned, everything else being equal. Strouse v. Strouse, 75 Ill. App. 2d 362, 220 N.E.2d 485 (4 Dist. 1966).

New conditions must arise to warrant change in circumstances and it is usual in custody cases, due to the tender years of the child and in consideration of its best interest, to entrust the care and custody to the mother, if a fit person. Each case stands on its own facts. Szczawinski v. Szczawinski, 37 Ill. App. 2d 350, 185 N.E.2d 375 (1 Dist. 1962).

For a case decided under the presumption of the Tender Years Doctrine, see Dunning v. Dunning, 14 Ill. App. 2d 242, 144 N.E.2d 535 (2 Dist. 1957); Bulandr v. Bulandr, 23 Ill. App. 2d 299, 162 N.E.2d 585 (1 Dist. 1959); Leary v. Leary, 61 Ill. App. 2d 152, 209 N.E.2d 663 (5 Dist. 1965); Hahn v. Hahn, 69 Ill. App. 2d 302, 216 N.E.2d 229 (2 Dist. 1966); Frees v. Frees, 99 Ill. App. 2d 213, 240 N.E.2d 274 (1 Dist. 1968).

It is usual in cases of custody of minor children to take into account the tender years of the child and in consideration of its best interests, to entrust its care and custody to the mother, she being a fit and proper person to rear the child. Nye v. Nye, 411 Ill. 408, 105 N.E.2d 300 (1952).

Maternal affection, being more active, is better adapted to the care of a young child, especially in the case of a minor daughter, where the care and guidance of a mother's hand is doubly important; compelling evidence must be presented proving a mother to be an unfit person, to cause the custody of her minor daughter to be denied her, or there must be a positive showing that to deny custody to the mother would be for the best interests of the child. Nye v. Nye, 411 Ill. 408, 105 N.E.2d 300 (1952).

—Not Applied

Although the "tender years doctrine", a presumption favoring the mother, has been abrogated in this state, the importance of maintaining stability and continuity in a young child's environment has been repeatedly emphasized. Hall v. Hall, 226 Ill. App. 3d 686, 168 Ill. Dec. 153, 589 N.E.2d 553 (3 Dist. 1991), cert. denied, 146 Ill. 2d 627, 176 Ill. Dec. 797, 602 N.E.2d 451 (1992).

Where there was evidence of the many times the mother left the children overnight and for extensive periods, that she resorted to intoxicants when real or imagined problems arose, and that she had a distaste and dislike for the confusing duties of a wife and mother to the point of running away from these duties on many occasions, the best interests of the children were served by granting custody of them to the father. Wachowski v. Wachowski, 86 Ill. App. 2d 145, 229 N.E.2d 149 (2 Dist. 1967).

—Not Inflexible

There is today no inflexible rule which requires that custody of children, especially of tender age, be vested in the mother. Marcus v. Marcus, 24 Ill. App. 3d 401, 320 N.E.2d 581 (1 Dist. 1974).

While it is usual to place small children in the care of their mother, this is not an inflexible rule, since the welfare of the child is the prime consideration. Wachowski v. Wachowski, 86 Ill. App. 2d 145, 229 N.E.2d 149 (2 Dist. 1967).

For a case which states the tender years doctrine is not inflexible, see Wolfrum v. Wolfrum, 5 Ill. App. 2d 471, 126 N.E.2d 34 (3 Dist. 1955).

—Presumption

For a case decided under the presumption of the tender years doctrine, see King v. Vancil, 34 Ill. App. 3d 831, 341 N.E.2d 65 (5 Dist. 1975); Strand v. Strand, 41 Ill. App. 3d 651, 355 N.E.2d 47 (2 Dist. 1976); Gren v. Gren, 59 Ill. App. 3d 624, 16 Ill. Dec. 892, 375 N.E.2d 999 (2 Dist. 1978); Jines v. Jines, 63 Ill. App. 3d 564, 20 Ill. Dec. 462, 380 N.E.2d 440 (5 Dist. 1978); In re Farris, 69 Ill. App. 3d 1042, 26 Ill. Dec. 608, 388 N.E.2d 232 (4 Dist. 1979); In re Mangan, 182 Ill. App. 3d 140, 130 Ill. Dec. 631, 537 N.E.2d 960 (1 Dist. 1989).

Tender Years Doctrine (Cont'd)

—Validity

The tender year doctrine, which recognizes that where all things are equal the best interest of a young child of tender years requires the care and custody of the mother, is no longer universally accepted. Melear v. Melear, 76 Ill. App. 3d 706, 32 Ill. Dec. 261, 395 N.E.2d 208 (3 Dist. 1979).

The fact that a mother is fit, standing by itself, does not authorize a denial of custody to the father, when this appears necessary because of other considerations. Marcus v. Marcus, 24 Ill. App. 3d 401, 320 N.E.2d 581 (1 Dist. 1974).

While giving custody to the mother may be the usual result of a custody hearing, there is no rule in Illinois that unless she is shown to be unfit, custody should be given to the mother. Anagnostopoulos v. Anagnostopoulos, 22 Ill. App. 3d 479, 317 N.E.2d 681 (1 Dist. 1974).

In Illinois there is no arbitrary rule that unless there is evidence that a mother is unfit, she should have the custody of young children. Carlson v. Carlson, 80 Ill. App. 2d 251, 225 N.E.2d 130 (1 Dist. 1967).

For a case discussing the validity of the tender years doctrine, see Stafford v. Stafford, 299 Ill. 438, 132 N.E. 452 (1921); Frees v. Frees, 99 Ill. App. 2d 213, 240 N.E.2d 274 (1 Dist. 1968); Akin v. Akin, 109 Ill. App. 2d 150, 248 N.E.2d 829 (5 Dist. 1969); Pratt v. Pratt, 29 Ill. App. 3d 214, 330 N.E.2d 244 (4 Dist. 1975); People ex rel. Irby v. Dubois, 41 Ill. App. 3d 609, 354 N.E.2d 562 (1 Dist. 1976); Strand v. Strand, 41 Ill. App. 3d 651, 355 N.E.2d 47 (2 Dist. 1976); Jines v. Jines, 63 Ill. App. 3d 564, 20 Ill. Dec. 462, 380 N.E.2d 440 (5 Dist. 1978); De Franco v. De Franco, 67 Ill. App. 3d 760, 24 Ill. Dec. 130, 384 N.E.2d 997 (1 Dist. 1978); In re Sieck, 78 Ill. App. 3d 204, 33 Ill. Dec. 490, 396 N.E.2d 1214 (1 Dist. 1979); In re Ramer, 84 Ill. App. 3d 213, 39 Ill. Dec. 648, 405 N.E.2d 401 (5 Dist. 1980); In re Lovejoy, 84 Ill. App. 3d 53, 39 Ill. Dec. 501, 404 N.E.2d 1092 (3 Dist. 1980); In re Kennedy, 94 Ill. App. 3d 537, 49 Ill. Dec. 927, 418 N.E.2d 947 (1 Dist. 1981); In re Rizzo, 95 Ill. App. 3d 636, 51 Ill. Dec. 141, 420 N.E.2d 555 (1 Dist. 1981); In re Stevens, 183 Ill. App. 3d 160, 131 Ill. Dec. 723, 538 N.E.2d 1279 (5 Dist. 1989).

Unmarried Parents

Regardless of whether the parents have ever been married, the statutory factors listed in this section are relevant in determining a child's custody. Hall v. Hall, 226 Ill. App. 3d 686, 168 Ill. Dec. 153, 589 N.E.2d 553 (3 Dist. 1991), cert. denied, 146 Ill. 2d 627, 176 Ill. Dec. 797, 602 N.E.2d 451 (1992).

In the application of the best interest of the child test to a custody dispute between unmarried parents, there is no longer a presumption in favor of either parent. Giagnoni v. Bourey, 127 Ill. App. 3d 530, 82 Ill. Dec. 852, 469 N.E.2d 386 (2 Dist. 1984).

Visitation

Modification of a visitation order was permitted when the modification would be in the child's best interests, and thus, the trial court should have considered the best interest determination factors set forth in 750 ILCS 5/602 before deciding whether the mother's petition to modify visitation to allow the mother and child to move to Florida should have been granted. DeBilio v. Rodgers, 337 Ill. App. 3d 614, 272 Ill. Dec. 9, 786 N.E.2d 548, 2002 Ill. App. LEXIS 947 (3 Dist. 2002).

The fact that respondent had moved to this state, that she would not allow the children to visit another state, that the children's father was confined to a wheelchair, that grandmother was able to travel to this state to visit her grandchildren with their father only at tremendous inconvenience due to her age and her husband's inability to accompany her, all established the inadequacy of visitation under a previous judgment. Lyons v. Lyons, 228 Ill. App. 3d 407, 169 Ill. Dec. 502, 591 N.E.2d 1006 (5 Dist. 1992).

A petition seeking visitation with a child who has been moved from one county to another is not an appropriate issue to be raised or decided on a motion to dismiss, and may properly be resolved by a hearing to determine what is in the child's best interest. Padin v. Padin, 193 Ill. App. 3d 554, 140 Ill. Dec. 640, 550 N.E.2d 276 (3 Dist.), cert. denied, 132 Ill. 2d 547, 144 Ill. Dec. 259, 555 N.E.2d 378 (1990).

Evidence of failure to visit is insufficient, of itself, to support a finding of unfitness. Chick v. Massey, 35 Ill. App. 3d 518, 341 N.E.2d 405 (4 Dist. 1976).

For a case discussing custody and visitation, see Lawyer v. Lawyer, 19 Ill. App. 3d 571, 312 N.E.2d 7 (2 Dist. 1974).

When visitation rights are substantially decreased, it is such a change of condition that it does not, ipso facto, establish a base for a change in custody. Johnson v. Johnson, 105 Ill. App. 2d 399, 245 N.E.2d 580 (1 Dist. 1969).

A grant of visitation rights of necessity involves a grant of "control" over a minor child. De Phillips v. De Phillips, 35 Ill. 2d 154, 219 N.E.2d 465 (1966).

A decree denying the right of visitation was temporary in character, and to alleviate a condition which had been contrary to the best interests of the children, and was designed to impress upon both of the parents that any visitation rights must be consistent with the best interests of the children at all times; therefore, the decree was not contrary to the best interests of the children. Malone v. Malone, 5 Ill. App. 2d 425, 126 N.E.2d 505 (4 Dist. 1955).

Where the parties continually and repeatedly sought relief from the courts in connection with the custody of the minor children, brought the children into court on numerous occasions and conducted themselves in a manner which was contrary to the best interests of the minor children, it was in the best interests of all the minor children that each of the parents did not have visitation periods with the child or children awarded to the other until the further order of the court. Malone v. Malone, 5 Ill. App. 2d 425, 126 N.E.2d 505 (4 Dist. 1955).

In the absence of a constitutionally valid grandparent visitation statute, a noncustodial parent's request that visitation be modified to permit grandparent visitation in lieu of the parent's visitation while the parent was on active military duty was governed by Illinois common law, which allowed such modifications under special circumstances, including military duty; therefore, the trial court had subject matter jurisdiction over the parent's modification petition and should have conducted a best interests proceeding. In re Marriage of Sullivan, 342 Ill. App. 3d 560, 277 Ill. Dec. 25, 795 N.E.2d 392, 2003 Ill. App. LEXIS 1012 (2 Dist. 2003).

Witnesses

—Children

Court's ruling denying counsel's attempt to question children in open court as to a specific preference for one parent over the other was not error. Wurm v. Howard, 82 Ill. App. 3d 116, 37 Ill. Dec. 517, 402 N.E.2d 407 (3 Dist. 1980).

If competent as a witness in other respects, the child may testify to his custodial preferences in a custody proceeding. In re Combs, 78 Ill. App. 3d 533, 33 Ill. Dec. 922, 397 N.E.2d 255 (5 Dist. 1979).

In determining whether a child should testify at a custody proceeding, the trial court should take great pains to conduct an in camera conference with the child to determine the competency of the child, as well as the competency of any evidence which the child might present and then determine whether the best interests of the child would be served by permitting her to testify or be sheltered from testifying and being subjected to vigorous cross-examination, and a report of the essential material matters developed at the in camera conference should be made of record by the trial court and the court should state the reasons for allowing or disallowing the testimony of the child, and also note the factual information which the court developed from the conference with the child which would be considered by the court in its ultimate determinations in the case. Crownover v. Crownover, 33 Ill. App. 3d 327, 337 N.E.2d 56 (3 Dist. 1975).

The trial court's refusal to hear a six-year old child as a witness in a custody hearing was neither prejudicial or an abuse of discretion in view of the age of the child. Osman v. Osman, 130 Ill. App. 2d 830, 264 N.E.2d 263 (5 Dist. 1970).

—Cross-Examination

Where no new evidence was elicited from either witnesses on redirect examination and recross-examination of witnesses would simply have covered areas addressed and answered in direct, cross and redirect examination, the trial court did not abuse its discretion in precluding father from recross-examining witnesses in custody dispute. In re Felson, 171 Ill. App. 3d 923, 121 Ill. Dec. 796, 525 N.E.2d 1103 (1 Dist. 1988).

—Experts

Even assuming that the witness was an expert, however, the trial

Witnesses (Cont'd)

—Experts (Cont'd)
court clearly would not be bound by her opinion because custody is a judicial determination. In re Milovich, 105 Ill. App. 3d 596, 61 Ill. Dec. 456, 434 N.E.2d 811 (1 Dist. 1982).

There was no error with respect to the exclusion of a psychologist from respondent's witness list, where the record indicated that the mother sought to add the doctor as a witness long after discovery was closed, trial was underway, and ten witnesses had already testified, the attorneys for petitioner and the children objected to the witness, partly on the basis of surprise and their lack of time to depose the witness, and respondent did not offer reasons why the witness had not been available earlier, nor did she explain why it was necessary to belatedly call in another psychologist after apparently deciding not to submit testimony from the court appointed psychologist. In re Milovich, 105 Ill. App. 3d 596, 61 Ill. Dec. 456, 434 N.E.2d 811 (1 Dist. 1982).

—Testimony of Doctor
That the children's pediatrician may have disagreed with the court appointed psychiatrist did not in and of itself render the trial court's award of custody to the mother an abuse of discretion. In re Ford, 91 Ill. App. 3d 1066, 47 Ill. Dec. 541, 415 N.E.2d 546 (1 Dist. 1980).

LEGAL PERIODICALS

For article, "Baby Richard and Beyond: The Future for Adopted Children", see 18 N. Ill. U.L. Rev. 445 (1999).

For article, "Conference on Ethical Issues in the Legal Representation of Children in Illinois: Reconsidering the Need for Counsel for Children in Custody, Visitation and Child Protection Proceedings", see 29 Loy. U. Chi. L.J. 299 (1998).

For comment, "Paternity Actions in Illinois: Why Not Consider What is in the Best Interest of the Child?," see 21 S. Ill. U.L.J. 613 (1997).

For article, "The Potential Impact of Homosexual Parenting on Children," see 1997 U. Ill. L. Rev. 833.

For article, "Child Custody in a Changing World: A Study of Postdivorce Arrangements," see 1997 U. Ill. L. Rev. 773.

For note, "Best Interest of the Child: The Case for Joint Custody Even in Contested Divorce," 84 Ill. B.J. 348 (1996).

For article, "Child Custody: Assessing Your Client's Case, see 9 CBA Rec. 44 (1995).

For article "Judicial Discretion in Child Custody: The Wisdom of Solomon?" see 81 Ill. B.J. 650 (1993).

For article, "Out of the Mouths of Babes: Determination of Child Custodial Preference in Illinois," see 23 Loy. U. Chi. L.J. 383 (1991-92).

For article, "The Need to Consider Children's Rights in Biological Parent v. Third Party Custody Disputes," see 67 Chi.-Kent L. Rev. 1077 (1991).

For article, "Family Law: 1988-89 Illinois Law Survey," see 21 Loy. U. Chi. L.J. 417 (1989-90).

For article, "Family Law: 1987-88 Illinois Law Survey," see Loy. U. Chi. L.J. 461 (1988-89).

For article, "Illinois Child Custody Law: An Overview," see 76 Ill. B.J. 732 (1987).

For article, "Divorce Illinois Style: Ten Years Under the Marriage and Dissolution of Marriage Act," see 75 Ill. B.J. 606 (1987).

For article, "Family Law: 1986-87 Illinois Law Survey," see 19 Loy. U. Chi. L.J. 489 (1987-88).

For article, "An Interpretation of Illinois New Joint Custody Amendments," see 75 Ill. B.J. 332 (1986).

For note, "Judicial Treatment of Parental Cohabitation after Jarrett v. Jarrett," see 15 Loy. U. Chi. L.J. 337 (1983-84).

For case note, "In re Custody of Christy Elizabeth Townsend, 413 N.E.2d 428 (1980): Applying the 'Best Interests' Doctrine to Custody Disputes Between a Biological Parent and a Third Party," see 15 J. Marshall L. Rev. 213 (1982).

For article, "The Ambiguous Role of the Lawyer Representing the Minor in Domestic Relations Litigation," see 70 Ill. B.J. 510 (1982).

For article, "The Folly of Joint Custody," see 69 Ill. B.J. 412 (1981).

For note, "Child Custody: Parental Cohabitational Relationships and the Best Interest of the Child Standard — Jarrett v. Jarrett," see 29 De Paul L. Rev. 1141 (1980).

For comment, "Modifying Child Custody Awards: A Substantial Change Under the Illinois Marriage and Dissolution of Marriage Act," see 1980 S. Ill U. L.J. 439.

For note, "Best Interest of the Child in Custody Proceedings and Waiver of Jurisdictional Objection — Sommer v. Bororis," see 27 De Paul L. Rev. 853 (1978).

RESEARCH REFERENCES

Parent's physical disability or handicap as factor in custody award or proceedings. 3 ALR4th 1044.

Propriety of awarding custody of child to parent residing or intending to reside in foreign country. 20 ALR4th 677.

Effect of remarriage of spouses to each other on child custody and support provisions of prior divorce decree. 26 ALR4th 325.

Continuity of residence as factor in contest between parent and non-parent for custody of child who has been residing with non-parent — modern status. 15 ALR5th 692.

Parent's use of drugs as factor in award of custody of children, visitation rights, or termination of parental rights. 20 ALR5th 534.

Age of parent as factor in awarding custody. 34 ALR5th 57.

Smoking as factor in child custody and visitation cases. 36 ALR5th 377.

Rights and remedies of parents inter se with respect to the names of their children. 40 ALR5th 697.

Construction and effect of statutes mandating consideration of, or creating presumptions regarding, domestic violence in awarding custody of children. 51 ALR5th 241.

Mental health of contesting parent as factor in award of child custody. 53 ALR5th 375.

Initial award or denial of child custody to homosexual or lesbian parent. 62 ALR5th 591.

Custodial parent's homosexual or lesbian relationship with third person as justifying modification of child custody order. 65 ALR5th 591.

Custodial parent's relocation as grounds for change of custody. 70 ALR5th 377.

Child custody and visitation rights arising from same-sex relationship. 80 ALR5th 1.

Religion as factor in child custody cases. 124 ALR5th 203.

750 ILCS 5/602.1 [Parental powers, rights and responsibilities; joint custody; access to child's records]

Sec. 602.1. (a) The dissolution of marriage, the declaration of invalidity of marriage, the legal separation of the parents, or the parents living separate and apart shall not diminish parental powers, rights, and responsibilities except as the court for good reason may determine under the standards of Section 602 [750 ILCS 5/602].

(b) Upon the application of either or both parents, or upon its own motion, the court shall consider an award of joint custody. Joint custody means custody determined pursuant to a Joint Parenting Agreement or a Joint Parenting Order. In such cases, the court shall initially request the parents to produce a Joint Parenting Agreement. Such Agreement shall specify each parent's powers, rights and responsibilities for the personal care of the child and for major decisions such as education, health care, and religious training. The Agreement shall further specify a procedure by which proposed changes, disputes and alleged breaches may be mediated or otherwise resolved and shall provide for a periodic review of its terms by the parents. In producing a Joint Parenting Agreement, the parents shall be flexible in arriving at resolutions which further the policy of this State as expressed in Sections 102 and 602 [750 ILCS 5/102 and 750 ILCS 5/602]. For the purpose of assisting the court in making a determination whether an award of joint custody is appropriate, the court may order mediation and may direct that an investigation be conducted pursuant to the provisions of Section 605 [750 ILCS 5/605]. In the event the parents fail to produce a Joint Parenting Agreement, the court may enter an appropriate Joint Parenting Order under the standards of Section 602 [750 ILCS 5/602] which shall specify and contain the same elements as a Joint Parenting Agreement, or it may award sole custody under the standards of Sections 602, 607, and 608 [750 ILCS 5/602, 750 ILCS 5/607, and 750 ILCS 5/608].

(c) The court may enter an order of joint custody if it determines that joint custody would be in the best interests of the child, taking into account the following:

(1) the ability of the parents to cooperate effectively and consistently in matters that directly affect the joint parenting of the child. "Ability of the parents to cooperate" means the parents' capacity to substantially comply with a Joint Parenting Order. The court shall not consider the inability of the parents to cooperate effectively and consistently in matters that do not directly affect the joint parenting of the child;

(2) The residential circumstances of each parent; and

(3) all other factors which may be relevant to the best interest of the child.

(d) Nothing within this section shall imply or presume that joint custody shall necessarily mean equal parenting time. The physical residence of the child in joint custodial situations shall be determined by:

(1) express agreement of the parties; or

(2) order of the court under the standards of this Section.

(e) Notwithstanding any other provision of law, access to records and information pertaining to a child, including but not limited to medical, dental, child care and school records, shall not be denied to a parent for the reason that such parent is not the child's custodial parent; however, no parent shall have access to the school records of a child if the parent is prohibited by an order of protection from inspecting or obtaining such records pursuant to the Illinois Domestic Violence Act of 1986, as now or hereafter amended [750 ILCS 60/101 et seq.].

(Source: P.A. 86-966; 88-409, § 1.)

Note.

This section was Ill.Rev.Stat., Ch. 40, para. 602.1.

CASE NOTES

ANALYSIS

Best Interests of Child
Custody
—Award Improper
—Award Upheld
—Effect on Homestead
Default Judgment
—Delay in Seeking Relief
Exclusive Custody
Joint Custody
—Arrangements Improper
—Award
—Court Order
—Definition
—Parental Cooperation
Joint Custody Agreement
Legislative Intent
Modification
—Agreement
Order
—Improper
Removal
Summary Termination
Support Modification
Testimony Required
Trust

Best Interests of Child

In determining custody, the trial court must assess what is in the "best interest" of the child, and in doing so, must consider all relevant factors. In re Marcello, 247 Ill. App. 3d 304, 187 Ill. Dec. 81, 617 N.E.2d 289 (1 Dist. 1993).

Where a change in custody did not appear to be a real change from the arrangement that was in effect before the order, the mother's rights were not prejudiced by the lack of a hearing on whether the change was in the child's best interests. In re Clarke, 194 Ill. App. 3d 248, 141 Ill. Dec. 174, 550 N.E.2d 1220 (1 Dist. 1990).

This section provides that upon agreement of the parties, the court may award joint custody if it determines joint custody to be in the best interest of the child. In re Hanson, 112 Ill. App. 3d 564, 68 Ill. Dec. 268, 445 N.E.2d 912 (5 Dist. 1983).

Custody

—Award Improper

Trial court's award of custody to husband was against the manifest weight of the evidence where the evidence established at trial regarding custody indicated that wife should be awarded custody. In re Drummond, 156 Ill. App. 3d 672, 109 Ill. Dec. 46, 509 N.E.2d 707 (4 Dist. 1987).

Where both parents sought absolute custody of both children throughout the entire trial, and there was testimony regarding noncooperation and discord during the period of separation and trial, the trial court abused its discretion in making a joint custodial award. In re Pool, 118 Ill. App. 3d 1035, 74 Ill. Dec. 458, 455 N.E.2d 887 (3 Dist. 1983), overruled on other grounds, In re Wycoff, 266 Ill. App. 3d 408 203 Ill. Dec. 338, 639 N.E.2d 897 (4 Dist. 1994).

Where parents disagreed as to who should have custody of daughter, but agreed that custody should be in only one parent, the trial court erred in not granting custody of daughter to only one parent; therefore, the provision of the order awarding custody to the parents jointly was reversed. Imes v. Imes, 52 Ill. App. 3d 792, 10 Ill. Dec. 466, 367 N.E.2d 1075 (3 Dist. 1977).

—Award Upheld

Trial court determination that joint custody would not be in the best interests of the children, in large part, because the husband resided far from his children, was not against the manifest weight of the evidence or an abuse of discretion. In re Hahin, 266 Ill. App. 3d 168, 205 Ill. Dec. 788, 644 N.E.2d 4 (2 Dist. 1994).

While the parties shared custody, the judgment for dissolution gave mother the primary physical custody of son and thus, the trial court properly could have considered this factor in maintaining the primary physical custody of son with mother. In re Kartholl, 143 Ill. App. 3d 228, 97 Ill. Dec. 347, 492 N.E.2d 1006 (2 Dist. 1986).

—Effect on Homestead

A decree awarding the care, custody, and education of children to their mother, and her taking the children to live with her away from

Custody (Cont'd)

—Effect on Homestead (Cont'd)
the premises, did not mean that the children lost or forfeited the homestead estate therein; by the divorce proceeding and decree thereunder, the children were not given a new or separate home. Walker v. Walker, 181 Ill. 260, 54 N.E. 956 (1899).

Default Judgment

—Delay in Seeking Relief
Although respondent could have obtained relief from the default judgment in dissolution of marriage proceeding had she diligently pursued a hearing on her motion to vacate, where she sat on her rights for 18 months before filing a notice of hearing, she simply waited too long to pursue relief and offered no satisfactory explanation for her delay nor any reason why the trial court erred in enforcing the rule against her. In re Jackson, 259 Ill. App. 3d 538, 197 Ill. Dec. 626, 631 N.E.2d 848 (4 Dist. 1994).

Exclusive Custody
A parent is entitled to the exclusive care and custody of his own child unless he has forfeited that right by some act of his own or unless he is deemed a person unfit to have the care and custody of the child. Bush v. Bush, 342 Ill. App. 86, 95 N.E.2d 121 (3 Dist. 1950).

Joint Custody

—Arrangements Improper
Joint parenting order that established a schedule whereby boys would move between parents twice each month was not in the children's best interest. In re Swanson, 275 Ill. App. 3d 519, 212 Ill. Dec. 62, 656 N.E.2d 215 (4 Dist. 1995), appeal denied, 165 Ill. 2d 566, 214 Ill. Dec. 866, 662 N.E.2d 432 (1996).

The decision to order joint custody was not necessarily erroneous but the decision to have the children live with one parent one week and another the next week was error; no testimony concerning the workability of such a program was presented; the constant shifting would obviously be detrimental to the minor children, who were seven, five, and three years of age at the time of the decree, moreover, each home would have to make arrangements and undergo many of the same expenses that would arise if the children were there on a permanent basis. In re Hacker, 239 Ill. App. 3d 658, 179 Ill. Dec. 816, 606 N.E.2d 648 (4 Dist. 1992), appeal denied, 151 Ill. 2d 563, 186 Ill. Dec. 380, 616 N.E.2d 333 (1993).

—Award
Either party can move for an award of joint custody, or the court can make the award on its own motion. In re Marcello, 247 Ill. App. 3d 304, 187 Ill. Dec. 81, 617 N.E.2d 289 (1 Dist. 1993); In re Bush, 191 Ill. App. 3d 249, 138 Ill. Dec. 423, 547 N.E.2d 590 (4 Dist. 1989).

—Court Order
In no instance should the court enter a joint-custody order when the respondent is in default. In re Jackson, 259 Ill. App. 3d 538, 197 Ill. Dec. 626, 631 N.E.2d 848 (4 Dist. 1994).

—Definition
An oxymoron, "joint custody" is a term that is so susceptible to varying meanings that it defies definition. In re Pool, 118 Ill. App. 3d 1035, 74 Ill. Dec. 458, 455 N.E.2d 887 (3 Dist. 1983), overruled on other grounds, In re Wycoff, 266 Ill. App. 3d 408 203 Ill. Dec. 338, 639 N.E.2d 897 (4 Dist. 1994).

—Parental Cooperation
Court would modify trial court's order which made husband who had joint custody responsible for decisions affecting his daughter's schooling and wife who had joint custody and primary physical custody responsible for decisions affecting her daughter's religious development, and would order that husband and wife share decision-making authority on schooling and religion. Seitzinger v. Seitzinger, 333 Ill. App. 3d 103, 266 Ill. Dec. 720, 775 N.E.2d 282, 2002 Ill. App. LEXIS 763 (4 Dist. 2002).

Parties did not demonstrate an "unusual ability to cooperate", where 1) mother did not want joint custody and; 2) the parties participated in mediation several times and established some guidelines for raising the children at their first mediation sessions but subsequent mediation proved ineffective. In re Swanson, 275 Ill. App. 3d 519, 212 Ill. Dec. 62, 656 N.E.2d 215 (4 Dist. 1995), appeal denied, 165 Ill. 2d 566, 214 Ill. Dec. 866, 662 N.E.2d 432 (1996).

The trial court did not abuse its discretion in denying joint custody where, although husband testified that he was able to cooperate with wife, she contradicted this testimony and presented evidence that husband was quick-tempered, violent, depressive, and "cooperated" only when he got his way. In re McCoy, 272 Ill. App. 3d 125, 208 Ill. Dec. 732, 650 N.E.2d 3 (4 Dist. 1995).

Joint custody orders are appropriate only where both parents have displayed an unusual capacity to cooperate; where the record clearly supported the court's determination that the parties were unable to cooperate, the trial court did not abuse its discretion when it declined to order joint custody. In re Heinze, 257 Ill. App. 3d 782, 197 Ill. Dec. 506, 631 N.E.2d 728 (3 Dist. 1994).

The statutory prerequisites of this section evidence an intent that joint custody only be awarded where circumstances indicate that the parents are willing to cooperate in the upbringing of their children. In re Marcello, 247 Ill. App. 3d 304, 187 Ill. Dec. 81, 617 N.E.2d 289 (1 Dist. 1993).

Joint Custody Agreement
Because a trial court is authorized to enter a joint parenting order on its own motion, if the parties fail to produce one, the court may also modify the parties' proposed joint parenting agreement if it fails to protect the best interest of the children. In re Duffy, 307 Ill. App. 3d 257, 240 Ill. Dec. 805, 718 N.E.2d 286 (2 Dist. 1999).

Where the parties were unable to produce a joint parenting agreement, the trial court should have prepared and executed a joint parenting order; remand to trial court for further proceedings was necessary. McCoy v McCoy, 225 Ill. App. 3d 966, 168 Ill. Dec. 27, 589 N.E.2d 141 (3 Dist. 1992).

The parents are to determine the terms of the agreement, which specifies each parent's powers, rights, and responsibilities for the care of the child and for major decisions such as education, health care, and religious training. In re Bush, 191 Ill. App. 3d 249, 138 Ill. Dec. 423, 547 N.E.2d 590 (4 Dist. 1989).

Custody is determined pursuant to the terms of a joint parenting agreement or order. In re Bush, 191 Ill. App. 3d 249, 138 Ill. Dec. 423, 547 N.E.2d 590 (4 Dist. 1989).

Legislative Intent
The effect of this section is to create a legislative presumption in favor of the present custodial arrangement, thereby promoting the stability and continuity of the child's custodial and environmental relationship which should not be lightly overturned. In re Burke, 185 Ill. App. 3d 253, 133 Ill. Dec. 408, 541 N.E.2d 245 (2 Dist. 1989).

Statutory prerequisites evidence an intent that joint custody should only be awarded where circumstances indicate that the parents are willing to cooperate in the upbringing of their children. In re Drummond, 156 Ill. App. 3d 672, 109 Ill. Dec. 46, 509 N.E.2d 707 (4 Dist. 1987).

The legislature has seen fit to amend this Act to make joint custody awards appropriate only where it is in the best interest of the child and both parties agree to the arrangement. In re Pool, 118 Ill. App. 3d 1035, 74 Ill. Dec. 458, 455 N.E.2d 887 (3 Dist. 1983), overruled on other grounds, In re Wycoff, 266 Ill. App. 3d 408 203 Ill. Dec. 338, 639 N.E.2d 897 (4 Dist. 1994).

Modification

—Agreement
Father's request for modification of joint custody award was governed by this section where the parties agreed in writing in their judgment for dissolution that the court would be bound by the statute in force at the time any request was made for modification of the joint custody award. In re Kartholl, 143 Ill. App. 3d 228, 97 Ill. Dec. 347, 492 N.E.2d 1006 (2 Dist. 1986).

Order

—Improper
Where the court did not specifically incorporate any type of "joint parenting agreement" or make any provisions for dispute resolution in the event of conflict, joint custody order was erroneously entered. In re Drummond, 156 Ill. App. 3d 672, 109 Ill. Dec. 46, 509 N.E.2d 707 (4 Dist. 1987).

Removal

The possibility that removal of a child from the jurisdiction of this state to another may adversely affect the noncustodial parent's interaction with the child does not compel the conclusion that a removal petition is, as a matter of law, a petition for modification of custody. Instead, the impact of removal upon the rights of the nonresidential custodial parent is a significant and important factor the trial court considers in its adjudication of whether removal would be in the child's best interests. In re Bednar, 146 Ill. App. 3d 704, 100 Ill. Dec. 84, 496 N.E.2d 1149 (1 Dist. 1986).

Summary Termination

Since the joint custody provisions found in this section expressly grant the trial court broad discretion to impose joint custody in the best interests of the child even over the objections of the parties, the summary termination of joint custody upon the petition of parties who agree to such a termination is clearly in conflict with the intent and purposes of this section. In re Burke, 185 Ill. App. 3d 253, 133 Ill. Dec. 408, 541 N.E.2d 245 (2 Dist. 1989).

Support Modification

There is no provision allowing the parents or the court to include as part of a joint custody agreement or order any provision regarding child support or any modification of any child support award. In re Grabarek, 175 Ill. App. 3d 1045, 125 Ill. Dec. 522, 530 N.E.2d 680 (2 Dist. 1988).

Testimony Required

Where no testimony was presented relating to the custody of the children an award of joint custody was inappropriate. In re Birt, 157 Ill. App. 3d 363, 109 Ill. Dec. 363, 109 Ill. Dec. 691, 510 N.E.2d 559 (2 Dist. 1987).

Trust

Proceeds of a life insurance policy for the benefit of the children of decedent's first marriage could be placed in a trust for the children's benefit; such proceeds need not be directly paid to the children or their guardian. Downey v. Downey, 293 Ill. App. 3d 234, 227 Ill. Dec. 265, 687 N.E.2d 339 (4 Dist. 1997).

LEGAL PERIODICALS

For note, "Guardians Ad Litem: The Guardian Angels of Our Children in Domestic Violence Courts", see 30 Loy. U. Chi. L.J. 281 (1999).

For note, "Best Interest of the Child: The Case for Joint Custody Even in Contested Divorce," 84 Ill. B.J. 348 (1996).

For article, "Joint Custody in Illinois: From Panacea to Placebo," see 83 Ill. B.J. 178 (1995).

For article, "The Need to Consider Children's Rights in Biological Parent v. Third Party Custody Disputes," see 67 Chi.-Kent L. Rev. 1077 (1991).

For article, "Joint Child Custody—An Exception," see 64 Chi. B. Rec. 406 (1983).

RESEARCH REFERENCES

Parent's use of drugs as factor in award of custody of children, visitation rights, or termination of parental rights. 20 ALR5th 534.

Smoking as factor in child custody and visitation cases. 36 ALR5th 377.

Propriety of awarding joint custody of children. 17 ALR4th 1013.

750 ILCS 5/603 Temporary Orders

Sec. 603. *Temporary Orders.* (a) A party to a custody proceeding, including a proceeding to modify custody, may move for a temporary custody order. The court may award temporary custody under the standards of Section 602 [750 ILCS 5/602] and the standards and procedures of Section 602.1 [750 ILCS 5/602.1], after a hearing, or, if there is no objection, solely on the basis of the affidavits.

(b) If a proceeding for dissolution of marriage or legal separation or declaration of invalidity of marriage is dismissed, any temporary custody order is vacated unless a parent or the child's custodian moves that the proceeding continue as a custody proceeding and the court finds, after a hearing, that the circumstances of the parents and the best interest of the child requires that a custody judgment be issued.

(c) If a custody proceeding commenced in the absence of a petition for dissolution of marriage or legal separation, under either subparagraph (ii) of paragraph (1), or paragraph (2), of subsection (d) of Section 601 [750 ILCS 5/601], is dismissed, any temporary custody order is vacated.

(Source: P.A. 86-530; 87-1255, § 1.)

Note.

This section was Ill.Rev.Stat., Ch. 40, para. 603.

CASE NOTES

ANALYSIS

In General
Death of Party
Final Order
—Appeal
—Not Shown
—Shown
Maintaining Status Quo
Modification of Order
Presumption
Purpose
Scope of Review
Specific Findings
—Not Required
Visitation

In General

A temporary order by its very nature is provisional in character and continues only during the pendency of the action. In re Fields, 283 Ill. App. 3d 894, 219 Ill. Dec. 420, 671 N.E.2d 85 (4 Dist. 1996).

An order of child custody is temporary or final according to its substance and not its form. Levy v. Skilling, 136 Ill. App. 3d 727, 91 Ill. Dec. 431, 483 N.E.2d 917 (1 Dist. 1985).

Death of Party

Child custody proceedings are not jurisdictionally precluded by the absence or termination of dissolution proceedings, hence, the general principle that death of a party abates the divorce action should not be too hastily applied to child custody matters. Milenkovic v. Milenkovic, 93 Ill. App. 3d 204, 48 Ill. Dec. 618, 416 N.E.2d 1140 (1 Dist. 1981).

Final Order

Once the trial court enters the final order, an assumption arises that the court has thereby adjusted for any inequity in its temporary orders. In re Fields, 283 Ill. App. 3d 894, 219 Ill. Dec. 420, 671 N.E.2d 85 (4 Dist. 1996).

When the matter that is the subject of the temporary order comes before the court for a hearing on the merits, the temporary order has fulfilled its purpose and is superseded by the final, or permanent, order. In re Fields, 283 Ill. App. 3d 894, 219 Ill. Dec. 420, 671 N.E.2d 85 (4 Dist. 1996).

—Appeal

It was clear from the substance of a custody order that it was a final custody decision which could be modified only pursuant to the strict standards set forth in 750 ILCS 5/610, even though the order was not final for purposes of appeal. In re Goldman, 196 Ill. App. 3d 785, 143 Ill. Dec. 944, 554 N.E.2d 1016 (1 Dist.), cert. denied, 132 Ill. 2d 544, 144 Ill. Dec. 257, 555 N.E.2d 376 (1990).

Final Order (Cont'd)

—Appeal (Cont'd)

An order for the custody of a child, even though partial and temporary, is an appealable order. Schneeman v. Schneeman, 317 Ill. App. 286, 45 N.E.2d 1016 (1 Dist. 1942).

—Not Shown

The trial court should have applied this section involving temporary orders, to the facts where the court stated the order was temporary and there was never a final order. Levy v. Skilling, 136 Ill. App. 3d 727, 91 Ill. Dec. 431, 483 N.E.2d 917 (1 Dist. 1985).

—Shown

A custody decree which provided that husband should have custody of the child for one year at which time, "the question of custody of the minor child of the parties shall be re-examined by the court to ascertain if any change is necessary for the best interests of said child at said time" was a final order and appealable. Pratt v. Pratt, 29 Ill. App. 3d 214, 330 N.E.2d 244 (4 Dist. 1975).

Maintaining Status Quo

Court's order of temporary custody merely maintained the status quo of the parties until the permanent custody hearing was held. In re Hanson, 112 Ill. App. 3d 564, 68 Ill. Dec. 268, 445 N.E.2d 912 (5 Dist. 1983).

Modification of Order

Litigation that is neither a motion for temporary custody nor an initial custody determination, but rather a modification of the original custody order, is governed by the dictates of 750 ILCS 5/610 and not by this section. In re Strader, 101 Ill. App. 3d 779, 57 Ill. Dec. 232, 428 N.E.2d 912 (5 Dist. 1981).

A divorce decree that was modified to provide that the defendant have the sole custody of the minor children of the parties until one week after the close of school, and that plaintiff and defendant have temporary custody on alternate holidays, was continued, but where the judge died before the hearing, the order was temporary and a permanent change of custody was dependent upon a further hearing to be held on the continued date. Frees v. Frees, 99 Ill. App. 2d 213, 240 N.E.2d 274 (1 Dist. 1968).

Presumption

A court may consider the period of time that a child has spent with a parent by virtue of a temporary custody order but there is no presumption in favor of the existing custodian under 750 ILCS 5/602 as there is in modification cases under 750 ILCS 5/610. In re Hefer, 282 Ill. App. 3d 73, 217 Ill. Dec. 701, 667 N.E.2d 1094 (4 Dist. 1996).

Purpose

If the findings at a temporary hearing were binding at the final hearing, the purposes of this section would be defeated and the best interests of the children would not be served, parties would no longer be willing to have the trial court enter a temporary order based solely on affidavits or on evidence adduced during truncated hearings. In re Fields, 283 Ill. App. 3d 894, 219 Ill. Dec. 420, 671 N.E.2d 85 (4 Dist. 1996).

This section was implemented to 1) encourage informal and agreed determinations of temporary custody and visitation, 2) accelerate the process of awarding temporary custody and visitation through the use of affidavits, and 3) minimize disruptions in children's lives by providing stability in their living environment and relationships with their parents as quickly as possible. In re Fields, 283 Ill. App. 3d 894, 219 Ill. Dec. 420, 671 N.E.2d 85 (4 Dist. 1996).

Scope of Review

The appellate court may review orders enjoining the wife in a marriage dissolution from entering and residing in the marital home, having custody of and unsupervised visitation with her children. In re Lombaer, 200 Ill. App. 3d 712, 146 Ill. Dec. 425, 558 N.E.2d 388 (1 Dist. 1990).

Specific Findings

—Not Required

Subsection (a) of this section does not require specific findings to accompany a temporary custody order. Levy v. Skilling, 136 Ill. App. 3d 727, 91 Ill. Dec. 431, 483 N.E.2d 917 (1 Dist. 1985).

Visitation

Although this section refers only to a custody proceeding, visitation is a form of custody and is subject to the custody rules set forth in this Act. In re Fields, 283 Ill. App. 3d 894, 219 Ill. Dec. 420, 671 N.E.2d 85 (4 Dist. 1996).

The temporary order of visitation was based on a petition and was not to be regarded as res judicata of the issues raised by the pleadings; on a final hearing of the suit in chancery, all previously rendered interlocutory orders were before the court and were altered or vacated, as justice required. Smith v. Smith, 36 Ill. App. 2d 55, 183 N.E.2d 559 (1 Dist. 1962).

LEGAL PERIODICALS

For article, "An Interpretation of Illinois New Joint Custody Amendments," see 75 Ill. B. J. 332 (1986).

750 ILCS 5/604 Interviews

Sec. 604. *Interviews.* (a) The court may interview the child in chambers to ascertain the child's wishes as to his custodian and as to visitation. Counsel shall be present at the interview unless otherwise agreed upon by the parties. The court shall cause a court reporter to be present who shall make a complete record of the interview instantaneously to be part of the record in the case.

(b) The court may seek the advice of professional personnel, whether or not employed by the court on a regular basis. The advice given shall be in writing and made available by the court to counsel. Counsel may examine, as a witness, any professional personnel consulted by the court, designated as a court's witness.

(Source: P.A. 80-923.)

Note.

This section was Ill.Rev.Stat., Ch. 40, para. 604.

CASE NOTES

ANALYSIS

Absence of Transcript
—Prejudicial
Construction
—Instantaneously
Court Reporter
—Presence Mandatory
Child as Witness
Discretion of Court
Doctor's Testimony
Due Process
Evidence Held Sufficient
In Camera Proceeding
—Persons Present
—Purpose
Illustrative Cases
Presence of Counsel
—Purpose
Psychologist's Testimony
Record of Interview
—Error
—Release
Scope of Inquiry
—Held Proper
Use of Videos

Waiver
Witness Fees

Absence of Transcript

—Prejudicial

The absence of a transcript of the interviews with the children was clearly prejudicial to defendant, and provided no means for the appellate court to determine whether the trial court's decision was correct. DeYoung v. DeYoung, 62 Ill. App. 3d 837, 19 Ill. Dec. 732, 379 N.E.2d 396 (3 Dist. 1978).

Construction

—Instantaneously

The word "instantaneously" in this section refers to the making of the record rather than the filing of the transcript in the record. In re Hindenburg, 227 Ill. App. 3d 228, 169 Ill. Dec. 187, 591 N.E.2d 67 (2 Dist. 1992).

Court Reporter

—Presence Mandatory

A court reporter must be present for an in camera interview of a child, and a transcript of the interview must be made part of the record; thus, a court committed reversible error when it interviewed a child without the presence of a court reporter, and the matter was remanded for proceedings in compliance with the requirements of the statute. Gingrey v. Lamer, 15 Ill. App. 3d 486, 248 Ill. Dec. 478, 734 N.E.2d 186, 2000 Ill. App. LEXIS 651 (3 Dist. 2000).

The requirement for a court reporter to be present during an interview with the child is mandatory. DeYoung v. DeYoung, 62 Ill. App. 3d 837, 19 Ill. Dec. 732, 379 N.E.2d 396 (3 Dist. 1978).

Child as Witness

If competent as a witness in other respects, the child may testify to his custodial preferences in a custody proceeding. In re Combs, 78 Ill. App. 3d 533, 33 Ill. Dec. 922, 397 N.E.2d 255 (5 Dist. 1979).

Discretion of Court

Where this section states that "the court may interview the child in chambers to ascertain the child's wishes as to his custodian and as to visitation," the use of the word "may" indicates that the choice of whether or not to conduct an interview is a matter within the discretion of the trial court. In re Padiak, 101 Ill. App. 3d 306, 56 Ill. Dec. 826, 427 N.E.2d 1372 (2 Dist. 1981).

The choice of conducting an interview with the child is a matter within the trial court's discretion. DeYoung v. DeYoung, 62 Ill. App. 3d 837, 19 Ill. Dec. 732, 379 N.E.2d 396 (3 Dist. 1978); In re Smith, 114 Ill. App. 3d 47, 69 Ill. Dec. 827, 448 N.E.2d 545 (1 Dist. 1983).

The trial court did not abuse its discretion in ordering psychiatric tests of both parents. In re Sieck, 78 Ill. App. 3d 204, 33 Ill. Dec. 490, 396 N.E.2d 1214 (1 Dist. 1979).

Doctor's Testimony

That the children's pediatrician may have disagreed with the court appointed psychiatrist did not in and of itself render the trial court's award of custody to the mother an abuse of discretion. In re Ford, 91 Ill. App. 3d 1066, 47 Ill. Dec. 541, 415 N.E.2d 546 (1 Dist. 1980).

Due Process

In a case decided prior to the effective date of this Act, in a proceeding for modification of custody, there was no violation of due process resulting from the court's interview with a child in chambers with both counsel present where the child was sworn and testified in open court and expressed his views and feelings at considerable length both on direct and cross-examination. Levy v. Levy, 117 Ill. App. 2d 194, 254 N.E.2d 108 (1 Dist. 1969).

Evidence Held Sufficient

Although it was error, the respondent was not prejudiced by failing to have the in camera interview on record since there was ample evidence in the record to provide a means of determining whether the trial court's decision was an abuse of discretion. In re Slavenas, 139 Ill. App. 3d 581, 93 Ill. Dec. 914, 487 N.E.2d 739 (2 Dist. 1985).

In Camera Proceeding

—Persons Present

In a proceeding to change custody in which the mother appeared pro se, the trial court did not abuse its discretion in not allowing the mother in chambers when the child was testifying, notwithstanding that the mother had no counsel to be allowed in chambers. In re Knoche, 322 Ill. App. 3d 297, 255 Ill. Dec. 716, 750 N.E.2d 297, 2001 Ill. App. LEXIS 389 (5 Dist. 2001).

—Purpose

In review of a custody modification hearing, the court could not say the balance struck by the trial court in not conducting an in camera hearing with the child under § 604(a) of the Illinois Marriage and Dissolution of Marriage Act, 750 ILCS 5/604(a) was an abuse of discretion where the trial court had a concern that the child would be put in the position of blaming herself for the outcome. In re Marriage of De Bates, 212 Ill. 2d 489, 289 Ill. Dec. 218, 819 N.E.2d 714, 2004 Ill. LEXIS 1619 (2004).

The entire purpose of the in camera interview procedure is to permit the court to ascertain the children's preferences free from the pressures and acrimony of open court. In re Hindenburg, 227 Ill. App. 3d 228, 169 Ill. Dec. 187, 591 N.E.2d 67 (2 Dist. 1992).

Illustrative Cases

The trial court did not abuse its discretion in refusing to interview the parties' son to assist in determining custody; the record supported the trial court's finding that it would not be in the son's best interest to be interviewed in camera and, furthermore, there was evidence of the son's "preference" entered into evidence. In re Doty, 255 Ill. App. 3d 1087, 196 Ill. Dec. 134, 629 N.E.2d 679 (5 Dist. 1994).

The trial court stated that the probative value of what the children might say in an in camera interview would be far outweighed by the possible damage of requiring them to testify as to a choice between their parents, this determination was not an abuse of discretion. In re Johnson, 245 Ill. App. 3d 545, 185 Ill. Dec. 617, 614 N.E.2d 1302 (3 Dist.), appeal denied, 152 Ill. 2d 560, 190 Ill. Dec. 891, 622 N.E.2d 1208 (1993).

Trial court did not err in refusing to interview six year old child regarding his custodial preferences as such interviews are discretionary. In re McKeever, 117 Ill. App. 3d 905, 73 Ill. Dec. 164, 453 N.E.2d 1153 (3 Dist. 1983).

The statutory admonition to the trial court that the purpose of the interview was to ascertain the child's wishes as to his custodian and as to visitation did not limit the trial judge to questioning the child directly as to where he wished to live and what visitation he would desire. In re Ford, 91 Ill. App. 3d 1066, 47 Ill. Dec. 541, 415 N.E.2d 546 (1 Dist. 1980).

The court did not err in interviewing the child and considering her wishes as to her custodian. In re Piccirilli, 88 Ill. App. 3d 621, 43 Ill. Dec. 953, 410 N.E.2d 1086 (1 Dist. 1980).

Presence of Counsel

—Purpose

The right of counsel to be present given by this section is intended to assure fairness in the interview; the added protection afforded to the litigants by the presence of counsel permits the court to exercise considerable discretion in setting the scope of the interview in order to best determine the child's intelligence, understanding, and basis for any preference for a custodian. In re Willis, 234 Ill. App. 3d 156, 174 Ill. Dec. 633, 599 N.E.2d 179 (3 Dist. 1992).

Psychologist's Testimony

The testimony of psychologists is generally acceptable in child custody cases. In re Auer, 86 Ill. App. 3d 84, 41 Ill. Dec. 536, 407 N.E.2d 1034 (1 Dist. 1980).

The trial court did not err in allowing psychologist to testify as to what the children allegedly told father's witness and in allowing father's witness to testify as to what the children allegedly told her about their relationship to the mother because those statements were not hearsay and influenced the trial court's decision. In re Sieck, 78 Ill. App. 3d 204, 33 Ill. Dec. 490, 396 N.E.2d 1214 (1 Dist. 1979).

Record of Interview

—Error

It was error to conduct an in chambers interview without making a record. In re Slavenas, 139 Ill. App. 3d 581, 93 Ill. Dec. 914, 487 N.E.2d 739 (2 Dist. 1985).

Record of Interview (Cont'd)

—Release

The court did not err by not immediately releasing the transcript of an in camera interview or at least making findings of fact on the record where a court reporter was present at the interview and the transcript was eventually made available to the parties. In re Hindenburg, 227 Ill. App. 3d 228, 169 Ill. Dec. 187, 591 N.E.2d 67 (2 Dist. 1992).

Scope of Inquiry

—Held Proper

Where the trial judge asked the child general questions about his school, friends, health, age, hobbies, and what he liked to do, tried to ascertain whether the child knew the difference between right and wrong, and, finally, asked the child what do you think ought to be done here today and the child responded that he did not know, so that after a short discussion about making paper spaceships the judge concluded the interview, the trial court did not abuse its discretion in fixing the scope of inquiry during an in camera conference. In re Ford, 91 Ill. App. 3d 1066, 47 Ill. Dec. 541, 415 N.E.2d 546 (1 Dist. 1980).

Use of Videos

The procedure of using day-in-the-life videotapes of young children in child custody proceedings must not be allowed. In re Willis, 234 Ill. App. 3d 156, 174 Ill. Dec. 633, 599 N.E.2d 179 (3 Dist. 1992).

Waiver

Where there is absolutely nothing in the record to contradict the court's detailed recollection of a waiver by both attorneys, the appellate court must presume the trial court acted properly. In re Hindenburg, 227 Ill. App. 3d 228, 169 Ill. Dec. 187, 591 N.E.2d 67 (2 Dist. 1992).

Parties are presumed to act through their attorneys, and the action of an attorney in the conduct of a case is binding on his client, so an attorney's waiver would bind the party under this section. In re Hindenburg, 227 Ill. App. 3d 228, 169 Ill. Dec. 187, 591 N.E.2d 67 (2 Dist. 1992).

Nothing in this section requires that a waiver be in any particular form. In re Hindenburg, 227 Ill. App. 3d 228, 169 Ill. Dec. 187, 591 N.E.2d 67 (2 Dist. 1992).

Where respondent's counsel was present at and participated in the in camera conference with the parties' older children but made no objection to the scope of inquiry at that time, his objection was waived for purposes of appeal. In re Ford, 91 Ill. App. 3d 1066, 47 Ill. Dec. 541, 415 N.E.2d 546 (1 Dist. 1980).

Where this new statute, which made broad changes in Illinois marital law, took effect ten days before the hearing and its text was not yet readily available, the parties could not have waived a requirement of which they had no knowledge. DeYoung v. DeYoung, 62 Ill. App. 3d 837, 19 Ill. Dec. 732, 379 N.E.2d 396 (3 Dist. 1978).

Witness Fees

The court did not err in holding a husband in contempt of court for failure to pay an expert witness fee under subsection (b) as the expert witness was appointed for the ultimate benefit of the minor children and was necessary to protect the interests of the minor children regarding issues of custody and visitation. It was within the circuit court's inherent plenary powers to order the husband to pay the expert witness fees. In re Petersen, 319 Ill. App. 3d 325, 253 Ill. Dec. 144, 744 N.E.2d 877, 2001 Ill. App. LEXIS 46 (1 Dist. 2001), appeal denied sub nom. Petersen v. Petersen, 195 Ill. 2d 597, 258 Ill. Dec. 100, 755 N.E.2d 483 (2001).

LEGAL PERIODICALS

For article, "Out of the Mouths of Babes: Determination of Child Custodial Preference in Illinois," see 23 Loy. U. Chi. L. J. 383 (1991-92).

750 ILCS 5/604.5 Evaluation of child's best interest

Sec. 604.5. *Evaluation of child's best interest.* (a) In a proceeding for custody, visitation, or removal of a child from Illinois, upon notice and motion made within a reasonable time before trial, the court may order an evaluation concerning the best interest of the child as it relates to custody, visitation, or removal. The motion may be made by a party, a parent, the child's custodian, the attorney for the child, the child's guardian ad litem, or the child's representative. The requested evaluation may be in place of or in addition to an evaluation conducted under subsection (b) of Section 604 [750 ILCS 5/604].

The motion shall state the identity of the proposed evaluator and set forth the evaluator's specialty or discipline. The court may refuse to order an evaluation by the proposed evaluator, but in that event, the court may permit the party seeking the evaluation to propose one or more other evaluators.

(b) An order for an evaluation shall fix the time, place, conditions, and scope of the evaluation and shall designate the evaluator. A party or person shall not be required to travel an unreasonable distance for the evaluation.

(c) The person requesting an evaluator shall pay the fee for the evaluation unless otherwise ordered by the court.

(d) Within 21 days after the completion of the evaluation, if the moving party or person intends to call the evaluator as a witness, the evaluator shall prepare and mail or deliver to the attorneys of record duplicate originals of the written evaluation. The evaluation shall set forth the evaluator's findings, the results of all tests administered, and the evaluator's conclusions and recommendations. If the written evaluation is not delivered or mailed to the attorneys within 21 days or within any extensions or modifications granted by the court, the written evaluation and the evaluator's testimony, conclusions, and recommendations may not be received into evidence.

(e) The person calling an evaluator to testify at trial shall disclose the evaluator as an opinion witness in accordance with the Supreme Court Rules.

(f) Subject to compliance with the Supreme Court Rules, nothing in this Section bars a person who did not request the evaluation from calling the evaluator as a witness. In that case, however, that person shall pay the evaluator's fee for testifying unless otherwise ordered by the court.

(Source: P.A. 91-746, § 5.)

Effective Date.

Section 99 of P.A. 91-746 made this section effective upon becoming law.

RESEARCH REFERENCES

Religion as factor in child custody cases. 124 ALR5th 203.

750 ILCS 5/605 Investigations and Reports

Sec. 605. *Investigations and Reports.* (a) In contested custody proceedings, and in other custody proceedings if a parent or the child's custodian so requests, the court may order an investigation and report concerning custodial arrangements for the child. The investigation and report may be made by a child welfare agency approved by the Department of Children and Family Services, but shall not be made by that Department unless the court determines either that there is no child welfare agency available or that the parent or the child's custodian is financially unable to pay for the investigation or report.

(b) In preparing his report concerning a child, the investigator may consult any person who may have information about the child and his potential custodial arrangements. Under order of the court, the investigator may refer the child to professional personnel for diagnosis. The investigator may consult with and obtain information from medical, psychiatric or other expert persons who have served the child in the past, without obtaining the consent of the parent or the child's custodian. The child's consent must be obtained if he has reached the age of 16, unless the court finds that he lacks mental capacity to consent.

(c) The investigator shall mail the report to counsel, and to any party not represented by counsel, at least 10 days prior to the hearing. The court may examine and consider the investigator's report in determining custody. The investigator shall make available to counsel, and to any party not represented by counsel, the investigator's file of underlying data, reports, and the complete texts of diagnostic reports made to the investigator pursuant to the provisions of subsection (b) of this Section, and the names and addresses of all persons whom the investigator has consulted. Any party to the proceeding may call the investigator, or any person whom he has consulted, as a court's witness, for cross-examination. A party may not waive his right of cross-examination prior to the hearing.
(Source: P.A. 86-659.)

Note.
This section was Ill.Rev.Stat., Ch. 40, para. 605.

CASE NOTES

Analysis

Child As Witness
Cross-Examination of Investigator
Discretion of Court
Domestic Violence Cases
Hearsay
Impeachment of Psychologist
Independent Investigation
Mental Condition of Parent
Post-Judgment Order

Child As Witness
If competent as a witness in other respects, the child may testify to his custodial preferences in a custody proceeding. In re Combs, 78 Ill. App. 3d 533, 33 Ill. Dec. 922, 397 N.E.2d 255 (5 Dist. 1979).

Cross-Examination of Investigator
When a court receives a report pursuant to this section, the court can consider the report as if the contents of that report had been given as direct testimony during a hearing; thus, subsection (c) provides that a report submitted under this section is an exception to the hearsay rule, however, subsection (c) further provides that the court must allow either party the opportunity to cross-examine the investigator who made the report, unless the party waives that opportunity at a hearing on the matter. Helderbrandt v. Helderbrandt, 251 Ill. App. 3d 950, 191 Ill. Dec. 190, 623 N.E.2d 780 (4 Dist. 1993).

Discretion of Court
Ordering an investigation and using the report at trial is clearly within the trial court's discretion. In re Slavenas, 139 Ill. App. 3d 581, 93 Ill. Dec. 914, 487 N.E.2d 739 (2 Dist. 1985).

Nothing of record required the court to proceed sua sponte to cause an investigation to be made under this section; therefore, since no specific request for such an investigation was made, the circuit court's failure to order an investigation was not an abuse of discretion. Hollo v. Hollo, 131 Ill. App. 3d 119, 85 Ill. Dec. 867, 474 N.E.2d 827 (5 Dist. 1985).

The trial court did not abuse its discretion in failing to appoint a guardian ad litem, sua sponte, or in ordering an investigation and report by the Department of Children and Family Services in an action modifying the custody provisions of a divorce decree. De Franco v. De Franco, 67 Ill. App. 3d 760, 24 Ill. Dec. 130, 384 N.E.2d 997 (1 Dist. 1978).

Domestic Violence Cases
Because temporary custody may be awarded under the Domestic Violence Act, and because the act makes specific reference to the Marriage Act, a court in a domestic violence case can order a home study pursuant to this section; however, such a study should only be ordered in exceptional cases because of the substantial possibility of causing delay and, further, such a study cannot be ordered in connection with an emergency order of protection as such an order may not include an award of legal custody. Wilson v. Jackson, 312 Ill. App. 3d 1156, 245 Ill. Dec. 750, 728 N.E.2d 832, 2000 Ill. App. LEXIS 267 (3 Dist. 2000).

Hearsay
This subsection, which provides an exception to the hearsay rule, allows the court to consider the report of a court appointed investigator, who may then be called for cross-examination. In re Noble, 192 Ill. App. 3d 501, 139 Ill. Dec. 133, 548 N.E.2d 518 (2 Dist. 1989).

The information contained in a report which was received by third parties or otherwise was outside the personal knowledge of witness, was hearsay, and was properly stricken by the trial court. In re Hazard, 167 Ill. App. 3d 61, 117 Ill. Dec. 770, 520 N.E.2d 1121 (1 Dist. 1988).

A report may be used by the trial court as evidence of what an investigator observed and his conclusions concerning custodial arrangements. In re Slavenas, 139 Ill. App. 3d 581, 93 Ill. Dec. 914, 487 N.E.2d 739 (2 Dist. 1985).

Investigative report could not encompass finding of fact concerning who abused child; the report was only evidence of what the investigator observed and of his conclusions concerning suggested custody arrangements based upon those observations and any underlying facts contained in the report which were outside the personal knowledge of the investigator were hearsay. In re Theis, 121 Ill. App. 3d 1092, 77 Ill. Dec. 608, 460 N.E.2d 912 (3 Dist. 1984).

Impeachment of Psychologist
Impeachment of a psychologist of the preparer of a report is valid when, and only when, that psychologist's work product was entered verbatim in its entirety into the overall report prepared by the investigator. In re Auer, 86 Ill. App. 3d 84, 41 Ill. Dec. 536, 407 N.E.2d 1034 (1 Dist. 1980).

Independent Investigation
Where the parties agreed at the temporary custody hearing to an independent investigation, it was not the responsibility of the trial court to insure that the investigation took place. In re Slavenas, 139 Ill. App. 3d 581, 93 Ill. Dec. 914, 487 N.E.2d 739 (2 Dist. 1985).

Mental Condition of Parent
Where the mother requested a Supreme Court Rule 215 examination, but did not request an examination under this section, the court properly limited the scope of the examination to the mental

Mental Condition of Parent (Cont'd)
status of the parties and stated that the examination would not result in a custody evaluation. In re Divelbiss, 308 Ill. App. 3d 198, 241 Ill. Dec. 514, 719 N.E.2d 375 (2 Dist. 1999).

The trial court committed error when it allowed into evidence a doctor's diagnosis about a parent's mental condition; however, it did not adversely affect the outcome of the proceedings and was a failed attempt on the parties to use this section. In re Willis, 234 Ill. App. 3d 156, 174 Ill. Dec. 633, 599 N.E.2d 179 (3 Dist. 1992).

Post-Judgment Order
The trial court did not err in ordering a home study investigation and report after a dissolution judgment had been entered because the trial court still had jurisdiction due to the pending post trial motion; the preferred practice for the trial court would have been to order the investigation prior to final disposition. Knight v. Knight, 165 Ill. App. 3d 403, 116 Ill. Dec. 516, 519 N.E.2d 106 (3 Dist. 1988).

750 ILCS 5/606 Hearings

Sec. 606. *Hearings.* (a) Custody proceedings shall receive priority in being set for hearing.

(b) The court may tax as costs the payment of necessary travel and other expenses incurred by any person whose presence at the hearing the court deems necessary to determine the best interest of the child.

(c) The court, without a jury, shall determine questions of law and fact. If it finds that a public hearing may be detrimental to the child's best interest, the court may exclude the public from a custody hearing, but may admit any person who has a direct and legitimate interest in the particular case or a legitimate educational or research interest in the work of the court.

(d) If the court finds it necessary, in order to protect the child's welfare, that the record of any interview, report, investigation, or testimony in a custody proceeding be kept secret, the court may make an appropriate order sealing the record.

(e) Previous statements made by the child relating to any allegations that the child is an abused or neglected child within the meaning of the Abused and Neglected Child Reporting Act [325 ILCS 5/1 et seq.], or an abused or neglected minor within the meaning of the Juvenile Court Act of 1987 [705 ILCS 405/1-1 et seq.], shall be admissible in evidence in a hearing concerning custody of or visitation with the child. No such statement, however, if uncorroborated and not subject to cross-examination, shall be sufficient in itself to support a finding of abuse or neglect.

(Source: P.A. 80-923; 87-1081, § 1.)

Note.
This section was Ill.Rev.Stat., Ch. 40, para. 606.

CASE NOTES

ANALYSIS

Allegations of Abuse
Construction
Evidence
Hearing Required

Allegations of Abuse
Allegations of abuse do not become irrelevant in a visitation proceeding merely because a finding of guilt has not been entered against the accused party; clearly a parent's alleged sexual misconduct toward a child, whether or not his or her own, is relevant in determining the visitation rights of that parent. In re Rudd, 293 Ill. App. 3d 367, 227 Ill. Dec. 861, 688 N.E.2d 342 (4 Dist. 1997).

Construction
The language of subsection (e) explicitly refers to statements made by the child who is the subject of the custody or visitation proceeding and does not support a finding that the hearsay exception encompasses statements made by a child who is a third party to those proceedings. In re Rudd, 293 Ill. App. 3d 367, 227 Ill. Dec. 861, 688 N.E.2d 342 (4 Dist. 1997).

Evidence
Four-year-old child's out-of-court statements, in which she alleged that she had been sexually abused by her father, were properly admitted and considered in hearing conducted after an ex parte order of protection was issued against the father; the statements were corroborated by testimony from a police detective, a child advocate, and an observer of supervised visitation the father had with the child. In re Marriage of Gilbert, Ill. App. 3d , 290 Ill. Dec. 834, 822 N.E.2d 116, 2004 Ill. App. LEXIS 1563 (1 Dist. 2004).

Trial courts are not required to conduct reliability hearings for hearsay statements admitted in proceedings under subsection (e) of this section. In re Marriage of Gilbert, Ill. App. 3d , 290 Ill. Dec. 834, 822 N.E.2d 116, 2004 Ill. App. LEXIS 1563 (1 Dist. 2004).

Where the relief sought in a petition refers to the Illinois Domestic Violence Act, but the essence of a court's ruling clearly implicates questions of custody and visitation, subsection (e) of this section, applies to the issue regarding the admissibility of previous statements made by a child about allegations that the child was an abused or neglected child. In re Marriage of Gilbert, Ill. App. 3d , 290 Ill. Dec. 834, 822 N.E.2d 116, 2004 Ill. App. LEXIS 1563 (1 Dist. 2004).

In a proceeding commenced by a mother for an order of protection on behalf of her minor child against the father of the child, the court properly applied subsection (e) to admit hearsay statements of the child that the father sexually abused her during an overnight visit; although both that statute and this section concern the admission of hearsay statements by abused children in civil proceedings, the former statute addresses the admission of those statements when the alleged abuser is the parent and specifically mentions that it applies to hearings concerning visitation with the child. Daria W. v. Bradley W., 317 Ill. App. 3d 194, 250 Ill. Dec. 505, 738 N.E.2d 974, 2000 Ill. App. LEXIS 830 (3 Dist. 2000).

Neither this section not 750 ILCS 5/607 contains any language limiting the introduction of evidence to facts that have arisen since prior judgment. In re Fields, 283 Ill. App. 3d 894, 219 Ill. Dec. 420, 671 N.E.2d 85 (4 Dist. 1996).

Hearing Required
Unfitness does not follow conclusively from a failure to comply with of rights visitation or other orders which may be entered in a divorce proceeding nor can the child be used as a basis for punishing the contumacy of a party in a contempt proceeding; nothing short of a hearing relating to unfitness and the interests of the child and a finding thereon is adequate support for an order changing custody. Szczawinski v. Szczawinski, 37 Ill. App. 2d 350, 185 N.E.2d 375 (1 Dist. 1962).

Evidence of the father's unfitness was sufficient to require a hearing on the issue of child custody. Szewczyk v. Szewczyk, 320 Ill. App. 562, 51 N.E.2d 801 (1 Dist. 1943).

LEGAL PERIODICALS

For article, "Survey of Illinois Law: Evidence," see 26 S. Ill. U.L.J. 795 (2002).

RESEARCH REFERENCES

Necessity of requiring presence in court of both parties in proceedings relating to custody or visitation of children. 15 ALR4th 864.

750 ILCS 5/607 Visitation

Sec. 607. *Visitation.* (a) A parent not granted custody of the child is entitled to reasonable visitation rights unless the court finds, after a hearing, that visitation would endanger seriously the child's physical, mental, moral or emotional health. If the custodian's street address is not identified, pursuant to Section 708 [750 ILCS 5/708], the court shall require the parties to identify reasonable alternative arrangements for visitation by a non-custodial parent, including but not limited to visitation of the minor child at the residence of another person or at a local public or private facility.

(a-3) Nothing in subsection (a-5) of this Section shall apply to a child in whose interests a petition under Section 2-13 of the Juvenile Court Act of 1987 [705 ILCS 405/2-13] is pending.

(a-5) (1) Except as otherwise provided in this subsection (a-5), any grandparent, great-grandparent, or sibling may file a petition for visitation rights to a minor child if there is an unreasonable denial of visitation by a parent and at least one of the following conditions exists:

(A) one parent of the child is incompetent as a matter of law or deceased or has been sentenced to a period of imprisonment for more than 1 year;

(B) the child's mother and father are divorced or have been legally separated from each other during the 3 month period prior to the filing of the petition and at least one parent does not object to the grandparent, great-grandparent, or sibling having visitation with the child. The visitation of the grandparent, great-grandparent, or sibling must not diminish the visitation of the parent who is not related to the grandparent, great-grandparent, or sibling seeking visitation;

(C) the court, other than a Juvenile Court, has terminated a parent-child relationship and the grandparent, great-grandparent, or sibling is the parent of the person whose parental rights have been terminated, except in cases of adoption. The visitation must not be used to allow the parent who lost parental rights to unlawfully visit with the child;

(D) the child is illegitimate, the parents are not living together, and the petitioner is a maternal grandparent, great-grandparent, or sibling of the illegitimate child; or

(E) the child is illegitimate, the parents are not living together, the petitioner is a paternal grandparent, great-grandparent, or sibling, and the paternity has been established by a court of competent jurisdiction.

(2) The grandparent, great-grandparent, or sibling of a parent whose parental rights have been terminated through an adoption proceeding may not petition for visitation rights.

(3) In making a determination under this subsection (a-5), there is a rebuttable presumption that a fit parent's actions and decisions regarding grandparent, great-grandparent, or sibling visitation are not harmful to the child's mental, physical, or emotional health. The burden is on the party filing a petition under this Section to prove that the parent's actions and decisions regarding visitation times are harmful to the child's mental, physical, or emotional health.

(4) In determining whether to grant visitation, the court shall consider the following:

(A) the preference of the child if the child is determined to be of sufficient maturity to express a preference;

(B) the mental and physical health of the child;

(C) the mental and physical health of the grandparent, great-grandparent, or sibling;

(D) the length and quality of the prior relationship between the child and the grandparent, great-grandparent, or sibling;

(E) the good faith of the party in filing the petition;

(F) the good faith of the person denying visitation;

(G) the quantity of the visitation time requested and the potential adverse impact that visitation would have on the child's customary activities;

(H) whether the child resided with the petitioner for at least 6 consecutive months with or without the current custodian present;

(I) whether the petitioner had frequent or regular contact with the child for at least 12 consecutive months; and

(J) any other fact that establishes that the loss of the relationship between the petitioner and the child is likely to harm the child's mental, physical, or emotional health.

(5) The court may order visitation rights for the grandparent, great-grandparent, or sibling that include reasonable access without requiring overnight or possessory visitation.

(a-7) (1) Unless by stipulation of the parties, no motion to modify a grandparent, great-grandparent, or sibling visitation order may be made earlier than 2 years after the date the order was filed, unless the court permits it to be made on the basis of affidavits that there is reason to believe the child's present environment may endanger seriously the child's mental, physical, or emotional health.

(2) The court shall not modify a prior grandparent, great-grandparent, or sibling visitation order unless it finds by clear and convincing evidence, upon the basis of facts that have arisen since the prior visitation order or that were unknown to the court at the time of entry of the prior visitation, that a change has occurred in the circumstances of the child or his or her custodian, and that the modification is necessary to protect the mental, physical, or emotional health of the child. The court shall state in its decision specific findings of fact in support of its modification or termination of the grandparent, great-grandparent, or sibling visitation.

(3) Attorney fees and costs shall be assessed against a party seeking modification of the visitation order if the court finds that the modification action is vexatious and constitutes harassment.

(4) Notice under this subsection (a-7) shall be given as provided in subsections (c) and (d) of Section 601 [750 ILCS 5/601].

(b) (1) (Blank.)

(1.5) The Court may grant reasonable visitation privileges to a stepparent upon petition to the court by the stepparent, with notice to the parties required to be notified under Section 601 of this Act [750 ILCS 5/601], if the court determines that it is in the best interests and welfare of the child, and may issue any necessary orders to enforce those visitation privileges. A petition for visitation privileges may be filed under this paragraph (1.5) whether or not a petition pursuant to this Act has been previously filed or is currently pending if the following circumstances are met:

(A) the child is at least 12 years old;

(B) the child resided continuously with the parent and stepparent for at least 5 years;

(C) the parent is deceased or is disabled and is unable to care for the child;

(D) the child wishes to have reasonable visitation with the stepparent; and

(E) the stepparent was providing for the care, control, and welfare to the child prior to the initiation of the petition for visitation.

(2)(A) A petition for visitation privileges shall not be filed pursuant to this subsection (b) by the parents or grandparents of a putative father if the paternity of the putative father has not been legally established.

(B) A petition for visitation privileges may not be filed under this subsection (b) if the child who is the subject of the grandparents' or great-grandparents' petition has been voluntarily surrendered by the parent or parents, except for a surrender to the Illinois Department of Children and Family Services or a foster care facility, or has been previously adopted by an individual or individuals who are not related to the biological parents of the child or is the subject of a pending adoption petition by an individual or individuals who are not related to the biological parents of the child.

(3) (Blank).

(c) The court may modify an order granting or denying visitation rights of a parent whenever modification would serve the best interest of the child; but the court shall not restrict a parent's visitation rights unless it finds that the visitation would endanger seriously the child's physical, mental, moral or emotional health. The court may modify an order granting, denying, or limiting visitation rights of a grandparent, great-grandparent, or sibling of any minor child whenever a change of circumstances has occurred based on facts occurring subsequent to the judgment and the court finds by clear and convincing evidence that the modification is in the best interest of the minor child.

(d) If any court has entered an order prohibiting a non-custodial parent of a child from any contact with a child or restricting the non-custodial parent's contact with the child, the following provisions shall apply:

(1) If an order has been entered granting visitation privileges with the child to a grandparent or great-grandparent who is related to the child through the non-custodial parent, the visitation privileges of the grandparent or great-grandparent may be revoked if:

(i) a court has entered an order prohibiting the non-custodial parent from any contact with the child, and the grandparent or great-grandparent is found to have used his or her visitation privileges to facilitate contact between the child and the non-custodial parent; or

(ii) a court has entered an order restricting the non-custodial parent's contact with the child, and the grandparent or great-grandparent is found to have used his or her visitation privileges to facilitate contact between the child and the non-custodial parent in a manner that violates the terms of the order restricting the non-custodial parent's contact with the child.

Nothing in this subdivision (1) limits the authority of the court to enforce its orders in any manner permitted by law.

(2) Any order granting visitation privileges with the child to a grandparent or great-grandparent who is related to the child through the non-custodial parent shall contain the following provision:

"If the (grandparent or great-grandparent, whichever is applicable) who has been granted visitation privileges under this order uses the visitation privileges to facilitate contact between the child and the child's non-custodial parent, the visitation privileges granted under this order shall be permanently revoked."

(e) No parent, not granted custody of the child, or grandparent, or great-grandparent, or stepparent, or sibling of any minor child, convicted of any offense involving an illegal sex act perpetrated upon a victim less than 18 years of age including but not limited to offenses for violations of Article 12 of the Criminal Code of 1961 [720 ILCS 5/12-1 et seq.], is entitled to visitation rights while incarcerated or while on parole, probation, conditional discharge, periodic imprisonment, or mandatory supervised release for that offense, and upon discharge from incarceration for a misdemeanor offense or upon discharge from parole, probation, conditional discharge, periodic imprisonment, or mandatory supervised release for a felony offense, visitation shall be denied until the person successfully completes a treatment program approved by the court.

(f) Unless the court determines, after considering all relevant factors, including but not limited to those set forth in Section 602(a) [750 ILCS 5/602], that it would be in the best interests of the child to allow visitation, the court shall not enter an order providing visitation rights and pursuant to a motion to modify visitation shall revoke visitation rights previously granted to any person who would otherwise be entitled to petition for visitation rights under this Section who has been convicted of first degree murder of the parent, grandparent, great-grandparent, or sibling of the child who is the subject of the order. Until an order is entered pursuant to this subsection, no person shall visit, with the child present, a person who has been convicted of first degree murder of the parent, grandparent, great-grandparent, or sibling of the child without the consent of the child's parent, other than a parent convicted of first degree murder as set forth herein, or legal guardian.

(g) If an order has been entered limiting, for cause, a minor child's contact or visitation with a grandparent, great-grandparent, or sibling on the grounds that it was in the best interest of the child to do so, that order may be modified only upon a showing of a substantial change in circumstances occurring subsequent to the entry of the order with proof by clear and convincing evidence that modification is in the best interest of the minor child.

(Source: P.A. 86-855; 86-917; 86-1028; 86-1452; 88-23, § 5; 88-267, § 5; 88-670, § 2-68; 89-488, § 5; 90-782, § 5; 90-801, § 5; 91-357, § 256; 91-610, § 5; 93-911, § 5.)

Note.

This section was Ill.Rev.Stat., Ch. 40, para. 607.

Illinois Administrative Code.

See 89 Illinois Administrative Code, § 301.240.

Effect of Amendments.

The 1994 amendment by P.A. 88-670, effective December 2, 1994, combined the amendments by P.A. 88-23 and P.A. 88-267.

The 1996 amendment by P.A. 89-488, effective June 21, 1996, in subsection (e) inserted "while incarcerated or", inserted "incarceration for a misdemeanor offense or upon discharge from" and inserted "for a felony offense".

The 1998 amendment by P.A. 90-782, effective August 14, 1998, in subsection (b)(1) substituted "paragraph (1)" for "subsection (b)"; added subsection (b)(1.5); and in subsection (e) inserted "or step-parent," and twice inserted ", probation, conditional discharge, periodic imprisonment," and made a minor stylistic change.

The 1998 amendment by P.A. 90-801, effective June 1, 1999, added subsection (f).

The 1999 amendment by P.A. 91-357, effective July 7, 1999, incorporated the amendments by P.A. 90-782 and P.A. 90-801.

The 1999 amendment by P.A. 91-610, effective August 19, 1999, in subsection (c) inserted "of a parent" in the first sentence, and added the present last sentence; and added subsection (g).

Although the amendments made to this section by P.A. 91-357, § 256 and P.A. 91-610, § 5 did not take into account the amendments made by the other, the amendments have been combined into a single version by the publisher.

The 2004 amendment by P.A. 93-911, effective January 1, 2005, inserted subsections (a-3), (a-5) and (a-7), and deleted the text from subsections (b)(1) and (b)(3).

CASE NOTES

Analysis

Constitutionality
In General
Adoption
—Court Ordered Visitation
—Visitation by Natural Relatives
Applicability
—Adult Disabled Persons
—Grandparents
Basis for Visitation
Best Interests of the Child
Burden of Proof
Cost of Visitation
Counseling
Custody Award
De Novo Review
Denial of Visitation
—Extreme Circumstances
—Not Proper
—Proper
—Reluctance of Courts
—Test
Discretion of Court
—In General
—Abuse Not Shown
—Appellate Review
—Delegation of Duties
Entitlement
Evidence
Grandparent Visitation
—In General
—Agreement
—Burden of Proof
—Common Law
—Court's Authority
—Death of Parent
—Determination
—Discretion of Court
—Effect of Adoption
—Improper
—Increased Visitation
—Proper
—Rights
—Special Circumstances
Imprisoned Parent
Liberal Visitation
Mental Condition of Parent
Modification
—Best Interest of Child
—Burden of Proof
—Move Out-of-State
—Properly Allowed
—Properly Denied
—Time Constraints
Noncustodial Parent
—In General
—Burden of Proof
—Evidence
—Rights of
Overnight Visitation
Parent's Cohabitation
Parentage Act
Past Conduct
Prejudicial Comments
Public Policy
Punishment
Reinstatement of Visitation
Religious Services
Restricted Visitation
—In General
—Burden of Proof
—Counseling
—Court's Findings
—Determination
—Discretion of Court
—Endangerment Standard
—Erroneous Standard
—Failure to File Petition
—Failure to Use Proper Standard
—Improper
—Manifest Injustice
—Not Shown
—Place
—Reluctance of Courts

—Sexual Orientation of Parent
—Shown
—Supervision
Scope
Sexual Abuse
Standing
Stepparent Visitation
Termination
—Not Proper
—Proper
Visitation Order
—Finality

Constitutionality

Provisions of this section authorizing the court to order grandparent visitation privileges, against a parent's wishes, were declared unconstitutional, and the prior common law that authorized the same is equally unconstitutional. In re Ross, Ill. App. 3d , Ill. Dec. , N.E.2d , 2005 Ill. App. LEXIS 128 (5 Dist. Feb. 16, 2005).

Subdivision (b)(1.5) of this section, which states that the court may grant visitation to a stepparent if it would be in the best interest of the child, places a fit parent on equal footing with the stepparent in their attempts to convince the court that visitation is or is not in the child's best interest; therefore, it is unconstitutional on its face. In re Marriage of Engelkens, Ill. App. 3d , 290 Ill. Dec. 487, 821 N.E.2d 799, 2004 Ill. App. LEXIS 1559 (3 Dist. 2004).

Where an order granting grandparent visitation was based on an agreement between a father and the grandparents, the order was in the nature of a consent decree, which did not require scrutiny under the principles outlined in the Illinois Supreme Court's decision in Wickham v. Byrne; however, while the agreement could generally only be modified or terminated based upon the consent of all of the parties, modification would be appropriate if a showing was made that modification was in the best interest of the child involved. Johnson v. Duncan (In re M.M.D.), 213 Ill. 2d 105, 289 Ill. Dec. 616, 820 N.E.2d 392, 2004 Ill. LEXIS 1674 (2004).

Supreme Court's ruling in Wickham v. Byrne that 750 ILCS 5/607(b) was unconstitutional did not affect a grandparent visitation order entered prior to that ruling because the order was based on an agreement between the parties and did not constitute a situation in which a judge had imposed the visitation against a father's wishes. Johnson v. Duncan (In re M.M.D.), 213 Ill. 2d 105, 289 Ill. Dec. 616, 820 N.E.2d 392, 2004 Ill. LEXIS 1674 (2004).

The state supreme court upheld the trial court's order prohibiting the grandparents from filing for visitation with their granddaughter after the death of one of the parents not because the statute was unconstitutional as applied, but because it was facially unconstitutional in its entirety. Schweigert v. Schweigert, 201 Ill. 2d 42, 265 Ill. Dec. 191, 772 N.E.2d 229, 2002 Ill. LEXIS 329 (2002).

Statutory provisions used to impose grandparent visitation against the will of a parent, 750 ILCS 5/607(b)(1) and 750 ILCS 5/607(b)(3), were facially unconstitutional as a presumption existed that fit parents acted in the best interests of their children and those statutory provisions violated that presumption by putting the grandparents seeking visitation on an equal footing with the parents in determining the best interests of the children; accordingly, the statutory provisions violated the substantive due process rights of the parents to raise their children as they saw fit, which included whom children would visit and under what circumstances. Wickham v. Byrne, 199 Ill. 2d 309, 263 Ill. Dec. 799, 769 N.E.2d 1, 2002 Ill. LEXIS 313 (2002).

The application of 750 ILCS 5/607(b)(1) to the case was unconstitutional since: (1) neither the grandparents nor the trial court alleged that the parent of the children at issue was unfit; (2) the grandparents did not allege that the parent sought to entirely terminate their visitation with the children and, instead, she sought only to limit their visitation to supervised visits in her home; and (3) the trial court did not give any special weight to the parent's determination of the her children's best interests. Langman v. Langman, 325 Ill. App. 3d 101, 258 Ill. Dec. 816, 757 N.E.2d 505, 2001 Ill. App. LEXIS 553 (3 Dist. 2001).

Subsection (b)(1), which allows grandparents to petition for court-ordered visitation with the grandchildren when both parents have decided not to allow such visitation, improperly impinges upon the fundamental constitutional right of parents to make decisions regarding the upbringing of their children by allowing the state to interfere with the parents' decision in this regard. Lulay v. Lulay, 193 Ill. 2d 455, 250 Ill. Dec. 758, 739 N.E.2d 521, 2000 Ill. LEXIS 1694 (2000).

It is not a violation of divorced or parents' equal protection rights for the State to allow grandparents to seek visitation privileges, and the grandparental visitation provision of subsection (b) is constitutional. West v. West, 294 Ill. App. 3d 356, 228 Ill. Dec. 794, 689 N.E.2d 1215 (5 Dist. 1998).

In General

Legislature's intent in enacting 750 ILCS 5/608 of the Illinois Marriage and Dissolution of Marriage Act (Dissolution Act), giving a custodial parent the right to determine a child's religious upbringing, is to provide a guideline for the parties and the court in the general area of child welfare and upbringing, and the legislature granted the custodial parent the authority to make the initial decision on such matters and placed the burden upon the noncustodial parent to establish the fault of any such custodial determination, but section 608 does not exist in a vacuum as that section must be read in conjunction with other sections of the Dissolution Act, including 750 ILCS 5/607(c), which grants to a noncustodial parent the right to unrestricted visitation. and, more important, 750 ILCS 5/608 must yield to the best interest and general welfare of the child. Minix v. Dunaven-Minix, 344 Ill. App. 3d 801, 280 Ill. Dec. 256, 801 N.E.2d 1201, 2003 Ill. App. LEXIS 1559 (4 Dist. 2003).

Absent exigent circumstances, all biological parents enjoy a presumption that they are entitled to visitation with their children, whether visitation is requested under the Illinois Marriage and Dissolution of Marriage Act, 750 ILCS 5/101 et seq., or the Illinois Parentage Act of 1984, 750 ILCS 45/1 et seq. Wenzelman v. Bennett, 322 Ill. App. 3d 262, 255 Ill. Dec. 196, 748 N.E.2d 1266, 2001 Ill. App. LEXIS 365 (3 Dist. 2001).

In matters of visitation, the primary concern of the court is the welfare of the child. In re Blanchard, 162 Ill. App. 3d 202, 113 Ill. Dec. 197, 514 N.E.2d 1208 (5 Dist. 1987).

Adoption

—Court Ordered Visitation

Subsection (b) of this section, as amended, cannot, by its silence, be construed to authorize court ordered visitation in the situation wherein the parental rights of both biological parents have been terminated by consent to the child's adoption by other relatives. Bush v. Squellati, 154 Ill. App. 3d 727, 107 Ill. Dec. 81, 506 N.E.2d 972 (3 Dist. 1987).

—Visitation by Natural Relatives

A court rendering a judgment of adoption has no jurisdiction to simultaneously grant visitation rights to natural relatives of the adopted child, and such provisions in adoption orders are void. Krystek v. Schumacher, 120 Ill. App. 3d 50, 75 Ill. Dec. 926, 458 N.E.2d 94 (2 Dist. 1983).

Applicability

—Adult Disabled Persons

A court does not have authority under this section to grant an order of visitation as to an adult disabled person. In re Casarotto, 316 Ill. App. 3d 567, 249 Ill. Dec. 731, 736 N.E.2d 1169, 2000 Ill. App. LEXIS 769 (2 Dist. 2000).

—Grandparents

This provision is applicable when the grandparents are seeking visitation and the custodial parent or parents are resisting such visitation. In re Spomer, 123 Ill. App. 3d 31, 78 Ill. Dec. 605, 462 N.E.2d 724 (5 Dist. 1984).

Basis for Visitation

The visitation privilege is founded on the belief that it is for the welfare of the child that he have a healthy and close relationship with both of his parents. Keefer v. Keefer, 107 Ill. App. 2d 74, 245 N.E.2d 784 (2 Dist. 1969).

Best Interests of the Child

The best interest of the child is normally fostered by having a healthy and close relationship with both parents. In re Blanchard, 162 Ill. App. 3d 202, 113 Ill. Dec. 197, 514 N.E.2d 1208 (5 Dist. 1987).

Best Interests of the Child (Cont'd)

The trial court's determination that both parties had demonstrated a genuine and honest concern for the best interests of their minor children, despite the friction generated between the parents as a result of the Tuesday night visitation, was amply supported by the record and the trial court did not err by retaining the existing Tuesday night custody schedule. In re Kessler, 110 Ill. App. 3d 61, 65 Ill. Dec. 707, 441 N.E.2d 1221 (1 Dist. 1982).

The terms of visitation are not to be limited as a punishment for the past conduct of a parent, but determined in the light of present circumstances relevant to the present welfare and best interests of the child. In re Lawver, 82 Ill. App. 3d 198, 37 Ill. Dec. 540, 402 N.E.2d 430 (3 Dist. 1980).

It has been said that to deny all right of visitation to the noncustodial parent would be inequitable and unjust, but it should be kept in mind that the child's welfare, not the interest of the parents, is paramount. Valencia v. Valencia, 46 Ill. App. 3d 741, 4 Ill. Dec. 951, 360 N.E.2d 1384 (5 Dist. 1977), modified on other grounds, 71 Ill. 2d 220, 16 Ill. Dec. 467, 375 N.E.2d 98 (1978).

It is believed to be in the best interest of a child — the touchstone against which all the court's determinations as to visitation must be evaluated — that he or she have a healthy and close relationship with both parents. Valencia v. Valencia, 46 Ill. App. 3d 741, 4 Ill. Dec. 951, 360 N.E.2d 1384 (5 Dist. 1977), modified on other grounds, 71 Ill. 2d 220, 16 Ill. Dec. 467, 375 N.E.2d 98 (1978).

Children's best interests who were in father's custody demanded that visitation with their mother be scheduled even though she was imprisoned for conviction of a felony for physical abuse where arrangements could be made at the visits with the children in a non-prison atmosphere. Frail v. Frail, 54 Ill. App. 3d 1013, 12 Ill. Dec. 680, 370 N.E.2d 303 (3 Dist. 1977).

A circuit court, in granting visitation rights to a parent who does not have custody of a child, must seek primarily to promote the child's welfare; the welfare of the child usually requires that the parent who does not have custody of the child be given liberal visitation rights so the child will not be estranged from that parent. McManus v. McManus, 38 Ill. App. 3d 645, 348 N.E.2d 507 (5 Dist. 1976).

In view of the evidence showing father to be unfit, and his lack of good health, it was adequately shown that allowing visitation or any further contact between him and his son would be detrimental to the child. Ice v. Department of Children & Family Servs., 35 Ill. App. 3d 783, 342 N.E.2d 460 (3 Dist. 1976).

Burden of Proof

Trial court properly placed the burden on the mother to overcome the presumption that the father would be entitled to visitation and it properly concluded the mother fell short of proving that visitation was not warranted pursuant to 750 ILCS 5/607 as there was no evidence of endangerment. Jines v. Jurich, 335 Ill. App. 3d 1156, 270 Ill. Dec. 572, 783 N.E.2d 147, 2002 Ill. App. LEXIS 1279 (5 Dist. 2002).

Where mother petitioned for temporary custody, which was granted, and prior to the final hearing, the parties stipulated that mother would have sole custody, the trial court did not err by placing burden on mother, as custodial parent, of proving visitation with father would seriously endanger the children. In re Fields, 283 Ill. App. 3d 894, 219 Ill. Dec. 420, 671 N.E.2d 85 (4 Dist. 1996).

The custodial parent bears the burden of proving by a preponderance of the evidence that visitation with the noncustodial parent would seriously endanger the child. In re Diehl, 221 Ill. App. 3d 410, 164 Ill. Dec. 73, 582 N.E.2d 281 (2 Dist. 1991), cert. denied, 144 Ill. 2d 632, 169 Ill. Dec. 140, 591 N.E.2d 20 (1992).

Cost of Visitation

Apportionment of transportation responsibilities connected with visitation to the noncustodial parent was held not to have been an abuse of discretion. In re Nuechterlien, 225 Ill. App. 3d 1, 167 Ill. Dec. 139, 587 N.E.2d 21 (4 Dist.), cert. denied, 145 Ill. 2d 636, 173 Ill. Dec. 6, 596 N.E.2d 630 (1992).

An order of visitation at the mother's expense for one week in the months of September, December and July in Illinois each year with father, was within the court's discretion where the mother had removed the child to Panama. Crawley v. Bauchens, 13 Ill. App. 3d 791, 300 N.E.2d 603 (5 Dist. 1973), aff'd, 57 Ill. 2d 360, 312 N.E.2d 236 (1974).

Counseling

Because requiring a noncustodial parent to participate in counseling is not a restriction, a trial court should apply the best interest of the child standard in determining whether to order the noncustodial parent to participate in counseling. In re Fields, 283 Ill. App. 3d 894, 219 Ill. Dec. 420, 671 N.E.2d 85 (4 Dist. 1996).

Custody Award

In custody proceeding, under the terms of custody order, the noncustodial parent would have authority over the children's clothing, education, and medical care and virtually no area of decisional authority was allotted exclusively to the custodial parent and, perhaps most significant, over a typical 14 day period, the custodial parent would have contact with his children for only two full days, plus two evening sessions and Sunday morning for church; this order was not an award of custody, it was an award of visitation and clearly and unequivocally awarded authority for the children's upbringing to the noncustodial parent which had no justification under the Act. In re Ivey, 261 Ill. App. 3d 200, 198 Ill. Dec. 510, 632 N.E.2d 1121 (4 Dist.), appeal denied, 157 Ill. 2d 502, 205 Ill. Dec. 164, 642 N.E.2d 1281 (1994).

De Novo Review

Because a temporary visitation order means just that, particularly when a different judge presides at the hearing on the merits which will result in a permanent or final order, a trial court must conduct a hearing regarding permanent custody or visitation de novo; during the final hearing the court should consider all factors which relate to the best interests of the children. In re Fields, 283 Ill. App. 3d 894, 219 Ill. Dec. 420, 671 N.E.2d 85 (4 Dist. 1996).

Denial of Visitation

—Extreme Circumstances

The endangerment standard has been described as onerous, stringent and rigorous; parents have a natural or inherent right of access to their children, and because sound public policy encourages the maintenance of strong family relationships, even in post-divorce situations only extreme circumstances allow courts to deprive a parent of visitation. In re L. R., 202 Ill. App. 3d 69, 147 Ill. Dec. 439, 559 N.E.2d 779 (1 Dist. 1990).

Courts are reluctant to deny all visitation rights because of the underlying rationale that parents have a natural or inherent right of access to their children and the sound public policy that this state encourages the maintenance of strong interfamily relationships, even in post-divorce situations; only very extreme circumstances require and allow the trial court to permanently deprive a parent of visitation. Frail v. Frail, 54 Ill. App. 3d 1013, 12 Ill. Dec. 680, 370 N.E.2d 303 (3 Dist. 1977).

—Not Proper

Where no suggestion was made that the exercise of visitation privileges by the father or grandparents had in any way been harmful to the child and no specific reason was given why such visitation was not in the child's best interest, no showing was made that would justify vacation of the provisions of the dissolution decree relating to visitation. In re Spomer, 123 Ill. App. 3d 31, 78 Ill. Dec. 605, 462 N.E.2d 724 (5 Dist. 1984).

Evidence of endangerment was insufficient to justify denying visitation to non-custodial parent. In re Neat, 101 Ill. App. 3d 1046, 57 Ill. Dec. 413, 428 N.E.2d 1093 (1 Dist. 1981).

—Proper

Trial court's finding that visitation by defendant with the child "would seriously endanger the physical, mental and emotional health of the minor child" was sufficiently supported by the evidence where defendant had repeatedly violated previous orders by harassing his former wife and, concomitantly, visitation would be very difficult to arrange without creating situations where defendant's tendency to lose control of himself would be likely to have occurred with unpredictable results. People v. Hazelwonder, 138 Ill. App. 3d 213, 93 Ill. Dec. 1, 485 N.E.2d 1211 (4 Dist. 1985).

—Reluctance of Courts

The courts of Illinois have been reluctant to deny visitation rights because of the principle that parents have a natural or inherent right of access to their children, and because sound public policy encourages the maintenance of strong family relationships, even in

Denial of Visitation (Cont'd)

—Reluctance of Courts (Cont'd)
post-divorce situations; only extreme circumstances allow courts to deprive a parent of visitation. In re Diehl, 221 Ill. App. 3d 410, 164 Ill. Dec. 73, 582 N.E.2d 281 (2 Dist. 1991), cert. denied, 144 Ill. 2d 632, 169 Ill. Dec. 140, 591 N.E.2d 20 (1992).

—Test
While it is the trial judge's function to observe the demeanor of witnesses in the courtroom, the primacy of the parent-child relationship in the area of visitation rights demands that endangerment to the child, not courtroom demeanor, be the test for denying visitation to a non-custodial parent. In re Neat, 101 Ill. App. 3d 1046, 57 Ill. Dec. 413, 428 N.E.2d 1093 (1 Dist. 1981).

Discretion of Court

—In General
The court has broad discretion in determining visitation rights of the noncustodial parent, with the best interest of the child being the primary concern. In re Dobey, 258 Ill. App. 3d 874, 196 Ill. Dec. 267, 629 N.E.2d 812 (4 Dist. 1994).

The matter of visitation privileges rests in the broad discretion of the trial court. Frail v. Frail, 54 Ill. App. 3d 1013, 12 Ill. Dec. 680, 370 N.E.2d 303 (3 Dist. 1977); In re Lawver, 82 Ill. App. 3d 198, 37 Ill. Dec. 540, 402 N.E.2d 430 (3 Dist. 1980); In re Marriage of Roberts, 151 Ill. App. 3d 65, 104 Ill. Dec. 806, 503 N.E.2d 363, 1986 Ill. App. LEXIS 3290 (3 Dist. 1986), cert. denied, 106 Ill. Dec. 55, 505 N.E.2d 361 (1987), appeal denied, 106 Ill. Dec. 55, 505 N.E.2d 361 (1987) cert denied, 485 U.S. 963, 108 S. Ct. 1230, 99 L. Ed. 2d 430 (1988); In re Tisckos, 161 Ill. App. 3d 302, 112 Ill. Dec. 860, 514 N.E.2d 523 (4 Dist. 1987).

The burden of determining visitation rights of the non-custodial parent falls initially on the circuit court, which has been endowed by the General Assembly with broad discretion. Valencia v. Valencia, 46 Ill. App. 3d 741, 4 Ill. Dec. 951, 360 N.E.2d 1384 (5 Dist. 1977), modified on other grounds, 71 Ill. 2d 220, 16 Ill. Dec. 467, 375 N.E.2d 98 (1978).

The trial court has broad discretion to adjust the privileges of visitation, that discretion to be exercised only in the interest of the children and not as a punishment or reward to either parent. Keefer v. Keefer, 107 Ill. App. 2d 74, 245 N.E.2d 784 (2 Dist. 1969).

—Abuse Not Shown
There was no abuse of discretion in the circuit court's resolution of visitation issues where father was granted visitation with daughter pursuant to the report of the court-appointed psychiatrist. In re Campbell, 261 Ill. App. 3d 483, 199 Ill. Dec. 1, 633 N.E.2d 797 (1 Dist. 1993), appeal denied, 156 Ill. 2d 556, 202 Ill. Dec. 919, 638 N.E.2d 1113 (1994).

The trial court properly exercised its discretion in modifying the visitation provisions of the divorce decree. Flanagan v. Flanagan, 123 Ill. App. 2d 17, 259 N.E.2d 610 (1 Dist. 1970).

—Appellate Review
The trial court is vested with wide discretion in resolving visitation issues; the appellate court will not interfere with the lower court's determination unless an abuse of discretion occurred, or where manifest injustice has been done to the child or parent. In re Diehl, 221 Ill. App. 3d 410, 164 Ill. Dec. 73, 582 N.E.2d 281 (2 Dist. 1991), cert. denied, 144 Ill. 2d 632, 169 Ill. Dec. 140, 591 N.E.2d 20 (1992).

A circuit court possesses broad discretion in awarding visitation rights, and the court's award will be modified on appeal only if it causes manifest injustice to the child or either of the parents. McManus v. McManus, 38 Ill. App. 3d 645, 348 N.E.2d 507 (5 Dist. 1976).

—Delegation of Duties
Trial court abused its discretion by delegating its responsibility regarding the modification of a father's supervised monthly visitation schedule unless clearly authorized by law; courts have no power to delegate any of their duties. In re Stribling, 219 Ill. App. 3d 105, 161 Ill. Dec. 749, 579 N.E.2d 6 (5 Dist. 1991).

Entitlement
This section creates something of an "entitlement" to reasonable visitation. Lyons v. Lyons, 228 Ill. App. 3d 407, 169 Ill. Dec. 502, 591 N.E.2d 1006 (5 Dist. 1992).

Evidence
Neither this section nor 750 ILCS 5/606 contains any language limiting the introduction of evidence to facts that have arisen since prior judgment. In re Fields, 283 Ill. App. 3d 894, 219 Ill. Dec. 420, 671 N.E.2d 85 (4 Dist. 1996).

Grandparent Visitation

—In General
Judgment finding 750 ILCS 5/607(b)(1), (3) of the Illinois Marriage and Dissolution of Marriage Act unconstitutional did not void grandparents' visitation rights under a previous order as a matter of law; however, as a matter of fact, the visitation order had to pass scrutiny under the principles articulated in Wickham v. Byrne, 199 Ill. 2d 309, 263 Ill. Dec. 799, 769 N.E.2d 1. Johnson v. Duncan (In re M.M.D.), 344 Ill. App. 3d 345, 279 Ill. Dec. 543, 800 N.E.2d 831, 2003 Ill. App. LEXIS 1373 (3 Dist. 2003).

Subsection (b)(1) permits a grandparent to file a petition for visitation where the grandparent's own child, i.e., the parent, objects to the visitation between the grandparent and grandchild. Lulay v. Lulay, 193 Ill. 2d 455, 250 Ill. Dec. 758, 739 N.E.2d 521, 2000 Ill. LEXIS 1694 (2000).

—Agreement
The court's power to grant grandparental visitation is not limited where the parties have by agreement requested the court to grant such visitation. In re Spomer, 123 Ill. App. 3d 31, 78 Ill. Dec. 605, 462 N.E.2d 724 (5 Dist. 1984).

—Burden of Proof
A grandparent whose child has died and who seeks visitation under subsection (b) must show that it is in the best interest of the grandchild that the visitation request be granted. Weybright v. Puckett, 262 Ill. App. 3d 605, 200 Ill Dec. 18, 635 N.E.2d 119 (4 Dist. 1994).

—Common Law
At common law, grandparents could be entitled to court-ordered visitation with a minor child only in special, limited circumstances. Bush v. Squellati, 154 Ill. App. 3d 727, 107 Ill. Dec. 81, 506 N.E.2d 972 (3 Dist. 1987).

—Court's Authority
Under the Parentage Act, (750 ILCS 45/1 et seq.), custody and visitation is to be determined in accordance with all of the factors set forth in the Marriage and Dissolution Act, including those contained in this section; thus, grandparent visitation is available under the Parentage Act. People ex rel. Farina v. Sensor, 299 Ill. App. 3d 333, 233 Ill. Dec. 873, 701 N.E.2d 1147 (2 Dist. 1998).

Where a grandmother brought suit against her son and his wife, who were not involved in a dissolution of marriage proceeding, seeking a court ordered granting her visitation with their daughter, the trial court lacked authority to grant visitation rights. Towne v. Cole, 133 Ill. App. 3d 380, 88 Ill. Dec. 404, 478 N.E.2d 895 (2 Dist. 1985).

—Death of Parent
An amendment to subsection (b) of this section was inserted to provide a remedy for grandparent visitation when there was no dissolution proceedings but where one of the parents had died. Towne v. Cole, 133 Ill. App. 3d 380, 88 Ill. Dec. 404, 478 N.E.2d 895 (2 Dist. 1985).

—Determination
There are only two ways for a trial court to award grandparent visitation: (1) when there are special circumstances, and (2) when a grandparent petitions the court under subsection (b) of this section. In re Balzell, 207 Ill. App. 3d 310, 152 Ill. Dec. 492, 566 N.E.2d 20 (3 Dist. 1991).

The existence of the best interest standard does not guarantee that grandparents have visitation; normally, the loving, caring, and reasonable grandparent should be given visitation, and, normally, this visitation should not be restricted. Lindsey v. Lindsey, 158 Ill. App. 3d 769, 110 Ill. Dec. 363, 511 N.E.2d 198 (4 Dist. 1987).

Child's best interest is not entirely severable from the interests of the parents in a reconstituted family, and certainly the parents'

Grandparent Visitation (Cont'd)

—Determination (Cont'd)
attitude toward grandparental visitation is an important factor for the court to consider in determining whether such visitation should be ordered, however, their attitude is not the only, or even the paramount consideration and such factors as the length and quality of the relationship between grandparents and child, the child's need for continuity in his relationships with people who may have played a significant nurturing role in his life, and the effect of the termination of the child's relationship with the parent who has relinquished his rights and responsibilities must also be considered. Lingwall v. Hoener, 108 Ill. 2d 206, 91 Ill. Dec. 166, 483 N.E.2d 512 (1985).

In order to grant visitation to a grandparent or great-grandparent, subdivision (b)(1) of this section requires that the court determine that visitation is in "the best interests and welfare of the child." Lingwall v. Hoener, 124 Ill. App. 3d 986, 80 Ill. Dec. 265, 464 N.E.2d 1248 (4 Dist. 1984).

In cases of dissolution of marriage or death of a parent, a court is empowered to grant grandparent visitation when it is in the child's best interest to do so. Krystek v. Schumacher, 120 Ill. App. 3d 50, 75 Ill. Dec. 926, 458 N.E.2d 94 (2 Dist. 1983).

—Discretion of Court
A trial court's determination regarding grandparent's visitation is within its sound discretion and will not be disturbed on review. McVey v. Fredrickson, 226 Ill. App. 3d 1082, 169 Ill. Dec. 77, 590 N.E.2d 996 (3 Dist. 1992).

—Effect of Adoption
Where the biological parents of a minor child both consented to the adoption of the child by his biological maternal great-aunt and her husband, visitation privileges could not be granted to the child's biological grandparents under subsection (b) of this section. Bush v. Squellati, 122 Ill. 2d 153, 119 Ill. Dec. 366, 522 N.E.2d 1225 (1988).

The legislature, by narrowly delimiting those situations in which grandparental visitation may be granted following a child's adoption, intended to promote the public policy underlying this State's adoption law, maximizing the pool of potential adoptive parents by guaranteeing, through the termination of the rights and responsibilities of the natural parents, that the adoptive parents will have the opportunity to create a stable family relationship free from unnecessary intrusions. Bush v. Squellati, 154 Ill. App. 3d 727, 107 Ill. Dec. 81, 506 N.E.2d 972 (3 Dist. 1987).

Absent an adoption of an infant by strangers, there is no reason to assume from the outset that termination of a grandparental relationship is in an adopted child's best interest, nor is there any reason to view grandparental visitation as an "unnecessary intrusion" in the lives of a reconstituted family. Lingwall v. Hoener, 108 Ill. 2d 206, 91 Ill. Dec. 166, 483 N.E.2d 512 (1985).

Where parent of child through whom grandparent sought visitation had lost all parental rights in the child through adoption proceedings whereby the child was adopted by his mother's husband, the ties of the grandparent need not be severed unless the visitation causes disruption or disunity. Lingwall v. Hoener, 124 Ill. App. 3d 986, 80 Ill. Dec. 265, 464 N.E.2d 1248 (4 Dist. 1984).

As a grandparent's status as such is derived from the relationship between the child and the natural parent, an adoption, which terminates the rights of the natural parent, also removes the basis for the relationship of the grandparent and thereby ends the status on which the statutory right to visitation rests. Krystek v. Schumacher, 120 Ill. App. 3d 50, 75 Ill. Dec. 926, 458 N.E.2d 94 (2 Dist. 1983).

An order of adoption will operate to divest natural relatives, such as grandparents, of the right to visitation with the adopted child. Krystek v. Schumacher, 120 Ill. App. 3d 50, 75 Ill. Dec. 926, 458 N.E.2d 94 (2 Dist. 1983).

The grandparent visitation provision should be construed as subject to the adoption laws, such that a completed adoption proceeding supersedes any rights which could have been obtained pursuant to subsection (b) of this statute. Krystek v. Schumacher, 120 Ill. App. 3d 50, 75 Ill. Dec. 926, 458 N.E.2d 94 (2 Dist. 1983).

—Improper
Visitation order granting a grandmother overnight and summer vacation visitation was rendered void by the Illinois Supreme Court's ruling that 750 ILCS 5/607(b) was facially unconstitutional; no common law right to grandparent visitation existed as such a right would be in direct conflict with a fit parent's constitutionally protected right to make decisions regarding the best interest of his or her child. Beurksen v. Graff, 351 Ill. App. 3d 148, 286 Ill. Dec. 325, 813 N.E.2d 1018, 2004 Ill. App. LEXIS 745 (1 Dist. 2004).

Trial court did not abuse its discretion in granting grandmother visitation of deceased son's children one day per month where evidence showed she was hostile toward the children's mother, which she relayed to the children, and there was concern over how that conduct adversely affected her relationship with the children. In re Gollahon, 303 Ill. App. 3d 254, 236 Ill. Dec. 608, 707 N.E.2d 735 (4 Dist. 1999).

Where petitioner had no contact with her young granddaughter for over four years, the trial court did not err in ruling petitioner had not shown it was in grandchild's best interest to grant the requested visitation. Weybright v. Puckett, 262 Ill. App. 3d 605, 200 Ill Dec. 18, 635 N.E.2d 119 (4 Dist. 1994).

The giving of the visitation rights to the grandfather over the objections of the mother in the absence of any special circumstances justifying the interference with the superior custodial right to the natural parent was error. Chodzko v. Chodzko, 66 Ill. 2d 28, 4 Ill. Dec. 313, 360 N.E.2d 60 (1976).

—Increased Visitation
Grandmother did not present that increased visitation with her was within the best interests of her grandchild where the parties had agreed on a visitation schedule just eight months before the hearing and the only new evidence before the court at the hearing was the psychologist's testimony, and that testimony was adverse to the grandmother's position. Sarchet ex rel. Candler v. Zeigler, 278 Ill. App. 3d 460, 215 Ill. Dec. 275, 663 N.E.2d 25 (3 Dist. 1996).

—Proper
Where the trial court granted the plaintiffs visitation with their two grandchildren, on a limited basis, one Saturday per month from 8 a.m. to 8 p.m. or at any other time the parties agreed, the trial court's decision was not an abuse of discretion because the circumstances of the family changed substantially from the time of the mother's divorce until her remarriage and after the mother remarried, the children gradually enjoyed more and more of a normal family life. McVey v. Fredrickson, 226 Ill. App. 3d 1082, 169 Ill. Dec. 77, 590 N.E.2d 996 (3 Dist. 1992).

Since plaintiff had previously agreed that visitation by paternal grandparents would be in the best interest of the child, and since the trial court had made that agreement a part of its decree, testimony by plaintiff that she sometimes had difficulty with the child's conduct after his visits with the grandparents, did not require the appellate court to overturn the finding of the trial court that paternal grandparents had right to visitation as contrary to the manifest weight of the evidence. Loveless v. Michalak, 168 Ill. App. 3d 598, 119 Ill. Dec. 211, 522 N.E.2d 873 (3 Dist. 1988).

Manifest weight of the evidence supported the trial court's ruling that child's welfare would be best served by giving her adoptive father permanent custody and granting visitation rights to the grandparents. People ex rel. Lutz v. Lutz, 24 Ill. App. 3d 948, 322 N.E.2d 62 (2 Dist. 1975).

The granting of visitation rights to the maternal grandparents in a custody decree was neither void nor erroneous, in a case where the mother had died; consequently, the custodial father was not free to disregard the provision of the valid decree. Boyles v. Boyles, 14 Ill. App. 3d 602, 302 N.E.2d 199 (3 Dist. 1973).

—Rights
Grandparents have the right to seek visitation with their grandchildren pursuant to a petition for the dissolution of the parents' marriage, and the court may grant such visitation if it is in the children's best interest and welfare. Lingwall v. Hoener, 108 Ill. 2d 206, 91 Ill. Dec. 166, 483 N.E.2d 512 (1985).

Long standing common law tradition clearly establishes authority for extending visitation privileges to grandparents in special, limited circumstances. Hawkins v. Hawkins, 102 Ill. App. 3d 1037, 58 Ill. Dec. 620, 430 N.E.2d 652 (3 Dist. 1981).

If circumstances warrant visitation, grandparents may be granted a right to visit their grandchild. Boyles v. Boyles, 14 Ill. App. 3d 602, 302 N.E.2d 199 (3 Dist. 1973).

Grandparent Visitation (Cont'd)

—Special Circumstances

Where the child had been abandoned by both natural parents, that constituted "special circumstances" which justified the trial court's recognition of the grandparents' right to visitation. Loveless v. Michalak, 168 Ill. App. 3d 598, 119 Ill. Dec. 211, 522 N.E.2d 873 (3 Dist. 1988).

Imprisoned Parent

Imprisonment of the noncustodial parent does not create a per se right to visitation at a prison or at a particular place chosen by the noncustodial parent. Woods v. Woods, 147 Ill. App. 3d 772, 101 Ill. Dec. 582, 498 N.E.2d 906 (5 Dist. 1986).

Imprisonment of a parent does not, of itself, require that visitation between child and parent be barred or restricted. Griffiths v. Griffiths, 127 Ill. App. 3d 126, 82 Ill. Dec. 220, 468 N.E.2d 482 (4 Dist. 1984).

Liberal Visitation

Courts favor liberal visitation for the noncustodial parent because the child is entitled to a healthy, close relationship with both parents. In re Dobey, 258 Ill. App. 3d 874, 196 Ill. Dec. 267, 629 N.E.2d 812 (4 Dist. 1994).

Liberal visitation is the rule; restricted visitation is the exception. In re Diehl, 221 Ill. App. 3d 410, 164 Ill. Dec. 73, 582 N.E.2d 281 (2 Dist. 1991), cert. denied, 144 Ill. 2d 632, 169 Ill. Dec. 140, 591 N.E.2d 20 (1992).

Mental Condition of Parent

A petition to regain visitation rights is appropriate whenever a parent can show an improvement in his or her mental condition, particularly if he or she obtains psychiatric treatment. In re Neat, 101 Ill. App. 3d 1046, 57 Ill. Dec. 413, 428 N.E.2d 1093 (1 Dist. 1981).

Modification

—Best Interest of Child

Since any modification of a visitation order was required to be in accordance with the relevant factors specified in the Illinois Marriage and Dissolution of Marriage Act, 750 ILCS 5/101, the trial court erred in not considering whether the mother's proposed move to Florida was in the best interest of the child, which was a modification factor. DeBilio v. Rodgers, 337 Ill. App. 3d 614, 272 Ill. Dec. 9, 786 N.E.2d 548, 2002 Ill. App. LEXIS 947 (3 Dist. 2002).

This Act creates, in the case of child visitation rights, an exception to the general requirement that modification of a dissolution of marriage decree be preceded by a petition requesting modification, by providing that visitation rights may be modified whenever modification would serve the best interest of the child. In re Stanley, 133 Ill. App. 3d 963, 89 Ill. Dec. 146, 479 N.E.2d 1152 (4 Dist. 1985).

The best interest of the child standard governs the modification of visiting rights whereas the endangerment standard governs the restriction of such rights where the court finds that the visitation as it exists seriously endangers the child's physical, mental, moral, or emotional health. In re Anderson, 130 Ill. App. 3d 684, 85 Ill. Dec. 951, 474 N.E.2d 911 (2 Dist. 1985).

A court may amend visitation privileges previously established, or, in extreme cases, temporarily deny them altogether if the privilege is abused. Keefer v. Keefer, 107 Ill. App. 2d 74, 245 N.E.2d 784 (2 Dist. 1969).

An order of visitation is not final; it can be modified as circumstances require, if it should appear reasonable and proper to do so, upon motion of either parent, and if the best interests of the child make it advisable. Smith v. Smith, 36 Ill. App. 2d 55, 183 N.E.2d 559 (1 Dist. 1962).

—Burden of Proof

The party seeking to increase or otherwise modify visitation rights originally granted by the dissolution decree bears the burden of showing such alteration is in the best interests of the child. In re Tisckos, 161 Ill. App. 3d 302, 112 Ill. Dec. 860, 514 N.E.2d 523 (4 Dist. 1987).

The custodial parent bears the burden of proving by a preponderance of the evidence that visitation would endanger the children. In re Neat, 101 Ill. App. 3d 1046, 57 Ill. Dec. 413, 428 N.E.2d 1093 (1 Dist. 1981); In re Blanchard, 162 Ill. App. 3d 202, 113 Ill. Dec. 197, 514 N.E.2d 1208 (5 Dist. 1987).

The burden of proving that a modification would be in the best interest of the child is on the party seeking the modification. Valencia v. Valencia, 46 Ill. App. 3d 741, 4 Ill. Dec. 951, 360 N.E.2d 1384 (5 Dist. 1977), modified on other grounds, 71 Ill. 2d 220, 16 Ill. Dec. 467, 375 N.E.2d 98 (1978).

Where a circuit court is called upon to alter previously established visitation rights, it need not find (as it must where a change of custody is sought) that there has been a material change of circumstances since the original order; its decision is to be guided solely by what it perceives to be in the best interest of the child. Valencia v. Valencia, 46 Ill. App. 3d 741, 4 Ill. Dec. 951, 360 N.E.2d 1384 (5 Dist. 1977), modified on other grounds, 71 Ill. 2d 220, 16 Ill. Dec. 467, 375 N.E.2d 98 (1978).

—Move Out-of-State

A reduction of weekend visitation from 50 hours to 31 hours, and reduction of summer visitation from four weeks to two weeks (because of the children's activities), was not a restriction which had to meet the serious endangerment standard; the trial court could have changed visitation in this case to accommodate mother's move without violating subsection (c). In re Wycoff, 266 Ill. App. 3d 408, 203 Ill. Dec. 338, 639 N.E.2d 897 (4 Dist.), appeal denied, 158 Ill. 2d 566, 206 Ill. Dec. 847, 645 N.E.2d 1369 (1994).

Although husband complained that the number of his visitation days was reduced by 29%, the fact the number of days of visitation was reduced was not dispositive; what was important was whether, in a given case, a realistic and reasonable visitation schedule could be reached if move out-of-state was allowed. In re Deckard, 246 Ill. App. 3d 427, 186 Ill. Dec. 270, 615 N.E.2d 1327 (4 Dist. 1993).

—Properly Allowed

Visitation schedule was unjust due to the unusual circumstances involved; in a two-month period, father was home only 20 days, but during those 20 days, he was available the entire day, therefore, child's father had daytime visitation in place of baby-sitter during the weeks he was home. In re Dobey, 258 Ill. App. 3d 874, 196 Ill. Dec. 267, 629 N.E.2d 812 (4 Dist. 1994).

The trial court did not err in a child custody proceeding where the evidence was held sufficient to sustain a judge's order that expanded the mother's visitation rights but left custody with the father. Patton v. Armstrong, 16 Ill. App. 3d 881, 307 N.E.2d 178 (5 Dist. 1974).

Where there was evidence that considerable difficulty arose under the "reasonable" visitation provisions of the original decree, the court did not abuse his discretion in spelling out specific provisions for visitation in the modified decree. Lewis v. Lewis, 120 Ill. App. 2d 263, 256 N.E.2d 660 (3 Dist. 1970).

The trial court, reasonably concluded, that the plaintiff's interest in caring for the children had deteriorated during the last two years, and that their future care by the plaintiff would be neglected insofar as an estimate of the future might be projected from the evidence as to plaintiff's manner of living. Froman v. Froman, 73 Ill. App. 2d 421, 218 N.E.2d 808 (4 Dist. 1966).

—Properly Denied

Petitioner/prisoner who presented no evidence of a strong relationship with his child plus the fact that child would have to enter the prison grounds, be searched by guards, and observe the general prison environment to see his father was not in the child's best interests and thus petitioner's modification of visitation rights was denied. Woods v. Woods, 147 Ill. App. 3d 772, 101 Ill. Dec. 582, 498 N.E.2d 906 (5 Dist. 1986).

Evidence was held insufficient to sustain a motion of change of visitation rights because of the mother's alleged associations and the child's falling grades. Keefer v. Keefer, 107 Ill. App. 2d 74, 245 N.E.2d 784 (2 Dist. 1969).

The court erred in its order modifying the decree of divorce which in effect provided that the defendant father need pay no more for the support of the minor children except when he requested that they be brought to his home and then he was required to pay plaintiff $30 on each and every occasion, where he was financially able to support the children. Kemp v. Kemp, 332 Ill. App. 432, 75 N.E.2d 385 (1 Dist. 1947).

—Time Constraints

The two-year limitation against custody modification does not

Modification (Cont'd)

—Time Constraints (Cont'd)

apply to modification of visitation rights. Mueller v. Weis, 76 Ill. App. 3d 860, 32 Ill. Dec. 447, 395 N.E.2d 677 (5 Dist. 1979).

Noncustodial Parent

—In General

In the absence of a constitutionally valid grandparent visitation statute, a noncustodial parent's request that visitation be modified to permit grandparent visitation in lieu of the parent's visitation while the parent was on active military duty was governed by Illinois common law, which allowed such modifications under special circumstances, including military duty; therefore, the trial court had subject matter jurisdiction over the parent's modification petition and should have conducted a best interests proceeding. In re Marriage of Sullivan, 342 Ill. App. 3d 560, 277 Ill. Dec. 25, 795 N.E.2d 392, 2003 Ill. App. LEXIS 1012 (2 Dist. 2003).

The Parentage Act (750 ILCS 45/1 et seq.) does not incorporate this section requiring a court to award visitation to a noncustodial parent unless the court finds, after a hearing, that visitation would endanger seriously the child's physical, mental, moral or emotional health. Illinois Dep't of Pub. Aid ex rel. Gagnon-Dix v. Gagnon, 288 Ill. App. 3d 424, 223 Ill. Dec. 776, 680 N.E.2d 509 (4 Dist. 1997).

—Burden of Proof

When a noncustodial parent seeks to modify visitation rights, that parent has the burden of showing the modification is in the best interest of the child or children. Lyons v. Lyons, 228 Ill. App. 3d 407, 169 Ill. Dec. 502, 591 N.E.2d 1006 (5 Dist. 1992); Woods v. Woods, 147 Ill. App. 3d 772, 101 Ill. Dec. 582, 498 N.E.2d 906 (5 Dist. 1986).

—Evidence

Although there was evidence that child, born during marriage between wife and ex-husband but not ex-husband's biological child, resented the interruption caused by visitation with the ex-husband, the trial court could reasonably conclude that this anger did not amount to a serious threat to the child's emotional development. In re Slayton, 292 Ill. App. 3d 379, 226 Ill. Dec. 583, 685 N.E.2d 1038 (4 Dist. 1997), appeal denied, 176 Ill. 2d 593, 229 Ill. Dec. 60, 690 N.E.2d 1387 (1998).

—Rights of

When a court designates one parent as the custodial parent, that designation does not and should not deprive the noncustodial parent of all rights and privileges as a parent. In re Dobey, 258 Ill. App. 3d 874, 196 Ill. Dec. 267, 629 N.E.2d 812 (4 Dist. 1994).

Overnight Visitation

Where the child was of such a young age, it was difficult to perceive how he could have been influenced by his father's choice of living arrangements where the father, who planned to marry the unmarried woman he was living with, was entitled to overnight visitation. In re Hanson, 112 Ill. App. 3d 564, 68 Ill. Dec. 268, 445 N.E.2d 912 (5 Dist. 1983).

Facts that limited pattern of visitation, whereby husband was not allowed to have daughter for overnight visits in home shared with woman outside of marriage, had been voluntarily followed for two years subsequent to the parties' separation and that wife found it distasteful to have any contact with or knowledge of the woman for whom the husband left the marital home did not justify limiting father's contact with his daughter. In re Lawver, 82 Ill. App. 3d 198, 37 Ill. Dec. 540, 402 N.E.2d 430 (3 Dist. 1980).

Because respondent alleged that petitioner's overnight visitation would so endanger their minor daughter in her affirmative defense and reply to her ex-husband's petition, respondent then had to carry the burden of proving the allegation by a preponderance of the evidence to succeed in restricting the petitioner's visitation rights. Crichton v. Crichton, 75 Ill. App. 3d 326, 31 Ill. Dec. 12, 393 N.E.2d 1319 (3 Dist. 1979).

The manifest weight of the evidence did support the trial court's rejection of mother's contention that overnight visitation be denied father when the evidence offered by the mother indicated no demonstrative depravity which would place child in danger on father's part. Crichton v. Crichton, 75 Ill. App. 3d 326, 31 Ill. Dec. 12, 393 N.E.2d 1319 (3 Dist. 1979).

It was incumbent on the defendant to show by competent evidence that it was in the best interests of the child to change the visitation rights provided in the order. Keefer v. Keefer, 107 Ill. App. 2d 74, 245 N.E.2d 784 (2 Dist. 1969).

Parent's Cohabitation

Under the best interests standard in custody cases, the presumption that a parent's cohabitation establishes harm to the child has been rejected; this approach, which is sexual orientation neutral, is extended to visitation, which involves the more rigorous serious endangerment standard. Pleasant v. Pleasant, 256 Ill. App. 3d 742, 195 Ill. Dec. 169, 628 N.E.2d 633 (1 Dist. 1993).

Parentage Act

The Parentage Act incorporates the factors specified in section 607(c) of the Marriage and Dissolution of Marriage Act, 750 ILCS 5/607, for modification of visitation; that is, the court may modify visitation whenever the modification would serve the child's best interests, but the court should not restrict the noncustodial parent's visitation unless it finds that the visitation would endanger seriously the child's physical, mental, moral or emotional health. Hall v. Melton, 314 Ill. App. 3d 476, 247 Ill. Dec. 295, 732 N.E.2d 11, 2000 Ill. App. LEXIS 584 (1 Dist. 2000).

Past Conduct

It is not the past conduct of the petitioner that is controlling in an action for visitation rights, but rather the present circumstances and the present welfare of the children. Aud v. Etienne, 47 Ill. 2d 110, 264 N.E.2d 196 (1970).

Prejudicial Comments

Although the trial court made various comments in evaluating the evidence, those comments did not have any prejudicial effect on the trial court's decision on the law or as to the lack of detrimental effect of the petitioner's exercising overnight visitation privileges with his preschool age daughter. Crichton v. Crichton, 75 Ill. App. 3d 326, 31 Ill. Dec. 12, 393 N.E.2d 1319 (3 Dist. 1979).

Public Policy

Although the legislature has manifested an intent to protect intact nuclear families from interfering with visitation by nonparents and although a "no visitation except for compelling reason" standard might be a reasonable rule, there is no statutory support for grafting such a rule onto subsection (a). In re Slayton, 292 Ill. App. 3d 379, 226 Ill. Dec. 583, 685 N.E.2d 1038 (4 Dist. 1997), appeal denied, 176 Ill. 2d 593, 229 Ill. Dec. 60, 690 N.E.2d 1387 (1998).

This section states a strong public policy designed to preserve the relationship of parent and child. In re Blanchard, 162 Ill. App. 3d 202, 113 Ill. Dec. 197, 514 N.E.2d 1208 (5 Dist. 1987).

The policy of this state is to grant liberal visitation rights. In re Blanchard, 162 Ill. App. 3d 202, 113 Ill. Dec. 197, 514 N.E.2d 1208 (5 Dist. 1987).

Based on the belief that the best interests of the child are usually fostered by maintaining a close relationship with both parents, the policy in Illinois is to grant liberal visitation rights to the noncustodial parent which are not to be restricted as punishment for past conduct of the parent. In re Marriage of Roberts, 151 Ill. App. 3d 65, 104 Ill. Dec. 806, 503 N.E.2d 363, 1986 Ill. App. LEXIS 3290 (3 Dist. 1986), cert. denied, 106 Ill. Dec. 55, 505 N.E.2d 361 (1987), appeal denied, 106 Ill. Dec. 55, 505 N.E.2d 361 (1987) cert denied, 485 U.S. 963, 108 S. Ct. 1230, 99 L. Ed. 2d 430 (1988).

This statute's aim is to promote the best interests and welfare of the child, a purpose which generally is served by giving the adopted child the status of a natural child of the adoptive parents and completely breaking all ties with the natural family. Krystek v. Schumacher, 120 Ill. App. 3d 50, 75 Ill. Dec. 926, 458 N.E.2d 94 (2 Dist. 1983).

Punishment

Matters of visitation and custody are not to be used as means of punishing either parent. Hock v. Hock, 50 Ill. App. 3d 583, 8 Ill. Dec. 639, 365 N.E.2d 1025 (2 Dist. 1977).

Reinstatement of Visitation

Judge did not err in failing to modify the judgment for dissolution with respect to the provision concerning custody and visitation even though the psychologist examining the parties' daughter, who was

Reinstatement of Visitation (Cont'd)
solely responsible for establishing a procedure for visitation until relieved of that responsibility by further order of the court, resigned prior to the entry of the judgment and was deceased prior to the hearing, because the judge appointed a doctor to consult with the minor child and each of the parties in order to establish a procedure to reinstate defendant's visitation, if any, with his daughter. In re Hartian, 172 Ill. App. 3d 440, 122 Ill. Dec. 565, 526 N.E.2d 1104 (1 Dist.), appeal denied, 123 Ill. 2d 558, 128 Ill. Dec. 890, 535 N.E.2d 401 (1988).

Religious Services
Custodial mother did not have an absolute right, under 750 ILCS 5/608(a), to prohibit the noncustodial father from taking the parties' child to his religious services during his visitation, over her objection, without some proof that this action by the father was harmful to the child, given the father's right to unrestricted visitation, under 750 ILCS 5/607(c), and his right to the free exercise of his religion. Minix v. Dunaven-Minix, 344 Ill. App. 3d 801, 280 Ill. Dec. 256, 801 N.E.2d 1201, 2003 Ill. App. LEXIS 1559 (4 Dist. 2003).

Restricted Visitation

—In General
Not every condition which a trial court may place upon a noncustodial parent is a restriction; a restriction of visitation is an action which limits, restrains, or confines visitation within bounds. In re Fields, 283 Ill. App. 3d 894, 219 Ill. Dec. 420, 671 N.E.2d 85 (4 Dist. 1996).

—Burden of Proof
A restriction on a noncustodial parent's visitation rights is inappropriate absent a finding of serious endangerment. In re Fields, 283 Ill. App. 3d 894, 219 Ill. Dec. 420, 671 N.E.2d 85 (4 Dist. 1996).

The custodial parent bears the burden of proving by a preponderance of the evidence that visitation with the noncustodial parent would seriously endanger the child. In re Diehl, 221 Ill. App. 3d 410, 164 Ill. Dec. 73, 582 N.E.2d 281 (2 Dist. 1991), cert. denied, 144 Ill. 2d 632, 169 Ill. Dec. 140, 591 N.E.2d 20 (1992).

Restriction of visitation rights requires a showing that the visitation endangers the physical or emotional welfare of the child. In re Lewis, 188 Ill. App. 3d 142, 135 Ill. Dec. 667, 544 N.E.2d 24 (5 Dist. 1989).

—Counseling
Requiring a noncustodial parent to participate in counseling is not a restriction on visitation. In re Fields, 283 Ill. App. 3d 894, 219 Ill. Dec. 420, 671 N.E.2d 85 (4 Dist. 1996).

—Court's Findings
This section does not require a formalistic recital by the trial court that a danger was posed to the child before visitation rights could be restricted, where the trial court's reasoning for restriction of visitation rights was undeniably and explicitly set forth in the record, and those findings were supported by the evidence. In re Johnson, 100 Ill. App. 3d 767, 56 Ill. Dec. 294, 427 N.E.2d 374 (5 Dist. 1981).

—Determination
The welfare and best interests of the child is the paramount consideration in determining whether visitation rights should be restricted and visitation rights will not be restricted merely because the custodial parent considers such restriction to be advisable. Blazina v. Blazina, 42 Ill. App. 3d 159, 1 Ill. Dec. 164, 356 N.E.2d 164 (2 Dist. 1976).

—Discretion of Court
A prohibition of overnight visitation, a requirement that visitation occur in the custodial parent's home, or a requirement that visitation occur outside the home of the non-custodial parent if made with children's best interests in mind and fully supported by the testimony at the hearing is well within the broad measure of discretionary authority given the trial court. Gibson v. Barton, 118 Ill. App. 3d 576, 74 Ill. Dec. 252, 455 N.E.2d 282 (4 Dist. 1983).

The matter of visitation privileges rests in the broad discretion of the trial court. Frail v. Frail, 54 Ill. App. 3d 1013, 12 Ill. Dec. 680, 370 N.E.2d 303 (3 Dist. 1977).

—Endangerment Standard
A parent is entitled to visitation unless the visits would endanger the child; the endangerment standard is an extraordinary finding that is onerous, stringent, and rigorous and is more stringent than the best interests standard, which is used to determine custody. Pleasant v. Pleasant, 256 Ill. App. 3d 742, 195 Ill. Dec. 169, 628 N.E.2d 633 (1 Dist. 1993).

Visitation rights cannot be restricted unless the court finds that the visitation would "endanger seriously the child's physical, mental, moral or emotional health." Woods v. Woods, 147 Ill. App. 3d 772, 101 Ill. Dec. 582, 498 N.E.2d 906 (5 Dist. 1986).

To restrict visitation rights the trial court must find that the visitation as it exists endangers seriously the child's physical, mental, moral or emotional health, not merely that a restriction would be in the best interest of the child. In re Solomon, 84 Ill. App. 3d 901, 40 Ill. Dec. 197, 405 N.E.2d 1289 (1 Dist. 1980).

—Erroneous Standard
Where the trial court did not make the requisite finding that the visitation would seriously endanger the child's physical, mental, moral or emotional health but rather found that the restriction in visitation was in "the best interests of the minor child," it erred in restricting the respondent's visitation rights. In re Anderson, 130 Ill. App. 3d 684, 85 Ill. Dec. 951, 474 N.E.2d 911 (2 Dist. 1985).

—Failure to File Petition
Attorney's failure to petition the trial court for an order pursuant to subsection (a) of this section resulted in the trial court never having had the opportunity to consider whether father's threats and conduct posed a danger to child's health and well-being sufficient to justify an order limiting father's visitation with child. Shehade v. Gerson, 148 Ill. App. 3d 1026, 102 Ill. Dec. 617, 500 N.E.2d 510 (1 Dist. 1986).

—Failure to Use Proper Standard
Where the trial court's docket entry did not explicitly reveal whether it used a best interest standard or the serious endangerment standard, but the court did not make a specific finding that father's visitation with the children would seriously endanger the physical, mental, moral, or emotional health of any of the children and furthermore, the court stated in its February 1993 order that visitation would not be "in the best interest of the children," the trial court used the incorrect standard when reviewing father's visitation rights; use of a best interests standard, rather than the serious endangerment standard, constitutes reversible error. Helderbrandt v. Helderbrandt, 251 Ill. App. 3d 950, 191 Ill. Dec. 190, 623 N.E.2d 780 (4 Dist. 1993).

The trial court erred by restricting the mother's visitation rights because the court applied the best interests of the child standard rather than the serious endangerment standard embodied in subsections (a) and (c) of this section. In re Diehl, 221 Ill. App. 3d 410, 164 Ill. Dec. 73, 582 N.E.2d 281 (2 Dist. 1991), cert. denied, 144 Ill. 2d 632, 169 Ill. Dec. 140, 591 N.E.2d 20 (1992).

The judge's discretion is limited by the requirement that the evidence fit the higher standard of endangerment prior to visitation restriction and that such a finding be explicitly set out before proceeding to modify in the best interests. In re Solomon, 84 Ill. App. 3d 901, 40 Ill. Dec. 197, 405 N.E.2d 1289 (1 Dist. 1980).

Without the threshold inquiry of whether the visitation as it existed endangered seriously the child's physical, mental, moral or emotional health, the judge erred in restricting respondent's visitation privileges under the lesser standard of best interests of the child. In re Solomon, 84 Ill. App. 3d 901, 40 Ill. Dec. 197, 405 N.E.2d 1289 (1 Dist. 1980).

—Improper
Where the restriction on visitation did not merely shorten visitation to accommodate the activities of the children, rather, the condition operated to grant the ultimate determination of whether father may exercise his visitation rights to wife, and where the parties' had a history of discord and inability to communicate and reach agreements, the court's restriction was in error. In re LaTour, 241 Ill. App. 3d 500, 181 Ill. Dec. 865, 608 N.E.2d 1339 (4 Dist. 1993).

—Manifest Injustice
A grant of visitation rights, which allowed the defendant four hours per month to visit his daughter, was so restricted as to cause

Restricted Visitation (Cont'd)

—Manifest Injustice (Cont'd)

manifest injustice to the defendant. McManus v. McManus, 38 Ill. App. 3d 645, 348 N.E.2d 507 (5 Dist. 1976).

An award of visitation rights, which provided the defendant about one full day per month to visit the child, is limited, but not so limited as to cause manifest injustice to the defendant or child; the award falls within the area of the circuit court's broad discretion and must be affirmed. McManus v. McManus, 38 Ill. App. 3d 645, 348 N.E.2d 507 (5 Dist. 1976).

—Not Shown

The "denial" of husband's requests did not amount to a restriction on visitation where he was granted visitation with son; such visitation included weekend overnight stays, and two weeks in the summer, as well as provision for holidays and other special events. In re Yong Sun Lee, 246 Ill. App. 3d 628, 186 Ill. Dec. 257, 615 N.E.2d 1314 (4 Dist.), cert. denied, 153 Ill. 2d 560, 191 Ill. Dec. 620, 624 N.E.2d 808 (1993).

—Place

The trial court abused its discretion in allowing the child's father only very limited visitation with his child, and then only in the home of the maternal grandparents where the restrictions imposed were not shown to be necessary for the child's physical, mental, moral or emotional health or otherwise required in the best interests of the child. Becton v. Sanders, 130 Ill. App. 3d 763, 86 Ill. Dec. 121, 474 N.E.2d 1318 (1 Dist. 1985).

Absent allegations of impropriety or misconduct, equity and good conscience require that the parent who is permitted to visit should be able to do so under some arrangement which does not require him, or her, to stay in the home of the parent having custody under this parent's watchful eye or even in his absence. Patton v. Armstrong, 6 Ill. App. 3d 998, 286 N.E.2d 351 (5 Dist. 1972).

—Reluctance of Courts

Courts are reluctant to restrict visitation rights; such reluctance is based on a recognition of the parental feelings of a divorced spouse who has not been granted custody or on the theory that restriction should be limited to cases where extraordinary circumstances are present or where the unfitness of the parent being denied is clearly shown. Blazina v. Blazina, 42 Ill. App. 3d 159, 1 Ill. Dec. 164, 356 N.E.2d 164 (2 Dist. 1976).

—Sexual Orientation of Parent

Court order restricting respondent's visitation rights by requiring that visitation be supervised by heterosexual employees of the Illinois Department of Children and Family Services, reducing her visitation to alternate weekends, eliminating overnight visitation, and requiring that she enroll in regular psychotherapy was against the manifest weight of the evidence; there was no evidence in the record that respondent was a defiant and hostile lesbian or that child had any confusion about having "two mothers." Pleasant v. Pleasant, 256 Ill. App. 3d 742, 195 Ill. Dec. 169, 628 N.E.2d 633 (1 Dist. 1993).

Sexual orientation is not relevant to a parent's visitation rights. Pleasant v. Pleasant, 256 Ill. App. 3d 742, 195 Ill. Dec. 169, 628 N.E.2d 633 (1 Dist. 1993).

—Shown

A termination of visitation is a restriction, as is prohibition on overnight visitation; likewise, a requirement that visitation is supervised, occur in the home of the custodial parent, or outside the home of the noncustodial parent is a restriction. In re Fields, 283 Ill. App. 3d 894, 219 Ill. Dec. 420, 671 N.E.2d 85 (4 Dist. 1996).

An order which provided, in pertinent part, that respondent was entitled to one week's summertime visitation, excluding overnight visitation, and supervised overnight weekend visitation with his minor son, amounted to a restriction of his visitation rights under subsection (c) of this section. In re Anderson, 130 Ill. App. 3d 684, 85 Ill. Dec. 951, 474 N.E.2d 911 (2 Dist. 1985).

—Supervision

Evidence was sufficient to require supervised visitations by divorced father for the first six months where even the husband's adoptive father could not recommend that the husband have unrestricted visitation. In re Johnson, 100 Ill. App. 3d 767, 56 Ill. Dec. 294, 427 N.E.2d 374 (5 Dist. 1981).

The trial court properly demonstrated concern for the Illinois policy for liberal visitation by ruling that the order requiring supervised visitations of an abusive father, with his son would be reviewed in six months, to give the father an opportunity to rehabilitate himself. In re Johnson, 100 Ill. App. 3d 767, 56 Ill. Dec. 294, 427 N.E.2d 374 (5 Dist. 1981).

Scope

This Act continues to govern other issues connected with divorce, such as spousal support and property settlements and also continues to govern the issue of grandparental visitation when, subsequent to a divorce, a child is adopted by one of the natural parents and that parent's new spouse. Lingwall v. Hoener, 108 Ill. 2d 206, 91 Ill. Dec. 166, 483 N.E.2d 512 (1985).

Sexual Abuse

Evidence of sexual abuse and transmission of sexually transmitted disease satisfied the rigorous endangerment standard of this section. In re Woppel, 178 Ill. App. 3d 781, 127 Ill. Dec. 920, 533 N.E.2d 1002 (1 Dist. 1989).

In order to prevail on the motion to terminate visitation rights, petitioner had to convince the trier of fact that the sexual abuse had in fact occurred, and that the abuse seriously endangered to child's physical, mental, moral or emotional health. In re Dunn, 155 Ill. App. 3d 247, 108 Ill. Dec. 89, 508 N.E.2d 250 (4 Dist. 1987).

Standing

Where domestic partner made no argument that she had standing under any subsection of 750 ILCS 5/607 to seek visitation of three children born during her relationship with the children's mother, the trial court did not abuse its discretion when it denied the partner's petition for visitation. R.H. v. E.W. (In re A.W.), 343 Ill. App. 3d 396, 277 Ill. Dec. 643, 796 N.E.2d 729, 2003 Ill. App. LEXIS 1113 (2 Dist. 2003).

Standing to petition for visitation, if it exists, must be found solely within the specific provisions of this section as the statute supersedes and supplants the common law of visitation in Illinois. A.B. v. H.L., 309 Ill. App. 3d 888, 243 Ill. Dec. 284, 723 N.E.2d 316 (1 Dist. 1999).

Stepparent Visitation

Trial court erred in refusing to terminate a former wife's stepparent visitation, as the statute on which the parties' visitation agreement was based, subsection (b)(1.5) of this section, was facially unconstitutional, and the former husband's agreement to allow her visitation was a gratuitous undertaking that was unenforceable. In re Marriage of Engelkens, Ill. App. 3d , 290 Ill. Dec. 487, 821 N.E.2d 799, 2004 Ill. App. LEXIS 1559 (3 Dist. 2004).

Trial court erred in refusing to terminate a former wife's stepparent visitation, as the statute on which the parties' visitation agreement was based, subsection (b)(1.5) of this section, was facially unconstitutional, and the husband was not equitably estopped from renouncing the agreement because the wife did not claim she was induced to provide health care coverage for the child based on his representations. In re Marriage of Engelkens, Ill. App. 3d , 290 Ill. Dec. 487, 821 N.E.2d 799, 2004 Ill. App. LEXIS 1559 (3 Dist. 2004).

Trial court erred in refusing to terminate a former wife's stepparent visitation, as the statute on which the parties' visitation agreement was based, subsection (b)(1.5) of this section, was facially unconstitutional, and estoppel by remarriage did not apply because the wife's challenge was not to the judgment of dissolution as a whole, but only that portion granting her visitation. In re Marriage of Engelkens, Ill. App. 3d , 290 Ill. Dec. 487, 821 N.E.2d 799, 2004 Ill. App. LEXIS 1559 (3 Dist. 2004).

As subsection (b)(1.5) of this section was facially unconstitutional, it was void ab initio, and a trial court erred in finding an "exception" to its unconstitutionality — the natural parent's unfitness — and in refusing to terminate the stepparent's visitation rights. In re Marriage of Engelkens, Ill. App. 3d , 290 Ill. Dec. 487, 821 N.E.2d 799, 2004 Ill. App. LEXIS 1559 (3 Dist. 2004).

A provision in a marital settlement that provided for stepparent visitation was unenforceable where both of the child's parents were living and she had wholesome relationships with both of them, and the child was not consulted about her desires with regard to

Stepparent Visitation (Cont'd)
visitation with her former stepparent. In re Booth, 325 Ill. App. 3d 92, 258 Ill. Dec. 572, 756 N.E.2d 846, 2001 Ill. App. LEXIS 269 (3 Dist. 2001), appeal denied, 195 Ill. 2d 575, 258 Ill. Dec. 93, 755 N.E.2d 476 (2001).

Termination

—Not Proper
The evidence did not support a finding that the visitation with non-custodial parent seriously endangered the welfare of the children so as to warrant termination of visiting rights. In re Blanchard, 162 Ill. App. 3d 202, 113 Ill. Dec. 197, 514 N.E.2d 1208 (5 Dist. 1987).

Where father presented evidence that mother rather than he sexually abused child and psychologists concluded that visitation between child and father would not harm the child, trial court's decision to terminate dissolution decree visitation rights of father was abuse of discretion. In re Dunn, 155 Ill. App. 3d 247, 108 Ill. Dec. 89, 508 N.E.2d 250 (4 Dist. 1987).

There was no showing of an abuse of the trial court's discretion in awarding the mother visitation rights, even though she left them at a very young age, where the evidence showed that she had married at 16, that she had matured since that time, and that she had left her family due to her husband's drinking and gambling problem. Aud v. Etienne, 47 Ill. 2d 110, 264 N.E.2d 196 (1970).

—Proper
The trial court did not abuse its discretion in terminating father's visitation privileges with his two year old daughter on the basis that sexual abuse committed by father on daughter during those visitation periods seriously endangered daughter's physical, mental, moral or emotional health. In re Ashby, 193 Ill. App. 3d 366, 140 Ill. Dec. 272, 549 N.E.2d 923 (5 Dist. 1990).

The trial court did not abuse its discretion in determining that the weekend joint custody schedule was detrimental to the children's best interests where its frequency prevented a balanced relationship, or recreation time, with their mother and new family unit. In re Kessler, 110 Ill. App. 3d 61, 65 Ill. Dec. 707, 441 N.E.2d 1221 (1 Dist. 1982).

Visitation Order

—Finality
Where matters closely related to the issue of visitation are pending, petitioner's petition for custody, and respondent's petition to modify the judgment of dissolution with respect to visitation and relocation, the appealed visitation order was not a final order from which an appeal would lie. In re Bresnahan, 189 Ill. App. 3d 159, 136 Ill. Dec. 515, 544 N.E.2d 1290 (2 Dist. 1989).

LEGAL PERIODICALS

For article, "Survey of Illinois Law: Constitutional Law," see 25 S. Ill. U. L.J. 733 (2001).

For comment, "Paternity Actions in Illinois: Why Not Consider What is in the Best Interest of the Child?," see 21 S. Ill. U.L.J. 613 (1997).

For article, "The Potential Impact of Homosexual Parenting on Children," see 1997 U. Ill. L. Rev. 833.

For article, "Child Custody in a Changing World: A Study of Postdivorce Arrangements," see 1997 U. Ill. L. Rev. 773.

For comment, "Grandparent Visitation and the Intact Family," see 16 S. Ill. U.L.J. 133 (1991).

For article, "Survey of Illinois Law [1988-89] — Family Law," see 14 S. Ill. U.L.J. 1007 (1990).

For article, "Family Law: 1987-88 Illinois Law Survey," see Loy. U. Chi. L.J. 461 (1988-89).

For article, "Family Law: 1985-86 Survey," see 11 S. Ill. U.L.J. 741 (1987).

For article, "Grandparents' Right to Visitation," see 75 Ill. B.J. 26 (1986).

For article, "Suggested Guidelines for Supervisual Visitation," see 74 Ill. B.J. 244 (1986).

For article, "Family Law: 1986-87 Illinois Law Survey," see 19 Loy. U. Chi. L.J. 489 (1987-88).

RESEARCH REFERENCES

Visitation rights of persons other than natural parents or grandparents. 1 ALR4th 1270.

Interference by custodian of child with noncustodial parent's visitation rights as ground for change of custody. 28 ALR4th 9.

Visitation rights of homosexual or lesbian parent. 36 ALR4th 997.

Withholding visitation rights for failure to make alimony or support payments. 65 ALR4th 1155.

Parent's use of drugs as factor in award of custody of children, visitation rights, or termination of parental rights. 20 ALR5th 534.

Smoking as factor in child custody and visitation cases. 36 ALR5th 377.

Initial award or denial of child custody to homosexual or lesbian parent. 62 ALR5th 591.

Custodial parent's homosexual or lesbian relationship with third person as justifying modification of child custody order. 65 ALR5th 591.

Grandparents' visitation rights where child's parents are deceased, or where status of parents is unspecified. 69 ALR5th 1.

Grandparent's visitation rights where child's parents are living. 71 ALR5th 99.

Child custody and visitation rights arising from same-sex relationship. 80 ALR5th 1.

Religion as factor in visitation cases. 95 ALR5th 533.

Restrictions on parent's child visitation rights based on parent's sexual conduct. 99 ALR5th 475.

750 ILCS 5/607.1 Enforcement of visitation orders; visitation abuse

Sec. 607.1. *Enforcement of visitation orders; visitation abuse.* (a) The circuit court shall provide an expedited procedure for enforcement of court ordered visitation in cases of visitation abuse. Visitation abuse occurs when a party has willfully and without justification: (1) denied another party visitation as set forth by the court; or (2) exercised his or her visitation rights in a manner that is harmful to the child or child's custodian.

(b) An Action may be commenced by filing a petition setting forth: (i) the petitioner's name, residence address or mailing address, and telephone number; (ii) respondent's name and place of residence, place of employment, or mailing address; (iii) the nature of the visitation abuse, giving dates and other relevant information; (iv) that a reasonable attempt was made to resolve the dispute; and (v) the relief sought.

Notice of the filing of the petitions shall be given as provided in Section 511 [750 ILCS 5/511].

(c) After hearing all of the evidence, the court may order one or more of the following:

(1) Modification of the visitation order to specifically outline periods of visitation or restrict visitation as provided by law.

(2) Supervised visitation with a third party or public agency.

(3) Make up visitation of the same time period, such as weekend for weekend, holiday for holiday.

(4) Counseling or mediation, except in cases where there is evidence of domestic violence, as defined in Section 1 of the Domestic Violence Shelters Act [20 ILCS 1310/1], occurring between the parties.

(5) Other appropriate relief deemed equitable.

(d) Nothing contained in this Section shall be construed to limit the court's contempt power, except as provided in subsection (g) of this Section.

(e) When the court issues an order holding a party in contempt of court for violation of a visitation order, the clerk shall transmit a copy of the contempt order to the sheriff of the county. The sheriff shall furnish a copy of each contempt order to the Department of State Police on a daily basis in the form and manner required by the Department. The Department shall maintain a complete record and index of the contempt orders and make this data available to all local law enforcement agencies.

(f) Attorney fees and costs shall be assessed against a party if the court finds that the enforcement action is vexatious and constitutes harassment.

(g) A person convicted of unlawful visitation interference under Section 10-5.5 of the Criminal Code of 1961 [720 ILCS 5/10-5.5] shall not be subject to the provisions of this Section and the court may not enter a contempt order for visitation abuse against any person for the same conduct for which the person was convicted of unlawful visitation interference or subject that person to the sanctions provided for in this Section.

(Source: P.A. 87-895; 88-96, § 10.)

Note.

This section was Ill.Rev.Stat., Ch. 40, para. 607.1.

CASE NOTES

Analysis

Best Interests of Child
Change of Custody
Contempt
—Construed as Indirect
—Evidence Held Sufficient
—Purging
—Willful
Duty of Court
Mediation
Modification
Visitation Abuse
—Not Wilful

Best Interests of Child

In contempt proceedings involving visitation abuse issues, the importance of the children's best interests must not be lost. Pryweller v. Pryweller, 218 Ill. App. 3d 619, 161 Ill. Dec. 884, 579 N.E.2d 432 (1 Dist. 1991), cert. denied, 143 Ill. 2d 648, 167 Ill. Dec. 409, 587 N.E.2d 1024 (1992).

Change of Custody

Change of custody is an improper remedy to punish a custodial parent's contumacious interference with visitation rights. In re Fox, 191 Ill. App. 3d 514, 138 Ill. Dec. 841, 548 N.E.2d 71 (4 Dist. 1989).

Contempt

—Construed as Indirect

Where a parent is charged with contempt for failure to turn a child over to the other parent for visitation or custody, the conduct occurs outside of the court's presence and must be construed as indirect contempt and thus proof of facts of which the court cannot take judicial notice must be presented in order for the court to make a finding of contempt. Pryweller v. Pryweller, 218 Ill. App. 3d 619, 161 Ill. Dec. 884, 579 N.E.2d 432 (1 Dist. 1991), cert. denied, 143 Ill. 2d 648, 167 Ill. Dec. 409, 587 N.E.2d 1024 (1992).

—Evidence Held Sufficient

There was ample evidence in the record in support of the trial court's finding that appellant wife was guilty of contempt for failure to comply with the visitation provisions of the divorce decree; the decree vested her with the care, custody and control of the children ranging in age from five to nine years and they had neither the level of requisite maturity nor the obligation to make their own decisions, and thus wife could not escape her duty to comply with the provisions of the decree by attempting to shift this burden to the discretion of her children or to some other person in her absence. Doggett v. Doggett, 51 Ill. App. 3d 868, 9 Ill. Dec. 474, 366 N.E.2d 985 (5 Dist. 1977).

An order finding the husband guilty of contempt of court for withholding custody of children awarded to the wife by divorce decree was simply an interlocutory order, made by the court in the process of a suit at law, and was in no sense definite. Flaningam v. Flaningam, 331 Ill. App. 418, 73 N.E.2d 652 (2 Dist. 1947).

—Purging

In civil contempt proceedings, the contemner must have the opportunity to purge the contempt, and contempt will not lie when the alleged contemner, through no fault of his own, is in a position where he cannot comply with the order of the court. Pryweller v. Pryweller, 218 Ill. App. 3d 619, 161 Ill. Dec. 884, 579 N.E.2d 432 (1 Dist. 1991), cert. denied, 143 Ill. 2d 648, 167 Ill. Dec. 409, 587 N.E.2d 1024 (1992).

—Willful

In a proceeding for civil contempt for failure to produce children for therapy and visitation, it was necessary to show that petitioner's alleged contemptuous conduct was willful. Pryweller v. Pryweller, 218 Ill. App. 3d 619, 161 Ill. Dec. 884, 579 N.E.2d 432 (1 Dist. 1991), cert. denied, 143 Ill. 2d 648, 167 Ill. Dec. 409, 587 N.E.2d 1024 (1992).

Duty of Court

The trial court abused its discretion and denied petitioner her due process rights by denying petitioner the opportunity to present evidence in her own behalf before holding her in contempt for visitation abuse. Pryweller v. Pryweller, 218 Ill. App. 3d 619, 161 Ill. Dec. 884, 579 N.E.2d 432 (1 Dist. 1991), cert. denied, 143 Ill. 2d 648, 167 Ill. Dec. 409, 587 N.E.2d 1024 (1992).

Mediation

The language "after hearing all of the evidence" means that the trial court may order mediation only after assessing whether mediation would be useful in resolving a specific dispute before the court, therefore, this section does not authorize trial courts to order mediation of prospective visitation disputes. In re Aleshire, 273 Ill. App. 3d 81, 209 Ill. Dec. 843, 652 N.E.2d 383 (3 Dist. 1995).

Modification

The court cannot modify custody under this section absent a petition to modify pursuant to 750 ILCS 5/602 or 750 ILCS 5/610. In re M.M.W., 296 Ill. App. 3d 877, 231 Ill. Dec. 238, 695 N.E.2d 1357 (2 Dist. 1998).

Visitation Abuse

—Not Wilful

Petitioner committed visitation abuse by threatening to withhold visitation unless respondent signed the parental declaration, however, petitioner's actions stemmed from her concern about how respondent was treating the children, rather than from an intent to interfere with his rights and there was no evidence in the record that she actually denied respondent an opportunity to visit the children based upon his failure to sign the document; therefore, petitioner's conduct did not amount to a wilful and unjustifiable denial of respondent's visitation rights. In re Aleshire, 273 Ill. App. 3d 81, 209 Ill. Dec. 843, 652 N.E.2d 383 (3 Dist. 1995).

LEGAL PERIODICALS

For note, "In re Interest of Z.J.H.: Are Two Moms Too Many?," see 42 De Paul L. Rev. 1125 (1993).

RESEARCH REFERENCES

Denial or restriction of visitation rights to parent charged with sexually abusing child. 1 ALR5th 776.

750 ILCS 5/608 Judicial Supervision

Sec. 608. *Judicial Supervision.* (a) Except as otherwise agreed by the parties in writing at the time of the custody judgment or as otherwise ordered by the court, the custodian may determine the child's upbringing, including but not limited to, his education, health care and religious training, unless the court, after hearing, finds, upon motion by the noncustodial parent, that the absence of a specific limitation of the custodian's authority would clearly be contrary to the best interests of the child.

(b) If both parents or all contestants agree to the order, or if the court finds that in the absence of agreement the child's physical health would be endangered or his emotional development significantly impaired, the court may order the Department of Children and Family Services to exercise continuing supervision over the case to assure that the custodial or visitation terms of the judgment are carried out. Supervision shall be carried out under the provisions of Section 5 of the Children and Family Services Act [20 ILCS 505/5].
(Source: P.A. 87-824.)

Note.
This section was Ill.Rev.Stat., Ch. 40, para. 608.

CASE NOTES

ANALYSIS

In General
Applicability
Authority of Custodian
—In General
—Trust Proceeds
Consent for Medical Procedure
—Available Parent
—Best Interests of Child
—Burden of Proof
Private Cause of Action
—Third Party
Purpose
Religious Services
Restrict Defined
Restrictions
—Examples
Suit on Child's Behalf

In General
This section speaks in terms of a single custodian with substantial authority. In re Tisckos, 161 Ill. App. 3d 302, 112 Ill. Dec. 860, 514 N.E.2d 523 (4 Dist. 1987).

Applicability
Only if the provisions of the court's order in question are deemed a "restriction" of the non-custodial parent's visitation rights does the endangerment standard come into play. In re Tisckos, 161 Ill. App. 3d 302, 112 Ill. Dec. 860, 514 N.E.2d 523 (4 Dist. 1987).

Authority of Custodian

—In General
Legislature's intent in enacting 750 ILCS 5/608 of the Illinois Marriage and Dissolution of Marriage Act (Dissolution Act), giving a custodial parent the right to determine a child's religious upbringing, is to provide a guideline for the parties and the court in the general area of child welfare and upbringing, and the legislature granted the custodial parent the authority to make the initial decision on such matters and placed the burden upon the noncustodial parent to establish the fault of any such custodial determination, but section 608 does not exist in a vacuum as that section must be read in conjunction with other sections of the Dissolution Act, including 750 ILCS 5/607(c), which grants to a noncustodial parent the right to unrestricted visitation. and, more important, 750 ILCS 5/608 must yield to the best interest and general welfare of the child. Minix v. Dunaven-Minix, 344 Ill. App. 3d 801, 280 Ill. Dec. 256, 801 N.E.2d 1201, 2003 Ill. App. LEXIS 1559 (4 Dist. 2003).

—Trust Proceeds
Proceeds of a life insurance policy for the benefit of the children of decedent's first marriage could be placed in a trust for the children's benefit; such proceeds need not be directly paid to the children or their guardian. Downey v. Downey, 293 Ill. App. 3d 234, 227 Ill. Dec. 265, 687 N.E.2d 339 (4 Dist. 1997).

Consent for Medical Procedure

—Available Parent
While the power to consent to surgical procedures on a child ordinarily rests exclusively with the custodial parent, when that parent is not available, the parent who has actual custody and is available may consent to the surgery. Taylor v. R.D. Morgan & Assoc., 205 Ill. App. 3d 682, 151 Ill. Dec. 80, 563 N.E.2d 1186 (5 Dist. 1990).

—Best Interests of Child
A parent or guardian may give consent on behalf of a minor daughter or son for the child to donate bone marrow to a sibling, only when to do so would be in the minor's best interest. Curran v. Bosze, 141 Ill. 2d 473, 153 Ill. Dec. 213, 566 N.E.2d 1319 (1990).

—Burden of Proof
The noncustodial parent has the burden of persuading the court that the withholding of consent by custodial parent to medical procedure is clearly contrary to the best interests of the child. Curran v. Bosze, 141 Ill. 2d 473, 153 Ill. Dec. 213, 566 N.E.2d 1319 (1990).

Private Cause of Action

—Third Party
A private cause of action against a psychiatrist, a third party to a custody proceeding, was implied from subsection (a) of this section where the psychiatrist had no authority to subject a young child to psychotherapy twice a month for a period of one year, without the lawful consent of either the child's father, as child's custodial parent, or the court having authority under this subsection. Dymek v. Nyquist, 128 Ill. App. 3d 859, 83 Ill. Dec. 52, 469 N.E.2d 659 (1 Dist. 1984).

Purpose
Subsection (a) of this section was intended to help reconcile the conflicting interests of estranged parents. In re Tisckos, 161 Ill. App. 3d 302, 112 Ill. Dec. 860, 514 N.E.2d 523 (4 Dist. 1987).

Religious Services
750 ILCS 5/608 of the Illinois Marriage and Dissolution of Marriage Act (Dissolution Act) permits a custodial parent to control a child's religious upbringing absent proof that involvement in any other religion is not harmful to the child, and trial courts have the authority to set forth accommodations during lawful visitation periods with a showing that such accommodations are necessary to eliminate or prevent any harm to the child and are in the child's best interest, but absent proof of harm or that attendance at religious services with the noncustodial parent somehow interferes with the custodial parent's selection of the child's religion, the noncustodial parent is entitled to his or her visitation period without interference from the custodial parent despite the authority granted to the custodian in section 608. Minix v. Dunaven-Minix, 344 Ill. App. 3d 801, 280 Ill. Dec. 256, 801 N.E.2d 1201, 2003 Ill. App. LEXIS 1559 (4 Dist. 2003).

Custodial mother did not have an absolute right, under 750 ILCS 5/608(a), to prohibit the noncustodial father from taking the parties' child to his religious services during his visitation, over her objection, without some proof that this action by the father was harmful to the child, given the father's right to unrestricted visitation, under 750 ILCS 5/607(c), and his right to the free

Religious Services (Cont'd)
exercise of his religion. Minix v. Dunaven-Minix, 344 Ill. App. 3d 801, 280 Ill. Dec. 256, 801 N.E.2d 1201, 2003 Ill. App. LEXIS 1559 (4 Dist. 2003).

In dissolution proceedings, the circuit court is not bound by a premarital agreement purporting to fix the religion in which the parties' children will be raised. In re Bennett, 225 Ill. App. 3d 828, 167 Ill. Dec. 308, 587 N.E.2d 577 (4 Dist.), appeal denied, 145 Ill. 2d 631, 173 Ill. Dec. 2, 596 N.E.2d 626 (1992).

A premarital agreement relating to the religious upbringing of the children was not binding on the court in dissolution proceedings. In re Nuechterlien, 225 Ill. App. 3d 1, 167 Ill. Dec. 139, 587 N.E.2d 21 (4 Dist.), cert. denied, 145 Ill. 2d 636, 173 Ill. Dec. 6, 596 N.E.2d 630 (1992).

The court's order directing a father as noncustodial parent to take his daughter to the Roman Catholic church and not to his Baptist church being in the nature of an accommodation to be made on behalf of the child by the noncustodial parent, and involving the noncustodial parent to a degree when the child's obligation occurs during a period of visitation, was governed by this section and was not a restriction governed by 750 ILCS 5/607. In re Tisckos, 161 Ill. App. 3d 302, 112 Ill. Dec. 860, 514 N.E.2d 523 (4 Dist. 1987).

An order directing that a child be enrolled in the public school system was not erroneous, where the child was born into the Jewish faith, but following the parents divorce, the child was enrolled in a Lutheran day school. Stern v. Stern, 40 Ill. App. 2d 374, 188 N.E.2d 97 (1 Dist. 1963).

Restrict Defined
The word "restrict," given its ordinary and everyday meaning, indicates action to limit, restrain, or confine within bounds. In re Tisckos, 161 Ill. App. 3d 302, 112 Ill. Dec. 860, 514 N.E.2d 523 (4 Dist. 1987).

Restrictions

—Examples
"Restrictions" have been found to include a prohibition of overnight visitation, a requirement that visitation occur in the custodial parent's home, or outside the home of the noncustodial parent, or the requirements that summertime visitation exclude overnight visitation and weekend visitation be supervised. In re Tisckos, 161 Ill. App. 3d 302, 112 Ill. Dec. 860, 514 N.E.2d 523 (4 Dist. 1987).

Suit on Child's Behalf
The custodial parent may maintain a legal action on behalf of the child; however, the award of custody does not per se exclude the rights of the noncustodial parent to sue on behalf of the child. Stevenson ex rel. Magna Bank v. Hawthorne Elementary Sch., 144 Ill. 2d 294, 162 Ill. Dec. 38, 579 N.E.2d 852 (1991).

Where the father owed back child-support, he could not maintain an action as "next friend" of the child and, at the same time, defend against the child as a judgment-creditor. Stevenson ex rel. Magna Bank v. Hawthorne Elementary Sch., 144 Ill. 2d 294, 162 Ill. Dec. 38, 579 N.E.2d 852 (1991).

Absent a proper showing, the custodial parent's plenary authority over the child includes the right to prosecute litigation on the minor's behalf as next friend of the minor. Stevenson ex rel. Magna Bank v. Hawthorne Elementary Sch., 144 Ill. 2d 294, 162 Ill. Dec. 38, 579 N.E.2d 852 (1991).

LEGAL PERIODICALS

For note, "Best Interest of the Child: The Case for Joint Custody Even in Contested Divorce," 84 Ill. B.J. 348 (1996).

RESEARCH REFERENCES

Propriety of surgically invading incompetent or minor for benefit of third party. 4 ALR5th 1000.

Religion as factor in child custody cases. 124 ALR5th 203.

750 ILCS 5/609 Leave to Remove Children

Sec. 609. *Leave to Remove Children.* (a) The court may grant leave, before or after judgment, to any party having custody of any minor child or children to remove such child or children from Illinois whenever such approval is in the best interests of such child or children. The burden of proving that such removal is in the best interests of such child or children is on the party seeking the removal. When such removal is permitted, the court may require the party removing such child or children from Illinois to give reasonable security guaranteeing the return of such children.

(b) Before a minor child is temporarily removed from Illinois, the parent responsible for the removal shall inform the other parent, or the other parent's attorney, of the address and telephone number where the child may be reached during the period of temporary removal, and the date on which the child shall return to Illinois.

The State of Illinois retains jurisdiction when the minor child is absent from the State pursuant to this subsection.

(Source: P.A. 85-768.)

Note.
This section was Ill.Rev.Stat., Ch. 40, para. 609.

CASE NOTES

ANALYSIS

In General
Address of New Location
Applicability
Attorney Fees
Basis of Decision
Best Interests of Child
—In General
—Appeal
—Determination of Custody Award
—Emotional Health of Child
—Enhancement of Life
—Enhancement of Parent's Life
—Factors
—Factual Circumstances
—Health of Child
—Hearing Required
—Illegitimate
—Motives of Custodian
—Motives of Non-Custodian
—Not Shown
—Shown
—Visitation Rights
—Visitation Schedule
Best Interests of Custodial Parent
Burden of Proof
—In General
—Met
—Not Met
Change of Custody
Cohabitation
Consolidation
—Improper
—Of Petitions
Construction With Parentage Act
Contempt
Desire of Parents
Discretion of Court
Evidence
—Additional Evidence
—Held Insufficient
—Held Sufficient
Factors Considered
Final Orders

Harm to Child
Housing
Illustrative Cases
Indirect Benefits
Parental Involvement
Petition Not Required
Preservation of Family
Removal
—Allowed
—Circumstances Supporting
—Denial
—Denied
—Distinguished from Custody
—Domicile
—From Country
—Jurisdiction
—Permitted
—Petition
Standard of Review
Time Since Divorce
Venue
Visitation Rights

In General

Section 609 of the Illinois Marriage and Dissolution of Marriage Act, 750 ILCS 5/609, is not incorporated by reference into the Illinois Parentage Act of 1984, 750 ILCS 45/1 et seq., and does not apply to unmarried parents. Harbour v. Melton, 333 Ill. App. 3d 124, 266 Ill. Dec. 729, 775 N.E.2d 291, 2002 Ill. App. LEXIS 762 (4 Dist. 2002).

The policy of this section is to insure the maximum involvement of both parents in matters involving the physical, mental, moral and emotional well being of the child. In re Coss, 247 Ill. App. 3d 51, 187 Ill. Dec. 94, 617 N.E.2d 302 (1 Dist. 1993).

In joint custody cases, this section applies to petitions to remove a child from Illinois, rather than 750 ILCS 5/610, which deals with the more general matter of modifications of custody judgments. In re Carlson, 216 Ill. App. 3d 1077, 159 Ill. Dec. 909, 576 N.E.2d 578 (3 Dist.), cert. denied, 142 Ill. 2d 651, 164 Ill. Dec. 915, 584 N.E.2d 127 (1991).

In removal cases, the paramount question is whether the move is in the best interests of the child. In re Eckert, 119 Ill. 2d 316, 116 Ill. Dec. 220, 518 N.E.2d 1041 (1988).

The test of whether minor child should be removed from this state is not singly the best interest of the child, but also whether the general quality of life for both the custodial parent and the child will be improved by the removal; so long as the court is satisfied with the motives of the custodial parent in seeking the move and reasonable visitation is available to the remaining parent, removal should be granted. Arquilla v. Arquilla, 85 Ill. App. 3d 1090, 41 Ill. Dec. 450, 407 N.E.2d 948 (1 Dist. 1980); Winebright v. Winebright, 155 Ill. App. 3d 722, 108 Ill. Dec. 463, 508 N.E.2d 774 (3 Dist. 1987).

Pursuant to this section, the trial court is empowered to allow any party having custody of a child to remove him from Illinois whenever such removal is in the best interests of the child. Hickey v. Hickey, 31 Ill. App. 3d 257, 333 N.E.2d 271 (1 Dist. 1975); Gray v. Gray, 57 Ill. App. 3d 1, 14 Ill. Dec. 630, 372 N.E.2d 909 (1 Dist. 1978).

Address of New Location

It is impractical to require that parties seeking removal provide a new address since parties seeking removal often do not know where they will live. In re Shalashnow, 159 Ill. App. 3d 760, 111 Ill. Dec. 535, 512 N.E.2d 1076 (2 Dist. 1987).

Applicability

This section applies to cases where the party seeking custody has moved to another state before the permanent order of custody is entered. In re Hefer, 282 Ill. App. 3d 73, 217 Ill. Dec. 701, 667 N.E.2d 1094 (4 Dist. 1996).

Petitions to remove a child from Illinois are governed by this section, despite any provisions in a joint parenting agreement purporting to limit the right of removal. In re Yndestad, 232 Ill. App. 3d 1, 173 Ill. Dec. 507, 597 N.E.2d 215 (2 Dist. 1992).

Even where the parties have been awarded joint custody, a petition to remove the child from Illinois does not constitute a petition to modify custody; hence, the removal petition is governed by this section, and not 750 ILCS 5/610. Winebright v. Winebright, 155 Ill. App. 3d 722, 108 Ill. Dec. 463, 508 N.E.2d 774 (3 Dist. 1987).

While the trial court applied the wrong statute, it did apply the correct legal standard, of whether the best interests of the children would be served by remaining in Illinois or moving to Colorado; 705 ILCS 5/609, of the Illinois Marriage and Dissolution of Marriage Act, applied as it addressed a potential out-of-state move. In re Marriage of Sobol, 342 Ill. App. 3d 623, 277 Ill. Dec. 468, 796 N.E.2d 183, 2003 Ill. App. LEXIS 1097 (4 Dist. 2003).

Attorney Fees

Where a petition for removal of minor child from this state was strictly for the benefit of custodial parent and child, to require non-custodial parent to pay attorney's fees and costs would be harsh and unjust. Arquilla v. Arquilla, 85 Ill. App. 3d 1090, 41 Ill. Dec. 450, 407 N.E.2d 948 (1 Dist. 1980).

Where the record did not show any waiver and the court in its hearing stated that plaintiff's former attorney had told the court that he would not request attorney fees, the court should have granted a hearing to determine whether or not there was a waiver. Johnson v. Johnson, 105 Ill. App. 2d 399, 245 N.E.2d 580 (1 Dist. 1969).

Basis of Decision

Each removal case must be reviewed on its own facts and the judge's ruling denying custodial parent's petition to remove the child was not against the manifest weight of the evidence. In re Gibbs, 268 Ill. App. 3d 962, 206 Ill. Dec. 502, 645 N.E.2d 507 (1 Dist. 1994), appeal denied, 162 Ill. 2d 566, 209 Ill. Dec. 801, 652 N.E.2d 341 (1995).

Where the petitioner wished to remove her children from Illinois, the fact that the court did not list specifically the impact on the petitioner's quality of life, and thus that of the children, does not mean that the court did not consider it. In re Berk, 215 Ill. App. 3d 459, 158 Ill. Dec. 971, 574 N.E.2d 1364 (2 Dist.), cert. denied, 141 Ill. 2d 536, 162 Ill. Dec. 482, 580 N.E.2d 108 (1991).

Best Interests of Child

—In General

Determination of a child's best interests cannot be reduced to a simple bright-line test but rather must be made on a case-by-case basis, depending, to a great extent, upon the circumstances of each case. Parr v. Parr, 345 Ill. App. 3d 371, 280 Ill. Dec. 468, 802 N.E.2d 393, 2003 Ill. App. LEXIS 1620 (4 Dist. 2003).

Cases decided under 750 ILCS 5/609 provided guidance for determining when a child's interests might warrant moving the child out-of-state even though the move might adversely affect the noncustodial parent's visitation, and thus, the trial court erred in not considering that guidance and concluding that it had no choice but to grant the mother's petition to modify visitation that requested she be allowed to move with the child to Florida. DeBilio v. Rodgers, 337 Ill. App. 3d 614, 272 Ill. Dec. 9, 786 N.E.2d 548, 2002 Ill. App. LEXIS 947 (3 Dist. 2002).

The paramount question in a removal case is whether the move is in the best interest of the child. In re Taylor, 251 Ill. App. 3d 58, 190 Ill. Dec. 404, 621 N.E.2d 273 (3 Dist. 1993).

The Illinois Supreme Court identified five factors for the court to consider in determining whether a proposed removal is in the best interests of the child sought to be removed. The factors to be considered are (1) the likelihood that the move will enhance the general quality of life for both the custodial parent and the child; (2) the motives of the custodial parent in seeking the move to determine whether the removal is merely a ruse intended to defeat or frustrate visitation; (3) the motives of the noncustodial parent in resisting the removal; (4) the visitation rights of the noncustodial parent; and (5) whether a realistic and reasonable visitation schedule can be reached if the move is allowed. In re Branham, 248 Ill. App. 3d 898, 187 Ill. Dec. 596, 617 N.E.2d 1317 (4 Dist. 1993).

Court approval is required where minor children subject to the jurisdiction of the court are to be removed permanently from the state; custodial parent is authorized to obtain court permission to remove the minor child from Illinois where the permanent removal is in the best interests of the children. In re Roppo, 225 Ill. App. 3d 721, 167 Ill. Dec. 416, 587 N.E.2d 1031 (1 Dist. 1991).

This state's courts are in place to protect the children's interests and will not be intimidated or threatened by "irrevocable" actions of

Best Interests of Child (Cont'd)

—In General (Cont'd)

parents, such as the decision of petitioner to move regardless of the outcome of the petition for removal. In re Berk, 215 Ill. App. 3d 459, 158 Ill. Dec. 971, 574 N.E.2d 1364 (2 Dist.), cert. denied, 141 Ill. 2d 536, 162 Ill. Dec. 482, 580 N.E.2d 108 (1991).

A trial court may grant removal of a child from the state when it is in the child's best interest. In re Shalashnow, 159 Ill. App. 3d 760, 111 Ill. Dec. 535, 512 N.E.2d 1076 (2 Dist. 1987).

Where the divorce decree, by reason of an agreement of the parties, limited even further the area to which a child may be removed without approval, the standard to be applied was the best interests of the child. Falk v. Falk, 77 Ill. App. 3d 13, 32 Ill. Dec. 520, 395 N.E.2d 750 (3 Dist. 1979).

Not only may a court approve the removal of the child whenever removal is in the best interests of the child, but where there is no showing that an award of custody is against the child's best interests, a court should not oppose the removal of the child unless there is a specific showing that the move would be against the child's best interest. Falk v. Falk, 77 Ill. App. 3d 13, 32 Ill. Dec. 520, 395 N.E.2d 750 (3 Dist. 1979).

The court may grant leave, before or after judgment, to any party having custody of the minor child or children to remove such child or children from Illinois whenever such approval is in the best interest of such child or children. Gallagher v. Gallagher, 60 Ill. App. 3d 26, 17 Ill. Dec. 280, 376 N.E.2d 279 (1 Dist. 1978).

It is generally in a child's best interest to remain with the parent in whose custody the court has determined to place it. Gray v. Gray, 57 Ill. App. 3d 1, 14 Ill. Dec. 630, 372 N.E.2d 909 (1 Dist. 1978).

—Appeal

Trial court's determination on a petition to remove a child from the State of Illinois after a dissolution of the marriage of the child's parents is not to be disturbed unless it is clear that its decision was against the manifest weight of the evidence. In re Marriage of Sale, 347 Ill. App. 3d 1083, 283 Ill. Dec. 837, 808 N.E.2d 1125, 2004 Ill. App. LEXIS 418 (5 Dist. 2004).

A determination by the trial court as to what serves the best interests of the child will not be held error on appeal unless it is against the manifest weight of the evidence. Gray v. Gray, 57 Ill. App. 3d 1, 14 Ill. Dec. 630, 372 N.E.2d 909 (1 Dist. 1978).

—Determination of Custody Award

Paramount consideration in awarding the custody of a minor child to one parent or the other must necessarily be the welfare and best interest of the child. Gallagher v. Gallagher, 60 Ill. App. 3d 26, 17 Ill. Dec. 280, 376 N.E.2d 279 (1 Dist. 1978).

—Emotional Health of Child

Where removal of children from Illinois to New Jersey was shown to be detrimental to childrens' emotional health, circuit court's decision to deny mother's request for removal of children was not against manifest weight of evidence. In re Smith, 172 Ill. 2d 312, 216 Ill. Dec. 652, 665 N.E.2d 1209 (1996).

—Enhancement of Life

In considering whether a move will enhance the quality of life of a minor child, a court may consider the direct benefit to the child as well as the direct benefit to the custodial parent. In re Coss, 247 Ill. App. 3d 51, 187 Ill. Dec. 94, 617 N.E.2d 302 (1 Dist. 1993).

The court should consider the proposed move in terms of likelihood for enhancing the general quality of life for both the custodial parent and the children. In re Eckert, 119 Ill. 2d 316, 116 Ill. Dec. 220, 518 N.E.2d 1041 (1988).

—Enhancement of Parent's Life

Where mother claimed that a move out-of-state would enhance her quality of life, such claim was insufficient, standing alone, to merit the granting of a petition for a child's removal. In re Johnson, 277 Ill. App. 3d 675, 214 Ill. Dec. 421, 660 N.E.2d 1370 (5 Dist. 1996).

—Factors

Because a child has an important interest in maintaining significant contact with both parents following a divorce, a custodial parent must prove more than his or her own desire to live with a new spouse to show that a child's best interests will be served by a removal. In re Marriage of Sale, 347 Ill. App. 3d 1083, 283 Ill. Dec. 837, 808 N.E.2d 1125, 2004 Ill. App. LEXIS 418 (5 Dist. 2004).

In custody matters, the factors the Illinois Supreme Court has outlined for determining the removal of a child from the State are by no means exclusive; a circuit court may validly consider other relevant factors, as dictated by the specific circumstances of each case, in arriving at a best interests determination. In re Marriage of Sale, 347 Ill. App. 3d 1083, 283 Ill. Dec. 837, 808 N.E.2d 1125, 2004 Ill. App. LEXIS 418 (5 Dist. 2004).

While removal cases must be judged on their own unique set of facts, the Illinois Supreme Court has provided guidance for determining whether a removal of a child from the state would be in the child's best interests; the five factors that should be considered in determining whether a removal is in the child's best interests are (1) whether the proposed move will enhance the quality of life for both the custodial parent and the child, (2) whether the proposed move is a ruse designed to frustrate or defeat the noncustodial parent's visitation, (3) the motives of the noncustodial parent in resisting removal, (4) the visitation rights of the noncustodial parent, and (5) whether a reasonable visitation schedule can be achieved if the move is allowed. In re Marriage of Sale, 347 Ill. App. 3d 1083, 283 Ill. Dec. 837, 808 N.E.2d 1125, 2004 Ill. App. LEXIS 418 (5 Dist. 2004).

Five factors have been identified by the Illinois Supreme Court that should be considered in determining whether removal form the state is in a child's best interests: (1) whether the proposed move will enhance the quality of life for both the custodial parent and the children, (2) whether the proposed move is a ruse designed to frustrate or defeat the noncustodial parent's visitation, (3) the noncustodial parent's motives in resisting removal, (4) the noncustodial parent's visitation rights, and (5) whether a reasonable visitation schedule can be worked out; a reasonable visitation schedule is one that would preserve and foster the children's relationship with the noncustodial parent. Parr v. Parr, 345 Ill. App. 3d 371, 280 Ill. Dec. 468, 802 N.E.2d 393, 2003 Ill. App. LEXIS 1620 (4 Dist. 2003).

A court should not confine its consideration only to the direct benefits a child may receive from removal; a child may also receive indirect benefits from a proposed move and such benefits should be considered where they are established by the evidence. In re Davis, 229 Ill. App. 3d 653, 171 Ill. Dec. 590, 594 N.E.2d 734 (4 Dist.), cert. denied, 146 Ill. 2d 625, 176 Ill. Dec. 795, 602 N.E.2d 449 (1992).

A mobile society, by itself, is not a compelling reason to grant a custodial parent's petition for removal; custodial parents and their spouses do not make decisions in a vacuum, and decisions must be made in an environment in which the best interests of the child is paramount. In re Davis, 229 Ill. App. 3d 653, 171 Ill. Dec. 590, 594 N.E.2d 734 (4 Dist.), cert. denied, 146 Ill. 2d 625, 176 Ill. Dec. 795, 602 N.E.2d 449 (1992).

Five factors should be considered in determining whether removal is in the best interests of the child or children sought to be removed: (1) the likelihood for enhancing the general quality of life for both the custodial parent and the children; (2) the motives of the custodial parent in seeking the move; (3) the motives of the noncustodial parent in resisting the removal; (4) the visitation rights of the noncustodial parents; and (5) whether a realistic and reasonable visitation schedule can be reached if the move is allowed. In re Davis, 229 Ill. App. 3d 653, 171 Ill. Dec. 590, 594 N.E.2d 734 (4 Dist.), cert. denied, 146 Ill. 2d 625, 176 Ill. Dec. 795, 602 N.E.2d 449 (1992).

Trial court's conclusion that remaining in Illinois, rather than relocating to Colorado, was in the children's best interests was supported by the record, as the father tried to find employment in Colorado and was unable to, he needed to work for his emotional well-being, neither party had improper motives, and the children were happy and adjusted; the mother did not exercise all of her visitation under the Illinois visitation schedule, and she had not effectively and consistently cooperated with petitioner on matters in the children's best interests. In re Marriage of Sobol, 342 Ill. App. 3d 623, 277 Ill. Dec. 468, 796 N.E.2d 183, 2003 Ill. App. LEXIS 1097 (4 Dist. 2003).

—Factual Circumstances

Denial of a mother's petition to remove her son from Illinois so that they could live with her new husband was not against the manifest weight of the evidence, where the evidence failed to establish that the child's quality of life would be enhanced by the

Best Interests of Child (Cont'd)

—Factual Circumstances (Cont'd)

move and the creation of a reasonable visitation schedule for the boy's father was impossible. In re Marriage of Sale, 347 Ill. App. 3d 1083, 283 Ill. Dec. 837, 808 N.E.2d 1125, 2004 Ill. App. LEXIS 418 (5 Dist. 2004).

A determination of the best interests of the child cannot be reduced to a simple brightline test, but rather must be made on a case-by-case basis, depending, to a great extent, upon the circumstances of each case. In re Eckert, 119 Ill. 2d 316, 116 Ill. Dec. 220, 518 N.E.2d 1041 (1988); In re Berk, 215 Ill. App. 3d 459, 158 Ill. Dec. 971, 574 N.E.2d 1364 (2 Dist.), cert. denied, 141 Ill. 2d 536, 162 Ill. Dec. 482, 580 N.E.2d 108 (1991).

—Health of Child

Where child's asthmatic condition was greatly mitigated by Arizona climate there was no error in the trial court's decision to allow the mother to move him there. Hickey v. Hickey, 31 Ill. App. 3d 257, 333 N.E.2d 271 (1 Dist. 1975).

—Hearing Required

While the appellate court did not hold that the discretionary power of the trial court was abused when an order was entered denying the plaintiff's request to take the children to Texas, the court did recognize the fact that the children were in Texas and had been there for a period of months and deemed it to be in the best interests of the children that the trial court conduct a further hearing regarding their removal from the State of Illinois. Reddig v. Reddig, 12 Ill. App. 3d 1009, 299 N.E.2d 353 (3 Dist. 1973).

—Illegitimate

A court adjudicating a dispute between parents over custody of a legitimate child would be guided by what is in the best interest of the child and would best promote its welfare; there is no justification for proceeding differently with a child born out of wedlock. People ex rel. Elmore v. Elmore, 46 Ill. App. 3d 504, 5 Ill. Dec. 292, 361 N.E.2d 615 (1 Dist. 1977).

—Motives of Custodian

So long as the trial court is satisfied with the motives of the custodial parent in seeking the move, and reasonable visitation is available to the remaining parent, removal should be granted. In re Roppo, 225 Ill. App. 3d 721, 167 Ill. Dec. 416, 587 N.E.2d 1031 (1 Dist. 1991).

In examining what will likely enhance the general quality of life for the child, it is permissible for the trial court to analyze the benefits to be derived by the custodial parent who desires to move because the existence of such direct benefits will indirectly enhance the quality of life enjoyed by the child involved. In re Roppo, 225 Ill. App. 3d 721, 167 Ill. Dec. 416, 587 N.E.2d 1031 (1 Dist. 1991).

The court should consider the motives of the custodial parent in seeking the move to determine whether the removal is merely a ruse intended to defeat or frustrate visitation. In re Eckert, 119 Ill. 2d 316, 116 Ill. Dec. 220, 518 N.E.2d 1041 (1988).

A court was mindful of the difficulties faced by a divorced mother who, often with an inadequate income, has the burden of taking care of the children. Laughlin v. Laughlin, 97 Ill. App. 2d 480, 240 N.E.2d 323 (1 Dist. 1968).

—Motives of Non-Custodian

The court should consider the motives of the non-custodial parent in resisting the removal. In re Eckert, 119 Ill. 2d 316, 116 Ill. Dec. 220, 518 N.E.2d 1041 (1988).

—Not Shown

The trial court properly denied a mother's request to move the parties' children to Texas where (1) she testified part of the reason she wanted to move to Texas was to improve her financial position, but the evidence simply did not reveal any significant financial advantage flowing from such a move, (2) the father had assiduously exercised his visitation rights, and (3) the children's relationship with extended family members from both sides of the family would have been disrupted by a move to Texas. Lange v. Lange, 307 Ill. App. 3d 303, 240 Ill. Dec. 414, 717 N.E.2d 507 (4 Dist. 1999).

Where father had diligently established and maintained a close relationship with child ever since her birth, most of child's relatives resided within close proximity to her home, the removal of child some 550 miles away, which may have improved the relationship between mother and her new husband, would have a damaging effect on the relationship of child and father, as well as her relationship with her extended family, the circuit court's finding that removal was in child's best interests was clearly against the manifest weight of the evidence, and upon removal, a manifest injustice would occur. In re Johnson, 277 Ill. App. 3d 675, 214 Ill. Dec. 421, 660 N.E.2d 1370 (5 Dist. 1996).

Where petitioner's income at new job was speculative, she had not looked in immediate area for new job, and father would lose substantial visitation rights, removal was not in the children's best interest. Anderson v. Anderson, 145 Ill. App. 3d 746, 99 Ill. Dec. 770, 496 N.E.2d 345 (2 Dist. 1986).

—Shown

Facts which showed that a 10-year-old child would benefit indirectly by moving with his mother to Massachusetts because he and his mother would become part of a new family when his mother remarried and his mother would earn a higher income while having more time for her son, and that the child would still be able to visit his father in Illinois, supported the trial court's judgment that the move was in the child's best interests, and the intermediate appellate court erred by reversing the trial court's judgment permitting the move. In re Marriage of Collingbourne, 204 Ill. 2d 498, 274 Ill. Dec. 440, 791 N.E.2d 532, 2003 Ill. LEXIS 780 (2003).

Where reasons for the move of child were not frivolous and proposed move to Texas would have improved the standard of living and general quality of life for child, it therefore could be found to be in child's best interest. In re Brady, 115 Ill. App. 3d 521, 71 Ill. Dec. 297, 450 N.E.2d 985 (2 Dist. 1983).

Chancellor should grant permission to take the children out of the jurisdiction, if he deems that to be for the best interests of the children, and make such provisions as are reasonably necessary to protect the rights given to the noncustodial parent of divorce. Trimble v. Trimble, 16 Ill. App. 2d 408, 148 N.E.2d 612 (1 Dist. 1958).

—Visitation Rights

Where evidence did not support a finding that upon removal child's quality of life would be improved and that a reasonable visitation schedule could be reached, removal to another state was not in the child's best interest. In re Johnson, 277 Ill. App. 3d 675, 214 Ill. Dec. 421, 660 N.E.2d 1370 (5 Dist. 1996).

Where the trial court's visitation schedule granted respondent approximately 91 days of visitation per year, in light of the "extraordinary involvement" on the part of respondent with child's life, this visitation was unreasonable. In re Johnson, 277 Ill. App. 3d 675, 214 Ill. Dec. 421, 660 N.E.2d 1370 (5 Dist. 1996).

It is in the best interests of a child to have a healthy and close relationship with both parents, as well as other family members; therefore, the visitation rights of the non-custodial parent should be carefully considered. In re Eckert, 119 Ill. 2d 316, 116 Ill. Dec. 220, 518 N.E.2d 1041 (1988).

Where a petitioner arranged for housing, child care facilities and looked into the schools the child was to attend, and the trial court specifically found that the move would not adversely affect the father's visitation rights as the petitioner stated she would transport the child, at her expense, to the respondent for the respondent's visitation and the custodial parent would be able to spend more time with her child, the move was in the child's best interests. Falk v. Falk, 77 Ill. App. 3d 13, 32 Ill. Dec. 520, 395 N.E.2d 750 (3 Dist. 1979).

—Visitation Schedule

Removal of the children of divorced parents outside of Illinois will always have some impact on visitation, however, the pivotal question under 750 ILCS 5/609(a) was whether a reasonable visitation schedule could be created. In re Marriage of Repond, 349 Ill. App. 3d 910, 285 Ill. Dec. 491, 812 N.E.2d 80, 2004 Ill. App. LEXIS 724 (2 Dist. 2004).

Because in all instances the removal of a child from the State of Illinois will have some adverse effect on visitation by a noncustodial parent, the question in considering a petition for removal becomes whether or not a reasonable and realistic visitation schedule can be developed. In re Marriage of Sale, 347 Ill. App. 3d 1083, 283 Ill. Dec. 837, 808 N.E.2d 1125, 2004 Ill. App. LEXIS 418 (5 Dist. 2004).

Best Interests of Child (Cont'd)

—Visitation Schedule (Cont'd)

It is in the best interest of the child if a realistic and reasonable visitation schedule can be reached if the move is allowed. In re Eckert, 119 Ill. 2d 316, 116 Ill. Dec. 220, 518 N.E.2d 1041 (1988).

Best Interests of Custodial Parent

Custodial parent's interests should not be automatically subordinated to those of the noncustodial parent in a removal of children from Illinois issue; the best interests of children cannot be fully understood without also considering the best interests of the custodial parent. Parr v. Parr, 345 Ill. App. 3d 371, 280 Ill. Dec. 468, 802 N.E.2d 393, 2003 Ill. App. LEXIS 1620 (4 Dist. 2003).

The best interests of children cannot be fully understood without also considering the best interests of the custodial parent. In re Eaton, 269 Ill. App. 3d 507, 207 Ill. Dec. 69, 646 N.E.2d 635 (4 Dist. 1995).

Burden of Proof

—In General

Trial court erred in denying father's petition for a permanent injunction preventing the mother from removing their child from Illinois; the burden of proof should have been on mother to establish that it was in child's best interest to remain with her and the evidence showed that removal was not in the child's best interest because of the effect it would have on the child's relationship with father. Fisher v. Waldrop, Ill. App. 3d , 291 Ill. Dec. 365, 823 N.E.2d 657, 2005 Ill. App. LEXIS 157 (4 Dist. 2005).

The burden of proving that removal from the state is in the child's best interest lies with the party seeking removal. Elliott v. Elliott, 279 Ill. App. 3d 1061, 216 Ill. Dec. 625, 665 N.E.2d 883 (3 Dist. 1996).

In removal cases, the paramount question is whether the move is in the best interest of the child; as stated by this section, the burden is on the custodial parent to show that removal of the child from the state is in the best interest of the child. In re Davis, 229 Ill. App. 3d 653, 171 Ill. Dec. 590, 594 N.E.2d 734 (4 Dist.), cert. denied, 146 Ill. 2d 625, 176 Ill. Dec. 795, 602 N.E.2d 449 (1992).

A custodial parent must prove more than his or her own desire to live with a new spouse to prove that a child's best interests will be served by removal. In re Berk, 215 Ill. App. 3d 459, 158 Ill. Dec. 971, 574 N.E.2d 1364 (2 Dist.), cert. denied, 141 Ill. 2d 536, 162 Ill. Dec. 482, 580 N.E.2d 108 (1991).

Irrespective of whether the trial court grants the right to remove a child from the state or refuses it, the prime considerations remain the best interests of the child and the burden of proof to be borne as a prerequisite to permission to remove. In re Eckert, 148 Ill. App. 3d 512, 102 Ill. Dec. 70, 499 N.E.2d 627 (5 Dist. 1986), rev'd on other grounds, 119 Ill. 2d 316, 116 Ill. Dec. 220, 518 N.E.2d 1041 (1988).

The burden of proof was on the party seeking judicial approval of the proposed removal. Quirin v. Quirin, 50 Ill. App. 3d 785, 7 Ill. Dec. 941, 365 N.E.2d 226 (5 Dist. 1977); Gallagher v. Gallagher, 60 Ill. App. 3d 26, 17 Ill. Dec. 280, 376 N.E.2d 279 (1 Dist. 1978); In re Burgham, 86 Ill. App. 3d 341, 41 Ill. Dec. 691, 408 N.E.2d 37 (4 Dist. 1980); In re Feliciano, 103 Ill. App. 3d 666, 59 Ill. Dec. 363, 431 N.E.2d 1120 (1 Dist. 1981); In re Brady, 115 Ill. App. 3d 521, 71 Ill. Dec. 297, 450 N.E.2d 985 (2 Dist. 1983); Anderson v. Anderson, 145 Ill. App. 3d 746, 99 Ill. Dec. 770, 496 N.E.2d 345 (2 Dist. 1986); Winebright v. Winebright, 155 Ill. App. 3d 722, 108 Ill. Dec. 463, 508 N.E.2d 774 (3 Dist. 1987); In re Eckert, 119 Ill. 2d 316, 116 Ill. Dec. 220, 518 N.E.2d 1041 (1988); In re Taylor, 202 Ill. App. 3d 740, 147 Ill. Dec. 810, 559 N.E.2d 1150 (3 Dist. 1990).

—Met

The trial court's order to allow the custodial parent to remove children was supported by the evidence. In re Herkert, 245 Ill. App. 3d 1068, 186 Ill. Dec. 29, 615 N.E.2d 833 (4 Dist. 1993).

—Not Met

Eckert factors, which the court considered in evaluating a mother's petition to remove her and her ex-husband's children out of Illinois and to Arizona, weighed in favor of denying her petition because, although the move would enhance the mother's quality of life, the children would lose more than they would gain by the move because they would be leaving their father and his new wife, with whom they had extremely positive visits, their large extended families, and their school, friends, and activities, moreover, the move would drastically affect the father's visitation rights, which he exercised in full in addition to calling the children on days when he did not visit with them and attending their extracurricular activities. In re Marriage of Johnson, 352 Ill. App. 3d 605, 287 Ill. Dec. 480, 815 N.E.2d 1283, 2004 Ill. App. LEXIS 1121 (2 Dist. 2004).

Where the evidence was mixed in the case of a parent who wished to remove the parties' children from Illinois to Wisconsin, a trial court did not go against the manifest weight of the evidence in determining that relocation was not against the manifest weight of the evidence. In re Marriage of Stahl, 348 Ill. App. 3d 602, 284 Ill. Dec. 606, 810 N.E.2d 259, 2004 Ill. App. LEXIS 582 (2 Dist. 2004), appeal denied sub nom. Stahl v. Deleo, 2004 Ill. LEXIS 1552 (2004).

Trial court's order denying permission to remove minor children to Colorado was upheld where petitioner failed to meet her burden of proof that the removal to Colorado would be in the best interests of the children. In re Stone, 201 Ill. App. 3d 238, 147 Ill. Dec. 92, 559 N.E.2d 92 (1 Dist. 1990).

Plaintiff failed to set forth a prima facie case that removal of herself and her two children to Florida was in the best interests of her children, although plaintiff claimed that Florida's climate would benefit her health, as well as the health of her son, and that, because she did not drive, Florida's public transportation system was better than what she had been using, plaintiff failed to meet her burden of proof with regard to the petition for removal. In re Kutinac, 182 Ill. App. 3d 377, 131 Ill. Dec. 487, 538 N.E.2d 862 (2 Dist. 1989).

Change of Custody

After the judgment for divorce, the question of the custody of a child remains subject to the order of the court and could be reviewed and modified from time to time as the unfolding circumstances and the best interest of the child may require. Gallagher v. Gallagher, 60 Ill. App. 3d 26, 17 Ill. Dec. 280, 376 N.E.2d 279 (1 Dist. 1978).

In ruling on an application for a change of custody, the trial court is entrusted with wide discretion. Gallagher v. Gallagher, 60 Ill. App. 3d 26, 17 Ill. Dec. 280, 376 N.E.2d 279 (1 Dist. 1978).

Evidence of facts that existed prior to the divorce will not be admitted unless the proponent lays a foundation which shows it is relevant to the change of circumstances being urged to justify a change in the custody. Gallagher v. Gallagher, 60 Ill. App. 3d 26, 17 Ill. Dec. 280, 376 N.E.2d 279 (1 Dist. 1978).

Father's remarriage and having a larger house than mother were factors to be considered by the court but were not sufficient reasons for a change of custody. Gallagher v. Gallagher, 60 Ill. App. 3d 26, 17 Ill. Dec. 280, 376 N.E.2d 279 (1 Dist. 1978).

Decree fixing custody is final as to the conditions then existing, and should not subsequently be changed unless on altered conditions or on material facts existing at the time of the decree but unknown to the court. Langin v. Langin, 2 Ill. App. 3d 544, 276 N.E.2d 822 (5 Dist. 1971).

Cohabitation

Where in considering a petition by former wife to remove children from the state, the trial court considered the effect of petitioner's cohabitation upon the best interest of the children in light of overruled precedent, the trial court misinterpreted the law and the case was reversed and remanded for rehearing. In re Burgham, 86 Ill. App. 3d 341, 41 Ill. Dec. 691, 408 N.E.2d 37 (4 Dist. 1980).

In deciding petition by former wife to remove children from state, the court should recognize that past improper cohabitation, if discontinued, does not, of itself, disqualify a spouse for custody and the court must also weigh the possible detriment to the boys from reduced opportunities of visitation that would result from the added expenses and time involved in travel between the husband's home on the east coast and wife's on the west coast. In re Burgham, 86 Ill. App. 3d 341, 41 Ill. Dec. 691, 408 N.E.2d 37 (4 Dist. 1980).

Consolidation

—Improper

Father's petition for change of custody was predicated upon mother's anticipated petition to move with child to Virginia; the court allowed both petitions to be consolidated into one hearing; the trial court issued one order discussing its findings of fact and its decision denying mother's petition to remove and allowing father's

Consolidation (Cont'd)

—Improper (Cont'd)

petition for change in physical custody; the trial court was in error; the trial court should have ruled on mother's petition first; had the trial court denied mother's petition, the basis for father's petition would have been eliminated; father then would have been required to prove, by clear and convincing evidence, that another change, other than the move to Virginia, had occurred such that child should be removed from mother's physical custody. In re Taylor, 202 Ill. App. 3d 740, 147 Ill. Dec. 810, 559 N.E.2d 1150 (3 Dist. 1990).

—Of Petitions

Where the custody petition was predicated upon the removal petition and the two petitions were tried together, the trial court should have considered the merits of the removal petition before ruling on the custody petition. In re Benson, 217 Ill. App. 3d 564, 160 Ill. Dec. 542, 577 N.E.2d 867 (3 Dist. 1991).

Construction With Parentage Act

The Parentage Act (750 ILCS 45/1 et seq.) does not contain any provision requiring that actions for removal be resolved pursuant to this section which is not implicitly incorporated into that Act. In re M.M.W., 296 Ill. App. 3d 877, 231 Ill. Dec. 238, 695 N.E.2d 1357 (2 Dist. 1998).

Contempt

Before a person could be held in contempt, the action of that party must have clearly arisen from an attempt to show willful defiance of a rule of law. Voss v. Voss, 23 Ill. App. 3d 312, 319 N.E.2d 72 (3 Dist. 1974).

Where plaintiff testified at the hearing that she was unaware of the statutory requirement or the procedure for obtaining consent when taking the minor from the state, to find plaintiff in contempt for an unintentional violation of this section would seem to be contrary to the purpose of the procedure which was designed to punish for a willful defiance of a rule of law or provisions of a decree known to the party charged. Voss v. Voss, 23 Ill. App. 3d 312, 319 N.E.2d 72 (3 Dist. 1974).

Desire of Parents

The mere desire of the parent having custody to move to another state, without more, is insufficient to establish that the move would be in the best interests of the children. Quirin v. Quirin, 50 Ill. App. 3d 785, 7 Ill. Dec. 941, 365 N.E.2d 226 (5 Dist. 1977); In re Eckert, 119 Ill. 2d 316, 116 Ill. Dec. 220, 518 N.E.2d 1041 (1988); In re Stone, 201 Ill. App. 3d 238, 147 Ill. Dec. 92, 559 N.E.2d 92 (1 Dist. 1990).

Where one of the parents has been awarded custody of the parties' child and there is no showing that award was against the child's best interests, a court should not oppose removal of the child from Illinois where the parent granted custody has moved or desires to move to another jurisdiction unless there is a specific showing that the move would be against the child's best interests. Tandy v. Tandy, 42 Ill. App. 3d 87, 355 N.E.2d 585 (1 Dist. 1976).

Discretion of Court

The trial court acted properly when it approved the mother's petition to remove the parties' child from the jurisdiction even though joint custody of the child had been awarded to the parties upon the dissolution of their marriage, and there was no abuse by the trial court of its broad discretion. Gallagher v. Gallagher, 60 Ill. App. 3d 26, 17 Ill. Dec. 280, 376 N.E.2d 279 (1 Dist. 1978).

The discretion given by this statute to the courts is limited only by the best interests of such child. Johnson v. Johnson, 105 Ill. App. 2d 399, 245 N.E.2d 580 (1 Dist. 1969).

Evidence

—Additional Evidence

Where respondent presented new and additional evidence not brought out during petitioner's case-in-chief, specifically as to how often he had residency of the children, in far greater detail and additional facts, the respondent did meet his burden of going forward with the evidence, and motion to remove children was properly denied. Anderson v. Anderson, 145 Ill. App. 3d 746, 99 Ill. Dec. 770, 496 N.E.2d 345 (2 Dist. 1986).

—Held Insufficient

Evidence was held insufficient to deny custodial parent's request to remove child to another state. In re Taylor, 202 Ill. App. 3d 740, 147 Ill. Dec. 810, 559 N.E.2d 1150 (3 Dist. 1990).

—Held Sufficient

In light of the uncertainty of petitioner's future employment, the fact that petitioner might well be able to find similar employment in the present area, and the fact that removal would severely intrude upon respondent's joint custody rights, the trial court's denial of petitioner's motion to remove was not against the manifest weight of the evidence. Anderson v. Anderson, 145 Ill. App. 3d 746, 99 Ill. Dec. 770, 496 N.E.2d 345 (2 Dist. 1986).

Factors Considered

When a removal of a child to a distant jurisdiction impaired a noncustodial parent's involvement with the child, the potential harm to the child was to be assessed under 750 ILCS 5/609(a). In re Marriage of Repond, 349 Ill. App. 3d 910, 285 Ill. Dec. 491, 812 N.E.2d 80, 2004 Ill. App. LEXIS 724 (2 Dist. 2004).

Illinois trial court considering a petition to remove children of divorced parents from Illinois, under 750 ILCS 5/609(a), had to hear any and all relevant evidence, and the factors that a trial court was to consider in determining whether a removal would be in the child's best interests included (1) the likelihood that the move would enhance the general quality of life for both the custodial parent and the child, (2) the custodial parent's motives in seeking the removal, to determine whether the removal is a ruse intended to defeat or frustrate visitation, (3) the noncustodial parent's motives in resisting the removal, (4) the removal's effect on the visitation rights of the noncustodial parent, and (5) whether a realistic and reasonable visitation schedule could be created if the move was allowed; these factors are not exclusive, and the weight to be given each factor varies according to the facts of each case, as the purpose of these factors not to establish a test but, rather, is to be considered and balanced by the trial court in arriving at a best interests determination. In re Marriage of Repond, 349 Ill. App. 3d 910, 285 Ill. Dec. 491, 812 N.E.2d 80, 2004 Ill. App. LEXIS 724 (2 Dist. 2004).

Supreme court has identified five factors to consider in determining whether removal is in the child's best interests: the likelihood that the proposed move will enhance the general quality of life for both the custodial parent and the child, the motives of the custodial parent in seeking the move, the motives of the noncustodial parent in resisting the removal, the visitation rights of the noncustodial parent, and whether a realistic and reasonable visitation schedule can be reached if the move is allowed. In re Taylor, 251 Ill. App. 3d 58, 190 Ill. Dec. 404, 621 N.E.2d 273 (3 Dist. 1993).

The factors contained in In re Marriage of Eckert, 119 Ill.2d 316, 116 Ill.Dec. 220, 518 N.E.2d 1041 (1988) are not elements of a prima facie case that must be proven in order to avoid a directed judgment; a prima facie case for removal of a child from the state is made by proving that the move is in the child's best interests. In re Firkus, 223 Ill. App. 3d 94, 165 Ill. Dec. 602, 584 N.E.2d 1036 (5 Dist. 1991).

To aid the circuit court's determination whether removal of a child from a state is in the child's best interest, the court should consider the following factors: (1) the likelihood that the move will enhance the quality of life and general welfare of both the custodial parent and the child; (2) the custodial parent's motive in seeking removal; (3) the motives of the noncustodial parent in resisting removal; (4) whether a realistic and reasonable visitation schedule can be reached if removal is allowed; and (5) if the move is to a distant jurisdiction, the harm to the child which may result. In re Firkus, 223 Ill. App. 3d 94, 165 Ill. Dec. 602, 584 N.E.2d 1036 (5 Dist. 1991).

In deciding whether removal is in the child's best interest, courts look primarily at three factors: whether there is a sensible reason for the move, whether the move is consistent with the child's best interest, and whether the removal will prevent reasonable visitation by the second parent. Anderson v. Anderson, 145 Ill. App. 3d 746, 99 Ill. Dec. 770, 496 N.E.2d 345 (2 Dist. 1986); In re Gratz, 193 Ill. App. 3d 142, 139 Ill. Dec. 611, 548 N.E.2d 1325 (2 Dist. 1989); In re Taylor, 202 Ill. App. 3d 740, 147 Ill. Dec. 810, 559 N.E.2d 1150 (3 Dist. 1990); In re Shelton, 217 Ill. App. 3d 26, 159 Ill. Dec. 939, 576 N.E.2d 862 (5 Dist. 1991).

Final Orders

Where the trial judge determined as a matter of law that, under the circumstances of the case, the mother's petition for removal amounted to a petition to modify a custody judgment, and dismissed the petition because she presented no affidavits showing potential serious endangerment to her daughter's health if the petition was not granted, such dismissal was a final order, appealable by the mother. In re Yndestad, 232 Ill. App. 3d 1, 173 Ill. Dec. 507, 597 N.E.2d 215 (2 Dist. 1992).

Harm to Child

When removal to a distant jurisdiction will substantially impair the non-custodial parent's involvement with the child, the trial court should examine the potential harm to the child which may result from the move. In re Eckert, 119 Ill. 2d 316, 116 Ill. Dec. 220, 518 N.E.2d 1041 (1988).

Housing

While it is true that good housing is in the best interest of children and is, therefore, relevant to the determination of whether a removal petition should be granted, the courts do not require that housing be shown as a prerequisite to removal. In re Shalashnow, 159 Ill. App. 3d 760, 111 Ill. Dec. 535, 512 N.E.2d 1076 (2 Dist. 1987).

Illustrative Cases

In balancing the various factors set out in In re Marriage of Eckert, 119 Ill. 2d 316, 518 N.E.2d 1041, 116 Ill. Dec. 220 (1988), the denial of the petition to remove was against the manifest weight of the evidence and the judgment was reversed. In re Ludwinski, 312 Ill. App. 3d 495, 245 Ill. Dec. 166, 727 N.E.2d 419, 2000 Ill. App. LEXIS 219 (4 Dist. 2000).

Petitioner failed to prove that moving the children 850 miles away from their father was in their best interests: 1) there was no evidence the move would enhance their quality of life; 2) only motive for move by custodial parent was to be close to family; 3) there were no improper motives on noncustodial parents part in resisting move; 4) move 850 miles away would have great negative impact on respondent's visitation rights; and 5) great distance greatly impaired a visitation schedule that would give respondent any meaningful contact with his children. In re Krivi, 283 Ill. App. 3d 772, 219 Ill. Dec. 274, 670 N.E.2d 1162 (5 Dist. 1996).

Evidence of any benefit to child was overwhelmingly insufficient to support a petition for removal out-of-state; the benefits of the move accruing to the custodial parent were unsubstantiated and the benefits to the child, which appeared to be nothing more than relief from a mild allergy, were not only unsubstantiated, but insignificant as well. In re Clark, 246 Ill. App. 3d 479, 186 Ill. Dec. 335, 616 N.E.2d 2 (4 Dist. 1993).

Where at the time of the hearing on the petition, the petitioner had remarried, her husband became employed in Florida, the evidence presented established that the children's lifestyle in both Florida and Illinois would be comparable, and where the petitioner's motive for moving was to be with her husband, a legitimate reason, and one which cannot be deemed as an attempt to frustrate the respondent's visitation, the decision of the court was not against the manifest weight of the evidence. In re Shelton, 217 Ill. App. 3d 26, 159 Ill. Dec. 939, 576 N.E.2d 862 (5 Dist. 1991).

The finding that the move to Germany was consistent with the best interests of the children was not against the manifest weight of the evidence where the children would be staying with their mother, who had primary custody since the divorce, petitioner would have more time because she did not plan to work outside the home, and there was sufficient evidence to show petitioner was a fit parent and would continue to be. In re Lichtenstein, 139 Ill. App. 3d 881, 94 Ill. Dec. 416, 487 N.E.2d 1293 (5 Dist. 1986).

Wife established that move was in the best interests of the child and met her burden of proof; evidence adduced at the hearing established that there was a general overall improvement in the child's living conditions and health and the action of the court was correct in granting the wife leave to remove the child to Tennessee. In re Feliciano, 103 Ill. App. 3d 666, 59 Ill. Dec. 363, 431 N.E.2d 1120 (1 Dist. 1981).

Indirect Benefits

If only direct benefits to affected children were considered, there would almost never arise a situation where removal from Illinois would be permitted where children were in a good environment with good schools, good parents, and good friends; however, it is necessary to also consider indirect benefits to the children from the proposed move. Such indirect benefits include the benefit the children would derive from the effect on their mother from the establishing of a new and successful marriage relationship; the mother's quality of life would be significantly improved, both by being able to live with her new husband and by not needing to work outside the home, and in the new arrangement the mother would have the time and energy to be a part of her children's life in ways that had not been possible in the past, which would certainly enhance the mother's quality of life. In re Carlson, 216 Ill. App. 3d 1077, 159 Ill. Dec. 909, 576 N.E.2d 578 (3 Dist.), cert. denied, 142 Ill. 2d 651, 164 Ill. Dec. 915, 584 N.E.2d 127 (1991).

Parental Involvement

It is the province of the trial court to determine whether removal of child from Illinois to Colorado would permit a degree of involvement and cooperation between parents and child that would foster their son's physical, mental, moral and emotional well-being. In re Bednar, 146 Ill. App. 3d 704, 100 Ill. Dec. 84, 496 N.E.2d 1149 (1 Dist. 1986).

Petition Not Required

In cases where the parties were never married, the custodial parent is not required to file a petition for removal, thus, the court will not yet have engaged in a best interest of the child analysis to determine whether the custodial parent should be allowed to remove the minor child from the state, therefore, where the parties were never married, the fact that a custodial parent wishes to move out of the state with the minor child is sufficient to show a change of circumstances which would satisfy the first prong of 750 ILCS 5/610 and the court would then be required to engage in a best interests of the child analysis, utilizing the factors enumerated in 750 ILCS 5/602. In re R.M.F., 275 Ill. App. 3d 43, 211 Ill. Dec. 754, 655 N.E.2d 1137 (2 Dist. 1995).

Preservation of Family

The preservation of the existing family unit is an element to be considered in determining the best interests of the children, with regard to a petition for removal but it is only one of many elements. In re Berk, 215 Ill. App. 3d 459, 158 Ill. Dec. 971, 574 N.E.2d 1364 (2 Dist.), cert. denied, 141 Ill. 2d 536, 162 Ill. Dec. 482, 580 N.E.2d 108 (1991).

Removal

Where 750 ILCS 5/609(a) allowed the trial court to require a party removing a child from Illinois to give reasonable security guaranteeing the child's return to Illinois, but the judgment of dissolution, incorporating by reference the parties' agreement, required the mother to pay liquidated damages if the mother and child did not return to Illinois, neither § 609(a) nor any other provision of the Illinois Marriage and Dissolution of Marriage Act, 750 ILCS 5/101 et seq., authorized the trial court to require a reasonable security to guarantee the mother's return to Illinois; because the trial court lacked the authority to incorporate the agreement by reference into the divorce judgment, that portion of the judgment was void, and res judicata did not bar the mother's challenge to the liquidated damages provision. In re Marriage of Roe, 352 Ill. App. 3d 1155, 288 Ill. Dec. 186, 817 N.E.2d 544, 2004 Ill. App. LEXIS 1205 (2 Dist. 2004).

—Allowed

Trial court erred when it denied a former wife's request that she be allowed to remove her children to Colorado based on a ruling that the wife had failed to carry her burden of establishing that a reasonable visitation schedule could be worked out; the wife was not required to prove each of the five Eckert factors before removal could be granted, rather, the factors were to be weighed against each other to determine whether removal was in the best interests of the wife's children. Parr v. Parr, 345 Ill. App. 3d 371, 280 Ill. Dec. 468, 802 N.E.2d 393, 2003 Ill. App. LEXIS 1620 (4 Dist. 2003).

The trial court properly granted the petition to remove the minor child from the State of Illinois with the following specific findings: (1) petitioner and her husband would both be able to find higher paying jobs in Arizona; (2) petitioner's plan to stay home with the child for an initial period of time would enhance the child's quality of life; (3) the living conditions in Arizona would be comparable to

Removal (Cont'd)

—Allowed (Cont'd)

those in hometown; (4) respondent's motivation in resisting the petition was not improper; (5) petitioner's motivation in seeking the removal was not to frustrate respondent's visitation rights; and (6) the visitation with respondent could be enhanced by allowing longer blocks of visitation with the child. In re R.M.F., 275 Ill. App. 3d 43, 211 Ill. Dec. 754, 655 N.E.2d 1137 (2 Dist. 1995).

Denial of petitioner's request for removal was against the manifest weight of the evidence and reversed. In re Eaton, 269 Ill. App. 3d 507, 207 Ill. Dec. 69, 646 N.E.2d 635 (4 Dist. 1995).

Where a move to Colorado significantly enhanced the general quality of life for the mother by her job promotion, and therefore indirectly benefitted the child's quality of life, mother was willing to allow liberal visitation, including extended summer and Christmas visitations, and in addition, further opportunities for visitation would exist at times when mother returned to Illinois to visit with her family, the trial court's decision denying petition for removal was against the manifest weight of the evidence. In re Ballegeer, 236 Ill. App. 3d 941, 176 Ill. Dec. 906, 602 N.E.2d 852 (3 Dist. 1992).

Wife met her burden of showing that the move was in the best interests of the child. In re Pfeiffer, 237 Ill. App. 3d 510, 178 Ill. Dec. 546, 604 N.E.2d 1069 (3 Dist. 1992), appeal denied, 149 Ill. 2d 660, 183 Ill. Dec. 871, 612 N.E.2d 523 (1993); In re Pribble, 239 Ill. App. 3d 761, 180 Ill. Dec. 455, 607 N.E.2d 349 (5 Dist. 1993).

Removal of two minor children to Michigan was upheld as being in the best interests of the children despite increased distance from the noncustodial father. In re Miroballi, 225 Ill. App. 3d 1094, 168 Ill. Dec. 165, 589 N.E.2d 565 (1 Dist. 1991).

The trial court agreed that petitioner should have custody of four minor children, that petitioner had made excellent arrangements concerning housing and schooling in Florida, that petitioner was a competent mother; therefore, in the absence of a showing that the petitioner's move to Florida would be against the best interests of the children, the move was allowed. In re Siklossy, 87 Ill. App. 3d 124, 42 Ill. Dec. 534, 409 N.E.2d 29 (1 Dist. 1980).

—Circumstances Supporting

All other things being equal, it was an abuse of discretion to deny a custodial parent permission to remove a child when the removal would allow the custodial parent to terminate reliance on state aid, establish economic self-sufficiency and advance her career. In re Young, 263 Ill. App. 3d 901, 201 Ill. Dec. 660, 636 N.E.2d 1092 (3 Dist. 1994).

Where a move by a custodial parent, new spouse and minor child to another state does not appear to be based on financial considerations alone, and would enhance the general quality of life for the family, and the court could assess a realistic and reasonable visitation schedule for the noncustodial parent remaining in Illinois, the custodial parent would not be precluded from removing the child from the state of Illinois. In re Zamarripa-Gesundheit, 175 Ill. App. 3d 184, 124 Ill. Dec. 799, 529 N.E.2d 780 (1 Dist. 1988).

—Denial

Denial of petition to remove children from the state was not against the manifest weight of the evidence; thus, circuit court decision was affirmed. Elliott v. Elliott, 279 Ill. App. 3d 1061, 216 Ill. Dec. 625, 665 N.E.2d 883 (3 Dist. 1996).

—Denied

The court stayed the judgment denying custodial spouse's petition to remove which required her to move back to Illinois, and preserving the status quo after the stay would have allowed custodial parent to retain custody, while the trial judge's order, entered after the stay and granting non-custodial parent further visitation for an unspecified number of dates, was in effect an attempt to change custody which would have violated the status quo, was a direct violation of the stay and the trial court did not have jurisdiction over it. In re Gibbs, 268 Ill. App. 3d 962, 206 Ill. Dec. 502, 645 N.E.2d 507 (1 Dist. 1994), appeal denied, 162 Ill. 2d 566, 209 Ill. Dec. 801, 652 N.E.2d 341 (1995).

—Distinguished from Custody

Where the court allowed both a petition for removal under this section and one for change in custody under 750 ILCS 5/610 to be consolidated into one hearing, the trial court erred in issuing one order discussing its findings of fact and its decision denying the petition to remove and allowing the petition for change in physical custody; the trial court should have ruled on the petition to remove first, because had the court denied the petition, the basis for change in custody petition would have been eliminated. In re Ballegeer, 236 Ill. App. 3d 941, 176 Ill. Dec. 906, 602 N.E.2d 852 (3 Dist. 1992).

This section and 750 ILCS 5/610 clearly distinguish between petitions for removal and petitions to modify custody, and evidence that the father was a more suitable custodian and that the father's town was a better place for the child to live than Arizona, the location where the mother intended to move, was irrelevant with regard to the removal petition; the trial court should have focused instead on whether the child's best interests would be served by living with his mother, the custodial parent, in Illinois or moving with her to Arizona. In re Gratz, 193 Ill. App. 3d 142, 139 Ill. Dec. 611, 548 N.E.2d 1325 (2 Dist. 1989).

Where the evidence showed that the move to Arizona would likely directly benefit the child by significantly improving his allergies and enabling him to spend more time with his mother, where the child would also indirectly benefit from the likely improvement in the health of his mother's husband and resultant reduction in marital tensions, and where the child would additionally be able to spend more time with his mother since she would not have to work full time, since these benefits could be achieved while still allowing the child ample opportunity to visit his friends and father, the removal petitions should have been granted. In re Gratz, 193 Ill. App. 3d 142, 139 Ill. Dec. 611, 548 N.E.2d 1325 (2 Dist. 1989).

—Domicile

A question of domicile, standing alone, was insufficient as a matter of law to warrant a change of custody; the finding of the trial court based on that proposition alone was against the manifest weight of the evidence. Dokos v. Dokos, 88 Ill. App. 2d 330, 232 N.E.2d 508 (1 Dist. 1967).

—From Country

Under 750 ILCS 5/609(a), a trial court's denial of a mother's petition to remove her children from Illinois to Switzerland was against the manifest weight of the evidence because (1) the move would enhance the mother's and children's quality of life; (2) the mother had a valid motive in seeking removal, as she lost her employment in Illinois, was unable to find substitute employment in the United States, and found such employment in Switzerland, and was not trying to defeat the father's visitation; (3) the father had not used half of his scheduled visitation in the past several years, and the mother's visitation proposal was reasonable in light of the father's relationship with the children; and (4) there was no reason to believe the mother would not comply with court-ordered visitation. In re Marriage of Repond, 349 Ill. App. 3d 910, 285 Ill. Dec. 491, 812 N.E.2d 80, 2004 Ill. App. LEXIS 724 (2 Dist. 2004).

This statute authorizing the removal of a child or children from Illinois whenever such removal is in the best interest of such child or children is not expressly nor by necessary implication limited to a removal to another state in the Union; the court may authorize removal to another country. Dokos v. Dokos, 88 Ill. App. 2d 330, 232 N.E.2d 508 (1 Dist. 1967).

—Jurisdiction

The court had jurisdiction to consider issues related to removal of the children to Texas and visitation, notwithstanding that the mother had already received implicit approval to move the children to Indiana in the original dissolution decree; the trial court's authority to deny the mother's request to move the children to Texas was an inherent part of the trial court's authority to enforce the custody and visitation provisions of the judgment of dissolution. Lange v. Lange, 307 Ill. App. 3d 303, 240 Ill. Dec. 414, 717 N.E.2d 507 (4 Dist. 1999).

—Permitted

Order of the circuit court granting a petition for leave to remove the parties' minor child from the state of Illinois was properly granted as the move to Texas would enhance the general quality of life for both the custodial parent and the child. In re Taylor, 251 Ill. App. 3d 58, 190 Ill. Dec. 404, 621 N.E.2d 273 (3 Dist. 1993).

Where the custodial parent seeking permission to relocate a minor child had made arrangements concerning both housing and child care facilities in the new area, she had inquired about schools in the area of her proposed residence, and there was no showing

Removal (Cont'd)

—Permitted (Cont'd)
that these schools were inferior and could not provide the minor child with an education similar in quality to that he was then obtaining the trial court erred in denying custodial parent's petition for removal of the minor child to another state. Gray v. Gray, 57 Ill. App. 3d 1, 14 Ill. Dec. 630, 372 N.E.2d 909 (1 Dist. 1978).

—Petition

Ordinarily, petitions to remove a minor from the jurisdiction address the issue of removing that child from the state. Falk v. Falk, 77 Ill. App. 3d 13, 32 Ill. Dec. 520, 395 N.E.2d 750 (3 Dist. 1979).

Standard of Review

Trial court's determination of what is in the children's best interests should not be reversed unless it is clearly against the manifest weight of the evidence and it appears that a manifest injustice has occurred. Parr v. Parr, 345 Ill. App. 3d 371, 280 Ill. Dec. 468, 802 N.E.2d 393, 2003 Ill. App. LEXIS 1620 (4 Dist. 2003).

In removal cases, a trial court's decision is not to be disturbed unless it is clear its decision was against the manifest weight of the evidence and that a manifest injustice has occurred, and although the trial court has broad discretion in these cases, that discretion is not unlimited and, when the decision is against the manifest weight of the evidence, it will be reversed. In re Davis, 229 Ill. App. 3d 653, 171 Ill. Dec. 590, 594 N.E.2d 734 (4 Dist.), cert. denied, 146 Ill. 2d 625, 176 Ill. Dec. 795, 602 N.E.2d 449 (1992).

The reviewing court should not disturb the trial court's determination of what is in the best interests of the child in a removal action unless such determination has resulted in manifest injustice or is against the weight of the evidence. In re Roppo, 225 Ill. App. 3d 721, 167 Ill. Dec. 416, 587 N.E.2d 1031 (1 Dist. 1991).

The trial court's determination of what is in the best interests of the child should not be reversed unless it is clearly against the manifest weight of the evidence and it appears that a manifest injustice has occurred. Hickey v. Hickey, 31 Ill. App. 3d 257, 333 N.E.2d 271 (1 Dist. 1975); Quirin v. Quirin, 50 Ill. App. 3d 785, 7 Ill. Dec. 941, 365 N.E.2d 226 (5 Dist. 1977); In re Eckert, 119 Ill. 2d 316, 116 Ill. Dec. 220, 518 N.E.2d 1041 (1988); In re Gratz, 193 Ill. App. 3d 142, 139 Ill. Dec. 611, 548 N.E.2d 1325 (2 Dist. 1989).

Time Since Divorce

Fact that less than two years had elapsed since the trial court's initial custody determination was also a matter for the trial court to consider in its examination of whether removal would serve the best interests of the child. In re Bednar, 146 Ill. App. 3d 704, 100 Ill. Dec. 84, 496 N.E.2d 1149 (1 Dist. 1986).

The two year limitation against custody modification does not apply to the provision governing leave to remove minor children from Illinois. Mueller v. Weis, 76 Ill. App. 3d 860, 32 Ill. Dec. 447, 395 N.E.2d 677 (5 Dist. 1979).

Venue

Where the parties were married in Kane County they lived and cohabited together in Kane County until the day before plaintiff commenced this action in Cook County, the defendant continued to reside in Kane County, the two counties were physically proximate to each other, and there would be no inconvenience to the parties or to witnesses if the matter proceeded in Kane County, the trial court erred in dismissing the complaint, and in not transferring the cause to Kane County. Carlson v. Carlson, 39 Ill. App. 3d 234, 350 N.E.2d 213 (1 Dist. 1976).

Visitation Rights

In examining, under 750 ILCS 5/609(a), the impact of removal of the children of divorced parents outside of Illinois on the non-custodial parent's visitation, it was proper to consider the degree to which the non-custodial parent had exercised visitation in the past. In re Marriage of Repond, 349 Ill. App. 3d 910, 285 Ill. Dec. 491, 812 N.E.2d 80, 2004 Ill. App. LEXIS 724 (2 Dist. 2004).

It is in the best interests of children to have a healthy and close relationship with both parents, as well as with other family members, and thus the visitation rights of the noncustodial parent should be carefully considered. In re Stone, 201 Ill. App. 3d 238, 147 Ill. Dec. 92, 559 N.E.2d 92 (1 Dist. 1990).

A reasonable visitation schedule is one that will preserve and foster the child's relationship with the noncustodial parent. In re Eckert, 119 Ill. 2d 316, 116 Ill. Dec. 220, 518 N.E.2d 1041 (1988).

When a parent has assiduously exercised his or her visitation rights, a court should be loath to interfere with it by permitting removal of the children for frivolous or unpersuasive or inadequate reasons. In re Eckert, 119 Ill. 2d 316, 116 Ill. Dec. 220, 518 N.E.2d 1041 (1988).

If the best interests of the children would not be affected by a move to another state, the custodial parent should be free to move; thus, if the noncustodial parent objects to the removal but has not exercised his or her visitation rights, this fact should be considered in determining whether to grant the custodial parent's desire to move. In re Eckert, 119 Ill. 2d 316, 116 Ill. Dec. 220, 518 N.E.2d 1041 (1988).

The visitation difficulties of the non-custodial parent are not alone sufficient to deny a petition for removal. Gray v. Gray, 57 Ill. App. 3d 1, 14 Ill. Dec. 630, 372 N.E.2d 909 (1 Dist. 1978).

LEGAL PERIODICALS

For article, "Post-Eckert Trends in Child Removal: A Review of Appellate Cases," see 84 Ill. B.J. 76 (1996).

For article, "Family Law: 1987-88 Illinois Law Survey," see Loy. U. Chi. L. J. 461 (1988-89).

For article, "Family Law: 1985-86 Survey," see 11 S. Ill. U. L. J. 741 (1987).

RESEARCH REFERENCES

Propriety of awarding custody of child to parent residing or intending to reside in foreign country. 20 ALR4th 677.

Court-authorized permanent or temporary removal of child by parent to foreign county. 30 ALR4th 548.

750 ILCS 5/610 Modification

Sec. 610. *Modification.* (a) Unless by stipulation of the parties, no motion to modify a custody judgment may be made earlier than 2 years after its date, unless the court permits it to be made on the basis of affidavits that there is reason to believe the child's present environment may endanger seriously his physical, mental, moral or emotional health.

(b) The court shall not modify a prior custody judgment unless it finds by clear and convincing evidence, upon the basis of facts that have arisen since the prior judgment or that were unknown to the court at the time of entry of the prior judgment, that a change has occurred in the circumstances of the child or his custodian, or in the case of a joint custody arrangement that a change has occurred in the circumstances of the child or either or both parties having custody, and that the modification is necessary to serve the best interest of the child. In the case of joint custody, if the parties agree to a termination of a joint custody arrangement, the court shall so terminate the joint custody and make any modification which is in the child's best interest. The court shall state in its decision specific findings of fact in support of its modification or termination of joint custody if either parent opposes the modification or termination.

(c) Attorney fees and costs shall be assessed against a party seeking modification if the court finds that the modification action is vexatious and constitutes harassment.

(d) Notice under this Section shall be given as provided in subsections (c) and (d) of Section 601 [750 ILCS 5/601].
(Source: P.A. 85-746; 87-1255, § 1.)

Note.
This section was Ill.Rev.Stat., Ch. 40, para. 610.

CASE NOTES

Analysis

In General
Abortion
Abuse
—In General
—Detrimental to Welfare
—Not Shown
—Shown
Abuse of Discretion
Acts of Parents
Adultery
Affidavits
—In General
—Failure to File
—Form of Word
—Not Deficient
—Not Jurisdictional Prerequisites
—Specificity
—Sufficient Facts
—Waiver
Agreement
Alternating Custody
—Not Experimentation
—Not Joint Custody
—Upheld
Anxiety of Child
Appellate Review
—In General
—Remand Required
Applicability
Application and Construction
—In General
—Burden of Proof
—Custody Proceedings
—Limitation Period
—Petitions Included
—Physical Custody
—Procedure
Attorney Fees
Balancing Test
Best Interest of the Child
—In General
—Custody Hearing
—Drug Use
—Evidence Held Insufficient
—Evidence Held Sufficient
—Father Versus Grandparents
—Fitness of Parent
—Maternal Affection
—Natural Parent's Right
—Nonparental Custody
—Primary Consideration
—Race of Parent
—Relocation of Parent
—Scope of Determination
—Stability of Environment
—Weekend Custody
Bigamous Remarriage
Burden of Proof
Change in Circumstances
—In General
—Allegations
—Burden of Proof
—Clear and Convincing Evidence
—Criteria
—Custodian's Unfitness
—Death of Custodial Parent
—Discretion of Court
—Divorce Decree
—Facts
—Failure to Comply
—Home Schooling
—Medical Care
—Mother's Actions
—New Information
—Noncustodial Parent
—Not Required
—Not Sufficient
—Parental Alienation
—Parental Illness
—Preference of Child
—Religious Activity
—Relocation
—Remarriage
—Removal of Child
—Reversal of Original Decree
—Scope of Inquiry
—Shown
—Statutory Construction
—Sworn
—Welfare of Child
Change of Custody
—Birth of Illegitimate Child
—Burden of Proof
—Change in Circumstances
—Child's Preference
—Custodian's Fitness
—Endangerment
—Factors
—Homosexuality of Custodial Parent
—Improper
—Incarceration of Custodial Parent
—Insufficient Analysis
—Misconduct
—Not Warranted
—Relative Affluence
—Remanded for Further Proceedings
—Reversed
—Social Condemnation
—Temporary
—Warranted
Change of Environment
—Harm
Character
Clear and Convincing Evidence
Cohabitation
Compliance
Conditions
Consent
Criminal Contempt
Custody Judgments
—In General
—Change in Circumstances
—Change of Venue
—Evidence
—Final Order
—Incomplete Determination
—Interim Remedial Period
—Limitation Period
—Modification
—Not Shown
—Permanent Custody
—Petition to Remove Child from State
—Prior Judgments
—Purpose
—Res Judicata
—Unconditional Decree
Custody Proceedings
—Modification Not Shown
—Private Interviews in Chambers

—Separate Issues
Decision of Court
Determination of Custody
—Best Interest of the Child
—Factors
—Scope of Inquiry
Discretion of Court
—In General
—Abuse Not Shown
—Abuse Shown
—Duty of Court
—Prior Order Improper
Effect of Amendment
Endangerment
—Showing Not Required
—Shown
—Standard of Proof
Evidence
—In General
—Events Prior to Decree
—Financial Circumstances
—Held Insufficient
—Held Sufficient
—Preference of Child
—Previous Orders
—Probation Report
—Religion
—Social Service's Report
—Sufficiency
Factors
Final Order
Findings
—Exact Language Not Required
—Forfeiture of Privileges
—Modification Denied
—Required
—Specific
—Void Judgment
Foreign Court's Modification
Fraud
Guardianship
Illustrative Cases
Integration
Joint Custody
—Abuse of Discretion
—Burden of Proof
—Findings Sufficient
—Removal of Child
—Termination
—Termination by Agreement
Jurisdiction
Legislative Intent
Loss of Parent
Mandatory Provision
Moral Fitness
Parentage Order
Permanent Order
Physical Custody
—Award to Father Upheld
—Award to Mother
—Child's Welfare
Pleadings
—Timeliness
Preference of Child
—Evidence Held Insufficient
—Immaturity
—Transfer Unwarranted
Preservation of Family
Presumption
—Present Custodian
Previous Orders
Psychologist's Testimony
Punitive Remedy
Purpose
Religion
Remarriage
—Effect on Custody
—Of Custodial Parent
—Preference of Child
—Sufficient
Removal of Child
—In General
—Burden of Proof
—Close Scrutiny Required
—Distinguished from Custody
—From Jurisdiction
—Jurisdiction
—Limitation Period
—Not Modification
—Out-of-State Residence
—Petition Not Required
Res Judicata
Residence
Revocation
School Attendance
—In General
—Parent Attending School
Scope
Stability
Statute of Limitations
Stipulation
Technical Defect in Order
Temporary Award
Terms Used
Transfer of Custody
Vacation of Order
Visitation
—Upheld
Waiver

In General

This section reflects an underlying policy favoring the finality of child custody judgments and creating a presumption in favor of the present custody so as to promote stability and continuity in the child's custodial and environmental relationships. In re Fuesting, 228 Ill. App. 3d 339, 169 Ill. Dec. 456, 591 N.E.2d 960 (5 Dist. 1992); In re Andersen, 236 Ill. App. 3d 679, 177 Ill. Dec. 289, 603 N.E.2d 70 (2 Dist. 1992).

It is evident from the language of this section that the section is operative in cases of child custody modifications, and it is clear that the court shall not modify a prior custody judgment unless this section's requirements are met. In re Gibbons, 158 Ill. App. 3d 998, 111 Ill. Dec. 148, 512 N.E.2d 52 (4 Dist. 1987).

This section does not differentiate between contested and agreed custody judgments. In re Gibbons, 158 Ill. App. 3d 998, 111 Ill. Dec. 148, 512 N.E.2d 52 (4 Dist. 1987).

The ill effects of changes need not manifest themselves before a court can alter a child's custody. In re Pease, 106 Ill. App. 3d 617, 62 Ill. Dec. 389, 435 N.E.2d 1361 (2 Dist. 1982).

The law favors the preservation of the existing custody judgment. In re Pease, 106 Ill. App. 3d 617, 62 Ill. Dec. 389, 435 N.E.2d 1361 (2 Dist. 1982).

Reviewing courts are reluctant to interfere with the disposition of the trial court in child custody matters. In re Pease, 106 Ill. App. 3d 617, 62 Ill. Dec. 389, 435 N.E.2d 1361 (2 Dist. 1982).

Post-decree divorce matters are not new proceedings; they are simply an extension of the same proceedings. Santos v. Santos, 97 Ill. App. 3d 629, 52 Ill. Dec. 776, 422 N.E.2d 985 (3 Dist. 1981).

The commands of this section to consider only whether the child's environment endangers his physical, mental, moral and emotional health and to disregard any conduct of the custodian that does not affect his relationship with the child reemphasize the principle that the focus of custody determinations must be the welfare of the child. Jarrett v. Jarrett, 78 Ill. 2d 337, 36 Ill. Dec. 1, 400 N.E.2d 421 (1979), cert. denied, 449 U.S. 927, 101 S. Ct. 329, 66 L. Ed. 2d 155 (1980).

A custody decree may be changed by order of the court from time to time as the best interests of the child demand. Marcus v. Marcus, 109 Ill. App. 2d 423, 248 N.E.2d 800 (1 Dist. 1969); Maroney v. Maroney, 109 Ill. App. 2d 162, 249 N.E.2d 871 (3 Dist. 1969).

Abortion

Although the trial court erroneously considered evidence of a

Abortion (Cont'd)
mother's previous abortion such consideration was not reversible error where the trial court reached a proper decision. Thompson v. Thompson, 83 Ill. App. 3d 97, 38 Ill. Dec. 485, 403 N.E.2d 716 (3 Dist. 1980).

Abuse

—In General
The trial court had a right and duty to consider the child abuse question in deciding the proper award of custody. Hinton v. Searles, 53 Ill. App. 3d 433, 11 Ill. Dec. 329, 368 N.E.2d 937 (5 Dist. 1977).

Where the custodial parent permitted her new spouse to commit indecent liberties with her minor daughter, after he had confessed to earlier acts of indecent liberties, rendered plaintiff an improper person at that time to have the custody of her children. Day v. Day, 33 Ill. App. 2d 247, 178 N.E.2d 203 (2 Dist. 1961).

—Detrimental to Welfare
Where a plaintiff, the custodial parent, exercised poor judgment in permitting contacts between her daughter and her new spouse subsequent to the time he admitted acts of indecent liberties with her daughter, and these contacts were detrimental to her welfare, the plaintiff properly lost custody. Day v. Day, 33 Ill. App. 2d 247, 178 N.E.2d 203 (2 Dist. 1961).

—Not Shown
Where evidence with regard to stepfather's disciplining of the children indicated a rather strict approach to such matters, there was no indication that the discipline administered caused serious physical or emotional harm to stepson or the other children and where there was no testimony that stepson ever suffered any injury as a result of the discipline from his stepfather or that it was administered arbitrarily or without some justification, the court was unable to say that the punishment was anything outside the bounds of normal, albeit strict, parental discipline and therefore, the requirement of serious dangers to their health had not been met. In re Poston, 77 Ill. App. 3d 689, 33 Ill. Dec. 187, 396 N.E.2d 576 (3 Dist. 1979).

—Shown
In light of the evidence produced by respondent and petitioner on the question of child abuse, the allegations of child abuse were verified to the extent that the petitioner should have been awarded custody of the children under all the facts presented to the trial court. Hinton v. Searles, 53 Ill. App. 3d 433, 11 Ill. Dec. 329, 368 N.E.2d 937 (5 Dist. 1977).

Abuse of Discretion
Where a child lived with defendant for seven of his eight years of life, and since the trial court could have considered evidence existing prior to the entry of the default judgment, the defendant's petition for child custody modification was not vexatious under this section and the trial court's finding to the contrary was an abuse of discretion. Padgett v. Padgett, 157 Ill. App. 3d 492, 109 Ill. Dec. 567, 510 N.E.2d 435 (5 Dist. 1987).

Acts of Parents
Trial court correctly changed the custody of the parties' children from that of the mother to the father where evidence showed that mother was a shoplifter and the minor children aided and abetted her in such conduct. Stark v. Stark, 13 Ill. App. 3d 35, 299 N.E.2d 605 (3 Dist. 1973).

Adultery
Where no showing is made of detriment resulting to the children, evidence of a parent's extramarital relationship with another is insufficient upon which to base a change of custody. In re Farris, 69 Ill. App. 3d 1042, 26 Ill. Dec. 608, 388 N.E.2d 232 (4 Dist. 1979).

Previous open adulterous conduct, once the mother has married the paramour and reestablished a good home, is not grounds for change of custody. Rippon v. Rippon, 64 Ill. App. 3d 465, 21 Ill. Dec. 135, 381 N.E.2d 70 (3 Dist. 1978).

Even though a wife has been dating other men prior to divorce, it is not an abuse of discretion for the trial court to award custody of the children to her. Rippon v. Rippon, 64 Ill. App. 3d 465, 21 Ill. Dec. 135, 381 N.E.2d 70 (3 Dist. 1978).

Only when an open adulterous relationship exists with no possibility of marriage, as when the paramour is and remains married to another woman, is there sufficient grounds to remove custody from the mother. Rippon v. Rippon, 64 Ill. App. 3d 465, 21 Ill. Dec. 135, 381 N.E.2d 70 (3 Dist. 1978).

Where the flagrant adulterous relationship between the custodial mother and a married man did affect the relationship of mother and children within the meaning of 750 ILCS 5/602(b), and negatively affected the moral health of children, the trial court did not err or abuse its discretion in transferring custody of the minor children to their father, despite the mother's remorse over her actions. De Franco v. De Franco, 67 Ill. App. 3d 760, 24 Ill. Dec. 130, 384 N.E.2d 997 (1 Dist. 1978).

Affidavits

—In General
This provision does not set forth the standard which must be reached before a change of custody may be made, but rather requires the filing of affidavits in instances where custody modification is sought within two years of an original custody determination. In re Farris, 69 Ill. App. 3d 1042, 26 Ill. Dec. 608, 388 N.E.2d 232 (4 Dist. 1979).

—Failure to File
The failure to file affidavits with regard to child custody does not render a judgment subsequently entered in the same proceeding void for lack of jurisdiction. Sexton v. Sexton, 84 Ill. 2d 312, 49 Ill. Dec. 709, 418 N.E.2d 729 (1981).

Where Louisiana custody judgment that was entered in connection with legal separation was a final order, the husband and wife in Illinois were subject to the structures of this section; even though neither parent filed the affidavit required by subsection (a) of this section, stating that there was reason to believe the child was endangered by his present environment, the parents' proceedings in the circuit court adequately petitioned the court to modify the Louisiana custody judgment. In re Herron, 74 Ill. App. 3d 748, 30 Ill. Dec. 806, 393 N.E.2d 1153 (1 Dist. 1979).

—Form of Word
The use of the plural "affidavits" in this section does not necessitate a filing of two or more such affidavits. In re Braje, 85 Ill. App. 3d 744, 41 Ill. Dec. 593, 407 N.E.2d 1091 (2 Dist. 1980).

—Not Deficient
Father's petition for removal was not deficient as a matter of law because of its failure to include affidavits alleging that there was reason to believe the child's present environment might endanger seriously his physical, mental, moral or emotional health. In re Bednar, 146 Ill. App. 3d 704, 100 Ill. Dec. 84, 496 N.E.2d 1149 (1 Dist. 1986).

—Not Jurisdictional Prerequisites
The provisions of subdivision (a) of this section, at least with regard to its reference to "affidavits," are not jurisdictional prerequisites; a failure to file more than one affidavit is not fatal to a request for modification of a custody order. In re Braje, 85 Ill. App. 3d 744, 41 Ill. Dec. 593, 407 N.E.2d 1091 (2 Dist. 1980).

—Specificity
A party requesting that the court modify a prior custody order within two years of its enactment must comply through the procedural requirements of this section; the court must be informed by affidavit that there is reason to believe the child's present environment may endanger seriously his physical, mental, moral or emotional health; an affidavit is sufficient to so inform the court if it is attached to and supports the petition requesting modification of a prior custody judgment; perfect specificity is desired, but is not always required. In re Eleopoulos, 186 Ill. App. 3d 374, 134 Ill. Dec. 326, 542 N.E.2d 505 (4 Dist. 1989).

—Sufficient Facts
Where the verified petition and domestic violence order of protection contained the exact statutory language of this section, and the attached affidavit reported a specific instance wherein the respondent struck his daughter with a belt, causing her to suffer a large bruise on her buttocks, it was sufficient to inform the court and parties of the facts relied upon for a custody change, even

Affidavits (Cont'd)

—Sufficient Facts (Cont'd)
though the affidavit did not repeat the statutory language. In re Eleopoulos, 186 Ill. App. 3d 374, 134 Ill. Dec. 326, 542 N.E.2d 505 (4 Dist. 1989).

—Waiver
The requirement that affidavits be filed was waived where appellant had not objected to holding the hearing on the petition; appellant sought to gain advantage on appeal by silence in the trial court; petitioner's verified complaint set forth specific facts informing the court of the basis for custody change; and the facts not sworn to by affidavit were testified to in open court. In re Noble, 192 Ill. App. 3d 501, 139 Ill. Dec. 133, 548 N.E.2d 518 (2 Dist. 1989).

Petitioner's inaction in not objecting to the lack of affidavit appeared to constitute a waiver. In re Kading, 150 Ill. App. 3d 623, 103 Ill. Dec. 654, 501 N.E.2d 971 (2 Dist. 1986).

Agreement
Father's request for modification of joint custody award was governed by this section where the parties agreed in writing in their judgment for dissolution that the court would be bound by the statute in force at the time any request was made for modification of the joint custody award. In re Kartholl, 143 Ill. App. 3d 228, 97 Ill. Dec. 347, 492 N.E.2d 1006 (2 Dist. 1986).

A court may use initial discretion in deciding custody questions where the original custody order is achieved by agreement of the parties, but this discretion is limited to the issue of a change of circumstances. LaMarca v. LaMarca, 78 Ill. App. 3d 26, 33 Ill. Dec. 698, 397 N.E.2d 31 (1 Dist. 1979).

The petitioned court had the right to know the circumstances surrounding the custody agreement by the parties, when those circumstances did not appear of record, and had the right to consider them in rendering a decision on a petition seeking change of custody. Randolph v. Dean, 27 Ill. App. 3d 913, 327 N.E.2d 473 (3 Dist. 1975).

Alternating Custody

—Not Experimentation
Modification order granting father sole custody during school year, and mother sole custody during summer provided predictable, periodic changes in the children's residence; therefore, that modification cannot be termed "experimentation." In re Dullard, 176 Ill. App. 3d 817, 126 Ill. Dec. 227, 531 N.E.2d 854 (1 Dist. 1988).

—Not Joint Custody
Modification order granting sole custody to father during the school year, and sole custody to mother during the summer did not constitute joint custody. In re Dullard, 176 Ill. App. 3d 817, 126 Ill. Dec. 227, 531 N.E.2d 854 (1 Dist. 1988).

—Upheld
Modification of joint custody agreement, which awarded the father sole custody of the minor children during the school year, and gave the mother sole custody of the children during the summer months, was in the best interest of the children. In re Dullard, 176 Ill. App. 3d 817, 126 Ill. Dec. 227, 531 N.E.2d 854 (1 Dist. 1988).

Anxiety of Child
The mother argued that the evidence indicated that the cause of child's problems originated with the custody dispute; no doubt the custody dispute contributed to child's anxiety and other problems, but those problems were nonetheless matters affecting his welfare and thus were properly considered by the trial court regardless of their origin. In re Eldert, 158 Ill. App. 3d 798, 110 Ill. Dec. 768, 511 N.E.2d 945 (3 Dist. 1987), appeal denied, 117 Ill. Dec. 224, 520 N.E.2d 385 (Ill. 1988).

Appellate Review

—In General
Once the trial court has made its determination that the necessary proof for a change of custody is established by clear and convincing evidence, the appellate court should overturn that determination only if it is contrary to the manifest weight of the evidence. In re England, 158 Ill. App. 3d 1005, 111 Ill. Dec. 191, 512 N.E.2d 95 (4 Dist. 1987).

A grant of relief under this section by a trial court during the pendency of an appeal from a prior custody order differs in a significant aspect from other situations where a trial court is requested to "modify" a prior order pending its appeal; this section retains the common law rule that a final custody order is res judicata as to facts presented to the court at the time of the entry of that order. In re Spangler, 124 Ill. App. 3d 1023, 80 Ill. Dec. 137, 464 N.E.2d 1120 (4 Dist. 1984).

The trial court, as the party closest to the litigation and with the best opportunity to observe and decide, is presumed to have made the correct placement decision; the presumption is both strong and compelling, and absent a clear abuse of discretion will not be overturned. In re Pool, 118 Ill. App. 3d 1035, 74 Ill. Dec. 458, 455 N.E.2d 887 (3 Dist. 1983), overruled on other grounds, In re Wycoff, 266 Ill. App. 3d 408 203 Ill. Dec. 338, 639 N.E.2d 897 (4 Dist. 1994).

Subsection (b) of this section creates a presumption in favor of the present custodian, thus promoting the important factors of stability and continuity in the child's life; but once a trial court has determined that the presumption has been overcome, an appellate court will disturb that determination on review only where the trial court's decision was contrary to the manifest weight of the evidence or amounted to an abuse of its discretion. In re Friedman, 100 Ill. App. 3d 794, 56 Ill. Dec. 181, 427 N.E.2d 261 (1 Dist. 1981).

Where nearly three years had elapsed since the trial court rendered its custody decision and the delay appeared to have been principally related to petitioner's failure to proceed expeditiously with his appeal, the appellate court would enter an order directing the trial court to conduct proceedings and to advise of the current status of the children whose best interests are of paramount importance; child custody cases should not be decided on such a stale record. In re Manley, 83 Ill. App. 3d 633, 39 Ill. Dec. 319, 404 N.E.2d 910 (1 Dist. 1980).

The trial court's determination of custody will not be set aside unless there has been an abuse of discretion or the decision was contrary to the manifest weight of the evidence. In re Manley, 83 Ill. App. 3d 633, 39 Ill. Dec. 319, 404 N.E.2d 910 (1 Dist. 1980).

The trial court's determination of custody will not be reversed unless there has been a clear abuse of discretion or the decision was contrary to the manifest weight of the evidence. In re Piccirilli, 88 Ill. App. 3d 621, 43 Ill. Dec. 953, 410 N.E.2d 1086 (1 Dist. 1980).

The trial court's determination on the question of the change of custody will not be set aside unless there is an abuse of discretion, or the determination is shown to be against the manifest weight of the evidence. LaMarca v. LaMarca, 78 Ill. App. 3d 26, 33 Ill. Dec. 698, 397 N.E.2d 31 (1 Dist. 1979).

The appellate court will not disturb the determination of the trial court in custody proceedings unless it has resulted in manifest injustice or is against the manifest weight of the evidence. Courson v. Courson, 47 Ill. App. 3d 318, 5 Ill. Dec. 645, 361 N.E.2d 1173 (3 Dist. 1977).

A reviewing court will not disturb the award of the trial court in a child custody case unless it appears that manifest injustice has been done. Drake v. Hohimer, 35 Ill. App. 3d 529, 341 N.E.2d 399 (4 Dist. 1976).

In reviewing orders bearing upon child custody, it is the duty of the court to give constant and unswerving attention to the best interests of the child, entrusting the trial court with broad discretion. Marcus v. Marcus, 24 Ill. App. 3d 401, 320 N.E.2d 581 (1 Dist. 1974).

The trial judge in an action to modify custody observes the witnesses and is better able, on the basis of his observation, to assess the value of the testimony and study the personalities involved, than is a court of review; the order of the trial court should not be disturbed unless there is an obvious abuse of discretion or unless the order is contrary to the manifest weight of the evidence. Windhorn v. Windhorn, 131 Ill. App. 2d 785, 264 N.E.2d 531 (3 Dist. 1970).

Normally, in matters involving custody of infant children, the determination of a trial judge is not to be disturbed unless it appears that a manifest injustice has been done and the trial court's determination should not be reversed unless it is clearly against the manifest weight of the evidence. Carstens v. Carstens, 108 Ill. App. 2d 439, 248 N.E.2d 135 (3 Dist. 1969).

Where an appellate court determined the issue and decided the question of custody of a minor child, the trial court had no power

Appellate Review (Cont'd)

—In General (Cont'd)
but to issue final order or decree. Nye v. Nye, 411 Ill. 408, 105 N.E.2d 300 (1952).

A wide latitude is properly given to a court to exercise its sound discretion in matters of custody modification, and the appellate court would not be at liberty to disturb the finding of the trial court, unless it were able to say that proper and sufficient evidence had not been produced to warrant the modifying of the decree. Kent v. Kent, 315 Ill. App. 284, 42 N.E.2d 958 (4 Dist. 1942).

—Remand Required
In a case regarding modification of custody, where the allegations in the petitioner's motion for modification were mere conclusion, not affirmative evidence, remand was necessary to reconsider the evidence, hear additional testimony from witnesses and make explicit findings supporting a change of custody, if a change proves necessary. In re Godwin, 104 Ill. App. 3d 790, 60 Ill. Dec. 513, 433 N.E.2d 310 (3 Dist. 1982).

Applicability
This section was not implicated by husband's amended motion to reconsider, as nothing in the section restricts the power of the court to vacate or revise a final judgment upon a timely posttrial motion of a party made pursuant to 735 ILCS 5/2-1203. In re Wolff, Ill. App. 3d , 290 Ill. Dec. 1011, 822 N.E.2d 596, 2005 Ill. App. LEXIS 59 (2 Dist. 2005).

In joint custody cases, it is 750 ILCS 5/609 of this Act that applies to petitions to remove a child from Illinois, rather than this section which deals with the more general matter of modifications of custody judgments. In re Carlson, 216 Ill. App. 3d 1077, 159 Ill. Dec. 909, 576 N.E.2d 578 (3 Dist.), cert. denied, 142 Ill. 2d 651, 164 Ill. Dec. 915, 584 N.E.2d 127 (1991).

The policy favoring finality and stability in children's lives would be endangered if the custody standards in 750 ILCS 5/602 were used to modify custody judgments; it is clear that in order to modify an existing custody judgment, this section should be used. In re Gibbons, 158 Ill. App. 3d 998, 111 Ill. Dec. 148, 512 N.E.2d 52 (4 Dist. 1987).

Where a father's petition for change of custody was filed prior to the effective date of this Act, but judgment was not entered until more than two months after the Act had taken effect, the provisions of subdivisions (b)(1), (2), (3) of this section applied and some effort should have been pursued by court and counsel to articulate the reasons requiring the change of custody in light of the strong legislative policy. In re Sweet, 104 Ill. App. 3d 738, 60 Ill. Dec. 199, 432 N.E.2d 1098 (1 Dist. 1982).

A permanent award of custody is not a modification merely because the permanent custodian differs from the temporary custodian; therefore, the permanent award must be made under the best interest standard of 750 ILCS 5/602, not this section. In re Kennedy, 94 Ill. App. 3d 537, 49 Ill. Dec. 927, 418 N.E.2d 947 (1 Dist. 1981).

Although custody order conditioned mother's continued retention of physical custody during the school year upon her efforts to obtain special help for the boys' learning difficulties, it did not alter the basic arrangement created by the prior custody judgment, and father's petition was not a petition for temporary custody, governed by 750 ILCS 5/602(a) and 750 ILCS 5/603(a) since he was seeking modification of the prior custody judgment which, although awarding joint custody, gave actual physical custody of the four children during the school year to mother; consequently, this section governed modification of prior custody judgment. In re Batchelor, 89 Ill. App. 3d 781, 45 Ill. Dec. 13, 412 N.E.2d 49 (3 Dist. 1980).

Denial of the wife's petition to terminate joint custody did not modify the original custody judgment; thus, the ruling was not an order affecting custody, and 750 ILCS 5/610 did not apply. In re Marriage of Spent, 342 Ill. App. 3d 643, 277 Ill. Dec. 476, 796 N.E.2d 191, 2003 Ill. App. LEXIS 1096 (4 Dist. 2003).

Application and Construction

—In General
Once custody has been determined initially, any further proceedings must perforce constitute a modification of that judgment under this section. People ex rel. Bukovic v. Smith, 98 Ill. App. 3d 144, 53 Ill. Dec. 498, 423 N.E.2d 1302 (1 Dist. 1981).

—Burden of Proof
Subsection (b) of this section requires a more exacting burden of proof than did the former version of this section, which employed only a preponderance of the evidence test. In re Jones, 160 Ill. App. 3d 593, 112 Ill. Dec. 572, 513 N.E.2d 1181 (3 Dist. 1987).

—Custody Proceedings
750 ILCS 5/601(b) and this section are not mutually exclusive since 750 ILCS 5/601(b) applies to both initial determinations of custody and modification of judgments. People ex rel. Bukovic v. Smith, 98 Ill. App. 3d 144, 53 Ill. Dec. 498, 423 N.E.2d 1302 (1 Dist. 1981).

—Limitation Period
The custody judgment, granting custody to the mother, issued less than two years before the father's motion to modify, was entitled to the statute's two year protection from modification; therefore, because father's petition was premature, it should have been dismissed by the trial court. In re Miller, 170 Ill. App. 3d 1044, 121 Ill. Dec. 17, 524 N.E.2d 1065 (1 Dist. 1988).

The two year prohibition on motions for modification of custody in subsection (a) of this section is not invoked by motions for modification of visitation rights. Mueller v. Weis, 76 Ill. App. 3d 860, 32 Ill. Dec. 447, 395 N.E.2d 677 (5 Dist. 1979).

—Petitions Included
The plain language of subsection (b) applies to all petitions, regardless of whether they are filed and heard before or after two years from the date of entry of the custody judgment. Department of Pub. Aid ex rel. Davis v. Brewer, 183 Ill. 2d 540, 234 Ill. Dec. 223, 702 N.E.2d 563 (1998).

—Physical Custody
Although the custodian had chosen not to retain physical custody of her children, she did not change the finality of the judgment upon which she relied; the court must apply this section. People ex rel. Bukovic v. Smith, 98 Ill. App. 3d 144, 53 Ill. Dec. 498, 423 N.E.2d 1302 (1 Dist. 1981).

—Procedure
Subsection (a) serves an important gatekeeping function, as only those cases which satisfy the initial procedural prerequisite contained in subsection (a) proceed to an evidentiary hearing conducted pursuant to the provisions of subsection (b). Department of Pub. Aid ex rel. Davis v. Brewer, 183 Ill. 2d 540, 234 Ill. Dec. 223, 702 N.E.2d 563 (1998).

Attorney Fees
Former wife was properly awarded attorney fees under subsection (c) where former husband explicitly disclosed his motive in seeking to modify custody order in his letter to former wife's brother: "If you pursue a claim for further financial assistance for Margy from me, I will have no recourse but to petition the court to terminate the award of custody to Margy ...." In re Campbell, 252 Ill. App. 3d 653, 191 Ill. Dec. 852, 624 N.E.2d 1230 (1 Dist. 1993), appeal denied, 155 Ill. 2d 562, 198 Ill. Dec. 540, 633 N.E.2d 2 (1994).

An abuse of discretion in allowing attorney fees will be found only where it can be said that no reasonable person would adopt the view taken by the trial court. In re Kramer, 211 Ill. App. 3d 401, 155 Ill. Dec. 909, 570 N.E.2d 422 (1 Dist. 1991).

Although the father might have been financially better able to pay the fees, the court's award of attorney fees was based in part upon its view that the mother's actions were the cause of a substantial portion of the litigation; trial court did not abuse its discretion in allocating the father's attorney fees equally between the parties. In re Kramer, 211 Ill. App. 3d 401, 155 Ill. Dec. 909, 570 N.E.2d 422 (1 Dist. 1991).

Attorney's fees awarded in a divorce decree have been held to be in the nature of alimony and therefore not dischargeable in bankruptcy. In re Kramer, 211 Ill. App. 3d 401, 155 Ill. Dec. 909, 570 N.E.2d 422 (1 Dist. 1991).

Where the court found the ex-wife's repeated attempts at modification and her continual interference with her ex-husband's visitation rights to be vexatious and to constitute harassment, the decision to award attorney's fees to the ex-husband rested with the discretion of the trial court. In re Lewis, 188 Ill. App. 3d 142, 135 Ill. Dec. 667, 544 N.E.2d 24 (5 Dist. 1989).

Attorney Fees (Cont'd)

Where petitioner was ordered to pay only a portion of respondent's attorney fees, such a finding constituted an abuse of discretion since the bystander's report did not support a finding that the financial resources of the parties were such that petitioner was able to pay, and respondent was unable to pay, his attorney fees. In re Kading, 150 Ill. App. 3d 623, 103 Ill. Dec. 654, 501 N.E.2d 971 (2 Dist. 1986).

The legislature made vexation and harassment relevant considerations in the award of attorney's fees for the cost of a proceeding to modify a dissolution order, but it did not do so in the award of fees for the defense of an action to distribute marital property. In re Stewart, 79 Ill. App. 3d 1125, 35 Ill. Dec. 249, 398 N.E.2d 1199 (1 Dist. 1979).

Where post-decree proceedings are brought to modify the custodial provisions of the decree, the husband is liable for legal services rendered necessary to properly present the needs of the children to the court; however, where the custodial modification is sought primarily for the convenience of the parties and not the welfare of the children, the attorney's allowance will be disallowed. Horwitz v. Horwitz, 130 Ill. App. 2d 424, 264 N.E.2d 723 (1 Dist. 1970).

Attorney fees can be awarded to a divorced wife in subsequent proceedings to modify the decree under proper circumstances; the allowance of the aforesaid attorney fees depends not upon who initiates the proceeding but rather upon the circumstances peculiar to the individual case. Mabbatt v. Mabbatt, 78 Ill. App. 2d 455, 223 N.E.2d 191 (1 Dist. 1967).

Allowance of attorney fees was proper where petition for modification of custody was in the best interests of children and not for the convenience of the parties. Williams v. Williams, 320 Ill. App. 354, 51 N.E.2d 284 (3 Dist. 1943).

Balancing Test

The evidence of respondent's inability to devote sufficient time to the children and her lack of concern for their well-being together with the evidence of the advantages to the children of living with their father, support the trial court's conclusions, implicit in its ruling, that the children's present environment endangers seriously their physical, mental, moral, or emotional health and that the harm likely to be caused by a change of environment was outweighed by its advantages to them. In re Farris, 69 Ill. App. 3d 1042, 26 Ill. Dec. 608, 388 N.E.2d 232 (4 Dist. 1979).

Best Interest of the Child

—In General

The custody of a child of divorced parents is always subject to modification by the court as the best interest of the child demands. Brady v. Brady, 26 Ill. App. 3d 131, 324 N.E.2d 645 (5 Dist. 1975).

Subsequent to a divorce decree, custody of a child of the parties is subject to the order of the court and may be changed from time to time as the child's best interest and welfare demand. Levy v. Levy, 117 Ill. App. 2d 194, 254 N.E.2d 108 (1 Dist. 1969).

In a situation involving a change of custody, the interest of the child is preeminently the thing to be considered. Martinec v. Sharapata, 328 Ill. App. 339, 66 N.E.2d 103 (1 Dist. 1946).

—Custody Hearing

In order to make the proper determination as to what decision is in the child's best interest, there should be a hearing on the question of custody. Nothing short of a hearing relating to unfitness and the best interest of the child and a finding thereon is adequate support for an order changing custody. Henrikson v. Henrikson, 26 Ill. App. 3d 37, 324 N.E.2d 473 (3 Dist. 1975).

—Drug Use

Although the record clearly and convincingly established that a change had occurred in the circumstances of the custodial parent which would permit modification, such as the past sexual promiscuity and drug use of the mother, the record did not hold that the best interests of the children would necessarily be served by allowing them to go to live with their father in Iowa. In re Dilley, 127 Ill. App. 3d 992, 83 Ill. Dec. 67, 469 N.E.2d 674 (5 Dist. 1984).

—Evidence Held Insufficient

Evidence adduced during the hearing on the petition for modification established only that the custodial parent might have used poor judgment in assessing the danger of sexual abuse by the babysitter's son but failed to make a specific finding, as required by subsection (b), that the non-custodial parent had proven, by clear and convincing evidence, that the modification was necessary to serve the best interest of the child. Department of Pub. Aid ex rel. Davis v. Brewer, 183 Ill. 2d 540, 234 Ill. Dec. 223, 702 N.E.2d 563 (1998).

—Evidence Held Sufficient

Custody was properly transferred from the mother to the father where the mother violated the father's visitation rights, made unfounded allegations of sexual abuse against the father's new wife's father, married four men after her marriage to the father, lived with numerous other men, and forced the child to move numerous times in order to accommodate her numerous relationships. In re Knoche, 322 Ill. App. 3d 297, 255 Ill. Dec. 716, 750 N.E.2d 297, 2001 Ill. App. LEXIS 389 (5 Dist. 2001).

The circuit court did not abuse its discretion in determining that a transfer of custody to the father was necessary to serve the child's best interests where the mother had bad judgment and was impulsive, was convicted of indirect criminal contempt, permitted improper supervision of the child by her heavy-drinking boyfriend and out-of-control half-sister, improperly instructed the child's school to deny the father access to records and information, and had been charged with driving under the influence. Brudd v. Brudd, 307 Ill. App. 3d 57, 240 Ill. Dec. 218, 716 N.E.2d 812 (3 Dist. 1999).

The trial court's determination that both parties had demonstrated a genuine and honest concern for the best interests of their minor children, despite the friction generated between the parents as a result of the Tuesday night visitation, was amply supported by the record and the trial court did not err by retaining the existing Tuesday night custody schedule. In re Kessler, 110 Ill. App. 3d 61, 65 Ill. Dec. 707, 441 N.E.2d 1221 (1 Dist. 1982).

Defendant sustained his burden of proof and the trial court properly exercised its discretion in determining that an emotionally disturbed child would be afforded more promise to regain his health if custody were changed from plaintiff, who sent the child to a school for emotionally disturbed children, who was single, and who employed a child care provider, to defendant, who could afford a stable family structure, permanent family roots and out-patient treatment, if necessary, whereas the continuation of the status quo revealed not only a lack of substantial recovery, but an actual regression touching directly upon the best interest and welfare of their son. Levy v. Levy, 117 Ill. App. 2d 194, 254 N.E.2d 108 (1 Dist. 1969).

—Father Versus Grandparents

The law presumes that it is in the child's best interest to be raised by the natural parent, and ordinarily the natural right of the father will prevail in a contest between him and the grandparents where both parties are equally fit to care for the child. In re Piccirilli, 88 Ill. App. 3d 621, 43 Ill. Dec. 953, 410 N.E.2d 1086 (1 Dist. 1980).

Where father petitioned to modify the divorce decree so as to award custody of his daughter to him, the finding of the chancellor that it was in the best interest of the child to remain with her grandmother was not against the manifest weight of the evidence. Kokotekian v. Kokotekian, 23 Ill. App. 2d 171, 161 N.E.2d 712 (1 Dist. 1959).

For a case discussing modification of divorce decree awarding custody of child to father instead of grandparents, see Liles v. Liles, 336 Ill. App. 159, 83 N.E.2d 35 (3 Dist. 1948).

—Fitness of Parent

It is not necessary that the natural father be found unfit or be found to have legally forfeited his right to custody if it is in the child's best interests that she be placed in the custody of someone other than the natural parent. In re Piccirilli, 88 Ill. App. 3d 621, 43 Ill. Dec. 953, 410 N.E.2d 1086 (1 Dist. 1980).

While the court should exercise restraint in depriving a mother of custody of a child, a change of custody does not require a showing of unfitness on the part of the mother. Carstens v. Carstens, 108 Ill. App. 2d 439, 248 N.E.2d 135 (3 Dist. 1969).

The fact that the mother could offer the children a more modern and perhaps more comfortable residence than could the father, did not of itself justify the conclusion that their welfare demands that they live permanently with her; there was no arbitrary rule that required custody to be awarded the mother in every case in which

Best Interest of the Child (Cont'd)

—Fitness of Parent (Cont'd)
she is found to be a fit parent. Vysoky v. Vysoky, 85 Ill. App. 2d 306, 230 N.E.2d 3 (1 Dist. 1967).

—Maternal Affection
Although for most of the period since a decree granting custody to petitioner had been entered, respondent had had actual custody, and there was no showing of changed circumstances in rendering its decision in a habeas corpus proceeding to award custody to petitioner, the court took into consideration not only the best interests of the parties' children but also the petitioner's children by a prior marriage and the petitioner's child out-of-wedlock, and with the benefit of observation as well as consultation, decided that it was in keeping with the interests of all the children concerned to allow the children to grow up, to know their brothers and sisters, and to try to keep the bond of the family unit throughout their lives; implicit in the court's decision was the fact that the two children of the parties were of tender years, and that the maternal affection was better adapted to the care of the children. People ex rel. Morris v. Morris, 44 Ill. 2d 66, 254 N.E.2d 478 (1969).

—Natural Parent's Right
The natural parent's superior right to custody of a child is not absolute and must yield to the best interest of the child. In re Piccirilli, 88 Ill. App. 3d 621, 43 Ill. Dec. 953, 410 N.E.2d 1086 (1 Dist. 1980).

—Nonparental Custody
It was essential for the child to have the benefit of a stable and secure home with his paternal aunt and uncle and the company of three other children, his cousins, slightly older than he, with the important realization that his father would be a part of the same household with ample opportunity for companionship between the two. Marcus v. Marcus, 24 Ill. App. 3d 401, 320 N.E.2d 581 (1 Dist. 1974).

—Primary Consideration
The primary consideration in determining custody is the best interest and welfare of the child. In re Piccirilli, 88 Ill. App. 3d 621, 43 Ill. Dec. 953, 410 N.E.2d 1086 (1 Dist. 1980).

—Race of Parent
The trial court erred in awarding custody of children from an interracial marriage to the African-American father based on the fact that the children's racial characteristics were more like the father's than like the Caucasian mother's. Fountaine v. Fountaine, 9 Ill. App. 2d 482, 133 N.E.2d 532 (1 Dist.), aff'd, 9 Ill. 2d 616, 138 N.E.2d 495 (1956).

—Relocation of Parent
Trial court erred when it required wife who was given joint custody and primary physical custody of her daughter to remain in one of two counties as a condition for retaining joint custody and primary physical custody. Seitzinger v. Seitzinger, 333 Ill. App. 3d 103, 266 Ill. Dec. 720, 775 N.E.2d 282, 2002 Ill. App. LEXIS 763 (4 Dist. 2002).

Because the parties' joint-parenting agreement did not restrict the mother's right as the children's primary physical custodian to make an intrastate move, the fact that the father spent nearly as much time with children as the mother, did not require court permission for the move. In re Means, 329 Ill. App. 3d 392, 264 Ill. Dec. 797, 771 N.E.2d 501, 2002 Ill. App. LEXIS 337 (4 Dist. 2002).

The trial court properly modified a joint parenting agreement by naming the father the residential parent and modifying visitation arrangements where: (1) the terms of the joint parenting agreement provided for reconsideration of the residential parent in the event that the mother moved from the county in which the parties lived; (2) the majority of the children's family and friends were in that county; (3) both children expressed a desire to live in that county; (4) although the children were doing well in their new location, they were better adjusted to their old schools; (5) there were no indications that mental and physical health or physical abuse was an issue; and (6) both parties were willing to promote a strong and continuing bond with the other parent. In re McGillicuddy, 315 Ill. App. 3d 939, 249 Ill. Dec. 203, 735 N.E.2d 1028, 2000 Ill. App. LEXIS 712 (3 Dist. 2000).

—Scope of Determination
The best interest of the child is of paramount importance and consideration thereof cannot be limited to a transitory factual setting but must be viewed in its entirety. In re Manley, 83 Ill. App. 3d 633, 39 Ill. Dec. 319, 404 N.E.2d 910 (1 Dist. 1980).

—Stability of Environment
Stability of environment is an important factor in determining what is in the best interest of a child. Holloway v. Holloway, 10 Ill. App. 3d 662, 294 N.E.2d 759 (1 Dist. 1973).

—Weekend Custody
The trial court did not abuse its discretion in determining that the weekend custody schedule was detrimental to the children's best interests where its frequency prevented a balanced relationship, or recreation time, with their mother and new family unit. In re Kessler, 110 Ill. App. 3d 61, 65 Ill. Dec. 707, 441 N.E.2d 1221 (1 Dist. 1982).

Bigamous Remarriage
The trial court did not abuse its discretion in transferring custody of children from their mother to their father where the mother's subsequent bigamous marriage was a change in circumstances of the child or their custodian that seriously endangered the children's physical, mental, moral or emotional health under this section. In re Gunter, 93 Ill. App. 3d 1043, 49 Ill. Dec. 505, 418 N.E.2d 149 (1 Dist. 1981).

Burden of Proof
The plain language of the statute supports the conclusion that the legislature did not intend for a parent seeking modification of a custody judgment within two years of the judgment's entry to prove serious endangerment by clear and convincing evidence; rather, modifications may be made after clear and convincing proof has been presented that the best interests of the child require modification. Department of Pub. Aid ex rel. Davis v. Brewer, 183 Ill. 2d 540, 234 Ill. Dec. 223, 702 N.E.2d 563 (1998).

Where husband filed petition for modification less than two years after the date of the entry of prior custody judgment and the hearing was held prior to the expiration of the two-year period, he was required to meet the "endangerment" section of subsection (a) of this section and additionally, the standards of subsection (b) had to be met. McClelland v. McClelland, 231 Ill. App. 3d 214, 172 Ill. Dec. 461, 595 N.E.2d 1131 (1 Dist. 1992).

The party seeking a change in custody has the burden of demonstrating that the child's best interests warrant the change and that circumstances have changed sufficiently to permit the modification. Katzer v. Katzer, 61 Ill. App. 3d 299, 18 Ill. Dec. 852, 378 N.E.2d 316 (1 Dist. 1978); In re Godwin, 104 Ill. App. 3d 790, 60 Ill. Dec. 513, 433 N.E.2d 310 (3 Dist. 1982).

Change in Circumstances

—In General
Trial court abused its discretion by declining to hold a hearing on a mother's request to modify visitation when her child, whose custody was split between the mother and the child's father, who lived in different towns, reached school age, as the court's determination of where the child would attend school was a change in circumstances and, once that decision was made, it created instability for the child, which was an additional change in circumstances, so the trial court was authorized to hold a hearing on the mother's request, under 750 ILCS 5/610(b). Davis v. Davis, Ill. App. 3d , Ill. Dec. , N.E.2d , 2003 Ill. App. LEXIS 874 (3 Dist. July 15, 2003).

Changes in custody should neither be arbitrarily made nor be subject to constant or even occasional variation merely to follow fluctuations in the health, employment, or residence of the party last deprived of custody, barring specific provision to that effect in the divorce decree, however, such factors as remarriage or securing permanent employment and living quarters, while not controlling, are sufficiently related to the child's welfare, even when involving the parent not then having custody. Randolph v. Dean, 27 Ill. App. 3d 913, 327 N.E.2d 473 (3 Dist. 1975).

New and changed conditions must arise to warrant the court in changing its prior custody determination. Eggemeyer v. Eggemeyer, 86 Ill. App. 2d 224, 229 N.E.2d 144 (2 Dist. 1967).

Change in Circumstances (Cont'd)

—Allegations

The allegations of neglect, a violent environment, thievery, failing in school and emotional disorders due to the home environment, if true, could constitute a sufficient change in circumstances to support a change in custody. In re Godwin, 104 Ill. App. 3d 790, 60 Ill. Dec. 513, 433 N.E.2d 310 (3 Dist. 1982).

—Burden of Proof

The trial court did not improperly alter the statutory standard of proof for modification of custody. In re Diddens, 255 Ill. App. 3d 850, 192 Ill. Dec. 878, 625 N.E.2d 1033 (3 Dist. 1993).

This Act codifies the rule that a party seeking a change in custody has to prove that there has been a material change in the circumstances of either parent which affects the well-being of the child, with the added guidelines of the existence of any agreement between the parties, integration into the family of the petitioner with the consent of the custodian, and a finding as to whether the child's present environment seriously endangers its physical, mental, moral or emotional health. Thompson v. Thompson, 83 Ill. App. 3d 97, 38 Ill. Dec. 485, 403 N.E.2d 716 (3 Dist. 1980).

In matters involving the custody of children, every presumption is indulged in the continuing validity of the original decree and, if its provisions are to be changed, the burden of proof is on the moving party. Brady v. Brady, 26 Ill. App. 3d 131, 324 N.E.2d 645 (5 Dist. 1975).

To justify a modification of the original decree awarding custody to the mother, it was incumbent upon the father to show some change in circumstances affecting the welfare of the child. Jacobs v. Jacobs, 25 Ill. App. 3d 175, 323 N.E.2d 21 (1 Dist. 1974).

—Clear and Convincing Evidence

This statute works to discourage the filing of frequent custody petitions by requiring that specific standards be proved by clear and convincing evidence before any modification may be made. Valliere v. Valliere, 275 Ill. App. 3d 1095, 212 Ill. Dec. 696, 657 N.E.2d 1041 (1 Dist. 1995).

To prohibit the modification of a custody judgment, the court must find "by clear and convincing evidence" that a change has occurred in the circumstances of the child or his or her custodian and that modification is necessary to serve the best interests of the child. This finding is to be based on facts that have arisen since the prior judgment or facts that were unknown to the court at the time of entry of the prior judgment. In re Burke, 185 Ill. App. 3d 253, 133 Ill. Dec. 408, 541 N.E.2d 245 (2 Dist. 1989).

This Act requires the petitioner to establish by clear and convincing evidence that a change in circumstances has occurred and that the modification was in the best interests of the child. In re Wechselberger, 115 Ill. App. 3d 779, 71 Ill. Dec. 506, 450 N.E.2d 1385 (2 Dist. 1983); Vollmer v. Mattox, 137 Ill. App. 3d 1, 91 Ill. Dec. 752, 484 N.E.2d 311 (5 Dist. 1985); In re Eleopoulos, 186 Ill. App. 3d 374, 134 Ill. Dec. 326, 542 N.E.2d 505 (4 Dist. 1989); In re Dall, 191 Ill. App. 3d 652, 138 Ill. Dec. 879, 548 N.E.2d 109 (5 Dist. 1989); In re Good, 208 Ill. App. 3d 775, 153 Ill. Dec. 151, 566 N.E.2d 1001 (3 Dist. 1991).

—Criteria

When a non-custodial parent seeks under this section to modify a stipulated custody judgment the court must weigh the evidence and find if the circumstances existing at the time of the prior custody hearing were different than they appeared; if the evidence indicates the custodial parent was fit and acceptable at the time of the prior hearing, then modification must rest on subsequent change of circumstances of the child or of the child's custodian. In re Gibbons, 158 Ill. App. 3d 998, 111 Ill. Dec. 148, 512 N.E.2d 52 (4 Dist. 1987).

Courts will not amend a child custody award unless there has been an actual change in circumstances occurring after entry of the decree, which change makes it apparent that the welfare of the child requires modification of the decree's custody provisions. Stickler v. Stickler, 57 Ill. App. 2d 286, 206 N.E.2d 720 (1 Dist. 1965).

—Custodian's Unfitness

A custodial judgment cannot be modified unless the evidence establishes that the parent to whom custody was originally awarded is either unfit to retain custody or that the change in conditions is directly related to the child's needs. Ipema v. Dykhuis, 131 Ill. App. 3d 371, 86 Ill. Dec. 728, 475 N.E.2d 1107 (3 Dist. 1985).

A change in circumstances justifying a modification of a child custody award need not relate solely to the custodial parent, nor is it necessary for the court to find that the custodial parent is an unfit person if other circumstances warrant modification. Kjellesvik v. Shannon, 41 Ill. App. 3d 674, 355 N.E.2d 120 (3 Dist. 1976).

In order to change custody of a child from the mother to the father, it is not necessary to find that the mother is unfit; the court must merely find that conditions have changed to such an extent that a change of custody is in the best interest of the child. Brady v. Brady, 26 Ill. App. 3d 131, 324 N.E.2d 645 (5 Dist. 1975).

The change of conditions which will justify altering the custody provisions of a divorce not limited to conditions relating solely to the custodial parent, or evidence that he or she has become unfit for custody. Collings v. Collings, 120 Ill. App. 2d 125, 256 N.E.2d 108 (2 Dist. 1970).

—Death of Custodial Parent

The death of the parent having custody is a significant change in circumstances, such that the custodial portion of the judgment would require modification. In re Piccirilli, 88 Ill. App. 3d 621, 43 Ill. Dec. 953, 410 N.E.2d 1086 (1 Dist. 1980).

The death of the parent having custody is a significant and substantial change in circumstances, and it is obvious in such case that the custodial portion of the divorce decree requires modification, in that custody must be awarded to a different person; in so doing, the court must consider the circumstances as they presently exist and cannot be limited to a consideration of the circumstances existing at the time of the original custodial order. Sholty v. Sholty, 67 Ill. App. 2d 60, 214 N.E.2d 15 (3 Dist. 1966).

—Discretion of Court

Where custody was originally granted based solely on stipulation by the parties, upon a petition for change of custody, there need not be a showing of a substantial change in circumstances; the court may, in effect, determine, for the first time, in its own discretion, what custody provisions would be in the best interests of the child. Randolph v. Dean, 27 Ill. App. 3d 913, 327 N.E.2d 473 (3 Dist. 1975).

—Divorce Decree

Where the court, at the time of entering the divorce decree, knew only that the parties had agreed that defendant should take custody of the 2½ year old boy and that plaintiff considered defendant fit and proper to have custody, it was proper for the court, in hearing the petition for the change in custody, to consider for the first time other facts existing at the time of the decree, such as plaintiff's circumstances and her reasons for signing the custody agreement, together with the oral agreement to which she testified. Randolph v. Dean, 27 Ill. App. 3d 913, 327 N.E.2d 473 (3 Dist. 1975).

—Facts

A court may not modify a custody award unless it finds, based on facts arising since the prior decree or facts unknown at the time of the prior decree, that a change has occurred in the circumstances of the child or his custodian which necessitates the modification to serve the child's best interests. In re Strader, 101 Ill. App. 3d 779, 57 Ill. Dec. 232, 428 N.E.2d 912 (5 Dist. 1981).

—Failure to Comply

Where the only material change in circumstances, as apparently shown by the record, was that the father completely refused to comply with the decree which provided for liberal and reasonable visitation with the mother, the child was to remain in custody of the mother pending final determination by the trial court as to what was in the best interests of the child. Schultz v. Schultz, 38 Ill. App. 3d 678, 347 N.E.2d 749 (3 Dist. 1976).

—Home Schooling

Removing child from school and initiating home schooling constitutes a change in circumstances for purposes of subsection (b). In re Riess, 260 Ill. App. 3d 210, 198 Ill. Dec. 305, 632 N.E.2d 635 (2 Dist. 1994).

—Medical Care

The failure of the mother to seek out medical care for her son was a sufficient change in circumstance to warrant a change of custody, especially because there was medical testimony indicating deteri-

Change in Circumstances (Cont'd)

—Medical Care (Cont'd)
oration of the child's physical condition. People ex rel. Rathbun v. Rathbun, 48 Ill. App. 3d 328, 6 Ill. Dec. 314, 362 N.E.2d 1136 (4 Dist. 1977).

—Mother's Actions
The trial court's decision that there had been a change of circumstances which required a modification of an earlier custody order was against the manifest weight of the evidence where a mother's actions seriously endangered the mental or emotional health of the child and that the harm if any which might be caused by a change of environment to the custody of the father was outweighed by the advantages of that change to the child. Thompson v. Thompson, 83 Ill. App. 3d 97, 38 Ill. Dec. 485, 403 N.E.2d 716 (3 Dist. 1980).

—New Information
At the time the agreed order for joint custody was entered, the court had no knowledge that wife's hostility toward husband endangered the well-being of her children, but where subsequently the court did have knowledge of numerous incidents of hostility and physical violence occurring since the divorce, that justified a finding of a change in circumstances. In re Johnson, 245 Ill. App. 3d 545, 185 Ill. Dec. 617, 614 N.E.2d 1302 (3 Dist.), appeal denied, 152 Ill. 2d 560, 190 Ill. Dec. 891, 622 N.E.2d 1208 (1993).

—Noncustodial Parent
The only change in circumstances had occurred in the life of the noncustodial parent, and under subsection (b), custody cannot be changed on that basis alone. In re Webber, 249 Ill. App. 3d 892, 189 Ill. Dec. 67, 619 N.E.2d 768 (3 Dist. 1993).

If a divorce decree awards custody unconditionally, a mere showing of change in conditions of the person deprived of custody is not sufficient to set aside or drastically modify such decree, in the absence of proof that the welfare of the children requires such a change. Dunning v. Dunning, 14 Ill. App. 2d 242, 144 N.E.2d 535 (2 Dist. 1957).

—Not Required
Where the mother filed a counter petition seeking sole custody of the child, thus agreeing to termination of the previous joint custody arrangement, the father was not required to show that a change in circumstances had occurred. In re Lovejoy, 158 Ill. App. 3d 1, 109 Ill. Dec. 768, 510 N.E.2d 636 (3 Dist. 1987).

—Not Sufficient
Record did not show such changed conditions that child's welfare would dictate a modification of the custody provisions of a divorce decree. Collings v. Collings, 120 Ill. App. 2d 125, 256 N.E.2d 108 (2 Dist. 1970).

The contumacy of the husband in his failure to conscientiously respect wife's visitation rights and his obdurate refusal to make child support payments, as provided in the decree, as well as the litigiousness of the parties, all contributed in causing the trial court to modify the custody provisions of the decree; however, these circumstances alone did not constitute a change in conditions sufficient to warrant a change in the custody of the children. Eggemeyer v. Eggemeyer, 86 Ill. App. 2d 224, 229 N.E.2d 144 (2 Dist. 1967).

—Parental Alienation
The trial court did not err in finding that the father met his burden of proof by clear and convincing evidence on the basis of new circumstances or previously unknown facts and properly instituted a rotating custody arrangement and ongoing therapy in an attempt to break the cycle of parental alienation and to assist the parties' child in her adjustment. In re Divelbiss, 308 Ill. App. 3d 198, 241 Ill. Dec. 514, 719 N.E.2d 375 (2 Dist. 1999).

—Parental Illness
Trial court properly found in favor of wife on the issue of custody where testimony was uncontradicted that wife's severe illness was a singular event and that she had returned to a "normal" state since. In re Campbell, 252 Ill. App. 3d 653, 191 Ill. Dec. 852, 624 N.E.2d 1230 (1 Dist. 1993), appeal denied, 155 Ill. 2d 562, 198 Ill. Dec. 540, 633 N.E.2d 2 (1994).

—Preference of Child
Although the children's preference for their mother's custody by itself was not sufficient change in circumstance to warrant a change of custody, when considered in connection with their apparent fear of their father, their emotional instability, and the older daughter's desperate attempt to be free of him through falsification of a criminal charge against him, the court was justified in finding sufficient change in circumstances related to the children's welfare to warrant a change in their custody. Wells v. Wells, 36 Ill. App. 3d 488, 344 N.E.2d 37 (2 Dist. 1976).

A change in the child's preference is not a sufficient change in circumstances to warrant modification of a custody award. Stickler v. Stickler, 57 Ill. App. 2d 286, 206 N.E.2d 720 (1 Dist. 1965).

—Religious Activity
A father's recent activity as an orthodox religionist was not a material change of circumstances affecting the child's welfare so as to justify modification of the original decree. Jacobs v. Jacobs, 25 Ill. App. 3d 175, 323 N.E.2d 21 (1 Dist. 1974).

—Relocation
Where the only change in circumstances found by the trial court was the relocation of the defendant without first obtaining leave of court, this, in and of itself, was not sufficient grounds for revoking defendant's custody. Mathey v. Mathey, 1 Ill. App. 3d 1008, 274 N.E.2d 501 (2 Dist. 1971).

—Remarriage
Remarriage of one or both of the parents, while a changed circumstance, is not sufficient to authorize modification of a custodial arrangement unless such remarriage affects the welfare of the child. Swanson v. Swanson, 1 Ill. App. 3d 753, 274 N.E.2d 465 (3 Dist. 1971).

Remarriage in and of itself would not be a sufficient change in circumstance to warrant a change in custody unless the remarriage also affected the welfare of the child. Windhorn v. Windhorn, 131 Ill. App. 2d 785, 264 N.E.2d 531 (3 Dist. 1970).

Relinquishment of custody on a voluntary basis together with a remarriage is normally a sufficient change of circumstance to warrant an examination into the custody question; in all such cases, however, the paramount rule is to determine what is in the best interest of the child. Carstens v. Carstens, 108 Ill. App. 2d 439, 248 N.E.2d 135 (3 Dist. 1969).

The new marriage status of the husband did not constitute sufficient cause to change the custody of the children in question. Eggemeyer v. Eggemeyer, 86 Ill. App. 2d 224, 229 N.E.2d 144 (2 Dist. 1967).

The relinquishment of custody and the subsequent remarriage of the mother were sufficient changes of circumstances as to warrant an examination into the custody question in the sense of a hearing to determine the necessity of a change in custody. Stingley v. Wesch, 77 Ill. App. 2d 472, 222 N.E.2d 505 (4 Dist. 1966).

—Removal of Child
A custodian parent's removal of her children to another state was not such a change which would so affect the welfare of the children as to warrant a modification of the original decree of custody. Garland v. Garland, 19 Ill. App. 3d 951, 312 N.E.2d 811 (1 Dist. 1974).

—Reversal of Original Decree
Where order was a complete reversal of the original decree it must have been based on a substantial change of circumstances. Hinton v. Searles, 53 Ill. App. 3d 433, 11 Ill. Dec. 329, 368 N.E.2d 937 (5 Dist. 1977).

—Scope of Inquiry
In considering a permanent change of custody, the court is concerned with all circumstances that are changed from the time of the original award of custody. In re McIntyre, 97 Ill. App. 3d 777, 53 Ill. Dec. 89, 423 N.E.2d 281 (3 Dist. 1981).

—Shown
There was clear and convincing evidence that a change in circumstances had occurred, and that modification of custody was in the best interest of the child, where although mother retained legal custody of the child, she relinquished physical custody of the child to father when the child was only four years of age, where the

Change in Circumstances (Cont'd)

—Shown (Cont'd)

child continued to live with father until the time of the hearing, when he was eight years of age, where during the almost four years in which he lived with father, the child saw mother only on two occasions and only for brief periods of time, and where during that time, the child became well integrated into father's new family, home, school and community. Shoff v. Shoff, 179 Ill. App. 3d 178, 128 Ill. Dec. 280, 534 N.E.2d 462 (5 Dist. 1989).

The loss of one stepmother, substitution of babysitters, and final introduction of a new stepmother and stepsisters can be a substantial change in the circumstances and surroundings of a child. In re Valter, 191 Ill. App. 3d 584, 138 Ill. Dec. 799, 548 N.E.2d 29 (5 Dist. 1989).

The trial court did not find the mother to be unfit, rather the court found that there had been a change in the circumstances of the child since the original custody decree; those changes included problem behavior in school, disciplinary problems at home, and hyperactivity and other emotional problems requiring professional treatment. In re Eldert, 158 Ill. App. 3d 798, 110 Ill. Dec. 768, 511 N.E.2d 945 (3 Dist. 1987), appeal denied, 117 Ill. Dec. 224, 520 N.E.2d 385 (Ill. 1988).

—Statutory Construction

The wording of this section is constructed in such a way as to indicate that evidence of both newly arisen facts and those previously unknown to the court can be considered not only on the question of the child's best interests but also on the change of circumstances requirement. Boggs v. Boggs, 65 Ill. App. 3d 965, 22 Ill. Dec. 645, 383 N.E.2d 9 (4 Dist. 1978).

As used in subsection (b) of this section, the words "a change has occurred in the circumstances of the child or his custodian" were construed to mean, that a change in circumstances as previously shown to the court has occurred, and that construction would enable the court hearing the petition to modify and exercise its judicial discretion rather than to be bound by the previous order based upon an agreement. Boggs v. Boggs, 65 Ill. App. 3d 965, 22 Ill. Dec. 645, 383 N.E.2d 9 (4 Dist. 1978).

—Sworn

Mother's frequent changes in residence, the instability of her second marriage, and the uncertainty of her vocational and child care plans were facts that arose since the prior initial judgment awarding her custody judgment which constituted a change in circumstances warranting modification of custody. Russell v. Kellum, 80 Ill. App. 3d 41, 35 Ill. Dec. 378, 399 N.E.2d 212 (5 Dist. 1979).

—Welfare of Child

A custody decree is not to be modified, unless a substantial change of circumstances has occurred subsequent to the original custody order, and the change of circumstances affects the welfare of the child. Brady v. Brady, 26 Ill. App. 3d 131, 324 N.E.2d 645 (5 Dist. 1975); Randolph v. Dean, 27 Ill. App. 3d 913, 327 N.E.2d 473 (3 Dist. 1975); De Franco v. De Franco, 67 Ill. App. 3d 760, 24 Ill. Dec. 130, 384 N.E.2d 997 (1 Dist. 1978); In re Lichtenstein, 139 Ill. App. 3d 881, 94 Ill. Dec. 416, 487 N.E.2d 1293 (5 Dist. 1986); In re Eldert, 158 Ill. App. 3d 798, 110 Ill. Dec. 768, 511 N.E.2d 945 (3 Dist. 1987), appeal denied, 117 Ill. Dec. 224, 520 N.E.2d 385 (Ill. 1988).

A material change in circumstances, which occurs after entry of a decree granting custody, may be sufficient basis to change custody; however, the court may not change custody unless the altered conditions are of such a nature that a change is necessary for the welfare of the child. Mathey v. Mathey, 1 Ill. App. 3d 1008, 274 N.E.2d 501 (2 Dist. 1971).

Changed circumstances do not in and of themselves authorize changes in custodial arrangements; such changed circumstances must affect the welfare of the child. Swanson v. Swanson, 1 Ill. App. 3d 753, 274 N.E.2d 465 (3 Dist. 1971); Brandt v. Brandt, 99 Ill. App. 3d 1089, 55 Ill. Dec. 78, 425 N.E.2d 1251 (1 Dist. 1981).

The welfare of the child is the cardinal consideration in determining the custodial arrangements for such child; once custody has been decreed it will not be modified unless there are changed circumstances affecting the welfare of the child requiring a modification of the custodial arrangement. Swanson v. Swanson, 1 Ill. App. 3d 753, 274 N.E.2d 465 (3 Dist. 1971).

The mere fact there has been a change in conditions is not sufficient in itself to modify a decree unless those changed conditions affect the welfare of the child. Dunning v. Dunning, 14 Ill. App. 2d 242, 144 N.E.2d 535 (2 Dist. 1957); Maupin v. Maupin, 339 Ill. App. 484, 90 N.E.2d 234 (4 Dist. 1950); Eggemeyer v. Eggemeyer, 86 Ill. App. 2d 224, 229 N.E.2d 144 (2 Dist. 1967).

In determining whether there have been changed conditions the court must keep in view primarily the welfare of the child. Dunning v. Dunning, 14 Ill. App. 2d 242, 144 N.E.2d 535 (2 Dist. 1957).

Where a divorce decree awarded custody unconditionally, a mere showing of change in conditions of the person deprived of custody was not sufficient to set aside or drastically modify such decree, in the absence of proof that the welfare of the children required such a change. Maupin v. Maupin, 339 Ill. App. 484, 90 N.E.2d 234 (4 Dist. 1950).

Change of Custody

—Birth of Illegitimate Child

Giving birth to an illegitimate child by a mother who has custody of minor children by a dissolved marriage is not of itself a basis for changing the custody. Jayroe v. Jayroe, 58 Ill. App. 2d 79, 206 N.E.2d 266 (4 Dist. 1965).

—Burden of Proof

Petitioner, as the party seeking to change the custody judgment, has the burden to show a material change in circumstances which would justify a modification, since respondent has custody. In re Manley, 83 Ill. App. 3d 633, 39 Ill. Dec. 319, 404 N.E.2d 910 (1 Dist. 1980).

A father did not meet his burden of proof in that a change of circumstances was not shown which would warrant a change of custody. Perisich v. Perisich, 6 Ill. App. 3d 97, 284 N.E.2d 654 (1 Dist. 1972).

Where the trial court found that both parties were fit and proper persons to have the care, control and custody of the children, the person seeking to alter the custody judgment has the burden of proving altered conditions before the court can modify the custody provisions. Perisich v. Perisich, 6 Ill. App. 3d 97, 284 N.E.2d 654 (1 Dist. 1972).

Every presumption is indulged in the validity of the decree and if its provisions are to be changed, the burden of proof is on the moving party to show why the change should be made. Eggemeyer v. Eggemeyer, 86 Ill. App. 2d 224, 229 N.E.2d 144 (2 Dist. 1967).

In a post-decree hearing to modify the child custody provisions of the decree, the party seeking the modification has the burden of proving altered conditions. Eggemeyer v. Eggemeyer, 86 Ill. App. 2d 224, 229 N.E.2d 144 (2 Dist. 1967).

If provisions of a custody disposition are to be changed, the burden of proof is on the party so moving to show why it should be done. Martinec v. Sharapata, 328 Ill. App. 339, 66 N.E.2d 103 (1 Dist. 1946).

—Change in Circumstances

Trial court abused its discretion in dismissing the portion of the mother's petition regarding custody without holding a hearing because the trial court's decision that the daughter attend school in Ottawa, Illinois, was a change in circumstances not clearly contemplated by the parties, and once the school problem was resolved, the custody agreement created instability for the daughter, which created a change of circumstances permitting a hearing on modification under 750 ILCS 5/610(b). In re Marriage of Davis, 341 Ill. App. 3d 356, 275 Ill. Dec. 160, 792 N.E.2d 391, 2003 Ill. App. LEXIS 825 (3 Dist. 2003).

Changes in the custodial parent's residence and employment may be relevant factors in determining the children's best interest; these factors are not controlling, however, unless they adversely affect the children. Nolte v. Nolte, 241 Ill. App. 3d 320, 182 Ill. Dec. 78, 609 N.E.2d 381 (3 Dist. 1993).

New conditions must have arisen since the decree to warrant the court changing its prior custody determination and these changed conditions must have affected the welfare of the child. Maroney v. Maroney, 109 Ill. App. 2d 162, 249 N.E.2d 871 (3 Dist. 1969).

—Child's Preference

While a child's preferences need not be deemed as controlling in

Change of Custody (Cont'd)

—Child's Preference (Cont'd)
a custodial hearing, the preferences of mature children should be given considerable weight when they are based on sound reasoning. Nolte v. Nolte, 241 Ill. App. 3d 320, 182 Ill. Dec. 78, 609 N.E.2d 381 (3 Dist. 1993).

—Custodian's Fitness
Divorce decree, which awarded custody to the defendant father, was res judicata of the defendant's fitness as determined by the known facts in existence at the time of the decree; to justify a modification of the decree and a change of custody, the evidence must establish that the parent to whom the children were originally awarded was unfit to retain custody or that a change of conditions would make a change of custody in their best interests; the party seeking to alter the custody provisions had the burden of proving that the children's best interests required such a change. Vysoky v. Vysoky, 85 Ill. App. 2d 306, 230 N.E.2d 3 (1 Dist. 1967).

—Endangerment
Without proof of endangerment and specific findings to that effect, an order modifying custody within two years of the latest order is void. Department of Pub. Aid ex rel. Davis v. Brewer, 292 Ill. App. 3d 416, 226 Ill. Dec. 555, 685 N.E.2d 1010 (5 Dist. 1997), aff'd in part and rev'd in part on other grounds, 183 Ill. 2d 540, 234 Ill. Dec. 223, 702 N.E.2d 563 (1998).

—Factors
The trial court erred in not finding by clear and convincing evidence that the changes in circumstances indicated that it would be in the best interests of the minor children to modify the custody arrangement where most of the statutory factors weighed heavily in favor of finding that the best interests of the minor children would be served by transferring residential custody of the children to the father. In re Martins, 269 Ill. App. 3d 380, 206 Ill. Dec. 562, 645 N.E.2d 567 (2 Dist.), appeal denied, 161 Ill. 2d 528, 208 Ill. Dec. 362, 649 N.E.2d 418 (1995).

Before a change in custody should be approved, there must be a substantial change in conditions which also affects the welfare of the child involved. Windhorn v. Windhorn, 131 Ill. App. 2d 785, 264 N.E.2d 531 (3 Dist. 1970).

—Homosexuality of Custodial Parent
Where court appointed psychologist testified that there was no empirical evidence which suggested that children growing up in a homosexual environment would experience increased psychological problems, the mother's homosexual relationship standing alone was not enough to justify modification of custody. In re R.S., 286 Ill. App. 3d 1046, 222 Ill. Dec. 498, 677 N.E.2d 1297 (3 Dist. 1996).

—Improper
Where evidence established that the children were thriving in their mother's care and the only evidence the children would be better off with their father was psychologist's opinion that there was slight advantage to him having custody, the father failed to meet the burden of proving by clear and convincing evidence that the proposed arrangement was necessary to serve the best interest's of the children. In re R.S., 286 Ill. App. 3d 1046, 222 Ill. Dec. 498, 677 N.E.2d 1297 (3 Dist. 1996).

While the father could provide a good home for the children, the children's relationship with his new family, standing alone, did not support a modification of custody. In re R.S., 286 Ill. App. 3d 1046, 222 Ill. Dec. 498, 677 N.E.2d 1297 (3 Dist. 1996).

The trial court's decision to change custody from mother after terminating joint custody was an abuse of discretion where mother had been the primary physical custodian for more than six years, ever since the marriage of the parties was dissolved, child testified in camera that she preferred to live with her mother and guardian ad litem recommended that the custody of child remain with mother. In re Wycoff, 266 Ill. App. 3d 408, 203 Ill. Dec. 338, 639 N.E.2d 897 (4 Dist.), appeal denied, 158 Ill. 2d 566, 206 Ill. Dec. 847, 645 N.E.2d 1369 (1994).

—Incarceration of Custodial Parent
While an incarcerated parent has the right to make emergency arrangements for the child's immediate care, the incarcerated parent cannot dictate that a third party continue to act as temporary custodian for the child for the duration of his or her incarceration, defeating the noncustodial parent's right to custody. Naylor v. Kindred, 250 Ill. App. 3d 997, 189 Ill. Dec. 552, 620 N.E.2d 520 (4 Dist. 1993).

When the custodial parent has been incarcerated, the noncustodial parent need not show serious endangerment to prevail on a motion for modification of custody. Naylor v. Kindred, 250 Ill. App. 3d 997, 189 Ill. Dec. 552, 620 N.E.2d 520 (4 Dist. 1993).

—Insufficient Analysis
Where the record indicated that the trial court made its custody modification determination based on information that defendant was out of state with the children without court permission, there was no stipulation to a change of custody between the parties nor were there affidavits presented indicating a reason to believe there was a serious endangerment to the children, the trial court's analysis on the change of custody order was insufficient and did not meet the required standards of subsections (a) and (b). People v. Olsewski, 257 Ill. App. 3d 1018, 196 Ill. Dec. 434, 630 N.E.2d 131 (2 Dist.), appeal denied, 156 Ill. 2d 564, 202 Ill. Dec. 928, 638 N.E.2d 1122 (1994).

—Misconduct
Father was not entitled to a change of custody on the basis that his ex-wife was cohabiting with a man who was not her husband; a petitioner seeking a change of custody is required to show the relevance between a custodial parent's alleged misconduct and the children's best interests. Nolte v. Nolte, 241 Ill. App. 3d 320, 182 Ill. Dec. 78, 609 N.E.2d 381 (3 Dist. 1993).

—Not Warranted
Trial court erred in transferring custody of children from mother to father where no evidence of endangerment was shown; evidence established only that the mother might have used poor judgment in assessing the danger of sexual abuse by the children's babysitter. Department of Pub. Aid ex rel. Davis v. Brewer, 292 Ill. App. 3d 416, 226 Ill. Dec. 555, 685 N.E.2d 1010 (5 Dist. 1997), aff'd in part and rev'd in part on other grounds, 183 Ill. 2d 540, 234 Ill. Dec. 223, 702 N.E.2d 563 (1998).

The trial judge could not have found serious danger to the minor child in her present environment to justify his modification of the original custody judgment where the child's report cards from her religious school and public school and the testimony of her first grade teacher indicated that she had been a very good student and had a mature demeanor. Kraft v. Kraft, 108 Ill. App. 3d 590, 64 Ill. Dec. 240, 439 N.E.2d 491 (1 Dist. 1982).

Where the mother placed her children temporarily with the children's grandparents, asked for their return for the first time in less than one year, reasonably agreed to allow them to finish the school year, continued to seek the children's return thereafter, and remained in contact with them, custody was not modified in favor of grandparents. People ex rel. Bukovic v. Smith, 98 Ill. App. 3d 144, 53 Ill. Dec. 498, 423 N.E.2d 1302 (1 Dist. 1981).

Where evidence did not support a finding that boy's living with his mother and stepfather seriously endangered his physical, mental, emotional, or moral health, where it was not established that his best interests were served by placing him with his father, where there was an insufficient basis upon which to modify the then existing custodial arrangement, and where the circuit court overemphasized the seriousness of the parental discipline received by the children, the decision of the circuit court was contrary to the manifest weight of the evidence, which fell far short of the statutory standard justifying a custody change. In re Poston, 77 Ill. App. 3d 689, 33 Ill. Dec. 187, 396 N.E.2d 576 (3 Dist. 1979).

Where there was no evidence of grandmother's unfitness to have custody of the child, and there was no showing of a substantial change in conditions, a modification of the custody decree was not warranted. Marcus v. Marcus, 109 Ill. App. 2d 423, 248 N.E.2d 800 (1 Dist. 1969).

Denial of petition to modify a divorce decree so as to grant mother the custody of her son upheld. Jenkins v. Jenkins, 81 Ill. App. 2d 67, 225 N.E.2d 698 (1 Dist. 1967).

—Relative Affluence
The relative affluence of one parent over another, without more, is not a sufficient cause to transfer custody. Nolte v. Nolte, 241 Ill. App. 3d 320, 182 Ill. Dec. 78, 609 N.E.2d 381 (3 Dist. 1993).

Change of Custody (Cont'd)

—Remanded for Further Proceedings

Decision to remand custody case for a full hearing to decide what would be best for child was the preferred route for two reasons, both intertwined with the child's best interests; first, 18 months had passed since the custody change during which time the child went from a 10 year old being home schooled in Arizona to a girl of almost 12 attending a traditional school in Illinois and how the child had adjusted to those changes would be a crucial factor to consider in determining her future and second, it was never clearly determined whether home schooling was having a positive or negative effect on the child. In re Riess, 260 Ill. App. 3d 210, 198 Ill. Dec. 305, 632 N.E.2d 635 (2 Dist. 1994).

—Reversed

Where there was no evidence to suggest that plaintiff was unfit as a mother, or evidence of any change of circumstances sufficient to justify a change in custody awarding custody to defendant father, the order of the circuit court modifying the divorce decree granting custody to the father would be reversed. Brady v. Brady, 26 Ill. App. 3d 131, 324 N.E.2d 645 (5 Dist. 1975).

—Social Condemnation

The potential for social condemnation, standing alone, cannot justify a change in custody. In re R.S., 286 Ill. App. 3d 1046, 222 Ill. Dec. 498, 677 N.E.2d 1297 (3 Dist. 1996).

—Temporary

Even though the custody relief requested by father was temporary, where such relief was a modification of an existing custody judgment which was not more than two years old, subsection (a) was the governing statute rather than section 5/501(a)(3) (750 ILCS 5/501). In re Oehm, 252 Ill. App. 3d 311, 192 Ill. Dec. 74, 625 N.E.2d 34 (1 Dist. 1993).

—Warranted

Where the presumption in favor of the present custodian was overcome because the daughter had been living with the father for a year, and the changed circumstances were that the mother threw the daughter out of the house, and the daughter was angry with the mother, the daughter expressed a preference to live with the father, and the court found that it would be in the daughter's best interests if custody were awarded to the father, in light of the age of the daughter, who was 17, and the deterioration of the relationship between mother and daughter, the trial court's decision to modify custody was not an abuse of discretion. In re Metz, 233 Ill. App. 3d 50, 174 Ill. Dec. 172, 598 N.E.2d 369 (2 Dist. 1992).

Trial court's modification of a prior order which had given ex-wife custody of the children, to now grant ex-husband and ex-wife joint custody of the younger son was not against the manifest weight of the evidence when the younger son's emotional problems, bed-wetting and nightmares disappeared after living with ex-husband. In re Richmond, 171 Ill. App. 3d 506, 121 Ill. Dec. 919, 525 N.E.2d 1226 (4 Dist. 1988).

Changes in the situation of the custodial parent which were detrimental to the child's best interest, including living with an unstable boyfriend who was unemployed and used force against the child, and evidence that the child underwent "a change" during the custody clearly and convincingly rebutted the presumption in favor of the original custodial order and established that a change in custody was necessary to serve the child's best interest. Boyd v. Sussenbach, 108 Ill. 2d 489, 92 Ill. Dec. 556, 485 N.E.2d 367 (1985).

Trial court was not in error in changing custody of child to wife with visitation rights to husband, where even though there was a court order establishing custody with husband, child had been with wife, where previously there had been no hearing with respect to best interests of child, where divorced husband had mistreated child and where his situation had changed since custody was granted to him. In re Sweet, 119 Ill. App. 3d 1033, 75 Ill. Dec. 846, 458 N.E.2d 14 (1 Dist. 1983).

Where a pattern of unstable, volatile and erratic behavior was demonstrated that the mother, although remarried at the time of the trial court proceedings, had lived in an open and adulterous relationship in her home with the children prior to the marriage, and the father was remarried, employed, and could have provided a stable emotional and physical environment for the two children, then a change of custody from the mother to the father was not against the manifest weight of the evidence. In re McIntyre, 97 Ill. App. 3d 777, 53 Ill. Dec. 89, 423 N.E.2d 281 (3 Dist. 1981).

Where the trial court was presented with evidence that the child was substantially in the care of a child care provider and had a close relationship with the father; that the mother intended to go to Indonesia, perhaps South America and then to France, apparently out of devotion to her new husband and a personal desire for travel; and that their departure for Jakarta was unavoidable and in her new husband's case, imminent; the situation presented was such that the court might well have concluded the stability and continuity of the child's relationships and environment could be maintained only by a change in custody, satisfying the requirements of subsection (b) of this section. Nodot v. Nodot, 81 Ill. App. 3d 883, 37 Ill. Dec. 96, 401 N.E.2d 1189 (1 Dist. 1980).

Where there was substantial evidence indicating that the long-range interests of the children would be served by a modification of the prior custody judgment, where the children's mother, the legal custodian, had given her parents actual physical custody of the children where the mother clearly was unable to assume responsibility for the care of her children, and her parents' age made it quite unlikely that they could continue indefinitely to raise the children, despite their willingness to do so where father of the children was remarried, steadily employed, and owned a three bedroom house and his present wife wanted the children to live with them, the trial judge's order granting petition to change custody to father was not against the manifest weight of the evidence. Harne v. Johnson, 77 Ill. 2d 414, 33 Ill. Dec. 110, 396 N.E.2d 499 (1979).

Father's petition for custody of minor children from his ex-wife to himself was affirmed, where wife never seriously attempted to provide a home and children primarily lived with wife's parents while husband had remarried and his new wife was willing to provide a home for the children, and change of custody from mother to father would serve the best interests of the children. Hazelwood v. Hazelwood, 20 Ill. App. 3d 223, 313 N.E.2d 485 (4 Dist. 1974).

Order modifying custody of child was not contrary to the manifest weight of the evidence. Windhorn v. Windhorn, 131 Ill. App. 2d 785, 264 N.E.2d 531 (3 Dist. 1970).

Modification of a custody agreement in favor of father, even though he had ignored the terms of the original decree by taking the child from the mother, was not against the manifest weight of the evidence where the evidence showed that the mother was an unfit parent. Maroney v. Maroney, 109 Ill. App. 2d 162, 249 N.E.2d 871 (3 Dist. 1969).

Although there was no showing of unfitness, where plaintiff, who had custody, left the child with the defendant for a period of years, the trial court awarded custody to the defendant. Carstens v. Carstens, 108 Ill. App. 2d 439, 248 N.E.2d 135 (3 Dist. 1969).

Change of Environment

—Harm

House where mother and her husband lived had no toilet, bathtub or phone and its only running water was in the kitchen, the house was heated with a coal and wood burning stove and the house was over two miles from the nearest neighbor, other evidence indicated that the daughter had been molested by her stepfather's older son while she was in the mother's custody, the children had been whipped by their stepfather, and neither the mother nor the stepfather worked, leaving the children without a role model to provide guidance and support toward becoming productive members of society, and the only family income came from social security disability payments, the trial court's finding that the harm likely to be caused by the change of environment was outweighed by the advantages of such change was not contrary to the manifest weight of the evidence. Caulkins v. Caulkins, 68 Ill. App. 3d 284, 24 Ill. Dec. 827, 385 N.E.2d 1117 (3 Dist. 1979).

Where the children had been away from the permanent custodian for a substantial period of time and in the temporary custody of the parent seeking permanent custody and where no evidence was presented which indicated that ending the plaintiff's permanent custody would harm the children in any way, in fact, the trial court's order actually provided for them to continue in their environment, and comported with the clear intent of this section to stabilize custodial arrangements. Doyle v. Doyle, 62 Ill. App. 3d 786, 19 Ill. Dec. 723, 379 N.E.2d 387 (4 Dist. 1978).

Character

Where the record, as a whole, supported the trial court's conclu-

Character (Cont'd)
sion that the mother's new husband had certain "flaws" in his personality that could cause serious harm to the children, the trial court was correct in finding that mother's marriage to him was an important consideration in modifying the custody decree. In re Gunter, 93 Ill. App. 3d 1043, 49 Ill. Dec. 505, 418 N.E.2d 149 (1 Dist. 1981).

One factor which will be considered is the character of the person with whom the party presently having custody is living and his probable effect on the child's home life and development. Katzer v. Katzer, 61 Ill. App. 3d 299, 18 Ill. Dec. 852, 378 N.E.2d 316 (1 Dist. 1978).

Where the evidence established that the character and conduct of the person to whom the mother subsequently married was unsatisfactory, that the children's interests were adversely affected by earlier divorce decree awarding custody to their mother, and the children's father was of good moral character, the evidence was sufficient to support the decree of modification granting custody to the father. Kline v. Kline, 57 Ill. App. 2d 244, 205 N.E.2d 775 (3 Dist. 1965).

Clear and Convincing Evidence

Clear and convincing evidence does not require the degree of proof necessary to convict a person of a criminal offense, but it requires more than a preponderance of the evidence. In re Dall, 191 Ill. App. 3d 652, 138 Ill. Dec. 879, 548 N.E.2d 109 (5 Dist. 1989).

The new evidence produced by father to support allegations of sexual abuse did not meet the requisite clear and convincing standard where, in addition to the guardian's and a physician's report that the father had suborned the child to make false allegations of sexual abuse by his maternal half brothers, the father's own expert could not conclude who, in fact, was the perpetrator, and the board-certified child psychologist could not discern the perpetrator. In re Dall, 191 Ill. App. 3d 652, 138 Ill. Dec. 879, 548 N.E.2d 109 (5 Dist. 1989).

Cohabitation

Illinois courts cannot presume that a custodial parent's cohabitation is harmful to a child. In re R.S., 286 Ill. App. 3d 1046, 222 Ill. Dec. 498, 677 N.E.2d 1297 (3 Dist. 1996).

A per se rule requiring a change in custody of minor children where the custodial parent cohabits, in the children's presence, with a member of the opposite sex openly and on a continuing conjugal basis, has not been established, although the trial court should give due consideration to the custodial parent's living arrangement and its effect on the well-being of the children in determining whether a change in custody is warranted. Brandt v. Brandt, 99 Ill. App. 3d 1089, 55 Ill. Dec. 78, 425 N.E.2d 1251 (1 Dist. 1981).

A decision directing a change of custody must be buttressed on more than the fact that the custodial parent resides with a member of the opposite sex in an open and continuing cohabitation, since a decision on the issue of custody includes the evaluation of the totality of the evidence submitted along with a consideration of the elements and principles enunciated in prior decisions of the courts of Illinois and the relevant statutory provisions. Brandt v. Brandt, 99 Ill. App. 3d 1089, 55 Ill. Dec. 78, 425 N.E.2d 1251 (1 Dist. 1981).

The resident presence of the custodial mother's paramour must be considered in light of the moral values which the parent is actually demonstrating to the children. In re Olson, 98 Ill. App. 3d 316, 53 Ill. Dec. 751, 424 N.E.2d 386 (3 Dist. 1981).

The fornication statute, the violation of which is relevant to child custody matters, requires that the cohabitation or intercourse be "open and notorious"; mere notoriety is not enough, as notoriety is not an independent issue, and the notoriety of the behavior must be a result of its openness. In re Olson, 98 Ill. App. 3d 316, 53 Ill. Dec. 751, 424 N.E.2d 386 (3 Dist. 1981).

The trial court did not err in transferring custody of the child to a non-custodial parent living with a person to whom he was not married, since the circumstances of the case at bar in which the father had represented in his brief and oral argument that he and the woman with whom he lived, both unmarried at the time of the hearing, had married, pursuant to his intention as expressed to the trial court, were distinguished from a prior case where there was an adulterous relationship between a custodial parent and a married man and evidence that the children whose custody was at issue were aware of and had observed their sexual conduct. Nodot v. Nodot, 81 Ill. App. 3d 883, 37 Ill. Dec. 96, 401 N.E.2d 1189 (1 Dist. 1980).

Trial court's transfer of custody to father, based on mother's cohabitation with boyfriend, was not contrary to the manifest weight of the evidence, and tangible manifestations of damage to the children's character were not required to effectuate the custody modification. Jarrett v. Jarrett, 78 Ill. 2d 337, 36 Ill. Dec. 1, 400 N.E.2d 421 (1979), cert. denied, 449 U.S. 927, 101 S. Ct. 329, 66 L. Ed. 2d 155 (1980).

Compliance

Subsection (a) of this section does not specify at what point stipulations by the parties must be made or entered; in a custody proceeding, once the parties stipulated prior to the beginning of the hearing that joint custody should be terminated and a substantial change in circumstance had occurred, compliance with the requirements of subsection (a) had been met. In re Stevens, 183 Ill. App. 3d 160, 131 Ill. Dec. 723, 538 N.E.2d 1279 (5 Dist. 1989).

Conditions

Respondent failed to show that the parent to whom custody was originally awarded was either unfit to retain custody or that the change in conditions was directly related to the child's needs. In re Lichtenstein, 139 Ill. App. 3d 881, 94 Ill. Dec. 416, 487 N.E.2d 1293 (5 Dist. 1986).

Consent

The consent requirement is intended to ensure that the custodian acquiesced in the transfer of physical custody and the integration into the new family, and should be viewed in that narrow context. Stearns v. Stearns, 84 Ill. App. 3d 195, 39 Ill. Dec. 704, 405 N.E.2d 457 (3 Dist. 1980).

Mother who gave consent to child to stay with his father for the school year did not consent to the boy's integration into the father's family. Stearns v. Stearns, 84 Ill. App. 3d 195, 39 Ill. Dec. 704, 405 N.E.2d 457 (3 Dist. 1980).

The consent requirement in this section is intended to ensure that the custodian acquiesced in the transfer of physical custody and the integration into the family of the petitioner, and should be viewed in that narrow context. Burnett v. Burnett, 75 Ill. App. 3d 998, 31 Ill. Dec. 142, 394 N.E.2d 58 (2 Dist. 1979); In re Pease, 106 Ill. App. 3d 617, 62 Ill. Dec. 389, 435 N.E.2d 1361 (2 Dist. 1982).

Criminal Contempt

Where the custody order did not require telephone communication between the parents except in an emergency or during the extended summer vacation, and husband's testimony established only that the wife did not answer the telephone or return his calls during spring vacation, the wife was not guilty of contempt. In re Kramer, 211 Ill. App. 3d 401, 155 Ill. Dec. 909, 570 N.E.2d 422 (1 Dist. 1991).

Custody Judgments

—In General

Where the divorce decree awarding the custody of a child to the mother was final as to the conditions then existing, it should not be altered unless there had been a substantial change of conditions thereafter, or unless there were existing material facts, unknown to the court at the time of the decree, which affected the child's welfare. Collings v. Collings, 120 Ill. App. 2d 125, 256 N.E.2d 108 (2 Dist. 1970).

After a divorce decree in this state, the custody of the children is always subject to the order of the court which enters the decree and may be changed from time to time as the best interests of the children demand; the decree is res judicata as to the facts which existed at the time it was entered but not as to facts arising thereafter. Nye v. Nye, 411 Ill. 408, 105 N.E.2d 300 (1952).

—Change in Circumstances

This section is designed to maximize finality and ensure continuity for the child without jeopardizing his best interest; to this end, a prior custody judgment should not be modified unless a court first finds upon the basis of facts that have arisen since the prior judgment that a change has occurred in the circumstances of the child and that the modification is necessary to serve the best interest of the child. Iverson v. Iverson, 83 Ill. App. 3d 493, 39 Ill. Dec. 27, 404 N.E.2d 411 (1 Dist. 1980).

Custody Judgments (Cont'd)

—Change of Venue

Where petitions for modification of the divorce decree and for change of venue, under former Ill.Rev.Stat., ch. 40, para. 19 (see now this section) were filed on the same day where the venue petition was timely and notice thereof was served on the plaintiff who filed an answer thereto, and where the petition alleged that the prejudice of the trial judge came to defendant's knowledge the day the custody of the children was obtained by the plaintiff through the writ of attachment; even though her conduct was reprehensible, the defendant had the right to have the custody issue, presented by her petition, heard and determined by a judge who was not, according to her belief, prejudiced against her. Smith v. Smith, 87 Ill. App. 2d 21, 230 N.E.2d 474 (2 Dist. 1967).

—Evidence

Although original custody judgment had resulted from an agreement of the parties and the trial court had not heard evidence concerning the child's best interest, the court will not hear all the evidence de novo when one party subsequently petitions for modification. In re Gargus, 97 Ill. App. 3d 598, 53 Ill. Dec. 1, 423 N.E.2d 193 (1 Dist. 1981).

—Final Order

A decree fixing the custody of a child is final on the conditions then existing and should not be changed afterwards, unless on altered conditions since the decree, or on material facts existing at the time of the decree, but unknown by the court, and then only for the welfare of the child. Maupin v. Maupin, 339 Ill. App. 484, 90 N.E.2d 234 (4 Dist. 1950); Dunning v. Dunning, 14 Ill. App. 2d 242, 144 N.E.2d 535 (2 Dist. 1957).

—Incomplete Determination

An order did not represent a complete determination based on the facts as they existed at that time, where the testimony of a witness on the date of the order was the only additional evidence considered, and since the entry of the original decree, two of the three children whose custody had been awarded to the petitioner were no longer in her custody. Klitzing v. Gottemoller, 76 Ill. App. 3d 783, 32 Ill. Dec. 246, 395 N.E.2d 193 (3 Dist. 1979).

—Interim Remedial Period

In modification of child custody action the circuit court erred by creating a "interim remedial period" during which mother could resolve her problems and improperly ordered a second hearing in which the court shifted mother's burden of proof from clear and convincing to a preponderance of the evidence. Valliere v. Valliere, 275 Ill. App. 3d 1095, 212 Ill. Dec. 696, 657 N.E.2d 1041 (1 Dist. 1995).

—Limitation Period

Although the decree entered by the court on August 12, 1977 was less than two years from its subsequent modification on December 12, 1977, the determination by the court in August, 1977 was not a new consideration of the custody issue but rather represented a determination as of the date of the initial custody decree in 1974; the additional evidence considered by the trial court did not refer to circumstances of the parties in 1977 but rather to the circumstances which took place prior to the initial custody order, and for that reason the spirit and intent of this section did not preclude a reconsideration of the custody issue. Klitzing v. Gottemoller, 76 Ill. App. 3d 783, 32 Ill. Dec. 246, 395 N.E.2d 193 (3 Dist. 1979).

—Modification

For a case discussing modification of custody decree, see Fears v. Fears, 5 Ill. App. 3d 610, 283 N.E.2d 709 (5 Dist. 1972); Girolamo v. Girolamo, 5 Ill. App. 3d 627, 283 N.E.2d 713 (5 Dist. 1972); Breedlove v. Breedlove, 5 Ill. App. 3d 774, 283 N.E.2d 919 (2 Dist. 1972).

—Not Shown

An order that allowed removal of minor children to a foreign jurisdiction by the parent with custody and granted modification of the other parent's visitation rights did not constitute a "custody judgment" under subsection (a) of this section. Mueller v. Weis, 76 Ill. App. 3d 860, 32 Ill. Dec. 447, 395 N.E.2d 677 (5 Dist. 1979).

—Permanent Custody

In the absence of proof that the welfare of the child requires a change in its custody, permanent custody should not be subject to constant or spasmodic variation, where the decree granting custody was not conditional. Collings v. Collings, 120 Ill. App. 2d 125, 256 N.E.2d 108 (2 Dist. 1970).

Changes in permanent custody (as distinguished from visitation privileges) should not be subject either to constant or spasmodic variation, merely to follow fluctuations in the health, employment, or residence of the party last deprived of custody, where the order was not conditional with respect to such changes. Dunning v. Dunning, 14 Ill. App. 2d 242, 144 N.E.2d 535 (2 Dist. 1957).

—Petition to Remove Child from State

An order denying a petition for leave to remove a child from the state is not a "custody judgment" as that phrase is used in subsection (b). In re Shaddle, 317 Ill. App. 3d 428, 251 Ill. Dec. 444, 740 N.E.2d 525, 2000 Ill. App. LEXIS 919 (4 Dist. 2000).

—Prior Judgments

By its terms, a former version of this section required a two step approach to the modification of prior custody judgments: the court had to first determine whether one of the statutory prerequisites listed in former subdivisions (b)(1) through (b)(3) (see now subsections (a) and (b)) existed, and if only subdivision (b)(3) was applicable (the child's environment endangered him), the court had to determine whether the modification was necessary to serve the best interest of the child. In re Friedman, 100 Ill. App. 3d 794, 56 Ill. Dec. 181, 427 N.E.2d 261 (1 Dist. 1981).

The substance of prior court proceedings should be determined before a modification of custody occurs. Mueller v. Weis, 76 Ill. App. 3d 860, 32 Ill. Dec. 447, 395 N.E.2d 677 (5 Dist. 1979).

—Purpose

The custody of the child is not awarded for the purpose of gratifying the feelings of either parent or with any idea of punishing or rewarding either parent. Dunning v. Dunning, 14 Ill. App. 2d 242, 144 N.E.2d 535 (2 Dist. 1957).

—Res Judicata

A divorce decree granting custody is res judicata as to the facts which existed at the time of divorce but custody may be changed from time to time as the best interests of the children demand; however, new conditions must arise to warrant a custody change. Frees v. Frees, 99 Ill. App. 2d 213, 240 N.E.2d 274 (1 Dist. 1968).

A decree fixing the custody of children is final and res judicata and should not be altered or amended unless new facts have arisen since the entry of the decree that make it necessary for the welfare of the child that the custody be changed. Dunning v. Dunning, 14 Ill. App. 2d 242, 144 N.E.2d 535 (2 Dist. 1957).

Order sustaining the master's report and awarding custody to the plaintiff's sister, from which there was no appeal, was res judicata as to all circumstances and conditions of the parties existing up to the time of the entry of that order, and the same holds true with respect to the order denying a petition to vacate the order. Stark v. Stark, 7 Ill. App. 2d 442, 129 N.E.2d 776 (1 Dist. 1955).

—Unconditional Decree

Where the agreement entered into by the parties in anticipation of the divorce decree contained a provision to the effect that the children had been living with their father, that they were of a suitable age to exercise their discretion concerning the parent with whom they would reside, and that the father should have their custody, subject, of course, to order of court, the decree was clearly unconditional in its award of custody to the father. Stickler v. Stickler, 57 Ill. App. 2d 286, 206 N.E.2d 720 (1 Dist. 1965).

Custody Proceedings

—Modification Not Shown

The trial court decision properly constituted an initial custody proceeding under 750 ILCS 5/602 and not a post-decree modification of an earlier temporary child support order under this section where the parties had an ongoing dispute as to custody and during the pendency of this dispute, the trial court entered various orders modifying the temporary custodial, residential, and visitation arrangements. In re Balzell, 207 Ill. App. 3d 310, 152 Ill. Dec. 492, 566 N.E.2d 20 (3 Dist. 1991).

Custody Proceedings (Cont'd)

—Private Interviews in Chambers

The purpose of an in camera hearing is to lessen the ordeal for the child and does not extend to the parties, nor is it intended to make a secret of the basis for the court's findings. Stickler v. Stickler, 57 Ill. App. 2d 286, 206 N.E.2d 720 (1 Dist. 1965).

—Separate Issues

Since the matter at issue was a permanent change of custody, and the former proceeding was summer custody, then the parties were not relitigating issues decided in the prior proceeding. In re McIntyre, 97 Ill. App. 3d 777, 53 Ill. Dec. 89, 423 N.E.2d 281 (3 Dist. 1981).

Decision of Court

A trial court should not be allowed to evade the effects of this section by making a custody order temporary, especially where all the other issues in the case have been resolved and all the evidence is in; a trial judge must make a permanent decision based on the evidence presented and cannot continue temporary custody from time to time either to avoid making a difficult decision or to avoid the requirements of this section. In re Cesaretti, 203 Ill. App. 3d 347, 149 Ill. Dec. 28, 561 N.E.2d 306 (2 Dist. 1990).

Determination of Custody

—Best Interest of the Child

Custody will be awarded consistent with the welfare and best interest of the child. People ex rel. Morris v. Morris, 44 Ill. 2d 66, 254 N.E.2d 478 (1969).

—Factors

In a dispute between a natural parent and a non-parent, the two most significant elements are the superior right of parents to custody of their children and the concern of the court for the best interests of the child; courts should also give significance to the claim of a non-parent who has had actual or legal custody of the child for a substantial period of time, especially if the evidence shows that the child has become an integral member of a true family unit. Wadman v. Kirsten, York, 110 Ill. App. 3d 302, 66 Ill. Dec. 61, 442 N.E.2d 333 (4 Dist. 1982).

The guiding star in a hearing to modify child custody provisions of a decree is at all times the best interest of the child. Maroney v. Maroney, 109 Ill. App. 2d 162, 249 N.E.2d 871 (3 Dist. 1969).

Where father permitted the children to remain in the custody of mother for nearly four years following the entry of the divorce decree, notwithstanding that (1) custody of all the children was awarded to the father, and (2) father had remarried, the proper inquiry was as to the conditions surrounding the children in the mother's home. Mabbatt v. Mabbatt, 78 Ill. App. 2d 455, 223 N.E.2d 191 (1 Dist. 1967).

Where both principals to a divorce proceeding are fit persons, they have equal right to custody of their minor children, and the paramount consideration in settling the issue of child custody is the welfare and best interests of the children themselves, without any purpose of penalizing the parent upon whom the blame for the dissolution of the marital union may be fixed. Kline v. Kline, 57 Ill. App. 2d 244, 205 N.E.2d 775 (3 Dist. 1965).

—Scope of Inquiry

While the court, in a petition to modify a decree as to custody of a minor child, is not limited in the scope of its inquiry, it may not override the findings in the original decree and may not use the transcript of the evidence in the divorce proceeding as a basis for a ruling on the modification question. Arden v. Arden, 25 Ill. App. 2d 181, 166 N.E.2d 111 (3 Dist. 1960).

Discretion of Court

—In General

Change in the custody of the child rests in the sound discretion of the trial court, whose determination in that regard will not be disturbed on review unless contrary to the manifest weight of the evidence. Katzer v. Katzer, 61 Ill. App. 3d 299, 18 Ill. Dec. 852, 378 N.E.2d 316 (1 Dist. 1978).

Where there was not a full hearing by the trial court at the time of the original placement of the child but custody was achieved by the stipulation of the parties upon their divorce, the trial court may use initial discretion in deciding what custody provisions provide for the children's best interests. De Franco v. De Franco, 67 Ill. App. 3d 760, 24 Ill. Dec. 130, 384 N.E.2d 997 (1 Dist. 1978).

In a petition, a change in custody of minor children incident to a divorce, the trier of fact has significant opportunity to observe both parents, the children and other witnesses and thus evaluate their temperaments, personalities, demeanor and capabilities, this is a vital and important link in the chain of judicial decision. Courson v. Courson, 47 Ill. App. 3d 318, 5 Ill. Dec. 645, 361 N.E.2d 1173 (3 Dist. 1977).

In child custody matters, the trial court is vested with broad discretion, subject to review, in determining where the best interests of the child lie. Kjellesvik v. Shannon, 41 Ill. App. 3d 674, 355 N.E.2d 120 (3 Dist. 1976); De Franco v. De Franco, 67 Ill. App. 3d 760, 24 Ill. Dec. 130, 384 N.E.2d 997 (1 Dist. 1978); Caulkins v. Caulkins, 68 Ill. App. 3d 284, 24 Ill. Dec. 827, 385 N.E.2d 1117 (3 Dist. 1979); Applegate v. Applegate, 80 Ill. App. 3d 81, 35 Ill. Dec. 496, 399 N.E.2d 330 (5 Dist. 1980); In re Piccirilli, 88 Ill. App. 3d 621, 43 Ill. Dec. 953, 410 N.E.2d 1086 (1 Dist. 1980); Markham v. Markham, 91 Ill. App. 3d 1122, 47 Ill. Dec. 235, 414 N.E.2d 1351 (3 Dist. 1981); In re Richmond, 171 Ill. App. 3d 506, 121 Ill. Dec. 919, 525 N.E.2d 1226 (4 Dist. 1988); In re Dullard, 176 Ill. App. 3d 817, 126 Ill. Dec. 227, 531 N.E.2d 854 (1 Dist. 1988); In re Engelbach, 181 Ill. App. 3d 563, 130 Ill. Dec. 305, 537 N.E.2d 372 (2 Dist. 1989); In re Apperson, 215 Ill. App. 3d 378, 158 Ill. Dec. 864, 574 N.E.2d 1257 (4 Dist. 1991).

The trial court properly exercised its discretion in modifying the visitation provisions of the divorce decree. Flanagan v. Flanagan, 123 Ill. App. 2d 17, 259 N.E.2d 610 (1 Dist. 1970).

Under the divorce statute, the court is clothed with a large discretion in determining to which parent a child will be given, however, such discretion is a judicial one, not unlimited and subject to review. Nye v. Nye, 411 Ill. 408, 105 N.E.2d 300 (1952).

—Abuse Not Shown

Trial court's decision to keep mother as the custodian of children was not contrary to the manifest weight of the evidence and did not constitute an abuse of discretion since no substantial diminution took place in the quality of children's environment which seriously endangered their mental, moral, or emotional health. Farm v. Farm, 93 Ill. App. 3d 332, 48 Ill. Dec. 838, 417 N.E.2d 240 (3 Dist. 1981).

The court did not abuse its discretion in awarding custody of child to grandparents, instead of to natural father, following the death of the custodial parent (mother). In re Piccirilli, 88 Ill. App. 3d 621, 43 Ill. Dec. 953, 410 N.E.2d 1086 (1 Dist. 1980).

The trial court did not abuse its discretion in denying father's petition for a modification of custody where it was determined that it was in the best interest of the child that she remain with her mother despite the fact that the mother had been living with a man who was not her husband. Boyer v. Boyer, 83 Ill. App. 3d 52, 38 Ill. Dec. 565, 403 N.E.2d 796 (3 Dist. 1980).

—Abuse Shown

Where the trial court, in entering a modification of a child custody decree, relied on changed conditions, but a subsequent review indicated that there was no showing of change in conditions warranting a modification of the custody decree, nor was there a proper determination of unfitness on the part of the mother, the modification of the custody decree was thus an abuse of discretion by the chancellor. Nye v. Nye, 411 Ill. 408, 105 N.E.2d 300 (1952).

—Duty of Court

Where there was no hearing on the merits of the mother's petition to change the custody of the child and the custodial father was not permitted to introduce testimony bearing on the dispute as to the proper person to have the care and custody of the child, as the child was treated as a ward of the court, it was the duty of the court to hear testimony in order to ascertain whether a change in the custody should be made; therefore, the trial court committed reversible error in declining to hear the witnesses tendered by the custodial father on the issue of custody. Gerst v. Gerst, 349 Ill. App. 201, 110 N.E.2d 470 (1 Dist. 1953).

—Prior Order Improper

Where the previous order changing custody of a child was improper, no change of circumstances was necessary before the trial

Discretion of Court (Cont'd)

—Prior Order Improper (Cont'd)

judge could alter it, and it was not an abuse of discretion for him to vacate the order after he had heard from all the parties. Norris v. Norris, 121 Ill. App. 2d 226, 257 N.E.2d 545 (1 Dist. 1970).

Effect of Amendment

The second sentence of subsection (b) was not repealed by implication through the enactment of 750 ILCS 5/602.1. In re Lasky, 176 Ill. 2d 75, 223 Ill. Dec. 27, 678 N.E.2d 1035 (1997).

Endangerment

Where the evidence presented at trial showed that plaintiff had made very good progress in eliminating her abuse of alcohol and that her ability to function and cope with stress had greatly improved, but when the children had been taken from her earlier she had often been intoxicated and unable to care for the children and unable to properly relate to them and there was no assurance that plaintiff's abuse of alcohol would not recur or that her inability to relate to the children would not continue, the court could have concluded that to allow the children to live with their mother would severely endanger their physical and emotional health. Doyle v. Doyle, 62 Ill. App. 3d 786, 19 Ill. Dec. 723, 379 N.E.2d 387 (4 Dist. 1978).

—Showing Not Required

An incarcerated custodial parent, by virtue of his or her incarceration, does not have physical custody of a child and there is no longer a presumption in favor of retaining him or her as the custodial parent; since the purpose of establishing serious endangerment is to rebut a presumption in favor of retaining the custodial parent, it is therefore unnecessary to establish serious endangerment. Naylor v. Kindred, 250 Ill. App. 3d 997, 189 Ill. Dec. 552, 620 N.E.2d 520 (4 Dist. 1993).

—Shown

Judge clearly permitted respondent's motion to modify the custody judgment even though it was less than two years old because there was reason to believe that the children's environment, when in the custody of petitioner, was a serious endangerment to them physically, emotionally, psychologically or mentally. In re Oehm, 252 Ill. App. 3d 311, 192 Ill. Dec. 74, 625 N.E.2d 34 (1 Dist. 1993).

Evidence of the child's need for psychiatric counseling and the trial court's conclusion that this could not be accomplished while he remained with his mother provided a sufficient basis for establishing a harmful environment as required by subsection (b) of this section (see now subsection (a)). In re Friedman, 100 Ill. App. 3d 794, 56 Ill. Dec. 181, 427 N.E.2d 261 (1 Dist. 1981).

—Standard of Proof

This section does not require that the court find endangerment by clear and convincing evidence; the statute requires that there must be "reason to believe" that the child's present environment may endanger him in some way. In re Oehm, 252 Ill. App. 3d 311, 192 Ill. Dec. 74, 625 N.E.2d 34 (1 Dist. 1993).

Evidence

—In General

In an action by a father to obtain custody of his two children, testimony given by maternal grandmother as to what the children supposedly told her about the father's conduct and living conditions was inadmissible; such evidence was from a party who attempted to obtain legal custody and was rebuffed. In re Gustafson, 187 Ill. App. 3d 551, 135 Ill. Dec. 192, 543 N.E.2d 575 (4 Dist. 1989).

The evidentiary ingredients in a custody dispute, by the very nature of the contest and the individuality of the disputants are, indeed, numerous, varied, and interrelated and thus each factor must be weighed and considered in its relationship to all of the others shown to exist. Brandt v. Brandt, 99 Ill. App. 3d 1089, 55 Ill. Dec. 78, 425 N.E.2d 1251 (1 Dist. 1981).

—Events Prior to Decree

The court originally based the custody award to the father on the stipulation of the parties, without taking evidence as to the circumstances of the parents or their ability to take care of the children; therefore, there was no error in the trial court's consideration of facts which were unknown to the court at the time of entry of the previous custody order in making its determination of modification under this section. In re Kleiboeker, 262 Ill. App. 3d 644, 199 Ill. Dec. 975, 634 N.E.2d 1329 (5 Dist. 1994).

In post-decretal proceedings in which the issue is custody of children, evidence which tends to prove change of circumstances may make relevant, and thus admissible, evidence proving facts which existed prior to the divorce, despite the rule that a divorce decree is res judicata of the facts existing at the time it was entered. Johnson v. Johnson, 34 Ill. App. 3d 356, 340 N.E.2d 68 (1 Dist. 1975).

At a hearing on the father's petition for modification of a divorce decree to give him custody of his children, evidence of facts pre-dating that decree could not be heard for the purpose of impeaching the mother's fitness, but such evidence was not inadmissible for every purpose, for such evidence was competent where it related to other new circumstances having bearing on the question of the children's welfare. Kline v. Kline, 57 Ill. App. 2d 244, 205 N.E.2d 775 (3 Dist. 1965).

—Financial Circumstances

While evidence of wife's boyfriend's financial circumstances may have been irrelevant to a determination of the maintenance issue, it may have been relevant to the court's full understanding of the circumstances at wife's residence in connection with the custody issue. Junge v. Junge, 73 Ill. App. 3d 767, 29 Ill. Dec. 756, 392 N.E.2d 313 (5 Dist. 1979).

—Held Insufficient

Evidence presented did not support the trial court's conclusion that termination of joint custody and allowance of sole custody to mother was necessary for the best interest of son. In re Kartholl, 143 Ill. App. 3d 228, 97 Ill. Dec. 347, 492 N.E.2d 1006 (2 Dist. 1986).

Modification judgment awarding custody to the father was against the manifest weight of the evidence. Ipema v. Dykhuis, 131 Ill. App. 3d 371, 86 Ill. Dec. 728, 475 N.E.2d 1107 (3 Dist. 1985).

Nothing in the record suggested that the children's present welfare was seriously endangered, and there was a lack of evidence that the children's welfare would be endangered in the future. In re Pease, 106 Ill. App. 3d 617, 62 Ill. Dec. 389, 435 N.E.2d 1361 (2 Dist. 1982).

Petitioner failed to satisfy subdivision (b)(3) of this section where the evidence failed to support a finding that the children's environment seriously endangered their physical, mental, moral or emotional health. In re Gebis, 100 Ill. App. 3d 710, 56 Ill. Dec. 280, 427 N.E.2d 360 (1 Dist. 1981).

Evidence was insufficient to order change of custody to establish the present environment did not endanger the physical, mental, moral, or emotional health of the children and that the conduct of the mother did not affect her relationship with them. Holt v. Holt, 71 Ill. App. 3d 87, 27 Ill. Dec. 304, 388 N.E.2d 1353 (4 Dist. 1979).

—Held Sufficient

The findings of fact by the trial court supported the modification of custody where the trial court found respondent father had beat his daughter with a belt since the prior custody judgment, causing her to bruise and to fear her father. In re Eleopoulos, 186 Ill. App. 3d 374, 134 Ill. Dec. 326, 542 N.E.2d 505 (4 Dist. 1989).

Evidence was held to be sufficient that father established by clear and convincing evidence that a change had occurred in child's circumstances, therefore prompting a change in custody. In re Eldert, 158 Ill. App. 3d 798, 110 Ill. Dec. 768, 511 N.E.2d 945 (3 Dist. 1987), appeal denied, 117 Ill. Dec. 224, 520 N.E.2d 385 (Ill. 1988).

Where only respondent father chose to appear and where it was apparent, that respondent was credible, the decision that the children's environment may seriously endanger their physical, mental, moral, and emotional health was proper. In re Kading, 150 Ill. App. 3d 623, 103 Ill. Dec. 654, 501 N.E.2d 971 (2 Dist. 1986).

The trial court's conclusion that modification was of a custody judgment was unnecessary to serve the best interest of child was not against the manifest weight of the evidence. In re Kartholl, 143 Ill. App. 3d 228, 97 Ill. Dec. 347, 492 N.E.2d 1006 (2 Dist. 1986).

Where the trial court's findings were not contrary to the manifest weight of the evidence and they satisfied the statutory requirements of this section, the order of the trial court transferring custody of the minor children to petitioner was affirmed. Mullins v.

Evidence (Cont'd)

—Held Sufficient (Cont'd)
Mullins, 142 Ill. App. 3d 57, 96 Ill. Dec. 170, 490 N.E.2d 1375 (1 Dist. 1986).

There was ample evidentiary support for the trial court's determination that custody should remain with the father because he never consented to a change in that custody. In re Hill, 105 Ill. App. 3d 473, 61 Ill. Dec. 374, 434 N.E.2d 527 (1 Dist. 1982).

The trial court's judgment was not against the manifest weight of the evidence when the evidence was clear that child's stepmother had slapped child on the face causing child's nose to bleed and resulting in bruises and when child had made it clear that she wanted to live with her own mother and that her relationship with her stepmother was deteriorating. Hoskins v. Yuhas, 87 Ill. App. 3d 521, 42 Ill. Dec. 653, 409 N.E.2d 148 (3 Dist. 1980).

Where minor was not shown to be endangered, the drinking problem of minor's stepfather had abated with counseling, she was well-adjusted, doing well in school and involved in extracurricular activities, the determination of the trial court that a change in custody to father was not against the manifest weight of the evidence. LaMarca v. LaMarca, 78 Ill. App. 3d 26, 33 Ill. Dec. 698, 397 N.E.2d 31 (1 Dist. 1979).

Where ample evidence was presented that while living with husband and his new wife, the children were under constant supervision, appeared happy, and were better behaved than previously, as well as other evidence which indicated that children's schoolwork improved during the period they lived with father finding that modification was necessary to serve the children's best interest was correct. In re Farris, 69 Ill. App. 3d 1042, 26 Ill. Dec. 608, 388 N.E.2d 232 (4 Dist. 1979).

No evidence indicated that wife's living arrangement with man to whom she was not married has adversely affected the children, therefore there was insufficient evidence that a change in custody would have been in the best interest of the children. Burris v. Burris, 70 Ill. App. 3d 503, 26 Ill. Dec. 810, 388 N.E.2d 811 (5 Dist. 1979).

Evidence was sufficient for the court to have found that the circumstances existing at the time of the hearing were greatly changed from the way they appeared to be at the time of the prior agreed upon custody judgment; thus, a change was for the best interest of the child, the child's present environment seriously endangered its emotional health, and the advantages of any change would outweigh any harm to the child. Boggs v. Boggs, 65 Ill. App. 3d 965, 22 Ill. Dec. 645, 383 N.E.2d 9 (4 Dist. 1978).

The evidence was held sufficient to sustain the trial court's order changing custody of a son from his father to his paternal grandparents where the award of custody to the grandparents was not a change of custody but merely a modification of the custody order to conform to the realities of the situation and the trial court's order complied with the standards provided by this section. Barclay v. Barclay, 66 Ill. App. 3d 1028, 23 Ill. Dec. 770, 384 N.E.2d 564 (3 Dist. 1978).

—Preference of Child
Preference of child, indicated in a family services report, was improperly considered by trial court in making a custody modification proceeding. In re Zucco, 150 Ill. App. 3d 146, 103 Ill. Dec. 558, 501 N.E.2d 875 (5 Dist. 1986).

—Previous Orders
Where the court entertained evidence of child abuse by the father previous to a foreign modification, but stated that it was prevented from considering the evidence because it occurred prior to the modification, this was error, for the court had the duty to consider all facts and circumstances which related to the well-being of the children. Hinton v. Searles, 53 Ill. App. 3d 433, 11 Ill. Dec. 329, 368 N.E.2d 937 (5 Dist. 1977).

—Probation Report
A trial judge who granted a modified decree of divorce awarding custody of the children to the husband erred in basing his decree upon the probation officer's report of investigation, and wife's motion for a rehearing should have been granted. Harris v. Spencer, 86 Ill. App. 2d 41, 229 N.E.2d 16 (5 Dist. 1967).

—Religion
Where a father sought modification to educate his child in the Jewish faith, the court should have considered the possible effect on the child of the reaction of the stepfather and the stepbrothers and/or stepsisters with whom the child resided during the greater portion of the year, rather than a report of a psychiatrist who felt the mother could adjust more easily to the child being raised Jewish than the father could adjust to the child being raised Catholic, and as a result he felt that instruction in the Jewish faith would improve the child's relationship with her natural father. Jacobs v. Jacobs, 25 Ill. App. 3d 175, 323 N.E.2d 21 (1 Dist. 1974).

—Social Service's Report
The trial court erred in using a report submitted to it by the Department of Welfare in making its decision regarding whether to change custody of children from mother to father. Perisich v. Perisich, 6 Ill. App. 3d 97, 284 N.E.2d 654 (1 Dist. 1972).

A confidential report from the social service department could not be considered during a custody modification hearing. Des Chatelets v. Des Chatelets, 292 Ill. App. 357, 11 N.E.2d 13 (1 Dist. 1937).

—Sufficiency
It is not necessary for the validity of an order changing custody to another parent that the evidence of new facts establish the present unfitness of the parent to whom custody has been previously entrusted, if other circumstances are clearly shown which require a modification for the welfare of the children. Kline v. Kline, 57 Ill. App. 2d 244, 205 N.E.2d 775 (3 Dist. 1965).

Factors
Although a custodian's suicide attempt may present concerns about a child's welfare, a court may consider the fact the suicide attempt was prompted by the wrongful conduct of the noncustodial parent. In re Gustavson, 247 Ill. App. 3d 797, 187 Ill. Dec. 592, 617 N.E.2d 1313 (4 Dist. 1993), appeal denied, 154 Ill. 2d 559, 197 Ill. Dec. 486, 631 N.E.2d 708 (1994).

While changes in the parent's residence, employment and choice of babysitters are relevant factors in determining the child's best interest, they are not controlling unless they adversely affect the child's welfare. In re Pease, 106 Ill. App. 3d 617, 62 Ill. Dec. 389, 435 N.E.2d 1361 (2 Dist. 1982).

The trial court was correct in stating that, in addition to a finding of the best interests of the children, there are other considerations under this section. Willcutts v. Willcutts, 88 Ill. App. 3d 813, 43 Ill. Dec. 924, 410 N.E.2d 1057 (3 Dist. 1980).

One factor the court may consider before modifying an award is the effect of a parent's work schedule on the ability to care for the child, but the fact that one parent must work outside the home is not controlling, especially when the child at issue has reached school age. Blonsky v. Blonsky, 84 Ill. App. 3d 810, 40 Ill. Dec. 20, 405 N.E.2d 1112 (1 Dist. 1980).

Where the trial court was presented with testimony relating to the factors outlined in subsection (a) of this section, the fact that the court did not explicitly explore its conclusions as to each factor in issuing its order does not establish that the criteria were not utilized. Blonsky v. Blonsky, 84 Ill. App. 3d 810, 40 Ill. Dec. 20, 405 N.E.2d 1112 (1 Dist. 1980).

The list of criteria outlined in subsection (a) of this section was not intended to be exhaustive or necessarily controlling. Blonsky v. Blonsky, 84 Ill. App. 3d 810, 40 Ill. Dec. 20, 405 N.E.2d 1112 (1 Dist. 1980).

Trial court erred in denying father's petition for modification of divorce decree where the evidence showed that, at the father's home, the children would be entering a friendly and loving environment where they would receive proper treatment and attention; they would have the opportunity to spend time with their father and stepmother, who had demonstrated their willingness and desire to care for them and the children would also be near to their friends unlike their present situation where friendships were lacking. Applegate v. Applegate, 80 Ill. App. 3d 81, 35 Ill. Dec. 496, 399 N.E.2d 330 (5 Dist. 1980).

Factors such as remarriage and living quarters, while not controlling, are sufficiently related to a child's welfare, even when involving the parent not then having custody, and those factors can be considered in determining whether there has been a change in circumstances. Caulkins v. Caulkins, 68 Ill. App. 3d 284, 24 Ill. Dec. 827, 385 N.E.2d 1117 (3 Dist. 1979).

It is not necessary for the party seeking a change in custody to show the other party is unfit as a parent, although consideration

Factors (Cont'd)
will be given to the stability of the child's current environment and the ability of each party to provide him with a good home life. Katzer v. Katzer, 61 Ill. App. 3d 299, 18 Ill. Dec. 852, 378 N.E.2d 316 (1 Dist. 1978).

Final Order
It was clear from the substance of a custody order that it was a final custody decision which could be modified only pursuant to the strict standards set forth in this section, even though the order was not final for purposes of appeal. In re Goldman, 196 Ill. App. 3d 785, 143 Ill. Dec. 944, 554 N.E.2d 1016 (1 Dist.), cert. denied, 132 Ill. 2d 544, 144 Ill. Dec. 257, 555 N.E.2d 376 (1990).

Where the appeal was from an order denying a motion to dismiss the petition to modify custody, such an order was not final and appealable; it did not dispose of the controversy or any definite part thereof and no determination as to the custody of the child was made. Jedynak v. Lawrecki, 123 Ill. App. 3d 185, 78 Ill. Dec. 789, 462 N.E.2d 908 (1 Dist. 1984).

Subsection (b) of this section reflects the judgment that in post-dissolution custody proceedings, the finality of the original custody order is more important than a redetermination of which parent should be the custodian. Kraft v. Kraft, 108 Ill. App. 3d 590, 64 Ill. Dec. 240, 439 N.E.2d 491 (1 Dist. 1982).

Findings

—Exact Language Not Required
Although the court did not recite the exact language of this Act pertaining to custody modification, it set forth extensive, detailed findings of fact supporting its decision to modify custody which was sufficient to fulfill the requirements of the statute. In re Kramer, 211 Ill. App. 3d 401, 155 Ill. Dec. 909, 570 N.E.2d 422 (1 Dist. 1991).

—Forfeiture of Privileges
Where former wife had visited children only twice in ten years since divorce decree awarding custody to former husband, the trial court's finding that she had forfeited her rights to custody and visitation privileges and its refusal to modify the original divorce decree was not inequitable, unjust, or erroneous. Huber v. Huber, 26 Ill. App. 2d 207, 167 N.E.2d 431 (2 Dist. 1960).

—Modification Denied
The trial court did not err in failing to make specific findings of fact in support of its decision where a modification was denied, it was sufficient that the court found only that a change in circumstances requiring modification had not been proved. In re Diddens, 255 Ill. App. 3d 850, 192 Ill. Dec. 878, 625 N.E.2d 1033 (3 Dist. 1993).

—Required
This section merely requires the court to state in its decision specific findings of fact which have arisen since the prior judgment or that were unknown to the court at the time of entry of the prior judgment, demonstrating that a change has occurred in the circumstances of the child or his custodian; in addition, the court must find that the modification is necessary to serve the best interest of the child. In re Valter, 191 Ill. App. 3d 584, 138 Ill. Dec. 799, 548 N.E.2d 29 (5 Dist. 1989).

A trial court is required to make explicit findings in support of any modification of custody under the provisions of subsection (b) of this section. Vollmer v. Mattox, 137 Ill. App. 3d 1, 91 Ill. Dec. 752, 484 N.E.2d 311 (5 Dist. 1985).

Where a circuit court specifically found that it would be in the child's best interest to live with his father but failed to find any change of circumstances, which is required to overcome the legislative presumption in favor of respondent who was the present custodial parent, the level of specificity required by subsection (b) of this section was not met. Vollmer v. Mattox, 137 Ill. App. 3d 1, 91 Ill. Dec. 752, 484 N.E.2d 311 (5 Dist. 1985).

—Specific
The initial award of permanent custody under 750 ILCS 5/602 must be distinguished from a later modification of custody under this section; the latter requires findings of fact upon the record but that is because this Act only allows modification for three specified reasons, specific findings of fact by the trial court are needed to insure that the modification rests on a proper basis, however, initial custody awards, are made after an exercise of the trial judge's broad discretion, taking into account all relevant factors. In re Kennedy, 94 Ill. App. 3d 537, 49 Ill. Dec. 927, 418 N.E.2d 947 (1 Dist. 1981).

—Void Judgment
Where a trial court failed to make any specific finding that the children's present environment endangered seriously their physical, mental, moral or emotional health, the failure to expressly make the required findings rendered its judgment void and required that the modification of custody be reversed. Carter v. Carter, 137 Ill. App. 3d 439, 92 Ill. Dec. 320, 484 N.E.2d 1175 (2 Dist. 1985).

Foreign Court's Modification
Appellant, by her conduct in seeking a second custody decree by a California court, was not estopped from asserting her right to recover a money judgment against appellee for past due installments awarded her under the provisions of an Illinois decree. Hallett v. Hallett, 10 Ill. App. 2d 513, 135 N.E.2d 224 (2 Dist. 1956).

Although appellant accepted a lesser sum from a second custody decree rendered in California, she did not abandon the provisions made for her by the decree of an Illinois court. Hallett v. Hallett, 10 Ill. App. 2d 513, 135 N.E.2d 224 (2 Dist. 1956).

Fraud
Fraud which occurs after the court acquires jurisdiction, such as false testimony or concealment, renders the judgment voidable only, subject to collateral attack only under the procedure set out in 735 ILCS 5/2-1401. In re Noble, 192 Ill. App. 3d 501, 139 Ill. Dec. 133, 548 N.E.2d 518 (2 Dist. 1989).

Guardianship
The trial court properly denied the respondent's motion to dismiss the petition brought by minor's mother to terminate the guardianship and return the minor to her which was brought under this Act, where the case did not involve a custody dispute incident to marriage or dissolution of, but rather involved a custody arrangement under the Probate Act (755 ILCS 5/1-1), and mother failed to show how the Act applied to her proceeding. Lyons v. Bute, 107 Ill. 2d 169, 90 Ill. Dec. 892, 483 N.E.2d 210 (1985).

Illustrative Cases
There was no error in decision to change custody to father where: 1) mother had acrimonious reaction to the breakup of her marriage which caused her on several occasions to make immature choices and to put her own welfare ahead of the children's; 2) mother was working with a counselor to help with her own problems and that of her older daughter; and 3) mother would continue to play a significant role in children's lives. In re Melton, 288 Ill. App. 3d 1084, 224 Ill. Dec. 425, 681 N.E.2d 1046 (5 Dist. 1997).

It was not simply the denial of visitation, or the mother's decision to change the child's surname, or any other single factor that prompted the custody change from the mother to the father; these factors were simply outward manifestations of a comprehensive scheme by the mother to deny the child any type of relationship whatsoever with his father. In re Kramer, 211 Ill. App. 3d 401, 155 Ill. Dec. 909, 570 N.E.2d 422 (1 Dist. 1991).

While plaintiff's overall level of attentiveness and concern for her children's welfare left much to be desired, the trial court was correct in basing its ruling on the lack of evidence that the mother's shortcomings had a serious physical, mental, moral, or emotional effect upon the children. In re Clark, 149 Ill. App. 3d 613, 103 Ill. Dec. 21, 500 N.E.2d 1092 (3 Dist. 1986).

Respondent's contention that his children had been integrated into his family with petitioner's consent was without merit. In re Pease, 106 Ill. App. 3d 617, 62 Ill. Dec. 389, 435 N.E.2d 1361 (2 Dist. 1982).

Viewing the evidence in light of the requirements of subsection (b) of this section, judgment of the circuit court denying father's petition to modify the prior custody judgment and award to him physical custody of sons during the school year was not against the manifest weight of the evidence although both sons admitted in camera that they preferred to stay with father, mother had several residences since her divorce, and was remarried during the summer to a man whom the children had never met; there was no indication in the record that these moves had an adverse effect. In re Batchelor, 89 Ill. App. 3d 781, 45 Ill. Dec. 13, 412 N.E.2d 49 (3 Dist. 1980).

Integration

The integration of a child into a family with its various relationships, while no longer a statutory factor, may be considered by a court on a petition for custody; a showing of integration, however, requires more than moving in with parent under the same roof. Ipema v. Dykhuis, 131 Ill. App. 3d 371, 86 Ill. Dec. 728, 475 N.E.2d 1107 (3 Dist. 1985).

Children had not been integrated into father's family with mother's consent during the summers of 1980 and 1981, periods during which the mother entrusted the children to the father's care, in part, because she wanted to afford them a greater opportunity to visit their father and because she was experiencing financial difficulties. In re Wechselberger, 115 Ill. App. 3d 779, 71 Ill. Dec. 506, 450 N.E.2d 1385 (2 Dist. 1983).

Mother's generosity in allowing the father to exercise greater visitation rights than mandated by the court order did not demonstrate that she consented to the integration of her children into the father's family. In re Wechselberger, 115 Ill. App. 3d 779, 71 Ill. Dec. 506, 450 N.E.2d 1385 (2 Dist. 1983).

The consent requirement set forth in former subdivision (b)(2) of this section was intended to ensure that the custodian acquiesce in the transfer of physical custody as a guard against noncustodial kidnapping and should be viewed within that narrow context. People ex rel. Bukovic v. Smith, 98 Ill. App. 3d 144, 53 Ill. Dec. 498, 423 N.E.2d 1302 (1 Dist. 1981).

Although the mother willingly placed the children with their grandparents, since the record did not show that she willingly permitted them to become integrated into their family, the consent requirement of former subdivision (b)(2) of this section was not met. People ex rel. Bukovic v. Smith, 98 Ill. App. 3d 144, 53 Ill. Dec. 498, 423 N.E.2d 1302 (1 Dist. 1981).

When a child of five years spends in excess of a year within a natural parent's home, integration, as that term was used in a former version of this section, can be inferred as a matter of law. Iverson v. Iverson, 83 Ill. App. 3d 493, 39 Ill. Dec. 27, 404 N.E.2d 411 (1 Dist. 1980).

The trial court did not err in considering a child's integration into his father's home without his mother's consent, where the child's integration would not have occurred except for the mother's actions, and the integration was not considered separately but as a part of the home environment. Thompson v. Thompson, 83 Ill. App. 3d 97, 38 Ill. Dec. 485, 403 N.E.2d 716 (3 Dist. 1980).

Joint Custody

—Abuse of Discretion

The trial court abused its discretion under these circumstances in allowing the shifting physical custody of the child to continue. In re Oros, 256 Ill. App. 3d 167, 194 Ill. Dec. 604, 627 N.E.2d 1246 (4 Dist. 1994).

—Burden of Proof

A joint custody arrangement does not alter the burden of proof; the plain language of subsection (b) of this section imposes a "clear and convincing" standard of proof on petitioners who would modify a joint custody arrangement, as well as on those who seek to change a single custody arrangement. In re Jones, 160 Ill. App. 3d 593, 112 Ill. Dec. 572, 513 N.E.2d 1181 (3 Dist. 1987).

—Findings Sufficient

Where the trial judge specifically found that after the marriage had been dissolved, the parties were unable to agree on important aspects of child's care and the judge further found that it was in the best interests of the child to terminate the joint custody order; based on those statements, the trial court made findings that were specific enough to satisfy subsection (b) although the better procedure would have been to reduce those findings to a written order. In re Pfaff, 250 Ill. App. 3d 265, 189 Ill. Dec. 174, 619 N.E.2d 875 (3 Dist. 1993).

—Removal of Child

Trial court's denial of father's request for modification of joint custody and removal of children to Florida would be upheld where father had chosen to move to Florida for the benefit of his relationship with his new wife and in the hope of finding better employment opportunities for himself. In re Jones, 160 Ill. App. 3d 593, 112 Ill. Dec. 572, 513 N.E.2d 1181 (3 Dist. 1987).

—Termination

Where both parents sought to terminate joint custody arrangement, each seeking sole custody, the trial court properly treated it as an agreement to terminate joint custody and did not require clear and convincing evidence that the child would be seriously harmed in the absence of termination. In re Ricketts, 329 Ill. App. 3d 173, 263 Ill. Dec. 753, 768 N.E.2d 834, 2002 Ill. App. LEXIS 321 (2 Dist. 2002).

Where both parties seek to terminate joint custody and stipulate that a change in circumstances has occurred, it is a given that a change in circumstances has occurred and at that juncture the court should move to consider what custody modification is in the child's best interests. In re Lasky, 176 Ill. 2d 75, 223 Ill. Dec. 27, 678 N.E.2d 1035 (1997).

The directive of the second sentence of subsection (b), immediately following the sentence allowing termination of joint custody if both parties agree, indicates that the legislature anticipated a comprehensive scheme whereby a joint custody arrangement may be terminated either by the wishes of the parties or by an order of the court. In re Lasky, 176 Ill. 2d 75, 223 Ill. Dec. 27, 678 N.E.2d 1035 (1997).

Even where the joint custody arrangement is terminated by agreement there is no justification for ignoring the bond which has developed between the child and the primary physical custodian, whether the case is decided under the presumption favoring the present custodian of this section or as an initial award of custody based on the best interest of the child under 750 ILCS 5/602. In re Wycoff, 266 Ill. App. 3d 408, 203 Ill. Dec. 338, 639 N.E.2d 897 (4 Dist.), appeal denied, 158 Ill. 2d 566, 206 Ill. Dec. 847, 645 N.E.2d 1369 (1994).

—Termination by Agreement

Once the parties agreed to terminate the joint parenting agreement, there was no need to show any serious endangerment to the children's physical, mental, moral, or emotional health; subsection (b) clearly provides the trial court shall make any modification which is in the children's best interests. In re Melton, 288 Ill. App. 3d 1084, 224 Ill. Dec. 425, 681 N.E.2d 1046 (5 Dist. 1997).

The legislature changed this section when it enacted the new joint custody statute in 1986, but apparently chose not to eliminate the agreement clause, instead the legislature directed the court to make specific findings "if either parent opposes the modification or termination" language, which indicates the legislature still believed that joint custody could be terminated by agreement. In re Wycoff, 266 Ill. App. 3d 408, 203 Ill. Dec. 338, 639 N.E.2d 897 (4 Dist.), appeal denied, 158 Ill. 2d 566, 206 Ill. Dec. 847, 645 N.E.2d 1369 (1994).

Jurisdiction

The fact alone that there was no pending petition or motion before the court did not deprive the court of the authority to modify custody where the parties agreed in a stipulation concerning some matters that required resolution by the court and agreed to joint legal and physical custody. People ex rel. Gibbs v. Ketchum, 284 Ill. App. 3d 70, 219 Ill. Dec. 696, 671 N.E.2d 1149 (4 Dist. 1996), appeal denied, 171 Ill. 2d 584, 222 Ill. Dec. 437, 677 N.E.2d 971 (1997).

Court views with suspicion any major modification of a custody decree rendered while the children and other parent are not present in the jurisdiction. Hinton v. Searles, 53 Ill. App. 3d 433, 11 Ill. Dec. 329, 368 N.E.2d 937 (5 Dist. 1977).

Where the modification of the decree in the foreign court was obtained without the presence of respondent or the children, there could be no informed decision of what action was in the best interests of the children. Hinton v. Searles, 53 Ill. App. 3d 433, 11 Ill. Dec. 329, 368 N.E.2d 937 (5 Dist. 1977).

The court's jurisdiction to alter custody and support of the children is exclusive and continuing until the child or children attain their majority, and the decree or order fixing the custody of the child or children is final only as to the conditions then existing. Eggemeyer v. Eggemeyer, 86 Ill. App. 2d 224, 229 N.E.2d 144 (2 Dist. 1967).

Parents ought to be bound by the custodial features of a decree to which they were both parties if the court rendering the decree had jurisdiction of the subject matter and of them. Sharpe v. Sharpe, 77 Ill. App. 2d 295, 222 N.E.2d 340 (4 Dist. 1966).

Legislative Intent

The limitation on custody modification within two years, absent

Legislative Intent (Cont'd)
serious endangerment, is a legislative attempt to provide stability and continuity in the child's life by preventing the "ping-pong" litigation of custody disputes, yet provide a "safety valve" for the modification of custody in emergency situations. Naylor v. Kindred, 250 Ill. App. 3d 997, 189 Ill. Dec. 552, 620 N.E.2d 520 (4 Dist. 1993).

A former version of subsection (b) of this section reflected an underlying policy favoring the finality of child custody judgments and making their modification more difficult; this subsection further created a presumption in favor of the present custodian in order to promote stability and continuity in the child's custodial and environmental relationships, which were not to be lightly overturned. In re Padiak, 101 Ill. App. 3d 306, 56 Ill. Dec. 826, 427 N.E.2d 1372 (2 Dist. 1981).

By creating a presumption in favor of the custodian appointed pursuant to the prior judgment, the legislature has sought to promote stability and continuity in the child's custodial and environmental relationship which is not to be lightly overturned. In re Gebis, 100 Ill. App. 3d 710, 56 Ill. Dec. 280, 427 N.E.2d 360 (1 Dist. 1981).

Subsection (b) of this section reflects an underlying policy favoring the finality of child custody judgments, and making their modification more difficult. Harne v. Johnson, 77 Ill. 2d 414, 33 Ill. Dec. 110, 396 N.E.2d 499 (1979); In re Poston, 77 Ill. App. 3d 689, 33 Ill. Dec. 187, 396 N.E.2d 576 (3 Dist. 1979); In re Gebis, 100 Ill. App. 3d 710, 56 Ill. Dec. 280, 427 N.E.2d 360 (1 Dist. 1981); In re Wechselberger, 115 Ill. App. 3d 779, 71 Ill. Dec. 506, 450 N.E.2d 1385 (2 Dist. 1983); Vollmer v. Mattox, 137 Ill. App. 3d 1, 91 Ill. Dec. 752, 484 N.E.2d 311 (5 Dist. 1985); In re Lichtenstein, 139 Ill. App. 3d 881, 94 Ill. Dec. 416, 487 N.E.2d 1293 (5 Dist. 1986); In re Eldert, 158 Ill. App. 3d 798, 110 Ill. Dec. 768, 511 N.E.2d 945 (3 Dist. 1987), appeal denied, 117 Ill. Dec. 224, 520 N.E.2d 385 (Ill. 1988); In re Gibbons, 158 Ill. App. 3d 998, 111 Ill. Dec. 148, 512 N.E.2d 52 (4 Dist. 1987); In re Miller, 170 Ill. App. 3d 1044, 121 Ill. Dec. 17, 524 N.E.2d 1065 (1 Dist. 1988); In re Engelbach, 181 Ill. App. 3d 563, 130 Ill. Dec. 305, 537 N.E.2d 372 (2 Dist. 1989); In re Valter, 191 Ill. App. 3d 584, 138 Ill. Dec. 799, 548 N.E.2d 29 (5 Dist. 1989); In re Noble, 192 Ill. App. 3d 501, 139 Ill. Dec. 133, 548 N.E.2d 518 (2 Dist. 1989); In re Cesaretti, 203 Ill. App. 3d 347, 149 Ill. Dec. 28, 561 N.E.2d 306 (2 Dist. 1990); In re Dunn, 208 Ill. App. 3d 1033, 153 Ill. Dec. 805, 567 N.E.2d 763 (5 Dist. 1991).

Loss of Parent
A significant change occurred in the circumstances of children who lost their custodial parent. Markham v. Markham, 91 Ill. App. 3d 1122, 47 Ill. Dec. 235, 414 N.E.2d 1351 (3 Dist. 1981).

Mandatory Provision
This subsection is a mandatory, rather than a directory, provision, because the consequence of noncompliance, that the child custody modification motion be disallowed, is clearly provided. In re Noble, 192 Ill. App. 3d 501, 139 Ill. Dec. 133, 548 N.E.2d 518 (2 Dist. 1989).

The affidavit requirement of subsection (a) of this section is a mandatory, rather than a directory, provision, because the consequence of noncompliance, that the child custody modification motion be disallowed, is clearly provided in this Act; however, holding this provision mandatory, does not establish that subsection (a) of this section as a jurisdictional requirement in the sense that it cannot be waived. Sexton v. Sexton, 84 Ill. 2d 312, 49 Ill. Dec. 709, 418 N.E.2d 729 (1981).

Moral Fitness
Allegedly immoral conduct, in and of itself, without a showing of detriment to the children, was insufficient proof of unfitness for petition for custody change. Burris v. Burris, 70 Ill. App. 3d 503, 26 Ill. Dec. 810, 388 N.E.2d 811 (5 Dist. 1979).

Indulgence in moral indiscretions alone is not grounds for a change of custody where the children are leading a normal life. Rippon v. Rippon, 64 Ill. App. 3d 465, 21 Ill. Dec. 135, 381 N.E.2d 70 (3 Dist. 1978).

Evidence concerning the moral fitness of a divorced woman's second husband is relevant to the issue whether she should continue to have custody of her children. Johnson v. Johnson, 34 Ill. App. 3d 356, 340 N.E.2d 68 (1 Dist. 1975).

Parentage Order
A parentage order did not constitute a prior custody order where the order did not address the issues of custody, visitation and amount of support, and it explicitly provided for further proceedings in the case. Upmann ex rel. Upmann-Terhark v. Terhark, 200 Ill. App. 3d 827, 146 Ill. Dec. 605, 558 N.E.2d 568 (2 Dist. 1990).

Permanent Order
While a custody order may not have been final for appeal purposes, (i.e., the property arrangements had yet to be determined and it was not a written order), it was a conscious modification of the two year old temporary custody arrangement where it came after the grant of divorce and after several days of testimony devoted solely to the custody question; thus subsequent custody order should have been viewed as a modification of a permanent order, requiring non-custodial parent to prove unfitness by the custodial parent. Carroll v. Carroll, 64 Ill. App. 3d 925, 21 Ill. Dec. 713, 382 N.E.2d 7 (1 Dist. 1978).

Physical Custody

—Award to Father Upheld
In case in which both parents had joint custody of child, change awarding physical custody to father would be upheld. In re England, 158 Ill. App. 3d 1005, 111 Ill. Dec. 191, 512 N.E.2d 95 (4 Dist. 1987).

Court did not err in awarding custody of boy to his father even though the parties with whom the boy was living could do more for the boy in a financial way than his father could. Kent v. Kent, 315 Ill. App. 284, 42 N.E.2d 958 (4 Dist. 1942).

—Award to Mother
While the parties shared custody, the judgment for dissolution gave mother the primary physical custody of son and thus, the trial court properly could have considered this factor in maintaining the primary physical custody of son with mother. In re Kartholl, 143 Ill. App. 3d 228, 97 Ill. Dec. 347, 492 N.E.2d 1006 (2 Dist. 1986).

Despite a defendant's attempts to demonstrate that his child had been so integrated into the defendant's family life that to return the child to his mother in Arizona would be detrimental to his well-being, the trial judge's ruling giving custody to the mother was not against the manifest weight of the evidence. Santos v. Santos, 97 Ill. App. 3d 629, 52 Ill. Dec. 776, 422 N.E.2d 985 (3 Dist. 1981).

It used to be usual in custody cases, due to the tender years of the child and in consideration of its best interest, to entrust the care and custody to the mother, if a fit person. Frees v. Frees, 99 Ill. App. 2d 213, 240 N.E.2d 274 (1 Dist. 1968).

—Child's Welfare
Where a child's welfare is at stake, care must be taken that its welfare is not impaired by being shuttled between contesting parents. Collings v. Collings, 120 Ill. App. 2d 125, 256 N.E.2d 108 (2 Dist. 1970).

Pleadings
The court cannot modify custody under 750 ILCS 5/607.1 absent a petition to modify pursuant to this section or 750 ILCS 5/602. In re M.M.W., 296 Ill. App. 3d 877, 231 Ill. Dec. 238, 695 N.E.2d 1357 (2 Dist. 1998).

Petitioner should not have been barred from raising certain allegations in a petition to modify a custody order merely because some of the same allegations were included in earlier pleadings which were dismissed for failure to follow technical procedures of this section. In re Weaver, 228 Ill. App. 3d 609, 170 Ill. Dec. 207, 592 N.E.2d 643 (4 Dist. 1992).

A petition to change the primary custody of a child, though not a petition to undo joint custody, is a modification under this section. In re Noble, 192 Ill. App. 3d 501, 139 Ill. Dec. 133, 548 N.E.2d 518 (2 Dist. 1989).

Although respondent's verified petition does not use the term "endangerment" in the allegations, it does represent by its allegations that petitioner's present husband has a past history of criminal charges relating to the abuse of minors and that respondent's children are, in effect, being exposed to danger or harm by residing with petitioner and her husband. In re Kading, 150 Ill. App. 3d 623, 103 Ill. Dec. 654, 501 N.E.2d 971 (2 Dist. 1986).

Where a petition in the instant case was filed within two years but did not allege the required statutory grounds under subsection (a) of this section of endangerment to the child by present environment, the petition was subject to a dismissal motion. Ipema v.

Pleadings (Cont'd)
Dykhuis, 131 Ill. App. 3d 371, 86 Ill. Dec. 728, 475 N.E.2d 1107 (3 Dist. 1985).

The matter of visitation was placed in issue by husband's filing a petition requesting, inter alia, that because of wife's cohabiting with another on a resident, continuing conjugal basis, custody be changed to him, as well as husband's petition that wife be held in contempt for failure to accord him visitation. In re Stanley, 133 Ill. App. 3d 963, 89 Ill. Dec. 146, 479 N.E.2d 1152 (4 Dist. 1985).

—Timeliness
Where the trial court issued the permanent custody order in October 2001 and a final judgment in the custody case in September 2002, the father's September 2002 motion to reconsider, filed pursuant to 735 ILCS 5/2-1203, was not timely filed, as it should have been filed within 30 days of the October 2001 order; furthermore, the motion did not satisfy the requirements of 750 ILCS 5/610 for a motion seeking a modification of custody, as the two-year proscription on motions to modify custody, which started to run in October 2001, had not expired. Marsh v. Marsh, 343 Ill. App. 3d 1235, 279 Ill. Dec. 234, 799 N.E.2d 1037, 2003 Ill. App. LEXIS 1389 (4 Dist. 2003).

Preference of Child
Preferences of a child are only appropriate when based on reasons related to their best welfare. In re Jones, 160 Ill. App. 3d 593, 112 Ill. Dec. 572, 513 N.E.2d 1181 (3 Dist. 1987).

The preferences of young children, though entitled to consideration, are not binding upon the court. In re Kush, 106 Ill. App. 3d 233, 62 Ill. Dec. 123, 435 N.E.2d 921 (3 Dist. 1982).

A child's preference for a change of custodial parent, without showing that the welfare of the child is affected, is not a sufficient change of circumstances to warrant a custody change. Wells v. Wells, 36 Ill. App. 3d 488, 344 N.E.2d 37 (2 Dist. 1976); Hinton v. Searles, 53 Ill. App. 3d 433, 11 Ill. Dec. 329, 368 N.E.2d 937 (5 Dist. 1977); Caulkins v. Caulkins, 68 Ill. App. 3d 284, 24 Ill. Dec. 827, 385 N.E.2d 1117 (3 Dist. 1979); Applegate v. Applegate, 80 Ill. App. 3d 81, 35 Ill. Dec. 496, 399 N.E.2d 330 (5 Dist. 1980); In re Valter, 191 Ill. App. 3d 584, 138 Ill. Dec. 799, 548 N.E.2d 29 (5 Dist. 1989); In re Apperson, 215 Ill. App. 3d 378, 158 Ill. Dec. 864, 574 N.E.2d 1257 (4 Dist. 1991).

Preferences of a child for change in custodial arrangements should be considered only when based on reasons related to a child's best welfare. Swanson v. Swanson, 1 Ill. App. 3d 753, 274 N.E.2d 465 (3 Dist. 1971).

The positive refusal of the child, a young man of 14 years of age, and his stated preference to remain with his paternal grandmother, was certainly entitled to serious consideration by the trial court. Marcus v. Marcus, 109 Ill. App. 2d 423, 248 N.E.2d 800 (1 Dist. 1969).

A child's preference may properly be a factor to be considered by the court to determine custody, but when custody has once been awarded, it may not properly be changed on that ground alone. Stickler v. Stickler, 57 Ill. App. 2d 286, 206 N.E.2d 720 (1 Dist. 1965).

—Evidence Held Insufficient
The evidence that son wished to live with his father and the father's testimony that son's feelings were so strong that he threatened to run away if not permitted to do so was not sufficient by itself to warrant change in custody. Blankenship v. Blankenship, 63 Ill. App. 3d 803, 20 Ill. Dec. 956, 380 N.E.2d 1165 (4 Dist. 1978).

—Immaturity
The desires of immature children are not controlling. In re Riess, 260 Ill. App. 3d 210, 198 Ill. Dec. 305, 632 N.E.2d 635 (2 Dist. 1994).

—Transfer Unwarranted
Where the children told the court that they were happy and preferred to live with their mother, the children mentioned that they liked school where they were living and had made some friends there, and respondent testified that the younger boy was receiving special help for a speech problem, and that the school in which the children were enrolled had special classes for just such problems, it was against the manifest weight of the evidence for the trial court to transfer custody to the father. Hinton v. Searles, 53 Ill. App. 3d 433, 11 Ill. Dec. 329, 368 N.E.2d 937 (5 Dist. 1977).

Preservation of Family
The preservation of the existing family unit is an element to be considered in determining the best interests of the children, with regard to a petition for removal but it is only one of many elements. In re Berk, 215 Ill. App. 3d 459, 158 Ill. Dec. 971, 574 N.E.2d 1364 (2 Dist.), cert. denied, 141 Ill. 2d 536, 162 Ill. Dec. 482, 580 N.E.2d 108 (1991).

Presumption

—Present Custodian
The presumption of continued custody remained with the child's mother as the parent having the right of physical possession under the terms of the court ordered custody arrangement and did not shift to favor the father simply because he had de facto physical custody pursuant to the agreement of the parties. In re Childers, 305 Ill. App. 3d 70, 238 Ill. Dec. 353, 711 N.E.2d 456 (2 Dist. 1999).

The statute creates a legislative presumption in favor of the present custodian and environmental relationship that is not to be overturned lightly. In re Childers, 305 Ill. App. 3d 70, 238 Ill. Dec. 353, 711 N.E.2d 456 (2 Dist. 1999).

By creating a presumption in favor of the present custodian, the legislature in this section has sought to promote stability and continuity in the child's custodial and environmental relationships which is not to be lightly overturned. In re Wycoff, 266 Ill. App. 3d 408, 203 Ill. Dec. 338, 639 N.E.2d 897 (4 Dist.), appeal denied, 158 Ill. 2d 566, 206 Ill. Dec. 847, 645 N.E.2d 1369 (1994).

Previous Orders
The trial court in its consideration of the best interest of the children can make a just determination without being hindered by a previous order in another court. Hinton v. Searles, 53 Ill. App. 3d 433, 11 Ill. Dec. 329, 368 N.E.2d 937 (5 Dist. 1977).

Psychologist's Testimony
Although it was found that the submission of a child's representative's report without the mother being allowed to cross-examine in a custody hearing denied the mother due process, the error was harmless because the mother received the report prior to the modification hearing under § 610 of the Illinois Marriage and Dissolution of Marriage Act, 750 ILCS 5/610, and presented no evidence to rebut the report, and there was substantial expert testimony that supported the conclusion that the mother had consistently failed to facilitate and encourage a close and continuing relationship between the child and the father under 750 ILCS 5/602. In re Marriage of De Bates, 212 Ill. 2d 489, 289 Ill. Dec. 218, 819 N.E.2d 714, 2004 Ill. LEXIS 1619 (2004).

In custody modification proceedings, the examining psychologist's testimony is entitled to great weight. In re Dunn, 208 Ill. App. 3d 1033, 153 Ill. Dec. 805, 567 N.E.2d 763 (5 Dist. 1991).

Punitive Remedy
Change of custody is an improper remedy to punish a custodial parent's contumacious interference with visitation rights. In re Fox, 191 Ill. App. 3d 514, 138 Ill. Dec. 841, 548 N.E.2d 71 (4 Dist. 1989).

Where order made no finding of unfitness, nor did it recite anything from which that finding was implicit, nor did it show that it would be in the best interest of a six year old child to place her in a boarding school until she had completed her high school education, and it appeared that the child was used as the basis for punishing the mother for the mother's alleged wilful disregard of the court's orders; this method of securing obedience to a court's order was not in the best interest of the child and the record failed to show justification for a change of custody. Szczawinski v. Szczawinski, 37 Ill. App. 2d 350, 185 N.E.2d 375 (1 Dist. 1962).

Purpose
The rationale for this provision was to provide stability and permanency in children's custodial and environmental relationships. In re Pease, 106 Ill. App. 3d 617, 62 Ill. Dec. 389, 435 N.E.2d 1361 (2 Dist. 1982).

Religion
The trial court's judgment that the mother had displayed a tendency to make rigid unilateral decisions concerning the child without adequate deliberation or consultation, which involved religious matters to some extent, was an improper consideration of religious issues by the court since it was not determining the

Religion (Cont'd)
validity of the choices made, only the manner in which they were made. Blonsky v. Blonsky, 84 Ill. App. 3d 810, 40 Ill. Dec. 20, 405 N.E.2d 1112 (1 Dist. 1980).

It was not an abuse of discretion to modify divorce decree by transferring custody of child from father to mother, even though child had been brought up as a Catholic by father, and mother was married to Protestant by whom she was pregnant when she divorced former husband and with whom she had raised the second child in Protestant home, where she promised she would raise child of first marriage as a Catholic. Frank v. Frank, 26 Ill. App. 2d 16, 167 N.E.2d 577 (1 Dist. 1960).

Remarriage

A subsequent marriage of a parent and stability of environment are important considerations in child custody modification proceedings. Kjellesvik v. Shannon, 41 Ill. App. 3d 674, 355 N.E.2d 120 (3 Dist. 1976).

—Effect on Custody

The court did not err in allowing former husband to maintain custody of the two minor children even though former wife had remarried and could provide a better home for the children than she could at the time when they were placed in defendant's custody and defendant at times had been in arrears of his support payments. Vanderlaan v. Vanderlaan, 9 Ill. App. 3d 260, 292 N.E.2d 145 (1 Dist.), cert. granted, 405 U.S. 1051, 92 S. Ct. 1488, 31 L. Ed. 2d 787 (1972).

—Of Custodial Parent

While the admissibility of a criminal conviction in a subsequent civil proceeding has been limited to use against the party convicted, such a strict application of the rule in a child custody proceeding following one parent's remarriage would bar introduction of any evidence of the new spouse's criminal record, and such a result in a proceeding primarily concerned with the best interests of the children ignores the purpose of the proceeding and is contrary to common sense. In re Engelbach, 181 Ill. App. 3d 563, 130 Ill. Dec. 305, 537 N.E.2d 372 (2 Dist. 1989).

A change in circumstances justifying a modification of child custody need not relate solely to the custodial parent, and the remarriage of the custodial parent and subsequent stability of environment are important considerations. In re Engelbach, 181 Ill. App. 3d 563, 130 Ill. Dec. 305, 537 N.E.2d 372 (2 Dist. 1989).

Modification of custody may be proper where the remarriage of the custodial parent affects the welfare of the child. In re Engelbach, 181 Ill. App. 3d 563, 130 Ill. Dec. 305, 537 N.E.2d 372 (2 Dist. 1989).

Because the remarriage of the custodial parent results in the children living and associating with the new spouse, evidence bearing on the character of that person is relevant in a custody proceeding. In re Engelbach, 181 Ill. App. 3d 563, 130 Ill. Dec. 305, 537 N.E.2d 372 (2 Dist. 1989).

Respondent should have been permitted to rebut the evidence of her new husband's criminal convictions when such evidence was introduced for purposes of petitioner's motion for a custodial change. In re Engelbach, 181 Ill. App. 3d 563, 130 Ill. Dec. 305, 537 N.E.2d 372 (2 Dist. 1989).

—Preference of Child

Where each parent remarried but neither the father nor the trial court indicated how or in what manner such remarriages had an adverse effect on the existing custodial provision awarding custody of the child to her mother, although the child preferred to live with her father, the child's preference was not an appropriate basis for modifying the custodial provisions in a decree. Swanson v. Swanson, 1 Ill. App. 3d 753, 274 N.E.2d 465 (3 Dist. 1971).

—Sufficient

The chancellor was amply justified in modifying the decree by awarding the custody of the children to the plaintiff, where defendant had hastily married an unfit party. Serotzke v. Serotzke, 335 Ill. App. 485, 82 N.E.2d 375 (1 Dist. 1948).

Removal of Child

—In General

The removal of child to another jurisdiction, standing alone, is not sufficient grounds to warrant a change in custody and where record was devoid of any evidence of findings which would warrant a change in custody pursuant to this section, trial court's denial of petition to modify custody was proper. In re Feliciano, 103 Ill. App. 3d 666, 59 Ill. Dec. 363, 431 N.E.2d 1120 (1 Dist. 1981).

—Burden of Proof

A custodial parent petitioning to remove a child from Illinois has the burden of proving that removal is in the child's best interest. Winebright v. Winebright, 155 Ill. App. 3d 722, 108 Ill. Dec. 463, 508 N.E.2d 774 (3 Dist. 1987).

—Close Scrutiny Required

Where the parents have shared physical custody and parenting time almost equally and where father's removal request would alter children's environment in a material way, the request of one parent to remove the child from Illinois should be given particularly close judicial scrutiny. In re Jones, 160 Ill. App. 3d 593, 112 Ill. Dec. 572, 513 N.E.2d 1181 (3 Dist. 1987).

—Distinguished from Custody

Where the court allowed both a petition for removal under 750 ILCS 5/609 and one for change in custody under this section to be consolidated into one hearing, the trial court erred in issuing one order discussing its findings of fact and its decision denying the petition to remove and allowing the petition for change in physical custody; the trial court should have ruled on the petition to remove first, because had the court denied the petition, the basis for the change in custody petition would have been eliminated. In re Ballegeer, 236 Ill. App. 3d 941, 176 Ill. Dec. 906, 602 N.E.2d 852 (3 Dist. 1992).

This section and 750 ILCS 5/609 clearly distinguish between petitions for removal and petitions to modify custody, and evidence that the father was a more suitable custodian and that the father's town was a better place for the child to live than Arizona, the location where the mother intended to move, was irrelevant with regard to the removal petition; the trial court should have focused instead on whether the child's best interests would be served by living with his mother, the custodial parent, in Illinois or moving with her to Arizona. In re Gratz, 193 Ill. App. 3d 142, 139 Ill. Dec. 611, 548 N.E.2d 1325 (2 Dist. 1989).

—From Jurisdiction

While removal of a child from the jurisdiction was not alone sufficient grounds for a change of custody, this conduct indicated that mother placed her children in a secondary position to that of her new husband and career, and supported the trial court's determination to modify custody. In re Gunter, 93 Ill. App. 3d 1043, 49 Ill. Dec. 505, 418 N.E.2d 149 (1 Dist. 1981).

Where the father, who had custody of the minor child, had moved to Mississippi with the child since the hearing, any modification of the custody order because of changes in circumstances arising since the hearing should have been initiated in the trial court pursuant to this section. Melear v. Melear, 76 Ill. App. 3d 706, 32 Ill. Dec. 261, 395 N.E.2d 208 (3 Dist. 1979).

In view of modern living conditions, to say that as a fixed rule of law, without exception, a child may never be taken from the state out of the jurisdiction of the court seems harsh and absurd, and this is especially true where the court has retained jurisdiction in the matter and appellee has entered into a bond to carry out the terms of the decree. Schmidt v. Schmidt, 346 Ill. App. 436, 105 N.E.2d 117 (2 Dist. 1952).

—Jurisdiction

There were insufficient facts presented to the court to support any change in custody even though respondent removed the children to another state without the permission of the court, and even though such conduct cannot be condoned, the removal of the child from the jurisdiction was not alone sufficient grounds for a change of custody. Potts v. Potts, 83 Ill. App. 3d 518, 39 Ill. Dec. 62, 404 N.E.2d 446 (1 Dist. 1980).

—Limitation Period

Since the two year limitation in subsection (a) of this section applies to custody modification, and since removal is no more a matter of custody than is modification of visitation rights, the two year prohibition to removal petitions does not apply; the legislature chose not to impose the prohibition in either the provision of the Act

Removal of Child (Cont'd)

—Limitation Period (Cont'd)
governing modification of visitation rights (750 ILCS 5/607) or the provision governing leave to remove minor children from Illinois (750 ILCS 5/609). Mueller v. Weis, 76 Ill. App. 3d 860, 32 Ill. Dec. 447, 395 N.E.2d 677 (5 Dist. 1979).

—Not Modification
The possibility that removal of a child from the jurisdiction of this state to another may adversely affect the non-custodial parent's interaction with the child does not compel the conclusion that a removal petition is, as a matter of law, a petition for modification of custody. Instead, the impact of removal upon the rights of the nonresidential custodial parent is a significant and important factor the trial court considers in its adjudication of whether removal would be in the child's best interests. In re Bednar, 146 Ill. App. 3d 704, 100 Ill. Dec. 84, 496 N.E.2d 1149 (1 Dist. 1986).

—Out-of-State Residence
There was nothing unusual or harsh in permitting a child to leave the state to be with his mother, if the child would thereby have a good home, the best of care, and the love of his mother and stepfather. Schmidt v. Schmidt, 346 Ill. App. 436, 105 N.E.2d 117 (2 Dist. 1952).

—Petition Not Required
In cases where the parties were never married, the custodial parent is not required to file a petition for removal, thus, the court will not yet have engaged in a best interest of the child analysis to determine whether the custodial parent should be allowed to remove the minor child from the state, therefore, where the parties were never married, the fact that a custodial parent wishes to move out of the state with the minor child is sufficient to show a change of circumstances which would satisfy the first prong of this section and the court would then be required to engage in a best interests of the child analysis, utilizing the factors enumerated in 750 ILCS 5/602. In re R.M.F., 275 Ill. App. 3d 43, 211 Ill. Dec. 754, 655 N.E.2d 1137 (2 Dist. 1995).

Res Judicata
A petition to modify custody of child was not barred by res judicata or collateral estoppel even though the appeal was filed more than two years after the order. In re Weaver, 228 Ill. App. 3d 609, 170 Ill. Dec. 207, 592 N.E.2d 643 (4 Dist. 1992).
If the trial court that entered the original custody order hears a petition pursuant to this section while the original order is on appeal and denies relief, the appeal would not suffer interference since, if the trial court grants relief, the original appeal may become moot. In re Spangler, 124 Ill. App. 3d 1023, 80 Ill. Dec. 137, 464 N.E.2d 1120 (4 Dist. 1984).
Because of the res judicata effect that the trial court must give to the original order on appeal, the authority of the reviewing court to pass on the propriety of the original order is not infringed upon by the trial court. In re Spangler, 124 Ill. App. 3d 1023, 80 Ill. Dec. 137, 464 N.E.2d 1120 (4 Dist. 1984).

Residence
While a change in the custodial parent's residence is a relevant factor in determining a child's best interest, it is not controlling unless it adversely affects the child's welfare. In re Lichtenstein, 139 Ill. App. 3d 881, 94 Ill. Dec. 416, 487 N.E.2d 1293 (5 Dist. 1986).

Revocation
It would be inconsistent with the policies of stability and continuity underlying this section to allow revocation of consent by one parent once the child has become settled into her new family with the acquiescence of the custodial parent. Burnett v. Burnett, 75 Ill. App. 3d 998, 31 Ill. Dec. 142, 394 N.E.2d 58 (2 Dist. 1979).

School Attendance

—In General
Where the onset of the child's school years required a change in custody arrangements in order to serve child's best interest, the trial court did not err in failing to articulate the change in circumstances upon which its order was based. In re Zucco, 150 Ill. App. 3d 146, 103 Ill. Dec. 558, 501 N.E.2d 875 (5 Dist. 1986).

The trial court's conclusion that there was a connection between stepson's chores on the farm and his showing in school was incorrect where there is no indication that his chores tired him out so that he was unable to do the work assigned to him or that his chores left him no time to do school work and especially where the boy's poor performance in the fifth grade, up until the time of the hearing, could be attributed to other factors besides his chores, including his relationship with his teacher and the principal and the pressure and disturbance caused by the custody proceedings. In re Poston, 77 Ill. App. 3d 689, 33 Ill. Dec. 187, 396 N.E.2d 576 (3 Dist. 1979).
Where the original decree awarded the mother the right to control the education of the child, that right encompassed the right to select the schools the child shall attend. Jacobs v. Jacobs, 25 Ill. App. 3d 175, 323 N.E.2d 21 (1 Dist. 1974).

—Parent Attending School
The fact that mother must leave the children when she works or attends school does not, alone, require a court to award custody to the father as a matter of law. In re Kush, 106 Ill. App. 3d 233, 62 Ill. Dec. 123, 435 N.E.2d 921 (3 Dist. 1982).

Scope
Litigation that is neither a motion for temporary custody nor an initial custody determination, but rather a modification of the original custody order, is governed by the dictates of this section and not by 750 ILCS 5/602 and 750 ILCS 5/603. In re Strader, 101 Ill. App. 3d 779, 57 Ill. Dec. 232, 428 N.E.2d 912 (5 Dist. 1981).

Stability
Stability of environment is an important factor in determining a child's best interest for the purposes of awarding custody. Russell v. Kellum, 80 Ill. App. 3d 41, 35 Ill. Dec. 378, 399 N.E.2d 212 (5 Dist. 1979).
In a custody modification, the court can consider the stability of the children's environment in judging their best interests. De Franco v. De Franco, 67 Ill. App. 3d 760, 24 Ill. Dec. 130, 384 N.E.2d 997 (1 Dist. 1978).
In determining what is in a child's best interest, stability of environment is an important factor. Rippon v. Rippon, 64 Ill. App. 3d 465, 21 Ill. Dec. 135, 381 N.E.2d 70 (3 Dist. 1978); In re Pease, 106 Ill. App. 3d 617, 62 Ill. Dec. 389, 435 N.E.2d 1361 (2 Dist. 1982).

Statute of Limitations
Two-year proscription under 750 ILCS 5/610(a) on motions to modify custody, absent affidavits showing serious endangerment, starts to run when the trial court enters a permanent custody order, regardless of whether such an order is entered contemporaneously to the final judgment of dissolution or earlier in the dissolution proceedings; accordingly, if a trial court bifurcates proceedings and a previously entered custody order goes unchallenged for many months, the date upon which the final judgment of dissolution is entered is irrelevant for purposes of calculating the § 610(a) two-year proscription period. Marsh v. Marsh, 343 Ill. App. 3d 1235, 279 Ill. Dec. 234, 799 N.E.2d 1037, 2003 Ill. App. LEXIS 1389 (4 Dist. 2003).

Stipulation
This section forecloses the practice of hearing a modification petition de novo if the original custody judgment had been entered by stipulation. In re Strader, 101 Ill. App. 3d 779, 57 Ill. Dec. 232, 428 N.E.2d 912 (5 Dist. 1981).

Technical Defect in Order
Where the evidence clearly and convincingly rebutted the presumption in favor of the original custodial order and established that a change in custody was necessary to serve the child's best interest, the trial court did not err in transferring custody even though it failed to specifically state in its order that it had found a change in circumstances. Boyd v. Sussenbach, 108 Ill. 2d 489, 92 Ill. Dec. 556, 485 N.E.2d 367 (1985).

Temporary Award
Where the only custody order in effect at the time of custody award was a temporary award of custody to respondent until a custody hearing was held, the order from which respondent appealed was not a modification of a previous custody judgment; therefore, subsection (a) of the Act was inapplicable. In re Arcaute,

Temporary Award (Cont'd)
261 Ill. App. 3d 263, 198 Ill. Dec. 471, 632 N.E.2d 1082 (3 Dist. 1994).

Terms Used

The terms "custody judgment" and "prior custody judgment" as stated in this section refer to final rather than temporary orders of custody. Doyle v. Doyle, 62 Ill. App. 3d 786, 19 Ill. Dec. 723, 379 N.E.2d 387 (4 Dist. 1978).

Transfer of Custody

Where support obligation and visitation rights were established in the respondent, along with a prior judgment of parentage, when respondent filed petition to transfer custody it should have been treated as a motion to modify custody under this section rather than treated as if it were an initial custody determination under 750 ILCS 5/602. In re M.M.W., 296 Ill. App. 3d 877, 231 Ill. Dec. 238, 695 N.E.2d 1357 (2 Dist. 1998).

Vacation of Order

Where neither the court nor the petitioner cited a lack of jurisdiction, never moved to vacate the judgment, and made no allegation of fraud or misrepresentation, where petitioner asserted only that in the best interest of his child, he should be granted primary custody, the court erred in vacating its original custody order granting equitable relief where it was not prayed for. In re Noble, 192 Ill. App. 3d 501, 139 Ill. Dec. 133, 548 N.E.2d 518 (2 Dist. 1989).

Visitation

The trial court did not err in a child custody proceeding where the evidence was held sufficient to sustain a judge's order that expanded the mother's visitation rights but left custody with the father. Patton v. Armstrong, 16 Ill. App. 3d 881, 307 N.E.2d 178 (5 Dist. 1974).

The order of the trial court allowing defendant to take the child out of plaintiff's home every Sunday between 11:30 a.m. and 5:30 p.m. would not materially abridge plaintiff's rights to the custody of the child; neither would it interfere with the general welfare of the child, nor with the regular care and sleep needed by the child. Blonsley v. Blonsley, 52 Ill. App. 2d 391, 202 N.E.2d 70 (1 Dist. 1964).

An order allowing the father to have the children in his home for a month in the summers and two days in each October and March was a modification of the visitation privilege rather than a change in custody. Ruberts v. Ruberts, 4 Ill. App. 2d 134, 123 N.E.2d 737 (2 Dist. 1955).

The court erred in its order modifying the decree of divorce which in effect provided that the defendant father need pay no more for the support of the minor children except when he requested that they be brought to his home, when he was required to pay plaintiff $30 on each and every occasion. Kemp v. Kemp, 332 Ill. App. 432, 75 N.E.2d 385 (1 Dist. 1947).

—Upheld

The trial court could properly find that mother's home environment endangered her child's health, yet still permit her liberal visitation, including a month-long visit at her home, because even though the trial court found that the home environment was not sufficiently stable for the child's needs, it did not find that the mother was unfit to have any control over the child. Thompson v. Thompson, 83 Ill. App. 3d 97, 38 Ill. Dec. 485, 403 N.E.2d 716 (3 Dist. 1980).

Waiver

A mother's objections under subsection (a) of this section to the father's petition for custody modification was waived by her participation in the hearing and her failure to cite the correct statute in support of dismissal. In re Noble, 192 Ill. App. 3d 501, 139 Ill. Dec. 133, 548 N.E.2d 518 (2 Dist. 1989).

In a case as serious and delicate as a child custody proceeding, the waiver rule should not be strictly enforced. In re Godwin, 104 Ill. App. 3d 790, 60 Ill. Dec. 513, 433 N.E.2d 310 (3 Dist. 1982).

LEGAL PERIODICALS

For article, "Illinois Supreme Court Civil '98: Back to the Nuts and Bolts", see 87 Ill. B.J. 250 (1998).

For article, "Joint Custody in Illinois: From Panacea to Placebo," see 83 Ill. B.J. 178 (1995).

For article "Judicial Discretion in Child Custody: The Wisdom of Solomon?", see 81 Ill. B.J. 650 (1993).

For article, "Survey of Illinois Law [1988-89] — Family Law," see 14 S. Ill. U. L. J. 1007 (1990).

For article, "Family Law: 1985-86 Survey," see 11 S. Ill. U. L. J. 741 (1987).

For article, "Divorce Illinois Style: Ten Years Under the Marriage and Dissolution of Marriage Act," see 75 Ill. B. J. 606 (1987).

For article, "Family Law: 1986-87 Illinois Law Survey," see 19 Loy. U. Chi. L. J. 489 (1987-88).

For article, "An Interpretation of Illinois New Joint Custody Amendments," see 75 Ill. B. J. 332 (1986).

For note, "Judicial Treatment of Parental Cohabitation after Jarrett v. Jarrett," see 15 Loy. U. Chi. L. J. 337 (1983-84).

For comment, "Modifying Child Custody Awards: A Substantial Change Under the Illinois Marriage and Dissolution of Marriage Act," see 1980 S. Ill. U. L. J. 439.

For note, "Child Custody: Parental Cohabitational Relationships and the Best Interest of the Child Standard — Jarrett v. Jarrett," see 29 De Paul L. Rev. 1141 (1980).

For article, "'Twas Brillig, and the Court did Gyre, Gimble, and Out Grable," see 69 Ill. B.J. 154 (1980).

For note, "Best Interest of the Child in Custody Proceedings and Waiver of Jurisdictional Objection — Sommer v. Bororis," see 27 De Paul L. Rev. 853 (1978).

RESEARCH REFERENCES

Retirement of husband as change of circumstances warranting modification of divorce decree — Prospective retirement. 110 ALR5th 237.

Propriety of awarding joint custody of children. 17 ALR4th 1013.

Interference by custodian of child with noncustodial parent's visitation rights as ground for change of custody. 28 ALR4th 9.

Withholding visitation rights for failure to make alimony or support payments. 65 ALR4th 1155.

Child custody: separating children by custody awards to different parents — post-1975 cases. 67 ALR4th 354.

750 ILCS 5/611 Enforcement of custody order or order prohibiting removal of child from the jurisdiction of the court

Sec. 611. *Enforcement of custody order or order prohibiting removal of child from the jurisdiction of the court.* (a) The court may enter a judgment to enforce a custody order or a court order prohibiting removal of the child from the jurisdiction of the court if it finds that the respondent has violated the terms of the court order by having improperly removed the child from the physical custody of the petitioner or another person entitled to custody or by having improperly retained the child after a visit or other temporary relinquishment of physical custody.

If the general whereabouts of the child are known, the judgment shall direct any sheriff or law enforcement officer to provide assistance to the petitioner in apprehending the child and shall further authorize any child care personnel, babysitter, teacher or any person having physical custody of the child to surrender the child to such sheriff or law enforcement officer.

(b) The court may enter a judgment pursuant to subsection (a) of this Section without prior notice to the respondent if the court finds that prior notice would be likely to cause the respondent's flight from the jurisdiction or cause further removal or concealment of the child. If an ex parte order is entered pursuant to this subsection, the respondent may, upon 2 days notice to the petitioner or upon such shorter notice as the court may prescribe, appear and move for the dissolution or modification of the judgment and in that event the court shall proceed to hear and determine such motion as expeditiously as possible.

(c) Nothing contained in this Section shall be construed to limit the court's contempt power.
(Source: P.A. 83-1396.)

Note.
This section was Ill.Rev.Stat., Ch. 40, para. 611.

Cross References.
As to the enforcement of orders of protection, specifically for violation of custody or support orders, see 750 ILCS 60/223.

CASE NOTES

Appeal

—Conditional
Litigant may not disobey a decree of the court with reference to the custody of a child, take the child to a place unknown and defy the orderly legal processes of the courts, and then seek the aid of appellate court in determining whether or not his rights were adequately protected by the trial court; however, instead of dismissing the appeal, appellate court entered an order that the appeal would be dismissed 30 days after the date of filing of opinion, unless, within that period, the defendant filed in appellate court a supplementary record showing that he had appeared in his own proper person in the trial court and had returned the custody of the minor to his mother, and if he failed to file such supplementary record, an order would thereupon be entered dismissing the appeal. Burns v. Burns, 35 Ill. App. 2d 34, 181 N.E.2d 605 (1 Dist. 1962).

PART VII.
MISCELLANEOUS

750 ILCS 5/701 Marital Residence — Order Granting Possession to Spouse

Sec. 701. *Marital Residence — Order Granting Possession to Spouse.* Where there is on file a verified complaint or verified petition seeking temporary eviction from the marital residence, the court may, during the pendency of the proceeding, only in cases where the physical or mental well being of either spouse or their children is jeopardized by occupancy of the marital residence by both spouses, and only upon due notice and full hearing, unless waived by the court on good cause shown, enter orders of injunction, mandatory or restraining, granting the exclusive possession of the marital residence to either spouse, by eviction from, or restoration of, the marital residence, until the final determination of the cause. No such order shall in any manner affect any estate in homestead property of either party.
(Source: P.A. 80-923.)

Note.
This section was Ill.Rev.Stat., Ch. 40, para. 701.

Cross References.
As to the applicability of this section to the Criminal Code, specifically to the granting of exclusive possession of a residence, see 725 ILCS 5/112A-14.

CASE NOTES

ANALYSIS

Concurrent Remedies
Exclusive Possession
—Granted
—Improperly Granted
—Pending Outcome
Pleadings
Review

Concurrent Remedies
The Illinois Domestic Violence Act (750 ILCS 60/101 et seq.) provides a concurrent remedy to that available under this section and the definition of abuse under the Domestic Violence Act differs substantially from the test contained in this section. In re Hagaman, 123 Ill. App. 3d 549, 78 Ill. Dec. 922, 462 N.E.2d 1276 (4 Dist. 1984).

Exclusive Possession

—Granted
There was sufficient evidence to determine that the wife should have exclusive possession of the marital home where the husband's presence would jeopardize the wife's physical and emotional well-being and the trial judge did not abuse his discretion by awarding her exclusive possession of the marital home. In re Hofstetter, 102 Ill. App. 3d 392, 58 Ill. Dec. 137, 430 N.E.2d 79 (1 Dist. 1981).

—Improperly Granted
It was clear from the evidence adduced at trial there was no jeopardy to either the physical or mental well-being of wife prior to dated court order nor was there evidence of any future jeopardy to the physical or mental well-being of wife, thus no rational trier of fact viewing the evidence most favorable to wife could have agreed with the trial court's order of exclusive possession of the marital residence to the wife. In re Lima, 265 Ill. App. 3d 753, 203 Ill. Dec. 60, 638 N.E.2d 1186 (2 Dist. 1994).

—Pending Outcome
Trial court's order of exclusive possession of marital home to the wife pending outcome of the cause was irrelevant to the later disposition of the home as marital or non-marital property. In re Hofstetter, 102 Ill. App. 3d 392, 58 Ill. Dec. 137, 430 N.E.2d 79 (1 Dist. 1981).

Pleadings
One of the two types of pleadings must be on file for former section 23 of the Divorce Act (see now this section) to apply. Hoda v. Hoda, 122 Ill. App. 2d 283, 258 N.E.2d 386 (2 Dist. 1970).

Review
The Appellate Court may review orders enjoining the wife in a marriage dissolution case from entering and residing in the marital home and having custody of or participating in unsupervised visitation with her children. In re Lombaer, 200 Ill. App. 3d 712, 146 Ill. Dec. 425, 558 N.E.2d 388 (1 Dist. 1990).

750 ILCS 5/702 Maintenance in Case of Bigamy

Sec. 702. *Maintenance in Case of Bigamy.* When a dissolution of marriage is granted to a person who shall, in good faith, have intermarried with a person having at the time of such marriage, another spouse or spouses living, the court may, nevertheless, allow the petitioner maintenance in the same manner as in other cases of dissolution of marriage; but no such allowance shall be made as will be inconsistent with

the rights of such other spouse or spouses, which shall first be ascertained by the court before the granting of such maintenance.
(Source: P.A. 80-923.)

Note.
This section was Ill.Rev.Stat., Ch. 40, para. 702.

CASE NOTES

Good Faith

—Maintenance Allowed
Where the evidence strongly supported the fact that plaintiff married defendant in good faith with the honest belief that there was no impediment to their marriage, the judgment of annulment was reversed, with directions for entry of a proper divorce in favor of wife, and the trial court was directed to determine the nature, amount and duration of alimony allowance. Belluomini v. Belluomini, 73 Ill. App. 3d 836, 30 Ill. Dec. 14, 392 N.E.2d 669 (1 Dist. 1979).

750 ILCS 5/703 Lien of judgment — Sales

Sec. 703. *Lien of judgment — Sales.* Whenever, in any case of dissolution of marriage, a judgment orders that maintenance be made, a lien on any real estate to arise to secure the payment of any money to become due by installments, and a sale of such real estate to be made if necessary to satisfy any of such installments, the property shall be sold subject to the lien of the installments not then due, unless the court shall at the same time direct otherwise, and subsequent sales may, from time to time, be made to enforce such lien as the installments may become due, until all installments are paid.
(Source: P.A. 81-231.)

Note.
This section was Ill.Rev.Stat., Ch. 40, para. 703.

CASE NOTES

Analysis

Injunction
Lien on Personal Property
Lien on Real Estate
—Not Allowed
—Property Settlement
Maintenance Payment

Injunction
An injunction is tantamount to a lien on the husband's personal property and therefore cannot be sustained. In re Rochford, 91 Ill. App. 3d 769, 46 Ill. Dec. 943, 414 N.E.2d 1096 (1 Dist. 1980).

Lien on Personal Property
Decree awarding alimony cannot be a lien against a husband's personal property. In re Rochford, 91 Ill. App. 3d 769, 46 Ill. Dec. 943, 414 N.E.2d 1096 (1 Dist. 1980).
Although a decree for alimony or maintenance may be made a lien on any real estate to secure the payment of any money to become due by installments, the court in a divorce case has no power to make a money decree a lien on personal property. Lenz v. Lenz, 33 Ill. App. 3d 568, 337 N.E.2d 195 (2 Dist. 1975).

Lien on Real Estate

—Not Allowed
Although the installment payments provided for in the agreement were not specifically labeled "maintenance," they were intended to be so, but as the decree itself did not recite that it was to become a lien, a lien never arose. Interstate Bank v. Cardona, 167 Ill. App. 3d 214, 118 Ill. Dec. 72, 521 N.E.2d 140 (3 Dist. 1988).

—Property Settlement
The legislature has made no provision for the creation of a judgment lien on past due payments for the "settlement of property." Saldeen v. Hamelberg, 198 Ill. App. 3d 146, 144 Ill. Dec. 384, 555 N.E.2d 743 (4 Dist. 1990).

Maintenance Payment
A judgment ordering payment of maintenance may be made a lien on real estate, but only if the decree itself recites that it shall become a lien. Interstate Bank v. Cardona, 167 Ill. App. 3d 214, 118 Ill. Dec. 72, 521 N.E.2d 140 (3 Dist. 1988).

750 ILCS 5/704 Public Aid Provisions

Sec. 704. *Public Aid Provisions.* Except as provided in Sections 709 through 712 [750 ILCS 5/709 through 750 ILCS 5/712], if maintenance, child support or both, is awarded to persons who are recipients of aid under "The Illinois Public Aid Code" [305 ILCS 5/1-1 et seq.], the court shall direct the husband or wife, as the case may be, to make the payments to (1) the Illinois Department of Public Aid if the persons are recipients under Articles III, IV or V of the Code [305 ILCS 5/3-1 et seq., 305 ILCS 5/4-1 et seq. or 305 ILCS 5/5-1 et seq.], or (2) the local governmental unit responsible for their support if they are recipients under Article VI or VII of the Code [305 ILCS 5/6-1 et seq.]. The order shall permit the Illinois Department of Public Aid or the local governmental unit, as the case may be, to direct that subsequent payments be made directly to the former spouse, the children, or both, or to some person or agency in their behalf, upon removal of the former spouse or children from the public aid rolls; and upon such direction and removal of the recipients from the public aid rolls, the Illinois Department or local governmental unit, as the case requires, shall give written notice of such action to the court.
(Source: P.A. 81-1474.)

Note.
This section was Ill.Rev.Stat., Ch. 40, para. 704.
Article VII of The Illinois Public Aid Code, referred to above, has been repealed.

750 ILCS 5/705 Support payments; receiving and disbursing agents

Sec. 705. *Support payments; receiving and disbursing agents.* (1) The provisions of this Section shall apply, except as provided in Sections 709 through 712 [750 ILCS 5/709 through 750 ILCS 5/712].

(2) In a dissolution of marriage action filed in a county of less than 3 million population in which an order or judgment for child support is entered, and in supplementary proceedings in any such county to enforce or vary the terms of such order or judgment arising out of an action for dissolution of marriage filed in such county, the court, except as it otherwise

orders, under subsection (4) of this Section, may direct that child support payments be made to the clerk of the court.

(3) In a dissolution of marriage action filed in any county of 3 million or more population in which an order or judgment for child support is entered, and in supplementary proceedings in any such county to enforce or vary the terms of such order or judgment arising out of an action for dissolution of marriage filed in such county, the court, except as it otherwise orders under subsection (4) of this Section, may direct that child support payments be made either to the clerk of the court or to the Court Service Division of the County Department of Public Aid. After the effective date of this Act, the court, except as it otherwise orders under subsection (4) of this Section, may direct that child support payments be made either to the clerk of the court or to the Illinois Department of Public Aid.

(4) In a dissolution of marriage action or supplementary proceedings involving maintenance or child support payments, or both, to persons who are recipients of aid under the Illinois Public Aid Code [305 ILCS 5/1-1 et seq.], the court shall direct that such payments be made to (a) the Illinois Department of Public Aid if the persons are recipients under Articles III, IV, or V of the Code [305 ILCS 5/3-1 et seq., 305 ILCS 5/4-0.5 et seq., or 305 ILCS 5/5-1 et seq.], or (b) the local governmental unit responsible for their support if they are recipients under Articles VI or VII of the Code [305 ILCS 5/6-1 et seq. or 305 ILCS 5/7-1 et seq.]. In accordance with federal law and regulations, the Illinois Department of Public Aid may continue to collect current maintenance payments or child support payments, or both, after those persons cease to receive public assistance and until termination of services under Article X of the Illinois Public Aid Code [305 ILCS 5/10-1 et seq.]. The Illinois Department of Public Aid shall pay the net amount collected to those persons after deducting any costs incurred in making the collection or any collection fee from the amount of any recovery made. The order shall permit the Illinois Department of Public Aid or the local governmental unit, as the case may be, to direct that payments be made directly to the former spouse, the children, or both, or to some person or agency in their behalf, upon removal of the former spouse or children from the public aid rolls or upon termination of services under Article X of the Illinois Public Aid Code [305 ILCS 5/10-1 et seq.]; and upon such direction, the Illinois Department or local governmental unit, as the case requires, shall give notice of such action to the court in writing or by electronic transmission.

(5) All clerks of the court and the Court Service Division of a County Department of Public Aid and, after the effective date of this Act, all clerks of the court and the Illinois Department of Public Aid, receiving child support payments under subsections (2) and (3) of this Section shall disburse the payments to the person or persons entitled thereto under the terms of the order or judgment. They shall establish and maintain current records of all moneys received and disbursed and of defaults and delinquencies in required payments. The court, by order or rule, shall make provision for the carrying out of these duties.

Upon notification in writing or by electronic transmission from the Illinois Department of Public Aid to the clerk of the court that a person who is receiving support payments under this Section is receiving services under the Child Support Enforcement Program established by Title IV-D of the Social Security Act [42 U.S.C. § 651 et seq.], any support payments subsequently received by the clerk of the court shall be transmitted in accordance with the instructions of the Illinois Department of Public Aid until the Department gives notice to the clerk of the court to cease the transmittal. After providing the notification authorized under this paragraph, the Illinois Department of Public Aid shall be entitled as a party to notice of any further proceedings in the case. The clerk of the court shall file a copy of the Illinois Department of Public Aid's notification in the court file. The failure of the clerk to file a copy of the notification in the court file shall not, however, affect the Illinois Department of Public Aid's right to receive notice of further proceedings.

Payments under this Section to the Illinois Department of Public Aid pursuant to the Child Support Enforcement Program established by Title IV-D of the Social Security Act [42 U.S.C. § 651 et seq.] shall be paid into the Child Support Enforcement Trust Fund. All payments under this Section to the Illinois Department of Human Services shall be deposited in the DHS Recoveries Trust Fund. Disbursements from these funds shall be as provided in the Illinois Public Aid Code [305 ILCS 5/1-1 et seq.]. Payments received by a local governmental unit shall be deposited in that unit's General Assistance Fund. Any order of court directing payment of child support to a clerk of court or the Court Service Division of a County Department of Public Aid, which order has been entered on or after August 14, 1961, and prior to the effective date of this Act, may be amended by the court in line with this Act; and orders involving payments of maintenance or child support to recipients of public aid may in like manner be amended to conform to this Act.

(6) No filing fee or costs will be required in any action brought at the request of the Illinois Department of Public Aid in any proceeding under this Act. However, any such fees or costs may be assessed by the court against the respondent in the court's order of support or any modification thereof in a proceeding under this Act.

(7) For those cases in which child support is payable to the clerk of the circuit court for transmittal to the Illinois Department of Public Aid by order of court or upon notification by the Illinois Department of Public Aid, the clerk shall transmit all such

payments, within 4 working days of receipt, to insure that funds are available for immediate distribution by the Department to the person or entity entitled thereto in accordance with standards of the Child Support Enforcement Program established under Title IV-D of the Social Security Act [42 U.S.C. § 651 et seq.]. The clerk shall notify the Department of the date of receipt and amount thereof at the time of transmittal. Where the clerk has entered into an agreement of cooperation with the Department to record the terms of child support orders and payments made thereunder directly into the Department's automated data processing system, the clerk shall account for, transmit and otherwise distribute child support payments in accordance with such agreement in lieu of the requirements contained herein.

In any action filed in a county with a population of 1,000,000 or less, the court shall assess against the respondent in any order of maintenance or child support any sum up to $36 annually authorized by ordinance of the county board to be collected by the clerk of the court as costs for administering the collection and disbursement of maintenance and child support payments. Such sum shall be in addition to and separate from amounts ordered to be paid as maintenance or child support.

(8) To the extent the provisions of this Section are inconsistent with the requirements pertaining to the State Disbursement Unit under Section 507.1 of this Act [750 ILCS 5/507.1] and Section 10-26 of the Illinois Public Aid Code [305 ILCS 5/10-26], the requirements pertaining to the State Disbursement Unit shall apply.

(Source: P.A. 86-1184; 88-687, § 13; 90-18, § 100; 90-673, § 915; 90-790, § 10; 91-24, § 30; 91-212, § 25; 91-357, § 256; 92-16, § 96.)

Note.

This section was Ill.Rev.Stat., Ch. 40, para. 705.

Article VII of the Illinois Public Aid Code, referred to above, has been repealed.

Section 996 of P.A. 92-16 contains a "no acceleration or delay" provision, and Section 997 contains a "no revival or extension" provision.

Effect of Amendments.

The 1994 amendment by P.A. 88-687, effective January 24, 1995, in subsection (4) substituted the present second and third sentences for the former second and third sentences on the same subject matter and in the fourth sentence deleted "subsequent" preceding "payments", substituted "services under Article X of the Illinois Public Aid Code" for "any extended collection period", deleted "written" preceding "notice" and added at the end "in writing or by electronic transmission"; in subsection (5) added the second paragraph; and in subsection (7), in the first paragraph, in the first sentence, inserted "or upon notification by the Illinois Department of Public Aid".

The 1997 amendment by P.A. 90-18, effective July 1, 1997, in subsection (5) added the second paragraph.

The 1998 amendment by P.A. 90-673, effective January 1, 1999, incorporated the amendment by P.A. 90-18; and substituted "in accordance with the Income Withholding for Support Act" for "under Section 706.1 of this Act" in the second paragraph of subsection (5).

The 1998 amendment by P.A. 90-790, effective August 14, 1998, deleted the former second paragraph in subsection (5), relating to support orders pursuant to Article X of the Illinois Public Aid Act.

The 1999 amendment by P.A. 91-24, effective July 1, 1999, incorporated the amendments by P.A. 90-673 and P.A. 90-790; in subsection (5) deleted "in effect in accordance with the Income Withholding for Support" at the end of the first paragraph; and in the second sentence of the last paragraph deleted "other" following "All", and substituted "Human Services" for "Public Aid" and "DHS" for "Public Assistance".

The 1999 amendment by P.A. 91-212, effective July 20, 1999, incorporated the amendments by P.A. 90-673 and P.A. 90-790; deleted "in effect in accordance with the Income Withholding for Support" at the end of the first paragraph in subsection (5); and added subsection (8).

The 1999 amendment by P.A. 91-357, effective July 29, 1999, incorporated the amendments by P.A. 90-673 and 90-790; deleted "in effect in accordance with the Income Withholding for Support" at the end of the first paragraph in subsection (5).

The 2001 amendment by P.A. 92-16, effective June 28, 2001, combined the amendments by P.A. 91-24, P.A. 91-212 and P.A. 91-357.

LEGAL PERIODICALS

For article, "Family Law: 1985-86 Survey," see 11 S. Ill. U. L. J. 741 (1987).

RESEARCH REFERENCES

Right to credit against child support arrearages for time child spent in custody of noncustodial parent, other than for visitation or under court order, without custodial parent's approval. 108 ALR5th 359.

Right to credit on child support arrearages for time parties resided together after separation or divorce. 104 ALR5th 605.

750 ILCS 5/706.1 Withholding of Income to Secure Payment of Support

Sec. 706.1. *Withholding of Income to Secure Payment of Support.* Orders for support entered under this Act are subject to the Income Withholding for Support Act [750 ILCS 28/1 et seq.].

(Source: P.A. 86-496; 86-546; 86-649; 86-746; 86-911; 86-1028; 86-1184; 87-529; 87-935, § 2; 87-988, § 2; 87-1105, § 2; 88-26, § 2; 88-45, § 2-59; 88-94, § 2; 88-131, § 10; 88-307, § 10; 88-670, § 2-68; 89-507, § 90D-93; 90-18, § 100; 90-425, § 91; 90-655, § 170; 91-357, § 256; 90-673, § 915; 90-790, § 10.)

Note.

This section was Ill.Rev.Stat., Ch. 40, para. 706.1.

Effect of Amendments.

The 1994 amendment by P.A. 88-670, effective December 2, 1994, combined the amendments by P.A. 88-26, P.A. 88-45, P.A. 88-94, P.A. 88-131 and P.A. 88-307.

The 1996 amendment by P.A. 89-507, effective July 1, 1997, in subsection (A)(8) substituted "Human Services" for "Mental Health and Developmental Disabilities".

The 1997 amendment by P.A. 90-18, effective July 1, 1997, rewrote this section.

The 1997 amendment by P.A. 90-425, effective August 15, 1997, in subdivision (E)(3), in the first sentence, inserted "regular or" and substituted "facsimile" for "personal delivery"; in subdivision (F)(2), in the second sentence, inserted "regular or" and substituted "facsimile" for "personal delivery"; added subdivision (F)(4); and in the first paragraph of subdivision (G)(1), inserted the eighth sentence.

The 1998 amendment by P.A. 90-655, effective July 30, 1998, incorporated the amendments made by P.A. 90-18 and P.A. 90-425, substituted the subsection (B)(9) designation for the (B)(4) designation, and in subsection (B)(9) twice substituted "an income withholding notice" for "an order for withholding" and once in subsection (E)(1); and in subsection (D)(4) deleted "regular or facsimile regular or facsimile" following "subsection (F)." at the end.

The 1998 amendment by P.A. 90-673, effective January 1, 1999, incorporated the amendments by P.A. 90-18 and P.A. 90-425; and rewrote this section.

The 1998 amendment by P.A. 90-790, effective August 14, 1998, added subsection (A)(2.5); in subsection (B), added subsections (B)(3)(a-5) and (B)(3)(k), inserted "A copy of the income withholding notice together with" in subsection (B)(7) and the last sentence in subsection (B)(8), and substituted "income withholding notice" for "order for withholding" twice in subsection (B)(9); deleted "a computation of" and "period and" from subsection (C)(1)(b); substituted "income withholding notice" for "order for withholding" in the first paragraph of subsection (E)(1); and deleted "or who has been served with a notice of delinquency" preceding "pursuant" in subsection (G)(4).

The 1999 amendment by P.A. 91-357, effective July 29, 1999, incorporated the amendments by P.A. 90-655, P.A. 90-673, and P.A. 90-790; and rewrote the section to the extent that a detailed comparison would be impracticable.

CASE NOTES

Analysis

In General
Arrearages
—Amount Owed
—Collection
Employer Penalty
—Failure to Withhold
—Mandatory
—Warranted
Future Child Support
Garnishment Proceedings
Government Employee
Income
Interest
Legislative Intent
Military Pension
Net Income
—Definition in Other Sections
Order of Withholding
—Issuance
Public Policy
Purpose
Spendthrift Trusts

In General

Conceptually the granting of lien status is nothing more than the giving of one creditor priority over another creditor. In re Salaway, 126 Bankr. 58 (Bankr. C.D. Ill. 1991).

Arrearages

—Amount Owed

The question of the amount of child support arrearages owed petitioner by respondent is a factual question for the determination of the trial court, and its decision will not be disturbed unless it is contrary to the manifest weight of the evidence. In re Belluomini, 104 Ill. App. 3d 301, 60 Ill. Dec. 59, 432 N.E.2d 958 (1 Dist. 1982).

—Collection

Courts may apply this statute to collect an arrearage that accumulated before the effective date of the Act. In re Wyant, 197 Ill. App. 3d 538, 143 Ill. Dec. 847, 554 N.E.2d 782 (2 Dist. 1990).

Employer Penalty

—Failure to Withhold

Subdivision (G)(1) does not impose a penalty upon an employer which, after receiving an order of withholding, fails to withhold child support payments from its employee's paycheck. Vrombaut v. Norcross Safety Prods., L.L.C., 298 Ill. App. 3d 560, 232 Ill. Dec. 708, 699 N.E.2d 155 (3 Dist. 1998), appeal denied, 181 Ill. 2d 590, 235 Ill. Dec. 948, 706 N.E.2d 503 (1998).

—Mandatory

The context of this section supports a mandatory reading of the employer penalty provision. Dunahee v. Chenoa Welding & Fabrication, Inc., 273 Ill. App. 3d 201, 209 Ill. Dec. 898, 652 N.E.2d 438 (4 Dist. 1995).

—Warranted

Defendant/employer proffered no compelling excuse for its noncompliance, but instead merely claimed ignorance coupled with a wish to avoid the paltry cost of three additional postage stamps per month, although defendant wrote out a check each week, by mailing the checks only once each month, defendant maintained access to the withheld child support funds in its account, to its own benefit and in the meantime, plaintiff and her children suffered hardship waiting for the overdue payments, moreover, defendant's practice continued even after plaintiff informed defendant's treasurer of her need for timely receipt of the withheld child support payment; in short, the trial court's failure to apply the penalty was an abuse of discretion. Dunahee v. Chenoa Welding & Fabrication, Inc., 273 Ill. App. 3d 201, 209 Ill. Dec. 898, 652 N.E.2d 438 (4 Dist. 1995).

Future Child Support

Spendthrift trusts may be reached only to satisfy child support arrearages, and not future child support payments. In re Chapman, 297 Ill. App. 3d 611, 231 Ill. Dec. 811, 697 N.E.2d 365 (1 Dist. 1998), (decided under former 750 ILCS 15/4.1).

Garnishment Proceedings

Subsection (B) does not require that an order of withholding be served upon a garnishee but merely provides a method for recovery of sums due pursuant to an order of support, and the statutory requirements for garnishment proceedings impose no requirement for service of an order of withholding. Miller v. Miller, 268 Ill. App. 3d 132, 205 Ill. Dec. 337, 643 N.E.2d 288 (4 Dist. 1994), appeal denied, 159 Ill. 2d 570, 207 Ill. Dec. 518, 647 N.E.2d 1011 (1995).

The legislature, in enacting this section, which contains exactly the same language as Section 4.1 of the Nonsupport of Spouse and Children Act (750 ILCS 15/4.1) and Section 26.1 of the Revised Uniform Reciprocal Enforcement of Support Act (750 ILCS 20/26.1), established that it is in the public policy of Illinois to ensure the enforcement of support judgments through all available means. Keeler v. Keeler, 156 Ill. App. 3d 513, 108 Ill. Dec. 716, 509 N.E.2d 142 (2 Dist. 1987).

Government Employee

City was not exempt from complying with wage assignment under former Ill.Rev.Stat., ch 40, para. 21.1 (see now this section), granted in favor of ex-wife in satisfaction of certain alimony and child support obligations owed to her by her ex-husband, an employee of the city, and was liable for the amounts which it failed to withhold between the date of the service of the assignment and the date of its order. Fair v. City of Chicago, 45 Ill. App. 3d 240, 3 Ill. Dec. 914, 359 N.E.2d 773 (1 Dist. 1977).

Income

This section governs the withholding of income in order to secure payment of support, and the definition of income found in subdivision (A)(4) of this section is intended to define the term for the purposes of this section only; there is no indication that it is intended to define the term for any other purpose of this Act. In re Dodds, 222 Ill. App. 3d 99, 164 Ill. Dec. 692, 583 N.E.2d 608 (2 Dist. 1991), cert. denied, 144 Ill. 2d 632, 169 Ill. Dec. 140, 591 N.E.2d 20 (1992).

Interest

For a case discussing interest owed on an unpaid preliminary award, decided under prior provisions, see Harding v. Harding, 180 Ill. 592, 54 N.E. 604 (1899).

Legislative Intent

This section is intended to secure the payment of child support through third parties who are normally obligated to pay income to the supporting parent in the form of periodic payments. In re Dodds, 222 Ill. App. 3d 99, 164 Ill. Dec. 692, 583 N.E.2d 608 (2 Dist. 1991), cert. denied, 144 Ill. 2d 632, 169 Ill. Dec. 140, 591 N.E.2d 20 (1992).

Legislative Intent (Cont'd)

The plain language of this section reveals no intent by the legislature to vest a trial court with the discretion to refuse to issue an order for withholding once an obligor becomes delinquent; if a court determines an obligor has become delinquent, this section directs the court to immediately order the service of the order for withholding. In re Bergman, 183 Ill. App. 3d 897, 132 Ill. Dec. 309, 539 N.E.2d 872 (4 Dist. 1989).

Military Pension

At the time of dissolution, plaintiff's pension was partially earned, with a known value, but had not yet been collected and the pension was clearly marital property; however the fact of its classification as marital property prior to the date plaintiff began collecting it in monthly installments did not bar it from use in determining net income for child support. In re Klomps, 286 Ill. App. 3d 710, 221 Ill. Dec. 883, 676 N.E.2d 686 (5 Dist. 1997).

Like pay for active duty military service, plaintiff's military pension was income for child support purposes. In re Klomps, 286 Ill. App. 3d 710, 221 Ill. Dec. 883, 676 N.E.2d 686 (5 Dist. 1997).

Net Income

—Definition in Other Sections

The definition of net income found in this section does not limit the definition of net income in 750 ILCS 5/505. Illinois Dep't of Public Aid ex rel. Jennings v. White, 286 Ill. App. 3d 213, 221 Ill. Dec. 561, 675 N.E.2d 985 (2 Dist. 1997).

Order of Withholding

—Issuance

Where there was no alternative arrangement evidenced by a written agreement approved by the court, the order of withholding to take effect immediately was proper. People ex rel. Stokely v. Goodenow, 211 Ill. App. 3d 802, 164 Ill. Dec. 548, 583 N.E.2d 102 (4 Dist. 1991).

The court had no discretion in issuing an order for withholding where former husband was already in arrears on his child support obligation. In re Wyant, 197 Ill. App. 3d 538, 143 Ill. Dec. 847, 554 N.E.2d 782 (2 Dist. 1990).

This section mandates a court to order the immediate issuance and service of an order for withholding once it finds an obligor is in arrears in child support, and the arrearage exceeds one month's obligation. In re Bergman, 183 Ill. App. 3d 897, 132 Ill. Dec. 309, 539 N.E.2d 872 (4 Dist. 1989).

Public Policy

The legislature, in enacting this section, which contains exactly the same language as Section 4.1 of the Nonsupport of Spouse and Children Act (750 ILCS 15/4.1) and Section 26.1 of the Revised Uniform Reciprocal Enforcement of Support Act (750 ILCS 20/26.1), established that it is the public policy of Illinois to ensure the enforcement of support judgments through all available means. Keeler v. Keeler, 156 Ill. App. 3d 513, 108 Ill. Dec. 716, 509 N.E.2d 142 (2 Dist. 1987).

Purpose

The purpose of this provision for a contingent deduction is to comply with federal law and regulations, which require that withholding occur without the need for any amendment to the support order or any further action by the court issuing the withholding order; should respondent become delinquent in his current support payments, petitioner or the Department of Public Aid must still comply with the statutory procedures for serving a notice of delinquency on respondent and his employer thus giving respondent an opportunity to be heard should there be a bona fide dispute concerning the alleged delinquency. In re Holmes, 260 Ill. App. 3d 836, 198 Ill. Dec. 669, 633 N.E.2d 131 (4 Dist. 1994).

Spendthrift Trusts

Court ruled in error that spendthrift trust income or principal could not be reached at all to satisfy a child support judgment; the language of the trust showed the settlor of the trust clearly contemplated that income or principal of the trust could be used for the benefit of appellee's children. In re Chapman, 297 Ill. App. 3d 611, 231 Ill. Dec. 811, 697 N.E.2d 365 (1 Dist. 1998), (decided under former 750 ILCS 15/4.1).

RESEARCH REFERENCES

Enforcement of claim for alimony or support, or for attorneys' fees and costs incurred in connection therewith, against exemption. 52 ALR5th 221.

750 ILCS 5/706.2 Posting Security, Bond or Guarantee to Secure Payment

Sec. 706.2. *Posting Security, Bond or Guarantee to Secure Payment.* The court may require a parent to post security, bond or give some other guarantee of a character and amount sufficient to assure payment of any amount of support due.
(Source: P.A. 84-758.)

Note.

This section was Ill.Rev.Stat., Ch. 40, para. 706.2.

750 ILCS 5/706.3 Information concerning obligors

Sec. 706.3. *Information concerning obligors.* (a) In this Section:

"Arrearage", "delinquency", "obligor", and "order for support" have the meanings attributed to those terms in the Income Withholding for Support Act [750 ILCS 28/1 et seq.].

"Consumer reporting agency" has the meaning attributed to that term in Section 603(f) of the Fair Credit Reporting Act, 15 U.S.C. 1681a(f).

(b) Whenever a court of competent jurisdiction finds that an obligor either owes an arrearage of more than $10,000, is delinquent in payment of an amount equal to at least 3 months' support obligation pursuant to an order for support, or fails to pay the child support annual fee for a period of 3 years, the court shall direct the clerk of the court to make information concerning the obligor available to consumer reporting agencies.

(c) Whenever a court of competent jurisdiction finds that an obligor either owes an arrearage of more than $10,000 or is delinquent in payment of an amount equal to at least 3 months' support obligation pursuant to an order for support, the court shall direct the clerk of the court to cause the obligor's name and address to be published in a newspaper of general circulation in the area in which the obligor resides. The clerk shall cause the obligor's name and address to be published only after sending to the obligor at the obligor's last known address, by certified mail, return receipt requested, a notice of intent to publish the information. This subsection (c) applies only if the obligor resides in the county in which the clerk of the court holds office.
(Source: P.A. 90-466, § 10; 90-673, § 915; 93-836, § 20.)

Effective Date.

This section became effective January 1, 1998 pursuant to Ill. Const. (1970), Art. IV, § 10 and 5 ILCS 75/1.

Effect of Amendments.

The 1998 amendment by P.A. 90-673, effective January 1, 1999,

incorporated the amendment by P.A. 90-466; and substituted "the Income Withholding for Support Act" for "Section 706.1 of this Act" in subsection (a).

The 2004 amendment by P.A. 93-836, effective January 1, 2005, inserted "or fails to pay the child support annual fee for a period of 3 years" in subsection (b).

750 ILCS 5/707 Certificate of Dissolution or Invalidity of Marriage — Filing with Department of Public Health

Sec. 707. *Certificate of Dissolution or Invalidity of Marriage — Filing with Department of Public Health.* A certificate of each dissolution of marriage or declaration of invalidity of marriage ordered in this State shall be filed with the Illinois Department of Public Health on a form furnished by such Department. The form shall contain the social security numbers of the parties whose marriage has been dissolved or declared invalid. This form shall be prepared by the person filing the petition for dissolution of marriage or declaration of invalidity of marriage and shall be presented to the judge of the court for his inspection prior to the entry of the final order. Failure to comply with this Act shall not invalidate any judgment of dissolution of marriage or declaration of invalidity of marriage. Immediately after the judgment is granted, the clerk of the court shall complete the remaining entries on the certificate. Within 45 days after the close of the month in which the judgment is rendered, the clerk shall forward the certificate to the Illinois Department of Public Health.
(Source: P.A. 81-399; 90-18, § 100.)

Note.
This section was Ill.Rev.Stat., Ch. 40, para. 707.

Effect of Amendments.
The 1997 amendment by P.A. 90-18, effective July 1, 1997, added the second sentence.

750 ILCS 5/708 [Address disclosure]

Sec. 708. In any proceeding brought under this Act, the identification of a party's street address shall not be required for any purpose if the court finds that the physical, mental or emotional health of a party or that of a minor child, or both, would be seriously endangered by disclosure of the party's address.
(Source: P.A. 81-419.)

Note.
This section was Ill.Rev.Stat., Ch. 40, para. 708.

750 ILCS 5/709 Mandatory child support payments to clerk

Sec. 709. *Mandatory child support payments to clerk.* (a) As of January 1, 1982, child support orders entered in any county covered by this subsection shall be made pursuant to the provisions of Sections 709 through 712 of this Act [750 ILCS 5/709 through 750 ILCS 5/712]. For purposes of these Sections, the term "child support payment" or "payment" shall include any payment ordered to be made solely for the purpose of the support of a child or children or any payment ordered for general support which includes any amount for support of any child or children.

The provisions of Sections 709 through 712 [750 ILCS 5/709 through 750 ILCS 5/712] shall be applicable to any county with a population of 2 million or more and to any other county which notifies the Supreme Court of its desire to be included within the coverage of these Sections and is certified pursuant to Supreme Court Rules.

The effective date of inclusion, however, shall be subject to approval of the application for reimbursement of the costs of the support program by the Department of Public Aid as provided in Section 712 [750 ILCS 5/712].

(b) In any proceeding for a dissolution of marriage, legal separation, or declaration of invalidity of marriage, or in any supplementary proceedings in which a judgment or modification thereof for the payment of child support is entered on or after January 1, 1982, in any county covered by Sections 709 through 712 [750 ILCS 5/709 through 750 ILCS 5/712], and the person entitled to payment is receiving a grant of financial aid under Article IV of the Illinois Public Aid Code [305 ILCS 5/4-0.5 et seq.] or has applied and qualified for child support enforcement services under Section 10-1 of that Code [305 ILCS 5/10-1], the court shall direct: (1) that such payments be made to the clerk of the court and (2) that the parties affected shall each thereafter notify the clerk of any change of address or change in other conditions that may affect the administration of the order, including the fact that a party who was previously not on public aid has become a recipient of public aid, within 10 days of such change. All notices sent to the obligor's last known address on file with the clerk shall be deemed sufficient to proceed with enforcement pursuant to the provisions of Sections 709 through 712 [750 ILCS 5/709 through 750 ILCS 5/712].

In all other cases, the court may direct that payments be made to the clerk of the court.

(c) Except as provided in subsection (d) of this Section, the clerk shall disburse the payments to the person or persons entitled thereto under the terms of the order or judgment.

(d) The court shall determine, prior to the entry of the support order, if the party who is to receive the support is presently receiving public aid or has a current application for public aid pending and shall enter the finding on the record.

If the person entitled to payment is a recipient of aid under the Illinois Public Aid Code [305 ILCS 5/1-1 et seq.], the clerk, upon being informed of this fact by finding of the court, by notification by the party entitled to payment, by the Illinois Department of Public Aid or by the local governmental unit, shall make all payments to: (1) the Illinois Department of Public Aid if the person is a recipient under Article III, IV, or V of the Code [305 ILCS 5/3-1 et seq., 305 ILCS 5/4-0.5 et seq., or 305 ILCS 5/5-1 et seq.] or (2) the local governmental unit responsible for his or her support if the person is a recipient under Article VI [305 ILCS 5/6-1 et seq.] or VII of the Code [repealed]. In accordance with federal law and regulations, the Illinois Department of Public Aid may continue to collect current maintenance payments or child support payments, or both, after those persons cease to receive public assistance and until termination of services under Article X of the Illinois Public Aid Code [305 ILCS 5/10-1 et seq.]. The Illinois Department of Public Aid shall pay the net amount collected to those persons after deducting any costs incurred in making the collection or any collection fee from the amount of any recovery made. Upon termination of public aid payments to such a recipient or termination of services under Article X of the Illinois Public Aid Code [305 ILCS 5/10-1 et seq.], the Illinois Department of Public Aid or the appropriate local governmental unit shall notify the clerk in writing or by electronic transmission that all subsequent payments are to be sent directly to the person entitled thereto.

Upon notification in writing or by electronic transmission from the Illinois Department of Public Aid to the clerk of the court that a person who is receiving support payments under this Section is receiving services under the Child Support Enforcement Program established by Title IV-D of the Social Security Act [42 U.S.C. § 651 et seq.], any support payments subsequently received by the clerk of the court shall be transmitted in accordance with the instructions of the Illinois Department of Public Aid until the Department gives notice to the clerk of the court to cease the transmittal. After providing the notification authorized under this paragraph, the Illinois Department of Public Aid shall be entitled as a party to notice of any further proceedings in the case. The clerk of the court shall file a copy of the Illinois Department of Public Aid's notification in the court file. The failure of the clerk to file a copy of the notification in the court file shall not, however, affect the Illinois Department of Public Aid's right to receive notice of further proceedings.

Payments under this Section to the Illinois Department of Public Aid pursuant to the Child Support Enforcement Program established by Title IV-D of the Social Security Act [42 U.S.C. § 651 et seq.] shall be paid into the Child Support Enforcement Trust Fund. All payments under this Section to the Illinois Department of Human Services shall be deposited in the DHS Recoveries Trust Fund. Disbursements from these funds shall be as provided in the Illinois Public Aid Code [305 ILCS 5/1-1 et seq.]. Payments received by a local governmental unit shall be deposited in that unit's General Assistance Fund.

(e) Any order or judgment may be amended by the court, upon its own motion or upon the motion of either party, to conform with the provisions of Sections 709 through 712 [750 ILCS 5/709 through 750 ILCS 5/712], either as to the requirement of making payments to the clerk or, where payments are already being made to the clerk, as to the statutory fees provided for under Section 711 [750 ILCS 5/711].

(f) The clerk may invest in any interest bearing account or in any securities, monies collected for the benefit of a payee, where such payee cannot be found; however, the investment may be only for the period until the clerk is able to locate and present the payee with such monies. The clerk may invest in any interest bearing account, or in any securities, monies collected for the benefit of any other payee; however, this does not alter the clerk's obligation to make payments to the payee in a timely manner. Any interest or capital gains accrued shall be for the benefit of the county and shall be paid into the special fund established in subsection (b) of Section 711 [750 ILCS 5/711].

(g) The clerk shall establish and maintain a payment record of all monies received and disbursed and such record shall constitute prima facie evidence of such payment and non-payment, as the case may be.

(h) For those cases in which child support is payable to the clerk of the circuit court for transmittal to the Illinois Department of Public Aid by order of court or upon notification by the Illinois Department of Public Aid, the clerk shall transmit all such payments, within 4 working days of receipt, to insure that funds are available for immediate distribution by the Department to the person or entity entitled thereto in accordance with standards of the Child Support Enforcement Program established under Title IV-D of the Social Security Act [42 U.S.C. § 651 et seq.]. The clerk shall notify the Department of the date of receipt and amount thereof at the time of transmittal. Where the clerk has entered into an agreement of cooperation with the Department to record the terms of child support orders and payments made thereunder directly into the Department's automated data processing system, the clerk shall account for, transmit and otherwise distribute child support payments in accordance with such agreement in lieu of the requirements contained herein.

(i) To the extent the provisions of this Section are inconsistent with the requirements pertaining to the State Disbursement Unit under Section 507.1 of this Act [750 ILCS 5/507.1] and Section 10-26 of the Illinois Public Aid Code [305 ILCS 5/10-26], the requirements pertaining to the State Disbursement Unit shall apply.

(Source: P.A. 86-582; 86-1184; 87-1252, § 1; 88-687, § 13; 91-24, § 30; 91-212, § 25; 92-16, § 96; 92-590, § 10.)

Note.

This section was Ill.Rev.Stat., Ch. 40, para. 709.

Article VII of the Illinois Public Aid Code, referred to in subsection (d), is reserved.

Section 996 of P.A. 92-16 contains a "no acceleration or delay" provision, and Section 997 contains a "no revival or extension" provision.

Effect of Amendments.

The 1994 amendment by P.A. 88-687, effective January 24, 1995, in subsection (b), in the first paragraph, in the first sentence, deleted the quotation marks around "Illinois Public Aid Code"; in subsection (d), in the second paragraph, added the present second and third sentences for the former second and third sentences on the same subject matter and in the fourth sentence inserted "or termination of services under Article X of the Illinois Public Aid Code" and inserted "in writing or by electronic transmission" and added the third paragraph; and in subsection (h), in the first sentence, inserted "or upon notification by the Illinois Department of Public Aid".

The 1999 amendment by P.A. 91-24, effective July 1, 1999, in the second sentence of the last paragraph of subsection (d) deleted "other" following "All", substituted "Human Services" for "Public Aid", and "DHS" for "Public Assistance".

The 1999 amendment by P.A. 91-212, effective July 20, 1999, added subsection (i).

The 2001 amendment by P.A. 92-16, effective June 28, 2001, combined the amendments by P.A. 91-24 and P.A. 91-212.

The 2002 amendment by P.A. 92-590, effective July 1, 2002, substituted "child support enforcement services" for "support services" in subsection (b).

CASE NOTES

Date of Collection

The proper "date of collection" for purposes of "pass through" payments is the date of collection by the circuit court clerk's office. Golden v. Department of Pub. Aid, 150 Ill. App. 3d 617, 103 Ill. Dec. 473, 501 N.E.2d 790 (3 Dist. 1986).

750 ILCS 5/710 Enforcement; Penalties

Sec. 710. *Enforcement; Penalties.* (a) In counties certified as included under the provisions of Sections 709 through 712 [750 ILCS 5/709 through 750 ILCS 5/712] and whose application for reimbursement is approved, there shall be instituted a child support enforcement program to be conducted by the clerk of the circuit court and the state's attorney of the county. The program is to be limited to enforcement of child support orders entered pursuant to this Act.

The child support enforcement program is to be conducted only on behalf of dependent children included in a grant of financial aid under Article IV of The Illinois Public Aid Code [305 ILCS 5/4-1 et seq.] and parties who apply and qualify for child support enforcement services pursuant to Section 10-1 of such Code [305 ILCS 5/10-1].

Nothing in this Section shall be construed to prohibit the establishment of a child support enforcement program by the clerk of the circuit court in cooperation with the State's Attorney of the county.

(b) In the event of a delinquency in payment, as determined from the record maintained by the clerk in a county covered by the child support enforcement program, such clerk shall notify both the party obligated to make the payment, hereinafter called the payor, and the recipient of such payment, hereinafter called the payee, of such delinquency and that if the amount then due and owing is not remitted in the time period required by circuit court rules, the matter will be referred to the state's attorney for enforcement proceedings. Upon failure of the payor to remit as required, the clerk shall refer the matter to the state's attorney, except as provided by rule of the circuit court.

(c) Upon referral from the clerk, the state's attorney shall promptly initiate enforcement proceedings against the payor. Legal representation by the state's attorney shall be limited to child support and shall not extend to visitation, custody, property or other matters; however, if the payor properly files pleadings raising such matters during the course of the child support hearing and the court finds that it has jurisdiction of such matters, the payee shall be granted the opportunity to obtain a continuance in order to secure representation for those other matters, and the court shall not delay entry of an appropriate support order pending the disposition of such other matters.

If the state's attorney does not commence enforcement proceedings within 30 days, the clerk shall inform the court which, upon its own motion, shall appoint counsel for purposes of enforcement. The fees and expenses of such counsel shall be paid by the payor and shall not be paid by the State.

Nothing in this Section shall be construed to prevent a payee from instituting independent enforcement proceedings or limit the remedies available to payee in such proceedings. However, absent the exercise under this provision of a private right of enforcement, enforcement shall be as otherwise provided in this Section.

(d) At the time any support order is entered, the payee shall be informed of the procedure used for enforcement and shall be given the address and telephone number both of the clerk and of the Child and Spouse Support Unit as provided in Section 712 [750 ILCS 5/712].

The payee shall be informed that, if no action is taken within 2 months of any complaint to the clerk, payee may contact the Unit to seek assistance in obtaining enforcement.

(e) Upon a finding that payor is in default and that such non-payment is for a period of two months and that such non-payment is without good cause, the court shall order the payor to pay a sum equal to 2% of the arrearage as a penalty along with his payment.

The court may further assess against the payor any fees and expenses incurred in the enforcement of any order or the reasonable value thereof and may impose any penalty otherwise available to it in a case of contempt.

All penalties, fees and expenses assessed against the payor pursuant to this subsection are to cover the expenses of enforcement, are to be paid to the clerk and are to be placed by him in the special fund provided for in Section 711 [750 ILCS 5/711].

(f) Any person not covered by the child support enforcement program may institute private and

independent proceedings to enforce payment of support.
(Source: P.A. 86-522; 88-284, § 5; 92-590, § 10.)

Note.
This section was Ill.Rev.Stat., Ch. 40, para. 710.

Effect of Amendments.
The 2002 amendment by P.A. 92-590, effective July 1, 2002, substituted "child support enforcement services" for "support services" in the second paragraph of subsection (a).

CASE NOTES

Interest

—Discretion of Court
The assessment of interest upon child support is a matter of discretion for the trial court. In re Belluomini, 104 Ill. App. 3d 301, 60 Ill. Dec. 59, 432 N.E.2d 958 (1 Dist. 1982).

750 ILCS 5/711 Fees

Sec. 711. *Fees.* (a) To reimburse any covered county for the cost of maintaining the child support enforcement program pursuant to Section 710 [750 ILCS 5/710], the court shall order any payor making payments directly to the clerk to pay the clerk a fee at the rate of $3.00 per month for every month the order is in effect. However, any fee collected for any case not included in such program as provided in subsection (a) of Section 710 [750 ILCS 5/710(a)] may be used by the county for any purpose.

The fee shall be payable semi-annually, being due with the support payment due on or next immediately following January 1 and July 1. The fee shall be payable in advance as herein provided, except for the initial payment which shall be paid at the time of the initial child support payment to the clerk. The amount of the fee due for the initial period shall be computed from the date the support order first takes effect to the next January 1 or July 1, whichever occurs first.

Unless paid in cash, the payment of the fee shall be by a separate instrument from the support payment and shall be made to the order of the clerk.

(b) All monies collected in fees by the clerk and all monies received by him upon assessment under Section 710 [750 ILCS 5/710] for reimbursement for the costs of enforcement shall be held in a special fund, the contents of which the clerk shall pay over to the county treasury every month or at such other period as the treasurer shall determine.
(Source: P.A. 82-1002.)

Note.
This section was Ill.Rev.Stat., Ch. 40, para. 711.

750 ILCS 5/712 [Rules for certification; reimbursement; comparison report; supervision by the Child and Spouse Support Unit]

Sec. 712. (a) The Supreme Court may make Rules concerning the certification of counties for inclusion in the child support enforcement program and the application of the procedures created by Sections 709 through 712 [750 ILCS 5/709 through 750 ILCS 5/712] in the various counties.

The Supreme Court shall inform each circuit court and clerk of the court of the availability of the program to reimburse counties desiring to participate in the program of enforcement of child support payments.

The Supreme Court shall also distribute to each circuit court and clerk of the court any materials prepared by the Child and Spouse Support Unit comparing child support enforcement in counties included and not included in this program.

(b) The Illinois Department of Public Aid, through the Child and Spouse Support Unit provided for by Section 10-3.1 of The Illinois Public Aid Code [305 ILCS 5/10-3.1], shall have general supervision of the child support programs created by Sections 709 through 712 [750 ILCS 5/709 through 750 ILCS 5/712] and shall have the powers and duties provided in this Section, including the following:

(1) to make advance payments to any county included in the program for expenses in preparing programs to enforce payment of child support to the clerk from appropriations made for such purposes by the General Assembly;

(2) to make payments to each covered county to pay for its reasonable expenses actually necessary to maintain a continuing program not paid for by fees, penalties, or other monies; provided that, with respect to that portion of the program on behalf of dependent children included in a grant of financial aid under Article IV of The Illinois Public Aid Code [305 ILCS 5/4-1 et seq.] the Unit shall pay only such expenses as is its current practice or as it may deem appropriate; provided further that the Unit shall only pay expenses of the entire program subject to the availability of federal monies to pay the majority of expenses of the entire child support enforcement program; provided further that the Unit or Department may set standards relating to enforcement which have to be met by any county seeking to enter a contract with the Department for reimbursement of expenses of the entire enforcement program prior to an application for reimbursement being approved and the contract granted; and provided further that such standards may relate to, but are not limited to the following factors: maintenance of the payment record, the definition of delinquency; the period of time in which a delinquency must be determined, the payor notified, the remittance received, the referral to the state's attorney made, and the payment remitted by the clerk to the payee or other party entitled to the payment; the conditions under which referral will not be made to the state's attorney; and the definitions and procedures for other matters necessary for the conduct and operation of the program;

(3) to monitor the various local programs for enforcement of child support payments to the clerk;

(4) to act to encourage enforcement whenever local enforcement procedures are inadequate;

(5) to receive monies from any source for assistance in enforcement of child support; and

(6) to assist any county desirous of assistance in establishing and maintaining a child support enforcement program.

(c) Any county may apply for financial assistance to the Unit to initiate or maintain a program of child support enforcement. Every county which desires such assistance shall apply according to procedures established by the Unit. In its application, it shall state the following: financial needs, personnel requirements, anticipated caseloads, any amounts collected or anticipated in fees or penalties, and any other information required by the Unit.

(d) In the case that any advance money is given to any county under this Section to initiate an enforcement system, the county shall reimburse the state within 2 years from the date such monies are given to it. The Unit may establish an appropriate schedule of reimbursement for any county.

(e) In the event of the unavailability of federal monies to pay for the greater part of the costs to a county of the child support enforcement program under Sections 709 through 712 [750 ILCS 5/709 through 750 ILCS 5/712] and the resulting cessation of state participation, the operation of the child support enforcement program under Sections 709 through 712 [750 ILCS 5/709 through 750 ILCS 5/712] shall terminate. The date and the method of termination shall be determined by Supreme Court Rule.

(Source: P.A. 84-1395.)

Note.

This section was Ill.Rev.Stat., Ch. 40, para. 712.

750 ILCS 5/713 Attachment of the Body

Sec. 713. *Attachment of the Body.* As used in this Section, "obligor" has the same meaning ascribed to such term in the Income Withholding for Support Act [750 ILCS 28/1 et seq.].

(a) In any proceeding to enforce an order for support, where the obligor has failed to appear in court pursuant to order of court and after due notice thereof, the court may enter an order for the attachment of the body of the obligor. Notices under this Section shall be served upon the obligor by any means authorized under subsection (a-5) of Section 505 [750 ILCS 5/505]. The attachment order shall fix an amount of escrow which is equal to a minimum of 20% of the total child support arrearage alleged by the obligee in sworn testimony to be due and owing. The attachment order shall direct the Sheriff of any county in Illinois to take the obligor into custody and shall set the number of days following release from custody for a hearing to be held at which the obligor must appear, if he is released under subsection (b) of this Section.

(b) If the obligor is taken into custody, the Sheriff shall take the obligor before the court which entered the attachment order. However, the Sheriff may release the person after he or she has deposited the amount of escrow ordered by the court pursuant to local procedures for the posting of bond. The Sheriff shall advise the obligor of the hearing date at which the obligor is required to appear.

(c) Any escrow deposited pursuant to this Section shall be transmitted to the Clerk of the Circuit Court for the county in which the order for attachment of the body of the obligor was entered. Any Clerk who receives money deposited into escrow pursuant to this Section shall notify the obligee, public office or legal counsel whose name appears on the attachment order of the court date at which the obligor is required to appear and the amount deposited into escrow. The Clerk shall disburse such money to the obligee only under an order from the court that entered the attachment order pursuant to this Section.

(d) Whenever an obligor is taken before the court by the Sheriff, or appears in court after the court has ordered the attachment of his body, the court shall:

(1) hold a hearing on the complaint or petition that gave rise to the attachment order. For purposes of determining arrearages that are due and owing by the obligor, the court shall accept the previous sworn testimony of the obligee as true and the appearance of the obligee shall not be required. The court shall require sworn testimony of the obligor as to his or her Social Security number, income, employment, bank accounts, property and any other assets. If there is a dispute as to the total amount of arrearages, the court shall proceed as in any other case as to the undisputed amounts; and

(2) order the Clerk of the Circuit Court to disburse to the obligee or public office money held in escrow pursuant to this Section if the court finds that the amount of arrearages exceeds the amount of the escrow. Amounts received by the obligee or public office shall be deducted from the amount of the arrearages.

(e) If the obligor fails to appear in court after being notified of the court date by the Sheriff upon release from custody, the court shall order any monies deposited into escrow to be immediately released to the obligee or public office and shall proceed under subsection (a) of this Section by entering another order for the attachment of the body of the obligor.

(f) This Section shall apply to any order for support issued under the "Illinois Marriage and Dissolution of Marriage Act", approved September 22, 1977, as amended [750 ILCS 5/101 et seq.]; the "Illinois Parentage Act of 1984", effective July 1, 1985, as amended [750 ILCS 45/1 et seq.]; the "Revised Uniform Reciprocal Enforcement of Support Act", approved August 28, 1969, as amended [repealed]; "The Illinois Public Aid Code", approved April 11, 1967, as amended [305 ILCS 5/1-1 et seq.]; the Non-Support Punishment Act [750 ILCS 16/1 et seq.]; and the "Non-support of Spouse and Children Act", approved June 8, 1953, as amended [repealed].

(g) Any escrow established pursuant to this Section for the purpose of providing support shall not be subject to fees collected by the Clerk of the Circuit Court for any other escrow.
(Source: P.A. 85-219; 90-673, § 915; 91-113, § 5; 91-613, § 970; 92-16, § 96.)

Note.

This section was Ill.Rev.Stat., Ch. 40, para. 713.

Section 70 of P.A. 91-613 contains a severability provision.

The Revised Uniform Reciprocal Enforcement of Support Act, referred to in subsection (f), has been repealed.

The Non-Support of Spouse and Children Act, referred to in subsection (f), is repealed. For similar provisions, see 750 ILCS 16/1 et seq.

Section 996 of P.A. 92-16 contains a "no acceleration or delay" provision, and Section 997 contains a "no revival or extension" provision.

Effect of Amendments.

The 1998 amendment by P.A. 90-673, effective January 1, 1999, substituted "the Income Withholding for Support Act" for "Section 706.1 of this Act" in the introductory paragraph.

The 1999 amendment by P.A. 91-113, effective July 15, 1999, in the second sentence of subdivision (a) substituted "by any means authorized under subsection (a-5) of Section 505" for "either (1) by prepaid certified mail with delivery restricted to the obligor, or (2) by personal service on the obligor".

The 1999 amendment by P.A. 91-613, effective October 1, 1999, inserted "the Non-Support Punishment Act" in subdivision (f).

The 2001 amendment by P.A. 92-16, effective June 28, 2001, combined the amendments by P.A. 91-113 and P.A. 91-613.

CASE NOTES

Bond to Department of Public Aid

Trial court had the power to hold a father in contempt when the father did not appear at a hearing scheduled to determine whether the father should be held in contempt for failing to pay child support, to order the father's arrest and set bond in an amount that was roughly equivalent to child support arrearages the father owed, and to order payment of the bond to the Illinois Department of Public Aid after the father was arrested and a hearing was held to determine whether the father owed past-due child support. In re Marriage of Verstreater, 337 Ill. App. 3d 1112, 273 Ill. Dec. 14, 788 N.E.2d 323, 2003 Ill. App. LEXIS 402 (5 Dist. 2003).

750 ILCS 5/714 Information to locate putative fathers and noncustodial parents

Sec. 714. *Information to locate putative fathers and noncustodial parents.* (a) Upon request by a public office, employers, labor unions, and telephone companies shall provide location information concerning putative fathers and noncustodial parents for the purpose of establishing a child's paternity or establishing, enforcing, or modifying a child support obligation. The term "public office" is defined as set forth in the Income Withholding for Support Act [750 ILCS 28/1 et seq.]. In this Section, "location information" means information about (i) the physical whereabouts of a putative father or noncustodial parent, (ii) the employer of the putative father or noncustodial parent, or (iii) the salary, wages, and other compensation paid and the health insurance coverage provided to the putative father or noncustodial parent by the employer of the putative father or noncustodial parent or by a labor union of which the putative father or noncustodial parent is a member. An employer, labor union, or telephone company shall respond to the request of the public office within 15 days after receiving the request. Any employer, labor union, or telephone company that willfully fails to fully respond within the 15-day period shall be subject to a penalty of $100 for each day that the response is not provided to the public office after the 15-day period has expired. The penalty may be collected in a civil action, which may be brought against the employer, labor union, or telephone company in favor of the public office.

(b) Upon being served with a subpoena (including an administrative subpoena as authorized by law), a utility company or cable television company must provide location information to a public office for the purpose of establishing a child's paternity or establishing, enforcing, or modifying a child support obligation.

(c) Notwithstanding the provisions of any other State or local law to the contrary, an employer, labor union, telephone company, utility company, or cable television company shall not be liable to any person for disclosure of location information under the requirements of this Section, except for willful and wanton misconduct.
(Source: P.A. 93-116, § 10.)

Effective Date.

Section 99 of P.A. 93-116 made this Act effective upon becoming law. The Act was approved July 10, 2003.

PART VIII.

APPLICATION AND SEVERABILITY

750 ILCS 5/801 Application

Sec. 801. *Application.* (a) This Act applies to all proceedings commenced on or after its effective date.

(b) This Act applies to all pending actions and proceedings commenced prior to its effective date with respect to issues on which a judgment has not been entered. Evidence adduced after the effective date of this Act shall be in compliance with this Act.

(c) This Act applies to all proceedings commenced after its effective date for the modification of a judgment or order entered prior to the effective date of this Act. Alimony in gross or settlements in lieu of alimony provided for in judgments entered prior to October 1, 1977 shall not be modifiable or terminable as maintenance thereafter.

(d) In any action or proceeding in which an appeal was pending or a new trial was ordered prior to the effective date of this Act, the law in effect at the time of the order sustaining the appeal or the new trial governs the appeal, the new trial, and any subsequent trial or appeal.
(Source: P.A. 82-566.)

Note.

This section was Ill.Rev.Stat., Ch. 40, para. 801.

CASE NOTES

Analysis

Constitutionality
Agreement
—Act Applicable
Alimony Determination
—Act Applicable
Appeal
—Act Applicable
—Act Not Applicable
—Rehearing Required
Application and Construction
Commenced Action
—Act Applicable
—Act Not Applicable
Custody
—Act Applicable
Legislative Intent
Modification
—Act Applicable
New Trial
Order Sustaining Appeal
Orders
—Act Applicable
Pending Actions
—Act Applicable
Post-Decree Proceedings
—Act Applicable
Property Disposition
—Act Applicable
Purpose
Relitigation Not Required
Remand
—Act Applicable
Retroactive Application
Rights Under Dissolution
—Act Applicable

Constitutionality

Petitioner had no vested right to modification of his alimony obligations; rather, he had a mere expectation that he could seek such relief under the preexisting divorce laws. Thus his claim that subsection (c) of this section retroactively deprived him of a vested right was unfounded. In re Josic, 78 Ill. App. 3d 347, 33 Ill. Dec. 871, 397 N.E.2d 204 (1 Dist. 1979).

Subsection (c) of this section did not impair the obligations arising out of a marital agreement regarding its subsequent modification, and was not in violation of Ill. Const. (1970), Art. I, § 16. In re Josic, 78 Ill. App. 3d 347, 33 Ill. Dec. 871, 397 N.E.2d 204 (1 Dist. 1979).

Subsection (b) of this section does not unconstitutionally prevent the court from determining facts in cases pending before it. The section does not dictate the resolution of facts in pending actions, but merely mandates which law the court is to apply to the facts in pending cases. Kujawinski v. Kujawinski, 71 Ill. 2d 563, 17 Ill. Dec. 801, 376 N.E.2d 1382 (1978).

Agreement

—Act Applicable

Although maintenance agreement was entered into prior to adoption of this Act, the Act was applicable to the agreement. In re Martino, 166 Ill. App. 3d 692, 117 Ill. Dec. 788, 520 N.E.2d 1139 (2 Dist. 1988).

Alimony Determination

—Act Applicable

Although decree of divorce and petition to modify alimony were both filed prior to the effective date of this Act, the Act was applicable to the issue of changed circumstances, because the evidence adduced at the hearing on the petition to modify and the order terminating alimony both occurred after the new law was in effect. Pierce v. Pierce, 69 Ill. App. 3d 42, 25 Ill. Dec. 511, 386 N.E.2d 1175 (5 Dist. 1979).

Appeal

—Act Applicable

This Act was applicable to an appeal from the denial of a request that respondent be ordered to pay the college education expenses of two of the parties' children and to reimburse petitioner for such related expenses already paid by her, where the order appealed from was entered after the effective date of the Act. Singer v. Singer, 70 Ill. App. 3d 472, 27 Ill. Dec. 88, 388 N.E.2d 1051 (1 Dist. 1979).

—Act Not Applicable

Where notice of the cross-appeal in a divorce case was filed before the effective date of this Act, the appeal was governed by the prior Divorce Act pursuant to subsection (d). Belluomini v. Belluomini, 73 Ill. App. 3d 836, 30 Ill. Dec. 14, 392 N.E.2d 669 (1 Dist. 1979).

For purposes of subsection (b) of this section, a judgment on post-trial motion contesting a divorce decree was entered when the written judgment order was filed, rather than when the post-trial motions were denied, such that the appeal had to be decided on the basis of the former Divorce Act rather than the newly effective Marriage and Dissolution of Marriage Act. Staub v. Staub, 67 Ill. App. 3d 1004, 24 Ill. Dec. 630, 385 N.E.2d 771 (5 Dist. 1978).

The new Illinois Marriage and Divorce Act, effective October 1, 1977, was not applicable to an appeal which was pending on the effective date of the Act. Prenzler v. Prenzler, 55 Ill. App. 3d 244, 12 Ill. Dec. 838, 370 N.E.2d 642 (3 Dist. 1977).

Where the appeal from judgment in action for divorce was perfected on a date well in advance of the effective date of this Act, this Act did not apply to the appeal, which was remanded to the trial court to apply the law which existed at the time the orders were entered. McArdle v. McArdle, 55 Ill. App. 3d 829, 13 Ill. Dec. 282, 370 N.E.2d 1309 (3 Dist. 1977).

—Rehearing Required

Where both plaintiff and defendant indicated that they would have liked to have had a hearing on all issues but that there was no opportunity to do so because they were limited by the trial court's declarations that the only point it was concerned with was whether or not it had jurisdiction to permit the filing of the petition and complaint under the "cooling off" provisions of the former Divorce Act, the mistake would be rectified and the case would be remanded with directions to permit the plaintiff to plead over if he so desired, to conduct a hearing on the issues formulated if he denied the defendant's allegations, or to enter an order based on those allegations if they were not denied or remained admitted. Haney v. Haney, 37 Ill. App. 2d 216, 185 N.E.2d 409 (1 Dist. 1962).

Application and Construction

This section refers to this whole Act whereas § 2 of P.A. 83-129 although similar, applies only to 750 ILCS 5/401 and 750 ILCS 5/503 (amended by P.A. 83-129); therefore subsection (d) of this section applies to determine the appropriate law on retrial. In re Smith, 162 Ill. App. 3d 792, 114 Ill. Dec. 622, 516 N.E.2d 777 (5 Dist. 1987).

Commenced Action

—Act Applicable

Subsection (b) of this section applies to all actions commenced before this Act's effective date with respect to issues on which a judgment has not been entered. Legan v. Legan, 69 Ill. App. 3d 304, 25 Ill. Dec. 757, 387 N.E.2d 413 (3 Dist. 1979).

Where an action was commenced in June, trial was held in September, and the written decree was not signed and filed until October 31, 1977, with respect to all the issues, a judgment was not entered until after the effective date of this Act, and because the decree was entered after October 1, 1977, this Act applied. Schubert v. Schubert, 66 Ill. App. 3d 29, 22 Ill. Dec. 790, 383 N.E.2d 266 (3 Dist. 1978).

—Act Not Applicable

Where the specific amount of attorney fees was not fixed by a court's written decision, but the substantive issues of marital status, alimony, and custody and support of minor children had been litigated and were determined before the effective date of this Act, it was error for the appellate court to reverse the judgment of the circuit court and remand the cause for consideration under this

Commenced Action (Cont'd)

—Act Not Applicable (Cont'd)

Act. West v. West, 76 Ill. 2d 226, 28 Ill. Dec. 521, 390 N.E.2d 880 (1979).

Custody

—Act Applicable

Inasmuch as the judgment resolving the issue of custody was not rendered until after the effective date of this Act, the statutory standard for determining the best interest of the child had to be as set forth in this Act. Wurm v. Wurm, 68 Ill. App. 3d 168, 24 Ill. Dec. 753, 385 N.E.2d 894 (3 Dist. 1979).

Legislative Intent

The legislature attempted through subsection (b) of this section to allow only those issues which had not been fully litigated prior to the effective date of this Act to be decided under the new law. It is not this section's intent to require the relitigation of issues already decided under the previous law simply because post-trial motions are pending or filed after the effective date of this Act. West v. West, 76 Ill. 2d 226, 28 Ill. Dec. 521, 390 N.E.2d 880 (1979).

Modification

—Act Applicable

Although the parties were divorced prior to the enactment of this Act, modification proceedings were governed by this Act, because the stipulation and modification order were filed after the effective date of the Act. Hartman v. Hartman, 89 Ill. App. 3d 969, 45 Ill. Dec. 360, 412 N.E.2d 711 (4 Dist. 1980).

This Act applies to all proceedings commenced after its effective date for the modification of a judgment or order entered prior to the effective date. In re Gammons, 78 Ill. App. 3d 1001, 34 Ill. Dec. 655, 398 N.E.2d 330 (3 Dist. 1979).

New Trial

Where the mandate issued in the first appeal of the case required the circuit court to conduct necessary hearings in order to establish a proper basis for the custodial award under 750 ILCS 5/610(b), further hearings would be treated as equivalent to a new trial under subsection (d) of this section. In re Brown, 127 Ill. App. 3d 831, 83 Ill. Dec. 5, 469 N.E.2d 612 (5 Dist. 1984).

Order Sustaining Appeal

The phrase "order sustaining the appeal," as used in subsection (d) of this section, refers not to the judgment entered by the reviewing court upon the appeal, but rather the order of the trial court which forms the basis of the appeal. In re Brown, 127 Ill. App. 3d 831, 83 Ill. Dec. 5, 469 N.E.2d 612 (5 Dist. 1984).

Orders

—Act Applicable

Although complaint was filed prior to the effective date of the present Illinois Marriage and Dissolution of Marriage Act, decree and orders issued after its effective date and the proceedings would be controlled by that statute. In re Lawver, 82 Ill. App. 3d 198, 37 Ill. Dec. 540, 402 N.E.2d 430 (3 Dist. 1980).

Pending Actions

—Act Applicable

This Act was applicable to actions pending prior to its effective date, but in which judgment was not entered until after that effective date. In re Sweet, 104 Ill. App. 3d 738, 60 Ill. Dec. 199, 432 N.E.2d 1098 (1 Dist. 1982).

Post-Decree Proceedings

—Act Applicable

Even though the parties' divorce decree was entered prior to the effective date of this Act, the Act was held applicable to the post-decree proceeding. Ihle v. Ihle, 92 Ill. App. 3d 893, 48 Ill. Dec. 335, 416 N.E.2d 366 (3 Dist. 1981).

Property Disposition

—Act Applicable

Where a complaint was filed on March 22, 1977, but no hearing on the merits was held until October 7, 1977, and a written judgment order was filed thereafter, the trial court properly applied the new Act which took effect on October 1, 1977, to the distribution of the parties' property and petitioner was not deprived of due process. Marsh v. Marsh, 64 Ill. App. 3d 572, 21 Ill. Dec. 477, 381 N.E.2d 804 (4 Dist. 1978).

Purpose

The purpose of subsection (d) of this section is to allow the correction on appeal or in a new trial of errors made in applying the law in effect at the time of the original hearing pursuant to that law. In re Brown, 127 Ill. App. 3d 831, 83 Ill. Dec. 5, 469 N.E.2d 612 (5 Dist. 1984).

The purpose of this provision is to allow the correction on appeal or in a new trial of errors made in applying the law in effect at the time of the original hearing pursuant to that law; therefore changing the rules on appeal or at the new trial would be unfair to the party prejudiced by the error. In re Sweet, 119 Ill. App. 3d 1033, 75 Ill. Dec. 846, 458 N.E.2d 14 (1 Dist. 1983).

Relitigation Not Required

Issues already decided in the trial court before the 1977 version of this Act became effective could not be relitigated. Cuneo v. Cuneo, 80 Ill. App. 3d 141, 35 Ill. Dec. 856, 399 N.E.2d 1384 (2 Dist. 1980).

This section was not intended to require the relitigation of issues already decided under the previous Divorce Act simply because post-trial motions were pending or filed after the effective date of this Act. Staub v. Staub, 67 Ill. App. 3d 1004, 24 Ill. Dec. 630, 385 N.E.2d 771 (5 Dist. 1978).

Remand

—Act Applicable

Where a judgment of divorce was entered without a new hearing, that judgment, other than the portion decreeing the divorce, was reversed and the cause remanded for a new hearing to determine the circumstances of the parties and to frame a judgment which reflected current circumstances regarding the necessity of alimony and child support; under this section, the issues of alimony and child support were to be considered "issues on which a judgment has not been entered" for the purpose of application of the new Act. Smith v. Smith, 73 Ill. App. 3d 423, 29 Ill. Dec. 735, 392 N.E.2d 292 (1 Dist. 1979).

Retroactive Application

Subsection (d) of this section does not apply retroactively to orders issued prior to January 1, 1986. In re Zucco, 150 Ill. App. 3d 146, 103 Ill. Dec. 558, 501 N.E.2d 875 (5 Dist. 1986).

A right of action which stems purely from statutory enactments may be abrogated by the retrospective application of legislation, and since dissolution of marriage, including modification of settlements, is entirely statutory in origin and nature retrospective application of this Act did not deprive petitioner of any vested common-law right of action. In re Josic, 78 Ill. App. 3d 347, 33 Ill. Dec. 871, 397 N.E.2d 204 (1 Dist. 1979).

Rights Under Dissolution

—Act Applicable

Where judgment dissolving the marriage and dividing the property was entered five months after this Act became effective, this Act controlled the rights of the parties. In re Pieper, 79 Ill. App. 3d 835, 34 Ill. Dec. 877, 398 N.E.2d 868 (1 Dist. 1979).

LEGAL PERIODICALS

For case note, "Hewitt v. Hewitt—Contract Cohabitation and 'Equitable Expectations' Relief for Meretricious Spouses," see 12 J. Marshall J. Prac. & Proc. 435 (1979).

750 ILCS 5/802 Court Rules

Sec. 802. *Court Rules.* The Supreme Court and, subject to the Rules of the Supreme Court, the respective circuit courts, may adopt such rules as

they deem necessary and expedient to carry out the provisions of this Act.
(Source: P.A. 80-923.)

Note.
This section was Ill.Rev.Stat., Ch. 40, para. 802.

CASE NOTES

Necessary and Expedient
Sixth Judicial Circuit Court Rule 7.1(g) is both necessary and expedient when resolving marital disputes involving financial matters; when a trial court receives financial affidavits, it can consider them as if their contents had been presented as direct testimony during a hearing. In re Kocher, 282 Ill. App. 3d 655, 218 Ill. Dec. 167, 668 N.E.2d 651 (4 Dist. 1996).

ILLINOIS UNIFORM PREMARITAL AGREEMENT ACT

750 ILCS 10/1 [Short title]

Sec. 1. This Article shall be known and may be cited as the Illinois Uniform Premarital Agreement Act.
(Source: P.A. 86-966.)

Derivation.
Title: An Act pertaining to domestic matters, and amending named Acts.
Cite: 750 ILCS 10/1 et seq.
Source: P.A. 86-966.
Date: Certified December 13, 1989.

Note.
This section was Ill.Rev.Stat., Ch. 40, para. 2601.

CASE NOTES

ANALYSIS

Public Policy
—Prior Law
Validity of Antenuptial Agreement

Public Policy

—Prior Law
There was little empirical evidence to show that agreements limiting alimony encouraged or incited divorce or separation. Volid v. Volid, 6 Ill. App. 3d 386, 286 N.E.2d 42 (1 Dist. 1972).

Validity of Antenuptial Agreement
Prenuptial agreements should be considered in their entirety to ascertain the general scope or purpose and to give effect to the real intentions of the parties. Anderson v. Anderson, 195 Ill. App. 3d 644, 142 Ill. Dec. 79, 552 N.E.2d 429 (4 Dist. 1990).
Although the law prescribed the rights of a husband and a wife in the property of each other, persons possessing the requisite legal capacity could, by an agreement made in contemplation of marriage, exclude the operation of the law and determine for themselves what rights they would have in each other's property during the marriage and after its termination by death. Volid v. Volid, 6 Ill. App. 3d 386, 286 N.E.2d 42 (1 Dist. 1972).

RESEARCH REFERENCES

Modern status of views as to validity of premarital agreements contemplating divorce or separation. 53 ALR4th 22.
Enforceability of premarital agreements governing support or property rights upon divorce or separation as affected by circumstances surrounding execution—modern status. 53 ALR4th 85.
Enforceability of premarital agreements governing support or property rights upon divorce or separation as affected by fairness or adequacy of those terms—modern status. 53 ALR4th 161.

750 ILCS 10/2 Definitions

Sec. 2. *Definitions.* As used in this Article:
(1) "Premarital agreement" means an agreement between prospective spouses made in contemplation of marriage and to be effective upon marriage.
(2) "Property" means an interest, present or future, legal or equitable, vested or contingent, in real or personal property, including income and earnings.
(Source: P.A. 86-966.)

Note.
This section was Ill.Rev.Stat., Ch. 40, para. 2602.

750 ILCS 10/3 Formalities

Sec. 3. *Formalities.* A premarital agreement must be in writing and signed by both parties. It is enforceable without consideration.
(Source: P.A. 86-966.)

Note.
This section was Ill.Rev.Stat., Ch. 40, para. 2603.

CASE NOTES

Oral Agreement

—Prior Law
A written instrument that was not executed until a considerable time after the parties' marriage was a sufficient memorandum of the parties' oral antenuptial agreement that neither party would claim any interest in the property of the other to remove the oral antenuptial agreement from the bar of the Statute of Frauds. Lee v. Central Nat'l Bank & Trust Co., 56 Ill. 2d 394, 308 N.E.2d 605 (1974).

750 ILCS 10/4 Content

Sec. 4. *Content.* (a) Parties to a premarital agreement may contract with respect to:
(1) the rights and obligations of each of the parties in any of the property of either or both of them whenever and wherever acquired or located;
(2) the right to buy, sell, use, transfer, exchange, abandon, lease, consume, expend, assign, create a security interest in, mortgage, encumber, dispose of, or otherwise manage and control property;
(3) the disposition of property upon separation, marital dissolution, death, or the occurrence or nonoccurrence of any other event;
(4) the modification or elimination of spousal support;
(5) the making of a will, trust, or other arrangement to carry out the provisions of the agreement;
(6) the ownership rights in and disposition of the death benefit from a life insurance policy;
(7) the choice of law governing the construction of the agreement; and

(8) any other matter, including their personal rights and obligations, not in violation of public policy or a statute imposing a criminal penalty.

(b) The right of a child to support may not be adversely affected by a premarital agreement.

(Source: P.A. 86-966.)

Note.

This section was Ill.Rev.Stat., Ch. 40, para. 2604.

CASE NOTES

Analysis

Agreement Upheld
Knowledge of Assets
—Prior Law
Reciprocal Provisions
Support Obligation
—Prior Law

Agreement Upheld

An antenuptial agreement which provided that the wife, if she survived the husband, should receive only certain money and real estate in lieu of all rights which she might have had as a widow, was upheld. Petru v. Petru, 4 Ill. App. 2d 1, 123 N.E.2d 352 (1 Dist. 1954).

Knowledge of Assets

—Prior Law

Information as to the nature and extent of the holdings of the husband need not have come directly from him, and surrounding circumstances may have been such as to charge the wife with knowledge of his property; general reputation was not sufficient to supply that knowledge. Watson v. Watson, 5 Ill. 2d 526, 126 N.E.2d 220 (1955).

Reciprocal Provisions

The validity of an antenuptial agreement was not impaired where the intended wife failed or omitted to waive the interest she would have acquired in her prospective husband's property, since it was not essential that the agreement contain reciprocal provisions. Lee v. Central Nat'l Bank & Trust Co., 56 Ill. 2d 394, 308 N.E.2d 605 (1974).

Support Obligation

—Prior Law

Under prior law, a husband and wife could contract with each other as to their mutual property rights, but the husband could not by contract, either before or after marriage, relieve himself of the obligation imposed upon him by law to support his wife. Hallam v. Hallam, 298 Ill. App. 445, 19 N.E.2d 101 (1 Dist. 1939).

750 ILCS 10/5 Effect of marriage

Sec. 5. *Effect of marriage.* A premarital agreement becomes effective upon marriage.

(Source: P.A. 86-966.)

Note.

This section was Ill.Rev.Stat., Ch. 40, para. 2605.

750 ILCS 10/6 Amendment, revocation

Sec. 6. *Amendment, revocation.* After marriage, a premarital agreement may be amended or revoked only by a written agreement signed by the parties. The amended agreement or the revocation is enforceable without consideration.

(Source: P.A. 86-966.)

Note.

This section was Ill.Rev.Stat., Ch. 40, para. 2606.

750 ILCS 10/7 Enforcement

Sec. 7. *Enforcement.* (a) A premarital agreement is not enforceable if the party against whom enforcement is sought proves that:

(1) that party did not execute the agreement voluntarily; or

(2) the agreement was unconscionable when it was executed and, before execution of the agreement, that party:

(i) was not provided a fair and reasonable disclosure of the property or financial obligations of the other party;

(ii) did not voluntarily and expressly waive, in writing, any right to disclosure of the property or financial obligations of the other party beyond the disclosure provided; and

(iii) did not have, or reasonably could not have had, an adequate knowledge of the property or financial obligations of the other party.

(b) If a provision of a premarital agreement modifies or eliminates spousal support and that modification or elimination causes one party to the agreement undue hardship in light of circumstances not reasonably foreseeable at the time of the execution of the agreement, a court, notwithstanding the terms of the agreement, may require the other party to provide support to the extent necessary to avoid such hardship.

(c) An issue of unconscionability of a premarital agreement shall be decided by the court as a matter of law.

(Source: P.A. 86-966.)

Note.

This section was Ill.Rev.Stat., Ch. 40, para. 2607.

CASE NOTES

Analysis

Attorney Fees
Confidential Relationship
—Prior Law
Declaratory Judgments
Duress and Coercion
—Not Shown
Incomplete Disclosure
Limitation of Support
—Prior Law
Review by Court
—In General
—Agreement Upheld
—Maintenance and Support
—Time of Review
Validity

Attorney Fees

Where husband instituted the proceedings to determine the validity of the antenuptial agreement and financially was in a far superior position to wife, the provision that each party pay his or her own attorney fees upon dissolution was not fair and reasonable. Warren v. Warren, 169 Ill. App. 3d 226, 119 Ill. Dec. 924, 523 N.E.2d 680 (5 Dist. 1988).

Confidential Relationship

—Prior Law

Where parties to an antenuptial contract were engaged to be married, before the contract was entered into, a confidential relationship existed and if the provision made for the wife was disproportionate to the extent and value of the husband's estate, a presumption was raised of an intended concealment by the intended husband, which constituted a prima facie case of concealment and cast upon those who would sustain the agreement the burden of showing the absence of concealment and that the intended wife had full knowledge of the nature and extent of the husband's property. Watson v. Watson, 5 Ill. 2d 526, 126 N.E.2d 220 (1955).

Where widow brought action to set aside antenuptial agreement, testimony that the parties were engaged prior to signing the agreement, taken with the language of the antenuptial agreement that the parties "contemplated a marriage ceremony" which was "soon to be solemnized," was sufficient to show an engagement to be married; therefore, a confidential or fiduciary relationship existed between the parties at the time the antenuptial agreement was executed. Watson v. Watson, 5 Ill. 2d 526, 126 N.E.2d 220 (1955).

Declaratory Judgments

There was an actual controversy, definite and concrete, and the parties to an antenuptial contract had adverse legal interests, where the contention of the defendant was that the contract was invalid, thus preventing a comprehensive plan being made on the part of the plaintiff to dispose of his estate; such a dispute under the declaratory judgment statute could be tried at its inception before it had accumulated the asperity, distemper, animosity, passion, and violence of the full-blown battle which loomed ahead. Trossman v. Trossman, 24 Ill. App. 2d 521, 165 N.E.2d 368 (1 Dist. 1960).

Duress and Coercion

—Not Shown

Where wife claimed that she entered into agreement under conditions of stress and coercion, and the record showed (1) that husband encouraged her to seek independent legal counsel, (2) that the marriage did not take place until about two months after the agreement was executed, and (3) that wife appeared to be in good spirits at the time of execution, the circuit court properly found that the agreement was made in the absence of duress or coercion. Warren v. Warren, 169 Ill. App. 3d 226, 119 Ill. Dec. 924, 523 N.E.2d 680 (5 Dist. 1988).

Incomplete Disclosure

Where there was no showing that the subsequent acceptance of the consideration of $1,000 by wife was preceded by a full disclosure of the nature and extent of the property holdings of the husband, there was no ratification of the antenuptial agreement. Watson v. Watson, 5 Ill. 2d 526, 126 N.E.2d 220 (1955).

A circuit court was correct in concluding that a confidential relationship existed between the parties to an antenuptial agreement prior to the execution thereof, and that the husband did not make a complete and adequate disclosure to the wife of the nature and extent of his holdings, which required setting aside the antenuptial agreement. Watson v. Watson, 5 Ill. 2d 526, 126 N.E.2d 220 (1955).

Limitation of Support

—Prior Law

Where the parties agreed in an antenuptial agreement to a sum of $600 per month for 125 successive months to be paid to the wife in lieu of all rights to alimony or support, and the court, in the exercise of its discretion, awarded temporary alimony in the amount of $1,250 per month, the order should have contained a provision that any temporary sums for her support which were paid would ultimately be deducted from the lump sum settlement agreed to by the parties. Volid v. Volid, 6 Ill. App. 3d 386, 286 N.E.2d 42 (1 Dist. 1972).

Review by Court

—In General

A court should uphold the validity of clauses in an antenuptial agreement when they are fair and reasonable. In re Burgess, 138 Ill. App. 3d 13, 92 Ill. Dec. 693, 485 N.E.2d 504 (3 Dist. 1985).

—Agreement Upheld

Evidence clearly showed that at the time the divorce decree was entered, plaintiff knowingly waived and relinquished all her rights under the antenuptial agreement. Friend v. Northern Trust Co., 314 Ill. App. 596, 42 N.E.2d 330 (1 Dist. 1942).

—Maintenance and Support

Where premarital agreement provided no financial settlement whatsoever for wife, and for several years wife and husband lived a lifestyle far more extravagant than wife could hope to afford on her own, provision for total waiver of wife's right to maintenance was not fair and reasonable due to wife's financial circumstances. Warren v. Warren, 169 Ill. App. 3d 226, 119 Ill. Dec. 924, 523 N.E.2d 680 (5 Dist. 1988).

At the time of dissolution, courts may consider whether some untoward circumstance, one not contemplated by the parties, has occurred such that justice requires a re-examination of the issue of maintenance to mitigate the potential harm to spouses which could result from the strict enforcement of maintenance provisions of antenuptial agreements. In re Burgess, 138 Ill. App. 3d 13, 92 Ill. Dec. 693, 485 N.E.2d 504 (3 Dist. 1985).

—Time of Review

The parties in a case involving an antenuptial contract should have the matter decided by the courts during the lifetime of both of the parties, when both plaintiff and defendant can, without any restrictions imposed by the Dead Man's Act, 735 ILCS 5/8-201, fully and adequately present their case as to the validity of the contract. Trossman v. Trossman, 24 Ill. App. 2d 521, 165 N.E.2d 368 (1 Dist. 1960).

Validity

An antenuptial agreement is valid at the time of execution if it was entered with full knowledge and without fraud, duress or coercion. In re Burgess, 138 Ill. App. 3d 13, 92 Ill. Dec. 693, 485 N.E.2d 504 (3 Dist. 1985).

750 ILCS 10/8 Enforcement: void marriage

Sec. 8. *Enforcement: void marriage.* If a marriage is determined to be void, an agreement that would otherwise have been a premarital agreement is enforceable only to the extent necessary to avoid an inequitable result.
(Source: P.A. 86-966.)

Note.

This section was Ill.Rev.Stat., Ch. 40, para. 2608.

750 ILCS 10/9 Limitation of actions

Sec. 9. *Limitation of actions.* Any statute of limitations applicable to an action asserting a claim for relief under a premarital agreement is tolled during the marriage of the parties to the agreement. However, equitable defenses limiting the time for enforcement, including laches and estoppel, are available to either party.
(Source: P.A. 86-966.)

Note.

This section was Ill.Rev.Stat., Ch. 40, para. 2609.

750 ILCS 10/10 Application and construction

Sec. 10. *Application and construction.* This Act shall be applied and construed to effectuate its general purpose to make uniform the law with

respect to the subject of this Act among states enacting it.
(Source: P.A. 86-966.)

Note.
This section was Ill.Rev.Stat., Ch. 40, para. 2610.

750 ILCS 10/11 Time of taking effect

Sec. 11. *Time of taking effect.* This Article applies to any premarital agreement executed on or after January 1, 1990.
(Source: P.A. 86-966; 86-1028.)

Note.
This section was Ill.Rev.Stat., Ch. 40, para. 2611.

NON-SUPPORT OF SPOUSE AND CHILDREN ACT

750 ILCS 15/1 through 750 ILCS 15/12.2: Repealed by P.A. 91-613, § 992, effective October 1, 1999.

Note.
The Non-Support of Spouse and Children Act was repealed by P.A. 91-613, § 992. For similar provisions, see 750 ILCS 16/1 et seq.

A number of sections within the Non-Support of Spouse and Children Act were amended by 1999 legislation. Due to the repeal of this Act, the amendments made to those sections are not set out, but are described below.

750 ILCS 15/2.1 was amended by P.A. 91-24, § 35, effective July 1, 1999, which incorporated the amendments by P.A. 90-673 and P.A. 90-790, deleted "in effect in accordance with the Income Withholding for Support" at the end of the first paragraph of subsection (3), and, in the second sentence of subsection (4), deleted "other" following "All", and substituted "Human Services" for "Public Aid" and "DHS" for "Public Assistance".

750 ILCS 15/2.1 was amended by P.A. 91-212, § 30, effective July 20, 1999, which deleted "in accordance with the Income Withholding for Support" at the end of the first paragraph of subsection (3), and added subsection (7), relating to requirements of the State Disbursement Unit.

750 ILCS 15/2.1 was amended by P.A. 91-357, § 257, effective July 29, 1999, which deleted "in accordance with the Income Withholding for Support" at the end of the first paragraph of subsection (3).

750 ILCS 15/2.2, which was enacted by P.A. 91-212, § 30, effective July 20, 1999, concerned payment of support to the State Disbursement Unit.

750 ILCS 15/4.1 was amended by P.A. 91-357, § 257, effective July 29, 1999, which rewrote the section.

750 ILCS 15/4.3 which was enacted by P.A. 91-397, § 15, effective July 29, 1999, concerned interest on support obligations accruing at a rate of 9% per annum.

750 ILCS 15/12 was amended by P.A. 91-357, § 257, effective July 29, 1999, which substituted "Job" for "Jobs" in the second sentence of subsection (a).

750 ILCS 15/12.2, which was enacted by P.A. 91-212, § 30, effective July 20, 1999, concerned information provided to the state case registry.

NON-SUPPORT PUNISHMENT ACT

750 ILCS 16/1 Short title

Sec. 1. *Short title.* This Act may be cited as the Non-Support Punishment Act.
(Source: P.A. 91-613, § 1.)

Effective Date.
Section 999 of P.A. 91-613 made this Act effective October 1, 1999.

750 ILCS 16/5 Prosecutions by State's Attorneys

Sec. 5. *Prosecutions by State's Attorneys.* A proceeding for enforcement of this Act may be instituted and prosecuted by the several State's Attorneys only upon the filing of a verified complaint by the person or persons receiving child or spousal support.
(Source: P.A. 91-613, § 5.)

CASE NOTES

Public Aid

—Not Necessary
A complainant under former 750 ILCS 15/16 need not be a public aid recipient to pursue the action through the State's attorney. People ex rel. Wright v. Wright, 67 Ill. App. 3d 586, 24 Ill. Dec. 347, 385 N.E.2d 114 (1 Dist. 1978).

750 ILCS 16/7 Prosecutions by Attorney General

Sec. 7. *Prosecutions by Attorney General.* In addition to enforcement proceedings by the several State's Attorneys, a proceeding for the enforcement of this Act may be instituted and prosecuted by the Attorney General in cases referred by the Illinois Department of Public Aid involving persons receiving child support enforcement services under Article X of the Illinois Public Aid Code [305 ILCS 5/10-1 et seq.]. Before referring a case to the Attorney General for enforcement under this Act, the Department of Public Aid shall notify the person receiving child support enforcement services under Article X of the Illinois Public Aid Code [305 ILCS 5/10-1 et seq.] of the Department's intent to refer the case to the Attorney General under this Section for prosecution.
(Source: P.A. 91-613, § 7; 92-590, § 15.)

Effect of Amendments.
The 2002 amendment by P.A. 92-590, effective July 1, 2002, substituted "child support enforcement services" for "child and spouse support services" twice.

750 ILCS 16/10 Proceedings

Sec. 10. *Proceedings.* Proceedings under this Act may be by indictment or information. No proceeding may be brought under Section 15 [750 ILCS 16/15] against a person whose court or administrative order for support was entered by default, unless the indictment or information specifically alleges that the person has knowledge of the existence of the order for support and that the person has the ability to pay the support.
(Source: P.A. 91-613, § 10.)

CASE NOTES

Review
While former Ill.Rev.Stat., ch. 68, para. 24 was a criminal

Review (Cont'd)
statute, and for any order entered thereunder a review could only be had by abolished writ of error, former Ill.Rev.Stat., ch. 26, para. 68 was chiefly in the interest of the wife and children, and proceedings pursuant to its terms were civil in their character; as a consequence, a person who felt himself aggrieved by an order entered for support pendente lite might question its propriety or correctness by appeal. People v. Riggs, 296 Ill. App. 136, 15 N.E.2d 914 (4 Dist. 1938).

750 ILCS 16/15 Failure to support

Sec. 15. *Failure to support.* (a) A person commits the offense of failure to support when he or she:

(1) willfully, without any lawful excuse, refuses to provide for the support or maintenance of his or her spouse, with the knowledge that the spouse is in need of such support or maintenance, or, without lawful excuse, deserts or willfully refuses to provide for the support or maintenance of his or her child or children in need of support or maintenance and the person has the ability to provide the support; or

(2) willfully fails to pay a support obligation required under a court or administrative order for support, if the obligation has remained unpaid for a period longer than 6 months, or is in arrears in an amount greater than $5,000, and the person has the ability to provide the support; or

(3) leaves the State with the intent to evade a support obligation required under a court or administrative order for support, if the obligation, regardless of when it accrued, has remained unpaid for a period longer than 6 months, or is in arrears in an amount greater than $10,000; or

(4) willfully fails to pay a support obligation required under a court or administrative order for support, if the obligation has remained unpaid for a period longer than one year, or is in arrears in an amount greater than $20,000, and the person has the ability to provide the support.

(a-5) Presumption of ability to pay support. The existence of a court or administrative order of support that was not based on a default judgment and was in effect for the time period charged in the indictment or information creates a rebuttable presumption that the obligor has the ability to pay the support obligation for that time period.

(b) Sentence. A person convicted of a first offense under subdivision (a)(1) or (a)(2) is guilty of a Class A misdemeanor. A person convicted of an offense under subdivision (a)(3) or (a)(4) or a second or subsequent offense under subdivision (a)(1) or (a)(2) is guilty of a Class 4 felony.

(c) Expungement. A person convicted of a first offense under subdivision (a)(1) or (a)(2) who is eligible for the Earnfare program, shall, in lieu of the sentence prescribed in subsection (b), be referred to the Earnfare program. Upon certification of completion of the Earnfare program, the conviction shall be expunged. If the person fails to successfully complete the Earnfare program, he or she shall be sentenced in accordance with subsection (b).

(d) Fine. Sentences of imprisonment and fines for offenses committed under this Act shall be as provided under Articles 8 and 9 of Chapter V of the Unified Code of Corrections [730 ILCS 5/5-8-1 et seq. and 730 ILCS 5/5-9-1 et seq.], except that the court shall order restitution of all unpaid support payments and may impose the following fines, alone, or in addition to a sentence of imprisonment under the following circumstances:

(1) from $1,000 to $5,000 if the support obligation has remained unpaid for a period longer than 2 years, or is in arrears in an amount greater than $1,000 and not exceeding $10,000;

(2) from $5,000 to $10,000 if the support obligation has remained unpaid for a period longer than 5 years, or is in arrears in an amount greater than $10,000 and not exceeding $20,000; or

(3) from $10,000 to $25,000 if the support obligation has remained unpaid for a period longer than 8 years, or is in arrears in an amount greater than $20,000.

(e) Restitution shall be ordered in an amount equal to the total unpaid support obligation as it existed at the time of sentencing. Any amounts paid by the obligor shall be allocated first to current support and then to restitution ordered and then to fines imposed under this Section.

(f) For purposes of this Act, the term "child" shall have the meaning ascribed to it in Section 505 of the Illinois Marriage and Dissolution of Marriage Act [750 ILCS 5/101 et seq.].

(Source: P.A. 91-613, § 15; 92-876, § 915.)

Effect of Amendments.

The 2002 amendment by P.A. 92-876, effective June 1, 2003, deleted "under the age of 18 years" after "children" in subsection (a)(1); and added the subsection (e) designation and subsection (f).

CASE NOTES

Analysis

In General
Ability to Pay
—New Spouse
Appeals
Failure to Pay
—Lawful Excuse Generally
—Lawful Excuse Not Shown
Jurisdiction
—Not Found
Jury Trial
Modification
—Denied
Need of Support or Maintenance
—Child's Financial Condition
—Evidence Held Sufficient
—Factors
Parentage
Reciprocal Spousal Support
Rights of Defendant
Sentencing
Venue

In General

Former Ill.Rev.Stat. ch. 40, para. 1101 (Non-Support of Spouse and Children Act) imposed liability on a spouse for nonsupport only when the other spouse was in need of such support or maintenance. McGloon v. Zmigrocki, 191 Ill. App. 3d 968, 139 Ill. Dec. 53, 548 N.E.2d 438 (1 Dist. 1989).

In General (Cont'd)

The obligation of one spouse to support the other and the obligation of a parent to support his children who are under the age of 18 and in need of support were recognized and required to be satisfied by former Ill.Rev.Stat. ch. 40, para. 1101 et seq. (Non-Support of Spouse and Children Act) In re Gan, 83 Ill. App. 3d 265, 38 Ill. Dec. 882, 404 N.E.2d 306 (5 Dist. 1980).

Ability to Pay

—New Spouse

Ex-husband's current wife's employment status was relevant to the issue of ex-husband's "available means," where it was clear that ex-wife's current husband had no obligation to support ex-husband's children, and it was equally clear that ex-husband did have an obligation to support his ex-wife should she be in need. In re Whitney, 90 Ill. App. 3d 734, 46 Ill. Dec. 118, 413 N.E.2d 872 (3 Dist. 1980).

Appeals

While former Ill.Rev.Stat., ch. 68, para. 24 (see now this section) was a criminal statute, and for any order entered thereunder a review could only be had by abolished writ of error, former Ill.Rev.Stat., ch. 68, para. 26 was chiefly in the interest of the wife and children, and proceedings pursuant to its terms were civil in their character; as a consequence, a person who felt himself aggrieved by an order entered for support pendente lite might question its propriety or correctness by appeal. People v. Riggs, 296 Ill. App. 136, 15 N.E.2d 914 (4 Dist. 1938).

Failure to Pay

—Lawful Excuse Generally

In order for a defendant to have a lawful excuse, the conditions giving rise to his failure to provide support must not have been of his own making nor as a result of a course of conduct which materially contributed to the frustration of this section. People v. James, 89 Ill. App. 3d 157, 44 Ill. Dec. 441, 411 N.E.2d 563 (4 Dist. 1980).

—Lawful Excuse Not Shown

Defendant was without any lawful excuse where the record demonstrated his ability to generate $19,000 in cash flow but he knowingly, and voluntarily, diverted it to his own purposes; however laudable his aspirations to assist and elevate unfortunates, it was not a lawful excuse for permitting his children to become public charges. People v. James, 89 Ill. App. 3d 157, 44 Ill. Dec. 441, 411 N.E.2d 563 (4 Dist. 1980).

Evidence in prosecution of husband for neglect showed reasonable cause for the wife leaving the husband since he removed his clothes from the domicile and informed his wife he was not going to live with her and the children, and refused to provide more than bread and milk for the family. People v. Rose, 350 Ill. App. 338, 113 N.E.2d 75 (4 Dist. 1953).

Jurisdiction

—Not Found

Order entered after the court found the defendant guilty of violation of former Ill.Rev.Stat., ch. 68, para. 22, which was repealed 17 days earlier, was void because the trial court lacked subject matter jurisdiction over the action. People ex rel. Wright v. Wright, 67 Ill. App. 3d 586, 24 Ill. Dec. 347, 385 N.E.2d 114 (1 Dist. 1978).

Jury Trial

The mere fact that in cases concerning the former crime of wife abandonment the legislature empowered the court, in its discretion, to inflict a punishment differing from that inflicted in other cases of misdemeanor did not affect the right of the defendant to a trial by jury. People v. Heise, 257 Ill. 443, 100 N.E. 1000 (1913).

Modification

—Denied

Where there was no showing of a substantial change in the father's ability to pay child support not already provided for by the flexible terms of the support decree then in effect, ex-wife's petition for modification was denied. In re Whitney, 90 Ill. App. 3d 734, 46 Ill. Dec. 118, 413 N.E.2d 872 (3 Dist. 1980).

Need of Support or Maintenance

—Child's Financial Condition

The financial condition of a child's estate was considered in determining whether she was destitute and in necessitous circumstances under former Ill.Rev.Stat., ch. 68, para. 24 (see now this section). People v. Booth, 390 Ill. 330, 61 N.E.2d 370 (1945).

—Evidence Held Sufficient

Evidence was sufficient to have established the destitution of defendant's child, and his conviction of criminal nonsupport would be upheld. People v. Powers, 340 Ill. App. 201, 91 N.E.2d 637 (1 Dist. 1950).

—Factors

The factors, the proof of which would show a child to be in destitute and necessitous circumstances under former Ill.Rev.Stat., ch. 68, para. 24 are factual conditions which are to be proved as any other fact essential to the establishment of a crime. People v. Booth, 390 Ill. 330, 61 N.E.2d 370 (1945).

Parentage

Former Ill.Rev.Stat., ch. 68, para. 24 does not explicitly provide for a determination of paternity; however, it does state that a parent is responsible for the support of "his or her child," which suggests that the determination of paternity is implicit. People v. Askew, 74 Ill. App. 3d 743, 30 Ill. Dec. 777, 393 N.E.2d 1124 (1 Dist. 1979).

Mere denial by the husband that he had access to his wife has been held to be insufficient proof to overcome the presumption of legitimacy of a child born during wedlock, and therefore precluding from husband from introducing results of blood tests has the effect of denying him a defense, which constitutes a violation of due process. People v. Askew, 74 Ill. App. 3d 743, 30 Ill. Dec. 777, 393 N.E.2d 1124 (1 Dist. 1979).

Under former Ill.Rev.Stat., ch. 68, para. 24, although it appeared that defendant had ample time prior to trial to have made his motion for blood tests and was possibly not diligent in making the motion, the evidence of paternity might obviously have been material to the case and could well have affected its outcome; therefore, a new trial was ordered in a criminal prosecution for nonsupport of child. People v. Askew, 74 Ill. App. 3d 743, 30 Ill. Dec. 777, 393 N.E.2d 1124 (1 Dist. 1979).

Reciprocal Spousal Support

Common-law doctrines which imposed a duty of support solely on the husband are inconsistent with the constitutional mandate and the statutory scheme recognizing equal rights and responsibilities, and are no longer valid. McGloon v. Zmigrocki, 191 Ill. App. 3d 968, 139 Ill. Dec. 53, 548 N.E.2d 438 (1 Dist. 1989).

Rights of Defendant

Because the court has the authority to make a determination of paternity in criminal prosecution for nonsupport of child, defendant must be accorded the same protections, including blood tests, which are available in civil proceedings; this is particularly true because in a civil proceeding, the relevant standard of proof is a preponderance of the evidence, while in a criminal proceeding, the standard is proof beyond a reasonable doubt. People v. Askew, 74 Ill. App. 3d 743, 30 Ill. Dec. 777, 393 N.E.2d 1124 (1 Dist. 1979).

Since violation of this section was a Class A misdemeanor and the defendant was subject to a prison sentence if found guilty, he was entitled to all rights which attach to a criminal proceeding, including the right to a jury trial and the right to counsel; therefore, defendant was entitled to be informed of his rights and to be given the opportunity to be tried by a jury and represented by counsel. People ex rel. Wright v. Wright, 67 Ill. App. 3d 586, 24 Ill. Dec. 347, 385 N.E.2d 114 (1 Dist. 1978).

Sentencing

It is not wrong per se to impose a sentence of incarceration upon one found guilty of failure to support his children. People v. Millsap, 8 Ill. App. 3d 1030, 291 N.E.2d 238 (3 Dist. 1972).

Venue

Where there was evidence in the record to show that the wife had

Venue (Cont'd)
returned to the home of her parents after considerable misconduct on part of the husband and after making demands for the rest of her clothes and personal property and replevying the clothes from the husband, it was clear that for prosecution of husband's neglect, venue was proper in the county where wife was residing as well as in the husband's county of residence. People v. Rose, 350 Ill. App. 338, 113 N.E.2d 75 (4 Dist. 1953).

LEGAL PERIODICALS

For note, "Making Form Follow Function: Considerations in Creating and Applying a Statutory Parent-Child Privilege," see U. Ill. L. Rev. 879 (1990).

RESEARCH REFERENCES

Constitutionality of gender-based classifications in criminal laws proscribing nonsupport of spouse or child. 14 ALR4th 717.

750 ILCS 16/20 Entry of order for support; income withholding

Sec. 20. *Entry of order for support; income withholding.* (a) In a case in which no court or administrative order for support is in effect against the defendant:

(1) at any time before the trial, upon motion of the State's Attorney, or of the Attorney General if the action has been instituted by his office, and upon notice to the defendant, or at the time of arraignment or as a condition of postponement of arraignment, the court may enter such temporary order for support as may seem just, providing for the support or maintenance of the spouse or child or children of the defendant, or both, pendente lite; or

(2) before trial with the consent of the defendant, or at the trial on entry of a plea of guilty, or after conviction, instead of imposing the penalty provided in this Act, or in addition thereto, the court may enter an order for support, subject to modification by the court from time to time as circumstances may require, directing the defendant to pay a certain sum for maintenance of the spouse, or for support of the child or children, or both.

(b) The court shall determine the amount of child support by using the guidelines and standards set forth in subsection (a) of Section 505 and in Section 505.2 of the Illinois Marriage and Dissolution of Marriage Act [750 ILCS 5/505 and 750 ILCS 5/505.2].

If (i) the non-custodial parent was properly served with a request for discovery of financial information relating to the non-custodial parent's ability to provide child support, (ii) the non-custodial parent failed to comply with the request, despite having been ordered to do so by the court, and (iii) the non-custodial parent is not present at the hearing to determine support despite having received proper notice, then any relevant financial information concerning the non-custodial parent's ability to provide support that was obtained pursuant to subpoena and proper notice shall be admitted into evidence without the need to establish any further foundation for its admission.

(c) The court shall determine the amount of maintenance using the standards set forth in Section 504 of the Illinois Marriage and Dissolution of Marriage Act [750 ILCS 5/504].

(d) The court may, for violation of any order under this Section, punish the offender as for a contempt of court, but no pendente lite order shall remain in effect longer than 4 months, or after the discharge of any panel of jurors summoned for service thereafter in such court, whichever is sooner.

(e) Any order for support entered by the court under this Section shall be deemed to be a series of judgments against the person obligated to pay support under the judgments, each such judgment to be in the amount of each payment or installment of support and each judgment to be deemed entered as of the date the corresponding payment or installment becomes due under the terms of the support order. Each judgment shall have the full force, effect, and attributes of any other judgment of this State, including the ability to be enforced. Each judgment is subject to modification or termination only in accordance with Section 510 of the Illinois Marriage and Dissolution of Marriage Act [750 ILCS 5/510]. A lien arises by operation of law against the real and personal property of the noncustodial parent for each installment of overdue support owed by the noncustodial parent.

(f) An order for support entered under this Section shall include a provision requiring the obligor to report to the obligee and to the clerk of the court within 10 days each time the obligor obtains new employment, and each time the obligor's employment is terminated for any reason. The report shall be in writing and shall, in the case of new employment, include the name and address of the new employer.

Failure to report new employment or the termination of current employment, if coupled with nonpayment of support for a period in excess of 60 days, is indirect criminal contempt. For any obligor arrested for failure to report new employment, bond shall be set in the amount of the child support that should have been paid during the period of unreported employment.

An order for support entered under this Section shall also include a provision requiring the obligor and obligee parents to advise each other of a change in residence within 5 days of the change except when the court finds that the physical, mental, or emotional health of a party or of a minor child, or both, would be seriously endangered by disclosure of the party's address.

(g) An order for support entered or modified in a case in which a party is receiving child and spouse support services under Article X of the Illinois Public Aid Code [305 ILCS 5/10-1 et seq.] shall include a provision requiring the noncustodial parent to notify the Illinois Department of Public Aid, within 7 days, of the name and address of any new employer of the noncustodial parent, whether the noncustodial parent has access to health insurance coverage through the employer or other group coverage and, if so, the policy name and number and the names of persons covered under the policy.

(h) In any subsequent action to enforce an order for support entered under this Act, upon sufficient showing that diligent effort has been made to ascertain the location of the noncustodial parent, service of process or provision of notice necessary in that action may be made at the last known address of the noncustodial parent, in any manner expressly provided by the Code of Civil Procedure [735 ILCS 5/1-101 et seq.] or in this Act, which service shall be sufficient for purposes of due process.

(i) An order for support shall include a date on which the current support obligation terminates. The termination date shall be no earlier than the date on which the child covered by the order will attain the age of 18. However, if the child will not graduate from high school until after attaining the age of 18, then the termination date shall be no earlier than the earlier of the date on which the child's high school graduation will occur or the date on which the child will attain the age of 19. The order for support shall state that the termination date does not apply to any arrearage that may remain unpaid on that date. Nothing in this subsection shall be construed to prevent the court from modifying the order or terminating the order in the event the child is otherwise emancipated.

(i-5) If there is an unpaid arrearage or delinquency (as those terms are defined in the Income Withholding for Support Act [750 ILCS 28/1 et seq.]) equal to at least one month's support obligation on the termination date stated in the order for support or, if there is no termination date stated in the order, on the date the child attains the age of majority or is otherwise emancipated, the periodic amount required to be paid for current support of that child immediately prior to that date shall automatically continue to be an obligation, not as current support but as periodic payment toward satisfaction of the unpaid arrearage or delinquency. That periodic payment shall be in addition to any periodic payment previously required for satisfaction of the arrearage or delinquency. The total periodic amount to be paid toward satisfaction of the arrearage or delinquency may be enforced and collected by any method provided by law for enforcement and collection of child support, including but not limited to income withholding under the Income Withholding for Support Act [750 ILCS 28/1 et seq.]. Each order for support entered or modified on or after the effective date of this amendatory Act of the 93rd General Assembly [P.A. 93-1061] must contain a statement notifying the parties of the requirements of this subsection. Failure to include the statement in the order for support does not affect the validity of the order or the operation of the provisions of this subsection with regard to the order. This subsection shall not be construed to prevent or affect the establishment or modification of an order for support of a minor child or the establishment or modification of an order for support of a non-minor child or educational expenses under Section 513 of the Illinois Marriage and Dissolution of Marriage Act [750 ILCS 5/513].

(j) A support obligation, or any portion of a support obligation, which becomes due and remains unpaid for 30 days or more shall accrue simple interest at the rate of 9% per annum. An order for support entered or modified on or after January 1, 2002 shall contain a statement that a support obligation required under the order, or any portion of a support obligation required under the order, that becomes due and remains unpaid for 30 days or more shall accrue simple interest at the rate of 9% per annum. Failure to include the statement in the order for support does not affect the validity of the order or the accrual of interest as provided in this Section.
(Source: P.A. 91-613, § 20; 91-767, § 15; 92-374, § 15; 92-590, § 15; 92-876, § 915; 93-1061, § 15.)

Effect of Amendments.

The 2000 amendment by P.A. 91-767, effective June 9, 2000, inserted the second paragraph of subsection (b).

The 2001 amendment by P.A. 92-374, effective August 15, 2001, added subsection (j).

The 2002 amendment by P.A. 92-590, effective July 1, 2002, substituted "child support enforcement services" for "child and spouse support services" in subsection (g).

The 2002 amendment by P.A. 92-876, effective June 1, 2003, in subsection (i) substituted "age of 18. However, if the child will not graduate from high school until after attaining the age of 18, then the termination date shall be no earlier than the earlier of the date on which the child's high school graduation will occur or the date on which the child will attain the age of 19" for "age of majority or is otherwise emancipated", and added "or terminating the order in the event the child is otherwise emancipated" at the end.

Although the amendments made to this section by P.A. 92-590, § 15, and P.A. 92-876, § 915 did not take into account the amendments made by the others, the amendments have been combined into a single version by the publisher.

The 2004 amendment by P.A. 93-1061, effective January 1, 2005, inserted subsection (i-5).

CASE NOTES

Analysis

Complaint
—Amendment
Fine
—Bring Back Orders
Review

Complaint

—Amendment

Because order requiring the defendant to pay $40.00 a week as support to his wife was temporary, an amendment of the complaint on its face was proper; however because the complaint was amended on its face to refer to a repealed statute, the amendment was a nullity. People ex rel. Wright v. Wright, 67 Ill. App. 3d 586, 24 Ill. Dec. 347, 385 N.E.2d 114 (1 Dist. 1978).

Fine

—Bring Back Orders

Where the trial judge merely agreed to stay imprisonment so that defendant could pay part of what he owed on his arrearage, and the

Fine (Cont'd)

—Bring Back Orders (Cont'd)
court retained the option to commit defendant, to further stay his commitment, or to suspend or vacate his sentence, the "bring back" order was not a pecuniary punishment and was not considered a fine under former Ill.Rev.Stat., ch. 68, para. 27. People ex rel. Doss v. Doss, 35 Ill. App. 3d 365, 342 N.E.2d 60 (1 Dist. 1975).

Review
While former Ill.Rev.Stat., ch. 68, para. 24 was a criminal statute, and for any order entered thereunder a review could only be had by abolished writ of error, former Ill.Rev.Stat., ch. 26, para. 68 was chiefly in the interest of the wife and children, and proceedings pursuant to its terms were civil in their character; as a consequence, a person who felt himself aggrieved by an order entered for support pendente lite might question its propriety or correctness by appeal. People v. Riggs, 296 Ill. App. 136, 15 N.E.2d 914 (4 Dist. 1938).

750 ILCS 16/22 Withholding of income to secure payment of support

Sec. 22. *Withholding of income to secure payment of support.* An order for support entered or modified under this Act is subject to the Income Withholding for Support Act.
(Source: P.A. 91-613, § 22.)

CASE NOTES

ANALYSIS

Construction
Future Child Support
Public Policy
Withholding
—Garnishment Proceedings
—Spendthrift Trust

Construction
This section prevails over all laws to the contrary, including section 2-1403 of the Code of Civil Procedure (735 ILCS 5/2-1403). Matt v. Matt, 105 Ill. 2d 330, 85 Ill. Dec. 505, 473 N.E.2d 1310 (1985).

Future Child Support
Spendthrift trusts may be reached only to satisfy child support arrearages, and not future child support payments. In re Chapman, 297 Ill. App. 3d 611, 231 Ill. Dec. 811, 697 N.E.2d 365 (1 Dist. 1998), (decided under former 750 ILCS 15/4.1).

Public Policy
The legislature, in enacting Section 706.1 of the Illinois Marriage and Dissolution of Marriage Act (750 ILCS 5/706.1), which contains exactly the same language as Section 4.1 of the Nonsupport of Spouse and Children Act (750 ILCS 15/4.1) and Section 26.1 of the Revised Uniform Reciprocal Enforcement of Support Act (750 ILCS 20/26.1), established that it is in the public policy of Illinois to ensure the enforcement of support judgments through all available means. Keeler v. Keeler, 156 Ill. App. 3d 513, 108 Ill. Dec. 716, 509 N.E.2d 142 (2 Dist. 1987).

It is the public policy of Illinois to ensure that support judgments are enforced by all available means. Matt v. Matt, 105 Ill. 2d 330, 85 Ill. Dec. 505, 473 N.E.2d 1310 (1985).

Withholding

—Garnishment Proceedings
Ex-wife was permitted to institute garnishment proceedings against ex-husband after he had an order of withholding entered against him under this section. Keeler v. Keeler, 156 Ill. App. 3d 513, 108 Ill. Dec. 716, 509 N.E.2d 142 (2 Dist. 1987).

—Spendthrift Trust
Court ruled in error that spendthrift trust income or principal could not be reached at all to satisfy a child support judgment; the language of the trust showed the settlor of the trust clearly contemplated that income or principal of the trust could be used for the benefit of appellee's children. In re Chapman, 297 Ill. App. 3d 611, 231 Ill. Dec. 811, 697 N.E.2d 365 (1 Dist. 1998), (decided under former 750 ILCS 15/4.1).

It is only in circumstances in which the obligor cannot be located or takes no steps to avoid garnishment that the income from a spendthrift trust would become subject to withholding. Matt v. Matt, 105 Ill. 2d 330, 85 Ill. Dec. 505, 473 N.E.2d 1310 (1985).

Income from a spendthrift trust, which is generally exempt from invasion under section 2-1403 of the Code of Civil Procedure (see 735 ILCS 5/2-1403) is subject to garnishment to collect past-due child support under this section. Matt v. Matt, 105 Ill. 2d 330, 85 Ill. Dec. 505, 473 N.E.2d 1310 (1985).

750 ILCS 16/23 Interest on support obligations

Sec. 23. *Interest on support obligations.* A support obligation, or any portion of a support obligation, which becomes due and remains unpaid for 30 days or more shall accrue interest at the rate of 9% per annum.
(Source: P.A. 92-16, § 97.)

Note.
Section 996 of P.A. 92-16 contains a "no acceleration or delay" provision, and Section 997 contains a "no revival or extension" provision.

Effective Date.
Section 999 of P.A. 92-16 made this section effective upon becoming law. The Act was approved June 28, 2001.

750 ILCS 16/25 Payment of support to State Disbursement Unit; clerk of the court

Sec. 25. *Payment of support to State Disbursement Unit; clerk of the court.* (a) As used in this Section, "order for support", "obligor", "obligee", and "payor" mean those terms as defined in the Income Withholding for Support Act [750 ILCS 28/1 et seq.].

(b) Each order for support entered or modified under Section 20 of this Act [750 ILCS 16/20] shall require that support payments be made to the State Disbursement Unit established under the Illinois Public Aid Code [305 ILCS 5/1-1 et seq.], under the following circumstances:

(1) when a party to the order is receiving child support enforcement services under Article X of the Illinois Public Aid Code [305 ILCS 5/10-1 et seq.]; or

(2) when no party to the order is receiving child support enforcement services, but the support payments are made through income withholding.

(c) When no party to the order is receiving child support enforcement services, and payments are not being made through income withholding, the court shall order the obligor to make support payments to the clerk of the court.

(d) At any time, and notwithstanding the existence of an order directing payments to be made elsewhere, the Department of Public Aid may provide notice to the obligor and, where applicable, to the obligor's payor:

(1) to make support payments to the State Disbursement Unit if:

(A) a party to the order for support is receiving child support enforcement services under Article X of the Illinois Public Aid Code [305 ILCS 5/10-1 et seq.]; or

(B) no party to the order for support is receiving child support enforcement services under Article X of the Illinois Public Aid Code [305 ILCS 5/10-1 et seq.], but the support payments are made through income withholding; or

(2) to make support payments to the State Disbursement Unit of another state upon request of another state's Title IV-D child support enforcement agency, in accordance with the requirements of Title IV, Part D of the Social Security Act [42 U.S.C. § 601 et seq.] and regulations promulgated under that Part D.

The Department of Public Aid shall provide a copy of the notice to the obligee and to the clerk of the circuit court.

(e) If a State Disbursement Unit as specified by federal law has not been created in Illinois upon the effective date of this Act, then, until the creation of a State Disbursement Unit as specified by federal law, the following provisions regarding payment and disbursement of support payments shall control and the provisions in subsections (a), (b), (c), and (d) shall be inoperative. Upon the creation of a State Disbursement Unit as specified by federal law, the payment and disbursement provisions of subsections (a), (b), (c), and (d) shall control, and this subsection (e) shall be inoperative to the extent that it conflicts with those subsections.

(1) In cases in which an order for support is entered under Section 20 of this Act [750 ILCS 16/20], the court shall order that maintenance and support payments be made to the clerk of the court for remittance to the person or agency entitled to receive the payments. However, the court in its discretion may direct otherwise where exceptional circumstances so warrant.

(2) The court shall direct that support payments be sent by the clerk to (i) the Illinois Department of Public Aid if the person in whose behalf payments are made is receiving aid under Articles III, IV, or V of the Illinois Public Aid Code [305 ILCS 5/3-1 et seq., 305 ILCS 5/4-1 et seq., or 305 ILCS 5/5-1 et seq.] or child support enforcement services under Article X of the Code [305 ILCS 5/10-1 et seq.], or (ii) to the local governmental unit responsible for the support of the person if he or she is a recipient under Article VI of the Code [305 ILCS 5/6-1 et seq.]. In accordance with federal law and regulations, the Illinois Department of Public Aid may continue to collect current maintenance payments or child support payments, or both, after those persons cease to receive public assistance and until termination of services under Article X of the Illinois Public Aid Code [305 ILCS 5/10-1 et seq.]. The Illinois Department shall pay the net amount collected to those persons after deducting any costs incurred in making the collection or any collection fee from the amount of any recovery made. The order shall permit the Illinois Department of Public Aid or the local governmental unit, as the case may be, to direct that support payments be made directly to the spouse, children, or both, or to some person or agency in their behalf, upon removal of the spouse or children from the public aid rolls or upon termination of services under Article X of the Illinois Public Aid Code [305 ILCS 5/10-1 et seq.]; and upon such direction, the Illinois Department or the local governmental unit, as the case requires, shall give notice of such action to the court in writing or by electronic transmission.

(3) The clerk of the court shall establish and maintain current records of all moneys received and disbursed and of delinquencies and defaults in required payments. The court, by order or rule, shall make provision for the carrying out of these duties.

(4) Upon notification in writing or by electronic transmission from the Illinois Department of Public Aid to the clerk of the court that a person who is receiving support payments under this Section is receiving services under the Child Support Enforcement Program established by Title IV-D of the Social Security Act [42 U.S.C. § 601 et seq.], any support payments subsequently received by the clerk of the court shall be transmitted in accordance with the instructions of the Illinois Department of Public Aid until the Department gives notice to cease the transmittal. After providing the notification authorized under this paragraph, the Illinois Department of Public Aid shall be a party and entitled to notice of any further proceedings in the case. The clerk of the court shall file a copy of the Illinois Department of Public Aid's notification in the court file. The failure of the clerk to file a copy of the notification in the court file shall not, however, affect the Illinois Department of Public Aid's rights as a party or its right to receive notice of further proceedings.

(5) Payments under this Section to the Illinois Department of Public Aid pursuant to the Child Support Enforcement Program established by Title IV-D of the Social Security Act [42 U.S.C. § 601 et seq.] shall be paid into the Child Support Enforcement Trust Fund. All other payments under this Section to the Illinois Department of Public Aid shall be deposited in the Public Assistance Recoveries Trust Fund. Disbursements from these funds shall be as provided in the Illinois Public Aid Code [305 ILCS 5/1-1 et seq.]. Payments received by a local governmental unit shall be deposited in that unit's General Assistance Fund.

(6) For those cases in which child support is payable to the clerk of the circuit court for transmittal to the Illinois Department of Public Aid by order of court or upon notification by the Illinois Department of Public Aid, the clerk shall transmit all such payments, within 4 working days of receipt, to insure that funds are available for immediate distribution by the Department to the person or entity entitled thereto in accordance with standards of the

Child Support Enforcement Program established under Title IV-D of the Social Security Act [42 U.S.C. § 601 et seq.]. The clerk shall notify the Department of the date of receipt and amount thereof at the time of transmittal. Where the clerk has entered into an agreement of cooperation with the Department to record the terms of child support orders and payments made thereunder directly into the Department's automated data processing system, the clerk shall account for, transmit and otherwise distribute child support payments in accordance with such agreement in lieu of the requirements contained herein.

(Source: P.A. 91-613, § 25; 92-590, § 15.)

Illinois Administrative Code.

See 89 Illinois Administrative Code, § 160.60.

Effect of Amendments.

The 2002 amendment by P.A. 92-590, effective July 1, 2002, substituted "child support enforcement services" throughout the section; rewrote subsection (d); and in the second sentence of subsection (e) deleted "this subsection (e) shall be inoperative and" following "(d) shall control" and inserted "and this subsection (e) shall be inoperative to the extent that it conflicts with those subsections".

750 ILCS 16/30 Information to State Case Registry

Sec. 30. *Information to State Case Registry.* (a) In this Section:

"Order for support", "obligor", "obligee", and "business day" are defined as set forth in the Income Withholding for Support Act.

"State Case Registry" means the State Case Registry established under Section 10-27 of the Illinois Public Aid Code [305 ILCS 5/10-27].

(b) Each order for support entered or modified by the circuit court under this Act shall require that the obligor and obligee (i) file with the clerk of the circuit court the information required by this Section (and any other information required under Title IV, Part D of the Social Security Act [42 U.S.C. § 601 et seq.] or by the federal Department of Health and Human Services) at the time of entry or modification of the order for support and (ii) file updated information with the clerk within 5 business days of any change. Failure of the obligor or obligee to file or update the required information shall be punishable as in cases of contempt. The failure shall not prevent the court from entering or modifying the order for support, however.

(c) The obligor shall file the following information: the obligor's name, date of birth, social security number, and mailing address.

If either the obligor or the obligee receives child support enforcement services from the Illinois Department of Public Aid under Article X of the Illinois Public Aid Code [305 ILCS 5/10-1 et seq.], the obligor shall also file the following information: the obligor's telephone number, driver's license number, and residential address (if different from the obligor's mailing address), and the name, address, and telephone number of the obligor's employer or employers.

(d) The obligee shall file the following information:

(1) The names of the obligee and the child or children covered by the order for support.

(2) The dates of birth of the obligee and the child or children covered by the order for support.

(3) The social security numbers of the obligee and the child or children covered by the order for support.

(4) The obligee's mailing address.

(e) In cases in which the obligee receives child support enforcement services from the Illinois Department of Public Aid under Article X of the Illinois Public Aid Code [305 ILCS 5/10-1 et seq.], the order for support shall (i) require that the obligee file the information required under subsection (d) with the Illinois Department of Public Aid for inclusion in the State Case Registry, rather than file the information with the clerk, and (ii) require that the obligee include the following additional information:

(1) The obligee's telephone and driver's license numbers.

(2) The obligee's residential address, if different from the obligee's mailing address.

(3) The name, address, and telephone number of the obligee's employer or employers.

The order for support shall also require that the obligee update the information filed with the Illinois Department of Public Aid within 5 business days of any change.

(f) The clerk shall provide the information filed under this Section, together with the court docket number and county in which the order for support was entered, to the State Case Registry within 5 business days after receipt of the information.

(g) In a case in which a party is receiving child support enforcement services under Article X of the Illinois Public Aid Code [305 ILCS 5/10-1 et seq.], the clerk shall provide the following additional information to the State Case Registry within 5 business days after entry or modification of an order for support or request from the Illinois Department of Public Aid:

(1) The amount of monthly or other periodic support owed under the order for support and other amounts, including arrearage, interest, or late payment penalties and fees, due or overdue under the order.

(2) Any such amounts that have been received by the clerk, and the distribution of those amounts by the clerk.

(h) Information filed by the obligor and obligee under this Section that is not specifically required to be included in the body of an order for support under other laws is not a public record and shall be treated as confidential and subject to disclosure only in accordance with the provisions of this Section, Section 10-27 of the Illinois Public Aid Code [305 ILCS 5/10-27], and Title IV, Part D of the Social Security Act [42 U.S.C. § 601 et seq.].

(Source: P.A. 91-613, § 30; 92-463, § 15.)

Effect of Amendments.

The 2001 amendment by P.A. 92-463, effective August 22, 2001, rewrote this section to the extent that a detailed comparison would be impracticable.

750 ILCS 16/33 Information to locate putative fathers and noncustodial parents

Sec. 33. *Information to locate putative fathers and noncustodial parents.* (a) Upon request by a public office, employers, labor unions, and telephone companies shall provide location information concerning putative fathers and noncustodial parents for the purpose of establishing a child's paternity or establishing, enforcing, or modifying a child support obligation. The term "public office" is defined as set forth in the Income Withholding for Support Act [750 ILCS 28/1 et seq.]. In this Section, "location information" means information about (i) the physical whereabouts of a putative father or noncustodial parent, (ii) the employer of the putative father or noncustodial parent, or (iii) the salary, wages, and other compensation paid and the health insurance coverage provided to the putative father or noncustodial parent by the employer of the putative father or noncustodial parent or by a labor union of which the putative father or noncustodial parent is a member. An employer, labor union, or telephone company shall respond to the request of the public office within 15 days after receiving the request. Any employer, labor union, or telephone company that willfully fails to fully respond within the 15-day period shall be subject to a penalty of $100 for each day that the response is not provided to the public office after the 15-day period has expired. The penalty may be collected in a civil action, which may be brought against the employer, labor union, or telephone company in favor of the public office.

(b) Upon being served with a subpoena (including an administrative subpoena as authorized by law), a utility company or cable television company must provide location information to a public office for the purpose of establishing a child's paternity or establishing, enforcing, or modifying a child support obligation.

(c) Notwithstanding the provisions of any other State or local law to the contrary, an employer, labor union, telephone company, utility company, or cable television company shall not be liable to any person for disclosure of location information under the requirements of this Section, except for willful and wanton misconduct.

(Source: P.A. 93-116, § 15.)

Effective Date.

Section 99 of P.A. 93-116 made this Act effective upon becoming law. The Act was approved July 10, 2003.

750 ILCS 16/35 Fine; release of defendant on probation; violation of order for support; forfeiture of recognizance

Sec. 35. *Fine; release of defendant on probation; violation of order for support; forfeiture of recognizance.* (a) Whenever a fine is imposed it may be directed by the court to be paid, in whole or in part, to the spouse, ex-spouse, or if the support of a child or children is involved, to the custodial parent, to the clerk, probation officer, or to the Illinois Department of Public Aid if a recipient of child support enforcement services under Article X of the Illinois Public Aid Code [305 ILCS 5/10-1 et seq.] is involved as the case requires, to be disbursed by such officers or agency under the terms of the order.

(b) The court may also relieve the defendant from custody on probation for the period fixed in the order or judgment upon his or her entering into a recognizance, with or without surety, in the sum as the court orders and approves. The condition of the recognizance shall be such that if the defendant makes his or her personal appearance in court whenever ordered to do so by the court, during such period as may be so fixed, and further complies with the terms of the order for support, or any subsequent modification of the order, then the recognizance shall be void; otherwise it will remain in full force and effect.

(c) If the court is satisfied by testimony in open court, that at any time during the period of one year the defendant has violated the terms of the order for support, it may proceed with the trial of the defendant under the original charge, or sentence him or her under the original conviction, or enforce the suspended sentence, as the case may be. In case of forfeiture of recognizance, and enforcement of recognizance by execution, the sum so recovered may, in the discretion of the court, be paid, in whole or in part, to the spouse, ex-spouse, or if the support of a child or children is involved, to the custodial parent, to the clerk, or to the Illinois Department of Public Aid if a recipient of child support enforcement services under Article X of the Illinois Public Aid Code [305 ILCS 5/10-1 et seq.] is involved as the case requires, to be disbursed by the clerk or the Department under the terms of the order.

(Source: P.A. 91-613, § 35; 92-590, § 15.)

Effect of Amendments.

The 2002 amendment by P.A. 92-590, effective July 1, 2002, substituted "child support enforcement services" for "child and spouse support services" throughout.

750 ILCS 16/40 Evidence

Sec. 40. *Evidence.* No other or greater evidence shall be required to prove the marriage of a husband and wife, or that the defendant is the father or mother of the child or children than is or shall be required to prove that fact in a civil action.

(Source: P.A. 91-613, § 40.)

750 ILCS 16/45 Husband or wife as competent witness

Sec. 45. *Husband or wife as competent witness.* In no prosecution under this Act shall any existing statute or rule of law prohibiting the disclosure of

confidential communications between husband and wife apply. And both husband and wife shall be competent witnesses to testify to any and all relevant matters, including the fact of such marriage and of the parentage of such child or children, provided that neither shall be compelled to give evidence incriminating himself or herself.
(Source: P.A. 91-613, § 45.)

750 ILCS 16/50 Community service; work alternative program

Sec. 50. *Community service; work alternative program.* (a) In addition to any other penalties imposed against an offender under this Act, the court may order the offender to perform community service for not less than 30 and not more than 120 hours per month, if community service is available in the jurisdiction and is funded and approved by the county board of the county where the offense was committed. In addition, whenever any person is placed on supervision for committing an offense under this Act, the supervision shall be conditioned on the performance of the community service.

(b) In addition to any other penalties imposed against an offender under this Act, the court may sentence the offender to service in a work alternative program administered by the sheriff. The conditions of the program are that the offender obtain or retain employment and participate in a work alternative program administered by the sheriff during non-working hours. A person may not be required to participate in a work alternative program under this subsection if the person is currently participating in a work program pursuant to another provision of this Act, Section 10-11.1 of the Illinois Public Aid Code [305 ILCS 5/10-11.1], Section 505.1 of the Illinois Marriage and Dissolution of Marriage Act [750 ILCS 5/505.1], or Section 15.1 of the Illinois Parentage Act of 1984 [750 ILCS 45/15.1].

(c) In addition to any other penalties imposed against an offender under this Act, the court may order, in cases where the offender has been in violation of this Act for 90 days or more, that the offender's Illinois driving privileges be suspended until the court determines that the offender is in compliance with this Act.

The court may determine that the offender is in compliance with this Act if the offender has agreed (i) to pay all required amounts of support and maintenance as determined by the court or (ii) to the garnishment of his or her income for the purpose of paying those amounts.

The court may also order that the offender be issued a family financial responsibility driving permit that would allow limited driving privileges for employment and medical purposes in accordance with Section 7-702.1 of the Illinois Vehicle Code [625 ILCS 5/7-702.1]. The clerk of the circuit court shall certify the order suspending the driving privileges of the offender or granting the issuance of a family financial responsibility driving permit to the Secretary of State on forms prescribed by the Secretary. Upon receipt of the authenticated documents, the Secretary of State shall suspend the offender's driving privileges until further order of the court and shall, if ordered by the court, subject to the provisions of Section 7-702.1 of the Illinois Vehicle Code [625 ILCS 5/7-702.1], issue a family financial responsibility driving permit to the offender.

(d) If the court determines that the offender has been in violation of this Act for more than 60 days, the court may determine whether the offender has applied for or been issued a professional license by the Department of Professional Regulation or another licensing agency. If the court determines that the offender has applied for or been issued such a license, the court may certify to the Department of Professional Regulation or other licensing agency that the offender has been in violation of this Act for more than 60 days so that the Department or other agency may take appropriate steps with respect to the license or application as provided in Section 10-65 of the Illinois Administrative Procedure Act [5 ILCS 100/10-65] and Section 2105-15 of the Department of Professional Regulation Law of the Civil Administrative Code of Illinois [20 ILCS 2105/2105-15]. The court may take the actions required under this subsection in addition to imposing any other penalty authorized under this Act.
(Source: P.A. 91-613, § 50; 92-651, § 88.)

Note.
Section 997 of P.A. 92-651 is a no acceleration or delay provision, and Section 998 is a no revival or extension provision.

Effect of Amendments.
The 2002 amendment by P.A. 92-651, effective July 11, 2002, substituted "Section 2105-15 of the Department of Professional Regulation Law" for "Section 60" in the next-to-last sentence of subsection (d).

750 ILCS 16/55 Offenses; how construed

Sec. 55. *Offenses; how construed.* It is hereby expressly declared that the offenses set forth in this Act shall be construed to be continuing offenses.
(Source: P.A. 91-613, § 55.)

750 ILCS 16/60 Unemployed persons owing duty of support

Sec. 60. *Unemployed persons owing duty of support.* (a) Whenever it is determined in a proceeding to establish or enforce a child support or maintenance obligation that the person owing a duty of support is unemployed, the court may order the person to seek employment and report periodically to the court with a diary, listing or other memorandum of his or her efforts in accordance with such order. Additionally, the court may order the unemployed person to report to the Department of Employment Security for job search services or to make application with the local Job Training Partnership Act [29 U.S.C. § 1501 et seq.] provider for participation in job search, training, or work programs and where the duty of support is owed to a child receiving child support enforcement services under Article X of the Illinois Public Aid Code [305 ILCS 5/10-1 et seq.] the court may order the unemployed person to report to the Illinois Department of Public Aid for participation in job search, training, or work programs established under Section 9-6 and Article IXA of that Code [305 ILCS 5/9-6 and 305 ILCS 5/9A-1 et seq].

(b) Whenever it is determined that a person owes past due support for a child or for a child and the parent with whom the child is living, and the child is receiving assistance under the Illinois Public Aid Code [305 ILCS 5/1-1 et seq.], the court shall order at the request of the Illinois Department of Public Aid:

(1) that the person pay the past-due support in accordance with a plan approved by the court; or

(2) if the person owing past-due support is unemployed, is subject to such a plan, and is not incapacitated, that the person participate in such job search, training, or work programs established under Section 9-6 and Article IXA of the Illinois Public Aid Code [305 ILCS 5/9-6 and 305 ILCS 5/9A-1 et seq.] as the court deems appropriate.

(Source: P.A. 91-613, § 60; 92-16, § 97; 92-590, § 15.)

Note.

Section 996 of P.A. 92-16 contains a "no acceleration or delay" provision, and Section 997 contains a "no revival or extension" provision.

Effect of Amendments.

The 2001 amendment by P.A. 92-16, effective June 28, 2001, made a typographical correction.

The 2002 amendment by P.A. 92-590, effective July 1, 2002, substituted "child support enforcement services" for "child and spouse support services" in subsection (a).

RESEARCH REFERENCES

Basis for imputing income for purpose of determining child support where obligor spouse is voluntarily unemployed or underemployed. 76 ALR5th 191.

750 ILCS 16/65 Order of protection; status

Sec. 65. *Order of protection; status.* Whenever relief sought under this Act is based on allegations of domestic violence, as defined in the Illinois Domestic Violence Act of 1986 [750 ILCS 60/101 et seq.], the court, before granting relief, shall determine whether any order of protection has previously been entered in the instant proceeding or any other proceeding in which any party, or a child of any party, or both, if relevant, has been designated as either a respondent or a protected person.

(Source: P.A. 91-613, § 65.)

750 ILCS 16/70 Severability.

Sec. 70. *Severability.* If any provision of this Act or its application provision or application does not affect other provisions or applications of this Act that can be given effect without the invalid provision or application.

(Source: P.A. 91-613, § 70.)

750 ILCS 16/905 through 750 ILCS 16/992 [Not Set Out]

Note.

These sections, as contained in P.A. 91-613, §§ 905 through 992, contained amendatory provisions.

750 ILCS 16/995 Certain actions to be determined under prior law

Sec. 995. *Certain actions to be determined under prior law.* An action that was commenced under the Non-Support of Spouse and Children Act and is pending on the effective date of this Act shall be decided in accordance with the Non-Support of Spouse and Children Act as it existed immediately before its repeal by this Act.

(Source: P.A. 91-613, § 995.)

750 ILCS 16/999 Effective date

Sec. 999. *Effective date.* This Act takes effect on October 1, 1999, except that Section 945 takes effect July 1, 2000.

(Source: P.A. 91-613, § 999.)

Revised Uniform Reciprocal Enforcement of Support Act

750 ILCS 20/1 through 750 ILCS 20/42: Repealed by P.A. 90-240, § 5, effective July 28, 1997.

Uniform Interstate Family Support Act

ARTICLE 1. GENERAL PROVISIONS

(PRIOR TO RENUMBERING BY P.A. 93-479; SEE NOTES UNDER 750 ILCS 22/100)

750 ILCS 22/100 (Prior to Renumbering by P.A. 93-479; see notes) Short title

Sec. 100. *Short title.* This Act may be cited as the Uniform Interstate Family Support Act.

(Source: P.A. 88-550, § 100.)

Article 1 Set Out Twice.

Article 1 of The Uniform Interstate Family Support Act, 750 ILCS 22/100 through 750 ILCS 22/103, has been set out twice to reflect postponed amendments and renumbering by P.A. 93-479.

Note.

"This Act shall become operative upon at least one of the

following 2 events taking place, whichever occurs first, but in no event prior to July 1, 2004:

"(1) The amendment by Congress of subdivision (f) of 42 U.S.C. Sec. 666 to statutorily require or authorize, in connection with the approval of state plans for purposes of federal funding, the adoption of the Uniform Interstate Family Support Act as promulgated by the National Conference of Commissioners on Uniform State Laws in 2001.

"(2) The approval, either generally or with specific application to Illinois, by the federal office of Child Support Enforcement or by the Secretary of Health and Human Services, of a waiver, exemption, finding, or other indicia of regulatory approval of the Uniform Interstate Family Support Act, as promulgated by the National Conference of Commissioners on Uniform State Laws in 2001, in connection with the approval of state plans for purposes of federal funding."

Derivation.

Title: An act relating to children, amending named Acts.

Cite: 750 ILCS 22/100 et seq.

Source: P.A. 88-550, effective July 3, 1994 (some parts effective January 1, 1995).

Date: Approved July 3, 1994.

Effective Date.

Section 999 of P.A. 88-550, as amended by P.A. 88-691, made this Act effective January 1, 1996, except for sections 955, 960, 970, 975 and 999 which are effective upon becoming law, and section 965 which is effective January 1, 1995. The Act was approved July 3, 1994.

LEGAL PERIODICALS

For article, "Child Support Reassessed: Federalization of Enforcement Nears Completion," see 1997 U. Ill. L. Rev. 695.

For article, "Highlights of the Uniform Interstate Family Support Act," see 83 Ill. B.J. 647 (1995).

RESEARCH REFERENCES

Construction and application of Uniform Interstate Family Support Act. 90 ALR5th 1.

750 ILCS 22/101 (Prior to Renumbering by P.A. 93-479; see notes) Definitions

Sec. 101. *Definitions.* In this Act:

"Child" means an individual, whether over or under the age of 18, who is or is alleged to be owed a duty of support by the individual's parent or who is or is alleged to be the beneficiary of a support order directed to the parent.

"Child-support order" means a support order for a child, including a child who has attained the age of 18.

"Duty of support" means an obligation imposed or imposable by law to provide support for a child, spouse, or former spouse including an unsatisfied obligation to provide support.

"Home state" means the state in which a child lived with a parent or a person acting as parent for at least 6 consecutive months immediately preceding the time of filing of a petition or comparable pleading for support, and if a child is less than 6 months old, the state in which the child lived from birth with any of them. A period of temporary absence of any of them is counted as part of the 6-month or other period.

"Income" includes earnings or other periodic entitlements to money from any source and any other property subject to withholding for support under the law of this State.

"Income-withholding order" means an order or other legal process directed to an obligor's employer or other debtor, as defined by the Illinois Marriage and Dissolution of Marriage Act [750 ILCS 5/101 et seq.], the Non-Support of Spouse and Children Act [750 ILCS 15/1 et seq.], the Non-Support Punishment Act [750 ILCS 16/1 et seq.], the Illinois Public Aid Code [305 ILCS 5/1-1 et seq.], and the Illinois Parentage Act of 1984 [750 ILCS 45/1 et seq.], to withhold support from the income of the obligor.

"Initiating state" means a state from which a proceeding is forwarded or in which a proceeding is filed for forwarding to a responding state under this Act or a law or procedure substantially similar to this Act.

"Initiating tribunal" means the authorized tribunal in an initiating state.

"Issuing state" means the state in which a tribunal issues a support order or renders a judgment determining parentage.

"Issuing tribunal" means the tribunal that issues a support order or renders a judgment determining parentage.

"Obligee" means:

(i) an individual to whom a duty of support is or is alleged to be owed or in whose favor a support order has been issued or a judgment determining parentage has been rendered;

(ii) a state or political subdivision to which the rights under a duty of support or support order have been assigned or which has independent claims based on financial assistance provided to an individual obligee; or

(iii) an individual seeking a judgment determining parentage of the individual's child.

"Obligor" means an individual, or the estate of a decedent: (i) who owes or is alleged to owe a duty of support; (ii) who is alleged but has not been adjudicated to be a parent of a child; or (iii) who is liable under a support order.

"Register" means to record a support order or judgment determining parentage in the appropriate Registry of Foreign Support Orders.

"Registering tribunal" means a tribunal in which a support order is registered.

"Responding state" means a state in which a proceeding is filed or to which a proceeding is forwarded for filing from an initiating state under this Act or a law or procedure substantially similar to this Act.

"Responding tribunal" means the authorized tribunal in a responding state.

"Spousal-support order" means a support order for a spouse or former spouse of the obligor.

"State" means a state of the United States, the District of Columbia, Puerto Rico, the United States Virgin Islands, or any territory or insular possession subject to the jurisdiction of the United States. The term includes:

(i) an Indian tribe; and

(ii) a foreign jurisdiction that has enacted a law or established procedures for issuance and enforcement of support orders which are substantially similar to the procedures under this Act, the Uniform Reciprocal Enforcement of Support Act, or the Revised Uniform Reciprocal Enforcement of Support Act [750 ILCS 20/1 et seq.].

"Support enforcement agency" means a public official or agency authorized to seek:

(1) enforcement of support orders or laws relating to the duty of support;

(2) establishment or modification of child support;

(3) determination of parentage; or

(4) to locate obligors or their assets.

"Support order" means a judgment, decree, or order, whether temporary, final, or subject to modification, for the benefit of a child, a spouse, or a former spouse, which provides for monetary support, health care, arrearages, or reimbursement, and may include related costs and fees, interest, income withholding, attorney's fees, and other relief.

"Tribunal" means a court, administrative agency, or quasi-judicial entity authorized to establish, enforce, or modify support orders or to determine parentage.

(Source: P.A. 88-550, § 101; 90-240, § 5; 91-613, § 975.)

Article 1 Set Out Twice.

Article 1 of The Uniform Interstate Family Support Act, 750 ILCS 22/101 through 750 ILCS 22/103, has been set out twice to reflect postponed amendments and renumbering by P.A. 93-479.

Note.

Section 70 of P.A. 91-613 contains a severability provision.

The Non-Support of Spouse and Children Act, 750 ILCS 15/1 et seq., referred to in the definition of "income-withholding order", is repealed. Current similar provisions are found as the Non-Support Punishment Act, 750 ILCS 16/1 et seq.

"This Act shall become operative upon at least one of the following 2 events taking place, whichever occurs first, but in no event prior to July 1, 2004:

"(1) The amendment by Congress of subdivision (f) of 42 U.S.C. Sec. 666 to statutorily require or authorize, in connection with the approval of state plans for purposes of federal funding, the adoption of the Uniform Interstate Family Support Act as promulgated by the National Conference of Commissioners on Uniform State Laws in 2001.

"(2) The approval, either generally or with specific application to Illinois, by the federal office of Child Support Enforcement or by the Secretary of Health and Human Services, of a waiver, exemption, finding, or other indicia of regulatory approval of the Uniform Interstate Family Support Act, as promulgated by the National Conference of Commissioners on Uniform State Laws in 2001, in connection with the approval of state plans for purposes of federal funding."

Effect of Amendments.

The 1997 amendment by P.A. 90-240, effective July 28, 1997, in the definition of Child-support order substituted "Child-support" for "Child support"; in the definition of Initiating state" substituted "from" for "in", inserted "is forwarded or in which a proceeding is filed for forwarding to a responding state", inserted "or procedure" and deleted from the end "is filed for forwarding to a responding state"; in the definition of Responding state substituted "in" for "to", inserted "filed or to which a proceeding is", inserted "for filing from an initiating state" and inserted "or procedure"; and in the definition of State, in the introductory language, in the first sentence, deleted "the Commonwealth of" preceding "Puerto Rico", inserted "the United States Virgin Islands" and in the second sentence, deleted "'state"' preceding "includes", added the subsection designations, in subdivision (i) inserted a semicolon and deleted "includes" from the end and in subdivision (ii) inserted "enacted by a law or" and added at the end "the Uniform Reciprocal Enforcement of Support Act, or the Revised Uniform Reciprocal Enforcement of Support Act".

The 1999 amendment by P.A. 91-613, effective October 1, 1999, inserted "the Non-Support Punishment Act" in the definition of Income-withholding order.

750 ILCS 22/102 (Prior to Renumbering by P.A. 93-479; see notes under 750 ILCS 22/100) Tribunal of State

Sec. 102. *Tribunal of State.* The circuit court is a tribunal of this State. The Illinois Department of Public Aid is an initiating tribunal. The Illinois Department of Public Aid is also a responding tribunal of this State to the extent that it can administratively establish paternity and establish, modify, and enforce an administrative child-support order under authority of Article X of the Illinois Public Aid Code [305 ILCS 5/10-1 et seq.].

(Source: P.A. 88-550, § 102; 88-691, § 20; 90-240, § 5.)

Article 1 Set Out Twice.

Article 1 of The Uniform Interstate Family Support Act, 750 ILCS 22/100 through 750 ILCS 22/103, has been set out twice to reflect postponed amendments and renumbering by P.A. 93-479.

Note.

"This Act shall become operative upon at least one of the following 2 events taking place, whichever occurs first, but in no event prior to July 1, 2004:

"(1) The amendment by Congress of subdivision (f) of 42 U.S.C. Sec. 666 to statutorily require or authorize, in connection with the approval of state plans for purposes of federal funding, the adoption of the Uniform Interstate Family Support Act as promulgated by the National Conference of Commissioners on Uniform State Laws in 2001.

"(2) The approval, either generally or with specific application to Illinois, by the federal office of Child Support Enforcement or by the Secretary of Health and Human Services, of a waiver, exemption, finding, or other indicia of regulatory approval of the Uniform Interstate Family Support Act, as promulgated by the National Conference of Commissioners on Uniform State Laws in 2001, in connection with the approval of state plans for purposes of federal funding."

Effect of Amendments.

The 1994 amendment by P.A. 88-691, effective January 24, 1995, in the section catchline substituted "Tribunals" for "Tribunal"; in the first sentence substituted "a" for "the"; and added the second and third sentences.

The 1997 amendment by P.A. 90-240, effective July 28, 1997, in the section catchline substituted "Tribunal" for "Tribunals" and deleted "this" preceding "State"; and in the third sentence substituted "child-support" for "child support".

750 ILCS 22/103 (Prior to Renumbering by P.A. 93-479; see notes under 750 ILCS 22/100) Remedies cumulative

Sec. 103. *Remedies cumulative.* Remedies provided by this Act are cumulative and do not affect the availability of remedies under other law.

(Source: P.A. 88-550, § 103; 93-479, § 5.)

Article 1 Set Out Twice.

Article 1 of The Uniform Interstate Family Support Act, 750 ILCS 22/100 through 750 ILCS 22/103, has been set out twice to reflect postponed amendments and renumbering by P.A. 93-479.

Note.

"This Act shall become operative upon at least one of the following 2 events taking place, whichever occurs first, but in no event prior to July 1, 2004:

"(1) The amendment by Congress of subdivision (f) of 42 U.S.C. Sec. 666 to statutorily require or authorize, in connection with the approval of state plans for purposes of federal funding, the adoption of the Uniform Interstate Family Support Act as promulgated by the National Conference of Commissioners on Uniform State Laws in 2001.

"(2) The approval, either generally or with specific application to Illinois, by the federal office of Child Support Enforcement or by the Secretary of Health and Human Services, of a waiver, exemption, finding, or other indicia of regulatory approval of the Uniform Interstate Family Support Act, as promulgated by the National Conference of Commissioners on Uniform State Laws in 2001, in connection with the approval of state plans for purposes of federal funding."

CASE NOTES

Illustrative Cases

A husband was not unfairly subjected to the simultaneous jurisdiction of judicial systems in two separate states where (1) a Florida court registered a prior Illinois support order and ordered the husband to make support payments, and (2) an Illinois court subsequently recalculated the husband's arrearage and ordered substantial additional payments toward the arrearage. In re Hartman, 305 Ill. App. 3d 338, 238 Ill. Dec. 645, 712 N.E.2d 367 (2 Dist. 1999).

ARTICLE 1.
GENERAL PROVISIONS

(AS AMENDED AND RENUMBERED BY P.A. 93-479; SEE NOTES UNDER 750 ILCS 22/101)

750 ILCS 22/101 (As renumbered by P.A. 93-479; see notes) Short title

Sec. 101. *Short title.* This Act may be cited as the Uniform Interstate Family Support Act.
(Source: P.A. 88-550, § 100.)

Article 1 Set Out Twice.

Article 1 of The Uniform Interstate Family Support Act, 750 ILCS 22/101 through 750 ILCS 22/103, has been set out twice to reflect postponed amendments and renumbering by P.A. 93-479.

Note.

"This Act shall become operative upon at least one of the following 2 events taking place, whichever occurs first, but in no event prior to July 1, 2004:

"(1) The amendment by Congress of subdivision (f) of 42 U.S.C. Sec. 666 to statutorily require or authorize, in connection with the approval of state plans for purposes of federal funding, the adoption of the Uniform Interstate Family Support Act as promulgated by the National Conference of Commissioners on Uniform State Laws in 2001.

"(2) The approval, either generally or with specific application to Illinois, by the federal office of Child Support Enforcement or by the Secretary of Health and Human Services, of a waiver, exemption, finding, or other indicia of regulatory approval of the Uniform Interstate Family Support Act, as promulgated by the National Conference of Commissioners on Uniform State Laws in 2001, in connection with the approval of state plans for purposes of federal funding."

Derivation.

Title: An act relating to children, amending named Acts.

Cite: 750 ILCS 22/101 et seq.

Source: P.A. 88-550, effective July 3, 1994 (some parts effective January 1, 1995).

Date: Approved July 3, 1994.

Effective Date.

Section 999 of P.A. 88-550, as amended by P.A. 88-691, made this Act effective January 1, 1996, except for sections 955, 960, 970, 975 and 999 which are effective upon becoming law, and section 965 which is effective January 1, 1995. The Act was approved July 3, 1994.

LEGAL PERIODICALS

For article, "Child Support Reassessed: Federalization of Enforcement Nears Completion," see 1997 U. Ill. L. Rev. 695.

For article, "Highlights of the Uniform Interstate Family Support Act," see 83 Ill. B.J. 647 (1995).

RESEARCH REFERENCES

Construction and application of Uniform Interstate Family Support Act. 90 ALR5th 1.

750 ILCS 22/102 (As amended and renumbered by P.A. 93-479; see notes under 750 ILCS 22/101) Definitions

Sec. 102. *Definitions.* In this Act:

"Child" means an individual, whether over or under the age of 18, who is or is alleged to be owed a duty of support by the individual's parent or who is or is alleged to be the beneficiary of a support order directed to the parent.

"Child-support order" means a support order for a child, including a child who has attained the age of 18.

"Duty of support" means an obligation imposed or imposable by law to provide support for a child, spouse, or former spouse including an unsatisfied obligation to provide support.

"Home state" means the state in which a child lived with a parent or a person acting as parent for at least 6 consecutive months immediately preceding the time of filing of a petition or comparable pleading for support, and if a child is less than 6 months old, the state in which the child lived from birth with any of them. A period of temporary absence of any of them is counted as part of the 6-month or other period.

"Income" includes earnings or other periodic entitlements to money from any source and any other property subject to withholding for support under the law of this State.

"Income-withholding order" means an order or other legal process directed to an obligor's employer or other debtor, as defined by the Illinois Marriage and Dissolution of Marriage Act [750 ILCS 5/101 et seq.], the Non-Support of Spouse and Children Act [750 ILCS 15/1 et seq.], the Non-Support Punishment Act [750 ILCS 16/1 et seq.], the Illinois Public

Aid Code [305 ILCS 5/1-1 et seq.], and the Illinois Parentage Act of 1984 [750 ILCS 45/1 et seq.], to withhold support from the income of the obligor.

"Initiating state" means a state from which a proceeding is forwarded or in which a proceeding is filed for forwarding to a responding state under this Act or a law or procedure substantially similar to this Act.

"Initiating tribunal" means the authorized tribunal in an initiating state.

"Issuing state" means the state in which a tribunal issues a support order or renders a judgment determining parentage.

"Issuing tribunal" means the tribunal that issues a support order or renders a judgment determining parentage.

"Obligee" means:

(A) an individual to whom a duty of support is or is alleged to be owed or in whose favor a support order has been issued or a judgment determining parentage has been rendered;

(B) a state or political subdivision to which the rights under a duty of support or support order have been assigned or which has independent claims based on financial assistance provided to an individual obligee; or

(C) an individual seeking a judgment determining parentage of the individual's child.

"Obligor" means an individual, or the estate of a decedent:

(i) who owes or is alleged to owe a duty of support;

(ii) who is alleged but has not been adjudicated to be a parent of a child; or

(iii) who is liable under a support order.

"Person means an individual, corporation, business trust, estate, trust, partnership, limited liability company, association, joint venture, government, governmental subdivision, agency, instrumentality, public corporation, or any other legal or commercial entity.

"Record" means information that is inscribed on a tangible medium or that is stored in an electronic or other medium and is retrievable in perceivable form.

"Register" means to record a support order or judgment determining parentage in the appropriate Registry of Foreign Support Orders.

"Registering tribunal" means a tribunal in which a support order is registered.

"Responding state" means a state in which a proceeding is filed or to which a proceeding is forwarded for filing from an initiating state under this Act or a law or procedure substantially similar to this Act.

"Responding tribunal" means the authorized tribunal in a responding state.

"Spousal-support order" means a support order for a spouse or former spouse of the obligor.

"State" means a state of the United States, the District of Columbia, Puerto Rico, the United States Virgin Islands, or any territory or insular possession subject to the jurisdiction of the United States. The term includes:

(A) an Indian tribe; and

(B) a foreign country or political subdivision that:

(i) has been declared to be a foreign reciprocating country or political subdivision under federal law;

(ii) has established a reciprocal arrangement for child support with this State as provided in Section 308 [750 ILCS 22/308]; or

(iii) has enacted a law or established procedures for issuance and enforcement of support orders which are substantially similar to the procedures under this Act.

"Support enforcement agency" means a public official or agency authorized to seek:

(A) enforcement of support orders or laws relating to the duty of support;

(B) establishment or modification of child support;

(C) determination of parentage;

(D) to locate obligors or their assets; or

(E) determination of the controlling child support order.

"Support order" means a judgment, decree, order, or directive, whether temporary, final, or subject to modification, issued by a tribunal for the benefit of a child, a spouse, or a former spouse, which provides for monetary support, health care, arrearages, or reimbursement, and may include related costs and fees, interest, income withholding, attorney's fees, and other relief.

"Tribunal" means a court, administrative agency, or quasi-judicial entity authorized to establish, enforce, or modify support orders or to determine parentage.

(Source: P.A. 88-550, § 101; 90-240, § 5; 91-613, § 975; 93-479, § 5.)

Article 1 Set Out Twice.

Article 1 of The Uniform Interstate Family Support Act, 750 ILCS 22/101 through 750 ILCS 22/103, has been set out twice to reflect postponed amendments and renumbering by P.A. 93-479.

Note.

Section 70 of P.A. 91-613 contains a severability provision.

The Non-Support of Spouse and Children Act, 750 ILCS 15/1 et seq., referred to in the definition of "income-withholding order", is repealed. Current similar provisions are found as the Non-Support Punishment Act, 750 ILCS 16/1 et seq.

"This Act shall become operative upon at least one of the following 2 events taking place, whichever occurs first, but in no event prior to July 1, 2004:

"(1) The amendment by Congress of subdivision (f) of 42 U.S.C. Sec. 666 to statutorily require or authorize, in connection with the approval of state plans for purposes of federal funding, the adoption of the Uniform Interstate Family Support Act as promulgated by the National Conference of Commissioners on Uniform State Laws in 2001.

"(2) The approval, either generally or with specific application to Illinois, by the federal office of Child Support Enforcement or by the Secretary of Health and Human Services, of a waiver, exemption, finding, or other indicia of regulatory approval of the Uniform Interstate Family Support Act, as promulgated by the National Conference of Commissioners on Uniform State Laws in 2001, in connection with the approval of state plans for purposes of federal funding."

Effect of Amendments.

The 1997 amendment by P.A. 90-240, effective July 28, 1997, in the definition of Child-support order substituted "Child-support" for "Child support"; in the definition of Initiating state" substituted "from" for "in", inserted "is forwarded or in which a proceeding is filed for forwarding to a responding state", inserted "or procedure" and deleted from the end "is filed for forwarding to a responding state"; in the definition of Responding state substituted "in" for "to", inserted "filed or to which a proceeding is", inserted "for filing from an initiating state" and inserted "or procedure"; and in the definition of State, in the introductory language, in the first sentence, deleted "the Commonwealth of" preceding "Puerto Rico", inserted "the United States Virgin Islands" and in the second sentence, deleted "'state"' preceding "includes", added the subsection designations, in subdivision (i) inserted a semicolon and deleted "includes" from the end and in subdivision (ii) inserted "enacted by a law or" and added at the end "the Uniform Reciprocal Enforcement of Support Act, or the Revised Uniform Reciprocal Enforcement of Support Act".

The 1999 amendment by P.A. 91-613, effective October 1, 1999, inserted "the Non-Support Punishment Act" in the definition of Income-withholding order.

The 2003 amendment by P.A. 93-479 (see editor's note as to effective date), rewrote and renumbered the section, which was formerly 750 ILCS 22/101.

750 ILCS 22/103 (As renumbered by P.A. 93-479; see notes under 750 ILCS 22/101) Tribunal of State

Sec. 103. *Tribunal of State.* The circuit court is a tribunal of this State. The Illinois Department of Public Aid is an initiating tribunal. The Illinois Department of Public Aid is also a responding tribunal of this State to the extent that it can administratively establish paternity and establish, modify, and enforce an administrative child-support order under authority of Article X of the Illinois Public Aid Code [305 ILCS 5/10-1 et seq.].
(Source: P.A. 88-550, § 102; 88-691, § 20; 90-240, § 5; 93-479, § 5.)

Article 1 Set Out Twice.

Article 1 of The Uniform Interstate Family Support Act, 750 ILCS 22/101 through 750 ILCS 22/103, has been set out twice to reflect postponed amendments and renumbering by P.A. 93-479.

Note.

"This Act shall become operative upon at least one of the following 2 events taking place, whichever occurs first, but in no event prior to July 1, 2004:

"(1) The amendment by Congress of subdivision (f) of 42 U.S.C. Sec. 666 to statutorily require or authorize, in connection with the approval of state plans for purposes of federal funding, the adoption of the Uniform Interstate Family Support Act as promulgated by the National Conference of Commissioners on Uniform State Laws in 2001.

"(2) The approval, either generally or with specific application to Illinois, by the federal office of Child Support Enforcement or by the Secretary of Health and Human Services, of a waiver, exemption, finding, or other indicia of regulatory approval of the Uniform Interstate Family Support Act, as promulgated by the National Conference of Commissioners on Uniform State Laws in 2001, in connection with the approval of state plans for purposes of federal funding."

Effect of Amendments.

The 1994 amendment by P.A. 88-691, effective January 24, 1995, in the section catchline substituted "Tribunals" for "Tribunal"; in the first sentence substituted "a" for "the"; and added the second and third sentences.

The 1997 amendment by P.A. 90-240, effective July 28, 1997, in the section catchline substituted "Tribunal" for "Tribunals" and deleted "this" preceding "State"; and in the third sentence substituted "child-support" for "child support".

The 2003 amendment by P.A. 93-479, (see 750 ILCS 22/101 for effective date), renumbered the section, which is now 750 ILCS 22/104.

750 ILCS 22/104 (As amended and renumbered by P.A. 93-479; see notes under 750 ILCS 22/101) Remedies cumulative

Sec. 104. *Remedies cumulative.* (a) Remedies provided by this Act are cumulative and do not affect the availability of remedies under other law, including the recognition of a support order of a foreign country or political subdivision on the basis of comity.

(b) This Act does not:

(1) provide the exclusive method of establishing or enforcing a support order under the law of this State; or

(2) grant a tribunal of this State jurisdiction to render judgment or issue an order relating to child custody or visitation in a proceeding under this Act.
(Source: P.A. 88-550, § 103; 93-479, § 5.)

Article 1 Set Out Twice.

Article 1 of The Uniform Interstate Family Support Act, 750 ILCS 22/101 through 750 ILCS 22/103, has been set out twice to reflect postponed amendments and renumbering by P.A. 93-479.

Note.

"This Act shall become operative upon at least one of the following 2 events taking place, whichever occurs first, but in no event prior to July 1, 2004:

"(1) The amendment by Congress of subdivision (f) of 42 U.S.C. Sec. 666 to statutorily require or authorize, in connection with the approval of state plans for purposes of federal funding, the adoption of the Uniform Interstate Family Support Act as promulgated by the National Conference of Commissioners on Uniform State Laws in 2001.

"(2) The approval, either generally or with specific application to Illinois, by the federal office of Child Support Enforcement or by the Secretary of Health and Human Services, of a waiver, exemption, finding, or other indicia of regulatory approval of the Uniform Interstate Family Support Act, as promulgated by the National Conference of Commissioners on Uniform State Laws in 2001, in connection with the approval of state plans for purposes of federal funding."

Effect of Amendments.

The 2003 amendment by P.A. 93-479 (see 750 ILCS 22/101 as to effective date), rewrote and renumbered the section, which was formerly 750 ILCS 22/103.

CASE NOTES

Illustrative Cases

A husband was not unfairly subjected to the simultaneous jurisdiction of judicial systems in two separate states where (1) a Florida court registered a prior Illinois support order and ordered the husband to make support payments, and (2) an Illinois court subsequently recalculated the husband's arrearage and ordered substantial additional payments toward the arrearage. In re Hart-

Illustrative Cases (Cont'd)
man, 305 Ill. App. 3d 338, 238 Ill. Dec. 645, 712 N.E.2d 367 (2 Dist. 1999).

ARTICLE 2. JURISDICTION

Part 1. Extended Personal Jurisdiction

750 ILCS 22/201 (Without amendments by P.A. 93-479; see notes for effective date) Bases for jurisdiction over nonresident

Sec. 201. *Bases for jurisdiction over nonresident.* In a proceeding to establish, enforce, or modify a support order or to determine parentage, a tribunal of this State may exercise personal jurisdiction over a nonresident individual or the individual's guardian or conservator if:

(1) the individual is personally served with notice within this State;

(2) the individual submits to the jurisdiction of this State by consent, by entering a general appearance, or by filing a responsive document having the effect of waiving any contest to personal jurisdiction;

(3) the individual resided with the child in this State;

(4) the individual resided in this State and provided prenatal expenses or support for the child;

(5) the child resides in this State as a result of the acts or directives of the individual;

(6) the individual engaged in sexual intercourse in this State and the child may have been conceived by that act of intercourse;

(7) (Blank); or

(8) there is any other basis consistent with the constitutions of this State and the United States for the exercise of personal jurisdiction.

(Source: P.A. 88-550, § 201.)

Section Set Out Twice.
The section above is without the amendments by P.A. 93-479 (see notes for effective date). For the version of this section with the amendments by P.A. 93-479, see the following version, also numbered 750 ILCS 22/201.

Note.
P.A. 90-240, § 5 redesignated this Part A. as Part 1.

750 ILCS 22/201 (As amended by P.A. 93-479, see notes for effective date) Bases for jurisdiction over nonresident

Sec. 201. *Bases for jurisdiction over nonresident.* (a) In a proceeding to establish or enforce a support order or to determine parentage, a tribunal of this State may exercise personal jurisdiction over a nonresident individual or the individual's guardian or conservator if:

(1) the individual is personally served with notice within this State;

(2) the individual submits to the jurisdiction of this State by consent, by entering a general appearance, or by filing a responsive document having the effect of waiving any contest to personal jurisdiction;

(3) the individual resided with the child in this State;

(4) the individual resided in this State and provided prenatal expenses or support for the child;

(5) the child resides in this State as a result of the acts or directives of the individual;

(6) the individual engaged in sexual intercourse in this State and the child may have been conceived by that act of intercourse;

(7) (Blank); or

(8) there is any other basis consistent with the constitutions of this State and the United States for the exercise of personal jurisdiction.

(b) The bases of personal jurisdiction set forth in subsection (a) or in any other law of this State may not be used to acquire personal jurisdiction for a tribunal of the State to modify a child support order of another state unless the requirements of Section 611 or 615 [750 ILCS 22/611 or 750 ILCS 22/615] are met.

(Source: P.A. 88-550, § 201; 93-479, § 5.)

Section Set Out Twice.
Multiple versions of this section have been created by the editor to reflect conflicting or postponed legislation.

Note.
Section 99 of P.A. 93-479, which amended this section, provides:
Operative date. This Act shall become operative upon at least one of the following 2 events taking place, whichever occurs first, but in no event prior to July 1, 2004:

"(1) The amendment by Congress of subdivision (f) of 42 U.S.C. Sec. 666 to statutorily require or authorize, in connection with the approval of state plans for purposes of federal funding, the adoption of the Uniform Interstate Family Support Act as promulgated by the National Conference of Commissioners on Uniform State Laws in 2001.

"(2) The approval, either generally or with specific application to Illinois, by the federal office of Child Support Enforcement or by the Secretary of Health and Human Services, of a waiver, exemption, finding, or other indicia of regulatory approval of the Uniform Interstate Family Support Act, as promulgated by the National Conference of Commissioners on Uniform State Laws in 2001, in connection with the approval of state plans for purposes of federal funding."

Effect of Amendments.
The 2003 amendment by P.A. 93-479 (see editor's note as to effective date), added the subsection (a) designation and added subsection (b); and substituted "or enforce" for "enforce, or modify" in the first paragraph of subsection (a).

750 ILCS 22/202 (Without amendments by P.A. 93-479; see notes for effective date) Procedure when exercising jurisdiction over nonresident

Sec. 202. *Procedure when exercising jurisdiction over nonresident.* A tribunal of this State exercising personal jurisdiction over a nonresident under Section 201 [750 ILCS 22/201] may apply Section 316 [750 ILCS 22/316] to receive evidence from another state, and Section 318 [750 ILCS 22/318] to obtain discovery through a tribunal of another state. In all

other respects, Articles 3 through 7 do not apply and the tribunal shall apply the procedural and substantive law of this State, including the rules on choice of law other than those established by this Act.
(Source: P.A. 88-550, § 202.)

Section Set Out Twice.
The section above is without amendments by P.A. 93-479 (see notes for effective date). For the version of this section containing amendments by P.A. 93-479, see the following section, also numbered 750 ILCS 22/202.

750 ILCS 22/202 (As amended by P.A. 93-479; see notes for effective date) Duration of personal jurisdiction

Sec. 202. *Duration of personal jurisdiction.* Personal jurisdiction acquired by a tribunal of this State in a proceeding under this Act or other law of this State relating to a support order continues as long as a tribunal of this State has continuing, exclusive jurisdiction to modify its order or continuing jurisdiction to enforce its order as provided by Sections 205, 206, and 211 [750 ILCS 22/205, 750 ILCS 22/206, and 750 ILCS 22/211].
(Source: P.A. 88-550, § 202; 93-479, § 5.)

Section Set Out Twice.
Multiple versions of this section have been created by the editor to reflect conflicting or postponed legislation.

Note.
Section 99 of P.A. 93-479, which amended this section, provides:
"Operative date. This Act shall become operative upon at least one of the following 2 events taking place, whichever occurs first, but in no event prior to July 1, 2004:
"(1) The amendment by Congress of subdivision (f) of 42 U.S.C. Sec. 666 to statutorily require or authorize, in connection with the approval of state plans for purposes of federal funding, the adoption of the Uniform Interstate Family Support Act as promulgated by the National Conference of Commissioners on Uniform State Laws in 2001.
"(2) The approval, either generally or with specific application to Illinois, by the federal office of Child Support Enforcement or by the Secretary of Health and Human Services, of a waiver, exemption, finding, or other indicia of regulatory approval of the Uniform Interstate Family Support Act, as promulgated by the National Conference of Commissioners on Uniform State Laws in 2001, in connection with the approval of state plans for purposes of federal funding."

Effect of Amendments.
The 2003 amendment by P.A. 93-479 (see editor's note as to effective date), revised the section heading and rewrote the section to the extent that a detailed comparison would be impracticable.

Part 2.
Proceedings Involving Two or More States

750 ILCS 22/203 Initiating and responding tribunal of State

Sec. 203. *Initiating and responding tribunal of State.* Under this Act, a tribunal of this State may serve as an initiating tribunal to forward proceedings to another state and as a responding tribunal for proceedings initiated in another state.
(Source: P.A. 88-550, § 203; 90-240, § 5.)

Effect of Amendments.
The 1997 amendment by P.A. 90-240, effective July 28, 1997, redesignated Part B as Part 2; and in section catchline deleted "this" preceding "State".

750 ILCS 22/204 (Without amendments by P.A. 93-479; see notes for effective date) Simultaneous proceedings in another state

Sec. 204. *Simultaneous proceedings in another state.* (a) A tribunal of this State may exercise jurisdiction to establish a support order if the petition is filed after a petition or comparable pleading is filed in another state only if:
(1) the petition in this State is filed before the expiration of the time allowed in the other state for filing a responsive pleading challenging the exercise of jurisdiction by the other state;
(2) the contesting party timely challenges the exercise of jurisdiction in the other state; and
(3) if relevant, this State is the home state of the child.
(b) A tribunal of this State may not exercise jurisdiction to establish a support order if the petition is filed before a petition or comparable pleading is filed in another state if:
(1) the petition or comparable pleading in the other state is filed before the expiration of the time allowed in this State for filing a responsive pleading challenging the exercise of jurisdiction by this State;
(2) the contesting party timely challenges the exercise of jurisdiction in this State; and
(3) if relevant, the other state is the home state of the child.
(Source: P.A. 88-550, § 204.)

Section Set Out Twice.
The section above is without amendments by P.A. 93-479 (see notes for effective date). For the version of this section as amended by P.A. 93-479, see the following section, also numbered 750 ILCS 22/204.

750 ILCS 22/204 (As amended by P.A. 93-479; see notes for effective date) Simultaneous proceedings

Sec. 204. *Simultaneous proceedings.* (a) A tribunal of this State may exercise jurisdiction to establish a support order if the petition is filed after a petition or comparable pleading is filed in another state only if:
(1) the petition in this State is filed before the expiration of the time allowed in the other state for filing a responsive pleading challenging the exercise of jurisdiction by the other state;
(2) the contesting party timely challenges the exercise of jurisdiction in the other state; and
(3) if relevant, this State is the home state of the child.

(b) A tribunal of this State may not exercise jurisdiction to establish a support order if the petition is filed before a petition or comparable pleading is filed in another state if:

(1) the petition or comparable pleading in the other state is filed before the expiration of the time allowed in this State for filing a responsive pleading challenging the exercise of jurisdiction by this State;

(2) the contesting party timely challenges the exercise of jurisdiction in this State; and

(3) if relevant, the other state is the home state of the child.

(Source: P.A. 88-550, § 204; 93-479, § 5.)

Section Set Out Twice.

Multiple versions of this section have been created by the editor to reflect conflicting or postponed legislation.

Note.

Section 99 of P.A. 93-479, which amended this section, provides: "Operative date. This Act shall become operative upon at least one of the following 2 events taking place, whichever occurs first, but in no event prior to July 1, 2004:

"(1) The amendment by Congress of subdivision (f) of 42 U.S.C. Sec. 666 to statutorily require or authorize, in connection with the approval of state plans for purposes of federal funding, the adoption of the Uniform Interstate Family Support Act aspromulgated by the National Conference of Commissioners on Uniform State Laws in 2001.

"(2) The approval, either generally or with specific application to Illinois, by the federal office of Child Support Enforcement or by the Secretary of Health and Human Services, of a waiver, exemption, finding, or other indicia of regulatory approval of the Uniform Interstate Family Support Act, as promulgated by the National Conference of Commissioners on Uniform State Laws in 2001, in connection with the approval of state plans for purposes of federal funding."

Effect of Amendments.

The 2003 amendment by P.A. 93-479 (see editor's note as to effective date), revised the section heading.

750 ILCS 22/205 (Without amendments by P.A. 93-479; see notes for effective date) Continuing, exclusive jurisdiction

Sec. 205. *Continuing, exclusive jurisdiction.* (a) A tribunal of this State issuing a support order consistent with the law of this State has continuing, exclusive jurisdiction over a child-support order:

(1) as long as this State remains the residence of the obligor, the individual obligee, or the child for whose benefit the support order is issued; or

(2) until all of the parties who are individuals have filed written consents with the tribunal of this State for a tribunal of another state to modify the order and assume continuing, exclusive jurisdiction.

(b) A tribunal of this State issuing a child-support order consistent with the law of this State may not exercise its continuing jurisdiction to modify the order if the order has been modified by a tribunal of another state pursuant to a law substantially similar to this Act.

(c) If a child-support order of this State is modified by a tribunal of another state pursuant to a law substantially similar to this Act, a tribunal of this State loses its continuing, exclusive jurisdiction with regard to prospective enforcement of the order issued in this State, and may only:

(1) enforce the order that was modified as to amounts accruing before the modification;

(2) enforce nonmodifiable aspects of that order; and

(3) provide other appropriate relief for violations of that order which occurred before the effective date of the modification.

(d) A tribunal of this State shall recognize the continuing, exclusive jurisdiction of a tribunal of another state which has issued a child-support order pursuant to a law substantially similar to this Act.

(e) A temporary support order issued ex parte or pending resolution of a jurisdictional conflict does not create continuing, exclusive jurisdiction in the issuing tribunal.

(f) A tribunal of this State issuing a support order consistent with the law of this State has continuing, exclusive jurisdiction over a spousal-support order throughout the existence of the support obligation. A tribunal of this State may not modify a spousal-support order issued by a tribunal of another state having continuing, exclusive jurisdiction over that order under the law of that state.

(Source: P.A. 88-550, § 205; 90-240, § 5.)

Section Set Out Twice.

The section above is without the amendments by P.A. 93-479 (see notes for effective date). For the version of this section as amended by P.A. 93-479, see the following section, also numbered 750 ILCS 22/205.

Effect of Amendments.

The 1997 amendment by P.A. 90-240, effective July 28, 1997, substituted "child-support" for "child support" throughout the section; in subdivision (a)(2) substituted "all of the parties who are individuals have" for "each individual party has" and substituted "consents" for "consent"; and in subsection (f), in the first and second sentences, substituted "spousal-support" for "spousal support".

CASE NOTES

ANALYSIS

Applicability
Full Faith and Credit
Illustrative Cases
Modification

Applicability

750 ILCS 22/205(a) does not apply to a circuit court's jurisdiction to enforce its support order. Zaabel v. Konetski, 209 Ill. 2d 127, 282 Ill. Dec. 748, 807 N.E.2d 372, 2004 Ill. LEXIS 359 (2004).

Full Faith and Credit

Illinois trial court's exercise of jurisdiction was proper under the Full Faith and Credit for Child Support Orders Act, 28 U.S.C.S. § 1738B, in light of the decision of the Indiana state court, where the marriage dissolution had occurred, to decline jurisdiction, and where there was no evidence the ex-wife was forum shopping. Mattmuller v. Mattmuller, 336 Ill. App. 3d 984, 271 Ill. Dec. 545, 785 N.E.2d 196, 2003 Ill. App. LEXIS 119 (5 Dist. 2003).

The constitutional requirement of full faith and credit did not prevent the Illinois trial court from recalculating the arrearage amount and ordering the husband to make substantial additional payments towards the arrearage; despite the Florida court's express reservation of jurisdiction to determine subsequent arrearage amounts, the Illinois trial court nonetheless retained continuing

Full Faith and Credit (Cont'd)
exclusive jurisdiction to enforce its earlier order of support. In re Hartman, 305 Ill. App. 3d 338, 238 Ill. Dec. 645, 712 N.E.2d 367 (2 Dist. 1999).

Illustrative Cases
Under 750 ILCS 22/205(a), the circuit court lost jurisdiction to modify the support order when all of the effected parties moved outside of Illinois, but the circuit court continued to have jurisdiction to enforce its prior order. Zaabel v. Konetski, 209 Ill. 2d 127, 282 Ill. Dec. 748, 807 N.E.2d 372, 2004 Ill. LEXIS 359 (2004).

Where the wife and the parties' child continued to reside in Illinois and there was no evidence that the parties entered into a written agreement consenting to the transfer of jurisdiction over the case to another state, the trial court retained continuing, exclusive jurisdiction over the child support order it entered. In re Hartman, 305 Ill. App. 3d 338, 238 Ill. Dec. 645, 712 N.E.2d 367 (2 Dist. 1999).

Modification
A Florida court order which registered an Illinois support order and ordered the husband to make ongoing payments did not "modify" the support order and thereby remove the order from the jurisdiction of Illinois courts; further, even if the Florida court had modified the order, the Illinois courts could still have properly entered appropriate orders compelling the husband to pay his arrearage accruing prior to the modification. In re Hartman, 305 Ill. App. 3d 338, 238 Ill. Dec. 645, 712 N.E.2d 367 (2 Dist. 1999).

750 ILCS 22/205 (As amended by P.A. 93-479; see notes for effective date) Continuing, exclusive jurisdiction to modify child-support order

Sec. 205. *Continuing, exclusive jurisdiction to modify child-support order.* (a) A tribunal of this State that has issued a support order consistent with the law of this State has and shall exercise continuing, exclusive jurisdiction to modify its child-support order if the order is the controlling order and:

(1) at the time of the filing of a request for modification this State is the residence of the obligor, the individual obligee, or the child for whose benefit the support order is issued; or

(2) even if this State is not the residence of the obligor, the individual obligee, or the child for whose benefit the support order is issued, the parties consent in a record or in open court that the tribunal of this State may continue to exercise the jurisdiction to modify its order.

(b) A tribunal of this State that has issued a child-support order consistent with the law of this State may not exercise continuing exclusive jurisdiction to modify the order if:

(1) all of the parties who are individuals file consent in a record with the tribunal of this State that a tribunal of another state that has jurisdiction over at least one of the parties who is an individual or that is located in the state of residence of the child may modify the order and assume continuing, exclusive jurisdiction; or

(2) its order is not the controlling order.

(c) If a tribunal of another state has issued a child-support order pursuant to the Uniform Interstate Family Support Act [750 ILCS 22/101 et seq.] or a law substantially similar to that Act which modifies a child-support order of a tribunal of this State, tribunals of this State shall recognize the continuing, exclusive jurisdiction of the tribunal of the other state.

(d) A tribunal of this State that lacks continuing, exclusive jurisdiction to modify a child-support order may serve as an initiating tribunal to request a tribunal of another state to modify a support order issued in that state.

(e) A temporary support order issued ex parte or pending resolution of a jurisdictional conflict does not create continuing, exclusive jurisdiction in the issuing tribunal.

(Source: P.A. 88-550, § 205; 90-240, § 5; 93-479, § 5.)

Section Set Out Twice.
The section above contains the amendments by P.A. 93-479 (see notes for effective date). For the version of this section without the amendments by P.A. 93-479, see the preceding section, also numbered 750 ILCS 22/205.

Note.
Section 99 of P.A. 93-479, which amended this section, provides: "Operative date. This Act shall become operative upon at least one of the following 2 events taking place, whichever occurs first, but in no event prior to July 1, 2004:

"(1) The amendment by Congress of subdivision (f) of 42 U.S.C. Sec. 666 to statutorily require or authorize, in connection with the approval of state plans for purposes of federal funding, the adoption of the Uniform Interstate Family Support Act aspromulgated by the National Conference of Commissioners on Uniform State Laws in 2001.

"(2) The approval, either generally or with specific application to Illinois, by the federal office of Child Support Enforcement or by the Secretary of Health and Human Services, of a waiver, exemption, finding, or other indicia of regulatory approval of the Uniform Interstate Family Support Act, as promulgated by the National Conference of Commissioners on Uniform State Laws in 2001, in connection with the approval of state plans for purposes of federal funding."

Effect of Amendments.
The 2003 amendment by P.A. 93-479 (see editor's note as to effective date), rewrote the section to the extent that a detailed comparison would be impracticable.

750 ILCS 22/206 (Without amendments by P.A. 93-479; see notes for effective date) Enforcement and modification of support order by tribunal having continuing jurisdiction

Sec. 206. *Enforcement and modification of support order by tribunal having continuing jurisdiction.* (a) A tribunal of this State may serve as an initiating tribunal to request a tribunal of another state to enforce or modify a support order issued in that state.

(b) A tribunal of this State having continuing, exclusive jurisdiction over a support order may act as a responding tribunal to enforce or modify the order. If a party subject to the continuing, exclusive jurisdiction of the tribunal no longer resides in the issuing state, in subsequent proceedings the tribunal may apply Section 316 (Special Rules of Evidence and Procedure) [750 ILCS 22/316] to receive evidence from another state and Section 318 (Assistance with Discovery) [750 ILCS 22/318] to obtain discovery through a tribunal of another state.

(c) A tribunal of this State which lacks continuing, exclusive jurisdiction over a spousal-support order may not serve as a responding tribunal to modify a spousal-support order of another state.
(Source: P.A. 88-550, § 206; 90-240, § 5.)

Section Set Out Twice.
The section above is without amendments by P.A. 93-479 (see notes for effective date). For the version of this section as amended by P.A. 93-479, see the following section, also numbered 750 ILCS 22/206.

Effect of Amendments.
The 1997 amendment by P.A. 90-240, effective July 28, 1997, in subsection (c) substituted "spousal-support" for "spousal support" twice.

750 ILCS 22/206 (As amended by P.A. 93-479; see notes for effective date) Continuing jurisdiction to enforce child-support order

Sec. 206. *Continuing jurisdiction to enforce child-support order.* (a) A tribunal of this State that has issued a child-support order consistent with the law of this State may serve as an initiating tribunal to request a tribunal of another state to enforce:

(1) the order if the order is the controlling order and has not been modified by a tribunal of another state that assumed jurisdiction pursuant to the Uniform Interstate Family Support Act [750 ILCS 22/101 et seq.]; or

(2) a money judgment for arrears of support and interest on the order accrued before a determination that an order of another state is the controlling order.

(b) A tribunal of this State having continuing jurisdiction over a support order may act as a responding tribunal to enforce the order.
(Source: P.A. 88-550, § 206; 90-240, § 5; 93-479, § 5.)

Section Set Out Twice.
Multiple versions of this section have been created by the editor to reflect conflicting or postponed legislation.

Note.
Section 99 of P.A. 93-479, which amended this section, provides: "Operative date. This Act shall become operative upon at least one of the following 2 events taking place, whichever occurs first, but in no event prior to July 1, 2004:

"(1) The amendment by Congress of subdivision (f) of 42 U.S.C. Sec. 666 to statutorily require or authorize, in connection with the approval of state plans for purposes of federal funding, the adoption of the Uniform Interstate Family Support Act as promulgated by the National Conference of Commissioners on Uniform State Laws in 2001.

"(2) The approval, either generally or with specific application to Illinois, by the federal office of Child Support Enforcement or by the Secretary of Health and Human Services, of a waiver, exemption, finding, or other indicia of regulatory approval of the Uniform Interstate Family Support Act, as promulgated by the National Conference of Commissioners on Uniform State Laws in 2001, in connection with the approval of state plans for purposes of federal funding."

Effect of Amendments.
The 2003 amendment by P.A. 93-479 (see editor's note as to effective date), rewrote the section to the extent that a detailed comparison would be impracticable.

Part 3. Reconciliation of Multiple Orders

750 ILCS 22/207 (Without amendments by P.A. 93-479; see notes for effective date) Recognition of controlling child-support order

Sec. 207. *Recognition of controlling child-support order.* (a) If a proceeding is brought under this Act and only one tribunal has issued a child-support order, the order of that tribunal controls and must be so recognized.

(b) If a proceeding is brought under this Act, and two or more child-support orders have been issued by tribunals of this State or another state with regard to the same obligor and child, a tribunal of this State shall apply the following rules in determining which order to recognize for purposes of continuing, exclusive jurisdiction:

(1) If only one of the tribunals would have continuing, exclusive jurisdiction under this Act, the order of that tribunal controls and must be so recognized.

(2) If more than one of the tribunals would have continuing, exclusive jurisdiction under this Act, an order issued by a tribunal in the current home state of the child controls and must be so recognized, but if an order has not been issued in the current home state of the child, the order most recently issued controls and must be so recognized.

(3) If none of the tribunals would have continuing, exclusive jurisdiction under this Act, the tribunal of this State having jurisdiction over the parties shall issue a child-support order, which controls and must be so recognized.

(c) If two or more child-support orders have been issued for the same obligor and child and if the obligor or the individual obligee resides in this State, a party may request a tribunal of this State to determine which order controls and must be so recognized under subsection (b). The request must be accompanied by a certified copy of every support order in effect. The requesting party shall give notice of the request to each party whose rights may be affected by the determination.

(d) The tribunal that issued the controlling order under subsection (a), (b), or (c) is the tribunal that has continuing, exclusive jurisdiction under Section 205 [750 ILCS 22/205].

(e) A tribunal of this State which determines by order the identity of the controlling order under subsection (b)(1) or (2) or which issues a new controlling order under subsection (b)(3) shall state in that order the basis upon which the tribunal made its determination.

(f) Within 30 days after issuance of an order determining the identity of the controlling order, the party obtaining the order shall file a certified copy of it with each tribunal that issued or registered an earlier order of child support. A party who obtains the order and fails to file a certified copy is subject to

appropriate sanctions by a tribunal in which the issue of failure to file arises. The failure to file does not affect the validity or enforceability of the controlling order.
(Source: P.A. 88-550, § 207; 90-240, § 5.)

Section Set Out Twice.
The section above is without amendments by P.A. 93-479 (see notes for effective date). For the version of this section as amended by P.A. 93-479, see the following section, also numbered 750 ILCS 22/207.

Effect of Amendments.
The 1997 amendment by P.A. 90-240, effective July 28, 1997, redesignated Part C as Part 3 and in the Part head inserted "Of Multiple", deleted "With" preceding "Orders" and deleted from the end "Of Other States"; in the section catchline substituted "controlling child-support order" for "child support orders"; in subsection (a) deleted from the beginning "If a proceeding is brought under this Act, and one or more child support orders have been issued in this or another state with regard to an obligor and a child, a tribunal of this State shall apply the following rules in determining which order to recognize for purposes of continuing, exclusive jurisdiction: (1)", inserted "a proceeding is brought under this Act and", substituted "child-support" for "child support", inserted "controls and" and inserted "so"; added present subsection (b); redesignated subdivisions (a)(2) through (a)(4) as subdivisions (b)(1) through (b)(3); in subdivision (b)(1) deleted "two or more tribunals have issued child support orders for the same obligor and child, and" preceding "only", inserted "controls and" and inserted "so"; in subdivision (b)(2) deleted "two or more tribunals have issued child support orders for the same obligor and child, and" preceding "more", inserted "controls and" twice and inserted "so" twice; in subdivision (b)(3) deleted "two or more tribunals have issued child support orders for the same obligor and child, and" preceding "none", substituted "having jurisdiction over the parties shall" for "may", substituted "child-support" for "child support", inserted "controls and" and inserted "so"; added subsection (c); redesignated former subsection (b) as subsection (d); in subsection (d) deleted "has" preceding "issued", substituted "the controlling" for "an", deleted "recognized" preceding "under", inserted "(b), or (c)", substituted "that has" for "having" and added at the end "under Section 205"; and added subsections (e) and (f).

750 ILCS 22/207 (As amended by P.A. 93-479; see notes for effective date) Determination of controlling child-support order

Sec. 207. *Determination of controlling child-support order.* (a) If a proceeding is brought under this Act and only one tribunal has issued a child-support order, the order of that tribunal controls and must be so recognized.

(b) If a proceeding is brought under this Act, and two or more child-support orders have been issued by tribunals of this State or another state with regard to the same obligor and same child, a tribunal of this State having personal jurisdiction over both the obligor and individual obligee shall apply the following rules and by order shall determine which order controls:

(1) If only one of the tribunals would have continuing, exclusive jurisdiction under this Act, the order of that tribunal controls and must be so recognized.

(2) If more than one of the tribunals would have continuing, exclusive jurisdiction under this Act:

(A) an order issued by a tribunal in the current home state of the child controls; but

(B) if an order has not been issued in the current home state of the child, the order most recently issued controls.

(3) If none of the tribunals would have continuing, exclusive jurisdiction under this Act, the tribunal of this State shall issue a child-support order, which controls.

(c) If two or more child-support orders have been issued for the same obligor and same child, upon request of a party who is an individual or a support enforcement agency, a tribunal of this State having personal jurisdiction over both the obligor and the obligee who is an individual shall determine which order controls under subsection (b). The request may be filed with a registration for enforcement or registration for modification pursuant to Article 6, or may be filed as a separate proceeding.

(d) A request to determine which is the controlling order must be accompanied by a copy of every child-support order in effect and the applicable record of payments. The requesting party shall give notice of the request to each party whose rights may be affected by the determination.

(e) The tribunal that issued the controlling order under subsection (a), (b), or (c) has continuing jurisdiction to the extent provided in Section 205 or 206.

(f) A tribunal of this State that determines by order which is the controlling order under subsection (b)(1) or (2) or (c), or that issues a new controlling order under subsection (b)(3), shall state in that order:

(1) the basis upon which the tribunal made its determination;

(2) the amount of prospective support, if any; and

(3) the total amount of consolidated arrears and accrued interest, if any, under all of the orders after all payments made are credited as provided by Section 209 [750 ILCS 22/209].

(g) Within 30 days after issuance of an order determining which is the controlling order, the party obtaining the order shall file a certified copy of it in each tribunal that issued or registered an earlier order of child support. A party or support enforcement agency obtaining the order that fails to file a certified copy is subject to appropriate sanctions by a tribunal in which the issue of failure to file arises. The failure to file does not affect the validity or enforceability of the controlling order.

(h) An order that has been determined to be the controlling order, or a judgment for consolidated arrears of support and interest, if any, made pursuant to this Section must be recognized in proceedings under this Act.
(Source: P.A. 88-550, § 207; 90-240, § 5; 93-479, § 5.)

Section Set Out Twice.
Multiple versions of this section have been created by the editor to reflect conflicting or postponed legislation.

Note.
Section 99 of P.A. 93-479, which amended this section, provides:

"Operative date. This Act shall become operative upon at least one of the following 2 events taking place, whichever occurs first, but in no event prior to July 1, 2004:

"(1) The amendment by Congress of subdivision (f) of 42 U.S.C. Sec. 666 to statutorily require or authorize, in connection with the approval of state plans for purposes of federal funding, the adoption of the Uniform Interstate Family Support Act as promulgated by the National Conference of Commissioners on Uniform State Laws in 2001.

"(2) The approval, either generally or with specific application to Illinois, by the federal office of Child Support Enforcement or by the Secretary of Health and Human Services, of a waiver, exemption, finding, or other indicia of regulatory approval of the Uniform Interstate Family Support Act, as promulgated by the National Conference of Commissioners on Uniform State Laws in 2001, in connection with the approval of state plans for purposes of federal funding."

Effect of Amendments.

The 2003 amendment by P.A. 93-479 (see editor's note as to effective date), rewrote the section to the extent that a detailed comparison would be impracticable.

750 ILCS 22/208 (Without amendments by P.A. 93-479; see notes for effective date) Multiple child-support orders for two or more obligees

Sec. 208. *Multiple child-support orders for two or more obligees.* In responding to multiple registrations or petitions for enforcement of two or more child support orders in effect at the same time with regard to the same obligor and different individual obligees, at least one of which was issued by a tribunal of another state, a tribunal of this State shall enforce those orders in the same manner as if the multiple orders had been issued by a tribunal of this State.

(Source: P.A. 88-550, § 208; 90-240, § 5.)

Section Set Out Twice.

The section above is without amendments by P.A. 93-479 (see notes for effective date). For the version of this section as amended by P.A. 93-479, see the following section, also numbered 750 ILCS 22/208.

Effect of Amendments.

The 1997 amendment by P.A. 90-240, effective July 28, 1997, in the section catchline substituted "child-support" for "child support".

750 ILCS 22/208 (As amended by P.A. 93-479; see notes for effective date) Child-support orders for two or more obligees

Sec. 208. *Child-support orders for two or more obligees.* In responding to registrations or petitions for enforcement of two or more child support orders in effect at the same time with regard to the same obligor and different individual obligees, at least one of which was issued by a tribunal of another state, a tribunal of this State shall enforce those orders in the same manner as if the orders had been issued by a tribunal of this State.

(Source: P.A. 88-550, § 208; 90-240, § 5; 93-479, § 5.)

Section Set Out Twice.

Multiple versions of this section have been created by the editor to reflect conflicting or postponed legislation.

Note.

Section 99 of P.A. 93-479, which amended this section, provides:

"Operative date. This Act shall become operative upon at least one of the following 2 events taking place, whichever occurs first, but in no event prior to July 1, 2004:

"(1) The amendment by Congress of subdivision (f) of 42 U.S.C. Sec. 666 to statutorily require or authorize, in connection with the approval of state plans for purposes of federal funding, the adoption of the Uniform Interstate Family Support Act as promulgated by the National Conference of Commissioners on Uniform State Laws in 2001.

"(2) The approval, either generally or with specific application to Illinois, by the federal office of Child Support Enforcement or by the Secretary of Health and Human Services, of a waiver, exemption, finding, or other indicia of regulatory approval of the Uniform Interstate Family Support Act, as promulgated by the National Conference of Commissioners on Uniform State Laws in 2001, in connection with the approval of state plans for purposes of federal funding."

Effect of Amendments.

The 2003 amendment by P.A. 93-479 (see editor's note as to effective date), deleted "multiple" from the beginning of the section heading and preceding "registrations or" and preceding "orders had been".

750 ILCS 22/209 (Without amendments by P.A. 93-479; see notes for effective date) Credit for payments

Sec. 209. *Credit for payments.* Amounts collected and credited for a particular period pursuant to a support order issued by a tribunal of another state must be credited against the amounts accruing or accrued for the same period under a support order issued by the tribunal of this State.

(Source: P.A. 88-550, § 209.)

Section Set Out Twice.

The section above is without amendments by P.A. 93-479 (see notes for effective date). For the version of this section as amended by P.A. 93-479, see the following section, also numbered 750 ILCS 22/209.

750 ILCS 22/209 (As amended by P.A. 93-479; see notes for effective date) Credit for payments

Sec. 209. *Credit for payments.* A tribunal of this State shall credit amounts collected for a particular period pursuant to any child-support order against the amounts owed for the same period under any other child-support order for support of the same child issued by a tribunal of this or another state.

(Source: P.A. 88-550, § 209; 93-479, § 5.)

Section Set Out Twice.

Multiple versions of this section have been created by the editor to reflect conflicting or postponed legislation.

Note.

Section 99 of P.A. 93-479, which amended this section, provides:

"Operative date. This Act shall become operative upon at least one of the following 2 events taking place, whichever occurs first, but in no event prior to July 1, 2004:

"(1) The amendment by Congress of subdivision (f) of 42 U.S.C. Sec. 666 to statutorily require or authorize, in connection with the approval of state plans for purposes of federal funding, the adoption of the Uniform Interstate Family Support Act as promulgated by the National Conference of Commissioners on Uniform State Laws in 2001.

"(2) The approval, either generally or with specific application to Illinois, by the federal office of Child Support Enforcement or by the Secretary of Health and Human Services, of a waiver, exemption, finding, or other indicia of regulatory approval of the Uniform Interstate Family Support Act, as promulgated by the National Conference of Commissioners on Uniform State Laws in 2001, in connection with the approval of state plans for purposes of federal funding."

Effect of Amendments.

The 2003 amendment by P.A. 93-479 (see editor's note as to effective date), rewrote the section to the extent that a detailed comparison would be impracticable.

750 ILCS 22/210 (See notes for effective date) Application of Act to nonresident subject to personal jurisdiction

Sec. 210. *Application of Act to nonresident subject to personal jurisdiction.* A tribunal of this State exercising personal jurisdiction over a nonresident in a proceeding under this Act, under other law of this State relating to a support order, or recognizing a support order of a foreign country or political subdivision on the basis of comity may receive evidence from another state pursuant to Section 316 [750 ILCS 22/316], communicate with a tribunal of another state pursuant to Section 317 [750 ILCS 22/317], and obtain discovery through a tribunal of another state pursuant to Section 318 [750 ILCS 22/218]. In all other respects, Articles 3 through 7 [750 ILCS 22/301 et seq. through 750 ILCS 22/701 et seq.] do not apply and the tribunal shall apply the procedural and substantive law of this State.
(Source: P.A. 93-479, § 5.)

Note.

Section 99 of P.A. 93-479, which enacted this section, provides:

"Operative date. This Act shall become operative upon at least one of the following 2 events taking place, whichever occurs first, but in no event prior to July 1, 2004:

"(1) The amendment by Congress of subdivision (f) of 42 U.S.C. Sec. 666 to statutorily require or authorize, in connection with the approval of state plans for purposes of federal funding, the adoption of the Uniform Interstate Family Support Act as promulgated by the National Conference of Commissioners on Uniform State Laws in 2001.

"(2) The approval, either generally or with specific application to Illinois, by the federal office of Child Support Enforcement or by the Secretary of Health and Human Services, of a waiver, exemption, finding, or other indicia of regulatory approval of the Uniform Interstate Family Support Act, as promulgated by the National Conference of Commissioners on Uniform State Laws in 2001, in connection with the approval of state plans for purposes of federal funding."

750 ILCS 22/211 (See notes for effective date) Continuing, exclusive jurisdiction to modify spousal-support order

Sec. 211. *Continuing, exclusive jurisdiction to modify spousal-support order.* (a) A tribunal of this State issuing a spousal-support order consistent with the law of this State has continuing, exclusive jurisdiction to modify the spousal-support order throughout the existence of the support obligation.

(b) A tribunal of this State may not modify a spousal-support order issued by a tribunal of another state having continuing, exclusive jurisdiction over that order under the law of that state.

(c) A tribunal of this State that has continuing, exclusive jurisdiction over a spousal-support order may serve as:

(1) an initiating tribunal to request a tribunal of another state to enforce the spousal-support order issued in this State; or

(2) a responding tribunal to enforce or modify its own spousal-support order.
(Source: P.A. 93-479, § 5.)

Note.

Section 99 of P.A. 93-479, which enacted this section, provides:

"Operative date. This Act shall become operative upon at least one of the following 2 events taking place, whichever occurs first, but in no event prior to July 1, 2004:

"(1) The amendment by Congress of subdivision (f) of 42 U.S.C. Sec. 666 to statutorily require or authorize, in connection with the approval of state plans for purposes of federal funding, the adoption of the Uniform Interstate Family Support Act as promulgated by the National Conference of Commissioners on Uniform State Laws in 2001.

"(2) The approval, either generally or with specific application to Illinois, by the federal office of Child Support Enforcement or by the Secretary of Health and Human Services, of a waiver, exemption, finding, or other indicia of regulatory approval of the Uniform Interstate Family Support Act, as promulgated by the National Conference of Commissioners on Uniform State Laws in 2001, in connection with the approval of state plans for purposes of federal funding."

ARTICLE 3.

CIVIL PROVISIONS OF GENERAL APPLICATION

750 ILCS 22/301 (Without amendments by P.A. 93-479; see notes for effective date) Proceedings under Act

Sec. 301. *Proceedings under Act.* (a) Except as otherwise provided in this Act, this Article applies to all proceedings under this Act.

(b) This Act provides for the following proceedings:

(1) establishment of an order for spousal support or child support pursuant to Article 4;

(2) enforcement of a support order and income-withholding order of another state without registration pursuant to Article 5;

(3) registration of an order for spousal support or child support of another state for enforcement pursuant to Article 6;

(4) modification of an order for child support or spousal support issued by a tribunal of this State pursuant to Article 2, Part 2;

(5) registration of an order for child support of another state for modification pursuant to Article 6;

(6) determination of parentage pursuant to Article 7; and

(7) assertion of jurisdiction over nonresidents pursuant to Article 2, Part 1.

(c) An individual obligee or a support enforcement agency may commence a proceeding authorized un-

der this Act by filing a petition in an initiating tribunal for forwarding to a responding tribunal or by filing a petition or a comparable pleading directly in a tribunal of another state which has or can obtain personal jurisdiction over the obligor.
(Source: P.A. 88-550, § 301; 90-240, § 5.)

Section Set Out Twice.
The section above is without amendments by P.A. 93-479 (see effective date for notes). For the version of this section as amended by P.A. 93-479, see the following section, also numbered 750 ILCS 22/301.

Effect of Amendments.
The 1997 amendment by P.A. 90-240, effective July 28, 1997, in the section catchline deleted "this" preceding "Act"; in subdivision (b)(4) substituted "Part 2" for "Part B"; and in subdivision (b)(7) substituted "Part 1" for "Part A".

750 ILCS 22/301 (As amended by P.A. 93-479; see notes for effective date) Proceedings under Act

Sec. 301. *Proceedings under Act.* (a) Except as otherwise provided in this Act, this Article applies to all proceedings under this Act.

(b) An individual obligee or a support enforcement agency may initiate a proceeding authorized under this Act by filing a petition in an initiating tribunal for forwarding to a responding tribunal or by filing a petition or a comparable pleading directly in a tribunal of another state which has or can obtain personal jurisdiction over the obligor.
(Source: P.A. 88-550, § 301; 90-240, § 5; 93-479, § 5.)

Section Set Out Twice.
Multiple versions of this section have been created by the editor to reflect conflicting or postponed legislation.

Note.
Section 99 of P.A. 93-479, which amended this section, provides: "Operative date. This Act shall become operative upon at least one of the following 2 events taking place, whichever occurs first, but in no event prior to July 1, 2004:

"(1) The amendment by Congress of subdivision (f) of 42 U.S.C. Sec. 666 to statutorily require or authorize, in connection with the approval of state plans for purposes of federal funding, the adoption of the Uniform Interstate Family Support Act as promulgated by the National Conference of Commissioners on Uniform State Laws in 2001.

"(2) The approval, either generally or with specific application to Illinois, by the federal office of Child Support Enforcement or by the Secretary of Health and Human Services, of a waiver, exemption, finding, or other indicia of regulatory approval of the Uniform Interstate Family Support Act, as promulgated by the National Conference of Commissioners on Uniform State Laws in 2001, in connection with the approval of state plans for purposes of federal funding."

Effect of Amendments.
The 2003 amendment by P.A. 93-479 (see editor's note as to effective date), rewrote the section to the extent that a detailed comparison would be impracticable.

750 ILCS 22/302 (As amended by P.A. 93-479; see notes for effective date) Proceeding by minor parent

Sec. 302. *Proceeding by minor parent.* A minor parent or a guardian or other legal representative of a minor parent may maintain a proceeding on behalf of or for the benefit of the minor's child.
(Source: P.A. 88-550, § 302; 93-479, § 5.)

Note.
Section 99 of P.A. 93-479, which amended this section, provides: "Operative date. This Act shall become operative upon at least one of the following 2 events taking place, whichever occurs first, but in no event prior to July 1, 2004:

"(1) The amendment by Congress of subdivision (f) of 42 U.S.C. Sec. 666 to statutorily require or authorize, in connection with the approval of state plans for purposes of federal funding, the adoption of the Uniform Interstate Family Support Act as promulgated by the National Conference of Commissioners on Uniform State Laws in 2001.

"(2) The approval, either generally or with specific application to Illinois, by the federal office of Child Support Enforcement or by the Secretary of Health and Human Services, of a waiver, exemption, finding, or other indicia of regulatory approval of the Uniform Interstate Family Support Act, as promulgated by the National Conference of Commissioners on Uniform State Laws in 2001, in connection with the approval of state plans for purposes of federal funding."

Section Set Out Twice.
The 2003 amendment by P.A. 93-479 (see editor's note for effective date), revised the section heading.
Multiple versions of this section have been created by the editor to reflect conflicting or postponed legislation.

750 ILCS 22/303 (Without amendments by P.A. 93-479; see notes for effective date) Application of law of State

Sec. 303. *Application of law of State.* Except as otherwise provided by this Act, a responding tribunal of this State:

(1) shall apply the procedural and substantive law, including the rules on choice of law, generally applicable to similar proceedings originating in this State and may exercise all powers and provide all remedies available in those proceedings; and

(2) shall determine the duty of support and the amount payable in accordance with the law and support guidelines of this State.
(Source: P.A. 88-550, § 303; 90-240, § 5.)

Section Set Out Twice.
The section above is without amendments by P.A. 93-479 (see notes for effective date). For the version of this section as amended by P.A. 93-479, see the following section, also numbered 750 ILCS 22/303.

Effect of Amendments.
The 1997 amendment by P.A. 90-240, effective July 28, 1997, in the section catchline deleted "this" preceding "State".

750 ILCS 22/303 (As amended by P.A. 93-479; see notes for effective date) Application of law of State

Sec. 303. *Application of law of State.* Except as otherwise provided in this Act, a responding tribunal of this State shall:

(1) apply the procedural and substantive law generally applicable to similar proceedings originating in this State and may exercise all powers and provide all remedies available in those proceedings; and

(2) determine the duty of support and the amount payable in accordance with the law and support guidelines of this State.
(Source: P.A. 88-550, § 303; 90-240, § 5; 93-479, § 5.)

Section Set Out Twice.
Multiple versions of this section have been created by the editor to reflect conflicting or postponed legislation.

Note.
Section 99 of P.A. 93-479, which amended this section, provides:
"Operative date. This Act shall become operative upon at least one of the following 2 events taking place, whichever occurs first, but in no event prior to July 1, 2004:
"(1) The amendment by Congress of subdivision (f) of 42 U.S.C. Sec. 666 to statutorily require or authorize, in connection with the approval of state plans for purposes of federal funding, the adoption of the Uniform Interstate Family Support Act as promulgated by the National Conference of Commissioners on Uniform State Laws in 2001.
"(2) The approval, either generally or with specific application to Illinois, by the federal office of Child Support Enforcement or by the Secretary of Health and Human Services, of a waiver, exemption, finding, or other indicia of regulatory approval of the Uniform Interstate Family Support Act, as promulgated by the National Conference of Commissioners on Uniform State Laws in 2001, in connection with the approval of state plans for purposes of federal funding."

Effect of Amendments.
The 2003 amendment by P.A. 93-479 (see editor's note as to effective date), rewrote the section to the extent that a detailed comparison would be impracticable.

750 ILCS 22/304 (Without amendments by PA 93-479) Duties of initiating tribunal

Sec. 304. *(Without amendments by PA 93-479) Duties of initiating tribunal.* (a) Upon the filing of a petition authorized by this Act, an initiating tribunal of this State shall forward three copies of the petition and its accompanying documents:
(1) to the responding tribunal or appropriate support enforcement agency in the responding state; or
(2) if the identity of the responding tribunal is unknown, to the state information agency of the responding state with a request that they be forwarded to the appropriate tribunal and that receipt be acknowledged.
(b) If a responding state has not enacted this Act or a law or procedure substantially similar to this Act, a tribunal of this State may issue a certificate or other document and make findings required by the law of the responding state. If the responding state is a foreign jurisidction, the tribunal may specify the amount of support sought and provide other documents necessary to satisfy the requirements of the responding state.
(Source: P.A. 88-550, § 304; 90-240, § 5.)

Note.
Section 99 of P.A. 93-479, which amended this section, provides:
"Operative date. This Act shall become operative upon at least one of the following 2 events taking place, whichever occurs first, but in no event prior to July 1, 2004:
"(1) The amendment by Congress of subdivision (f) of 42 U.S.C. Sec. 666 to statutorily require or authorize, in connection with the approval of state plans for purposes of federal funding, the adoption of the Uniform Interstate Family Support Act as promulgated by the National Conference of Commissioners on Uniform State Laws in 2001.
"(2) The approval, either generally or with specific application to Illinois, by the federal office of Child Support Enforcement or by the Secretary of Health and Human Services, of a waiver, exemption, finding, or other indicia of regulatory approval of the Uniform Interstate Family Support Act, as promulgated by the National Conference of Commissioners on Uniform State Laws in 2001, in connection with the approval of state plans for purposes of federal funding."

Effect of Amendments.
The 1997 amendment by P.A. 90-240, effective July 28, 1997, added the subsection (a) designation; and added subsection (b).

Section Set Out Twice.
Multiple versions of this section have been created by the editor to reflect conflicting or postponed legislation.

750 ILCS 22/304 (As amended by P.A. 93-479; see notes for effective date) Duties of initiating tribunal

Sec. 304. *Duties of initiating tribunal.* (a) Upon the filing of a petition authorized by this Act, an initiating tribunal of this State shall forward the petition and its accompanying documents:
(1) to the responding tribunal or appropriate support enforcement agency in the responding state; or
(2) if the identity of the responding tribunal is unknown, to the state information agency of the responding state with a request that they be forwarded to the appropriate tribunal and that receipt be acknowledged.
(b) If requested by the responding tribunal, a tribunal of this State shall issue a certificate or other document and make findings required by the law of the responding state. If the responding state is a foreign country or political subdivision, upon request the tribunal shall specify the amount of support sought, convert that amount into the equivalent amount in the foreign currency under applicable official or market exchange rate as publicly reported, and provide any other documents necessary to satisfy the requirements of the responding state.
(Source: P.A. 88-550, § 304; 90-240, § 5; 93-479, § 5.)

Note.
Section 99 of P.A. 93-479, which amended this section, provides:
"Operative date. This Act shall become operative upon at least one of the following 2 events taking place, whichever occurs first, but in no event prior to July 1, 2004:
"(1) The amendment by Congress of subdivision (f) of 42 U.S.C. Sec. 666 to statutorily require or authorize, in connection with the approval of state plans for purposes of federal funding, the adoption of the Uniform Interstate Family Support Act as promulgated by the National Conference of Commissioners on Uniform State Laws in 2001.
"(2) The approval, either generally or with specific application to Illinois, by the federal office of Child Support Enforcement or by the Secretary of Health and Human Services, of a waiver, exemption, finding, or other indicia of regulatory approval of the Uniform Interstate Family Support Act, as promulgated by the National Conference of Commissioners on Uniform State Laws in 2001, in connection with the approval of state plans for purposes of federal funding."

Effect of Amendments.

The 1997 amendment by P.A. 90-240, effective July 28, 1997, added the subsection (a) designation; and added subsection (b).

The 2003 amendment by P.A. 93-479 (see editor's note as to effective date), rewrote the section to the extent that a detailed comparison would be impracticable.

Section Set Out Twice.

Multiple versions of this section have been created by the editor to reflect conflicting or postponed legislation.

750 ILCS 22/305 Duties and powers of responding tribunal

Sec. 305. *Duties and powers of responding tribunal.* (a) *(Without amendments by P.A. 93-479)* When a responding tribunal of this State receives a petition or comparable pleading from an initiating tribunal or directly pursuant to Section 301(c) [750 ILCS 22/301], it shall cause the petition or pleading to be filed and notify the obligee where and when it was filed.

(a) *(As amended by P.A. 93-479; see notes for effective date)* When a responding tribunal of this State receives a petition or comparable pleading from an initiating tribunal or directly pursuant to Section 301(b) [750 ILCS 22/301], it shall cause the petition or pleading to be filed and notify the obligee where and when it was filed.

(b) *(Without amendments by P.A. 93-479)* A responding tribunal of this State, to the extent otherwise authorized by law, may do one or more of the following:

(b) *(As amended by P.A. 93-479; see notes for effective date)* A responding tribunal of this State, to the extent not prohibited by other law, may do one or more of the following:

(1) *(Without amendments by P.A. 93-479)* issue or enforce a support order, modify a child-support order, or render a judgment to determine parentage;

(1) *(As amended by P.A. 93-479; see notes for effective date)* issue or enforce a support order, modify a child-support order, determine the controlling child-support order, or determine parentage;

(2) order an obligor to comply with a support order, specifying the amount and the manner of compliance;

(3) order income withholding;

(4) determine the amount of any arrearages, and specify a method of payment;

(5) enforce orders by civil or criminal contempt, or both;

(6) set aside property for satisfaction of the support order;

(7) place liens and order execution on the obligor's property;

(8) order an obligor to keep the tribunal informed of the obligor's current residential address, telephone number, employer, address of employment, and telephone number at the place of employment;

(9) issue a bench warrant for an obligor who has failed after proper notice to appear at a hearing ordered by the tribunal and enter the bench warrant in any local and state computer systems for criminal warrants;

(10) order the obligor to seek appropriate employment by specified methods;

(11) award reasonable attorney's fees and other fees and costs; and

(12) grant any other available remedy.

(c) A responding tribunal of this State shall include in a support order issued under this Act, or in the documents accompanying the order, the calculations on which the support order is based.

(d) A responding tribunal of this State may not condition the payment of a support order issued under this Act upon compliance by a party with provisions for visitation.

(e) If a responding tribunal of this State issues an order under this Act, the tribunal shall send a copy of the order to the obligee and the obligor and to the initiating tribunal, if any.

(f) *(Added by P.A. 93-479; see notes for effective date)* If requested to enforce a support order, arrears, or judgement or modify a support order stated in a foreign currency, a responding tribunal of this State shall convert the amount stated in the foreign currency to the equivalent amount in dollars under the applicable official or market exchange rate as publicly reported.

(Source: P.A. 88-550, § 305; 90-240, § 5; 93-479, § 5.)

Subsections (a), (b) and (b)(1) Set Out Twice.

Subsections (a), (b) and (b)(1) are set out twice. The first version is without amendments by P.A. 93-479, and the second version is as amended by P.A. 93-479 (see notes for effective date).

Note.

Section 99 of P.A. 93-479, which amended this section, provides: "Operative date. This Act shall become operative upon at least one of the following 2 events taking place, whichever occurs first, but in no event prior to July 1, 2004:

"(1) The amendment by Congress of subdivision (f) of 42 U.S.C. Sec. 666 to statutorily require or authorize, in connection with the approval of state plans for purposes of federal funding, the adoption of the Uniform Interstate Family Support Act as promulgated by the National Conference of Commissioners on Uniform State Laws in 2001.

"(2) The approval, either generally or with specific application to Illinois, by the federal office of Child Support Enforcement or by the Secretary of Health and Human Services, of a waiver, exemption, finding, or other indicia of regulatory approval of the Uniform Interstate Family Support Act, as promulgated by the National Conference of Commissioners on Uniform State Laws in 2001, in connection with the approval of state plans for purposes of federal funding."

Effect of Amendments.

The 1997 amendment by P.A. 90-240, effective July 28, 1997, in subsection (a) deleted "by first class mail" preceding "where"; in subdivision (b)(1) substituted "child-support" for "child support"; and in subsection (e) deleted "by first class mail" preceding "to the obligee".

The 2003 amendment by P.A. 93-479 (see editor's note as to effective date), subsituted "301(b)" for "301(c)" in subsection (a); rewrote the introductory paragraph of subsection (b) and subsection (b)(1); and added subsection (f).

750 ILCS 22/306 (Without amendments by P.A. 93-479, see notes for effective date) Inappropriate tribunal

Sec. 306. *Inappropriate tribunal.* If a petition or comparable pleading is received by an inappropriate tribunal of this State, it shall forward the pleading and accompanying documents to an appropriate tribunal in this State or another state and notify the obligee where and when the pleading was sent.
(Source: P.A. 88-550, § 306; 90-240, § 5.)

Section Set Out Twice.
The section above is set out twice. The first is without amendments by P.A. 93-479, and the second is as amended by P.A. 93-479 (see notes for effective date).

Effect of Amendments.
The 1997 amendment by P.A. 90-240, effective July 28, 1997, deleted "by first class mail" preceding "where".

750 ILCS 22/306 (As amended by P.A. 93-479; see notes for effective date) Inappropriate tribunal

Sec. 306. *Inappropriate tribunal. (As amended by P.A. 93-479; see notes for effective date)* If a petition or comparable pleading is received by an inappropriate tribunal of this State, the tribunal shall forward the pleading and accompanying documents to an appropriate tribunal in this State or another state and notify the obligee where and when the pleading was sent.
(Source: P.A. 88-550, § 306; 90-240, § 5; 93-479, § 5.)

Section Set Out Twice.
The section above is set out twice. The first is without amendments by P.A. 93-479, and the second is as amended by P.A. 93-479 (see notes for effective date).

Note.
Section 99 of P.A. 93-479, which amended this section, provides:
"Operative date. This Act shall become operative upon at least one of the following 2 events taking place, whichever occurs first, but in no event prior to July 1, 2004:
"(1) The amendment by Congress of subdivision (f) of 42 U.S.C. Sec. 666 to statutorily require or authorize, in connection with the approval of state plans for purposes of federal funding, the adoption of the Uniform Interstate Family Support Act as promulgated by the National Conference of Commissioners on Uniform State Laws in 2001.
"(2) The approval, either generally or with specific application to Illinois, by the federal office of Child Support Enforcement or by the Secretary of Health and Human Services, of a waiver, exemption, finding, or other indicia of regulatory approval of the Uniform Interstate Family Support Act, as promulgated by the National Conference of Commissioners on Uniform State Laws in 2001, in connection with the approval of state plans for purposes of federal funding."

Effect of Amendments.
The 1997 amendment by P.A. 90-240, effective July 28, 1997, deleted "by first class mail" preceding "where".
The 2003 amendment by P.A. 93-479 (see editor's note as to effective date), substituted "the tribunal" for "it".

750 ILCS 22/307 (Without amendments by P.A. 93-479; see notes for effective date) Duties of support enforcement agency

Sec. 307. *Duties of support enforcement agency.* (a) A support enforcement agency of this State, upon request, shall provide services to a petitioner in a proceeding under this Act. This subsection does not affect any ability the support enforcement agency may have to require an application for services, charge fees, or recover costs in accordance with federal or State law and regulations.

(b) A support enforcement agency that is providing services to the petitioner as appropriate shall:

(1) take all steps necessary to enable an appropriate tribunal in this State or another state to obtain jurisdiction over the respondent;

(2) request an appropriate tribunal to set a date, time, and place for a hearing;

(3) make a reasonable effort to obtain all relevant information, including information as to income and property of the parties;

(4) within 10 days, exclusive of Saturdays, Sundays, and legal holidays, after receipt of a written notice from an initiating, responding, or registering tribunal, send a copy of the notice to the petitioner;

(5) within 10 days, exclusive of Saturdays, Sundays, and legal holidays, after receipt of a written communication from the respondent or the respondent's attorney, send a copy of the communication to the petitioner; and

(6) notify the petitioner if jurisdiction over the respondent cannot be obtained.

(c) This Act does not create or negate a relationship of attorney and client or other fiduciary relationship between a support enforcement agency or the attorney for the agency and the individual being assisted by the agency.
(Source: P.A. 88-550, § 307; 88-691, § 20; 90-240, § 5.)

Section Set Out Twice.
The section above is without amendments by P.A. 93-479 (see notes for effective date). For the version as amended by P.A. 93-479, see the following section, also numbered 750 ILCS 22/307.

Effect of Amendments.
The 1994 amendment by P.A. 88-691, effective January 24, 1995, substituted "petitioner" for "obligee" and "respondent" for "obligor" throughout the section; and in subsection (a), in the first sentence, substituted "a petitioner" for "an obligee".
The 1997 amendment by P.A. 90-240, effective July 28, 1997, in subdivisions (b)(4) and (b)(5) deleted "by first class mail" preceding "to the petitioner".

750 ILCS 22/307 (As amended by P.A. 93-479; see notes for effective date) Duties of support enforcement agency

Sec. 307. *Duties of support enforcement agency.* (a) A support enforcement agency of this State, upon request, shall provide services to a petitioner in a proceeding under this Act. This subsection does not affect any ability the support enforcement agency may have to require an application for services, charge fees, or recover costs in accordance with federal or State law and regulations.

(b) A support enforcement agency that is providing services to the petitioner shall:

(1) take all steps necessary to enable an appropriate tribunal in this State or another state to obtain jurisdiction over the respondent;

(2) request an appropriate tribunal to set a date, time, and place for a hearing;

(3) make a reasonable effort to obtain all relevant information, including information as to income and property of the parties;

(4) within 10 days, exclusive of Saturdays, Sundays, and legal holidays, after receipt of a written notice in a record from an initiating, responding, or registering tribunal, send a copy of the notice to the petitioner;

(5) within 10 days, exclusive of Saturdays, Sundays, and legal holidays, after receipt of a written communication in a record from the respondent or the respondent's attorney, send a copy of the communication to the petitioner; and

(6) notify the petitioner if jurisdiction over the respondent cannot be obtained.

(c) A support enforcement agency of this State that requests registration of a child-support order in this State for enforcement or for modification shall make reasonable efforts:

(1) to ensure that the order to be registered is the controlling order; or

(2) if two or more child-support orders exist and the identity of the controlling order has not been determined, to ensure that a request for such a determination is made in a tribunal having jurisdiction to do so.

(d) A support enforcement agency of this State that requests registration and enforcement of a support order, arrears, or judgement stated in a foreign currency shall convert the amounts stated in the foreign currency into the equivalent amounts in dollars under the applicable official or market exchange rate as publicly reported.

(e) A support enforcement agency of this State shall issue or request a tribunal of this State to issue a child-support order and an income-withholding order that redirect payment of current support, arrears, and interest if requested to do so by a support enforcement agency of another state pursuant to Section 319 of the Uniform Interstate Family Support Act [150 ILCS 22/319].

(f) This Act does not create or negate a relationship of attorney and client or other fiduciary relationship between a support enforcement agency or the attorney for the agency and the individual being assisted by the agency.

(Source: P.A. 88-550, § 307; 88-691, § 20; 90-240, § 5; 93-479, § 5.)

Section Set Out Twice.

Multiple versions of this section have been created by the editor to reflect conflicting or postponed legislation.

Note.

Section 99 of P.A. 93-479, which amended this section, provides: "Operative date. This Act shall become operative upon at least one of the following 2 events taking place, whichever occurs first, but in no event prior to July 1, 2004:

"(1) The amendment by Congress of subdivision (f) of 42 U.S.C. Sec. 666 to statutorily require or authorize, in connection with the approval of state plans for purposes of federal funding, the adoption of the Uniform Interstate Family Support Act as promulgated by the National Conference of Commissioners on Uniform State Laws in 2001.

"(2) The approval, either generally or with specific application to Illinois, by the federal office of Child Support Enforcement or by the Secretary of Health and Human Services, of a waiver, exemption, finding, or other indicia of regulatory approval of the Uniform Interstate Family Support Act, as promulgated by the National Conference of Commissioners on Uniform State Laws in 2001, in connection with the approval of state plans for purposes of federal funding."

Effect of Amendments.

The 2003 amendment by P.A. 93-479 (see editor's note as to effective date), rewrote the section to the extent that a detailed comparison would be impracticable.

750 ILCS 22/308 Duty of Attorney General

Sec. 308. *Duty of Attorney General.* If the support enforcement agency is a prosecuting attorney of this State and if the Attorney General determines that the support enforcement agency is neglecting or refusing to provide services to an individual, the Attorney General may order the agency to perform its duties under this Act or may provide those services directly to the individual.

(Source: P.A. 88-550, § 308.)

750 ILCS 22/309 Private counsel

Sec. 309. *Private counsel.* An individual may employ private counsel to represent the individual in proceedings authorized by this Act.

(Source: P.A. 88-550, § 309.)

750 ILCS 22/310 Duties of the Illinois Department of Public Aid

Sec. 310. *Duties of the Illinois Department of Public Aid.* (a) The Illinois Department of Public Aid is the state information agency under this Act.

(b) The state information agency shall:

(1) compile and maintain a current list, including addresses, of the tribunals in this State which have jurisdiction under this Act and any support enforcement agencies in this State and transmit a copy to the state information agency of every other state;

(2) *(Without amendments by P.A. 93-479)* maintain a register of tribunals and support enforcement agencies received from other states;

(2) *(As amended by P.A. 93-479; see notes for effective date)* maintain a register of names and addresses of tribunals and support enforcement agencies received from other states;

(3) *(Without amendments by P.A. 93-479)* forward to the appropriate tribunal in the place in this State in which the individual obligee or the obligor resides, or in which the obligor's property is believed to be located, all documents concerning a proceeding under this Act received from an initiating tribunal or the state information agency of the initiating state; and

(3) *(As amended by P.A. 93-479; see notes for effective date)* forward to the appropriate tribunal in the county in this State in which the obligee who is an individual or the obligor resides, or in which the obligor's property is believed to be located, all documents concerning a proceeding under this Act received from an initiating tribunal or the state information agency of the initiating state; and

(4) obtain information concerning the location of the obligor and the obligor's property within this State not exempt from execution, by such means as postal verification and federal or state locator services, examination of telephone directories, requests for the obligor's address from employers, and examination of governmental records, including, to the extent not prohibited by other law, those relating to real property, vital statistics, law enforcement, taxation, motor vehicles, driver's licenses, and social security.

(c) The Illinois Department of Public Aid may determine that a foreign country or political subdivision has established a reciprocal arrangement for child support with Illinois and take appropriate action for notification of this determination.
(Source: P.A. 88-550, § 310; 93-479, § 5.)

Subsections (b)(2) and (b)(3) Set Out Twice.
Subsections (b)(2) and (b)(3) are set out twice. The first versions are without amendments by P.A. 93-479, and the second versions are as amended by P.A. 93-479 (see notes for effective date).

Note.
Section 99 of P.A. 93-479, which amended this section, provides:
"Operative date. This Act shall become operative upon at least one of the following 2 events taking place, whichever occurs first, but in no event prior to July 1, 2004:
"(1) The amendment by Congress of subdivision (f) of 42 U.S.C. Sec. 666 to statutorily require or authorize, in connection with the approval of state plans for purposes of federal funding, the adoption of the Uniform Interstate Family Support Act as promulgated by the National Conference of Commissioners on Uniform State Laws in 2001.
"(2) The approval, either generally or with specific application to Illinois, by the federal office of Child Support Enforcement or by the Secretary of Health and Human Services, of a waiver, exemption, finding, or other indicia of regulatory approval of the Uniform Interstate Family Support Act, as promulgated by the National Conference of Commissioners on Uniform State Laws in 2001, in connection with the approval of state plans for purposes of federal funding."

Effect of Amendments.
The 2003 amendment by P.A. 93-479 (see editor's note as to effective date), inserted "names and addresses of" in subsection (b)(2); substituted "county in this State in which the obligee who is an individual" for "place in this State in which the individual obligee" in subsection (b)(3); and added subsection (c).

750 ILCS 22/311 Pleadings and accompanying documents

Sec. 311. *Pleadings and accompanying documents.* (a) *(Without amendments by P.A. 93-479)* A petitioner seeking to establish or modify a support order or to determine parentage in a proceeding under this Act must verify the petition. Unless otherwise ordered under Section 312 [750 ILCS 22/312], the petition or accompanying documents must provide, so far as known, the name, residential address, and social security numbers of the respondent and the petitioner, and the name, sex, residential address, social security number, and date of birth of each child for whom support is sought. The petition must be accompanied by a certified copy of any support order in effect. The petition may include any other information that may assist in locating or identifying the respondent.

(a) *(As amended by P.A. 93-479; see notes for effective date)* In a proceeding under this Act, a petitioner seeking to establish a support order to determine parentage or to register and modify a support order of another state must file a petition. Unless otherwise ordered under Section 312 [750 ILCS 22/312], the petition or accompanying documents must provide, so far as known, the name, residential address, and social security numbers of the respondent and the petitioner or the parent and alleged parent, and the name, sex, residential address, social security number, and date of birth of each child for whose benefit support is sought or whose parentage is to be determined. Unless filed at the time of registration, the petition must be accompanied by a copy of any support order known to have been issued by another tribunal. The petition may include any other information that may assist in locating or identifying the respondent.

(b) The petition must specify the relief sought. The petition and accompanying documents must conform substantially with the requirements imposed by the forms mandated by federal law for use in cases filed by a support enforcement agency.
(Source: P.A. 88-550, § 311; 88-691, § 20; 93-479, § 5.)

Subsection (a) Set Out Twice.
Subsection (a) is set out twice. The first version is without amendments by P.A. 93-479, and the second version is as amended by P.A. 93-479 (see notes for effective date).

Note.
Section 99 of P.A. 93-479, which amended this section, provides:
"Operative date. This Act shall become operative upon at least one of the following 2 events taking place, whichever occurs first, but in no event prior to July 1, 2004:
"(1) The amendment by Congress of subdivision (f) of 42 U.S.C. Sec. 666 to statutorily require or authorize, in connection with the approval of state plans for purposes of federal funding, the adoption of the Uniform Interstate Family Support Act as promulgated by the National Conference of Commissioners on Uniform State Laws in 2001.
"(2) The approval, either generally or with specific application to Illinois, by the federal office of Child Support Enforcement or by the Secretary of Health and Human Services, of a waiver, exemption, finding, or other indicia of regulatory approval of the Uniform Interstate Family Support Act, as promulgated by the National Conference of Commissioners on Uniform State Laws in 2001, in connection with the approval of state plans for purposes of federal funding."

Effect of Amendments.
The 1994 amendment by P.A. 88-691, effective January 24, 1995, substituted "petitioner" for "obligee" and "respondent" for "obligor" throughout the section.
The 2003 amendment by P.A. 93-479 (see editor's note as to effective date), rewrote the section to the extent that a detailed comparison would be impracticable.

750 ILCS 22/312 (Without amendments by P.A. 93-479; see notes for effective date) Nondisclosure of information in exceptional circumstances

Sec. 312. *Nondisclosure of information in exceptional circumstances.* Upon a finding, which may be made ex parte, that the health, safety, or liberty of a party or child would be unreasonably put at risk by the disclosure of identifying information, or if an existing order so provides, a tribunal shall order that the address of the child or party or other identifying information not be disclosed in a pleading or other document filed in a proceeding under this Act.
(Source: P.A. 88-550, § 312.)

Section Set Out Twice.
The section above is without amendments by P.A. 93-479 (see notes for effective date). For the version of this section as amended by P.A. 93-479, see the following section, also numbered 750 ILCS 22/312.

750 ILCS 22/312 (As amended by P.A. 93-479; see notes for effective date) Nondisclosure of information in exceptional circumstances

Sec. 312. *Nondisclosure of information in exceptional circumstances.* If a party alleges in an affidavit or a pleading under oath that the health, safety, or liberty of a party or child would be jeopardized by disclosure of specific identifying information, that information must be sealed and may not be disclosed to the other party or public. After a hearing in which a tribunal takes into consideration the health, safety, or liberty of the party or child, the tribunal may order disclosure of information that the tribunal determines to be in the interest of justice.
(Source: P.A. 88-550, § 312; 93-479, § 5.)

Section Set Out Twice.
Multiple versions of this section have been created by the editor to reflect conflicting or postponed legislation.

Note.
Section 99 of P.A. 93-479, which amended this section, provides:
"Operative date. This Act shall become operative upon at least one of the following 2 events taking place, whichever occurs first, but in no event prior to July 1, 2004:
"(1) The amendment by Congress of subdivision (f) of 42 U.S.C. Sec. 666 to statutorily require or authorize, in connection with the approval of state plans for purposes of federal funding, the adoption of the Uniform Interstate Family Support Act as promulgated by the National Conference of Commissioners on Uniform State Laws in 2001.
"(2) The approval, either generally or with specific application to Illinois, by the federal office of Child Support Enforcement or by the Secretary of Health and Human Services, of a waiver, exemption, finding, or other indicia of regulatory approval of the Uniform Interstate Family Support Act, as promulgated by the National Conference of Commissioners on Uniform State Laws in 2001, in connection with the approval of state plans for purposes of federal funding."

Effect of Amendments.
The 2003 amendment by P.A. 93-479 (see editor's note as to effective date), rewrote the section to the extent that a detailed comparison would be impracticable.

750 ILCS 22/313 Costs and fees

Sec. 313. *Costs and fees.* (a) The petitioner may not be required to pay a filing fee or other costs.
(b) If a petitioner prevails, a responding tribunal may assess against a respondent filing fees, reasonable attorney's fees, other costs, and necessary travel and other reasonable expenses incurred by the petitioner and the petitioner's witnesses. The tribunal may not assess fees, costs, or expenses against the petitioner or the support enforcement agency of either the initiating or the responding state, except as provided by other law. Attorney's fees may be taxed as costs, and may be ordered paid directly to the attorney, who may enforce the order in the attorney's own name. Payment of support owed to the petitioner has priority over fees, costs and expenses.
(c) The tribunal shall order the payment of costs and reasonable attorney's fees if it determines that a hearing was requested primarily for delay. In a proceeding under Article 6 [750 ILCS 22/601 et seq.], a hearing is presumed to have been requested primarily for delay if a registered support order is confirmed or enforced without change.
(Source: P.A. 88-550, § 313; 88-691, § 20.)

Effect of Amendments.
The 1994 amendment by P.A. 88-691, effective January 24, 1995, substituted "petitioner" for "obligee" in subsection (b), in the first sentence, substituted "a petitioner" for "an obligee", substituted "a respondent" for "an obligor" and substituted "petitioner's" for "obligee's".

750 ILCS 22/314 Limited immunity of petitioner

Sec. 314. *Limited immunity of petitioner.* (a) *(Without amendments by P.A. 93-479)* Participation by a petitioner in a proceeding before a responding tribunal, whether in person, by private attorney, or through services provided by the support enforcement agency, does not confer personal jurisdiction over the petitioner in another proceeding.
(a) *(As amended by P.A. 93-479; see notes for effective date)* Participation by a petitioner in a proceeding under this Act before a responding tribunal, whether in person, by private attorney, or through services provided by the support enforcement agency, does not confer personal jurisdiction over the petitioner in another proceeding.
(b) A petitioner is not amenable to service of civil process while physically present in this State to participate in a proceeding under this Act.
(c) The immunity granted by this Section does not extend to civil litigation based on acts unrelated to a proceeding under this Act committed by a party while present in this State to participate in the proceeding.
(Source: P.A. 88-550, § 314; 88-691, § 20; 93-479, § 5.)

Subsection (a) Set Out Twice.
Subsection (a) is set out twice. The first version is without

amendments by P.A. 93-479, and the second version is as amended by P.A. 93-479 (see notes for effective date).

Note.

Section 99 of P.A. 93-479, which amended this section, provides:

"Operative date. This Act shall become operative upon at least one of the following 2 events taking place, whichever occurs first, but in no event prior to July 1, 2004:

"(1) The amendment by Congress of subdivision (f) of 42 U.S.C. Sec. 666 to statutorily require or authorize, in connection with the approval of state plans for purposes of federal funding, the adoption of the Uniform Interstate Family Support Act as promulgated by the National Conference of Commissioners on Uniform State Laws in 2001.

"(2) The approval, either generally or with specific application to Illinois, by the federal office of Child Support Enforcement or by the Secretary of Health and Human Services, of a waiver, exemption, finding, or other indicia of regulatory approval of the Uniform Interstate Family Support Act, as promulgated by the National Conference of Commissioners on Uniform State Laws in 2001, in connection with the approval of state plans for purposes of federal funding."

Effect of Amendments.

The 1994 amendment by P.A. 88-691, effective January 24, 1995, substituted "petitioner" for "obligee"; and in subsection (a) substituted "a petitioner" for "an obligee".

The 2003 amendment by P.A. 93-479 (see editor's note as to effective date), inserted "under this Act" in subsection (a).

750 ILCS 22/315 Nonparentage as defense

Sec. 315. *Nonparentage as defense.* A party whose parentage of a child has been previously determined by or pursuant to law may not plead nonparentage as a defense to a proceeding under this Act.
(Source: P.A. 88-550, § 315.)

750 ILCS 22/316 Special rules of evidence and procedure

Sec. 316. *Special rules of evidence and procedure.* (a) *(Without amendments by P.A. 93-479)* The physical presence of the petitioner in a responding tribunal of this State is not required for the establishment, enforcement, or modification of a support order or the rendition of a judgment determining parentage.

(a) *(As amended by P.A. 93-479; see notes for effective date)* The physical presence of a nonresident party who is an individual in a tribunal of this State is not required for the establishment, enforcement, or modification of a support order or the rendition of a judgment determining parentage.

(b) *(Without amendments by P.A. 93-479)* A verified petition, affidavit, document substantially complying with federally mandated forms, and a document incorporated by reference in any of them, not excluded under the hearsay rule if given in person, is admissible in evidence if given under oath by a party or witness residing in another state.

(b) *(As amended by P.A. 93-479; see notes for effective date)* An affidavit, a document substantially complying with federally mandated forms, or a document incorporated by reference in any of them, which would not be excluded under the hearsay rule if given in person, is admissible in evidence if given under penalty of perjury by a party or witness residing in another state.

(c) A copy of the record of child-support payments certified as a true copy of the original by the custodian of the record may be forwarded to a responding tribunal. The copy is evidence of facts asserted in it, and is admissible to show whether payments were made.

(d) Copies of bills for testing for parentage, and for prenatal and postnatal health care of the mother and child, furnished to the adverse party at least 10 days before trial, are admissible in evidence to prove the amount of the charges billed and that the charges were reasonable, necessary, and customary.

(e) *(Without amendments by P.A. 93-479)* Documentary evidence transmitted from another state to a tribunal of this State by telephone, telecopier, or other means that do not provide an original writing may not be excluded from evidence on an objection based on the means of transmission.

(e) *(As amended by P.A. 93-479; see notes for effective date)* Documentary evidence transmitted from another state to a tribunal of this State by telephone, telecopier, or other means that do not provide an original record may not be excluded from evidence on an objection based on the means of transmission.

(f) *(Without amendments by P.A. 93-479)* In a proceeding under this Act, a tribunal of this State may permit a party or witness residing in another state to be deposed or to testify by telephone, audiovisual means, or other electronic means at a designated tribunal or other location in that state. A tribunal of this State shall cooperate with tribunals of other states in designating an appropriate location for the deposition or testimony.

(f) *(As amended by P.A. 93-479; see notes for effective date)* In a proceeding under this Act, a tribunal of this State shall permit a party or witness residing in another state to be deposed or to testify by telephone, audiovisual means, or other electronic means at a designated tribunal or other location in that state. A tribunal of this State shall cooperate with tribunals of other states in designating an appropriate location for the deposition or testimony.

(g) If a party called to testify at a civil hearing refuses to answer on the ground that the testimony may be self-incriminating, the trier of fact may draw an adverse inference from the refusal.

(h) A privilege against disclosure of communications between spouses does not apply in a proceeding under this Act.

(i) The defense of immunity based on the relationship of husband and wife or parent and child does not apply in a proceeding under this Act.

(j) *(Added by P.A. 93-479; see notes for effective date)* A voluntary acknowledgment of paternity, certified as a true copy, is admissible to establish parentage of the child.
(Source: P.A. 88-550, § 316; 88-691, § 20; 90-240, § 5; 93-479, § 5.)

Subsections (a), (b), (e), and (f) Set Out Twice.

Subsections (a), (b), (e), and (f) are set out twice. The first versions are without amendments by P.A. 93-479, and the second versions are as amended by P.A. 93-479 (see notes for effective date).

Note.

Section 99 of P.A. 93-479, which amended this section, provides: "Operative date. This Act shall become operative upon at least one of the following 2 events taking place, whichever occurs first, but in no event prior to July 1, 2004:

"(1) The amendment by Congress of subdivision (f) of 42 U.S.C. Sec. 666 to statutorily require or authorize, in connection with the approval of state plans for purposes of federal funding, the adoption of the Uniform Interstate Family Support Act as promulgated by the National Conference of Commissioners on Uniform State Laws in 2001.

"(2) The approval, either generally or with specific application to Illinois, by the federal office of Child Support Enforcement or by the Secretary of Health and Human Services, of a waiver, exemption, finding, or other indicia of regulatory approval of the Uniform Interstate Family Support Act, as promulgated by the National Conference of Commissioners on Uniform State Laws in 2001, in connection with the approval of state plans for purposes of federal funding."

Effect of Amendments.

The 1994 amendment by P.A. 88-691, effective January 24, 1995, substituted "petitioner" for "obligee" in subsection (a).

The 1997 amendment by P.A. 90-240, effective July 28, 1997, in subsection (c), in the first sentence, substituted "child-support" for "child support".

The 2003 amendment by P.A. 93-479 (see editor's note as to effective date), rewrote the section to the extent that a detailed comparison would be impracticable.

750 ILCS 22/317 (Without amendments by P.A. 93-479; see notes for effective date) Communications between tribunals

Sec. 317. *Communications between tribunals.* A tribunal of this State may communicate with a tribunal of another state in writing, or by telephone or other means, to obtain information concerning the laws of that state, the legal effect of a judgment, decree, or order of that tribunal, and the status of a proceeding in the other state. A tribunal of this State may furnish similar information by similar means to a tribunal of another state.
(Source: P.A. 88-550, § 317.)

Section Set Out Twice.

The section above is without amendments by P.A. 93-479 (see notes for effective date). For the version of this section as amended by P.A. 93-479, see the following section, also numbered 750 ILCS 22/317.

750 ILCS 22/317 (As amended by P.A. 93-479; see notes for effective date) Communications between tribunals

Sec. 317. *Communications between tribunals.* A tribunal of this State may communicate with a tribunal of another state or foreign country or political subdivision in a record, or by telephone or other means, to obtain information concerning the laws, the legal effect of a judgment, decree, or order of that tribunal, and the status of a proceeding in the other state or foreign country or political subdivision. A tribunal of this State may furnish similar information by similar means to a tribunal of another state or foreign country or political subdivision.
(Source: P.A. 88-550, § 317; 93-479, § 5.)

Section Set Out Twice.

Multiple versions of this section have been created by the editor to reflect conflicting or postponed legislation.

Note.

Section 99 of P.A. 93-479, which amended this section, provides: "Operative date. This Act shall become operative upon at least one of the following 2 events taking place, whichever occurs first, but in no event prior to July 1, 2004:

"(1) The amendment by Congress of subdivision (f) of 42 U.S.C. Sec. 666 to statutorily require or authorize, in connection with the approval of state plans for purposes of federal funding, the adoption of the Uniform Interstate Family Support Act as promulgated by the National Conference of Commissioners on Uniform State Laws in 2001.

"(2) The approval, either generally or with specific application to Illinois, by the federal office of Child Support Enforcement or by the Secretary of Health and Human Services, of a waiver, exemption, finding, or other indicia of regulatory approval of the Uniform Interstate Family Support Act, as promulgated by the National Conference of Commissioners on Uniform State Laws in 2001, in connection with the approval of state plans for purposes of federal funding."

Effect of Amendments.

The 2003 amendment by P.A. 93-479 (see editor's note as to effective date), rewrote the section to the extent that a detailed comparison would be impracticable.

750 ILCS 22/318 Assistance with discovery

Sec. 318. *Assistance with discovery.* A tribunal of this State may:

(1) request a tribunal of another state to assist in obtaining discovery; and

(2) upon request, compel a person over whom it has jurisdiction to respond to a discovery order issued by a tribunal of another state.
(Source: P.A. 88-550, § 318.)

750 ILCS 22/319 Receipt and disbursement of payments

Sec. 319. *Receipt and disbursement of payments.* A support enforcement agency or tribunal of this State shall disburse promptly any amounts received pursuant to a support order, as directed by the order. The agency or tribunal shall furnish to a requesting party or tribunal of another state a certified statement by the custodian of the record of the amounts and dates of all payments received.

(b) *(Added by P.A. 93-479; see notes for effective date)* If neither the obligor, nor the obligee who is an individual, nor the child resides in this State, upon request from the support enforcement agency of this State or another state, the support enforcement agency of this State or a tribunal of this State shall:

(1) direct that the support payment be made to the support enforcement agency in the state in which the obligee is receiving services; and

(2) issue and send to the obligor's employer a conforming income-withholding order or an administrative notice of change of payee, reflecting the redirected payments.

(3) The support enforcement agency of this State receiving redirected payments from another state pursuant to a law similar to subsection (b) shall furnish to a requesting party or tribunal of the other state a certified statement by the custodian of the record of the amount and dates of all payments received.
(Source: P.A. 88-550, § 319; 93-479, § 5.)

Note.

P.A. 93-479 apparently enacted subsection (b) in error, since the section has no subsection (a).

Section 99 of P.A. 93-479, which amended this section, provides: "Operative date. This Act shall become operative upon at least one of the following 2 events taking place, whichever occurs first, but in no event prior to July 1, 2004:

"(1) The amendment by Congress of subdivision (f) of 42 U.S.C. Sec. 666 to statutorily require or authorize, in connection with the approval of state plans for purposes of federal funding, the adoption of the Uniform Interstate Family Support Act as promulgated by the National Conference of Commissioners on Uniform State Laws in 2001.

"(2) The approval, either generally or with specific application to Illinois, by the federal office of Child Support Enforcement or by the Secretary of Health and Human Services, of a waiver, exemption, finding, or other indicia of regulatory approval of the Uniform Interstate Family Support Act, as promulgated by the National Conference of Commissioners on Uniform State Laws in 2001, in connection with the approval of state plans for purposes of federal funding."

Effect of Amendments.

The 2003 amendment by P.A. 93-479 (see editor's note as to effective date), added subsection (b).

750 ILCS 22/320 Payment of Support to State Disbursement Unit

Sec. 320. *Payment of Support to State Disbursement Unit.* (a) As used in this Section:

"Order for support", "obligor", "obligee", and "payor" mean those terms as defined in the Income Withholding for Support Act [750 ILCS 28/1 et seq.], except that "order for support" means an order entered by any tribunal of this State but shall not mean orders providing for spousal maintenance under which there is no child support obligation.

(b) Notwithstanding any other provision of this Act to the contrary, each order for support entered or modified on or after October 1, 1999 shall require that support payments be made to the State Disbursement Unit established under Section 10-26 of the Illinois Public Aid Code if [305 ILCS 5/10-26]:

(1) a party to the order is receiving child support enforcement services under Article X of the Illinois Public Aid Code [305 ILCS 5/10-1 et seq.]; or

(2) no party to the order is receiving child support enforcement services, but the support payments are made through income withholding.

(c) Support payments shall be made to the State Disbursement Unit if:

(1) the order for support was entered before October 1, 1999, and a party to the order is receiving child support enforcement services under Article X of the Illinois Public Aid Code [305 ILCS 5/10-1 et seq.]; or

(2) no party to the order is receiving child support enforcement services, and the support payments are being made through income withholding.

(c-5) If no party to the order is receiving child support enforcement services under Article X of the Illinois Public Aid Code [305 ILCS 5/10-1 et seq.], and the support payments are not made through income withholding, then support payments shall be made as directed by the order for support.

(c-10) At any time, and notwithstanding the existence of an order directing payments to be made elsewhere, the Department of Public Aid may provide notice to the obligor and, where applicable, to the obligor's payor:

(1) to make support payments to the State Disbursement Unit if:

(A) a party to the order for support is receiving child support enforcement services under Article X of the Illinois Public Aid Code [305 ILCS 5/10-1 et seq]; or

(B) no party to the order for support is receiving child support enforcement services under Article X of the Illinois Public Aid Code [305 ILCS 5/10-1 et seq], but the support payments are made through income withholding; or

(2) to make support payments to the State Disbursement Unit of another state upon request of another state's Title IV-D child support enforcement agency, in accordance with the requirements of Title IV, Part D of the Social Security Act [42 U.S.C. § 601 et seq.] and regulations promulgated under that Part D.

The Department of Public Aid shall provide a copy of the notice to the obligee and to the clerk of the circuit court.

(c-15) Within 15 days after the effective date of this amendatory Act of the 91st General Assembly [P.A. 91-677], the clerk of the circuit court shall provide written notice to the obligor to make payments directly to the clerk of the circuit court if no party to the order is receiving child support enforcement services under Article X of the Illinois Public Aid Code [305 ILCS 5/10-1 et seq], the support payments are not made through income withholding, and the order for support requires support payments to be made directly to the clerk of the circuit court. The clerk shall provide a copy of the notice to the obligee.

(c-20) If the State Disbursement Unit receives a support payment that was not appropriately made to the Unit under this Section, the Unit shall immediately return the payment to the sender, including, if possible, instructions detailing where to send the support payments.

(d) The notices under subsections (c-10) and (c-15) may be sent by ordinary mail, certified mail, return receipt requested, facsimile transmission, or other electronic process, or may be served upon the obligor or payor using any method provided by law for service of a summons.
(Source: P.A. 91-677, § 20; 92-590, § 20.)

Illinois Administrative Code.

See 89 Illinois Administrative Code, § 160.60.

Effective Date.

Section 99 of P.A. 91-677 made this section effective upon becoming law. The Act was approved January 5, 2000.

Effect of Amendments.

The 2002 amendment by P.A. 92-590, effective July 1, 2002, substituted "child support enforcement services" for "child and spouse support services" throughout the section; rewrote subsection (c-10); added the last sentence to subsection (c-15); and deleted the former last sentence in subsection (c-20), which read: "The Illinois Department of Public Aid shall provide a copy of the notice to the obligee and to the clerk of the court."

ARTICLE 4.

ESTABLISHMENT OF SUPPORT ORDER

750 ILCS 22/401 Petition to establish support order

Sec. 401. *Petition to establish support order.* (a) If a support order entitled to recognition under this Act has not been issued, a responding tribunal of this State may issue a support order if:

(1) the individual seeking the order resides in another state; or

(2) the support enforcement agency seeking the order is located in another state.

(b) *(Without amendments by P.A. 93-479)* The tribunal may issue a temporary child-support order if:

(1) the respondent has signed a verified statement acknowledging parentage;

(2) the respondent has been determined by or pursuant to law to be the parent; or

(3) there is other clear and convincing evidence that the respondent is the child's parent.

(b) *(As amended by P.A. 93-479; see notes for effective date)* The tribunal may issue a temporary child-support order if the tribunal determines that such an order is appropriate and the individual ordered to pay is:

(1) a presumed father of the child;

(2) petitioning to have his paternity adjudicated;

(3) identified as the father of the child through genetic testing;

(4) an alleged father who has declined to submit to genetic testing;

(5) shown by clear and convincing evidence to be the father of the child;

(6) an acknowledged father as provided by applicable State law;

(7) the mother of the child; or

(8) an individual who has been ordered to pay child support in a previous proceeding and the order has not been reversed or vacated.

(c) Upon finding, after notice and opportunity to be heard, that a respondent owes a duty of support, the tribunal shall issue a support order directed to the respondent and may issue other orders pursuant to Section 305 [750 ILCS 22/305].

(Source: P.A. 88-550, § 401; 88-691, § 20; 90-240, § 5; 93-479, § 5.)

Subsection (b) Set Out Twice.

Subsection (b) is set out twice. The first version is without amendments by P.A. 93-479, and the second is as amended by P.A. 93-479 (see notes for effective date).

Note.

Section 99 of P.A. 93-479, which amended this section, provides:

"Operative date. This Act shall become operative upon at least one of the following 2 events taking place, whichever occurs first, but in no event prior to July 1, 2004:

"(1) The amendment by Congress of subdivision (f) of 42 U.S.C. Sec. 666 to statutorily require or authorize, in connection with the approval of state plans for purposes of federal funding, the adoption of the Uniform Interstate Family Support Act as promulgated by the National Conference of Commissioners on Uniform State Laws in 2001.

"(2) The approval, either generally or with specific application to Illinois, by the federal office of Child Support Enforcement or by the Secretary of Health and Human Services, of a waiver, exemption, finding, or other indicia of regulatory approval of the Uniform Interstate Family Support Act, as promulgated by the National Conference of Commissioners on Uniform State Laws in 2001, in connection with the approval of state plans for purposes of federal funding."

Effect of Amendments.

The 1994 amendment by P.A. 88-691, effective January 24, 1995, substituted "respondent" for "obligor" throughout the section; and in subsection (c) substituted "a respondent" for "an obligor".

The 1997 amendment by P.A. 90-240, effective July 28, 1997, in subsection (b), in the introductory language, substituted "child-support" for "child support".

The 2003 amendment by P.A. 93-479 (see editor's note as to effective date), rewrote subsection (b).

ARTICLE 5.

ENFORCEMENT OF ORDER OF ANOTHER STATE WITHOUT REGISTRATION

750 ILCS 22/501 Employer's receipt of income-withholding order of another state

Sec. 501. *Employer's receipt of income-withholding order of another state. (Without amendments by P.A. 93-479)* An income-withholding order issued in another state may be sent to the person or entity defined as the obligor's employer without first filing a petition or comparable pleading or registering the order with a tribunal of this State.

(As amended by P.A. 93-479; see notes for effective date) An income-withholding order issued in another state may be sent by or on behalf of the obligee, or by the support enforcement agency, to the person defined as the obligor's employer under the income-withholding law of this State without first filing a petition or comparable pleading or registering the order with a tribunal of this State.

(Source: P.A. 88-550, § 501; 90-240, § 5; 93-479, § 5.)

Paragraph Set Out Twice.

The paragraph above is set out twice. The first is without

amendments by P.A. 93-479, and the second is as amended by P.A. 93-479 (see notes for effective date).

Note.

Section 99 of P.A. 93-479, which amended this section, provides: "Operative date. This Act shall become operative upon at least one of the following 2 events taking place, whichever occurs first, but in no event prior to July 1, 2004:

"(1) The amendment by Congress of subdivision (f) of 42 U.S.C. Sec. 666 to statutorily require or authorize, in connection with the approval of state plans for purposes of federal funding, the adoption of the Uniform Interstate Family Support Act as promulgated by the National Conference of Commissioners on Uniform State Laws in 2001.

"(2) The approval, either generally or with specific application to Illinois, by the federal office of Child Support Enforcement or by the Secretary of Health and Human Services, of a waiver, exemption, finding, or other indicia of regulatory approval of the Uniform Interstate Family Support Act, as promulgated by the National Conference of Commissioners on Uniform State Laws in 2001, in connection with the approval of state plans for purposes of federal funding."

Effect of Amendments.

The 1997 amendment by P.A. 90-240, effective July 28, 1997, in the Article head deleted "Direct" from the beginning; in the section catchline substituted "Employer's receipt" for "Recognition"; deleted the subsection (a) designation preceding "An income"; deleted "by first class mail" preceding "to the person"; deleted the former second sentence of the introductory language of subsection (a) which read "Upon receipt of the order, the employer shall:"; deleted subdivision (a)(1) which read "treat an income withholding order issued in another state which appears regular on its face as if it had been issued by a tribunal of this State"; deleted subdivision (a)(2) which read "immediately provide a copy of the order to the obligor; and"; deleted subdivision (a)(3) which read "distribute the funds as directed in the withholding order"; and deleted subsection (b) regarding contesting the validity or enforcement of an income withholding order.

The 2003 amendment by P.A. 93-479 (see editor's note as to effective date), rewrote the section to the extent that a detailed comparison would be impracticable.

750 ILCS 22/502 Employer's compliance with income-withholding order of another state

Sec. 502. *Employer's compliance with income-withholding order of another state.* (a) Upon receipt of an income-withholding order, the obligor's employer shall immediately provide a copy of the order to the obligor.

(b) The employer shall treat an income-withholding order issued in another state which appears regular on its face as if it had been issued by a tribunal of this State.

(c) Except as otherwise provided in subsection (d) and Section 503 [750 ILCS 22/503] the employer shall withhold and distribute the funds as directed in the withholding order by complying with terms of the order which specify:

(1) the duration and amount of periodic payments of current child-support, stated as a sum certain;

(2) *(Without amendments by P.A. 93-479)* the person or agency designated to receive payments and the address to which the payments are to be forwarded;

(2) *(As amended by P.A. 93-479; see notes for effective date)* the person designated to receive payments and the address to which the payments are to be forwarded;

(3) medical support, whether in the form of periodic cash payment, stated as a sum certain, or ordering the obligor to provide health insurance coverage for the child under a policy available through the obligor's employment;

(4) the amount of periodic payments of fees and costs for a support enforcement agency, the issuing tribunal, and the obligee's attorney, stated as sums certain; and

(5) the amount of periodic payments of arrearages and interest on arrearages, stated as sums certain.

(d) An employer shall comply with the law of the state of the obligor's principal place of employment for withholding from income with respect to:

(1) the employer's fee for processing an income-withholding order;

(2) the maximum amount permitted to be withheld from the obligor's income; and

(3) the times within which the employer must implement the withholding order and forward the child support payment.

(Source: P.A. 88-550, § 502; 90-240, § 5; 93-479, § 5.)

Subsection (c)(2) Set Out Twice.

Subsection (c)(2) is set out twice. The first is without amendments by P.A. 93-479, and the second is as amended by P.A. 93-479 (see notes for effective date).

Note.

Section 99 of P.A. 93-479, which amended this section, provides: "Operative date. This Act shall become operative upon at least one of the following 2 events taking place, whichever occurs first, but in no event prior to July 1, 2004:

"(1) The amendment by Congress of subdivision (f) of 42 U.S.C. Sec. 666 to statutorily require or authorize, in connection with the approval of state plans for purposes of federal funding, the adoption of the Uniform Interstate Family Support Act as promulgated by the National Conference of Commissioners on Uniform State Laws in 2001.

"(2) The approval, either generally or with specific application to Illinois, by the federal office of Child Support Enforcement or by the Secretary of Health and Human Services, of a waiver, exemption, finding, or other indicia of regulatory approval of the Uniform Interstate Family Support Act, as promulgated by the National Conference of Commissioners on Uniform State Laws in 2001, in connection with the approval of state plans for purposes of federal funding."

Effect of Amendments.

The 1997 amendment by P.A. 90-240, effective July 28, 1997, rewrote this section.

The 2003 amendment by P.A. 93-479 (see editor's note as to effective date), deleted "or agency" after "the person" in subsection (c)(2).

750 ILCS 22/503 Employer's compliance with two or more income-withholding orders

Sec. 503. *Employer's compliance with two or more income-withholding orders. (Without amendments by P.A. 93-479)* If an obligor's employer receives multiple income-withholding orders with respect to the earnings of the same obligor, the employer satisfies the terms of the multiple orders if the employer complies with the law of the state of the obligor's principal place of employment to establish the priorities for withholding and allocating income withheld for multiple child support obligees.

(As amended by P.A. 93-479; see notes for effective date) If an obligor's employer receives two or more income-withholding orders with respect to the earnings of the same obligor, the employer satisfies the terms of the orders if the employer complies with the law of the state of the obligor's principal place of employment to establish the priorities for withholding and allocating income withheld for two or more child support obligees.
(Source: P.A. 90-240, § 5; 93-479, § 5.)

Paragraph Set Out Twice.
The paragraph above is set out twice. The first version is without amendments by P.A. 93-479, and the second version is as amended by P.A. 93-479 (see notes for effective date).

Note.
Section 99 of P.A. 93-479, which amended this section, provides: "Operative date. This Act shall become operative upon at least one of the following 2 events taking place, whichever occurs first, but in no event prior to July 1, 2004:

"(1) The amendment by Congress of subdivision (f) of 42 U.S.C. Sec. 666 to statutorily require or authorize, in connection with the approval of state plans for purposes of federal funding, the adoption of the Uniform Interstate Family Support Act as promulgated by the National Conference of Commissioners on Uniform State Laws in 2001.

"(2) The approval, either generally or with specific application to Illinois, by the federal office of Child Support Enforcement or by the Secretary of Health and Human Services, of a waiver, exemption, finding, or other indicia of regulatory approval of the Uniform Interstate Family Support Act, as promulgated by the National Conference of Commissioners on Uniform State Laws in 2001, in connection with the approval of state plans for purposes of federal funding."

Effective Date.
Section 99 of P.A. 90-240 made this section effective upon becoming law. The Act was approved July 28, 1997.

Effect of Amendments.
The 2003 amendment by P.A. 93-479 (see editor's note as to effective date), revised the section heading, and twice substituted "two or more" for "multiple".

750 ILCS 22/504 Immunity from civil liability

Sec. 504. *Immunity from civil liability.* An employer who complies with an income-withholding order issued in another state in accordance with this Article is not subject to civil liability to an individual or agency with regard to the employer's withholding of child support from the obligor's income.
(Source: P.A. 90-240, § 5.)

Effective Date.
Section 99 of P.A. 90-240 made this section effective upon becoming law. The Act was approved July 28, 1997.

750 ILCS 22/505 Penalties for noncompliance

Sec. 505. *Penalties for noncompliance.* An employer who willfully fails to comply with an income-withholding order issued by another state and received for enforcement is subject to the same penalties that may be imposed for noncompliance with an order issued by a tribunal of this State.
(Source: P.A. 90-240, § 5.)

Effective Date.
Section 99 of P.A. 90-240 made this section effective upon becoming law. The Act was approved July 28, 1997.

750 ILCS 22/506 (Without amendments by P.A. 93-479) Contest by obligor

Sec. 506. *(Without amendments by P.A. 93-479) Contest by obligor.* (a) An obligor may contest the validity or enforcement of an income-withholding order issued in another state and received directly by an employer in this State in the same manner as if the order had been issued by a tribunal of this State. Section 604 [750 ILCS 22/604] applies to the contest.

(b) The obligor shall give notice of the contest to:

(1) a support enforcement agency providing services to the obligee;

(2) each employer that has directly received an income-withholding order; and

(3) the person or agency designated to receive payments in the income-withholding order or if no person or agency is designated, to the obligee.
(Source: P.A. 90-240, § 5.)

Section Set Out Twice.
The section above is without amendments by P.A. 93-479 (see notes for effective date). For the version of this section as amended by P.A. 93-479, see the following section, also numbered 750 ILCS 22/507.

Effective Date.
Section 99 of P.A. 90-240 made this section effective upon becoming law. The Act was approved July 28, 1997.

750 ILCS 22/506 (As amended by P.A. 93-479; see notes for effective date) Contest by obligor

Sec. 506. *Contest by obligor.* (a) An obligor may contest the validity or enforcement of an income-withholding order issued in another state and received directly by an employer in this State by registering the order in a tribunal of this State and filing a contest to that order as provided in Article 6 [750 ILCS 22/601 et seq.], or otherwise contesting the order in the same manner as if the order had been issued by a tribunal of this State.

(b) The obligor shall give notice of the contest to:

(1) a support enforcement agency providing services to the obligee;

(2) each employer that has directly received an income-withholding order relating to the obligor; and

(3) the person designated to receive payments in the income-withholding order or if no person is designated, to the obligee.
(Source: P.A. 90-240, § 5; 93-479, § 5.)

Section Set Out Twice.
Multiple versions of this section have been created by the editor to reflect conflicting or postponed legislation.

Note.
Section 99 of P.A. 93-479, which renumbered this section, provides:

"Operative date. This Act shall become operative upon at least one of the following 2 events taking place, whichever occurs first, but in no event prior to July 1, 2004:

"(1) The amendment by Congress of subdivision (f) of 42 U.S.C. Sec. 666 to statutorily require or authorize, in connection with the approval of state plans for purposes of federal funding, the adoption of the Uniform Interstate Family Support Act as promulgated by the National Conference of Commissioners on Uniform State Laws in 2001.

"(2) The approval, either generally or with specific application to Illinois, by the federal office of Child Support Enforcement or by the Secretary of Health and Human Services, of a waiver, exemption, finding, or other indicia of regulatory approval of the Uniform Interstate Family Support Act, as promulgated by the National Conference of Commissioners on Uniform State Laws in 2001, in connection with the approval of state plans for purposes of federal funding."

Effect of Amendments.

The 2003 amendment by P.A. 93-479 (see editor's note as to effective date), rewrote the section to the extent that a detailed comparison would be impracticable.

750 ILCS 22/507 Administrative enforcement of orders

Sec. 507. *Administrative enforcement of orders.* (a) *(Without amendments by P.A. 93-479)* A party seeking to enforce a support order or an income-withholding order, or both, issued by a tribunal of another state may send the documents required for registering the order to a support enforcement agency of this State.

(a) *(As amended by P.A. 93-479; see notes for effective date)* A party or support enforcement agency seeking to enforce a support order or an income-withholding order, or both, issued by a tribunal of another state may send the documents required for registering the order to a support enforcement agency of this State.

(b) Upon receipt of the documents, the support enforcement agency, without initially seeking to register the order, shall consider and, if appropriate, use any administrative procedure authorized by the law of this State to enforce a support order or an income-withholding order, or both. If the obligor does not contest administrative enforcement, the order need not be registered. If the obligor contests the validity or administrative enforcement of the order, the support enforcement agency shall register the order pursuant to this Act.

(Source: P.A. 90-240, § 5; 93-479, § 5.)

Subsection (a) Set Out Twice.

Subsection (a) is set out twice. The first is without amendments by P.A. 93-479, and the second is as amended by P.A. 93-479 (see notes for effective date).

Note.

Section 99 of P.A. 93-479, which amended this section, provides:

"Operative date. This Act shall become operative upon at least one of the following 2 events taking place, whichever occurs first, but in no event prior to July 1, 2004:

"(1) The amendment by Congress of subdivision (f) of 42 U.S.C. Sec. 666 to statutorily require or authorize, in connection with the approval of state plans for purposes of federal funding, the adoption of the Uniform Interstate Family Support Act as promulgated by the National Conference of Commissioners on Uniform State Laws in 2001.

"(2) The approval, either generally or with specific application to Illinois, by the federal office of Child Support Enforcement or by the Secretary of Health and Human Services, of a waiver, exemption, finding, or other indicia of regulatory approval of the Uniform Interstate Family Support Act, as promulgated by the National Conference of Commissioners on Uniform State Laws in 2001, in connection with the approval of state plans for purposes of federal funding."

Effective Date.

Section 99 of P.A. 90-240 made this section effective upon becoming law. The Act was approved July 28, 1997.

Effect of Amendments.

The 2003 amendment by P.A. 93-479 (see editor's note as to effective date), inserted "or support enforcement agency" near the beginning of subsection (a).

ARTICLE 6.

REGISTRATION, ENFORCEMENT, AND MODIFICATION OF SUPPORT ORDER

Part 1.

Registration and Enforcement of Support Order

750 ILCS 22/601 Registration of order for enforcement

Sec. 601. *Registration of order for enforcement.* A support order or income-withholding order issued by a tribunal of another state may be registered in this State for enforcement.

(Source: P.A. 88-550, § 601; 93-479, § 5.)

Note.

P.A. 90-240, § 5 redesignated Part A. as Part 1.

Section 99 of P.A. 93-479, which amended this section, provides:

"Operative date. This Act shall become operative upon at least one of the following 2 events taking place, whichever occurs first, but in no event prior to July 1, 2004:

"(1) The amendment by Congress of subdivision (f) of 42 U.S.C. Sec. 666 to statutorily require or authorize, in connection with the approval of state plans for purposes of federal funding, the adoption of the Uniform Interstate Family Support Act as promulgated by the National Conference of Commissioners on Uniform State Laws in 2001.

"(2) The approval, either generally or with specific application to Illinois, by the federal office of Child Support Enforcement or by the Secretary of Health and Human Services, of a waiver, exemption, finding, or other indicia of regulatory approval of the Uniform Interstate Family Support Act, as promulgated by the National Conference of Commissioners on Uniform State Laws in 2001, in connection with the approval of state plans for purposes of federal funding."

Effect of Amendments.

The 2003 amendment by P.A. 93-479 (see editor's note as to effective date), deleted "an" after "order or".

750 ILCS 22/602 (Without amendments by P.A. 93-479) Procedure to register order for enforcement

Sec. 602. *(Without amendments by P.A. 93-479) Procedure to register order for enforcement.* (a) A support order or income-withholding order of another state may be registered in this State by sending the following documents and information to the appropriate tribunal in this State:

(1) a letter of transmittal to the tribunal requesting registration and enforcement;

(2) 2 copies, including one certified copy, of all orders to be registered, including any modification of an order;

(3) a sworn statement by the party seeking registration or a certified statement by the custodian of the records showing the amount of any arrearage;

(4) the name of the obligor and, if known:

(i) the obligor's address and social security number;

(ii) the name and address of the obligor's employer and any other source of income of the obligor; and

(iii) a description and the location of property of the obligor in this State not exempt from execution; and

(5) the name and address of the obligee and, if applicable, the agency or person to whom support payments are to be remitted.

(b) On receipt of a request for registration, the registering tribunal shall cause the order to be filed as a foreign judgment, together with one copy of the documents and information, regardless of their form.

(c) A petition or comparable pleading seeking a remedy that must be affirmatively sought under other law of this State may be filed at the same time as the request for registration or later. The pleading must specify the grounds for the remedy sought.
(Source: P.A. 88-550, § 602; 92-463, § 17.)

Section Set Out Twice.
Multiple versions of this section have been created by the editor to reflect conflicting or postponed legislation.

Effect of Amendments.
The 2001 amendment by P.A. 92-463, effective August 22, 2001, substituted "tribunal" for "circuit court" in the first paragraph of subsection (a).

750 ILCS 22/602 (As amended by P.A. 93-479; see notes for effective date) Procedure to register order for enforcement

Sec. 602. *Procedure to register order for enforcement.* (a) A support order or income-withholding order of another state may be registered in this State by sending the following records and information to the appropriate tribunal in this State:

(1) a letter of transmittal to the tribunal requesting registration and enforcement;

(2) 2 copies, including one certified copy, of the order to be registered, including any modification of the order;

(3) a sworn statement by the person requesting registration or a certified statement by the custodian of the records showing the amount of any arrearage;

(4) the name of the obligor and, if known:

(i) the obligor's address and social security number;

(ii) the name and address of the obligor's employer and any other source of income of the obligor; and

(iii) a description and the location of property of the obligor in this State not exempt from execution; and

(5) except as otherwise provided in Section 312 [750 ILCS 22/312], the name and address of the obligee and, if applicable, the person to whom support payments are to be remitted.

(b) On receipt of a request for registration, the registering tribunal shall cause the order to be filed as a foreign judgment, together with one copy of the documents and information, regardless of their form.

(c) A petition or comparable pleading seeking a remedy that must be affirmatively sought under other law of this State may be filed at the same time as the request for registration or later. The pleading must specify the grounds for the remedy sought.

(d) If two or more orders are in effect, the person requesting registration shall:

(1) furnish to the tribunal a copy of every support order asserted to be in effect in addition to the documents specified in this Section;

(2) specify the order alleged to be the controlling order, if any; and

(3) specify the amount of consolidated arrears, if any.

(e) A request for a determination of which is the controlling order may be filed separately or with a request for registration and enforcement or for registration and modification. The person requesting registration shall give notice of the request to each party whose rights may be affected by the determination.
(Source: P.A. 88-550, § 602; 92-463, § 17; 93-479, § 5.)

Section Set Out Twice.
Multiple versions of this section have been created by the editor to reflect conflicting or postponed legislation.

Note.
Section 99 of P.A. 93-479, which amended this section, provides: "Operative date. This Act shall become operative upon at least one of the following 2 events taking place, whichever occurs first, but in no event prior to July 1, 2004:

"(1) The amendment by Congress of subdivision (f) of 42 U.S.C. Sec. 666 to statutorily require or authorize, in connection with the approval of state plans for purposes of federal funding, the adoption of the Uniform Interstate Family Support Act as promulgated by the National Conference of Commissioners on Uniform State Laws in 2001.

"(2) The approval, either generally or with specific application to Illinois, by the federal office of Child Support Enforcement or by the Secretary of Health and Human Services, of a waiver, exemption, finding, or other indicia of regulatory approval of the Uniform Interstate Family Support Act, as promulgated by the National Conference of Commissioners on Uniform State Laws in 2001, in connection with the approval of state plans for purposes of federal funding."

Effect of Amendments.
The 2003 amendment by P.A. 93-479 (see editor's note as to

effective date), rewrote the section to the extent that a detailed comparison would be impracticable.

750 ILCS 22/603 Effect of registration for enforcement

Sec. 603. *Effect of registration for enforcement.* (a) A support order or income-withholding order issued in another state is registered when the order is filed in the registering tribunal of this State.

(b) A registered order issued in another state is enforceable in the same manner and is subject to the same procedures as an order issued by a tribunal of this State.

(c) Except as otherwise provided in this article, a tribunal of this State shall recognize and enforce, but may not modify, a registered order if the issuing tribunal had jurisdiction.

(Source: P.A. 88-550, § 603.)

750 ILCS 22/604 (Without amendments by P.A. 93-479) Choice of law

Sec. 604. *(Without amendments by P.A. 93-479) Choice of law.* (a) The law of the issuing state governs the nature, extent, amount, and duration of current payments and other obligations of support and the payment of arrearages under the order.

(b) In a proceeding for arrearages, the statute of limitation under the laws of this State or of the issuing state, whichever is longer, applies.

(Source: P.A. 88-550, § 604.)

Section Set Out Twice.

The section above is without amendments by P.A. 93-479 (see notes for effective date). For the version of this section as amended by P.A. 93-479, see the following section, also numbered 750 ILCS 22/604.

750 ILCS 22/604 (As amended by P.A. 93-479; see notes for effective date) Choice of law

Sec. 604. *Choice of law.* (a) Except as otherwise provided in subsection (d), the law of the issuing state governs:

(1) the nature, extent, amount, and duration of current payments under a registered support order;

(2) the computation and payment of arrearages and accrual of interest on the arrearages under the support order; and

(3) the existence and satisfaction of other obligations under the support order.

(b) In a proceeding for arrears under a registered support order, the statute of limitation of this State or of the issuing state, whichever is longer, applies.

(c) A responding tribunal of this State shall apply the procedures and remedies of this State to enforce current support and collect arrears and interest due on a support order of another state registered in this State.

(d) After a tribunal of this or another state determines which is the controlling order and issues an order consolidating arrears, if any, a tribunal of this State shall prospectively apply the law of the state issuing the controlling order, including its law on interest on arrears, on current and future support, and on consolidated arrears.

(Source: P.A. 88-550, § 604; 93-479, § 5.)

Section Set Out Twice.

Multiple versions of this section have been created by the editor to reflect conflicting or postponed legislation.

Note.

Section 99 of P.A. 93-479, which amended this section, provides: "Operative date. This Act shall become operative upon at least one of the following 2 events taking place, whichever occurs first, but in no event prior to July 1, 2004:

"(1) The amendment by Congress of subdivision (f) of 42 U.S.C. Sec. 666 to statutorily require or authorize, in connection with the approval of state plans for purposes of federal funding, the adoption of the Uniform Interstate Family Support Act as promulgated by the National Conference of Commissioners on Uniform State Laws in 2001.

"(2) The approval, either generally or with specific application to Illinois, by the federal office of Child Support Enforcement or by the Secretary of Health and Human Services, of a waiver, exemption, finding, or other indicia of regulatory approval of the Uniform Interstate Family Support Act, as promulgated by the National Conference of Commissioners on Uniform State Laws in 2001, in connection with the approval of state plans for purposes of federal funding."

Effect of Amendments.

The 2003 amendment by P.A. 93-479 (see editor's note as to effective date), rewrote the section to the extent that a detailed comparison would be impracticable.

Part 2. Contest of Validity or Enforcement

750 ILCS 22/605 (Without amendments by P.A. 93-479) Notice of registration of order

Sec. 605. *(Without amendments by P.A. 93-479) Notice of registration of order.* (a) When a support order or income-withholding order issued in another state is registered, the registering tribunal shall notify the nonregistering party. The notice must be accompanied by a copy of the registered order and the documents and relevant information accompanying the order.

(b) The notice must inform the nonregistering party:

(1) that a registered order is enforceable as of the date of registration in the same manner as an order issued by a tribunal of this State;

(2) that a hearing to contest the validity or enforcement of the registered order must be requested within 20 days after the date of mailing or personal service of the notice;

(3) that failure to contest the validity or enforcement of the registered order in a timely manner will result in confirmation of the order and enforcement of the order and the alleged arrearages and precludes further contest of that order with respect to any matter that could have been asserted; and

(4) of the amount of any alleged arrearages.

(c) Upon registration of an income-withholding order for enforcement, the registering tribunal shall notify the obligor's employer pursuant to the Income Withholding for Support Act [750 ILCS 28/1 et seq.].

(Source: P.A. 88-550, § 605; 90-240, § 5; 90-655, § 172; 90-673, § 925; 91-357, § 259.)

Section Set Out Twice.

The section above is without the amendments by P.A. 93-479. For the version of this section as amended by P.A. 93-479 (see notes for effective date), see the following section, also numbered 750 ILCS 22/605.

Effect of Amendments.

The 1997 amendment by P.A. 90-240, effective July 28, 1997, redesignated Part B as Part 2; and in subsection (a) deleted the former second sentence which read "Notice must be given by first class, certified, or registered mail or by any means of personal service authorized by the law of this State".

The 1998 amendment by P.A. 90-655, effective July 30, 1998, in subsection (c) substituted "the Illinois Parentage Act of 1984" for "the Illinois Parentage Act of 1989".

The 1998 amendment by P.A. 90-673, effective January 1, 1999, incorporated the amendment by P.A. 90-240; and substituted "the Income Withholding for Support Act" for "Section 10-16.2 of the Illinois Public Aid Code, Section 706.1 of the Illinois Marriage and Dissolution of Marriage Act, Section 4.1 of the Non-Support of Spouse and Children Act, and Section 20 of the Illinois Parentage Act of 1989" in subsection (c).

The 1999 amendment by P.A. 91-357, effective July 29, 1999, combined the amendments by P.A. 90-655 and P.A. 90-673.

CASE NOTES

Effect of Noncompliance

In an action for enforcement of an Israeli judgment in Illinois, where none of the documents the wife served on the husband complied with the language of 750 ILCS 22/605, the requirement in 750 ILCS 22/606 that the husband file a request for a hearing within 20 days of being personally served was never triggered. Kohl v. Kohl, 334 Ill. App. 3d 867, 268 Ill. Dec. 547, 778 N.E.2d 1169, 2002 Ill. App. LEXIS 931 (1 Dist. 2002).

750 ILCS 22/605 (As amended by P.A. 93-479; see notes for effective date) Notice of registration of order

Sec. 605. *Notice of registration of order.* (a) When a support order or income-withholding order issued in another state is registered, the registering tribunal shall notify the nonregistering party. The notice must be accompanied by a copy of the registered order and the documents and relevant information accompanying the order.

(b) A notice must inform the nonregistering party:

(1) that a registered order is enforceable as of the date of registration in the same manner as an order issued by a tribunal of this State;

(2) that a hearing to contest the validity or enforcement of the registered order must be requested within 20 days after the date of mailing or personal service of the notice;

(3) that failure to contest the validity or enforcement of the registered order in a timely manner will result in confirmation of the order and enforcement of the order and the alleged arrearages and precludes further contest of that order with respect to any matter that could have been asserted; and

(4) of the amount of any alleged arrearages.

(c) If the registering party asserts that two or more orders are in effect, a notice must also:

(1) identify the two or more orders and the order alleged by the registering person to be the controlling order and the consolidated arrears, if any;

(2) notify the nonregistering party of the right to a determination of which is the controlling order;

(3) state that the procedures provided in subsection (b) apply to the determination of which is the controlling order; and

(4) state that failure to contest the validity or enforcement of the order alleged to be the controlling order in a timely manner may result in confirmation that the order is the controlling order.

(d) Upon registration of an income-withholding order for enforcement, the registering tribunal shall notify the obligor's employer pursuant to the Income Withholding for Support Act [750 ILCS 28/1 et seq.].

(Source: P.A. 88-550, § 605; 90-240, § 5; 90-655, § 172; 90-673, § 925; 91-357, § 259; 93-479, § 5.)

Section Set Out Twice.

The section above contains the amendments by P.A. 93-479 (see notes for effective date). For the version of this section without the amendments by P.A. 93-479, see the preceding version, also numbered 750 ILCS 22/605.

Note.

Section 99 of P.A. 93-479, which amended this section, provides: "Operative date. This Act shall become operative upon at least one of the following 2 events taking place, whichever occurs first, but in no event prior to July 1, 2004:

"(1) The amendment by Congress of subdivision (f) of 42 U.S.C. Sec. 666 to statutorily require or authorize, in connection with the approval of state plans for purposes of federal funding, the adoption of the Uniform Interstate Family Support Act as promulgated by the National Conference of Commissioners on Uniform State Laws in 2001.

"(2) The approval, either generally or with specific application to Illinois, by the federal office of Child Support Enforcement or by the Secretary of Health and Human Services, of a waiver, exemption, finding, or other indicia of regulatory approval of the Uniform Interstate Family Support Act, as promulgated by the National Conference of Commissioners on Uniform State Laws in 2001, in connection with the approval of state plans for purposes of federal funding."

Effect of Amendments.

The 2003 amendment by P.A. 93-479 (see editor's note as to effective date), inserted subsection (c) and redesignated former subsection (c) as subsection (d).

750 ILCS 22/606 Procedure to contest validity or enforcement of registered order

Sec. 606. *Procedure to contest validity or enforcement of registered order.* (a) A nonregistering party seeking to contest the validity or enforcement of a registered order in this State shall request a hearing within 20 days after the date of mailing or personal service of notice of the registration. The nonregistering party may seek to vacate the registration, to assert any defense to an allegation of noncompliance with the registered order, or to contest the remedies being sought or the amount of any alleged arrearages pursuant to Section 607 [750 ILCS 22/607].

(b) If the nonregistering party fails to contest the validity or enforcement of the registered order in a timely manner, the order is confirmed by operation of law.

(c) If a nonregistering party requests a hearing to contest the validity or enforcement of the registered order, the registering tribunal shall schedule the matter for hearing and give notice to the parties of the date, time, and place of the hearing.

(Source: P.A. 88-550, § 606; 90-240, § 5.)

Effect of Amendments.

The 1997 amendment by P.A. 90-240, effective July 28, 1997, in subsection (c) deleted "by first class mail" preceding "of the date".

CASE NOTES

Applicability

In an action for enforcement of an Israeli judgment in Illinois, where none of the documents the wife served on the husband complied with the language of 750 ILCS 22/605, the requirement in 750 ILCS 22/606 that the husband file a request for a hearing within 20 days of being personally served was never triggered. Kohl v. Kohl, 334 Ill. App. 3d 867, 268 Ill. Dec. 547, 778 N.E.2d 1169, 2002 Ill. App. LEXIS 931 (1 Dist. 2002).

750 ILCS 22/607 Contest of registration or enforcement

Sec. 607. *Contest of registration or enforcement.* (a) A party contesting the validity or enforcement of a registered order or seeking to vacate the registration has the burden of proving one or more of the following defenses:

(1) the issuing tribunal lacked personal jurisdiction over the contesting party;

(2) the order was obtained by fraud;

(3) the order has been vacated, suspended, or modified by a later order;

(4) the issuing tribunal has stayed the order pending appeal;

(5) there is a defense under the law of this State to the remedy sought;

(6) *(Without amendments by P.A. 93-479)* full or partial payment has been made; or

(6) *(As amended by P.A. 93-479; see notes for effective date)* full or partial payment has been made;

(7) *(Without amendments by P.A. 93-479)* the statute of limitation under Section 604 [750 ILCS 22/604] precludes enforcement of some or all of the arrearages.

(7) *(As amended by P.A. 93-479; see notes for effective date)* the statute of limitation under Section 604 [750 ILCS 22/604] precludes enforcement of some or all of the alleged arrearages; or

(8) *(Added by P.A. 93-479; see notes for effective date)* the alleged controlling order is not the controlling order.

(b) If a party presents evidence establishing a full or partial defense under subsection (a), a tribunal may stay enforcement of the registered order, continue the proceeding to permit production of additional relevant evidence, and issue other appropriate orders. An uncontested portion of the registered order may be enforced by all remedies available under the law of this State.

(c) If the contesting party does not establish a defense under subsection (a) to the validity or enforcement of the order, the registering tribunal shall issue an order confirming the order.

(Source: P.A. 88-550, § 607; 93-479, § 5.)

Subsections (a)(6) and (a)(7) Set Out Twice.

Subsections (a)(6) and (a)(7) are set out twice. The first is without amendments by P.A. 93-479, and the second is as amended by P.A. 93-479 (see notes for effective date).

Note.

Section 99 of P.A. 93-479, which amended this section, provides: "Operative date. This Act shall become operative upon at least one of the following 2 events taking place, whichever occurs first, but in no event prior to July 1, 2004:

"(1) The amendment by Congress of subdivision (f) of 42 U.S.C. Sec. 666 to statutorily require or authorize, in connection with the approval of state plans for purposes of federal funding, the adoption of the Uniform Interstate Family Support Act as promulgated by the National Conference of Commissioners on Uniform State Laws in 2001.

"(2) The approval, either generally or with specific application to Illinois, by the federal office of Child Support Enforcement or by the Secretary of Health and Human Services, of a waiver, exemption, finding, or other indicia of regulatory approval of the Uniform Interstate Family Support Act, as promulgated by the National Conference of Commissioners on Uniform State Laws in 2001, in connection with the approval of state plans for purposes of federal funding."

Effect of Amendments.

The 2003 amendment by P.A. 93-479 (see editor's note as to effective date), inserted "alleged" in subsection (a)(7); and added subsection (a)(8) and made a related change.

750 ILCS 22/608 Confirmed order

Sec. 608. *Confirmed order.* Confirmation of a registered order, whether by operation of law or after notice and hearing, precludes further contest of the order with respect to any matter that could have been asserted at the time of registration.

(Source: P.A. 88-550, § 608.)

Part 3.

Registration and Modification of Child Support Order

750 ILCS 22/609 Procedure to register child-support order of another state for modification

Sec. 609. *Procedure to register child-support order of another state for modification.* A party or support enforcement agency seeking to modify, or to modify and enforce, a child-support order issued in another state shall register that order in this State in the same manner provided in Part 1 if the order has not been registered. A petition for modification may be filed at the same time as a request for registration,

or later. The pleading must specify the grounds for modification.
(Source: P.A. 88-550, § 609; 90-240, § 5.)

Effect of Amendments.
The 1997 amendment by P.A. 90-240, effective July 28, 1997, redesignated Part C as Part 3; in the section catchline substituted "child-support" for "child support"; and in the first sentence substituted "child-support" for "child support" and substituted "Part 1" for "Part A of this Article".

750 ILCS 22/610 (Without amendments by P.A. 93-479) Effect of registration for modification

Sec. 610. *(Without amendments by P.A. 93-479) Effect of registration for modification.* A tribunal of this State may enforce a child-support order of another state registered for purposes of modification, in the same manner as if the order had been issued by a tribunal of this State, but the registered order may be modified only if the requirements of Section 611 [750 ILCS 22/611] have been met.
(Source: P.A. 88-550, § 610; 90-240, § 5.)

Section Set Out Twice.
The section above is set out twice. The first version is without amendments by P.A. 93-479, and the second version is as amended by P.A. 93-479 (see notes for effective date).

Effect of Amendments.
The 1997 amendment by P.A. 90-240, effective July 28, 1997, substituted "child-support" for "child support".

750 ILCS 22/610 (As amended by P.A. 93-479; see notes for effective date) Effect of registration for modification

Sec. 610. *Effect of registration for modification.* A tribunal of this State may enforce a child-support order of another state registered for purposes of modification, in the same manner as if the order had been issued by a tribunal of this State, but the registered order may be modified only if the requirements of Section 611, 613, or 615 [750 ILCS 22/611, 750 ILCS 22/613, or 750 ILCS 22/615] have been met.
(Source: P.A. 88-550, § 610; 90-240, § 5; 93-479, § 5.)

Section Set Out Twice.
The section above is set out twice. The first version is without amendments by P.A. 93-479, and the second version is as amended by P.A. 93-479 (see notes for effective date).

Note.
Section 99 of P.A. 93-479, which amended this section, provides: "Operative date. This Act shall become operative upon at least one of the following 2 events taking place, whichever occurs first, but in no event prior to July 1, 2004:

"(1) The amendment by Congress of subdivision (f) of 42 U.S.C. Sec. 666 to statutorily require or authorize, in connection with the approval of state plans for purposes of federal funding, the adoption of the Uniform Interstate Family Support Act as promulgated by the National Conference of Commissioners on Uniform State Laws in 2001.

"(2) The approval, either generally or with specific application to Illinois, by the federal office of Child Support Enforcement or by the Secretary of Health and Human Services, of a waiver, exemption, finding, or other indicia of regulatory approval of the Uniform Interstate Family Support Act, as promulgated by the National Conference of Commissioners on Uniform State Laws in 2001, in connection with the approval of state plans for purposes of federal funding."

Effect of Amendments.
The 1997 amendment by P.A. 90-240, effective July 28, 1997, substituted "child-support" for "child support".
The 2003 amendment by P.A. 93-479 (see editor's note as to effective date), inserted "613, or 615".

750 ILCS 22/611 (Without amendments by P.A. 93-479) Modification of Child-Support Order of Another State

Sec. 611. *(Without amendments by P.A. 93-479) Modification of Child-Support Order of Another State.* (a) After a child-support order issued in another state has been registered in this State, the responding tribunal of this State may modify that order only if Section 613 [750 ILCS 22/613] does not apply and after notice and hearing it finds that:

(1) the following requirements are met:

(i) the child, the individual petitioner, and the respondent do not reside in the issuing state;

(ii) a petitioner who is a nonresident of this State seeks modification; and

(iii) the respondent is subject to the personal jurisdiction of the tribunal of this State; or

(2) the child, or a party who is an individual, is subject to the personal jurisdiction of the tribunal of this State and all of the parties who are individuals have filed written consents in the issuing tribunal for a tribunal of this State to modify the support order and assume continuing, exclusive jurisdiction over the order. However, if the issuing state is a foreign jurisdiction that has not enacted a law or established procedures substantially similar to the procedures under this Act, the consent otherwise required of an individual residing in this State is not required for the tribunal to assume jurisdiction to modify the child-support order.

(b) Modification of a registered child-support order is subject to the same requirements, procedures, and defenses that apply to the modification of an order issued by a tribunal of this State and the order may be enforced and satisfied in the same manner.

(c) A tribunal of this State may not modify any aspect of a child-support order that may not be modified under the law of the issuing state. If two or more tribunals have issued child-support orders for the same obligor and child, the order that controls and must be so recognized under Section 207 [750 ILCS 22/207] establishes the aspects of the support order which are nonmodifiable.

(d) On issuance of an order modifying a child-support order issued in another state, a tribunal of this State becomes the tribunal having continuing, exclusive jurisdiction.
(Source: P.A. 88-550, § 611; 88-691, § 20; 90-240, § 5.)

Section Set Out Twice.
The section above is as amended by P.A. 93-479 (see notes for

effective date). For the version of this section as amended by P.A. 93-479, see the following section, also numbered 750 ILCS 22/611.

Effect of Amendments.

The 1994 amendment by P.A. 88-691, effective January 24, 1995, substituted "petitioner" for "obligee" and "respondent" for "obligor" throughout subdivision (a)(1); and in subdivision (a)(1)(ii) substituted "a petitioner" for "an obligee".

The 1997 amendment by P.A. 90-240, effective July 28, 1997, in the section catchline substituted "Child-Support" for "Child Support"; substituted "child-support" for "child support" throughout the section; in subsection (a), in the introductory language inserted "Section 613 does not apply and" and deleted a comma after "hearing"; in subdivision (a)(2), in the first sentence, deleted "an individual party or" from the beginning, inserted "or a party who is an individual", inserted "of this State", deleted "individual" preceding "parties", inserted "who are individuals", deleted "a" preceding "written", substituted "consents" for "consent", substituted "for" for "providing that" and substituted "to modify" for "may modify" and added the second sentence; in subsection (c) added the second sentence; in subsection (d) substituted "having" for "of"; and deleted subsection (e) regarding filing of copy of certified modified support order.

750 ILCS 22/611 (As amended by P.A. 93-479; see notes for effective date) Modification of Child-Support Order of Another State

Sec. 611. *Modification of Child-Support Order of Another State.* (a) If Section 613 [750 ILCS 22/613] does no apply, except as otherwise provided in Section 615 [750 ILCS 22/615], upon petition a tribunal of this State may modify a child-support order issued in another state which is registered in this State if, after notice and hearing, the tribunal finds that:

(1) the following requirements are met:

(A) neither the child, nor the petitioner who is an individual, nor the respondent resides in the issuing state;

(B) a petitioner who is a nonresident of this State seeks modification; and

(C) the respondent is subject to the personal jurisdiction of the tribunal of this State; or

(2) this State is the State of residence of the child, or a party who is an individual is subject to the personal jurisdiction of the tribunal of this State and all of the parties who are individuals have filed consents in a record in the issuing tribunal for a tribunal of this State to modify the support order and assume continuing, exclusive jurisdiction.

(b) Modification of a registered child-support order is subject to the same requirements, procedures, and defenses that apply to the modification of an order issued by a tribunal of this State and the order may be enforced and satisfied in the same manner.

(c) Except as otherwise provided in Section 615 [750 ILCS 22/615], a tribunal of this State may not modify any aspect of a child-support order that may not be modified under the law of the issuing state, including the duration of the obligation of support. If two or more tribunals have issued child-support orders for the same obligor and same child, the order that controls and must be so recognized under Section 207 [750 ILCS 22/207] establishes the aspects of the support order which are nonmodifiable.

(d) In a proceeding to modify a child-support order, the law of the state that is determined to have issued the initial controlling order governs the duration of the obligation of support. The obligor's fulfillment of the duty of support established by that order precludes imposition of a further obligation of support by a tribunal of this State.

(e) On issuance of an order by a tribunal of this State modifying a child-support order issued in another state, the tribunal of this State becomes the tribunal having continuing, exclusive jurisdiction.
(Source: P.A. 88-550, § 611; 88-691, § 20; 90-240, § 5; 93-479, § 5.)

Section Set Out Twice.

Multiple versions of this section have been created by the editor to reflect conflicting or postponed legislation.

Note.

Section 99 of P.A. 93-479, which amended this section, provides: "Operative date. This Act shall become operative upon at least one of the following 2 events taking place, whichever occurs first, but in no event prior to July 1, 2004:

"(1) The amendment by Congress of subdivision (f) of 42 U.S.C. Sec. 666 to statutorily require or authorize, in connection with the approval of state plans for purposes of federal funding, the adoption of the Uniform Interstate Family Support Act as promulgated by the National Conference of Commissioners on Uniform State Laws in 2001.

"(2) The approval, either generally or with specific application to Illinois, by the federal office of Child Support Enforcement or by the Secretary of Health and Human Services, of a waiver, exemption, finding, or other indicia of regulatory approval of the Uniform Interstate Family Support Act, as promulgated by the National Conference of Commissioners on Uniform State Laws in 2001, in connection with the approval of state plans for purposes of federal funding."

Effect of Amendments.

The 2003 amendment by P.A. 93-479 (see editor's note as to effective date), rewrote the section to the extent that a detailed comparison would be impracticable.

750 ILCS 22/612 (Without amendments by P.A. 93-479) Recognition of order modified in another state

Sec. 612. *(Without amendments by P.A. 93-479) Recognition of order modified in another state.* A tribunal of this State shall recognize a modification of its earlier child-support order by a tribunal of another state which assumed jurisdiction pursuant to a law substantially similar to this Act and, upon request, except as otherwise provided in this Act, shall:

(1) enforce the order that was modified only as to amounts accruing before the modification;

(2) enforce only nonmodifiable aspects of that order;

(3) provide other appropriate relief only for violations of that order which occurred before the effective date of the modification; and

(4) recognize the modifying order of the other state, upon registration, for the purpose of enforcement.

(Source: P.A. 88-550, § 612; 90-240, § 5.)

Section Set Out Twice.

The section above is without amendments by P.A. 93-479 (see

notes for effective dates). For the version of this section as amended by P.A. 93-479, see the following section, also numbered 750 ILCS 22/612.

Effect of Amendments.

The 1997 amendment by P.A. 90-240, effective July 28, 1997, in the introductory language substituted "child-support" for "child support".

750 ILCS 22/612 (As amended by P.A. 93-479; see notes for effective date) Recognition of order modified in another state

Sec. 612. *Recognition of order modified in another state.* If a child-support order issued by a tribunal of this State is modified by a tribunal of another state which assumed jurisdiction pursuant to the Uniform Interstate Family Support Act [750 ILCS 22/101 et seq.], a tribunal of this State:

(1) may enforce its order that was modified only as to arrears and interest accruing before the modification;

(2) provide appropriate relief for violations of its order which occurred before the effective date of the modification; and

(3) recognize the modifying order of the other state, upon registration, for the purpose of enforcement.

(Source: P.A. 88-550, § 612; 90-240, § 5; 93-479, § 5.)

Section Set Out Twice.

The section above contains the amendments by P.A. 93-479 (see notes for effective date). For the version of this section without the amendments by P.A. 93-479, see the preceding version, also numbered 750 ILCS 22/612.

Note.

Section 99 of P.A. 93-479, which amended this section, provides: "Operative date. This Act shall become operative upon at least one of the following 2 events taking place, whichever occurs first, but in no event prior to July 1, 2004:

"(1) The amendment by Congress of subdivision (f) of 42 U.S.C. Sec. 666 to statutorily require or authorize, in connection with the approval of state plans for purposes of federal funding, the adoption of the Uniform Interstate Family Support Act as promulgated by the National Conference of Commissioners on Uniform State Laws in 2001.

"(2) The approval, either generally or with specific application to Illinois, by the federal office of Child Support Enforcement or by the Secretary of Health and Human Services, of a waiver, exemption, finding, or other indicia of regulatory approval of the Uniform Interstate Family Support Act, as promulgated by the National Conference of Commissioners on Uniform State Laws in 2001, in connection with the approval of state plans for purposes of federal funding."

Effect of Amendments.

The 2003 amendment by P.A. 93-479 (see editor's note as to effective date), rewrote the section to the extent that a detailed comparison would be impracticable.

750 ILCS 22/613 Jurisdiction to modify child-support order of another state when individual parties reside in this State

Sec. 613. *Jurisdiction to modify child-support order of another state when individual parties reside in this State.* (a) If all of the parties who are individuals reside in this State and the child does not reside in the issuing state, a tribunal of this State has jurisdiction to enforce and to modify the issuing state's child-support order in a proceeding to register that order.

(b) A tribunal of this State exercising jurisdiction under this Section shall apply the provisions of Articles 1 and 2, this Article, and the procedural and substantive law of this State to the proceeding for enforcement or modification. Articles 3, 4, 5, 7, and 8 do not apply.

(Source: P.A. 90-240, § 5.)

Effective Date.

Section 99 of P.A. 90-240 made this section effective upon becoming law. The Act was approved July 28, 1997.

750 ILCS 22/614 Notice to issuing tribunal of modification

Sec. 614. *Notice to issuing tribunal of modification.* Within 30 days after issuance of a modified child-support order, the party obtaining the modification shall file a certified copy of the order with the issuing tribunal that had continuing, exclusive jurisdiction over the earlier order, and in each tribunal in which the party knows the earlier order has been registered. A party who obtains the order and fails to file a certified copy is subject to appropriate sanctions by a tribunal in which the issue of failure to file arises. The failure to file does not affect the validity or enforceability of the modified order of the new tribunal having continuing, exclusive jurisdiction.

(Source: P.A. 90-240, § 5.)

Effective Date.

Section 99 of P.A. 90-240 made this section effective upon becoming law. The Act was approved July 28, 1997.

750 ILCS 22/615 (See notes for effective date) Jurisdiction to modify child-support order of foreign country or political subdivision

Sec. 615. *Jurisdiction to modify child-support order of foreign country or political subdivision.* (a) If a foreign country or political subdivision that otherwise meets the requirements for inclusion under this Act as set forth in subpart (B) of the definition of "State" contained in Section 102 [750 ILCS 22/102] will not or may not modify its order pursuant to its laws, a tribunal of this State may assume jurisdiction to modify the child-support order and bind all individuals subject to the personal jurisdiction of the tribunal whether or not the consent to modification of a child-support order otherwise required of the individual pursuant to Section 611 [750 ILCS 22/611] has been given or whether the individual seeking modification is a resident of this State or of the foreign country or political subdivision.

(b) An order issued pursuant to this Section is the controlling order.

(Source: P.A. 93-479, § 5.)

Note.

750 ILCS 22/102, referred to above, was repealed.

Section 99 of P.A. 93-479, which enacted this section, provides:
"Operative date. This Act shall become operative upon at least one of the following 2 events taking place, whichever occurs first, but in no event prior to July 1, 2004:
"(1) The amendment by Congress of subdivision (f) of 42 U.S.C. Sec. 666 to statutorily require or authorize, in connection with the approval of state plans for purposes of federal funding, the adoption of the Uniform Interstate Family Support Act as promulgated by the National Conference of Commissioners on Uniform State Laws in 2001.
"(2) The approval, either generally or with specific application to Illinois, by the federal office of Child Support Enforcement or by the Secretary of Health and Human Services, of a waiver, exemption, finding, or other indicia of regulatory approval of the Uniform Interstate Family Support Act, as promulgated by the National Conference of Commissioners on Uniform State Laws in 2001, in connection with the approval of state plans for purposes of federal funding."

ARTICLE 7.

DETERMINATION OF PARENTAGE

750 ILCS 22/701 (Without amendments by P.A. 93-479) Proceeding to determine parentage

Sec. 701. *(Without amendments by P.A. 93-479) Proceeding to determine parentage.* (a) A tribunal of this State may serve as an initiating or responding tribunal in a proceeding brought under this Act or a law substantially similar to this Act, to determine that the obligee is a parent of a particular child or to determine that an obligor is a parent of that child.

(b) In a proceeding to determine parentage, a responding tribunal of this State shall apply the Illinois Parentage Act of 1984 [750 ILCS 45/1 et seq.], and the rules of this State on choice of law.
(Source: P.A. 88-550, § 701.)

Section Set Out Twice.
The section above is without amendments by P.A. 93-479 (see notes for effective date). For the version of this section as amended by P.A. 93-479, see the following section, also numbered 750 ILCS 22/701.

750 ILCS 22/701 (As amended by P.A. 93-479; see notes for effective date) Proceeding to determine parentage

Sec. 701. *Proceeding to determine parentage.* A tribunal of this State authorized to determine parentage of a child may serve as a responding tribunal in a proceeding to determine parentage brought under this Act or a law substantially similar to this Act.
(Source: P.A. 88-550, § 701; 93-479, § 5.)

Section Set Out Twice.
Multiple versions of this section have been created by the editor to reflect conflicting or postponed legislation.

Note.
Section 99 of P.A. 93-479, which amended this section, provides:
"Operative date. This Act shall become operative upon at least one of the following 2 events taking place, whichever occurs first, but in no event prior to July 1, 2004:
"(1) The amendment by Congress of subdivision (f) of 42 U.S.C. Sec. 666 to statutorily require or authorize, in connection with the approval of state plans for purposes of federal funding, the adoption of the Uniform Interstate Family Support Act as promulgated by the National Conference of Commissioners on Uniform State Laws in 2001.
"(2) The approval, either generally or with specific application to Illinois, by the federal office of Child Support Enforcement or by the Secretary of Health and Human Services, of a waiver, exemption, finding, or other indicia of regulatory approval of the Uniform Interstate Family Support Act, as promulgated by the National Conference of Commissioners on Uniform State Laws in 2001, in connection with the approval of state plans for purposes of federal funding."

Effect of Amendments.
The 2003 amendment by P.A. 93-479 (see editor's note as to effective date), rewrote the section to the extent that a detailed comparison would be impracticable.

ARTICLE 8.

INTERSTATE RENDITION

750 ILCS 22/801 Grounds for rendition

Sec. 801. *Grounds for rendition.* (a) For purposes of this article, "governor" includes an individual performing the functions of governor or the executive authority of a state covered by this Act.

(b) The governor of this State may:

(1) demand that the governor of another state surrender an individual found in the other state who is charged criminally in this State with having failed to provide for the support of an obligee; or

(2) *(Without amendments by P.A. 93-479)* on the demand by the governor of another state, surrender an individual found in this State who is charged criminally in the other state with having failed to provide for the support of an obligee.

(2) *(As amended by P.A. 93-479; see notes for effective date)* on the demand of the governor of another state, surrender an individual found in this State who is charged criminally in the other state with having failed to provide for the support of an obligee.

(c) A provision for extradition of individuals not inconsistent with this Act applies to the demand even if the individual whose surrender is demanded was not in the demanding state when the crime was allegedly committed and has not fled therefrom.
(Source: P.A. 88-550, § 801; 93-479, § 5.)

Subsection (b)(2) Set Out Twice.
Subsection (b)(2) is set out twice. The first version is without amendments by P.A. 93-479, and the second version is as amended by P.A. 93-479 (see notes for effective date).

Note.
Section 99 of P.A. 93-479, which amended this section, provides:
"Operative date. This Act shall become operative upon at least one of the following 2 events taking place, whichever occurs first, but in no event prior to July 1, 2004:
"(1) The amendment by Congress of subdivision (f) of 42 U.S.C. Sec. 666 to statutorily require or authorize, in connection with the approval of state plans for purposes of federal funding, the adoption of the Uniform Interstate Family Support Act as promulgated by the National Conference of Commissioners on Uniform State Laws in 2001.

"(2) The approval, either generally or with specific application to Illinois, by the federal office of Child Support Enforcement or by the Secretary of Health and Human Services, of a waiver, exemption, finding, or other indicia of regulatory approval of the Uniform Interstate Family Support Act, as promulgated by the National Conference of Commissioners on Uniform State Laws in 2001, in connection with the approval of state plans for purposes of federal funding."

Effect of Amendments.

The 2003 amendment by P.A. 93-479 (see editor's note as to effective date), made a stylistic change.

750 ILCS 22/802 Conditions of rendition

Sec. 802. *Conditions of rendition.* (a) Before making demand that the governor of another state surrender an individual charged criminally in this State with having failed to provide for the support of an obligee, the Governor of this State may require a prosecutor of this State to demonstrate that at least 60 days previously the obligee had initiated proceedings for support pursuant to this Act or that the proceeding would be of no avail.

(b) *(Without amendments by P.A. 93-479)* If, under this Act or a law substantially similar to this Act, the Uniform Reciprocal Enforcement of Support Act [repealed], or the Revised Uniform Reciprocal Enforcement of Support Act [repealed], the Governor of another state makes a demand that the governor of this State surrender an individual charged criminally in that state with having failed to provide for the support of a child or other individual to whom a duty of support is owed, the governor may require a prosecutor to investigate the demand and report whether a proceeding for support has been initiated or would be effective. If it appears that a proceeding would be effective but has not been initiated, the governor may delay honoring the demand for a reasonable time to permit the initiation of a proceeding.

(b) *(As amended by P.A. 93-479; see notes for effective date)* If, under this Act or a law substantially similar to this Act, the Governor of another state makes a demand that the governor of this State surrender an individual charged criminally in that state with having failed to provide for the support of a child or other individual to whom a duty of support is owed, the governor may require a prosecutor to investigate the demand and report whether a proceeding for support has been initiated or would be effective. If it appears that a proceeding would be effective but has not been initiated, the governor may delay honoring the demand for a reasonable time to permit the initiation of a proceeding.

(c) If a proceeding for support has been initiated and the individual whose rendition is demanded prevails, the governor may decline to honor the demand. If the obligee prevails and the individual whose rendition is demanded is subject to a support order, the governor may decline to honor the demand if the individual is complying with the support order.
(Source: P.A. 88-550, § 802; 93-479, § 5.)

Subsection (b) Set Out Twice.

Subsection (b) is set out twice. The first version is without amendments by P.A. 93-479, and the second version is as amended by P.A. 93-479 (see notes for effective dates).

Note.

The Uniform Reciprocal Enforcement of Support Act, and the Revised Uniform Reciprocal Enforcement of Support Act, referred to above, was repealed. See now the Uniform Interstate Family Support Act, 750 ILCS 22/101, et seq.

Section 99 of P.A. 93-479, which amended this section, provides:

"Operative date. This Act shall become operative upon at least one of the following 2 events taking place, whichever occurs first, but in no event prior to July 1, 2004:

"(1) The amendment by Congress of subdivision (f) of 42 U.S.C. Sec. 666 to statutorily require or authorize, in connection with the approval of state plans for purposes of federal funding, the adoption of the Uniform Interstate Family Support Act as promulgated by the National Conference of Commissioners on Uniform State Laws in 2001.

"(2) The approval, either generally or with specific application to Illinois, by the federal office of Child Support Enforcement or by the Secretary of Health and Human Services, of a waiver, exemption, finding, or other indicia of regulatory approval of the Uniform Interstate Family Support Act, as promulgated by the National Conference of Commissioners on Uniform State Laws in 2001, in connection with the approval of state plans for purposes of federal funding."

Effect of Amendments.

The 2003 amendment by P.A. 93-479 (see editor's note as to effective date), deleted "the Uniform Reciprocal Enforcement of Support Act, or the Revised Uniform Reciprocal Enforcement of Support Act" in the first sentence of subsection (b) following "similar to this Act".

ARTICLE 9.
MISCELLANEOUS PROVISIONS

750 ILCS 22/901 (Without amendments by P.A. 93-479) Uniformity of application and construction

Sec. 901. *(Without amendments by P.A. 93-479) Uniformity of application and construction.* This Act shall be applied and construed to effectuate its general purpose to make uniform the law with respect to the subject of this Act among states enacting it.
(Source: P.A. 88-550, § 901.)

Section Set Out Twice.

The section above is without amendments by P.A. 93-479. For the version of this section as amended by P.A. 93-479 (see notes for effective date), see the following section, also numbered 750 ILCS 22/901.

750 ILCS 22/901 (As amended by P.A. 93-479; see notes for effective date) Uniformity of application and construction

Sec. 901. *Uniformity of application and construction.* In applying and construing this Uniform Act [750 ILCS 22/100 et seq.] consideration must be given to the need to promote uniformity of the law with respect to its subject matter among states that enact it.
(Source: P.A. 88-550, § 901; 93-479, § 5.)

Section Set Out Twice.

The section above contains the amendments by P.A. 93-479 (see notes for effective date). For the version of this section without the amendments by P.A. 93-479, see the preceding version, also numbered 750 ILCS 22/901.

Note.

Section 99 of P.A. 93-479, which amended this section, provides:

"Operative date. This Act shall become operative upon at least one of the following 2 events taking place, whichever occurs first, but in no event prior to July 1, 2004:

"(1) The amendment by Congress of subdivision (f) of 42 U.S.C. Sec. 666 to statutorily require or authorize, in connection with the approval of state plans for purposes of federal funding, the adoption of the Uniform Interstate Family Support Act as promulgated by the National Conference of Commissioners on Uniform State Laws in 2001.

"(2) The approval, either generally or with specific application to Illinois, by the federal office of Child Support Enforcement or by the Secretary of Health and Human Services, of a waiver, exemption, finding, or other indicia of regulatory approval of the Uniform Interstate Family Support Act, as promulgated by the National Conference of Commissioners on Uniform State Laws in 2001, in connection with the approval of state plans for purposes of federal funding."

Effect of Amendments.

The 2003 amendment by P.A. 93-479 (see editor's note as to effective date), rewrote the section to the extent that a detailed comparison would be impracticable.

750 ILCS 22/902 (Repealed by P.A. 93-479; see notes for effective date) Short title

Sec. 902. *Short title.* (See Section 100 [750 ILCS 22/101] for short title.)
(Source: P.A. 88-550, § 902; 93-479, § 5.)

Note.

Section 99 of P.A. 93-479, which repealed this section and renumbered 750 ILCS 22/903 as 750 ILCS 22/902, provides:

"Operative date. This Act shall become operative upon at least one of the following 2 events taking place, whichever occurs first, but in no event prior to July 1, 2004:

"(1) The amendment by Congress of subdivision (f) of 42 U.S.C. Sec. 666 to statutorily require or authorize, in connection with the approval of state plans for purposes of federal funding, the adoption of the Uniform Interstate Family Support Act as promulgated by the National Conference of Commissioners on Uniform State Laws in 2001.

"(2) The approval, either generally or with specific application to Illinois, by the federal office of Child Support Enforcement or by the Secretary of Health and Human Services, of a waiver, exemption, finding, or other indicia of regulatory approval of the Uniform Interstate Family Support Act, as promulgated by the National Conference of Commissioners on Uniform State Laws in 2001, in connection with the approval of state plans for purposes of federal funding."

750 ILCS 22/903 (Prior to renumbering by P.A. 93-479; see notes for effective date) Severability clause

Sec. 903. *Severability clause.* If any provision of this Act or its application to any person or circumstance is held invalid, the invalidity does not affect other provisions or applications of this Act which can be given effect without the invalid provision or application, and to this end the provisions of this Act are severable.
(Source: P.A. 88-550, § 903.)

Note.

This section is subject to a postponed renumbering as 750 ILCS 22/902, by P.A. 93-479. Section 99 of P.A. 93-479 provides:

"This Act shall become operative upon at least one of the following 2 events taking place, whichever occurs first, but in no event prior to July 1, 2004:

"(1) The amendment by Congress of subdivision (f) of 42 U.S.C. Sec. 666 to statutorily require or authorize, in connection with the approval of state plans for purposes of federal funding, the adoption of the Uniform Interstate Family Support Act as promulgated by the National Conference of Commissioners on Uniform State Laws in 2001.

"(2) The approval, either generally or with specific application to Illinois, by the federal office of Child Support Enforcement or by the Secretary of Health and Human Services, of a waiver, exemption, finding, or other indicia of regulatory approval of the Uniform Interstate Family Support Act, as promulgated by the National Conference of Commissioners on Uniform State Laws in 2001, in connection with the approval of state plans for purposes of federal funding."

750 ILCS 22/904 (Prior to renumbering by P.A. 93-479; see notes for effective date) Effective date

Sec. 904. *Effective date.* (See Section 999 [750 ILCS 22/999] for effective date.)
(Source: P.A. 88-550, § 904.)

Note.

This section is subject to a postponed renumbering as 750 ILCS 22/903, by P.A. 93-479. Section 99 of P.A. 93-479 provides:

"This Act shall become operative upon at least one of the following 2 events taking place, whichever occurs first, but in no event prior to July 1, 2004:

"(1) The amendment by Congress of subdivision (f) of 42 U.S.C. Sec. 666 to statutorily require or authorize, in connection with the approval of state plans for purposes of federal funding, the adoption of the Uniform Interstate Family Support Act as promulgated by the National Conference of Commissioners on Uniform State Laws in 2001.

"(2) The approval, either generally or with specific application to Illinois, by the federal office of Child Support Enforcement or by the Secretary of Health and Human Services, of a waiver, exemption, finding, or other indicia of regulatory approval of the Uniform Interstate Family Support Act, as promulgated by the National Conference of Commissioners on Uniform State Laws in 2001, in connection with the approval of state plans for purposes of federal funding."

This section is set out as it appears in P.A. 88-550. Section 999, as amended by P.A. 88-691, made the Act effective January 1, 1996, except for sections 955, 960, 970, 975 and 999 (750 ILCS 22/955, 750 ILCS 22/960, 750 ILCS 22/970, 750 ILCS 22/975 and 750 ILCS 22/999) which are effective upon becoming law and section 965 (750 ILCS 22/965), effective January 1, 1995. The Act was approved July 3, 1994.

750 ILCS 22/905 (Prior to renumbering by P.A. 93-479; see notes for effective date) Repeal

Sec. 905. *Repeal.* The Revised Uniform Reciprocal Enforcement of Support Act [750 ILCS 20/1 et seq.] is repealed on the effective date of this amendatory Act of 1997. An action that was commenced under the Revised Uniform Reciprocal Enforcement of Support Act [750 ILCS 20/1 et seq.] and is pending on the effective date of this amendatory Act of 1997 shall be decided in accordance with that Act as it existed immediately before its repeal by this amendatory Act of 1997.
(Source: P.A. 88-550, § 905; 90-240, § 5.)

Note.

This section is subject to a postponed renumbering as 750 ILCS 22/904, by P.A. 93-479. Section 99 of P.A. 93-479 provides:

"This Act shall become operative upon at least one of the following 2 events taking place, whichever occurs first, but in no event prior to July 1, 2004:

"(1) The amendment by Congress of subdivision (f) of 42 U.S.C. Sec. 666 to statutorily require or authorize, in connection with the approval of state plans for purposes of federal funding, the adoption of the Uniform Interstate Family Support Act as promulgated by the National Conference of Commissioners on Uniform State Laws in 2001.

"(2) The approval, either generally or with specific application to Illinois, by the federal office of Child Support Enforcement or by the Secretary of Health and Human Services, of a waiver, exemption, finding, or other indicia of regulatory approval of the Uniform Interstate Family Support Act, as promulgated by the National Conference of Commissioners on Uniform State Laws in 2001, in connection with the approval of state plans for purposes of federal funding."

Effect of Amendments.

The 1997 amendment by P.A. 90-240, effective July 28, 1997, added the language of this section which was blank before.

750 ILCS 22/910 Conflict

Sec. 910. *Conflict.* If there is an apparent conflict between a provision of this Act and a provision of any other law of this State, those provisions must be construed so as to give effect to both of them if possible. If the conflict is irreconcilable, the later of the provisions as passed by the General Assembly governs.
(Source: P.A. 88-550, § 910.)

750 ILCS 22/950 [Not Set Out]

Note.

This section, as found in P.A. 88-550, § 950, contained amendatory provisions.

750 ILCS 22/955 [Not Set Out]

Note.

This section was compiled at 20 ILCS 505/7.2, however 20 ILCS 505/7.2 was repealed effective July 9, 2000.

750 ILCS 22/960 through 750 ILCS 22/975 [Not Set Out]

Note.

These sections, as found in P.A. 88-550, §§ 960 through 975, contained amendatory provisions.

750 ILCS 22/999 Effective date

Sec. 999. *Effective date.* This Act takes effect upon becoming law, except that Sections 100 through 910 [750 ILCS 22/100 through 750 ILCS 22/910], and the provisions amending Section 24 of the Revised Uniform Reciprocal Enforcement of Support Act [750 ILCS 20/24] take effect January 1, 1996, and Section 965 [750 ILCS 22/965] takes effect January 1, 1995.
(Source: P.A. 88-550, § 999; 88-691, § 20.)

Effect of Amendments.

The 1994 amendment by P.A. 88-691, effective January 24, 1995, inserted "1996, and Section 965 takes effect January 1,".

UNIFIED CHILD SUPPORT SERVICES ACT

750 ILCS 24/1 [Short title]

Sec. 1. This Act may be cited as the Unified Child Support Services Act.
(Source: P.A. 92-876, § 1.)

Effective Date.

This Act is effective June 1, 2003, pursuant to Ill. Const. (1970) Art. IV, § 10 and 5 ILCS 75/2.

750 ILCS 24/5 Definitions

Sec. 5. *Definitions.* In this Act:

"Child support services" mean any services provided with respect to parentage establishment, support establishment, medical support establishment, support modification, or support enforcement.

"Child support specialist" means a paralegal, attorney, or other staff member with specialized training in child support services.

"Current child support case" means a case that is pending in the IV-D Child Support Program for which any action is being taken by a Unified Child Support Services Program.

"Department" means the Illinois Department of Public Aid.

"IV-D Child Support Program" means the child support enforcement program established pursuant to Title IV, Part D of the federal Social Security Act and Article X of the Illinois Public Aid Code [305 ILCS 5/10-1 et seq.].

"KIDS" means the Key Information Delivery System that includes a statewide database of all cases in the IV-D Child Support Program.

"Medicaid" means the medical assistance program under Article V of the Illinois Public Aid Code [305 ILCS 5/5-1 et seq.].

"Obligor" and "obligee" mean those terms as defined in the Income Withholding for Support Act.

"Plan" means a plan for a Unified Child Support Services Program.

"Program" means the Unified Child Support Services Program in a county or group of counties.

"State Disbursement Unit" means the State Disbursement Unit established under Section 10-26 of the Illinois Public Aid Code [305 ILCS 5/10-26].

"State's Attorney" means the duly elected State's Attorney of an Illinois county or 2 or more State's Attorneys who have formed a consortium for purposes of managing a Unified Child Support Services Program within a specific region of the State.

"Temporary Assistance for Needy Families" means the Temporary Assistance for Needy Families (TANF) program under Article IV of the Illinois Public Aid Code [305 ILCS 5/4-1 et seq.].
(Source: P.A. 92-876, § 5.)

750 ILCS 24/10 Plan for Unified Child Support Services

Sec. 10. *Plan for Unified Child Support Services.* (a) By July 1, 2003 and by July 1 of each subsequent year, a State's Attorney, in cooperation with the appropriate county officials, may submit to the Department a Plan for a Unified Child Support Services Program that includes all of the components set forth in Section 15 of this Act [750 ILCS 24/15] and that includes a projected budget of the necessary and reasonable direct and indirect costs for operation of the Program. The Plan may provide for phasing in the Program with different implementation dates.

(b) By December 1 of the year in which a Plan is submitted, the Department shall approve or reject the Plan. If the Plan is approved, the Department and the State's Attorney shall enter into an intergovernmental agreement incorporating the Plan, subject to the approval of the Attorney General and the appropriate county board. If the Plan is rejected, the Department must set forth (i) specific reasons that the Plan fails to satisfy the specific goals and requirements of this Act or other State or federal requirements and (ii) specific reasons that the necessary and reasonable costs for operation of the Plan could not be agreed upon.

(c) Any State's Attorney who submits a Plan pursuant to this Act shall commit to manage the Program for a period of no less than 3 years.

(d) If a Plan is rejected, or if for any reason an intergovernmental agreement is not signed, the prior agreement under this Act shall continue in effect until a new intergovernmental agreement is signed or the agreement is terminated.

(e) The Department may impose a restriction that no more than 3 State's Attorneys may begin operating a Program in a given year. The Department shall develop a procedure for fair and orderly consideration of Plans as they are submitted or as interest by a State's Attorney is otherwise demonstrated.

(f) In any county in which a Unified Child Support Services Program is operating, the Clerk of the Circuit Court may submit to the Department a plan for filing, recording, and making available for retrieval all administrative orders of parentage and administrative orders setting, modifying, or terminating child support obligations for all IV-D cases pending in the county on the implementation date of the Program and all new cases in the IV-D Child Support Program. The Department shall approve or reject the plan, according to the criteria set forth in subsection (b), and shall enter into the appropriate intergovernmental agreement incorporating the plan unless the Department can demonstrate that it has an alternative approach.

(Source: P.A. 92-876, § 10.)

750 ILCS 24/15 Components of a Unified Child Support Services Program

Sec. 15. *Components of a Unified Child Support Services Program.* (a) Any intergovernmental agreement incorporating an approved Plan under this Act must provide that the State's Attorney shall create and manage a Program offering child support services in all IV-D cases pending in the county as of the approval date of the Plan and all new cases in the Department's IV-D Child Support Program, based upon the jurisdiction of the case and in accordance with all relevant laws or Department policies.

(b) The child support services offered by each Program and incorporated in the State's Attorney's Plan must comply with the Department's approved Title IV, Part D State Plan and, except as provided in Section 35 [750 ILCS 24/35], must include, but need not be limited to, the following:

(1) Accepting applications for child support services from private parties or referrals from any State agency that submits information to KIDS, and providing for the conducting of initial interviews with applicants by telephone or other electronic means.

(2) Maintaining flexible office hours, including evening or weekend hours for in-person or telephone appointments, or any other appropriate means in order to meet customer service demands.

(3) Providing for a staffing plan that includes assigning cases to a child support specialist who is responsible for coordinating child support services for the case, receiving new and updated information about the case and forwarding that information to all relevant persons and agencies, responding to parents' inquiries and requests in a timely manner, and making appropriate referrals as specified in paragraph (12) of this subsection.

(4) Assessing each case for child support services by determining the status of the case and the necessary steps appropriate for the case, including establishing and following standards for determining whether to use judicial or administrative processes for child support services, and establishing and following standards for seeking cooperation from the parties before invoking other enforcement mechanisms.

(5) Taking all necessary steps identified in paragraph (4) of this subsection as appropriate for the case, whether by use of judicial or administrative processes, and making appropriate referrals to the Department to follow agency processes for which it is responsible under Section 35 of this Act [750 ILCS 24/35].

(6) Offering genetic testing to determine parentage at the site of the unified child support services operations or near the county courthouse or administrative hearing office where proceedings to establish parentage are conducted.

(7) Obtaining identified cases that have moved into non-compliance with obligations set forth in an order involving a child support case and taking steps necessary to bring the case into compliance, including investigating sources of income and the location and type of assets of child support obligors who are in arrears in the payment of support.

(8) Obtaining information to provide for periodic or other review of administrative and court orders for support consistent with federal guidelines to determine whether a modification of the order should be sought.

(9) Taking responsibility for using KIDS, for entering data with respect to a current child support case into KIDS and editing that data, and for having conflicting or incorrect data reconciled with respect to a current child support case.

(10) Reporting cooperation or the circumstances for lack of cooperation with child support services by recipients of public aid under Temporary Assistance for Needy Families or Medicaid.

(11) Conducting account reviews and redeterminations with respect to a current child support case in accordance with Department policies and federal guidelines.

(12) Establishing referral procedures and making appropriate referrals for programs such as voluntary mediation on custody and visitation, domestic violence, employment and training, child care, and governmental benefits such as Temporary Assistance for Needy Families and Medicaid.

(13) Establishing and maintaining a separate, impartial, and independent administrative process for parentage establishment, support establishment, and support modification that affords due process of law to alleged fathers and custodial and non-custodial parents; and furnishing copies of all such administrative orders to the clerk of the circuit court and the Department.

(14) Providing all information on the Program's operation needed by the Department to satisfy the Department's reporting requirements to the State and federal governments on a timely basis.

(15) Responding to requests for Administrative Accountability Analyses under Article X of the Illinois Public Aid Code [305 ILCS 5/10-1 et seq.], for State's Attorney cases as of the effective date of the approved Plan, and reporting final determinations to the Department.

(16) Marketing the Program within the county in which it is operating so that potential applicants learn about child support services offered.

(17) Appointing a local, unpaid child support advisory board, with the State's Attorney operating the Program as the chair, that meets at least quarterly.

(18) Establishing procedures for referral to the Illinois Attorney General of designated child support cases brought by non-custodial parents.

(19) Conducting all operations in accordance with any applicable State or federal laws and regulations and the Plan.

(Source: P.A. 92-876, § 15.)

750 ILCS 24/20 Subcontracts

Sec. 20. *Subcontracts.* A Plan submitted by a State's Attorney for approval to manage a Program must include those subcontracts and intergovernmental agreements necessary for the provision of any components of child support services under the Plan. The Plan must also include a copy of each signed subcontract or intergovernmental agreement or other evidence of the proposed subcontractor or other local governmental entity's intent to perform the services covered by the subcontract or intergovernmental agreement. The subcontract or intergovernmental agreement may be approved by the Department only if the subcontractor or other intergovernmental entity's services are fully integrated into the Program and the subcontractor or other intergovernmental entity's services enhance the efficiency, accessibility, and effectiveness of child support services.

(Source: P.A. 92-876, § 20.)

750 ILCS 24/25 Performance standards

Sec. 25. *Performance standards.* (a) In consultation with the Department's statewide Child Support Advisory Committee and a designated representative of the Illinois State's Attorneys Association, the Department shall establish the following by rule:

(1) Measures of performance for all State's Attorneys operating a program and contractors and local governmental entities providing child support services in the IV-D Child Support Program with respect to parentage establishment, support order establishment, current support collections, arrearage collections, cost-effectiveness, or any other measures used by the federal government or as set forth by the Department.

(2) Procedures for apportioning any projected incentive funding between any eligible contractors or local governmental entities.

(b) Once each year, the Department shall estimate the total State and federal incentive funding that will be available for distribution under this subsection during the following year. Any State's Attorney operating a program and a contractor or local governmental entity providing child support services in the IV-D Child Support Program are eligible to earn incentive payments, based on the score received for performance standards required under this Section and the amount available for that year under this subsection.

(c) Once each year, the Department shall apply the performance standards to all State's Attorneys operating a program and contractors and local governmental entities providing child support services in the IV-D Child Support Program, and shall publish a report of such performance levels and corresponding scores used in calculating the incentive payment amount.

(Source: P.A. 92-876, § 25.)

750 ILCS 24/30 Annual report to General Assembly

Sec. 30. *Annual report to General Assembly.* The Department shall submit to the General Assembly an annual report on the operation of Programs during the preceding State fiscal year. The annual report must include, but need not be limited to, the following:

(1) The report of performance levels and corresponding scores used in calculating the incentive payment amounts under Section 20 [750 ILCS 24/20].

(2) A narrative description of each Program operating in the State, including (i) the manner in which a State's Attorney complied or failed to comply with each assurance included in the applicable Plan and (ii) the Program's annual budget and staffing.

(Source: P.A. 92-876, § 30.)

750 ILCS 24/35 IV-D Child Support Program responsibilities

Sec. 35. *IV-D Child Support Program responsibilities.* (a) The Department has the authority and responsibility for administering the IV-D Child Support Program in compliance with Title IV, Part D of the federal Social Security Act.

(b) The Department may enter into agreements with contractors or local governmental entities to manage any services provided by the IV-D Child Support Program in counties in which the State's Attorney is not operating a Program. All contractors or local governmental entities entering into agreements with the Department must meet the applicable performance standards set forth in Section 25 [750 ILCS 24/25].

(c) In all counties, whether or not the State's Attorney in a county is operating a Program, the Department must, at a minimum, fulfill its responsibilities under Title IV, Part D of the federal Social Security Act and Article X of the Illinois Public Aid Code [305 ILCS 5/10-1 et seq.] in connection with the following:

(1) Operation of a statewide toll free telephone number that refers parties to the appropriate contact as established by a Plan.

(2) Management and supervision of the State Disbursement Unit.

(3) Management and supervision of KIDS and the State Case Registry established under Section 10-27 of the Illinois Public Aid Code [305 ILCS 5/10-27], including the responsibility (i) for entering and editing data for activities being conducted by the Department with respect to a current child support case and (ii) for having conflicting or incorrect data reconciled with respect to those activities. A State's Attorney operating a Program, however, must be able to enter data directly into KIDS with respect to any current child support cases for which the State's Attorney is responsible and must be able to edit that data when necessary.

(4) Federal income tax refund intercepts.

(5) State income tax refund and other payment intercepts.

(6) Sending notices required by law to parents, except as otherwise provided in a Plan.

(7) Submitting past due support information to licensing agencies.

(8) Notifying the Illinois Department of Public Health of parentage establishments and acknowledgments.

(9) Maintaining the Central Case Registry with respect to interstate cases, and taking any necessary actions that are not otherwise specified in a Plan.

(10) Submittal of past-due support information to the Illinois Department of Revenue.

(11) Requests for data matches with financial institutions.

(12) Account reviews and redeterminations for any child support cases in which administrative processes are utilized by the Department under this Section.

(13) Reports to the federal government.

(14) All other duties required under Title IV, Part D of the federal Social Security Act that are not otherwise included in a Plan.

(d) To the extent that the provisions of this Act are inconsistent with the responsibilities or requirements imposed on the IV-D Child Support Program under Article X of the Illinois Public Aid Code [305 ILCS 5/10-1 et seq.], the provisions of this Act shall control, unless doing so violates Title IV, Part D of the federal Social Security Act.

(Source: P.A. 92-876, § 35.)

750 ILCS 24/905 through 750 ILCS 24/920 [Not Set Out]

(Source: P.A. 92-876, § 905.)

Note.

Sections 905 through 920, as enacted by P.A. 92-876, contain amendatory provisions.

EXPEDITED CHILD SUPPORT ACT OF 1990

750 ILCS 25/1 Short title

Sec. 1. *Short title.* This Act may be cited as the Expedited Child Support Act of 1990.

(Source: P.A. 86-1401.)

Derivation.

Title: An Act in relation to child support.
Cite: 750 ILCS 25/1 et seq.
Source: P.A. 86-1401.
Date: Approved September 10, 1990.

Note.

This section was Ill.Rev.Stat., Ch. 40, para. 2701.

750 ILCS 25/2 Purpose

Sec. 2. *Purpose.* It is the express public policy of this State to ensure the expeditious establishment, enforcement and modification of child support orders and to ensure the expeditious establishment of parentage.

(Source: P.A. 86-1401.)

Note.

This section was Ill.Rev.Stat., Ch. 40, para. 2702.

750 ILCS 25/3 Definitions

Sec. 3. *Definitions.* For the purposes of this Act, the following terms shall have the following meaning:

(a) "Administrative Hearing Officer" shall mean the person employed by the Chief Judge of the Circuit Court of each county establishing an Expedited Child Support System for the purpose of hearing child support and parentage matters and making recommendations.

(b) "Administrative expenses" shall mean, but not be limited to, the costs of personnel, travel, equipment, telecommunications, postage, space, contractual services, and other related costs necessary to implement the provisions of this Act.

(c) "Arrearage" shall mean the total amount of unpaid child support obligations.

(d) "Department" shall mean the Illinois Department of Public Aid.

(e) "Expedited child support hearing" shall mean a hearing before an Administrative Hearing Officer pursuant to this Act.

(f) "Federal time frames" shall mean the time frames established for the IV-D program in regulations promulgated by the United States Department of Health and Human Services, Office of Child Support Enforcement, (codified at 45 C.F.R. 303), for the disposition of parentage and child support cases and shall, for purposes of this Act, apply to all parentage and child support matters, whether IV-D or non-IV-D.

(g) "System" shall mean the procedures and personnel created by this Act for the expedited establishment, modification, and enforcement of child support orders, and for the expedited establishment of parentage.

(h) "IV-D program" shall mean the Child Support Enforcement Program established pursuant to Title IV, Part D of the Social Security Act, (42 U.S.C. 651 et seq.) as administered by the Illinois Department of Public Aid.

(i) "Medical support" shall mean support provided pursuant to Section 505.2 of the Illinois Marriage and Dissolution of Marriage Act [750 ILCS 5/505.2].

(j) "Obligee" shall mean the individual to whom a duty of support is owed or that individual's legal representative.

(k) "Obligor" shall mean the individual who owes a duty to make payments under an order of support.

(l) "Plan" shall mean the plan submitted by the Chief Judge of a Judicial Circuit to the Supreme Court for the creation of an Expedited Child Support System in such circuit pursuant to this Act.

(m) "Pre-hearing motions" shall mean all motions, the disposition of which requires a court order, except motions for the ultimate relief requested in the petition to commence the action.

(n) "Recommendations" shall mean the Administrative Hearing Officer's proposed findings of fact, recommended orders and any other recommendations made by the Administrative Hearing Officer. (Source: P.A. 86-1401.)

Note.

This section was Ill.Rev.Stat., Ch. 40, para. 2703.

750 ILCS 25/4 Establishment of the Expedited Child Support System

Sec. 4. *Establishment of the Expedited Child Support System.* (a) Creation of Expedited Child Support System.

(1) Beginning July 1, 1991, an Expedited Child Support System may be established in accordance with this Act in one or more counties for actions to establish parentage and to establish, modify, and enforce child support obligations. The System shall be available to all participants in the IV-D program, and may be made available to all persons, regardless of participation in the IV-D program, in accordance with subsection (d) of this Section.

(2) Implementation. To implement this System, the Chief Judge of any Circuit shall develop and submit to the Supreme Court a Plan for the creation of a System.

(3) The Plan. The Plan shall indicate whether the System is to be available to non-participants in the IV-D program; designate the number of Administrative Hearing Officers to be employed; describe the facilities to be made available for Expedited Child Support Hearings, including days and hours of availability; describe the procedure for presentation to a judge of contested pre-hearing motions that require a court order; describe the procedure for transmittal of recommendations to a judge; describe the procedure for action on recommendations by a judge; describe the procedure for transfer of matters from a judge to an Administrative Hearing Officer; and describe the procedure for referral of matters from an Administrative Hearing Officer to a judge. The Plan shall otherwise be in accordance with the provisions of this Act, with Supreme Court rules promulgated pursuant to this Act, and with the standards, policies and rules of the IV-D program to the extent federal reimbursement is sought. At the option of the Chief Judge, the Plan may create a circuit-wide System or may create a separate System for each county within the circuit. The Chief Judges of 2 or more contiguous judicial circuits may jointly submit a Plan that creates a single System for those judicial circuits.

(4) Supreme Court Review and Approval. The Supreme Court shall review and approve or modify any submitted Plan to assure that it is consistent with the standards, policies and rules of the Supreme Court, the provisions and policies of this Act, and with the standards, policies and rules of the IV-D program to the extent federal reimbursement

is sought, but shall not require Department or county approval.

(5) Implementation. The System shall be administered by the Supreme Court. The Supreme Court may delegate, to the Chief Judge of each Judicial Circuit, the day-to-day administration of the System in the county or counties in such circuit in a manner consistent with the standards, policies, and rules established by the Supreme Court. Day-to-day administration includes, but is not limited to, engagement and termination of services, and periodic evaluation and assessment of work performed by all Administrative Hearing Officers.

(6) Hearing officers. At a minimum, Administrative Hearing Officers must be licensed to practice law in Illinois and shall otherwise meet the qualifications established by the Supreme Court in rules promulgated pursuant to this Act.

(7) Reporting.

(A) The Supreme Court may promulgate rules for the collection and reporting of data with respect to compliance with the Federal time frames for all counties within the State. The reports shall be submitted at such intervals as the Supreme Court may prescribe and shall otherwise be in accordance with rules promulgated by the Supreme Court pursuant to this Act.

(B) Beginning in 1992, the Supreme Court shall file with the General Assembly a report no later than April 1, of each year, describing the implementation status of this Act, which shall include, but not be limited to, an assessment of the System's effectiveness in all implementing counties, data reported pursuant to subparagraph (A) of this paragraph, and recommendations regarding continuation of the System in the implementing counties and expansion of the System into other counties.

(b) Demonstration Program. The Department may establish a demonstration program in one or more counties selected by the Department for the use of the Expedited Child Support System in IV-D cases beginning July 1, 1991, or as soon thereafter as practicable. The program shall remain operative until June 30, 1994; provided, that if funds become unavailable the program shall terminate. The portion of the administrative expenses for such program attributable to use by the IV-D program which is not funded by the federal government shall be paid out of funds in the Child Support Enforcement Trust Fund as established in Section 12-10.2 of the Illinois Public Aid Code [305 ILCS 5/12-10.2].

The Supreme Court shall notify the Chief Judge of each judicial circuit of the Department's intent to establish a demonstration program in one or more counties. Any Chief Judge may submit a demonstration Plan to the Supreme Court for its review; approval or modification pursuant to subsection (a) of this Section; and for potential submission to the Department. The demonstration Plan, in addition to the elements described in subsection (a) of this Section, shall include a projected budget for the operation of the System and may provide for participation in the System by parties who are not participants in the IV-D program provided that the portion of administrative expenses attributable to use by non-participants in the IV-D program has been appropriated by the respective county and the conditions of subsection (d) of this Section shall apply. The Department may select, after reviewing the submitted Plans, one or more counties to participate in a demonstration program and shall notify the Supreme Court of its decision.

The Department shall file, no later than April 1, 1993, an interim report assessing the effectiveness of the program in the demonstration county or counties, including specific data on the disposition of child support cases covered by this Act. The Department shall file no later than April 1, 1994, a final report updating the assessment and data provided in the interim report, making recommendations regarding continuation of the program in the participating county or counties and making recommendations regarding implementation in non-participating counties.

(c) Non-Demonstration Counties. Upon Supreme Court approval of a submitted Plan, any non-demonstration county, circuit or multi-circuit area may implement an Expedited Child Support System, provided that funding has been appropriated by the respective County Board or Boards for administrative expenses incurred in the establishment and maintenance of the non-IV-D portion of the System and the IV-D portion that is not subject to federal reimbursement and that a plan for cost sharing has been filed with and approved by the Department. The Chief Judge of each implementing circuit shall maintain records of the number of IV-D and non-IV-D cases pending and disposed of in the System. The administrative expenses that are subject to federal reimbursement shall be documented and recorded in such a fashion as to insure eligibility for federal reimbursement under the IV-D program. The Supreme Court shall co-operate with the Department in providing information necessary to obtain reimbursement from the federal government pursuant to the IV-D program.

(d) Use of the Expedited Child Support System when neither party is a IV-D participant. Any Plan submitted by the Chief Judge of a Judicial Circuit may provide, but may not require, that the Expedited Child Support System be available, on a case by case basis, when neither party is a participant in the IV-D program, provided that funding for administrative expenses relating to non-IV-D participants has been appropriated by the respective County Board or Boards and that a plan for cost sharing has been filed with and approved by the Department. Provided that, the petitioner may elect to file an action under this Act before the Administrative Hearing Officer; in such a case, the other party, notwithstanding any other provision of this Act, on

or before the hearing date, may elect to have the case transferred for judicial hearing.
(Source: P.A. 86-1401.)

Note.
This section was Ill.Rev.Stat., Ch. 40, para. 2704.

750 ILCS 25/5 Actions Subject to Expedited Child Support Hearings

Sec. 5. *Actions Subject to Expedited Child Support Hearings.* (a) The Chief Judge of each Judicial Circuit that establishes a System shall delegate to the Administrative Hearing Officer the authority to hear the following actions:

(1) Petitions for child support and for medical support, pursuant to Section 505.2 of the Illinois Marriage and Dissolution of Marriage Act [750 ILCS 5/505.2], for post-judgment dissolution of marriage and post-judgment parentage actions where child support or medical support was reserved or could not be ordered at the time of entry of the judgment because the court lacked personal jurisdiction over the obligor.

(2) Petitions for modification of child support and medical support in post-judgment dissolution of marriage and post-judgment parentage actions.

(3) Parentage actions, including the establishment of child support orders after parentage has been acknowledged.

(4) Actions for the enforcement of any existing order for child support or medical support in post-judgment dissolution of marriage and post-judgment parentage actions.

(5) Actions for the establishment of child support and medical support orders involving parties who are married and living separately, pursuant to Section 402 of the Marriage and Dissolution of Marriage Act [750 ILCS 5/402].

(6) Temporary orders for support in any action in which the custodial parent is a participant in the IV-D program.

(7) Any other child support matter provided for in the Plan for the creation of the System approved by the Illinois Supreme Court.

(8) Actions brought pursuant to Article X of the Illinois Public Aid Code [305 ILCS 5/10-1 et seq.].

(b) Notwithstanding the provisions of subsection (a) of this Section, if the custodial parent is not a participant in the IV-D program and maintenance is in issue, the case shall be presented directly to the court.

(c) Except as provided in subsection (b), the Plan may provide that the System be available in pre-judgment proceedings for dissolution of marriage, declaration of invalidity of marriage and legal separation.
(Source: P.A. 86-1401.)

Note.
This section was Ill.Rev.Stat., Ch. 40, para. 2705.

750 ILCS 25/6 Authority of hearing officers

Sec. 6. *Authority of hearing officers.* (a) With the exception of judicial functions exclusively retained by the court in Section 8 of this Act [750 ILCS 25/8] and in accordance with Supreme Court rules promulgated pursuant to this Act, Administrative Hearing Officers shall be authorized to:

(1) Accept voluntary agreements reached by the parties setting the amount of child support to be paid and medical support liability and recommend the entry of orders incorporating such agreements.

(2) Accept voluntary acknowledgments of parentage and recommend entry of an order establishing parentage based on such acknowledgement. Prior to accepting such acknowledgment, the Administrative Hearing Officer shall advise the putative father of his rights and obligations in accordance with Supreme Court rules promulgated pursuant to this Act.

(3) Manage all stages of discovery, including setting deadlines by which discovery must be completed; and directing the parties to submit to appropriate tests pursuant to Section 11 of the Illinois Parentage Act of 1984 [750 ILCS 45/11].

(4) Cause notices to be issued requiring the Obligor to appear either before the Administrative Hearing Officer or in court.

(5) Administer the oath or affirmation and take testimony under oath or affirmation.

(6) Analyze the evidence and prepare written recommendations based on such evidence, including but not limited to: (i) proposed findings as to the amount of the Obligor's income; (ii) proposed findings as to the amount and nature of appropriate deductions from the Obligor's income to determine the Obligor's net income; (iii) proposed findings as to the existence of relevant factors as set forth in subsection (a)(2) of Section 505 of the Illinois Marriage and Dissolution of Marriage Act [750 ILCS 5/505], which justify setting child support payment levels above or below the guidelines; (iv) recommended orders for temporary child support; (v) recommended orders setting the amount of current child support to be paid; (vi) proposed findings as to the existence and amount of any arrearages; (vii) recommended orders reducing any arrearages to judgement and for the payment of amounts towards such arrearages; (viii) proposed findings as to whether there has been a substantial change of circumstances since the entry of the last child support order, or other circumstances justifying a modification of the child support order; and (ix) proposed findings as to whether the Obligor is employed.

(7) With respect to any unemployed Obligor who is not making child support payments or is otherwise unable to provide support, recommend that the Obligor be ordered to seek employment and report periodically of his or her efforts in accordance with such order. Additionally, the Administrative Hearing Officer may recommend that the Obligor be ordered to report to the Department of Employment Security

for job search services or to make application with the local Job Training Partnership Act [29 U.S.C. § 1501 et seq.] provider for participation in job search, training or work programs and, where the duty of support is owed to a child receiving child support enforcement services under Article X of The Illinois Public Aid Code [305 ILCS 5/10-1 et seq.], the Administrative Hearing Officer may recommend that the Obligor be ordered to report to the Illinois Department of Public Aid for participation in the job search, training or work programs established under Section 9-6 of the Public Aid Code [305 ILCS 5/9-6].

(8) Recommend the registration of any foreign support judgments or orders as the judgments or orders of Illinois.

(b) In any case in which the Obligee is not participating in the IV-D program or has not applied to participate in the IV-D program, the Administrative Hearing Officer shall:

(1) inform the Obligee of the existence of the IV-D program and provide applications on request; and

(2) inform the Obligee and the Obligor of the option of requesting payment to be made through the Clerk of the Circuit Court.

If a request for payment through the Clerk is made, the Administrative Hearing Officer shall note this fact in the recommendations to the court.

(c) The Administrative Hearing Officer may make recommendations in addition to the proposed findings of fact and recommended order to which the parties have agreed.

(Source: P.A. 86-1401; 92-16, § 97.4; 92-590, § 22.)

Note.

This section was Ill.Rev.Stat., Ch. 40, para. 2706.

Section 996 of P.A. 92-16 contains a "no acceleration or delay" provision, and Section 997 contains a "no revival or extension" provision.

Effect of Amendments.

The 2001 amendment by P.A. 92-16, effective June 28, 2001, in subsection (a)(7) made a typographical correction and deleted "and" from the end of the subsection and made a related change.

The 2002 amendment by P.A. 92-590, effective July 1, 2002, substituted "child support enforcement services" for "support services" in the last sentence of subsection (a)(7).

750 ILCS 25/7 Expedited Child Support Hearings

Sec. 7. *Expedited Child Support Hearings.* (a) Service. Except as otherwise provided in this subsection and in Section 11 of this Act [750 ILCS 25/11], the service of notice to commence an action under this Act may be made by regular mail. The notice shall be sent to the last known address of the Obligor. Parentage actions, actions for the establishment of child support orders involving parties who are married and living separately, and any other proceedings in which no court has yet acquired jurisdiction over the subject matter shall be commenced as provided in the Code of Civil Procedure [735 ILCS 5/1-101 et seq.] and Supreme Court Rules. The notice or summons shall indicate the date set for hearing.

(b) Rules of Evidence. Except as provided in this Section, the established rules of evidence shall be followed in all Expedited Child Support Hearings. A party may offer in evidence, without foundation or other proof:

(1) the Obligor's pay stubs or other employer-provided statement of gross income, deductions, and net income prepared by the employer in the usual course of business;

(2) documents provided by the Obligor's insurance company that describe the dependent care coverage available to the Obligor; and

(3) records kept by the Clerk of the Circuit Court as to payment of child support.

(c) Other domestic relations matters. Petitions for visitation, custody, distribution of property, petitions pursuant to Section 513 of the Illinois Marriage and Dissolution of Marriage Act [750 ILCS 5/513], spousal maintenance as otherwise provided, and any domestic relations matters other than parentage and child support shall be transferred by the Administrative Hearing Officer for a judicial hearing as provided in the Plan. Transfer of such matters shall not delay the proceeding before the Administrative Hearing Officer relative to parentage or child support.

(d) Transfers for judicial hearings. All actions and matters requiring a judicial hearing, as provided for in this Act and in Supreme Court rules promulgated pursuant to this Act, shall be transferred to the court as provided in the Plan.

(e) All pre-hearing motions and other matters that require a court order, as defined in this Act and in the Supreme Court rules promulgated pursuant to this Act, shall be presented to the court for resolution and the court shall make every effort to dispose of the motion in an expeditious manner. However, if the parties are in agreement with respect to the pre-hearing motion or other matters, the Administrative Hearing Officer shall transmit a recommended order, signed by both parties, to the court.

(f) Notice to parties and transmittal of recommendations. The Administrative Hearing Officer shall provide each party with a copy of the recommendations, together with a notice informing the parties of their right to request a judicial hearing. The recommendations and notice shall be given to the parties at the time of the hearing. If either party is not present at the time of the hearing, either in person or through his or her attorney, the provisions of Section 10 of this Act [750 ILCS 25/10] shall apply. If both parties are present at the hearing and agree to the recommended order of the Administrative Hearing Officer, they shall sign the recommended order and the Administrative Hearing Officer shall transmit the recommendations to the Court as provided in the Plan.

(1) If either party does not agree to the recommended order or any part thereof, a judicial hearing

shall immediately be scheduled as to those matters on which the parties disagree. The Administrative Hearing Officer shall record the date, time, and place of the judicial hearing on a notice and provide a copy of the notice to each party either in person at the time of the expedited hearing or by regular mail. The Administrative Hearing Officer shall transmit to the court a written statement indicating that the parties do not agree to all or part of the recommendations.

No part of the recommendations on which the parties disagree shall be made a part of the record in court unless both parties stipulate to its admission and the court so orders. However, those matters on which the parties agree may be made a part of the record in court.

(2) If either party does not agree to the Administrative Hearing Officer's recommendations and the case is transferred for a judicial hearing, neither the parties nor the court may compel the Administrative Hearing Officer to testify at the judicial hearing.

(g) Forms. The Supreme Court may develop and provide a standard form for proposed findings and recommended orders, and any other necessary standard forms, for use by Administrative Hearing Officers in Expedited Child Support Hearings.
(Source: P.A. 86-1401.)

Note.
This section was Ill.Rev.Stat., Ch. 40, para. 2707.

750 ILCS 25/8 Authority retained by the court

Sec. 8. *Authority retained by the court.* The following shall be deemed judicial functions and shall only be performed by a judge or associate judge:

(a) review the recommendations of the Administrative Hearing Officer and enter such order as it deems appropriate;

(b) conduct judicial hearings on all pre-hearing motions and other matters that require a court order and enter such orders as it deems appropriate;

(c) conduct judicial hearings on all child support matters in which the parties disagree with the Administrative Hearing Officer's recommendations;

(d) conduct trials in contested parentage cases;

(e) issue body attachment orders and rules to show cause, conduct contempt proceedings, and impose such sanctions or relief as may be appropriate;

(f) conduct judicial hearings on visitation, custody, distribution of property, petitions pursuant to Section 513 of the Illinois Marriage and Dissolution of Marriage Act [750 ILCS 5/513], spousal maintenance as otherwise provided, and any domestic relations matters other than parentage and child support;

(g) conduct judicial hearings on objections to the entry of orders pursuant to Section 10 of this Act [750 ILCS 25/10], where the hearing has been requested by the absent party in a timely manner;

(h) conduct judicial hearings on such other matters as are provided in Supreme Court Rules promulgated pursuant to this Act; and

(i) impose sanctions pursuant to Supreme Court Rule 137.
(Source: P.A. 86-1401.)

Note.
This section was Ill.Rev.Stat., Ch. 40, para. 2708.

750 ILCS 25/9 Judicial hearings

Sec. 9. *Judicial hearings.* (a) Upon receipt of any recommended order to which both parties agree, the court shall review the Administrative Hearing Officer's recommendations. The court may enter an order consistent with these recommendations, may refer the matter to the Administrative Hearing Officer for further proceedings, or may hold such additional hearing as it deems necessary.

(b) Upon receipt of a statement from the Administrative Hearing Officer indicating that the parties do not agree to the Administrative Hearing Officer's recommended order, or any part thereof, the court shall conduct a judicial hearing on those matters to which the parties do not agree and enter such orders following the hearing as it deems appropriate.

(c) A copy of all court orders shall be mailed to the parties within 5 days of entry, unless the parties were present in court at the time the order was entered, in which case the parties shall be given a copy of the order in open court. The specially certified copy of the order for withholding, if any, shall be mailed only to the Obligee or his or her attorney, and not the Obligor.
(Source: P.A. 86-1401.)

Note.
This section was Ill.Rev.Stat., Ch. 40, para. 2709.

750 ILCS 25/10 Failure to Appear

Sec. 10. *Failure to Appear.* (a) In any case in which the responding party fails to appear at the hearing, the Administrative Hearing Officer shall proceed to hear the case based upon the testimony of the petitioning party and other evidence presented, and shall recommend that the court enter an appropriate order. If the petitioning party agrees to the Administrative Hearing Officer's recommended order, a copy of such order signed by the petitioning party and a notice advising the absent party of his or her right to object shall be served upon the absent party in the following manner:

(1) If service to commence the proceeding before the Administrative Hearing Officer was by regular mail, the notice and recommended order shall be served in the same manner as summonses are served in other civil proceedings, or, in lieu of personal service, by certified mail, return receipt requested, mailed to the absent party's last known address. If service is made by certified mail, the return receipt shall constitute proof of service.

(2) If service to commence the proceeding before the Administrative Hearing Officer was as provided

in the Code of Civil Procedure [735 ILCS 5/1-101 et seq.] and Supreme Court Rules, the notice and recommended order shall be served by regular mail to the absent party's last known address.

(b) At any time within 14 days after the recommended order has been mailed, the absent party may file a written objection with the court to the entry of the recommended order. The court shall hold a hearing on the objection and enter the appropriate orders. If the court determines that the recommended order not be entered, the court may refer the case back to the Administrative Hearing Officer for further proceedings or may conduct a judicial hearing.

(c) If the petitioning party does not agree to the recommended order or any part thereof, a judicial hearing shall immediately be scheduled. The Administrative Hearing Officer shall record the date, time and place of the judicial hearing on a notice and provide a copy of the notice to the petitioning party at the time of the expedited hearing and to the responding party by regular mail.
(Source: P.A. 86-1401.)

Note.
This section was Ill.Rev.Stat., Ch. 40, para. 2710.

750 ILCS 25/13 [Effective date]

Sec. 13. This Act takes effect upon becoming law.
(Source: P.A. 86-1401.)

Note.
This section was Ill.Rev.Stat., Ch. 40, para. 2713.

Income Withholding for Support Act

750 ILCS 28/1 Short title

Sec. 1. *Short title.* This Act may be cited as the Income Withholding for Support Act.
(Source: P.A. 90-673, § 1.)

Effective Date.
Section 99 of P.A. 90-673 made this Act effective January 1, 1999.

750 ILCS 28/5 Purpose; intent

Sec. 5. *Purpose; intent.* This Act consolidates into a single new Act the lengthy and nearly identical provisions relating to income withholding for support that were formerly contained in Section 10-16.2 of the Illinois Public Aid Code [305 ILCS 5/10-16.2], Section 706.1 of the Illinois Marriage and Dissolution of Marriage Act [750 ILCS 5/706.1], Section 4.1 of the Non-Support of Spouse and Children Act [750 ILCS 15/4.1], and Section 20 of the Illinois Parentage Act of 1984 [750 ILCS 45/20]. It also divides the consolidated provisions into smaller Sections for ease of use and future amendment and makes technical corrections. This Act is intended as a continuation of the consolidated provisions, and the consolidation is not intended to make any substantive change in the law nor to affect any order issued under any of the consolidated provisions.
(Source: P.A. 90-673, § 5.)

Note.
The Non-Support of Spouse and Children Act, 750 ILCS 15/1 et seq., referred to above, is repealed. Current similar provisions are found as the Non-Support Punishment Act, 750 ILCS 16/1 et seq.

750 ILCS 28/15 Definitions

Sec. 15. *Definitions.* (a) "Order for support" means any order of the court which provides for periodic payment of funds for the support of a child or maintenance of a spouse, whether temporary or final, and includes any such order which provides for:

(1) modification or resumption of, or payment of arrearage accrued under, a previously existing order;

(2) reimbursement of support;

(3) payment or reimbursement of the expenses of pregnancy and delivery (for orders for support entered under the Illinois Parentage Act of 1984 [750 ILCS 45/1 et seq.] or its predecessor the Paternity Act); or

(4) enrollment in a health insurance plan that is available to the obligor through an employer or labor union or trade union.

(b) "Arrearage" means the total amount of unpaid support obligations as determined by the court and incorporated into an order for support.

(b-5) "Business day" means a day on which State offices are open for regular business.

(c) "Delinquency" means any payment under an order for support which becomes due and remains unpaid after entry of the order for support.

(d) "Income" means any form of periodic payment to an individual, regardless of source, including, but not limited to: wages, salary, commission, compensation as an independent contractor, workers' compensation, disability, annuity, pension, and retirement benefits, lottery prize awards, insurance proceeds, vacation pay, bonuses, profit-sharing payments, interest, and any other payments, made by any person, private entity, federal or state government, any unit of local government, school district or any entity created by Public Act; however, "income" excludes:

(1) any amounts required by law to be withheld, other than creditor claims, including, but not limited to, federal, State and local taxes, Social Security and other retirement and disability contributions;

(2) union dues;

(3) any amounts exempted by the federal Consumer Credit Protection Act [15 U.S.C. § 1601 et seq.];

(4) public assistance payments; and

(5) unemployment insurance benefits except as provided by law.

Any other State or local laws which limit or exempt income or the amount or percentage of income that can be withheld shall not apply.

(e) "Obligor" means the individual who owes a duty to make payments under an order for support.

(f) "Obligee" means the individual to whom a duty of support is owed or the individual's legal representative.

(g) "Payor" means any payor of income to an obligor.

(h) "Public office" means any elected official or any State or local agency which is or may become responsible by law for enforcement of, or which is or may become authorized to enforce, an order for support, including, but not limited to: the Attorney General, the Illinois Department of Public Aid, the Illinois Department of Human Services, the Illinois Department of Children and Family Services, and the various State's Attorneys, Clerks of the Circuit Court and supervisors of general assistance.

(i) "Premium" means the dollar amount for which the obligor is liable to his employer or labor union or trade union and which must be paid to enroll or maintain a child in a health insurance plan that is available to the obligor through an employer or labor union or trade union.

(j) "State Disbursement Unit" means the unit established to collect and disburse support payments in accordance with the provisions of Section 10-26 of the Illinois Public Aid Code [305 ILCS 5/10-26].

(k) "Title IV-D Agency" means the agency of this State charged by law with the duty to administer the child support enforcement program established under Title IV, Part D of the Social Security Act and Article X of the Illinois Public Aid Code [42 U.S.C. § 601 et seq. and 305 ILCS 5/10-1 et seq.].

(l) "Title IV-D case" means a case in which an obligee or obligor is receiving child support enforcement services under Title IV, Part D of the Social Security Act and Article X of the Illinois Public Aid Code [42 U.S.C. § 601 et seq. and 305 ILCS 5/10-1 et seq.].

(m) "National Medical Support Notice" means the notice required for enforcement of orders for support providing for health insurance coverage of a child under Title IV, Part D of the Social Security Act [42 U.S.C. § 601 et seq], the Employee Retirement Income Security Act of 1974 [29 U.S.C. § 1001 et seq.], and federal regulations promulgated under those Acts.

(n) "Employer" means a payor or labor union or trade union with an employee group health insurance plan and, for purposes of the National Medical Support Notice, also includes but is not limited to:

(1) any State or local governmental agency with a group health plan; and

(2) any payor with a group health plan or "church plan" covered under the Employee Retirement Income Security Act of 1974 [29 U.S.C. § 1001 et seq.].
(Source: P.A. 90-673, § 15; impl. am. 90-790; 91-212, § 35; 91-357, § 260; 92-590, § 25.)

Illinois Administrative Code.
See 89 Illinois Administrative Code, § 160.75.

Effect of Amendments.
The 1999 amendment by P.A. 91-212, effective July 20, 1999, added subsections (b-5) and (j).

The 1999 amendment by P.A. 91-357, effective July 29, 1999, added subsection (b-5).

The 2002 amendment by P.A. 92-590, effective July 1, 2002, added subsections (k) through (n).

CASE NOTES

Analysis

"Income"
Delinquency

"Income"
Trial court properly ordered a father to turn over a certificate of deposit purchased with past due military retirement benefits to satisfy child support arrearages because the general exemption from judgment for payments under a government retirement plan, in 735 ILCS 5/12-1006(a) and (b)(2) was subject to the exception in 750 ILCS 28/15(d), regarding enforcement of support obligations, which included these retirement benefits as income and provided that any state or local law exempting them from execution to satisfy such an obligation did not apply. In re Marriage of Murphy, 338 Ill. App. 3d 1095, 274 Ill. Dec. 917, 792 N.E.2d 12, 2003 Ill. App. LEXIS 757 (4 Dist. 2003).

Delinquency
Penalties for late mailing of withheld child support should not have been imposed against employer that mailed checks on the Saturday following each pay period since weekends did not count in computing the seven-day mailing requirement, the checks should have been regarded as mailed when (according to uncontradicted evidence) they were put out for pick-up by the letter carrier, and mailing, not date of receipt by the enforcement unit, was the controlling date for purposes of determining compliance. Thomas v. Diener, 351 Ill. App. 3d 645, 286 Ill. Dec. 537, 814 N.E.2d 187, 2004 Ill. App. LEXIS 940 (4 Dist. 2004).

750 ILCS 28/20 Entry of order for support containing income withholding provisions; income withholding notice

Sec. 20. *Entry of order for support containing income withholding provisions; income withholding notice.* (a) In addition to any content required under other laws, every order for support entered on or after July 1, 1997, shall:

(1) Require an income withholding notice to be prepared and served immediately upon any payor of the obligor by the obligee or public office, unless a written agreement is reached between and signed by both parties providing for an alternative arrangement, approved and entered into the record by the court, which ensures payment of support. In that case, the order for support shall provide that an income withholding notice is to be prepared and

served only if the obligor becomes delinquent in paying the order for support; and

(2) Contain a dollar amount to be paid until payment in full of any delinquency that accrues after entry of the order for support. The amount for payment of delinquency shall not be less than 20% of the total of the current support amount and the amount to be paid periodically for payment of any arrearage stated in the order for support; and

(3) Include the obligor's Social Security Number, which the obligor shall disclose to the court. If the obligor is not a United States citizen, the obligor shall disclose to the court, and the court shall include in the order for support, the obligor's alien registration number, passport number, and home country's social security or national health number, if applicable.

(b) At the time the order for support is entered, the Clerk of the Circuit Court shall provide a copy of the order to the obligor and shall make copies available to the obligee and public office.

(c) The income withholding notice shall:

(1) be in the standard format prescribed by the federal Department of Health and Human Services; and

(1.1) state the date of entry of the order for support upon which the income withholding notice is based; and

(2) direct any payor to withhold the dollar amount required for current support under the order for support; and

(3) direct any payor to withhold the dollar amount required to be paid periodically under the order for support for payment of the amount of any arrearage stated in the order for support; and

(4) direct any payor or labor union or trade union to enroll a child as a beneficiary of a health insurance plan and withhold or cause to be withheld, if applicable, any required premiums; and

(5) state the amount of the payor income withholding fee specified under this Section; and

(6) state that the amount actually withheld from the obligor's income for support and other purposes, including the payor withholding fee specified under this Section, may not be in excess of the maximum amount permitted under the federal Consumer Credit Protection Act [15 U.S.C. § 1601 et seq]; and

(7) state the duties of the payor and the fines and penalties for failure to withhold and pay over income and for discharging, disciplining, refusing to hire, or otherwise penalizing the obligor because of the duty to withhold and pay over income under this Section; and

(8) state the rights, remedies, and duties of the obligor under this Section; and

(9) include the Social Security Numbers of the obligor, the obligee, and the child or children included in the order for support; and

(10) include the date that withholding for current support terminates, which shall be the date of termination of the current support obligation set forth in the order for support; and

(11) contain the signature of the obligee or the printed name and telephone number of the authorized representative of the public office, except that the failure to contain the signature of the obligee or the printed name and telephone number of the authorized representative of the public office shall not affect the validity of the income withholding notice; and

(12) direct any payor to pay over amounts withheld for payment of support to the State Disbursement Unit.

(d) The accrual of a delinquency as a condition for service of an income withholding notice, under the exception to immediate withholding in subsection (a) of this Section, shall apply only to the initial service of an income withholding notice on a payor of the obligor.

(e) Notwithstanding the exception to immediate withholding contained in subsection (a) of this Section, if the court finds at the time of any hearing that an arrearage has accrued, the court shall order immediate service of an income withholding notice upon the payer.

(f) If the order for support, under the exception to immediate withholding contained in subsection (a) of this Section, provides that an income withholding notice is to be prepared and served only if the obligor becomes delinquent in paying the order for support, the obligor may execute a written waiver of that condition and request immediate service on the payor.

(g) The obligee or public office may serve the income withholding notice on the payor or its superintendent, manager, or other agent by ordinary mail or certified mail return receipt requested, by facsimile transmission or other electronic means, by personal delivery, or by any method provided by law for service of a summons. At the time of service on the payor and as notice that withholding has commenced, the obligee or public office shall serve a copy of the income withholding notice on the obligor by ordinary mail addressed to his or her last known address. A copy of the income withholding notice together with proofs of service on the payor and the obligor shall be filed with the Clerk of the Circuit Court.

(h) At any time after the initial service of an income withholding notice, any other payor of the obligor may be served with the same income withholding notice without further notice to the obligor. A copy of the income withholding notice together with a proof of service on the other payor shall be filed with the Clerk of the Circuit Court.

(i) New service of an income withholding notice is not required in order to resume withholding of income in the case of an obligor with respect to whom an income withholding notice was previously served on the payor if withholding of income was terminated because of an interruption in the obligor's employment of less than 180 days.

(Source: P.A. 90-673, § 20; impl. am 90-790; 91-212, § 35; 91-357, § 260.)

Effect of Amendments.

The 1999 amendment by P.A. 91-212, effective July 20, 1999, inserted subsection (c)(1.1), rewrote subsection (c)(9) and added subsections (c)(11) and (c)(12); inserted "A copy of the income withholding notice together with" in the third sentence of subsection (g); and added the last sentence in subsection (h).

The 1999 amendment by P.A. 91-357, effective July 29, 1999, added subsections (c)(1.1) and (c)(11); inserted "A copy of the income withholding notice together with" at the beginning of the last sentence in subsection (g); added the second sentence in subsection (h) and made a stylistic change.

Although the amendments made to this section by P.A. 91-212, § 35 and P.A. 91-357, § 260 did not take into account the amendments made by the other, the amendments have been combined into a single version by the publisher.

CASE NOTES

Service of Notice

In petitioner's action against an employer pursuant to 750 ILCS 28/35, for failure to pay child support from its employee's wages, in light of the legislature's use of the word "may" in subsection (g) of this section, personal delivery of the support order by the employee/obligor on the employer satisfied the purpose of the provision to the same extent as notice served by petitioner or the public office. In re Marriage of Chen, Ill. App. 3d , 290 Ill. Dec. 69, 820 N.E.2d 1136, 2004 Ill. App. LEXIS 1496 (2 Dist. 2004).

750 ILCS 28/22 Use of National Medical Support Notice to enforce health insurance coverage

Sec. 22. *Use of National Medical Support Notice to enforce health insurance coverage.* (a) Notwithstanding the provisions of subdivision (c)(4) of Section 20 [750 ILCS 28/20], when an order for support is being enforced by the Title IV-D Agency under this Act, any requirement for health insurance coverage to be provided through an employer, including withholding of premiums from the income of the obligor, shall be enforced through use of a National Medical Support Notice instead of through provisions in an income withholding notice.

(b) A National Medical Support Notice may be served on the employer in the manner and under the circumstances provided for serving an income withholding notice under this Act, except that an order for support that conditions service of an income withholding notice on the obligor becoming delinquent in paying the order for support, as provided under subdivision (a)(1) of Section 20 [750 ILCS 28/20], shall not prevent immediate service of a National Medical Support Notice by the Title IV-D Agency. The Title IV-D Agency may serve a National Medical Support Notice on an employer in conjunction with service of an income withholding notice. Service of an income withholding notice is not a condition for service of a National Medical Support Notice, however.

(c) At the time of service of a National Medical Support Notice on the employer, the Title IV-D Agency shall serve a copy of the Notice on the obligor by ordinary mail addressed to the obligor's last known address. The Title IV-D Agency shall file a copy of the National Medical Support Notice, together with proofs of service on the employer and the obligor, with the clerk of the circuit court.

(d) Within 20 business days after the date of a National Medical Support Notice, an employer served with the Notice shall transfer the severable notice to plan administrator to the appropriate group health plan providing any health insurance coverage for which the child is eligible. As required in the part of the National Medical Support Notice directed to the employer, the employer shall withhold any employee premium necessary for coverage of the child and shall send any amount withheld directly to the plan. The employer shall commence the withholding no later than the next payment of income that occurs 14 days following the date the National Medical Support Notice was mailed, sent by facsimile or other electronic means, or placed for personal delivery to or service on the employer.

Notwithstanding the requirement to withhold premiums from the obligor's income, if the plan administrator informs the employer that the child is enrolled in an option under the plan for which the employer has determined that the obligor's premium exceeds the amount that may be withheld from the obligor's income due to the withholding limitation or prioritization contained in Section 35 of this Act [750 ILCS 28/35], the employer shall complete the appropriate item in the part of the National Medical Support Notice directed to the employer according to the instructions in the Notice and shall return that part to the Title IV-D Agency.

(e) If one of the following circumstances exists, an employer served with a National Medical Support Notice shall complete the part of the Notice directed to the employer in accordance with the instructions in the Notice and shall return that part to the Title IV-D Agency within 20 business days after the date of the Notice:

(1) The employer does not maintain or contribute to plans providing dependent or family health insurance coverage.

(2) The obligor is among a class of employees that is not eligible for family health insurance coverage under any group health plan maintained by the employer or to which the employer contributes.

(3) Health insurance coverage is not available because the obligor is no longer employed by the employer.

(f) The administrator of a health insurance plan to whom an employer has transferred the severable notice to plan administrator part of a National Medical Support Notice shall complete that part with the health insurance coverage information required under the instructions in the Notice and shall return that part to the Title IV-D Agency within 40 business days after the date of the Notice.

(g) The obligor may contest withholding under this Section based only on a mistake of fact and may contest withholding by filing a petition with the clerk of the circuit court within 20 days after service of a copy of the National Medical Support Notice on the obligor. The obligor must serve a copy of the petition on the Title IV-D Agency at the address stated in the National Medical Support Notice. The National Medical Support Notice, including the requirement to withhold any required premium, shall continue to be binding on the employer until the employer is served with a court order resolving the contest or until notified by the Title IV-D Agency.

(h) Whenever the obligor is no longer receiving income from the employer, the employer shall return a copy of the National Medical Support Notice to the Title IV-D Agency and shall provide information for the purpose of enforcing health insurance coverage under this Section.

(i) The Title IV-D Agency shall promptly notify the employer when there is no longer a current order for health insurance coverage in effect which the Title IV-D Agency is responsible for enforcing.

(j) Unless stated otherwise in this Section, all of the provisions of this Act relating to income withholding for support shall pertain to income withholding for health insurance coverage under a National Medical Support Notice, including but not limited to the duties of the employer and obligor, and the penalties contained in Section 35 and Section 50 [750 ILCS 28/35 and 750 ILCS 28/50]. In addition, an employer who willfully fails to transfer the severable notice to plan administrator part of a National Medical Support Notice to the appropriate group health plan providing health insurance coverage for which the child is eligible, within 20 business days after the date of the Notice, is liable for the full amount of medical expenses incurred by or on behalf of the child which would have been paid or reimbursed by the health insurance coverage had the severable notice to plan administrator part of the Notice been timely transferred to the group health insurance plan. This penalty may be collected in a civil action that may be brought against the employer in favor of the obligee or the Title IV-D Agency.

(k) To the extent that any other State or local law may be construed to limit or prevent compliance by an employer or health insurance plan administrator with the requirements of this Section and federal law and regulations pertaining to the National Medical Support Notice, that State or local law shall not apply.

(l) As the Title IV-D Agency, the Department of Public Aid shall adopt any rules necessary for use of and compliance with the National Medical Support Notice.

(Source: P.A. 92-590, § 25.)

Effective Date.

Section 99 of P.A. 92-590, made this section effective July 1, 2002.

750 ILCS 28/25 Income withholding after accrual of delinquency

Sec. 25. *Income withholding after accrual of delinquency.* (a) Whenever an obligor accrues a delinquency, the obligee or public office may prepare and serve upon the obligor's payor an income withholding notice that:

(1) contains the information required under subsection (c) of Section 20 [750 ILCS 28/20]; and

(2) contains the total amount of the delinquency as of the date of the notice; and

(3) directs the payor to withhold the dollar amount required to be withheld periodically under the order for support for payment of the delinquency.

(b) The income withholding notice and the obligor's copy of the income withholding notice shall be served as provided in subsection (g) of Section 20 [750 ILCS 28/20].

(c) The obligor may contest withholding commenced under this Section by filing a petition to contest withholding with the Clerk of the Circuit Court within 20 days after service of a copy of the income withholding notice on the obligor. However, the grounds for the petition to contest withholding shall be limited to:

(1) a dispute concerning the existence or amount of the delinquency; or

(2) the identity of the obligor.

The Clerk of the Circuit Court shall notify the obligor and the obligee or public office of the time and place of the hearing on the petition to contest withholding. The court shall hold the hearing pursuant to the provisions of Section 40 [750 ILCS 28/40].

(Source: P.A. 90-673, § 25; 91-357, § 260.)

Effect of Amendments.

The 1999 amendment by P.A. 91-357, effective July 29, 1999, in subsection (a)(2) deleted "a computation of" following "contains" and "period and" preceding "total".

750 ILCS 28/30 Initiated withholding

Sec. 30. *Initiated withholding.* (a) Notwithstanding any other provision of this Act, if the court has not required that income withholding take effect immediately, the obligee or public office may initiate withholding, regardless of whether a delinquency has accrued, by preparing and serving an income withholding notice on the payor that contains the information required under subsection (c) of Section 20 [750 ILCS 28/20] and states that the parties' written agreement providing an alternative arrangement to immediate withholding under subsection (a) of Section 20 [750 ILCS 28/20] no longer ensures payment of support due and the reason or reasons why it does not.

(b) The income withholding notice and the obligor's copy of the income withholding notice shall be served as provided in subsection (g) of Section 20 [750 ILCS 28/20].

(c) The obligor may contest withholding commenced under this Section by filing a petition to contest withholding with the Clerk of the Circuit Court within 20 days after service of a copy of the income withholding notice on the obligor. However, the grounds for the petition shall be limited to a dispute concerning.

(1) whether the parties' written agreement providing an alternative arrangement to immediate withholding under subsection (a) of Section 20 [750 ILCS 28/20] continues to ensure payment of support; or

(2) the identity of the obligor.

It shall not be grounds for filing a petition that the obligor has made all payments due by the date of the petition.

(d) If the obligor files a petition contesting withholding within the 20-day period required under subsection (c), the Clerk of the Circuit Court shall notify the obligor and the obligee or public office, as appropriate, of the time and place of the hearing on the petition. The court shall hold the hearing pursuant to the provisions of Section 40 [750 ILCS 28/40].

(Source: P.A. 90-673, § 30.)

750 ILCS 28/32 Unpaid arrearage or delinquency after current support obligation terminates

Sec. 32. *Unpaid arrearage or delinquency after current support obligation terminates.* (a) When current support terminates on the date stated in the order for support, or because the child attains the age of majority or is otherwise emancipated, and the amount previously required to be paid for current support of that child automatically continues as an obligation for periodic payment toward satisfaction of unpaid arrearage or delinquency as provided for by law, the obligee or public office may prepare and serve upon the obligor's payor an income withholding notice that:

(1) contains the information required under subsection (c) of Section 20 [720 ILCS 28/20]; and

(2) contains the total amount of the unpaid arrearage or delinquency as of the date of the notice; and

(3) directs the payor to withhold, as a periodic payment toward satisfaction of the unpaid arrearage or delinquency, the total of:

(A) the periodic amount required to be paid as current support immediately prior to the date the current support obligation terminated under the order, or by the child becoming emancipated by age or otherwise, and

(B) any periodic amount previously required for satisfaction of the arrearage or delinquency.

(b) The income withholding notice and the obligor's copy of the income withholding notice shall be served as provided in subsection (g) of Section 20 [750 ILCS 28/20].

(c) The obligor may contest withholding commenced under this Section by filing a petition to contest withholding with the Clerk of the Circuit Court within 20 days after service of a copy of the income withholding notice on the obligor. The grounds for the petition to contest withholding shall be limited to:

(1) a dispute concerning the existence or amount of the unpaid arrearage or delinquency; or

(2) the accuracy of the periodic amount required to be withheld for payments of the unpaid arrearage or delinquency under the income withholding notice; or

(3) the identity of the obligor.

The Clerk of the Circuit Court shall notify the obligor and the obligee or public office of the time and place of the hearing on the petition to contest withholding. The court shall hold the hearing pursuant to the provisions of Section 40 [750 ILCS 20/40].

(Source: P.A. 93-1061, § 20.)

Effective Date.

Section 99 of P.A. 93-1061 made this section effective January 1, 2005.

750 ILCS 28/35 Duties of payor

Sec. 35. *Duties of payor.* (a) It shall be the duty of any payor who has been served with an income withholding notice to deduct and pay over income as provided in this Section. The payor shall deduct the amount designated in the income withholding notice, as supplemented by any notice provided pursuant to subsection (f) of Section 45 [750 ILCS 28/45], beginning no later than the next payment of income which is payable or creditable to the obligor that occurs 14 days following the date the income withholding notice was mailed, sent by facsimile or other electronic means, or placed for personal delivery to or service on the payor. The payor may combine all amounts withheld for the benefit of an obligee or public office into a single payment and transmit the payment with a listing of obligors from whom withholding has been effected. The payor shall pay the amount withheld to the State Disbursement Unit within 7 business days after the date the amount would (but for the duty to withhold income) have been paid or credited to the obligor. If the payor knowingly fails to withhold the amount designated in the income withholding notice or to pay any amount withheld to the State Disbursement Unit within 7 business days after the date the amount would have been paid or credited to the obligor, then the payor shall pay a penalty of $100 for each day that the amount designated in the income withholding notice (whether or not withheld by the payor) is not paid to the State Disbursement Unit after the period of 7 business days has expired. The failure of a payor, on more than one occasion, to pay amounts withheld to the State Disbursement Unit within 7 business days after the date the amount would have been paid or credited to the obligor creates a presumption that the payor knowingly failed to pay over the amounts. This penalty may be collected in a civil action which may be brought against the payor in favor of the obligee or public office. A finding of a payor's nonperformance within the time required under this Act must be documented by a certified mail return receipt showing the date the income withholding notice was served on the payor. For purposes of this Act, a withheld amount shall be considered paid by a payor on the date it is mailed by the payor, or on the date an electronic funds transfer of the amount has been initiated by the payor, or on the date delivery of the amount has been initiated by the payor. For each deduction, the payor shall provide the State Disbursement Unit, at the time of transmittal, with the date the amount would (but for the duty to withhold income) have been paid or credited to the obligor.

After June 30, 2000, every payor that has 250 or more employees shall use electronic funds transfer to pay all amounts withheld under this Section. During the year 2001 and during each year thereafter, every payor that has fewer than 250 employees and that withheld income under this Section pursuant to 10 or more income withholding notices during December of the preceding year shall use electronic funds transfer to pay all amounts withheld under this Section.

Upon receipt of an income withholding notice requiring that a minor child be named as a beneficiary of a health insurance plan available through an employer or labor union or trade union, the employer or labor union or trade union shall immediately enroll the minor child as a beneficiary in the health insurance plan designated by the income withholding notice. The employer shall withhold any required premiums and pay over any amounts so withheld and any additional amounts the employer pays to the insurance carrier in a timely manner. The employer or labor union or trade union shall mail to the obligee, within 15 days of enrollment or upon request, notice of the date of coverage, information on the dependent coverage plan, and all forms necessary to obtain reimbursement for covered health expenses, such as would be made available to a new employee. When an order for dependent coverage is in effect and the insurance coverage is terminated or changed for any reason, the employer or labor union or trade union shall notify the obligee within 10 days of the termination or change date along with notice of conversion privileges.

For withholding of income, the payor shall be entitled to receive a fee not to exceed $5 per month to be taken from the income to be paid to the obligor.

(b) Whenever the obligor is no longer receiving income from the payor, the payor shall return a copy of the income withholding notice to the obligee or public office and shall provide information for the purpose of enforcing this Act.

(c) Withholding of income under this Act shall be made without regard to any prior or subsequent garnishments, attachments, wage assignments, or any other claims of creditors. Withholding of income under this Act shall not be in excess of the maximum amounts permitted under the federal Consumer Credit Protection Act [15 U.S.C. § 1601 et seq]. Income available for withholding shall be applied first to the current support obligation, then to any premium required for employer, labor union, or trade union-related health insurance coverage ordered under the order for support, and then to payments required on past-due support obligations. If there is insufficient available income remaining to pay the full amount of the required health insurance premium after withholding of income for the current support obligation, then the remaining available income shall be applied to payments required on past-due support obligations. If the payor has been served with more than one income withholding notice pertaining to the same obligor, the payor shall allocate income available for withholding on a proportionate share basis, giving priority to current support payments. A payor who complies with an income withholding notice that is regular on its face shall not be subject to civil liability with respect to any individual, any agency, or any creditor of the obligor for conduct in compliance with the notice.

(d) No payor shall discharge, discipline, refuse to hire or otherwise penalize any obligor because of the duty to withhold income.

(Source: P.A. 90-673, § 35; 91-212, § 35; 91-677, § 22; 92-590, § 25; 93-294, § 5.)

Effect of Amendments.

The 1999 amendment by P.A. 91-212, effective July 20, 1999, substituted "State Disbursement Unit" for "obligee or public office" throughout the section.

The 1999 amendment by P.A. 91-677, effective January 5, 2000, added the second paragraph in subsection (a).

The 2002 amendment by P.A. 92-590, effective July 1, 2002, in subsection (c) in the first paragraph inserted the second and third sentences and deleted the former fourth sentence concerning allocation of available income for past due support payments.

The 2003 amendment by P.A. 93-294, effective January 1, 2004, in subsection (a), inserted "withhold the amount designated in the income withholding notice or to" preceding "pay any amount", inserted "then" preceding "the payor shall", deleted "withheld" preceding "amounts designated", and inserted "designated in the income withholding notice (whether or not withheld by the payor)".

CASE NOTES

Analysis

Constitutionality
Penalty for Failure to Pay

Constitutionality

In petitioner's suit against an employer for knowingly failing to pay child support from its employee's wages pursuant to § 35 of the Income Withholding for Support Act, 750 ILCS 28/35, § 35 was not unconstitutionally vague simply because a $100-per-day penalty was not referenced in the penalties provision of the Support Act (750 ILCS 28/50); the legislature chose to include the $100-per-day penalty provision in the section detailing the duties of an employer to withhold and pay over income upon being served with an income withholding notice (750 ILCS 28/35), and as the employer admitted, the language in § 35 was clear and unambiguous. In re Marriage of Chen, Ill. App. 3d , 290 Ill. Dec. 69, 820 N.E.2d 1136, 2004 Ill. App. LEXIS 1496 (2 Dist. 2004).

Penalty for Failure to Pay

In petitioner's suit against an employer for knowingly failing to pay child support from its employee's wages, the trial court's finding that the employer "knowingly" failed to pay over income on the employee's final three paychecks was not against the manifest weight of the evidence, as the trial court expressly found that the employer knowingly failed to pay over amounts withheld from the

Penalty for Failure to Pay (Cont'd)
employee's final three paychecks and the employer's controller acknowledged that at some point he became aware that the money being withheld from the employee's paychecks was not being paid over. In re Marriage of Chen, Ill. App. 3d , 290 Ill. Dec. 69, 820 N.E.2d 1136, 2004 Ill. App. LEXIS 1496 (2 Dist. 2004).

In petitioner's action against an employer for failure to pay child support from its employee's wages pursuant to § 35 of the Income Withholding for Support Act, 750 ILCS 28/35, four paychecks issued prior to service of a 2000 support order were not subject to the § 35 penalty provision. The employer did not receive notice of a $100-per-day penalty until it was served with the 2000 support order by certified mail, and any paychecks issued to its employee, the obligor, prior to that date were not subject to the penalty. In re Marriage of Chen, Ill. App. 3d , 290 Ill. Dec. 69, 820 N.E.2d 1136, 2004 Ill. App. LEXIS 1496 (2 Dist. 2004).

Penalties for late mailing of withheld child support should not have been imposed against employer that mailed checks on the Saturday following each pay period since weekends did not count in computing the seven-day mailing requirement, the checks should have been regarded as mailed when (according to uncontradicted evidence) they were put out for pick-up by the letter carrier, and mailing, not date of receipt by the enforcement unit, was the controlling date for purposes of determining compliance. Thomas v. Diener, 351 Ill. App. 3d 645, 286 Ill. Dec. 537, 814 N.E.2d 187, 2004 Ill. App. LEXIS 940 (4 Dist. 2004).

The statute requires the imposition of a separate penalty of $100 per day against an employer for each consecutive withholding from an employee's paycheck that is not timely forwarded to the recipient. Grams v. Autozone, Inc., 319 Ill. App. 3d 567, 253 Ill. Dec. 564, 745 N.E.2d 687, 2001 Ill. App. LEXIS 136 (3 Dist. 2001).

750 ILCS 28/40 Petitions to contest withholding or to modify, suspend, terminate, or correct income withholding notices

Sec. 40. *Petitions to contest withholding or to modify, suspend, terminate, or correct income withholding notices.* (a) When an obligor files a petition to contest withholding, the court, after due notice to all parties, shall hear the matter as soon as practicable and shall enter an order granting or denying relief, ordering service of an amended income withholding notice, where applicable, or otherwise resolving the matter.

The court shall deny the obligor's petition if the court finds that when the income withholding notice was mailed, sent by facsimile transmission or other electronic means, or placed for personal delivery to or service on the payor:

(1) a delinquency existed; or

(2) the parties' written agreement providing an alternative arrangement to immediate withholding under subsection (a) of Section 20 [750 ILCS 28/20] no longer ensured payment of support.

(b) At any time, an obligor, obligee, public office or Clerk of the Circuit Court may petition the court to:

(1) modify, suspend or terminate the income withholding notice because of a modification, suspension or termination of the underlying order for support; or

(2) modify the amount of income to be withheld to reflect payment in full or in part of the delinquency or arrearage by income withholding or otherwise; or

(3) suspend the income withholding notice because of inability to deliver income withheld to the obligee due to the obligee's failure to provide a mailing address or other means of delivery.

(c) At any time an obliger may petition the court to correct a term contained in an income withholding notice to conform to that stated in the underlying order for support for:

(1) the amount of current support;

(2) the amount of the arrearage;

(3) the periodic amount for payment of the arrearage; or

(4) the periodic amount for payment of the delinquency.

(d) The obliger, obligee or public office shall serve on the payor, in the manner provided for service of income withholding notices in subsection (g) of Section 20 [750 ILCS 28/20], a copy of any order entered pursuant to this Section that affects the duties of the payor.

(e) At any time, a public office or Clerk of the Circuit Court may serve a notice on the payor to:

(1) cease withholding of income for payment of current support for a child when the support obligation for that child has automatically ceased under the order for support through emancipation or otherwise; or

(2) cease withholding of income for payment of delinquency or arrearage when the delinquency or arrearage has been paid in full.

(f) The notice provided for under subsection (e) of this Section shall be served on the payor in the manner provided for service of income withholding notices in subsection (g) of Section 20 [750 ILCS 28/20], and a copy shall be provided to the obliger and the obligee.

(g) The income withholding notice shall continue to be binding upon the payor until service of an amended income withholding notice or any order of the court or notice entered or provided for under this Section.

(Source: P.A. 90-673, § 40.)

750 ILCS 28/45 Additional duties

Sec. 45. *Additional duties.* (a) An obligee who is receiving income withholding payments under this Act shall notify the State Disbursement Unit and the Clerk of the Circuit Court of any change of address within 7 days of such change.

(b) An obligee who is a recipient of public aid shall send a copy of any income withholding notice served by the obligee to the Division of Child Support Enforcement of the Illinois Department of Public Aid.

(c) Each obligor shall notify the obligee, the public office, and the Clerk of the Circuit Court of any change of address within 7 days.

(d) An obligor whose income is being withheld pursuant to this Act shall notify the obligee, the public office, and the Clerk of the Circuit Court of any new payor, within 7 days.

(e) (Blank.)

(f) The obligee or public office shall provide notice to the payor and Clerk of the Circuit Court of any other support payment made, including but not limited to, a set-off under federal and State law or partial payment of the delinquency or arrearage, or both.

(g) The State Disbursement Unit shall maintain complete, accurate, and clear records of all income withholding payments and their disbursements. Certified copies of payment records maintained by the State Disbursement Unit, a public office, or the Clerk of the Circuit Court shall, without further proof, be admitted into evidence in any legal proceedings under this Act.

(h) The Illinois Department of Public Aid shall design suggested legal forms for proceeding under this Act and shall make available to the courts such forms and informational materials which describe the procedures and remedies set forth herein for distribution to all parties in support actions.

(i) At the time of transmitting each support payment, the State Disbursement Unit shall provide the obligee or public office, as appropriate, with any information furnished by the payor as to the date the amount would (but for the duty to withhold income) have been paid or credited to the obliger.

(Source: P.A. 90-673, § 45; impl. am. 90-790; 91-212, § 35; 91-357, § 260.)

Effect of Amendments.

The 1999 amendment by P.A. 91-212, effective July 20, 1999, rewrote the section to the extent that a detailed comparison would be impracticable.

The 1999 amendment by P.A. 91-357, effective July 29, 1999, deleted "or who has been served with a notice of delinquency" following "is being withheld" in subsection (d).

Although the amendments made to this section by P.A. 91-212, § 35 and P.A. 91-357, § 260 did not take into account the amendments made by the other, the amendments have been combined into a single version by the publisher.

750 ILCS 28/50 Penalties

Sec. 50. *Penalties.* (a) Where a payor wilfully fails to withhold or pay over income pursuant to a properly served income withholding notice, or wilfully discharges, disciplines, refuses to hire or otherwise penalizes an obligor as prohibited by Section 40 [750 ILCS 28/40], or otherwise fails to comply with any duties imposed by this Act, the obligee, public office or obligor, as appropriate, may file a complaint with the court against the payor. The Clerk of the Circuit Court shall notify the obligee or public office, as appropriate, and the obligor and payor of the time and place of the hearing on the complaint. The court shall resolve any factual dispute including, but not limited to, a denial that the payor is paying or has paid income to the obligor. Upon a finding in favor of the complaining party, the court:

(1) shall enter judgment and direct the enforcement thereof for the total amount that the payor wilfully failed to withhold or pay over; and

(2) may order employment or reinstatement of or restitution to the obligor, or both, where the obligor has been discharged, disciplined, denied employment or otherwise penalized by the payor and may impose a fine upon the payor not to exceed $200.

(b) Any obligee, public office or obligor who wilfully initiates a false proceeding under this Act or who wilfully fails to comply with the requirements of this Act shall be punished as in cases of contempt of court.

(Source: P.A. 90-673, § 50.)

CASE NOTES

Improper Withholding Beyond Termination Date

Trial court erred in dismissing an employee's claims for negligence, breach of contract, conversion, and punitive damages against his employer for improperly withholding part of his wages after the termination date of a withholding order issued under the Illinois Income Withholding for Support Act, 750 ILCS 28/1 et seq., because the Act was not applicable to the situation, and, thus, did not afford a proper basis to dismiss the employee's claims; furthermore, the employee's punitive damages claim was sufficiently supported by the negligence and conversion claims. Giles v. GMC, 344 Ill. App. 3d 1191, 280 Ill. Dec. 607, 802 N.E.2d 858, 2004 Ill. App. LEXIS 59 (5 Dist. 2004).

750 ILCS 28/55 Alternative procedures for service of an income withholding notice

Sec. 55. *Alternative procedures for service of an income withholding notice.* (a) The procedures of this Section may be used in any matter to serve an income withholding notice on a payor if:

(1) for any reason the most recent order for support entered does not contain the income withholding provisions required under Section 20 [750 ILCS 28/20], irrespective of whether a separate order for withholding was entered prior to July 1, 1997; and

(2) the obligor has accrued a delinquency after entry of the most recent order for support.

(b) The obligee or public office shall prepare and serve the income withholding notice in accordance with the provisions of Section 25 [750 ILCS 28/25], except that the notice shall contain a periodic amount for payment of the delinquency equal to 20% of the total of the current support amount and the amount to be paid periodically for payment of any arrearage stated in the most recent order for support.

(c) If the obligor requests in writing that income withholding become effective prior to the obligor accruing a delinquency under the most recent order for support, the obligee or public office may prepare and serve an income withholding notice on the payor as provided in Section 20 [750 ILCS 28/20]. In addition to filing proofs of service of the income withholding notice on the payor and the obligor, the obligee or public office shall file a copy of the obligor's written request for income withholding with the Clerk of the Circuit Court.

(d) All other provisions of this Act shall be applicable with respect to the provisions of this Section 55 [750 ILCS 28/55].

(Source: P.A. 90-673, § 55.)

750 ILCS 28/60 Remedies in addition to other laws

Sec. 60. *Remedies in addition to other laws.* (a) The rights, remedies, duties and penalties created by this Act are in addition to and not in substitution for any other rights, remedies, duties and penalties created by any other law.

(b) Nothing in this Act shall be construed as invalidating any assignment of wages or benefits executed prior to January 1, 1984 (or July 1, 1985 with respect to invalidity under the Illinois Parentage Act of 1984 [750 ILCS 45/1 et seq.]) or any order for withholding served prior to July 1, 1997.
(Source: P.A. 90-673, § 60.)

CASE NOTES

Improper Withholding Beyond Termination Date
Trial court erred in dismissing an employee's claims for negligence, breach of contract, conversion, and punitive damages against his employer for improperly withholding part of his wages after the termination date of a withholding order issued under the Illinois Income Withholding for Support Act, 750 ILCS 28/1 et seq., because the Act was not applicable to the situation, and, thus, did not afford a proper basis to dismiss the employee's claims; furthermore, the employee's punitive damages claim was sufficiently supported by the negligence and conversion claims. Giles v. GMC, 344 Ill. App. 3d 1191, 280 Ill. Dec. 607, 802 N.E.2d 858, 2004 Ill. App. LEXIS 59 (5 Dist. 2004).

750 ILCS 28/905 through 750 ILCS 28/930 [Not Set Out]

Note.
These sections, as found in P.A. 90-673, §§ 905 to 930, contained amendatory provisions.

750 ILCS 28/999 Effective date

Sec. 999. *Effective date.* This Act takes effect January 1, 1999.
(Source: P.A. 90-673, § 99; 91-357, § 260.)

Effect of Amendments.
The 1999 amendment by P.A. 91-357, effective July 29, 1999, renumbered the section.

Emancipation of Mature Minors Act

750 ILCS 30/1 Short title

Sec. 1. *Short title.* This Act may be cited as the Emancipation of Minors Act.
(Source: P.A. 81-833; 93-105, § 10.)

Derivation.
Title: An Act relating to the emancipation of certain minors.
Cite: 750 ILCS 30/1 et seq.
Source: P.A. 81-833.
Date: Approved September 19, 1979.

Note.
This section was Ill.Rev.Stat., Ch. 40, para. 2201.

Effect of Amendments.
The 2003 amendment by P.A. 93-105, effective July 8, 2003, deleted "shall be know and" following "This Act" and substituted 'Emancipation of Minors Act" for "Emancipation of Mature Minors Act".

CASE NOTES

Analysis

Refusal of Medical Treatment
—Legislative Intent
—Partial Emancipation

Refusal of Medical Treatment

—Legislative Intent
This Act, when read together in a complementary fashion with the Consent by Minors to Medical Procedures Act (410 ILCS 210/1 et seq.), indicates that the legislature did not intend that there be an absolute 18 year old age barrier prohibiting minors from consenting to medical treatment. People v. E.G., 133 Ill. 2d 98, 139 Ill. Dec. 810, 549 N.E.2d 322 (1989).

—Partial Emancipation
A Jehovah's Witness, found to be mature and to have made the decision to refuse blood transfusions independently, could not be denied her constitutional right to the free exercise of religion solely because of her minority; upon finding that the minor was medically neglected, she should have been partially emancipated and granted the right to accept or refuse transfusions based on her religious belief. People v. E.G., 161 Ill. App. 3d 765, 113 Ill. Dec. 477, 515 N.E.2d 286 (1 Dist. 1987).

LEGAL PERIODICALS

For comment, "Minors, Medical Treatment, and Interspousal Disagreement: Should Solomon Split the Child?" see 41 De Paul L. Rev. 841 (1992).
For note, "In re E.G.: The Right of Mature Minors in Illinois to Refuse Lifesaving Medical Treatment," see 21 Loy. U. Chi. L.J. 1199 (1989-90).
For article, "New Laws Okay Jail and Work for Juveniles," see 68 Ill. B.J. 514 (1980).

750 ILCS 30/2 Purpose and policy

Sec. 2. *Purpose and policy.* The purpose of this Act is to provide a means by which a mature minor who has demonstrated the ability and capacity to manage his own affairs and to live wholly or partially independent of his parents or guardian, may obtain the legal status of an emancipated person with power to enter into valid legal contracts. This Act is also intended (i) to provide a means by which a homeless minor who is seeking assistance may have the authority to consent, independent of his or her parents or guardian, to receive shelter, housing, and services provided by a licensed agency that has the ability and willingness to serve the homeless minor and (ii) to do so without requiring the delay or difficulty of first holding a hearing.

This Act is not intended to interfere with the integrity of the family or the rights of parents and their children. No order of complete or partial emancipation may be entered under this Act if there is any objection by the minor, his parents or guardian. No petition may be filed for the partial emancipation of a homeless minor unless appropriate attempts have been made to reunify the homeless minor with

his or her family through the services of a Comprehensive Community Based Youth Services Agency. This Act does not limit or exclude any other means either in statute or case law by which a minor may become emancipated.
(Source: P.A. 81-833; 93-105, § 10.)

Note.
This section was Ill.Rev.Stat., Ch. 40, para. 2202.

Effect of Amendments.
The 2003 amendment by P.A. 93-105, effective July 8, 2003, added the second sentences in both the first and second paragraphs.

750 ILCS 30/3 Definitions

Sec. 3. *Definitions.* Terms used in this Act, unless the context otherwise requires, have the meanings ascribed to them in Sections 3-1 through 3-5 [750 ILCS 30/3-1 through 750 ILCS 30/3-5].
(Source: P.A. 81-833.)

Note.
This section was Ill.Rev.Stat., Ch. 40, para. 2203.

750 ILCS 30/3-1 Minor

Sec. 3-1. *Minor.* "Minor" means a person 16 years of age or over, and under the age of 18 years, subject to this Act.
(Source: P.A. 81-833.)

Note.
This section was Ill.Rev.Stat., Ch. 40, para. 2203-1.

750 ILCS 30/3-2 Mature minor

Sec. 3-2. *Mature minor.* "Mature minor" means a person 16 years of age or over and under the age of 18 years who has demonstrated the ability and capacity to manage his own affairs and to live wholly or partially independent of his parents or guardian.
(Source: P.A. 81-833.)

Note.
This section was Ill.Rev.Stat., Ch. 40, para. 2203-2.

750 ILCS 30/3-2.5 Homeless minor

Sec. 3-2.5. *Homeless minor.* "Homeless minor" means a person at least 16 years of age but less than 18 years of age who lacks a regular, fixed, and adequate place to live and who desires to participate in a youth transitional housing program. The term includes, but is not limited to, a minor who is sharing the dwelling of another or living in a temporary shelter or who is unable or unwilling to return to the residence of a parent. The term does not include a minor in the custody or under the guardianship of the Department of Children and Family Services. No child may be terminated from the custody or guardianship of the Department of Children and Family Services for the purpose of obtaining emancipation as a homeless minor.
(Source: P.A. 93-105, § 10.)

Effective Date.
Section 99 of P.A. 93-105 made this section effective upon becoming law. The Act was approved July 8, 2003.

750 ILCS 30/3-2.10 Youth transitional housing program

Sec. 3-2.10. *Youth transitional housing program.* "Youth transitional housing program" means a program licensed by the Department of Children and Family Services to provide services, shelter, or housing to a minor.
(Source: P.A. 93-105, § 10.)

Effective Date.
Section 99 of P.A. 93-105 made this section effective upon becoming law. The Act was approved July 8, 2003.

750 ILCS 30/3-3 Parents

Sec. 3-3. *Parents.* "Parent" means the father or mother of a legitimate or illegitimate child, and includes any adoptive parent. It does not include a parent whose rights in respect to the minor have been terminated in any manner provided by law.
(Source: P.A. 81-833.)

Note.
This section was Ill.Rev.Stat., Ch. 40, para. 2203-3.

750 ILCS 30/3-4 Guardian

Sec. 3-4. *Guardian.* "Guardian" means any person, association or agency appointed guardian of the person of the minor under the Juvenile Court Act, the Juvenile Court Act of 1987 [705 ILCS 405/1-1 et seq.], the "Probate Act of 1975" [755 ILCS 5/1-1 et seq.], or any other statute or court order.
(Source: P.A. 85-1440.)

Note.
This section was Ill.Rev.Stat., Ch. 40, para. 2203-4.
The Juvenile Court Act, referred to above, has been repealed. See now the Juvenile Court Act of 1987, 705 ILCS 405/1-1 et seq.

750 ILCS 30/3-5 Petition

Sec. 3-5. *Petition.* "Petition" means the petition provided for in Section 7 of this Act [750 ILCS 30/7], or any other petition filed under the Juvenile Court Act or the Juvenile Court Act of 1987 [705 ILCS 405/1-1 et seq.], seeking the emancipation of a minor in accordance with the provisions of this Act.
(Source: P.A. 85-1209.)

Note.
This section was Ill.Rev.Stat., Ch. 40, para. 2203-5.
The Juvenile Court Act referred to above, was repealed. See now the Juvenile Court Act of 1987, 705 ILCS 405/1-1 et seq.

750 ILCS 30/4 Jurisdiction

Sec. 4. *Jurisdiction.* The circuit court in the county where the minor resides, is found, owns property, or in which a court action affecting the interests of the

minor is pending, may, upon the filing of a petition on behalf of the minor by his next friend, parent or guardian and after any hearing or notice to all persons as set forth in Sections 7, 8, and 9 of this Act [750 ILCS 30/7, 750 ILCS 30/8 and 750 ILCS 30/9], enter a finding that the minor is a mature minor or a homeless minor as defined in this Act and order complete or partial emancipation of the minor. The court in its order for partial emancipation may specifically limit the rights and responsibilities of the minor seeking emancipation. In the case of a homeless minor, the court shall restrict the order of emancipation to allowing the minor to consent to the receipt of transitional services and shelter or housing from a specified youth transitional program and its referral agencies only.
(Source: P.A. 81-833; 93-105, § 10.)

Note.
This section was Ill.Rev.Stat., Ch. 40, para. 2204.

Effect of Amendments.
The 2003 amendment by P.A. 93-105, effective July 8, 2003, in the first sentence, substituted "any hearing or notice" for "a hearing on notice," inserted "9" and inserted "or a homeless minor" and added the last sentence.

750 ILCS 30/5 Rights and responsibilities of an emancipated minor

Sec. 5. *Rights and responsibilities of an emancipated minor.* (a) A mature minor ordered emancipated under this Act shall have the right to enter into valid legal contracts, and shall have such other rights and responsibilities as the court may order that are not inconsistent with the specific age requirements of the State or federal constitution or any State or federal law.

(b) A mature minor or homeless minor who is partially emancipated under this Act shall have only those rights and responsibilities specified in the order of the court.
(Source: P.A. 81-833; 93-105, § 10.)

Note.
This section was Ill.Rev.Stat., Ch. 40, para. 2205.

Effect of Amendments.
The 2003 amendment by P.A. 93-105, effective July 8, 2003, inserted "or homeless minor" in subsection (b).

CASE NOTES

Earnings
The right of parents to emancipate their child, and relinquish their right to his wages and earnings during the child's minority, is recognized; this may be done by a written instrument or implied by acquiescence on the part of the parent in allowing the child to receive his wages and earnings, or from conduct inconsistent with his claim for the further services of the child. Romine v. City of Watseka, 341 Ill. App. 370, 91 N.E.2d 76 (2 Dist. 1950).

Where a minor has been emancipated, the parent will be barred from his right to claim the child's earnings, and they may be sued for and recovered in a suit by the minor's guardian or next friend, and in such a suit the minor does not sue as assignee of his parents' right of action, as they have lost that right by emancipation, but the minor sues for wages and earnings due and owing him in his own right. Romine v. City of Watseka, 341 Ill. App. 370, 91 N.E.2d 76 (2 Dist. 1950).

750 ILCS 30/6 Duration of emancipation and discharge of proceedings

Sec. 6. *Duration of emancipation and discharge of proceedings.* The court shall retain continuing jurisdiction over the proceedings until the emancipated minor reaches age 18, and may modify or terminate its previous emancipation orders. However, any subsequent modification or termination of a previous order shall be effective only prospectively and shall not affect any rights, duties, obligations or causes of action existing prior to the modification or termination of any order under this Act.
(Source: P.A. 81-833.)

Note.
This section was Ill.Rev.Stat., Ch. 40, para. 2206.

750 ILCS 30/7 Petition

Sec. 7. *Petition.* The petition for emancipation shall be verified and shall set forth: (1) the age of the minor; (2) that the minor is a resident of Illinois at the time of the filing of the petition, or owns real estate in Illinois, or has an interest or is a party in any case pending in Illinois; (3) the cause for which the minor seeks to obtain partial or complete emancipation; (4) the names of the minor's parents, and the address, if living; (5) the names and addresses of any guardians or custodians appointed for the minor; (6) that the minor is (i) a mature minor who has demonstrated the ability and capacity to manage his own affairs or (ii) a homeless minor who is located in this State; and (7) that the minor has lived wholly or partially independent of his parents or guardian. If the minor seeks emancipation as a homeless minor, the petition shall also set forth the name of the youth transitional housing program that is willing and able to provide services and shelter or housing to the minor, the address of the program, and the name and phone number of the contact person at the program. The petition shall also briefly assert the reason that the services and shelter or housing to be offered are appropriate and necessary for the well-being of the homeless minor.
(Source: P.A. 81-833; 93-105, § 10.)

Note.
This section was Ill.Rev.Stat., Ch. 40, para. 2207.

Effect of Amendments.
The 2003 amendment by P.A. 93-105, effective July 8, 2003, in the first sentence, added the (i) designation and added (ii) and added the second sentence.

750 ILCS 30/8 Notice

Sec. 8. *Notice.* All persons named in the petition shall be given written notice within 21 days after the filing of the petition for emancipation. Those persons shall have a right to be present if a hearing is sought or scheduled and to be represented by counsel.

All notices shall be served on persons named in the petition by personal service or by "certified mail, return receipt requested, addressee only". If personal service cannot be made in accordance with the provisions of this Act, substitute service or service by publication shall be made in accordance with the Civil Practice Law [735 ILCS 5/2-101 et seq.].
(Source: P.A. 83-1539; 93-105, § 10.)

Note.
This section was Ill.Rev.Stat., Ch. 40, para. 2208.

Effect of Amendments.
The 2003 amendment by P.A. 93-105, effective July 8, 2003, substituted the present first paragraph for the former which read "All persons named in the petition shall be given written notice 21 days prior to the hearing and shall have a right to be present and be represented by counsel".

750 ILCS 30/9 Hearing on petition

Sec. 9. *Hearing on petition.* (a) Mature minor. Before proceeding to a hearing on the petition for emancipation of a mature minor the court shall advise all persons present of the nature of the proceedings, and their rights and responsibilities if an order of emancipation should be entered.

If, after the hearing, the court determines that the minor is a mature minor who is of sound mind and has the capacity and maturity to manage his own affairs including his finances, and that the best interests of the minor and his family will be promoted by declaring the minor an emancipated minor, the court shall enter a finding that the minor is an emancipated minor within the meaning of this Act, or that the mature minor is partially emancipated with such limitations as the court by order deems appropriate. No order of complete or partial emancipation may be entered under this Act if there is any objection by the minor, his parents or guardian.

(b) Homeless minor. Upon the verified petition of a homeless minor, the court shall immediately grant partial emancipation for the sole purpose of allowing the homeless minor to consent to the receipt of services and shelter or housing provided by the youth transitional housing program named in the petition and to other services that the youth transitional housing program may arrange by referral. The court may require that a youth transitional housing program employee appear before the court at the time of the filing of the petition and may inquire into the facts asserted in the petition. No other hearing shall be scheduled in the case of a petition affecting a homeless minor, unless, after notice, a parent or guardian requests such a hearing. If such a hearing is requested, then the homeless minor must be present at the hearing. After the granting of partial emancipation to a homeless youth, if the youth transitional housing program determines that its facility and services are no longer appropriate for the minor or that another program is more appropriate for the minor, the program shall notify the court and the court, after a hearing, may modify its order.
(Source: P.A. 81-833; 93-105, § 10.)

Note.
This section was Ill.Rev.Stat., Ch. 40, para. 2209.

Effect of Amendments.
The 2003 amendment by P.A. 93-105, effective July 8, 2003, added "on petition" in the section heading; in subsection (a) added the subsection (a) designation and the heading and inserted "for emancipation of a mature minor"; and added subsection (b).

750 ILCS 30/10 Joinder, Juvenile Court Proceedings

Sec. 10. *Joinder, Juvenile Court Proceedings.* The petition for declaration of emancipation may, with leave of the court, be joined with any pending litigation affecting the interests of the minor including a petition filed under the Juvenile Court Act or the Juvenile Court Act of 1987 [705 ILCS 405/1-1 et seq.].

If any minor seeking emancipation as a mature minor is a ward of the court under the Juvenile Court Act or the Juvenile Court Act of 1987 [705 ILCS 405/1-1 et seq.] at the time of the filing of the petition for emancipation, the petition shall be set for hearing in the juvenile court.
(Source: P.A. 85-1209; 93-105, § 10.)

Note.
This section was Ill.Rev.Stat., Ch. 40, para. 2210.
The Juvenile Court Act, referred to above, was repealed. See now the Juvenile Court Act of 1987, 705 ILCS 405/1-1 et seq.

Effect of Amendments.
The 2003 amendment by P.A. 93-105, effective July 8, 2003, inserted "as a mature minor" in the second paragraph.

750 ILCS 30/11 Appeal

Sec. 11. *Appeal.* Any judgment or order allowing or denying a complete or partial emancipation is a final order for purposes of appeal.
(Source: P.A. 81-833.)

Note.
This section was Ill.Rev.Stat., Ch. 40, para. 2211.

Uniform Child Custody Jurisdiction Act

750 ILCS 35/1 through 750 ILCS 35/26: Repealed by P.A. 93-108, § 403, effective January 1, 2004.

Uniform Child-Custody Jurisdiction and Enforcement Act

ARTICLE 1.

GENERAL PROVISIONS

750 ILCS 36/101 Short Title

Sec. 101. *Short Title.* This Act may be cited as the Uniform Child-Custody Jurisdiction and Enforcement Act.
(Source: P.A. 93-108, § 101.)

Note.
750 ILCS 36/401 of this Act contains an application and construction provision, and 750 ILCS 36/402 contains a severability clause.

Effective Date.
Section 403 of P.A. 93-108 made this Act effective January 1, 2004.

CASE NOTES

Analysis

In General
Applicability
—Support Orders
Federal Preemption
Removal from State
Split Residence
Waiver

In General
This Act applies to matters of child custody and visitation and does not contemplate determinations relating to child support or any other monetary obligation. *(Decided under former Uniform Child Custody Jurisdiction Act, repealed 750 ILCS 35/1 et seq.)* In re Buchanio, 262 Ill. App. 3d 910, 200 Ill. Dec. 641, 635 N.E.2d 980 (1 Dist.), appeal denied, 157 Ill. 2d 496, 205 Ill. Dec. 157, 642 N.E.2d 1274 (1994).

The purposes of this Act are primarily to avoid jurisdictional competition and conflicts with other states, to protect the best interests of the child, and to discourage forum shopping. *(Decided under former Uniform Child Custody Jurisdiction Act, repealed 750 ILCS 35/1 et seq.)* In re Rizza, 237 Ill. App. 3d 83, 177 Ill. Dec. 353, 603 N.E.2d 134 (2 Dist. 1992).

The principal purposes of this Act are to avoid conflicts with courts of other states, to protect the best interests of the child, and to discourage forum shopping. *(Decided under former Uniform Child Custody Jurisdiction Act, repealed 750 ILCS 35/1 et seq.)* In re Mauro, 187 Ill. App. 3d 794, 135 Ill. Dec. 288, 543 N.E.2d 856 (1 Dist. 1989).

The purposes of this Act clearly reflect the concern that an interstate custody dispute be resolved in the one forum with the closest connection to the child, the family of the child, and the evidence required to make an informed decision. *(Decided under former Uniform Child Custody Jurisdiction Act, repealed 750 ILCS 35/1 et seq.)* Bellefont v. Wright, 179 Ill. App. 3d 1036, 129 Ill. Dec. 390, 536 N.E.2d 74 (4 Dist. 1989).

Adjudication of interstate and international custody issues involved in child custody proceedings before courts in the State of Illinois is governed by this Act. *(Decided under former Uniform Child Custody Jurisdiction Act, repealed 750 ILCS 35/1 et seq.)* In re Silvestri-Gagliardoni, 186 Ill. App. 3d 46, 134 Ill. Dec. 106, 542 N.E.2d 106 (1 Dist. 1989).

This Act was aimed at resolving the conflicts arising out of interstate custody disputes: children not returned after out of state visits, conflicting custody awards in two states, child abductions and concealments by fugitive parents, and denials of visitation rights in a distant state. *(Decided under former Uniform Child Custody Jurisdiction Act, repealed 750 ILCS 35/1 et seq.)* Bellefont v. Wright, 179 Ill. App. 3d 1036, 129 Ill. Dec. 390, 536 N.E.2d 74 (4 Dist. 1989).

One of the purposes of this Act is to assure that litigation concerning the custody of a child takes place in the state in which the child and his or her family have the closest connection; another is to deter abductions and other unilateral removals of children undertaken to obtain custody awards. *(Decided under former Uniform Child Custody Jurisdiction Act, repealed 750 ILCS 35/1 et seq.)* In re Thompson, 96 Ill. 2d 67, 70 Ill. Dec. 214, 449 N.E.2d 88 (1983).

Applicability
Illinois courts did not have subject matter jurisdiction over an unborn child in the context of a future child custody matter or other marital dissolution issue, and the home state of the child at issue was determined by the child's birth in Texas. In re Marriage of Skelton, 352 Ill. App. 3d 348, 287 Ill. Dec. 373, 815 N.E.2d 1176, 2004 Ill. App. LEXIS 1057 (5 Dist. 2004).

—Support Orders
This Act has been found applicable for modifying custody and visitation orders, but not applicable to modify support orders pursuant to its provisions. *(Decided under former Uniform Child Custody Jurisdiction Act, repealed 750 ILCS 35/1 et seq.)* In re Schuham, 120 Ill. App. 3d 339, 76 Ill. Dec. 159, 458 N.E.2d 559 (1 Dist. 1983).

Federal Preemption
The federal Parental Kidnapping Prevention Act of 1980 (28 U.S.C. § 1738A (1994)) preempts the Uniform Child Custody Jurisdiction Act in cases of conflict. *(Decided under former Uniform Child Custody Jurisdiction Act, repealed 750 ILCS 35/1 et seq.)* In re Wiseman, 316 Ill. App. 3d 631, 737 N.E.2d 325, 2000 Ill. App. LEXIS 823 (2 Dist. 2000).

Removal from State
Where child was removed from Illinois to Texas without the trial court's knowledge or consent, to transfer custody proceedings to Texas would condone behavior contrary to the purposes of this act; one of act's stated purposes is to deter unilateral removals of children. *(Decided under former Uniform Child Custody Jurisdiction Act, repealed 750 ILCS 35/1 et seq.)* In re Breyley, 247 Ill. App. 3d 486, 187 Ill. Dec. 215, 617 N.E.2d 423 (3 Dist. 1993).

If a court lost its jurisdiction because respondent removed herself and the child from this state without the court's permission, the respondent would subvert the clear intention of the General Assembly as well as profit from her own misbehavior. *(Decided under former Uniform Child Custody Jurisdiction Act, repealed 750 ILCS 35/1 et seq.)* In re Godwin, 104 Ill. App. 3d 790, 60 Ill. Dec. 513, 433 N.E.2d 310 (3 Dist. 1982).

Split Residence
Where Illinois would not have jurisdiction to determine the custody of the youngest child of three who remained in California, the purposes of this Act would be better served by declining jurisdiction in Illinois, so that custody of all three children could be determined at the same time in California. *(Decided under former Uniform Child Custody Jurisdiction Act, repealed 750 ILCS 35/1 et seq.)* In re Miche, 131 Ill. App. 3d 1029, 87 Ill. Dec. 72, 476 N.E.2d 774 (2 Dist. 1985).

Waiver
Party may object to subject matter jurisdiction without waiving objections to personal jurisdiction. *(Decided under former Uniform Child Custody Jurisdiction Act, repealed 750 ILCS 35/1 et seq.)* In re Stack, 281 Ill. App. 3d 423, 217 Ill. Dec. 290, 666 N.E.2d 1228 (2 Dist. 1996), appeal denied, 168 Ill. 2d 626, 219 Ill. Dec. 577, 671 N.E.2d 744 (1996).

LEGAL PERIODICALS

For article, "Survey of Illinois Law [1988-89]—Family Law," see 14 S. Ill. U.L.J. 1007 (1990).

For article, "Family Law: 1985-86 Survey," see 11 S. Ill. U.L.J 741 (1987).

For article, "Illinois Child Custody Law: An Overview," see 76 Ill. B.J. 732 (1987).

For comment, "Prohibiting Payments to Surrogate Mothers: Love's Labor Lost and the Constitutional Right of Privacy," see 20 J. Marshall L. Rev. 715 (1987).

For comment, "Tortious Interference with Visitation Rights: A New and Important Remedy for Non-Custodial Parents," see 20 J. Marshall L. Rev. 307 (1986).

For article, "Uniform Child Custody Litigation in Light of Siegel and New Legislation," see 65 Chi. B. Rec. 72 (1983).

For article, "The Continuing Jurisdiction Dilemma in Interstate Child Custody Disputes," see 70 Ill. B.J. 304 (1982).

For article, "Law, Social Change and Child Snatching," see 14 Loy. U. Chi. L.J. 677 (1982-83).

RESEARCH REFERENCES

What types of proceedings or determinations are governed by the Uniform Child Custody Jurisdiction Act (UCCJA) or the Parental Kidnapping Prevention Act (PKPA). 78 ALR4th 1028.

Applicability of Uniform Child Custody Jurisdiction Act (UCCJA) to temporary custody orders. 81 ALR4th 1101.

Child custody: when does state that issued previous custody determination have continuing jurisdiction under Uniform Child Custody Jurisdiction Act (UCCJA) or Parental Kidnapping Prevention Act (PKPA), 28 USCS § 1738A. 83 ALR4th 742.

Significant connection jurisdiction of court under section 3(a)(2) of the Uniform Child Custody Jurisdiction Act (UCCJA) and the Parental Kidnapping Prevention Act (PKPA), 28 USCS § 1738A(c)(2)(B). 5 ALR5th 550.

Abandonment and emergency jurisdiction of court under section 3(a)(3) of the Uniform Child Custody Jurisdiction Act (UCCJA) and the Parental Kidnapping Prevention Act (PKPA), 28 USCS § 1738A(c)(2)(C). 5 ALR5th 788.

Parties' misconduct as ground for declining jurisdiction under § 8 of the Uniform Child Custody Jurisdiction Act (UCCJA). 16 ALR5th 650.

Recognition and enforcement of out-of-state custody decree under § 13 of the Uniform Child Custody Jurisdiction Act (UCCJA) or the Parental Kidnapping Prevention Act (PKPA), 28 USCS § 1738A(a). 40 ALR5th 227.

Abandonment jurisdiction of court under §§ 3(a)(3)(i) and 14(a) of Uniform Child Custody Jurisdiction Act and Parental Kidnapping Prevention Act, 28 U.S.C.A. §§ 1738A(c)(2)(C)(i) and 1738A(f), notwithstanding existence of prior valid custody decree rendered by second state. 78 ALR5th 465.

Appealability of interlocutory or pendente lite order for temporary child custody. 82 ALR5th 389.

Construction and operation of Uniform Child Custody Jurisdiction and Enforcement Act. 100 ALR5th 1.

750 ILCS 36/102 Definitions

Sec. 102. *Definitions.* In this Act:

(1) "Abandoned" means left without provision for reasonable and necessary care or supervision.

(2) "Child" means an individual who has not attained 18 years of age.

(3) "Child-custody determination" means a judgment, decree, or other order of a court providing for the legal custody, physical custody, or visitation with respect to a child. The term includes a permanent, temporary, initial, and modification order. The term does not include an order relating to child support or other monetary obligation of an individual.

(4) "Child-custody proceeding" means a proceeding in which legal custody, physical custody, or visitation with respect to a child is an issue. The term includes a proceeding for divorce, separation, neglect, abuse, dependency, guardianship, paternity, termination of parental rights, and protection from domestic violence, in which the issue may appear. The term does not include a proceeding involving juvenile delinquency, contractual emancipation, or enforcement under Article 3.

(5) "Commencement" means the filing of the first pleading in a proceeding.

(6) "Court" means an entity authorized under the law of a state to establish, enforce, or modify a child-custody determination.

(7) "Home state" means the state in which a child lived with a parent or a person acting as a parent for at least six consecutive months immediately before the commencement of a child-custody proceeding. In the case of a child less than six months of age, the term means the state in which the child lived from birth with any of the persons mentioned. A period of temporary absence of any of the mentioned persons is part of the period.

(8) "Initial determination" means the first child-custody determination concerning a particular child.

(9) "Issuing court" means the court that makes a child-custody determination for which enforcement is sought under this Act.

(10) "Issuing state" means the state in which a child-custody determination is made.

(11) "Modification" means a child-custody determination that changes, replaces, supersedes, or is otherwise made after a previous determination concerning the same child, whether or not it is made by the court that made the previous determination.

(12) "Person" means an individual, corporation, business trust, estate, trust, partnership, limited liability company, association, joint venture, government; governmental subdivision, agency, or instrumentality; public corporation; or any other legal or commercial entity.

(13) "Person acting as a parent" means a person, other than a parent, who:

(A) has physical custody of the child or has had physical custody for a period of six consecutive months, including any temporary absence, within one year immediately before the commencement of a child-custody proceeding; and

(B) has been awarded legal custody by a court or claims a right to legal custody under the law of this State.

(14) "Physical custody" means the physical care and supervision of a child.

(15) "State" means a state of the United States, the District of Columbia, Puerto Rico, the United States Virgin Islands, or any territory or insular possession subject to the jurisdiction of the United States.

(16) "Tribe" means an Indian tribe or band, or Alaskan Native village, which is recognized by federal law or formally acknowledged by a state.

(17) "Warrant" means an order issued by a court authorizing law enforcement officers to take physical custody of a child.

(Source: P.A. 93-108, § 102.)

CASE NOTES

Analysis

Closer Connections
Deprivation of Custody
—In General
—Not Shown
Illinois as Home State
Illustrative Cases
Jurisdiction
—Foreign Court
Inadequate Parenting
Reconciliation
Temporary Absences
Temporary Loss of Possession and Control

Closer Connections

Although Illinois may have been the home state of the child, because the petitioner stated the child had lived in Illinois with petitioner for more than six consecutive months immediately preceding the filing of the petition, petitioner could not deny that North Dakota recently was the child's home state where the petition indicated that for more than six consecutive months preceding the child's move to Illinois, and for most of the child's life, he had lived in North Dakota. *(Decided under former Uniform Child Custody Jurisdiction Act, repealed 750 ILCS 35/1 et seq.)* Flesner v. Houser, 104 Ill. App. 3d 904, 60 Ill. Dec. 678, 433 N.E.2d 720 (4 Dist. 1982).

Deprivation of Custody

—In General

A natural parent's superior right to the care, custody and control of his child should not be deprived absent strict compliance with the statutory provisions involved. *(Decided under former Uniform Child Custody Jurisdiction Act, repealed 750 ILCS 35/1 et seq.)* Feuer v. Barokas, 109 Ill. App. 3d 536, 65 Ill. Dec. 181, 440 N.E.2d 1036 (1 Dist. 1982).

—Not Shown

Petitioners could not deprive respondent of physical custody of her child so as to acquire standing by taking the child from the home of her adult sister where respondent had placed her. *(Decided under former Uniform Child Custody Jurisdiction Act, repealed 750 ILCS 35/1 et seq.)* Feuer v. Barokas, 109 Ill. App. 3d 536, 65 Ill. Dec. 181, 440 N.E.2d 1036 (1 Dist. 1982).

Illinois as Home State

Where the facts alleged by both parties established that the child had resided with the petitioner in Illinois for the past three years, and the child was in the physical custody of the petitioner, who was clearly a "person acting as parent" within the meaning of 750 ILCS 35/3.09, Illinois was the child's "home state" as she has resided in this state for at least six months immediately preceding the initiation of the petition, thus satisfying the requirements of this section. *(Decided under former Uniform Child Custody Jurisdiction Act, repealed 750 ILCS 35/1 et seq.)* McKerr v. Bozarth, 182 Ill. App. 3d 345, 131 Ill. Dec. 410, 538 N.E.2d 785 (2 Dist. 1989).

Illustrative Cases

A proceeding in which the husband sought to punish the wife for violating the terms of the judgment for dissolution of their marriage by moving to Georgia with their child was a proceeding in which a custody determination was one of several issues where the husband asserted that the wife improperly relocated to Georgia and thereby interfered with his visitation rights. *(Decided under former Uniform Child Custody Jurisdiction Act, repealed 750 ILCS 35/1 et seq.)* In re Blanchard, 305 Ill. App. 3d 348, 238 Ill. Dec. 652, 712 N.E.2d 374 (2 Dist. 1999).

Jurisdiction

—Foreign Court

Trial court's decision not to decline jurisdiction to a foreign court will be affirmed absent an abuse of discretion. *(Decided under former Uniform Child Custody Jurisdiction Act, repealed 750 ILCS 35/1 et seq.)* In re Stack, 281 Ill. App. 3d 423, 217 Ill. Dec. 290, 666 N.E.2d 1228 (2 Dist. 1996), appeal denied, 168 Ill. 2d 626, 219 Ill. Dec. 577, 671 N.E.2d 744 (1996).

Inadequate Parenting

Physical custody may not be relinquished by default if a parent performs the task of parenting in a less than adequate manner. *(Decided under former Uniform Child Custody Jurisdiction Act, repealed 750 ILCS 35/1 et seq.)* Feuer v. Barokas, 109 Ill. App. 3d 536, 65 Ill. Dec. 181, 440 N.E.2d 1036 (1 Dist. 1982).

Reconciliation

Trial court properly found that Illinois was not the home state of the children at the time of, or six months prior to, the commencement of the proceedings when mother and the children moved to New York seven months before the date she filed an action for custody in New York and the mother and the children did not abandon their New York domicile when the parties attempted reconciliation. *(Decided under former Uniform Child Custody Jurisdiction Act, repealed 750 ILCS 35/1 et seq.)* In re Schoeffel, 268 Ill. App. 3d 839, 206 Ill. Dec. 59, 644 N.E.2d 827 (4 Dist. 1994).

Temporary Absences

Minor child's absence from Florida for educational purposes was temporary and did not divest Florida of jurisdiction as the child's home state. *(Decided under former Uniform Child Custody Jurisdiction Act, repealed 750 ILCS 35/1 et seq.)* In re Howard, 291 Ill. App. 3d 675, 225 Ill. Dec. 703, 684 N.E.2d 178 (5 Dist. 1997).

Where California judgment provided that child's primary residence was with her father, child stayed with her mother in Illinois while her father moved to Arizona to pursue employment opportunities, and the understanding of all parties was that child would not remain in this state, her 11 month stay in Illinois constituted a "temporary absence" from California. *(Decided under former Uniform Child Custody Jurisdiction Act, repealed 750 ILCS 35/1 et seq.)* Richardson v. Richardson, 255 Ill. App. 3d 1099, 193 Ill. Dec. 1, 625 N.E.2d 1122 (3 Dist. 1993).

Temporary Loss of Possession and Control

Overnight contact with third parties fails to fulfill the statutory provision that the child not be in the physical custody of one of her parents; a parent's actual possession and control of a child is not lost every time the child visits or spends a vacation with a relative or friend. *(Decided under former Uniform Child Custody Jurisdiction Act, repealed 750 ILCS 35/1 et seq.)* Feuer v. Barokas, 109 Ill. App. 3d 536, 65 Ill. Dec. 181, 440 N.E.2d 1036 (1 Dist. 1982).

RESEARCH REFERENCES

Primary caretaker role of respective parents as factor in awarding custody of child. 41 ALR4th 1129.

Child custody and visitation rights of person infected with AIDS. 86 ALR4th 211.

Home state jurisdiction of court under § 3(a)(1) of the Uniform Child Custody Jurisdiction Act (UCCJA) or the Parental Kidnapping Prevention Act (PKPA), 28 U.S.C.S. § 1738A(c)(2)(a). 6 ALR5th 1.

750 ILCS 36/103 Proceedings Governed By Other Law

Sec. 103. *Proceedings Governed By Other Law.* This Act does not govern an adoption proceeding or a proceeding pertaining to the authorization of emergency medical care for a child.
(Source: P.A. 93-108, § 103.)

750 ILCS 36/104 Application To Indian Tribes

Sec. 104. *Application To Indian Tribes.* (a) A child-custody proceeding that pertains to an Indian child as defined in the Indian Child Welfare Act, 25 U.S.C. 1901 et seq., is not subject to this Act to the extent that it is governed by the Indian Child Welfare Act.

(b) A court of this State shall treat a tribe as if it were a state of the United States for the purpose of applying Articles 1 and 2.

(c) A child-custody determination made by a tribe under factual circumstances in substantial conformity with the jurisdictional standards of this Act must be recognized and enforced under Article 3.

(Source: P.A. 93-108, § 104.)

750 ILCS 36/105 International Application Of Act

Sec. 105. *International Application Of Act.* (a) A court of this State shall treat a foreign country as if it were a state of the United States for the purpose of applying Articles 1 and 2.

(b) Except as otherwise provided in subsection (c), a child-custody determination made in a foreign country under factual circumstances in substantial conformity with the jurisdictional standards of this Act must be recognized and enforced under Article 3.

(c) A court of this State need not apply this Act if the child custody law of a foreign country violates fundamental principles of human rights.

(Source: P.A. 93-108, § 105.)

CASE NOTES

ANALYSIS

In General
Custody Judgment
—Visitation Rights
Enforcement of Foreign Judgment
—Held Proper
Judicial Authority
—In General
—Contempt
Modifications
—Household Conditions
Personal Jurisdiction
—Upon Commencement of Action
Registration and Recognition
—Denied
—Requirements

In General

In a case involving the custody decree of a foreign nation, the provisions of this Act become operational to determine whether the trial court had jurisdiction. In re Silvestri-Gagliardoni, 186 Ill. App. 3d 46, 134 Ill. Dec. 106, 542 N.E.2d 106 (1 Dist. 1989).

Custody Judgment

—Visitation Rights

The term "custody judgment" includes court orders providing for visitation rights. In re Alush, 172 Ill. App. 3d 646, 122 Ill. Dec. 694, 527 N.E.2d 66 (2 Dist. 1988).

Enforcement of Foreign Judgment

—Held Proper

Italy qualified as the proper forum to assume jurisdiction because it was "in the best interest of the child," since both of the child's parents had a significant connection with Italy and there was available in Italy substantial evidence concerning the child's housing, support, education, medical and dental care and personal relationship; therefore, the judgment entered in the Italian court was subject to enforcement in the Illinois courts, and the trial court did not err in dismissing petition for dissolution of the marriage and in transferring the cause back to the courts of Milan, Italy. In re Silvestri-Gagliardoni, 186 Ill. App. 3d 46, 134 Ill. Dec. 106, 542 N.E.2d 106 (1 Dist. 1989).

Judicial Authority

—In General

Trial court's decision not to decline jurisdiction to a foreign court will be affirmed absent an abuse of discretion. In re Stack, 281 Ill. App. 3d 423, 217 Ill. Dec. 290, 666 N.E.2d 1228 (2 Dist. 1996), appeal denied, 168 Ill. 2d 626, 219 Ill. Dec. 577, 671 N.E.2d 744 (1996).

—Contempt

This section and former 750 ILCS 35/16 authorize the court to recognize and enforce the custody provisions of a foreign country's decree, but do not authorize the power to hold a party in contempt for conduct which occurred prior to the recognition of the decree by the circuit court. In re Alush, 172 Ill. App. 3d 646, 122 Ill. Dec. 694, 527 N.E.2d 66 (2 Dist. 1988).

Modifications

—Household Conditions

This Act compels Illinois courts not only to recognize proper custody decrees from foreign nations, but also to decline to accept jurisdiction to modify custody decrees in the absence of the showing of conditions in the custodial household that are physically or emotionally harmful to the child. In re Silvestri-Gagliardoni, 186 Ill. App. 3d 46, 134 Ill. Dec. 106, 542 N.E.2d 106 (1 Dist. 1989).

Personal Jurisdiction

—Upon Commencement of Action

Where non-resident father commenced custody action rather than defend against wife's action, father submitted himself to court's general jurisdiction and could not object to personal jurisdiction. In re Stack, 281 Ill. App. 3d 423, 217 Ill. Dec. 290, 666 N.E.2d 1228 (2 Dist. 1996), appeal denied, 168 Ill. 2d 626, 219 Ill. Dec. 577, 671 N.E.2d 744 (1996).

Registration and Recognition

—Denied

Where the circuit court's registration and recognition of Greek custody orders was not based upon this Act, the respondent had not been given the opportunity to contest this registration and recognition under the standards of this Act, and the circuit court erroneously deprived itself of further jurisdiction, the orders of the circuit court purporting to register and recognize the orders of the Greek court were reversed and the cause remanded for further proceedings. In re Agathos, 194 Ill. App. 3d 168, 141 Ill. Dec. 115, 550 N.E.2d 1161 (1 Dist. 1990).

—Requirements

The elements required to establish a prima facie case of entitlement to recognition of a foreign country judgment are that the rendering court had jurisdiction over the person and subject matter, there was timely notice and an opportunity to present a defense, no fraud was involved, and the proceedings were according to a civilized jurisprudence. In re Silvestri-Gagliardoni, 186 Ill. App. 3d 46, 134 Ill. Dec. 106, 542 N.E.2d 106 (1 Dist. 1989).

750 ILCS 36/106 Effect Of Child-Custody Determination

Sec. 106. *Effect Of Child-Custody Determination.* A child-custody determination made by a court of this State that had jurisdiction under this Act binds all persons who have been served in accordance with the laws of this State or notified in accordance with Section 108 [750 ILCS 36/108] or who have submitted to the jurisdiction of the court, and who have been given an opportunity to be heard. As to those persons, the determination is conclusive as to all

decided issues of law and fact except to the extent the determination is modified.
(Source: P.A. 93-108, § 106.)

CASE NOTES

ANALYSIS

Applicability
—Final Custody Judgments
Enforcement of Judgment
—Stay
Res Judicata
—In General
—Shown
—Strict Application

Applicability

—Final Custody Judgments

This section expressly provides that custody determinations by courts of this state are binding and conclusive until modified and applies only to final custody judgments which were not appealed within the statutory period or to those in which appellate review has concluded. *(Decided under former Uniform Child Custody Jurisdiction Act, repealed 750 ILCS 35/1 et seq.)* In re Maroon, 165 Ill. App. 3d 529, 116 Ill. Dec. 459, 519 N.E.2d 49 (5 Dist. 1988).

Enforcement of Judgment

—Stay

This section was not meant to supersede or alter the general rule of 735 ILCS 5/2-1203, which states that a motion after judgment filed in apt time stays enforcement of a judgment. *(Decided under former Uniform Child Custody Jurisdiction Act, repealed 750 ILCS 35/1 et seq.)* In re Maroon, 165 Ill. App. 3d 529, 116 Ill. Dec. 459, 519 N.E.2d 49 (5 Dist. 1988).

Where wife's post-trial motion was pending at the time she is claimed to have violated the child custody terms of the dissolution judgment, such judgment was stayed and could not serve as the predicate for contempt. *(Decided under former Uniform Child Custody Jurisdiction Act, repealed 750 ILCS 35/1 et seq.)* In re Maroon, 165 Ill. App. 3d 529, 116 Ill. Dec. 459, 519 N.E.2d 49 (5 Dist. 1988).

Res Judicata

—In General

This Act provides for application of res judicata. *(Decided under former Uniform Child Custody Jurisdiction Act, repealed 750 ILCS 35/1 et seq.)* Klumpner v. Klumpner, 182 Ill. App. 3d 22, 130 Ill. Dec. 585, 537 N.E.2d 914 (1 Dist.), appeal denied, 136 Ill. Dec. 588, 545 N.E.2d 112 (1989), cert. denied, 494 U.S. 1004, 110 S. Ct. 1298, 108 L. Ed. 2d 475 (1990).

—Shown

In child custody action, Illinois courts' decisions were res judicata of Minnesota juvenile court proceeding and, additionally, the Minnesota court lacked jurisdiction to enter its judgment because the exercise of its jurisdiction was in contravention of the purposes for which this Act was enacted. *(Decided under former Uniform Child Custody Jurisdiction Act, repealed 750 ILCS 35/1 et seq.)* Klumpner v. Klumpner, 182 Ill. App. 3d 22, 130 Ill. Dec. 585, 537 N.E.2d 914 (1 Dist.), appeal denied, 136 Ill. Dec. 588, 545 N.E.2d 112 (1989), cert. denied, 494 U.S. 1004, 110 S. Ct. 1298, 108 L. Ed. 2d 475 (1990).

—Strict Application

It is of paramount importance that where child custody and visitation rights are involved, the doctrine of res judicata must be strictly applied prior to a second forum assuming jurisdiction over such matters involving the same facts and same parties, in compliance with the purposes of this Act, so that a third action between the same parties based on the same facts cannot arise. *(Decided under former Uniform Child Custody Jurisdiction Act, repealed 750 ILCS 35/1 et seq.)* Klumpner v. Klumpner, 182 Ill. App. 3d 22, 130 Ill. Dec. 585, 537 N.E.2d 914 (1 Dist.), appeal denied, 136 Ill. Dec. 588, 545 N.E.2d 112 (1989), cert. denied, 494 U.S. 1004, 110 S. Ct. 1298, 108 L. Ed. 2d 475 (1990).

750 ILCS 36/107 Priority

Sec. 107. *Priority.* If a question of existence or exercise of jurisdiction under this Act is raised in a child-custody proceeding, the question, upon request of a party, must be given priority on the calendar and handled expeditiously.
(Source: P.A. 93-108, § 107.)

750 ILCS 36/108 Notice To Persons Outside State

Sec. 108. *Notice To Persons Outside State.* (a) Notice required for the exercise of jurisdiction when a person is outside this State may be given in a manner prescribed by the law of this State for service of process or by the law of the state in which the service is made. Notice must be given in a manner reasonably calculated to give actual notice but may be by publication if other means are not effective.

(b) Proof of service may be made in the manner prescribed by the law of this State or by the law of the state in which the service is made.

(c) Notice is not required for the exercise of jurisdiction with respect to a person who submits to the jurisdiction of the court.
(Source: P.A. 93-108, § 108.)

LEGAL PERIODICALS

For article, "The Continuing Jurisdiction Dilemma in Interstate Child Custody Disputes," see 70 Ill. B. J. 304 (1982).

750 ILCS 36/109 Appearance And Limited Immunity

Sec. 109. *Appearance And Limited Immunity.* (a) A party to a child-custody proceeding, including a modification proceeding, or a petitioner or respondent in a proceeding to enforce or register a child-custody determination, is not subject to personal jurisdiction in this State for another proceeding or purpose solely by reason of having participated, or of having been physically present for the purpose of participating, in the proceeding.

(b) A person who is subject to personal jurisdiction in this State on a basis other than physical presence is not immune from service of process in this State. A party present in this State who is subject to the jurisdiction of another state is not immune from service of process allowable under the laws of that state.

(c) The immunity granted by subsection (a) does not extend to civil litigation based on acts unrelated to the participation in a proceeding under this Act committed by an individual while present in this State.
(Source: P.A. 93-108, § 109.)

750 ILCS 36/110 Communication Between Courts

Sec. 110. *Communication Between Courts.* (a) A court of this State may communicate with a court in another state concerning a proceeding arising under this Act.

(b) The court may allow the parties to participate in the communication. If the parties are not able to participate in the communication, they must be given the opportunity to present facts and legal arguments before a decision on jurisdiction is made.

(c) Communication between courts on schedules, calendars, court records, and similar matters may occur without informing the parties. A record need not be made of the communication.

(d) Except as otherwise provided in subsection (c), a record must be made of a communication under this Section. The parties must be informed promptly of the communication and granted access to the record.

(e) For the purposes of this Section, "record" means information that is inscribed on a tangible medium or that is stored in an electronic or other medium and is retrievable in perceivable form.

(Source: P.A. 93-108, § 110.)

750 ILCS 36/111 Taking Testimony In Another State

Sec. 111. *Taking Testimony In Another State.* (a) In addition to other procedures available to a party, a party to a child-custody proceeding may offer testimony of witnesses who are located in another state, including testimony of the parties and the child, by deposition or other means allowable in this State for testimony taken in another state. The court on its own motion may order that the testimony of a person be taken in another state and may prescribe the manner in which and the terms upon which the testimony is taken.

(b) A court of this State may permit an individual residing in another state to be deposed or to testify by telephone, audiovisual means, or other electronic means before a designated court or at another location in that state. A court of this State shall cooperate with courts of other states in designating an appropriate location for the deposition or testimony.

(c) Documentary evidence transmitted from another state to a court of this State by technological means that do not produce an original writing may not be excluded from evidence on an objection based on the means of transmission.

(Source: P.A. 93-108, § 111.)

750 ILCS 36/112 Cooperation Between Courts; Preservation Of Records

Sec. 112. *Cooperation Between Courts; Preservation Of Records.* (a) A court of this State may request the appropriate court of another state to:

(1) hold an evidentiary hearing;

(2) order a person to produce or give evidence pursuant to procedures of that state;

(3) order that an evaluation be made with respect to the custody of a child involved in a pending proceeding;

(4) forward to the court of this State a certified copy of the transcript of the record of the hearing, the evidence otherwise presented, and any evaluation prepared in compliance with the request; and

(5) order a party to a child-custody proceeding or any person having physical custody of the child to appear in the proceeding with or without the child.

(b) Upon request of a court of another state, a court of this State may hold a hearing or enter an order described in subsection (a).

(c) Travel and other necessary and reasonable expenses incurred under subsections (a) and (b) may be assessed against the parties according to the law of this State.

(d) A court of this State shall preserve the pleadings, orders, decrees, records of hearings, evaluations, and other pertinent records with respect to a child-custody proceeding until the child attains 18 years of age. Upon appropriate request by a court or law enforcement official of another state, the court shall forward a certified copy of those records.

(Source: P.A. 93-108, § 112.)

ARTICLE 2.

JURISDICTION

750 ILCS 36/201 Initial Child-Custody Jurisdiction

Sec. 201. *Initial Child-Custody Jurisdiction.* (a) Except as otherwise provided in Section 204 [750 ILCS 36/204], a court of this State has jurisdiction to make an initial child-custody determination only if:

(1) this State is the home state of the child on the date of the commencement of the proceeding, or was the home state of the child within six months before the commencement of the proceeding and the child is absent from this State but a parent or person acting as a parent continues to live in this State;

(2) a court of another state does not have jurisdiction under paragraph (1), or a court of the home state of the child has declined to exercise jurisdiction on the ground that this State is the more appropriate forum under Section 207 or 208 [750 ILCS 36/207 or 750 ILCS 36/208], and:

(A) the child and the child's parents, or the child and at least one parent or a person acting as a parent, have a significant connection with this State other than mere physical presence; and

(B) substantial evidence is available in this State concerning the child's care, protection, training, and personal relationships;

(3) all courts having jurisdiction under paragraph (1) or (2) have declined to exercise jurisdiction on the ground that a court of this State is the more appro-

priate forum to determine the custody of the child under Section 207 or 208 [750 ILCS 36/207 or 750 ILCS 36/208]; or

(4) no court of any other state would have jurisdiction under the criteria specified in paragraph (1), (2), or (3).

(b) Subsection (a) is the exclusive jurisdictional basis for making a child-custody determination by a court of this State.

(c) Physical presence of, or personal jurisdiction over, a party or a child is not necessary or sufficient to make a child-custody determination.

(Source: P.A. 93-108, § 201.)

CASE NOTES

Analysis

In General
Best Interest of the Child
—Jurisdiction Assumed
—Jurisdiction Not Assumed
—Jurisdiction Proper
—Legislative Intent
—Substantial Evidence
Compliance
—Required
Construction
Discretion of Court
—In General
Emergency Provision
—Authority of Court
Filing
—Commencement of Time
Home State
—Not Shown
—Shown
—Test
Inconvenient Forum
—Declining Jurisdiction
Jurisdiction
—In General
—First State
—Lack of Personal Jurisdiction
—Not Shown
—Parties' Motions
—Registration of Divorce Decree
—Removal of Child from State
—Residency
—Shown
Modification
—Continuing Jurisdiction Shown
—Foreign Custody Judgment
—Jurisdiction Over Parents
Most Appropriate Forum
—Shown
Out-of-State Courts
Personal Jurisdiction
—In General
—Upon Commencement of Action
Presence in State
—Lacking
—Prospective Custodians
Purpose
Review
—Abuse of Discretion
Significant Connection
—In General
—Lack of Recent Connection
—Not Shown
—Shown
Special Appearance
—Jurisdiction Not Shown
Temporary Absence

In General

If another state in substantial accordance with the jurisdictional standards of this Act modifies a custody order, Illinois courts will recognize and enforce such modification. *(Decided under former Uniform Child Custody Jurisdiction Act, repealed 750 ILCS 35/1 et seq.)* In re Rizza, 237 Ill. App. 3d 83, 177 Ill. Dec. 353, 603 N.E.2d 134 (2 Dist. 1992).

In order to exercise original jurisdiction as well as continuing jurisdiction over child custody and visitation determinations, a trial court must meet certain jurisdictional criteria, regardless of whether that court entered the original decree and specifically retained jurisdiction for enforcement thereof. *(Decided under former Uniform Child Custody Jurisdiction Act, repealed 750 ILCS 35/1 et seq.)* Klumpner v. Klumpner, 182 Ill. App. 3d 22, 130 Ill. Dec. 585, 537 N.E.2d 914 (1 Dist.), appeal denied, 136 Ill. Dec. 588, 545 N.E.2d 112 (1989), cert. denied, 494 U.S. 1004, 110 S. Ct. 1298, 108 L. Ed. 2d 475 (1990).

In the context of this Act, "jurisdiction" refers not to the due process limits of potential subject matter or personal jurisdiction, but rather to the legislature's discretionary limitation upon the exercise of existing jurisdiction. *(Decided under former Uniform Child Custody Jurisdiction Act, repealed 750 ILCS 35/1 et seq.)* Noga v. Noga, 111 Ill. App. 3d 328, 67 Ill. Dec. 18, 443 N.E.2d 1142 (2 Dist. 1982); In re Slate, 181 Ill. App. 3d 110, 129 Ill. Dec. 844, 536 N.E.2d 894 (1 Dist. 1989).

This Act involves a process in which the court must first resolve whether it has jurisdiction under this section and, after such a finding, it must determine under 750 ILCS 35/7 and 750 ILCS 35/8, whether it should decline to exercise jurisdiction. *(Decided under former Uniform Child Custody Jurisdiction Act, repealed 750 ILCS 35/1 et seq.)* In re Levy, 105 Ill. App. 3d 355, 61 Ill. Dec. 247, 434 N.E.2d 400 (1 Dist. 1982).

This Act appears to confer subject matter jurisdiction of child custody determinations, the term "jurisdiction" is not used in its traditional sense but as a limitation on the existing jurisdiction conferred on the courts by the Illinois Constitution. *(Decided under former Uniform Child Custody Jurisdiction Act, repealed 750 ILCS 35/1 et seq.)* In re Levy, 105 Ill. App. 3d 355, 61 Ill. Dec. 247, 434 N.E.2d 400 (1 Dist. 1982).

Best Interest of the Child

—Jurisdiction Assumed

The best interests of the child were served, and the requirements of this Act were satisfied, by permitting mother to proceed with her motion in the Illinois circuit court. *(Decided under former Uniform Child Custody Jurisdiction Act, repealed 750 ILCS 35/1 et seq.)* In re Kitchen, 126 Ill. App. 3d 192, 81 Ill. Dec. 644, 467 N.E.2d 344 (3 Dist. 1984).

It was in the best interest of the minor that Illinois assume jurisdiction where the record showed that the minor spent his entire life and had all of his schooling in Illinois prior to the divorce proceeding, that most of his school records were in Illinois as were his brother, sister, grandmother, and an aunt and uncle who lived with the family for a number of years, and not only were potential witnesses concerning the minor's education, personal relationships, and well-being in Illinois, but respondent also lived and worked in the state and had done so since the minor's birth. *(Decided under former Uniform Child Custody Jurisdiction Act, repealed 750 ILCS 35/1 et seq.)* In re Levy, 105 Ill. App. 3d 355, 61 Ill. Dec. 247, 434 N.E.2d 400 (1 Dist. 1982).

—Jurisdiction Not Assumed

Although children had connections with both Illinois and Virginia, their best interests indicated that Virginia was the proper forum to contest modification of custody since all prior court proceedings had occurred there, including a subsequent award of custody to the father. *(Decided under former Uniform Child Custody Jurisdiction Act, repealed 750 ILCS 35/1 et seq.)* Carlsten v. Robertson, 295 Ill. App. 3d 369, 230 Ill. Dec. 177, 692 N.E.2d 1343 (3 Dist. 1998).

The trial court lacked subject matter jurisdiction under subdivision (a)(2), where, at the time the mother filed her petition in Illinois, child had returned to live with her father in accordance with the California judgment and the written agreement of the

Best Interest of the Child (Cont'd)

—Jurisdiction Not Assumed (Cont'd)
parents. *(Decided under former Uniform Child Custody Jurisdiction Act, repealed 750 ILCS 35/1 et seq.)* Richardson v. Richardson, 255 Ill. App. 3d 1099, 193 Ill. Dec. 1, 625 N.E.2d 1122 (3 Dist. 1993).

It was not in the best interest of the children that Illinois retain jurisdiction over the custody determination where the minor children had spent nearly their entire lives in California and have had all of their schooling in California prior to the divorce proceeding. *(Decided under former Uniform Child Custody Jurisdiction Act, repealed 750 ILCS 35/1 et seq.)* In re Miche, 131 Ill. App. 3d 1029, 87 Ill. Dec. 72, 476 N.E.2d 774 (2 Dist. 1985).

—Jurisdiction Proper
The children and their mother had a significant connection to Illinois and had no connection at all to the state where their father currently resided, therefore jurisdiction was proper in Illinois. *(Decided under former Uniform Child Custody Jurisdiction Act, repealed 750 ILCS 35/1 et seq.)* Arulpragasam v. Eisele, 304 Ill. App. 3d 139, 237 Ill. Dec. 470, 709 N.E.2d 725 (4 Dist. 1999), appeal denied, 185 Ill. 2d 617, 242 Ill. Dec. 134, 720 N.E.2d 1089 (1999).

—Legislative Intent
This Act is written to protect the child's best interest; any hardships faced by the parents must give way to what is in the best interest of the child. *(Decided under former Uniform Child Custody Jurisdiction Act, repealed 750 ILCS 35/1 et seq.)* Doehner v. Jessup, 215 Ill. App. 3d 570, 158 Ill. Dec. 987, 574 N.E.2d 1380 (3 Dist. 1991).

—Substantial Evidence
Where the minor children spent most of their entire life in the state of Illinois and the father, his parents, and other relatives continued to reside within the state of Illinois, the fact that the father could be the potential custodian of the children indicated that there would be substantial evidence concerning the children's future care and a significant interest and connection with the state of Illinois. *(Decided under former Uniform Child Custody Jurisdiction Act, repealed 750 ILCS 35/1 et seq.)* In re Bass, 176 Ill. App. 3d 249, 125 Ill. Dec. 559, 530 N.E.2d 717 (3 Dist. 1988).

Compliance

—Required
The substantial criteria of this section must be met before the court can acquire subject matter jurisdiction. *(Decided under former Uniform Child Custody Jurisdiction Act, repealed 750 ILCS 35/1 et seq.)* In re Rogers, 141 Ill. App. 3d 561, 95 Ill. Dec. 908, 490 N.E.2d 1000 (5 Dist. 1986).

Construction
As long as jurisdiction is established under this section, the trial court may enter an order of protection even though it might have been required to decline to exercise its jurisdiction under section 7 of the Child Custody Act (750 ILCS 35/7) if it had instead been faced only with a petition to modify an out-of-state custody judgment. *(Decided under former Uniform Child Custody Jurisdiction Act, repealed 750 ILCS 35/1 et seq.)* Gasaway v. Gasaway, 246 Ill. App. 3d 531, 186 Ill. Dec. 420, 616 N.E.2d 610 (3 Dist. 1993).

When read in the context of the remaining portions of this Act, it is clear that subsection (b) is intended to determine jurisdiction as between Illinois and another state, not among the circuit courts of Illinois; further, it would be inconsistent to construe the statute governing jurisdiction as vesting exclusive jurisdiction in the circuit court first acquiring jurisdiction where the venue statute plainly provides that actions for modification may be brought in other circuits. *(Decided under former Uniform Child Custody Jurisdiction Act, repealed 750 ILCS 35/1 et seq.)* Bashwiner v. Bashwiner, 126 Ill. App. 3d 365, 81 Ill. Dec. 359, 466 N.E.2d 1161 (1 Dist. 1984).

Discretion of Court

—In General
This Act permits some discretion in the trial court's determination of its jurisdiction to ensure that litigation takes place in the forum where the ties between the state and the child and his family are the closest. *(Decided under former Uniform Child Custody Jurisdiction Act, repealed 750 ILCS 35/1 et seq.)* In re Slate, 181 Ill. App. 3d 110, 129 Ill. Dec. 844, 536 N.E.2d 894 (1 Dist. 1989).

Emergency Provision

—Authority of Court
A trial court may not issue a permanent custody order when its jurisdiction is based solely upon the emergency provision in subdivision (a)(3)(ii). *(Decided under former Uniform Child Custody Jurisdiction Act, repealed 750 ILCS 35/1 et seq.)* In re Alexander, 921 Ill. App. 3d 70, 191 Ill. Dec. 331, 623 N.E.2d 921 (4 Dist. 1993).

Filing

—Commencement of Time
While the child may have resided in the new state for a period of six months or longer, the six month period within which the parent in the original state would not begin to run until that parent had reason to recognize the permanency of the out of state absence. *(Decided under former Uniform Child Custody Jurisdiction Act, repealed 750 ILCS 35/1 et seq.)* In re Frost, 289 Ill. App. 3d 95, 224 Ill. Dec. 409, 681 N.E.2d 1030 (1 Dist. 1997).

Home State

—Not Shown
Trial court properly found that Illinois was not the home state of the children at the time of, or six months prior to, the commencement of the proceedings when mother and the children moved to New York seven months before the date she filed an action for custody in New York and the mother and the children did not abandon their New York domicile when the parties attempted reconciliation. *(Decided under former Uniform Child Custody Jurisdiction Act, repealed 750 ILCS 35/1 et seq.)* In re Schoeffel, 268 Ill. App. 3d 839, 206 Ill. Dec. 59, 644 N.E.2d 827 (4 Dist. 1994).

Illinois was not the home state of the minor children at the time of commencement of the proceeding since only three months had elapsed since the children moved from California; therefore, jurisdiction in the Illinois circuit court was lacking. *(Decided under former Uniform Child Custody Jurisdiction Act, repealed 750 ILCS 35/1 et seq.)* In re Miche, 131 Ill. App. 3d 1029, 87 Ill. Dec. 72, 476 N.E.2d 774 (2 Dist. 1985).

Illinois did not qualify as the home state where the minor clearly had not lived in Illinois for a period of six consecutive months immediately preceding commencement of the action, nor had Illinois been the home state within six months before commencement of the proceeding. *(Decided under former Uniform Child Custody Jurisdiction Act, repealed 750 ILCS 35/1 et seq.)* In re Levy, 105 Ill. App. 3d 355, 61 Ill. Dec. 247, 434 N.E.2d 400 (1 Dist. 1982).

—Shown
Illinois was the home state of the children at the time the mother's petition for modification of custody was filed, since they had lived with the mother for the prior two years in Illinois, even though this was under a temporary order of the court of another state. *(Decided under former Uniform Child Custody Jurisdiction Act, repealed 750 ILCS 35/1 et seq.)* Arulpragasam v. Eisele, 304 Ill. App. 3d 139, 237 Ill. Dec. 470, 709 N.E.2d 725 (4 Dist. 1999), appeal denied, 185 Ill. 2d 617, 242 Ill. Dec. 134, 720 N.E.2d 1089 (1999).

—Test
The test for a "home state" is where has a child lived with a person acting as a parent for the last six months; the "temporary absence" provision is designed to prevent lapses in the six consecutive months required of a "home state,", caused by brief interstate visits by the child, and does not incorporate all the nuances of domicile into the definition of "home state." *(Decided under former Uniform Child Custody Jurisdiction Act, repealed 750 ILCS 35/1 et seq.)* In re Schoeffel, 268 Ill. App. 3d 839, 206 Ill. Dec. 59, 644 N.E.2d 827 (4 Dist. 1994).

Inconvenient Forum

—Declining Jurisdiction
Even where the requirements of this section are met and the court has jurisdiction to make a child custody determination, it may decline to exercise it if it finds that court to be an inconvenient forum for the determination under the circumstances of the case, and that a court of another state is a more appropriate forum.

Inconvenient Forum (Cont'd)

—Declining Jurisdiction (Cont'd)
(Decided under former Uniform Child Custody Jurisdiction Act, repealed 750 ILCS 35/1 et seq.) Noga v. Noga, 111 Ill. App. 3d 328, 67 Ill. Dec. 18, 443 N.E.2d 1142 (2 Dist. 1982).

Jurisdiction

—In General
Maximum rather than minimum contacts with Illinois are required in order for jurisdiction to exist under subdivision (a)(2). *(Decided under former Uniform Child Custody Jurisdiction Act, repealed 750 ILCS 35/1 et seq.)* In re Frost, 289 Ill. App. 3d 95, 224 Ill. Dec. 409, 681 N.E.2d 1030 (1 Dist. 1997).

A habeas corpus action is a proper method for bringing a collateral attack against an order entered in another court which was void for lack of jurisdiction. *(Decided under former Uniform Child Custody Jurisdiction Act, repealed 750 ILCS 35/1 et seq.)* McGuane v. McGuane, 268 Ill. App. 3d 751, 206 Ill. Dec. 570, 645 N.E.2d 575 (2 Dist. 1995).

The jurisdictional standards of this Act permit the exercise of jurisdiction on four bases: first, a court has jurisdiction based on being a child's home state, either at the time the proceeding was commenced or within the prior six months if one parent continues to reside within the state and the other parent removed the child from the state; a forum may also exert jurisdiction if it is in the best interests of the child either because one of the contestants or the child has significant contacts with the forum, or because the necessary evidence is located there; if a child has been abandoned in a state or there is an emergency requiring protection of the child, such state may exert jurisdiction; and finally, if no other state has jurisdiction based on the above factual situations or has declined jurisdiction and it is in the best interests of the child, a forum may exercise its jurisdiction. *(Decided under former Uniform Child Custody Jurisdiction Act, repealed 750 ILCS 35/1 et seq.)* In re Rizza, 237 Ill. App. 3d 83, 177 Ill. Dec. 353, 603 N.E.2d 134 (2 Dist. 1992).

A contestant's failure to act does not vest an inappropriate court with jurisdiction, nor does the fact that one court has succeeded in issuing a custody order sooner than another court endow it with jurisdiction if it does not meet the requirements of this Act. *(Decided under former Uniform Child Custody Jurisdiction Act, repealed 750 ILCS 35/1 et seq.)* McKerr v. Bozarth, 182 Ill. App. 3d 345, 131 Ill. Dec. 410, 538 N.E.2d 785 (2 Dist. 1989).

While this Act, and subsection (b) of this section in particular, were intended to operate as limitations on a court's continuing jurisdiction in custody matters, the subsection was not intended to divest a court of jurisdiction in the midst of a custody modification proceeding based on a change in circumstances occurring after the proceeding had commenced but prior to final determination; the jurisdiction of a court over the subject matter and parties in a case, once fully attached, continues until all issues of fact and law have been decided, and once jurisdiction has been vested, it cannot be divested by subsequent events. *(Decided under former Uniform Child Custody Jurisdiction Act, repealed 750 ILCS 35/1 et seq.)* Kelly v. Warner, 119 Ill. App. 3d 217, 77 Ill. Dec. 273, 460 N.E.2d 329 (3 Dist. 1983).

—First State
The Uniform Child Custody Jurisdiction Act achieves certainty by its provision that the first such state to exercise jurisdiction has the exclusive right to proceed; once the action is filed jurisdiction attaches, and it makes no difference where the children are then taken. *(Decided under former Uniform Child Custody Jurisdiction Act, repealed 750 ILCS 35/1 et seq.)* In re Schoeffel, 268 Ill. App. 3d 839, 206 Ill. Dec. 59, 644 N.E.2d 827 (4 Dist. 1994).

—Lack of Personal Jurisdiction
Personal jurisdiction over either parent is not required for a circuit court to decide the custody status of a child; the court may proceed quasi in rem so long as the jurisdictional requirements of this section are met. *(Decided under former Uniform Child Custody Jurisdiction Act, repealed 750 ILCS 35/1 et seq.)* McGuane v. McGuane, 268 Ill. App. 3d 751, 206 Ill. Dec. 570, 645 N.E.2d 575 (2 Dist. 1995).

This Act's policies and purposes may be effectuated without in personam jurisdiction, and as long as certain other jurisdictional criteria are met, a court may grant relief under the Act despite a lack of personal jurisdiction over one of the parents. *(Decided under former Uniform Child Custody Jurisdiction Act, repealed 750 ILCS 35/1 et seq.)* In re Buchanio, 262 Ill. App. 3d 910, 200 Ill. Dec. 641, 635 N.E.2d 980 (1 Dist.), appeal denied, 157 Ill. 2d 496, 205 Ill. Dec. 157, 642 N.E.2d 1274 (1994).

—Not Shown
Where minor children had lived in Illinois for over 18 months when the petition to transfer custody was filed, they attended school in Illinois, and there was a significant connection with the state by the children and their parent, the fact that one child was in Oregon because the other parent refused to return her to petitioner after her summer visit did not deprive Illinois of jurisdiction. *(Decided under former Uniform Child Custody Jurisdiction Act, repealed 750 ILCS 35/1 et seq.)* Lewis v. Canty, 115 Ill. App. 3d 306, 71 Ill. Dec. 176, 450 N.E.2d 864 (1 Dist. 1983).

—Parties' Motions
Mere movement of the parties cannot serve to divest a court of its jurisdiction once acquired during modification proceedings which are underway but unconcluded. *(Decided under former Uniform Child Custody Jurisdiction Act, repealed 750 ILCS 35/1 et seq.)* Kelly v. Warner, 119 Ill. App. 3d 217, 77 Ill. Dec. 273, 460 N.E.2d 329 (3 Dist. 1983).

—Registration of Divorce Decree
Lack of jurisdiction of the circuit court to register a Scottish decree of divorce did not preclude the court from entering a valid custody order upon the request in respondent's response and the personal appearance of petitioner and respondent. *(Decided under former Uniform Child Custody Jurisdiction Act, repealed 750 ILCS 35/1 et seq.)* In re Mullins, 135 Ill. App. 3d 279, 89 Ill. Dec. 771, 481 N.E.2d 322 (4 Dist. 1985).

—Removal of Child from State
Where a court has proper jurisdiction under the provisions of this section, it cannot be divested of jurisdiction by removal of the child from the state. *(Decided under former Uniform Child Custody Jurisdiction Act, repealed 750 ILCS 35/1 et seq.)* Lewis v. Canty, 115 Ill. App. 3d 306, 71 Ill. Dec. 176, 450 N.E.2d 864 (1 Dist. 1983).

—Residency
The action of the circuit court in exercising jurisdiction over matter was a patent violation of this Act where neither the child nor the defendant father was ever a resident of Illinois. *(Decided under former Uniform Child Custody Jurisdiction Act, repealed 750 ILCS 35/1 et seq.)* In re Rogers, 141 Ill. App. 3d 561, 95 Ill. Dec. 908, 490 N.E.2d 1000 (5 Dist. 1986).

—Shown
Custodial parent who removed children from Illinois to Louisiana and obtained a Louisiana court order that prohibited visitation by the other parent the day prior to a scheduled visitation was properly found in contempt of the Illinois visitation order because the Louisiana order did not excuse the custodial parent's noncompliance where it was intentionally procured as a way not to follow the order with which the custodial parent disagreed and because the Illinois court retained exclusive jurisdiction over the matter, regardless of where the children were taken. *(Decided under former Uniform Child Custody Jurisdiction Act, repealed 750 ILCS 35/1 et seq.)* In re Marriage of Kneitz, 341 Ill. App. 3d 299, 276 Ill. Dec. 229, 793 N.E.2d 988, 2003 Ill. App. LEXIS 922 (2 Dist. 2003).

Under subsection (b) court had jurisdiction where petitioner allegedly moved with child to Kentucky but this state had jurisdiction when petitioner filed a motion for order to show cause, alleging respondent failed to pay part of child support and medical expenses; since that motion respondent continued to reside in Illinois and state continued to retain jurisdiction over custody and support issues. *(Decided under former Uniform Child Custody Jurisdiction Act, repealed 750 ILCS 35/1 et seq.)* In re Tatham, 293 Ill. App. 3d 471, 228 Ill. Dec. 166, 688 N.E.2d 864 (5 Dist. 1997).

In a custody determination proceeding Illinois had jurisdiction when wife commenced dissolution proceedings, because it was the home state of the child and, since husband continued to reside in Illinois, Illinois retained jurisdiction to determine custody of the child. *(Decided under former Uniform Child Custody Jurisdiction*

Jurisdiction (Cont'd)

—Shown (Cont'd)

Act, repealed 750 ILCS 35/1 et seq.) In re Breyley, 247 Ill. App. 3d 486, 187 Ill. Dec. 215, 617 N.E.2d 423 (3 Dist. 1993).

Where child's mother was born in Illinois, lived there until she was 13, returned to Illinois upon the failure of her first marriage, lived in Illinois for three years until she enlisted in the armed services, then continued to list Illinois as her permanent residence and to vote in Illinois elections, and where her mother, her mother's mother, her mother's other children and numerous other relatives lived in Illinois, she established jurisdiction in Illinois under subdivision (a)(2) of this section. *(Decided under former Uniform Child Custody Jurisdiction Act, repealed 750 ILCS 35/1 et seq.)* In re Mobley, 210 Ill. App. 3d 936, 155 Ill. Dec. 323, 569 N.E.2d 323 (5 Dist. 1991).

Where, at the time custody proceedings were commenced, the child was 13 months old and had lived in both Illinois and North Carolina, but had not lived in either state for the six consecutive months necessary for either state to be considered his home state, only the circuit court of Montgomery County, Illinois, where the marriage dissolution proceedings took place, had jurisdiction to make the child custody determination under subdivision (a)(4) of this section. *(Decided under former Uniform Child Custody Jurisdiction Act, repealed 750 ILCS 35/1 et seq.)* Hollo v. Hollo, 131 Ill. App. 3d 119, 85 Ill. Dec. 867, 474 N.E.2d 827 (5 Dist. 1985).

The trial court correctly declined to assert jurisdiction over grandparents' visitation petition where the children had not been residents of Illinois for over two years, it appeared Arkansas was now their home state, the record did not disclose whether the children's natural father continued to reside in Illinois, and the natural father submitted to the jurisdiction of the Arkansas courts in an adoption proceeding in which his parental rights were being determined. *(Decided under former Uniform Child Custody Jurisdiction Act, repealed 750 ILCS 35/1 et seq.)* Noga v. Noga, 111 Ill. App. 3d 328, 67 Ill. Dec. 18, 443 N.E.2d 1142 (2 Dist. 1982).

Modification

—Continuing Jurisdiction Shown

Once the circuit court obtains jurisdiction over a child, it shall retain jurisdiction unless it concedes jurisdiction to a foreign state or none of the parties, including the child, remains in Illinois; thus the court properly denied mother's motion to transfer jurisdiction to California where Illinois jurisdiction had been established in the original action. *(Decided under former Uniform Child Custody Jurisdiction Act, repealed 750 ILCS 35/1 et seq.)* In re Hilliard, 178 Ill. App. 3d 620, 127 Ill. Dec. 671, 533 N.E.2d 543 (3 Dist. 1989).

Where wife filed a petition to modify the initial child custody order in Illinois even though her former husband had relocated to a different state, and at no time did the Illinois court concede jurisdiction of this matter to a foreign state, it is clear that Illinois has continuing subject matter jurisdiction over this cause. *(Decided under former Uniform Child Custody Jurisdiction Act, repealed 750 ILCS 35/1 et seq.)* In re Stafeil, 169 Ill. App. 3d 630, 120 Ill. Dec. 92, 523 N.E.2d 1003 (1 Dist. 1988).

The court had jurisdiction to enter an order requiring husband to pay child support and his wife's attorney fees, as the wife filed her petition in the county where the original orders were entered, the court retained personal jurisdiction over the husband to modify the judgment by ordering the husband to pay child support and the wife's attorney fees. *(Decided under former Uniform Child Custody Jurisdiction Act, repealed 750 ILCS 35/1 et seq.)* In re Stafeil, 169 Ill. App. 3d 630, 120 Ill. Dec. 92, 523 N.E.2d 1003 (1 Dist. 1988).

—Foreign Custody Judgment

An Illinois court may modify a foreign custody judgment even if the other state has jurisdiction, so long as the Illinois court has jurisdiction under this section. *(Decided under former Uniform Child Custody Jurisdiction Act, repealed 750 ILCS 35/1 et seq.)* In re Bueche, 193 Ill. App. 3d 594, 140 Ill. Dec. 566, 550 N.E.2d 48 (2 Dist. 1990).

—Jurisdiction Over Parents

Personal jurisdiction over either parent is not necessary for a circuit court to modify a custody order so long as the jurisdictional requirements of this section are met. *(Decided under former Uniform Child Custody Jurisdiction Act, repealed 750 ILCS 35/1 et seq.)* In re Bueche, 193 Ill. App. 3d 594, 140 Ill. Dec. 566, 550 N.E.2d 48 (2 Dist. 1990).

Most Appropriate Forum

—Shown

Where the children moved to Illinois four years earlier, both parents were from Illinois, the petitioner, the parents' extended families, the three children and the children's guardian all lived in Illinois, any relevant information about petitioner was in Illinois, any out-of-state agency was no longer in contact with petitioner, and all of petitioner's contacts were in Illinois including her mother, with whom she resided, the social worker with whom she met, her psychiatrists, her job, her Red Cross caseworker and her attorney, Illinois, rather than the state from which the children had moved four years ago, was the most appropriate forum to litigate any possible alteration in custody. *(Decided under former Uniform Child Custody Jurisdiction Act, repealed 750 ILCS 35/1 et seq.)* In re Slate, 181 Ill. App. 3d 110, 129 Ill. Dec. 844, 536 N.E.2d 894 (1 Dist. 1989).

Out-of-State Courts

Illinois could not assert jurisdiction over the mother's petition for modification of a custody order since Virginia had original jurisdiction and had subsequently modified custody in favor of the father. The fact that father had moved from Virginia did not affect its jurisdiction. *(Decided under former Uniform Child Custody Jurisdiction Act, repealed 750 ILCS 35/1 et seq.)* Carlsten v. Robertson, 295 Ill. App. 3d 369, 230 Ill. Dec. 177, 692 N.E.2d 1343 (3 Dist. 1998).

Trial court did not have subject matter jurisdiction pursuant to subdivision (a)(4), because California possessed jurisdiction at the time that the divorce decree was entered, while the child lived in California thereafter, and during the child's temporary visit with her mother in Illinois. *(Decided under former Uniform Child Custody Jurisdiction Act, repealed 750 ILCS 35/1 et seq.)* Richardson v. Richardson, 255 Ill. App. 3d 1099, 193 Ill. Dec. 1, 625 N.E.2d 1122 (3 Dist. 1993).

Since subsection (b) of this section is not part of the Uniform Child Custody Jurisdiction Act (750 ILCS 35/1) but is strictly an Illinois enactment, it does not apply to a court in another state modifying a decree from that state where the other state court would have otherwise lost jurisdiction, nor would subsection (b) of this section preclude a transfer of jurisdiction under forum non conveniens. *(Decided under former Uniform Child Custody Jurisdiction Act, repealed 750 ILCS 35/1 et seq.)* In re Bueche, 193 Ill. App. 3d 594, 140 Ill. Dec. 566, 550 N.E.2d 48 (2 Dist. 1990).

Personal Jurisdiction

—In General

Party may object to subject matter jurisdiction without waiving objections to personal jurisdiction. *(Decided under former Uniform Child Custody Jurisdiction Act, repealed 750 ILCS 35/1 et seq.)* In re Stack, 281 Ill. App. 3d 423, 217 Ill. Dec. 290, 666 N.E.2d 1228 (2 Dist. 1996), appeal denied, 168 Ill. 2d 626, 219 Ill. Dec. 577, 671 N.E.2d 744 (1996).

Although personal jurisdiction is necessary to impose child support obligations, the same is not true with regard to orders establishing or modifying custody arrangements under this Act. *(Decided under former Uniform Child Custody Jurisdiction Act, repealed 750 ILCS 35/1 et seq.)* In re Mobley, 210 Ill. App. 3d 936, 155 Ill. Dec. 323, 569 N.E.2d 323 (5 Dist. 1991).

—Upon Commencement of Action

Where non-resident father commenced custody action rather than defend against wife's action, father submitted himself to court's general jurisdiction and could not object to personal jurisdiction. *(Decided under former Uniform Child Custody Jurisdiction Act, repealed 750 ILCS 35/1 et seq.)* In re Stack, 281 Ill. App. 3d 423, 217 Ill. Dec. 290, 666 N.E.2d 1228 (2 Dist. 1996), appeal denied, 168 Ill. 2d 626, 219 Ill. Dec. 577, 671 N.E.2d 744 (1996).

Presence in State

—Lacking

Where the child and both parents had a significant connection with Illinois, all having resided, as opposed to having been merely

Presence in State (Cont'd)

—Lacking (Cont'd)

present, within Illinois immediately prior to the commencement of proceedings, and where petitioner's continued residence in Illinois and the fact that he represented a potential custodian indicated that there was available within the state substantial evidence concerning the child's future care, the fact that the child was no longer physically present within the state was not fatal to the circuit court's jurisdiction; therefore, the trial court had jurisdiction to make the custody determination. *(Decided under former Uniform Child Custody Jurisdiction Act, repealed 750 ILCS 35/1 et seq.)* Hollo v. Hollo, 131 Ill. App. 3d 119, 85 Ill. Dec. 867, 474 N.E.2d 827 (5 Dist. 1985).

—Prospective Custodians

Where both prospective custodians are present in a state and there is an opportunity for a full hearing on the custody issue, the jurisdictional requirements of this Act may be satisfied. *(Decided under former Uniform Child Custody Jurisdiction Act, repealed 750 ILCS 35/1 et seq.)* In re Weinstein, 87 Ill. App. 3d 101, 42 Ill. Dec. 243, 408 N.E.2d 952 (1 Dist. 1980).

Purpose

The purpose of this section is to limit jurisdiction rather than to proliferate it, and the interest of the child is served when the forum has optimum access to relevant evidence about the child and the family. *(Decided under former Uniform Child Custody Jurisdiction Act, repealed 750 ILCS 35/1 et seq.)* In re Miche, 131 Ill. App. 3d 1029, 87 Ill. Dec. 72, 476 N.E.2d 774 (2 Dist. 1985).

Review

—Abuse of Discretion

A trial court's decision not to decline jurisdiction will be affirmed absent an abuse of that discretion. *(Decided under former Uniform Child Custody Jurisdiction Act, repealed 750 ILCS 35/1 et seq.)* In re Hilliard, 178 Ill. App. 3d 620, 127 Ill. Dec. 671, 533 N.E.2d 543 (3 Dist. 1989).

Significant Connection

—In General

There are two requirements for the exercise of jurisdiction over a custody determination which emerge from the provisions of this Act and 750 ILCS 5/601: a significant connection with the state by the children and one of both custodial contestants and substantial evidence bearing upon their future environment. *(Decided under former Uniform Child Custody Jurisdiction Act, repealed 750 ILCS 35/1 et seq.)* In re Weinstein, 87 Ill. App. 3d 101, 42 Ill. Dec. 243, 408 N.E.2d 952 (1 Dist. 1980).

—Lack of Recent Connection

Where children were present in Illinois, the parties had been raised, married, lived several years and borne their older child in Illinois, both maternal and paternal grandparents resided in Illinois, and the father intended to do so for an indefinite period in the future, the absence of immediate past connections with this state directly by the parties did not preclude its jurisdiction over the custody issue. *(Decided under former Uniform Child Custody Jurisdiction Act, repealed 750 ILCS 35/1 et seq.)* In re Weinstein, 87 Ill. App. 3d 101, 42 Ill. Dec. 243, 408 N.E.2d 952 (1 Dist. 1980).

—Not Shown

Husband did not establish sufficient contacts under subdivision (a)(2)(i) with the State of Illinois for a court here to accept child custody jurisdiction. *(Decided under former Uniform Child Custody Jurisdiction Act, repealed 750 ILCS 35/1 et seq.)* In re Alexander, 921 Ill. App. 3d 70, 191 Ill. Dec. 331, 623 N.E.2d 921 (4 Dist. 1993).

—Shown

Evidence supported jurisdiction under subsection (a)(2), notwithstanding that the mother and children lived in Indiana, where (1) the children's father was a lifetime resident of Illinois, (2) the children visited him in Illinois on a regular basis, (3) numerous extended family members with whom the children had close relationships lived in Illinois, (4) the parties lived in Illinois during their marriage, (5) the children lived in Illinois until the dissolution of their parents' marriage, (6) an Illinois court dissolved the marriage and made the original custody and visitation determinations, (7) five of the seven witnesses who testified in the matter were Illinois residents, and (8) the mother's home and those of the mother's principal witnesses were less than an hour drive from the father's Illinois home. *(Decided under former Uniform Child Custody Jurisdiction Act, repealed 750 ILCS 35/1 et seq.)* Lange v. Lange, 307 Ill. App. 3d 303, 240 Ill. Dec. 414, 717 N.E.2d 507 (4 Dist. 1999).

Special Appearance

—Jurisdiction Not Shown

Circuit court did not have jurisdiction where defendant's only appearance was a special appearance contesting the jurisdiction of the court. *(Decided under former Uniform Child Custody Jurisdiction Act, repealed 750 ILCS 35/1 et seq.)* In re Rogers, 141 Ill. App. 3d 561, 95 Ill. Dec. 908, 490 N.E.2d 1000 (5 Dist. 1986).

Temporary Absence

An evidentiary hearing must be held in order to determine whether minor's absence from Illinois qualified as a temporary absence, based upon an agreement between his parents that minor would return to Illinois, such that Illinois was minor's home state at the time the petitioner filed his action. *(Decided under former Uniform Child Custody Jurisdiction Act, repealed 750 ILCS 35/1 et seq.)* In re Frost, 289 Ill. App. 3d 95, 224 Ill. Dec. 409, 681 N.E.2d 1030 (1 Dist. 1997).

LEGAL PERIODICALS

For article, "The Continuing Jurisdiction Dilemma in Interstate Child Custody Disputes," see 70 Ill. B. J. 304 (1982).

RESEARCH REFERENCES

Significant connection jurisdiction of court under section 3(a)(2) of the Uniform Child Custody Jurisdiction Act (UCCJA) and the Parental Kidnapping Prevention Act (PKPA), 28 USCS § 1738A(c)(2)(B). 5 ALR5th 550.

Abandonment and emergency jurisdiction of court under section 3(a)(3) of the Uniform Child Custody Jurisdiction Act (UCCJA) and the Parental Kidnapping Prevention Act (PKPA), 28 USCS § 1738A(c)(2)(C). 5 ALR5th 788.

Pending proceeding in another state as ground for declining jurisdiction under § 6(a) of the Uniform Child Custody Jurisdiction Act (UCCJA) or the Parental Kidnapping Prevention Act (PKPA), 28 USCS § 1738A(g). 20 ALR5th 700.

Inconvenience of forum as ground for declining jurisdiction under § 7 of the Uniform Child Custody Jurisdiction Act (UCCJA). 21 ALR5th 396.

Significant connection jurisdiction of court to modify foreign child custody decree under §§ 3(a)(2) and 14(b) of the Uniform Child Custody Jurisdiction Act (UCCJA) and the Parental Kidnapping Prevention Act (PICPA), 28 U.S.C.A. §§ 1738A(c)(2)(b) and 1738A(f)(1). 67 ALR5th 1.

Home state jurisdiction of court to modify foreign child custody decree under §§ 3(a)(1) and 14(a)(2) of Uniform Child Custody Jurisdiction Act (UCCJA) and Parental Kidnapping Prevention Act (PKPA), §§ 28 U.S.C.A. 1738A(c)(2)(A) and 1738A(f)(1). 72 ALR5th 249.

Declining jurisdiction to modify prior child custody decree under § 14(a)(1) of Uniform Child Custody Jurisdiction Act (UCCJA) and Parental Kidnapping Prevention Act (PKPA), 28 U.S.C.A. § 1738A(f)(2). 73 ALR5th 185.

Abandonment jurisdiction of court under §§ 3(a)(3)(i) and 14(a) of Uniform Child Custody Jurisdiction Act and Parental Kidnapping Prevention Act, 28 U.S.C.A. §§ 1738A(c)(2)(C)(i) and 1738A(f), notwithstanding existence of prior valid custody decree rendered by second state. 78 ALR5th 465.

Emergency jurisdiction of court under §§ 3(a)(3)(ii) and 14(a) of Uniform Child Custody Jurisdiction Act and Parental Kidnapping Prevention Act, 28 U.S.C.A. §§ 1738A(c)(2)(C)(ii) and 1738A(f), to protect interests of child notwithstanding existence of prior, valid custody decree rendered by another state. 80 ALR5th 117.

Home state jurisdiction of court under § 3(a)(1) of the Uniform Child Custody Jurisdiction Act (UCCJA) or the Parental Kidnapping Prevention Act (PKPA), 28 U.S.C.S. § 1738A(c)(2)(a). 6 ALR5th 1.

Default jurisdiction of court under § 3(a)(4) of the Uniform Child Custody Jurisdiction Act (UCCJA) or the Parental Kidnapping Prevention Act (PKPA), 28 U.S.C.S. § 1738A(c)(2)(D). 6 ALR5th 69.

750 ILCS 36/202 Exclusive, Continuing Jurisdiction

Sec. 202. *Exclusive, Continuing Jurisdiction.* (a) Except as otherwise provided in Section 204 [750 ILCS 36/204], a court of this State which has made a child-custody determination consistent with Section 201 or 203 [750 ILCS 36/201 or 750 ILCS 36/203] has exclusive, continuing jurisdiction over the determination until:

(1) a court of this State determines that neither the child, the child's parents, and any person acting as a parent do not have a significant connection with this State and that substantial evidence is no longer available in this State concerning the child's care, protection, training, and personal relationships; or

(2) a court of this State or a court of another state determines that the child, the child's parents, and any person acting as a parent do not presently reside in this State.

(b) A court of this State which has made a child-custody determination and does not have exclusive, continuing jurisdiction under this Section may modify that determination only if it has jurisdiction to make an initial determination under Section 201 [750 ILCS 36/201].

(Source: P.A. 93-108, § 202.)

750 ILCS 36/203 Jurisdiction To Modify Determination

Sec. 203. *Jurisdiction To Modify Determination.* Except as otherwise provided in Section 204 [750 ILCS 36/204], a court of this State may not modify a child-custody determination made by a court of another state unless a court of this State has jurisdiction to make an initial determination under Section 201(a)(1) or (2) [750 ILCS 36/201] and:

(1) the court of the other state determines it no longer has exclusive, continuing jurisdiction under Section 202 [750 ILCS 36/202] or that a court of this State would be a more convenient forum under Section 207 [750 ILCS 36/207]; or

(2) a court of this State or a court of the other state determines that the child, the child's parents, and any person acting as a parent do not presently reside in the other state.

(Source: P.A. 93-108, § 203.)

CASE NOTES

ANALYSIS

Construction
Personal Jurisdiction
—Not Necessary

Construction

An Illinois court may modify a foreign custody judgment even if another state has jurisdiction so long as the Illinois court has jurisdiction under 750 ILCS 35/4. *(Decided under former Uniform Child Custody Jurisdiction Act, repealed 750 ILCS 35/1 et seq.)* In re Bueche, 193 Ill. App. 3d 594, 140 Ill. Dec. 566, 550 N.E.2d 48 (2 Dist. 1990).

Personal Jurisdiction

—Not Necessary

Personal jurisdiction is not necessary for a circuit court to modify the judgment as long as the jurisdictional requirements of 750 ILCS 35/4 are met. *(Decided under former Uniform Child Custody Jurisdiction Act, repealed 750 ILCS 35/1 et seq.)* In re Los, 229 Ill. App. 3d 357, 170 Ill. Dec. 584, 593 N.E.2d 126 (2 Dist. 1992).

LEGAL PERIODICALS

For article, "The Continuing Jurisdiction Dilemma in Interstate Child Custody Disputes," see 70 Ill. B. J. 304 (1982).

750 ILCS 36/204 Temporary Emergency Jurisdiction

Sec. 204. *Temporary Emergency Jurisdiction.* (a) A court of this State has temporary emergency jurisdiction if the child is present in this State and the child has been abandoned or it is necessary in an emergency to protect the child because the child, or a sibling or parent of the child, is subjected to or threatened with mistreatment or abuse.

(b) If there is no previous child-custody determination that is entitled to be enforced under this Act and a child-custody proceeding has not been commenced in a court of a state having jurisdiction under Sections 201 through 203 [750 ILCS 36/201 through 750 ILCS 36/203], a child-custody determination made under this Section remains in effect until an order is obtained from a court of a state having jurisdiction under Sections 201 through 203 [750 ILCS 36/201 through 750 ILCS 36/203]. If a child-custody proceeding has not been or is not commenced in a court of a state having jurisdiction under Sections 201 through 203 [750 ILCS 36/201 through 750 ILCS 36/203], a child-custody determination made under this Section becomes a final determination, if it so provides and this State becomes the home state of the child.

(c) If there is a previous child-custody determination that is entitled to be enforced under this Act, or a child-custody proceeding has been commenced in a court of a state having jurisdiction under Sections 201 through 203 [750 ILCS 36/201 through 750 ILCS 36/203], any order issued by a court of this State under this Section must specify in the order a period that the court considers adequate to allow the person seeking an order to obtain an order from the state having jurisdiction under Sections 201 through 203 [750 ILCS 36/201 through 750 ILCS 36/203]. The order issued in this State remains in effect until an order is obtained from the other state within the period specified or the period expires.

(d) A court of this State which has been asked to make a child-custody determination under this Sec-

tion, upon being informed that a child-custody proceeding has been commenced in, or a child-custody determination has been made by, a court of a state having jurisdiction under Sections 201 through 203 [750 ILCS 36/201 through 750 ILCS 36/203], shall immediately communicate with the other court. A court of this State which is exercising jurisdiction pursuant to Sections 201 through 203 [750 ILCS 36/201 through 750 ILCS 36/203], upon being informed that a child-custody proceeding has been commenced in, or a child-custody determination has been made by, a court of another state under a statute similar to this Section shall immediately communicate with the court of that state to resolve the emergency, protect the safety of the parties and the child, and determine a period for the duration of the temporary order.
(Source: P.A. 93-108, § 204.)

750 ILCS 36/205 Notice; Opportunity To Be Heard; Joinder

Sec. 205. *Notice; Opportunity To Be Heard; Joinder.* (a) Before a child-custody determination is made under this Act, notice and an opportunity to be heard in accordance with the standards of Section 108 [750 ILCS 36/108] must be given to all persons entitled to notice under the law of this State as in child-custody proceedings between residents of this State, any parent whose parental rights have not been previously terminated, and any person having physical custody of the child.

(b) This Act does not govern the enforceability of a child-custody determination made without notice or an opportunity to be heard.

(c) The obligation to join a party and the right to intervene as a party in a child-custody proceeding under this Act are governed by the law of this State as in child-custody proceedings between residents of this State.
(Source: P.A. 93-108, § 205.)

CASE NOTES

Personal Jurisdiction

Party may object to subject matter jurisdiction without waiving objections to personal jurisdiction. *(Decided under former Uniform Child Custody Jurisdiction Act, repealed 750 ILCS 35/1 et seq.)* In re Stack, 281 Ill. App. 3d 423, 217 Ill. Dec. 290, 666 N.E.2d 1228 (2 Dist. 1996), appeal denied, 168 Ill. 2d 626, 219 Ill. Dec. 577, 671 N.E.2d 744 (1996).

LEGAL PERIODICALS

For article, "The Continuing Jurisdiction Dilemma in Interstate Child Custody Disputes," see 70 Ill. B. J. 304 (1982).

750 ILCS 36/206 Simultaneous Proceedings

Sec. 206. *Simultaneous Proceedings.* (a) Except as otherwise provided in Section 204 [750 ILCS 36/204], a court of this State may not exercise its jurisdiction under this Article if, at the time of the commencement of the proceeding, a proceeding concerning the custody of the child has been commenced in a court of another state having jurisdiction substantially in conformity with this Act, unless the proceeding has been terminated or is stayed by the court of the other state because a court of this State is a more convenient forum under Section 207 [750 ILCS 36/207].

(b) Except as otherwise provided in Section 204 [750 ILCS 36/204], a court of this State, before hearing a child-custody proceeding, shall examine the court documents and other information supplied by the parties pursuant to Section 209 [750 ILCS 36/209]. If the court determines that a child-custody proceeding has been commenced in a court in another state having jurisdiction substantially in accordance with this Act, the court of this State shall stay its proceeding and communicate with the court of the other state. If the court of the state having jurisdiction substantially in accordance with this Act does not determine that the court of this State is a more appropriate forum, the court of this State shall dismiss the proceeding.

(c) In a proceeding to modify a child-custody determination, a court of this State shall determine whether a proceeding to enforce the determination has been commenced in another state. If a proceeding to enforce a child-custody determination has been commenced in another state, the court may:

(1) stay the proceeding for modification pending the entry of an order of a court of the other state enforcing, staying, denying, or dismissing the proceeding for enforcement;

(2) enjoin the parties from continuing with the proceeding for enforcement; or

(3) proceed with the modification under conditions it considers appropriate.
(Source: P.A. 93-108, § 206.)

CASE NOTES

ANALYSIS

In General
Applicability
—Stay of Proceedings
Construction
—With Other Section
Consultation Provision
Forum Determination
—Interstate Communication
Overlapping Suits
Presence in State
—Lacking

In General

Custodial parent who removed children from Illinois to Louisiana and obtained a Louisiana court order that prohibited visitation by the other parent the day prior to a scheduled visitation was properly found in contempt of the Illinois visitation order because the Louisiana order did not excuse the custodial parent's noncompliance where it was intentionally procured as a way not to follow the order with which the custodial parent disagreed and because the Illinois court retained exclusive jurisdiction over the matter, regardless of where the children were taken. *(Decided under former Uniform Child Custody Jurisdiction Act, repealed 750 ILCS 35/1 et*

In General (Cont'd)
seq.) In re Marriage of Kneitz, 341 Ill. App. 3d 299, 276 Ill. Dec. 229, 793 N.E.2d 988, 2003 Ill. App. LEXIS 922 (2 Dist. 2003).

This Act involves a process in which the court must first resolve whether it has jurisdiction under 750 ILCS 35/4, and after such a finding, it must determine under this section and 750 ILCS 35/8 whether it should decline to exercise jurisdiction. *(Decided under former Uniform Child Custody Jurisdiction Act, repealed 750 ILCS 35/1 et seq.)* In re Levy, 105 Ill. App. 3d 355, 61 Ill. Dec. 247, 434 N.E.2d 400 (1 Dist. 1982).

Applicability

—Stay of Proceedings

Subsection (c) of this section applies only where the court learns of another pending action after assuming jurisdiction. *(Decided under former Uniform Child Custody Jurisdiction Act, repealed 750 ILCS 35/1 et seq.)* Jennings v. Jennings, 133 Ill. App. 3d 753, 88 Ill. Dec. 806, 479 N.E.2d 419 (5 Dist. 1985).

Construction

—With Other Section

As long as jurisdiction is established under section 4 of the Child Custody Act (750 ILCS 35/4), the trial court may enter an order of protection even though it might have been required to decline to exercise its jurisdiction under this section if it had instead been faced only with a petition to modify an out-of-state custody judgment. *(Decided under former Uniform Child Custody Jurisdiction Act, repealed 750 ILCS 35/1 et seq.)* Gasaway v. Gasaway, 246 Ill. App. 3d 531, 186 Ill. Dec. 420, 616 N.E.2d 610 (3 Dist. 1993).

Consultation Provision

The question of whether an Illinois court has a jurisdictional base is separate from the question of whether it complied with the mandatory consultation provision of subsection (c). *(Decided under former Uniform Child Custody Jurisdiction Act, repealed 750 ILCS 35/1 et seq.)* McGuane v. McGuane, 268 Ill. App. 3d 751, 206 Ill. Dec. 570, 645 N.E.2d 575 (2 Dist. 1995).

Forum Determination

—Interstate Communication

In child custody proceeding where five month old child was born in Texas, was hospitalized there, her mother died there and her father was incarcerated there and custody proceedings were filed there by maternal grandparent prior to Illinois proceeding, the trial judge in Illinois recognized the importance of contacting the Texas court which consisted of two phone calls; the Illinois judge was informed by the Texas judge that home studies had been ordered and, in due time, a final hearing would be held and the Illinois judge was assured by the Texas judge that the interests of all parties would be fairly considered; therefore the Illinois judge properly determined jurisdiction should remain with the Texas court. *(Decided under former Uniform Child Custody Jurisdiction Act, repealed 750 ILCS 35/1 et seq.)* In re Horne, 259 Ill. App. 3d 325, 197 Ill. Dec. 560, 631 N.E.2d 782 (4 Dist. 1994).

Overlapping Suits

As there was another proceeding concerning the custody of the children pending in a district court in Kansas, and that proceeding had not been stayed, Kansas' exercise of jurisdiction substantially in conformity with this Act prevented Illinois from exercising jurisdiction under this Act. *(Decided under former Uniform Child Custody Jurisdiction Act, repealed 750 ILCS 35/1 et seq.)* Jennings v. Jennings, 133 Ill. App. 3d 753, 88 Ill. Dec. 806, 479 N.E.2d 419 (5 Dist. 1985).

Presence in State

—Lacking

Where petitioner chose the courts of Kansas as the venue for determination of her controversy concerning custody, respondent resided in Kansas, and the children spent their summers with respondent, there was available in Kansas substantial evidence concerning the children's present and future care; therefore, the fact that the children were not physically present in Kansas did not affect that court's jurisdiction. *(Decided under former Uniform Child Custody Jurisdiction Act, repealed 750 ILCS 35/1 et seq.)* Jennings v. Jennings, 133 Ill. App. 3d 753, 88 Ill. Dec. 806, 479 N.E.2d 419 (5 Dist. 1985).

RESEARCH REFERENCES

Pending proceeding in another state as ground for declining jurisdiction under § 6(a) of the Uniform Child Custody Jurisdiction Act (UCCJA) or the Parental Kidnapping Prevention Act (PKPA), 28 USCS § 1738A(g). 20 ALR5th 700.

750 ILCS 36/207 Inconvenient Forum

Sec. 207. *Inconvenient Forum.* (a) A court of this State which has jurisdiction under this Act to make a child-custody determination may decline to exercise its jurisdiction at any time if it determines that it is an inconvenient forum under the circumstances and that a court of another state is a more appropriate forum. The issue of inconvenient forum may be raised upon motion of a party, the court's own motion, or request of another court.

(b) Before determining whether it is an inconvenient forum, a court of this State shall consider whether it is appropriate for a court of another state to exercise jurisdiction. For this purpose, the court shall allow the parties to submit information and shall consider all relevant factors, including:

(1) whether domestic violence has occurred and is likely to continue in the future and which state could best protect the parties and the child;

(2) the length of time the child has resided outside this State;

(3) the distance between the court in this State and the court in the state that would assume jurisdiction;

(4) the relative financial circumstances of the parties;

(5) any agreement of the parties as to which state should assume jurisdiction;

(6) the nature and location of the evidence required to resolve the pending litigation, including testimony of the child;

(7) the ability of the court of each state to decide the issue expeditiously and the procedures necessary to present the evidence; and

(8) the familiarity of the court of each state with the facts and issues in the pending litigation.

(c) If a court of this State determines that it is an inconvenient forum and that a court of another state is a more appropriate forum, it shall stay the proceedings upon condition that a child-custody proceeding be promptly commenced in another designated state and may impose any other condition the court considers just and proper.

(d) A court of this State may decline to exercise its jurisdiction under this Act if a child-custody determination is incidental to an action for divorce or another proceeding while still retaining jurisdiction over the divorce or other proceeding.

(Source: P.A. 93-108, § 207.)

CASE NOTES

ANALYSIS

In General

Appropriate Forum
—Other Country
—Other State
Best Interests of the Child
—In General
Discretion of Court
Factors Considered
Inconvenience
—Not Shown
Interstate Communication by Judges
Jurisdiction
—Conceding
—Proper
—Significant Connections
Purpose
Review
—Abuse of Discretion
Settlement Agreements
—Jurisdictional Limitations
—Superseding Facts
Unilateral Removal of Child

In General

Custodial parent who removed children from Illinois to Louisiana and obtained a Louisiana court order that prohibited visitation by the other parent the day prior to a scheduled visitation was properly found in contempt of the Illinois visitation order because the Louisiana order did not excuse the custodial parent's noncompliance where it was intentionally procured as a way not to follow the order with which the custodial parent disagreed and because the Illinois court retained exclusive jurisdiction over the matter, regardless of where the children were taken. *(Decided under former Uniform Child Custody Jurisdiction Act, repealed 750 ILCS 35/1 et seq.)* In re Marriage of Kneitz, 341 Ill. App. 3d 299, 276 Ill. Dec. 229, 793 N.E.2d 988, 2003 Ill. App. LEXIS 922 (2 Dist. 2003).

Even if a court meets jurisdictional criteria, it may decline to exercise its jurisdiction, and it must in some cases if it finds that it is an inconvenient forum for making such determinations under the circumstances of the case and that a court of another state is a more appropriate forum. *(Decided under former Uniform Child Custody Jurisdiction Act, repealed 750 ILCS 35/1 et seq.)* Klumpner v. Klumpner, 182 Ill. App. 3d 22, 130 Ill. Dec. 585, 537 N.E.2d 914 (1 Dist.), appeal denied, 136 Ill. Dec. 588, 545 N.E.2d 112 (1989), cert. denied, 494 U.S. 1004, 110 S. Ct. 1298, 108 L. Ed. 2d 475 (1990).

This Act requires that the trial court decline jurisdiction once it is aware that it may be an inconvenient forum, and that the court of another state is more appropriate. *(Decided under former Uniform Child Custody Jurisdiction Act, repealed 750 ILCS 35/1 et seq.)* In re Pavelcik, 138 Ill. App. 3d 1060, 93 Ill. Dec. 589, 487 N.E.2d 33 (1 Dist. 1985).

Even where the requirements of 750 ILCS 35/4 are met and the court has jurisdiction to make a child custody determination, it may decline to exercise it if it finds that court to be an inconvenient forum for the determination under the circumstances of the case, and that a court of another state is a more appropriate forum. *(Decided under former Uniform Child Custody Jurisdiction Act, repealed 750 ILCS 35/1 et seq.)* Noga v. Noga, 111 Ill. App. 3d 328, 67 Ill. Dec. 18, 443 N.E.2d 1142 (2 Dist. 1982).

This Act involves a process in which the court must first resolve whether it has jurisdiction under 750 ILCS 35/4, and after such a finding, it must determine under this section and 750 ILCS 35/7 whether it should decline to exercise jurisdiction. *(Decided under former Uniform Child Custody Jurisdiction Act, repealed 750 ILCS 35/1 et seq.)* In re Levy, 105 Ill. App. 3d 355, 61 Ill. Dec. 247, 434 N.E.2d 400 (1 Dist. 1982).

Appropriate Forum

—Other Country

Italy qualified as the proper forum to assume jurisdiction because it was "in the best interest of the child," since both of the child's parents had a significant connection with Italy and there was available in Italy substantial evidence concerning the child's housing, support, education, medical and dental care and personal relationships; therefore, the judgment entered in the Italian court was subject to enforcement in the Illinois courts and the trial court did not err in dismissing petition for dissolution of the marriage and transferring the cause back to the courts of Milan, Italy. *(Decided under former Uniform Child Custody Jurisdiction Act, repealed 750 ILCS 35/1 et seq.)* In re Silvestri-Gagliardoni, 186 Ill. App. 3d 46, 134 Ill. Dec. 106, 542 N.E.2d 106 (1 Dist. 1989).

—Other State

Where an appeal involved an application of the inconvenient forum provisions of this act, although the court granted a divorce, it declined to address the child custody matter and deferred to the jurisdiction of the New York court; the court found New York to be the more convenient forum since both sides were represented in that court, and the New York court had already received evidence from both sides regarding the forum issue. *(Decided under former Uniform Child Custody Jurisdiction Act, repealed 750 ILCS 35/1 et seq.)* In re Elblkasy, 241 Ill. App. 3d 662, 182 Ill. Dec. 715, 610 N.E.2d 139 (3 Dist. 1993).

North Carolina has found the forum with the greatest access to relevant evidence concerning the subject child's present and future well-being where her minister and teachers were present in that state to comment on her religious and academic performance, and friends and acquaintances were available to testify concerning her personal relationships. *(Decided under former Uniform Child Custody Jurisdiction Act, repealed 750 ILCS 35/1 et seq.)* Doehner v. Jessup, 215 Ill. App. 3d 570, 158 Ill. Dec. 987, 574 N.E.2d 1380 (3 Dist. 1991).

Where proceedings had been pending for over a year in another state's court, the minor's interests were represented in those court proceedings through the appointment of a guardian ad litem, and petitioner's actions were a hindrance to and not a help to the resolution of the matter in the other forum, the Illinois court properly declined jurisdiction. *(Decided under former Uniform Child Custody Jurisdiction Act, repealed 750 ILCS 35/1 et seq.)* Bellefont v. Wright, 179 Ill. App. 3d 1036, 129 Ill. Dec. 390, 536 N.E.2d 74 (4 Dist. 1989).

No abuse of discretion existed in the trial court's conclusion that it should decline to exercise its jurisdiction where the child resided in another state and had never permanently resided in Illinois, evidence regarding father's ability to care for his daughter was located in another state, and wife's petition did not indicate that the child's living environment with her father posed an immediate, grave risk to the child's physical or emotional well-being. *(Decided under former Uniform Child Custody Jurisdiction Act, repealed 750 ILCS 35/1 et seq.)* Kuehl v. Kuehl, 186 Ill. App. 3d 31, 134 Ill. Dec. 75, 542 N.E.2d 75 (1 Dist. 1989).

The facts amply supported trial court's conclusion that Missouri was the most appropriate forum to litigate the child custody matter. *(Decided under former Uniform Child Custody Jurisdiction Act, repealed 750 ILCS 35/1 et seq.)* In re Pavelcik, 138 Ill. App. 3d 1060, 93 Ill. Dec. 589, 487 N.E.2d 33 (1 Dist. 1985).

The trial court correctly declined to assert jurisdiction over grandparents' visitation petition where the children had not been residents of Illinois for over two years, it appeared Arkansas was now their home state, the record did not disclose whether the children's natural father continued to reside in Illinois, and the natural father submitted to the jurisdiction of the Arkansas courts in an adoption proceeding in which his parental rights were being determined. *(Decided under former Uniform Child Custody Jurisdiction Act, repealed 750 ILCS 35/1 et seq.)* Noga v. Noga, 111 Ill. App. 3d 328, 67 Ill. Dec. 18, 443 N.E.2d 1142 (2 Dist. 1982).

Circuit court's order of dismissal stating that it had jurisdiction but would decline to exercise it, because North Dakota courts were in a better position to determine the issues, was within its discretion where the main thrust of petitioner's affidavit was directed to the situation in North Dakota and as to how respondent would provide for the child there. *(Decided under former Uniform Child Custody Jurisdiction Act, repealed 750 ILCS 35/1 et seq.)* Flesner v. Houser, 104 Ill. App. 3d 904, 60 Ill. Dec. 678, 433 N.E.2d 720 (4 Dist. 1982).

Best Interests of the Child

—In General

The primary objective of the trial court is to determine which court can most capably act in the best interests of the child. *(Decided under former Uniform Child Custody Jurisdiction Act, repealed 750 ILCS 35/1 et seq.)* Doehner v. Jessup, 215 Ill. App. 3d 570, 158 Ill. Dec. 987, 574 N.E.2d 1380 (3 Dist. 1991).

Discretion of Court

The above principles cannot be applied in a rigid or mechanical fashion but require the trial court to exercise discretion. *(Decided under former Uniform Child Custody Jurisdiction Act, repealed 750 ILCS 35/1 et seq.)* In re Tatham, 293 Ill. App. 3d 471, 228 Ill. Dec. 166, 688 N.E.2d 864 (5 Dist. 1997).

The standards applicable to determining jurisdiction cannot be applied in a mechanical fashion, but require the exercise of discretion by the trial court. *(Decided under former Uniform Child Custody Jurisdiction Act, repealed 750 ILCS 35/1 et seq.)* In re Kehres, 164 Ill. App. 3d 148, 115 Ill. Dec. 206, 517 N.E.2d 617 (5 Dist. 1987).

Factors Considered

The child's home state, the location of necessary evidence of the child's well-being, and the significant relationships of the child or parties to the competing states are considerations to be weighed in determining whether Illinois is an inconvenient forum. *(Decided under former Uniform Child Custody Jurisdiction Act, repealed 750 ILCS 35/1 et seq.)* In re Rizza, 237 Ill. App. 3d 83, 177 Ill. Dec. 353, 603 N.E.2d 134 (2 Dist. 1992).

Inconvenience

—Not Shown

Circuit court abused its discretion by declining to exercise jurisdiction on the basis of an inconvenient forum; no other state was or recently had been the home state of the children, no other state had a closer connection than Illinois to the children or their mother, and all evidence regarding the children's present circumstances was available in Illinois. *(Decided under former Uniform Child Custody Jurisdiction Act, repealed 750 ILCS 35/1 et seq.)* Arulpragasam v. Eisele, 304 Ill. App. 3d 139, 237 Ill. Dec. 470, 709 N.E.2d 725 (4 Dist. 1999), appeal denied, 185 Ill. 2d 617, 242 Ill. Dec. 134, 720 N.E.2d 1089 (1999).

Since petitioner agreed that Illinois was the proper forum as late as December of 1994, the trial court did not abuse its discretion in deciding not to decline jurisdiction. *(Decided under former Uniform Child Custody Jurisdiction Act, repealed 750 ILCS 35/1 et seq.)* In re Tatham, 293 Ill. App. 3d 471, 228 Ill. Dec. 166, 688 N.E.2d 864 (5 Dist. 1997).

Interstate Communication by Judges

Interstate communication by the trial judges is authorized by subsection (d). *(Decided under former Uniform Child Custody Jurisdiction Act, repealed 750 ILCS 35/1 et seq.)* In re Horne, 259 Ill. App. 3d 325, 197 Ill. Dec. 560, 631 N.E.2d 782 (4 Dist. 1994).

Jurisdiction

—Conceding

In a proceeding in which the husband sought to punish the wife for violating the terms of the judgment for dissolution of their marriage by moving to Georgia with their child, the court properly conceded jurisdiction to Georgia where the mother alleged, and the husband offered to evidence to dispute, (1) that Georgia was the child's home state, (2) that all the evidence concerning the child's care, protection, training, and personal relationships was available in Georgia rather than in Illinois; and (3) that she had filed a motion in the Georgia court to enroll the Illinois judgment of dissolution of marriage. *(Decided under former Uniform Child Custody Jurisdiction Act, repealed 750 ILCS 35/1 et seq.)* In re Blanchard, 305 Ill. App. 3d 348, 238 Ill. Dec. 652, 712 N.E.2d 374 (2 Dist. 1999).

Trial court did not abuse its discretion in conceding jurisdiction to another state where other state was child's home, had a closer connection with the child and with respondent than did Illinois and there was substantial evidence there, as settlement agreement provided that post decree proceedings would be construed under Illinois law not filed only in Illinois. *(Decided under former Uniform Child Custody Jurisdiction Act, repealed 750 ILCS 35/1 et seq.)* In re Walker, 287 Ill. App. 3d 634, 222 Ill. Dec. 833, 678 N.E.2d 705 (1 Dist. 1997).

—Proper

In a motion for forum non conveniens under this section, the court correctly asserted jurisdiction under this Act where an alternate court had already determined that it would not exercise jurisdiction, and where the children who were the subject of the action had lived most of their lives in the state and were absent less than six months before the first action was filed. *(Decided under former Uniform Child Custody Jurisdiction Act, repealed 750 ILCS 35/1 et seq.)* In re Kehres, 164 Ill. App. 3d 148, 115 Ill. Dec. 206, 517 N.E.2d 617 (5 Dist. 1987).

—Significant Connections

Although child of the parties was residing in Texas pursuant to an agreed order granting mother temporary custody and a number of witnesses were located in Texas, where father was present in Illinois, had visitation with the child in Illinois, had family and friends in Illinois who would be called as witnesses and, in addition a doctor conducting an evaluation of the parties and the child was located in Illinois, retained a significant connection with Illinois. *(Decided under former Uniform Child Custody Jurisdiction Act, repealed 750 ILCS 35/1 et seq.)* In re Breyley, 247 Ill. App. 3d 486, 187 Ill. Dec. 215, 617 N.E.2d 423 (3 Dist. 1993).

Purpose

The "inconvenient forum" paragraph of this Act was plainly designed to effectuate its policy objectives by granting authority to the trial court to yield jurisdiction to another court which is in a superior position to determine the merits of the dispute. *(Decided under former Uniform Child Custody Jurisdiction Act, repealed 750 ILCS 35/1 et seq.)* In re Pavelcik, 138 Ill. App. 3d 1060, 93 Ill. Dec. 589, 487 N.E.2d 33 (1 Dist. 1985).

Review

—Abuse of Discretion

As the application of this section requires exercise of the trial court's discretion, a decision not to decline jurisdiction will be affirmed absent an abuse of that discretion. *(Decided under former Uniform Child Custody Jurisdiction Act, repealed 750 ILCS 35/1 et seq.)* Doehner v. Jessup, 215 Ill. App. 3d 570, 158 Ill. Dec. 987, 574 N.E.2d 1380 (3 Dist. 1991).

A trial court's decision to decline jurisdiction will be affirmed absent an abuse of that discretion. *(Decided under former Uniform Child Custody Jurisdiction Act, repealed 750 ILCS 35/1 et seq.)* Kuehl v. Kuehl, 186 Ill. App. 3d 31, 134 Ill. Dec. 75, 542 N.E.2d 75 (1 Dist. 1989).

A trial court's decision not to decline jurisdiction to a foreign court will be affirmed absent an abuse of that discretion. *(Decided under former Uniform Child Custody Jurisdiction Act, repealed 750 ILCS 35/1 et seq.)* In re Kehres, 164 Ill. App. 3d 148, 115 Ill. Dec. 206, 517 N.E.2d 617 (5 Dist. 1987).

Settlement Agreements

—Jurisdictional Limitations

A trial court's order refusing to transfer jurisdiction pursuant to the doctrine of forum non conveniens was correct where the parties' settlement agreement, which was incorporated into the dissolution judgment, provided that any further post-decree proceedings would only be filed in Illinois, provided the husband resides in Illinois. *(Decided under former Uniform Child Custody Jurisdiction Act, repealed 750 ILCS 35/1 et seq.)* In re Hilliard, 178 Ill. App. 3d 620, 127 Ill. Dec. 671, 533 N.E.2d 543 (3 Dist. 1989).

—Superseding Facts

Although the trial court retained continuing jurisdiction of the matter of visitation rights in the dissolution decree, and the father validly invoked that jurisdiction when he filed his petition to modify visitation, that fact was superseded by the intervening fact that the children and petitioner-mother had absented themselves from Illinois, with the permission of the court, after the dissolution decree was entered; this intervening fact, coupled with the length of the children's stay in Missouri, obviated the language of the dissolution decree, at least to the extent that compliance with that decree would frustrate the objectives of this Act. *(Decided under former Uniform Child Custody Jurisdiction Act, repealed 750 ILCS 35/1 et seq.)* In re Pavelcik, 138 Ill. App. 3d 1060, 93 Ill. Dec. 589, 487 N.E.2d 33 (1 Dist. 1985).

Unilateral Removal of Child

Where child was removed from Illinois to Texas without the trial court's knowledge or consent, to transfer custody proceedings to

Unilateral Removal of Child (Cont'd)
Texas would condone behavior contrary to the purposes of this Act; one of Act's stated purposes is to deter unilateral removals of children. *(Decided under former Uniform Child Custody Jurisdiction Act, repealed 750 ILCS 35/1 et seq.)* In re Breyley, 247 Ill. App. 3d 486, 187 Ill. Dec. 215, 617 N.E.2d 423 (3 Dist. 1993).

RESEARCH REFERENCES

Court-authorized permanent or temporary removal of child by parent to foreign country. 30 ALR4th 548.

Inconvenience of forum as ground for declining jurisdiction under § 7 of the Uniform Child Custody Jurisdiction Act (UCCJA). 21 ALR5th 396.

750 ILCS 36/208 Jurisdiction Declined By Reason Of Conduct

Sec. 208. *Jurisdiction Declined By Reason Of Conduct.* (a) Except as otherwise provided in Section 204 [750 ILCS 36/204] or by other law of this State, if a court of this State has jurisdiction under this Act because a person seeking to invoke its jurisdiction has engaged in unjustifiable conduct, the court shall decline to exercise its jurisdiction unless:

(1) the parents and all persons acting as parents have acquiesced in the exercise of jurisdiction;

(2) a court of the state otherwise having jurisdiction under Sections 201 through 203 [750 ILCS 36/201 through 750 ILCS 36/203] determines that this State is a more appropriate forum under Section 207 [750 ILCS 36/207]; or

(3) no court of any other state would have jurisdiction under the criteria specified in Sections 201 through 203 [750 ILCS 36/201 through 750 ILCS 36/203].

(b) If a court of this State declines to exercise its jurisdiction pursuant to subsection (a), it may fashion an appropriate remedy to ensure the safety of the child and prevent a repetition of the unjustifiable conduct, including staying the proceeding until a child-custody proceeding is commenced in a court having jurisdiction under Sections 201 through 203 [750 ILCS 36/201 through 750 ILCS 36/203].

(c) If a court dismisses a petition or stays a proceeding because it declines to exercise its jurisdiction pursuant to subsection (a), it shall assess against the party seeking to invoke its jurisdiction necessary and reasonable expenses including costs, communication expenses, attorney's fees, investigative fees, expenses for witnesses, travel expenses, and child care during the course of the proceedings, unless the party from whom fees are sought establishes that the assessment would be clearly inappropriate. The court may not assess fees, costs, or expenses against this State unless authorized by law other than this Act.

(Source: P.A. 93-108, § 208.)

CASE NOTES

ANALYSIS

Conduct Disapproved
—Jurisdiction Denied
Misconduct Not Shown

Conduct Disapproved

—Jurisdiction Denied

Where counsel for the mother failed to request deference to the Michigan courts prior to the commencement of the proceeding in this case, and since the merits of the case had been heard prior to the request that that defense be entertained by the Illinois circuit court, the court properly rejected such a consideration, even though the father's conduct in forcibly obtaining physical custody of the child from the mother in Michigan was strongly disapproved. *(Decided under former Uniform Child Custody Jurisdiction Act, repealed 750 ILCS 35/1 et seq.)* In re Thompson, 96 Ill. 2d 67, 70 Ill. Dec. 214, 449 N.E.2d 88 (1983).

Misconduct Not Shown

Where mother did not abduct or unilaterally remove the children from the foreign state but she complied with the requirement of the dissolution judgment that she seek permission of the court before taking the children to another state, she did not engage in forum shopping or other similar reprehensible conduct; therefore the circuit court abused its discretion by declining to exercise otherwise proper jurisdiction on this basis. *(Decided under former Uniform Child Custody Jurisdiction Act, repealed 750 ILCS 35/1 et seq.)* Arulpragasam v. Eisele, 304 Ill. App. 3d 139, 237 Ill. Dec. 470, 709 N.E.2d 725 (4 Dist. 1999), appeal denied, 185 Ill. 2d 617, 242 Ill. Dec. 134, 720 N.E.2d 1089 (1999).

750 ILCS 36/209 Information To Be Submitted To Court

Sec. 209. *Information To Be Submitted To Court.* (a) Subject to any other law providing for the confidentiality of procedures, addresses, and other identifying information, in a child-custody proceeding, each party, in its first pleading or in an attached affidavit, shall give information, if reasonably ascertainable, under oath as to the child's present address or whereabouts, the places where the child has lived during the last five years, and the names and present addresses of the persons with whom the child has lived during that period. The pleading or affidavit must state whether the party:

(1) has participated, as a party or witness or in any other capacity, in any other proceeding concerning the custody of or visitation with the child and, if so, identify the court, the case number, and the date of the child-custody determination, if any;

(2) knows of any proceeding that could affect the current proceeding, including proceedings for enforcement and proceedings relating to domestic violence, protective orders, termination of parental rights, and adoptions and, if so, identify the court, the case number, and the nature of the proceeding; and

(3) knows the names and addresses of any person not a party to the proceeding who has physical custody of the child or claims rights of legal custody or physical custody of, or visitation with, the child and, if so, the names and addresses of those persons.

(b) If the information required by subsection (a) is not furnished, the court, upon motion of a party or its own motion, may stay the proceeding until the information is furnished.

(c) If the declaration as to any of the items described in subsection (a)(1) through (3) is in the affirmative, the declarant shall give additional information under oath as required by the court. The court may examine the parties under oath as to details of the information furnished and other matters pertinent to the court's jurisdiction and the disposition of the case.

(d) Each party has a continuing duty to inform the court of any proceeding in this or any other state that could affect the current proceeding.

(e) (Blank).

(Source: P.A. 93-108, § 209.)

CASE NOTES

Failure to Inform

—Equitable Action Inappropriate

Where mother had been informed by the father prior to his filing for divorce in Illinois that he intended to bring suit there, she filed her special appearance in the Illinois action prior to entry of a Montana dissolution decree, and neither that decree nor any prior pleadings in the Montana action of record indicated that court's knowledge of a pending Illinois suit, the mother did not inform the Montana court of the Illinois action, as required under this section, even after her knowledge of it was irrefutably shown by her active participation; therefore, invocation of equitable principles on her behalf was inappropriate, particularly since the father did not violate any court order by removing the children to Illinois. *(Decided under former Uniform Child Custody Jurisdiction Act, repealed 750 ILCS 35/1 et seq.)* In re Weinstein, 87 Ill. App. 3d 101, 42 Ill. Dec. 243, 408 N.E.2d 952 (1 Dist. 1980).

750 ILCS 36/210 Appearance Of Parties And Child

Sec. 210. *Appearance Of Parties And Child.* (a) In a child-custody proceeding in this State, the court may order a party to the proceeding who is in this State to appear before the court in person with or without the child. The court may order any person who is in this State and who has physical custody or control of the child to appear in person with the child.

(b) If a party to a child-custody proceeding whose presence is desired by the court is outside this State, the court may order that a notice given pursuant to Section 108 [750 ILCS 36/108] include a statement directing the party to appear in person with or without the child and informing the party that failure to appear may result in a decision adverse to the party.

(c) The court may enter any orders necessary to ensure the safety of the child and of any person ordered to appear under this Section.

(d) If a party to a child-custody proceeding who is outside this State is directed to appear under subsection (b) or desires to appear personally before the court with or without the child, the court may require another party to pay reasonable and necessary travel and other expenses of the party so appearing and of the child.

(Source: P.A. 93-108, § 210.)

ARTICLE 3. ENFORCEMENT

750 ILCS 36/301 Definitions

Sec. 301. *Definitions.* In this Article:

(1) "Petitioner" means a person who seeks enforcement of an order for return of a child under the Hague Convention on the Civil Aspects of International Child Abduction or enforcement of a child-custody determination.

(2) "Respondent" means a person against whom a proceeding has been commenced for enforcement of an order for return of a child under the Hague Convention on the Civil Aspects of International Child Abduction or enforcement of a child-custody determination.

(Source: P.A. 93-108, § 301.)

750 ILCS 36/302 Enforcement Under Hague Convention

Sec. 302. *Enforcement Under Hague Convention.* Under this Article a court of this State may enforce an order for the return of the child made under the Hague Convention on the Civil Aspects of International Child Abduction as if it were a child-custody determination.

(Source: P.A. 93-108, § 302.)

750 ILCS 36/303 Duty To Enforce

Sec. 303. *Duty To Enforce.* (a) A court of this State shall recognize and enforce a child-custody determination of a court of another state if the latter court exercised jurisdiction in substantial conformity with this Act or the determination was made under factual circumstances meeting the jurisdictional standards of this Act and the determination has not been modified in accordance with this Act.

(b) A court of this State may utilize any remedy available under other law of this State to enforce a child-custody determination made by a court of another state. The remedies provided in this Article are cumulative and do not affect the availability of other remedies to enforce a child-custody determination.

(Source: P.A. 93-108, § 303.)

750 ILCS 36/304 Temporary Visitation

Sec. 304. *Temporary Visitation.* (a) A court of this State which does not have jurisdiction to modify a child-custody determination, may issue a temporary order enforcing:

(1) a visitation schedule made by a court of another state; or

(2) the visitation provisions of a child-custody determination of another state that does not provide for a specific visitation schedule.

(b) If a court of this State makes an order under subsection (a)(2), it shall specify in the order a period that it considers adequate to allow the petitioner to obtain an order from a court having jurisdiction under the criteria specified in Article 2. The order remains in effect until an order is obtained from the other court or the period expires.

(Source: P.A. 93-108, § 304.)

750 ILCS 36/305 Registration Of Child-Custody Determination

Sec. 305. *Registration Of Child-Custody Determination.* (a) A child-custody determination issued by a court of another state may be registered in this State, with or without a simultaneous request for enforcement, by sending to the circuit court in this State:

(1) a letter or other document requesting registration;

(2) two copies, including one certified copy, of the determination sought to be registered, and a statement under penalty of perjury that to the best of the knowledge and belief of the person seeking registration the order has not been modified; and

(3) except as otherwise provided in Section 209 [750 ILCS 36/209], the name and address of the person seeking registration and any parent or person acting as a parent who has been awarded custody or visitation in the child-custody determination sought to be registered.

(b) On receipt of the documents required by subsection (a), the registering court shall:

(1) cause the determination to be filed as a foreign judgment, together with one copy of any accompanying documents and information, regardless of their form; and

(2) serve notice upon the persons named pursuant to subsection (a)(3) and provide them with an opportunity to contest the registration in accordance with this Section.

(c) The notice required by subsection (b)(2) must state that:

(1) a registered determination is enforceable as of the date of the registration in the same manner as a determination issued by a court of this State;

(2) a hearing to contest the validity of the registered determination must be requested within 20 days after service of notice; and

(3) failure to contest the registration will result in confirmation of the child-custody determination and preclude further contest of that determination with respect to any matter that could have been asserted.

(d) A person seeking to contest the validity of a registered order must request a hearing within 20 days after service of the notice. At that hearing, the court shall confirm the registered order unless the person contesting registration establishes that:

(1) the issuing court did not have jurisdiction under Article 2;

(2) the child-custody determination sought to be registered has been vacated, stayed, or modified by a court having jurisdiction to do so under Article 2; or

(3) the person contesting registration was entitled to notice, but notice was not given in accordance with the standards of Section 108 [750 ILCS 36/108], in the proceedings before the court that issued the order for which registration is sought.

(e) If a timely request for a hearing to contest the validity of the registration is not made, the registration is confirmed as a matter of law and the person requesting registration and all persons served must be notified of the confirmation.

(f) Confirmation of a registered order, whether by operation of law or after notice and hearing, precludes further contest of the order with respect to any matter that could have been asserted at the time of registration.

(Source: P.A. 93-108, § 305.)

750 ILCS 36/306 Enforcement Of Registered Determination

Sec. 306. *Enforcement Of Registered Determination.* (a) A court of this State may grant any relief normally available under the law of this State to enforce a registered child-custody determination made by a court of another state.

(b) A court of this State shall recognize and enforce, but may not modify, except in accordance with Article 2, a registered child-custody determination of a court of another state.

(Source: P.A. 93-108, § 306.)

750 ILCS 36/307 Simultaneous Proceedings

Sec. 307. *Simultaneous Proceedings.* If a proceeding for enforcement under this Article is commenced in a court of this State and the court determines that a proceeding to modify the determination is pending in a court of another state having jurisdiction to modify the determination under Article 2, the enforcing court shall immediately communicate with the modifying court. The proceeding for enforcement continues unless the enforcing court, after consultation with the modifying court, stays or dismisses the proceeding.

(Source: P.A. 93-108, § 307.)

750 ILCS 36/308 Expedited Enforcement Of Child-Custody Determination

Sec. 308. *Expedited Enforcement Of Child-Custody Determination.* (a) A petition under this Article must be verified. Certified copies of all orders sought to be enforced and of any order confirming registration must be attached to the petition. A copy of a certified copy of an order may be attached instead of the original.

(b) A petition for enforcement of a child-custody determination must state:

(1) whether the court that issued the determination identified the jurisdictional basis it relied upon in exercising jurisdiction and, if so, what the basis was;

(2) whether the determination for which enforcement is sought has been vacated, stayed, or modified by a court whose decision must be enforced under this Act and, if so, identify the court, the case number, and the nature of the proceeding;

(3) whether any proceeding has been commenced that could affect the current proceeding, including proceedings relating to domestic violence, protective orders, termination of parental rights, and adoptions and, if so, identify the court, the case number, and the nature of the proceeding;

(4) the present physical address of the child and the respondent, if known;

(5) whether relief in addition to the immediate physical custody of the child and attorney's fees is sought, including a request for assistance from law enforcement officials and, if so, the relief sought; and

(6) if the child-custody determination has been registered and confirmed under Section 305 [750 ILCS 36/305], the date and place of registration.

(c) Upon the filing of a petition, the court shall issue an order directing the respondent to appear in person with or without the child at a hearing and may enter any order necessary to ensure the safety of the parties and the child. The hearing must be held on the next judicial day after service of the order unless that date is impossible. In that event, the court shall hold the hearing on the first judicial day possible. The court may extend the date of hearing at the request of the petitioner.

(d) An order issued under subsection (c) must state the time and place of the hearing and advise the respondent that at the hearing the court will order that the petitioner may take immediate physical custody of the child and the payment of fees, costs, and expenses under Section 312 [750 ILCS 36/312], and may schedule a hearing to determine whether further relief is appropriate, unless the respondent appears and establishes that:

(1) the child-custody determination has not been registered and confirmed under Section 305 [750 ILCS 36/305] and that:

(A) the issuing court did not have jurisdiction under Article 2;

(B) the child-custody determination for which enforcement is sought has been vacated, stayed, or modified by a court having jurisdiction to do so under Article 2;

(C) the respondent was entitled to notice, but notice was not given in accordance with the standards of Section 108 [750 ILCS 36/108], in the proceedings before the court that issued the order for which enforcement is sought; or

(2) the child-custody determination for which enforcement is sought was registered and confirmed under Section 304 [750 ILCS 36/304], but has been vacated, stayed, or modified by a court of a state having jurisdiction to do so under Article 2.

(Source: P.A. 93-108, § 308.)

750 ILCS 36/309 Service Of Petition And Order

Sec. 309. *Service Of Petition And Order.* Except as otherwise provided in Section 311 [750 ILCS 36/311], the petition and order must be served, by any method authorized by the law of this State, upon respondent and any person who has physical custody of the child.

(Source: P.A. 93-108, § 309.)

750 ILCS 36/310 Hearing And Order

Sec. 310. *Hearing And Order.* (a) Unless the court issues a temporary emergency order pursuant to Section 204 [750 ILCS 36/204], upon a finding that a petitioner is entitled to immediate physical custody of the child, the court shall order that the petitioner may take immediate physical custody of the child unless the respondent establishes that:

(1) the child-custody determination has not been registered and confirmed under Section 305 [750 ILCS 36/305] and that:

(A) the issuing court did not have jurisdiction under Article 2;

(B) the child-custody determination for which enforcement is sought has been vacated, stayed, or modified by a court of a state having jurisdiction to do so under Article 2; or

(C) the respondent was entitled to notice, but notice was not given in accordance with the standards of Section 108 [750 ILCS 36/108], in the proceedings before the court that issued the order for which enforcement is sought; or

(2) the child-custody determination for which enforcement is sought was registered and confirmed under Section 305 [750 ILCS 36/305] but has been vacated, stayed, or modified by a court of a state having jurisdiction to do so under Article 2.

(b) The court shall award the fees, costs, and expenses authorized under Section 312 [750 ILCS 36/312] and may grant additional relief, including a request for the assistance of law enforcement officials, and set a further hearing to determine whether additional relief is appropriate.

(c) If a party called to testify refuses to answer on the ground that the testimony may be self-incriminating, the court may draw an adverse inference from the refusal.

(d) A privilege against disclosure of communications between spouses and a defense of immunity based on the relationship of husband and wife or parent and child may not be invoked in a proceeding under this Article.

(Source: P.A. 93-108, § 310.)

750 ILCS 36/311 Warrant To Take Physical Custody Of Child

Sec. 311. *Warrant To Take Physical Custody Of Child.* (a) Upon the filing of a petition seeking enforcement of a child-custody determination, the petitioner may file a verified application for the issuance of a warrant to take physical custody of the child if the child is immediately likely to suffer serious physical harm or be removed from this State.

(b) If the court, upon the testimony of the petitioner or other witness, finds that the child is imminently likely to suffer serious physical harm or be removed from this State, it may issue a warrant to take physical custody of the child. The petition must be heard on the next judicial day after the warrant is executed unless that date is impossible. In that event, the court shall hold the hearing on the first judicial day possible. The application for the warrant must include the statements required by Section 308(b) [750 ILCS 36/308].

(c) A warrant to take physical custody of a child must:

(1) recite the facts upon which a conclusion of imminent serious physical harm or removal from the jurisdiction is based;

(2) direct law enforcement officers to take physical custody of the child immediately; and

(3) provide for the placement of the child pending final relief.

(d) The respondent must be served with the petition, warrant, and order immediately after the child is taken into physical custody.

(e) A warrant to take physical custody of a child is enforceable throughout this State. If the court finds on the basis of the testimony of the petitioner or other witness that a less intrusive remedy is not effective, it may authorize law enforcement officers to enter private property to take physical custody of the child. If required by exigent circumstances of the case, the court may authorize law enforcement officers to make a forcible entry at any hour.

(f) The court may impose conditions upon placement of a child to ensure the appearance of the child and the child's custodian.

(Source: P.A. 93-108, § 311.)

750 ILCS 36/312 Costs, Fees, And Expenses

Sec. 312. *Costs, Fees, And Expenses.* (a) The court shall award the prevailing party, including a state, necessary and reasonable expenses incurred by or on behalf of the party, including costs, communication expenses, attorney's fees, investigative fees, expenses for witnesses, travel expenses, and child care during the course of the proceedings, unless the party from whom fees or expenses are sought establishes that the award would be clearly inappropriate.

(b) The court may not assess fees, costs, or expenses against a state unless authorized by law other than this Act.

(Source: P.A. 93-108, § 312.)

750 ILCS 36/313 Recognition And Enforcement

Sec. 313. *Recognition And Enforcement.* A court of this State shall accord full faith and credit to an order issued by another state and consistent with this Act which enforces a child-custody determination by a court of another state unless the order has been vacated, stayed, or modified by a court having jurisdiction to do so under Article 2.

(Source: P.A. 93-108, § 313.)

CASE NOTES

Analysis

In General
Full Faith and Credit
—Not Warranted
—Properly Extended
Judicial Authority
—Contempt
Notice and Opportunity to be Heard

In General

This section requires that Illinois courts recognize and enforce an initial custody judgment of a court of another state, or a modification thereof, which had assumed jurisdiction under statutory provisions substantially in accordance with the provisions of this Act, just as this Act requires that its custody judgments be considered conclusive unless and until that determination is modified pursuant to law. *(Decided under former Uniform Child Custody Jurisdiction Act, repealed 750 ILCS 35/1 et seq.)* Moseley v. Goldstone, 89 Ill. App. 3d 360, 44 Ill. Dec. 779, 411 N.E.2d 1145 (1 Dist. 1980).

Full Faith and Credit

—Not Warranted

The trial court was not compelled to recognize and enforce the custody order of the Washington court pursuant to this section as it was plain that that court had not properly assumed jurisdiction under this Act, nor was its order made under factual circumstances meeting the jurisdictional standards of this Act. *(Decided under former Uniform Child Custody Jurisdiction Act, repealed 750 ILCS 35/1 et seq.)* McKerr v. Bozarth, 182 Ill. App. 3d 345, 131 Ill. Dec. 410, 538 N.E.2d 785 (2 Dist. 1989).

Under former Ill.Rev.Stat., ch. 3, para. 132 (see now this section), where a child was taken from the mother by order of a California court and had since resided in the home of the paternal grandparents, and where neither the child nor the defendants were heard at the California hearing to grant custody to the mother, there was at best grave doubt as to whether California could exercise jurisdiction over the child, and an even more serious question as to whether the California court had acquired jurisdiction over the defendants, and therefore, an order of the California court granting custody to the mother was not entitled to full faith and credit in Illinois. *(Decided under former Uniform Child Custody Jurisdiction Act, repealed 750 ILCS 35/1 et seq.)* People ex rel. Strand v. Harnetiaux, 46 Ill. 2d 424, 263 N.E.2d 30 (1970).

—Properly Extended

Michigan court had jurisdiction to modify its custody order in accordance with the purposes of this Act to discourage forum shopping and to deter removal of children to obtain custody awards; therefore, the trial court properly extended full faith and credit to the Michigan court order. *(Decided under former Uniform Child Custody Jurisdiction Act, repealed 750 ILCS 35/1 et seq.)* In re Mauro, 187 Ill. App. 3d 794, 135 Ill. Dec. 288, 543 N.E.2d 856 (1 Dist. 1989).

In absence of an adequate showing that Nevada no longer retained jurisdiction to modify a prior custody decree, the trial court properly denied petitioner's motion to vacate the granting of full faith and credit to a Nevada modification order as well as her request for an evidentiary hearing. *(Decided under former Uniform*

Full Faith and Credit (Cont'd)

—Properly Extended (Cont'd)

Child Custody Jurisdiction Act, repealed 750 ILCS 35/1 et seq.) In re Dagher, 145 Ill. App. 3d 379, 99 Ill. Dec. 269, 495 N.E.2d 1004 (1 Dist. 1986).

Judicial Authority

—Contempt

This section and 750 ILCS 35/24 authorize the court to recognize and enforce the custody provisions of a foreign country's decree, but do not authorize the power to hold a party in contempt for conduct which occurred prior to the recognition of the decree by the circuit court. *(Decided under former Uniform Child Custody Jurisdiction Act, repealed 750 ILCS 35/1 et seq.)* In re Alush, 172 Ill. App. 3d 646, 122 Ill. Dec. 694, 527 N.E.2d 66 (2 Dist. 1988).

Notice and Opportunity to be Heard

Although the Illinois Uniform Child Custody Jurisdiction Act does not specify that notice and an opportunity to be heard on jurisdictional prerequisites, both constitutional and statutory, must precede enforcement of an out-of-state order, some opportunity to object to jurisdiction and sufficiency of notice must be provided, in order to allow the adverse party the opportunity to contest recognition and enforcement. *(Decided under former Uniform Child Custody Jurisdiction Act, repealed 750 ILCS 35/1 et seq.)* Morrell v. Mock, 270 F.3d 1090, 2001 U.S. App. LEXIS 23632 (7th Cir. 2001), cert. denied, 537 U.S. 812, 123 S. Ct. 71, 154 L. Ed. 2d 14 (2002).

LEGAL PERIODICALS

For article, "The Continuing Jurisdiction Dilemma in Interstate Child Custody Disputes," see 70 Ill. B. J. 304 (1982).

750 ILCS 36/314 Appeals

Sec. 314. *Appeals.* An appeal may be taken from a final order in a proceeding under this Article in accordance with expedited appellate procedures which are or may be established by Supreme Court Rule. Unless the court enters a temporary emergency order under Section 204 [750 ILCS 36/204], the enforcing court may not stay an order enforcing a child-custody determination pending appeal.
(Source: P.A. 93-108, § 314.)

750 ILCS 36/315 Role Of State's Attorney

Sec. 315. *Role Of State's Attorney.* (a) In a case arising under this Act or involving the Hague Convention on the Civil Aspects of International Child Abduction, the State's Attorney or other appropriate public official may take any lawful action, including resort to a proceeding under this Article or any other available civil proceeding to locate a child, obtain the return of a child, or enforce a child-custody determination if there is:

(1) an existing child-custody determination;

(2) a request to do so from a court in a pending child-custody proceeding;

(3) a reasonable belief that a criminal statute has been violated; or

(4) a reasonable belief that the child has been wrongfully removed or retained in violation of the Hague Convention on the Civil Aspects of International Child Abduction.

(b) A State's Attorney or appropriate public official acting under this Section acts on behalf of the court and may not represent any party.
(Source: P.A. 93-108, § 315.)

750 ILCS 36/316 Role Of Law Enforcement

Sec. 316. *Role Of Law Enforcement.* At the request of a State's Attorney or other appropriate public official acting under Section 315 [750 ILCS 36/315], a law enforcement officer may take any lawful action reasonably necessary to locate a child or a party and assist a State's Attorney or appropriate public official with responsibilities under Section 315 [750 ILCS 36/315].
(Source: P.A. 93-108, § 316.)

750 ILCS 36/317 Costs And Expenses

Sec. 317. *Costs And Expenses.* If the respondent is not the prevailing party, the court may assess against the respondent all direct expenses and costs incurred by the State's Attorney or other appropriate public official and law enforcement officers under Section 315 or 316 [750 ILCS 36/315 or 750 ILCS 36/316].
(Source: P.A. 93-108, § 317.)

ARTICLE 4.
MISCELLANEOUS PROVISIONS

750 ILCS 36/401 Application And Construction

Sec. 401. *Application And Construction.* In applying and construing this Uniform Act [750 ILCS 36/101 et seq.], consideration must be given to the need to promote uniformity of the law with respect to its subject matter among states that enact it.
(Source: P.A. 93-108, § 401.)

Note.

Article 4 of this Act, as enacted by P.A. 93-108, also contained amendatory provisions which are not set out in this Article.

750 ILCS 36/402 Severability Clause

Sec. 402. *Severability Clause.* If any provision of this Act or its application to any person or circumstance is held invalid, the invalidity does not affect other provisions or applications of this Act which can be given effect without the invalid provision or application, and to this end the provisions of this Act are severable.
(Source: P.A. 93-108, § 402.)

750 ILCS 36/403 Effective Date

Sec. 403. *Effective Date.* This Act takes effect on January 1, 2004.
(Source: P.A. 93-108, § 403.)

750 ILCS 36/405 Transitional Provision

Sec. 405. *Transitional Provision.* A motion or other request for relief made in a child-custody proceeding or to enforce a child-custody determination which was commenced before the effective date of this Act is governed by the law in effect at the time the motion or other request was made.
(Source: P.A. 93-108, § 405.)

Effective Date.
Section 403 of P.A. 93-108 made this Act effective July 1, 2004.

ILLINOIS PARENTAGE ACT

750 ILCS 40/1 [Short title]

Sec. 1. This Act may be cited as the Illinois Parentage Act.
(Source: P.A. 86-1475.)

Derivation.
Title: An Act to define the legal relationships of a child born to a wife and husband requesting and consenting to heterologous artificial insemination.
Cite: 750 ILCS 40/1 et seq.
Source: P.A. 83-1026.
Date: Certified January 5, 1984.

Note.
This section was Ill.Rev.Stat., Ch. 40, para. 1451.

CASE NOTES

Relationship to Other Theories of Recovery
Although a mother was precluded from obtaining a declaration of parentage and child support under the Illinois Parentage Act, 750 ILCS 40/1 et seq., because she did not obtain a boyfriend's written consent before becoming pregnant through artificial insemination, the Parentage Act did not preclude the mother from asserting common law claims for breach of an oral contract to provide child support and promissory estoppel. Mitchell v. Banary (In re M.J.), 203 Ill. 2d 526, 272 Ill. Dec. 329, 787 N.E.2d 144, 2003 Ill. LEXIS 21 (2003).

LEGAL PERIODICALS

Student Note: Abandoned Equity and the Best Interests of the Child: Why Illinois Courts Must Recognize Same-Sex Parents Seeking Visitation, 76 Chi.-Kent. L. Rev. 1933 (2001).

For article, "The Call of The Child," see 6 Chi. B. Rec. 26 (1992).

For note, "The AID Child and In re Marriage of Adams: Ambiguities in the Illinois Parentage Act (or Who's Your Daddy?)," see 21 Loy. U. Chi. L.J. 1173 (1989-90).

For article, "The Constitutional Right to Privacy and Emerging Tort Liability for Deceit in Interpersonal Relationships," see U. Ill. L. Rev. 779 (1986).

For article, "Surrogate Parenthood: A Need for Legislative Direction," see 71 Ill. B. J. 412 (1983).

For article, "An Illegitimate Gripe: Unequal Protection Under the Illinois Paternity Limitation Provision," see 69 Ill. B. J. 738 (1981).

For recent development, "The Legal Incubation of Artificial Insemination: A Proposal to Amend the Illinois Parentage Act," see 18 J. Marshall L. Rev. 797 (1985).

RESEARCH REFERENCES

Validity and construction of surrogate parenting agreement. 77 ALR4th 70.

Rights and obligations resulting from human artificial insemination. 83 ALR4th 295.

Sexual partner's tort liability to other partner for fraudulent misrepresentation regarding sterility or user of birth control resulting in pregnancy. 2 ALR5th 301.

Parent's child support liability as affected by other parent's fraudulent misrepresentation regarding sterility or use of birth control, or refusal to abort pregnancy. 2 ALR5th 337.

Liability of Father for Retroactive Child Support on Judicial Determination of Paternity. 87 ALR5th 361.

750 ILCS 40/2 [Status of child conceived by artificial insemination]

Sec. 2. Any child or children born as the result of heterologous artificial insemination shall be considered at law in all respects the same as a naturally conceived legitimate child of the husband and wife so requesting and consenting to the use of such technique.
(Source: P.A. 83-1026.)

Note.
This section was Ill.Rev.Stat., Ch. 40, para. 1452.

750 ILCS 40/3 [Status of husband of artificially inseminated wife; consent]

Sec. 3. (a) If, under the supervision of a licensed physician and with the consent of her husband, a wife is inseminated artificially with semen donated by a man not her husband, the husband shall be treated in law as if he were the natural father of a child thereby conceived. The husband's consent must be in writing executed and acknowledged by both the husband and wife. The physician who is to perform the technique shall certify their signatures and the date of the insemination, and file the husband's consent in the medical record where it shall be kept confidential and held by the patient's physician. However, the physician's failure to do so shall not affect the legal relationship between father and child. All papers and records pertaining to the insemination, whether part of the permanent medical record held by the physician or not, are subject to inspection only upon an order of the court for good cause shown.

(b) The donor of semen provided to a licensed physician for use in artificial insemination of a woman other than the donor's wife shall be treated in law as if he were not the natural father of a child thereby conceived.
(Source: P.A. 83-1026.)

Note.
This section was Ill.Rev.Stat., Ch. 40, para. 1453.

CASE NOTES

ANALYSIS

In General
Choice of Law
Husband's Consent
Unmarried Couples

In General

It is the Supreme Court's duty to ensure, in an action involving a minor's interests, that the rights of the child are adequately protected. In re Adams, 133 Ill. 2d 437, 141 Ill. Dec. 448, 551 N.E.2d 635 (1990).

Where the interests of a minor are at stake, it is appropriate for a court to recognize irregularities occurring in the proceedings below, despite the absence of an appropriate objection by the minor's counsel. In re Adams, 133 Ill. 2d 437, 141 Ill. Dec. 448, 551 N.E.2d 635 (1990).

Choice of Law

In an action to determine legitimacy where the State of Florida bore a more substantial relationship to the parties than did Illinois, and since Florida law is not repugnant to Illinois public policy, Florida law governed the determination of the questions whether a parent and child relationship would be recognized and whether one spouse had a duty to support the child; accordingly, the parties' stipulation that Illinois law should govern those determinations should have been rejected by the court. In re Adams, 133 Ill. 2d 437, 141 Ill. Dec. 448, 551 N.E.2d 635 (1990).

Husband's Consent

Where wife was impregnated by the sperm of a man other than her husband by artificial insemination procedure, without husband's knowledge or consent, and apparently without any intention of raising the child, it would be inconsistent with public policy to force upon husband parental obligations which he declined to undertake. In re Witbeck-Wildhagen, 281 Ill. App. 3d 502, 217 Ill. Dec. 329, 667 N.E.2d 122 (4 Dist. 1996).

The legislature intended a husband's written consent to be a prerequisite to the establishment of a legal father-child relationship and the imposition of a support obligation, and the husband's written consent is required each time his wife is to undergo an artificial insemination procedure. In re Witbeck-Wildhagen, 281 Ill. App. 3d 502, 217 Ill. Dec. 329, 667 N.E.2d 122 (4 Dist. 1996).

Unmarried Couples

Artificial insemination agreement was insufficient to establish parental rights in a would-be transsexual who had signed the consent a agreement as the mother's husband, since the parties' marriage was an invalid attempt at a same-sex marriage and the statute specifically referenced husbands and wives; furthermore, the consent form had not been re-executed, as required by law, at the time of the insemination attempt that worked. In re Simmons, Ill. App. 3d , Ill. Dec. , N.E.2d , 2005 Ill. App. LEXIS 127 (1 Dist. Feb. 16, 2005).

Although a mother was precluded from obtaining a declaration of parentage and child support under the Illinois Parentage Act, 750 ILCS 40/1 et seq., because she did not obtain a boyfriend's written consent before becoming pregnant through artificial insemination, the Parentage Act did not preclude the mother from asserting common law claims for breach of an oral contract to provide child support and promissory estoppel. Mitchell v. Banary (In re M.J.), 203 Ill. 2d 526, 272 Ill. Dec. 329, 787 N.E.2d 144, 2003 Ill. LEXIS 21 (2003).

At a minimum, 750 ILCS 40/3(a) requires written consent before an unmarried man becomes legally obligated to support a child born as a result of heterologous artificial insemination; the act does not discriminate against unmarried women or children born to unmarried women. Mitchell v. Banary, 325 Ill. App. 3d 826, 259 Ill. Dec. 641, 759 N.E.2d 121, 2001 Ill. App. LEXIS 813 (1 Dist. 2001).

Illinois Parentage Act of 1984

750 ILCS 45/1 Short Title

Sec. 1. *Short Title.* This Act shall be known and may be cited as the "Illinois Parentage Act of 1984". (Source: P.A. 83-1372.)

Derivation.

Title: An Act in relation to parentage.
Cite: 750 ILCS 45/1 et seq.
Source: P.A. 83-1372.
Date: Approved September 12, 1984.

Note.

This section was Ill.Rev.Stat., Ch. 40, para. 2501.

CASE NOTES

Analysis

Constitutionality
—Prior Law
In General
Best Interest of Child
Construction
—Prior Law
Construction with Marriage Act
Legislative Intent
—Retroactivity
Marriage and Dissolution of Marriage Act
Paternity Act
—Applicability
Purpose
—Prior Law
—Support of Child
Removal Actions
Res Judicata
—Paternity Action
Visitation

Constitutionality

—Prior Law

The former Paternity Act (see now this Act) did not violate equal protection as a father who had established paternity was not barred from instituting an action under the Act. Happel v. Mecklenburger, 101 Ill. App. 3d 107, 56 Ill. Dec. 569, 427 N.E.2d 974 (1 Dist. 1981).

In General

A paternity proceeding, although criminal in form, is a civil proceeding to determine the identity of the putative father, provide support for the illegitimate child, and prevent the child from becoming a public charge. People ex rel. Cizek v. Azzarello, 81 Ill. App. 3d 1102, 37 Ill. Dec. 84, 401 N.E.2d 1177 (1 Dist. 1980).

Best Interest of Child

The Illinois Parentage Act contains no express requirement that a trial court consider a child's best interest before allowing a paternity action to proceed. In re Slayton, 277 Ill. App. 3d 574, 214 Ill. Dec 117, 660 N.E.2d 562 (3 Dist. 1996).

Construction

—Prior Law

Under the former Paternity Act (see now this Act), a paternity action was solely statutory and compliance with the procedure outlined in the statute was required. People ex rel. Blackmon v. Brent, 97 Ill. App. 2d 438, 240 N.E.2d 255 (1 Dist. 1968).

Construction with Marriage Act

References in the Parentage Act to the Marriage and Dissolution Act do not confer all of the powers conferred by the latter act; in particular, in proceedings under the Parentage Act, the court lacks the power to enjoin a party from removing the child at issue from the state. Hall v. Melton, 314 Ill. App. 3d 476, 247 Ill. Dec. 295, 732 N.E.2d 11, 2000 Ill. App. LEXIS 420 (1 Dist. 2000).

Legislative Intent

—Retroactivity

The legislature intended this Act to apply retroactively. Klawitter v. Crawford, 185 Ill. App. 3d 778, 133 Ill. Dec. 721, 541 N.E.2d 1159 (1 Dist. 1989).

Marriage and Dissolution of Marriage Act

Although the Illinois Parentage Act of 1984, 750 ILCS 45/1 et seq., has adopted some of the provisions of the Illinois Marriage and Dissolution of Marriage Act, 750 ILCS 5/101 et seq., it does not

Marriage and Dissolution of Marriage Act (Cont'd)
incorporate the entire Marriage Act and does not confer the same broad powers on a court. Harbour v. Melton, 333 Ill. App. 3d 124, 266 Ill. Dec. 729, 775 N.E.2d 291, 2002 Ill. App. LEXIS 762 (4 Dist. 2002).

References in the Parentage Act to the Marriage and Dissolution of Marriage Act, 750 ILCS 5/101 et seq., do not confer on the courts all of the powers conferred by the latter Act; in particular, in proceedings under the Parentage Act the court lacks the power to enjoin a party from removing the child from the state. Hall v. Melton, 314 Ill. App. 3d 476, 247 Ill. Dec. 295, 732 N.E.2d 11, 2000 Ill. App. LEXIS 584 (1 Dist. 2000).

Paternity Act

—Applicability

The former Paternity Act (see now this Act) applied only to children born out of wedlock, and it expressly excluded children born into a marriage which was subsequently declared void, such as a bigamous marriage. People ex rel. Valle v. Valle, 113 Ill. App. 3d 682, 69 Ill. Dec. 510, 447 N.E.2d 945 (1 Dist. 1983).

The former Paternity Act (see now this Act), which replaced the Bastardy Act, materially enlarged the responsibility of the putative father by making him liable for the support, maintenance, education, and welfare of the child until its attainment of age 18 or until it was legally adopted, and the putative father was likewise liable for the reasonable expenses of the mother during the period of her pregnancy, confinement and recovery. People ex rel. v. Starks, 23 Ill. App. 2d 430, 163 N.E.2d 544 (1 Dist. 1959).

Purpose

—Prior Law

The objective of the former Paternity Act (see now this Act) was support for a minor child; if the child was being supported by a legal father who had assumed the parenting responsibility of daily supervision, education, protection and care of the child, then the provisions of the Act did not apply. Happel v. Mecklenburger, 101 Ill. App. 3d 107, 56 Ill. Dec. 569, 427 N.E.2d 974 (1 Dist. 1981).

The purpose of a paternity proceeding under the former Paternity Act (see now this Act) was to determine the identity of the putative father, provide support for the illegitimate child, and prevent the child from becoming a public charge. Happel v. Mecklenburger, 101 Ill. App. 3d 107, 56 Ill. Dec. 569, 427 N.E.2d 974 (1 Dist. 1981).

Although a proceeding pursuant to the former Paternity Act (see now this Act) may have had the appearance of a criminal prosecution, it was actually a civil proceeding to determine the identity of the putative father, to provide support for the illegitimate child, and to prevent the child from becoming a public charge. People ex rel. Mathis v. Brown, 44 Ill. App. 3d 783, 3 Ill. Dec. 475, 358 N.E.2d 1160 (1 Dist. 1976).

The Paternity Act (see now this Act) was not punitive. People ex rel. Blackmon v. Brent, 97 Ill. App. 2d 438, 240 N.E.2d 255 (1 Dist. 1968).

The purpose of the former Paternity Act (see now this Act) was to provide for the support, maintenance and education of illegitimate children so that the latter would not become wards of the state. People ex rel. Blackmon v. Brent, 97 Ill. App. 2d 438, 240 N.E.2d 255 (1 Dist. 1968).

The purpose of the former Paternity Act (see now this Act) was to determine the putative father and to provide support for the illegitimate child so as to prevent said child from becoming a public charge. Cornmesser v. Laken, 43 Ill. App. 2d 324, 193 N.E.2d 337 (2 Dist. 1963).

—Support of Child

The purpose of a paternity proceeding is not to impose a penalty as in criminal actions, but to convert a father's moral obligation to support his illegitimate children into a legal obligation. People ex rel. Cizek v. Azzarello, 81 Ill. App. 3d 1102, 37 Ill. Dec. 84, 401 N.E.2d 1177 (1 Dist. 1980).

Removal Actions

The Illinois Parentage Act of 1984, 750 ILCS 45/1 et seq., does not give courts the power to enjoin a parent with joint custody from removing her child from the state. In re Adams, 324 Ill. App. 3d 177, 257 Ill. Dec. 767, 754 N.E.2d 425, 2001 Ill. App. LEXIS 622 (3 Dist. 2001).

A custodial parent in a case where the parents are not married is not required to file an action for removal prior to removing the minor from the state. In re M.M.W., 296 Ill. App. 3d 877, 231 Ill. Dec. 238, 695 N.E.2d 1357 (2 Dist. 1998).

This Act does not contain any provision requiring that actions for removal be resolved pursuant to 750 ILCS 5/609 which is not implicitly incorporated into this Act. In re M.M.W., 296 Ill. App. 3d 877, 231 Ill. Dec. 238, 695 N.E.2d 1357 (2 Dist. 1998).

Res Judicata

—Paternity Action

Where a mother's action to establish paternity was adjudicated upon the merits for purposes of the doctrine of res judicata, child had no right to bring another action where there was no new evidence. Draper ex rel. Crutcher v. Truitt, 250 Ill. App. 3d 654, 190 Ill. Dec. 333, 621 N.E.2d 202 (1 Dist. 1993).

Visitation

While it was true that the Illinois Parentage Act of 1984, 750 ILCS 45/1 et seq., did not empower a trial court to enjoin a parent from removing her child from the state, a trial court is not required to grant a petition to modify visitation simply because one parent desired to modify, and thus, trial court should have considered whether modification of visitation would have been in child's best interest. DeBilio v. Rodgers, 337 Ill. App. 3d 614, 272 Ill. Dec. 9, 786 N.E.2d 548, 2002 Ill. App. LEXIS 947 (3 Dist. 2002).

Absent exigent circumstances, all biological parents enjoy a presumption that they are entitled to visitation with their children, whether visitation is requested under the Illinois Marriage and Dissolution of Marriage Act, 750 ILCS 5/101 et seq., or the Illinois Parentage Act of 1984, 750 ILCS 45/1 et seq. Wenzelman v. Bennett, 322 Ill. App. 3d 262, 255 Ill. Dec. 196, 748 N.E.2d 1266, 2001 Ill. App. LEXIS 365 (3 Dist. 2001).

LEGAL PERIODICALS

For article, "Who's Your Daddy?: An Analysis of Illinois' Law of Parentage and the Meaning of Parenthood," see 35 Loy. U. Chi. L.J. 811 (2004).

Student Note: Abandoned Equity and the Best Interests of the Child: Why Illinois Courts Must Recognize Same-Sex Parents Seeking Visitation, 76 Chi.-Kent. L. Rev. 1933 (2001).

For comment, "Paternity Actions in Illinois: Why Not Consider What is in the Best Interest of the Child?," see 21 S. Ill. U.L.J. 613 (1997).

For article, "The Illinois Parentage Act: Constitutional?" see 15 N. Ill. U.L. Rev. 63 (1994).

For article, "Survey of Illinois Law: Family Law," see 17 S. Ill. U.L.J. 903 (1993).

For article, "Bringing Up Baby: Settling Parentage Act Suits (And Making Sure They Stay Settled)," see 5 Chi. B. Rec. 14 (1991).

For case note, "Illinois ex rel. Sheppard v. Money: Income Withholding Provision of the Illinois Parentage Act of 1984 Expedites Child Support Enforcement At Employers' Expense," see 23 J. Marshall L. Rev. 285 (1990).

For article, "Paternity Blood Testing: Analysis Interpretation and Selection of a Program to Verify Parentage," see 75 Ill. B. J. 276 (1987).

For article, "The Constitutional Right to Privacy and Emerging Tort Liability for Deceit in Interpersonal Relationships," see U. Ill. L. Rev. 779 (1986).

For article, "The Illinois Parentage Act of 1984: The Continuing Shift Toward Civil Enforcement," see 73 Ill. B. J. 564 (1985).

RESEARCH REFERENCES

Sexual partner's tort liability to other partner for fraudulent misrepresentation regarding sterility or user of birth control resulting in pregnancy. 2 ALR5th 301.

Parent's child support liability as affected by other parent's fraudulent misrepresentation regarding sterility or use of birth control, or refusal to abort pregnancy. 2 ALR5th 337.

Liability of Father for Retroactive Child Support on Judicial Determination of Paternity. 87 ALR5th 361.

750 ILCS 45/1.1 Public Policy

Sec. 1.1. *Public Policy.* Illinois recognizes the right of every child to the physical, mental, emotional and monetary support of his or her parents under this Act.
(Source: P.A. 83-1372.)

Note.
This section was Ill.Rev.Stat., Ch. 40, para. 2501.1.

CASE NOTES

Analysis

Father's Rights
—In General
Legislative Intent
Purpose
—Child's Equal Protection Rights

Father's Rights

—In General
Although this Act addresses the establishment of the parent and child relationship, its focus and main purpose centers on the interests of the illegitimate child and does not propose to extend any further than it does, any rights for alleged fathers, presumed fathers, or natural mothers. Klawitter v. Crawford, 185 Ill. App. 3d 778, 133 Ill. Dec. 721, 541 N.E.2d 1159 (1 Dist. 1989).

Legislative Intent
This Act is intended to provide for the support, maintenance and education of illegitimate children so that they will not become wards of the state; in seeking to effectuate this strong public policy, a trial court should take every step reasonably necessary to assure that an adjudication on the merits is obtained. Berg ex rel. Berg v. Garrett, 224 Ill. App. 3d 619, 167 Ill. Dec. 119, 587 N.E.2d 1 (1992).

Purpose

—Child's Equal Protection Rights
The main objective of this Act of 1984 concerns the rights of the child involved, in remedying past denials of equal protection rights existing under the old Paternity Act. Klawitter v. Crawford, 185 Ill. App. 3d 778, 133 Ill. Dec. 721, 541 N.E.2d 1159 (1 Dist. 1989).

LEGAL PERIODICALS

For comment, "Paternity Actions in Illinois: Why Not Consider What is in the Best Interest of the Child?," see 21 S. Ill. U.L.J. 613 (1997).

For article, "What's Good for the Goose is Good for the Gander: Toward Recognition of Men's Reproductive Rights," see 15 N. Ill. U.L. Rev. 141 (1994).

750 ILCS 45/2 Parent and Child Relationship Defined

Sec. 2. *Parent and Child Relationship Defined.* As used in this Act, "parent and child relationship" means the legal relationship existing between a child and his natural or adoptive parents incident to which the law confers or imposes rights, privileges, duties, and obligations. It includes the mother and child relationship and the father and child relationship.
(Source: P.A. 83-1372.)

Note.
This section was Ill.Rev.Stat., Ch. 40, para. 2502.

CASE NOTES

Analysis

Control Over Child
Death of Child
Divorced Father
Scope of Act
Support
—Prior Law
Visitation
—Nonparent

Control Over Child
A grant of visitation rights of necessity involved a grant of "control" over a minor child, and the former Bastardy Act (see now this Act) clearly embodied a legislative determination that a putative father should have no right to the society of his illegitimate child. De Phillips v. De Phillips, 35 Ill. 2d 154, 219 N.E.2d 465 (1966).

Death of Child
If an illegitimate child is born dead, no liability attaches to its father; if a child should die after birth, the father's liability ceases at the time of its death. People ex rel. Blackmon v. Brent, 97 Ill. App. 2d 438, 240 N.E.2d 255 (1 Dist. 1968).

Divorced Father
Where respondent failed to establish that he had sired the minor child, a divorce decree which required him to pay child support but which was obtained by misrepresenting to the divorce court that he was the biological father of the child did not give respondent the status of a parent, and he did not become vested with the rights of a natural parent to withhold consent to the child's adoption. In re Weller, 47 Ill. App. 3d 492, 5 Ill. Dec. 760, 362 N.E.2d 73 (3 Dist. 1977).

Scope of Act
This Act governs the legal relationship between a child and the natural parent and delineates, among other things, the obligations arising incident to such relationship. Ivanyi v. Granoff, 171 Ill. App. 3d 411, 122 Ill. Dec. 49, 526 N.E.2d 189 (2 Dist. 1988).

Support

—Prior Law
Where plaintiff testified that she paid no rent nor had she obtained a babysitter for her child, but stated that expenses for rent and child care attributable to the child were $125 a month, that sum obviously did not represent an actual outlay of funds, and where she sought to hold defendant responsible for the rent as part of the support payments, as in a separate maintenance or divorce case, there was no provision in the former Paternity Act (see now this Act) for such payment, express or implied, nor did it appear that it was intended that the mother of a child be equated with the wife in a divorce or separate maintenance action. People ex rel. Perz v. Schneemilch, 82 Ill. App. 2d 371, 227 N.E.2d 132 (1 Dist. 1967).

Visitation

—Nonparent
Where plaintiff claims he was deceived into believing he was child's father and consequently developed a mutually loving and nurturing relationship with child, trial court erred in ruling that because this Act and Illinois Marriage and Dissolution of Marriage Act (750 ILCS 5/101 et seq.) do not authorize visitation privileges for a nonparent, plaintiff was not entitled to such privileges. Koelle v. Zwiren, 284 Ill. App. 3d 778, 220 Ill. Dec. 51, 672 N.E.2d 868 (1 Dist. 1996).

RESEARCH REFERENCES

Right of putative father to visitation with child born out of wedlock. 58 ALR5th 669.

750 ILCS 45/2.5 Definitions

Sec. 2.5. *Definitions.* As used in this Act, the terms "gestational surrogacy", "gestational surrogate", and "intended parent" have the same meanings as the terms are defined in Section 10 of the Gestational Surrogacy Act [750 ILCS 47/10].
(Source: P.A. 93-921, § 800.)

Effective Date.
This section is effective January 1, 2005, pursuant to Ill. Const. (1970) Art. IV, § 10 and 5 ILCS 75/1.

750 ILCS 45/3 Relationship and Support Not Dependent on Marriage

Sec. 3. *Relationship and Support Not Dependent on Marriage.* The parent and child relationship, including support obligations, extends equally to every child and to every parent, regardless of the marital status of the parents.
(Source: P.A. 83-1372.)

Note.
This section was Ill.Rev.Stat., Ch. 40, para. 2503.

CASE NOTES

Analysis

Construction
—Prior Law
Duty of Support
—Constitutionality
—Estates of Children
—Minor's Education Expenses
—Parent and Child Relationship
—Parties' Marital Status
—Pregnancy Expenses
—Sexual Assault Damages
Illegitimate Children
—Prior Law
Intent

Construction

—Prior Law
Under the former Bastardy Act (see now this Act), the marriage of the mother of an illegitimate child, after delivery, to one not the father, could not affect the status of the child, and her husband was liable for its support. People ex rel. Wilmers v. Volksdorf, 112 Ill. 292 (1884).

Duty of Support

—Constitutionality
Defendant's argument that because he was tricked into fathering a child that he did not want, the state violated his constitutional right of procreative choice by requiring him to support that child, was deemed to be without merit, as there is no right which would require such discrimination against an innocent minor. Department of Pub. Aid ex rel. McFarland v. Thompsen, 218 Ill. App. 3d 1099, 161 Ill. Dec. 854, 579 N.E.2d 402 (2 Dist. 1991).

—Estates of Children
Where a mother had ample assets to support and maintain her children, she was not entitled to reimbursement from the minor's estates for the cost of supporting her children, including food, clothing, medical care, camp, religious school, the purchase of a piano for her daughter and a proportionate share of the taxes, maintenance and insurance for the family home. Stillerman v. Schultz, 39 Ill. App. 2d 380, 188 N.E.2d 726 (1 Dist. 1963).

—Minor's Education Expenses
A court, in a parentage proceeding, can apply section 513 of the Dissolution Act (750 ILCS 5/513) so as to provide for the education of a non-minor, illegitimate child as equity requires, thereby effectuating the legislative intent to treat all children equally in matters of support, such intent being manifested in this section of the Parentage Act. Rawles v. Hartman, 172 Ill. App. 3d 931, 123 Ill. Dec. 217, 527 N.E.2d 680 (2 Dist. 1988).

—Parent and Child Relationship
Under this section, the appropriate inquiry in a paternity action was not whether the relator was married, but whether the child was born out of wedlock, and whether defendant was the natural father of that child. People ex rel. Raines v. Biggs, 135 Ill. App. 3d 200, 90 Ill. Dec. 99, 481 N.E.2d 899 (5 Dist. 1985).

—Parties' Marital Status
All that is required to be shown in a paternity action is that the mother and father were not married to each other at the time of the child's birth; consequently, both married and unmarried women are given the benefit of this Act. People ex rel. Raines v. Biggs, 135 Ill. App. 3d 200, 90 Ill. Dec. 99, 481 N.E.2d 899 (5 Dist. 1985).

—Pregnancy Expenses
A father whose paternity is established shall also be liable for the reasonable expenses of the mother during the period of her pregnancy, confinement, and recovery. Schultz v. Peeler, 10 Ill. App. 3d 937, 295 N.E.2d 252 (5 Dist. 1973), aff'd, 56 Ill. 2d 318, 307 N.E.2d 380 (1974).

—Sexual Assault Damages
Where the continuing tort damage plaintiff sought for defendant's failure to support her son, allegedly born as a result of defendant's sexual assault upon her, would not have been incurred had she pursued an act for paternity on her minor son's behalf, the inescapable conclusion was that plaintiff's action was one for damages resulting from the injuries she sustained due to the act of sexual assault alleged against defendant, which action was barred by the statute of limitations. Williams v. Ali, 145 Ill. App. 3d 458, 99 Ill. Dec. 317, 495 N.E.2d 1052 (1 Dist. 1986).

Illegitimate Children

—Prior Law
Under former sections 52 and 62 of the Paternity Act (see now 750 ILCS 45/1.1, 750 ILCS 45/3 and 750 ILCS 45/21), a father had absolutely no right to the custody or society of his illegitimate minor child. Wallace ex rel. Wallace v. Wallace, 60 Ill. App. 2d 300, 210 N.E.2d 4 (1 Dist. 1965).

Intent
Former section 62 of the Paternity Act, read in conjunction with former section 52 of that Act (see now 750 ILCS 45/1.1, 750 ILCS 45/3 and 750 ILCS 45/21), revealed the legislature's view of the relationship of an illegitimate child and its father; the father had the duties to his illegitimate child equal to the duties of a father of a legitimate child, but he had none of the rights enjoyed by the father of a child born in wedlock. Wallace ex rel. Wallace v. Wallace, 60 Ill. App. 2d 300, 210 N.E.2d 4 (1 Dist. 1965).

750 ILCS 45/3.1 [Duty of minor parent to support]

Sec. 3.1. A child's mother or a person found to be the father of a child under this Act, is not relieved of support and maintenance obligations to the child because he or she is a minor.
(Source: P.A. 87-537.)

Note.
This section was Ill.Rev.Stat., Ch. 40, para. 2503.1.

CASE NOTES

Duty of Support

—Public Policy
Where respondent was a 15 year old minor when his child was

Duty of Support (Cont'd)

—Public Policy (Cont'd)
conceived, the public policy mandating parental support of children overrode any policy of protecting a minor from improvident acts, and the trial court properly found that the respondent was financially responsible for his child. Stone v. Williams, 193 Ill. App. 3d 563, 140 Ill. Dec. 621, 550 N.E.2d 257 (3 Dist. 1990).

750 ILCS 45/4 How Parent and Child Relationship Established

Sec. 4. *How Parent and Child Relationship Established.* The parent and child relationship between a child and

(1) the natural mother may be established by proof of her having given birth to the child, or under this Act;

(2) the natural father may be established under this Act;

(3) an adoptive parent may be established by proof of adoption, or by records established pursuant to Section 16 of the "Vital Records Act", approved August 8, 1961, as amended [410 ILCS 535/16].
(Source: P.A. 83-1372.)

Note.
This section was Ill.Rev.Stat., Ch. 40, para. 2504.

CASE NOTES

Analysis

Burden of Proof
—In General
Crimes
—Abduction
Evidence of Paternity
—In General
—Held Insufficient
—Held Sufficient
Living Children
Proceedings by Father
—Statute of Limitations
Summary Judgment
—Held Proper

Burden of Proof

—In General
In a paternity action, the burden is on the mother to establish paternity by a preponderance of the evidence, and this does not depend on the number of witnesses for each side, but depends on the weight to be afforded to the witnesses' testimony. People ex rel. Raines v. Price, 37 Ill. App. 3d 921, 347 N.E.2d 29 (4 Dist. 1976).

Crimes

—Abduction
The state's failure to grant the same measure of recognition of legal parentage at birth to an unwed father as that accorded an unwed mother is based merely upon the biological reality that motherhood is obviously more apparent and therefore more easily established; once an unwed father complies with the statutory procedure of legally establishing his biological relationship with the child, he cannot be convicted under the child abduction statute (720 ILCS 5/10-5). People v. Morrison, 223 Ill. App. 3d 176, 165 Ill. Dec. 330, 584 N.E.2d 509 (3 Dist. 1991), cert. denied, 144 Ill. 2d 640, 169 Ill. Dec. 148, 591 N.E.2d 28 (1992).

Evidence of Paternity

—In General
The fact that there was testimony that other men had had intercourse with complainant during the period of conception was not determinative of the issue of putative father's non-paternity. People ex rel. Raines v. Price, 37 Ill. App. 3d 921, 347 N.E.2d 29 (4 Dist. 1976).

—Held Insufficient
The trial court's decision that defendant was the natural father of plaintiff's child was against the manifest weight of the evidence where plaintiff's version of the facts was rife with inconsistencies. People ex rel. Barbour v. Hatchett, 131 Ill. App. 3d 540, 86 Ill. Dec. 734, 475 N.E.2d 1113 (4 Dist. 1985).

The jury's verdict finding that the defendant was not the father of plaintiff's child was held not to be erroneous. People ex rel. Reynolds v. Aldridge, 107 Ill. App. 3d 679, 63 Ill. Dec. 346, 437 N.E.2d 1268 (4 Dist. 1982).

Where mother's testimony was clear that defendant's penis never entered her vagina, trial court was correct in deciding that, on the basis of this evidence only, no verdict finding defendant to be the father of her child could ever stand. People ex rel. Adams v. Kite, 48 Ill. App. 3d 828, 6 Ill. Dec. 653, 363 N.E.2d 182 (5 Dist. 1977).

Evidence supported the finding that defendant was not the putative father of the child. People ex rel. Mathis v. Brown, 44 Ill. App. 3d 783, 3 Ill. Dec. 475, 358 N.E.2d 1160 (1 Dist. 1976).

—Held Sufficient
Evidence held sufficient to establish that defendant was the father of the child. People ex rel. Gomez v. Wedech, 58 Ill. App. 3d 518, 16 Ill. Dec. 74, 374 N.E.2d 849 (1 Dist. 1978).

Where there was an admittedly existing intimate relationship between the parties, the testimony of the complainant was corroborated as to the time, place and opportunity, and the defendant admitted under oath that he was the father, the circuit court's decision pursuant to the former Paternity Act (see now 750 ILCS 45/1 et seq.) that the defendant was not the father of the child in question was against the manifest weight of the evidence. People ex rel. Walsh v. Kilbride, 16 Ill. App. 3d 820, 306 N.E.2d 879 (3 Dist. 1974).

In a proceeding under the former Paternity Act (see now this Act), where the relatrix stated she had intercourse with the defendant during July, August and September of 1969; she stated when she informed him she was pregnant, he discussed supporting the child and gave her ten dollars; after the child was born he visited her and the child once a week until the end of October, 1970; and a friend of the relatrix was present during some of these visits, testified she saw the defendant playing with the child and once asked him if he wanted to hold his daughter, and he answered "Yes," the evidence was sufficient to find that defendant was the father of the child. People ex rel. Bucaro v. Johnson, 8 Ill. App. 3d 618, 291 N.E.2d 9 (1 Dist. 1972).

Under the former Paternity Act (see now this Act), the evidence was sufficient to support the finding that defendant was father of a child, even though at the time of the child's conception, the mother was married and living in her husband's home with her husband. People ex rel. Jones v. Schmitt, 101 Ill. App. 2d 183, 242 N.E.2d 275 (3 Dist. 1968).

Living Children
Children were born alive and to be living at the time of trial where a complaining witness testified that the children were born, her testimony was uncontradicted, and the record was replete with testimony which could be interpreted in no other way than that they were alive at the time she was testifying. People ex rel. Blackmon v. Brent, 97 Ill. App. 2d 438, 240 N.E.2d 255 (1 Dist. 1968).

When a child has been born alive, it is presumed that the child continues to live until the contrary is shown. People ex rel. Blackmon v. Brent, 97 Ill. App. 2d 438, 240 N.E.2d 255 (1 Dist. 1968).

Proceedings by Father

—Statute of Limitations
This Act's statute of limitations applies to complaint brought by unmarried, but undisputed natural father seeking a finding that a father and child relationship existed, where previously the plaintiff had never been acknowledged to be the father, by either party, in any official document, or proceeding. Kapp v. Alexander, 218 Ill. App. 3d 412, 161 Ill. Dec. 158, 578 N.E.2d 285 (3 Dist. 1991).

Summary Judgment

—Held Proper

Where plaintiff filed an action under this Act requesting a finding of paternity, and she had compiled a plethora of evidence supporting her motion for summary judgment to which the defendant at no time had offered evidence by opposing affidavits or other pleadings or proof which would have presented the trial court with a genuine issue of material fact, summary judgment of paternity on plaintiff's motion was proper. Breese ex rel. Breese v. Dewey, 223 Ill. App. 3d 356, 165 Ill. Dec. 490, 584 N.E.2d 924 (4 Dist. 1991).

LEGAL PERIODICALS

For comment, "Prohibiting Payments to Surrogate Mothers: Love's Labor Lost and the Constitutional Right of Privacy," see 20 J. Marshall L. Rev. 715 (1987).

750 ILCS 45/4.1 Administrative paternity determinations

Sec. 4.1. *Administrative paternity determinations.* Notwithstanding any other provision of this Act, the Illinois Department of Public Aid may make administrative determinations of paternity and nonpaternity in accordance with Section 10-17.7 of the Illinois Public Aid Code [305 ILCS 5/10-17.7]. These determinations of paternity or nonpaternity shall have the full force and effect of judgments entered under this Act.

(Source: P.A. 88-687, § 20.)

Effective Date.

Section 99 of P.A. 88-687 made this section effective upon becoming law. The Act was approved January 24, 1995.

750 ILCS 45/5 Presumption of Paternity

Sec. 5. *Presumption of Paternity.* (a) A man is presumed to be the natural father of a child if:

(1) he and the child's natural mother are or have been married to each other, even though the marriage is or could be declared invalid, and the child is born or conceived during such marriage;

(2) after the child's birth, he and the child's natural mother have married each other, even though the marriage is or could be declared invalid, and he is named, with his written consent, as the child's father on the child's birth certificate;

(3) he and the child's natural mother have signed an acknowledgment of paternity in accordance with rules adopted by the Illinois Department of Public Aid under Section 10-17.7 of the Illinois Public Aid Code [305 ILCS 5/10-17.7]; or

(4) he and the child's natural mother have signed an acknowledgment of parentage or, if the natural father is someone other than one presumed to be the father under this Section, an acknowledgment of parentage and denial of paternity in accordance with Section 12 of the Vital Records Act [410 ILCS 535/12].

(b) A presumption under subdivision (a)(1) or (a)(2) of this Section may be rebutted only by clear and convincing evidence. A presumption under subdivision (a)(3) or (a)(4) is conclusive, unless the acknowledgment of parentage is rescinded under the process provided in Section 12 of the Vital Records Act [410 ILCS 535/12], upon the earlier of:

(1) 60 days after the date the acknowledgment of parentage is signed, or

(2) the date of an administrative or judicial proceeding relating to the child (including a proceeding to establish a support order) in which the signatory is a party;

except that if a minor has signed the acknowledgment of paternity or acknowledgment of parentage and denial of paternity, the presumption becomes conclusive 6 months after the minor reaches majority or is otherwise emancipated.

(Source: P.A. 83-1372; 88-687, § 20; 89-641, § 30; 90-18, § 120.)

Note.

This section was Ill.Rev.Stat., Ch. 40, para. 2505.

Illinois Administrative Code.

See 89 Illinois Administrative Code, §§ 160.61, 315.20, 160.60, 301.20, 301.20, 315.20.

Effect of Amendments.

The 1994 amendment by P.A. 88-687, effective January 24, 1995, in subdivision (a)(2) substituted "Vital Records Act" for "'Vital Records Act', approved August 8, 1961, as amended"; and added subdivisions (a)(3) and (a)(4).

The 1996 amendment by P.A. 89-641, effective August 9, 1996, in subdivision (a)(2) inserted "written" and deleted from the end "pursuant to Section 12 of the Vital Records Act"; in subdivision (a)(4) substituted "an acknowledgment of parentage or, if the natural father is someone other than one presumed to be the father under this Section, an acknowledgment of parentage and denial of paternity" for "a petition to establish the parent and child relationship by consent of the parties" and substituted "12 of the Vital Records" for "6 of this"; and in subsection (b), in the first sentence inserted "subdivision (a)(1) or (a)(2) of" and added the second sentence.

The 1997 amendment by P.A. 90-18, effective July 1, 1997, in subsection (b), in the introductory language, added at the end "unless the acknowledgment of parentage is rescinded under the process provided in Section 12 of the Vital Records Act, upon the earlier of"; and added subdivisions (b)(1) and (b)(2).

CASE NOTES

Analysis

Blood Test Results
—Not Conclusive of Paternity
Exceptions
Jurisdiction
—Personal
—Visitation Order
Level of Proof
Marriage of Parents
Presumption of Legitimacy
—In General
—Blood Tests
—Omissions Not Conclusive
—Prior Law
Rebuttable Presumption
—Child Born During Marriage
—Presumption Not Overcome
—Presumption Overcome
—Putative Fathers
Standing
—Presumed Parent
Visitation Order
—Natural Father

Blood Test Results

—Not Conclusive of Paternity

Despite a blood test that assessed the relative chance of respondent's paternity to be 99.99%, there was evidence that clearly demonstrated a genuine issue on the question of paternity that remained for trial. Smith ex rel. Smith v. Barbre, 179 Ill. App. 3d 473, 128 Ill. Dec. 487, 534 N.E.2d 669 (5 Dist. 1989).

Where a first blood test indicated a 100% "relative chance of non-paternity," or a 0% "relative chance of paternity," and a second test found the probability of paternity would be very high, and a third test indicated "the likelihood of defendant being the father" at 99.764%, all the tests were inadmissible. Watkins v. Martin, 115 Ill. App. 3d 417, 71 Ill. Dec. 178, 450 N.E.2d 866 (1 Dist. 1983).

Exceptions

Jurisdiction

—Personal

The visitation order granting visitation to husband was not void even though the trial court lacked personal jurisdiction over the natural father. In re Allen, 265 Ill. App. 3d 208, 202 Ill. Dec. 694, 638 N.E.2d 340 (4 Dist.), appeal denied, 158 Ill. 2d 549, 206 Ill. Dec. 834, 645 N.E.2d 1356 (1994).

—Visitation Order

When action for dissolution was brought, there existed a legal presumption that child was a child of the parties, since she was conceived and born during their marriage and that presumption was not subject to attack in any action, except an action brought on behalf of child since more than two years had passed since her birth; therefore, the trial court indisputably had jurisdiction to enter the visitation order agreed to by the parties as part of the supplemental judgment. In re Allen, 265 Ill. App. 3d 208, 202 Ill. Dec. 694, 638 N.E.2d 340 (4 Dist.), appeal denied, 158 Ill. 2d 549, 206 Ill. Dec. 834, 645 N.E.2d 1356 (1994).

Level of Proof

Administrative law judge erred by (1) denying child insurance benefits where the applicant submitted a probate order declaring the deceased insured the biological father of the child, and (2) questioning the validity of a DNA test which was 99.99 percent conclusive as to paternity. Malone v. Barnhart, F. Supp. 2d , 2004 U.S. Dist. LEXIS 15187 (N.D. Ill. Aug. 4, 2004).

The level of proof for legitimacy cases should be at the high end of the clear and convincing range; between the word "irrefragable" and the importance of the state interest, proof against legitimacy has to be extremely strong to overcome the presumption. Binion v. Chater, 108 F.3d 780 (7th Cir. 1997).

Marriage of Parents

Presumption of paternity did not apply to a would-be transsexual who had not completed sex change surgeries and therefore did not qualify as a "man" for purposes of the statute; moreover, that same failure to complete the surgical transformation had also caused the transsexual's purported marriage to the child's mother to be held void, so there was no basis for classifying the transsexual as the mother's husband. In re Simmons, Ill. App. 3d , Ill. Dec. , N.E.2d , 2005 Ill. App. LEXIS 127 (1 Dist. Feb. 16, 2005).

Seeking to have the plaintiff mother admit to a lack of maternity when defendant had participated in the divorce and finding of maternity bordered on fraud; the divorce decree and finding that the child was born of the marriage of plaintiff, and defendant was proper on its face. Sanders v. Sanders, 55 Ill. App. 3d 248, 13 Ill. Dec. 426, 371 N.E.2d 121 (3 Dist. 1978).

Where the parties' child was conceived before their marriage, and born after the parties' divorce, and where defendant denied a lawful marriage, denied the consummation of the marriage, and denied the possibility of issue to the parties, it could properly have been found that the child was legitimate, and that the defendant was liable in an action for its care and support. Sturdy v. Sturdy, 67 Ill. App. 2d 469, 214 N.E.2d 607 (4 Dist. 1966).

Under a prior similar provision, an illegitimate child has to deemed legitimate upon the marriage of the mother and the reputed father. Dunlavy v. Lowrie, 372 Ill. 622, 25 N.E.2d 67 (1939).

Presumption of Legitimacy

—In General

Petition for reimbursement of child support failed because respondent did not allege that child support order was invalid when entered, nor did he challenge the statutory principle that a man is presumed to be the father of the child born to the child's mother during marriage. In re Smak, 267 Ill. App. 3d 231, 204 Ill. Dec. 551, 641 N.E.2d 981 (2 Dist. 1994).

This section confers upon a man the presumption of paternity, if he was married to the mother of the child at the time the child was born or conceived, or if he marries the child's mother after the child's birth, and consents to being named as the child's father on the birth certificate. In re Klebs, 196 Ill. App. 3d 472, 143 Ill. Dec. 363, 554 N.E.2d 298 (1 Dist. 1990).

The marital status of the mother affects only her burden of proof in a paternity action; should the mother be married, she must overcome the presumption of legitimacy that thereby attaches. People ex rel. Raines v. Biggs, 135 Ill. App. 3d 200, 90 Ill. Dec. 99, 481 N.E.2d 899 (5 Dist. 1985).

—Blood Tests

Blood tests performed on mother, former husband, and child excluding husband from the paternity of the child, along with testimony by mother, corroborated by husband, that she did not have intercourse with husband during the period of conception, represented proof necessary to overcome presumption of legitimacy. Santiago v. Silva, 90 Ill. App. 3d 554, 45 Ill. Dec. 806, 413 N.E.2d 139 (1 Dist. 1980).

—Omissions Not Conclusive

Presumption of legitimacy can not be overcome by fact that child is not named in divorce decree standing alone. Binion v. Chater, 108 F.3d 780 (7th Cir. 1997).

Omissions on a birth certificate and divorce decree, while implying that the husband may not be the father, are not dispositive. Binion v. Chater, 108 F.3d 780 (7th Cir. 1997).

—Prior Law

In a paternity case under the former Paternity Act (see now this Act), the burden of proof was on the mother and the charge against the defendant was to be proven by a preponderance or greater weight of the evidence. People ex rel. Lyke v. Rucker, 2 Ill. App. 3d 113, 276 N.E.2d 139 (1 Dist. 1971).

Where an alleged father denied paternity, denied sexual intercourse with the mother, and alleged that the mother was married at the time of conception and at the time of the birth of the child, such allegations in a paternity action under the former Paternity Act (see now this Act) raised the rebuttable presumption of legitimacy, which was required to be overcome by clear and convincing proof, and defendant's denials of paternity presented factual determinations for the jury's consideration. Clark v. Brown, 121 Ill. App. 2d 280, 257 N.E.2d 565 (1 Dist. 1970).

Rebuttable Presumption

—Child Born During Marriage

If a woman is lawfully married at the time a child is born to her, there is a strong presumption that the husband is the father of the child, and a party seeking to rebut that presumption has the burden of introducing evidence that clearly and conclusively proves that the child's father is someone other than the mother's husband. Dillon v. Industrial Comm'n, 195 Ill. App. 3d 599, 142 Ill. Dec. 341, 552 N.E.2d 1082 (1 Dist. 1990).

Where plaintiff had separated from her husband, and plaintiff and defendant were admittedly engaging in acts of sexual intercourse during plaintiff's separation from her husband, there was clear and convincing proof to overcome the presumption that plaintiff's husband was the father of the child. People ex rel. Davis v. Clark, 99 Ill. App. 3d 979, 55 Ill. Dec. 319, 426 N.E.2d 294 (4 Dist. 1981).

There is a strong presumption that a child born during marriage was fathered by the husband; however, the presumption is not conclusive, and it may be rebutted by clear, convincing, and irrefutable proof, such as proof that the husband had no access to his wife during the period of possible conception, or by blood tests. People v. Askew, 74 Ill. App. 3d 743, 30 Ill. Dec. 777, 393 N.E.2d 1124 (1 Dist. 1979); People ex rel. Davis v. Clark, 99 Ill. App. 3d 979, 55 Ill. Dec. 319, 426 N.E.2d 294 (4 Dist. 1981); People ex rel. Brown v. Bloodworth, 155 Ill. App. 3d 901, 108 Ill. Dec. 575, 508 N.E.2d 1152 (5 Dist. 1987).

Rebuttable Presumption (Cont'd)

—Presumption Not Overcome

Pursuant to former Ill.Rev.Stat., ch. 106 ¾, para. 1 et seq. (see now this Act), the evidence produced failed to sufficiently overcome the presumption that a child was legitimate, since the relator was married to a third party at the time of the conception of the child. People ex rel. Repsel v. Kirk, 133 Ill. App. 2d 771, 273 N.E.2d 86 (3 Dist. 1971).

—Presumption Overcome

Where there was no evidence contradicting plaintiff's testimony that the man she was married to was not the father of her child, there was sufficient testimony, as a matter of law, to overcome the presumption of legitimacy. People ex rel. Davis v. Clark, 99 Ill. App. 3d 979, 55 Ill. Dec. 319, 426 N.E.2d 294 (4 Dist. 1981).

—Putative Fathers

If the presumption of paternity, as set forth in this section, is sufficiently rebutted, then paternity of the child by another man may be established if that man has been made a party to the proceedings. In re Klebs, 196 Ill. App. 3d 472, 143 Ill. Dec. 363, 554 N.E.2d 298 (1 Dist. 1990).

The provisions of this Act do not distinguish between putative fathers, and married fathers, in determining the existence of the father and child relationship. Klawitter v. Crawford, 185 Ill. App. 3d 778, 133 Ill. Dec. 721, 541 N.E.2d 1159 (1 Dist. 1989).

Standing

—Presumed Parent

Since petitioner was the child's presumed father at the time petitioner first sought custody of the child, petitioner retained standing to seek custody of the child even after a trial court adjudicated another to be the child's biological father. In re Slayton, 277 Ill. App. 3d 574, 214 Ill. Dec 117, 660 N.E.2d 562 (3 Dist. 1996).

Visitation Order

—Natural Father

Visitation order granting visitation to husband did not become void when the trial court made paternity findings. In re Allen, 265 Ill. App. 3d 208, 202 Ill. Dec. 694, 638 N.E.2d 340 (4 Dist.), appeal denied, 158 Ill. 2d 549, 206 Ill. Dec. 834, 645 N.E.2d 1356 (1994).

LEGAL PERIODICALS

For article, "Independent Evidence: A New Tool for Paternity Cases", see 86 Ill. B.J. 476 (1998).

For comment, "Paternity Actions in Illinois: Why Not Consider What is in the Best Interest of the Child?," see 21 S. Ill. U.L.J. 613 (1997).

For article, "Survey of Illinois Law [1988-89]—Family Law," see 14 S. Ill. U. L. J. 1007 (1990).

RESEARCH REFERENCES

Right of putative father to visitation with child born out of wedlock. 58 ALR5th 669.

750 ILCS 45/6 Establishment of Parent and Child Relationship by Consent of the Parties

Sec. 6. *Establishment of Parent and Child Relationship by Consent of the Parties.* (a) A parent and child relationship may be established voluntarily by the signing and witnessing of a voluntary acknowledgment of parentage in accordance with Section 12 of the Vital Records Act [410 ILCS 535/12], Section 10-17.7 of the Illinois Public Aid Code [305 ILCS 5/10-17.7], or the provisions of the Gestational Surrogacy Act [750 ILCS 47/1 et seq.]. The voluntary acknowledgment of parentage shall contain the social security numbers of the persons signing the voluntary acknowledgment of parentage; however, failure to include the social security numbers of the persons signing a voluntary acknowledgment of parentage does not invalidate the voluntary acknowledgment of parentage.

(1) A parent-child relationship may be established in the event of gestational surrogacy if all of the following conditions are met prior to the birth of the child:

(A) The gestational surrogate certifies that she is not the biological mother of the child, and that she is carrying the child for the intended parents.

(B) The husband, if any, of the gestational surrogate certifies that he is not the biological father of the child.

(C) The intended mother certifies that she provided or an egg donor donated the egg from which the child being carried by the gestational surrogate was conceived.

(D) The intended father certifies that he provided or a sperm donor donated the sperm from which the child being carried by the gestational surrogate was conceived.

(E) A physician licensed to practice medicine in all its branches in the State of Illinois certifies that the child being carried by the gestational surrogate is the biological child of the intended mother or the intended father or both and that neither the gestational surrogate nor the gestational surrogate's husband, if any, is a biological parent of the child being carried by the gestational surrogate.

(E-5) The attorneys for the intended parents and the gestational surrogate each certifies that the parties entered into a gestational surrogacy contract intended to satisfy the requirements of Section 25 of the Gestational Surrogacy Act [750 ILCS 47/25] with respect to the child.

(F) All certifications shall be in writing and witnessed by 2 competent adults who are not the gestational surrogate , gestational surrogate's husband, if any, intended mother, or intended father. Certifications shall be on forms prescribed by the Illinois Department of Public Health, shall be executed prior to the birth of the child, and shall be placed in the medical records of the gestational surrogate prior to the birth of the child. Copies of all certifications shall be delivered to the Illinois Department of Public Health prior to the birth of the child.

(2) Unless otherwise determined by order of the Circuit Court, the child shall be presumed to be the child of the gestational surrogate and of the gestational surrogate's husband, if any, if all requirements of subdivision (a)(1) are not met prior to the birth of the child. This presumption may be rebutted by clear and convincing evidence. The circuit court may order the gestational surrogate , gestational surrogate's husband, intended mother, intended father, and child to submit to such medical examinations and testing as the court deems appropriate.

(b) Notwithstanding any other provisions of this Act, paternity established in accordance with subsection (a) has the full force and effect of a judgment entered under this Act and serves as a basis for seeking a child support order without any further proceedings to establish paternity.

(c) A judicial or administrative proceeding to ratify paternity established in accordance with subsection (a) is neither required nor permitted.

(d) A signed acknowledgment of paternity entered under this Act may be challenged in court only on the basis of fraud, duress, or material mistake of fact, with the burden of proof upon the challenging party. Pending outcome of the challenge to the acknowledgment of paternity, the legal responsibilities of the signatories shall remain in full force and effect, except upon order of the court upon a showing of good cause.

(e) Once a parent and child relationship is established in accordance with subsection (a), an order for support may be established pursuant to a petition to establish an order for support by consent filed with the clerk of the circuit court. A copy of the properly completed acknowledgment of parentage form shall be attached to the petition. The petition shall ask that the circuit court enter an order for support. The petition may ask that an order for visitation, custody, or guardianship be entered. The filing and appearance fees provided under the Clerks of Courts Act [705 ILCS 105/0.01 et seq.] shall be waived for all cases in which an acknowledgment of parentage form has been properly completed by the parties and in which a petition to establish an order for support by consent has been filed with the clerk of the circuit court. This subsection shall not be construed to prohibit filing any petition for child support, visitation, or custody under this Act, the Illinois Marriage and Dissolution of Marriage Act [750 ILCS 5/101 et seq.], or the Non-Support Punishment Act [750 ILCS 16/1 et seq.]. This subsection shall also not be construed to prevent the establishment of an administrative support order in cases involving persons receiving child support enforcement services under Article X of the Illinois Public Aid Code [305 ILCS 5/10-1 et seq.].

(Source: P.A. 84-848; 88-687, § 20; 89-641, § 30; 90-18, § 120; 91-308, § 10; 91-613, § 980; 92-16, § 98; 93-921, § 800; 93-1095, § 5.)

Note.

This section was Ill.Rev.Stat., Ch. 40, para. 2506.

Section 70 of P.A. 91-613 contains a severability provision.

Section 996 of P.A. 92-16 contains a "no acceleration or delay" provision, and Section 997 contains a "no revival or extension" provision.

Illinois Administrative Code.

See 89 Illinois Administrative Code, § 160.60.

Effect of Amendments.

The 1994 amendment by P.A. 88-687, effective January 24, 1995, in subsection (a), in the introductory language, inserted "addresses, social security numbers"; in subsection (b), deleted the second sentence which read "In any case where a public agency is providing assistance to the child, the parties requesting an order for support shall serve a copy of the petition and proposed order upon the agency" and in the present second sentence substituted "the Clerks of Courts Act" for "'An Act to Revise the Law in Relation to Clerks of Court', as now or hereafter amended"; in subsection (c) added the second sentence; in subsection (e), in the first sentence, deleted "suggested" preceding "legal" and added the second and third sentences; added subsection (e-5); and in subsection (f), inserted "a" preceding "proceeding" and substituted "the Criminal Code of 1961" for "'Criminal Code of 1961', approved July 28, 1961, as amended".

The 1996 amendment by P.A. 89-641, effective August 9, 1996, rewrote subsections (a) and (b); and deleted subsections (c) through (f).

The 1997 amendment by P.A. 90-18, effective July 1, 1997, in subsection (a) added the second sentence; and added subsections (c) through (e).

The 1999 amendment by P.A. 91-308, effective July 29, 1999, added subsections (a)(1) and (a)(2).

The 1999 amendment by P.A. 91-613, effective October 1, 1999, substituted "Non-Support Punishment Act" for "Non-Support of Spouse and Children Act" in the next to last sentence of subsection (e).

The 2001 amendment by P.A. 92-16, effective June 28, 2001, combined the amendments by P.A. 91-308 and P.A. 91-613.

The 2004 amendment by P.A. 93-921, effective January 1, 2005, rewrote the section to the extent that a detailed comparison would be impracticable.

The 2005 amendment by P.A. 93-1095, effective March 29, 2005, in (a)(1)(E) substituted "or the intended" for "and the intended" and inserted "or both".

CASE NOTES

ANALYSIS

Challenges to Paternity Adjudication
Genetic Testing
Rescission of Acknowledgment

Challenges to Paternity Adjudication

Genetic Testing

In the absence of fraud, duress, or material mistake of fact, a man who had voluntarily acknowledged paternity was bound by a conclusive presumption of paternity and could not attempt to rebut the presumption by DNA testing once the short period in which rescission was allowed had expired; the option to petition for a declaration of nonexistence of a parent-child relationship was only available where the original presumption had not been conclusive, as in the case where a mother and putative father had been married. People ex rel. Dep't of Pub. Aid v. Smith, 212 Ill. 2d 389, 289 Ill. Dec. 1, 818 N.E.2d 1204, 2004 Ill. LEXIS 1027 (2004).

Following the execution of a voluntary acknowledgment of paternity, the putative father could not successfully seek an order requiring genetic testing in the absence of fraud, duress, or material mistake of fact. Department of Pub. Aid ex rel. Allen v. Dixson, 323 Ill. App. 3d 600, 256 Ill. Dec. 905, 752 N.E.2d 1147, 2001 Ill. App. LEXIS 547 (3 Dist. 2001).

Rescission of Acknowledgment

A presumed father who signed a voluntary acknowledgment of paternity but failed to rescind the acknowledgment within the statutory period cannot challenge paternity in a subsequent child support action; he must file a motion under 735 ILCS 5/2-1401 to challenge his acknowledgment of paternity on the limited grounds of fraud, duress, or material mistake of fact. Ill. Dep't of Pub. Aid ex rel. Howard v. Graham, Ill. App. 3d , 262 Ill. Dec. 652, 766 N.E.2d 272, 2002 Ill. App. LEXIS 150 (3 Dist. 2002).

LEGAL PERIODICALS

For comment, "Prohibiting Payments to Surrogate Mothers: Love's Labor Lost and the Constitutional Right of Privacy," see 20 J. Marshall L. Rev. 715 (1987).

750 ILCS 45/7 Determination of Father and Child Relationship; Who May Bring Action; Parties

Sec. 7. *Determination of Father and Child Relationship; Who May Bring Action; Parties.* (a) An action to determine the existence of the father and child relationship, whether or not such a relationship is already presumed under Section 5 of this Act [750 ILCS 45/5], may be brought by the child; the mother; a pregnant woman; any person or public agency who has custody of, or is providing or has provided financial support to, the child; the Illinois Department of Public Aid if it is providing or has provided financial support to the child or if it is assisting with child support collection services; or a man presumed or alleging himself to be the father of the child or expected child. The complaint shall be verified and shall name the person or persons alleged to be the father of the child.

(b) An action to declare the non-existence of the parent and child relationship may be brought by the child, the natural mother, or a man presumed to be the father under subdivision (a)(1) or (a)(2) of Section 5 of this Act [750 ILCS 45/5]. Actions brought by the child, the natural mother or a presumed father shall be brought by verified complaint.

After the presumption that a man presumed to be the father under subdivision (a)(1) or (a)(2) of Section 5 [750 ILCS 45/5] has been rebutted, paternity of the child by another man may be determined in the same action, if he has been made a party.

(b-5) An action to declare the non-existence of the parent and child relationship may be brought subsequent to an adjudication of paternity in any judgment by the man adjudicated to be the father pursuant to the presumptions in Section 5 of this Act [750 ILCS 45/5] if, as a result of deoxyribonucleic acid (DNA) tests, it is discovered that the man adjudicated to be the father is not the natural father of the child. Actions brought by the adjudicated father shall be brought by verified complaint. If, as a result of the deoxyribonucleic acid (DNA) tests, the plaintiff is determined not to be the father of the child, the adjudication of paternity and any orders regarding custody, visitation, and future payments of support may be vacated.

(c) If any party is a minor, he or she may be represented by his or her general guardian or a guardian ad litem appointed by the court, which may include an appropriate agency. The court may align the parties.

(d) Regardless of its terms, an agreement, other than a settlement approved by the court, between an alleged or presumed father and the mother or child, does not bar an action under this Section.

(e) If an action under this Section is brought before the birth of the child, all proceedings shall be stayed until after the birth, except for service or process, the taking of depositions to perpetuate testimony, and the ordering of blood tests under appropriate circumstances.

(Source: P.A. 83-1372; 87-1058, § 1; 89-674, § 50; 90-18, § 120; 90-715, § 5.)

Note.

This section was Ill.Rev.Stat., Ch. 40, para. 2507.

Cross References.

As to settlement orders, specifically in cases where the alleged father has not consented to a finding of paternity and where the parties have requested a settlement, see 750 ILCS 45/12.1.

Effect of Amendments.

The 1996 amendment by P.A. 89-674, effective August 14, 1996, in subsection (a), in the first sentence, inserted "the Illinois Department of Public Aid if it is providing or has provided financial support to the child or if it is assisting with child support collection services".

The 1997 amendment by P.A. 90-18, effective July 1, 1997, in subsection (b), in the introductory language, in the first sentence, inserted "or", inserted "subdivision (a)(1) or (a)(2) of" and deleted from the end "or a man determined to be the father under Section 6" and deleted the third sentence, subdivisions (b)(1) and (b)(2) and the former second paragraph regarding action to declare the non existence of parent and child relationship brought by a man determined to be the father and in the present second paragraph inserted "subdivision (a)(1) or (a)(2) of" and deleted "or after a man determined to be the father under Section 6 has been determined under this Section to not be the father" preceding "paternity of the child".

The 1998 amendment by P.A. 90-715, effective August 7, 1998, added subsection (b-5).

CASE NOTES

Analysis

Constitutionality
Action by Father
—Custody
—Interest, Concern or Responsibility
—Interference
Appointment of Guardian Ad Litem
—Trial Court's Duty
Challenges to Paternity Adjudication
Construction
—Prior Law
Establishment of Paternity
—Eligible
—Statute of Limitations
—Sufficiency of Complaint
—Sufficiency of Evidence
—Unrebutted Statement by Party
General Guardian
—Qualification
Nonmarital Children
—Equal Protection
Parties
—Children
—Privity
—Putative Fathers
Paternity Action
Petition to Declare Nonexistence of Parent-Child Relationship
—DNA Test Results Required
—Not Shown
—Shown
—Standing
Presumption of Paternity
—Rebuttal
Prior Proceedings
—Privity
—Res Judicata
Res Judicata
—Paternity Action

Settlement Orders
—Failure to Comply with Statutory Requirements
—Parties
—Preclusive Effect
Standing to Bring Paternity Action
—In General
—By Child
—By Natural Father
—By Natural Mother
—By Public Agency
—Physical Custody
Support Actions
Time limitations.
Vacation of Paternity Order

Constitutionality

Subsection (b-5) is not unconstitutional, notwithstanding the contention that to deny a cause of action under the subsection to the mother is discrimination on the basis of gender and a denial of due process guaranteed by the Illinois and United States Constitutions. The subsection is designed to provide a remedy for a person who has already been determined by the court to be the father of the child based on certain presumptions in the Illinois Parentage Act, and a mother can challenge a father's parentage under a different subsection of the statute. Donath v. Buckley, 319 Ill. App. 3d 83, 253 Ill. Dec. 103, 744 N.E.2d 385, 2001 Ill. App. LEXIS 83 (3 Dist. 2001).

Action by Father

—Custody

As custody is obviously an aspect of the legal relationship between a father and child, the legislature has provided the procedural course for a putative father to file an action seeking custody within the framework of the Parentage Act; courts in parentage proceedings are thus bound to consider custody determinations upon the proper filing of an action and in accordance with the best interests of the child. Ligon ex rel. Williams v. Williams, 264 Ill. App. 3d 701, 202 Ill. Dec. 94, 637 N.E.2d 633 (1 Dist. 1994).

—Interest, Concern or Responsibility

Section 7(a) of the Illinois Parentage Act, codified at 750 ILCS 45/7(a), is not facially invalid to the extent that it permits, without a prior best interests hearing, a paternity action to be brought by a man alleging himself to be the biological father of a child who was born during the marriage of the mother to another man. Valdivia v. Izaguirre (In re John M.), 212 Ill. 2d 253, 288 Ill. Dec. 142, 817 N.E.2d 500, 2004 Ill. LEXIS 1024 (2004).

The filing of paternity action under subsection (e) establishes the alleged father's status of record and entitles him to service of process in proceedings involving the child; had respondent simply availed himself of the provisions of subsection (e), he would not have had to rely upon the cooperation of mother and her family, which he was aware was unreliable, to express his concern for his child and he would have demonstrated concern for his child under 750 ILCS 50/1 D.(l). In re J.R.G., 247 Ill. App. 3d 104, 187 Ill. Dec. 169, 617 N.E.2d 377 (1 Dist. 1993).

—Interference

Interference with biological father's right to bring action to establish paternity was not a deprivation of a federal constitutional right, though it might have given rise to state law claims for abuse of process and malicious prosecution. Pena v. Mattox, 84 F.3d 894 (7th Cir. 1996).

Appointment of Guardian Ad Litem

—Trial Court's Duty

Where it was established by DNA that a child was not the biological child of the mother's husband, the child was not a party in the divorcing parties' parentage proceeding; therefore, the appointment of a guardian for the child by the court was not mandatory under the Illinois Parentage Act. In re Marriage of Nienhouse, Ill. App. 3d , 290 Ill. Dec. 654, 821 N.E.2d 1228, 2004 Ill. App. LEXIS 1551 (1 Dist. 2004).

A trial court has the inherent power, and statutory authority, to appoint a guardian ad litem for a child subject to paternity proceedings. Denofrio v. Kuc, 201 Ill. App. 3d 810, 146 Ill. Dec. 1021, 558 N.E.2d 1355 (1 Dist. 1990).

It is not mandatory that the trial court appoint a guardian ad litem for a child, in an action under this Act. Klawitter v. Crawford, 185 Ill. App. 3d 778, 133 Ill. Dec. 721, 541 N.E.2d 1159 (1 Dist. 1989).

Where a trial court has notice that a minor's interests are not properly represented, it is the duty of the trial court to appoint a guardian ad litem to safeguard and protect those interests. In re Tzoumas, 187 Ill. App. 3d 723, 135 Ill. Dec. 525, 543 N.E.2d 1093 (2 Dist. 1989).

Where it was apparent to the trial court that respondent did not wish to promote the child's interest in visitation with, and child support from her father, the trial court had an obligation under these circumstances to appoint a guardian ad litem. Majidi v. Palmer, 175 Ill. App. 3d 679, 125 Ill. Dec. 148, 530 N.E.2d 66 (2 Dist. 1988).

Challenges to Paternity Adjudication

Father's challenge to adjudication of paternity was properly dismissed where he failed to allege DNA test results excluding him as the father and, therefore, failed to state a cause of action under subsection (b-5) of this section. In re Lubbs, 313 Ill. App. 3d 968, 246 Ill. Dec. 674, 730 N.E.2d 1139, 2000 Ill. App. LEXIS 137 (3 Dist. 2000).

Subsection (b-5) of this section, as amended in 1998, provides a new cause of action allowing an adjudicated father to challenge the adjudication of paternity only if DNA testing has established, prior to the filing of the petition, that the adjudicated father is not the natural father; it does not authorize such action to be brought in the absence of DNA testing, nor does it provide a mechanism for compelling the mother or child to undergo DNA testing. In re Lubbs, 313 Ill. App. 3d 968, 246 Ill. Dec. 674, 730 N.E.2d 1139, 2000 Ill. App. LEXIS 137 (3 Dist. 2000).

Construction

—Prior Law

Under the former Bastardy Act (see now this Act), a mother was to have been unmarried at the time a child was born, and the word "unmarried" did not relate to the time of making a complaint. People ex rel. Wilmers v. Volksdorf, 112 Ill. 292 (1884).

Establishment of Paternity

—Eligible

A hearing to determine whether the father was the stillborn baby's natural father was appropriate under 755 ILCS 5/2-2; as the statute does not have a blanket effect of debarring all illegitimate fathers from recovering for the wrongful deaths of their children. Rather it insures that fathers have to prove they are "eligible," before they can take under the line of intestate distribution. Poole v. Clausen (In re Estate of Poole), 207 Ill. 2d 393, 278 Ill. Dec. 532, 799 N.E.2d 250, 2003 Ill. LEXIS 1492 (2003).

—Statute of Limitations

The statute of limitations applied to complaint brought by unmarried, but undisputed natural father seeking a finding that a father and child relationship existed, and custody of, or rights of visitation with the child, where prior to the lawsuit, the plaintiff had never been acknowledged to be the father by either party in any official document, or proceeding. Kapp v. Alexander, 218 Ill. App. 3d 412, 161 Ill. Dec. 158, 578 N.E.2d 285 (3 Dist. 1991).

Regardless of any legal presumptions of paternity, a man alleging he is the father of a child may bring an action to determine a parent-child relationship if the action is brought within the limitations of 750 ILCS 45/8, that is, no later than two years after the child reaches the age majority and where a child, who was born to a woman who was married at the time of conception and birth, had not yet reached the age of majority, a potential father's petition to determine a parent-child relationship, rather than an action to declare the non-existence of a parent-child relationship, was proper. J.S.A. v. M.H., 343 Ill. App. 3d 217, 278 Ill. Dec. 110, 797 N.E.2d 705, 2003 Ill. App. LEXIS 1066 (3 Dist. 2003), appeal denied, 207 Ill. 2d 604, 283 Ill. Dec. 134, 807 N.E.2d 975 (2004).

—Sufficiency of Complaint

In paternity action pursuant to former Paternity Act (see now this Act), state was not required to allege facts demonstrating that it had authority to bring the action and that the child had not been

Establishment of Paternity (Cont'd)

—Sufficiency of Complaint (Cont'd)
supported and provided for by the defendant; the defendant was accused of fathering the child and was obviously on notice of the nature of the claim against him. People ex rel. Moore v. McIntosh, 134 Ill. App. 3d 1070, 90 Ill. Dec. 33, 481 N.E.2d 833 (5 Dist. 1985).

Under the former Paternity Act (see now this Act), where each of two complaints contained the signature of the complaining witness, which was preceded by a statement that she, being sworn under oath, read the complaint and that it was true and accurate, but the space provided for the signature of a person authorized to administer oaths was blank on both complaints, where the complaining witness and the defendant were present in open court, and two orders entered on that date recited that the complaining witness presented the complaint under oath, the requirements of the Act were followed. People ex rel. Blackmon v. Brent, 97 Ill. App. 2d 438, 240 N.E.2d 255 (1 Dist. 1968).

—Sufficiency of Evidence
Where defendant never alleged that relator was married, nor denied that she was unmarried, relator testified that she had not lived with any other man, and had not had sexual intercourse with any other man, and defendant made no effort to rebut this testimony, the evidence adduced at trial was sufficient to support the trial court's finding under the former Paternity Act (see now this Act) that defendant was proved by a preponderance of the evidence to be the father of a child born out of wedlock. People ex rel. Raines v. Biggs, 135 Ill. App. 3d 200, 90 Ill. Dec. 99, 481 N.E.2d 899 (5 Dist. 1985).

Where mother testified that she had sexual intercourse with the putative father, and that he signed a hospital document stating he was the father of the child, and that he held out the child as his own, this testimony was sufficient to corroborate finding of paternity. Watkins v. Martin, 115 Ill. App. 3d 417, 71 Ill. Dec. 178, 450 N.E.2d 866 (1 Dist. 1983).

Where defendant did not argue that the evidence was insufficient to prove paternity, and that he was not the father of the child, the trial court's determination that defendant was the father of the child born to plaintiff was not against the manifest weight of the evidence. People ex rel. Davis v. Clark, 99 Ill. App. 3d 979, 55 Ill. Dec. 319, 426 N.E.2d 294 (4 Dist. 1981).

Although plaintiff did present evidence of a physical relationship with defendant, the jury found that he was not the father of her child, and in viewing all the evidence most favorably, the trial court did not err in denying plaintiff's motions for a directed verdict and judgment n.o.v. People ex rel. Johnson v. Hampton, 70 Ill. App. 3d 555, 26 Ill. Dec. 781, 388 N.E.2d 782 (1 Dist. 1979).

Where under section 56 of the former Paternity Act (see now this section), the judgment of the trial court that defendant was the father of plaintiff's illegitimate child was not contrary to the manifest weight of the evidence, the judgment of paternity would be affirmed. People ex rel. Wider v. Johnson, 26 Ill. App. 3d 192, 324 N.E.2d 722 (5 Dist. 1975).

Evidence was sufficient to justify court's verdict which found defendant to be baby's father. People ex rel. Morton v. Woolen, 322 Ill. App. 182, 54 N.E.2d 419 (3 Dist. 1944).

—Unrebutted Statement by Party
The jury in a paternity suit was not required to believe complainant's statement merely because it was unrebutted. People ex rel. Martin v. Presswood, 85 Ill. App. 3d 975, 41 Ill. Dec. 272, 407 N.E.2d 770 (1 Dist. 1980).

General Guardian

—Qualification
Natural mother of child did not qualify as child's general guardian, where the mother's former husband was given the sole permanent care, custody, control and education of the minor child in the couple's divorce settlement and agreed judgment. Koenig ex rel. Koenig v. Koenig, 211 Ill. App. 3d 1045, 156 Ill. Dec. 385, 570 N.E.2d 861 (1 Dist. 1991).

Nonmarital Children

—Equal Protection
A settlement order entered pursuant to the settlement provisions of a paternity statute should not bar a subsequent support action brought on behalf of a nonmarital child; equal protection of the law would be violated if a right to seek support from their parents during the whole of their minority were granted to marital children but denied to nonmarital children. Department of Public Aid ex rel. Cox v. Miller, 146 Ill. 2d 399, 166 Ill. Dec. 922, 586 N.E.2d 1251 (1992).

Parties

—Children
A child under the age of 18 may not file a petition to determine the existence of a parent and child relationship on her or his own behalf without a guardian or next friend. Klak v. Skellion, 317 Ill. App. 3d 1092, 251 Ill. Dec. 694, 741 N.E.2d 288, 2000 Ill. App. LEXIS 928 (1 Dist. 2000).

—Privity
There was no privity between a minor and her mother even though an action could be brought by a child or a parent, because the mere filing of a complaint by one or more of the parties able to bring an action did not in and of itself suggest privity with the nonfiling party or parties. Mayberry ex rel. Mayberry v. Kovas, 222 Ill. App. 3d 1008, 165 Ill. Dec. 354, 584 N.E.2d 533 (2 Dist. 1991), cert. denied, 144 Ill. 2d 634, 169 Ill. Dec. 142, 591 N.E.2d 22 (1992).

This Act and the former Paternity Act did not establish privity between a minor and her mother, even though they allowed an action to be brought by the child or a parent, because the mere filing of a complaint by one or more of the parties able to bring an action did not in and of itself suggest privity with the nonfiling party or parties. Mayberry ex rel. Mayberry v. Kovas, 222 Ill. App. 3d 1008, 165 Ill. Dec. 354, 584 N.E.2d 533 (2 Dist. 1991), cert. denied, 144 Ill. 2d 634, 169 Ill. Dec. 142, 591 N.E.2d 22 (1992).

Children are not privies of their parents in dissolution proceedings, and, as such, are not bound by findings of paternity in such proceedings unless they are parties to the proceedings. Simcox ex rel. Dear v. Simcox, 131 Ill. 2d 491, 137 Ill. Dec. 664, 546 N.E.2d 609 (1989).

—Putative Fathers
The trial court did not err in failing to appoint the putative father as the alleged child's guardian ad litem, since, there was a potential conflict between the putative father's interests and the child's; the putative father was not a proper person to represent the child, so the trial court could not interpret his petition as a petition brought on the child's behalf and correctly dismissed the petition. McDonald v. McGowan, 163 Ill. App. 3d 697, 114 Ill. Dec. 779, 516 N.E.2d 934 (1 Dist. 1987).

This section evidences an intent, on the part of the General Assembly to permit a man "alleging himself to be the father" of a child, to bring an action for determination of the existence of a father and child relationship. LeHew v. Mellyn, 131 Ill. App. 3d 314, 86 Ill. Dec. 534, 475 N.E.2d 913 (1 Dist. 1985).

Paternity Action
Social services agency had standing to bring an action to determine paternity of children for whom the agency had assumed responsibility, even though its initial pleading was characterized as a petition instead of a complaint. People v. Ras M., 344 Ill. App. 3d 503, 279 Ill. Dec. 836, 801 N.E.2d 128, 2003 Ill. App. LEXIS 1375 (1 Dist. 2003).

Unwed biological father who lost parental rights when minor mother took child out of state and put her up for adoption could have commenced paternity action prior to the birth of the child and established the father-child relationship; the judgment rendered would contain or explicitly reserve provisions concerning the custody and guardianship of the child, and visitation privileges with the child. Pena v. Mattox, 880 F. Supp. 567 (N.D. Ill. 1995), aff'd, 84 F.3d 894 (7th Cir. 1996).

Petition to Declare Nonexistence of Parent-Child Relationship

—DNA Test Results Required
An adjudicated father must obtain deoxyribonucleic acid (DNA) test results disproving paternity as a condition precedent to filing an action to declare the nonexistence of a parent/child relationship.

Petition to Declare Nonexistence of Parent-Child Relationship (Cont'd)

—DNA Test Results Required (Cont'd)
In re Kates, 198 Ill. 2d 156, 260 Ill. Dec. 309, 761 N.E.2d 153, 2001 Ill. LEXIS 1437 (2001).

—Not Shown
Petitioner did not bring an "action to declare the nonexistence of the parent and child relationship," where petitioner brought an action to, inter alia, gain permanent custody of his child. In re Ingram, 176 Ill. App. 3d 413, 125 Ill. Dec. 918, 531 N.E.2d 97 (5 Dist. 1988).

—Shown
Action to vacate paternity acknowledgement order was proper under § 7(b-5) of the Parentage Act, codified at 750 ILCS 45/7(b-5), where paternity had originally been established through acknowledgement filed in a court proceeding. Jackson v. Newsome, 325 Ill. App. 3d 372, 259 Ill. Dec. 219, 758 N.E.2d 342, 2001 Ill. App. LEXIS 750 (1 Dist. 2001).

—Standing
A mother lacked standing to bring an action under subsection (b-5) as she clearly was not "the man adjudicated to be the father." Donath v. Buckley, 319 Ill. App. 3d 83, 253 Ill. Dec. 103, 744 N.E.2d 385, 2001 Ill. App. LEXIS 83 (3 Dist. 2001).

Presumption of Paternity
In the absence of fraud, duress, or material mistake of fact, a man who had voluntarily acknowledged paternity was bound by a conclusive presumption of paternity and could not attempt to rebut the presumption by DNA testing once the short period in which rescission was allowed had expired; the option to petition for a declaration of nonexistence of a parent-child relationship was only available where the original presumption had not been conclusive, as in the case where a mother and putative father had been married. People ex rel. Dep't of Pub. Aid v. Smith, 212 Ill. 2d 389, 289 Ill. Dec. 1, 818 N.E.2d 1204, 2004 Ill. LEXIS 1027 (2004).

—Rebuttal
This Act allows a biological father to rebut the statutory presumption that a child born during marriage is the husband's issue; there is a two-year limitation period on this right that commences with the child's birth. Allen v. Allen, 48 F.3d 259 (7th Cir. 1995).

If the presumption of paternity, as set forth in section 5 of this Act (750 ILCS 45/5), is sufficiently rebutted, then paternity of the child by another man may be established if that man has been made a party to the proceedings. In re Klebs, 196 Ill. App. 3d 472, 143 Ill. Dec. 363, 554 N.E.2d 298 (1 Dist. 1990).

Prior Proceedings

—Privity
In mother's filing of the action to establish that defendant was the father of a minor child, four years prior to the child's subsequent paternity action, there was no privity between mother and child. Maller ex rel. Maller v. Cohen, 176 Ill. App. 3d 987, 126 Ill. Dec. 402, 531 N.E.2d 1029 (1 Dist. 1988).

—Res Judicata
Children are not in privity with their mothers and thus not barred from bringing paternity actions under the doctrine of res judicata when their mothers have filed previous paternity or support actions. Department of Public Aid ex rel. Stark v. Wheeler, 248 Ill. App. 3d 749, 188 Ill. Dec. 741, 618 N.E.2d 1311 (5 Dist. 1993).

A child's paternity action is not barred by the dismissal of the mother's paternity action, because the child was neither a party, nor in privity with a party, in the earlier proceeding. Illinois Dep't of Pub. Aid ex rel. Skelton v. Liesman, 218 Ill. App. 3d 437, 161 Ill. Dec. 183, 578 N.E.2d 310 (4 Dist. 1991).

The doctrine of res judicata did not bar the claim of the Department of Public Aid, a public agency providing financial support to minor children, to intervene in minor child's paternity action, where paternity action by child's mother was dismissed four years earlier. Maller ex rel. Maller v. Cohen, 176 Ill. App. 3d 987, 126 Ill. Dec. 402, 531 N.E.2d 1029 (1 Dist. 1988).

Res Judicata

—Paternity Action
Where a mother's action to establish paternity was adjudicated upon the merits for purposes of the doctrine of res judicata, child had no right to bring another action where there was no new evidence. Draper ex rel. Crutcher v. Truitt, 250 Ill. App. 3d 654, 190 Ill. Dec. 333, 621 N.E.2d 202 (1 Dist. 1993).

Settlement Orders

—Failure to Comply with Statutory Requirements
When first action was brought and settled under the former Paternity Act but the settlement agreement did not comport with the requirements of that Act, it was not properly considered a settlement within the meaning of the Paternity Act, and did not preclude any subsequent action under this Act. Illinois Dep't. of Pub. Aid ex rel. McGee v. Kennedy, 211 Ill. App. 3d 158, 155 Ill. Dec. 792, 570 N.E.2d 12 (4 Dist. 1991).

—Parties
The trial court erred in dismissing a minor's paternity action where a previous paternity action between her mother and the putative father resulted in a court-approved settlement without an adjudication of paternity; the trial court's dismissal was vacated because the minor was not made a party to the prior settlement and therefore was not bound by its restrictions. Mayberry ex rel. Mayberry v. Kovas, 222 Ill. App. 3d 1008, 165 Ill. Dec. 354, 584 N.E.2d 533 (2 Dist. 1991), cert. denied, 144 Ill. 2d 634, 169 Ill. Dec. 142, 591 N.E.2d 22 (1992).

—Preclusive Effect
The phrase "settlement approved by the court" in subsection (d) of this section is properly construed as referring to the settlement orders of 750 ILCS 45/12.1 and unless such an order complies with this section, it has no preclusive effect under this Act. Illinois Dep't. of Pub. Aid ex rel. McGee v. Kennedy, 211 Ill. App. 3d 158, 155 Ill. Dec. 792, 570 N.E.2d 12 (4 Dist. 1991).

This section continues to preserve the finality afforded to court-approved settlement orders as was provided by former sections of this Act, and it does not permit the mother, alleged father, or a public agency which has supported the child, to bring an action after a court approved settlement has been reached. Illinois Dep't of Pub. Aid ex rel. Spurgetis v. Newburg, 181 Ill. App. 3d 424, 130 Ill. Dec. 317, 537 N.E.2d 384 (3 Dist. 1989).

Standing to Bring Paternity Action

—In General
The standing provisions embodied in 750 ILCS 5/601(b)(2) apply to those seeking custody under this Act regardless of whether they are intervenors or interested parties. Brumfield v. Yard, 284 Ill. App. 3d 950, 220 Ill. Dec. 549, 673 N.E.2d 461 (4 Dist. 1996), appeal denied, 172 Ill. 2d 548, 223 Ill. Dec. 193, 679 N.E.2d 378 (1997).

—By Child
A finding of paternity included in a divorce decree explicitly or by implication was not binding upon a child in a subsequent proceeding involving the child and the former husband of the child's mother because the child had not been a party to the divorce action. Simcox ex rel. Dear v. Simcox, 175 Ill. App. 3d 473, 124 Ill. Dec. 915, 529 N.E.2d 1032 (1 Dist. 1988).

—By Natural Father
Where the child's natural mother was not her general guardian, nor was she the child's guardian ad litem, the natural mother lacked standing to bring a paternity petition on the child's behalf. Koenig ex rel. Koenig v. Koenig, 211 Ill. App. 3d 1045, 156 Ill. Dec. 385, 570 N.E.2d 861 (1 Dist. 1991).

Although the former Paternity Act (see now this Act) provided that actions for support, maintenance, education and welfare could be instituted by the mother or by the Illinois Department of Public Aid on behalf of a minor child, a father was not barred by this Act from having his paternity established when he had overcome the presumption of legitimacy. Happel v. Mecklenburger, 101 Ill. App. 3d 107, 56 Ill. Dec. 569, 427 N.E.2d 974 (1 Dist. 1981).

—By Natural Mother
Absent her judicial admission as to her former husband's pater-

Standing to Bring Paternity Action (Cont'd)

—By Natural Mother (Cont'd)
nity the child's natural mother might have challenged the existence of a parent and child relationship between the former husband and the child on her own behalf, without involving the child. Koenig ex rel. Koenig v. Koenig, 211 Ill. App. 3d 1045, 156 Ill. Dec. 385, 570 N.E.2d 861 (1 Dist. 1991).

There was no language in former Act (see now this Act) making it mandatory for a woman seeking relief under the Act to call upon the Attorney General or the State's Attorney to institute her action; rather, the legislature intended to provide a prosecutrix with an alternative procedure to retaining private counsel. People ex rel. Foster v. Louder, 97 Ill. App. 3d 1104, 53 Ill. Dec. 468, 423 N.E.2d 1272 (1 Dist. 1981).

—By Public Agency
Just as children in paternity actions are not in privity with their mothers, public agencies which have provided financial support are also not in privity with the mothers; just as the interests of children are different from those of their mothers, the interests of public agencies providing aid are separate from the caretakers of the children. Department of Public Aid ex rel. Stark v. Wheeler, 248 Ill. App. 3d 749, 188 Ill. Dec. 741, 618 N.E.2d 1311 (5 Dist. 1993).

—Physical Custody
Child was in the "physical custody" of father at time non-parents seeking adoption filed petition to intervene, thus denying non-parents standing to seek child's custody, where father acted to protect his interest and establish his relationship with child, father had not been declared father of child when child was placed with persons seeking adoption, father brought suit for declaration of paternity before child was born, and non-parents who took possession of child had no contact with father to determine his desires. Brumfield v. Yard, 284 Ill. App. 3d 950, 220 Ill. Dec. 549, 673 N.E.2d 461 (4 Dist. 1996), appeal denied, 172 Ill. 2d 548, 223 Ill. Dec. 193, 679 N.E.2d 378 (1997).

Support Actions
A support order is not complete and appealable until the issue of health insurance is resolved and a paternity judgment is not final and appealable until all issues regarding child support are fully resolved. People ex rel. Davis v. Washington, 283 Ill. App. 3d 437, 218 Ill. Dec. 689, 669 N.E.2d 1215 (1 Dist. 1996).

A settlement order and dismissal entered in a paternity action do not bar a subsequent action brought by or on behalf of the illegitimate minor for support. Department of Public Aid ex rel. Cox v. Miller, 146 Ill. 2d 399, 166 Ill. Dec. 922, 586 N.E.2d 1251 (1992).

Time limitations.
Two-year limitations period for § 7(b-5) actions to vacate paternity order must be filed within two years of the obtaining of actual knowledge of relevant facts and does not require knowledge of the results of a DNA test. The period is tolled if the mother or child refuses to submit to the DNA test. Jackson v. Newsome, 325 Ill. App. 3d 372, 259 Ill. Dec. 219, 758 N.E.2d 342, 2001 Ill. App. LEXIS 750 (1 Dist. 2001).

Vacation of Paternity Order
Section 12 of the Vital Records Act, codified at 410 ILCS 535/12 was not incorporated into § 7(b-5) of the Parentage Act, codified at 750 ILCS 45/7(b-5). Jackson v. Newsome, 325 Ill. App. 3d 372, 259 Ill. Dec. 219, 758 N.E.2d 342, 2001 Ill. App. LEXIS 750 (1 Dist. 2001).

LEGAL PERIODICALS

For article, "Baby Richard and Beyond: The Future for Adopted Children", see 18 N. Ill. U.L. Rev. 445 (1999).

For comment, "Paternity Actions in Illinois: Why Not Consider What is in the Best Interest of the Child?," see 21 S. Ill. U.L.J. 613 (1997).

For comment, "Prohibiting Payments to Surrogate Mothers: Love's Labor Lost and the Constitutional Right of Privacy," see 20 J. Marshall L. Rev. 715 (1987).

RESEARCH REFERENCES

Necessity or propriety of appointment of independent guardian for child who is subject of paternity proceedings. 70 ALR4th 1033.

Right of Illegitimate Child to Maintain Action to Determine Paternity. 86 ALR5th 637.

750 ILCS 45/8 Statute of limitations

Sec. 8. *Statute of limitations.* (a)(1) An action brought by or on behalf of a child, an action brought by a party alleging that he or she is the child's natural parent, or an action brought by the Illinois Department of Public Aid, if it is providing or has provided financial support to the child or if it is assisting with child support collection services, shall be barred if brought later than 2 years after the child reaches the age of majority; however, if the action on behalf of the child is brought by a public agency, other than the Illinois Department of Public Aid if it is providing or has provided financial support to the child or if it is assisting with child support collection services, it shall be barred 2 years after the agency has ceased to provide assistance to the child.

(2) Failure to bring an action within 2 years shall not bar any party from asserting a defense in any action to declare the non-existence of the parent and child relationship.

(3) An action to declare the non-existence of the parent and child relationship brought under subsection (b) of Section 7 of this Act [750 ILCS 45/7] shall be barred if brought later than 2 years after the petitioner obtains knowledge of relevant facts. The 2-year period for bringing an action to declare the nonexistence of the parent and child relationship shall not extend beyond the date on which the child reaches the age of 18 years. Failure to bring an action within 2 years shall not bar any party from asserting a defense in any action to declare the existence of the parent and child relationship.

(4) An action to declare the non-existence of the parent and child relationship brought under subsection (b-5) of Section 7 of this Act [750 ILCS 45/7] shall be barred if brought more than 6 months after the effective date of this amendatory Act of 1998 or more than 2 years after the petitioner obtains actual knowledge of relevant facts, whichever is later. The 2-year period shall not apply to periods of time where the natural mother or the child refuses to submit to deoxyribonucleic acid (DNA) tests. The 2-year period for bringing an action to declare the nonexistence of the Parent and child relationship shall not extend beyond the date on which the child reaches the age of 18 years. Failure to bring an action within 2 years shall not bar any arty from asserting a defense in any action to declare the existence of the parent and child relationship.

(b) The time during which any party is not subject to service of process or is otherwise not subject to the jurisdiction of the courts of this State shall toll the aforementioned periods.

(c) This Act does not affect the time within which any rights under the Probate Act of 1975 [755 ILCS 5/1-1 et seq.] may be asserted beyond the time provided by law relating to distribution and closing of decedent's estates or to the determination of heirship, or otherwise.

(Source: P.A. 84-848; 87-1058, § 1; 88-538, § 10; 88-687, § 20; 89-674, § 50; 90-18, § 120; 90-715, § 5.)

Note.

This section was Ill.Rev.Stat., Ch. 40, para. 2508.

Effect of Amendments.

The 1994 amendment by P.A. 88-538, effective January 1, 1995, in subdivision (a)(1), added the second paragraph; in subdivision (a)(2), deleted the former first sentence, which read "An action brought on behalf of any person other than the child shall be barred if brought later than 2 years after the birth of the child"; and in subsection (c) deleted "as amended" following "Act of 1975".

The 1994 amendment by P.A. 88-687, effective January 24, 1995, incorporated the amendments by P.A. 88-538 and in subdivision (a)(3), in the first sentence, deleted from the end "except that an action brought by a man determined to be the father under Section 6 shall be brought, in any event, no later than the date on which the child reaches the age of 10 years" and added the second sentence.

The 1996 amendment by P.A. 89-674, effective August 14, 1996, in subdivision (a)(1), in the first paragraph, inserted "or an action brought by the Illinois Department of Public Aid, if it is providing or has provided financial support to the child or if it is assisting with child support collection services" and inserted "other than the Illinois Department of Public Aid if it is providing or has provided financial support to the child or if it is assisting with child support collection services".

The 1997 amendment by P.A. 90-18, effective July 1, 1997, in subdivision (a)(1) inserted "an action brought by a party alleging that he or she is the child's natural parent" and deleted the second paragraph regarding statute of limitations period.

The 1998 amendment by P.A. 90-715, effective August 7, 1998, inserted "brought under subsection (b) of Section 7 of this Act" in subsection (a)(3); and added subsection (a)(4).

CASE NOTES

Analysis

Constitutionality
—Prior Law
—Retroactive Application
—Statutory Classification
—Two Year Limitations
Action Brought on Child's Behalf
—Action "Ex Rel."
—Not Shown
Affirmative Defense
—Estoppel
Applicability of Limitations Period
—In General
—Action by Child
—Construction of Trust
—Custody Suit
—Dismissal with Leave to Reinstate
—Former Paternity Act
—Lack of Standing
—Parentage Not at Issue
—Prior Law
—Purpose
—Retroactive Application
—Rights Under Probate Act
—Strict Construction
Effective Date of Act
—Filing Untimely
—Pending Actions
—Petition Untimely
Petition to Declare Nonexistence of Parent-Child Relationship
—Time Limitation
Petition Properly Dismissed
Posthumous Actions
Presumption of Paternity
—Rebuttal
Reasonable Time
Retroactive Application
Tolling
—Limitations Period Not Tolled
—Notice of Intent to File
—Paternity Affirmed in Answer
Unreasonable Delay
Waiver

Constitutionality

—Prior Law

The two year limitations period on paternity actions under section 1354 of the former Paternity Act, replaced by this section, violated the equal protection clause of the Fourteenth Amendment. People ex rel. McCoy v. Sherman, 123 Ill. App. 3d 444, 78 Ill. Dec. 698, 462 N.E.2d 817 (4 Dist. 1984).

The two year limitations period of the former Paternity Act (see now this section) was unconstitutional. Azzone v. Bricco, 125 Ill. App. 3d 818, 81 Ill. Dec. 85, 466 N.E.2d 671 (2 Dist. 1984).

—Retroactive Application

The two year statute of limitations applicable to an action brought on behalf of any person, other than the child, did not violate plaintiff's due process rights in that it was applied retroactively, as he still had a reasonable time period following the effective date of the Parentage Act in which to file his claim. Majidi v. Palmer, 175 Ill. App. 3d 679, 125 Ill. Dec. 148, 530 N.E.2d 66 (2 Dist. 1988).

—Statutory Classification

The statute of limitations classification in this section of this Act is rationally related to a legitimate governmental purpose, and does not violate equal protection. Klawitter v. Crawford, 185 Ill. App. 3d 778, 133 Ill. Dec. 721, 541 N.E.2d 1159 (1 Dist. 1989).

The statute of limitations classification in this section of this Act is rationally related to a legitimate governmental purpose, and therefore does not violate equal protection. Majidi v. Palmer, 175 Ill. App. 3d 679, 125 Ill. Dec. 148, 530 N.E.2d 66 (2 Dist. 1988).

—Two Year Limitations

The two year limitations period provided in this section of this Act is not unconstitutional under United States Constitution, Amend. 14. Denofrio v. Kuc, 201 Ill. App. 3d 810, 146 Ill. Dec. 1021, 558 N.E.2d 1355 (1 Dist. 1990).

Action Brought on Child's Behalf

—Action "Ex Rel."

An action brought by the state "ex rel." the mother, seeking to find the putative father liable for the support, education, maintenance, and welfare of the child, was an action brought on behalf of the child, within the meaning of this Act and could be brought until two years after the child's majority. People ex rel. Todd v. Harvey, 154 Ill. App. 3d 296, 107 Ill. Dec. 446, 507 N.E.2d 110 (1 Dist. 1987).

—Not Shown

Where defendant sought to deprive the child of the only father he had known, thereby depriving the child of a source of financial and emotional support, defendant's actions could not have been interpreted as pursued on the child's behalf. In re Ingram, 176 Ill. App. 3d 413, 125 Ill. Dec. 918, 531 N.E.2d 97 (5 Dist. 1988).

Affirmative Defense

—Estoppel

Where a mother testified that she lived with the putative father defendant continuously for over several years, and that during that time, the putative father contributed to the expenses of herself and the children, and that the putative father gave the children presents, took them places, and never denied or disclaimed being their father, such evidence was sufficient to warrant estoppel of a putative father's assertion of the two year limitation period as a

Affirmative Defense (Cont'd)

—Estoppel (Cont'd)

defense to a paternity action under former section 4 of the Paternity Act (see now this section). People ex rel. Andrews v. Andrews, 94 Ill. App. 3d 84, 49 Ill. Dec. 616, 418 N.E.2d 470 (2 Dist. 1981).

Where a prior judge concluded that defendant was equitably estopped to assert the defense of the statute of limitations, since he had supported the children, and held them out as his children, a second judge was barred from concluding that the paternity statute of limitations had run prior to commencement of the paternity action, absent a proffer of new evidence. People ex rel. Belisle v. McField, 95 Ill. App. 3d 655, 51 Ill. Dec. 159, 420 N.E.2d 573 (1 Dist. 1981).

Applicability of Limitations Period

—In General

The statute of limitations applies to complaint brought by unmarried, but undisputed natural father, seeking a finding that a father and child relationship existed, and custody of, or rights of visitation with the child, where prior to suit under this Act, the plaintiff had never been acknowledged to be the father by either party, in any official document or proceeding. Kapp v. Alexander, 218 Ill. App. 3d 412, 161 Ill. Dec. 158, 578 N.E.2d 285 (3 Dist. 1991).

The limitation included in this section attempts to limit the spectre of lurking problems with respect to proof of paternity, and at the same time, however, it triggers a two year statute of limitations only when a child reaches the age of majority so that such children have a reasonable opportunity to assert their rights. Tersavich v. First Nat'l Bank & Trust Co., 194 Ill. App. 3d 972, 141 Ill. Dec. 628, 551 N.E.2d 815 (2 Dist. 1990).

A reasonable time for bringing an action in cases under this Act cannot be greater than the statutory limitation period itself, since a longer period would defeat the purpose of the statute. In re Johnson, 206 Ill. App. 3d 992, 151 Ill. Dec. 891, 565 N.E.2d 162 (1 Dist. 1990).

—Action by Child

A child can bring an action to ascertain paternity anytime during the limitations period. Department of Public Aid ex rel. Cox v. Miller, 146 Ill. 2d 399, 166 Ill. Dec. 922, 586 N.E.2d 1251 (1992).

—Construction of Trust

This section's period of limitations should not run with respect to an illegitimate child seeking to construe a trust, until the latter of two triggering events occurs: (1) the child reaches the age of majority, or (2) the child knows, or should know, that a trustee has repudiated, disavowed or acted in hostility to the trust. Tersavich v. First Nat'l Bank & Trust Co., 194 Ill. App. 3d 972, 141 Ill. Dec. 628, 551 N.E.2d 815 (2 Dist. 1990).

—Custody Suit

Where respondent attempted to make parentage an issue in the custody controversy, the statute of limitations in this Act applied. In re Ingram, 176 Ill. App. 3d 413, 125 Ill. Dec. 918, 531 N.E.2d 97 (5 Dist. 1988).

—Dismissal with Leave to Reinstate

Trial court had authority to enter order reinstating paternity cause to the trial calendar, even though the paternity complaint had been dismissed approximately three years earlier, where the case was removed from the docket with leave to reinstate; therefore, subsequent paternity judgment was not void because the court had jurisdiction over defendant's person. People ex rel. Pranske v. Lowe, 74 Ill. App. 3d 734, 30 Ill. Dec. 629, 393 N.E.2d 665 (1 Dist. 1979).

—Former Paternity Act

The two year limitation period for paternity actions as provided by section 1354 of the former Paternity Act (see now this section), was not, technically speaking, a statute of limitations. People ex rel. Getz v. Lang, 61 Ill. App. 3d 933, 18 Ill. Dec. 934, 378 N.E.2d 398 (3 Dist. 1978).

—Lack of Standing

Since the nonexistence of a parent-child relationship was raised by a custodial parent as a defense to petitioner's action seeking custody, the statute of limitations was not a bar to the argument that petitioner, as a female whose transformation into a male had never been completed, lacked standing as a parent to seek custody. In re Simmons, Ill. App. 3d , Ill. Dec. , N.E.2d , 2005 Ill. App. LEXIS 127 (1 Dist. Feb. 16, 2005).

—Parentage Not at Issue

Where parentage is not at issue, due to the fact that decedent openly acknowledged paternity of child, the limitations period of this Act does not apply. Tersavich v. First Nat'l Bank & Trust Co., 143 Ill. 2d 74, 156 Ill. Dec. 753, 571 N.E.2d 733 (1991).

Where child's birth certificate, which the mother signed, listed petitioner as the father, and the child's last name was the same as petitioner, which had never been disputed, parentage was not an issue and the statute of limitations found in this section did not apply. Padin v. Padin, 193 Ill. App. 3d 554, 140 Ill. Dec. 640, 550 N.E.2d 276 (3 Dist.), cert. denied, 132 Ill. 2d 547, 144 Ill. Dec. 259, 555 N.E.2d 378 (1990).

—Prior Law

Although a complaint was filed more than two years after a child's birth, in contravention of the requirement set out in former section 16 of the Bastardy Act (see now this section), where there was no affirmative showing in the record that the case came within the exception, the two year provision of the Bastardy Act did not affect the court's general jurisdiction, but merely constituted a condition of the right to maintain an action. People ex rel. Person v. Miller, 56 Ill. App. 3d 450, 13 Ill. Dec. 920, 371 N.E.2d 1012 (1 Dist. 1977).

—Purpose

The two year statute of limitations which applies to the plaintiff serves its intended purpose, which is to avoid fraudulent, or stale claims, and provide repose for defendants. Klawitter v. Crawford, 185 Ill. App. 3d 778, 133 Ill. Dec. 721, 541 N.E.2d 1159 (1 Dist. 1989).

—Retroactive Application

The general rule that an amendment shortening a statute of limitations period will not be retroactively applied, so as to terminate a cause of action, unless the party has had a reasonable period of time after the effective date of the amendment in which to file his action, was found to be specifically applicable to the limitations provisions in this section. In re Johnson, 206 Ill. App. 3d 992, 151 Ill. Dec. 891, 565 N.E.2d 162 (1 Dist. 1990).

Petitioner's suggested reason for his delay in filing his suit, that he was allowed to visit the child without legal action, did not render the 20 month delay reasonable for purposes of avoiding retroactive application of the statute of limitations. Majidi v. Palmer, 175 Ill. App. 3d 679, 125 Ill. Dec. 148, 530 N.E.2d 66 (2 Dist. 1988).

The legislature intended a retroactive application of the statute of limitations. In re Ingram, 176 Ill. App. 3d 413, 125 Ill. Dec. 918, 531 N.E.2d 97 (5 Dist. 1988).

—Rights Under Probate Act

This section does not mandate a paternity action before a court can consider heirship under the Probate Act of 1975 (755 ILCS 5/1-1 et seq.). In re Estate of Willis, 214 Ill. App. 3d 683, 158 Ill. Dec. 378, 574 N.E.2d 172 (1 Dist.), cert. denied, 141 Ill. 2d 539, 162 Ill. Dec. 486, 580 N.E.2d 112 (1991).

—Strict Construction

Where plaintiff did not advance any substantive arguments (such as an estoppel argument) which would equitably indicate that the limitation period should not be strictly applied, it was clear that the trial court properly applied the two year limitation provision in dismissing a complaint under the former Paternity Act (see now this section). People ex rel. Getz v. Lang, 61 Ill. App. 3d 933, 18 Ill. Dec. 934, 378 N.E.2d 398 (3 Dist. 1978).

Effective Date of Act

—Filing Untimely

Where husband, in marriage dissolution proceeding, disputed parentage of two minor children, first mentioned parentage dispute two months before effective date of this Act, but the first pleading relating to the issue was filed more than two years after the effective date of the Act, filing was beyond the time when the

Effective Date of Act (Cont'd)

—Filing Untimely (Cont'd)
statute of limitations would have run. In re Beckett, 195 Ill. App. 3d 424, 142 Ill. Dec. 25, 552 N.E.2d 375 (4 Dist. 1990).

—Pending Actions
The extended limitations period in this section applies to actions pending at the time this section became effective. People ex rel. Kelly v. Pasko, 184 Ill. App. 3d 528, 132 Ill. Dec. 722, 540 N.E.2d 462 (1 Dist. 1989).

—Petition Untimely
The filing of a petition three years after the enactment of the statute, and 15 years after the expiration of the limitations period, cannot be construed as reasonable when a parent possessed the relevant facts upon which to base his petition at the time of the child's birth. In re Johnson, 206 Ill. App. 3d 992, 151 Ill. Dec. 891, 565 N.E.2d 162 (1 Dist. 1990).

Where paternity action was filed later than two years after the birth of the child, and the plaintiff waited for almost two years after this Act was passed, and almost a year after it became effective, before bringing a paternity action, the cause of action was time-barred. Klawitter v. Crawford, 185 Ill. App. 3d 778, 133 Ill. Dec. 721, 541 N.E.2d 1159 (1 Dist. 1989).

Petition to Declare Nonexistence of Parent-Child Relationship
An action to declare the non-existence of a parent/child relationship was barred by the statute of limitations where the mother testified that she always knew that respondent was not the child's father, yet the child was over three years old by the time the mother filed her petition. Donath v. Buckley, 319 Ill. App. 3d 83, 253 Ill. Dec. 103, 744 N.E.2d 385, 2001 Ill. App. LEXIS 83 (3 Dist. 2001).

—Time Limitation
Regardless of any legal presumptions of paternity, a man alleging he is the father of a child may bring an action under 750 ILCS 45/7(a) to determine a parent-child relationship if the action is brought no later than two years after the child reaches the age majority; where a child, who was born to a woman who was married at the time of conception and birth, had not yet reached the age of majority, a potential father's petition to determine a parent-child relationship, rather than an action to declare the non-existence of a parent-child relationship, was proper. J.S.A. v. M.H., 343 Ill. App. 3d 217, 278 Ill. Dec. 110, 797 N.E.2d 705, 2003 Ill. App. LEXIS 1066 (3 Dist. 2003), appeal denied, 207 Ill. 2d 604, 283 Ill. Dec. 134, 807 N.E.2d 975 (2004).

Subsection (a)(3) did not apply to an action to establish paternity, notwithstanding the putative father's assertion that the action also implicitly sought to prove the "nonexistence" of a parent-child relationship between the child and the mother's husband. In re Adams, 297 Ill. App. 3d 156, 233 Ill. Dec. 857, 701 N.E.2d 1131 (4 Dist. 1998).

A petition to declare the nonexistence of a parent-child relationship is barred, if brought by someone other than the child, more than two years after that party obtains knowledge of relevant facts. In re Klebs, 196 Ill. App. 3d 472, 143 Ill. Dec. 363, 554 N.E.2d 298 (1 Dist. 1990).

Petition Properly Dismissed
Alleged father's petition for visitation and to establish paternity was properly dismissed. McDonald v. McGowan, 163 Ill. App. 3d 697, 114 Ill. Dec. 779, 516 N.E.2d 934 (1 Dist. 1987).

Posthumous Actions
Under former provision (see now this section), paternity could not be laid at the door of a putative father posthumously, nor could liability be imposed on his estate in the absence of an adjudication of paternity during the lifetime of the father. Toms v. Lohrentz, 37 Ill. App. 2d 414, 185 N.E.2d 708 (2 Dist. 1962).

Presumption of Paternity

—Rebuttal
This Act allows a biological father to rebut the statutory presumption that a child born during marriage is the husband's issue; there is a two-year limitation period on this right that commences with the child's birth. Allen v. Allen, 48 F.3d 259 (7th Cir. 1995).

Reasonable Time
What constitutes a reasonable time to commence an action will depend on the facts of each case. Sakellariadis v. Spanos, 163 Ill. App. 3d 1084, 115 Ill. Dec. 122, 517 N.E.2d 324 (2 Dist. 1987), appeal denied, 119 Ill. 2d 575, 119 Ill. Dec. 397, 522 N.E.2d 1256 (1988).

Retroactive Application
Paternity action was timely filed, although child was over five years of age, because two year statute of limitations under former Paternity Act governing paternity actions had been declared unconstitutional, and dismissal would have abrogated expressed intent of the legislature in this Act. People ex rel. Moore v. McIntosh, 134 Ill. App. 3d 1070, 90 Ill. Dec. 33, 481 N.E.2d 833 (5 Dist. 1985).

Tolling

—Limitations Period Not Tolled
Running of the limitations period was not tolled under subsection (b) of this section where the defendant continued to return to Illinois, where his wife lived and where he kept his clothes, and because the defendant was a resident of Illinois and thus subject to personal service outside the state. Sakellariadis v. Spanos, 163 Ill. App. 3d 1084, 115 Ill. Dec. 122, 517 N.E.2d 324 (2 Dist. 1987), appeal denied, 119 Ill. 2d 575, 119 Ill. Dec. 397, 522 N.E.2d 1256 (1988).

—Notice of Intent to File
The filing of a notice of an intent to file a motion is not a filing of a motion within a required time. In re Beckett, 195 Ill. App. 3d 424, 142 Ill. Dec. 25, 552 N.E.2d 375 (4 Dist. 1990).

—Paternity Affirmed in Answer
When defendant moved to dismiss paternity suit under the former Paternity Act, he admitted all facts well pled, thereby affirming that (1) he was the natural father of the parties' two children, (2) all official public records pertaining to the children indicate that he was their father, and (3) for approximately six and one half years, he had lived with, supported, and maintained the children as his own; consequently this affirmation extended the time in which plaintiff could commence a paternity action to within two years from the last time the person accused contributed to the support, maintenance, education and welfare of the child[ren] subsequent to such acknowledgment. Cook v. Askew, 34 Ill. App. 3d 1055, 341 N.E.2d 13 (1 Dist. 1975).

Unreasonable Delay
Plaintiff's delay in commencing an action one year and eight days after the effective date of this section and more than 2 years after the child's birth was not reasonable where the plaintiff had knowledge of his cause of action for a considerable period of time and defendant refused to discuss the matter, which should have suggested to plaintiff that his only recourse was legal action. Sakellariadis v. Spanos, 163 Ill. App. 3d 1084, 115 Ill. Dec. 122, 517 N.E.2d 324 (2 Dist. 1987), appeal denied, 119 Ill. 2d 575, 119 Ill. Dec. 397, 522 N.E.2d 1256 (1988).

Waiver
Trial court would not consider father's argument that mother's recovery for pregnancy and delivery expenses was barred by the statute of limitations where the father raised the argument for the first time on appeal. Janssen ex rel. Janssen v. Turner, 292 Ill. App. 3d 219, 226 Ill. Dec. 202, 685 N.E.2d 16 (4 Dist. 1997).

LEGAL PERIODICALS

For article, "The Illinois Parentage Act: Constitutional?," see 15 N. Ill. U.L. Rev. 63 (1994).

For article, "Survey of Illinois Law [1989-90]—Trusts and Estates," see 15 S. Ill. U. L. J. 1191 (1991).

For article, "Survey of Illinois Law [1988-89]—Family Law," see 14 S. Ill. U. L. J. 1007 (1990).

For case note, "Limitation Period on Paternity Actions Constitutional," see 1977 U. Ill. L.F. 282.

RESEARCH REFERENCES

Statutes limiting time for commencement of action to establish paternity of illegitimate child as violating child's constitutional rights. 16 ALR4th 926.

750 ILCS 45/9 Jurisdiction; Venue

Sec. 9. *Jurisdiction; Venue.* (a) The circuit courts shall have jurisdiction of an action brought under this Act. In any civil action not brought under this Act, the provisions of this Act shall apply if parentage is at issue. The Court may join any action under this Act with any other civil action where applicable.

(b) The action may be brought in the county in which any party resides or is found or, if the father is deceased, in which proceedings for probate of his estate have been or could be commenced.

(c) The summons that is served on a defendant shall include the return date on or by which the defendant must appear and shall contain the following information, in a prominent place and in conspicuous language, in addition to the information required to be provided by the laws of this State: "If you do not appear as instructed in this summons, you may be required to support the child named in this petition until the child is at least 18 years old. You may also have to pay the pregnancy and delivery costs of the mother."

(Source: P.A. 84-848.)

Note.

This section was Ill.Rev.Stat., Ch. 40, para. 2509.

CASE NOTES

Analysis

Applicability
—Parentage Not at Issue
Challenges to Jurisdiction
Death of Father
Heirship Actions Distinguished
Improper Venue
—Not Waived
Jurisdiction
—Prior Law
—Sufficiency of Complaint
—Sufficiency of Court Order
Tortious Acts

Applicability

—Parentage Not at Issue

Parentage was not an issue within the terms of this section, where plaintiff filed affidavits of mother and uncle alleging decedent's open acknowledgment of paternity, and defendant did not specifically refute the facts alleged therein, but only made a general denial in the pleadings. Tersavich v. First Nat'l Bank & Trust Co., 143 Ill. 2d 74, 156 Ill. Dec. 753, 571 N.E.2d 733 (1991).

Where child's birth certificate, which the mother signed, listed petitioner as the father, and the child's last name was the same as petitioner's, which had never been disputed, parentage was not an issue, and the statute of limitations found in 750 ILCS 45/8 did not apply. Padin v. Padin, 193 Ill. App. 3d 554, 140 Ill. Dec. 640, 550 N.E.2d 276 (3 Dist.), cert. denied, 132 Ill. 2d 547, 144 Ill. Dec. 259, 555 N.E.2d 378 (1990).

Challenges to Jurisdiction

Defendant was bound and could not now challenge the court's jurisdiction where the original child support matter had been adjudicated to a final judgment without objection to the court's right to hear the cause. People ex rel. Person v. Miller, 56 Ill. App. 3d 450, 13 Ill. Dec. 920, 371 N.E.2d 1012 (1 Dist. 1977).

Death of Father

Subsection (b) contemplates a paternity action surviving the death of the putative father, and the argument that paternity cannot be established after death is no longer the law in Illinois. In re Estate of Medlen, 286 Ill. App. 3d 860, 222 Ill. Dec. 220, 677 N.E.2d 33 (2 Dist. 1997).

Heirship Actions Distinguished

Paternity proceedings after death are recognized by the Parentage Act, (750 ILCS 45/1 et seq.) and are separate and distinct from heirship actions in remedy. Reddick v. Murray, 266 Ill. App. 3d 333, 203 Ill. Dec. 739, 640 N.E.2d 659 (3 Dist. 1994).

Improper Venue

—Not Waived

Where the fact plaintiff commenced paternity action in the wrong county was not apparent from the face of the pleading, and could not be ascertained until discovery had been undertaken by the parties, and where the trial court did not set a time for the appearance and answer of defendant, defendant did not waive his objections to the trial being conducted in the wrong venue. Ehorn v. Podraza, 51 Ill. App. 3d 816, 9 Ill. Dec. 866, 367 N.E.2d 300 (2 Dist. 1977).

Jurisdiction

—Prior Law

Since section 16 of the former Bastardy Act (see now this Act) required that acknowledgment of paternity in open court precede the institution of a paternity action, where there was neither allegation nor proof of any prior acknowledgment, but the only acknowledgment was that which was elicited from the defendant upon questioning by the trial judge after the complaint had been filed, the court had no jurisdiction under this Act. Brown v Box, 38 Ill. 2d 80, 230 N.E.2d 204 (1967).

—Sufficiency of Complaint

Even assuming that the complaint under former Paternity Act (see now this Act) defectively stated a cause of action, by failing to allege that the child had not been legally adopted, the court nevertheless had subject matter jurisdiction where the complaint clearly sounded in paternity. People ex rel. Tillery v. Ginsberg, 141 Ill. App. 3d 634, 96 Ill. Dec. 8, 490 N.E.2d 1044 (2 Dist. 1986).

—Sufficiency of Court Order

In a paternity action under of the former Paternity Act (see now this Act), which specifically required the court, following a judgment of paternity, to take evidence upon the requirements of the child for its support, maintenance, education and welfare, where the trial court's order adjudging defendant the father of the child contained no provisions for support of child, court retained jurisdiction of the case, and necessarily, the authority to make further determinations. People ex rel. Irby v. Homyer, 135 Ill. App. 3d 161, 90 Ill. Dec. 128, 481 N.E.2d 928 (5 Dist. 1985).

Tortious Acts

In an action brought under the former Paternity Act (see now this Act), the failure of a nonresident father to support an illegitimate child constituted a tortious act within the meaning of former Ill.Rev.Stat., ch. 110, para. 17(1)(b) (see now 735 ILCS 5/2-209), and subjected him to the jurisdiction of the Illinois courts. Poindexter v. Willis, 87 Ill. App. 2d 213, 231 N.E.2d 1 (5 Dist. 1967).

LEGAL PERIODICALS

For article, "Survey of Illinois Law [1989-90]—Trusts and Estates," see 15 S. Ill. U.L.J. 1191 (1991).

750 ILCS 45/9.1 Notice to Presumed Father

Sec. 9.1. *Notice to Presumed Father.* (a) In any action brought under Section 6 or 7 of this Act [750 ILCS 45/6 or 750 ILCS 45/7] where the man signing the petition for an order establishing the existence of the parent and child relationship by consent or the man alleged to be the father in a complaint is different from a man who is presumed to be father of the child under Section 5 [750 ILCS 45/5], a notice shall be served on the presumed father in the same manner as summonses are served in other civil proceedings or, in lieu of personal service, service may be made as follows:

(1) The person requesting notice shall pay to the Clerk of the Court a mailing fee of $1.50 and furnish to the Clerk an original and one copy of a notice together with an affidavit setting forth the presumed father's last known address. The original notice shall be retained by the Clerk.

(2) The Clerk shall promptly mail to the presumed father, at the address appearing in the affidavit, the copy of the notice, certified mail, return receipt requested. The envelope and return receipt shall bear the return address of the Clerk. The receipt for certified mail shall state the name and address of the addressee, and the date of mailing, and shall be attached to the original notice.

(3) The return receipt, when returned to the Clerk, shall be attached to the original notice, and shall constitute proof of service.

(4) The Clerk shall note the fact of service in a permanent record.

(b) The notice shall read as follows:

IN THE MATTER OF NOTICE TO .... PRESUMED FATHER.

You have been identified as the presumed father of .... born on ....

The mother of the child is ....

An action is being brought to establish the parent and child relationship between the named child and a man named by the mother, ...

Under the law, you are presumed to be the father if (1) you and the child's mother are or have been married to each other, and the child was born or conceived during the marriage; or if (2) upon the child's birth, you and the child's mother married each other and you were named, with your consent, as the child's father on the child's birth certificate.

As the presumed father, you have certain legal rights with respect to the named child, including the right to notice of the filing of proceedings instituted for the establishment of parentage of said child and if named as the father in a petition to establish parentage, the right to submit, along with the mother and child, to deoxyribonucleic acid (DNA) tests to determine inherited characteristics. If you wish to retain your rights with respect to said child, you must file with the Clerk of this Circuit Court of .... County, Illinois whose address is ...., Illinois, within 30 days after the date of receipt of this notice, a declaration of parentage stating that you are, in fact, the father of said child and that you intend to retain your legal rights with respect to said child, or request to be notified of any further proceedings with respect to the parentage of said child.

If you do not file such declaration of parentage, or a request for notice, then whatever legal rights you have with respect to the named child, including the right to notice of any future proceedings for the establishment of parentage of the child, may be terminated without any further notice to you. When your legal rights with respect to the named child are so terminated, you will not be entitled to notice of any future proceedings.

(c) The notice to presumed fathers provided for in this Section in any action brought by a public agency shall be prepared and mailed by such public agency and the mailing fee to the Clerk shall be waived.

(Source: P.A. 84-848; 90-23, § 5.)

Note.

This section was Ill.Rev.Stat., Ch. 40, para. 2509.1.

Effect of Amendments.

The 1997 amendment by P.A. 90-23, effective January 1, 1998, in subsection (b), in the fourth paragraph of the notice, in the first sentence, added at the end "and if named as the father in a petition to establish parentage, the right to submit, along with the mother and child, to deoxyribonucleic acid (DNA) tests to determine inherited characteristics".

CASE NOTES

ANALYSIS

Adjudication of Paternity
—Death of Putative Father
Applicability of Cases
Bonds
—Prior Law
Failure to Declare Parentage
—Prior Law
Failure to Serve Summons
—Effect
Summons Requirement
—Probate Proceedings

Adjudication of Paternity

—Death of Putative Father

Under former Paternity Act (see now this Act), respondent's due process rights were not violated by permitting adjudication of paternity after the death of an alleged father. Metropolitan Life Ins. Co. v. Johnson, 92 Ill. App. 3d 208, 47 Ill. Dec. 818, 415 N.E.2d 1131 (1 Dist. 1980).

Applicability of Cases

Cases construing the procedures in the former Bastardy Act were held applicable to the subsequent statute entitled Paternity Act (see now this Act). People v. Johnson, 79 Ill. App. 2d 266, 224 N.E.2d 664 (1 Dist. 1967).

Bonds

—Prior Law

There was no provision in the former Paternity Act (see now this Act) for a method of enforcement of an appearance bond; the method provided in former section 20 of the Bail in Civil Cases Act was not applicable because it presupposed an original judgment, for payment of which the bond was given, but there was no judgment to satisfy which a capias ad satisfaciendum, as required by section 20, could issue, and the bond in the suit was conditioned only on the appearance of the paternity suit defendant. People v. White, 26 Ill. App. 2d 279, 168 N.E.2d 48 (1 Dist. 1960).

Failure to Declare Parentage

—Prior Law

A proceeding was not contrary to the provisions of the former

Failure to Declare Parentage (Cont'd)

—Prior Law (Cont'd)
Paternity Act (see now this Act) where defendant did not file a written acknowledgment that he was the father of the child, and the court by its order stated that defendant had been tried on the issue of paternity and found guilty of being the father of the child. People v. Johnson, 79 Ill. App. 2d 266, 224 N.E.2d 664 (1 Dist. 1967).

Failure to Serve Summons

—Effect
Failure to serve summons on presumed father renders adjudication of parentage null and void. Lewis v. Newsome, 173 Ill. App. 3d 376, 123 Ill. Dec. 61, 527 N.E.2d 524 (4 Dist. 1988).

Summons Requirement

—Probate Proceedings
The summons requirement in this section does not apply in a probate action establishing heirship for purposes of inheritance. In re Estate of Willis, 214 Ill. App. 3d 683, 158 Ill. Dec. 378, 574 N.E.2d 172 (1 Dist.), cert. denied, 141 Ill. 2d 539, 162 Ill. Dec. 486, 580 N.E.2d 112 (1991).

750 ILCS 45/10 Pre-trial Proceedings

Sec. 10. *Pre-trial Proceedings.* (a) As soon as practicable after an action to declare the existence or non-existence of the father and child relationship has been brought, and the parties are at issue, the court may conduct a pre-trial conference.
(Source: P.A. 83-1372.)

Note.
This section was Ill.Rev.Stat., Ch. 40, para. 2510.

750 ILCS 45/11 Tests to determine inherited characteristics

Sec. 11. *Tests to determine inherited characteristics.* (a) As soon as practicable, the court or Administrative Hearing Officer in an Expedited Child Support System may, and upon request of a party shall, order or direct the mother, child and alleged father to submit to deoxyribonucleic acid (DNA) tests to determine inherited characteristics. If any party refuses to submit to the tests, the court may resolve the question of paternity against that party or enforce its order if the rights of others and the interests of justice so require.

(b) The tests shall be conducted by an expert qualified as an examiner of blood or tissue types and appointed by the court. The expert shall determine the testing procedures. However, any interested party, for good cause shown, in advance of the scheduled tests, may request a hearing to object to the qualifications of the expert or the testing procedures. The expert appointed by the court shall testify at the pre-test hearing at the expense of the party requesting the hearing, except as provided in subsection (h) of this Section for an indigent party. An expert not appointed by the court shall testify at the pre-test hearing at the expense of the party retaining the expert. Inquiry into an expert's qualifications at the pre-test hearing shall not affect either parties' right to have the expert qualified at trial.

(c) The expert shall prepare a written report of the test results. If the test results show that the alleged father is not excluded, the report shall contain a combined paternity index relating to the probability of paternity. The expert may be called by the court as a witness to testify to his or her findings and, if called, shall be subject to cross-examination by the parties. If the test results show that the alleged father is not excluded, any party may demand that other experts, qualified as examiners of blood or tissue types, perform independent tests under order of court, including, but not limited to, blood types or other tests of genetic markers such as those found by Human Leucocyte Antigen (HLA) tests. The results of the tests may be offered into evidence. The number and qualifications of the experts shall be determined by the court.

(d) Documentation of the chain of custody of the blood or tissue samples, accompanied by an affidavit or certification in accordance with Section 1-109 of the Code of Civil Procedure [735 ILCS 5/1-109], is competent evidence to establish the chain of custody.

(e) The report of the test results prepared by the appointed expert shall be made by affidavit or by certification as provided in Section 1-109 of the Code of Civil Procedure [735 ILCS 5/1-109] and shall be mailed to all parties. A proof of service shall be filed with the court. The verified report shall be admitted into evidence at trial without foundation testimony or other proof of authenticity or accuracy, unless a written motion challenging the admissibility of the report is filed by either party within 28 days of receipt of the report, in which case expert testimony shall be required. A party may not file such a motion challenging the admissibility of the report later than 28 days before commencement of trial. Before trial, the court shall determine whether the motion is sufficient to deny admission of the report by verification. Failure to make that timely motion constitutes a waiver of the right to object to admission by verification and shall not be grounds for a continuance of the hearing to determine paternity.

(f) Tests taken pursuant to this Section shall have the following effect:

(1) If the court finds that the conclusion of the expert or experts, as disclosed by the evidence based upon the tests, is that the alleged father is not the parent of the child, the question of paternity shall be resolved accordingly.

(2) If the experts disagree in their findings or conclusions, the question shall be weighed with other competent evidence of paternity.

(3) If the tests show that the alleged father is not excluded and that the combined paternity index is less than 500 to 1, this evidence shall be admitted by the court and shall be weighed with other competent evidence of paternity.

(4) If the tests show that the alleged father is not excluded and that the combined paternity index is at least 500 to 1, the alleged father is presumed to be the father, and this evidence shall be admitted. This

presumption may be rebutted by clear and convincing evidence.

(g) Any presumption of parentage as set forth in Section 5 of this Act [750 ILCS 45/5] is rebutted if the court finds that the conclusion of the expert or experts excludes paternity of the presumed father.

(h) The expense of the tests shall be paid by the party who requests the tests. Where the tests are requested by the party seeking to establish paternity and that party is found to be indigent by the court, the expense shall be paid by the public agency providing representation; except that where a public agency is not providing representation, the expense shall be paid by the county in which the action is brought. Where the tests are ordered by the court on its own motion or are requested by the alleged or presumed father and that father is found to be indigent by the court, the expense shall be paid by the county in which the action is brought. Any part of the expense may be taxed as costs in the action, except that no costs may be taxed against a public agency that has not requested the tests.

(i) The compensation of each expert witness appointed by the court shall be paid as provided in subsection (h) of this Section. Any part of the payment may be taxed as costs in the action, except that no costs may be taxed against a public agency that has not requested the services of the expert witness.

(j) Nothing in this Section shall prevent any party from obtaining tests of his or her own blood or tissue independent of those ordered by the court or from presenting expert testimony interpreting those tests or any other blood tests ordered pursuant to this Section. Reports of all the independent tests, accompanied by affidavit or certification pursuant to Section 1-109 of the Code of Civil Procedure [735 ILCS 5/1-109], and notice of any expert witnesses to be called to testify to the results of those tests shall be submitted to all parties at least 30 days before any hearing set to determine the issue of parentage.

(Source: P.A. 86-1339; 86-1401; 86-1452; 87-428; 87-435; 88-353, § 5; 88-687, § 20.)

Note.

This section was Ill.Rev.Stat., Ch. 40, para. 2511.

Cross References.

As to the powers of administrative hearing officers, see Rule 100.4, Supreme Court Rules.

Illinois Administrative Code.

See 89 Illinois Administrative Code, § 104.249.

Effect of Amendments.

The 1994 amendment by P.A. 88-687, effective January 24, 1995, in subsection (e), in the third sentence, inserted "without foundation testimony or other proof of authenticity or accuracy" and added the fourth sentence.

CASE NOTES

Analysis

Applicability
Blood Test Request
—Admissibility
—Failure to Produce
—Found Reliable
—Not Conclusive of Paternity
—Paternity Indexes
—Summary Judgment
Challenge
—Time Limitation
Construction
Court Order to Submit to Blood Test
—Discretion of Court
—Divorce Action
—Prior Law
—Test Requirements
Evidence of Paternity
—Failure to Challenge
—Held Sufficient
—Presumption Not Overcome
—Twins
Prejudice
Rebuttal Evidence
—Insufficient
Refusal to Submit to Blood Test
—Admissibility
—Sanctions
Refusal to Submit to Blood Tests
—Sanctions

Applicability

ILCS 45/11(a) does not apply to actions by an adjudicated father to disprove paternity under 750 ILCS 45/7(b-5). In re Kates, 198 Ill. 2d 156, 260 Ill. Dec. 309, 761 N.E.2d 153, 2001 Ill. LEXIS 1437 (2001).

Blood Test Request

Either party to a paternity action may request blood testing for the mother, child, or alleged father to determine inherited characteristics; in addition, any party may demand that other experts, qualified as examiners of blood or tissue types, may perform independent tests under order of court, the results of which may be offered in evidence. Department of Pub. Aid ex rel. Moutria v. Roach, 258 Ill. App. 3d 491, 196 Ill. Dec. 616, 630 N.E.2d 551 (5 Dist. 1994).

—Admissibility

Where there was ample foundation for concluding that the results of blood tests performed by two physicians were not in disagreement, trial court did not err in admitting the results of the blood tests into evidence. Daubach v. Ishihara, 103 Ill. App. 3d 750, 59 Ill. Dec. 426, 431 N.E.2d 1183 (1 Dist. 1981).

In paternity proceedings under former Ill.Rev.Stat., ch. 40, paras. 1401 and 1404 (see now this section), evidence of the alleged father's blood type was admissible only if it excluded him as being the father of the child. People v. Henderson, 83 Ill. App. 3d 854, 39 Ill. Dec. 8, 404 N.E.2d 392 (1 Dist. 1980).

—Failure to Produce

The failure of the state to produce the results of the blood tests at trial did not raise the presumption that the results would have been unfavorable to the state. People ex rel. Gomez v. Wedech, 58 Ill. App. 3d 518, 16 Ill. Dec. 74, 374 N.E.2d 849 (1 Dist. 1978).

—Found Reliable

Jury's finding that blood test was reliable was not manifestly erroneous. People ex rel. Forrest v. Winston-Bey, 252 Ill. App. 3d 924, 192 Ill. Dec. 553, 625 N.E.2d 708 (1 Dist. 1993).

—Not Conclusive of Paternity

Evidence construed most favorably to defendant, was held insufficient to support the finding of paternity under the former Paternity Act (see now this Act). People ex rel. Martin v. Presswood, 85 Ill. App. 3d 975, 41 Ill. Dec. 272, 407 N.E.2d 770 (1 Dist. 1980).

—Paternity Indexes

Test results include the paternity indexes. People ex rel. Kelly v. Pasko, 184 Ill. App. 3d 528, 132 Ill. Dec. 722, 540 N.E.2d 462 (1 Dist. 1989).

—Summary Judgment

Summary judgment could not be granted in a paternity action

Blood Test Request (Cont'd)

—Summary Judgment (Cont'd)
solely on the basis of the results of blood tests, pursuant to the former Act on Blood Tests to Determine Paternity (see now this section). Daubach v. Ishihara, 103 Ill. App. 3d 750, 59 Ill. Dec. 426, 431 N.E.2d 1183 (1 Dist. 1981).

Challenge

—Time Limitation
The 28 day limitation is reasonable. People ex rel. Black v. Neby, 265 Ill. App. 3d 203, 202 Ill. Dec. 630, 638 N.E.2d 276 (4 Dist.), appeal denied, 157 Ill. 2d 520, 205 Ill. Dec. 184, 642 N.E.2d 1301 (1994).

Construction
Illinois Parentage Act of 1984 does not give a court authority to order a best interest hearing prior to a blood test dismissal of a petition seeking the determination of a parent-child relationship after a court held a best interest hearing was error. J.S.A. v. M.H., 343 Ill. App. 3d 217, 278 Ill. Dec. 110, 797 N.E.2d 705, 2003 Ill. App. LEXIS 1066 (3 Dist. 2003), appeal denied, 207 Ill. 2d 604, 283 Ill. Dec. 134, 807 N.E.2d 975 (2004).

Court Order to Submit to Blood Test

—Discretion of Court
The former Act on blood tests did not require the trial court to order blood tests, rather the court has discretion in the matter. People ex rel. Cizek v. Azzarello, 81 Ill. App. 3d 1102, 37 Ill. Dec. 84, 401 N.E.2d 1177 (1 Dist. 1980).

In a paternity proceeding the trial court had the discretion under Rule 215, Supreme Court Rules, to determine whether a second blood test of a putative father was warranted, thus, where the trial court believed that this rule was inapplicable to the paternity proceedings, and therefore did not exercise its discretion thereunder, the trial court's order dismissing the plaintiff mother's complaint was reversed. People ex rel. Yarn v. Yarn, 73 Ill. App. 3d 454, 29 Ill. Dec. 909, 392 N.E.2d 606 (1 Dist. 1979).

—Divorce Action
A trial court in a divorce proceeding had the authority to order blood tests for the mother, and the minor child of the parties, to aid in determining the paternity of the minor child, and the mother was properly held in contempt for her failure to comply with the court's order. Zavaleta v. Zavaleta, 43 Ill. App. 3d 1017, 3 Ill. Dec. 13, 358 N.E.2d 13 (1 Dist. 1976).

—Prior Law
Under former section 55 of the Paternity Act (see now this section), a defendant in a paternity action could not be compelled to submit to a blood test and could not be required to submit to a second blood test merely because he volunteered to take an initial test; thus, an order directing the defendant to submit to a second blood test was improper and the defendant's refusal to abide by such order was not contempt. People ex rel. Hawthorne v. Hamilton, 9 Ill. App. 3d 551, 292 N.E.2d 563 (3 Dist. 1973).

—Test Requirements
Although the court ordered a type IV blood test, the most accurate type of test, when that type of test was not being performed due to budget constraints this section did not require a type IV test and the test performed, between a type III and IV, complied with the statute's requirements. People ex rel. Forrest v. Winston-Bey, 252 Ill. App. 3d 924, 192 Ill. Dec. 553, 625 N.E.2d 708 (1 Dist. 1993).

Evidence of Paternity

—Failure to Challenge
In paternity action, defendant at no time offered a scintilla of evidence by opposing affidavits or other pleadings and proof which would present the trial court with a genuine issue of material fact; defendant failed to challenge the probable period of conception, failed to rebut mother's sworn affidavit that he was the only man with whom she had had intercourse during that period, failed to reconcile his own inconsistent statements regarding whether he engaged in sexual relations with mother during that period, and failed to question the blood test experts and testing procedures. People ex rel. Stockwill v. Keller, 251 Ill. App. 3d 796, 191 Ill. Dec. 226, 623 N.E.2d 816 (4 Dist. 1993).

—Held Sufficient
Where defendant's combined paternity index was 611 to 1, the rebuttable presumption that defendant was the father of petitioner's child arose. Illinois Dep't of Pub. Aid ex rel. Galbraith v. Jones, 281 Ill. App. 3d 115, 216 Ill. Dec. 844, 666 N.E.2d 12 (4 Dist. 1996).

Under the former Paternity Act (see now this Act), where a suit was brought on the mother's complaint, the putative father was required to support the minor child until he or she became 18 years old, and to pay not only support money but all expenses of the mother during pregnancy, confinement, and recovery; this obligation could not be voided by settlement. People v. Makar, 25 Ill. App. 2d 246, 166 N.E.2d 467 (1 Dist. 1960).

—Presumption Not Overcome
Where defendant did not deny having sexual relations with the mother during the period of conception nor challenge the test results, nor contend he was sterile or impotent, the mere existence of access to the mother during the relevant period by another male whose paternity index was unknown did not rebut the statutory presumption based on genetic testing. People ex rel. Hughes v. Walker, 278 Ill. App. 3d 116, 214 Ill. Dec. 823, 662 N.E.2d 177 (4 Dist. 1996).

—Twins
Where putative father had an identical twin and the paternity indexes created a rebuttable presumption against the rest of the world that one of the twins was the father and the court then relied on the nongenetic evidence to conclude that, as between the two twins, more likely than not, defendant was the father of the child, the presumption was properly applied. Illinois Dep't of Public Aid ex rel. Masinelli v. Whitworth, 273 Ill. App. 3d 156, 209 Ill. Dec. 918, 652 N.E.2d 458 (4 Dist. 1995).

Prejudice
Trial court error in not appointing experts to perform blood tests, as required by former Ill.Rev.Stat., ch. 40, para. 1402 (see now this section), absent showing of prejudice was not a basis for reversal. People ex rel. Tillery v. Ginsberg, 141 Ill. App. 3d 634, 96 Ill. Dec. 8, 490 N.E.2d 1044 (2 Dist. 1986).

Rebuttal Evidence

—Insufficient
The defendant failed to rebut the statutory presumption of parentage that arose from a CPI of 2,582 to 1 where he presented expert testimony that a CPI of 10,000 to 1 was required to show parentage, but his expert admitted that a majority of other experts would disagree with him. Villareal ex rel. Villareal v. Peebles, 299 Ill. App. 3d 556, 233 Ill. Dec. 502, 701 N.E.2d 145 (1 Dist. 1998), appeal denied, 181 Ill. 2d 590, 235 Ill. Dec. 948, 706 N.E.2d 503 (1998).

Where respondent's rebuttal evidence did not constitute clear and convincing evidence necessary to rebut presumption of paternity, respondent's motion for summary judgment was properly denied. Illinois Dep't of Pub. Aid ex rel. Galbraith v. Jones, 281 Ill. App. 3d 115, 216 Ill. Dec. 844, 666 N.E.2d 12 (4 Dist. 1996).

Refusal to Submit to Blood Test

—Admissibility
Under section 1401 of the former Act on blood tests (see now this section) the focus was on the results of the tests, and not the reluctance of the defendant to submit to them, and the rationale for excluding evidence of such refusal to submit to the examination is similar to that which compels exclusion of testimony of silence after being advised of one's rights under the Fifth Amendment. People ex rel. Aldworth v. Dutkanych, 112 Ill. 2d 505, 98 Ill. Dec. 16, 493 N.E.2d 1037 (1986).

—Sanctions
Rule 215, Supreme Court Rules, authorizes blood tests as a matter of discovery, and the court may properly cite an alleged father for contempt for failure to comply with a court order, to submit to a blood test. People ex rel. Aldworth v. Dutkanych, 112 Ill. 2d 505, 98 Ill. Dec. 16, 493 N.E.2d 1037 (1986).

Refusal to Submit to Blood Test (Cont'd)

—Sanctions (Cont'd)

Circuit court did not abuse its discretion in ordering defendant to submit to a blood test pursuant to former paragraph 1401 of chapter 40 (see now this section), nor in holding defendant in contempt and sentencing him as a result of his refusal to obey the court's order. People ex rel. Aldworth v. Dutkanych, 131 Ill. App. 3d 1007, 87 Ill. Dec. 103, 476 N.E.2d 805 (2 Dist. 1985), aff'd, 112 Ill. 2d 505, 98 Ill. Dec. 16, 493 N.E.2d 1037 (1986).

Prior to the adoption of this Act, the ordering of a blood test was a matter of discovery regulated by the Supreme Court Rules, and a trial court had broad discretion to order a party to submit to such a blood test, and although section 1 of the former Act on Blood Tests (see now this section) appeared to give a defendant a right to refuse to submit to a blood test, any right of refusal was contrary to the court's broad powers to compel discovery, and was therefore an invalid exercise of the legislative power. Thus, a trial court had authority to order a defendant to submit to a blood test, and to hold that defendant in contempt for failure to comply with the court's order. People ex rel. Coleman v. Ely, 71 Ill. App. 3d 701, 28 Ill. Dec. 158, 390 N.E.2d 140 (1 Dist. 1979).

Refusal to Submit to Blood Tests

—Sanctions

Sanction of declaring uncooperative putative fathers to be the fathers of the subject children was an abuse of discretion because it was not required by the rights of others (particularly the children) or in the interests of justice; prospects of obtaining support from those possible parents were almost nil, and an adjudication could have prevented future paternity actions against the children's true fathers. People v. Ras M., 344 Ill. App. 3d 503, 279 Ill. Dec. 836, 801 N.E.2d 128, 2003 Ill. App. LEXIS 1375 (1 Dist. 2003).

LEGAL PERIODICALS

For article, "Using Summary Judgment in Illinois Paternity Cases", see 86 Ill. B.J. 483 (1998).

For article, "Independent Evidence: A New Tool for Paternity Cases", see 86 Ill. B.J. 476 (1998).

RESEARCH REFERENCES

Admissibility, weight and sufficiency of human leukocyte antigen (HLA) tissue typing tests in paternity cases. 37 ALR4th 167.

Admissibility and weight of blood-grouping tests in disputed paternity cases. 43 ALR4th 579.

Admissibility or compellability of blood test to establish testee's nonpaternity for purpose of challenging testee's parental rights. 87 ALR4th 572.

Authentication of blood sample taken from human body for purposes other than determining blood alcohol content. 77 ALR5th 201.

750 ILCS 45/12 Pre-Trial Recommendations

Sec. 12. *Pre-Trial Recommendations.* (a) On the basis of the information produced at a pretrial conference, the court shall evaluate the probability of determining the existence or non-existence of the father and child relationship in a trial and whether a judicial declaration of the relationship would be in the best interest of the child. On the basis of the evaluation, an appropriate recommendation for settlement shall be made to the parties, which may include that the alleged father consent to a finding of his paternity of the child, or that the action be dismissed with or without prejudice.

(b) If the parties accept a recommendation made in accordance with subsection (a) of this Section, judgment shall be entered accordingly.

(Source: P.A. 83-1372.)

Note.

This section was Ill.Rev.Stat., Ch. 40, para. 2512.

CASE NOTES

Authority of Court

—Authority to Hold Best Interest Hearing

While 750 ILCS 45/12 requires a court to determine whether it is in a child's best interest to make a judicial declaration of the parent-child relationship, nothing in this section gives the court the authority to hold a "best interest" hearing or to order the parties to do anything; this section only gives the court the power to recommend a settlement and the best interest determination is based on a pretrial conference and is merely a predicate to that recommendation. J.S.A. v. M.H., 343 Ill. App. 3d 217, 278 Ill. Dec. 110, 797 N.E.2d 705, 2003 Ill. App. LEXIS 1066 (3 Dist. 2003), appeal denied, 207 Ill. 2d 604, 283 Ill. Dec. 134, 807 N.E.2d 975 (2004).

LEGAL PERIODICALS

For comment, "Paternity Actions in Illinois: Why Not Consider What is in the Best Interest of the Child?," see 21 S. Ill. U.L.J. 613 (1997).

750 ILCS 45/12.1 Settlement Orders

Sec. 12.1. *Settlement Orders.* In cases where the alleged father has not consented to a finding of paternity and where the parties have requested a settlement, the court shall review the proposed settlement in light of the allegations made, the probable evidence and the circumstances of the parties. If the court is satisfied that the best interests of the child and of the parties will be served by entry of an order incorporating the settlement, and if the court is satisfied that the financial security of the child is adequately provided for and that the child and its mother are not likely to become public charges, it may enter an order so incorporating the settlement. The order may be directed to the defendant, or the mother, or both. Notwithstanding subsection (d) of Section 7 of this Act [750 ILCS 45/7], neither the entry of a settlement order, nor the terms of a settlement order shall bar an action brought under this Act by a child to ascertain paternity.

(Source: P.A. 83-1372.)

Note.

This section was Ill.Rev.Stat., Ch. 40, para. 2512.1.

CASE NOTES

Analysis

Amendments to Settlement Orders
Applicability
—Prior Law
Effect of Settlement
Nonmarital Children
—Equal Protection
Support Actions

Amendments to Settlement Orders

Settlement agreements entered under the former Paternity Act (see now this Act) were not amendable after the order approving the settlement became final, as the legislature intended to deprive courts of jurisdiction to modify such settlement orders. Fitzgerald v.

Amendments to Settlement Orders (Cont'd)

Theisen, 101 Ill. App. 3d 193, 56 Ill. Dec. 639, 427 N.E.2d 1044 (2 Dist. 1981).

Applicability

—Prior Law

Since former Ill.Rev.Stat., ch. 40, para. 1360 (see now this section) only applied to cases where the father did not acknowledge paternity, it was not controlling and could not have deprived the trial court of jurisdiction to modify the support provision of a stipulation where defendant and the mother agreed that he was the father. Fink v. Roller, 76 Ill. App. 3d 818, 32 Ill. Dec. 387, 395 N.E.2d 617 (5 Dist. 1979).

Two factors must have occurred before former Ill.Rev.Stat., ch. 40, para. 1360 (see now this section) was applicable: the putative father must not have acknowledged paternity and he must have entered into a settlement with the party bringing the action. Fink v. Roller, 76 Ill. App. 3d 818, 32 Ill. Dec. 387, 395 N.E.2d 617 (5 Dist. 1979).

Where defendant had acknowledged paternity through a stipulation, one of the statutory prerequisites of former Ill.Rev.Stat., ch. 40, para. 1360 (see now this section) was absent and placed the action outside the purview of that section. Fink v. Roller, 76 Ill. App. 3d 818, 32 Ill. Dec. 387, 395 N.E.2d 617 (5 Dist. 1979).

Effect of Settlement

Under this Act, a settlement approved by the court will bar further judicial action on the matter. Mayberry ex rel. Mayberry v. Kovas, 222 Ill. App. 3d 1008, 165 Ill. Dec. 354, 584 N.E.2d 533 (2 Dist. 1991), cert. denied, 144 Ill. 2d 634, 169 Ill. Dec. 142, 591 N.E.2d 22 (1992).

Nonmarital Children

—Equal Protection

A settlement order entered pursuant to the settlement provisions of a paternity statute should not bar a subsequent support action brought on behalf of a nonmarital child; equal protection of the law would be violated if a right to seek support from their parents during the whole of their minority were granted to marital children but denied to nonmarital children. Department of Public Aid ex rel. Cox v. Miller, 146 Ill. 2d 399, 166 Ill. Dec. 922, 586 N.E.2d 1251 (1992).

Support Actions

This section, which allows a child to bring an action to ascertain paternity, also allows that child to bring an action seeking support from his or her parent. Department of Public Aid ex rel. Cox v. Miller, 146 Ill. 2d 399, 166 Ill. Dec. 922, 586 N.E.2d 1251 (1992).

A settlement order and dismissal entered in a paternity action do not bar a subsequent action brought by or on behalf of the illegitimate minor for support. Department of Public Aid ex rel. Cox v. Miller, 146 Ill. 2d 399, 166 Ill. Dec. 922, 586 N.E.2d 1251 (1992).

750 ILCS 45/13 Civil Action

Sec. 13. *Civil Action.* (a) An action under this Act is a civil action governed by the provisions of the "Code of Civil Procedure", approved August 19, 1981, as amended [735 ILCS 5/1-101 et seq.], and the Supreme Court rules applicable thereto, except where otherwise specified in this Act.

(b) Trial by jury is not available under this Act.

(c) Certified copies of the bills for costs incurred for pregnancy and childbirth shall be admitted into evidence at judicial or administrative proceedings without foundation testimony or other proof of authenticity or accuracy.

(Source: P.A. 83-1372; 90-18, § 120.)

Note.

This section was Ill.Rev.Stat., Ch. 40, para. 2513.

Effect of Amendments.

The 1997 amendment by P.A. 90-18, effective July 1, 1997, in the section catchline deleted "Jury" from the end; rewrote subsection (b) which read "Any party who desires a trial by jury on the issue of parentage must file a demand therefor pursuant to and within the time limits set forth in the 'Code of Civil Procedure', approved August 19, 1981, as amended"; and added subsection (c).

CASE NOTES

Analysis

In General
Bonds
—Prior Law
Burden of Proof
Civil Actions
Continuances
—Denied
Elements of Proof
Evidence
—Birth Certificate
—Gestation Period
—Mother's Testimony
—Sexual Activity
Judgment Notwithstanding the Verdict
Jury Trial
—Construction of Section
—Denial of Jury Trial
—Failure to Pay Jury Fee
—Late Motions
—No Waiver
—Waiver
Self-Incrimination
Standard of Review
Witnesses
—Competency

In General

A paternity action is considered a proceeding that is civil in nature although criminal in form. Clark v. Brown, 121 Ill. App. 2d 280, 257 N.E.2d 565 (1 Dist. 1970).

A paternity proceeding was a civil proceeding, and was governed by the former Civil Practice Act (see now 735 ILCS 5/1-101 et seq.). People v. Rimicci, 97 Ill. App. 2d 470, 240 N.E.2d 195 (1 Dist. 1968).

Bonds

—Prior Law

The former Paternity Act (see now this Act), which repealed the Bastardy Act in 1957, expressly provided that the Civil Practice Act (see now 735 ILCS 5/1-101 et seq.) should apply to all proceedings under its provision; accordingly, the appropriate action to enforce an appearance bond was by a plain and concise statement of a cause of action on the bond, as in other civil cases. Upon forfeiture, an action to recover the amount of the bond accrued to the People, and the principal and surety need not be summoned to show cause but summoned to defend as in other civil cases, and substituted service on paternity defendants was sufficient. People v. White, 26 Ill. App. 2d 279, 168 N.E.2d 48 (1 Dist. 1960).

There was no provision in the former Paternity Act (see now this Act) for a method of enforcement of an appearance bond; the method provided in former section 20 of the Bail in Civil Cases Act was not applicable because it presupposed an original judgment, for payment of which the bond was given, but there was no judgment to satisfy which a capias ad satisfaciendum, as required by section 20, could issue, and the bond in the suit was conditioned only on the appearance of the paternity suit defendant. People v. White, 26 Ill. App. 2d 279, 168 N.E.2d 48 (1 Dist. 1960).

Burden of Proof

In a paternity action, the burden is on the mother, as plaintiff, to establish paternity by a preponderance of the evidence. People ex rel. Mathis v. Brown, 44 Ill. App. 3d 783, 3 Ill. Dec. 475, 358 N.E.2d 1160 (1 Dist. 1976); People ex rel. Cizek v. Azzarello, 81 Ill. App. 3d 1102, 37 Ill. Dec. 84, 401 N.E.2d 1177 (1 Dist. 1980); People ex rel.

Burden of Proof (Cont'd)
Barbour v. Hatchett, 131 Ill. App. 3d 540, 86 Ill. Dec. 734, 475 N.E.2d 1113 (4 Dist. 1985).

The plaintiff in a paternity case must prove the charge against the defendant by a preponderance of the evidence. Schultz v. Peeler, 10 Ill. App. 3d 937, 295 N.E.2d 252 (5 Dist. 1973), aff'd, 56 Ill. 2d 318, 307 N.E.2d 380 (1974).

An action under the former Paternity Act (see now this Act) was a civil action and the rules of evidence applicable in civil cases were applicable to it; the law placed upon the plaintiff in a paternity suit the burden of proving her case by the greater weight of the evidence. People ex rel. Jones v. Schmitt, 101 Ill. App. 2d 183, 242 N.E.2d 275 (3 Dist. 1968).

Civil Actions
A paternity action under the former Paternity Act (see now this Act) was civil for the recovery of money. People v. White, 26 Ill. App. 2d 279, 168 N.E.2d 48 (1 Dist. 1960).

Continuances

—Denied
Trial court's denial of the state's motion for a continuance pending arrival of out-of-state expert witness was held to be an abuse of discretion. Berg ex rel. Berg v. Garrett, 224 Ill. App. 3d 619, 167 Ill. Dec. 119, 587 N.E.2d 1 (1992).

Elements of Proof
An essential element of a paternity case is that a child was born and was born out of wedlock. Ashford v. Ziemann, 99 Ill. 2d 353, 76 Ill. Dec. 805, 459 N.E.2d 940 (1984).

Evidence

—Birth Certificate
In a paternity action, a birth certificate which listed the alleged father's age and place of birth, both of which matched those of the defendant, constituted relevant and proper evidence to prove the name, sex, date and place of birth of a child, along with the fact that it was born out of wedlock, and therefore the trial court erred in refusing its admission. Ashford v. Ziemann, 99 Ill. 2d 353, 76 Ill. Dec. 805, 459 N.E.2d 940 (1984).

A birth certificate with the father's name not entered was probative of the fact that a child was born out of wedlock; thus, the birth certificate was relevant evidence and the trial court erred in refusing its admission. People ex rel. Ashford v. Ziemann, 110 Ill. App. 3d 34, 65 Ill. Dec. 741, 441 N.E.2d 1255 (1 Dist. 1982), aff'd, 99 Ill. 2d 353, 76 Ill. Dec. 805, 459 N.E.2d 940 (1984).

—Gestation Period
It is not a matter outside of common experience, nor is proof required to show, that the normal gestation period is "approximately" nine months, not exactly nine months, and a mother giving birth to a baby a couple of weeks before or after the approximate due date cannot be said to have had an abnormally long pregnancy. People ex rel. Cizek v. Azzarello, 81 Ill. App. 3d 1102, 37 Ill. Dec. 84, 401 N.E.2d 1177 (1 Dist. 1980).

—Mother's Testimony
The jury findings, that inconsistencies in mother's testimony or the delay in filing paternity suit did not warrant discrediting her testimony, would not be disturbed. People ex rel. Forrest v. Winston-Bey, 252 Ill. App. 3d 924, 192 Ill. Dec. 553, 625 N.E.2d 708 (1 Dist. 1993).

—Sexual Activity
Evidence which showed that the relatrix had intercourse with other men was to be limited to the period of time within which, in the course of nature, the child could have been begotten; evidence regarding the relatrix' sexual activity outside the period of conception had no rational bearing on the issue of paternity. People ex rel. Mehorczyk v. Kelley, 137 Ill. App. 3d 1074, 92 Ill. Dec. 777, 485 N.E.2d 588 (1 Dist. 1985).

Proof of acts of impropriety or other conduct on the part of the relatrix had no relation to the issue of paternity and was incompetent, and the fact that the relatrix was an unchaste woman was not a defense in a paternity proceeding. People ex rel. Mehorczyk v. Kelley, 137 Ill. App. 3d 1074, 92 Ill. Dec. 777, 485 N.E.2d 588 (1 Dist. 1985).

Judgment Notwithstanding the Verdict
Former section 68.1 of the Civil Practice Act (see now 735 ILCS 5/2-1202), providing for judgments notwithstanding the verdict, applied to the former Paternity Act (see now this Act), because to hold that judgment should not be entered contrary to a jury verdict in favor of a defendant in a paternity suit would be to deny review of the findings of the trier of fact, either the jury or the court alone, in such cases. Petrous v. Roberts, 12 Ill. App. 3d 992, 299 N.E.2d 322 (2 Dist. 1973).

Jury Trial

—Construction of Section
There was nothing in the former Paternity Act (see now this Act) which placed any limits on the time for filing a jury demand; therefore, the provisions of the former Civil Practice Law (see now 735 ILCS 5/1-101 et seq.) controlled. People ex rel. Raines v. Biggs, 135 Ill. App. 3d 200, 90 Ill. Dec. 99, 481 N.E.2d 899 (5 Dist. 1985).

This provision has been construed to refer to the right of trial by jury, as it existed at common law, and as enjoyed at the adoption of the Constitution, it neither provides for a jury trial in every case, or precludes all restrictions on the exercise of that right. People ex rel. Cizek v. Azzarello, 81 Ill. App. 3d 1102, 37 Ill. Dec. 84, 401 N.E.2d 1177 (1 Dist. 1980).

—Denial of Jury Trial
Trial court abused its discretion in an action brought pursuant to the former Paternity Act (see now this Act) by refusing to grant a jury trial. People ex rel. Raines v. Biggs, 135 Ill. App. 3d 200, 90 Ill. Dec. 99, 481 N.E.2d 899 (5 Dist. 1985).

Where in a paternity suit the defendant was never required to appear, and answer and no issue was ever formed by the trial court prior to the scheduled trial date, defendant did not waive his right to trial by jury, and the trial court erred by denying defendant's request for a jury trial on the trial date, even though the trial date was six months after the complaint was filed. Ehorn v. Podraza, 51 Ill. App. 3d 816, 9 Ill. Dec. 866, 367 N.E.2d 300 (2 Dist. 1977).

When no motion, oral or written, for a jury trial was made for the defendant, the defendant was not deprived of a jury trial. LaLacker v. Stuckey, 40 Ill. App. 2d 341, 189 N.E.2d 676 (3 Dist. 1963).

A trial court should not deny the right to a jury trial when there is no showing of inconvenience to the court or to the parties litigant or prejudice to any rights in any manner whatsoever. Hartsock v. Bress, 40 Ill. App. 2d 66, 189 N.E.2d 673 (4 Dist. 1963).

—Failure to Pay Jury Fee
A jury in a paternity proceeding is not constitutionally mandated; therefore the trial judge did not err in striking indigent defendant's jury request for lack of payment of the jury fee. People ex rel. Lockwood v. McDaniel, 180 Ill. App. 3d 13, 129 Ill. Dec. 396, 536 N.E.2d 80 (4 Dist. 1989).

—Late Motions
Former section 59 of the Civil Practice Act (see now 735 ILCS 5/2-1007) allowed a late motion for a jury trial in a paternity action under both the statute and Rule 183, Supreme Court Rules, but the motion would be granted only for good cause shown. People v. Stephens, 132 Ill. App. 2d 586, 270 N.E.2d 212 (1 Dist. 1971).

—No Waiver
In a paternity action where the alleged father was adjudged the father, such judgment order was void since the case was tried at an ex parte hearing, without a jury, while the case was at issue upon the complaint and answer of the parties and a jury demand by the alleged father was of record; notice of the hearing should have been given to the alleged father, and without notice, the jury demand was not waived at the ex parte hearing. Clark v. Brown, 121 Ill. App. 2d 280, 257 N.E.2d 565 (1 Dist. 1970).

—Waiver
Where defendant in a paternity suit did not demand a jury until after commencement of the trial, his failure to file a timely demand resulted in a waiver of his statutory right to a trial by jury. People ex rel. Chrisco v. Carnes, 114 Ill. App. 3d 417, 70 Ill. Dec. 333, 449 N.E.2d 207 (3 Dist. 1983).

A defendant in an action brought under the former Paternity Act (see now this Act) may, after making a jury demand, waive his

Jury Trial (Cont'd)

—Waiver (Cont'd)

statutory right to a jury trial. Adkins v. Shannon, 83 Ill. App. 3d 384, 38 Ill. Dec. 736, 403 N.E.2d 1340 (3 Dist. 1980).

Where a defendant appeared and testified at a hearing without complaining about his counsel's withdrawal of a jury demand, the defendant waived his statutory right to a jury trial. Adkins v. Shannon, 83 Ill. App. 3d 384, 38 Ill. Dec. 736, 403 N.E.2d 1340 (3 Dist. 1980).

A defendant must file a jury demand no later than the filing of his answer, or else he waives a jury. People ex rel. Cizek v. Azzarello, 81 Ill. App. 3d 1102, 37 Ill. Dec. 84, 401 N.E.2d 1177 (1 Dist. 1980).

Where there was nothing in the record to show that the defendant either in person, or by his attorney, at any time requested a jury trial, defendant's right to trial by jury was waived. People ex rel. Cizek v. Azzarello, 81 Ill. App. 3d 1102, 37 Ill. Dec. 84, 401 N.E.2d 1177 (1 Dist. 1980).

Because defendant's right to trial was not constitutionally derived, but was based upon section 1355 of the former Paternity Act (see now this section), which provided for a jury trial only upon demand, without which waiver of the right occurred, no affirmative showing of waiver was required. People ex rel. Cizek v. Azzarello, 81 Ill. App. 3d 1102, 37 Ill. Dec. 84, 401 N.E.2d 1177 (1 Dist. 1980).

Under former section 56 of the Paternity Act (see now this section), where a defendant went to trial without filing an answer and made no demand for a jury in his five appearances prior to trial, he waived his right to a jury. People ex rel. Harris v. Williams, 8 Ill. App. 3d 821, 291 N.E.2d 323 (1 Dist. 1972).

Under former section 56 of the Paternity Act (see now this section), where a defendant's demand for a jury trial should have been made when he appeared and made his plea of not guilty, because of his failure to do so at that time, he waived his right and the judge did not abuse his discretion when he denied the request at a later date. People ex rel. Bucaro v. Johnson, 8 Ill. App. 3d 618, 291 N.E.2d 9 (1 Dist. 1972).

Self-Incrimination

In a paternity proceeding in which the defendant was found to be the father, calling the defendant to the stand as an adverse witness under 735 ILCS 5/2-1102 did not violate his privilege against self-incrimination because the Fifth Amendment does not disallow the asking of potentially incriminating questions, nor does it allow the person of whom the questions are asked to refuse to answer them without expressly asserting that his answer may tend to incriminate him; his failure to claim the privilege during his questioning by the State's attorney waived his right to assert it on appeal. People v. Rimicci, 97 Ill. App. 2d 470, 240 N.E.2d 195 (1 Dist. 1968).

Standard of Review

In a paternity case, questions of the credibility of the witnesses and the weight to be given their testimony are for the trier of fact, and these findings must be affirmed on review unless they are clearly and palpably erroneous. People ex rel. Gomez v. Wedech, 58 Ill. App. 3d 518, 16 Ill. Dec. 74, 374 N.E.2d 849 (1 Dist. 1978).

Witnesses

—Competency

In a paternity suit under the former Paternity Act (see now this Act), both the complainant mother, and the defendant are competent witnesses, and their credibility is determined by the trier of fact. People ex rel. Martin v. Presswood, 85 Ill. App. 3d 975, 41 Ill. Dec. 272, 407 N.E.2d 770 (1 Dist. 1980).

RESEARCH REFERENCES

Paternity proceedings: right to jury trial. 51 ALR4th 565.

750 ILCS 45/13.1 Temporary order for child support

Sec. 13.1. *Temporary order for child support.* Notwithstanding any other law to the contrary, pending the outcome of a judicial determination of parentage, the court shall issue a temporary order for child support, upon motion by a party and a showing of clear and convincing evidence of paternity. In determining the amount of the temporary child support award, the court shall use the guidelines and standards set forth in subsection (a) of Section 505 and in Section 505.2 of the Illinois Marriage and Dissolution of Marriage Act [750 ILCS 5/505 and 750 ILCS 5/505.2].

Any new or existing support order entered by the court under this Section shall be deemed to be a series of judgments against the person obligated to pay support thereunder, each such judgment to be in the amount of each payment or installment of support and each judgment to be deemed entered as of the date the corresponding payment or installment becomes due under the terms of the support order. Each such judgment shall have the full force, effect, and attributes of any other judgment of this State, including the ability to be enforced. Any such judgment is subject to modification or termination only in accordance with Section 510 of the Illinois Marriage and Dissolution of Marriage Act [750 ILCS 5/510]. A lien arises by operation of law against the real and personal property of the noncustodial parent for each installment of overdue support owed by the noncustodial parent.

All orders for support, when entered or modified, shall include a provision requiring the non-custodial parent to notify the court, and in cases in which a party is receiving child support enforcement services under Article X of the Illinois Public Aid Code [305 ILCS 5/10-1 et seq.], the Illinois Department of Public Aid, within 7 days, (i) of the name, address, and telephone number of any new employer of the non-custodial parent, (ii) whether the non-custodial parent has access to health insurance coverage through the employer or other group coverage, and, if so, the policy name and number and the names of persons covered under the policy, and (iii) of any new residential or mailing address or telephone number of the non-custodial parent.

In any subsequent action to enforce a support order, upon sufficient showing that diligent effort has been made to ascertain the location of the non-custodial parent, service of process or provision of notice necessary in that action may be made at the last known address of the non-custodial parent, in any manner expressly provided by the Code of Civil Procedure [735 ILCS 5/1-101 et seq.] or in this Act, which service shall be sufficient for purposes of due process.

An order for support shall include a date on which the current support obligation terminates. The termination date shall be no earlier than the date on which the child covered by the order will attain the age of majority or is otherwise emancipated. The order for support shall state that the termination date does not apply to any arrearage that may remain unpaid on that date. Nothing in this paragraph shall be construed to prevent the court from modifying the order.

If there is an unpaid arrearage or delinquency (as those terms are defined in the Income Withholding for Support Act [750 ILCS 28/1 et seq.]) equal to at least one month's support obligation on the termination date stated in the order for support or, if there is no termination date stated in the order, on the date the child attains the age of majority or is otherwise emancipated, then the periodic amount required to be paid for current support of that child immediately prior to that date shall automatically continue to be an obligation, not as current support but as periodic payment toward satisfaction of the unpaid arrearage or delinquency. That periodic payment shall be in addition to any periodic payment previously required for satisfaction of the arrearage or delinquency. The total periodic amount to be paid toward satisfaction of the arrearage or delinquency may be enforced and collected by any method provided by law for the enforcement and collection of child support, including but not limited to income withholding under the Income Withholding for Support Act [750 ILCS 28/1 et seq.]. Each order for support entered or modified on or after the effective date of this amendatory Act of the 93rd General Assembly [P.A. 93-1061] must contain a statement notifying the parties of the requirements of this paragraph. Failure to include the statement in the order for support does not affect the validity of the order or the operation of the provisions of this paragraph with regard to the order. This paragraph shall not be construed to prevent or affect the establishment or modification of an order for the support of a minor child or the establishment or modification of an order for the support of a non-minor child or educational expenses under Section 513 of the Illinois Marriage and Dissolution of Marriage Act [750 ILCS 5/513].
(Source: P.A. 90-18, § 120; 92-590, § 30; 93-1061, § 25.)

Effective Date.

Section 999 of P.A. 90-18 made this section effective July 1, 1997.

Effect of Amendments.

The 2002 amendment by P.A. 92-590, effective July 1, 2002, substituted "child support enforcement services" for "child and spouse support services" in the third paragraph.

The 2004 amendment by P.A. 93-1061, effective January 1, 2005, added the last paragraph.

750 ILCS 45/13.5 Injunctive relief

Sec. 13.5. *Injunctive relief.* (a) In any action brought under this Act for the initial determination of custody or visitation of a child or for modification of a prior custody or visitation order, the court, upon application of any party, may enjoin a party having physical possession or custody of a child from temporarily or permanently removing the child from Illinois pending the adjudication of the issues of custody and visitation. When deciding whether to enjoin removal of a child, the Court shall consider the following factors including, but not limited to:

(1) the extent of previous involvement with the child by the party seeking to enjoin removal;

(2) the likelihood that parentage will be established; and

(3) the impact on the financial, physical, and emotional health of the party being enjoined from removing the child.

(b) Injunctive relief under this Act shall be governed by the relevant provisions of the Code of Civil Procedure [735 ILCS 5/1-101 et seq.].

(c) Notwithstanding the provisions of subsection (a), the court may decline to enjoin a domestic violence victim having physical possession or custody of a child from temporarily or permanently removing the child from Illinois pending the adjudication of the issues of custody and visitation. In determining whether a person is a domestic violence victim, the court shall consider the following factors:

(1) a sworn statement by the person that the person has good reason to believe that he or she is the victim of domestic violence or stalking;

(2) a sworn statement that the person fears for his or her safety or the safety of his or her children;

(3) evidence from police, court or other government agency records or files;

(4) documentation from a domestic violence program if the person is alleged to be a victim of domestic violence;

(5) documentation from a legal, clerical, medical, or other professional from whom the person has sought assistance in dealing with the alleged domestic violence; and

(6) any other evidence that supports the sworn statements, such as a statement from any other individual with knowledge of the circumstances that provides the basis for the claim, or physical evidence of the act or acts of domestic violence.
(Source: P.A. 93-139, § 5.)

Effective Date.

Section 99 of P.A. 93-139, made this section effective upon becoming law. The Act was approved July 10, 2003.

CASE NOTES

Removal

—Burden of Proof

Trial court improperly placed on father the burden of proof to establish that removal by mother was not in the child's best interests rather than applying the injunction standard; the burden of proof should have been on mother to establish that it was in child's best interest to remain with her. Fisher v. Waldrop, Ill. App. 3d , 291 Ill. Dec. 365, 823 N.E.2d 657, 2005 Ill. App. LEXIS 157 (4 Dist. 2005).

750 ILCS 45/14 Judgment

Sec. 14. *Judgment.* (a)(1) The judgment shall contain or explicitly reserve provisions concerning any duty and amount of child support and may contain provisions concerning the custody and guardianship of the child, visitation privileges with the child, the furnishing of bond or other security for the payment of the judgment, which the court shall determine in accordance with the relevant factors set forth in the Illinois Marriage and Dissolution of Marriage Act [750 ILCS 5/101 et seq.] and any other applicable law of Illinois, to guide the court in a finding in the best interests of the child. In determining custody, joint custody, removal, or visitation, the court shall apply the relevant standards of the Illinois Marriage and Dissolution of Marriage Act [750 ILCS 5/101 et seq.], including Section 609 [750 ILCS 5/609]. Specifically, in determining the amount of any child support award, the court shall use the guidelines and standards set forth in subsection (a) of Section 505 and in Section 505.2 of the Illinois Marriage and Dissolution of Marriage Act [750 ILCS 5/505 and 750 ILCS 5/505.2]. For purposes of Section 505 of the Illinois Marriage and Dissolution of Marriage Act [750 ILCS 5/505], "net income" of the non-custodial parent shall include any benefits available to that person under the Illinois Public Aid Code [305 ILCS 5/1-1 et seq.] or from other federal, State or local government-funded programs. The court shall, in any event and regardless of the amount of the non-custodial parent's net income, in its judgment order the non-custodial parent to pay child support to the custodial parent in a minimum amount of not less than $10 per month. In an action brought within 2 years after a child's birth, the judgment or order may direct either parent to pay the reasonable expenses incurred by either parent related to the mother's pregnancy and the delivery of the child. The judgment or order shall contain the father's social security number, which the father shall disclose to the court; however, failure to include the father's social security number on the judgment or order does not invalidate the judgment or order.

(2) If a judgment of parentage contains no explicit award of custody, the establishment of a support obligation or of visitation rights in one parent shall be considered a judgment granting custody to the other parent. If the parentage judgment contains no such provisions, custody shall be presumed to be with the mother; however, the presumption shall not apply if the father has had physical custody for at least 6 months prior to the date that the mother seeks to enforce custodial rights.

(b) The court shall order all child support payments, determined in accordance with such guidelines, to commence with the date summons is served. The level of current periodic support payments shall not be reduced because of payments set for the period prior to the date of entry of the support order. The Court may order any child support payments to be made for a period prior to the commencement of the action. In determining whether and the extent to which the payments shall be made for any prior period, the court shall consider all relevant facts, including the factors for determining the amount of support specified in the Illinois Marriage and Dissolution of Marriage Act [750 ILCS 5/101 et seq.] and other equitable factors including but not limited to:

(1) The father's prior knowledge of the fact and circumstances of the child's birth.

(2) The father's prior willingness or refusal to help raise or support the child.

(3) The extent to which the mother or the public agency bringing the action previously informed the father of the child's needs or attempted to seek or require his help in raising or supporting the child.

(4) The reasons the mother or the public agency did not file the action earlier.

(5) The extent to which the father would be prejudiced by the delay in bringing the action.

For purposes of determining the amount of child support to be paid for any period before the date the order for current child support is entered, there is a rebuttable presumption that the father's net income for the prior period was the same as his net income at the time the order for current child support is entered.

If (i) the non-custodial parent was properly served with a request for discovery of financial information relating to the non-custodial parent's ability to provide child support, (ii) the non-custodial parent failed to comply with the request, despite having been ordered to do so by the court, and (iii) the non-custodial parent is not present at the hearing to determine support despite having received proper notice, then any relevant financial information concerning the non-custodial parent's ability to provide child support that was obtained pursuant to subpoena and proper notice shall be admitted into evidence without the need to establish any further foundation for its admission.

(c) Any new or existing support order entered by the court under this Section shall be deemed to be a series of judgments against the person obligated to pay support thereunder, each judgment to be in the amount of each payment or installment of support and each such judgment to be deemed entered as of the date the corresponding payment or installment becomes due under the terms of the support order. Each judgment shall have the full force, effect and attributes of any other judgment of this State, including the ability to be enforced. A lien arises by operation of law against the real and personal property of the noncustodial parent for each installment of overdue support owed by the noncustodial parent.

(d) If the judgment or order of the court is at variance with the child's birth certificate, the court shall order that a new birth certificate be issued under the Vital Records Act [410 ILCS 535/1 et seq.].

(e) On request of the mother and the father, the court shall order a change in the child's name. After hearing evidence the court may stay payment of support during the period of the father's minority or period of disability.

(f) If, upon a showing of proper service, the father fails to appear in court, or otherwise appear as provided by law, the court may proceed to hear the cause upon testimony of the mother or other parties taken in open court and shall enter a judgment by default. The court may reserve any order as to the amount of child support until the father has received notice, by regular mail, of a hearing on the matter.

(g) A one-time charge of 20% is imposable upon the amount of past-due child support owed on July 1, 1988 which has accrued under a support order entered by the court. The charge shall be imposed in accordance with the provisions of Section 10-21 of the Illinois Public Aid Code [305 ILCS 5/10-21] and shall be enforced by the court upon petition.

(h) All orders for support, when entered or modified, shall include a provision requiring the non-custodial parent to notify the court and, in cases in which party is receiving child and spouse support services under Article X of the Illinois Public Aid Code [305 ILCS 5/10-1 et seq.], the Illinois Department of Public Aid, within 7 days, (i) of the name and address of any new employer of the non-custodial parent, (ii) whether the non-custodial parent has access to health insurance coverage through the employer or other group coverage and, if so, the policy name and number and the names of persons covered under the policy, and (iii) of any new residential or mailing address or telephone number of the non-custodial parent. In any subsequent action to enforce a support order, upon a sufficient showing that a diligent effort has been made to ascertain the location of the non-custodial parent, service of process or provision of notice necessary in the case may be made at the last known address of the non-custodial parent in any manner expressly provided by the Code of Civil Procedure [735 ILCS 5/1-101 et seq.] or this Act, which service shall be sufficient for purposes of due process.

(i) An order for support shall include a date on which the current support obligation terminates. The termination date shall be no earlier than the date on which the child covered by the order will attain the age of 18. However, if the child will not graduate from high school until after attaining the age of 18, then the termination date shall be no earlier than the earlier of the date on which the child's high school graduation will occur or the date on which the child will attain the age of 19. The order for support shall state that the termination date does not apply to any arrearage that may remain unpaid on that date. Nothing in this subsection shall be construed to prevent the court from modifying the order or terminating the order in the event the child is otherwise emancipated.

(i-5) If there is an unpaid arrearage or delinquency (as those terms are defined in the Income Withholding for Support Act [750 ILCS 28/1 et seq.]) equal to at least one month's support obligation on the termination date stated in the order for support or, if there is no termination date stated in the order, on the date the child attains the age of majority or is otherwise emancipated, the periodic amount required to be paid for current support of that child immediately prior to that date shall automatically continue to be an obligation, not as current support but as periodic payment toward satisfaction of the unpaid arrearage or delinquency. That periodic payment shall be in addition to any periodic payment previously required for satisfaction of the arrearage or delinquency. The total periodic amount to be paid toward satisfaction of the arrearage or delinquency may be enforced and collected by any method provided by law for enforcement and collection of child support, including but not limited to income withholding under the Income Withholding for Support Act [750 ILCS 28/1 et seq.]. Each order for support entered or modified on or after the effective date of this amendatory Act of the 93rd General Assembly [P.A. 93-1061] must contain a statement notifying the parties of the requirements of this subsection. Failure to include the statement in the order for support does not affect the validity of the order or the operation of the provisions of this subsection with regard to the order. This subsection shall not be construed to prevent or affect the establishment or modification of an order for support of a minor child or the establishment or modification of an order for support of a non-minor child or educational expenses under Section 513 of the Illinois Marriage and Dissolution of Marriage Act [750 ILCS 5/513].

(j) An order entered under this Section shall include a provision requiring the obligor to report to the obligee and to the clerk of court within 10 days each time the obligor obtains new employment, and each time the obligor's employment is terminated for any reason. The report shall be in writing and shall, in the case of new employment, include the name and address of the new employer. Failure to report new employment or the termination of current employment, if coupled with nonpayment of support for a period in excess of 60 days, is indirect criminal contempt. For any obligor arrested for failure to report new employment bond shall be set in the amount of the child support that should have been paid during the period of unreported employment. An order entered under this Section shall also include a provision requiring the obligor and obligee parents to advise each other of a change in residence within 5 days of the change except when the court finds that the physical, mental, or emotional health of a party or that of a minor child, or both, would be seriously endangered by disclosure of the party's address.

(Source: P.A. 86-312; 86-649; 86-714; 86-859; 86-1028; 88-307, § 25; 88-538, § 10; 88-687, § 20; 90-18, § 120; 90-539, § 25; 90-655, § 173; 91-767, § 20; 92-590, § 30; 92-876, § 920; 93-139, § 5; 93-1061, § 25.)

Note.

This section was Ill.Rev.Stat., Ch. 40, para. 2514.

Illinois Administrative Code.

See 89 Illinois Administrative Code, §§ 160.60, 160.60.

Effect of Amendments.

The 1994 amendment by P.A. 88-538, effective January 1, 1995,

in subdivision (a)(1), in the first and third sentences, deleted "approved September 22, 1977, as amended" following "Marriage Act", added the second and sixth sentences and deleted the former last sentence, which read "Subject to the limitations on actions brought on behalf of persons other than the child as provided in Section 8 of this Act, the judgment or order may direct the father to pay the reasonable expenses of the mother's pregnancy and delivery"; in subsection (b), in the fourth sentence, deleted "approved September 22, 1977, as amended" following "Marriage Act"; in subsection (d) deleted "approved August 8, 1961, as amended" from the end and made other stylistic and punctuation changes.

The 1994 amendment by P.A. 88-687, effective January 24, 1995, incorporated the amendments by P.A. 88-538 and in subdivision (a)(1), added the last sentence; in subsection (b), in the introductory language, in the third sentence deleted from the end "including payments to reimburse any public agency for assistance granted on behalf of the child" and added the last paragraph.

The 1997 amendment by P.A. 90-18, effective July 1, 1997, in subdivision (a)(1), in the seventh sentence added at the end "however, failure to include the father's social security number on the judgment or order does not invalidate the judgment or order"; in subsection (c) added the third sentence; in subsection (f), in the first sentence, inserted "a showing of"; and in subsection (h), in the first sentence, substituted "All orders" for "An order", inserted "when", deleted "in a case in which a party is receiving child and spouse support services under Article X of the Illinois Public Aid Code" preceding "shall include", inserted "the court and, in cases in which a party is receiving child and spouse support services under Article X of the Illinois Public Aid Code", inserted "(i)", inserted "(ii)" deleted a comma after "other group coverage" and added at the end "and (iii) of any new residential or mailing address or telephone number of the non-custodial parent" and added the second sentence.

The 1997 amendment by P.A. 90-539, effective June 1, 1998, added subsection (j).

The 1998 amendment by P.A. 90-655, effective July 30, 1998, incorporated the amendments by P.A. 90-18 and P.A. 90-539.

The 2000 amendment by P.A. 91-767, effective June 9, 2000, inserted the last paragraph of subsection (b).

The 2002 amendment by P.A. 92-590, effective July 1, 2002, substituted "child support enforcement services" for "child and spouse support services" in subsection (h).

The 2002 amendment by P.A. 92-876, effective June 1, 2003, in subsection (i) substituted "age of 18. However, if the child will not graduate from high school until after attaining the age of 18, then the termination date shall be no earlier than the earlier of the date on which the child's high school graduation will occur or the date on which the child will attain the age of 19" for "age of majority or is otherwise emancipated", and added "or terminating the order in the event the child is otherwise emancipated" at the end.

The 2003 amendment by P.A. 93-139, effective July 10, 2003, in the second sentence of subsection (a)(1), inserted "removal" and "including Section 609"

The 2004 amendment by P.A. 93-1061, effective January 1, 2005, inserted subsection (i-5).

CASE NOTES

Analysis

Bankruptcy Proceedings
Child Support
—Award Guidelines
—Commencement
—Deviation from Guidelines
—Finality of Award
—Judicial Review
—Proper Award
—Retroactive Support
Construction
Educational Expenses
—In General
Joint Custody
Judgment of Parentage
—Child Custody
—Court Rulings
—Summary Judgment
Life Insurance
Minor's Medical Expenses
—Health Insurance
—Trial Court Discretion
Necessaries
—Reimbursement to Third Party
Pregnancy Expenses
—Collateral Source Rule
—Lost Wages
—Trial Court Discretion
Retroactivity
Statute of Limitations
—Waiver
Visitation

Bankruptcy Proceedings

Attorney's fee award in paternity action was a support debt under 11 U.S.C. § 522(f)(1)(A). In re Allen, 217 Bankr. 247 (Bankr. S.D. Ill. 1998).

Child Support

—Award Guidelines

The standards and guidelines in the marriage and Dissolution of Marriage Act (750 ILCS 5/505), apply to paternity cases and this section of this Act requires a parent to pay a minimum of 20% of his or her net income for the support of one child, and a trial court may not deviate from the statutory minimum, unless it finds reason to, and if so, the court must enter express findings upon which such deviation rests. Jiles v. Spratt, 195 Ill. App. 3d 354, 142 Ill. Dec. 21, 552 N.E.2d 371 (4 Dist. 1990); Carnes v. Dressen, 215 Ill. App. 3d 166, 158 Ill. Dec. 732, 574 N.E.2d 845 (4 Dist. 1991).

In a paternity action, the court must consider the totality of circumstances in determining the amount of support payments. People ex rel. Holland v. DeMichael, 79 Ill. App. 3d 974, 35 Ill. Dec. 188, 398 N.E.2d 1138 (1 Dist. 1979).

—Commencement

The intention of this section is that support should begin no later than the date the summons is served, after the action is commenced. Carnes v. Dressen, 215 Ill. App. 3d 166, 158 Ill. Dec. 732, 574 N.E.2d 845 (4 Dist. 1991).

—Deviation from Guidelines

Trial court deviating from child support guidelines is required to consider evidence on such factors as the financial resources, and needs of child and custodial, and noncustodial parent, the standard of living the child would have enjoyed if the household had been one, and the physical and emotional condition of the child, and his educational needs. Parks ex rel. Parks v. Romans, 187 Ill. App. 3d 445, 135 Ill. Dec. 42, 543 N.E.2d 277 (1 Dist. 1989).

—Finality of Award

Where trial court set retroactive support at 20% of defendant's net income, but had not yet determined what the amount would be, and where the method of payment was not addressed by the trial court, but was delayed until defendant submitted proof of income, the lower court's order would not constitute a final judgment for appeal purposes. Department of Pub. Aid ex rel. Chiapelli v. Viviano, 195 Ill. App. 3d 1033, 142 Ill. Dec. 747, 553 N.E.2d 97 (5 Dist. 1990).

For purposes of appeal in a paternity action, the final order is the order establishing the father's support obligation. People ex rel. Raines v. Biggs, 135 Ill. App. 3d 200, 90 Ill. Dec. 99, 481 N.E.2d 899 (5 Dist. 1985).

—Judicial Review

The finding of the trial court as to the proper level of child support will not be reversed unless it is against the manifest weight of the evidence. Milligan ex rel. Cange v. Cange, 200 Ill. App. 3d 284, 146 Ill. Dec. 667, 558 N.E.2d 630 (4 Dist. 1990).

—Proper Award

The trial court did not abuse its discretion in requiring father who netted income of $1128 a month to pay unemployed mother $225 a month for child support. People ex rel. Holland v. DeMichael, 79 Ill. App. 3d 974, 35 Ill. Dec. 188, 398 N.E.2d 1138 (1 Dist. 1979).

Child Support (Cont'd)

—Retroactive Support

An award of retroactive support was not an abuse of discretion; the father conceded that he knew of the child's birth, the father participated in the child's support to the extent he saw fit, the mother tried to work out an agreement with the father before filing suit, and the father was not prejudiced by the delay in bringing suit. Janssen ex rel. Janssen v. Turner, 292 Ill. App. 3d 219, 226 Ill. Dec. 202, 685 N.E.2d 16 (4 Dist. 1997).

The first sentence of subsection (b) does not control the rest of the section such that an award of child support may only be retroactive to the date of service of summons, not to the date of a child's birth. Janssen ex rel. Janssen v. Turner, 292 Ill. App. 3d 219, 226 Ill. Dec. 202, 685 N.E.2d 16 (4 Dist. 1997).

Defendant's argument, that this Act does not allow for retroactive payments of child support, failed in that this section plainly states that the court may order child support payments to be made "for a period prior to the commencement of the action." Department of Pub. Aid ex rel. McFarland v. Thompsen, 218 Ill. App. 3d 1099, 161 Ill. Dec. 854, 579 N.E.2d 402 (2 Dist. 1991).

Where plaintiff filed an action against defendant under this Act prior, to the birth of the child, and where defendant took two blood tests, both of which conclusively determined the child's parentage, and where a motion for summary judgment was granted less than two months after the birth of the child which found defendant to be the father, there was no reason child support should not have been ordered retroactive to the date of birth and any other decision would have encouraged delay tactics in litigation, and defeated the obvious intent of the legislature. Carnes v. Dressen, 215 Ill. App. 3d 166, 158 Ill. Dec. 732, 574 N.E.2d 845 (4 Dist. 1991).

Retroactive child support is authorized by subsection (b) of this section; in so finding, the appellate court overruled its prior decision in People ex rel. Causley v. Jackson, 171 Ill. App. 3d 464, 122 Ill. Dec. 644, 527 N.E.2d 16 (1988). Milligan ex rel. Cange v. Cange, 200 Ill. App. 3d 284, 146 Ill. Dec. 667, 558 N.E.2d 630 (4 Dist. 1990).

Where the only factors considered by the trial court were that the father was employed at a salary of approximately $19,000 per year, and that he was economically assisting a disabled sister in Jamaica, and another child in college in New York, the requisite statutory factors were not adequately addressed to determine whether retroactive benefits were appropriate. Parks ex rel. Parks v. Romans, 187 Ill. App. 3d 445, 135 Ill. Dec. 42, 543 N.E.2d 277 (1 Dist. 1989).

Construction

Because 750 ILCS 45/14 and 750 ILCS 45/16 expressly adopt relevant provisions of the Illinois Marriage and Dissolution of Marriage Act to apply to the Illinois Parentage Act, 750 ILCS 45/1 et seq., provisions from the Marriage Act do not apply to the Parentage Act unless expressly adopted. Stella v. Garcia (In re Stella), 339 Ill. App. 3d 610, 274 Ill. Dec. 391, 791 N.E.2d 187, 2003 Ill. App. LEXIS 650 (1 Dist. 2003).

The reference in subdivision (a)(1) to the factors set forth in the Marriage Act is a reference to 750 ILCS 5/602. Illinois Dep't of Pub. Aid ex rel. Gagnon-Dix v. Gagnon, 288 Ill. App. 3d 424, 223 Ill. Dec. 776, 680 N.E.2d 509 (4 Dist. 1997).

Educational Expenses

—In General

When read together, this Act and the Marriage and Dissolution of Marriage Act (750 ILCS 5/513) establish that the court has broad discretion to determine any award of child support, including support for educational expenses beyond the age of majority, despite the absence of a specific provision for the education of nonminor, illegitimate children. Rawles v. Hartman, 172 Ill. App. 3d 931, 123 Ill. Dec. 217, 527 N.E.2d 680 (2 Dist. 1988).

Joint Custody

Joint custody orders are appropriate only where both parents have displayed an unusual capacity to cooperate. Kocal v. Holt, 229 Ill. App. 3d 1023, 172 Ill. Dec. 106, 595 N.E.2d 169 (3 Dist. 1992).

Where petitioner and respondent have a history of disagreement, imposing a joint custody arrangement, even though limited, is against the best interests of the child. Kocal v. Holt, 229 Ill. App. 3d 1023, 172 Ill. Dec. 106, 595 N.E.2d 169 (3 Dist. 1992).

Judgment of Parentage

—Child Custody

Trial court's order determining paternity and granting the child's father custody and the child's mother visitation rights did not prohibit the father from removing the child from Illinois, and the trial court erred by holding the father in contempt for removing the child from Illinois without getting the mother's permission or the court's permission because the court's order did not prohibit that conduct and the mother did not show that the father's conduct violated her visitation rights. Harbour v. Melton, 333 Ill. App. 3d 124, 266 Ill. Dec. 729, 775 N.E.2d 291, 2002 Ill. App. LEXIS 762 (4 Dist. 2002).

A parentage order did not constitute a prior custody order where the order did not address the issues of custody, visitation and amount of support, and it explicitly provided for further proceedings in the case. Upmann ex rel. Upmann-Terhark v. Terhark, 200 Ill. App. 3d 827, 146 Ill. Dec. 605, 558 N.E.2d 568 (2 Dist. 1990).

—Court Rulings

When a plaintiff requests relief directly tied to a finding of paternity, such as child support and birth expenses, the circuit court must make an initial ruling upon those matters, even though it may retain jurisdiction to enforce its orders, or to modify the relief granted a plaintiff. People ex rel. Driver v. Taylor, 152 Ill. App. 3d 413, 105 Ill. Dec. 416, 504 N.E.2d 516 (4 Dist. 1987).

—Summary Judgment

Where a genuine issue remained for trial, as to the paternity of a child, the trial court erred, as a matter of law, in granting summary judgment upon this issue. Smith ex rel. Smith v. Barbre, 179 Ill. App. 3d 473, 128 Ill. Dec. 487, 534 N.E.2d 669 (5 Dist. 1989).

Life Insurance

The trial court did not abuse its discretion in ordering the father to maintain a life insurance policy for the benefit of his child; no finding of special circumstances is necessary to support such an order. Janssen ex rel. Janssen v. Turner, 292 Ill. App. 3d 219, 226 Ill. Dec. 202, 685 N.E.2d 16 (4 Dist. 1997).

Minor's Medical Expenses

—Health Insurance

Where health insurance coverage is requested, question of support cannot be regarded as fully resolved until court has ruled on issue of health insurance; duty to provide health insurance is an integral part of parent's current and future support obligations. Franson ex rel. Franson v. Micelli, 172 Ill. 2d 352, 217 Ill. Dec. 250, 666 N.E.2d 1188 (1996).

—Trial Court Discretion

The court did not abuse its discretion in ordering respondent to pay child's medical expenses. Stone v. Williams, 193 Ill. App. 3d 563, 140 Ill. Dec. 621, 550 N.E.2d 257 (3 Dist. 1990).

Necessaries

—Reimbursement to Third Party

There was no authority for the proposition that a natural father must reimburse third persons who provided support and maintenance to a child, without the natural parent's knowledge or authority, or promise, either express or implied, that such necessities would be paid for. Evink v. Pekin Ins. Co., 122 Ill. App. 3d 246, 77 Ill. Dec. 647, 460 N.E.2d 1211 (2 Dist. 1984).

Pregnancy Expenses

—Collateral Source Rule

Where trial court read the collateral source rule into this Act, it erred by granting mother's expenses in paternity suit, where an insurance company paid the mother's medical expenses. Jiles v. Spratt, 195 Ill. App. 3d 354, 142 Ill. Dec. 21, 552 N.E.2d 371 (4 Dist. 1990).

—Lost Wages

This section does not authorize a recovery of the mother's lost wages as an expense related to the mother's pregnancy and the delivery of the child. Stockton v. Oldenburg, 305 Ill. App. 3d 897, 238 Ill. Dec. 1013, 713 N.E.2d 259 (4 Dist. 1999).

Pregnancy Expenses (Cont'd)

—Trial Court Discretion

In an action decided under the former Paternity Act (see now this Act), the trial court considered both the father's and the mother's financial condition and circumstances in determining who should pay the mother's pregnancy expenses and, in view of the substantial payments already made by plaintiff-father, who was attempting to establish paternity in an action under that Act, it was not an abuse of discretion to fail to order plaintiff to pay defendant-mother's expenses. Sullivan v. McGaw, 134 Ill. App. 3d 455, 89 Ill. Dec. 540, 480 N.E.2d 1283 (2 Dist. 1985).

Retroactivity

The provision of subdivision (a)(2), added in 1989, stating that the establishment of a support obligation or visitation rights for one parent shall be considered a judgment granting custody to the other parent, did not apply retroactively. In re D.R., 295 Ill. App. 3d 115, 229 Ill. Dec. 583, 692 N.E.2d 356 (2 Dist. 1998).

The legislature intended to allow children born prior to the passage of this Act of 1984 to obtain retroactive support under the Paternity Act of 1957. Thompson v. Yancey, 186 Ill. App. 3d 234, 134 Ill. Dec. 253, 542 N.E.2d 432 (2 Dist. 1989).

Statute of Limitations

—Waiver

Trial court would not consider father's argument that mother's recovery for pregnancy and delivery expenses was barred by the statute of limitations where the father raised the argument for the first time on appeal. Janssen ex rel. Janssen v. Turner, 292 Ill. App. 3d 219, 226 Ill. Dec. 202, 685 N.E.2d 16 (4 Dist. 1997).

Visitation

Trial court properly placed the burden on the mother to overcome the presumption that the father would be entitled to visitation. Jines v. Jurich, 335 Ill. App. 3d 1156, 270 Ill. Dec. 572, 783 N.E.2d 147, 2002 Ill. App. LEXIS 1279 (5 Dist. 2002).

Under the Parentage Act, (750 ILCS 45/1 et seq.); custody and visitation is to be determined in accordance with all of the factors set forth in the Marriage and Dissolution Act, including those contained in 750 ILCS 5/607; thus, grandparent visitation is available under the Parentage Act. People ex rel. Farina v. Sensor, 299 Ill. App. 3d 333, 233 Ill. Dec. 873, 701 N.E.2d 1147 (2 Dist. 1998).

Burden of proof is on the noncustodial parent seeking visitation. Illinois Dep't of Pub. Aid ex rel. Gagnon-Dix v. Gagnon, 288 Ill. App. 3d 424, 223 Ill. Dec. 776, 680 N.E.2d 509 (4 Dist. 1997).

The fact that the Department has obtained an order establishing paternity and setting child support does not mean that the father is automatically entitled to visitation. Illinois Dep't of Pub. Aid ex rel. Gagnon-Dix v. Gagnon, 288 Ill. App. 3d 424, 223 Ill. Dec. 776, 680 N.E.2d 509 (4 Dist. 1997).

This Act does not incorporate 750 ILCS 5/607 requiring a court to award visitation to a noncustodial parent unless the court finds, after a hearing, that visitation would endanger seriously the child's physical, mental, moral or emotional health. Illinois Dep't of Pub. Aid ex rel. Gagnon-Dix v. Gagnon, 288 Ill. App. 3d 424, 223 Ill. Dec. 776, 680 N.E.2d 509 (4 Dist. 1997).

RESEARCH REFERENCES

Liability of Father for Retroactive Child Support on Judicial Determination of Paternity. 87 ALR5th 361.

750 ILCS 45/14.1 Information to State Case Registry

Sec. 14.1. *Information to State Case Registry.* (a) In this Section:

"Order for support", "obligor", "obligee", and "business day" are defined as set forth in the Income Withholding for Support Act [750 ILCS 28/1 et seq.].

"State Case Registry" means the State Case Registry established under Section 10-27 of the Illinois Public Aid Code [305 ILCS 5/10-27].

(b) Each order for support entered or modified by the circuit court under this Act shall require that the obligor and obligee (i) file with the clerk of the circuit court the information required by this Section (and any other information required under Title IV, Part D of the Social Security Act [42 U.S.C. § 601 et seq.] or by the federal Department of Health and Human Services) at the time of entry or modification of the order for support and (ii) file updated information with the clerk within 5 business days of any change. Failure of the obligor or obligee to file or update the required information shall be punishable as in cases of contempt. The failure shall not prevent the court from entering or modifying the order for support, however.

(c) The obligor shall file the following information: the obligor's name, date of birth, social security number, and mailing address.

If either the obligor or the obligee receives child support enforcement services from the Illinois Department of Public Aid under Article X of the Illinois Public Aid Code, [305 ILCS 5/10-1 et seq.] the obligor shall also file the following information: the obligor's telephone number, driver's license number, and residential address (if different from the obligor's mailing address), and the name, address, and telephone number of the obligor's employer or employers.

(d) The obligee shall file the following information:

(1) The names of the obligee and the child or children covered by the order for support.

(2) The dates of birth of the obligee and the child or children covered by the order for support.

(3) The social security numbers of the obligee and the child or children covered by the order for support.

(4) The obligee's mailing address.

(e) In cases in which the obligee receives child support enforcement services from the Illinois Department of Public Aid under Article X of the Illinois Public Aid Code [305 ILCS 5/10-1 et seq.], the order for support shall (i) require that the obligee file the information required under subsection (d) with the Illinois Department of Public Aid for inclusion in the State Case Registry, rather than file the information with the clerk, and (ii) require that the obligee include the following additional information:

(1) The obligee's telephone and driver's license numbers.

(2) The obligee's residential address, if different from the obligee's mailing address.

(3) The name, address, and telephone number of the obligee's employer or employers.

The order for support shall also require that the obligee update the information filed with the Illinois Department of Public Aid within 5 business days of any change.

(f) The clerk shall provide the information filed under this Section, together with the court docket number and county in which the order for support was entered, to the State Case Registry within 5 business days after receipt of the information.

(g) In a case in which a party is receiving child support enforcement services under Article X of the Illinois Public Aid Code [305 ILCS 5/10-1 et seq.], the clerk shall provide the following additional information to the State Case Registry within 5 business days after entry or modification of an order for support or request from the Illinois Department of Public Aid:

(1) The amount of monthly or other periodic support owed under the order for support and other amounts, including arrearage, interest, or late payment penalties and fees, due or overdue under the order.

(2) Any such amounts that have been received by the clerk, and the distribution of those amounts by the clerk.

(h) Information filed by the obligor and obligee under this Section that is not specifically required to be included in the body of an order for support under other laws is not a public record and shall be treated as confidential and subject to disclosure only in accordance with the provisions of this Section, Section 10-27 of the Illinois Public Aid Code [305 ILCS 5/10-27], and Title IV, Part D of the Social Security Act [42 U.S.C. § 601 et seq.].

(Source: P.A. 91-212, § 40; 92-463, § 20.)

Effective Date.

Section 999 of P.A. 91-212 made this section effective upon becoming law. The Act was approved July 20, 1999.

Effect of Amendments.

The 2001 amendment by P.A. 92-463, effective August 22, 2001, rewrote this section to the extent that a detailed comparison would be impracticable.

750 ILCS 45/14.5 Information to locate putative fathers and noncustodial parents

Sec. 14.5. *Information to locate putative fathers and noncustodial parents.* (a) Upon request by a public office, employers, labor unions, and telephone companies shall provide location information concerning putative fathers and noncustodial parents for the purpose of establishing a child's paternity or establishing, enforcing, or modifying a child support obligation. The term "public office" is defined as set forth in the Income Withholding for Support Act [750 ILCS 28/1 et seq.]. In this Section, "location information" means information about (i) the physical whereabouts of a putative father or noncustodial parent, (ii) the employer of the putative father or noncustodial parent, or (iii) the salary, wages, and other compensation paid and the health insurance coverage provided to the putative father or noncustodial parent by the employer of the putative father or noncustodial parent or by a labor union of which the putative father or noncustodial parent is a member. An employer, labor union, or telephone company shall respond to the request of the public office within 15 days after receiving the request. Any employer, labor union, or telephone company that willfully fails to fully respond within the 15-day period shall be subject to a penalty of $100 for each day that the response is not provided to the public office after the 15-day period has expired. The penalty may be collected in a civil action, which may be brought against the employer, labor union, or telephone company in favor of the public office.

(b) Upon being served with a subpoena (including an administrative subpoena as authorized by law), a utility company or cable television company must provide location information to a public office for the purpose of establishing a child's paternity or establishing, enforcing, or modifying a child support obligation.

(c) Notwithstanding the provisions of any other State or local law to the contrary, an employer, labor union, telephone company, utility company, or cable television company shall not be liable to any person for disclosure of location information under the requirements of this Section, except for willful and wanton misconduct.

(Source: P.A. 93-116, § 20.)

Effective Date.

Section 99 of P.A. 93-116 made this Act effective upon becoming law. The Act was approved July 10, 2003.

750 ILCS 45/15 Enforcement of Judgment or Order

Sec. 15. *Enforcement of Judgment or Order.* (a) If existence of the parent and child relationship is declared, or paternity or duty of support has been established under this Act or under prior law or under the law of any other jurisdiction, the judgment rendered thereunder may be enforced in the same or other proceedings by any party or any person or agency that has furnished or may furnish financial assistance or services to the child. The Income Withholding for Support Act [750 ILCS 28/1 et seq.] and Sections 14 and 16 of this Act [750 ILCS 45/14 and 750 ILCS 45/16] shall also be applicable with respect to entry, modification and enforcement of any support judgment entered under provisions of the "Paternity Act", approved July 5, 1957, as amended, repealed July 1, 1985.

(b) Failure to comply with any order of the court shall be punishable as contempt as in other cases of failure to comply under the "Illinois Marriage and Dissolution of Marriage Act", as now or hereafter amended [750 ILCS 5/101 et seq.]. In addition to other penalties provided by law, the court may, after finding the party guilty of contempt, order that the party be:

(1) Placed on probation with such conditions of probation as the court deems advisable;

(2) Sentenced to periodic imprisonment for a period not to exceed 6 months. However, the court may permit the party to be released for periods of time during the day or night to work or conduct business or other self-employed occupation. The court may further order any part of all the earnings of a party during a sentence of periodic imprisonment to be

paid to the Clerk of the Circuit Court or to the person or parent having custody of the minor child for the support of said child until further order of the court.

(2.5) The court may also pierce the ownership veil of a person, persons, or business entity to discover assets of a non-custodial parent held in the name of that person, those persons, or that business entity if there is a unity of interest and ownership sufficient to render no financial separation between the non-custodial parent and that person, those persons, or the business entity. The following circumstances are sufficient for a court to order discovery of the assets of a person, persons, or business entity and to compel the application of any discovered assets toward payment on the judgment for support:

(A) the non-custodial parent and the person, persons, or business entity maintain records together.

(B) the non-custodial parent and the person, persons, or business entity fail to maintain an arms length relationship between themselves with regard to any assets.

(C) the non-custodial parent transfers assets to the person, persons, or business entity with the intent to perpetrate a fraud on the custodial parent.

With respect to assets which are real property, no order entered under this subdivision (2.5) shall affect the rights of bona fide purchasers, mortgagees, judgment creditors, or other lien holders who acquire their interests in the property prior to the time a notice of lis pendens pursuant to the Code of Civil Procedure [735 ILCS 5/1-101 et seq.] or a copy of the order is placed of record in the office of the recorder of deeds for the county in which the real property is located.

(3) The court may also order that in cases where the party is 90 days or more delinquent in payment of support or has been adjudicated in arrears in an amount equal to 90 days obligation or more, that the party's Illinois driving privileges be suspended until the court determines that the party is in compliance with the judgement or duty of support. The court may also order that the parent be issued a family financial responsibility driving permit that would allow limited driving privileges for employment and medical purposes in accordance with Section 7-702.1 of the Illinois Vehicle Code [625 ILCS 5/7-702.1]. The clerk of the circuit court shall certify the order suspending the driving privileges of the parent or granting the issuance of a family financial responsibility driving permit to the Secretary of State on forms prescribed by the Secretary. Upon receipt of the authenticated documents, the Secretary of State shall suspend the party's driving privileges until further order of the court and shall, if ordered by the court, subject to the provisions of Section 7-702.1 of the Illinois Vehicle Code [625 ILCS 5/7-702.1], issue a family financial responsibility driving permit to the parent.

In addition to the penalties or punishment that may be imposed under this Section, any person whose conduct constitutes a violation of Section 15 of the Non-Support Punishment Act [750 ILCS 16/15] may be prosecuted under that Act, and a person convicted under that Act may be sentenced in accordance with that Act. The sentence may include but need not be limited to a requirement that the person perform community service under Section 50 of that Act [750 ILCS 16/50] or participate in a work alternative program under Section 50 of that Act [750 ILCS 16/50]. A person may not be required to participate in a work alternative program under Section 50 of that Act [750 ILCS 16/50] if the person is currently participating in a work program pursuant to Section 15.1 of this Act [750 ILCS 45/15.1].

(c) In any post-judgment proceeding to enforce or modify the judgment the parties shall continue to be designated as in the original proceeding.

(Source: P.A. 85-2; 89-92, § 25; 90-476, § 15; 90-673, § 930; 90-733, § 40; 91-357, § 261; 92-16, § 98.)

Note.

This section was Ill.Rev.Stat., Ch. 40, para. 2515.

The Non-Support of Spouse and Children Act, 750 ILCS 15/1 et seq., referred to in the last paragraph of subsection (b), is repealed. Current similar provisions are found as the Non-Support Punishment Act, 750 ILCS 16/1 et seq.

Section 996 of P.A. 92-16 contains a "no acceleration or delay" provision, and Section 997 contains a "no revival or extension" provision.

Effect of Amendments.

The 1995 amendment by P.A. 89-92, effective July 1, 1996, added subdivision (b)(3).

The 1997 amendment by P.A. 90-476, effective January 1, 1998, added subdivision (b)(2.5).

The 1998 amendment by P.A. 90-673, effective January 1, 1999, substituted "The Income Withholding for Support Act" for "Sections 14, 16 and 20 of this Act" in subsection (a).

The 1998 amendment by P.A. 90-733, effective August 11, 1998, added the last paragraph of subsection (b).

The 1999 amendment by P.A. 91-357, effective July 29, 1999, incorporated the changes made by P.A. 90-673 and P.A. 90-733.

The 2001 amendment by P.A. 92-16, effective June 28, 2001, all in the last paragraph of subsection (b): substituted references to "Act" for references to "Section" throughout the paragraph, in the first sentence substituted "Section 15" for "Section 1", and "Punishment" for "of Spouse and Children", in the second sentence substituted the first instance of "Section 50" for "subsection (b)" and the second instance of "Section 50" for "subsection (c)", and in the last sentence substituted "Section 50" for "subsection (c)".

CASE NOTES

Analysis

In General
Attorney fees
Child Support
—Award Upheld
—Sanctions for Arrearages

In General

If paternity is established, the father's duty of support will be imposed and enforced. People ex rel. Moore v. McIntosh, 134 Ill. App. 3d 1070, 90 Ill. Dec. 33, 481 N.E.2d 833 (5 Dist. 1985).

Attorney fees

Standard provided for under 750 ILCS 5/508(b) was used in a determination of a mother's request for attorneys fees incurred in

Attorney fees (Cont'd)
seeking to enforce a prior order of the trial court. Jennifer B. v. King, 324 Ill. App. 3d 1, 257 Ill. Dec. 822, 754 N.E.2d 480, 2001 Ill. App. LEXIS 663 (2 Dist. 2001).

Child Support

—Award Upheld
Where mother filed an affidavit specifying net monthly income of $974 and expenses of $1,320, however, only $240 of those expenses were attributed directly to the child, and father filed an affidavit specifying net monthly income of $2,838.72 and monthly expenses of $2,833, which included a $567 payment for a $28,000 automobile purchased between the time of the finding of paternity and the support hearing, trial court's order to defendant to pay $300 monthly child support which represented approximately 11% of defendant's net income was sustained. Watkins v. Martin, 115 Ill. App. 3d 417, 71 Ill. Dec. 178, 450 N.E.2d 866 (1 Dist. 1983).

—Sanctions for Arrearages
Where the husband had no legal relationship to the child, the court was without authority to order him to pay alleged child support arrearage, or to find him in contempt of court for failing to pay said arrearage. In re Watling, 183 Ill. App. 3d 18, 131 Ill. Dec. 718, 538 N.E.2d 1274 (2 Dist. 1989).

750 ILCS 45/15.1 [Unemployed obligor; court's powers]

Sec. 15.1. (a) Whenever it is determined in a proceeding to establish or enforce a child support obligation that the person owing a duty of support is unemployed, the court may order the person to seek employment and report periodically to the court with a diary, listing or other memorandum of his or her efforts in accordance with such order. Additionally, the court may order the unemployed person to report to the Department of Employment Security for job search services or to make application with the local Job Training Partnership Act [29 U.S.C. § 1501 et seq.] provider for participation in job search, training or work programs and where the duty of support is owed to a child receiving child support enforcement services under Article X of The Illinois Public Aid Code, as amended [305 ILCS 5/10-1 et seq.], the court may order the unemployed person to report to the Illinois Department of Public Aid for participation in job search, training or work programs established under Section 9-6 and Article IXA of that Code [305 ILCS 5/9-6 and 305 ILCS 5/9A-1 et seq.].

(b) Whenever it is determined that a person owes past-due support for a child, and the child is receiving assistance under the Illinois Public Aid Code [305 ILCS 5/1-1 et seq.], the court shall order the following at the request of the Illinois Department of Public Aid:

(1) that the person pay the past-due support in accordance with a plan approved by the court; or

(2) if the person owing past-due support is unemployed, is subject to such a plan, and is not incapacitated, that the person participate in such job search, training, or work programs established under Section 9-6 and Article IXA of the Illinois Public Aid Code [305 ILCS 5/9-6 and 305 ILCS 5/9A-1 et seq.] as the court deems appropriate.
(Source: P.A. 85-1155; 90-18, § 120; 91-357, § 261; 92-590, § 30.)

Note.
This section was Ill.Rev.Stat., Ch. 40, para. 2515.1.

Effect of Amendments.
The 1997 amendment by P.A. 90-18, effective July 1, 1997, added the subsection (a) designation; in subsection (a), in the second sentence, inserted "and Article IXA"; and added subsection (b).

The 1999 amendment by P.A. 91-357, effective July 29, 1999, substituted "Job" for "Jobs" in the second sentence of subsection (a).

The 2002 amendment by P.A. 92-590, effective July 1, 2002, substituted "child support enforcement services" for "child and spouse support services" throughout the section.

750 ILCS 45/15.2 Order of protection; status

Sec. 15.2. *Order of protection; status.* Whenever relief is sought under this Act, the court, before granting relief, shall determine whether any order of protection has previously been entered in the instant proceeding or any other proceeding in which any party, or a child of any party, or both, if relevant, has been designated as either a respondent or a protected person.
(Source: P.A. 87-743.)

Note.
This section was Ill.Rev.Stat., Ch. 40, para. 2515.2.

750 ILCS 45/16 Modification of Judgment

Sec. 16. *Modification of Judgment.* The court has continuing jurisdiction to modify an order for support, custody, visitation, or removal included in a judgment entered under this Act. Any custody, visitation, or removal judgment modification shall be in accordance with the relevant factors specified in the Illinois Marriage and Dissolution of Marriage Act [750 ILCS 5/101 et seq.], including Section 609 [750 ILCS 5/609]. Any support judgment is subject to modification or termination only in accordance with Section 510 of the Illinois Marriage and Dissolution of Marriage Act [750 ILCS 5/510].
(Source: P.A. 85-2; 93-139, § 5.)

Note.
This section was Ill.Rev.Stat., Ch. 40, para. 2516.

Effect of Amendments.
The 2003 amendment by P.A. 93-139, effective July 10, 2003, inserted "or removal" twice and "including Section 609" and deleted "approved September 22, 1977, as now or hereafter amended" at the end of the first sentence.

CASE NOTES

Analysis

Change in Circumstances
—Presumption
—Special Finding
Child Support Modification
—Attorney Fees
—Factors
Estoppel
Marriage and Dissolution of Marriage Act
Removal of Child
—Petition Not Required
Retroactive Support
Visitation

Change in Circumstances

—Presumption

An increase in the child's needs can be presumed on the basis that the child has grown older and the cost of living has risen. People ex rel. Stokely v. Goodenow, 211 Ill. App. 3d 802, 164 Ill. Dec. 548, 583 N.E.2d 102 (4 Dist. 1991).

—Special Finding

A previous special finding made in a support order, which varies from the guidelines and which is no longer found to be a factor, is a proper consideration in determining a substantial change in circumstances. People ex rel. Stokely v. Goodenow, 211 Ill. App. 3d 802, 164 Ill. Dec. 548, 583 N.E.2d 102 (4 Dist. 1991).

Child Support Modification

—Attorney Fees

Section 1359 of the former Paternity Act (see now this section) did not authorize trial court to assess attorney's fees for proceedings incident to modification of child support. Fink v. Roller, 113 Ill. App. 3d 1084, 69 Ill. Dec. 744, 448 N.E.2d 204 (5 Dist. 1983).

—Factors

Trial court did not abuse its discretion in concluding that the evidence adduced concerning increased cost of living, from 1967 to 1981, warranted increase in defendant's support obligation from $75 to $150 per month. Fink v. Roller, 113 Ill. App. 3d 1084, 69 Ill. Dec. 744, 448 N.E.2d 204 (5 Dist. 1983).

Although section 1359 of the former Paternity Act (see now this section) did not purport to set forth a standard to be used in determining requests for modifications of child support, it has been construed as requiring the same showing for a support modification as is required under the Marriage and Dissolution of Marriage Act (750 ILCS 5/101 et seq.), i.e., a substantial change in circumstances. Fink v. Roller, 113 Ill. App. 3d 1084, 69 Ill. Dec. 744, 448 N.E.2d 204 (5 Dist. 1983).

Estoppel

Under the doctrine of estoppel, an award for child support arrearages was improper where petitioner failed to make a demand for child support payments during an extended period; for 12½ years the petitioner and the children lived in an apartment in a building owned by respondent; respondent charged them no rent; respondent testified that he allowed petitioner and the children to live in the apartment without paying rent based upon his agreement with petitioner that she would not prosecute him for arrearages; defendant frequently bought groceries and gave petitioner money; he testified that this money was being used to support the children; and he paid the children's medical and dental bills, bought them clothes and gave them money. People ex rel. Foster v. Louder, 97 Ill. App. 3d 1104, 53 Ill. Dec. 468, 423 N.E.2d 1272 (1 Dist. 1981).

Marriage and Dissolution of Marriage Act

Because 750 ILCS 45/14 and 750 ILCS 45/16 expressly adopt relevant provisions of the Illinois Marriage and Dissolution of Marriage Act to apply to the Illinois Parentage Act, 750 ILCS 45/1 et seq., provisions from the Marriage Act do not apply to the Parentage Act unless expressly adopted. Stella v. Garcia (In re Stella), 339 Ill. App. 3d 610, 274 Ill. Dec. 391, 791 N.E.2d 187, 2003 Ill. App. LEXIS 650 (1 Dist. 2003).

The Parentage Act incorporates the factors specified in section 607(c) of the Marriage and Dissolution of Marriage Act, 750 ILCS 5/607, for modification of visitation; that is, the court may modify visitation whenever the modification would serve the child's best interests, but the court should not restrict the noncustodial parent's visitation unless it finds that the visitation would endanger seriously the child's physical, mental, moral or emotional health. Hall v. Melton, 314 Ill. App. 3d 476, 247 Ill. Dec. 295, 732 N.E.2d 11, 2000 Ill. App. LEXIS 584 (1 Dist. 2000).

Removal of Child

—Petition Not Required

In cases where the parties were never married, the custodial parent is not required to file a petition for removal, thus, the court will not yet have engaged in a best interest of the child analysis to determine whether the custodial parent should be allowed to remove the minor child from the state, therefore, where the parties were never married, the fact that a custodial parent wishes to move out of the state with the minor child is sufficient to show a change of circumstances which would satisfy the first prong of 750 ILCS 5/610 and the court would then be required to engage in a best interests of the child analysis utilizing the factors enumerated in 750 ILCS 5/602. In re R.M.F., 275 Ill. App. 3d 43, 211 Ill. Dec. 754, 655 N.E.2d 1137 (2 Dist. 1995).

Retroactive Support

Trial court did not err in making support obligation under section 1359 the former Paternity Act (see now this section) retroactive to the date the petition for modification was filed. Fink v. Roller, 113 Ill. App. 3d 1084, 69 Ill. Dec. 744, 448 N.E.2d 204 (5 Dist. 1983).

Visitation

The Parentage Act incorporates section 607 of the Marriage Act, 750 ILCS 5/607, for modification of visitation, and a presumption of visitation applies unless the court sees evidence of grounds to terminate parental rights. Hall v. Melton, 314 Ill. App. 3d 476, 247 Ill. Dec. 295, 732 N.E.2d 11, 2000 Ill. App. LEXIS 420 (1 Dist. 2000).

750 ILCS 45/17 Costs

Sec. 17. *Costs.* Except as otherwise provided in this Act, the court may order reasonable fees of counsel, experts, and other costs of the action, pre-trial proceedings, post-judgment proceedings to enforce or modify the judgment, and the appeal or the defense of an appeal of the judgment, to be paid by the parties in accordance with the relevant factors specified in Section 508 of the Illinois Marriage and Dissolution of Marriage Act, as amended [750 ILCS 5/508].
(Source: P.A. 85-1417; 86-1339.)

Note.

This section was Ill.Rev.Stat., Ch. 40, para. 2517.

CASE NOTES

Analysis

Attorney Fees
—Inability to Pay
—Interim Fees
—On Appeal
—Payable Directly to Attorney
—Payment After Discharge
—Payment After Settlement
—Post-Trial Proceedings
—Private Counsel
—Proper
—Retention Agreement
—Settlement Provision Void
—Standard for Award
—Suit for Fees by Attorney
—Trial Court Discretion
—Venue
Fee Shifting
—Illustrative Cases
—Strict Construction

Attorney Fees

—Inability to Pay

Propriety of an award of attorney fees in child support actions is dependent upon a showing by the party seeking the award of an inability to pay and a demonstration of the ability of the other party to do so. Hall v. Clark (In re Keon C.), 344 Ill. App. 3d 1137, 279 Ill. Dec. 674, 800 N.E.2d 1257, 2003 Ill. App. LEXIS 1498 (4 Dist. 2003), appeal denied sub nom. In re Keon C., 208 Ill. 2d 538, 284 Ill. Dec. 340, 809 N.E.2d 1286 (2004).

Attorney Fees (Cont'd)

—Inability to Pay (Cont'd)

Standard provided for under 750 ILCS 5/508(b) is not proper for use in a determination of a mother's request for attorneys fees incurred in seeking to enforce a prior order of the trial court. Jennifer B. v. King, 324 Ill. App. 3d 1, 257 Ill. Dec. 822, 754 N.E.2d 480, 2001 Ill. App. LEXIS 663 (2 Dist. 2001).

An award of attorney fees was not an abuse of discretion where the court found that the mother did not have the financial ability to pay all of her attorney fees. Janssen ex rel. Janssen v. Turner, 292 Ill. App. 3d 219, 226 Ill. Dec. 202, 685 N.E.2d 16 (4 Dist. 1997).

In order to justify an attorney fee award, a party must show financial inability to pay, and the ability of the other party to pay. Pacheco v. Silva, 194 Ill. App. 3d 620, 141 Ill. Dec. 323, 551 N.E.2d 316 (1 Dist. 1990).

It is not necessary that one party be destitute in order to support an attorney fee award, it is sufficient that disbursement of the petitioner's funds would exhaust her own estate, or undermine her economic stability. Pacheco v. Silva, 194 Ill. App. 3d 620, 141 Ill. Dec. 323, 551 N.E.2d 316 (1 Dist. 1990).

If defendant is financially unable to pay attorney fees, appropriate adjustments may be made. Jiles v. Spratt, 195 Ill. App. 3d 354, 142 Ill. Dec. 21, 552 N.E.2d 371 (4 Dist. 1990).

—Interim Fees

Trial court erred in ruling that interim attorney's fees could not be recovered under the Illinois Parentage Act as 750 ILCS 45/17 allowed for attorney's fees based on the factors found in 750 ILCS 5/508, which allowed for interim attorney's fees based on the factors listed in 750 ILCS 5/501(c-1)(1),(2),(3). Stella v. Garcia (In re Stella), 353 Ill. App. 3d 415, 288 Ill. Dec. 889, 818 N.E.2d 824, 2004 Ill. App. LEXIS 1265 (1 Dist. 2004).

Interim attorney's fees can be awarded under the Illinois Parentage Act by using the methods, factors, and procedures set forth in § 501 of the Illinois Marriage Act, 750 ILCS 5/501(c-1)(1),(2),(3); and disgorgement cannot be considered or used in a Parentage Act proceeding. Stella v. Garcia (In re Stella), 353 Ill. App. 3d 415, 288 Ill. Dec. 889, 818 N.E.2d 824, 2004 Ill. App. LEXIS 1265 (1 Dist. 2004).

—On Appeal

The fact that the legislature specifically authorized recovery of appellate attorney fees in the Marriage and Dissolution of Marriage Act (750 ILCS 5/508) suggests that it did not intend that such fees be recoverable in this section which is silent on the subject. Saltzman Printers, Inc. v. Gunthorp-Warren Printing Co., 192 Ill. App. 3d 130, 139 Ill. Dec. 200, 548 N.E.2d 585 (1 Dist. 1989).

—Payable Directly to Attorney

By allowing courts in paternity suits to award attorney fees "in accordance with the relevant factors" in this section, this act permits awards of attorney fees payable directly to attorneys. Heiden v. Ottinger, 245 Ill. App. 3d 612, 186 Ill. Dec. 563, 616 N.E.2d 1005 (2 Dist.), appeal denied, 152 Ill. 2d 559, 190 Ill. Dec. 888, 622 N.E.2d 1205 (1993).

—Payment After Discharge

Attorney could pursue the mother in a still pending paternity suit for the payment of his fees after the mother had discharged him. Heiden v. Ottinger, 245 Ill. App. 3d 612, 186 Ill. Dec. 563, 616 N.E.2d 1005 (2 Dist.), appeal denied, 152 Ill. 2d 559, 190 Ill. Dec. 888, 622 N.E.2d 1205 (1993).

The fact that attorney was discharged by the mother would not prohibit him from pursuing the father for payment of his fees in a still pending paternity action. Heiden v. Ottinger, 245 Ill. App. 3d 612, 186 Ill. Dec. 563, 616 N.E.2d 1005 (2 Dist.), appeal denied, 152 Ill. 2d 559, 190 Ill. Dec. 888, 622 N.E.2d 1205 (1993).

—Payment After Settlement

A settlement of the merits of a paternity suit would not have prevented wife's attorney from seeking payment of his fees by the father. Heiden v. Ottinger, 245 Ill. App. 3d 612, 186 Ill. Dec. 563, 616 N.E.2d 1005 (2 Dist.), appeal denied, 152 Ill. 2d 559, 190 Ill. Dec. 888, 622 N.E.2d 1205 (1993).

—Post-Trial Proceedings

This section, as amended in 1988, now allows an award of attorney fees in a post-trial proceeding to modify child support in a paternity suit. Pacheco v. Silva, 194 Ill. App. 3d 620, 141 Ill. Dec. 323, 551 N.E.2d 316 (1 Dist. 1990).

—Private Counsel

This section entitling a mother to representation by a State's Attorney in a paternity action was intended to provide an alternative procedure to retaining private counsel, and it does not preclude her from retaining private counsel and petitioning the court for the related attorney fees. Milligan ex rel. Cange v. Cange, 200 Ill. App. 3d 284, 146 Ill. Dec. 667, 558 N.E.2d 630 (4 Dist. 1990).

Allowance of attorney fees under former section 9 of the Paternity Act (see now this section) for private counsel retained by mother was not inconsistent with former section 4 of the Paternity Act (see now 750 ILCS 45/18), which provided that an action was to be commenced by State's attorney upon request of the mother. People ex rel. Adams v. Sanes, 41 Ill. 2d 381, 243 N.E.2d 233 (1968).

—Proper

Trial court did not abuse its discretion in awarding attorney fees to a mother in a proceeding regarding child support where the mother made less than $10 per hour in a part-time job while the father was a professional basketball player with a seven figure income. Hall v. Clark (In re Keon C.), 344 Ill. App. 3d 1137, 279 Ill. Dec. 674, 800 N.E.2d 1257, 2003 Ill. App. LEXIS 1498 (4 Dist. 2003), appeal denied sub nom. In re Keon C., 208 Ill. 2d 538, 284 Ill. Dec. 340, 809 N.E.2d 1286 (2004).

—Retention Agreement

Retention agreements stating hourly rates are commonplace in divorce cases, and such agreements have never precluded the courts of this state from reducing attorney fees, where a court deems such fees were not reasonable for the services rendered, or necessary. Gitlin v. Hartmann, 175 Ill. App. 3d 805, 125 Ill. Dec. 426, 530 N.E.2d 584 (2 Dist. 1988).

—Settlement Provision Void

Where settlement agreement in a paternity action was drawn up by the father's lawyer and executed by the parties, all without plaintiff's knowledge and while he was attorney of record for the mother, the provision in the settlement agreement requiring each party to pay his or her own attorney fees was void; the record revealed a strong inference that there was a concerted effort made to place obstacles in the path to plaintiff's reimbursement. Heiden v. Ottinger, 245 Ill. App. 3d 612, 186 Ill. Dec. 563, 616 N.E.2d 1005 (2 Dist.), appeal denied, 152 Ill. 2d 559, 190 Ill. Dec. 888, 622 N.E.2d 1205 (1993).

—Standard for Award

In awarding attorney fees in paternity cases, factors such as the relative financial abilities of the parties, the nature of the controversy, and the skill of the attorney become evident during the proceedings, and no independent proofs need be made concerning such factors, however, factors such as the amount of time and labor involved in a case require independent proof. Jiles v. Spratt, 195 Ill. App. 3d 354, 142 Ill. Dec. 21, 552 N.E.2d 371 (4 Dist. 1990).

Although this section contains no express provision linking the award of attorney fees, incurred in enforcing support orders, to similar provisions of the Marriage and Dissolution of Marriage Act (750 ILCS 5/508) as is the case with contempt proceedings to enforce support orders, because of the close relationship between the two acts, it is appropriate that the attorney fees awarded under this section of the Act are awarded under the same standard as those awarded under 750 ILCS 5/508. Davis v. Sprague, 186 Ill. App. 3d 249, 133 Ill. Dec. 620, 541 N.E.2d 831 (4 Dist. 1989).

The financial position of the parties, the skill and standing of the attorneys employed, the importance, novelty and difficulty of the questions raised, especially from the family law standpoint, the degree of responsibility involved from a management perspective, the time and labor required, the usual and customary charge in the community, and the benefits resulting to the client, of these, the time factor is probably given the same weight or greater weight than any other factor. The fee allowance should provide for fair compensation, but only for those services which were both reasonable, and necessary to the action. Ivanyi v. Granoff, 171 Ill. App. 3d 411, 122 Ill. Dec. 49, 526 N.E.2d 189 (2 Dist. 1988).

The trial court is not bound by an attorney's opinion as to what constitutes a reasonable fee, and an attorney's generalized state-

Attorney Fees (Cont'd)

—Standard for Award (Cont'd)

ment as to the time spent is an insufficient basis for a fee award, and the usual practice is for the attorney to submit detailed records as to the time spent. Ivanyi v. Granoff, 171 Ill. App. 3d 411, 122 Ill. Dec. 49, 526 N.E.2d 189 (2 Dist. 1988).

—Suit for Fees by Attorney

While dissolution proceedings or proceedings under this Act are ongoing, no separate action for fees may be maintained, however, nothing precludes an attorney, whether discharged or not, from bringing a separate suit against his or her own client for fees earned in a dissolution proceeding or proceeding under this Act, after the circuit court has lost jurisdiction of those statutory proceedings, nor will an attorney be barred from bringing such a separate action because that issue was not raised in the underlying proceedings. Myers v. Brantley, 204 Ill. App. 3d 832, 149 Ill. Dec. 891, 562 N.E.2d 355 (4 Dist. 1990).

—Trial Court Discretion

The awarding of attorney fees under this Act is within the discretion of the trial court, and will not be reversed absent a clear abuse of such discretion. Jiles v. Spratt, 195 Ill. App. 3d 354, 142 Ill. Dec. 21, 552 N.E.2d 371 (4 Dist. 1990).

—Venue

Plaintiff's application for attorney fees, and costs, must be made in the pending parentage proceeding, and may not, during the period of the proceeding, be brought as a new action in another court. Gitlin v. Hartmann, 175 Ill. App. 3d 805, 125 Ill. Dec. 426, 530 N.E.2d 584 (2 Dist. 1988).

Fee Shifting

—Illustrative Cases

Because nothing in 750 ILCS 45/17, 750 ILCS 5/508, or 750 ILCS5⁄501(c-1)(3) gave trial judges the power to order disgorgement of interim fees in parentage cases, the trial court improperly ordered the attorney to disgorge $ 20,000 to the opposing attorney. Stella v. Garcia (In re Stella), 339 Ill. App. 3d 610, 274 Ill. Dec. 391, 791 N.E.2d 187, 2003 Ill. App. LEXIS 650 (1 Dist. 2003).

—Strict Construction

Courts generally construe fee shifting provisions, like this section, as they are in derogation of the common law. Saltzman Printers, Inc. v. Gunthorp-Warren Printing Co., 192 Ill. App. 3d 130, 139 Ill. Dec. 200, 548 N.E.2d 585 (1 Dist. 1989).

750 ILCS 45/18 Right to Counsel; Free Transcript on Appeal

Sec. 18. *Right to Counsel; Free Transcript on Appeal.* (a) Any party may be represented by counsel at all proceedings under this Act.

(a-5) In any proceedings involving the support, custody, visitation, education, parentage, property interest, or general welfare of a minor or dependent child, the court may, on its own motion or that of any party, and subject to the terms or specifications the court determines, appoint an attorney to serve in one of the following capacities:

(1) as an attorney to represent the child;

(2) as a guardian ad litem to address issues the court delineates;

(3) as a child's representative whose duty shall be to advocate what the representative finds to be in the best interests of the child after reviewing the facts and circumstances of the case. The child's representative shall have the same power and authority to take part in the conduct of the litigation as does an attorney for a party and shall possess all the powers of investigation and recommendation as does a guardian ad litem. The child's representative shall consider, but not be bound by, the expressed wishes of the child. A child's representative shall have received training in child advocacy or shall possess such experience as determined to be equivalent to such training by the chief judge of the circuit where the child's representative has been appointed. The child's representative shall not disclose confidential communications made by the child, except as required by law or by the Rules of Professional Conduct. The child's representative shall not be called as a witness regarding the issues set forth in this subsection.

During the proceedings the court may appoint an additional attorney to serve in another of the capacities described in subdivisions (1), (2), or (3) of the preceding paragraph on its own motion or that of a party only for good cause shown and when the reasons for the additional appointment are set forth in specific findings.

The court shall enter an order as appropriate for costs, fees, and disbursements, including a retainer, when the attorney, guardian ad litem, or child's representative is appointed, and thereafter as necessary. Such orders shall require payment by either or both parents, by any other party or source, or from the marital estate or the child's separate estate. The court may not order payment by the Illinois Department of Public Aid in cases in which the Department is providing child support enforcement services under Article X of the Illinois Public Aid Code [305 ILCS 5/10-1 et seq.]. Unless otherwise ordered by the court at the time fees and costs are approved, all fees and costs payable to an attorney, guardian ad litem, or child's representative under this Section are by implication deemed to be in the nature of support of the child and are within the exceptions to discharge in bankruptcy under 11 U.S.C.A. 523. The provisions of Sections 501 and 508 of this Act [750 ILCS 5/501 and 750 ILCS 5/508] shall apply to fees and costs for attorneys appointed under this Section.

(b) Upon the request of a mother or child seeking to establish the existence of a father and child relationship, the State's Attorney shall represent the mother or child in the trial court. If the child is an applicant for or a recipient of assistance as defined in Section 2-6 of "The Illinois Public Aid Code", approved April 11, 1967, as amended [305 ILCS 5/2-6], or has applied to the Illinois Department of Public Aid for services under Article X of such Code [305 ILCS 5/10-1 et seq.], the Department may file a complaint in the child's behalf under this Act. The Department shall refer the complaint to the Public Aid Claims Enforcement Division of the Office of the Attorney General as provided in Section 12-16 of "The Illinois Public Aid Code" [305 ILCS 5/12-16] for enforcement by the Attorney General. Legal representation by the State's Attorney or the Attorney General shall be limited to the establishment and enforcement of an order for support, and shall not extend to visitation, custody, property or other matters. If visitation, custody, property or other matters are raised by a party and considered by the court in any proceeding under this Act, the court shall provide a continuance sufficient to enable the mother or child to obtain representation for such matters.

(c) The Court may appoint counsel to represent any indigent defendant in the trial court, except that this representation shall be limited to the establishment of a parent and child relationship and an order for support, and shall not extend to visitation, custody, property, enforcement of an order for support, or other matters. If visitation, custody, property or other matters are raised by a party and considered by the court in any proceeding under this Act, the court shall provide a continuance sufficient to enable the defendant to obtain representation for such matters.

(d) The court shall furnish on request of any indigent party a transcript for purposes of appeal.

(Source: P.A. 86-522; 90-23, § 5; 91-410, § 10; 92-590, § 30.)

Note.

This section was Ill.Rev.Stat., Ch. 40, para. 2518.

Effect of Amendments.

The 1997 amendment by P.A. 90-23, effective January 1, 1998, in subsection (c), in the first sentence, substituted "may" for "shall", deleted "the Public Defender, or if there is no Public Defender other" preceding "counsel" and deleted a comma after "counsel".

The 1999 amendment by P.A. 91-410, effective January 1, 2000, deleted the second sentence of subsection (a), which read "In the best interests of the child, the court may appoint counsel to represent a child whose parentage is at issue"; and added subsection (a-5).

The 2002 amendment by P.A. 92-590, effective July 1, 2002, substituted "child support enforcement services" for "child and spouse support services" in the last paragraph of subsection (a-5).

CASE NOTES

ANALYSIS

Attorney Fees
—Private Counsel
Claim of Error
—Incomplete Record
Construction
—Former Paternity Act
Failure to Admonish
—Attorney
—Prejudice
—Transcript

Attorney Fees

—Private Counsel

This section entitles a mother to representation by a State's Attorney in a paternity action, in order to provide an alternative procedure to retaining private counsel, and does not preclude her from retaining private counsel, and petitioning the court for the related attorney fees. Ivanyi v. Granoff, 171 Ill. App. 3d 411, 122 Ill. Dec. 49, 526 N.E.2d 189 (2 Dist. 1988).

Claim of Error

—Incomplete Record

Where defendant did not supply a sufficiently complete record to support his claim of error, there was a presumption that the trial court conformed to the law. People ex rel. Tillery v. Ginsberg, 141 Ill. App. 3d 634, 96 Ill. Dec. 8, 490 N.E.2d 1044 (2 Dist. 1986).

Construction

—Former Paternity Act

The reference to the defendant's right to counsel, to a complete transcript of the proceedings, to plead not guilty, to be proven guilty by a preponderance of evidence, and to a trial by jury was deemed to be mandatory under section 1355 of the former Paternity Act (see now this section), because these rights depend on giving the word "shall" a mandatory construction, it cannot be given a merely directory meaning. Serpico v. Urso, 127 Ill. App. 3d 667, 82 Ill. Dec. 821, 469 N.E.2d 355 (1 Dist. 1984).

Failure to Admonish

—Attorney

Where defendant appealed and retained private appellate counsel under section 1366 of the former Paternity Act (see now this section), any failure of the trial court to admonish him of his right to appeal, and to have counsel without cost, was not prejudicial. People ex rel. Tillery v. Ginsberg, 141 Ill. App. 3d 634, 96 Ill. Dec. 8, 490 N.E.2d 1044 (2 Dist. 1986).

—Prejudice

Where the trial court failed to "fully advise" defendant of his statutorily granted rights set out in section 1355 of the former Paternity Act (see now this section), the court failed to substantially comply with the mandate of this section. Serpico v. Urso, 127 Ill. App. 3d 667, 82 Ill. Dec. 821, 469 N.E.2d 355 (1 Dist. 1984).

—Transcript

Failure to admonish defendant of his right to a free copy of the trial transcript, if indigent, was not prejudicial where defendant's ability to retain private counsel demonstrated that defendant would not have qualified for the free trial transcript. People ex rel. Tillery v. Ginsberg, 141 Ill. App. 3d 634, 96 Ill. Dec. 8, 490 N.E.2d 1044 (2 Dist. 1986).

LEGAL PERIODICALS

For article, "Conference on Ethical Issues in the Legal Representation of Children in Illinois", see 29 Loy. U. Chi. L.J. 289 (1998).

RESEARCH REFERENCES

Right of indigent defendant in paternity suit to have assistance of counsel at state expense. 4 ALR4th 363.

750 ILCS 45/19 Action to Declare Mother and Child Relationship

Sec. 19. *Action to Declare Mother and Child Relationship.* Any interested party may bring an action to determine the existence or non-existence of a mother and child relationship. Insofar as practicable, the provisions of this Act applicable to the father and child relationship shall apply to the mother and child relationship, including, but not limited to the obligation to support.

(Source: P.A. 83-1372.)

Note.

This section was Ill.Rev.Stat., Ch. 40, para. 2519.

750 ILCS 45/20 Withholding of Income to Secure Payment of Support

Sec. 20. *Withholding of Income to Secure Payment of Support.* Orders for support entered under this

Act are subject to the Income Withholding for Support Act [750 ILCS 28/1 et seq.].
(Source: P.A. 86-496; 86-546; 86-649; 86-746; 86-911; 86-1028; 86-1184; 87-529; 87-935, § 5; 87-988, § 5; 87-1105, § 5; 88-26, § 5; 88-45, § 2-62; 88-94, § 5; 88-131, § 25; 88-307, § 25; 88-670, § 2-71; 89-507, § 90D-96; 90-425, § 94; 90-655, § 173; 90-673, § 930; 90-790, § 20; 91-357, § 261.)

Note.

This section was Ill.Rev.Stat., Ch. 40, para. 2520.

Effect of Amendments.

The 1994 amendment by P.A. 88-670, effective December 2, 1994, combined the amendments by P.A. 88-26, P.A. 88-45, P.A. 88-94, P.A. 88-131 and P.A. 88-307.

The 1996 amendment by P.A. 89-507, effective July 1, 1997, in subdivision (A)(8) substituted "Human Services" for "Mental Health and Developmental Disabilities".

The 1997 amendment by P.A. 90-18, effective July 1, 1997, rewrote this section.

The 1998 amendment by P.A. 90-655, effective July 30, 1998, incorporated the amendments made by P.A. 90-18 and P.A. 90-425; substituted the present subdivision (B)(9) designation for the former subdivision (B)(4) designation, and in present subdivision (B)(9) twice substituted "income withholding notice" for "order for withholding" and once in subdivision (E)(1); in subdivision (D)(4) deleted "regular or facsimile regular or facsimile" following "subsection (F)." at the end.

The 1998 amendment by P.A. 90-673, effective January 1, 1999, incorporated the amendments by P.A. 90-18 and P.A. 90-425; and rewrote this section.

The 1998 amendment by P.A. 90-790, effective August 14, 1998, added subdivision (A)(2.5); in subdivision (B), added (3)(a-5) and (k), inserted "A copy of the income withholding notice together with" in (7) and the last sentence in (8) and substituted "income withholding notice" for "order for withholding" twice in (9); substituted "income withholding notice" for "order for withholding" in the first paragraph of subdivision (E)(1); deleted "a computation of" and "period and" in subdivision (C)(1)(b); deleted "regular or facsimile regular or facsimile" at the end of subdivision (D)(4); and deleted "or who has been served with a notice of delinquency" from subdivision (G)(4).

The 1999 amendment by P.A. 91-357, effective July 29, 1999, combined the amendments by P.A. 90-655, P.A. 90-673 and P.A. 90-790.

CASE NOTES

ANALYSIS

Mandatory Income Withholding
—Constitutionality
—Court Order
Specific Delinquency Amount
—Constitutionality

Mandatory Income Withholding

—Constitutionality

The mandatory income withholding procedures contained in this Act do not violate the federal and state constitutional provisions for separation of powers. People ex rel. Sheppard v. Money, 124 Ill. 2d 265, 124 Ill. Dec. 561, 529 N.E.2d 542 (1988).

—Court Order

Court's order for withholding, showing the name and address of defendant's current employer, rather than making the order applicable to "any payor," as requested by plaintiff, was improper. Parks ex rel. Parks v. Romans, 187 Ill. App. 3d 445, 135 Ill. Dec. 42, 543 N.E.2d 277 (1 Dist. 1989).

Specific Delinquency Amount

—Constitutionality

Subsection (B)(3) of this section, which requires the delinquency amount be specified when the withholding order is entered, does not interfere with the trial court's prerogative in entering orders. People ex rel. Massey v. Jones, 233 Ill. App. 3d 411, 174 Ill. Dec. 502, 599 N.E.2d 48 (4 Dist. 1992).

LEGAL PERIODICALS

For case note, "Illinois ex rel. Sheppard v. Money: Income Withholding Provision of the Illinois Parentage Act of 1984 Expedites Child Support Enforcement At Employers' Expense," see 23 J. Marshall L. Rev. 285 (1990).

750 ILCS 45/20.5 Information concerning obligors

Sec. 20.5. *Information concerning obligors.* (a) In this Section:

"Arrearage", "delinquency", "obligor", and "order for support" have the meanings attributed to those terms in the Income Withholding for Support Act [750 ILCS 28/1 et seq.].

"Consumer reporting agency" has the meaning attributed to that term in Section 603(f) of the Fair Credit Reporting Act, 15 U.S.C. 1681a(f).

(b) Whenever a court of competent jurisdiction finds that an obligor either owes an arrearage of more than $10,000 or is delinquent in payment of an amount equal to at least 3 months' support obligation pursuant to an order for support, the court shall direct the clerk of the court to make information concerning the obligor available to consumer reporting agencies.

(c) Whenever a court of competent jurisdiction finds that an obligor either owes an arrearage of more than $10,000 or is delinquent in payment of an amount equal to at least 3 months' support obligation pursuant to an order for support, the court shall direct the clerk of the court to cause the obligor's name and address to be published in a newspaper of general circulation in the area in which the obligor resides. The clerk shall cause the obligor's name and address to be published only after sending to the obligor at the obligor's last known address, by certified mail, return receipt requested, a notice of intent to publish the information. This subsection (c) applies only if the obligor resides in the county in which the clerk of the court holds office.
(Source: P.A. 90-466, § 25; 90-673, § 930.)

Effective Date.

This section became effective January 1, 1998 pursuant to Ill. Const. (1970), Art. IV, § 10 and 5 ILCS 75/1.

Effect of Amendments.

The 1998 amendment by P.A. 90-673, effective January 1, 1999, incorporated the amendment by P.A. 90-466; and substituted "the Income Withholding for Support Act" for "Section 20 of this Act" in subsection (a).

750 ILCS 45/20.7 Interest on support obligations

Sec. 20.7. *Interest on support obligations.* A support obligation, or any portion of a support obligation, which becomes due and remains unpaid for 30

days or more shall accrue simple interest at the rate of 9% per annum. An order for support entered or modified on or after January 1, 2002 shall contain a statement that a support obligation required under the order, or any portion of a support obligation required under the order, that becomes due and remains unpaid for 30 days or more shall accrue simple interest at the rate of 9% per annum. Failure to include the statement in the order for support does not affect the validity of the order or the accrual of interest as provided in this Section.
(Source: P.A. 91-397, § 20; 92-374, § 20.)

Effective Date.

This section became effective January 1, 2000, pursuant to Ill. Const. (1970), Art. IV, § 10 and 5 ILCS 75/1.

Effect of Amendments.

The 2001 amendment by P.A. 92-374, effective August 15, 2001, inserted "simple" preceding "interest" in the first sentence and added the second and third sentences.

750 ILCS 45/21 Support payments; receiving and disbursing agents

Sec. 21. *Support payments; receiving and disbursing agents.* (1) In an action filed in a county of less than 3 million population in which an order for child support is entered, and in supplementary proceedings in such a county to enforce or vary the terms of such order arising out of an action filed in such a county, the court, except in actions or supplementary proceedings in which the pregnancy and delivery expenses of the mother or the child support payments are for a recipient of aid under the Illinois Public Aid Code [305 ILCS 5/1-1 et seq.], shall direct that child support payments be made to the clerk of the court unless in the discretion of the court exceptional circumstances warrant otherwise. In cases where payment is to be made to persons other than the clerk of the court the judgment or order of support shall set forth the facts of the exceptional circumstances.

(2) In an action filed in a county of 3 million or more population in which an order for child support is entered, and in supplementary proceedings in such a county to enforce or vary the terms of such order arising out of an action filed in such a county, the court, except in actions or supplementary proceedings in which the pregnancy and delivery expenses of the mother or the child support payments are for a recipient of aid under the Illinois Public Aid Code [305 ILCS 5/1-1 et seq.], shall direct that child support payments be made either to the clerk of the court or to the Court Service Division of the County Department of Public Aid, or to the clerk of the court or to the Illinois Department of Public Aid, unless in the discretion of the court exceptional circumstances warrant otherwise. In cases where payment is to be made to persons other than the clerk of the court, the Court Service Division of the County Department of Public Aid, or the Illinois Department of Public Aid, the judgment or order of support shall set forth the facts of the exceptional circumstances.

(3) Where the action or supplementary proceeding is in behalf of a mother for pregnancy and delivery expenses or for child support, or both, and the mother, child, or both, are recipients of aid under the Illinois Public Aid Code [305 ILCS 5/1-1 et seq.], the court shall order that the payments be made directly to (a) the Illinois Department of Public Aid if the mother or child, or both, are recipients under Articles IV or V of the Code [305 ILCS 5/4-0.5 et seq. or 305 ILCS 5/5-1 et seq.], or (b) the local governmental unit responsible for the support of the mother or child, or both, if they are recipients under Articles VI [305 ILCS 5/6-1 et seq.] or VII of the Code [repealed]. In accordance with federal law and regulations, the Illinois Department of Public Aid may continue to collect current maintenance payments or child support payments, or both, after those persons cease to receive public assistance and until termination of services under Article X of the Illinois Public Aid Code [305 ILCS 5/10-1 et seq.]. The Illinois Department of Public Aid shall pay the net amount collected to those persons after deducting any costs incurred in making the collection or any collection fee from the amount of any recovery made. The Illinois Department of Public Aid or the local governmental unit, as the case may be, may direct that payments be made directly to the mother of the child, or to some other person or agency in the child's behalf, upon the removal of the mother and child from the public aid rolls or upon termination of services under Article X of the Illinois Public Aid Code [305 ILCS 5/10-1 et seq.]; and upon such direction, the Illinois Department or the local governmental unit, as the case requires, shall give notice of such action to the court in writing or by electronic transmission.

(4) All clerks of the court and the Court Service Division of a County Department of Public Aid and the Illinois Department of Public Aid, receiving child support payments under paragraphs (1) or (2) shall disburse the same to the person or persons entitled thereto under the terms of the order. They shall establish and maintain clear and current records of all moneys received and disbursed and of defaults and delinquencies in required payments. The court, by order or rule, shall make provision for the carrying out of these duties.

Upon notification in writing or by electronic transmission from the Illinois Department of Public Aid to the clerk of the court that a person who is receiving support payments under this Section is receiving services under the Child Support Enforcement Program established by Title IV-D of the Social Security Act [42 U.S.C. § 651 et seq.], any support payments subsequently received by the clerk of the court shall be transmitted in accordance with the instructions of the Illinois Department of Public Aid until the Department gives notice to cease the transmittal. After providing the notification authorized under this paragraph, the Illinois Department of Public Aid shall be entitled as a party to notice of any further proceedings in the case. The clerk of the court shall file a copy of the Illinois Department of Public Aid's notification in the court file. The failure of the clerk to file a copy of the notification in the court file shall not, however, affect the Illinois Department of Public Aid's right to receive notice of further proceedings.

Payments under this Section to the Illinois Department of Public Aid pursuant to the Child Support Enforcement Program established by Title IV-D of the Social Security Act [42 U.S.C. § 651 et seq.] shall be paid into the Child Support Enforcement Trust Fund. All payments under this Section to the Illinois Department of Human Services shall be deposited in the DHS Recoveries Trust Fund. Disbursement from these funds shall be as provided in the Illinois Public Aid Code [305 ILCS 5/1-1 et seq.]. Payments received by a local governmental unit shall be deposited in that unit's General Assistance Fund.

(5) The moneys received by persons or agencies designated by the court shall be disbursed by them in accordance with the order. However, the court, on petition of the state's attorney, may enter new orders designating the clerk of the court or the Illinois Department of Public Aid, as the person or agency authorized to receive and disburse child support payments and, in the case of recipients of public aid, the court, on petition of the Attorney General or State's Attorney, shall direct subsequent payments to be paid to the Illinois Department of Public Aid or to the appropriate local governmental unit, as provided in paragraph (3). Payments of child support by principals or sureties on bonds, or proceeds of any sale for the enforcement of a judgment shall be made to the clerk of the court, the Illinois Department of Public Aid or the appropriate local governmental unit, as the respective provisions of this Section require.

(6) For those cases in which child support is payable to the clerk of the circuit court for transmittal to the Illinois Department of Public Aid by order of court or upon notification by the Illinois Department of Public Aid, the clerk shall transmit all such payments, within 4 working days of receipt, to insure that funds are available for immediate distribution by the Department to the person or entity entitled thereto in accordance with standards of the Child Support Enforcement Program established under Title IV-D of the Social Security Act [42 U.S.C. § 651 et seq.]. The clerk shall notify the Department of the date of receipt and amount thereof at the time of transmittal. Where the clerk has entered into an agreement of cooperation with the Department to record the terms of child support orders and payments made thereunder directly into the Department's automated data processing system, the clerk shall account for, transmit and otherwise distribute child support payments in accordance with such agreement in lieu of the requirements contained herein.

(7) To the extent the provisions of this Section are inconsistent with the requirements pertaining to the State Disbursement Unit under Section 21.1 of this Act [750 ILCS 45/21.1] and Section 10-26 of the Illinois Public Aid Code [305 ILCS 5/10-26], the requirements pertaining to the State Disbursement Unit shall apply.

(Source: P.A. 86-1184; 88-687, § 20; 90-18, § 120; 90-673, § 930; 90-790, § 20; 91-24, § 40; 91-212, § 40; 91-357, § 261; 92-16, § 98.)

Note.

This section was Ill.Rev.Stat., Ch. 40, para. 2521.

Article VII of the Public Aid Code, referred to in subsection (3), has been repealed.

Section 996 of P.A. 92-16 contains a "no acceleration or delay" provision, and Section 997 contains a "no revival or extension" provision.

Effect of Amendments.

The 1994 amendment by P.A. 88-687, effective January 24, 1995, added the section catchline; in subsection (1), in the first sentence, substituted "Illinois Public Aid Code" for "'Illinois Public Aid Code', approved April 11, 1967, as amended"; in subsection (3), substituted the present second and third sentences for the former second and third sentences on the same subject matter and in the fourth sentence deleted "subsequent" preceding "payments" substituted "services under Article X of the Illinois Public Aid Code" for "any extended collection period", deleted "written" preceding "notice" and added "in writing or by electronic transmission" at the end; in subsection (4), in the second paragraph, in the first sentence, substituted "or by electronic transmission from" for "by", inserted "to the clerk of the court", substituted "receiving services under the Child Support Enforcement Program established by Title IV-D of the Social Security Act" for "a public aid recipient", substituted "in accordance with the instructions of" for "to" and substituted "the transmittal" for "such transmittal" and added the second through fourth sentences; and in subsection (6), in the first sentence, inserted "or upon notification by the Illinois Department of Public Aid".

The 1997 amendment by P.A. 90-18, effective July 1, 1997, in subsection (4) added the second paragraph.

The 1998 amendment by P.A. 90-673, effective January 1, 1999, incorporated the amendment by P.A. 90-18; and substituted "in accordance with the Income Withholding for Support Act" for "under Section 20 of this Act" in the second paragraph of subsection (4).

The 1998 amendment by P.A. 90-790, effective August 14, 1998, deleted the former second paragraph from subsection (4), relating to orders for support issued pursuant to Article X of the Illinois Public Aid Code.

The 1999 amendment by P.A. 91-24, effective July 1, 1999, incorporated the amendments by P.A. 90-673 and P.A. 90-790; substituted "a county" for "counties" throughout the section; deleted "date" following "filed" in the first sentence of subsection (2); and in subsection (4), deleted "in accordance with the Income Withholding for Support" following the first paragraph, and in the second sentence of the last paragraph, deleted "other" following "All", and substituted "Human Services" for "Public Aid" and "DHS" for "Public Assistance".

The 1999 amendment by P.A. 91-212, effective July 20, 1999, substituted "a county" for "counties" throughout subsections (1) and (2); deleted "date" following "of an action filed" in subsection (2); deleted "in accordance with the Income Withholding for Support" at the end of the first paragraph in subsection (4); and added subsection (7).

The 1999 amendment by P.A. 91-357, effective July 29, 1999, substituted "a county" for "counties" throughout subsections (1) and (2); deleted "date" following "of an action filed" in subsection (2); and deleted "in accordance with the Income Withholding for Support" in subsection (4).

The 2001 amendment by P.A. 92-16, effective June 28, 2001, combined the amendments by P.A. 91-24, P.A. 91-212 and P.A. 91-357.

750 ILCS 45/21.1 Payment of Support to State Disbursement Unit

Sec. 21.1. *Payment of Support to State Disbursement Unit.* (a) As used in this Section:

"Order for support", "obligor", "obligee", and "payor" mean those terms as defined in the Income Withholding for Support Act [750 ILCS 28/1 et seq.], except that "order for support" shall not mean orders providing for spousal maintenance under which there is no child support obligation.

(b) Notwithstanding any other provision of this Act to the contrary, each order for support entered or modified on or after October 1, 1999 shall require that support payments be made to the State Disbursement Unit established under Section 10-26 of the Illinois Public Aid Code [305 ILCS 10-26] if:

(1) a party to the order is receiving child support enforcement services under Article X of the Illinois Public Aid Code [305 ILCS 5/10-1 et seq.]; or

(2) no party to the order is receiving child support enforcement services, but the support payments are made through income withholding.

(c) Support payments shall be made to the State Disbursement Unit if:

(1) the order for support was entered before October 1, 1999, and a party to the order is receiving child support enforcement services under Article X of the Illinois Public Aid Code [305 ILCS 5/10-1 et seq.]; or

(2) no party to the order is receiving child support enforcement services, and the support payments are being made through income withholding.

(c-5) If no party to the order is receiving child support enforcement services under Article X of the Illinois Public Aid Code [305 ILCS 5/10-1 et seq.], and the support payments are not made through income withholding, then support payments shall be made as directed by the order for support.

(c-10) At any time, and notwithstanding the existence of an order directing payments to be made elsewhere, the Department of Public Aid may provide notice to the obligor and, where applicable, to the obligor's payor:

(1) to make support payments to the State Disbursement Unit if:

(A) a party to the order for support is receiving child support enforcement services under Article X of the Illinois Public Aid Code [305 ILCS 5/10-1 et seq]; or

(B) no party to the order for support is receiving child support enforcement services under Article X of the Illinois Public Aid Code [305 ILCS 5/10-1 et seq.], but the support payments are made through income withholding; or

(2) to make support payments to the State Disbursement Unit of another state upon request of another state's Title IV-D child support enforcement agency, in accordance with the requirements of Title IV, Part D of the Social Security Act [42 U.S.C. § 601 et seq.] and regulations promulgated under that Part D.

The Department of Public Aid shall provide a copy of the notice to the obligee and to the clerk of the circuit court.

(c-15) Within 15 days after the effective date of this amendatory Act of the 91st General Assembly [P.A. 91-677], the clerk of the circuit court shall provide written notice to the obligor to directly to the clerk of the circuit court if no party to the order is receiving child support enforcement services under Article X of the Illinois Public Aid Code [305 ILCS 5/10-1 et seq.], the support payments are not made through income withholding, and the order for support requires support payments to be made directly to the clerk of the circuit court. The clerk shall provide a copy of the notice to the obligee.

(c-20) If the State Disbursement Unit receives a support payment that was not appropriately made to the Unit under this Section, the Unit shall immediately return the payment to the sender, including, if possible, instructions detailing where to send the support payments.

(d) The notices under subsections (c-10) and (c-15) may be sent by ordinary mail, certified mail, return receipt requested, facsimile transmission, or other electronic process, or may be served upon the obligor or payor using any method provided by law for service of a summons.

(Source: P.A. 91-212, § 40; 91-677, § 25; 92-590, § 30.)

Illinois Administrative Code.

See 89 Illinois Administrative Code, § 160.60.

Effective Date.

Section 999 of P.A. 91-212 made this section effective upon becoming law. The Act was approved July 20, 1999.

Effect of Amendments.

The 1999 amendment by P.A. 91-677, effective January 5, 2000, in subsection (a) inserted "except that 'order for support' shall not mean orders providing for spousal maintenance under which there is no child support obligation"; in subsection (c) deleted "The Illinois Department of Public Aid shall provide notice to the obligor and, where applicable, to the obligor's payor to make" and inserted "shall be made"; in subsection (c)(2) deleted "the order for support was entered after January 1, 1994"; added subsections (c-5), (c-10), (c-15) and (c-20); and in subsection (d) substituted "subsections (c-10) and (c-15)" for "subsection (c)" and made stylistic changes.

The 2002 amendment by P.A. 92-590, effective July 1, 2002, substituted "child support enforcement services" for "child and spouse support services" throughout; rewrote subsection (c-10) to the extent that a detailed comparison would be impracticable; added the last sentence to subsection (c-15); and deleted the former last sentence in subsection (d), which read: "The Illinois Department of Public Aid shall provide a copy of the notice to the obligee and to the clerk of the court".

750 ILCS 45/22 [Collection fee]

Sec. 22. In all cases instituted by the Illinois Department of Public Aid on behalf of a child or spouse, other than one receiving a grant of financial aid under Article IV of The Illinois Public Aid Code

[305 ILCS 5/4-1 et seq.], on whose behalf an application has been made and approved for child support enforcement services as provided by Section 10-1 of that Code [305 ILCS 5/10-1], the court shall impose a collection fee on the individual who owes a child or spouse support obligation in an amount equal to 10% of the amount so owed as long as such collection is required by federal law, which fee shall be in addition to the support obligation. The imposition of such fee shall be in accordance with provisions of Title IV, Part D, of the Social Security Act [42 U.S.C. § 651 et seq.] and regulations duly promulgated thereunder. The fee shall be payable to the clerk of the circuit court for transmittal to the Illinois Department of Public Aid and shall continue until support services are terminated by that Department.
(Source: P.A. 83-1372; 92-590, § 30.)

Note.
This section was Ill.Rev.Stat., Ch. 40, para. 2522.

Effect of Amendments.
The 2002 amendment by P.A. 92-590, effective July 1, 2002, substituted "child support enforcement services" for "support services" in the first sentence.

750 ILCS 45/23 Notice to Clerk of Circuit Court of Payment Received by Illinois Department of Public Aid for Recording

Sec. 23. *Notice to Clerk of Circuit Court of Payment Received by Illinois Department of Public Aid for Recording.* For those cases in which support is payable to the clerk of the circuit court for transmittal to the Illinois Department of Public Aid by order of court, and the Illinois Department of Public Aid collects support by assignment offset, withhold, deduction or other process permitted by law, the Illinois Department of Public Aid shall notify the clerk of the date and amount of such collection. Upon notification, the clerk shall record the collection on the payment record for the case.
(Source: P.A. 83-1372.)

Note.
This section was Ill.Rev.Stat., Ch. 40, para. 2523.

750 ILCS 45/25 [Repeal of Paternity Act; effect]

Sec. 25. Except as provided in Section 8 of this Act, the repeal of the "Paternity Act" [750 ILCS 45/8], approved July 5, 1957, as amended, shall not affect rights or liabilities which have accrued thereunder and which have been determined, settled or adjudicated prior to the effective date of this Act or which are the subject of proceedings pending thereunder on such effective date. Provided further, this Act shall not be construed to bar an action which would have been barred because the action had not been filed within the then applicable time limitation, or which could not have been maintained under the "Paternity Act," approved July 5, 1957 and repealed hereunder, as long as the limitations periods set forth in Section 8 of this Act [750 ILCS 45/8] are complied with.
(Source: P.A. 83-1372.)

Note.
This section was Ill.Rev.Stat., Ch. 40, para. 2525.

CASE NOTES

Analysis

Legislative Intent
Parties
—Putative Fathers
Prior Proceedings
Retroactive Support
—Effect of Parentage Act
Rights and Liabilities
—Effect of Parentage Act

Legislative Intent
This section clearly expresses an intent on the part of the legislature that the new limitations period for the filing of a paternity action would be retroactively applied and could revive an action which had been previously barred; because the former two year statute of limitations was found to be unconstitutional, it is void ab initio and confers no rights, imposes no duties, and affords no protections. Department of Public Aid ex rel. Evans v. Lively, 246 Ill. App. 3d 216, 186 Ill. Dec. 324, 615 N.E.2d 1381 (5 Dist. 1993).

The savings provision of this Act reinforces the conclusion that the legislature intended to: (1) allow persons to bring actions to establish paternity who were not previously allowed to do so under the old Paternity Act, and (2) extend the statutory limitations period for causes of action brought by or on behalf of the child. Klawitter v. Crawford, 185 Ill. App. 3d 778, 133 Ill. Dec. 721, 541 N.E.2d 1159 (1 Dist. 1989).

The legislature intended a retroactive application of the statute of limitations. In re Ingram, 176 Ill. App. 3d 413, 125 Ill. Dec. 918, 531 N.E.2d 97 (5 Dist. 1988).

Parties

—Putative Fathers
This Act established that putative fathers were no longer barred—as they were under the Paternity Act of 1958—from bringing suit to determine the parent-child relationship as long as they met the statutory requirements, and statute of limitations contained in this Act. Klawitter v. Crawford, 185 Ill. App. 3d 778, 133 Ill. Dec. 721, 541 N.E.2d 1159 (1 Dist. 1989).

Prior Proceedings
Dismissal of the mother's paternity suit under the former Paternity Act had no effect on the right of the child to bring an action under this Act. Chiapelli ex rel. Ashton v. Viviano, 225 Ill. App. 3d 1026, 168 Ill. Dec. 84, 589 N.E.2d 198 (5 Dist. 1992).

Retroactive Support

—Effect of Parentage Act
The concept of retroactive support was new to this Act in 1984, and such a provision cannot be implied into the earlier Paternity Act of 1957; thus, where child was born prior to the effective date of this Act, an order imposing retroactive liability for support would be vacated. People ex rel. Causley v. Jackson, 171 Ill. App. 3d 464, 122 Ill. Dec. 644, 527 N.E.2d 16 (4 Dist. 1988).

Rights and Liabilities

—Effect of Parentage Act
This Act provides that the repeal of the Paternity Act shall not affect rights or liabilities which were determined, settled or adjudicated prior to the effective date of the Parentage Act. Illinois Dep't of Pub. Aid ex rel. Spurgetis v. Newburg, 181 Ill. App. 3d 424, 130 Ill. Dec. 317, 537 N.E.2d 384 (3 Dist. 1989).

Rights and Liabilities (Cont'd)

—Effect of Parentage Act (Cont'd)

This Act excepts rights and liabilities which accrued under the former Paternity Act of 1957, or which were the subject of proceedings on the effective date of the new Act, which proceedings are to be governed by the Paternity Act of 1957. People ex rel. Causley v. Jackson, 171 Ill. App. 3d 464, 122 Ill. Dec. 644, 527 N.E.2d 16 (4 Dist. 1988).

The rights and liabilities of the father of an illegitimate child are to be determined by the statute in effect at the time of the child's birth. People ex rel. Causley v. Jackson, 171 Ill. App. 3d 464, 122 Ill. Dec. 644, 527 N.E.2d 16 (4 Dist. 1988).

750 ILCS 45/26 [Severability]

Sec. 26. If any provision of this Act or the application thereof to any person or circumstance is held invalid, the invalidity does not affect other provisions or applications of the Act which can be given effect without the invalid provision or application, and to this end the provisions of this Act are severable.
(Source: P.A. 83-1372.)

Note.

This section was Ill.Rev.Stat., Ch. 40, para. 2526.

750 ILCS 45/27 Other states' establishments of paternity

Sec. 27. *Other states' establishments of paternity.* Establishments of paternity made under the laws of other states shall be given full faith and credit in this State regardless of whether paternity was established through voluntary acknowledgment, tests to determine inherited characteristics, or judicial or administrative processes.
(Source: P.A. 90-18, § 120.)

Effective Date.

Section 999 of P.A. 90-18 made this section effective July 1, 1997.

CASE NOTES

Full Faith and Credit

When a child was born in California and the California statutes in effect at the time the child was born did not require that an alleged father sign a declaration of paternity to be named on the child's birth certificate, the fact that a person was so named did not require an Illinois court to find that person to be the child's father, under its obligation to give another state's establishment of paternity full faith and credit, or preclude the trial court from finding that another person was the child's father. People ex rel. Shockley v. Hoyle, 338 Ill. App. 3d 1046, 273 Ill. Dec. 850, 789 N.E.2d 1282, 2003 Ill. App. LEXIS 687 (2 Dist. 2003).

GESTATIONAL SURROGACY ACT

750 ILCS 47/1 Short title

Sec. 1. *Short title.* This Act may be cited as the Gestational Surrogacy Act.
(Source: P.A. 93-921, § 1.)

Effective Date.

This Act is effective January 1, 2005, pursuant to Ill. Const. (1970) Art. IV, § 10 and 5 ILCS 75/1.

750 ILCS 47/5 Purpose

Sec. 5. *Purpose.* The purpose of this Act is to establish consistent standards and procedural safeguards for the protection of all parties involved in a gestational surrogacy contract in this State and to confirm the legal status of children born as a result of these contracts. These standards and safeguards are meant to facilitate the use of this type of reproductive contract in accord with the public policy of this State.
(Source: P.A. 93-921, § 5.)

750 ILCS 47/10 Definitions

Sec. 10. *Definitions.* As used in this Act:

"Compensation" means payment of any valuable consideration for services in excess of reasonable medical and ancillary costs.

"Donor" means an individual who contributes a gamete or gametes for the purpose of in vitro fertilization or implantation in another.

"Gamete" means either a sperm or an egg.

"Gestational surrogacy" means the process by which a woman attempts to carry and give birth to a child created through in vitro fertilization using the gamete or gametes of at least one of the intended parents and to which the gestational surrogate has made no genetic contribution.

"Gestational surrogate" means a woman who agrees to engage in a gestational surrogacy.

"Gestational surrogacy contract" means a written agreement regarding gestational surrogacy.

"Health care provider" means a person who is duly licensed to provide health care, including all medical, psychological, or counseling professionals.

"Intended parent" means a person or persons who enters into a gestational surrogacy contract with a gestational surrogate pursuant to which he or she will be the legal parent of the resulting child. In the case of a married couple, any reference to an intended parent shall include both husband and wife for all purposes of this Act. This term shall include the intended mother, intended father, or both.

"In vitro fertilization" means all medical and laboratory procedures that are necessary to effectuate the extracorporeal fertilization of egg and sperm.

"Medical evaluation" means an evaluation and consultation of a physician meeting the requirements of Section 60.

"Mental health evaluation" means an evaluation and consultation of a mental health professional meeting the requirements of Section 60.

"Physician" means a person licensed to practice medicine in all its branches in Illinois.

"Pre-embryo" means a fertilized egg prior to 14 days of development.

"Pre-embryo transfer" means all medical and laboratory procedures that are necessary to effectuate the transfer of a pre-embryo into the uterine cavity.
(Source: P.A. 93-921, § 10.)

750 ILCS 47/15 Rights of parentage

Sec. 15. *Rights of parentage.* (a) Except as provided in this Act, the woman who gives birth to a child is presumed to be the mother of that child for purposes of State law.

(b) In the case of a gestational surrogacy satisfying the requirements set forth in subsection (d) of this Section:

(1) the intended mother shall be the mother of the child for purposes of State law immediately upon the birth of the child;

(2) the intended father shall be the father of the child for purposes of State law immediately upon the birth of the child;

(3) the child shall be considered the legitimate child of the intended parent or parents for purposes of State law immediately upon the birth of the child;

(4) parental rights shall vest in the intended parent or parents immediately upon the birth of the child;

(5) sole custody of the child shall rest with the intended parent or parents immediately upon the birth of the child; and

(6) neither the gestational surrogate nor her husband, if any, shall be the parents of the child for purposes of State law immediately upon the birth of the child.

(c) In the case of a gestational surrogacy meeting the requirements set forth in subsection (d) of this Section, in the event of a laboratory error in which the resulting child is not genetically related to either of the intended parents, the intended parents will be the parents of the child for purposes of State law unless otherwise determined by a court of competent jurisdiction.

(d) The parties to a gestational surrogacy shall assume the rights and obligations of subsections (b) and (c) of this Section if:

(1) the gestational surrogate satisfies the eligibility requirements set forth in subsection (a) of Section 20 [750 ILCS 47/20];

(2) the intended parent or parents satisfy the eligibility requirements set forth in subsection (b) of Section 20 [750 ILCS 47/20]; and

(3) the gestational surrogacy occurs pursuant to a gestational surrogacy contract meeting the requirements set forth in Section 25 [750 ILCS 47/25].

(Source: P.A. 93-921, § 15.)

750 ILCS 47/20 Eligibility

Sec. 20. *Eligibility.* (a) A gestational surrogate shall be deemed to have satisfied the requirements of this Act if she has met the following requirements at the time the gestational surrogacy contract is executed:

(1) she is at least 21 years of age;

(2) she has given birth to at least one child;

(3) she has completed a medical evaluation;

(4) she has completed a mental health evaluation;

(5) she has undergone legal consultation with independent legal counsel regarding the terms of the gestational surrogacy contract and the potential legal consequences of the gestational surrogacy; and

(6) she has obtained a health insurance policy that covers major medical treatments and hospitalization and the health insurance policy has a term that extends throughout the duration of the expected pregnancy and for 8 weeks after the birth of the child; provided, however, that the policy may be procured by the intended parents on behalf of the gestational surrogate pursuant to the gestational surrogacy contract.

(b) The intended parent or parents shall be deemed to have satisfied the requirements of this Act if he, she, or they have met the following requirements at the time the gestational surrogacy contract is executed:

(1) he, she, or they contribute at least one of the gametes resulting in a pre-embryo that the gestational surrogate will attempt to carry to term;

(2) he, she, or they have a medical need for the gestational surrogacy as evidenced by a qualified physician's affidavit attached to the gestational surrogacy contract and as required by the Illinois Parentage Act of 1984 [750 ILCS 45/1 et seq.];

(3) he, she, or they have completed a mental health evaluation; and

(4) he, she, or they have undergone legal consultation with independent legal counsel regarding the terms of the gestational surrogacy contract and the potential legal consequences of the gestational surrogacy.

(Source: P.A. 93-921, § 20.)

750 ILCS 47/25 Requirements for a gestational surrogacy contract

Sec. 25. *Requirements for a gestational surrogacy contract.* (a) A gestational surrogacy contract shall be presumed enforceable for purposes of State law only if:

(1) it meets the contractual requirements set forth in subsection (b) of this Section; and

(2) it contains at a minimum each of the terms set forth in subsection (c) of this Section.

(b) A gestational surrogacy contract shall meet the following requirements:

(1) it shall be in writing;

(2) it shall be executed prior to the commencement of any medical procedures (other than medical or mental health evaluations necessary to determine eligibility of the parties pursuant to Section 20 of this Act [750 ILCS 47/20]) in furtherance of the gestational surrogacy:

(i) by a gestational surrogate meeting the eligibility requirements of subsection (a) of Section 20 of this Act [750 ILCS 47/20] and, if married, the gestational surrogate's husband; and

(ii) by the intended parent or parents meeting the eligibility requirements of subsection (b) of Section

20 of this Act [750 ILCS 47/20]. In the event an intended parent is married, both husband and wife must execute the gestational surrogacy contract;

(3) each of the gestational surrogate and the intended parent or parents shall have been represented by separate counsel in all matters concerning the gestational surrogacy and the gestational surrogacy contract;

(3.5) each of the gestational surrogate and the intended parent or parents shall have signed a written acknowledgement that he or she received information about the legal, financial, and contractual rights, expectations, penalties, and obligations of the surrogacy agreement;

(4) if the gestational surrogacy contract provides for the payment of compensation to the gestational surrogate, the compensation shall have been placed in escrow with an independent escrow agent prior to the gestational surrogate's commencement of any medical procedure (other than medical or mental health evaluations necessary to determine the gestational surrogate's eligibility pursuant to subsection (a) of Section 20 of this Act [750 ILCS 47/20]); and

(5) it shall be witnessed by 2 competent adults.

(c) A gestational surrogacy contract shall provide for:

(1) the express written agreement of the gestational surrogate to:

(i) undergo pre-embryo transfer and attempt to carry and give birth to the child; and

(ii) surrender custody of the child to the intended parent or parents immediately upon the birth of the child;

(2) if the gestational surrogate is married, the express agreement of her husband to:

(i) undertake the obligations imposed on the gestational surrogate pursuant to the terms of the gestational surrogacy contract;

(ii) surrender custody of the child to the intended parent or parents immediately upon the birth of the child;

(3) the right of the gestational surrogate to utilize the services of a physician of her choosing, after consultation with the intended parents, to provide her care during the pregnancy; and

(4) the express written agreement of the intended parent or parents to:

(i) accept custody of the child immediately upon his or her birth; and

(ii) assume sole responsibility for the support of the child immediately upon his or her birth.

(d) A gestational surrogacy contract shall be presumed enforceable for purposes of State law even though it contains one or more of the following provisions:

(1) the gestational surrogate's agreement to undergo all medical exams, treatments, and fetal monitoring procedures that the physician recommended for the success of the pregnancy;

(2) the gestational surrogate's agreement to abstain from any activities that the intended parent or parents or the physician reasonably believes to be harmful to the pregnancy and future health of the child, including, without limitation, smoking, drinking alcohol, using nonprescribed drugs, using prescription drugs not authorized by a physician aware of the gestational surrogate's pregnancy, exposure to radiation, or any other activities proscribed by a health care provider;

(3) the agreement of the intended parent or parents to pay the gestational surrogate reasonable compensation; and

(4) the agreement of the intended parent or parents to pay for or reimburse the gestational surrogate for reasonable expenses (including, without limitation, medical, legal, or other professional expenses) related to the gestational surrogacy and the gestational surrogacy contract.

(e) In the event that any of the requirements of this Section are not met, a court of competent jurisdiction shall determine parentage based on evidence of the parties' intent.

(Source: P.A. 93-921, § 25.)

750 ILCS 47/30 Duty to support

Sec. 30. *Duty to support.* (a) Any person who is considered to be the parent of a child pursuant to Section 15 of this Act [750 ILCS 47/15] shall be obligated to support the child.

(b) The breach of the gestational surrogacy contract by the intended parent or parents shall not relieve such intended parent or parents of the support obligations imposed by this Act.

(c) A gamete donor may be liable for child support only if he or she fails to enter into a legal agreement with the intended parent or parents in which the intended parent or parents agree to assume all rights and responsibilities for any resulting child, and the gamete donor relinquishes his or her rights to any gametes, resulting embryos, or children.

(Source: P.A. 93-921, § 30.)

750 ILCS 47/35 Establishment of the parent-child relationship

Sec. 35. *Establishment of the parent-child relationship.* (a) For purposes of the Illinois Parentage Act of 1984, a parent-child relationship shall be established prior to the birth of a child born through gestational surrogacy if, in addition to satisfying the requirements of Sections 5 and 6 of the Illinois Parentage Act of 1984 [750 ILCS 45/5 and 750 ILCS 45/6], the attorneys representing both the gestational surrogate and the intended parent or parents certify that the parties entered into a gestational surrogacy contract intended to satisfy the requirements of Section 25 of this Act [750 ILCS 47/25] with respect to the child.

(b) The attorneys' certifications required by subsection (a) of this Section shall be filed on forms prescribed by the Illinois Department of Public Health and in a manner consistent with the require-

ment of the Illinois Parentage Act of 1984 [750 ILCS 45/1 et seq.].
(Source: P.A. 93-921, § 35.)

750 ILCS 47/40 Immunities

Sec. 40. *Immunities.* Except as provided in this Act, no person shall be civilly or criminally liable for non-negligent actions taken pursuant to the requirements of this Act.
(Source: P.A. 93-921, § 40.)

750 ILCS 47/45 Noncompliance

Sec. 45. *Noncompliance.* Noncompliance by the gestational surrogate or the intended parent or parents occurs when that party breaches a provision of the gestational surrogacy contract.
(Source: P.A. 93-921, § 45.)

750 ILCS 47/50 Effect of Noncompliance

Sec. 50. *Effect of Noncompliance.* (a) Except as otherwise provided in this Act, in the event of noncompliance with the requirements of subsection (d) of Section 15 of this Act [750 ILCS 47/15], a court of competent jurisdiction shall determine the respective rights and obligations of the parties.

(b) There shall be no specific performance remedy available for a breach by the gestational surrogate of a gestational surrogacy contract term that requires her to be impregnated.
(Source: P.A. 93-921, § 50.)

750 ILCS 47/55 Damages

Sec. 55. *Damages.* (a) Except as expressly provided in the gestational surrogacy contract, the intended parent or parents shall be entitled to all remedies available at law or equity.

(b) Except as expressly provided in the gestational surrogacy contract, the gestational surrogate shall be entitled to all remedies available at law or equity.
(Source: P.A. 93-921, § 55.)

750 ILCS 47/60 Rulemaking

Sec. 60. *Rulemaking.* The Department of Public Health may adopt rules pertaining to the required medical and mental health evaluations for a gestational surrogacy contract. Until the Department of Public Health adopts such rules, medical and mental health evaluations and procedures shall be conducted in accordance with the recommended guidelines published by the American Society for Reproductive Medicine and the American College of Obstetricians and Gynecologists. The rules may adopt these guidelines or others by reference.
(Source: P.A. 93-921, § 60.)

750 ILCS 47/65 Severability

Sec. 65. *Severability.* If any provision of this Act or its application to any person or circumstance is held invalid, the invalidity of that provision or application does not affect other provisions or applications of this Act that can be given effect without the invalid provision or application.
(Source: P.A. 93-921, § 65.)

750 ILCS 47/70 Irrevocability

Sec. 70. *Irrevocability.* No action to invalidate a gestational surrogacy meeting the requirements of subsection (d) of Section 15 of this Act [750 ILCS 47/15] or to challenge the rights of parentage established pursuant to Section 15 of this Act [750 ILCS 47/15] and the Illinois Parentage Act of 1984 [750 ILCS 45/1 et seq.] shall be commenced after 12 months from the date of birth of the child.
(Source: P.A. 93-921, § 70.)

750 ILCS 47/75 Application

Sec. 75. *Application.* The provisions of this Act shall apply only to gestational surrogacy contracts entered into after the effective date of this Act.
(Source: P.A. 93-921, § 75.)

750 ILCS 47/800 [Not set out]

(Source: P.A. 93-921, § 800.)

Note.
These sections, as found in P.A. 93-921, § 800, contained amendatory provisions.

ADOPTION ACT

750 ILCS 50/0.01 Short title

Sec. 0.01. *Short title.* This Act may be cited as the Adoption Act.
(Source: P.A. 86-1324.)

Derivation.
Title: An Act in relation to the adoption of persons, and to repeal an act therein named.
Cite: 750 ILCS 50/0.01 et seq.
Source: L. 1959, p. 1269.
Date: Approved July 17, 1959.

Note.
This section was Ill.Rev.Stat., Ch. 40, para. 1500.

CASE NOTES

ANALYSIS

Constitutionality
In General
Adoptive Parents
—Characteristics

Constitutionality
This Act does not violate the due process rights of minor parents, but is reasonably related to the public policy purposes sought to be protected by the legislature. Kathy O. v. Counseling & Family Servs., 107 Ill. App. 3d 920, 63 Ill. Dec. 764, 438 N.E.2d 695 (3 Dist. 1982).

In General

To acquire standing to petition for custody of a minor child under 750 ILCS 5/601(b)(2), a non-parent must show that the child is not in the physical possession of one of his or her parents and a non-parent failing to satisfy the standing requirement of 750 ILCS 5/601(b)(2) must proceed under the stricter requirements imposed by the Adoption or Juvenile Court Acts. In re Cannon, 268 Ill. App. 3d 937, 206 Ill. Dec. 343, 645 N.E.2d 348 (1 Dist. 1994).

Adoption is a question for the state, in the discharge of its duty as parens patriae, to regulate through its legislature as it seems wise; hence, judicial proceedings are not essential to the validity of statutes providing for the adoption of minors. In re Simaner, 15 Ill. 2d 568, 155 N.E.2d 555 (1959).

Adoption was unknown at common law and it is governed entirely by statute. Simaner v. Simonick, 16 Ill. App. 2d 48, 147 N.E.2d 419 (1 Dist. 1957), aff'd, 15 Ill. 2d 568, 155 N.E.2d 555 (1959).

Adoption, which changes the course of inheritance, deprives the child of the place in which it was placed by nature, and by force of law, thrusts the child into another relationship, and is a very different matter from change of custody. Hill v. Allabaugh, 333 Ill. App. 602, 78 N.E.2d 127 (2 Dist. 1948).

Adoptive Parents

—Characteristics

Because by its own terms the Act must be liberally construed; because the Act specifically allows for the singular to include the plural; because the "related child" provisions of the Act must be meaningfully interpreted; because considerations concerning the best interests of the child must be applied in construing the Act; and because nothing in the Act specifically precludes it, the Act must be construed to give standing to unmarried persons, regardless of sex or sexual orientation, to petition for adoption jointly. In re K.M., 274 Ill. App. 3d 189, 210 Ill. Dec. 693, 653 N.E.2d 888 (1 Dist. 1995).

LEGAL PERIODICALS

Student Note: Abandoned Equity and the Best Interests of the Child: Why Illinois Courts Must Recognize Same-Sex Parents Seeking Visitation, 76 Chi.-Kent. L. Rev. 1933 (2001).

For essay, "The Criminal Courtroom: Is it Child Proof?," see 26 Loy. U. Chi. L.J. 681 (1995).

For article, "It's Time to be Fair—All Adopted Children Should Have Equal Rights," see 75 Ill. B. J. 224 (1986).

RESEARCH REFERENCES

Admissibility of social worker's expert testimony on child custody issues. 1 ALR4th 837.

Marital status of prospective adopting parents as factor in adoption proceedings. 2 ALR4th 555.

Desire of child as to geographical location of residence or domicile as factor in awarding custody or terminating parental rights. 10 ALR4th 827.

Right of incarcerated mother to retain custody of infant in penal institution. 14 ALR4th 748.

Race as factor in adoption proceedings. 34 ALR4th 167.

Action for wrongful adoption based on misrepresentation of child's mental or physical condition or parentage. 56 ALR4th 375.

Adoption of child by same-sex partners. 27 ALR5th 54.

Admissibility of expert testimony regarding questions of domestic law. 66 ALR5th 135.

"Wrongful adoption" causes of action against adoption agencies where children have or develop mental or physical problems that are misrepresented or not disclosed to adoptive parents. 74 ALR5th 1.

750 ILCS 50/1 Definitions

Sec. 1. *Definitions.* When used in this Act, unless the context otherwise requires:

A. "Child" means a person under legal age subject to adoption under this Act.

B. "Related child" means a child subject to adoption where either or both of the adopting parents stands in any of the following relationships to the child by blood or marriage: parent, grand-parent, brother, sister, step-parent, step-grandparent, step-brother, step-sister, uncle, aunt, great-uncle, great-aunt, or cousin of first degree. A child whose parent has executed a final irrevocable consent to adoption or a final irrevocable surrender for purposes of adoption, or whose parent has had his or her parental rights terminated, is not a related child to that person, unless the consent is determined to be void or is void pursuant to subsection O of Section 10 [750 ILCS 50/10].

C. "Agency" for the purpose of this Act means a public child welfare agency or a licensed child welfare agency.

D. "Unfit person" means any person whom the court shall find to be unfit to have a child, without regard to the likelihood that the child will be placed for adoption. The grounds of unfitness are any one or more of the following, except that a person shall not be considered an unfit person for the sole reason that the person has relinquished a child in accordance with the Abandoned Newborn Infant Protection Act:

(a) Abandonment of the child.

(a-1) Abandonment of a newborn infant in a hospital.

(a-2) Abandonment of a newborn infant in any setting where the evidence suggests that the parent intended to relinquish his or her parental rights.

(b) Failure to maintain a reasonable degree of interest, concern or responsibility as to the child's welfare.

(c) Desertion of the child for more than 3 months next preceding the commencement of the Adoption proceeding.

(d) Substantial neglect of the child if continuous or repeated.

(d-1) Substantial neglect, if continuous or repeated, of any child residing in the household which resulted in the death of that child.

(e) Extreme or repeated cruelty to the child.

(f) Two or more findings of physical abuse to any children under Section 4-8 of the Juvenile Court Act [repealed] or Section 2-21 of the Juvenile Court Act of 1987 [705 ILCS 405/2-21], the most recent of which was determined by the juvenile court hearing the matter to be supported by clear and convincing evidence; a criminal conviction or a finding of not guilty by reason of insanity resulting from the death of any child by physical child abuse; or a finding of physical child abuse resulting from the death of any child under Section 4-8 of the Juvenile Court Act [repealed] or Section 2-21 of the Juvenile Court Act of 1987 [705 ILCS 405/2-21].

(g) Failure to protect the child from conditions within his environment injurious to the child's welfare.

(h) Other neglect of, or misconduct toward the child; provided that in making a finding of unfitness the court hearing the adoption proceeding shall not be bound by any previous finding, order or judgment affecting or determining the rights of the parents toward the child sought to be adopted in any other proceeding except such proceedings terminating parental rights as shall be had under either this Act, the Juvenile Court Act or the Juvenile Court Act of 1987 [705 ILCS 405/1-1 et seq.].

(i) Depravity. Conviction of any one of the following crimes shall create a presumption that a parent is depraved which can be overcome only by clear and convincing evidence: (1) first degree murder in violation of paragraph 1 or 2 of subsection (a) of Section 9-1 of the Criminal Code of 1961 [720 ILCS 5/9-1] or conviction of second degree murder in violation of subsection (a) of Section 9-2 of the Criminal Code of 1961 [720 ILCS 5/9-2] of a parent of the child to be adopted; (2) first degree murder or second degree murder of any child in violation of the Criminal Code of 1961 [720 ILCS 5/1-1 et seq.]; (3) attempt or conspiracy to commit first degree murder or second degree murder of any child in violation of the Criminal Code of 1961 [720 ILCS 5/1-1 et seq.]; (4) solicitation to commit murder of any child, solicitation to commit murder of any child for hire, or solicitation to commit second degree murder of any child in violation of the Criminal Code of 1961 [720 ILCS 5/1-1 et seq.]; or (5) aggravated criminal sexual assault in violation of Section 12-14(b)(1) of the Criminal Code of 1961 [720 ILCS 5/12-14].

There is a rebuttable presumption that a parent is depraved if the parent has been criminally convicted of at least 3 felonies under the laws of this State or any other state, or under federal law, or the criminal laws of any United States territory; and at least one of these convictions took place within 5 years of the filing of the petition or motion seeking termination of parental rights.

There is a rebuttable presumption that a parent is depraved if that parent has been criminally convicted of either first or second degree murder of any person as defined in the Criminal Code of 1961 [720 ILCS 5/1-1 et seq.] within 10 years of the filing date of the petition or motion to terminate parental rights.

(j) Open and notorious adultery or fornication.

(j-1) (Blank).

(k) Habitual drunkenness or addiction to drugs, other than those prescribed by a physician, for at least one year immediately prior to the commencement of the unfitness proceeding.

There is a rebuttable presumption that a parent is unfit under this subsection with respect to any child to which that parent gives birth where there is a confirmed test result that at birth the child's blood, urine, or meconium contained any amount of a controlled substance as defined in subsection (f) of Section 102 of the Illinois Controlled Substances Act [720 ILCS 570/102] or metabolites of such substances, the presence of which in the newborn infant was not the result of medical treatment administered to the mother or the newborn infant; and the biological mother of this child is the biological mother of at least one other child who was adjudicated a neglected minor under subsection (c) of Section 2-3 of the Juvenile Court Act of 1987 [705 ILCS 405/2-3].

(l) Failure to demonstrate a reasonable degree of interest, concern or responsibility as to the welfare of a new born child during the first 30 days after its birth.

(m) Failure by a parent (i) to make reasonable efforts to correct the conditions that were the basis for the removal of the child from the parent, or (ii) to make reasonable progress toward the return of the child to the parent within 9 months after an adjudication of neglected or abused minor under Section 2-3 of the Juvenile Court Act of 1987 [705 ILCS 405/2-3] or dependent minor under Section 2-4 of that Act [705 ILCS 405/2-4], or (iii) to make reasonable progress toward the return of the child to the parent during any 9-month period after the end of the initial 9-month period following the adjudication of neglected or abused minor under Section 2-3 of the Juvenile Court Act of 1987 [705 ILCS 405/2-3] or dependent minor under Section 2-4 of that Act [705 ILCS 405/2-4]. If a service plan has been established as required under Section 8.2 of the Abused and Neglected Child Reporting Act [325 ILCS 5/8.2] to correct the conditions that were the basis for the removal of the child from the parent and if those services were available, then, for purposes of this Act, "failure to make reasonable progress toward the return of the child to the parent" includes (I) the parent's failure to substantially fulfill his or her obligations under the service plan and correct the conditions that brought the child into care within 9 months after the adjudication under Section 2-3 or 2-4 of the Juvenile Court Act of 1987 [705 ILCS 405/2-3 or 705 ILCS 405/2-4] and (II) the parent's failure to substantially fulfill his or her obligations under the service plan and correct the conditions that brought the child into care during any 9-month period after the end of the initial 9-month period following the adjudication under Section 2-3 or 2-4 of the Juvenile Court Act of 1987 [705 ILCS 405/2-3 or 705 ILCS 405/2-4].

(m-1) Pursuant to the Juvenile Court Act of 1987 [705 ILCS 405/1-1 et seq.], a child has been in foster care for 15 months out of any 22 month period which begins on or after the effective date of this amendatory Act of 1998 unless the child's parent can prove by a preponderance of the evidence that it is more likely than not that it will be in the best interests of the child to be returned to the parent within 6 months of the date on which a petition for termination of parental rights is filed under the Juvenile Court Act of 1987 [705 ILCS 405/1-1 et seq.]. The 15 month time limit is tolled during any period for which there is a court finding that the appointed custodian or guardian failed to make reasonable efforts to reunify the child with his or her family, provided that (i) the finding of no reasonable efforts is made within 60 days of the period when reasonable efforts were not made or (ii) the parent filed a motion requesting a finding of no reasonable efforts within 60 days of the period when reasonable efforts were not made. For purposes of this subdivision (m-1), the date of entering foster care is the earlier of: (i) the date of a judicial finding at an adjudicatory hearing that the child is an abused, neglected, or dependent minor; or (ii) 60 days after the date on which the child is removed from his or her parent, guardian, or legal custodian.

(n) Evidence of intent to forgo his or her parental rights, whether or not the child is a ward of the court, (1) as manifested by his or her failure for a period of 12 months: (i) to visit the child, (ii) to communicate with the child or agency, although able to do so and not prevented from doing so by an agency or by court order, or (iii) to maintain contact with or plan for the future of the child, although physically able to do so, or (2) as manifested by the father's failure, where he and the mother of the child were unmarried to each other at the time of the child's birth, (i) to commence legal proceedings to establish his paternity under the Illinois Parentage Act of 1984 [750 ILCS 45/1 et seq.] or the law of the jurisdiction of the child's birth within 30 days of being informed, pursuant to Section 12a of this Act [750 ILCS 50/12a], that he is the father or the likely father of the child or, after being so informed where the child is not yet born, within 30 days of the child's birth, or (ii) to make a good faith effort to pay a reasonable amount of the expenses related to the birth of the child and to provide a reasonable amount for the financial support of the child, the court to consider in its determination all relevant circumstances, including the financial condition of both parents; provided that the ground for termination provided in this subparagraph (n)(2)(ii) shall only be available where the petition is brought by the mother or the husband of the mother.

Contact or communication by a parent with his or her child that does not demonstrate affection and concern does not constitute reasonable contact and planning under subdivision (n). In the absence of evidence to the contrary, the ability to visit, communicate, maintain contact, pay expenses and plan for the future shall be presumed. The subjective intent of the parent, whether expressed or otherwise, unsupported by evidence of the foregoing parental acts manifesting that intent, shall not preclude a determination that the parent has intended to forgo his or her parental rights. In making this determination, the court may consider but shall not require a showing of diligent efforts by an authorized agency to encourage the parent to perform the acts specified in subdivision (n).

It shall be an affirmative defense to any allegation under paragraph (2) of this subsection that the father's failure was due to circumstances beyond his control or to impediments created by the mother or any other person having legal custody. Proof of that fact need only be by a preponderance of the evidence.

(o) Repeated or continuous failure by the parents, although physically and financially able, to provide the child with adequate food, clothing, or shelter.

(p) Inability to discharge parental responsibilities supported by competent evidence from a psychiatrist, licensed clinical social worker, or clinical psychologist of mental impairment, mental illness or mental retardation as defined in Section 1-116 of the Mental Health and Developmental Disabilities Code [405 ILCS 5/1-116], or developmental disability as defined in Section 1-106 of that Code [405 ILCS 5/1-106], and there is sufficient justification to believe that the inability to discharge parental responsibilities shall extend beyond a reasonable time period. However, this subdivision (p) shall not be construed so as to permit a licensed clinical social worker to conduct any medical diagnosis to determine mental illness or mental impairment.

(q) The parent has been criminally convicted of aggravated battery, heinous battery, or attempted murder of any child.

(r) The child is in the temporary custody or guardianship of the Department of Children and Family Services, the parent is incarcerated as a result of criminal conviction at the time the petition or motion for termination of parental rights is filed, prior to incarceration the parent had little or no contact with the child or provided little or no support for the child, and the parent's incarceration will prevent the parent from discharging his or her parental responsibilities for the child for a period in excess of 2 years after the filing of the petition or motion for termination of parental rights.

(s) The child is in the temporary custody or guardianship of the Department of Children and Family Services, the parent is incarcerated at the time the petition or motion for termination of parental rights is filed, the parent has been repeatedly incarcerated as a result of criminal convictions, and the parent's repeated incarceration has prevented the parent from discharging his or her parental responsibilities for the child.

(t) A finding that at birth the child's blood, urine, or meconium contained any amount of a controlled substance as defined in subsection (f) of Section 102 of the Illinois Controlled Substances Act [720 ILCS 570/102], or a metabolite of a controlled substance, with the exception of controlled substances or metabolites of such substances, the presence of which in the newborn infant was the result of medical treatment administered to the mother or the newborn infant, and that the biological mother of this child is the biological mother of at least one other child who was adjudicated a neglected minor under subsection (c) of Section 2-3 of the Juvenile Court Act of 1987 [705 ILCS 405/2-3], after which the biological mother had the opportunity to enroll in and participate in a clinically appropriate substance abuse counseling, treatment, and rehabilitation program.

E. "Parent" means the father or mother of a legitimate or illegitimate child. For the purpose of this Act, a person who has executed a final and irrevocable consent to adoption or a final and irrevocable surrender for purposes of adoption, or whose parental rights have been terminated by a court, is not a parent of the child who was the subject of the consent or surrender, unless the consent is void pursuant to subsection O of Section 10 [750 ILCS 50/10].

F. A person is available for adoption when the person is:

(a) a child who has been surrendered for adoption to an agency and to whose adoption the agency has thereafter consented;

(b) a child to whose adoption a person authorized by law, other than his parents, has consented, or to whose adoption no consent is required pursuant to Section 8 of this Act [750 ILCS 50/8];

(c) a child who is in the custody of persons who intend to adopt him through placement made by his parents;

(c-1) a child for whom a parent has signed a specific consent pursuant to subsection O of Section 10 [750 ILCS 50/10]; or

(d) an adult who meets the conditions set forth in Section 3 of this Act [750 ILCS 50/3]; or

(e) a child who has been relinquished as defined in Section 10 of the Abandoned Newborn Infant Protection Act [325 ILCS 2/10].

A person who would otherwise be available for adoption shall not be deemed unavailable for adoption solely by reason of his or her death.

G. The singular includes the plural and the plural includes the singular and the "male" includes the "female", as the context of this Act may require.

H. "Adoption disruption" occurs when an adoptive placement does not prove successful and it becomes necessary for the child to be removed from placement before the adoption is finalized.

I. "Foreign placing agency" is an agency or individual operating in a country or territory outside the United States that is authorized by its country to place children for adoption either directly with families in the United States or through United States based international agencies.

J. "Immediate relatives" means the biological parents, the parents of the biological parents and siblings of the biological parents.

K. "Intercountry adoption" is a process by which a child from a country other than the United States is adopted.

L. "Intercountry Adoption Coordinator" is a staff person of the Department of Children and Family Services appointed by the Director to coordinate the provision of services by the public and private sector to prospective parents of foreign-born children.

M. "Interstate Compact on the Placement of Children" is a law enacted by most states for the purpose of establishing uniform procedures for handling the interstate placement of children in foster homes, adoptive homes, or other child care facilities.

N. "Non-Compact state" means a state that has not enacted the Interstate Compact on the Placement of Children.

O. "Preadoption requirements" are any conditions established by the laws or regulations of the Federal Government or of each state that must be met prior to the placement of a child in an adoptive home.

P. "Abused child" means a child whose parent or immediate family member, or any person responsible for the child's welfare, or any individual residing in the same home as the child, or a paramour of the child's parent:

(a) inflicts, causes to be inflicted, or allows to be inflicted upon the child physical injury, by other than accidental means, that causes death, disfigurement, impairment of physical or emotional health, or loss or impairment of any bodily function;

(b) creates a substantial risk of physical injury to the child by other than accidental means which would be likely to cause death, disfigurement, impairment of physical or emotional health, or loss or impairment of any bodily function;

(c) commits or allows to be committed any sex offense against the child, as sex offenses are defined in the Criminal Code of 1961 [720 ILCS 5/1-1 et seq.] and extending those definitions of sex offenses to include children under 18 years of age;

(d) commits or allows to be committed an act or acts of torture upon the child; or

(e) inflicts excessive corporal punishment.

Q. "Neglected child" means any child whose parent or other person responsible for the child's welfare withholds or denies nourishment or medically indicated treatment including food or care denied solely on the basis of the present or anticipated mental or physical impairment as determined by a physician acting alone or in consultation with other physicians or otherwise does not provide the proper or necessary support, education as required by law, or medical or other remedial care recognized under State law as necessary for a child's well-being, or other care necessary for his or her well-being, including adequate food, clothing and shelter; or who is abandoned by his or her parents or other person responsible for the child's welfare.

A child shall not be considered neglected or abused for the sole reason that the child's parent or other person responsible for his or her welfare depends upon spiritual means through prayer alone for the treatment or cure of disease or remedial care as provided under Section 4 of the Abused and Neglected Child Reporting Act [325 ILCS 5/4]. A child shall not be considered neglected or abused for the sole reason that the child's parent or other person responsible for the child's welfare failed to vaccinate, delayed vaccination, or refused vaccination for the child due to a waiver on religious or medical grounds as permitted by law.

R. "Putative father" means a man who may be a child's father, but who (1) is not married to the child's mother on or before the date that the child was or is to be born and (2) has not established paternity of the child in a court proceeding before the filing of a petition for the adoption of the child. The term includes a male who is less than 18 years of age. "Putative father" does not mean a man who is the child's father as a result of criminal sexual abuse or assault as defined under Article 12 of the Criminal Code of 1961 [720 ILCS 5/12-1 et seq.].

S. "Standby adoption" means an adoption in which a parent consents to custody and termination of parental rights to become effective upon the occurrence of a future event, which is either the death of the parent or the request of the parent for the entry of a final judgment of adoption.

T. (Blank).

(Source: P.A. 86-403; 86-659; 86-883; 86-1028; 87-617; 87-1158, § 2; 88-20, § 5; 88-550, § 975; 88-691, § 15; 89-235, § 2-160; 90-13, § 5; 90-15, § 20; 90-27, § 45; 90-28, § 10-25; 90-443, § 15; 90-608, § 40; 90-655, § 174; 91-357, § 262; 91-373, § 5; 91-572, § 5; 92-16, § 99; 92-375, § 5; 92-408, § 97; 92-432, § 97; 92-651, § 89; 93-732, § 5.)

Note.

This section was Ill.Rev.Stat., Ch. 40, para. 1501.

The Juvenile Court Act, referred to above, was repealed and replaced with the Juvenile Court Act of 1987, 705 ILCS 405/1-1 et seq.

Section 95 of P.A. 90-15 provided "Where this Act makes changes in a statute that is represented in this Act by text that is not yet or no longer in effect (for example, a Section represented by multiple versions), the use of that text does not accelerate or delay the taking effect of (i) the changes made by this Act or (ii) provisions derived from any other Public Act".

Section 996 of P.A. 92-16 contains a "no acceleration or delay" provision, and Section 997 contains a "no revival or extension" provision.

Section 997 of P.A. 92-651 is a no acceleration or delay provision, and Section 998 is a no revival or extension provision.

Cross References.

As to consents to adoptions, see 750 ILCS 50/8.

Illinois Administrative Code.

See 89 Illinois Administrative Code, §§ 315.215, 309.50.

Effect of Amendments.

The 1994 amendment by P.A. 88-550, effective July 3, 1994, in subdivision D. (m), in the first sentence substituted "adjudication of neglected or abused minor under Section 2-3 or dependent minor under Section 2-4 of" for "adjudication of neglected minor, abused minor or dependent minor under the Juvenile Court Act or" and added the second sentence; and added subsection R.

The 1994 amendment by P.A. 88-691, effective January 24, 1995, effective retroactively to July 3, 1994, incorporated the amendments by P.A. 88-550; in subdivision D.(m), substituted "minor" for "or", deleted "under Section 2-3" preceding "or dependent minor" and substituted "the Juvenile Court Act or" for "Section 2-4 of" and deleted the second sentence which read "For purposes of this Act, failure to make reasonable progress toward the return of the child to the parents may be defined as failure to complete the service plan established to correct the conditions that were the basis for the removal of the child from his or her parents as required under Section 8.2 of the Abused and Neglected Child Reporting Act within 12 months after the adjudication under Section 2-3 or 2-4 of the Juvenile Court Act of 1987".

The 1995 amendment by P.A. 89-235, effective August 4, 1995, combined the amendments by P.A. 88-20, § 5 and P.A. 88-550, § 975.

The 1997 amendment by P.A. 90-13, effective June 13, 1997, combined the amendments by P.A. 88-691 and P.A. 89-235; and added subdivision 1.D.(r).

The 1997 amendment by P.A. 90-15, effective June 13, 1997, combined the amendments by P.A. 88-691 and P.A. 89-235; and in subsection R. added the third sentence.

The 1997 amendment by P.A. 90-27, effective January 1, 1998, combined the amendments by P.A. 88-691 and P.A. 89-235; incorporated the amendments by P.A. 90-28; and in subdivision D.(m), in the second sentence, deleted "the parent's", substituted "substantially fulfill his or her obligations under the" for "complete that" and inserted "and correct the conditions that brought the child into care".

The 1997 amendment by P.A. 90-28, effective January 1, 1998, combined the amendments by P.A. 88-691 and P.A. 89-235; and in subdivision D.(m), in the first sentence, substituted "9" for "12", substituted "or" for minor", inserted "under Section 2-3 of the Juvenile Court Act of 1987" and substituted "Section 2-4 of that Act" for "the Juvenile Court Act or the Juvenile Court Act of 1987" and added the second sentence.

The 1997 amendment by P.A. 90-443, effective July 1, 1997, approved August 16, 1997, in subsection B, in the second sentence, inserted "determined to be void or is".

The 1998 amendment by P.A. 90-608, effective June 30, 1998, incorporated the amendments by P.A. 90-13, P.A. 90-15, P.A. 90-27, P.A. 90-28, and P.A. 90-443; in subdivision D.(i), added the second sentence in the first paragraph and added the last two paragraphs; deleted subdivision D.(j-1), which contained content similar to that now in subdivision D.(i); added the second paragraph in subdivision D.(k); added subdivision D.(m-1); rewrote subdivision D.(q); redesignated the former second subdivision D.(r) as subdivision D.(t); and in subdivision D.(t), inserted "or meconium" and made a related change near the beginning, and substituted "to enroll in and participate in a clinically appropriate substance abuse counseling" for "to participate in a drug counseling".

The 1998 amendment by P.A. 90-655, effective July 30, 1998, substituted the present subdivision D.(t) designation for the former subdivision D.(r) designation, and in present subdivision D.(t) substituted "blood, urine, or meconium" for "blood or urine" and "to enroll in and participate in a clinically appropriate substance abuse counseling" for "to participate in a drug counseling".

The 1999 amendment by P.A. 91-357, effective July 29, 1999, in subdivision D.(n) substituted "forgo" for "forego" in the first and second paragraphs.

The 1999 amendment by P.A. 91-373, effective January 1, 2000, in subdivision D.(m) in the first sentence inserted the item (i) and (ii) designations and item (iii); inserted the item (I) designation and item (II); in subdivision D.(n) substituted "forgo" for "forego" in the first and second paragraphs; and made stylistic changes.

The 1999 amendment by P.A. 91-572, effective January 1, 2000, in subdivision D.(n) substituted "forgo" for "forego" in the first and second paragraphs; added subdivisions S. and T., and made stylistic changes.

The 2001 amendment by P.A. 92-16, effective June 28, 2001, combined the amendments by P.A. 91-357, P.A. 91-373 and P.A. 91-572.

The 2001 amendment by P.A. 92-375, effective January 1, 2002, added the last sentence in the second paragraph of subsection Q.

The 2001 amendment by P.A. 92-408, effective August 17, 2001, inserted "except that a person shall not be considered an unfit person for the sole reason that the person has relinquished a child in accordance with the Abandoned Newborn Infant Protection Act" in subsection D; and inserted subsection F(e) and made related changes.

The 2001 amendment by P.A. 92-432, effective August 17, 2001, at the end of subsection D added "except that a person shall not be considered an unfit person for the sole reason that the person has relinquished a child in accordance with the Abandoned Newborn Infant Protection Act"; inserted subsection F(e); and made stylistic changes.

The 2002 amendment by P.A. 92-651, effective July 11, 2002, deleted "the" preceding "law" at the end of subdivision R; and combined the amendments by P.A. 92-16, P.A. 92-375, P.A. 92-408, and P.A. 92-432.

The 2004 amendment by P.A. 93-732, effective January 1, 2005, deleted the former last sentence in subsection R concerning refusal to vaccinate a child; in subsection S twice deleted "terminally ill" before "parent"; and deleted the text from subsection T, which defined "Terminally ill parent".

CASE NOTES

Analysis

Constitutionality
—In General
—Due Process
—Equal Protection
—Mental Illness or Mental Retardation
—Mentally Retarded Parent
—Prior Law
In General
Abandonment
—Not Shown
Abused Minors
Adoption Agreements
—Held Void
Adoption and Custody Distinguished
Adoption Proceeding
—Collateral Attack
Adult Adoption
Application and Construction
Attorney
—Motion to Withdraw
Availability for Adoption
—Best Interests of Child
—Consent Form
—Filing of Petition
—Legal Counsel
—Non-Consenting Parent's Fitness
—Parental Rights Termination
—Shown
—Single Hearing
—Termination of Consent
—Without Parental Consent
Best Interests of Child
—Not Independent Grounds
—Petition Denied
—Petition Granted
—Priority of Interests
—Separate Hearing
Biological Parent
Compliance
—Prior Law
Construction With Other Laws
Custody Proceeding Distinguished
Depravity
—In General
—Child Out of Wedlock
—Conduct Required
—Defined
—Felony Convictions
—Illustrative Cases
—Murder Conviction
—Not Shown
—Rehabilitative Potential
—Shown
—Standard
—Witness Demeanor
Desertion
—Adoption by Foster Parents
—Burden of Proof
—Defined
—Imprisonment
—Intent of Parent
—Not Shown
—Shown
Effect of Amendment
Efforts or Reasonable Progress
—Lack of
Final Order
Habeas Corpus Distinguished
Illness
—Medical Testimony
Intent of Parent
—Imprisonment
Interest, Concern or Responsibility
—Clear and Convincing Evidence
—Denial of Visitation
—Drug Abuse
—Illustrative Cases
—Importance of Effort
—Incarcerated Parent
—Lack of Conduct
—Lack of Effort
—Mitigating Circumstances Not Shown
—Murder Conviction
—Newborn Children
—Not Shown
—Paternity Action
—Shown
Juvenile Proceedings
—No Jury Trial
Legislative Intent
Mental Illness
—In General
—Before Age of 18
—Illustrative Cases
—Impairment vs Retardation
—Length of Time
—Medical Testimony
—Mental Impairment
—Mental Retardation
—Required
Mootness
Parent
—Related Child
Petition to Adopt
Presumption
Private Placement
Purpose
Reasonable Efforts or Progress
—In General
—Actual Progress
—Appointment of Guardian
—Best Interests of Child
—Correction of Conditions
—Defined
—Denial of Shortcomings
—Drug Abuse
—Establishment of Home Life
—Future Events
—Goal of Reunification
—Illustrative Cases
—Importance of Effort

—Incarcerated Parent
—Independent Grounds for Unfitness
—Judicial Admission Admissible
—Legislative Intent
—Mental Retardation
—Noncustodial Parent
—Not Shown
—Objective Standard
—Observable Progress
—Original Adjudication
—Original Situation as Benchmark
—Parental Conduct
—Parental Understanding of Requirements
—Parenting Classes
—Prior Proceeding
—Purpose
—Removal of Child from Parent
—Sexual Conduct
—Shown
—Standard of Evidence
—Subjective Standard
—Surrender by Custodial Parent
—Suitable Housing
—Time Limits
—Time Period
—Unfitness Order Reversed
Relation to Other Laws
Scope of Review
—Standard Inapplicable
Standard of Review
Substantial Neglect
—Factors
—Mentally Retarded Parents
Summary Judgment
—Denied
—Proper
Termination of Parental Rights
—In General
—Best Interest of Child
—Burden of Proof
—Construction
—Conviction
—Decision Unaffected by Appeal
—Drug Abuse
—Failure to Pay Child Support
—Illustrative Cases
—Reversed
—Right to Counsel
—Substantial Progress
—Unfitness
—Ward of Court
Unfitness
—In General
—Abandonment
—Absence of Fault
—Acknowledgment of Abuse
—Adjudicating Order Entry Date
—Admissible Evidence
—Admissions by Parent
—Adultery
—Appointment of Guardian
—Argument Waived
—Basis of Finding
—Best Interests of Child
—Cases Unique
—Child Out of Wedlock
—Clear and Convincing Evidence
—Conduct Over Time
—Considerations
—Consolidated Hearings
—Construction with Similar Case
—Corrections Record
—Criminal Conviction
—Cruelty
—Death of One Parent
—Deficient Record
—Denial of Visitation
—Depravity
—Drug Addiction
—Evidence Held Sufficient
—Failure to Protect
—Failure to Support
—Fault of Parent
—Fornication
—Habitual Drunkenness
—Illustrative Cases
—Inability to Nurture or Interact
—Incarceration
—Independent Grounds
—Individual Consideration
—Initial Determination
—Injurious Environment
—Intent to Contact
—Killing by Parent
—Lack of Contact
—Legislative Intent
—Mental Illness
—Mental Impairment
—Mental Retardation
—Minor Parent
—Non-Consenting Parent
—Not Found
—Passive Neglect
—Planning for the Future
—Pleading
—Reasonable Degree of Interest
—Reasonable Efforts to Correct Conditions
—Reasonable Progress Toward Return of Child
—Relinquishment of Child
—Removal from Home
—Sexual Abuse
—Shown
—Single Hearing
—Standard of Evidence
—Standard of Review
—Standing
—State Interest
—Strict Compliance
—Subsequent Children
—Substantial Neglect
—Sufficiency of Evidence
—Termination of Parental Rights
—Termination of Rights Order Reversed
—Validity of Petition
—Visitation
—Warning About Spouse
—Withdrawal of Petition to Terminate
Unknown Fathers
Unwed Father
—Procedural Safeguards
Waiver

Constitutionality

—In General

Since the mother's claim to raise her own child was a liberty interest but not a vested right, 750 ILCS 50/1(D)(q) did not violate Due Process or Equal Protection Clauses under a heightened protection strict scrutiny analysis; section 1(D)(q)'s presumption that the mother was unfit, since she was convicted of a crime, abuse of any child (not limited to the child for whom termination was sought), that was a per se (not rebuttable) factor to establish parental unfitness, and could be applied retroactively to effect an overriding State interest. People v. W.B., 328 Ill. App. 3d 175, 262 Ill. Dec. 485, 765 N.E.2d 1093, 2002 Ill. App. LEXIS 131 (1 Dist. 2002).

Since Illinois law does not create an expectation of a continued relationship, foster parents have no constitutionally protected liberty interest in the continued custody of their charges. Johnson v. Burnett, 182 Ill. App. 3d 574, 131 Ill. Dec. 517, 538 N.E.2d 892 (3 Dist. 1989).

—Due Process

By the time of the best interest phase of a termination of parental

Constitutionality (Cont'd)

—Due Process (Cont'd)

rights proceeding, the parent has been found unfit by clear and convincing evidence, and while the parent retains a fundamental interest, the proper focus of this hearing is on the child; once a finding of unfitness has been made, all considerations, including the parent's rights, must yield to the best interest of the child. People v. Michelle L. (In re Brandon L.), 348 Ill. App. 3d 315, 284 Ill. Dec. 197, 809 N.E.2d 763, 2004 Ill. App. LEXIS 458 (2 Dist. 2004).

In the best interest phase of a termination of parental rights proceeding, the interests of the parent and the child diverge and due process does not require standards as strict as in the unfitness phase; due process requires only a preponderance of the evidence burden of proof in the best interest phase versus a clear and convincing evidence standard in the unfitness phase. People v. Michelle L. (In re Brandon L.), 348 Ill. App. 3d 315, 284 Ill. Dec. 197, 809 N.E.2d 763, 2004 Ill. App. LEXIS 458 (2 Dist. 2004).

Parents have a fundamental due process right to the care, custody and control of their children, but that right is subject to termination; a parental rights termination proceeding must comport with the guarantees of procedural due process because such a proceeding implicates a fundamental liberty interest. People v. Michelle L. (In re Brandon L.), 348 Ill. App. 3d 315, 284 Ill. Dec. 197, 809 N.E.2d 763, 2004 Ill. App. LEXIS 458 (2 Dist. 2004).

Since 750 ILCS 50/1(D)(t) required the State to prove that the mother failed to take advantage of available drug treatment by clear and convincing evidence it did not violate the mother's constitutional due process rights. People v. Mitchell C. (In re Jamarqon C.), 338 Ill. App. 3d 639, 273 Ill. Dec. 35, 788 N.E.2d 344, 2003 Ill. App. LEXIS 441 (2 Dist. 2003).

Parent's right to his children was not always a vested right within the due process clause of the Illinois Constitution, so an amendment to the statute authorizing termination of parental rights that added incarceration as ground for an unfitness finding could be applied retroactively. People v. E.C. (In re E.C.), 337 Ill. App. 3d 391, 272 Ill. Dec. 51, 786 N.E.2d 590, 2003 Ill. App. LEXIS 272 (1 Dist. 2003).

Unfitness presumption applied under 750 ILCS 50/1(D)(m-1) to parents whose children had been in foster care for 15 out of the preceding 22 months did not survive strict scrutiny for due process violations, because it was not narrowly tailored to further the State's compelling interest in child welfare; it did not bear any necessary relationship to parental competence at all. People v. E.W., 197 Ill. 2d 317, 259 Ill. Dec. 1, 757 N.E.2d 864, 2001 Ill. LEXIS 1068 (2001).

There was no violation of the constitutional guarantee of due process where father's depravity was proved by clear and convincing evidence of his murder of the mother of his children in an exceptionally brutal and heinous fashion and his sentence to a 55 year term of imprisonment. In re T.H., 255 Ill. App. 3d 247, 193 Ill. Dec. 370, 626 N.E.2d 403 (5 Dist. 1993), appeal denied, 155 Ill. 2d 577, 198 Ill. Dec. 554, 633 N.E.2d 16, cert. denied, 513 U.S. 905, 115 S. Ct. 269, 130 L. Ed. 2d 187 (1994).

This subsection does not satisfy the requirement of due process because it authorizes the termination of parental rights upon proof of physical abuse by a preponderance of the evidence; if the state seeks to terminate parental rights on the ground that the parent has physically abused his or her child on two separate or more occasions, or another ground, it must prove, to satisfy due process, those allegations by clear and convincing evidence. People v. Enis, 121 Ill. 2d 124, 117 Ill. Dec. 201, 520 N.E.2d 362 (1988).

When a statute makes provisions for conditions and procedures to be followed in creating the relationship of a parent and child between persons not so related by nature, followed by a trial of the issue by a court of general jurisdiction at the election of the party was aggrieved, with the right of ultimate appeal to the highest court of the state, the requirements for due process of law are discharged. Bland v. Department of Children & Family Servs., 141 Ill. App. 3d 818, 96 Ill. Dec. 122, 490 N.E.2d 1327 (3 Dist. 1986).

Former Section 9.1-1(D)(b) of the Adoption Act (see now this section) was valid and did not violate due process. People v. Ladewig, 34 Ill. App. 3d 393, 340 N.E.2d 150 (1 Dist. 1975).

—Equal Protection

Statute narrowly tailored to identify parents dangerous to children and meet compelling state interest of protecting child from abuse using least restrictive means did not violate equal protection clause or due process. People v. A.R., 328 Ill. App. 3d 955, 263 Ill. Dec. 146, 767 N.E.2d 872, 2002 Ill. App. LEXIS 244 (2 Dist. 2002).

Statute does not discriminate against a suspect class, it does not burden a fundamental right and it is rationally related to a legitimate state goal, therefore there is no equal protection violation. In re A.S.B., 293 Ill. App. 3d 836, 228 Ill. Dec. 238, 688 N.E.2d 1215 (2 Dist. 1997).

A state does not violate the guarantee merely because the classifications made by its laws are imperfect, and a statutory discrimination will not be set aside if any state of facts reasonably may be believed to justify it. Bland v. Department of Children & Family Servs., 141 Ill. App. 3d 818, 96 Ill. Dec. 122, 490 N.E.2d 1327 (3 Dist. 1986).

Subdivision (D)(h) of this section properly promotes an overriding state interest and thus withstands constitutional attack, whether viewed as rationally related to a legitimate state purpose or necessary to promote a compelling state interest. People v. Ray, 88 Ill. App. 3d 1010, 44 Ill. Dec. 182, 411 N.E.2d 88 (5 Dist. 1980), appeal dismissed, 452 U.S. 956, 101 S. Ct. 3102, 69 L. Ed. 2d 967 (1981).

—Mental Illness or Mental Retardation

Subsection (D)(p) does not violate equal protection either because it impermissibly distinguishes between parents who are unable to discharge parental responsibilities because of mental conditions and parents who are unable to discharge their responsibilities for other reasons or because parents facing the loss of their parental rights are treated differently depending on whether their fitness is challenged under the Juvenile Court Act, 705 ILCS 405/1-1 et seq., or the Adoption Act since the statute does require a causal link between a mental impairment and the inability to discharge parental responsibilities, and the Juvenile Court Act did not pertain to similarly situated individuals. R.W. v. D.C., 195 Ill. 2d 291, 253 Ill. Dec. 699, 745 N.E.2d 1233, 2001 Ill. LEXIS 239 (2001).

Subsection (D)(p) does not violate due process because it does not require the court to consider less restrictive alternatives to termination of parental rights or because it does not require proof that the inability to discharge parental responsibilities be related to the parent's mental condition or proof that the mental condition cannot be treated as it is apparent that termination of parental rights should not be the default option in proceedings under the Adoption Act in which a parent contests an allegation of unfitness, and it is clear from the statutory language that the mental condition must be the cause of the inability to discharge parental responsibilities which forms the basis for the finding of unfitness. R.W. v. D.C., 195 Ill. 2d 291, 253 Ill. Dec. 699, 745 N.E.2d 1233, 2001 Ill. LEXIS 239 (2001).

Subsection (D)(p) is not constitutionally infirm for allowing a parent to be declared unfit without proving that the parent has or is about to neglect or harm the child. The state's interest in protecting minors is sufficiently compelling to satisfy strict due process scrutiny when a child is being raised by a parent who is and will remain, for an unreasonable time mentally unable to give the child proper care. R.W. v. D.C., 195 Ill. 2d 291, 253 Ill. Dec. 699, 745 N.E.2d 1233, 2001 Ill. LEXIS 239 (2001).

Subsection (D)(p) does not violate procedural due process on the basis that it alters the burden of proof for termination of parental rights to something less than clear and convincing evidence since the section is definitional and does not even purport to alter the burden of proof. R.W. v. D.C., 195 Ill. 2d 291, 253 Ill. Dec. 699, 745 N.E.2d 1233, 2001 Ill. LEXIS 239 (2001).

The trial court improperly determined that subsection (D)(p) was unconstitutional due to vagueness as applied to the parent at issue in that it failed to define the term "parental responsibilities" where there had been no fact-finding in the case R.W. v. D.C., 195 Ill. 2d 291, 253 Ill. Dec. 699, 745 N.E.2d 1233, 2001 Ill. LEXIS 239 (2001).

—Mentally Retarded Parent

Subsection (E) of this section, so far as it pertains to the appointment of a guardian ad litem with power to consent to adoption for a parent who has been adjudged to be mentally retarded, is in violation of the equal protection and due process clauses of the Fourteenth Amendment of the Constitution of the United States (U.S. Const., Amend. 14) as well as Article 1 § 2 of the Illinois Constitution (Ill. Const., Art. I, § 2 (1970)). Helvey v.

Constitutionality (Cont'd)

—Mentally Retarded Parent (Cont'd)
Rednour, 86 Ill. App. 3d 154, 41 Ill. Dec. 671, 408 N.E.2d 17 (5 Dist. 1980).

—Prior Law
Former Ill.Rev.Stat., ch. 4, para. 9.1.1E and former Ill.Rev.Stat., ch. 4, para. 9.1-8 (see now this section and 750 ILCS 50/8), which prevented the father of an illegitimate child from asserting any right to the child in adoption proceedings and denying the father of such a child custody in the absence of an attempt to adopt were unconstitutional and denied equal protection of the law. People ex rel. Slawek v. Covenant Children's Home, 52 Ill. 2d 20, 284 N.E.2d 291 (1972).

In General
Indigent parent facing involuntary termination of parental rights in a proceeding under the Adoption Act, 750 ILCS 50/1 et seq., was entitled to court-appointed counsel as equal protection grounds dictated that she receive the same procedural safeguards as a similarly situated parent in a proceeding under the Juvenile Court Act of 1987, 705 ILCS 405/1 et seq., which permitted appointment of counsel. R.R.E. v. R.P., 198 Ill. 2d 448, 261 Ill. Dec. 492, 763 N.E.2d 741, 2002 Ill. LEXIS 8 (2002).

Abandonment
Abandonment, as that term was used in the former Adoption Act (see now this section), was conduct on the part of the parent which indicated a settled purpose to forego all parental duties and to relinquish all parental claims to the child. Hill v. Allabaugh, 333 Ill. App. 602, 78 N.E.2d 127 (2 Dist. 1948); Thorpe v. Thorpe, 48 Ill. App. 2d 455, 198 N.E.2d 743 (4 Dist. 1964); Robinson v. Neubauer, 79 Ill. App. 2d 362, 223 N.E.2d 705 (4 Dist. 1967); In re Smith, 4 Ill. App. 3d 261, 280 N.E.2d 770 (1 Dist. 1972); Bergstedt v. Cech, 8 Ill. App. 3d 642, 291 N.E.2d 21 (1 Dist. 1972); Moriarity v. People, 14 Ill. App. 3d 553, 302 N.E.2d 491 (2 Dist. 1973); Peyla v. Martin, 40 Ill. App. 3d 373, 352 N.E.2d 407 (5 Dist. 1976); Markham v. Markham, 91 Ill. App. 3d 1122, 47 Ill. Dec. 235, 414 N.E.2d 1351 (3 Dist. 1981); Estes v. Garrison, 93 Ill. App. 3d 670, 49 Ill. Dec. 97, 417 N.E.2d 787 (1 Dist. 1981); N.H. v. A.A., 222 Ill. App. 3d 73, 164 Ill. Dec. 696, 583 N.E.2d 612 (2 Dist. 1991).

—Not Shown
Considering respondent's testimony concerning child support, visitation, and other contacts with his son such as telephone calls, cards and gifts—much of which was corroborated and very little contradicted by petitioner— the trial court's finding of abandonment was contrary to the manifest weight of the evidence. Estes v. Garrison, 93 Ill. App. 3d 670, 49 Ill. Dec. 97, 417 N.E.2d 787 (1 Dist. 1981).

Where minors were voluntarily placed with the Department of Children and Family Services, and during the 18 months that the children were with the DCFS, the mother testified that she visited with the children a total of 15 times (the DCFS only allowed one visit per month during placement), additionally, the mother also stated that she gave the children Christmas presents in 1977 and 1978 and birthday presents in 1978, the trial court correctly found that the mother had not abandoned or deserted her children. People ex rel. Department of Children & Family Servs. v. Sanders, 77 Ill. App. 3d 78, 32 Ill. Dec. 847, 395 N.E.2d 1228 (4 Dist. 1979).

Where a father, upon his release from incarceration, set up residence with the respondent mother in Indiana, and while incarcerated, had made a weekend visit with the children, had sent letters and drawings to the children prior to their involvement with the Department of Children and Family Services, and prior to his incarceration, had cooked meals and read to the children on numerous occasions, the trial court properly concluded that the respondent father had not abandoned or deserted the children. People ex rel. Department of Children & Family Servs. v. Sanders, 77 Ill. App. 3d 78, 32 Ill. Dec. 847, 395 N.E.2d 1228 (4 Dist. 1979).

The state failed to establish clearly and convincingly that the plaintiff intended to abandon her children. Moriarity v. People, 14 Ill. App. 3d 553, 302 N.E.2d 491 (2 Dist. 1973).

Although grandparents offered more stability and a better environment than its parents, the court could not disregard the established law in an effort to do what it might like to do for the child because there had been no abandonment as required under former Ill.Rev.Stat., ch. 4, para. 4-1 (see now this section). Jackson v. Russell, 342 Ill. App. 637, 97 N.E.2d 584 (3 Dist. 1951).

Abused Minors
Prior to the 1989 amendment adding the term "abused minor," the state could not use subdivision (D)(m) of this section to terminate the parental rights on grounds of being an unfit parent of a child adjudicated abused; "abuse" was not subsumed within "neglect" and/or "dependency." People v. Strode, 198 Ill. App. 3d 633, 144 Ill. Dec. 801, 556 N.E.2d 268 (3 Dist. 1990).

Adoption Agreements

—Held Void
An agreement between the natural parent and adopting parents whereby the latter, for a consideration payable to them, agreed to adopt children of the natural parent was contrary to public policy and void, and a note given to evidence the obligation to pay a part of that consideration was void. Willey v. Lawton, 8 Ill. App. 2d 344, 132 N.E.2d 34 (1 Dist. 1956).

Adoption and Custody Distinguished
Custody and adoption proceedings are distinguishable in that adoption severs the rights and interests of the natural parents; it permanently terminates the relation between parent and child. Wittig v. Atherton, 107 Ill. App. 3d 1006, 63 Ill. Dec. 582, 438 N.E.2d 513 (1 Dist. 1982).

Adoption Proceeding

—Collateral Attack
Where the record in an adoption proceeding shows at least substantial compliance with the statute, a judgment of adoption is secure from collateral attack. Dahl v. Grenier, 126 Ill. App. 3d 891, 81 Ill. Dec. 870, 467 N.E.2d 992 (1 Dist. 1984).

Adult Adoption
There is no statutory distinction between an adopted adult and an adopted minor with respect to the nature of the legal relationship created between the adoptee and the adopting parent, namely, a parent-child relationship; the adoptee regardless of his age upon adoption, attains the status of a natural child of the adopting parents. In re Estate of Brittin, 279 Ill. App. 3d 512, 216 Ill. Dec. 50, 664 N.E.2d 687 (5 Dist. 1996).

Application and Construction
Subsection (D)(m) limits the evidence that may be considered under this section of the Adoption Act to matters concerning the parent's conduct in the 12 months following the applicable adjudication of neglect, abuse, or dependency. People v. Tawanda R., 191 Ill. 2d 1, 245 Ill. Dec. 256, 727 N.E.2d 990, 2000 Ill. LEXIS 329 (2000).

Because the parties to a custody proceeding were never married, the former Divorce Act (see now 750 ILCS 5/101 et seq.) did not provide a vehicle for determining custody of their child, nor did the former Adoption Act (see now 750 ILCS 50/0.01 et seq.) where plaintiff was not eligible to seek adoption of her natural child, or the Juvenile Court Act (705 ILCS 405/1-1 et seq.) when plaintiff was not claiming her child was neglected, dependent, delinquent or in need of supervision. People ex rel. Elmore v. Elmore, 46 Ill. App. 3d 504, 5 Ill. Dec. 292, 361 N.E.2d 615 (1 Dist. 1977).

Attorney

—Motion to Withdraw
Although an attorney who was appointed to represent a father who appealed a trial court's judgment terminating the father's parental rights stated that the attorney's review of the record showed that the trial court's judgment was correct, the attorney's memorandum of law in support of the attorney's motion to withdraw as appellate counsel did not discuss the basis for that conclusion or identify any arguments in support of issues the father could have argued on appeal, and the appellate court denied the attorney's motion to withdraw, and directed the attorney to file a new brief in support of the father's appeal or a new motion to withdraw that followed the procedure outlined by the United States Supreme Court in its Anders decision. People v. L.J. (In re Alexa J.), 345 Ill. App. 3d 985, 280 Ill. Dec. 777, 803 N.E.2d 7, 2003 Ill. App. LEXIS 473 (2 Dist. 2003).

Availability for Adoption

—Best Interests of Child

A court cannot grant an adoption solely on the basis of the best interests of the child, without a consent or a finding of unfitness, but a court must give prime consideration to the welfare and best interests of the child involved. Tiernan v. Stewart, 33 Ill. App. 3d 545, 338 N.E.2d 153 (2 Dist. 1975).

—Consent Form

Where father completed "consent to adoption" form for relatives to adopt his son, but such adoption didn't occur, father's completion of form did not surrender his rights so as to allow the placement of his son with others unknown; the consent form here did not follow statutory form, even though father gave up his rights and custody. People v. Mitchell, 115 Ill. App. 3d 169, 70 Ill. Dec. 895, 450 N.E.2d 368 (5 Dist. 1983).

—Filing of Petition

This Act does not authorize the filing of an adoption petition by a nonrelated party prior to the child becoming available for adoption; a party who is not related to the child may not file a petition to adopt that child until after any of the acts contained in this section has occurred and, specifically, they may not file seeking to prove the unfitness of the parent in a subsequent hearing. Johnson v. Burnett, 182 Ill. App. 3d 574, 131 Ill. Dec. 517, 538 N.E.2d 892 (3 Dist. 1989).

—Legal Counsel

While it may be desirable for the parents to have legal counsel prior to consenting to the adoption of the child, it is neither constitutionally required nor statutorily required by the Adoption Act. People v. Nolan, 94 Ill. App. 3d 1081, 50 Ill. Dec. 442, 419 N.E.2d 550 (1 Dist. 1981).

—Non-Consenting Parent's Fitness

Under this Act, the court must first determine whether a non-consenting parent is unfit and then decide whether adoption is in the best interest of the child. Lael v. Warga, 155 Ill. App. 3d 1005, 108 Ill. Dec. 518, 508 N.E.2d 1095 (4 Dist. 1987).

Before a third party can adopt the child of a non-consenting parent pursuant to this Act, he or she is required to prove by clear and convincing evidence that the parent is unfit; only after this showing has been made, will the court apply the best interests of the child standard to determine whether custody should be awarded to the third party. Menconi v. Menconi, 117 Ill. App. 3d 394, 73 Ill. Dec. 10, 453 N.E.2d 835 (1 Dist. 1983).

—Parental Rights Termination

In an action for adoption, one must establish the statutory ground for termination of parental rights before the best interests of the child or children can be considered. People v. Allen, 34 Ill. App. 3d 603, 340 N.E.2d 269 (1 Dist. 1975).

—Shown

A child was available for adoption where the child's biological mother voluntarily surrendered her parental rights to the child by executing a final and irrevocable surrender to an agency for purposes of adoption, the form of that surrender complied with the statutory requirements, the biological mother acknowledged her surrender before a judge, and the adoption agency consented to an adoption by third parties. Doe v. Noe, 317 Ill. App. 3d 419, 251 Ill. Dec. 103, 739 N.E.2d 1036, 2000 Ill. App. LEXIS 922 (4 Dist. 2000), cert. denied, 535 U.S. 932, 122 S. Ct. 1308, 152 L. Ed. 2d 218 (2002).

Where one of the child's parents is deceased and the other parent is found to be unfit, the child is available for adoption. In re C.M.J., 278 Ill. App. 3d 885, 215 Ill. Dec. 487, 663 N.E.2d 498 (5 Dist. 1996).

—Single Hearing

This Act contains no requirement that separate hearings be held in instances where the petition is for the adoption of a related child; therefore, the trial court is required to find that a parent is unfit, absent his consent, before considering the welfare of the child; nevertheless, these determinations may be made at a single hearing. Freeman v. Settle, 75 Ill. App. 3d 799, 31 Ill. Dec. 78, 393 N.E.2d 1385 (5 Dist. 1979).

—Termination of Consent

The court may consider whether the termination of the parent's residual right to consent to adoption is in the best interests of the minor only after a finding of parental consent or unfitness. People v. Rogers, 54 Ill. App. 3d 627, 12 Ill. Dec. 756, 370 N.E.2d 560 (1 Dist. 1977).

—Without Parental Consent

In order for the court to empower a guardian to consent to an adoption without the consent of the natural parent, the natural parent must be found to be an unfit person. People v. Drescher, 91 Ill. App. 3d 658, 47 Ill. Dec. 631, 415 N.E.2d 636 (1 Dist. 1980).

Best Interests of Child

—Not Independent Grounds

Absent parental consent or an order finding parental unfitness under the statute, the best interest of the child are not independent grounds for a decree of adoption. Culkin v. Culkin, 30 Ill. App. 3d 1073, 333 N.E.2d 698 (4 Dist. 1975).

—Petition Denied

Where child sought to be adopted had been separated from petitioners for over four-and-one-half years, had established a new lifestyle with his foster parents, and looked upon them as his natural parents, where the court found that the child's memories and recollections of his stay in petitioners' home were extremely vague, where the court took specific note of testimony given by a clinical psychologist, who contended that the child was beginning to make adjustments to his present home situation although the adjustments were marginal and indicated that a removal from his current environment would abort any positive adjustments and could result in severe emotional disturbance, because of the favorable adjustment in the child's foster home and the length of time that he had been out of petitioners' home, it would not serve the child's best interests to grant the adoption petition. Stines v. Vaughn, 23 Ill. App. 3d 511, 319 N.E.2d 561 (4 Dist. 1974).

—Petition Granted

The circuit court's termination of a mother's parental rights with respect to her three children did not constitute an abuse of discretion since it was in the best interests of the children to terminate her rights, notwithstanding testimony that the mother loved the children and that they loved her, in the light of testimony that the children also loved their foster mothers, had developed bonds with their respective foster families, and wanted to remain with those families. People v. Wanda H. (In re D.H.), 323 Ill. App. 3d 1, 256 Ill. Dec. 1, 751 N.E.2d 54, 2001 Ill. App. LEXIS 374 (1 Dist. 2001).

Termination of a father's parental rights was in the child's best interests where: (1) the father was responsible for the child's permanent injuries and would not be in a position to have the child returned to him at any time in the near future, as he was in prison serving a sentence of 25 years for aggravated battery of a child; (2) the child was in the custody of his maternal grandmother, who provided the child with the aid he needed and stability; and (3) the child's mother was involved in the child's care and was working toward regaining custody of him. People v. Musson, 314 Ill. App. 3d 682, 247 Ill. Dec. 424, 732 N.E.2d 140, 2000 Ill. App. LEXIS 536 (4 Dist. 2000).

—Priority of Interests

All of the parental rights must yield to the best interests of the child. People v. Hobbs, 215 Ill. App. 3d 522, 159 Ill. Dec. 32, 575 N.E.2d 261 (4 Dist.), appeal denied, 142 Ill. 2d 651, 164 Ill. Dec 914, 584 N.E.2d 126 (1991).

—Separate Hearing

Although a separate hearing and determination of the child's best interests is mandatory, the best interests hearing may be held immediately after the fitness hearing. In re B.R., 282 Ill. App. 3d 665, 218 Ill. Dec. 404, 669 N.E.2d 347 (3 Dist. 1996), appeal denied, 169 Ill. 2d 568, 221 Ill. Dec. 438, 675 N.E.2d 633 (1996).

A separate hearing and determination on the best interests issue is not a significant burden, but its importance is very significant. In re J.T.C., 273 Ill. App. 3d 193, 209 Ill. Dec. 881, 652 N.E.2d 421 (4 Dist. 1995).

Biological Parent

Trial court correctly interpreted the term "parents" to mean

Biological Parent (Cont'd)
biological and legally adoptive parents; husband who was not the biological father of wife's child was not a "parent" and had no right to contest the adoption of child. In re McFadyen, 108 Ill. App. 3d 329, 64 Ill. Dec. 43, 438 N.E.2d 1362 (1 Dist. 1982), cert. denied, 460 U.S. 1015, 103 S. Ct. 1259, 75 L. Ed. 2d 486 (1983).

The language used in this Act does not require the interpretation that a biological parent is not related to her child because she has consented to its adoption. Partington v. Department of Children & Family Servs., 91 Ill. App. 3d 205, 46 Ill. Dec. 656, 414 N.E.2d 540 (2 Dist. 1980).

Under former Ill.Rev.Stat., ch. 4, para. 1 (see now this section), unless the proof was clear that the natural parents were unfit to have the care, custody and control of a child, the contest for control of the child's future between persons having no vested interest in the child, and having had little or no opportunity of developing love, affection and attachment for the child, as against the natural law which bound a mother to her child, was to be solved in favor of the mother. Dickholtz v. Littfin, 341 Ill. App. 400, 94 N.E.2d 89 (1 Dist. 1950).

Compliance

—Prior Law

Substantial compliance with the former Adoption Act (see now 750 ILCS 50/0.01 et seq.) was sufficient. Simaner v. Simonick, 16 Ill. App. 2d 48, 147 N.E.2d 419 (1 Dist. 1957), aff'd, 15 Ill. 2d 568, 155 N.E.2d 555 (1959).

Construction With Other Laws

Parental rights could be terminated under former section 5-9 of the Juvenile Court Act (see now 705 ILCS 405/2-29, 705 ILCS 405/3-30, 705 ILCS 405/4-27, and 705 ILCS 403/5-31) independent of any adoption proceeding. People v. Welch, 164 Ill. App. 3d 142, 115 Ill. Dec. 211, 517 N.E.2d 622 (5 Dist. 1987).

Custody Proceeding Distinguished

Custody determination and adoption proceedings are two distinct procedures; a determination in the former does not affect the determination of parental fitness for the latter, therefore, neither res judicata or collateral estoppel apply. Lael v. Warga, 155 Ill. App. 3d 1005, 108 Ill. Dec. 518, 508 N.E.2d 1095 (4 Dist. 1987).

The distinction between a custody proceeding and an adoption is essential because adoption severs conclusively the rights and interests of natural parents; accordingly, a clear case must be made establishing the statutory grounds before a consideration of the best interests of the child can be made. Shuman v. Shuman, 22 Ill. App. 3d 151, 319 N.E.2d 287 (3 Dist. 1974).

Depravity

—In General

A 1998 amendment to the statute, which created a rebuttable presumption that a parent is depraved if he has been criminally convicted of at least three felonies, as long as one of the convictions occurred within five years of the filing of the petition to terminate parental rights, applied retroactively as the amendment only clarified existing law concerning proof of depravity. People v. T.T., Ill. App. 3d , 255 Ill. Dec. 561, 749 N.E.2d 1043, 2001 Ill. App. LEXIS 346 (1 Dist. May 14, 2001).

Subsection (D)(i), as amended, was properly applied to a parent, notwithstanding that his three felony convictions were entered prior to June 30, 1998 and his contention that the application of the amended statute to him would be an impermissible retroactive application of a new law, since the subsection did not create a new ground of unfitness and only created a rebuttable presumption of depravity. People v. Rosado, 316 Ill. App. 3d 553, 249 Ill. Dec. 484, 736 N.E.2d 678, 2000 Ill. App. LEXIS 754 (1 Dist. 2000).

In construing "depravity," both the rights of the parent and the best interests of the child must be considered. People v. Abdullah, 85 Ill. 2d 300, 53 Ill. Dec. 246, 423 N.E.2d 915 (1981).

—Child Out of Wedlock

In an adoption contest, there is no presumption of depravity arising from the fact that the child was born out of wedlock. Oeth v. Erwin, 6 Ill. App. 2d 18, 126 N.E.2d 526 (4 Dist. 1955).

—Conduct Required

A criminal conviction is neither necessary for a finding of unfitness based on depravity nor sufficient for a finding of unfitness based on depravity. In re T.H., 255 Ill. App. 3d 247, 193 Ill. Dec. 370, 626 N.E.2d 403 (5 Dist. 1993), appeal denied, 155 Ill. 2d 577, 198 Ill. Dec. 554, 633 N.E.2d 16, cert. denied, 513 U.S. 905, 115 S. Ct. 269, 130 L. Ed. 2d 187 (1994).

To support a finding of unfitness based on depravity, it must be established by clear and convincing evidence that the parent committed repetitious acts of sufficient duration to establish a deficiency in a moral sense and either an inability or unwillingness to conform to accepted moral standards. People v. Green, 173 Ill. App. 3d 922, 123 Ill. Dec. 693, 528 N.E.2d 238 (2 Dist. 1988).

—Defined

In order to find a person unfit on the ground of depravity, the court must find that the person suffers from an inherent deficiency of moral sense and rectitude. In re T.H., 255 Ill. App. 3d 247, 193 Ill. Dec. 370, 626 N.E.2d 403 (5 Dist. 1993), appeal denied, 155 Ill. 2d 577, 198 Ill. Dec. 554, 633 N.E.2d 16, cert. denied, 513 U.S. 905, 115 S. Ct. 269, 130 L. Ed. 2d 187 (1994).

Depravity is an inherent deficiency of moral sense and rectitude. Stalder v. Stone, 412 Ill. 488, 107 N.E.2d 696, 35 A.L.R.2d 653 (1952); Smith v. Andrews ex rel. Andrews, 54 Ill. App. 2d 51, 203 N.E.2d 160 (2 Dist. 1965).

—Felony Convictions

Finding of parental unfitness by reason of depravity was not against the manifest weight of the evidence in the case of a mother with five felony drug convictions whose child was born with cocaine exposure problems and syphilis. People v. Dorothy W. (In re Shanna W.), 343 Ill. App. 3d 1155, 279 Ill. Dec. 40, 799 N.E.2d 843, 2003 Ill. App. LEXIS 1267 (1 Dist. 2003).

Clear and convincing evidence supported a finding of parental unfitness by reason of depraved conduct, where the parent failed to offer any evidence to counter evidence of the parent's seven felony convictions. People v. Herman O. (In re Travarius O.), 343 Ill. App. 3d 844, 278 Ill. Dec. 792, 799 N.E.2d 510, 2003 Ill. App. LEXIS 1262 (1 Dist. 2003).

Respondent's conviction of two counts of aggravated criminal sexual assault of his daughter was vicious and perverted conduct constituting by itself overwhelming evidence that respondent was unfit within the meaning of this Act and termination of parental rights was in the child's best interest; respondent was subject to being found unfit due to depravity based solely upon that conduct, and thereby forever forfeited any claim to any further contact with that child or her siblings. People v. Heiman, 284 Ill. App. 3d 392, 219 Ill. Dec. 895, 672 N.E.2d 403 (4 Dist. 1996).

The mere fact that a parent has been convicted of a felony, even a number of felonies, is not sufficient to establish depravity which would render a parent unfit to have the child sought to be adopted. People v. Green, 173 Ill. App. 3d 922, 123 Ill. Dec. 693, 528 N.E.2d 238 (2 Dist. 1988).

A father's convictions of rape in 1951 and 1953 were relevant and were not so remote as to be immaterial where he served 20 years for these convictions and, once released, was again arrested and convicted of rape, deviate sexual assault and intimidation. Such acts constituting depravity were of sufficient duration and repetition to establish moral deficiency and either an inability or unwillingness to conform to accepted morality. Kellum v. Cornes, 125 Ill. App. 3d 512, 80 Ill. Dec. 821, 466 N.E.2d 273 (5 Dist. 1984), appeal dismissed, 471 U.S. 1062, 105 S. Ct. 2129, 85 L. Ed. 2d 493 (1985).

Where defendant had exhausted all state appeals from his conviction for murdering the mother of his child, and was unable to show that he was prejudiced when the court proceeded to trial in the determination of depravity before those appeals took place, then it was proper to use defendant's conviction in the determination of depravity. People v. Abdullah, 85 Ill. 2d 300, 53 Ill. Dec. 246, 423 N.E.2d 915 (1981).

One prior felony conviction alone is insufficient to automatically constitute depravity. Bryant v. Lenza, 90 Ill. App. 3d 275, 45 Ill. Dec. 572, 412 N.E.2d 1154 (3 Dist. 1980).

In adoption proceeding where on appeal the court was provided with a certified copy of the decision of Missouri Court of Appeals containing details of facts underlying natural father's conviction for murder of natural mother, which was not available to trial court, appellate court chose to remand issue to the trial court with instructions that it take judicial notice of the underlying facts of natural father's conviction and make its depravity determination

Depravity (Cont'd)

—Felony Convictions (Cont'd)

accordingly. Bryant v. Lenza, 90 Ill. App. 3d 275, 45 Ill. Dec. 572, 412 N.E.2d 1154 (3 Dist. 1980).

There must be some allowance for an individual to become rehabilitated; otherwise, the court merely compounds the punishment for the crime by declaring the perpetrator an unfit person and terminating his parental rights. People ex rel. Department of Children & Family Servs. v. Sanders, 77 Ill. App. 3d 78, 32 Ill. Dec. 847, 395 N.E.2d 1228 (4 Dist. 1979).

While a criminal record reveals a rejection of societal mores in the past, it is not conclusive. People ex rel. Department of Children & Family Servs. v. Sanders, 77 Ill. App. 3d 78, 32 Ill. Dec. 847, 395 N.E.2d 1228 (4 Dist. 1979).

The mere fact that a parent has been convicted of a felony, or even a number of felonies, is not sufficient to establish depravity; the criminal record of a person, while highly persuasive, is only one factor to be considered. People ex rel. Department of Children & Family Servs. v. Sanders, 77 Ill. App. 3d 78, 32 Ill. Dec. 847, 395 N.E.2d 1228 (4 Dist. 1979).

Where during the 11 years prior to the termination of his parental rights, appellant was convicted of six felonies and, at the time of the hearing appealed from, was incarcerated in the penitentiary serving a three to nine year sentence, the finding of depravity in the trial court was not palpably contrary to the manifest weight of the evidence. People ex rel. Dep't of Children & Family Servs., v. Buttram, 56 Ill. App. 3d 950, 14 Ill. Dec. 856, 372 N.E.2d 1135 (3 Dist. 1978).

Conviction of a felony alone is not a statutory ground for adoption without the consent of a natural parent, and a finding of depravity cannot be based exclusively on the fact of a criminal conviction. Ornstead v. Kleba, 37 Ill. App. 3d 163, 345 N.E.2d 714 (1 Dist. 1976).

A father was found to be an unfit parent, by reason of depravity, where he had been convicted of the crime of robbery, received a sentence of one to seven years in the penitentiary, and had been found guilty of the crime of forcible rape, for which he received a sentence of ten years in the penitentiary, to run concurrently with the sentence on the robbery conviction. Smith v. Andrews ex rel. Andrews, 54 Ill. App. 2d 51, 203 N.E.2d 160 (2 Dist. 1965).

The fact that a defendant had committed a robbery and a forcible rape was obviously relevant to the question of whether he had an inherent deficiency of moral sense and rectitude. Smith v. Andrews ex rel. Andrews, 54 Ill. App. 2d 51, 203 N.E.2d 160 (2 Dist. 1965).

—Illustrative Cases

Where a father had been incarcerated or involved in criminal activities for all but 1 of the last 14 years, was unable to provide emotional or financial support or stability to his daughter due to his repeated incarceration, had anger management issues, and lied to receive preferential treatment in prison, the trial court's finding him unfit under 750 ILCS 50/1(D)(s) was not against the manifest weight of the evidence. People v. Andre D. (In re Andrea D.), 342 Ill. App. 3d 233, 276 Ill. Dec. 793, 794 N.E.2d 1043, 2003 Ill. App. LEXIS 1006 (2 Dist. 2003), appeal denied, Ill. 2d , 282 Ill. Dec. 478, 806 N.E.2d 1066 (2003).

Where evidence before the court consisted of 20 convictions in a ten year period, this lengthy series of offenses demonstrated by clear and convincing evidence that mother was unable to cope with the norms of society in a lawful manner and that she was either unable or unwilling to conform to accepted morality; each time she was released from prison, she resumed the same sort of criminal activity in which she previously engaged and her continuing course of criminal conduct during the entire lifetimes of the four children at issue was more than sufficient to establish depravity. In re R.K., 247 Ill. App. 3d 512, 187 Ill. Dec. 294, 617 N.E.2d 502 (3 Dist. 1993).

In an adoption proceeding where defendant, child's natural father lived and cohabited with the mother of the baby for a substantial time both prior to her divorce from her former husband and subsequent to that divorce, without benefit of marriage, was in trouble in the navy and in more serious trouble afterwards, and had a drinking problem which the trial judge may not have been persuaded he had mastered, under former section 1 of the Adoption Act (see now this section) evidence at trial presented enough instances of misconduct of various degrees of seriousness to permit the trial judge, who could also observe the witnesses, to find the defendant unfit by reason of depravity. Tiernan v. Stewart, 33 Ill. App. 3d 545, 338 N.E.2d 153 (2 Dist. 1975).

The evidence was sufficient to support a trial court's finding that a defendant was an unfit parent due to depravity as evidenced by his continued pattern of extreme and repeated physical cruelty towards the women in his life, his conduct and actions in formerly living in open and notorious adultery with the deceased mother of the child, his mental condition relative to distrust for women, the untrustworthiness of the testimony given by the defendant at the trial regarding certain matters of child support, and prior conduct between the defendant and his present wife. Taylor v. Starkey, 20 Ill. App. 3d 630, 314 N.E.2d 620 (5 Dist. 1974).

Testimony fell short of clear and convincing evidence that depravity on the part of the mother existed at the time of the adoption petition or at the time of the decree. Young v. Prather, 120 Ill. App. 2d 395, 256 N.E.2d 670 (4 Dist. 1970).

Bearing a child out of wedlock did not alone indicate depravity, but where the affair resulting in the birth of the child was but one of a series, conducted both before and after the birth, with different persons, some of whom were known to be already married, and where abortion and perjury were resorted to without moral trepidation, then it could properly be found that there was an inherent deficiency of moral sense and rectitude constituting the "depravity" of character contemplated by the statute. Stalder v. Stone, 412 Ill. 488, 107 N.E.2d 696, 35 A.L.R.2d 653 (1952).

—Murder Conviction

A father met the statutory requirements of depravity where he was convicted of murder within ten years prior to the filing of the petition to terminate his parental rights, notwithstanding pleadings indicating that he was young at the time of the murder and was attempting rehabilitation while incarcerated, as well as the testimony of the child at issue's case manager, who testified that the father wrote letters to the child for approximately five months. People v. Rashon W., 315 Ill. App. 3d 1153, 249 Ill. Dec. 102, 735 N.E.2d 706, 2000 Ill. App. LEXIS 688 (1 Dist. 2000).

The application of the 1998 amendment to subsection 1(D)(i), which created a rebuttable presumption that a parent is depraved if the parent has been convicted of either first or second degree murder of any person within ten years of the filing date of the petition or motion to terminate parental rights, applied to a parent who was so convicted prior to the effective date of the amendment. People v. Rashon W., 315 Ill. App. 3d 1153, 249 Ill. Dec. 102, 735 N.E.2d 706, 2000 Ill. App. LEXIS 688 (1 Dist. 2000).

—Not Shown

The trial court properly found that a child's biological father was not depraved, notwithstanding his three prior felony convictions, where the trial court specifically found that the father had rebutted the presumption of depravity by clear and convincing evidence and noted that it was impressed with testimony by the father's wife that they had prepared a room in their home for the child in case the father was awarded custody and with testimony by the father's son that the father had been a good father to him, who provided for both his physical and emotional needs. People v. Rosado, 316 Ill. App. 3d 553, 249 Ill. Dec. 484, 736 N.E.2d 678, 2000 Ill. App. LEXIS 754 (1 Dist. 2000).

Where the father repeatedly and consistently kept in contact with the Department of Children and Family Services after the children were first removed, was incarcerated, and while incarcerated, he petitioned for appointment of counsel and succeeded in obtaining visitation with his children throughout his incarceration, he was not unfit by reason of depravity. People v. Green, 173 Ill. App. 3d 922, 123 Ill. Dec. 693, 528 N.E.2d 238 (2 Dist. 1988).

—Rehabilitative Potential

Trial court erred in terminating parental rights of mother even though she had been found to be a depraved person; the record clearly showed that mother and children loved each other and that mother had rehabilitative potential in that she was taking classes and receiving counseling to make a better life for herself and her children. B.C. & W.C. v. Cheryl C., 247 Ill. App. 3d 803, 187 Ill. Dec. 486, 617 N.E.2d 1207 (3 Dist.), appeal allowed, 153 Ill. 2d 559, 191 Ill. Dec. 619, 624 N.E.2d 807 (1993).

—Shown

Finding by circuit court that a father was depraved and unfit was

Depravity (Cont'd)

—Shown (Cont'd)
not against the manifest weight of the evidence where the father did not rebut the statutory presumption in subdivision (D)(i) of this section that a conviction and sentence the father was serving for murder of his stepfather established that he was depraved and an unfit parent. Jeffrey D.B. v. Stacy L.B. (In re Alyssa Jo B.), 2005 Ill. App. LEXIS 20 (3 Dist. Jan. 19, 2005).

The trial court's finding of depravity was not against the manifest weight of the evidence where the respondent was convicted of first degree murder for the murder of the mother of his children, he was also convicted of two counts of aggravated battery for the injury of two persons who were passengers with his wife when he killed her, respondent's bigotry was well documented and, in addition, the record showed his cruelty to his victim before the incident that ended her life. In re A.L., 301 Ill. App. 3d 198, 234 Ill. Dec. 367, 702 N.E.2d 1021 (3 Dist. 1998).

Proof of respondent's criminal conduct against his stepchildren, as known to the court by certified copies of his convictions and the indictment, was alone sufficient proof of his depravity and inherent deficiency of moral sense and rectitude to prove his unfitness as a parent. People v. Deerwester, 298 Ill. App. 3d 250, 232 Ill. Dec. 459, 698 N.E.2d 550, 1998 Ill. App. LEXIS 370 (4 Dist. 1998), appeal denied, 181 Ill. 2d 571, 235 Ill. Dec. 942, 706 N.E.2d 497 (1998), cert. denied, 528 U.S. 811, 120 S. Ct. 45, 145 L. Ed. 2d 40 (1999).

Where father, over a 20-year period, had been convicted five times for a series of crimes, all but one of which was violent, this pattern of conduct showed depravity, without potential for rehabilitation. In re Dawn H., 281 Ill. App. 3d 746, 217 Ill. Dec. 396, 667 N.E.2d 485 (1 Dist. 1996).

The fact the father did not visit daughter for almost five years or attempt to discover her whereabouts during that time supported the trial court's finding of desertion, an intent to forgo parental rights, lack of interest in daughter and failure to work towards her return and was a sufficient basis for finding father an unfit parent on grounds other than depravity due to his incarcerations. In re Dawn H., 281 Ill. App. 3d 746, 217 Ill. Dec. 396, 667 N.E.2d 485 (1 Dist. 1996).

The trial court correctly held that the testimony of credible witnesses concerning father's use of drugs and alcohol demonstrated that his lifestyle categorized him as being depraved; therefore, as father was properly found to be an unfit person in accordance with subdivisions (D)(b) and (D)(i) of the Act, his consent to the adoption of baby was unnecessary. In re Casale, 266 Ill. App. 3d 656, 203 Ill. Dec. 135, 639 N.E.2d 174 (1 Dist. 1994).

—Standard
Depravity may be established by a series of acts or a course of conduct indicating a deficiency in a moral sense and showing either an inability or a unwillingness to conform to accepted morality; however, the mere fact of a felony criminal conviction is not sufficient to justify a finding of depravity. In re T.H., 255 Ill. App. 3d 247, 193 Ill. Dec. 370, 626 N.E.2d 403 (5 Dist. 1993), appeal denied, 155 Ill. 2d 577, 198 Ill. Dec. 554, 633 N.E.2d 16, cert. denied, 513 U.S. 905, 115 S. Ct. 269, 130 L. Ed. 2d 187 (1994).

The statutory ground of depravity requires the trier of fact to closely scrutinize the character and credibility of the person. People ex rel. Department of Children & Family Servs. v. Sanders, 77 Ill. App. 3d 78, 32 Ill. Dec. 847, 395 N.E.2d 1228 (4 Dist. 1979).

—Witness Demeanor
The court could properly take into consideration father's demeanor on the stand while giving evidence when it determined whether or not he was depraved at the time of the hearing in adoption proceeding. Ornstead v. Kleba, 37 Ill. App. 3d 163, 345 N.E.2d 714 (1 Dist. 1976).

Desertion

—Adoption by Foster Parents
There could be no other conclusion but that a natural mother deserted her child when she sold him; therefore, the trial court should have considered adoption by the foster parents because of the bonding which has occurred since the child was placed with the foster parents. People v. Tamburini, 192 Ill. App. 3d 477, 139 Ill. Dec. 529, 548 N.E.2d 1085 (4 Dist. 1989), cert. denied, 132 Ill. 2d 545, 144 Ill. Dec. 266, 555 N.E.2d 385 (1990).

—Burden of Proof
Evidence of desertion must be proved by very clear and convincing evidence. Green v. Department of Children & Family Servs., 131 Ill. App. 2d 952, 267 N.E.2d 505 (4 Dist. 1971).

—Defined
The mere fact of physical separation does not necessarily constitute desertion. People v. Overton, 21 Ill. App. 3d 1014, 316 N.E.2d 201 (2 Dist. 1974).

Desertion is any conduct on the part of a parent which indicates an intention to permanently terminate custody over the child but not to relinquish all parental duties and claims to the child. Bergstedt v. Cech, 8 Ill. App. 3d 642, 291 N.E.2d 21 (1 Dist. 1972); Thorpe v. Thorpe, 48 Ill. App. 2d 455, 198 N.E.2d 743 (4 Dist. 1964); People v. Overton, 21 Ill. App. 3d 1014, 316 N.E.2d 201 (2 Dist. 1974); Markham v. Markham, 91 Ill. App. 3d 1122, 47 Ill. Dec. 235, 414 N.E.2d 1351 (3 Dist. 1981); People v. Tamburini, 192 Ill. App. 3d 477, 139 Ill. Dec. 529, 548 N.E.2d 1085 (4 Dist. 1989), cert. denied, 132 Ill. 2d 545, 144 Ill. Dec. 266, 555 N.E.2d 385 (1990).

Desertion is any conduct on the part of a parent which would indicate an intention to permanently terminate custody over the child but not to relinquish all parental duties and parental claims to the child. In re Smith, 4 Ill. App. 3d 261, 280 N.E.2d 770 (1 Dist. 1972).

Desertion must necessarily have a far broader meaning than physical separation. Green v. Department of Children & Family Servs., 131 Ill. App. 2d 952, 267 N.E.2d 505 (4 Dist. 1971).

Desertion is something less than abandonment, but necessarily requires the establishment of the existence of an intention by the parent to terminate permanently custody over the child but not to relinquish all parental duties. Robinson v. Neubauer, 79 Ill. App. 2d 362, 223 N.E.2d 705 (4 Dist. 1967).

"Desertion" was described as action by a parent that would indicate an intention to terminate custody permanently but not to relinquish all parental duties and claim to the child, and "abandonment" was described as conduct on the part of a parent which evinced a settled purpose to forego parental duties and relinquish all parental claims to the child; in both, intent and an examination of the conduct toward the child were proper areas of judicial inquiry. Carlson v. Oberling, 73 Ill. App. 2d 412, 218 N.E.2d 820 (4 Dist. 1966).

The legislature, having added the word "abandonment" to the former Adoption Act (see now subdivision (D)(a) of this section), recognized some difference between abandonment under subdivision (D)(a) and desertion under subdivision (D)(c) of this section. Hill v. Allabaugh, 333 Ill. App. 602, 78 N.E.2d 127 (2 Dist. 1948).

—Imprisonment
Natural father had not voluntarily left his children; his imprisonment was certainly involuntary and would not support a charge of unfitness based upon desertion for a period in excess of three months. Bryant v. Lenza, 90 Ill. App. 3d 275, 45 Ill. Dec. 572, 412 N.E.2d 1154 (3 Dist. 1980).

If the only reason that the respondent had not visited or cared for the children was his imprisonment, he could not be held to have the intent to abandon or desert. People ex rel. Department of Children & Family Servs. v. Sanders, 77 Ill. App. 3d 78, 32 Ill. Dec. 847, 395 N.E.2d 1228 (4 Dist. 1979).

—Intent of Parent
Where the court expressly stated that the question of desertion was not a matter of intent, thereby basing its decision only on the mother's physical separation from her children for a three month period, the finding of the court that the mother deserted her children was reversed. People v. Overton, 21 Ill. App. 3d 1014, 316 N.E.2d 201 (2 Dist. 1974).

Appellant's periodic inquiries to and appointments with her son's caseworkers and her plans to visit her son negated any alleged intention on her part to desert her son. Green v. Department of Children & Family Servs., 131 Ill. App. 2d 952, 267 N.E.2d 505 (4 Dist. 1971).

—Not Shown
Petitioners failed to prove by clear and convincing evidence under the former Adoption Act (see now this section), that natural father was unfit by reason of desertion. Rich v. Rich, 51 Ill. App. 3d 174, 9 Ill. Dec. 318, 366 N.E.2d 575 (1 Dist. 1977).

Desertion (Cont'd)

—Shown

Where the evidence, including the natural mother's own testimony, clearly established that she intended to permanently give up custody of her child for purposes of adoption, even though she testified that she thought she could retain some contact with the child, that the trial court's failure to terminate parental rights on the ground of desertion was against the manifest weight of the evidence. People v. Tamburini, 192 Ill. App. 3d 477, 139 Ill. Dec. 529, 548 N.E.2d 1085 (4 Dist. 1989), cert. denied, 132 Ill. 2d 545, 144 Ill. Dec. 266, 555 N.E.2d 385 (1990).

Effect of Amendment

An amendment to subsection (1)(D)(m) of this section, which provides that a parent of a child adjudicated neglected is given only nine months to correct the conditions that were the basis for removal of the child before his parental rights can be terminated, applies retroactively to pending actions because it does not affect any vested rights. In re K.P., 305 Ill. App. 3d 175, 238 Ill. Dec. 375, 711 N.E.2d 478 (4 Dist. 1999).

Efforts or Reasonable Progress

—Lack of

Mother was found unfit under both parts of subdivision (D)(m) for failing to make reasonable efforts to correct the conditions which were the basis for removal of the children, and failing to make measurable progress toward the return of her children. In re Y.B., 285 Ill. App. 3d 385, 221 Ill. Dec. 26, 674 N.E.2d 819 (3 Dist. 1996).

A lack of reasonable progress toward the return of her children is a ground for termination of parental rights, but is not involved with termination of proceedings under the Act; the appropriate standard is the child's best interests. In re M.K., 271 Ill. App. 3d 820, 208 Ill. Dec. 242, 649 N.E.2d 74 (4 Dist. 1995), appeal denied, 163 Ill. 2d 558, 212 Ill. Dec. 421, 657 N.E.2d 622 (1995).

Final Order

Although petitioner had motions pending to modify and clarify visitation and to obtain a restraining order against the respondent's spouse, these matters were ancillary and incidental to the orders transferring custody and establishing a support obligation and a visitation schedule; therefore the order ruling on respondent's motion for sanctions was a final order. In re M.M.W., 296 Ill. App. 3d 877, 231 Ill. Dec. 238, 695 N.E.2d 1357 (2 Dist. 1998).

Habeas Corpus Distinguished

A habeas corpus action brought by foster parents for the sole legal purpose of reacquiring custody of their foster child differed from an adoption proceeding, because the purpose of an adoption petition is not to simply reacquire physical custody, but rather to determine the permanent de facto and de jure custody, whereas the critical issue in a habeas corpus action is whether the petitioner can show a prima facie legal right to custody. Stines v. Vaughn, 23 Ill. App. 3d 511, 319 N.E.2d 561 (4 Dist. 1974).

Illness

—Medical Testimony

The testimony of two doctors who gave similarly negative prognoses for mother's future hope of being a successful parent, testified that respondent was grossly psychotic, indicated that she had periods of hospitalization for paranoid schizophrenia, although she had made improvement through medication, was sufficient to show that the mother would probably never be able to function normally outside of a supervised living situation. People v. Freeman, 161 Ill. App. 3d 325, 112 Ill. Dec. 881, 514 N.E.2d 544 (4 Dist. 1987).

Intent of Parent

—Imprisonment

The trial court may properly consider imprisonment as it relates to intent. People ex rel. Department of Children & Family Servs. v. Sanders, 77 Ill. App. 3d 78, 32 Ill. Dec. 847, 395 N.E.2d 1228 (4 Dist. 1979).

While incarcerated, there are a number of things a person can do which would indicate a lack of intent to abandon or desert. People ex rel. Department of Children & Family Servs. v. Sanders, 77 Ill. App. 3d 78, 32 Ill. Dec. 847, 395 N.E.2d 1228 (4 Dist. 1979).

The trial court's finding that the mother failed to maintain a reasonable degree of interest, concern or responsibility as to the children's welfare was not based upon clear and convincing evidence. People v. Overton, 21 Ill. App. 3d 1014, 316 N.E.2d 201 (2 Dist. 1974).

Interest, Concern or Responsibility

—Clear and Convincing Evidence

Parental rights should be terminated on the basis of unfitness only if there is clear and convincing evidence that the parent has not maintained a reasonable degree of interest, concern, or responsibility as to the welfare of the children, and in making this determination, a court should evaluate the parent's conduct in the context of the circumstances in which it occurred and, in addition, the court should consider the parent's efforts to show interest in the children or communicate with them and not necessarily the success of those efforts. N.H. v. A.A., 222 Ill. App. 3d 73, 164 Ill. Dec. 696, 583 N.E.2d 612 (2 Dist. 1991).

In order to find that a parent is unfit under subdivision 1(D)(b) of this section, thereby avoiding the necessity of obtaining that parent's consent to the adoption of his or her child, the trial court must find clear and convincing evidence that the parent failed to maintain a reasonable degree of interest, concern, or responsibility as to the child's welfare. Syck v. Snyder, 138 Ill. 2d 255, 149 Ill. Dec. 710, 562 N.E.2d 174 (1990).

Judgment of the trial court should be reversed where the finding by the trial court that the mother had failed to maintain a reasonable degree of interest, concern and responsibility for her children's welfare was not based on clear and convincing evidence. Gibson v. People, 24 Ill. App. 3d 981, 322 N.E.2d 223 (2 Dist. 1975).

The trial court's finding that the mother failed to maintain a reasonable degree of interest, concern or responsibility as to the children's welfare was not based upon clear and convincing evidence. People v. Overton, 21 Ill. App. 3d 1014, 316 N.E.2d 201 (2 Dist. 1974).

—Denial of Visitation

Where father admitted that he had denied or restricted mother's visitation, and dictated the circumstances of what visitation he permitted, he may not then argue it is evidence of the mother's indifference to the child that she did not immediately ask to see the child upon her return to Illinois for the adoption hearing. Culkin v. Culkin, 30 Ill. App. 3d 1073, 333 N.E.2d 698 (4 Dist. 1975).

—Drug Abuse

Facts including mother's continued addiction to drugs, her repeated failure to obtain treatment for that addiction, and her infrequent and irregular visitation with her child are more than sufficient to warrant a finding that the mother lacked interest, concern or responsibility for her child. People v. Gill, 201 Ill. App. 3d 792, 147 Ill. Dec. 236, 559 N.E.2d 236 (1 Dist. 1990).

—Illustrative Cases

Noncompliance with an imposed service plan, a continued addiction to drugs, a repeated failure to obtain treatment for an addiction, and infrequent or irregular visitation with the child have all been held to be sufficient evidence warranting a finding of unfitness under 750 ILCS 50/1(D)(b); thus, a trial court's determination that a mother was unfit under this section was not against the manifest weight of the evidence where her lack of interaction with social workers, her children's special needs, her continued refusal to participate in even the most minor aspects of drug treatment and the imposed service plans, and her repeated failure to maintain frequent and regular visitation more than sufficiently demonstrated that she had not maintained a reasonable degree of responsibility toward the welfare of her children. People v. Lynette H.F. (In re Jaron Z.), 348 Ill. App. 3d 239, 284 Ill. Dec. 455, 810 N.E.2d 108, 2004 Ill. App. LEXIS 457 (1 Dist. 2004).

Evidence was sufficient to establish that parents failed to maintain a reasonable degree of interest, concern, or responsibility as to their children's welfare since when and if the father visited, he would stay for only a portion of the already brief visit and sometimes showed up after the time allotted for the visit was already expired, and although the mother visited frequently, she could not seem to manage to control her inappropriate behavior including her angry outbursts despite the fact that such behavior

Interest, Concern or Responsibility (Cont'd)

—Illustrative Cases (Cont'd)

was profoundly upsetting. In re C.M., 319 Ill. App. 3d 344, 253 Ill. Dec. 183, 744 N.E.2d 916, 2001 Ill App. LEXIS 59 (1 Dist. 2001).

The finding that the father had not shown a reasonable degree of interest in the child was not supported by the evidence, in fact, he made various attempts to locate the child, all of which were either frustrated or blocked by the actions of the mother. In re Doe, 159 Ill. 2d 347, 202 Ill. Dec. 535, 638 N.E.2d 181, cert. denied, 513 U.S. 994, 115 S. Ct. 499, 130 L. Ed. 2d 408 (1994).

Where the mother was unable to properly clothe, feed and bathe the child, although the father was capable, he was nonetheless unfit as he simply failed to rectify the home situation, including allowing dirty and unsafe living conditions, lack of food, and inappropriate clothing. People v. Sandvik, 128 Ill. App. 3d 449, 83 Ill. Dec. 880, 470 N.E.2d 1300 (5 Dist. 1984).

A natural parent who has validly consented to the adoption of her child may, prior to the specific placement of the child for adoption by others, properly petition to adopt as the parent of a related child. Partington v. Department of Children & Family Servs., 91 Ill. App. 3d 205, 46 Ill. Dec. 656, 414 N.E.2d 540 (2 Dist. 1980).

—Importance of Effort

Mother's efforts to contact her children rather than her lack of success should be considered in determining the correctness of a finding of unfitness under subsection 9.1-1(D)(b) of the former Adoption Act (see now subdivision (b) of this section), particularly where the mother's attempts to fulfill her parental duties were prevented by the policies or personnel, or both, of the Department of Children and Family Services. People v. Taylor, 30 Ill. App. 3d 906, 334 N.E.2d 194 (1 Dist. 1975).

—Incarcerated Parent

Because the father's contacts with his children were both "small in number" and "lacking distinction" while he was incarcerated, his parental rights were properly terminated. People v. T.T.R., 326 Ill. App. 3d 356, 260 Ill. Dec. 225, 760 N.E.2d 998, 2001 Ill. App. LEXIS 834 (2 Dist. 2001).

In adoption proceeding, evidence indicated that even while natural father was imprisoned he made numerous attempts to contact his children through letters and certified mail and also by personal contacts in his behalf by his family, his attorney, and the Department of Children and Family Services, sent birthday cards and presents as well as Christmas presents to the children, evidence was clear and convincing that the natural father made numerous attempts to contact his children and maintained more than a reasonable degree of interest, concern and responsibility for the children's welfare under the circumstances in which he found himself; it is the natural father's efforts to carry out his responsibilities rather than the success with which he meets them that is determinative. Bryant v. Lenza, 90 Ill. App. 3d 275, 45 Ill. Dec. 572, 412 N.E.2d 1154 (3 Dist. 1980).

The evidence did not clearly and convincingly demonstrate that respondent had failed to maintain a reasonable degree of interest, concern, or responsibility toward the welfare of her children to warrant the termination of her parental rights; although the record was replete with evidence of respondent's shortcomings and failures, it was her efforts to carry out her parental responsibilities, and not her success, which would measure the standard of fitness. People v. Fay, 44 Ill. App. 3d 260, 2 Ill. Dec. 595, 357 N.E.2d 815 (2 Dist. 1976).

The evidence was held insufficient to sustain the trial court's finding that an incarcerated putative father was an unfit parent within the former Adoption Act (see now this section). People v. Allen, 34 Ill. App. 3d 603, 340 N.E.2d 269 (1 Dist. 1975).

—Lack of Conduct

Where the respondent's efforts to visit son were halfhearted and easily abandoned, when he was faced with standard Department of Children and Family Services procedures regarding visitation and did, in fact, sign a service plan, he lacked the commitment necessary to complete its terms, keeping only two of the six counseling sessions he agreed to attend; the evidence was sufficient to show that the respondent failed to maintain a reasonable degree of interest, concern or responsibility as to son's welfare. People v. Autio, 135 Ill. App. 3d 1017, 90 Ill. Dec. 553, 482 N.E.2d 372 (1 Dist. 1985).

Petitioners proved by clear and convincing evidence that natural father failed to maintain a reasonable degree of interest, concern or responsibility as to the welfare of his two minor children where, while he did suffer financial difficulties and episodes of mental illness, the former were not so great and the latter were not so long as to justify the lack of contact with his children over an extended period of time. Pyatt v. Pyatt, 88 Ill. App. 3d 8, 43 Ill. Dec. 241, 410 N.E.2d 241 (5 Dist. 1980).

Even though respondent occasionally visited her children and on two occasions bought them gifts and that traveling from respondent's home to the children's foster home may have caused the respondent some difficulty as well as expense, it could not be said that these factors excused her from her palpable lack of a reasonable degree of interest, concern or responsibility for their welfare in accordance with the statutory standard of the former Adoption Act (see now this section), in that she never had any type of communication or contact with children from date of their birth until 1972, a period of five years. People v. Grant, 29 Ill. App. 3d 731, 331 N.E.2d 219 (1 Dist. 1975).

—Lack of Effort

Clear and convincing evidence supported the conclusion that father had not shown adequate interest and concern for his children, where his efforts to contact his children were not even minimal, he made no attempt to contact the Department of Children and Family Services (DCFS) to arrange visits with them or to inquire as to their welfare, and he never informed DCFS of his whereabouts while in prison, nor did he take the opportunity to contact DCFS during the six month period that he was not incarcerated. T.D. v. Baldwin, 268 Ill. App. 3d 239, 205 Ill. Dec. 708, 643 N.E.2d 1315 (1 Dist. 1994).

—Mitigating Circumstances Not Shown

A father's desire to escape arrest is not a circumstance mitigating the failure to demonstrate a reasonable level of interest, concern and responsibility for a child; public policy requires that a parent not be able to turn his desire to evade justice into a valid excuse for his failure to pay crucial (and statutorily required) attention to his neglected child. People v. T.J., 233 Ill. App. 3d 88, 174 Ill. Dec. 159, 598 N.E.2d 456 (2 Dist. 1992).

—Murder Conviction

A putative father's conviction for the murder of the woman who had given birth to his illegitimate offspring, the children whose adoption he had refused to approve, was not relevant or material to the state's charge that he had failed to maintain a reasonable degree of interest, concern or responsibility as to his children's welfare. People v. Allen, 34 Ill. App. 3d 603, 340 N.E.2d 269 (1 Dist. 1975).

—Newborn Children

Where the state proved by at least clear and convincing evidence that respondent failed to demonstrate any interest, concern, or responsibility for his newborn child not only during the first 30 days of her life but during the first four and one-half months of her life, the trial court's decision that respondent's parental rights should not be terminated was against the manifest weight of the evidence. In re A.S.V., 268 Ill. App. 3d 549, 205 Ill. Dec. 944, 644 N.E.2d 500 (5 Dist. 1994), appeal denied, 161 Ill. 2d 526, 208 Ill. Dec. 360, 649 N.E.2d 416 (1995).

—Not Shown

Trial court's finding that father's parental rights should be terminated based on his failure to maintain a reasonable degree of interest, concern or responsibility for his son was not against the manifest weight of the evidence where the evidence showed that the father only saw his son when the boy's mother initiated contact, that the father did not know where his son lived or how to contact him, that the father was unaware that the son had been in foster care for six years, and that there was a period of six months prior to the father's incarceration when the father could not have had any contact with his son because the mother had died. People v. Rodney S. (In re Rodney T.), 352 Ill. App. 3d 496, 287 Ill. Dec. 774, 816 N.E.2d 741, 2004 Ill. App. LEXIS 1089 (1 Dist. 2004).

Child welfare agency presented sufficient evidence to establish that a father's habitual drunkenness prevented him from showing

Interest, Concern or Responsibility (Cont'd)

—Not Shown (Cont'd)

required levels of interest, concern, or responsibility for his children, where his frequent attempts to quit drinking were unavailing and he often showed up for visitation while drunk. People v. J.Y., 334 Ill. App. 3d 894, 268 Ill. Dec. 590, 778 N.E.2d 1212, 2002 Ill. App. LEXIS 969 (1 Dist. 2002).

The trial court's finding of father's parental unfitness, based on his failure to maintain a reasonable degree of care, concern, or responsibility for his child's welfare in accordance with subdivision (D)(b) was not against the manifest weight of the evidence where it was apparent that father's sole interest in baby was to use her as a tool to convince mother to resume their relationship. In re Casale, 266 Ill. App. 3d 656, 203 Ill. Dec. 135, 639 N.E.2d 174 (1 Dist. 1994).

Where a father failed to visit or otherwise show concern for a child before he went to prison and after he was released, missed 11 scheduled visits in a period of slightly over two months without excuse, and where there was no evidence that the father had found gainful employment or even tried to do so, his conduct was sufficient for the trial court to conclude that he had not shown reasonable concern, interest or responsibility as to the child's welfare. People v. T.J., 233 Ill. App. 3d 88, 174 Ill. Dec. 159, 598 N.E.2d 456 (2 Dist. 1992).

—Paternity Action

The filing of paternity action under 750 ILCS 45/7(e) establishes the alleged father's status of record and entitles him to service of process in proceedings involving the child; had respondent simply availed himself of the provisions of that section, he would not have had to rely upon the cooperation of mother and her family, which he was aware was unreliable, to express his concern for his child and he would have demonstrated concern for his child under subdivision D.(l). In re J.R.G., 247 Ill. App. 3d 104, 187 Ill. Dec. 169, 617 N.E.2d 377 (1 Dist. 1993).

—Shown

Parents showed a reasonable interest, concern, and responsibility under 750 ILCS 50/1(D)(6), given the parents' personal circumstances and the subject child's profound medical problems, where both parents had multiple visits with the child, the father involved himself in decisions regarding medical treatment, and the mother asked many questions about the child's health. People v. Brownlee, 334 Ill. App. 3d 651, 268 Ill. Dec. 458, 778 N.E.2d 724, 2002 Ill. App. LEXIS 1044 (4 Dist. 2002).

Where a mother, who had several other children, made substantial efforts at visitation and had a plausible explanation for most of her absences, and where she spent some of her limited income on gifts and toys and made substantial efforts to make her home suitable for her daughter, the trial court's finding that there was clear and convincing evidence that she failed to demonstrate a reasonable level of concern, interest or responsibility for the child was not upheld. People v. T.J., 233 Ill. App. 3d 88, 174 Ill. Dec. 159, 598 N.E.2d 456 (2 Dist. 1992).

A finding of unfitness was premised entirely upon father's failure to provide financial support for his child for a period of over two years, despite the fact that he had made reasonable efforts to visit the child, which were frustrated by lack of cooperation from the mother, was not supported by clear and convincing evidence, and was overturned. Perkins v. Breitbarth, 99 Ill. App. 3d 135, 54 Ill. Dec. 458, 424 N.E.2d 1361 (3 Dist. 1981).

Where respondent-mother visited child six times in 18 months, where caseworkers testified that respondent expressed her desire to have son returned to her, and there was evidence that she had sent cards to son on at least two occasions, the trial court's determination, that respondent-mother failed to show a reasonable degree of interest and concern, was against the manifest weight of the evidence. People v. Foster, 95 Ill. App. 3d 169, 50 Ill. Dec. 605, 419 N.E.2d 713 (4 Dist. 1981).

Clear and convincing evidence sufficient to justify the termination of the natural rights between mother and child was not offered in case where mother's neglect was excusable due to transportation problems, and after judge's order was entered to assist mother with transportation, her visits dramatically increased. Gibson v. People, 24 Ill. App. 3d 981, 322 N.E.2d 223 (2 Dist. 1975).

Juvenile Proceedings

—No Jury Trial

Under the former Juvenile Court Act, (Ill.Rev.Stat., ch. 37, para. 701-1 et seq., (see now 705 ILCS 405/1-1 et seq.), and the former Adoption Act (see now this section), the use of "the court" by the legislature suggested that the court is to be the trier of fact in juvenile proceedings. In re Weinstein, 68 Ill. App. 3d 883, 25 Ill. Dec. 322, 386 N.E.2d 593 (1 Dist. 1979).

In a proceeding seeking a finding of unfitness and termination of parental rights under former Juvenile Court Act (Ill.Rev.Stat., ch. 37, para. 705-9 (1975)), (see now 705 ILCS 405/2-29), and former Adoption Act (Ill.Rev.Stat., ch. 4, para. 9.1-1 (1975)), (see now 750 ILCS 50/1), no right to a jury trial exists. In re Weinstein, 68 Ill. App. 3d 883, 25 Ill. Dec. 322, 386 N.E.2d 593 (1 Dist. 1979).

Legislative Intent

Under subsection (D)(q), the legislature intended that there be a criminal conviction for some type of aggravated battery and that the victim be "the child" that is at issue in the unfitness proceedings. People v. C.L.F., 311 Ill. App. 3d 1049, 244 Ill. Dec. 686, 726 N.E.2d 661, 2000 Ill. App. LEXIS 140 (5 Dist. 2000).

Mental Illness

—In General

In order to find a parent unfit it must first be shown by competent evidence that the parent suffers from a mental inability sufficient to prevent her from discharging a parent's normal responsibilities, and there must also be sufficient evidence to conclude that the inability will extend beyond a reasonable time period. In re J.A.S., 255 Ill. App. 3d 822, 194 Ill. Dec. 433, 627 N.E.2d 770 (5 Dist. 1994).

—Before Age of 18

In light of a clinical psychologist's testimony regarding respondent's low intelligence and personality problems, a reasonable fact finder could have inferred that respondent's mental retardation existed from the time she was 18 years old. People v. C.S., 303 Ill. App. 3d 559, 237 Ill. Dec. 273, 709 N.E.2d 259 (2 Dist. 1999), appeal denied, 184 Ill. 2d 557, 239 Ill. Dec. 608, 714 N.E.2d 527 (1999).

—Illustrative Cases

There was clear and convincing evidence of unfitness due to mental impairment and that such impairment would extend beyond a reasonable time. In re J.A.S., 255 Ill. App. 3d 822, 194 Ill. Dec. 433, 627 N.E.2d 770 (5 Dist. 1994).

Mother had a mental impairment which prohibited her from discharging her parental responsibilities where doctor concluded that mother was of limited intellectual ability; that she had severe, chronic borderline personality disorder; that she was emotionally and behaviorally unstable; that she consistently demonstrated a severe and repeated neglect of the child; that she demonstrated self absorption to the exclusion of her protection of the child; and most importantly, that she had been unable to meet the demands of her adult life so as to care for herself, let alone her dependent children. People v. D.D., 198 Ill. App. 3d 495, 144 Ill. Dec. 679, 555 N.E.2d 1198 (5 Dist. 1990).

Where, under the care of his mother, who had limited mental ability, a child was developmentally retarded, but under foster care, was able to overcome, to a considerable extent, the handicap visited upon him by the deprived environment in which he had lived, even though the mother loved her son and wanted him returned to her, the evidence also clearly supported a finding that she failed, since the child was adjudged neglected and dependent, to make measurable progress toward his safe return. People v. Edmonds, 85 Ill. App. 3d 229, 40 Ill. Dec. 530, 406 N.E.2d 231 (3 Dist. 1980).

—Impairment vs Retardation

The state was not required to prove the respondent was mentally retarded as a finding of unfitness could be based on the respondent's mental impairment sufficient to prevent her from discharging a parent's normal responsibilities. People v. C.S., 303 Ill. App. 3d 559, 237 Ill. Dec. 273, 709 N.E.2d 259 (2 Dist. 1999), appeal denied, 184 Ill. 2d 557, 239 Ill. Dec. 608, 714 N.E.2d 527 (1999).

—Length of Time

The state presented ample evidence that respondent's mental impairment would extend beyond a reasonable period of time where there was testimony that her poor prognosis was not likely to change within a year. People v. C.S., 303 Ill. App. 3d 559, 237 Ill. Dec. 273, 709 N.E.2d 259 (2 Dist. 1999), appeal denied, 184 Ill. 2d 557, 239 Ill. Dec. 608, 714 N.E.2d 527 (1999).

Mental Illness (Cont'd)

—Medical TestimonyPeople v. Williams, 218 Ill. App. 3d 431, 161 Ill. Dec. 179, 578 N.E.2d 306 (4 Dist. 1991).

Medical testimony which was consistent and strongly weighted against respondent was a sufficient justification for the trial court's finding that respondent's mental impairment would extend beyond a reasonable time. People v. Freeman, 161 Ill. App. 3d 325, 112 Ill. Dec. 881, 514 N.E.2d 544 (4 Dist. 1987).

—Mental Impairment

Evidence was sufficient to establish that a mother was unable to discharge her parental responsibilities due to mental impairment where she was diagnosed with a borderline personality disorder which caused her to become psychotic and/or paranoid under periods of stress. In re C.M., 319 Ill. App. 3d 344, 253 Ill. Dec. 183, 744 N.E.2d 916, 2001 Ill App. LEXIS 59 (1 Dist. 2001).

Psychiatric evidence of parent's long term inability to perform parental duties held sufficient to sustain finding of unfitness. People v. Fontana, 178 Ill. App. 3d 662, 127 Ill. Dec. 870, 533 N.E.2d 952 (2 Dist. 1989).

—Mental Retardation

Clear and convincing evidence that respondent was an unfit parent existed where respondent repeatedly tried to learn how to care for her child, yet she was unable to learn such elementary skills as feeding and diapering; respondent, a resident of a group home, with an IQ of 65 and problem solving skills at the level of a seven or eight year old, was barely able to meet her own basic needs, let alone those of a young child. People v. T.S., 187 Ill. App. 3d 41, 134 Ill. Dec. 816, 542 N.E.2d 1323 (5 Dist. 1989).

Although an adjudication that a parent is mentally retarded may not in and of itself render that parent unfit, evidence of such adjudication may be considered, along with all other pertinent evidence bearing upon the question of that parent's fitness. Helvey v. Rednour, 86 Ill. App. 3d 154, 41 Ill. Dec. 671, 408 N.E.2d 17 (5 Dist. 1980).

—Required

Before mentally retarded mother could be deprived of her right to raise her child, a hearing had to be held to determine her fitness. Helvey v. Rednour, 86 Ill. App. 3d 154, 41 Ill. Dec. 671, 408 N.E.2d 17 (5 Dist. 1980).

Mootness

Appeal of the termination of the parent's parental rights was dismissed because the appellate court lacked the authority to consider the merits of the substantive questions raised, as the appeal was moot upon the adoption of the children where the parent did not seek a stay of the trial court's termination order. People v. Wanda B. (In re J.B.), 204 Ill. 2d 382, 273 Ill. Dec. 827, 789 N.E.2d 1259, 2003 Ill. LEXIS 771 (2003).

Parent

—Related Child

A natural parent who has validly consented to the adoption of her child may, prior to the specific placement of the child for adoption by others, properly petition to adopt as the parent of a related child. Partington v. Department of Children & Family Servs., 91 Ill. App. 3d 205, 46 Ill. Dec. 656, 414 N.E.2d 540 (2 Dist. 1980).

Petition to Adopt

Appellate court found nothing in either the Adoption Act or the Juvenile Court Act (705 ILCS 405/1-1 et seq.) which mandated that a subsequently filed petition to adopt with consent be heard prior to a previously filed petition to terminate parental rights. In re T.H., 255 Ill. App. 3d 247, 193 Ill. Dec. 370, 626 N.E.2d 403 (5 Dist. 1993), appeal denied, 155 Ill. 2d 577, 198 Ill. Dec. 554, 633 N.E.2d 16, cert. denied, 513 U.S. 905, 115 S. Ct. 269, 130 L. Ed. 2d 187 (1994).

Presumption

This section does not impose an impermissible "irrebuttable" or conclusive presumption; this section does not constitute a conclusive presumption or a presumption in any sense. People v. Ray, 88 Ill. App. 3d 1010, 44 Ill. Dec. 182, 411 N.E.2d 88 (5 Dist. 1980), appeal dismissed, 452 U.S. 956, 101 S. Ct. 3102, 69 L. Ed. 2d 967 (1981).

Private Placement

Even with private placement the court may decide that the adoption is not in the best interests of the child and return the child to the parents. In re L.R.B., 278 Ill. App. 3d 1091, 215 Ill. Dec. 950, 664 N.E.2d 347 (4 Dist. 1996), appeal denied, 168 Ill. 2d 591, 219 Ill. Dec. 564, 671 N.E.2d 731 (1996).

Private placement is not available where the parents are unable to transfer custody, as in the case where a child is a ward of the court. In re L.R.B., 278 Ill. App. 3d 1091, 215 Ill. Dec. 950, 664 N.E.2d 347 (4 Dist. 1996), appeal denied, 168 Ill. 2d 591, 219 Ill. Dec. 564, 671 N.E.2d 731 (1996).

Purpose

The overriding concern of both the Adoption Act and the Juvenile Court Act (705 ILCS 405/1-1 et seq.) is the best interests of the child. In re T.H., 255 Ill. App. 3d 247, 193 Ill. Dec. 370, 626 N.E.2d 403 (5 Dist. 1993), appeal denied, 155 Ill. 2d 577, 198 Ill. Dec. 554, 633 N.E.2d 16, cert. denied, 513 U.S. 905, 115 S. Ct. 269, 130 L. Ed. 2d 187 (1994).

The essence of former ch. 4, section 9.1-1 (see now this section) was that the parents whose child has been taken from their custody to protect the child are unfit if they do not make reasonable efforts to change themselves and their circumstances so that they can give the child the care it needs. Chick v. Massey, 35 Ill. App. 3d 518, 341 N.E.2d 405 (4 Dist. 1976).

Reasonable Efforts or Progress

When making a determination of a parent's unfitness on the basis of failure to make reasonable efforts to correct the conditions that were the basis of removal of the child, a remand was required because the parents' alleged unfitness under 750 ILCS 50/1(D)(m) could only be assessed with respect to events within the statutory time frame of nine months, counting from the filing of the dispositional order. People v. Brownlee, 334 Ill. App. 3d 651, 268 Ill. Dec. 458, 778 N.E.2d 724, 2002 Ill. App. LEXIS 1044 (4 Dist. 2002).

—In General

The court rejected the narrow view that in measuring a parent's progress toward the return of a child, a court should focus solely on the parent's compliance with the service plans of the department of children and family services; the benchmark for measuring a parent's progress toward the return of the child under 750 ILCS 50/1(D)(m) encompasses the parent's compliance with the service plans and the court's directives, in light of the condition which gave rise to the removal of the child, and in light of other conditions which later become known and which would prevent the court from returning custody of the child to the parent. People v. Diane N., 196 Ill. 2d 181, 256 Ill. Dec. 788, 752 N.E.2d 1030, 2001 Ill. LEXIS 484 (2001).

The court rejected the narrow view that a court may only look to the situation that triggered a minor's initial removal, or the conditions existing at the time custody was taken, in measuring a parent's progress under 750 ILCS 50/1(D)(m); a court may also consider other conditions that later come to light. People v. Diane N., 196 Ill. 2d 181, 256 Ill. Dec. 788, 752 N.E.2d 1030, 2001 Ill. LEXIS 484 (2001).

Applying the "reasonable efforts" standard involves a subjective judgment based upon the amount of effort reasonable for the particular person; deciding whether a parent has made "reasonable progress" toward the return of the child involves an objective judgment based upon progress measured from the conditions existing when the parent was deprived of custody. People v. T.J., 233 Ill. App. 3d 88, 174 Ill. Dec. 159, 598 N.E.2d 456 (2 Dist. 1992).

"Reasonable progress" is an objective standard which exists when the court, based on the evidence before it, can conclude that the progress being made by a parent to comply with directives given for the return of the child is sufficiently demonstrable and of such a quality that the court, in the near future, will be able to order the child returned to parental custody, because, in the near future the parent will have fully complied with the directives previously given to the parent in order to regain custody of the child. People v. Sallee, 218 Ill. App. 3d 444, 160 Ill. Dec. 804, 577 N.E.2d 1375 (4 Dist.), cert. denied, 142 Ill. 2d 655, 164 Ill. Dec. 918, 584 N.E.2d 130 (1991).

A parent may be found unfit if he or she fails to make reasonable efforts to correct the conditions which were the basis for the removal of the child or fails to make reasonable progress toward the

Reasonable Efforts or Progress (Cont'd)

—In General (Cont'd)

return of the child within 12 months after an adjudication of abused minor. People v. Clarence H. B., 215 Ill. App. 3d 85, 158 Ill. Dec. 765, 574 N.E.2d 878 (2 Dist. 1991).

At a minimum, reasonable progress requires measurable or demonstrable movement toward the goal of reunification. People v. Gill, 201 Ill. App. 3d 792, 147 Ill. Dec. 236, 559 N.E.2d 236 (1 Dist. 1990).

—Actual Progress

While the mother made an effort to remedy the conditions that were the basis for the removal of her son, the appellate court noted that there was a difference between effort and progress; although the mother had made an effort to learn good parenting techniques, her ability to implement the information she garnered proved unsuccessful and, thus, termination of her parental rights was upheld. People v. Laura V. (In re R.L.), 352 Ill. App. 3d 985, 288 Ill. Dec. 304, 817 N.E.2d 954, 2004 Ill. App. LEXIS 1127 (1 Dist. 2004).

The crucial consideration in determining whether "reasonable progress" has been made since a neglect adjudication is the actual progress made, in light of all the circumstances, from the conditions at the time of the neglect adjudication, and a parent might succeed at reaching a goal envisioned by the Department of Children and Family Services without following its specific directives. People v. T.J., 233 Ill. App. 3d 88, 174 Ill. Dec. 159, 598 N.E.2d 456 (2 Dist. 1992).

—Appointment of Guardian

Where mother refused to enter into an agreement with social workers which could enable return of her child, and refused to cooperate by entering a treatment program and the child had spent the greater part of his life with the foster parents, the judgment appointing a guardian who could authorize adoption due to mother's failure to make progress was affirmed. People v. Saadoon, 78 Ill. App. 3d 319, 33 Ill. Dec. 845, 397 N.E.2d 178 (1 Dist. 1979).

—Best Interests of Child

The assumption that the best interests of the child are the "paramount consideration" in the construction of subdivision D.(m) of this section is highly suspect at best, given the unequivocal pronouncements of the Supreme Court that a trial court is not to consider what would serve the "best interests of the child" until after the trial court has found, by clear and convincing evidence, that the parent or parents are unfit. People v. T.J., 233 Ill. App. 3d 88, 174 Ill. Dec. 159, 598 N.E.2d 456 (2 Dist. 1992).

Reasonable progress requires measurable movement toward the goal of returning the child and whether a small amount of progress is reasonable must be determined with proper regard for the best interest of the child. People v. Daniels, 197 Ill. App. 3d 821, 144 Ill. Dec. 383, 555 N.E.2d 402 (4 Dist. 1990).

—Correction of Conditions

Subdivision D.(m) requires the parent to make the necessary effort or progress toward correcting the injurious conditions underlying the neglect finding in order to regain custody of the children. In re D.J., 262 Ill. App. 3d 584, 199 Ill. Dec. 952, 634 N.E.2d 1306 (4 Dist. 1994).

The proper first basis for a finding of parental unfitness is failure by a parent to make reasonable efforts to correct the conditions which were the basis for the removal of the child; "progress" is not an element of this basis. In re S.G., 216 Ill. App. 3d 668, 159 Ill. Dec. 125, 575 N.E.2d 932 (2 Dist.), cert. denied, 142 Ill. 2d 665, 164 Ill. Dec. 928, 584 N.E.2d 140 (1991).

—Defined

Subdivision (D)(m) and 325 ILCS 5/8.2 together indicate that the measure of reasonable progress encompasses those conditions which could give rise to a finding of abuse or neglect (not merely those conditions which led to the initial removal of the child), and support a holding that "the standard by which progress is to be measured is parental compliance with the court's directives, the service plan, or both." In re C.S., 294 Ill. App. 3d 780, 229 Ill. Dec. 225, 691 N.E.2d 161 (4 Dist. 1998).

This section requires proof of either a failure to make a reasonable effort or a failure to make reasonable progress in order to support a finding of unfitness; the question of what is a reasonable effort involves a subjective judgment based upon the amount of effort which is reasonable for a particular person, while the question of what is reasonable progress is more objective, depending upon the amount of progress measured from the conditions existing at the time custody was taken from the parent. People v. Doolan, 101 Ill. App. 3d 322, 56 Ill. Dec. 802, 427 N.E.2d 1348 (3 Dist. 1981).

—Denial of Shortcomings

Although the parents had visited the child their refusal to face their shortcomings was a sufficient basis for the court to conclude that they had not made "reasonable progress" toward the return of the child. People v. Boolman, 141 Ill. App. 3d 508, 96 Ill. Dec. 187, 491 N.E.2d 1 (4 Dist. 1986).

—Drug Abuse

Evidence was sufficient to establish unfitness on the basis of a mother's failure to make reasonable progress towards the return of her children, although she began a drug treatment program within the applicable 12-month period, as she did not begin to make any progress until after that period had expired. People v. Wanda H. (In re D.H.), 323 Ill. App. 3d 1, 256 Ill. Dec. 1, 751 N.E.2d 54, 2001 Ill. App. LEXIS 374 (1 Dist. 2001).

It was error to terminate the parental rights of a mother following the removal of the child at issue because of the mother's drug abuse and poor parenting skills evidenced by a filthy home and allegations of inadequate supervision and food where (1) the state presented no evidence concerning the mother's parenting skills or the cleanliness of her home at the end of the relevant time period, and (2) the mother found a drug and alcohol abuse program that helped her and she had ingested no drugs or alcohol for almost three months at the end of the relevant time period. People v. S.K., Ill. App. 3d , 255 Ill. Dec. 551, 749 N.E.2d 1033, 2001 Ill. App. LEXIS 347 (1 Dist. 2001).

Where the trial court found that the mother had failed to make "reasonable progress" toward the return of her children within 12 months after the adjudication of their neglect, and where her abuse of drugs led not only to the neglect of her children, but endangered them as well, the trial court's finding was not contrary to the manifest weight of the evidence. People v. Smith, 203 Ill. App. 3d 586, 148 Ill. Dec. 682, 560 N.E.2d 1380 (4 Dist. 1990).

—Establishment of Home Life

Evidence that mother was not making "reasonable progress" in establishing an adequate home life for children, a prerequisite for the children's return to their natural home after a finding of neglect, was not sufficient to overturn trial court's ruling that return of child was not warranted. People v. Knell, 153 Ill. App. 3d 704, 106 Ill. Dec. 653, 506 N.E.2d 360 (4 Dist. 1987).

—Future Events

Anticipated future events are an insufficient basis on which to measure progress. People v. Allen, 172 Ill. App. 3d 950, 123 Ill. Dec. 184, 527 N.E.2d 647 (2 Dist. 1988).

—Goal of Reunification

The record demonstrated considerable progress made by respondent toward the goal of reunification with her child where she: 1) divorced the man accused of molesting the child; 2) reported abuse by other family members; 3) maintained a regular visitation schedule; 4) kept moving whenever Department of Children and Family Services was not satisfied with her living situation; 5) obtained employment; 6) attended counseling; and 7) attended a parenting class. In re L.N., 278 Ill. App. 3d 46, 214 Ill. Dec. 798, 662 N.E.2d 152 (3 Dist. 1996).

Whether a parent's efforts to correct conditions are reasonable involves a subjective judgment of the particular parent's efforts; however, the reasonableness of a parent's progress toward the child's return is measured objectively by the amount of movement toward the goal of reunification. In re S.O., 272 Ill. App. 3d 144, 208 Ill. Dec. 637, 649 N.E.2d 997 (3 Dist. 1995).

—Illustrative Cases

Juvenile court did not abuse its discretion in finding that a mother was unfit and that it was in her three children's best interests to terminate the mother's parental rights and place them up for adoption, as the mother, despite making reasonable efforts, failed to make reasonable progress toward a return home within

Reasonable Efforts or Progress (Cont'd)

—Illustrative Cases (Cont'd)
nine months after adjudication, and she failed to maintain a reasonable degree of concern or responsibility as to the children's welfare; furthermore, the children were suffering from anxiety because they had been in foster care for a long time, and wished to have the permanency of adoption. People v. Kathleen C. (In re April C.), 345 Ill. App. 3d 872, 281 Ill. Dec. 312, 803 N.E.2d 933, 2004 Ill. App. LEXIS 21 (1 Dist. 2004).

Evidence supported a termination of parental rights on the basis that the parents failed to make reasonable progress toward the return of the child at issue within 12 months of the adjudication of neglect, and that it was in the child's best interests that parental rights be terminated where (1) the mother failed to comply with the terms of the service plan, as ordered by the circuit court, failed to participate meaningfully in available services, and disclaimed all responsibility for the abuse of the child; and (2) the father was reluctant to engage in recommended services and, although he eventually obtained alcohol and psychological assessments, he failed to attend any appointments at Family Advocate, notwithstanding his prior agreement and the circuit court's order. People v. Diane N., 196 Ill. 2d 181, 256 Ill. Dec. 788, 752 N.E.2d 1030, 2001 Ill. LEXIS 484 (2001).

The court contravened the manifest weight of the evidence in finding that the state carried its burden of proving by clear and convincing evidence that the respondent failed to make the requisite reasonable efforts and progress during the appropriate nine month period where testimony covering the relevant period addressed the service plan ratings with very little focus on the respondent's specific acts, but indicated that the respondent subsequently regained custody of the children at issue, which would not have occurred without the respondent previously making reasonable progress toward that goal and reasonable efforts to overcome her alcoholism. People v. Phyllis J., 316 Ill. App. 3d 817, 250 Ill. Dec. 103, 737 N.E.2d 1080, 2000 Ill. App. LEXIS 819 (3 Dist. 2000).

Parents' flurry of activity regarding child immediately prior to the adjudicatory hearing on the petition to terminate their parental rights can hardly overcome the many months of their demonstrable disinterest. People v. Sallee, 218 Ill. App. 3d 444, 160 Ill. Dec. 804, 577 N.E.2d 1375 (4 Dist.), cert. denied, 142 Ill. 2d 655, 164 Ill. Dec. 918, 584 N.E.2d 130 (1991).

Where Department of Children and Family Services provided respondent with five different client-service plans in an attempt to allow respondent to regain custody of her children, respondent received an "unsatisfactory" grade as to one or more of the conditions for each of the plans, never did regularly attend counseling and was apparently still consuming alcohol during the time she was directed to abstain from alcohol and drugs, and did not secure housing suitable for her and the children, the trial court's finding that she failed to make reasonable progress toward the return of her children in the nearly 14 months since the order adjudicating neglect was not contrary to the manifest weight of the evidence. People v. Stiarwalt, 190 Ill. App. 3d 547, 137 Ill. Dec. 420, 546 N.E.2d 44 (2 Dist. 1989).

The finding that respondent failed to make a reasonable effort to correct the conditions which were the basis of removal of her child was not contrary to the manifest weight of the evidence where respondent did not cooperate with the social workers, did not follow through with counseling, refused to attend parenting classes, cancelled many of her visits with the child and failed to interact with him when she did visit. People v. Williams, 187 Ill. App. 3d 988, 135 Ill. Dec. 406, 543 N.E.2d 974 (1 Dist. 1989).

—Importance of Effort
Whether a parent has made reasonable efforts to correct the conditions which were the basis for the child's removal involves a subjective judgment based upon the amount of effort which is reasonable for a particular person. In re S.G., 216 Ill. App. 3d 668, 159 Ill. Dec. 125, 575 N.E.2d 932 (2 Dist.), cert. denied, 142 Ill. 2d 665, 164 Ill. Dec. 928, 584 N.E.2d 140 (1991).

Whether a parent's efforts to correct the conditions are reasonable involves a subjective judgment based upon the amount of effort which is reasonable for a particular person. People v. Gill, 201 Ill. App. 3d 792, 147 Ill. Dec. 236, 559 N.E.2d 236 (1 Dist. 1990).

—Incarcerated Parent
Trial court's finding that father failed to make reasonable progress towards the return of his children from foster care was not contrary to the manifest weight of the evidence, even where the father was an inmate of the Illinois Department of Corrections on the date of the adjudicatory hearing, when his three children were found to be neglected minors. People v. Smith, 203 Ill. App. 3d 586, 148 Ill. Dec. 682, 560 N.E.2d 1380 (4 Dist. 1990).

The period of time in which a mother was incarcerated at the county correctional center should be considered in determining whether she has made reasonable progress toward the return of her child where the mother rejected all efforts to cooperate with social worker in participating in visitation, in establishing and maintaining a home capable of sustaining a child, and in undergoing evaluations for chemical dependency and mental fitness. People v. Freeman, 161 Ill. App. 3d 325, 112 Ill. Dec. 881, 514 N.E.2d 544 (4 Dist. 1987).

The mere fact of incarceration is not evidence of failure to make reasonable progress, but the incarceration did not provide the father immunity from a petition to terminate parental rights under subdivision (D)(m) of this Act. People v. Yelliott, 157 Ill. App. 3d 396, 109 Ill. Dec. 673, 510 N.E.2d 541 (4 Dist. 1987).

—Independent Grounds for Unfitness
The two standards of reasonable progress and reasonable efforts as set forth in this subdivision are disjunctive, so that failure to make either reasonable efforts or reasonable progress constitutes a ground for unfitness. People v. Harvey, 61 Ill. App. 3d 344, 19 Ill. Dec. 37, 378 N.E.2d 538 (1 Dist. 1978); People v. Bennett, 80 Ill. App. 3d 207, 35 Ill. Dec. 669, 399 N.E.2d 735 (3 Dist. 1980); People v. Edmonds, 85 Ill. App. 3d 229, 40 Ill. Dec. 530, 406 N.E.2d 231 (3 Dist. 1980); People v. Drescher, 91 Ill. App. 3d 658, 47 Ill. Dec. 631, 415 N.E.2d 636 (1 Dist. 1980); People v. Allen, 172 Ill. App. 3d 950, 123 Ill. Dec. 184, 527 N.E.2d 647 (2 Dist. 1988); People v. Green, 173 Ill. App. 3d 922, 123 Ill. Dec. 693, 528 N.E.2d 238 (2 Dist. 1988); People v. Gill, 201 Ill. App. 3d 792, 147 Ill. Dec. 236, 559 N.E.2d 236 (1 Dist. 1990); In re S.G., 216 Ill. App. 3d 668, 159 Ill. Dec. 125, 575 N.E.2d 932 (2 Dist.), cert. denied, 142 Ill. 2d 665, 164 Ill. Dec. 928, 584 N.E.2d 140 (1991).

—Judicial Admission Admissible
Where father pleaded guilty to a residential burglary, this amounted to a judicial admission which was admissible in the proceeding to terminate parental rights because of its relevance to the issue of whether the father was making reasonable progress in bringing about the child's return to his home. People v. Yelliott, 157 Ill. App. 3d 396, 109 Ill. Dec. 673, 510 N.E.2d 541 (4 Dist. 1987).

—Legislative Intent
Subdivision (D)(m) of this section evidences both the legislature's recognition of the problem of children removed from their parents but ineligible for adoption, and the legislature's intent to better protect the interests of such children. People v. Sepulveda, 174 Ill. App. 3d 132, 123 Ill. Dec. 641, 528 N.E.2d 25 (3 Dist. 1988).

—Mental Retardation
The evidence showed that respondent was mildly mentally retarded and this fact must be taken into consideration in any determination as to whether her efforts were reasonable, and even though respondent testified at the hearing on her own behalf and seemed to have no difficulty understanding questions asked her and also seemed to understand why the children had been taken from her and why she was being required to fulfill the goals set for her by Department of Children and Family Services (DCFS) the trial court's finding of unfitness as to the reasonable efforts standard was not against the manifest weight of the evidence. In re J.P., 261 Ill. App. 3d 165, 198 Ill. Dec. 565, 633 N.E.2d 27 (4 Dist. 1994).

—Noncustodial Parent
The parental rights of a noncustodial parent can be terminated under the provisions of this section. People v. Yelliott, 157 Ill. App. 3d 396, 109 Ill. Dec. 673, 510 N.E.2d 541 (4 Dist. 1987).

A noncustodial parent is required to step in during a guardianship administered by the Department of Children and Family Service and correct conditions of neglect and make reasonable efforts to help the minor return to the custody of one of the natural parents; a noncustodial parent is charged with as much responsibility as a custodial parent for the support, protection, and care of a child. People v. Yelliott, 157 Ill. App. 3d 396, 109 Ill. Dec. 673, 510 N.E.2d 541 (4 Dist. 1987).

Reasonable Efforts or Progress (Cont'd)

—Not Shown

While the mother complied with many of the service goals and received some satisfactory ratings, she did not comply with the most important goals, i.e., she refused homemaker services to remedy the defects in her living arrangements, she often failed to satisfy the therapy goals, and she refused visitation when it suited her needs; thus, the evidence supported a finding that the mother failed to make reasonable progress toward the return of the child and was unfit. People v. Carmen D. (In re Kenneth J.), 352 Ill. App. 3d 967, 288 Ill. Dec. 290, 817 N.E.2d 940, 2004 Ill. App. LEXIS 1128 (1 Dist. 2004).

Evidence was insufficient to support a determination of a mother's unfitness based on a lack of reasonable efforts or progress; the state presented no evidence as to the mother's progress or efforts during the initial 12 month period following the dispositional order that completed the adjudication of her child as a neglected minor, and the state's evidence commenced with a time period more than three years after the child's adjudication. People v. Crowder, 314 Ill. App. 3d 739, 247 Ill. Dec. 866, 732 N.E.2d 1198, 2000 Ill. App. LEXIS 570 (4 Dist. 2000).

A mother's parental rights were properly terminated on the basis of her failure to make reasonable progress toward the return of her children within 12 months after they had been adjudicated neglected where: (1) the children were removed from her custody and adjudicated neglected because one child was born with cocaine in his system, (2) from that time until the fitness hearing, the mother never successfully completed a drug treatment program as required in her service plans, and (3) even when she was accepted into a program, she did not enroll because she had to "take care of some things." In re T.S., 312 Ill. App. 3d 875, 245 Ill. Dec. 367, 728 N.E.2d 98, 2000 Ill. App. LEXIS 248 (2000).

A mother's parental rights were properly terminated for failure to make reasonable efforts or progress toward the return of her children where (1) the children were removed from the mother's home because she was in a drug treatment program and was unable to care for them, (2) at the time of the fitness hearing, which was over five years later, the mother had never successfully completed a drug treatment program and continued to abuse alcohol and drugs, and (3) she had not visited her children in over three years. People v. Kimberline B., 307 Ill. App. 3d 71, 240 Ill. Dec. 252, 716 N.E.2d 846 (3 Dist. 1999).

Trial court properly found that respondent failed to make reasonable efforts to correct the conditions that were the basis for child's removal from her custody where evidence demonstrated respondent failed to complete parenting classes, failed to attend and complete counseling, missed many visitations and failed to demonstrate appropriate supervision. In re J.G., 298 Ill. App. 3d 617, 232 Ill. Dec. 720, 699 N.E.2d 167 (4 Dist. 1998).

Where respondent was ordered to undergo sex abuse counseling in July of 1992 and was periodically admonished that participation in weekly sex abuse counseling sessions was required if he was to regain custody of his children but, nonetheless failed to take more than passive interest in the 18 sessions he attended between November of 1992 and May of 1993, and he made no progress whatsoever in addressing the issues of pedophilia, admitted that he only resumed attending the scheduled sessions in January of 1994 because he was told he would lose his parental rights if he did not, the trial court's finding of unfitness was not contrary to the manifest weight of the evidence. In re S.O., 272 Ill. App. 3d 144, 208 Ill. Dec. 637, 649 N.E.2d 997 (3 Dist. 1995).

While it was true that the evidence showed respondent partially met some of the objectives of her service plans at various times during the post-adjudication period, the Department of Children and Family Services (DCFS) caseworker testified this merely meant respondent was trying; the final outcome of all respondent's service plans was unsatisfactory and there was no error in the trial court's conclusion that respondent had not made reasonable progress toward return of her children to her custody. In re J.P., 261 Ill. App. 3d 165, 198 Ill. Dec. 565, 633 N.E.2d 27 (4 Dist. 1994).

Respondent's failure to terminate her relationship with child molester and remove him from the children's environment herself, as opposed to the criminal justice system's doing so for her, constituted a failure to make reasonable efforts or reasonable progress. In re D.J., 262 Ill. App. 3d 584, 199 Ill. Dec. 952, 634 N.E.2d 1306 (4 Dist. 1994).

The trial court's finding that defendant failed to make reasonable progress toward the return of the children within 12 months of the adjudication of neglect was not against the manifest weight of the evidence where he was uncooperative in counseling, sporadically attended AA meetings, and failed to acknowledge responsibility for the sexual abuse. C. R. v. Richardson, 221 Ill. App. 3d 373, 163 Ill. Dec. 779, 581 N.E.2d 1202 (4 Dist. 1991).

Where the respondent mother had no residence at which the children could live, no employment, and was apparently undertaking no treatment, in-patient or otherwise, to address her substance abuse and dependency problem, reasonable progress had to be made to justify returning her children. People v. Houston, 219 Ill. App. 3d 269, 162 Ill. Dec. 343, 579 N.E.2d 1157 (4 Dist. 1991).

Father's visits with his children did not enable him to meet the "reasonable progress" standard when he failed to make progress in other areas, such as providing housing for his children. People v. Phillips, 191 Ill. App. 3d 237, 138 Ill. Dec. 437, 547 N.E.2d 604 (4 Dist. 1989).

Where respondent sought to excuse her failure to make progress in completing the tasks by citing her limited financial resources, poor health, and lack of transportation, the handicaps had little or no bearing on her ability to complete most of the tasks set forth in the client service plans. People v. Munjak, 175 Ill. App. 3d 778, 125 Ill. Dec. 413, 530 N.E.2d 571 (2 Dist. 1988).

Mother's efforts to correct conditions were not reasonable when they were only the result of actions by her social workers or based on court orders. People v. Allen, 172 Ill. App. 3d 950, 123 Ill. Dec. 184, 527 N.E.2d 647 (2 Dist. 1988).

The failure of respondent to make reasonable progress toward the return of her child coupled with her failure to maintain a reasonable degree of interest in her child were sufficient to constitute unfitness. People v. Drescher, 91 Ill. App. 3d 658, 47 Ill. Dec. 631, 415 N.E.2d 636 (1 Dist. 1980).

In proceeding to terminate parental rights, the evidence in the record clearly and convincingly showed that mother had failed to make reasonable efforts to correct conditions of neglect. People v. Berry, 86 Ill. App. 3d 522, 42 Ill. Dec. 150, 408 N.E.2d 728 (5 Dist. 1980).

Trial court's conclusion that there was a lack of reasonable progress toward the return of the minor within 12 months after the adjudication of neglect was not against the manifest weight of the evidence. People v. Bentsen, 90 Ill. App. 3d 269, 45 Ill. Dec. 585, 412 N.E.2d 1167 (3 Dist. 1980).

—Objective Standard

An assessment as to whether respondent had made reasonable progress toward return of the children involved an objective judgment based upon the amount of progress made by the parent. In re J.P., 261 Ill. App. 3d 165, 198 Ill. Dec. 565, 633 N.E.2d 27 (4 Dist. 1994).

Whether a parent's efforts to correct the conditions which were the basis for removing her children are reasonable involves subjective standards based upon the amount of effort which is reasonable for a particular parent, but whether a parent's progress toward return of the children within 12 months of being adjudicated neglected is reasonable requires an objective standard based upon the amount of progress measured from the conditions existing at the time custody was taken from the parent, and not what is reasonable for the parent. People v. Sallee, 218 Ill. App. 3d 444, 160 Ill. Dec. 804, 577 N.E.2d 1375 (4 Dist.), cert. denied, 142 Ill. 2d 655, 164 Ill. Dec. 918, 584 N.E.2d 130 (1991).

Determining whether parents have made reasonable progress toward the return of their children involves an objective judgment based on measurable progress from the conditions present at the time custody was taken from the parents and requires demonstrable movement toward the goal of reunification. In re S.G., 216 Ill. App. 3d 668, 159 Ill. Dec. 125, 575 N.E.2d 932 (2 Dist.), cert. denied, 142 Ill. 2d 665, 164 Ill. Dec. 928, 584 N.E.2d 140 (1991).

The question of whether or not a parent has made reasonable progress is an objective standard; the court may consider any particular shortcomings or handicaps with which the parent struggles, but the question is whether or not that parent has made reasonable progress, not whether or not the parent has tried. People v. Houston, 219 Ill. App. 3d 269, 162 Ill. Dec. 343, 579 N.E.2d 1157 (4 Dist. 1991).

Whether a particular parent's progress towards return of the child within 12 months of being adjudicated neglected is reasonable

Reasonable Efforts or Progress (Cont'd)

—Objective Standard (Cont'd)
involves an objective judgment based upon the amount of progress measured from the conditions existing at the time custody was taken from the parent. People v. Gill, 201 Ill. App. 3d 792, 147 Ill. Dec. 236, 559 N.E.2d 236 (1 Dist. 1990).

Whether a parent's progress toward the return of the children was reasonable involves an objective determination based upon the amount of progress measured from the conditions existing at the time custody was taken from the parent. People v. Stiarwalt, 190 Ill. App. 3d 547, 137 Ill. Dec. 420, 546 N.E.2d 44 (2 Dist. 1989).

At a minimum, reasonable progress requires measurable or demonstrable movement toward the goal of reunification. People v. Stiarwalt, 190 Ill. App. 3d 547, 137 Ill. Dec. 420, 546 N.E.2d 44 (2 Dist. 1989).

Reasonable progress requires at a minimum measurable or demonstrable movement toward the goal of return of the child. People v. Green, 173 Ill. App. 3d 922, 123 Ill. Dec. 693, 528 N.E.2d 238 (2 Dist. 1988).

To make "reasonable progress" toward the return of a child, parents must make a minimum measurable or demonstrable movement toward that goal. People v. Boolman, 141 Ill. App. 3d 508, 96 Ill. Dec. 187, 491 N.E.2d 1 (4 Dist. 1986).

The term "reasonable progress" requires at a minimum measurable or demonstrable movement toward the goal of return of the child; whether a small amount of progress is "reasonable" must be determined with proper regard for the best interests of the child. People v. Harvey, 61 Ill. App. 3d 344, 19 Ill. Dec. 37, 378 N.E.2d 538 (1 Dist. 1978).

—Observable Progress
The court is to demand measurable, observable progress if it is to conclude that, in fact, reasonable progress has been made. People v. Houston, 219 Ill. App. 3d 269, 162 Ill. Dec. 343, 579 N.E.2d 1157 (4 Dist. 1991).

—Original Adjudication
A determination of reasonable progress relates to the goal of return of the child and such a determination is not constrained by the original adjudication of neglect. People v. Green, 173 Ill. App. 3d 922, 123 Ill. Dec. 693, 528 N.E.2d 238 (2 Dist. 1988).

—Original Situation as Benchmark
It is essential for the trial court to consider the situation triggering the minor children's initial removal as a benchmark for measuring reasonable progress. People v. Stiarwalt, 190 Ill. App. 3d 547, 137 Ill. Dec. 420, 546 N.E.2d 44 (2 Dist. 1989).

Reasonable progress is measurable or demonstrable progress toward return of the child, and to measure reasonable progress, evidence concerning the initial status of the parent at the time of removal is required in order to determine progress toward return of the child. People v. Green, 173 Ill. App. 3d 922, 123 Ill. Dec. 693, 528 N.E.2d 238 (2 Dist. 1988).

Where there is evidence in the record that respondent mother failed to make progress as to the conditions imposed upon her at the dispositional hearing, this failure only relates to her progress after the children were removed. The trial court could not properly find, nor the appellate court review, whether reasonable progress toward return of the children had been made without evidence as to respondent mother's status at the time of removal of the children. People v. Green, 173 Ill. App. 3d 922, 123 Ill. Dec. 693, 528 N.E.2d 238 (2 Dist. 1988).

—Parental Conduct
Where more than 12 months have passed after an adjudication of a child's neglect or dependency and the child has not been returned to the parent, if the state alleges a parent's unfitness under this subdivision, it is clearly in the best interest of the child to consider the parent's conduct during the entire post-adjudication period; further, not merely evidence indicating unfitness need be considered but probative evidence favorable to the parents' progress would also be entitled to consideration. People v. Sepulveda, 174 Ill. App. 3d 132, 123 Ill. Dec. 641, 528 N.E.2d 25 (3 Dist. 1988).

—Parental Understanding of Requirements
Because the Juvenile Court Act (see 705 ILCS 405/1-1 et seq.) intends the involvement of a parent in all proceedings under that Act, and because the father actually participated in the underlying neglect proceedings through which his children were placed in foster homes, he was fully subject to the requirements regarding "reasonable progress" he had to demonstrate or risk having his parental rights terminated. People v. Smith, 203 Ill. App. 3d 586, 148 Ill. Dec. 682, 560 N.E.2d 1380 (4 Dist. 1990).

—Parenting Classes
A mother's failure to take parenting classes, as had been directed by the Department of Children and Family Services, was not to be given great weight where (1) any lack of "parenting skills" as such was not the reason for the initial neglect adjudication; (2) she was never shown, at the initial adjudication, to have lacked these parenting skills; (3) the weight of the evidence was that she kept her house satisfactorily furnished and cared responsibly for the children in her custody; and (4) the vast majority of parents are never required by the state to take parenting classes. People v. T.J., 233 Ill. App. 3d 88, 174 Ill. Dec. 159, 598 N.E.2d 456 (2 Dist. 1992).

—Prior Proceeding
Order of circuit court terminating the parental rights of mother was vacated where trial court did not consider the record of the prior proceeding which determined mother unfit since it is essential that the trial court consider the situations triggering the minor's initial removal as a benchmark for measuring progress. People v. Bennett, 80 Ill. App. 3d 207, 35 Ill. Dec. 669, 399 N.E.2d 735 (3 Dist. 1980).

—Purpose
A major purpose for requiring a natural parent to make reasonable progress toward the return of child within 12 months of being adjudicated neglected, pursuant to this subdivision, is so the child will not be left for an unnecessarily long time without a permanent parental relationship. People v. Allen, 172 Ill. App. 3d 950, 123 Ill. Dec. 184, 527 N.E.2d 647 (2 Dist. 1988).

—Removal of Child from Parent
The statutory language of subsection (D)(m) of both "reasonable efforts" and "reasonable progress" is not premised upon the child actually having been removed from the parent; the subsection can apply to cases where the child was never in substitute care during the nine months following the adjudication of neglect. People v. Edwards, 317 Ill. App. 3d 227, 250 Ill. Dec. 538, 738 N.E.2d 1007, 2000 Ill. App. LEXIS 854 (4 Dist. 2000).

—Sexual Conduct
A mother failed to make reasonable efforts to correct the conditions that were the basis for the removal of her children where the children were removed because they were sexually abused by their father and were at substantial risk of physical injury, but the mother continued to reside with the father and, despite counseling, refused to admit that he had sexually molested the children. People v. Nereida S., 322 Ill. App. 3d 81, 255 Ill. Dec. 25, 748 N.E.2d 729, 2001 Ill. App. LEXIS 296 (1 Dist. 2001).

Evidence respondent was engaging in sexual conduct in the presence of other children entrusted in her care eight months after the adjudication of neglect of her own children bears directly upon the efforts and progress respondent was making to rehabilitate herself and as such, this evidence was not irrelevant. People v. Daniels, 197 Ill. App. 3d 821, 144 Ill. Dec. 383, 555 N.E.2d 402 (4 Dist. 1990).

—Shown
A father made reasonable efforts and reasonable progress toward reunification with his child where: (1) he visited the child on a weekly basis, as the court ordered, and usually visited more often than that, (2) he took a drug test, the results of which were negative, (3) he submitted himself to a psychological evaluation and a substance abuse assessment, and (4) he underwent anger management counseling as a follow-up to his psychological evaluation. People v. Rosado, 316 Ill. App. 3d 553, 249 Ill. Dec. 484, 736 N.E.2d 678, 2000 Ill. App. LEXIS 754 (1 Dist. 2000).

Based on the mother's diligent cooperation with the Department of Children and Family Services, her acknowledgment that her former boyfriend was a risk to her children, and the uncontradicted evidence that she was no longer living with or dating her former boyfriend, the mother made reasonable efforts to correct the condition that was the basis of the removal of her children, notwith-

Reasonable Efforts or Progress (Cont'd)

—Shown (Cont'd)

standing that the mother had several brief public contacts with the former boyfriend after he moved out of her home. People v. Head, 305 Ill. App. 3d 869, 239 Ill. Dec. 253, 713 N.E.2d 784 (4 Dist. 1999), appeal denied, 185 Ill. 2d 627, 242 Ill. Dec. 138, 720 N.E.2d 1093 (1999).

Respondent made reasonable efforts to correct the conditions that were the basis for removal, sexual conduct perpetrated on the child, where respondent reported three incidents of abuse by family members, two of which were prosecuted and she divorced her husband after she found out he was abusing the child. In re L.N., 278 Ill. App. 3d 46, 214 Ill. Dec. 798, 662 N.E.2d 152 (3 Dist. 1996).

Where parents were observed to have made satisfactory progress at six-month reviews, including maintaining a safe, clean, hazard-free home, regularly visiting with their children and regularly attending counseling sessions and parenting classes, there can be little doubt that the parents made substantial measurable progress from the conditions which necessitated the removal of the children. In re S.G., 216 Ill. App. 3d 668, 159 Ill. Dec. 125, 575 N.E.2d 932 (2 Dist.), cert. denied, 142 Ill. 2d 665, 164 Ill. Dec. 928, 584 N.E.2d 140 (1991).

—Standard of Evidence

In a case where children were originally taken away from their parents because of the "injurious" environment at home and having made progress toward correcting that problem, the parents should not have their parental rights terminated for these other nebulous, uncharged reasons; to decide otherwise would allow the state to terminate parental rights for nonstatutory reasons which were originally uncharged and which parents have no reason to know are possible bases for removal of their children. In re S.G., 216 Ill. App. 3d 668, 159 Ill. Dec. 125, 575 N.E.2d 932 (2 Dist.), cert. denied, 142 Ill. 2d 665, 164 Ill. Dec. 928, 584 N.E.2d 140 (1991).

To prove unfitness of a parent on the ground of failure to make reasonable progress towards return of the child within 12 months of an adjudication of neglect, the state need not establish that the conditions of the dispositional order entered after an adjudication of neglect were reasonably related to the basis of the petition to adjudicate the child a neglected minor in a proceeding to terminate parental rights based on parental unfitness as defined in subdivision (m) of subsection D. of this section. People v. Green, 173 Ill. App. 3d 922, 123 Ill. Dec. 693, 528 N.E.2d 238 (2 Dist. 1988).

—Subjective Standard

Whether a parent's efforts to correct conditions which were the basis for removal of the child are reasonable involves a subjective judgment based upon the amount of effort reasonable for the parent whose rights are sought to be terminated. In re J.P., 261 Ill. App. 3d 165, 198 Ill. Dec. 565, 633 N.E.2d 27 (4 Dist. 1994).

—Surrender by Custodial Parent

The surrender of parental rights by the child's mother does not eliminate the father's obligation to make reasonable progress in bringing about the return of the child to his home. People v. Yelliott, 157 Ill. App. 3d 396, 109 Ill. Dec. 673, 510 N.E.2d 541 (4 Dist. 1987).

—Suitable Housing

Mother's failure to obtain and maintain housing suitable for the minors after more than three years was unreasonable, particularly when the lack of suitable housing was a primary factor in the removal of the minors. People v. Allen, 172 Ill. App. 3d 950, 123 Ill. Dec. 184, 527 N.E.2d 647 (2 Dist. 1988).

—Time Limits

The provision of subdivision (D)(m) regarding the time limit within which a parent's failure to make reasonable efforts to correct conditions which were the basis of a child's removal could be considered as a ground for a determination of parental unfitness did not apply in a permanency planning hearing under the Juvenile Court Act. In re D.H., 295 Ill. App. 3d 981, 230 Ill. Dec. 469, 693 N.E.2d 1220 (1 Dist. 1998).

—Time Period

750 ILCS 50/1(D)(m) does not require that a parent lose guardianship or custody of her children for the statutory period for making progress toward return of the child to toll; the statutory nine-month period begins to toll when a trial court adjudicates children abused, neglected or dependent. People v. Teresa R. (In re Cheyenne S.), 351 Ill. App. 3d 1042, 287 Ill. Dec. 383, 815 N.E.2d 1186, 2004 Ill. App. LEXIS 1064 (3 Dist. 2004).

Nine-month period for assessment of parental fitness begins to run on the date the trial court entered its order adjudging the minors neglected, abused, or dependent, not on the date the trial court entered its dispositional order. People v. Lashawn F. (In re D.F.), 208 Ill. 2d 223, 280 Ill. Dec. 549, 802 N.E.2d 800, 2003 Ill. LEXIS 2606 (2003).

Nine-month period for assessment of parental fitness applied to both the reasonable-efforts and reasonable-progress grounds since an inspection of both the Adoption Act and the Juvenile Court Act, as well as the legislative history of this section, indicated the legislature's ongoing desire to shorten the period of time during which a parent must make reasonable efforts and progress or be deemed unfit. People v. Lashawn F. (In re D.F.), 208 Ill. 2d 223, 280 Ill. Dec. 549, 802 N.E.2d 800, 2003 Ill. LEXIS 2606 (2003).

Since mother did not raise at trial the issue of whether State's petition to terminate parental rights sufficiently alleged that the mother had not made reasonable progress toward the son's return during the time period identified in 750 ILCS 50/1(D)(m)(iii), and because the evidence was not closely balanced and the alleged error did affect substantial rights, the issue was waived on appeal. People v. Tamara J. (In re Christopher J.), 338 Ill. App. 3d 1057, 273 Ill. Dec. 707, 789 N.E.2d 881, 2003 Ill. App. LEXIS 575 (2 Dist. 2003).

Shortening of the period for making reasonable progress toward the return of a parent's child, pursuant to 750 ILCS 50/1 (D)(m), to nine months, instead of twelve months, applied to a termination of parental rights proceeding even though the longer period of time had been applicable at the time the proceeding was initiated. People v. J.Y., 334 Ill. App. 3d 894, 268 Ill. Dec. 590, 778 N.E.2d 1212, 2002 Ill. App. LEXIS 969 (1 Dist. 2002).

Subsections 1(D)(m)(ii) and 1(D)(m)(iii) designate two separate non-overlapping time periods; thus, when the state alleges grounds for unfitness under both of these subsections, a trial court must decide each allegation based only on the evidence pertaining to the designated time period and should make explicit the beginning and ending dates upon which it bases its findings. People v. Fleming, 317 Ill. App. 3d 461, 251 Ill. Dec. 230, 740 N.E.2d 60, 2000 Ill. App. LEXIS 925 (4 Dist. 2000).

Where the trial court based its decision as to each of the alleged grounds of unfitness, i.e., lack of reasonable efforts or reasonable progress, on evidence pertaining to occurrences outside the time periods applicable to those grounds, the order terminating parental rights was vacated and the matter was remanded with directions for the court to review the evidence presented and determine parental fitness under the statute by reference only to the evidence of events that occurred within each of the relevant time periods. People v. Fleming, 317 Ill. App. 3d 461, 251 Ill. Dec. 230, 740 N.E.2d 60, 2000 Ill. App. LEXIS 925 (4 Dist. 2000).

Because the trial court obviously based its decision on evidence pertaining to matters outside the relevant time period, and the record contained essentially no probative evidence regarding the relevant time period, the court reversed the trial court's termination of parental rights based on the mother's alleged failure to make reasonable progress toward the return of her children. People v. Ellis, 315 Ill. App. 3d 944, 248 Ill. Dec. 850, 735 N.E.2d 170, 2000 Ill. App. LEXIS 706 (4 Dist. 2000).

With respect to allegations of both a lack of reasonable efforts and a lack of reasonable progress, a court may only consider a parent's conduct that occurs within the initial 12 month period following adjudication, which period starts on the date that the trial court files its dispositional order completing the adjudication of the minor as neglected, abused, or dependent; any evidence subsequent to that time period is irrelevant in establishing parental unfitness. People v. Crowder, 314 Ill. App. 3d 739, 247 Ill. Dec. 866, 732 N.E.2d 1198, 2000 Ill. App. LEXIS 570 (4 Dist. 2000).

Whether a parent made reasonable progress toward the return of his or her child within nine months after an adjudication of neglect refers to the date that the court files its dispositional order on the state's petition for adjudication of neglect, abuse, or dependency, that is, the date on which the trial court completes the adjudication of neglected, abused, or dependent minor. People v. Sherman, 313

Reasonable Efforts or Progress (Cont'd)

—Time Period (Cont'd)

Ill. App. 3d 1020, 246 Ill. Dec. 612, 730 N.E.2d 637, 2000 Ill. App. LEXIS 438 (4 Dist. 2000).

The court found respondents unfit based upon their failure to maintain a reasonable degree of interest, concern, or responsibility as to the welfare of the children and they were not entitled to 12 months in which to make reasonable progress toward the return of the children, based upon subdivision (D)(m). In re M.M., 261 Ill. App. 3d 71, 199 Ill. Dec. 436, 634 N.E.2d 36 (5 Dist. 1994).

Although this statute can be interpreted to give a parent only 12 months in which to make "reasonable progress," the weight of recent authority is that 12 months is the minimum period in which a parent has to make reasonable progress, and that in evaluating whether a parent has made reasonable progress, the trial court should consider the parent's conduct during the entire period after the neglect adjudication. People v. T.J., 233 Ill. App. 3d 88, 174 Ill. Dec. 159, 598 N.E.2d 456 (2 Dist. 1992).

The time frame in which the parent has to make reasonable progress is not limited to the 12 months after the adjudication of neglect, rather, the court may consider the parent's conduct during the entire post-adjudication period. C. R. v. Richardson, 221 Ill. App. 3d 373, 163 Ill. Dec. 779, 581 N.E.2d 1202 (4 Dist. 1991).

A determination of unfitness must be based upon parenting efforts or progress made during the entire period between adjudication and filing of the termination petition and is not limited to only the first 12 months following an adjudication. People v. Daniels, 197 Ill. App. 3d 821, 144 Ill. Dec. 383, 555 N.E.2d 402 (4 Dist. 1990).

The designated time period of subdivision (D)(m) of this section reflects the rehabilitation period before which unfitness may not be proved under that provision; it does not terminate the period from which evidence may be considered. People v. Sepulveda, 174 Ill. App. 3d 132, 123 Ill. Dec. 641, 528 N.E.2d 25 (3 Dist. 1988).

In spite of the 12 month analysis which runs from the date of the adjudication of neglect, evidence of a parent's ability to care for a minor child, prior to the adjudicatory hearing, is admissible on the issue of parental unfitness if it bears on the issue of a parent's ability in caring for the minor prior to removal. People v. Green, 173 Ill. App. 3d 922, 123 Ill. Dec. 693, 528 N.E.2d 238 (2 Dist. 1988).

—Unfitness Order Reversed

In a case involving the termination of parental rights, where the parents made both reasonable efforts and reasonable progress to remedy the situation that led to an earlier adjudication of unfitness, an order terminating the respondents' parental rights should be reversed. In re S.G., 216 Ill. App. 3d 668, 159 Ill. Dec. 125, 575 N.E.2d 932 (2 Dist.), cert. denied, 142 Ill. 2d 665, 164 Ill. Dec. 928, 584 N.E.2d 140 (1991).

Relation to Other Laws

There were differing consequences in determining unfitness under the former Adoption Act (see now 750 ILCS 50/0.01 et seq.) and unfitness for purposes of child custody under the Illinois Marriage and Dissolution of Marriage Act (750 ILCS 5/101 et seq.) divorced spouses who lost custody of their children could still retain visitation rights and the legal status of parents; they retained rights to their child, subservient to the custodial spouse but greater than those of the rest of the world. But a parent who, because of a finding of depravity, was held unfit under this Act lost not only the custody of the child, but also all residual parental rights; the child was given to new parents without the consent of the old, and for all practical purposes, the natural parent became a nonperson to the child. People v. Abdullah, 85 Ill. 2d 300, 53 Ill. Dec. 246, 423 N.E.2d 915 (1981).

Scope of Review

Where petition for adoption was originally made in the county court it was not the province of the trial judge, nor was it the privilege or duty of the appellate court on review, to determine if the natural parents or the petitioners could better provide for the child; the court was to decide solely if the statutory grounds for adoption had been proven. Jackson v. Russell, 342 Ill. App. 637, 97 N.E.2d 584 (3 Dist. 1951); Oeth v. Erwin, 6 Ill. App. 2d 18, 126 N.E.2d 526 (4 Dist. 1955).

—Standard Inapplicable

Where there was no finding that child's injuries were inflicted by respondent, since they could have been inflicted by someone else or incurred in a manner not involving the parents, even assuming that respondent was responsible for inflicting the injuries, she could not make a "reasonable effort" to correct the condition of physically abusing the child since she did not have custody of the child after the adjudicatory and dispositional hearings; therefore, the "reasonable efforts" basis of unfitness did not apply here. People v. LaShay, 81 Ill. App. 3d 962, 36 Ill. Dec. 833, 401 N.E.2d 971 (1 Dist. 1979).

Standard of Review

A reviewing court cannot upset the decision of the lower court in an adoption proceeding granting custody to the natural mother unless such holding is palpably against the manifest weight of the evidence. Shuman v. Shuman, 22 Ill. App. 3d 151, 319 N.E.2d 287 (3 Dist. 1974).

The correctness of the trial court's determination will not be disturbed on appeal unless it is against the manifest weight of the evidence. In re Smith, 4 Ill. App. 3d 261, 280 N.E.2d 770 (1 Dist. 1972).

In adoption proceedings, the correctness of the trial court's determination should not be disturbed unless it is palpably against the manifest weight of the evidence. Thorpe v. Thorpe, 48 Ill. App. 2d 455, 198 N.E.2d 743 (4 Dist. 1964).

Substantial Neglect

—Factors

Leaving a child with neighbors for indefinite periods of time and failing to provide sufficient food for the child are further factors which the court may consider in determining whether substantial and repeated neglect exists. People v. Berry, 86 Ill. App. 3d 522, 42 Ill. Dec. 150, 408 N.E.2d 728 (5 Dist. 1980).

—Mentally Retarded Parents

Where mentally retarded parents substantially neglected their child continuously and repeatedly and failed to maintain a reasonable degree of interest, concern or responsibility as to his welfare, despite efforts to care for the child, parental rights were properly terminated. Department of Children & Family Servs. v. Devine, 81 Ill. App. 3d 314, 36 Ill. Dec. 775, 401 N.E.2d 616 (5 Dist. 1980).

Subdivision (D)(l) of the former Adoption Act (see now this section) was enacted by the legislature to apply only to children who were adjudicated neglected under section 2-4 of the former Juvenile Court Act (Ill.Rev.Stat., ch. 37, para. 702-4) (see now 705 ILCS 405/2-3). People v. Jankowski, 38 Ill. App. 3d 95, 347 N.E.2d 474 (1 Dist. 1976).

Summary Judgment

—Denied

In a termination of rights proceeding, the juvenile court did not err in denying an incarcerated parent's motion to dismiss the proceeding, sought on grounds of retroactive application of a new grounds for termination—long-term parental incarceration; parents did not have vested rights in parenting in all situations, so summary judgment terminating the parent's rights was properly ordered where the children's best interests required it, even though the foster parents, fearful of the parent's reaction, said they did not wish to adopt the children. People v. E.C. (In re E.C.), 337 Ill. App. 3d 391, 272 Ill. Dec. 51, 786 N.E.2d 590, 2003 Ill. App. LEXIS 272 (1 Dist. 2003).

—Proper

The state bore the burden of proving and did prove the respondent's unfitness on a proper ground; as argued by the state, the "irrebuttable presumption" challenged by the respondent was nothing more than the relation between a fact and its legal result; in light of the undisputed facts that the defendant had a criminal conviction resulting from the death of any child by physical child abuse, the court correctly determined that there was no material issue of fact and granted summary judgment finding her unfit and terminating her parental rights. People v. Ray, 88 Ill. App. 3d 1010, 44 Ill. Dec. 182, 411 N.E.2d 88 (5 Dist. 1980), appeal dismissed, 452 U.S. 956, 101 S. Ct. 3102, 69 L. Ed. 2d 967 (1981).

Termination of Parental Rights

Mother's action under this Act, which necessitated termination of

Termination of Parental Rights (Cont'd)
the father's parental rights, was an action by a private party and did not involve state action for constitutional due process purposes; therefore, the indigent father's due process rights were not implicated when the circuit court denied his request for court-appointed counsel. Jeffrey D.B. v. Stacy L.B. (In re Alyssa Jo B.), 2005 Ill. App. LEXIS 20 (3 Dist. Jan. 19, 2005).

—In General
Termination of a mother's parental rights to a minor child was reversed because the trial court applied the wrong nine-month period for determining whether the mother had made the reasonable efforts required in 750 ILCS 50/1(D)(m) to correct the conditions that led to the removal of the child from her custody. The trial court looked at a nine-month period commencing with the dispositional order when it should have looked a nine-month period commencing with the adjudication of neglect, which occurred three months earlier. People v. Teresa N.-S. (In re Jacien B.), 341 Ill. App. 3d 876, 276 Ill. Dec. 250, 793 N.E.2d 1009, 2003 Ill. App. LEXIS 932 (2 Dist. 2003), appeal denied sub nom. In re Jacien B., 207 Ill. 2d 603, 283 Ill. Dec. 134, 807 N.E.2d 975 (2004).

The termination of parental rights is as drastic and permanent an action as can be taken by a court. In re S.G., 216 Ill. App. 3d 668, 159 Ill. Dec. 125, 575 N.E.2d 932 (2 Dist.), cert. denied, 142 Ill. 2d 665, 164 Ill. Dec. 928, 584 N.E.2d 140 (1991).

Subdivision (D)(m) of this section does not require a showing at a termination hearing that the conditions imposed upon a parent at a dispositional hearing, designed to achieve return to the parent of a minor adjudged a ward of the court and placed with the Department of Children and Family Services, are reasonably related to the initial basis for adjudging the minor neglected. People v. Green, 173 Ill. App. 3d 922, 123 Ill. Dec. 693, 528 N.E.2d 238 (2 Dist. 1988).

Because the common law did not provide for the adoption of children, adoption rights and duties are determined by statute. Evink v. Edwards ex rel. Gregory, 106 Ill. App. 3d 635, 62 Ill. Dec. 407, 435 N.E.2d 1379 (2 Dist. 1982).

There is an inherent right which all parents have to the society and custody of their own child, and this right should not be abrogated without compelling reasons. People v. Drescher, 91 Ill. App. 3d 658, 47 Ill. Dec. 631, 415 N.E.2d 636 (1 Dist. 1980).

An adoption permanently severs not only custodial rights but all rights and interests of the natural parent. People v. Drescher, 91 Ill. App. 3d 658, 47 Ill. Dec. 631, 415 N.E.2d 636 (1 Dist. 1980).

A natural parent who has validly consented to the adoption of her child may, prior to the specific placement of the child for adoption by others, properly petition to adopt as the parent of a related child. Partington v. Department of Children & Family Servs., 91 Ill. App. 3d 205, 46 Ill. Dec. 656, 414 N.E.2d 540 (2 Dist. 1980).

Provisions in the former Juvenile Court Act (see now 705 ILCS 405/1-1 et seq.) and the former Adoption Act (see now 750 ILCS 50/0.01 et seq.) are, and should be, the exclusive authority by which parental rights may be terminated. Patrick v. Patrick, 59 Ill. App. 3d 11, 16 Ill. Dec. 309, 374 N.E.2d 1084 (4 Dist. 1978).

An adoption severs the rights and interests of natural parents; it permanently terminates the relation between parent and child. People v. Allen, 34 Ill. App. 3d 603, 340 N.E.2d 269 (1 Dist. 1975).

Adoption, which affects the course of inheritance, deprives a child of the place in which it was placed by nature, and by force of law thrusts the child into another relationship, while severing conclusively the rights and interests of the natural parents, is a very different and more drastic matter than a change of custody; the rights of natural parents to their children must not be terminated unless a clear and convincing case is made in strict compliance with the adoption statute. People ex rel. Buell v. Bell, 20 Ill. App. 2d 82, 155 N.E.2d 104 (2 Dist. 1959).

—Best Interest of Child
Even though the court made sufficient findings that termination of a father's parental rights would be in the child's best interest, a separate hearing on that issue was mandatory and, because the court did not hold a separate hearing, its order terminating the father's parental rights was reversed and the case was remanded for a best interest of the child hearing. Jeffrey D.B. v. Stacy L.B. (In re Alyssa Jo B.), 2005 Ill. App. LEXIS 20 (3 Dist. Jan. 19, 2005).

Trial court's decision to terminate parents' rights to two small children was in the best interests of the children where the evidence showed that the children were in a safe and happy foster home, that the children had bonded with the foster mother, that it would be traumatic for the children to be removed from their foster home, that reunification attempts in the past had failed, and that the parents were unable to provide a home that was safe and secure or to provide for the children's health or to give them love. People v. Lacina B. (In re J.B.), 346 Ill. App. 3d 77, 281 Ill. Dec. 376, 803 N.E.2d 997, 2004 Ill. App. LEXIS 22 (1 Dist. 2004), appeal denied sub nom. In re J.B., 208 Ill. 2d 538, 284 Ill. Dec. 340, 809 N.E.2d 1286 (2004).

Trial court properly terminated a mother's parental rights to her son, pursuant to 705 ILCS 405/2-29(2) and 750 ILCS 50/1(D)(q), because based on testimony at the best interest hearing indicating that the child had been physically and sexually abused, and in light of the required considerations of 705 ILCS 405/1-3(4.05), the termination of the mother's parental rights was in the best interest of the child. People v. L.M. (In re D.W.), 344 Ill. App. 3d 30, 278 Ill. Dec. 692, 799 N.E.2d 410, 2003 Ill. App. LEXIS 1238 (1 Dist. 2003).

Under former Ill.Rev.Stat., ch. 37, paras. 701-2(3)(c) and 705-9, (see now 705 ILCS 405/1-2 and 705 ILCS 405/2-29) as well as former Ill.Rev.Stat., ch. 4, paras. 9.1-1 and 9.1-20a, (see now 750 ILCS 50/4 and this section), in the type of situation involving the issue of terminating the interest and rights of a natural parent so that the court may in the future proceed with examination of the merits of an adoption, the courts were required to consider the best interests of the minor. People v. Grant, 29 Ill. App. 3d 731, 331 N.E.2d 219 (1 Dist. 1975).

Determination that termination of parental rights was in a child's best interest was not an abuse of discretion or against the manifest weight of the evidence where the trial court went beyond the parent's felony conviction record and considered the desirability of the parent's two children being raised together, the particular child's special needs, and the fact that the child had bonded well with the foster family that wished to adopt. People v. Herman O. (In re Travarius O.), 343 Ill. App. 3d 844, 278 Ill. Dec. 792, 799 N.E.2d 510, 2003 Ill. App. LEXIS 1262 (1 Dist. 2003).

—Burden of Proof
The rights of natural parents to their children cannot be severed unless the movant presents a clear and convincing case. People v. Overton, 21 Ill. App. 3d 1014, 316 N.E.2d 201 (2 Dist. 1974).

The rights and interest of natural parents should not be terminated unless a clear and convincing case has been made in strict compliance with the adoption statute. Bergstedt v. Cech, 8 Ill. App. 3d 642, 291 N.E.2d 21 (1 Dist. 1972); Jackson v. Russell, 342 Ill. App. 637, 97 N.E.2d 584 (3 Dist. 1951).

—Construction
Trial court did not act unlawfully by terminating a mother's parental rights after it found that the mother was unfit under 750 ILCS 50/1(D)(g) but not unfit under 750 ILCS 50/1(D)(m), and the state supreme court affirmed the trial court's finding that the mother, who made a conscious choice to remain in abusive relationships with different men, was an unfit parent. People v. Rosanna W., 199 Ill. 2d 198, 262 Ill. Dec. 802, 766 N.E.2d 1105, 2002 Ill. LEXIS 297 (2002).

—Conviction
Trial court properly terminated a mother's parental rights to her son, pursuant to 750 ILCS 50/1(D)(q), as that statute did not violate the due process clause or the equal protection clause of the Illinois Constitution, Ill. Const. Art. 1, § 2; the statute did not violate a party's due process rights merely because the statute required a finding of unfitness as a matter of law based on a prior conviction involving the attempted murder of a child; the statute created a method for the State to have a parent declared unfit for the protection of children because of a prior conviction, and did not create classifications for administering direct punishment for convictions. People v. L.M. (In re D.W.), 344 Ill. App. 3d 30, 278 Ill. Dec. 692, 799 N.E.2d 410, 2003 Ill. App. LEXIS 1238 (1 Dist. 2003).

Father's contention that it was precipitous to terminate his parental rights on the basis of a conviction which might be overturned on appeal, was meritless, as the likelihood that his conviction will yet be reversed was slight, and the evidence relied upon in the trial court was unimpeached, and the finding of father's parental unfitness was unshaken. In re T.H., 255 Ill. App. 3d 247, 193 Ill. Dec. 370, 626 N.E.2d 403 (5 Dist. 1993), appeal denied, 155

Termination of Parental Rights (Cont'd)

—Conviction (Cont'd)
Ill. 2d 577, 198 Ill. Dec. 554, 633 N.E.2d 16, cert. denied, 513 U.S. 905, 115 S. Ct. 269, 130 L. Ed. 2d 187 (1994).

—Decision Unaffected by Appeal
The Adoption Act does not call for the courts to reserve ruling on termination until parent judged unfit exhausts the appeal process. In re C.M.J., 278 Ill. App. 3d 885, 215 Ill. Dec. 487, 663 N.E.2d 498 (5 Dist. 1996).

—Drug Abuse
Where the basis of the removal of a child was her birth with cocaine in her system, such a condition could happen only once, and nothing the mother could have done after the neglect adjudication would have corrected this condition, or would have brought about the recurrence of this unique event; thus, where all the relevant evidence at the hearing was that the mother had given up cocaine before the birth of the child, her conduct relating to the use or possession of marijuana did not suffice as a basis for judicial action as sweeping and devastating as the termination of her parental rights in her child. People v. T.J., 233 Ill. App. 3d 88, 174 Ill. Dec. 159, 598 N.E.2d 456 (2 Dist. 1992).

—Failure to Pay Child Support
Where a father had not relinquished all parental interests, but rather had maintained those interests even though he was delinquent in his support payments, failure to supply support, however reprehensible, did not mean that his parental rights would be extinguished by adoption; therefore, the decision of the circuit court denying a petition for adoption of his child could not be said to be against the manifest weight of the evidence. Carlson v. Oberling, 73 Ill. App. 2d 412, 218 N.E.2d 820 (4 Dist. 1966).

—Illustrative Cases
In a proceeding by mother and her husband under the this Act, to terminate respondent father's parental rights, the trial court violated his equal protection rights by failing to provide him with a written "Notice of Rights," as required by 705 ILCS 405/1-5(1), including including notice that he had the right to request appointed counsel at trial. In re K.M., Ill. App. 3d , Ill. Dec. , N.E.2d , 2005 Ill. App. LEXIS 116 (3 Dist. Feb. 10, 2005).

In a proceeding for termination of a father's parental rights because of substantial neglect and depravity, his due process rights were not violated by his telephonic participation in a hearing held on his fitness as a parent where he was in an Iowa jail at the time of the hearing and was periodically allowed throughout the hearing to confer privately with his attorney. People v. Anthony C. (In re A.C.), Ill. App. 3d , 290 Ill. Dec. 679, 821 N.E.2d 1253, 2005 Ill. App. LEXIS 2 (3 Dist. 2005).

Trial court did not err by finding that it was in a child's best interest to terminate her father's parental rights because he did not provide for her safety or welfare since he failed to provide support or an adequate home due to his frequent criminal trouble and because she felt a sense of attachment to her foster parents and her half-siblings in a foster home while the foster parents wished to provide guardianship for her. People v. Anthony C. (In re A.C.), Ill. App. 3d , 290 Ill. Dec. 679, 821 N.E.2d 1253, 2005 Ill. App. LEXIS 2 (3 Dist. 2005).

Termination of the mother's parental rights was not against the manifest weight of the evidence where there was evidence in the record supporting the trial court's determination that the mother failed to protect the children from the father and failed to make reasonable progress to remedy the situation. People v. Anderson (In re Janine M.A.), 342 Ill. App. 3d 1041, 277 Ill. Dec. 809, 796 N.E.2d 1175, 2003 Ill. App. LEXIS 1160 (4 Dist. 2003).

Where the State alleged that respondent father was an unfit parent under 750 ILCS 50/1(D)(b), (D)(i), (D)(r), (D)(s), and recited the statutory language, without more, the pleadings were sufficiently specific. People v. Andre D. (In re Andrea D.), 342 Ill. App. 3d 233, 276 Ill. Dec. 793, 794 N.E.2d 1043, 2003 Ill. App. LEXIS 1006 (2 Dist. 2003), appeal denied, Ill. 2d , 282 Ill. Dec. 478, 806 N.E.2d 1066 (2003).

Although the State's petition seeking an order terminating the parental rights of a mother who was convicted of murder did not state that the mother could lose her rights "permanently," that omission did not require reversal of the trial court's judgment terminating her rights. People v. Griffin (In re J.R.), 342 Ill. App. 3d 310, 276 Ill. Dec. 519, 794 N.E.2d 414, 2003 Ill. App. LEXIS 976 (4 Dist. 2003).

Father was properly found to be unfit under 750 ILCS 50/1 (D)(m) where he had three prior felonies, had visited his son only twice since his birth, never made any inquiries to his son's caseworker about his son, and never sent his son any letters, gifts, or financial assistance; thus the father failed to demonstrate a reasonable degree of interest in his son. People v. Mitchell C. (In re Jamarqon C.), 338 Ill. App. 3d 639, 273 Ill. Dec. 35, 788 N.E.2d 344, 2003 Ill. App. LEXIS 441 (2 Dist. 2003).

Father's failure to register with the Putative Father Registry was not evidence of unfitness for purposes of terminating parental rights; the termination was not set aside, however, because the record established statutory grounds for termination that included abandonment and lack of interest. People v. Quinella W., Ill. App. 3d , 262 Ill. Dec. 606, 765 N.E.2d 1214, 2002 Ill. App. LEXIS 186 (2 Dist. 2002).

The trial court did not abuse its discretion in terminating the respondent's parental rights where the state proved by clear and convincing evidence that respondent was an unfit parent; she failed to visit her children for months at a time, failed to demonstrate a reasonable degree of interest, concern or responsibility and showed a lack of progress in working towards the return of her children. In re M.S., 302 Ill. App. 3d 998, 235 Ill. Dec. 969, 706 N.E.2d 524 (2 Dist. 1999).

Where the trial court waited almost four years and still the mother was not close to being able to provide for the needs of her children, there was no error in the trial court's decision to terminate the mother's parental rights. In re C.C., 299 Ill. App. 3d 827, 234 Ill. Dec. 258, 702 N.E.2d 598 (5 Dist. 1998).

The fact that mother's current attempt at rehabilitation from drug use was overshadowed by her longstanding drug dependency and all children were developing well in foster homes, trial court's decision to terminate parental rights was not against the manifest weight of the evidence. In re D.M., 298 Ill. App. 3d 574, 232 Ill. Dec. 765, 699 N.E.2d 212 (3 Dist. 1998).

Where evidence clearly indicated that respondent would be unable to provide a stable home environment in the foreseeable future and child's foster family wished to adopt him, a family with which he was content and bonded, court did not err in terminating respondent's parental rights. In re J.G., 298 Ill. App. 3d 617, 232 Ill. Dec. 720, 699 N.E.2d 167 (4 Dist. 1998).

Where the state noted that one of the two reasons for the neglect finding was the marital discord between the respondent and her spouse, while the state conceded that this condition did not exist during the time her spouse was incarcerated, it noted that respondent had observable bruises on her face and arms on the day of the fitness hearing which may have been caused by a fight between respondent and her husband, this evidence was highly speculative and was not sufficient to support a termination of parental rights. People v. Foster, 95 Ill. App. 3d 169, 50 Ill. Dec. 605, 419 N.E.2d 713 (4 Dist. 1981).

A trial court's decision not to terminate parental rights was not against the manifest weight of the evidence, despite a lack of contact between father and child, where the father had been given advice not to attempt visitation and the father was never ordered to pay child support. Blakey v. Blakey, 72 Ill. App. 3d 946, 29 Ill. Dec. 63, 391 N.E.2d 222 (4 Dist. 1979).

Since the proceedings which terminated defendant's parental rights were not conducted under the auspices of either the former Juvenile Court Act (see now 705 ILCS 405/1-1 et seq.) or the former Adoption Act (see now 750 ILCS 50/0.01 et seq.), the procedures outlined to terminate parental rights were not followed, since the order terminating defendant's parental rights was inappropriate and insufficient to support the order of the court. Patrick v. Patrick, 59 Ill. App. 3d 11, 16 Ill. Dec. 309, 374 N.E.2d 1084 (4 Dist. 1978).

—Reversed
Trial court's termination of parental rights was reversed where the record showed the mother made some objective, demonstrable movement toward accomplishing the goal of return of the child. People v. Doolan, 101 Ill. App. 3d 322, 56 Ill. Dec. 802, 427 N.E.2d 1348 (3 Dist. 1981).

—Right to Counsel
Parent whose rights had been terminated had not been deprived

Termination of Parental Rights (Cont'd)

—Right to Counsel (Cont'd)

of an indigent parent's guarantee of counsel where the parent had been provided with three successive lawyers, each of whom had been fired or forced to withdraw rather than commit ethical violations; it did not violate the parent's rights to decline to appoint yet another lawyer. People v. Herman O. (In re Travarius O.), 343 Ill. App. 3d 844, 278 Ill. Dec. 792, 799 N.E.2d 510, 2003 Ill. App. LEXIS 1262 (1 Dist. 2003).

—Substantial Progress

Where a parent has made substantial progress toward correcting the condition that led to the removal of the child, the lack of what Department of Children and Family Services deems satisfactory interaction between parent and child is not justification for the termination of parental rights. People v. T.J., 233 Ill. App. 3d 88, 174 Ill. Dec. 159, 598 N.E.2d 456 (2 Dist. 1992).

—Unfitness

Finding of a father's unfitness based on § 1(D)(m), 750 ILCS 50/1(D)(m), of the Adoption Act was not against the manifest weight of the evidence, as the father failed to complete any recommended substance abuse treatment, tested positive for cocaine at least once per month from January to May 2003, was unemployed and did not obtain a lawful means of support as directed, and he continued to reside with a woman struggling with her own substance abuse issues. People v. J.M. (In re Tiffany M.), 353 Ill. App. 3d 883, 289 Ill. Dec. 317, 819 N.E.2d 813, 2004 Ill. App. LEXIS 1464 (2 Dist. 2004).

State of Illinois failed to establish a mother's unfitness where no finding of neglect was entered against the mother in an initial neglect proceeding, and a finding that the mother neglected her children made in a second proceeding was improper because it was based on the mother's violation of an order of protection she was ordered to obtain; however, the trial court was without authority to require the mother to obtain the order of protection. People v. Teresa R. (In re Cheyenne S.), 351 Ill. App. 3d 1042, 287 Ill. Dec. 383, 815 N.E.2d 1186, 2004 Ill. App. LEXIS 1064 (3 Dist. 2004).

Statutory section that State cited as the sole basis for finding the mother unfit as a parent, 750 ILCS 50/1(D)(q), was an unconstitutional violation of the mother's substantive due process rights as that statutory section permitted a finding of unfitness merely on a person's conviction for aggravated battery, without consideration of other relevant factors that might show fitness, such as rehabilitation, fitness, or change of circumstance; while the State had an interest in the welfare of children, that statutory section was not narrowly tailored to achieve that end as it made irrelevant factors that might show a parent, such as the mother, was a fit parent. People v. Lisa Z. (In re Amanda D.), 349 Ill. App. 3d 941, 285 Ill. Dec. 358, 811 N.E.2d 1237, 2004 Ill. App. LEXIS 763 (2 Dist. 2004).

Child welfare agency met its burden to prove that the mother would not be able to meet her parental responsibilities due to chronic bipolar disorder, which included manifestations of hyperactivity and depression, including suicide attempts. People v. J.Y., 334 Ill. App. 3d 894, 268 Ill. Dec. 590, 778 N.E.2d 1212, 2002 Ill. App. LEXIS 969 (1 Dist. 2002).

Father was deemed unfit due to his incarceration at the time of the custody petition and the father's efforts to take control of his life were not relevant in considering his fitness. People v. Putman, Ill. App. 3d , 258 Ill. Dec. 244, 755 N.E.2d 1063, 2001 Ill. App. LEXIS 731 (5 Dist. 2001).

State met its burden of proving by clear and convincing evidence that mother was unfit because of her failure to protect the minor from an environment injurious to his welfare; mother failed to protect minor's sibling from the father, admitted to beating the sibling herself, and failed to seek medical attention for the sibling after beating him. In re G.V., 292 Ill. App. 3d 301, 226 Ill. Dec. 303, 685 N.E.2d 406 (2 Dist. 1997).

The trial court properly found father to be an unfit parent and terminated his parental rights to his two minor daughters who had lived with their foster parents since their infancy. In re J.F., 248 Ill. App. 3d 1, 187 Ill. Dec. 698, 618 N.E.2d 289 (1 Dist. 1992).

A finding of unfitness may lead to the termination of parental rights and a court may take such action after finding it to be in the best interests of the minor. People v. Walters, 226 Ill. App. 3d 805, 168 Ill. Dec. 570, 589 N.E.2d 970 (4 Dist. 1992).

In a case proceeding under subsection (D)(b) of this section, the issue is whether a parent maintained concern, interest and responsibility as to his or her child's welfare that, under the circumstances, was of a reasonable degree. To terminate a particular parent's parental rights, a court must find the negative of the proposition and it must find that there is clear and convincing evidence that such a level of reasonable interest and concern was not maintained. Syck v. Snyder, 138 Ill. 2d 255, 149 Ill. Dec. 710, 562 N.E.2d 174 (1990).

State's evidence was sufficient to establish the father's unfitness under 750 ILCS 50/1(D)(h), as the daughter testified clearly and consistently to multiple acts of sexual abuse by the father to which the father admitted to authorities. People v. James L. (In re Diana L.), 343 Ill. App. 3d 419, 278 Ill. Dec. 116, 797 N.E.2d 711, 2003 Ill. App. LEXIS 1100 (3 Dist. 2003).

—Ward of Court

Once there has been a finding of neglect and a child has been adjudged a ward of the court pursuant to the Juvenile Court Act (705 ILCS 405/1-1 et seq.) the proceedings by which parental rights are terminated are governed by this Act. People ex rel. Dep't of Children & Family Servs. v. Tolbert, 62 Ill. App. 3d 927, 19 Ill. Dec. 64, 378 N.E.2d 565 (5 Dist. 1978).

Unfitness

—In General

In Illinois, a finding of parental unfitness may be based on evidence sufficient to support any one statutory ground. People v. Velez (In re Jordan V.), 347 Ill. App. 3d 1057, 283 Ill. Dec. 630, 808 N.E.2d 596, 2004 Ill. App. LEXIS 411 (4 Dist. 2004).

When the evidence supports a finding that one parent is unfit and it is in the best interests of the child that the parental rights of that parent be terminated, the trial court may so order even though the parental rights of the child's other parent have not been terminated or are not, as of that moment, even subject to a petition for termination. People v. Houston, 219 Ill. App. 3d 269, 162 Ill. Dec. 343, 579 N.E.2d 1157 (4 Dist. 1991).

A finding of unfitness may lead to the termination of parental rights and a court may take such action after finding it to be in the best interests of the minor. C. R. v. Richardson, 221 Ill. App. 3d 373, 163 Ill. Dec. 779, 581 N.E.2d 1202 (4 Dist. 1991).

In situations in which unfitness under subdivision (D)(p) of this section are in question, a two part analysis is required: first, the evidence must indicate a parent is mentally unable to discharge her normal parental responsibilities and second, there must be sufficient justification to find that the inability shall extend beyond a reasonable time period. People v. D.D., 198 Ill. App. 3d 495, 144 Ill. Dec. 679, 555 N.E.2d 1198 (5 Dist. 1990).

While parental rights and responsibilities are matters of deep human importance and will not be lightly terminated, the parental rights of a non-consenting parent may be terminated if the parent is adjudicated unfit for one or more of the grounds listed in this section. People v. Phillips, 191 Ill. App. 3d 237, 138 Ill. Dec. 437, 547 N.E.2d 604 (4 Dist. 1989).

Unfitness under this Act is different than unfitness for the purpose of child custody under the Illinois Marriage and Dissolution of Marriage Act (750 ILCS 5/101 et seq.). Tranel v. Lutgen, 177 Ill. App. 3d 954, 127 Ill. Dec. 147, 532 N.E.2d 976 (2 Dist. 1988).

Where either both natural parents are proved unfit or one parent consents to the adoption and the other is proved unfit, it is desirable for the child to acquire new parents through adoption, and the court will ordinarily appoint a guardian empowered to consent to the adoption. People v. Autio, 135 Ill. App. 3d 1017, 90 Ill. Dec. 553, 482 N.E.2d 372 (1 Dist. 1985).

The termination of parental rights is an extreme action, justified only upon clear and convincing evidence of unfitness presented in strict compliance with this Act. Davis v. Bughdadi, 120 Ill. App. 3d 236, 76 Ill. Dec. 38, 458 N.E.2d 177 (5 Dist. 1983).

A finding of parental unfitness, absent parental consent, is a prerequisite and must be determined before the court can consider what placement, if any will suit the best interests of the child. People ex rel. Dep't of Children & Family Servs., v. Buttram, 56 Ill. App. 3d 950, 14 Ill. Dec. 856, 372 N.E.2d 1135 (3 Dist. 1978).

—Abandonment

Because the natural father was found to have abandoned his

Unfitness (Cont'd)

—Abandonment (Cont'd)

child, that did not mean he was unfit. Flangel v. Flangel, 87 Ill. App. 3d 1100, 42 Ill. Dec. 906, 409 N.E.2d 521 (2 Dist. 1980).

—Absence of Fault

Where Department of Children and Family Services (DCFS) failed to inform father of the various service plans which were created to enable him to work towards visitation and/ custody of his children and there was no indication in the record that any of the DCFS workers involved in this case ever contacted the Department of Corrections in an effort to locate the father who had informed DCFS of his incarceration, DCFS' handling of the case was inexcusably clumsy, and since DCFS did not keep the father apprised of the service plans, his failure to complete the tasks within those plans could not alone support a finding of unfitness. T.D. v. Baldwin, 268 Ill. App. 3d 239, 205 Ill. Dec. 708, 643 N.E.2d 1315 (1 Dist. 1994).

A parent can be unfit without fault. People v. Edmonds, 85 Ill. App. 3d 229, 40 Ill. Dec. 530, 406 N.E.2d 231 (3 Dist. 1980).

A parent can be unfit without fault; and such a conclusion is necessary if it is to accord with the legislative intent of an act manifestly concerned with the best interests of the child. Department of Children & Family Servs. v. Devine, 81 Ill. App. 3d 314, 36 Ill. Dec. 775, 401 N.E.2d 616 (5 Dist. 1980).

—Acknowledgment of Abuse

The trial court's termination of the parental rights of the defendant was not against the manifest weight of the evidence where the father had yet to unequivocally accept responsibility for the sexual abuse. C. R. v. Richardson, 221 Ill. App. 3d 373, 163 Ill. Dec. 779, 581 N.E.2d 1202 (4 Dist. 1991).

Where the evidence established respondent completed some of the goals established in the DCFS client-service plans but adamantly refused to admit to sexually abusing the child and the counsellors involved in the case established respondent's acknowledgment of the abuse was critical to the full recovery for child from the trauma she suffered from the abuse and was required before respondent would be reunited with child and, further, failure to admit the abuse could lead to additional incidents of sexual abuse if respondent and child were reunited, the trial court's order finding respondent an unfit parent in terminating his parental rights was supported by the evidence. People v. Dillman, 213 Ill. App. 3d 284, 157 Ill. Dec. 143, 571 N.E.2d 1162 (1991).

A parent's failure to acknowledge that sexual abuse has occurred and, therefore, failure to take steps to prevent the children's exposure to that abuse, is sufficient to support a finding of unfitness by clear and convincing evidence. People v. Clarence H. B., 215 Ill. App. 3d 85, 158 Ill. Dec. 765, 574 N.E.2d 878 (2 Dist. 1991).

—Adjudicating Order Entry Date

Trial court erred in finding the mother unfit pursuant to 750 ILCS 50/1(D)(m)(iii) with regard to her youngest child, who was born within the statutory nine-month period used to assess the mother's fitness as to her other children, because the youngest child was not adjudicated neglected until April 27, 2001; thus, the nine-month period chosen by the State to demonstrate the mother's unfitness, i.e., November 1, 2000, to July 31, 2001, was not, with respect to the youngest child, a nine-month period after the end of the initial nine-month period following the adjudication. People v. Tontorya C. (In re D.C.), 209 Ill. 2d 287, 282 Ill. Dec. 848, 807 N.E.2d 472, 2004 Ill. LEXIS 364 (2004).

For purposes of the twelve-month (now nine-month) period in subdivision (D)(m) of this section, an adjudication order is entered as of the date of the docket entry. People v. R.B., 195 Ill. App. 3d 919, 142 Ill. Dec. 366, 552 N.E.2d 1107 (5 Dist. 1990).

—Admissible Evidence

Evidence of mother's relationships with her other children was admissible as it was probative of her progress in correcting conditions which were basis for removal of child. People v. Bentsen, 90 Ill. App. 3d 269, 45 Ill. Dec. 585, 412 N.E.2d 1167 (3 Dist. 1980).

—Admissions by Parent

Due process requires a circuit court to determine whether a factual basis exists for an admission of parental unfitness before it accepts the admission; a factual-basis determination safeguards against an erroneous deprivation of the respondent's fundamental right to parent her children, and such a requirement does not impose any increased burden on the state, but fosters just and accurate decisionmaking. People v. V.D., 196 Ill. 2d 356, 256 Ill. Dec. 297, 751 N.E.2d 1134, 2001 Ill. LEXIS 491 (2001).

Where a parent makes an admission of unfitness, the trial court must determine that there is a factual basis for such admission since, otherwise, there is a danger that a parent may understand the state's alleged grounds of unfitness, but may not realize that his or her conduct does not fall within those allegations; however, the factual basis that is required before the court may accept an admission of unfitness need not rise to the level of the state's burden of proof, and the trial court may determine the best method for ascertaining whether a sufficient factual basis exists. People v. V.D., 313 Ill. App. 3d 205, 246 Ill. Dec. 86, 729 N.E.2d 86, 2000 Ill. App. LEXIS 274 (2 Dist. 2000).

—Adultery

As in cases of divorce, the critical conduct for purposes of unfitness must be found in acts occurring after the marriage; fact that mother gave birth to two children out of wedlock prior to marriage is not probative of father's claim of "open and notorious" adultery subsequent to the marriage. Culkin v. Culkin, 30 Ill. App. 3d 1073, 333 N.E.2d 698 (4 Dist. 1975).

In view of the fact that the welfare of the child was the prime consideration in an adoption proceeding, the court abused its discretion in not permitting an amendment to an adoption petition to charge depravity and open and notorious adultery or fornication and to consider evidence upon those two charges of unfitness. Thorpe v. Thorpe, 48 Ill. App. 2d 455, 198 N.E.2d 743 (4 Dist. 1964).

—Appointment of Guardian

A trial court may appoint a guardian with the authority to consent to the adoption of a minor under the Juvenile Court Act (705 ILCS 405/2-29), whenever it finds by clear and convincing evidence that a nonconsenting parent is unfit as defined in this section. Walker v. State, 199 Ill. App. 3d 1050, 146 Ill. Dec. 17, 557 N.E.2d 959 (3 Dist. 1990).

The trial court's order which specifically appointed a guardian with specific power to consent to adoption was sufficient to terminate the parental rights of respondent and his wife, even though the order did not specifically state it was terminating parental rights. People v. R.B., 195 Ill. App. 3d 919, 142 Ill. Dec. 366, 552 N.E.2d 1107 (5 Dist. 1990).

Where petitioner sought leave to amend the petition for adjudication of wardship orally to include a prayer for appointment of a guardian with power to consent to adoption, the amendment adequately notified defendants of the nature of the proceedings and allegations against them, adequately described the grounds for the filing of the petition, and was sufficient to allow the court's specific finding that defendants were unfit and that appointment of a guardian with power to consent to adoption was necessary to protect the best interests of the children. People v. Berry, 86 Ill. App. 3d 522, 42 Ill. Dec. 150, 408 N.E.2d 728 (5 Dist. 1980).

Only if the trial court finds a nonconsenting parent unfit, after a minor child is adjudged a ward of the court under the Act, may a guardian with power to consent to an adoption be appointed. People v. Nitz, 76 Ill. App. 3d 15, 31 Ill. Dec. 685, 394 N.E.2d 887 (3 Dist. 1979).

—Argument Waived

Arguments that the state failed to furnish a bill of particulars in a case involving termination of parental rights which was raised for the first time in a reply brief, were waived. People v. Mikel, 205 Ill. App. 3d 497, 150 Ill. Dec. 872, 563 N.E.2d 999 (4 Dist. 1990).

—Basis of Finding

Trial court's finding that a mother was an unfit parent because she was convicted on charges of aggravated battery of a child and the felony murder of the same child was not against the manifest weight of the evidence based on the fact that the murder conviction was vacated; 750 ILCS 50/1(D)(f) did not require that death be an element of an underlying criminal conviction and the aggravated battery conviction was sufficient to form a basis for the unfitness finding. People v. Sherry L.S. (In re A.L.C.), 346 Ill. App. 3d 763, 282 Ill. Dec. 202, 805 N.E.2d 1219, 2004 Ill. App. LEXIS 162 (3 Dist. 2004).

Unfitness (Cont'd)

—Basis of Finding (Cont'd)

Trial court erred in finding the mother unfit pursuant to 750 ILCS 50/1(D)(m)(iii) with regard to her youngest child, who was born within the statutory nine-month period used to assess the mother's fitness as to her other children, because the youngest child was not adjudicated neglected until April 27, 2001; thus, the nine-month period chosen by the State to demonstrate the mother's unfitness, i.e., November 1, 2000, to July 31, 2001, was not, with respect to the youngest child, a nine-month period after the end of the initial nine-month period following the adjudication. People v. Tontorya C. (In re D.C.), 209 Ill. 2d 287, 282 Ill. Dec. 848, 807 N.E.2d 472, 2004 Ill. LEXIS 364 (2004).

For a finding of parental unfitness, 750 ILCS 50/1(D)(f) does not require death to be an element of the offense for which a respondent is convicted; the plain language of the statute only requires the conviction to "result" from a death by physical child abuse. People v. Sherry L.S. (In re A.L.C.), 346 Ill. App. 3d 763, 282 Ill. Dec. 202, 805 N.E.2d 1219, 2004 Ill. App. LEXIS 162 (3 Dist. 2004).

A finding of parental unfitness may be based on evidence sufficient to support any one statutory ground, even if the evidence is not sufficient to support other grounds alleged. People v. Walters, 226 Ill. App. 3d 805, 168 Ill. Dec. 570, 589 N.E.2d 970 (4 Dist. 1992).

It was in the child's best interests that mother's parental rights be terminated where a clinical psychologist noted that the child suffered severe emotional trauma, found the child to be very delayed in developmental skills and described her general behavior as chaotic. People v. D.D., 198 Ill. App. 3d 495, 144 Ill. Dec. 679, 555 N.E.2d 1198 (5 Dist. 1990).

When the evidence of unfitness is clear and satisfactory, the best interests of the children should out-weigh the residual parental rights. People ex rel. Dep't of Children & Family Servs., v. Buttram, 56 Ill. App. 3d 950, 14 Ill. Dec. 856, 372 N.E.2d 1135 (3 Dist. 1978).

—Best Interests of Child

The trial court should not consider the child's best interests when determining whether the parent is unfit. People v. Clarence H. B., 215 Ill. App. 3d 85, 158 Ill. Dec. 765, 574 N.E.2d 878 (2 Dist. 1991).

When ruling on parental unfitness, a court is not to consider the child's "best interests"; only evidence that bears on the issue of unfitness is to be considered. Syck v. Snyder, 138 Ill. 2d 255, 149 Ill. Dec. 710, 562 N.E.2d 174 (1990).

A finding of unfitness is a prerequisite to addressing the question of the child's best interest. People v. Williams, 187 Ill. App. 3d 988, 135 Ill. Dec. 406, 543 N.E.2d 974 (1 Dist. 1989).

Where as here, there was clear and convincing evidence of the unfitness of a natural parent, then it was necessary that the natural right of the parent must yield to the best interest of the child. In re Dixon, 81 Ill. App. 3d 493, 36 Ill. Dec. 750, 401 N.E.2d 591 (3 Dist. 1980).

—Cases Unique

Each case concerning parental unfitness is sui generis, and factual comparisons between cases are inherently suspect. People v. T.J., 233 Ill. App. 3d 88, 174 Ill. Dec. 159, 598 N.E.2d 456 (2 Dist. 1992).

Each case of an adjudication of parental unfitness is unique, and comparisons with other causes are not appropriate. People v. Clarence H. B., 215 Ill. App. 3d 85, 158 Ill. Dec. 765, 574 N.E.2d 878 (2 Dist. 1991).

—Child Out of Wedlock

Under former Ill.Rev.Stat., ch. 4, para. 1 (see now this section), the fact that a child was born out of wedlock did not alone prove the unfitness of the mother to have the custody of the child. Dickholtz v. Littfin, 341 Ill. App. 400, 94 N.E.2d 89 (1 Dist. 1950).

—Clear and Convincing Evidence

Trial court erred in finding the parents unfit and in terminating their parental rights to two of their children because the State failed to prove by clear and convincing evidence that the parents were unfit under 750 ILCS 50/1(D)(p); the parents had mental disabilities sufficient to prevent them from discharging normal parental duties and the State's case rested almost entirely on the testimony of one expert. People v. Tonya L. (In re Cornica J.), 351 Ill. App. 3d 557, 286 Ill. Dec. 630, 814 N.E.2d 618, 2004 Ill. App. LEXIS 951 (2 Dist. 2004).

State of Illinois must prove parental unfitness by clear and convincing evidence, and a trial court's findings must be given great deference because of its superior opportunity to observe the witnesses and evaluate their credibility. People v. Velez (In re Jordan V.), 347 Ill. App. 3d 1057, 283 Ill. Dec. 630, 808 N.E.2d 596, 2004 Ill. App. LEXIS 411 (4 Dist. 2004).

The state proved by clear and convincing evidence that the respondents failed to maintain a reasonable degree of interest, concern, or responsibility as to the future of their children, therefore the trial court's findings of unfitness and termination of parental rights was fully supported by the weight of the evidence. In re M.M., 261 Ill. App. 3d 71, 199 Ill. Dec. 436, 634 N.E.2d 36 (5 Dist. 1994).

Parental rights are of deep human importance and must not be lightly terminated, and a finding of parental fitness must be supported by clear and convincing evidence. People v. McIntosh, 214 Ill. App. 3d 545, 158 Ill. Dec. 296, 574 N.E.2d 90 (1 Dist. 1991).

Where a minor adjudicated a ward of the court and removed from his parents is the subject of a petition for adoption as authorized by 705 ILCS 405/2-29, it is that section which requires proof by clear and convincing evidence that a parent or legal guardian is unfit as defined in subsection D of this section. People v. Green, 173 Ill. App. 3d 922, 123 Ill. Dec. 693, 528 N.E.2d 238 (2 Dist. 1988).

The unfitness of a parent must be proved by clear and convincing evidence. People v. Green, 118 Ill. 2d 512, 115 Ill. Dec. 390, 517 N.E.2d 1076 (1987).

Parental rights are not lightly terminated, because the state must show the existence of one or more of the statutory grounds by clear and convincing evidence. People v. Foster, 95 Ill. App. 3d 169, 50 Ill. Dec. 605, 419 N.E.2d 713 (4 Dist. 1981).

To justify termination of parental rights, the parent's unfitness for the exercise of parental rights must be established not merely by a preponderance of the evidence but by clear and convincing evidence presented in strict compliance with this Act. Pyatt v. Pyatt, 88 Ill. App. 3d 8, 43 Ill. Dec. 241, 410 N.E.2d 241 (5 Dist. 1980).

General finding of unfitness of nonconsenting mother was sufficient to sustain the judgment where the petition alleges her unfitness, the specific grounds therefor were set forth with particularity, and the evidence in the record clearly and convincingly supported the judgment. People v. Berry, 86 Ill. App. 3d 522, 42 Ill. Dec. 150, 408 N.E.2d 728 (5 Dist. 1980).

The language of subdivision 1(D)(m) of this section indicates that the two standards therein are disjunctive, making either a failure to make reasonable efforts or reasonable progress a ground for an adjudication of unfitness. People v. Edmonds, 85 Ill. App. 3d 229, 40 Ill. Dec. 530, 406 N.E.2d 231 (3 Dist. 1980).

Proof of unfitness of a natural parent must be made by clear and convincing evidence, and the court's determination should not be disturbed unless it is against the manifest weight of the evidence. People v. Saadoon, 78 Ill. App. 3d 319, 33 Ill. Dec. 845, 397 N.E.2d 178 (1 Dist. 1979).

The evidence of a parent's unfitness must be clear and convincing in a termination of parental rights case. Blakey v. Blakey, 72 Ill. App. 3d 946, 29 Ill. Dec. 63, 391 N.E.2d 222 (4 Dist. 1979).

Where there is clear and convincing evidence of the unfitness of a natural parent, then the natural right of the parent must yield to the best interest of the child. Ornstead v. Kleba, 37 Ill. App. 3d 163, 345 N.E.2d 714 (1 Dist. 1976).

Under the former Adoption Act (see now this section), to justify termination of the rights of natural parents to the custody of their own children, their unfitness for the exercise of their parental rights had to be established by clear and convincing evidence. People v. Grant, 29 Ill. App. 3d 731, 331 N.E.2d 219 (1 Dist. 1975).

A finding of parental unfitness must be supported by clear and convincing evidence. Kubisz v. Johnson, 29 Ill. App. 3d 381, 329 N.E.2d 815 (4 Dist. 1975); Culkin v. Culkin, 30 Ill. App. 3d 1073, 333 N.E.2d 698 (4 Dist. 1975); People v. Allen, 34 Ill. App. 3d 603, 340 N.E.2d 269 (1 Dist. 1975); Peyla v. Martin, 40 Ill. App. 3d 373, 352 N.E.2d 407 (5 Dist. 1976); In re Dixon, 81 Ill. App. 3d 493, 36 Ill. Dec. 750, 401 N.E.2d 591 (3 Dist. 1980); People v. Berry, 86 Ill. App. 3d 522, 42 Ill. Dec. 150, 408 N.E.2d 728 (5 Dist. 1980); People v. Bentsen, 90 Ill. App. 3d 269, 45 Ill. Dec. 585, 412 N.E.2d 1167 (3 Dist. 1980); People v. Drescher, 91 Ill. App. 3d 658, 47 Ill. Dec. 631, 415 N.E.2d 636 (1 Dist. 1980); People v. Brown, 86 Ill. 2d 147, 56 Ill. Dec. 4, 427 N.E.2d 84 (1981); Lael v. Warga, 155 Ill. App. 3d 1005,

Unfitness (Cont'd)

—Clear and Convincing Evidence (Cont'd)
108 Ill. Dec. 518, 508 N.E.2d 1095 (4 Dist. 1987); People v. Williams, 187 Ill. App. 3d 988, 135 Ill. Dec. 406, 543 N.E.2d 974 (1 Dist. 1989); People v. Phillips, 191 Ill. App. 3d 237, 138 Ill. Dec. 437, 547 N.E.2d 604 (4 Dist. 1989); People v. Tamburini, 192 Ill. App. 3d 477, 139 Ill. Dec. 529, 548 N.E.2d 1085 (4 Dist. 1989), cert. denied, 132 Ill. 2d 545, 144 Ill. Dec. 266, 555 N.E.2d 385 (1990); People v. Dorsey, 205 Ill. App. 3d 543, 151 Ill. Dec. 94, 563 N.E.2d 1200 (4 Dist. 1990); People v. B.S., 210 Ill. App. 3d 1085, 155 Ill. Dec. 671, 569 N.E.2d 1282 (2 Dist. 1991).

To prove unfitness by reason of abandonment or desertion, there must be clear and convincing proof supported by evidence of conduct in accordance with the definitions of such conduct. In re Smith, 4 Ill. App. 3d 261, 280 N.E.2d 770 (1 Dist. 1972).

The unfitness of a natural parent must be supported by clear and convincing evidence. Thorpe v. Thorpe, 48 Ill. App. 2d 455, 198 N.E.2d 743 (4 Dist. 1964).

A parent has a right to his child against all the world unless he has forfeited that right under subsection (D) of this section, or the welfare of the child demands that he be deprived of it, and the rights of a natural parent will not be disturbed unless petitioners make out a case by clear and satisfactory evidence. Hill v. Allabaugh, 333 Ill. App. 602, 78 N.E.2d 127 (2 Dist. 1948).

—Conduct Over Time
In determining fitness a court must look not to the conduct of the parent during any single, isolated period of time but to the conduct of the parent over the entire period of time in question, that is, to the entirety of the parent's conduct. Adams v. Adams, 103 Ill. App. 3d 126, 58 Ill. Dec. 712, 430 N.E.2d 744 (5 Dist. 1982).

—Considerations
Trial courts must undertake a two-step process in ruling on adoption petitions: the first step is to determine whether the parent whose parental rights petitioners are seeking to terminate is unfit, and at this stage it is the parent's past conduct which is under scrutiny and evidence of whether allowing the adoption would be in the children's best interests is not to be considered; then, if the court determines that petitioners have met their burden of establishing by clear and convincing evidence the existence of one or more grounds for unfitness, it must then determine whether termination of parental rights and allowance of the adoption petition would be in the children's best interests. N.H. v. A.A., 222 Ill. App. 3d 73, 164 Ill. Dec. 696, 583 N.E.2d 612 (2 Dist. 1991).

It is the efforts of the parent to carry out parental responsibilities, rather than their success, which should be considered in determining the correctness of a finding of unfitness. People v. Drescher, 91 Ill. App. 3d 658, 47 Ill. Dec. 631, 415 N.E.2d 636 (1 Dist. 1980).

—Consolidated Hearings
To establish prejudice resulting from a consolidated hearing, a respondent must show: 1) that a timely objection was made in the trial court; 2) that there is reason to believe that the trial judge considered incompetent evidence in its unfitness determination; and 3) that erroneous commingling of evidence of the parent's unfitness and the child's best interests was not reversible, or harmless error. In re V.S., 285 Ill. App. 3d 372, 220 Ill. Dec. 894, 674 N.E.2d 437 (3 Dist. 1996), appeal denied, 172 Ill. 2d 552, 223 Ill. Dec. 195, 679 N.E.2d 380 (1997).

Unless it clearly appears that no prejudice resulted from consolidating hearings on the issues of unfitness and best interests, the conduct of a single hearing commingling the issues is reversible error. In re V.S., 285 Ill. App. 3d 372, 220 Ill. Dec. 894, 674 N.E.2d 437 (3 Dist. 1996), appeal denied, 172 Ill. 2d 552, 223 Ill. Dec. 195, 679 N.E.2d 380 (1997).

A single hearing consolidating issues of unfitness and best interests carries a risk of prejudice from considering evidence irrelevant to the unfitness question before determining that issue. In re V.S., 285 Ill. App. 3d 372, 220 Ill. Dec. 894, 674 N.E.2d 437 (3 Dist. 1996), appeal denied, 172 Ill. 2d 552, 223 Ill. Dec. 195, 679 N.E.2d 380 (1997).

—Construction with Similar Case
Where father was convicted of voluntary manslaughter, not murder, and where the victim was the mother of the children he sought custody of, and where he received the minimum sentence of imprisonment for voluntary manslaughter, and was released at the end of 13 months, and where the trial court determined that the father was a fit and proper person for the custody of the children and that it was in the best interests of the children that they be placed with the father, the factors cited by the Supreme Court in In re Abdullah 85 Ill.2d. 306, 423 N.E.2d 915 that support the finding of unfitness based upon depravity were not present. Tranel v. Lutgen, 177 Ill. App. 3d 954, 127 Ill. Dec. 147, 532 N.E.2d 976 (2 Dist. 1988).

—Corrections Record
Department of Correction hearings (and the procedures which underlie them) are not sufficiently reliable to provide the sole basis for a trial court to conclude that an inmate is an unfit parent because of findings adverse to that inmate at those hearings. In re M.S., 239 Ill. App. 3d 938, 179 Ill. Dec. 936, 606 N.E.2d 768 (4 Dist. 1992).

—Criminal Conviction
The Adoption Act states that a ground for unfitness includes a criminal conviction resulting from the death of any child by physical abuse; the Act does not state that the child must be related to the parent alleged to be unfit. In re J.H., 292 Ill. App. 3d 1102, 227 Ill. Dec. 182, 687 N.E.2d 105 (1 Dist. 1997).

The trial court did not err in granting State's motion for summary judgment in a proceeding to terminate a mother's parental rights based on the finding that she was an unfit parent where the mother had been convicted of first degree murder of a child, although not her own child. In re J.H., 292 Ill. App. 3d 1102, 227 Ill. Dec. 182, 687 N.E.2d 105 (1 Dist. 1997).

Subsection (D)(f) of this section requires only that there be a criminal conviction resulting from the death of any child by physical child abuse. People v. Simmons, 196 Ill. App. 3d 107, 142 Ill. Dec. 735, 553 N.E.2d 85 (4 Dist. 1990).

Conviction of a felony alone is not a statutory ground for adoption without the consent of a natural parent, but such evidence could be submitted on the subject of fitness of that parent in the adoption proceedings under former Ill.Rev.Stat., ch. 4, para. 9.1-1 (see now this section). Townsend v. Curtis, 15 Ill. App. 3d 209, 303 N.E.2d 566 (3 Dist. 1973).

—Cruelty
The result rather than intent are more important in defining cruelty. People v. Hollis, 135 Ill. App. 3d 585, 90 Ill. Dec. 523, 482 N.E.2d 230 (4 Dist. 1985).

—Death of One Parent
The state established by clear and convincing evidence that at the time of placement the parents displayed a disturbing lack of interest in and concern for their children and that the children's condition was rapidly approaching a critical and dangerous level where for two years after the adjudication of neglect, there was no request by either parent to visit the children, and no inquiry was made regarding their health and well-being; mother's unfitness was established by clear and convincing evidence, however, after father's death a new hearing was required to determine mother's fitness. People v. Bredendick, 74 Ill. App. 3d 946, 30 Ill. Dec. 639, 393 N.E.2d 675 (1 Dist. 1979).

—Deficient Record
Where the record was deficient as to a finding of neglect, such as whether there was physical abuse by respondent, and that deficiency was not cured at the hearing to terminate parental rights, the cause was remanded to the trial court for a new hearing. People v. LaShay, 81 Ill. App. 3d 962, 36 Ill. Dec. 833, 401 N.E.2d 971 (1 Dist. 1979).

—Denial of Visitation
The fact that a custodial parent denies or hinders the visitation rights of a non-custodial parent may be a significant element weighing against the clear and convincing determination of the non-custodial parent's indifference to his or her child. Davis v. Bughdadi, 120 Ill. App. 3d 236, 76 Ill. Dec. 38, 458 N.E.2d 177 (5 Dist. 1983).

—Depravity
A father's parental rights were properly terminated on the basis

Unfitness (Cont'd)

—Depravity (Cont'd)

of his depravity where: (1) he had six prior felony convictions, and four of those convictions occurred within five years of the filing of the petition to terminate his parental rights, (2) although he testified that he was going to change when he got out of prison because his child needed him, he continued to commit crimes when he had three other children who presumably needed him, and (3) he gave the child's mother a black eye while she was pregnant with him. In re T.S., 312 Ill. App. 3d 875, 245 Ill. Dec. 367, 728 N.E.2d 98, 2000 Ill. App. LEXIS 248 (2000).

When the state relies solely upon a finding of depravity to support the termination of parental rights, it must establish some connection between the depraved conduct and the alleged need to terminate parental rights. B.C. & W.C. v. Cheryl C., 247 Ill. App. 3d 803, 187 Ill. Dec. 486, 617 N.E.2d 1207 (3 Dist.), appeal allowed, 153 Ill. 2d 559, 191 Ill. Dec. 619, 624 N.E.2d 807 (1993).

Depravity is one such ground whereby a person may be found unfit and has been defined as an inherent deficiency of moral sense and rectitude. People v. Daniels, 165 Ill. App. 3d 112, 116 Ill. Dec. 69, 518 N.E.2d 691 (2 Dist. 1988).

Termination of parental rights on the basis of depravity is constitutionally permissible and is not overly vague. Kellum v. Cornes, 125 Ill. App. 3d 512, 80 Ill. Dec. 821, 466 N.E.2d 273 (5 Dist. 1984), appeal dismissed, 471 U.S. 1062, 105 S. Ct. 2129, 85 L. Ed. 2d 493 (1985).

Even in combination, the alleged violent temper and other alleged parental and moral defects of natural father could give rise to either a finding of depravity or parental unfitness. Bryant v. Lenza, 90 Ill. App. 3d 275, 45 Ill. Dec. 572, 412 N.E.2d 1154 (3 Dist. 1980).

Depravity may be established by a series of acts or a course of conduct indicating a deficiency in a moral sense and showing either an inability or an unwillingness to conform to accepted morality. People ex rel. Dep't of Children & Family Servs., v. Buttram, 56 Ill. App. 3d 950, 14 Ill. Dec. 856, 372 N.E.2d 1135 (3 Dist. 1978).

Depravity is defined as an inherent deficiency of moral sense and rectitude and it may be established by a series of acts or a course of conduct indicating a deficiency in moral sense and showing either an inability or an unwillingness to conform to accepted morality. Tiernan v. Stewart, 33 Ill. App. 3d 545, 338 N.E.2d 153 (2 Dist. 1975).

—Drug Addiction

A circuit court's decision that a mother was not unfit was against the manifest weight of the evidence where the state proved by clear and convincing evidence that she was addicted to drugs for at least one year prior to the commencement of the termination proceedings. People v. Veronica P., 315 Ill. App. 3d 1122, 249 Ill. Dec. 179, 735 N.E.2d 1004, 2000 Ill. App. LEXIS 686 (1 Dist. 2000).

For purposes of subsection 1(D)(k), which requires the state to prove by clear and convincing evidence that the parent was addicted to drugs, other than those prescribed by a physician, for at least one year immediately prior to the commencement of the unfitness proceeding, the date upon which the unfitness proceeding commenced is the date that the petition of termination of parental rights is filed, rather than the date on which the hearing commenced. People v. Veronica P., 315 Ill. App. 3d 1122, 249 Ill. Dec. 179, 735 N.E.2d 1004, 2000 Ill. App. LEXIS 686 (1 Dist. 2000).

Evidence established that the father was unfit based on his addiction to drugs for at least one year immediately prior to the commencement of the unfitness proceeding; the fact that the father completed a drug treatment program subsequent to the filing of the state's petition did not make this ground for unfitness inapplicable. People v. Arthur M., 307 Ill. App. 3d 865, 241 Ill. Dec. 334, 719 N.E.2d 195 (1 Dist. 1999).

Evidence of indulgence without intermission is not necessary to prove drug addiction. In re D.M., 298 Ill. App. 3d 574, 232 Ill. Dec. 765, 699 N.E.2d 212 (3 Dist. 1998).

Addiction to drugs under subdivision (D)(k) is the inability or unwillingness to refrain from the use of drugs because frequent indulgence has instilled in the person an habitual craving which is manifested in an ongoing pattern of drug use. In re D.M., 298 Ill. App. 3d 574, 232 Ill. Dec. 765, 699 N.E.2d 212 (3 Dist. 1998).

—Evidence Held Sufficient

Trial court's finding of the mother's unfitness based on 750 ILCS 50/1(D)(b) was not against the manifest weight of the evidence because the trial court was not precluded from considering evidence of the mother's conduct after the State filed its petitions for termination, and the mother did not dispute that there was sufficient evidence after that date to support the finding of unfitness. People v. Tieriel (In re Dominique W.), 347 Ill. App. 3d 557, 283 Ill. Dec. 471, 808 N.E.2d 21, 2004 Ill. App. LEXIS 276 (1 Dist. 2004).

Trial court properly terminated the parental rights of a mother and father to three minor children pursuant to the Illinois Adoption Act, 750 ILCS 50/1, et seq.; the evidence, including testimony by a daughter that the mother had forced her to have sex with many men in order to support the mother's drug habit, and the fact that the father had no relationship with the children for some time, supported the findings of unfitness as to both parents, and neither parent had completed required social service programs. People v. Marilyn D. (In re S.B.), 348 Ill. App. 3d 61, 283 Ill. Dec. 806, 808 N.E.2d 1094, 2004 Ill. App. LEXIS 357 (1 Dist. 2004).

Evidence was sufficient to establish the unfitness of the mother of two children where, notwithstanding that the mother's mental illness sometimes required her to be hospitalized and necessitated the regular and prolonged use of prescription medicines, there was still strong evidence that the mother did not make reasonable efforts to act responsibly toward her children and that, at several crucial points, her voluntary decisions actually distanced her, literally and figuratively, from her children. People v. P.O., 311 Ill. App. 3d 720, 244 Ill. Dec. 165, 724 N.E.2d 1053, 2000 Ill. App. LEXIS 75 (2 Dist. 2000).

Respondent did not make reasonable progress toward minor's return; instead of making arrangements for drug and alcohol assessment or a psychological evaluation he committed retail theft, he participated in gang activities, used drugs on a daily basis and committed armed robbery; therefore there was sufficient evidence respondent was an unfit parent. In re S.E., 296 Ill. App. 3d 412, 231 Ill. Dec. 248, 695 N.E.2d 1367 (3 Dist. 1998), appeal denied, 179 Ill. 2d 583, 235 Ill. Dec. 564, 705 N.E.2d 437 (1998).

Termination of father's parental rights was proper where it was shown that he did not attend most scheduled visits with his children while they were in foster care, he did not fully comply with agency services, and his efforts to communicate with and show interest in his children were minimal. In re A.M., 294 Ill. App. 3d 616, 229 Ill. Dec. 165, 691 N.E.2d 101 (1 Dist. 1998).

The trial court's finding of unfitness as to mother was not against the manifest weight of the evidence where she was uncooperative in her counseling, had a hostile attitude, often was sullen and uncommunicative during the sessions, and her failure to believe her child and accept the fact that her husband abused her child. C. R. v. Richardson, 221 Ill. App. 3d 373, 163 Ill. Dec. 779, 581 N.E.2d 1202 (4 Dist. 1991).

Evidence of the failure of a parent to visit or communicate with a child was clear and convincing proof of unfitness where the parent did not offer a reasonable explanation for her failure, and it appeared that she made no serious effort to visit or contact the child or the caseworker during the ten months prior to the filing of the petition for supplemental relief. People v. Martin, 48 Ill. App. 3d 341, 6 Ill. Dec. 500, 363 N.E.2d 29 (1 Dist. 1977).

—Failure to Protect

Where the children at issue were in foster care for several years, the statutory ground of failure to protect them from an injurious environment was not available as a basis for terminating parental rights. People v. Demuth, 314 Ill. App. 3d 1109, 248 Ill. Dec. 385, 734 N.E.2d 93, 2000 Ill. App. LEXIS 624 (4 Dist. 2000).

This section does not entitle a parent a specific period of time to correct a problem before the court may find a parent unfit on the grounds listed under subdivision (D)(g). In re B.R., 282 Ill. App. 3d 665, 218 Ill. Dec. 404, 669 N.E.2d 347 (3 Dist. 1996), appeal denied, 169 Ill. 2d 568, 221 Ill. Dec. 438, 675 N.E.2d 633 (1996).

Where mother had adequate warning about the violent tendencies of the child's father toward herself and her children, the trial court's finding that she was unfit for failing to protect the minors from conditions within their environment under subdivision (D)(g) was not against the manifest weight of the evidence. In re B.R., 282 Ill. App. 3d 665, 218 Ill. Dec. 404, 669 N.E.2d 347 (3 Dist. 1996), appeal denied, 169 Ill. 2d 568, 221 Ill. Dec. 438, 675 N.E.2d 633 (1996).

Unfitness (Cont'd)

—Failure to Support

Where mother had not inquired at clerk's office regarding support checks, had not given clerk's office her address and stated she did not need the checks and never made demand on defendant for any payment, these facts were inconsistent with court's finding of unfitness based on failure to contribute support. Regan v. Joseph P., 286 Ill. App. 3d 889, 222 Ill. Dec. 231, 677 N.E.2d 434 (3 Dist. 1996).

—Fault of Parent

In light of the evidence supporting defendant's intent to establish and/ maintain contact with the child, coupled with the ex parte and the plenary orders of protection that officially frustrated defendant's visitation with the child, these facts were inconsistent with the court's finding of unfitness based on failure to maintain a reasonable degree of interest concerning responsibility as to child's welfare. Regan v. Joseph P., 286 Ill. App. 3d 889, 222 Ill. Dec. 231, 677 N.E.2d 434 (3 Dist. 1996).

Where respondent did not visit with her son between May 16, 1978, and the filing of the petition to terminate her parental rights on February 14, 1979, and never sent her son a birthday card or Christmas card, nor inquired about his well-being during the intervals between her visits with him, respondent's failure to maintain a reasonable amount of contact with her son over the length of time involved in this case did not result from the Department of Children and Family Services failure to warn her of the consequences of her inaction. People v. Drescher, 91 Ill. App. 3d 658, 47 Ill. Dec. 631, 415 N.E.2d 636 (1 Dist. 1980).

The father of a child must either consent to that child's adoption or must have been guilty of conduct detrimental to the best interests of the child to warrant a judicial determination of unfitness so that his consent was not required by reason of that detrimental conduct. Robinson v. Neubauer, 79 Ill. App. 2d 362, 223 N.E.2d 705 (4 Dist. 1967).

—Fornication

Evidence of fornication, of substantial and repeated neglect, and of failure to make reasonable efforts to correct the conditions which led to the original adjudication of neglect was clear and convincing, and supported the finding of appellant's mother's unfitness. People v. Berry, 86 Ill. App. 3d 522, 42 Ill. Dec. 150, 408 N.E.2d 728 (5 Dist. 1980).

—Habitual Drunkenness

Once the state had established that the parent's dependence on alcohol and, to a lesser extent, drugs was uncontrollable during the one-year period preceding the filing of the petition to terminate parental rights, the trial court did not abuse its discretion in considering evidence of alcohol and drug abuse from an earlier period. People v. Blanche B., 333 Ill. App. 3d 893, 267 Ill. Dec. 422, 776 N.E.2d 794, 2002 Ill. App. LEXIS 780 (3 Dist. 2002).

To prove the first prong of the test for habitual drunkenness for purposes of terminating parental rights the State is required to present enough evidence to show that the parent drank to excess frequently enough for drinking to be deemed "a fixed habit;" similarly, to prove the second prong of the test, the State has to present clear and convincing evidence that the parent drank frequently enough to demonstrate an inability to control the craving for alcohol. People v. Phyllis J., 201 Ill. 2d 236, 267 Ill. Dec. 1, 776 N.E.2d 138, 2002 Ill. LEXIS 341 (2002).

To prove the first prong of the test for habitual drunkenness for purposes of terminating parental rights, the State must first show that the parent drank alcohol "to excess;" while the exact amount of alcohol consumed in any specific instance need not be established, there must be clear and convincing evidence showing that the parent suffered significant impairment in her ability to supervise and parent her children due to the consumption of alcohol. People v. Phyllis J., 201 Ill. 2d 236, 267 Ill. Dec. 1, 776 N.E.2d 138, 2002 Ill. LEXIS 341 (2002).

State failed to prove habitual drunkenness by clear and convincing evidence where the record showed only that the mother admitted drinking some unspecified amount of alcohol during the review period even though she knew her service plan required abstinence; this admission, although relevant to an analysis of the mother's inability to control her craving for alcohol, was weak evidence of the addiction, and provided no evidence of a fixed habit of drinking to excess. People v. Phyllis J., 201 Ill. 2d 236, 267 Ill. Dec. 1, 776 N.E.2d 138, 2002 Ill. LEXIS 341 (2002).

Critical time period for presenting evidence of habitual drunkenness for purposes of the termination of a parent's rights is the one year just prior to the filing of the State's termination petition, without any reference to evidence either before or after that period; if this initial burden is met, the State may also present evidence showing that the parent was habitually drunk prior to or after that period as well. People v. Phyllis J., 201 Ill. 2d 236, 267 Ill. Dec. 1, 776 N.E.2d 138, 2002 Ill. LEXIS 341 (2002).

Evidence was insufficient to establish habitual drunkenness; at most, the evidence showed that the respondent drank alcohol and failed to attend her treatment sessions during the relevant period, but the state did not establish the required frequency and extent elements of a habitual drunkenness finding. People v. Phyllis J., 316 Ill. App. 3d 817, 250 Ill. Dec. 103, 737 N.E.2d 1080, 2000 Ill. App. LEXIS 819 (3 Dist. 2000).

Where defendant had been clean and sober three months prior to commencement of adoption, seven months prior to his awareness of the proceedings and ten months prior to the fitness hearing, these facts were inconsistent with court's finding of unfitness based on his habitual addiction to drugs and alcohol. Regan v. Joseph P., 286 Ill. App. 3d 889, 222 Ill. Dec. 231, 677 N.E.2d 434 (3 Dist. 1996).

Habitual drunkenness under this act should be defined as it was under the former Divorce Act (see now this section). Lael v. Warga, 155 Ill. App. 3d 1005, 108 Ill. Dec. 518, 508 N.E.2d 1095 (4 Dist. 1987).

Habitual drunkenness has the same meaning in the Illinois Marriage and Dissolution of Marriage Act (750 ILCS 5/101 et seq.) and in determining whether a parent is unfit. People ex rel. Department of Children & Family Servs. v. Sanders, 77 Ill. App. 3d 78, 32 Ill. Dec. 847, 395 N.E.2d 1228 (4 Dist. 1979).

Where a mother stated that she had a drinking problem and that she had indulged to excess three times in 1978; on at least two occasions since May of 1976, she was a resident of an alcohol and drug treatment center and she was also treated on occasion as an outpatient; the program director of the treatment center, whose expertise was derived from being a recovered alcoholic, spoke to the mother on a number of occasions but was not her counselor, and the director believed that the mother behaved like an alcoholic because of her impatient, and impetuous actions, but could not state that the mother was an alcoholic; the trial court's findings of habitual drunkenness were not against the manifest weight of the evidence. People ex rel. Department of Children & Family Servs. v. Sanders, 77 Ill. App. 3d 78, 32 Ill. Dec. 847, 395 N.E.2d 1228 (4 Dist. 1979).

—Illustrative Cases

Trial court's order terminating a mother's parental rights to three children because the mother was unfit was not against the manifest weight of the evidence; the evidence established that the mother failed to make reasonable progress towards reunification with her children when she failed to comply with directives to complete individual and couple's counseling even though she knew that successful completion of such counseling was a requirement for reunification. People v. Velez (In re Jordan V.), 347 Ill. App. 3d 1057, 283 Ill. Dec. 630, 808 N.E.2d 596, 2004 Ill. App. LEXIS 411 (4 Dist. 2004).

There was sufficient evidence to prove the mother's parental unfitness on the basis of depravity where (1) at age 10, the mother was adjudicated delinquent for the offenses of involuntary manslaughter, aggravated battery, and aggravated criminal sexual assault, (2) the mother was placed on probation for eight years, (3) during probation, the mother was guilty of numerous probation violations, including curfew violations, truancy, and stealing her mother's car, (4) the mother failed to provide necessary medical care for a three-month-old child left in the mother's care, and (5) the mother committed felony retail theft on two occasions. People v. Elunder D. (In re J'America B.), 346 Ill. App. 3d 1034, 282 Ill. Dec. 317, 806 N.E.2d 292, 2004 Ill. App. LEXIS 266 (2 Dist. 2004).

The court properly determined that a father failed to maintain a reasonable degree of interest, concern, or responsibility as to his daughter's welfare; deserted her for more than three months next preceding the termination proceedings; failed to maintain a reasonable degree of interest, concern or responsibility as to her welfare within the first 30 days of her birth; failed to make reasonable efforts to correct the conditions that were the basis for her removal or to make reasonable progress toward her return within nine

Unfitness (Cont'd)

—Illustrative Cases (Cont'd)

months after the adjudication of abuse and neglect; manifested an intent to forego his parental rights; was depraved due to his repeated convictions; and that his repeated incarceration prevented him from discharging his parental responsibilities. People v. Brent, 309 Ill. App. 3d 941, 243 Ill. Dec. 441, 723 N.E.2d 744, 1999 Ill. App. LEXIS 880 (1 Dist. 1999).

A mother's failure to cooperate with the department as to visitation of the minors, to complete parenting classes, to complete treatment for any drug or alcohol problems, and to keep the department informed of her whereabouts evidenced her failure to maintain a reasonable degree of interest, concern, or responsibility as to the welfare of the minors; in addition, and her failure to appear for the termination hearing proved the allegation of unfitness was not against the manifest weight of the evidence. In re C.L.T., 302 Ill. App. 3d 770, 235 Ill. Dec. 863, 706 N.E.2d 123 (5 Dist. 1999).

Trial court's decision finding respondent unfit was not against the manifest weight of the evidence, where his children were removed from his home due to his wife's drug abuse problem, he allowed them to see their mother after being ordered by the court not to, repeatedly failed to complete a 12-step program, lived with his wife while he was supposed to be working toward return of his children, and failed to attend visits to see his children, demonstrating both a lack of reasonable effort and reasonable progress. In re V.O., 284 Ill. App. 3d 686, 220 Ill. Dec. 527, 673 N.E.2d 439 (3 Dist. 1996).

The trial court's finding that mother was an unfit parent was not against the manifest weight of the evidence where she made no reasonable efforts to correct the conditions which were the basis for the removal of the children after the children were removed for environmental neglect and inadequate shelter; during the entire time between the filing of the petition alleging neglect through the termination of her parental rights, she failed to maintain a permanent, suitable home for herself and her four children, she did not avail herself of any homemaking services in order to learn better housekeeping skills, which were in essence part of the basis for removing the children, she made no reasonable progress toward the return of the children in the 12 months after the children were adjudicated neglected and she failed to comply with any objectives in the client service plan except the regular visitation with the children and in fact on occasion failed to comply with that objective. In re E.S., 246 Ill. App. 3d 330, 186 Ill. Dec. 289, 615 N.E.2d 1346 (4 Dist. 1993).

Finding of unfitness and termination of parental rights was proper when the evidence clearly and convincingly established that the parents failed to make reasonable progress toward the return of the children, failed to make reasonable efforts to correct the conditions which were the basis for the removal of the children, and both parents refused to acknowledge that any sexual abuse of the children had occurred and refused to seek counseling regarding that abuse. People v. Hobbs, 215 Ill. App. 3d 522, 159 Ill. Dec. 32, 575 N.E.2d 261 (4 Dist.), appeal denied, 142 Ill. 2d 651, 164 Ill. Dec. 914, 584 N.E.2d 126 (1991).

The evidence was sufficient to prove respondent father an unfit parent where the record shows that respondent had a longstanding history of mental instability, having been admitted for psychiatric care twice and having made repeated references to suicide; he also suffered from what was described as a psychosexual disorder manifesting itself as transvestism and at the time of the hearing on the supplemental petition, did not have a permanent address, having changed addresses frequently in the months preceding the hearing, further, respondent demonstrated an almost complete lack of parenting skills and showed little progress despite extensive counseling offered by numerous state agencies. People v. R.B., 195 Ill. App. 3d 919, 142 Ill. Dec. 366, 552 N.E.2d 1107 (5 Dist. 1990).

Finding of unfitness on the part of minor parent was predicated upon clear and convincing proof, and thus was not contrary to the manifest weight of the evidence as mother was slightly retarded, lived in hazardous conditions, showed little interest in child during visitations, and acted hostile toward child. People v. J.B., 146 Ill. App. 3d 523, 100 Ill. Dec. 183, 496 N.E.2d 1248 (4 Dist. 1986).

Where parents failed to make reasonable efforts to correct conditions which were the basis for their child's removal or to make reasonable progress toward the return of the child, and failed to maintain a reasonable degree of interest, concern, or responsibility as to the child's welfare, and repeatedly failed to provide the child with adequate food, clothing or shelter although physically and financially able to do so, the evidence adduced at the hearings amply sustained the finding of unfitness as defined in the Adoption Act. People v. Sandvik, 128 Ill. App. 3d 449, 83 Ill. Dec. 880, 470 N.E.2d 1300 (5 Dist. 1984).

Evidence that a mother failed to contact the Department of Children and Family Services for purpose of visitation, she failed to supervise the children properly with regard to school attendance, and she failed to maintain a clean and healthy household for the children was sufficient to establish the mother's unfitness and to support a termination of her parental rights. People v. Hillyer, 82 Ill. App. 3d 505, 38 Ill. Dec. 21, 403 N.E.2d 36 (3 Dist. 1980).

Evidence supported a finding of unfitness and termination of a mother's parental rights under the former Adoption Act (see now this Act) where the same regrettable series of events which had prevented her from being able to fulfill the responsibilities of parenthood at the time of her original relinquishment of custody had not abated, but had in fact been aggravated by yet another unsuccessful marriage, no successful reconciliation was achieved between the mother and her second husband, and the circuit court correctly analyzed her prospects for establishing any kind of a stable home life, as she drifted through a succession of jobs and addresses. In re Workman, 76 Ill. 2d 256, 28 Ill. Dec. 541, 390 N.E.2d 900 (1979).

Where very little responsibility was shown by a mother, and rather than cooperating with the caseworkers, the mother appeared to be hiding from them, appearing periodically to make requests, although the court recognized the hardship of one in the mother's position, the evidence was sufficient to support the finding of the trial court that the mother was unfit. People ex rel. Patterson v. Patterson, 36 Ill. App. 3d 484, 344 N.E.2d 226 (4 Dist. 1976).

Where petitioner's conduct consisted not only of a denial of paternity and lack of support, but an inexcusable lack of interest, concern and responsibility for his son's welfare, the petitioner's conduct was of a culpable nature and clear and convincing proof of his unfitness was supported by the evidence. Ice v. Department of Children & Family Servs., 35 Ill. App. 3d 783, 342 N.E.2d 460 (3 Dist. 1976).

The evidence presented at trial was sufficient to support the findings of unfitness based upon section 9.1-1(D)(b) of the former Adoption Act (see now subdivision (b) of this section): mother frequently failed to attend court proceedings she had initiated, she failed to visit her child even after special visits had been arranged, and she ignored the child for long periods of time. People v. Taradash, 31 Ill. App. 3d 133, 334 N.E.2d 187 (1 Dist. 1975).

—Inability to Nurture or Interact

The inability of parents to nurture or interact with their children is not a proper statutory basis for the removal of children in this state. In re S.G., 216 Ill. App. 3d 668, 159 Ill. Dec. 125, 575 N.E.2d 932 (2 Dist.), cert. denied, 142 Ill. 2d 665, 164 Ill. Dec. 928, 584 N.E.2d 140 (1991).

—Incarceration

In order for a parent to be unfit based on his or her repeated incarcerations, it is not necessary to show that the parent was unable to fulfill his or her parental duties as a result of being repeatedly unavailable during the lifetime of the child due to incarceration; the incarceration of a parent before the birth of the child can be considered in determining whether a parent is unfit. People v. M.D., 196 Ill. 2d 405, 256 Ill. Dec. 870, 752 N.E.2d 1112, 2001 Ill. LEXIS 775 (2001).

750 ILCS 50/1(D)(s), pertaining to the repeated incarceration of a parent, does not violate either substantive or procedural due process. People v. Deanthony B., 318 Ill. App. 3d 554, 253 Ill. Dec. 597, 745 N.E.2d 720, 2001 Ill. App. LEXIS 150 (3 Dist. 2001).

The parental rights of a father were properly terminated since he had been repeatedly incarcerated as a result of criminal convictions and his repeated incarcerations prevented him from providing the emotional and financial support and stability the child needed and deserved. People v. Johnson, 313 Ill. App. 3d 352, 245 Ill. Dec. 880, 728 N.E.2d 1237, 2000 Ill. App. LEXIS 289 (4 Dist. 2000).

A parent was properly deemed unfit based on a two incarcerations which occurred before the birth of the child at issue and a single continuous incarceration since the child's birth. People v.

Unfitness (Cont'd)

—Incarceration (Cont'd)

M.D., 309 Ill. App. 3d 581, 243 Ill. Dec. 365, 723 N.E.2d 397 (2 Dist. 2000).

A parent's comprehensive history of repeated incarceration, rather than just his or her history of repeated incarceration during the life of the child at issue, is appropriately considered in the determination of unfitness. People v. Caldwell, 309 Ill. App. 3d 493, 242 Ill. Dec. 671, 721 N.E.2d 1202 (4 Dist. 1999).

The mere fact of incarceration is insufficient to establish unfitness. People ex rel. Department of Children & Family Servs. v. Sanders, 77 Ill. App. 3d 78, 32 Ill. Dec. 847, 395 N.E.2d 1228 (4 Dist. 1979).

Where defendant was convicted of a crime and imprisoned prior to the time the child was born and had little contact with the child after it was born, the trial court could properly find him unfit. Townsend v. Curtis, 15 Ill. App. 3d 209, 303 N.E.2d 566 (3 Dist. 1973).

—Independent Grounds

Any of the grounds contained in subdivisions (b), (m) and (n) of subsection (D) of this section will sustain a finding of unfitness. People v. Drescher, 91 Ill. App. 3d 658, 47 Ill. Dec. 631, 415 N.E.2d 636 (1 Dist. 1980).

—Individual Consideration

The trial court did not abuse its discretion in terminating parental rights for youngest child where such a decision was supported by clear and convincing evidence termination was in the best interests of that child, while finding it not to be in the best interests of the two eldest children to terminate parental rights. People v. Johnson, 199 Ill. App. 3d 320, 145 Ill. Dec. 269, 556 N.E.2d 887 (4 Dist. 1990).

—Initial Determination

When a petition for adoption alleges that a parent is unfit, abrogating the need for that parent's consent to the adoption, the trial court is initially to determine the parental unfitness, basing that determination on any evidence relevant to the particular grounds of unfitness alleged. Syck v. Snyder, 138 Ill. 2d 255, 149 Ill. Dec. 710, 562 N.E.2d 174 (1990).

—Injurious Environment

Evidence was sufficient to establish that parents failed to protect their children from injurious conditions in the environment based on the parents' history of domestic disputes accompanied by violence. In re C.M., 319 Ill. App. 3d 344, 253 Ill. Dec. 183, 744 N.E.2d 916, 2001 Ill App. LEXIS 59 (1 Dist. 2001).

It was improper for the state to allege as one of the grounds for termination that respondent failed to protect the child from an environment injurious to her welfare when the child had been in foster care; while respondent's alleged failure to protect the child could form the basis for the initial removal of the child from the home, such an allegation was irrelevant in a subsequent termination proceeding. In re L.N., 278 Ill. App. 3d 46, 214 Ill. Dec. 798, 662 N.E.2d 152 (3 Dist. 1996).

Respondent's conduct clearly and convincingly demonstrated a failure to protect the child from conditions in her environment that were injurious to her welfare, thereby demonstrating his unfitness as defined by subdivision (D)(g) of this section, where two examining physicians testified that when the child was brought to the hospital by police, she had between 20 and 30 bruises covering almost her entire body that were from two days to several weeks old and that had been inflicted, rather than accidental. People v. Brown, 86 Ill. 2d 147, 56 Ill. Dec. 4, 427 N.E.2d 84 (1981).

The trial court's determination that the father was an unfit parent was not against the manifest weight of the evidence where all three of the parents' children were suffering from various degrees of mistreatment and neglect while in the custody of their parents and where the environment of the parents' home presented the children with little more than a host of physical and psychological problems that were cured only by removal to a foster home. In re Dixon, 81 Ill. App. 3d 493, 36 Ill. Dec. 750, 401 N.E.2d 591 (3 Dist. 1980).

—Intent to Contact

Where the parents' attempts to see the child have been officially frustrated, it is the intent to establish and/or maintain contact with the child rather than actual contact which is determinative in a proceeding to determine whether parents are unfit. People v. Bredendick, 74 Ill. App. 3d 946, 30 Ill. Dec. 639, 393 N.E.2d 675 (1 Dist. 1979).

—Killing by Parent

Regardless of whether a parent is likely to prevail on appeal, if he was convicted of murdering the children's other parent, then he is unfit and his parental rights are to be terminated immediately, unless he can overcome the presumption of unfitness by clear and convincing evidence. In re C.M.J., 278 Ill. App. 3d 885, 215 Ill. Dec. 487, 663 N.E.2d 498 (5 Dist. 1996).

Where defendant was convicted of killing his wife, the mother of his three children, the trial court correctly applied the clear words of this section when it terminated defendant's parental rights regardless of the status of any appeal right respondent might choose to exercise. In re C.M.J., 278 Ill. App. 3d 885, 215 Ill. Dec. 487, 663 N.E.2d 498 (5 Dist. 1996).

The court in states neither the legislature nor case law in Illinois has seen fit to set forth a rule of law that the killing of one parent by the other in the presence of the children no matter what the circumstances is sufficient to deprive that parent of his or her children on the basis of unfitness. Tranel v. Lutgen, 177 Ill. App. 3d 954, 127 Ill. Dec. 147, 532 N.E.2d 976 (2 Dist. 1988).

—Lack of Contact

Where defendant had no contact with either of his sons for approximately 2½ years after they were removed from their home, appellate court upheld the trial court's ruling that the defendant was an unfit parent. People v. McIntosh, 214 Ill. App. 3d 545, 158 Ill. Dec. 296, 574 N.E.2d 90 (1 Dist. 1991).

—Legislative Intent

The legislature did not intend to preclude a trial court from terminating the parental rights of a parent who was proved unfit by clear and convincing evidence. People v. Autio, 135 Ill. App. 3d 1017, 90 Ill. Dec. 553, 482 N.E.2d 372 (1 Dist. 1985).

—Mental Illness

The trial court properly determined that a mother was an unfit parent under 750 ILCS 50/1(D)(p), because the mother was a diagnosed schizophrenic, and were the mother to have a psychotic episode, she would pose a risk to a child in her care, and further, her ability to protect her children from harm was limited due to her failure or inability to acknowledge or identify potential harm. People v. Ferrell, Ill. App. 3d , 261 Ill. Dec. 132, 762 N.E.2d 701, 2002 Ill. App. LEXIS 44 (4 Dist. 2002).

Not every parent with a psychiatric illness or condition is per se unfit to be a parent and to maintain custody of her children. People v. Yvonne J., 269 Ill. App. 3d 824, 207 Ill. Dec. 152, 646 N.E.2d 1239 (1 Dist. 1994).

The testimony of the mother, two mental health professionals, and her caseworkers was sufficient to support the court's finding of inability to discharge parental responsibilities due to mental illness, and her history of psychiatric hospitalizations, the poor prognosis for improvement, and the testimony she would always suffer from schizophrenia provided sufficient justification for finding that her mental illness would extend beyond a reasonable time period. People v. Williams, 218 Ill. App. 3d 431, 161 Ill. Dec. 179, 578 N.E.2d 306 (4 Dist. 1991).

—Mental Impairment

Psychiatric evidence of parent's long term inability to perform parental duties held sufficient to sustain finding of unfitness. People v. Fontana, 178 Ill. App. 3d 662, 127 Ill. Dec. 870, 533 N.E.2d 952 (2 Dist. 1989).

—Mental Retardation

Clear and convincing evidence that respondent was an unfit parent existed where respondent repeatedly tried to learn how to care for her child, yet she was unable to learn such elementary skills as feeding and diapering; respondent, a resident of a group home, with an IQ of 65 and problem solving skills at the level of a seven or eight year old, was barely able to meet her own basic needs, let alone those of a young child. People v. T.S., 187 Ill. App. 3d 41, 134 Ill. Dec. 816, 542 N.E.2d 1323 (5 Dist. 1989).

Unfitness (Cont'd)

—Mental Retardation (Cont'd)

Although, an adjudication that a parent is mentally retarded may not in and of itself render that parent unfit, evidence of such adjudication may be considered, along with all other pertinent evidence bearing upon the question of that parent's fitness. Helvey v. Rednour, 86 Ill. App. 3d 154, 41 Ill. Dec. 671, 408 N.E.2d 17 (5 Dist. 1980).

—Minor Parent

Minor parent's parental rights could be terminated even though she herself was a minor and her parents, although present, were not parties to the proceeding. People v. J.B., 146 Ill. App. 3d 523, 100 Ill. Dec. 183, 496 N.E.2d 1248 (4 Dist. 1986).

—Non-Consenting Parent

Under this section parental rights of a non-consenting parent can be terminated only if the parent is found unfit. People v. Berry, 86 Ill. App. 3d 522, 42 Ill. Dec. 150, 408 N.E.2d 728 (5 Dist. 1980).

—Not Found

The state failed to present clear and convincing evidence to support any of the three alleged grounds of a mother's unfitness and, therefore, the termination of her parental rights would be reversed. In re M.F., 304 Ill. App. 3d 236, 237 Ill. Dec. 889, 710 N.E.2d 519 (5 Dist. 1999).

It could not be properly concluded that respondent failed to make a good faith effort to pay a reasonable amount of the expenses related to the birth of the child and was therefore unfit. In re M.M.W., 296 Ill. App. 3d 877, 231 Ill. Dec. 238, 695 N.E.2d 1357 (2 Dist. 1998).

Where father stated that his failure to make frequent contact with his child was a result of wife's interference with his visitation rights and where he withheld support because of his inability to visit his child, there was insufficient evidence to justify termination of parental rights. Davis v. Bughdadi, 120 Ill. App. 3d 236, 76 Ill. Dec. 38, 458 N.E.2d 177 (5 Dist. 1983).

A mother was not unfit where she was living in a foster home herself at the time of her child's birth and was not given a chance at the outset to care for her child, and where she was interested in her child and visited him fairly frequently; her failure to express more of an interest may have in great part stemmed from the state's failure to inculcate into her the need for maintaining greater and more consistent contact with her child, and she was unaware of her child's plight. People v. Barber, 55 Ill. App. 3d 587, 13 Ill. Dec. 582, 371 N.E.2d 299 (1 Dist. 1977).

Trial court's findings that defendant failed to maintain a reasonable degree of interest, concern or responsibility for his child, and was unfit was against the manifest weight of the evidence. Peyla v. Martin, 40 Ill. App. 3d 373, 352 N.E.2d 407 (5 Dist. 1976).

Where the evidence showed that appellant had maintained her interest and concern regarding her son's welfare since the original dependency decree, the evidence failed to justify finding the appellant to be an unfit person. Green v. Department of Children & Family Servs., 131 Ill. App. 2d 952, 267 N.E.2d 505 (4 Dist. 1971).

—Passive Neglect

Where the father knew very well that his children were being mistreated and neglected by his wife and expressed concern to a number of people for his children's welfare, this concern never evolved into purposeful action to remedy the situation and although there was circumstantial evidence of actual mistreatment by the father, the type of passive neglect he exhibited toward his children was sufficient to render him unfit. In re Dixon, 81 Ill. App. 3d 493, 36 Ill. Dec. 750, 401 N.E.2d 591 (3 Dist. 1980).

—Planning for the Future

The evidence did not show failure on the part of defendant to plan for her child's future within the meaning of the statute where there was evidence that the agency discouraged or frustrated a promotion of the parent-child relationship. People v. Steele, 101 Ill. 2d 345, 78 Ill. Dec. 149, 461 N.E.2d 983 (1984).

—Pleading

In order to terminate parental rights for unfitness, the grounds of unfitness must be alleged with particularity. People v. Knell, 153 Ill. App. 3d 704, 106 Ill. Dec. 653, 506 N.E.2d 360 (4 Dist. 1987).

—Reasonable Degree of Interest

It was error to terminate the parental rights of a mother, notwithstanding the assertion that the mother failed to show a reasonable degree of interest, concern, or responsibility as to the child's welfare, where (1) evidence showed that the mother initiated visits with her child and that she always interacted appropriately, with care for her child, whenever she was permitted to visit; and (2) the fact that she missed several visits was explained by her participation in a restrictive drug and alcohol abuse program. People v. S.K., Ill. App. 3d , 255 Ill. Dec. 551, 749 N.E.2d 1033, 2001 Ill. App. LEXIS 347 (1 Dist. 2001).

The trial court's finding of parental unfitness based upon a mother's failure to maintain a reasonable degree of interest, concern, or responsibility concerning her children's welfare was not against the manifest weight of the evidence where she consistently attended scheduled visitations with her children, but failed to comply with the remainder of the service plan despite her knowing that the compliance was necessary in order for her children to be returned home. People v. K.J., 314 Ill. App. 3d 649, 247 Ill. Dec. 735, 732 N.E.2d 790, 2000 Ill. App. LEXIS 577 (2 Dist. 2000).

Evidence established that the father failed to maintain a reasonable degree of interest as to his child's welfare where, during the first five years the child was in foster care, the father demonstrated an almost total lack of interest, concern, or responsibility as to the child's welfare; the father's conduct during the year or so immediately prior to the hearing did not require a contrary result. People v. Arthur M., 307 Ill. App. 3d 865, 241 Ill. Dec. 334, 719 N.E.2d 195 (1 Dist. 1999).

In an adoption proceeding brought by the deceased mother's sister, the court improperly found that the father was not unfit where, although he knew of the mother's pregnancy at least seven months before the birth of the child at issue, he did not pay any pregnancy expenses, made no effort to prepare for the birth of the child or her future, and did nothing within the first 30 days of the child's life to demonstrate any interest, concern, or responsibility for the child or her welfare. M.R.G. v. M.C., 307 Ill. App. 3d 953, 240 Ill. Dec. 879, 718 N.E.2d 360 (2 Dist. 1999).

The failure of a mother to make reasonable progress toward the return of her child coupled with her failure to manifest any interest in her child for a period of six years was sufficient to constitute unfitness. People v. Ladewig, 34 Ill. App. 3d 393, 340 N.E.2d 150 (1 Dist. 1975).

Under the former Adoption Act (see now this section), before a court could empower a guardian to consent to an adoption without the consent of the natural parent, there had to be clear and convincing evidence of unfitness, where the record reflected a doleful picture of a widow in ill health and on welfare, whose children were taken from her originally through no fault of hers, and while it may have been in the best interests of child to require that he remain in the custody of someone other than respondent, there had to be clear and convincing evidence that the respondent failed to maintain a reasonable degree of interest, concern or a responsibility as to child's welfare and there was no such clear and convincing evidence sufficient to terminate forever the right of a mother to her child. People v. Ybarra, 29 Ill. App. 3d 725, 331 N.E.2d 224 (1 Dist. 1975).

—Reasonable Efforts to Correct Conditions

The state failed to prove by clear and convincing evidence that the respondent mother failed to make reasonable efforts to correct the conditions that were the basis for the removal of her children from her custody where (1) the conditions which led to the removal of the children were the mother's evictions, resulting homelessness, and inability to provide the children with shelter, (2) the mother subsequently secured an apartment, continuously sought better housing, and moved several times during the litigation, (3) instead of addressing the evidence head on, the state instead attempted to show that the mother could not control her children because she lacked disciplinary skills. People v. Ringer, 305 Ill. App. 3d 154, 238 Ill. Dec. 422, 711 N.E.2d 809 (4 Dist. 1999), appeal denied, 185 Ill. 2d 626, 242 Ill. Dec. 138, 720 N.E.2d 1093 (1999).

—Reasonable Progress Toward Return of Child

"Reasonable progress" toward the return of the child under 750 ILCS 50/1(D)(m) exists when a trial court can conclude that the court, in the near future, will be able to order the child returned to parental custody; the court will be able to order the child returned

Unfitness (Cont'd)

—Reasonable Progress Toward Return of Child (Cont'd)

to parental custody in the near future because, at that point, the parent will have fully complied with the directives previously given to the parent. People v. Velez (In re Jordan V.), 347 Ill. App. 3d 1057, 283 Ill. Dec. 630, 808 N.E.2d 596, 2004 Ill. App. LEXIS 411 (4 Dist. 2004).

Benchmark for measuring a parent's progress toward the return of the child under 750 ILCS 50/1(D)(m) encompasses the parent's compliance with the service plans and the court's directives, in light of the condition which gave rise to the removal of the child, and in light of other conditions which later become known and which would prevent the court from returning custody of the child to the parent. People v. Velez (In re Jordan V.), 347 Ill. App. 3d 1057, 283 Ill. Dec. 630, 808 N.E.2d 596, 2004 Ill. App. LEXIS 411 (4 Dist. 2004).

Reasonable progress, as used in 750 ILCS 50/1(D)(m)(iii), is an objective review of the steps the parent has taken toward the goal of reunification. People v. Velez (In re Jordan V.), 347 Ill. App. 3d 1057, 283 Ill. Dec. 630, 808 N.E.2d 596, 2004 Ill. App. LEXIS 411 (4 Dist. 2004).

The benchmark for measuring a parent's "progress toward the return of the child" of the Adoption Act encompassed the parent's compliance with the service plans and the court's directives, in light of the condition which gave rise to the removal of the child, and in light of other conditions which later become known and which would prevent the court from returning custody to the parent; trial court's finding of mother's unfitness was supported by the evidence. People v. S.R., Ill. App. 3d , 258 Ill. Dec. 924, 757 N.E.2d 613, 2001 Ill. App. LEXIS 723 (1 Dist. 2001).

While the yardstick to measure a parent's progress toward return of a child need not necessarily be the condition which caused the child's removal in the first place, it must bear some relationship to a parental shortcoming that would inhibit the return of the child to the parent. People v. M.D., 309 Ill. App. 3d 581, 243 Ill. Dec. 365, 723 N.E.2d 397 (2 Dist. 2000).

Evidence established a father's failure to make reasonable progress toward the return of the child at issue where the father was unaware of the birth of the child and, upon learning of the child's existence and the neglect proceeding, he failed to make any reasonable progress toward unification. People v. Caldwell, 309 Ill. App. 3d 493, 242 Ill. Dec. 671, 721 N.E.2d 1202 (4 Dist. 1999).

Evidence was sufficient to show unfitness of the father on the basis of failure to make reasonable efforts to correct the conditions that were the basis for the removal of the child from the father and the failure to make reasonable progress toward the return of the child where the only effort the father ever made was to visit with the child on several occasions in late 1993 and early 1994 and one time in December 1994, he did not attend parenting classes, he did not obtain an alcohol or psychological evaluation, and he did not attempt to maintain contact with the child from December 1994 until late 1998. People v. William J.S., 308 Ill. App. 3d 291, 241 Ill. Dec. 765, 719 N.E.2d 1168 (3 Dist. 1999).

Notwithstanding disagreement among the appellate districts as to whether a court may consider the parent's conduct only as to the 12-month period immediately following the adjudication of neglect, or if it may consider the parent's conduct during the entire post-adjudication period, the statutory language is plain and unambiguous that it is the parent's efforts "within 12 months after an adjudication of neglected minor" that is determinative of unfitness. People v. Arthur M., 307 Ill. App. 3d 865, 241 Ill. Dec. 334, 719 N.E.2d 195 (1 Dist. 1999).

Evidence established that the father was unfit based on his failure to make reasonable progress toward the return of his child within 12 months after the adjudication of neglect. People v. Arthur M., 307 Ill. App. 3d 865, 241 Ill. Dec. 334, 719 N.E.2d 195 (1 Dist. 1999).

Whether a parent's efforts are reasonable involves a subjective judgment based upon the amount of effort that is reasonable for a particular person; however, whether a parent's progress is reasonable involves an objective judgment based upon the amount of progress measured from the conditions existing at the time custody was taken from the parent. In re K.P., 305 Ill. App. 3d 175, 238 Ill. Dec. 375, 711 N.E.2d 478 (4 Dist. 1999).

Respondent was determined unfit because she failed to make reasonable progress toward the return of her child within 12 months of the adjudication of neglect. In re B.W., 282 Ill. App. 3d 680, 218 Ill. Dec. 422, 669 N.E.2d 365 (3 Dist. 1996).

—Relinquishment of Child

Appellant was not an unfit person because she willingly gave up the care and custody of her son for the apparent reason that he needed medical treatment and care that she was unable to provide. Green v. Department of Children & Family Servs., 131 Ill. App. 2d 952, 267 N.E.2d 505 (4 Dist. 1971).

—Removal from Home

Where the basis for the removal of a child from his mother's home was the financial inability of the mother to purchase new eyeglasses for him, plainly, this subsection was not applicable to that situation. People v. Steele, 101 Ill. 2d 345, 78 Ill. Dec. 149, 461 N.E.2d 983 (1984).

—Sexual Abuse

Where each of the minors testified separately and in detail concerning the litany of sexual "family touching" practices which occurred at the instigation of the respondent and her husband and there was expert testimony that the children had been sexually abused and that they were still either undergoing treatment or had been placed in a treatment facility as a result of the sexual abuse, the trial court's finding of respondent's unfitness was not against the weight of the evidence. People v. Daniels, 165 Ill. App. 3d 112, 116 Ill. Dec. 69, 518 N.E.2d 691 (2 Dist. 1988).

—Shown

Trial court's finding of unfitness was supported by clear and convincing evidence where a clinical psychologist testified respondent was mildly retarded and there were numerous other witnesses that provided testimony regarding respondent's limited mental capabilities. People v. C.S., 303 Ill. App. 3d 559, 237 Ill. Dec. 273, 709 N.E.2d 259 (2 Dist. 1999), appeal denied, 184 Ill. 2d 557, 239 Ill. Dec. 608, 714 N.E.2d 527 (1999).

Record established mother was an unfit parent where she failed to maintain a reasonable degree of interest, concern or responsibility as to child's welfare, failed to make reasonable progress toward the return of child within 12 months after the adjudication of neglect and was addicted to drugs for at least one year preceding the commencement of the unfitness proceeding. People v. Tawanda R., 298 Ill. App. 3d 905, 232 Ill. Dec. 877, 699 N.E.2d 1062 (1 Dist. 1998), aff'd, 191 Ill. 2d 1, 245 Ill. Dec. 256, 727 N.E.2d 990 (2000).

Even accepting mother's testimony that she had two periods of abstinence from cocaine use during the previous year, which the trial court found unbelievable, it would not negate the overwhelming evidence that she had been dominated by her addiction for the past six years, therefore, trial court's finding of unfitness was not against the manifest weight of the evidence. In re D.M., 298 Ill. App. 3d 574, 232 Ill. Dec. 765, 699 N.E.2d 212 (3 Dist. 1998).

Where doctor testified that without appropriate treatment, respondent would not be able to parent her children in the foreseeable future, the record demonstrated that respondent's condition had deteriorated since 1987 and respondent had a lengthy history of mental illness, received treatment in the past and needed a prolonged course of treatment in the future, the trial court's finding of respondent's parental unfitness was based upon clear and convincing evidence. People v. Yvonne J., 269 Ill. App. 3d 824, 207 Ill. Dec. 152, 646 N.E.2d 1239 (1 Dist. 1994).

Where for a period of over three years, a father's efforts to see or communicate with his children were minimal or nonexistent, and he provided little financial support for the children and even tried at one point to cut off their primary means of support, public aid, there was clear and convincing evidence that the father failed to maintain a reasonable degree of interest, concern, and responsibility with regard to the welfare of his children and he was therefore an unfit parent, and the trial court's contrary conclusion was against the manifest weight of the evidence. N.H. v. A.A., 222 Ill. App. 3d 73, 164 Ill. Dec. 696, 583 N.E.2d 612 (2 Dist. 1991).

There was clear and convincing evidence of mother's unfitness due to mental impairment and that such impairment would extend beyond a reasonable time where there was no evidence on the record that the mother had sought any treatment and that even with substantial treatment, the doctor stated he would not expect significant improvement in the foreseeable future. People v. D.D.,

Unfitness (Cont'd)

—Shown (Cont'd)

198 Ill. App. 3d 495, 144 Ill. Dec. 679, 555 N.E.2d 1198 (5 Dist. 1990).

Evidence was held sufficient to sustain finding that a natural father was an unfit parent because of his failure to maintain a reasonable degree of interest, concern, or responsibility for the four minor children and it was to the best interest of the minors that defendant's parental rights be terminated. People v. Adams, 175 Ill. App. 3d 343, 125 Ill. Dec. 39, 529 N.E.2d 1115 (4 Dist. 1988).

Although respondent professed love for his children he offered no significant evidence to show his rehabilitation and the series of felonies over a lengthy period of time established by clear and convincing evidence that respondent was unfit. Kellum v. Cornes, 125 Ill. App. 3d 512, 80 Ill. Dec. 821, 466 N.E.2d 273 (5 Dist. 1984), appeal dismissed, 471 U.S. 1062, 105 S. Ct. 2129, 85 L. Ed. 2d 493 (1985).

Failure to keep eight visits, which was not shown to have been caused sheerly by neglect or indifference, did not constitute clear and convincing evidence of a lack of concern for the child. People v. Steele, 101 Ill. 2d 345, 78 Ill. Dec. 149, 461 N.E.2d 983 (1984).

Trial court found parental unfitness on the ground that a mother failed to make reasonable progress toward the return of the minor to her within 12 months after the minor was adjudged a neglected minor under former sections 702-4 and 702-5 of the Juvenile Court Act (see now Ill.Rev.Stat., ch. 37, paras. 802-3 and 802-4), such a finding alone was sufficient to support a judgment of parental unfitness. People v. Edmonds, 85 Ill. App. 3d 229, 40 Ill. Dec. 530, 406 N.E.2d 231 (3 Dist. 1980).

Father failed to maintain a reasonable degree of interest, concern or responsibility as to the child's welfare and was therefore an unfit person within the terms of this Act. Freeman v. Settle, 75 Ill. App. 3d 799, 31 Ill. Dec. 78, 393 N.E.2d 1385 (5 Dist. 1979).

Under the former Adoption Act (see now this section), where it was clear that the evidence supported a finding that prior to the removal of the minors from their custody, the respondents almost totally failed to maintain a reasonable degree of interest in and concern for their children, the state met the burden of proving the respondents to be unfit parents. Department of Children & Family Servs. v. Love, 50 Ill. App. 3d 1018, 9 Ill. Dec. 25, 366 N.E.2d 139 (3 Dist. 1977).

The failure of the mother to manifest any interest in her child for a period of five years, when taken in to consideration with other evidence, was sufficient to constitute unfitness by clear and convincing evidence. People v. Perez, 14 Ill. App. 3d 1019, 304 N.E.2d 109 (1 Dist. 1973).

—Single Hearing

The court recognized its responsibility to determine whether or not the father was an unfit parent before considering what placement would suit the best interest and welfare of the child; since both determinations may be made at the same hearing, the procedure followed by the trial court was proper. Freeman v. Settle, 75 Ill. App. 3d 799, 31 Ill. Dec. 78, 393 N.E.2d 1385 (5 Dist. 1979).

—Standard of Evidence

The language of subdivision D.(m) indicates the two standards for unfitness are disjunctive, meaning that either ground may be established as a basis for unfitness. In re J.P., 261 Ill. App. 3d 165, 198 Ill. Dec. 565, 633 N.E.2d 27 (4 Dist. 1994).

The burden of proving unfitness under subdivision D.(l) lies with the parties petitioning to adopt the child; because a finding of unfitness will operate to permanently sever a parent-child relationship, it must be based upon clear and convincing evidence. In re J.R.G., 247 Ill. App. 3d 104, 187 Ill. Dec. 169, 617 N.E.2d 377 (1 Dist. 1993).

A finding of parental unfitness may be based on evidence sufficient to support any one statutory ground, even if the evidence is not sufficient to support other grounds alleged. C. R. v. Richardson, 221 Ill. App. 3d 373, 163 Ill. Dec. 779, 581 N.E.2d 1202 (4 Dist. 1991).

Finding to terminate parental rights was insufficient where it was made on a preponderance of the evidence standard and not on the required standard of clear and convincing evidence. People v. Enis, 121 Ill. 2d 124, 117 Ill. Dec. 201, 520 N.E.2d 362 (1988).

If clear and convincing evidence of unfitness on one or more of the grounds specified in the former Adoption Act (see now this section) is not forthcoming, the petition for termination of parental rights should be denied. Neal v. Burton, 43 Ill. App. 3d 294, 1 Ill. Dec. 946, 356 N.E.2d 1279 (5 Dist. 1976).

—Standard of Review

Appellate courts will not reverse a trial court's finding of parental unfitness unless it was contrary to the manifest weight of the evidence, meaning that the correctness of the opposite conclusion is clearly evident from a review of the evidence. People v. Velez (In re Jordan V.), 347 Ill. App. 3d 1057, 283 Ill. Dec. 630, 808 N.E.2d 596, 2004 Ill. App. LEXIS 411 (4 Dist. 2004).

A court will not reverse a finding of unfitness unless it is against the manifest weight of the evidence. Ice v. Department of Children & Family Servs., 35 Ill. App. 3d 783, 342 N.E.2d 460 (3 Dist. 1976); Ornstead v. Kleba, 37 Ill. App. 3d 163, 345 N.E.2d 714 (1 Dist. 1976); People v. Nitz, 76 Ill. App. 3d 15, 31 Ill. Dec. 685, 394 N.E.2d 887 (3 Dist. 1979); People v. Bennett, 80 Ill. App. 3d 207, 35 Ill. Dec. 669, 399 N.E.2d 735 (3 Dist. 1980); People v. Berry, 86 Ill. App. 3d 522, 42 Ill. Dec. 150, 408 N.E.2d 728 (5 Dist. 1980); People v. Drescher, 91 Ill. App. 3d 658, 47 Ill. Dec. 631, 415 N.E.2d 636 (1 Dist. 1980); People v. Dalton, 98 Ill. App. 3d 902, 54 Ill. Dec. 323, 424 N.E.2d 1226 (2 Dist. 1981); Lael v. Warga, 155 Ill. App. 3d 1005, 108 Ill. Dec. 518, 508 N.E.2d 1095 (4 Dist. 1987); People v. Fontana, 178 Ill. App. 3d 662, 127 Ill. Dec. 870, 533 N.E.2d 952 (2 Dist. 1989); People v. Williams, 187 Ill. App. 3d 988, 135 Ill. Dec. 406, 543 N.E.2d 974 (1 Dist. 1989); C. R. v. Richardson, 221 Ill. App. 3d 373, 163 Ill. Dec. 779, 581 N.E.2d 1202 (4 Dist. 1991).

The decision to terminate parental rights and appoint a guardian rests within the sound discretion of the trial judge, and a reviewing court should not interfere with the trial judge's decision absent an abuse of discretion. People v. McIntosh, 214 Ill. App. 3d 545, 158 Ill. Dec. 296, 574 N.E.2d 90 (1 Dist. 1991).

A finding of unfitness will not be reversed unless it is against the manifest weight of the evidence; the rationale underlying this standard is that the trial court's opportunity to view and evaluate the parties and their testimony is superior to that of a reviewing court, accordingly, the trial court's findings should be given great deference. People v. Brown, 86 Ill. 2d 147, 56 Ill. Dec. 4, 427 N.E.2d 84 (1981).

—Standing

Where unfitness was not an issue, a third party could not challenge custody under this Act or the Juvenile Court Act (Ill.Rev.Stat., ch. 37, para. 801-1 et seq (1981)). In re Peterson, 112 Ill. 2d 48, 96 Ill. Dec. 690, 491 N.E.2d 1150 (1986).

—State Interest

Where the court affirmed the respondent's conviction of murder and cruelty to children on evidence of common design and participation in her boyfriend's course of torture and abuse that resulted in the death of her child, the conflict inherent in parental fitness legislation between the state's interest in legislation for the protection of children and the continuation of parental rights was resolved in favor of the state's interest. People v. Ray, 88 Ill. App. 3d 1010, 44 Ill. Dec. 182, 411 N.E.2d 88 (5 Dist. 1980), appeal dismissed, 452 U.S. 956, 101 S. Ct. 3102, 69 L. Ed. 2d 967 (1981).

The state interest in providing suitable homes for children and the administrative burden of conducting an additional hearing do not justify the termination of a parent's fundamental right in the absence of a showing of unfitness. Helvey v. Rednour, 86 Ill. App. 3d 154, 41 Ill. Dec. 671, 408 N.E.2d 17 (5 Dist. 1980).

—Strict Compliance

The rights of natural parents to their children cannot be severed unless a clear and convincing case is presented in strict compliance with this Act. Culkin v. Culkin, 30 Ill. App. 3d 1073, 333 N.E.2d 698 (4 Dist. 1975).

—Subsequent Children

Evidence supporting a parent's unfitness towards some of her children may serve as a basis for termination of parental rights toward all of that party's children, even where that evidence relates to events occurring prior to the birth of some of the children; thus, notwithstanding the fact that two children arrived after the other children were taken from respondent's custody, the trial court had an adequate basis for returning a finding of unfitness as to those

Unfitness (Cont'd)

—Subsequent Children (Cont'd)
two children. People v. Munjak, 175 Ill. App. 3d 778, 125 Ill. Dec. 413, 530 N.E.2d 571 (2 Dist. 1988).

—Substantial Neglect
Evidence was sufficient to show substantial neglect where the respondent abandoned her children and left the state since she could not have provided proper or necessary support, education, or medical or other remedial care recognized under state law as necessary for a minor's well-being, including adequate food, clothing, and shelter. People v. C.B., 308 Ill. App. 3d 227, 241 Ill. Dec. 487, 719 N.E.2d 348 (2 Dist. 1999).

It is insufficient to find a parent unfit based upon neglect alone or an isolated incident of neglect; instead, the neglect must be both substantial and continuous or repeated. People v. C.B., 308 Ill. App. 3d 227, 241 Ill. Dec. 487, 719 N.E.2d 348 (2 Dist. 1999).

Evidence of parental unfitness was clear and convincing, where the parents voluntarily refused to show a reasonable degree of concern and responsibility toward their son for perhaps as long as ten years. People v. Bales, 83 Ill. App. 3d 348, 38 Ill. Dec. 740, 403 N.E.2d 1344 (3 Dist. 1980).

Under the former Adoption Act (seen now this section) evidence presented at a hearing on petitions asking for the termination of parental rights which alleged substantial, repeated neglect were sufficient to sustain such an allegation. People ex rel. Department of Children & Family Servs. v. Sparrow, 59 Ill. App. 3d 731, 17 Ill. Dec. 237, 376 N.E.2d 236 (5 Dist. 1978).

Where respondent's failure to contact his children by phone or letter, lack of diligent inquiry regarding their affairs and failure to send them gifts for a period of eight years made the children want to remain with their foster parents, the evidence unequivocally satisfied the clear and convincing standard. In re Woods, 54 Ill. App. 3d 729, 12 Ill. Dec. 342, 369 N.E.2d 1356 (1 Dist. 1977).

—Sufficiency of Evidence
Clear and convincing evidence supported trial court's determination that parent whose rights were being terminated had given birth to many successive children born with drug exposure, including the two referenced in the petition, that the parent continued to have such a problem, failed to acknowledge it, and had not completed any treatment program, and these findings were sufficient to support a finding of unfitness; further, the trial court's second finding, that the children were doing well with the family that wished to adopt them and that such a course was in their best interest, was not against the manifest weight of the evidence. People v. R.S. (In re M.S.), 351 Ill. App. 3d 799, 286 Ill. Dec. 712, 814 N.E.2d 938, 2004 Ill. App. LEXIS 953 (1 Dist. 2004).

Where mother challenged two of the five statutory grounds for a finding of unfitness as deficient as a matter of law, if any of the remaining three grounds were sufficiently supported by the evidence to warrant finding parents unfit, the mother's challenge to the legal sufficiency of two of the findings would not be considered. People v. Mikel, 205 Ill. App. 3d 497, 150 Ill. Dec. 872, 563 N.E.2d 999 (4 Dist. 1990).

The evidence was sufficient to support a finding of unfitness. People v. Hrusosky, 39 Ill. App. 3d 954, 351 N.E.2d 386 (3 Dist. 1976).

—Termination of Parental Rights
Findings of parental unfitness and that termination of parental rights was in the child's best interests were upheld as not against the manifest weight of the evidence, even though it was clear that parent and child loved each other; the record was clear that the parent had failed to make any progress toward addressing domestic violence issues in more than three years since the child's injuries at the parent's paramour's hands had first been noticed. People v. Tabitha H. (In re K.H.), 346 Ill. App. 3d 443, 281 Ill. Dec. 813, 804 N.E.2d 1108, 2004 Ill. App. LEXIS 154 (2 Dist. 2004).

Trial court found mother to be unfit and affirmed the termination of her parental rights where the record reflected that one child had been in foster care for six of his seven years of life and had been cared for by his foster mother for years and the youngest child was removed from mother's custody less than two weeks after birth. People v. M.P., 329 Ill. App. 3d 18, 263 Ill. Dec. 607, 768 N.E.2d 367, 2002 Ill. App. LEXIS 246 (1 Dist. 2002).

Where respondent testified that she agreed the goals set for her were appropriate, and she even stated that it was "obvious" what she had to do to regain custody of her son, it was not necessary for the trial court to have evidence of respondent's status at the time of her son's adjudication. In re J.T.C., 273 Ill. App. 3d 193, 209 Ill. Dec. 881, 652 N.E.2d 421 (4 Dist. 1995).

A parent's right to a minor child may be terminated by a trial court after a finding that the child has been neglected under the Juvenile Court Act (705 ILCS 405/2-3) and after the parent has been found unfit under this section. People v. M.R., 191 Ill. App. 3d 607, 138 Ill. Dec. 837, 548 N.E.2d 67 (5 Dist. 1989).

Where respondent had steadfastly refused to undertake nutritional planning, had failed to attend child's school as suggested, had made no effort to attend parenting classes, had missed the children's medical appointments, resisted and refused vocational and educational assistance and had made no real attempt to obtain housing, termination of her parental rights was proper. People v. Miller, 169 Ill. App. 3d 357, 120 Ill. Dec. 235, 523 N.E.2d 1146 (4 Dist. 1988).

The termination of parental rights requires a finding of unfitness fully supported by clear and convincing evidence. People v. Sandvik, 128 Ill. App. 3d 449, 83 Ill. Dec. 880, 470 N.E.2d 1300 (5 Dist. 1984).

Evidence sufficiently justified the trial judge's conclusion that termination of parental rights of both natural parents was in the best interest of the children. People v. Dalton, 98 Ill. App. 3d 902, 54 Ill. Dec. 323, 424 N.E.2d 1226 (2 Dist. 1981).

Since parental rights were properly terminated because of the findings of dependency and unfitness, it was not necessary that the child be found a neglected minor pursuant to former section 2-4 of the Juvenile Act (Ill.Rev.Stat., ch. 37, para. 702-4 (1977)) (now contained in 705 ILCS 405/2-3) for parental rights to have been terminated. Department of Children & Family Servs. v. Devine, 81 Ill. App. 3d 314, 36 Ill. Dec. 775, 401 N.E.2d 616 (5 Dist. 1980).

—Termination of Rights Order Reversed
Where there is a failure to produce clear and convincing evidence that a parent is unfit within the statutory definition, it is proper to reverse the order terminating parental rights. Peyla v. Martin, 40 Ill. App. 3d 373, 352 N.E.2d 407 (5 Dist. 1976).

—Validity of Petition
For a petition attempting to declare parents as unfit to be valid, it is necessary that it set forth with particularity the grounds for such a determination and these grounds must be supported by clear and convincing evidence. People v. Harvey, 61 Ill. App. 3d 344, 19 Ill. Dec. 37, 378 N.E.2d 538 (1 Dist. 1978).

—Visitation
Failure to visit a child is not proof of unfitness if the parent offers a reasonable explanation. People v. McIntosh, 214 Ill. App. 3d 545, 158 Ill. Dec. 296, 574 N.E.2d 90 (1 Dist. 1991).

—Warning About Spouse
Mother should not have been found to be an unfit parent based on fact that her husband was still a substance abuser, the reason the children had been removed, when mother was never warned that she would have to choose between husband and children if husband's substance abuse did not stop. In re R.B., 297 Ill. App. 3d 97, 231 Ill. Dec. 688, 696 N.E.2d 1259 (2 Dist. 1998), appeal denied, 179 Ill. 2d 583, 235 Ill. Dec. 564, 705 N.E.2d 437 (1998).

—Withdrawal of Petition to Terminate
A finding of parental unfitness made during a proceeding to terminate parental rights, cannot stand when the petition to terminate parental rights is withdrawn. In re Chilean D., 304 Ill. App. 3d 580, 237 Ill. Dec. 601, 710 N.E.2d 24 (1 Dist. 1999).

Unknown Fathers
Juvenile court correctly terminated the parental rights of all unknown fathers where records showed no fathers ever surfaced or had any contact with minor within 30 days of birth. In re A.S.B., 293 Ill. App. 3d 836, 228 Ill. Dec. 238, 688 N.E.2d 1215 (2 Dist. 1997).

Unwed Father

—Procedural Safeguards
Where an unwed father is fit and willing to develop a relationship

Unwed Father (Cont'd)

—Procedural Safeguards (Cont'd)

with and raise his child, but is prevented from doing so through deceit and an invalid adoption proceeding, that father is entitled to the care, custody and control of his child upon the subsequent vacatur of the invalid adoption; a hearing under 750 ILCS 5/601(b)(2) would be improper because it would contravene the safeguards afforded unwed fathers in the Adoption Act. In re Kirchner, 164 Ill. 2d 468, 208 Ill. Dec. 268, 649 N.E.2d 324 (1995), cert. denied, 515 U.S. 1152, 115 S. Ct. 2599, 132 L. Ed. 2d 846 (1995).

Adoptive parents cannot, once an invalid adoption is vacated, attempt to circumvent the rights afforded fathers under the Adoption Act by seeking a custody hearing under 750 ILCS 5/601 which, unlike the Adoption Act, could result in a father's being divested of his right to the care, custody and control of his child without being found unfit by clear and convincing evidence. In re Kirchner, 164 Ill. 2d 468, 208 Ill. Dec. 268, 649 N.E.2d 324 (1995), cert. denied, 515 U.S. 1152, 115 S. Ct. 2599, 132 L. Ed. 2d 846 (1995).

Waiver

Father's contention that the termination of his parental rights based solely on the fact of his conviction violated the federal constitutional prohibition against cruel and unusual punishment, U.S. Const., amends. VIII, XIV and the Illinois constitutional prohibition against corruption of blood, Ill. Const. (1970), Art. I, § 11, was rejected for he failed to raise these constitutional arguments before the trial court, as such, he waived them for purposes of appeal; moreover, the termination of his parental rights was not based solely on his conviction but on a finding of unfitness grounded in depravity based on his murder of the mother of his children in an exceptionally brutal and heinous manner indicating wanton cruelty. In re T.H., 255 Ill. App. 3d 247, 193 Ill. Dec. 370, 626 N.E.2d 403 (5 Dist. 1993), appeal denied, 155 Ill. 2d 577, 198 Ill. Dec. 554, 633 N.E.2d 16, cert. denied, 513 U.S. 905, 115 S. Ct. 269, 130 L. Ed. 2d 187 (1994).

LEGAL PERIODICALS

For article, "Survey of Illinois Law: Constitutional Law," see 25 S. Ill. U. L.J. 733 (2001).

For comment, "The Illinois Adoption Act: Should a Child's Length of Time in Foster Care Measure Parental Unfitness", see 30 Loy. U. Chi. L.J. 727 (1999).

For note, "Putting Reason back in the Reasonable Efforts Requirement in Child Abuse and Neglect Cases", see 1999 U. Ill. L. Rev. 287 (1999).

For article, "Baby Richard and Beyond: The Future for Adopted Children", see 18 N. Ill. U.L. Rev. 445 (1999).

For note, "The Best Interests of Children in the Cultural Context of the Indian Child Welfare Act in In re S.S. and R.S.," see 28 Loy. U. Chi. L.J. 839 (1997).

For casenote, "Born to Lose: The Illinois 'Baby Richard' Case — How Examining His Father's Pre-Birth Conduct Might Have Led to a Different Ending for Richard," see 16 N. Ill. U.L. Rev. 543 (1996).

For casenote, "Babies, Jessica, Richard and Emily: The Need for Legislative Reform of Adoption Laws," 70 Chi. Kent L. Rev. 1851 (1996).

For casenote, "Baby Richard: The Case That Won't Go Away," see 9 CBA Rec. 8 (1995).

For article, "A Primer on the Juvenile Court Act of 1987," see 9 CBA Rec. 33 (1995).

For comment, "Rights of Unwed Fathers and the Best Interests of the Child: Can These Competing Interests be Harmonized? Illinois Putative Father Registry Provides an Answer," see 26 Loy. U. Chi. L.J. 703 (1995).

For article, "Terminating Parental Rights of Incarcerated Parents," see 6 Chi. B. Rec. 22 (1992).

For article, "Ending Family Ties: Termination of Parental Rights in Illinois," see 79 Ill. B. J. 572 (1991).

For article, "Defining the Best Interest of Children: Parents v. Others in Custody Proceedings," see 79 Ill. B. J. 566 (1991).

For article, "Family Law: 1987-88 Illinois Law Survey," see Loy. U. Chi. L. J. 461 (1988-89).

For article, "Recent Developments and Proposed Legislative Reform of the Illinois Adoption Act," see 19 Loy. U. Chi. L. J. 971 (1987-88).

For article, "Juvenile Law: 1985-86 Illinois Law Survey," see 18 Loy. U. Chi. L. J. 633 (1986-87).

For comment, "Severed Roots: The Sealed Adoption Records Controversy," see 6 N. Ill. U.L. Rev. 103 (1986).

For note, "The Termination of Parental Rights: Lassiter and the New Illinois Termination Law," see 13 Loy. U. Chi. L. J. 135 (1981-82).

For article, "Twas , and the Court did Gyre, Gimble, and Outgrable," see 69 Ill. B. J. 154 (1980).

For note, "Delineating the Reasonable Progress Ground as a Basis for Termination of Parental Rights—In re Austin," see 28 De Paul L. Rev. 819 (1979).

For comments, "Illegitimacy and the Rights of Unwed Fathers in Adoption Proceedings After Quillian v. Walcott," see 12 J. Marshall J. Prac. & Proc. 383 (1979).

For comment, "Children in Limbo: The Illinois Solution," see 73 Nw. U.L. Rev. 180 (1978).

For comment, "Child Abuse: The Role of Adoption as a Preventative Measure," see 10 J. Marshall J. Prac. & Proc. 546 (1977).

RESEARCH REFERENCES

Parent's mental deficiency as factor in termination of parental rights—modern status. 1 ALR5th 469.

Sufficiency of evidence to establish parent's knowledge or allowance of child's sexual abuse by another under statute permitting termination of parental rights for "allowing" or "knowingly allowing" such abuse to occur. 53 ALR5th 499.

Comment Note: Natural parent's indigence as precluding finding that failure to support child waived requirement of consent to adoption — general principles. 82 ALR5th 443.

Natural parent's indigence resulting from unemployment or underemployment as precluding finding that failure to support child waived requirement of consent to adoption. 83 ALR5th 375.

Construction and application of Indian Child Welfare Act of 1978 (ICWA) (25 U.S.C.A. §§ 1901 et seq.) upon child custody determinations. 89 ALR5th 195.

Right of indigent parent to appointed counsel in proceeding for involuntary termination of parental rights. 92 ALR5th 379.

Standing of foster parent to seek termination of rights of foster child's natural parents. 21 ALR4th 535.

750 ILCS 50/2 Who may adopt a child

Sec. 2. *Who may adopt a child.* A. Any of the following persons, who is under no legal disability (except the minority specified in sub-paragraph (b) and who has resided in the State of Illinois continuously for a period of at least 6 months immediately preceding the commencement of an adoption proceeding, or any member of the armed forces of the United States who has been domiciled in the State of Illinois for 90 days, may institute such proceeding:

(a) A reputable person of legal age and of either sex, provided that if such person is married and has not been living separate and apart from his or her spouse for 12 months or longer, his or her spouse shall be a party to the adoption proceeding, including a husband or wife desiring to adopt a child of the other spouse, in all of which cases the adoption shall be by both spouses jointly;

(b) A minor, by leave of court upon good cause shown.

B. The residence requirement specified in paragraph A of this Section shall not apply to an adoption of a related child or to an adoption of a child placed by an agency.

(Source: P.A. 83-62; 90-608, § 40.)

Note.
This section was Ill.Rev.Stat., Ch. 40, para. 1502.

Illinois Administrative Code.
See 89 Illinois Administrative Code, § 309.105.

Effect of Amendments.
The 1998 amendment by P.A. 90-608, effective June 30, 1998, inserted "and has not been living separate and apart from his or her spouse for 12 months or longer" in subsection (a).

CASE NOTES

ANALYSIS

Age Not a Bar
Authority to Petition
Reputable Person
Vacation of Adoption

Age Not a Bar
Under former Ill.Rev.Stat., ch. 4, para. 9.1-1 (see now this section), the trial court erred in determining that the sole factor of the age of the petitioners (53 years and 58 years) should be a bar to adoption. Madsen v. Chasten, 7 Ill. App. 3d 21, 286 N.E.2d 505 (4 Dist. 1972).

Authority to Petition
A prior similar provision authorized any resident of the state to petition the circuit or county court for leave to adopt a child not his own, and for a change of the name of the child, if desired. McNabb v. Irvington, 308 Ill. 214, 139 N.E. 64 (1923).

Reputable Person
Father's criminal history, his continuing pattern of deception, and employment instability justified finding that he was not a reputable person for the purposes of this Act. Nees v. Doan, 185 Ill. App. 3d 122, 133 Ill. Dec. 180, 540 N.E.2d 1046 (4 Dist. 1989).

Vacation of Adoption
Where a petition to vacate an adoption rested solely on the statement that the marriage of the petitioner and his former wife was annulled subsequent to their joint adoption of the minors, it would have been improper to apply the doctrine which declares an annulled marriage void from the beginning to the validity of the adoption because it would have affected the rights of minors, who were third parties to the annulment action. The adopted minors were not parties to the alleged fraud the petitioner's former wife may have perpetrated upon the petitioner, and they should not have suffered for the acts of another, and in light of concern for the best interests of the adopted children, the petitioner's contention that he and his former wife were not married at the time they adopted former wife's three children was rejected, the petition to vacate the adoption did not state a valid cause of action, and the trial court's dismissal of the petition was proper. Cowhey v. Tator, 36 Ill. App. 3d 962, 344 N.E.2d 501 (1 Dist. 1976).

750 ILCS 50/2.1 [Relation to other laws]

Sec. 2.1. This Act shall be construed in concert with the Juvenile Court Act of 1987 [705 ILCS 405/1-1 et seq.], the Child Care Act of 1969 [225 ILCS 10/1 et seq.], and the Interstate Compact on the Placement of Children [45 ILCS 15/0.01 et seq.].
(Source: P.A. 85-1209.)

Note.
This section was Ill.Rev.Stat., Ch. 40, para. 1503.

CASE NOTES

Application
Putative fathers are not treated disparately under the Adoption Act and the Illinois Juvenile Court Act (705 ILCS 405/1-1 et seq.); the Adoption Act specifically states that it should be construed in concert with the Juvenile Court Act (705 ILCS 405/1-1 et seq.), and § 2-29 of the Juvenile Court Act (705 ILCS 405/2-29) incorporates by reference many of the provisions in the Adoption Act, including those with respect to notice and consent. In re K.J.R., 293 Ill. App. 3d 49, 227 Ill. Dec. 190, 687 N.E.2d 113 (1 Dist. 1997).

750 ILCS 50/3 Who may be adopted

Sec. 3. *Who may be adopted.* A male or female child, or an adult, may be adopted, provided the other conditions set forth in this Act are met, and further provided, with respect to an adult, that such adult has resided in the home of the persons intending to adopt him at any time for more than 2 years continuously preceding the commencement of an adoption proceeding, or in the alternative that such persons are related to him within a degree set forth in the definition of a related child in Section 1 of this Act [750 ILCS 50/1].
(Source: Laws 1959, p. 1269.)

Note.
This section was Ill.Rev.Stat., Ch. 40, para. 1504.

CASE NOTES

ANALYSIS

In General
Construction with Other Laws

In General
There is no statutory distinction between an adopted adult and an adopted minor with respect to the nature of the legal relationship created between the adoptee and the adopting parent, namely, a parent-child relationship; the adoptee regardless of his age upon adoption, attains the status of a natural child of the adopting parents. In re Estate of Brittin, 279 Ill. App. 3d 512, 216 Ill. Dec. 50, 664 N.E.2d 687 (5 Dist. 1996).

Construction with Other Laws
The word "child" as used in 755 ILCS 5/2-4(a) cannot be interpreted fairly as meaning a minor in light of this section which permits adult adoptions. In re Estate of Brittin, 279 Ill. App. 3d 512, 216 Ill. Dec. 50, 664 N.E.2d 687 (5 Dist. 1996).
There is nothing in 755 ILCS 5/2-4(a) indicating a distinction between the adoptee's status as an adult or a minor at the time of adoption with regard to the adoptee's classification as a descendant of the adopting parent; the only qualification set forth is that the adoptee be legally adopted, nothing more is required. In re Estate of Brittin, 279 Ill. App. 3d 512, 216 Ill. Dec. 50, 664 N.E.2d 687 (5 Dist. 1996).

750 ILCS 50/4 Jurisdiction and venue

Sec. 4. *Jurisdiction and venue.* An adoption proceeding may be commenced in the circuit court of the county in which petitioners reside, or the county in which the person to be adopted resides, or was born, or the county in which the parents of such person reside, provided, however, if an agency has acquired the custody and control of a child and such agency is authorized to consent to the adoption of such child, the proceeding may be commenced in any county, and provided further that if a guardian of the person of such child has been appointed by a court of competent jurisdiction, the proceeding may be commenced in any county.
(Source: Laws 1965, p. 3308.)

Note.
This section was Ill.Rev.Stat., Ch. 40, para. 1505.

CASE NOTES

Analysis

Challenges to Jurisdiction
Collateral Attacks on Jurisdiction
Compliance
—Substantial
Continuing Jurisdiction
No Presumption of Jurisdiction
Subject Matter Jurisdiction
—Improper
—Proper

Challenges to Jurisdiction

Where one has invoked the jurisdiction of a court in an adoption proceeding, she cannot question such jurisdiction in a subsequent proceeding, especially where the defects were procedural and not substantial. Carter Oil Co. v. Norman, 131 F.2d 451 (7th Cir. 1942).

Collateral Attacks on Jurisdiction

In a collateral attack on an adoption, the party attacking collaterally could only question the jurisdiction of the court granting the adoption. Burke v. Wallace, 339 Ill. App. 162, 89 N.E.2d 197 (3 Dist. 1949).

Compliance

—Substantial

Under the former Adoption Act (see now this section), substantial compliance with the jurisdictional requirements of the adoption statutes was sufficient. Perl v. Baby Boy, 38 Ill. App. 2d 430, 187 N.E.2d 303 (1 Dist. 1963).

Continuing Jurisdiction

Where a mother had been deprived of the custody of her child at a time when the child was declared neglected and dependent, court's jurisdiction was a continuing one and the mother could petition for restoration of custody based on a change of circumstances at any time prior to the consummation of adoption by decree, if she had not been deprived of such right by prior order of court. Oeth v. Erwin, 6 Ill. App. 2d 18, 126 N.E.2d 526 (4 Dist. 1955).

No Presumption of Jurisdiction

Jurisdiction is not presumed, but a petition for adoption must show sufficient facts on its face to give the court jurisdiction of an adoption matter. In re Simaner, 15 Ill. 2d 568, 155 N.E.2d 555 (1959).

Subject Matter Jurisdiction

—Improper

The trial court's order of continued postadoption visitation with the adopted boy's biological family was without legal authority and was vacated because the trial court lacked subject matter jurisdiction to enter such an order. Harold K. v. Ryan B., Ill. App. 3d , Ill. Dec. , N.E.2d , 2000 Ill. App. LEXIS 318 (5 Dist. May 12, 2000).

Under a prior similar provision, a motion to dismiss an adoption petition was properly granted where the county court did not obtain jurisdiction of the subject matter as to consent when it failed to find and place of record the statutory ground or test of unfitness of the mother when she withheld her consent to the adoption. Oeth v. Erwin, 6 Ill. App. 2d 18, 126 N.E.2d 526 (4 Dist. 1955).

—Proper

The trial court did not lack subject matter jurisdiction to enter the adoption decree even though it initially erroneously found the natural father to have consented to the adoption in accordance with this Act. Flangel v. Flangel, 87 Ill. App. 3d 1100, 42 Ill. Dec. 906, 409 N.E.2d 521 (2 Dist. 1980).

750 ILCS 50/4.1 [Compliance with the Child Care Act of 1969 and the Interstate Compact on the Placement of Children]

Sec. 4.1. Except for children placed with relatives by the Department of Children and Family Services pursuant to subsection (b) of Section 7 of the Children and Family Services Act [20 ILCS 505/7], placements under this Act shall comply with the Child Care Act of 1969 [225 ILCS 10/1 et seq.] and the Interstate Compact on the Placement of Children [45 ILCS 15/0.01 et seq.]. Placements of children born outside the United States or a territory thereof shall comply with rules promulgated by the United States Department of Immigration and Naturalization.

Rules promulgated by the Department of Children and Family Services shall include but not be limited to the following:

(a) Any agency which places such children for adoption in this State:

(i) Shall be licensed in this State as a child welfare agency as defined in Section 2.08 of the Child Care Act of 1969 [225 ILCS 10/2.08]; or

(ii) Shall be licensed as a child placement agency in a state which is a party to the Interstate Compact on the Placement of Children; or

(iii) Shall be licensed as a child placement agency in a country other than the United States or, if located in such a country but not so licensed, shall provide information such as a license or court document which authorizes that agency to place children for adoption and to establish that such agency has legal authority to place children for adoption; or

(iv) Shall be a child placement agency which is so licensed in a non-compact state, if such agency first files with the Department of Children and Family Services a bond with surety in the amount of $5,000 for each such child to ensure that such child shall not become a public charge upon this State. Such bond shall remain in effect until a judgment for adoption is entered with respect to such child pursuant to this Act. The Department of Children and Family Services may accept, in lieu of such bond, a written agreement with such agency which provides that such agency shall be liable for all costs associated with the placement of such child in the event a judgement of adoption is not entered, upon such terms and conditions as the Department deems appropriate.

The rules shall also provide that any agency that places children for adoption in this State may not, in any policy or practice relating to the placement of children for adoption, discriminate against any child or prospective adoptive parent on the basis of race.

(b) As an alternative to requiring the bond provided for in paragraph (a)(iv) of this Section, the Department of Children and Family Services may require the filing of such a bond by the individual or individuals seeking to adopt such a child through placement of such child by a child placement agency located in a state which is not a party to the Interstate Compact on the Placement of Children.

(c) In the case of any foreign-born child brought to the United States for adoption in this State, the following preadoption requirements shall be met:

(1) Documentation that the child is legally free for adoption prior to entry into the United States shall be submitted.

(2) A medical report on the child, by authorized medical personnel in the country of the child's origin, shall be provided when such personnel are available.

(3) Verification that the adoptive family has been licensed as a foster family home pursuant to the Child Care Act of 1969, as now or hereafter amended [225 ILCS 10/1 et seq.], shall be provided.

(4) A valid home study conducted by a licensed child welfare agency that complies with guidelines established by the United States Immigration and Naturalization Service at 8 CFR 204.4(d)(2)(i), as now or hereafter amended, shall be submitted. A home study is considered valid if it contains:

(i) A factual evaluation of the financial, physical, mental and moral capabilities of the prospective parent or parents to rear and educate the child properly.

(ii) A detailed description of the living accommodations where the prospective parent or parents currently reside.

(iii) A detailed description of the living accommodations in the United States where the child will reside, if known.

(iv) A statement or attachment recommending the proposed adoption signed by an official of the child welfare agency which has conducted the home study.

(5) The placing agency located in a non-compact state or a family desiring to adopt through an authorized placement party in a non-compact state or a foreign country shall file with the Department of Children and Family Services a bond with surety in the amount of $5,000 as protection that a foreign-born child accepted for care or supervision not become a public charge upon the State of Illinois.

(6) In lieu of the $5,000 bond, the placement agency may sign a binding agreement with the Department of Children and Family Services to assume full liability for all placements should, for any reason, the adoption be disrupted or not be completed, including financial and planning responsibility until the child is either returned to the country of its origin or placed with a new adoptive family in the United States and that adoption is finalized.

(7) Compliance with the requirements of the Interstate Compact on the Placement of Children, when applicable, shall be demonstrated.

(8) When a child is adopted in a foreign country and a final, complete and valid Order of Adoption is issued in that country, as determined by both the United States Department of State and the United States Department of Justice, this State shall not impose any additional preadoption requirements. The adoptive family, however, must comply with applicable requirements of the United States Department of Immigration and Naturalization as provided in 8 CFR 204.4 (d)(2)(ii), as now or hereafter amended.

(d) The Department of Children and Family Services shall maintain the office of Intercountry Adoption Coordinator, shall maintain and protect the rights of families and children participating in adoption of foreign born children, and shall develop ongoing programs of support and services to such families and children. The Intercountry Adoption Coordinator shall determine that all preadoption requirements have been met and report such information to the Department of Immigration and Naturalization.

(Source: P.A. 85-517; 89-21, § 15-20; 89-422, § 5; 89-626, § 2-79.)

Note.

This section was Ill.Rev.Stat., Ch. 40, para. 1506.

Effect of Amendments.

The 1995 amendment by P.A. 89-21, effective July 1, 1995, in the introductory paragraph, in the first sentence, added at the beginning "Except for children placed with relatives by the Department of Children and Family Services pursuant to subsection (b) of Section 7 of the Children and Family Services Act".

The 1995 amendment by P.A. 89-422, effective December 4, 1995, added the last paragraph in subsection (a).

The 1996 amendment by P.A. 89-626, effective August 9, 1996, combined the amendments by P.A. 89-21 and P.A. 89-422.

CASE NOTES

Visitation

—Grandparents

The statutes permitting grandparent visitation in certain circumstances do not authorize the court to order such visitation in an adoption judgment. Krystek v. Schumacher, 120 Ill. App. 3d 50, 75 Ill. Dec. 926, 458 N.E.2d 94 (2 Dist. 1983).

The adoption statute cannot serve as authority for the inclusion of a grant of grandparent visitation in an adoption judgment because it contains no express provision for grandparent visitation. Krystek v. Schumacher, 120 Ill. App. 3d 50, 75 Ill. Dec. 926, 458 N.E.2d 94 (2 Dist. 1983).

750 ILCS 50/5 Petition, contents, verification, filing

Sec. 5. *Petition, contents, verification, filing.* A. A proceeding to adopt a child, other than a related child, shall be commenced by the filing of a petition within 30 days after such child has become available for adoption, provided that such petition may be filed at a later date by leave of court upon a showing that the failure to file such petition within such 30 day period was not due to the petitioners' culpable negligence or their wilful disregard of the provisions of this Section. In the case of a child born outside the United States or a territory thereof, if the prospective adoptive parents of such child have been appointed guardians of such child by a court of competent jurisdiction in a country other than the United States or a territory thereof, such parents shall file a petition as provided in this Section within 30 days after entry of the child into the United States. A petition to adopt an adult or a related child may be filed at any time. A petition for adoption may include more than one person sought to be adopted.

B. A petition to adopt a child other than a related child shall state:

(a) The full names of the petitioners and, if minors, their respective ages;

(b) The place of residence of the petitioners and the length of residence of each in the State of Illinois immediately preceding the filing of the petition;

(c) When the petitioners acquired, or intend to acquire, custody of the child, and the name and address of the persons or agency from whom the child was or will be received;

(d) The name, the place and date of birth if known, and the sex of the child sought to be adopted;

(e) The relationship, if any, of the child to each petitioner;

(f) The names, if known, and the place of residence, if known, of the parents; and whether such parents are minors, or otherwise under any legal disability. The names and addresses of the parents shall be omitted and they shall not be made parties defendant to the petition if (1) the rights of the parents have been terminated by a court of competent jurisdiction, or (2) if the child has been surrendered to an agency, or (3) if the parent or parents have been served with the notice provided in Section 12a of this Act [750 ILCS 50/12a] and said parent or parents have filed a disclaimer of paternity as therein provided or have failed to file such declaration of paternity or a request for notice as provided in said Section;

(g) If it is alleged that the child has no living parent, then the name of the guardian, if any, of such child and the court which appointed such guardian;

(h) If it is alleged that the child has no living parent and that no guardian of such child is known to petitioners, then the name of a near relative, if known, shall be set forth, or an allegation that no near relative is known and on due inquiry cannot be ascertained by petitioners;

(i) The name to be given the child or adult;

(j) That the person or agency, having authority to consent under Section 8 of this Act [750 ILCS 50/8], has consented, or has indicated willingness to consent, to the adoption of the child by the petitioners, or that the person having authority to consent is an unfit person and the ground therefor, or that no consent is required under paragraph (f) of Section 8 of this Act [750 ILCS 50/8];

(k) Whatever orders, judgments or decrees have heretofore been entered by any court affecting (1) adoption or custody of the child, or (2) the adoptive, custodial or parental rights of either petitioner, including the prior denial of any petition for adoption pertaining to such child, or to the petitioners, or either of them.

C. A petition to adopt a related child shall include the information specified in sub-paragraphs (a), (b), (d), (e), (f), (i) and (k) of paragraph B and a petition to adopt an adult shall contain the information required by sub-paragraphs (a), (b) and (i) of paragraph B in addition to the name, place, date of birth and sex of such adult.

D. The petition shall be verified by the petitioners.

E. Upon the filing of the petition the petitioners shall furnish the Clerk of the Court in which the petition is pending such information not contained in such petition as shall be necessary to enable the Clerk of such Court to complete a certificate of adoption as hereinafter provided.

F. A petition for standby adoption shall conform to the requirements of this Act with respect to petition contents, verification, and filing. The petition for standby adoption shall also state the facts concerning the consent of the child's parent to the standby adoption. A petition for standby adoption shall include the information in paragraph B if the petitioner seeks to adopt a child other than a related child. A petition for standby adoption shall include the information in paragraph C if the petitioner seeks to adopt a related child or adult.

(Source: P.A. 85-517; 87-1129, § 2; 88-148, § 10; 91-357, § 262; 91-572, § 5.)

Note.

This section was Ill.Rev.Stat., Ch. 40, para. 1507.

Effect of Amendments.

The 1999 amendment by P.A. 91-357, effective July 29, 1999, made stylistic changes.

The 1999 amendment by P.A. 91-572, effective January 1, 2000, added subsection F. and made stylistic changes.

Although the amendments made to this section by P.A. 91-357, § 262 and P.A. 91-572, § 5 did not take into account the amendments made by the other, the amendments have been combined into a single version by the publisher.

CASE NOTES

ANALYSIS

In General
Ability to Care for Child
Amended Complaint
Available for Adoption
Evidence
—Held Sufficient
Grounds for Adoption
—Failure to Allege
Legal Status
Legislative Intent
Nonrelated Party
Notice
Oral Contract
Parties
—Child
—Petitioners
Petition to Intervene
—Dismissed
Petitions
—In General
—Against Both Parents
—Allegation of Unfitness
Refusal to Consent
Standing
Stepparents
Unfit Person

In General

It has been held that this Act contemplates a two-step process: first, the filing of a petition, followed as soon as possible by a hearing, and then if consent or unfitness is found, the entry of an interim order; second, ordinarily after a six-month waiting period, the final decree of adoption. This procedure appears to be the only method under this Act by which an adoption can be accomplished where the parents are unfit and refuse to consent. In re Filippelli, 207 Ill. App. 3d 813, 152 Ill. Dec. 725, 566 N.E.2d 412 (1 Dist. 1990).

Ability to Care for Child

While it was technically error to refuse defense testimony relating to the mother's ability to care for her child, the remoteness of the testimony, along with mother's marriage to the abuser, indicated that any error was harmless and the judge did, even though excluding evidence, make a totally informed decision about the child's best interests and what physical abuse might occur to the minor if the child were not made a ward of the court under former Adoption Act (Ill.Rev.Stat., ch. 4, para. 9.1-1 (1975)) (see now this section). In re Willis, 57 Ill. App. 3d 381, 14 Ill. Dec. 948, 373 N.E.2d 79 (4 Dist. 1978).

Amended Complaint

Where trial court dismissed an adoption complaint due to failure to comply with former paragraph 9.1-5B of chapter 4 (see now this section) and allowed 21 days for the filing of an amended complaint, the trial court could allow the amended complaint to be filed after the expiration of that period, pursuant to former section 46(1) of chapter 110 (see now 735 ILCS 5/2-617) since the dismissal of the complaint with leave to correct the deficiency did not amount to a final judgment. Gray v. Starkey, 41 Ill. App. 3d 555, 353 N.E.2d 703 (5 Dist. 1976).

Available for Adoption

Related parties do not have to allege in their petition to adopt that a child is unavailable for adoption. In re L.R.B., 278 Ill. App. 3d 1091, 215 Ill. Dec. 950, 664 N.E.2d 347 (4 Dist. 1996), appeal denied, 168 Ill. 2d 591, 219 Ill. Dec. 564, 671 N.E.2d 731 (1996).

Evidence

—Held Sufficient

There was clear and convincing evidence upon which the trial court could find that the respondent failed to exhibit sufficient interest in her child to be considered a fit parent, where she relinquished custody of the child less than five weeks after she was born, had only minimal contact with the child, and made no discernible effort to regain custody of the child for approximately four years. In re Richards, 104 Ill. App. 3d 406, 60 Ill. Dec. 138, 432 N.E.2d 1037 (1 Dist. 1982).

Grounds for Adoption

—Failure to Allege

Where petitioners contended that the evidence adduced at trial showed depravity of the respondent, but did not allege depravity as a ground for finding respondent unfit, failure to allege depravity as a ground of unfitness was never placed in issue in the trial court, was not ruled upon there and could not, therefore, be urged for the first time on appeal. In re Smith, 4 Ill. App. 3d 261, 280 N.E.2d 770 (1 Dist. 1972).

Legal Status

The trial court was correct in ruling that the best interest of the children required that their legal status be determined with certainty especially where foster parents, who had cared for the boys for five years, were waiting for the final termination of petitioner's rights before filing a petition to adopt. In re Workman, 56 Ill. App. 3d 1007, 14 Ill. Dec. 908, 373 N.E.2d 39 (3 Dist. 1978), aff'd, 76 Ill. 2d 256, 28 Ill. Dec. 541, 390 N.E.2d 900 (1979).

Legislative Intent

This section clearly contemplates that a petition to adopt may be filed alleging unfitness and the basis for the allegation. This statutory provision does not require that the petition allege that a court of competent jurisdiction had previously entered a finding of unfitness, but only that unfitness be alleged along with the ground therefore. In re Filippelli, 207 Ill. App. 3d 813, 152 Ill. Dec. 725, 566 N.E.2d 412 (1 Dist. 1990).

Under former section 11 of the Adoption Act Ill.Rev.Stat., ch. 4, para. 9.1-11 (see now this section) a consent to adoption executed and acknowledged was deemed to be irrevocable unless it was shown to have been obtained by fraud or duress and this section was construed to be a reflection of a clear legislative recognition of the strong public policy favoring the finality and stability of adoptions. Hale v. Hale, 57 Ill. App. 3d 730, 15 Ill. Dec. 85, 373 N.E.2d 431 (5 Dist. 1978).

Nonrelated Party

This Act (750 ILCS 50/1) does not authorize the filing of an adoption petition by a nonrelated party prior to the child becoming available for adoption; a party who is not related to the child may not file a petition to adopt that child until after any of the acts contained in 750 ILCS 50/1 has occurred and, specifically, they may not file seeking to prove the unfitness of the parent in a subsequent hearing. Johnson v. Burnett, 182 Ill. App. 3d 574, 131 Ill. Dec. 517, 538 N.E.2d 892 (3 Dist. 1989).

Notice

Where the State's Attorney's petition to terminate parental rights alleged that the mother was "unknown"; notice was given by publication for unknowns in accordance with the statute; the court in the order terminating parental rights expressly found that the natural mother and father were both unknown and that the child was abandoned by both and was dependent on the public for support; and the adoption decree was entered upon the consent of the Department of Probation, appointed to consent upon the termination of parental rights, the trial court acquired jurisdiction of both the subject matter and the parties and its judgment was presumptively valid under former Adoption Act (Ill.Rev.Stat., ch. 4, para. 9.1-1) (see now this section) and under former Juvenile Court Act (Ill.Rev.Stat., ch. 37, para. 704-2) (see now 705 ILCS 405/2-16). Rodriguez v. Koschny, 57 Ill. App. 3d 355, 14 Ill. Dec. 916, 373 N.E.2d 47 (2 Dist. 1978).

It was unreasonable to believe that petitioner did not know that her parental rights were subject to dispute where according to her own testimony she repeatedly confronted her sister demanding return of the child, asking to see him and to know his whereabouts where in view of her age, intelligence and education it seemed incredulous that she would not be on notice that her parental rights were not recognized where it was even more incredulous that petitioner so trusted her sister that she believed she had done nothing to jeopardize petitioner's parental rights when over a nine year period her sister totally denied petitioner any information as to the child's whereabouts and where it was incredible that a woman seriously interested in regaining custody of her child would refrain from seeking legal enforcement of her parental rights over a nine year period for fear of upsetting her own ethnic family relationship under former Ill.Rev.Stat., ch. 4, para. 9.1-20 (see now this section). Rodriguez v. Koschny, 57 Ill. App. 3d 355, 14 Ill. Dec. 916, 373 N.E.2d 47 (2 Dist. 1978).

Oral Contract

Proof of the elements of an oral contract to adopt merely permits the enforcement of contract rights; it does not create a parent-child relationship or afford all of the legal consequences of a statutory adoption. Evink v. Edwards ex rel. Gregory, 106 Ill. App. 3d 635, 62 Ill. Dec. 407, 435 N.E.2d 1379 (2 Dist. 1982).

Parties

—Child

It was not the intention of the legislature that the child should be made a party defendant in an adoption proceeding. McConnell v. McConnell, 345 Ill. 70, 177 N.E. 692 (1931).

—Petitioners

Petitioners seeking to adopt a child can prosecute a proceeding to terminate parental rights; it is not the case that only the state can prosecute such a proceeding. In re K.L.P., 316 Ill. App. 3d 110, 249 Ill. Dec. 246, 735 N.E.2d 1071, 2000 Ill. App. LEXIS 734 (2 Dist. 2000).

Petition to Intervene

—Dismissed

Trial court did not err in dismissing natural father's petition to

Petition to Intervene (Cont'd)

—Dismissed (Cont'd)
intervene where his parental rights had been terminated pursuant to former paragraph 9.1-17 of chapter 4 (see now this section) despite fact that natural father's parental rights were terminated in an earlier adoption proceeding which was abandoned by the other petitioners before that adoption was finalized. Gray v. Starkey, 41 Ill. App. 3d 555, 353 N.E.2d 703 (5 Dist. 1976).

Petitions

—In General
Under a prior similar provision, a petition of adoption required to put the court in motion and give it jurisdiction was required to be in conformity with the statute and the requisite facts must have appeared upon the face of the petition itself. Burke v. Wallace, 339 Ill. App. 162, 89 N.E.2d 197 (3 Dist. 1949).

—Against Both Parents
A petition seeking to terminate the parental rights of one parent may be brought after such a petition has already been successfully brought against the other parent; that one parent has not been (and may never be) found unfit is merely one additional factor which the trial court may give whatever weight it believes appropriate when it is deciding at a dispositional hearing whether it is in the best interest of the child that the parental rights of the first parent be terminated. People v. Houston, 219 Ill. App. 3d 269, 162 Ill. Dec. 343, 579 N.E.2d 1157 (4 Dist. 1991).

—Allegation of Unfitness
This Act allows the filing of a petition which alleges unfitness, and the ground therefore, and a subsequent hearing by the court in the adoption proceeding at which the court determines whether the allegation of unfitness has been proved; the statute does not provide that a finding of unfitness is a condition precedent to the filing of a petition to adopt. In re Filippelli, 207 Ill. App. 3d 813, 152 Ill. Dec. 725, 566 N.E.2d 412 (1 Dist. 1990).

If it is alleged that consent is not required because the person having the authority to consent is an unfit person, the ground of unfitness must also be alleged. In re Smith, 4 Ill. App. 3d 261, 280 N.E.2d 770 (1 Dist. 1972).

Refusal to Consent
Even though mother was the victim of frequent warnings concerning her son's physical condition, the court could not say conclusively that such statements were fraudulent and that she was faced with no other choice but to consent to her child's adoption under former Ill.Rev.Stat., ch. 4, para. 9.1 (see now this section) especially where it was apparent from the record that child had received medical care on at least two occasions in the months preceding his adoption by grandparents and on both of these occasions claims were filed with his father's medical insurer. Hale v. Hale, 57 Ill. App. 3d 730, 15 Ill. Dec. 85, 373 N.E.2d 431 (5 Dist. 1978).

An agency cannot deprive a court of its jurisdiction to review an adoption petition by merely refusing to give its consent. Stines v. Vaughn, 23 Ill. App. 3d 511, 319 N.E.2d 561 (4 Dist. 1974).

Under a prior similar provision, where written consent of the parents to an adoption of a child was attached to adoption petition, and the consent stated the parents' residence, there was compliance with the requirement that the petition contain the parents' residence. Flannigan v. Howard, 200 Ill. 396, 65 N.E. 782 (1902).

Under a prior similar provision, it was required, in an adoption proceeding that the name of the father be stated, and that he consented to the adoption; but only if he were alive and had not abandoned the child; if he were dead, or if he were alive and had abandoned the child, it was necessary to state the name of the mother and that she consented to the adoption. Barnard v. Barnard, 119 Ill. 92, 8 N.E. 320 (1886).

Standing
A mother has standing to appeal an adjudication of wardship under the former Adoption Act (Ill.Rev.Stat., ch. 4, para. 9.1-1) (see now this section). In re Willis, 57 Ill. App. 3d 381, 14 Ill. Dec. 948, 373 N.E.2d 79 (4 Dist. 1978).

Stepparents
Stepmother was a related person for purposes of adopting a child after the father died and was, therefore, not required to give notice of the adoption petition to the grandparents or uncle of the child. Christine A.T. v. H.T., 326 Ill. App. 3d 569, 260 Ill. Dec. 455, 761 N.E.2d 299, 2001 Ill. App. LEXIS 900 (3 Dist. 2001).

Unfit Person
Although proof of unfitness must be clear and convincing, the finding of unfitness is a question of fact and the decision of the trial court should not be disturbed on appeal unless against the manifest weight of the evidence. In re Richards, 104 Ill. App. 3d 406, 60 Ill. Dec. 138, 432 N.E.2d 1037 (1 Dist. 1982).

To terminate the parental rights of a biological mother she must be found an unfit person by clear and convincing evidence. In re Richards, 104 Ill. App. 3d 406, 60 Ill. Dec. 138, 432 N.E.2d 1037 (1 Dist. 1982).

Where the appellant's failure to learn to care for the medical needs of child led to the original order finding child to be a minor in need of supervision and declaring her a ward of the court, where in the ensuing months the appellant made no effort to undergo training by the hospital personnel or by surgical technicians trained to care for child even though such training was offered, where on two occasions she attempted to feed child, once causing a coughing spell because of her inability to properly position the feeding tube, and where the appellant's failure to arrange more frequent visits with her child, although insufficient to establish unfitness by reason of lack of interest, could be considered in assessing her progress toward the correction of the conditions which led to the original decree, the factors were sufficient to support the trial court's findings that the appellant was unfit under the former Adoption Act ch. 4, para. 9.1-1 (1975) (see now this section). People v. Gates, 57 Ill. App. 3d 844, 15 Ill. Dec. 222, 373 N.E.2d 568 (5 Dist. 1978).

Where, under former Ill.Rev.Stat., ch. 4, para. 9.1-5 (see now this section), the petitioners contended that the trial court should have found the natural father unfit on the ground of depravity, drunkenness, adultery, fornication, and should have based its determination upon the natural father's course of conduct over many years of his adult life but did not plead these contentions in either the original or the amended petition, they could not be urged in appellate court for the first time. Rich v. Rich, 51 Ill. App. 3d 174, 9 Ill. Dec. 318, 366 N.E.2d 575 (1 Dist. 1977).

750 ILCS 50/6 Investigation; all cases

Sec. 6. *Investigation; all cases.* A. Investigation; all cases. Within 10 days after the filing of a petition for the adoption or standby adoption of a child other than a related child, the court shall appoint a child welfare agency approved by the Department of Children and Family Services, or a person deemed competent by the court, or in Cook County the Court Services Division of the Cook County Department of Public Aid, or the Department of Children and Family Services if the court determines that no child welfare agency is available or that the petitioner is financially unable to pay for the investigation, to investigate accurately, fully and promptly, the allegations contained in the petition; the character, reputation, health and general standing in the community of the petitioners; the religious faith of the petitioners and, if ascertainable, of the child sought to be adopted; and whether the petitioners are proper persons to adopt the child and whether the child is a proper subject of adoption. The investigation required under this Section shall include a fingerprint based criminal background check with a review of fingerprints by the Illinois State Police and Federal Bureau of Investigation. Each petitioner subject to this investigation, shall submit his or her fingerprints to the Department of State Police in the form and manner prescribed by the Department of State Police. These fingerprints shall be checked against the fingerprint records now and hereafter filed in the Department of State Police and Federal Bureau of Investigation criminal history records databases. The Department of State Police shall charge a fee for conducting the criminal history records check, which shall be deposited in the State Police Services Fund and shall not exceed the actual cost of the records check. The criminal background check required by this Section shall include a listing of when, where and by whom the criminal background check was prepared. The criminal background check required by this Section shall not be more than two years old.

Neither a clerk of the circuit court nor a judge may require that a criminal background check or fingerprint review be filed with, or at the same time as, an initial petition for adoption.

B. Investigation; foreign-born child. In the case of a child born outside the United States or a territory thereof, in addition to the investigation required under subsection (A) of this Section, a post-placement investigation shall be conducted in accordance with the requirements of the Child Care Act of 1969 [225 ILCS 10/1 et seq.], the Interstate Compact on the Placement of Children [45 ILCS 15/0.01 et seq.], and regulations of the foreign placing agency and the supervising agency.

The requirements of a post-placement investigation shall be deemed to have been satisfied if a valid final order or judgment of adoption has been entered by a court of competent jurisdiction in a country other than the United States or a territory thereof with respect to such child and the petitioners.

C. Report of investigation. The court shall determine whether the costs of the investigation shall be charged to the petitioners. The information obtained as a result of such investigation shall be presented to the court in a written report. The results of the criminal background check required under subsection (A) shall be provided to the court for its review. The court may, in its discretion, weigh the significance of the results of the criminal background check against the entirety of the background of the petitioners. The Court, in its discretion, may accept the report of the investigation previously made by a licensed child welfare agency, if made within one year prior to the entry of the judgment. Such report shall be treated as confidential and withheld from inspection unless findings adverse to the petitioners or to the child sought to be adopted are contained therein, and in that event the court shall inform the petitioners of the relevant portions pertaining to the adverse findings. In no event shall any facts set forth in the report be considered at the hearing of the proceeding, unless established by competent evidence. The report shall be filed with the record of the proceeding. If the file relating to the proceeding is not impounded, the report shall be impounded by the clerk of the court and shall be made available for inspection only upon order of the court.

D. Related adoption. Such investigation shall not be made when the petition seeks to adopt a related child or an adult unless the court, in its discretion, shall so order. In such an event the court may appoint a person deemed competent by the court.
(Source: P.A. 86-522; 86-659; 86-1028; 87-1129, § 2; 88-148, § 10; 91-429, § 10; 91-572, § 5; 91-740, § 5; 93-418, § 50.)

Note.
This section was Ill.Rev.Stat., Ch. 40, para. 1508.

Effect of Amendments.
The 1999 amendment by P.A. 91-429, effective January 1, 2000, deleted "or a probation officer of the court" preceding "or in Cook County" near the beginning of subsection A.

The 1999 amendment by P.A. 91-572, effective January 1, 2000, inserted "or standby adoption" in the first sentence of subsection A. near the beginning.

The 2000 amendment by P.A. 91-740, effective June 2, 2000, incorporated the amendments by P.A. 91-429 and P.A. 91-572 and inserted "or a person deemed competent by the court" in the first sentence of the introductory paragraph.

The 2003 amendment by P.A. 93-418, effective January 1, 2004, in the second sentence of subsection A., inserted "fingerprint based", "the Illinois", and "Police", and substituted "authorities" for "Bureau of Investigation"; and added the second through fifth sentences.

CASE NOTES

Analysis

Investigative Reports
Related Adoption
Results
—Use as Evidence

Investigative Reports
Neither foster-care home study performed in another state nor Department of Children and Family Services client service plans were investigative reports within the meaning of subsection (C). Bonnie S.P. v. Phillip P., 313 Ill. App. 3d 301, 246 Ill. Dec. 180, 729 N.E.2d 553, 2000 Ill. App. LEXIS 372 (4 Dist. 2000).

Related Adoption
Where natural mother surrendered child for adoption, then subsequently sought to adopt the child as a related child, judicial discretion would dictate that a social investigation be ordered to determine whether the best interests of the child would be served by allowing the adoption. Partington v. Department of Children & Family Servs., 91 Ill. App. 3d 205, 46 Ill. Dec. 656, 414 N.E.2d 540 (2 Dist. 1980).

Results

—Use as Evidence
The denial of consent to adoption based on the contents of agency's file alone was an excessive reaction by the agency, and exceeded the bounds of reasonableness. Bland v. Department of Children & Family Servs., 141 Ill. App. 3d 818, 96 Ill. Dec. 122, 490 N.E.2d 1327 (3 Dist. 1986).

LEGAL PERIODICALS

For article, "Baby Richard and Beyond: The Future for Adopted Children", see 18 N. Ill. U.L. Rev. 445 (1999).

750 ILCS 50/7 Process

Sec. 7. *Process.* A. All persons named in the petition for adoption or standby adoption, other than the petitioners and any party who has previously either denied being a parent pursuant to Section 12a of this Act [750 ILCS 50/12a] or whose rights have been terminated pursuant to Section 12a of this Act [750 ILCS 50/12a], but including the person sought to be adopted, shall be made parties defendant by name, and if the name or names of any such persons are alleged in the petition to be unknown such persons shall be made parties defendant under the name and style of "All whom it may concern". In all such actions petitioner or his attorney shall file, at the office of the clerk of the court in which the action is pending, an affidavit showing that the defendant resides or has gone out of this State, or on due inquiry cannot be found, or is concealed within this State, so that process cannot be served upon him, and stating the place of residence of the defendant, if known, or that upon diligent inquiry his place of residence cannot be ascertained, the clerk shall cause publication to be made in some newspaper published in the county in which the action is pending. If there is no newspaper published in that county, then the publication shall be in a newspaper published in an adjoining county in this State, having a circulation in the county in which such action is pending. In the event there is service on any of the parties by publication, the publication shall contain notice of pendency of the action, the name of the person to be adopted and the name of the parties to be served by publication, and the date on or after which default may be entered against such parties. Neither the name of petitioners nor the name of any party who has either surrendered said child, has given their consent to the adoption of the child, or whose parental rights have been terminated by a court of competent jurisdiction shall be included in the notice of publication. The Clerk shall also, within ten (10) days of the first publication of the notice, send a copy thereof by mail, addressed to each defendant whose place of residence is stated in such affidavit. The certificate of the Clerk that he sent the copies pursuant to this section is evidence that he has done so. Except as provided in this section pertaining to service by publication, all parties defendant shall be notified of the proceedings in the same manner as is now or may hereafter be required in other civil cases or proceedings. Any party defendant who is of age of 14 years or upward may waive service of process by entering an appearance in writing. The form to be used for publication shall be substantially as follows:

"ADOPTION NOTICE

STATE OF ILLINOIS)
) ss.
COUNTY OF ....)
Circuit Court of .... County.

In the matter of the Petition for the Adoption of ...., a .... male child. Adoption No. .... To .... (whom it may concern or the named parent) Take notice that a petition was filed in the Circuit Court of .... County, Illinois, for the adoption of a child named .... Now, therefore, unless you ...., and all whom it may concern, file your answer to the Petition in the action or otherwise file your appearance therein, in the said Circuit Court of ...., County, Room ...., ..., in the City of ...., Illinois, on or before the .... day of ...., a default may be entered against you at any time after that day and a judgment entered in accordance with the prayer of said Petition.

Dated, ..., Illinois, ..., Clerk. (Name and address of attorney for petitioners.)

B. A minor defendant who has been served in accordance with this Section may be defaulted in the same manner as any other defendant.

C. Notwithstanding any inconsistent provision of this or any other law, and in addition to the notice requirements of any law pertaining to persons other than those specified in this subsection, the persons entitled to notice that a petition has been filed under Section 5 of this Act [750 ILCS 50/5] shall include:

(a) any person adjudicated by a court in this State to be the father of the child;

(b) any person adjudicated by a court of another state or territory of the United States to be the father of the child, when a certified copy of the court order has been filed with the Putative Father Registry under Section 12.1 of this Act [750 ILCS 50/12.1];

(c) any person who at the time of the filing of the petition is registered in the Putative Father Registry under Section 12.1 of this Act [750 ILCS 50/12.1] as the putative father of the child;

(d) any person who is recorded on the child's birth certificate as the child's father;

(e) any person who is openly living with the child or the child's mother at the time the proceeding is initiated and who is holding himself out to be the child's father;

(f) any person who has been identified as the child's father by the mother in a written, sworn statement, including an Affidavit of Identification as specified under Section 11 of this Act [750 ILCS 50/11];

(g) any person who was married to the child's mother on the date of the child's birth or within 300 days prior to the child's birth.

The sole purpose of notice under this Section shall be to enable the person receiving notice to appear in the adoption proceedings to present evidence to the court relevant to the best interests of the child.

(Source: P.A. 84-452; 89-315, § 5; 91-572, § 5.)

Note.

This section was Ill.Rev.Stat., Ch. 40, para. 1509.

Effect of Amendments.

The 1995 amendment by P.A. 89-315, effective January 1, 1996, added subsection C.

The 1999 amendment by P.A. 91-572, effective January 1, 2000, inserted "or standby adoption" in the first sentence of subsection A.

CASE NOTES

Analysis

Constitutionality
—Putative Fathers
Registration

Constitutionality

—Putative Fathers

Putative fathers are not treated disparately under the Adoption Act and the Illinois Juvenile Court Act (705 ILCS 405/1-1 et seq.); the Adoption Act specifically states that it should be construed in concert with the Juvenile Court Act (705 ILCS 405/1-1 et seq.), and § 2-29 of the Juvenile Court Act (705 ILCS 405/2-29) incorporates by reference many of the provisions in the Adoption Act, including those with respect to notice and consent. In re K.J.R., 293 Ill. App. 3d 49, 227 Ill. Dec. 190, 687 N.E.2d 113 (1 Dist. 1997).

Registration

Because putative father failed to timely register with the Putative Father Registry and did not allege facts that would bring him within the exceptions to 750 ILCS 50/12.1(g), he waived the right to bring or maintain a parentage petition. In re K.J.R., 293 Ill. App. 3d 49, 227 Ill. Dec. 190, 687 N.E.2d 113 (1 Dist. 1997).

LEGAL PERIODICALS

For casenote, "Born to Lose: The Illinois 'Baby Richard' Case — How Examining His Father's Pre-Birth Conduct Might Have Led to a Different Ending for Richard," see 16 N. Ill. U.L. Rev. 543 (1996).

For note, "Incorporating Thwarted Putative Fathers into the Adoptive Scheme: Illinois Proposes a Solution after the 'Baby Richard' Case," 1996 U. Ill. L. Rev. 189.

RESEARCH REFERENCES

Required parties in adoption proceedings. 48 ALR4th 860.

750 ILCS 50/8 Consents to adoption and surrenders for purposes of adoption

Sec. 8. *Consents to adoption and surrenders for purposes of adoption.* (a) Except as hereinafter provided in this Section consents or surrenders shall be required in all cases, unless the person whose consent or surrender would otherwise be required shall be found by the court:

(1) to be an unfit person as defined in Section 1 of this Act [750 ILCS 50/1], by clear and convincing evidence; or

(2) not to be the biological or adoptive father of the child; or

(3) to have waived his parental rights to the child under Section 12a or 12.1 of this Act [750 ILCS 50/12a or 750 ILCS 50/12.1]; or

(4) to be the parent of an adult sought to be adopted; or

(5) to be the father of the child as a result of criminal sexual abuse or assault as defined under Article 12 of the Criminal Code of 1961 [720 ILCS 5/12-1 et seq.]; or

(6) to have been indicated for child sexual abuse as defined in the Abused and Neglected Child Reporting Act [325 ILCS 5/1 et seq.] that involved sexual penetration of the mother; or

(7) to be at least 5 years older than the mother and the mother was under the age 17 at the time of conception of the child to be adopted.

(b) Where consents are required in the case of an adoption of a minor child, the consents of the following persons shall be sufficient:

(1)(A) The mother of the minor child; and

(B) The father of the minor child, if the father:

(i) was married to the mother on the date of birth of the child or within 300 days before the birth of the child, except for a husband or former husband who has been found by a court of competent jurisdiction not to be the biological father of the child; or

(ii) is the father of the child under a judgment for adoption, an order of parentage, or an acknowledgment of parentage or paternity pursuant to subsection (a) of Section 5 of the Illinois Parentage Act of 1984 [750 ILCS 45/5]; or

(iii) in the case of a child placed with the adopting parents less than 6 months after birth, openly lived with the child, the child's biological mother, or both, and held himself out to be the child's biological father during the first 30 days following the birth of the child; or

(iv) in the case of a child placed with the adopting parents less than 6 months after birth, made a good faith effort to pay a reasonable amount of the expenses related to the birth of the child and to provide a reasonable amount for the financial support of the child before the expiration of 30 days following the birth of the child, provided that the court may consider in its determination all relevant circumstances, including the financial condition of both biological parents; or

(v) in the case of a child placed with the adopting parents more than 6 months after birth, has maintained substantial and continuous or repeated contact with the child as manifested by: (I) the payment by the father toward the support of the child of a fair and reasonable sum, according to the father's means, and either (II) the father's visiting the child at least monthly when physically and financially able to do so and not prevented from doing so by the person or authorized agency having lawful custody of the child, or (III) the father's regular communication with the child or with the person or agency having the care or custody of the child, when physically and financially unable to visit the child or prevented from doing so by the person or authorized agency having lawful custody of the child. The subjective intent of the father, whether expressed or otherwise unsupported by evidence of acts specified in this sub-paragraph as manifesting such intent, shall not preclude a determination that the father failed to maintain substantial and continuous or repeated contact with the child; or

(vi) in the case of a child placed with the adopting parents more than six months after birth, openly lived with the child for a period of six months within the one year period immediately preceding the placement of the child for adoption and openly held himself out to be the father of the child; or

(vii) has timely registered with Putative Father Registry, as provided in Section 12.1 of this Act [750 ILCS 50/12.1], and prior to the expiration of 30 days from the date of such registration, commenced legal proceedings to establish paternity under the Illinois Parentage Act of 1984 [750 ILCS 45/1 et seq.] or under the law of the jurisdiction of the child's birth; or

(2) The legal guardian of the person of the child, if there is no surviving parent; or

(3) An agency, if the child has been surrendered for adoption to such agency; or

(4) Any person or agency having legal custody of a child by court order if the parental rights of the parents have been judicially terminated, and the court having jurisdiction of the guardianship of the child has authorized the consent to the adoption; or

(5) The execution and verification of the petition by any petitioner who is also a parent of the child sought to be adopted shall be sufficient evidence of such parent's consent to the adoption.

(c) Where surrenders to an agency are required in the case of a placement for adoption of a minor child by an agency, the surrenders of the following persons shall be sufficient:

(1)(A) The mother of the minor child; and

(B) The father of the minor child, if the father:

(i) was married to the mother on the date of birth of the child or within 300 days before the birth of the child, except for a husband or former husband who has been found by a court of competent jurisdiction not to be the biological father of the child; or

(ii) is the father of the child under a judgment for adoption, an order of parentage, or an acknowledgment of parentage or paternity pursuant to subsection (a) of Section 5 of the Illinois Parentage Act of 1984 [750 ILCS 45/5]; or

(iii) in the case of a child placed with the adopting parents less than 6 months after birth, openly lived with the child, the child's biological mother, or both, and held himself out to be the child's biological father during the first 30 days following the birth of a child; or

(iv) in the case of a child placed with the adopting parents less than 6 months after birth, made a good faith effort to pay a reasonable amount of the expenses related to the birth of the child and to provide a reasonable amount for the financial support of the child before the expiration of 30 days following the birth of the child, provided that the court may consider in its determination all relevant circumstances, including the financial condition of both biological parents; or

(v) in the case of a child placed with the adopting parents more than six months after birth, has maintained substantial and continuous or repeated contact with the child as manifested by: (I) the payment by the father toward the support of the child of a fair and reasonable sum, according to the father's means, and either (II) the father's visiting the child at least monthly when physically and financially able to do so and not prevented from doing so by the person or authorized agency having lawful custody of the child or (III) the father's regular communication with the child or with the person or agency having the care or custody of the child, when physically and financially unable to visit the child or prevented from doing so by the person or authorized agency having lawful custody of the child. The subjective intent of the father, whether expressed or otherwise, unsupported by evidence of acts specified in this sub-paragraph as manifesting such intent, shall not preclude a determination that the father failed to maintain substantial and continuous or repeated contact with the child; or

(vi) in the case of a child placed with the adopting parents more than six months after birth, openly lived with the child for a period of six months within the one year period immediately preceding the placement of the child for adoption and openly held himself out to be the father of the child; or

(vii) has timely registered with the Putative Father Registry, as provided in Section 12.1 of this Act [750 ILCS 50/12.1], and prior to the expiration of 30 days from the date of such registration, commenced legal proceedings to establish paternity under the Illinois Parentage Act of 1984 [750 ILCS 45/1 et seq.], or under the law of the jurisdiction of the child's birth.

(d) In making a determination under subparagraphs (b)(1) and (c)(1), no showing shall be required of diligent efforts by a person or agency to encourage the father to perform the acts specified therein.

(e) In the case of the adoption of an adult, only the consent of such adult shall be required.

(Source: P.A. 84-1403; 88-550, § 975; 89-315, § 5; 89-641, § 35; 90-15, § 20; 91-357, § 262; 93-510, § 5.)

Note.

This section was Ill.Rev.Stat., Ch. 40, para. 1510.

Effect of Amendments.

The 1994 amendment by P.A. 88-550, effective July 3, 1994, added "and surrenders for purposes of adoption" at the end of the section catchline; rewrote subsection (a); in the introductory language of subsection (b) inserted "minor"; added the subdivision (b)(1)(A) designation; in subdivision (b)(1)(A) substituted "mother of the minor child; and" for "parents or"; added subdivision (b)(1)(B) and subsections (c) and (d); and redesignated former subsection (c) as present subsection (e).

The 1995 amendment by P.A. 89-315, effective January 1, 1996, in subdivisions (b)(1)(vii) and (c)(1)(B)(vii) substituted "prior to the expiration of 30 days from" for "within 30 days of".

The 1996 amendment by P.A. 89-641, effective August 9, 1996, in subdivisions (b)(B)(ii) and (c)(1)(B)(ii) substituted a comma for "or" preceding "an order" and added at the end "or an acknowledgment of parentage or paternity pursuant to subsection (a) of Section 5 of the Illinois Parentage Act of 1984".

The 1997 amendment by P.A. 90-15, effective June 13, 1997, in subdivision (a)(4) added "or" at the end; and added subdivision (a)(5).

The 1999 amendment by P.A. 91-357, effective July 29, 1999, made a stylistic change.

The 2003 amendment by P.A. 93-510, effective January 1, 2004, added subsections (a)(6) and (a)(7); and made a related change.

CASE NOTES

Analysis

Constitutionality
—Advice of Counsel Not Required
—Father of Illegitimate
—Mentally Retarded Parent
—Putative Fathers
In General
Abandonment
—Not Shown
Consent
—In General
—Condition Precedent
—Guardians
—Limitation
—Not Required
—Prior Law
—Refusal to Consent
Illustrative Cases
Jurisdiction
Legislative Intent
Marriage of Father and Mother
Petitions
—Allegation of Unfitness
—Failure to Allege Consent
Prerequisites to Adoption
Proof of Parentage
Selection of Adopting Parents
Standard of Review
Unfit Person
Unwed Father
—Procedural Safeguards
Waiver of Rights

Constitutionality

—Advice of Counsel Not Required

Signing of the consents to adoption without the advice of counsel did not constitute a violation of the equal protection and due process clauses of the United States and Illinois Constitutions; while it may be desirable for the natural parents of a child to have legal counsel prior to consenting to the adoption of the child, it was not constitutionally required, particularly in view of the safeguards contained in former section 8 of the Adoption Act (see now this section), which specified the form of the consent, and former section 10(F) (see now 750 ILCS 50/10), which requires all consents of this type to be acknowledged by a parent before a judge or other person designated or approved by the court. Hoffman v. Hoffman, 61 Ill. 2d 569, 338 N.E.2d 862 (1975).

—Father of Illegitimate

Former Ill.Rev.Stat., ch. 4, para. 9.1-1E and former Ill.Rev.Stat., ch. 4, para. 9.1-8 (see now 750 ILCS 50/1 and this section), which prevented the father of an illegitimate child from asserting any right to the child in adoption proceedings and denying the father of such a child custody in the absence of an attempt to adopt were unconstitutional and denied equal protection of the law. People ex rel. Slawek v. Covenant Children's Home, 52 Ill. 2d 20, 284 N.E.2d 291 (1972).

—Mentally Retarded Parent

Former subsection (e) of this section, so far as it pertained to the appointment of a guardian ad litem with power to consent to adoption for a parent who has been adjudged to be mentally retarded, it was in violation of the equal protection and due process clauses of the Fourteenth Amendment of the Constitution of the United States (U.S. Const., Amend. 14) as well as Article 1, § 2 of the Illinois Constitution (Ill.Const. (1970), Art. I, § 2). Helvey v. Rednour, 86 Ill. App. 3d 154, 41 Ill. Dec. 671, 408 N.E.2d 17 (5 Dist. 1980).

—Putative Fathers

Putative fathers are not treated disparately under the Adoption Act and the Illinois Juvenile Court Act (705 ILCS 405/1-1 et seq.); the Adoption Act specifically states that it should be construed in concert with the Juvenile Court Act (705 ILCS 405/1-1 et seq.), and § 2-29 of the Juvenile Court Act (705 ILCS 405/2-29 et seq.) incorporates by reference many of the provisions in the Adoption Act, including those with respect to notice and consent. In re K.J.R., 293 Ill. App. 3d 49, 227 Ill. Dec. 190, 687 N.E.2d 113 (1 Dist. 1997).

In General

The courts have no right to expand the terms of this statute. Bland v. Department of Children & Family Servs., 141 Ill. App. 3d 818, 96 Ill. Dec. 122, 490 N.E.2d 1327 (3 Dist. 1986).

When dealing with parental rights termination cases, it is not a question of searching for fixed standards or binding precedent; each case is sui generis. It is of little use to compare frequency of visits, cards, or gifts with the frequency in other cases. Blakey v. Blakey, 72 Ill. App. 3d 946, 29 Ill. Dec. 63, 391 N.E.2d 222 (4 Dist. 1979).

Under this section, a child may not be adopted without the consent of his parents unless his parents have been declared unfit persons. People v. Harvey, 61 Ill. App. 3d 344, 19 Ill. Dec. 37, 378 N.E.2d 538 (1 Dist. 1978).

Abandonment

—Not Shown

Considering respondent's testimony concerning child support, visitation, and other contacts with his son such as telephone calls, cards and gifts—much of which was corroborated and very little contradicted by petitioner—the trial court's finding of abandonment, one of the grounds by which lack of fitness may be demonstrated, was contrary to the manifest weight of the evidence. Estes v. Garrison, 93 Ill. App. 3d 670, 49 Ill. Dec. 97, 417 N.E.2d 787 (1 Dist. 1981).

Consent

—In General

Where the valid consents of the natural parents to an adoption by related persons have been executed and filed in such a proceeding, and petitioners are fit persons, there should be no occasion whatever for subsequently inquiring in a juvenile proceeding as to the fitness of those natural parents; their residual parental rights were already surrendered to the court by valid consents. Smith v. Smith, 38 Ill. App. 3d 217, 347 N.E.2d 292 (4 Dist. 1976).

It is important that consent should not be forced, but it is also important that the regret and misgiving which always arise after a decision born of emotional and moral conflict should not be permitted to create instability and confusion. In re Wojtkowiak, 14 Ill. App. 2d 344, 144 N.E.2d 760 (1 Dist. 1957).

Consent to adoption or excuse thereof must be in conformity with the mandatory requirements of the adoption statute and are jurisdictional. Oeth v. Erwin, 6 Ill. App. 2d 18, 126 N.E.2d 526 (4 Dist. 1955).

—Condition Precedent

A condition precedent to an adoption is either consent of the parent or a finding by the court that consent is not required for the reason of unfitness. In re Smith, 4 Ill. App. 3d 261, 280 N.E.2d 770 (1 Dist. 1972).

—Guardians

Children were available for adoption, and the parent whose parental rights had been terminated could not challenge the adoption once a year had passed from the entry of the adoption, where the parent had not sought to stay the termination of rights order, which had named a welfare agency as the children's guardian, the agency had consented to the foster parents' adoption petition, and an adoption decree had been properly entered. People v. Denise S., 202 Ill. 2d 522, 270 Ill. Dec. 30, 782 N.E.2d 224, 2002 Ill. LEXIS 964 (2002).

Consent (Cont'd)

—Guardians (Cont'd)

In order for the court to empower a guardian to consent to adoption without the consent of the natural parent, the natural parent must be found to be unfit and such unfitness must be proven by clear and convincing evidence. People v. Perez, 14 Ill. App. 3d 1019, 304 N.E.2d 109 (1 Dist. 1973); Green v. Department of Children & Family Servs., 131 Ill. App. 2d 952, 267 N.E.2d 505 (4 Dist. 1971).

—Limitation

A parent whose parental rights are about to be terminated may not execute consents in favor of his relatives in an attempt to control the placement of his children and to prevent the court from choosing the placement which the court believes is in the best interests of the child. In re L.R.B., 278 Ill. App. 3d 1091, 215 Ill. Dec. 950, 664 N.E.2d 347 (4 Dist. 1996), appeal denied, 168 Ill. 2d 591, 219 Ill. Dec. 564, 671 N.E.2d 731 (1996).

Father could not control the selection of adoptive parents of his child by executing a specific consent in their favor when that child was a ward of the court. In re L.R.B., 278 Ill. App. 3d 1091, 215 Ill. Dec. 950, 664 N.E.2d 347 (4 Dist. 1996), appeal denied, 168 Ill. 2d 591, 219 Ill. Dec. 564, 671 N.E.2d 731 (1996).

Consent of the natural parents is necessary for adoption of a child unless the parents are judged "unfit." In re Peterson, 112 Ill. 2d 48, 96 Ill. Dec. 690, 491 N.E.2d 1150 (1986).

—Not Required

The trial court correctly held that the testimony of credible witnesses concerning father's use of drugs and alcohol demonstrated that his lifestyle categorized him as being depraved; therefore, as father was properly found to be an unfit person in accordance with 750 ILCS 50/1(D)(b) and 750 ILCS 50/1(D)(i) of the Act, his consent to the adoption of baby was unnecessary. In re Casale, 266 Ill. App. 3d 656, 203 Ill. Dec. 135, 639 N.E.2d 174 (1 Dist. 1994).

Because respondent was specifically found unfit, his consent was not required for child's adoption and his parental rights were properly terminated. In re J.R.G., 247 Ill. App. 3d 104, 187 Ill. Dec. 169, 617 N.E.2d 377 (1 Dist. 1993).

Natural father's consent to adoption was not required where natural parents failed to enter into a common law marriage in Iowa before the child's birth and the formal marriage took place after the adoption petition was filed. Jambrone v. David, 16 Ill. 2d 32, 156 N.E.2d 569 (1959).

—Prior Law

Under former Ill.Rev. Stat., ch. 4, paras. 2-1, 3-7, and 4-1 (see now 750 ILCS 50/7 and 750 ILCS 50/11), it was an essential element of an acknowledgment taken in open court that the person who had signed the consent in some form of words admit the current validity and binding force of the instrument evidencing the parent's consent, a declaration by the parent signing an adoption consent, admitting the previous signing; the consent coupled with a denial that the parent currently consented to the adoption of her child was not such an acknowledgement in open court as required by the statute. Thompson v. Burns, 337 Ill. App. 354, 86 N.E.2d 155 (2 Dist. 1949).

—Refusal to Consent

When an agency withholds its consent to an adoption, the courts look to the reasonableness of the agency's refusal as the important factor in deciding whether the court will act in compliance with or opposition to, the agency's determination. Bland v. Department of Children & Family Servs., 141 Ill. App. 3d 818, 96 Ill. Dec. 122, 490 N.E.2d 1327 (3 Dist. 1986).

Where the court considers the refusal to consent to be arbitrary, capricious, or unreasonable and without merit, the adoption petitions are allowed or determined to be allowable. Bland v. Department of Children & Family Servs., 141 Ill. App. 3d 818, 96 Ill. Dec. 122, 490 N.E.2d 1327 (3 Dist. 1986).

An agency cannot deprive a court of its jurisdiction to review an adoption petition by merely refusing to give its consent. Stines v. Vaughn, 23 Ill. App. 3d 511, 319 N.E.2d 561 (4 Dist. 1974).

Where a child is born of her mother's prior marriage and the father consents to the adoption, but the mother opposes and contests the adoption, the evidence must show by its preponderance that the natural parent is unfit for one of the reasons set forth in the statute to authorize adoption without the parents' consent. Young v. Prather, 120 Ill. App. 2d 395, 256 N.E.2d 670 (4 Dist. 1970).

In a habeas corpus action against a foundling home and its administrator, to obtain custody of an infant which had been surrendered to the home with adoption rights, where petitioners charged that respondents abused their discretion by arbitrarily detaining the child and withholding final consent to adoption by them, aside from some vague, veiled accusations against the administrator of the home and assertions that she bore personal animosity toward them and general statements that respondents acted arbitrarily, and capriciously, the allegations of the petition were insufficient to justify intervention by the court, under former Ill.Rev.Stat., ch. 4, para. 9.1-1 H(a) (see now 750 ILCS 5/510), and former Ill.Rev.Stat., ch. 4, para. 9.1-8 (see now this section). Greco v. Chicago Foundlings Home, 38 Ill. 2d 289, 230 N.E.2d 865 (1967).

Illustrative Cases

Clear and convincing evidence supported the conclusion that father had not shown adequate interest and concern for his children, where his efforts to contact his children were not even minimal, he made no attempt to contact the Department of Children and Family Services (DCFS) to arrange visits with them or to inquire as to their welfare, and he never informed DCFS of his whereabouts while in prison, nor did he take the opportunity to contact DCFS during the six month period that he was not incarcerated. T.D. v. Baldwin, 268 Ill. App. 3d 239, 205 Ill. Dec. 708, 643 N.E.2d 1315 (1 Dist. 1994).

Where the unmarried father never lived with his child, contributed to the child's support in only three out of her some eleven and a half years of life, and waited about two years after she was adopted to begin his attack on the adoption proceedings, he was not entitled to retroactive application because such would allow any unwed father whose child was adopted in conformity with existing laws to contest the adoption of their children. In re Negron, 33 Ill. App. 3d 112, 337 N.E.2d 375 (1 Dist. 1975).

Jurisdiction

When the father failed to consent to the adoption of his child, it was then necessary to obtain jurisdiction of his person by following the provisions of the former Civil Practice Act (see now Code of Civil Procedure, 735 ILCS 5/1-101 et seq.). Markham v. Markham, 50 Ill. App. 3d 1061, 8 Ill. Dec. 70, 365 N.E.2d 308 (3 Dist. 1977).

Legislative Intent

The phrase "shall be found" in subsection (a) of this section is prospective and manifests a legislative intent that the court hold the hearing on fitness within the adoption proceeding following the filing of the petition to adopt. In re Filippelli, 207 Ill. App. 3d 813, 152 Ill. Dec. 725, 566 N.E.2d 412 (1 Dist. 1990).

Marriage of Father and Mother

It would be a repudiation of the public policy as declared by the legislature, and contrary to the best interest of the child, to allow a laggard putative father, by a marriage with the mother occurring at any time before the filing of a petition for adoption, to be vested with the right to control the adoption proceedings by either giving or refraining from giving his consent thereto. Simaner v. Simonick, 16 Ill. App. 2d 48, 147 N.E.2d 419 (1 Dist. 1957), aff'd, 15 Ill. 2d 568, 155 N.E.2d 555 (1959).

Petitions

—Allegation of Unfitness

If it is alleged that consent is not required because the person having the authority to consent is an unfit person, the ground of unfitness must also be alleged. In re Smith, 4 Ill. App. 3d 261, 280 N.E.2d 770 (1 Dist. 1972).

—Failure to Allege Consent

The fact that a petition for adoption failed to allege that the appropriate agency consented to the adoption of the infant did not deprive the trial court of its jurisdiction. Stines v. Vaughn, 23 Ill. App. 3d 511, 319 N.E.2d 561 (4 Dist. 1974).

Failure of petition to allege that the natural mother had consented to the adoption of her child was not fatal where the mother did consent to the adoption, her consent was filed of record in the

Petitions (Cont'd)

—Failure to Allege Consent (Cont'd)
proceedings, and the county court found in its decree that she had consented to the adoption of her minor child. Wolfner v. Bidwill, 44 Ill. App. 2d 77, 194 N.E.2d 1 (1 Dist. 1963).

Prerequisites to Adoption
Counseling by an attorney was not a prerequisite to valid parental consent under the Adoption Act (see now 750 ILCS 50/0.01 et seq.). People v. Kerwood, 44 Ill. App. 3d 1040, 3 Ill. Dec. 773, 359 N.E.2d 183 (1 Dist. 1976).

Only after proof of the existence of one of the statutory conditions precedent to adoption, either consent or unfitness, could the court properly consider the best interests of the child under former Ill.Rev.Stat., ch. 4, para. 9.1-8 (1975) (see now this section). Neal v. Burton, 43 Ill. App. 3d 294, 1 Ill. Dec. 946, 356 N.E.2d 1279 (5 Dist. 1976).

A finding of unfitness of a natural mother was required in the absence of consent on her part to the petition for adoption of her children. Shuman v. Shuman, 22 Ill. App. 3d 151, 319 N.E.2d 287 (3 Dist. 1974).

In an action on a petition for adoption, the petitioner must establish either that there has been a valid consent to the adoption or that consent is not required because the person of whom consent is normally required is, among other things, an unfit person. In re Smith, 4 Ill. App. 3d 261, 280 N.E.2d 770 (1 Dist. 1972).

Proof of Parentage
Where respondent failed to establish that he had sired the minor child, a divorce decree which required him to pay child support but which was obtained by misrepresenting to the divorce court that he was the biological father of the child did not give respondent the status of a parent, and he did not become vested with the rights of a natural parent to withhold consent to the child's adoption. In re Weller, 47 Ill. App. 3d 492, 5 Ill. Dec. 760, 362 N.E.2d 73 (3 Dist. 1977).

Selection of Adopting Parents
When a petition for adoption is approved by the court, the child becomes a ward of the court and custody of the child is determined by that court, and the selection of the adopting parents is beyond the control of the consenting parent. Cohen v. Janic, 57 Ill. App. 2d 309, 207 N.E.2d 89 (1 Dist. 1965).

Standard of Review
On a direct appeal from a decree of adoption, the decree must be supported by facts appearing in the evidence preserved in the record that the mother acknowledged her consent to the adoption of the child by the petitioners. Thompson v. Burns, 337 Ill. App. 354, 86 N.E.2d 155 (2 Dist. 1949).

Unfit Person
Evidence that the father had not made reasonable efforts to see or support his child provided the clear and convincing proof necessary to support a finding that the father was unfit and thus, his consent to adoption was not necessary. Jo Ellen J. v. John M. (In re L.T.M.), Ill. 2d , 291 Ill. Dec. 645, 824 N.E.2d 221, 2005 Ill. LEXIS 4 (2005).

State met its burden of proving by clear and convincing evidence that mother was unfit because of her failure to protect the minor from an environment injurious to his welfare; mother failed to protect minor's sibling from the father, admitted to beating the sibling herself, and failed to seek medical attention for the sibling after beating him. In re G.V., 292 Ill. App. 3d 301, 226 Ill. Dec. 303, 685 N.E.2d 406 (2 Dist. 1997).

The evidentiary standard in cases of parental unfitness is proof by clear and convincing evidence and the trial court's decision should not be disturbed on appeal unless contrary to the manifest weight of the evidence. Markham v. Markham, 91 Ill. App. 3d 1122, 47 Ill. Dec. 235, 414 N.E.2d 1351 (3 Dist. 1981).

Before mentally retarded mother could be deprived of her right to raise her child, a hearing had to be held to determine her fitness. Helvey v. Rednour, 86 Ill. App. 3d 154, 41 Ill. Dec. 671, 408 N.E.2d 17 (5 Dist. 1980).

The state interest in providing suitable homes for children and the administrative burden of conducting an additional hearing do not justify the termination of a parent's fundamental right in the absence of a showing of unfitness. Helvey v. Rednour, 86 Ill. App. 3d 154, 41 Ill. Dec. 671, 408 N.E.2d 17 (5 Dist. 1980).

Although, an adjudication that a parent is mentally retarded may not in and of itself render that parent unfit, evidence of such adjudication may be considered, along with all other pertinent evidence bearing upon the question of that parent's fitness. Helvey v. Rednour, 86 Ill. App. 3d 154, 41 Ill. Dec. 671, 408 N.E.2d 17 (5 Dist. 1980).

This Act contains no requirement that separate hearings be held in instances where the petition is for the adoption of a related child; therefore, the trial court is required to find that a parent is unfit, absent his consent, before considering the welfare of the child, nevertheless, these determinations may be made at a single hearing. Freeman v. Settle, 75 Ill. App. 3d 799, 31 Ill. Dec. 78, 393 N.E.2d 1385 (5 Dist. 1979).

The court recognized its responsibility to determine whether or not the father was an unfit parent before considering what placement would suit the best interest and welfare of the child since both determinations may be made at the same hearing, and the procedure followed by the trial court was proper. Freeman v. Settle, 75 Ill. App. 3d 799, 31 Ill. Dec. 78, 393 N.E.2d 1385 (5 Dist. 1979).

A primary purpose of this provision which defines "unfit" is to give greater protection to the best interests of the child. People v. Saadoon, 78 Ill. App. 3d 319, 33 Ill. Dec. 845, 397 N.E.2d 178 (1 Dist. 1979).

Unwed Father

—Procedural Safeguards
Adoptive parents cannot, once an invalid adoption is vacated, attempt to circumvent the rights afforded fathers under the Adoption Act by seeking a custody hearing under 750 ILCS 5/601 which, unlike the Adoption Act, could result in a father's being divested of his right to the care, custody and control of his child without being found unfit by clear and convincing evidence. In re Kirchner, 164 Ill. 2d 468, 208 Ill. Dec. 268, 649 N.E.2d 324 (1995), cert. denied, 515 U.S. 1152, 115 S. Ct. 2599, 132 L. Ed. 2d 846 (1995).

Where an unwed father is fit and willing to develop a relationship with and raise his child, but is prevented from doing so through deceit and an invalid adoption proceeding, that father is entitled to the care, custody and control of his child upon the subsequent vacatur of the invalid adoption; a hearing under 750 ILCS 5/601(b)(2) would be improper because it would contravene the safeguards afforded unwed fathers in the Adoption Act. In re Kirchner, 164 Ill. 2d 468, 208 Ill. Dec. 268, 649 N.E.2d 324 (1995), cert. denied, 515 U.S. 1152, 115 S. Ct. 2599, 132 L. Ed. 2d 846 (1995).

Waiver of Rights
Because putative father failed to timely register with the Putative Father Registry and did not allege facts that would bring him within the exceptions to 750 ILCS 50/12.1(g), he waived the right to bring or maintain a parentage petition. In re K.J.R., 293 Ill. App. 3d 49, 227 Ill. Dec. 190, 687 N.E.2d 113 (1 Dist. 1997).

LEGAL PERIODICALS

For article, "Baby Richard and Beyond: The Future for Adopted Children", see 18 N. Ill. U.L. Rev. 445 (1999).

For casenote, "Born to Lose: The Illinois 'Baby Richard' Case — How Examining His Father's Pre-Birth Conduct Might Have Led to a Different Ending for Richard," see 16 N. Ill. U.L. Rev. 543 (1996).

For note, "Incorporating Thwarted Putative Fathers into the Adoptive Scheme: Illinois Proposes a Solution after the 'Baby Richard' Case," 1996 U. Ill. L. Rev. 189.

For note, "Babies, Jessica, Richard and Emily: The Need for Legislative Reform of Adoption Laws," 70 Chi-Kent L. Rev. 1851 (1996).

For comment, "Rights of Unwed Fathers and the Best Interests of the Child: Can These Competing Interests be Harmonized? Illinois Putative Father Registry Provides an Answer," see 26 Loy. U. Chi. L.J. 703 (1995).

For article, "Survey of Illinois Law [1988-89]—Family Law," see 14 S. Ill. U. L.J. 1007 (1990).

For comment, "Terminating the Rights of Mentally Retarded Parents: Severing the Ties that Bind," see 22 J. Marshall L. Rev. 133 (1988-89).

For article, "Surrogate Parenthood: A Need for Legislative Direction," see 71 Ill. B.J. 412 (1983).

For note, "The Termination of Parental Rights: Lassiter and the New Illinois Termination Law," see 13 Loy. U. Chi. L.J. 135 (1981-82).

For comment, "Illegitimacy and the Rights of Unwed Fathers in Adoption Proceedings After Quillian v. Walcott," see 12 J. Marshall J. Prac. & Proc. 383 (1979).

RESEARCH REFERENCES

Natural parent's parental rights as affected by consent to child's adoption by other natural parent. 37 ALR4th 724.

Necessity and sufficiency of consent to adoption by spouse of adopting parent. 38 ALR4th 768.

Validity of agreement to pay expenses attendant on birth of child on condition that natural parents consent to adoption of child. 43 ALR4th 935.

Rights of unwed father to obstruct adoption of his child by withholding consent. 61 ALR5th 151.

Comment Note: Natural parent's indigence as precluding finding that failure to support child waived requirement of consent to adoption — general principles. 82 ALR5th 443.

Natural parent's indigence resulting from unemployment or underemployment as precluding finding that failure to support child waived requirement of consent to adoption. 83 ALR5th 375.

Natural Parent's Indigence as Precluding Finding That Failure to Support Child Waived Requirement of Consent to Adoption — Factors Other Than Employment Status. 84 ALR5th 191.

Parents' mental illness or mental deficiency as ground for termination of parental rights — Issues concerning guardian ad litem and counsel. 118 ALR5th 561.

Parents' mental illness or mental deficiency as ground for termination of parental rights — Applicability of Americans With Disabilities Act. 119 ALR5th 351.

Parents' mental illness or mental deficiency as ground for termination of parental rights — Evidentiary issues. 122 ALR5th 385.

750 ILCS 50/9 Time for taking a consent or surrender

Sec. 9. *Time for taking a consent or surrender.* A. A consent or a surrender taken not less than 72 hours after the birth of the child is irrevocable except as provided in Section 11 of this Act [750 ILCS 50/11].

B. No consent or surrender shall be taken within the 72 hour period immediately following the birth of the child.

C. A consent or a surrender may be taken from the father prior to the birth of the child. Such consent or surrender shall be revoked if, within 72 hours after the birth of the child, the father who gave such consent or surrender, notifies in writing the person, agency or court representative who took the surrender or consent or any individual representing or connected with such person, agency or court representative of the revocation of the consent or surrender.

D. Any consent or surrender taken in accordance with paragraph C above which is not revoked within 72 hours after the birth of the child is irrevocable except as provided in Section 11 of this Act [750 ILCS 50/11].

E. Consent may be given to a standby adoption by a parent whose consent is required pursuant to Section 8 of this Act [750 ILCS 50/8] to become effective when the consenting parent of the child dies or that parent requests that the final judgment of adoption be entered.
(Source: P.A. 78-854; 91-572, § 5; 93-732, § 5.)

Note.
This section was Ill.Rev.Stat., Ch. 40, para. 1511.

Effect of Amendments.
The 1999 amendment by P.A. 91-572, effective January 1, 2000, added paragraph E.

The 2004 amendment by P.A. 93-732, effective January 1, 2005, in subsection E twice deleted "terminally ill" before "parent", and inserted "consenting".

LEGAL PERIODICALS

For article, "Surrogate Parenthood: A Need for Legislative Direction," see 71 Ill. B. J. 412 (1983).

750 ILCS 50/10 Forms of consent and surrender; execution and acknowledgment thereof

Sec. 10. *Forms of consent and surrender; execution and acknowledgment thereof.* A. The form of consent required for the adoption of a born child shall be substantially as follows:

FINAL AND IRREVOCABLE CONSENT TO ADOPTION

I, ..., (relationship, e.g., mother, father, relative, guardian) of ...., a .... male child, state:

That such child was born on .... at ....

That I reside at ...., County of .... and State of ....

That I am of the age of .... years.

That I hereby enter my appearance in this proceeding and waive service of summons on me.

That I do hereby consent and agree to the adoption of such child.

That I wish to and understand that by signing this consent I do irrevocably and permanently give up all custody and other parental rights I have to such child.

That I understand such child will be placed for adoption and that I cannot under any circumstances, after signing this document, change my mind and revoke or cancel this consent or obtain or recover custody or any other rights over such child. That I have read and understand the above and I am signing it as my free and voluntary act.

Dated (insert date).

....
signature

If under Section 8 [750 ILCS 50/8] the consent of more than one person is required, then each such person shall execute a separate consent.

B. The form of consent required for the adoption of an unborn child shall be substantially as follows:

CONSENT TO ADOPTION OF UNBORN CHILD

I, ..., state:

That I am the father of a child expected to be born on or about .... to .... (name of mother).

That I reside at .... County of ...., and State of ....

That I am of the age of .... years.

That I hereby enter my appearance in such adoption proceeding and waive service of summons on me.

That I do hereby consent and agree to the adoption of such child, and that I have not previously executed a consent or surrender with respect to such child.

That I wish to and do understand that by signing this consent I do irrevocably and permanently give up all custody and other parental rights I have to such child, except that I have the right to revoke this consent by giving written notice of my revocation not later than 72 hours after the birth of the child.

That I understand such child will be placed for adoption and that, except as hereinabove provided, I cannot under any circumstances, after signing this document, change my mind and revoke or cancel this consent or obtain or recover custody or any other rights over such child.

That I have read and understand the above and I am signing it as my free and voluntary act.

Dated (insert date).

....

B-5.(1) The parent of a child may execute a consent to standby adoption by a specified person or persons. A consent under this subsection B-5 shall be acknowledged by a parent pursuant to subsection H and subsection K of this Section. The form of consent required for the standby adoption of a born child effective at a future date when the consenting parent of the child dies or requests that a final judgment of adoption be entered shall be substantially as follows:

FINAL AND IRREVOCABLE CONSENT TO STANDBY ADOPTION

I, ... (relationship, e.g. mother or father) of .... a .... male child, state:

That the child was born on .... at ....

That I reside at ...., County of ...., and State of ....

That I am of the age of .... years.

That I hereby enter my appearance in this proceeding and waive service of summons on me in this action only.

That I do hereby consent and agree to the standby adoption of the child, and that I have not previously executed a consent or surrender with respect to the child.

That I wish to and understand that by signing this consent I do irrevocably and permanently give up all custody and other parental rights I have to the child, effective upon (my death) (the child's other parent's death) or upon (my) (the other parent's) request for the entry of a final judgment for adoption if .... (specified person or persons) adopt my child.

That I understand that until (I die) (the child's other parent dies), I retain all legal rights and obligations concerning the child, but at the time, I irrevocably give all custody and other parental rights to .... (specified person or persons).

I understand my child will be adopted by .... (specified person or persons) only and that I cannot, under any circumstances, after signing this document, change my mind and revoke or cancel this consent or obtain or recover custody or any other rights over my child if .... (specified person or persons) adopt my child.

I understand that this consent to standby adoption is valid only if the petition for standby adoption is filed and that if .... (specified person or persons), for any reason, cannot or will not file a petition for standby adoption or if his, her, or their petition for standby adoption is denied, then this consent is void. I have the right to notice of any other proceeding that could affect my parental rights.

That I have read and understand the above and I am signing it as my free and voluntary act.

Dated (inserted date).

....

If under Section 8 [750 ILCS 50/8] the consent of more than one person is required, then each such person shall execute a separate consent. A separate consent shall be executed for each child.

(2) If the parent consents to a standby adoption by 2 specified persons, then the form shall contain 2 additional paragraphs in substantially the following form:

If .... (specified persons) obtain a judgment of dissolution of marriage before the judgment for adoption is entered, then .... (specified person) shall adopt my child. I understand that I cannot change my mind and revoke this consent or obtain or recover custody of my child if .... (specified persons) obtain a judgment of dissolution of marriage and .... (specified person) adopts my child. I understand that I cannot change my mind and revoke this consent if .... (specified persons) obtain a judgment of dissolution of marriage before the adoption is final. I understand that this consent to adoption has no effect on who will get custody of my child if .... (specified persons) obtain a judgment of dissolution of marriage after the adoption is final. I understand that if either .... (specified persons) dies before the petition to adopt my child is granted, then the surviving person may adopt my child. I understand that I cannot change my mind and revoke this consent or obtain or recover custody of my child if the surviving person adopts my child.

A consent to standby adoption by specified persons on this form shall have no effect on a court's determination of custody or visitation under the Illinois Marriage and Dissolution of Marriage Act [750 ILCS 5/101 et seq.] if the marriage of the specified persons is dissolved before the adoption is final.

(3) The form of the certificate of acknowledgement for a Final and Irrevocable Consent for Standby Adoption shall be substantially as follows:

STATE OF .... }
COUNTY OF .... } ss.

I, ... (name of Judge or other person) .... (official title, name, and address), certify that ...., personally known to me to be the same person whose name is subscribed to the foregoing Final and Irrevocable Consent to Standby Adoption, appeared before me this day in person and acknowledged that (she)(he) signed and delivered the consent as (her)(his) free and voluntary act, for the specified purpose.

I have fully explained that this consent to adoption is valid only if the petition to adopt is filed, and that if the specified person or persons, for any reason, cannot or will not adopt the child or if the adoption petition is denied, then this consent will be void. I have fully explained that if the specified person or persons adopt the child, by signing this consent (she)(he) is irrevocably and permanently relinquishing all parental rights to the child, and (she)(he) has stated that such is (her)(his) intention and desire.

Dated (insert date).

Signature ....

(4) If a consent to standby adoption is executed in this form, the consent shall be valid only if the specified person or persons adopt the child. The consent shall be void if:

(a) the specified person or persons do not file a petition for standby adoption of the child; or

(b) a court denies the standby adoption petition.

The parent shall not need to take further action to revoke the consent if the standby adoption by the specified person or persons does not occur, notwithstanding the provisions of Section 11 of this Act [750 ILCS 50/11].

C. The form of surrender to any agency given by a parent of a born child who is to be subsequently placed for adoption shall be substantially as follows and shall contain such other facts and statements as the particular agency shall require.

FINAL AND IRREVOCABLE SURRENDER FOR PURPOSES OF ADOPTION

I, ... (relationship, e.g., mother, father, relative, guardian) of ...., a .... male child, state:

That such child was born on ...., at ....

That I reside at ...., County of ...., and State of ....

That I am of the age of .... years.

That I do hereby surrender and entrust the entire custody and control of such child to the .... (the "Agency"), a (public) (licensed) child welfare agency with its principal office in the City of ...., County of .... and State of ...., for the purpose of enabling it to care for and supervise the care of such child, to place such child for adoption and to consent to the legal adoption of such child.

That I hereby grant to the Agency full power and authority to place such child with any person or persons it may in its sole discretion select to become the adopting parent or parents and to consent to the legal adoption of such child by such person or persons; and to take any and all measures which, in the judgment of the Agency, may be for the best interests of such child, including authorizing medical, surgical and dental care and treatment including inoculation and anaesthesia for such child.

That I wish to and understand that by signing this surrender I do irrevocably and permanently give up all custody and other parental rights I have to such child.

That I understand I cannot under any circumstances, after signing this surrender, change my mind and revoke or cancel this surrender or obtain or recover custody or any other rights over such child.

That I have read and understand the above and I am signing it as my free and voluntary act.

Dated (insert date).

....

D. The form of surrender to an agency given by a parent of an unborn child who is to be subsequently placed for adoption shall be substantially as follows and shall contain such other facts and statements as the particular agency shall require.

SURRENDER OF UNBORN CHILD FOR PURPOSES OF ADOPTION

I, ... (father), state:

That I am the father of a child expected to be born on or about .... to .... (name of mother).

That I reside at ...., County of ...., and State of ....

That I am of the age of .... years.

That I do hereby surrender and entrust the entire custody and control of such child to the .... (the "Agency"), a (public) (licensed) child welfare agency with its principal office in the City of ...., County of .... and State of ...., for the purpose of enabling it to care for and supervise the care of such child, to place such child for adoption and to consent to the legal adoption of such child, and that I have not previously executed a consent or surrender with respect to such child.

That I hereby grant to the Agency full power and authority to place such child with any person or persons it may in its sole discretion select to become the adopting parent or parents and to consent to the legal adoption of such child by such person or persons; and to take any and all measures which, in the judgment of the Agency, may be for the best interests of such child, including authorizing medical, surgical and dental care and treatment, including inoculation and anaesthesia for such child.

That I wish to and understand that by signing this surrender I do irrevocably and permanently give up all custody and other parental rights I have to such child.

That I understand I cannot under any circumstances, after signing this surrender, change my mind and revoke or cancel this surrender or obtain or recover custody or any other rights over such child, except that I have the right to revoke this surrender by giving written notice of my revocation not later than 72 hours after the birth of such child.

That I have read and understand the above and I am signing it as my free and voluntary act.

Dated (insert date).

....

E. The form of consent required from the parents for the adoption of an adult, when such adult elects to obtain such consent, shall be substantially as follows:

CONSENT

I, ..., (father) (mother) of ...., an adult, state:

That I reside at ...., County of .... and State of ....

That I do hereby consent and agree to the adoption of such adult by .... and ....

Dated (insert date).

....

F. The form of consent required for the adoption of a child of the age of 14 years or upwards, or of an adult, to be given by such person, shall be substantially as follows:

CONSENT

I, ..., state:

That I reside at ...., County of .... and State of .... That I am of the age of .... years. That I consent and agree to my adoption by .... and ....

Dated (insert date).

....

G. The form of consent given by an agency to the adoption by specified persons of a child previously surrendered to it shall set forth that the agency has the authority to execute such consent. The form of consent given by a guardian of the person of a child sought to be adopted, appointed by a court of competent jurisdiction, shall set forth the facts of such appointment and the authority of the guardian to execute such consent.

H. A consent (other than that given by an agency, or guardian of the person of the child sought to be adopted appointed by a court of competent jurisdiction) shall be acknowledged by a parent before the presiding judge of the court in which the petition for adoption has been, or is to be filed or before any other judge or hearing officer designated or subsequently approved by the court, or the circuit clerk if so authorized by the presiding judge or, except as otherwise provided in this Act, before a representative of the Department of Children and Family Services or a licensed child welfare agency, or before social service personnel under the jurisdiction of a court of competent jurisdiction, or before social service personnel of the Cook County Department of Supportive Services designated by the presiding judge.

I. A surrender, or any other document equivalent to a surrender, by which a child is surrendered to an agency shall be acknowledged by the person signing such surrender, or other document, before a judge or hearing officer or the clerk of any court of record, either in this State or any other state of the United States, or before a representative of an agency or before any other person designated or approved by the presiding judge of the court in which the petition for adoption has been, or is to be, filed.

J. The form of the certificate of acknowledgment for a consent, a surrender, or any other document equivalent to a surrender, shall be substantially as follows:

STATE OF .... }
} ss.
COUNTY OF .... }

I, ... (Name of judge or other person), ... (official title, name and location of court or status or position of other person), certify that ...., personally known to me to be the same person whose name is subscribed to the foregoing (consent) (surrender), appeared before me this day in person and acknowledged that (she) (he) signed and delivered such (consent) (surrender) as (her) (his) free and voluntary act, for the specified purpose.

I have fully explained that by signing such (consent) (surrender) (she) (he) is irrevocably relinquishing all parental rights to such child or adult and (she) (he) has stated that such is (her) (his) intention and desire.

Dated (insert date).

Signature ....

K. When the execution of a consent or a surrender is acknowledged before someone other than a judge or the clerk of a court of record, such other person shall have his signature on the certificate acknowledged before a notary public, in form substantially as follows:

STATE OF .... }
} ss.
COUNTY OF .... }

I, a Notary Public, in and for the County of ...., in the State of ...., certify that ...., personally known to me to be the same person whose name is subscribed to the foregoing certificate of acknowledgment, appeared before me in person and acknowledged that (she) (he) signed such certificate as (her) (his) free and voluntary act and that the statements made in the certificate are true.

Dated (insert date).

Signature .... Notary Public
(official seal)

There shall be attached a certificate of magistracy, or other comparable proof of office of the notary public satisfactory to the court, to a consent signed and acknowledged in another state.

L. A surrender or consent executed and acknowledged outside of this State, either in accordance with the law of this State or in accordance with the law of the place where executed, is valid.

M. Where a consent or a surrender is signed in a foreign country, the execution of such consent shall be acknowledged or affirmed in a manner conformable to the law and procedure of such country.

N. If the person signing a consent or surrender is in the military service of the United States, the execution of such consent or surrender may be acknowledged before a commissioned officer and the signature of such officer on such certificate shall be verified or acknowledged before a notary public or by such other procedure as is then in effect for such division or branch of the armed forces.

O. (1) The parent or parents of a child in whose interests a petition under Section 2-13 of the Juvenile Court Act of 1987 [705 ILCS 405/2-13] is pending may, with the approval of the designated representative of the Department of Children and Family Services, execute a consent to adoption by a specified person or persons:

(a) in whose physical custody the child has resided for at least 6 months; or

(b) in whose physical custody at least one sibling of the child who is the subject of this consent has resided for at least 6 months, and the child who is the subject of this consent is currently residing in this foster home; or

(c) in whose physical custody a child under one year of age has resided for at least 3 months.

A consent under this subsection O shall be acknowledged by a parent pursuant to subsection H and subsection K of this Section.

(2) The consent to adoption by a specified person or persons shall have the caption of the proceeding in which it is to be filed and shall be substantially as follows:

FINAL AND IRREVOCABLE CONSENT TO ADOPTION BY A SPECIFIED PERSON OR PERSONS

I, ..., the .... (mother or father) of a .... male child, state:

1. My child .... (name of child) was born on (insert date) at .... Hospital in .... County, State of ....

2. I reside at ...., County of .... and State of ....

3. I, ..., am .... years old.

4. I enter my appearance in this action to adopt my child by the person or persons specified herein by me and waive service of summons on me in this action only.

5. I consent to the adoption of my child by .... (specified person or persons) only.

6. I wish to sign this consent and I understand that by signing this consent I irrevocably and permanently give up all parental rights I have to my child if my child is adopted by .... (specified person or persons).

7. I understand my child will be adopted by .... (specified person or persons) only and that I cannot under any circumstances, after signing this document, change my mind and revoke or cancel this consent or obtain or recover custody or any other rights over my child if .... (specified person or persons) adopt my child.

8. I understand that this consent to adoption is valid only if the petition to adopt is filed within one year from the date that I sign it and that if .... (specified person or persons), for any reason, cannot or will not file a petition to adopt my child within that one year period or if their adoption petition is denied, then this consent will be voidable after one year upon the timely filing of my motion. If I file this motion before the filing of the petition for adoption, I understand that the court shall revoke this specific consent. I have the right to notice of any other proceeding that could affect my parental rights, except for the proceeding for .... (specified person or persons) to adopt my child.

9. I have read and understand the above and I am signing it as my free and voluntary act.

Dated (insert date).

....

Signature of parent

(3) If the parent consents to an adoption by 2 specified persons, then the form shall contain 2 additional paragraphs in substantially the following form:

10. If .... (specified persons) get a divorce before the petition to adopt my child is granted, then .... (specified person) shall adopt my child. I understand that I cannot change my mind and revoke this consent or obtain or recover custody over my child if .... (specified persons) divorce and .... (specified person) adopts my child. I understand that I cannot change my mind and revoke this consent or obtain or recover custody over my child if .... (specified persons) divorce after the adoption is final. I understand that this consent to adoption has no effect on who will get custody of my child if they divorce after the adoption is final.

11. I understand that if either .... (specified persons) dies before the petition to adopt my child is granted, then the surviving person can adopt my child. I understand that I cannot change my mind and revoke this consent or obtain or recover custody over my child if the surviving person adopts my child.

A consent to adoption by specified persons on this form shall have no effect on a court's determination of custody or visitation under the Illinois Marriage and Dissolution of Marriage Act if the marriage of the specified persons is dissolved after the adoption is final.

(4) The form of the certificate of acknowledgement for a Final and Irrevocable Consent for Adoption by a Specified Person or Persons shall be substantially as follows:

STATE OF ....)
) ss.
COUNTY OF ....)

I, ... (Name of Judge or other person), ... (official title, name, and address), certify that ...., personally known to me to be the same person whose name is subscribed to the foregoing Final and Irrevocable Consent for Adoption by a Specified Person or Persons, appeared before me this day in person and acknowledged that (she) (he) signed and delivered the consent as (her) (his) free and voluntary act, for the specified purpose.

I have fully explained that this consent to adoption is valid only if the petition to adopt is filed within one year from the date that it is signed, and that if the specified person or persons, for any reason, cannot or will not adopt the child or if the adoption petition is denied, then this consent will be voidable after one year upon the timely filing of a motion by the parent to revoke the consent. I explained that if this motion is filed before the filing of the petition for adoption, the court shall revoke this specific consent. I have fully explained that if the specified person or persons adopt the child, by signing this consent this parent is irrevocably and permanently relinquishing all parental rights to the child, and this parent has stated that such is (her) (his) intention and desire.

Dated (insert date).

....

Signature

(5) If a consent to adoption by a specified person or persons is executed in this form, the following provisions shall apply. The consent shall be valid only if that specified person or persons adopt the child. The consent shall be voidable after one year if:

(a) the specified person or persons do not file a petition to adopt the child within one year after the consent is signed and the parent files a timely motion to revoke this consent. If this motion is filed before the filing of the petition for adoption the court shall revoke this consent; or

(b) a court denies the adoption petition; or

(c) the Department of Children and Family Services Guardianship Administrator determines that the specified person or persons will not or cannot complete the adoption, or in the best interests of the child should not adopt the child.

Within 30 days of the consent becoming void, the Department of Children and Family Services Guardianship Administrator shall make good faith attempts to notify the parent in writing and shall give written notice to the court and all additional parties in writing that the adoption has not occurred or will not occur and that the consent is void. If the adoption by a specified person or persons does not occur, no proceeding for termination of parental rights shall be brought unless the biological parent who executed the consent to adoption by a specified person or persons has been notified of the proceeding pursuant to Section 7 of this Act [750 ILCS 50/7] or subsection (4) of Section 2-13 of the Juvenile Court Act of 1987 [705 ILCS 405/2-13]. The parent shall not need to take further action to revoke the consent if the specified adoption does not occur, notwithstanding the provisions of Section 11 of this Act [750 ILCS 50/11].

(6) The Department of Children and Family Services is authorized to promulgate rules necessary to implement this subsection O.

(7) The Department shall collect and maintain data concerning the efficacy of specific consents. This data shall include the number of specific consents executed and their outcomes, including but not limited to the number of children adopted pursuant to the consents, the number of children for whom adoptions are not completed, and the reason or reasons why the adoptions are not completed.

(Source: P.A. 84-550; 89-704, § 5; 90-443, § 20; 90-608, § 40; 90-655, § 174; 91-357, § 262; 91-572, § 5; 92-320, § 10; 93-732, § 5.)

Note.

This section was Ill.Rev.Stat., Ch. 40, para. 1512.

Illinois Administrative Code.

See 89 Illinois Administrative Code, § 309.70.

Effect of Amendments.

The 1996 amendment by P.A. 89-704, effective July 1, 1997 as amended by P.A. 90-443, added subsection O.

The 1998 amendment by P.A. 90-608, effective June 30, 1998, deleted an ending parenthesis at the end of the section heading; inserted "or hearing officer" in subsections H and I; and made stylistic changes in the form in subsection K.

The 1998 amendment by P.A. 90-655, effective July 30, 1998, deleted an ending parenthesis at the end of the section heading; and in subsection K, in the first paragraph of the form, inserted "of ......" following "County" and "State", and in the second paragraph substituted "Dated .... 19..." for "Dated 19 ".

The 1999 amendment by P.A. 91-357, effective July 29, 1999, changed the date blanks in the forms and inserted a signature line in the forms in subsections A., E., J. and K.

The 1999 amendment by P.A. 91-572, effective January 1, 2000, changed the date blanks in the forms; added a signature line at the end of the forms in subsections A., E., and J.; and inserted subsection B-5;

The 2001 amendment by P.A. 92-320, effective January 1, 2002, in subsections O(1)(a) and O(1)(b) substituted "6 months" for "one year"; in subsection O(2), in item 8 of the form and in the last paragraph of subsection O(4), substituted "voidable after one year upon the timely filing of a motion by the parent to revoke the consent. I explained that if this motion is filed before the filing of the petition for adoption, the court shall revoke this specific consent" for "void"; in the last paragraph of subsection O(4) substituted "this parent" for "(she)(he)" in two places; at the end of subsection O(5), substituted "voidable after one year" for "void"; and, in subsection O(5)(a), inserted "and the parent files a timely motion to revoke this consent. If this motion is filed before the filing of the petition for adoption the court shall revoke this consent" following "signed".

The 2004 amendment by P.A. 93-732, effective January 1, 2005, in subsection B-5, in the first paragraph substituted "consenting" for "terminally ill", deleted "That (I am terminally ill) (the child's other parent is terminally ill)" from the Standby Adoption form and substituted "other" for "terminally ill" from the paragraph beginning "That I wish".

CASE NOTES

Analysis

Constitutionality
—Advice of Counsel Not Required
Acknowledgements
—Prior Law
—Proper
Burden of Proof
Compliance
Consent
—General Surrender
—Not Valid
—Proper Form
—Third-Party Beneficiary
—Voidable
Construction
Fraud
—Not Shown
Mental Incompetence
Taking of Consent or Surrender
Unenforceable Agreement
Unfitness
—Consolidated Hearings
Waiver

Constitutionality

This section does not impermissibly delegate the right to terminate parental rights to a representative of a child welfare agency, especially as a natural parent retains an opportunity to have a court review the voluntariness of his or her surrender. Meza v. Rodriguez, 305 Ill. App. 3d 777, 239 Ill. Dec. 233, 713 N.E.2d 764 (2 Dist. 1999).

—Advice of Counsel Not Required

Signing of the consents to adoption without the advice of counsel did not constitute a violation of the equal protection and due process clauses of the United States and Illinois Constitutions; while it may be desirable for the natural parents of a child to have legal counsel prior to consenting to the adoption of the child, it was not constitutionally required, particularly in view of the safeguards contained in former section 8 of the Adoption Act (see now 750 ILCS 50/8), which specified the form of the consent and former Ill.Rev.Stat., ch. 4, para. 9.1-10(F) (see now this section), which requires all consents of this type to be acknowledged by a parent before a judge or other person designated or approved by the court. Hoffman v. Hoffman, 61 Ill. 2d 569, 338 N.E.2d 862 (1975).

Acknowledgements

—Prior Law

Where the consent filed with an adoption petition was not in compliance with the mandatory requirements of the former Adoption Act (see now 750 ILCS 50/0.01 et seq.) requiring the acknowledging or witnessing of the signing of the consent by mother, the purported consent furnished no valid ground or reason for a finding by the court that the mother had consented to the adoption of her child. Thompson v. Burns, 337 Ill. App. 354, 86 N.E.2d 155 (2 Dist. 1949).

—Proper

A certificate of acknowledgment was adequate, even though it deviated in two ways from the statutory language contained in subsection (J), as the form was in substantial compliance with the subsection. Meza v. Rodriguez, 305 Ill. App. 3d 777, 239 Ill. Dec. 233, 713 N.E.2d 764 (2 Dist. 1999).

Under former Ill.Rev.Stat., ch. 4, para. 9.1-10 (see now this section), where the order entered appointing a guardian and authorizing her to consent to the adoption of the children found that the mother signed the consents before the court, there was no reason to question the validity of the manner in which consents to adoption were acknowledged. In re Jennings, 68 Ill. 2d 125, 11 Ill. Dec. 256, 368 N.E.2d 864 (1977).

Burden of Proof

A court should not set aside a consent or a surrender executed in accordance with the former Adoption Act (Ill.Rev.Stat., ch. 4, para. 9.1-10) (see now this section) unless the one seeking to invalidate the document proves by clear and convincing evidence that its execution was procured by fraud or duress; the natural mother did not sustain this burden of proof. Regenold v. Baby Fold, Inc., 68 Ill. 2d 419, 12 Ill. Dec. 151, 369 N.E.2d 858 (1977).

Compliance

While a liberal rule of construction applied under the former Adoption Act (see now 750 ILCS 50/0.01 et seq.), substantial compliance with the suggested forms of consent and surrender was required. Chiapelli ex rel. Ashton v. Viviano, 225 Ill. App. 3d 1026, 168 Ill. Dec. 84, 589 N.E.2d 198 (5 Dist. 1992).

A court order purporting to memorialize the termination of the putative father's parental rights, which met none of the formalities of the consent and surrender forms and did not refer to any such documents, did not terminate his parental rights, and the father was open to paternity and support suits. Chiapelli ex rel. Ashton v. Viviano, 225 Ill. App. 3d 1026, 168 Ill. Dec. 84, 589 N.E.2d 198 (5 Dist. 1992).

Only substantial compliance with this Act is required regarding the forms for consents and surrenders for adoption; exact conformity is not mandatory for the form of the consent if the irrevocable nature of the consent to adoption was made sufficiently clear and if the parents understood the consequences of their acts. Kathy O. v. Counseling & Family Servs., 107 Ill. App. 3d 920, 63 Ill. Dec. 764, 438 N.E.2d 695 (3 Dist. 1982).

Under a prior similar provision, even though the names of the adopting parents may have been omitted from the adoption consent form, the form was acceptable where it substantially complied with the requirements of the form of consent. Cohen v. Janic, 57 Ill. App. 2d 309, 207 N.E.2d 89 (1 Dist. 1965).

Consent

—General Surrender

Consent by parents of child to permit the child's aunt and uncle to adopt the child was specific to the case it was prepared for, and did not act as a general surrender, so as to permit the filing of adoption petition by nonrelatives. Johnson v. Burnett, 182 Ill. App. 3d 574, 131 Ill. Dec. 517, 538 N.E.2d 892 (3 Dist. 1989).

—Not Valid

A mother's direct consent to adopt by her mother under subsection (Q)(1) was invalid since: (1) subparagraph (a) was inapplicable because the child at issue was never in the grandmother's physical custody, (2) subparagraph (b) was inapplicable because, although the grandmother eventually had custody of the child's half-brother, she did not have that custody at the time the consent was signed, and (3) subparagraph (c) was inapplicable because the child was not 'child under one year of age" at any pertinent time and never resided with the grandmother for three months. Bonnie S.P. v. Phillip P., 313 Ill. App. 3d 301, 246 Ill. Dec. 180, 729 N.E.2d 553, 2000 Ill. App. LEXIS 372 (4 Dist. 2000).

Where the consent by the natural father was executed in Michigan and was not acknowledged; it was the consent document, not a certificate of acknowledgement, that was notarized; moreover, the requirement of a certificate of magistracy was not met; therefore the consent was not acknowledged by the natural father as his free and voluntary act and was not valid. Flangel v. Flangel, 87 Ill. App. 3d 1100, 42 Ill. Dec. 906, 409 N.E.2d 521 (2 Dist. 1980).

—Proper Form

Where children were not the subject of currently pending petitions for adoption, but were to be placed for future adoption, under former Ill.Rev.Stat., ch. 4, para. 9.1-10 (see now this section), the proper form for parental consent was the surrender form. People v. Kerwood, 44 Ill. App. 3d 1040, 3 Ill. Dec. 773, 359 N.E.2d 183 (1 Dist. 1976).

—Third-Party Beneficiary

The sister of the biological mother of the child at issue did not have standing as a third-party beneficiary to specifically enforce the terms of an alleged oral contract of adoption between an adoption agency and the biological mother which provided that the child would be adopted by the sister since: (1) the biological mother's

Consent (Cont'd)

—Third-Party Beneficiary (Cont'd)

surrender of parental rights gave the adoption agency the right to place the child with any person selected by the agency; and (2) the biological mother had no power to execute a consent to adoption as the child was a ward of the court when she signed the surrender. Doe v. Noe, 317 Ill. App. 3d 419, 251 Ill. Dec. 103, 739 N.E.2d 1036, 2000 Ill. App. LEXIS 922 (4 Dist. 2000), cert. denied, 535 U.S. 932, 122 S. Ct. 1308, 152 L. Ed. 2d 218 (2002).

—Voidable

Subsection (A) of this section must be read to provide for irrevocable consent to a specific adoption only; when the circuit court denies the petition for adoption, the natural mother's consent to an irrevocable termination of her parental rights becomes voidable. Nees v. Doan, 185 Ill. App. 3d 122, 133 Ill. Dec. 180, 540 N.E.2d 1046 (4 Dist. 1989).

Construction

The difference between consent under subsection (A) of this section and surrender under subsection (C) of this section is that the latter contains language indicating the child is surrendered to an agency for adoption at the discretion of the agency, and the former does not contain this language and indicates the parent is giving consent to a specific adoption. Nees v. Doan, 185 Ill. App. 3d 122, 133 Ill. Dec. 180, 540 N.E.2d 1046 (4 Dist. 1989).

Where the father completed a "consent to adoption" form for relatives to adopt his son, but such adoption did not occur, the father's completion of form did not surrender his rights so as to allow the placement of his son with others unknown. People v. Mitchell, 115 Ill. App. 3d 169, 70 Ill. Dec. 895, 450 N.E.2d 368 (5 Dist. 1983).

By providing different forms for different routes of adoption, the legislature did not intend that no distinction be drawn between the different forms and that a consent to adoption be interchangeable with a surrender to an agency. People v. Mitchell, 115 Ill. App. 3d 169, 70 Ill. Dec. 895, 450 N.E.2d 368 (5 Dist. 1983).

Fraud

—Not Shown

Acceptance of surrender from a person subject to the assorted pressures that faced her, did not rise to the level of fraud. Regenold v. Baby Fold, Inc., 68 Ill. 2d 419, 12 Ill. Dec. 151, 369 N.E.2d 858 (1977).

Mental Incompetence

Mother's petition brought pursuant to former section 72 of chapter 110 (see now 735 ILCS 5/2-1401) was properly denied by the trial court where she sought to vacate surrender of her parental rights made pursuant to former section 9.1-11 of chapter 4 (see now 750 ILCS 50/12) where she claimed mental incompetence at the time of the surrender brought on by taking pills prescribed for a cerebral disturbance reflected by an EEG, a recent abortion and a long history of psychiatric illness and where there was no allegation that these facts were not known to the court at the time the surrender was executed and the order entered. In re Keiss, 40 Ill. App. 3d 1071, 353 N.E.2d 13 (3 Dist. 1976).

A surrender for adoption executed by a mentally incompetent person pursuant to former section 9.1-10 of chapter 4 (see now this section) was voidable to the same extent as a contractual undertaking entered into by a person lacking capacity to contract. In re Keiss, 40 Ill. App. 3d 1071, 353 N.E.2d 13 (3 Dist. 1976).

Taking of Consent or Surrender

The taking of a consent or surrender does not constitute the practice of law; thus, a child welfare agency representative does not commit the unauthorized practice of law when he or she explains the content of a consent or surrender and takes such a consent or surrender from a natural parent. Meza v. Rodriguez, 305 Ill. App. 3d 777, 239 Ill. Dec. 233, 713 N.E.2d 764 (2 Dist. 1999).

Unenforceable Agreement

Parties attempted to alter custody of child by means of an agreement among themselves bypassing the custody decisions of the court, notwithstanding the previous termination of all parental rights of the natural parents; the purpose of formal statutory requirements in adoption cases is to add stability and certainty to adoption proceedings and thus, such determinations could not be circumvented by an alleged agreement without judicial sanction. Wittig v. Atherton, 107 Ill. App. 3d 1006, 63 Ill. Dec. 582, 438 N.E.2d 513 (1 Dist. 1982).

Unfitness

—Consolidated Hearings

Based on the record the court could not say evidence of unfitness was so overwhelming that no prejudice resulted from the consolidated hearing on unfitness and best interests; defendant's failure to cooperate with the Department of Children and Family Services or complete its service plans might not by itself require a finding of unfitness thus, the court could not conclude the trial court would have found sufficient evidence of defendant's unfitness without considering improperly admitted testimony of his childhood sexual misconduct. In re V.S., 285 Ill. App. 3d 372, 220 Ill. Dec. 894, 674 N.E.2d 437 (3 Dist. 1996), appeal denied, 172 Ill. 2d 552, 223 Ill. Dec. 195, 679 N.E.2d 380 (1997).

Waiver

Mother did not waive the issue of incompetency by her failure to raise it in surrender proceeding pursuant to former section 9.1-10 of chapter 4 (see now this section). In re Keiss, 40 Ill. App. 3d 1071, 353 N.E.2d 13 (3 Dist. 1976).

LEGAL PERIODICALS

For article, "Survey of Illinois Law [1988-89]—Family Law," see 14 S. Ill. U. L. J. 1007 (1990).

For comment, "Prohibiting Payments to Surrogate Mothers: Love's Labor Lost and the Constitutional Right of Privacy," see 20 J. Marshall L. Rev. 715 (1987).

RESEARCH REFERENCES

Validity and construction of surrogate parenting agreement. 77 ALR4th 70.

750 ILCS 50/11 Consents, surrenders, irrevocability

Sec. 11. *Consents, surrenders, irrevocability.* (a) A consent to adoption or standby adoption by a parent, including a minor, executed and acknowledged in accordance with the provisions of Section 8 of this Act [750 ILCS 50/8], or a surrender of a child by a parent, including a minor, to an agency for the purpose of adoption shall be irrevocable unless it shall have been obtained by fraud or duress on the part of the person before whom such consent, surrender, or other document equivalent to a surrender is acknowledged pursuant to the provisions of Section 10 of this Act [750 ILCS 50/10] or on the part of the adopting parents or their agents and a court of competent jurisdiction shall so find. No action to void or revoke a consent to or surrender for adoption, including an action based on fraud or duress, may be commenced after 12 months from the date the consent or surrender was executed. The consent or surrender of a parent who is a minor shall not be voidable because of such minority.

(b) The petitioners in an adoption proceeding are entitled to rely upon a sworn statement of the biological mother of the child to be adopted identifying the father of her child. The affidavit shall be conclusive evidence as to the biological mother regarding the facts stated therein, and shall create a rebuttable presumption of truth as to the biological father only. Except as provided in Section 11 of this Act, the biological mother of the child shall be permanently barred from attacking the proceeding thereafter. The biological mother shall execute such affidavit in writing and under oath. The affidavit shall be executed by the biological mother before or at the time of execution of the consent or surrender, and shall be retained by the court and be a part of the Court's files. The form of affidavit shall be substantially as follows:

AFFIDAVIT OF IDENTIFICATION

I, ..., the mother of a (male or female) child, state under oath or affirm as follows:

(1) That the child was born, or is expected to be born, on (insert date), at ...., in the State of ....

(2) That I reside at ...., in the City or Village of ...., State of ....

(3) That I am of the age of .... years.

(4) That I acknowledge that I have been asked to identify the father of my child.

(5) (CHECK ONE)

.... I know and am identifying the biological father.

.... I do not know the identity of the biological father.

.... I am unwilling to identify the biological father.

(6A) If I know and am identifying the father:

That the name of the biological father is ....; his last known home address is ....; his last known work address is ....; and he is ... years of age; or he is deceased, having died on (insert date) at ...., in the State of ....

(6B) If I do not know the identity of the biological father:

I do not know who the biological father is; the following is an explanation of why I am unable to identify him:

....

....

....

(6C) If I am unwilling to identify the biological father:

I do not wish to name the biological father of the child for the following reasons:

....

....

....

(7) The physical description of the biological father is: ....

....

....

(8) I reaffirm that the information contained in paragraphs 5, 6, and 7, inclusive, is true and correct.

(9) I have been informed and understand that if I am unwilling, refuse to identify, or misidentify the biological father of the child, absent fraud or duress, I am permanently barred from attacking the proceedings for the adoption of the child at any time after I sign a final and irrevocable consent to adoption or surrender for purposes of adoption.

(10) I have read this Affidavit and have had the opportunity to review and question it; it was explained to me by .; and I am signing it as my free and voluntary act and understand the contents and the results of signing it.

Dated (insert date).

....
Signature

Under penalties as provided by law under Section 1-109 of the Code of Civil Procedure [735 ILCS 5/1-109], the undersigned certifies that the statements set forth in this Affidavit are true and correct.

....
Signature

(Source: P.A. 83-138; 88-550, § 975; 89-315, § 5; 91-357, § 262; 91-572, § 5.)

Note.

This section was Ill.Rev.Stat., Ch. 40, para. 1513.

Cross References.

Concerning the time for taking a consent or surrender, see 750 ILCS 50/9.

Illinois Administrative Code.

See 89 Illinois Administrative Code, § 309.120.

Effect of Amendments.

The 1994 amendment by P.A. 88-550, effective July 3, 1994, added the subsection (a) designation and added subsection (b).

The 1995 amendment by P.A. 89-315, effective January 1, 1996, in subdivision (b)(6B), in the introductory language, substituted "not know" for "now know"; in subdivision (b)(9) substituted "a final and irrevocable consent to adoption or surrender for purposes of adoption" for "this document".

The 1999 amendment by P.A. 91-357, effective July 29, 1999, changed the date blanks in the form.

The 1999 amendment by P.A. 91-572, effective January 1, 2000, inserted "or standby adoption" near the beginning of the first sentence of subsection (a); and changed the date blank three times in the form in subsection (b).

Although the amendments made to this section by P.A. 91-357, § 262 and P.A. 91-572, § 5 did not take into account the amendments made by the other, the amendments have been combined into a single version by the publisher.

CASE NOTES

Analysis

Constitutionality
—Equal Protection
In General
Consent
—Acknowledgement
—Underage Parents
—Valid
—Withdrawal
Duress
—Defined
—Not Shown
Financial Compensation
Fraud
—Not Shown

Fraud and Duress
—Burden of Proof
—Discovery Rule
—Not Shown
—Review
—Shown
Legislative Intent
Limitations Period
Scope

Constitutionality

—Equal Protection

The legislative restriction on the revocability of consent imposed by the 1973 amendment of former Ill.Rev.Stat., ch. 4, para. 9.1-11 (see now this section) is reasonably related to the state's authority to legislate with regard to the adoption of children and for their general welfare. Regenold v. Baby Fold, Inc., 68 Ill. 2d 419, 12 Ill. Dec. 151, 369 N.E.2d 858 (1977).

In General

The 1973 amendment, which required that the fraud or duress be "on the part of the person before whom such consent, surrender, or other document is acknowledged or on the part of the adopting parents or their agents" (Ill.Rev.Stat., ch. 4, para. 9.1-11) (see now this section) was a repudiation by the legislature of the totality approach. Regenold v. Baby Fold, Inc., 68 Ill. 2d 419, 12 Ill. Dec. 151, 369 N.E.2d 858 (1977).

The consent provision of this section has evolved over the years in response to the recognized need for providing a stable and secure environment for the adopted child and to protect the parties from the complex psychological problems inherent in permitting a natural parent to withdraw consent. Regenold v. Baby Fold, Inc., 42 Ill. App. 3d 39, 355 N.E.2d 361 (4 Dist. 1976), aff'd, 68 Ill. 2d 419, 12 Ill. Dec. 151, 369 N.E.2d 858 (1977).

Consent

—Acknowledgement

Under former Ill.Rev. Stat., ch. 4, paras. 2-1, 3-7, and 4-1, (see now 750 ILCS 50/7, 750 ILCS 50/5 and this section), it was an essential element of an acknowledgment taken in open court that the person who had signed the consent in some form of words admit the current validity and binding force of the instrument evidencing the parent's consent; a declaration by the parent signing an adoption consent admitting the previous signing of the consent, coupled with a denial that she currently consented to the adoption of her child, was not such an acknowledgement in open court as required by the statute. Thompson v. Burns, 337 Ill. App. 354, 86 N.E.2d 155 (2 Dist. 1949).

—Underage Parents

Neither the courts nor the legislature require that unmarried minor parents receive any counseling prior to executing a valid consent to adoption; the law requires only that the consent be executed knowingly and as a free and voluntary act before a person authorized to obtain a consent. Kathy O. v. Counseling & Family Servs., 107 Ill. App. 3d 920, 63 Ill. Dec. 764, 438 N.E.2d 695 (3 Dist. 1982).

Where the consent signed by the 15 year old parents quite clearly indicated that the consents were irrevocable and that all parental rights were being given up permanently and both parents testified that the document was explained to them, that they understood what the consent meant, and that they knew they could not later change their minds, the evidence was clear and convincing that these parents knew the legal effect and consequences of the consent documents and that they were fully advised that they were permanently surrendering their parental rights to their child; thus, the purpose of the statute was met, even though the form was somewhat deficient. Kathy O. v. Counseling & Family Servs., 107 Ill. App. 3d 920, 63 Ill. Dec. 764, 438 N.E.2d 695 (3 Dist. 1982).

—Valid

The stress a petitioner established, regardless of its source, as a matter of law did not amount to the duress which was necessary to vitiate her consent where, although the record reflected a number of disturbing and vexing problems which she faced, there was no evidence suggesting that the petitioner's consent was the product of third party persuasion, inducement, deception, or domination. Regenold v. Baby Fold, Inc., 42 Ill. App. 3d 39, 355 N.E.2d 361 (4 Dist. 1976), aff'd, 68 Ill. 2d 419, 12 Ill. Dec. 151, 369 N.E.2d 858 (1977).

—Withdrawal

Under former Ill.Rev.Stat., ch. 4, para. 9.1-10 (see now this section and 750 ILCS 50/8) once consent to adoption or a surrender for adoption was acknowledged in the prescribed manner, it was irrevocable unless obtained by fraud or duress on the part of the person before whom the document was acknowledged. People v. Kerwood, 44 Ill. App. 3d 1040, 3 Ill. Dec. 773, 359 N.E.2d 183 (1 Dist. 1976).

Under former Ill.Rev.Stat., ch. 4, para. 9.1-11 (see now this section), consent to an adoption was irrevocable in the absence of fraud or duress even in instances where the consenting parent was a minor; this clear expression of public policy could not be restricted by the courts, and where the evidence indicated no fraud or duress was present, the consent was to be held effective. People ex rel. Drury v. Catholic Home Bureau, 34 Ill. 2d 84, 213 N.E.2d 507 (1966).

The right to withdraw a consent should not be declared absolute, but should be left to the sound discretion of the trial court, depending upon the particular circumstances in each case. Weisbart v. Brezin, 347 Ill. App. 13, 105 N.E.2d 814 (1 Dist. 1952).

A mother had the right to withdraw her consent to the adoption of her minor child any time before the court had actually acted upon the petition under former Ill.Rev. Stat., ch. 4, paras. 2-1, 3-7, and 4-1, (see now 750 ILCS 50/7 and this section). Thompson v. Burns, 337 Ill. App. 354, 86 N.E.2d 155 (2 Dist. 1949).

Duress

—Defined

Where it was not contended that the surrender of child was executed under duress, thus leaving as the issue the question of whether mother had proved by clear and convincing evidence that her execution of the surrender was procured by fraud, the mother had not sustained a burden of clear and convincing proof. People v. Nolan, 94 Ill. App. 3d 1081, 50 Ill. Dec. 442, 419 N.E.2d 550 (1 Dist. 1981).

Duress has been universally defined as a condition which exists where one is induced by the unlawful act of another to make a contract or perform or forego an act under circumstances which will deprive him of the exercise of his free will. There must be such compulsion affecting the mind to show that the execution of the contract or other instrument was not the voluntary act of the maker and such compulsion must be present and operate at the time the instrument was executed; moreover, the burden of proving such duress is on the person asserting it. Regenold v. Baby Fold, Inc., 42 Ill. App. 3d 39, 355 N.E.2d 361 (4 Dist. 1976), aff'd, 68 Ill. 2d 419, 12 Ill. Dec. 151, 369 N.E.2d 858 (1977).

Duress is defined as personal restraint, or fear of personal injury or imprisonment, or the deprivation of one's freedom of will by the unlawful act of another, or where one is induced by another's unlawful act to perform some act under circumstances which prevent his exercising free will. In re Wojtkowiak, 14 Ill. App. 2d 344, 144 N.E.2d 760 (1 Dist. 1957).

—Not Shown

Under former Ill.Rev.Stat., ch. 4, para. 3-7 (see now this section), although a mother was mentally upset at the time her child was placed for adoption, this did not constitute duress; her act was deliberate and undoubtedly, as she felt at the time, in the best interests of the child. Simaner v. Simonick, 16 Ill. App. 2d 48, 147 N.E.2d 419 (1 Dist. 1957), aff'd, 15 Ill. 2d 568, 155 N.E.2d 555 (1959).

Defendant's argument that duress prevented her from freely deciding whether to put her child up for adoption was not supported by the evidence where, if any duress existed, it was in the statement alleged to have been made by her doctor that if defendant retained her baby, her ex-husband would probably be able to take her three children born of their marriage. In re Wojtkowiak, 14 Ill. App. 2d 344, 144 N.E.2d 760 (1 Dist. 1957).

Financial Compensation

A consent given in exchange for a payment of money in violation of section 1702 of this Act (720 ILCS 525/2) renders such consent

Financial Compensation (Cont'd)
void as against public policy. Samuel v. Kindgren, 184 Ill. App. 3d 661, 132 Ill. Dec. 745, 540 N.E.2d 485 (2 Dist. 1989).

Fraud

—Not Shown
In a habeas corpus proceeding to regain custody of their son given up for adoption, the petition of the child's natural parents was denied where there was no proof of fraud or constructive fraud, the consents were voluntarily given, and petitioners were fully apprised by the Welfare Department of the finality and irrevocability of their consents. People ex rel. Filipkowski v. Gusterine, 16 Ill. App. 2d 336, 148 N.E.2d 1 (1 Dist. 1958).

Fraud and Duress
In order to set aside a consent or a surrender, the fraud or duress must have been accomplished by the person before whom the consent or surrender was acknowledged. Meza v. Rodriguez, 305 Ill. App. 3d 777, 239 Ill. Dec. 233, 713 N.E.2d 764 (2 Dist. 1999).

To constitute fraud, the misrepresentation must be of a material fact and must be relied upon by the parent in executing the consent or surrender document. Meza v. Rodriguez, 305 Ill. App. 3d 777, 239 Ill. Dec. 233, 713 N.E.2d 764 (2 Dist. 1999).

—Burden of Proof
The burden of proving fraud or duress rests upon the party challenging the validity of the consent. Hoffman v. Hoffman, 61 Ill. 2d 569, 338 N.E.2d 862 (1975).

Pursuant to former section 9.1-11 of the Adoption Act (see now this section), the burden of proving fraud or duress rested upon the petitioner. People ex rel. Karr v. Weihe, 30 Ill. App. 2d 361, 174 N.E.2d 897 (2 Dist. 1961).

Under former Ill.Rev.Stat., ch. 4, para. 3-7 (see now this section), the burden of showing whether consent was obtained by fraud or duress rested upon those asserting duress or fraud. Balota v. Handlon, 7 Ill. App. 2d 178, 129 N.E.2d 234 (4 Dist. 1955).

—Discovery Rule
The discovery rule does not apply to termination of parental rights case and respondent mother could not raise an affirmative defense of fraud and duress more than 12 months after the signing of the surrender of adoption. In re D.B., 246 Ill. App. 3d 484, 186 Ill. Dec. 279, 615 N.E.2d 1336 (4 Dist. 1993).

—Not Shown
The putative father failed to show fraud or duress, notwithstanding evidence concerning his preparations for the birth of the child at issue and his desire to keep the child, as such was not relevant to the question of a social worker's conduct in obtaining a surrender from him; similarly, evidence concerning alleged misrepresentations by the natural mother regarding the adoption of the child was also not relevant. Meza v. Rodriguez, 305 Ill. App. 3d 777, 239 Ill. Dec. 233, 713 N.E.2d 764 (2 Dist. 1999).

Where the evidence clearly showed that natural mother initiated the contact with Department of Children and Family Services (DCFS) which led to execution of the surrender of her children for adoption when she told her DCFS homemaker that she had decided to surrender the children and where DCFS lawfully removed the children from her home, the trial court's finding that appellant failed to prove fraud or duress on the part of DCFS by clear and convincing evidence was not against the manifest weight of the evidence. In re Jackson, 243 Ill. App. 3d 631, 183 Ill. Dec. 708, 611 N.E.2d 1356 (5 Dist. 1993).

To set aside a consent to adoption, the fraud and duress must have been accomplished by the person before whom the consent or surrender is acknowledged; where both parents testified that they felt pressure to sign from the parents of the mother but not from counselor, the fact that duress or fraud was practiced by some third party did not affect the validity of the consent. Kathy O. v. Counseling & Family Servs., 107 Ill. App. 3d 920, 63 Ill. Dec. 764, 438 N.E.2d 695 (3 Dist. 1982).

While the petitioner claimed her consent to adoption was procured by both fraud and duress, there was no proof that any hospital staff member, doctor, caseworker, relative or friend sought to take advantage of petitioner or misrepresent facts to her, and while it was undisputed that her family and fiance advised her to surrender the child and that the hospital staff thought this course of action best, it was also clear that her doctors and the caseworkers in their frequent discussions with her repeatedly impressed upon petitioner the fact that the decision was hers to make, explaining to her the possible plans and alternatives. People ex rel. Drury v. Catholic Home Bureau, 34 Ill. 2d 84, 213 N.E.2d 507 (1966).

Where there was no evidence of duress or fraud, the court could not properly permit the consent to adoption to be withdrawn unless it had been improperly executed. Cohen v. Janic, 57 Ill. App. 2d 309, 207 N.E.2d 89 (1 Dist. 1965).

—Review
The findings of a trial court as to issue of fraud or duress may not be set aside on appeal unless contrary to the manifest weight of the evidence. Hoffman v. Hoffman, 61 Ill. 2d 569, 338 N.E.2d 862 (1975).

—Shown
Consent of natural mother to adoption held obtained by duress and fraud and vacated as null and void. Huebert v. Marshall, 132 Ill. App. 2d 793, 270 N.E.2d 464 (1 Dist. 1971).

Under former section 9.1-11 of the Adoption Act (see now this section), where natural mother signed her surrender or consent under the mistaken belief and misapprehension that she had one year to get the baby back, both she and her husband and offices of licensed child welfare agency knew of mistaken belief and made no effort to clarify or dispel that mistaken notion, given her age and experience, the time and place where the signing occurred, her then physical condition, that she had never been in a hospital before, and this being her first child, and the fact that she was obviously not familiar with the laws of adoption, the failure to fully inform her and remove the mistaken belief or misapprehension on a material point was calculated to deceive and amounted to deception and fraud, and thus her surrender or consent to adoption was obtained by fraud and was revocable. People ex rel. Karr v. Weihe, 30 Ill. App. 2d 361, 174 N.E.2d 897 (2 Dist. 1961).

Legislative Intent
The purpose of formal statutory requirements in adoption cases is to add stability and certainty to adoption proceedings and thus, court determinations could not be circumvented by an alleged agreement without judicial sanction. Wittig v. Atherton, 107 Ill. App. 3d 1006, 63 Ill. Dec. 582, 438 N.E.2d 513 (1 Dist. 1982).

This section clearly reflects a legislative recognition of the public policy favoring the finality and stability of adoptions. People v. Nolan, 94 Ill. App. 3d 1081, 50 Ill. Dec. 442, 419 N.E.2d 550 (1 Dist. 1981).

The legislature has balanced the needs of the adoption system against the natural inclinations of consenting parents and concluded that such consent is irrevocable in the absence of fraud or duress. Regenold v. Baby Fold, Inc., 42 Ill. App. 3d 39, 355 N.E.2d 361 (4 Dist. 1976), aff'd, 68 Ill. 2d 419, 12 Ill. Dec. 151, 369 N.E.2d 858 (1977).

Former section 11 of the Adoption Act (Ill.Rev.Stat., ch. 4, para. 9.1-11) (see now this section) clearly reflected a legislative recognition of the public policy favoring the finality and stability of adoptions. Hoffman v. Hoffman, 61 Ill. 2d 569, 338 N.E.2d 862 (1975).

Limitations Period
One cannot seek to enforce an oral contract for adoption and challenge a trial court's jurisdiction to enter an adoption judgment after the time for setting aside the adoption judgment and consent have passed. Doe v. Noe, 317 Ill. App. 3d 445, 251 Ill. Dec. 110, 739 N.E.2d 1043, 2000 Ill. App. LEXIS 923 (4 Dist. 2000).

The sister of the biological mother of the child at issue could not challenge an adoption judgment more than 12 months after the mother signed a surrender of parental rights. Doe v. Noe, 317 Ill. App. 3d 419, 251 Ill. Dec. 103, 739 N.E.2d 1036, 2000 Ill. App. LEXIS 922 (4 Dist. 2000), cert. denied, 535 U.S. 932, 122 S. Ct. 1308, 152 L. Ed. 2d 218 (2002).

The one year statute of limitations contained in this section has consistently been interpreted by courts as being absolute. Joseph B. v. Angela S., 258 Ill. App. 3d 954, 197 Ill. Dec. 56, 630 N.E.2d 1180 (1 Dist. 1994).

Where natural mother failed to challenge the validity of her surrenders for adoption within 12 months of their execution, the appellate court affirmed the decision of the trial court denying her

Limitations Period (Cont'd)
third application for restoration of the minors to custody of the mother. In re Jackson, 243 Ill. App. 3d 631, 183 Ill. Dec. 708, 611 N.E.2d 1356 (5 Dist. 1993).

Where petitioner wished to challenge the validity of her consent to adoption, she was required to do so within the time period prescribed in this section, and having failed to do so, petitioner could not have subsequently circumvented this limitation by characterizing her action as a challenge to the judgment of adoption when her position was bottomed entirely on a challenge to the validity of her consent. Mandell v. Doe, 213 Ill. App. 3d 670, 157 Ill. Dec. 290, 572 N.E.2d 359 (2 Dist.), cert. denied, 141 Ill. 2d 541, 162 Ill. Dec. 489, 580 N.E.2d 115 (1991).

Scope

This section does not limit actions seeking to void a consent to those based on fraud or duress. Joseph B. v. Angela S., 258 Ill. App. 3d 954, 197 Ill. Dec. 56, 630 N.E.2d 1180 (1 Dist. 1994).

LEGAL PERIODICALS

For casenote, "Born to Lose: The Illinois 'Baby Richard' Case — How Examining His Father's Pre-Birth Conduct Might Have Led to a Different Ending for Richard," see 16 N. Ill. U.L. Rev. 543 (1996).

For note, "Babies, Jessica, Richard and Emily: The Need for Legislative Reform of Adoption Laws," 70 Chi-Kent L. Rev. 1851 (1996).

For article, "Surrogate Parenthood: A Need for Legislative Direction," see 71 Ill. B. J. 412 (1983).

750 ILCS 50/12 Consent of child or adult

Sec. 12. *Consent of child or adult.* If, upon the date of the entry of the judgment the person sought to be adopted is of the age of 14 years or upwards, the adoption shall not be made without the consent of such person. Such consent shall be in writing and shall be acknowledged by such person as provided in Section 10 of this Act [750 ILCS 50/10], provided, that if such person is in need of mental treatment or mentally retarded, the court may waive the provisions of this Section. No consent shall be required under this Section if the person sought to be adopted has died before giving such consent.
(Source: P.A. 85-517.)

Note.

This section was Ill.Rev.Stat., Ch. 40, para. 1514.

CASE NOTES

ANALYSIS

Consent of Child
—Former Act
—Presence in Court

Consent of Child

—Former Act

In a collateral attack on an adoption, the fact that nowhere in the record for adoption, or in the decree of adoption, was there any evidence or intimation that the defendant, then a child aged 17 years, consented to the adoption was irrelevant, as nowhere in the former Adoption Act was it required that the petition or the decree state or find that the child consented to the adoption. Burke v. Wallace, 339 Ill. App. 162, 89 N.E.2d 197 (3 Dist. 1949).

—Presence in Court

Under the former Adoption Act (see now 750 ILCS 50/0.01 et seq.), minors over 14 years of age who were residing in a foreign country could not be adopted where they could not be not present in open court to consent to their adoptions. Noel v. Olszerski v. Mannka, 350 Ill. App. 264, 112 N.E.2d 727 (1 Dist. 1953).

LEGAL PERIODICALS

For article, "Baby Richard and Beyond: The Future for Adopted Children", see 18 N. Ill. U.L. Rev. 445 (1999).

For casenote, "Born to Lose: The Illinois 'Baby Richard' Case — How Examining His Father's Pre-Birth Conduct Might Have Led to a Different Ending for Richard," see 16 N. Ill. U.L. Rev. 543 (1996).

For article, "What's Good for the Goose is Good for the Gander: Toward Recognition of Men's Reproductive Rights," see 15 N. Ill. U.L. Rev. 141 (1994).

RESEARCH REFERENCES

Validity of birth parent's "blanket" consent to adoption which fails to identify adoptive parents. 15 ALR5th 1.

750 ILCS 50/12.1 Putative Father Registry

Sec. 12.1. *Putative Father Registry.* The Department of Children and Family Services shall establish a Putative Father Registry for the purpose of determining the identity and location of a putative father of a minor child who is, or is expected to be, the subject of an adoption proceeding, in order to provide notice of such proceeding to the putative father. The Department of Children and Family Services shall establish rules and informational material necessary to implement the provisions of this Section. The Department shall have the authority to set reasonable fees for the use of the Registry.

(a) The Department shall maintain the following information in the Registry:

(1) With respect to the putative father:

(i) Name, including any other names by which the putative father may be known and that he may provide to the Registry;

(ii) Address at which he may be served with notice of a petition under this Act, including any change of address;

(iii) Social Security Number;

(iv) Date of birth; and

(v) If applicable, a certified copy of an order by a court of this State or of another state or territory of the United States adjudicating the putative father to be the father of the child.

(2) With respect to the mother of the child:

(i) Name, including all other names known to the putative father by which the mother may be known;

(ii) If known to the putative father, her last address;

(iii) Social Security Number; and

(iv) Date of birth.

(3) If known to the putative father, the name, gender, place of birth, and date of birth or anticipated date of birth of the child.

(4) The date that the Department received the putative father's registration.

(5) Other information as the Department may by rule determine necessary for the orderly administration of the Registry.

(b) A putative father may register with the Department before the birth of the child but shall register no later than 30 days after the birth of the child. All registrations shall be in writing and signed by the putative father. No fee shall be charged for the initial registration. The Department shall have no independent obligation to gather the information to be maintained.

(c) An interested party, including persons intending to adopt a child, a child welfare agency with whom the mother has placed or has given written notice of her intention to place a child for adoption, the mother of the child, or an attorney representing an interested party may request that the Department search the Registry to determine whether a putative father is registered in relation to a child who is or may be the subject to an adoption petition.

(d) A search of the Registry may be proven by the production of a certified copy of the registration form, or by the certified statement of the administrator of the Registry that after a search, no registration of a putative father in relation to a child who is or may be the subject of an adoption petition could be located.

(e) Except as otherwise provided, information contained within the Registry is confidential and shall not be published or open to public inspection.

(f) A person who knowingly or intentionally registers false information under this Section commits a Class B misdemeanor. A person who knowingly or intentionally releases confidential information in violation of this Section commits a Class B misdemeanor.

(g) Except as provided in subsections (b) or (c) of Section 8 of this Act [750 ILCS 50/8], a putative father who fails to register with the Putative Father Registry as provided in this Section is barred from thereafter bringing or maintaining any action to assert any interest in the child, unless he proves by clear and convincing evidence that:

(1) it was not possible for him to register within the period of time specified in subsection (b) of this Section; and

(2) his failure to register was through no fault of his own; and

(3) he registered within 10 days after it became possible for him to file.

A lack of knowledge of the pregnancy or birth is not an acceptable reason for failure to register.

(h) Except as provided in subsection (b) or (c) of Section 8 of this Act [750 ILCS 50/8], failure to timely register with the Putative Father Registry (i) shall be deemed to be a waiver and surrender of any right to notice of any hearing in any judicial proceeding for the adoption of the child, and the consent or surrender of that person to the adoption of the child is not required, and (ii) shall constitute an abandonment of the child and shall be prima facie evidence of sufficient grounds to support termination of such father's parental rights under this Act.

(i) In any adoption proceeding pertaining to a child born out of wedlock, if there is no showing that a putative father has executed a consent or surrender or waived his rights regarding the proposed adoption, certification as specified in subsection (d) shall be filed with the court prior to entry of a final judgment order of adoption.

(j) The Registry shall not be used to notify a putative father who is the father of a child as a result of criminal sexual abuse or assault as defined under Article 12 of the Criminal Code of 1961 [720 ILCS 5/12-1 et seq.].

(Source: P.A. 88-550, § 975; 89-315, § 5; 90-15, § 20.)

Illinois Administrative Code.
See 89 Illinois Administrative Code, § 309.90.

Effective Date.
Section 999 of P.A. 88-550 made this section effective upon becoming law. The Act was approved July 3, 1994.

Effect of Amendments.
The 1995 amendment by P.A. 89-315, effective January 1, 1996, in subdivision (a)(1)(v) inserted "of this State or"; and in subsection (d) deleted "by the certified statement of the administrator of the Registry form, or"; in subsections (g) and (h), in the introductory language, substituted "subsections (b) or (c) of Section 8" for "Section 8(b)"; in subsection (h), in the introductory language, inserted "the preceding "adoption" and inserted "or surrender"; and in subsection (i) substituted "executed a consent or surrender" for "consented to".

The 1997 amendment by P.A. 90-15, effective June 13, 1997, added subsection (j).

CASE NOTES

Analysis

Constitutionality
Due Process
Failure to Register
Waiver

Constitutionality
The statute is a gender based classification substantially related to important state interests and does not violate equal protection rights. In re A.S.B., 293 Ill. App. 3d 836, 228 Ill. Dec. 238, 688 N.E.2d 1215 (2 Dist. 1997).

The Illinois adoption laws provide a statutory scheme that protects a putative father's interest in assuming a responsible role in the future of his child. In re K.J.R., 293 Ill. App. 3d 49, 227 Ill. Dec. 190, 687 N.E.2d 113 (1 Dist. 1997).

Due Process
Where petitioner did not establish any relationship with minor during her life and did not avail himself of the statutory scheme designed to protect his inchoate interest in minor, not registering with the Putative Father Registry, he was not entitled to receive special notice of the adoption proceeding when he was presumptively capable of protecting his interest in such notice and his due process rights were not violated. In re A.S.B., 293 Ill. App. 3d 836, 228 Ill. Dec. 238, 688 N.E.2d 1215 (2 Dist. 1997).

Failure to Register
Father's failure to register with the Putative Father Registry was not evidence of unfitness for purposes of terminating parental rights; the termination was not set aside, however, because the record established statutory grounds for termination that included abandonment and lack of interest. People v. Quinella W., Ill. App. 3d , 262 Ill. Dec. 606, 765 N.E.2d 1214, 2002 Ill. App. LEXIS 186 (2 Dist. 2002).

Putative father failed to act to preserve his inchoate interest in establishing a relationship with his child by registering and initiating a parentage action, and thus was not entitled to notice or an

Failure to Register (Cont'd)
opportunity to be heard in the adoption proceedings. In re K.J.R., 293 Ill. App. 3d 49, 227 Ill. Dec. 190, 687 N.E.2d 113 (1 Dist. 1997).

Even if putative father could have relied on mother's misrepresentation of parentage and such reliance could have excused putative father from registering during the statutory time period, putative father's subsequent knowledge of mother's alleged fraud and his failure to register within 10 days after receipt of that knowledge barred him from pursuing his parentage claim. In re K.J.R., 293 Ill. App. 3d 49, 227 Ill. Dec. 190, 687 N.E.2d 113 (1 Dist. 1997).

Waiver
Because putative father failed to timely register with the Putative Father Registry and did not allege facts that would bring him within the exceptions to subsection (g), he waived the right to bring or maintain a parentage petition. In re K.J.R., 293 Ill. App. 3d 49, 227 Ill. Dec. 190, 687 N.E.2d 113 (1 Dist. 1997).

LEGAL PERIODICALS

For comment, "Implementing a National Putative Father Registry by Utilizing Existing Federal/State Collaborative Databases," see 36 J. Marshall L. Rev. 1033 (2003).

For comment, "Paternity Actions in Illinois: Why Not Consider What is in the Best Interest of the Child?," see 21 S. Ill. U.L.J. 613 (1997).

For note, "Babies Jessica, Richard, and Emily: The need for Legislative Reform of Adoption Laws," see 70 Chi. Kent L. Rev. 1851 (1997).

For casenote, "Born to Lose: The Illinois 'Baby Richard' Case — How Examining His Father's Pre-Birth Conduct Might Have Led to a Different Ending for Richard," see 16 N. Ill. U.L. Rev. 543 (1996).

For note, "Incorporating Thwarted Putative Fathers into the Adoptive Scheme: Illinois Proposes a Solution after the 'Baby Richard' Case," 1996 U. Ill. L. Rev. 189.

For article, "What's Good for the Goose is Good for the Gander: Toward Recognition of Men's Reproductive Rights," see 15 N. Ill. U.L. Rev. 141 (1994).

750 ILCS 50/12a Notice to putative father

Sec. 12a. *Notice to putative father.* 1. Upon the written request to any Clerk of any Circuit Court, and upon the payment of a filing fee of $10.00, by any interested party, including persons intending to adopt a child, a child welfare agency with whom the mother has placed or has given written notice of her intention to place a child for adoption, the mother of a child, or any attorney representing an interested party, a notice, the declaration of paternity and the disclaimer of paternity may be served on a putative father in the same manner as Summons is served in other civil proceedings, or, in lieu of personal service, service may be made as follows:

(a) The person requesting notice shall pay to the Clerk of the Court a mailing fee of $2 plus the cost of U. S. postage for certified or registered mail and furnish to the Clerk an original and one copy of a notice, the declaration of paternity and the disclaimer of paternity together with an Affidavit setting forth the putative father's last known address. The original notice, the declaration of paternity and the disclaimer of paternity shall be retained by the Clerk.

(b) The Clerk shall forthwith mail to the putative father, at the address appearing in the Affidavit, the copy of the notice, the declaration of paternity and the disclaimer of paternity, by certified mail, return receipt requested; the envelope and return receipt shall bear the return address of the Clerk. The receipt for certified mail shall state the name and address of the addressee, and the date of mailing, and shall be attached to the original notice.

(c) The return receipt, when returned to the Clerk, shall be attached to the original notice, the declaration of paternity and the disclaimer of paternity, and shall constitute proof of service.

(d) The Clerk shall note the fact of service in a permanent record.

2. The notice shall be signed by the Clerk, and may be served on the putative father at any time after conception, and shall read as follows:

"IN THE MATTER OF NOTICE TO ...., PUTATIVE FATHER.

You have been identified as the father of a child born on or expected to be born on or about (insert date).

The mother of the child is ....

The mother has indicated that she intends to place the child for adoption.

As the alleged father of the child, you have certain legal rights with respect to the child, including the right to notice of the filing of proceedings instituted for the adoption of the child. If you wish to retain your rights with respect to the child, you must file with the Clerk of this Circuit Court of .... County, Illinois, whose address is ...., Illinois, within 30 days after the date of receipt of this notice, the declaration of paternity enclosed herewith stating that you are, in fact, the father of the child and that you intend to retain your legal rights with respect to the child, or request to be notified of any further proceedings with respect to custody or adoption of the child.

If you do not file such a declaration of paternity, or a request for notice, then whatever legal rights you have with respect to the child, including the right to notice of any future proceedings for the adoption of the child, may be terminated without any further notice to you. When your legal rights with respect to the child are so terminated, you will not be entitled to notice of any proceeding instituted for the adoption of the child.

If you are not the father of the child, you may file with the Clerk of this Court the disclaimer of paternity enclosed herewith which will be noted in the Clerk's file and you will receive no further notice with respect to the child."

The declaration of paternity shall be substantially as follows:

"IN THE CIRCUIT COURT OF THE
....
JUDICIAL CIRCUIT, ILLINOIS
.... County

)
)
) No.
)
)

DECLARATION OF PATERNITY WITH ENTRY OF APPEARANCE

I, ..., state as follows:

(1) That I am .... years of age; and I reside at .... in the County of ...., State of ....

(2) That I have been advised that .... is the mother of a .... male child named .... born or expected to be born on or about .... and that such mother has stated that I am the father of this child.

(3) I declare that I am the father of this child.

(4) I understand that the mother of this child wishes to consent to the adoption of this child. I do not consent to the adoption of this child, and I understand that I must return this initial declaration of parentage form to the Clerk of the Circuit Court of .... County, located at ...., within 30 days of receipt of this notice.

(5) I further understand that I am also obligated to establish my paternity pursuant to the Parentage Act of 1984 [750 ILCS 45/1 et seq.] within 30 days of my receiving this notice or, if the child is not yet born, within 30 days after the birth of the child. This proceeding is separate and distinct from the above mailing of initial declaration of paternity; in this second notice, I must state that I am, in fact, the father of said child, and that I intend to retain my legal rights with respect to said child, and request to be notified of any further proceedings with respect to custody or adoption of the child.

(6) I hereby enter my appearance in the above entitled cause.

OATH

I have been duly sworn and I say under oath that I have read and understand this Declaration of Paternity With Entry of Appearance. The facts that it contains are true and correct to the best of my knowledge, and I understand that by signing this document I admit my paternity. I have signed this document as my free and voluntary act.

....
(signature)

Dated (insert date).
Signed and sworn before me on (insert date).

....
(notary public)".

The disclaimer of paternity shall be substantially as follows:

"IN THE CIRCUIT COURT OF THE
....
JUDICIAL CIRCUIT, ILLINOIS
.... County

)
)
) No.
)
)

DENIAL OF PATERNITY WITH ENTRY OF APPEARANCE AND CONSENT TO ADOPTION

I, ..., state as follows:

(1) That I am .... years of age; and I reside at .... in the County of ...., State of ....

(2) That I have been advised that .... is the mother of a .... male child named .... born or expected to be born on or about .... and that such mother has stated that I am the father of this child.

(3) I deny that I am the father of this child.

(4) I further understand that the mother of this child wishes to consent to the adoption of the child. I hereby consent to the adoption of this child, and waive any rights, remedies and defenses that I may now or in the future have as a result of the mother's allegation of the paternity of this child. This consent is being given in order to facilitate the adoption of the child and so that the court may terminate what rights I may have to the child as a result of being named the father by the mother. This consent is not in any manner an admission of paternity.

(5) I hereby enter my appearance in the above entitled cause and waive service of summons and other pleading.

OATH

I have been duly sworn and I say under oath that I have read and understood this Denial of Paternity With Entry of Appearance and Consent to Adoption. The facts it contains are true and correct to the best of my knowledge, and I understand that by signing this document I have not admitted paternity. I have signed this document as my free and voluntary act in order to facilitate the adoption of the child.

....
(signature)

Dated (insert date).
Signed and sworn before me on (insert date).

....
(notary public)".

The names of adoptive parents shall not be included in the notice.

3. If the putative father files a disclaimer of paternity, he shall be deemed not to be the father of the child with respect to any adoption or other proceeding held to terminate the rights of parents as respects such child.

4. In the event the putative father does not file a declaration of paternity of the child or request for notice within 30 days of service of the above notice, he need not be made a party to or given notice of any proceeding brought for the adoption of the child. An Order or judgment may be entered in such proceeding terminating all of his rights with respect to the child without further notice to him.

5. If the putative father files a declaration of paternity or a request for notice in accordance with subsection 2, with respect to the child, he shall be given notice in event any proceeding is brought for the adoption of the child.

6. The Clerk shall maintain separate numbered files and records of requests and proofs of service and all other documents filed pursuant to this article. All such records shall be impounded.

(Source: P.A. 86-744; 88-550, § 975; 89-315, § 5; 91-357, § 262.)

Note.

This section was Ill.Rev.Stat., Ch. 40, para. 1515.

Effect of Amendments.

The 1994 amendment by P.A. 88-550, effective July 3, 1994, added subsection 1.5.

The 1995 amendment by P.A. 89-315, effective January 1, 1996, deleted former subsection 1.5 listing the people entitled to notice that a petition has been filed under Section 5.

The 1999 amendment by P.A. 91-357, effective July 29, 1999, changed the date blanks in the forms.

CASE NOTES

Petition

—Defective

In an adoption proceeding based on the ground that the father had deserted the child for 17 years, where the petition did not give the place of residence of the father, but merely alleged that he resided in the state of Michigan, which allegation was not in compliance with the statute, this allegation was not equivalent to an allegation that his place of residence was unknown; in addition, the petition did not allege that the father consented to the adoption, and his willingness to consent if knowledge could be conveyed to him was not equivalent to an allegation that he did consent. Hook v. Wright, 329 Ill. 299, 160 N.E. 579 (1928).

LEGAL PERIODICALS

For casenote, "Born to Lose: The Illinois 'Baby Richard' Case — How Examining His Father's Pre-Birth Conduct Might Have Led to a Different Ending for Richard," see 16 N. Ill. U.L. Rev. 543 (1996).

For note, "Incorporating Thwarted Putative Fathers into the Adoptive Scheme: Illinois Proposes a Solution after the 'Baby Richard' Case," 1996 U. Ill. L. Rev. 189.

For note, "The Termination of Parental Rights: Lassiter and the New Illinois Termination Law," see 13 Loy. U. Chi. L. J. 135 (1981-82).

For Comments, "Illegitimacy and the Rights of Unwed Fathers in Adoption Proceedings After Quillian v. Walcott," see 12 J. Marshall J. Prac. & Proc. 383 (1979).

750 ILCS 50/13 Interim order

Sec. 13. *Interim order.* As soon as practicable after the filing of a petition for adoption the court shall hold a hearing for the following purposes:

A. In other than an adoption of a related child or an adoption through an agency or of an adult:

(a) To determine the validity of the consent, provided that the execution of a consent pursuant to this Act shall be prima facie evidence of its validity, and provided that the validity of a consent shall not be affected by the omission therefrom of the names of the petitioners or adopting parents at the time the consent is executed or acknowledged, and further provided that the execution of a consent prior to the filing of a petition for adoption shall not affect its validity.

(b) To determine whether there is available suitable temporary custodial care for a child sought to be adopted.

B. In all cases except standby adoptions:

(a) The court shall appoint some licensed attorney other than the State's attorney acting in his or her official capacity as guardian ad litem to represent a child sought to be adopted. Such guardian ad litem shall have power to consent to the adoption of the child, if such consent is required.

(b) The court shall appoint a guardian ad litem for all named minors or defendants who are persons under legal disability, if any.

(c) If the petition alleges a person to be unfit pursuant to the provisions of subparagraph (p) of paragraph D of Section 1 of this Act [750 ILCS 50/1], such person shall be represented by counsel. If such person is indigent or an appearance has not been entered on his behalf at the time the matter is set for hearing, the court shall appoint as counsel for him either the Guardianship and Advocacy Commission, the public defender, or, only if no attorney from the Guardianship and Advocacy Commission or the public defender is available, an attorney licensed to practice law in this State.

(d) If it is proved to the satisfaction of the court, after such investigation as the court deems necessary, that termination of parental rights and temporary commitment of the child to an agency or to a person deemed competent by the court, including petitioners, will be for the welfare of the child, the court may order the child to be so committed and may terminate the parental rights of the parents and declare the child a ward of the court or, if it is not so proved, the court may enter such other order as it shall deem necessary and advisable.

(e) Before an interim custody order is granted under this Section, service of summons shall be had upon the parent or parents whose rights have not been terminated, except as provided in subsection (f). Reasonable notice and opportunity to be heard shall be given to the parent or parents after service of summons when the address of the parent or parents is available. The party seeking an interim custody order shall make all reasonable efforts to locate the parent or parents of the child or children they are seeking to adopt and to notify the parent or parents of the party's request for an interim custody order pursuant to this Section.

(f) An interim custody order may be granted without notice upon presentation to the court of a written petition, accompanied by an affidavit, stating that there is an immediate danger to the child and that irreparable harm will result to the child if notice is given to the parent or parents or legal guardian. Upon making a finding that there is an immediate danger to the child if service of process is had upon and notice of hearing is given to the parent or parents or legal guardian prior to the entry of an order granting temporary custody to someone other than a parent or legal guardian, the court may enter an order of temporary custody which shall expire not more than 10 days after its entry. Every ex parte custody order granted without notice shall state the injury which the court sought to avoid by granting the order, the irreparable injury that would have occurred had notice been given, and the reason the order was granted without notice. The matter shall be set down for full hearing before the expiration of the ex parte order and will be heard after service of summons is had upon and notice of hearing is given to the parent or parents or legal guardian. At the hearing the burden of proof shall be upon the party seeking to extend the interim custody order to show that the order was properly granted without notice and that custody should remain with the party seeking to adopt during the pendency of the adoption proceeding. If the interim custody order is extended, the reasons for granting the extension shall be stated in the order.

C. In the case of a child born outside the United States or a territory thereof, if the petitioners have previously been appointed guardians of such child by a court of competent jurisdiction in a country other than the United States or a territory thereof, the court may order that the petitioners continue as guardians of such child.

D. In standby adoption cases:

(a) The court shall appoint a licensed attorney other than the State's Attorney acting in his or her official capacity as guardian ad litem to represent a child sought to be adopted. The guardian ad litem shall have power to consent to the adoption of the child, if consent is required.

(b) The court shall appoint a guardian ad litem for all named minors or defendants who are persons under legal disability, if any.

(c) The court lacks jurisdiction to proceed on the petition for standby adoption if the child has a living parent, adoptive parent, or adjudicated parent whose rights have not been terminated and whose whereabouts are known, unless the parent consents to the standby adoption or, after receiving notice of the hearing on the standby adoption petition, fails to object to the appointment of a standby adoptive parent at the hearing on the petition.

(d) The court shall investigate as needed for the welfare of the child and shall determine whether the petitioner or petitioners shall be permitted to adopt.

(Source: P.A. 85-1440; 89-644, § 5; 89-686, § 12-5; 90-14, § 2-270; 90-349, § 5; 91-572, § 5.)

Note.

This section was Ill.Rev.Stat., Ch. 40, para. 1516.

Effect of Amendments.

The 1996 amendment by P.A. 89-644, effective January 1, 1997, in subdivision B.(a), in the first sentence, deleted "the State's Attorney of the county in which the proceeding is pending, or" following "appoint", deleted "other" preceding "licensed attorney" and inserted "other than the State's attorney acting in his official capacity".

The 1996 amendment by P.A. 89-686, effective June 1, 1997, in the first sentence of subdivision B.(a) substituted "some licensed attorney other than the State's attorney acting in his or her official capacity" for "the State's Attorney of the county in which the proceeding is pending, or some other licensed attorney".

The 1997 amendment by P.A. 90-14, effective July 1, 1997, combined the amendments by P.A. 89-644 and P.A. 89-686.

The 1997 amendment by P.A. 90-349, effective January 1, 1998, combined the amendments by P.A. 89-644 and P.A. 89-686; and added subdivisions B.(e) and B.(f).

The 1999 amendment by P.A. 91-572, effective January 1, 2000, inserted "except standby adoptions" at the beginning of subdivision B., and added subdivision D.

CASE NOTES

Analysis

Consent
—Failure to Consent
Guardian Ad Litem
Right to Counsel

Consent

—Failure to Consent

The primary issue in the hearing mandated by former section 9.1-13 of the Adoption Act (see now this section) is the validity of the parent's consent to the adoption and where the parent does not consent, he or she must be determined unfit within the statutory definition. Neal v. Burton, 43 Ill. App. 3d 294, 1 Ill. Dec. 946, 356 N.E.2d 1279 (5 Dist. 1976).

Guardian Ad Litem

An organization based in Washington, D.C. was not subject to the jurisdiction of the court and was not qualified to act as guardian ad litem in an adoption proceeding. In re C.M.A., 306 Ill. App. 3d 1061, 239 Ill. Dec. 920, 715 N.E.2d 674 (1 Dist. 1999).

Right to Counsel

Enactment of a statutory scheme that provided appointed counsel for indigent parents facing termination of parental rights under the Juvenile Court Act, but not under the Adoption Act, violated the equal protection clause of the Fourteenth Amendment. Jo Ellen J. v. John M. (In re L.T.M.), Ill. 2d , 291 Ill. Dec. 645, 824 N.E.2d 221, 2005 Ill. LEXIS 4 (2005).

Allowing the involuntary termination of the parental rights of an indigent parent without the appointment of counsel through an adoption proceeding violates the equal protection clause; thus, the court construed the Adoption Act as requiring the same procedural safeguards required by the Juvenile Court Act in cases where indigent parents are facing the involuntary termination of their parental rights. In re K.L.P., 316 Ill. App. 3d 110, 249 Ill. Dec. 246, 735 N.E.2d 1071, 2000 Ill. App. LEXIS 734 (2 Dist. 2000).

The trial court did not err in failing to appoint counsel for the respondent natural mother on procedural due process grounds where: (1) there was no claim that criminal charges could be brought based on the allegations of neglect and abuse; (2) no expert witnesses testified; (3) the case did not present any troublesome points of law; and (4) the evidence was not closely balanced so that the presence of counsel would have made a determinative difference. In re K.L.P., 316 Ill. App. 3d 110, 249 Ill. Dec. 246, 735 N.E.2d 1071, 2000 Ill. App. LEXIS 734 (2 Dist. 2000).

Under subdivision (B)(c) of this section, the biological mother was never alleged to be unfit due to any mental or physical illness, and she did not fall within the category of those persons entitled to appointment of counsel under the Adoption Act. Rosewell v.

Right to Counsel (Cont'd)
Hanrahan, 168 Ill. App. 3d 329, 119 Ill. Dec. 542, 523 N.E.2d 10 (1 Dist. 1988).

In a proceeding for termination for parental rights, where most of the evidence before the court as to the mother's unfitness consisted of clinical psychologists' report and medical records of her periodic bouts with mental illness and drug problems, she had a right to counsel under either former section 1-20 of the Juvenile Court Act (Ill.Rev.Stat., ch. 37, para. 701-20) (see now 705 ILCS 405/1-5), or subdivision (B)(c) of this Act. Pack v. Ellul, 130 Ill. App. 3d 398, 85 Ill. Dec. 685, 474 N.E.2d 413 (3 Dist. 1985).

750 ILCS 50/13.1 Order for standby adoption

Sec. 13.1. *Order for standby adoption.* (a) If it is proved to the satisfaction of the court, after such investigation as the court deems necessary, that the child's parent consents to or fails to object to the standby adoption and adoption by the petitioner will be for the welfare of the child, the court may enter an order for standby adoption. However, the consenting parent's parental rights may not be terminated until consent becomes effective.

(b) The order for standby adoption shall be final as to all findings and shall be followed in the judgment of adoption unless the court finds by clear and convincing evidence that it is no longer in the best interest of the child for the adoption to be finalized.

(c) Once the standby adoptive parent receives knowledge of the death of the consenting parent, or the consenting parent requests that a final judgment for adoption be entered, the standby adoptive parent shall have 60 days to apply for a judgment for adoption.
(Source: P.A. 91-572, § 5; 93-732, § 5.)

Effective Date.
This section became effective January 1, 2000, pursuant to Ill. Const. (1970), Art. IV, § 10 and 5 ILCS 75/1.

Effect of Amendments.
The 2004 amendment by P.A. 93-732, effective January 1, 2005, substituted "consenting parent" for "terminally ill parent" throughout the section.

750 ILCS 50/14 Judgment

Sec. 14. *Judgment.* (a) Prior to the entry of the judgment for order of adoption in any case other than an adoption of a related child or of an adult, each petitioner and each person, agency, association, corporation, institution, society or organization involved in the adoption of the child, except a child welfare agency, shall execute an affidavit setting forth the hospital and medical costs, legal fees, counseling fees, and any other fees or expenditures paid in accordance with the Adoption Compensation Prohibition Act [720 ILCS 525/0.01 et seq.].

(b) Before the entry of the judgment for adoption, each child welfare agency involved in the adoption of the child shall file an affidavit concerning the costs, expenses, contributions, fees, compensation, or other things of value which have been given, promised, or received including but not limited to hospital and medical costs, legal fees, social services, living expenses, or any other expenses related to the adoption paid in accordance with the Adoption Compensation Prohibition Act [720 ILCS 525/0.01 et seq.].

If the total amount paid by the child welfare agency is $4,500 or more, the affidavit shall contain an itemization of expenditures.

If the total amount paid by the child welfare agency is less than $4,500, the agency may file an unitemized affidavit stating that the total amount paid is less than $4,500 unless the court, in its discretion, requires that agency to file an itemized affidavit.

(c) No affidavit need be filed in the case of an adoption of a related child or an adult, nor shall an affidavit be required to be filed by a non-consenting parent, or by any judge, or clerk, involved in an official capacity in the adoption proceedings.

(d) All affidavits filed in accordance with this Section shall be under penalty of perjury and shall include, but are not limited to, hospital and medical costs, legal fees, social services, living expenses or any other expenses related to the adoption or to the placement of the child, whether or not the payments are permitted by applicable laws.

(e) Upon the expiration of 6 months after the date of any interim order vesting temporary care, custody and control of a child, other than a related child, in the petitioners, entered pursuant to this Act, the petitioners may apply to the court for a judgment of adoption. Notice of such application shall be served by the petitioners upon the investigating agency or the person making such investigation, and the guardian ad litem. After the hearing on such application, at which the petitioners and the child shall appear in person, unless their presence is waived by the court for good cause shown, the court may enter a judgment for adoption, provided the court is satisfied from the report of the investigating agency or the person making the investigation, and from the evidence, if any, introduced, that the adoption is for the welfare of the child and that there is a valid consent, or that no consent is required as provided in Section 8 of this Act [750 ILCS 50/8].

(f) A judgment for adoption of a related child, an adult, or a child as to whose adoption an agency or person authorized by law has the right of authority to consent may be entered at any time after service of process and after the return day designated therein.

(f-5) A standby adoption judgment may be entered upon notice of the death of the consenting parent or upon the consenting parent's request that a final judgment for adoption be entered. The notice must be provided to the court within 60 days after the standby adoptive parent's receipt of knowledge of death of the consenting parent or the consenting parent's request that a final judgment for adoption be entered. If the court finds that adoption is for the welfare of the child and that there is a valid consent, including consent for standby adoption, which is still in effect, or that no consent is required under Section 8 of the Act [750 ILCS 50/8], a judgment for adoption shall be entered unless the court finds by clear and convincing evidence that it is no longer in the best interest of the child for the adoption to be finalized.

(g) No special findings of fact or certificate of evidence shall be necessary in any case to support the judgment.

(h) Only the circuit court that entered the judgment of the adoption may order the issuance of any contents of the court file or that the original birth record of the adoptee be provided to any persons.

(Source: P.A. 84-452; 88-148, § 10; 91-572, § 5; 93-732, § 5.)

Note.

This section was Ill.Rev.Stat., Ch. 40, para. 1517.

Effect of Amendments.

The 1999 amendment by P.A. 91-572, effective January 1, 2000, inserted subsection (f-5).

The 2004 amendment by P.A. 93-732, effective January 1, 2005, substituted "consenting parent" for "consenting terminally ill parent" throughout subsection (f-5).

CASE NOTES

Analysis

Appearance in Court
Decree
Parental Consent
Single Hearing

Appearance in Court

Former section 14 of the Adoption Act (see now this section) suggested the presence of the child at the final adoption hearing, but allowed the court to waive this requirement for good cause shown. Donlon v. Miller, 42 Ill. App. 3d 64, 355 N.E.2d 195 (3 Dist. 1976).

Where the child is of such age as to be incapable of understanding the nature of the proceedings except in very broad and simple terms, normally the decision of the legal custodian or guardian determines whether the child appears in court. Donlon v. Miller, 42 Ill. App. 3d 64, 355 N.E.2d 195 (3 Dist. 1976).

Decree

An adoption decree clearly does not fit the definition of a consent decree; rather, its entry is dependent on the court's finding from the evidence, if any, introduced, that the adoption is for the welfare of the child. Flangel v. Flangel, 87 Ill. App. 3d 1100, 42 Ill. Dec. 906, 409 N.E.2d 521 (2 Dist. 1980).

Parental Consent

In the absence of valid parental consent, a finding of parental unfitness and a determination that adoption is for the welfare of the child are required before the court may enter an order of adoption. Freeman v. Settle, 75 Ill. App. 3d 799, 31 Ill. Dec. 78, 393 N.E.2d 1385 (5 Dist. 1979).

Single Hearing

This Act contains no requirement that separate hearings be held in instances where the petition is for the adoption of a related child; therefore, the trial court is required to find that a parent is unfit, absent his consent, before considering the welfare of the child, nevertheless, these determinations may be made at a single hearing. Freeman v. Settle, 75 Ill. App. 3d 799, 31 Ill. Dec. 78, 393 N.E.2d 1385 (5 Dist. 1979).

LEGAL PERIODICALS

For article, "Baby Richard and Beyond: The Future for Adopted Children", see 18 N. Ill. U.L. Rev. 445 (1999).

For note, "The Termination of Parental Rights: Lassiter and the New Illinois Termination Law," see 13 Loy. U. Chi. L. J. 135 (1981-82).

750 ILCS 50/14a [Death of child during proceedings]

Sec. 14a. After any court has acquired jurisdiction over the person of any child in an adoption proceeding, if such child dies before entry of final judgment, upon petition by the intended adoptive parent or parents suggesting the death of the child and asking that the court proceed in absence of the child to enter a final judgment, in the presence of the adoptive parent or parents who are parties to the record, the court shall proceed to hearing and final judgment to enable the child to have the intended name by adoption. Otherwise the court may dismiss the proceeding.

In the case of an adoption proceeding commenced after the death of the person sought to be adopted, the intended adoptive parent or parents shall not, by reason of such adoption, acquire any interest in the estate of such deceased person, nor shall the intended adoptive parent or parents acquire any other right or incur any duty or obligation with respect to such deceased person.

(Source: P.A. 85-517; 89-644, § 5.)

Note.

This section was Ill.Rev.Stat., Ch. 40, para. 1518.

Effect of Amendments.

The 1996 amendment by P.A. 89-644, effective January 1, 1997, in the first paragraph deleted "and the State's attorney" preceding "who are parties to the record".

750 ILCS 50/14b Death of intended adoptive parent prior to entry of judgment

Sec. 14b. *Death of intended adoptive parent prior to entry of judgment.* After any court has acquired jurisdiction over the person of any intended adoptive parent in an adoption proceeding, if the intended adoptive parent dies before entry of final judgment, upon petition by the other intended adoptive parent or the child's guardian ad litem suggesting the death of the intended adoptive parent and asking that the court proceed in absence of the deceased intended adoptive parent to enter a final judgment, in the presence of the other intended adoptive parent or the child to be adopted who is a party to the record, the court shall proceed to hearing and final judgment to enable the child to have the intended name by adoption. Otherwise the court may dismiss the proceeding.

This amendatory Act of the 91st General Assembly [P.A. 91-573] shall apply to all cases in which the court acquired jurisdiction of the person of any intended adoptive parent in an adoption proceeding, if such jurisdiction was acquired on or after November 1, 1997.

(Source: P.A. 91-573, § 5.)

Effective Date.
This section became effective January 1, 2000, pursuant to Ill. Const. (1970), Art. IV, § 10 and 5 ILCS 75/1.

750 ILCS 50/15 [Prime consideration]

Sec. 15. The welfare of the child shall be the prime consideration in all adoption proceedings. The court in entering a judgment of adoption shall, whenever possible, give custody through adoption to a petitioner or petitioners of the same religious belief as that of the child.
(Source: P.A. 84-452.)

Note.
This section was Ill.Rev.Stat., Ch. 40, para. 1519.

Illinois Administrative Code.
See 89 Illinois Administrative Code, § 309.130.

CASE NOTES

Analysis

In General
Best Interest
—Not Found
Construction
Effect of Religious Belief
Legislative Intent

In General
A court cannot grant an adoption solely on the basis of the best interests of the child, without a consent or a finding of unfitness, but a court must give prime consideration to the welfare and best interests of the child involved. Tiernan v. Stewart, 33 Ill. App. 3d 545, 338 N.E.2d 153 (2 Dist. 1975).

Best Interest

—Not Found
Despite the excellent care which petitioners provided for the child and the voluntary nature of the consent provided by the child's natural parents, evidence of petitioners financial instability and ongoing health problems supported the finding that the adoption would not be in the best interest of the child. Nees v. Doan, 185 Ill. App. 3d 122, 133 Ill. Dec. 180, 540 N.E.2d 1046 (4 Dist. 1989).

Construction
The use of the words "whenever possible" after the word "shall" in former Ill.Rev.Stat., ch. 4, para. 4-2 (see now this section) suggested that the legislature contemplated that identity of religion between adopting parents and children would not be followed in all adoptions. Cooper v. Hinrichs, 10 Ill. 2d 269, 140 N.E.2d 293 (1957).

The word "shall" does not have an exclusive, fixed or inviolate connotation, and has been construed as meaning both "must" and "may," depending upon the legislative intent. Cooper v. Hinrichs, 10 Ill. 2d 269, 140 N.E.2d 293 (1957).

Effect of Religious Belief
The religious faith of the adopting parents is a matter for consideration, among all the circumstances of gradational significance in promoting the welfare of the child, but a difference in the religion of adopting parents and children will not per se bar the adoption. Cooper v. Hinrichs, 10 Ill. 2d 269, 140 N.E.2d 293 (1957).

Legislative Intent
Former Ill.Rev.Stat., ch. 4, para. 4-2 (see now this section) indicated a legislative intention to stress the religious factor and to direct the court to give preferences to persons of the same religion as the child to be adopted, where they were otherwise qualified to promote the welfare of the child, but did not bar adoption irrespective of all other factors merely because the adopting parents were of a different religious persuasion than the child. Cooper v. Hinrichs, 10 Ill. 2d 269, 140 N.E.2d 293 (1957).

750 ILCS 50/15.1 [Foster parent; application for consent from guardian]

Sec. 15.1. (a) Any person over the age of 18, who has cared for a child for a continuous period of one year or more as a foster parent licensed under the Child Care Act of 1969 [225 ILCS 10/1 et seq.] to operate a foster family home, may apply to the child's guardian with the power to consent to adoption, for such guardian's consent.

(b) Such guardian shall give preference and first consideration to that application over all other applications for adoption of the child but the guardian's final decision shall be based on the welfare and best interest of the child. In arriving at this decision, the guardian shall consider all relevant factors including but not limited to:

(1) the wishes of the child;

(2) the interaction and interrelationship of the child with the applicant to adopt the child;

(3) the child's need for stability and continuity of relationship with parent figures;

(4) the wishes of the child's parent as expressed in writing prior to that parent's execution of a consent or surrender for adoption;

(5) the child's adjustment to his present home, school and community;

(6) the mental and physical health of all individuals involved;

(7) the family ties between the child and the applicant to adopt the child and the value of preserving family ties between the child and the child's relatives, including siblings;

(8) the background, age and living arrangements of the applicant to adopt the child;

(9) the criminal background check report presented to the court as part of the investigation required under Section 6 of this Act [750 ILCS 50/6].

(c) The final determination of the propriety of the adoption shall be within the sole discretion of the court, which shall base its decision on the welfare and best interest of the child. In arriving at this decision, the court shall consider all relevant factors including but not limited to the factors in subsection (b).

(d) If the court specifically finds that the guardian has abused his discretion by withholding consent to an adoption in violation of the child's welfare and best interests, then the court may grant an adoption, after all of the other provisions of this Act have been complied with, with or without the consent of the guardian with power to consent to adoption. If the court specifically finds that the guardian has abused his discretion by granting consent to an adoption in violation of the child's welfare and best interests, then the court may deny an adoption even though the guardian with power to consent to adoption has consented to it.
(Source: P.A. 85-497; 87-1129, § 2; 90-608, § 40.)

Note.
This section was Ill.Rev.Stat., Ch. 40, para. 1519.1.

Effect of Amendments.

The 1998 amendment by P.A. 90-608, effective June 30, 1998, deleted "race, ethnic heritage, behavior" following "background" in subdivision (b)(8).

CASE NOTES

ANALYSIS

Constitutionality
—Due Process
—Equal Protection
—Liberty Interest
Determination Upheld
Expectancy Interest
Family Ties
—Sibling Visitation Rights
Foster Parents
—Adoption
—Wrongful Death Action

Constitutionality

—Due Process

The foster parent preference contained in subsection (b) does not violate the due process rights of out-of-state relatives. Bonnie S.P. v. Phillip P., 313 Ill. App. 3d 301, 246 Ill. Dec. 180, 729 N.E.2d 553, 2000 Ill. App. LEXIS 372 (4 Dist. 2000).

—Equal Protection

The foster parent preference contained in subsection (b) is rationally related to the legitimate goal of providing a stable adoptive home for children in need and does not violate the equal protection rights of out-of-state relatives. Bonnie S.P. v. Phillip P., 313 Ill. App. 3d 301, 246 Ill. Dec. 180, 729 N.E.2d 553, 2000 Ill. App. LEXIS 372 (4 Dist. 2000).

—Liberty Interest

The foster family's existence is subject to the state's determination that it should continue, and Illinois law can create no expectancy of a constitutionally protected liberty interest in family relationship. Procopio v. Johnson, 994 F.2d 325 (7th Cir. 1993).

Determination Upheld

The trial court's decision to allow one petition to adopt a child, and to disallow another petition by biological relatives, was in the child's best interests and was appropriately granted where: (1) the decision was in accord with the child's preference, (2) the child had bonded with his adoptive parents and considered them to be his parents, (3) the child had already lived with his adoptive parents for three years, and (4) while the families' income levels were virtually identical, the adoptive parents had four children less to support. Harold K. v. Ryan B., 313 Ill. App. 3d 692, 246 Ill. Dec. 408, 730 N.E.2d 88, 2000 Ill. App. LEXIS 319 (5 Dist. 2000), appeal denied, 191 Ill. 2d 529, 250 Ill. Dec. 456, 738 N.E.2d 925 (2000).

Expectancy Interest

Notwithstanding the preference state law grants to foster families seeking to adopt their foster children, this priority does not rise to the level of an entitlement or expectancy. Procopio v. Johnson, 994 F.2d 325 (7th Cir. 1993).

Family Ties

—Sibling Visitation Rights

Since the adoption court can sever all family ties as part of the adoption process, even those rights to sibling visitation that unadopted children may have may be severed as to their adopted siblings. In re Donte, 259 Ill. App. 3d 246, 197 Ill. Dec. 254, 631 N.E.2d 257 (1 Dist. 1994).

Foster Parents

—Adoption

The trial court did not commit reversible error by its application of subsection (b), notwithstanding the grandparents' argument that the the application of subsection (b) circumvented public policy favoring relatives in adoption proceedings, where the court appropriately considered all the testimony and evidence presented, as well as the factors set forth in the Adoption Act, in granting the foster parents' petition. Bonnie S.P. v. Phillip P., 313 Ill. App. 3d 301, 246 Ill. Dec. 180, 729 N.E.2d 553, 2000 Ill. App. LEXIS 372 (4 Dist. 2000).

Once an adoptive placement is determined to be in the best interests of the child, the responsibilities concerning the care, custody, and control of the child vest, solely, in the adoptive parents and it is up to them to decide whether to permit or deny continued contact with the child's biological family; biological family ties do not continue to receive protected status in the face of an adoption. In re Donte, 259 Ill. App. 3d 246, 197 Ill. Dec. 254, 631 N.E.2d 257 (1 Dist. 1994).

—Wrongful Death Action

Foster parents were not entitled to bring an action for wrongful death of a child on theories of an agreement to adopt or "equitable adoption." Evink v. Edwards ex rel. Gregory, 106 Ill. App. 3d 635, 62 Ill. Dec. 407, 435 N.E.2d 1379 (2 Dist. 1982).

RESEARCH REFERENCES

Standing of foster parent to seek termination of rights of foster child's natural parents. 21 ALR4th 535.

750 ILCS 50/16 Entry of Judgment

Sec. 16. *Entry of Judgment.* If, after examination of the report required by Section 6 [750 ILCS 50/6], the court finds a waiver to be for the welfare of the child, the court may, in its discretion, waive the waiting period of 6 months provided in Section 14 [750 ILCS 50/14] and enter a judgment of adoption. (Source: P.A. 84-452.)

Note.

This section was Ill.Rev.Stat., Ch. 40, para. 1520.

CASE NOTES

ANALYSIS

Adoption Orders
—Motion to Vacate
Legislative Intent
Waiver

Adoption Orders

—Motion to Vacate

The trial court properly denied petitioner's motion to vacate an adoption order and reopen the case on the basis of newly discovered evidence regarding the petitioner's competency where such evidence was discoverable before the original trial. People ex rel. Drury v. Catholic Home Bureau, 34 Ill. 2d 84, 213 N.E.2d 507 (1966).

Legislative Intent

The best interests and welfare of the child has been declared by the legislature to be of paramount consideration in the construction and interpretation of the former Adoption Act (see now 750 ILCS 50/0.01 et seq.). Neal v. Burton, 43 Ill. App. 3d 294, 1 Ill. Dec. 946, 356 N.E.2d 1279 (5 Dist. 1976).

Waiver

Petitioners who specifically waived the waiting period had no grounds to complain where their petition was denied within the six-month period. Nees v. Doan, 185 Ill. App. 3d 122, 133 Ill. Dec. 180, 540 N.E.2d 1046 (4 Dist. 1989).

750 ILCS 50/17 Effect of order terminating parental rights or Judgment of Adoption

Sec. 17. *Effect of order terminating parental rights or Judgment of Adoption.* After either the entry of an order terminating parental rights or the entry of

a judgment of adoption, the natural parents of a child sought to be adopted shall be relieved of all parental responsibility for such child and shall be deprived of all legal rights as respects the child, and the child shall be free from all obligations of maintenance and obedience as respects such natural parents.
(Source: P.A. 84-452; 91-357, § 262.)

Note.
This section was Ill.Rev.Stat., Ch. 40, para. 1521.

Illinois Administrative Code.
See 20 Illinois Administrative Code, § 107.320.

Effect of Amendments.
The 1999 amendment by P.A. 91-357, effective July 29, 1999, substituted "After either the entry" for "After the entry either" and made a stylistic change in the section heading.

CASE NOTES

Analysis

In General
Construction
Duty to Support
—Natural Father
Estoppel
Habeas Corpus
Illustrative Cases
Intervention
Jurisdiction
Parental Rights
—Not Terminated
Remaining Connections
Support Obligations
Visitation by Grandparents
Workers' Compensation Benefits

In General
Once an order terminating parental rights is entered, the natural parent is relieved of all parental responsibility for that child. Chiapelli ex rel. Ashton v. Viviano, 225 Ill. App. 3d 1026, 168 Ill. Dec. 84, 589 N.E.2d 198 (5 Dist. 1992).

After an order of adoption is entered, the natural parents of the adopted child are relieved of all parental responsibilities for the child and deprived of all parental rights with regard to the child and these parental rights and responsibilities are assumed by the adoptive parents. Krystek v. Schumacher, 120 Ill. App. 3d 50, 75 Ill. Dec. 926, 458 N.E.2d 94 (2 Dist. 1983).

Adoption constitutes a complete and permanent severance of all rights and interests of the natural parent and child which includes a termination of custodial rights, as well as all rights of the natural parent to visitation. Krystek v. Schumacher, 120 Ill. App. 3d 50, 75 Ill. Dec. 926, 458 N.E.2d 94 (2 Dist. 1983).

Construction
After a parent's parental rights have been terminated under this Act, that parent has no remaining residual rights of any kind, nor does that parent have any standing to raise any concerns or state any references regarding the ultimate placement of his or her child for adoption; when viewed from the perspective of the child, the parent whose parental rights have been terminated no longer exists. People v. Longshaw, 211 Ill. App. 3d 686, 164 Ill. Dec. 553, 583 N.E.2d 107 (4 Dist. 1991).

Duty to Support

—Natural Father
Under a prior provision of the Adoption Act, (see now this section) the primary duty of supporting, caring for and maintaining a child was on the adoptive parents; however, an adoption did not relieve the natural father, from his duty to support his offspring, and if necessity arose, he could be required to perform that duty. From the record it could not be said that the necessity had arisen so as to require the defendant to carry out his obligation as the natural father, and further evidence regarding that obligation was required. Anderson v. Anderson, 320 Ill. App. 75, 49 N.E.2d 841 (1 Dist. 1943).

Estoppel
Where wife was or should have been aware that ex-husband had stopped seeing his children because of the consent to adoption, it was her duty to inform him in no uncertain terms that there would be no adoption, that he could begin seeing his children again, and that he should start paying support. Because she did not so inform within a reasonable time, her silence contributed to ex-husband's harboring a misconception concerning his parental rights and responsibilities, and wife's failure to speak alone might well constitute a legitimate estoppel. Bodine v. Bodine, 141 Ill. App. 3d 21, 95 Ill. Dec. 349, 489 N.E.2d 911 (3 Dist. 1986).

Habeas Corpus
A decree of adoption of a minor child entered under former Ill.Rev.Stat., ch. 4, para. 9.1-17 (see now this section) terminated the authority of the court sitting in the original divorce action insofar as the custody and control of said child was concerned, and that court's order purporting to award joint custody of a child to respondents and petitioners was subject to attack in a habeas corpus proceeding. People ex rel. Bachleda v. Dean, 48 Ill. 2d 16, 268 N.E.2d 11 (1971).

Illustrative Cases
In adoptions involving strangers, the primary policy concern has traditionally been with maximizing the pool of potential adoptive parents by guaranteeing, through the termination of the rights and responsibilities of the natural parents, that the adoptive parents will have the opportunity to create a stable family relationship free from unnecessary intrusion. Lingwall v. Hoener, 108 Ill. 2d 206, 91 Ill. Dec. 166, 483 N.E.2d 512 (1985).

Intervention
Trial court did not err in dismissing natural father's petition to intervene where his parental rights had been terminated pursuant to former section 9.1-17 of chapter 4 (see now this section) despite fact that natural father's parental rights were terminated in an earlier adoption proceeding which was abandoned by the other petitioners before that adoption was finalized. Gray v. Starkey, 41 Ill. App. 3d 555, 353 N.E.2d 703 (5 Dist. 1976).

Jurisdiction
Appellate court lacked jurisdiction where the petitioners' notices of appeal were filed before entry of the written judgments, although after the trial judge's oral announcement that he would enter judgment terminating petitioners' parental rights. People v. Dunbar, 212 Ill. App. 3d 251, 156 Ill. Dec. 462, 570 N.E.2d 1184 (2 Dist. 1991).

Parental Rights

—Not Terminated
Because an interim order terminating parental rights had not become final at the time the adoption proceeding was dismissed, dismissal of the main proceeding of which it was a part, rendered it functus officio or without effect. Therefore, the respondent's parental rights were not altered by the interim order in the unsuccessful adoption proceeding and the court's order in the estate proceeding, excluding the respondent as an heir by virtue of this interim order, was erroneous. McGathey v. Griffin, 160 Ill. App. 3d 670, 112 Ill. Dec. 635, 514 N.E.2d 31 (5 Dist. 1987), appeal denied, 117 Ill. Dec. 226, 520 N.E.2d 387 (Ill. 1988).

Remaining Connections
There was no absurdity in an adopted child's inheriting from both of his or her natural parents, and 755 ILCS 5/2-4(d)(1) of the Probate Act of 1975, clearly required a court to hold that a deceased's purported illegitimate natural children were the deceased's heirs, if they were in fact the deceased's natural children. Estate of Snodgrass v. Snodgrass, 336 Ill. App. 3d 619, 271 Ill. Dec. 213, 784 N.E.2d 431, 2003 Ill. App. LEXIS 175 (4 Dist. 2003), appeal denied sub nom. Parr v. Snodgrass (In re Estate of Snodgrass), 204 Ill. 2d 683, 275 Ill. Dec. 83, 792 N.E.2d 314 (2003).

Remaining Connections (Cont'd)

Following an adoption, the only connections remaining between the natural parent and the child are that the natural parent may be required to support the child if the adoptive parent is unable to do so and that the child may inherit from the natural parent. Krystek v. Schumacher, 120 Ill. App. 3d 50, 75 Ill. Dec. 926, 458 N.E.2d 94 (2 Dist. 1983).

Support Obligations

A prior similar provision was not construed as relieving the natural parents from all obligation to support their minor children. Dwyer v. Dwyer, 366 Ill. 630, 10 N.E.2d 344 (1937).

Visitation by Grandparents

The Marriage and Dissolution of Marriage Act (see 750 ILCS 5/101 et seq.) and this Act share the common goal of proceeding in the child's best interest and welfare, and the statutes should be read together to give effect to their common goal, thus, when an adoption by a natural parent and a new spouse has occurred, the court must examine all relevant factors to determine whether grandparental visitation is in the child's best interest. Lingwall v. Hoener, 108 Ill. 2d 206, 91 Ill. Dec. 166, 483 N.E.2d 512 (1985).

While the best interests of the adopted child are to be a paramount concern in adoption proceedings and the adoption statute is to be liberally construed, these principles do not constitute authorization for an order of grandparent visitation given the fact that the adoption judgment has the effect of terminating the rights of the natural parent. Krystek v. Schumacher, 120 Ill. App. 3d 50, 75 Ill. Dec. 926, 458 N.E.2d 94 (2 Dist. 1983).

Workers' Compensation Benefits

In order to award death benefits to minors under subsection 7(a) of the Workers' Compensation Act (820 ILCS 305/7) it must be established that a legally enforceable basis for the dependency existed at the time of the employee's accident and, at time of the accident causing his death, legal obligation of decedent to support his minor daughter did not exist, pursuant to former section 17 of the Adoption Act (Ill.Rev.Stat., ch. 4, para. 9.1-17) (see now this section) since she had been adopted by her stepfather; thus, daughter was not entitled to recover compensation benefits due to the accidental death of her natural father from work-related injuries. Inventory Serv. Corp. v. Industrial Comm'n, 62 Ill. 2d 34, 338 N.E.2d 377 (1975).

LEGAL PERIODICALS

For article, "Family Law: 1985-86 Illinois Law Survey," see 18 Loy. U. Chi. L. J. 549 (1986-87).

For article, "Surrogate Parenthood: A Need for Legislative Direction," see 71 Ill. B. J. 412 (1983).

For article: "Toward the Concept of Future Parental Capacity, Under the Illinois Adoption Act," see 66 Ill. B. J. 638 (1978).

RESEARCH REFERENCES

Validity of state statute providing for termination of parental rights. 22 ALR4th 774.

Postadoption visitation by natural parent. 78 ALR4th 218.

750 ILCS 50/18 Records confidential

Sec. 18. *Records confidential.* (a) The word "illegitimate", the words "born out of wedlock", and words of similar import shall not be used in any adoption proceeding in any respect.

(b) The court call of adoption proceedings shall not identify any of the parties by name. The parties may be identified by initials or pseudonyms. The case shall be identified by its general number. The names of the lawyers representing the parties may appear on the court call, and the type of application that is being made to the court may also be identified.

(c) All adoption records maintained by each circuit clerk shall be impounded in accordance with the procedures provided by the Illinois Supreme Court's General Administrative Order on Recordkeeping and shall be opened for examination only upon specific order of the court, which order shall name the person or persons who are to be permitted to examine the file. Certified copies of all papers and documents contained in any file so impounded shall be made only on like order. The guardian ad litem for a minor sought to be adopted shall have the right to inspect the court file without leave of court during the pendency of the proceeding. The attorney of record for the petitioners and other parties may inspect the file only with leave of court. The petitioners to the adoption, the attorney of record for the petitioners, and the guardian ad litem of the person who is the subject of the proceeding shall be entitled to receive certified copies of the order of adoption in the proceeding at any time within 30 days after the entry of the judgment of adoption without order of court. After 30 days from the entry of the judgment of adoption, no copies may be obtained without prior order of court, but good cause is not necessary to be shown by one of the petitioners to the adoption.

(d) If an appeal is taken from an adoption proceeding, the papers filed in the court of review and the opinion of the reviewing court shall not identify the true names of the parties; instead, initials or pseudonyms shall be used to identify the parties.

(Source: P.A. 86-493; 87-620.)

Note.

This section was Ill.Rev.Stat., Ch. 40, para. 1522.

CASE NOTES

Analysis

Constitutionality
In General
Applicability
Good Cause
—Adulthood
—Inheritance

Constitutionality

This statute is rationally related to the legitimate legislative purpose of protecting the adoption process, consequently, this section does not unconstitutionally infringe upon an adoptee's right to discover his own identity. In re Roger B., 84 Ill. 2d 323, 49 Ill. Dec. 731, 418 N.E.2d 751, appeal dismissed, 454 U.S. 806, 102 S. Ct. 80, 70 L. Ed. 2d 76 (1981).

Section 18 of the former Adoption Act does not create a suspect classification. In re Roger B., 84 Ill. 2d 323, 49 Ill. Dec. 731, 418 N.E.2d 751, appeal dismissed, 454 U.S. 806, 102 S. Ct. 80, 70 L. Ed. 2d 76 (1981).

This section does not violate one's constitutional right to receive information under the First Amendment. In re Roger B., 84 Ill. 2d 323, 49 Ill. Dec. 731, 418 N.E.2d 751, appeal dismissed, 454 U.S. 806, 102 S. Ct. 80, 70 L. Ed. 2d 76 (1981).

This section contains no equal protection violation of the United States Constitution. In re Roger B., 84 Ill. 2d 323, 49 Ill. Dec. 731, 418 N.E.2d 751, appeal dismissed, 454 U.S. 806, 102 S. Ct. 80, 70 L. Ed. 2d 76 (1981).

This statute does not violate an adoptee's right to receive important information and his right to privacy; nor his due process rights; nor his right to equal protection of the laws; nor does the

Constitutionality (Cont'd)
statute violate the U.S. Const., Amend. IX. Roger B. v. People, 85 Ill. App. 3d 1064, 41 Ill. Dec. 386, 407 N.E.2d 884 (1 Dist. 1980), aff'd, 84 Ill. 2d 323, 418 N.E.2d 751, cert. denied, 454 U.S. 806, 102 S. Ct. 80, 70 L. Ed. 2d 76 (1981).

In General

This section represents a considered legislative judgment that confidentiality promotes the integrity of the adoption process. In re Roger B., 84 Ill. 2d 323, 49 Ill. Dec. 731, 418 N.E.2d 751, appeal dismissed, 454 U.S. 806, 102 S. Ct. 80, 70 L. Ed. 2d 76 (1981).

This statute, by providing for release of adoption records only upon issuance of a court order, does no more than allow the court to balance the interests of all the parties and make a determination based on the facts and circumstances of each individual case. In re Roger B., 84 Ill. 2d 323, 49 Ill. Dec. 731, 418 N.E.2d 751, appeal dismissed, 454 U.S. 806, 102 S. Ct. 80, 70 L. Ed. 2d 76 (1981).

The discretion conferred by this statute upon the courts was intended to be exercised upon a showing of good cause. In re Roger B., 84 Ill. 2d 323, 49 Ill. Dec. 731, 418 N.E.2d 751, appeal dismissed, 454 U.S. 806, 102 S. Ct. 80, 70 L. Ed. 2d 76 (1981).

Applicability

The use of pseudonyms in accordance with subsection (d) was appropriate in an action which was related to an adoption proceeding, even though the underlying petition was filed on the trial court's MR calendar and not in the adoption case number. Doe v. Noe, 317 Ill. App. 3d 419, 251 Ill. Dec. 103, 739 N.E.2d 1036, 2000 Ill. App. LEXIS 922 (4 Dist. 2000), cert. denied, 535 U.S. 932, 122 S. Ct. 1308, 152 L. Ed. 2d 218 (2002).

Good Cause

—Adulthood

Adulthood of the adoptee is not of itself good cause to have access to sealed adoption records; good cause requires an analysis of many factors, which will necessarily vary depending upon the facts of each case. Roger B. v. People, 85 Ill. App. 3d 1064, 41 Ill. Dec. 386, 407 N.E.2d 884 (1 Dist. 1980), aff'd, 84 Ill. 2d 323, 418 N.E.2d 751, cert. denied, 454 U.S. 806, 102 S. Ct. 80, 70 L. Ed. 2d 76 (1981).

—Inheritance

The expectation of a possibility that an adopted person may inherit from her natural parents was not a sufficient cause to open sealed adoption files, as a possible inheritance did not outweigh the policy considerations for keeping adoption files under seal. Aimone v. Finley, 113 Ill. App. 3d 507, 69 Ill. Dec. 433, 447 N.E.2d 868 (1 Dist. 1983), appeal dismissed, 465 U.S. 1095, 104 S. Ct. 1583, 80 L. Ed. 2d 117 (1984).

LEGAL PERIODICALS

For comment, "Severed Roots: The Sealed Adoption Records Controversy," see 6 N. Ill. U.L. Rev. 103 (1986).

RESEARCH REFERENCES

Natural parent's parental rights as affected by consent to child's adoption by other natural parent. 37 ALR4th 724.

Restricting access to judicial records of concluded adoption proceedings. 103 ALR5th 255.

750 ILCS 50/18.04 The Illinois Adoption Registry and Medical Information Exchange; legislative intent

Sec. 18.04. *The Illinois Adoption Registry and Medical Information Exchange; legislative intent.* The General Assembly recognizes the importance of creating a procedure by which mutually consenting adult members of birth families, adoptive parents and legal guardians of adopted and surrendered children, and adult adopted or surrendered persons may voluntarily exchange vital medical information throughout the life of the adopted or surrendered person. The General Assembly supports public policy that requires explicit mutual consent prior to the release of confidential information. The General Assembly further recognizes that it is in the best interest of adopted and surrendered persons that birth family medical histories and the preferences regarding contact of all parties to an adoption be compiled, preserved and provided to mutually consenting adoptive parents and legal guardians of adopted or surrendered children and to adult adopted or surrendered persons and their birth parents and siblings. The purpose of this amendatory Act of 1999 [P.A. 91-417] is to respond to these concerns by enhancing the Adoption Registry and creating the voluntary Medical Information Exchange.

(Source: P.A. 91-417, § 10.)

Effective Date.

This section became effective January 1, 2000 pursuant to Ill. Const. (1970), Art. IV, § 10 and 5 ILCS 75/2.

750 ILCS 50/18.05 The Illinois Adoption Registry and Medical Information Exchange

Sec. 18.05. *The Illinois Adoption Registry and Medical Information Exchange.* (a) General function. Subject to appropriation, the Department of Public Health shall redefine the function of the Illinois Adoption Registry and create the Medical Information Exchange in the manner outlined in subsections (b) and (c) for the purpose of facilitating the voluntary exchange of medical information between mutually consenting birth parents or birth siblings and mutually consenting adoptive parents or legal guardians of adopted or surrendered persons under the age of 21 or adopted or surrendered persons 21 years of age or over. The Department shall establish rules for the confidential operation of the Illinois Adoption Registry. Beginning January 1, 2000, the Department shall conduct a public information campaign through public service announcements and other forms of media coverage and, for a minimum of 4 years, through notices enclosed with driver's license renewal applications, shall inform adopted and surrendered persons born, surrendered, or adopted in Illinois and their adoptive parents, legal guardians, birth parents and birth siblings of the Illinois Adoption Registry and Medical Information Exchange. The Department shall notify all parties who registered with the Illinois Adoption Registry prior to January 1, 2000 of the provisions of this amendatory Act of 1999 [P.A. 91-417]. The Illinois Adoption Registry shall also maintain an informational Internet site where interested parties may access information about the Illinois Adoption Registry and Medical Information Exchange and download all necessary application forms. The Illinois Adoption Registry shall maintain statistical records regarding Registry participation and publish and circulate to the public informational material about the function and operation of the Registry.

(b) Establishment of the Adoption/Surrender Records File. When a person has voluntarily registered with the Illinois Adoption Registry and completed an Illinois Adoption Registry Application or a Registration Identification Form, the Registry shall establish a new Adoption/Surrender Records File. Such file may concern an adoption that was finalized by a court action in the State of Illinois, an adoption of a person born in Illinois finalized by a court action in a state other than Illinois or in a foreign country, or a surrender taken in the State of Illinois. Such file may be established for adoptions or surrenders finalized prior to as well as after the effective date of this amendatory Act of 1999 [P.A. 91-417]. A file may be created in any manner to preserve documents including but not limited to microfilm, optical imaging, or electronic documents.

(c) Contents of the Adoption/Surrender Records File. An established Adoption/Surrender Records File shall be limited to the following items, to the extent that they are available:

(1) The General Information Section and Medical Information Exchange Questionnaire of any Illinois Adoption Registry Application or a Registration Identification Form which has been voluntarily completed by the adopted or surrendered person or his or her adoptive parents, legal guardians, birth parents, or birth siblings.

(2) Any photographs voluntarily provided by any registrant for the adopted or surrendered person or his or her adoptive parents, legal guardians, birth parents, or birth siblings at the time of registration or any time thereafter. All such photographs shall be submitted in an unsealed envelope no larger than 8 ½″ x 11″, and shall not include identifying information pertaining to any person other than the registrant who submitted them. Any such identifying information shall be redacted by the Department or the information shall be returned for removal of identifying information.

(3) Any Information Exchange Authorization or Denial of Information Exchange which has been filed by a registrant.

(4) For all adoptions finalized after January 1, 2000, copies of the original certificate of live birth and the certificate of adoption.

(5) Any updated address submitted by any registered party about himself or herself.

(6) Any proof of death which has been submitted by an adopted or surrendered person, adoptive parent, legal guardian, birth parent, or birth sibling.
(Source: P.A. 91-417, § 10.)

Effective Date.
This section became effective January 1, 2000 pursuant to Ill. Const. (1970), Art. IV, § 10 and 5 ILCS 75/2.

750 ILCS 50/18.06 Definitions

Sec. 18.06. *Definitions.* When used in Sections 18.05 through Section 18.6 [750 ILCS 50/18.05 through 750 ILCS 50/18.6], for the purposes of the Registry:

"Adopted person" means a person who was adopted pursuant to the laws in effect at the time of the adoption.

"Adoptive parent" means a person who has become a parent through the legal process of adoption.

"Agency" means a public child welfare agency or a licensed child welfare agency.

"Birth father" means the biological father of an adopted or surrendered person who is named on the original certificate of live birth or on a consent or surrender document, or a biological father whose paternity has been established by a judgment or order of the court, pursuant to the Illinois Parentage Act of 1984 [750 ILCS 45/1 et seq.].

"Birth mother" means the biological mother of an adopted or surrendered person.

"Birth parent" means a birth mother or birth father of an adopted or surrendered person.

"Birth sibling" means the adult full or half sibling of an adopted or surrendered person.

"Denial of Information Exchange" means an affidavit completed by a registrant with the Illinois Adoption Registry and Medical Information Exchange denying the release of identifying information.

"Information Exchange Authorization" means an affidavit completed by a registrant with the Illinois Adoption Registry and Medical Information Exchange authorizing the release of identifying information.

"Medical Information Exchange Questionnaire" means the medical history questionnaire completed by a registrant of the Illinois Adoption Registry and Medical Information Exchange.

"Proof of death" means a death certificate.

"Registrant" or "Registered Party" means a birth parent, birth sibling, adopted or surrendered person over the age of 21, or adoptive parent or legal guardian of an adopted or surrendered person under the age of 21 who has filed an Illinois Adoption Registry Application or Registration Identification Form with the Registry.

"Surrendered person" means a person whose parents' rights have been surrendered or terminated but who has not been adopted.
(Source: P.A. 91-417, § 10.)

Effective Date.
This section became effective January 1, 2000 pursuant to Ill. Const. (1970), Art. IV, § 10 and 5 ILCS 75/2.

750 ILCS 50/18.07 Adoption Registry Advisory Council

Sec. 18.07. *Adoption Registry Advisory Council.* There is established an Adoption Registry Advisory Council. The Council shall be chaired by the Director of the Department of Public Health or his designee. The Council shall include the Director of the Department of Children and Family Services or his designee. The Council shall also include one representative from each of the following organizations: Adoption Advocates of Illinois, Adoptive Families Today, American Adoption Congress, Catholic Conference of Illinois, Chicago Area Families for Adoption, Chicago Bar Association, Child Care Association of Illinois, Children Remembered, Inc., Children's Home and Aid Society of Illinois, Child Welfare Advisory Council, The Cradle, Healing Hearts, Illinois Foster Parents Association, Illinois State Bar Association, Illinois State Medical Society, Jewish Children's Bureau, Kids Help Foundation, LDS Social Services, Lutheran Social Services of Illinois, Maryville Academy, Midwest Adoption Center, St. Mary's Services, Stars of David, and Truthseekers in Adoption.

If any one of the above named organizations notifies the Director of the Department of Public Health in writing that the organization does not wish to participate on the Advisory Council or that the organization is no longer functioning, the Director shall appoint another organization that represents the same constituency as the named organization to replace the named organization on the Council.

The Council's responsibilities shall include the following:

1) Advising the Department on the development of rules, procedures, and forms utilized by the Illinois Adoption Registry and Medical Information Exchange;

2) Making recommendations regarding the procedures, tools and technology that will ensure efficient and effective operation of the Registry;

3) Submitting a report to the Governor and the General Assembly no later than January 1, 2001, on the status of the Registry, an evaluation of the effectiveness of the Registry, and pertinent statistics regarding the Registry;

4) Assisting the Department with the development, publication, and circulation of an informational pamphlet that describes the purpose, function, and mechanics of the Illinois Adoption Registry and Medical Information Exchange, including information about who is eligible to register and how to register; information about the questions and concerns that registrants may develop when they register or when they receive information from the Registry; and a list of services, programs, groups, and informational websites that are available to assist registrants with their questions and concerns.
(Source: P.A. 91-417, § 10.)

Effective Date.
This section became effective January 1, 2000 pursuant to Ill. Const. (1970), Art. IV, § 10 and 5 ILCS 75/1.

750 ILCS 50/18.1 Disclosure of identifying information

Sec. 18.1. *Disclosure of identifying information.* (a) The Department of Public Health shall establish and maintain a Registry for the purpose of providing identifying information to mutually consenting adult adopted or surrendered persons, birth parents, adoptive parents, legal guardians and birth siblings. Identifying information for the purpose of this Act shall mean any one or more of the following:

(1) The name and last known address of the consenting person or persons.

(2) A copy of the Illinois Adoption Registry Application of the consenting person or persons.

(3) A copy of the original certificate of live birth of the adopted person.

Written authorization from all parties identified must be received prior to disclosure of any identifying information.

(b) At any time after a child is surrendered for adoption, or at any time during the adoption proceedings or at any time thereafter, either birth parent or both of them may file with the Registry a Birth Parent Registration Identification Form and an Information Exchange Authorization or a Denial of Information Exchange.

(b-5) A birth sibling 21 years of age or over who was not surrendered for adoption and who has submitted proof of death for a deceased birth parent and such birth parent did not file a Denial of Information Exchange with the Registry prior to his or her death may file a Registration Identification Form and an Information Exchange Authorization or a Denial of Information Exchange.

(c) Any adopted person over the age of 21, any surrendered person over the age of 21, or any adoptive parent or legal guardian of an adopted or surrendered person under the age of 21 may file with the Registry a Registration Identification Form and an Information Exchange Authorization or a Denial of Information Exchange.

(d) The Department of Public Health shall supply to the adopted or surrendered person or his or her adoptive parents or legal guardians and to the birth parents identifying information only if both the adopted or surrendered person or his or her adoptive parents or legal guardians and the birth parents have filed with the Registry an Information Exchange Authorization and the information at the Registry indicates that the consenting adopted or surrendered person or the child of the consenting adoptive parents or legal guardians is the child of the consenting birth parents.

The Department of Public Health shall supply to adopted or surrendered persons who are birth siblings identifying information only if both siblings have filed with the Registry an Information Exchange Authorization and the information at the Registry indicates that the consenting siblings have one or both birth parents in common. Identifying information shall be supplied to consenting birth siblings who were adopted or surrendered if any such sibling is 21 years of age or over. Identifying information shall be supplied to consenting birth siblings who were not adopted or surrendered if any such sibling is 21 years of age or over and has proof of death of the common birth parent and such birth parent did not file a Denial of Information Exchange with the Registry prior to his or her death.

(e) A birth parent, birth sibling, adopted or surrendered person or their adoptive parents or legal guardians may notify the Registry of his or her desire not to have his or her identity revealed or may revoke any previously filed Information Exchange Authorization by completing and filing with the Registry a Registry Identification Form along with a Denial of Information Exchange. The Illinois Adoption Registry Application does not need to be completed in order to file a Denial of Information Exchange. Any adopted or, surrendered person or his or her adoptive parents or legal guardians, birth sibling or birth parent may revoke a Denial of Information Exchange by filing an Information Exchange Authorization. The Department of Public Health shall act in accordance with the most recently filed Authorization.

(f) Identifying information ascertained from the Registry shall be confidential and may be disclosed only (1) upon a Court Order, which order shall name the person or persons entitled to the information, or (2) to the adopted or surrendered person, adoptive parents or legal guardians, birth sibling, or birth parent if both the adopted or surrendered person or his or her adoptive parents or legal guardians, and his or her birth parent, or both, birth siblings, have filed with the Registry an Information Exchange Authorization, or (3) as authorized under subsection (h) of Section 18.3 of this Act [750 ILCS 50/18.3]. A copy of the certificate of live birth shall only be released to an adopted person who was born in Illinois and who is the subject of an Information Exchange Authorization filed by one of his or her birth parents or non-surrendered birth siblings. Any person who willfully provides unauthorized disclosure of any information filed with the Registry or who knowingly or intentionally files false information with the Registry shall be guilty of a Class A misdemeanor and shall be liable for damages.

(g) If information is disclosed pursuant to this Act, the Department shall redact it to remove any identifying information about any party who has not consented to the disclosure of such identifying information.

(Source: P.A. 86-1451; 91-417, § 10; 92-16, § 99.)

Note.

This section was Ill.Rev.Stat., Ch. 40, para. 1522.1.

Section 996 of P.A. 92-16 contains a "no acceleration or delay" provision, and Section 997 contains a "no revival or extension" provision.

Effect of Amendments.

The 1999 amendment by P.A. 91-417, effective January 1, 2000, rewrote subsections (a) through (f) to the extent that a detailed comparison would be impracticable; inserted subsection (b-5); and added subsection (g).

The 2001 amendment by P.A. 92-16, effective June 28, 2001, made a typographical correction and a stylistic change.

750 ILCS 50/18.1a Registry matches

Sec. 18.1a. *Registry matches.* (a) The Registry shall release identifying information, as specified on the Information Exchange Authorization, to the following mutually consenting registered parties and provide them with any photographs which have been placed in the Adoption/Surrender Records File and are specifically intended for the registered parties:

(i) an adult adopted or surrendered person and one of his or her birth parents or birth siblings who have both filed an applicable Information Exchange Authorization specifying the other consenting party with the Registry, if information available to the Registry confirms that the consenting adopted or surrendered person is a birth relative of the consenting birth parent or sibling;

(ii) the adoptive parent or legal guardian of an adopted or surrendered person under the age of 21 and one of his or her birth parents or birth siblings who have both filed an Information Exchange Authorization specifying the other consenting party with the Registry, if information available to the Registry confirms that the child of the consenting adoptive parent or legal guardian is a birth relative of the consenting birth parent or birth sibling.

(b) If a registrant is the subject of a Denial of Information Exchange filed by another party to the adoption, the Registry shall not release identifying information to either registrant.

(c) If a registrant has completed a Medical Information Exchange Questionnaire and has consented to its disclosure, that Questionnaire shall be released to any registered party who has indicated their desire to receive such information on his or her Illinois Adoption Registry Application, if information available to the Registry confirms that the consenting parties are birth relatives or that the consenting birth relative and the child of the consenting, adoptive parents or legal guardians are birth relatives.

(Source: P.A. 91-417, § 10.)

Effective Date.

This section became effective January 1, 2000 pursuant to Ill. Const. (1970), Art. IV, § 10 and 5 ILCS 75/2.

750 ILCS 50/18.1b The Illinois Adoption Registry Application

Sec. 18.1b. *The Illinois Adoption Registry Application.* The Illinois Adoption Registry Application shall substantially include the following:

(a) General Information. The Illinois Adoption Registry Application shall include the space to provide Information about the registrant including his or her surname, given name or names, social security number (optional), mailing address, home telephone number, gender, date and place of birth, and the date of registration. If applicable and known to the registrant, he or she may include the maiden surname of the birth mother, any subsequent surnames of the birth mother, the surname of the birth father, the given name or names of the birth parents, the dates and places of birth of the birth parents, the surname and given name or names of the adopted person prior to adoption, the gender and date and place of birth of the adopted or surrendered person, the name of the adopted person following his or her adoption and the state and county where the judgment of adoption was finalized.

(b) Medical Information Exchange Questionnaire. In recognition of the importance of medical information and of recent discoveries regarding the genetic origin of many medical conditions and diseases all registrants shall be asked to voluntarily complete a Medical Information Exchange Questionnaire.

(1) For birth parents or birth siblings, the Medical Information Exchange Questionnaire shall include a comprehensive check-list of medical conditions and diseases including those of genetic origin. Birth parents and birth siblings shall be asked to indicate all genetically-inherited diseases and conditions on this list which are known to exist in the adopted or surrendered person's birth family at the time of registration. In addition, all birth parents and birth siblings shall be apprised of the Registry's provisions for voluntarily submitting information about their and their family's medical histories on a confidential, ongoing basis.

(2) Adopted and surrendered persons and their adoptive parents or legal guardians shall be asked to indicate all genetically-inherited diseases and medical conditions with which the adopted or surrendered person or, if applicable, his or her children have been diagnosed since birth.

(3) The Medical Information Exchange Questionnaire shall include a space where the registrant may authorize the release of the Medical Information Exchange Questionnaire to specified parties and a disclaimer informing registrants that the Department of Public Health cannot guarantee the accuracy of medical information exchanged through the Registry.

(c) Written statement. All registrants shall be given the opportunity to voluntarily file a written statement with the Registry. This statement shall be submitted in the space provided. No written statement submitted to the Registry shall include identifying information pertaining to any person other than the registrant who submitted it. Any such identifying information shall be redacted by the Department or returned for removal of identifying information.

(d) Contact information. All registrants may indicate their wishes regarding contact with any other registrant by completing an Information Exchange Authorization or a Denial of Information Exchange.

(1) Information Exchange Authorization. Adopted or surrendered persons 21 years of age or over who would welcome contact with one or more of their birth parents or birth siblings; birth parents who would welcome contact with an adopted or surrendered person, or one or more of his or her adoptive parents or legal guardians; birth siblings 21 years of age or over who were adopted or surrendered and who would welcome contact with an adopted or surrendered person, or one or more of his or her adoptive parents or legal guardians; birth siblings 21 years of age or over who were not surrendered and who have submitted proof of death for any common birth parent who did not file a Denial of Information Exchange prior to his or her death, and who would welcome contact with an adopted or surrendered person, or one or more of his or her adoptive parents or legal guardians; and adoptive parents or legal guardians of adopted or surrendered persons under the age of 21 who would welcome contact with one or more of the adopted or surrendered person's birth parents or birth siblings may specify with whom they wish to exchange identifying information by filing an Information Exchange Authorization at the time of the adoption or surrender, or any time thereafter.

(2) Denial of Information Exchange. Adopted or surrendered persons 21 years of age or over who do not wish to establish contact with one or more of their birth parents or birth siblings may specify with whom they do not wish to exchange identifying information by filing a Denial of Information Exchange. Birth parents or birth siblings who do not wish to establish contact with an adopted or surrendered person or one or more of his or her adoptive parents or legal guardians may specify with whom they do not wish to exchange identifying information by filing a Denial of Information Exchange at the time of the adoption or surrender, or any time thereafter. Adoptive parents or legal guardians of adopted or surrendered persons under the age of 21 who do not wish to establish contact with one or more of the adopted or surrendered person's birth parents or birth siblings may specify with whom they do not wish to exchange identifying information by filing a Denial of Information Exchange at the time of the adoption or surrender, or any time thereafter. The Illinois Adoption Registry Application does not need to be completed in order to file a Denial of Information Exchange.

(e) A registrant may complete all or any part of the Illinois Adoption Registry Application. All Illinois Adoption Registry Applications, Information Exchange Authorizations, Denials of Information Exchange, requests to revoke an Information Exchange Authorization or Denial of Information Exchange, and affidavits submitted to the Registry shall be accompanied by proof of identification.

(f) The Department shall establish the Illinois Adoption Registry Application form including the Medical Information Exchange Questionnaire by rule.

(Source: P.A. 91-417, § 10.)

Effective Date.

This section became effective January 1, 2000 pursuant to Ill. Const. (1970), Art. IV, § 10 and 5 ILCS 75/2.

750 ILCS 50/18.1c Effective date of registration

Sec. 18.1c. *Effective date of registration.* Registration with the Illinois Adoption Registry and Medical Information Exchange shall become effective as soon as the applicant's completed Illinois Adoption Registry Application has been filed with the Registry. (Source: P.A. 91-417, § 10.)

Effective Date.
This section became effective January 1, 2000 pursuant to Ill. Const. (1970), Art. IV, § 10 and 5 ILCS 75/2.

750 ILCS 50/18.2 Forms

Sec. 18.2. *Forms.* (a) The form of the Birth Parent Registration Identification Form shall be substantially as follows:

BIRTH PARENT REGISTRATION IDENTIFICATION

(Insert all known information)

I, ..., state that I am the .... (mother or father) of the following child:

Child's original name: .... (first) .... (middle) .... (last), ... (hour of birth), ... (date of birth), ... (city and state of birth), ... (name of hospital).

Father's full name: .... (first) .... (middle) .... (last), ... (date of birth), ... (city and state of birth).

Name of mother inserted on birth certificate: .... (first) .... (middle) .... (last), ... (race), ... (date of birth), ... (city and state of birth).

That I surrendered my child to: .... (name of agency), ... (city and State of agency), ... (approximate date child surrendered).

That I placed my child by private adoption: .... (date), ... (city and state).

Name of adoptive parents, if known: ....

Other identifying information: ....

....
(Signature of parent)

....
(date) (printed name of parent)

(b) The form of the Adopted Person Registration Identification shall be substantially as follows:

ADOPTED PERSON REGISTRATION IDENTIFICATION

(Insert all known information)

I, ..., state the following:

Adopted Person's name at birth (if known): .... (first) .... (middle) .... (last).

Adopted Person's name at birth (if known): .... (first) .... (middle) .... (last), ... (birth date), ... (city and state of birth), ... (sex), ... (race).

Name of adoptive father: .... (first) .... (middle) .... (last, ... (race).

Maiden name of adoptive mother: .... (first) .... (middle) .... (last) .... (race).

Name of birth mother (if known): .... (first) .... (middle) .... (last), ... (race).

Name of birth father (if known): .... (first) .... (middle) .... (last), ... (race).

Name(s) at birth of sibling(s) having a common birth parent with adoptee (if known): .... (first) .... (middle) .... (last), ... (race), and name of common birth parent: .... (first) .... (middle) .... (last), ... (race).

I was adopted through: .... (name of agency).

I was adopted privately: .... (state "yes" if known).

I was adopted in .... (city and state), ... (approximate date).

Other identifying information: ....

....
(signature of adoptee)

....
(date) (printed name of adoptee)

(c) The form of the Surrendered Person Registration Identification shall be substantially as follows:

SURRENDERED PERSON REGISTRATION IDENTIFICATION

(Insert all known information)

I, ..., state the following:

Surrendered Person's name at birth (if known): .... (first) .... (middle) .... (last).

Surrendered Person's name at birth (if known): .... (first) .... (middle) .... (last), ... (birth date), ... (city and state of birth), ... (sex), ... (race).

Name of guardian father: .... (first) .... (middle) .... (last, ... (race).

Maiden name of guardian mother: .... (first) .... (middle) .... (last) .... (race).

Name of birth mother (if known): .... (first) .... (middle) .... (last), ... (race).

Name of birth father (if known): .... (first) .... (middle) .... (last), ... (race).

Name(s) at birth of sibling(s) having a common birth parent with surrendered person (if known): .... (first) .... (middle) .... (last), ... (race), and name of common birth parent: .... (first) .... (middle) .... (last), ... (race).

I was surrendered for adoption to: .... (name of agency).

I was surrendered for adoption in .... (city and state), ... (approximate date).

Other identifying information: ....

....

(signature of surrendered person)

....
(date) (printed name of person surrendered for adoption)

(d) The form of the Information Exchange Authorization shall be substantially as follows:

INFORMATION EXCHANGE AUTHORIZATION

I, ..., state that I am the person who completed the Registration Identification; that I am of the age of .... years; that I hereby authorize the Department of Public Health to give to my (birth parent) (birth sibling) (surrendered child) the following (please check the information authorized for exchange):

[ ] 1. Only my name and last known address.

[ ] 2. A copy of my Illinois Adoption Registry Application.

[ ] 3. A copy of the original certificate of live birth.

I am fully aware that I can only be supplied with any information about my (birth parent) (birth sibling) (surrendered child) if such person has duly executed an Information Exchange Authorization for such information which has not been revoked; that I can be contacted by writing to: ...... (own name or name of person to contact) (address) (phone number).

Dated (insert date).

....
(signature)

(e) The form of the Denial of Information Exchange shall be substantially as follows:

DENIAL OF INFORMATION EXCHANGE

I, ..., state that I am the person who completed the Registration Identification; that I am of the age of .... years; that I hereby instruct the Department of Public Health not to give any identifying information about me to my (birth parent) (birth sibling) (surrendered child); that I do not wish to be contacted.

Dated (insert date).

....
(signature)

(f) The Information Exchange Authorization and the Denial of Information Exchange shall be acknowledged by the birth parent, birth sibling, adopted or surrendered person, adoptive parent, or legal guardian before a notary public, in form substantially as follows:
State of ....
County of ....

I, a Notary Public, in and for the said County, in the State aforesaid, do hereby certify that .... personally known to me to be the same person whose name is subscribed to the foregoing certificate of acknowledgement, appeared before me in person and acknowledged that (he or she) signed such certificate as (his or her) free and voluntary act and that the statements in such certificate are true.

Given under my hand and notarial seal on (insert date).

....
(signature)

(g) When the execution of an Information Exchange Authorization or a Denial of Information Exchange is acknowledged before a representative of an agency, such representative shall have his signature on said Certificate acknowledged before a notary public, in form substantially as follows:
State of ....
County of ....

I, a Notary Public, in and for the said County, in the State aforesaid, do hereby certify that .... personally known to me to be the same person whose name is subscribed to the foregoing certificate of acknowledgement, appeared before me in person and acknowledged that (he or she) signed such certificate as (his or her) free and voluntary act and that the statements in such certificate are true.

Given under my hand and notarial seal on (insert date).

....
(signature)

(h) When an Illinois Adoption Registry Application, Information Exchange Authorization or a Denial of Information Exchange is executed in a foreign country, the execution of such document shall be acknowledged or affirmed before an officer of the United States consular services.

(i) If the person signing an Information Exchange Authorization or a Denial of Information is in the military service of the United States, the execution of such document may be acknowledged before a commissioned officer and the signature of such officer on such certificate shall be verified or acknowledged before a notary public or by such other procedure as is then in effect for such division or branch of the armed forces.

(j) The Department shall modify these forms as necessary to implement the provisions of this Amendatory Act of 1999 [P.A. 91-417] including creating Registration Identification Forms for non-surrendered birth siblings, adoptive parents and legal guardians.

(Source: P.A. 86-304; 87-413; 87-895; 88-45, § 2-62.5; 91-357, § 262; 91-417, § 10; 93-189, § 5.)

Note.

This section was Ill.Rev.Stat., Ch. 40, para. 1522.2.

Effect of Amendments.

The 1999 amendment by P.A. 91-357, effective July 29, 1999, in subsections (d), (e), (f) and (g) changed the date blank.

The 1999 amendment by P.A. 91-417, effective January 1, 2000, retitled the forms in subsections (a) through (c), rewrote subsections (a) through (h) to the extent that a detailed comparison would be impracticable; and added subsection (j).

The 2003 amendment by P.A. 93-189, effective January 1, 2004, deleted "witness" at the end of the forms in subsections (d) and (e).

750 ILCS 50/18.3 [Sharing of identifying information; written statement]

Sec. 18.3. (a) The agency, Department of Children and Family Services, Court Supportive Services, Juvenile Division of the Circuit Court, and any other party to the surrender of a child for adoption or in an adoption proceeding shall obtain from any birth parent or parents giving up a child for purposes of adoption after the effective date of this Act a written statement which indicates: (1) a desire to have identifying information shared with the adopted or surrendered person at a later date; (2) a desire not to have identifying information revealed; or (3) that no decision is made at that time. In addition, the agency, Department of Children and Family Services, Court Supportive Services, Juvenile Division of the Circuit Court, and any other organization involved in the surrender of a child for adoption in an adoption proceeding shall inform the birth parent or parents of a child born, adopted or surrendered in Illinois of the existence of the Illinois Adoption Registry and Medical Information Exchange and provide them with the necessary application forms and if requested, assistance with completing the forms.

(b) When the written statement is signed, the birth parent or parents shall be informed in writing that their decision regarding the sharing of identifying information can be made or changed by such birth parent or parents at any future date.

(c) The birth parent shall be informed in writing that if sharing of identifying information with the adopted or surrendered person is to occur, that he or she must be 21 years of age or over.

(d) If the birth parent or parents indicate a desire to share identifying information with the adopted or surrendered person, the birth parent shall complete an Information Exchange Authorization.

(e) Any birth parent or parents requesting that no identifying information be revealed to the adopted or surrendered person shall be informed that such request will be conveyed to the adopted or surrendered person if he or she requests such information; and such identifying information shall not be revealed.

(f) Any adopted or surrendered person 21 years of age or over, may also indicate in writing his or her desire or lack of desire to share identifying information with the birth parent or parents or birth sibling or siblings. Any adopted or surrendered person requesting that no identifying information be revealed to the birth parent or birth sibling shall be informed that such request shall be conveyed to the parent if such birth parent or birth sibling requests such information; and such identifying information shall not be revealed.

(g) Any birth parents, birth sibling and adopted or surrendered person, adoptive parent or legal guardian indicating their desire to receive identifying or medical information shall be informed of the existence of the Registry and assistance shall be given to such person to legally record his or her name with the Registry.

(h) The agency, Department of Children and Family Services, Court Supportive Services, Juvenile Division of the Circuit Court, and any other organization involved in the surrender of a child for adoption in an adoption proceeding which has written statements from an adopted or surrendered person and the birth parent or a birth sibling indicating a desire to receive identifying information shall supply such information to the mutually consenting parties, except that no identifying information shall be supplied to consenting birth siblings if any such sibling is under 21 years of age. However, both the Registry having an Information Exchange Authorization and the organization having a written statement requesting identifying information shall communicate with each other to determine if the adopted or surrendered person or the birth parent or birth sibling has signed a form at a later date indicating a change in his or her desires regarding the sharing of information. The agreement of the birth parent shall be binding.

(i) On and after January 1, 2000, any licensed child welfare agency which provides post-adoption search assistance to adoptive parents, adopted persons, birth parents, or birth siblings shall require that any person requesting post-adoption search assistance complete an Illinois Adoption Registry Application prior to the commencement of the search.

(Source: P.A. 86-1451; 91-417, § 10.)

Note.

This section was Ill.Rev.Stat., Ch. 40, para. 1522.3.

Illinois Administrative Code.

See 89 Illinois Administrative Code, §§ 309.20, 309.170, 309.20.

Effect of Amendments.

The 1999 amendment by P.A. 91-417, effective January 1, 2000, rewrote the section to the extent that a detailed comparison would be impracticable.

750 ILCS 50/18.3a Confidential intermediary

Sec. 18.3a. *Confidential intermediary.* (a) General purposes. Notwithstanding any other provision of this Act, any adopted person 21 years of age or over, any adoptive parent or legal guardian of an adopted person under the age of 21, or any birth parent of an adopted person who is 21 years of age or over may petition the court in any county in the State of Illinois for appointment of a confidential intermediary as provided in this Section for the purpose of exchanging medical information with one or more mutually consenting biological relatives, obtaining identifying information about one or more mutually consenting biological relatives, or arranging contact with one or more mutually consenting biological relatives. Additionally, in cases where an adopted or surrendered person is deceased, an adult child of the adopted or surrendered person may file a petition under this Section and in cases where the birth parent is deceased, an adult birth sibling of the adopted person or of the deceased birth parent may file a petition under this Section for the purpose of exchanging medical information with one or more mutually consenting biological relatives, obtaining identifying information about one or more mutually consenting biological relatives, or arranging contact with one or more mutually consenting biological relatives.

(b) Petition. Upon petition by an adopted person 21 years of age or over, an adoptive parent or legal guardian of an adopted person under the age of 21, or a birth parent of an adopted person who is 21 years of age or over, the court shall appoint a confidential intermediary. Upon petition by an adult child of an adopted person who is deceased or by an adult birth sibling of an adopted person whose birth parent is deceased or by an adult sibling of a birth parent who is deceased, the court may appoint a confidential intermediary if the court finds that the disclosure is of greater benefit than nondisclosure. The petition shall state which biological relative or relatives are being sought and shall indicate if the petitioner wants to do any one or more of the following: exchange medical information with the biological relative or relatives, obtain identifying information from the biological relative or relatives, or to arrange contact with the biological relative.

(c) Order. The order appointing the confidential intermediary shall allow that intermediary to conduct a search for the sought-after relative by accessing those records described in subsection (g) of this Section.

(d) Fees and expenses. The court shall condition the appointment of the confidential intermediary on the petitioner's payment of the intermediary's fees and expenses in advance of the commencement of the work of the confidential intermediary.

(e) Eligibility of intermediary. The court may appoint as confidential intermediary either an employee of the Illinois Department of Children and Family Services designated by the Department to serve as such, any other person certified by the Department as qualified to serve as a confidential intermediary, or any employee of a licensed child welfare agency certified by the agency as qualified to serve as a confidential intermediary. Certification shall be dependent upon the confidential intermediary completing a course of training including, but not limited to, applicable federal and State privacy laws.

(f) Confidential Intermediary Council. There shall be established under the Department of Children and Family Services a Confidential Intermediary Advisory Council. One member shall be an attorney representing the Attorney General's Office appointed by the Attorney General. One member shall be a currently certified confidential intermediary appointed by the Director of the Department of Children and Family Services. The Director shall also appoint 5 additional members. When making those appointments, the Director shall consider advocates for adopted persons, adoptive parents, birth parents, lawyers who represent clients in private adoptions, lawyers specializing in privacy law, and representatives of agencies involved in adoptions. The Director shall appoint one of the 7 members as the chairperson. An attorney from the Department of Children and Family Services and the person directly responsible for administering the confidential intermediary program shall serve as ex-officio, non-voting advisors to the Council. Council members shall serve at the discretion of the Director and shall receive no compensation other than reasonable expenses approved by the Director. The Council shall meet no less than twice yearly, and shall make recommendations to the Director regarding the development of rules, procedures, and forms that will ensure efficient and effective operation of the confidential intermediary process, including:

(1) Standards for certification for confidential intermediaries.

(2) Oversight of methods used to verify that intermediaries are complying with the appropriate laws.

(3) Training for confidential intermediaries, including training with respect to federal and State privacy laws.

(4) The relationship between confidential intermediaries and the court system, including the development of sample orders defining the scope of the intermediaries' access to information.

(5) Any recent violations of policy or procedures by confidential intermediaries and remedial steps, including decertification, to prevent future violations.

(g) Access. Subject to the limitations of subsection (i) of this Section, the confidential intermediary shall have access to vital records maintained by the Department of Public Health and its local designees for the maintenance of vital records and all records of the court or any adoption agency, public or private, which relate to the adoption or the identity and location of an adopted person, of an adult child of a deceased adopted person, or of a birth parent, birth sibling, or the sibling of a deceased birth parent. The confidential intermediary shall not have access to any personal health information protected by the Standards for Privacy of Individually Identifiable Health Information adopted by the U.S. Department of Health and Human Services under the Health Insurance Portability and Accountability Act of 1996 [42 U.S.C. § 201 et seq.] unless the confidential intermediary has obtained written consent from the person whose information is being sought or, if that person is a minor child, that person's parent or guardian. Confidential intermediaries shall be authorized to inspect confidential relinquishment and adoption records. The confidential intermediary shall not be authorized to access medical records, financial records, credit records, banking records, home studies, attorney file records, or other personal records. In cases where a birth parent is being sought, an adoption agency shall inform the confidential intermediary of any statement filed pursuant to Section 18.3 [750 ILCS 50/18.3] indicating a desire of the surrendering birth parent to have identifying information shared or to not have identifying information shared. If there was a clear statement of intent by the sought-after birth parent not to have identifying information shared, the confidential intermediary shall discontinue the search and inform the petitioning party of the sought-after relative's intent. Additional information provided to the confidential intermediary by an adoption agency shall be restricted to the full name, date of birth, place of birth, last known address, and last known telephone number of the sought-after relative or, if applicable, of the children or siblings of the sought-after relative.

(h) Adoption agency disclosure of medical information. If the petitioner is an adult adopted person or the adoptive parent of a minor and if the petitioner has signed a written authorization to disclose personal medical information, an adoption agency disclosing information to a confidential intermediary shall disclose available medical information about the adopted person from birth through adoption.

(i) Duties of confidential intermediary in conducting a search. In conducting a search under this Section, the confidential intermediary shall first confirm that there is no Denial of Information Exchange on file with the Illinois Adoption Registry. If the petitioner is an adult child of an adopted person who is deceased, the confidential intermediary shall additionally confirm that the adopted person did not file a Denial of Information Exchange with the Illinois Adoption Registry during his or her life. If the petitioner is an adult birth sibling of an adopted person or an adult sibling of a birth parent who is deceased, the confidential intermediary shall additionally confirm that the birth parent did not file a Denial of Information Exchange with the Registry during his or her life. If the confidential intermediary learns that a sought-after birth parent signed a statement indicating his or her intent not to have identifying information shared, and did not later file an Information Exchange Authorization with the Adoption Registry, the confidential intermediary shall discontinue the search and inform the petitioning party of the birth parent's intent.

In conducting a search under this Section, the confidential intermediary shall attempt to locate the relative or relatives from whom the petitioner has requested information. If the sought-after relative is deceased or cannot be located after a diligent search, the confidential intermediary may contact adult biological relatives of the sought-after relative.

The confidential intermediary shall contact a sought-after relative on behalf of the petitioner in a manner that respects the sought-after relative's privacy and shall inform the sought-after relative of the petitioner's request for medical information, identifying information or contact as stated in the petition. Based upon the terms of the petitioner's request, the confidential intermediary shall contact a sought-after relative on behalf of the petitioner and inform the sought-after relative of the following options:

(1) The sought-after relative may totally reject one or all of the requests for medical information, identifying information or contact. The sought-after relative shall be informed that they can provide a medical questionnaire to be forwarded to the petitioner without releasing any identifying information. The confidential intermediary shall inform the petitioner of the sought-after relative's decision to reject the sharing of information or contact.

(2) The sought-after relative may consent to completing a medical questionnaire only. In this case, the confidential intermediary shall provide the questionnaire and ask the sought-after relative to complete it. The confidential intermediary shall forward the completed questionnaire to the petitioner and inform the petitioner of the sought-after relative's desire to not provide any additional information.

(3) The sought-after relative may communicate with the petitioner without having his or her identity disclosed. In this case, the confidential intermediary shall arrange the desired communication in a manner that protects the identity of the sought-after relative. The confidential intermediary shall inform the petitioner of the sought-after relative's decision to communicate but not disclose his or her identity.

(4) The sought after relative may consent to initiate contact with the petitioner. If both the petitioner and the sought-after relative or relatives are eligible to register with the Illinois Adoption Registry, the confidential intermediary shall provide the necessary application forms and request that the sought-after relative register with the Illinois Adoption Registry. If either the petitioner or the sought-after relative or relatives are ineligible to register with the Illinois Adoption Registry, the confidential intermediary shall obtain written consents from both parties that they wish to disclose their identities to each other and to have contact with each other.

(j) Oath. The confidential intermediary shall sign an oath of confidentiality substantially as follows: "I, ..., being duly sworn, on oath depose and say: As a condition of appointment as a confidential intermediary, I affirm that:

(1) I will not disclose to the petitioner, directly or indirectly, any confidential information except in a manner consistent with the law.

(2) I recognize that violation of this oath subjects me to civil liability and to a potential finding of contempt of court. ....

SUBSCRIBED AND SWORN to before me, a Notary Public, on (insert date)

..............................."

(k) Sanctions.

(1) Any confidential intermediary who improperly discloses confidential information identifying a sought-after relative shall be liable to the sought-after relative for damages and may also be found in contempt of court.

(2) Any person who learns a sought-after relative's identity, directly or indirectly, through the use of procedures provided in this Section and who improperly discloses information identifying the sought-after relative shall be liable to the sought-after relative for actual damages plus minimum punitive damages of $10,000.

(3) The Department shall fine any confidential intermediary who improperly discloses confidential information in violation of item (1) or (2) of this subsection (k) an amount up to $2,000 per improper disclosure. This fine does not affect civil liability under item (2) of this subsection (k). The Department shall deposit all fines and penalties collected under this Section into the Illinois Adoption Registry and Medical Information Fund.

(l) Death of person being sought. Notwithstanding any other provision of this Act, if the confidential intermediary discovers that the person being sought has died, he or she shall report this fact to the court, along with a copy of the death certificate.

(m) Any confidential information obtained by the confidential intermediary during the course of his or her search shall be kept strictly confidential and shall be used for the purpose of arranging contact between the petitioner and the sought-after birth relative. At the time the case is closed, all identifying information shall be returned to the court for inclusion in the impounded adoption file.

(n) If the petitioner is an adopted person 21 years of age or over or the adoptive parent or legal guardian of an adopted person under the age of 21, any non-identifying information, as defined in Section 18.4 [750 ILCS 50/18.4], that is ascertained during the course of the search may be given in writing to the petitioner before the case is closed.

(o) Except as provided in subsection (k) of this Section, no liability shall accrue to the State, any State agency, any judge, any officer or employee of the court, any certified confidential intermediary, or any agency designated to oversee confidential intermediary services for acts, omissions, or efforts made in good faith within the scope of this Section.

(Source: P.A. 86-1451; 91-357, § 262; 91-417, § 10; 93-189, § 5.)

Note.

This section was Ill.Rev.Stat., Ch. 40, para. 1522.3a.

Effect of Amendments.

The 1999 amendment by P.A. 91-357, effective July 29, 1999, changed the date blank in subsection (g).

The 1999 amendment by P.A. 91-417, effective January 1, 2000, substituted "adopted person" for "adoptee", and "birth parent" for "biological parent" throughout the section; substituted "age of 21" for "age of 18" twice in subsection (a); changed the date blank in subsection (g)(2); deleted "physician or other" preceding "person who learns" in subsection (h)(2); and deleted "if possible" following "death certificate" in subsection (i).

The 2003 amendment by P.A. 93-189, effective January 1, 2004, rewrote the section to the extent that a detailed comparison would be impracticable.

750 ILCS 50/18.4 [Information for adoptive parents]

Sec. 18.4. (a) The agency, Department of Children and Family Services, Court Supportive Services, Juvenile Division of the Circuit Court, or the Probation Officers of the Circuit Court involved in the adoption proceedings shall give in writing the following non-identifying information, if known, to the adoptive parents not later than the date of placement with the petitioning adoptive parents: (i) age of biological parents; (ii) their race, religion and ethnic background; (iii) general physical appearance of biological parents; (iv) their education, occupation, hobbies, interests and talents; (v) existence of any other children born to the biological parents; (vi) information about biological grandparents; reason for emigrating into the United States, if applicable, and country of origin; (vii) relationship between biological parents; (viii) detailed medical and mental health histories of the child, the biological parents, and their immediate relatives; and (ix) the actual date and place of birth of the adopted person. However, no information provided under this subsection shall disclose the name or last known address of the biological parents, grandparents, the siblings of the biological parents, the adopted person, or any other relative of the adopted person.

(b) Any adoptee 18 years of age or over shall be given the information in subsection (a) upon request.

(c) The Illinois Adoption Registry shall release any non-identifying information listed in (a) of this Section that appears on the certified copy of the original birth certificate or the Certificate of Adoption to an adopted person, adoptive parent, or legal guardian who is a registrant of the Illinois Adoption Registry.

(d) The Illinois Adoption Registry shall release the actual date and place of birth of an adopted person who is 21 years of age or over to the birth parent if the birth parent is a registrant of the Illinois Adoption Registry and has completed a Medical Information Exchange Authorization.

(e) The Illinois Adoption Registry shall release information regarding the date the adoption was finalized and the county in which the adoption was finalized to a certified confidential intermediary upon submission of a court order.

(f) In cases where the Illinois Adoption Registry possesses information indicating that an adopted person who is 21 years of age or over was adopted in a state other than Illinois or a country other than the United States, the Illinois Adoption Registry shall release the name of the state or country where the adoption was finalized and, if available, the agency involved in the adoption to a registrant of the

Illinois Adoption Registry, provided the registrant is not the subject of a Denial of Information Exchange and the registrant has completed a Medical Information Exchange Authorization.

(g) Any of the above available information for any adoption proceedings completed before the effective date of this Act shall be supplied to the adoptive parents or an adoptee 18 years of age or over upon request.

(h) The agency, Department of Children and Family Services, Court Supportive Services, Juvenile Division of the Circuit Court, the Probation Officers of the Circuit Court and any other governmental bodies having any of the above information shall retain the file until the adoptee would have reached the age of 99 years.

(Source: P.A. 87-617; 93-189, § 5.)

Note.

This section was Ill.Rev.Stat., Ch. 40, para. 1522.4.

Illinois Administrative Code.

See 89 Illinois Administrative Code, § 309.190.

Effect of Amendments.

The 2003 amendment by P.A. 93-189, effective January 1, 2004, in subsection (a), inserted "non-identifying" and "and (ix) the actual date and place of birth of the adopted person" in the first sentence and inserted "the adopted person" and "person" in the second sentence; inserted subsections (c) through (f) and made related designation changes.

LEGAL PERIODICALS

For article, "Secrecy and Genetics in Adoption Law and Practice," 27 Loy. U. Chi. L.J. 277 (1996).

750 ILCS 50/18.4a Medical and mental health histories

Sec. 18.4a. *Medical and mental health histories.* (a) Notwithstanding any other provision of law to the contrary, to the extent currently in possession of the agency, the medical and mental health histories of a child legally freed for adoption and of the birth parents, with information identifying the birth parents eliminated, shall be provided by an agency to the child's prospective adoptive parent and shall be provided upon request to an adoptive parent when a child has been adopted. The medical and mental health histories shall include all the following available information:

(1) Conditions or diseases believed to be hereditary.

(2) Drugs or medications taken by the child's birth mother during pregnancy.

(3) Psychological and psychiatric information.

(4) Any other information that may be a factor influencing the child's present or future health.

(b) The Department of Children and Family Services may promulgate rules and regulations governing the release of medical histories under this Section.

(Source: P.A. 87-617; 91-417, § 10.)

Note.

This section was Ill.Rev.Stat., Ch. 40, para. 1522.4a.

Effect of Amendments.

The 1999 amendment by P.A. 91-417, effective January 1, 2000, added the section heading; and substituted "birth" for "biological" twice in the introductory language in subsection (a) and once in subsection (a)(2).

CASE NOTES

Disclosure of Medical Information

Adoption agency was held to have breached a duty of care when it failed to disclose necessary medical and psychological information to adoptive parents. Roe v. Catholic Charities, 225 Ill. App. 3d 519, 167 Ill. Dec. 713, 588 N.E.2d 354 (5 Dist.), appeal denied, 146 Ill. 2d 651, 176 Ill. Dec. 821, 602 N.E.2d 475 (1992).

750 ILCS 50/18.5 Liability

Sec. 18.5. *Liability.* No liability shall attach to the State, any agency thereof, any licensed agency, any judge, any officer or employee of the court, or any party or employee thereof involved in the surrender of a child for adoption or in an adoption proceeding for acts or efforts made within the scope of Sections 18.05 thru 18.5, inclusive, of this Act [750 ILCS 50/18.05 thru 750 ILCS 50/18.5] and under its provisions, except for subsection (f) of Section 18.1 [750 ILCS 50/18.1].

(Source: P.A. 86-304; 91-417, § 10.)

Note.

This section was Ill.Rev.Stat., Ch. 40, para. 1522.5.

Effect of Amendments.

The 1999 amendment by P.A. 91-417, effective January 1, 2000, added the section heading; substituted "18.05" for "18.1" and substituted "under" for "pursuant to".

750 ILCS 50/18.6 Registry fees

Sec. 18.6. *Registry fees.* The Department of Public Health shall levy a fee for each registrant under Sections 18.05 through 18.5 [750 ILCS 50/18.05 through 750 ILCS 50/18.5]. A $40 fee shall be charged for registering with the Illinois Adoption Registry and Medical Information Exchange. However, this fee shall be waived for all adopted or surrendered persons, adoptive parents, legal guardians, birth parents, and birth siblings who complete a Medical Information Exchange Questionnaire at the time of registration and authorize its release to specified registered parties, and for adoptive parents registering within 12 months of the finalization of the adoption. All persons who were registered with the Illinois Adoption Registry prior to the effective date of this amendatory Act of 1999 [P.A. 91-417] and who wish to update their registration may do so without charge. No charge of any kind shall be made for the withdrawal of any form provided in Section 18.2 [750 ILCS 50/18.2].

(Source: P.A. 87-318; 91-417, § 10.)

Note.

This section was Ill.Rev.Stat., Ch. 40, para. 1522.6.

Effect of Amendments.

The 1999 amendment by P.A. 91-417, effective January 1, 2000, added the section heading; substituted "18.05" for "18.1"; added the second through fourth sentences; and substituted "any form provided in Section 18.2" for "a registration or consent form" in the last sentence.

750 ILCS 50/18.7 Illinois Adoption Registry and Medical Information Exchange Fund

Sec. 18.7. *Illinois Adoption Registry and Medical Information Exchange Fund.* There is created in the State treasury a special fund to be known as the Illinois Adoption Registry and Medical Information Exchange Fund. All fees collected by the Illinois Adoption Registry under this amendatory Act of 1999 [P.A. 91-417] shall be deposited into the Fund. Subject to appropriation, the amounts in the Fund shall be used by the Department of Public Health to conduct activities related to maintaining the Illinois Adoption Registry and Medical Information Exchange and issuing any documents and forms related to the Illinois Adoption Registry and Medical Information Exchange.
(Source: P.A. 91-417, § 10.)

Effective Date.

This section became effective January 1, 2000 pursuant to Ill. Const. (1970), Art. IV, § 10 and 5 ILCS 75/2.

750 ILCS 50/18.8 Improper disclosure of identifying information

Sec. 18.8. *Improper disclosure of identifying information.* All information submitted to the Registry is confidential and gathered by the State solely for the purpose of facilitating the exchange of updated medical data and contact information between adopted and surrendered persons and other registered parties. Information exchanged through the Registry shall not be admissible as evidence nor discoverable in any action of any kind in any court or before any tribunal, board, agency, or commission. Disclosure of identifying information in violation of this Act is a Class A misdemeanor.
(Source: P.A. 91-417, § 10.)

Effective Date.

This section became effective January 1, 2000 pursuant to Ill. Const. (1970), Art. IV, § 10 and 5 ILCS 75/2.

750 ILCS 50/19 Registration new birth certificate

Sec. 19. *Registration new birth certificate.* Upon the entry of a judgment of adoption, the clerk of the court that entered the judgment shall prepare a certificate of adoption and send the certificate to the Department of Public Health, pursuant to Sections 16 and 17 of the Vital Records Act [410 ILCS 535/16 and 410 ILCS 535/17]. The statutory fee of the clerk of the court for that certificate shall be paid by the petitioners.

Nothing in this Act shall be construed to prohibit the amendment of a birth certificate in accordance with subsection (6) of Section 22 of the Vital Records Act [410 ILCS 535/22].
(Source: P.A. 87-895; 89-257, § 10.)

Note.

This section was Ill.Rev.Stat., Ch. 40, para. 1523.

Effect of Amendments.

The 1995 amendment by P.A. 89-257, effective January 1, 1996, added the second paragraph.

750 ILCS 50/20 Practice

Sec. 20. *Practice.* The provisions of the Civil Practice Law and all existing and future amendments of that Law [735 ILCS 5/2-101 et seq.] and the Supreme Court Rules now or hereafter adopted in relation to that Law shall apply to all adoption proceedings except as otherwise specifically provided in this Act.

Proceedings under this Act shall receive priority over other civil cases in being set for hearing.

No matters not germane to the distinctive purpose of a proceeding under this Act shall be introduced by joinder, counterclaim or otherwise.

An appeal from a judgment order for adoption or other appealable orders under this Act shall be prosecuted and heard on an expedited basis, unless good cause for doing otherwise is shown.

In the event a judgment order for adoption is vacated or a petition for adoption is denied, the court shall promptly conduct a hearing as to the temporary and permanent custody of the minor child who is the subject of the proceedings pursuant to Part VI of the Illinois Marriage and Dissolution of Marriage Act [750 ILCS 5/601 et seq.]. The parties to said proceedings shall be the petitioners to the adoption proceedings, the minor child, any biological parents whose parental rights have not been terminated, and other parties who have been granted leave to intervene in the proceedings.

This Act shall be liberally construed, and the rule that statutes in derogation of the common law must be strictly construed shall not apply to this Act.

All defects in pleadings, either in form or substance, not objected to prior to the entry of final judgment, shall be deemed to be waived.

As to persons over whom the court had jurisdiction or persons claiming under them, it shall be no basis for attack as to the validity of an adoption judgment that the court lacked jurisdiction over some other person or persons over whom it should have had jurisdiction. If, upon attack by a person or persons over whom the court lacked jurisdiction, or persons claiming under them, an adoption judgment is set aside, it shall be set aside only insofar as it affects such person or persons.

The provisions of this Section shall apply to all cases pending on or after July 3, 1994.
(Source: P.A. 82-783; 88-550, § 975; 89-315, § 5; 90-655, § 174.)

Note.

This section was Ill.Rev.Stat., Ch. 40, para. 1524.

Effect of Amendments.

The 1994 amendment by P.A. 88-550, effective July 3, 1994, added the second and fourth paragraphs; substituted the present language of the fifth paragraph for "Appeals may be taken as in other civil cases"; and added the last paragraph.

The 1995 amendment by P.A. 89-315, effective January 1, 1996, substituted the present last paragraph for the former which read "This amendatory Act of 1994 applies to cases pending on and after its effective date".

The 1998 amendment by P.A. 90-655, effective July 30, 1998, in the seventh paragraph substituted "objected to prior" for "objected 45 prior".

CASE NOTES

Analysis

In General
Collateral Attacks
Custody Hearing
Final Orders
Injunction
Jury Trials
Mootness

In General

Although termination-of-parental-rights proceedings are civil in nature and 735 ILCS 5/2-612(c) of the Illinois Code of Civil Procedure, provides that all defects in pleadings, either in form or substance, not objected to in the trial court are waived, in some circumstances, justice will require relaxation of the forfeiture rule. People v. Griffin (In re J.R.), 342 Ill. App. 3d 310, 276 Ill. Dec. 519, 794 N.E.2d 414, 2003 Ill. App. LEXIS 976 (4 Dist. 2003).

Collateral Attacks

An adoption decree rendered by a court having jurisdiction of adoption proceedings is not subject to collateral attack where the record shows substantial compliance with the essential provisions of the statute. Wolfner v. Bidwill, 44 Ill. App. 2d 77, 194 N.E.2d 1 (1 Dist. 1963).

Custody Hearing

The plain language of the statute does not require a custody hearing to be conducted where the judgment order for adoption and proceedings have been held to be void ab initio; further, the intent of the legislature in amending the statute was not to require a custody hearing where an adoption order and proceedings have been held void ab initio due to lack of jurisdiction and fraud. In re E.L., 315 Ill. App. 3d 137, 248 Ill. Dec. 171, 733 N.E.2d 846, 2000 Ill. App. LEXIS 557 (1 Dist. 2000).

Final Orders

An order finding the natural father to be unfit and making a temporary custody arrangement was not a final and appealable order of the court. Valentin v. Morehead, 64 Ill. App. 2d 469, 212 N.E.2d 250 (1 Dist. 1965).

Injunction

An injunction may be germane to an adoption proceeding and may be granted in the appropriate case. In re Scraggs, 125 Ill. 2d 382, 126 Ill. Dec. 559, 532 N.E.2d 244 (1988).

Jury Trials

The denial of the father's demand for a jury trial on the issue of his unfitness was a matter within the sound discretion of the trial court; in the absence of any showing of abuse of such discretion or necessity for trial of such issue by a jury, the trial court committed no error in denying the demand for a trial by jury. Houston v. Brackett, 38 Ill. App. 2d 463, 187 N.E.2d 545 (2 Dist. 1963).

Mootness

Appeal of the termination of the parent's parental rights was dismissed because the appellate court lacked the authority to consider the merits of the substantive questions raised, as the appeal was moot upon the adoption of the children where the parent did not seek a stay of the trial court's termination order. People v. Wanda B. (In re J.B.), 204 Ill. 2d 382, 273 Ill. Dec. 827, 789 N.E.2d 1259, 2003 Ill. LEXIS 771 (2003).

LEGAL PERIODICALS

For article, "Baby Richard and Beyond: The Future for Adopted Children", see 18 N. Ill. U.L. Rev. 445 (1999).

For casenote, "Born to Lose: The Illinois 'Baby Richard' Case — How Examining His Father's Pre-Birth Conduct Might Have Led to a Different Ending for Richard," see 16 N. Ill. U.L. Rev. 543 (1996).

For note, "Babies, Jessica, Richard and Emily: The Need for Legislative Reform of Adoption Laws," 70 Chi-Kent L. Rev. 1851 (1996).

For comment, "Rights of Unwed Fathers and the Best Interests of the Child: Can These Competing Interests be Harmonized? Illinois Putative Father Registry Provides an Answer," see 26 Loy. U. Chi. L.J. 703 (1995).

For article, "Family Law: 1988-89 Illinois Law Survey," see 21 Loy. U. Chi. L. J. 417 (1989-90).

RESEARCH REFERENCES

Marital or sexual relationship between parties as affecting right to adopt. 42 ALR4th 776.

Attorney malpractice in connection with services related to adoption of child. 18 ALR5th 892.

750 ILCS 50/20a Construction of Act

Sec. 20a. *Construction of Act.* The best interests and welfare of the person to be adopted shall be of paramount consideration in the construction and interpretation of this Act. It is in the best interests of persons to be adopted that this Act be construed and interpreted so as not to result in extending time limits beyond those set forth herein.
(Source: P.A. 78-854; 88-550, § 975.)

Note.

This section was Ill.Rev.Stat., Ch. 40, para. 1525.

Effect of Amendments.

The 1994 amendment by P.A. 88-550, effective July 3, 1994, added the section catchline and the second sentence.

CASE NOTES

Analysis

In General
Adoption Judgment
—Grandparents' Rights Terminated
Cruelty
Evidence Held Sufficient
Grounds for Adoption
Illustrative Cases
Inability to Provide Care
Interests
Rights of Natural Parents
Unfitness
—Shown
Vacation of Adoption

In General

The paramount consideration in the construction and interpretation of this statute is the best interests and welfare of the person to be adopted. In re Scraggs, 125 Ill. 2d 382, 126 Ill. Dec. 559, 532 N.E.2d 244 (1988).

In construing this Act, the best interests and welfare of the child are of paramount consideration. People v. Hollis, 135 Ill. App. 3d 585, 90 Ill. Dec. 523, 482 N.E.2d 230 (4 Dist. 1985).

In General (Cont'd)

Before there can be consideration of the best interests of the child, there must be a finding of parental unfitness. Blakey v. Blakey, 72 Ill. App. 3d 946, 29 Ill. Dec. 63, 391 N.E.2d 222 (4 Dist. 1979).

A court cannot grant an adoption solely on the basis of the best interests of the child, without a consent or a finding of unfitness, but a court must give prime consideration to the welfare and best interests of the child involved. Bergstedt v. Cech, 8 Ill. App. 3d 642, 291 N.E.2d 21 (1 Dist. 1972); Tiernan v. Stewart, 33 Ill. App. 3d 545, 338 N.E.2d 153 (2 Dist. 1975); Lehmann v. Shapkoff, 37 Ill. App. 3d 217, 345 N.E.2d 742 (1 Dist. 1976).

In a case where the natural parents were not contestants, the welfare of the child was the trial court's only concern. Stines v. Vaughn, 23 Ill. App. 3d 511, 319 N.E.2d 561 (4 Dist. 1974).

When the trial court reviews facts in making its final determination, the welfare of the child should be the prime consideration in all adoption proceedings. Stines v. Vaughn, 23 Ill. App. 3d 511, 319 N.E.2d 561 (4 Dist. 1974).

The question of paramount importance in any adoption proceeding is what will be in the best interests of the child. Thorpe v. Thorpe, 48 Ill. App. 2d 455, 198 N.E.2d 743 (4 Dist. 1964).

Under former Ill.Rev.Stat., ch. 4, para. 1 (see now 750 ILCS 50/0.01 et seq.), the welfare of the child was the paramount interest in adoption proceedings. Dickholtz v. Littfin, 341 Ill. App. 400, 94 N.E.2d 89 (1 Dist. 1950).

Adoption Judgment

—Grandparents' Rights Terminated

This statute's aim is to promote the best interests and welfare of the child, a purpose which generally is served by giving the adopted child the status of a natural child of the adoptive parents and completely breaking all ties with the natural family. Krystek v. Schumacher, 120 Ill. App. 3d 50, 75 Ill. Dec. 926, 458 N.E.2d 94 (2 Dist. 1983).

An order of adoption will operate to divest natural relatives, such as grandparents, of the right to visitation with the adopted child. Krystek v. Schumacher, 120 Ill. App. 3d 50, 75 Ill. Dec. 926, 458 N.E.2d 94 (2 Dist. 1983).

Cruelty

When a parent engages in extreme or repeated cruelty, his conduct at other times is largely irrelevant. People v. Hollis, 135 Ill. App. 3d 585, 90 Ill. Dec. 523, 482 N.E.2d 230 (4 Dist. 1985).

Evidence Held Sufficient

In proceeding on petition by mother and her husband for adoption of daughter, record did not show by clear and convincing evidence father abandoned the child, however, the evidence showed in a most clear and convincing manner the intention of father had deserted his daughter for more than three months before the adoption proceeding began. Lehmann v. Shapkoff, 37 Ill. App. 3d 217, 345 N.E.2d 742 (1 Dist. 1976).

Grounds for Adoption

Absent parental consent or an order finding parental unfitness, the best interests of the child are not independent grounds for a decree of adoption. Culkin v. Culkin, 30 Ill. App. 3d 1073, 333 N.E.2d 698 (4 Dist. 1975).

Illustrative Cases

The trial court's decision granting foster parents' petition for adoption was within its discretion and not against the manifest weight of the evidence, notwithstanding the assertion by grandparents that they were the child's blood relatives and currently had custody the child' younger half-brother and that they were financially more stable than the foster parents. Bonnie S.P. v. Phillip P., 313 Ill. App. 3d 301, 246 Ill. Dec. 180, 729 N.E.2d 553, 2000 Ill. App. LEXIS 372 (4 Dist. 2000).

Trial court could have properly found that it was not in the best interests of the children to place them in the home of a 25 year old man who had to leave them in the care of a babysitter during his hours of employment, but that the interests of the children would best be served by returning them to their natural father, where they would live with him in the home of their paternal grandparents. Middlecoff v. Leofanti, 133 Ill. App. 2d 822, 272 N.E.2d 289 (5 Dist. 1971).

Inability to Provide Care

A child is no less exposed to danger, no less dirty or hungry because his parent is unable rather than unwilling to give him care. Department of Children & Family Servs. v. Devine, 81 Ill. App. 3d 314, 36 Ill. Dec. 775, 401 N.E.2d 616 (5 Dist. 1980).

Interests

The overriding interest in any adoption proceeding is that of the child. In re Scraggs, 125 Ill. 2d 382, 126 Ill. Dec. 559, 532 N.E.2d 244 (1988).

There must be an appraisal of the effect of the adoption on the natural parent whose relationship is sought to be terminated and these rights should only be terminated after unfitness has been established by clear and convincing evidence. In re Scraggs, 125 Ill. 2d 382, 126 Ill. Dec. 559, 532 N.E.2d 244 (1988).

Rights of Natural Parents

A parent's right to custody of his child is superior to that of any other person if the parent is fit to have custody of his children, although such right is not absolute and must yield to the best interests of the child. In re Smith, 4 Ill. App. 3d 261, 280 N.E.2d 770 (1 Dist. 1972).

Unfitness

—Shown

The trial court properly considered the best interests of the child in conjunction with making the general finding of unfitness. People v. Berry, 86 Ill. App. 3d 522, 42 Ill. Dec. 150, 408 N.E.2d 728 (5 Dist. 1980).

Vacation of Adoption

Where a petition to vacate an adoption rested solely on the statement that the marriage of the petitioner and his former wife was annulled subsequent to their joint adoption of the minors, it would have been improper to apply the doctrine which declares an annulled marriage void from the beginning to the validity of the adoption because it would have affected the rights of minors, who were third parties to the annulment action. The adopted minors were not parties to the alleged fraud the petitioner's former wife may have perpetrated upon the petitioner, and they should not have suffered for the acts of another, and in light of concern for the best interests of the adopted children, the petitioner's contention that he and his former wife were not married at the time they adopted former wife's three children was rejected, the petition to vacate the adoption, did not state a valid cause of action, and the trial court's dismissal of the petition was proper. Cowhey v. Tator, 36 Ill. App. 3d 962, 344 N.E.2d 501 (1 Dist. 1976).

RESEARCH REFERENCES

Parent's mental deficiency as factor in termination of parental rights—modern status. 1 ALR5th 469.

750 ILCS 50/20b Time limit for relief from final judgment or order

Sec. 20b. *Time limit for relief from final judgment or order.* A petition for relief from a final order or judgment entered in a proceeding under this Act, after 30 days from the entry thereof under the provisions of Section 2-1401 of the Code of Civil Procedure [735 ILCS 5/2-1401] or otherwise, must be filed not later than one year after the entry of the order or judgment.
(Source: P.A. 88-550, § 975; 89-315, § 5.)

Effective Date.

Section 999 of P.A. 88-550 made this section effective upon becoming law. The Act was approved July 3, 1994.

Effect of Amendments.

The 1995 amendment by P.A. 89-315, effective January 1, 1996,

deleted the former second paragraph which read "An appeal from a judgment order for adoption or other appealable order under this Act shall be heard on an expedited basis. In the event that an order for adoption is vacated, the court shall promptly conduct a hearing as to the temporary and permanent custody of the minor child who is the subject of the proceeding pursuant to Part VI of the Illinois Marriage and Dissolution Act. The parties to the proceeding shall be the petitioners to the adoption proceeding, the minor child, the biological parents whose rights have been terminated, and other parties who have been granted leave to intervene in the proceeding. The provisions of this Section shall apply to all cases pending on and after the effective date of this amendatory Act of 1994."

CASE NOTES

Illustrative Cases

Children were available for adoption, and the parent whose parental rights had been terminated could not challenge the adoption once a year had passed from the entry of the adoption, where the parent had not sought to stay the termination of rights order, which had named a welfare agency as the children's guardian, the agency had consented to the foster parents' adoption petition, and an adoption decree had been properly entered. People v. Denise S., 202 Ill. 2d 522, 270 Ill. Dec. 30, 782 N.E.2d 224, 2002 Ill. LEXIS 964 (2002).

750 ILCS 50/21 Compensation for placing of children prohibited

Sec. 21. *Compensation for placing of children prohibited.* No person, agency, association, corporation, institution, society or other organization, except a child welfare agency as defined by the "Child Care Act", approved July 10, 1957, as now or hereafter amended [225 ILCS 10/1 et seq.], shall receive or accept, or pay or give any compensation or thing of value, directly or indirectly, for placing out of a child as is more specifically provided in "An Act to prevent the payment or receipt of compensation for placing out children for adoption or for the purpose of providing care", approved July 14, 1955, as now or hereafter amended [720 ILCS 525/1 et seq.].
(Source: Laws, 1959, p. 1269.)

Note.
This section was Ill.Rev.Stat., Ch. 40, para. 1526.

CASE NOTES

Hospital Expenses

Where the mother consented to the adoption of child, but there were no allegations regarding payments received by her, and from the testimony of the respondent, it appeared that a $200 payment was made as reimbursement for hospital and medical expenses, it was error to find that the laws as to illegal placement were violated by either party. Cohen v. Janic, 57 Ill. App. 2d 309, 207 N.E.2d 89 (1 Dist. 1965).

LEGAL PERIODICALS

For article, "Compensation for Birth Mothers: A Challenge to the Adoption Laws," see 23 Loy. U. Chi. L.J. 25 (1991-92).

750 ILCS 50/22 Partial invalidity

Sec. 22. *Partial invalidity.* If any part of this Act is held by any court to be unconstitutional or invalid, such decision or judgment shall not affect the validity of the remaining portions of this Act.
(Source: Laws 1959, p. 1269.)

Note.
This section was Ill.Rev.Stat., Ch. 40, para. 1527.

750 ILCS 50/23: Repeal — Saving

Sec. 23. *Repeal — Saving.* "An Act in relation to the adoption of children and to repeal an Act therein named", approved June 30, 1945, as amended is repealed.

Such repeal shall not in any way affect an act done or a right, power or remedy given or accrued under any statute in force prior to the effective date of this Act.

The execution of a consent or surrender, prior to the effective date of this Act, shall not affect its validity for use in a proceeding under this Act, if such consent or surrender was executed in accordance with law then in effect.
(Source: Laws 1959, p. 1269.)

Note.
This section was Ill.Rev.Stat., Ch. 40, para. 1528.

750 ILCS 50/24 Effective date

Sec. 24. *Effective date.* This Act shall take effect January 1, 1960.
(Source: Laws 1959, p. 1269.)

Note.
This section was Ill.Rev.Stat., Ch. 40, para. 1529.

CONTEST OF ADOPTIONS ACT

750 ILCS 55/0.01 Short title

Sec. 0.01. *Short title.* This Act may be cited as the Contest of Adoptions Act.
(Source: P.A. 86-1324.)

Derivation.
Title: An Act to fix the time for attacking or bringing proceedings to contest the validity of adoption decrees heretofore entered, because of the failure to serve notice on or give notice to the reputed father.
Cite: 750 ILCS 55/0.01 et seq.
Source: L. 1949, p. 12.
Date: Approved August 3, 1949.

Note.
This section was Ill.Rev.Stat., Ch. 40, para. 1600.

750 ILCS 55/1 [Failure to give notice; attack]

Sec. 1. No attack upon or proceedings contesting the validity of an adoption decree heretofore entered shall be made either directly or collaterally because of the failure to serve notice on or give notice to the reputed father, unless such attack or proceedings shall be instituted within one year after the effective date of this Act.
(Source: Laws 1949, p. 12.)

Note.
This section was Ill.Rev.Stat., Ch. 40, para. 1601.

ILLINOIS DOMESTIC VIOLENCE ACT OF 1986

ARTICLE I. GENERAL PROVISIONS

750 ILCS 60/101 Short Title

Sec. 101. *Short Title.* This Act shall be known and may be cited as the "Illinois Domestic Violence Act of 1986".
(Source: P.A. 84-1305.)

Derivation.
Title: An Act concerning domestic violence, amending and repealing certain Acts and parts of Acts herein named.
Cite: 750 ILCS 60/101 et seq.
Source: P.A. 84-1305.
Date: Approved August 21, 1986.

Note.
This section was Ill.Rev.Stat., Ch. 40, para. 2311-1.

CASE NOTES

ANALYSIS

Concurrent Remedies
Construction
Special Duty Exception

Concurrent Remedies
Where a plaintiff alleged that police officers willfully and wantonly violated the Illinois Domestic Violence Act of 1986, 750 ILCS 60/101 et seq., the court held that she alleged the same cause of action in two different counts despite her argument that she had a distinct tort claim of willful and wanton behavior. Farrar v. City of Chicago, 291 F. Supp. 2d 747, 2003 U.S. Dist. LEXIS 20478 (N.D. Ill. 2003).

This Act provides a concurrent remedy to that available under 750 ILCS 5/701, which allows for an order granting possession of the marital residence to one spouse, and the definition of abuse under this Act differs substantially from the test contained in 750 ILCS 5/701. In re Hagaman, 123 Ill. App. 3d 549, 78 Ill. Dec. 922, 462 N.E.2d 1276 (4 Dist. 1984).

Construction
Because temporary custody may be awarded under the Domestic Violence Act, and because the act makes specific reference to the Marriage Act, a court in a domestic violence case can order a home study pursuant to this section; however, such a study should only be ordered in exceptional cases because of the substantial possibility of causing delay and, further, such a study cannot be ordered in connection with an emergency order of protection as such an order may not include an award of legal custody. Wilson v. Jackson, 312 Ill. App. 3d 1156, 245 Ill. Dec. 750, 728 N.E.2d 832, 2000 Ill. App. LEXIS 267 (3 Dist. 2000).

Special Duty Exception
This Act which is to be construed together with 725 ILCS 5/112A-1 et seq., carves out an exception to the public duty doctrine and elevates the holder of an order of protection to a status above that of other members of the general public; it singles out those who are victims of domestic violence as persons in need of special protection by law enforcement officials. Calloway v. Kinkelaar, 261 Ill. App. 3d 63, 199 Ill. Dec. 389, 633 N.E.2d 1380 (5 Dist. 1994), aff'd, 168 Ill. 2d 312, 213 Ill. Dec. 675, 659 N.E.2d 1322 (1995).

LEGAL PERIODICALS

For article, "Defending the Indefensible to Further a Later Case: Sanctioning Respondents in Illinois Domestic Violence Cases," see 23 N. Ill. U. L. Rev. 403 (2003).

For note, "Guardians Ad Litem: The Guardian Angels of Our Children in Domestic Violence Courts", see 30 Loy. U. Chi. L.J. 281 (1999).

For article, "The Death of the Special Duty Exception to Statutory Governmental Immunity", see 86 Ill. B.J. 372 (1998).

For article, "Survey of Illinois Law: Tort Developments," see 19 S. Ill. U.L.J. 945 (1996).

For essay, "The Criminal Courtroom: Is it Child Proof?," see 26 Loy. U. Chi. L.J. 681 (1995).

For essay, "Enforcement in Domestic Violence Cases," see 26 Loy. U. Chi. L.J. 663 (1995).

For note, "Beyond Self-Defense: The Use of Battered Women Syndrome in Duress Defenses," see 1994 Ill. L. Rev. 955 (1994).

For article, "Battered Women Syndrome, Expert Testimony, and the Distinction Between Justification and Excuse," see 1994 U. Ill. L. Rev. 45 (1994).

For article, "Orders of Protection and the Battered Woman Syndrome," see 23 Loy. U. Chi. L.J. 397 (1991-92).

For practice tip, "Handling Complaints Under the Illinois Domestic Violence Act," see 79 Ill. B.J. 296 (1991).

For article, "The Illinois Domestic Violence Act of 1986: A Selective Critique," see 19 Loy. U. Chi. L.J. 797 (1987-88).

For article, "Domestic Abuse Legislation in Illinois and Other States: A Survey and Suggestions for Reform," see U. Ill. L. Rev. 261 (1983).

For comment, "Domestic Violence: Illinois Responds to the Plight of the Battered Wife—The Illinois Domestic Violence Act," see 16 J. Marshall L. Rev. 77 (1982-83).

RESEARCH REFERENCES

Admissibility of expert or opinion testimony on battered wife or battered woman syndrome. 18 ALR4th 1153.

Liability of municipality or other governmental unit for failure to provide police protection from crime. 90 ALR5th 273.

750 ILCS 60/102 Purposes; rules of construction

Sec. 102. *Purposes; rules of construction.* This Act shall be liberally construed and applied to promote its underlying purposes, which are to:

(1) Recognize domestic violence as a serious crime against the individual and society which produces family disharmony in thousands of Illinois families, promotes a pattern of escalating violence which frequently culminates in intra-family homicide, and creates an emotional atmosphere that is not conducive to healthy childhood development;

(2) Recognize domestic violence against high risk adults with disabilities, who are particularly vulnerable due to impairments in ability to seek or obtain protection, as a serious problem which takes on many forms, including physical abuse, sexual abuse, neglect, and exploitation, and facilitate accessibility of remedies under the Act in order to provide immediate and effective assistance and protection.

(3) Recognize that the legal system has ineffectively dealt with family violence in the past, allowing abusers to escape effective prosecution or financial liability, and has not adequately acknowledged the criminal nature of domestic violence; that, although many laws have changed, in practice there is still widespread failure to appropriately protect and assist victims;

(4) Support the efforts of victims of domestic violence to avoid further abuse by promptly entering and diligently enforcing court orders which prohibit

abuse and, when necessary, reduce the abuser's access to the victim and address any related issues of child custody and economic support, so that victims are not trapped in abusive situations by fear of retaliation, loss of a child, financial dependence, or loss of accessible housing or services;

(5) Clarify the responsibilities and support the efforts of law enforcement officers to provide immediate, effective assistance and protection for victims of domestic violence, recognizing that law enforcement officers often become the secondary victims of domestic violence, as evidenced by the high rates of police injuries and deaths that occur in response to domestic violence calls; and

(6) Expand the civil and criminal remedies for victims of domestic violence; including, when necessary, the remedies which effect physical separation of the parties to prevent further abuse.

(Source: P.A. 86-542; 87-1186, § 3.)

Note.

This section was Ill.Rev.Stat., Ch. 40, para. 2311-2.

CASE NOTES

Analysis

Constitutionality
—Vagueness
Civil Damages
Construction
Misuse of Act
Ordinary Negligence
Public Policy
Purpose

Constitutionality

—Vagueness

Former Ill.Rev.Stat., ch. 40, para. 2301-1 (see now this section) was not unconstitutionally vague or overbroad as a statute which had as its objective a safety net against physical and psychological abuses which only someone as close as a relative could inflict, since it could not be expected to address every conceivable form of abuse. People v. Blackwood, 131 Ill. App. 3d 1018, 87 Ill. Dec. 40, 476 N.E.2d 742 (3 Dist. 1985).

Civil Damages

To give effect to the legislature's purposes and intent in enacting the Domestic Violence Act, judicial recognition of a right of action for civil damages is necessary, provided that the injured party can establish that he or she is a person in need of protection under the Act, the statutory law enforcement duties owed to him or her were breached by the wilful and wanton acts or omissions of law enforcement officers, and such conduct proximately caused plaintiff's injuries. Calloway v. Kinkelaar, 168 Ill. 2d 312, 213 Ill. Dec. 675, 659 N.E.2d 1322 (1995).

Construction

Primary purpose of the Illinois Domestic Violence Act of 1986 is to aid victims of domestic violence and to prevent further violence. 750 ILCS 60/102; obtaining an order of protection is not the proper procedure for resolving child custody or visitation issues, and those issues should be resolved under the Illinois Marriage and Dissolution of Marriage Act, 750 ILCS 5/101 et seq. Radke v. Radke, 349 Ill. App. 3d 264, 285 Ill. Dec. 420, 812 N.E.2d 9, 2004 Ill. App. LEXIS 528 (3 Dist. 2004).

While the Illinois Domestic Violence Act is to be liberally construed, it also serves a penal purpose, and as such, must be strictly construed in favor of an accused. Alison C. v. Westcott, 343 Ill. App. 3d 648, 278 Ill. Dec. 429, 798 N.E.2d 813, 2003 Ill. App. LEXIS 1280 (2 Dist. 2003).

This Act should be liberally construed to support the efforts of victims of domestic violence to avoid further abuse by promptly entering and diligently enforcing court orders which prohibit abuse so that victims are not trapped in abusive situations. Gasaway v. Gasaway, 246 Ill. App. 3d 531, 186 Ill. Dec. 420, 616 N.E.2d 610 (3 Dist. 1993).

Because temporary custody may be awarded under the Domestic Violence Act, and because the act makes specific reference to the Marriage Act, a court in a domestic violence case can order a home study pursuant to this section; however, such a study should only be ordered in exceptional cases because of the substantial possibility of causing delay and, further, such a study cannot be ordered in connection with an emergency order of protection as such an order may not include an award of legal custody. Wilson v. Jackson, 312 Ill. App. 3d 1156, 245 Ill. Dec. 750, 728 N.E.2d 832, 2000 Ill. App. LEXIS 267 (3 Dist. 2000).

Misuse of Act

Entry of an order of protection prohibiting a father from abusing or harassing his daughter was error where the father's actions in prohibiting his daughter from using the phone and in physically returning her to her room when she tried to leave during regularly scheduled visitation constituted a "reasonable direction" of the daughter; use of the order of protection to deal with what was basically a custody/visitation issue was improper. Radke v. Radke, 349 Ill. App. 3d 264, 285 Ill. Dec. 420, 812 N.E.2d 9, 2004 Ill. App. LEXIS 528 (3 Dist. 2004).

An ex parte order of protection obtained by a father was properly reversed where the father misused the Domestic Violence Act in seeking an order of protection not to prevent abuse, but to obtain visitation with and custody of the child, and because there was a dearth of evidence of abuse. Wilson v. Jackson, 312 Ill. App. 3d 1156, 245 Ill. Dec. 750, 728 N.E.2d 832, 2000 Ill. App. LEXIS 267 (3 Dist. 2000).

Ordinary Negligence

The Domestic Violence Act bars recognition of a cause of action sounding in ordinary negligence. Calloway v. Kinkelaar, 168 Ill. 2d 312, 213 Ill. Dec. 675, 659 N.E.2d 1322 (1995).

Public Policy

It violates public policy to evict a woman from her home merely because she got an order of protection against her husband who was physically abusing her. Wood v. Wood, 284 Ill. App. 3d 718, 219 Ill. Dec. 877, 672 N.E.2d 385 (4 Dist. 1996).

Purpose

This Act was enacted to prevent abuse and harassment between family or household members. Glater v. Fabianich, 252 Ill. App. 3d 372, 192 Ill. Dec. 136, 625 N.E.2d 96 (1 Dist. 1993).

The express legislative purpose of this Act is to prevent and alleviate domestic violence. People v. Whitfield, 147 Ill. App. 3d 675, 101 Ill. Dec. 80, 498 N.E.2d 262 (4 Dist. 1986).

750 ILCS 60/103 Definitions

Sec. 103. *Definitions.* For the purposes of this Act, the following terms shall have the following meanings:

(1) "Abuse" means physical abuse, harassment, intimidation of a dependent, interference with personal liberty or willful deprivation but does not include reasonable direction of a minor child by a parent or person in loco parentis.

(2) "Adult with disabilities" means an elder adult with disabilities or a high-risk adult with disabilities. A person may be an adult with disabilities for purposes of this Act even though he or she has never been adjudicated an incompetent adult. However, no court proceeding may be initiated or continued on behalf of an adult with disabilities over that adult's objection, unless such proceeding is approved by his or her legal guardian, if any.

(3) "Domestic violence" means abuse as defined in paragraph (1).

(4) "Elder adult with disabilities" means an adult prevented by advanced age from taking appropriate action to protect himself or herself from abuse by a family or household member.

(5) "Exploitation" means the illegal, including tortious, use of a high-risk adult with disabilities or of the assets or resources of a high-risk adult with disabilities. Exploitation includes, but is not limited to, the misappropriation of assets or resources of a high-risk adult with disabilities by undue influence, by breach of a fiduciary relationship, by fraud, deception, or extortion, or the use of such assets or resources in a manner contrary to law.

(6) "Family or household members" include spouses, former spouses, parents, children, stepchildren and other persons related by blood or by present or prior marriage, persons who share or formerly shared a common dwelling, persons who have or allegedly have a child in common, persons who share or allegedly share a blood relationship through a child, persons who have or have had a dating or engagement relationship, persons with disabilities and their personal assistants, and caregivers as defined in paragraph (3) of subsection (b) of Section 12-21 of the Criminal Code of 1961 [720 ILCS 5/12-21]. For purposes of this paragraph, neither a casual acquaintanceship nor ordinary fraternization between 2 individuals in business or social contexts shall be deemed to constitute a dating relationship. In the case of a high-risk adult with disabilities, "family or household members" includes any person who has the responsibility for a high-risk adult as a result of a family relationship or who has assumed responsibility for all or a portion of the care of a high-risk adult with disabilities voluntarily, or by express or implied contract, or by court order.

(7) "Harassment" means knowing conduct which is not necessary to accomplish a purpose that is reasonable under the circumstances; would cause a reasonable person emotional distress; and does cause emotional distress to the petitioner. Unless the presumption is rebutted by a preponderance of the evidence, the following types of conduct shall be presumed to cause emotional distress:

(i) creating a disturbance at petitioner's place of employment or school;

(ii) repeatedly telephoning petitioner's place of employment, home or residence;

(iii) repeatedly following petitioner about in a public place or places;

(iv) repeatedly keeping petitioner under surveillance by remaining present outside his or her home, school, place of employment, vehicle or other place occupied by petitioner or by peering in petitioner's windows;

(v) improperly concealing a minor child from petitioner, repeatedly threatening to improperly remove a minor child of petitioner's from the jurisdiction or from the physical care of petitioner, repeatedly threatening to conceal a minor child from petitioner, or making a single such threat following an actual or attempted improper removal or concealment, unless respondent was fleeing an incident or pattern of domestic violence; or

(vi) threatening physical force, confinement or restraint on one or more occasions.

(8) "High-risk adult with disabilities" means a person aged 18 or over whose physical or mental disability impairs his or her ability to seek or obtain protection from abuse, neglect, or exploitation.

(9) "Interference with personal liberty" means committing or threatening physical abuse, harassment, intimidation or willful deprivation so as to compel another to engage in conduct from which she or he has a right to abstain or to refrain from conduct in which she or he has a right to engage.

(10) "Intimidation of a dependent" means subjecting a person who is dependent because of age, health or disability to participation in or the witnessing of: physical force against another or physical confinement or restraint of another which constitutes physical abuse as defined in this Act, regardless of whether the abused person is a family or household member.

(11)(A) "Neglect" means the failure to exercise that degree of care toward a high-risk adult with disabilities which a reasonable person would exercise under the circumstances and includes but is not limited to:

(i) the failure to take reasonable steps to protect a high-risk adult with disabilities from acts of abuse;

(ii) the repeated, careless imposition of unreasonable confinement;

(iii) the failure to provide food, shelter, clothing, and personal hygiene to a high-risk adult with disabilities who requires such assistance;

(iv) the failure to provide medical and rehabilitative care for the physical and mental health needs of a high-risk adult with disabilities; or

(v) the failure to protect a high-risk adult with disabilities from health and safety hazards.

(B) Nothing in this subsection (10) shall be construed to impose a requirement that assistance be provided to a high-risk adult with disabilities over his or her objection in the absence of a court order, nor to create any new affirmative duty to provide support to a high-risk adult with disabilities.

(12) "Order of protection" means an emergency order, interim order or plenary order, granted pursuant to this Act, which includes any or all of the remedies authorized by Section 214 of this Act [750 ILCS 60/214].

(13) "Petitioner" may mean not only any named petitioner for the order of protection and any named victim of abuse on whose behalf the petition is brought, but also any other person protected by this Act.

(14) "Physical abuse" includes sexual abuse and means any of the following:

(i) knowing or reckless use of physical force, confinement or restraint;

(ii) knowing, repeated and unnecessary sleep deprivation; or

(iii) knowing or reckless conduct which creates an immediate risk of physical harm.

(14.5) "Stay away" means for the respondent to refrain from both physical presence and nonphysical contact with the petitioner whether direct, indirect (including, but not limited to, telephone calls, mail, email, faxes, and written notes), or through third parties who may or may not know about the order of protection.

(15) "Willful deprivation" means willfully denying a person who because of age, health or disability requires medication, medical care, shelter, accessible shelter or services, food, therapeutic device, or other physical assistance, and thereby exposing that person to the risk of physical, mental or emotional harm, except with regard to medical care or treatment when the dependent person has expressed an intent to forgo such medical care or treatment. This paragraph does not create any new affirmative duty to provide support to dependent persons.

(Source: P.A. 86-542; 87-1186, § 3; 92-253, § 10; 93-811, § 10.)

Note.

This section was Ill.Rev.Stat., Ch. 40, para. 2311-3.

Cross References.

For the contents of an order of protection, see 750 ILCS 60/221.

Illinois Administrative Code.

See 89 Illinois Administrative Code, § 337.10.

Effect of Amendments.

The 2001 amendment by P.A. 92-253, effective January 1, 2002, in subdivision (6) inserted "and caregivers as defined in paragraph (3) of subsection (b) of Section 12-21 of the Criminal Code of 1961" in the first sentence and made a related change.

The 2004 amendment by P.A. 93-811, effective January 1, 2005, inserted paragraph (14.5).

CASE NOTES

ANALYSIS

Abuse
—Court's Discretion
—Not Shown
—Review of Finding
—Shown
—Vagueness of Definition
Appealable Orders
—Factors Considered
Applicability
—Dating Relationship
—Intimate Relationships
Common Household
Construction
Harassment
—Knowing Conduct
—Not Shown
—Overbroad
—Shown
Interference with Personal Liberty
—Not Shown

Abuse

—Court's Discretion

It is the duty of the trial court, in its broad discretion, to determine whether a particular individual's actions constitute abuse on a case-by-case basis; the trial judge will assess the credibility of the witnesses and the acts and statements described, and in doing so, the trial judge necessarily considers the potential for future abuse. People v. Whitfield, 147 Ill. App. 3d 675, 101 Ill. Dec. 80, 498 N.E.2d 262 (4 Dist. 1986).

—Not Shown

Entry of an order of protection prohibiting a father from abusing or harassing his daughter was error where the father's actions in prohibiting his daughter from using the phone and in physically returning her to her room when she tried to leave during regularly scheduled visitation constituted a "reasonable direction" of the daughter; "reasonable direction" was not abuse of the daughter under 750 ILCS 60/103(7). Radke v. Radke, 349 Ill. App. 3d 264, 285 Ill. Dec. 420, 812 N.E.2d 9, 2004 Ill. App. LEXIS 528 (3 Dist. 2004).

Even assuming that the trial court resolved all questions of credibility in favor of the petitioner father, the respondent mother's conduct on a specified date did not constitute physical abuse of the parties' infant child since there was no indication that her actions created an immediate risk of physical harm to the child where, according to the father, after the mother refused his offer of $40 for baby pictures, she became "angry, upset and loud," she screamed at him and told him to leave, and when he did not leave, she "grabbed" the child and "jerked" him from father's hands. Wilson v. Jackson, 312 Ill. App. 3d 1156, 245 Ill. Dec. 750, 728 N.E.2d 832, 2000 Ill. App. LEXIS 267 (3 Dist. 2000).

—Review of Finding

Trial court abused its discretion in refusing to add non-pattern language to an instruction on domestic battery to allow jurors to consider whether a parent accused of violence against an older teen-aged child was actually attempting to exercise reasonable discipline. People v. Roberts, 351 Ill. App. 3d 684, 286 Ill. Dec. 524, 814 N.E.2d 174, 2004 Ill. App. LEXIS 921 (4 Dist. 2004).

Where the record supported the trial court's finding of abuse within the meaning of former Ill.Rev.Stat., ch. 40, para. 2301-3(1) (see now subsection (1) of this section), a reviewing court would not overturn the court's order solely for the reason that the trial judge did not make specific findings on the factors referenced in former Ill.Rev.Stat., ch. 40, para. 2302-8(d)(1) (see now 750 ILCS 60/214). In re Hagaman, 123 Ill. App. 3d 549, 78 Ill. Dec. 922, 462 N.E.2d 1276 (4 Dist. 1984).

—Shown

Mother's sexual exploitation of her minor child by involving the child in sexual acts with men for money, constituted abuse under 750 ILCS 60/103(1), (14) and supported the entry of an order of protection against the mother and in favor of the child, who had been made a ward of the court. People v. L.S. (In re T.H.), 354 Ill. App. 3d 301, 289 Ill. Dec. 902, 820 N.E.2d 977, 2004 Ill. App. LEXIS 1407 (1 Dist. 2004).

The court did not abuse its discretion in entering an interim order of protection; the evidence was sufficient to allow the court to find that respondent's conduct exceeded reasonable discipline of the minor child and was in fact physical abuse as defined in this section. Whitten v. Whitten, 292 Ill. App. 3d 780, 226 Ill. Dec. 670, 686 N.E.2d 19 (3 Dist. 1997), appeal denied, 176 Ill. 2d 594, 229 Ill. Dec. 61, 690 N.E.2d 1388 (1998).

Where court found that petitioner had been abused and that there had been threats, harassment, and interference with her living, there was testimony to support a finding of abuse within the meaning of former Ill.Rev.Stat, ch. 40, para. 2301-3(1) (see now subsection (1) of this section). In re Hagaman, 123 Ill. App. 3d 549, 78 Ill. Dec. 922, 462 N.E.2d 1276 (4 Dist. 1984).

—Vagueness of Definition

While the statutory definition of abuse under former Ill.Rev.Stat., ch. 40, para. 2301-3(1) (see now subsection (1) of this section) encompassed a broad range of conduct, it was not so unclear that courts were unable to determine the legislature's intent. In re Hagaman, 123 Ill. App. 3d 549, 78 Ill. Dec. 922, 462 N.E.2d 1276 (4 Dist. 1984).

Appealable Orders

—Factors Considered

In determining appealability under this Act, other matters pend-

Appealable Orders (Cont'd)

—Factors Considered (Cont'd)

ing in dissolution proceedings are not relevant, such as petitions for visitation, filed by child's grandparents, and the father's petition for permanent custody which was filed after the notice of appeal was filed. In re Gordon, 233 Ill. App. 3d 617, 175 Ill. Dec. 137, 599 N.E.2d 1151 (1 Dist.), appeal denied, 147 Ill. 2d 626, 180 Ill. Dec. 149, 606 N.E.2d 1226 (1992).

Applicability

—Dating Relationship

Female teenager who had only gone on one "date" with a male teenager, during which he assaulted her, was not in a dating relationship for purposes of the Illinois Domestic Violence Act; therefore, she could not obtain an order of protection. Alison C. v. Westcott, 343 Ill. App. 3d 648, 278 Ill. Dec. 429, 798 N.E.2d 813, 2003 Ill. App. LEXIS 1280 (2 Dist. 2003).

—Intimate Relationships

This Act does not apply only to persons related by marriage or blood; the Act was designed to prevent abuse between persons sharing intimate relationships. Glater v. Fabianich, 252 Ill. App. 3d 372, 192 Ill. Dec. 136, 625 N.E.2d 96 (1 Dist. 1993).

Common Household

Where incontrovertible evidence revealed that petitioner stayed at respondent's apartment for at least seven to 10 days during 1990 and during this time, petitioner ate and slept there every night and also contributed to household expenses such as buying food, along with controverted evidence that petitioner stayed at respondent's apartment every night for three months in 1989, kept a full complement of clothes there and performed some household chores, there was sufficient basis in the evidence to find that the parties had shared a common household. Glater v. Fabianich, 252 Ill. App. 3d 372, 192 Ill. Dec. 136, 625 N.E.2d 96 (1 Dist. 1993).

Construction

Because temporary custody may be awarded under the Domestic Violence Act, and because the act makes specific reference to the Marriage Act, a court in a domestic violence case can order a home study pursuant to this section; however, such a study should only be ordered in exceptional cases because of the substantial possibility of causing delay and, further, such a study cannot be ordered in connection with an emergency order of protection as such an order may not include an award of legal custody. Wilson v. Jackson, 312 Ill. App. 3d 1156, 245 Ill. Dec. 750, 728 N.E.2d 832, 2000 Ill. App. LEXIS 267 (3 Dist. 2000).

Harassment

—Knowing Conduct

Mother's unexpected and improper contact with her child, a ward of the court, as the child was arriving for a counseling session at a family assistance agency, which resulted in severe emotional distress to the child, constituted harassment for purposes of 750 ILCS 60/103(7) and supported the entry of an order of protection against the mother and in favor of the child. People v. L.S. (In re T.H.), 354 Ill. App. 3d 301, 289 Ill. Dec. 902, 820 N.E.2d 977, 2004 Ill. App. LEXIS 1407 (1 Dist. 2004).

Harassment occurs when a protagonist knowingly causes his victim to suffer undue distress; the protagonist must act with knowledge of the protective order for there to be a violation. People v. Whitfield, 147 Ill. App. 3d 675, 101 Ill. Dec. 80, 498 N.E.2d 262 (4 Dist. 1986).

—Not Shown

Where there was no evidence in the record that husband's conduct was knowing, or that it was not necessary to accomplish a purpose which was reasonable under the circumstances, nor was there evidence that his conduct would have caused a reasonable person emotional distress, the order of protection was not warranted on the basis of harassment. In re Healy, 263 Ill. App. 3d 596, 200 Ill. Dec. 327, 635 N.E.2d 666 (1 Dist. 1994).

—Overbroad

The speech that subsection (7) would inhibit must not be necessary to accomplish a reasonable purpose, must be such that it would cause another reasonable person emotional distress and actually causes emotional distress; it is speech which is not constitutionally protected, therefore the statute is not overbroad. People v. Reynolds, 302 Ill. App. 3d 722, 235 Ill. Dec. 789, 706 N.E.2d 49 (4 Dist. 1999).

—Shown

Father's act in coming home after drinking, and breaking and throwing things, constituted harassment that was sufficient to show "abuse" under the domestic violence statute as such conduct was not necessary to accomplish a purpose that was reasonable under the circumstances, such conduct would cause a reasonable person emotional distress, and such conduct did cause emotional distress to the father's minor son even though no physical violence occurred. Peck v. Otten, 329 Ill. App. 3d 266, 263 Ill. Dec. 688, 768 N.E.2d 769, 2002 Ill. App. LEXIS 279 (3 Dist. 2002).

The evidence was sufficient for a jury to find the defendant guilty where the jury could reasonably believe a note was sent as an act of retaliation and was an intimidation tactic. People v. Reynolds, 302 Ill. App. 3d 722, 235 Ill. Dec. 789, 706 N.E.2d 49 (4 Dist. 1999).

The order prohibited the defendant from intimidating his ex-wife and the defendant should have known that the note he sent with the intent of deterring his ex-wife from filing more charges did not have a reasonable purpose and therefore fell under the definition of harassment in subsection (7). People v. Reynolds, 302 Ill. App. 3d 722, 235 Ill. Dec. 789, 706 N.E.2d 49 (4 Dist. 1999).

Where the petitioner made it abundantly clear that she wanted no further contact with the respondent, the respondent's stated purpose of reestablishing the parties' relationship was not reasonable and his actions therefore constituted harassment under the Act. Shields v. Fry, 301 Ill. App. 3d 570, 234 Ill. Dec. 821, 703 N.E.2d 921 (4 Dist. 1998).

Non-custodial parent's conduct repeatedly directing the children to ask the custodial parent for visitation, as well as numerous phone calls for that same purpose, was harassment of the children and supported court's order of protection including the children. In re McCoy, 253 Ill. App. 3d 958, 192 Ill. Dec. 728, 625 N.E.2d 883 (4 Dist. 1993).

Husband's removal of phone cords to prevent wife from calling the police over to calm a domestic dispute was harassment. In re Blitstein, 212 Ill. App. 3d 124, 155 Ill. Dec. 746, 569 N.E.2d 1357 (2 Dist. 1991).

Evidence supported jury's verdict that defendant harassed his wife and knowingly violated the order of protection under former Ill.Rev.Stat., ch. 40, para. 2301-1 (see now this section) by entering the residence with knowledge that wife was present and, in her presence, engaging in a shouting match with her guest and ordering him out of the house; this conduct, especially when coupled with his act of approaching wife before exiting the premises, could certainly be found by a jury to constitute "harassment." People v. Zarebski, 186 Ill. App. 3d 285, 134 Ill. Dec. 266, 542 N.E.2d 445 (2 Dist. 1989).

Interference with Personal Liberty

—Not Shown

Where there was no evidence in the record that husband compelled wife or the children to refrain from eating or drinking, or did any act that would have led to that result, order of protection was not warranted on the basis of interference with personal liberty. In re Healy, 263 Ill. App. 3d 596, 200 Ill. Dec. 327, 635 N.E.2d 666 (1 Dist. 1994).

RESEARCH REFERENCES

"Cohabitation" for purposes of domestic violence statutes. 71 ALR5th 285.

ARTICLE II.

ORDERS OF PROTECTION

750 ILCS 60/201 Persons protected by this Act

Sec. 201. *Persons protected by this Act.* (a) The following persons are protected by this Act:

(i) any person abused by a family or household member;

(ii) any high-risk adult with disabilities who is abused, neglected, or exploited by a family or household member;

(iii) any minor child or dependent adult in the care of such person; and

(iv) any person residing or employed at a private home or public shelter which is housing an abused family or household member.

(b) A petition for an order of protection may be filed only: (i) by a person who has been abused by a family or household member or by any person on behalf of a minor child or an adult who has been abused by a family or household member and who, because of age, health, disability, or inaccessibility, cannot file the petition, or (ii) by any person on behalf of a high-risk adult with disabilities who has been abused, neglected, or exploited by a family or household member. However, any petition properly filed under this Act may seek protection for any additional persons protected by this Act.

(Source: P.A. 86-542; 87-1186, § 3.)

Note.

This section was Ill.Rev.Stat., Ch. 40, para. 2312-1.

CASE NOTES

ANALYSIS

Appealable Orders
—Factors Considered
Applicability
Domestic Violence
—Battered Woman's Syndrome
Family or Household Members
Notice
—Unified Code of Corrections
Petition
—Third Party
Pleading
—Mental State
Protection of Minor

Appealable Orders

—Factors Considered

In determining appealability under this Act, other matters pending in dissolution proceedings are not relevant, such as petitions for visitation, filed by child's grandparents, and the father's petition for permanent custody which was filed after the notice of appeal was filed. In re Gordon, 233 Ill. App. 3d 617, 175 Ill. Dec. 137, 599 N.E.2d 1151 (1 Dist.), appeal denied, 147 Ill. 2d 626, 180 Ill. Dec. 149, 606 N.E.2d 1226 (1992).

Applicability

Female teenager who had only gone on one "date" with a male teenager, during which he assaulted her, was not in a dating relationship for purposes of the Illinois Domestic Violence Act; therefore, she could not obtain an order of protection. Alison C. v. Westcott, 343 Ill. App. 3d 648, 278 Ill. Dec. 429, 798 N.E.2d 813, 2003 Ill. App. LEXIS 1280 (2 Dist. 2003).

Domestic Violence

—Battered Woman's Syndrome

When the defendant is a victim of battered woman's syndrome in a case involving the homicide of her husband, and the homicide was committed during the course of another beating, the law can no longer ignore the fact that in reality what occurred involved two victims; the law must step up to the times and itself comprehend the reality of domestic violence cases which involve victims of battered woman's syndrome. People v. Evans, 259 Ill. App. 3d 195, 197 Ill. Dec. 278, 631 N.E.2d 281 (1 Dist. 1994).

Family or Household Members

Once one member of a household is abused, the court has maximum discretionary power to fashion the scope of an order of protection to include other household members or relatives who may be at risk of retaliatory acts by the abuser. In re McCoy, 253 Ill. App. 3d 958, 192 Ill. Dec. 728, 625 N.E.2d 883 (4 Dist. 1993).

Notice

—Unified Code of Corrections

Although this section requires the issuance of summons to a respondent before a protective order may be entered when the request is initiated by a petition, it makes no requirement for notice or summons when the order is entered pursuant to a proceeding under the Unified Code of Corrections (730 ILCS 5/1-1-1 et seq.). People v. Hazelwonder, 138 Ill. App. 3d 213, 93 Ill. Dec. 1, 485 N.E.2d 1211 (4 Dist. 1985).

Petition

—Third Party

A high-risk adult with disabilities is allowed to bring a petition for an order of protection either in her own name or through another acting on her behalf. Anderson v. Schlosser, 267 Ill. App. 3d 351, 204 Ill. Dec. 732, 642 N.E.2d 194 (3 Dist. 1994), appeal denied, 159 Ill. 2d 563, 207 Ill. Dec. 513, 647 N.E.2d 1006 (1995).

Pleading

—Mental State

Mental state was not an element which had to be alleged in a complaint alleging violation of a protective order entered under a former version of this Act. People v. Blackwood, 131 Ill. App. 3d 1018, 87 Ill. Dec. 40, 476 N.E.2d 742 (3 Dist. 1985).

Protection of Minor

In an action which a father filed against his ex-wife and the ex-wife's new husband, the trial court properly considered the fact that the ex-wife's new husband was charged with abusing his own daughter and that the new husband's daughter and the father's daughter lived in the same house. Mowen v. Holland, 336 Ill. App. 3d 368, 270 Ill. Dec. 605, 783 N.E.2d 180, 2003 Ill. App. LEXIS 29 (4 Dist. 2003).

Protective orders could be entered against persons who have abused a minor child in their care, and, thus, it was not an abuse of discretion to enter a protective order against the father where the trial court found he had abused his minor son by coming home after drinking, and breaking and throwing things, as such conduct constituted harassment under the domestic violence statute even though no physical injury was involved. Peck v. Otten, 329 Ill. App. 3d 266, 263 Ill. Dec. 688, 768 N.E.2d 769, 2002 Ill. App. LEXIS 279 (3 Dist. 2002).

An order of protection under this Act may be entered against a minor. Wright v. Wright, 211 Ill. App. 3d 659, 164 Ill. Dec. 543, 583 N.E.2d 97 (4 Dist. 1991).

LEGAL PERIODICALS

For article, "Defending the Indefensible to Further a Later Case: Sanctioning Respondents in Illinois Domestic Violence Cases," see 23 N. Ill. U. L. Rev. 403 (2003).

For note, "Guardians Ad Litem: The Guardian Angels of Our Children in Domestic Violence Courts", see 30 Loy. U. Chi. L.J. 281 (1999).

For article, "Orders of Protection and the Battered Woman Syndrome," see 23 Loy. U. Chi. L.J. 397 (1991-92).

750 ILCS 60/201.1 Access of high-risk adults

Sec. 201.1. *Access of high-risk adults.* No person shall obstruct or impede the access of a high-risk adult with disabilities to any agency or organization

authorized to file a petition for an order of protection under Section 201 of this Act [750 ILCS 60/201] for the purpose of a private visit relating to legal rights, entitlements, claims and services under this Act and Section 1 of "An Act in relation to domestic relations and domestic violence shelters and service programs", approved September 24, 1981, as now or hereafter amended [20 ILCS 1310/0.01 et seq.]. If a person does so obstruct or impede such access of a high-risk adult with disabilities, local law enforcement agencies shall take all appropriate action to assist the party seeking access in petitioning for a search warrant or an ex parte injunctive order. Such warrant or order may issue upon a showing of probable cause to believe that the high-risk adult with disabilities is the subject of abuse, neglect, or exploitation which constitutes a criminal offense or that any other criminal offense is occurring which affects the interests or welfare of the high-risk adult with disabilities. When, from the personal observations of a law enforcement officer, it appears probable that delay of entry in order to obtain a warrant or order would cause the high-risk adult with disabilities to be in imminent danger of death or great bodily harm, entry may be made by the law enforcement officer after an announcement of the officer's authority and purpose.
(Source: P.A. 86-542.)

Note.
This section was Ill.Rev.Stat., Ch. 40, para. 2312-1.1.

750 ILCS 60/202 Commencement of action; filing fees; dismissal

Sec. 202. *Commencement of action; filing fees; dismissal.* (a) How to commence action. Actions for orders of protection are commenced:

(1) Independently: By filing a petition for an order of protection in any civil court, unless specific courts are designated by local rule or order.

(2) In conjunction with another civil proceeding: By filing a petition for an order of protection under the same case number as another civil proceeding involving the parties, including but not limited to: (i) any proceeding under the Illinois Marriage and Dissolution of Marriage Act [750 ILCS 5/101 et seq.], Illinois Parentage Act of 1984 [750 ILCS 45/1 et seq.], Nonsupport of Spouse and Children Act [750 ILCS 15/1 et seq.], Revised Uniform Reciprocal Enforcement of Support Act [750 ILCS 20/1 et seq.] or an action for nonsupport brought under Article 10 of the Illinois Public Aid Code [305 ILCS 5/10-1 et seq.], provided that a petitioner and the respondent are a party to or the subject of that proceeding or (ii) a guardianship proceeding under the Probate Act of 1975 [755 ILCS 5/1-1 et seq.], or a proceeding for involuntary commitment under the Mental Health and Developmental Disabilities Code [405 ILCS 5/1-100 et seq.], or any proceeding, other than a delinquency petition, under the Juvenile Court Act of 1987 [705 ILCS 405/1-1 et seq.], provided that a petitioner or the respondent is a party to or the subject of such proceeding.

(3) In conjunction with a delinquency petition or a criminal prosecution: By filing a petition for an order of protection, under the same case number as the delinquency petition or criminal prosecution, to be granted during pre-trial release of a defendant, with any dispositional order issued under Section 5-710 of the Juvenile Court Act of 1987 [705 ILCS 405/5-710] or as a condition of release, supervision, conditional discharge, probation, periodic imprisonment, parole or mandatory supervised release, or in conjunction with imprisonment or a bond forfeiture warrant; provided that:

(i) the violation is alleged in an information, complaint, indictment or delinquency petition on file, and the alleged offender and victim are family or household members or persons protected by this Act; and

(ii) the petition, which is filed by the State's Attorney, names a victim of the alleged crime as a petitioner.

(b) Filing, certification, and service fees. No fee shall be charged by the clerk for filing, amending, vacating, certifying, or photocopying petitions or orders; or for issuing alias summons; or for any related filing service. No fee shall be charged by the sheriff for service by the sheriff of a petition, rule, motion, or order in an action commenced under this Section.

(c) Dismissal and consolidation. Withdrawal or dismissal of any petition for an order of protection prior to adjudication where the petitioner is represented by the State shall operate as a dismissal without prejudice. No action for an order of protection shall be dismissed because the respondent is being prosecuted for a crime against the petitioner. An independent action may be consolidated with another civil proceeding, as provided by paragraph (2) of subsection (a) of this Section. For any action commenced under paragraph (2) or (3) of subsection (a) of this Section, dismissal of the conjoined case (or a finding of not guilty) shall not require dismissal of the action for the order of protection; instead, it may be treated as an independent action and, if necessary and appropriate, transferred to a different court or division. Dismissal of any conjoined case shall not affect the validity of any previously issued order of protection, and thereafter subsections (b)(1) and (b)(2) of Section 220 [750 ILCS 60/220] shall be inapplicable to such order.

(d) Pro se petitions. The court shall provide, through the office of the clerk of the court, simplified forms and clerical assistance to help with the writing and filing of a petition under this Section by any person not represented by counsel. In addition, that assistance may be provided by the state's attorney.
(Source: P.A. 85-1209; 86-1300; 87-1186, § 3; 88-306, § 5; 90-590, § 2001-50; 93-458, § 5.)

Note.
This section was Ill.Rev.Stat., Ch. 40, para. 2312-2.

The Non-Support of Spouse and Children Act, 750 ILCS 15/1 et seq., referred to in subsection (a)(2), is repealed. Current similar provisions are found as the Non-Support Punishment Act, 750 ILCS 16/1 et seq.

Cross References.

As to the necessary requirements of an emergency order of protection, see 750 ILCS 60/217.

As to the duration and extension of emergency interim orders, see 750 ILCS 60/220.

Effect of Amendments.

The 1998 amendment by P.A. 90-590, effective January 1, 1999, substituted "Section 5-710" for "Section 5-23" in subdivision (a)(3).

The 2003 amendment by P.A. 93-458, effective January 1, 2004, in the second sentence of subsection (b), inserted "amending, vacating, certifying, or photocopying" preceding "petitions", deleted "certifying" preceding "orders", and added "or for issuing alias summons; or for any related filing service" at the end.

CASE NOTES

Analysis

Appealability
—Separate Claims
Right to Counsel
—Failure to Appoint Counsel

Appealability

—Separate Claims

Because petitions for orders of protection may be filed in conjunction with other civil proceedings, in connection with criminal proceedings, or independently, a petition for a protective order in a marital dissolution case is a separate claim, is not an ancillary part of the claim for dissolution, and is immediately appealable. In re Blitstein, 212 Ill. App. 3d 124, 155 Ill. Dec. 746, 569 N.E.2d 1357 (2 Dist. 1991).

Right to Counsel

—Failure to Appoint Counsel

Indigent defendant's due process rights were not violated by court's failure to appoint counsel to represent him in action by defendant's wife for an order of protection. People ex rel. Williams v. Rhodes, 185 Ill. App. 3d 114, 133 Ill. Dec. 248, 540 N.E.2d 1114 (4 Dist. 1989).

OPINIONS OF ATTORNEY GENERAL

Legislative Intent

The amendments to this section by P.A. 87-1186 and P.A. 88-306 taken together, clearly express a legislative intent that no filing or service fees are to be charged with respect to petitions for, or orders of, protection, and related documents. 1994 Op. Atty. Gen. (94-003).

750 ILCS 60/203 Pleading; non-disclosure of address; non-disclosure of schools

Sec. 203. *Pleading; non-disclosure of address; non-disclosure of schools.* (a) A petition for an order of protection shall be in writing and verified or accompanied by affidavit and shall allege that petitioner has been abused by respondent, who is a family or household member. The petition shall further set forth whether there is any other pending action between the parties. During the pendency of this proceeding, each party has a continuing duty to inform the court of any subsequent proceeding for an order of protection in this or any other state.

(b) If the petition states that disclosure of petitioner's address would risk abuse of petitioner or any member of petitioner's family or household or reveal the confidential address of a shelter for domestic violence victims, that address may be omitted from all documents filed with the court. If disclosure is necessary to determine jurisdiction or consider any venue issue, it shall be made orally and in camera. If petitioner has not disclosed an address under this subsection, petitioner shall designate an alternative address at which respondent may serve notice of any motions.

(c) If the petitioner is seeking to have a child protected by the order of protection, and if that child is enrolled in any day-care facility, pre-school, pre-kindergarten, private school, public school district, college, or university, the petitioner may provide the name and address of the day-care facility, pre-school, pre-kindergarten, private school, public school district, college, or university to the court. However, if the petition states that disclosure of this information would risk abuse to petitioner or to the child protected under the order, this information may be omitted from all documents filed with the court.

(Source: P.A. 84-1305; 87-1186, § 3; 92-90, § 5.)

Note.

This section was Ill.Rev.Stat., Ch. 40, para. 2312-3.

Effect of Amendments.

The 2001 amendment by P.A. 92-90, effective July 18, 2001, revised the section heading, and added subsection (c).

CASE NOTES

Protective Order

—Forcible Removal of Child

Where father attempted to remove the child from the State of Illinois and take custody of the child, this was an improper attempt to remove the child from mother and his conduct warranted the imposition of a protective order. Gasaway v. Gasaway, 246 Ill. App. 3d 531, 186 Ill. Dec. 420, 616 N.E.2d 610 (3 Dist. 1993).

750 ILCS 60/204: Repealed by P.A. 88-306, § 10, January 1, 1994.

750 ILCS 60/205 Application of rules of civil procedure; Domestic abuse advocates

Sec. 205. *Application of rules of civil procedure; Domestic abuse advocates.* (a) Any proceeding to obtain, modify, reopen or appeal an order of protection, whether commenced alone or in conjunction with a civil or criminal proceeding, shall be governed by the rules of civil procedure of this State. The standard of proof in such a proceeding is proof by a preponderance of the evidence, whether the proceeding is heard in criminal or civil court. The Code of Civil Procedure [735 ILCS 5/1-101 et seq.] and Supreme Court and local court rules applicable to civil proceedings, as now or hereafter amended, shall apply, except as otherwise provided by this law.

(b)(1) In all circuit court proceedings under this Act, domestic abuse advocates shall be allowed to attend and sit at counsel table and confer with the victim, unless otherwise directed by the court.

(2) In criminal proceedings in circuit courts, domestic abuse advocates shall be allowed to accompany the victim and confer with the victim, unless otherwise directed by the court.

(3) Court administrators shall allow domestic abuse advocates to assist victims of domestic violence in the preparation of petitions for orders of protection.

(4) Domestic abuse advocates are not engaged in the unauthorized practice of law when providing assistance of the types specified in this subsection (b).

(Source: P.A. 84-1305; 87-1186, § 3; 87-1255, § 2; 88-45, § 2-63.)

Note.

This section was Ill.Rev.Stat., Ch. 40, para. 2312-5.

CASE NOTES

Evidence

Trial court properly considered the fact that an ex-wife's new husband was charged with abusing his own daughter when it granted a petition filed by the ex-wife's former husband for an order protecting his daughter because both children lived in the same house. Mowen v. Holland, 336 Ill. App. 3d 368, 270 Ill. Dec. 605, 783 N.E.2d 180, 2003 Ill. App. LEXIS 29 (4 Dist. 2003).

Evidence during the ex parte hearing should not have been considered to relieve petitioner of her burden of proving by a preponderance of the evidence that respondent had abused her; court should have considered only the evidence presented at the later hearing, where both parties were present, before determining whether petitioner met her burden of proving by a preponderance of the evidence that respondent had abused her. People ex rel. Minteer v. Kozin, 297 Ill. App. 3d 1038, 232 Ill. Dec. 149, 697 N.E.2d 891 (1 Dist. 1998).

RESEARCH REFERENCES

Crimes against spouse within exception permitting testimony by one spouse against other in criminal prosecution—modern state cases. 74 ALR4th 223.

750 ILCS 60/206 Trial by jury

Sec. 206. *Trial by jury.* There shall be no right to trial by jury in any proceeding to obtain, modify, vacate or extend any order of protection under this Act. However, nothing in this Section shall deny any existing right to trial by jury in a criminal proceeding.

(Source: P.A. 84-1305; 87-1186, § 3.)

Note.

This section was Ill.Rev.Stat., Ch. 40, para. 2312-6.

750 ILCS 60/207 Subject matter jurisdiction

Sec. 207. *Subject matter jurisdiction.* Each of the circuit courts shall have the power to issue orders of protection.

(Source: P.A. 84-1305.)

Note.

This section was Ill.Rev.Stat., Ch. 40, para. 2312-7.

750 ILCS 60/208 Jurisdiction over persons

Sec. 208. *Jurisdiction over persons.* In child custody proceedings, the court's personal jurisdiction is determined by this State's Uniform Child-Custody Jurisdiction and Enforcement Act [750 ILCS 36/101 et seq.]. Otherwise, the courts of this State have jurisdiction to bind (i) State residents and (ii) nonresidents having minimum contacts with this State, to the extent permitted by the long-arm statute, Section 2-209 of the Code of Civil Procedure, as now or hereafter amended [735 ILCS 5/2-209].

(Source: P.A. 84-1305; 93-108, § 402.6.)

Note.

This section was Ill.Rev.Stat., Ch. 40, para. 2312-8.

Effect of Amendments.

The 2003 amendment by P.A. 93-108, effective January 1, 2004, in the first sentence, substituted "Uniform Child-Custody Jurisdiction and Enforcement Act" for "Uniform Child Custody Jurisdiction Act" and deleted "as now or hereafter amended" at the end.

CASE NOTES

Construction

Because temporary custody may be awarded under the Domestic Violence Act, and because the act makes specific reference to the Marriage Act, a court in a domestic violence case can order a home study pursuant to this section; however, such a study should only be ordered in exceptional cases because of the substantial possibility of causing delay and, further, such a study cannot be ordered in connection with an emergency order of protection as such an order may not include an award of legal custody. Wilson v. Jackson, 312 Ill. App. 3d 1156, 245 Ill. Dec. 750, 728 N.E.2d 832, 2000 Ill. App. LEXIS 267 (3 Dist. 2000).

750 ILCS 60/209 Venue

Sec. 209. *Venue.* (a) Filing. A petition for an order of protection may be filed in any county where (i) petitioner resides, (ii) respondent resides, (iii) the alleged abuse occurred or (iv) the petitioner is temporarily located if petitioner left petitioner's residence to avoid further abuse and could not obtain safe, accessible, and adequate temporary housing in the county of that residence.

(b) Exclusive Possession. With respect to requests for exclusive possession of the residence under this Act, venue is proper only in the county where the residence is located, except in the following circumstances:

(1) If a request for exclusive possession of the residence is made under this Act in conjunction with a proceeding under the Illinois Marriage and Dissolution of Marriage Act [750 ILCS 5/101 et seq.], venue is proper in the county or judicial circuit where the residence is located or in a contiguous county or judicial circuit.

(2) If a request for exclusive possession of the residence is made under this Act in any other proceeding, provided the petitioner meets the requirements of item (iv) of subsection (a), venue is proper in the county or judicial circuit where the residence is located or in a contiguous county or

judicial circuit. In such case, however, if the court is not located in the county where the residence is located, it may grant exclusive possession of the residence under subdivision (b)(2) of Section 214 [750 ILCS 60/214] only in an emergency order under Section 217 [750 ILCS 60/217], and such grant may be extended thereafter beyond the maximum initial period only by a court located in the county where the residence is located.

(c) Inconvenient forum. If an order of protection is issued by a court in a county in which neither of the parties resides, the court may balance hardships to the parties and accordingly transfer any proceeding to extend, modify, re-open, vacate or enforce any such order to a county wherein a party resides.

(d) Objection. Objection to venue is waived if not made within such time as respondent's response is due, except as otherwise provided in subsection (b). In no event shall venue be deemed jurisdictional.

(Source: P.A. 86-966; 87-1186, § 3.)

Note.

This section was Ill.Rev.Stat., Ch. 40, para. 2312-9.

750 ILCS 60/210 Process

Sec. 210. *Process.* (a) Summons. Any action for an order of protection, whether commenced alone or in conjunction with another proceeding, is a distinct cause of action and requires that a separate summons be issued and served, except that in pending cases the following methods may be used:

(1) By delivery of the summons to respondent personally in open court in pending civil or criminal cases.

(2) By notice in accordance with Section 210.1 [750 ILCS 60/210.1] in civil cases in which the defendant has filed a general appearance.

The summons shall be in the form prescribed by Supreme Court Rule 101(d), except that it shall require respondent to answer or appear within 7 days. Attachments to the summons or notice shall include the petition for order of protection and supporting affidavits, if any, and any emergency order of protection that has been issued. The enforcement of an order of protection under Section 223 [750 ILCS 60/223] shall not be affected by the lack of service, delivery, or notice, provided the requirements of subsection (d) of that Section are otherwise met.

(b) Blank.

(c) Expedited service. The summons shall be served by the sheriff or other law enforcement officer at the earliest time and shall take precedence over other summonses except those of a similar emergency nature. Special process servers may be appointed at any time, and their designation shall not affect the responsibilities and authority of the sheriff or other official process servers.

(d) Remedies requiring actual notice. The counseling, payment of support, payment of shelter services, and payment of losses remedies provided by paragraphs 4, 12, 13, and 16 of subsection (b) of Section 214 [750 ILCS 60/214] may be granted only if respondent has been personally served with process, has answered or has made a general appearance.

(e) Remedies upon constructive notice. Service of process on a member of respondent's household or by publication shall be adequate for the remedies provided by paragraphs 1, 2, 3, 5, 6, 7, 8, 9, 10, 11, 14, 15, and 17 of subsection (b) of Section 214 [750 ILCS 60/214], but only if: (i) petitioner has made all reasonable efforts to accomplish actual service of process personally upon respondent, but respondent cannot be found to effect such service and (ii) petitioner files an affidavit or presents sworn testimony as to those efforts.

(f) Default. A plenary order of protection may be entered by default as follows:

(1) For any of the remedies sought in the petition, if respondent has been served or given notice in accordance with subsection (a) and if respondent then fails to appear as directed or fails to appear on any subsequent appearance or hearing date agreed to by the parties or set by the court; or

(2) For any of the remedies provided in accordance with subsection (e), if respondent fails to answer or appear in accordance with the date set in the publication notice or the return date indicated on the service of a household member.

(Source: P.A. 84-1305; 87-1186, § 3; 88-306, § 5.)

Note.

This section was Ill.Rev.Stat., Ch. 40, para. 2312-10.

CASE NOTES

Modification

—Permitted

Despite the fact that the wife was not given prior notice of the trial court's consideration of the issue of modification of a protective order against the husband, in accordance with 750 ILCS 60/224(b) of the Illinois Domestic Violence Act, the appellate court concluded that the power to make such a change in the previously ordered visitation was inherent in the trial court's authority; as the trial court had jurisdiction of the subject matter and of the parties, it further had the power to make such modifications of the visitation under the circumstances presented, consistent with the best interest of the child. In re Marriage of Munger, 339 Ill. App. 3d 1104, 274 Ill. Dec. 481, 791 N.E.2d 573, 2003 Ill. App. LEXIS 717 (4 Dist. 2003).

750 ILCS 60/210.1 Service of notice in conjunction with a pending civil case

Sec. 210.1. *Service of notice in conjunction with a pending civil case.* (a) Notice. When an action for an order of protection is sought in conjunction with a pending civil case in which the court has obtained jurisdiction over respondent, and respondent has filed a general appearance, then a separate summons need not issue. Original notice of a hearing on a petition for an order of protection may be given, and the documents served, in accordance with Illinois Supreme Court Rules 11 and 12. When, however, an emergency order of protection is sought in such a case on an ex parte application, then the procedure set forth in subsection (a) of Section 210 [750 ILCS 60/210] (other than in subsection (a)(2)) shall be followed. If an order of protection is issued using the notice provisions of this Section, then the order of protection or extensions of that order may survive the disposition of the main civil case. The enforcement of any order of protection under Section 223 [750 ILCS 60/223] shall not be affected by the lack of notice under this Section, provided the requirements of subsection (d) of that Section are otherwise met.

(b) Default. The form of notice described in subsection (a) shall include the following language directed to the respondent:

A 2-year plenary order of protection may be entered by default for any of the remedies sought in the petition if you fail to appear on the specified hearing date or on any subsequent hearing date agreed to by the parties or set by the court.

(c) Party to give notice. Notice in the pending civil cases shall be given (i) by either party under this Section, with respect to extensions, modifications, hearings, or other relief pertinent to an order of protection, in accordance with Illinois Supreme Court Rules 11 and 12 or (ii) by the respondent as provided in subsection (c) of Section 224 [750 ILCS 60/224].
(Source: P.A. 87-1186, § 3.)

Effective Date.
This section became effective January 1, 1993, pursuant to Ill. Const. (1970), Art. IV, § 10 and 5 ILCS 75/1.

750 ILCS 60/211 Service of notice of hearings

Sec. 211. *Service of notice of hearings.* Except as provided in Sections 210 and 210.1 [750 ILCS 60/210 and 750 ILCS 60/210.1], notice of hearings on petitions or motions shall be served in accordance with Supreme Court Rules 11 and 12, unless notice is excused by Section 217 of this Act [750 ILCS 60/217], or by the Code of Civil Procedure [735 ILCS 5/1-101 et seq.], Supreme Court Rules, or local rules, as now or hereafter amended.
(Source: P.A. 84-1305; 87-1186, § 3.)

Note.
This section was Ill.Rev.Stat., Ch. 40, para. 2312-11.

750 ILCS 60/212 Hearings

Sec. 212. *Hearings.* (a) A petition for an order of protection shall be treated as an expedited proceeding, and no court shall transfer or otherwise decline to decide all or part of such petition except as otherwise provided herein. Nothing in this Section shall prevent the court from reserving issues when jurisdiction or notice requirements are not met.

(b) Any court or a division thereof which ordinarily does not decide matters of child custody and family support may decline to decide contested issues of physical care, custody, visitation, or family support unless a decision on one or more of those contested issues is necessary to avoid the risk of abuse, neglect, removal from the state or concealment within the state of the child or of separation of the child from the primary caretaker. If the court or division thereof has declined to decide any or all of these issues, then it shall transfer all undecided issues to the appropriate court or division. In the event of such a transfer, a government attorney involved in the criminal prosecution may, but need not, continue to offer counsel to petitioner on transferred matters.

(c) If the court transfers or otherwise declines to decide any issue, judgment on that issue shall be expressly reserved and ruling on other issues shall not be delayed or declined.
(Source: P.A. 84-1305; 87-1186, § 3.)

Note.
This section was Ill.Rev.Stat., Ch. 40, para. 2312-12.

750 ILCS 60/213 Continuances

Sec. 213. *Continuances.* (a) Petitions for emergency orders. Petitions for emergency remedies shall be granted or denied in accordance with the standards of Section 217 [750 ILCS 60/217], regardless of respondent's appearance or presence in court.

(b) Petitions for interim and plenary orders. Any action for an order of protection is an expedited proceeding. Continuances should be granted only for good cause shown and kept to the minimum reasonable duration, taking into account the reasons for the continuance. If the continuance is necessary for some, but not all, of the remedies requested, hearing on those other remedies shall not be delayed.
(Source: P.A. 84-1305; 87-1186, § 3.)

Note.
This section was Ill.Rev.Stat., Ch. 40, para. 2312-13.

750 ILCS 60/213.1 Hearsay exception

Sec. 213.1. *Hearsay exception.* In an action for an order of protection on behalf of a high-risk adult with disabilities, a finding of lack of capacity to testify shall not render inadmissible any statement as long as the reliability of the statement is ensured by circumstances bringing it within the scope of a hearsay exception. The following evidence shall be admitted as an exception to the hearsay rule whether or not the declarant is available as a witness:

(1) A statement relating to a startling event or condition made spontaneously while the declarant was under the contemporaneous or continuing stress of excitement caused by the event or condition.

(2) A statement made for the purpose of obtaining, receiving, or promoting medical diagnosis or treatment, including psychotherapy, and describing med-

ical history, or past or present symptoms, pain, or sensations, or the inception or general character of the cause or external source thereof insofar as reasonably pertinent to diagnosis or treatment. For purposes of obtaining a protective order, the identity of any person inflicting abuse or neglect as defined in this Act shall be deemed reasonably pertinent to diagnosis or treatment.

(3) A statement not specifically covered by any of the foregoing exceptions but having equivalent circumstantial guarantees of trustworthiness, if the court determines that (A) the statement is offered as evidence of a material fact, and (B) the statement is more probative on the point for which it is offered than any other evidence which the proponent can procure through reasonable efforts.

Circumstantial guarantees of trustworthiness include:

(1) the credibility of the witness who testifies the statement was made;

(2) assurance of the declarant's personal knowledge of the event;

(3) the declarant's interest or bias and the presence or absence of capacity or motive to fabricate;

(4) the presence or absence of suggestiveness or prompting at the time the statement was made;

(5) whether the declarant has ever reaffirmed or recanted the statement; and

(6) corroboration by physical evidence or behavioral changes in the declarant.

The record shall reflect the court's findings of fact and conclusions of law as to the trustworthiness requirement.

A statement shall not be admitted under the exception set forth in this Section unless its proponent gives written notice stating his or her intention to offer the statement and the particulars of it to the adverse party sufficiently in advance of offering the statement to provide the adverse party with a fair opportunity to prepare to meet the statement.
(Source: P.A. 86-542.)

Note.

This section was Ill.Rev.Stat., Ch. 40, para. 2312-13.1.

RESEARCH REFERENCES

Admissibility of statements made for purposes of medical diagnosis or treatment as hearsay exception under Rule 803(4) of the Uniform Rules of Evidence. 38 ALR5th 433.

750 ILCS 60/213.2 Waiver of privilege

Sec. 213.2. *Waiver of privilege.* When the subject of any proceeding under this Act is a high-risk adult with disabilities for whom no guardian has been appointed, no party other than the high-risk adult or the attorney for the high-risk adult shall be entitled to invoke or waive a common law or statutory privilege on behalf of the high-risk adult which results in the exclusion of evidence.
(Source: P.A. 86-542.)

Note.

This section was Ill.Rev.Stat., Ch. 40, para. 2312-13.2.

750 ILCS 60/213.3 Independent counsel; temporary substitute guardian

Sec. 213.3. *Independent counsel; temporary substitute guardian.* If the petitioner is a high-risk adult with disabilities for whom a guardian has been appointed, the court shall appoint independent counsel other than a guardian ad litem and, may appoint a temporary substitute guardian under the provisions of Article XIa of the Probate Act of 1975 [755 ILCS 5/11a-1 et seq.]. The court shall appoint a temporary substitute guardian if the guardian is named as a respondent in a petition under this Act.
(Source: P.A. 86-542.)

Note.

This section was Ill.Rev.Stat., Ch. 40, para. 2312-13.3.

Illinois Administrative Code.

See 59 Illinois Administrative Code, § 51.70.

750 ILCS 60/214 Order of protection; remedies

Sec. 214. *Order of protection; remedies.* (a) Issuance of order. If the court finds that petitioner has been abused by a family or household member or that petitioner is a high-risk adult who has been abused, neglected, or exploited, as defined in this Act, an order of protection prohibiting the abuse, neglect, or exploitation shall issue; provided that petitioner must also satisfy the requirements of one of the following Sections, as appropriate: Section 217 [750 ILCS 60/217] on emergency orders, Section 218 [750 ILCS 60/218] on interim orders, or Section 219 [750 ILCS 60/219] on plenary orders. Petitioner shall not be denied an order of protection because petitioner or respondent is a minor. The court, when determining whether or not to issue an order of protection, shall not require physical manifestations of abuse on the person of the victim. Modification and extension of prior orders of protection shall be in accordance with this Act.

(b) Remedies and standards. The remedies to be included in an order of protection shall be determined in accordance with this Section and one of the following Sections, as appropriate: Section 217 [750 ILCS 60/217] on emergency orders, Section 218 [750 ILCS 60/218] on interim orders, and Section 219 [750 ILCS 60/219] on plenary orders. The remedies listed in this subsection shall be in addition to other civil or criminal remedies available to petitioner.

(1) Prohibition of abuse, neglect, or exploitation. Prohibit respondent's harassment, interference with personal liberty, intimidation of a dependent, physical abuse, or willful deprivation, neglect or exploitation, as defined in this Act, or stalking of the petitioner, as defined in Section 12-7.3 of the Criminal Code of 1961 [720 ILCS 5/12-7.3], if such abuse, neglect, exploitation, or stalking has occurred or otherwise appears likely to occur if not prohibited.

(2) Grant of exclusive possession of residence. Prohibit respondent from entering or remaining in any residence or household of the petitioner, including one owned or leased by respondent, if petitioner has a right to occupancy thereof. The grant of exclusive possession of the residence shall not affect title to real property, nor shall the court be limited by the standard set forth in Section 701 of the Illinois Marriage and Dissolution of Marriage Act [750 ILCS 5/701].

(A) Right to occupancy. A party has a right to occupancy of a residence or household if it is solely or jointly owned or leased by that party, that party's spouse, a person with a legal duty to support that party or a minor child in that party's care, or by any person or entity other than the opposing party that authorizes that party's occupancy (e.g., a domestic violence shelter). Standards set forth in subparagraph (B) shall not preclude equitable relief.

(B) Presumption of hardships. If petitioner and respondent each has the right to occupancy of a residence or household, the court shall balance (i) the hardships to respondent and any minor child or dependent adult in respondent's care resulting from entry of this remedy with (ii) the hardships to petitioner and any minor child or dependent adult in petitioner's care resulting from continued exposure to the risk of abuse (should petitioner remain at the residence or household) or from loss of possession of the residence or household (should petitioner leave to avoid the risk of abuse). When determining the balance of hardships, the court shall also take into account the accessibility of the residence or household. Hardships need not be balanced if respondent does not have a right to occupancy.

The balance of hardships is presumed to favor possession by petitioner unless the presumption is rebutted by a preponderance of the evidence, showing that the hardships to respondent substantially outweigh the hardships to petitioner and any minor child or dependent adult in petitioner's care. The court, on the request of petitioner or on its own motion, may order respondent to provide suitable, accessible, alternate housing for petitioner instead of excluding respondent from a mutual residence or household.

(3) Stay away order and additional prohibitions. Order respondent to stay away from petitioner or any other person protected by the order of protection, or prohibit respondent from entering or remaining present at petitioner's school, place of employment, or other specified places at times when petitioner is present, or both, if reasonable, given the balance of hardships. Hardships need not be balanced for the court to enter a stay away order or prohibit entry if respondent has no right to enter the premises.

If an order of protection grants petitioner exclusive possession of the residence, or prohibits respondent from entering the residence, or orders respondent to stay away from petitioner or other protected persons, then the court may allow respondent access to the residence to remove items of clothing and personal adornment used exclusively by respondent, medications, and other items as the court directs. The right to access shall be exercised on only one occasion as the court directs and in the presence of an agreed-upon adult third party or law enforcement officer.

(4) Counseling. Require or recommend the respondent to undergo counseling for a specified duration with a social worker, psychologist, clinical psychologist, psychiatrist, family service agency, alcohol or substance abuse program, mental health center guidance counselor, agency providing services to elders, program designed for domestic violence abusers or any other guidance service the court deems appropriate.

(5) Physical care and possession of the minor child. In order to protect the minor child from abuse, neglect, or unwarranted separation from the person who has been the minor child's primary caretaker, or to otherwise protect the well-being of the minor child, the court may do either or both of the following: (i) grant petitioner physical care or possession of the minor child, or both, or (ii) order respondent to return a minor child to, or not remove a minor child from, the physical care of a parent or person in loco parentis.

If a court finds, after a hearing, that respondent has committed abuse (as defined in Section 103 [750 ILCS 60/103]) of a minor child, there shall be a rebuttable presumption that awarding physical care to respondent would not be in the minor child's best interest.

(6) Temporary legal custody. Award temporary legal custody to petitioner in accordance with this Section, the Illinois Marriage and Dissolution of Marriage Act [750 ILCS 5/101 et seq.], the Illinois Parentage Act of 1984 [750 ILCS 45/1 et seq.], and this State's Uniform Child-Custody Jurisdiction and Enforcement Act [750 ILCS 36/101 et seq.].

If a court finds, after a hearing, that respondent has committed abuse (as defined in Section 103 [750 ILCS 60/103]) of a minor child, there shall be a rebuttable presumption that awarding temporary legal custody to respondent would not be in the child's best interest.

(7) Visitation. Determine the visitation rights, if any, of respondent in any case in which the court awards physical care or temporary legal custody of a minor child to petitioner. The court shall restrict or deny respondent's visitation with a minor child if the court finds that respondent has done or is likely to do any of the following: (i) abuse or endanger the minor child during visitation; (ii) use the visitation as an opportunity to abuse or harass petitioner or petitioner's family or household members; (iii) improperly conceal or detain the minor child; or (iv) otherwise act in a manner that is not in the best

interests of the minor child. The court shall not be limited by the standards set forth in Section 607.1 of the Illinois Marriage and Dissolution of Marriage Act [750 ILCS 5/607.1]. If the court grants visitation, the order shall specify dates and times for the visitation to take place or other specific parameters or conditions that are appropriate. No order for visitation shall refer merely to the term "reasonable visitation".

Petitioner may deny respondent access to the minor child if, when respondent arrives for visitation, respondent is under the influence of drugs or alcohol and constitutes a threat to the safety and well-being of petitioner or petitioner's minor children or is behaving in a violent or abusive manner.

If necessary to protect any member of petitioner's family or household from future abuse, respondent shall be prohibited from coming to petitioner's residence to meet the minor child for visitation, and the parties shall submit to the court their recommendations for reasonable alternative arrangements for visitation. A person may be approved to supervise visitation only after filing an affidavit accepting that responsibility and acknowledging accountability to the court.

(8) Removal or concealment of minor child. Prohibit respondent from removing a minor child from the State or concealing the child within the State.

(9) Order to appear. Order the respondent to appear in court, alone or with a minor child, to prevent abuse, neglect, removal or concealment of the child, to return the child to the custody or care of the petitioner or to permit any court-ordered interview or examination of the child or the respondent.

(10) Possession of personal property. Grant petitioner exclusive possession of personal property and, if respondent has possession or control, direct respondent to promptly make it available to petitioner, if:

(i) petitioner, but not respondent, owns the property; or

(ii) the parties own the property jointly; sharing it would risk abuse of petitioner by respondent or is impracticable; and the balance of hardships favors temporary possession by petitioner.

If petitioner's sole claim to ownership of the property is that it is marital property, the court may award petitioner temporary possession thereof under the standards of subparagraph (ii) of this paragraph only if a proper proceeding has been filed under the Illinois Marriage and Dissolution of Marriage Act, as now or hereafter amended [750 ILCS 5/101 et seq.].

No order under this provision shall affect title to property.

(11) Protection of property. Forbid the respondent from taking, transferring, encumbering, concealing, damaging or otherwise disposing of any real or personal property, except as explicitly authorized by the court, if:

(i) petitioner, but not respondent, owns the property; or

(ii) the parties own the property jointly, and the balance of hardships favors granting this remedy.

If petitioner's sole claim to ownership of the property is that it is marital property, the court may grant petitioner relief under subparagraph (ii) of this paragraph only if a proper proceeding has been filed under the Illinois Marriage and Dissolution of Marriage Act, as now or hereafter amended [750 ILCS 5/101 et seq.].

The court may further prohibit respondent from improperly using the financial or other resources of an aged member of the family or household for the profit or advantage of respondent or of any other person.

(12) Order for payment of support. Order respondent to pay temporary support for the petitioner or any child in the petitioner's care or custody, when the respondent has a legal obligation to support that person, in accordance with the Illinois Marriage and Dissolution of Marriage Act [750 ILCS 5/101 et seq.], which shall govern, among other matters, the amount of support, payment through the clerk and withholding of income to secure payment. An order for child support may be granted to a petitioner with lawful physical care or custody of a child, or an order or agreement for physical care or custody, prior to entry of an order for legal custody. Such a support order shall expire upon entry of a valid order granting legal custody to another, unless otherwise provided in the custody order.

(13) Order for payment of losses. Order respondent to pay petitioner for losses suffered as a direct result of the abuse, neglect, or exploitation. Such losses shall include, but not be limited to, medical expenses, lost earnings or other support, repair or replacement of property damaged or taken, reasonable attorney's fees, court costs and moving or other travel expenses, including additional reasonable expenses for temporary shelter and restaurant meals.

(i) Losses affecting family needs. If a party is entitled to seek maintenance, child support or property distribution from the other party under the Illinois Marriage and Dissolution of Marriage Act, as now or hereafter amended [750 ILCS 5/101 et seq.], the court may order respondent to reimburse petitioner's actual losses, to the extent that such reimbursement would be "appropriate temporary relief", as authorized by subsection (a)(3) of Section 501 of that Act [750 ILCS 5/501].

(ii) Recovery of expenses. In the case of an improper concealment or removal of a minor child, the court may order respondent to pay the reasonable expenses incurred or to be incurred in the search for and recovery of the minor child, including but not limited to legal fees, court costs, private investigator fees, and travel costs.

(14) Prohibition of entry. Prohibit the respondent from entering or remaining in the residence or household while the respondent is under the influence of alcohol or drugs and constitutes a threat to the safety and well-being of the petitioner or the petitioner's children.

(14.5) Prohibition of firearm possession.

(a) When a complaint is made under a request for an order of protection, that the respondent has threatened or is likely to use firearms illegally against the petitioner, and the respondent is present in court, or has failed to appear after receiving actual notice, the court shall examine on oath the petitioner, and any witnesses who may be produced. If the court is satisfied that there is any danger of the illegal use of firearms, it shall issue an order that any firearms in the possession of the respondent, except as provided in subsection (b), be turned over to the local law enforcement agency for safekeeping. If the respondent has failed to appear, the court shall issue a warrant for seizure of any firearm in the possession of the respondent. The period of safekeeping shall be for a stated period of time not to exceed 2 years. The firearm or firearms shall be returned to the respondent at the end of the stated period or at expiration of the order of protection, whichever is sooner.

(b) If the respondent is a peace officer as defined in Section 2-13 of the Criminal Code of 1961 [720 ILCS 5/2-13], the court shall order that any firearms used by the respondent in the performance of his or her duties as a peace officer be surrendered to the chief law enforcement executive of the agency in which the respondent is employed, who shall retain the firearms for safekeeping for the stated period not to exceed 2 years as set forth in the court order.

(15) Prohibition of access to records. If an order of protection prohibits respondent from having contact with the minor child, or if petitioner's address is omitted under subsection (b) of Section 203 [750 ILCS 60/203], or if necessary to prevent abuse or wrongful removal or concealment of a minor child, the order shall deny respondent access to, and prohibit respondent from inspecting, obtaining, or attempting to inspect or obtain, school or any other records of the minor child who is in the care of petitioner.

(16) Order for payment of shelter services. Order respondent to reimburse a shelter providing temporary housing and counseling services to the petitioner for the cost of the services, as certified by the shelter and deemed reasonable by the court.

(17) Order for injunctive relief. Enter injunctive relief necessary or appropriate to prevent further abuse of a family or household member or further abuse, neglect, or exploitation of a high-risk adult with disabilities or to effectuate one of the granted remedies, if supported by the balance of hardships. If the harm to be prevented by the injunction is abuse or any other harm that one of the remedies listed in paragraphs (1) through (16) of this subsection is designed to prevent, no further evidence is necessary that the harm is an irreparable injury.

(c) Relevant factors; findings.

(1) In determining whether to grant a specific remedy, other than payment of support, the court shall consider relevant factors, including but not limited to the following:

(i) the nature, frequency, severity, pattern and consequences of the respondent's past abuse, neglect or exploitation of the petitioner or any family or household member, including the concealment of his or her location in order to evade service of process or notice, and the likelihood of danger of future abuse, neglect, or exploitation to petitioner or any member of petitioner's or respondent's family or household; and

(ii) the danger that any minor child will be abused or neglected or improperly removed from the jurisdiction, improperly concealed within the State or improperly separated from the child's primary caretaker.

(2) In comparing relative hardships resulting to the parties from loss of possession of the family home, the court shall consider relevant factors, including but not limited to the following:

(i) availability, accessibility, cost, safety, adequacy, location and other characteristics of alternate housing for each party and any minor child or dependent adult in the party's care;

(ii) the effect on the party's employment; and

(iii) the effect on the relationship of the party, and any minor child or dependent adult in the party's care, to family, school, church and community.

(3) Subject to the exceptions set forth in paragraph (4) of this subsection, the court shall make its findings in an official record or in writing, and shall at a minimum set forth the following:

(i) That the court has considered the applicable relevant factors described in paragraphs (1) and (2) of this subsection.

(ii) Whether the conduct or actions of respondent, unless prohibited, will likely cause irreparable harm or continued abuse.

(iii) Whether it is necessary to grant the requested relief in order to protect petitioner or other alleged abused persons.

(4) For purposes of issuing an ex parte emergency order of protection, the court, as an alternative to or as a supplement to making the findings described in paragraphs (c)(3)(i) through (c)(3)(iii) of this subsection, may use the following procedure:

When a verified petition for an emergency order of protection in accordance with the requirements of Sections 203 and 217 [750 ILCS 60/203 and 750 ILCS 60/217] is presented to the court, the court shall examine petitioner on oath or affirmation. An emergency order of protection shall be issued by the court if it appears from the contents of the petition and the examination of petitioner that the averments are sufficient to indicate abuse by respondent and to support the granting of relief under the issuance of the emergency order of protection.

(5) Never married parties. No rights or responsibilities for a minor child born outside of marriage attach to a putative father until a father and child relationship has been established under the Illinois Parentage Act of 1984 [750 ILCS 45/1 et seq.], the

Illinois Public Aid Code [305 ILCS 5/1-1 et seq.], Section 12 of the Vital Records Act [410 ILCS 535/12], the Juvenile Court Act of 1987 [705 ILCS 405/1-1 et seq.], the Probate Act of 1985 [755 ILCS 5/1-1 et seq.], the Revised Uniform Reciprocal Enforcement of Support Act [750 ILCS 20/1 et seq.], the Uniform Interstate Family Support Act [750 ILCS 22/101 et seq.], the Expedited Child Support Act of 1990 [750 ILCS 25/1 et seq.], any judicial, administrative, or other act of another state or territory, any other Illinois statute, or by any foreign nation establishing the father and child relationship, any other proceeding substantially in conformity with the Personal Responsibility and Work Opportunity Reconciliation Act of 1996 (Pub. L. 104-193) [8 U.S.C. § 1610 et seq.], or where both parties appeared in open court or at an administrative hearing acknowledging under oath or admitting by affirmation the existence of a father and child relationship. Absent such an adjudication, finding, or acknowledgement, no putative father shall be granted temporary custody of the minor child, visitation with the minor child, or physical care and possession of the minor child, nor shall an order of payment for support of the minor child be entered.

(d) Balance of hardships; findings. If the court finds that the balance of hardships does not support the granting of a remedy governed by paragraph (2), (3), (10), (11), or (16) of subsection (b) of this Section, which may require such balancing, the court's findings shall so indicate and shall include a finding as to whether granting the remedy will result in hardship to respondent that would substantially outweigh the hardship to petitioner from denial of the remedy. The findings shall be an official record or in writing.

(e) Denial of remedies. Denial of any remedy shall not be based, in whole or in part, on evidence that:

(1) Respondent has cause for any use of force, unless that cause satisfies the standards for justifiable use of force provided by Article VII of the Criminal Code of 1961 [720 ILCS 5/7-1 et seq.];

(2) Respondent was voluntarily intoxicated;

(3) Petitioner acted in self-defense or defense of another, provided that, if petitioner utilized force, such force was justifiable under Article VII of the Criminal Code of 1961 [720 ILCS 5/7-1 et seq.];

(4) Petitioner did not act in self-defense or defense of another;

(5) Petitioner left the residence or household to avoid further abuse, neglect, or exploitation by respondent;

(6) Petitioner did not leave the residence or household to avoid further abuse, neglect, or exploitation by respondent;

(7) Conduct by any family or household member excused the abuse, neglect, or exploitation by respondent, unless that same conduct would have excused such abuse, neglect, or exploitation if the parties had not been family or household members. (Source: P.A. 86-542; 86-966; 86-1028; 87-743; 87-870; 87-871; 87-1186, § 3; 88-45, § 2-63; 89-367, § 20; 90-118, § 5; 93-108, § 402.6.)

Note.

750 ILCS 35/1 et seq., was repealed. See now 750 ILCS 36/101 et seq.

This section was Ill.Rev.Stat., Ch. 40, para. 2312-14.

Cross References.

Concerning the violation of an order of protection, and certain criminal penalties, see 720 ILCS 5/12-30.

For the definition of order of protection, see 750 ILCS 60/103.

Concerning the enforcement of an order of protection, see 750 ILCS 60/223.

Concerning the modification and re-opening of order, see 750 ILCS 60/224.

Effect of Amendments.

The 1995 amendment by P.A. 89-367, effective January 1, 1996, added subdivision (b)(14.5).

The 1997 amendment by P.A. 90-118, effective January 1, 1998, in subdivision (c)(5), in the first sentence, added at the end "the Illinois Public Aid Code, Section 12 of the Vital Records Act, the Juvenile Court Act of 1987, the Probate Act of 1985, the Revised Uniform Reciprocal Enforcement of Support Act, the Uniform Interstate Family Support Act, the Expedited Child Support Act of 1990, any judicial, administrative, or other act of another state or territory, any other Illinois statute, or by any foreign nation establishing the father and child relationship, any other proceeding substantially in conformity with the Personal Responsibility and Work Opportunity Reconciliation Act of 1996 (Pub. L. 104-193), or where both parties appeared in open court or at an administrative hearing acknowledging under oath or admitting by affirmation the existence of a father and child relationship" and in the second sentence, inserted "finding, or acknowledgement".

The 2003 amendment by P.A. 93-108, effective January 1, 2004, substituted "Uniform Child-Custody Jurisdiction and Enforcement Act" for "Uniform Child Custody Jurisdiction Act" in the first sentence of subsection (b)(6).

CASE NOTES

ANALYSIS

Attorney's Fees
Exclusive Possession of Residence
—Factors to Consider
—Held Proper
Findings
Future Abuse
Injunctive Relief
—Mandatory Contact
—Prohibiting Verbal Contact
Legislative Intent
Marriage
—No Exception
Nonphysical Contact
Order to Appear
—Notice
Prohibited Entry
—Homeowner
Protection
—Not Warranted
—Of Family or Household Members
—Of Minor
—Types
Relevant Factors
—Residence in Family Shelter
Right to Counsel
—Failure to Appoint Counsel
Self-Defense
—Use of Deadly Force
Specific Findings Required

Attorney's Fees

As 750 ILCS 60/214(b)(13) authorizes a trial court to order a respondent who committed domestic violence to pay the petitioner's attorney's fees, that the petitioner's attorney was court-appointed and that her fees were paid by the county did not bar the trial court from ordering the father to reimburse the county for those fees.

Attorney's Fees (Cont'd)
Steward v. Schluter, 352 Ill. App. 3d 1196, 289 Ill. Dec. 89, 819 N.E.2d 1, 2004 Ill. App. LEXIS 1387 (4 Dist. 2004).

Exclusive Possession of Residence

—Factors to Consider
Where the record supported the trial court's finding of abuse within the meaning of former Ill.Rev.Stat., ch. 40, para. 2301-3(1) (see now 750 ILCS 60/103), a reviewing court would not overturn the court's order solely for the reason that the trial judge did not make specific findings on the factors referenced in former Ill.Rev.Stat., ch. 40, para. 2302-8(d)(1) (see now subdivision (b)(2) of this section). In re Hagaman, 123 Ill. App. 3d 549, 78 Ill. Dec. 922, 462 N.E.2d 1276 (4 Dist. 1984).

—Held Proper
The trial court did not err in excluding husband from the marital residence as his conduct justified the harsh remedy ordered under former Ill.Rev.Stat., ch. 40, para. 2302-8 (see now subdivision (b)(2) of this section). In re Hagaman, 123 Ill. App. 3d 549, 78 Ill. Dec. 922, 462 N.E.2d 1276 (4 Dist. 1984).

Findings
Where a mother accused a father of physically abusing the parties' child, the trial court did not abuse its discretion by not allowing the child's mental health counselor to testify. While the trial court had not been bound by the parties' stipulation in their divorce action that the counselor could not be called as a witness in any proceeding, since hearing such evidence might have been in the child's best interest, as no legal factors compelled the testimony, that determination was for the trial court to make. Steward v. Schluter, 352 Ill. App. 3d 1196, 289 Ill. Dec. 89, 819 N.E.2d 1, 2004 Ill. App. LEXIS 1387 (4 Dist. 2004).

Where the trial court issed the orders of protection against the former boyfriend protecting the former girlfriend, but there was no transcript containing the trial court's oral findings pursuant to 750 ILCS 60/214(c), and, likewise, there was no transcript indicating that the trial court complied with 750 ILCS 60/214(c)(4) by examining the girlfriend under oath or affirmation as an alternative to making specific findings, the appellate court remanded the case for the requisite findings. Hedrick-Koroll v. Bagley, 352 Ill. App. 3d 590, 287 Ill. Dec. 882, 816 N.E.2d 849, 2004 Ill. App. LEXIS 1204 (2 Dist. 2004).

Future Abuse
The trial court's finding that a risk of future abuse existed was not an abuse of discretion when the trial judge found that although no physical abuse had taken place, actions were still violent and could easily have led to physical violence between the couple. In re Blitstein, 212 Ill. App. 3d 124, 155 Ill. Dec. 746, 569 N.E.2d 1357 (2 Dist. 1991).

Injunctive Relief
Order of protection entered under 750 ILCS 60/214 against a mother and in favor of her minor child, which was entered based on the mother's sexual exploitation of the child during visitations and which prohibited the mother from making contact with the child, was injunctive in nature and therefore was an appealable order under Ill. Sup. Ct. R. 307(a)(1). People v. L.S. (In re T.H.), 354 Ill. App. 3d 301, 289 Ill. Dec. 902, 820 N.E.2d 977, 2004 Ill. App. LEXIS 1407 (1 Dist. 2004).

—Mandatory Contact
Requiring plaintiff to call and visit his mother was not necessary or appropriate to prevent further harassment. Rosenbaum v. Rosenbaum, 184 Ill. App. 3d 987, 133 Ill. Dec. 661, 541 N.E.2d 872 (1 Dist.), appeal denied, 136 Ill. Dec. 606, 545 N.E.2d 130 (1989), cert. denied, 494 U.S. 1004, 110 S. Ct. 1297, 108 L. Ed. 2d 474 (1990).

—Prohibiting Verbal Contact
Enjoining defendant from telephoning or "verbally" contacting plaintiff, while allowing her to communicate with him through written correspondence, was clearly within the trial court's authority. Rosenbaum v. Rosenbaum, 184 Ill. App. 3d 987, 133 Ill. Dec. 661, 541 N.E.2d 872 (1 Dist.), appeal denied, 136 Ill. Dec. 606, 545 N.E.2d 130 (1989), cert. denied, 494 U.S. 1004, 110 S. Ct. 1297, 108 L. Ed. 2d 474 (1990).

Legislative Intent
Legislature intentionally distinguished between the physical care and possession of a child, which a court could award under 750 ILCS 60/214(b)(5) and temporary custody of a child, under 750 ILCS 60/214(b)(6). In re Flannery, 328 Ill. App. 3d 602, 263 Ill. Dec. 274, 768 N.E.2d 34, 2002 Ill. App. LEXIS 238 (2 Dist. 2002), appeal denied, 201 Ill. 2d 565, 271 Ill. Dec. 924, 786 N.E.2d 182 (2002).

It is apparent from the language of subsection (a) of this section that the legislature intended that orders of protection may be entered against minors, as well as against adults. Wright v. Wright, 211 Ill. App. 3d 659, 164 Ill. Dec. 543, 583 N.E.2d 97 (4 Dist. 1991).

Marriage

—No Exception
Where the defendant was charged with residential burglary upon violating a protective order by entering his wife's residence, the marriage between the resident or custodian and the invader did not create any exception under the residential burglary statute, nor did their joint ownership of the residence obviate the court-imposed restrictions on the defendant. People v. Williams, 222 Ill. App. 3d 129, 164 Ill. Dec. 214, 582 N.E.2d 1158 (1 Dist. 1991), appeal denied, 144 Ill. 2d 642, 169 Ill. Dec. 150, 591 N.E.2d 30 (1992).

Nonphysical Contact
Court found that a stay-away order can encompass both physical presence and nonphysical contact and a trial court erred in dismissing a charge against a defendant who violated a protective order forbidding telephone contact by making a single phone call. People v. Olsson, 335 Ill. App. 3d 372, 269 Ill. Dec. 344, 780 N.E.2d 816, 2002 Ill. App. LEXIS 1180 (4 Dist. 2002), appeal denied, 203 Ill. 2d 562, 273 Ill. Dec. 142, 788 N.E.2d 733 (2003).

Order to Appear

—Notice
Where mother requested that respondent be ordered to appear in court, with a minor child, to prevent concealment of the child, and the mother's affidavit in support of the emergency order of protection recited that she feared prior notice to the father of the petition for the emergency protection order would cause him to further conceal the child, the absence of prior notice did not violate procedural due process. Sanders v. Shephard, 185 Ill. App. 3d 719, 133 Ill. Dec. 712, 541 N.E.2d 1150 (1 Dist. 1989).

Prohibited Entry

—Homeowner
Where emergency protection order granted to wife the exclusive possession of the house being leased from husband's parents, parents could not prevail in forcible entry and detainer action, because parents were intentionally attempting to aid husband in his violation of the order of protection. Wood v. Wood, 284 Ill. App. 3d 718, 219 Ill. Dec. 877, 672 N.E.2d 385 (4 Dist. 1996).

Under this Act, the owner of a home may be prohibited from entering the premises if the protected party has a right to exclusive occupancy of the residence. People v. Williams, 222 Ill. App. 3d 129, 164 Ill. Dec. 214, 582 N.E.2d 1158 (1 Dist. 1991), appeal denied, 144 Ill. 2d 642, 169 Ill. Dec. 150, 591 N.E.2d 30 (1992).

Protection
Appellate Court construed 750 ILCS 60/214(b)(5), in pari materia with the definition of neglect of a minor in 705 ILCS 405/2-3(1), and in an action which a father filed against his ex-wife and the ex-wife's new husband, pursuant to the Illinois Domestic Violence Act, 750 ILCS 60/101 et seq., the appellate court held that trial court properly considered the fact that the ex-wife's new husband was charged with abusing his own daughter and that the new husband's daughter and the father's daughter lived in the same house. Mowen v. Holland, 336 Ill. App. 3d 368, 270 Ill. Dec. 605, 783 N.E.2d 180, 2003 Ill. App. LEXIS 29 (4 Dist. 2003).

—Not Warranted
Where petitioner claimed that respondent was at bar she frequented, she saw respondent leave notes on her car once and respondent was arrested for telephone harassment for telephoning petitioner at her place of employment, this was insufficient to prove by a preponderance of the evidence that respondent abused peti-

Protection (Cont'd)

—Not Warranted (Cont'd)

tioner. People ex rel. Minteer v. Kozin, 297 Ill. App. 3d 1038, 232 Ill. Dec. 149, 697 N.E.2d 891 (1 Dist. 1998).

The report of proceedings of the hearing fully supported the lower court's remarks concerning the parties' respective personalities, attitudes, and conduct, as well as the court's observation that both parties bore some responsibility for creating conflict; judging from the record, it was little wonder the trial court had great difficulty in assessing the parties' credibility and under the circumstances the court acted well within its discretion in deciding that neither party had shown the abuse which would warrant an order of protection. In re Lichtenstein, 263 Ill. App. 3d 266, 202 Ill. Dec. 522, 637 N.E.2d 1258 (2 Dist. 1994).

—Of Family or Household Members

Once one member of a household is abused, the court has maximum discretionary power to fashion the scope of an order of protection to include other household members or relatives who may be at risk of retaliatory acts by the abuser. In re McCoy, 253 Ill. App. 3d 958, 192 Ill. Dec. 728, 625 N.E.2d 883 (4 Dist. 1993).

—Of Minor

Mother's unexpected and improper contact with her child, a ward of the court, as the child was arriving for a counseling session at a family assistance agency, which resulted in severe emotional distress to the child, constituted harassment for purposes of 750 ILCS 60/103(7) and supported the entry of an order of protection against the mother and in favor of the child. People v. L.S. (In re T.H.), 354 Ill. App. 3d 301, 289 Ill. Dec. 902, 820 N.E.2d 977, 2004 Ill. App. LEXIS 1407 (1 Dist. 2004).

Mother's sexual exploitation of her minor child by involving the child in sexual acts with men for money, constituted abuse under 750 ILCS 60/103(1), (14) and supported the entry of an order of protection against the mother and in favor of the child, who had been made a ward of the court. People v. L.S. (In re T.H.), 354 Ill. App. 3d 301, 289 Ill. Dec. 902, 820 N.E.2d 977, 2004 Ill. App. LEXIS 1407 (1 Dist. 2004).

Entering order of protection that deprived father of any contact with his minor son, effectively for two years, was an abuse of discretion and the trial court was ordered on remand to consider issuing an order of protection that would allow some contact between the father and minor son; appropriate remedies towards that end could include counseling and visitation. Peck v. Otten, 329 Ill. App. 3d 266, 263 Ill. Dec. 688, 768 N.E.2d 769, 2002 Ill. App. LEXIS 279 (3 Dist. 2002).

Non-custodial parent's conduct repeatedly directing the children to ask the custodial parent for visitation, as well as numerous phone calls for that same purpose, was harassment of the children and supported court's order of protection including the children. In re McCoy, 253 Ill. App. 3d 958, 192 Ill. Dec. 728, 625 N.E.2d 883 (4 Dist. 1993).

An order of protection under this Act may be entered against a minor. Wright v. Wright, 211 Ill. App. 3d 659, 164 Ill. Dec. 543, 583 N.E.2d 97 (4 Dist. 1991).

—Types

Under this Act, three types of orders of protection may be issued: plenary, emergency and interim orders. People v. Williams, 222 Ill. App. 3d 129, 164 Ill. Dec. 214, 582 N.E.2d 1158 (1 Dist. 1991), appeal denied, 144 Ill. 2d 642, 169 Ill. Dec. 150, 591 N.E.2d 30 (1992).

Relevant Factors

—Residence in Family Shelter

In a prosecution for violation of a protection order pursuant to former Ill.Rev.Stat., ch. 40, para. 2301-1 (see now this section), reference to defendant's estranged wife's staying at a family shelter did not prejudice the jury, particularly since the trial court immediately sustained defendant's objection to that reference and admonished the jury to disregard it. People v. Zarebski, 186 Ill. App. 3d 285, 134 Ill. Dec. 266, 542 N.E.2d 445 (2 Dist. 1989).

Right to Counsel

—Failure to Appoint Counsel

Indigent defendant's due process rights were not violated by court's failure to appoint counsel to represent him in action by defendant's wife for an order of protection. People ex rel. Williams v. Rhodes, 185 Ill. App. 3d 114, 133 Ill. Dec. 248, 540 N.E.2d 1114 (4 Dist. 1989).

Self-Defense

—Use of Deadly Force

The law does not require that a woman exercise infallible judgment when she uses deadly force to repel her attacker if she has reasonable grounds to believe that she is in danger of suffering great bodily injury or losing her life; rather, the law only requires that she use reasonable judgment under the existing circumstances and, reasonable judgment means that a woman's right of self-defense arises before she is caused to spout blood. People v. Evans, 259 Ill. App. 3d 195, 197 Ill. Dec. 278, 631 N.E.2d 281 (1 Dist. 1994).

Specific Findings Required

Trial court satisfied the requirements of 750 ILCS 60/214(c)(3) by referencing findings it made in previous orders suspending a mother's visitation rights, by finding the mother in violation of those orders, and by taking judicial notice of its previous visitation orders, an interim order of protection, and a pending termination of parental rights proceeding at the hearing on a plenary order of protection. People v. L.S. (In re T.H.), 354 Ill. App. 3d 301, 289 Ill. Dec. 902, 820 N.E.2d 977, 2004 Ill. App. LEXIS 1407 (1 Dist. 2004).

Where trial court made no findings, oral or written, regarding the relevant factors, entry of order of protection was reversed because trial court failed to make specific findings as required by the Act. People ex rel. Minteer v. Kozin, 297 Ill. App. 3d 1038, 232 Ill. Dec. 149, 697 N.E.2d 891 (1 Dist. 1998).

Trial court failed to set forth its findings as required by subdivision (c)(1)(i) where it simply stated that it believed that it was inappropriate for the parties' children to be around weapons and that children were aware of volatile circumstances. In re Henry, 297 Ill. App. 3d 139, 231 Ill. Dec. 610, 696 N.E.2d 1181 (2 Dist. 1998).

The current statute plainly requires specific findings for an order of protection. In re Healy, 263 Ill. App. 3d 596, 200 Ill. Dec. 327, 635 N.E.2d 666 (1 Dist. 1994).

LEGAL PERIODICALS

For article, "Defending the Indefensible to Further a Later Case: Sanctioning Respondents in Illinois Domestic Violence Cases," see 23 N. Ill. U. L. Rev. 403 (2003).

For note, "Guardians Ad Litem: The Guardian Angels of Our Children in Domestic Violence Courts", see 30 Loy. U. Chi. L.J. 281 (1999).

For essay, "Enforcement in Domestic Violence Cases," see 26 Loy. U. Chi. L.J. 663 (1995).

750 ILCS 60/215 Mutual orders of protection; correlative separate orders

Sec. 215. *Mutual orders of protection; correlative separate orders.* Mutual orders of protection are prohibited. Correlative separate orders of protection undermine the purposes of this Act and are prohibited unless both parties have properly filed written pleadings, proved past abuse by the other party, given prior written notice to the other party unless excused under Section 217 [750 ILCS 60/217], satisfied all prerequisites for the type of order and each remedy granted, and otherwise complied with this Act. In these cases, the court shall hear relevant evidence, make findings, and issue separate orders in accordance with Sections 214 and 221 [750 ILCS 60/214 and 750 ILCS 60/221]. The fact that correlative separate orders are issued shall not be a sufficient basis to deny any remedy to petitioner or to

prove that the parties are equally at fault or equally endangered.
(Source: P.A. 84-1305; 87-1186, § 3.)

Note.
This section was Ill.Rev.Stat., Ch. 40, para. 2312-15.

CASE NOTES

Fraudulently Obtained Order
Trial court did not err in finding defendant's order of protection, taken out several days after the woman defendant had been dating took one out against defendant and defendant was informed of that fact, was a fraud as mutual orders of protection were prohibited and the evidence showed that defendant only obtained defendant's order of protection by not informing the court holding a hearing on defendant's order of protection that the woman whom defendant had obtained an order against had already obtained an order against defendant. People v. Stiles, 334 Ill. App. 3d 953, 268 Ill. Dec. 783, 779 N.E.2d 397, 2002 Ill. App. LEXIS 994 (1 Dist. 2002), appeal denied, 202 Ill. 2d 695, 272 Ill. Dec. 365, 787 N.E.2d 180 (2003).

750 ILCS 60/216 Accountability for Actions of Others

Sec. 216. *Accountability for Actions of Others.* For the purposes of issuing an order of protection, deciding what remedies should be included and enforcing the order, Article 5 of the Criminal Code of 1961 [720 ILCS 5/5-1 et seq.] shall govern whether respondent is legally accountable for the conduct of another person.
(Source: P.A. 84-1305.)

Note.
This section was Ill.Rev.Stat., Ch. 40, para. 2312-16.

CASE NOTES

Eviction from Residence
Where emergency protection order granted to wife exclusive possession of house being leased from husband's parents, parents could not prevail in forcible entry and detainer action, because parents were intentionally attempting to aid husband in his violation of the order of protection. Wood v. Wood, 284 Ill. App. 3d 718, 219 Ill. Dec. 877, 672 N.E.2d 385 (4 Dist. 1996).

750 ILCS 60/217 Emergency order of protection

Sec. 217. *Emergency order of protection.* (a) Prerequisites. An emergency order of protection shall issue if petitioner satisfies the requirements of this subsection for one or more of the requested remedies. For each remedy requested, petitioner shall establish that:

(1) The court has jurisdiction under Section 208 [750 ILCS 60/208];

(2) The requirements of Section 214 [750 ILCS 60/214] are satisfied; and

(3) There is good cause to grant the remedy, regardless of prior service of process or of notice upon the respondent, because:

(i) For the remedies of "prohibition of abuse" described in Section 214(b)(1) [750 ILCS 60/214], "stay away order and additional prohibitions" described in Section 214(b)(3) [750 ILCS 60/214], "removal or concealment of minor child" described in Section 214(b)(8) [750 ILCS 60/214], "order to appear" described in Section 214(b)(9) [750 ILCS 60/214], "physical care and possession of the minor child" described in Section 214(b)(5) [750 ILCS 60/214], "protection of property" described in Section 214(b)(11) [750 ILCS 60/214], "prohibition of entry" described in Section 214(b)(14) [750 ILCS 60/214], "prohibition of access to records" described in Section 214(b)(15) [750 ILCS 60/214], and "injunctive relief" described in Section 214(b)(16) [750 ILCS 60/214], the harm which that remedy is intended to prevent would be likely to occur if the respondent were given any prior notice, or greater notice than was actually given, of the petitioner's efforts to obtain judicial relief;

(ii) For the remedy of "grant of exclusive possession of residence" described in Section 214(b)(2) [750 ILCS 60/214], the immediate danger of further abuse of petitioner by respondent, if petitioner chooses or had chosen to remain in the residence or household while respondent was given any prior notice or greater notice than was actually given of petitioner's efforts to obtain judicial relief, outweighs the hardships to respondent of an emergency order granting petitioner exclusive possession of the residence or household. This remedy shall not be denied because petitioner has or could obtain temporary shelter elsewhere while prior notice is given to respondent, unless the hardships to respondent from exclusion from the home substantially outweigh those to petitioner;

(iii) For the remedy of "possession of personal property" described in Section 214(b)(10) [750 ILCS 60/214], improper disposition of the personal property would be likely to occur if respondent were given any prior notice, or greater notice than was actually given, of petitioner's efforts to obtain judicial relief, or petitioner has an immediate and pressing need for possession of that property.

An emergency order may not include the counseling, legal custody, payment of support or monetary compensation remedies.

(b) Appearance by respondent. If respondent appears in court for this hearing for an emergency order, he or she may elect to file a general appearance and testify. Any resulting order may be an emergency order, governed by this Section. Notwithstanding the requirements of this Section, if all requirements of Section 218 [750 ILCS 60/218] have been met, the court may issue a 30-day interim order.

(c) Emergency orders: court holidays and evenings.

(1) Prerequisites. When the court is unavailable at the close of business, the petitioner may file a petition for a 21-day emergency order before any available circuit judge or associate judge who may

grant relief under this Act. If the judge finds that there is an immediate and present danger of abuse to petitioner and that petitioner has satisfied the prerequisites set forth in subsection (a) of Section 217 [750 ILCS 60/217], that judge may issue an emergency order of protection.

(1.5) Issuance of order. The chief judge of the circuit court may designate for each county in the circuit at least one judge to be reasonably available to issue orally, by telephone, by facsimile, or otherwise, an emergency order of protection at all times, whether or not the court is in session.

(2) Certification and transfer. Any order issued under this Section and any documentation in support thereof shall be certified on the next court day to the appropriate court. The clerk of that court shall immediately assign a case number, file the petition, order and other documents with the court, and enter the order of record and file it with the sheriff for service, in accordance with Section 222 [750 ILCS 60/222]. Filing the petition shall commence proceedings for further relief under Section 202 [750 ILCS 60/202]. Failure to comply with the requirements of this subsection shall not affect the validity of the order.

(Source: P.A. 86-966; 87-1186, § 3; 90-392, § 10.)

Note.

This section was Ill.Rev.Stat., Ch. 40, para. 2312-17.

Cross References.

Concerning the assistance by law enforcement officers, see 750 ILCS 60/304.

Effect of Amendments.

The 1997 amendment by P.A. 90-392, effective January 1, 1998, added subdivision (b)(1.5).

CASE NOTES

ANALYSIS

Constitutionality
—Due Process
Custody
Evidence
—Requirements
—Sufficient
Jurisdiction

Constitutionality

—Due Process

There is no procedural due process defect in obtaining an emergency order of protection without notice to a respondent, when the petition for the emergency protection order is supported by affidavits that demonstrate exigent circumstances justifying entry of an emergency order without prior notice. Sanders v. Shephard, 185 Ill. App. 3d 719, 133 Ill. Dec. 712, 541 N.E.2d 1150 (1 Dist. 1989).

Custody

Custody is not a remedy that may be granted under an emergency order under this Act. In re Gordon, 233 Ill. App. 3d 617, 175 Ill. Dec. 137, 599 N.E.2d 1151 (1 Dist.), appeal denied, 147 Ill. 2d 626, 180 Ill. Dec. 149, 606 N.E.2d 1226 (1992).

Evidence

—Requirements

The Illinois Domestic Violence Act does not require that actual affidavits be attached to the petition; instead the Act requires the petitioner to show good cause to grant the remedy without prior notice to respondent, although the Act does not specify the manner in which good cause can be shown. Whitten v. Whitten, 292 Ill. App. 3d 780, 226 Ill. Dec. 670, 686 N.E.2d 19 (3 Dist. 1997), appeal denied, 176 Ill. 2d 594, 229 Ill. Dec. 61, 690 N.E.2d 1388 (1998).

—Sufficient

In an action which a father filed against his ex-wife and the ex-wife's new husband, pursuant to the Illinois Domestic Violence Act of 1986, 750 ILCS 60/101 et seq., the trial court properly considered the fact that the ex-wife's new husband was charged with abusing his own daughter and that the new husband's daughter and the father's daughter lived in the same house, and the appellate court upheld the trial court's judgment awarding custody of the father's daughter to the father and ordering the ex-wife and her new husband to stay away from the father's daughter. Mowen v. Holland, 336 Ill. App. 3d 368, 270 Ill. Dec. 605, 783 N.E.2d 180, 2003 Ill. App. LEXIS 29 (4 Dist. 2003).

Petitioner's verified petition, sworn testimony, and pictures were sufficient proof of exigent circumstances justifying the issuance of an emergency protective order of protection without prior notice; petitioner's failure to attach a separate affidavit did not violate respondent's procedural due process rights. Whitten v. Whitten, 292 Ill. App. 3d 780, 226 Ill. Dec. 670, 686 N.E.2d 19 (3 Dist. 1997), appeal denied, 176 Ill. 2d 594, 229 Ill. Dec. 61, 690 N.E.2d 1388 (1998).

Jurisdiction

Given the public interest in protecting victims of domestic violence and the likelihood that this question will reappear, the appellate court had jurisdiction to hear respondent's interlocutory appeal to clarify and provide authoritative determination of what the Illinois Domestic Violence Act requires prior to issuance of an ex-parte emergency order of protection, notwithstanding petitioner's allegation of mootness. Whitten v. Whitten, 292 Ill. App. 3d 780, 226 Ill. Dec. 670, 686 N.E.2d 19 (3 Dist. 1997), appeal denied, 176 Ill. 2d 594, 229 Ill. Dec. 61, 690 N.E.2d 1388 (1998).

750 ILCS 60/218 30-day interim order of protection

Sec. 218. *30-day interim order of protection.* (a) Prerequisites. An interim order of protection shall issue if petitioner has served notice of the hearing for that order on respondent, in accordance with Section 211 [750 ILCS 60/211], and satisfies the requirements of this subsection for one or more of the requested remedies. For each remedy requested, petitioner shall establish that:

(1) The court has jurisdiction under Section 208 [750 ILCS 60/208];

(2) The requirements of Section 214 [750 ILCS 60/214] are satisfied; and

(3) A general appearance was made or filed by or for respondent; or process was served on respondent in the manner required by Section 210 [750 ILCS 60/210]; or the petitioner is diligently attempting to complete the required service of process.

An interim order may not include the counseling, payment of support or monetary compensation remedies, unless the respondent has filed a general appearance or has been personally served.

(b) Appearance by respondent. If respondent appears in court for this hearing for an interim order, he or she may elect to file a general appearance and testify. Any resulting order may be an interim order, governed by this Section. Notwithstanding the requirements of this Section, if all requirements of Section 219 [750 ILCS 60/219] have been met, the Court may issue a plenary order of protection.

(Source: P.A. 84-1305; 87-1186, § 3.)

Note.
This section was Ill.Rev.Stat., Ch. 40, para. 2312-18.

CASE NOTES

ANALYSIS

General Appearance
—Related Proceedings
—Shown
Jurisdiction
—Requirements

General Appearance

—Related Proceedings
The filing of pleadings in relation to a petition to modify custody did not amount to a general entry of appearance in a domestic violence proceeding where a separate special and limited appearance was filed in the domestic violence proceeding, since domestic violence proceedings and custody proceedings are separate proceedings, even though filed under the same case number, so long as the pleadings in the custody case have no connection with the petition for a domestic violence order of protection. In re Lenhardt, 176 Ill. App. 3d 429, 125 Ill. Dec. 944, 531 N.E.2d 123 (5 Dist. 1988).

—Shown
Where respondent, in his special and limited appearance, argued that the court lacked jurisdiction in the domestic violence proceeding because no service had been obtained, but then went on to challenge the emergency order of protection in several respects, the respondent recognized the case as being in court and did much more than merely challenge jurisdiction; therefore, there was a general appearance. In re Lenhardt, 176 Ill. App. 3d 429, 125 Ill. Dec. 944, 531 N.E.2d 123 (5 Dist. 1988).

Jurisdiction

—Requirements
There must be service of process or a general entry of appearance before the court can exercise jurisdiction over respondent in a domestic violence matter and issue an order under this section. In re Lenhardt, 176 Ill. App. 3d 429, 125 Ill. Dec. 944, 531 N.E.2d 123 (5 Dist. 1988).

750 ILCS 60/219 Plenary Order of Protection

Sec. 219. *Plenary Order of Protection.* A plenary order of protection shall issue if petitioner has served notice of the hearing for that order on respondent, in accordance with Section 211 [750 ILCS 60/211], and satisfies the requirements of this Section for one or more of the requested remedies. For each remedy requested, petitioner must establish that:

(1) The court has jurisdiction under Section 208 [750 ILCS 60/208];

(2) The requirements of Section 214 [750 ILCS 60/214] are satisfied; and

(3) A general appearance was made or filed by or for respondent or process was served on respondent in the manner required by Section 210 [750 ILCS 60/210]; and

(4) Respondent has answered or is in default.

(Source: P.A. 84-1305.)

Note.
This section was Ill.Rev.Stat., Ch. 40, para. 2312-19.

CASE NOTES

ANALYSIS

Constitutionality
—Due Process
Due Process Violations
—Waiver
Plenary Order
—Not Shown

Constitutionality

—Due Process
This section is not unconstitutional on its face for lack of adequate procedural due process guarantees. Sanders v. Shephard, 185 Ill. App. 3d 719, 133 Ill. Dec. 712, 541 N.E.2d 1150 (1 Dist. 1989).

Due Process Violations

—Waiver
The court's plenary order of protection was not obtained in violation of defendant's procedural due process rights, because defendant waived this claim for purposes of review by failing to alert the court that he was entitled to a new hearing. Sanders v. Shephard, 185 Ill. App. 3d 719, 133 Ill. Dec. 712, 541 N.E.2d 1150 (1 Dist. 1989).

Plenary Order

—Not Shown
Order of protection was not a plenary order where the judge and counsel recognized the time limitations for plenary orders and because there is no provision in this Act for an order of indefinite duration. In re Gordon, 233 Ill. App. 3d 617, 175 Ill. Dec. 137, 599 N.E.2d 1151 (1 Dist.), appeal denied, 147 Ill. 2d 626, 180 Ill. Dec. 149, 606 N.E.2d 1226 (1992).

750 ILCS 60/220 Duration and extension of orders

Sec. 220. *Duration and extension of orders.* (a) Duration of emergency and interim orders. Unless re-opened or extended or voided by entry of an order of greater duration:

(1) Emergency orders issued under Section 217 [750 ILCS 60/217] shall be effective for not less than 14 nor more than 21 days;

(2) Interim orders shall be effective for up to 30 days.

(b) Duration of plenary orders. Except as otherwise provided in this Section, a plenary order of protection shall be valid for a fixed period of time, not to exceed two years.

(1) A plenary order of protection entered in conjunction with another civil proceeding shall remain in effect as follows:

(i) if entered as preliminary relief in that other proceeding, until entry of final judgment in that other proceeding;

(ii) if incorporated into the final judgment in that other proceeding, until the order of protection is vacated or modified; or

(iii) if incorporated in an order for involuntary commitment, until termination of both the involuntary commitment and any voluntary commitment, or for a fixed period of time not exceeding 2 years.

(2) A plenary order of protection entered in conjunction with a criminal prosecution shall remain in effect as follows:

(i) if entered during pre-trial release, until disposition, withdrawal, or dismissal of the underlying charge; if, however, the case is continued as an independent cause of action, the order's duration may be for a fixed period of time not to exceed 2 years;

(ii) if in effect in conjunction with a bond forfeiture warrant, until final disposition or an additional period of time not exceeding 2 years; no order of protection, however, shall be terminated by a dismissal that is accompanied by the issuance of a bond forfeiture warrant;

(iii) until expiration of any supervision, conditional discharge, probation, periodic imprisonment, parole or mandatory supervised release and for an additional period of time thereafter not exceeding 2 years; or

(iv) until the date set by the court for expiration of any sentence of imprisonment and subsequent parole or mandatory supervised release and for an additional period of time thereafter not exceeding 2 years.

(c) Computation of time. The duration of an order of protection shall not be reduced by the duration of any prior order of protection.

(d) Law enforcement records. When a plenary order of protection expires upon the occurrence of a specified event, rather than upon a specified date as provided in subsection (b), no expiration date shall be entered in Department of State Police records. To remove the plenary order from those records, either party shall request the clerk of the court to file a certified copy of an order stating that the specified event has occurred or that the plenary order has been vacated or modified with the Sheriff, and the Sheriff shall direct that law enforcement records shall be promptly corrected in accordance with the filed order.

(e) Extension of orders. Any emergency, interim or plenary order may be extended one or more times, as required, provided that the requirements of Section 217, 218 or 219 [750 ILCS 60/217, 750 ILCS 60/218 or 750 ILCS 60/219], as appropriate, are satisfied. If the motion for extension is uncontested and petitioner seeks no modification of the order, the order may be extended on the basis of petitioner's motion or affidavit stating that there has been no material change in relevant circumstances since entry of the order and stating the reason for the requested extension. Extensions may be granted only in open court and not under the provisions of subsection (c) of Section 217 [750 ILCS 60/217], which applies only when the court is unavailable at the close of business or on a court holiday.

(f) Termination date. Any order of protection which would expire on a court holiday shall instead expire at the close of the next court business day.

(g) Statement of purpose. The practice of dismissing or suspending a criminal prosecution in exchange for the issuance of an order of protection undermines the purposes of this Act. This Section shall not be construed as encouraging that practice.

(Source: P.A. 86-966; 87-1186, § 3.)

Note.

This section was Ill.Rev.Stat., Ch. 40, para. 2312-20.

CASE NOTES

ANALYSIS

Extension of Order
Fixed Period

Extension of Order

Evidence sufficed to support the extension of an order of protection, notwithstanding the argument by the respondent that he "agreed" to the original plenary order of protection, but did not "stipulate" to a factual basis of abuse, where the parties' consent to the original plenary order of protection essentially conceded the factual basis necessary to support that order. Lutz v. Lutz, 313 Ill. App. 3d 286, 245 Ill. Dec. 877, 728 N.E.2d 1234, 2000 Ill. App. LEXIS 291 (4 Dist. 2000).

Fixed Period

Trial court abused its discretion in entering a plenary order of protection that had no time limit as a plenary order of protection was valid only for a fixed period of time not to exceed two years. Peck v. Otten, 329 Ill. App. 3d 266, 263 Ill. Dec. 688, 768 N.E.2d 769, 2002 Ill. App. LEXIS 279 (3 Dist. 2002).

750 ILCS 60/221 Contents of orders

Sec. 221. *Contents of orders.* (a) Any order of protection shall describe the following:

(1) Each remedy granted by the court, in reasonable detail and not by reference to any other document, so that respondent may clearly understand what he or she must do or refrain from doing. Pre-printed form orders of protection shall include the definitions of the types of abuse, neglect, and exploitation, as provided in Section 103 [750 ILCS 60/103]. Remedies set forth in pre-printed form orders shall be numbered consistently with and corresponding to the numerical sequence of remedies listed in Section 214 [750 ILCS 60/214] (at least as of the date the form orders are printed).

(2) The reason for denial of petitioner's request for any remedy listed in Section 214 [750 ILCS 60/214].

(b) An order of protection shall further state the following:

(1) The name of each petitioner that the court finds was abused, neglected, or exploited by respondent, and that respondent is a member of the family or household of each such petitioner, and the name of each other person protected by the order and that such person is protected by this Act.

(2) For any remedy requested by petitioner on which the court has declined to rule, that that remedy is reserved.

(3) The date and time the order of protection was issued, whether it is an emergency, interim or plenary order and the duration of the order.

(4) The date, time and place for any scheduled hearing for extension of that order of protection or for another order of greater duration or scope.

(5) For each remedy in an emergency order of protection, the reason for entering that remedy without prior notice to respondent or greater notice than was actually given.

(6) For emergency and interim orders of protection, that respondent may petition the court, in accordance with Section 224 [750 ILCS 60/224], to re-open that order if he or she did not receive actual

prior notice of the hearing, in accordance with Section 211 [750 ILCS 60/211], and alleges that he or she had a meritorious defense to the order or that the order or any of its remedies was not authorized by this Act.

(c) Any order of protection shall include the following notice, printed in conspicuous type: "Any knowing violation of an order of protection forbidding physical abuse, neglect, exploitation, harassment, intimidation, interference with personal liberty, willful deprivation, or entering or remaining present at specified places when the protected person is present, or granting exclusive possession of the residence or household, or granting a stay away order is a Class A misdemeanor. Grant of exclusive possession of the residence or household shall constitute notice forbidding trespass to land. Any knowing violation of an order awarding legal custody or physical care of a child or prohibiting removal or concealment of a child may be a Class 4 felony. Any willful violation of any order is contempt of court. Any violation may result in fine or imprisonment."

(d) An emergency order of protection shall state, "This Order of Protection is enforceable, even without registration, in all 50 states, the District of Columbia, tribal lands, and the U.S. territories pursuant to the Violence Against Women Act (18 U.S.C. 2265). Violating this Order of Protection may subject the respondent to federal charges and punishment (18 U.S.C. 2261-2262)."

(e) An interim or plenary order of protection shall state, "This Order of Protection is enforceable, even without registration, in all 50 states, the District of Columbia, tribal lands, and the U.S. territories pursuant to the Violence Against Women Act (18 U.S.C. 2265). Violating this Order of Protection may subject the respondent to federal charges and punishment (18 U.S.C. 2261-2262). The respondent may be subject to federal criminal penalties for possessing, transporting, shipping, or receiving any firearm or ammunition under the Gun Control Act (18 U.S.C. 922(g)(8) and (9))."

(Source: P.A. 86-542; 86-1300; 87-1186, § 3; 93-944, § 10.)

Note.

This section was Ill.Rev.Stat., Ch. 40, para. 2312-21.

Effect of Amendments.

The 2004 amendment by P.A. 93-944, effective January 1, 2005, added subsections (d) and (e).

CASE NOTES

Reference to Other Documents

The clearest way to require compliance with a plenary order of protection based on provisions of prior orders was to refer to them in a plenary order rather than to attempt a summarization. In re McCoy, 253 Ill. App. 3d 958, 192 Ill. Dec. 728, 625 N.E.2d 883 (4 Dist. 1993).

750 ILCS 60/222 Notice of orders

Sec. 222. *Notice of orders.* (a) Entry and issuance. Upon issuance of any order of protection, the clerk shall immediately, or on the next court day if an emergency order is issued in accordance with subsection (c) of Section 217 [750 ILCS 60/217], (i) enter the order on the record and file it in accordance with the circuit court procedures and (ii) provide a file stamped copy of the order to respondent, if present, and to petitioner.

(b) Filing with sheriff. The clerk of the issuing judge shall, or the petitioner may, on the same day that an order of protection is issued, file a certified copy of that order with the sheriff or other law enforcement officials charged with maintaining Department of State Police records or charged with serving the order upon respondent. If the order was issued in accordance with subsection (c) of Section 217 [750 ILCS 60/217], the clerk shall on the next court day, file a certified copy of the order with the Sheriff or other law enforcement officials charged with maintaining Department of State Police records.

(c) Service by sheriff. Unless respondent was present in court when the order was issued, the sheriff, other law enforcement official or special process server shall promptly serve that order upon respondent and file proof of such service, in the manner provided for service of process in civil proceedings. Instead of serving the order upon the respondent, however, the sheriff, other law enforcement official, or special process server may serve the respondent with a short form notification as provided in Section 222.10 [750 ILCS 60/222.10]. If process has not yet been served upon the respondent, it shall be served with the order or short form notification. A single fee may be charged for service of an order obtained in civil court, or for service of such an order together with process, unless waived or deferred under Section 210 [750 ILCS 60/210].

(c-5) If the person against whom the order of protection is issued is arrested and the written order is issued in accordance with subsection (c) of Section 217 [750 ILCS 60/217] and received by the custodial law enforcement agency before the respondent or arrestee is released from custody, the custodial law enforcement agent shall promptly serve the order upon the respondent or arrestee before the respondent or arrestee is released from custody. In no event shall detention of the respondent or arrestee be extended for hearing on the petition for order of protection or receipt of the order issued under Section 217 of this Act [750 ILCS 60/217].

(d) Extensions, modifications and revocations. Any order extending, modifying or revoking any order of protection shall be promptly recorded, issued and served as provided in this Section.

(e) Notice to schools. Upon the request of the petitioner, within 24 hours of the issuance of an order of protection, the clerk of the issuing judge shall send written notice of the order of protection along with a certified copy of the order of protection to the day-care facility, pre-school or pre-kindergarten, or private school or the principal office of the public school district or any college or university in which any child who is a protected person under the order of protection or any child of the petitioner is enrolled. If the child transfers enrollment to another day-care facility, pre-school, pre-kindergarten, private school, public school, college, or university, the petitioner may, within 24 hours of the transfer, send to the clerk written notice of the transfer, including the name and address of the institution to which the child is transferring. Within 24 hours of receipt of notice from the petitioner that a child is transferring to another day-care facility, pre-school, pre-kindergarten, private school, public school, college, or university, the clerk shall send written notice of the order of protection, along with a certified copy of the order, to the institution to which the child is transferring.

(f) Disclosure by schools. After receiving a certified copy of an order of protection that prohibits a respondent's access to records, neither a day-care facility, pre-school, pre-kindergarten, public or private school, college, or university nor its employees shall allow a respondent access to a protected child's records or release information in those records to the respondent. The school shall file the copy of the order of protection in the records of a child who is a protected person under the order of protection. When a child who is a protected person under the order of protection transfers to another day-care facility, pre-school, pre-kindergarten, public or private school, college, or university, the institution from which the child is transferring may, at the request of the petitioner, provide, within 24 hours of the transfer, written notice of the order of protection, along with a certified copy of the order, to the institution to which the child is transferring.

(Source: P.A. 87-437; 87-1186, § 3; 88-306, § 5; 89-106, § 20; 90-392, § 10; 92-90, § 5; 92-162, § 10; 92-651, § 90.)

Note.

This section was Ill.Rev.Stat., Ch. 40, para. 2312-22.

Section 997 of P.A. 92-651 is a no acceleration or delay provision, and Section 998 is a no revival or extension provision.

Illinois Administrative Code.

See 23 Illinois Administrative Code, § 375.40.

Effect of Amendments.

The 1995 amendment by P.A. 89-106, effective July 1, 1995 and approved July 7, 1995, in subsection (e) inserted "public"; and in subsection (f) added the present first sentence, deleted the former first sentence which read "A private school may prohibit the disclosure by any school employee to any person against whom the school has received a certified copy of an order of protection the location or address of the petitioner for the order of protection", in the present second sentence, substituted "file" for "maintain" and substituted "a child who is a protected person under the" for "the child or children enrolled in the school whose parent is the petitioner of an" and deleted the former last sentence which read "A public school district may prohibit disclosure in accordance with Section 10-22.3c or 34-18.6a of the School Code".

The 1997 amendment by P.A. 90-392, effective January 1, 1998, in subsection (a), inserted "or on the next court day if an emergency order is issued in accordance with subsection (c) of Section 217"; in subsection (b) added the second sentence; and added subsection (c-5).

The 2001 amendment by P.A. 92-90, effective July 18, 2001, rewrote subsection (e), which formerly read: "Upon request the clerk of the issuing judge shall file a certified copy of an order of protection with the private school or schools or the principal office of the public school district or districts in which any children of the petitioner are enrolled"; in subsection (f), in the first sentence, inserted "day-care facility, pre-school, pre-kindergarten", "college, or university", and added the last sentence.

The 2001 amendment by P.A. 92-162, effective January 1, 2002, in subsection (c) inserted the second sentence, and at the end of the third sentence added "or short form notification."

The 2002 amendment by P.A. 92-651, effective July 11, 2002, combined the amendments by P.A. 92-90 and P.A. 92-162.

750 ILCS 60/222.5 Filing of an order of protection issued in another state

Sec. 222.5. *Filing of an order of protection issued in another state.* (a) A person entitled to protection under an order of protection issued by the court of another state, tribe, or United States territory may file a certified copy of the order of protection with the clerk of the court in a judicial circuit in which the person believes that enforcement may be necessary.

(b) The clerk shall:

(1) treat the foreign order of protection in the same manner as a judgment of the circuit court for any county of this State in accordance with the provisions of the Uniform Enforcement of Foreign Judgments Act [735 ILCS 5/12-650 et seq.], except that the clerk shall not mail notice of the filing of the foreign order to the respondent named in the order; and

(2) on the same day that a foreign order of protection is filed, file a certified copy of that order with the sheriff or other law enforcement officials charged with maintaining Department of State Police records as set forth in Section 222 of this Act [750 ILCS 60/222].

(c) Neither residence in this State nor filing of a foreign order of protection shall be required for enforcement of the order by this State. Failure to file the foreign order shall not be an impediment to its treatment in all respects as an Illinois order of protection.

(d) The clerk shall not charge a fee to file a foreign order of protection under this Section.

(e) The sheriff shall inform the Department of State Police as set forth in Section 302 of this Act [750 ILCS 60/302].

(Source: P.A. 91-903, § 20.)

Effective Date.

This section is effective January 1, 2001, pursuant to Ill. Const. (1970), Art. IV, § 10 and 5 ILCS 75/1.

750 ILCS 60/222.10 Short form notification

Sec. 222.10. *Short form notification.* (a) Instead of personal service of an order of protection under Section 112A-22 [725 ILCS 5/112A-22], a sheriff, other law enforcement official, or special process server may serve a respondent with a short form notification. The short form notification must include the following items:

(1) The respondent's name.
(2) The respondent's date of birth, if known.
(3) The petitioner's name.
(4) The names of other protected parties.
(5) The date and county in which the order of protection was filed.
(6) The court file number.
(7) The hearing date and time, if known.
(8) The conditions that apply to the respondent, either in checklist form or handwritten.
(9) The name of the judge who signed the order.

(b) The short form notification must contain the following notice in bold print:

"The order of protection is now enforceable. You must report to the office of the sheriff or the office of the circuit court in (name of county) County to obtain a copy of the order of protection. You are subject to arrest and may be charged with a misdemeanor or felony if you violate any of the terms of the order of protection."

(c) Upon verification of the identity of the respondent and the existence of an unserved order of protection against the respondent, a sheriff or other law enforcement official may detain the respondent for a reasonable time necessary to complete and serve the short form notification.

(d) When service is made by short form notification under this Section, it may be proved by the affidavit of the sheriff, other law enforcement official, or special process server making the service.

(e) The Attorney General shall provide adequate copies of the short form notification form to law enforcement agencies in this State.

(Source: P.A. 92-162, § 10.)

Effective Date.
This section is effective January 1, 2002, pursuant to Ill. Const. (1970) Art. IV, § 10 and 5 ILCS 75/1.

750 ILCS 60/223 Enforcement of orders of protection

Sec. 223. *Enforcement of orders of protection.* (a) When violation is crime. A violation of any order of protection, whether issued in a civil or criminal proceeding, shall be enforced by a criminal court when:

(1) The respondent commits the crime of violation of an order of protection pursuant to Section 12-30 of the Criminal Code of 1961 [720 ILCS 5/12-30], by having knowingly violated:

(i) remedies described in paragraphs (1), (2), (3), (14), or (14.5) of subsection (b) of Section 214 of this Act [750 ILCS 60/214]; or

(ii) a remedy, which is substantially similar to the remedies authorized under paragraphs (1), (2), (3), (14), and (14.5) of subsection (b) of Section 214 of this Act [750 ILCS 60/214], in a valid order of protection which is authorized under the laws of another state, tribe, or United States territory; or

(iii) any other remedy when the act constitutes a crime against the protected parties as defined by the Criminal Code of 1961 [720 ILCS 5/1-1 et seq.].

Prosecution for a violation of an order of protection shall not bar concurrent prosecution for any other crime, including any crime that may have been committed at the time of the violation of the order of protection; or

(2) The respondent commits the crime of child abduction pursuant to Section 10-5 of the Criminal Code of 1961 [720 ILCS 5/10-5], by having knowingly violated:

(i) remedies described in paragraphs (5), (6) or (8) of subsection (b) of Section 214 of this Act [750 ILCS 60/214]; or

(ii) a remedy, which is substantially similar to the remedies authorized under paragraphs (5), (6), or (8) of subsection (b) of Section 214 of this Act [750 ILCS 60/214], in a valid order of protection which is authorized under the laws of another state, tribe, or United States territory.

(b) When violation is contempt of court. A violation of any valid Illinois order of protection, whether issued in a civil or criminal proceeding, may be enforced through civil or criminal contempt procedures, as appropriate, by any court with jurisdiction, regardless where the act or acts which violated the order of protection were committed, to the extent consistent with the venue provisions of this Act. Nothing in this Act shall preclude any Illinois court from enforcing any valid order of protection issued in another state. Illinois courts may enforce orders of protection through both criminal prosecution and contempt proceedings, unless the action which is second in time is barred by collateral estoppel or the constitutional prohibition against double jeopardy.

(1) In a contempt proceeding where the petition for a rule to show cause sets forth facts evidencing an immediate danger that the respondent will flee the jurisdiction, conceal a child, or inflict physical abuse on the petitioner or minor children or on dependent adults in petitioner's care, the court may order the attachment of the respondent without prior service of the rule to show cause or the petition for a rule to show cause. Bond shall be set unless specifically denied in writing.

(2) A petition for a rule to show cause for violation of an order of protection shall be treated as an expedited proceeding.

(c) Violation of custody or support orders. A violation of remedies described in paragraphs (5), (6), (8), or (9) of subsection (b) of Section 214 of this Act [750 ILCS 60/214] may be enforced by any remedy provided by Section 611 of the Illinois Marriage and Dissolution of Marriage Act [750 ILCS 5/611]. The court may enforce any order for support issued under paragraph (12) of subsection (b) of Section 214 [750 ILCS 5/214] in the manner provided for under Articles V and VII of the Illinois Marriage and Dissolution of Marriage Act [750 ILCS 5/501 et seq. and 750 ILCS 5/701 et seq.].

(d) Actual knowledge. An order of protection may be enforced pursuant to this Section if the respondent violates the order after the respondent has actual knowledge of its contents as shown through one of the following means:

(1) By service, delivery, or notice under Section 210 [750 ILCS 60/210].

(2) By notice under Section 210.1 or 211 [750 ILCS 60/210.1 or 750 ILCS 60/211].

(3) By service of an order of protection under Section 222 [750 ILCS 60/222].

(4) By other means demonstrating actual knowledge of the contents of the order.

(e) The enforcement of an order of protection in civil or criminal court shall not be affected by either of the following:

(1) The existence of a separate, correlative order, entered under Section 215 [750 ILCS 60/215].

(2) Any finding or order entered in a conjoined criminal proceeding.

(f) Circumstances. The court, when determining whether or not a violation of an order of protection has occurred, shall not require physical manifestations of abuse on the person of the victim.

(g) Penalties.

(1) Except as provided in paragraph (3) of this subsection, where the court finds the commission of a crime or contempt of court under subsections (a) or (b) of this Section, the penalty shall be the penalty that generally applies in such criminal or contempt proceedings, and may include one or more of the following: incarceration, payment of restitution, a fine, payment of attorneys' fees and costs, or community service.

(2) The court shall hear and take into account evidence of any factors in aggravation or mitigation before deciding an appropriate penalty under paragraph (1) of this subsection.

(3) To the extent permitted by law, the court is encouraged to:

(i) increase the penalty for the knowing violation of any order of protection over any penalty previously imposed by any court for respondent's violation of any order of protection or penal statute involving petitioner as victim and respondent as defendant;

(ii) impose a minimum penalty of 24 hours imprisonment for respondent's first violation of any order of protection; and

(iii) impose a minimum penalty of 48 hours imprisonment for respondent's second or subsequent violation of an order of protection

unless the court explicitly finds that an increased penalty or that period of imprisonment would be manifestly unjust.

(4) In addition to any other penalties imposed for a violation of an order of protection, a criminal court may consider evidence of any violations of an order of protection:

(i) to increase, revoke or modify the bail bond on an underlying criminal charge pursuant to Section 110-6 of the Code of Criminal Procedure of 1963 [725 ILCS 5/110-6];

(ii) to revoke or modify an order of probation, conditional discharge or supervision, pursuant to Section 5-6-4 of the Unified Code of Corrections [730 ILCS 5/5-6-4];

(iii) to revoke or modify a sentence of periodic imprisonment, pursuant to Section 5-7-2 of the Unified Code of Corrections [730 ILCS 5/5-7-2].

(5) In addition to any other penalties, the court shall impose an additional fine of $20 as authorized by Section 5-9-1.11 of the Unified Code of Corrections [730 ILCS 5/5-9-1.11] upon any person convicted of or placed on supervision for a violation of an order of protection. The additional fine shall be imposed for each violation of this Section.

(Source: P.A. 86-1300; 87-743; 87-1186, § 3; 90-241, § 20; 91-903, § 20; 93-359, § 10.)

Note.

This section was Ill.Rev.Stat., Ch. 40, para. 2312-23.

Effect of Amendments.

The 1997 amendment by P.A. 90-241, effective January 1, 1998, added subdivision (g)(5).

The 2000 amendment by P.A. 91-903, effective January 1, 2001, rewrote subsection (a).

The 2003 amendment by P.A. 93-359, effective January 1, 2004, substituted "shall" for "may" in the introductory language of subsection (a).

CASE NOTES

Constitutionality

—Due Process

Subdivision (b)(1) of this section is not unconstitutional on its face for lack of adequate procedural due process guarantees. Sanders v. Shephard, 185 Ill. App. 3d 719, 133 Ill. Dec. 712, 541 N.E.2d 1150 (1 Dist. 1989).

750 ILCS 60/223.1 Order of protection status

Sec. 223.1. *Order of protection status.* Whenever relief is sought under this Act, the court, before granting relief, shall determine whether any order of protection has previously been entered in the instant proceeding or any other proceeding in which any party, or a child of any party, or both, if relevant, has been designated as either a respondent or a protected person.

(Source: P.A. 87-743.)

Note.

This section was Ill.Rev.Stat., Ch. 40, para. 2312-23.1.

750 ILCS 60/224 Modification and re-opening of orders

Sec. 224. *Modification and re-opening of orders.* (a) Except as otherwise provided in this Section, upon motion by petitioner, the court may modify an emergency, interim, or plenary order of protection:

(1) If respondent has abused petitioner since the hearing for that order, by adding or altering one or more remedies, as authorized by Section 214 [750 ILCS 60/214]; and

(2) Otherwise, by adding any remedy authorized by Section 214 [750 ILCS 60/214] which was:

(i) reserved in that order of protection;

(ii) not requested for inclusion in that order of protection; or

(iii) denied on procedural grounds, but not on the merits.

(b) Upon motion by petitioner or respondent, the court may modify any prior order of protection's remedy for custody, visitation or payment of support in accordance with the relevant provisions of the Illinois Marriage and Dissolution of Marriage Act [750 ILCS 5/101 et seq.]. Each order of protection shall be entered in the Law Enforcement Automated Data System on the same day it is issued by the court.

(c) After 30 days following entry of a plenary order of protection, a court may modify that order only when changes in the applicable law or facts since that plenary order was entered warrant a modification of its terms.

(d) Upon 2 days' notice to petitioner, in accordance with Section 211 of this Act [750 ILCS 60/211], or such shorter notice as the court may prescribe, a respondent subject to an emergency or interim order of protection issued under this Act may appear and petition the court to re-hear the original or amended petition. Any petition to re-hear shall be verified and shall allege the following:

(1) that respondent did not receive prior notice of the initial hearing in which the emergency, interim, or plenary order was entered under Sections 211 and 217 [750 ILCS 60/211 and 750 ILCS 60/217]; and

(2) that the respondent had a meritorious defense to the order or any of its remedies or that the order or any of its remedies was not authorized by this Act.

(e) In the event that the emergency or interim order granted petitioner exclusive possession and the petition of respondent seeks to re-open or vacate that grant, the court shall set a date for hearing within 14 days on all issues relating to exclusive possession. Under no circumstances shall a court continue a hearing concerning exclusive possession beyond the 14th day, except by agreement of the parties. Other issues raised by the pleadings may be consolidated for the hearing if neither party nor the court objects.

(f) This Section does not limit the means, otherwise available by law, for vacating or modifying orders of protection.

(Source: P.A. 84-1305; 87-1186, § 3.)

Note.

This section was Ill.Rev.Stat., Ch. 40, para. 2312-24.

CASE NOTES

Modification

—Permitted

Despite the fact that the wife was not given prior notice of the trial court's consideration of the issue of modification of a protective order against the husband, in accordance with 750 ILCS 60/224(b) of the Illinois Domestic Violence Act, the appellate court concluded that the power to make such a change in the previously ordered visitation was inherent in the trial court's authority; as the trial court had jurisdiction of the subject matter and of the parties, it further had the power to make such modifications of the visitation under the circumstances presented, consistent with the best interest of the child. In re Marriage of Munger, 339 Ill. App. 3d 1104, 274 Ill. Dec. 481, 791 N.E.2d 573, 2003 Ill. App. LEXIS 717 (4 Dist. 2003).

750 ILCS 60/225 Immunity from prosecution

Sec. 225. *Immunity from prosecution.* Any individual or organization acting in good faith to report the abuse of any person 60 years of age or older or to do any of the following in complying with the provisions of this Act shall not be subject to criminal prosecution or civil liability as a result of such action: providing any information to the appropriate law enforcement agency, providing that the giving of any information does not violate any privilege of confidentiality under law; assisting in any investigation; assisting in the preparation of any materials for distribution under this Act; or by providing services ordered under an order of protection.

Any individual, agency, or organization acting in good faith to report or investigate alleged abuse, neglect, or exploitation of a high-risk adult with disabilities, to testify in any proceeding on behalf of a high-risk adult with disabilities, to take photographs or perform an examination, or to perform any other act in compliance with the provisions of this Act shall not be the subject of criminal prosecution, civil liability, or other penalty, sanction, restriction, or retaliation as a result of such action.

(Source: P.A. 86-542; 87-1186, § 3.)

Note.

This section was Ill.Rev.Stat., Ch. 40, para. 2312-25.

750 ILCS 60/226 Untrue statements

Sec. 226. *Untrue statements.* Allegations and denials, made without reasonable cause and found to be untrue, shall subject the party pleading them to the payment of reasonable expenses actually incurred by the other party by reason of the untrue pleading, together with a reasonable attorney's fee, to be summarily taxed by the court upon motion made within 30 days of the judgment or dismissal, as provided in Supreme Court Rule 137. The court may direct that a copy of an order entered under this Section be provided to the State's Attorney so that he or she may determine whether to prosecute for perjury. This Section shall not apply to proceedings heard in Criminal Court or to criminal contempt of court proceedings, whether heard in Civil or Criminal Court.

(Source: P.A. 84-1305; 87-1186, § 3.)

Note.

This section was Ill.Rev.Stat., Ch. 40, para. 2312-26.

750 ILCS 60/227 Privileged communications between domestic violence counselors and victims

Sec. 227. *Privileged communications between domestic violence counselors and victims.* (a) As used in this Section:

(1) "Domestic violence program" means any unit of local government, organization, or association whose major purpose is to provide one or more of the following: information, crisis intervention, emergency shelter, referral, counseling, advocacy, or emotional support to victims of domestic violence.

(2) "Domestic violence advocate or counselor" means any person (A) who has undergone a minimum of forty hours of training in domestic violence advocacy, crisis intervention, and related areas, and (B) who provides services to victims through a domestic violence program either on an employed or volunteer basis.

(3) "Confidential communication" means any communication between an alleged victim of domestic violence and a domestic violence advocate or counselor in the course of providing information, counseling, or advocacy. The term includes all records kept by the advocate or counselor or by the domestic violence program in the course of providing services to an alleged victim concerning the alleged victim and the services provided. The confidential nature of the communication is not waived by the presence at the time of the communication of any additional persons, including but not limited to an interpreter, to further express the interests of the domestic violence victim or by the advocate's or counselor's disclosure to such an additional person with the consent of the victim when reasonably necessary to accomplish the purpose for which the advocate or counselor is consulted.

(4) "Domestic violence victim" means any person who consults a domestic violence counselor for the purpose of securing advice, counseling or assistance related to one or more alleged incidents of domestic violence.

(5) "Domestic violence" means abuse as defined in the Illinois Domestic Violence Act [750 ILCS 60/101 et seq.].

(b) No domestic violence advocate or counselor shall disclose any confidential communication or be examined as a witness in any civil or criminal case or proceeding or in any legislative or administrative proceeding without the written consent of the domestic violence victim except (1) in accordance with the provisions of the Abused and Neglected Child Reporting Act [325 ILCS 5/1 et seq.] or (2) in cases where failure to disclose is likely to result in an imminent risk of serious bodily harm or death of the victim or another person.

(c) A domestic violence advocate or counselor who knowingly discloses any confidential communication in violation of this Act commits a Class A misdemeanor.

(d) When a domestic violence victim is deceased or has been adjudged incompetent by a court of competent jurisdiction, the guardian of the domestic violence victim or the executor or administrator of the estate of the domestic violence victim may waive the privilege established by this Section except where the guardian, executor or administrator of the estate has been charged with a violent crime against the domestic violence victim or has had an Order of Protection entered against him or her at the request of or on behalf of the domestic violence victim or otherwise has an interest adverse to that of the domestic violence victim with respect to the waiver of the privilege. In that case, the court shall appoint an attorney for the estate of the domestic violence victim.

(e) A minor may knowingly waive the privilege established by this Section. Where a minor is, in the opinion of the court, incapable of knowingly waiving the privilege, the parent or guardian of the minor may waive the privilege on behalf of the minor, except where such parent or guardian has been charged with a violent crime against the minor or has had an Order of Protection entered against him or her on request of or on behalf of the minor or otherwise has any interest adverse to that of the minor with respect to the waiver of the privilege. In that case, the court shall appoint an attorney for the minor child who shall be compensated in accordance with Section 506 of the Illinois Marriage and Dissolution of Marriage Act [750 ILCS 5/506].

(f) Nothing in this Section shall be construed to limit in any way any privilege that might otherwise exist under statute or common law.

(g) The assertion of any privilege under this Section shall not result in an inference unfavorable to the State's cause or to the cause of the domestic violence victim.

(Source: P.A. 84-1305; 87-1186, § 3.)

Note.

This section was Ill.Rev.Stat., Ch. 40, para. 2312-27.

750 ILCS 60/227.1 Other privileged information

Sec. 227.1. *Other privileged information.* Except as otherwise provided in this Section, no court or administrative or legislative body shall compel any person or domestic violence program to disclose the location of any domestic violence program or the identity of any domestic violence advocate or counselor in any civil or criminal case or proceeding or in any administrative or legislative proceeding. A court may compel disclosure of the location of a domestic violence program or the identity of a domestic violence advocate or counselor if the court finds, following a hearing, that there is clear and convincing evidence that failure to disclose would be likely to result in an imminent risk of serious bodily harm or death to a domestic violence victim or another person. If the court makes such a finding, then disclo-

sure shall take place in camera, under a restrictive protective order that does not frustrate the purposes of compelling the disclosure, and the information disclosed shall not be made a part of the written record of the case.
(Source: P.A. 87-1186, § 3.)

Effective Date.
This section became effective January 1, 1993, pursuant to Ill. Const. (1970), Art. IV, § 10 and 5 ILCS 75/1.

ARTICLE III. LAW ENFORCEMENT RESPONSIBILITY

750 ILCS 60/301 Arrest without warrant

Sec. 301. *Arrest without warrant.* (a) Any law enforcement officer may make an arrest without warrant if the officer has probable cause to believe that the person has committed or is committing any crime, including but not limited to violation of an order of protection, under Section 12-30 of the Criminal Code of 1961 [720 ILCS 5/12-30], even if the crime was not committed in the presence of the officer.

(b) The law enforcement officer may verify the existence of an order of protection by telephone or radio communication with his or her law enforcement agency or by referring to the copy of the order provided by the petitioner or respondent.

(c) Any law enforcement officer may make an arrest without warrant if the officer has reasonable grounds to believe a defendant at liberty under the provisions of subdivision (d)(1) or (d)(2) of Section 110-10 of the Code of Criminal Procedure of 1963 [725 ILCS 5/110-10] has violated a condition of his or her bail bond or recognizance.
(Source: P.A. 84-1305; 88-624, § 5.)

Note.
This section was Ill.Rev.Stat., Ch. 40, para. 2313-1.

Effect of Amendments.
The 1994 amendment by P.A. 88-624, effective January 1, 1995, added subsection (c).

CASE NOTES

Special Protection

—Duty of Law Enforcement
Plaintiff obtained an order of protection and, thus, was singled out by the judicial process as a person in need of special protection; the sheriff had a duty to provide her with such protection. Calloway v. Kinkelaar, 261 Ill. App. 3d 63, 199 Ill. Dec. 389, 633 N.E.2d 1380 (5 Dist. 1994), aff'd, 168 Ill. 2d 312, 213 Ill. Dec. 675, 659 N.E.2d 1322 (1995).

LEGAL PERIODICALS

For essay, "Enforcement in Domestic Violence Cases," see 26 Loy. U. Chi. L.J. 633 (1995).

750 ILCS 60/301.1 Law enforcement policies

Sec. 301.1. *Law enforcement policies.* Every law enforcement agency shall develop, adopt, and implement written policies regarding arrest procedures for domestic violence incidents consistent with the provisions of this Act. In developing these policies, each law enforcement agency is encouraged to consult with community organizations and other law enforcement agencies with expertise in recognizing and handling domestic violence incidents.
(Source: P.A. 87-1186, § 3.)

Effective Date.
This section became effective January 1, 1993, pursuant to Ill. Const. (1970), Art. IV, § 10 and 5 ILCS 75/1.

750 ILCS 60/302 Data maintenance by law enforcement agencies

Sec. 302. *Data maintenance by law enforcement agencies.* (a) All sheriffs shall furnish to the Department of State Police, on the same day as received, in the form and detail the Department requires, copies of any recorded emergency, interim, or plenary orders of protection issued by the court, and any foreign orders of protection filed by the clerk of the court, and transmitted to the sheriff by the clerk of the court pursuant to subsection (b) of Section 222 of this Act [750 ILCS 60/222]. Each order of protection shall be entered in the Law Enforcement Automated Data System on the same day it is issued by the court. If an emergency order of protection was issued in accordance with subsection (c) of Section 217 [750 ILCS 60/217], the order shall be entered in the Law Enforcement Automated Data System as soon as possible after receipt from the clerk.

(b) The Department of State Police shall maintain a complete and systematic record and index of all valid and recorded orders of protection issued pursuant to this Act. The data shall be used to inform all dispatchers and law enforcement officers at the scene of an alleged incident of abuse, neglect, or exploitation or violation of an order of protection of any recorded prior incident of abuse, neglect, or exploitation involving the abused, neglected, or exploited party and the effective dates and terms of any recorded order of protection.

(c) The data, records and transmittals required under this Section shall pertain to any valid emergency, interim or plenary order of protection, whether issued in a civil or criminal proceeding or authorized under the laws of another state, tribe, or United States territory.
(Source: P.A. 86-542; 87-1186, § 3; 90-392, § 10; 91-903, § 20.)

Note.
This section was Ill.Rev.Stat., Ch. 40, para. 2313-2.

Effect of Amendments.
The 1997 amendment by P.A. 90-392, effective January 1, 1998, in subsection (a) added the third sentence.

The 2000 amendment by P.A. 91-903, effective January 1, 2001, inserted "and any foreign orders of protection filed by the clerk of the court" in the first sentence of subsection (a), and inserted "or authorized under the laws of another state, tribe, or United States territory" in subsection (c).

750 ILCS 60/303 Reports by law enforcement officers

Sec. 303. *Reports by law enforcement officers.* (a) Every law enforcement officer investigating an alleged incident of abuse, neglect, or exploitation between family or household members shall make a written police report of any bona fide allegation and the disposition of such investigation. The police report shall include the victim's statements as to the frequency and severity of prior incidents of abuse, neglect, or exploitation by the same family or household member and the number of prior calls for police assistance to prevent such further abuse, neglect, or exploitation.

(b) Every police report completed pursuant to this Section shall be recorded and compiled as a domestic crime within the meaning of Section 5.1 of the Criminal Identification Act [20 ILCS 2630/5.1].
(Source: P.A. 86-542; 87-1186, § 3.)

Note.
This section was Ill.Rev.Stat., Ch. 40, para. 2313-3.

CASE NOTES

Illustrative Cases
Court dismissed plaintiff's claim that police officers violated the Illinois Domestic Violence Act of 1986, 750 ILCS 60/101 et seq., where she stated in her complaint that they wrote up a police report and informed her how to initiate a criminal proceeding against her sister who had threatened her. Farrar v. City of Chicago, 291 F. Supp. 2d 747, 2003 U.S. Dist. LEXIS 20478 (N.D. Ill. 2003).

750 ILCS 60/304 Assistance by law enforcement officers

Sec. 304. *Assistance by law enforcement officers.* (a) Whenever a law enforcement officer has reason to believe that a person has been abused, neglected, or exploited by a family or household member, the officer shall immediately use all reasonable means to prevent further abuse, neglect, or exploitation, including:

(1) Arresting the abusing, neglecting and exploiting party, where appropriate;

(2) If there is probable cause to believe that particular weapons were used to commit the incident of abuse, subject to constitutional limitations, seizing and taking inventory of the weapons;

(3) Accompanying the victim of abuse, neglect, or exploitation to his or her place of residence for a reasonable period of time to remove necessary personal belongings and possessions;

(4) Offering the victim of abuse, neglect, or exploitation immediate and adequate information (written in a language appropriate for the victim or in Braille or communicated in appropriate sign language), which shall include a summary of the procedures and relief available to victims of abuse under subsection (c) of Section 217 [750 ILCS 60/217] and the officer's name and badge number;

(5) Providing the victim with one referral to an accessible service agency;

(6) Advising the victim of abuse about seeking medical attention and preserving evidence (specifically including photographs of injury or damage and damaged clothing or other property); and

(7) Providing or arranging accessible transportation for the victim of abuse (and, at the victim's request, any minors or dependents in the victim's care) to a medical facility for treatment of injuries or to a nearby place of shelter or safety; or, after the close of court business hours, providing or arranging for transportation for the victim (and, at the victim's request, any minors or dependents in the victim's care) to the nearest available circuit judge or associate judge so the victim may file a petition for an emergency order of protection under subsection (c) of Section 217 [750 ILCS 60/217]. When a victim of abuse chooses to leave the scene of the offense, it shall be presumed that it is in the best interests of any minors or dependents in the victim's care to remain with the victim or a person designated by the victim, rather than to remain with the abusing party.

(b) Whenever a law enforcement officer does not exercise arrest powers or otherwise initiate criminal proceedings, the officer shall:

(1) Make a police report of the investigation of any bona fide allegation of an incident of abuse, neglect, or exploitation and the disposition of the investigation, in accordance with subsection (a) of Section 303 [750 ILCS 60/303];

(2) Inform the victim of abuse neglect, or exploitation of the victim's right to request that a criminal proceeding be initiated where appropriate, including specific times and places for meeting with the State's Attorney's office, a warrant officer, or other official in accordance with local procedure; and

(3) Advise the victim of the importance of seeking medical attention and preserving evidence (specifically including photographs of injury or damage and damaged clothing or other property).

(c) Except as provided by Section 24-6 of the Criminal Code of 1961 [720 ILCS 5/24-6] or under a court order, any weapon seized under subsection (a)(2) shall be returned forthwith to the person from whom it was seized when it is no longer needed for evidentiary purposes.
(Source: P.A. 86-542; 87-1186, § 3; 88-498, § 10.)

Note.
This section was Ill.Rev.Stat., Ch. 40, para. 2313-4.

CASE NOTES

ANALYSIS

Qualified Immunity
Reasonable Means

—Examples Not Exclusive
—Shown
Unlawful Arrest
—Not Shown

Qualified Immunity

In light of the officers' duty under this Act, the officers were certainly on notice that their conduct was unlawful and the officers were also aware that their deliberate omission to act was in violation of victim's clearly established constitutional right to equal protection, therefore the officers were denied qualified immunity. Didzerekis v. Stewart, 41 F. Supp. 2d 840 (N.D. Ill. 1999).

Reasonable Means

—Examples Not Exclusive

Although this section enumerates specific examples of authorized conduct by law enforcement officers in the event of an abusive domestic situation, the section is inclusive rather than exclusive in requiring an officer to use all reasonable methods necessary to prevent further abuse. People v. Hetzel, 176 Ill. App. 3d 630, 126 Ill. Dec. 141, 531 N.E.2d 436 (2 Dist. 1988).

—Shown

Where police officer was informed by victim that defendant had pushed and shoved her and that she wanted him removed from her home, police officer was authorized under this section to remove from defendant the two keys which would have given defendant access to victim's home. People v. Hetzel, 176 Ill. App. 3d 630, 126 Ill. Dec. 141, 531 N.E.2d 436 (2 Dist. 1988).

Unlawful Arrest

—Not Shown

A reasonable officer would have thought that there was ample basis to believe that defendant committed the crime of battery and that the filing of a complaint was warranted; plaintiff thus failed to establish an essential element of his unlawful arrest claim, and summary judgment was appropriate. Simmons v. Pryor, 9 F.3d 555 (7th Cir. 1993), modified, 26 F.3d 650 (7th Cir.), cert. denied, 511 U.S. 1082, 114 S. Ct. 1833, 128 L. Ed. 2d 461 (1994).

750 ILCS 60/305 Limited law enforcement liability

Sec. 305. *Limited law enforcement liability.* Any act of omission or commission by any law enforcement officer acting in good faith in rendering emergency assistance or otherwise enforcing this Act shall not impose civil liability upon the law enforcement officer or his or her supervisor or employer, unless the act is a result of willful or wanton misconduct.
(Source: P.A. 84-1305.)

Note.

This section was Ill.Rev.Stat., Ch. 40, para. 2313-5.

CASE NOTES

ANALYSIS

Federal Law
Legislative Intent
Ordinary Negligence
Qualified Immunity
Wilful and Wanton Misconduct

Federal Law

The statute does not affect an officer's liability under federal law for the violation of a person's federal constitutional rights. Reich v. Hanrahan, F. Supp. 2d , 2000 U.S. Dist. LEXIS 9481 (N.D. Ill. July 6, 2000).

Legislative Intent

Partial immunity of law enforcement agents provided by this section is a direct expression of the legislative intent to reconcile the strongly worded purposes of this Act — protection of and assistance to victims of abuse — with the recognition that officers performing their legal duties should not be held civilly liable when their efforts to enforce the Act fall short, unless the conduct in question can be viewed as willful or wanton. Moore v. Green, Ill. App. 3d , 290 Ill. Dec. 787, 822 N.E.2d 69, 2004 Ill. App. LEXIS 1549 (1 Dist. 2004).

The legislature unambiguously intended to limit the liability of law enforcement personnel to wilful and wanton acts or omissions in enforcing the Domestic Violence Act. Calloway v. Kinkelaar, 168 Ill. 2d 312, 213 Ill. Dec. 675, 659 N.E.2d 1322 (1995).

The language of this section plainly intends that officers are not to be held civilly liable for mere negligence in the good faith performance of their duties under the Domestic Violence Act; however, the express limitation on liability does not apply if the act or omission in question is a result of "wilful or wanton misconduct." Calloway v. Kinkelaar, 168 Ill. 2d 312, 213 Ill. Dec. 675, 659 N.E.2d 1322 (1995).

The General Assembly intended to make a law enforcement officer and/or his employer liable, but only for wilful and wanton acts of misfeasance or nonfeasance in the exercise of police power, with respect to the enforcement of this Act; only actions alleging wilful and wanton misconduct can survive a motion to dismiss. Calloway v. Kinkelaar, 261 Ill. App. 3d 63, 199 Ill. Dec. 389, 633 N.E.2d 1380 (5 Dist. 1994), aff'd, 168 Ill. 2d 312, 213 Ill. Dec. 675, 659 N.E.2d 1322 (1995).

Ordinary Negligence

The Domestic Violence Act bars recognition of a cause of action sounding in ordinary negligence. Calloway v. Kinkelaar, 168 Ill. 2d 312, 213 Ill. Dec. 675, 659 N.E.2d 1322 (1995).

Qualified Immunity

In light of the officers' duty under this Act, the officers were certainly on notice that their conduct was unlawful and the officers were also aware that their deliberate omission to act was in violation of victim's clearly established constitutional right to equal protection, therefore the officers were denied qualified immunity. Didzerekis v. Stewart, 41 F. Supp. 2d 840 (N.D. Ill. 1999).

Wilful and Wanton Misconduct

Where police officers were accused of willfully and wantonly failing to prevent a crime against a victim of domestic violence, this section, not 745 ILCS 10/4-102 or 745 ILCS 10/4-107, controlled in a wrongful death and survival action brought by plaintiff adminstrator against the officers and their city employer. Moore v. Green, Ill. App. 3d , 290 Ill. Dec. 787, 822 N.E.2d 69, 2004 Ill. App. LEXIS 1549 (1 Dist. 2004).

The complaint sufficiently pled facts constituting willful and wanton action by the inaction of the police department of the defendant city where (1) the complaint stated repeated instances where the decedent reported abuse by her ex-husband, (2) the decedent took the proper steps to protect herself by obtaining a plenary order of protection, (3) after having taken the proper steps to establish herself as a person in special need of protection, she again reported repeated stalking on the part of her ex-husband, and (4) she even had an eyewitness corroborate her claims of harassment. Sneed v. Howell, 306 Ill. App. 3d 1149, 240 Ill. Dec. 203, 716 N.E.2d 336, 1999 Ill. App. LEXIS 603 (5 Dist. 1999), appeal denied, 187 Ill. 2d 590, 244 Ill. Dec. 191, 724 N.E.2d 1275 (2000).

Plaintiff adequately pleaded a cause of action in wilful and wanton misconduct against both sheriff and county. Calloway v. Kinkelaar, 168 Ill. 2d 312, 213 Ill. Dec. 675, 659 N.E.2d 1322 (1995).

RESEARCH REFERENCES

Right to compensation for real property damaged by law enforcement personnel in course of apprehending suspect. 23 ALR5th 834.

750 ILCS 60/306: Repealed by P.A. 87-1255, effective September 1, 1994.

Note.

This section was repealed by its own terms which read "This Section is repealed on September 1, 1994".

The 1994 amendment to this section by P.A. 88-586, effective August 12, 1994 has not been set out due to the repeal. The amendment, in the first sentence of subsection (a) substituted "the Illinois Law Enforcement Training Standards Board" for "the Illinois Local Governmental Law Enforcement Officers Training Board".

ARTICLE IV. HEALTH CARE PROVIDERS

750 ILCS 60/401 [Providing information on services; liability]

Sec. 401. Any person who is licensed, certified or otherwise authorized by the law of this State to administer health care in the ordinary course of business or practice of a profession shall offer to a person suspected to be a victim of abuse immediate and adequate information regarding services available to victims of abuse.

Any person who is licensed, certified or otherwise authorized by the law of this State to administer health care in the ordinary course of business, or practice of a profession and who in good faith offers to a person suspected to be a victim of abuse information regarding services available to victims of abuse shall not be civilly liable for any act or omission of the agency providing those services to the victims of abuse or for the inadequacy of those services provided by the agency.
(Source: P.A. 87-436.)

Note.
This section was Ill.Rev.Stat., Ch. 40, para. 2314-1.

ADDRESS CONFIDENTIALITY FOR VICTIMS OF DOMESTIC VIOLENCE ACT

750 ILCS 61/1 Short title

Sec. 1. *Short title.* This Act may be cited as the Address Confidentiality for Victims of Domestic Violence Act.
(Source: P.A. 91-494, § 1.)

Effective Date.
This Act became effective January 1, 2000 pursuant to Ill. Const. (1970), Art. IV § 10 and 5 ILCS 75/1.

750 ILCS 61/5 Legislative findings

Sec. 5. *Legislative findings.* The General Assembly finds that persons attempting to escape from actual or threatened domestic violence frequently establish new addresses in order to prevent their assailants or probable assailants from finding them. The purpose of this Act is to enable State and local agencies to respond to requests for public records without disclosing the location of a victim of domestic violence, to enable interagency cooperation with the Attorney General in providing address confidentiality for victims of domestic violence, and to enable State and local agencies to accept a program participant's use of an address designated by the Attorney General as a substitute mailing address.
(Source: P.A. 91-494, § 5.)

750 ILCS 61/10 Definitions

Sec. 10. *Definitions.* In this Act, unless the context otherwise requires:

"Address" means a residential street address, school address, or work address of an individual, as specified on the individual's application to be a program participant under this Act.

"Program participant" means a person certified as a program participant under this Act.

"Domestic violence" has the same meaning as in the Illinois Domestic Violence Act of 1986 [750 ILCS 60/1 et seq.] and includes a threat of domestic violence against an individual in a domestic situation, regardless of whether the domestic violence or threat has been reported to law enforcement officers.
(Source: P.A. 91-494, § 10.)

750 ILCS 61/11 Address confidentiality program; administration

Sec. 11. *Address confidentiality program; administration.* Subject to appropriations for the purposes of this Act, the Attorney General shall administer an address confidentiality program for victims of domestic violence.
(Source: P.A. 91-494, § 11.)

750 ILCS 61/15 Address confidentiality program; application; certification

Sec. 15. *Address confidentiality program; application; certification.* (a) An adult person, a parent or guardian acting on behalf of a minor, or a guardian acting on behalf of a disabled person, as defined in Article 11a of the Probate Act of 1975 [755 ILCS 5/11a-1 et seq.], may apply to the Attorney General to have an address designated by the Attorney General serve as the person's address or the address of the minor or disabled person. The Attorney General shall approve an application if it is filed in the manner and on the form prescribed by him or her and if it contains:

(1) a sworn statement by the applicant that the applicant has good reason to believe (i) that the applicant, or the minor or disabled person on whose behalf the application is made, is a victim of domestic violence; and (ii) that the applicant fears for his or her safety or his or her children's safety, or the safety of the minor or disabled person on whose behalf the application is made;

(2) a designation of the Attorney General as agent for purposes of service of process and receipt of mail;

(3) the mailing address where the applicant can be contacted by the Attorney General, and the phone number or numbers where the applicant can be called by the Attorney General;

(4) the new address or addresses that the applicant requests not be disclosed for the reason that disclosure will increase the risk of domestic violence; and

(5) the signature of the applicant and of any individual or representative of any office designated in writing under Section 40 of this Act [750 ILCS 61/40] who assisted in the preparation of the application, and the date on which the applicant signed the application.

(b) Applications shall be filed with the office of the Attorney General.

(c) Upon filing a properly completed application, the Attorney General shall certify the applicant as a program participant. Applicants shall be certified for 4 years following the date of filing unless the certification is withdrawn or invalidated before that date. The Attorney General shall by rule establish a renewal procedure.

(d) A person who falsely attests in an application that disclosure of the applicant's address would endanger the applicant's safety or the safety of the applicant's children or the minor or incapacitated person on whose behalf the application is made, or who knowingly provides false or incorrect information upon making an application, is guilty of a Class 3 felony.

(Source: P.A. 91-494, § 15.)

750 ILCS 61/20 Certification cancellation

Sec. 20. *Certification cancellation.* (a) If the program participant obtains a name change, he or she loses certification as a program participant.

(b) The Attorney General may cancel a program participant's certification if there is a change in the residential address from the one listed on the application, unless the program participant provides the Attorney General within 7 days notice before the change of address.

(c) The Attorney General may cancel certification of a program participant if mail forwarded by the Attorney General to the program participant's address is returned as nondeliverable.

(d) The Attorney General shall cancel certification of a program participant who applies using false information.

(Source: P.A. 91-494, § 20.)

750 ILCS 61/25 Agency use of designated address

Sec. 25. *Agency use of designated address.* (a) A program participant may request that State and local agencies use the address designated by the Attorney General as his or her address. When creating a new public record, State and local agencies shall accept the address designated by the Attorney General as a program participant's substitute address, unless the Attorney General has determined that:

(1) the agency has a bona fide statutory or administrative requirement for the use of the address that would otherwise be confidential under this Act; and

(2) this address will be used only for those statutory and administrative purposes.

(b) A program participant may use the address designated by the Attorney General as his or her work address.

(c) The office of the Attorney General shall forward all first class mail to the appropriate program participants.

(Source: P.A. 91-494, § 25.)

750 ILCS 61/30 Voting by program participant; use of designated address by election authority

Sec. 30. *Voting by program participant; use of designated address by election authority.* (a) A program participant who is otherwise qualified to vote may apply to vote under Article 20 of the Election Code [10 ILCS 5/20-1 et seq.]. The program participant shall automatically receive absentee ballots for all elections in the jurisdictions for which that individual resides in the same manner as absentee voters who qualify under Article 20 of the Election Code [10 ILCS 5/20-1 et seq.]. The Attorney General shall adopt rules to ensure the integrity of the voting process and the confidentiality of the program participant. The election authority shall transmit the absentee ballot to the program participant at the address designated by the participant in his or her application. Neither the name nor the address of a program participant shall be included in any list of registered voters available to the public.

(b) The election authority may not make the participant's address contained in voter registration records available for public inspection or copying except under the following circumstances:

(1) if requested by a law enforcement agency, to the law enforcement agency; and

(2) if directed by a court order, to a person identified in the order.

(Source: P.A. 91-494, § 30.)

750 ILCS 61/35 Disclosure of address prohibited; exceptions

Sec. 35. *Disclosure of address prohibited; exceptions.* The Attorney General may not make a program participant's address, other than the address designated by the Attorney General, available for inspection or copying, except under the following circumstances:

(a) if requested by a law enforcement agency, to the law enforcement agency;

(b) if directed by a court order, to a person identified in the order; and

(c) if certification has been canceled.
(Source: P.A. 91-494, § 35.)

750 ILCS 61/40 Assistance for program applicants

Sec. 40. *Assistance for program applicants.* The Attorney General shall designate State and local agencies and nonprofit agencies that provide counseling and shelter services to victims of domestic violence to assist persons applying to be program participants. Any assistance and counseling rendered by the office of the Attorney General or its designees to applicants shall in no way be construed as legal advice.
(Source: P.A. 91-494, § 40.)

750 ILCS 61/45 Rules

Sec. 45. *Rules.* The Attorney General may adopt rules to facilitate the administration of this Act by State and local agencies.
(Source: P.A. 91-494, § 45.)

RIGHTS OF MARRIED PERSONS ACT

750 ILCS 65/0.01 Short title

Sec. 0.01. *Short title.* This Act may be cited as the Rights of Married Persons Act.
(Source: P.A. 86-1324; 87-286.)

Derivation.
Title: An Act to revise the law in relation to husband and wife.
Cite: 750 ILCS 65/0.01 et seq.
Source: R.S. 1874, p. 576.
Date: Approved March 30, 1874.

Note.
This section was Ill.Rev.Stat., Ch. 40, para. 1000.

CASE NOTES

Constitutionality
This Act is not unconstitutional because the purpose is not expressed in the title, and this Act contains more than one subject. Steffa v. Stanley, 39 Ill. App. 3d 915, 350 N.E.2d 886 (2 Dist. 1976).

LEGAL PERIODICALS

For article, "Recent Trends in School Tort Immunity," see 71 Ill. B. J. 240 (1982).

RESEARCH REFERENCES

Recovery for loss of consortium for injury occurring prior to marriage. 5 ALR4th 300.

Injured party's release of tortfeasor as barring spouse's action for loss of consortium. 29 ALR4th 1200.

Action for loss of consortium based on nonmarital cohabitation. 40 ALR4th 553.

750 ILCS 65/1 Rights to sue and be sued

Sec. 1. *Rights to sue and be sued.* A married person may, in all cases, sue and be sued without joining his or her spouse as if unmarried. A husband or wife may sue the other for a tort committed during the marriage. No finding by any court under Section 401 of the Illinois Marriage and Dissolution of Marriage Act [750 ILCS 5/401] shall be admissible or be used as prima facie evidence of a tort in any civil action brought under this Act. An attachment or judgment in an action may be enforced by or against a married person as if unmarried.
(Source: P.A. 87-286.)

Note.
This section was Ill.Rev.Stat., Ch. 40, para. 1001.

CASE NOTES

ANALYSIS

Constitutionality
In General
Application and Construction
—In General
—Personal Injury
—Premarital Tort
—Prior Law
—Wrongful Death
Arbitration
Effect of Amendment
Insurance Contracts
Interspousal Tort Immunity
Law of Domicile
Legislative Intent
Public Policy
Purpose
Retroactivity

Constitutionality
The intermediate level of scrutiny standard, which requires that a classification which affects important, as opposed to fundamental, rights must be substantially related to important governmental objectives sought to be achieved by the legislation does not apply to this statute since it does not significantly burden the fundamental right to marry. Nicpon ex rel. Urbanski v. Nicpon, 145 Ill. App. 3d 464, 99 Ill. Dec. 458, 495 N.E.2d 1193 (1 Dist. 1986).

This section has been upheld under equal protection utilizing the minimum scrutiny analysis. Nicpon ex rel. Urbanski v. Nicpon, 145 Ill. App. 3d 464, 99 Ill. Dec. 458, 495 N.E.2d 1193 (1 Dist. 1986).

The former interspousal tort immunity statute was held unconstitutional. Moran v. Beyer, 734 F.2d 1245 (7th Cir. 1984).

The purpose of this section is not to control or otherwise abridge the rights of married women but, rather, to allow rights denied under the common law and elevate married women to a legal parity with married men; thus, this section does not deny plaintiff equal protection of the law. Steffa v. Stanley, 39 Ill. App. 3d 915, 350 N.E.2d 886 (2 Dist. 1976).

In General
This Act removes the common-law disabilities of married women and places married women in the same status as single women; however, it does not remove the statutory disability of minority. Kowalski v. Liska, 78 Ill. App. 3d 64, 33 Ill. Dec. 706, 397 N.E.2d 39 (1 Dist. 1979).

Wrongful death actions brought for the benefit of surviving children of a deceased mother are not within the contemplation of the rule that a wife cannot sue her husband under former Ill.Rev.Stat., ch. 68, para. 1 (1973) (see now 750 ILCS 65/1). Herget Nat'l Bank v. Berardi, 64 Ill. 2d 467, 1 Ill. Dec. 341, 356 N.E.2d 529 (1976).

In General (Cont'd)

Although this Act provides that a wife may contract, own property, receive, use and possess her own earnings, and may sue her husband for property belonging to her which he unlawfully obtained or retained, she could not sue him for her services, nor for a tort committed by him to her person (but see now this section) and therefore her right to sue her husband, except for those limitations, was the same as her right against a stranger, and this was not contrary to this state's public policy. Boker v. Boker, 17 Ill. App. 2d 260, 149 N.E.2d 774 (4 Dist. 1958).

A wife could maintain an appropriate action against her husband, at law or in equity, depending on the factual situation, the same as if she were an unmarried woman, and even while the marriage relation subsisted she could maintain an action against her husband under former Ill.Rev.Stat., ch. 68, para. 1 (see now this section). Glennon v. Glennon, 299 Ill. App. 13, 19 N.E.2d 412 (1 Dist. 1939).

Application and Construction

—In General

Prior to the 1953 amendment of former Ill.Rev.Stat., ch. 68, para. 1 (see now this section), one spouse could bring an action in tort against the other during coverture, and the effect of the 1953 amendment was not to destroy the cause of action of the injured spouse, but to confer immunity on the tortfeasor spouse, which, like a defense based upon the statute of limitations, could be waived by the defendant spouse. Allstate Ins. Co. v. Elkins, 77 Ill. 2d 384, 33 Ill. Dec. 139, 396 N.E.2d 528 (1979).

At common law a married woman had no separate identity before the law; she was regarded as a chattel with neither property nor other rights which were enforceable against anyone, and her husband owned all her property and asserted all of her legal and equitable right; it therefore followed that a husband was immune from suits by his wife, either in tort or contract. Heckendorn v. First Nat'l Bank, 19 Ill. 2d 190, 166 N.E.2d 571 (1960).

—Personal Injury

Under the former Married Women's Act of 1874 (former Ill.Rev.Stat., ch. 68, paras. 1 to 21) (see now this Act), a married woman could maintain an action for damages against her husband for personal injuries caused by his wilful and wanton misconduct. Brandt v. Keller, 413 Ill. 503, 109 N.E.2d 729 (1952).

—Premarital Tort

Wife was permitted to maintain action against husband, pursuant to former § 1 of the former Married Women's Act (see now this section) for premarital tort. Packenham v. Miltimore, 89 Ill. App. 2d 452, 232 N.E.2d 42 (2 Dist. 1967).

—Prior Law

Former § 1 of the Married Women's Act (see now this section), which would have precluded the wife, had she survived, from suing her husband or his estate for a tort committed during coverture, did not preclude her personal representative, where her death ensued from such injuries, from recovering from her spouse or his estate under the death statute (740 ILCS 180/1) for the use and benefit of her children. Herget Nat'l Bank v. Berardi, 31 Ill. App. 3d 608, 335 N.E.2d 39 (3 Dist. 1975), aff'd, 64 Ill. 2d 467, 1 Ill. Dec. 341, 356 N.E.2d 529 (1976).

A 1953 amendment to former Ill.Rev.Stat., ch. 68, para. 1 (see now this section), which prohibited a husband or wife from suing the other for a tort committed during coverture, barred wife's tort action against husband, even though the action was commenced prior to enactment of the amendment. Hindman v. Holmes, 4 Ill. App. 2d 279, 124 N.E.2d 344 (4 Dist. 1955).

—Wrongful Death

Administrator of estate of woman killed in automobile accident could bring wrongful death action against woman's husband, who was driver of the car in which she was riding. Rogers v. Jackson, 416 F. Supp. 1125 (N.D. Ill. 1976).

Under prior similar provision, an administrator of estate of wife killed unlawfully by her husband, who then took his own life, could maintain an action against the husband's estate for pecuniary loss suffered by the children of wife from former marriage through the unlawful killing of the mother. Calvert v. Morgan, 41 Ill. App. 2d 23, 190 N.E.2d 1 (2 Dist. 1963).

The administrator of the wife's estate could maintain an action for wrongful death which derived from the wrongful act of deceased's husband. Welch v. Davis, 410 Ill. 130, 101 N.E.2d 547 (1951).

Arbitration

Arbitrator was without authority to resolve an insurance coverage dispute involving the question of whether interspousal immunity under former Ill.Rev.Stat., ch. 68, para. 1 (see now this section) precluded defendant from receiving benefits under the uninsured motorist provision of her husband's insurance policy and his decision concerning defendant was therefore vacated. Allstate Ins. Co. v. Elkins, 63 Ill. App. 3d 62, 21 Ill. Dec. 66, 381 N.E.2d 1 (1 Dist. 1978), aff'd, 77 Ill. 2d 384, 33 Ill. Dec. 139, 396 N.E.2d 528 (1979).

Effect of Amendment

The 1987 amendment to this Act did not expand tort liability between husband and wife, but merely abolished the defense of interspousal tort immunity. Kukla v. Kukla, 184 Ill. App. 3d 585, 132 Ill. Dec. 770, 540 N.E.2d 510 (1 Dist. 1989).

Insurance Contracts

To the extent that a family exclusion clause in an insurance policy does not prevent a lawsuit brought by one spouse against the other, it does not contravene the public policy espoused by the unambiguously worded former Married Women's Act (see now this Act). Safeco Ins. Co. v. Seck, 225 Ill. App. 3d 397, 167 Ill. Dec. 636, 587 N.E.2d 1251 (2 Dist. 1992).

The abrogation of interspousal immunity for intentional torts did not automatically invalidate a family exclusion clause when the clause was used to bar coverage in the face of an intentional tort action. Safeco Ins. Co. v. Seck, 225 Ill. App. 3d 397, 167 Ill. Dec. 636, 587 N.E.2d 1251 (2 Dist. 1992).

Interspousal Tort Immunity

The former interspousal tort immunity provision of this section barred a tort action between a husband and wife although they were separated and living apart. Soedler v. Soedler, 89 Ill. App. 3d 74, 44 Ill. Dec. 425, 411 N.E.2d 547 (3 Dist. 1980).

Law of Domicile

Because under Illinois' conflict of law rules, the law of the marital domicile must be applied to determine whether one spouse may maintain an action in tort against the other, wife injured in automobile accident which occurred in Illinois was permitted to sue her husband in tort because the couple's domicile was in Ontario, Canada, and the law of Ontario permitted the suit. Nelson v. Hix, 122 Ill. 2d 343, 119 Ill. Dec. 355, 522 N.E.2d 1214, cert. denied, 488 U.S. 925, 109 S. Ct. 309, 102 L. Ed. 2d 327 (1988).

The law of a married couple's domicile controlled their capacity to sue one another in tort where Canadian wife sued husband for injuries arising from accident in Illinois. Nelson v. Hix, 146 Ill. App. 3d 486, 99 Ill. Dec. 960, 496 N.E.2d 1052 (2 Dist. 1986), cert. denied, 488 U.S. 925, 109 S. Ct. 309, 102 L. Ed. 2d 327 (1988).

Legislative Intent

Former Ill.Rev.Stat., ch. 68, para. 1 (see now this section) reflected a legislative intent to remove a married woman's common-law disability with reference to suing and being sued, so that she would be placed in the same status as if she were unmarried. Heckendorn v. First Nat'l Bank, 19 Ill. 2d 190, 166 N.E.2d 571 (1960).

Public Policy

Insurance policy's member of the household exclusion did not violate the public policy of Illinois as expressed in the amended Married Women Act, 750 ILCS 65/1 et seq., and the Financial Responsibility Law, 625 ILCS 5/7-100 et seq. State Farm Mut. Auto. Ins. Co. v. Collins, 258 Ill. App. 3d 1, 196 Ill. Dec. 217, 629 N.E.2d 762 (1 Dist.), appeal denied, 156 Ill. 2d 567, 202 Ill. Dec. 932, 638 N.E.2d 1126 (1994).

Purpose

The policy underlying the former Married Women's Act is one which seeks to increase the legal rights, entitlements, and powers of married women (and men) rather than one which seeks to assure

Purpose (Cont'd)
the compensation of injured parties. Safeco Ins. Co. v. Seck, 225 Ill. App. 3d 397, 167 Ill. Dec. 636, 587 N.E.2d 1251 (2 Dist. 1992).

Retroactivity
This Act was approved on September 20, 1987, but did not become effective until January 1, 1988, thus, the legislature intended a later, rather than an earlier, effective date; had the legislature intended retroactive application, it would not have provided for an effective date more than three months after approval of the act and without any evidence of a contrary intent by the legislature, there was no error in the trial court's prospective application of the act. Glaves v. Glaves, 193 Ill. App. 3d 651, 140 Ill. Dec. 570, 550 N.E.2d 52 (2 Dist.), cert. denied, 132 Ill. 2d 544, 144 Ill. Dec. 257, 555 N.E.2d 376 (1990).

The 1987 amendment to this section conferred the new ability upon a spouse the right to file a cause of action for nonintentional torts and exposed spouses to liability for nonintentional torts for which their spouses could not have sued them prior to its enactment and therefore was not a matter of procedure or remedy but related to substantive rights, and could not be applied retroactively. Kim v. Kim, 196 Ill. App. 3d 1095, 143 Ill. Dec. 686, 554 N.E.2d 621 (1 Dist. 1990).

LEGAL PERIODICALS

For article, "Illinois Tort Law: A Rich History of Cooperation and Respect Between the Courts and the Legislature," see 28 Loy. U. Chi. L.J. 745 (1997).

For note, "Making Form Follow Function: Considerations in Creating and Applying a Statutory Parent-Child Privilege," see U. Ill. L. Rev. 879 (1990).

For comment, "Husband and Wife — Illinois Law as a Catalyst for Hollow Interspousal Tort Recoveries," see 13 S. Ill. U. L.J. 337 (1989).

For article, "Torts: 1987-88 Illinois Law Survey," see 20 Loy. U. Chi. L.J. 679 (1988-89).

For article, "Family Law: 1987-88 Illinois Law Survey," see Loy. U. Chi. L.J. 461 (1988-89).

For article, "Family Law: 1987-88 Illinois Law Survey," see Loy. U. Chi. L.J. 461 (1988-89).

For article, "Interspousal Tort Immunity and the Family Exclusion Clause in Liability Insurance Policies," see 66 Chi. B. Rec. 186 (1985).

For article, "Domestic Abuse Legislation in Illinois and Other States: a Survey and Suggestions for Reform," see U. Ill. L. Rev. 261 (1983).

For article, "Abolishing the Marital Exemption for Rape: a Statutory Proposal," see U. Ill. L. Rev. 201 (1983).

750 ILCS 65/2 Defending in own right or for other

Sec. 2. *Defending in own right or for other.* If husband and wife are sued together, either may defend for his or her own right and, if either neglects to defend, the other may defend for both.
(Source: P.A. 87-286.)

Note.
This section was Ill.Rev.Stat., Ch. 40, para. 1002.

750 ILCS 65/3 [Defending in name of spouse]

Sec. 3. When the husband has deserted his family, the wife may prosecute or defend, in his name, any action which he might have prosecuted or defended, and, under like circumstances, the same right shall apply to the husband upon the desertion of the wife.
(Source: R.S. 1874, p. 576.)

Note.
This section was Ill.Rev.Stat., Ch. 40, para. 1003.

750 ILCS 65/4 Recovery of damages

Sec. 4. *Recovery of damages.* For all civil injuries committed by a married person, damages may be recovered from that person alone, and his or her spouse shall not be responsible for those damages, except in cases where he or she would be jointly responsible with that person if the marriage did not exist.
(Source: P.A. 87-286.)

Note.
This section was Ill.Rev.Stat., Ch. 40, para. 1004.

CASE NOTES

Agency
If wife, at the time of the commission of the tort, was acting in the capacity of agent of the husband, the husband may be held responsible for the wife's tort. O'Haran v. Leiner, 306 Ill. App. 230, 28 N.E.2d 315 (4 Dist. 1940).

RESEARCH REFERENCES

Action for loss of consortium based on nonmarital cohabitation. 40 ALR4th 553.

750 ILCS 65/5 [Responsibility for liabilities of spouse]

Sec. 5. Neither husband or wife shall be liable for the debts or liabilities of the other incurred before marriage, and (except as herein otherwise provided) they shall not be liable for the separate debts of each other, nor shall the wages, earnings or property of either, nor the rent or income of such property, be liable for the separate debts of the other.
(Source: R.S. 1874, p. 576.)

Note.
This section was Ill.Rev.Stat., Ch. 40, para. 1005.

750 ILCS 65/6 Contracts

Sec. 6. *Contracts.* Contracts may be made and liabilities incurred by any married person and may be enforced against that person to the same extent and in the same manner as if unmarried.
(Source: P.A. 87-286.)

Note.
This section was Ill.Rev.Stat., Ch. 40, para. 1006.

CASE NOTES

ANALYSIS

Illustrative Case
Prior Law

Illustrative Case
Under a prior similar provision, a married woman had the power to contract with an elderly bachelor to provide a home for him, and

Illustrative Case (Cont'd)
the contract was enforceable, but her husband had the power to compel her to cease the performance of the agreement at any time. Casner v. Preston, 109 Ill. 531 (1884).

Prior Law
For a case discussing former restrictions on the power of husband and wife to contract with each other, see Thomas v. Mueller, 106 Ill. 36 (1883).

750 ILCS 65/7 Earnings

Sec. 7. *Earnings.* A married person may receive, use, and possess his or her own earnings and sue for those earnings in his or her own name, free from the interference of his or her spouse or the creditors of his or her spouse.
(Source: P.A. 87-286.)

Note.
This section was Ill.Rev.Stat., Ch. 40, para. 1007.

750 ILCS 65/9 Property

Sec. 9. *Property.* A married person may own in his or her own right real and personal property obtained by descent, gift, or purchase and may manage, sell, and convey that property to the same extent and in the same manner as an unmarried person. When husband and wife live together, however, no transfer or conveyance of goods and chattels between the husband and wife shall be valid as against the rights and interests of any third person unless the transfer or conveyance is in writing and filed in the same manner as security interests are required to be filed by the laws of this State in cases where the possession of the property is to remain with the person giving the security.
(Source: P.A. 87-286.)

Note.
This section was Ill.Rev.Stat., Ch. 40, para. 1009.

CASE NOTES

Analysis

In General
Conveyances
Divorce Proceeding
Illustrative Cases
Mortgages
Purpose
Witnesses

In General
Husband and wife, as respects her separate estate, stand before the law as strangers. Wolkau v. Wolkau, 299 Ill. 176, 132 N.E. 507 (1921).

Conveyances
The payments by the husband of one-half of his salary to his wife, did not constitute transfers which were void as to creditors, irrespective of the transferor's solvency. Knowles v. Crow, 289 Ill. App. 108, 6 N.E.2d 892 (4 Dist. 1937).

Divorce Proceeding
Although property rights are not involved in a suit for separate maintenance, they cannot be adjudicated in a divorce action if divorce is denied, but this rule only pertains to the form of the action; it does not deny the wife's right to separate property, nor preclude her from asserting her rights in an appropriate form of action under former Ill.Rev.Stat., ch. 68, para. 1 (see now this section). Boker v. Boker, 17 Ill. App. 2d 260, 149 N.E.2d 774 (4 Dist. 1958).

Illustrative Cases
Where the husband no longer had control and management of the separate property of his wife, she was under no obligation to furnish her husband with a home, even though she had one and he did not. Jones v. Kilfether, 12 Ill. App. 2d 390, 139 N.E.2d 801 (1 Dist. 1956).

Mortgages
Under a prior similar provision, a married woman could mortgage her land by joining with her husband in the execution of a mortgage to pay his debts. Edwards v. Schoeneman, 104 Ill. 278 (1882).

Purpose
The purpose of a former similar provision which required the transfer of property be acknowledged and recorded like chattel mortgages was to prevent the defrauding of creditors through reliance upon apparent ownership of tangible chattels. Knowles v. Crow, 289 Ill. App. 108, 6 N.E.2d 892 (4 Dist. 1937).

Witnesses
Under a former similar law (see now this Act), husband and wife could be witnesses for and against each other where the litigation concerned the separate property of the wife. Cassem v. Heustis, 201 Ill. 208, 66 N.E. 283 (1903).

LEGAL PERIODICALS

For article, "Pour-Over Lives: Estate Planning for the Second Marriage," see 74 Ill. B.J. 92 (1985).
For comment, "Tenancy by the Entirety in Illinois: A Reexamination," see 1980 S. Ill. U. L.J. 83.

750 ILCS 65/10 [Unlawful possession of property by spouse]

Sec. 10. Should either the husband or wife unlawfully obtain or retain possession or control of property belonging to the other, either before or after marriage, the owner of the property may maintain an action therefor, or for any right growing out of the same, in the same manner and to the same extent as if they were unmarried.
(Source: R.S. 1874, p. 576.)

Note.
This section was Ill.Rev.Stat., Ch. 40, para. 1010.

750 ILCS 65/11 [Abandoned spouse; control over property]

Sec. 11. In case the husband or wife abandons the other and leaves the state, and is absent therefrom for one year, without providing for the maintenance and support of his or her family, or is imprisoned in the penitentiary, the circuit court in the county where the husband or wife so abandoned or, not confined, resides, may, on application by petition, setting forth fully the facts, if the court is satisfied of the necessity by the evidence, authorize him or her to manage, control, sell or incumber the property of the other, as shall be necessary, in the judgment of the court, for the support and maintenance of the

family, and for the purpose of paying debts of the other, or debts contracted for the support of the family. Notice of such proceedings shall be given as in other civil actions, and anything done under or by virtue of the order or judgment of the court, shall be valid to the same extent as if the same were done by the party owning the property.
(Source: P.A. 84-1308.)

Note.
This section was Ill.Rev.Stat., Ch. 40, para. 1011.

CASE NOTES

Analysis

Abandonment
—In General
Disposition of Property
—Absolute Right of Disposal
—Inter Vivos Gift

Abandonment

—In General
Abandonment requires conduct which evinces a settled purpose to forego all parental duties and relinquish all familial claims to a child. In re Bartha, 107 Ill. App. 2d 214, 245 N.E.2d 779 (2 Dist. 1969).

Disposition of Property

—Absolute Right of Disposal
Under former Ill.Rev.Stat., ch. 68, para. 11 (see now this section), insofar as the statutory marital right is concerned, the abandoned spouse, in the lifetime of both spouses, has the absolute right actually and really to dispose of his or her own property in any manner he or she sees fit without the concurrence or even the knowledge of the other spouse; moreover, he or she may do so even though he or she does so for the precise purpose of thereby minimizing or completely defeating the interest which the other spouse would otherwise have obtained by reason of the statutory marital right. Toman v. Svoboda, 39 Ill. App. 3d 394, 349 N.E.2d 668 (1 Dist. 1976).

—Inter Vivos Gift
Under former Ill.Rev.Stat., ch. 68, para. 11 (see now this section) the effective method by which to minimize or defeat the statutory marital right is by making a real inter vivos gift to another person. Toman v. Svoboda, 39 Ill. App. 3d 394, 349 N.E.2d 668 (1 Dist. 1976).

750 ILCS 65/12 [Contracts, sales or incumbrances made by spouse]

Sec. 12. All contracts, sales or incumbrances made by either the husband or wife, by virtue of the power contemplated in the preceding section, shall be binding on both, and during such absence or confinement, the person acting under such power may sue and be sued thereon; and for all acts done the property of both shall be liable, and execution may be levied or attachment issued accordingly. No suit or proceeding shall abate, or be in anywise affected, by the return or release of the person absent or confined, but he or she shall be permitted to prosecute or defend jointly with the other.
(Source: R.S. 1874, p. 576.)

Note.
This section was Ill.Rev.Stat., Ch. 40, para. 1012.

750 ILCS 65/13 [Setting aside judgment]

Sec. 13. The husband or wife affected by the proceedings contemplated in the 2 preceding sections may have the order or judgment of the court set aside or annulled, by filing a petition therefor and serving a notice on the person in whose favor the same was granted, as in other civil actions. But the setting aside of such judgment or order shall in nowise affect any act done thereunder.
(Source: P.A. 84-1308.)

Note.
This section was Ill.Rev.Stat., Ch. 40, para. 1013.

750 ILCS 65/14 [Power of attorney]

Sec. 14. A husband or wife may constitute the other his or her attorney in fact, to control and dispose of his or her property for their mutual benefit or otherwise, and may revoke the same to the same extent and in the same manner as other persons.
(Source: R.S. 1874, p. 576.)

Note.
This section was Ill.Rev.Stat., Ch. 40, para. 1014.

750 ILCS 65/15 [Creditor's rights]

Sec. 15. (a)(1) The expenses of the family and of the education of the children shall be chargeable upon the property of both husband and wife, or of either of them, in favor of creditors therefor, and in relation thereto they may be sued jointly or separately.

(2) No creditor, who has a claim against a spouse or former spouse for an expense incurred by that spouse or former spouse which is not a family expense, shall maintain an action against the other spouse or former spouse for that expense except:

(A) an expense for which the other spouse or former spouse agreed, in writing, to be liable; or

(B) an expense for goods or merchandise purchased by or in the possession of the other spouse or former spouse, or for services ordered by the other spouse or former spouse.

(3) Any creditor who maintains an action in violation of this subsection (a) for an expense other than a family expense against a spouse or former spouse other than the spouse or former spouse who incurred the expense, shall be liable to the other spouse or former spouse for his or her costs, expenses and attorney's fees incurred in defending the action.

(4) No creditor shall, with respect to any claim against a spouse or former spouse for which the creditor is prohibited under this subsection (a) from maintaining an action against the other spouse or former spouse, engage in any collection efforts against the other spouse or former spouse, including, but not limited to, informal or formal collection attempts, referral of the claim to a collector or

collection agency for collection from the other spouse or former spouse, or making any representation to a credit reporting agency that the other spouse or former spouse is any way liable for payment of the claim.

(b) No spouse shall be liable for any expense incurred by the other spouse when an abortion is performed on such spouse, without the consent of such other spouse, unless the physician who performed the abortion certifies that such abortion is necessary to preserve the life of the spouse who obtained such abortion.

(c) No parent shall be liable for any expense incurred by his or her minor child when an abortion is performed on such minor child without the consent of both parents of such child, if they both have custody, or the parent having custody, or legal guardian of such child, unless the physician who performed the abortion certifies that such abortion is necessary to preserve the life of the minor child who obtained such abortion.

(Source: P.A. 86-689.)

Note.

This section was Ill.Rev.Stat., Ch. 40, para. 1015.

Illinois Administrative Code.

See 83 Illinois Administrative Code, §§ 280.50, 280.130, 735.100, 735.130, 735.100, 735.130.

CASE NOTES

ANALYSIS

Constitutionality
In General
Action Against Tortfeasor
Application and Construction
—In General
—Borrowed Money
—Derivative Claims
—Divorces
—Public Utilities Act
—Representative Capacity
Assignment
Attorney Fees
Cause of Action
Creditors
Disclosure of Public Facts
Dismissal
—Inappropriate
Expenses of the Family
—Adult Children
—Business Expenses
—Carpet
—Consent Not Required
—Credit Card Debt
—Dwelling
—Fur Coat
—Liability Not Shown
—Minor Children
—Rent
—Utilities
Family in Fact
—Not Shown
—Required
Funeral and Medical Expenses
Hospital Lien
Items of Luxury
—Jewelry
Judgment Reduced
Legislative Intent
Liability Between Parents
Liability for Support
Liability of Spouse
Limitations Period
Necessaries
Necessity Requirement
No Consent Requirement
Parental Responsibility
Procedure
Recovery
—Not Allowed
Reimbursement
—Direct Payment Allowed
—Not Allowed
Standing
—Jurisdiction
—No Liability During Estrangement
Voluntary Payment

Constitutionality

This section held constitutional. Carson Pirie Scott & Co. v. Hyde, 39 Ill. 2d 433, 235 N.E.2d 643 (1968).

In General

A creditor may hold a divorced, non-custodial parent liable under the Expense Statute for expenses incurred on behalf of his or her children. Proctor Hosp. v. Taylor, 279 Ill. App. 3d 624, 216 Ill. Dec. 614, 665 N.E.2d 872 (3 Dist. 1996).

An expense is an expense of the family when it is incurred for an article which contributes to the welfare of the family generally and tends to maintain the integrity of the family. Lyman v. Harbaugh, 117 Ill. App. 3d 732, 73 Ill. Dec. 81, 453 N.E.2d 906 (4 Dist. 1983).

A former section which charged expenses of the family and of the education of the children upon the property of both husband and wife, or either of them, was adopted from a similar statute of the State of Iowa (1882), and was interpreted as creating a primary right against husband and wife, or both, for family expenses incurred by either. Walker v. Houghteling, 107 F. 619 (7th Cir. 1901).

Subdivision (a)(1) of this section was adopted from an Iowa statute, and the Illinois Supreme Court adopted the interpretation placed upon it by the Iowa Supreme Court. Houghteling v. Walker, 100 F. 253 (N.D. Ill. 1900), aff'd, 107 F. 619 (7th Cir. 1901).

Action Against Tortfeasor

This section allows one spouse to maintain a cause of action against a tortfeasor for injuries to the other spouse, for expenses for which the suing spouse has become liable under this section; claims under this section are derivative and depend on the establishment of tortfeasor's liability for the injuries to the other spouse. Boesl v. Suburban Trust & Sav. Bank, 642 F. Supp. 1503 (N.D. Ill. 1986).

A cause of action is maintainable against a tortfeasor by the deprived spouse for family expenses arising from the injuries to the impaired spouse for which the deprived spouse has become liable under this section. Brown v. Metzger, 118 Ill. App. 3d 855, 74 Ill. Dec. 405, 455 N.E.2d 834 (2 Dist. 1983).

An original complaint which sought recovery from defendants only for injuries sustained by plaintiff as a result of a shooting incident, but was amended so as to also sue defendants for alleged loss of means of support sustained by his wife and three minor children resulting from his injuries, and an additional count seeking reimbursement for medical and hospital expenses incurred by the family under the former Ill.Rev.Stat., ch. 68, para. 15 (see now this section) was properly allowed and the subsequent amended and additional complaints related back to the time of filing of the original complaint. McCullough v. Tomaich, 20 Ill. App. 3d 262, 314 N.E.2d 643 (3 Dist. 1974).

Where wife sued to recover medical expenses incurred due to personal injuries sustained in an automobile accident and was denied recovery because the jury in effect found that the defendant was not guilty of negligence, the plaintiff's husband was barred from seeking the same property rights which were litigated in the wife's suit. Houghton v. Novak, 9 Ill. App. 3d 699, 292 N.E.2d 905 (2 Dist. 1973).

Parents are liable for the medical and funeral expenses incurred by them on behalf of a minor child, but, if such expenses result from

Action Against Tortfeasor (Cont'd)
injuries inflicted on the minor child by the wrongful act of another, the parents may recover such expenses incurred by them from the tortfeasor in a separate action and in addition to any recovery allowable under the Wrongful Death Act (740 ILCS 180/0.01). Graul v. Adrian, 49 Ill. App. 2d 101, 199 N.E.2d 631 (5 Dist. 1964), aff'd, 32 Ill. 2d 345, 205 N.E.2d 444 (1965).

A parent cannot maintain, separately, and in addition to an action to recover under the Wrongful Death Act (740 ILCS 185/0.01), a suit to recover the costs of medical expenses and funeral bills paid by the parent on behalf of the child. Wright v. Royse, 43 Ill. App. 2d 267, 193 N.E.2d 340 (3 Dist. 1963).

Widow's cause of action for medical and funeral expenses as a result of fatal injuries caused to her husband by defendant in an automobile collision was for a separate wrong done to her by the defendant, and her cause of action was not extinguished by her husband's death, although he died from the wrongful injury. Saunders v. Schultz, 22 Ill. App. 2d 402, 161 N.E.2d 129 (2 Dist. 1959), aff'd, 20 Ill. 2d 301, 170 N.E.2d 163 (1960).

A married woman did not have a cause of action for loss of consortium of her husband against third parties. Seymour v. Union News Co., 217 F.2d 168 (7th Cir. 1954).

Plaintiff, in her capacity as a widow, had a right to bring an action in negligence against a city for damages such as medical, hospital and nursing services furnished to her husband prior to his death; the cause of action of plaintiff was predicated upon her liability under former Ill.Rev.Stat., ch. 68, para. 15 (see now this section). Thompson v. City of Bushnell, 346 Ill. App. 352, 105 N.E.2d 311 (3 Dist. 1952).

Application and Construction

—In General
Any common law rights parents may have had to recover for expenses incurred on behalf of their children have been abrogated by this section and the Illinois Marriage and Dissolution of Marriage Act (750 ILCS 5/101 et seq.); the former applicable prior to divorce and the latter thereafter. In re Van Winkle, 107 Ill. App. 3d 73, 62 Ill. Dec. 831, 437 N.E.2d 358 (3 Dist. 1982).

This section applies to the expenses of the family, without limitation or qualification as to kind or amount, and without reference to the wealth, habits, or social position of the party. Houghteling v. Walker, 100 F. 253 (N.D. Ill. 1900), aff'd, 107 F. 619 (7th Cir. 1901).

—Borrowed Money
Borrowed money obtained from a bank and secured by a promissory note does not constitute a family expense and therefore one spouse cannot be held responsible for the default of the payment of the note executed by the other spouse under the Act. North Shore Community Bank & Trust Co. v. Kollar, 304 Ill. App. 3d 838, 237 Ill. Dec. 683, 710 N.E.2d 106 (1 Dist. 1999).

—Derivative Claims
The 1987 amendment to 735 ILCS 5/13-203 applies to claims under this section because they are derivative claims within the meaning of the language in 735 ILCS 5/13-203 referring to "other actions deriving from the injury of another." Dewey v. Zack, 272 Ill. App. 3d 742, 209 Ill. Dec. 465, 651 N.E.2d 643 (2 Dist. 1995).

—Divorces
This section, which requires parents to pay for the necessary expenses of their minor children, including reasonable attorney fees, does not apply where the parents are divorced. In re Van Winkle, 107 Ill. App. 3d 73, 62 Ill. Dec. 831, 437 N.E.2d 358 (3 Dist. 1982).

If a wife is guilty of conduct subsequent to the separation that would entitle the husband to a divorce, the husband should avail himself of his remedy in order to absolve himself from liability for her necessities under this section. Abraham Lincoln Mem. Hosp. Corp. v. Gordon, 111 Ill. App. 2d 179, 249 N.E.2d 311 (4 Dist. 1969).

—Public Utilities Act
The civil damages section of the Illinois Public Utilities Act (220 ILCS 5/5-201) is independent of the Wrongful Death Act (740 ILCS 180/1 et seq.), the survival section (see now 755 ILCS 5/27-6), or former section 15 of "An Act to revise the law in relation to husband and wife" (the family expense statute) (see now this section). Churchill v. Norfolk & W. Ry., 46 Ill. App. 3d 781, 5 Ill. Dec. 885, 362 N.E.2d 356 (4 Dist. 1977), aff'd, 73 Ill. 2d 127, 23 Ill. Dec. 58, 383 N.E.2d 929 (1978).

A widow, as plaintiff, seeking to recover under this section, was entitled under the Public Utilities Act (see now 625 ILCS 5/18c-7401 et seq.) to recover punitive damages as a person affected by the wilful and wanton tortious conduct of the defendant railroads in violating the safety rule promulgated by the Illinois Commerce Commission. National Bank v. Norfolk & W. Ry., 46 Ill. App. 3d 757, 5 Ill. Dec. 898, 362 N.E.2d 369 (4 Dist. 1977), aff'd, 73 Ill. 2d 160, 23 Ill. Dec. 48, 383 N.E.2d 919 (1978).

—Representative Capacity
Plaintiff shop owner was a competent witness at the trial under the Dead Man's Statute as the defendant was not being sued in any representative capacity, but rather was being sued for her own separate liability under this section; the Dead Man's Statute was not involved, because even if defendant's husband were alive, the defendant could still be sued alone for her separate liability under this section. Pope v. Kaleta, 90 Ill. App. 2d 61, 234 N.E.2d 109 (1 Dist. 1967).

Assignment
Even if plaintiff's second amended complaint had alleged an assignment to minor plaintiff of his parents' right to recover for medical expenses necessitated by his injuries, which it did not, any action brought upon such an assignment would be circumscribed by his parents' right of recovery which was nonexistent. Cullotta ex rel. Cullotta v. Cullotta, 287 Ill. App. 3d 967, 222 Ill. Dec. 845, 678 N.E.2d 717 (1 Dist. 1997).

Attorney Fees
The subrogee had no subrogation rights because of its ambiguous insurance policy language; therefore, it did not benefit from any common fund that was created and the insureds' attorney was not entitled to fees out of the fund. Garcia v. Gutierrez, 331 Ill. App. 3d 127, 264 Ill. Dec. 531, 770 N.E.2d 1227, 2002 Ill. App. LEXIS 457 (3 Dist. 2002).

The attorney fees provision in subdivision (a)(3) of this section is mandatory. North Shore Community Bank & Trust Co. v. Kollar, 304 Ill. App. 3d 838, 237 Ill. Dec. 683, 710 N.E.2d 106 (1 Dist. 1999).

Cause of Action
A cause of action to recover for the expenses of minors, including medical expenses, lies in the parents, not in the child. Dewey v. Zack, 272 Ill. App. 3d 742, 209 Ill. Dec. 465, 651 N.E.2d 643 (2 Dist. 1995).

Creditors
This section does not bar a creditor from bringing an action for recovering family expenses. Carle Clinic Ass'n v. Seten, 176 Ill. App. 3d 590, 125 Ill. Dec. 948, 531 N.E.2d 127 (4 Dist. 1988).

The burden rests on a creditor suing under this section to prove that the wife or husband is entitled to live separate and apart by mutual agreement or because of the misconduct of the spouse. Berenson v. Berenson, 34 Ill. App. 2d 376, 181 N.E.2d 357 (1 Dist. 1962).

A prior similar provision created a right in favor of the creditor and a liability against the husband and wife. Walker v. Houghteling, 107 F. 619 (7th Cir. 1901).

Disclosure of Public Facts
Plaintiff's spouse had a natural and proper interest in knowing about the credit card debts of her spouse and creditor's disclosure of said information to her did not satisfy the publicity element for the tort of public disclosure of private facts. Doe v. TCF Bank Ill., 302 Ill. App. 3d 839, 236 Ill. Dec. 375, 707 N.E.2d 220 (1 Dist. 1999), appeal denied, 183 Ill 2d 567, 238 Ill. Dec. 712, 712 N.E.2d 816 (1999).

Dismissal

—Inappropriate
The action against defendant, not being dependent upon his wife's presence in the lawsuit for the hospital services, could not have been dismissed even had the dismissal of the hospital's complaint against defendant been an appropriate sanction under

Dismissal (Cont'd)

—Inappropriate (Cont'd)

the circumstances. Presbyterian St. Luke's Hosp. v. Feil, 75 Ill. App. 3d 438, 31 Ill. Dec. 335, 394 N.E.2d 537 (1 Dist. 1979).

Expenses of the Family

—Adult Children

Parents, however, are not liable for expenses incurred by their adult children under this statute. Rodgers v. Consolidated R.R., 136 Ill. App. 3d 191, 90 Ill. Dec. 797, 482 N.E.2d 1080 (4 Dist. 1985).

—Business Expenses

Anything that is used as a general thing to carry on the farm of a farmer or the trade of a tradesman or mechanic is not to be regarded as a family expense within the meaning of subsection (a) of this section. Dunn v. Pickard Bros., 24 Ill. App. 423 (2 Dist. 1887).

—Carpet

Carpeting in the family home clearly benefits the entire family and consequently is an "expense of the family" as that phrase is used in the statute. Lyman v. Harbaugh, 117 Ill. App. 3d 732, 73 Ill. Dec. 81, 453 N.E.2d 906 (4 Dist. 1983).

—Consent Not Required

When making purchases for the support and welfare of the family, the consent and action of both husband and wife is not required to constitute a family expense. Hudson v. King Bros., 23 Ill. App. 118 (2 Dist. 1886).

—Credit Card Debt

Under former Ill.Rev.Stat., ch. 68, para. 15 (see now this section), a person having a charge account is liable for all purchases made by those authorized to buy on the account prior to a cancellation or withdrawal of the authority. Saks & Co. v. Brown, 347 Ill. App. 289, 106 N.E.2d 755 (1 Dist. 1952).

—Dwelling

The use and occupation of a house for a family dwelling under prior similar provisions is a legitimate family expense, and fell within the meaning of that term. Walker v. Houghteling, 107 F. 619 (7th Cir. 1901).

Where there was a written lease, executed by the husband alone, covering the period for which the suit was brought, and the suit was founded upon the provision of similar prior provisions that the wife, as well as the husband, shall be liable for family expenses, and upon the fact that the use of a dwelling house is, within the meaning of similar prior provisions, a family expense, the circumstance that the subject matter was the use and occupation of real estate was an incident only, the suit against both the husband and the wife was proper. Walker v. Houghteling, 107 F. 619 (7th Cir. 1901).

—Fur Coat

A fur coat was a family expense, so as to render the husband liable under former Family Expense Act (see now this section) where evidence did not tend to prove that his wife had a separate business in which fur coat was used and where, although defendant and his wife had separate homes, then lived together as husband and wife and were, therefore, a family. Louis Berman & Co. v. Dahlberg, 336 Ill. App. 233, 83 N.E.2d 380 (1 Dist. 1948).

—Liability Not Shown

Because there was no evidence to prove what services were rendered to defendant's son, how much the services were worth, and whether they were necessary and reasonable, defendant was not liable under this Act. Dreyer Medical Clinic v. Corral, 227 Ill. App. 3d 221, 169 Ill. Dec. 231, 591 N.E.2d 111 (2 Dist. 1992).

—Minor Children

Parents' medical expense claim under this section was tolled during the minority of an injured child pursuant to the tolling provision found in § 13-211 of the Code of Civil Procedure (735 ILCS 5/13-211). Beck v. Yatvin, 235 Ill. App. 3d 1085, 177 Ill. Dec. 488, 603 N.E.2d 558 (1 Dist. 1992), appeal denied, 149 Ill. 2d 647, 183 Ill. Dec. 858, 612 N.E.2d 510 (1993).

This section requires parents to pay for the necessary expenses of their minor children; this obligation includes the payment of the minor child's medical payments. Beck v. Yatvin, 235 Ill. App. 3d 1085, 177 Ill. Dec. 488, 603 N.E.2d 558 (1 Dist. 1992), appeal denied, 149 Ill. 2d 647, 183 Ill. Dec. 858, 612 N.E.2d 510 (1993).

—Rent

Where wife was sued, after the death of the husband, for house rent accruing under a lease with the husband prior to his death, the rent was a family expense properly chargeable to wife. Houghteling v. Walker, 100 F. 253 (N.D. Ill. 1900), aff'd, 107 F. 619 (7th Cir. 1901).

—Utilities

It is within the scope of the Illinois Commerce Commission's authority to pass upon a utility's "attribution" of an outstanding gas bill to the spouse of the customer of record — based upon the family expense statute — for the limited purpose of passing on his or her application for service; a utility should not be required to extend service to an applicant who by all appearances is liable for an outstanding gas bill under the family expense statute, even if the service for that time was in the spouse's name. DiBello v. Illinois Commerce Comm'n, 241 Ill. App. 3d 1088, 182 Ill. Dec. 861, 610 N.E.2d 730 (4 Dist. 1993).

Where the provision of gas service was an expenditure which benefited the family, a utility company could look to the wife for the payment of gas service, even though the husband was the customer of record. Peoples Gas Light & Coke Co. v. Illinois Commerce Comm'n, 222 Ill. App. 3d 738, 165 Ill. Dec. 162, 584 N.E.2d 341 (1 Dist. 1991).

Utility costs incurred by a husband were not "family expenses" where they were incurred after the parties had separated, in homes where the wife never resided; where it could not be said that the utility expenses contributed to the welfare of the family generally or that the expenses served to maintain the integrity of the family unit; and where the husband alone benefitted from the expenditures. Central Ill. Light Co. v. Illinois Commerce Comm'n, 204 Ill. App. 3d 1, 149 Ill. Dec. 697, 562 N.E.2d 4 (3 Dist. 1990).

Family in Fact

—Not Shown

Where the appellees, husband and wife, had ceased to live together for some months before purchasing ladies' and children's apparel from the appellants, even though the appellants had no notice of such separation, the trial court rightly decided that the appellees were not liable under subsection (a) of this section for family expenses since there was no family. Schlesinger & Mayer v. Keifer, 30 Ill. App. 253 (1 Dist. 1888).

—Required

It is essential to the liability of a husband or wife, for family expenses, that they constitute a family in fact. Schlesinger & Mayer v. Keifer, 30 Ill. App. 253 (1 Dist. 1888).

Funeral and Medical Expenses

Surviving spouse's recovery of the medical, hospital, and funeral expenses for which he or she is liable under 750 ILCS 65/15 of the Rights of Married Persons Act is not a cause of action for injuries to the intoxicated person himself (235 ILCS 5/6—21) and is not barred by the 1985 amendment to the Dramshop Act, Ill. Pub. Act 84-271. Schramer v. Tiger Ath. Ass'n, 351 Ill. App. 3d 1016, 287 Ill. Dec. 350, 815 N.E.2d 994, 2004 Ill. App. LEXIS 1099 (2 Dist. 2004).

The medical expenses of the defendant's deceased husband, including interest and reasonable attorney's fees, were a family expense within the meaning of the statute where: (1) upon entering the hospital shortly before his death, the deceased husband signed an admission agreement which required him to pay 18 percent interest annually on any medical costs he failed to pay before he left the hospital and also permitted the plaintiff to recover reasonable attorney fees it might incur while seeking payment; and (2) there was no evidence to support the defendant's contention that her deceased husband suffered from a "life-threatening illness" when he entered the hospital and, therefore, could not freely assent to the admission agreement. Boswell Mem. Hosp. v. Bongiorno, 314 Ill. App. 3d 620, 247 Ill. Dec. 421, 732 N.E.2d 137, 2000 Ill. App. LEXIS 519 (2 Dist. 2000).

Inasmuch as it is the parents of the minor who receive a benefit from the payment of medical expenses by an insurer, the insurer may not recover those expenses from the minor's estate. Estate of

Funeral and Medical Expenses (Cont'd)
Aimone v. State Health Benefit Plan/Equicor, 248 Ill. App. 3d 882, 188 Ill. Dec. 821, 619 N.E.2d 185 (3 Dist. 1993), cert. denied, 154 Ill. 2d 559, 197 Ill. Dec. 485, 631 N.E.2d 707 (1994).

Since the obligation to pay the child's medical expense is on the parent, a cause of action to recover for medical expenses lies in the parent, rather than the child. Beck v. Yatvin, 235 Ill. App. 3d 1085, 177 Ill. Dec. 488, 603 N.E.2d 558 (1 Dist. 1992), appeal denied, 149 Ill. 2d 647, 183 Ill. Dec. 858, 612 N.E.2d 510 (1993).

A noncustodial divorced parent is legally liable for the hospital and medical expenses of his or her minor child regardless of the parent's marital status. Mercy Ctr. For Health Care Servs. V. Lemke, 199 Ill. App. 3d 958, 146 Ill. Dec. 1, 557 N.E.2d 943 (2 Dist. 1990).

This section has been held to authorize a mother to sue a third-party tortfeasor to recover medical expenses incurred by her son, but makes no provision for the liability of one spouse to another, since at common law only the husband was liable for family expenses. Setinc v. Masny, 185 Ill. App. 3d 15, 133 Ill. Dec. 71, 540 N.E.2d 937 (3 Dist. 1989).

Since the parents of a minor child are responsible for the child's medical expenses, and a minor child is neither the beneficiary of payments under an insurance contract, nor a third-party beneficiary as to such payments, minor had no legal interest in the payment of insurance proceeds for her medical treatment. International Union of Operating Eng'rs Local 841 v. Hickman, 190 Ill. App. 3d 658, 138 Ill. Dec. 1, 546 N.E.2d 1056 (5 Dist. 1989).

Parents are liable for the medical expenses of their minor children. Estate of Hammon v. Aetna Life & Cas. Co., 141 Ill. App. 3d 963, 96 Ill. Dec. 270, 491 N.E.2d 84 (1 Dist. 1986).

The obligation to pay medical expenses is on the parent, and the cause of action to recover for the medical expenses lies in the parent, not in the child. Estate of Hammon v. Aetna Life & Cas. Co., 141 Ill. App. 3d 963, 96 Ill. Dec. 270, 491 N.E.2d 84 (1 Dist. 1986).

The parents' action for recovery of medical expenses was derivative, where it arose from an injury to their minor child and from their obligation to pay those expenses under the former Husband and Wife Act (see now this section); the parents' action, however, was not tolled during the injured child's minority. Curtis v. Womeldorff, 145 Ill. App. 3d 1006, 99 Ill. Dec. 807, 496 N.E.2d 500 (4 Dist. 1986).

Parents are liable for the medical expenses of their minor children, and any cause of action to recover for medical expenses is that of the parent and not the child; and is governed by the applicable limitations period for derivative causes of action. Reimers v. Honda Motor Co., 150 Ill. App. 3d 840, 104 Ill. Dec. 165, 502 N.E.2d 428 (1 Dist. 1986).

Recovery of funeral expenses based upon out-of-pocket payment for which there was a legal liability have been allowed under this section. Rodgers v. Consolidated R.R., 136 Ill. App. 3d 191, 90 Ill. Dec. 797, 482 N.E.2d 1080 (4 Dist. 1985).

In order for one parent to recover for his child's medical expenses against the other parent, the parent must not only be legally liable, but the basis for such liability must exist prior to the creation of the charges and not arise due to a voluntary assumption of financial responsibility after the fact. Tully v. Cuddy, 139 Ill. App. 3d 697, 94 Ill. Dec. 218, 487 N.E.2d 1095 (1 Dist. 1985).

The parents' suit for the injuries suffered by their minor daughter was derivative where the right of action arose out of the injury to the person of another and their obligation under the former Husband and Wife Act (Ill.Rev.Stat., ch. 68, para. 1 (1973), see now this section) to pay for medical expenses. Severe v. Miller, 120 Ill. App. 3d 550, 76 Ill. Dec. 34, 458 N.E.2d 173 (4 Dist. 1983).

Medical expenses are properly considered expenses of the family under this section. St. John's Hosp. v. Enloe ex rel. Enloe, 109 Ill. App. 3d 1089, 65 Ill. Dec. 553, 441 N.E.2d 868 (4 Dist. 1982).

Recovery of funeral and medical expenses is based on the survivors' liability for them under this Act and is not grounded in the Wrongful Death Act (740 ILCS 180/0.01). Elliott v. Willis, 89 Ill. App. 3d 1144, 45 Ill. Dec. 287, 412 N.E.2d 638 (4 Dist. 1980), rev'd on other grounds, 92 Ill. 2d 530, 65 Ill. Dec. 852, 442 N.E.2d 163 (1982).

Since the obligation to pay medical payments is on the parent, the cause of action to recover for the medical expenses lies in the parent not in the child, and while the parents may assign their cause of action to the child, the assignee must prove that the assignor had a cause of action and the assignee is subject to any defense which might have been raised against the assignor; thus a child cannot recover for medical expenses where the parent could not. Kennedy ex rel. Kennedy v. Kiss, 89 Ill. App. 3d 890, 45 Ill. Dec. 273, 412 N.E.2d 624 (1 Dist. 1980).

Rule that parents are responsible for medical expenses of minor child is not affected by the fact that an insurance company paid at least part of the expenses since the payment of those expenses was to the benefit of the parents, who were liable for the expenses, rather than for the benefit of the child, who was not. Kennedy ex rel. Kennedy v. Kiss, 89 Ill. App. 3d 890, 45 Ill. Dec. 273, 412 N.E.2d 624 (1 Dist. 1980).

Since the cause of action for medical expenses lay in the plaintiff's parents, in order to recover such expenses the plaintiff was required to prove her parents free from contributory negligence. Kennedy ex rel. Kennedy v. Kiss, 89 Ill. App. 3d 890, 45 Ill. Dec. 273, 412 N.E.2d 624 (1 Dist. 1980).

Deceased child's medical expenses were necessaries, for which her parents were primarily liable; but, because it was the minor's estate which was recovering under a settlement agreement with tortfeasor, and the minor's estate received no benefit from the payment of the medical expenses by parent's insurance company, the company had no subrogation right against a payment by the tortfeasor as part of the settlement of a claim by the minor's estate. Estate of Woodring v. Liberty Mut. Fire Ins. Co., 71 Ill. App. 3d 158, 27 Ill. Dec. 399, 389 N.E.2d 211 (2 Dist. 1979); Estate of Hammon v. Aetna Life & Cas. Co., 141 Ill. App. 3d 963, 96 Ill. Dec. 270, 491 N.E.2d 84 (1 Dist. 1986).

It makes no sense whatsoever to permit a recovery by the widow individually when she has paid funeral expenses and deny recovery to the administrator of the estate when those expenses have been paid by the administrator, and by this proceeding the administrator seeks to recover the expenditures that decreased the decedent's estate. National Bank v. Norfolk & W. Ry., 46 Ill. App. 3d 757, 5 Ill. Dec. 898, 362 N.E.2d 369 (4 Dist. 1977), aff'd, 73 Ill. 2d 160, 23 Ill. Dec. 48, 383 N.E.2d 919 (1978).

Right of recovery by hospital for services performed on wife still exist by force of the common law, if the wife is living separate from the husband because of his fault or wrong, or with his consent. Abraham Lincoln Mem. Hosp. Corp. v. Gordon, 111 Ill. App. 2d 179, 249 N.E.2d 311 (4 Dist. 1969).

Under the former Husband and Wife Act (former Ill.Rev.Stat., ch. 68, para. 15) (see now this section), funeral expenses were within the meaning of family expenses as between spouses and such necessarily applied as between a minor child and parent. Graul v. Adrian, 32 Ill. 2d 345, 205 N.E.2d 444 (1965).

The common law should be construed to permit the recovery of funeral and medical expenses in an action either by the decedent's estate, or by the surviving spouse. Saunders v. Schultz, 20 Ill. 2d 301, 170 N.E.2d 163 (1960).

The expense of hospital care for treatment, detention and training at a state operated institution for the mentally ill, fell within the category of necessaries, and patient's husband was liable for expenses incurred by his wife while in a state mental hospital, which would also have been true as to private hospitals. Bennett v. Bennett, 27 Ill. App. 2d 24, 169 N.E.2d 172 (2 Dist. 1960).

At common law and independent of the former Family Expense Act the husband was liable for his wife's funeral expenses. Staken v. Shanle, 23 Ill. App. 2d 269, 162 N.E.2d 604 (3 Dist. 1959).

This section imposed a legal liability upon the plaintiff for the hospital, medical and funeral expenses of her husband even though they may have been living apart. Fortner v. Norris, 19 Ill. App. 2d 212, 153 N.E.2d 433 (3 Dist. 1958).

Under a similar prior provision, a divorced father was not liable for medical services performed for his child who was in the custody of the mother. Hess v. Slutsky, 224 Ill. App. 419 (1 Dist. 1922).

Hospital Lien

Family Expenses Statute was not an exclusive remedy for a hospital nor did it conflict with the Hospital Lien Statute (770 ILCS 35/1); therefore, hospital was not precluded from enforcing a lien on minor's personal injury claim. St. John's Hosp. v. Enloe ex rel. Enloe, 109 Ill. App. 3d 1089, 65 Ill. Dec. 553, 441 N.E.2d 868 (4 Dist. 1982).

Items of Luxury

—Jewelry

The question of whether articles of jewelry or similar items of

Items of Luxury (Cont'd)

—Jewelry (Cont'd)
luxury constitute a family expense depends upon the nature and actual use of the item in question and trial court erred in determining as a matter of law that certain jewelry purchased by defendant wife conferred no substantial benefit to her family. White v. Neeland, 114 Ill. App. 3d 174, 69 Ill. Dec. 931, 448 N.E.2d 649 (3 Dist. 1983).

Judgment Reduced
Since plaintiff's cause of action here was based upon the Family Expense Statute, the five year statute of limitations applied to the various sales slips introduced into evidence; all sales slips dated five years prior to filing date were barred by the five year statute of limitations, reducing the judgment. Pope v. Kaleta, 90 Ill. App. 2d 61, 234 N.E.2d 109 (1 Dist. 1967).

Legislative Intent
This section is based on a legislative intent that a parent be held responsible if the claim is for a family expense, which was necessary and reasonable. Carle Clinic Ass'n v. Seten, 176 Ill. App. 3d 590, 125 Ill. Dec. 948, 531 N.E.2d 127 (4 Dist. 1988).

Liability Between Parents
A mother who had not paid son's medical expenses but is liable for them had neither a common law nor a statutory basis for a cause of action against the father. Setinc v. Masny, 185 Ill. App. 3d 15, 133 Ill. Dec. 71, 540 N.E.2d 937 (3 Dist. 1989).

A father is not liable under this section, where the son is not a minor nor when the parents divorced. Sapp v. Johnston, 15 Ill. App. 3d 119, 303 N.E.2d 429 (3 Dist. 1973).

Husband was barred from seeking child's medical expenses because his wife, by acquiescing in the guardian's claim for this item of damages, waived the parents' claim for such family expenses. Houghton v. Novak, 9 Ill. App. 3d 699, 292 N.E.2d 905 (2 Dist. 1973).

Liability for Support
Where the father contended that the former Family Expense Act (Ill.Rev.Stat., ch. 68, para. 15) (see now 750 ILCS 65/15) was relevant to the establishment of his liability for the support of a minor, the argument had no bearing on a case brought under the former Juvenile Court Act (Ill.Rev.Stat., ch. 37, para. 704-1, et. seq.) (see now 705 ILCS 405/3-15). People v. Nelsen, 54 Ill. App. 3d 412, 12 Ill. Dec. 18, 369 N.E.2d 515 (2 Dist. 1977).

Where mother had ample assets to support and maintain her children, she was not entitled to reimbursement from the minors' estates for the cost of supporting her children, including food, clothing, medical care, camp, religious school, the purchase of a piano for her daughter and a proportionate share of the taxes, maintenance and insurance for the family home. Stillerman v. Schultz, 39 Ill. App. 2d 380, 188 N.E.2d 726 (1 Dist. 1963).

Liability of Spouse
A wife's individual liability under this statute precluded an action against her husband's estate for reimbursement for payments she made for her own support. McGloon v. Zmigrocki, 191 Ill. App. 3d 968, 139 Ill. Dec. 53, 548 N.E.2d 438 (1 Dist. 1989).

A spouse may be legally liable for the hospital and medical expenses of the other spouse. St. Mary of Nazareth Hosp. v. Kuczaj, 174 Ill. App. 3d 268, 123 Ill. Dec. 745, 528 N.E.2d 290 (1 Dist. 1988).

A husband may be liable for expenses incurred by a wife irrespective of whether they were living separately or whether the husband consented to the expense. St. Mary of Nazareth Hosp. v. Kuczaj, 174 Ill. App. 3d 268, 123 Ill. Dec. 745, 528 N.E.2d 290 (1 Dist. 1988).

Where a wife's counteraffidavit rebutted her husband's assertion that she deserted him and thus he could not be held liable for her medical expenses under this section, and a judgment for dissolution required him to maintain adequate hospital insurance coverage for the time period covering the costs in issue, negating any inference that the separation of the parties barred his liability, the wife's affidavit raised a question of fact as to the husband's liability and summary judgment should not have been granted as a matter of law. St. Mary of Nazareth Hosp. v. Kuczaj, 174 Ill. App. 3d 268, 123 Ill. Dec. 745, 528 N.E.2d 290 (1 Dist. 1988).

All this statute does is give to third parties for expenses of the family a remedy against both husband and wife, and that is all, for to ascribe a larger import is to deny the meaning of plain words and accepted canons of construction. Bennett v. Bennett, 27 Ill. App. 2d 24, 169 N.E.2d 172 (2 Dist. 1960).

Liability under this section is not limited to necessaries. Louis Berman & Co. v. Dahlberg, 336 Ill. App. 233, 83 N.E.2d 380 (1 Dist. 1948).

This section imposes upon the wife a personal liability for indebtedness incurred for the expenses of the family, and not merely a charge upon her property to be enforced by proceedings in rem. Houghteling v. Walker, 100 F. 253 (N.D. Ill. 1900), aff'd, 107 F. 619 (7th Cir. 1901).

The liability of the wife for family expenses is not limited to necessary family expenses. Houghteling v. Walker, 100 F. 253 (N.D. Ill. 1900), aff'd, 107 F. 619 (7th Cir. 1901).

Money or securities in the hands of a married woman were held properly subjected to the payment of a personal judgment for family expenses. Myers v. Field, 146 Ill. 50, 34 N.E. 424 (1893).

Subsection (a) of this section does not limit the liability of the property of the wife to expenditures for necessary family expenses; it applies to the expenses of the family without limitation or qualification as to kind or amount, and does not depend upon the wealth, habits or social position of the party. Hudson v. King Bros., 23 Ill. App. 118 (2 Dist. 1886).

Limitations Period
Under the extended limitations period applicable to plaintiffs' claims, pursuant to the 1987 amendment to 735 ILCS 5/13-203, plaintiffs' Family Expense Act claims were timely where plaintiffs alleged that they discovered the injuries giving rise to their claims in 1992 and filed their claims on June 1, 1993, within two years of the discovery of the injuries, thereby satisfying the general statute of limitations provided by 735 ILCS 5/13-212, even if it still applied to plaintiffs' claims; injuries allegedly occurred at birth on September 19 to 20, 1987 and thus, plaintiffs filed their claims less than eight years after the date of the occurrences which allegedly caused infant's injuries, i.e., within the applicable period of repose under the 1987 amendment to 735 ILCS 5/13-203. Accordingly, under the 1987 amendment to 735 ILCS 5/13-203, plaintiffs timely filed their Family Expense Act claims. Dewey v. Zack, 272 Ill. App. 3d 742, 209 Ill. Dec. 465, 651 N.E.2d 643 (2 Dist. 1995).

Where the cause of action for expenses alleged in an amended complaint, in which plaintiffs sought to recover expenses pursuant to this Act, arose out of the same transaction as set forth in the original complaint, filed pursuant to the Illinois Wrongful Death Act (740 ILCS 180/1), the amended claim was not time barred since it was clear that plaintiffs intended to bring the cause of action for medical and funeral expenses in their original complaint because they made substantially the same allegations in their amended complaint as they did in the original complaint; defendants were not prejudiced because they were informed by plaintiffs' original complaint of the facts which formed the basis of the claim asserted in the amended pleading. Joyce v. Wilner, 156 Ill. App. 3d 702, 109 Ill. Dec. 108, 509 N.E.2d 769 (3 Dist. 1987).

Father's claim for reimbursement for his medical expenditures under the Husband and Wife Act (see now this section) was subject to the two year limitation, and the minor-assignee took assignment subject to that limitation period which was not tolled; therefore, the court did not err in failing to allow plaintiff leave to file an amended, verified complaint. Curtis v. Womeldorff, 145 Ill. App. 3d 1006, 99 Ill. Dec. 807, 496 N.E.2d 500 (4 Dist. 1986).

Where the complaint and summons show when the action for payment was commenced and the allegations of the complaint gave the various dates on which the causes of action accrued, and the answer showed the defendant was relying on the five year statute of limitations, from these two pleadings some of the invoices were barred by the statute of limitations, if the five year statute was adopted; therefore plaintiff shop owner did not admit the truth of the affirmative defenses raised for the first time in defendant's answer by not filing a reply, and a reply was not required in the circumstances. Pope v. Kaleta, 90 Ill. App. 2d 61, 234 N.E.2d 109 (1 Dist. 1967).

Since this section does not contain a statute of limitations section, the general statute of limitations controls. Pope v. Kaleta, 90 Ill. App. 2d 61, 234 N.E.2d 109 (1 Dist. 1967).

Necessaries

Although the wife and her husband lived apart, expenses incurred to supply the wife with necessaries were family expenses under the statute if she was living apart from her husband through no fault of her own. McGloon v. Zmigrocki, 191 Ill. App. 3d 968, 139 Ill. Dec. 53, 548 N.E.2d 438 (1 Dist. 1989).

A minor is liable for necessaries only if the sale is on his own credit, and not on the credit of another, including his parents. Estate of Hammon v. Aetna Life & Cas. Co., 141 Ill. App. 3d 963, 96 Ill. Dec. 270, 491 N.E.2d 84 (1 Dist. 1986).

Nothing in either the Mental Health Code (see 405 ILCS 5/1-100 et seq.) or this section detracts from the common law duty of a husband to supply his wife with necessaries, which, of course, includes support. Bennett v. Bennett, 27 Ill. App. 2d 24, 169 N.E.2d 172 (2 Dist. 1960).

The fact that the wife may have ample means to finance necessaries in no wise alters or detracts from the responsibility and obligation of the husband to her, and the responsibility or duty does not, to state it another way, depend upon the inadequacy of the wife's means but on the marriage relation. Bennett v. Bennett, 27 Ill. App. 2d 24, 169 N.E.2d 172 (2 Dist. 1960).

Necessity Requirement

Whether or not the expense of an item is a family expense does not depend on whether that item is a necessity. Lyman v. Harbaugh, 117 Ill. App. 3d 732, 73 Ill. Dec. 81, 453 N.E.2d 906 (4 Dist. 1983).

No Consent Requirement

The statute contains neither an express spousal consent requirement nor an implicit spousal consent requirement. Lyman v. Harbaugh, 117 Ill. App. 3d 732, 73 Ill. Dec. 81, 453 N.E.2d 906 (4 Dist. 1983).

Parental Responsibility

The primary responsibility for family expenses of minor children, regardless of the marital status of the parents, remains with the parents. Carle Clinic Ass'n v. Seten, 176 Ill. App. 3d 590, 125 Ill. Dec. 948, 531 N.E.2d 127 (4 Dist. 1988).

Procedure

Defendant's denial of any liability under this section did not require the plaintiff to reply in order to avoid an admission. Pope v. Kaleta, 90 Ill. App. 2d 61, 234 N.E.2d 109 (1 Dist. 1967).

Recovery

—Not Allowed

The trial court properly dismissed plaintiff's claim under this Act to recover for injuries sustained by his 19 year old daughter, despite his assertions that she was not fully emancipated. Tully v. Cuddy, 139 Ill. App. 3d 697, 94 Ill. Dec. 218, 487 N.E.2d 1095 (1 Dist. 1985).

Reimbursement

—Direct Payment Allowed

The "for the benefit of the injured person" language which appeared in the policy appeared to contemplate direct payment by the insurer to providers of services for the injured person, and if such amounts are payable under the policy, a parent who has made the initial payment to the provider can be paid directly. Gattorna v. American States Ins. Co., 122 Ill. App. 3d 582, 78 Ill. Dec. 91, 461 N.E.2d 675 (2 Dist. 1984).

—Not Allowed

Insurer was not entitled to a lien on any monies paid to or on behalf of injured minor and was not entitled to receive monies from settlement fund. Klem v. Mann, 279 Ill. App. 3d 735, 216 Ill. Dec. 454, 665 N.E.2d 514 (1 Dist. 1996), appeal denied, 168 Ill. 2d 594, 219 Ill. Dec. 565, 671 N.E.2d 732 (1996).

Standing

Adult child did not plead she was obligated individually to pay for father's medical expenses and therefore could not bring an individual claim under this Act. Gragg v. Calandra, 297 Ill. App. 3d 639, 231 Ill. Dec. 711, 696 N.E.2d 1282 (2 Dist. 1998), appeal denied, 181 Ill. 2d 570, 235 Ill. Dec. 941, 706 N.E.2d 496 (1998).

—Jurisdiction

Because this section is a state statute which clearly affected a utility company's ability to collect revenue for its service, the Illinois Commerce Commission was authorized to determine the utility's right to bill a spouse who had not been directly billed under 220 ILCS 5/4-201 for outstanding gas bills. Peoples Gas Light & Coke Co. v. Illinois Commerce Comm'n, 222 Ill. App. 3d 738, 165 Ill. Dec. 162, 584 N.E.2d 341 (1 Dist. 1991).

—No Liability During Estrangement

A wife was not liable under this section for a utility service debt incurred by her husband while the parties were separated and maintaining separate houses. Central Ill. Light Co. v. Illinois Commerce Comm'n, 204 Ill. App. 3d 1, 149 Ill. Dec. 697, 562 N.E.2d 4 (3 Dist. 1990).

Voluntary Payment

When one obligated under this statute voluntarily pays family expenses, those voluntary payments are not reimbursable. McGloon v. Zmigrocki, 191 Ill. App. 3d 968, 139 Ill. Dec. 53, 548 N.E.2d 438 (1 Dist. 1989).

LEGAL PERIODICALS

For article, "Illinois Courts: Vital Developers of Tort Law as Constitutional Vanguards, Statutory Interpreters, and Common Law Adjudicators", see 30 Loy. U. Chi. L.J. 183 (1999).

For note and comment, "Wrongful Death in Illinois: a Statute Comes of Age," see 62 Chi.-Kent L. Rev. (1985).

RESEARCH REFERENCES

Wife's liability for necessaries furnished husband. 11 ALR4th 1160.

What constitutes "extraordinary" or similar medical or dental expenses for purposes of divorce decree requiring one parent to pay such expenses for child in custody of other parent. 39 ALR4th 502.

Postsecondary education as within nondivorced parent's child support obligation. 42 ALR4th 819.

Support Provisions of Judicial Decree or Order as Limit of Parent's Liability for Expenses of Child. 35 ALR5th 757.

750 ILCS 65/16 [Removal of children from homestead]

Sec. 16. Neither the husband nor wife can remove the other or their children from their homestead without the consent of the other, unless the owner of the property shall, in good faith, provide another homestead suitable to the condition in life of the family; and if he abandons her, she is entitled to the custody of their minor children, unless a court of competent jurisdiction, upon application for that purpose, shall otherwise direct.
(Source: R.S. 1874, p. 576.)

Note.

This section was Ill.Rev.Stat., Ch. 40, para. 1016.

CASE NOTES

Analysis

Abandonment
Divorce Decree
Homestead Rights
Partition
Right to Occupancy
Setoff

Abandonment

Where wife obtained a divorce, and no mention of homestead was made in the decree and she then removed from the premises, and

Abandonment (Cont'd)
where prior to abandoning the premises, she could have obtained a homestead in the divorce proceeding, but failed to do so, the husband was vested with a homestead in the real estate, and his former wife abandoned any homestead rights which she might have had by quitting the premises and failing to have a homestead awarded to her in the divorce proceeding. Taylor v. Bukowski, 19 Ill. 2d 586, 169 N.E.2d 89 (1960).

Divorce Decree
Unless a decree for divorce specifically disposes of the homestead estate as authorized by 735 ILCS 5/12-905, the disposition of the homestead right is subject to the further provisions of the code and other pertinent statutory enactments. Taylor v. Bukowski, 19 Ill. 2d 586, 169 N.E.2d 89 (1960).

Homestead Rights
The Rights of Married Persons Act, 750 ILCS 65/16, did not bestow upon the non-titled spouse an absolute right in a particular piece of property; a titleholder is free to convey the homestead so long as another homestead is provided. In re Carver, Bankr. , 2003 Bankr. LEXIS 70 (Bankr. S.D. Ill. Jan. 24, 2003).

This section and the Release of Homestead statute (765 ILCS 5/27), when read in conjunction with the exemption statute (735 ILCS 5/12-901), conclusively entitle a nonowner spouse to claim a homestead exemption in the marital residence owned by the other spouse. In re Miller, 174 Bankr. 279 (Bankr. N.D. Ill. 1994).

Where the wife continued to reside in the property as her homestead, she thereby acquired, under former Ill.Rev.Stat., ch. 68, para. 16 (see now this section), certain rights which she was entitled to, and of which she could not be deprived, unless another homestead is provided or unless an estate of homestead were set apart for her. Cohn v. Litwin, 311 Ill. App. 55, 35 N.E.2d 410 (1 Dist. 1941).

Partition
Under section 1 of the Homestead Act, former Ill.Rev.Stat., ch. 52, para. 1, (see now 735 ILCS 5/12-901) homestead exemption was not available between co-tenants, and this prohibition encompassed situations in which the exemption was sought to be asserted by one spouse against another in the course of partition proceedings, since prohibition barred a co-tenant from claiming the monetary equivalent of a homestead exemption under former section 16, Ill.Rev.Stat., ch. 68, para. 16 (see now this section). Phillips v. Phillips, 74 Ill. 2d 27, 23 Ill. Dec. 102, 383 N.E.2d 973 (1978).

Premises which were subject to a divorce proceeding could be partitioned even though they were occupied as a home by the minor children. Tucker v. Tucker, 29 Ill. App. 3d 489, 330 N.E.2d 274 (4 Dist. 1975).

As between a husband and wife, each occupying the premises, there is authority that the homestead is owned jointly; if, however, a husband seeks by partition to deprive his wife of the right of occupancy, he must either provide another suitable homestead for her, or set off to her the statutory homestead in cash. Taylor v. Bukowski, 19 Ill. 2d 586, 169 N.E.2d 89 (1960).

Depending on the circumstances, it may not be inequitable to equally partition jointly owned property in which both the husband and wife have a right of homestead, without setting off a homestead to either. Taylor v. Bukowski, 19 Ill. 2d 586, 169 N.E.2d 89 (1960).

Right to Occupancy
It is within the power of the court to grant the right to occupy the homestead property to either party in a divorce action, thus the court may award the right to occupy the homestead to the party into whose custody the children are given, even though the title thereto is in the name of the other party; nevertheless, where a homestead exists, neither can change the residence of the other from that homestead without such other's consent, or unless another suitable homestead is provided. Klebba v. Klebba, 108 Ill. App. 2d 32, 246 N.E.2d 681 (5 Dist. 1969).

Setoff
Under former Ill.Rev.Stat., ch. 52, para. 1 and 16 (see now this section) the trial court properly ruled that defendant, in an action seeking the partition of the premises where plaintiff and defendant had lived and which was owned by them equally as joint tenants, was not entitled to setoff for homestead on her behalf before any division of the property or proceeds of the sale thereof. Phillips v. Phillips, 56 Ill. App. 3d 276, 14 Ill. Dec. 293, 372 N.E.2d 98 (4 Dist. 1977), aff'd, 74 Ill. 2d 27, 23 Ill. Dec. 102, 383 N.E.2d 973 (1978).

The trial court properly denied a wife's motion to set off homestead, where the equities between the parties had been considered in a prior divorce decree which provided that the parties should share the homestead equally. Tucker v. Tucker, 29 Ill. App. 3d 489, 330 N.E.2d 274 (4 Dist. 1975).

750 ILCS 65/17 [Spouse under legal disability]

Sec. 17. When the husband or wife is under legal disability and therefore incapable of executing a deed or mortgage, and relinquishing or conveying his or her right to homestead in the real property of the other, such other person may present his or her petition to the circuit court in the county where the petitioner resides, or where the real estate to be affected is situated, setting forth the facts, and particularly describing the real estate sought to be conveyed or mortgaged, and asking for an order authorizing the petitioner, or some other person, to execute a deed or mortgage for the person who is under legal disability, and thereby relinquish his or her right of homestead in the real estate.
(Source: P.A. 83-706.)

Note.
This section was Ill.Rev.Stat., Ch. 40, para. 1017.

CASE NOTES

Purpose
The object of a proceeding authorized by a former similar provision was to enable a husband or wife whose spouse had become insane to sell the real estate of the insane spouse when circumstances required it and to convey the title free of any claim of the insane spouse; the purchaser of the real estate was not a proper party to this type of proceeding as he had no rights to be enforced, and the proceeding was not for his benefit, but was for the benefit of the owner of the property. Vyverberg v. Vyverberg, 310 Ill. 599, 142 N.E. 191 (1923).

750 ILCS 65/18 [Petition to convey real estate; notice]

Sec. 18. The petition shall be verified by the oath of the petitioner, and shall be filed in the office of the clerk of the circuit court. Notice of the filing of such petition shall be given to such person who is under disability, by service of summons or by publication, as provided in other civil cases. The court shall appoint some discreet person or attorney as guardian for the person alleged to be under disability, and the appointed person shall ascertain as to the propriety, good faith and necessity of the petition, and shall have power to resist such application and subpoena witnesses and take depositions to disprove any of the matters in the petition, or show the impropriety of granting the same.
(Source: P.A. 83-706.)

Note.
This section was Ill.Rev.Stat., Ch. 40, para. 1018.

750 ILCS 65/19 [Granting petition to convey]

Sec. 19. If the court is satisfied upon the hearing that the petition was made in good faith, and the prayer thereof ought to be granted, then the court shall enter a judgment granting such prayer, and authorizing some discreet and proper person to make, execute, acknowledge and deliver jointly with said petitioner all such conveyances or mortgages, and of such parcels of land as shall in said judgment be specified.
(Source: P.A. 79-1365.)

Note.
This section was Ill.Rev.Stat., Ch. 40, para. 1019.

750 ILCS 65/20 [Security for petition]

Sec. 20. The court shall require of the petitioner, at the time and as one of the conditions of entering the judgment, such security for the protection of the interests, and for the proper support of such person under legal disability, as the court deems satisfactory, and may from time to time renew or change the same, or require additional security. Such security shall be deposited with the clerk of the court, and actions may be maintained thereon for the benefit of such person under legal disability in any court of competent jurisdiction; or the court may order such portion of the money received from the sale of such property as the court deems just, to be set apart in such manner as the court shall direct, for the use and benefit of such person under legal disability; and such sum so set apart shall be and remain subject to the control and order of the court.
(Source: P.A. 84-1308.)

Note.
This section was Ill.Rev.Stat., Ch. 40, para. 1020.

CASE NOTES

Analysis

Appellate Review
Protection of Purchaser

Appellate Review
Whether the trial court correctly estimated the extent and value of an appellee's interest in real property was not a question to be considered on a bill of review as against purchasers in good faith for value, but where the court had jurisdiction, it was authorized to decide upon the security that was necessary, and whether the bond presented was satisfactory. Vyverberg v. Vyverberg, 310 Ill. 599, 142 N.E. 191 (1923).

Protection of Purchaser
A purchaser of real property subject to a right of the seller's insane spouse under former Ill.Rev.Stat., ch. 68, para. 17, (see now this section) would be protected if the facts necessary to give the court jurisdiction appeared on the face of the record, and the fact that a bond was forged would not affect those subsequently dealing with the property. Vyverberg v. Vyverberg, 310 Ill. 599, 142 N.E. 191 (1923).

750 ILCS 65/21 [Validity of deeds or mortgages]

Sec. 21. All deeds or mortgages authorized by and executed under the order of any court, made as hereinbefore provided, shall be valid and shall convey all the homestead interest of such person under legal disability in and to the real estate so conveyed or mortgaged, as fully as if such person had been under no legal disability, and executed and acknowledged the same in due form of law.
(Source: P.A. 83-706.)

Note.
This section was Ill.Rev.Stat., Ch. 40, para. 1021.

750 ILCS 65/22 [Estate of tenancy by the entirety]

Sec. 22. Nothing in this Act abolishes or prevents the creation and enjoyment of the estate of tenancy by the entirety with respect to any devise, conveyance, assignment, or other transfer of property, including a beneficial interest in a land trust, maintained or intended for maintenance as a homestead by both husband and wife during coverture made or executed on or after October 1, 1990.

This amendatory Act of 1995 is declarative of existing law.
(Source: P.A. 86-966; 86-1028; 87-421; 89-88, § 10; 89-438, § 10.)

Note.
This section was Ill.Rev.Stat., Ch. 40, para. 1022.
There were two effective date sections listed in P.A. 89-438. One made the amendments to this section effective December 15, 1995 and one made the amendments to this section effective June 1, 1996.

Effect of Amendments.
The 1995 amendment by P.A. 89-88, effective June 30, 1995 and P.A. 89-438, effective December 15, 1995 made identical changes, they each: in the first paragraph, deleted "homestead" preceding "property", inserted "including a beneficial interest in a land trust" and inserted "or intended for maintenance"; and added a second paragraph.

CASE NOTES

Bankruptcy
Although this section, the entireties statute, is not found among the exemptions sections of the Illinois Code of Civil Procedure (735 ILCS 5/1-101 et seq.), the practical function of the statute can be interpreted to qualify entireties property as exempt from process under bankruptcy law. In re Allard, 196 Bankr. 402 (Bankr. N.D. Ill. 1996), aff'd, 202 Bankr. 938 (N.D. Ill. 1996).

RESEARCH REFERENCES

Proceeds or derivatives of real property held by entirety as themselves held by entirety. 22 ALR4th 459.

Parental Notice of Abortion Act of 1995

750 ILCS 70/1 Short title

Sec. 1. *Short title.* This Act may be cited as the Parental Notice of Abortion Act of 1995.
(Source: P.A. 89-18, § 1.)

Derivation.
Title: An Act concerning parental notice of abortion.
Cite: 750 ILCS 70/1 et seq.
Source: P.A. 89-18, eff. 6-1-95.
Date: Approved June 1, 1995.

Effective Date.
Section 99 of P.A. 89-18 made this Act effective upon becoming law. The Act was approved June 1, 1995.

CASE NOTES

ANALYSIS

Constitutionality
Standing

Constitutionality
The former Illinois Parental Notice of Abortion Act of 1983 (720 ILCS 520/1 et seq.) as supplemented by Rule 307, Supreme Court Rules, was unconstitutional by failing to assure that a minor received an expeditious and confidential appeal of a circuit court denial of a waiver of notice, and that such an appeal focused solely on her maturity and best interests, and that the appeal proceedings comported with due process. Zbaraz v. Hartigan, 776 F. Supp. 375 (N.D. Ill. 1991).

Standing
Plaintiff physicians, engaged in the practice of obstetrics and gynecology that rendered and performed pregnancy termination procedures for minor women as part of their medical practice, had standing to challenge the constitutionality of the parental consent provision. Wynn v. Scott, 448 F. Supp. 997 (N.D. Ill.), aff'd, 582 F.2d 1375 (7th Cir. 1978).

LEGAL PERIODICALS

For comment, "The Illinois Parental Notice Abortion Act: Legal and Ethical Ramifications of A Physician's Decision to Give Parental Notification," see J. Marshall L. Rev. 475 (1985).

For casenote, "Zbaraz v. Hartigan, 763 F.2d 1532 (7th Circ. 1985): Manadatory Twenty-Four Hour Waiting Period After Parental Notification Unconstitutionally Burdens a Minor's Abortion Decision," see 19 J. Marshall L. Rev. 1071.

For note and comment, "Spousal Notification and the Right of Privacy — Scheinberg v. Smith 659 F.2d 476 (5th Cir. 1981)," see 59 Chi.-Kent L. Rev. 1129 (1983).

For comment, "The Illinois Abortion Parental Consent Act of 1977: A Far Cry From Permissible Consultation," see 12 J. Marshall J. Prac. & Proc. 135 (1978).

RESEARCH REFERENCES

Validity, construction, and application of statutes requiring parental notification of or consent to minor's abortion. 77 ALR5th 1.

750 ILCS 70/5 Legislative findings and purpose

Sec. 5. *Legislative findings and purpose.* The General Assembly finds that notification of a family member as defined in this Act is in the best interest of an unemancipated minor, and the General Assembly's purpose in enacting this parental notice law is to further and protect the best interests of an unemancipated minor.

The medical, emotional, and psychological consequences of abortion are sometimes serious and long-lasting, and immature minors often lack the ability to make fully informed choices that consider both the immediate and long-range consequences.

Parental consultation is usually in the best interest of the minor and is desirable since the capacity to become pregnant and the capacity for mature judgment concerning the wisdom of an abortion are not necessarily related.
(Source: P.A. 89-18, § 5.)

750 ILCS 70/10 Definitions

Sec. 10. *Definitions.* As used in this Act:

"Abortion" means the use of any instrument, medicine, drug, or any other substance or device to terminate the pregnancy of a woman known to be pregnant with an intention other than to increase the probability of a live birth, to preserve the life or health of a child after live birth, or to remove a dead fetus.

"Actual notice" means the giving of notice directly, in person, or by telephone.

"Adult family member" means a person over 21 years of age who is the parent, grandparent, step-parent living in the household, or legal guardian.

"Constructive notice" means notice by certified mail to the last known address of the person entitled to notice with delivery deemed to have occurred 48 hours after the certified notice is mailed.

"Incompetent" means any person who has been adjudged as mentally ill or developmentally disabled and who, because of her mental illness or developmental disability, is not fully able to manage her person and for whom a guardian of the person has been appointed under Section 11a-3(a)(1) of the Probate Act of 1975 [755 ILCS 5/11a-3].

"Medical emergency" means a condition that, on the basis of the physician's good faith clinical judgment, so complicates the medical condition of a pregnant woman as to necessitate the immediate abortion of her pregnancy to avert her death or for which a delay will create serious risk of substantial and irreversible impairment of major bodily function.

"Minor" means any person under 18 years of age who is not or has not been married or who has not been emancipated under the Emancipation of Mature Minors Act [750 ILCS 30/1 et seq.].

"Neglect" means the failure of an adult family member to supply a child with necessary food, clothing, shelter, or medical care when reasonably able to do so or the failure to protect a child from conditions or actions that imminently and seriously endanger the child's physical or mental health when reasonably able to do so.

"Physical abuse" means any physical injury intentionally inflicted by an adult family member on a child.

"Physician" means any person licensed to practice medicine in all its branches under the Illinois Medical Practice Act of 1987 [225 ILCS 60/1 et seq.].

"Sexual abuse" means any sexual conduct or sexual penetration as defined in Section 12-12 of the Criminal Code of 1961 [720 ILCS 5/12-12] that is

prohibited by the criminal laws of the State of Illinois and committed against a minor by an adult family member as defined in this Act.
(Source: P.A. 89-18, § 10.)

750 ILCS 70/15 Notice to adult family member

Sec. 15. *Notice to adult family member.* No person shall knowingly perform an abortion upon a minor or upon an incompetent person unless the physician or his or her agent has given at least 48 hours actual notice to an adult family member of the pregnant minor or incompetent person of his or her intention to perform the abortion, unless that person or his or her agent has received a written statement by a referring physician certifying that the referring physician or his or her agent has given at least 48 hours notice to an adult family member of the pregnant minor or incompetent person. If actual notice is not possible after a reasonable effort, the physician or his or her agent must give 48 hours constructive notice.
(Source: P.A. 89-18, § 15.)

750 ILCS 70/20 Exceptions

Sec. 20. *Exceptions.* Notice shall not be required under this Act if:

(1) the minor or incompetent person is accompanied by a person entitled to notice; or

(2) notice is waived in writing by a person who is entitled to notice; or

(3) the attending physician certifies in the patient's medical record that a medical emergency exists and there is insufficient time to provide the required notice; or

(4) the minor declares in writing that she is a victim of sexual abuse, neglect, or physical abuse by an adult family member as defined in this Act. The attending physician must certify in the patient's medical record that he or she has received the written declaration of abuse or neglect. Any notification of public authorities of abuse that may be required under other laws of this State need not be made by the person performing the abortion until after the minor receives an abortion that otherwise complies with the requirements of this Act; or

(5) notice is waived under Section 25 [750 ILCS 70/25].
(Source: P.A. 89-18, § 20.)

750 ILCS 70/25 Procedure for judicial waiver of notice

Sec. 25. *Procedure for judicial waiver of notice.* (a) The requirements and procedures under this Section are available to minors and incompetent persons whether or not they are residents of this State.

(b) The minor or incompetent person may petition any circuit court for a waiver of the notice requirement and may participate in proceedings on her own behalf. The court shall appoint a guardian ad litem for her. Any guardian ad litem appointed under this Act shall act to maintain the confidentiality of the proceedings. The circuit court shall advise her that she has a right to court-appointed counsel and shall provide her with counsel upon her request.

(c) Court proceedings under this Section shall be confidential and shall ensure the anonymity of the minor or incompetent person. All court proceedings under this Section shall be sealed. The minor or incompetent person shall have the right to file her petition in the circuit court using a pseudonym or using solely her initials. All documents related to this petition shall be confidential and shall not be made available to the public.

These proceedings shall be given precedence over other pending matters to the extent necessary to ensure that the court reaches a decision promptly. The court shall rule and issue written findings of fact and conclusions of law within 48 hours of the time that the petition is filed, except that the 48-hour limitation may be extended at the request of the minor or incompetent person. If the court fails to rule within the 48-hour period and an extension is not requested, then the petition shall be deemed to have been granted, and the notice requirement shall be waived.

(d) Notice shall be waived if the court finds by a preponderance of the evidence either:

(1) that the minor or incompetent person is sufficiently mature and well enough informed to decide intelligently whether to have an abortion, or

(2) that notification under Section 15 of this Act [750 ILCS 70/15] would not be in the best interests of the minor or incompetent person.

(e) A court that conducts proceedings under this Section shall issue written and specific factual findings and legal conclusions supporting its decision and shall order that a confidential record of the evidence and the judge's findings and conditions be maintained.

(f) An expedited confidential appeal shall be available, as the Supreme Court provides by rule, to any minor or incompetent person to whom the circuit court denies a waiver of notice. An order authorizing an abortion without notice shall not be subject to appeal.

(g) The Supreme Court is respectfully requested to promulgate any rules and regulations necessary to ensure that proceedings under this Act are handled in an expeditious and confidential manner.

(h) No fees shall be required of any minor or incompetent person who avails herself of the procedures provided by this Section.
(Source: P.A. 89-18, § 25.)

750 ILCS 70/30 Minor's consent to abortion

Sec. 30. *Minor's consent to abortion.* A person may not perform an abortion on a minor without the minor's consent, except in a medical emergency.
(Source: P.A. 89-18, § 30.)

CASE NOTES

ANALYSIS

Constitutionality
—Equal Protection Clause
—Waiting Period
In General
Informed Consent
Judicial Inquiry
—Minor's Comprehension

Constitutionality

—Equal Protection Clause

The 48 hour waiting period of former 720 ILCS 515/4 violated the equal protection clause of the Fourteenth Amendment; it was underinclusive because it excluded married minors and overinclusive because it included mature, emancipated minors. Wynn v. Carey, 599 F.2d 193 (7th Cir. 1979).

—Waiting Period

The waiting requirement imposed by former 720 ILCS 520/4, standing alone, was unconstitutional, and former section 7 of this Act (720 ILCS 520/7) did not alleviate the burden imposed but merely offered an alternative, and apparently greater, burden to that which the case law held unconstitutional. Zbaraz v. Hartigan, 763 F.2d 1532 (7th Cir. 1985), aff'd, 484 U.S. 171, 108 S. Ct. 479, 98 L. Ed. 2d 478 (1987).

The twenty-four hour waiting period imposed by former 720 ILCS 520/4(a) was unconstitutional as unduly burdening a minor's right to have an abortion in the absence of a compelling state interest. Zbaraz v. Hartigan, 584 F. Supp. 1452 (N.D. Ill. 1984), modified on other grounds, 763 F.2d 1532 (7th Cir. 1985), aff'd, 484 U.S. 171, 98 L. Ed. 2d 478, 108 S. Ct. 479 (1987).

In General

The former Illinois Abortion Parental Consent Act of 1977 (720 ILCS 515/4) was found to be deficient because it failed to provide for minors who did not understand the consequences of an abortion; the only judicial inquiry permitted by the Act is whether "the pregnant minor fully understands the consequences of an abortion to her and her unborn child". Wynn v. Carey, 582 F.2d 1375 (7th Cir. 1978).

Informed Consent

The former Illinois Abortion Parental Consent Act of 1977 (720 ILCS 515/1 et seq.) was found to be substantively deficient in failing to provide a standard under which a judicial order can be obtained where the minor is incapable of giving informed consent. Wynn v. Carey, 582 F.2d 1375 (7th Cir. 1978).

While parental consent is a device the state may utilize to safeguard against a minor's uninformed, coerced consent, an alternative without parental consultation must be provided to the mature minor capable of voluntarily giving informed consent; furthermore, the alternative without parental consultation must also accommodate the right of the minor incapable of giving informed consent upon a showing that an abortion is in her best interests. Wynn v. Scott, 448 F. Supp. 997 (N.D. Ill.), aff'd, 582 F.2d 1375 (7th Cir. 1978).

Judicial Inquiry

—Minor's Comprehension

Where an abortion involves termination of the potentiality of human life, a late abortion, and the termination of prenatal life, these are immediate consequences of an abortion and are appropriate elements of an inquiry as to whether the minor's consent is informed; thus, judicial inquiry does not recognize only the constitutionally permissible inquiries, but rather, it provides that the court must inquire as to whether the pregnant minor fully understands the consequences of an abortion to her and to her unborn child. Wynn v. Scott, 448 F. Supp. 997 (N.D. Ill.), aff'd, 582 F.2d 1375 (7th Cir. 1978).

RESEARCH REFERENCES

Requisites and conditions of judicial consent to minor's abortion. 23 ALR4th 1061.

750 ILCS 70/35 Reports

Sec. 35. *Reports.* The Department of Public Health shall comply with the reporting requirements set forth in the consent decree in Herbst v. O'Malley, case no. 84-C-5602 in the U.S. District Court for the Northern District of Illinois, Eastern Division.
(Source: P.A. 89-18, § 35.)

750 ILCS 70/40 Penalties

Sec. 40. *Penalties.* (a) Any physician who willfully fails to provide notice as required under this Act before performing an abortion on a minor or an incompetent person shall be referred to the Illinois State Medical Disciplinary Board for action in accordance with Section 22 of the Medical Practice Act of 1987 [225 ILCS 60/22].

(b) Any person, not authorized under this Act, who signs any waiver of notice for a minor or incompetent person seeking an abortion, is guilty of a Class C misdemeanor.
(Source: P.A. 89-18, § 40.)

750 ILCS 70/45 Immunity

Sec. 45. *Immunity.* Any physician who, in good faith, provides notice in accordance with Section 15 [750 ILCS 70/15] or relies on an exception under Section 20 [750 ILCS 70/20] shall not be subject to any type of civil or criminal liability or discipline for unprofessional conduct for failure to give required notice.
(Source: P.A. 89-18, § 45.)

750 ILCS 70/50 Severability and inseverability

Sec. 50. *Severability and inseverability.* If any provision of this Act or its application to any person or circumstance is held invalid, the invalidity of that provision or application does not affect other provisions or applications of the Act that can be given effect without the invalid provision or application, except that Section 25 [750 ILCS 70/25] is inseverable to the extent that if all or any substantial and material part of Section 25 [750 ILCS 70/25] is held invalid, then the entire Act is invalid.
(Source: P.A. 89-18, § 50.)

CASE NOTES

Severability

Although the twenty-four hour waiting period imposed by former 720 ILCS 520/4 was unconstitutional, it could be severed from the Act, thereby removing the constitutional infirmity of that provision from the statute without affecting the essential purpose of the entire Act. Zbaraz v. Hartigan, 763 F.2d 1532 (7th Cir. 1985), aff'd, 484 U.S. 171, 108 S. Ct. 479, 98 L. Ed. 2d 478 (1987).

750 ILCS 70/85 through 750 ILCS 70/95 [Not Set Out]

Note.

These sections, as found in P.A. 89-18, §§ 85 through 95, contained amendatory provisions.

750 ILCS 70/99 Effective date

Sec. 99. *Effective date.* This Act takes effect upon becoming law.
(Source: P.A. 89-18, § 99.)

Note.
The Act was approved June 1, 1995.

Related Laws

CHAPTER 20
EXECUTIVE BRANCH

DEPARTMENT OF CHILDREN AND FAMILY SERVICES

CHILDREN AND FAMILY SERVICES ACT

20 ILCS 505/7 Placement of children; considerations
20 ILCS 505/7.1 One Church One Child Advisory Board
20 ILCS 505/7.2 [Repealed]
20 ILCS 505/7.3 Placement plan
20 ILCS 505/7.4 Placement of siblings
20 ILCS 505/7.7 Limit on multiple placements

CIVIL ADMINISTRATIVE CODE OF ILLINOIS

ARTICLE 510.

DEPARTMENT OF CHILDREN AND FAMILY SERVICES

20 ILCS 510/510-1 Article short title
20 ILCS 510/510-5 Definition
20 ILCS 510/510-10 Powers, generally
20 ILCS 510/510-15 Children and Family Services Act
20 ILCS 510/510-20 Juveniles
20 ILCS 510/510-25 Child Care Act of 1969; injunction
20 ILCS 510/510-30 Escaped inmates
20 ILCS 510/510-35 State agency employees child care services
20 ILCS 510/510-95 Statutory responsibilities pertaining to children
20 ILCS 510/510-100 Criminal history record information
20 ILCS 510/510-200 Police and security force

DEPARTMENT OF HUMAN SERVICES

DOMESTIC VIOLENCE SHELTERS ACT

20 ILCS 1310/0.01 Short title
20 ILCS 1310/1 [Definitions]
20 ILCS 1310/2 [Administration of shelters]
20 ILCS 1310/3 [Funding for shelters]
20 ILCS 1310/3.2 [Domestic Violence Shelter and Service Fund]

DEPARTMENT OF CHILDREN AND FAMILY SERVICES

CHILDREN AND FAMILY SERVICES ACT

20 ILCS 505/7 Placement of children; considerations

Sec. 7. *Placement of children; considerations.* (a) In placing any child under this Act, the Department shall place such child, as far as possible, in the care and custody of some individual holding the same religious belief as the parents of the child, or with some child care facility which is operated by persons of like religious faith as the parents of such child.

(b) In placing a child under this Act, the Department may place a child with a relative if the Department has reason to believe that the relative will be able to adequately provide for the child's safety and welfare. The Department may not place a child with a relative, with the exception of certain circumstances which may be waived as defined by the Department in rules, if the results of a check of the Law Enforcement Agency Data System (LEADS) identifies a prior criminal conviction of the relative or any adult member of the relative's household for any of the following offenses under the Criminal Code of 1961 [720 ILCS 5/1-1 et seq.]:

(1) murder;
(1.1) solicitation of murder;
(1.2) solicitation of murder for hire;
(1.3) intentional homicide of an unborn child;
(1.4) voluntary manslaughter of an unborn child;
(1.5) involuntary manslaughter;
(1.6) reckless homicide;
(1.7) concealment of a homicidal death;
(1.8) involuntary manslaughter of an unborn child;
(1.9) reckless homicide of an unborn child;
(1.10) drug-induced homicide;
(2) a sex offense under Article 11 [720 ILCS 11-6 et seq.], except offenses described in Sections 11-7, 11-8, 11-12, and 11-13 [720 ILCS 5/11-7, 720 ILCS 5/11-8, 720 ILCS 5/11-12, and 720 ILCS 5/11-13];
(3) kidnapping;
(3.1) aggravated unlawful restraint;
(3.2) forcible detention;
(3.3) aiding and abetting child abduction;
(4) aggravated kidnapping;
(5) child abduction;
(6) aggravated battery of a child;
(7) criminal sexual assault;
(8) aggravated criminal sexual assault;
(8.1) predatory criminal sexual assault of a child;
(9) criminal sexual abuse;
(10) aggravated sexual abuse;
(11) heinous battery;
(12) aggravated battery with a firearm;
(13) tampering with food, drugs, or cosmetics;
(14) drug-induced infliction of great bodily harm;
(15) aggravated stalking;
(16) home invasion;
(17) vehicular invasion;
(18) criminal transmission of HIV;
(19) criminal abuse or neglect of an elderly or disabled person;
(20) child abandonment;
(21) endangering the life or health of a child;
(22) ritual mutilation;
(23) ritualized abuse of a child;
(24) an offense in any other state the elements of which are similar and bear a substantial relationship to any of the foregoing offenses.

For the purpose of this subsection, "relative" shall include any person, 21 years of age or over, other than the parent, who (i) is currently related to the child in any of the following ways by blood or adoption: grandparent, sibling, great-grandparent, uncle, aunt, nephew, niece, first cousin, second cousin, godparent, great-uncle, or great-aunt; or (ii) is the spouse of such a relative; or (iii) is the child's step-father, step-mother, or adult step-brother or step-sister; "relative" also includes a person related in any of the foregoing ways to a sibling of a child, even though the person is not related to the child, when the child and its sibling are placed together with that person. A relative with whom a child is placed pursuant to this subsection may, but is not required to, apply for licensure as a foster family home pursuant to the Child Care Act of 1969 [225 ILCS 10/1 et seq.]; provided, however, that as of July 1, 1995, foster care payments shall be made only to licensed foster family homes pursuant to the terms of Section 5 of this Act [20 ILCS 505/5].

(c) In placing a child under this Act, the Department shall ensure that the child's health, safety, and best interests are met in making a family foster care placement. The Department shall consider the individual needs of the child and the capacity of the prospective foster or adoptive parents to meet the needs of the child. When a child must be placed outside his or her home and cannot be immediately returned to his or her parents or guardian, a comprehensive, individualized assessment shall be performed of that child at which time the needs of the child shall be determined. Only if race, color, or national origin is identified as a legitimate factor in advancing the child's best interests shall it be considered. Race, color, or national origin shall not be routinely considered in making a placement decision. The Department shall make special efforts for the diligent recruitment of potential foster and adoptive families that reflect the ethnic and racial diversity of the children for whom foster and adoptive homes are needed. "Special efforts" shall include contacting and working with community organizations and religious organizations and may include contracting with those organizations, utilizing local media and other local resources, and conducting outreach activities.

(c-1) At the time of placement, the Department shall consider concurrent planning, as described in subsection (l-1) of Section 5 [20 ILCS 505/5], so that permanency may occur at the earliest opportunity. Consideration should be given so that if reunification fails or is delayed, the placement made is the best available placement to provide permanency for the child.

(d) The Department may accept gifts, grants, offers of services, and other contributions to use in making special recruitment efforts.

(e) The Department in placing children in adoptive or foster care homes may not, in any policy or practice relating to the placement of children for adoption or foster care, discriminate against any child or prospective adoptive or foster parent on the basis of race.

(Source: P.A. 85-1403; 86-1482; 89-21, § 5-15; 89-422, § 2; 89-428, § 210; 89-462, § 210; 89-626, § 2-11; 90-27, § 5; 90-28, § 10-5; 90-608, § 5; 92-192, § 5; 92-328, § 5; 92-334, § 5; 92-651, § 11.)

Note.

This section was Ill.Rev.Stat., Ch. 23, para. 5007.

Section 997 of P.A. 92-651 is a no acceleration or delay provision, and Section 998 is a no revival or extension provision.

Illinois Administrative Code.

See 89 Illinois Administrative Code, §§ 304.2, 338.20, 359.2, 300.20, 315.20, 309.30, 301.20, 302.20, 337.20, 402.2, 301.20, 315.20, 337.20, 402.2.

Effect of Amendments.

The 1998 amendment by P.A. 90-608, effective June 30, 1998, rewrote the first two sentences in subsection (c).

The 2001 amendment by P.A. 92-192, effective January 1, 2002, in subsection (b) inserted "second cousin, godparent" in the first sentence.

The 2001 amendment by P.A. 92-328, effective January 1, 2002, in subsection (b)(19) inserted "abuse or".

The 2001 amendment by P.A. 92-334, effective August 10, 2001, inserted the third, fourth and fifth sentences of subsection (c).

The 2002 amendment by P.A. 92-651, effective July 11, 2002, combined the amendments by P.A. 92-192, P.A. 92-328 and P.A. 92-334.

CASE NOTES

ANALYSIS

Constitutionality
Best Interests of Child
—Paramount
—Relevant Factors
—Violated by Order
Bonding
—Evidence
Custody Award
—Reversed
Due Process
—Home of Relative Reform

Constitutionality

Public Act 89-428 was enacted in violation of the single subject rule of the state constitution and is therefore invalid in its entirety. Johnson v. Edgar, 176 Ill. 2d 499, 224 Ill. Dec. 1, 680 N.E.2d 1372 (1997).

Best Interests of Child

—Paramount

This section does not explicitly state what the Department must prove in order to meet its burden of placing child with someone other than a close relative. However, it is well established that the paramount consideration in all guardianship and child custody cases is the best interest of the child, which takes precedence over even a natural parent's superior right to custody of his child. Violetta B. v. Stanciel, 210 Ill. App. 3d 521, 154 Ill. Dec. 896, 568 N.E.2d 1345 (1 Dist.), cert. denied, 139 Ill. 2d 605, 159 Ill. Dec. 118, 575 N.E.2d 925 (1991).

—Relevant Factors

When the best interests of the child conflicts with the statutory preference for placement with a close relative or even a natural parent's right to have custody restored, the best interests of the child takes precedence and will defeat all other considerations. In re C.B., 248 Ill. App. 3d 168, 188 Ill. Dec. 28, 618 N.E.2d 598 (1 Dist. 1993).

Among the appropriate matters to be considered when assessing the best interests of the child in matters of custody are the nature

Best Interests of Child (Cont'd)

—Relevant Factors (Cont'd)
and length of the child's relationship with the present caretaker and the effect that a change of placement would have upon the emotional and psychological well-being of the child. Violetta B. v. Stanciel, 210 Ill. App. 3d 521, 154 Ill. Dec. 896, 568 N.E.2d 1345 (1 Dist.), cert. denied, 139 Ill. 2d 605, 159 Ill. Dec. 118, 575 N.E.2d 925 (1991).

—Violated by Order
The trial court's order vacating the guardianship of the Department of Child and Family Services and appointing the child's grandmother as private guardian and custodian of the child was contrary to what the evidence showed to be in the child's best interests where a transfer of custody from foster parent would cause severe and irreparable psychological trauma to the child. Violetta B. v. Stanciel, 210 Ill. App. 3d 521, 154 Ill. Dec. 896, 568 N.E.2d 1345 (1 Dist.), cert. denied, 139 Ill. 2d 605, 159 Ill. Dec. 118, 575 N.E.2d 925 (1991).

Bonding

—Evidence
Whether or not the bonding between the child and her foster mother was caused by misconduct on the part of the Department of Child and Family Services, the clear and convincing evidence showed that such bonding did in fact occur and that a transfer of custody to the child's grandmother would cause severe and irreparable psychological trauma to the child; it was not permissible to ignore or discount this evidence as a means of punishing the Department for its perceived misconduct when considering the issue of the child's best interests. Violetta B. v. Stanciel, 210 Ill. App. 3d 521, 154 Ill. Dec. 896, 568 N.E.2d 1345 (1 Dist.), cert. denied, 139 Ill. 2d 605, 159 Ill. Dec. 118, 575 N.E.2d 925 (1991).

Custody Award

—Reversed
Where the trial court unreasonably relied upon expert testimony that was not shown to be relevant, the trial court's award of permanent custody was reversed and remanded for further proceedings to determine what was in child's best interest. In re C.B., 248 Ill. App. 3d 168, 188 Ill. Dec. 28, 618 N.E.2d 598 (1 Dist. 1993).

Due Process

—Home of Relative Reform
Children had a legitimate claim of entitlement to foster care benefits they were receiving prior to the implementation of home of relative reform; therefore, Department of Children and Family Services' blanket determination that all approved and preapproved relative homes did not satisfy new requirements because they were unlicensed violated the due process rights of these children by discontinuing their benefits without providing an opportunity for an unlicensed home to submit a timely license application, and the Director could not terminate the benefits of resident children unless they were provided an opportunity to have a license application considered on its merits. Youakim v. McDonald, 71 F.3d 1274 (7th Cir. 1995), cert. denied, 518 U.S. 1028, 116 S. Ct. 2571, 135 L. Ed. 2d 1087 (1996).

RESEARCH REFERENCES

Religion as factor in child custody and visitation cases. 22 ALR4th 971.

20 ILCS 505/7.1 One Church One Child Advisory Board

Sec. 7.1. *One Church One Child Advisory Board.* There is created the One Church One Child Advisory Board to advise the Department in the placement of children by encouraging black churches to help find permanent homes for black children waiting to be adopted. The Advisory Board shall consist of 25 members appointed by the Governor, with at least one member representing each region of the State as determined by the Department. Members of the Advisory Board shall be reimbursed for their expenses incurred in performing their duties as determined by the Department.
(Source: P.A. 87-1148, § 1.)

Illinois Administrative Code.
See 89 Illinois Administrative Code, § 428.35.

Effective Date.
Section 3 of P.A. 87-1148 made this section effective January 1, 1993.

20 ILCS 505/7.2: Repealed by P.A. 91-798, § 25, effective July 9, 2000.

20 ILCS 505/7.3 Placement plan

Sec. 7.3. *Placement plan.* The Department shall develop and implement a written plan for placing children. The plan shall include at least the following features:

(1) A plan for recruiting minority adoptive and foster families. The plan shall include strategies for using existing resources in minority communities, use of minority outreach staff whenever possible, use of minority foster homes for placements after birth and before adoption, and other techniques as appropriate.

(2) A plan for training adoptive and foster families of minority children.

(3) A plan for employing social workers in adoption and foster care. The plan shall include staffing goals and objectives.

(4) A plan for ensuring that adoption and foster care workers attend training offered or approved by the Department regarding the State's goal of encouraging cultural diversity and the needs of special needs children.

(5) A plan that includes policies and procedures for determining for each child requiring placement outside of his or her home, and who cannot be immediately returned to his or her parents or guardian, the placement needs of that child. In the rare instance when an individualized assessment identifies, documents, and substantiates that race, color, or national origin is a factor that needs to be considered in advancing a particular child's best interests, it shall be considered in making a placement.
(Source: P.A. 89-422, § 2; 92-334, § 5.)

Effective Date.
Section 99 of P.A. 89-422 made this section effective upon becoming law. The Act was approved December 4, 1995.

Effect of Amendments.
The 2001 amendment by P.A. 92-334, effective August 10, 2001, added subsection (5).

20 ILCS 505/7.4 Placement of siblings

Sec. 7.4. *Placement of siblings.* (a) When a child is in need of an adoptive placement, the Department shall examine its files and other available resources and attempt to determine whether any biological sibling of the child has been adopted. If the Department determines that a biological sibling of the child has been adopted, the Department shall make a good faith effort to locate the adoptive parents of the sibling and inform them of the availability of the child for adoption.

(b) If the adoptive parents of a biological sibling of a child available for adoption apply to adopt that child, the Department shall consider them as adoptive applicants for the adoption of the child. The Department's final decision, however, shall be based upon the welfare and best interest of the child. In arriving at its decision, the Department shall consider all relevant factors, including but not limited to:

(1) the wishes of the child;

(2) the interaction and interrelationship of the child with the applicant to adopt the child;

(3) the child's need for stability and continuity of relationship with parent figures;

(4) the child's adjustment to his or her present home, school, and community;

(5) the mental and physical health of all individuals involved;

(6) the family ties between the child and the child's relatives, including siblings;

(7) the background, age, and living arrangements of the applicant to adopt the child;

(8) a criminal background report of the applicant to adopt the child.

(c) The Department may refuse to inform the adoptive parents of a biological sibling of a child that the child is available for adoption, as required under subsection (a), only for a reason permitted under criteria adopted by the Department by rule.

(Source: P.A. 92-666, § 5.)

Effective Date.

Section 99 of P.A. 92-666 made this section effective upon becoming law. The Act was approved July 16, 2002.

20 ILCS 505/7.7 Limit on multiple placements

Sec. 7.7. *Limit on multiple placements.* If the Department has placed a child in substitute care pursuant to a court order, the Department may not change the child's placement unless the Department specifically documents that the current placement is unsafe or unsuitable or that another placement is in the child's best interests or unless the new placement is in an adoptive home or other permanent placement.

(Source: P.A. 89-422, § 2; 90-28, § 10-5.)

Effective Date.

Section 99 of P.A. 89-422 made this section effective upon becoming law. The Act was approved December 4, 1995.

CIVIL ADMINISTRATIVE CODE OF ILLINOIS

ARTICLE 510.

DEPARTMENT OF CHILDREN AND FAMILY SERVICES

20 ILCS 510/510-1 Article short title

Sec. 510-1. *Article short title.* This Article 510 of the Civil Administrative Code of Illinois may be cited as the Department of Children and Family Services Powers Law.

(Source: P.A. 91-239, § 5-5.)

Effective Date.

Section 99-5 of P.A. 91-239 made this section effective January 1, 2000.

20 ILCS 510/510-5 Definition

Sec. 510-5. *Definition.* As used in this Article 510, "Department" means the Department of Children and Family Services.

(Source: P.A. 91-239, § 5-5; 92-16, § 15.)

Note.

Section 996 of P.A. 92-16 contains a "no acceleration or delay" provision, and Section 997 contains a "no revival or extension" provision.

Effective Date.

Section 99-5 of P.A. 91-239 made this section effective January 1, 2000.

Effect of Amendments.

The 2001 amendment by P.A. 92-16, effective June 28, 2001, substituted "Article 510" for "Article 30".

20 ILCS 510/510-10 Powers, generally

Sec. 510-10. *Powers, generally.* The Department has the powers enumerated in the following Sections.

(Source: P.A. 86-610; 91-239, § 5-5.)

Derivation.

Title: An Act in relation to the civil administration of the State government, and to repeal certain acts therein named.

Cite: 20 ILCS 510/65 et seq.

Source: L. 1917, p. 2.

Date: Approved March 7, 1917.

Note.

This section was Ill.Rev.Stat., Ch. 127, para. 63b11.

Effect of Amendments.

The 1999 amendment by P.A. 91-239, effective January 1, 2000, renumbered this section, which was formerly 20 ILCS 510/65, and made stylistic changes.

CASE NOTES

Contracting Power

—Authority

The provisions of the Code giving power to Department of Children and Family Services give that entity no express power to contract for services from a private entity; however, their general authority to perform its statutory duties implies contracting power pursuant to these duties. Illinois State Employees Ass'n v. Department of Children & Family Servs., 178 Ill. App. 3d 712, 127 Ill. Dec. 694, 533 N.E.2d 566 (4 Dist. 1989).

20 ILCS 510/510-15 Children and Family Services Act

Sec. 510-15. *Children and Family Services Act.* The Department has the power to administer the Children and Family Services Act [20 ILCS 505/1 et seq.].
(Source: Laws 1967, p. 4089; 91-239, § 5-5.)

Note.

This section was Ill.Rev.Stat., Ch. 127, para. 63b11.1.

Effect of Amendments.

The 1999 amendment by P.A. 91-239, effective January 1, 2000, renumbered this section, which was formerly 20 ILCS 510/65.1, and made stylistic changes.

CASE NOTES

Probationary Employee

A probationary employee was not entitled to a hearing. Swanson v. Visotsky, 97 Ill. App. 2d 305, 240 N.E.2d 444 (1 Dist. 1968).

20 ILCS 510/510-20 Juveniles

Sec. 510-20. *Juveniles.* The Department has the power to exercise the powers and fulfill the duties assigned the Department by the Juvenile Court Act of 1987 [705 ILCS 405/1-1].
(Source: P.A. 85-1209; 90-372, § 5-75; 91-239, § 5-5.)

Note.

This section was Ill.Rev.Stat., Ch. 127, para. 63b11.4.

Effect of Amendments.

The 1999 amendment by P.A. 91-239, effective January 1, 2000, renumbered this section, which was formerly 20 ILCS 510/65.4; and added the section heading and "The Department has the power" at the beginning.

20 ILCS 510/510-25 Child Care Act of 1969; injunction

Sec. 510-25. *Child Care Act of 1969; injunction.* The Department has the power to initiate injunction proceedings whenever it appears to the Director of Children and Family Services that any person, group of persons, or corporation is engaged or about to engage in any acts or practices that constitute or will constitute a violation of the Child Care Act of 1969 [225 ILCS 10/1 et seq.] or any rule or regulation prescribed under the authority of that Act. The Director of Children and Family Services may, in his or her discretion, through the Attorney General apply for an injunction to enforce the Act, rule, or regulation. Upon a proper showing, any circuit court may enter a permanent or preliminary injunction or a temporary restraining order without bond to enforce the Act, rule, or regulation in addition to the penalties and other remedies provided in the Act, rule, or regulation. Appeals may be taken as in other civil cases.
(Source: P.A. 83-1362; 91-239, § 5-5.)

Note.

This section was Ill.Rev.Stat., Ch. 127, para. 63b11.5.

Effect of Amendments.

The 1999 amendment by P.A. 91-239, effective January 1, 2000, renumbered this section, which was formerly 20 ILCS 510/65.5, added the section heading, inserted "to enforce the Act, rule, or regulation" in the second sentence, twice substituted "the Act, rule, or regulation" for "those Acts" in the last sentence, and made stylistic changes.

20 ILCS 510/510-30 Escaped inmates

Sec. 510-30. *Escaped inmates.* The Department has the power to exercise the powers and fulfill the duties assigned the Department by the Escaped Inmate Damages Act [740 ILCS 60/0.01 et seq.].
(Source: Laws 1967, p. 4089; 91-239, § 5-5.)

Note.

This section was Ill.Rev.Stat., Ch. 127, para. 63b11.6.

Effect of Amendments.

The 1999 amendment by P.A. 91-239, effective January 1, 2000, renumbered this section, which was formerly 20 ILCS 510/65.6, added the section heading, and made a stylistic change.

20 ILCS 510/510-35 State agency employees child care services

Sec. 510-35. *State agency employees child care services.* The Department has the power to advise the Department of Central Management Services concerning the provision of child care services pursuant to the State Agency Employees Child Care Services Act [30 ILCS 590/1 et seq.].
(Source: P.A. 84-652; 91-239, § 5-5.)

Note.

This section was Ill.Rev.Stat., Ch. 127, para. 63b11.7.

Effect of Amendments.

The 1999 amendment by P.A. 91-239, effective January 1, 2000, renumbered this section, which was formerly 20 ILCS 510/65.7; added the section heading and "The Department has the power" at the beginning; deleted ", enacted by the 84th General Assembly" at the end of the section; and made stylistic changes.

20 ILCS 510/510-95 Statutory responsibilities pertaining to children

Sec. 510-95. *Statutory responsibilities pertaining to children.* The Department has the power to administer the Child Care Act (repealed) and the other responsibilities pertaining to children that are delegated to the Department by statute.
(Source: Laws 1967, p. 4089; P.A. 91-239, § 5-5.)

Note.
This section was Ill.Rev.Stat., Ch. 127, para. 63b11.3.
The Child Care Act, referred to in this section, has been repealed. See now the Child Care Act of 1969, 225 ILCS 10/1 et seq.

Effect of Amendments.
The 1999 amendment by P.A. 91-239, effective January 1, 2000, renumbered this section, which was formerly 20 ILCS 510/65.3, inserted the section heading, inserted "(repealed)", and made stylistic changes.

20 ILCS 510/510-100 Criminal history record information

Sec. 510-100. *Criminal history record information.* Whenever the Department is authorized or required by law to consider some aspect of criminal history record information for the purpose of carrying out its statutory powers and responsibilities, then, upon request and payment of fees in conformance with the requirements of Section 2605-400 of the Department of State Police Law (20 ILCS 2605/2605-400), the Department of State Police is authorized to furnish, pursuant to positive identification, the information contained in State files that is necessary to fulfill the request.
(Source: P.A. 86-610; 91-239, § 5-5.)

Note.
This section was Ill.Rev.Stat., Ch. 127, para. 63b11.8.

Effect of Amendments.
The 1999 amendment by P.A. 91-239, effective January 1, 2000, renumbered this section, which was formerly 20 ILCS 510/65.8, added the section heading, made a renumbering change, and made stylistic changes.

20 ILCS 510/510-200 Police and security force

Sec. 510-200. *Police and security force.* (a) The Department has the power to appoint, subject to the Personnel Code, persons to be members of a police and security force. Members of the police and security force shall be peace officers and as such have all powers possessed by policemen in cities and sheriffs, including the power to make arrests on view or on warrants of violations of State statutes or city or county ordinances. These powers may, however, be exercised only in counties of more than 500,000 population when required for the protection of Department properties, interests, and personnel or when specifically requested by appropriate State or local law enforcement officials. Members of the police and security force may not serve and execute civil process.

(b) The Director must authorize to each member of the police and security force and to any other employee of the Department exercising the powers of a peace officer a distinct badge that, on its face, (i) clearly states that the badge is authorized by the Department and (ii) contains a unique identifying number. No other badge shall be authorized by the Department.
(Source: P.A. Laws 1967, p. 4089; 91-239, § 5-5; 91-883, § 20.)

Note.
This section was Ill.Rev.Stat., Ch. 127, para. 63b11.2.

Effect of Amendments.
The 1999 amendment by P.A. 91-239, effective January 1, 2000, renumbered this section, which was formerly 20 ILCS 510/65.2; and inserted "The Department has the power" at the beginning and made stylistic changes.
The 2000 amendment by P.A. 91-883, effective January 1, 2001, inserted the subsection designations and added subsection (b).

DEPARTMENT OF HUMAN SERVICES

Domestic Violence Shelters Act

20 ILCS 1310/0.01 Short title

Sec. 0.01. *Short title.* This Act may be cited as the Domestic Violence Shelters Act.
(Source: P.A. 86-1324.)

Derivation.
Title: An Act in relation to domestic relations and domestic violence shelters and service programs.
Cite: 20 ILCS 1310/0.01 et seq.
Source: P.A. 82-645.
Date: Approved September 24, 1981.

Note.
This section was Ill.Rev.Stat., Ch. 40, para. 2400.
This Act was renumbered from 20 ILCS 2210/0.01 et seq.

CASE NOTES

Challenge to Validity

—Waived
Defendant's failure to raise and preserve properly his constitutional challenge to provisions of this Act as unconstitutionally vague constituted a waiver thereof. People v. Whitfield, 147 Ill. App. 3d 675, 101 Ill. Dec. 80, 498 N.E.2d 262 (4 Dist. 1986).

20 ILCS 1310/1 [Definitions]

Sec. 1. The terms used in this Act shall have the following meanings ascribed to them:

(a) "Domestic violence" means attempting to cause or causing abuse of a family or household member or high-risk adult with disabilities, or attempting to cause or causing neglect or exploitation of a high-risk adult with disabilities which threatens the adult's health and safety, as defined in Section 103 of the Illinois Domestic Violence Act of 1986 [750 ILCS 60/103].

(b) "Family or household member" means a spouse, person living as a spouse, parent, or other adult person related by consanguinity or affinity, who is residing or has resided with the person committing domestic violence. "Family or household member"includes a high-risk adult with disabilities who resides with or receives care from any person who has the responsibility for a high-risk adult as a result of a family relationship or who has assumed responsibility for all or a portion of the care of an adult with disabilities voluntarily, by express or implied contract, or by court order.

(c) "Shelter" means a facility including, but not limited to, a facility providing temporary residential facilities to family or household members who are victims of domestic violence and their children and to high-risk adults with disabilities.

(d) "High-risk adult with disabilities" means a person aged 18 or over whose physical or mental disability impairs his or her ability to seek or obtain protection from abuse, neglect, or exploitation.
(Source: P.A. 86-542.)

Note.
This section was Ill.Rev.Stat., Ch. 40, para. 2401.

Cross References.
As to domestic violence as a basis for counseling or mediation in visitation matters, see 750 ILCS 5/607.1.

LEGAL PERIODICALS

For article, "Domestic Abuse Legislation in Illinois and Other States: A Survey and Suggestions for Reform," see U. Ill. L. Rev. 261 (1983).

20 ILCS 1310/2 [Administration of shelters]

Sec. 2. The Department of Human Services shall administer domestic violence shelters and service programs, or shall provide for their administration by not-for-profit corporations with whom the Department has contracts, for adults and their dependents who are the subjects of domestic violence.
(Source: P.A. 82-645; 89-507, § 90L-21.)

Note.
This section was Ill.Rev.Stat., Ch. 40, para. 2402.

20 ILCS 1310/3 [Funding for shelters]

Sec. 3. The Department of Human Services shall provide for the funding of domestic violence shelters and service programs in part from the Domestic Violence Shelter and Service Fund and in part from the General Revenue Fund. In allotting monies from such fund, the Department shall give priority to shelters or programs offering or proposing to offer the broadest range of services and referrals to the community served. Such shelters or programs may be operated by community-based organizations or units of local government. The Department shall require shelters or programs eligible for funding under this Act to provide matching funds in such percentage as the Department shall by rule determine and such percentage shall be uniform throughout the State.
(Source: P.A. 84-1480; 89-507, § 90L-21.)

Note.
This section was Ill.Rev.Stat., Ch. 40, para. 2403.

CASE NOTES

Marriage License Tax

—Constitutionality
The imposition of a special tax on the issuance of a marriage license for the purpose of contributing to the Domestic Violence Shelter and Service Fund imposed a significant interference with the fundamental right to marriage, and since it could not pass the strict scrutiny test of due process, it was unconstitutional. Boynton v. Kusper, 112 Ill. 2d 356, 98 Ill. Dec. 208, 494 N.E.2d 135 (1986).

LEGAL PERIODICALS

For article, "Domestic Abuse Legislation in Illinois and Other States: A Survey and Suggestions for Reform," see U. Ill. L. Rev. 261 (1983).

20 ILCS 1310/3.2 [Domestic Violence Shelter and Service Fund]

Sec. 3.2. All funds collected pursuant to P.A. 82-645, which are held in escrow for refund and for which a refund is not approved by September 1, 1988, shall be forwarded to the State Treasurer for deposit into the Domestic Violence Shelter and Service Fund. The Domestic Violence Shelter and Service Fund shall also include fines received by the State Treasurer from circuit clerks in accordance with Section 5-9-1.5 of the Unified Code of Corrections [730 ILCS 5/5-9-1.5]. Monies deposited in the Fund pursuant to this Section and the income tax check-off for the Domestic Violence Shelter and Service Fund authorized by Section 507F of the Illinois Income Tax Act [35 ILCS 5/507F] shall be appropriated to the Department of Human Services for the purpose of providing services specified by this Act; however, the Department may waive the matching funds requirement of this Act with respect to such monies. Any such waiver shall be uniform throughout the State. This amendatory Act of 1987 applies to all funds collected pursuant to PA 82-645, held in escrow and for which no refund is approved by September 1, 1988, whether those funds are administered by the State, a county, a court, or any other unit or agency of government.
(Source: P.A. 86-559; 87-342; 87-791; 87-895; 89-507, § 90L-21.)

Note.
This section was Ill.Rev.Stat., Ch. 40, para. 2403.2.

CHAPTER 55
COUNTIES

NEUTRAL SITE CUSTODY EXCHANGE FUNDING ACT

55 ILCS 82/1 Short title
55 ILCS 82/5 Legislative findings
55 ILCS 82/10 Definition
55 ILCS 82/15 Fund; fee; administration
55 ILCS 82/20 Grant disbursements
55 ILCS 82/25 Rules
55 ILCS 82/99 Effective date

NEUTRAL SITE CUSTODY EXCHANGE FUNDING ACT

55 ILCS 82/1 Short title

Sec. 1. *Short title.* This Act may be cited as the Neutral Site Custody Exchange Funding Act.
(Source: P.A. 91-811, § 1.)

Effective Date.
Section 99 of P.A. 91-811 made this Act effective upon becoming law. The Act was approved June 13, 2000.

55 ILCS 82/5 Legislative findings

Sec. 5. *Legislative findings.* The General Assembly finds that the domestic relations area of law, and particularly child custody matters, frequently involves seemingly minor disputes between individuals that escalate into major social and legal problems without the intervention of neutral parties; these problems often result in emotional damage to the children involved and create an extra burden for the courts; there are compelling reasons for providing neutral sites for parents to exchange the physical custody of a child for purposes of visitation; and not-for-profit charitable organizations can make a substantial contribution to the expeditious implementation of child custody and visitation orders in this State.
(Source: P.A. 91-811, § 5.)

55 ILCS 82/10 Definition

Sec. 10. *Definition.* In this Act:

"Custody exchange" means an exchange of the physical custody of a child at the commencement or conclusion of visitation with the child or at other times pursuant to an order for child custody or visitation.

"Neutral site" means a place not under the ownership or control of any party to an order for child custody or visitation, where a custody exchange takes place.
(Source: P.A. 91-811, § 10.)

55 ILCS 82/15 Fund; fee; administration

Sec. 15. *Fund; fee; administration.* (a) In any county, a neutral site custody exchange fund may be established by the passage of an ordinance by the county board.

(b) In each county in which a county board has enacted an ordinance authorizing a neutral site custody exchange fund to be established, the county board shall set a fee to be collected by the clerk of the circuit court on all civil case filings of not less than $1 nor more than $8 to be paid by the plaintiff at the time of the filing of the case and by the defendant at the time of filing an appearance. The county board shall review the amount of the fee on an annual basis and shall increase the amount of the fee, not to exceed the $8 maximum, if the demand for neutral site custody exchanges requires additional funding.

(c) In each county in which a county board has enacted an ordinance authorizing a neutral site custody exchange fund to be established, the clerk of the circuit court shall charge and collect a neutral site custody exchange fund fee as established by the county ordinance. The fee shall be paid by the parties to the action at the time of filing the first pleading in all civil cases. The fees shall not be charged in any proceeding commenced by or on behalf of a unit of local government.

The fees shall be in addition to all other fees and charges of the clerk, shall be assessable as costs, shall be remitted by the clerk monthly to the county treasurer, and shall be deposited monthly by the county treasurer in the neutral site custody exchange fund established under this Section. Each such clerk shall commence the charging and collection of the fee upon receipt of written notice from the county board that a neutral site custody exchange fund has been established.
(Source: P.A. 91-811, § 15; 93-746, § 5.)

Effect of Amendments.
The 2004 amendment by P.A. 93-746, effective July 15, 2004, substituted "In any county" for "In a county with a population of over 100,000 and less than 1,000,000 inhabitants" in subsection (a).

55 ILCS 82/20 Grant disbursements

Sec. 20. *Grant disbursements.* (a) The county board in a county that has established a neutral site custody exchange fund shall annually make grant disbursements from the fund to one or more qualified not-for-profit organizations for the purpose of implementing a neutral site custody exchange program, provided that the expenditure is approved by the chief judge of the judicial circuit in which the county is located.

(b) Disbursements by the county board shall be made to one or more qualified not-for-profit organizations that operate within the county based on each such organization's proportionate share of the total number of neutral site custody exchanges handled by all such organizations in that county during the year prior to the grant application.

(c) In no event shall the disbursements to any not-for-profit organization in one year exceed $500,000. Any amounts collected under Section 15

[55 ILCS 82/15] but not disbursed in a particular year shall be paid to the county treasurer for the administration of justice in the county.
(Source: P.A. 91-811, § 20.)

55 ILCS 82/25 Rules

Sec. 25. *Rules.* (a) The county board in a county in which a neutral site custody exchange fund has been established shall make rules pertaining to the operation and standards to be adhered to by a not-for-profit organization in that county in order to qualify for a grant under Section 20 [55 ILCS 82/20]. The rules shall provide for the following:

(1) All work performed by the not-for-profit organization, its staff, and volunteers shall be performed without collecting a fee or charge from the parties involved in a custody exchange.

(2) Each not-for-profit organization receiving a grant under this Act shall maintain records as required by the county board. The records shall be available for inspection by the office of the Chief Judge and shall demonstrate adherence to applicable requirements.

(b) The county board in a county in which a neutral site custody exchange fund has been established may make additional rules necessary for the operation of this Act in that county.
(Source: P.A. 91-811, § 25.)

55 ILCS 82/99 Effective date

Sec. 99. *Effective date.* This Act takes effect upon becoming law.
(Source: P.A. 91-811, § 99.)

Note.

P.A. 91-811 was approved June 13, 2000.

CHAPTER 305
PUBLIC AID

Illinois Public Aid Code

ARTICLE IV.

TEMPORARY ASSISTANCE FOR NEEDY FAMILIES

305 ILCS 5/4-1.7 Enforcement of Parental Child Support Obligation

ARTICLE X.

DETERMINATION AND ENFORCEMENT OF SUPPORT RESPONSIBILITY OF RELATIVES

305 ILCS 5/10-1 Declaration of Public Policy — Persons Eligible for Child Support Enforcement Services — Fees for Non-Applicants and Non-Recipients
305 ILCS 5/10-2 Extent of Liability
305 ILCS 5/10-3 Standard and Regulations for Determining Ability to Support
305 ILCS 5/10-3.1 Child and Spouse Support Unit
305 ILCS 5/10-3.2 Parent Locator Service
305 ILCS 5/10-3.3 Locating support obligor and others; penalties
305 ILCS 5/10-3.4 Obtaining location information
305 ILCS 5/10-4 Notification of Support Obligation
305 ILCS 5/10-5 Declarations by Responsible Relatives — Penalty
305 ILCS 5/10-6 Investigation and Determination
305 ILCS 5/10-7 Notice of support due
305 ILCS 5/10-8 Support Payments — Partial Support — Full Support
305 ILCS 5/10-8.1 Temporary order for child support
305 ILCS 5/10-9 Alternative Actions to Enforce Support
305 ILCS 5/10-10 Court enforcement; applicability also to persons who are not applicants or recipients
305 ILCS 5/10-10.1 Public Aid Collection Fee
305 ILCS 5/10-10.2 Notice to Clerk of Circuit Court of Payment Received by the Illinois Department for Recording
305 ILCS 5/10-10.3 [Child support payments payable to clerk of circuit court]
305 ILCS 5/10-10.4 Payment of Support to State Disbursement Unit
305 ILCS 5/10-10.5 Information to State Case Registry
305 ILCS 5/10-11 Administrative Orders
305 ILCS 5/10-11.1 [Unemployed responsible relative ordered to participate in job search, training or work programs]
305 ILCS 5/10-11.2 Administrative support order information for State Case Registry
305 ILCS 5/10-12 Petition by responsible relative for release from or modification of administrative support order or administrative determination of paternity
305 ILCS 5/10-12.1 Petition by person receiving child support enforcement services for release from or modification of administrative support order or administrative determination of paternity
305 ILCS 5/10-13 Hearing on Petition
305 ILCS 5/10-13.1 Examination of records
305 ILCS 5/10-13.2 Hearings not subject to technical rules of evidence or procedure
305 ILCS 5/10-13.3 Authority to administer oaths
305 ILCS 5/10-13.4 Proof of records
305 ILCS 5/10-13.5 Proof of necessitous circumstances
305 ILCS 5/10-13.6 Subpoenas
305 ILCS 5/10-13.7 Witness fees
305 ILCS 5/10-13.8 Compelling attendance of witness and production of records
305 ILCS 5/10-13.9 Penalty for non-compliance with subpoena
305 ILCS 5/10-13.10 Depositions
305 ILCS 5/10-14 Review of Illinois department decision on petition for hearing
305 ILCS 5/10-14.1 Relief from administrative orders
305 ILCS 5/10-15 Enforcement of administrative order; costs and fees
305 ILCS 5/10-16 Judicial enforcement of court and administrative support orders
305 ILCS 5/10-16.2 Withholding of Income to Secure Payment of Support
305 ILCS 5/10-16.3 Posting Security, Bond or Guarantee to Secure Payment
305 ILCS 5/10-16.4 Information concerning obligors
305 ILCS 5/10-16.5 Interest on support obligations
305 ILCS 5/10-16.6 Electronic Funds Transfer Committee
305 ILCS 5/10-16.7 Child support enforcement debit authorization
305 ILCS 5/10-17 Other Actions and Remedies for Support
305 ILCS 5/10-17.1 Administrative Order by Registration
305 ILCS 5/10-17.2 Income Withholding By Administrative Order
305 ILCS 5/10-17.3 Federal Income Tax Refund Intercept
305 ILCS 5/10-17.4 Security, Bond or Guarantee to Secure Payment
305 ILCS 5/10-17.5 State Income Tax Refund and Other Payment Intercept
305 ILCS 5/10-17.6 Past Due Support Information to Licensing Agencies
305 ILCS 5/10-17.7 Administrative determination of paternity
305 ILCS 5/10-17.8 New birth certificate
305 ILCS 5/10-17.9 Past due support information to State Department of Revenue
305 ILCS 5/10-17.11 Requests to other states for administrative enforcement
305 ILCS 5/10-18 Recoveries — Deductibility of Direct Relatives' Support Payment
305 ILCS 5/10-19 Support Payments Ordered Under Other Laws; where deposited
305 ILCS 5/10-20, 305 ILCS 5/10-21 [Repealed]
305 ILCS 5/10-22 [Repealed]
305 ILCS 5/10-23 Employer obligations
305 ILCS 5/10-24 Definitions
305 ILCS 5/10-24.5 Financial institutions data matches
305 ILCS 5/10-24.30 Types of accounts to be reported
305 ILCS 5/10-24.35 Accommodation of financial institutions
305 ILCS 5/10-24.40 Financial institution's charges on account
305 ILCS 5/10-24.45 Confidentiality
305 ILCS 5/10-24.50 Financial institution's freedom from liability
305 ILCS 5/10-25 Administrative liens and levies on real property for past-due child support
305 ILCS 5/10-25.5 Administrative liens and levies on personal property for past-due child support
305 ILCS 5/10-26 State Disbursement Unit
305 ILCS 5/10-26.2 Contracts concerning the operation of the State Disbursement Unit
305 ILCS 5/10-26.5 Delayed payment from State Disbursement Unit
305 ILCS 5/10-27 State Case Registry

Illinois Public Aid Code

ARTICLE IV.

TEMPORARY ASSISTANCE FOR NEEDY FAMILIES

305 ILCS 5/4-1.7 Enforcement of Parental Child Support Obligation

Sec. 4-1.7. *Enforcement of Parental Child Support Obligation.* If the parent or parents of the child are failing to meet or are delinquent in their legal obligation to support the child, the parent or other person having custody of the child or the Illinois Department of Public Aid may request the law enforcement officer authorized or directed by law to so act to file action for the enforcement of such remedies as the law provides for the fulfillment of the child support obligation.

If a parent has a judicial remedy against the other parent to compel child support, or if, as the result of an action initiated by or in behalf of one parent against the other, a child support order has been entered in respect to which there is noncompliance or delinquency, or where the order so entered may be changed upon petition to the court to provide additional support, the parent or other person having custody of the child or the Illinois Department of Public Aid may request the appropriate law enforcement officer to seek enforcement of the remedy, or of the support order, or a change therein to provide additional support. If the law enforcement officer is not authorized by law to so act in these instances, the parent, or if so authorized by law the other person having custody of the child, or the Illinois Department of Public Aid may initiate an action to enforce these remedies.

A parent or other person having custody of the child must comply with the requirements of Title IV of the federal Social Security Act [42 U.S.C. § 601 et seq.], and the regulations duly promulgated thereunder, and any rules promulgated by the Illinois Department regarding enforcement of the child support obligation. The Illinois Department of Public Aid and the Department of Human Services may provide by rule for the grant or continuation of aid to the person for a temporary period if he or she accepts counseling or other services designed to increase his or her motivation to seek enforcement of the child support obligation.

In addition to any other definition of failure or refusal to comply with the requirements of Title IV of the federal Social Security Act [42 U.S.C. § 601 et seq.], or Illinois Department rule, in the case of failure to attend court hearings, the parent or other person can show cooperation by attending a court hearing or, if a court hearing cannot be scheduled within 14 days following the court hearing that was missed, by signing a statement that the parent or other person is now willing to cooperate in the child support enforcement process and will appear at any later scheduled court date. The parent or other person can show cooperation by signing such a statement only once. If failure to attend the court hearing or other failure to cooperate results in the case being dismissed, such a statement may be signed after 2 months.

No denial or termination of medical assistance pursuant to this Section shall commence during pregnancy of the parent or other person having custody of the child or for 30 days after the termination of such pregnancy. The termination of medical assistance may commence thereafter if the Illinois Department of Public Aid determines that the failure or refusal to comply with this Section persists. Postponement of denial or termination of medical assistance during pregnancy under this paragraph shall be effective only to the extent it does not conflict with federal law or regulation.

Any evidence a parent or other person having custody of the child gives in order to comply with the requirements of this Section shall not render him or her liable to prosecution under Sections 11-7 or 11-8 of the "Criminal Code of 1961", approved July 28, 1961, as amended [720 ILCS 5/11-7 or 720 ILCS 5/11-8].

When so requested, the Illinois Department of Public Aid and the Department of Human Services shall provide such services and assistance as the law enforcement officer may require in connection with the filing of any action hereunder.

The Illinois Department of Public Aid and the Department of Human Services, as an expense of administration, may also provide applicants for and recipients of aid with such services and assistance, including assumption of the reasonable costs of prosecuting any action or proceeding, as may be necessary to enable them to enforce the child support liability required hereunder.

Nothing in this Section shall be construed as a requirement that an applicant or recipient file an action for dissolution of marriage against his or her spouse.

(Source: P.A. 85-1308; 89-507, § 90L-61; 90-17, § 10; 92-651, § 64.)

Note.

This section was Ill.Rev.Stat., Ch. 23, para. 4-1.7.

Section 997 of P.A. 92-651 is a no acceleration or delay provision, and Section 998 is a no revival or extension provision.

Effect of Amendments.

The 1996 amendment by P.A. 89-507, effective July 1, 1997, in the first paragraph, the first and second sentences of the second paragraph and the second sentence of the sixth paragraph inserted "of Public Aid"; and in the third paragraph, in the second sentence, and in the eighth and ninth paragraphs, inserted "of Public Aid and the Department of Human Services".

The 1997 amendment by P.A. 90-17, effective July 1, 1997, in the third paragraph, in the first sentence, substituted "must" for "who fails or refuses to", inserted "and any rules promulgated by the Illinois Department" and deleted from the end "shall be denied aid or aid for that person shall be terminated for as long as the failure or refusal persists"; deleted the former fourth paragraph which read "A child shall not be denied aid under this Article either initially or subsequently because a parent or other person having custody of the child fails or refuses to comply with the requirements of this Section"; and in the present fourth paragraph, in the first sentence, inserted "or Illinois Department rule" and substituted "14 days" for "30 days".

The 2002 amendment by P.A. 92-651, effective July 11, 2002, made a typographical correction and a stylistic change.

ARTICLE X.

DETERMINATION AND ENFORCEMENT OF SUPPORT RESPONSIBILITY OF RELATIVES

305 ILCS 5/10-1 Declaration of Public Policy — Persons Eligible for Child Support Enforcement Services — Fees for Non-Applicants and Non-Recipients

Sec. 10-1. *Declaration of Public Policy — Persons Eligible for Child Support Enforcement Services — Fees for Non-Applicants and Non-Recipients.* It is the intent of this Code that the financial aid and social welfare services herein provided supplement rather than supplant the primary and continuing obligation of the family unit for self-support to the fullest extent permitted by the resources available to it. This primary and continuing obligation applies whether the family unit of parents and children or of husband and wife remains intact and resides in a common household or whether the unit has been broken by absence of one or more members of the unit. The obligation of the family unit is particularly applicable when a member is in necessitous circumstances and lacks the means of a livelihood compatible with health and well-being.

It is the purpose of this Article to provide for locating an absent parent or spouse, for determining his financial circumstances, and for enforcing his legal obligation of support, if he is able to furnish support, in whole or in part. The Illinois Department of Public Aid shall give priority to establishing, enforcing and collecting the current support obligation, and then to past due support owed to the family unit, except with respect to collections effected through the intercept programs provided for in this Article.

The child support enforcement services provided hereunder shall be furnished dependents of an absent parent or spouse who are applicants for or recipients of financial aid under this Code. It is not, however, a condition of eligibility for financial aid that there be no responsible relatives who are reasonably able to provide support. Nor, except as provided in Sections 4-1.7 and 10-8 [305 ILCS 5/4-1.7 and 305 ILCS 5/10-8], shall the existence of such relatives or their payment of support contributions disqualify a needy person for financial aid.

By accepting financial aid under this Code, a spouse or a parent or other person having custody of a child shall be deemed to have made assignment to the Illinois Department for aid under Articles III, IV, V and VII or to a local governmental unit for aid under Article VI of any and all rights, title, and interest in any support obligation up to the amount of financial aid provided. The rights to support assigned to the Illinois Department of Public Aid or local governmental unit shall constitute an obligation owed the State or local governmental unit by the person who is responsible for providing the support, and shall be collectible under all applicable processes.

The Illinois Department of Public Aid shall also furnish the child support enforcement services established under this Article in behalf of persons who are not applicants for or recipients of financial aid under this Code in accordance with the requirements of Title IV, Part D of the Social Security Act [42 U.S.C. § 601 et seq.]. The Department may establish a schedule of reasonable fees, to be paid for the services provided and may deduct a collection fee, not to exceed 10% of the amount collected, from such collection. The Illinois Department of Public Aid shall cause to be published and distributed publications reasonably calculated to inform the public that individuals who are not recipients of or applicants for public aid under this Code are eligible for the child support enforcement services under this Article X. Such publications shall set forth an explanation, in plain language, that the child support enforcement services program is independent of any public aid program under the Code and that the receiving of child support enforcement services in no way implies that the person receiving such services is receiving public aid.

(Source: P.A. 85-597; 90-18, § 65; 92-590, § 5.)

Note.

This section was Ill.Rev.Stat., Ch. 23, para. 10-1.

Article VII of this Code, referred to above, has been repealed.

Cross References.

As for deductions from warrants and payments for satisfaction of past due child support, see 15 ILCS 405/10.05a.

As for the employment and job training obligations of an unemployed person owing a duty of child support or maintenance, see 750 ILCS 5/505.1, 750 ILCS 16/60, and 750 ILCS 20/24.1.

As for actions brought pursuant to this Article subject to expedited child support hearings, see 750 ILCS 25/5.

As for deductions from unemployment benefits for payment of past due child support, see 820 ILCS 405/1300.

Illinois Administrative Code.

See 89 Illinois Administrative Code, §§ 160.20, 160.5.

Effect of Amendments.

The 1997 amendment by P.A. 90-18, effective July 1, 1997, in the fifth paragraph added the present first sentence, deleted the former first sentence which read "At the discretion of the Illinois Department of Public Aid, the child and spouse support services established under this Article may also be furnished in behalf of spouses and dependent children who are not applicants for or recipients of financial aid under this Code", deleted the former second sentence which read "The Department may limit eligibility of these persons to designated income classes" and in the present second sentence deleted from the beginning "If non applicants and non recipients are included".

The 2002 amendment by P.A. 92-590, effective July 1, 2002, substituted references to "child support enforcement services" for references to "child and spouse support services" throughout the section.

CASE NOTES

ANALYSIS

Arrearage Proceedings
—Remarriage of Parties
Assignment by Recipient

—Arrearages Accrued at Time of Assignment
—Authority
—Automatic
Bankruptcy
Financial Status
No Notice to Department
—Effect
Notice to Recipient
Public Purpose
Responsibility for Support
—Effect of Leaving Home
—Grandparents
—Legal Relationship
—Marital Assets
Standing
Support Service

Arrearage Proceedings

—Remarriage of Parties

Since the Illinois Department of Public Aid timely intervened in petition alleging that respondent was in arrears on child support and alleged a present and substantial monetary interest, and since an intervenor has a right to have his claims litigated on their own merits even when the primary issue is dismissed, the relief sought by the Department should not have been denied on the grounds that the underlying proceedings had been terminated by the remarriage of the parties. In re Conway, 139 Ill. App. 3d 1062, 94 Ill. Dec. 363, 487 N.E.2d 1240 (5 Dist. 1986).

Assignment by Recipient

—Arrearages Accrued at Time of Assignment

Under the statute, a public aid recipient assigns the right to both arrearages accrued at the time of the assignment and support payments which become due after the assignment. Department of Pub. Aid v. Peavy, 307 Ill. App. 3d 16, 240 Ill. Dec. 314, 716 N.E.2d 1261 (2 Dist. 1999).

—Authority

There was sufficient statutory authority for the Illinois Department of Public Aid to have required an assignment of child support as a condition of the mother's receipt of AFDC benefits; therefore, there was no abuse of discretion in an order of the circuit court denying the mother's motion to vacate a prior order directing child support payments from the father to the Department. Winchell v. Winchell, 144 Ill. App. 3d 988, 99 Ill. Dec. 151, 495 N.E.2d 598 (3 Dist. 1986).

—Automatic

By accepting Aid to Families with Dependent Children, the recipient automatically assigns, to the extent of the amount of such aid furnished by the governmental unit, all rights, title, and interest in support payments to the governmental unit furnishing the aid; furthermore, an obligation to pay support owed to the governmental unit is imposed upon the person responsible for furnishing support to the recipient. In re Conway, 139 Ill. App. 3d 1062, 94 Ill. Dec. 363, 487 N.E.2d 1240 (5 Dist. 1986).

Under this section and a corresponding provision of the Illinois Administrative Code (see now 5 ILCS 100/1-1 et seq.), a person with custody of a child, who accepts Aid to Families with Dependent Children, is deemed to have assigned to the Illinois Department of Public Aid any support obligation to the child, up to the amount of assistance provided; the person responsible for providing the child support is correspondingly obligated to the state. Winchell v. Winchell, 144 Ill. App. 3d 988, 99 Ill. Dec. 151, 495 N.E.2d 598 (3 Dist. 1986).

Bankruptcy

Child support debts which had been assigned to the Department of Public Aid pursuant to the Social Security Act, 42 U.S.C. § 602(a)(26), were not dischargeable in bankruptcy. In re Stovall, 721 F.2d 1133 (7th Cir. 1983).

Financial Status

This section and 305 ILCS 5/10-10 authorize the department to provide child support enforcement services to any individual who applies for such services, regardless of his financial status. In re Lappe, 176 Ill. 2d 414, 223 Ill. Dec. 647, 680 N.E.2d 380 (1997).

No Notice to Department

—Effect

Where an order which represented a compromise between parents of the amount of child support arrearage owed by the father during much, if not all, of the time mother was on public aid and where the Department of Public Aid did not receive notice of any motions or hearings which affected rights of the Department, the order was void. In re Johnson, 97 Ill. App. 3d 634, 53 Ill. Dec. 72, 423 N.E.2d 264 (3 Dist. 1981).

Notice to Recipient

Where Department of Public Aid intervened in recipient's dissolution action to require ex-spouse to pay child support payments to the county and the recipient made an assignment of her rights to receive child support, the Department of Public Aid was not required to give recipient notice of its actions. In re Clark, 170 Ill. App. 3d 690, 121 Ill. Dec. 343, 525 N.E.2d 149 (5 Dist. 1988).

Public Purpose

This section and 305 ILCS 5/10-10 serve a public purpose by advancing the welfare of children and this public service is served by the extension of these services to all children, regardless of the financial circumstances of their custodial parents. In re Lappe, 176 Ill. 2d 414, 223 Ill. Dec. 647, 680 N.E.2d 380 (1997).

Responsibility for Support

—Effect of Leaving Home

A finding that one spouse left the marital home does not affect the determination that the other spouse is a legally responsible relative under the statute. Therefore, plaintiff's responsibility for his wife's support continued until their marriage was dissolved, even though she voluntarily left the home. Neff v. Miller, 146 Ill. App. 3d 395, 100 Ill. Dec. 8, 496 N.E.2d 1073 (1 Dist. 1986).

—Grandparents

Where there was no allegation in the complaint that the minors were paupers, nor were facts stated from which it could be inferred that they were liable in the immediate future to become paupers, complaint seeking the monetary support of the minor's grandparents was insufficient. Brown v. Vankeuren, 340 Ill. 118, 172 N.E. 1 (1930).

—Legal Relationship

The legislature clearly indicated that it is the legal relationship between the spouses which controls the responsibility for support, regardless of whether they reside together. Neff v. Miller, 146 Ill. App. 3d 395, 100 Ill. Dec. 8, 496 N.E.2d 1073 (1 Dist. 1986).

—Marital Assets

Proposal of petitioner that court should award her all marital assets up to the point where her comatose ex-husband would be available for public assistance was without merit, as such an award would be in violation of this Code and would leave comatose spouse with no means of support. In re Click, 169 Ill. App. 3d 48, 119 Ill. Dec. 701, 523 N.E.2d 169 (2 Dist.), appeal denied, 122 Ill. 2d 571, 125 Ill. Dec. 213, 530 N.E.2d 241 (1988).

Standing

The Department of Public Aid had standing to bring a petition to a modify child support obligation on behalf of public aid recipients without regard to any assignment of an arrearage to the Department. Illinois Dep't of Pub. Aid ex rel. Marshall v. Ringo, 303 Ill. App. 3d 250, 236 Ill. Dec. 173, 706 N.E.2d 1047 (3 Dist. 1999).

Support Service

The filing of a petition to modify a child support obligation is a support service contemplated under the Code. Illinois Dep't of Pub. Aid ex rel. Marshall v. Ringo, 303 Ill. App. 3d 250, 236 Ill. Dec. 173, 706 N.E.2d 1047 (3 Dist. 1999).

LEGAL PERIODICALS

For article, "Independent Evidence: A New Tool for Paternity Cases", see 86 Ill. B.J. 476 (1998).

For article, "Child Support Enforcement and the Illinois Department of Public Aid," see 81 Ill. B.J. 638 (1993).

305 ILCS 5/10-2 Extent of Liability

Sec. 10-2. *Extent of Liability.* A husband is liable for the support of his wife and a wife for the support of her husband. Unless the child is otherwise emancipated, the parents are severally liable for the support of any child under age 18, and for any child aged 18 who is attending high school, until that child graduates from high school, or attains the age of 19, whichever is earlier. The term "child" includes a child born out of wedlock, or legally adopted child.

In addition to the primary obligation of support imposed upon responsible relatives, such relatives, if individually or together in any combination they have sufficient income or other resources to support a needy person, in whole or in part, shall be liable for any financial aid extended under this Code to a person for whose support they are responsible, including amounts expended for funeral and burial costs.

(Source: P.A. 86-431; 88-687, § 5; 89-641, § 15; 90-18, § 65; 92-876, § 905.)

Note.

This section was Ill.Rev.Stat., Ch. 23, para. 10-2.

Effect of Amendments.

The 1996 amendment by P.A. 89-641, effective August 9, 1996, in the first paragraph, in the fourth sentence, substituted "accordance with Section 10-17.7 of this Code or Section 12 of the Vital Records Act" for "open court or by a verified written statement".

The 1997 amendment by P.A. 90-18, effective July 1, 1997, in the first paragraph, in the fourth sentence, deleted from the end "but the liability of the father of a child born out of wedlock shall not be enforceable unless he has been determined to be the child's father in a judicial or administrative proceeding, or he has or shall acknowledge paternity of the child in accordance with Section 10-17.7 of this Code or Section 12 of the Vital Records Act".

The 2002 amendment by P.A. 92-876, effective June 1, 2003, rewrote the second sentence of the first paragraph, which formerly read: "the parents are severally liable for the support of any child under age 21, except that a parent is not liable for a child age 18 or over if such child is not living with the parent or parents, and a parent is not liable for a child of any age if the child has married and is not living with the parent or parents. A child shall be considered to be living with the parent or parents if such child is absent from the parent's or parents' home only in order to regularly attend a school, college or university or to receive technical training designed for preparation for gainful employment."

CASE NOTES

Analysis

Constitutionality
Dismissal Upheld
Reciprocal Spousal Support
Responsibility for Support
—Adult Children

Constitutionality

The distinction drawn by this section between parents whose 18- through 20-year-old children reside with them and those whose 18- through 20-year-old children reside elsewhere violates the equal protection clause and is therefore invalid because it exempts some parents from support obligations completely based on reasons that have no rational relationship to the purpose of the section, strengthening the family unit. Jacobson v. Department of Pub. Aid, 171 Ill. 2d 314, 216 Ill. Dec. 96, 664 N.E.2d 1024 (1996).

Parents of 18 to 21 year old Aid to Families with Dependent Children recipients who live at home are not similarly situated with those whose children live separately, but this distinction affords a rational basis for the classifications in the statute. Brown v. Illinois Dep't of Pub. Aid, 274 Ill. App. 3d 410, 211 Ill. Dec. 120, 654 N.E.2d 582 (4 Dist. 1995).

In light of the stated purposes of the code, there is no rational basis for distinguishing between those parents whose 18 to 21 year old children live with them and those whose children do not in the determination of support liability. Jacobson v. Department of Pub. Aid, 269 Ill. App. 3d 359, 207 Ill. Dec. 115, 646 N.E.2d 949 (2 Dist. 1995), appeal granted, 162 Ill. 2d 568, 209 Ill. Dec. 802, 652 N.E.2d 342 (1995), modified on other grounds, 171 Ill. 2d 314, 216 Ill. Dec. 96, 664 N.E.2d 1024 (1996).

This section does not "directly and substantially" interfere with family living arrangements so as to interfere with a family's fundamental right to live in the type of family unit it chooses. Jacobson v. Department of Pub. Aid, 269 Ill. App. 3d 359, 207 Ill. Dec. 115, 646 N.E.2d 949 (2 Dist. 1995), appeal granted, 162 Ill. 2d 568, 209 Ill. Dec. 802, 652 N.E.2d 342 (1995), modified on other grounds, 171 Ill. 2d 314, 216 Ill. Dec. 96, 664 N.E.2d 1024 (1996).

Dismissal Upheld

Where plaintiff failed to plead sufficient facts to support his claim that he was required to pay his daughter's medical expenses, the trial court properly dismissed his complaint seeking relief under this section for failure to state a cause of action. Tully v. Cuddy, 139 Ill. App. 3d 697, 94 Ill. Dec. 218, 487 N.E.2d 1095 (1 Dist. 1985).

Reciprocal Spousal Support

Common-law doctrines which impose a duty of support solely on the husband are inconsistent with the constitutional mandate and the statutory scheme recognizing equal rights and responsibilities, and are no longer valid. McGloon v. Zmigrocki, 191 Ill. App. 3d 968, 139 Ill. Dec. 53, 548 N.E.2d 438 (1 Dist. 1989).

Responsibility for Support

—Adult Children

Where parents have the ability to and demonstrate the willingness to continue supporting a child between the ages of 18 and 21 years of age by allowing the child to remain at home, then the state should be relieved of any burden of assisting with that child's support, allowing for the allocation of limited public aid funds to persons who really need them even if those other persons are also between the ages of 18 and 21 years, but are not living in their parents' home because their parents are unable or unwilling to support them. Brown v. Illinois Dep't of Pub. Aid, 274 Ill. App. 3d 410, 211 Ill. Dec. 120, 654 N.E.2d 582 (4 Dist. 1995).

Where the pleadings disclosed no special circumstances which would extend defendant's obligation to support his children into their majority, defendant's obligation to support his daughters terminated respectively on the dates of their eighteenth birthdays. Snip v. Snip, 35 Ill. App. 2d 427, 183 N.E.2d 175 (1 Dist. 1962).

305 ILCS 5/10-3 Standard and Regulations for Determining Ability to Support

Sec. 10-3. *Standard and Regulations for Determining Ability to Support.* The Illinois Department shall establish a standard by which shall be measured the ability of responsible relatives to provide support, and shall implement the standard by rules governing its application. The standard and the rules shall take into account the buying and consumption patterns of self-supporting persons of modest income, present or future contingencies having direct bearing on maintenance of the relative's self-support status and fulfillment of his obligations to his immediate family, and any unusual or exceptional circumstances including estrangement or other personal or social factors, that have a bearing on family relationships and the relative's ability to meet his support obligations. The standard shall be recomputed periodically to reflect changes in the cost of living and other pertinent factors.

In addition to the standard, the Illinois Department may establish guidelines to be used exclusively to measure the ability of responsible relatives to provide support on behalf of applicants for or recipients of financial aid under Article IV of this Act and other persons who are given access to the child support enforcement services of this Article as provided in Section 10-1 [305 ILCS 5/10-1]. In such case, the Illinois Department shall base the guidelines upon the applicable provisions of Sections 504, 505 and 505.2 of the Illinois Marriage and Dissolution of Marriage Act, as amended [750 ILCS 5/504, 750 ILCS 5/505 and 750 ILCS 5/505.2], and shall implement such guidelines by rules governing their application.

The term "administrative enforcement unit", when used in this Article, means local governmental units or the Child and Spouse Support Unit established under Section 10-3.1 [305 ILCS 5/10-3.1] when exercising the powers designated in this Article. The administrative enforcement unit shall apply the standard or guidelines, rules and procedures provided for by this Section and Sections 10-4 through 10-8 [305 ILCS 5/10-4 through 305 ILCS 5/10-8] in determining the ability of responsible relatives to provide support for applicants for or recipients of financial aid under this Code, except that the administrative enforcement unit may apply such standard or guidelines, rules and procedures at its discretion with respect to those applicants for or recipients of financial aid under Article IV and other persons who are given access to the child support enforcement services of this Article as provided by Section 10-1 [305 ILCS 5/10-1].
(Source: P.A. 86-649; 92-590, § 5; 92-651, § 64.)

Note.

This section was Ill.Rev.Stat., Ch. 23, para. 10-3.

Section 997 of P.A. 92-651 is a no acceleration or delay provision, and Section 998 is a no revival or extension provision.

Effect of Amendments.

The 2002 amendment by P.A. 92-590, effective July 1, 2002, substituted references to "child support enforcement services" for references to "child and spouse support services" and made stylistic and related changes throughout the section.

The 2002 amendment by P.A. 92-651, effective July 11, 2002, substituted "administrative enforcement" for "administration enforcement" in the first sentence of the last paragraph, and made a stylistic change.

Although the amendments made to this section by P.A. 92-590, § 5, and P.A. 92-651, § 64 did not take into account the amendments made by the other, the amendments have been combined into a single version by the publisher.

CASE NOTES

Analysis

Circumstances Considered
Guidelines
—Deviation
—Reevaluation
Responsibility for Support
—Age of Children

Circumstances Considered

There is nothing in this section which requires that all plaintiff's expenses and circumstances be considered in the determination of his support obligation. Neff v. Miller, 146 Ill. App. 3d 395, 100 Ill. Dec. 8, 496 N.E.2d 1073 (1 Dist. 1986).

Guidelines

—Deviation

Petitioner was allowed to contend for the first time on appeal that the trial court erred in failing to set forth in its order the reasons for deviating from the child support guidelines. In re Wright, 212 Ill. App. 3d 392, 156 Ill. Dec. 610, 571 N.E.2d 197 (5 Dist. 1991).

—Reevaluation

Failure of state to recompute statutory requirements in five year period since its adoption did not constitute an arbitrary or capricious exercise of authority. Neff v. Miller, 146 Ill. App. 3d 395, 100 Ill. Dec. 8, 496 N.E.2d 1073 (1 Dist. 1986).

Responsibility for Support

—Age of Children

A father was not liable for the cost of medical services under this section because "legally responsible relative" no longer includes a parent of any child who is over 21. Sapp v. Johnston, 15 Ill. App. 3d 119, 303 N.E.2d 429 (3 Dist. 1973).

305 ILCS 5/10-3.1 Child and Spouse Support Unit

Sec. 10-3.1. *Child and Spouse Support Unit.* The Illinois Department shall establish within its administrative staff a Child and Spouse Support Unit to search for and locate absent parents and spouses liable for the support of persons resident in this State and to exercise the support enforcement powers and responsibilities assigned the Department by this Article. The unit shall cooperate with all law enforcement officials in this State and with the authorities of other States in locating persons responsible for the support of persons resident in other States and shall invite the cooperation of these authorities in the performance of its duties.

In addition to other duties assigned the Child and Spouse Support Unit by this Article, the Unit may refer to the Attorney General or units of local government with the approval of the Attorney General, any actions under Sections 10-10 and 10-15 [305 ILCS 5/10-10 and 305 ILCS 5/10-15] for judicial enforcement of the support liability. The Child and Spouse Support Unit shall act for the Department in referring to the Attorney General support matters requiring judicial enforcement under other laws. If requested by the Attorney General to so act, as provided in Section 12-16 [305 ILCS 5/12-16], attorneys of the Unit may assist the Attorney General or themselves institute actions in behalf of the Illinois Department under the Revised Uniform Reciprocal Enforcement of Support Act [repealed]; under the Illinois Parentage Act of 1984 [750 ILCS 45/1 et seq.]; under the Non-Support of Spouse and Children Act [repealed]; under the Non-Support Punishment Act [750 ILCS 16/1 et seq.]; or under any other law, State or Federal, providing for support of a spouse or dependent child.

The Illinois Department shall also have the authority to enter into agreements with local governmental units or individuals, with the approval of the Attorney General, for the collection of moneys owing because of the failure of a parent to make child support payments for any child receiving services under this Article. Such agreements may be on a contingent fee basis, but such contingent fee shall not exceed 25% of the total amount collected.

An attorney who provides representation pursuant to this Section shall represent the Illinois Department exclusively. Regardless of the designation of the plaintiff in an action brought pursuant to this Section, an attorney-client relationship does not exist for purposes of that action between that attorney and (i) an applicant for or recipient of child support enforcement services or (ii) any other party to the action other than the Illinois Department. Nothing in this Section shall be construed to modify any power or duty (including a duty to maintain confidentiality) of the Child and Spouse Support Unit or the Illinois Department otherwise provided by law.

The Illinois Department may also enter into agreements with local governmental units for the Child and Spouse Support Unit to exercise the investigative and enforcement powers designated in this Article, including the issuance of administrative orders under Section 10-11 [305 ILCS 5/10-11], in locating responsible relatives and obtaining support for persons applying for or receiving aid under Article VI. Payments for defrayment of administrative costs and support payments obtained shall be deposited into the DHS Recoveries Trust Fund. Support payments shall be paid over to the General Assistance Fund of the local governmental unit at such time or times as the agreement may specify.

With respect to those cases in which it has support enforcement powers and responsibilities under this Article, the Illinois Department may provide by rule for periodic or other review of each administrative and court order for support to determine whether a modification of the order should be sought. The Illinois Department shall provide for and conduct such review in accordance with any applicable federal law and regulation.

As part of its process for review of orders for support, the Illinois Department, through written notice, may require the responsible relative to disclose his or her Social Security Number and past and present information concerning the relative's address, employment, gross wages, deductions from gross wages, net wages, bonuses, commissions, number of dependent exemptions claimed, individual and dependent health insurance coverage, and any other information necessary to determine the relative's ability to provide support in a case receiving child support enforcement services under this Article X.

The Illinois Department may send a written request for the same information to the relative's employer. The employer shall respond to the request for information within 15 days after the date the employer receives the request. If the employer willfully fails to fully respond within the 15-day period, the employer shall pay a penalty of $100 for each day that the response is not provided to the Illinois Department after the 15-day period has expired. The penalty may be collected in a civil action which may be brought against the employer in favor of the Illinois Department.

A written request for information sent to an employer pursuant to this Section shall consist of (i) a citation of this Section as the statutory authority for the request and for the employer's obligation to provide the requested information, (ii) a returnable form setting forth the employer's name and address and listing the name of the employee with respect to whom information is requested, and (iii) a citation of this Section as the statutory authority authorizing the employer to withhold a fee of up to $20 from the wages or income to be paid to each responsible relative for providing the information to the Illinois Department within the 15-day period. If the employer is withholding support payments from the responsible relative's income pursuant to an order for withholding, the employer may withhold the fee provided for in this Section only after withholding support as required under the order. Any amounts withheld from the responsible relative's income for payment of support and the fee provided for in this Section shall not be in excess of the amounts permitted under the federal Consumer Credit Protection Act [15 U.S.C. § 1601 et seq.].

In a case receiving child support enforcement services, the Illinois Department may request and obtain information from a particular employer under this Section no more than once in any 12-month period, unless the information is necessary to conduct a review of a court or administrative order for support at the request of the person receiving child support enforcement services.

The Illinois Department shall establish and maintain an administrative unit to receive and transmit to the Child and Spouse Support Unit information supplied by persons applying for or receiving child support enforcement services under Section 10-1 [305 ILCS 5/10-1]. In addition, the Illinois Department shall address and respond to any alleged deficiencies that persons receiving or applying for services from the Child and Spouse Support Unit may identify concerning the Child and Spouse Support Unit's provision of child support enforcement services. Within 60 days after an action or failure to act by the Child and Spouse Support Unit that affects his or her case, a recipient of or applicant for child support enforcement services under Article X of this Code may request an explanation of the Unit's handling of the case. At the requestor's option, the explanation may be provided either orally in an interview, in writing, or both. If the Illinois Department fails to respond to the request for an explanation or fails to respond in a manner satisfactory to the applicant or recipient within 30 days from the date of the request for an explanation, the applicant or recipient may request a conference for further review of the matter by the Office of the Administrator of the Child and Spouse Support Unit. A request for a conference may be submitted at any time within 60 days after the explanation has been provided by the Child and Spouse Support Unit or within 60 days after the time for providing the explanation has expired.

The applicant or recipient may request a conference concerning any decision denying or terminating child support enforcement services under Article X of this Code [305 ILCS 5/10-1 et seq.], and the applicant or recipient may also request a conference concerning the Unit's failure to provide services or the provision of services in an amount or manner that is considered inadequate. For purposes of this Section, the Child and Spouse Support Unit includes all local governmental units or individuals with whom the Illinois Department has contracted under Section 10-3.1 [305 ILCS 5/10-3.1].

Upon receipt of a timely request for a conference, the Office of the Administrator shall review the case. The applicant or recipient requesting the conference shall be entitled, at his or her option, to appear in person or to participate in the conference by telephone. The applicant or recipient requesting the conference shall be entitled to be represented and to be afforded a reasonable opportunity to review the Illinois Department's file before or at the conference. At the conference, the applicant or recipient requesting the conference shall be afforded an opportunity to present all relevant matters in support of his or her claim. Conferences shall be without cost to the applicant or recipient requesting the conference and shall be conducted by a representative of the Child or Spouse Support Unit who did not participate in the action or inaction being reviewed.

The Office of the Administrator shall conduct a conference and inform all interested parties, in writing, of the results of the conference within 60 days from the date of filing of the request for a conference.

In addition to its other powers and responsibilities established by this Article, the Child and Spouse Support Unit shall conduct an annual assessment of each institution's program for institution based paternity establishment under Section 12 of the Vital Records Act [410 ILCS 535/12].

(Source: P.A. 86-752; 88-307, § 5; 88-687, § 5; 90-18, § 65; 91-24, § 25; 91-613, § 935; 92-16, § 76; 92-590, § 5.)

Note.

This section was Ill.Rev.Stat., Ch. 23, para. 10-3.1.

The Revised Uniform Reciprocal Enforcement of Support Act, referred to above, has been repealed.

Section 70 of P.A. 91-613 contains a severability provision.

The Non-Support of Spouse and Children Act, 750 ILCS 15/1 et seq., referred to in the second paragraph, is repealed. Current similar provisions are found as the Non-Support Punishment Act, 750 ILCS 16/1 et seq.

Section 996 of P.A. 92-16 contains a "no acceleration or delay" provision, and Section 997 contains a "no revival or extension" provision.

Illinois Administrative Code.

See 89 Illinois Administrative Code, § 160.65.

Effect of Amendments.

The 1994 amendment by P.A. 88-687, effective January 24, 1995, in the second paragraph, in the third sentence substituted "Revised Uniform Reciprocal Enforcement of Support Act; under the Illinois Parentage Act of 1984; under the Non-Support of Spouse and Children Act" for "'Revised Uniform Reciprocal Enforcement of Support Act', approved August 28, 1969, as amended; under Section 4 of the 'Paternity Act', approved July 5, 1957, as amended, where the Department files action in behalf of a child to determine the paternity of that child and to obtain support from the person adjudicated to be the father; under the 'Non-Support of Spouse and Children Act', approved June 24, 1915, as amended"; in the third paragraph, in the first sentence substituted "moneys" for "monies"; added the fourth paragraph; and added the fifteenth paragraph.

The 1997 amendment by P.A. 90-18, effective July 1, 1997, in the eighth paragraph, in the first sentence, deleted from the beginning "If the responsible relative fails to fully respond to the notice for information within 15 days after the date the relative receives the notice".

The 1999 amendment by P.A. 91-24, effective July 1, 1999, substituted "DHS" for "Public Assistance" preceding "Recoveries Trust Fund" in the second sentence of the fifth paragraph.

The 1999 amendment by P.A. 91-613, effective October 1, 1999, inserted "under the Non-Support Punishment Act" in the last sentence of the second paragraph.

The 2001 amendment by P.A. 92-16, effective June 28, 2001, combined the amendments by P.A. 91-24 and P.A. 91-613.

The 2002 amendment by P.A. 92-590, effective July 1, 2002, substituted "child support enforcement services" for "child and spouse support services" throughout.

305 ILCS 5/10-3.2 Parent Locator Service

Sec. 10-3.2. *Parent Locator Service.* The Illinois Department through its Child and Spouse Support Unit shall enter into agreements with the Secretary of Health and Human Services or his designee under which the services of the federal Parent Locator Service established by the Social Security Act [42 U.S.C. § 301 et seq.] are made available to this State and the Illinois Department for the purpose of locating an absent parent or child when the child has been abducted or otherwise improperly removed or retained from the physical custody of a parent or other person entitled to custody of the child, or in connection with the making or enforcing of a child custody determination in custody proceedings instituted under the Uniform Child Custody Jurisdiction Act [750 ILCS 35/1 et seq.] or the Uniform Child-Custody Jurisdiction and Enforcement Act [repealed], or otherwise in accordance with law. The Illinois Department shall provide general information to the public about the availability and use of the Parent Locator Service in relation to child abduction and custody determination proceedings, shall promptly respond to inquiries made by those parties specified by federal regulations upon receipt of information as to the location of an absent parent or child from the federal Parent Locator Service and

shall maintain accurate records as to the number of such inquiries received and processed by the Department.
(Source: P.A. 83-1396; 93-108, § 402.1.)

Note.
750 ILCS 35/1 et seq., was repealed. See now 750 ILCS 36/101 et seq.
This section was Ill.Rev.Stat., Ch. 23, para. 10-3.2.

Effect of Amendments.
The 2003 amendment by P.A. 93-108, effective January 1, 2004, inserted "or the Uniform Child-Custody Jurisdiction and Enforcement Act" in the first sentence.

305 ILCS 5/10-3.3 Locating support obligor and others; penalties

Sec. 10-3.3. *Locating support obligor and others; penalties.* (a) Upon request by the Child and Spouse Support Unit, employers, labor unions, and telephone companies shall provide location information concerning putative fathers and noncustodial parents for the purpose of establishing a child's paternity or establishing, enforcing, or modifying a child support obligation. In this Section, "location information" means information about (i) the physical whereabouts of a putative father or noncustodial parent, (ii) the putative father or noncustodial parent's employer, or (iii) the salary, wages, and other compensation paid and the health insurance coverage provided to the putative father or noncustodial parent by the employer of the putative father or noncustodial parent or by a labor union of which the putative father or noncustodial parent is a member.

An employer, labor union, or telephone company shall respond to the request of the Child and Spouse Support Unit within 15 days after receiving the request. Any employer, labor union, or telephone company that willfully fails to fully respond within the 15-day period shall be subject to a penalty of $100 for each day that the response is not provided to the Illinois Department after the 15-day period has expired. The penalty may be collected in a civil action, which may be brought against the employer, labor union, or telephone company in favor of the Illinois Department.

(b) Upon being served with an administrative subpoena as authorized under this Code, a utility company or cable television company must provide location information to the Child and Spouse Support Unit for the purpose of establishing a child's paternity or establishing, enforcing, or modifying a child support obligation.

(c) Notwithstanding the provisions of any other State or local law to the contrary, an employer, labor union, telephone company, utility company, or cable television company shall not be liable to any person for disclosure of location information under the requirements of this Section, except for willful and wanton misconduct.
(Source: P.A. 89-395, § 15; 90-18, § 65; 93-116, § 5.)

Effective Date.
This section became effective January 1, 1996 pursuant to Ill. Const. (1970), Art. IV, § 10 and 5 ILCS 75/1.

Effect of Amendments.
The 1997 amendment by P.A. 90-18, effective July 1, 1997, in the section catchline added at the end "and others; penalties"; added the subsection (a) designation; added the second paragraph in subsection (a); and added subsection (b).
The 2003 amendment by P.A. 93-116, effective July 10, 2003, rewrote the section to the extent that a detailed comparison would be impracticable.

305 ILCS 5/10-3.4 Obtaining location information

Sec. 10-3.4. *Obtaining location information.* (a) The Illinois Department shall enter into agreements with the Department of State Police and the Secretary of State to obtain location information on persons for the purpose of establishing paternity, and establishing, modifying, and enforcing child support obligations.

(b) Upon request, the Illinois Department shall provide information obtained pursuant to this Section to federal agencies and other states' agencies conducting child support enforcement activities under Title IV, Part D of the Social Security Act [42 U.S.C. § 601 et seq.].
(Source: P.A. 90-18, § 65.)

Effective Date.
Section 999 of P.A. 90-18 made this section effective July 1, 1997.

305 ILCS 5/10-4 Notification of Support Obligation

Sec. 10-4. *Notification of Support Obligation.* The administrative enforcement unit within the authorized area of its operation shall notify each responsible relative of an applicant or recipient, or responsible relatives of other persons given access to the child support enforcement services of this Article, of his legal obligation to support and shall request such information concerning his financial status as may be necessary to determine whether he is financially able to provide such support, in whole or in part. In cases involving a child born out of wedlock, the notification shall include a statement that the responsible relative has been named as the biological father of the child identified in the notification.

In the case of applicants, the notification shall be sent as soon as practical after the filing of the application. In the case of recipients, the notice shall be sent at such time as may be established by rule of the Illinois Department.

The notice shall be accompanied by the forms or questionnaires provided in Section 10-5 [305 ILCS 5/10-5]. It shall inform the relative that he may be liable for reimbursement of any support furnished from public aid funds prior to determination of the relative's financial circumstances, as well as for future support. In the alternative, when support is sought on behalf of applicants for or recipients of financial aid under Article IV of this Code [305 ILCS 5/4-0.5 et seq.] and other persons who are given access to the child support enforcement services of this Article as provided in Section 10-1 [305 ILCS 5/10-1], the notice shall inform the relative that the relative may be required to pay support for a period before the date an administrative support order is entered, as well as future support.

Neither the mailing nor receipt of such notice shall be deemed a jurisdictional requirement for the subsequent exercise of the investigative procedures undertaken by an administrative enforcement unit or the entry of any order or determination of paternity or support or reimbursement by the administrative enforcement unit; except that notice shall be served by certified mail addressed to the responsible relative at his or her last known address, return receipt requested, or by any method provided by law for service of summons, in cases where a determination of paternity or support by default is sought on behalf of applicants for or recipients of financial aid under Article IV of this Act [305 ILCS 5/4-0.5 et seq.] and other persons who are given access to the child support enforcement services of this Article as provided in Section 10-1 [305 ILCS 5/10-1].
(Source: P.A. 84-758; 88-687, § 5; 92-590, § 5.)

Note.
This section was Ill.Rev.Stat., Ch. 23, para. 10-4.

Effect of Amendments.
The 1994 amendment by P.A. 88-687, effective January 24, 1995, in the first paragraph added the second sentence; in the third paragraph added the third sentence; and in the fourth paragraph, substituted "of paternity or" for "for" and inserted "a determination of paternity or".
The 2002 amendment by P.A. 92-590, effective July 1, 2002, substituted references to "child support enforcement services" for references to "child and spouse support services" throughout the section.

305 ILCS 5/10-5 Declarations by Responsible Relatives — Penalty

Sec. 10-5. *Declarations by Responsible Relatives — Penalty.* Information requested of responsible relatives shall be submitted on forms or questionnaires prescribed by the Illinois Department or local governmental units, as the case may be, and shall contain a written declaration to be signed by the relative in substantially the following form:

"I declare under penalties of perjury that I have examined this form (or questionnaire) and all accompanying statements or documents pertaining to my income, resources, or any other matter having bearing upon my status and ability to provide support, and to the best of my knowledge and belief the information supplied is true, correct, and complete".

A person who makes and subscribes a form or questionnaire which contains, as hereinabove provided, a written declaration that it is made under the penalties of perjury, knowing it to be false, incorrect or incomplete, in respect to any material statement or representation bearing upon his status as a responsible relative, or upon his income, resources, or other matter concerning his ability to provide support, shall be subject to the penalties for perjury provided for in Section 32-2 of the "Criminal Code of 1961", approved July 28, 1961, as amended [720 ILCS 5/32-2].
(Source: Laws 1967, p. 122.)

Note.
This section was Ill.Rev.Stat., Ch. 23, para. 10-5.

305 ILCS 5/10-6 Investigation and Determination

Sec. 10-6. *Investigation and Determination.* The administrative enforcement unit shall review the forms or questionnaires returned by each responsible relative and supplement the information provided therein, where required, by such additional consultations with the responsible relative and such other investigations as may be necessary, including genetic testing if paternity is an issue and, applying the standard or guidelines and regulations established by the Illinois Department, shall determine whether and the extent to which, the responsible relative individually or together in any combination, are reasonably able to provide support. If the child was born out of wedlock and the case is subject to the voluntary acknowledgment of paternity or the administrative determination of paternity under rules established under Section 10-17.7 [305 ILCS 5/10-17.7], the Child and Spouse Support Unit of the Illinois Department shall determine the child support obligation under subsection (b) of Section 10-7 [305 ILCS 5/10-7] upon establishing the child's paternity. If the child's paternity was established by judicial or administrative process in any other state, the Illinois Department may use administrative processes contained in this Article X to establish a child support order.

In aid of its investigative authority, the Child and Spouse Support Unit of the Illinois Department may use the subpoena power as set forth in this Article.

The Illinois Department, by rule, may authorize the administrative enforcement units to conduct periodic or other reinvestigations and redeterminations of the financial ability of responsible relatives. Any redeterminations shall have the effect of altering, amending, or modifying previous determinations and administrative orders entered pursuant to Sections 10-7 and 10-11 [305 ILCS 5/10-7 and 305 ILCS 5/10-11]. However, any redetermination which establishes liability for support or reimbursement, or which modifies the support or reimbursement liability specified in a prior order, shall be subject to the provisions of Section 10-12 [305 ILCS 5/10-12] and the administrative and judicial review procedures herein provided for original orders.
(Source: P.A. 84-758; 88-687, § 5; 89-641, § 15; 90-18, § 65.)

Note.
This section was Ill.Rev.Stat., Ch. 23, para. 10-6.

Effect of Amendments.

The 1994 amendment by P.A. 88-687, effective January 24, 1995, in the first paragraph, in the first sentence, inserted "including genetic testing if paternity is an issue" and added the second sentence.

The 1996 amendment by P.A. 89-641, effective August 9, 1996, in the first paragraph, in the second sentence, inserted "the voluntary acknowledgment of paternity or"; and substituted "establishing" for "determining".

The 1997 amendment by P.A. 90-18, effective July 1, 1997, in the first paragraph added the third sentence.

305 ILCS 5/10-7 Notice of support due

Sec. 10-7. *Notice of support due.* (a) When an administrative enforcement unit has determined that a responsible relative is financially able to contribute to the support of an applicant or recipient, the responsible relative shall be notified by mailing him a copy of the determination by United States registered or certified mail, advising him of his legal obligation to make support payments for such period or periods of time, definite in duration or indefinite, as the circumstances require. The notice shall direct payment as provided in Section 10-8 [305 ILCS 5/10-8]. Where applicable, the determination and notice may include a demand for reimbursement for emergency aid granted an applicant or recipient during the period between the application and determination of the relative's obligation for support and for aid granted during any subsequent period the responsible relative was financially able to provide support but failed or refused to do so.

(b) In the alternative, when support is sought on behalf of applicants for or recipients of financial aid under Article IV of this Act [305 ILCS 5/4-0.5 et seq.] and other persons who are given access to the child support enforcement services of this Article as provided in Section 10-1 [305 ILCS 5/10-1], the administrative enforcement unit shall not be required to send the notice and may enter an administrative order immediately under the provisions of Section 10-11 [305 ILCS 5/10-11]. The order shall be based upon the determination made under the provisions of Section 10-6 [305 ILCS 5/10-6] or, in instances of default, upon the needs of the persons for whom support is sought. In addition to requiring payment of future support, the administrative order may require payment of support for a period before the date the order is entered. The amount of support to be paid for the prior period shall be determined under the guidelines established by the Illinois Department pursuant to Section 10-3 [305 ILCS 5/10-3]. The order shall direct payment as provided in Section 10-10 [305 ILCS 5/10-10].

(Source: P.A. 84-1389; 88-687, § 5; 92-590, § 5.)

Note.

This section was Ill.Rev.Stat., Ch. 23, para. 10-7.

Effect of Amendments.

The 1994 amendment by P.A. 88-687, effective January 24, 1995, moved the subsection (a) designation from in front of "Notice" to its present location; and in subsection (b), in the first sentence substituted "when" for "where" and added the third and fourth sentences.

The 2002 amendment by P.A. 92-590, effective July 1, 2002, substituted "child support enforcement services" for "child and spouse support services" in subsection (b).

305 ILCS 5/10-8 Support Payments — Partial Support — Full Support

Sec. 10-8. *Support Payments — Partial Support — Full Support.* The notice to responsible relatives issued pursuant to Section 10-7 [305 ILCS 5/10-7] shall direct payment (a) to the Illinois Department in cases of applicants and recipients under Articles III, IV, V and VII, (b) except as provided in Section 10-3.1 [305 ILCS 5/10-3.1], to the local governmental unit in the case of applicants and recipients under Article VI, and (c) to the Illinois Department in cases of non-applicants and non-recipients given access to the child support enforcement services of this Article, as provided by Section 10-1 [305 ILCS 5/10-1]. However, if the support payments by responsible relatives are sufficient to meet needs of a recipient in full, including current and anticipated medical needs, and the Illinois Department or the local governmental unit, as the case may be, has reasonable grounds to believe that such needs will continue to be provided in full by the responsible relatives, the relatives may be directed to make subsequent support payments to the needy person or to some person or agency in his behalf and the recipient shall be removed from the rolls. In such instance the recipient also shall be notified by registered or certified mail of the action taken. If a recipient removed from the rolls requests the Illinois Department to continue to collect the support payments in his behalf, the Department, at its option, may do so and pay amounts so collected to the person. The Department may provide for deducting any costs incurred by it in making the collection from the amount of any recovery made and pay only the net amount to the person.

Payments under this Section to the Illinois Department pursuant to the Child Support Enforcement Program established by Title IV-D of the Social Security Act [42 U.S.C. § 651 et seq.] shall be paid into the Child Support Enforcement Trust Fund. All payments under this Section to the Illinois Department of Human Services shall be deposited in the DHS Recoveries Trust Fund. Disbursements from these funds shall be as provided in Sections 12-9.1 and 12-10.2 of this Code [305 ILCS 5/12-9.1 and 305 ILCS 5/12-10.2]. Payments received by a local governmental unit shall be deposited in that unit's General Assistance Fund.

To the extent the provisions of this Section are inconsistent with the requirements pertaining to the State Disbursement Unit under Sections 10-10.4 and 10-26 of this Code [305 ILCS 5/10-10.4 and 305 ILCS 5/10-26], the requirements pertaining to the State Disbursement Unit shall apply.

(Source: P.A. 83-1126; 91-24, § 25; 91-212, § 20; 92-16, § 76; 92-590, § 5.)

Note.

This section was Ill.Rev.Stat., Ch. 23, para. 10-8.

Article VII of this Code, referred to in (a) above, has been repealed.

Section 996 of P.A. 92-16 contains a "no acceleration or delay" provision, and Section 997 contains a "no revival or extension" provision.

Effect of Amendments.

The 1999 amendment by P.A. 91-24, effective July 1, 1999, in the second paragraph deleted "other" following "All", inserted "of Human Services" preceding "shall be deposited in the", and substituted "DHS" for "Public Assistance" in the second sentence, and substituted "12-9.1" for "12-9" in the third sentence.

The 1999 amendment by P.A. 91-212, effective July 20, 1999, added the last paragraph.

The 2001 amendment by P.A. 92-16, effective June 28, 2001, combined the amendments by P.A. 91-24 and P.A. 91-212.

The 2002 amendment by P.A. 92-590, effective July 1, 2002, substituted "child support enforcement services" for "child and spouse support services" in the first sentence of the first paragraph.

305 ILCS 5/10-8.1 Temporary order for child support

Sec. 10-8.1. *Temporary order for child support.* Notwithstanding any other law to the contrary, pending the outcome of an administrative determination of parentage, the Illinois Department shall issue a temporary order for child support, upon motion by a party and a showing of clear and convincing evidence of paternity. In determining the amount of the temporary child support award, the Illinois Department shall use the guidelines and standards set forth in subsection (a) of Section 505 and in Section 505.2 of the Illinois Marriage and Dissolution of Marriage Act [750 ILCS 5/505 and 750 ILCS 5/505.2].

Any new or existing support order entered by the Illinois Department under this Section shall be deemed to be a series of judgments against the person obligated to pay support thereunder, each such judgment to be in the amount of each payment or installment of support and each judgment to be deemed entered as of the date the corresponding payment or installment becomes due under the terms of the support order. Each such judgment shall have the full force, effect, and attributes of any other judgment of this State, including the ability to be enforced. Any such judgment is subject to modification or termination only in accordance with Section 510 of the Illinois Marriage and Dissolution of Marriage Act [750 ILCS 5/510]. A lien arises by operation of law against the real and personal property of the noncustodial parent for each installment of overdue support owed by the noncustodial parent.

All orders for support entered or modified in a case in which a party is receiving child support enforcement services under this Article X shall include a provision requiring the non-custodial parent to notify the Illinois Department, within 7 days, (i) of the name, address, and telephone number of any new employer of the non-custodial parent, (ii) whether the non-custodial parent has access to health insurance coverage through the employer or other group coverage, and, if so, the policy name and number and the names of persons covered under the policy, and (iii) of any new residential or mailing address or telephone number of the non-custodial parent.

In any subsequent action to enforce a support order, upon sufficient showing that diligent effort has been made to ascertain the location of the non-custodial parent, service of process or provision of notice necessary in that action may be made at the last known address of the non-custodial parent, in any manner expressly provided by the Code of Civil Procedure [735 ILCS 5/1-101 et seq.] or this Act, which service shall be sufficient for purposes of due process.

An order for support shall include a date on which the current support obligation terminates. The termination date shall be no earlier than the date on which the child covered by the order will attain the age of 18. However, if the child will not graduate from high school until after attaining the age of 18, then the termination date shall be no earlier than the earlier of the date on which the child's high school graduation will occur or the date on which the child will attain the age of 19. The order for support shall state that the termination date does not apply to any arrearage that may remain unpaid on that date. Nothing in this paragraph shall be construed to prevent the Illinois Department from modifying the order or terminating the order in the event the child is otherwise emancipated.

If there is an unpaid arrearage or delinquency (as those terms are defined in the Income Withholding for Support Act [750 ILCS 28/1 et seq.]) equal to at least one month's support obligation on the termination date stated in the order for support or, if there is no termination date stated in the order, on the date the child attains the age of majority or is otherwise emancipated, then the periodic amount required to be paid for current support of that child immediately prior to that date shall automatically continue to be an obligation, not as current support but as periodic payment toward satisfaction of the unpaid arrearage or delinquency. That periodic payment shall be in addition to any periodic payment previously required for satisfaction of the arrearage or delinquency. The total periodic amount to be paid toward satisfaction of the arrearage or delinquency may be enforced and collected by any method provided by law for the enforcement and collection of child support, including but not limited to income withholding under the Income Withholding for Support Act [750 ILCS 28/1 et seq.]. Each order for support entered or modified on or after the effective date of this amendatory Act of the 93rd General Assembly [P.A. 93-1061] must contain a statement notifying the parties of the requirements of this paragraph. Failure to include the statement in the order for support does not affect the validity of the order or the operation of the provisions of this paragraph with regard to the order. This paragraph shall not be construed to prevent or affect the establishment or modification of an order for the

support of a minor child or the establishment or modification of an order for the support of a non-minor child or educational expenses under Section 513 of the Illinois Marriage and Dissolution of Marriage Act [750 ILCS 5/513].
(Source: P.A. 90-18, § 65; 92-590, § 5; 92-876, § 905; 93-1061, § 5.)

Illinois Administrative Code.
See 89 Illinois Administrative Code, § 160.88.

Effective Date.
Section 999 of P.A. 90-18 made this Section effective July 1, 1997.

Effect of Amendments.
The 2002 amendment by P.A. 92-590, effective July 1, 2002, substituted "child support enforcement services" for references to "child and spouse support services" in the third paragraph.
The 2002 amendment by P.A. 92-876, effective June 1, 2003, in the last paragraph substituted "age of 18. However, if the child will not graduate from high school until after attaining the age of 18, then the termination date shall be no earlier than the earlier of the date on which the child's high school graduation will occur or the date on which the child will attain the age of 19" for "age of majority or is otherwise emancipated", and added "or terminating the order in the event the child is otherwise emancipated" at the end.
The 2004 amendment by P.A. 93-1061, effective January 1, 2005, added the last paragraph.

305 ILCS 5/10-9 Alternative Actions to Enforce Support

Sec. 10-9. *Alternative Actions to Enforce Support.* If a responsible relative fails or refuses to furnish support, or contributes less than the amount indicated by the determination, the administrative enforcement unit shall take action to enforce support in accordance with Section 10-10 or Section 10-11 [305 ILCS 5/10-10 or 305 ILCS 5/10-11].
(Source: Laws 1967, p. 122.)

Note.
This section was Ill.Rev.Stat., Ch. 23, para. 10-9.

305 ILCS 5/10-10 Court enforcement; applicability also to persons who are not applicants or recipients

Sec. 10-10. *Court enforcement; applicability also to persons who are not applicants or recipients.* Except where the Illinois Department, by agreement, acts for the local governmental unit, as provided in Section 10-3.1 [305 ILCS 5/10-3.1], local governmental units shall refer to the State's Attorney or to the proper legal representative of the governmental unit, for judicial enforcement as herein provided, instances of non-support or insufficient support when the dependents are applicants or recipients under Article VI. The Child and Spouse Support Unit established by Section 10-3.1 [305 ILCS 5/10-3.1] may institute in behalf of the Illinois Department any actions under this Section for judicial enforcement of the support liability when the dependents are (a) applicants or recipients under Articles III, IV, V or VII; (b) applicants or recipients in a local governmental unit when the Illinois Department, by agreement, acts for the unit; or (c) non-applicants or non-recipients who are receiving child support enforcement services under this Article X, as provided in Section 10-1 [305 ILCS 5/10-1]. Where the Child and Spouse Support Unit has exercised its option and discretion not to apply the provisions of Sections 10-3 through 10-8 [305 ILCS 5/10-3 through 305 ILCS 5/10-8], the failure by the Unit to apply such provisions shall not be a bar to bringing an action under this Section.

Action shall be brought in the circuit court to obtain support, or for the recovery of aid granted during the period such support was not provided, or both for the obtainment of support and the recovery of the aid provided. Actions for the recovery of aid may be taken separately or they may be consolidated with actions to obtain support. Such actions may be brought in the name of the person or persons requiring support, or may be brought in the name of the Illinois Department or the local governmental unit, as the case requires, in behalf of such persons.

The court may enter such orders for the payment of moneys for the support of the person as may be just and equitable and may direct payment thereof for such period or periods of time as the circumstances require, including support for a period before the date the order for support is entered. The order may be entered against any or all of the defendant responsible relatives and may be based upon the proportionate ability of each to contribute to the person's support.

The Court shall determine the amount of child support (including child support for a period before the date the order for child support is entered) by using the guidelines and standards set forth in subsection (a) of Section 505 and in Section 505.2 of the Illinois Marriage and Dissolution of Marriage Act [750 ILCS 5/505 and 750 ILCS 5/505.2]. For purposes of determining the amount of child support to be paid for a period before the date the order for child support is entered, there is a rebuttable presumption that the responsible relative's net income for that period was the same as his or her net income at the time the order is entered.

If (i) the responsible relative was properly served with a request for discovery of financial information relating to the responsible relative's ability to provide child support, (ii) the responsible relative failed to comply with the request, despite having been ordered to do so by the court, and (iii) the responsible relative is not present at the hearing to determine support despite having received proper notice, then any relevant financial information concerning the responsible relative's ability to provide child support that was obtained pursuant to subpoena and proper notice shall be admitted into evidence without the need to establish any further foundation for its admission.

An order entered under this Section shall include a provision requiring the obligor to report to the obligee and to the clerk of court within 10 days each time the obligor obtains new employment, and each time the obligor's employment is terminated for any reason. The report shall be in writing and shall, in the case of new employment, include the name and address of the new employer. Failure to report new employment or the termination of current employment, if coupled with nonpayment of support for a period in excess of 60 days, is indirect criminal contempt. For any obligor arrested for failure to report new employment bond shall be set in the amount of the child support that should have been paid during the period of unreported employment. An order entered under this Section shall also include a provision requiring the obligor and obligee parents to advise each other of a change in residence within 5 days of the change except when the court finds that the physical, mental, or emotional health of a party or that of a minor child, or both, would be seriously endangered by disclosure of the party's address.

The Court shall determine the amount of maintenance using the standards set forth in Section 504 of the Illinois Marriage and Dissolution of Marriage Act [750 ILCS 5/504].

Any new or existing support order entered by the court under this Section shall be deemed to be a series of judgments against the person obligated to pay support thereunder, each such judgment to be in the amount of each payment or installment of support and each such judgment to be deemed entered as of the date the corresponding payment or installment becomes due under the terms of the support order. Each such judgment shall have the full force, effect and attributes of any other judgment of this State, including the ability to be enforced. Any such judgment is subject to modification or termination only in accordance with Section 510 of the Illinois Marriage and Dissolution of Marriage Act [750 ILCS 5/510]. A lien arises by operation of law against the real and personal property of the noncustodial parent for each installment of overdue support owed by the noncustodial parent.

When an order is entered for the support of a minor, the court may provide therein for reasonable visitation of the minor by the person or persons who provided support pursuant to the order. Whoever willfully refuses to comply with such visitation order or willfully interferes with its enforcement may be declared in contempt of court and punished therefor.

Except where the local governmental unit has entered into an agreement with the Illinois Department for the Child and Spouse Support Unit to act for it, as provided in Section 10-3.1 [305 ILCS 5/10-3.1], support orders entered by the court in cases involving applicants or recipients under Article VI shall provide that payments thereunder be made directly to the local governmental unit. Orders for the support of all other applicants or recipients shall provide that payments thereunder be made directly to the Illinois Department. In accordance with federal law and regulations, the Illinois Department may continue to collect current maintenance payments or child support payments, or both, after those persons cease to receive public assistance and until termination of services under Article X. The Illinois Department shall pay the net amount collected to those persons after deducting any costs incurred in making the collection or any collection fee from the amount of any recovery made. In both cases the order shall permit the local governmental unit or the Illinois Department, as the case may be, to direct the responsible relative or relatives to make support payments directly to the needy person, or to some person or agency in his behalf, upon removal of the person from the public aid rolls or upon termination of services under Article X.

If the notice of support due issued pursuant to Section 10-7 [305 ILCS 5/10-7] directs that support payments be made directly to the needy person, or to some person or agency in his behalf, and the recipient is removed from the public aid rolls, court action may be taken against the responsible relative hereunder if he fails to furnish support in accordance with the terms of such notice.

Actions may also be brought under this Section in behalf of any person who is in need of support from responsible relatives, as defined in Section 2-11 of Article II [305 ILCS 5/2-11] who is not an applicant for or recipient of financial aid under this Code. In such instances, the State's Attorney of the county in which such person resides shall bring action against the responsible relatives hereunder. If the Illinois Department, as authorized by Section 10-1 [305 ILCS 5/10-1], extends the child support enforcement services provided by this Article to spouses and dependent children who are not applicants or recipients under this Code, the Child and Spouse Support Unit established by Section 10-3.1 [305 ILCS 5/10-3.1] shall bring action against the responsible relatives hereunder and any support orders entered by the court in such cases shall provide that payments thereunder be made directly to the Illinois Department.

Whenever it is determined in a proceeding to establish or enforce a child support or maintenance obligation that the person owing a duty of support is unemployed, the court may order the person to seek employment and report periodically to the court with a diary, listing or other memorandum of his or her efforts in accordance with such order. Additionally, the court may order the unemployed person to report to the Department of Employment Security for job search services or to make application with the local Job Training Partnership Act [29 U.S.C. § 1501 et seq.] provider for participation in job search, training or work programs and where the duty of support is owed to a child receiving child support enforcement services under this Article X, the court may order the unemployed person to report to the Illinois Department for participation in job search, training or work programs established under Section 9-6 and Article IXA of this Code [305 ILCS 5/9-6 and 305 ILCS 5/9A-1 et seq.].

Whenever it is determined that a person owes past-due support for a child receiving assistance under this Code, the court shall order at the request of the Illinois Department:

(1) that the person pay the past-due support in accordance with a plan approved by the court; or

(2) if the person owing past-due support is unemployed, is subject to such a plan, and is not incapacitated, that the person participate in such job search, training, or work programs established under Section 9-6 and Article IXA of this Code [305 ILCS 5/9-6 and 305 ILCS 5/9A-1 et seq.] as the court deems appropriate.

A determination under this Section shall not be administratively reviewable by the procedures specified in Sections 10-12, and 10-13 to 10-13.10 [305 ILCS 5/10-12, and 305 ILCS 5/10-13 to 305 ILCS 5/10-13.10]. Any determination under these Sections, if made the basis of court action under this Section, shall not affect the de novo judicial determination required under this Section.

A one-time charge of 20% is imposable upon the amount of past-due child support owed on July 1, 1988 which has accrued under a support order entered by the court. The charge shall be imposed in accordance with the provisions of Section 10-21 of this Code [305 ILCS 5/10-21] and shall be enforced by the court upon petition.

All orders for support, when entered or modified, shall include a provision requiring the non-custodial parent to notify the court and, in cases in which a party is receiving child support enforcement services under this Article X, the Illinois Department, within 7 days, (i) of the name, address, and telephone number of any new employer of the non-custodial parent, (ii) whether the non-custodial parent has access to health insurance coverage through the employer or other group coverage and, if so, the policy name and number and the names of persons covered under the policy, and (iii) of any new residential or mailing address or telephone number of the non-custodial parent. In any subsequent action to enforce a support order, upon a sufficient showing that a diligent effort has been made to ascertain the location of the non-custodial parent, service of process or provision of notice necessary in the case may be made at the last known address of the non-custodial parent in any manner expressly provided by the Code of Civil Procedure [735 ILCS 5/1-101 et seq.] or this Code, which service shall be sufficient for purposes of due process.

An order for support shall include a date on which the current support obligation terminates. The termination date shall be no earlier than the date on which the child covered by the order will attain the age of 18. However, if the child will not graduate from high school until after attaining the age of 18, then the termination date shall be no earlier than the earlier of the date on which the child's high school graduation will occur or the date on which the child will attain the age of 19. The order for support shall state that the termination date does not apply to any arrearage that may remain unpaid on that date. Nothing in this paragraph shall be construed to prevent the court from modifying the order or terminating the order in the event the child is otherwise emancipated.

If there is an unpaid arrearage or delinquency (as those terms are defined in the Income Withholding for Support Act [750 ILCS 28/1 et seq.]) equal to at least one month's support obligation on the termination date stated in the order for support or, if there is no termination date stated in the order, on the date the child attains the age of majority or is otherwise emancipated, then the periodic amount required to be paid for current support of that child immediately prior to that date shall automatically continue to be an obligation, not as current support but as periodic payment toward satisfaction of the unpaid arrearage or delinquency. That periodic payment shall be in addition to any periodic payment previously required for satisfaction of the arrearage or delinquency. The total periodic amount to be paid toward satisfaction of the arrearage or delinquency may be enforced and collected by any method provided by law for the enforcement and collection of child support, including but not limited to income withholding under the Income Withholding for Support Act [750 ILCS 28/1 et seq.]. Each order for support entered or modified on or after the effective date of this amendatory Act of the 93rd General Assembly [P.A. 93-1061] must contain a statement notifying the parties of the requirements of this paragraph. Failure to include the statement in the order for support does not affect the validity of the order or the operation of the provisions of this paragraph with regard to the order. This paragraph shall not be construed to prevent or affect the establishment or modification of an order for the support of a minor child or the establishment or modification of an order for the support of a non-minor child or educational expenses under Section 513 of the Illinois Marriage and Dissolution of Marriage Act [750 ILCS 5/513].

Upon notification in writing or by electronic transmission from the Illinois Department to the clerk of the court that a person who is receiving support payments under this Section is receiving services under the Child Support Enforcement Program established by Title IV-D of the Social Security Act [42 U.S.C. § 651 et seq.], any support payments subsequently received by the clerk of the court shall be transmitted in accordance with the instructions of the Illinois Department until the Illinois Department gives notice to the clerk of the court to cease the transmittal. After providing the notification authorized under this paragraph, the Illinois Department shall be entitled as a party to notice of any further proceedings in the case. The clerk of the court shall file a copy of the Illinois Department's notification in the court file. The clerk's failure to file a copy of the notification in the court file shall not, however, affect the Illinois Department's right to receive notice of further proceedings.

Payments under this Section to the Illinois Department pursuant to the Child Support Enforcement Program established by Title IV-D of the Social Security Act [42 U.S.C. § 651 et seq.] shall be paid into the Child Support Enforcement Trust Fund. All payments under this Section to the Illinois Department of Human Services shall be deposited in the DHS Recoveries Trust Fund. Disbursements from these funds shall be as provided in Sections 12-9.1 and 12-10.2 of this Code [305 ILCS 5/12-9.1 and 305 ILCS 5/12-10.2]. Payments received by a local governmental unit shall be deposited in that unit's General Assistance Fund.

To the extent the provisions of this Section are inconsistent with the requirements pertaining to the State Disbursement Unit under Sections 10-10.4 and 10-26 of this Code [305 ILCS 5/10-10.4 and 305 ILCS 5/10-26], the requirements pertaining to the State Disbursement Unit shall apply.

(Source: P.A. 86-649; 88-307, § 5; 88-687, § 5; 90-18, § 65; 90-539, § 5; 90-655, § 127; 90-673, § 910; 90-790, § 5; 91-24, § 25; 91-212, § 20; 91-357, § 168; 91-767, § 5; 92-16, § 76; 92-590, § 5; 92-876, § 905; 93-1061, § 5.)

Note.

This section was Ill.Rev.Stat., Ch. 23, para. 10-10.

P.A. 91-357, § 996, contains a "no acceleration or delay" provision, and P.A. 91-357, § 997, contains a "no revival or extension" provision.

Article VII, referred to above, has been repealed.

Section 996 of P.A. 92-16 contains a "no acceleration or delay" provision, and Section 997 contains a "no revival or extension" provision.

Illinois Administrative Code.

See 89 Illinois Administrative Code, § 160.88.

Effect of Amendments.

The 1994 amendment by P.A. 88-687, effective January 24, 1995, in the second paragraph, in the second sentence, deleted "future" preceding "support"; in the third paragraph, in the first sentence, added at the end "including support for a period before the date the order for support is entered"; in the fourth paragraph, in the first sentence inserted "(including child support for a period before the date the order for child support is entered)" and added the second sentence; in the eighth paragraph, added the present third and fourth sentences for the former third and fourth sentences on the same subject and in the fifth sentence substituted "services under Article X" for "any extended collection period, as provided in Section 10-8"; in the thirteenth paragraph, in the second sentence, substituted "this Code" for "the Illinois Public Aid Code"; in the fourteenth paragraph, substituted "and the names" for "of the names"; and added the sixteenth paragraph.

The 1997 amendment by P.A. 90-539, effective June 1, 1998, added the fifth paragraph.

The 1998 amendment by P.A. 90-655, effective July 30, 1998, incorporated the amendments by P.A. 90-18 and P.A. 90-539.

The 1998 amendment by P.A. 90-673, effective January 1, 1999, incorporated the amendments by P.A. 90-18 and P.A. 90-539; and substituted "in accordance with the Income Withholding for Support Act" for "under Section 10-16.2" in the eighteenth paragraph (later deleted by P.A. 90-790).

The 1998 amendment by P.A. 90-790, effective August 14, 1998, deleted the eighteenth paragraph, relating to payments made by income withholding.

The 1999 amendment by P.A. 91-24, effective July 1, 1999, deleted "in accordance with the Income Withholding for Support Act" following the sixteenth paragraph; and in the next-to-last paragraph, deleted "other" following "All", and inserted "of Human Services" and substituted "DHS" for "Public Assistance" in the second sentence, and substituted "12-9.1" for "12-9" in the third sentence.

The 1999 amendment by P.A. 91-212, effective July 20, 1999, deleted "in accordance with the Income Withholding for Support Act" at the end of the sixteenth paragraph; and added the last paragraph.

The 1999 amendment by P.A. 91-357, effective July 29, 1999, deleted "in accordance with the Income Withholding for Support Act" at the end of the sixteenth paragraph, which begins "All orders".

The 2000 amendment by P.A. 91-767, effective June 9, 2000, combined the amendments by P.A. 91-24, P.A. 91-212 and P.A. 91-357; and inserted the fifth paragraph.

The 2001 amendment by P.A. 92-16, effective June 28, 2001, made a grammatical correction; and combined the amendments by P.A. 91-24, P.A. 91-212, P.A. 91-357 and P.A. 91-767.

The 2002 amendment by P.A. 92-590, effective July 1, 2002, substituted references to "child support enforcement services" for references to "child and spouse support services" throughout the section.

The 2002 amendment by P.A. 92-876, effective June 1, 2003, in the fourth paragraph from the end substituted "age of 18. However, if the child will not graduate from high school until after attaining the age of 18, then the termination date shall be no earlier than the earlier of the date on which the child's high school graduation will occur or the date on which the child will attain the age of 19" for "age of majority or is otherwise emancipated", and added "or terminating the order in the event the child is otherwise emancipated" at the end.

Although the amendments made to this section by P.A. 92-590, § 5, and P.A. 92-876, § 905 did not take into account the amendments made by the other, the amendments have been combined into a single version by the publisher.

The 2004 amendment by P.A. 93-1061, effective January 1, 2005, inserted the fourth paragraph from the end.

CASE NOTES

ANALYSIS

Equitable Estoppel
—Availability
—Shown
Financial Status
Public Purpose
Statutory Guidelines
—Applicability
—Deviation Generally
—Deviation Not Authorized

Equitable Estoppel

—Availability

Doctrine of equitable estoppel as a defense to liability for past due child support has been restricted but not abolished. Johnston v. Johnston, 196 Ill. App. 3d 101, 142 Ill. Dec. 743, 553 N.E.2d 93 (4 Dist. 1990).

—Shown

Mother was equitably estopped from obtaining court ordered support which was in arrears as to son when (1) son was in the actual custody of his father on a permanent basis; (2) son's rights of support were not infringed as his father actually supported him; (3) mother led father to believe he did not need to provide support for son; and (4) mother would be getting a windfall for support she did not actually furnish. Johnston v. Johnston, 196 Ill. App. 3d 101, 142 Ill. Dec. 743, 553 N.E.2d 93 (4 Dist. 1990).

Financial Status

This section and 305 ILCS 5/10-1 authorize the department to provide child support enforcement services to any individual who applies for such services, regardless of his financial status. In re Lappe, 176 Ill. 2d 414, 223 Ill. Dec. 647, 680 N.E.2d 380 (1997).

Public Purpose

This section and 305 ILCS 5/10-1 serve a public purpose by advancing the welfare of children and this public service is served by the extension of these services to all children, regardless of the financial circumstances of their custodial parents. In re Lappe, 176 Ill. 2d 414, 223 Ill. Dec. 647, 680 N.E.2d 380 (1997).

Statutory Guidelines

—Applicability

The guidelines for determining child support contained in 750 ILCS 5/505 must be followed when a court determines support in cases brought under this section. People ex rel. Browning v. Melton, 180 Ill. App. 3d 519, 129 Ill. Dec. 449, 536 N.E.2d 133 (5 Dist. 1989).

—Deviation Generally

In appropriate cases, the court may enter an order for child support in an amount less than that prescribed in 750 ILCS 5/505. However, in that instance, the court must enter express findings upon which the deviation rests. People ex rel. Browning v. Melton, 180 Ill. App. 3d 519, 129 Ill. Dec. 449, 536 N.E.2d 133 (5 Dist. 1989).

—Deviation Not Authorized

Fact that demands were placed upon defendant from other jurisdictions for other children and for debts other than the standard debts of his personal household did not justify an order for child support in an amount less than the guidelines prescribed by 750 ILCS 5/505. People ex rel. Browning v. Melton, 180 Ill. App. 3d 519, 129 Ill. Dec. 449, 536 N.E.2d 133 (5 Dist. 1989).

305 ILCS 5/10-10.1 Public Aid Collection Fee

Sec. 10-10.1. *Public Aid Collection Fee.* In all cases instituted by the Illinois Department on behalf of a child or spouse, other than one receiving a grant of financial aid under Article IV, on whose behalf an application has been made and approved for child support enforcement services as provided by Section 10-1 [305 ILCS 5/10-1], the court shall impose a collection fee on the individual who owes a child or spouse support obligation in an amount equal to 10% of the amount so owed as long as such collection is required by federal law, which fee shall be in addition to the support obligation. The imposition of such fee shall be in accordance with provisions of Title IV, Part D, of the Social Security Act [42 U.S.C. § 651 et seq.] and regulations duly promulgated thereunder. The fee shall be payable to the clerk of the circuit court for transmittal to the Illinois Department and shall continue until child support enforcement services are terminated by the Department.
(Source: P.A. 82-979; 92-590, § 5.)

Note.

This section was Ill.Rev.Stat., Ch. 23, para. 10-10.1.

Effect of Amendments.

The 2002 amendment by P.A. 92-590, effective July 1, 2002, substituted "child support enforcement services" for "support services" twice.

305 ILCS 5/10-10.2 Notice to Clerk of Circuit Court of Payment Received by the Illinois Department for Recording

Sec. 10-10.2. *Notice to Clerk of Circuit Court of Payment Received by the Illinois Department for Recording.* For those cases in which support is payable to the clerk of the circuit court for transmittal to the Illinois Department by order of court, and the Illinois Department collects support by assignment, offset, withholding, deduction or other process permitted by law, the Illinois Department shall notify the clerk of the date and amount of such collection. Upon notification, the clerk shall record the collection on the payment record for the case.
(Source: P.A. 82-1057.)

Note.

This section was Ill.Rev.Stat., Ch. 23, para. 10-10.2.

305 ILCS 5/10-10.3 [Child support payments payable to clerk of circuit court]

Sec. 10-10.3. For those cases in which child support is payable to the clerk of the circuit court for transmittal to the Illinois Department by order of court, the clerk shall transmit all such payments, within 4 working days of receipt, to insure that funds are available for immediate distribution by the Department to the person or entity entitled thereto in accordance with standards of the Child Support Enforcement Program established under Title IV-D of the Social Security Act [42 U.S.C. § 651 et seq.]. The clerk shall notify the Department of the date of receipt and amount thereof at the time of transmittal. Where the clerk has entered into an agreement of cooperation with the Department to record the terms of child support orders and payments made thereunder directly into the Department's automated data processing system, the clerk shall account for, transmit and otherwise distribute child support payments in accordance with such agreement in lieu of the requirements contained herein.

To the extent the provisions of this Section are inconsistent with the requirements pertaining to the State Disbursement Unit under Sections 10-10.4 and 10-26 of this Code [305 ILCS 5/10-10.4 and 305 ILCS 5/10-26], the requirements pertaining to the State Disbursement Unit shall apply.
(Source: P.A. 86-1184; 91-212, § 20.)

Note.

This section was Ill.Rev.Stat., Ch. 23, para. 10-10.3.

Effect of Amendments.

The 1999 amendment by P.A. 91-212, effective July 20, 1999, added the last sentence.

305 ILCS 5/10-10.4 Payment of Support to State Disbursement Unit

Sec. 10-10.4. *Payment of Support to State Disbursement Unit.* (a) As used in this Section:

"Order for support", "obligor", "obligee", and "payor" mean those terms as defined in the Income Withholding for Support Act [750 ILCS 28/1 et seq.], except that "order for support" shall not mean orders providing for spousal maintenance under which there is no child support obligation.

(b) Notwithstanding any other provision of this Code to the contrary, each court or administrative order for support entered or modified on or after October 1, 1999 shall require that support payments be made to the State Disbursement Unit established under Section 10-26 [305 ILCS 5/10-26] if:

(1) a party to the order is receiving child support enforcement services under this Article X; or

(2) no party to the order is receiving child support enforcement services, but the support payments are made through income withholding.

(c) Support payments shall be made to the State Disbursement Unit if:

(1) the order for support was entered before October 1, 1999, and a party to the order is receiving child support enforcement services under this Article X; or

(2) no party to the order is receiving child support enforcement services, and the support payments are being made through income withholding.

(c-5) If no party to the order is receiving child support enforcement services under this Article X, and the support payments are not being made through income withholding, then support payments shall be made as directed in the order for support.

(c-10) At any time, and notwithstanding the existence of an order directing payments to be made elsewhere, the Department of Public Aid may provide notice to the obligor and, where applicable, to the obligor's payor:

(1) to make support payments to the State Disbursement Unit if:

(A) a party to the order for support is receiving child support enforcement services under this Article X; or

(B) no party to the order for support is receiving child support enforcement services under this Article X, but the support payments are made through income withholding; or

(2) to make support payments to the State Disbursement Unit of another state upon request of another state's Title IV-D child support enforcement agency, in accordance with the requirements of Title IV, Part D of the Social Security Act and regulations promulgated under that Part D.

(c-15) Within 15 days after the effective date of this amendatory Act of the 91st General Assembly [P.A. 91-677], the clerk of the circuit court shall provide written notice to the obligor to make payments directly to the clerk of the circuit court if no party to the order is receiving child support enforcement services under this Article X, the support payments are not made through income withholding, and the order for support requires support payments to be made directly to the clerk of the circuit court.

(c-20) If the State Disbursement Unit receives a support payment that was not appropriately made to the Unit under this Section, the Unit shall immediately return the payment to the sender, including, if possible, instructions detailing where to send the support payments.

(d) The notices under subsections (c-10) and (c-15) may be sent by ordinary mail, certified mail, return receipt requested, facsimile transmission, or other electronic process, or may be served upon the obligor or payor using any method provided by law for service of a summons. A copy of the notice shall be provided to the obligee and, when the order for support was entered by the court, to the clerk of the court.

(Source: P.A. 91-212, § 20; 91-677, § 5; 92-590, § 5.)

Illinois Administrative Code.
See 89 Illinois Administrative Code, § 160.60.

Effective Date.
Section 999 of P.A. 91-212 made this section effective upon becoming law. The Act was approved July 20, 1999.

Effect of Amendments.
The 1999 amendment by P.A. 91-677, effective January 5, 2000, inserted "except that 'order for support' shall not mean orders providing for spousal maintenance under which there is no child support obligation" at the end of subsection (a); in subsection (c), deleted "The Illinois Department shall provide notice to the obligor and, where applicable, to the obligor's payor to make" at the beginning and inserted "shall be made" following "support payments"; deleted "the order for support was entered after January 1, 1994" at the beginning of subsection (c)(2); added subsections (c-5), (c-10), (c-15), and (c-20); and substituted "subsections (c-10) and (c-15)" for "subsection (c)" in subsection (d) and made a related change.

The 2002 amendment by P.A. 92-590, effective July 1, 2002, substituted references to "child support enforcement services" for references to "child and spouse support services" throughout the section; rewrote subsection (c-10) and deleted "required" following notices in subsection (d).

305 ILCS 5/10-10.5 Information to State Case Registry

Sec. 10-10.5. *Information to State Case Registry.*
(a) In this Section:

"Order for support", "obligor", "obligee", and "business day" are defined as set forth in the Income Withholding for Support Act [750 ILCS 28/1 et seq.].

"State Case Registry" means the State Case Registry established under Section 10-27 of this Code [305 ILCS 5/10-27].

(b) Each order for support entered or modified by the circuit court under Section 10-10 [305 ILCS 5/10-10] shall require that the obligor and obligee (i) file with the clerk of the circuit court the information required by this Section (and any other information required under Title IV, Part D of the Social Security Act [42 U.S.C. § 601 et seq.] or by the federal Department of Health and Human Services) at the time of entry or modification of the order for support and (ii) file updated information with the clerk within 5 business days of any change. Failure of the obligor or obligee to file or update the required information shall be punishable as in cases of contempt. The failure shall not prevent the court from entering or modifying the order for support, however.

(c) The obligor shall file the following information: the obligor's name, date of birth, social security number, and mailing address.

If either the obligor or the obligee receives child support enforcement services from the Illinois Department under Article X of this Code [305 ILCS 5/10 et seq.], the obligor shall also file the following information: the obligor's telephone number, driver's license number, and residential address (if different from the obligor's mailing address), and the name, address, and telephone number of the obligor's employer or employers.

(d) The obligee shall file the following information:

(1) The names of the obligee and the child or children covered by the order for support.

(2) The dates of birth of the obligee and the child or children covered by the order for support.

(3) The social security numbers of the obligee and the child or children covered by the order for support.

(4) The obligee's mailing address.

(e) In cases in which the obligee receives child support enforcement services from the Illinois Department under Article X of this Code [305 ILCS 5/10 et seq.], the order for support shall (i) require that the obligee file the information required under subsection (d) with the Illinois Department for inclusion in the State Case Registry, rather than file the information with the clerk, and (ii) require that the obligee include the following additional information:

(1) The obligee's telephone and driver's license numbers.

(2) The obligee's residential address, if different from the obligee's mailing address.

(3) The name, address, and telephone number of the obligee's employer or employers.

The order for support shall also require that the obligee update the information filed with the Illinois Department within 5 business days of any change.

(f) The clerk shall provide the information filed under this Section, together with the court docket number and county in which the order for support was entered, to the State Case Registry within 5 business days after receipt of the information.

(g) In a case in which a party is receiving child support enforcement services under Article X of this Code [305 ILCS 5/10 et seq.], the clerk shall provide the following additional information to the State Case Registry within 5 business days after entry or modification of an order for support or request from the Illinois Department:

(1) The amount of monthly or other periodic support owed under the order for support and other amounts, including arrearage, interest, or late payment penalties and fees, due or overdue under the order.

(2) Any such amounts that have been received by the clerk, and the distribution of those amounts by the clerk.

(h) Information filed by the obligor and obligee under this Section that is not specifically required to be included in the body of an order for support under other laws is not a public record and shall be treated as confidential and subject to disclosure only in accordance with the provisions of this Section, Section 10-27 of this Code [305 ILCS 5/10-27], and Title IV, Part D of the Social Security Act [42 U.S.C. § 601 et seq.].

(Source: P.A. 91-212, § 20; 92-16, § 76; 92-463, § 5; 92-651, § 64.)

Note.

Section 996 of P.A. 92-16 contains a "no acceleration or delay" provision, and Section 997 contains a "no revival or extension" provision.

Section 997 of P.A. 92-651 is a no acceleration or delay provision, and Section 998 is a no revival or extension provision.

Effective Date.

Section 999 of P.A. 91-212 made this section effective upon becoming law. The Act was approved July 20, 1999.

Effect of Amendments.

The 2001 amendment by P.A. 92-16, effective June 28, 2001, made a grammatical correction.

The 2001 amendment by P.A. 92-463, effective August 22, 2001, rewrote this section to the extent that a detailed comparison would be impracticable.

The 2002 amendment by P.A. 92-651, effective July 11, 2002, combined the amendments by P.A. 92-16 and P.A. 92-463 and made a typographical correction.

305 ILCS 5/10-11 Administrative Orders

Sec. 10-11. *Administrative Orders.* In lieu of actions for court enforcement of support under Section 10-10 [305 ILCS 5/10-10], the Child and Spouse Support Unit of the Illinois Department, in accordance with the rules of the Illinois Department, may issue an administrative order requiring the responsible relative to comply with the terms of the determination and notice of support due, determined and issued under Sections 10-6 and 10-7 [305 ILCS 5/10-6 and 305 ILCS 5/10-7]. The Unit may also enter an administrative order under subsection (b) of Section 10-7 [305 ILCS 5/10-7]. The administrative order shall be served upon the responsible relative by United States registered or certified mail. In cases in which the responsible relative appeared at the office of the Child and Spouse Support Unit in response to the notice of support obligation issued under Section 10-4 [305 ILCS 5/10-4], however, or in cases of default in which the notice was served on the responsible relative by certified mail, return receipt requested, or by any method provided by law for service of summons, the administrative determination of paternity or administrative support order may be sent to the responsible relative by ordinary mail addressed to the responsible relative's last known address.

If a responsible relative or a person receiving child support enforcement services under this Article fails to petition the Illinois Department for release from or modification of the administrative order, as provided in Section 10-12 or Section 10-12.1 [305 ILCS 5/10-12 or 305 ILCS 5/10-12.1], the order shall become final and there shall be no further administrative or judicial remedy. Likewise a decision by the Illinois Department as a result of an administrative hearing, as provided in Sections 10-13 to 10-13.10 [305 ILCS 5/10-13 to 305 ILCS 5/10-13.10], shall become final and enforceable if not judicially reviewed under the Administrative Review Law [735 ILCS 5/3-101 et seq.], as provided in Section 10-14 [305 ILCS 5/10-14].

Any new or existing support order entered by the Illinois Department under this Section shall be deemed to be a series of judgments against the person obligated to pay support thereunder, each such judgment to be in the amount of each payment or installment of support and each such judgment to be deemed entered as of the date the corresponding payment or installment becomes due under the terms of the support order. Each such judgment shall have the full force, effect and attributes of any other judgment of this State, including the ability to be enforced. Any such judgment is subject to modification or termination only in accordance with Section 510 of the Illinois Marriage and Dissolution of Marriage Act [750 ILCS 5/510]. A lien arises by operation of law against the real and personal property of the noncustodial parent for each installment of overdue support owed by the noncustodial parent.

An order for support shall include a date on which the current support obligation terminates. The termination date shall be no earlier than the date on which the child covered by the order will attain the age of majority or is otherwise emancipated. The order for support shall state that the termination date does not apply to any arrearage that may remain unpaid on that date. Nothing in this paragraph shall be construed to prevent modification of the order by the Department.

If there is an unpaid arrearage or delinquency (as those terms are defined in the Income Withholding for Support Act [750 ILCS 28/1 et seq.]) equal to at least one month's support obligation on the termination date stated in the order for support or, if there is no termination date stated in the order, on the date the child attains the age of majority or is otherwise emancipated, then the periodic amount required to be paid for current support of that child immediately prior to that date shall automatically continue to be an obligation, not as current support but as periodic payment toward satisfaction of the unpaid arrearage or delinquency. That periodic payment shall be in addition to any periodic payment previously required for satisfaction of the arrearage or delinquency. The total periodic amount to be paid toward satisfaction of the arrearage or delinquency may be enforced and collected by any method provided by law for the enforcement and collection of child support, including but not limited to income withholding under the Income Withholding for Support Act [750 ILCS 28/1 et seq.]. Each order for support entered or modified on or after the effective date of this amendatory Act of the 93rd General Assembly [P.A. 93-1061] must contain a statement notifying the parties of the requirements of this paragraph. Failure to include the statement in the order for support does not affect the validity of the order or the operation of the provisions of this paragraph with regard to the order. This paragraph shall not be construed to prevent or affect the establishment or modification of an order for the support of a minor child or the establishment or modification of an order for the support of a non-minor child or educational expenses under Section 513 of the Illinois Marriage and Dissolution of Marriage Act [750 ILCS 5/513].

An order for support shall include a date on which the support obligation terminates. The termination date shall be no earlier than the date on which the child covered by the order will attain the age of 18. However, if the child will not graduate from high school until after attaining the age of 18, then the termination date shall be no earlier than the earlier of the date that the child's graduation will occur or the date on which the child will attain the age of 19. The order for support shall state that the termination date does not apply to any arrearage that may remain unpaid on that date. Nothing in this paragraph shall be construed to prevent the Illinois Department from modifying the order or terminating the order in the event the child is otherwise emancipated.

(Source: P.A. 85-1156; 90-18, § 65; 90-539, § 5; 90-655, § 127; 90-790, § 5; 91-212, § 20; 92-590, § 5; 92-876, § 905; 93-1061, § 5.)

Note.

This section was Ill.Rev.Stat., Ch. 23, para. 10-11.

Effect of Amendments.

The 1997 amendment by P.A. 90-18, effective July 1, 1997, in the third paragraph added the fourth sentence.

The 1997 amendment by P.A. 90-539, effective June 1, 1998, added the fourth paragraph.

The 1998 amendment by P.A. 90-655, effective July 30, 1998, appears to have made no discernible changes to this section.

The 1998 amendment by P.A. 90-790, effective August 14, 1998, added the last sentence in the first paragraph; and inserted "or a person receiving child and spouse support services under this Article" and "or Section 10-12.1" in the first sentence of the second paragraph.

The 1999 amendment by P.A. 91-212, effective July 20, 1999, deleted "or by a private person as authorized under Section 10-4" following "return receipt requested" in the fourth sentence of the first paragraph.

The 2002 amendment by P.A. 92-590, effective July 1, 2002, substituted "child support enforcement services" for "child and spouse support services" in the second paragraph.

The 2002 amendment by P.A. 92-876, effective June 1, 2003, added the last paragraph.

The 2004 amendment by P.A. 93-1061, effective January 1, 2005, rewrote the section to the extent that a detailed comparison would be impracticable.

305 ILCS 5/10-11.1 [Unemployed responsible relative ordered to participate in job search, training or work programs]

Sec. 10-11.1. (a) Whenever it is determined in a proceeding under Sections 10-6, 10-7, 10-11 or 10-17.1 [305 ILCS 5/10-6, 305 ILCS 5/10-7, 305 ILCS 5/10-11 or 305 ILCS 5/10-17.1] that the responsible relative is unemployed, and support is sought on behalf of applicants for or recipients of financial aid under Article IV of this Code [305 ILCS 5/4-0.5 et seq.] or other persons who are given access to the child support enforcement services of this Article as provided in Section 10-1 [305 ILCS 5/10-1], the administrative enforcement unit may order the responsible relative to report to the Illinois Department for participation in job search, training or work programs established under Section 9-6 [305 ILCS 5/9-6] and Article IXA of this Code [305 ILCS 5/9A-1 et seq.] or to the Illinois Department of Employment Security for job search services or to make application with the local Job Training Partnership Act [29 U.S.C. § 1501 et seq.] provider for participation in job search, training or work programs.

(b) Whenever it is determined that a responsible relative owes past-due support for a child under an administrative support order entered under subsection (b) of Section 10-7 [305 ILCS 5/10-7] or under Section 10-11 or 10-17.1 [305 ILCS 5/10-11 or 305 ILCS 5/10-17.1] and the child is receiving assistance under this Code, the administrative enforcement unit shall order the following:

(1) that the responsible relative pay the past-due support in accordance with a plan approved by the administrative enforcement unit; or

(2) if the responsible relative owing past-due support is unemployed, is subject to such a plan, and is not incapacitated, that the responsible relative participate in job search, training, or work programs established under Section 9-6 [305 ILCS 5/9-6] and Article IXA of this Code [305 ILCS 5/9A-1 et seq.].

(Source: P.A. 85-1155; 90-18, § 65; 92-16, § 76; 92-590, § 5.)

Note.

This section was Ill.Rev.Stat., Ch. 23, para. 10-11.1.

Section 996 of P.A. 92-16 contains a "no acceleration or delay" provision, and Section 997 contains a "no revival or extension" provision.

Effect of Amendments.

The 1997 amendment by P.A. 90-18, effective July 1, 1997, added the subsection (a) designation; in subsection (a) inserted "and Article IXA"; and added subsection (b).

The 2001 amendment by P.A. 92-16, effective June 28, 2001, made a grammatical correction.

The 2002 amendment by P.A. 92-590, effective July 1, 2002, substituted "child support enforcement services" for "child and spouse support services" in subsection (a).

305 ILCS 5/10-11.2 Administrative support order information for State Case Registry

Sec. 10-11.2. *Administrative support order information for State Case Registry.* (a) In this Section, "business day" is defined as set forth in the Income Withholding for Support Act [750 ILCS 28/1 et seq.].

(b) Each administrative support order entered or modified under Section 10-8.1 or Section 10-11 [305 ILCS 5/10-8.1 or 305 ILCS 5/10-11] shall require the following:

(1) That the non-custodial parent file with the Illinois Department the information required by subsection (c) of this Section (and any other information required under Title IV, Part D of the Social Security Act [42 U.S.C. § 601 et seq.] or by the federal Department of Health and Human Services) within 5 business days after entry or modification of the administrative support order, and that the parent file updated information with the Illinois Department within 5 business days of any change.

(2) That the custodial parent file with the Illinois Department the information required by subsection (d) of this Section (and any other information required under Title IV, Part D of the Social Security Act [42 U.S.C. § 601 et seq.] or by the federal Department of Health and Human Services) within 5 business days after entry or modification of the administrative support order (unless the custodial parent already filed the information during the child support case intake process), and that the parent file updated information with the Illinois Department within 5 business days of any change.

(c) The non-custodial parent shall file the following information:

(1) The name and date of birth of the non-custodial parent.

(2) The non-custodial parent's social security number, driver's license number, and telephone number.

(3) The mailing address (and the residential address, if different from the mailing address) of the non-custodial parent.

(4) The name, address, and telephone number of the non-custodial parent's employer or employers.

(d) The custodial parent shall file the following information:

(1) The names and dates of birth of the custodial parent and the child or children covered by the administrative support order.

(2) The social security numbers of the custodial parent and the child or children covered by the administrative support order.

(3) The custodial parent's driver's license number and telephone number.

(4) The custodial parent's mailing address (and residential address, if different from the mailing address).

(5) The name, address, and telephone number of the custodial parent's employer or employers.

(e) The information filed with the Illinois Department under this Section shall be included in the State Case Registry established under Section 10-27 of this Code [305 ILCS 5/10-27].

(f) Information filed by the non-custodial parent and custodial parent under this Section that is not specifically required to be included in the body of an administrative support order under other laws or under rules of the Illinois Department shall be treated as confidential and subject to disclosure only in accordance with the provisions of this Section, Section 10-27 [305 ILCS 5/10-27] of this Code, and Title IV, Part D of the Social Security Act [42 U.S.C. § 601 et seq.].

(Source: P.A. 91-212, § 20; 92-463, § 5.)

Effective Date.

Section 999 of P.A. 91-212 made this section effective upon becoming law. The Act was approved July 20, 1999.

Effect of Amendments.

The 2001 amendment by P.A. 92-463, effective August 22, 2001, rewrote this section to the extent that a detailed comparison would be impracticable.

305 ILCS 5/10-12 Petition by responsible relative for release from or modification of administrative support order or administrative determination of paternity

Sec. 10-12. *Petition by responsible relative for release from or modification of administrative support order or administrative determination of paternity.* (a) Any responsible relative aggrieved by an administrative order entered under Section 10-11 or 10-11.1 [305 ILCS 5/10-11 or 305 ILCS 5/10-11.1] or an administrative determination of paternity entered under Section 10-17.7 [305 ILCS 5/10-17.7] who has been duly notified of such order or determination may, within 30 days from the date of mailing of such order or determination, petition the Illinois Department for a release from or modification of the order or determination. The day immediately subsequent to the mailing of the order or determination shall be considered as the first day, and the day such petition is received by the Illinois Department shall be considered as the last day in computing the 30 day appeal period.

The Illinois Department shall, upon receipt of a petition within the 30 day appeal period, provide for a hearing to be held thereon.

(b) Notwithstanding the 30-day appeal period set forth in subsection (a), a man against whom a default administrative determination of paternity has been entered may have the determination vacated if, within 30 days after being served with the determination, he appears in person at the office to which he was given notice to appear for an interview and files a written request for relief from the determination. The Illinois Department shall then proceed with the establishment of paternity. A man may obtain relief under this subsection from an administrative determination of paternity only once in any proceeding to establish paternity.

(Source: P.A. 85-1155; 90-790, § 5.)

Note.

This section was Ill.Rev.Stat., Ch. 23, para. 10-12.

Effect of Amendments.

The 1998 amendment by P.A. 90-790, effective August 14, 1998, inserted "by responsible relative" and "or administrative determination of paternity" in the section catchline, added the subsection (a) designation, inserted references to administrative determinations throughout the first paragraph of subsection (a), and added subsection (b).

305 ILCS 5/10-12.1 Petition by person receiving child support enforcement services for release from or modification of administrative support order or administrative determination of paternity

Sec. 10-12.1. *Petition by person receiving child support enforcement services for release from or modification of administrative support order or administrative determination of paternity.* Any person receiving child support enforcement services under this Article who is aggrieved by an administrative order entered under Section 10-11 or 10-11.1 [305 ILCS 5/10-11 or 305 ILCS 5/10-11.1] or an administrative determination of paternity entered under Section 10-17.7 [305 ILCS 5/10-17.7] who has been duly notified of the order or determination may, within 30 days after the date of mailing of the order or determination, petition the Illinois Department for release from or modification of the order or determination. The day immediately subsequent to the mailing of the order or determination shall be considered as the first day and the day the petition is received by the Illinois Department shall be considered as the last day in computing the 30-day appeal period. Upon receiving a petition within the 30-day appeal period, the Illinois Department shall provide for a hearing to be held on the petition.

(Source: P.A. 90-790, § 5; 92-590, § 5.)

Effective Date.

Section 99 of P.A. 90-790 makes this section effective upon becoming law. The Act was approved August 14, 1998.

Effect of Amendments.

The 2002 amendment by P.A. 92-590, effective July 1, 2002, substituted "child support enforcement services" for to "child and spouse support services" in the section catchline and the first sentence.

305 ILCS 5/10-13 Hearing on Petition

Sec. 10-13. *Hearing on Petition.* The Illinois Department, or any officer or employee thereof designated in writing by the Illinois Department, shall conduct hearings and investigations in connection with petitions filed pursuant to Section 10-12 or Section 10-12.1 [305 ILCS 5/10-12 or 305 ILCS 5/10-12.1]. Responsible relatives and persons receiving child support enforcement services under this Article shall be entitled to appear in person, to be represented by counsel at the hearing and to present all relevant matter in support of their petitions. The provisions of Sections 10-13.1 through 10-13.10 [305 ILCS 5/10-13.1 through 305 ILCS 5/10-13.10] shall govern the hearing.

The hearing shall be de novo and the Illinois Department's determination of liability or non-liability shall be independent of the determination of the administrative enforcement unit.

(Source: Laws 1967, p. 122; P.A. 90-790, § 5; 92-590, § 5.)

Note.

This section was Ill.Rev.Stat., Ch. 23, para. 10-13.

Illinois Administrative Code.

See 89 Illinois Administrative Code, § 14.100.

Effect of Amendments.

The 1998 amendment by P.A. 90-790, effective August 14, 1998, in the first paragraph, substituted "pursuant to" for "pursuant with," inserted "and persons receiving child and spouse support services under this Article," and substituted "through 10-13.10" for "to 10-13.10."

The 2002 amendment by P.A. 92-590, effective July 1, 2002, substituted "child support enforcement services" for "child and spouse support services" in the first paragraph.

305 ILCS 5/10-13.1 Examination of records

Sec. 10-13.1. *Examination of records.* The Illinois Department, or any properly designated officer or employee thereof, may examine any books, papers, records or memoranda bearing upon the determination of ability to support and the order for support and upon any matter pertinent to the relative's petition and may compel the attendance and testimony of any person or persons, including the petitioning responsible relative, having knowledge of matters germane to the determination order, or the petition.
(Source: Laws 1967, p. 122.)

Note.
This section was Ill.Rev.Stat., Ch. 23, para. 10-13.1.

305 ILCS 5/10-13.2 Hearings not subject to technical rules of evidence or procedure

Sec. 10-13.2. *Hearings not subject to technical rules of evidence or procedure.* In the conduct of any hearing or investigation, neither the Illinois Department nor a person duly authorized to conduct such hearing or investigation, shall be bound by the technical rules of evidence, common law or statutory, or by technical or formal rules of procedure, but shall conduct the hearing or make the investigation in such manner as seems best calculated to conform to substantial justice and the spirit of this Code. No informality in any proceedings, or in the manner of taking testimony, shall invalidate any order or decision made by the Illinois Department pursuant to such hearing or investigation.
(Source: Laws 1967, p. 122.)

Note.
This section was Ill.Rev.Stat., Ch. 23, para. 10-13.2.

305 ILCS 5/10-13.3 Authority to administer oaths

Sec. 10-13.3. *Authority to administer oaths.* The Illinois Department, or any person duly authorized to conduct such hearing or investigation, shall have power to administer oaths. Every person who, having taken an oath or made affirmation before the Illinois Department, or any duly authorized officer or employee thereof, shall wilfully swear or affirm falsely, shall be guilty of perjury, and upon conviction shall be punished accordingly.
(Source: Laws 1967, p. 122.)

Note.
This section was Ill.Rev.Stat., Ch. 23, para. 10-13.3.

305 ILCS 5/10-13.4 Proof of records

Sec. 10-13.4. *Proof of records.* The books, papers, records and memoranda of the Illinois Department or of the administrative enforcement unit, or parts thereof, may be proved in any hearing, investigation, or legal proceeding by a photostatic or other copy thereof under the certificate of the Director of the Illinois Department. Such certified copy shall, without further proof, be admitted into evidence in the hearing before the Illinois Department or in any other legal proceeding.
(Source: P.A. 79-474.)

Note.
This section was Ill.Rev.Stat., Ch. 23, para. 10-13.4.

CASE NOTES

Analysis

Certificate
—Admissibility
Computer Records
—Admissibility
—Sufficient Foundation
Facsimile Signature
—Sufficiency
Proof of Lien
Purpose

Certificate

—Admissibility
Where as its only proof in support of a claim against the estate of a public aid recipient, the Department of Public Aid offered the certificate of the Director of the Department which listed the payments made on behalf of the decedent by the Department, the certificate constituted sufficient proof of the payments made to or on behalf of the decedent and it was properly admitted into evidence under the public records exception to the hearsay rule and by this section. Department of Pub. Aid v. Estate of Wall, 81 Ill. App. 3d 394, 36 Ill. Dec. 798, 401 N.E.2d 639 (5 Dist. 1980).

This section is at least as broad as the common law exception of the hearsay rule exempting public records and Rule 803(8)(A), F.R.Evid.; it requires admission of the Director's certificate into evidence and, in the absence of countervailing evidence, acceptance as credibly proved of the information the certificate contains. Department of Pub. Aid v. Estate of Wall, 81 Ill. App. 3d 394, 36 Ill. Dec. 798, 401 N.E.2d 639 (5 Dist. 1980).

Computer Records

—Admissibility
Computer documents which showed that decedent received medical payments for the department were properly admitted because they were not documents prepared in anticipation of litigation. In re Estate of Huffmon, 265 Ill. App. 3d 225, 202 Ill. Dec. 589, 638 N.E.2d 235 (4 Dist. 1994).

Where computer generated documents constituted the Department of Public Aid's entire file on the decedent with a few handwritten notations and the records were not prepared in anticipation of litigation, the computer records certified by the director were admissible pursuant to this section. Estate of Zander v. Illinois Dep't of Pub. Aid, 242 Ill. App. 3d 774, 183 Ill. Dec. 233, 611 N.E.2d 86 (4 Dist.), appeal denied, 152 Ill. 2d 560, 190 Ill. Dec. 890, 622 N.E.2d 1207 (1993).

—Sufficient Foundation
When official records are available only in the form of computer records, a proper foundation is required before the computer records can be admitted into evidence, under the official records exception to the hearsay rule; the certificate of the director provides the necessary foundation. Estate of Zander v. Illinois Dep't of Pub.

Computer Records (Cont'd)

—Sufficient Foundation (Cont'd)
Aid, 242 Ill. App. 3d 774, 183 Ill. Dec. 233, 611 N.E.2d 86 (4 Dist.), appeal denied, 152 Ill. 2d 560, 190 Ill. Dec. 890, 622 N.E.2d 1207 (1993).

Facsimile Signature

—Sufficiency
Recognizing the burden of requiring department heads to place their original signatures on (or personally stamp) all documents, the trial court properly ruled the director's facsimile signature was sufficient under this section in Department of Public Aid's claim against estate for medical supplies and/or services. Estate of Zander v. Illinois Dep't of Pub. Aid, 242 Ill. App. 3d 774, 183 Ill. Dec. 233, 611 N.E.2d 86 (4 Dist.), appeal denied, 152 Ill. 2d 560, 190 Ill. Dec. 890, 622 N.E.2d 1207 (1993).

Proof of Lien
A certification regarding direct medical payments, with attachments, was admissible into evidence and competent proof of a Department of Public Aid lien against a plaintiff's settlement recovery. Connor v. Shaw, 138 Ill. App. 3d 429, 92 Ill. Dec. 941, 485 N.E.2d 1184 (5 Dist. 1985).

Purpose
This section does not require the Department of Public Aid to produce copies of every document utilized in every payment to a public aid recipient; what gives reliability to certifications made under this section is not the detail of the supporting documentation, but the fact that they are attested to by a public official, the Director of the Department of Public Aid, in connection with performance of his statutory duties. Connor v. Shaw, 138 Ill. App. 3d 429, 92 Ill. Dec. 941, 485 N.E.2d 1184 (5 Dist. 1985).

305 ILCS 5/10-13.5 Proof of necessitous circumstances

Sec. 10-13.5. *Proof of necessitous circumstances.* Proof in any hearing before the Illinois Department that a person is an applicant for or recipient of assistance shall be prima facie proof that he is a "person who is in necessitous circumstances by reason of infirmity, unemployment, or other cause depriving him of the means of a livelihood compatible with health and well-being", within the meaning of this Code.
(Source: Laws 1967, p. 122.)

Note.
This section was Ill.Rev.Stat., Ch. 23, para. 10-13.5.

305 ILCS 5/10-13.6 Subpoenas

Sec. 10-13.6. *Subpoenas.* (a) The Illinois Department, or any officer or employee thereof designated in writing by the Illinois Department, shall at its or his own instance, or on the written request of any other party to the proceeding, issue subpoenas requiring the attendance of and the giving of testimony by witnesses, and subpoenas duces tecum requiring the production of books, papers, records or memoranda. The subpoenas and subpoenas duces tecum may be served by any person of full age. Any subpoena may be served in the same manner as a subpoena issued out of a circuit court, and may also be served by United States registered or certified mail, addressed to the person concerned at his last known address, and proof of such mailing shall be sufficient for the purposes of the Article.

(b) Subpoenas duces tecum issued in other states shall be afforded full faith and credit in this State. Every such subpoena shall have the full force, effect, and attributes of a subpoena issued in this State, including the ability to be enforced.
(Source: Laws 1967, p. 122; P.A. 90-790, § 5.)

Note.
This section was Ill.Rev.Stat., Ch. 23, para. 10-13.6.

Effect of Amendments.
The 1998 amendment by P.A. 90-790, effective August 14, 1998, added the subsection (a) designation and added subsection (b).

305 ILCS 5/10-13.7 Witness fees

Sec. 10-13.7. *Witness fees.* The fees of witnesses for attendance and travel shall be the same as the fees of witnesses before the Circuit Court of this State; such fees to be paid when the witness is excused from further attendance. When the witness is subpoenaed at the instance of the Illinois Department or any employee thereof, the fees shall be paid in the same manner as other expenses of the Illinois Department. If the witness is subpoenaed at the instance of any other party to the proceeding, the Illinois Department may require that the cost of service of the subpoena or subpoena duces tecum and the fee of the witness be borne by the party at whose instance the witness is summoned. In such case, the Illinois Department may require a deposit to cover the cost of such service and witness fees.
(Source: Laws 1967, p. 122.)

Note.
This section was Ill.Rev.Stat., Ch. 23, para. 10-13.7.

305 ILCS 5/10-13.8 Compelling attendance of witness and production of records

Sec. 10-13.8. *Compelling attendance of witness and production of records.* The circuit court, of the county wherein the investigation or administrative hearing is held, upon the application of the Illinois Department or any duly authorized officer or employee thereof, or upon the application of any other party to the proceeding, may, in its discretion, compel the attendance of witnesses, the production of books, papers, records or memorandum and the giving of testimony before the Illinois Department or any duly authorized officer or employee thereof conducting an investigation or holding a hearing authorized by this Act, by an attachment for contempt, or otherwise, in the same manner as production of evidence may be compelled before the court.
(Source: P.A. 83-334.)

Note.
This section was Ill.Rev.Stat., Ch. 23, para. 10-13.8.

305 ILCS 5/10-13.9 Penalty for non-compliance with subpoena

Sec. 10-13.9. *Penalty for non-compliance with subpoena.* Any person who is served with a subpoena or subpoena duces tecum, issued by the Illinois Department or any duly authorized officer or employee thereof, to appear and testify or to produce books and papers, in the course of an investigation or hearing authorized by law, and who refuses or neglects to appear, or to testify, or to produce books and papers relevant to such investigation or hearing, as commanded in such subpoena, shall, be guilty of a Class B misdemeanor.
(Source: P.A. 77-2344.)

Note.
This section was Ill.Rev.Stat., Ch. 23, para. 10-13.9.

305 ILCS 5/10-13.10 Depositions

Sec. 10-13.10. *Depositions.* The Illinois Department or any duly authorized officer or employee thereof, or any other party in an investigation or hearing before the Illinois Department, may cause the depositions of witnesses within or without the State to be taken in the manner prescribed by law for like depositions in civil actions in courts of this State, and to that end compel the attendance of witnesses and the production of books, papers, records or memoranda.
(Source: Laws 1967, p. 122.)

Note.
This section was Ill.Rev.Stat., Ch. 23, para. 10-13.10.

305 ILCS 5/10-14 Review of Illinois department decision on petition for hearing

Sec. 10-14. *Review of Illinois department decision on petition for hearing.* Any responsible relative or person receiving child support enforcement services under this Article affected by a final administrative decision of the Illinois Department in a hearing, conducted pursuant to Sections 10-13 through 10-13.10 [305 ILCS 5/10-13 through 305 ILCS 5/10-13.10] in which such relative or person receiving services was a party, may have the decision reviewed only under and in accordance with the Administrative Review Law, as amended [735 ILCS 5/3-101 et seq.]. The provisions of the Administrative Review Law [735 ILCS 5/3-101 et seq.], and the rules adopted pursuant thereto, shall apply to and govern all proceedings for the judicial review of such final administrative decisions of the Illinois Department. The term "administrative decision" is defined as in Section 3-101 of the Code of Civil Procedure [735 ILCS 5/3-101].

Appeals from all final orders and judgments entered by a court upon review of the Illinois Department's order in any case may be taken by either party to the proceeding and shall be governed by the rules applicable to appeals in civil cases.

The remedy herein provided for appeal shall be exclusive, and no court shall have jurisdiction to review the subject matter of any order made by the Illinois Department except as herein provided.
(Source: P.A. 82-783; 90-790, § 5; 92-590, § 5.)

Note.
This section was Ill.Rev.Stat., Ch. 23, para. 10-14.

Effect of Amendments.
The 1998 amendment by P.A. 90-790, effective August 14, 1998, in the first paragraph, inserted "or person receiving child and spouse support services under this Article", substituted "through 10-13.10" for "to 10-13.10," and inserted "or person receiving services".
The 2002 amendment by P.A. 92-590, effective July 1, 2002, substituted "child support enforcement services" for "child and spouse support services" in the first sentence of the first paragraph.

305 ILCS 5/10-14.1 Relief from administrative orders

Sec. 10-14.1. *Relief from administrative orders.* Notwithstanding the 30-day appeal period provided in Sections 10-12 and 10-12.1 [305 ILCS 5/10-12 and 305 ILCS 5/10-12.1] and the limitation on review of final administrative decisions contained in Section 10-14 [305 ILCS 5/10-14], a responsible relative or a person receiving child support enforcement services under this Article who is aggrieved by an administrative order entered under Section 10-11 or 10-11.1 [305 ILCS 5/10-11 or 305 ILCS 5/10-11.1] or an administrative determination of paternity entered under Section 10-17.7 [305 ILCS 5/10-17.7] and who did not petition within the 30-day appeal period may petition the Illinois Department for relief from the administrative order or determination on the same grounds as are provided for relief from judgments under Section 2-1401 of the Code of Civil Procedure [735 ILCS 5/2-1401]. The petition must be filed not later than 2 years after the entry of the order or determination by the Illinois Department. The day immediately subsequent to the mailing of the order or determination shall be considered as the first day and the day the petition is received by the Illinois Department shall be considered as the last day in computing the 2-year period. Any period during which the person seeking relief is under a legal disability or duress or during which the grounds for relief are fraudulently concealed shall be excluded in computing the period of 2 years.

Upon receiving a petition within the 2-year period, the Illinois Department shall provide for a hearing to be held on the petition.
(Source: P.A. 90-790, § 5; 92-590, § 5.)

Effective Date.
Section 99 of P.A. 90-790 makes this section effective upon becoming law. The Act was approved August 14, 1998.

Effect of Amendments.
The 2002 amendment by P.A. 92-590, effective July 1, 2002, substituted "child support enforcement services" for "child and spouse support services" in the first sentence of the first paragraph.

305 ILCS 5/10-15 Enforcement of administrative order; costs and fees

Sec. 10-15. *Enforcement of administrative order; costs and fees.* If a responsible relative refuses, neglects, or fails to comply with a final administrative support or reimbursement order of the Illinois Department entered by the Child and Spouse Support Unit pursuant to Sections 10-11 or 10-11.1 [305 ILCS 5/10-11 or 305 ILCS 5/10-11.1] or registered pursuant to Section 10-17.1 [305 ILCS 5/10-17.1], the Child and Spouse Support Unit may file suit against the responsible relative or relatives to secure compliance with the administrative order.

Suits shall be instituted in the name of the People of the State of Illinois on the relation of the Department of Public Aid of the State of Illinois and the spouse or dependent children for whom the support order has been issued.

The court shall order the payment of the support obligation, or orders for reimbursement of moneys for support provided, directly to the Illinois Department but the order shall permit the Illinois Department to direct the responsible relative or relatives to make payments of support directly to the spouse or dependent children, or to some person or agency in his or their behalf, as provided in Section 10-8 or 10-10 [305 ILCS 5/10-8 or 305 ILCS 5/10-10], as applicable.

Whenever it is determined in a proceeding to enforce an administrative order that the responsible relative is unemployed, and support is sought on behalf of applicants for or recipients of financial aid under Article IV of this Code [305 ILCS 5/4-0.5 et seq.] or other persons who are given access to the child support enforcement services of this Article as provided in Section 10-1 [305 ILCS 5/10-1], the court may order the responsible relative to seek employment and report periodically to the court with a diary, listing or other memorandum of his or her efforts in accordance with such order. In addition, the court may order the unemployed responsible relative to report to the Illinois Department for participation in job search, training or work programs established under Section 9-6 of this Code [305 ILCS 5/9-6] or to the Illinois Department of Employment Security for job search services or to make application with the local Job Training Partnership Act [29 U.S.C. § 1501 et seq.] provider for participation in job search, training or work programs.

Charges imposed in accordance with the provisions of Section 10-21 [305 ILCS 5/10-21] shall be enforced by the Court in a suit filed under this Section.

To the extent the provisions of this Section are inconsistent with the requirements pertaining to the State Disbursement Unit under Sections 10-10.4 and 10-26 of this Code [305 ILCS 5/10-10.4 and 305 ILCS 5/10-26], the requirements pertaining to the State Disbursement Unit shall apply.

(Source: P.A. 85-1440; 91-212, § 20; 92-16, § 76; 92-590, § 5.)

Note.

This section was Ill.Rev.Stat., Ch. 23, para. 10-15.

Section 996 of P.A. 92-16 contains a "no acceleration or delay" provision, and Section 997 contains a "no revival or extension" provision.

Effect of Amendments.

The 1999 amendment by P.A. 91-212, effective July 20, 1999, added the last paragraph.

The 2001 amendment by P.A. 92-16, effective June 28, 2001, made a grammatical correction.

The 2002 amendment by P.A. 92-590, effective July 1, 2002, substituted "child support enforcement services" for "child and spouse support services" in the first sentence of the fourth paragraph.

305 ILCS 5/10-16 Judicial enforcement of court and administrative support orders

Sec. 10-16. *Judicial enforcement of court and administrative support orders.* Court orders entered in proceedings under Section 10-10 [305 ILCS 5/10-10] and court orders for enforcement of an administrative order under Section 10-15 [305 ILCS 5/10-15] and for the payment of money may be enforced by attachment as for contempt against the persons of the defendants, and in addition, as other judgments for the payment of money, and costs may be adjudged against the defendants and apportioned among them; but if the complaint is dismissed, costs shall be borne by the Illinois Department or the local governmental unit, as the case may be. If a responsible relative is directed by the Illinois Department, or the local governmental unit, under the conditions stated in Section 10-8 [305 ILCS 5/10-8], to make support payments directly to the person, or to some person or agency in his behalf, the court order entered against him under this Section or Section 10-10 [305 ILCS 5/10-10] may be enforced as herein provided if he thereafter fails to furnish support in accordance with its terms. The State of Illinois shall not be required to make a deposit for or pay any costs or fees of any court or officer thereof in any proceeding instituted under this Section.

The provisions of the Civil Practice Law [735 ILCS 5/2-101 et seq.], and all amendments and modifications thereof, shall apply to and govern all actions instituted under this Section and Section 10-10 [305 ILCS 5/10-10]. In such actions proof that a person is an applicant for or recipient of public aid under any Article of this Code shall be prima facie proof that he is a person in necessitous circumstances by reason of infirmity, unemployment or other cause depriving him of the means of a livelihood compatible with health and well-being.

Payments under this Section to the Illinois Department pursuant to the Child Support Enforcement Program established by Title IV-D of the Social Security Act [42 U.S.C. § 651 et seq.] shall be paid into the Child Support Enforcement Trust Fund. All payments under this Section to the Illinois Department of Human Services shall be deposited in the DHS Recoveries Trust Fund. Disbursements from these funds shall be as provided in Sections 12-9.1 and 12-10.2 of this Code [305 ILCS 5/12-9.1 and 305

ILCS 5/12-10.2]. Payments received by a local governmental unit shall be deposited in that unit's General Assistance Fund.

In addition to the penalties or punishment that may be imposed under this Section, any person whose conduct constitutes a violation of Section 15 of the Non-Support Punishment Act [750 ILCS 16/15] may be prosecuted under that Act, and a person convicted under that Act may be sentenced in accordance with that Act. The sentence may include but need not be limited to a requirement that the person perform community service under Section 50 of that Act [750 ILCS 16/50] or participate in a work alternative program under Section 50 of that Act [750 ILCS 16/50]. A person may not be required to participate in a work alternative program under Section 50 of that Act [750 ILCS 16/50] if the person is currently participating in a work program pursuant to Section 10-11.1 of this Code [305 ILCS 5/10-11.1].

To the extent the provisions of this Section are inconsistent with the requirements pertaining to the State Disbursement Unit under Sections 10-10.4 and 10-26 of this Code [305 ILCS 5/10-10.4 and 305 ILCS 5/10-26], the requirements pertaining to the State Disbursement Unit shall apply.
(Source: P.A. 83-1126; 90-733, § 5; 91-24, § 25; 91-212, § 20; 92-16, § 76.)

Note.

This section was Ill.Rev.Stat., Ch. 23, para. 10-16.

Section 996 of P.A. 92-16 contains a "no acceleration or delay" provision, and Section 997 contains a "no revival or extension" provision.

Effect of Amendments.

The 1998 amendment by P.A. 90-733, effective August 11, 1998, added the fourth paragraph to the section.

The 1999 amendment by P.A. 91-24, effective July 1, 1999, in the third paragraph, deleted "other" following "All", inserted "of Human Services" and substituted "DHS" for "Public Assistance" in the second sentence, and substituted "12-9.1" for "12-9" in the third sentence.

The 1999 amendment by P.A. 91-212, effective July 20, 1999, added the last paragraph.

The 2001 amendment by P.A. 92-16, effective June 28, 2001, in the fourth paragraph: substituted "Section 15" for "Section 1" and "Non-Support Punishment Act" for "Non-Support of Spouse and Children Act" in the first sentence; substituted "Act" for "Section" three times in the first sentence, twice in the second sentence and once in the last sentence; substituted "Section 50" for "subsection (b) in the second sentence and substituted "Section (50)" for "subsection (c)" in the second and third sentences; and combined the amendments by P.A. 91-24 and P.A. 91-212.

305 ILCS 5/10-16.2 Withholding of Income to Secure Payment of Support

Sec. 10-16.2. *Withholding of Income to Secure Payment of Support.* Orders for support entered under this Code are subject to the Income Withholding for Support Act [750 ILCS 28/1 et seq.].
(Source: P.A. 86-496; 86-546; 86-649; 86-746; 86-911; 86-1028; 86-1184; 87-529; 87-935, § 1; 87-988, § 1; 87-1105, § 1; 88-26, § 1; 88-45, § 2-47; 88-94, § 1; 88-131, § 5; 88-307, § 5; 88-670, § 2-51; 89-507, § 90D-63; 90-18, § 65; 90-425, § 90; 90-655, § 127; 90-673, § 910; 91-357, § 168.)

Note.

P.A. 91-357, § 996, contains a "no acceleration or delay" provision, and P.A. 91-357, § 997, contains a "no revival or extension" provision.

This section was Ill.Rev.Stat., Ch. 23, para. 10-16.2.

Effect of Amendments.

The 1994 amendment by P.A. 88-670, effective December 2, 1994, combined the amendments by P.A. 88-26, P.A. 88-45, P.A. 88-94, P.A. 88-131 and P.A. 88-307.

The 1996 amendment by P.A. 89-507, effective July 1, 1997, in subdivision (A)(8) inserted "Human Services (as successor to the Department of" and inserted a closing parenthesis following "Developmental Disabilities".

The 1997 amendment by P.A. 90-18, effective July 1, 1997, rewrote this section.

The 1997 amendment by P.A. 90-425, effective August 15, 1997, in subdivision (E)(3), in the first sentence, inserted "regular or" and substituted "facsimile" for "personal delivery"; in subdivision (F)(2), in the first sentence, inserted "regular or" and substituted "facsimile" for "personal delivery"; added subdivision (F)(4); and in the first paragraph of subdivision (G)(1), added the eighth sentence.

The 1998 amendment by P.A. 90-655, effective July 30, 1998, in present subsection (B)(9) substituted "(9) New service of an income withholding notice" for "(4) New service of an order for withholding", in subsections (B)(9) and (E)(1) substituted "income withholding notice" for "order for withholding"; and in subsection (D)(4) deleted "regular or facsimile regular or facsimile" following "provisions of subsection (F)."

The 1998 amendment by P.A. 90-790, effective August 14, 1998, added subsection (A)(2.5); in (B), added subsections (a-5) and (k), inserted "A copy of the income withholding notice together with" in subsection (7) and the last sentence in subsection (8); in subsection (B)(9), substituted "income withholding" for "order for withholding" throughout and inserted "notice" throughout; deleted "a computation of" and "period and" in subsection (C)(1)(b); deleted "or who has been served with a notice of delinquency" following "withheld" in subsection (G)(4).

The 1998 amendment by P.A. 90-673, effective January 1, 1999, incorporated the amendments by P.A. 90-18 and P.A. 90-425; and rewrote this section.

The 1999 amendment by P.A. 91-357, effective July 29, 1999, combined the 1998 amendments by P.A. 90-655, § 127 and P.A. 90-790, § 5 and rewrote the section to the extent that a detailed comparison would be impracticable.

CASE NOTES

Periodic Payment

—Lump Sum

A lump sum payment of a personal injury judgment is not a periodic payment. Brinegar v. Reeves, 289 Ill. App. 3d 405, 224 Ill. Dec. 459, 681 N.E.2d 1080 (4 Dist. 1997).

305 ILCS 5/10-16.3 Posting Security, Bond or Guarantee to Secure Payment

Sec. 10-16.3. *Posting Security, Bond or Guarantee to Secure Payment.* The court may require the responsible relative to post security, bond or give some other guarantee of a character and amount sufficient to assure payment of any amount of support due.
(Source: P.A. 84-758.)

Note.

This section was Ill.Rev.Stat., Ch. 23, para. 10-16.3.

305 ILCS 5/10-16.4 Information concerning obligors

Sec. 10-16.4. *Information concerning obligors.* (a) In this Section:

"Arrearage", "delinquency", "obligor", and "order for support" have the meanings attributed to those terms in the Income Withholding for Support Act [750 ILCS 28/1 et seq.].

"Consumer reporting agency" has the meaning attributed to that term in Section 603(f) of the Fair Credit Reporting Act, 15 U.S.C. 1681a(f).

(b) Whenever a court of competent jurisdiction finds that an obligor either owes an arrearage of more than $10,000 or is delinquent in payment of an amount equal to at least 3 months' support obligation pursuant to an order for support, the court shall direct the clerk of the court to make information concerning the obligor available to consumer reporting agencies.

(c) Whenever a court of competent jurisdiction finds that an obligor either owes an arrearage of more than $10,000 or is delinquent in payment of an amount equal to at least 3 months' support obligation pursuant to an order for support, the court shall direct the clerk of the court to cause the obligor's name and address to be published in a newspaper of general circulation in the area in which the obligor resides. The clerk shall cause the obligor's name and address to be published only after sending to the obligor at the obligor's last known address, by certified mail, return receipt requested, a notice of intent to publish the information. This subsection (c) applies only if the obligor resides in the county in which the clerk of the court holds office.
(Source: P.A. 90-466, § 5; 90-673, § 910.)

Effective Date.
This section became effective January 1, 1998 pursuant to Ill. Const. (1970), Art. IV, § 10 and 5 ILCS 75/1.

Effect of Amendments.
The 1998 amendment by P.A. 90-673, effective January 1, 1999, incorporated the amendment by P.A. 90-466; and substituted "the Income Withholding for Support Act" for "Section 10-16.2 of this Code" in subsection (a).

305 ILCS 5/10-16.5 Interest on support obligations

Sec. 10-16.5. *Interest on support obligations.* A support obligation, or any portion of a support obligation, which becomes due and remains unpaid for 30 days or more shall accrue simple interest at the rate of 9% per annum. An order for support entered or modified on or after January 1, 2002 shall contain a statement that a support obligation required under the order, or any portion of a support obligation required under the order, that becomes due and remains unpaid for 30 days or more shall accrue simple interest at the rate of 9% per annum. Failure to include the statement in the order for support does not affect the validity of the order or the accrual of interest as provided in this Section.
(Source: P.A. 91-397, § 5; 92-374, § 5.)

Effective Date.
This section became effective January 1, 2000, pursuant to Ill. Const. (1970), Art. IV, § 10 and 5 ILCS 75/1.

Effect of Amendments.
The 2001 amendment by P.A. 92-374, effective August 15, 2001, inserted "simple" in the first sentence and added the last two sentences.

305 ILCS 5/10-16.6 Electronic Funds Transfer Committee

Sec. 10-16.6. *Electronic Funds Transfer Committee.* (a) The Director of Public Aid shall establish within the Department an Electronic Funds Transfer Committee. The Director or his or her designee shall be a member of the committee and shall serve as chairperson of the committee. The Director shall appoint 4 other members of the committee, 2 of whom shall represent employers in this State and 2 of whom shall represent the banking industry in this State. The administrator of the State Disbursement Unit established under Section 10-26 [305 ILCS 5/10-26] shall be an ex officio member of the committee.

(b) The committee shall study ways to modify or expand the use of electronic funds transfers for the payment of child support. The committee shall report its findings and recommendations to the Governor and the General Assembly before December 1, 2001.

(c) The committee is abolished on December 1, 2001.
(Source: P.A. 91-677, § 5.)

Effective Date.
Section 99 of P.A. 91-677 made this section effective upon becoming law. The Act was approved January 5, 2000.

305 ILCS 5/10-16.7 Child support enforcement debit authorization

Sec. 10-16.7. *Child support enforcement debit authorization.* (a) For purposes of this Section:

"Financial institution" and "account" are defined as set forth in Section 10-24 [305 ILCS 5/10-24].

"Payor" is defined as set forth in Section 15 of the Income Withholding for Support Act [750 ILCS 28/15].

"Order for support" means any order for periodic payment of funds to the State Disbursement Unit for the support of a child or, where applicable, for support of a child and a parent with whom the child resides, that is entered or modified under this Code or under the Illinois Marriage and Dissolution of Marriage Act [750 ILCS 5/101 et seq.], the Non-Support of Spouse and Children Act [750 ILCS 20/1 et seq.], the Non-Support Punishment Act [750 ILCS 16/1 et seq.], or the Illinois Parentage Act of 1984 [750 ILCS 45/1 et seq.], or that is entered or registered for modification or enforcement under the Uniform Interstate Family Support Act [750 ILCS 22/101 et seq.].

"Obligor" means an individual who owes a duty to make payments under an order for support in a case in which child support enforcement services are being provided under this Article X.

(b) The Department of Public Aid shall adopt a child support enforcement debit authorization form that, upon being signed by an obligor, authorizes a financial institution holding an account on the obligor's behalf to debit the obligor's account periodically in an amount equal to the amount of child support that the obligor is required to pay periodically and transfer that amount to the State Disbursement Unit. The form shall include instructions to the financial institution concerning the debiting of accounts held on behalf of obligors and the transfer of the debited amounts to the State Disbursement Unit. In adopting the form, the Department may consult with the Office of Banks and Real Estate and the Department of Financial Institutions. The Department must adopt the form within 6 months after the effective date of this amendatory Act of the 93rd General Assembly [P.A. 93-736]. Promptly after adopting the form, the Department must notify each financial institution conducting business in this State that the form has been adopted and is ready for use.

(c) An obligor who does not have a payor may sign a child support debit authorization form adopted by the Department under this Section. The obligor may sign a form in relation to any or all of the financial institutions holding an account on the obligor's behalf. Promptly after an obligor signs a child support debit authorization form, the Department shall send the original signed form to the appropriate financial institution. Subject to subsection (e), upon receiving the form, the financial institution shall debit the account and transfer the debited amounts to the State Disbursement Unit according to the instructions in the form. A financial institution that complies with a child support debit authorization form signed by an obligor and issued under this Section shall not be subject to civil liability with respect to any individual or any agency.

(d) The signing and issuance of a child support debit authorization form under this Section does not relieve the obligor from responsibility for compliance with any requirement under the order for support.

(e) A financial institution is obligated to debit the account of an obligor pursuant to this Section only if or to the extent:

(1) the financial institution reasonably believes the debit authorization form is a true and authentic original document;

(2) there are finally collected funds in the account; and

(3) the account is not subject to offsetting claims of the financial institution, whether due at the time of receipt of the debit authorization form or thereafter to become due and whether liquidated or unliquidated.

To the extent the account of the obligor is pledged or held by the financial institution as security for a loan or other obligation, or that the financial institution has any other claim or lien against the account, the financial institution is entitled to retain the account.

(Source: P.A. 93-736, § 30.)

Effective Date.

Section 99 of P.A. 93-736 made this section effective upon becoming law. The Act was approved July 14, 2004.

305 ILCS 5/10-17 Other Actions and Remedies for Support

Sec. 10-17. *Other Actions and Remedies for Support.* The procedures, actions and remedies provided in this Article shall in no way be exclusive, but shall be available in addition to other actions and remedies of support, including, but not by way of limitation, the remedies provided in (a) the "Paternity Act", approved July 5, 1957, as amended; (b) the "Non-Support of Spouse and Children Act", approved June 24, 1915, as amended [750 ILCS 15/1 et seq.]; (b-5) the Non-Support Punishment Act [750 ILCS 16/1 et seq.]; and (c) the "Revised Uniform Reciprocal Enforcement of Support Act", approved August 28, 1969, as amended [750 ILCS 20/1 et seq.].

(Source: P.A. 79-474; 91-613, § 935.)

Note.

This section was Ill.Rev.Stat., Ch. 23, para. 10-17.

The Paternity Act, referred to in this section, has been repealed. Similar present provisions may be found in the Illinois Parentage Act of 1984, 750 ILCS 45/1 et seq.

Section 70 of P.A. 91-613 contains a severability provision.

The Non-Support of Spouse and Children Act, 750 ILCS 15/1 et seq., referred to above, is repealed. Current similar provisions are found as the Non-Support Punishment Act, 750 ILCS 16/1 et seq.

Effect of Amendments.

The 1999 amendment by P.A. 91-613, effective October 1, 1999, inserted "(b-5) the Non-Support Punishment Act"; and made a stylistic change.

305 ILCS 5/10-17.1 Administrative Order by Registration

Sec. 10-17.1. *Administrative Order by Registration.* The Illinois Department may provide by rule for the administrative registration of a support order entered by a court or administrative body of another state. The purpose of registration shall be to enforce or modify the order in accordance with the provisions of the Uniform Interstate Family Support Act [750 ILCS 22/100 et seq.]. Upon registration, such support order shall become an administrative order of the Child and Spouse Support Unit by operation of law. The rule shall provide for notice to and an opportunity to be heard by the responsible relative and custodial parent affected, and any final administrative decision rendered by the Department shall be reviewed only under and in accordance with the Administrative Review Law [735 ILCS 5/3-101 et seq.].

Any new or existing support order registered by the Illinois Department under this Section shall be deemed to be a series of judgments against the person obligated to pay support thereunder, each such judgment to be in the amount of each payment or installment of support and each such judgment to be deemed entered as of the date the corresponding payment or installment becomes due under the terms of the support order. Each such judgment shall be enforceable in the same manner as any other judgment in this State. A lien arises by operation of law against the real and personal property of the noncustodial parent for each installment of overdue support owed by the noncustodial parent.

A one-time charge of 20% is imposable upon the amount of past-due child support owed on July 1, 1988, which has accrued under a support order registered by the Illinois Department under this Section. The charge shall be imposed in accordance with the provisions of Section 10-21 [305 ILCS 5/10-21] and shall be enforced by the court in a suit filed under Section 10-15 [305 ILCS 5/10-15].
(Source: P.A. 85-1156; 88-687, § 5; 90-18, § 65; 90-790, § 5.)

Note.
This section was Ill.Rev.Stat., Ch. 23, para. 10-17.1.

Effect of Amendments.
The 1994 amendment by P.A. 88-687, effective January 24, 1995, in the first paragraph, added the second sentence; and in the second paragraph, added the present second sentence and deleted the former second and third sentences which read "Each such judgment shall have the full force, effect and attributes of any other judgment of this State, including the ability to be enforced. Any such judgment is subject to modification or termination only in accordance with Section 510 of the Illinois Marriage and Dissolution of Marriage Act".

The 1997 amendment by P.A. 90-18, effective July 1, 1997, in the second paragraph, added the third sentence.

The 1998 amendment by P.A. 90-790, effective August 14, 1998, in the first paragraph, inserted "administrative" preceding "registration," substituted "another state" for "this or any other state," rewrote the second sentence, and inserted "and custodial parent in the last sentence.

305 ILCS 5/10-17.2 Income Withholding By Administrative Order

Sec. 10-17.2. *Income Withholding By Administrative Order.* The Illinois Department may provide by rule for entry of an administrative support order containing income withholding provisions and for service and enforcement of an income withholding notice and a National Medical Support Notice, by the Child and Spouse Support Unit based upon and in the same manner as prescribed by the Income Withholding for Support Act [750 ILCS 28/1 et seq.]. The penalties provided in the Income Withholding for Support Act [750 ILCS 28/1 et seq.] shall apply hereto and shall be enforced by filing an action under that Act. The rule shall provide for notice to and an opportunity to be heard by the responsible relative affected and any final administrative decision rendered by the Department shall be reviewed only under and in accordance with the Administrative Review Law [735 ILCS 5/3-101 et seq.].
(Source: P.A. 84-1389; 90-18, § 65; 90-673, § 910; 92-590, § 5.)

Note.
This section was Ill.Rev.Stat., Ch. 23, para. 10-17.2.

Effect of Amendments.
The 1997 amendment by P.A. 90-18, effective July 1, 1997, in the first sentence, inserted "support", substituted "containing income" for "for", inserted "provisions", substituted "for service" for "its subsequent service" and inserted "of an income withholding notice".

The 1998 amendment by P.A. 90-673, effective January 1, 1999, incorporated the amendment by P.A. 90-18; substituted "the Income Withholding for Support Act" for "Section 10-16.2 of this Code" twice; and substituted "Act" for "Section" in the second sentence.

The 2002 amendment by P.A. 92-590, effective July 1, 2002, inserted "and a National Medical Support Notice" following "withholding notice" in the first sentence.

305 ILCS 5/10-17.3 Federal Income Tax Refund Intercept

Sec. 10-17.3. *Federal Income Tax Refund Intercept.* The Illinois Department may provide by rule for certification to the Department of Health and Human Services of past due support owed by responsible relatives under a support order entered by a court or administrative body of this or any other State on behalf of resident or non-resident persons. The purpose of certification shall be to intercept Federal Income Tax refunds due such relatives in order to satisfy such past due support in whole or in part.

The rule shall provide for notice to and an opportunity to be heard by the responsible relative affected and any final administrative decision rendered by the Department shall be reviewed only under and in accordance with the Administrative Review Law. Certification shall be accomplished in accordance with Title IV, Part D of the federal Social Security Act [42 U.S.C. § 651 et seq.] and rules and regulations promulgated thereunder.
(Source: P.A. 84-758.)

Note.
This section was Ill.Rev.Stat., Ch. 23, para. 10-17.3.

CASE NOTES

Jurisdiction
A circuit court did not have jurisdiction to order the Department of Public Aid to refund an overpayment of child support collected through tax intercepts. James v. Mims, 316 Ill. App. 3d 1179, 250 Ill. Dec. 249, 738 N.E.2d 213, 2000 Ill. App. LEXIS 792 (1 Dist. 2000).

305 ILCS 5/10-17.4 Security, Bond or Guarantee to Secure Payment

Sec. 10-17.4. *Security, Bond or Guarantee to Secure Payment.* The Illinois Department may provide by rule for the requiring of, or for the requesting of the court to require, a responsible relative to post security, bond or give some other guarantee of a character and amount sufficient to assure payment of any amount due under a support order entered by a court or administrative body of this or any other State on behalf of resident or non-resident persons. The rule shall provide for notice to and an opportunity to be heard by each responsible relative affected and any final administrative decision rendered by

the Department shall be reviewed only under and in accordance with the Administrative Review Law [735 ILCS 5/3-101 et seq.].
(Source: P.A. 84-758.)

Note.
This section was Ill.Rev.Stat., Ch. 23, para. 10-17.4.

Illinois Administrative Code.
See 89 Illinois Administrative Code, § 160.70.

305 ILCS 5/10-17.5 State Income Tax Refund and Other Payment Intercept

Sec. 10-17.5. *State Income Tax Refund and Other Payment Intercept.* The Illinois Department may provide by rule for certification to the Comptroller of past due support owed by responsible relatives under a support order entered by a court or administrative body of this or any other State on behalf of resident or non-resident persons. The purpose of certification shall be to intercept state income tax refunds and other payments due such relatives in order to satisfy such past due support, in whole or in part, whether or not such support is owed to the State. The rule shall provide for notice to and an opportunity to be heard by the responsible relative and any joint payee affected and any final administrative decision rendered by the Department shall be reviewed only under and in accordance with the Administrative Review Law [735 ILCS 5/3-101 et seq.]. In any case where a state income tax refund is intercepted wrongfully or erroneously, the Department shall pay to such relative and any joint payee affected the amount of the refund plus interest, if any, on such amount at the rate of 9% per annum (or at such adjusted rate as is established under Section 6621(b) of the Internal Revenue Code [26 U.S.C. § 6621]). Interest shall be calculated from the date the Department receives the refund or from 60 days following the date the Department receives a request to be heard, whichever is later, until the date of payment to such relative and joint payee.
(Source: P.A. 85-1440.)

Note.
This section was Ill.Rev.Stat., Ch. 23, para. 10-17.5.

Cross References.
As for withholding of lottery prize money by the state for payment of past due support, see 20 ILCS 1605/13.

CASE NOTES

Jurisdiction
A circuit court did not have jurisdiction to order the Department of Public Aid to refund an overpayment of child support collected through tax intercepts. James v. Mims, 316 Ill. App. 3d 1179, 250 Ill. Dec. 249, 738 N.E.2d 213, 2000 Ill. App. LEXIS 792 (1 Dist. 2000).

305 ILCS 5/10-17.6 Past Due Support Information to Licensing Agencies

Sec. 10-17.6. *Past Due Support Information to Licensing Agencies.* The Illinois Department may provide by rule for certification to any State licensing agency of past due support owed by responsible relatives under a support order entered by a court or administrative body of this or any other State on behalf of resident or non-resident persons. The rule shall provide for notice to and an opportunity to be heard by each responsible relative affected and any final administrative decision rendered by the Department shall be reviewed only under and in accordance with the Administrative Review Law [735 ILCS 5/3-101 et seq.].
(Source: P.A. 87-412.)

Note.
This section was Ill.Rev.Stat., Ch. 23, para. 10-17.6.

305 ILCS 5/10-17.7 Administrative determination of paternity

Sec. 10-17.7. *Administrative determination of paternity.* The Illinois Department may provide by rule for the administrative determination of paternity by the Child and Spouse Support Unit in cases involving applicants for or recipients of financial aid under Article IV of this Act [305 ILCS 5/4-0.5 et seq.] and other persons who are given access to the child support enforcement services of this Article as provided in Section 10-1 [305 ILCS 5/10-1], including persons similarly situated and receiving similar services in other states. The rules shall extend to cases in which the mother and alleged father voluntarily acknowledge paternity in the form required by the Illinois Department or agree to be bound by the results of genetic testing or in which the alleged father has failed to respond to a notification of support obligation issued under Section 10-4 [305 ILCS 5/10-4] and to cases of contested paternity. Any presumption provided for under the Illinois Parentage Act of 1984 [750 ILCS 45/1 et seq.] shall apply to cases in which paternity is determined under the rules of the Illinois Department. The rules shall provide for notice and an opportunity to be heard by the responsible relative and the person receiving child support enforcement services under this Article if paternity is not voluntarily acknowledged, and any final administrative decision rendered by the Illinois Department shall be reviewed only under and in accordance with the Administrative Review Law [735 ILCS 5/3-101 et seq.]. Determinations of paternity made by the Illinois Department under the rules authorized by this Section shall have the full force and effect of a court judgment of paternity entered under the Illinois Parentage Act of 1984 [750 ILCS 45/1 et seq.].

In determining paternity in contested cases, the Illinois Department shall conduct the evidentiary hearing in accordance with Section 11 of the Parentage Act of 1984 [750 ILCS 40/11], except that references in that Section to "the court" shall be deemed to mean the Illinois Department's hearing officer in cases in which paternity is determined administratively by the Illinois Department.

Notwithstanding any other provision of this Article, a default determination of paternity may be made if service of the notice under Section 10-4 [305 ILCS 5/10-4] was made by publication under the rules for administrative paternity determination authorized by this Section. The rules as they pertain to service by publication shall (i) be based on the provisions of Section 2-206 and 2-207 of the Code of Civil Procedure [735 ILCS 5/2-206 and 735 ILCS 5/2-207], (ii) provide for service by publication in cases in which the whereabouts of the alleged father are unknown after diligent location efforts by the Child and Spouse Support Unit, and (iii) provide for publication of a notice of default paternity determination in the same manner that the notice under Section 10-4 [305 ILCS 5/10-4] was published.

The Illinois Department may implement this Section through the use of emergency rules in accordance with Section 5-45 of the Illinois Administrative Procedure Act [5 ILCS 100/5-45]. For purposes of the Illinois Administrative Procedure Act [5 ILCS 100/1-1 et seq.], the adoption of rules to implement this Section shall be considered an emergency and necessary for the public interest, safety, and welfare.
(Source: P.A. 88-687, § 5; 89-6, § 25; 89-641, § 15; 90-790, § 5; 92-590, § 5.)

Effective Date.
Section 99 of P.A. 88-687 made this section effective upon becoming law. The Act was approved January 24, 1995.

Effect of Amendments.
The 1995 amendment by P.A. 89-6, effective March 6, 1995, in the first paragraph, in the second sentence, inserted "by affidavit in the form required by the Illinois Department" and added at the end "and for purposes of the program provided for under Section 12-4.31 to cases of contested paternity involving only applicants for or recipients of assistance under Articles IV, V and VI of this Code"; and added the second through fifth paragraphs.
The 1996 amendment by P.A. 89-641, effective August 9, 1996, in the first paragraph, in the second sentence, deleted "by affidavit" following "voluntarily acknowledge paternity" and in the fourth sentence inserted "if paternity is not voluntarily acknowledged".
The 1998 amendment by P.A. 90-790, effective August 14, 1998, in the first paragraph, deleted "for purposes of the program provided for under Section 12-4.31" and "involving only applicants for or recipients of assistance under Articles IV, V and VI of this Code," and substituted "relative and the person receiving child and spouse support services under this Article" for "relative affected"; deleted "regarding only cases included in the program provided for under Section 12-4.31 of this Code" from the third paragraph; and deleted the fourth paragraph, relating to petitions for relief from a default administrative finding of paternity.
The 2002 amendment by P.A. 92-590, effective July 1, 2002, substituted "child support enforcement services" for "child and spouse support services" twice.

305 ILCS 5/10-17.8 New birth certificate

Sec. 10-17.8. *New birth certificate.* The Illinois Department shall notify the Department of Public Health of a final determination of parentage and a voluntary acknowledgment of paternity made under the rules authorized by Section 10-17.7 [305 ILCS 5/10-17.7], and the Department of Public Health shall issue a new certificate of birth pursuant to Section 17 of the Vital Records Act [410 ILCS 535/17].
(Source: P.A. 89-6, § 25; 89-641, § 15.)

Effective Date.
Section 99 of P.A. 89-6 made this section effective upon becoming law. The Act was approved March 6, 1995.

Effect of Amendments.
The 1996 amendment by P.A. 89-641, effective August 9, 1996, inserted "and a voluntary acknowledgment of paternity".

305 ILCS 5/10-17.9 Past due support information to State Department of Revenue

Sec. 10-17.9. *Past due support information to State Department of Revenue.* (a) The Illinois Department may provide by rule for certification to the Illinois Department of Revenue of past due support owed by responsible relatives under a support order entered by a court or administrative body of this or any other State on behalf of resident or non-resident persons. The rule shall provide for notice to and an opportunity to be heard by each responsible relative affected. Any final administrative decision rendered by the Department shall be reviewed only under and in accordance with the Administrative Review Law [735 ILCS 5/3-101 et seq.]. A responsible relative may avoid certification to the Illinois Department of Revenue by establishing a satisfactory repayment record as determined by the Illinois Department of Public Aid.

(b) A certified past due support amount shall be final. The certified amount shall be payable to the Illinois Department of Revenue upon written notification of the certification to the responsible relative by the Illinois Department of Revenue.

(c) In the event a responsible relative overpays pursuant to collection under this Section and the applicable Sections of the Illinois Income Tax Act [35 ILCS 5/101 et seq.], the overpayment shall be a credit against future support obligations. If the current support obligation of the responsible relative has terminated under operation of law or court order, any moneys overpaid but still in the possession of the Department shall be promptly returned to the responsible relative.

(d) Except as otherwise provided in this Article, any child support delinquency certified to the Illinois Department of Revenue shall be treated as a child support delinquency for all other purposes, and any collection action by the State's Attorney or the Illinois Department of Revenue with respect to any delinquency certified under this Article shall have the same priority against attachment, execution, assignment, or other collection action as is provided by any other provision of State law.

(e) Any child support delinquency collected by the Illinois Department of Revenue, including those amounts that result in overpayment of a child support delinquency, shall be paid to the State Disbursement Unit established under Section 10-26 [305 ILCS 5/10-26].
(Source: P.A. 89-6, § 25; 91-212, § 20.)

Illinois Administrative Code.
See 89 Illinois Administrative Code, § 160.70.

Effective Date.

Section 99 of P.A. 89-6 made this section effective December 31, 1995.

Effect of Amendments.

The 1999 amendment by P.A. 91-212, effective July 20, 1999, substituted "paid to the State Disbursement Unit established under Section 10-26" for "deposited in, or transferred to, the Child Support Enforcement Trust Fund" in subsection (e).

305 ILCS 5/10-17.11 Requests to other states for administrative enforcement

Sec. 10-17.11. *Requests to other states for administrative enforcement.* The Illinois Department may provide by rule for certification to other states' child support enforcement agencies of past due support owed by responsible relatives under a support order entered by a court or administrative body of this or any other state on behalf of resident or non-resident persons. The purpose of certification shall be to request the other states' assistance in administrative enforcement of the support orders. The rule shall provide for notice to and an opportunity to be heard by the responsible relative affected and any final administrative decision rendered by the Illinois Department shall be reviewed only under and in accordance with the Administrative Review Law [735 ILCS 5/3-101 et seq.].
(Source: P.A. 90-18, § 65.)

Effective Date.

Section 999 of P.A. 90-18 made this section effective July 1, 1997.

305 ILCS 5/10-18 Recoveries — Deductibility of Direct Relatives' Support Payment

Sec. 10-18. *Recoveries — Deductibility of Direct Relatives' Support Payment.* In any actions for the recovery of the financial aid, including actions for the enforcement of estate and lien claims, amounts contributed by responsible relatives either voluntarily or by court or administrative order and paid to the Illinois Department or to a local governmental unit shall be deducted from the claim of the State or the governmental unit.
(Source: P.A. 79-474.)

Note.

This section was Ill.Rev.Stat., Ch. 23, para. 10-18.

305 ILCS 5/10-19 Support Payments Ordered Under Other Laws; where deposited

Sec. 10-19. *Support Payments Ordered Under Other Laws; where deposited.* The Illinois Department and local governmental units are authorized to receive payments directed by court order for the support of recipients, as provided in the following Acts:

1. "Non-Support of Spouse and Children Act", approved June 24, 1915, as amended [repealed],

1.5. The Non-Support Punishment Act [750 ILCS 16/1 et seq.],

2. "Illinois Marriage and Dissolution of Marriage Act", as now or hereafter amended [750 ILCS 5/101 et seq.],

3. The Illinois Parentage Act, as amended [750 ILCS 45/1 et seq.],

4. "Revised Uniform Reciprocal Enforcement of Support Act", approved August 28, 1969, as amended [repealed],

5. The Juvenile Court Act or the Juvenile Court Act of 1987, as amended [705 ILCS 405/1-1 et seq.],

6. The "Unified Code of Corrections", approved July 26, 1972, as amended [730 ILCS 5/1-1-1 et seq.],

7. Part 7 of Article XII of the Code of Civil Procedure, as amended [735 ILCS 5/12-701 et seq.],

8. Part 8 of Article XII of the Code of Civil Procedure, as amended [735 ILCS 5/12-801 et seq.], and

9. Other laws which may provide by judicial order for direct payment of support moneys.

Payments under this Section to the Illinois Department pursuant to the Child Support Enforcement Program established by Title IV-D of the Social Security Act [42 U.S.C. § 651 et seq.] shall be paid into the Child Support Enforcement Trust Fund. All payments under this Section to the Illinois Department of Human Services shall be deposited in the DHS Recoveries Trust Fund. Disbursements from these funds shall be as provided in Sections 12-9.1 and 12-10.2 of this Code [305 ILCS 5/12-9.1 and 305 ILCS 5/12-10.2]. Payments received by a local governmental unit shall be deposited in that unit's General Assistance Fund.

To the extent the provisions of this Section are inconsistent with the requirements pertaining to the State Disbursement Unit under Sections 10-10.4 and 10-26 of this Code [305 ILCS 5/10-10.4 and 305 ILCS 5/10-26], the requirements pertaining to the State Disbursement Unit shall apply.
(Source: P.A. 86-1028; 91-24, § 25; 91-212, § 20; 91-613, § 935; 92-16, § 76.)

Note.

This section was Ill.Rev.Stat., Ch. 23, para. 10-19.

The Revised Uniform Reciprocal Enforcement of Support Act, Illinois Parentage Act and the Juvenile Court Act have been repealed. Similar present provisions appear as the Uniform Interstate Family Support Act, 750 ILCS 22/101 et seq., the Illinois Parentage Act of 1984, 750 ILCS 45/1 et seq., and the Juvenile Court Act of 1987, 705 ILCS 405/1-1 et seq., respectively.

Section 70 of P.A. 91-613 contains a severability provision.

The Non-Support of Spouse and Children Act, 750 ILCS 15/1 et seq., referred to in paragraph 1., is repealed. Current similar provisions are found as the Non-Support Punishment Act, 750 ILCS 16/1 et seq.

Section 996 of P.A. 92-16 contains a "no acceleration or delay" provision, and Section 997 contains a "no revival or extension" provision.

Effect of Amendments.

The 1999 amendment by P.A. 91-24, effective July 1, 1999, in the next-to-last paragraph: in the second sentence, deleted "other" following "All", inserted "of Human Services", and substituted "DHS" for "Public Assistance"; and substituted "12-9.1" for "12-9" in the third sentence.

The 1999 amendment by P.A. 91-212, effective July 20, 1999, added the last paragraph and made stylistic changes.

The 1999 amendment by P.A. 91-613, effective October 1, 1999. inserted "1.5. The Non-Support Punishment Act".

The 2001 amendment by P.A. 92-16, effective June 28, 2001 combined the amendments by P.A. 91-24, P.A. 91-212 and P.A. 91-613.

305 ILCS 5/10-20, 305 ILCS 5/10-21: Repealed by P.A. 92-84, § 65, effective July 1, 2002.

305 ILCS 5/10-22: Repealed by P.A. 90-790, § 6, effective August 14, 1998.

305 ILCS 5/10-23 Employer obligations

Sec. 10-23. *Employer obligations.* If a parent is required by a court or administrative order for support to provide coverage for a child's health care expenses and if that coverage is available to the parent through an employer who does business in this State, the employer must do all of the following upon receipt of a copy of the order of support or order for withholding:

(1) The employer shall, upon the parent's request, permit the parent to include in that coverage a child who is otherwise eligible for that coverage, without regard to any enrollment season restrictions that might otherwise be applicable as to the time period within which the child may be added to that coverage.

(2) If the parent has health care coverage through the employer but fails to apply for coverage of the child, the employer shall include the child in the parent's coverage upon application by the child's other parent or the Illinois Department.

(3) The employer may not eliminate any child from the parent's health care coverage unless the employee is no longer employed by the employer and no longer covered under the employer's group health plan or unless the employer is provided with satisfactory written evidence of either of the following:

(A) The court or administrative order is no longer in effect.

(B) The child is or will be included in a comparable health care plan obtained by the parent under such order that is currently in effect or will take effect no later than the date the prior coverage is terminated.

The employer may eliminate a child from a parent's health care coverage if the employer has eliminated dependent health care coverage for all of its employees.

(Source: P.A. 89-183, § 35.)

Effective Date.

This section became effective January 1, 1996 pursuant to Ill. Const. (1970), Art. IV, § 10 and 5 ILCS 75/1.

305 ILCS 5/10-24 Definitions

Sec. 10-24. *Definitions.* In this Section through Section 10-24.50 [305 ILCS 5/10-24.50]:

"Account" means a demand deposit account, checking or negotiable withdrawal order account, savings account, time deposit account, or money market mutual fund account.

"Financial institution" includes:

(1) a depository institution, which is any bank or saving association;

(2) an insured depository institution, which is any bank or saving institution the deposits of which are insured pursuant to the Federal Deposit Insurance Act, or any uninsured branch or agency of a foreign bank or a commercial lending company owned or controlled by a foreign bank;

(3) a federal depository institution, which is any national bank, any federal savings association, or any federal branch;

(4) a state depository institution, which is any state bank, any state savings association, or any insured branch which is not a federal branch;

(5) a federal credit union, which is a cooperative association organized in accordance with the provisions of the Federal Credit Union Act [12 U.S.C. § 1751 et seq.];

(6) a state chartered credit union which is organized and operated according to the laws of this or any other state, which laws provide for the organization of credit unions similar in principle and objectives to federal credit unions; and

(7) any benefit association, insurance company, safe deposit company, money market mutual fund, or similar entity authorized to do business in this State.

"Financial record" has the meaning given to that term in Section 1101 of the federal Right to Financial Privacy Act of 1978 (12 U.S.C. 3401).

(Source: P.A. 90-18, § 65.)

Illinois Administrative Code.

See 89 Illinois Administrative Code, § 160.70.

Effective Date.

Section 999 of P.A. 90-18 made this Section effective July 1, 1997.

CASE NOTES

Money Market Mutual Fund

Where the department of public aid, pursuant to 305 ILCS 5/10-25.5(a), placed a child support lien on the investment account that was jointly owned by the debtor, who owed the support, and the debtor's father, the account, a money market mutual fund, was an account in a financial institution pursuant to 305 ILCS 5/10-24 that was subject to a lien, and the debtor was a responsible relative under 305 ILCS 5/2-11. Highsmith v. Dep't of Pub. Aid, 345 Ill. App. 3d 774, 281 Ill. Dec. 248, 803 N.E.2d 652, 2004 Ill. App. LEXIS 29 (2 Dist. 2004).

305 ILCS 5/10-24.5 Financial institutions data matches

Sec. 10-24.5. *Financial institutions data matches.* (a) The Illinois Department may design and implement a data match system pursuant to which the Illinois Department shall enter into agreements with financial institutions doing business in this State for the purpose of identifying accounts as defined in Section 10-24 [305 ILCS 5/10-24] of responsible relatives who owe past-due child support.

(b) Every agreement entered into with a financial institution under this Section shall provide, at the option of the financial institution, either (i) that the financial institution shall compare data concerning account holders, owners, or customers who maintain one or more accounts as defined in Section 10-24 [305 ILCS 5/10-24] at the financial institution with data concerning individuals identified by the Illinois Department as responsible relatives who owe past-due child support and for each of whom the Illinois Department shall provide the name, record address, and social security number or tax identification number, or (ii) that the financial institution shall provide the social security number or tax identification number of the account holders, owners, or customers who maintain one or more accounts as defined in Section 10-24 [305 ILCS 5/10-24] at the financial institution to the Illinois Department, which shall compare that data with data concerning individuals identified as responsible relatives who owe past-due child support.

(c) Every agreement shall provide that the Illinois Department shall pay to the financial institution providing or comparing the data a reasonable fee not to exceed the institution's actual cost of providing the data or performing the comparison.

(d) If the financial institution or Illinois Department determines that the name and either social security number or tax identification number of an individual identified by the Illinois Department under subsection (b) match the name and either social security number or tax identification number of the account holder, owner, or customer who maintains one or more accounts as defined in Section 10-24 [305 ILCS 5/10-24] at the financial institution, then the financial institution shall report the individual's name and either social security number or tax identification number to the Illinois Department, for each calendar quarter in which the individual is identified by the Illinois Department as a responsible relative who owes past-due child support.

(Source: P.A. 90-18, § 65.)

Effective Date.

Section 999 of P.A. 90-18 made this section effective July 1, 1997.

305 ILCS 5/10-24.30 Types of accounts to be reported

Sec. 10-24.30. *Types of accounts to be reported.* The reporting requirements of Section 10-24.5 [305 ILCS 5/10-24.5] regarding accounts as defined in Section 10-24 [305 ILCS 5/10-24] apply to individual accounts, joint accounts, and sole proprietorship accounts. In the case of a joint account, the account holder or owner shall be deemed to be the primary account holder or owner established by the financial institution in accordance with federal 1099 reporting requirements.

(Source: P.A. 90-18, § 65.)

Effective Date.

Section 999 of P.A. 90-18 made this section effective July 1, 1997.

305 ILCS 5/10-24.35 Accommodation of financial institutions

Sec. 10-24.35. *Accommodation of financial institutions.* The Illinois Department of Public Aid shall make a reasonable effort to accommodate those financial institutions on which the requirements of this Article X would impose a hardship. In the case of a non-automated financial institution, a paper copy including either social security numbers or tax identification numbers is an acceptable format. In order to allow for data processing implementation, no agreement shall become effective earlier than 90 days after its execution.

(Source: P.A. 90-18, § 65.)

Effective Date.

Section 999 of P.A. 90-18 made this section effective July 1, 1997.

305 ILCS 5/10-24.40 Financial institution's charges on account

Sec. 10-24.40. *Financial institution's charges on account.* (a) If the Illinois Department of Public Aid requests a financial institution to hold or encumber assets in an account as defined in Section 10-24 [305 ILCS 5/10-24], the financial institution at which the account as defined in Section 10-24 [305 ILCS 5/10-24] is maintained may charge and collect its normally scheduled account activity fees to maintain the account during the period of time the account assets are held or encumbered.

(b) If the Illinois Department of Public Aid takes any action to enforce a lien or levy imposed on an account, as defined in Section 10-24 [305 ILCS 5/10-24], under Section 10-25.5 [305 ILCS 5/10-25.5], the financial institution at which the account is maintained may charge to the account a fee of up to $50 and shall deduct the amount of the fee from the account before remitting any moneys from the account to the Illinois Department of Public Aid.

(Source: P.A. 90-18, § 65.)

Effective Date.

Section 999 of P.A. 90-18 made this section effective July 1, 1997.

305 ILCS 5/10-24.45 Confidentiality

Sec. 10-24.45. *Confidentiality.* All information provided by a financial institution under Sections 10-24 through 10-24.50 [305 ILCS 5/10-24 through 305 ILCS 5/10-24.50] is confidential and may be used only for the purpose of enforcing payment of child support. The Illinois Department shall adopt rules to safeguard any confidential information received from a financial institution.

(Source: P.A. 90-18, § 65.)

Effective Date.

Section 999 of P.A. 90-18 made this section effective July 1, 1997.

305 ILCS 5/10-24.50 Financial institution's freedom from liability

Sec. 10-24.50. *Financial institution's freedom from liability.* A financial institution that provides information under Sections 10-24 through 10-24.50 [305 ILCS 5/10-24 through 305 ILCS 5/10-24.50] shall not be liable to any account holder, owner, or other person in any civil, criminal, or administrative action for any of the following:

(1) Disclosing the required information to the Illinois Department of Public Aid, any other provisions of the law not withstanding.

(2) Holding, encumbering, or surrendering any of an individual's accounts as defined in Section 10-24 [305 ILCS 5/10-24] in response to a lien or order to withhold and deliver issued by:

(A) the Illinois Department of Public Aid under Sections 10-25 and 10-25.5 [305 ILCS 5/10-25 and 305 ILCS 5/10-25.5]; or

(B) a person or entity acting on behalf of the Illinois Department of Public Aid.

(3) Any other action taken or omission made in good faith to comply with Sections 10-24 through 10-24.50 [305 ILCS 5/10-24 through 305 ILCS 5/10-24.50], including individual or mechanical errors, provided that the action or omission does not constitute gross negligence or willful misconduct.

(Source: P.A. 90-18, § 65.)

Effective Date.

Section 999 of P.A. 90-18 made this section effective July 1, 1997.

CASE NOTES

Bank Immunity

Trial court properly dismissed bank account holder's claim against the bank after the bank transferred funds it held in a bank account with the bank account holder and nephew's name on the account based on a child support arrearage the nephew had, as the bank transferred the funds at the direction of the state department of public aid, which meant it was immune from liability pursuant to 305 ILCS 5/10-24.50 and that the bank account holder's complaint on that issue did not state a claim. Martinez v. Dep't of Pub. Aid, 348 Ill. App. 3d 788, 284 Ill. Dec. 818, 810 N.E.2d 608, 2004 Ill. App. LEXIS 591 (1 Dist. 2004).

305 ILCS 5/10-25 Administrative liens and levies on real property for past-due child support

Sec. 10-25. *Administrative liens and levies on real property for past-due child support.* (a) The State shall have a lien on all legal and equitable interests of responsible relatives in their real property in the amount of past-due child support owing pursuant to an order for child support entered under Sections 10-10 and 10-11 of this Code [305 ILCS 5/10-10 and 305 ILCS 5/10-11], or under the Illinois Marriage and Dissolution of Marriage Act [750 ILCS 5/101 et seq.], the Non-Support of Spouse and Children Act [750 ILCS 15/1 et seq.], the Non-Support Punishment Act [750 ILCS 16/1 et seq.], the Uniform Interstate Family Support Act [750 ILCS 22/101 et seq.], or the Illinois Parentage Act of 1984 [750 ILCS 45/1 et seq.].

(b) The Illinois Department shall provide by rule for notice to and an opportunity to be heard by each responsible relative affected, and any final administrative decision rendered by the Illinois Department shall be reviewed only under and in accordance with the Administrative Review Law [735 ILCS 5/3-101 et seq.].

(c) When enforcing a lien under subsection (a) of this Section, the Illinois Department shall have the authority to execute notices of administrative liens and levies, which shall contain the name and address of the responsible relative, a legal description of the real property to be levied, the fact that a lien is being claimed for past-due child support, and such other information as the Illinois Department may by rule prescribe. The Illinois Department shall record the notice of lien with the recorder or registrar of titles of the county or counties in which the real estate is located.

(d) The State's lien under subsection (a) shall be enforceable upon the recording or filing of a notice of lien with the recorder or registrar of titles of the county or counties in which the real estate is located. The lien shall be prior to any lien thereafter recorded or filed and shall be notice to a subsequent purchaser, assignor, or encumbrancer of the existence and nature of the lien. The lien shall be inferior to the lien of general taxes, special assessment, and special taxes heretofore or hereafter levied by any political subdivision or municipal corporation of the State.

In the event that title to the land to be affected by the notice of lien is registered under the Registered Titles (Torrens) Act [765 ILCS 35/0.01 et seq.], the notice shall be filed in the office of the registrar of titles as a memorial or charge upon each folium of the register of titles affected by the notice; but the State shall not have a preference over the rights of any bona fide purchaser, mortgagee, judgment creditor, or other lien holders registered prior to the registration of the notice.

(e) The recorder or registrar of titles of each county shall procure a file labeled "Child Support Lien Notices" and an index book labeled "Child Support Lien Notices". When notice of any lien is presented to the recorder or registrar of titles for filing, the recorder or registrar of titles shall file it in numerical order in the file and shall enter it alphabetically in the index. The entry shall show the name and last known address of the person named in the notice, the serial number of the notice, the date and hour of filing, and the amount of child support due at the time when the lien is filed.

(f) The Illinois Department shall not be required to furnish bond or make a deposit for or pay any costs or fees of any court or officer thereof in any legal proceeding involving the lien.

(g) To protect the lien of the State for past-due child support, the Illinois Department may, from funds that are available for that purpose, pay or provide for the payment of necessary or essential repairs, purchase tax certificates, pay balances due on land contracts, or pay or cause to be satisfied any prior liens on the property to which the lien hereunder applies.

(h) A lien on real property under this Section shall be released pursuant to Section 12-101 of the Code of Civil Procedure [735 ILCS 5/12-101].

(i) The Illinois Department, acting in behalf of the State, may foreclose the lien in a judicial proceeding to the same extent and in the same manner as in the enforcement of other liens. The process, practice, and procedure for the foreclosure shall be the same as provided in the Code of Civil Procedure [735 ILCS 5/1-101 et seq.].

(Source: P.A. 90-18, § 65; 91-613, § 935.)

Note.

Section 70 of P.A. 91-613 contains a severability provision.

The Non-Support of Spouse and Children Act, 750 ILCS 15/1 et seq., referred to in subsection (a), is repealed. Current similar provisions are found as the Non-Support Punishment Act, 750 ILCS 16/1 et seq.

Illinois Administrative Code.

See 89 Illinois Administrative Code, § 160.88.

Effective Date.

Section 999 of P.A. 90-18 made this section effective July 1, 1997.

Effect of Amendments.

The 1999 amendment by P.A. 91-613, effective October 1, 1999, inserted "the Non-Support Punishment Act" in subsection (a).

305 ILCS 5/10-25.5 Administrative liens and levies on personal property for past-due child support

Sec. 10-25.5. *Administrative liens and levies on personal property for past-due child support.* (a) The State shall have a lien on all legal and equitable interests of responsible relatives in their personal property, including any account in a financial institution as defined in Section 10-24 [305 ILCS 5/10-24], or in the case of an insurance company or benefit association only in accounts as defined in Section 10-24 [305 ILCS 5/10-24], in the amount of past-due child support owing pursuant to an order for child support entered under Sections 10-10 and 10-11 of this Code [305 ILCS 5/10-10 and 305 ILCS 5/10-11], or under the Illinois Marriage and Dissolution of Marriage Act [750 ILCS 5/101 et seq.], the Non-Support of Spouse and Children Act [repealed], the Non-Support Punishment Act [750 ILCS 16/1 et seq.], the Uniform Interstate Family Support Act [750 ILCS 22/101 et seq.], or the Illinois Parentage Act of 1984 [750 ILCS 45/1 et seq.].

(b) The Illinois Department shall provide by rule for notice to and an opportunity to be heard by each responsible relative affected, and any final administrative decision rendered by the Illinois Department shall be reviewed only under and in accordance with the Administrative Review Law [735 ILCS 5/3-101 et seq.].

(c) When enforcing a lien under subsection (a) of this Section, the Illinois Department shall have the authority to execute notices of administrative liens and levies, which shall contain the name and address of the responsible relative, a description of the property to be levied, the fact that a lien is being claimed for past-due child support, and such other information as the Illinois Department may by rule prescribe. The Illinois Department may serve the notice of lien or levy upon any financial institution where the accounts as defined in Section 10-24 [305 ILCS 5/10-24] of the responsible relative may be held, for encumbrance or surrender of the accounts as defined in Section 10-24 [305 ILCS 5/10-24] by the financial institution.

(d) The Illinois Department shall enforce its lien against the responsible relative's personal property, other than accounts as defined in Section 10-24 [305 ILCS 5/10-24] in financial institutions, and levy upon such personal property in the manner provided for enforcement of judgments contained in Article XII of the Code of Civil Procedure [735 ILCS 5/12-101 et seq.].

(e) The Illinois Department shall not be required to furnish bond or make a deposit for or pay any costs or fees of any court or officer thereof in any legal proceeding involving the lien.

(f) To protect the lien of the State for past-due child support, the Illinois Department may, from funds that are available for that purpose, pay or provide for the payment of necessary or essential repairs, purchase tax certificates, or pay or cause to be satisfied any prior liens on the property to which the lien hereunder applies.

(g) A lien on personal property under this Section shall be released in the manner provided under Article XII of the Code of Civil Procedure [735 ILCS 5/12-101 et seq.]. Notwithstanding the foregoing, a lien under this Section on accounts as defined in Section 10-24 [305 ILCS 5/10-24] shall expire upon the passage of 120 days from the date of issuance of the Notice of Lien or Levy by the Illinois Department. However, the lien shall remain in effect during the pendency of any appeal or protest.

(h) A lien created under this Section is subordinate to any prior lien of the financial institution or any prior lien holder or any prior right of set-off that the financial institution may have against the assets, or in the case of an insurance company or benefit association only in the accounts as defined in Section 10-24 [305 ILCS 5/10-24].

(i) A financial institution has no obligation under this Section to hold, encumber, or surrender the assets, or in the case of an insurance company or benefit association only the accounts as defined in Section 10-24 [305 ILCS 5/10-24], until the financial institution has been properly served with a subpoena, summons, warrant, court or administrative order, or administrative lien and levy requiring that action.

(Source: P.A. 90-18, § 65; 91-613, § 935.)

Note.

Section 70 of P.A. 91-613 contains a severability provision.

The Non-Support of Spouse and Children Act, 750 ILCS 15/1 et seq., referred to in subsection (a), is repealed. Current similar provisions are found as the Non-Support Punishment Act, 750 ILCS 16/1 et seq.

Effective Date.

Section 999 of P.A. 90-18 made this section effective July 1, 1997.

Effect of Amendments.

The 1999 amendment by P.A. 91-613, effective October 1, 1999, inserted "the Non-Support Punishment Act" in subsection (a).

CASE NOTES

Joint Ownership Account

Where the department of public aid, pursuant to 305 ILCS 5/10-25.5(a), placed a child support lien on the investment account that was jointly owned by the debtor, who owed the support, and the debtor's father, the account, a money market mutual fund, was an account in a financial institution pursuant to 305 ILCS 5/10-24 that was subject to a lien, and the debtor was a responsible relative under 305 ILCS 5/2-11. Highsmith v. Dep't of Pub. Aid, 345 Ill. App. 3d 774, 281 Ill. Dec. 248, 803 N.E.2d 652, 2004 Ill. App. LEXIS 29 (2 Dist. 2004).

Where the department of public aid, pursuant to 305 ILCS 5/10-25.5(a), placed a child support lien on the investment account that was jointly owned by the debtor, who owed the support, and the debtor's father, the father was permitted under 25.5(a) to put forth evidence that the assets in the account were the father's and not the debtor's. Highsmith v. Dep't of Pub. Aid, 345 Ill. App. 3d 774, 281 Ill. Dec. 248, 803 N.E.2d 652, 2004 Ill. App. LEXIS 29 (2 Dist. 2004).

305 ILCS 5/10-26 State Disbursement Unit

Sec. 10-26. *State Disbursement Unit.* (a) Effective October 1, 1999 the Illinois Department shall establish a State Disbursement Unit in accordance with the requirements of Title IV-D of the Social Security Act [42 U.S.C. § 651 et seq.]. The Illinois Department shall enter into an agreement with a State or local governmental unit or private entity to perform the functions of the State Disbursement Unit as set forth in this Section. The State Disbursement Unit shall collect and disburse support payments made under court and administrative support orders:

(1) being enforced in cases in which child and spouse support services are being provided under this Article X; and

(2) in all cases in which child and spouse support services are not being provided under this Article X and in which support payments are made under the provisions of the Income Withholding for Support Act [750 ILCS 28/1 et seq.].

(a-2) The contract entered into by the Illinois Department with a public or private entity or an individual for the operation of the State Disbursement Unit is subject to competitive bidding. In addition, the contract is subject to Section 10-26.2 of this Code [305 ILCS 5/10-26.2]. As used in this subsection (a-2), "contract" has the same meaning as in the Illinois Procurement Code [30 ILCS 500/1-1 et seq.].

(a-5) If the State Disbursement Unit receives a support payment that was not appropriately made to the Unit under this Section, the Unit shall immediately return the payment to the sender, including, if possible, instructions detailing where to send the support payments.

(b) All payments received by the State Disbursement Unit:

(1) shall be deposited into an account obtained by the Illinois Department, and

(2) distributed and disbursed by the State Disbursement Unit, in accordance with the directions of the Illinois Department, pursuant to Title IV-D of the Social Security Act [42 U.S.C. § 651 et seq.] and rules promulgated by the Department.

(c) All support payments assigned to the Illinois Department under Article X of this Code and rules promulgated by the Illinois Department that are disbursed to the Illinois Department by the State Disbursement Unit shall be paid into the Child Support Enforcement Trust Fund.

(d) If the agreement with the State or local governmental unit or private entity provided for in this Section is not in effect for any reason, the Department shall perform the functions of the State Disbursement Unit as set forth in this Section for a maximum of 12 months before July 1, 2001, and for a maximum of 24 months after June 30, 2001. If the Illinois Department is performing the functions of the State Disbursement Unit on July 1, 2001, then the Illinois Department shall make an award on or before December 31, 2002, to a State or local government unit or private entity to perform the functions of the State Disbursement Unit. Payments received by the Illinois Department in performance of the duties of the State Disbursement Unit shall be deposited into the State Disbursement Unit Revolving Fund established under Section 12-8.1 [5 ILCS 5/12-8.1]. Nothing in this Section shall prohibit the Illinois Department from holding the State Disbursement Unit Revolving Fund after June 30, 2003.

(e) By February 1, 2000, the Illinois Department shall conduct at least 4 regional training and educational seminars to educate the clerks of the circuit court on the general operation of the State Disbursement Unit, the role of the State Disbursement Unit, and the role of the clerks of the circuit court in the collection and distribution of child support payments.

(f) By March 1, 2000, the Illinois Department shall conduct at least 4 regional educational and training seminars to educate payors, as defined in the Income Withholding for Support Act [750 ILCS 28/1 et seq.], on the general operation of the State Disbursement Unit, the role of the State Disbursement Unit, and the distribution of income withholding payments pursuant to this Section and the Income Withholding for Support Act [750 ILCS 28/1 et seq.].

(Source: P.A. 91-212, § 20; 91-677, § 5; 91-712, § 55; 92-44, § 5; 93-20, § 15-5.)

Illinois Administrative Code.

See 89 Illinois Administrative Code, § 160.95.

Effective Date.

Section 999 of P.A. 91-212 made this section effective upon becoming law. The Act was approved July 20, 1999.

Effect of Amendments.

The 1999 amendment by P.A. 91-677, effective January 5, 2000, in subsection (a) deleted "purpose of the" preceding "State Disbursement Unit" and "be to" preceding "collect"; in subsection (a)(2) deleted "the order for support was entered after January 1, 1994" after "cases in which", added subsections (a-5), (e), and (f); and made stylistic changes.

The 2000 amendment by P.A. 91-712, effective July 1, 2000, added the last sentence in subsection (d).

The 2001 amendment by P.A. 92-44, effective July 1, 2001, inserted subsection (a-2); and inserted the language in the first sentence of subsection (d) beginning "before July 1, 2001" through the end of the sentence, and inserted the second sentence.

The 2003 amendment by P.A. 93-20, effective June 20, 2003, in subsection (b)(1) substituted "the Illinois Department" for "the State or local governmental unit or private entity, as the case may be"; and in subsection (d), in the third sentence inserted "Illinois", and added the last sentence.

305 ILCS 5/10-26.2 Contracts concerning the operation of the State Disbursement Unit

Sec. 10-26.2. *Contracts concerning the operation of the State Disbursement Unit.* (a) In this Section:

"Contract" has the same meaning as in the Illinois Procurement Code [30 ILCS 500/1-1 et seq.].

"SDU contractor" means any public or private entity or individual with whom the Illinois Department enters into a contract in connection with the operation of the State Disbursement Unit.

(b) The contract entered into by the Illinois Department with a public or private entity or an individual in connection with the operation of the State Disbursement Unit must contain, at a minimum, the provisions set forth in this Section.

(c) The contract must include standards and procedures to ensure that the data relied on by the State Disbursement Unit in performing its functions is accurate so that the State Disbursement Unit will be able to effectively administer the collection and disbursement of support payments.

(d) The contract must contain provisions to ensure that all clerks of the circuit court have access to non-custodial parents' support payment information in the possession of the State Disbursement Unit.

(e) The contract must contain provisions to ensure that notices to employers in connection with the collection of support are clear and consistent and that the SDU contractor will promptly inform an employer about any problems and any necessary changes in connection with the collection of support.

(f) The contract must contain appropriate management controls to ensure that (i) all of the SDU contractor's actions in performing the functions of the State Disbursement Unit are reasonably planned, timely implemented, and adequately controlled and (ii) all reports that are necessary to provide the Illinois Department with the information necessary to effectively monitor the quality and accuracy of the SDU contractor's actions in performing the functions of the State Disbursement Unit are timely filed.

(g) The contract must contain provisions specifying standards with respect to the level of performance expected of the SDU contractor. The contract may include provisions for incentives and penalties in connection with the SDU contractor's performance.

(h) The contract must contain provisions projecting the number of active support collection and disbursement cases to be handled by the State Disbursement Unit and estimating the number of support disbursement transactions to be handled each year.

(i) The contract must contain provisions requiring compliance with all applicable federal requirements concerning disbursement of support. The contract must also contain provisions for the Illinois Department's regular, periodic review of reports on disbursement performance.

(j) The contract must contain provisions requiring the SDU contractor to submit to the Illinois Department, within 45 days after the end of each State fiscal year, a completed American Institute of Certified Public Accountants Statement on Auditing Standards Number 88 (SAS 88) or its successor for the purpose of enabling the Illinois Department to appropriately monitor the State Disbursement Unit's performance as a service organization and to enable the Auditor General, as the external auditor of the State Disbursement Unit, to ensure that appropriate controls are present.

(k) The contract must contain provisions requiring the Illinois Department and the SDU contractor to examine the causes of untimely disbursement of support payments and inappropriate cost recovery and to take prompt action to ensure the timely and accurate disbursement of support payments. The contract must also contain provisions for the final disposition of support payments that cannot be processed by the State Disbursement Unit within 2 business days.

(l) The contract must contain provisions to ensure that neither the Illinois Department nor the SDU contractor uses moneys collected and held in trust for the payment of support for any purpose other than that for which the moneys were collected.

(m) The contract must contain provisions requiring the Illinois Department to audit the disbursement of all emergency support payments and report to the General Assembly the results of the audit, including, without limitation, the number of emergency support payment checks issued by the State Disbursement Unit, the amount of repayments received from recipients of those checks, and amounts for which the Illinois Department did not seek repayment.

(Source: P.A. 92-44, § 5.)

Effective Date.

Section 99 of P.A. 92-44 made this section effective July 1, 2001.

305 ILCS 5/10-26.5 Delayed payment from State Disbursement Unit

Sec. 10-26.5. *Delayed payment from State Disbursement Unit.* (a) In this Section, "adversely affected recipient of support" means a person who meets all of the following criteria:

(1) The person is entitled to disbursement of a child support payment from the State Disbursement Unit.

(2) The person either (i) does not receive from the State Disbursement Unit a disbursement of a child support payment to which he or she is entitled or (ii) receives a delayed disbursement of a child support payment from the State Disbursement Unit.

(3) As a result of the nonreceipt of the disbursement of the child support payment or the delayed disbursement of the child support payment, the person receives an adverse rating by a credit reporting agency based, for example, on the person's inability to make a timely payment of an amount owed to another person.

(b) Upon the request of an adversely affected recipient of support, the Illinois Department shall send a letter to the recipient verifying the delayed or undisbursed child support payment. The recipient may submit that letter to the appropriate credit reporting agency for placement in the recipient's credit file.

(c) The Illinois Department shall adopt rules necessary to implement this Section.

(Source: P.A. 91-793, § 5.)

Effect of Amendments.

Section 99 of P.A. 91-793 made this section effective upon becoming law. The Act was approved June 9, 2000.

305 ILCS 5/10-27 State Case Registry

Sec. 10-27. *State Case Registry.* (a) The Illinois Department shall establish an automated State Case Registry to contain records concerning child support orders for parties receiving child support enforcement services under this Article X, and for all child support orders entered or modified on or after October 1, 1998. The State Case Registry shall include (i) the information filed with the Illinois Department, or filed with the clerk of the circuit court and provided to the Illinois Department, under the provisions of Sections 10-10.5 and 10-11.2 of this Code [305 ILCS 5/10-10.5 and 305 ILCS 5/10-11.2], Section 505.3 of the Illinois Marriage and Dissolution of Marriage Act [750 ILCS 5/505.3], Section 30 of the Non-Support Punishment Act [750 ILCS 16/30], and Section 14.1 of the Illinois Parentage Act of 1984 [750 ILCS 45/14.1], and (ii) any other information required under Title IV, Part D of the Social Security Act [42 U.S.C. § 601 et seq.] or by the federal Department of Health and Human Services.

(b) (Blank).

(c) The Illinois Department shall maintain the following payment information on child support orders for parties receiving child support enforcement services under this Article X:

(1) the amount of monthly or other periodic support owed under the order and other amounts, including arrearages, interest or late payment penalties, and fees, due or overdue under the order;

(2) any amounts described in subdivision (1) of subsection (d) that have been collected;

(3) the distribution of the collected amounts; and

(4) the amount of any lien imposed with respect to the order pursuant to Section 10-25 or Section 10-25.5 of this Code [305 ILCS 5/10-25 or 305 ILCS 5/10-25.5].

(d) The Illinois Department shall establish, update, maintain, and monitor case records in the Registry of parties receiving child support enforcement services under this Article X, on the basis of:

(1) information on administrative actions and administrative and judicial proceedings and orders relating to paternity and support;

(2) information obtained from comparison with federal, State, and local sources of information;

(3) information on support collections and distribution; and

(4) any other relevant information.

(e) The Illinois Department shall use the automated State Case Registry to share and compare information with, and receive information from, other data bases and information comparison services in order to obtain (or provide) information necessary to enable the Illinois Department (or the federal Department of Health and Human Services or other State or federal agencies) to carry out the requirements of the child support enforcement program established under Title IV, Part D of the Social Security Act [42 U.S.C. § 601 et seq.]. Such information comparison activities shall include the following:

(1) Furnishing to the Federal Case Registry of Child Support Orders (and updating as necessary, with information including notice of expiration of orders) the information specified by the federal Department of Health and Human Services in regulations.

(2) Exchanging information with the Federal Parent Locator Service for the purposes specified in Section 453 of the Social Security Act.

(3) Exchanging information with State agencies (of this State and of other states) administering programs funded under Title IV, Part A and Title XIX of the Social Security Act and other programs designated by the federal Department of Health and Human Services, as necessary to perform responsibilities under Title IV, Part D of the Social Security Act [42 U.S.C. § 601 et seq.] and under such other programs.

(4) Exchanging information with other agencies of this State, agencies of other states, and interstate information networks, as necessary and appropriate to carry out (or assist other states to carry out) the purposes of Title IV, Part D of the Social Security Act [42 U.S.C. § 601 et seq.].

(5) Disclosing information to any other entities as required under Title IV, Part D of the Social Security Act [42 U.S.C. § 601 et seq.].

(f) The Illinois Department shall adopt rules establishing safeguards, applicable to all confidential information included in the State Case Registry, that are designed to protect the privacy rights of persons concerning whom information is on record in the State Case Registry. Such safeguards shall include, but not be limited to the following:

(1) Prohibitions against the release of information on the whereabouts of one party or the child to another party against whom a protective order with respect to the former party or the child has been entered.

(2) Prohibitions against the release of information on the whereabouts of one party or the child to another party if the Illinois Department has reasonable evidence of domestic violence or child abuse (that is, allegations of domestic violence or child abuse, unless the Illinois Department has an independent, reasonable basis to find the person making the allegation not credible) to the former party or child by the party requesting information.

(3) Prohibitions against the release of information on the whereabouts of one party or the child to another person if the Illinois Department has reason to believe the release of information to that person may result in physical or emotional harm to the party or child.

(Source: P.A. 90-790, § 5; 92-463, § 5.)

Note.

The Non-Support of Spouse and Children Act, 750 ILCS 15/1 et seq., referred to in subsection (a), is repealed. Current similar provisions are found as the Non-Support Punishment Act, 750 ILCS 16/1 et seq.

Illinois Administrative Code.

See 89 Illinois Administrative Code, § 160.88.

Effective Date.

Section 99 of P.A. 90-790 makes this section effective upon becoming law. The Act was approved August 14, 1998.

Effect of Amendments.

The 2001 amendment by P.A. 92-463, effective August 22, 2001, rewrote subsection (a) to the extent that a detailed comparison would be impracticable; deleted the text of subsection (b); in the first sentences of subsections (c) and (d), substituted "child support enforcement services" for "child and spouse support services"; and added subsection (e)(5).

CHAPTER 320
AGING

SENIOR CITIZENS ON STATE BOARDS AND COMMISSIONS ACT

320 ILCS 5/0.01 Short title
320 ILCS 5/1 [Findings of legislature; senior citizens as consumer representatives]

RESPITE PROGRAM ACT

320 ILCS 10/1 Short title
320 ILCS 10/1.5 Purpose
320 ILCS 10/2 Definitions
320 ILCS 10/3 Respite Program
320 ILCS 10/4 No Limit to Care
320 ILCS 10/5 Eligibility
320 ILCS 10/6 Responsibilities
320 ILCS 10/7 [Repealed]
320 ILCS 10/8 Funding
320 ILCS 10/9 [Repealed]
320 ILCS 10/10 [Repealed]
320 ILCS 10/11 Respite Care Worker Training
320 ILCS 10/12 Annual Report

ELDER ABUSE DEMONSTRATION PROJECT ACT

320 ILCS 15/0.01 through 320 ILCS 15/10.1 [Repealed]

ELDER ABUSE AND NEGLECT ACT

320 ILCS 20/1 Short title
320 ILCS 20/2 Definitions
320 ILCS 20/3 Responsibilities
320 ILCS 20/3.5 Other Responsibilities
320 ILCS 20/4 Reports of abuse or neglect
320 ILCS 20/4.1 Employer discrimination
320 ILCS 20/4.2 Testimony by mandated reporter and investigator
320 ILCS 20/5 Procedure
320 ILCS 20/6 Time
320 ILCS 20/7 (As amended by P.A. 93-300) Review
320 ILCS 20/7 (As amended by P.A. 93-301) Review
320 ILCS 20/8 Access to records
320 ILCS 20/9 Authority to consent to services
320 ILCS 20/9.5 Commencement of action for ex parte authorization orders; filing fees; process
320 ILCS 20/10 Rules
320 ILCS 20/11 Annual Reports
320 ILCS 20/12 [Repealed]
320 ILCS 20/13 Access
320 ILCS 20/13.5 Commencement of action for access; filing fees; process; notice; duration of orders

SENIOR CITIZENS AND DISABLED PERSONS PROPERTY TAX RELIEF AND PHARMACEUTICAL ASSISTANCE ACT

320 ILCS 25/1 Short title
320 ILCS 25/2 Purpose
320 ILCS 25/3 Definitions
320 ILCS 25/3.01 [Claimant defined]
320 ILCS 25/3.02 [Department defined]
320 ILCS 25/3.03 [Director defined]
320 ILCS 25/3.04 [Gross Rent defined]
320 ILCS 25/3.05 [Household defined]
320 ILCS 25/3.06 [Household income defined]
320 ILCS 25/3.07 [Income defined]
320 ILCS 25/3.08 [Internal Revenue Code defined]
320 ILCS 25/3.09 [Property taxes accrued defined]
320 ILCS 25/3.10 [Regulations defined]
320 ILCS 25/3.11 [Rent constituting property taxes accrued defined]
320 ILCS 25/3.12 [Residence defined]
320 ILCS 25/3.13 [Taxable year defined]
320 ILCS 25/3.14 [Disabled person defined]
320 ILCS 25/3.15 [Covered prescription drug defined]
320 ILCS 25/3.16 [Reasonable cost defined]
320 ILCS 25/3.17 [Authorized pharmacy defined]
320 ILCS 25/4 Amount of Grant
320 ILCS 25/4.1 Information to the Department
320 ILCS 25/5 Procedure
320 ILCS 25/5.1 [Eligibility to receive grant]
320 ILCS 25/6 Administration
320 ILCS 25/7 Payment and denial of claims
320 ILCS 25/7.1 [Repealed]
320 ILCS 25/8 Records
320 ILCS 25/8a Confidentiality
320 ILCS 25/9 [Fraud; penalties; barring of convicted person from program; recovery; time of prosecution]
320 ILCS 25/9.1 [Repealed]
320 ILCS 25/10 Arrangements and Captions
320 ILCS 25/11 Severability
320 ILCS 25/12 Regulations — Department on Aging
320 ILCS 25/13 [List of qualified persons; confidentiality; penalty for divulgence or misuse]

SENIOR CITIZENS REAL ESTATE TAX DEFERRAL ACT

320 ILCS 30/1 [Short title]
320 ILCS 30/2 Definitions
320 ILCS 30/3 [Application for deferral; tax deferral and recovery agreement]
320 ILCS 30/4 [Recording of tax deferral and recovery agreement]
320 ILCS 30/5 [Payment of tax bills]
320 ILCS 30/6 [Payments by taxpayer]
320 ILCS 30/7 [Collection of deferred taxes; foreclosure sales; remittance of funds received]
320 ILCS 30/8 [Instruments requiring payment of real estate taxes; eligibility for grants]

PARTNERSHIP FOR LONG-TERM CARE ACT

320 ILCS 35/1 Short title
320 ILCS 35/5 [Legislative findings and intent]
320 ILCS 35/10 Definitions
320 ILCS 35/15 Program
320 ILCS 35/20 Program participant eligibility for Medicaid
320 ILCS 35/25 Protection of resources
320 ILCS 35/30 Certification of policies and contracts
320 ILCS 35/35 [Repealed]
320 ILCS 35/40 Program
320 ILCS 35/45 Agency powers; regulations
320 ILCS 35/50 Task force
320 ILCS 35/55 Director of Aging
320 ILCS 35/60 Administrative costs

ALL-INCLUSIVE CARE FOR THE ELDERLY ACT

320 ILCS 40/1 Short title
320 ILCS 40/5 Legislative declaration
320 ILCS 40/10 Service for eligible persons
320 ILCS 40/15 Program implementation
320 ILCS 40/20 Duties of the Illinois Department
320 ILCS 40/25 Rules and regulations
320 ILCS 40/30 Rate of payment

OLDER ADULT SERVICES ACT

320 ILCS 42/1 Short title
320 ILCS 42/5 Purpose
320 ILCS 42/10 Definitions
320 ILCS 42/15 Designation of lead agency; annual report
320 ILCS 42/20 Priority service areas; service expansion
320 ILCS 42/25 Older adult services restructuring
320 ILCS 42/30 Nursing home conversion program
320 ILCS 42/35 Older Adult Services Advisory Committee
320 ILCS 42/90 through 320 ILCS 42/96 [Not Set Out]
320 ILCS 42/99 Effective date

SENIOR CITIZENS CHILD CARE SUPPORT ACT

320 ILCS 45/1 Short title

320 ILCS 45/5 [Purpose]
320 ILCS 45/10 Definitions
320 ILCS 45/15 [Information distribution system; demonstration training module]
320 ILCS 45/20 [Volunteer training program; availability; publicity]
320 ILCS 45/25 [Documentation for participants]

SENIOR PHARMACEUTICAL ASSISTANCE ACT

320 ILCS 50/1 Short title
320 ILCS 50/5 Findings
320 ILCS 50/10 Definitions
320 ILCS 50/15 Senior Pharmaceutical Assistance Review Committee
320 ILCS 50/20 Senior Health Assistance Program
320 ILCS 50/25 Study of catastrophic pharmaceutical assistance coverage
320 ILCS 50/99 Effective Date

SENIOR CITIZENS AND DISABLED PERSONS PRESCRIPTION DRUG DISCOUNT PROGRAM ACT

320 ILCS 55/1 Short title
320 ILCS 55/5 Findings
320 ILCS 55/10 Purpose
320 ILCS 55/15 Definitions
320 ILCS 55/17 Determination of disability
320 ILCS 55/20 The Senior Citizens and Disabled Persons Prescription Drug Discount Program
320 ILCS 55/25 Program administration
320 ILCS 55/30 Manufacturer rebate agreements
320 ILCS 55/35 Program eligibility
320 ILCS 55/40 Eligible pharmacies
320 ILCS 55/45 Rules
320 ILCS 55/47 Limit on State's obligation for cost of administration
320 ILCS 55/50 Report on administration of program
320 ILCS 55/99 Effective date
320 ILCS 55/990 [Not Set Out]

COMMUNITY SENIOR SERVICES AND RESOURCES ACT

320 ILCS 60/1 Short title
320 ILCS 60/5 Legislative findings
320 ILCS 60/10 Legislative intent
320 ILCS 60/15 Definitions
320 ILCS 60/20 Duties
320 ILCS 60/25 Community senior services and resource center grants
320 ILCS 60/30 Funding; waivers
320 ILCS 60/32 Bequests and gifts; awareness campaign
320 ILCS 60/35 Community Senior Services and Resource Center Advisory Committee
320 ILCS 60/40 Community Senior Services and Resources Fund
320 ILCS 60/99 Effective date

FAMILY CAREGIVER ACT

320 ILCS 65/1 Short title
320 ILCS 65/5 Legislative findings
320 ILCS 65/10 Legislative intent
320 ILCS 65/15 Definitions
320 ILCS 65/16 Family caregiver demonstration grant
320 ILCS 65/20 Powers and duties of the Department
320 ILCS 65/25 Provision of services
320 ILCS 65/30 Eligibility for respite and supplemental services
320 ILCS 65/35 Health care practitioners and facilities not impaired
320 ILCS 65/40 Entitlement not created; funding; waivers.
320 ILCS 65/90 [Not Set Out]
320 ILCS 65/99 Effective date

SENIOR CITIZENS ON STATE BOARDS AND COMMISSIONS ACT

320 ILCS 5/0.01 Short title

Sec. 0.01. *Short title.* This Act may be cited as the Senior Citizens on State Boards and Commissions Act.
(Source: P.A. 86-1324.)

Derivation.
Title: An Act in relation to senior citizens and certain Boards and Commissions.
Cite: 320 ILCS 5/0.01 et seq.
Source: P.A. 83-1538.
Date: Certified January 30, 1985.

Note.
This section was Ill.Rev.Stat., Ch. 23, para. 6150.

320 ILCS 5/1 [Findings of legislature; senior citizens as consumer representatives]

Sec. 1. It is hereby found and determined by the General Assembly that state boards and commissions exist for the singular purpose of protecting the public health and welfare; that citizens over 60 years of age represent a significant percentage of the population and have the time and experience to devote to the important issues which have a profound effect on the daily lives of older Illinoisans.

It is also hereby found that senior citizens shall hold their positions on boards and commissions by matter of right, not discretion. These positions shall be held by consumer representatives over the age of 60 who shall serve as spokespersons for the interests of the State's older population.
(Source: P.A. 83-1538.)

Note.
This section was Ill.Rev.Stat., Ch. 23, para. 6151.

RESPITE PROGRAM ACT

320 ILCS 10/1 Short title

Sec. 1. *Short title.* This Act may be cited as the Respite Program Act.
(Source: P.A. 83-826; 87-974, § 1.)

Derivation.
Title: An Act to create the Respite Program which gives families relief from their responsibilities of caring for frail and disabled adults.
Cite: 320 ILCS 10/1 et seq.
Source: P.A. 83-826. Title amended by P.A. 87-974.
Date: Approved September 24, 1983.

Note.
This section was Ill.Rev.Stat., Ch. 23, para. 6201.

320 ILCS 10/1.5 Purpose

Sec. 1.5. *Purpose.* It is hereby found and determined by the General Assembly that respite care provides relief and support to the primary care-giver of a frail or disabled adult and provides a break for the caregiver from the continuous responsibilities of care-giving. Without this support, the primary care-giver's ability to continue in his or her role would be jeopardized; thereby increasing the risk of institutionalization of the frail or disabled adult.

By providing respite care through intermittent planned or emergency relief to the care-giver during the regular week-day, evening, and weekend hours, both the special physical and psychological needs of the primary care-giver and the frail or disabled adult, who is the recipient of continuous care, shall be met reducing or preventing the need for institutionalization.

Furthermore, the primary care-giver providing continuous care is frequently under substantial financial stress. Respite care and other supportive services sustain and preserve the primary care-giver and family caregiving unit. It is the intent of the General Assembly that this Act ensure that Illinois primary care-givers of frail or disabled adults have access to affordable, appropriate in-home respite care services.

(Source: P.A. 87-974, § 1; 93-864, § 90.)

Note.

Section 99 of P.A. 93-864 made this amendment effective July 1, 2004; however, the Act was approved August 5, 2004.

Effective Date.

This section became effective January 1, 1993, pursuant to Ill. Const. (1970), Art. IV, § 10 and 5 ILCS 75/1.

Effect of Amendments.

The 2004 amendment by P.A. 93-864, effective August 5, 2004, rewrote the section, in part by deleting all references to "or abused or funtionally disabled or cognitively impaired older adult".

320 ILCS 10/2 Definitions

Sec. 2. *Definitions.* As used in this Act:

(1) "Respite care" means the provision of intermittent and temporary substitute care or supervision of frail or disabled adults on behalf of and in the absence of the primary care-giver, for the purpose of providing relief from the stress or responsibilities concomitant with providing constant care, so as to enable the care-giver to continue the provision of care in the home. Respite care should be available to sustain the care-giver throughout the period of care-giving, which can vary from several months to a number of years. Respite care can be provided in the home, in a day care setting during the day, overnight, in a substitute residential setting such as a long-term care facility required to be licensed under the Nursing Home Care Act or the Assisted Living and Shared Housing Act [210 ILCS 45/1-101 et seq. or 210 ILCS 9/1 et seq.], or for more extended periods of time on a temporary basis.

(1.5) "In-home respite care" means care provided by an appropriately trained paid worker providing short-term intermittent care, supervision, or companionship to the frail or disabled adult in the home while relieving the care-giver, by permitting a short-term break from the care-giver's care-giving role. This support may contribute to the delay, reduction, and prevention of institutionalization by enabling the care-giver to continue in his or her care-giving role. In-home respite care should be flexible and available in a manner that is responsive to the needs of the care-giver. This may consist of evening respite care services that are available from 6:00 p.m. to 8:00 a.m. Monday through Friday and weekend respite care services from 6:00 p.m. Friday to 8:00 a.m. Monday.

(2) "Care-giver" shall mean the family member or other natural person who normally provides the daily care or supervision of a frail or disabled adult. Such care-giver may, but need not, reside in the same household as the frail or disabled adult.

(3) (Blank).

(4) (Blank).

(5) (Blank).

(6) "Department" shall mean the Department on Aging.

(7) (Blank).

(8) "Frail or disabled adult" shall mean any person who is 60 years of age or older and who either (i) suffers from Alzheimers's disease or a related disorder or (ii) is unable to attend to his or her daily needs without the assistance or regular supervision of a care-giver due to mental or physical impairment and who is otherwise eligible for services on the basis of his or her level of impairment.

(9) "Emergency respite care" means the immediate placement of a trained, in-home respite care worker in the home during an emergency or unplanned event, or during a temporary placement outside the home, to substitute for the care-giver. Emergency respite care may be provided on one or more occasions unless an extension is deemed necessary by the case coordination unit or by another agency designated by the Department and area agencies on aging to conduct needs assessments for respite care services. When there is an urgent need for emergency respite care, procedures to accommodate this need must be determined. An emergency is:

(a) An unplanned event that results in the immediate and unavoidable absence of the care-giver from the home in an excess of 4 hours at a time when no other qualified care-giver is available.

(b) An unplanned situation that prevents the care-giver from providing the care required by a frail or disabled adult living at home.

(c) An unplanned event that threatens the health and safety of the frail or disabled adult.

(d) An unplanned event that threatens the health and safety of the care-giver thereby placing the frail or disabled adult in danger.

(10) (Blank).

(Source: P.A. 86-820; 87-974, § 1; 91-357, § 179; 92-16, § 76.5; 93-864, § 90.)

Note.

This section was Ill.Rev.Stat., Ch. 23, para. 6202.

P.A. 91-357, § 996 contains a "no acceleration or delay" provision, and P.A. 91-357, § 997 contains a "no revival or extension" provision.

Section 996 of P.A. 92-16 contains a "no acceleration or delay" provision, and Section 997 contains a "no revival or extension" provision.

Section 99 of P.A. 93-864 made this amendment effective July 1, 2004; however, the Act was approved August 5, 2004.

Effect of Amendments.

The 1999 amendment by P.A. 91-357, effective July 29, 1999, inserted "of 1986" at the end of subdivision (7).

The 2001 amendment by P.A. 92-16, effective June 28, 2001, made grammatical and gender-neutralizing changes.

The 2004 amendment by P.A. 93-864, effective August 5, 2004, rewrote the section, in part by deleting all references to "or abused or funtionally disabled or cognitively impaired older adult" and by inserting subsection (1.5) and deleting text from subsections (3), (4), (5), (7) and (10).

320 ILCS 10/3 Respite Program

Sec. 3. *Respite Program.* The Director is hereby authorized to administer a program of assistance to persons in need and to deter the institutionalization of frail or disabled adults.

(Source: P.A. 83-826; 87-974, § 1; 93-864, § 90.)

Note.

This section was Ill.Rev.Stat., Ch. 23, para. 6203.

Section 99 of P.A. 93-864 made this amendment effective July 1, 2004; however, the Act was approved August 5, 2004.

Effect of Amendments.

The 2004 amendment by P.A. 93-864, effective August 5, 2004, substituted "administer a program of" for "establish respite projects for the purposes of providing care and"; and deleted "or functionally disabled or cognitively impaired" after "disabled".

320 ILCS 10/4 No Limit to Care

Sec. 4. *No Limit to Care.* Nothing contained in this Act shall be construed so as to limit, modify or otherwise affect the provisions for in-home services being provided under Section 4.02 of the Illinois Act on the Aging [20 ILCS 105/4.02].

(Source: P.A. 83-826; 87-974, § 1; 93-864, § 90.)

Note.

This section was Ill.Rev.Stat., Ch. 23, para. 6204.

Section 99 of P.A. 93-864 made this amendment effective July 1, 2004; however, the Act was approved August 5, 2004.

Effect of Amendments.

The 2004 amendment by P.A. 93-864, effective August 5, 2004, deleted "long-term" before "in-home"; and inserted "being provided under" and made related and stylistic changes.

320 ILCS 10/5 Eligibility

Sec. 5. *Eligibility.* The Department may establish eligibility standards for respite services taking into consideration the unique economic and social needs of the population for whom they are to be provided. The population identified for the purposes of this Act includes persons suffering from Alzheimer's disease or a related disorder and persons who are 60 years of age or older with an identified service need. Priority shall be given in all cases to frail or disabled adults.

(Source: P.A. 84-511; 87-974, § 1; 93-864, § 90.)

Note.

This section was Ill.Rev.Stat., Ch. 23, para. 6205.

Section 99 of P.A. 93-864 made this amendment effective July 1, 2004; however, the Act was approved August 5, 2004.

Effect of Amendments.

The 2004 amendment by P.A. 93-864, effective August 5, 2004, substituted "or a related disorder and persons who are 60 years of age or older" for "and who are 55 years of age or older, or persons age 60 and older" in the first sentence; and in the last sentence substituted "or disabled" for "abused or funtionally disabled or cognitively impaired".

320 ILCS 10/6 Responsibilities

Sec. 6. *Responsibilities.* (a) The Department shall administer this Act and shall adopt rules and standards the Department deems necessary for that purpose.

(b) The Department shall make grants to or contract with Area Agencies on Aging and other appropriate community-based organizations to provide respite care under this Act.

(c) (Blank).

(d) (Blank).

(e) (Blank).

(f) Nothing in this Act shall be construed to limit, modify, or otherwise affect the provision of long-term in-home services under Section 4.02 of the Illinois Act on the Aging [20 ILCS 105/1 et seq.].

(Source: P.A. 83-826; 87-974, § 1; 93-864, § 90.)

Note.

This section was Ill.Rev.Stat., Ch. 23, para. 6206.

Section 99 of P.A. 93-864 made this amendment effective July 1, 2004; however, the Act was approved August 5, 2004.

Effect of Amendments.

The 2004 amendment by P.A. 93-864, effective August 5, 2004, rewrote the section to the extent that a detailed comparison would be impracticable.

320 ILCS 10/7: Repealed by P.A. 93-864, § 91, effective August 5, 2004.

Note.

Section 99 of P.A. 93-864 made this repeal effective July 1, 2004; however, the Act was approved August 5, 2004.

320 ILCS 10/8 Funding

Sec. 8. *Funding.* Services authorized under this Act shall be funded only to the extent of available appropriations for such purposes. The Director may seek and obtain State and federal funds that may be available to finance respite care under this Act, and may also seek and obtain other non-state resources

for which the State may be eligible. The Department may seek appropriate waivers of federal requirements from the U.S. Department of Health and Human Services.
(Source: P.A. 87-974, § 1; 93-864, § 90.)

Note.
Section 99 of P.A. 93-864 made this amendment effective July 1, 2004; however, the Act was approved August 5, 2004.

Effective Date.
This section became effective January 1, 1993, pursuant to Ill. Const. (1970), Art. IV, § 10 and 5 ILCS 75/1.

Effect of Amendments.
The 2004 amendment by P.A. 93-864, effective August 5, 2004, rewrote the section to the extent that a detailed comparison would be impracticable.

320 ILCS 10/9: Repealed by P.A. 93-864, § 91, effective August 5, 2004.

Note.
Section 99 of P.A. 93-864 made this repeal effective July 1, 2004; however, the Act was approved August 5, 2004.

320 ILCS 10/10: Repealed by P.A. 93-864, § 91, effective August 5, 2004.

Note.
Section 99 of P.A. 93-864 made this repeal effective July 1, 2004; however, the Act was approved August 5, 2004.

320 ILCS 10/11 Respite Care Worker Training

Sec. 11. *Respite Care Worker Training.* (a) A respite care worker shall be an appropriately trained individual whose duty it is to provide in-home supervision and assistance to a frail or disabled adult in order to allow the care-giver a break from his or her continuous care-giving responsibilities.

(b) The Director may prescribe minimum training guidelines for respite care workers to ensure that the special needs of persons receiving services under this Act and their caregivers will be met. The Director may designate Alzheimer's disease associations and community agencies to conduct such training. Nothing in this Act should be construed to exempt any individual providing a service subject to licensure or certification under State law from these requirements.
(Source: P.A. 87-974, § 1; 93-864, § 90.)

Note.
Section 99 of P.A. 93-864 made this amendment effective July 1, 2004; however, the Act was approved August 5, 2004.

Effective Date.
This section became effective January 1, 1993, pursuant to Ill. Const. (1970), Art. IV, § 10 and 5 ILCS 75/1.

Effect of Amendments.
The 2004 amendment by P.A. 93-864, effective August 5, 2004, in subsection (a) substituted "or disabled" for "or abused or functionally disabled or cognitively impaired older", and deleted "primary" after "allow the"; and in subsection (b) in the first sentence substituted "guidelines" for "standards" and deleted "primary" before "caregivers".

320 ILCS 10/12 Annual Report

Sec. 12. *Annual Report.* The Director shall submit a report each year to the Governor and the General Assembly detailing the progress of the respite care services provided under this Act.
(Source: P.A. 87-974, § 1; 93-864, § 90.)

Note.
Section 99 of P.A. 93-864 made this amendment effective July 1, 2004; however, the Act was approved August 5, 2004.

Effective Date.
This section became effective January 1, 1993, pursuant to Ill. Const. (1970), Art. IV, § 10 and 5 ILCS 75/1.

Effect of Amendments.
The 2004 amendment by P.A. 93-864, effective August 5, 2004, rewrote the section to the extent that a detailed comparison would be impracticable.

ELDER ABUSE DEMONSTRATION PROJECT ACT

320 ILCS 15/0.01 through 320 ILCS 15/10.1: Repealed by P.A. 92-84, § 70, effective July 1, 2002.

Cross References.
As to the offense of disorderly conduct with regard to transmitting a false report of abuse under this section, see 720 ILCS 5/26-1.

ELDER ABUSE AND NEGLECT ACT

320 ILCS 20/1 Short title

Sec. 1. *Short title.* This Act shall be known and may be cited as the "Elder Abuse and Neglect Act".
(Source: P.A. 85-1184.)

Derivation.
Title: An Act in relation to the abuse and neglect of elderly persons.
Cite: 320 ILCS 20/1 et seq.
Source: P.A. 85-1184.
Date: Approved August 13, 1988.

Note.
This section was Ill.Rev.Stat., Ch. 23, para. 6601.

CASE NOTES

Private Right of Action
Trial court erred in granting the terminated employee's motion to dismiss as to the employer for the terminated employee's discharge from employment, as the Elder Abuse and Neglect Act, 320 Ill. Comp. Stat. Ann. 20/1 et seq. (Act), provided an implied private cause of action for retaliatory discharge and the terminated employee alleged in her complaint both that the employer discharge her because she reported the criminal conduct of another employee who was abusing and financially exploiting a senior citizen and that the Act expressed the Illinois public policy of protecting senior citizens from abuse. King v. Senior Servs. Assocs., 341 Ill. App. 3d 264, 275 Ill. Dec. 181, 792 N.E.2d 412, 2003 Ill. App. LEXIS 853 (2 Dist. 2003).

320 ILCS 20/2 Definitions

Sec. 2. *Definitions.* As used in this Act, unless the context requires otherwise:

(a) "Abuse" means causing any physical, mental or sexual injury to an eligible adult, including exploitation of such adult's financial resources.

Nothing in this Act shall be construed to mean that an eligible adult is a victim of abuse or neglect for the sole reason that he or she is being furnished with or relies upon treatment by spiritual means through prayer alone, in accordance with the tenets and practices of a recognized church or religious denomination.

Nothing in this Act shall be construed to mean that an eligible adult is a victim of abuse because of health care services provided or not provided by licensed health care professionals.

(a-5) "Abuser" means a person who abuses, neglects, or financially exploits an eligible adult.

(a-7) "Caregiver" means a person who either as a result of a family relationship, voluntarily, or in exchange for compensation has assumed responsibility for all or a portion of the care of an eligible adult who needs assistance with activities of daily living.

(b) "Department" means the Department on Aging of the State of Illinois.

(c) "Director" means the Director of the Department.

(d) "Domestic living situation" means a residence where the eligible adult lives alone or with his or her family or a caregiver, or others, or a board and care home or other community-based unlicensed facility, but is not:

(1) A licensed facility as defined in Section 1-113 of the Nursing Home Care Act [210 ILCS 45/1-113];

(2) A "life care facility" as defined in the Life Care Facilities Act [210 ILCS 40/1 et seq.];

(3) A home, institution, or other place operated by the federal government or agency thereof or by the State of Illinois;

(4) A hospital, sanitarium, or other institution, the principal activity or business of which is the diagnosis, care, and treatment of human illness through the maintenance and operation of organized facilities therefor, which is required to be licensed under the Hospital Licensing Act [210 ILCS 85/1 et seq.];

(5) A "community living facility" as defined in the Community Living Facilities Licensing Act [210 ILCS 35/1 et seq.];

(6) A "community residential alternative" as defined in the Community Residential Alternatives Licensing Act [repealed]; and

(7) A "community-integrated living arrangement" as defined in the Community-Integrated Living Arrangements Licensure and Certification Act [210 ILCS 135/1 et seq.].

(e) "Eligible adult" means a person 60 years of age or older who resides in a domestic living situation and is, or is alleged to be, abused, neglected, or financially exploited by another individual.

(f) "Emergency" means a situation in which an eligible adult is living in conditions presenting a risk of death or physical, mental or sexual injury and the provider agency has reason to believe the eligible adult is unable to consent to services which would alleviate that risk.

(f-5) "Mandated reporter" means any of the following persons while engaged in carrying out their professional duties:

(1) a professional or professional's delegate while engaged in: (i) social services, (ii) law enforcement, (iii) education, (iv) the care of an eligible adult or eligible adults, or (v) any of the occupations required to be licensed under the Clinical Psychologist Licensing Act [225 ILCS 15/1 et seq.], the Clinical Social Work and Social Work Practice Act [225 ILCS 20/1 et seq.], the Illinois Dental Practice Act [225 ILCS 25/1 et seq.], the Dietetic and Nutrition Services Practice Act [225 ILCS 30/1 et seq.], the Marriage and Family Therapy Licensing Act [225 ILCS 55/1 et seq.], the Medical Practice Act of 1987 [225 ILCS 60/1 et seq.], the Naprapathic Practice Act [225 ILCS 63/1 et seq.], the Nursing and Advanced Practice Nursing Act [225 ILCS 65/5-1 et seq.], the Nursing Home Administrators Licensing and Disciplinary Act [225 ILCS 70/1 et seq.], the Illinois Occupational Therapy Practice Act [225 ILCS 75/1 et seq.], the Illinois Optometric Practice Act of 1987 [225 ILCS 80/1 et seq.], the Pharmacy Practice Act of 1987 [225 ILCS 85/1 et seq.], the Illinois Physical Therapy Act [225 ILCS 90/1 et seq.], the Physician Assistant Practice Act of 1987 [225 ILCS 95/1 et seq.], the Podiatric Medical Practice Act of 1987 [225 ILCS 100/1 et seq.], the Respiratory Care Practice Act [225 ILCS 106/1 et seq.], the Professional Counselor and Clinical Professional Counselor Licensing Act [225 ILCS 107/1 et seq.], the Illinois Speech-Language Pathology and Audiology Practice Act [225 ILCS 110/1 et seq.], the Veterinary Medicine and Surgery Practice Act of 2004 [225 ILCS 115/1 et seq.], and the Illinois Public Accounting Act [225 ILCS 450/0.01 et seq.];

(2) an employee of a vocational rehabilitation facility prescribed or supervised by the Department of Human Services;

(3) an administrator, employee, or person providing services in or through an unlicensed community based facility;

(4) a Christian Science Practitioner;

(5) field personnel of the Department of Public Aid, Department of Public Health, and Department of Human Services, and any county or municipal health department;

(6) personnel of the Department of Human Services, the Guardianship and Advocacy Commission, the State Fire Marshal, local fire departments, the Department on Aging and its subsidiary Area Agencies on Aging and provider

agencies, and the Office of State Long Term Care Ombudsman;

(7) any employee of the State of Illinois not otherwise specified herein who is involved in providing services to eligible adults, including professionals providing medical or rehabilitation services and all other persons having direct contact with eligible adults; or

(8) a person who performs the duties of a coroner or medical examiner.

(9) a person who performs the duties of a paramedic or an emergency medical technician.

(g) "Neglect" means another individual's failure to provide an eligible adult with or willful withholding from an eligible adult the necessities of life including, but not limited to, food, clothing, shelter or medical care. This subsection does not create any new affirmative duty to provide support to eligible adults. Nothing in this Act shall be construed to mean that an eligible adult is a victim of neglect because of health care services provided or not provided by licensed health care professionals.

(h) "Provider agency" means any public or nonprofit agency in a planning and service area appointed by the regional administrative agency with prior approval by the Department on Aging to receive and assess reports of alleged or suspected abuse, neglect, or financial exploitation.

(i) "Regional administrative agency" means any public or nonprofit agency in a planning and service area so designated by the Department, provided that the designated Area Agency on Aging shall be designated the regional administrative agency if it so requests. The Department shall assume the functions of the regional administrative agency for any planning and service area where another agency is not so designated.

(j) "Substantiated case" means a reported case of alleged or suspected abuse, neglect, or financial exploitation in which a provider agency, after assessment, determines that there is reason to believe abuse, neglect, or financial exploitation has occurred.

(Source: P.A. 86-820; 87-264; 90-628, § 5; 91-259, § 10; 91-357, § 180; 91-533, § 45; 92-16, § 77; 93-281, § 25; 93-300, § 5.)

Note.

This section was Ill.Rev.Stat., Ch. 23, para. 6602.

P.A. 91-357, § 996 contains a "no acceleration or delay" provision, and P.A. 91-357, § 997 contains a "no revival or extension" provision.

P.A. 91-533 § 990 contains a "no acceleration or delay" provision, and P.A. 91-533 § 995 contains a "no revival or extension" provision.

The Community Residential Alternatives Licensing Act, formerly at 210 ILCS 140/1 et seq. was repealed.

Section 996 of P.A. 92-16 contains a "no acceleration or delay" provision, and Section 997 contains a "no revival or extension" provision.

Illinois Administrative Code.

See 89 Illinois Administrative Code, §§ 10.268, 270.210, 10.268.

Effect of Amendments.

The 1998 amendment by P.A. 90-628, effective January 1, 1999, added the last paragraph in subsection (a); inserted subsections (a-5) and (a-7); rewrote the introductory paragraph of subsection (d); rewrote subsection (e); inserted "the provider agency has reason to believe the eligible adult" in subsection (f), inserted subsection (f-5); added the last sentence in subsection (g); substituted "abuse, neglect, or financial exploitation" for "abuse or neglect" in subsection (h) and twice in subsection (j); and added the last sentence in subsection (i).

The 1999 amendment by P.A. 91-259, effective January 1, 2000, in subdivision (f-5)(1) substituted "the Nursing and Advanced Practice Nursing Act" for "the Illinois Nursing Act of 1987", and inserted "the Respiratory Care Practice Act".

The 1999 amendment by P.A. 91-357, effective July 29, 1999, substituted "Nursing and Advanced Practice Nursing Act" for "Illinois Nursing Act of 1987" in subdivision (f-5)(1).

The 1999 amendment by P.A. 91-533, effective August 13, 1999, in subdivision (f-5), substituted "Nursing and Advanced Practice Nursing Act" for "Illinois Nursing Act of 1987" in subdivision (f-5)(1) and redesignated subdivision (f-5)(9) as (f-5)(8).

The 2001 amendment by P.A. 92-16, effective June 28, 2001, combined the amendments by P.A. 91-259, P.A. 91-357 and P.A. 91-533.

The 2003 amendment by P.A. 93-281, effective December 31, 2003, substituted "2004" for "1994" in subsection (f-5)(1).

The 2003 amendment by P.A. 93-300, effective January 1, 2004, in subsection (f-5) added subdivisions (1) and (9) and made a related change.

Although the amendments made to this section by P.A. 93-281, § 25 and P.A. 93-300, § 5 did not take into account the amendments made by the other, the amendments have been combined into a single version by the publisher.

CASE NOTES

In General

Elder Abuse and Neglect Act, 320 Ill. Comp. Stat. Ann. 20/1 et seq., gave the Department on Aging of the State of Illinois the responsibility to establish, design, and manage services for senior citizens in order to carry out the Illinois public policy of protecting senior citizens from abuse, and, thus, the trial court erred in dismissing the terminated employee's retaliatory discharge claim against the employer, a provider agency charged with implementing that public policy, as the terminated employee alleged she was discharged for reporting a fellow employee's elder abuse and that allegation, if proven, would show that the employer's action was contrary to the Illinois public policy of protecting senior citizens. King v. Senior Servs. Assocs., 341 Ill. App. 3d 264, 275 Ill. Dec. 181, 792 N.E.2d 412, 2003 Ill. App. LEXIS 853 (2 Dist. 2003).

320 ILCS 20/3 Responsibilities

Sec. 3. *Responsibilities.* (a) The Department shall establish, design and manage a program of response and services for persons 60 years of age and older who have been, or are alleged to be, victims of abuse, neglect, or financial exploitation. The Department shall contract with or fund or, contract with and fund, regional administrative agencies, provider agencies, or both, for the provision of those functions, and, contingent on adequate funding, with attorneys or legal services provider agencies for the provision of legal assistance pursuant to this Act.

(b) Each regional administrative agency shall designate provider agencies within its planning and service area with prior approval by the Department on Aging, monitor the use of services, provide technical assistance to the provider agencies and be involved in program development activities.

(c) Provider agencies shall assist, to the extent possible, eligible adults who need agency services to allow them to continue to function independently. Such assistance shall include but not be limited to receiving reports of alleged or suspected abuse, neglect, or financial exploitation, conducting face-to-face assessments of such reported cases, determination of substantiated cases, referral of substantiated cases for necessary support services, referral of criminal conduct to law enforcement in accordance with Department guidelines, and provision of case work and follow-up services on substantiated cases. (Source: P.A. 85-1184; 90-628, § 5.)

Note.

This section was Ill.Rev.Stat., Ch. 23, para. 6603.

Illinois Administrative Code.

See 89 Illinois Administrative Code, §§ 270.215, 270.220, 270.255, 270.255.

Effect of Amendments.

The 1998 amendment by P.A. 90-628, effective January 1, 1999, rewrote subsection (a); and in subsection (c), inserted "to the extent possible" in the first sentence, and in the second sentence, inserted "or financial exploitation" and made a related change, and inserted "referral of criminal conduct to law enforcement in accordance with Department guidelines".

CASE NOTES

In General

Elder Abuse and Neglect Act, 320 Ill. Comp. Stat. Ann. 20/1 et seq., gave the Department on Aging of the State of Illinois the responsibility to establish, design, and manage services for senior citizens in order to carry out the Illinois public policy of protecting senior citizens from abuse, and, thus, the trial court erred in dismissing the terminated employee's retaliatory discharge claim against the employer, a provider agency charged with implementing that public policy, as the terminated employee alleged she was discharged for reporting a fellow employee's elder abuse and that allegation, if proven, would show that the employer's action was contrary to the Illinois public policy of protecting senior citizens. King v. Senior Servs. Assocs., 341 Ill. App. 3d 264, 275 Ill. Dec. 181, 792 N.E.2d 412, 2003 Ill. App. LEXIS 853 (2 Dist. 2003).

320 ILCS 20/3.5 Other Responsibilities

Sec. 3.5. *Other Responsibilities.* The Department shall also be responsible for the following activities, contingent upon adequate funding:

(a) promotion of a wide range of endeavors for the purpose of preventing elder abuse, neglect, and financial exploitation in both domestic and institutional settings, including, but not limited to, promotion of public and professional education to increase awareness of elder abuse, neglect, and financial exploitation, to increase reports, and to improve response by various legal, financial, social, and health systems;

(b) coordination of efforts with other agencies, councils, and like entities, to include but not be limited to, the Office of the Attorney General, the State Police, the Illinois Law Enforcement Training Standards Board, the State Triad, the Criminal Justice Information Authority, the Departments of Public Health, Public Aid, and Human Services, the Family Violence Coordinating Council, the Violence Prevention Authority, and other entities which may impact awareness of, and response to, elder abuse, neglect, and financial exploitation;

(c) collection and analysis of data;

(d) monitoring of the performance of regional administrative agencies and elder abuse provider agencies;

(e) promotion of prevention activities;

(f) *(As added by P.A. 93-300)* establishment and coordination of an aggressive training program about the unique nature of elder abuse cases with other agencies, councils, and like entities, including but not limited to the Office of the Attorney General, the State Police, the Illinois Law Enforcement Training Standards Board, the State Triad, the Criminal Justice Information Authority, the Departments of Public Health, Public Aid, and Human Services, the Family Violence Coordinating Council, the Illinois Violence Prevention Authority, and other entities that may impact awareness of, and response to, elder abuse, neglect, and financial exploitation;

(f) *(As added by P.A. 93-301)* establishing and coordinating a training program on the unique nature of elder abuse cases with other agencies, councils, and like entities, to include but not be limited to the Office of the Attorney General, the State Police, the Illinois Law Enforcement Training Standards Board, the State Triad, the Illinois Criminal Justice Information Authority, the State departments of Public Health, Public Aid, and Human Services, the Family Violence Coordinating Council, the Illinois Violence Prevention Authority, and other entities that may impact awareness of, and response to elder abuse, neglect, and financial exploitation;

(g) *(As added by P.A. 93-300)* solicitation of financial institutions for the purpose of making information available to the general public warning of financial exploitation of the elderly and related financial fraud or abuse, including such information and warnings available through signage or other written materials provided by the Department on the premises of such financial institutions, provided that the manner of displaying or distributing such information is subject to the sole discretion of each financial institution; and

(g) *(As added by P.A. 93-301)* solicitation of financial institutions for the purpose of making information available to the general public warning of financial exploitation of the elderly and related financial fraud or abuse, including such information and warnings available through signage or other written materials provided by the Department on the premises of such financial institutions, provided that the manner of displaying or distributing such information is subject to the sole discretion of each financial institution; and

(h) *(As added by P.A. 93-300)* coordination of efforts with utility companies to send notices in utility bills which explain elder rights regarding telemarketing home repair frauds.

(h) *(As added by P.A. 93-301)* coordinating efforts with utility and electric companies to send notices in

utility bills to explain to persons 60 years of age or older their rights regarding telemarketing and home repair fraud.
(Source: P.A. 90-628, § 5; 92-16, § 77; 93-300, § 5; 93-301, § 5.)

Subsections (f), (g), and (h) Set Out Twice.
Subsections (f), (g), and (h) are set out twice. The first versions of each are as amended by P.A. 93-300, § 5, effective January 1, 2004. The second versions of each are as amended by P.A. 93-301, § 5, effective January 1, 2004.

Note.
Section 996 of P.A. 92-16 contains a "no acceleration or delay" provision, and Section 997 contains a "no revival or extension" provision.

Illinois Administrative Code.
See 89 Illinois Administrative Code, § 270.215.

Effective Date.
This section became effective January 1, 1999 pursuant to Ill. Const. (1970) Art. IV, § 10 and 5 ILCS 75/1.

Effect of Amendments.
The 2001 amendment by P.A. 92-16, effective June 28, 2001, made a grammatical correction.
The 2003 amendment by P.A. 93-300, effective January 1, 2004, added subsections (f), (g), and (h) and made a related change.
The 2003 amendment by P.A. 93-301, effective January 1, 2004, in subsection (b), inserted "Illinois" three times; added subsections (f), (g) and (h); and made a related change.

320 ILCS 20/4 Reports of abuse or neglect

Sec. 4. *Reports of abuse or neglect.* (a) Any person who suspects the abuse, neglect, or financial exploitation of an eligible adult may report this suspicion to an agency designated to receive such reports under this Act or to the Department.

(a-5) If any mandated reporter has reason to believe that an eligible adult, who because of dysfunction is unable to seek assistance for himself or herself, has, within the previous 12 months, been subjected to abuse, neglect, or financial exploitation, the mandated reporter shall, within 24 hours after developing such belief, report this suspicion to an agency designated to receive such reports under this Act or to the Department. Whenever a mandated reporter is required to report under this Act in his or her capacity as a member of the staff of a medical or other public or private institution, facility, board and care home, or agency, he or she shall make a report to an agency designated to receive such reports under this Act or to the Department in accordance with the provisions of this Act and may also notify the person in charge of the institution, facility, board and care home, or agency or his or her designated agent that the report has been made. Under no circumstances shall any person in charge of such institution, facility, board and care home, or agency, or his or her designated agent to whom the notification has been made, exercise any control, restraint, modification, or other change in the report or the forwarding of the report to an agency designated to receive such reports under this Act or to the Department. The privileged quality of communication between any professional person required to report and his or her patient or client shall not apply to situations involving abused, neglected, or financially exploited eligible adults and shall not constitute grounds for failure to report as required by this Act.

(a-7) A person making a report under this Act in the belief that it is in the alleged victim's best interest shall be immune from criminal or civil liability or professional disciplinary action on account of making the report, notwithstanding any requirements concerning the confidentiality of information with respect to such eligible adult which might otherwise be applicable.

(a-9) Law enforcement officers shall continue to report incidents of alleged abuse pursuant to the Illinois Domestic Violence Act of 1986 [750 ILCS 60/101 et seq.], notwithstanding any requirements under this Act.

(b) Any person, institution or agency participating in the making of a report, providing information or records related to a report, assessment, or services, or participating in the investigation of a report under this Act in good faith, or taking photographs or x-rays as a result of an authorized assessment, shall have immunity from any civil, criminal or other liability in any civil, criminal or other proceeding brought in consequence of making such report or assessment or on account of submitting or otherwise disclosing such photographs or x-rays to any agency designated to receive reports of alleged or suspected abuse or neglect. Any person, institution or agency authorized by the Department to provide assessment, intervention, or administrative services under this Act shall, in the good faith performance of those services, have immunity from any civil, criminal or other liability in any civil, criminal, or other proceeding brought as a consequence of the performance of those services. For the purposes of any civil, criminal, or other proceeding, the good faith of any person required to report, permitted to report, or participating in an investigation of a report of alleged or suspected abuse, neglect, or financial exploitation shall be presumed.

(c) The identity of a person making a report of alleged or suspected abuse or neglect under this Act may be disclosed by the Department or other agency provided for in this Act only with such person's written consent or by court order.

(d) The Department shall by rule establish a system for filing and compiling reports made under this Act.

(e) Any physician who willfully fails to report as required by this Act shall be referred to the Illinois State Medical Disciplinary Board for action in accordance with subdivision (A)(22) of Section 22 of the Medical Practice Act of 1987 [225 ILCS 60/22]. Any dentist or dental hygienist who willfully fails to report as required by this Act shall be referred to the Department of Professional Regulation for action in accordance with paragraph 19 of Section 23 of the Illinois Dental Practice Act [225 ILCS 25/23]. Any

other mandated reporter required by this Act to report suspected abuse, neglect, or financial exploitation who willfully fails to report the same is guilty of a Class A misdemeanor.
(Source: P.A. 87-264; 87-435; 90-628, § 5; 93-300, § 5; 93-301, § 5.)

Note.
This section was Ill.Rev.Stat., Ch. 23, para. 6604.

Cross References.
As to the wilful failure to report a suspected abuse under this Act with regard to refusal to issue a license under the Physical Therapy Act, see 225 ILCS 90/17.

Illinois Administrative Code.
See 89 Illinois Administrative Code, §§ 270.230, 270.235.

Effect of Amendments.
The 1998 amendment by P.A. 90-628, effective January 1, 1999, rewrote subsection (a); inserted subsection (a-5); added the subsection (a-7) and (a-9) designations; in subsection (a-7), substituted "eligible adult" for "patient"; and, in subsection (b), substituted "agency participating in the making of a report, providing information or records related to a report, assessment, or services, or participating in the investigation of a report" for "agency making a report" in the first sentence, and added the last sentence.

The 2003 amendment by P.A. 93-300, effective January 1, 2004, added subsection (e).

The 2003 amendment by P.A. 93-301, effective January 1, 2004, added subsection (e).

Although the amendments made to this section by P.A. 93-300, § 5 and P.A. 93-301, § 5 did not take into account the amendments made by the other, the amendments have been combined into a single version by the publisher.

LEGAL PERIODICALS

For article, "When Silence Resounds: Clergy and the Requirement to Report Elder Abuse and Neglect", see 49 DePaul L. Rev. 1 (1999).

320 ILCS 20/4.1 Employer discrimination

Sec. 4.1. *Employer discrimination.* No employer shall discharge, demote or suspend, or threaten to discharge, demote or suspend, or in any manner discriminate against any employee who makes any good faith oral or written report of suspected elder abuse, neglect, or financial exploitation or who is or will be a witness or testify in any investigation or proceeding concerning a report of suspected elder abuse, neglect, or financial exploitation.
(Source: P.A. 90-628, § 5.)

Effective Date.
This section became effective January 1, 1999 pursuant to Ill. Const. (1970) Art. IV. § 10 and 5 ILCS 75/1.

CASE NOTES

In General
Trial court erred in dismissing the terminated employee's complaint against the employer, as the terminated employee's allegations, if proven, established a private right of action pursuant to the Elder Abuse and Neglect Act, 320 ILCS 20/4.1 (Act) for retaliatory discharge since the allegations stated that she was terminated for reporting a fellow employee's abuse and financial exploitation of a senior citizen, even though the employer was charged with carrying out the Illinois public policy of protecting senior citizens victimized by that very conduct. King v. Senior Servs. Assocs., 341 Ill. App. 3d 264, 275 Ill. Dec. 181, 792 N.E.2d 412, 2003 Ill. App. LEXIS 853 (2 Dist. 2003).

320 ILCS 20/4.2 Testimony by mandated reporter and investigator

Sec. 4.2. *Testimony by mandated reporter and investigator.* Any mandated reporter who makes a report or any person who investigates a report under this Act shall testify fully in any judicial proceeding resulting from such report, as to any evidence of abuse, neglect, or financial exploitation or the cause thereof. Any mandated reporter who is required to report a suspected case of abuse, neglect, or financial exploitation under Section 4 of this Act [320 ILCS 20/4 et seq.] shall testify fully in any administrative hearing resulting from such report, as to any evidence of abuse, neglect, or financial exploitation or the cause thereof. No evidence shall be excluded by reason of any common law or statutory privilege relating to communications between the alleged abuser or the eligible adult subject of the report under this Act and the person making or investigating the report.
(Source: P.A. 90-628, § 5.)

Illinois Administrative Code.
See 89 Illinois Administrative Code, § 270.230.

Effective Date.
This section became effective January 1, 1999, pursuant to Ill. Const. (1970) Art. IV. § 10 and 5 ILCS 75/1.

CASE NOTES

In General
Trial court erred in dismissing the retaliatory discharge action that the terminated employee filed against the employer, a provider agency charged with implementing the Illinois public policy of protecting senior citizens, as the terminated employee stated a private right of action for retaliatory discharge pursuant to the Elder Abuse and Neglect Act, 320 ILCS 20/1 et seq. (Act) when she alleged in her complaint that she was discharged after she reported elder abuse being committed by a fellow employee; to hold otherwise would have a chilling effect on implementing the Illinois public policy to protect senior citizens because the reporter was required under the Act to testify at judicial proceedings about the report and would not want to make such a report if the consequence was being discharged from employment for making it. King v. Senior Servs. Assocs., 341 Ill. App. 3d 264, 275 Ill. Dec. 181, 792 N.E.2d 412, 2003 Ill. App. LEXIS 853 (2 Dist. 2003).

320 ILCS 20/5 Procedure

Sec. 5. *Procedure.* (a) A provider agency designated to receive reports of alleged or suspected abuse, neglect, or financial exploitation under this Act shall, upon receiving such a report, conduct a face-to-face assessment with respect to such report. The assessment shall include, but not be limited to, a visit to the residence of the eligible adult who is the subject of the report and may include interviews or consultations with service agencies or individuals who may have knowledge of the eligible adult's circumstances. If, after the assessment, the provider agency determines that the case is substantiated it shall develop a service care plan for the eligible adult. In developing the plan, the provider agency may consult with any other appropriate provider of services, and such providers shall be immune from civil or criminal liability on account of such acts. The plan shall include alternative suggested or recommended services which are appropriate to the needs of the eligible adult and which involve the least restriction of the eligible adult's activities commensurate with his or her needs. Only those services to which consent is provided in accordance with Section 9 of this Act [320 ILCS 20/9] shall be provided, contingent upon the availability of such services.

(b) A provider agency shall refer evidence of crimes against an eligible adult to the appropriate law enforcement agency according to Department policies. A referral to law enforcement may be made at intake or any time during the case. Where a provider agency has reason to believe the death of an eligible adult may be the result of abuse or neglect, the agency shall immediately report the matter to the coroner or medical examiner and shall cooperate fully with any subsequent investigation.
(Source: P.A. 85-1184; 90-628, § 5.)

Note.
This section was Ill.Rev.Stat., Ch. 23, para. 6605.

Illinois Administrative Code.
See 89 Illinois Administrative Code, §§ 270.250, 270.255, 270.250, 270.255.

Effect of Amendments.
The 1998 amendment by P.A. 90-628, effective January 1, 1999, added the subsection (a) designation (a); in subsection (a), inserted "or financial exploitation" and made a related change in the first sentence, and inserted "or her" in the next-to-last sentence; and added subsection (b).

CASE NOTES

In General
Trial court erred in dismissing the terminated employee's action against the employer, a provider agency charged with implementing the Illinois public policy of protecting senior citizens, as the allegations of the terminated employee's complaint that stated she was discharged because she reported a fellow employee's abuse and financial exploitation of a senior citizen, if proven, would show that the employer in terminating her acted in direct contravention of that public policy by disciplining an employee for lodging an abuse report. King v. Senior Servs. Assocs., 341 Ill. App. 3d 264, 275 Ill. Dec. 181, 792 N.E.2d 412, 2003 Ill. App. LEXIS 853 (2 Dist. 2003).

320 ILCS 20/6 Time

Sec. 6. *Time.* The Department shall by rule establish the period of time within which an assessment shall begin and within which a service care plan shall be implemented. Such rules shall provide for an expedited response to emergency situations.
(Source: P.A. 85-1184.)

Note.
This section was Ill.Rev.Stat., Ch. 23, para. 6606.

320 ILCS 20/7 (As amended by P.A. 93-300) Review

Sec. 7. *Review.* All services provided to an eligible adult shall be reviewed by the provider agency on at least a quarterly basis for up to one year to determine whether the service care plan should be continued or modified, except that the Department on Aging, upon review, may grant a waiver to extend the service care plan for up to an additional one year period.
(Source: P.A. 85-1184; 90-628, § 5; 93-300, § 5.)

Section Set Out Twice.
This section was separately amended by P.A. 93-300 and 93-301. The version above is as amended by P.A. 93-300, effective January 1, 2004. For the version as amended by P.A. 93-301, effective January 1, 2004, see the following section also numbered 320 ILCS 20/7.

Note.
This section was Ill.Rev.Stat., Ch. 23, para. 6607.

Illinois Administrative Code.
See 89 Illinois Administrative Code, §§ 270.255, 270.255.

Effect of Amendments.
The 1998 amendment by P.A. 90-628, effective January 1, 1999, substituted "up to one year" for "not less than one year".
The 2003 amendment by P.A. 93-300, effective January 1, 2004, inserted the language beginning "except that the" and ending "year period".

320 ILCS 20/7 (As amended by P.A. 93-301) Review

Sec. 7. *Review.* All services provided to an eligible adult shall be reviewed by the provider agency on at least a quarterly basis for up to one year to determine whether the service care plan should be continued or modified, except that, upon review, the Department may grant a waiver to extend the service care plan for up to one additional year.
(Source: P.A. 85-1184; 90-628, § 5; 93-301, § 5.)

Section Set Out Twice.
This section was separately amended by P.A. 93-300 and 93-301. The version above is as amended by P.A. 93-301, effective January 1, 2004. For the version as amended by P.A. 93-300, effective January 1, 2004, see the previous section also numbered 320 ILCS 20/7.

Note.
This section was Ill.Rev.Stat., Ch. 23, para. 6607.

Illinois Administrative Code.
See 89 Illinois Administrative Code, §§ 270.255, 270.255.

Effect of Amendments.
The 1998 amendment by P.A. 90-628, effective January 1, 1999, substituted "up to one year" for "not less than one year".
The 2003 amendment by P.A. 93-301 effective January 1, 2004, inserted the exception language at the end.

320 ILCS 20/8 Access to records

Sec. 8. *Access to records.* All records concerning reports of elder abuse, neglect, and financial exploitation and all records generated as a result of such reports shall be confidential and shall not be disclosed except as specifically authorized by this Act or other applicable law. Access to such records, but not access to the identity of the person or persons making a report of alleged abuse, neglect, or financial exploitation as contained in such records, shall be allowed to the following persons and for the following persons:

(1) Department staff, provider agency staff, other aging network staff, and regional administrative agency staff in the furtherance of their responsibilities under this Act;

(2) A law enforcement agency investigating known or suspected elder abuse, neglect, or financial exploitation. Where a provider agency has reason to believe that the death of an eligible adult may be the result of abuse or neglect, the agency shall immediately provide the appropriate law enforcement agency with all records pertaining to the eligible adult;

(3) A physician who has before him or her or who is involved in the treatment of an eligible adult whom he or she reasonably suspects may be abused, neglected, or financially exploited or who has been referred to the Elder Abuse and Neglect Program;

(4) An eligible adult reported to be abused, neglected, or financially exploited, or such adult's guardian unless such guardian is the abuser or the alleged abuser;

(5) A court or a guardian ad litem, upon its or his or her finding that access to such records may be necessary for the determination of an issue before the court. However, such access shall be limited to an in camera inspection of the records, unless the court determines that disclosure of the information contained therein is necessary for the resolution of an issue then pending before it;

(6) A grand jury, upon its determination that access to such records is necessary in the conduct of its official business;

(7) Any person authorized by the Director, in writing, for audit or bona fide research purposes;

(8) A coroner or medical examiner who has reason to believe that an eligible adult has died as the result of abuse, neglect, or financial exploitation. The provider agency shall immediately provide the coroner or medical examiner with all records pertaining to the eligible adult; and

(9) Department of Professional Regulation staff and members of the Social Work Examining and Disciplinary Board in the course of investigating alleged violations of the Clinical Social Work and Social Work Practice Act [225 ILCS 20/1 et seq.] by provider agency staff.

(Source: P.A. 85-1184; 89-387, § 100; 90-628, § 5.)

Note.

This section was Ill.Rev.Stat., Ch. 23, para. 6608.

Illinois Administrative Code.

See 89 Illinois Administrative Code, § 270.275.

Effect of Amendments.

The 1995 amendment by P.A. 89-387, effective August 20, 1995, substituted "and" for a period in subsection (h); and added subsection (i).

The 1998 amendment by P.A. 90-628, effective January 1, 1999, rewrote this section.

320 ILCS 20/9 Authority to consent to services

Sec. 9. *Authority to consent to services.* (a) If an eligible adult consents to services being provided according to the service care plan, such services shall be arranged to meet the adult's needs, based upon the availability of resources to provide such services. If an adult withdraws his or her consent or refuses to accept such services, the services shall not be provided.

(b) If it reasonably appears to the Department or other agency designated under this Act that a person is an eligible adult and lacks the capacity to consent to necessary services, including an assessment, the Department or other agency may seek the appointment of a guardian as provided in Article XIa of the Probate Act of 1975 [755 ILCS 5/11a-1 et seq.] for the purpose of consenting to such services.

(c) A guardian of the person of an eligible adult may consent to services being provided according to the service care plan. If a guardian withdraws his or her consent or refuses to allow services to be provided to the eligible adult, the Department, an agency designated under this Act, or the office of the Attorney General may request a court order seeking appropriate remedies, and may in addition request removal of the guardian and appointment of a successor guardian.

(d) If an emergency exists and the Department or other agency designated under this Act reasonably believes that a person is an eligible adult and lacks the capacity to consent to necessary services, the Department or other agency may request an ex parte order from the circuit court of the county in which the petitioner or respondent resides or in which the alleged abuse, neglect, or financial exploitation occurred, authorizing an assessment of a report of alleged or suspected abuse, neglect, or financial exploitation or the provision of necessary services, or both, including relief available under the Illinois Domestic Violence Act of 1986 [750 ILCS 60/101 et seq.]. Petitions filed under this subsection shall be treated as expedited proceedings.

(e) Within 15 days after the entry of the ex parte emergency order, the order shall expire, or, if the need for assessment or services continues, the provider agency shall petition for the appointment of a guardian as provided in Article XIa of the Probate Act of 1975 [755 ILCS 5/1-1 et seq.] for the purpose of consenting to such assessment or services or to protect the eligible adult from further harm.

(Source: P.A. 85-1184; 90-628, § 5.)

Note.

This section was Ill.Rev.Stat., Ch. 23, para. 6609.

Illinois Administrative Code.

See 89 Illinois Administrative Code, §§ 270.260, 270.260.

Effect of Amendments.
The 1998 amendment by P.A. 90-628, effective January 1, 1999, rewrote this section.

320 ILCS 20/9.5 Commencement of action for ex parte authorization orders; filing fees; process

Sec. 9.5. *Commencement of action for ex parte authorization orders; filing fees; process.* (a) Actions for ex parte authorization orders are commenced:

(1) independently, by filing a petition for an ex parte authorization order in the circuit court;

(2) in conjunction with other civil proceedings, by filing a petition for an ex parte authorization order under the same case number as a guardianship proceeding under the Probate Act of 1975 [755 ILCS 5/1-1 et seq.] where the eligible adult is the alleged disabled adult.

(b) No fee shall be charged by the clerk for filing petitions or certifying orders. No fee shall be charged by a sheriff for service by the sheriff of a petition, rule, motion, or order in an action commenced under this Section.

(c) Any action for an ex parte authorization order commenced independently is a distinct cause of action and requires that a separate summons be issued and served. Service of summons is not required prior to entry of emergency ex parte authorization orders.

(d) Summons may be served by a private person over 18 years of age and not a party to the action. The return by that private person shall be by affidavit. The summons may be served by a sheriff or other law enforcement officer, and if summons is placed for service by the sheriff, it shall be made at the earliest time practicable and shall take precedence over other summonses except those of a similar emergency nature.
(Source: P.A. 91-731, § 5.)

Effective Date.
Section 99 of P.A. 91-731 made this section effective upon becoming law. The Act was approved June 2, 2000.

320 ILCS 20/10 Rules

Sec. 10. *Rules.* The Department shall adopt such rules and regulations as it deems necessary to implement this Act.
(Source: P.A. 85-1184.)

Note.
This section was Ill.Rev.Stat., Ch. 23, para. 6610.

320 ILCS 20/11 Annual Reports

Sec. 11. *Annual Reports.* The Department shall file with the Governor and the General Assembly, within 270 days after the end of each fiscal year, a report concerning its implementation of this Act during such fiscal year, together with any recommendations for future implementation.
(Source: P.A. 85-1184; 90-628, § 5.)

Note.
This section was Ill.Rev.Stat., Ch. 23, para. 6611.

Illinois Administrative Code.
See 89 Illinois Administrative Code, § 270.215.

Effect of Amendments.
The 1998 amendment by P.A. 90-628, effective January 1, 1999, substituted "270 days" for "90 days".

320 ILCS 20/12: Repealed by P.A. 90-628, § 10, effective January 1, 1999.

320 ILCS 20/13 Access

Sec. 13. *Access.* (a) The designated provider agencies shall have access to eligible adults who have been reported or found to be victims of abuse, neglect, or financial exploitation in order to assess the validity of the report, assess other needs of the eligible adult, and provide services in accordance with this Act.

(b) Where access to an eligible adult is denied, the Office of the Attorney General, the Department, or the provider agency may petition the court for an order to require appropriate access where:

(1) a caregiver or third party has interfered with the assessment or service plan, or

(2) the agency has reason to believe that the eligible adult is denying access because of coercion, extortion, or justifiable fear of future abuse, neglect, or financial exploitation.

(c) The petition for an order requiring appropriate access shall be afforded an expedited hearing in the circuit court.

(d) If the elder abuse provider agency has substantiated financial exploitation against an eligible adult, and has documented a reasonable belief that the eligible adult will be irreparably harmed as a result of the financial exploitation, the Office of the Attorney General, the Department, or the provider agency may petition for an order freezing the assets of the eligible adult. The petition shall be filed in the county or counties in which the assets are located. The court's order shall prohibit the sale, gifting, transfer, or wasting of the assets of the eligible adult, both real and personal, owned by, or vested in, the eligible adult, without the express permission of the court. The petition to freeze the assets of the eligible adult shall be afforded an expedited hearing in the circuit court.
(Source: P.A. 90-628, § 5.)

Illinois Administrative Code.
See 89 Illinois Administrative Code, §§ 270.245, 270.260, 270.260.

Effective Date.
This section became effective January 1, 1999, pursuant to Ill. Const. (1970), Art. IV, § 10 and 5 ILCS 75/1.

320 ILCS 20/13.5 Commencement of action for access; filing fees; process; notice; duration of orders

Sec. 13.5. *Commencement of action for access; filing fees; process; notice; duration of orders.* (a) Actions for orders seeking access to an eligible adult or freezing assets of an eligible adult are commenced:

(1) independently, by filing a petition for access to an eligible adult or freezing the assets of an eligible adult in the circuit court;

(2) in conjunction with other civil proceedings, by filing a petition for access to an eligible adult or freezing the assets of an eligible adult under the same case number as another civil proceeding involving the parties, including, but not limited to:

(i) a guardianship proceeding under the Probate Act of 1975 [755 ILCS 5/1-1 et seq.];

(ii) a proceeding for involuntary commitment under the Mental Health and Developmental Disabilities Code [405 ILCS 5/1-100 et seq.];

(iii) any other proceeding, provided that the eligible adult or the respondent is a party to or the subject of that proceeding.

(b) No fee shall be charged by the clerk for filing petitions or certifying orders. No fee shall be charged by a sheriff for service by the sheriff of such a petition, rule, motion, or order in an action commenced under this Section.

(c) Any action for an order for access to an eligible adult or freezing assets of an eligible adult, whether commenced independently or in conjunction with another proceeding, is a distinct cause of action and requires that a separate summons be issued and served, except that in pending cases the following methods may be used:

(1) Delivery of the summons to respondent personally in open court in pending civil or criminal cases.

(2) Mailing to the defendant, or, if represented, to the defendant's attorney of record in the civil cases in which the defendant has filed a general appearance. The summons shall be in the form prescribed by subsection (d) of Supreme Court Rule 101, except that it shall require the respondent to answer or appear within 7 days. Attachments to the summons or notice shall include the petition for access to an eligible adult or freezing assets of an eligible adult and supporting affidavits, if any, and any emergency order for access to an eligible adult or freezing assets of an eligible adult that has been issued.

(d) Summons may be served by a private person over 18 years of age and not a party to the action. The return by that private person shall be by affidavit. The summons may be served by a sheriff or other law enforcement officer, and if summons is placed for service by the sheriff, it shall be made at the earliest time practicable and shall take precedence over other summonses except those of a similar emergency nature.

(e) Except as otherwise provided in this Section, notice of hearings on petitions or motions shall be served in accordance with Supreme Court Rules 11 and 12 unless notice is excused by the Code of Civil Procedure [735 ILCS 5/1-101 et seq.], Supreme Court Rules, or local rules, as now or hereafter amended.

(f) Original notice of a hearing on a petition for access to an eligible adult or freezing assets of an eligible adult may be given, and the documents served, in accordance with Supreme Court Rules 11 and 12. When, however, an emergency order is sought in such a case on an ex parte application, the notice rules set forth in Section 11-101 of the Code of Civil Procedure [735 ILCS 5/11-101] shall apply.

(g) An order entered in accordance with Sections 13 and 13.5 [320 ILCS 20/13] shall be valid for a fixed period of time, not to exceed 2 years.

(Source: P.A. 91-731, § 5.)

Effective Date.

Section 99 of P.A. 91-731 made this section effective upon becoming law. The Act was approved June 2, 2000.

SENIOR CITIZENS AND DISABLED PERSONS PROPERTY TAX RELIEF AND PHARMACEUTICAL ASSISTANCE ACT

320 ILCS 25/1 Short title

Sec. 1. *Short title.* This Article shall be known and may be cited as the "Senior Citizens and Disabled Persons Property Tax Relief and Pharmaceutical Assistance Act". As used in this Article, "this Act" means this Article.

(Source: P.A. 83-1531.)

Derivation.

Title: An Act in relation to the payment of grants to enable the elderly and the disabled to acquire or retain private housing and to acquire prescription drugs.

Cite: 320 ILCS 25/1 et seq.

Source: P.A. 77-2059. Title amended by P.A. 83-1531.

Date: Approved July 17, 1972.

Note.

This section was Ill.Rev.Stat., Ch. 67 ½, para. 401.

Illinois Administrative Code.

See 89 Illinois Administrative Code, § 113.113.

320 ILCS 25/2 Purpose

Sec. 2. *Purpose.* The purpose of this Act is to provide incentives to the senior citizens and disabled persons of this State to acquire and retain private housing of their choice and at the same time to relieve those citizens from the burdens of extraordinary property taxes against their increasingly restricted earning power, and thereby to reduce the requirements for public housing in this State.

(Source: P.A. 77-2059.)

Note.

This section was Ill.Rev.Stat., Ch. 67 ½, para. 402.

Cross References.

As to the lack of effect upon the eligibility of an applicant for or recipient of public aid under the aid to families with dependent children section of the Public Aid Code with regard to any grant made under this Act, see 305 ILCS 5/4-1.6.

As to the State Comptroller's inability to deduct payments owed the state from funds held by the State Treasurer under this Act, see 15 ILCS 405/10.05.

As to requests of the State Controller for replacement warrants issued for purpose specified in this Act, see 15 ILCS 405/10.10.

As to the effect of a payment of any grant under this Act upon this Act upon the eligibility of an applicant for or recipient of public aid under the Public Aid code see the following sections: for aid to the aged section, see 305 ILCS 5/3-1.2; for aid to families with dependent children section, see 305 ILCS 5/4-1.6; for medical assistance, see 305 ILCS 5/5-2; for general assistance, see 305 ILCS 5/6-1.2.

As to the effect of payment of a grant under this Act upon the amount and nature of any aid under the Public Aid Code see the following sections: with regard to aid to the aged, see 305 ILCS 5/3-5; with regard to aid to families with dependent children, see 305 ILCS 5/4-2; with regard to medical assistance, see 305 ILCS 5/5-4; with regard to general assistance, see 305 ILCS 5/6-2.

As to the ineligibility for benefits under this Act with regard to an individual who has been ordered deported, see 720 ILCS 5/17A-1.

As to a reduction in motor vehicle registration fees paid by a vehicle owner who has claimed and received a grant under this Act, see 625 ILCS 5/3-806.3.

As to the lack of effect the Senior Citizens Real Estate Tax Deferral Act has upon the eligibility of any person to receive any grant pursuant to this Act, see 320 ILCS 30/8.

320 ILCS 25/3 Definitions

Sec. 3. *Definitions.* As used in this Act, unless the context otherwise requires, words and phrases have the meanings set forth in the following Sections preceding Section 4 [320 ILCS 25/3.01 through 320 ILCS 25/4].
(Source: P.A. 87-895.)

Note.
This section was Ill.Rev.Stat., Ch. 67 ½, para. 403.

320 ILCS 25/3.01 [Claimant defined]

Sec. 3.01. "Claimant" means an individual who has filed a claim under this Act.
(Source: P.A. 77-2059.)

Note.
This section was Ill.Rev.Stat., Ch. 67 ½, para. 403.01.

Illinois Administrative Code.
See 86 Illinois Administrative Code, § 530.105.

320 ILCS 25/3.02 [Department defined]

Sec. 3.02. "Department" means the Department of Revenue of this State.
(Source: P.A. 77-2059.)

Note.
This section was Ill.Rev.Stat., Ch. 67 ½, para. 403.02.

Illinois Administrative Code.
See 86 Illinois Administrative Code, § 530.105.

320 ILCS 25/3.03 [Director defined]

Sec. 3.03. "Director" means the Director of Revenue of this State.
(Source: P.A. 77-2059.)

Note.
This section was Ill.Rev.Stat., Ch. 67 ½, para. 403.03.

Illinois Administrative Code.
See 86 Illinois Administrative Code, § 530.105.

320 ILCS 25/3.04 [Gross Rent defined]

Sec. 3.04. "Gross Rent" means the total amount paid solely for the right to occupy a residence.

If the residence is a nursing or sheltered care home, "gross rent" means the amount paid in a taxable year that is attributable to the cost of housing, but not of meals or care, for the claimant in that home, determined in accordance with regulations of the Department.
(Source: P.A. 78-1249; 78-1297.)

Note.
This section was Ill.Rev.Stat., Ch. 67 ½, para. 403.04.

320 ILCS 25/3.05 [Household defined]

Sec. 3.05. "Household" means a claimant or a claimant and his spouse living together in the same residence.
(Source: P.A. 77-2059.)

Note.
This section was Ill.Rev.Stat., Ch. 67 ½, para. 403.05.

Illinois Administrative Code.
See 86 Illinois Administrative Code, § 530.105.

320 ILCS 25/3.06 [Household income defined]

Sec. 3.06. "Household income" means the combined income of the members of a household.
(Source: P.A. 77-2059.)

Note.
This section was Ill.Rev.Stat., Ch. 67 ½, para. 403.06.

Illinois Administrative Code.
See 86 Illinois Administrative Code, § 530.105.

320 ILCS 25/3.07 [Income defined]

Sec. 3.07. "Income" means adjusted gross income, properly reportable for federal income tax purposes under the provisions of the Internal Revenue Code [26 U.S.C. § 1 et seq.], modified by adding thereto the sum of the following amounts to the extent deducted or excluded from gross income in the computation of adjusted gross income:

(A) An amount equal to all amounts paid or accrued as interest or dividends during the taxable year;

(B) An amount equal to the amount of tax imposed by the Illinois Income Tax Act [35 ILCS 5/101 et seq.] paid for the taxable year;

(C) An amount equal to all amounts received during the taxable year as an annuity under an annuity, endowment or life insurance contract or under any other contract or agreement;

(D) An amount equal to the amount of benefits paid under the Federal Social Security Act [42 U.S.C. § 301 et seq.] during the taxable year;

(E) An amount equal to the amount of benefits paid under the Railroad Retirement Act [45 U.S.C. § 231 et seq.] during the taxable year;

(F) An amount equal to the total amount of cash public assistance payments received from any governmental agency during the taxable year other than benefits received pursuant to this Act;

(G) An amount equal to any net operating loss carryover deduction or capital loss carryover deduction during the taxable year.

(H) For claim years beginning on or after January 1, 2002, an amount equal to any benefits received under the Workers' Compensation Act or the Workers' Occupational Diseases Act [820 ILCS 305/1 et seq. or 820 ILCS 310/1 et seq.] during the taxable year.

"Income" does not include any grant assistance received under the Nursing Home Grant Assistance Act [305 ILCS 40/1 et seq.] or any distributions or items of income described under subparagraph (X) of paragraph (2) of subsection (a) of Section 203 of the Illinois Income Tax Act [35 ILCS 5/203].

This amendatory Act of 1987 shall be effective for purposes of this Section for tax years ending on or after December 31, 1987.
(Source: P.A. 87-863; 90-491, § 75; 91-676, § 15; 92-131, § 5; 92-519, § 5.)

Note.

This section was Ill.Rev.Stat., Ch. 67 ½, para. 403.07.

Effect of Amendments.

The 1997 amendment by P.A. 90-491, effective January 1, 1998, added subsection (G).

The 1999 amendment by P.A. 91-676, effective December 23, 1999, inserted "or any distributions or items of income described under subparagraph (X) of paragraph (2) of subsection (a) of Section 203 of the Illinois Income Tax Act" at the end of the paragraph concerning "Income".

The 2001 amendment by P.A. 92-131 effective July 23, 2001, added subdivision (H).

The 2001 amendment by P.A. 92-519, effective January 1, 2002, added subdivision (H).

Although the amendments made to this section by P.A. 92-131, § 5 and P.A. 92-519, § 5 did not take into account the amendments made by the other, the amendments have been combined into a single version by the publisher.

320 ILCS 25/3.08 [Internal Revenue Code defined]

Sec. 3.08. "Internal Revenue Code" means the United States Internal Revenue Code of 1954 [26 U.S.C. § 1 et seq.] or any successor law or laws relating to federal income taxes in effect for the year.
(Source: P.A. 77-2059.)

Note.

This section was Ill.Rev.Stat., Ch. 67 ½, para. 403.08.

320 ILCS 25/3.09 [Property taxes accrued defined]

Sec. 3.09. "Property taxes accrued" means the ad valorem property taxes extended against a residence, but does not include special assessments, interest or charges for service. In the case of real estate improved with a multidwelling or multipurpose building, "property taxes accrued" extended against a residence within such a building is an amount equal to the same percentage of the total property taxes extended against that real estate as improved as the value of the residence is to the total value of the building. If the multidwelling building is owned and operated as a cooperative, the value of an individual residence is the value of the interest in the cooperative held by the owner of record of the legal or equitable interest, other than a leasehold interest, in the cooperative which confers the right to occupy that residence. In determining the amount of grant under Section 4 [320 ILCS 25/4] for 1976 and thereafter, the applicable "property taxes accrued", as determined under this Section, are those payable or paid in the last preceding taxable year.

In addition, if the residence is a mobile home as defined in and subject to the tax imposed by the Mobile Home Local Services Tax Act [35 ILCS 515 et seq.], "property taxes accrued" includes the amount of privilege tax paid during the calendar year for which benefits are claimed under that Act on that mobile home. Beginning in taxable year 1999, if (i) the residence is a mobile home, (ii) the resident is the record owner of the property upon which the mobile home is located, and (iii) the resident is liable for the taxes imposed under the Property Tax Code [35 ILCS 200/1 et seq.] for both the mobile home and the property, then "property taxes accrued" includes the amount of property taxes paid on both the mobile home and the property upon which the mobile home is located.
(Source: P.A. 79-1049; 91-357, § 181; 91-391, § 5.)

Note.

This section was Ill.Rev.Stat., Ch. 67 ½, para. 403.09.

An Act to provide for a privilege tax on mobile homes, referred to above, appears to be An Act to provide for a local services tax on mobile homes, approved August 28, 1973 [35 ILCS 515/1 et seq.].

P.A. 91-357, § 996 contains a "no acceleration or delay" provision, and P.A. 91-357, § 997 contains a "no revival or extension" provision.

Cross References.

The provisions of the Mobile Home Local Services Tax Act are set forth at 35 ILCS 515/1-14.

Effect of Amendments.

The 1999 amendment by P.A. 91-357, effective July 29, 1999 substituted "the Mobile Home Local Services Tax Act" for "'An Act to provide for a privilege tax on mobile homes', approved August 28, 1973" in the second paragraph of the section.

The 1999 amendment by P.A. 91-391, effective July 30, 1999, in the first sentence of the second paragraph, substituted "the Mobile Home Local Services Tax Act" for "'An Act to provide for a privilege tax on mobile homes' approved August 28, 1973"; and added the last sentence.

Although the amendments made to this section by P.A. 91-357, § 181 and P.A. 91-391, § 5 did not take into account the amendments made by the other, the amendments have been combined into a single version by the publisher.

320 ILCS 25/3.10 [Regulations defined]

Sec. 3.10. "Regulations" includes rules promulgated and forms prescribed by the Department.
(Source: P.A. 77-2059.)

Note.
This section was Ill.Rev.Stat., Ch. 67 ½, para. 403.10.

320 ILCS 25/3.11 [Rent constituting property taxes accrued defined]

Sec. 3.11. "Rent constituting property taxes accrued" means 25% of the amount of gross rent paid in a taxable year for a residence which was subject to ad valorem property taxes in that year under the Property Tax Code [35 ILCS 200/1-1 et seq.].
(Source: P.A. 87-860; 88-670, § 3-71.)

Note.
This section was Ill.Rev.Stat., Ch. 67 ½, para. 403.11.

Effect of Amendments.
The 1994 amendment by P.A. 88-670, effective December 2, 1994, substituted "Property Tax Code" for "Revenue Act of 1939".

320 ILCS 25/3.12 [Residence defined]

Sec. 3.12. "Residence" means the principal dwelling place occupied in this State by a household and so much of the surrounding land as is reasonably necessary for use of the dwelling as a home, and includes rental property, mobile homes, single family dwellings, and units in multifamily, multidwelling or multipurpose buildings. If the assessor has established a specific legal description for a portion of property constituting the residence, then that portion of property shall be deemed "residence" for the purposes of this Act. "Residence" also includes that portion of a nursing or sheltered care home occupied as a dwelling by a claimant, determined as prescribed in regulations of the Department.
(Source: P.A. 78-1249.)

Note.
This section was Ill.Rev.Stat., Ch. 67 ½, para. 403.12.

320 ILCS 25/3.13 [Taxable year defined]

Sec. 3.13. "Taxable year" means the calendar year during which ad valorem property taxes payable in the next succeeding calendar year were levied.
(Source: P.A. 77-2059.)

Note.
This section was Ill.Rev.Stat., Ch. 67 ½, para. 403.13.

320 ILCS 25/3.14 [Disabled person defined]

Sec. 3.14. "Disabled person" means a person unable to engage in any substantial gainful activity by reason of a medically determinable physical or mental impairment which can be expected to result in death or has lasted or can be expected to last for a continuous period of not less than 12 months. Disabled persons filing claims under this Act shall submit proof of disability in such form and manner as the Department shall by rule and regulation prescribe. Proof that a claimant is eligible to receive disability benefits under the Federal Social Security Act [42 U.S.C. § 301 et seq.] shall constitute proof of disability for purposes of this Act. Issuance of an Illinois Disabled Person Identification Card stating that the claimant is under a Class 2 disability, as defined in Section 4A of The Illinois Identification Card Act [15 ILCS 335/4A], shall constitute proof that the person named thereon is a disabled person for purposes of this Act. A disabled person not covered under the Federal Social Security Act [42 U.S.C. § 301 et seq.] and not presenting a Disabled Person Identification Card stating that the claimant is under a Class 2 disability shall be examined by a physician designated by the Department, and his status as a disabled person determined using the same standards as used by the Social Security Administration. The costs of any required examination shall be borne by the claimant.
(Source: P.A. 83-1421.)

Note.
This section was Ill.Rev.Stat., Ch. 67 ½, para. 403.14.

Cross References.
As to a reduction in the amount of local services tax for owners of mobile homes who are encompassed by this Act, see 315 ILCS 515/7.

Illinois Administrative Code.
See 86 Illinois Administrative Code, §§ 530.105, 530.117.

320 ILCS 25/3.15 [Covered prescription drug defined]

Sec. 3.15. "Covered prescription drug" means (1) any cardiovascular agent or drug; (2) any insulin or other prescription drug used in the treatment of diabetes, including syringe and needles used to administer the insulin; (3) any prescription drug used in the treatment of arthritis, (4) beginning on January 1, 2001, any prescription drug used in the treatment of cancer, (5) beginning on January 1, 2001, any prescription drug used in the treatment of Alzheimer's disease, (6) beginning on January 1, 2001, any prescription drug used in the treatment of Parkinson's disease, (7) beginning on January 1, 2001, any prescription drug used in the treatment of glaucoma, (8) beginning on January 1, 2001, any prescription drug used in the treatment of lung disease and smoking related illnesses, (9) beginning on July 1, 2001, any prescription drug used in the treatment of osteoporosis, and (10) beginning on January 1, 2004, any prescription drug used in the treatment of multiple sclerosis. The specific agents or products to be included under such categories shall be listed in a handbook to be prepared and distributed by the Department. The general types of covered prescription drugs shall be indicated by rule.
(Source: P.A. 85-1176; 91-699, § 15; 92-10, § 35; 92-790, § 40; 93-528, § 5.)

Note.
This section was Ill.Rev.Stat., Ch. 67 ½, para. 403.15.

Effect of Amendments.

The 2000 amendment by P.A. 91-699, effective January 1, 2001, added items (4) through (8) and made a stylistic change in the first sentence and added the last sentence.

The 2001 amendment by P.A. 92-10, effective June 11, 2001, at the end of the first sentence, added "and (9) beginning on July 1, 2001, any prescription drug used in the treatment of osteoporosis", and made a stylistic change.

The 2002 amendment by P.A. 92-790, effective August 6, 2002, deleted the last sentence which read, "The Department of Public Health shall promulgate a list of covered prescription drugs under this program that meet the definition of a narrow therapeutic index drug as described in subsection (f) of Section 4."

The 2003 amendment by P.A. 93-528, effective January 1, 2004, inserted "and (10) beginning on January 1, 2004, any prescription drug used in the treatment of multiple sclerosis"; and made a related change.

320 ILCS 25/3.16 [Reasonable cost defined]

Sec. 3.16. "Reasonable cost" means Average Wholesale Price (AWP) minus 10% for products provided by authorized pharmacies plus a professional dispensing fee determined by the Department in accordance with its findings in a survey of professional pharmacy dispensing fees conducted at least every 12 months. For the purpose of this Act, AWP shall be determined from the latest publication of the Blue Book, a universally subscribed pharmacist reference guide annually published by the Hearst Corporation. AWP may also be derived electronically from the drug pricing database synonymous with the latest publication of the Blue Book and furnished in the National Drug Data File (NDDF) by First Data Bank (FDB), a service of the Hearst Corporation. The elements of such fees and methodology of such survey shall be promulgated as an administrative rule. Effective July 1, 1986, the professional dispensing fee shall be $3.60 per prescription and such amount shall be adjusted on July 1st of each year thereafter in accordance with a survey of professional pharmacy dispensing fees. The Department may establish maximum acquisition costs from time to time based upon information as to the cost at which covered products may be readily acquired by authorized pharmacies. In no case shall the reasonable cost of any given pharmacy exceed the price normally charged to the general public by that pharmacy. In the event that generic equivalents for covered prescription drugs are available at lower cost, the Department shall establish the maximum acquisition costs for such covered prescription drugs at the lower generic cost unless, pursuant to the conditions described in subsection (f) of Section 4 [320 ILCS 25/4], a non-generic drug may be substituted.

Effective July 1, 2002, the rates paid for products provided by authorized pharmacies and a professional dispensing fee shall be determined by the Department by rule.

(Source: P.A. 87-114; 88-676, § 20; 91-699, § 15; 92-597, § 85.)

Note.

This section was Ill.Rev.Stat., Ch. 67 ½, para. 403.16.

Illinois Administrative Code.

See 86 Illinois Administrative Code, § 530.125.

Effect of Amendments.

The 1994 amendment by P.A. 88-676, effective December 14, 1994, in the first sentence, substituted "Average Wholesale Price (AWP) minus 10% for" for "the actual acquisition cost of"; and added the second and third sentences.

The 2000 amendment by P.A. 91-699, effective January 1, 2001, added "unless, pursuant to the conditions described in subsection (f) of Section 4, a non-generic drug may be substituted" to the end of the section.

The 2002 amendment by P.A. 92-597, effective June 28, 2002, added the second paragraph.

320 ILCS 25/3.17 [Authorized pharmacy defined]

Sec. 3.17. "Authorized pharmacy" means any pharmacy registered in this State under the Pharmacy Practice Act of 1987 [225 ILCS 85/1 et seq.].

(Source: P.A. 85-1209.)

Note.

This section was Ill.Rev.Stat., Ch. 67 ½, para. 403.17.

320 ILCS 25/4 Amount of Grant

Sec. 4. *Amount of Grant.* (a) In general. Any individual 65 years or older or any individual who will become 65 years old during the calendar year in which a claim is filed, and any surviving spouse of such a claimant, who at the time of death received or was entitled to receive a grant pursuant to this Section, which surviving spouse will become 65 years of age within the 24 months immediately following the death of such claimant and which surviving spouse but for his or her age is otherwise qualified to receive a grant pursuant to this Section, and any disabled person whose annual household income is less than $14,000 for grant years before the 1998 grant year, less than $16,000 for the 1998 and 1999 grant years, and less than (i) $21,218 for a household containing one person, (ii) $28,480 for a household containing 2 persons, or (iii) $35,740 for a household containing 3 or more persons for the 2000 grant year and thereafter and whose household is liable for payment of property taxes accrued or has paid rent constituting property taxes accrued and is domiciled in this State at the time he or she files his or her claim is entitled to claim a grant under this Act. With respect to claims filed by individuals who will become 65 years old during the calendar year in which a claim is filed, the amount of any grant to which that household is entitled shall be an amount equal to 1/12 of the amount to which the claimant would otherwise be entitled as provided in this Section, multiplied by the number of months in which the claimant was 65 in the calendar year in which the claim is filed.

(b) Limitation. Except as otherwise provided in subsections (a) and (f) of this Section, the maximum amount of grant which a claimant is entitled to claim is the amount by which the property taxes accrued which were paid or payable during the last preceding tax year or rent constituting property taxes accrued upon the claimant's residence for the last preceding taxable year exceeds 3 ½% of the claimant's household income for that year but in no event is the grant to exceed (i) $700 less 4.5% of household income for that year for those with a household income of $14,000 or less or (ii) $70 if household income for that year is more than $14,000.

(c) Public aid recipients. If household income in one or more months during a year includes cash assistance in excess of $55 per month from the Department of Public Aid or the Department of Human Services (acting as successor to the Department of Public Aid under the Department of Human Services Act [20 ILCS 1305/1-1 et seq.]) which was determined under regulations of that Department on a measure of need that included an allowance for actual rent or property taxes paid by the recipient of that assistance, the amount of grant to which that household is entitled, except as otherwise provided in subsection (a), shall be the product of (1) the maximum amount computed as specified in subsection (b) of this Section and (2) the ratio of the number of months in which household income did not include such cash assistance over $55 to the number twelve. If household income did not include such cash assistance over $55 for any months during the year, the amount of the grant to which the household is entitled shall be the maximum amount computed as specified in subsection (b) of this Section. For purposes of this paragraph (c), "cash assistance" does not include any amount received under the federal Supplemental Security Income (SSI) program.

(d) Joint ownership. If title to the residence is held jointly by the claimant with a person who is not a member of his or her household, the amount of property taxes accrued used in computing the amount of grant to which he or she is entitled shall be the same percentage of property taxes accrued as is the percentage of ownership held by the claimant in the residence.

(e) More than one residence. If a claimant has occupied more than one residence in the taxable year, he or she may claim only one residence for any part of a month. In the case of property taxes accrued, he or she shall prorate 1/12 of the total property taxes accrued on his or her residence to each month that he or she owned and occupied that residence; and, in the case of rent constituting property taxes accrued, shall prorate each month's rent payments to the residence actually occupied during that month.

(f) There is hereby established a program of pharmaceutical assistance to the aged and disabled which shall be administered by the Department in accordance with this Act, to consist of payments to authorized pharmacies, on behalf of beneficiaries of the program, for the reasonable costs of covered prescription drugs. Each beneficiary who pays $5 for an identification card shall pay no additional prescription costs. Each beneficiary who pays $25 for an identification card shall pay $3 per prescription. In addition, after a beneficiary receives $2,000 in benefits during a State fiscal year, that beneficiary shall also be charged 20% of the cost of each prescription for which payments are made by the program during the remainder of the fiscal year. To become a beneficiary under this program a person must: (1) be (i) 65 years of age or older, or (ii) the surviving spouse of such a claimant, who at the time of death received or was entitled to receive benefits pursuant to this subsection, which surviving spouse will become 65 years of age within the 24 months immediately following the death of such claimant and which surviving spouse but for his or her age is otherwise qualified to receive benefits pursuant to this subsection, or (iii) disabled, and (2) be domiciled in this State at the time he or she files his or her claim, and (3) have a maximum household income of less than $14,000 for grant years before the 1998 grant year, less than $16,000 for the 1998 and 1999 grant years, and less than (i) $21,218 for a household containing one person, (ii) $28,480 for a household containing 2 persons, or (iii) $35,740 for a household containing 3 more persons for the 2000 grant year and thereafter. In addition, each eligible person must (1) obtain an identification card from the Department, (2) at the time the card is obtained, sign a statement assigning to the State of Illinois benefits which may be otherwise claimed under any private insurance plans, and (3) present the identification card to the dispensing pharmacist.

The Department may adopt rules specifying participation requirements for the pharmaceutical assistance program, including copayment amounts, identification card fees, expenditure limits, and the benefit threshold after which a 20% charge is imposed on the cost of each prescription, to be in effect on and after July 1, 2004. Notwithstanding any other provision of this paragraph, however, the Department may not increase the identification card fee above the amount in effect on May 1, 2003 without the express consent of the General Assembly. To the extent practicable, those requirements shall be commensurate with the requirements provided in rules adopted by the Department of Public Aid to implement the pharmacy assistance program under Section 5-5.12a of the Illinois Public Aid Code [305 ILCS 5/5-5.12a].

Whenever a generic equivalent for a covered prescription drug is available, the Department shall reimburse only for the reasonable costs of the generic equivalent, less the co-pay established in this Section, unless (i) the covered prescription drug contains one or more ingredients defined as a narrow therapeutic index drug at 21 CFR 320.33, (ii) the prescriber indicates on the face of the prescription "brand medically necessary", and (iii) the prescriber specifies that a substitution is not permitted. When issuing an oral prescription for covered prescription medication described in item (i) of this paragraph, the prescriber shall stipulate "brand medically necessary" and that a substitution is not permitted. If the covered prescription drug and its authorizing prescription do not meet the criteria listed above, the beneficiary may purchase the non-generic equivalent of the covered prescription drug by paying the difference between the generic cost and the non-generic cost plus the beneficiary co-pay.

Any person otherwise eligible for pharmaceutical assistance under this Act whose covered drugs are covered by any public program for assistance in purchasing any covered prescription drugs shall be ineligible for assistance under this Act to the extent such costs are covered by such other plan.

The fee to be charged by the Department for the identification card shall be equal to $5 per coverage year for persons below the official poverty line as defined by the United States Department of Health and Human Services and $25 per coverage year for all other persons.

In the event that 2 or more persons are eligible for any benefit under this Act, and are members of the same household, (1) each such person shall be entitled to participate in the pharmaceutical assistance program, provided that he or she meets all other requirements imposed by this subsection and (2) each participating household member contributes the fee required for that person by the preceding paragraph for the purpose of obtaining an identification card.

(Source: P.A. 86-143; 87-14; 87-860; 87-868; 88-45, § 2-48; 89-507, § 90L-71; 90-650, § 5; 91-357, § 181; 91-699, § 15; 92-131, § 5; 92-519, § 5; 92-651, § 65; 93-130, § 5.)

Note.

This section was Ill.Rev.Stat., Ch. 67 ½, para. 404.

P.A. 91-357, § 996 contains a "no acceleration or delay" provision, and P.A. 91-357, § 997 contains a "no revival or extension" provision.

Section 997 of P.A. 92-651 is a no acceleration or delay provision, and Section 998 is a no revival or extension provision.

Illinois Administrative Code.

See 89 Illinois Administrative Code, §§ 240.815, 112.110, 114.210, 86 Illinois Administrative Code, §§ 530.115, 530.116, 530.135, 530.116.

Effect of Amendments.

The 1996 amendment by P.A. 89-507, effective July 1, 1997, in subsection (c), in the first sentence, inserted "or the Department of Human Services (acting as successor to the Department of Public Aid under the Department of Human Services Act)".

The 1998 amendment by 90-650, effective July 27, 1998, inserted "for grant years before the 1998 grant year and less than $16,000 for the 1998 grant year and thereafter" in the first sentence of subsection (a) and at the end of the fifth sentence of the first paragraph of subsection (f); and, in subsection (b), added the "(i)" designation, added "for those with a household income of $14,000 or less or" in present item (i), and added item (ii).

The 1999 amendment by P.A. 91-357, effective July 29, 1999 substituted "subsection (f)" for "subsection (g)" in the last sentence of the last paragraph.

The 2000 amendment by P.A. 91-699, effective January 1, 2001, substituted "and 1999 grant years, and less than (i) $21,218 for a household containing one person, (ii) $28,480 for a household containing 2 persons, or (iii) $35,740 for a household containing 3 or more persons for the 2000 grant" for "1998 grant" in subsections (a) and (f); deleted "but less than $16,000" from the end of subsection (b); and in subsection (f): substituted "$5" for "$40" and "$25" for "$80" near the beginning of the first paragraph and in the fourth paragraph, in the first paragraph, in the second sentence substituted "no additional prescription costs" for "the first $15 of prescription costs each month", in the third sentence substituted "$3 per prescription" for "the first $25 of prescription costs each month", and in the fourth sentence substituted "$2,000" for "$800", inserted the second paragraph, deleted the last sentence from the end of the last paragraph providing for an exclusion from the benefit for persons who become 65 years old in the calendar year they turn 65, and made stylistic changes.

The 2001 amendment by P.A. 92-131 effective July 23, 2001 in subsection (f) paragraph four inserted "per coverage year" in two places.

The 2001 amendment by P.A. 92-519, effective January 1, 2002, inserted "per coverage year" twice in the fourth paragraph of subsection (f).

The 2002 amendment by P.A. 92-651, effective July 11, 2002, combined the amendments by P.A. 92-131 and P.A. 92-519; and made spelling corrections, gender-neutralization and stylistic changes.

The 2003 amendment by P.A. 93-130, effective July 10, 2003, inserted the second paragraph in subsection (f).

CASE NOTES

Retroactivity

Amendment to this Act which was not made retroactive could not be retroactively applied. Lyons v. Department of Revenue, 116 Ill. App. 3d 1072, 72 Ill. Dec. 577, 452 N.E.2d 830 (1 Dist. 1983).

320 ILCS 25/4.1 Information to the Department

Sec. 4.1. *Information to the Department.* Notwithstanding any other law to the contrary, entities subject to the Illinois Insurance Code, Comprehensive Health Insurance Plan Act, Dental Service Plan Act, Children's Health Insurance Program Act, Health Care Purchasing Group Act, Health Maintenance Organization Act, Limited Health Service Organization Act, Voluntary Health Services Plans Act, and the Workers' Compensation Act [215 ILCS 5/1 et seq., 215 ILCS 105/1 et seq., 215 ILCS 110/1 et seq., 215 ILCS 106/1 et seq., 215 ILCS 123/1 et seq., 215 ILCS 125/1-1 et seq., 215 ILCS 130/1001 et seq., 215 ILCS 165/1 et seq., and the 820 ILCS 305/1 et seq.], including, but not limited to, insurers, health maintenance organizations, pharmacy benefit managers, third party administrators, fraternal benefit societies, group-funded workers' compensation pools, municipal group-funded pools, self-funded or self-insured welfare or benefit plans or programs, and any other entities that provide health coverage through an employer, union, trade association or other organization or source, or any other entities, must provide information to the Department, or its designee, that is necessary to carry out the purposes of this Act, including, but not limited to, the name, social security number, address, date of birth, and coverage of their policyholders, their subscribers, or the beneficiaries of their plans, benefits, or services who participate in the programs under this Act. The provision of this information to the Department or

its designee is subject to the confidentiality provisions in Section 8a of this Act [320 ILCS 25/8a].
(Source: P.A. 92-131, § 5; 92-519, § 5.)

Note.
Identical versions of this section were enacted by P.A. 92-131 and P.A. 92-519.

Illinois Administrative Code.
See 86 Illinois Administrative Code, § 530.155.

Effective Date.
Section 99 of P.A. 92-131 made this section effective upon becoming law. The Act was approved July 23, 2001.
Section 99 of P.A. 92-519 made this section effective upon becoming law. The Act was approved January 1, 2002.

320 ILCS 25/5 Procedure

Sec. 5. *Procedure.* (a) In general. Claims must be filed after January 1, on forms prescribed by the Department. No claim may be filed more than one year after December 31 of the year for which the claim is filed except that claims for 1976 may be filed until December 31, 1978. The pharmaceutical assistance identification card provided for in subsection (f) of Section 4 shall be valid for a period not to exceed one year. On and after January 1, 2002, however, to enable the Department to convert coverage for a pharmaceutical assistance program participant to a State fiscal year basis, a card shall be valid for a longer or shorter period than 12 months, depending on the date a timely claim is filed and as determined by the Department. All applicants for benefits under this program approved for benefits on or after July 1 but on or before December 31 of any State fiscal year are eligible for benefits through June 30 of that State fiscal year. All applicants for benefits under this program approved for benefits on or after January 1 but on or before June 30 of any State fiscal year are eligible for benefits through June 30 of the following State fiscal year.

(b) Claim is Personal. The right to file a claim under this Act shall be personal to the claimant and shall not survive his death, but such right may be exercised on behalf of a claimant by his legal guardian or attorney-in-fact. If a claimant dies after having filed a timely claim, the amount thereof shall be disbursed to his surviving spouse or, if no spouse survives, to his surviving dependent minor children in equal parts, provided the spouse or child, as the case may be, resided with the claimant at the time he filed his claim. If at the time of disbursement neither the claimant nor his spouse is surviving, and no dependent minor children of the claimant are surviving the amount of the claim shall escheat to the State.

(c) One claim per household. Only one member of a household may file a claim under this Act in any calendar year; where both members of a household are otherwise entitled to claim a grant under this Act, they must agree as to which of them will file a claim for that year.

(d) Content of application form. The form prescribed by the Department for purposes of paragraph (a) shall include a table, appropriately keyed to the parts of the form on which the claimant is required to furnish information, which will enable the claimant to determine readily the approximate amount of grant to which he is entitled by relating levels of household income to property taxes accrued or rent constituting property taxes accrued.

(e) Pharmaceutical Assistance Procedures. The Department shall establish the form and manner for application, and establish by January 1, 1986 a procedure to enable persons to apply for the additional grant or for the pharmaceutical assistance identification card on the same application form. The Department shall determine eligibility for pharmaceutical assistance using the applicant's current income. The Department shall determine a person's current income in the manner provided by the Department by rule.
(Source: P.A. 83-1531; 91-533, § 50; 91-699, § 15; 92-131, § 5; 92-519, § 5.)

Note.
This section was Ill.Rev.Stat., Ch. 67 ½, para. 405.
P.A. 91-533 § 990 contains a "no acceleration or delay" provision, and P.A. 91-533 § 995 contains a "no revival or extension" provision.

Illinois Administrative Code.
See 86 Illinois Administrative Code, §§ 530.117, 530.120, 530.120.

Effect of Amendments.
The 1999 amendment by P.A. 91-533, effective August 13, 1999, substituted "subsection (f)" for "subsection (g)" in the last sentence of subsection (a).
The 2000 amendment by P.A. 91-699, effective January 1, 2001, added the last sentence in subsection (e).
The 2001 amendment by P.A. 92-131, effective July 23, 2001 added the last sentence to subsection (a).
The 2001 amendment by P.A. 92-519, effective January 1, 2002, added the last three sentences of subsection (a).
Although the amendments to this section by P.A. 92-131, § 5 and P.A. 92-519, § 5 did not take into account the amendments made by the other, the amendments have been combined into a single version by the publisher.

OPINIONS OF ATTORNEY GENERAL

Replacement Warrant
The State Comptroller may issue a replacement warrant to heirs or legatees who have executed a small estate affidavit and requested a replacement for a warrant issued pursuant to the Senior Citizens and Disabled Persons Property Tax Relief and Pharmaceutical Assistance Act (320 ILCS 25/1 et seq.). 1979 Op. Atty. Gen. 16.

320 ILCS 25/5.1 [Eligibility to receive grant]

Sec. 5.1. Eligibility to receive a grant pursuant to this Act shall not be affected by participation in the "Senior Citizens Real Estate Tax Act" veto overridden November 2, 1983 [320 ILCS 30/1 et seq.].
(Source: P.A. 84-1308.)

Note.
This section was Ill.Rev.Stat., Ch. 67 ½, para. 405.1.

320 ILCS 25/6 Administration

Sec. 6. *Administration.* (a) In general. Upon receipt of a timely filed claim, the Department shall determine whether the claimant is a person entitled to a grant under this Act and the amount of grant to which he is entitled under this Act. The Department may require the claimant to furnish reasonable proof of the statements of domicile, household income, rent paid, property taxes accrued and other matters on which entitlement is based, and may withhold payment of a grant until such additional proof is furnished.

(b) Rental determination. If the Department finds that the gross rent used in the computation by a claimant of rent constituting property taxes accrued exceeds the fair rental value for the right to occupy that residence, the Department may determine the fair rental value for that residence and recompute rent constituting property taxes accrued accordingly.

(c) Fraudulent claims. The Department shall deny claims which have been fraudulently prepared or when it finds that the claimant has acquired title to his residence or has paid rent for his residence primarily for the purpose of receiving a grant under this Act.

(d) Pharmaceutical Assistance. The Department shall allow all pharmacies licensed under the Pharmacy Practice Act of 1987 [225 ILCS 85/1 et seq.] to participate as authorized pharmacies unless they have been removed from that status for cause pursuant to the terms of this Section. The Director of the Department may enter into a written contract with any State agency, instrumentality or political subdivision, or a fiscal intermediary for the purpose of making payments to authorized pharmacies for covered prescription drugs and coordinating the program of pharmaceutical assistance established by this Act with other programs that provide payment for covered prescription drugs. Such agreement shall establish procedures for properly contracting for pharmacy services, validating reimbursement claims, validating compliance of dispensing pharmacists with the contracts for participation required under this Section, validating the reasonable costs of covered prescription drugs, and otherwise providing for the effective administration of this Act.

The Department shall promulgate rules and regulations to implement and administer the program of pharmaceutical assistance required by this Act, which shall include the following:

(1) Execution of contracts with pharmacies to dispense covered prescription drugs. Such contracts shall stipulate terms and conditions for authorized pharmacies participation and the rights of the State to terminate such participation for breach of such contract or for violation of this Act or related rules and regulations of the Department;

(2) Establishment of maximum limits on the size of prescriptions, new or refilled, which shall be in amounts sufficient for 34 days, except as otherwise specified by rule for medical or utilization control reasons;

(3) Establishment of liens upon any and all causes of action which accrue to a beneficiary as a result of injuries for which covered prescription drugs are directly or indirectly required and for which the Director made payment or became liable for under this Act;

(4) Charge or collection of payments from third parties or private plans of assistance, or from other programs of public assistance for any claim that is properly chargeable under the assignment of benefits executed by beneficiaries as a requirement of eligibility for the pharmaceutical assistance identification card under this Act;

(4.5) Provision for automatic enrollment of beneficiaries into a Medicare Discount Card program authorized under the federal Medicare Modernization Act of 2003 (P.L. 108-391) to coordinate coverage including Medicare Transitional Assistance;

(5) Inspection of appropriate records and audit of participating authorized pharmacies to ensure contract compliance, and to determine any fraudulent transactions or practices under this Act;

(6) Annual determination of the reasonable costs of covered prescription drugs for which payments are made under this Act, as provided in Section 3.16 [305 ILCS 25/3.16];

(7) Payment to pharmacies under this Act in accordance with the State Prompt Payment Act [30 ILCS 540/0.01 et seq.].

The Department shall annually report to the Governor and the General Assembly by March 1st of each year on the administration of pharmaceutical assistance under this Act. By the effective date of this Act the Department shall determine the reasonable costs of covered prescription drugs in accordance with Section 3.16 of this Act [305 ILCS 25/3.16].

(Source: P.A. 85-797; 91-357, § 181; 92-651, § 65; 93-841, § 35.)

Note.

This section was Ill.Rev.Stat., Ch. 67 ½, para. 406.

P.A. 91-357, § 996 contains a "no acceleration or delay" provision, and P.A. 91-357, § 997 contains a "no revival or extension" provision.

Section 997 of P.A. 92-651 is a no acceleration or delay provision, and Section 998 is a no revival or extension provision.

Illinois Administrative Code.

See 86 Illinois Administrative Code, §§ 530.130, 530.140, 530.145, 530.155, 530.160, 530.155.

Effect of Amendments.

The 1999 amendment by P.A. 91-357, effective July 29, 1999, substituted "the State Prompt Payment Act" for "'An Act to require prompt payments by the State of Illinois for goods and services' approved December 19, 1975 in subsection (d)(7); and substituted "Section 3.16" for "Section 3-16" in the last sentence of the last paragraph.

The 2002 amendment by P.A. 92-651, effective July 11, 2002, inserted "of 1987" in the first sentence of the first paragraph of subsection (d).

The 2004 amendment by P.A. 93-841, effective July 30, 2004, inserted subsection (d)(4.5).

CASE NOTES

Class Action

Department of Revenue had no legal authority to certify a plaintiff class in administrative proceedings to settle dispute over tax relief grants, and the trial court acted properly in dismissing the class action aspects of plaintiffs' complaint. Lyons v. Department of Revenue, 116 Ill. App. 3d 1072, 72 Ill. Dec. 577, 452 N.E.2d 830 (1 Dist. 1983).

LEGAL PERIODICALS

For note, "Judicial Review of Welfare Policy Under the Illinois Administrative Review Act," see 1986 U. Ill. L. Rev. 199.

320 ILCS 25/7 Payment and denial of claims

Sec. 7. *Payment and denial of claims.* (a) In general. The Director shall order the payment from appropriations made for that purpose of grants to claimants under this Act in the amounts to which the Department has determined they are entitled, respectively. If a claim is denied, the Director shall cause written notice of that denial and the reasons for that denial to be sent to the claimant.

(b) Payment of claims one dollar and under. Where the amount of the grant computed under Section 4 [320 ILCS 25/4] is less than one dollar, the Department shall pay to the claimant one dollar.

(c) Right to appeal. Any claimant aggrieved by the action of the Department under this Act, whether in the reduction of the amount of the grant claimed or in the denial of the claim, may request in writing that the Department reconsider its prior determination, setting out the facts on which his request is based. The Department shall consider the request and either modify or affirm its prior determination.

(d) Administrative review. The decision of the Department to affirm its prior determination, or the failure of the Department to act on a request for reconsideration within 60 days, is a final administrative decision which is subject to judicial review under the Administrative Review Law [735 ILCS 5/3-101 et seq.], and all amendments and modifications thereof and the rules adopted thereto. The term "administrative decision" is defined as in Section 3-101 of the Code of Civil Procedure [735 ILCS 5/3-101].

(Source: P.A. 82-783.)

Note.

This section was Ill.Rev.Stat., Ch. 67 ½, para. 407.

Illinois Administrative Code.

See 86 Illinois Administrative Code, § 530.117.

320 ILCS 25/7.1: Repealed effective July 1, 1998.

Note.

This section was repealed by its own terms.

320 ILCS 25/8 Records

Sec. 8. *Records.* Every claimant of a grant under this Act shall keep such records, render such statements, file such forms and comply with such rules and regulations as the Department may from time to time prescribe. The Department may by regulations require landlords to furnish to tenants statements as to gross rent or rent constituting property taxes accrued.

(Source: P.A. 77-2059.)

Note.

This section was Ill.Rev.Stat., Ch. 67 ½, para. 408.

320 ILCS 25/8a Confidentiality

Sec. 8a. *Confidentiality.* (a) Except as otherwise provided in this Act all information received by the Department from claims filed under this Act, or from any investigation conducted under the provisions of this Act, shall be confidential, except for official purposes within the Department or pursuant to official procedures for collection of any State tax or enforcement of any civil or criminal penalty or sanction imposed by this Act or by any statute imposing a State tax, and any person who divulges any such information in any manner, except for such purposes and pursuant to order of the Director or in accordance with a proper judicial order, shall be guilty of a Class A misdemeanor.

(b) Nothing contained in this Act shall prevent the Director from publishing or making available reasonable statistics concerning the operation of the grant programs contained in this Act wherein the contents of claims are grouped into aggregates in such a way that information contained in any individual claim shall not be disclosed.

(c) The Department shall furnish to the Secretary of State such information as is reasonably necessary for the administration of reduced vehicle registration fees pursuant to Section 3-806.3 of "The Illinois Vehicle Code" [625 ILCS 5/3-806.3].

(Source: P.A. 83-1457; 89-399, § 30.)

Note.

This section was Ill.Rev.Stat., Ch. 67 ½, para. 408.1.

Effect of Amendments.

The 1995 amendment by P.A. 89-399, effective August 20, 1995, added the section catchline; and in subsection (a) deleted the subsection catchline of "Confidentiality", inserted "otherwise" and substituted "Act" for "Section".

320 ILCS 25/9 [Fraud; penalties; barring of convicted person from program; recovery; time of prosecution]

Sec. 9. Any person who files a fraudulent claim for a grant under this Act, or who for compensation prepares a claim for a grant and knowingly enters false information on a claim form for any claimant under this Act, or who fraudulently files multiple claim forms, or who fraudulently states that a

nondisabled person is disabled, or who fraudulently procures a pharmaceutical assistance identification card, or who fraudulently uses such card to procure covered prescription drugs, or who, on behalf of an authorized pharmacy, files a fraudulent claim for payment, is guilty of a Class 4 felony for the first offense and is guilty of a Class 3 felony for each subsequent offense. The Department shall immediately suspend the use of the pharmaceutical assistance identification card of any person suspected of fraudulent procurement or fraudulent use of such card, and shall revoke such card upon a conviction. A person convicted of such fraud shall be permanently barred from the program of pharmaceutical assistance established under this Act. The Department may recover from a claimant, including an authorized pharmacy, any amount paid under this Act on account of an erroneous or fraudulent claim, together with 6% interest per year. A prosecution for a violation of this Section may be commenced at any time within 3 years of the commission of that violation.
(Source: P.A. 85-299.)

Note.
This section was Ill.Rev.Stat., Ch. 67 ½, para. 409.

Illinois Administrative Code.
See 86 Illinois Administrative Code, § 530.165.

320 ILCS 25/9.1: Repealed by P.A. 92-84, § 75, effective July 1, 2002.

320 ILCS 25/10 Arrangements and Captions

Sec. 10. *Arrangements and Captions.* No inference, implication, or presumption of legislative construction shall be drawn or made by reason of the location or grouping of any particular section or provision of this Act, nor shall any caption be given any legal effect.
(Source: P.A. 77-2059.)

Note.
This section was Ill.Rev.Stat., Ch. 67 ½, para. 410.

320 ILCS 25/11 Severability

Sec. 11. *Severability.* If any clause, sentence, section, provision or part of this Act or the application thereof to any person or circumstance shall be adjudged to be unconstitutional, the remainder of this Act or its application to persons or circumstances other than those to which it is held invalid, shall not be affected thereby.
(Source: P.A. 77-2059.)

Note.
This section was Ill.Rev.Stat., Ch. 67 ½, para. 411.

320 ILCS 25/12 Regulations — Department on Aging

Sec. 12. *Regulations — Department on Aging.* (a) The Director shall promulgate such regulations as are necessary or desirable to effectuate the purposes of this Act, including but not limited to the method of computing "gross rent" in the case of a claimant living in a nursing or sheltered care home.

(b) The Department on Aging shall, to the extent of appropriations made for that purpose:

(1) attempt to secure the cooperation of appropriate federal, State and local agencies in securing the names and addresses of persons to whom this Act pertains;

(2) prepare a mailing list of persons eligible for grants under this Act;

(3) secure the cooperation of the Department of Revenue and of local business establishments to facilitate distribution of application forms under this Act to those eligible to file claims; and

(4) through use of direct mail, newspaper advertisements and radio and television advertisements, and all other appropriate means of communication, conduct an on-going public relations program to increase awareness of eligible citizens of the grants under this Act and the procedures for applying for them.
(Source: P.A. 78-1249.)

Note.
This section was Ill.Rev.Stat., Ch. 67 ½, para. 412.

320 ILCS 25/13 [List of qualified persons; confidentiality; penalty for divulgence or misuse]

Sec. 13. The Department of Revenue shall maintain a list of all persons who have qualified under this Act and shall make the list available to municipalities upon request.

All information received by a municipality under this Section shall be confidential, except for official purposes, and any person who divulges or uses that information in any manner, except in accordance with a proper judicial order, shall be guilty of a Class B misdemeanor.
(Source: P.A. 87-247.)

Note.
This section was Ill.Rev.Stat., Ch. 67 ½, para. 413.

SENIOR CITIZENS REAL ESTATE TAX DEFERRAL ACT

320 ILCS 30/1 [Short title]

Sec. 1. This Act shall be known and may be cited as the "Senior Citizens Real Estate Tax Deferral Act".
(Source: P.A. 83-895.)

Derivation.
Title: An Act in relation to the deferral of payment of real estate taxes by persons 65 years of age and over.
Cite: 320 ILCS 30/1 et seq.
Source: P.A. 83-895.
Date: Veto overridden November 2, 1983.

Note.
This section was Ill.Rev.Stat., Ch. 67 ½, para. 451.

320 ILCS 30/2 Definitions

Sec. 2. *Definitions.* As used in this Act:

(a) "Taxpayer" means an individual whose household income for the year is no greater than $40,000.

(b) "Tax deferred property" means the property upon which real estate taxes are deferred under this Act.

(c) "Homestead" means the land and buildings thereon, including a condominium or a dwelling unit in a multidwelling building that is owned and operated as a cooperative, occupied by the taxpayer as his residence or which are temporarily unoccupied by the taxpayer because such taxpayer is temporarily residing, for not more than 1 year, in a licensed facility as defined in Section 1-113 of the Nursing Home Care Act [210 ILCS 45/1-113].

(d) "Real estate taxes" or "taxes" means the taxes on real property for which the taxpayer would be liable under the Property Tax Code [35 ILCS 200/1-1 et seq.], including special service area taxes, and special assessments on benefited real property for which the taxpayer would be liable to a unit of local government.

(e) "Department" means the Department of Revenue.

(f) "Qualifying property" means a homestead which (a) the taxpayer or the taxpayer and his spouse own in fee simple or are purchasing in fee simple under a recorded instrument of sale, (b) is not income-producing property, (c) is not subject to a lien for unpaid real estate taxes when a claim under this Act is filed.

(g) "Equity interest" means the current assessed valuation of the qualified property times the fraction necessary to convert that figure to full market value minus any outstanding debts or liens on that property. In the case of qualifying property not having a separate assessed valuation, the appraised value as determined by a qualified real estate appraiser shall be used instead of the current assessed valuation.

(h) "Household income" has the meaning ascribed to that term in the Senior Citizens and Disabled Persons Property Tax Relief and Pharmaceutical Assistance Act [320 ILCS 25/1 et seq.].

(i) "Collector" means the county collector or, if the taxes to be deferred are special assessments, an official designated by a unit of local government to collect special assessments.

(Source: P.A. 86-147; 88-268, § 1; 88-509, § 5; 88-670, § 2-52; 92-639, § 5.)

Note.
This section was Ill.Rev.Stat., Ch. 67 ½, para. 452.

Effect of Amendments.
The 1994 amendment by P.A. 88-670, effective December 2, 1994, combined the amendments by P.A. 88-268 and P.A. 88-509; and in subsection (d) substituted "Property Tax Code" for "Revenue Act of 1939".

The 2002 amendment by P.A. 92-639, effective January 1, 2003, substituted "$40,000" for "$25,000" in subsection (a).

320 ILCS 30/3 [Application for deferral; tax deferral and recovery agreement]

Sec. 3. A taxpayer may, on or before March 1 of each year, apply to the county collector of the county where his qualifying property is located, or to the official designated by a unit of local government to collect special assessments on the qualifying property, as the case may be, for a deferral of all or a part of real estate taxes payable during that year for the preceding year in the case of real estate taxes other than special assessments, or for a deferral of any installments payable during that year in the case of special assessments, on all or part of his qualifying property. The application shall be on a form prescribed by the Department and furnished by the collector, (a) showing that the applicant will be 65 years of age or older by June 1 of the year for which a tax deferral is claimed, (b) describing the property and verifying that the property is qualifying property as defined in Section 2 [320 ILCS 30/2], (c) certifying that the taxpayer has owned and occupied as his residence such property or other qualifying property in the State for at least the last 3 years except for any periods during which the taxpayer may have temporarily resided in a nursing or sheltered care home, and (d) specifying whether the deferral is for all or a part of the taxes, and, if for a part, the amount of deferral applied for. As to qualifying property not having a separate assessed valuation, the taxpayer shall also file with the county collector a written appraisal of the property prepared by a qualified real estate appraiser together with a certificate signed by the appraiser stating that he has personally examined the property and setting forth the value of the land and the value of the buildings thereon occupied by the taxpayer as his residence.

The collector shall grant the tax deferral provided such deferral does not exceed funds available in the Senior Citizens Real Estate Deferred Tax Revolving Fund and provided that the owner or owners of such real property have entered into a tax deferral and recovery agreement with the collector on behalf of the county or other unit of local government, which agreement expressly states:

(1) That the total amount of taxes deferred under this Act, plus interest, for the year for which a tax deferral is claimed as well as for those previous years for which taxes are not delinquent and for which such deferral has been claimed may not exceed 80% of the taxpayer's equity interest in the property for which taxes are to be deferred and that, if the total deferred taxes plus interest equals 80% of the taxpayer's equity interest in the property, the taxpayer shall thereafter pay the annual interest due on such deferred taxes plus interest so that total deferred taxes plus interest will not exceed such 80% of the taxpayer's equity interest in the property.

(2) That any real estate taxes deferred under this Act and any interest accrued thereon at the rate of 6% per year are a lien on the real estate and improvements thereon until paid. No sale or transfer of such real property may be legally closed and recorded until the taxes which would otherwise have been due on the property, plus accrued interest, have been paid unless the collector certifies in writing that an arrangement for prompt payment of the amount due has been made with his office. The same shall apply if the property is to be made the subject of a contract of sale.

(3) That upon the death of the taxpayer claiming the deferral the heirs-at-law, assignees or legatees shall have first priority to the real property upon which taxes have been deferred by paying in full the total taxes which would otherwise have been due, plus interest. However, if such heir-at-law, assignee, or legatee is a surviving spouse, the tax deferred status of the property shall be continued during the life of that surviving spouse if the spouse is 55 years of age or older within 6 months of the date of death of the taxpayer and enters into a tax deferral and recovery agreement before the time when deferred taxes become due under this Section. Any additional taxes deferred, plus interest, on the real property under a tax deferral and recovery agreement signed by a surviving spouse shall be added to the taxes and interest which would otherwise have been due, and the payment of which has been postponed during the life of such surviving spouse, in determining the 80% equity requirement provided by this Section.

(4) That if the taxes due, plus interest, are not paid by the heir-at-law, assignee or legatee or if payment is not postponed during the life of a surviving spouse, the deferred taxes and interest shall be recovered from the estate of the taxpayer within one year of the date of his death. In addition, deferred real estate taxes and any interest accrued thereon are due within 90 days after any tax deferred property ceases to be qualifying property as defined in Section 2 [320 ILCS 30/2].

If payment is not made when required by this Section, foreclosure proceedings may be instituted under the Property Tax Code [35 ILCS 200/1-1 et seq.].

(5) That any joint owner has given written prior approval for such agreement, which written approval shall be made a part of such agreement.

(6) That a guardian for a person under legal disability appointed for a taxpayer who otherwise qualifies under this Act may act for the taxpayer in complying with this Act.

(7) That a taxpayer or his agent has provided to the satisfaction of the collector, sufficient evidence that the qualifying property on which the taxes are to be deferred is insured against fire or casualty loss for at least the total amount of taxes which have been deferred.

If the taxes to be deferred are special assessments, the unit of local government making the assessments shall forward a copy of the agreement entered into pursuant to this Section and the bills for such assessments to the county collector of the county in which the qualifying property is located.

(Source: P.A. 86-147; 88-670, § 3-72; 90-170, § 5; 91-357, § 182.)

Note.

This section was Ill.Rev.Stat., Ch. 67 ½, para. 453.

P.A. 91-357, § 996 contains a "no acceleration or delay" provision, and P.A. 91-357, § 997 contains a "no revival or extension" provision.

Cross References.

As to participation in this Act affecting the eligibility to receive a grant pursuant to the Senior Citizens and Disabled Persons Property Tax Relief and Pharmaceutical Assistance Act, see 320 ILCS 25/5.1.

Effect of Amendments.

The 1994 amendment by P.A. 88-670, effective December 2, 1994, in the second paragraph of subsection (4) substituted "Property Tax Code" for "Revenue Act of 1939".

The 1997 amendment by P.A. 90-170, effective July 23, 1997, in subsection (5) deleted "or mortgagee holding a mortgage on such property" preceding "has given written".

The 1999 amendment by P.A. 91-357, effective July 29, 1999, made two stylistic changes.

320 ILCS 30/4 [Recording of tax deferral and recovery agreement]

Sec. 4. In the case of each tax deferral and recovery agreement entered into between the collector and the owner or owners of qualifying property, the collector shall forthwith cause to be recorded with the recorder of the county in which the qualifying property is located a statement of their action which shall constitute a lien upon the real estate and improvements thereon covered by such agreement for such taxes as have been deferred under the provisions of this Act, plus accrued interest as provided for by Section 3 [320 ILCS 30/3]. In the case of a dwelling unit in a multidwelling building that is owned and operated as a cooperative, the lien shall be upon only that portion of the real estate that constitutes a homestead exemption occupied by the taxpayer. The statement shall name the owner or owners and shall include a description of the real estate adequate for identification. The filing fee for such statement shall be paid by the county or other unit of local government and shall be added to and become a part of the deferred taxes due.

(Source: P.A. 84-807; 88-268, § 1.)

Note.

This section was Ill.Rev.Stat., Ch. 67 ½, para. 454.

320 ILCS 30/5 [Payment of tax bills]

Sec. 5. The county collector shall note on his books each claim for deferral of real estate taxes which meets the requirements of Section 3 [320 ILCS 30/3] and, when taxes are extended, shall send to the Department the tax bills, including special assessment bills forwarded to the county collector under

Section 3 [320 ILCS 30/3], on all tax deferred property in that collector's county. The Department shall then pay by June 1 or within 30 days of the receipt of these tax bills, whichever is later, to the county collector, for distribution to the taxing bodies in his county, the total amount of taxes so deferred. The Department shall make these payments from the Senior Citizens Real Estate Deferred Tax Revolving Fund.
(Source: P.A. 84-807.)

Note.
This section was Ill.Rev.Stat., Ch. 67 ½, para. 455.

320 ILCS 30/6 [Payments by taxpayer]

Sec. 6. All or any part of taxes deferred under this Act and the accrued interest thereon, which are not due under a valid deferral and recovery agreement, may be paid to the collector at any time by the taxpayer or his spouse, or, if no objection is made by the taxpayer within 10 days after the collector mails him a written notice of the tender of such a payment, by a child, heir or next of kin of the taxpayer or other person claiming a legal or equitable interest in the property. In the absence of a valid agreement to the contrary and except as otherwise provided by law, such a payment by a person other than the taxpayer or his spouse confers no interest in the property nor claim against the estate. Payments made under this Section shall be applied first against accrued interest and any remainder against the deferred taxes and do not affect the deferred tax status of the property.
(Source: P.A. 84-807.)

Note.
This section was Ill.Rev.Stat., Ch. 67 ½, para. 456.

320 ILCS 30/7 [Collection of deferred taxes; foreclosure sales; remittance of funds received]

Sec. 7. When any deferred taxes, including interest, are collected, the moneys shall be credited to a special account in the treasury of the unit of local government and the collector shall notify the treasurer of the unit of local government of the properties for which the taxes were collected by setting forth a description of the property and the amount of taxes and interest collected for each property. The treasurer shall remit by the 10th day of each month the amount of deferred taxes and accrued interest paid during the preceding month, minus $50 or the total amount of deferred taxes and accrued interest collected, whichever is less, to the Department. The remittance shall be accompanied by a statement giving a description for each property for which the taxes were collected and setting out the amount of the taxes and interest collected for each property.

If the tax deferred property is sold by foreclosure under the Property Tax Code [35 ILCS 200/1-1 et seq.], the proceeds of the sale which may be applied under that Act to the payment of real estate taxes and interest shall be remitted by the county treasurer to the Department along with a description of the property and the amount of taxes and interest collected thereon.

When any deferred taxes and accrued interest are received by the Department, it shall enter the amounts received against the accounts which have been set up for the tax deferred properties and shall within 5 days remit such moneys to the State Treasurer for deposit in the Senior Citizens Real Estate Deferred Tax Revolving Fund.
(Source: P.A. 84-1308; 88-670, § 3-72.)

Note.
This section was Ill.Rev.Stat., Ch. 67 ½, para. 457.

Cross References.
As to appropriations from the Senior Citizens Real Estate Deferred Tax Revolving Fund, see 30 ILCS 105/6p-4.

Effect of Amendments.
The 1994 amendment by P.A. 88-670, effective December 2, 1994, in the second paragraph substituted "Property Tax Code" for "Revenue Act of 1939".

320 ILCS 30/8 [Instruments requiring payment of real estate taxes; eligibility for grants]

Sec. 8. Nothing in this Act (a) affects any provision of any mortgage or other instrument relating to land requiring a person to pay real estate taxes or (b) affects the eligibility of any person to receive any grant pursuant to the "Senior Citizens and Disabled Persons Property Tax Relief and Pharmaceutical Assistance Act" [320 ILCS 25/1 et seq.].
(Source: P.A. 84-807; 84-832.)

Note.
This section was Ill.Rev.Stat., Ch. 67 ½, para. 458.

Partnership for Long-Term Care Act

320 ILCS 35/1 Short title

Sec. 1. *Short title.* This Act may be cited as the Partnership for Long-Term Care Act.
(Source: P.A. 87-163.)

Derivation.
Title: An Act relating to long-term care.
Cite: 320 ILCS 35/1 et seq.
Source: P.A. 87-163.
Date: Approved August 22, 1991.

Note.
This section was Ill.Rev.Stat., Ch. 23, para. 6801-1.

320 ILCS 35/5 [Legislative findings and intent]

Sec. 5. The Legislature finds that chronic long-term care illnesses threaten the health and welfare of millions of families. Furthermore, most families have no private or public insurance to help pay the catastrophic expenses of an extended chronic episode requiring home, community, or institutional long-term care. The costs of care during an extended chronic illness are high and force tens of thousands of Illinoisans annually to spend-down their income and savings of a lifetime and become dependent upon public assistance programs.

The State cannot continue as the insurer of last resort for increasing numbers of middle-income Illinoisans while at the same time meeting its obligations to the poor who have no other means of caring for themselves.

The Legislature declares it is in the interest of the people of Illinois that individuals be encouraged to anticipate their potential long-term care needs by purchasing quality private long-term care insurance policies.

It is the intent of the Legislature that the State establish a private-public long-term care insurance partnership program in which individuals who purchase private long-term care insurance that meets State standards and who sustain extended episodes of chronic illnesses that exhaust all the benefits of their private insurance be eligible for continued care by in-home supportive services and by the Medicaid program on the basis of specific resource eligibility requirements.
(Source: P.A. 87-163; 89-525, § 10.)

Note.
This section was Ill.Rev.Stat., Ch. 23, para. 6801-5.

Effect of Amendments.
The 1996 amendment by P.A. 89-525, effective July 19, 1996, in the fourth paragraph deleted "demonstration pilot" preceding "program in which".

320 ILCS 35/10 Definitions

Sec. 10. *Definitions.* "Program" means the long-term care insurance partnership program established under this Act.
(Source: P.A. 87-163; 89-525, § 10.)

Note.
This section was Ill.Rev.Stat., Ch. 23, para. 6801-10.

Effect of Amendments.
The 1996 amendment by P.A. 89-525, effective July 19, 1996, deleted the definition of Department which read "means the Department on Aging"; deleted "Pilot" preceding "Program"; and substituted "program established under this Act" for "demonstration program".

320 ILCS 35/15 Program

Sec. 15. *Program.* (a) The Department on Aging, in cooperation with the Department of Insurance, and the Department of Public Aid, shall administer the program.

(b) The Departments shall seek any federal waivers and approvals necessary to accomplish the purposes of this Act.
(Source: P.A. 87-163; 88-328, § 5; 89-525, § 10.)

Note.
This section was Ill.Rev.Stat., Ch. 23, para. 6801-15.

Effect of Amendments.
The 1996 amendment by P.A. 89-525, effective July 19, 1996, in subsection (a) inserted "on Aging", inserted "Insurance, and the Department of" and substituted "the program" for "this pilot program"; and in subsection (b) substituted "Departments" for "Department".

320 ILCS 35/20 Program participant eligibility for Medicaid

Sec. 20. *Program participant eligibility for Medicaid.* (a) Individuals who participate in the program and have resources above the eligibility levels for receipt of medical assistance under Title XIX of the Social Security Act (Subchapter XIX (commencing with Section 1396) of Chapter 7 of Title 42 of the United States Code) shall be eligible to receive in-home supportive service benefits and Medicaid benefits through the Department of Public Aid if, before becoming eligible for benefits, they have purchased a long-term care insurance policy covering long-term care that has been certified by the Department of Insurance under Section 30 of this Act [320 ILCS 35/30].

(b) Individuals may purchase certified long-term care insurance policies which cover long-term care services in amounts equal to the resources they wish to protect.

(b-5) An individual may purchase a certified long-term care insurance policy which protects an individual's total assets. To be eligible for total asset protection, an amount equal to the average cost of 4 years of long-term care services in a nursing facility must be purchased.

(b-7) Although a resource has been protected by the Partnership Policy, income is to be applied to the cost of care when the insured becomes Medicaid eligible.

(c) The resource protection provided by this Act shall be effective only for long-term care policies which cover long-term care services, that are delivered, issued for delivery, or renewed on or after July 1, 1992.

(d) When an individual purchases a certified long-term care insurance policy, the issuer must notify the purchaser of the benefits of purchasing inflation protection for the long-term care insurance policy.

(e) An insurance company may offer for sale a policy as described in paragraph (b) of this Section or paragraph (b-5) of this Section or both types of policies.
(Source: P.A. 87-163; 89-507, § 90E-24; 89-525, § 10; 90-14, § 2-195.)

Note.
This section was Ill.Rev.Stat., Ch. 23, para. 6801-20.

Effect of Amendments.
The 1996 amendment by P.A. 89-507, effective July 1, 1997, in subsection (a) substituted "Human Services" for "Rehabilitation Services".

The 1996 amendment by P.A. 89-525, effective July 19, 1996, in the section catchline added "Program participant" at the beginning and added "for Medicaid" at the end; in subsection (a) deleted "pilot" preceding "program", deleted a comma after "Aid", deleted "or a health care service plan contract" preceding "covering long-term care" and substituted "of Insurance" for "or the Department of Rehabilitation Services"; in subsection (b) deleted "or health care service plan contracts" preceding "which cover" and deleted from the end "so long as the amount of insurance purchased exceeds the minimum level set by the program"; added subsections (b-5) and (b-7); in subsection (c) deleted "and health care service plan contracts" preceding "which cover long-term" and substituted "on or after July 1, 1992" for "between July 1, 1992, and June 30, 1997, inclusive, or before the termination of the pilot program, whichever is sooner"; and added subsections (d) and (e).

The 1997 amendment by P.A. 90-14, effective July 1, 1997, combined the amendments by P.A. 89-507 and P.A. 89-525.

320 ILCS 35/25 Protection of resources

Sec. 25. *Protection of resources.* (a) Notwithstanding any other provision of law, the resources, to the extent described in subsection (b), of an individual who (i) purchases a certified long-term care insurance policy which covers long-term care services and (ii) has received all the benefit payments that are payable under that policy or contract for items described in subsection (b) shall not be considered in determining:

(1) Medicaid eligibility.

(2) The amount of any Medicaid payment.

(3) The amount of any subsequent recovery by the State of payments made for medical services to the extent federal law permits.

(4) Eligibility for in-home supportive services.

(5) The amount of any payment for in-home supportive services.

(b) Benefit payments described in subsection (a) must be for one or more of the following:

(1) In-home supportive service benefits and Medicaid long-term care services specified in regulations by the Department of Public Aid.

(2) Long-term care services delivered to insured individuals in a community setting as part of an individual assessment and case management program provided by coordinating entities designated or approved by the Department on Aging.

(3) Services the insured individual received while meeting the disability criteria for eligibility for long-term care benefits established by the Departments.

(Source: P.A. 87-163; 89-525, § 10.)

Note.

This section was Ill.Rev.Stat., Ch. 23, para. 6801-25.

Illinois Administrative Code.

See 89 Illinois Administrative Code, § 240.815.

Effect of Amendments.

The 1996 amendment by P.A. 89-525, effective July 19, 1996, in the section catchline added "Protection of" at the beginning; in subsection (a), in the introductory language, inserted "(i)", deleted "or health care service plan contract" preceding "which covers" and inserted "and (ii) has received all the benefit payments that are payable under that policy or contract for items described in subsection (b)"; in subdivision (a)(3) added at the end "to the extent federal law permits"; and substituted the present language of subsection (b) for the former which read "The resources excluded from consideration by this Section shall be equal to, or in some proportion set by the Department that is less than equal to, the amount of long term care benefit payments made as described in Section 35 of this Act".

320 ILCS 35/30 Certification of policies and contracts

Sec. 30. *Certification of policies and contracts.* The Department of Insurance shall certify only long-term care insurance policies which cover long-term care that provide all of the following:

(1) Individual case management by a coordinating entity designated or approved by the Department on Aging.

(2) The levels and durations of benefits that meet minimum standards set by the Department of Insurance.

(3) A record keeping system including an explanation of benefit reports on insurance payments or benefits that count toward Medicaid resource exclusion.

(4) Approval of the insurance policy by the Department of Insurance.

(5) Compliance with any other requirements imposed by the Departments through regulations consistent with the purposes of this Act.

(Source: P.A. 87-163; 89-507, § 90E-24; 89-525, § 10; 90-14, § 2-195.)

Note.

This section was Ill.Rev.Stat., Ch. 23, para. 6801-30.

Effect of Amendments.

The 1996 amendment by P.A. 89-507, effective July 1, 1997, in subsection (e) substituted "Human Services" for "Rehabilitation Services".

The 1996 amendment by P.A. 89-525, effective July 19, 1996, added the section catchline; in the introductory language inserted "of Insurance", deleted "only" preceding "certify", inserted "only" and deleted "and health care service plan contracts" preceding "which cover"; redesignated subsections (a), (b) and (d) through (f) as subsections (1) through (5); in subsection (1) added "on Aging" at the end; in subsection (2) added "of Insurance" at the end; deleted former subsection (c) which read "Protection against loss of benefits due to inflation"; in subsection (4) deleted from the end "or approval of the health care service plan contract by the Department of Rehabilitation Services or the Department of Public Aid"; and in subsection (5) substituted "Departments" for "Department".

The 1997 amendment by P.A. 90-14, effective July 1, 1997, combined the amendments by P.A. 89-507 and P.A. 89-525.

320 ILCS 35/35: Repealed by P.A. 89-525, § 90, effective July 19, 1996.

320 ILCS 35/40 Program

Sec. 40. *Program.* (a) The program shall be designed so that the estimated aggregate State expenditures for long-term care services for individuals participating in the program do not exceed the aggregate expenditures that would be made for these services under the Medicaid program in effect prior to the implementation of the program.

(b) The Department of Insurance shall provide advice and counseling through a Health Insurance

Counseling and Advocacy Program to individuals interested in purchasing long-term care insurance that cover long-term care services certified under this Act.

(c) Insurers shall make available to the insureds the opportunity to purchase any traditional long-term care policy offered by the insurer which has benefits comparable to the benefits provided by a certified long-term care insurance policy provided for under this amendatory Act of 1996. The insurer shall make these policies available without requiring evidence of insurability in the event of the termination of the program.

(Source: P.A. 87-163; 89-525, § 10.)

Note.

This section was Ill.Rev.Stat., Ch. 23, para. 6801-40.

Effect of Amendments.

The 1996 amendment by P.A. 89-525, effective July 19, 1996, in the section catchline deleted "Pilot" preceding "Program"; in subsection (a) deleted "pilot" preceding "program shall" and substituted at the end "the program" for "this pilot program"; in subsection (b) inserted "of Insurance" and deleted "or health care service plan contracts" preceding "that cover"; and substituted the present language of subsection (c) for "Upon the termination of the pilot program, individuals who participated in the pilot program shall remain eligible for in home supportive service benefits and medicaid benefits provided by the pilot program for the life of the purchaser, as long as the insurance policy or health care service plan contract remains in force".

320 ILCS 35/45 Agency powers; regulations

Sec. 45. *Agency powers; regulations.* (a) The Departments shall adopt regulations to implement this Act, including, but not limited to the following:

(1) The population and age groups that are eligible to participate in the program.

(2) The minimum level of long-term care insurance that must be purchased to meet the requirement of subsection (b) of Section 20 of this Act [320 ILCS 35/20].

(3) The amount and types of services that a long-term care insurance policy that includes long-term care services must cover to meet the requirements of Section 30 of this Act [320 ILCS 35/30].

(4) Which coordinating entities are designated or approved to deliver individual assessment and case management services to individuals in a community setting as required by subdivision (b)(2) of Section 25 of this Act [320 ILCS 35/25].

(5) The disability criteria for eligibility for long-term care benefits as required by subdivision (b)(3) of Section 25 of this Act [320 ILCS 35/25].

(6) The specific eligibility requirements for receipt of the Medicaid benefits provided for by the program, and the Medicaid benefits for which participants in the program shall be eligible.

(b) The Departments shall also adopt regulations to implement this Act, including, but not limited to, regulations which establish the following:

(1) The specific eligibility requirements for in-home supportive service benefits.

(2) Those in-home supportive service benefits for which participants in the programs shall be eligible.

(c) (Blank).

(Source: P.A. 87-163; 89-525, § 10.)

Note.

This section was Ill.Rev.Stat., Ch. 23, para. 6801-45.

Effect of Amendments.

The 1996 amendment by P.A. 89-525, effective July 19, 1996, in the section catchline added "Agency" at the beginning and added "regulations" at the end; in subsection (a), in the introductory language, substituted "Departments" for "State Department on Aging"; in subdivision (a)(1) deleted "pilot" preceding "program"; in subdivision (a)(2) deleted "or long term care coverage included in health care service plan contracts"; in subdivision (c)(3) deleted "or health care service plan contract" preceding "that includes"; in subdivision (c)(4) substituted "subdivision (b)(2) of Section 25" for "subsection (b) of Section 35"; in subdivision (a)(5) substituted "subdivision (b)(3) of Section 25" for "subsection (c) of Section 35"; in subsection (b), in the introductory language, substituted "Departments" for "Department"; in subdivision (b)(2) deleted "pilot" preceding "programs"; and deleted subsection (c) regarding adoption of regulations.

320 ILCS 35/50 Task force

Sec. 50. *Task force.* (a) An executive and legislative advisory task force shall be created to provide advice and assistance in designing and implementing the Partnership for Long-term Care Program. The task force shall be composed of representatives, designated by the director of each of the following agencies or departments:

(1) The Department on Aging.

(2) The Department of Public Aid.

(3) (Blank).

(4) The Department of Insurance.

(5) The Department of Commerce and Community Affairs.

(6) The Legislative Research Unit.

(b) The task force shall consult with persons knowledgeable of and concerned with long-term care, including, but not limited to the following:

(1) Consumers.

(2) Health care providers.

(3) Representatives of long-term care insurance companies and administrators of health care service plans that cover long-term care services.

(4) Providers of long-term care.

(5) Private employers.

(6) Academic specialists in long-term care and aging.

(7) Representatives of the public employees' and teachers' retirement systems.

(c) The task force shall be established, and its members designated, not later than March 1, 1993. The task force shall make recommendations to the Department on Aging concerning the policy components of the program on or before September 1, 1993.

(Source: P.A. 87-163; 88-328, § 5; 89-507, § 90E-24; 89-525, § 10; 90-14, § 2-195.)

Note.

This section was Ill.Rev.Stat., Ch. 23, para. 6801-50.

Effect of Amendments.

The 1996 amendment by P.A. 89-507, effective July 1, 1997, in subsection (a), in the second sentence, inserted "(or Secretary)"; and in subdivision (a)(3) substituted "Human Services" for "Rehabilitation Services".

The 1996 amendment by P.A. 89-525, effective July 19, 1996, in subsection (a), in the introductory language, in the first sentence, deleted "Pilot" preceding "Program"; in subdivision (a)(1) added at the end "on Aging"; deleted subdivision (a)(3) which read "The Department of Rehabilitation Services"; and in subsection (c), in the second sentence, inserted "on Aging".

The 1997 amendment by P.A. 90-14, effective July 1, 1997, combined the amendments by P.A. 89-507 and P.A. 89-525; in the introductory language of the second sentence of subsection (a) deleted "(or Secretary)" preceding "of each of"; and deleted subdivision (a)(3) which read "Human".

320 ILCS 35/55 Director of Aging

Sec. 55. *Director of Aging.* The Director of Aging shall annually report to the General Assembly regarding the progress of the pilot program established under Public Act 87-163 and the permanent program established under this amendatory Act of 1996. The report regarding the pilot program shall be provided by January 1 of each year, commencing with 1993 and ending with 1996. The report regarding the permanent program shall be provided by January 1 of each year, commencing with 1997. The report shall include the following:

(a) The success in implementing the public and private partnership.

(b) The number and type of insurers and health care service plans with policies or contracts certified by the Departments.

(c) The number, age, and financial circumstances of participants in the pilot or permanent program who have purchased certified long-term care insurance policies which cover long-term care services.

(d) The number of individuals seeking consumer information services and advice from the Department on Aging under subsection (b) of Section 40 of this Act [320 ILCS 35/40].

(e) The number of participants actually receiving long-term care services, Medicaid benefits, and in-home supportive services provided by the program, and the type of benefits paid under certified policies which cover long-term care that could count toward Medicaid resource protection.

(f) Estimates of the impact on present and future Medicaid expenditures.

(g) The cost effectiveness of the program.

(h) A recommendation regarding the continuation of the program.

The Director of Aging shall report the following information to the General Assembly on or before March 31, 1998:

(1) For each department or agency set forth in subsection (a) of Section 50 [320 ILCS 35/50], the costs of implementing the program and the savings generated by the program.

(2) The details of the program proposed by the Department on Aging and Department of Insurance.

(3) The nature of any federal waivers or approvals sought by the Department on Aging, including any changes in the Medicaid State Plan proposed to the federal Health Care Finance Administration.

(Source: P.A. 87-163; 88-328, § 5; 89-525, § 10.)

Note.

This section was Ill.Rev.Stat., Ch. 23, para. 6801-55.

Effect of Amendments.

The 1996 amendment by P.A. 89-525, effective July 19, 1996, in the introductory paragraph, in the first sentence, added at the end "established under Public Act 87-163 and the permanent program established under this amendatory Act of 1996", in the second sentence, inserted "regarding the pilot program" and added at the end "and ending with 1996" and added the third sentence; in subsection (b) substituted "Departments" for "Department"; in subsection (c) inserted "or permanent" and deleted "and health care service loan contracts" preceding "which cover"; in subsection (d) inserted "on Aging"; in subsection (e) deleted "and health care service plan contracts" preceding "which cover"; in the second paragraph, in the introductory language, substituted "1998" for "1994"; in subsection (1) inserted "subsection (a) of" and substituted "50" for "50(a)"; in subsection (2) added at the end "on Aging and Department of Insurance"; and in subsection (3) inserted "on Aging".

320 ILCS 35/60 Administrative costs

Sec. 60. *Administrative costs.* (a) The Department on Aging, in conjunction with the Department of Public Aid, the Department of Insurance, and the Department of Commerce and Community Affairs, shall submit applications for State or federal grants or federal waivers, or funding from nationally distributed private foundation grants, or insurance reimbursements to be used to pay the administrative expenses of implementation of the program. The Department on Aging, in conjunction with those other departments, also shall seek moneys from these same sources for the purpose of implementing the program, including moneys appropriated for that purpose.

(b) In implementing this Act, the Department on Aging may negotiate contracts, on a nonbid basis, with long-term care insurers, health care insurers, health care service plans, or both, for the provision of coverage for long-term care services that will meet the certification requirements set forth in Section 30 and the other requirements of this Act.

(Source: P.A. 87-163; 88-328, § 5; 89-507, § 90E-24; 89-525, § 10; 90-14, § 2-195.)

Note.

This section was Ill.Rev.Stat., Ch. 23, para. 6801-60.

Effect of Amendments.

The 1996 amendment by P.A. 89-507, effective July 1, 1997, redesignated the former first paragraph as present subsection (a); in present subsection (a), in the first sentence, substituted "Human Services" for "Rehabilitation Services"; and redesignated former subsection (a) as present subsection (b).

The 1996 amendment by P.A. 89-525, effective July 19, 1996, in the first paragraph, in the first sentence, inserted "on Aging", deleted "the Department of Rehabilitation Services" and substituted "the program" for "this pilot program" and in the second sentence, inserted "on Aging"; and in subsection (a) inserted "on Aging".

The 1997 amendment by P.A. 90-14, effective July 1, 1997, combined the amendments by P.A. 89-507 and P.A. 89-525.

All-Inclusive Care for the Elderly Act

320 ILCS 40/1 Short title

Sec. 1. *Short title.* This Act may be cited as the All-Inclusive Care for the Elderly Act.
(Source: P.A. 87-411.)

Derivation.

Title: An Act concerning a program of all-inclusive care for the elderly.

Cite: 320 ILCS 40/1 et seq.

Source: P.A. 87-411.

Date: Approved September 10, 1991.

Note.

This section was Ill.Rev.Stat., Ch. 23, para. 6901.

320 ILCS 40/5 Legislative declaration

Sec. 5. *Legislative declaration.* The General Assembly finds and declares that it is the intent of this Act to replicate the ONLOK program in San Francisco, California, that has proven to be cost-effective at both the state and federal levels. The PACE program is part of a national replication project authorized in Section 9412(b)(2) of the federal Omnibus Reconciliation Act of 1986 [42 U.S.C. § 2601 et seq.], which instructs the Secretary of the federal Department of Health and Human Services to grant Medicare and Medicaid waivers to permit not more than 10 public or nonprofit private community-based organizations in the country to provide comprehensive health care services on a capitated basis to frail elderly who are at risk of institutionalization. The General Assembly finds that by coordinating an extensive array of medical and nonmedical services, the needs of the participants will be met primarily in an outpatient environment in an adult day health center, in their homes, or in an institutional setting. The General Assembly finds that such a service delivery system will enhance the quality of life for the participant and offers the potential to reduce and cap costs to Illinois of the medical needs of the participants, including hospital and nursing home admissions.

The General Assembly declares that the purpose of this Act is to provide services that would foster the following goals:

To maintain eligible persons at home as an alternative to long-term institutionalization;

To provide optimum accessibility to various important social and health resources that are available to assist eligible persons in maintaining independent living;

To provide that eligible persons who are frail elderly but who have the capacity to remain in an independent living situation have access to the appropriate social and health services without which independent living would not be possible;

To coordinate, integrate, and link these social and health services by removing obstacles that impede or limit improvements in delivery of these services;

To provide the most efficient and effective use of capitated funds for the delivery of these social and health services;

To assure that capitation payments amount to no more than 95% of the amount paid under the Medicaid fee-for-service structure of an actuarially similar population.
(Source: P.A. 87-411.)

Note.

This section was Ill.Rev.Stat., Ch. 23, para. 6905.

320 ILCS 40/10 Service for eligible persons

Sec. 10. *Service for eligible persons.* Within the context of the PACE program established under this Act, the Illinois Department of Public Aid may include any or all of the services in Article 5 of the Illinois Public Aid Code [305 ILCS 5/5-1 et seq.].

An eligible person may elect to receive services from the PACE program. If such an election is made, the eligible person shall not remain eligible for payment through the regular Medicare or Medicaid program. All services and programs provided through the PACE program shall be provided in accordance with this Act. An eligible person may elect to disenroll from the PACE program at any time.

For purposes of this Act, "eligible person" means a frail elderly individual who voluntarily enrolls in the PACE program, whose income and resources do not exceed limits established by the Illinois Department of Public Aid and for whom a licensed physician certifies that such a program provides an appropriate alternative to institutionalized care. The term "frail elderly" means an individual who meets functional eligibility requirements, as established by the Illinois Department of Public Aid and the Department on Aging for nursing home care, and who is 65 years of age or older.
(Source: P.A. 87-411.)

Note.

This section was Ill.Rev.Stat., Ch. 23, para. 6910.

320 ILCS 40/15 Program implementation

Sec. 15. *Program implementation.* (a) Upon receipt of federal waivers, the Illinois Department of Public Aid shall implement the PACE program as a demonstration program to provide the services set forth in Section 10 [320 ILCS 40/10] to eligible persons, as defined in Section 10 [320 ILCS 40/10], for a period of 3 years. After the 3 year demonstration, the General Assembly shall reexamine the PACE program and determine if the program should be implemented on a permanent basis.

(b) Using a risk-based financing model, the nonprofit organization providing the PACE program

shall assume responsibility for all costs generated by the PACE program participants, and it shall create and maintain a risk reserve fund that will cover any cost overages for any participant. The PACE program is responsible for the entire range of services in the consolidated service model, including hospital and nursing home care, according to participant need as determined by a multidisciplinary team. The nonprofit organization providing the PACE program is responsible for the full financial risk at the conclusion of the demonstration period and when permanent waivers from the federal Health Care Financing Administration are granted. Specific arrangements of the risk-based financing model shall be adopted and negotiated by the federal Health Care Financing Administration, the nonprofit organization providing the PACE program, and the Illinois Department.
(Source: P.A. 87-411.)

Note.
This section was Ill.Rev.Stat., Ch. 23, para. 6915.

320 ILCS 40/20 Duties of the Illinois Department

Sec. 20. *Duties of the Illinois Department.* (a) The Illinois Department shall provide a system for reimbursement for services to the PACE program.

(b) The Illinois Department shall develop and implement a contract with the nonprofit organization providing the PACE program that sets forth contractual obligations for the PACE program, including but not limited to reporting and monitoring of utilization of costs of the program as required by the Illinois Department.

(c) The Illinois Department shall acknowledge that it is participating in the national PACE project as initiated by Congress.

(d) The Illinois Department or its designee shall be responsible for certifying the eligibility for services of all PACE program participants.
(Source: P.A. 87-411.)

Note.
This section was Ill.Rev.Stat., Ch. 23, para. 6920.

320 ILCS 40/25 Rules and regulations

Sec. 25. *Rules and regulations.* The Illinois Department shall promulgate rules and regulations necessary to implement this Act.
(Source: P.A. 87-411.)

Note.
This section was Ill.Rev.Stat., Ch. 23, para. 6925.

320 ILCS 40/30 Rate of payment

Sec. 30. *Rate of payment.* The General Assembly shall make appropriations to the Illinois Department of Public Aid to fund services under this Act provided at a monthly capitated rate. The Illinois Department shall annually renegotiate a monthly capitated rate for the contracted services based on the 95% of the Medicaid fee-for-service costs of an actuarially similar population.
(Source: P.A. 87-411.)

Note.
This section was Ill.Rev.Stat., Ch. 23, para. 6930.

OLDER ADULT SERVICES ACT

320 ILCS 42/1 Short title

Sec. 1. *Short title.* This Act may be cited as the Older Adult Services Act.
(Source: P.A. 93-1031, § 1.)

Effective Date.
Section 99 of P.A. 93-1031 made this Act effective upon becoming law. The Act was approved August 27, 2004.

320 ILCS 42/5 Purpose

Sec. 5. *Purpose.* The purpose of this Act is to promote a transformation of Illinois' comprehensive system of older adult services from funding a primarily facility-based service delivery system to primarily a home-based and community-based system, taking into account the continuing need for 24-hour skilled nursing care and congregate housing with services. Such restructuring shall encompass the provision of housing, health, financial, and supportive older adult services. It is envisioned that this restructuring will promote the development, availability, and accessibility of a comprehensive, affordable, and sustainable service delivery system that places a high priority on home-based and community-based services. Such restructuring will encompass all aspects of the delivery system regardless of the setting in which the service is provided.
(Source: P.A. 93-1031, § 5.)

320 ILCS 42/10 Definitions

Sec. 10. *Definitions.* In this Act:

"Advisory Committee" means the Older Adult Services Advisory Committee.

"Certified nursing home" means any nursing home licensed under the Nursing Home Care Act [210 ILCS 45/1-101 et seq.] and certified under Title XIX of the Social Security Act [42 U.S.C. § 1396 et seq.] to participate as a vendor in the medical assistance program under Article V of the Illinois Public Aid Code [305 ILCS 5/5-1 et seq.].

"Comprehensive case management" means the assessment of needs and preferences of an older adult at the direction of the older adult or the older adult's designated representative and the arrangement, coordination, and monitoring of an optimum package of services to meet the needs of the older adult.

"Consumer-directed" means decisions made by an informed older adult from available services and care options, which may range from independently making all decisions and managing services directly to limited participation in decision-making, based upon the functional and cognitive level of the older adult.

"Coordinated point of entry" means an integrated access point where consumers receive information and assistance, assessment of needs, care planning, referral, assistance in completing applications, authorization of services where permitted, and follow-up to ensure that referrals and services are accessed.

"Department" means the Department on Aging, in collaboration with the departments of Public Health and Public Aid and other relevant agencies and in consultation with the Advisory Committee, except as otherwise provided.

"Departments" means the Department on Aging, the departments of Public Health and Public Aid, and other relevant agencies in collaboration with each other and in consultation with the Advisory Committee, except as otherwise provided.

"Family caregiver" means an adult family member or another individual who is an uncompensated provider of home-based or community-based care to an older adult.

"Health services" means activities that promote, maintain, improve, or restore mental or physical health or that are palliative in nature.

"Older adult" means a person age 60 or older and, if appropriate, the person's family caregiver.

"Person-centered" means a process that builds upon an older adult's strengths and capacities to engage in activities that promote community life and that reflect the older adult's preferences, choices, and abilities, to the extent practicable.

"Priority service area" means an area identified by the Departments as being less-served with respect to the availability of and access to older adult services in Illinois. The Departments shall determine by rule the criteria and standards used to designate such areas.

"Priority service plan" means the plan developed pursuant to Section 25 of this Act [320 ILCS 42/25].

"Provider" means any supplier of services under this Act.

"Residential setting" means the place where an older adult lives.

"Restructuring" means the transformation of Illinois' comprehensive system of older adult services from funding primarily a facility-based service delivery system to primarily a home-based and community-based system, taking into account the continuing need for 24-hour skilled nursing care and congregate housing with services.

"Services" means the range of housing, health, financial, and supportive services, other than acute health care services, that are delivered to an older adult with functional or cognitive limitations, or socialization needs, who requires assistance to perform activities of daily living, regardless of the residential setting in which the services are delivered.

"Supportive services" means non-medical assistance given over a period of time to an older adult that is needed to compensate for the older adult's functional or cognitive limitations, or socialization needs, or those services designed to restore, improve, or maintain the older adult's functional or cognitive abilities.

(Source: P.A. 93-1031, § 10.)

320 ILCS 42/15 Designation of lead agency; annual report

Sec. 15. *Designation of lead agency; annual report.* (a) The Department on Aging shall be the lead agency for: the provision of services to older adults and their family caregivers; restructuring Illinois' service delivery system for older adults; and implementation of this Act, except where otherwise provided. The Department on Aging shall collaborate with the departments of Public Health and Public Aid and any other relevant agencies, and shall consult with the Advisory Committee, in all aspects of these duties, except as otherwise provided in this Act.

(b) The Departments shall promulgate rules to implement this Act pursuant to the Illinois Administrative Procedure Act [5 ILCS 100/1-1 et seq.].

(c) On January 1, 2006, and each January 1 thereafter, the Department shall issue a report to the General Assembly on progress made in complying with this Act, impediments thereto, recommendations of the Advisory Committee, and any recommendations for legislative changes necessary to implement this Act. To the extent practicable, all reports required by this Act shall be consolidated into a single report.

(Source: P.A. 93-1031, § 15.)

320 ILCS 42/20 Priority service areas; service expansion

Sec. 20. *Priority service areas; service expansion.* (a) The requirements of this Section are subject to the availability of funding.

(b) The Department shall expand older adult services that promote independence and permit older adults to remain in their own homes and communities. Priority shall be given to both the expansion of services and the development of new services in priority service areas.

(c) Inventory of services. The Department shall develop and maintain an inventory and assessment of (i) the types and quantities of public older adult services and, to the extent possible, privately provided older adult services, including the unduplicated count, location, and characteristics of individuals served by each facility, program, or service and (ii) the resources supporting those services.

(d) Priority service areas. The Departments shall assess the current and projected need for older adult services throughout the State, analyze the results of the inventory, and identify priority service areas, which shall serve as the basis for a priority service plan to be filed with the Governor and the General Assembly no later than July 1, 2006, and every 5 years thereafter.

(e) Moneys appropriated by the General Assembly for the purpose of this Section, receipts from donations, grants, fees, or taxes that may accrue from any public or private sources to the Department for the purpose of this Section, and savings attributable to the nursing home conversion program as calculated in subsection (h) shall be deposited into the Department on Aging State Projects Fund. Interest earned by those moneys in the Fund shall be credited to the Fund.

(f) Moneys described in subsection (e) from the Department on Aging State Projects Fund shall be used for older adult services, regardless of where the older adult receives the service, with priority given to both the expansion of services and the development of new services in priority service areas. Fundable services shall include:

(1) Housing, health services, and supportive services:

(A) adult day care;

(B) adult day care for persons with Alzheimer's disease and related disorders;

(C) activities of daily living;

(D) care-related supplies and equipment;

(E) case management;

(F) community reintegration;

(G) companion;

(H) congregate meals;

(I) counseling and education;

(J) elder abuse prevention and intervention;

(K) emergency response and monitoring;

(L) environmental modifications;

(M) family caregiver support;

(N) financial;

(O) home delivered meals;

(P) homemaker;

(Q) home health;

(R) hospice;

(S) laundry;

(T) long-term care ombudsman;

(U) medication reminders;

(V) money management;

(W) nutrition services;

(X) personal care;

(Y) respite care;

(Z) residential care;

(AA) senior benefits outreach;

(BB) senior centers;

(CC) services provided under the Assisted Living and Shared Housing Act, or sheltered care services that meet the requirements of the Assisted Living and Shared Housing Act, or services provided under Section 5-5.01a of the Illinois Public Aid Code (the Supportive Living Facilities Pilot Program);

(DD) telemedicine devices to monitor recipients in their own homes as an alternative to hospital care, nursing home care, or home visits;

(EE) training for direct family caregivers;

(FF) transition;

(GG) transportation;

(HH) wellness and fitness programs; and

(II) other programs designed to assist older adults in Illinois to remain independent and receive services in the most integrated residential setting possible for that person.

(2) Older Adult Services Demonstration Grants, pursuant to subsection (g) of this Section.

(g) Older Adult Services Demonstration Grants. The Department shall establish a program of demonstration grants to assist in the restructuring of the delivery system for older adult services and provide funding for innovative service delivery models and system change and integration initiatives. The Department shall prescribe, by rule, the grant application process. At a minimum, every application must include:

(1) The type of grant sought;

(2) A description of the project;

(3) The objective of the project;

(4) The likelihood of the project meeting identified needs;

(5) The plan for financing, administration, and evaluation of the project;

(6) The timetable for implementation;

(7) The roles and capabilities of responsible individuals and organizations;

(8) Documentation of collaboration with other service providers, local community government leaders, and other stakeholders, other providers, and any other stakeholders in the community;

(9) Documentation of community support for the project, including support by other service providers, local community government leaders, and other stakeholders;

(10) The total budget for the project;

(11) The financial condition of the applicant; and

(12) Any other application requirements that may be established by the Department by rule.

Each project may include provisions for a designated staff person who is responsible for the development of the project and recruitment of providers.

Projects may include, but are not limited to: adult family foster care; family adult day care; assisted living in a supervised apartment; personal services in a subsidized housing project; evening and weekend home care coverage; small incentive grants to attract new providers; money following the person; cash and counseling; managed long-term care; and at least one respite care project that establishes a local coordinated network of volunteer and paid respite workers, coordinates assignment of respite workers to caregivers and older adults, ensures the health and safety of the older adult, provides training for caregivers, and ensures that support groups are available in the community.

A demonstration project funded in whole or in part by an Older Adult Services Demonstration Grant is exempt from the requirements of the Illinois Health Facilities Planning Act [20 ILCS 3960/1 et seq.]. To the extent applicable, however, for the purpose of maintaining the statewide inventory authorized by the Illinois Health Facilities Planning Act [20 ILCS 3960/1 et seq.], the Department shall send to the Health Facilities Planning Board a copy of each grant award made under this subsection (g).

The Department, in collaboration with the Departments of Public Health and Public Aid, shall evaluate the effectiveness of the projects receiving grants under this Section.

(h) No later than July 1 of each year, the Department of Public Health shall provide information to the Department of Public Aid to enable the Department of Public Aid to annually document and verify the savings attributable to the nursing home conversion program for the previous fiscal year to estimate an annual amount of such savings that may be appropriated to the Department on Aging State Projects Fund and notify the General Assembly, the Department on Aging, the Department of Human Services, and the Advisory Committee of the savings no later than October 1 of the same fiscal year.
(Source: P.A. 93-1031, § 20; 93-1031, § 25.)

320 ILCS 42/25 Older adult services restructuring

Sec. 25. *Older adult services restructuring.* No later than January 1, 2005, the Department shall commence the process of restructuring the older adult services delivery system. Priority shall be given to both the expansion of services and the development of new services in priority service areas. Subject to the availability of funding, the restructuring shall include, but not be limited to, the following:

(1) Planning. The Department shall develop a plan to restructure the State's service delivery system for older adults. The plan shall include a schedule for the implementation of the initiatives outlined in this Act and all other initiatives identified by the participating agencies to fulfill the purposes of this Act. Financing for older adult services shall be based on the principle that "money follows the individual". The plan shall also identify potential impediments to delivery system restructuring and include any known regulatory or statutory barriers.

(2) Comprehensive case management. The Department shall implement a statewide system of holistic comprehensive case management. The system shall include the identification and implementation of a universal, comprehensive assessment tool to be used statewide to determine the level of functional, cognitive, socialization, and financial needs of older adults. This tool shall be supported by an electronic intake, assessment, and care planning system linked to a central location. "Comprehensive case management" includes services and coordination such as (i) comprehensive assessment of the older adult (including the physical, functional, cognitive, psycho-social, and social needs of the individual); (ii) development and implementation of a service plan with the older adult to mobilize the formal and family resources and services identified in the assessment to meet the needs of the older adult, including coordination of the resources and services with any other plans that exist for various formal services, such as hospital discharge plans, and with the information and assistance services; (iii) coordination and monitoring of formal and family service delivery, including coordination and monitoring to ensure that services specified in the plan are being provided; (iv) periodic reassessment and revision of the status of the older adult with the older adult or, if necessary, the older adult's designated representative; and (v) in accordance with the wishes of the older adult, advocacy on behalf of the older adult for needed services or resources.

(3) Coordinated point of entry. The Department shall implement and publicize a statewide coordinated point of entry using a uniform name, identity, logo, and toll-free number.

(4) Public web site. The Department shall develop a public web site that provides links to available services, resources, and reference materials concerning caregiving, diseases, and best practices for use by professionals, older adults, and family caregivers.

(5) Expansion of older adult services. The Department shall expand older adult services that promote independence and permit older adults to remain in their own homes and communities.

(6) Consumer-directed home and community-based services. The Department shall expand the range of service options available to permit older adults to exercise maximum choice and control over their care.

(7) Comprehensive delivery system. The Department shall expand opportunities for older adults to receive services in systems that integrate acute and chronic care.

(8) Enhanced transition and follow-up services. The Department shall implement a program of transition from one residential setting to another and follow-up services, regardless of residential setting, pursuant to rules with respect to (i) resident eligibility, (ii) assessment of the resident's health, cognitive, social, and financial needs, (iii) development of transition plans, and (iv) the level of services that must be available before transitioning a resident from one setting to another.

(9) Family caregiver support. The Department shall develop strategies for public and private financing of services that supplement and support family caregivers.

(10) Quality standards and quality improvement. The Department shall establish a core set of uniform

quality standards for all providers that focus on outcomes and take into consideration consumer choice and satisfaction, and the Department shall require each provider to implement a continuous quality improvement process to address consumer issues. The continuous quality improvement process must benchmark performance, be person-centered and data-driven, and focus on consumer satisfaction.

(11) Workforce. The Department shall develop strategies to attract and retain a qualified and stable worker pool, provide living wages and benefits, and create a work environment that is conducive to long-term employment and career development. Resources such as grants, education, and promotion of career opportunities may be used.

(12) Coordination of services. The Department shall identify methods to better coordinate service networks to maximize resources and minimize duplication of services and ease of application.

(13) Barriers to services. The Department shall identify barriers to the provision, availability, and accessibility of services and shall implement a plan to address those barriers. The plan shall: (i) identify barriers, including but not limited to, statutory and regulatory complexity, reimbursement issues, payment issues, and labor force issues; (ii) recommend changes to State or federal laws or administrative rules or regulations; (iii) recommend application for federal waivers to improve efficiency and reduce cost and paperwork; (iv) develop innovative service delivery models; and (v) recommend application for federal or private service grants.

(14) Reimbursement and funding. The Department shall investigate and evaluate costs and payments by defining costs to implement a uniform, audited provider cost reporting system to be considered by all Departments in establishing payments. To the extent possible, multiple cost reporting mandates shall not be imposed.

(15) Medicaid nursing home cost containment and Medicare utilization. The Department of Public Aid, in collaboration with the Department on Aging and the Department of Public Health and in consultation with the Advisory Committee, shall propose a plan to contain Medicaid nursing home costs and maximize Medicare utilization. The plan must not impair the ability of an older adult to choose among available services. The plan shall include, but not be limited to, (i) techniques to maximize the use of the most cost-effective services without sacrificing quality and (ii) methods to identify and serve older adults in need of minimal services to remain independent, but who are likely to develop a need for more extensive services in the absense of those minimal services.

(16) Bed reduction. The Department of Public Health shall implement a nursing home conversion program to reduce the number of Medicaid-certified nursing home beds in areas with excess beds. The Department of Public Aid shall investigate changes to the Medicaid nursing facility reimbursement system in order to reduce beds. Such changes may include, but are not limited to, incentive payments that will enable facilities to adjust to the restructuring and expansion of services required by the Older Adult Services Act [320 ILCS 42/1 et seq.], including adjustments for the voluntary closure or layaway of nursing home beds certified under Title XIX of the federal Social Security Act [42 U.S.C. § 1396 et seq.]. Any savings shall be reallocated to fund home-based or community-based older adult services pursuant to Section 20 [320 ILCS 42/20].

(17) Financing. The Department shall investigate and evaluate financing options for older adult services and shall make recommendations in the report required by Section 15 concerning the feasibility of these financing arrangements. These arrangements shall include, but are not limited to:

(A) private long-term care insurance coverage for older adult services;

(B) enhancement of federal long-term care financing initiatives;

(C) employer benefit programs such as medical savings accounts for long-term care;

(D) individual and family cost-sharing options;

(E) strategies to reduce reliance on government programs;

(F) fraudulent asset divestiture and financial planning prevention; and

(G) methods to supplement and support family and community caregiving.

(18) Older Adult Services Demonstration Grants. The Department shall implement a program of demonstration grants that will assist in the restructuring of the older adult services delivery system, and shall provide funding for innovative service delivery models and system change and integration initiatives pursuant to subsection (g) of Section 20 [320 ILCS 42/20].

(19) Bed need methodology update. For the purposes of determining areas with excess beds, the Departments shall provide information and assistance to the Health Facilities Planning Board to update the Bed Need Methodology for Long-Term Care to update the assumptions used to establish the methodology to make them consistent with modern older adult services.

(Source: P.A. 93-1031, § 30.)

320 ILCS 42/30 Nursing home conversion program

Sec. 30. *Nursing home conversion program.* (a) The Department of Public Health, in collaboration with the Department on Aging and the Department of Public Aid, shall establish a nursing home conversion program. Start-up grants, pursuant to subsections (l) and (m) of this Section, shall be made available to nursing homes as appropriations permit as an incentive to reduce certified beds, retrofit, and retool operations to meet new service delivery expectations and demands.

(b) Grant moneys shall be made available for capital and other costs related to: (1) the conversion of all or a part of a nursing home to an assisted living establishment or a special program or unit for persons with Alzheimer's disease or related disorders licensed under the Assisted Living and Shared Housing Act [210 ILCS 9/1 et seq.] or a supportive living facility established under Section 5-5.01a of the Illinois Public Aid Code [305 ILCS 5/5-5.01a]; (2) the conversion of multi-resident bedrooms in the facility into single-occupancy rooms; and (3) the development of any of the services identified in a priority service plan that can be provided by a nursing home within the confines of a nursing home or transportation services. Grantees shall be required to provide a minimum of a 20% match toward the total cost of the project.

(c) Nothing in this Act shall prohibit the co-location of services or the development of multifunctional centers under subsection (f) of Section 20 [320 ILCS 42/20], including a nursing home offering community-based services or a community provider establishing a residential facility.

(d) A certified nursing home with at least 50% of its resident population having their care paid for by the Medicaid program is eligible to apply for a grant under this Section.

(e) Any nursing home receiving a grant under this Section shall reduce the number of certified nursing home beds by a number equal to or greater than the number of beds being converted for one or more of the permitted uses under item (1) or (2) of subsection (b). The nursing home shall retain the Certificate of Need for its nursing and sheltered care beds that were converted for 15 years. If the beds are reinstated by the provider or its successor in interest, the provider shall pay to the fund from which the grant was awarded, on an amortized basis, the amount of the grant. The Department shall establish, by rule, the bed reduction methodology for nursing homes that receive a grant pursuant to item (3) of subsection (b).

(f) Any nursing home receiving a grant under this Section shall agree that, for a minimum of 10 years after the date that the grant is awarded, a minimum of 50% of the nursing home's resident population shall have their care paid for by the Medicaid program. If the nursing home provider or its successor in interest ceases to comply with the requirement set forth in this subsection, the provider shall pay to the fund from which the grant was awarded, on an amortized basis, the amount of the grant.

(g) Before awarding grants, the Department of Public Health shall seek recommendations from the Department on Aging and the Department of Public Aid. The Department of Public Health shall attempt to balance the distribution of grants among geographic regions, and among small and large nursing homes. The Department of Public Health shall develop, by rule, the criteria for the award of grants based upon the following factors:

(1) the unique needs of older adults (including those with moderate and low incomes), caregivers, and providers in the geographic area of the State the grantee seeks to serve;

(2) whether the grantee proposes to provide services in a priority service area;

(3) the extent to which the conversion or transition will result in the reduction of certified nursing home beds in an area with excess beds;

(4) the compliance history of the nursing home; and

(5) any other relevant factors identified by the Department, including standards of need.

(h) A conversion funded in whole or in part by a grant under this Section must not:

(1) diminish or reduce the quality of services available to nursing home residents;

(2) force any nursing home resident to involuntarily accept home-based or community-based services instead of nursing home services;

(3) diminish or reduce the supply and distribution of nursing home services in any community below the level of need, as defined by the Department by rule; or

(4) cause undue hardship on any person who requires nursing home care.

(i) The Department shall prescribe, by rule, the grant application process. At a minimum, every application must include:

(1) the type of grant sought;

(2) a description of the project;

(3) the objective of the project;

(4) the likelihood of the project meeting identified needs;

(5) the plan for financing, administration, and evaluation of the project;

(6) the timetable for implementation;

(7) the roles and capabilities of responsible individuals and organizations;

(8) documentation of collaboration with other service providers, local community government leaders, and other stakeholders, other providers, and any other stakeholders in the community;

(9) documentation of community support for the project, including support by other service providers, local community government leaders, and other stakeholders;

(10) the total budget for the project;

(11) the financial condition of the applicant; and

(12) any other application requirements that may be established by the Department by rule.

(j) A conversion project funded in whole or in part by a grant under this Section is exempt from the requirements of the Illinois Health Facilities Planning Act [20 ILCS 3960/1 et seq.]. The Department of Public Health, however, shall send to the Health Facilities Planning Board a copy of each grant award made under this Section.

(k) Applications for grants are public information, except that nursing home financial condition and any proprietary data shall be classified as nonpublic data.

(l) The Department of Public Health may award grants from the Long Term Care Civil Money Penalties Fund established under Section 1919(h)(2)(A)(ii) of the Social Security Act [42 U.S.C. § 1919] and 42 CFR 488.422(g) [42 U.S.C. § 488.422] if the award meets federal requirements.
(Source: P.A. 93-1031, § 30.)

320 ILCS 42/35 Older Adult Services Advisory Committee

Sec. 35. *Older Adult Services Advisory Committee.* (a) The Older Adult Services Advisory Committee is created to advise the directors of Aging, Public Aid, and Public Health on all matters related to this Act and the delivery of services to older adults in general.

(b) The Advisory Committee shall be comprised of the following:

(1) The Director of Aging or his or her designee, who shall serve as chair and shall be an ex officio and nonvoting member.

(2) The Director of Public Aid and the Director of Public Health or their designees, who shall serve as vice-chairs and shall be ex officio and nonvoting members.

(3) One representative each of the Governor's Office, the Department of Public Aid, the Department of Public Health, the Department of Veterans' Affairs, the Department of Human Services, the Department of Insurance, the Department of Commerce and Economic Opportunity, the Department on Aging, the Department on Aging's State Long Term Care Ombudsman, the Illinois Housing Finance Authority, and the Illinois Housing Development Authority, each of whom shall be selected by his or her respective director and shall be an ex officio and nonvoting member.

(4) Thirty-two members appointed by the Director of Aging in collaboration with the directors of Public Health and Public Aid, and selected from the recommendations of statewide associations and organizations, as follows:

(A) One member representing the Area Agencies on Aging;

(B) Four members representing nursing homes or licensed assisted living establishments;

(C) One member representing home health agencies;

(D) One member representing case management services;

(E) One member representing statewide senior center associations;

(F) One member representing Community Care Program homemaker services;

(G) One member representing Community Care Program adult day services;

(H) One member representing nutrition project directors;

(I) One member representing hospice programs;

(J) One member representing individuals with Alzheimer's disease and related dementias;

(K) Two members representing statewide trade or labor unions;

(L) One advanced practice nurse with experience in gerontological nursing;

(M) One physician specializing in gerontology;

(N) One member representing regional long-term care ombudsmen;

(O) One member representing township officials;

(P) One member representing municipalities;

(Q) One member representing county officials;

(R) One member representing the parish nurse movement;

(S) One member representing pharmacists;

(T) Two members representing statewide organizations engaging in advocacy or legal representation on behalf of the senior population;

(U) Two family caregivers;

(V) Two citizen members over the age of 60;

(W) One citizen with knowledge in the area of gerontology research or health care law;

(X) One representative of health care facilities licensed under the Hospital Licensing Act; and

(Y) One representative of primary care service providers.

(c) Voting members of the Advisory Committee shall serve for a term of 3 years or until a replacement is named. All members shall be appointed no later than January 1, 2005. Of the initial appointees, as determined by lot, 10 members shall serve a term of one year; 10 shall serve for a term of 2 years; and 12 shall serve for a term of 3 years. Any member appointed to fill a vacancy occurring prior to the expiration of the term for which his or her predecessor was appointed shall be appointed for the remainder of that term. The Advisory Committee shall meet at least quarterly and may meet more frequently at the call of the Chair. A simple majority of those appointed shall constitute a quorum. The affirmative vote of a majority of those present and voting shall be necessary for Advisory Committee action. Members of the Advisory Committee shall receive no compensation for their services.

(d) The Advisory Committee shall have an Executive Committee comprised of the Chair, the Vice Chairs, and up to 15 members of the Advisory Committee appointed by the Chair who have demonstrated expertise in developing, implementing, or coordinating the system restructuring initiatives defined in Section 25. The Executive Committee shall have responsibility to oversee and structure the operations of the Advisory Committee and to create and appoint necessary subcommittees and subcommittee members.

(e) The Advisory Committee shall study and make recommendations related to the implementation of this Act, including but not limited to system restructuring initiatives as defined in Section 25 [320 ILCS 42/35] or otherwise related to this Act.
(Source: P.A. 93-1031, § 35.)

320 ILCS 42/90 through 320 ILCS 42/96 [Not Set Out]

(Source: P.A. 93-1031, § 90.)

Note.
These sections, as found in P.A. 93-1031, §§ 90-96, contained amendatory provisions.

320 ILCS 42/99 Effective date

Sec. 99. *Effective date.* This Act takes effect upon becoming law.
(Source: P.A. 93-1031, § 99.)

Note.
P.A. 93-1031 was approved August 27, 2004.

SENIOR CITIZENS CHILD CARE SUPPORT ACT

320 ILCS 45/1 Short title

Sec. 1. *Short title.* This Act may be cited as the Senior Citizens Child Care Support Act.
(Source: P.A. 87-672.)

Derivation.
Title: An Act to create a child care training program to establish a link between senior citizens and children in child care services.
Cite: 320 ILCS 45/1 et seq.
Source: P.A. 87-672.
Date: Approved September 23, 1991.

Note.
This section was Ill.Rev.Stat., Ch. 23, para. 7001.

320 ILCS 45/5 [Purpose]

Sec. 5. The purpose of this Act is to establish a link between senior citizens in need of additional income and children in child care.
(Source: P.A. 87-672.)

Note.
This section was Ill.Rev.Stat., Ch. 23, para. 7005.

320 ILCS 45/10 Definitions

Sec. 10. *Definitions.* In this Act:

"Resource and Referral System" means that organization as defined in Section 5 of the Children and Family Services Act [20 ILCS 505/5].

"Service area" means that organization as defined in Section 3.08 of the Illinois Act on the Aging [20 ILCS 105/3.08].

"Senior citizen" means a person of 55 years of age or older.
(Source: P.A. 87-672.)

Note.
This section was Ill.Rev.Stat., Ch. 23, para. 7010.

320 ILCS 45/15 [Information distribution system; demonstration training module]

Sec. 15. The Department on Aging shall develop and coordinate an information distribution system in conjunction with the Department of Children and Family Services to provide senior citizens with access to child care training. The Department of Children and Family Services shall develop a demonstration training module that shall be specifically designed for senior citizens contemplating employment or volunteer work in a day care center, day care home, or group day care home. The demonstration module shall include dissemination of information on employment and volunteer work opportunities; on available training programs in the geographic area including institutions of higher education through professional organizations, DCFS provider training, and Resource and Referral Systems. Additionally, information regarding license requirements, health and background checks, and a general introduction to child care shall be included in the demonstration module.
(Source: P.A. 87-672.)

Note.
This section was Ill.Rev.Stat., Ch. 23, para. 7015.

320 ILCS 45/20 [Volunteer training program; availability; publicity]

Sec. 20. The volunteer training program shall be available in every Resource and Referral Service area and publicized through service areas of the Department on Aging.
(Source: P.A. 87-672.)

Note.
This section was Ill.Rev.Stat., Ch. 23, para. 7020.

320 ILCS 45/25 [Documentation for participants]

Sec. 25. Participants shall be provided documentation of training by the Department of Children and Family Services.
(Source: P.A. 87-672.)

Note.
This section was Ill.Rev.Stat., Ch. 23, para. 7020.

SENIOR PHARMACEUTICAL ASSISTANCE ACT

320 ILCS 50/1 Short title

Sec. 1. *Short title.* This Act may be cited as the Senior Pharmaceutical Assistance Act.
(Source: P.A. 92-594, § 1.)

Effective Date.
Section 99 of P.A. 92-594 made this Act effective upon becoming law. P.A. 92-594 was approved June 27, 2002.

320 ILCS 50/5 Findings

Sec. 5. *Findings.* The General Assembly finds:

(1) Senior citizens identify pharmaceutical assistance as the single most critical factor to their health, well-being, and continued independence.

(2) The State of Illinois currently operates 2 pharmaceutical assistance programs that benefit seniors: (i) the program of pharmaceutical assistance under the Senior Citizens and Disabled Persons Property Tax Relief and Pharmaceutical Assistance Act [320 ILCS 25/1 et seq.] and (ii) the Aid to the Aged, Blind, or Disabled program under the Illinois Public Aid Code [305 ILCS 5/1-1 et seq.]. The State has been given authority to establish a third program, SeniorRx Care, through a federal Medicaid waiver.

(3) Each year, numerous pieces of legislation are filed seeking to establish additional pharmaceutical assistance benefits for seniors or to make changes to the existing programs.

(4) Establishment of a pharmaceutical assistance review committee will ensure proper coordination of benefits, diminish the likelihood of duplicative benefits, and ensure that the best interests of seniors are served.

(5) In addition to the State pharmaceutical assistance programs, several private entities, such as drug manufacturers and pharmacies, also offer prescription drug discount or coverage programs.

(6) Many seniors are unaware of the myriad of public and private programs available to them.

(7) Establishing a pharmaceutical clearinghouse with a toll-free hot-line and local outreach workers will educate seniors about the vast array of options available to them and enable seniors to make an educated and informed choice that is best for them.

(8) Estimates indicate that almost one-third of senior citizens lack prescription drug coverage. The federal government, states, and the pharmaceutical industry each have a role in helping these uninsured seniors gain access to life-saving medications.

(9) The State of Illinois has recognized its obligation to assist Illinois' neediest seniors in purchasing prescription medications, and it is now time for pharmaceutical manufacturers to recognize their obligation to make their medications affordable to seniors.

(Source: P.A. 92-594, § 5.)

320 ILCS 50/10 Definitions

Sec. 10. *Definitions.* In this Act:

"Manufacturer" includes:

(1) An entity that is engaged in (a) the production, preparation, propagation, compounding, conversion, or processing of prescription drug products (i) directly or indirectly by extraction from substances of natural origin, (ii) independently by means of chemical synthesis, or (iii) by combination of extraction and chemical synthesis; or (b) the packaging, repackaging, labeling or re-labeling, or distribution of prescription drug products.

(2) The entity holding legal title to or possession of the national drug code number for the covered prescription drug.

The term does not include a wholesale distributor of drugs, drugstore chain organization, or retail pharmacy licensed by the State.

"Prescription drug" means a drug that may be dispensed only upon prescription by an authorized prescriber and that is approved for safety and effectiveness as a prescription drug under Section 505 or 507 of the Federal Food, Drug and Cosmetic Act [21 U.S.C. § 505 or 21 U.S.C. § 507].

"Senior citizen" or "senior" means a person 65 years of age or older.

(Source: P.A. 92-594, § 10.)

320 ILCS 50/15 Senior Pharmaceutical Assistance Review Committee

Sec. 15. *Senior Pharmaceutical Assistance Review Committee.* (a) The Senior Pharmaceutical Assistance Review Committee is created. The Committee shall consist of 17 members as follows:

(1) Twelve members appointed as follows: 2 members of the General Assembly and 1 member of the general public, appointed by the President of the Senate; 2 members of the General Assembly and 1 member of the general public, appointed by the Minority Leader of the Senate; 2 members of the General Assembly and 1 member of the general public, appointed by the Speaker of the House of Representatives; and 2 members of the General Assembly and 1 member of the general public, appointed by the Minority Leader of the House of Representatives. These members shall serve at the pleasure of the appointing authority.

(2) The Director of Aging or his or her designee.

(3) The Director of Revenue or his or her designee.

(4) The Director of Public Aid or his or her designee.

(5) The Secretary of Human Services or his or her designee.

(6) The Director of Public Health or his or her designee.

(b) Members appointed from the general public shall represent the following associations, organizations, and interests: statewide membership-based senior advocacy organizations, pharmaceutical manufacturers, pharmacists, dispensing pharmacies, physicians, and providers of services to senior citizens. No single organization may have more than one representative appointed as a member from the general public.

(c) The President of the Senate and Speaker of the House of Representatives shall each designate one member of the Committee to serve as co-chairs.

(d) Committee members shall serve without compensation or reimbursement for expenses.

(e) The Committee shall meet at the call of the co-chairs, but at least quarterly.

(f) The Committee may conduct public hearings to gather testimony from interested parties regarding pharmaceutical assistance for Illinois seniors, including changes to existing and proposed programs.

(g) The Committee may advise appropriate State agencies regarding the establishment of proposed programs or changes to existing programs. The State agencies shall take into consideration any recommendations made by the Committee.

(h) The Committee shall report to the General Assembly and the Governor annually or as it deems necessary regarding proposed or recommended changes to pharmaceutical assistance programs that benefit Illinois seniors and any associated costs of those changes.

(i) In the event that a prescription drug benefit is added to the federal Medicare program, the Committee shall make recommendations for the realignment of State-operated senior prescription drug programs so that Illinois residents qualify for at least substantially the same level of benefits available to them prior to implementation of the Medicare prescription drug benefit, provided that a resident remains eligible for such a State-operated program. The Committee shall report its recommendations to the General Assembly and the Governor by January 1, 2005.
(Source: P.A. 92-594, § 15; 93-843, § 5.)

Effect of Amendments.
The 2004 amendment by P.A. 93-843, effective July 30, 2004, added subsection (i).

320 ILCS 50/20 Senior Health Assistance Program

Sec. 20. *Senior Health Assistance Program.* (a) The Senior Health Assistance Program is created within the Department on Aging, to become operational within 90 days after the effective date of this Act. The Senior Health Assistance Program shall provide outreach and education to senior citizens on available prescription drug coverage and discount programs.

(b) The Senior Health Assistance Program shall operate a Clearinghouse for all information regarding prescription drug coverage programs available to senior citizens in Illinois. The Clearinghouse shall operate in conjunction with the Department's toll-free senior information program.

(c) The purposes of the Clearinghouse include, but are not limited to:

(1) Maintaining information on public and private prescription assistance programs for Illinois seniors.

(2) Educating citizens on available public and private prescription assistance programs.

(3) Educating seniors on how to make an informed decision about participation in prescription drug assistance programs.

(d) The Clearinghouse has the following duties:

(1) Provide a one-stop resource for all information for seniors regarding public and private prescription drug discount and coverage programs.

(2) Perform outreach and education activities on public and private prescription drug discount and coverage programs.

(3) Maintain a toll-free telephone number staffed by trained customer service representatives.

(4) Maintain measurable data to identify the progress and success of the program, including, but not limited to, the number of individuals served, the type of assistance received, and overall program evaluation.

(e) The Department shall work cooperatively with other Departments that fund senior health assistance, including assistance with prescription drugs, to ensure maximum coordination.
(Source: P.A. 92-594, § 20.)

320 ILCS 50/25 Study of catastrophic pharmaceutical assistance coverage

Sec. 25. *Study of catastrophic pharmaceutical assistance coverage.* (a) The Illinois Comprehensive Health Insurance Board shall study a catastrophic pharmaceutical assistance coverage option. The Board may contract with a private entity for the completion of all or part of the study. Specifically, the study shall:

(1) Assess the need for a catastrophic pharmaceutical assistance coverage option, including information on the number of individuals in need of such a benefit.

(2) Estimate the cost of providing a catastrophic pharmaceutical assistance coverage option through the Illinois Comprehensive Health Insurance Plan or another public or private entity.

(3) Recommend ways to create a catastrophic pharmaceutical assistance coverage option.

(b) The Board may accept donations, in trust, from any legal source, public or private, for deposit into a specially created trust account and for expenditure, without the necessity of being appropriated, solely for the purpose of conducting all or part of the study.

(c) The Board may enter into intergovernmental agreements with other State agencies for the purpose of conducting all or part of the study.

(d) The Board shall issue a report with recommendations to the Governor and the General Assembly by January 1, 2003.
(Source: P.A. 92-594, § 25.)

320 ILCS 50/99 Effective Date

Sec. 99. *Effective Date.* This Act takes effect upon becoming law.
(Source: P.A. 92-594, § 99.)

Note.
P.A. 92-594 was approved June 27, 2002.

Senior Citizens and Disabled Persons Prescription Drug Discount Program Act

320 ILCS 55/1 Short title

Sec. 1. *Short title.* This Act may be cited as the Senior Citizens and Disabled Persons Prescription Drug Discount Program Act.
(Source: P.A. 93-18, § 1.)

Effective Date.
Section 99 of P.A. 93-18, made this Act effective July 1, 2003.

320 ILCS 55/5 Findings

Sec. 5. *Findings.* The General Assembly finds that:

(a) Although senior citizens represent 12% of the population, they use on average 37% of prescription drugs that are dispensed.

(b) Senior citizens in the United States without prescription drug insurance coverage pay the highest prices in the world for needed medications.

(c) High prescription drug prices force many Illinois seniors to go without proper medication or other necessities, thereby affecting their health and safety.

(d) Prescription drug prices in the United States are the world's highest, averaging 32% higher than in Canada, 40% higher than in Mexico, and 60% higher than in Great Britain.

(e) Regardless of household income, seniors without prescription drug coverage are often just one serious illness away from poverty.

(f) Reducing the price of prescription drugs would benefit the health and well-being of all Illinois senior citizens by providing more affordable access to needed drugs.
(Source: P.A. 93-18, § 5.)

320 ILCS 55/10 Purpose

Sec. 10. *Purpose.* The purpose of this program is to require the Department of Central Management Services to establish and administer a program that will enable eligible senior citizens and disabled persons to purchase prescription drugs at discounted prices.
(Source: P.A. 93-18, § 10.)

320 ILCS 55/15 Definitions

Sec. 15. *Definitions.* As used in this Act:

"Authorized pharmacy" means any pharmacy registered in this State under the Pharmacy Practice Act of 1987 [225 ILCS 85/1 et seq.] and approved by the Department or its program administrator.

"AWP" or "average wholesale price" means the amount determined from the latest publication of the Red Book, a universally subscribed pharmacist reference guide annually published by the Hearst Corporation. "AWP" or "average wholesale price" may also be derived electronically from the drug pricing database synonymous with the latest publication of the Red Book and furnished in the National Drug Data File (NDDF) by First Data Bank (FDB), a service of the Hearst Corporation.

"Department" means the Department of Central Management Services.

"Director" means the Director of Central Management Services.

"Disabled person" means a person unable to engage in any substantial gainful activity by reason of a medically determinable physical or mental impairment which can be expected to result in death or has lasted or can be expected to last for a continuous period of not less than 12 months.

"Drug manufacturer" means any entity (1) that is located within or outside Illinois that is engaged in (i) the production, preparation, propagation, compounding, conversion, or processing of prescription drug products covered under the program, either directly or indirectly by extraction from substances of natural origin, independently by means of chemical synthesis, or by a combination of extraction and chemical synthesis or (ii) the packaging, repackaging, leveling, labeling, or distribution of prescription drug products covered under the program and (2) that elects to provide prescription drugs either directly or under contract with any entity providing prescription drug services on behalf of the State of Illinois. "Drug manufacturer", however, does not include a wholesale distributor of drugs or a retail pharmacy licensed under Illinois law.

"Eligible senior" means a person who is (i) a resident of Illinois and (ii) 65 years of age or older.

"Prescription drug" means any prescribed drug that may be legally dispensed by an authorized pharmacy.

"Program" means the Senior Citizens and Disabled Persons Prescription Drug Discount Program created under this Act.

"Program administrator" means the entity that is chosen by the Department to administer the program. The program administrator may, in this case, be the Director or a Pharmacy Benefits Manager (PBM) chosen to subcontract with the Director.

"Rules" includes rules adopted and forms prescribed by the Department.
(Source: P.A. 93-18, § 15.)

320 ILCS 55/17 Determination of disability

Sec. 17. *Determination of disability.* Disabled persons filing applications for participation in the program shall submit proof of disability in such form and manner as the Department shall by rule prescribe. Proof that a claimant is eligible to receive disability benefits under the Federal Social Security Act [42 U.S.C. 301 et seq.] shall constitute proof of disability for purposes of this Act. Issuance of an

Illinois Disabled Person Identification Card stating that the claimant is under a Class 2 disability, as defined in Section 4A of the Illinois Identification Card Act [15 ILCS 335/4A], shall constitute proof that the person named thereon is a disabled person for purposes of this Act. A disabled person not covered under the Federal Social Security Act [42 U.S.C. § 301 et seq.] and not presenting a Disabled Person Identification Card stating that he or she is under a Class 2 disability shall be examined by a physician designated by the Department, and his or her status as a disabled person determined using the same standards as used by the Social Security Administration. The costs of any required examination shall be borne by the person claiming a disability.
(Source: P.A. 93-18, § 17.)

320 ILCS 55/20 The Senior Citizens and Disabled Persons Prescription Drug Discount Program

Sec. 20. *The Senior Citizens and Disabled Persons Prescription Drug Discount Program.* The Senior Citizens and Disabled Persons Prescription Drug Discount Program is established to protect the health and safety of senior citizens and disabled persons. The program shall be administered by the Department. The Department or its program administrator shall (i) enroll eligible seniors and disabled persons into the program, as provided in Section 35 of this Act [320 ILCS 55/35], to qualify them for a discount on the purchase of prescription drugs at an authorized pharmacy, (ii) enter into rebate agreements with drug manufacturers, as provided under Section 30 of this Act [320 ILCS 55/30], and (iii) subject to the provisions of Section 47 of this Act [320 ILCS 55/47], compensate pharmacies participating in the program as provided under Section 25 of this Act [320 ILCS 55/25].
(Source: P.A. 93-18, § 20.)

320 ILCS 55/25 Program administration

Sec. 25. *Program administration.* (a) The Department is authorized under this Act to be the program administrator. If the Department is not the program administrator, 90 days after the effective date of this Act, the Department must issue a request for proposals for bidders interested in administering the program. Bidders must compete on the basis of the following minimum criteria:

(1) The Director shall solicit and accept proposals from entities to provide for administration of a program or programs in accordance with rules adopted under Section 45 [320 ILCS 55/45]. Proposals must be submitted not later than a date established by the Director. The Director shall accept only those proposals that specify the following:

(A) The estimated amount of the discount based on the entity's previous experience and how the discount is to be achieved.

(B) The extent that discounts on prescription drugs are to be achieved through rebates, administrative fees, or other fees or discounts in prices that the entity negotiates with drug manufacturers. The proposals shall assure that rebates or discounts will be used to do the following:

(i) reduce costs to cardholders;

(ii) achieve discounts for cardholders; and

(iii) cover costs for administering the program.

(C) Any other benefits offered to cardholders.

(D) The estimated number and geographic distribution of participating pharmacies in the administrator's pharmacy network.

(E) The plan for pharmacy compensation, pursuant to subsection (e) of this Section.

(F) The method used for determining the prescription drugs to be covered by the program, including the criteria and process for establishing a preferred drug list, if applicable.

(G) How the entity proposes to improve medication management for cardholders, including any program of disease management.

(H) How cardholders and participating pharmacies will be informed of the discounted price negotiated by the entity.

(I) How the entity will handle complaints about the program's operation.

(J) The entity's previous experience in managing similar programs.

(K) Any additional information requested by the Director.

(2) The Director shall contract with one or more entities to administer a program or programs on the basis of the proposals submitted, but may require an administrator to modify its conduct of a program in accordance with rules adopted under Section 45 [320 ILCS 55/45].

The Director shall adopt rules specifying the period for which a contract will be in effect and may terminate a contract if an administrator fails to conduct a program in accordance with its proposal or with any modifications required by rule. When a contract period ends or a contract is terminated, the Director shall enter into a new contract in the manner specified in this Section for an original contract. Prior to making a new contract, the Director may modify the rules for administration of the program or programs.

(b) As used in this Section, "administrator" includes the administrator's parent company and any subsidiary of the parent company.

(1) No administrator shall sell any information concerning a person who holds a prescription drug discount card, other than aggregate information that does not identify the cardholder, without the cardholder's written consent.

(2) Unless an administrator has the cardholder's written consent, no administrator shall use any personally identifiable information that it obtains concerning a cardholder through the program to

promote or sell a program or product offered by the administrator that is not related to the administration of the program. This subsection (b) does not prohibit an administrator from contacting cardholders concerning participation in or administration of the program, including, but not limited to, mailing a list of pharmacies participating in the program's network or participating in disease management programs.

(3) To the extent that a discount is achieved through rebates, administrative fees, or any other fees or discounts in prices that an administrator negotiates with drug manufacturers, an administrator shall use the rebates or discounts to do the following:

(A) reduce costs to cardholders;

(B) achieve discounts for cardholders; and

(C) cover any administrative costs of the program.

(4) The administrator shall not use any funds generated from rebates, discounts, administrative fees, or other fees to promote its mail order pharmacy operation or the mail order pharmacy operation of an affiliate. This subdivision (b)(4) does not, however, limit the participation of an Illinois-licensed pharmacy under this Act if that pharmacy provides prescription drugs by mail order.

(c) Beginning on January 1, 2004, the amount paid by eligible seniors and disabled persons enrolled in the program to authorized pharmacies for prescription drugs may not exceed prices established as a result of the rebate agreements under Section 30 [320 ILCS 55/30]. The eligible seniors and disabled persons shall pay the price determined under Section 30 plus a dispensing fee of $3.50 per prescription for brand name drug products, single-source drug products, and, for a period of 6 months, newly released generic drug products and $4.25 per prescription for all other generic drug products, except that the total amount paid by the eligible senior or disabled person for each prescription drug under this program shall not exceed the usual and customary charge for such prescription.

(d) The contract between the Department and a pharmacy benefits manager must, at a minimum, meet the criteria of subsection (a). The contract must also require notification by the pharmacy benefits manager of any proposed or ongoing activity that involves, directly or indirectly, any conflict of interest on the part of the pharmacy benefits manager. The Department shall ensure that the pharmacy benefits manager complies with the contract and shall adopt all procedures necessary to enforce the contract.

(e) The Department or program administrator shall, subject to the funds available under Section 30 [320 ILCS 55/30] of this Act, compensate authorized pharmacies for prescription drugs dispensed under the program for the difference between the amount paid by the eligible senior or disabled person for prescription drugs dispensed under the program and (i) the AWP minus 12% for brand name drug products, single-source generic drug products, and, for a period of 6 months, newly released generic drug products and (ii) the AWP minus 35% for all other generic drug products. The Department shall compensate a pharmacy under this subsection (e) only if the amount paid by the eligible senior or disabled person has been discounted to a price, including the dispensing fees stated in subsection (c) of this Section, that is less than (i) the AWP minus 12% for brand name drug products, single-source generic drug products, and, for a period of 6 months, newly released generic drug products and (ii) the AWP minus 35% for all other generic drug products.

(f) Beginning on January 1, 2004, the Department or program administrator shall reimburse pharmacies under this Section within 30 days after adjudication of the claim.

(Source: P.A. 93-18, § 25.)

320 ILCS 55/30 Manufacturer rebate agreements

Sec. 30. *Manufacturer rebate agreements.* (a) Taking into consideration the extent to which the State pays for prescription drugs under various State programs and the provision of assistance to disabled persons or eligible seniors under patient assistance programs, prescription drug discount programs, or other offers for free or reduced price medicine, clinical research projects, limited supply distribution programs, compassionate use programs, or programs of research conducted by or for a drug manufacturer, the Department, its agent, or the program administrator shall negotiate and enter into rebate agreements with drug manufacturers, as defined in this Act, to effect prescription drug price discounts. The Department or program administrator may establish a preferred drug list as a basis for determining the discounts, administrative fees, or other fees or rebates under this Section.

(b) Rebate payment procedures. All rebates negotiated under agreements described in this Section shall be paid in accordance with procedures prescribed by the Department or the program administrator.

(c) Receipts from rebates shall be used to provide discounts for prescription drugs purchased by eligible seniors and disabled persons and to cover the cost of administering the program, including compensation to be paid to participating pharmacies by the Department or program administrator under subsection (e) of Section 25 [320 ILCS 55/25]. Any receipts to be allocated to the Department shall be deposited into the Senior Citizens and Disabled Persons Prescription Drug Discount Program Fund, a special fund hereby created in the State treasury.

(Source: P.A. 93-18, § 30.)

320 ILCS 55/35 Program eligibility

Sec. 35. *Program eligibility.* (a) Any person may apply to the Department or its program administrator for participation in the program in the form and manner required by the Department. The Department or its program administrator shall determine the eligibility of each applicant for the program within 30 days after the date of application. To participate in the program an eligible senior or disabled person whose application has been approved must pay $25 upon enrollment and annually thereafter and shall receive a program identification card. The card may be presented to an authorized pharmacy to assist the pharmacy in verifying eligibility under the program. The Department shall deposit the enrollment fees collected into the Senior Citizens and Disabled Persons Prescription Drug Discount Program Fund. The moneys collected by the Department for enrollment fees and deposited into the Senior Citizens and Disabled Persons Prescription Drug Discount Program Fund must be separately accounted for by the Department. If 2 or more persons are eligible for any benefit under this Act and are members of the same household, each participating household member shall apply to the Department and pay the fee required for the purpose of obtaining an identification card.

(b) Proceeds from annual enrollment fees shall be used by the Department to offset the administrative cost of this Act. The Department may reduce the annual enrollment fee by rule if the revenue from the enrollment fees is in excess of the costs to carry out the program.

(c) Any person who is eligible for pharmaceutical assistance under the Senior Citizens and Disabled Persons Property Tax Relief and Pharmaceutical Assistance Act [320 ILCS 25/1 et seq.] is presumed to be eligible for this program. The enrollment fee under this Act is not required for such persons. That person may purchase prescription drugs under this program that are not covered by the pharmaceutical assistance program under the Senior Citizens and Disabled Persons Property Tax Relief and Pharmaceutical Assistance Act [320 ILCS 55/35] by using the identification card issued under the pharmaceutical assistance program.
(Source: P.A. 93-18, § 35.)

320 ILCS 55/40 Eligible pharmacies

Sec. 40. *Eligible pharmacies.* (a) The Department or its program administrator shall adopt rules to establish standards and procedures for participation in the program and approve those pharmacies that apply to participate and meet the requirements for participation. Pharmacies in the program administrator's network must also comply with the Department's standards and procedures for participation.

(b) The Department shall establish procedures for properly contracting for pharmacy services, validating reimbursement claims, validating compliance of authorized pharmacies with the conditions for participation required under this Act, and otherwise providing for the effective administration of this Act. The Director, in consultation with pharmacists licensed under the Pharmacy Practice Act of 1987 [225 ILCS 85/1 et seq.], may enter into a written contract with any other State agency, instrumentality, or political subdivision or with a fiscal intermediary for the purpose of making payments to authorized pharmacies and coordinating the program with other programs that provide payments for prescription drugs covered under the program.
(Source: P.A. 93-18, § 40.)

320 ILCS 55/45 Rules

Sec. 45. *Rules.* The Department shall adopt rules to implement and administer the program, which shall include the following:

(1) Execution of contracts with pharmacies to participate in the program. The contracts shall stipulate terms and conditions for the participation of authorized pharmacies and the rights of the State to terminate participation for breach of the contract or for violation of this Act or rules adopted by the Department under this Act.

(2) Establishment of maximum limits on the size of prescriptions that are eligible for a discount under the program, up to a 90-day supply, except as may be necessary for utilization control reasons.

(3) Inspection of appropriate records and audits of participating authorized pharmacies to ensure contract compliance and to determine any fraudulent transactions or practices under this Act.

(4) Specify how a resident may apply to participate in the program.

(5) Specify the circumstances under which the Director may require an administrator to modify its conduct of the program.

(6) Specify the duration of a contract.

(7) Require that an administrator permit any Illinois-licensed pharmacy willing to comply with the requirements of this Act and terms and conditions for participation in the program's network to participate in any network used by the administrator for its program.

(8) Permit an administrator to negotiate with one or more drug manufacturers for discounts in drug prices or rebates.

(9) Permit an administrator to receive any rebate payments from drug manufacturers.

(10) Permit an administrator to develop, administer, and promote a program of disease management pursuant to written agreements between the administrator and pharmacies participating under the program established by this Act.
(Source: P.A. 93-18, § 45.)

320 ILCS 55/47 Limit on State's obligation for cost of administration

Sec. 47. *Limit on State's obligation for cost of administration.* The State of Illinois is obligated for the cost of administering this program only to the extent of the amount of money collected as enroll-

ment fees under Section 35 of this Act [320 ILCS 55/35], rebates collected under Section 30 of this Act [320 ILCS 55/30], and funds appropriated by the General Assembly for the purpose of this Act.
(Source: P.A. 93-18, § 47.)

320 ILCS 55/50 Report on administration of program

Sec. 50. *Report on administration of program.* The Department shall report to the Governor and the General Assembly by March 1st of each year on the administration of the program under this Act. The report shall include but not be limited to the following:

(1) the number of disabled persons and seniors eligible and enrolled in the program, by county;

(2) the activities undertaken by the State to inform disabled persons and seniors about the program;

(3) the number of prescriptions filled under the program for enrollees, and the estimated savings for enrollees;

(4) a listing of the manufacturers and pharmacies participating in the program;

(5) the amount of enrollment fees and rebates collected under the program, and any additional funds or resources made available to cover the cost of the program;

(6) the itemized annual cost of administering the program; and

(7) findings and recommendations regarding problems and solutions related to the program, together with proposals for changes in the rules, regulations, or laws necessary to improve the administration of the program.
(Source: P.A. 93-18, § 50.)

320 ILCS 55/99 Effective date

Sec. 99. *Effective date.* This Act takes effect on July 1, 2003.
(Source: P.A. 93-18, § 99.)

Effective Date.
Section 99 of P.A. 93-18, made this Act effective July 1, 2003.

320 ILCS 55/990 [Not Set Out]

(Source: P.A. 93-18, § 990.)

Note.
This section, as found in P.A. 93-18, § 990, contained amendatory provisions.

Community Senior Services and Resources Act

320 ILCS 60/1 Short title

Sec. 1. *Short title.* This Act may be cited as the Community Senior Services and Resources Act.
(Source: P.A. 93-246, § 1.)

Effective Date.
Section 99 of P.A. 93-246, made this Act effective upon becoming law. The Act was approved July 22, 2003.

320 ILCS 60/5 Legislative findings

Sec. 5. *Legislative findings.* The General Assembly recognizes that community senior services and resource centers:

(1) provide one-stop convenience for seniors and their families;

(2) assist seniors in avoiding inappropriate institutionalization; and

(3) address the health, safety, and well-being of those who receive senior services at home and those who receive them in an institutional setting.
(Source: P.A. 93-246, § 5.)

320 ILCS 60/10 Legislative intent

Sec. 10. *Legislative intent.* It is the intent of the General Assembly that the Department advocate on behalf of community senior services and resource centers and promote their financial stability through direct grants and identification of alternative funding sources.
(Source: P.A. 93-246, § 10.)

320 ILCS 60/15 Definitions

Sec. 15. *Definitions.* For the purposes of this Act:

"Advisory Committee" means the Community Senior Services and Resource Center Advisory Committee created under Section 35 [320 ILCS 60/35].

"Center" means a community senior services and resource center.

"Department" means the Department on Aging.

"Director" means the Director of Aging.

"Senior" means an individual 60 years of age or older.

"Home or community based services" includes the following: elder abuse; home-delivered meals; case management; wellness and fitness programs; counseling; adult day services; respite care; senior benefits outreach; congregate meals; long-term care ombudsman services; job training and placement; transportation; chore homemaker services; caregiver support; computer literacy; and any program that assists participants in avoiding inappropriate institutional placement or addresses participants' health, safety, or well-being, regardless of whether the service is received in a participant's home or in an institutional setting and a majority of participants are seniors or family of seniors.
(Source: P.A. 93-246, § 15.)

320 ILCS 60/20 Duties

Sec. 20. *Duties.* The Department shall perform all of the following duties:

(1) Administer this Act and promulgate any rules, regulations, guidelines, and directives necessary for its implementation.

(2) Establish a Community Senior Services and Resource Center Advisory Committee.

(3) Make grants to non-profit agencies and units of local government under Section 25 of this Act in consultation with the Advisory Committee.

(4) Facilitate access to government-issued bonds for the purpose of capital improvement.

(5) Provide technical assistance to centers.

(6) Develop a comprehensive list of centers and the senior services they offer for publication on the Department's web site and for distribution through other promotional opportunities.

(7) Develop a survey for annual distribution through the centers to gather information concerning the lack or inadequacy of senior services and to identify service demand trends and the unique needs of older Illinoisans and their families.

(8) Conduct an annual survey of centers to assess their facility, program, and operational needs.

(9) Report annually in conjunction with the Advisory Committee to the Governor and the General Assembly. The report shall include findings from all surveys conducted pursuant to this Act, a list of grantees by county (including amounts awarded), and recommendations concerning the ongoing financial stability of centers.

(10) Pursue alternative funding opportunities.

(Source: P.A. 93-246, § 20.)

320 ILCS 60/25 Community senior services and resource center grants

Sec. 25. *Community senior services and resource center grants.* (a) On and after January 1, 2005, the Department may award grants under this Act. It is the General Assembly's intent that grants awarded under this Act shall be made to the extent of the availability and level of appropriations made for this purpose by the General Assembly.

(b) A center must meet the following criteria to be eligible to receive a grant under this Section:

(1) It must be a non-profit agency or a unit of local government.

(2) It must be housed in a building or portion of a building that includes space for group activities offered to the community at large.

(3) It must be open 5 or more days each week, 7 or more hours per day.

(4) It must employ paid staff.

(5) It must offer 5 or more home or community-based services to the community at large on a daily basis.

(6) A majority of the participants in the center's programs must be seniors or family members of seniors.

(c) A center must apply for a grant in the manner prescribed by the Department. At a minimum, the application must do the following:

(1) Describe the services offered by the center.

(2) Identify the special needs of the center and how the grant will be used to alleviate identified funding problems.

(3) Demonstrate that the center addresses the service needs of seniors in the community served by the center.

(4) Describe other potential funding sources.

(5) Describe additional funding opportunities, if any, to be leveraged with grant funds.

(6) Provide proof of the center's involvement in the community's greater service delivery system.

(7) Provide documentation that funds were requested from other sources, including, but not limited to, units of local government, local donors, local Area Agencies on Aging, or private or religious foundations.

(8) Include letters of support for the awarding of the grant, from sources such as local government officials, community leaders, other human service providers, the local Area Agency on Aging, private or religious foundations, or local membership-based organizations.

(Source: P.A. 93-246, § 25.)

320 ILCS 60/30 Funding; waivers

Sec. 30. *Funding; waivers.* The Director may seek and obtain non-State resources for which the State may be eligible and other dedicated revenue streams and may also seek and obtain waivers of federal requirements from the U.S. Department of Health and Human Services.

(Source: P.A. 93-246, § 30.)

320 ILCS 60/32 Bequests and gifts; awareness campaign

Sec. 32. *Bequests and gifts; awareness campaign.* (a) The Director may accept monetary grants, gifts, and bequests for deposit into the Community Senior Services and Resources Fund.

(b) The Director may accept monetary grants, gifts, and bequests for the benefit of a specified center or distinct area of the State. Each such grant, gift, or bequest shall be kept in a distinct fund. The Department may make grants from these funds for the purposes established for the Community Senior Services and Resources Fund and in accordance with the terms and conditions of the grant, gift, or bequest. These funds are exempt from Section 8h of the State Finance Act [30 ILCS 105/8h].

(c) The Department, in conjunction with the Community Senior Services and Resource Center Advisory Committee, shall design an awareness campaign that can be implemented by senior services and resource centers at their individual expense.

(Source: P.A. 93-714, § 10.)

Effective Date.

Section 99 of P.A. 93-714 made this section effective upon becoming law. The Act was approved June 12, 2004.

320 ILCS 60/35 Community Senior Services and Resource Center Advisory Committee

Sec. 35. *Community Senior Services and Resource Center Advisory Committee.* (a) The Community

Senior Services and Resource Center Advisory Committee shall be established by the Department. The Advisory Committee shall advise the Director in all aspects of the administration of this Act, including the determination of grant awards.

(b) The Advisory Committee shall be composed of the Director, who shall serve as a nonvoting ex officio member, and 14 voting members. The voting members shall select a chairperson from among their number. The Governor shall appoint the 14 voting members as follows:

(1) Two members selected from recommendations provided by an association representing non-profit centers.

(2) Two members selected from recommendations provided by an association representing township governments.

(3) Two members selected from recommendations provided by an association representing park districts.

(4) Two members selected from recommendations provided by an association representing municipalities.

(5) Two members selected from recommendations provided by statewide membership-based organizations that engage solely in advocacy on behalf of the senior population.

(6) Two members selected from individuals who are active participants in programs at a center.

(7) Two members who are directors of Area Agencies on Aging.

(c) All voting members shall be appointed by January 1, 2004. As determined by lot at the time of their appointment, 4 of the initial appointee's terms shall expire in one year; 5 in 2 years; and 5 in 3 years. Thereafter, all voting members shall be appointed to serve for terms of 3 years. A voting member's term does not expire until a successor is appointed by the Governor. A voting member appointed to fill a vacancy occurring before the expiration of the term for which his or her predecessor was appointed shall be appointed for the remainder of that term.

(d) The Advisory Committee shall meet on a quarterly basis and at other times at the call of the chair. The affirmative vote of 7 members of the Advisory Committee shall be required to take action. Members of the Advisory Committee shall receive no compensation for their service and shall not be reimbursed for expenses related to their service.

(e) To the extent possible, members of the Advisory Committee shall assist the Department in reviewing grant applications.

(f) The Advisory Committee shall be provided with draft copies of proposed survey instruments for their review and comment before the survey is conducted.

(g) The Advisory Committee shall be provided with copies of all administrative rules and changes to administrative rules implementing this Act for their review and comment before notice of the proposed rules or changes is given as required under the Illinois Administrative Procedure Act [5 ILCS 100/1-1 et seq.]. If the Advisory Committee, having been asked for its review, fails to comment to the Department on the proposed rules or changes within 90 days, the Department may proceed as required for rulemaking under the Illinois Administrative Procedure Act [5 ILCS 100/1-1 et seq.].
(Source: P.A. 93-246, § 35.)

320 ILCS 60/40 Community Senior Services and Resources Fund

Sec. 40. *Community Senior Services and Resources Fund.* The Community Senior Services and Resources Fund is created as a special fund in the State treasury. All moneys received by the Department for the implementation of this Act shall be deposited into the Fund. Subject to appropriation, moneys in the Fund shall be used for grant awards and for the administration of this Act. Interest earned on moneys in the Fund shall be credited to the Fund.
(Source: P.A. 93-246, § 40.)

320 ILCS 60/99 Effective date

Sec. 99. *Effective date.* This Act takes effect upon becoming law.
(Source: P.A. 93-246, § 99.)

Note.

P.A. 93-246 was approved July 22, 2003.

FAMILY CAREGIVER ACT

320 ILCS 65/1 Short title

Sec. 1. *Short title.* This Act may be cited as the Family Caregiver Act.
(Source: P.A. 93-864, § 1.)

Effective Date.

Section 99 of P.A. 93-864 made this Act effective July 1, 2004, however P.A. 93-864 was approved August 5, 2004.

320 ILCS 65/5 Legislative findings

Sec. 5. *Legislative findings.* The General Assembly recognizes the following:

(1) Family caregivers, serving without compensation, have been the mainstay of the long-term care system in this country. Care provided by these informal caregivers is the most crucial factor in avoiding or postponing institutionalization of the State's residents.

(2) Among non-institutionalized persons needing assistance with personal care needs, two-thirds depend solely on family and friends for assistance. Another 25% supplement family care with services from paid providers. Only a little more than 5% rely exclusively on paid services.

(3) Family caregivers are frequently under substantial physical, psychological, and financial stress. Unrelieved by support services available to the caregiver, this stress may lead to premature or unnecessary institutionalization of the care recipient or deterioration in the health condition and family circumstances of the caregiver.

(4) Two out of 3 family caregivers, due to being employed outside the home, experience additional stress. Two-thirds of working caregivers report conflicts between work and caregiving, requiring them to rearrange their work schedules, work fewer than normal hours, or take an unpaid leave of absence. For this population, caregiver support services have the added benefit of allowing family caregivers to remain active members of our State's workforce.

(Source: P.A. 93-864, § 5.)

320 ILCS 65/10 Legislative intent

Sec. 10. *Legislative intent.* It is the intent of the General Assembly to establish a multi-faceted family caregiver support program to assist unpaid family caregivers and grandparents or other older individuals who are relative caregivers, who are informal providers of in-home and community care to older individuals or children.

Services provided under this program shall do the following:

(1) Provide information, relief, and support to family and other unpaid caregivers of older individuals and children.

(2) Encourage family members to provide care for their family members who are older individuals and children.

(3) Provide temporary substitute support services or living arrangements to allow a period of relief or rest for caregivers.

(4) Be provided in the least restrictive setting available consistent with the individually assessed needs of older individuals and children.

(5) Include services appropriate to the needs of family members caring for older individuals and children, including older individuals with dementia.

(6) Provide family caregivers with services that enable them to make informed decisions about current and future care plans, solve day-to-day caregiving problems, learn essential care giving skills, and locate services that may strengthen their capacity to provide care.

(Source: P.A. 93-864, § 10.)

320 ILCS 65/15 Definitions

Sec. 15. *Definitions.* In this Act:

"Caregiver" or "family caregiver" means an adult family member, or another individual, who is an informal provider of in-home and community care to an older individual, or a grandparent or older individual who is a relative caregiver.

"Child" or "children" means an individual or individuals 18 years of age or under.

"Department" means the Department on Aging.

"Eligible participant" means a family caregiver or a grandparent or older individual who is a relative caregiver.

"Family caregiver support services" includes, but is not limited to, the following:

(1) Information to caregivers about available services.

(2) Assistance to caregivers in gaining access to the services.

(3) Individual counseling, organization of support groups, and caregiver training for caregivers to assist the caregivers in making decisions and solving problems relating to their caregiving roles.

(4) Respite care to enable caregivers to be temporarily relieved from their caregiving responsibilities.

(5) Supplemental services, on a limited basis, to complement the care provided by the caregivers.

(6) Other services as identified by the Department and defined by rule.

"Frail individual" means an older individual who is determined to be functionally impaired because the individual (i) is unable to perform from at least 2 activities of daily living without substantial human assistance, including verbal reminding, physical cueing, or supervision or (ii) due to a cognitive or other mental impairment, requires substantial supervision because the individual behaves in a manner that poses a serious health or safety hazard to the individual or to another individual.

"Grandparent or older individual who is a relative caregiver" means a grandparent or step-grandparent of a child, or a relative of a child by blood or marriage, who:

(1) lives with the child;

(2) is the primary caregiver for the child because the child's biological or adoptive parents are unable or unwilling to serve as the primary caregiver for the child; and

(3) has a legal relationship to the child, such as legal custody or guardianship, or is raising the child informally.

"Informal provider" means an individual who is not compensated for the care he or she provides.

"Older individual" means an individual who is 60 years of age or older, except for a grandparent or older individual who is a relative caregiver.

"Respite care" means substitute supports or living arrangements provided on an intermittent, occasional basis. The term includes, but is not limited to, in-home respite care, adult day care, child care, and institutional care. The term also includes respite care as defined in Section 2 of the Respite Program Act [320 ILCS 10/2] to the extent that such services are allowable and participants are eligible under the National Family Caregiver Support Program.

(Source: P.A. 93-864, § 15.)

320 ILCS 65/16 Family caregiver demonstration grant

Sec. 16. *Family caregiver demonstration grant.* The Department shall seek federal funding for the

establishment and assessment of a Family Caregiver Training and Support Demonstration Project. The Department is authorized to fund 2 sites, one in a rural community and one in a more urban area. The Department shall adopt rules governing participation and oversight of the program. The Department shall seek technical assistance from the Department of Public Aid and the Department of Human Services. The Department shall advise the Governor and the General Assembly regarding the effectiveness of the program within 6 months after the conclusion of the demonstration period.
(Source: P.A. 93-864, § 16.)

320 ILCS 65/20 Powers and duties of the Department

Sec. 20. *Powers and duties of the Department.* The Department shall administer this Act and shall adopt rules and standards the Department deems necessary for that purpose. At a minimum, those rules and standards shall address the following:

(1) Standards and mechanisms designed to ensure the quality of services provided with assistance made available under this Act.

(2) Data collection and record maintenance.

The Department shall administer this Act in coordination with Section 4.02 [20 ILCS 105/4.02] and related provisions of the Illinois Act on the Aging.
(Source: P.A. 93-864, § 20.)

320 ILCS 65/25 Provision of services

Sec. 25. *Provision of services.* The Department shall contract with area agencies on aging and other appropriate agencies to conduct family caregiver support services to the extent of available State and federal funding. Services provided under this Act must be provided according to the requirements of federal law and rules, except for the provision of services to grandparents or older individuals who are relative caregivers when State funding is utilized to provide those services.
(Source: P.A. 93-864, § 25.)

320 ILCS 65/30 Eligibility for respite and supplemental services

Sec. 30. *Eligibility for respite and supplemental services.* When a family caregiver is providing in-home and community care to an older individual, the older individual must be a frail individual as defined in this Act in order for the family caregiver to be eligible to receive respite and supplemental services.
(Source: P.A. 93-864, § 30.)

320 ILCS 65/35 Health care practitioners and facilities not impaired

Sec. 35. *Health care practitioners and facilities not impaired.* Nothing in this Act shall impair the practice of any licensed health care practitioner or licensed health care facility.
(Source: P.A. 93-864, § 35.)

320 ILCS 65/40 Entitlement not created; funding; waivers.

Sec. 40. *Entitlement not created; funding; waivers.* (a) Nothing in this Act creates or provides any individual with an entitlement to services or benefits. It is the General Assembly's intent that services under this Act shall be made available only to the extent of the availability and level of appropriations made by the General Assembly.

(b) The Director may seek and obtain State and federal funds that may be available to finance services under this Act, and may also seek and obtain other non-State resources for which the State may be eligible.

(c) The Department may seek appropriate waivers of federal requirements from the U.S. Department of Health and Human Services.
(Source: P.A. 93-864, § 40.)

320 ILCS 65/90 [Not Set Out]

(Source: P.A. 93-864, § 90.)

Note.
These sections, as found in P.A. 93-864, §§ 90 and 91, contained amendatory provisions.

320 ILCS 65/99 Effective date

Sec. 99. *Effective date.* This Act takes effect on July 1, 2004.
(Source: P.A. 93-864, § 99.)

Note.
This Act was approved August 5, 2004.

CHAPTER 325
CHILDREN

ABANDONED NEWBORN INFANT PROTECTION ACT

325 ILCS 2/1 (For postponed repeal of this Act, see 325 ILCS 2/75) Short title
325 ILCS 2/5 (For postponed repeal of this Act, see 325 ILCS 2/75) Public policy
325 ILCS 2/10 (For postponed repeal of this Act, see 325 ILCS 2/75) Definitions
325 ILCS 2/15 (For postponed repeal of this Act, see 325 ILCS 2/75) Presumptions
325 ILCS 2/20 (For postponed repeal of this Act, see 325 ILCS 2/75) Procedures with respect to relinquished newborn infants
325 ILCS 2/25 (For postponed repeal of this Act, see 325 ILCS 2/75) Immunity for relinquishing person
325 ILCS 2/27 (For postponed repeal of this Act, see 325 ILCS 2/75) Immunity of facility and personnel
325 ILCS 2/30 (For postponed repeal of this Act, see 325 ILCS 2/75) Anonymity of relinquishing person
325 ILCS 2/35 (For postponed repeal of this Act, see 325 ILCS 2/75) Information for relinquishing person
325 ILCS 2/40 (For postponed repeal of this Act, see 325 ILCS 2/75) Reporting requirements
325 ILCS 2/45 (For postponed repeal of this Act, see 325 ILCS 2/75) Medical assistance
325 ILCS 2/50 (For postponed repeal of this Act, see 325 ILCS 2/75) Child-placing agency procedures
325 ILCS 2/55 (For postponed repeal of this Act, see 325 ILCS 2/75) Petition for return of custody
325 ILCS 2/60 (For postponed repeal of this Act, see 325 ILCS 2/75) Department's duties
325 ILCS 2/65 (For postponed repeal of this Act, see 325 ILCS 2/75) Evaluation
325 ILCS 2/70 (For postponed repeal of this Act, see 325 ILCS 2/75) Construction of Act
325 ILCS 2/75 Repeal
325 ILCS 2/90 [Not set out]
325 ILCS 2/999 Effective date

ABUSED AND NEGLECTED CHILD REPORTING ACT

325 ILCS 5/1 [Short title]
325 ILCS 5/2 [Scope of act]
325 ILCS 5/2.1 [Eligibility]
325 ILCS 5/3 [Definitions]
325 ILCS 5/4 Persons required to report; privileged communications; transmitting false report
325 ILCS 5/4.02 [Failure to report]
325 ILCS 5/4.1 [Reports to medical examiner or coroner]
325 ILCS 5/4.2 Departmental report on death of child
325 ILCS 5/4.3 DCFS duty to report
325 ILCS 5/5 [Temporary protective custody]
325 ILCS 5/6 [Photographs and x-rays]
325 ILCS 5/7 Time and manner of making reports
325 ILCS 5/7.1 [Cooperation with other agencies]
325 ILCS 5/7.2 [Child Protective Service Unit]
325 ILCS 5/7.3 [Investigations]
325 ILCS 5/7.3a [Perinatal Coordinator]
325 ILCS 5/7.3b [Addicted pregnant persons]
325 ILCS 5/7.3c Substance abuse services for women with children
325 ILCS 5/7.4 [Investigation procedures]
325 ILCS 5/7.5 [Access to child]
325 ILCS 5/7.6 [Posted telephone number]
325 ILCS 5/7.7 [Central register]
325 ILCS 5/7.8 [Notification of prior report]
325 ILCS 5/7.9 [Initial written reports; contents]
325 ILCS 5/7.10 [Preliminary report]
325 ILCS 5/7.12 [Determination]
325 ILCS 5/7.13 [Additional information]
325 ILCS 5/7.14 [Classification of reports]
325 ILCS 5/7.15 [Other information in central register]
325 ILCS 5/7.16 [Amendment, expunction or removal]
325 ILCS 5/7.17 [Notice]
325 ILCS 5/7.18 [Amending reports]
325 ILCS 5/7.19 [Copies]
325 ILCS 5/7.20 Inter-agency agreements for information
325 ILCS 5/7.21 Multidisciplinary Review Committee
325 ILCS 5/8.1 [Unfounded reports]
325 ILCS 5/8.2 [Service plan; report to General Assembly]
325 ILCS 5/8.3 [Assisting Circuit Court]
325 ILCS 5/8.4 [Rehabilitative services]
325 ILCS 5/8.5 [Child abuse and neglect index]
325 ILCS 5/8.6 Reports to a child's school
325 ILCS 5/9 [Immunity from liability]
325 ILCS 5/9.1 Employer discrimination
325 ILCS 5/10 [Testimony]
325 ILCS 5/11 [Confidentiality of records]
325 ILCS 5/11.1 Access to records
325 ILCS 5/11.1a Disclosure of information
325 ILCS 5/11.2 Disclosure to mandated reporting source
325 ILCS 5/11.2a Disclosure to extended family member
325 ILCS 5/11.3 [Information not to be publicized; exceptions]
325 ILCS 5/11.4 [Court and criminal justice system records]
325 ILCS 5/11.5 [Continuing education and training]
325 ILCS 5/11.6 [Review of administrative decisions]
325 ILCS 5/11.7 [State-wide Citizen's Committee on Child Abuse and Neglect]

BIRTH CONTROL SERVICES TO MINORS ACT

325 ILCS 10/0.01 Short title
325 ILCS 10/1 [Applicability]

CHILD SEXUAL ABUSE PREVENTION ACT

325 ILCS 15/0.01 Short title
325 ILCS 15/1 [Findings]
325 ILCS 15/2 [Department of Children and Family Services; duties]
325 ILCS 15/3 [Program functions and goals]
325 ILCS 15/4 [Child sexual abuse crisis intervention demonstration centers]
325 ILCS 15/5 [Confidentiality of records]
325 ILCS 15/6 [Funding of centers]
325 ILCS 15/7 [Annual reports]

CHILDREN'S PRIVACY PROTECTION AND PARENTAL EMPOWERMENT ACT

325 ILCS 17/1 Short title
325 ILCS 17/5 Definitions
325 ILCS 17/10 Prohibited act
325 ILCS 17/15 Information brokers
325 ILCS 17/20 Application of the Consumer Fraud and Deceptive Business Practices Act

EARLY INTERVENTION SERVICES SYSTEM ACT

325 ILCS 20/1 Short Title
325 ILCS 20/2 Legislative Findings and Policy
325 ILCS 20/3 Definitions
325 ILCS 20/4 Illinois Interagency Council on Early Intervention
325 ILCS 20/5 Lead Agency
325 ILCS 20/6 Local Structure and Interagency Councils
325 ILCS 20/7 Essential Components of the Statewide Service System
325 ILCS 20/8 Authority to Promulgate Rules and Regulations
325 ILCS 20/9 Role of Other State Entities
325 ILCS 20/10 Standards
325 ILCS 20/11 Individualized Family Service Plans
325 ILCS 20/12 Procedural Safeguards
325 ILCS 20/13 Funding and Fiscal Responsibility
325 ILCS 20/13.5 Other programs
325 ILCS 20/13.10 Private health insurance; assignment
325 ILCS 20/13.15 Billing of insurance carrier
325 ILCS 20/13.20 Families with insurance coverage
325 ILCS 20/13.25 Private insurance; exemption
325 ILCS 20/13.30 System of personnel development
325 ILCS 20/13.32 Contracting

325 ILCS 20/13.50 Early Intervention Legislative Advisory Committee
325 ILCS 20/14 [Repealed]
325 ILCS 20/15 [Evaluation]
325 ILCS 20/16 [Effect]
325 ILCS 20/20 Early Intervention Services Revolving Fund

HIGH RISK YOUTH CAREER DEVELOPMENT ACT

325 ILCS 25/0.01 Short title
325 ILCS 25/1 [Community-based programs]

FAMILY SUPPORT DEMONSTRATION PROJECT

325 ILCS 30/1 Short title
325 ILCS 30/2 Purpose
325 ILCS 30/3 Definitions
325 ILCS 30/4 Project
325 ILCS 30/5 Funding
325 ILCS 30/6 Council
325 ILCS 30/7 Reporting
325 ILCS 30/8 Literacy program
325 ILCS 30/9 [Effective date]

INTERAGENCY BOARD FOR CHILDREN WHO ARE DEAF OR HARD-OF-HEARING AND HAVE AN EMOTIONAL OR BEHAVIORAL DISORDER ACT

325 ILCS 35/1 Short title
325 ILCS 35/2 Purpose
325 ILCS 35/3 Definitions
325 ILCS 35/4 Appointment
325 ILCS 35/5 Term of office
325 ILCS 35/6 Organization
325 ILCS 35/7 Meetings
325 ILCS 35/8 Staff
325 ILCS 35/9 Compensation
325 ILCS 35/10 Powers and duties
325 ILCS 35/11 Reports
325 ILCS 35/12 [Effect]

INTERGOVERNMENTAL MISSING CHILD RECOVERY ACT OF 1984

325 ILCS 40/1 [Short title]
325 ILCS 40/2 [Definitions]
325 ILCS 40/3 [I SEARCH unit; powers]
325 ILCS 40/3.5 Contact with Department of Children and Family Services
325 ILCS 40/4 [Funding criteria]
325 ILCS 40/5 [State grants]
325 ILCS 40/6 [Department; powers and duties]
325 ILCS 40/7 [Law enforcement agencies; duties]
325 ILCS 40/7.1 [Custody judgments]
325 ILCS 40/8 [Duties of Director]

MINOR IDENTIFICATION AND PROTECTION ACT

325 ILCS 45/1 [Short title]
325 ILCS 45/2 [Definitions]
325 ILCS 45/3 [Fingerprint identification cards]

MISSING CHILDREN RECORDS ACT

325 ILCS 50/0.01 Short title
325 ILCS 50/1 Definitions
325 ILCS 50/2 Department duties
325 ILCS 50/3 Registrar duties
325 ILCS 50/4 Custodian duties
325 ILCS 50/5 School duties

MISSING CHILDREN REGISTRATION LAW

325 ILCS 55/0.01 Short title
325 ILCS 55/1 Definitions
325 ILCS 55/2 Department duties
325 ILCS 55/3 Registrar duties
325 ILCS 55/4 Custodian duties
325 ILCS 55/5 School duties
325 ILCS 55/6 Local law enforcement duties
325 ILCS 55/7 Home rule

SURGICAL INSTITUTE FOR CHILDREN ACT

325 ILCS 60/0.01 Short title
325 ILCS 60/1 [Establishment]
325 ILCS 60/2 [Name]
325 ILCS 60/3 [Purpose and object]
325 ILCS 60/4 [Management and control]
325 ILCS 60/5 [Admittance procedure]
325 ILCS 60/6 [Location]
325 ILCS 60/8 [General superintendent]
325 ILCS 60/11 [Gifts, donations and legacies]
325 ILCS 60/12 [Rules and regulations]

ABANDONED NEWBORN INFANT PROTECTION ACT

325 ILCS 2/1 (For postponed repeal of this Act, see 325 ILCS 2/75) Short title

Sec. 1. *Short title.* This Act may be cited as the Abandoned Newborn Infant Protection Act.
(Source: P.A. 92-408, § 1; 92-432, § 1.)

Note.

Section 75 of each of P.A. 92-408 and P.A. 92-432 provide that this Act is repealed July 1, 2007.

Identical versions of this Act were enacted by P.A. 92-408 and P.A. 92-432.

Effective Date.

Section 999 of P.A. 92-408 made this Act effective upon becoming law. The Act was approved August 17, 2001.

Section 999 of P.A. 92-432 made this Act effective upon becoming law. The Act was approved August 17, 2001.

325 ILCS 2/5 (For postponed repeal of this Act, see 325 ILCS 2/75) Public policy

Sec. 5. *Public policy.* Illinois recognizes that newborn infants have been abandoned to the environment or to other circumstances that may be unsafe to the newborn infant. These circumstances have caused injury and death to newborn infants and give rise to potential civil or criminal liability to parents who may be under severe emotional distress. This Act is intended to provide a mechanism for a newborn infant to be relinquished to a safe environment and for the parents of the infant to remain anonymous if they choose and to avoid civil or criminal liability for the act of relinquishing the infant. It is recognized that establishing an adoption plan is preferable to relinquishing a child using the procedures outlined in this Act, but to reduce the chance of injury to a newborn infant, this Act provides a safer alternative.

A public information campaign on this delicate issue shall be implemented to encourage parents considering abandonment of their newborn child to relinquish the child under the procedures outlined in this Act, to choose a traditional adoption plan, or to parent a child themselves rather than place the newborn infant in harm's way.
(Source: P.A. 92-408, § 5; 92-432, § 5.)

325 ILCS 2/10 (For postponed repeal of this Act, see 325 ILCS 2/75) Definitions

Sec. 10. *Definitions.* In this Act:

"Abandon" has the same meaning as in the Abused and Neglected Child Reporting Act [325 ILCS 5/1 et seq.].

"Abused child" has the same meaning as in the Abused and Neglected Child Reporting Act [325 ILCS 5/1 et seq.].

"Child-placing agency" means a licensed public or private agency that receives a child for the purpose of placing or arranging for the placement of the child in a foster family home or other facility for child care, apart from the custody of the child's parents.

"Department" or "DCFS" means the Illinois Department of Children and Family Services.

"Emergency medical facility" means a freestanding emergency center or trauma center, as defined in the Emergency Medical Services (EMS) Systems Act [210 ILCS 50/1 et seq.].

"Emergency medical professional" includes licensed physicians, and any emergency medical technician-basic, emergency medical technician-intermediate, emergency medical technician-paramedic, trauma nurse specialist, and pre-hospital RN, as defined in the Emergency Medical Services (EMS) Systems Act [210 ILCS 50/1 et seq.].

"Fire station" means a fire station within the State that is staffed with at least one full-time emergency medical professional.

"Hospital" has the same meaning as in the Hospital Licensing Act [210 ILCS 85/1 et seq.].

"Legal custody" means the relationship created by a court order in the best interest of a newborn infant that imposes on the infant's custodian the responsibility of physical possession of the infant, the duty to protect, train, and discipline the infant, and the duty to provide the infant with food, shelter, education, and medical care, except as these are limited by parental rights and responsibilities.

"Neglected child" has the same meaning as in the Abused and Neglected Child Reporting Act [325 ILCS 5/1 et seq.].

"Newborn infant" means a child who a licensed physician reasonably believes is 72 hours old or less at the time the child is initially relinquished to a hospital, police station, fire station, or emergency medical facility, and who is not an abused or a neglected child.

"Police station" means a municipal police station or a county sheriff's office.

"Relinquish" means to bring a newborn infant, who a licensed physician reasonably believes is 72 hours old or less, to a hospital, police station, fire station, or emergency medical facility and to leave the infant with personnel of the facility, if the person leaving the infant does not express an intent to return for the infant or states that he or she will not return for the infant. In the case of a mother who gives birth to an infant in a hospital, the mother's act of leaving that newborn infant at the hospital (i) without expressing an intent to return for the infant or (ii) stating that she will not return for the infant is not a "relinquishment" under this Act.

"Temporary protective custody" means the temporary placement of a newborn infant within a hospital or other medical facility out of the custody of the infant's parent.

(Source: P.A. 92-408, § 10; 92-432, § 10; 93-820, § 5.)

Effect of Amendments.

The 2004 amendment by P.A. 93-820, effective July 27, 2004, inserted the definition of "Police station"; and inserted "police station" in the first sentence of the definition of "Relinquish".

325 ILCS 2/15 (For postponed repeal of this Act, see 325 ILCS 2/75) Presumptions

Sec. 15. *Presumptions.* (a) There is a presumption that by relinquishing a newborn infant in accordance with this Act, the infant's parent consents to the termination of his or her parental rights with respect to the infant.

(b) There is a presumption that a person relinquishing a newborn infant in accordance with this Act:

(1) is the newborn infant's biological parent; and

(2) either without expressing an intent to return for the infant or expressing an intent not to return for the infant, did intend to relinquish the infant to the hospital, police station, fire station, or emergency medical facility to treat, care for, and provide for the infant in accordance with this Act.

(c) A parent of a relinquished newborn infant may rebut the presumption set forth in either subsection (a) or subsection (b) pursuant to Section 55 [325 ILCS 2/55], at any time before the termination of the parent's parental rights.

(Source: P.A. 92-408, § 15; 92-432, § 15; 93-820, § 5.)

Effect of Amendments.

The 2004 amendment by P.A. 93-820, effective July 27, 2004, inserted "police station" in subsection (b)(2).

325 ILCS 2/20 (For postponed repeal of this Act, see 325 ILCS 2/75) Procedures with respect to relinquished newborn infants

Sec. 20. *Procedures with respect to relinquished newborn infants.* (a) Hospitals. Every hospital must accept and provide all necessary emergency services and care to a relinquished newborn infant, in accordance with this Act. The hospital shall examine a relinquished newborn infant and perform tests that, based on reasonable medical judgment, are appropriate in evaluating whether the relinquished newborn infant was abused or neglected.

The act of relinquishing a newborn infant serves as implied consent for the hospital and its medical personnel and physicians on staff to treat and provide care for the infant.

The hospital shall be deemed to have temporary protective custody of a relinquished newborn infant until the infant is discharged to the custody of a child-placing agency or the Department.

(b) Fire stations and emergency medical facilities. Every fire station and emergency medical facility must accept and provide all necessary emergency services and care to a relinquished newborn infant, in accordance with this Act.

The act of relinquishing a newborn infant serves as implied consent for the fire station or emergency medical facility and its emergency medical professionals to treat and provide care for the infant, to the extent that those emergency medical professionals are trained to provide those services.

After the relinquishment of a newborn infant to a fire station or emergency medical facility, the fire station or emergency medical facility's personnel must arrange for the transportation of the infant to the nearest hospital as soon as transportation can be arranged.

If the parent of a newborn infant returns to reclaim the child within 72 hours after relinquishing the child to a fire station or emergency medical facility, the fire station or emergency medical facility must inform the parent of the name and location of the hospital to which the infant was transported.

(c) Police stations. Every police station must accept a relinquished newborn infant, in accordance with this Act. After the relinquishment of a newborn infant to a police station, the police station must arrange for the transportation of the infant to the nearest hospital as soon as transportation can be arranged. The act of relinquishing a newborn infant serves as implied consent for the hospital to which the infant is transported and that hospital's medical personnel and physicians on staff to treat and provide care for the infant.

If the parent of a newborn infant returns to reclaim the infant within 72 hours after relinquishing the infant to a police station, the police station must inform the parent of the name and location of the hospital to which the infant was transported.
(Source: P.A. 92-408, § 20; 92-432, § 20; 93-820, § 5.)

Effect of Amendments.
The 2004 amendment by P.A. 93-820, effective July 27, 2004, inserted subsection (c).

325 ILCS 2/25 (For postponed repeal of this Act, see 325 ILCS 2/75) Immunity for relinquishing person

Sec. 25. *Immunity for relinquishing person.* (a) The act of relinquishing a newborn infant to a hospital, police station, fire station, or emergency medical facility in accordance with this Act does not, by itself, constitute a basis for a finding of abuse, neglect, or abandonment of the infant pursuant to the laws of this State nor does it, by itself, constitute a violation of Section 12-21.5 or 12-21.6 of the Criminal Code of 1961 [720 ILCS 5/12-21.5 or 720 ILCS 5/12-21.6].

(b) If there is suspected child abuse or neglect that is not based solely on the newborn infant's relinquishment to a hospital, police station, fire station, or emergency medical facility, the personnel of the hospital, police station, fire station, or emergency medical facility who are mandated reporters under the Abused and Neglected Child Reporting Act [325 ILCS 5/1 et seq.] must report the abuse or neglect pursuant to that Act.

(c) Neither a child protective investigation nor a criminal investigation may be initiated solely because a newborn infant is relinquished pursuant to this Act.
(Source: P.A. 92-408, § 25; 92-432, § 25; 93-820, § 5.)

Effect of Amendments.
The 2004 amendment by P.A. 93-820, effective July 27, 2004, inserted references to "police station" throughout the section.

325 ILCS 2/27 (For postponed repeal of this Act, see 325 ILCS 2/75) Immunity of facility and personnel

Sec. 27. *Immunity of facility and personnel.* A hospital, police station, fire station, or emergency medical facility, and any personnel of a hospital, police station, fire station, or emergency medical facility, are immune from criminal or civil liability for acting in good faith in accordance with this Act. Nothing in this Act limits liability for negligence for care and medical treatment.
(Source: P.A. 92-408, § 27; 92-432, § 27; 93-820, § 5.)

Effect of Amendments.
The 2004 amendment by P.A. 93-820, effective July 27, 2004, inserted "police station" twice.

325 ILCS 2/30 (For postponed repeal of this Act, see 325 ILCS 2/75) Anonymity of relinquishing person

Sec. 30. *Anonymity of relinquishing person.* If there is no evidence of abuse or neglect of a relinquished newborn infant, the relinquishing person has the right to remain anonymous and to leave the hospital, police station, fire station, or emergency medical facility at any time and not be pursued or followed. Before the relinquishing person leaves the hospital, police station, fire station, or emergency medical facility, the hospital, police station, fire station, or emergency medical facility personnel shall (i) verbally inform the relinquishing person that by relinquishing the child anonymously, he or she will have to petition the court if he or she desires to prevent the termination of parental rights and regain custody of the child and (ii) shall offer the relinquishing person the information packet described in Section 35 of this Act [325 ILCS 2/35].

However, nothing in this Act shall be construed as precluding the relinquishing person from providing his or her identity or completing the application forms for the Illinois Adoption Registry and Medical Information Exchange and requesting that the hospital, police station, fire station, or emergency medical facility forward those forms to the Illinois Adoption Registry and Medical information Exchange.
(Source: P.A. 92-408, § 30; 92-432, § 30; 93-820, § 5.)

Effect of Amendments.
The 2004 amendment by P.A. 93-820, effective July 27, 2004, inserted "police station" throughout the section; and made related and stylistic changes.

325 ILCS 2/35 (For postponed repeal of this Act, see 325 ILCS 2/75) Information for relinquishing person

Sec. 35. *Information for relinquishing person.* A hospital, police station, fire station, or emergency medical facility that receives a newborn infant relinquished in accordance with this Act must offer an information packet to the relinquishing person and, if possible, must clearly inform the relinquishing person that his or her acceptance of the information is completely voluntary, that registration with the Illinois Adoption Registry and Medical Information Exchange is voluntary, that the person will remain anonymous if he or she completes a Denial of Information Exchange, and that the person has the option to provide medical information only and still remain anonymous. The information packet must include all of the following:

(1) All Illinois Adoption Registry and Medical Information Exchange application forms, including the Medical Information Exchange Questionnaire and the web site address and toll-free phone number of the Registry.

(2) Written notice of the following:

(A) No sooner than 60 days following the date of the initial relinquishment of the infant to a hospital, police station, fire station, or emergency medical facility, the child-placing agency or the Department will commence proceedings for the termination of parental rights and placement of the infant for adoption.

(B) Failure of a parent of the infant to contact the Department and petition for the return of custody of the infant before termination of parental rights bars any future action asserting legal rights with respect to the infant.

(3) A resource list of providers of counseling services including grief counseling, pregnancy counseling, and counseling regarding adoption and other available options for placement of the infant.

Upon request, the Department of Public Health shall provide the application forms for the Illinois Adoption Registry and Medical Information Exchange to hospitals, police stations, fire stations, and emergency medical facilities.
(Source: P.A. 92-408, § 35; 92-432, § 35; 93-820, § 5.)

Effect of Amendments.
The 2004 amendment by P.A. 93-820, effective July 27, 2004, inserted "police station" throughout the section.

325 ILCS 2/40 (For postponed repeal of this Act, see 325 ILCS 2/75) Reporting requirements

Sec. 40. *Reporting requirements.* (a) Within 12 hours after accepting a newborn infant from a relinquishing person or from a police station, fire station or emergency medical facility in accordance with this Act, a hospital must report to the Department's State Central Registry for the purpose of transferring physical custody of the infant from the hospital to either a child-placing agency or the Department.

(b) Within 24 hours after receiving a report under subsection (a), the Department must request assistance from law enforcement officials to investigate the matter using the National Crime Information Center to ensure that the relinquished newborn infant is not a missing child.

(c) Once a hospital has made a report to the Department under subsection (a), the Department must arrange for a licensed child-placing agency to accept physical custody of the relinquished newborn infant.

(d) If a relinquished child is not a newborn infant as defined in this Act, the hospital and the Department must proceed as if the child is an abused or neglected child.
(Source: P.A. 92-408, § 40; 92-432, § 40; 93-820, § 5.)

Effect of Amendments.
The 2004 amendment by P.A. 93-820, effective July 27, 2004, inserted "police station" in subsection (a).

325 ILCS 2/45 (For postponed repeal of this Act, see 325 ILCS 2/75) Medical assistance

Sec. 45. *Medical assistance.* Notwithstanding any other provision of law, a newborn infant relinquished in accordance with this Act shall be deemed eligible for medical assistance under the Illinois Public Aid Code [305 ILCS 5/1-1 et seq.], and a hospital providing medical services to such an infant shall be reimbursed for those services in accordance with the payment methodologies authorized under that Code. In addition, for any day that a hospital has custody of a newborn infant relinquished in accordance with this Act and the infant does not require medically necessary care, the hospital shall be reimbursed by the Illinois Department of Public Aid at the general acute care per diem rate, in accordance with 89 Ill. Adm. Code 148.270(c).
(Source: P.A. 92-408, § 45; 92-432, § 45.)

325 ILCS 2/50 (For postponed repeal of this Act, see 325 ILCS 2/75) Child-placing agency procedures

Sec. 50. *Child-placing agency procedures.* (a) The Department's State Central Registry must maintain a list of licensed child-placing agencies willing to take legal custody of newborn infants relinquished in accordance with this Act. The child-placing agencies on the list must be contacted by the Department on a rotating basis upon notice from a hospital that a newborn infant has been relinquished in accordance with this Act.

(b) Upon notice from the Department that a newborn infant has been relinquished in accordance with this Act, a child-placing agency must accept the newborn infant if the agency has the accommodations to do so. The child-placing agency must seek an order for legal custody of the infant upon its acceptance of the infant.

(c) Within 3 business days after assuming physical custody of the infant, the child-placing agency shall file a petition in the division of the circuit court in which petitions for adoption would normally be heard. The petition shall allege that the newborn infant has been relinquished in accordance with this Act and shall state that the child-placing agency intends to place the infant in an adoptive home.

(d) If no licensed child-placing agency is able to accept the relinquished newborn infant, then the Department must assume responsibility for the infant as soon as practicable.

(e) A custody order issued under subsection (b) shall remain in effect until a final adoption order based on the relinquished newborn infant's best interests is issued in accordance with this Act and the Adoption Act [750 ILCS 50/0.01 et seq.].

(f) When possible, the child-placing agency must place a relinquished newborn infant in a prospective adoptive home.

(g) The Department or child-placing agency must initiate proceedings to (i) terminate the parental rights of the relinquished newborn infant's known or unknown parents, (ii) appoint a guardian for the infant, and (iii) obtain consent to the infant's adoption in accordance with this Act no sooner than 60 days following the date of the initial relinquishment of the infant to the hospital, police station, fire station, or emergency medical facility.

(h) Before filing a petition for termination of parental rights, the Department or child-placing agency must do the following:

(1) Search its Putative Father Registry for the purpose of determining the identity and location of the putative father of the relinquished newborn infant who is, or is expected to be, the subject of an adoption proceeding, in order to provide notice of the proceeding to the putative father. At least one search of the Registry must be conducted, at least 30 days after the relinquished newborn infant's estimated date of birth; earlier searches may be conducted, however. Notice to any potential putative father discovered in a search of the Registry according to the estimated age of the relinquished newborn infant must be in accordance with Section 12a of the Adoption Act [750 ILCS 50/12a].

(2) Verify with law enforcement officials, using the National Crime Information Center, that the relinquished newborn infant is not a missing child.

(Source: P.A. 92-408, § 50; 92-432, § 50; 93-820, § 5.)

Effect of Amendments.

The 2004 amendment by P.A. 93-820, effective July 27, 2004, inserted "police station" in subsection (g).

325 ILCS 2/55 (For postponed repeal of this Act, see 325 ILCS 2/75) Petition for return of custody

Sec. 55. *Petition for return of custody.* (a) A parent of a newborn infant relinquished in accordance with this Act may petition for the return of custody of the infant before the termination of parental rights with respect to the infant.

(b) A parent of a newborn infant relinquished in accordance with this Act may petition for the return of custody of the infant by contacting the Department for the purpose of obtaining the name of the child-placing agency and then filing a petition for return of custody in the circuit court in which the proceeding for the termination of parental rights is pending.

(c) If a petition for the termination of parental rights has not been filed by the Department or the child-placing agency, the parent of the relinquished newborn infant must contact the Department, which must notify the parent of the appropriate court in which the petition for return of custody must be filed.

(d) The circuit court may hold the proceeding for the termination of parental rights in abeyance for a period not to exceed 60 days from the date that the petition for return of custody was filed without a showing of good cause. During that period:

(1) The court shall order genetic testing to establish maternity or paternity, or both.

(2) The Department shall conduct a child protective investigation and home study to develop recommendations to the court.

(3) When indicated as a result of the Department's investigation and home study, further proceedings under the Juvenile Court Act of 1987 [705 ILCS 405/1-1 et seq.] as the court determines appropriate, may be conducted. However, relinquishment of a newborn infant in accordance with this Act does not render the infant abused, neglected, or abandoned solely because the newborn infant was relinquished to a hospital, police station, fire station, or emergency medical facility in accordance with this Act.

(e) Failure to file a petition for the return of custody of a relinquished newborn infant before the termination of parental rights bars any future action asserting legal rights with respect to the infant unless the parent's act of relinquishment that led to the termination of parental rights involved fraud perpetrated against and not stemming from or involving the parent. No action to void or revoke the

termination of parental rights of a parent of a newborn infant relinquished in accordance with this Act, including an action based on fraud, may be commenced after 12 months after the date that the newborn infant was initially relinquished to a hospital, police station, fire station, or emergency medical facility.
(Source: P.A. 92-408, § 55; 92-432, § 55; 93-820, § 5.)

Effect of Amendments.
The 2004 amendment by P.A. 93-820, effective July 27, 2004, inserted "police station" twice.

325 ILCS 2/60 (For postponed repeal of this Act, see 325 ILCS 2/75) Department's duties

Sec. 60. *Department's duties.* The Department must implement a public information program to promote safe placement alternatives for newborn infants. The public information program must inform the public of the following:

(1) The relinquishment alternative provided for in this Act, which results in the adoption of a newborn infant under 72 hours of age and which provides for the parent's anonymity, if the parent so chooses.

(2) The alternative of adoption through a public or private agency, in which the parent's identity may or may not be known to the agency, but is kept anonymous from the adoptive parents, if the birth parent so desires, and which allows the parent to be actively involved in the child's adoption plan.

The public information program may include, but need not be limited to, the following elements:

(i) Educational and informational materials in print, audio, video, electronic or other media.

(ii) Establishment of a web site.

(iii) Public service announcements and advertisements.

(iv) Establishment of toll-free telephone hotlines to provide information.
(Source: P.A. 92-408, § 60; 92-432, § 60.)

325 ILCS 2/65 (For postponed repeal of this Act, see 325 ILCS 2/75) Evaluation

Sec. 65. *Evaluation.* (a) The Department shall collect and analyze information regarding the relinquishment of newborn infants and placement of children under this Act. Police stations, fire stations, emergency medical facilities, and medical professionals accepting and providing services to a newborn infant under this Act shall report to the Department data necessary for the Department to evaluate and determine the effect of this Act in the prevention of injury or death of newborn infants. Child-placing agencies shall report to the Department data necessary to evaluate and determine the effectiveness of these agencies in providing child protective and child welfare services to newborn infants relinquished under this Act.

(b) The information collected shall include, but need not be limited to: the number of newborn infants relinquished; the services provided to relinquished newborn infants; the outcome of care for the relinquished newborn infants; the number and disposition of cases of relinquished newborn infants subject to placement; the number of children accepted and served by child-placing agencies; and the services provided by child-placing agencies and the disposition of the cases of the children placed under this Act.

(c) The Department shall submit a report by January 1, 2002, and on January 1 of each year thereafter, to the Governor and General Assembly regarding the prevention of injury or death of newborn infants and the effect of placements of children under this Act. The report shall include, but need not be limited to, a summary of collected data, an analysis of the data and conclusions regarding the Act's effectiveness, a determination whether the purposes of the Act are being achieved, and recommendations for changes that may be considered necessary to improve the administration and enforcement of this Act.
(Source: P.A. 92-408, § 65; 92-432, § 65; 93-820, § 5.)

Effect of Amendments.
The 2004 amendment by P.A. 93-820, effective July 27, 2004, inserted "Police stations" in subsection (a).

325 ILCS 2/70 (For postponed repeal of this Act, see 325 ILCS 2/75) Construction of Act

Sec. 70. *Construction of Act.* Nothing in this Act shall be construed to preclude the courts of this State from exercising their discretion to protect the health and safety of children in individual cases. The best interests and welfare of a child shall be a paramount consideration in the construction and interpretation of this Act. It is in the child's best interests that this Act be construed and interpreted so as not to result in extending time limits beyond those set forth in this Act.
(Source: P.A. 92-408, § 70; 92-432, § 70.)

325 ILCS 2/75: Repeal

Sec. 75. *Repeal.* This Act is repealed on July 1, 2007.
(Source: P.A. 92-408, § 75; 92-432, § 75.)

325 ILCS 2/90 [Not set out]

(Source: P.A. 92-408, § 90; 92-432, § 90.)

Note.
Sections 90, 92, 95, 96, 96.5 and 97, as set out in each of P.A. 92-408 and P.A. 92-432, contain amendatory provisions.

325 ILCS 2/999 Effective date

Sec. 999. *Effective date.* This Act takes effect upon becoming law.
(Source: P.A. 92-408, § 999, 92-432, § 999.)

Note.
P.A. 92-408 and P.A. 92-432 were each approved August 17, 2001.

Abused and Neglected Child Reporting Act

325 ILCS 5/1 [Short title]

Sec. 1. This Act shall be known and may be cited as the Abused and Neglected Child Reporting Act.
(Source: P.A. 79-65.)

Derivation.
Title: An Act creating the Abused and Neglected Child Reporting Act and repealing and amending other Acts.
Cite: 325 ILCS 5/1 et seq.
Source: P.A. 79-65.
Date: Approved June 26, 1975.

Note.
This section was Ill.Rev.Stat., Ch. 23, para. 2051.

Cross References.
As to the administration of child abuse prevention shelters, under the Children and Family Services Act, see 20 ILCS 505/4a.
As to the admissibility of an Abused and Neglected Child report into evidence, see 705 ILCS 405/2-18.
As to disciplinary action by the Department of Professional Regulation for Violation of the Abused and Neglected Child Reporting Act see the following: as to athletic trainers, see 225 ILCS 10/16; as to hearing aid dispensers, see 225 ILCS 50/18; as to interior design professionals, see 225 ILCS 310/13; as to marriage and family therapists, see 225 ILCS 55/85; as to medical practice, see 225 ILCS 60/22; as to nursing, see 225 ILCS 65/25; as to optometrists, see 225 ILCS 80/24; as to physical therapists, see 225 ILCS 90/17; as to physician's assistants, see 225 ILCS 95/21; as to psychologists, see 225 ILCS 15/15; as to social workers, see 225 ILCS 20/19; as to speech language pathologists, see 225 ILCS 110/16.
As to suspension or revocation of a teacher's certification, for failure to file an abused and neglected child report under the School Code, see 105 ILCS 5/21-23.

CASE NOTES

Analysis

Due Process
School Board
Standing

Due Process
Due process rights of foster parents, who were the focus of an "indicated" report for the abuse of foster children in their care, were not violated as a result of a lengthy administrative hearing that stretched over several months and was interrupted by several continuances; the totality of the circumstances, including the number of witnesses, the gravity of the allegations, and the fact that the foster parent's counsel proposed or consented to the various hearing dates, showed that the length of the hearing was neither a violation of the Illinois Administrative Code nor unreasonable. Lehmann v. Dep't of Children & Family Servs., 342 Ill. App. 3d 1069, 277 Ill. Dec. 799, 796 N.E.2d 1165, 2003 Ill. App. LEXIS 1122 (1 Dist. 2003).
Due process rights of foster parents, who were the focus of an "indicated" report for the abuse of foster children in their care, were not violated by the fact that the administrative law judge filed his recommendation beyond the 30-day limit set out in Ill. Admin. Code 89, § 336.130(b)(14) (1996) because the foster parents failed to show that they were prejudiced in any way by the delay. Lehmann v. Dep't of Children & Family Servs., 342 Ill. App. 3d 1069, 277 Ill. Dec. 799, 796 N.E.2d 1165, 2003 Ill. App. LEXIS 1122 (1 Dist. 2003).

School Board
It was error to dismiss counts against a school board by a student alleging negligence, negligent infliction of emotional distress, and willful and wanton conduct, pursuant to 735 ILCS 5/2-619(a)(9), where the student had sufficiently pled the causes of action which revolved around the board's failure to report allegations of sexual harassment by a teacher, pursuant to its obligations under the Abused and Neglected Child Report Act, 325 ILCS 5/1 et seq.; Sections 2-201 and 3-108 of the Tort Immunity Act, 745 ILCS 10/2-201, 3-108 were inapplicable because the failure to report was not subject to the immunity of § 2-201 and the immunity under § 3-108 was applicable to failures to supervise. Doe v. Dimovski, 336 Ill. App. 3d 292, 270 Ill. Dec. 618, 783 N.E.2d 193, 2003 Ill. App. LEXIS 42 (2 Dist. 2003), appeal denied, 204 Ill. 2d 658, 275 Ill. Dec. 75, 792 N.E.2d 306 (2003).

Standing
Department of Children and Family Services had standing to contest circuit court's order that future interviews with parent's children regarding alleged sexual abuse be video recorded since the Department is responsible for investigating reports of suspected child abuse. In re R.V., 288 Ill. App. 3d 860, 224 Ill. Dec. 345, 681 N.E.2d 660 (1 Dist. 1997).

LEGAL PERIODICALS

For essay, "The Criminal Courtroom: Is It Child Proof?," see 26 Loy. U. Chi. L.J. 681 (1995).
For article "A Primer on the Juvenile Court Act of 1987," see 9 CBA Rec. 33 (1995).
For article, "Cocaine Babies: Meeting the Challenge," see 80 Ill. B.J. 348.
For article, "Child Abuse—Despite the Law It's Not Reported," see 5 CBA Rec. 24 (1991).
For comment, "When Self Abuse Becomes Child Abuse: The Need for Coercive Prenatal Government Act in Response to the Cocaine Baby Problem," see 11 N. Ill. U.L. Rev. 73 (1990).
For note, "Towards an Upstream Model of Child Abuse Legislation in Illinois," see 11 Loy. U. Chi. L.J. 251 (1979-80).

RESEARCH REFERENCES

Validity and construction of penal statute prohibiting child abuse. 1 ALR4th 38.
Validity, construction, and application of state statute requiring doctor or other person to report child abuse. 73 ALR4th 782.

325 ILCS 5/2 [Scope of act]

Sec. 2. The Illinois Department of Children and Family Services shall, upon receiving reports made under this Act, protect the health, safety, and best interests of the child in all situations in which the child is vulnerable to child abuse or neglect, offer protective services in order to prevent any further harm to the child and to other children in the same environment or family, stabilize the home environment, and preserve family life whenever possible. Recognizing that children also can be abused and neglected while living in public or private residential agencies or institutions meant to serve them, while attending day care centers, schools, or religious activities, or when in contact with adults who are responsible for the welfare of the child at that time, this Act also provides for the reporting and investigation of child abuse and neglect in such instances. In performing any of these duties, the Department may utilize such protective services of voluntary agencies as are available.
(Source: P.A. 84-1318; 90-28, § 10-15; 92-801, § 5.)

Note.
This section was Ill.Rev.Stat., Ch. 23, para. 2052.

Cross References.
As to home visits, interviews, or communications of the Department of Children and Family Services, for determining the amount of public assistance, see 305 ILCS 5/4-7.

As to reporting the mismanagement of funds, provided for assisting a child, under the Public Aid Code, see 305 ILCS 5/4-8.

As to the licensing of a child care facility, who fails to report suspected abuse or neglect, see 225 ILCS 10/8.

Effect of Amendments.
The 1997 amendment by P.A. 90-28, effective January 1, 1998, in the first sentence, inserted "health, safety, and", inserted "in all situations in which the child is vulnerable to child abuse or neglect", inserted "and" and deleted from the end "and protect the health and safety of children in all situations in which they are vulnerable to child abuse or neglect".

The 2002 amendment by P.A. 92-801, effective August 16, 2002, inserted "or religious activities", and made a stylistic change.

CASE NOTES

Analysis

Due Process
—Property Interest Insufficient
Preservation of Family Life
Termination of Parental Rights Upheld
Tort Duty of Hospital Employees

Due Process

—Property Interest Insufficient
Services to stabilize the home environment, preserve family life whenever possible, and protect the health and safety of children were not sufficiently precise to show a property interest sufficient to sustain a due process claim. B.H. v. Johnson, 715 F. Supp. 1387 (N.D. Ill. 1989).

Preservation of Family Life
Pursuant to the provisions in the Juvenile Court Act (705 ILCS 405/1-1 et seq.) and Department of Children and Family Services' (DCFS) mandate, the court may enter interim orders for services to the child and his or her family in order to prevent the unnecessary separation of children from their families and restoring to their families children who have been removed where it has found that they are in the best interest of the minor and his or her family and will help preserve the family. In re Lawrence M., 269 Ill. App. 3d 253, 206 Ill. Dec. 817, 645 N.E.2d 1069 (1 Dist.), aff'd, 172 Ill. 2d 523, 219 Ill. Dec. 32, 670 N.E.2d 710 (1996).

Termination of Parental Rights Upheld
Termination of parental rights held not against the manifest weight of the evidence. People ex rel. Greanias v. Holmes, 28 Ill. App. 3d 104, 328 N.E.2d 35 (4 Dist. 1975).

Tort Duty of Hospital Employees
Where the abuse victims filed suit against the psychological clinic alleging that it failed to report abuse, allegedly in violation of 325 ILCS 5/4, of which its therapist was informed by the abuser, the action was properly dismissed under 735 ILCS 5/2-615 as the Illinois Abused and Neglected Child Reporting Act granted no private right of action; while the Act, as stated in 325 ILCS 5/2, was meant to protect children from abuse, it did so by imposing a misdemeanor under 325 ILCS 5/4.02 if a person who was obligated to report abuse failed to do so rather than by granting a private right of action. Doe v. N. Cent. Behavioral Health Sys., 352 Ill. App. 3d 284, 287 Ill. Dec. 493, 816 N.E.2d 4, 2004 Ill. App. LEXIS 992 (3 Dist. 2004).

Judgment for plaintiff in a wrongful death action was reversed and the case was dismissed because Illinois' Abused and Neglected Child Reporting Act (ANCRA), 325 ILCS 5/2 et seq., did not impose a tort duty to report child abuse on hospital employees; nothing in the statute's text indicated that the legislature meant to expand the scope of tort liability to encompass people who failed to report child abuse, and a private right should not be implied because the fact that the only sanction the legislature had provided was for a willful violation (which was not alleged in plaintiff's case) suggested a reluctance to impose liability for merely negligent violations. Cuyler v. United States, 362 F.3d 949, 2004 U.S. App. LEXIS 5837 (7th Cir. 2004).

OPINIONS OF ATTORNEY GENERAL

Applicability
The reporting provisions of this Act are not limited only to cases of a child whose death occurs from suspected abuse or neglect before being found or brought to a hospital; this section contemplates the offering of protective services in order to prevent further harm to the child, and therefore clearly contemplates a situation where the child is alive. 1979 Op. Atty. Gen. 43.

LEGAL PERIODICALS

For comments, "Child Abuse: The Role of Adoption as a Preventative Measure," see 10 J. Marshall J. Prac. & Proc. 546 (1977).

325 ILCS 5/2.1 [Eligibility]

Sec. 2.1. Any person or family seeking assistance in meeting child care responsibilities may use the services and facilities established by this Act which may assist in meeting such responsibilities. Whether or not the problem presented constitutes child abuse or neglect, such persons or families shall be referred to appropriate resources or agencies. No person seeking assistance under this Section shall be required to give his name or any other identifying information.
(Source: P.A. 81-1077.)

Note.
This section was Ill.Rev.Stat., Ch. 23, para. 2052.1.

325 ILCS 5/3 [Definitions]

Sec. 3. As used in this Act unless the context otherwise requires:

"Child" means any person under the age of 18 years, unless legally emancipated by reason of marriage or entry into a branch of the United States armed services.

"Department" means Department of Children and Family Services.

"Local law enforcement agency" means the police of a city, town, village or other incorporated area or the sheriff of an unincorporated area or any sworn officer of the Illinois Department of State Police.

"Abused child" means a child whose parent or immediate family member, or any person responsible for the child's welfare, or any individual residing in the same home as the child, or a paramour of the child's parent:

(a) inflicts, causes to be inflicted, or allows to be inflicted upon such child physical injury, by other than accidental means, which causes death, disfigurement, impairment of physical or emotional health, or loss or impairment of any bodily function;

(b) creates a substantial risk of physical injury to such child by other than accidental means which would be likely to cause death, disfigurement, impairment of physical or emotional health, or loss or impairment of any bodily function;

(c) commits or allows to be committed any sex offense against such child, as such sex offenses are defined in the Criminal Code of 1961, as amended [720 ILCS 5/1-1 et seq.], and extending those definitions of sex offenses to include children under 18 years of age;

(d) commits or allows to be committed an act or acts of torture upon such child;

(e) inflicts excessive corporal punishment;

(f) commits or allows to be committed the offense of female genital mutilation, as defined in Section 12-34 of the Criminal Code of 1961 [720 ILCS 5/12-34], against the child; or

(g) causes to be sold, transferred, distributed, or given to such child under 18 years of age, a controlled substance as defined in Section 102 of the Illinois Controlled Substances Act [720 ILCS 570/102] in violation of Article IV of the Illinois Controlled Substances Act [720 ILCS 570/401 et seq.], except for controlled substances that are prescribed in accordance with Article III of the Illinois Controlled Substances Act [720 ILCS 570/301 et seq.] and are dispensed to such child in a manner that substantially complies with the prescription.

A child shall not be considered abused for the sole reason that the child has been relinquished in accordance with the Abandoned Newborn Infant Protection Act [325 ILCS 2/1 et seq.].

"Neglected child" means any child who is not receiving the proper or necessary nourishment or medically indicated treatment including food or care not provided solely on the basis of the present or anticipated mental or physical impairment as determined by a physician acting alone or in consultation with other physicians or otherwise is not receiving the proper or necessary support or medical or other remedial care recognized under State law as necessary for a child's well-being, or other care necessary for his or her well-being, including adequate food, clothing and shelter; or who is abandoned by his or her parents or other person responsible for the child's welfare without a proper plan of care; or who is a newborn infant whose blood, urine, or meconium contains any amount of a controlled substance as defined in subsection (f) of Section 102 of the Illinois Controlled Substances Act [720 ILCS 570/102] or a metabolite thereof, with the exception of a controlled substance or metabolite thereof whose presence in the newborn infant is the result of medical treatment administered to the mother or the newborn infant. A child shall not be considered neglected for the sole reason that the child's parent or other person responsible for his or her welfare has left the child in the care of an adult relative for any period of time. A child shall not be considered neglected for the sole reason that the child has been relinquished in accordance with the Abandoned Newborn Infant Protection Act [325 ILCS 2/1 et seq.]. A child shall not be considered neglected or abused for the sole reason that such child's parent or other person responsible for his or her welfare depends upon spiritual means through prayer alone for the treatment or cure of disease or remedial care as provided under Section 4 of this Act [325 ILCS 5/4]. A child shall not be considered neglected or abused solely because the child is not attending school in accordance with the requirements of Article 26 of The School Code, as amended [105 ILCS 5/26-1 et seq.].

"Child Protective Service Unit" means certain specialized State employees of the Department assigned by the Director to perform the duties and responsibilities as provided under Section 7.2 of this Act [325 ILCS 5/7.2].

"Person responsible for the child's welfare" means the child's parent; guardian; foster parent; relative caregiver; any person responsible for the child's welfare in a public or private residential agency or institution; any person responsible for the child's welfare within a public or private profit or not for profit child care facility; or any other person responsible for the child's welfare at the time of the alleged abuse or neglect, or any person who came to know the child through an official capacity or position of trust, including but not limited to health care professionals, educational personnel, recreational supervisors, members of the clergy, and volunteers or support personnel in any setting where children may be subject to abuse or neglect.

"Temporary protective custody" means custody within a hospital or other medical facility or a place previously designated for such custody by the Department, subject to review by the Court, including a licensed foster home, group home, or other institution; but such place shall not be a jail or other place for the detention of criminal or juvenile offenders.

"An unfounded report" means any report made under this Act for which it is determined after an investigation that no credible evidence of abuse or neglect exists.

"An indicated report" means a report made under this Act if an investigation determines that credible evidence of the alleged abuse or neglect exists.

"An undetermined report" means any report made under this Act in which it was not possible to initiate or complete an investigation on the basis of information provided to the Department.

"Subject of report" means any child reported to the central register of child abuse and neglect established under Section 7.7 of this Act [325 ILCS 5/7.7] and his or her parent, guardian or other person responsible who is also named in the report.

"Perpetrator" means a person who, as a result of investigation, has been determined by the Department to have caused child abuse or neglect.

"Member of the clergy" means a clergyman or practitioner of any religious denomination accredited by the religious body to which he or she belongs. (Source: P.A. 86-274; 86-601; 86-659; 86-1028; 88-85, § 80; 89-21, § 15-10; 90-239, § 10; 90-684, § 5; 91-802, § 5; 92-408, § 92; 92-432, § 92; 92-801, § 5.)

Note.

This section was Ill.Rev.Stat., Ch. 23, para. 2053.

Illinois Administrative Code.

See 89 Illinois Administrative Code, §§ 304.2, 304.2, 20 Illinois Administrative Code, §§ 801.150, 385.50, 300.20, 10.263, 117.10, 336.20, 10.263, 3-300.010.

Effect of Amendments.

The 1995 amendment by P.A. 89-21, effective July 1, 1995, in the definition of "neglected child", in the second sentence, deleted "as a plan of care" from the end; and in the definition of "person responsible" inserted "relative caregiver".

The 1997 amendment by P.A. 90-239, effective July 28, 1997, in the definition of neglected child, in the first sentence, substituted "blood, urine, or meconium" for "blood or urine".

The 1998 amendment by P.A. 90-684, effective July 31, 1998 in the definition of "Abused Child" added item f, and made related changes.

The 2000 amendment by P.A. 91-802, effective January 1, 2001, inserted subdivision g in the definition of "Abused child".

The 2001 amendment by P.A. 92-408, effective August 17, 2001, inserted the last paragraph in the definition of "Abused child" and inserted the third sentence in the definition of "Neglected child".

The 2001 amendment by P.A. 92-432, effective August 17, 2001, inserted the last paragraph in the definition of "Abused child" and inserted the third sentence in the definition of "Neglected child".

The 2002 amendment by P.A. 92-801, effective August 16, 2002, redesignated subsections a. through g. as (a) through (g); inserted "members of the clergy" in the paragraph defining "'Person responsible for the child's welfare'"; and added the last paragraph.

CASE NOTES

ANALYSIS

Abuse
—Corporal Punishment
—Inappropriate Behavior
—Shown
Religious Beliefs Exception
—Applicability
Subject of Report

Abuse

—Corporal Punishment

Where the actions by teacher caused marks but did not cause death, disfigurement, any impairment of health, or any loss of bodily function, his actions did not constitute excessive corporal punishment and did not amount to abuse. Korunka v. Department of Children & Family Servs., 259 Ill. App. 3d 527, 197 Ill. Dec. 537, 631 N.E.2d 759 (4 Dist. 1994).

—Inappropriate Behavior

Where the abuse victims filed suit against the psychological clinic alleging that it failed to report abuse, allegedly in violation of 325 ILCS 5/4, of which its therapist was informed by the abuser, the action was properly dismissed under 735 ILCS 5/2-615, as the clinic was not required to report the abuse; the children did not fall within the 325 ILCS 5/3 definition of abused children since there was no allegation that a parent or anyone else reponsible for the victims' welfare allowed the abuse to occur, and the clinic did not see the abuser in a professional or official capacity. Doe v. N. Cent. Behavioral Health Sys., 352 Ill. App. 3d 284, 287 Ill. Dec. 493, 816 N.E.2d 4, 2004 Ill. App. LEXIS 992 (3 Dist. 2004).

Inappropriate behavior does not necessarily amount to abuse. Korunka v. Department of Children & Family Servs., 259 Ill. App. 3d 527, 197 Ill. Dec. 537, 631 N.E.2d 759 (4 Dist. 1994).

—Shown

A kiss on the lips and a pat on the buttocks qualified as child abuse. Doe v. Illinois Dep't of Children & Family Servs., 265 Ill. App. 3d 907, 203 Ill. Dec. 110, 639 N.E.2d 149 (1 Dist.), appeal denied, 157 Ill. 2d 498, 205 Ill. Dec. 159, 642 N.E.2d 1276 (1994).

Religious Beliefs Exception

—Applicability

The religious beliefs exception in the definition of medical neglect in this section is not applicable to the definition of medical neglect in section 802-3 of the Juvenile Court Act (705 ILCS 405/2-3). People v. E.G., 161 Ill. App. 3d 765, 113 Ill. Dec. 477, 515 N.E.2d 286 (1 Dist. 1987).

Subject of Report

The legislature does not consider a person who makes a report a subject of the report. Kemp-Golden v. Department of Children & Family Servs., 281 Ill. App. 3d 869, 217 Ill. Dec. 594, 667 N.E.2d 688 (1 Dist. 1996).

Although the definition of Subject of Report in this section does include a parent named in the report, it refers only to a parent named as an alleged perpetrator of abuse or neglect. Kemp-Golden v. Department of Children & Family Servs., 281 Ill. App. 3d 869, 217 Ill. Dec. 594, 667 N.E.2d 688 (1 Dist. 1996).

LEGAL PERIODICALS

For article, "The Folly of Joint Custody," see 69 Ill. B.J. 412 (1981).

325 ILCS 5/4 Persons required to report; privileged communications; transmitting false report

Sec. 4. *Persons required to report; privileged communications; transmitting false report.* Any physician, resident, intern, hospital, hospital administrator and personnel engaged in examination, care and treatment of persons, surgeon, dentist, dentist hygienist, osteopath, chiropractor, podiatrist, physician assistant, substance abuse treatment personnel, funeral home director or employee, coroner, medical examiner, emergency medical technician, acupuncturist, crisis line or hotline personnel, school personnel, educational advocate assigned to a child pursuant to the School Code, truant officers, social worker, social services administrator, domestic violence program personnel, registered nurse, licensed practical nurse, genetic counselor, respiratory care practitioner, advanced practice nurse, home health aide, director or staff assistant of a nursery school or a child day care center, recreational program or facility personnel, law enforcement officer, licensed professional counselor, licensed clinical professional counselor, registered psychologist and assistants working under the direct supervision of a psychologist, psychiatrist, or field personnel of the Illinois Department of Public Aid, Public Health, Human Services (acting as successor to the Department of Mental Health and Developmental Disabilities, Rehabilitation Services, or Public Aid), Corrections, Human Rights, or Children and Family Services, supervisor and administrator of general assistance under the Illinois Public Aid Code [305 ILCS 5/1-1 et seq.], probation officer, or any other foster parent, homemaker or child care worker having reasonable cause to believe a child known to them in their professional or official capacity may be an abused child or a neglected child shall immediately report or cause a report to be made to the Department.

Any member of the clergy having reasonable cause to believe that a child known to that member of the clergy in his or her professional capacity may be an abused child as defined in item (c) of the definition of "abused child" in Section 3 of this Act [325 ILCS 5/3] shall immediately report or cause a report to be made to the Department.

Whenever such person is required to report under this Act in his capacity as a member of the staff of a medical or other public or private institution, school, facility or agency, or as a member of the clergy, he shall make report immediately to the Department in accordance with the provisions of this Act and may also notify the person in charge of such institution, school, facility or agency, or church, synagogue, temple, mosque, or other religious institution, or his designated agent that such report has been made. Under no circumstances shall any person in charge of such institution, school, facility or agency, or church, synagogue, temple, mosque, or other religious institution, or his designated agent to whom such notification has been made, exercise any control, restraint, modification or other change in the report or the forwarding of such report to the Department.

The privileged quality of communication between any professional person required to report and his patient or client shall not apply to situations involving abused or neglected children and shall not constitute grounds for failure to report as required by this Act.

A member of the clergy may claim the privilege under Section 8-803 of the Code of Civil Procedure [735 ILCS 5/8-803].

In addition to the above persons required to report suspected cases of abused or neglected children, any other person may make a report if such person has reasonable cause to believe a child may be an abused child or a neglected child.

Any person who enters into employment on and after July 1, 1986 and is mandated by virtue of that employment to report under this Act, shall sign a statement on a form prescribed by the Department, to the effect that the employee has knowledge and understanding of the reporting requirements of this Act. The statement shall be signed prior to commencement of the employment. The signed statement shall be retained by the employer. The cost of printing, distribution, and filing of the statement shall be borne by the employer.

The Department shall provide copies of this Act, upon request, to all employers employing persons who shall be required under the provisions of this Section to report under this Act.

Any person who knowingly transmits a false report to the Department commits the offense of disorderly conduct under subsection (a)(7) of Section 26-1 of the "Criminal Code of 1961" [720 ILCS 5/26-1]. Any person who violates this provision a second or subsequent time shall be guilty of a Class 3 felony.

Any person who knowingly and willfully violates any provision of this Section other than a second or subsequent violation of transmitting a false report as described in the preceding paragraph, is guilty of a Class A misdemeanor for a first violation and a Class 4 felony for a second or subsequent violation; except that if the person acted as part of a plan or scheme having as its object the prevention of discovery of an abused or neglected child by lawful authorities for the purpose of protecting or insulating any person or entity from arrest or prosecution, the person is guilty of a Class 4 felony for a first offense and a Class 3 felony for a second or subsequent offense (regardless of whether the second or subsequent offense involves any of the same facts or persons as the first or other prior offense).

A child whose parent, guardian or custodian in good faith selects and depends upon spiritual means through prayer alone for the treatment or cure of disease or remedial care may be considered neglected or abused, but not for the sole reason that his parent, guardian or custodian accepts and practices such beliefs.

A child shall not be considered neglected or abused solely because the child is not attending school in accordance with the requirements of Article 26 of the School Code, as amended [105 ILCS 5/26-1 et seq.].
(Source: P.A. 86-601; 86-716; 86-835; 86-1004; 86-1028; 89-363, § 15; 89-507, § 90L-74; 89-706, § 275; 90-116, § 20; 91-259, § 15; 91-516, § 5; 92-16, § 78; 92-801, § 5; 93-137, § 5; 93-356, § 5; 93-431, § 5; 93-1041, § 905.)

Note.

This section was Ill.Rev.Stat., Ch. 23, para. 2054.

Section 996 of P.A. 92-16 contains a "no acceleration or delay" provision, and Section 997 contains a "no revival or extension" provision.

Cross References.

As to the type of training a person needs, in order to report suspected child abuse or neglect, see 20 ILCS 505/34.8.

As to medical practitioners and immunity from suit for divulging information about a venereal disease contracted by a minor, see 745 ILCS 45/1.

Illinois Administrative Code.

See 77 Illinois Administrative Code, § 2200.60, 89 Illinois Administrative Code, § 300.30.

Effect of Amendments.

The 1995 amendment by P.A. 89-363, effective January 1, 1996, in the first paragraph, in the first sentence, inserted "funeral home director or employee".

The 1996 amendment by P.A. 89-507, effective July 1, 1997, in the first paragraph, in the first sentence, inserted "Human Services (acting as successor to the Department of", inserted "Rehabilitation Services, or Public Aid)" and deleted "Rehabilitation Services" following "Human Rights".

The 1996 amendment by P.A. 89-706, effective January 31, 1997, incorporated the amendments by P.A. 89-507; and inserted "acupuncturist" in the first sentence of the first paragraph.

The 1997 amendment by P.A. 90-116, effective July 14, 1997, in the first paragraph, in the first sentence, inserted "physician assistant".

The 1999 amendment by P.A. 91-259, effective January 1, 2000, added the section heading, and inserted "respiratory care practitioner" in the first sentence of the first paragraph.

The 1999 amendment by P.A. 91-516, effective August 13, 1999, inserted "advanced practice nurse, home health aide" near the middle of the first sentence in the first paragraph.

The 2001 amendment by P.A. 92-16, effective June 28, 2001, combined the amendments by P.A. 91-259 and P.A. 91-516.

The 2002 amendment by P.A. 92-801, effective August 16, 2002, added the second paragraph; in the third paragraph inserted "or as a member of the clergy", inserted "or church, synagogue, temple, mosque, or other religious institution" in two places; inserted the third paragraph; in the third-to-last paragraph substituted "is" for "shall be", inserted "for a first violation and a Class 4 felony for a second or subsequent violation", and made stylistic changes.

The 2003 amendment by P.A. 93-137, effective July 10, 2003, inserted "Licensed professional counselor, licensed clinical professional counselor" in the first sentence.

The 2003 amendment by P.A. 93-356, effective July 24, 2003, deleted "Christian Science practitioner" following "abuse treatment personnel" in the first paragraph.

The 2003 amendment by P.A. 93-431, effective August 5, 2003, substituted "3" for "4" in the ninth paragraph; and inserted the language beginning "except that if the person acted" and ending "persons as the first or other prior offense" in the tenth paragraph.

Although the amendments made to this section by P.A. 93-137, § 5, P.A. 93-356, § 5 and P.A. 93-431, § 5 did not take into account the amendments made by the other, the amendments have been combined into a single version by the publisher.

The 2004 amendment by P.A. 93-1041, effective September 29, 2004, inserted "genetic counselor" in the first paragraph.

CASE NOTES

ANALYSIS

Clergy Members
Confidentiality
—Negated
Constitutional Rights
—Not Violated
Duty to Report Abuse
Judicial Immunity
Neglect Finding
Privilege
—Negated
Suppression
—Not Required

Clergy Members

Since clergy members are not listed in the category of professionals who must immediately make a report to the Division of Child and Family Services when they have reasonable cause to believe a child known to them in their professional or official capacity may be abused or neglected, the clergy privilege is applicable to communications between clergyman and accused child abuser. People v. Burnidge, 279 Ill. App. 3d 127, 216 Ill. Dec. 19, 664 N.E.2d 656 (2 Dist. 1996), aff'd, 178 Ill. 2d 429, 227 Ill. Dec. 331, 687 N.E.2d 813 (1997).

Confidentiality

—Negated

The express language of this section destroys any confidentiality, for use in a criminal prosecution for child abuse, of information given by an accused to a therapist where the recipient was advised the conversation would not be confidential. People v. Morton, 188 Ill. App. 3d 95, 135 Ill. Dec. 619, 543 N.E.2d 1366 (4 Dist. 1989).

Constitutional Rights

—Not Violated

Teacher's claim under the Illinois Abused and Neglected Child Reporting Act failed for the same reason as her 42 U.S.C.S. § 1983 claim that she had been retaliated against for exercising her First Amendment rights by urging a school counselor to file a child abuse report failed for lack of evidence from which a reasonable jury could find a causal connection between the report of abuse and the school district's decision not to rehire her. Hausknecht v. Naperville Sch. Dist. Unit 203, F. Supp. 2d , 2004 U.S. Dist. LEXIS 8939 (N.D. Ill. May 19, 2004).

The requirement that a tenured teacher, school psychologist and others in similar positions of responsibility promptly report child abuse to a state agency does not unconstitutionally infringe any federal right to confidentiality, especially because this state has a compelling interest in protecting children. Pesce v. J. Sterling Morton High Sch., 830 F.2d 789 (7th Cir. 1987).

Where there was no evidence that a caseworker deliberately elicited defendant's statement for prosecutorial purposes, and defendant freely relayed information to caseworker in order to effect a return of his daughter to his home, neither defendant's right to counsel nor his privilege against self-incrimination was violated by the fact that he made the statement to the caseworker without his counsel being present. People v. Bradley, 128 Ill. App. 3d 372, 83 Ill. Dec. 701, 470 N.E.2d 1121 (4 Dist. 1984).

Duty to Report Abuse

Where the abuse victims filed suit against the psychological clinic alleging that it failed to report abuse, allegedly in violation of 325 ILCS 5/4, of which its therapist was informed by the abuser, the action was properly dismissed under 735 ILCS 5/2-615, as the clinic was not required to report the abuse; the children did not fall within the 325 ILCS 5/3 definition of abused children since there was no allegation that a parent or anyone else reponsible for the victims' welfare allowed the abuse to occur, and the clinic did not see the abuser in a professional or official capacity. Doe v. N. Cent. Behavioral Health Sys., 352 Ill. App. 3d 284, 287 Ill. Dec. 493, 816 N.E.2d 4, 2004 Ill. App. LEXIS 992 (3 Dist. 2004).

Where the abuse victims filed suit against the psychological clinic alleging that it failed to report abuse, allegedly in violation of 325 ILCS 5/4, of which its therapist was informed by the abuser, the action was properly dismissed under 735 ILCS 5/2-615 as the Illinois Abused and Neglected Child Reporting Act granted no private right of action; while the Act, as stated in 325 ILCS 5/2, was meant to protect children from abuse, it did so by imposing a misdemeanor under 325 ILCS 5/4.02 if a person who was obligated to report abuse failed to do so rather than by granting a private right of action. Doe v. N. Cent. Behavioral Health Sys., 352 Ill. App. 3d 284, 287 Ill. Dec. 493, 816 N.E.2d 4, 2004 Ill. App. LEXIS 992 (3 Dist. 2004).

Judicial Immunity

Where plaintiffs brought an action pursuant to 42 U.S.C. § 1983, based on a court order removing their son from their custody and appointing a guardian to consent to medical treatment and to the administration of blood transfusions to the child, and sued the judge who entered the order, the judge was protected by judicial immunity since his authority was based on, among other statutes, this Act. Staelens v. Yake, 432 F. Supp. 834 (N.D. Ill. 1977).

Neglect Finding

Fact that hospital failed to make a report pursuant to this section did not contradict a finding of neglect where school officials had already made a report. People v. Gomez, 53 Ill. App. 3d 353, 11 Ill. Dec. 224, 368 N.E.2d 775 (1 Dist. 1977).

Privilege

—Negated

Defendant's constitutional rights were not violated when the social worker to whom he admitted incestuous acts informed the authorities of his conduct; even if a "social worker-patient privilege" or a "therapist-patient privilege" otherwise existed, it was not applicable where abused or neglected children were involved. People v. McKean, 94 Ill. App. 3d 502, 50 Ill. Dec. 136, 418 N.E.2d 1130 (2 Dist. 1981).

Suppression

—Not Required

Suppression of evidence was not required where defendant's

Suppression (Cont'd)

—Not Required (Cont'd)

counselor, who was both a clergyman and a psychologist, reported to the Department of Children and Family Services the name of victim of abuse, but did not name the defendant. People v. Burnidge, 178 Ill. 2d 429, 227 Ill. Dec. 331, 687 N.E.2d 813 (1997).

OPINIONS OF ATTORNEY GENERAL

ANALYSIS

Applicability
Reasonable Cause to Believe

Applicability

The reporting provisions of this Act are not limited only to cases of a child whose death occurs from suspected abuse or neglect before being found or brought to a hospital, but contemplates the offering of protective services in order to prevent further harm to the child and therefore clearly contemplates a situation where the child is alive. 1979 Op. Atty. Gen. 43.

Reasonable Cause to Believe

The term "reasonable cause to believe" as used in the Abused and Neglected Child Reporting Act (325 ILCS 5/1 et seq.) is equivalent to the term "suspect" as used in the federal Child Abuse Prevention and Treatment Act (42 U.S.C. § 5101 et seq.) 1977 Op. Atty. Gen. 173.

LEGAL PERIODICALS

For article, "Survey of Illinois Law: Evidence," see 21 Ill. S. U.L.J. 847 (1997).

325 ILCS 5/4.02 [Failure to report]

Sec. 4.02. Any physician who willfully fails to report suspected child abuse or neglect as required by this Act shall be referred to the Illinois State Medical Disciplinary Board for action in accordance with paragraph 22 of Section 22 of the Medical Practice Act of 1987 [225 ILCS 60/22]. Any dentist or dental hygienist who willfully fails to report suspected child abuse or neglect as required by this Act shall be referred to the Department of Professional Regulation for action in accordance with paragraph 19 of Section 23 of the Illinois Dental Practice Act [225 ILCS 25/23]. Any other person required by this Act to report suspected child abuse and neglect who willfully fails to report such is guilty of a Class A misdemeanor for a first violation and a Class 4 felony for a second or subsequent violation.
(Source: P.A. 86-1004; 91-197, § 5; 92-801, § 5.)

Note.

This section was Ill.Rev.Stat., Ch. 23, para. 2054.02.

Cross References.

As to revocation of a dental license for failure to report suspected child abuse or neglect, see 225 ILCS 25/23.

Effect of Amendments.

The 1999 amendment by P.A. 91-197, effective January 1, 2000, inserted the second sentence.

The 2002 amendment by P.A. 92-801, effective August 16, 2002, in the last sentence substituted "is" for "shall be", and inserted "for a first violation and a Class 4 felony for a second or subsequent violation."

CASE NOTES

Duty To Report Abuse

Where the abuse victims filed suit against the psychological clinic alleging that it failed to report abuse, allegedly in violation of 325 ILCS 5/4, of which its therapist was informed by the abuser, the action was properly dismissed under 735 ILCS5/2-615 as the Illinois Abused and Neglected Child Reporting Act granted no private right of action; while the Act, as stated in 325 ILCS 5/2, was meant to protect children from abuse, it did so by imposing a misdemeanor under 325 ILCS 5/4.02 if a person who was obligated to report abuse failed to do so rather than by granting a private right of action. Doe v. N. Cent. Behavioral Health Sys., 352 Ill. App. 3d 284, 287 Ill. Dec. 493, 816 N.E.2d 4, 2004 Ill. App. LEXIS 992 (3 Dist. 2004).

325 ILCS 5/4.1 [Reports to medical examiner or coroner]

Sec. 4.1. Any person required to report under this Act who has reasonable cause to suspect that a child has died as a result of abuse or neglect shall also immediately report his suspicion to the appropriate medical examiner or coroner. Any other person who has reasonable cause to believe that a child has died as a result of abuse or neglect may report his suspicion to the appropriate medical examiner or coroner. The medical examiner or coroner shall investigate the report and communicate his apparent gross findings, orally, immediately upon completion of the gross autopsy, but in all cases within 72 hours and within 21 days in writing, to the local law enforcement agency, the appropriate State's attorney, the Department and, if the institution making the report is a hospital, the hospital. The child protective investigator assigned to the death investigation shall have the right to require a copy of the completed autopsy report from the coroner or medical examiner.
(Source: P.A. 85-193.)

Note.

This section was Ill.Rev.Stat., Ch. 23, para. 2054.1.

325 ILCS 5/4.2 Departmental report on death of child

Sec. 4.2. *Departmental report on death of child.* (a) In the case of the death of a child whose care and custody or custody and guardianship has been transferred to the Department, or in the case of a child abuse or neglect report made to the central register involving the death of a child, the Department shall (i) investigate or provide for an investigation of the cause of and circumstances surrounding the death, (ii) review the investigation, and (iii) prepare and issue a report on the death.

(b) The report shall include (i) the cause of death, whether from natural or other causes, (ii) identification of child protective or other services provided or actions taken regarding the child and his or her family, (iii) any extraordinary or pertinent information concerning the circumstances of the child's death, (iv) whether the child or the child's family had received assistance, care, or services from the social services district prior to the child's death, (v) any action or further investigation undertaken by the Department since the death of the child, and (vi) as appropriate, recommendations for State administrative or policy changes.

The report shall contain no information that would identify the name of the deceased child, his or her siblings, the parent or other person legally responsible for the child, or any other members of the child's household, but shall refer instead to the case, which may be denoted in any fashion determined appropriate by the Department. In making a fatality report available to the public pursuant to subsection (c) of this Section, the Department may respond to a child specific request for a report if the Department determines that the disclosure is not contrary to the best interests of the deceased child's siblings or other children in the household. Except as it may apply directly to the cause of the death of the child, nothing in this Section shall be deemed to authorize the release or disclosure to the public of the substance or content of any psychological, psychiatric, therapeutic, clinical, or medical reports, evaluation, or like materials or information pertaining to the child or the child's family.

(c) No later than 6 months after the date of the death of the child, the Department shall complete its report. The Department shall notify the President of the Senate, the Minority Leader of the Senate, the Speaker of the House of Representatives, the Minority Leader of the House of Representatives, and the members of the Senate and the House of Representatives in whose district the child's death occurred upon the completion of each report and shall submit an annual cumulative report to the Governor and the General Assembly incorporating the data in the above reports and including appropriate findings and recommendations. The reports concerning the death of a child and the cumulative reports shall be made available to the public after completion or submittal.

(d) To enable the Department to prepare the report, the Department may request and shall timely receive from departments, boards, bureaus, or other agencies of the State, or any of its political subdivisions, or any duly authorized agency, or any other agency which provided assistance, care, or services to the deceased child any information they are authorized to provide.
(Source: P.A. 90-15, § 13.)

Effective Date.
Section 99 of P.A. 90-15 made this section effective upon becoming law. The Act was approved June 13, 1997.

325 ILCS 5/4.3 DCFS duty to report

Sec. 4.3. *DCFS duty to report.* The Department shall report the disappearance of any child under its custody or guardianship to the local law enforcement agency working in cooperation with the I SEARCH Unit located nearest the last known whereabouts of the child.
(Source: P.A. 90-27, § 20.)

Effective Date.
This section became effective January 1, 1998 pursuant to Ill. Const. (1970), Art. IV, § 10 and 5 ILCS 75/1.

325 ILCS 5/5 [Temporary protective custody]

Sec. 5. An officer of a local law enforcement agency, designated employee of the Department, or a physician treating a child may take or retain temporary protective custody of the child without the consent of the person responsible for the child's welfare, if (1) he has reason to believe that the child cannot be cared for at home or in the custody of the person responsible for the child's welfare without endangering the child's health or safety; and (2) there is not time to apply for a court order under the Juvenile Court Act of 1987 [705 ILCS 405/1-1 et seq.] for temporary custody of the child. The person taking or retaining a child in temporary protective custody shall immediately make every reasonable effort to notify the person responsible for the child's welfare and shall immediately notify the Department. The Department shall provide to the temporary caretaker of a child any information in the Department's possession concerning the positive results of a test performed on the child to determine the presence of the antibody or antigen to Human Immunodeficiency Virus (HIV), or of HIV infection, as well as any communicable diseases or communicable infections that the child has. The temporary caretaker of a child shall not disclose to another person any information received by the temporary caretaker from the Department concerning the results of a test performed on the child to determine the presence of the antibody or antigen to HIV, or of HIV infection, except pursuant to Section 9 of the AIDS Confidentiality Act, as now or hereafter amended [410 ILCS 235/9]. The Department shall promptly initiate proceedings under the Juvenile Court Act of 1987 [705 ILCS 405/1-1 et seq.] for the continued temporary custody of the child.

Where the physician keeping a child in his custody does so in his capacity as a member of the staff of a hospital or similar institution, he shall notify the person in charge of the institution or his designated agent, who shall then become responsible for the further care of such child in the hospital or similar institution under the direction of the Department.

Said care includes, but is not limited to the granting of permission to perform emergency medical treatment to a minor where the treatment itself does not involve a substantial risk of harm to the minor and the failure to render such treatment will likely result in death or permanent harm to the minor, and there is not time to apply for a court order under the Juvenile Court Act of 1987 [705 ILCS 405/1-1 et seq.].

Any person authorized and acting in good faith in the removal of a child under this Section shall have immunity from any liability, civil or criminal that might otherwise be incurred or imposed as a result of such removal. Any physician authorized and acting in good faith and in accordance with acceptable medical practice in the treatment of a child under this Section shall have immunity from any liability, civil or criminal, that might otherwise be incurred or imposed as a result of granting permission for emergency treatment.

With respect to any child taken into temporary protective custody pursuant to this Section, the Department of Children and Family Services Guardianship Administrator or his designee shall be deemed the child's legally authorized representative for purposes of consenting to an HIV test if deemed necessary and appropriate by the Department's Guardianship Administrator or designee and obtaining and disclosing information concerning such test pursuant to the AIDS Confidentiality Act [410 ILCS 305/1 et seq.] if deemed necessary and appropriate by the Department's Guardianship Administrator or designee and for purposes of consenting to the release of information pursuant to the Illinois Sexually Transmissible Disease Control Act [410 ILCS 325/1 et seq.] if deemed necessary and appropriate by the Department's Guardianship Administrator or designee.

Any person who administers an HIV test upon the consent of the Department of Children and Family Services Guardianship Administrator or his designee, or who discloses the results of such tests to the Department's Guardianship Administrator or his designee, shall have immunity from any liability, civil, criminal or otherwise, that might result by reason of such actions. For the purpose of any proceedings, civil or criminal, the good faith of any persons required to administer or disclose the results of tests, or permitted to take such actions, shall be presumed.

(Source: P.A. 86-733; 86-904; 86-1028; 90-28, § 10-15.)

Note.

This section was Ill.Rev.Stat., Ch. 23, para. 2055.

Effect of Amendments.

The 1997 amendment by P.A. 90-28, effective January 1, 1998, in the first paragraph, in the first sentence, substituted "child cannot be cared for at home or in the" for "circumstances or conditions of the child are such that continuing in his place of residence or in the care and" and substituted "without endangering the child's health or safety" for "presents an imminent danger to that child's life or health".

CASE NOTES

Analysis

Constitutionality
—Due Process
—Good Faith Immunity

Constitutionality

—Due Process

This Act protects both the interest of the state and the parents while also minimizing the risk to erroneous deprivation of rights. The procedures and safeguards mandated by the Act strike a proper balance between the privacy rights involved while promoting important interests. Lehman v. Stephens, 148 Ill. App. 3d 538, 101 Ill. Dec. 736, 499 N.E.2d 103 (4 Dist. 1986).

—Good Faith Immunity

In light of the substantial state interest in uncovering child abuse or neglect, and in protecting the children of this state, the "good faith" immunity mandated and permitted under this Act is clearly justified and is in no way inconsistent with the Illinois Constitution. Lehman v. Stephens, 148 Ill. App. 3d 538, 101 Ill. Dec. 736, 499 N.E.2d 103 (4 Dist. 1986).

RESEARCH REFERENCES

Validity and application of statute allowing endangered child to be temporarily removed from parental custody. 38 ALR4th 756.

325 ILCS 5/6 [Photographs and x-rays]

Sec. 6. Any person required to investigate cases of suspected child abuse or neglect may take or cause to be taken, at Department expense, color photographs and x-rays of the child who is the subject of a report, and color photographs of the physical environment in which the alleged abuse or neglect has taken place. The person seeking to take such photographs or x-rays shall make every reasonable effort to notify the person responsible for the child's welfare.

(Source: P.A. 84-611.)

Note.

This section was Ill.Rev.Stat., Ch. 23, para. 2056.

325 ILCS 5/7 Time and manner of making reports

Sec. 7. *Time and manner of making reports.* All reports of suspected child abuse or neglect made under this Act shall be made immediately by telephone to the central register established under Section 7.7 [325 ILCS 5/7.7] on the single, Statewide, toll-free telephone number established in Section 7.6 [325 ILCS 5/7.6], or in person or by telephone through the nearest Department office. The Department shall, in cooperation with school officials, distribute appropriate materials in school buildings listing the toll-free telephone number established in Section 7.6 [325 ILCS 5/7.6], including methods of making a report under this Act. The Department may, in cooperation with appropriate members of the clergy, distribute appropriate materials in churches, synagogues, temples, mosques, or other religious buildings listing the toll-free telephone number established in Section 7.6 [325 ILCS 5/7.6], including methods of making a report under this Act.

Wherever the Statewide number is posted, there shall also be posted the following notice:

"Any person who knowingly transmits a false report to the Department commits the offense of disorderly conduct under subsection (a)(7) of Section 26-1 of the Criminal Code of 1961 [720 ILCS 5/26-1].

A first violation of this subsection is a Class A misdemeanor, punishable by a term of imprisonment for up to one year, or by a fine not to exceed $1,000, or by both such term and fine. A second or subsequent violation is a Class 4 felony."

The report required by this Act shall include, if known, the name and address of the child and his parents or other persons having his custody; the child's age; the nature of the child's condition including any evidence of previous injuries or disabilities; and any other information that the person filing the report believes might be helpful in establishing the cause of such abuse or neglect and the identity of the person believed to have caused such abuse or neglect. Reports made to the central register through the State-wide, toll-free telephone number shall be immediately transmitted to the appropriate Child Protective Service Unit. The Department shall within 24 hours orally notify local law enforcement personnel and the office of the State's Attorney of the involved county of the receipt of any report alleging the death of a child, serious injury to a child including, but not limited to, brain damage, skull fractures, subdural hematomas, and, internal injuries, torture of a child, malnutrition of a child, and sexual abuse to a child, including, but not limited to, sexual intercourse, sexual exploitation, sexual molestation, and sexually transmitted disease in a child age twelve and under. All oral reports made by the Department to local law enforcement personnel and the office of the State's Attorney of the involved county shall be confirmed in writing within 48 hours of the oral report. All reports by persons mandated to report under this Act shall be confirmed in writing to the appropriate Child Protective Service Unit, which may be on forms supplied by the Department, within 48 hours of any initial report.

Written confirmation reports from persons not required to report by this Act may be made to the appropriate Child Protective Service Unit. Written reports from persons required by this Act to report shall be admissible in evidence in any judicial proceeding relating to child abuse or neglect. Reports involving known or suspected child abuse or neglect in public or private residential agencies or institutions shall be made and received in the same manner as all other reports made under this Act.
(Source: P.A. 86-659; 86-1028; 86-1357; 89-187, § 40; 92-801, § 5.)

Note.
This section was Ill.Rev.Stat., Ch. 23, para. 2057.

Effect of Amendments.
The 1995 amendment by P.A. 89-187, effective July 19, 1995, added the section catchline; and in the third paragraph, in the third sentence, substituted "sexually transmitted" for "venereal".

The 2002 amendment by P.A. 92-801, effective August 16, 2002, added the last sentence in the first paragraph.

325 ILCS 5/7.1 [Cooperation with other agencies]

Sec. 7.1. (a) To the fullest extent feasible, the Department shall cooperate with and shall seek the cooperation and involvement of all appropriate public and private agencies, including health, education, social service and law enforcement agencies, religious institutions, courts of competent jurisdiction, and agencies, organizations, or programs providing or concerned with human services related to the prevention, identification or treatment of child abuse or neglect.

Such cooperation and involvement shall include joint consultation and services, joint planning, joint case management, joint public education and information services, joint utilization of facilities, joint staff development and other training, and the creation of multidisciplinary case diagnostic, case handling, case management, and policy planning teams. Such cooperation and involvement shall also include consultation and planning with the Illinois Department of Human Services regarding referrals to designated perinatal centers of newborn children requiring protective custody under this Act, whose life or development may be threatened by a developmental disability or handicapping condition.

For implementing such intergovernmental cooperation and involvement, units of local government and public and private agencies may apply for and receive federal or State funds from the Department under this Act or seek and receive gifts from local philanthropic or other private local sources in order to augment any State funds appropriated for the purposes of this Act.

(b) The Department may establish up to 5 demonstrations of multidisciplinary teams to advise, review and monitor cases of child abuse and neglect brought by the Department or any member of the team. The Director shall determine the criteria by which certain cases of child abuse or neglect are brought to the multidisciplinary teams. The criteria shall include but not be limited to geographic area and classification of certain cases where allegations are of a severe nature. Each multidisciplinary team shall consist of 7 to 10 members appointed by the Director, including, but not limited to representatives from the medical, mental health, educational, juvenile justice, law enforcement and social service fields.
(Source: P.A. 85-1440; 89-507, § 90M-5; 92-801, § 5.)

Note.
This section was Ill.Rev.Stat., Ch. 23, para. 2057.1.

Effect of Amendments.
The 1996 amendment by P.A. 89-507, effective July 1, 1997, in the second paragraph, in the second sentence, substituted "Human Services" for "Public Health".

The 2002 amendment by P.A. 92-801, effective August 16, 2002, inserted "religious institutions" in subsection (a) and made a stylistic change.

325 ILCS 5/7.2 [Child Protective Service Unit]

Sec. 7.2. The Department shall establish a Child Protective Service Unit within each geographic region as designated by the Director of the Department. The Child Protective Service Unit shall perform those functions assigned by this Act to it and only such others that would further the purposes of this Act. It shall have a sufficient staff of qualified personnel to fulfill the purpose of this Act and be organized in such a way as to maximize the continuity of responsibility, care and service of the individual workers toward the individual children and families.

The Child Protective Service Unit shall designate members of each unit to receive specialty training to serve as special consultants to unit staff and the public in the areas of child sexual abuse, child deaths and injuries, and out-of-home investigations. (Source: P.A. 85-1440.)

Note.
This section was Ill.Rev.Stat., Ch. 23, para. 2057.2.

325 ILCS 5/7.3 [Investigations]

Sec. 7.3. The Department shall be the sole agency responsible for receiving and investigating reports of child abuse or neglect made under this Act, except where investigations by other agencies may be required with respect to reports alleging the death of a child, serious injury to a child or sexual abuse to a child made pursuant to Sections 4.1 or 7 of this Act [325 ILCS 5/4.1 or 325 ILCS 5/7], and except that the Department may delegate the performance of the investigation to the Department of State Police, a law enforcement agency and to those private social service agencies which have been designated for this purpose by the Department prior to July 1, 1980. (Source: P.A. 85-1440.)

Note.
This section was Ill.Rev.Stat., Ch. 23, para. 2057.3.

CASE NOTES

Documentation

—Complete and Accurate
Inherent in the public policy of protecting children from abuse we find another public policy requiring accurate documentation of investigations; investigations into alleged cases of child abuse must necessarily be complete and accurate. Illinois Dept. of Cent. Mgt. Servs. v. AFSCME, 245 Ill. App. 3d 87, 185 Ill. Dec. 379, 614 N.E.2d 513 (4 Dist.), appeal denied, 152 Ill. 2d 556, 190 Ill. Dec. 886, 622 N.E.2d 1203 (1993).

325 ILCS 5/7.3a [Perinatal Coordinator]

Sec. 7.3a. The Director of the Department shall appoint a Perinatal Coordinator who shall be a physician licensed to practice medicine in all its branches with a specialty certification in pediatric care. Such coordinator, or other designated medical specialists, shall review all reports of suspected medical neglect involving newborns or infants, coordinate the evaluation of the subject of such report, and assist in necessary referrals to appropriate perinatal medical care and treatment. When the Perinatal Coordinator or other designated medical specialists, alone or in consultation with an infant care review committee established by a medical facility, determine that a newborn or infant child is being neglected as defined in Section 3 of this Act [325 ILCS 5/3], a designated employee of the Department shall take the steps necessary to protect such newborn or infant child's life or health, including but not limited to taking temporary protective custody. (Source: P.A. 83-1248.)

Note.
This section was Ill.Rev.Stat., Ch. 23, para. 2057.3a.

325 ILCS 5/7.3b [Addicted pregnant persons]

Sec. 7.3b. All persons required to report under Section 4 [325 ILCS 5/4] may refer to the Department of Human Services any pregnant person in this State who is addicted as defined in the Alcoholism and Other Drug Abuse and Dependency Act [20 ILCS 301/1-1 et seq.]. The Department of Human Services shall notify the local Infant Mortality Reduction Network service provider or Department funded prenatal care provider in the area in which the person resides. The service provider shall prepare a case management plan and assist the pregnant woman in obtaining counseling and treatment from a local substance abuse service provider licensed by the Department of Human Services or a licensed hospital which provides substance abuse treatment services. The local Infant Mortality Reduction Network service provider and Department funded prenatal care provider shall monitor the pregnant woman through the service program. The Department of Human Services shall have the authority to promulgate rules and regulations to implement this Section.
(Source: P.A. 86-1004; 88-670, § 3-73; 89-507, §§ 90C-25, 90M-5.)

Note.
This section was Ill.Rev.Stat., Ch. 23, para. 2057.3b.

Effect of Amendments.
The 1994 amendment by P.A. 88-670, effective December 2, 1994, in the first sentence deleted "Illinois" preceding "Alcoholism" and inserted "Abuse and".

The 1996 amendment by P.A. 89-507, § 90C-25, effective July 1, 1997, in the third sentence substituted "Human Services" for "Alcoholism and Substance Abuse".

The 1996 amendment by P.A. 89-507, § 90M-5, effective July 1, 1997, in the first, second and fifth sentences substituted "Human Services" for "Public Health"; and in the third sentence substituted "Human Services" for "Alcoholism and Substance Abuse".

Although the amendments to this section by P.A. 89-507, § 90C-25 and P.A. 89-507, § 90M-5 did not take into account the amendments made by the other, the amendments to this section have been combined into a single version by the publisher.

325 ILCS 5/7.3c Substance abuse services for women with children

Sec. 7.3c. *Substance abuse services for women with children.* The Department of Human Services and the Department of Children and Family Services shall develop a community based system of integrated child welfare and substance abuse services for the purpose of providing safety and protection for children, improving adult health and parenting outcomes, and improving family outcomes.

The Department of Children and Family Services, in cooperation with the Department of Human Services, shall develop case management protocols for DCFS clients with substance abuse problems. The Departments may establish pilot programs designed to test the most effective approaches to case-management. The Departments shall evaluate the effectiveness of these pilot programs and report to the Governor and the General Assembly on an annual basis.

(Source: P.A. 89-268, § 5; 89-507, § 90C-25.)

Effective Date.

This section became effective January 1, 1996 pursuant to Ill. Const. (1970), Art. IV, § 10 and 5 ILCS 75/1.

Effect of Amendments.

The 1996 amendment by P.A. 89-507, effective July 1, 1997, in the first paragraph substituted "Human Services" for "Alcoholism and Substance Abuse (DASA)" and deleted (DCFS)" following "Family Services"; and in the second paragraph, in the first sentence, substituted "The Department of Children and Family Services" for "DCFS" and substituted "The Department of Human Services" for "DASA" and in the second sentence substituted "The Departments shall" for "DCFS and DASA will".

325 ILCS 5/7.4 [Investigation procedures]

Sec. 7.4. (a) The Department shall be capable of receiving reports of suspected child abuse or neglect 24 hours a day, 7 days a week. Whenever the Department receives a report alleging that a child is a truant as defined in Section 26-2a of The School Code [105 ILCS 5/26-2a], as now or hereafter amended, the Department shall notify the superintendent of the school district in which the child resides and the appropriate superintendent of the educational service region. The notification to the appropriate officials by the Department shall not be considered an allegation of abuse or neglect under this Act.

(b)(1) The following procedures shall be followed in the investigation of all reports of suspected abuse or neglect of a child, except as provided in subsection (c) of this Section.

(2) If it appears that the immediate safety or well-being of a child is endangered, that the family may flee or the child disappear, or that the facts otherwise so warrant, the Child Protective Service Unit shall commence an investigation immediately, regardless of the time of day or night. In all other cases, investigation shall be commenced within 24 hours of receipt of the report. Upon receipt of a report, the Child Protective Service Unit shall make an initial investigation and an initial determination whether the report is a good faith indication of alleged child abuse or neglect.

(3) If the Unit determines the report is a good faith indication of alleged child abuse or neglect, then a formal investigation shall commence and, pursuant to Section 7.12 of this Act [325 ILCS 5/7.12], may or may not result in an indicated report. The formal investigation shall include: direct contact with the subject or subjects of the report as soon as possible after the report is received; an evaluation of the environment of the child named in the report and any other children in the same environment; a determination of the risk to such children if they continue to remain in the existing environments, as well as a determination of the nature, extent and cause of any condition enumerated in such report; the name, age and condition of other children in the environment; and an evaluation as to whether there would be an immediate and urgent necessity to remove the child from the environment if appropriate family preservation services were provided. After seeing to the safety of the child or children, the Department shall forthwith notify the subjects of the report in writing, of the existence of the report and their rights existing under this Act in regard to amendment or expungement. To fulfill the requirements of this Section, the Child Protective Service Unit shall have the capability of providing or arranging for comprehensive emergency services to children and families at all times of the day or night.

(4) If (i) at the conclusion of the Unit's initial investigation of a report, the Unit determines the report to be a good faith indication of alleged child abuse or neglect that warrants a formal investigation by the Unit, the Department, any law enforcement agency or any other responsible agency and (ii) the person who is alleged to have caused the abuse or neglect is employed or otherwise engaged in an activity resulting in frequent contact with children and the alleged abuse or neglect are in the course of such employment or activity, then the Department shall, except in investigations where the Director determines that such notification would be detrimental to the Department's investigation, inform the appropriate supervisor or administrator of that employment or activity that the Unit has commenced a formal investigation pursuant to this Act, which may or may not result in an indicated report. The Department shall also notify the person being investigated, unless the Director determines that such notification would be detrimental to the Department's investigation.

(c) In an investigation of a report of suspected abuse or neglect of a child by a school employee at a school or on school grounds, the Department shall make reasonable efforts to follow the following procedures:

(1) Investigations involving teachers shall not, to the extent possible, be conducted when the teacher is scheduled to conduct classes. Investigations involving other school employees shall be conducted so as to minimize disruption of the school day. The school employee accused of child abuse or neglect may have his superior, his association or union representative and his attorney present at any in-

terview or meeting at which the teacher or administrator is present. The accused school employee shall be informed by a representative of the Department, at any interview or meeting, of the accused school employee's due process rights and of the steps in the investigation process. The information shall include, but need not necessarily be limited to the right, subject to the approval of the Department, of the school employee to confront the accuser, if the accuser is 14 years of age or older, or the right to review the specific allegations which gave rise to the investigation, and the right to review all materials and evidence that have been submitted to the Department in support of the allegation. These due process rights shall also include the right of the school employee to present countervailing evidence regarding the accusations.

(2) If a report of neglect or abuse of a child by a teacher or administrator does not involve allegations of sexual abuse or extreme physical abuse, the Child Protective Service Unit shall make reasonable efforts to conduct the initial investigation in coordination with the employee's supervisor.

If the Unit determines that the report is a good faith indication of potential child abuse or neglect, it shall then commence a formal investigation under paragraph (3) of subsection (b) of this Section.

(3) If a report of neglect or abuse of a child by a teacher or administrator involves an allegation of sexual abuse or extreme physical abuse, the Child Protective Unit shall commence an investigation under paragraph (2) of subsection (b) of this Section.

(d) If the Department has contact with an employer, or with a religious institution or religious official having supervisory or hierarchical authority over a member of the clergy accused of the abuse of a child, in the course of its investigation, the Department shall notify the employer or the religious institution or religious official, in writing, when a report is unfounded so that any record of the investigation can be expunged from the employee's or member of the clergy's personnel or other records. The Department shall also notify the employee or the member of the clergy, in writing, that notification has been sent to the employer or to the appropriate religious institution or religious official informing the employer or religious institution or religious official that the Department's investigation has resulted in an unfounded report.

(e) Upon request by the Department, the Department of State Police and law enforcement agencies are authorized to provide criminal history record information as defined in the Illinois Uniform Conviction Information Act [20 ILCS 2635/1 et seq.] and information maintained in the adjudicatory and dispositional record system as defined in Section 2605-355 of the Department of State Police Law (20 ILCS 2605/2605-355) to properly designated employees of the Department of Children and Family Services if the Department determines the information is necessary to perform its duties under the Abused and Neglected Child Reporting Act [325 ILCS 5/1 et seq.], the Child Care Act of 1969 [225 ILCS 10/1 et seq.], and the Children and Family Services Act [20 ILCS 505/1 et seq.]. The request shall be in the form and manner required by the Department of State Police. Any information obtained by the Department of Children and Family Services under this Section is confidential and may not be transmitted outside the Department of Children and Family Services other than to a court of competent jurisdiction or unless otherwise authorized by law. Any employee of the Department of Children and Family Services who transmits confidential information in violation of this Section or causes the information to be transmitted in violation of this Section is guilty of a Class A misdemeanor unless the transmittal of the information is authorized by this Section or otherwise authorized by law.
(Source: P.A. 86-601; 87-400; 88-614, § 107; 91-239, § 5-480; 92-801, § 5.)

Note.

This section was Ill.Rev.Stat., Ch. 23, para. 2057.4.

Effect of Amendments.

The 1994 amendment by P.A. 88-614, effective September 7, 1994, added subsection (e).

The 1999 amendment by P.A. 91-239, effective January 1, 2000, in the first sentence of subsection (e), substituted "Section 2605-355 of the Department of State Police Law (20 ILCS 2605/2605-355)" for "subdivision (A)19 of Section 55a of the Civil Administrative Code of Illinois".

The 2002 amendment by P.A. 92-801, effective August 16, 2002, in subsection (d) in the first sentence inserted "or with a religious institution or religious official having supervisory or hierarchical authority over a member of the clergy accused of the abuse of a child", "or the religious institution or religious official", "or member of the clergy's", and "or other", in the second sentence inserted "or the member of the clergy", "or to the appropriate religious institution or religious official", and "or religious institution or religious official"; and made stylistic changes.

CASE NOTES

Videotaped Interviews

Circuit court did not have jurisdiction to compel Department of Children and Family Services to videotape interviews with allegedly sexually abused children. In re R.V., 288 Ill. App. 3d 860, 224 Ill. Dec. 345, 681 N.E.2d 660 (1 Dist. 1997).

325 ILCS 5/7.5 [Access to child]

Sec. 7.5. If the Child Protective Service Unit is denied reasonable access to a child by the parents or other persons and it deems that the health, safety, and best interests of the child so require, it shall request the intervention of a local law enforcement agency or seek an appropriate court order to examine and interview the child.
(Source: P.A. 81-1077; 90-28, § 10-15.)

Note.

This section was Ill.Rev.Stat., Ch. 23, para. 2057.5.

Effect of Amendments.

The 1997 amendment by P.A. 90-28, effective January 1, 1998, inserted "health , safety, and".

325 ILCS 5/7.6 [Posted telephone number]

Sec. 7.6. There shall be a single State-wide, toll-free telephone number established and maintained by the Department which all persons, whether or not mandated by law, may use to report suspected child abuse or neglect at any hour of the day or night, on any day of the week. Immediately upon receipt of such reports, the Department shall transmit the contents of the report, either orally or electronically, to the appropriate Child Protective Service Unit. Any other person may use the State-wide number to obtain assistance or information concerning the handling of child abuse and neglect cases.

Wherever the Statewide number is posted, there shall also be posted the following notice:

"Any person who knowingly transmits a false report to the Department commits the offense of disorderly conduct under subsection (a)(7) of Section 26-1 of the Criminal Code of 1961 [720 ILCS 5/26-1]. A violation of this subsection is a Class B misdemeanor, punishable by a term of imprisonment for not more than 6 months, or by a fine not to exceed $500, or by both such term and fine."
(Source: P.A. 84-1318.)

Note.
This section was Ill.Rev.Stat., Ch. 23, para. 2057.6.

325 ILCS 5/7.7 [Central register]

Sec. 7.7. There shall be a central register of all cases of suspected child abuse or neglect reported and maintained by the Department under this Act. Through the recording of initial, preliminary, and final reports, the central register shall be operated in such a manner as to enable the Department to: (1) immediately identify and locate prior reports of child abuse or neglect; (2) continuously monitor the current status of all reports of child abuse or neglect being provided services under this Act; and (3) regularly evaluate the effectiveness of existing laws and programs through the development and analysis of statistical and other information.

The Department shall maintain in the central register a listing of unfounded reports where the subject of the unfounded report requests that the record not be expunged because the subject alleges an intentional false report was made. Such a request must be made by the subject in writing to the Department, within 10 days of the investigation.

The Department shall also maintain in the central register a listing of unfounded reports where the report was classified as a priority one or priority two report in accordance with the Department's rules or the report was made by a person mandated to report suspected abuse or neglect under this Act.

The Department shall maintain in the central register for 3 years a listing of unfounded reports involving the death of a child, the sexual abuse of a child, or serious physical injury to a child as defined by the Department in rules.
(Source: P.A. 84-611; 88-614, § 107; 90-15, § 13.)

Note.
This section was Ill.Rev.Stat., Ch. 23, para. 2057.7.

Cross References.
As to the duty of an officer to register abused, or neglected minors, see 705 ILCS 405/2-6.

Effect of Amendments.
The 1994 amendment by P.A. 88-614, effective September 7, 1994, added the last paragraph.
The 1997 amendment by P.A. 90-15, effective June 13, 1997, added the fourth paragraph.

325 ILCS 5/7.8 [Notification of prior report]

Sec. 7.8. Upon receiving an oral or written report of suspected child abuse or neglect, the Department shall immediately notify, either orally or electronically, the Child Protective Service Unit of a previous report concerning a subject of the present report or other pertinent information. In addition, upon satisfactory identification procedures, to be established by Department regulation, any person authorized to have access to records under Section 11.1 [325 ILCS 5/11.1] relating to child abuse and neglect may request and shall be immediately provided the information requested in accordance with this Act. However, no information shall be released unless it prominently states the report is "indicated", and only information from "indicated" reports shall be released, except that information concerning pending reports may be released to any person authorized under paragraphs (1), (2), (3) and (11) of Section 11.1 [325 ILCS 5/11.1]. In addition, State's Attorneys are authorized to receive unfounded reports for prosecution purposes related to the transmission of false reports of child abuse or neglect in violation of subsection (a), paragraph (7) of Section 26-1 of the Criminal Code of 1961 [720 ILCS 5/26-1] and guardians ad litem appointed under Article II of the Juvenile Court Act of 1987 [705 ILCS 405/2-1 et seq.] shall receive the classified reports set forth in Section 7.14 of this Act [325 ILCS 5/7.14] in conformance with paragraph (19) of Section 11.1 and Section 7.14 of this Act [325 ILCS 5/11.1 and 325 ILCS 5/7.14]. The names and other identifying data and the dates and the circumstances of any persons requesting or receiving information from the central register shall be entered in the register record.
(Source: P.A. 86-904; 86-1293; 87-649.)

Note.
This section was Ill.Rev.Stat., Ch. 23, para. 2057.8.

325 ILCS 5/7.9 [Initial written reports; contents]

Sec. 7.9. The Department shall prepare, print, and distribute initial, preliminary, and final reporting forms to each Child Protective Service Unit. Initial

written reports from the reporting source shall contain the following information to the extent known at the time the report is made: (1) the names and addresses of the child and his parents or other persons responsible for his welfare; (1.5) the name and address of the school that the child attends (or the school that the child last attended, if the report is written during the summer when school is not in session), and the name of the school district in which the school is located, if applicable; (2) the child's age, sex, and race; (3) the nature and extent of the child's abuse or neglect, including any evidence of prior injuries, abuse, or neglect of the child or his siblings; (4) the names of the persons apparently responsible for the abuse or neglect; (5) family composition, including names, ages, sexes, and races of other children in the home; (6) the name of the person making the report, his occupation, and where he can be reached; (7) the actions taken by the reporting source, including the taking of photographs and x-rays, placing the child in temporary protective custody, or notifying the medical examiner or coroner; and (8) any other information the person making the report believes might be helpful in the furtherance of the purposes of this Act.
(Source: P.A. 84-611; 92-295, § 10; 92-651, § 66.)

Note.
This section was Ill.Rev.Stat., Ch. 23, para. 2057.9.
Section 997 of P.A. 92-651 is a no acceleration or delay provision, and Section 998 is a no revival or extension provision.

Effect of Amendments.
The 2001 amendment by P.A. 92-295, effective January 1, 2002, inserted item (1.5).
The 2002 amendment by P.A. 92-651, effective July 11, 2002, made a stylistic change.

325 ILCS 5/7.10 [Preliminary report]

Sec. 7.10. Upon the receipt of each oral report made under this Act, the Child Protective Service Unit shall immediately transmit a copy thereof to the state central register of child abuse and neglect. A preliminary report from a Child Protective Service Unit shall be made at the time of the first of any 30-day extensions made pursuant to Section 7.12 [325 ILCS 5/7.12] and shall describe the status of the related investigation up to that time, including an evaluation of the present family situation and danger to the child or children, corrections or updating of the initial report, and actions taken or contemplated.
(Source: P.A. 86-904.)

Note.
This section was Ill.Rev.Stat., Ch. 23, para. 2057.10.

325 ILCS 5/7.12 [Determination]

Sec. 7.12. The Child Protective Service Unit shall determine, within 60 days, whether the report is "indicated" or "unfounded" and report it forthwith to the central register; where it is not possible to initiate or complete an investigation within 60 days the report may be deemed "undetermined" provided every effort has been made to undertake a complete investigation. The Department may extend the period in which such determinations must be made in individual cases for additional periods of up to 30 days each for good cause shown. The Department shall by rule establish what shall constitute good cause.
(Source: P.A. 86-904.)

Note.
This section was Ill.Rev.Stat., Ch. 23, para. 2057.12.

325 ILCS 5/7.13 [Additional information]

Sec. 7.13. The reports made under this Act may contain such additional information in the furtherance of the purposes of this Act as the Department, by rule, may require.
(Source: P.A. 81-1077.)

Note.
This section was Ill.Rev.Stat., Ch. 23, para. 2057.13.

325 ILCS 5/7.14 [Classification of reports]

Sec. 7.14. All reports in the central register shall be classified in one of three categories: "indicated", "unfounded" or "undetermined", as the case may be. After the report is classified, the person making the classification shall determine whether the child named in the report is the subject of an action under Article II of the Juvenile Court Act of 1987 [705 ILCS 405/2-1 et seq.]. If the child is the subject of an action under Article II of the Juvenile Court Act [705 ILCS 405/2-1 et seq.], the Department shall transmit a copy of the report to the guardian ad litem appointed for the child under Section 2-17 of the Juvenile Court Act [705 ILCS 405/2-17]. All information identifying the subjects of an unfounded report shall be expunged from the register forthwith, except as provided in Section 7.7 [325 ILCS 5/7.7]. Unfounded reports may only be made available to the Child Protective Service Unit when investigating a subsequent report of suspected abuse or maltreatment involving a child named in the unfounded report; and to the subject of the report, provided that the subject requests the report within 60 days of being notified that the report was unfounded. The Child Protective Service Unit shall not indicate the subsequent report solely based upon the existence of the prior unfounded report or reports. Notwithstanding any other provision of law to the contrary, an unfounded report shall not be admissible in any judicial or administrative proceeding or action. Identifying information on all other records shall be removed from the register no later than 5 years after the report is indicated. However, if another report is received involving the same child, his sibling or offspring, or a child in the care of the persons responsible for the child's welfare, or involving the same alleged offender, the identifying information may be maintained in the register until 5 years after the subsequent case or report is closed.

Notwithstanding any other provision of this Section, identifying information in indicated reports involving the sexual abuse of a child, the death of a child, or serious physical injury to a child as defined by the Department in rules, may be retained longer than 5 years after the report is indicated or after the subsequent case or report is closed, and may not be removed from the register except as provided by the Department in rules.

(Source: P.A. 86-904; 87-649; 90-15, § 13; 92-801, § 5.)

Note.

This section was Ill.Rev.Stat., Ch. 23, para. 2057.14.

Effect of Amendments.

The 1997 amendment by P.A. 90-15, effective June 13, 1997, in the first paragraph, added the fifth through seventh sentences.

The 2002 amendment by P.A. 92-801, effective August 16, 2002, inserted "or involving the same alleged offender" in the last sentence of the first paragraph, and made a stylistic change.

325 ILCS 5/7.15 [Other information in central register]

Sec. 7.15. The central register may contain such other information which the Department determines to be in furtherance of the purposes of this Act. Pursuant to the provisions of Sections 7.14 and 7.16 [325 ILCS 5/7.14 and 325 ILCS 5/7.16], the Department may amend or remove from the central register appropriate records upon good cause shown and upon notice to the subjects of the report and the Child Protective Service Unit.

(Source: P.A. 81-1077; 90-15, § 13.)

Note.

This section was Ill.Rev.Stat., Ch. 23, para. 2057.15.

Cross References.

As to unfounded reports identifying an employee as the subject of an investigation by the Department of Children and Family Services, see 820 ILCS 40/13.

Effect of Amendments.

The 1997 amendment by P.A. 90-15, effective June 13, 1997, in the second sentence, deleted "expunge" preceding "or remove from".

325 ILCS 5/7.16 [Amendment, expunction or removal]

Sec. 7.16. For any investigation or appeal initiated on or after, or pending on July 1, 1998, the following time frames shall apply. Within 60 days after the notification of the completion of the Child Protective Service Unit investigation, determined by the date of the notification sent by the Department, a subject of a report may request the Department to amend the record or remove the record of the report from the register. Such request shall be in writing and directed to such person as the Department designates in the notification. If the Department disregards any request to do so or does not act within 10 days, the subject shall have the right to a hearing within the Department to determine whether the record of the report should be amended or removed on the grounds that it is inaccurate or it is being maintained in a manner inconsistent with this Act, except that there shall be no such right to a hearing on the ground of the report's inaccuracy if there has been a court finding of child abuse or neglect, the report's accuracy being conclusively presumed on such finding. Such hearing shall be held within a reasonable time after the subject's request and at a reasonable place and hour. The appropriate Child Protective Service Unit shall be given notice of the hearing. In such hearings, the burden of proving the accuracy and consistency of the record shall be on the Department and the appropriate Child Protective Service Unit. The hearing shall be conducted by the Director or his designee, who is hereby authorized and empowered to order the amendment or removal of the record to make it accurate and consistent with this Act. The decision shall be made, in writing, at the close of the hearing, or within 45 days thereof, and shall state the reasons upon which it is based. Decisions of the Department under this Section are administrative decisions subject to judicial review under the Administrative Review Law [735 ILCS 5/3-101 et seq.].

Should the Department grant the request of the subject of the report pursuant to this Section either on administrative review or after administrative hearing to amend an indicated report to an unfounded report, the report shall be released and expunged in accordance with the standards set forth in Section 7.14 of this Act [325 ILCS 5/7.14].

(Source: P.A. 86-904; 90-15, § 13; 90-608, § 20.)

Note.

This section was Ill.Rev.Stat., Ch. 23, para. 2057.16.

Illinois Administrative Code.

See 89 Illinois Administrative Code, § 300.160.

Effect of Amendments.

The 1997 amendment by P.A. 90-15, effective June 13, 1997, in the first paragraph, in the first sentence, substituted "the record" for "expunge identifying information from", in the fourth sentence deleted "expunged" preceding "or removed on" and in the eighth sentence deleted "expunction" preceding "or removal of"; and added the second paragraph.

The 1998 amendment by P.A. 90-608, effective June 30, 1998, added the present first sentence; rewrote the present fourth sentence; and substituted "45 days" for "30 days" in the present ninth sentence.

CASE NOTES

Analysis

Delay
Hearing
—Remedy for Refusal to Hold
Proof
Reconsideration
—Refused
Review
Standing
Time Limitations

Delay

Appellate court's judgment affirming the expungement of indicated findings of sexual abuse by a teacher from the Illinois State Central Register was affirmed because the teacher's due process rights were violated by the standard of proof used, the low credible-evidence standard to indicate the report against the teacher and to deny his first-stage appeal, and by the delays in the provision of the hearing and the final administrative decision. Lyon v. Dep't of Children & Family Servs., 209 Ill. 2d 264, 282 Ill. Dec. 799, 807 N.E.2d 423, 2004 Ill. LEXIS 361 (2004).

In a proceeding to expunge an indicated finding of sexual molestation, where the Department of Children and Family Services conceded that time periods established in this and the Illinois Administrative Code (5 ILCS 100/1-1 et seq.) were exceeded, and plaintiff did not seek mandamus relief and instead acquiesced throughout the proceedings, and the delay was reasonable, the delay did not constitute a violation of plaintiff's due process rights. S.W. v. Illinois Dep't of Children & Family Servs., 276 Ill. App. 3d 672, 213 Ill. Dec. 280, 658 N.E.2d 1301 (1 Dist. 1995).

Hearing

—Remedy for Refusal to Hold

The legislature did not intend that provision requiring the Department of Children and Family Services to hold a hearing within a reasonable time after request for expunction would limit the jurisdiction of the agency. Thus, the proper remedy for Department's refusal to hold a hearing is to proceed in mandamus. Shawgo v. Department of Children & Family Servs., 182 Ill. App. 3d 485, 131 Ill. Dec. 46, 538 N.E.2d 234 (4 Dist. 1989).

Proof

In an action for expunction, the burden of proving the accuracy and consistency of the record is upon the agency. Doe v. Illinois Dep't of Children & Family Servs., 265 Ill. App. 3d 907, 203 Ill. Dec. 110, 639 N.E.2d 149 (1 Dist.), appeal denied, 157 Ill. 2d 498, 205 Ill. Dec. 159, 642 N.E.2d 1276 (1994).

In an action for expunction under this section, the burden of proving the accuracy and consistency of the record is upon the agency. I.F. v. Department of Children & Family Servs., 146 Ill. App. 3d 68, 100 Ill. Dec. 97, 496 N.E.2d 1162 (1 Dist. 1986).

Where Department of Children and Family Services found that there was sufficient credible evidence which indicated child abuse based on excessive corporal punishment and recommended family counseling, and the circuit court affirmed the agency decision, petitioner's request to expunge the record was denied, as mother had admitted to striking the child and then discovering the blow had caused bleeding. I.F. v. Department of Children & Family Servs., 146 Ill. App. 3d 68, 100 Ill. Dec. 97, 496 N.E.2d 1162 (1 Dist. 1986).

Reconsideration

—Refused

Letter was not a notice of "intent to deny" but was a denial which anticipated no action in the future where it contained provisions indicating that the only recourse available to plaintiff was to wait 18 months and to then apply anew for the license. Teal v. Department of Children & Family Servs., 275 Ill. App. 3d 966, 212 Ill. Dec. 475, 657 N.E.2d 676 (4 Dist. 1995).

Review

Only if department refuses to amend, expunge or remove a report, or fails to act on a subject's request to do so, is the subject entitled to an administrative hearing, and potentially, judicial review of the department's decision. Kemp-Golden v. Department of Children & Family Servs., 281 Ill. App. 3d 869, 217 Ill. Dec. 594, 667 N.E.2d 688 (1 Dist. 1996).

Standing

Parent who made the report on alleged child abuse was not a subject of the report to have standing to seek judicial review of the department's decision to expunge report. Kemp-Golden v. Department of Children & Family Servs., 281 Ill. App. 3d 869, 217 Ill. Dec. 594, 667 N.E.2d 688 (1 Dist. 1996).

Time Limitations

Though the "credible-evidence" standard for recording an "indicated" report of child molestation by plaintiff was constitutional, the Department of Children and Family Services violated plaintiff's right to due process by failing to meet statutory and regulatory deadlines and thereby delaying his appeal. Lyon v. Dep't of Children & Family Servs., 335 Ill. App. 3d 376, 269 Ill. Dec. 276, 780 N.E.2d 748, 2002 Ill. App. LEXIS 1071 (4 Dist. 2002), aff'd, 209 Ill. 2d 264, 282 Ill. Dec. 799, 807 N.E.2d 423 (2004).

When the Department of Children and Family Services enters an "indicated" report in the central register on the basis of "credible evidence" rather than a preponderance of the evidence, due process requires the Department to strictly comply with its statutory and regulatory deadlines for processing the administrative appeal. Lyon v. Dep't of Children & Family Servs., 335 Ill. App. 3d 376, 269 Ill. Dec. 276, 780 N.E.2d 748, 2002 Ill. App. LEXIS 1071 (4 Dist. 2002), aff'd, 209 Ill. 2d 264, 282 Ill. Dec. 799, 807 N.E.2d 423 (2004).

Placement of the name of an individual who was the focus of an "indicated report" of child sex abuse on the Illinois State Central Register of suspected child abusers implicated both federal liberty interests and Illinois constitutional due process rights; a court decision upholding the Illinois Department of Children and Family Services indicated finding was reversed because the Department violated the individual's due process rights when it failed to comply with time requirements in Ill. Admin. Code ch. 89, § 336.220(a) (2001) and 325 ILCS 5/7.16 inasmuch as it failed to timely confirm the original "credible evidence" finding by a preponderance of evidence finding. Montalbano v. Ill. Dep't of Children & Family Servs., 343 Ill. App. 3d 471, 278 Ill. Dec. 160, 797 N.E.2d 1078, 2003 Ill. App. LEXIS 1220 (4 Dist. 2003), appeal denied, 209 Ill. 2d 583, 286 Ill. Dec. 166, 813 N.E.2d 223 (2004).

A gross deviation from time limitations would be deemed to be unreasonable and contrary to the legislative intent, evidenced by the setting of time limitations, that the agency act in a reasonably timely manner. Stull v. Department of Children & Family Servs., 239 Ill. App. 3d 325, 179 Ill. Dec. 954, 606 N.E.2d 786 (5 Dist. 1992), appeal denied, 149 Ill. 2d 661, 183 Ill. Dec. 872, 612 N.E.2d 524 (1993).

325 ILCS 5/7.17 [Notice]

Sec. 7.17. To the fullest extent possible, written notice of any amendment, expunction, or removal of any record made under this Act shall be served upon each subject of such report and the appropriate Child Protective Service Unit. Upon receipt of such notice, the Child Protective Service Unit shall take similar action in regard to the local child abuse and neglect index and shall inform, for the same purpose, any other individuals or agencies which received such record under this Act or in any other manner. Nothing in this Section is intended to require the destruction of case records.
(Source: P.A. 81-1077.)

Note.

This section was Ill.Rev.Stat., Ch. 23, para. 2057.17.

Illinois Administrative Code.

See 89 Illinois Administrative Code, §§ 431.30, 336.220, 336.220.

325 ILCS 5/7.18 [Amending reports]

Sec. 7.18. Pursuant to Sections 7.15 and 7.16 [325 ILCS 5/7.15 and 325 ILCS 5/7.16] and for good cause shown, the Child Protective Service Unit may amend any report previously sent to the State-wide center. Unless otherwise prescribed by this Act, the content, form, manner and timing of making the reports shall be established by rules of the Department.
(Source: P.A. 81-1077.)

Note.
This section was Ill.Rev.Stat., Ch. 23, para. 2057.18.

325 ILCS 5/7.19 [Copies]

Sec. 7.19. Upon request, a subject of a report shall be entitled to receive a copy of all information contained in the central register pertaining to his case. However, the Department may prohibit the release of data that would identify or locate a person who, in good faith, made a report or cooperated in a subsequent investigation. In addition, the Department may seek a court order from the circuit court prohibiting the release of any information which the court finds is likely to be harmful to the subject of the report.
(Source: P.A. 81-1077.)

Note.
This section was Ill.Rev.Stat., Ch. 23, para. 2057.19.

CASE NOTES

Confidentiality
A family's motion to require the state defendants to divulge the name of the person who reported abuse in their home was properly denied, since under this Act a mandatory reporter was given immunity from liability for good faith reporting of possible child abuse and the release of information concerning the identity of such persons was also prohibited as provided in this section. Darryl H. v. Coler, 585 F. Supp. 383 (N.D. Ill. 1984), modified on other grounds, 801 F.2d 893 (7th Cir. 1986).

325 ILCS 5/7.20 Inter-agency agreements for information

Sec. 7.20. *Inter-agency agreements for information.* The Department shall enter into an inter-agency agreement with the Secretary of State to establish a procedure by which employees of the Department may have immediate access to driver's license records maintained by the Secretary of State if the Department determines the information is necessary to perform its duties under the Abused and Neglected Child Reporting Act [325 ILCS 5/1 et seq.], the Child Care Act of 1969 [225 ILCS 10/1 et seq.], and the Children and Family Services Act [20 ILCS 505/1 et seq.]. The Department shall enter into an inter-agency agreement with the Illinois Department of Public Aid and the Department of Human Services (acting as successor to the Department of Public Aid under the Department of Human Services Act [20 ILCS 1305/1-1 et seq.]) to establish a procedure by which employees of the Department may have immediate access to records, files, papers, and communications (except medical, alcohol or drug assessment or treatment, mental health, or any other medical records) of the Illinois Department of Public Aid, county departments of public aid, the Department of Human Services, and local governmental units receiving State or federal funds or aid to provide public aid, if the Department determines the information is necessary to perform its duties under the Abused and Neglected Child Reporting Act [325 ILCS 5/1 et seq.], the Child Care Act of 1969 [225 ILCS 10/1 et seq.], and the Children and Family Services Act [20 ILCS 505/1 et seq.].
(Source: P.A. 88-614, § 107; 89-507, § 90L-74.)

Effective Date.
Section 999 of P.A. 88-614 made this section effective upon becoming law. The Act was approved September 7, 1994.

Effect of Amendments.
The 1996 amendment by P.A. 89-507, effective July 1, 1997, in the second sentence inserted "and the Department of Human Services (acting as successor to the Department of Public Aid under the Department of Human Services Act)", inserted "of Public Aid" following "Illinois Department" and inserted "the Department of Human Services".

325 ILCS 5/7.21 Multidisciplinary Review Committee

Sec. 7.21. *Multidisciplinary Review Committee.* (a) The Department may establish multidisciplinary review committees in each region of the State to assure that mandated reporters have the ability to have a review conducted on any situation where a child abuse or neglect report made by them was "unfounded", and they have concerns about the adequacy of the investigation. These committees shall draw upon the expertise of the Child Death Review Teams as necessary and practicable. Each committee will be composed of the following: a health care professional, a Department employee, a law enforcement official, a licensed social worker, and a representative of the State's attorney's office. In appointing members of a committee, primary consideration shall be given to a prospective member's prior experience in dealing with cases of suspected child abuse or neglect.

(b) Whenever the Department determines that a reported incident of child abuse or neglect from a mandated reporter is "unfounded", the mandated reporter may request a review of the investigation within 10 days of the notification of the final finding. Whenever the Department determines that a reported incident of child abuse or neglect from a mandated reporter or any other reporter is "unfounded", the minor's guardian ad litem appointed under the Juvenile Court Act of 1987 [705 ILCS 405/1-1 et seq.] may request a review of the investigation within 10 days of the notification of the final finding if the subject of the report is also the minor for whom the guardian ad litem has been appointed. The review of the investigation requested by the guardian ad litem may be conducted by the Regional Child Protection Manager.

A review under this subsection will be conducted by the committee, except those requests for review that are made by the guardian ad litem, which shall be conducted by the Regional Child Protection Manager. The Department shall make available to the committee all information in the Department's possession concerning the case. The committee shall make recommendations to the Department as to the adequacy of the investigation and of the accuracy of the final finding determination. These findings shall be forwarded to the Regional Child Protection Manager.

(c) The Department shall provide complete records of these investigations to the committee. Records provided to the committee and recommendation reports generated by the committee shall not be public record.

(c-5) On or before October 1 of each year, the Department shall prepare a report setting forth (i) the number of investigations reviewed by each committee during the previous fiscal year and (ii) the number of those investigations that the committee found to be inadequate. The report shall also include a summary of the committee's comments and a summary of the corrective action, if any, that was taken in response to the committee's recommendations. The report shall be a public record. The Department shall submit the report to the General Assembly and shall make the report available to the public upon request.

(d) The Department shall adopt rules to implement this Section.

(Source: P.A. 89-269, § 5; 90-239, § 10; 91-812, § 510.)

Note.

Section 995 of P.A. 91-812 contains a severability provision.

Effective Date.

This section became effective January 1, 1996 pursuant to Ill. Const. (1970), Art. IV, § 10 and 5 ILCS 75/1.

Effect of Amendments.

The 1997 amendment by P.A. 90-239, effective July 28, 1997, in subsection (a), rewrote the second sentence which read "These committees will serve under the auspices of the Child Death Review Teams".

The 2000 amendment by P.A. 91-812, effective July 13, 2000, in subsection (b) inserted the last two sentences in the first paragraph and rewrote the first sentence in the second paragraph, which formerly read: "This review will be conducted by the committee"; and inserted subsection (c-5).

325 ILCS 5/8.1 [Unfounded reports]

Sec. 8.1. If the Child Protective Service Unit determines after investigating a report that there is no credible evidence that a child is abused or neglected, it shall deem the report to be an unfounded report. However, if it appears that the child or family could benefit from other social services, the local service may suggest such services, including services under Section 8.2 [325 ILCS 5/8.2], for the family's voluntary acceptance or refusal. If the family declines such services, the Department shall take appropriate action in keeping with the best interest of the child, including referring a member of the child's family to a facility licensed by the Department of Human Services or the Department of Public Health.

(Source: P.A. 84-611; 88-85, § 80; 88-487, § 45; 88-670, § 2-53; 89-507, § 90C-25.)

Note.

This section was Ill.Rev.Stat., Ch. 23, para. 2058.1.

Effect of Amendments.

The 1994 amendment by P.A. 88-670, effective December 2, 1994, combined the amendments by P.A. 88-85 and P.A. 88-487.

The 1996 amendment by P.A. 89-507, effective July 1, 1997, in the third sentence substituted "Human Services" for "Alcoholism and Substance Abuse".

325 ILCS 5/8.2 [Service plan; report to General Assembly]

Sec. 8.2. If the Child Protective Service Unit determines, following an investigation made pursuant to Section 7.4 of this Act [325 ILCS 5/7.4], that there is credible evidence that the child is abused or neglected, the Department shall assess the family's need for services, and, as necessary, develop, with the family, an appropriate service plan for the family's voluntary acceptance or refusal. In any case where there is evidence that the perpetrator of the abuse or neglect is an addict or alcoholic as defined in the Alcoholism and Other Drug Abuse and Dependency Act [20 ILCS 301/1-1 et seq.], the Department, when making referrals for drug or alcohol abuse services, shall make such referrals to facilities licensed by the Department of Human Services or the Department of Public Health. The Department shall comply with Section 8.1 [325 ILCS 5/8.1] by explaining its lack of legal authority to compel the acceptance of services and may explain its concomitant authority to petition the Circuit court under the Juvenile Court Act of 1987 or refer the case to the local law enforcement authority or State's attorney for criminal prosecution.

For purposes of this Act, the term "family preservation services" refers to all services to help families, including adoptive and extended families. Family preservation services shall be offered, where safe and appropriate, to prevent the placement of children in substitute care when the children can be cared for at home or in the custody of the person responsible for the children's welfare without endangering the children's health or safety, to reunite them with their families if so placed when reunification is an appropriate goal, or to maintain an adoptive placement. The term "homemaker" includes emergency caretakers, homemakers, caretakers, housekeepers and chore services. The term "counseling" includes individual therapy, infant stimulation therapy, family therapy, group therapy, self-help groups, drug and alcohol abuse counseling, vocational counseling and post-adoptive services. The term "day care" includes protective day care and day care to meet educational, prevocational or vocational needs. The term "emergency assistance and advocacy" includes coordinated services to secure emergency cash, food, housing and medical assistance or advocacy for other subsistence and family protective needs.

Before July 1, 2000, appropriate family preservation services shall, subject to appropriation, be included in the service plan if the Department has determined that those services will ensure the child's health and safety, are in the child's best interests, and will not place the child in imminent risk of harm. Beginning July 1, 2000, appropriate family preservation services shall be uniformly available throughout the State. The Department shall promptly notify children and families of the Department's responsibility to offer and provide family preservation services as identified in the service plan. Such plans may include but are not limited to: case management services; homemakers; counseling; parent education; day care; emergency assistance and advocacy assessments; respite care; in-home health care; transportation to obtain any of the above services; and medical assistance. Nothing in this paragraph shall be construed to create a private right of action or claim on the part of any individual or child welfare agency.

The Department shall provide a preliminary report to the General Assembly no later than January 1, 1991, in regard to the provision of services authorized pursuant to this Section. The report shall include:

(a) the number of families and children served, by type of services;

(b) the outcome from the provision of such services, including the number of families which remained intact at least 6 months following the termination of services;

(c) the number of families which have been subjects of founded reports of abuse following the termination of services;

(d) an analysis of general family circumstances in which family preservation services have been determined to be an effective intervention;

(e) information regarding the number of families in need of services but unserved due to budget or program criteria guidelines;

(f) an estimate of the time necessary for and the annual cost of statewide implementation of such services;

(g) an estimate of the length of time before expansion of these services will be made to include families with children over the age of 6; and

(h) recommendations regarding any proposed legislative changes to this program.

Each Department field office shall maintain on a local basis directories of services available to children and families in the local area where the Department office is located.

The Department shall refer children and families served pursuant to this Section to private agencies and governmental agencies, where available.

Where there are 2 equal proposals from both a not-for-profit and a for-profit agency to provide services, the Department shall give preference to the proposal from the not-for-profit agency.

No service plan shall compel any child or parent to engage in any activity or refrain from any activity which is not reasonably related to remedying a condition or conditions that gave rise or which could give rise to any finding of child abuse or neglect. (Source: P.A. 86-425; 87-860; 87-895; 87-1199, § 2; 88-670, § 3-73; 89-21, § 15-10; 89-507, § 90C-25; 90-14, § 3-120; 90-28, § 10-15; 90-608, § 20.)

Note.

This section was Ill.Rev.Stat., Ch. 23, para. 2058.2.

Illinois Administrative Code.

See 89 Illinois Administrative Code, §§ 301.20, 301.20.

Effect of Amendments.

The 1994 amendment by P.A. 88-670, effective December 2, 1994, in the first paragraph, in the second sentence deleted "Illinois" preceding "Alcoholism", inserted "Abuse and" and deleted "as now or hereafter amended" following "Dependency Act".

The 1995 amendment by P.A. 89-21, effective June 6, 1995, in the third paragraph, added the first, second and fifth sentences, deleted the former fourth paragraph which read "The availability of family preservation services shall be phased in, so that orderly development may occur, during the first 5 fiscal years after the effective date (December 22, 1987) of this amendatory Act of 1987). The Department shall develop a phase in plan and rules in consultation with the Child Welfare Advisory Committee"; and deleted the former fifth paragraph which read "During the phase in period, any type of service enumerated in this Act and made available pursuant to the phase in plan to any client population in one geographic area shall be made equally available to the same client population throughout the State within 3 full years. By July 1, 1995, the family preservation services shall be uniformly available throughout the State".

The 1996 amendment by P.A. 89-507, effective July 1, 1997, in the first paragraph, in the second sentence, substituted "Human Services" for "Alcoholism and Substance Abuse".

The 1997 amendment by P.A. 90-14, effective July 1, 1997, in the first paragraph, in the third sentence, substituted "concomitant" for "noncommitant".

The 1997 amendment by P.A. 90-28, effective January 1, 1998, in the first paragraph, in the third sentence, substituted "concomitant" for "noncommitant"; in the second paragraph, in the first sentence, inserted "when the children can be cared for at home or in the custody of the person responsible for the children's welfare without endangering the children's health or safety" and substituted "when" for "and if"; and in the third paragraph, in the first sentence, inserted "will ensure the child's health and safety" added a comma after "interests" and substituted "will not place the child" for "when the child will not be".

The 1998 amendment by P.A. 90-608, effective June 30, 1998, incorporated the amendments by P.A. 90-14 and P.A. 90-28; and rewrote the former first sentence of the second paragraph to form the present first and second sentences.

CASE NOTES

Analysis

Construction with Other Laws
Family Preservation Services
Notice of Plans
—Failure to Notify Father
Payment for Services

Construction with Other Laws

Section 750 ILCS 50/1(D)(m) and this section together indicate that the measure of reasonable progress encompasses those conditions which could give rise to a finding of abuse or neglect (not merely those conditions which led to the initial removal of the child), and support a holding that "the standard by which progress is to be measured is parental compliance with the court's directives, the service plan, or both." In re C.S., 294 Ill. App. 3d 780, 229 Ill. Dec. 225, 691 N.E.2d 161 (4 Dist. 1998).

The Juvenile Court Act (705 ILCS 405/1-1 et seq.), this Act, the Children and Family Services Act (20 ILCS 505/1 et seq.) and to some extent the Illinois Alcoholism and Other Drug Dependency Act (20 ILCS 301/1-1 et seq.) must be construed in concert to determine the powers and responsibilities of Department of Children and Family Services in cases involving abuse or neglect resulting from parental drug abuse. In re Lawrence M., 172 Ill. 2d 523, 219 Ill. Dec. 32, 670 N.E.2d 710 (1996).

Family Preservation Services

Pursuant to the provisions in the Juvenile Court Act (705 ILCS

Family Preservation Services (Cont'd)
405/1-1 et seq.) and Department of Children and Family Services' (DCFS) mandate, the court may enter interim orders for services to the child and his or her family in order to prevent the unnecessary separation of children from their families and restoring to their families children who have been removed where it has found that they are in the best interest of the minor and his or her family and will help preserve the family. In re Lawrence M., 269 Ill. App. 3d 253, 206 Ill. Dec. 817, 645 N.E.2d 1069 (1 Dist.), aff'd, 172 Ill. 2d 523, 219 Ill. Dec. 32, 670 N.E.2d 710 (1996).

Orders were essential to the reunification of the families in question as in each case the Department of Children and Family Services did not dispute the need for inpatient treatment, but simply claimed that it should not be required to pay for such treatment and in all cases but one drug treatment was recommended by Department of Children and Family Services itself or by substance abuse professionals. In re Lawrence M., 172 Ill. 2d 523, 219 Ill. Dec. 32, 670 N.E.2d 710 (1996).

Notice of Plans

—Failure to Notify Father
Where Department of Children and Family Services (DCFS) failed to inform father of the various service plans which were created to enable him to work towards visitation and/or custody of his children and there was no indication in the record that any of the DCFS workers involved in case ever contacted the Department of Corrections in an effort to locate the father who had informed DCFS of his incarceration, DCFS' handling of the case was inexcusably clumsy, and since DCFS did not keep the father apprised of the service plans, his failure to complete the tasks within those plans could not alone support a finding of unfitness. T.D. v. Baldwin, 268 Ill. App. 3d 239, 205 Ill. Dec. 708, 643 N.E.2d 1315 (1 Dist. 1994).

Payment for Services
While it is true several statutory provisions allude to the Department of Children and Family Service's duty to make drug or alcohol abuse treatment recommendations in the family's case or service plan, these provisions do not abrogate its responsibility to provide and pay for drug and alcohol treatment services for parents who need these services. In re Lawrence M., 172 Ill. 2d 523, 219 Ill. Dec. 32, 670 N.E.2d 710 (1996).

325 ILCS 5/8.3 [Assisting Circuit Court]

Sec. 8.3. The Department shall assist a Circuit Court during all stages of the court proceeding in accordance with the purposes of this Act and the Juvenile Court Act of 1987 [705 ILCS 405/1-1 et seq.] by providing full, complete, and accurate information to the court and by appearing in court if requested by the court. Failure to provide assistance requested by a court shall be enforceable through proceedings for contempt of court.
(Source: P.A. 85-1209; 88-310, § 5.)

Note.
This section was Ill.Rev.Stat., Ch. 23, para. 2058.3.

325 ILCS 5/8.4 [Rehabilitative services]

Sec. 8.4. The Department shall provide or arrange for and monitor, as authorized by this Act, rehabilitative services for children and their families on a voluntary basis or under a final or intermediate order of the Court.
(Source: P.A. 84-611.)

Note.
This section was Ill.Rev.Stat., Ch. 23, para. 2058.4.

325 ILCS 5/8.5 [Child abuse and neglect index]

Sec. 8.5. The Child Protective Service Unit shall maintain a local child abuse and neglect index of all cases reported under this Act which will enable it to determine the location of case records and to monitor the timely and proper investigation and disposition of cases. The index shall include the information contained in the initial, progress, and final reports required under this Act, and any other appropriate information.
(Source: P.A. 81-1077.)

Note.
This section was Ill.Rev.Stat., Ch. 23, para. 2058.5.

325 ILCS 5/8.6 Reports to a child's school

Sec. 8.6. *Reports to a child's school.* Within 10 days after completing an investigation of alleged physical or sexual abuse under this Act, if the report is indicated, the Child Protective Service Unit shall send a copy of its final finding report to the school that the child who is the indicated victim of the report attends. If the final finding report is sent during the summer when the school is not in session, the report shall be sent to the last school that the child attended. The final finding report shall be sent as "confidential", and the school shall be responsible for ensuring that the report remains confidential in accordance with the Illinois School Student Records Act [105 ILCS 10/1 et seq.]. If an indicated finding is overturned in an appeal or hearing, or if the Department has made a determination that the child is no longer at risk of physical or sexual harm, the Department shall request that the final finding report be purged from the student's record, and the school shall purge the final finding report from the student's record and return the report to the Department. If an indicated report is expunged from the central register, and that report has been sent to a child's school, the Department shall request that the final finding report be purged from the student's record, and the school shall purge the final finding report from the student's record and return the report to the Department.
(Source: P.A. 92-295, § 10.)

Effective Date.
This section is effective January 1, 2002, pursuant to Ill. Const. (1970), Art. IV, § 10 and 5 ILCS 75/1.

325 ILCS 5/9 [Immunity from liability]

Sec. 9. Any person, institution or agency, under this Act, participating in good faith in the making of a report or referral, or in the investigation of such a report or referral or in the taking of photographs and x-rays or in the retaining a child in temporary protective custody or in making a disclosure of information concerning reports of child abuse and neglect in compliance with Sections 4.2 and 11.1 of

this Act [325 ILCS 5/4.2 and 325 ILCS 5/11.1] shall have immunity from any liability, civil, criminal or that otherwise might result by reason of such actions. For the purpose of any proceedings, civil or criminal, the good faith of any persons required to report or refer, or permitted to report, cases of suspected child abuse or neglect or permitted to refer individuals under this Act or required to disclose information concerning reports of child abuse and neglect in compliance with Sections 4.2 and 11.1 of this Act [325 ILCS 5/4.2 and 325 ILCS 5/11.1], shall be presumed.
(Source: P.A. 86-1004; 90-15, § 13.)

Note.
This section was Ill.Rev.Stat., Ch. 23, para. 2059.

Effect of Amendments.
The 1997 amendment by P.A. 90-15, effective June 13, 1997, in the first sentence inserted "or in making a disclosure of information concerning reports of child abuse and neglect in compliance with Sections 4.2 and 11.1 of this Act"; and in the second sentence added "or required to disclose information concerning reports of child abuse and neglect in compliance with Sections 4.2 and 11.1 of this Act" at the end.

CASE NOTES

ANALYSIS

Constitutionality
Immunity
—Not Granted
—Precluded by Allegations
Presumption
—Rebuttal
—To Whom Recorded
—Upheld

Constitutionality
In light of the substantial state interest in uncovering child abuse or neglect, and in protecting the children of this state, the "good faith" immunity provided for, mandated, and permitted reporters under this Act is clearly justified and is in no way inconsistent with the Illinois Constitution. Lehman v. Stephens, 148 Ill. App. 3d 538, 101 Ill. Dec. 736, 499 N.E.2d 103 (4 Dist. 1986).

Immunity

—Not Granted
Where trial court determined that defendant did not know a statement to be true and had no reasonable basis to know that it was true, that defendant's behavior in general was corroborative of an attitude of malice, and that defendant's subsequent explanations as to his making the statement were hollow with discordance, in light of the finding of lack of good faith, defendant was not entitled to immunity under this section. Brown v. Farkas, 158 Ill. App. 3d 772, 110 Ill. Dec. 823, 511 N.E.2d 1143 (1 Dist. 1986).

—Precluded by Allegations
Statute did not afford immunity where the plaintiff alleged personal injury resulting from medical care and treatment administered by a physician; however, a physician was protected from liability in reporting a diagnosis provided that he has acted in good faith in diagnosing the patient and reporting the information. Doe v. Winny, 327 Ill. App. 3d 668, 261 Ill. Dec. 852, 764 N.E.2d 143, 2002 Ill. App. LEXIS 73 (2 Dist. 2002).
Allegations that defendant grabbed plaintiff by the shoulders and threw her on a bed supported the conclusion that the defendant acted wilfully or recklessly and perhaps with malice, and was sufficient to preclude, on a motion to dismiss, the application of the good faith immunity provided by this section. Falk ex rel. Falk v. Martel, 210 Ill. App. 3d 557, 155 Ill. Dec. 248, 569 N.E.2d 248 (3 Dist. 1991).

Presumption

—Rebuttal
Allegations in a mother's complaint that a hospital continued to question a child about sexual abuse, conducted multiple vaginal examinations on the child, and refused to release the child to her mother until the Illinois Department of Children and Family Services gave its okay, even though at the time, the hospital had clear evidence that no sexual abuse involving the child had taken place, were sufficient to rebut any presumption of good faith by the hospital at the pleading stage of the mother's action and were sufficient to withstand a motion to dismiss. Lipscomb v. Sisters of St. Francis Health Servs., 343 Ill. App. 3d 1036, 278 Ill. Dec. 575, 799 N.E.2d 293, 2003 Ill. App. LEXIS 1135 (1 Dist. 2003).
The presumption of good faith afforded by this section on the part of the mandated reporter must be rebutted in order to have the name divulged. Darryl H. v. Coler, 585 F. Supp. 383 (N.D. Ill. 1984), modified on other grounds, 801 F.2d 893 (7th Cir. 1986).

—To Whom Recorded
The second sentence of this section grants a presumption of good faith to required and permitted reporters, and not to the other categories of persons mentioned in the first sentence. Thus, defendant, who was investigating a report of child abuse, was not entitled to a presumption of good faith. Falk ex rel. Falk v. Martel, 210 Ill. App. 3d 557, 155 Ill. Dec. 248, 569 N.E.2d 248 (3 Dist. 1991).

—Upheld
Court held that (1) the district court's finding that the parents did not rebut the Illinois statutory presumption of good faith, 325 ILCS 5/9, running in favor of the doctor, for reporting suspected child abuse with respect to their claim for defamation was proper; as the doctor did not have to have evidence of previous abuse per 325 ILCS 5/3, the doctor's belief that the parents might not be equipped to provide their child with the necessary medical care was sufficient. Franciski v. Univ. of Chi. Hosps., 338 F.3d 765, 2003 U.S. App. LEXIS 15430 (7th Cir. 2003).
Where a doctor followed proper procedures in conducting her examination of a child, and reported positive gonorrhea test results to the Illinois Department of Children and Family Services (DCFS) as required by statute, after notifying parents, the parents failed to overcome the statutory presumption that the doctor acted in good faith in reporting the child's test results to the DCFS. Poulos v. Lane, 276 Ill. App. 3d 524, 213 Ill. Dec. 404, 659 N.E.2d 34 (1 Dist. 1995), appeal denied, 166 Ill. 2d 553, 216 Ill. Dec. 10, 664 N.E.2d 647 (1996).

OPINIONS OF ATTORNEY GENERAL

Federal Compliance
The term "reasonable cause to believe" as used in the Abused and Neglected Child Reporting Act (325 ILCS 5/1 et seq.) is equivalent to the term "suspect" as used in the federal Child Abuse Prevention and Treatment Act (42 U.S.C. § 5101 et seq.) 1977 Op. Atty. Gen. 173.

LEGAL PERIODICALS

For article, "Survey of Illinois Law: Torts," see 25 S. Ill. U. L.J. 1001 (2001).
For article, "Survey of Illinois Law: Health Care," see 25 S. Ill. U. L.J. 873 (2001).

325 ILCS 5/9.1 Employer discrimination

Sec. 9.1. *Employer discrimination.* No employer shall discharge, demote or suspend, or threaten to discharge, demote or suspend, or in any manner discriminate against any employee who makes any good faith oral or written report of suspected child abuse or neglect, or who is or will be a witness or testify in any investigation or proceeding concerning a report of suspected child abuse or neglect.
(Source: P.A. 86-904.)

Note.
This section was Ill.Rev.Stat., Ch. 23, para. 2059.1.

Illinois Administrative Code.
See 89 Illinois Administrative Code, § 300.30.

325 ILCS 5/10 [Testimony]

Sec. 10. Any person who makes a report or who investigates a report under this Act shall testify fully in any judicial proceeding resulting from such report, as to any evidence of abuse or neglect, or the cause thereof. Any person who is required to report a suspected case of abuse or neglect under Section 4 of this Act [325 ILCS 5/4] shall testify fully in any administrative hearing resulting from such report, as to any evidence of abuse or neglect or the cause thereof. No evidence shall be excluded by reason of any common law or statutory privilege relating to communications between the alleged perpetrator of abuse or neglect, or the child subject of the report under this Act and the person making or investigating the report.
(Source: P.A. 86-904.)

Note.
This section was Ill.Rev.Stat., Ch. 23, para. 2060.

Cross References.
As to privileged communication of a clinical social worker or licensed social worker, see 225 ILCS 20/16.

CASE NOTES

ANALYSIS

Applicability
Status of Witness

Applicability
The statute does not apply to a custody proceeding brought pursuant to section 602 of the Illinois Marriage and Dissolution of Marriage Act (750 ILCS 5/602). In re Troy S., 319 Ill. App. 3d 61, 253 Ill. Dec. 335, 745 N.E.2d 109, 2001 Ill. App. LEXIS 84 (3 Dist. 2001).

Status of Witness
Although plaintiff filed the report of abuse and testified as a witness at the administrative hearing, such participation did not vest her with party status. Kemp-Golden v. Department of Children & Family Servs., 281 Ill. App. 3d 869, 217 Ill. Dec. 594, 667 N.E.2d 688 (1 Dist. 1996).

325 ILCS 5/11 [Confidentiality of records]

Sec. 11. All records concerning reports of child abuse and neglect or records concerning referrals under this Act and all records generated as a result of such reports or referrals, shall be confidential and shall not be disclosed except as specifically authorized by this Act or other applicable law. It is a Class A misdemeanor to permit, assist, or encourage the unauthorized release of any information contained in such reports, referrals or records.

Nothing contained in this Section prevents the sharing or disclosure of records relating or pertaining to the death of a minor under the care of or receiving services from the Department of Children and Family Services and under the jurisdiction of the juvenile court with the juvenile court, the State's Attorney, and the minor's attorney.
(Source: P.A. 86-1004; 90-15, § 13.)

Note.
This section was Ill.Rev.Stat., Ch. 23, para. 2061.

Cross References.
As to the disclosure of privileged communication, see 750 ILCS 60/227.
As to nondisclosure of information, under the School Code, see 105 ILCS 5/10-22.6b.

Effect of Amendments.
The 1997 amendment by P.A. 90-15, effective June 13, 1997, added the second paragraph.

CASE NOTES

ANALYSIS

Confidential Records
—In General
—Access
—Disclosure
Discoverability
—Discretion of Court

Confidential Records

—In General
The confidentiality provision applies not only to written records and reports but also to testimony regarding information contained in such reports. In re Troy S., 319 Ill. App. 3d 61, 253 Ill. Dec. 335, 745 N.E.2d 109, 2001 Ill. App. LEXIS 84 (3 Dist. 2001).

—Access
The right to confront and cross-examine does not entitle defendant to full access to confidential records in the hope of finding impeaching material. People v. Jennings, 254 Ill. App. 3d 14, 193 Ill. Dec. 232, 626 N.E.2d 265 (2 Dist. 1993), appeal denied, 156 Ill. 2d 562, 202 Ill. Dec. 927, 638 N.E.2d 1121 (1994).

—Disclosure
In the action against the parents of a 15 year old boy for negligent supervision, the parents' motion for a protective order was granted in that they were not required to provide copies of any child abuse records that they may have because Illinois's Abused and Neglected Child Reporting Act, 325 ILCS 5/11 provides that reports of child abuse and neglect or records concerning referrals under the Act and all records generated as a result of such reports or referrals, shall be confidential and shall not be disclosed except as specifically authorized by the Act or other applicable law. A.K. v. G.V., F. Supp. 2d , 2004 U.S. Dist. LEXIS 7570 (N.D. Ill. Apr. 29, 2004).

In a case involving criminal sexual assault of a child, the trial court did not abuse its discretion in refusing to turn over all of the records of the Department of Children and Family Services, for these records are confidential and generally they are not to be disclosed. People v. Jennings, 254 Ill. App. 3d 14, 193 Ill. Dec. 232, 626 N.E.2d 265 (2 Dist. 1993), appeal denied, 156 Ill. 2d 562, 202 Ill. Dec. 927, 638 N.E.2d 1121 (1994).

Discoverability

—Discretion of Court
Determination of whether material is discoverable and subject to disclosure is to be made by the circuit court; no error occurred where the circuit court conducted an in camera inspection of certain records without either defense counsel or the State's attorney present and permitted defendant to use certain portions of the documents for impeachment purposes. People v. Coates, 109 Ill. 2d 431, 94 Ill. Dec. 421, 488 N.E.2d 247 (1985), cert. denied, 475 U.S. 1088, 106 S. Ct. 1474, 89 L. Ed. 2d 729 (1986), overruled on other grounds, 145 Ill. 2d 188, 164 Ill. Dec. 127, 582 N.E.2d 690 (1991).

325 ILCS 5/11.1 Access to records

Sec. 11.1. *Access to records.* (a) A person shall have access to the records described in Section 11 [325

ILCS 5/11] only in furtherance of purposes directly connected with the administration of this Act or the Intergovernmental Missing Child Recovery Act of 1984 [325 ILCS 40/1 et seq.]. Those persons and purposes for access include:

(1) Department staff in the furtherance of their responsibilities under this Act, or for the purpose of completing background investigations on persons or agencies licensed by the Department or with whom the Department contracts for the provision of child welfare services.

(2) A law enforcement agency investigating known or suspected child abuse or neglect, known or suspected involvement with child pornography, known or suspected criminal sexual assault, known or suspected criminal sexual abuse, or any other sexual offense when a child is alleged to be involved.

(3) The Department of State Police when administering the provisions of the Intergovernmental Missing Child Recovery Act of 1984 [325 ILCS 40/1 et seq.].

(4) A physician who has before him a child whom he reasonably suspects may be abused or neglected.

(5) A person authorized under Section 5 of this Act [325 ILCS 5/5] to place a child in temporary protective custody when such person requires the information in the report or record to determine whether to place the child in temporary protective custody.

(6) A person having the legal responsibility or authorization to care for, treat, or supervise a child or a parent, guardian, or other person responsible for the child's welfare who is the subject of a report.

(7) Except in regard to harmful or detrimental information as provided in Section 7.19 [325 ILCS 5/7.19], any subject of the report, and if the subject of the report is a minor, his guardian or guardian ad litem.

(8) A court, upon its finding that access to such records may be necessary for the determination of an issue before such court; however, such access shall be limited to in camera inspection, unless the court determines that public disclosure of the information contained therein is necessary for the resolution of an issue then pending before it.

(8.1) A probation officer or other authorized representative of a probation or court services department conducting an investigation ordered by a court under the Juvenile Court Act of 1987 [705 ILCS 405/1-1 et seq.].

(9) A grand jury, upon its determination that access to such records is necessary in the conduct of its official business.

(10) Any person authorized by the Director, in writing, for audit or bona fide research purposes.

(11) Law enforcement agencies, coroners or medical examiners, physicians, courts, school superintendents and child welfare agencies in other states who are responsible for child abuse or neglect investigations or background investigations.

(12) The Department of Professional Regulation, the State Board of Education and school superintendents in Illinois, who may use or disclose information from the records as they deem necessary to conduct investigations or take disciplinary action, as provided by law.

(13) A coroner or medical examiner who has reason to believe that a child has died as the result of abuse or neglect.

(14) The Director of a State-operated facility when an employee of that facility is the perpetrator in an indicated report.

(15) The operator of a licensed child care facility or a facility licensed by the Department of Human Services (as successor to the Department of Alcoholism and Substance Abuse) in which children reside when a current or prospective employee of that facility is the perpetrator in an indicated child abuse or neglect report, pursuant to Section 4.3 of the Child Care Act of 1969 [225 ILCS 10/4.3].

(16) Members of a multidisciplinary team in the furtherance of its responsibilities under subsection (b) of Section 7.1 [325 ILCS 5/7.1]. All reports concerning child abuse and neglect made available to members of such multidisciplinary teams and all records generated as a result of such reports shall be confidential and shall not be disclosed, except as specifically authorized by this Act or other applicable law. It is a Class A misdemeanor to permit, assist or encourage the unauthorized release of any information contained in such reports or records. Nothing contained in this Section prevents the sharing of reports or records relating or pertaining to the death of a minor under the care of or receiving services from the Department of Children and Family Services and under the jurisdiction of the juvenile court with the juvenile court, the State's Attorney, and the minor's attorney.

(17) The Department of Human Services, as provided in Section 17 of the Disabled Persons Rehabilitation Act [20 ILCS 2405/17].

(18) Any other agency or investigative body, including the Department of Public Health and a local board of health, authorized by State law to conduct an investigation into the quality of care provided to children in hospitals and other State regulated care facilities. The access to and release of information from such records shall be subject to the approval of the Director of the Department or his designee.

(19) The person appointed, under Section 2-17 of the Juvenile Court Act of 1987 [705 ILCS 405/2-17], as the guardian ad litem of a minor who is the subject of a report or records under this Act.

(20) The Department of Human Services, as provided in Section 10 of the Early Intervention Services System Act [325 ILCS 20/10], and the operator of a facility providing early intervention services pursuant to that Act, for the purpose of determining whether a current or prospective employee who provides or may provide direct services under that Act is the perpetrator in an indicated report of child abuse or neglect filed under this Act. (b) Nothing contained in this Act prevents the sharing or disclo-

sure of information or records relating or pertaining to juveniles subject to the provisions of the Serious Habitual Offender Comprehensive Action Program when that information is used to assist in the early identification and treatment of habitual juvenile offenders.

(b) Nothing contained in this Act prevents the sharing or disclosure of information or records relating or pertaining to juveniles subject to the provisions of the Serious Habitual Offender Comprehensive Action Program when that information is used to assist in the early identification and treatment of habitual juvenile offenders.

(c) To the extent that persons or agencies are given access to information pursuant to this Section, those persons or agencies may give this information to and receive this information from each other in order to facilitate an investigation conducted by those persons or agencies.

(Source: P.A. 86-904; 86-1167; 86-1203; 86-1475; 87-649; 87-928, § 1; 87-1184, § 47; 88-45, § 2-49; 89-507, § 90C-25; 90-15, § 13; 91-357, § 183; 93-147, § 3.)

Note.

This section was Ill.Rev.Stat., Ch. 23, para. 2061.1.

Section 95 of P.A. 90-15 provided "Where this Act makes changes in a statute that is represented in this Act by text that is not yet or no longer in effect (for example, a Section represented by multiple versions), the use of that text does not accelerate or delay the taking effect of (i) the changes made by this Act or (ii) provisions derived from any other Public Act".

P.A. 91-357, § 996 contains a "no acceleration or delay" provision, and P.A. 91-357, § 997 contains a "no revival or extension" provision.

Cross References.

Concerning access to records by the guardian ad litem of an abused child, see 705 ILCS 405/2-17.

Illinois Administrative Code.

See 77 Illinois Administrative Code, § 2060.313, 89 Illinois Administrative Code, § 431.85.

Effect of Amendments.

The 1996 amendment by P.A. 89-507, effective July 1, 1997, in subsection (15) inserted "Human Services (as successor to the Department of" and inserted a closing parenthesis following "Alcoholism and Substance Abuse"; and in subsection (17) substituted "Human Services" for "Rehabilitation Services".

The 1997 amendment by P.A. 90-15, effective June 13, 1997, in subsection (16) added the fourth sentence; and added subsection (21).

The 1999 amendment by P.A. 91-357, effective July 29, 1999, inserted the subsection (a) designation; inserted "of 1987" following "Juvenile Court Act" in subsection (a)(19); and substituted the subsection designations (b) and (c) for the former subdivision designations (20) and (21).

The 2003 amendment by P.A. 93-147, effective January 1, 2004, added subsection (a)(20).

CASE NOTES

Access to Records

A court may gain limited access to Department of Children and Family Services records, but only if they may be necessary for the determination of an issue before the court. People v. Bell, 152 Ill. App. 3d 1007, 106 Ill. Dec. 59, 505 N.E.2d 365 (3 Dist. 1987).

325 ILCS 5/11.1a Disclosure of information

Sec. 11.1a. *Disclosure of information.* (a) The Director or a person designated in writing by the Director for this purpose may disclose information regarding the abuse or neglect of a child as set forth in this Section, the investigation thereof, and any services related thereto, if he or she determines that such disclosure is not contrary to the best interests of the child, the child's siblings, or other children in the household, and one of the following factors are present:

(1) The subject of the report has been criminally charged with committing a crime related to the child abuse or neglect report; or

(2) A law enforcement agency or official, a State's Attorney, or a judge of the State court system has publicly disclosed in a report as part of his or her official duty, information regarding the investigation of a report or the provision of services by the Department; or

(3) An adult subject of the report has knowingly and voluntarily made a public disclosure concerning a Child Abuse and Neglect Tracking System report; or

(4) The child named in the report has been critically injured or died.

(b) Information may be disclosed pursuant to this Section as follows:

(1) The name of the alleged abused or neglected child.

(2) The current status of the investigation, including whether a determination of credible evidence has been made.

(3) Identification of child protective or other services provided or actions taken regarding the child named in the report and his or her family as a result of this report.

(4) Whether there have been past reports of child abuse or neglect involving this child or family, or both. Any such reports shall be clearly identified as being "Indicated", "Unfounded", or "Pending".

(5) Whether the Department has a current or past open service case with the family, and a history of what types of services have been, or are being, provided.

(6) Any extraordinary or pertinent information concerning the circumstances of the report, if the Director determines such disclosure is consistent with the public interest.

(c) Any disclosure of information pursuant to this Section shall not identify the name of or provide identifying information regarding the source of the report.

(d) In determining pursuant to subsection (a) of this Section, whether disclosure will be contrary to the best interests of the child, the child's siblings, or other children in the household, the Director shall consider the interest in privacy of the child and the child's family and the effects which disclosure may have on efforts to reunite and provide services to the family.

(e) Except as it applies directly to the cause of the abuse or neglect of the child, nothing in this Section shall be deemed to authorize the release or disclosure of the substance or content of any psychological, psychiatric, therapeutic, clinical, or medical reports, evaluations, or like materials pertaining to the child or the child's family. Prior to the release or disclosure of any psychological, psychiatric, or therapeutic reports pursuant to this subsection, the Deputy Director of Clinical Services shall review such materials and make recommendations regarding its release. Any disclosure of information pursuant to this Section shall not identify the health care provider, health care facility or other maker of the report or source of any psychological, psychiatric, therapeutic, clinical, or medical reports, evaluations, or like materials.

(f) Regarding child abuse or neglect reports which occur at a facility licensed by the Department of Children and Family Services, only the following information may be disclosed or released:

(1) The name of the facility.

(2) The nature of the allegations of abuse or neglect.

(3) The number and ages of child victims involved, and their relationship to the perpetrator.

(4) Actions the Department has taken to ensure the safety of the children during and subsequent to the investigation.

(5) The final finding status of the investigation.

(Source: P.A. 90-75, § 5.)

Effective Date.

This section became effective January 1, 1998 pursuant to Ill. Const. (1970), Art. IV, § 10 and 5 ILCS 75/1.

325 ILCS 5/11.2 Disclosure to mandated reporting source

Sec. 11.2. *Disclosure to mandated reporting source.* A mandated reporting source as provided in Section 4 of this Act [325 ILCS 5/4] may receive appropriate information about the findings and actions taken by the Child Protective Service Unit in response to its report. The information shall include the actions taken by the Child Protective Service Unit to ensure a child's safety.

(Source: P.A. 81-1077; 92-319, § 5.)

Note.

This section was Ill.Rev.Stat., Ch. 23, para. 2061.2.

Effect of Amendments.

The 2001 amendment by P.A. 92-319, effective January 1, 2002, added the section heading, deleted "Upon request" from the beginning of the first sentence, made stylistic changes, and added the second sentence.

325 ILCS 5/11.2a Disclosure to extended family member

Sec. 11.2a. *Disclosure to extended family member.* Upon request, an extended family member interviewed for relevant information in the course of an investigation by the Child Protective Service Unit may receive appropriate information about the findings and actions taken by the Child Protective Service Unit to ensure the safety of the child or children who were the subjects of the investigation.

(Source: P.A. 92-319, § 5.)

Effective Date.

This section is effective January 1, 2002, pursuant to Ill. Const. (1970), Art. IV, § 10 and 5 ILCS 75/1.

325 ILCS 5/11.3 [Information not to be publicized; exceptions]

Sec. 11.3. A person given access to the names or other information identifying the subjects of the report, except the subject of the report, shall not make public such identifying information unless he is a State's attorney or other law enforcement official and the purpose is to initiate court action. Violation of this Section is a Class A misdemeanor.

(Source: P.A. 81-1077.)

Note.

This section was Ill.Rev.Stat., Ch. 23, para. 2061.3.

325 ILCS 5/11.4 [Court and criminal justice system records]

Sec. 11.4. Nothing in this Act affects existing policies or procedures concerning the status of court and criminal justice system records.

(Source: P.A. 81-1077.)

Note.

This section was Ill.Rev.Stat., Ch. 23, para. 2061.4.

325 ILCS 5/11.5 [Continuing education and training]

Sec. 11.5. Within the appropriation available, the Department shall conduct a continuing education and training program for State and local staff, persons and officials required to report, the general public, and other persons engaged in or intending to engage in the prevention, identification, and treatment of child abuse and neglect. The program shall be designed to encourage the fullest degree of reporting of known and suspected child abuse and neglect, and to improve communication, cooperation, and coordination among all agencies in the identification, prevention, and treatment of child abuse and neglect. The program shall inform the general public and professionals of the nature and extent of child abuse and neglect and their responsibilities, obligations, powers and immunity from liability under this Act. It may include information on the diagnosis of child abuse and neglect and the roles and procedures of the Child Protective Service Unit, the Department and central register, the courts and of the protective, treatment, and ameliorative services available to children and their families. Such information may also include special needs of mothers at risk of delivering a child whose life or development may be threatened by a handicapping condition, to ensure informed consent to treatment of the condition and understanding of the unique child care responsibilities required for such a child. The program may also encourage parents and other persons having responsibility for the welfare of children to seek assistance on their own in meeting their child care responsibilities and encourage the voluntary acceptance of available services when they are needed. It may also include publicity and dissemination of information on the existence and number of the 24 hour, State-wide, toll-free telephone service to assist persons seeking assistance and to receive reports of known and suspected abuse and neglect.

Within the appropriation available, the Department also shall conduct a continuing education and training program for State and local staff involved in investigating reports of child abuse or neglect made under this Act. The program shall be designed to train such staff in the necessary and appropriate procedures to be followed in investigating cases which it appears may result in civil or criminal charges being filed against a person. Program subjects shall include but not be limited to the gathering of evidence with a view toward presenting such evidence in court and the involvement of State or local law enforcement agencies in the investigation. The program shall be conducted in cooperation with State or local law enforcement agencies, State's Attorneys and other components of the criminal justice system as the Department deems appropriate.

(Source: P.A. 85-984.)

Note.
This section was Ill.Rev.Stat., Ch. 23, para. 2061.5.

325 ILCS 5/11.6 [Review of administrative decisions]

Sec. 11.6. All final administrative decisions of the Department under this Act are subject to judicial review under the Administrative Review Law [735 ILCS 5/3-101 et seq.], as now or hereafter amended, and the rules adopted pursuant thereto. The term "administrative decision" is defined as in Section 3-101 of the Code of Civil Procedure [735 ILCS 5/3-101].

(Source: P.A. 82-783.)

Note.
This section was Ill.Rev.Stat., Ch. 23, para. 2061.6.

325 ILCS 5/11.7 [State-wide Citizen's Committee on Child Abuse and Neglect]

Sec. 11.7. (a) The Director shall appoint the chairperson and members of a "State-wide Citizen's Committee on Child Abuse and Neglect" to consult with and advise the Director. The Committee shall be composed of individuals of distinction in human services, neonatal medical care, needs and rights of the disabled, law and community life, broadly representative of social and economic communities across the State, who shall be appointed to 3 year staggered terms. The chairperson and members of the Committee shall serve without compensation, although their travel and per diem expenses shall be reimbursed in accordance with standard State procedures. Under procedures adopted by the Committee, it may meet at any time, confer with any individuals, groups, and agencies; and may issue reports or recommendations on any aspect of child abuse or neglect it deems appropriate.

(b) The Committee shall advise the Director on setting priorities for the administration of child abuse prevention, shelters and service programs, as specified in Section 4a of "An Act creating the Department of Children and Family Services, codifying its powers and duties, and repealing certain Acts and Sections herein named", approved June 4, 1963, as amended [20 ILCS 505/4a].

(c) The Committee shall advise the Director on policies and procedures with respect to the medical neglect of newborns and infants.

(Source: P.A. 84-611.)

Note.
This section was Ill.Rev.Stat., Ch. 23, para. 2061.7.

Illinois Administrative Code.
See 89 Illinois Administrative Code, § 428.60.

Birth Control Services to Minors Act

325 ILCS 10/0.01 Short title

Sec. 0.01. *Short title.* This Act may be cited as the Birth Control Services to Minors Act.

(Source: P.A. 86-1324.)

Derivation.
Title: An Act to authorize medical doctors to supervise and control the rendering of birth control services to certain minors.
Cite: 325 ILCS 10/0.01 et seq.
Source: P.A. 76-1550.
Date: Approved September 22, 1969.

Note.
This section was Ill.Rev.Stat., Ch. 111 ½, para. 4650.

RESEARCH REFERENCES

Propriety of prophylactic availability programs. 52 ALR5th 477.

325 ILCS 10/1 [Applicability]

Sec. 1. Birth control services and information may be rendered by doctors licensed in Illinois to practice medicine in all of its branches to any minor:

1. who is married; or
2. who is a parent; or
3. who is pregnant; or

4. who has the consent of his parent or legal guardian; or

5. as to whom the failure to provide such services would create a serious health hazard; or

6. who is referred for such services by a physician, clergyman or a planned parenthood agency.

(Source: P.A. 76-1550.)

Note.

This section was Ill.Rev.Stat., Ch. 111 ½, para. 4651.

Illinois Administrative Code.

See 77 Illinois Administrative Code, § 2200.100.

CHILD SEXUAL ABUSE PREVENTION ACT

325 ILCS 15/0.01 Short title

Sec. 0.01. *Short title.* This Act may be cited as the Child Sexual Abuse Prevention Act.

(Source: P.A. 86-1324.)

Derivation.

Title: An Act in relation to programs and services for the prevention and treatment of child sexual abuse and exploitation.

Cite: 325 ILCS 15/0.01 et seq.

Source: P.A. 84-564.

Date: Approved September 19, 1985.

Note.

This section was Ill.Rev.Stat., Ch. 23, para. 2080.

325 ILCS 15/1 [Findings]

Sec. 1. The General Assembly finds that there is a need to develop programs to provide the kinds of innovative strategies and services which will prevent, ameliorate, reduce, and eliminate the trauma of child sexual abuse and exploitation.

The General Assembly also finds that for the purposes of developing and providing such programs and services, and for training and providing information to city, county and state personnel throughout the state, and otherwise educating the general public, about child sexual abuse and exploitation, prevention and treatment services and centers should be established.

(Source: P.A. 84-564.)

Note.

This section was Ill.Rev.Stat., Ch. 23, para. 2081.

RESEARCH REFERENCES

Sexual child abuser's civil liability to child's parent. 54 ALR4th 93.

325 ILCS 15/2 [Department of Children and Family Services; duties]

Sec. 2. The Department of Children and Family Services shall develop programs and services for the prevention of child sexual abuse and exploitation and shall provide for the treatment and counseling of sexually abused children and their families, where such sexual abuse or exploitation was inflicted by the child's immediate care giver, or any person responsible for the child's welfare, whenever possible, through community based child abuse grants or other appropriate means.

(Source: P.A. 84-564.)

Note.

This section was Ill.Rev.Stat., Ch. 23, para. 2082.

325 ILCS 15/3 [Program functions and goals]

Sec. 3. The functions and goals of the programs to be developed and provided by the Department of Children and Family Services shall include:

(a) Provision of counseling, treatment, rehabilitation and assistance to sexually abused and exploited children and their families, particularly to victims of predatory criminal sexual assault of a child, aggravated criminal sexual assault, criminal sexual assault, aggravated criminal sexual abuse and criminal sexual abuse and child pornography, and provision of training and education and professional counseling to other persons responsible for the child's welfare, personnel of the Department responsible for the licensure of facilities under the Child Care Act of 1969 [225 ILCS 10/1 et seq.], and persons required to file reports and conduct investigations of such reports under the Abused and Neglected Child Reporting Act [325 ILCS 5/1 et seq.];

(b) Hastening the process of reconstituting the family and the marriage, where such would be in the interest of the child;

(c) Marshaling and coordinating the services of all agencies responsible for the detection of a sexually abused and exploited child and for serving such a child, the child's family, or others responsible for the child's welfare, as well as for the development of other resources necessary to ensure a comprehensive program for the prevention of such abuse and exploitation, supportive case management;

(d) Responding to individual physical, emotional, and social needs of clients so that supportive services are individually tailored and applied as long as necessary;

(e) Informing the public at large and professional agencies about the problem of child sexual abuse and exploitation, methods of detecting and responding to such incidents, including those established under the Abused and Neglected Child Reporting Act [325 ILCS 5/1 et seq.], the availability of State service and other resources for responding to victims of such abuse and exploitation, and about the existence and supportive approach of treatment center programs; and

(f) Development of informational and training materials and seminars to assure the availability of such programs and services throughout the State, emphasizing the need for cooperation and coordina-

tion with all appropriate elements of the criminal justice system and law enforcement system.
(Source: P.A. 84-564; 89-428, § 240; 89-462, § 240.)

Note.
This section was Ill.Rev.Stat., Ch. 23, para. 2083.

Effect of Amendments.
The 1995 amendment by P.A. 89-428, effective December 13, 1995 and the 1996 amendment by P.A. 89-462, effective May 29, 1996, made identical amendments: they each, in subsection (a), inserted "predatory criminal sexual assault of a child".

CASE NOTES

Constitutionality
Public Act 89-428 was enacted in violation of the single subject rule of the state constitution and is therefore invalid in its entirety. Johnson v. Edgar, 176 Ill. 2d 499, 224 Ill. Dec. 1, 680 N.E.2d 1372 (1997).

325 ILCS 15/4 [Child sexual abuse crisis intervention demonstration centers]

Sec. 4. The Department of Children and Family Services shall support through a grant program a child sexual abuse crisis intervention demonstration center in Cook County and in other parts of the State as funding permits. The functions and goals of such crisis intervention centers shall be:

(a) To respond within 24 hours or as soon thereafter as possible to a report of child sexual abuse or exploitation by professional contact with the child and his family, and with those persons in the courts and police department involved in the case.

(b) The agents of such crisis intervention centers shall:

(1) refer the child, and his family if appropriate, to counseling services, including those provided by the treatment centers;

(2) accompany the victim through all stages of police investigation, case development and trial where necessary;

(3) provide advice to involved police, assistant district attorneys, and judges in the proper handling of a child subjected to sexual abuse and exploitation whenever possible. This advice will be made with consideration to the following priorities:

(i) the welfare of the child; and

(ii) improved chances for a successful prosecution;

(4) make every effort to develop an approach which meets the needs of developing a sound case by assisting the child to understand and cope with his role in the prosecution process.

(c) The crisis intervention demonstration centers shall develop and implement written procedures for case planning and case monitoring in relation to the processes of treatment and of investigation and prosecution.

(d) Crisis intervention agents should demonstrate evidence of professional knowledge of child development and a record of positive interaction with the police and courts.

(e) The centers shall develop training materials for city and county and State personnel through the State to enable emulation and adaptation of the program by other communities and to develop awareness of the problems faced by a child sexual abuse victim as he confronts the criminal justice system.

(f) The centers shall report to the director improvements in the criminal justice system and the interrelation of the criminal justice system and child support systems that would serve to meet the goals of this Act.

(g) Reports of child sexual abuse referred for investigation to a local law enforcement agency in Cook County by the State Central Registry of the Department of Children and Family Services must also be referred to the crisis intervention center. Reports of child sexual abuse made directly to a local law enforcement agency in Cook County may be referred by that agency to the crisis intervention center. All centers shall make local law enforcement agencies aware of their purposes and encourage their utilization.
(Source: P.A. 84-564.)

Note.
This section was Ill.Rev.Stat., Ch. 23, para. 2084.

325 ILCS 15/5 [Confidentiality of records]

Sec. 5. All records concerning reports of child sexual abuse or exploitation made to child sexual abuse and exploitation treatment center or to child sexual abuse crisis intervention demonstration centers and all records generated as a result of such reports, shall be confidential and shall not be disclosed except as specifically authorized by this Act or other applicable law. It is a Class A misdemeanor to permit, assist, or encourage the unauthorized release of any information contained in such reports or records.

Nothing contained in this Act prevents the sharing or disclosure of information or records relating or pertaining to juveniles subject to the provisions of the Serious Habitual Offender Comprehensive Action Program when that information is used to assist in the early identification and treatment of habitual juvenile offenders.
(Source: P.A. 84-564; 87-928, § 2.)

Note.
This section was Ill.Rev.Stat., Ch. 23, para. 2085.

325 ILCS 15/6 [Funding of centers]

Sec. 6. The centers may seek, receive, and make use of any funds which may be made available from federal, voluntary, philanthropic, or other sources in order to augment any state funds appropriated for the purposes of this Act.
(Source: P.A. 82-712.)

Note.
This section was Ill.Rev.Stat., Ch. 23, para. 2086.

325 ILCS 15/7 [Annual reports]

Sec. 7. The Director of the Department of Children and Family Services shall submit annual reports to the General Assembly concerning his findings regarding the degree of achievement of the goals of this Act.
(Source: P.A. 84-564.)

Note.
This section was Ill.Rev.Stat., Ch. 23, para. 2087.

CHILDREN'S PRIVACY PROTECTION AND PARENTAL EMPOWERMENT ACT

325 ILCS 17/1 Short title

Sec. 1. *Short title.* This Act may be cited as the Children's Privacy Protection and Parental Empowerment Act.
(Source: P.A. 93-462, § 1.)

Effective Date.
This Act is effective January 1, 2004, pursuant to Ill. Const. (1970) Art. IV, § 10 and 5 ILCS 75/1.

325 ILCS 17/5 Definitions

Sec. 5. *Definitions.* As used in this Act:

"Child" means a person under the age of 16. "Child" does not include a minor emancipated by operation of law.

"Parent" means a parent, step-parent, or legal guardian.

"Personal information" means any of the following:

(1) A person's name.

(2) A person's address.

(3) A person's telephone number.

(4) A person's driver's license number or State of Illinois identification card as assigned by the Illinois Secretary of State or by a similar agency of another state.

(5) A person's social security number.

(6) Any other information that can be used to locate or contact a specific individual.

"Personal information" does not include any of the following:

(1) Public records as defined by Section 2 of the Freedom of Information Act [5 ILCS 140/2].

(2) Court records.

(3) Information found in publicly available sources, including newspapers, magazines, and telephone directories.

(4) Any other information that is not known to concern a child.
(Source: P.A. 93-462, § 5.)

325 ILCS 17/10 Prohibited act

Sec. 10. *Prohibited act.* The sale or purchase of personal information concerning an individual known to be a child without parental consent is prohibited.
(Source: P.A. 93-462, § 10.)

325 ILCS 17/15 Information brokers

Sec. 15. *Information brokers.* (a) For the purpose of this Act, the consent of a parent to the sale or purchase of information concerning a child is presumed unless the parent withdraws consent under this Section.

A person who brokers or facilitates the sale of personal information concerning children must, upon written request from a parent that specifically identifies the child, provide to the parent within 20 days of the written request procedures that the parent must follow in order to withdraw consent to use personal information relating to that child. The person who brokers or facilitates the sale of personal information must discontinue disclosing a child's personal information within 20 days after the parent has completed the procedures to withdraw consent to use personal information relating to that child.

(b) This Section does not apply to any of the following:

(1) Any federal, state, or local government agency or any law enforcement agency.

(2) The National Center for Missing and Exploited Children.

(3) Any educational institution, consortium, organization, or professional association, including but not limited to, public community colleges, public universities, post-secondary educational institutions as defined in the Private College Act, and private business and vocational schools as defined in the Private Business and Vocational Schools Act.

(4) Any not-for-profit entity that is exempt from the payment of federal taxes under Section 501(c)(3) of the Internal Revenue Code of 1986.
(Source: P.A. 93-462, § 15.)

325 ILCS 17/20 Application of the Consumer Fraud and Deceptive Business Practices Act

Sec. 20. *Application of the Consumer Fraud and Deceptive Business Practices Act.* A violation of any provision of this Act is a violation of the Consumer Fraud and Deceptive Business Practices Act [815 ILCS 505/1 et seq.]. This Act, however, shall not be

considered or construed to provide any private right of action.
(Source: P.A. 93-462, § 20.)

EARLY INTERVENTION SERVICES SYSTEM ACT

325 ILCS 20/1 Short Title

Sec. 1. *Short Title.* This Act may be cited as the Early Intervention Services System Act.
(Source: P.A. 87-680.)

Derivation.
Title: An Act in relation to services for certain children.
Cite: 325 ILCS 20/1 et seq.
Source: P.A. 87-680.
Date: Approved September 23, 1991.

Note.
This section was Ill.Rev.Stat., Ch. 23, para. 4151.

LEGAL PERIODICALS

For article, "Survey of Illinois Law: Education Law," see 21 S. Ill. U.L.J. 815 (1997).

325 ILCS 20/2 Legislative Findings and Policy

Sec. 2. *Legislative Findings and Policy.* (a) The General Assembly finds that there is an urgent and substantial need to:

(1) enhance the development of all eligible infants and toddlers in the State of Illinois in order to minimize developmental delay and maximize individual potential for adult independence;

(2) enhance the capacity of families to meet the special needs of eligible infants and toddlers including the purchase of services when necessary;

(3) reduce educational costs by minimizing the need for special education and related services when eligible infants and toddlers reach school age;

(4) enhance the independence, productivity and integration with age-appropriate peers of eligible children and their families;

(5) reduce social services costs and minimize the need for institutionalization; and

(6) prevent secondary impairments and disabilities by improving the health of infants and toddlers, thereby reducing health costs for the families and the State.

(b) The General Assembly therefore intends that the policy of this State shall be to:

(1) affirm the importance of the family in all areas of the child's development and reinforce the role of the family as a participant in the decision making processes regarding their child;

(2) provide assistance and support to eligible infants and toddlers and their families to address the individual concerns and decisions of each family;

(3) develop and implement, on a statewide basis, locally based comprehensive, coordinated, interdisciplinary, interagency early intervention services for all eligible infants and toddlers;

(4) enhance the local communities' capacity to provide an array of quality early intervention services;

(5) identify and coordinate all available resources for early intervention within the State including those from federal, State, local and private sources;

(6) provide financial and technical assistance to local communities for the purposes of coordinating early intervention services in local communities and enhancing the communities' capacity to provide individualized early intervention services to all eligible infants and toddlers in their homes or in community environments; and

(7) affirm that eligible infants and toddlers have a right to receive early intervention services to the maximum extent appropriate, in natural environments in which infants and toddlers without disabilities would participate.

(c) The General Assembly further finds that early intervention services are cost-effective and effectively serve the developmental needs of eligible infants and toddlers and their families. Therefore, the purpose of this Act is to provide a comprehensive, coordinated, interagency, interdisciplinary early intervention services system for eligible infants and toddlers and their families by enhancing the capacity to provide quality early intervention services, expanding and improving existing services, and facilitating coordination of payments for early intervention services from various public and private sources.
(Source: P.A. 87-680; 91-538, § 5.)

Note.
This section was Ill.Rev.Stat., Ch. 23, para. 4152.

Effect of Amendments.
The 1999 amendment by P.A. 91-538, effective August 13, 1999, substituted "to the maximum extent appropriate, in natural environments in which infants and toddlers without disabilities would participate" for "in their own homes or, if provision of services at home is not possible or is rejected by the parents, in natural settings in local community environments" in subsection (b)(7).

325 ILCS 20/3 Definitions

Sec. 3. *Definitions.* As used in this Act:

(a) "Eligible infants and toddlers" means infants and toddlers under 36 months of age with any of the following conditions:

(1) Developmental delays.

(2) A physical or mental condition which typically results in developmental delay.

(3) Being at risk of having substantial developmental delays based on informed clinical judgment.

(4) Either (A) having entered the program under any of the circumstances listed in paragraphs (1) through (3) of this subsection but no longer meeting the current eligibility criteria under those paragraphs, and continuing to have any measurable delay, or (B) not having attained a level of develop-

ment in each area, including (i) cognitive, (ii) physical (including vision and hearing), (iii) language, speech, and communication, (iv) psycho-social, or (v) self-help skills, that is at least at the mean of the child's age equivalent peers; and, in addition to either item (A) or item (B), (C) having been determined by the multidisciplinary individualized family service plan team to require the continuation of early intervention services in order to support continuing developmental progress, pursuant to the child's needs and provided in an appropriate developmental manner. The type, frequency, and intensity of services shall differ from the initial individualized family services plan because of the child's developmental progress, and may consist of only service coordination, evaluation, and assessments.

(b) "Developmental delay" means a delay in one or more of the following areas of childhood development as measured by appropriate diagnostic instruments and standard procedures: cognitive; physical, including vision and hearing; language, speech and communication; psycho-social; or self-help skills. The term means a delay of 30% or more below the mean in function in one or more of those areas.

(c) "Physical or mental condition which typically results in developmental delay" means:

(1) a diagnosed medical disorder bearing a relatively well known expectancy for developmental outcomes within varying ranges of developmental disabilities; or

(2) a history of prenatal, perinatal, neonatal or early developmental events suggestive of biological insults to the developing central nervous system and which either singly or collectively increase the probability of developing a disability or delay based on a medical history.

(d) "Informed clinical judgment" means both clinical observations and parental participation to determine eligibility by a consensus of a multidisciplinary team of 2 or more members based on their professional experience and expertise.

(e) "Early intervention services" means services which:

(1) are designed to meet the developmental needs of each child eligible under this Act and the needs of his or her family;

(2) are selected in collaboration with the child's family;

(3) are provided under public supervision;

(4) are provided at no cost except where a schedule of sliding scale fees or other system of payments by families has been adopted in accordance with State and federal law;

(5) are designed to meet an infant's or toddler's developmental needs in any of the following areas:

(A) physical development, including vision and hearing,

(B) cognitive development,

(C) communication development,

(D) social or emotional development, or

(E) adaptive development;

(6) meet the standards of the State, including the requirements of this Act;

(7) include one or more of the following:

(A) family training,

(B) social work services, including counseling, and home visits,

(C) special instruction,

(D) speech, language pathology and audiology,

(E) occupational therapy,

(F) physical therapy,

(G) psychological services,

(H) service coordination services,

(I) medical services only for diagnostic or evaluation purposes,

(J) early identification, screening, and assessment services,

(K) health services specified by the lead agency as necessary to enable the infant or toddler to benefit from the other early intervention services,

(L) vision services,

(M) transportation, and

(N) assistive technology devices and services;

(8) are provided by qualified personnel, including but not limited to:

(A) child development specialists or special educators,

(B) speech and language pathologists and audiologists,

(C) occupational therapists,

(D) physical therapists,

(E) social workers,

(F) nurses,

(G) nutritionists,

(H) optometrists,

(I) psychologists, and

(J) physicians;

(9) are provided in conformity with an Individualized Family Service Plan;

(10) are provided throughout the year; and

(11) are provided in natural environments, including the home and community settings in which infants and toddlers without disabilities would participate to the extent determined by the multidisciplinary Individualized Family Service Plan.

(f) "Individualized Family Service Plan" or "Plan" means a written plan for providing early intervention services to a child eligible under this Act and the child's family, as set forth in Section 11 [325 ILCS 20/11].

(g) "Local interagency agreement" means an agreement entered into by local community and State and regional agencies receiving early intervention funds directly from the State and made in accordance with State interagency agreements providing for the delivery of early intervention services within a local community area.

(h) "Council" means the Illinois Interagency Council on Early Intervention established under Section 4 [325 ILCS 20/4].

(i) "Lead agency" means the State agency responsible for administering this Act and receiving and disbursing public funds received in accordance with State and federal law and rules.

(i-5) "Central billing office" means the central billing office created by the lead agency under Section 13 [325 ILCS 20/13].

(j) "Child find" means a service which identifies eligible infants and toddlers.

(k) "Regional intake entity" means the lead agency's designated entity responsible for implementation of the Early Intervention Services System within its designated geographic area.

(l) "Early intervention provider" means an individual who is qualified, as defined by the lead agency, to provide one or more types of early intervention services, and who has enrolled as a provider in the early intervention program.

(m) "Fully credentialed early intervention provider" means an individual who has met the standards in the State applicable to the relevant profession, and has met such other qualifications as the lead agency has determined are suitable for personnel providing early intervention services, including pediatric experience, education, and continuing education. The lead agency shall establish these qualifications by rule filed no later than 180 days after the effective date of this amendatory Act of the 92nd General Assembly [P.A. 92-307].

(Source: P.A. 87-680; 87-847; 90-158, § 5; 91-538, § 5; 92-307, § 5; 93-124, § 5.)

Note.

This section was Ill.Rev.Stat., Ch. 23, para. 4153.

Illinois Administrative Code.

See 59 Illinois Administrative Code, §§ 121.30, 122.20.

Effect of Amendments.

The 1997 amendment by P.A. 90-158, effective January 1, 1998, in subsection (i) deleted "as designated by the Governor" preceding "responsible for".

The 1999 amendment by P.A. 91-538, effective August 13, 1999, rewrote subsection (a)(1), which formerly read "Disabilities due to developmental delay"; in subsections (a)(2) and (c), substituted "typically results" for "has a high probability of resulting"; in subsection (a)(3), substituted "based on informed clinical judgment" for "due to a combination of serious factors"; rewrote subsection (d) to the extent that a detailed comparison would be impracticable; in subsection (e)(5)(A), added "including vision and hearing"; and in subsection (e)(11), inserted "including the home and community settings", and substituted "determined by the multidisciplinary Individualized Family Service Plan" for "desired by families".

The 2001 amendment by P.A. 92-307, effective August 9, 2001, added subsections (a)(4), (i-5), (k), (l), and (m).

The 2003 amendment by P.A. 93-124, effective July 10, 2003, deleted "as defined by the Department by rule" at the end of subsection (a)(1) and added the last sentence in subsection (b).

325 ILCS 20/4 Illinois Interagency Council on Early Intervention

Sec. 4. *Illinois Interagency Council on Early Intervention.* (a) There is established the Illinois Interagency Council on Early Intervention. The Council shall be composed of at least 15 but not more than 25 members. The members of the Council and the designated chairperson of the Council shall be appointed by the Governor. The Council member representing the lead agency may not serve as chairperson of the Council. The Council shall be composed of the following members:

(1) The Secretary of Human Services (or his or her designee) and 2 additional representatives of the Department of Human Services designated by the Secretary, plus the Directors (or their designees) of the following State agencies involved in the provision of or payment for early intervention services to eligible infants and toddlers and their families:

(A) Illinois State Board of Education;

(B) (Blank);

(C) (Blank);

(D) Illinois Department of Children and Family Services;

(E) University of Illinois Division of Specialized Care for Children;

(F) Illinois Department of Public Aid;

(G) Illinois Department of Public Health;

(H) (Blank);

(I) Illinois Planning Council on Developmental Disabilities; and

(J) Illinois Department of Insurance.

(2) Other members as follows:

(A) At least 20% of the members of the Council shall be parents, including minority parents, of infants or toddlers with disabilities or children with disabilities aged 12 or younger, with knowledge of, or experience with, programs for infants and toddlers with disabilities. At least one such member shall be a parent of an infant or toddler with a disability or a child with a disability aged 6 or younger;

(B) At least 20% of the members of the Council shall be public or private providers of early intervention services;

(C) One member shall be a representative of the General Assembly; and

(D) One member shall be involved in the preparation of professional personnel to serve infants and toddlers similar to those eligible for services under this Act.

The Council shall meet at least quarterly and in such places as it deems necessary. Terms of the initial members appointed under paragraph (2) shall be determined by lot at the first Council meeting as follows: of the persons appointed under subparagraphs (A) and (B), one-third shall serve one year terms, one-third shall serve 2 year terms, and one-third shall serve 3 year terms; and of the persons appointed under subparagraphs (C) and (D), one shall serve a 2 year term and one shall serve a 3 year term. Thereafter, successors appointed under paragraph (2) shall serve 3 year terms. Once appointed, members shall continue to serve until their successors are appointed. No member shall be appointed to serve more than 2 consecutive terms.

Council members shall serve without compensation but shall be reimbursed for reasonable costs incurred in the performance of their duties, including costs related to child care, and parents may be paid a stipend in accordance with applicable requirements.

The Council shall prepare and approve a budget using funds appropriated for the purpose to hire staff, and obtain the services of such professional, technical, and clerical personnel as may be necessary to carry out its functions under this Act. This funding support and staff shall be directed by the lead agency.

(b) The Council shall:

(1) advise and assist the lead agency in the performance of its responsibilities including but not limited to the identification of sources of fiscal and other support services for early intervention programs, and the promotion of interagency agreements which assign financial responsibility to the appropriate agencies;

(2) advise and assist the lead agency in the preparation of applications and amendments to applications;

(3) review and advise on relevant regulations and standards proposed by the related State agencies;

(4) advise and assist the lead agency in the development, implementation and evaluation of the comprehensive early intervention services system; and

(5) prepare and submit an annual report to the Governor and to the General Assembly on the status of early intervention programs for eligible infants and toddlers and their families in Illinois. The annual report shall include (i) the estimated number of eligible infants and toddlers in this State, (ii) the number of eligible infants and toddlers who have received services under this Act and the cost of providing those services, (iii) the estimated cost of providing services under this Act to all eligible infants and toddlers in this State, and (iv) data and other information as is requested to be included by the Legislative Advisory Committee established under Section 13.50 of this Act [325 ILCS 20/13.50]. The report shall be posted by the lead agency on the early intervention website as required under paragraph (f) of Section 5 [325 ILCS 20/5] of this Act.

No member of the Council shall cast a vote on or participate substantially in any matter which would provide a direct financial benefit to that member or otherwise give the appearance of a conflict of interest under State law. All provisions and reporting requirements of the Illinois Governmental Ethics Act [5 ILCS 420/1-101 et seq.] shall apply to Council members.

(Source: P.A. 87-680; 87-847; 89-294, § 5; 89-507, § 90D-65; 89-626, § 3-32; 91-357, § 184; 92-307, § 5.)

Note.

This section was Ill.Rev.Stat., Ch. 23, para. 4154.

P.A. 91-357, § 996 contains a "no acceleration or delay" provision, and P.A. 91-357, § 997 contains a "no revival or extension" provision.

Effect of Amendments.

The 1995 amendment by P.A. 89-294, effective January 1, 1996, in subdivision (b)(5) added the second sentence.

The 1996 amendment by P.A. 89-507, effective July 1, 1997, in subdivision (a)(1), in the introductory language, inserted "Secretary of Human Services (or his or her designee) and 2 additional representatives of the Department of Human Services designated by the Secretary plus the"; deleted subdivision (a)(1)(B) which read "Illinois Department of Rehabilitation Services"; deleted subdivision (a)(1)(C) which read "Illinois Department of Mental Health and Developmental Disabilities"; in subdivision (a)(1)(E) substituted "Specialized Care for Children" for "Services for Crippled Children"; and deleted subdivision (a)(1)(H) which read "Illinois Department of Alcoholism and Substance Abuse".

The 1996 amendment by P.A. 89-626, effective August 9, 1996, substituted "Specialized Care for Children" for "Services for Crippled Children" in subdivision (a)(1)(E); added a comma following "and (D)" in the second paragraph of subsection (a) in the second sentence; and inserted "a" preceding "direct financial" in the second paragraph of subsection (b).

Although the amendments to this section by P.A. 89-507, § 90D-65 and P.A. 89-626, § 3-32 did not take into account the amendments made by the other, the amendments to this section have been combined into a single version by the publisher.

The 1999 amendment by P.A. 91-357, effective July 29, 1999, made a stylistic change.

The 2001 amendment by P.A. 92-307, effective August 9, 2001, in subsection (b)(5), added item (iv).

325 ILCS 20/5 Lead Agency

Sec. 5. *Lead Agency.* The Department of Human Services is designated the lead agency and shall provide leadership in establishing and implementing the coordinated, comprehensive, interagency and interdisciplinary system of early intervention services. The lead agency shall not have the sole responsibility for providing these services. Each participating State agency shall continue to coordinate those early intervention services relating to health, social service and education provided under this authority.

The lead agency is responsible for carrying out the following:

(a) The general administration, supervision, and monitoring of programs and activities receiving assistance under Section 673 of the Individuals with Disabilities Education Act (20 United States Code 1473).

(b) The identification and coordination of all available resources within the State from federal, State, local and private sources.

(c) The development of procedures to ensure that services are provided to eligible infants and toddlers and their families in a timely manner pending the resolution of any disputes among public agencies or service providers.

(d) The resolution of intra-agency and interagency regulatory and procedural disputes.

(e) The development and implementation of formal interagency agreements, and the entry into such agreements, between the lead agency and (i) the Department of Public Aid, (ii) the University of Illinois Division of Specialized Care for Children, and (iii) other relevant State agencies that:

(1) define the financial responsibility of each agency for paying for early intervention services (consistent with existing State and federal law and rules, including the requirement that early

intervention funds be used as the payor of last resort), a hierarchical order of payment as among the agencies for early intervention services that are covered under or may be paid by programs in other agencies, and procedures for direct billing, collecting reimbursements for payments made, and resolving service and payment disputes; and

(2) include all additional components necessary to ensure meaningful cooperation and coordination.

Interagency agreements under this paragraph (e) must be reviewed and revised to implement the purposes of this amendatory Act of the 92nd General Assembly [P.A. 92-307] no later than 60 days after the effective date of this amendatory Act of the 92nd General Assembly [P.A. 92-307].

(f) The maintenance of an early intervention website. Within 30 days after the effective date of this amendatory Act of the 92nd General Assembly [P.A. 92-307], the lead agency shall post and keep posted on this website the following: (i) the current annual report required under subdivision (b)(5) of Section 4 of this Act [325 ILCS 20/4], and the annual reports of the prior 3 years, (ii) the most recent Illinois application for funds prepared under Section 637 of the Individuals with Disabilities Education Act [Section 637 of 20 U.S.C. § 1400 et seq.] filed with the United States Department of Education, (iii) proposed modifications of the application prepared for public comment, (iv) notice of Council meetings, Council agendas, and minutes of its proceedings for at least the previous year, (v) proposed and final early intervention rules, (vi) requests for proposals, and (vii) all reports created for dissemination to the public that are related to the early intervention program, including reports prepared at the request of the Council, the General Assembly, and the Legislative Advisory Committee established under Section 13.50 of this Act [325 ILCS 20/13.50]. Each such document shall be posted on the website within 3 working days after the document's completion.

(Source: P.A. 87-680; 90-158, § 5; 92-307, § 5.)

Note.

This section was Ill.Rev.Stat., Ch. 23, para. 4155.

Effect of Amendments.

The 1997 amendment by P.A. 90-158, effective January 1, 1998, in the first paragraph, in the first sentence, added at the beginning "The Department of Human Services is designated" and substituted "and shall" for "designated by the Governor shall".

The 2001 amendment by P.A. 92-307, effective August 9, 2001, added "the following" at the end of the second paragraph; in paragraph (e) inserted "and the entry into such agreements", added items (i) and (ii), and inserted the item designation (iii); in paragraph (e)(1), inserted "including the requirement that early intervention funds be used as the payor of last resort), a hierarchical order of payment as among the agencies for early intervention services that are covered under or may be paid by programs in other agencies", inserted "direct billing, collecting reimbursements for payments made, and", and inserted "and payment"; added the final undesignated paragraph of paragraph (e); added paragraph (f); and made stylistic changes.

325 ILCS 20/6 Local Structure and Interagency Councils

Sec. 6. *Local Structure and Interagency Councils.* The lead agency, in conjunction with the Council and as defined by administrative rule, shall define local service areas and define the geographic boundaries of each so that all areas of the State are included in a local service area but no area of the State is included in more than one service area. In each local service area, the lead agency shall designate a regional entity responsible for the assessment of eligibility and services and a local interagency council responsible for coordination and design of child find and public awareness. The regional entity shall be responsible for staffing the local council, carrying out child find and public awareness activities, and providing advocacy for eligible families within the given geographic area. The regional entity is the prime contractor responsible to the lead agency for implementation of this Act.

The lead agency, in conjunction with the Council, shall create local interagency councils. Members of each local interagency council shall include, but not be limited to, the following: parents; representatives from coordination and advocacy service providers; local education agencies; other local public and private service providers; representatives from State agencies at the local level; and others deemed necessary by the local council.

Local interagency councils shall:

(a) assist in the development of collaborative agreements between local service providers, diagnostic and other agencies providing additional services to the child and family;

(b) assist in conducting local needs assessments and planning efforts;

(c) identify and resolve local access issues;

(d) conduct collaborative child find activities;

(e) coordinate public awareness initiatives;

(f) coordinate local planning and evaluation;

(g) assist in the recruitment of specialty personnel;

(h) develop plans for facilitating transition and integration of eligible children and families into the community;

(i) facilitate conflict resolution at the local level; and

(j) report annually to the Council.

(Source: P.A. 87-680; 87-847; 91-538, § 5.)

Note.

This section was Ill.Rev.Stat., Ch. 23, para. 4156.

Illinois Administrative Code.

See 59 Illinois Administrative Code, § 121.30.

Effect of Amendments.

The 1999 amendment by P.A. 91-538, effective August 13, 1999, in the introductory language, inserted "and as defined by administrative rule"; and deleted "at least 40 and no more than 60" preceding "local service areas" in the first sentence, substituted "regional entity" for "core provider" in the second sentence, substituted "The regional entity" for "A coordination/advocacy provider" in the third sentence, and "regional entity" for "coordinating entity" in the last sentence.

325 ILCS 20/7 Essential Components of the Statewide Service System

Sec. 7. *Essential Components of the Statewide Service System.* As required by federal laws and regulations, a statewide system of coordinated, comprehensive, interagency and interdisciplinary programs shall be established and maintained. The framework of the statewide system shall be based on the components set forth in this Section. This framework shall be used for planning, implementation, coordination and evaluation of the statewide system of locally based early intervention services.

The statewide system shall include, at a minimum:

(a) a definition of the term "developmentally delayed", in accordance with the definition in Section 3 [325 ILCS 20/3], that will be used in Illinois in carrying out programs under this Act;

(b) timetables for ensuring that appropriate early intervention services will be available to all eligible infants and toddlers in this State after the effective date of this Act;

(c) a timely, comprehensive and interdisciplinary evaluation of the functioning of each infant and toddler with suspected disabilities in this State and the concerns, priorities and resource needs of the families to appropriately assist in the development of the infant and toddler with disabilities;

(d) for each eligible infant and toddler, an Individualized Family Service Plan, including case management services;

(e) a comprehensive child find system, consistent with Part B of the Individuals with Disabilities Education Act (20 United States Code 1411 through 1420), which includes timelines and provides for participation by primary referral sources;

(f) a public awareness program focusing on early identification of eligible infants and toddlers;

(g) a central directory which includes early intervention services, resources, and experts available in this State and early intervention research and demonstration projects being conducted in this State;

(h) a comprehensive system of personnel development;

(i) a policy pertaining to the contracting or making of other arrangements with public and private service providers to provide early intervention services in this State, consistent with the provisions of this Act, including the contents of the application used and the conditions of the contract or other arrangements;

(j) a procedure for securing timely reimbursement of funds;

(k) procedural safeguards with respect to programs under this Act;

(l) policies and procedures relating to the establishment and maintenance of standards to ensure that personnel necessary to carry out this Act are appropriately and adequately prepared and trained;

(m) a system of evaluation of, and compliance with, program standards;

(n) a system for compiling data on the numbers of eligible infants and toddlers and their families in this State in need of appropriate early intervention services; the numbers served; the types of services provided; and other information required by the State or federal government; and

(o) a single line of responsibility in a lead agency designated by the Governor to carry out its responsibilities as required by this Act.

In addition to these required components, linkages may be established within a local community area among the prenatal initiatives affording services to high risk pregnant women. Additional linkages among at risk programs and local literacy programs may also be established.

Within 60 days of the effective date of this Act, a five-fiscal-year implementation plan shall be submitted to the Governor by the lead agency with the concurrence of the Interagency Council on Early Intervention. The plan shall list specific activities to be accomplished each year, with cost estimates for each activity. No later than the second Monday in July of each year thereafter, the lead agency shall, with the concurrence of the Interagency Council, submit to the Governor's Office a report on accomplishments of the previous year and a revised list of activities for the remainder of the five-fiscal-year plan, with cost estimates for each. The Governor shall certify that specific activities in the plan for the previous year have been substantially completed before authorizing relevant State or local agencies to implement activities listed in the revised plan that depend substantially upon completion of one or more of the earlier activities.

(Source: P.A. 87-680.)

Note.

This section was Ill.Rev.Stat., Ch. 23, para. 4157.

325 ILCS 20/8 Authority to Promulgate Rules and Regulations

Sec. 8. *Authority to Promulgate Rules and Regulations.* The lead agency shall develop rules and regulations under this Act within one year of the effective date of this Act. These rules shall reflect the intent of federal regulations adopted under Part H of the Individuals with Disabilities Education Act (20 United States Code 1471 through 1485).

(Source: P.A. 87-680.)

Note.

This section was Ill.Rev.Stat., Ch. 23, para. 4158.

325 ILCS 20/9 Role of Other State Entities

Sec. 9. *Role of Other State Entities.* The Departments of Public Health, Human Services, Children and Family Services and Public Aid; the University of Illinois Division of Specialized Care for Children; the State Board of Education; and any other State agency which directly or indirectly provides or administers early intervention services shall adopt compatible rules for the provision of services to eligible infants and toddlers and their families within one year of the effective date of this Act.

These agencies shall enter into and maintain formal interagency agreements to enable the State and local agencies serving eligible children and their families to establish working relationships that will increase the efficiency and effectiveness of their early intervention services. The agreement shall outline the administrative, program and financial responsibilities of the relevant State agencies and shall implement a coordinated service delivery system through local interagency agreements.

There shall be created in the Office of the Governor an Early Childhood Intervention Ombudsman to assist families and local parties in ensuring that all State agencies serving eligible families do so in a comprehensive and collaborative manner.

(Source: P.A. 87-680; 89-507, § 90D-65; 89-626, § 3-32.)

Note.

This section was Ill.Rev.Stat., Ch. 23, para. 4159.

Effect of Amendments.

The 1996 amendment by P.A. 89-507, effective July 1, 1997, in the first paragraph substituted "Human Services" for "Rehabilitation Services, Mental Health and Developmental Disabilities, Alcoholism and Substance Abuse" and substituted "Specialized Care for Children" for "Services for Crippled Children".

The 1996 amendment by P.A. 89-626, effective August 9, 1996, substituted "Specialized Care for Children" for "Services for Crippled Children" in the first paragraph.

Although the amendments to this section by P.A. 89-507, § 90D-65 and P.A. 89-626, § 3-32 did not take into account the amendments made by the other, the amendments to this section have been combined into a single version by the publisher.

LEGAL PERIODICALS

For comment, "Universities, Corporations, and States Use Them Now It's Time To Protect Them: An Analysis of the Public and Private Sector Ombudsman and the Continued Need for a Privileged Relationship," see 27 S. Ill. U. L.J. 389 (2003).

325 ILCS 20/10 Standards

Sec. 10. *Standards.* The Council and the lead agency, with assistance from parents and providers, shall develop and promulgate policies and procedures relating to the establishment and implementation of program and personnel standards to ensure that services provided are consistent with any State-approved or recognized certification, licensing, registration, or other comparable requirements which apply to the area of early intervention program service standards. Only State-approved public or private early intervention service providers shall be eligible to receive State and federal funding for early intervention services. All early childhood intervention staff shall hold the highest entry requirement necessary for that position.

To be a State-approved early intervention service provider, an individual (i) shall not have served or completed, within the preceding 5 years, a sentence for conviction of any felony that the Department establishes by rule and (ii) shall not have been indicated as a perpetrator of child abuse or neglect, within the preceding 5 years, in an investigation by Illinois (pursuant to the Abused and Neglected Child Reporting Act [325 ILCS 5/1 et seq.]) or another state. The Department is authorized to receive criminal background checks for such providers and persons applying to be such a provider and to receive child abuse and neglect reports regarding indicated perpetrators who are applying to provide or currently authorized to provide early intervention services in Illinois. Beginning January 1, 2004, every provider of State-approved early intervention services and every applicant to provide such services must authorize, in writing and in the form required by the Department, a criminal background check and check of child abuse and neglect reports regarding the provider or applicant as a condition of authorization to provide early intervention services. The Department shall use the results of the checks only to determine State approval of the early intervention service provider and shall not re-release the information except as necessary to accomplish that purpose.

(Source: P.A. 87-680; 87-847; 93-147, § 5.)

Note.

This section was Ill.Rev.Stat., Ch. 23, para. 4160.

Effect of Amendments.

The 2003 amendment by P.A. 93-147, effective January 1, 2004, added the second paragraph.

325 ILCS 20/11 Individualized Family Service Plans

Sec. 11. *Individualized Family Service Plans.* (a) Each eligible infant or toddler and that infant's or toddler's family shall receive:

(1) timely, comprehensive, multidisciplinary assessment of the unique needs of each eligible infant and toddler, and assessment of the concerns and priorities of the families to appropriately assist them in meeting their needs and identify services to meet those needs; and

(2) a written Individualized Family Service Plan developed by a multidisciplinary team which includes the parent or guardian. The individualized family service plan shall be based on the multidisciplinary team's assessment of the resources, priorities, and concerns of the family and its identification of the supports and services necessary to enhance the family's capacity to meet the developmental needs of the infant or toddler, and shall include the identification of services appropriate to meet those needs, including the frequency, intensity, and method of delivering services. During and as part of the initial development of the individualized family services plan, and any periodic reviews of the

plan, the multidisciplinary team shall consult the lead agency's therapy guidelines and its designated experts, if any, to help determine appropriate services and the frequency and intensity of those services. All services in the individualized family services plan must be justified by the multidisciplinary assessment of the unique strengths and needs of the infant or toddler and must be appropriate to meet those needs. At the periodic reviews, the team shall determine whether modification or revision of the outcomes or services is necessary.

(b) The Individualized Family Service Plan shall be evaluated once a year and the family shall be provided a review of the Plan at 6 month intervals or more often where appropriate based on infant or toddler and family needs. The lead agency shall create a quality review process regarding Individualized Family Service Plan development and changes thereto, to monitor and help assure that resources are being used to provide appropriate early intervention services.

(c) The evaluation and initial assessment and initial Plan meeting must be held within 45 days after the initial contact with the early intervention services system. With parental consent, early intervention services may commence before the completion of the comprehensive assessment and development of the Plan.

(d) Parents must be informed that, at their discretion, early intervention services shall be provided to each eligible infant and toddler in the natural environment, which may include the home or other community settings. Parents shall make the final decision to accept or decline early intervention services. A decision to decline such services shall not be a basis for administrative determination of parental fitness, or other findings or sanctions against the parents. Parameters of the Plan shall be set forth in rules.

(e) The regional intake offices shall explain to each family, orally and in writing, all of the following:

(1) That the early intervention program will pay for all early intervention services set forth in the individualized family service plan that are not covered or paid under the family's public or private insurance plan or policy and not eligible for payment through any other third party payor.

(2) That services will not be delayed due to any rules or restrictions under the family's insurance plan or policy.

(3) That the family may request, with appropriate documentation supporting the request, a determination of an exemption from private insurance use under Section 13.25 [325 ILCS 20/13.25].

(4) That responsibility for co-payments or co-insurance under a family's private insurance plan or policy will be transferred to the lead agency's central billing office.

(5) That families will be responsible for payments of family fees, which will be based on a sliding scale according to income, and that these fees are payable to the central billing office, and that if the family encounters a catastrophic circumstance, as defined under subsection (f) of Section 13 of this Act [325 ILCS 20/13], making it unable to pay the fees, the lead agency may, upon proof of inability to pay, waive the fees.

(f) The individualized family service plan must state whether the family has private insurance coverage and, if the family has such coverage, must have attached to it a copy of the family's insurance identification card or otherwise include all of the following information:

(1) The name, address, and telephone number of the insurance carrier.

(2) The contract number and policy number of the insurance plan.

(3) The name, address, and social security number of the primary insured.

(4) The beginning date of the insurance benefit year.

(g) A copy of the individualized family service plan must be provided to each enrolled provider who is providing early intervention services to the child who is the subject of that plan.

(Source: P.A. 87-680; 91-538, § 5; 92-10, § 40; 92-307, § 5; 92-651, § 67.)

Note.

This section was Ill.Rev.Stat., Ch. 23, para. 4161.

Section 997 of P.A. 92-651 is a no acceleration or delay provision, and Section 998 is a no revival or extension provision.

Effect of Amendments.

The 1999 amendment by P.A. 91-538, effective August 13, 1999, substituted "multidisciplinary" for "interdisciplinary" in subsections (a) and (b); and substituted "natural environment, which may include the home or other community settings" for "parents' home" in the first sentence of the last paragraph.

The 2001 amendment by P.A. 92-10, effective June 11, 2001, added the last sentence in present subsection (b).

The 2001 amendment by P.A. 92-307, effective August 9, 2001, added the subsection designations; redesignated former subsections (a) and (b) as present subsections (a)(1) and (a)(2); in subsection (a)(2), added the second through fifth sentences; and added subsections (e), (f), and (g).

The 2002 amendment by P.A. 92-651, effective July 11, 2002, combined the amendments by P.A. 92-10 and P.A. 92-307.

325 ILCS 20/12 Procedural Safeguards

Sec. 12. *Procedural Safeguards.* The lead agency shall adopt procedural safeguards that meet federal requirements and ensure effective implementation of the safeguards for families by each public agency involved in the provision of early intervention services under this Act.

The procedural safeguards shall provide, at a minimum, the following:

(a) The timely administrative resolution of complaints by parents as defined by administrative rule.

(b) The right to confidentiality of personally identifiable information.

(c) The opportunity for parents and a guardian to examine and receive copies of records relating to assessment, screening, eligibility determinations, and the development and implementation of the Individualized Family Service Plan.

(d) Procedures to protect the rights of the eligible infant or toddler whenever the parents or guardians of the child are not known or unavailable or the child is a ward of the State, including the assignment of an individual (who shall not be an employee of the State agency or local agency providing services) to act as a surrogate for the parents or guardian.

(e) Timely written prior notice to the parents or guardian of the eligible infant or toddler whenever the State agency or public or private service provider proposes to initiate or change or refuses to initiate or change the identification, evaluation, placement, or the provision of appropriate early intervention services to the eligible infant or toddler.

(f) Written prior notice to fully inform the parents or guardians, in their primary language, in a comprehensible manner, of these procedural safeguards.

(g) During the pendency of any proceedings or action involving a complaint, unless the State agency and the parents or guardian otherwise agree, the child shall continue to receive the appropriate early intervention services currently being provided, or in the case of an application for initial services, the child shall receive the services not in dispute.
(Source: P.A. 87-680; 87-847; 91-538, § 5.)

Note.

This section was Ill.Rev.Stat., Ch. 23, para. 4162.

Effect of Amendments.

The 1999 amendment by P.A. 91-538, effective August 13, 1999, inserted "for families" in the first sentence of the first paragraph, and substituted "as defined by administrative rule" for "The process shall use formal mediation procedures used by the lead agency, as well as prescribed due process procedures, which may be used by families at their discretion" at the end of subsection (a).

325 ILCS 20/13 Funding and Fiscal Responsibility

Sec. 13. *Funding and Fiscal Responsibility.* (a) The lead agency and every other participating State agency may receive and expend funds appropriated by the General Assembly to implement the early intervention services system as required by this Act.

(b) The lead agency and each participating State agency shall identify and report on an annual basis to the Council the State agency funds utilized for the provision of early intervention services to eligible infants and toddlers.

(c) Funds provided under Section 633 of the Individuals with Disabilities Education Act (20 United States Code 1433) and State funds designated or appropriated for early intervention services or programs may not be used to satisfy a financial commitment for services which would have been paid for from another public or private source but for the enactment of this Act, except whenever considered necessary to prevent delay in receiving appropriate early intervention services by the eligible infant or toddler or family in a timely manner. "Public or private source" includes public and private insurance coverage.

Funds provided under Section 633 of the Individuals with Disabilities Education Act [20 U.S.C. § 1473] and State funds designated or appropriated for early intervention services or programs may be used by the lead agency to pay the provider of services (A) pending reimbursement from the appropriate State agency or (B) if (i) the claim for payment is denied in whole or in part by a public or private source, or would be denied under the written terms of the public program or plan or private plan, or (ii) use of private insurance for the service has been exempted under Section 13.25 [325 ILCS 20/13.25]. Payment under item (B)(i) may be made based on a pre-determination telephone inquiry supported by written documentation of the denial supplied thereafter by the insurance carrier.

(d) Nothing in this Act shall be construed to permit the State to reduce medical or other assistance available or to alter eligibility under Title V and Title XIX of the Social Security Act [42 U.S.C. § 701 et seq.] relating to the Maternal Child Health Program and Medicaid for eligible infants and toddlers in this State.

(e) The lead agency shall create a central billing office to receive and dispense all relevant State and federal resources, as well as local government or independent resources available, for early intervention services. This office shall assure that maximum federal resources are utilized and that providers receive funds with minimal duplications or interagency reporting and with consolidated audit procedures.

(f) The lead agency shall, by rule, create a system of payments by families, including a schedule of fees. No fees, however, may be charged for: implementing child find, evaluation and assessment, service coordination, administrative and coordination activities related to the development, review, and evaluation of Individualized Family Service Plans, or the implementation of procedural safeguards and other administrative components of the statewide early intervention system.

The system of payments, called family fees, shall be structured on a sliding scale based on family income. The family's coverage or lack of coverage under a public or private insurance plan or policy shall not be a factor in determining the amount of the family fees.

Each family's fee obligation shall be established annually, and shall be paid by families to the central billing office in installments. At the written request of the family, the fee obligation shall be adjusted prospectively at any point during the year upon proof of a change in family income or family size. The inability of the parents of an eligible child to pay family fees due to catastrophic circumstances or extraordinary expenses shall not result in the denial of services to the child or the child's family. A family must document its extraordinary expenses or other catastrophic circumstances by showing one of the following: (i) out-of-pocket medical expenses in excess of 15% of gross income; (ii) a fire, flood, or other disaster causing a direct out-of-pocket loss in excess of 15% of gross income; or (iii) other catastrophic circumstances causing out-of-pocket losses in excess of 15% of gross income. The family must present proof of loss to its service coordinator, who shall document it, and the lead agency shall determine whether the fees shall be reduced, forgiven, or suspended within 10 business days after the family's request.

(g) To ensure that early intervention funds are used as the payor of last resort for early intervention services, the lead agency shall determine at the point of early intervention intake, and again at any periodic review of eligibility thereafter or upon a change in family circumstances, whether the family is eligible for or enrolled in any program for which payment is made directly or through public or private insurance for any or all of the early intervention services made available under this Act. The lead agency shall establish procedures to ensure that payments are made either directly from these public and private sources instead of from State or federal early intervention funds, or as reimbursement for payments previously made from State or federal early intervention funds.

(Source: P.A. 87-680; 91-538, § 5; 92-10, § 40; 92-307, § 5; 92-651, § 67.)

Note.

This section was Ill.Rev.Stat., Ch. 23, para. 4163.

Section 997 of P.A. 92-651 is a no acceleration or delay provision, and Section 998 is a no revival or extension provision.

Effect of Amendments.

The 1999 amendment by P.A. 91-538, effective August 13, 1999, in the third paragraph, substituted "Section 633" for "Section 673" twice, and "20 United States Code 1433" for "20 United States Code 1473"; deleted the former fifth paragraph, which concerned the distribution of funds and community obligations; deleted "The lead agency shall also create a resource review committee on the use of public and private sector resources" from the end of the present fifth paragraph; and added the last paragraph.

The 2001 amendment by P.A. 92-10, effective June 11, 2001, inserted the last sentence in the third paragraph; and substituted "shall" for "may" in the first sentence of the last paragraph.

The 2001 amendment by P.A. 92-307, effective August 9, 2001, added the subsection designations; in subsection (c), in the first and second sentences, inserted "and State funds designated or appropriated for early intervention services or programs", inserted the item designation (A), and added item (B); in subsection (f) substituted "shall, by rule" for "may also" in the first sentence and added the last two paragraphs; and added subsection (g).

The 2002 amendment by P.A. 92-651, effective July 11, 2002, combined the amendments by P.A. 92-10 and P.A. 92-307.

325 ILCS 20/13.5 Other programs

Sec. 13.5. *Other programs.* (a) When an application or a review of eligibility for early intervention services is made, and at any eligibility redetermination thereafter, the family shall be asked if it is currently enrolled in Medicaid, KidCare, or the Title V program administered by the University of Illinois Division of Specialized Care for Children. If the family is enrolled in any of these programs, that information shall be put on the individualized family service plan and entered into the computerized case management system, and shall require that the individualized family services plan of a child who has been found eligible for services through the Division of Specialized Care for Children state that the child is enrolled in that program. For those programs in which the family is not enrolled, a preliminary eligibility screen shall be conducted simultaneously for (i) medical assistance (Medicaid) under Article V of the Illinois Public Aid Code [305 ILCS 5/5-1 et seq.], (ii) children's health insurance program (KidCare) benefits under the Children's Health Insurance Program Act [215 ILCS 106/1 et seq.], and (iii) Title V maternal and child health services provided through the Division of Specialized Care for Children of the University of Illinois.

(b) For purposes of determining family fees under subsection (f) of Section 13 [325 ILCS 20/13] and determining eligibility for the other programs and services specified in items (i) through (iii) of subsection (a), the lead agency shall develop and use, within 60 days after the effective date of this amendatory Act of the 92nd General Assembly [P.A. 92-307], with the cooperation of the Department of Public Aid and the Division of Specialized Care for Children of the University of Illinois, a screening device that provides sufficient information for the early intervention regional intake entities or other agencies to establish eligibility for those other programs and shall, in cooperation with the Illinois Department of Public Aid and the Division of Specialized Care for Children, train the regional intake entities on using the screening device.

(c) When a child is determined eligible for and enrolled in the early intervention program and has been found to at least meet the threshold income eligibility requirements for Medicaid or KidCare, the regional intake entity shall complete a KidCare/Medicaid application with the family and forward it to the Illinois Department of Public Aid's KidCare Unit for a determination of eligibility.

(d) With the cooperation of the Department of Public Aid, the lead agency shall establish procedures that ensure the timely and maximum allowable recovery of payments for all early intervention services and allowable administrative costs under Article V of the Illinois Public Aid Code [305 ILCS 5/5-1 et seq.] and the Children's Health Insurance Program Act [215 ILCS 106/1 et seq.] and shall include those procedures in the interagency agreement required under subsection (e) of Section 5 of this Act [325 ILCS 20/5].

(e) For purposes of making referrals for final determinations of eligibility for KidCare benefits under the Children's Health Insurance Program Act [215 ILCS 106/1 et seq.] and for medical assistance under Article V of the Illinois Public Aid Code [305 ILCS 5/5-1 et seq.], the lead agency shall require each early intervention regional intake entity to enroll as a "KidCare agent" in order for the entity to complete the KidCare application as authorized under Section 22 of the Children's Health Insurance Program Act [215 ILCS 106/22].

(f) For purposes of early intervention services that may be provided by the Division of Specialized Care for Children of the University of Illinois (DSCC), the lead agency shall establish procedures whereby the early intervention regional intake entities may determine whether children enrolled in the early intervention program may also be eligible for those services, and shall develop, within 60 days after the effective date of this amendatory Act of the 92nd General Assembly [P.A. 92-307], (i) the inter-agency agreement required under subsection (e) of Section 5 of this Act [325 ILCS 20/5], establishing that early intervention funds are to be used as the payor of last resort when services required under an individualized family services plan may be provided to an eligible child through the DSCC, and (ii) training guidelines for the regional intake entities and providers that explain eligibility and billing procedures for services through DSCC.

(g) The lead agency shall require that an individual applying for or renewing enrollment as a provider of services in the early intervention program state whether or not he or she is also enrolled as a DSCC provider. This information shall be noted next to the name of the provider on the computerized roster of Illinois early intervention providers, and regional intake entities shall make every effort to refer families eligible for DSCC services to these providers.
(Source: P.A. 92-307, § 5.)

Effective Date.
Section 99 of P.A. 92-307 made this section effective upon becoming law. The Act was approved August 9, 2001.

325 ILCS 20/13.10 Private health insurance; assignment

Sec. 13.10. *Private health insurance; assignment.* The lead agency shall determine, at the point of new applications for early intervention services, and for all children enrolled in the early intervention program, at the regional intake offices, whether the child is insured under a private health insurance plan or policy. An application for early intervention services shall serve as a right to assignment of the right of recovery against a private health insurance plan or policy for any covered early intervention services that may be billed to the family's insurance carrier and that are provided to a child covered under the plan or policy.
(Source: P.A. 92-307, § 5.)

Effective Date.
Section 99 of P.A. 92-307 made this section effective upon becoming law. The Act was approved August 9, 2001.

325 ILCS 20/13.15 Billing of insurance carrier

Sec. 13.15. *Billing of insurance carrier.* (a) Subject to the restrictions against private insurance use on the basis of material risk of loss of coverage, as determined under Section 13.25 [325 ILCS 20/13.25], each enrolled provider who is providing a family with early intervention services shall bill the child's insurance carrier for each unit of early intervention service for which coverage may be available. The lead agency may exempt from the requirement of this paragraph any early intervention service that it has deemed not to be covered by insurance plans. When the service is not exempted, providers who receive a denial of payment on the basis that the service is not covered under any circumstance under the plan are not required to bill that carrier for that service again until the following insurance benefit year. That explanation of benefits denying the claim, once submitted to the central billing office, shall be sufficient to meet the requirements of this paragraph as to subsequent services billed under the same billing code provided to that child during that insurance benefit year. Any time limit on a provider's filing of a claim for payment with the central billing office that is imposed through a policy, procedure, or rule of the lead agency shall be suspended until the provider receives an explanation of benefits or other final determination of the claim it files with the child's insurance carrier.

(b) In all instances when an insurance carrier has been billed for early intervention services, whether paid in full, paid in part, or denied by the carrier, the provider must provide the central billing office, within 90 days after receipt, with a copy of the explanation of benefits form and other information in the manner prescribed by the lead agency.

(c) When the insurance carrier has denied the claim or paid an amount for the early intervention service billed that is less that the current State rate for early intervention services, the provider shall submit the explanation of benefits with a claim for payment, and the lead agency shall pay the provider the difference between the sum actually paid by the insurance carrier for each unit of service provided under the individualized family service plan and the current State rate for early intervention services. The State shall also pay the family's co-payment or co-insurance under its plan, but only to the extent that those payments plus the balance of the claim do not exceed the current State rate for early intervention services. The provider may under no circumstances bill the family for the difference between its charge for services and that which has been paid by the insurance carrier or by the State.
(Source: P.A. 92-307, § 5.)

Effective Date.
Section 99 of P.A. 92-307 made this section effective upon becoming law. The Act was approved August 9, 2001.

325 ILCS 20/13.20 Families with insurance coverage

Sec. 13.20. *Families with insurance coverage.* (a) Families of children with insurance coverage, whether public or private, shall incur no greater or less direct out-of-pocket expenses for early intervention services than families who are not insured.

(b) Managed care plans.

(1) Use of managed care network providers. When a family's insurance coverage is through a managed care arrangement with a network of providers that includes one or more types of early intervention specialists who provide the services set forth in the family's individualized family service plan, the regional intake entity shall require the family to use those network providers, but only to the extent that:

(A) the network provider is immediately available to receive the referral and to begin providing services to the child;

(B) the network provider is enrolled as a provider in the Illinois early intervention system and fully credentialed under the current policy or rule of the lead agency;

(C) the network provider can provide the services to the child in the manner required in the individualized service plan;

(D) the family would not have to travel more than an additional 15 miles or an additional 30 minutes to the network provider than it would have to travel to a non-network provider who is available to provide the same service; and

(E) the family's managed care plan does not allow for billing (even at a reduced rate or reduced percentage of the claim) for early intervention services provided by non-network providers.

(2) Transfers from non-network to network providers. If a child has been receiving services from a non-network provider and the regional intake entity determines, at the time of enrollment in the early intervention program or at any point thereafter, that the family is enrolled in a managed care plan, the regional intake entity shall require the family to transfer to a network provider within 45 days after that determination, but within no more than 60 days after the effective date of this amendatory Act of the 92nd General Assembly [P.A. 92-307], if:

(A) all the requirements of subdivision (b)(1) of this Section have been met; and

(B) the child is less than 26 months of age.

(3) Waivers. The lead agency may fully or partially waive the network enrollment requirements of subdivision (b)(1) of this Section and the transfer requirements of subdivision (b)(2) of this Section as to a particular region, or narrower geographic area, if it finds that the managed care plans in that area are not allowing further enrollment of early intervention providers and it finds that referrals or transfers to network providers could cause an overall shortage of early intervention providers in that region of the State or could cause delays in families securing the early intervention services set forth in individualized family services plans.

(4) The lead agency, in conjunction with any entities with which it may have contracted for the training and credentialing of providers, the local interagency council for early intervention, the regional intake entity, and the enrolled providers in each region who wish to participate, shall cooperate in developing a matrix and action plan that (A) identifies both (i) which early intervention providers and which fully credentialed early intervention providers are members of the managed care plans that are used in the region by families with children in the early intervention program, and (ii) which early intervention services, with what restrictions, if any, are covered under those plans, (B) identifies which credentialed specialists are members of which managed care plans in the region, and (C) identifies the various managed care plans to early intervention providers, encourages their enrollment in the area plans, and provides them with information on how to enroll. These matrices shall be complete no later than 7 months after the effective date of this amendatory Act of the 92nd General Assembly [P.A. 92-307], and shall be provided to the Early Intervention Legislative Advisory Committee at that time. The lead agency shall work with networks that may have closed enrollment to additional providers to encourage their admission of early intervention providers, and shall report to the Early Intervention Legislative Advisory Committee on the initial results of these efforts no later than February 1, 2002.
(Source: P.A. 92-307, § 5.)

Effective Date.
Section 99 of P.A. 92-307 made this section effective upon becoming law. The Act was approved August 9, 2001.

325 ILCS 20/13.25 Private insurance; exemption

Sec. 13.25. *Private insurance; exemption.* (a) The lead agency shall establish procedures for a family, whose child is eligible to receive early intervention services, to apply for an exemption restricting the use of its private insurance plan or policy based on material risk of loss of coverage as authorized under subsection (c) of this Section.

(b) The lead agency shall make a final determination on a request for an exemption within 10 business days after its receipt of a written request for an exemption at the regional intake entity. During that 10 days, no claims may be filed against the insurance plan or policy. If the exemption is granted, it shall be noted on the individualized family service plan, and the family and the providers serving the family shall be notified in writing of the exemption.

(c) An exemption may be granted on the basis of material risk of loss of coverage only if the family submits documentation with its request for an exemption that establishes (i) that the insurance plan or policy covering the child is an individually purchased plan or policy and has been purchased by a head of a household that is not eligible for a group medical insurance plan, (ii) that the policy or plan has a lifetime cap that applies to one or more specific types of early intervention services specified in the family's individualized family service plan, and that coverage could be exhausted during the period covered by the individualized family service plan, or (iii) proof of another risk that the lead agency, in its discretion, may have additionally established and defined as a ground for exemption by rule.

(d) An exemption under this Section based on material risk of loss of coverage may apply to all early intervention services and all plans or policies insuring the child, may be limited to one or more plans or policies, or may be limited to one or more types of early intervention services in the child's individualized family services plan.

(Source: P.A. 92-307, § 5.)

Effective Date.

Section 99 of P.A. 92-307 made this section effective upon becoming law. The Act was approved August 9, 2001.

325 ILCS 20/13.30 System of personnel development

Sec. 13.30. *System of personnel development.* The lead agency shall provide training to early intervention providers and may enter into contracts to meet this requirement. If such contracts are let, they shall be bid under a public request for proposals that shall be posted on the lead agency's early intervention website for no less than 30 days. This training shall include, at minimum, the following types of instruction:

(a) Courses in birth-to-3 evaluation and treatment of children with developmental disabilities and delays (1) that are taught by fully credentialed early intervention providers or educators with substantial experience in evaluation and treatment of children from birth to age 3 with developmental disabilities and delays, (2) that cover these topics within each of the disciplines of audiology, occupational therapy, physical therapy, speech and language pathology, and developmental therapy, including the social-emotional domain of development, (3) that are held no less than twice per year, (4) that offer no fewer than 20 contact hours per year of course work, (5) that are held in no fewer than 5 separate locales throughout the State, and (6) that give enrollment priority to early intervention providers who do not meet the experience, education, or continuing education requirements necessary to be fully credentialed early intervention providers; and

(b) Courses held no less than twice per year for no fewer than 4 hours each in no fewer than 5 separate locales throughout the State each on the following topics:

(1) Practice and procedures of private insurance billing.

(2) The role of the regional intake entities; service coordination; program eligibility determinations; family fees; Medicaid, KidCare, and Division of Specialized Care applications, referrals, and coordination with Early Intervention; and procedural safeguards.

(3) Introduction to the early intervention program, including provider enrollment and credentialing, overview of Early Intervention program policies and regulations, and billing requirements.

(4) Evaluation and assessment of birth-to-3 children; individualized family service plan development, monitoring, and review; best practices; service guidelines; and quality assurance.

(Source: P.A. 92-307, § 5.)

Effective Date.

Section 99 of P.A. 92-307 made this section effective upon becoming law. The Act was approved August 9, 2001.

325 ILCS 20/13.32 Contracting

Sec. 13.32. *Contracting.* The lead agency may enter into contracts for some or all of its responsibilities under this Act, including but not limited to, credentialing and enrolling providers; training under Section 13.30 [325 ILCS 20/13.30]; maintaining a central billing office; data collection and analysis; establishing and maintaining a computerized case management system accessible to local referral offices and providers; creating and maintaining a system for provider credentialing and enrollment; creating and maintaining the central directory required under subsection (g) of Section 7 of this Act [325 ILCS 20/7]; and program operations. If contracted, the contract shall be subject to a public request for proposals as described in the Illinois Procurement Code, [30 ILCS 500/1-1 et seq.] notwithstanding any exemptions or alternative processes that may be allowed for such a contract under that Code, and, in addition to the posting requirements under that Code, shall be posted on the early intervention website maintained by the lead agency during the entire bid period. With the exception of contracts with or grants to regional intake entities, any of these listed responsibilities currently under contract or grant that have not met these requirements shall be subject to public bid under this request for proposal process no later than July 1, 2002 or the date of termination of any contract in place. Contracts with or grants to regional intake entities must be made subject to public bid under a request for proposals process no later than July 1, 2005.

(Source: P.A. 92-307, § 5; 93-147, § 5.)

Effective Date.

Section 99 of P.A. 92-307 made this section effective upon becoming law. The Act was approved August 9, 2001.

Effect of Amendments.

The 2003 amendment by P.A. 93-147, effective January 1, 2004, added "With the exception of contracts with or grants to regional intake entities" at the beginning of the second sentence and added the third sentence.

325 ILCS 20/13.50 Early Intervention Legislative Advisory Committee

Sec. 13.50. *Early Intervention Legislative Advisory Committee.* No later than 60 days after the effective

date of this amendatory Act of 92nd General Assembly [P.A. 92-307], there shall be convened the Early Intervention Legislative Advisory Committee. The majority and minority leaders of the General Assembly shall each appoint 2 members to the Committee. The Committee's term is for a period of 4 years, and the Committee shall publicly convene no less than 4 times per year. The Committee's responsibilities shall include, but not be limited to, providing guidance to the lead agency regarding programmatic and fiscal management and accountability, provider development and accountability, contracting, and program outcome measures. During the life of the Committee, on a quarterly basis, or more often as the Committee may request, the lead agency shall provide to the Committee, and simultaneously to the public, through postings on the lead agency's early intervention website, quarterly reports containing monthly data and other early intervention program information that the Committee requests. The first data report must be supplied no later than September 21, 2001, and must include the previous 2 quarters of data.
(Source: P.A. 92-307, § 5; 93-124, § 5.)

Effective Date.
Section 99 of P.A. 92-307 made this section effective upon becoming law. The Act was approved August 9, 2001.

Effect of Amendments.
The 2003 amendment by P.A. 93-124, effective July 10, 2003, substituted "4 years" for "2 years" in the fourth sentence.

325 ILCS 20/14: Repealed by P.A. 91-538, § 10, effective August 13, 1999.

325 ILCS 20/15 [Evaluation]

Sec. 15. The Auditor General of the State shall conduct a follow-up evaluation of the system established under this Act, in order to evaluate the effectiveness of the system in providing services that enhance the capacities of families throughout Illinois to meet the special needs of their eligible infants and toddlers, and provide a report of the evaluation to the Governor and the General Assembly no later than April 30, 2002. Upon receipt by the lead agency, this report shall be posted on the early intervention website.
(Source: P.A. 87-680; 92-307, § 5.)

Note.
This section was Ill.Rev.Stat., Ch. 23, para. 4165.

Effect of Amendments.
The 2001 amendment by P.A. 92-307, effective August 9, 2001, in the first sentence substituted "a follow-up" for "an" and substituted "April 30, 2002" for "April 30, 1993"; and added the second sentence.

325 ILCS 20/16 [Effect]

Sec. 16. This Act takes effect upon becoming law.
(Source: P.A. 87-680.)

Note.
This section was Ill.Rev.Stat., Ch. 23, para. 4166.

325 ILCS 20/20 Early Intervention Services Revolving Fund

Sec. 20. *Early Intervention Services Revolving Fund.* There is created a revolving fund to be known as the Early Intervention Services Revolving Fund, to be held by the lead agency.

The Early Intervention Services Revolving Fund shall be used to the extent determined necessary by the lead agency to pay for early intervention services.

Local Accounts for such purposes may be established by the lead agency.

Expenditures from the Early Intervention Services Revolving Fund shall be made in accordance with applicable program provisions and shall be limited to those purposes and amounts specified under applicable program guidelines. Funding of the Fund shall be from family fees, insurance company payments, federal financial participation received as reimbursement for expenditures from the Fund, and appropriations made to the State agencies involved in the payment for early intervention services under this Act.

Disbursements from the Early Intervention Services Revolving Fund shall be made as determined by the lead agency or its designee. Funds in the Early Intervention Services Revolving Fund or the local accounts created under this Section that are not immediately required for expenditure may be invested in certificates of deposit or other interest bearing accounts. Any interest earned shall be deposited in the Early Intervention Services Revolving Fund.
(Source: P.A. 89-106, § 15; 89-499, § 50.)

Effective Date.
Section 99 of P.A. 89-106 made this section effective July 1, 1995. The Act was approved July 7, 1995.

Effect of Amendments.
The 1996 amendment by P.A. 89-499, effective June 28, 1996, in the fourth paragraph, in the second sentence, inserted "family fees, insurance company payments, federal financial participation received as reimbursement for expenditures from the Fund, and".

HIGH RISK YOUTH CAREER DEVELOPMENT ACT

325 ILCS 25/0.01 Short title

Sec. 0.01. *Short title.* This Act may be cited as the High Risk Youth Career Development Act.
(Source: P.A. 86-1324.)

Derivation.
Title: An Act in relation to the provision of assistance to certain persons, amending Acts named therein.
Cite: 325 ILCS 25/0.01 et seq.
Source: P.A. 85-943.
Date: Certified December 2, 1987.

Note.
This section was Ill.Rev.Stat., Ch. 23, para. 6550.

325 ILCS 25/1 [Community-based programs]

Sec. 1. The Department of Human Services (acting as successor to the Illinois Department of Public Aid under the Department of Human Services Act [20 ILCS 1305/1-1 et seq.]), in cooperation with the Department of Commerce and Community Affairs, the Illinois State Board of Education, the Department of Children and Family Services, the Department of Employment Services and other appropriate State and local agencies, may establish and administer, on an experimental basis and subject to appropriation, community-based programs providing comprehensive, long-term intervention strategies to increase future employability and career development among high risk youth. The Department of Human Services, and the other cooperating agencies, shall establish provisions for community involvement in the design, development, implementation and administration of these programs. The programs may provide the following services: teaching of basic literacy and remedial reading and writing; vocational training programs which are realistic in terms of producing lifelong skills necessary for career development; and supportive services including transportation and child care during the training period and for up to one year after placement in a job. The programs shall be targeted to high risk youth residing in the geographic areas served by the respective programs. "High risk" means that a person is at least 16 years of age but not yet 21 years of age and possesses one or more of the following characteristics:

(1) Has low income;
(2) Is a member of a minority;
(3) Is illiterate;
(4) Is a school drop out;
(5) Is homeless;
(6) Is disabled;
(7) Is a parent; or
(8) Is a ward of the State.

The Department of Human Services and other cooperating State agencies shall promulgate rules and regulations, pursuant to the Illinois Administrative Procedure Act [5 ILCS 100/1-1 et seq.], for the implementation of this Act, including procedures and standards for determining whether a person possesses any of the characteristics specified in this Section.
(Source: P.A. 85-943; 89-507, § 90L-76.)

Note.
This section was Ill.Rev.Stat., Ch. 23, para. 6551.

Cross References.
As to contracts with nonprofit organizations, or units of local governments to implement career development programs, for high risk youths, see 305 ILCS 5/12-4.29.
As to the duties of the Department of Employment Security concerning high risk youth career development services such as job testing, job placement, and job referrals, see 20 ILCS 1015/15.

Effect of Amendments.
The 1996 amendment by P.A. 89-507, effective July 1, 1997, in the first paragraph, in the first sentence, inserted "Department of Human Services (acting as successor to the" and inserted "under the Department of Human Services Act)" and in the second sentence substituted "Human Services" for "Public Aid"; and in the second paragraph deleted "Illinois" preceding "Department" and substituted "Human Services" for "Public Aid".

Family Support Demonstration Project

325 ILCS 30/1 Short title

Sec. 1. *Short title.* This Act may be cited as the Family Support Demonstration Project.
(Source: P.A. 87-678.)

Derivation.
Title: An Act relating to community based family services.
Cite: 325 ILCS 30/1 et seq.
Source: P.A. 87-678.
Date: Approved September 23, 1991.

Note.
This section was Ill.Rev.Stat., Ch. 23, para. 4101.

325 ILCS 30/2 Purpose

Sec. 2. *Purpose.* The legislature finds that families and family structures have changed dramatically, and many families are suffering because of the stresses and strains of economic demands.

Many families are at high risk of becoming fragmented and dysfunctional, and a substantial number will be trapped in a cycle of poverty unless existing support systems designed to intervene and assist them in times of need are vastly improved.

Under the present system of services to families, families are required to be in trouble or dysfunctional before they can become eligible to receive services and assistance.

In order to reach out to families and successfully assist them, support services should be coordinated and provided in a community-based setting. These community-based centers should be responsive to and involved with the communities in which they are located to the extent that the communities feel a strong sense of ownership of and identification with the centers. In addition, the overall atmosphere of the facility, as well as the attitude of the staff, should project compassion, understanding, friendliness, and patience.

The purpose of this Act is to establish a family support center demonstration project to demonstrate the effectiveness of a community-based family support center concept, and to test different models of service delivery.
(Source: P.A. 87-678.)

Note.
This section was Ill.Rev.Stat., Ch. 23, para. 4102.

325 ILCS 30/3 Definitions

Sec. 3. *Definitions.* In this Act:

"Department" means the Department of Children and Family Services.

"Director" means director of the Department of Children and Family Services.

"Family" means the family as an enduring personal support system with the functions of nurturing, caring for, and educating children, youths, adults, and the elderly.

"Project" means the family support center demonstration project.

(Source: P.A. 87-678.)

Note.

This section was Ill.Rev.Stat., Ch. 23, para. 4103.

325 ILCS 30/4 Project

Sec. 4. *Project.* There is established, subject to available appropriations, a 2 year demonstration project, known as the family support center demonstration project. The Department of Children and Family Services shall be responsible for the planning, implementation and establishment of a family support center. The project shall coordinate the provision of core services to families at a community-based center in order to develop the community's capacity to identify and resolve its problems. The center shall be responsive to the community and involve the participants as equal partners in program development and execution.

The center shall offer an array of services tailored to the specific needs of its constituents. Services shall be developed pursuant to family support principles. Services must:

(1) Be offered at convenient times in accessible locations.

(2) Build on strengths, rather than search for deficits.

(3) Involve participants and the community in planning and implementation.

(4) Show respect for participants.

(5) Serve the best interests of children.

(6) Strengthen families.

(7) Be presented in coordination with other agencies and services in the community.

No single service shall overshadow the others, and services shall be provided in a coordinated manner. Because some services will be provided directly by the center and other services will be provided by other agencies, the center, with input from parent constituents, shall develop a service plan, using a systems management approach, for the provision of services. The staff of the center shall be responsible for ensuring that all components of the service plan are carried out. This may require interventions on the part of the staff, including but not limited to, accompanying parents to appointments with other agencies, advocating on behalf of parents, reminding parents of appointments with other agencies, and providing short-term counseling to parents concerning referrals for services.

The center shall consider the following services, activities, and components when developing its core services:

(a) Enhancement of parenting skills.

(b) Infant and child stimulation activities to maximize child growth and development.

(c) Outreach services targeted at community organizations, families, youth, and others to ensure community awareness, acceptance, and participation.

(d) Health care, family planning, counseling, and other services to avoid unwanted pregnancies.

(e) Assessment and treatment planning for developmental problems of the parent or the child.

(f) Temporary developmental child care for the offspring of parents receiving services on-site.

(g) Peer support activities, including recreational and social activities.

(h) Educational services, such as post-high school classes and instruction to those attempting to earn general equivalency diplomas.

(i) Job preparation and skill development services to assist young parents in preparing, securing, and maintaining employment.

(Source: P.A. 87-678.)

Note.

This section was Ill.Rev.Stat., Ch. 23, para. 4104.

325 ILCS 30/5 Funding

Sec. 5. *Funding.* The Department prior to establishing the family support center demonstration project shall seek funding from public and private sources. Funding received from private foundations or from other sources may be used by the Department to establish the demonstration project.

(Source: P.A. 87-678.)

Note.

This section was Ill.Rev.Stat., Ch. 23, para. 4105.

325 ILCS 30/6 Council

Sec. 6. *Council.* There is established the family support center council for the purpose of planning and implementing the establishment and development of a family support center. The council shall be appointed by the governor and consist of representatives from the public and private sectors of the community.

The council shall confer with the director who may:

(a) Enter into agreements with the federal government, other state departments and agencies, and the counties.

(b) Enter into assistance agreements with private persons, groups, institutions, or corporations.

(c) Purchase services required or appropriate under this Act from any private persons, groups, institutions, or corporations.

(d) Allocate and expend any resources available for the purposes of this Act.

(e) Encourage all agencies to cooperate with the Department in extending individual agency resources in order to develop the project.

(f) Enter into inter-agency agreements. All agreements entered into for the accomplishment of the purposes of this Act shall place a duty upon each affected agency to cooperate fully with the Department in making every effort to enter into the agreement.

(g) Do all things necessary to accomplish the purposes and provisions of this Act.

The center shall be required to complete an evaluation which includes, but is not limited to descriptive data on client status, program utilization data, profiles of participants, intervention plans, and participant and community satisfaction ratings.

The department may utilize a portion of its funds to conduct evaluations of the center.
(Source: P.A. 87-678.)

Note.
This section was Ill.Rev.Stat., Ch. 23, para. 4106.

325 ILCS 30/7 Reporting

Sec. 7. *Reporting.* The Department shall monitor and evaluate the demonstration project and shall submit a status report on its findings to the General Assembly on February 1, 1994 and 1995, and a final report on its findings to the General Assembly on February 1, 1996. Status and final reports shall include, but not be limited to:

(a) A descriptive summary of the operation of the family support center, including the services provided and a copy of the service plan developed by the center, the number of recipients of services at the center, the allocation of funds, staffing information, and the role and responsibility of the community family support center board.

(b) An assessment of the impact of the center upon the community served.

(c) The composition and role of the family support center.

(d) Recommendations regarding the continuance of the family support center demonstration project and plans for the implementation of other project sites.

(e) Recommendations regarding the process by which family support centers are allocated resources.

(f) A projected budget for the expenditures required to continue or to expand the demonstration project.

(g) Proposals for legislation necessary to facilitate the continuation or expansion of the demonstration project.
(Source: P.A. 87-678; 90-655, § 129.)

Note.
This section was Ill.Rev.Stat., Ch. 23, para. 4107.

Effect of Amendments.
The 1998 amendment by P.A. 90-655, effective July 30, 1998, in subdivision (a) substituted "recipients" for "receipients".

325 ILCS 30/8 Literacy program

Sec. 8. *Literacy program.* As part of the project, family literacy programs shall be provided for the purpose of addressing the family's need for educational, vocational, and parenting training. The family literacy program shall focus on learning sessions for preschool-aged children and their parents. The children shall receive preschool education while their parents receive education focusing on parenting skills; traditional subjects as reading, language, mathematics, and vocational training.
(Source: P.A. 87-678.)

Note.
This section was Ill.Rev.Stat., Ch. 23, para. 4108.

325 ILCS 30/9 [Effective date]

Sec. 9. This Act takes effect July 1, 1992.
(Source: P.A. 87-678.)

Note.
This section was Ill.Rev.Stat., Ch. 23, para. 4109.

Interagency Board for Children who are Deaf or Hard-of-Hearing and have an Emotional or Behavioral Disorder Act

325 ILCS 35/1 Short title

Sec. 1. *Short title.* This Act may be cited as the Interagency Board for Children who are Deaf or Hard-of-Hearing and have an Emotional or Behavioral Disorder Act.
(Source: P.A. 86-1200; 89-680, § 905.)

Derivation.
Title: An Act in relation to children who are deaf or hard-of-hearing and have an emotional or behavioral disorder.
Cite: 325 ILCS 35/1 et seq.
Source: P.A. 86-1200.
Date: Approved August 29, 1990.

Note.
This section was Ill.Rev.Stat., Ch. 23, para. 6701.

Effect of Amendments.
The 1996 amendment by P.A. 89-680, effective January 1, 1997 amended the Act title by deleting "hearing impaired and behavior disordered" preceding "children" and added at the end "who are deaf or hard-of-hearing and have an emotional or behavioral disorder" and in the section deleted "Hearing Impaired/Behavior Disordered" preceding "Children" and inserted "who are Deaf or Hard-of-Hearing and have an Emotional or Behavioral Disorder".

325 ILCS 35/2 Purpose

Sec. 2. *Purpose.* The State of Illinois recognizes the need to create an interagency board for services for children who are deaf or hard-of-hearing and have an emotional or behavioral disorder. The Board shall provide advice to the State Superintendent of Education, the Governor, and the General Assembly on all matters pertaining to policy on children who are deaf or hard-of-hearing and have an emotional or behavioral disorder, including, but not limited to:

(a) the need for diagnostic, referral, and placement assistance centers.

(b) a report on the implementation of legislation enacted for children who are deaf or hard-of-hearing and have an emotional or behavioral disorder.

(c) a status report on day and residential educational and mental health service providers for children who are deaf or hard-of-hearing and have an emotional or behavioral disorder.

(Source: P.A. 86-1200; 89-680, § 905.)

Note.

This section was Ill.Rev.Stat., Ch. 23, para. 6702.

Effect of Amendments.

The 1996 amendment by P.A. 89-680, effective January 1, 1997, inserted "who are deaf or hard-of-hearing and have an emotional or behavioral disorder" throughout the section; deleted "hearing impaired/behavior disordered" preceding "children" in the second sentence of the introductory language and in subsections (b) and (c); in the introductory language, in the first sentence, deleted "the hearing impaired/behavior disordered" preceding "children" and in the second sentence inserted a comma after "Governor"; and in subsection (a) inserted a comma after "referral".

325 ILCS 35/3 Definitions

Sec. 3. *Definitions.* As used in this Act:

"Board" means the Interagency Board.

"Children who are deaf or hard-of-hearing and have an emotional or behavioral disorder" means a child who has auditory impairment which is serious enough to warrant an array of special services and special education programs in order to assist the child both educationally and socially, and the behavior is seriously disruptive and unacceptable to peers, educational staff, and persons in the community or presents a danger to self or others.

(Source: P.A. 86-1200; 89-680, § 905.)

Note.

This section was Ill.Rev.Stat., Ch. 23, para. 6703.

Effect of Amendments.

The 1996 amendment by P.A. 89-680, effective January 1, 1997, in the second definition deleted "Hearing impaired/behavior disordered" preceding Children" and inserted "who are deaf or hard-of-hearing and have an emotional or behavioral disorder".

325 ILCS 35/4 Appointment

Sec. 4. *Appointment.* The Board shall consist of 12 members, one of whom shall be appointed by the Governor. The State Superintendent of Education shall appoint 2 members, one of whom shall be a parent of a child who is deaf or hard-of-hearing and has an emotional or behavioral disorder, and one of whom shall be an employee of the agency. The Director of Children and Family Services shall appoint 2 members, one of whom shall be a parent, foster parent, or legal guardian of a child who is deaf or hard-of-hearing and has an emotional or behavioral disorder, and one of whom shall be an employee of the agency. The Secretary of Human Services shall appoint 4 members, 2 of whom shall be parents of children who are deaf or hard-of-hearing and have an emotional or behavioral disorder, and 2 of whom shall be employees of the agency.

The Director of Public Aid shall appoint one member who shall be an employee of the agency. The Community and Residential Services Authority for Behavior Disturbed and Severe Emotionally Disturbed Students shall appoint one member who shall be an employee of the Authority, and the Director of the Division of Specialized Care for Children shall appoint one member who shall be an employee of that agency.

Each appointing authority shall give preference to any qualified deaf employee when making appointments to the Board.

(Source: P.A. 86-1200; 87-895; 87-1127, § 1; 89-507, § 90D-66; 89-680, § 905; 90-14, § 2-200.)

Note.

This section was Ill.Rev.Stat., Ch. 23, para. 6704.

Effect of Amendments.

The 1996 amendment by P.A. 89-507, effective July 1, 1997, in the first paragraph, in the fourth sentence, substituted "Secretary of Human Services" for "Director of Rehabilitation Services", substituted "4" for "2" and deleted "and one of whom shall be an employee of the agency". The Director of Mental Health and Developmental Disabilities shall appoint 2 members" preceding "one of whom", inserted a comma following the second occurrence of "hearing impaired/behavior disordered child", substituted "2" for "one" and substituted "employees" for "an employee".

The 1996 amendment by P.A. 89-680, effective January 1, 1997, deleted "hearing impaired/behavior disordered" preceding "child" and inserted "who is deaf or hard-of-hearing and has an emotional or behavioral disorder" throughout the first paragraph; in the first paragraph, in the third sentence, inserted "foster, parent, or legal guardian"; and in the third paragraph deleted the former second sentence which read "The initial Board members shall be appointed within 30 days of the effective date of this Act".

The 1997 amendment by P.A. 90-14, effective July 1, 1997, combined the amendments by P.A. 89-507 and P.A. 89-680; and in the first paragraph, in the fourth sentence, substituted "2" for "one", substituted "parents of children who are" for "a parent of a child who is", substituted "have" for "has" and deleted from the end "one of whom shall be a parent of a child who is deaf or hard of hearing and has an emotional or behavioral disorder".

325 ILCS 35/5 Term of office

Sec. 5. *Term of office.* Vacancies in terms shall be filled by the original appointing authority. All members shall be appointed for a term of 3 years.

(Source: P.A. 86-1200; 89-680, § 905.)

Note.

This section was Ill.Rev.Stat., Ch. 23, para. 6705.

Effect of Amendments.

The 1996 amendment by P.A. 89-680, effective January 1, 1997, deleted the former introductory language which read "The members initially appointed to the Board shall draw lots to determine their initial term of office"; deleted subsection (a) which read "Four members shall serve a term of 3 years"; deleted subsection (b) which read "Four members shall serve a term of 2 years"; deleted subsection (c) which read "Four members shall serve a term of 1 year"; and in the second sentence deleted "After the original terms" from the beginning.

325 ILCS 35/6 Organization

Sec. 6. *Organization.* The Board shall organize for the transaction of business by selecting a chairperson and a secretary from the members and adopt bylaws to govern its proceedings. The chairperson and secretary shall be elected by the Board from time to time from among members.
(Source: P.A. 86-1200; 89-680, § 905.)

Note.
This section was Ill.Rev.Stat., Ch. 23, para. 6706.

Effect of Amendments.
The 1996 amendment by P.A. 89-680, effective January 1, 1997, in the first sentence deleted "As soon as possible after the appointment of the initial members" from the beginning, substituted "by selecting" for "select", substituted "chairperson" for "chairman", deleted "temporary" preceding "secretary" and substituted "the members" for "its own number"; and in the second sentence substituted "chairperson and secretary" for "initial chairman and successors".

325 ILCS 35/7 Meetings

Sec. 7. *Meetings.* Regular meetings of the Board shall be held no less than 6 times the first year, the time and place of such meetings to be fixed by the Board. The Board shall meet at least quarterly thereafter but not more than 12 meetings per year thereafter. Special meetings may be called by the chairman or by any 8 members of the Board by giving notice thereof in writing, stating the time, place and purpose of the meeting. Such notice shall be served by special delivery letter deposited in the mail at least 48 hours before any special meeting. Eight members of the Board shall constitute a quorum. The affirmative vote of a majority of all members of the Board shall be necessary for any action taken by the Board.
(Source: P.A. 86-1200.)

Note.
This section was Ill.Rev.Stat., Ch. 23, para. 6707.

325 ILCS 35/8 Staff

Sec. 8. *Staff.* The State Board of Education shall designate employees to act as staff to the Board and shall furnish all professional and clerical assistance necessary for the performance of its powers and duties.
(Source: P.A. 86-1200.)

Note.
This section was Ill.Rev.Stat., Ch. 23, para. 6708.

325 ILCS 35/9 Compensation

Sec. 9. *Compensation.* Members of the Board shall not receive any compensation for service on the Board, but shall be reimbursed for necessary travel and other expenses incurred in the performance of their duties.
(Source: P.A. 86-1200.)

Note.
This section was Ill.Rev.Stat., Ch. 23, para. 6709.

325 ILCS 35/10 Powers and duties

Sec. 10. *Powers and duties.* The Board shall advise the State Superintendent of Education, the Governor and the General Assembly and make recommendations pertaining to but not limited to the following matters:

(a) Existing and proposed programs of services for children who are deaf or hard-of-hearing and have an emotional or behavioral disorder known to all State agencies.

(b) The State program and financial plan for services for children who are deaf or hard-of-hearing and have an emotional or behavioral disorder and the system of priorities to be developed by the State Board of Education.

(c) Standards for services in facilities serving children who are deaf or hard-of-hearing and have an emotional or behavioral disorder.

(d) Services and research activities in the field, including evaluation of services.

(e) Planning for professional training in a State university or college.

(f) The receipt and dispersal of State and federal funds designated for services to children who are deaf or hard-of-hearing and have an emotional or behavioral disorder.

(g) Statewide identification and tracking for this population.
(Source: P.A. 86-1200; 87-1127, § 1; 89-680, § 905.)

Note.
This section was Ill.Rev.Stat., Ch. 23, para. 6710.

Effect of Amendments.
The 1996 amendment by P.A. 89-680, effective January 1, 1997, deleted "hearing impaired/behavior disordered" preceding "children" in subsections (a) and (c); in subsection (a) inserted "who are deaf or hard-of-hearing and have an emotional or behavioral disorder"; in subsection (b) substituted "children who are deaf or hard-of-hearing and have an emotional or behavioral disorder" for "hearing impaired/behavior disordered"; in subsection (c) added at the end "who are deaf or hard-of-hearing and have an emotional or behavioral disorder"; and in subsection (f) substituted "deaf or hard-of-hearing and have an emotional or behavioral disorder" for "hearing impaired/behavior disordered".

325 ILCS 35/11 Reports

Sec. 11. *Reports.* The Board shall make a report of its work annually to the State Superintendent of Education and to the Governor and to each regular session of the General Assembly.

The requirement for reporting to the General Assembly shall be satisfied by filing copies of the report with the Speaker, the Minority Leader and the Clerk of the House of Representatives and the President, the Minority Leader and the Secretary of

the Senate and the Legislative Research Unit, as required by Section 3.1 of the General Assembly Organization Act [25 ILCS 5/3.1] and filing such additional copies with the State Government Report Distribution Center for the General Assembly as is required under paragraph (t) of Section 7 of the State Library Act [15 ILCS 320/7].
(Source: P.A. 86-1200; 87-1127, § 1.)

Note.
This section was Ill.Rev.Stat., Ch. 23, para. 6711.

325 ILCS 35/12 [Effect]

Sec. 12. This Act shall take effect upon becoming law.
(Source: P.A. 86-1200.)

Note.
This section was Ill.Rev.Stat., Ch. 23, para. 6712.

Intergovernmental Missing Child Recovery Act of 1984

325 ILCS 40/1 [Short title]

Sec. 1. This Act shall be known and may be cited as the "Intergovernmental Missing Child Recovery Act of 1984".
(Source: P.A. 83-1354.)

Derivation.
Title: An Act concerning the efforts of law enforcement agencies in locating lost, missing and runaway children, and amending an Act herein named.
Cite: 325 ILCS 40/1 et seq.
Source: P.A. 83-1354.
Date: Approved September 9, 1984.

Note.
This section was Ill.Rev.Stat., Ch. 23, para. 2251.

325 ILCS 40/2 [Definitions]

Sec. 2. As used in this Act: (a) "Department" means the Department of State Police.

(b) "Director" means the Director of the Department of State Police.

(c) "Unit of Local Government" is defined as in Article VII, Section 1 of the Illinois Constitution and includes both home rule units and units which are not home rule units. The term is also defined to include all public school districts subject to the provisions of The School Code [105 ILCS 5/1-1 et seq.].

(d) "Child" means a person under 21 years of age.

(e) A "LEADS terminal" is an interactive computerized communication and processing unit which permits a direct on-line communication with the Department of State Police's central data repository, the Law Enforcement Agencies Data System (LEADS).

(f) A "Primary contact agency" means a law enforcement agency which maintains a LEADS terminal, or has immediate access to one on a 24-hour-per-day, 7-day-per-week basis by written agreement with another law enforcement agency, and is designated by the I SEARCH policy board to be the agency responsible for coordinating the joint efforts between the Department of State Police and the I SEARCH program participants.

(g) "Illinois State Enforcement Agencies to Recover Children Unit" or "I SEARCH Unit" means a combination of units of local government within a contiguous geographical area served by one or more LEADS terminals and established to collectively address the missing and exploited children problem in their respective geographical areas.

(h) "Missing child" means any person under 21 years of age whose whereabouts are unknown to his or her parents or legal guardian.

(i) "Exploitation" means activities and actions which include, but are not limited to, child pornography, child prostitution, child sexual abuse, drug and substance abuse by children, and child suicide.

(j) "Participating agency" means a law enforcement agency that does not receive State funding, but signs an agreement of intergovernmental cooperation with the Department to perform the duties of an I SEARCH Unit.
(Source: P.A. 85-1209.)

Note.
This section was Ill.Rev.Stat., Ch. 23, para. 2252.

325 ILCS 40/3 [I SEARCH unit; powers]

Sec. 3. Each I SEARCH unit shall be established to promote an immediate and effective community response to missing children and may engage in, but shall not be limited to, the following activities:

(a) To establish and conduct programs to educate parents, children and communities in ways to prevent the abduction of children.

(b) To conduct training programs and distribute materials providing guidelines for children when dealing with strangers, casual acquaintances, or non-custodial parents, in order to avoid abduction or kidnapping situations.

(c) To compile, maintain and make available data upon the request of law enforcement agencies and other entities deemed appropriate by the Department to assist enforcement agencies in recovering missing children, including but not limited to data regarding the places of shelter commonly used by runaway children in the geographical area encompassed by the I SEARCH Unit.

(d) To draft and implement plans for the most efficient use of available resources to publicize and conduct searches for missing children.

(e) To establish and maintain contacts with other I SEARCH Units, law enforcement agencies, and the Department in order to increase the probability of locating and returning missing children, and to otherwise assist in the recovery and tracking of missing children.

(f) To coordinate the tracking and recovery of children under the custody or guardianship of the Department of Children and Family Services whose disappearance has been reported and to produce an annual report indicating the number of children under the custody or guardianship of that Department who have been reported missing and the number who have been recovered.

(g) To conduct other activities as may be necessary to achieve the goals established by this Act.

(Source: P.A. 83-1354; 90-27, § 25.)

Note.

This section was Ill.Rev.Stat., Ch. 23, para. 2253.

Effect of Amendments.

The 1997 amendment by P.A. 90-27, effective January 1, 1998, added present subsection (f); and redesignated former subsection (f) as subsection (g).

325 ILCS 40/3.5 Contact with Department of Children and Family Services

Sec. 3.5. *Contact with Department of Children and Family Services.* For each child reported missing and entered into the LEADS network as part of the I SEARCH program, the Department shall, in the form and manner it determines, contact the Department of Children and Family Services to provide it with the name, age, and sex of the child, and the geographic area from which the child was reported missing so that the Department of Children and Family Services can determine if that child had been abandoned within the previous 2 months.

(Source: P.A. 89-213, § 10.)

Effective Date.

This section became effective January 1, 1996 pursuant to Ill. Const. (1970), Art. IV, § 10 and 5 ILCS 75/1.

325 ILCS 40/4 [Funding criteria]

Sec. 4. To help defray the costs of operation, an I SEARCH program is eligible to receive State grants if the program meets the following minimum criteria:

(a) be established and operating pursuant to intergovernmental contracts between 2 or more units of local government written and executed in conformity with the Intergovernmental Cooperation Act [5 ILCS 220/1 et seq.].

(b) designate a primary contact agency.

(c) establish an I SEARCH policy board composed of the chief elected official or his designee from each participating unit of local government, the chief law enforcement officer or his designee from each participating police agency and a representative from each additional participating agency or organization as deemed appropriate by the primary contact agency to oversee the operation of the I SEARCH program and make such reports to the Department as the Department may require. At its discretion, the I SEARCH policy board may appoint public members to serve on the board.

(d) designate a single appropriate elected official or appointed local government finance officer of a participating unit of local government or his designee to act as the financial officer of the I SEARCH Unit for all participating units of local government and to receive funds for the operation of the I SEARCH program.

(e) limit its operations to locating missing children, preventing the running away, abduction and exploitation of children and diminishing the missing children problem.

(f) cooperate with the Department, in order to assure compliance with this Act and to enable the Department to fulfill its duties under this Act, and supply the Department with all information the Department deems necessary.

(g) receive funding of at least 50% of the total operating budget of the I SEARCH Unit from the participating units of local government.

(Source: P.A. 85-1209.)

Note.

This section was Ill.Rev.Stat., Ch. 23, para. 2254.

325 ILCS 40/5 [State grants]

Sec. 5. (a) The Department shall monitor the operations of all I SEARCH Units and determine the programs' eligibility to receive State grants under this Act. From the monies appropriated annually by the General Assembly for this purpose, the Director shall determine and certify to the Comptroller the amount of the grant to be made to each designated I SEARCH Unit. The amount of the State grant which an I SEARCH program may receive hereunder may not exceed 50% of the total operating budget of that I SEARCH Unit.

(b) The Department shall deposit any unexpended State grant funds remaining at the end of each fiscal year, which were originally disseminated to I-SEARCH Units but not expended by those units, into the Missing and Exploited Children Trust Fund.

(Source: P.A. 84-1366.)

Note.

This section was Ill.Rev.Stat., Ch. 23, para. 2255.

Cross References.

As to the distribution of money received by the Department of State Police for the purposes of promoting and conducting activities for the prevention of missing or exploited children, see 30 ILCS 105/6a-5.

325 ILCS 40/6 [Department; powers and duties]

Sec. 6. The Department shall:

(a) Establish and maintain a statewide Law Enforcement Agencies Data System (LEADS) for the purpose of effecting an immediate law enforcement response to reports of missing children. The Department shall implement an automated data exchange system to compile, to maintain and to make available for dissemination to Illinois and out-of-State law enforcement agencies, data which can assist appropriate agencies in recovering missing children.

(b) Establish contacts and exchange information regarding lost, missing or runaway children with nationally recognized "missing person and runaway" service organizations and monitor national research and publicize important developments.

(c) Provide a uniform reporting format for the entry of pertinent information regarding reports of missing children into LEADS.

(d) Develop and implement a policy whereby a statewide or regional alert would be used in situations relating to the disappearances of children, based on criteria and in a format established by the Department. Such a format shall include, but not be limited to, the age and physical description of the missing child and the suspected circumstances of the disappearance.

(e) Notify all law enforcement agencies that reports of missing persons shall be entered as soon as the minimum level of data specified by the Department is available to the reporting agency and that no waiting period for entry of such data exists.

(f) Provide a procedure for prompt confirmation of the receipt and entry of the missing child report into LEADS to the parent or guardian of the missing child.

(g) Compile and retain information regarding missing children in a separate data file, in a manner that allows such information to be used by law enforcement and other agencies deemed appropriate by the Director, for investigative purposes. Such files shall be updated to reflect and include information relating to the disposition of the case.

(h) Compile and maintain an historic data repository relating to missing children in order (1) to develop and improve techniques utilized by law enforcement agencies when responding to reports of missing children and (2) to provide a factual and statistical base for research that would address the problem of missing children.

(i) Create a quality control program to monitor timeliness of entries of missing children reports into LEADS and conduct performance audits of all entering agencies.

(j) Prepare a periodic information bulletin concerning missing children who it determines may be present in this State, compiling such bulletin from information contained in both the National Crime Information Center computer and from reports, alerts and other information entered into LEADS or otherwise compiled and retained by the Department pursuant to this Act. The bulletin shall indicate the name, age, physical description, suspected circumstances of disappearance if that information is available, a photograph if one is available, the name of the law enforcement agency investigating the case, and such other information as the Director considers appropriate concerning each missing child who the Department determines may be present in this State. The Department shall send a copy of each periodic information bulletin to the State Board of Education for its use in accordance with Section 2-3.48 of the School Code [105 ILCS 5/2-3.48]. The Department shall provide a copy of the bulletin, upon request, to law enforcement agencies of this or any other state or of the federal government, and may provide a copy of the bulletin, upon request, to other persons or entities, if deemed appropriate by the Director, and may establish limitations on its use and a reasonable fee for so providing the same, except that no fee shall be charged for providing the periodic information bulletin to the State Board of Education, appropriate units of local government, State agencies, or law enforcement agencies of this or any other state or of the federal government.

(k) Provide for the entry into LEADS of the names and addresses of sex offenders as defined in the Sex Offender Registration Act [730 ILCS 150/1 et seq.] who are required to register under that Act. The information shall be immediately accessible to law enforcement agencies and peace officers of this State or any other state or of the federal government. Similar information may be requested from any other state or of the federal government for purposes of this Act.

(Source: P.A. 84-171; 84-234; 87-1065, § 1; 88-76, § 5; 89-8, § 20-10.)

Note.

This section was Ill.Rev.Stat., Ch. 23, para. 2256.

Effect of Amendments.

The 1995 amendment by P.A. 89-8, effective January 1, 1996, in subsection (k), in the first sentence, deleted "habitual child" preceding "sex offenders" and deleted "Habitual Child" preceding "Sex Offender".

325 ILCS 40/7 [Law enforcement agencies; duties]

Sec. 7. (a) All law enforcement agencies and policing bodies of this State shall, upon receipt of a report of a missing person, enter that report into LEADS as soon as the minimum level of data specified pursuant to subsection (e) of Section 6 [325 ILCS 40/6] is available and shall furnish the Department, in the form and detail the Department requires, (1) reports of cases of lost, missing or runaway children as they arise and the disposition of such cases, (2) information relating to sex crimes which occurred in their respective jurisdictions and which they investigated, and (3) the names and addresses of sex offenders required to register in their respective jurisdictions under the Sex Offender Registration Act [730 ILCS 150/1 et seq.]. Such information shall be submitted on a regular basis, as deemed necessary by the Department, and shall be kept in a central automated data repository for the purpose of establishing profiles of sex offenders and victims and to assist all law enforcement agencies in the identification and apprehension of sex offenders.

(b) In addition to entering the report of a missing child into LEADS as prescribed by subsection (a), all law enforcement agencies shall, upon receipt of a report of a missing child:

(1) Immediately make a radio dispatch to officers on duty at the time of receipt of the report. The dispatch shall contain the name and approximate age of the missing child and any other pertinent information available at that time. In the event that the law enforcement agency receiving the report of the missing child does not operate a radio dispatch system, a geographically appropriate radio dispatch system shall be used, such as the Illinois State Police Emergency Radio Network or a similar multi-agency law enforcement radio communication system serving the area of the reporting agency.

In addition, in the event that a missing child is not recovered during the work shift in which the radio dispatch was made, the law enforcement agency receiving the report of the missing child shall disseminate the information relating to the missing child to all sworn personnel employed by the agency who work or are assigned to other shifts or time periods.

(2) Immediately contact I-SEARCH program personnel designated by the Department, by a means and in a manner and form prescribed by the Department, informing the personnel of the report of the missing child.

(Source: P.A. 84-1366; 87-1065, § 1; 89-8, § 20-10.)

Note.

This section was Ill.Rev.Stat., Ch. 23, para. 2257.

Cross References.

As to different purposes for the accessibility of an abused or neglected child's records, under the Abused and Neglected Child Reporting Act, see 325 ILCS 5/11.1.

Effect of Amendments.

The 1995 amendment by P.A. 89-8, effective January 1, 1996, in subsection (a), in the first sentence, deleted "habitual child" preceding "sex offenders" and deleted "Habitual Child" preceding "Sex Offender".

325 ILCS 40/7.1 [Custody judgments]

Sec. 7.1. In addition to any requirement of Section 601 or 611 of the Illinois Marriage and Dissolution of Marriage Act [75 ILCS 5/601 or 75 ILCS 5/611] or applicable provisions of the Uniform Child-Custody Jurisdiction and Enforcement Act [750 ILCS 36/101 et seq.] regarding a custody proceeding of an out-of-state party, every court in this State, prior to granting or modifying a custody judgment, shall inquire with LEADS and the National Crime Information Center to ascertain whether the child or children in question have been reported missing or have been involved in or are the victims of a parental or noncustodial abduction. Such inquiry may be conducted with any law enforcement agency in this State that maintains a LEADS terminal or has immediate access to one on a 24-hour-per-day, 7-day-per-week basis through a written agreement with another law enforcement agency.

(Source: P.A. 84-171; 93-108, § 402.2.)

Note.

This section was Ill.Rev.Stat., Ch. 23, para. 2257.1.

Effect of Amendments.

The 2003 amendment by P.A. 93-108, effective January 1, 2004, substituted "applicable provisions of the Uniform Child-Custody Jurisdiction and Enforcement Act" for "Section 9, 15 or 17 of the Uniform Child Custody Jurisdiction Act" in the first sentence.

325 ILCS 40/8 [Duties of Director]

Sec. 8. The Director shall report by December 31 of each year to the Governor and the General Assembly on the operations of the statewide I SEARCH program including a breakdown of the appropriation for the previous fiscal year indicating the amount of the State grant each I SEARCH unit received.

(Source: P.A. 85-214.)

Note.

This section was Ill.Rev.Stat., Ch. 23, para. 2258.

MINOR IDENTIFICATION AND PROTECTION ACT

325 ILCS 45/1 [Short title]

Sec. 1. This Act shall be known and may be cited as the Minor Identification and Protection Act.

(Source: P.A. 83-508.)

Derivation.

Title: An Act in relation to the fingerprinting of minors for identification purposes.

Cite: 325 ILCS 45/1 et seq.

Source: P.A. 83-508.

Date: Approved September 17, 1983.

Note.

This section was Ill.Rev.Stat., Ch. 23, para. 2451.

325 ILCS 45/2 [Definitions]

Sec. 2. For the purposes of this Act, unless the context otherwise requires, the terms used herein shall have the following meanings ascribed to them:

(a) "Fingerprints" mean the impressions of the lines upon the fingertips taken with ink and placed upon a paper or plastic card for the purpose of identification.

(b) "Local law enforcement agency" means the office of the county sheriff or a department of a municipality authorized by law or ordinance with the duties to maintain public order, make arrests, and enforce the criminal laws of this State or municipal ordinances;

(c) "Minor" means a person under 18 years of age; and

(d) "Parent" means the natural or adoptive parent who has legal custody of the minor.

(Source: P.A. 83-508.)

Note.

This section was Ill.Rev.Stat., Ch. 23, para. 2452.

325 ILCS 45/3 [Fingerprint identification cards]

Sec. 3. (a) Upon request of a parent or legal guardian of a minor and the presentation of the minor at a local law enforcement agency, the local law enforcement agency shall take a complete set of fingerprints of the minor and issue a fingerprint identification card to the parent or guardian which shall contain the fingerprints of such minor.

(b) The local law enforcement agency taking the fingerprints and issuing a fingerprint identification card may charge the requesting parent or guardian a reasonable fee sufficient to cover the costs incurred by that agency in complying with the provisions of this Act.

(Source: P.A. 83-508.)

Note.

This section was Ill.Rev.Stat., Ch. 23, para. 2453.

Cross References.

For compliance of corporate authorities of municipalities for minor identification, under the Municipal Code, see 65 ILCS 5/11-1-10.

MISSING CHILDREN RECORDS ACT

325 ILCS 50/0.01 Short title

Sec. 0.01. *Short title.* This Act may be cited as the Missing Children Records Act.

(Source: P.A. 86-1324.)

Derivation.

Title: An Act in relation to children.
Cite: 325 ILCS 50/0.01 et seq.
Source: P.A. 84-1430.
Date: Approved September 25, 1986.

Note.

This section was Ill.Rev.Stat., Ch. 23, para. 2280.

325 ILCS 50/1 Definitions

Sec. 1. *Definitions.* As used in this Act, unless the context requires otherwise:

(a) "Custodian" means the State Registrar of Vital Records, local registrars of vital records appointed by the State Registrar and county clerks.

(b) "Department" means the Illinois Department of State Police.

(c) "Missing person" means a person 17 years old or younger reported to any law enforcement authority as abducted, lost or a runaway.

(d) "Registrar" means the State Registrar of Vital Records.

(Source: P.A. 84-1430.)

Note.

This section was Ill.Rev.Stat., Ch. 23, para. 2281.

325 ILCS 50/2 Department duties

Sec. 2. *Department duties.* Upon entry of a report of a missing person born in Illinois into the Law Enforcement Agencies Data System (LEADS) established pursuant to the Intergovernmental Missing Child Recovery Act of 1984 [325 ILCS 40/1 et seq.], the Department shall notify the Registrar within 5 business days of the disappearance and shall provide the Registrar with information concerning the identity of the missing person. Upon entry of a report of a missing person born in a state other than Illinois into the Law Enforcement Agencies Data System (LEADS), the Department shall notify the registrar, or other state agency responsible for vital records, in that state within 5 business days of the disappearance and shall provide such registrar or other agency with information concerning the identity of the missing person.

If the Department has reason to believe that a missing person has been enrolled in a specific Illinois elementary or secondary school, it shall notify the last such known school as to the disappearance at which time the school shall flag the missing child's record pursuant to Section 5 [325 ILCS 50/5].

Upon learning of the recovery of a missing person, the Department shall so notify the Registrar and any school previously informed of the person's disappearance.

The Department shall by rule determine the manner and form of notices and information required by this Act.

(Source: P.A. 84-1430.)

Note.

This section was Ill.Rev.Stat., Ch. 23, para. 2282.

325 ILCS 50/3 Registrar duties

Sec. 3. *Registrar duties.* Upon notification by the Department that a person born in this State is missing, the Registrar shall flag the birth certificate record of that person in such a manner that whenever a copy of the birth certificate or information regarding the birth record is requested, the Registrar shall be alerted to the fact that the certificate is that of a missing person. The Registrar shall also notify the appropriate municipality or county custodians to likewise flag their records. Upon notification by the Department that the missing person has been recovered, the Registrar shall remove the flag from the person's birth certificate record and shall notify any other previously notified municipality or county custodian to remove the flag from his record.

(Source: P.A. 84-1430.)

Note.
This section was Ill.Rev.Stat., Ch. 23, para. 2283.

325 ILCS 50/4 Custodian duties

Sec. 4. *Custodian duties.* (a) In response to any inquiry, a custodian shall not provide a copy of a birth certificate or information concerning the birth record of any person whose record is flagged pursuant to Section 3 [325 ILCS 50/3] except as approved by the Department.

(b) When a copy of the birth certificate of a person whose record has been flagged is requested in person, the custodian's personnel accepting the request shall immediately notify his supervisor. The custodian's personnel shall then follow procedures prescribed by the Department to clearly ascertain the identity of the person making the request, his address and his physical description. Such procedures shall include requiring the person making the request to complete a standardized information form and to present at least one form of photo identification. The custodian's personnel shall inform the person making the request that a copy of the certificate shall be mailed to him, and, upon the latter's departure from the custodian's office, his supervisor shall immediately notify the Department or the local law enforcement authority as to the request and the information obtained pursuant to this subsection. The custodian shall retain the form completed by the person making the request.

(c) When a copy of the birth certificate of a person whose record has been flagged is requested in writing, the custodian's personnel receiving the request shall immediately notify his supervisor. The supervisor shall immediately notify the Department or local law enforcement authority as to the request and shall provide a copy of the written request. The custodian shall retain the original written request.
(Source: P.A. 84-1430.)

Note.
This section was Ill.Rev.Stat., Ch. 23, para. 2284.

325 ILCS 50/5 School duties

Sec. 5. *School duties.* (a) Upon notification by the Department of a person's disappearance, a school in which the person is currently or was previously enrolled shall flag the record of that person in such a manner that whenever a copy of or information regarding the record is requested, the school shall be alerted to the fact that the record is that of a missing person. The school shall immediately report to the Department any request concerning flagged records or knowledge as to the whereabouts of any missing person. Upon notification by the Department that the missing person has been recovered, the school shall remove the flag from the person's record.

(b)(1) Upon enrollment of a student for the first time in a particular elementary or secondary school, that school shall notify in writing the person enrolling the student that within 30 days he must provide either (i) a certified copy of the student's birth certificate or (ii) other reliable proof, as determined by the Department, of the student's identity and age and an affidavit explaining the inability to produce a copy of the birth certificate. Other reliable proof of the student's identity and age shall include a passport, visa or other governmental documentation of the child's identity.

(2) Upon the failure of a person enrolling a student to comply with subsection (b)(1), the school shall immediately notify the Department or local law enforcement agency of such failure, and shall notify the person enrolling the student in writing that he has 10 additional days to comply.

(3) The school shall immediately report to the Department any affidavit received pursuant to this subsection which appears inaccurate or suspicious in form or content.

(c) Within 14 days after enrolling a transfer student, the elementary or secondary school shall request directly from the student's previous school a certified copy of his record. The requesting school shall exercise due diligence in obtaining the copy of the record requested. Any elementary or secondary school requested to forward a copy of a transferring student's record to the new school shall comply within 10 days of receipt of the request unless the record has been flagged pursuant to subsection (a), in which case the copy shall not be forwarded and the requested school shall notify the Department or local law enforcement authority of the request.
(Source: P.A. 84-1430.)

Note.
This section was Ill.Rev.Stat., Ch. 23, para. 2285.

Illinois Administrative Code.
See 23 Illinois Administrative Code, § 375.75.

MISSING CHILDREN REGISTRATION LAW

325 ILCS 55/0.01 Short title

Sec. 0.01. *Short title.* This Article may be cited as the Missing Children Registration Law.
(Source: P.A. 86-1475.)

Derivation.
Title: An Act to require the registration of sex offenders and in relation to the confidentiality of information concerning minor victims of sex offenses and concerning missing children.
Cite: 325 ILCS 55/0.01 et seq.
Source: P.A. 84-1279. Title amended by P.A. 87-1064; P.A. 89-8, eff. 1-1-96.
Date: Approved August 15, 1986.

Note.
This section was Ill.Rev.Stat., Ch. 23, para. 2270.

325 ILCS 55/1 Definitions

Sec. 1. *Definitions.* As used in this Article, unless the context requires otherwise:

(a) "Custodian" means the State Registrar of Vital Records, local registrars of vital records appointed by the State Registrar and county clerks.

(b) "Department" means the Illinois Department of State Police.

(c) "Missing child" means a person under the age of 18 years, reported to any law enforcement authority as abducted, lost or a runaway, whose identity is entered into the Law Enforcement Agencies Data System.

(d) "Registrar" means the State Registrar of Vital Records.

(Source: P.A. 84-1279.)

Note.
This section was Ill.Rev.Stat., Ch. 23, para. 2271.

325 ILCS 55/2 Department duties

Sec. 2. *Department duties.* Upon entry of a report of a missing child born in Illinois into the Law Enforcement Agencies Data System, the Department shall notify the Registrar of the disappearance and shall provide the Registrar with information concerning the identity of the missing child.

If the Department has reason to believe that a missing child may be enrolled in an Illinois elementary or secondary school, it shall notify the last such known school as to the disappearance, at which time the school shall flag the missing child's record pursuant to Section 5 [325 ILCS 55/5].

Upon learning of the recovery of a missing child, the Department shall so notify the Registrar.

The Department shall by rule determine the manner and form of notices and information required by this Article.

(Source: P.A. 84-1279.)

Note.
This section was Ill.Rev.Stat., Ch. 23, para. 2272.

325 ILCS 55/3 Registrar duties

Sec. 3. *Registrar duties.* Upon notification by the Department that a person under the age of 18 years who was born in this State is missing, the Registrar shall flag the birth certificate record of that person in such a manner that whenever a copy of the birth certificate or information regarding the birth record is requested, the Registrar shall be alerted to the fact that the certificate is that of a missing child. The Registrar shall also notify the appropriate city or county custodian to likewise flag his records. Upon notification by the Department that the missing child has been recovered, the Registrar shall remove the flag from the person's birth certificate record and shall notify any other previously notified city or county custodian to remove the flag from his record.

(Source: P.A. 84-1279.)

Note.
This section was Ill.Rev.Stat., Ch. 23, para. 2273.

325 ILCS 55/4 Custodian duties

Sec. 4. *Custodian duties.* (a) In response to any inquiry, a custodian shall not provide a copy of a birth certificate or information concerning the birth record of any person whose record is flagged pursuant to Section 3 [325 ILCS 55/3] except as approved by the Department.

(b) When a copy of the birth certificate of a person whose record has been flagged is requested in person, the custodian's personnel accepting the request shall immediately notify his supervisor. The person making the request shall complete a form as prescribed by the Department, which may include the name, address, telephone number and social security number of the person making the request, his or her relationship to the missing child and the name, address and birth date of the missing child. The driver's license of the person making the request, if available, shall be photocopied and returned to him. He shall be informed that a copy of the certificate shall be mailed to him. The custodian's personnel shall note the physical description of the person making the request, and, upon the latter's departure from the custodian's office, his supervisor shall immediately notify the local law enforcement authority as to the request and the information obtained pursuant to this subsection. The custodian shall retain the form completed by the person making the request.

(c) When a copy of the birth certificate of a person whose record has been flagged is requested in writing, the custodian's personnel receiving the request shall immediately notify his supervisor. The supervisor shall immediately notify the local law enforcement authority as to the request and shall provide a copy of the written request. The custodian shall retain the original written request.

(Source: P.A. 84-1279.)

Note.
This section was Ill.Rev.Stat., Ch. 23, para. 2274.

325 ILCS 55/5 School duties

Sec. 5. *School duties.* (a) Upon notification by the Department of a child's disappearance, a school in which the child is currently or was previously enrolled shall flag the record of that child in such a manner that whenever a copy of or information regarding the record is requested, the school shall be alerted to the fact that the record is that of a missing child. The school shall immediately report to the local law enforcement authority any request concerning flagged records or knowledge as to the whereabouts of any missing child. Upon notification by the Department that the missing child has been recovered, the school shall remove the flag from the person's record.

(b) Upon enrollment of a student for the first time in a particular elementary or secondary school, that school shall notify in writing the person enrolling the student that within 30 days he must provide either (1) a certified copy of the student's birth certificate or (2) other reliable proof, as determined by the Department, of the student's identity and age, and an affidavit explaining the inability to produce a copy of the birth certificate.

Upon the failure of a person enrolling a student to comply with this subsection, the school shall immediately notify the local law enforcement agency and shall also notify the person enrolling the student in writing that, unless he complies within 10 days, the case shall be referred to the local law enforcement authority for investigation. If compliance is not obtained within that 10 day period, the school shall so refer the case.

The school shall immediately report to the local law enforcement authority any affidavit received pursuant to this subsection which appears inaccurate or suspicious in form or content.

(c) Within 14 days after enrolling a transfer student, the elementary or secondary school shall request directly from the student's previous school a certified copy of his record. The requesting school shall exercise due diligence in obtaining the copy of the record requested. Any elementary or secondary school requested to forward a copy of a transferring student's record to the new school shall comply within 10 days of receipt of such request unless the record has been flagged pursuant to subsection (a), in which case the copy shall not be forwarded and the requested school shall notify the local law enforcement authority of the request.
(Source: P.A. 84-1279.)

Note.
This section was Ill.Rev.Stat., Ch. 23, para. 2275.

Illinois Administrative Code.
See 23 Illinois Administrative Code, § 375.75.

325 ILCS 55/6 Local law enforcement duties

Sec. 6. *Local law enforcement duties.* Any local law enforcement authority notified pursuant to this Article of the request for the birth certificate or school record of or other information concerning a missing child shall immediately notify the Department of such request and shall investigate the request.
(Source: P.A. 84-1279.)

Note.
This section was Ill.Rev.Stat., Ch. 23, para. 2276.

325 ILCS 55/7 Home rule

Sec. 7. *Home rule.* This Article shall constitute the exercise of the State's exclusive jurisdiction pursuant to subsection (h) of Section 6 of Article VII of the Illinois Constitution and shall preempt the jurisdiction of any home rule unit.
(Source: P.A. 84-1279.)

Note.
This section was Ill.Rev.Stat., Ch. 23, para. 2277.

SURGICAL INSTITUTE FOR CHILDREN ACT

325 ILCS 60/0.01 Short title

Sec. 0.01. *Short title.* This Act may be cited as the Surgical Institute for Children Act.
(Source: P.A. 86-1324.)

Derivation.
Title: An Act to establish a surgical institution for children.
Cite: 325 ILCS 60/0.01 et seq.
Source: L. 1911, p. 129.
Date: Approved June 6, 1911.

Note.
This section was Ill.Rev.Stat., Ch. 23, para. 2200.

325 ILCS 60/1 [Establishment]

Sec. 1. There is hereby authorized to be established a surgical institute in and for the State of Illinois for the surgical treatment of children under the age of sixteen years, suffering from physical deformities or injuries of a nature which will likely yield to surgical skill and treatment and which unless so treated will probably make such children, in whole or in part, in after life, public charges.
(Source: Laws 1919, p. 246.)

Note.
This section was Ill.Rev.Stat., Ch. 23, para. 2201.

325 ILCS 60/2 [Name]

Sec. 2. Said institute shall be known as the Illinois Surgical Institute for Children; and by such name shall be and constitute a corporation, under the laws of the State of Illinois.
(Source: Laws 1911, p. 129.)

Note.
This section was Ill.Rev.Stat., Ch. 23, para. 2202.

325 ILCS 60/3 [Purpose and object]

Sec. 3. The purpose and object of said institute shall be to receive, treat and nurse such children whose parents or guardians may be financially unable to provide surgical treatment, as may be physically deformed, or suffering from injuries requiring surgical treatment, to the end that their physical disabilities may be removed, and that they may be thereby made able to become self-sustaining, instead of being or becoming, at some future time, public charges.
(Source: Laws 1911, p. 129.)

Note.
This section was Ill.Rev.Stat., Ch. 23, para. 2203.

325 ILCS 60/4 [Management and control]

Sec. 4. The management and control of said institution shall be vested in the Board of Trustees of the University of Illinois.
(Source: Laws 1951, p. 999.)

Note.
This section was Ill.Rev.Stat., Ch. 23, para. 2204.

325 ILCS 60/5 [Admittance procedure]

Sec. 5. Any child under the age of 16 years whose parents, or natural guardian, may be unable to furnish proper surgical treatment and who may be in need of the same, may be admitted to such institute, upon an order to that effect made by the circuit judge residing in the county in which the child may have had a legal residence for one year last past. The county treasurer of the county in which the child may have so resided shall, upon the order of the judge, furnish such child with transportation from the place where he may so reside to the place of such institution and return. The order admitting such child shall, when made, be filed with the superintendent of the institute, and the child shall be admitted thereto in the regular order of filing as soon thereafter as the institute can provide room, care and attendance therefor. The child, if deemed feasible, shall be treated, nursed in the institute, until a recovery is effected, or it becomes apparent that further treatment will be of no avail, whereupon he shall be discharged and returned to his former place of residence.
(Source: P.A. 77-1275.)

Note.
This section was Ill.Rev.Stat., Ch. 23, para. 2205.

325 ILCS 60/6 [Location]

Sec. 6. Said institution shall be located in that portion of Illinois which may be deemed most advantageous.
(Source: Laws 1911, p. 129.)

Note.
This section was Ill.Rev.Stat., Ch. 23, para. 2206.

325 ILCS 60/8 [General superintendent]

Sec. 8. The Board of Trustees of the University of Illinois shall appoint a skilled and capable surgeon, general superintendent, and may remove him for cause stated, first having given him a copy of the charges against him, and reasonable notice of the time and place when such charges will be heard, and an opportunity to defend himself.
(Source: Laws 1951, p. 999.)

Note.
This section was Ill.Rev.Stat., Ch. 23, para. 2207.

325 ILCS 60/11 [Gifts, donations and legacies]

Sec. 11. The Board of Trustees of the University of Illinois may, from time to time, accept, hold and use for the benefit of the institution, or the inmates thereof, any gift, donation or legacy of money, or real or personal property, and may agree to and perform any condition of such gift, donation or legacy not contrary to law.
(Source: P.A. 83-388.)

Note.
This section was Ill.Rev.Stat., Ch. 23, para. 2208.

325 ILCS 60/12 [Rules and regulations]

Sec. 12. The Board of Trustees of the University of Illinois shall establish all needful rules and regulations for the management of said institution and the inmates thereof.
(Source: Laws 1951, p. 999.)

Note.
This section was Ill.Rev.Stat., Ch. 23, para. 2209.

CHAPTER 410
PUBLIC HEALTH

HEALTH INFORMATION

MARRIAGE, DISSOLUTION, AND INVALIDITY RECORDS ACT

410 ILCS 530/0.01 Short title
410 ILCS 530/1 [Record-keeping by Department of Public Health]
410 ILCS 530/2 [Microfilm; electronic data]
410 ILCS 530/3 [Search of records; certified copies; use of files for research]
410 ILCS 530/3.1 [Administrative procedure]

HEALTH INFORMATION

MARRIAGE, DISSOLUTION, AND INVALIDITY RECORDS ACT

410 ILCS 530/0.01 Short title

Sec. 0.01. *Short title.* This Act may be cited as the Marriage, Dissolution, and Invalidity Records Act.
(Source: P.A. 86-1324.)

Derivation.
Title: An Act to provide for the registration of marriages, dissolutions of marriages and declarations of invalidity of marriages and making an appropriation therefor.
Cite: 410 ILCS 530/0.01 et seq.
Source: P.A. 81-230.
Date: Approved August 21, 1961.

Note.
This section was Ill.Rev.Stat., Ch. 40, para. 900.

410 ILCS 530/1 [Record-keeping by Department of Public Health]

Sec. 1. The Department of Public Health has charge of the registration of marriages, dissolutions of marriages and declarations of invalidity of marriages in the State. The Department has the authority and duty to

1. Install and maintain a state-wide system of registering, indexing, and preserving records of marriage, dissolution of marriage and declaration of invalidity of marriage;
2. Prescribe and furnish forms for collecting, transcribing, compiling, and preserving the records and statistics of marriage, dissolution of marriage and declaration of invalidity of marriage;
3. Make and publish a statistical report of the marriages, dissolutions of marriages and declarations of invalidity of marriages in the State at least annually.

Forms relating to dissolution of marriage shall, among other things, show the age of the individuals at the time of the marriage and at the time of the dissolution of marriage.

Information required to be filed under this Act relates only to marriages, dissolutions of marriages or declarations of invalidity of marriages which occur on or after January 1, 1962.
(Source: P.A. 81-230.)

Note.
This section was Ill.Rev.Stat., Ch. 40, para. 901.

410 ILCS 530/2 [Microfilm; electronic data]

Sec. 2. The Department may cause the records of marriage, dissolution of marriage and declaration of invalidity of marriage established under this Act to be reproduced on microfilm for permanent retention. Such microfilm shall comply with the minimum standards of quality approved for permanent photographic records by the National Bureau of Standards and the device used to reproduce such records on such film shall be one which accurately reproduces the original thereof in all its details.

Such microfilm or a computer print-out copy thereof, as provided herein shall be deemed to be an original record for all purposes, including introduction in evidence in all courts or administrative agencies. A transcript, exemplification, or certified copy thereof, shall, for all purposes recited herein, be deemed to be a transcript, exemplification, or certified copy of the original.

If the Department has records of marriage, divorce and annulment of marriage on computer tape, certified computer print-outs of such records shall have the same legal effect as certified copies of such documents would have for all purposes.

Whenever such microfilm has been properly and permanently filed for use and safekeeping, the Department may cause the original records from which the microfilm reproduction was made to be destroyed.

The Department is authorized to furnish a copy of the microfilm or computer print-out of the records relating to marriages, dissolutions of marriages and declarations of invalidity of marriages in a particular county to the Clerk of any court of that county, provided that this is done without cost to the State.

The Department shall cause its records of marriage, dissolution of marriage and declaration of invalidity of marriage to be permanently preserved and safeguarded in its offices at Springfield. The Secretary of State shall provide suitable quarters for the administration and the permanent and safe preservation of all records returned to the Department under this Act.
(Source: P.A. 81-0230; 81-0652; 81-1509.)

Note.
This section was Ill.Rev.Stat., Ch. 40, para. 902.

410 ILCS 530/3 [Search of records; certified copies; use of files for research]

Sec. 3. The Department shall search its files of records of marriage, dissolution of marriage or declaration of invalidity of marriage upon receipt of a written request and a fee of $5, and, if the record is found, shall verify the fact of marriage, dissolution of marriage or declaration of invalidity of marriage in writing to the applicant, and shall notify the applicant of the place where the original record is found, and that a certified copy thereof may be obtained only from such office. The Department shall not furnish a certified copy of the records filed with it under this Act except upon order of a court or upon the request of the clerk of any court in this State, in which event the Department shall furnish such certified copy without charge.

Whenever a certified copy is obtainable under this Section a certified computer print-out of such record shall have the same effect as a certified copy of such document.

The Department may authorize the use of the records filed under this Act and the information therein contained for any bona fide research purpose in the public interest. The Department is authorized to furnish information from, or transcripts of, its records to the United States Government for national statistics of marriage, dissolution of marriage and declaration of invalidity of marriage, provided that such is done without cost to the State.
(Source: P.A. 83-100.)

Note.
This section was Ill.Rev.Stat., Ch. 40, para. 903.

410 ILCS 530/3.1 [Administrative procedure]

Sec. 3.1. The provisions of the Illinois Administrative Procedure Act [5 ILCS 100/1-1 et seq.] are hereby expressly adopted and shall apply to all administrative rules and procedures of the Department of Public Health under this Act, except that Section 5-35 of the Illinois Administrative Procedure Act [5 ILCS 100/5-35] relating to procedures for rule-making does not apply to the adoption of any rule required by federal law in connection with which the Department is precluded by law from exercising any discretion.
(Source: P.A. 79-1347; 88-45, § 3-104.)

Note.
This section was Ill.Rev.Stat., Ch. 40, para. 904.

CHAPTER 720
CRIMINAL OFFENSES

CRIMINAL CODE

CRIMINAL CODE OF 1961

TITLE III.

SPECIFIC OFFENSES

Part B.

Offenses Directed Against the Person

Article 10.

Kidnapping and Related Offenses

720 ILCS 5/10-1 Kidnapping
720 ILCS 5/10-2 Aggravated kidnaping
720 ILCS 5/10-3 Unlawful restraint
720 ILCS 5/10-3.1 Aggravated Unlawful Restraint
720 ILCS 5/10-4 Forcible Detention
720 ILCS 5/10-5 Child Abduction
720 ILCS 5/10-5.5 Unlawful visitation interference
720 ILCS 5/10-6 Harboring a runaway
720 ILCS 5/10-7 Aiding and abetting child abduction
720 ILCS 5/10-8 Unlawful sale of a public conveyance travel ticket to a minor

Article 12.

Bodily Harm

720 ILCS 5/12-3.2 Domestic Battery
720 ILCS 5/12-3.3 Aggravated domestic battery
720 ILCS 5/12-4.10 (As enacted by P.A. 93-111) Endangering the life and health of an emergency service provider
720 ILCS 5/12-4.10 (As enacted by P.A. 93-340) Drug related child endangerment
720 ILCS 5/12-4.11 Aggravated drug related child endangerment

OFFENSES AGAINST PERSONS

NEGLECTED CHILDREN OFFENSE ACT

720 ILCS 130/0.01 Short title
720 ILCS 130/1 [Dependent and neglected child defined]
720 ILCS 130/1a [Delinquent child defined]
720 ILCS 130/2 [Contributing to dependency and neglect of children]
720 ILCS 130/2a [Contributing to the delinquency of children; penalty]
720 ILCS 130/3 [Testimony by spouse]

WRONGS TO CHILDREN ACT

720 ILCS 150/0.01 Short title
720 ILCS 150/1 [Using or employing a child for injurious, dangerous or immoral purposes prohibited]
720 ILCS 150/2 [Taking or employment of a child prohibited]
720 ILCS 150/3 [Placing a child in the custody of the court]
720 ILCS 150/3.1 [Single parents of children under 6; employment]
720 ILCS 150/4 [Repealed]
720 ILCS 150/4.1 [Abandonment of school bus by driver]
720 ILCS 150/5 [Sentence]
720 ILCS 150/5.1 Permitting sexual abuse of a child

OFFENSES AGAINST THE PUBLIC

ILLINOIS ABORTION LAW OF 1975

720 ILCS 510/10 [Reports on abortions]
720 ILCS 510/10.1 [Report of complications from abortion]
720 ILCS 510/11 [Penalty for violations of Law]
720 ILCS 510/11.1 [Referral fee prohibited]
720 ILCS 510/12 [Analysis of tissue removed]
720 ILCS 510/12.1 [Use of tissue from fetus or dead infant not obtained from abortion]
720 ILCS 510/13 [Refusal to participate in abortion]
720 ILCS 510/14 [Severability; regulations]
720 ILCS 510/15 [Short title]

ILLINOIS ABORTION PARENTAL CONSENT ACT OF 1977

720 ILCS 515/1 through 720 ILCS 515/5 [Repealed]

PARENTAL NOTICE OF ABORTION ACT OF 1983

720 ILCS 520/1 through 720 ILCS 520/10 [Repealed]

ADOPTION COMPENSATION PROHIBITION ACT

720 ILCS 525/0.01 Short title
720 ILCS 525/1 [Receipt of compensation for placing child prohibited]
720 ILCS 525/2 [Payment of compensation prohibited]
720 ILCS 525/3 [Placing out defined]
720 ILCS 525/4 [Compensation of licensed child welfare agency permitted; medical expenses permitted]
720 ILCS 525/4.1 Payment of certain expenses
720 ILCS 525/5 [Penalty]

CHILD CURFEW ACT

720 ILCS 555/0.01 Short title
720 ILCS 555/1 Curfew
720 ILCS 555/2 [More restrictive ordinances permitted]

CRIMINAL CODE

CRIMINAL CODE OF 1961

TITLE III.

SPECIFIC OFFENSES

Part B.

Offenses Directed Against the Person

Article 10.

Kidnapping and Related Offenses

720 ILCS 5/10-1 Kidnapping

Sec. 10-1. *Kidnapping.* (a) Kidnapping occurs when a person knowingly:

(1) And secretly confines another against his will, or

(2) By force or threat of imminent force carries another from one place to another with intent secretly to confine him against his will, or

(3) By deceit or enticement induces another to go from one place to another with intent secretly to confine him against his will.

(b) Confinement of a child under the age of 13 years is against his will within the meaning of this Section if such confinement is without the consent of his parent or legal guardian.

(c) Sentence. Kidnapping is a Class 2 felony.
(Source: P.A. 79-765.)

Note.
This section was Ill.Rev.Stat., Ch. 38, para. 10-1.

Cross References.
For provision regarding motions for continuance, see 725 ILCS 5/114-4.

Illinois Administrative Code.
See 59 Illinois Administrative Code, § 119.261, 77 Illinois Administrative Code, §§ 210.2250, 260.1750, 270.2250, 518.1610, 220.2800, 115.321, 250.435, 245.72, 350.681, 295.3040, 225.1050.

CASE NOTES

ANALYSIS

Constitutionality
—Sentencing
In General
Admonition
—Insufficient
Against Victim's Will
—Physical Evidence
Age
Application and Construction
Armed Violence
—Distinguished
Asportation
—Carry
—Duration
—Not Shown
Confinement
—In General
—Automobile
—Evidence Held Sufficient
—Not Incidental
Discretion of Prosecutor
Elements of Offense
—Against Victim's Will
—Asportation
—Assault
—Four Prong Test
—Length of Abduction
—Ransom Not Element
—Secret Confinement
—Significant Danger
Evidence
—Circumstantial
—Jury Question
—Photographic Display
—Photographs
—Question of Fact
Evidence Held Insufficient
Evidence Held Sufficient
Extradition Proceedings
Guardian
Identification
—Evidence Held Sufficient
Illustrative Cases
Inconsistent Verdicts
Indictment
—Conspiracy
—Held Sufficient
Lesser Included Offense
—Aggravated Kidnapping
—Unlawful Restraint
Mental State
—Intoxication
—Knowledge
Merger
—Armed Robbery
Methods of Commission
Parents
—Abductions
—Biological Father
—Parental Consent
Ransom
—In General
Secret Confinement
—Automobile
—Evidence Held Sufficient
—How Shown
—Not Shown
—Proof
—Shown
Sentencing
—Proper
—Set Aside
—Validity
Sexual Assault
—Distinguished
—Separate Offense
Single Course of Action
—In General
—Armed Violence
—Not Shown
Testimony
—Right to Confrontation
Unlawful Restraint
—Continuous Control
—Distinguished

Constitutionality

—Sentencing
Although the aggravated kidnaping statute provided for a 15-year enhancement in the sentence imposed where that crime involved a defendant armed with a firearm, the 15-year enhancement could not constitutionally be imposed where defendant was also convicted of armed violence predicated on the offense of kidnaping while carrying a category I weapon, such as a handgun, because imposition of the 15-year enhancement in that situation violated the proportionate penalties clause of the Illinois Constitution; the reason was that the enhancement allowed for the sentencing range for aggravated kidnaping to be 21 to 45 years in prison, while the armed violence with a category I weapon was 15 to 30 years, even though the statutes required the same elements for conviction. People v. Baker, 341 Ill. App. 3d 1083, 276 Ill. Dec. 458, 794 N.E.2d 353, 2003 Ill. App. LEXIS 532 (4 Dist. 2003).

In General
A person commits the offense of kidnaping when he knowingly secretly confines a person against his will. People v. Masterson, 79 Ill. App. 2d 117, 223 N.E.2d 252 (3 Dist. 1967).

Admonition

—Insufficient
Where defendant was not sufficiently admonished as to the consequences of his plea of guilty to the charge of kidnaping, it was error for the trial court to accept and enter the plea. People v. Berry, 2 Ill. App. 3d 760, 277 N.E.2d 328 (3 Dist. 1971).

Against Victim's Will

—Physical Evidence
The evidence sufficiently showed that the murder victim was confined by defendant against the victim's will where the victim had ligature marks on his wrists and the victim, a male prostitute, did not show any scarring which would indicate his engaging in bondage practices prior to the night of the incident. People v. Eyler, 133 Ill. 2d 173, 139 Ill. Dec. 756, 549 N.E.2d 268 (1989), cert. denied, 498 U.S. 881, 111 S. Ct. 215, 112 L. Ed. 2d 174 (1990).

Age
Subsection (b) of this section can be construed to refer to either mental or physical age since a mentally retarded adult who lacks both the intelligence and social maturity of a normal seven year old child is in no better position to exercise his will or consent to being taken from one place to another than that child, irrespective of his chronological age. People v. Castro, 113 Ill. App. 3d 265, 68 Ill. Dec. 870, 446 N.E.2d 1267 (1 Dist. 1983).

Application and Construction
The fact that an indictment which charged defendant with aggravated kidnaping was predicated upon intent secretly to con-

Application and Construction (Cont'd)
fine victim against his will, and the jury instructions focused on actual secret confinement of victim against his will, did not result in an indictment for one offense and an instruction for another offense, since the discrepancy is merely between two subdivisions of the same offense, and not sufficient to vitiate a conviction. People v. Singleton, 124 Ill. App. 3d 386, 79 Ill. Dec. 720, 464 N.E.2d 624 (1 Dist. 1984).

This section defines but one offense, kidnaping, and subdivisions (a)(1), (a)(2) and (a)(3) simply define three different ways that the crime may be committed. People v. Castro, 113 Ill. App. 3d 265, 68 Ill. Dec. 870, 446 N.E.2d 1267 (1 Dist. 1983).

Armed Violence

—Distinguished
Armed violence, based on the underlying felony of kidnaping, consists of the basic elements of kidnaping, plus the added factor of being armed with a dangerous weapon (720 ILCS 5/33A-2), and the only difference between aggravated kidnaping, and armed violence predicated upon kidnaping, is the penalty. People v. Moritz, 173 Ill. App. 3d 498, 123 Ill. Dec. 464, 527 N.E.2d 1102 (4 Dist. 1988).

Asportation
Victim's asportation for approximately 1 and ½ miles, lasting between 5 and 10 minutes, was sufficient to support defendants' convictions of kidnapping, apart from the victim's sexual assault. People v. Quintana, 332 Ill. App. 3d 96, 265 Ill. Dec. 462, 772 N.E.2d 833, 2002 Ill. App. LEXIS 518 (1 Dist. 2002).

—Carry
The word "carries," in subsection (a)(2) of this section simply, refers to the general legal concept of asportation. People v. Casiano, 212 Ill. App. 3d 680, 156 Ill. Dec. 762, 571 N.E.2d 742 (1 Dist.), cert. denied, 141 Ill. 2d 547, 162 Ill. Dec. 495, 580 N.E.2d 121 (1991).

Forcing a victim, at knifepoint, to walk approximately one-half block to an apartment is a carrying from one place to another. People v. Casiano, 212 Ill. App. 3d 680, 156 Ill. Dec. 762, 571 N.E.2d 742 (1 Dist.), cert. denied, 141 Ill. 2d 547, 162 Ill. Dec. 495, 580 N.E.2d 121 (1991).

—Duration
Although the distance of asportation was not great, the acts of kidnapping the victim and committing aggravated criminal sexual assault upon the victim were sufficient distinct to support conviction of, and imposition of mandatory consecutive sentences for, both kidnapping and sexual assault. People v. Watson, 342 Ill. App. 3d 1089, 277 Ill. Dec. 721, 796 N.E.2d 1087, 2003 Ill. App. LEXIS 1089 (1 Dist. 2003).

The brevity of the asportation does not preclude a kidnapping conviction. People v. Thomas, 163 Ill. App. 3d 670, 114 Ill. Dec. 746, 516 N.E.2d 901 (1 Dist. 1987).

—Not Shown
The asportation of the victim was not established beyond a reasonable doubt. People v. Lamkey, 240 Ill. App. 3d 435, 181 Ill. Dec. 333, 608 N.E.2d 406 (1 Dist. 1992).

Confinement

—In General
Although confinement usually means enclosure or confinement within something such as a car or a house, it is not strictly limited to those types of places. People v. Jackson, 281 Ill. App. 3d 759, 217 Ill. Dec. 185, 666 N.E.2d 854 (1 Dist. 1996).

—Automobile
Where defendant's confinement of victim in car was not merely incidental to capital murder offense, court properly convicted defendant separately of aggravated kidnapping. People v. Cole, 172 Ill. 2d 85, 216 Ill. Dec. 718, 665 N.E.2d 1275 (1996), cert. denied, 519 U.S. 1030, 117 S. Ct. 587, 136 L. Ed. 2d 517 (1996).

One can be secretly confined in an automobile within the meaning of this statute, whether the automobile is moving or parked. People v. Kittle, 140 Ill. App. 3d 951, 95 Ill. Dec. 260, 489 N.E.2d 481 (2 Dist. 1986).

A person may be secretly confined within the meaning of the kidnaping statute if confined in a car. People v. Masterson, 79 Ill. App. 2d 117, 223 N.E.2d 252 (3 Dist. 1967).

A person forcibly confined in an automobile constantly moving from place to place may be more secretly and effectively confined from the kidnaper's standpoint than one kept in a building or other place of incarceration. People v. Bishop, 1 Ill. 2d 60, 114 N.E.2d 566 (1953).

—Evidence Held Sufficient
Evidence was sufficient to show that defendant intended to secretly confine the victims where he approached two girls, nine and ten years old, in his car, offered them candy, told them he would take them wherever they wanted to go if they got in the car and, after being rebuffed, continued to prowl the neighborhood fleeing only when approached by the mother of one of the girls. People v. Williams, 295 Ill. App. 3d 663, 230 Ill. Dec. 369, 693 N.E.2d 498 (3 Dist. 1998).

Secret confinement may be shown by proof of either the secrecy of confinement or the place of confinement; in light of the concealment and enclosure of the victim in defendant's van, there was sufficient evidence in the present case to establish the element of secret confinement. People v. Riley, 219 Ill. App. 3d 482, 162 Ill. Dec. 194, 579 N.E.2d 1008 (1 Dist. 1991).

Where defendants told victim to get into the van, prevented her from making known her distress, repeatedly ordered her to lie down in back of the van, and one defendant instructed the other to sit on victim when she did not obey him immediately, the evidence was sufficient to establish the element of secret confinement. People v. Thomas, 163 Ill. App. 3d 670, 114 Ill. Dec. 746, 516 N.E.2d 901 (1 Dist. 1987).

—Not Incidental
Confinement was not merely incidental to the murder of the victim, but an independent crime, where the evidence supported the inference that when defendant induced the victim to go to defendant's apartment for the supposed purpose of prostitution, defendant had something else in mind: to bind, torture, and stab his victim before murdering him, in a place where the victim was beyond the reach of anyone who could help him. People v. Eyler, 133 Ill. 2d 173, 139 Ill. Dec. 756, 549 N.E.2d 268 (1989), cert. denied, 498 U.S. 881, 111 S. Ct. 215, 112 L. Ed. 2d 174 (1990).

Discretion of Prosecutor
The State's Attorney has discretion in choosing which offense, unlawful restraint, kidnaping, or aggravated kidnaping, should be prosecuted. People v. Mulcahey, 50 Ill. App. 3d 421, 8 Ill. Dec. 627, 365 N.E.2d 1013 (4 Dist. 1977), aff'd, 72 Ill. 2d 282, 21 Ill. Dec. 176, 381 N.E.2d 254 (1978).

Elements of Offense

—Against Victim's Will
There can be no kidnaping unless it occurs against the will of the victim. People v. Marin, 48 Ill. 2d 205, 269 N.E.2d 303 (1971).

—Asportation
Kidnaping can occur in relation to asportation, not merely detention, when such asportation is induced by deceit or enticement and accompanied with the requisite mental state. People v. Brown, 214 Ill. App. 3d 836, 158 Ill. Dec. 396, 574 N.E.2d 190 (1 Dist.), cert. denied, 141 Ill. 2d 547, 162 Ill. Dec. 495, 580 N.E.2d 121 (1991).

Asportation of the victim is not an element of kidnaping. People v. Mulcahey, 50 Ill. App. 3d 421, 8 Ill. Dec. 627, 365 N.E.2d 1013 (4 Dist. 1977), aff'd, 72 Ill. 2d 282, 21 Ill. Dec. 176, 381 N.E.2d 254 (1978).

—Assault
While defendant's act of grabbing the complainant and throwing her against the wall was not sufficient in itself to sustain the charge of kidnaping, it was a prerequisite to aggravated kidnaping. People v. Young, 115 Ill. App. 3d 455, 71 Ill. Dec. 259, 450 N.E.2d 947 (2 Dist. 1983).

—Four Prong Test
The four-part test to determine whether an act constitutes kidnaping includes: (1) the duration of the detention or asportation; (2) whether the detention or asportation occurred during the commission of a separate offense; (3) whether the detention or asportation which occurred was inherent in the separate offense;

Elements of Offense (Cont'd)

—Four Prong Test (Cont'd)

and (4) whether the asportation or detention created a significant danger to the victim independent of that posed by the separate offense. People v. Smith, 91 Ill. App. 3d 523, 47 Ill. Dec. 1, 414 N.E.2d 1117 (1 Dist. 1980); People v. Thomas, 163 Ill. App. 3d 670, 114 Ill. Dec. 746, 516 N.E.2d 901 (1 Dist. 1987); People v. Sherrod, 220 Ill. App. 3d 429, 163 Ill. Dec. 102, 581 N.E.2d 53 (1 Dist.), appeal denied, 142 Ill. 2d 662, 164 Ill. Dec. 925, 584 N.E.2d 137 (1991).

Where no other separate felony was committed, and it was not known whether any other crime was contemplated, it would be erroneous to apply the four prong test to determine whether defendant's conduct was kidnaping or unlawful restraint. People v. Kittle, 140 Ill. App. 3d 951, 95 Ill. Dec. 260, 489 N.E.2d 481 (2 Dist. 1986).

—Length of Abduction

The victim's escape negated the underlying value of the time factor in the four part test, primarily because it was not known whether any other crime was contemplated, or whether the victim would have been held for an lengthy period of time. People v. Thomas, 163 Ill. App. 3d 670, 114 Ill. Dec. 746, 516 N.E.2d 901 (1 Dist. 1987).

—Ransom Not Element

That a person be held for ransom or that a demand for ransom be made is not an element of the offense of kidnaping. People v. Masterson, 79 Ill. App. 2d 117, 223 N.E.2d 252 (3 Dist. 1967).

—Secret Confinement

The secret confinement element of kidnaping must be proved beyond a reasonable doubt. People v. Sykes, 161 Ill. App. 3d 623, 113 Ill. Dec. 444, 515 N.E.2d 253 (1 Dist. 1987).

Secret confinement is the gist of kidnaping and must be proved beyond a reasonable doubt. People v. Mulcahey, 50 Ill. App. 3d 421, 8 Ill. Dec. 627, 365 N.E.2d 1013 (4 Dist. 1977), aff'd, 72 Ill. 2d 282, 21 Ill. Dec. 176, 381 N.E.2d 254 (1978).

—Significant Danger

Forcing the victim into a van and leaving the scene of the robbery triggered a potential risk of harm to the victim which was substantially increased above that necessarily present in the crime of robbery itself, as the likelihood of her being seen by a passerby who might help was greatly decreased and, once the victim was confined within a moving vehicle, the possibility that an accident might occur or the victim might injure herself attempting to escape from a moving vehicle increased the risk of harm resulting from asportation. People v. Thomas, 163 Ill. App. 3d 670, 114 Ill. Dec. 746, 516 N.E.2d 901 (1 Dist. 1987).

Evidence

—Circumstantial

Circumstantial evidence that victim was taken across the street to codefendant's apartment without her coat or shoes while looking frightened and that she was last seen alive with defendant and codefendant supported defendant's conviction for aggravated kidnapping. People v. Turner, 282 Ill. App. 3d 770, 218 Ill. Dec. 226, 668 N.E.2d 1058 (1 Dist. 1996), appeal denied, 168 Ill. 2d 620, 219 Ill. Dec. 574, 671 N.E.2d 741 (1996).

—Jury Question

The evaluation of defendant's ex-girlfriend's testimony and of all the evidence in a kidnaping case was a question for the jury. People v. Mullen, 43 Ill. App. 3d 311, 2 Ill. Dec. 50, 356 N.E.2d 1337 (4 Dist. 1976).

—Photographic Display

The displaying of a photograph, which shows the suspect accused of kidnaping in custody, to a prospective witness before he views the suspect in a lineup is not considered objectionable. People v. Williams, 52 Ill. 2d 455, 288 N.E.2d 406 (1972).

—Photographs

Where defendant was convicted of kidnaping and felony murder the admission of photographs of the victim's jaw was not an abuse of discretion even though the color of the victim's teeth varied from pink to white in the photographs. People v. Jordan, 114 Ill. App. 3d 16, 69 Ill. Dec. 777, 448 N.E.2d 237 (3 Dist. 1983), rev'd on other grounds, 103 Ill. 2d 192, 82 Ill. Dec. 925, 469 N.E.2d 569 (1984).

—Question of Fact

The evaluation of defendant's ex-girlfriend's testimony and of all the evidence in a kidnaping case was a question for the jury. People v. Mullen, 43 Ill. App. 3d 311, 2 Ill. Dec. 50, 356 N.E.2d 1337 (4 Dist. 1976).

Evidence Held Insufficient

With the exception to the charge of criminal damage to property and kidnaping, the defendant was properly convicted and sentenced for attempted murder, robbery, attempted armed robbery, and theft, despite the single sentence provision of former section 1-7(m) of the Criminal Code (see now 730 ILCS 5/5-8-4), which stated that stated a conviction and sentence should be imposed only on the most serious one of a series of criminal acts resulting from the same conduct or transaction. People v. Berry, 2 Ill. App. 3d 760, 277 N.E.2d 328 (3 Dist. 1971).

Evidence Held Sufficient

Evidence was sufficient to support a conviction for kidnapping where the defendant forced the victim from a hallway into a bathroom and such asportation preceded a subsequent sexual assault; the forced movement of a victim from one place to another is not inherent in the offense of criminal sexual assault, and the asportation posed a significant danger to the victim independent of the danger created by the sexual assault. People v. Ware, 323 Ill. App. 3d 47, 256 Ill. Dec. 28, 751 N.E.2d 81, 2001 Ill. App. LEXIS 383 (1 Dist. 2001).

Where the victim testified that defendant, armed with a gun, accosted her in the street, threatened her life, forcibly moved her to several locations, compelled her to engage in sexual acts, and held her inside a van for hours, the trial court reasonably could find defendant guilty of aggravated criminal sexual assault and kidnaping. People v. Riley, 219 Ill. App. 3d 482, 162 Ill. Dec. 194, 579 N.E.2d 1008 (1 Dist. 1991).

Evidence was sufficient to support finding that defendant was guilty of kidnaping beyond a reasonable doubt. People v. Anthony, 38 Ill. App. 3d 190, 347 N.E.2d 179 (4 Dist. 1976); People v. Guyon, 101 Ill. App. 3d 799, 57 Ill. Dec. 318, 428 N.E.2d 998 (1 Dist. 1981).

Evidence was sufficient to support the conviction of kidnaping, aggravated kidnaping, and armed robbery against defendant where the defendant with others disarmed troopers and kept them for approximately thirty minutes during daylight, notwithstanding the fact that there was a conflict in the testimony of the troopers whether defendant had glasses on and as to the defendant's weight. People v. Del Genio, 10 Ill. App. 3d 432, 294 N.E.2d 332 (2 Dist. 1973).

Where the victim gave a physical description of her assailant and informed the police that her assailant was driving an avocado green 1967 Camaro, and that she had scratched her attacker on his face and arms, and a few minutes later and just a short distance away, the police observed a man fitting the description driving a 1968 Camaro, and where, as they halted, the Camaro the police observed fresh scratch marks on the face of the driver of the car, the totality of the facts was more than sufficient to create the probable cause necessary to support a lawful arrest for aggravated kidnapping, robbery, rape (now sexual assault) and battery. People v. Drayton, 7 Ill. App. 3d 812, 288 N.E.2d 922 (1 Dist. 1972).

The allegedly uncorroborated testimony of complaining witness that defendant, by use of force, pushed the complainant into his automobile, was sufficient to sustain defendant's conviction of the crime of attempted kidnaping, even in view of defendant's complete denial. People v. Sevastos, 117 Ill. App. 2d 104, 252 N.E.2d 745 (2 Dist. 1969).

Evidence established beyond a reasonable doubt a felonious concealment and imprisonment of children under the forerunner of this section. People v. Savage, 5 Ill. 2d 296, 125 N.E.2d 449 (1955).

By the defendant's confession and the other evidence in the case, the defendant was shown to be guilty of the crime of kidnaping an infant. People v. Diekelmann, 367 Ill. 372, 11 N.E.2d 420 (1937).

Evidence held sufficient to sustain defendant's conviction of kidnaping. People v. Siegal, 362 Ill. 389, 200 N.E. 72 (1935); People v. Landis, 66 Ill. App. 2d 458, 214 N.E.2d 343 (1 Dist. 1966); People v. Bravos, 114 Ill. App. 2d 298, 252 N.E.2d 776 (1 Dist. 1969); People

Evidence Held Sufficient (Cont'd)
v. Lingle, 122 Ill. App. 2d 87, 257 N.E.2d 243 (2 Dist. 1970); People v. Pierce, 9 Ill. App. 3d 153, 291 N.E.2d 58 (1 Dist. 1972), aff'd, 56 Ill. 2d 361, 308 N.E.2d 577 (1974); People v. Brandys, 15 Ill. App. 3d 379, 304 N.E.2d 471 (4 Dist. 1973); People v. Kubat, 94 Ill. 2d 437, 69 Ill. Dec. 30, 447 N.E.2d 247 (1983), vacated on other grounds, 679 F. Supp. 788 (N.D. Ill. 1988), aff'd, 867 F.2d 351 (7th Cir. 1989).

Where the verdict did not in direct terms state the specific intent of the parties engaged in the kidnaping, but it did refer to the indictment, which clearly stated the intent, verdict was sufficiently specific. People v. Gold, 343 Ill. 402, 175 N.E. 558 (1931).

Extradition Proceedings
For the purposes of extradition procedure, where respondents were charged with kidnapping and forcible seizure under Canadian law, both of the Canadian crimes would be comprehended within either the federal or state kidnapping statutes, since both statutes embrace confinement against the will of the victim by force or threat of force. In re Kulekowskis, 881 F. Supp. 1126 (N.D. Ill. 1995).

Guardian
To the extent ordered by the court and under its direction, the guardian of the person has legal custody of the ward, thus ward's power of decision regarding her care was vested in guardian and if ward had been living in Illinois, guardian could not be guilty of kidnapping or unlawful confinement in taking her to a medical examination against her will. In re Kulekowskis, 881 F. Supp. 1126 (N.D. Ill. 1995).

Identification

—Evidence Held Sufficient
Although defendant introduced evidence of an alibi and attacked the credibility of the victim's in-court identification of him, that identification testimony was nevertheless sufficient evidence to support defendant's conviction of kidnaping. People v. Bradley, 43 Ill. App. 3d 463, 2 Ill. Dec. 529, 357 N.E.2d 696 (4 Dist. 1976).

Illustrative Cases
The defendants' kidnaping convictions were proper where victim was forced off the street into an alley and then into a garage; the asportation from the street to a garage was not inherent in the sexual assault, and forcing an unwilling victim into the alley and into the garage posed a significant danger to her separate from that posed by the sexual assault. People v. Sherrod, 220 Ill. App. 3d 429, 163 Ill. Dec. 102, 581 N.E.2d 53 (1 Dist.), appeal denied, 142 Ill. 2d 662, 164 Ill. Dec. 925, 584 N.E.2d 137 (1991).

Complainant's testimony, the testimony of the other witnesses, and the physical evidence supported the finding that a kidnaping occurred when complainant was forcibly transported to a garage, and secretly confined there against her will. People v. Watts, 139 Ill. App. 3d 837, 94 Ill. Dec. 200, 487 N.E.2d 1077 (1 Dist. 1985).

Where the indictment not only charged an enticement with intent to conceal but in the second count it charged a felonious concealment and imprisonment as well, and all counts grew out of and related to the same transaction, the court found the defendant guilty as charged in the indictment. If the evidence established the guilt of the defendant under the second count, the judgment would be sustained regardless of a defense of intoxication. People v. Savage, 5 Ill. 2d 296, 125 N.E.2d 449 (1955).

Inconsistent Verdicts
Defendant's kidnaping conviction based on secret confinement was not legally inconsistent with the trial court's finding of not guilty of aggravated kidnaping (720 ILCS 5/10-2). People v. Riley, 219 Ill. App. 3d 482, 162 Ill. Dec. 194, 579 N.E.2d 1008 (1 Dist. 1991).

Indictment

—Conspiracy
As an indictment for conspiracy need not allege all the elements of the substantive offense which is the object of the conspiracy, in an indictment for attempt kidnaping the crime intended need not be set out as fully and specifically as would be required in an indictment for the actual commission of the crime. People v. Williams, 52 Ill. 2d 455, 288 N.E.2d 406 (1972).

—Held Sufficient
Where the record clearly showed that the defendants were not charged with any other offense except kidnaping for ransom, and where the indictment under which they were tried charged them with the crime of kidnaping the victim for the purpose of extorting from him a large sum of money, and charged them with no other crime, the trial court would have committed error if it had given the jury an instruction or form of verdict defining and prescribing the penalty for any other kind of kidnaping. People v. Resnick, 348 Ill. 544, 181 N.E. 415 (1932).

Lesser Included Offense

—Aggravated Kidnapping
Kidnaping, a class 2 felony, is a lesser included offense of aggravated kidnaping, a class 1 felony, since aggravated kidnaping requires the same elements as kidnaping plus one of the additional elements outlined in subsection (a) of 720 ILCS 5/10-2, such as being armed with a dangerous weapon. People v. Christy, 188 Ill. App. 3d 330, 135 Ill. Dec. 731, 544 N.E.2d 88 (3 Dist. 1989).

The offense of kidnaping of a victim is an included offense of any aggravated kidnaping of the victim. People v. Hines, 165 Ill. App. 3d 289, 116 Ill. Dec. 382, 518 N.E.2d 1362 (4 Dist.), cert. denied, 121 Ill. 2d 577, 122 Ill. Dec. 442, 526 N.E.2d 835, cert. denied, 488 U.S. 895, 109 S. Ct. 236, 102 L. Ed. 2d 225 (1988).

Where the offense of kidnaping, as a lesser included offense of aggravated kidnaping, arose from closely related acts, it was improper to convict defendant of both offenses. People v. Earl, 104 Ill. App. 3d 846, 60 Ill. Dec. 680, 433 N.E.2d 722 (2 Dist. 1982).

—Unlawful Restraint
Unlawful restraint is a lesser included offense of kidnaping. People v. Kittle, 140 Ill. App. 3d 951, 95 Ill. Dec. 260, 489 N.E.2d 481 (2 Dist. 1986).

Where judgment order incorrectly reflected convictions for both unlawful restraint and kidnaping, and the trial court ruled that the unlawful restraint conviction merged into the kidnaping conviction, and sentenced defendants only on the kidnaping conviction, the judgment order should have been amended to reflect only a conviction and sentence for kidnaping. People v. Eddington, 117 Ill. App. 3d 953, 73 Ill. Dec. 248, 453 N.E.2d 1383 (1 Dist. 1983).

Mental State

—Intoxication
To assert an intoxication defense, defendant must be able to show that drunkenness existed to such a degree that he was completely unable to form the specific intent required to commit the offense; thus, for a charge of kidnaping, the specific intent relevant to which is knowledge, a defendant would have to present the argument that he was so intoxicated that he did not know what he was doing. People v. Long, 30 Ill. App. 3d 815, 333 N.E.2d 534 (2 Dist. 1975).

Evidence of intoxication was insufficient to overcome verdict that defendant was responsible for his act of kidnaping. People v. Long, 30 Ill. App. 3d 815, 333 N.E.2d 534 (2 Dist. 1975).

—Knowledge
Kidnaping requires proof of knowledge, a particular form of general intent. People v. Utinans, 55 Ill. App. 3d 306, 13 Ill. Dec. 53, 370 N.E.2d 1080 (1 Dist. 1977).

Merger

—Armed Robbery
Offenses of armed robbery, kidnaping and aggravated kidnaping did not merge into a single conviction of armed robbery despite fact that they all arose out of the same conduct since where more than one offense arises from a series of closely related acts and the crimes are clearly distinct and require different elements of proof, the conviction and sentence for each offense must stand. People v. Boyce, 41 Ill. App. 3d 53, 353 N.E.2d 287 (1 Dist. 1976).

Methods of Commission
This section defines but one offense, kidnaping and subdivisions (a)(1), (2) and (3) simply define three different ways that the crime may be committed. People v. Castro, 113 Ill. App. 3d 265, 68 Ill. Dec. 870, 446 N.E.2d 1267 (1 Dist. 1983).

Parents

—Abductions

There is no reason to suppose that the legislature ever intended this section to encompass abductions by parents, as does the child abduction statute (720 ILCS 5/10-5). People v. Algarin, 200 Ill. App. 3d 740, 146 Ill. Dec. 494, 558 N.E.2d 457 (1 Dist. 1990).

—Biological Father

A victim's biological father was a parent under subsection (b) of this section and could not therefore be charged with the kidnaping of his own child. People v. Algarin, 200 Ill. App. 3d 740, 146 Ill. Dec. 494, 558 N.E.2d 457 (1 Dist. 1990).

—Parental Consent

Where one parent had consented to the taking and confinement of the child, this fact was of major consequence, although the defendants had acted for the purpose of obtaining ransom money. People v. Marin, 48 Ill. 2d 205, 269 N.E.2d 303 (1971).

There can be no kidnaping of a child under the age of 13 if the confinement occurs with the consent of his parent. People v. Marin, 48 Ill. 2d 205, 269 N.E.2d 303 (1971).

Ransom

—In General

Kidnaping for ransom is the unlawful seizure of a person, the secreting of that person, and the extortion of ransom or other valuable thing or concession from the person seized and secreted, or from his parent, guardian, or legal custodian; however, subdivision (a)(1) of this section does not require unlawful seizure if the secret confining is against the individual's will. People v. Long, 39 Ill. 2d 40, 233 N.E.2d 389 (1968).

Secret Confinement

—Automobile

Confinement in an automobile satisfies the requirement of secret confinement. People v. Harris, 68 Ill. App. 3d 12, 24 Ill. Dec. 648, 385 N.E.2d 789 (5 Dist. 1979).

—Evidence Held Sufficient

The evidence established that the victim was secretly confined and, therefore, defendant was properly convicted of aggravated kidnaping. People v. Enoch, 122 Ill. 2d 176, 119 Ill. Dec. 265, 522 N.E.2d 1124, cert. denied, 488 U.S. 917, 109 S. Ct. 274, 102 L. Ed. 2d 263 (1988).

—How Shown

The secret confinement contemplated by subsection (a) of this section may be shown by proof of either the secrecy of the confinement itself or by proof of the secrecy of the place of confinement. People v. Sykes, 161 Ill. App. 3d 623, 113 Ill. Dec. 444, 515 N.E.2d 253 (1 Dist. 1987); People v. Mulcahey, 72 Ill. 2d 282, 21 Ill. Dec. 176, 381 N.E.2d 254 (1978).

—Not Shown

The state failed to prove the element of secret confinement necessary to sustain a conviction for kidnapping. People v. Lamkey, 240 Ill. App. 3d 435, 181 Ill. Dec. 333, 608 N.E.2d 406 (1 Dist. 1992).

The state failed not only to establish the confinement element of kidnaping where the victim, who was grabbed by the defendant and pulled through the street, was not confined or enclosed within any place or any thing, but also failed to establish the component of this secrecy contained in section in that at no time was the victim concealed, hidden, or not made public. People v. Sykes, 161 Ill. App. 3d 623, 113 Ill. Dec. 444, 515 N.E.2d 253 (1 Dist. 1987).

—Proof

"Secret confinement" may be shown by proof of the secrecy of confinement or the place of confinement. People v. Jackson, 281 Ill. App. 3d 759, 217 Ill. Dec. 185, 666 N.E.2d 854 (1 Dist. 1996).

—Shown

Where victim was taken to secluded bridge and bound, kidnapping element of "secret confinement" was met. People v. Jackson, 281 Ill. App. 3d 759, 217 Ill. Dec. 185, 666 N.E.2d 854 (1 Dist. 1996).

Where the victim was dragged against her will from a well-lit parking lot to a place in a dark field, concealed from public view and not free to leave, secret confinement was proven. People v. Franzen, 251 Ill. App. 3d 813, 190 Ill. Dec. 847, 622 N.E.2d 877 (2 Dist. 1993), appeal denied, 154 Ill. 2d 564, 197 Ill. Dec. 490, 631 N.E.2d 712 (1994).

Where defendant forced entry into residence at gunpoint, inquired whether victim was home alone, searched the upstairs rooms for other persons, told victim's husband he was going to take victim on a trip and not to inform the police, and bound victim before he left the house in her car, defendant secretly confined his victim against her will. People v. Mulcahey, 50 Ill. App. 3d 421, 8 Ill. Dec. 627, 365 N.E.2d 1013 (4 Dist. 1977), aff'd, 72 Ill. 2d 282, 21 Ill. Dec. 176, 381 N.E.2d 254 (1978).

Sentencing

—Proper

Defendant's sentence of 30 years' imprisonment plus three months' mandatory supervised release for aggravated kidnapping for ransom was proper where the court found that serious harm was threatened, that the defendant had a history of delinquency, that the defendant was eligible for an extended term due to the age of the victim, that a prison sentence was not only mandated but necessary to protect the public and the public interest, and that the sentence to be imposed was necessary to deter others from committing the same crime. People v. Laliberte, 246 Ill. App. 3d 159, 186 Ill. Dec. 9, 615 N.E.2d 813 (2 Dist.), appeal denied, 152 Ill. 2d 570, 190 Ill. Dec. 901, 622 N.E.2d 1218 (1993).

—Set Aside

Where a kidnaping was effected to commit a rape and the penalty for rape was more severe than the sentence for aggravated kidnaping, the conviction and sentence for aggravated kidnaping was set aside, and the conviction and sentence for rape were affirmed. People v. Sims, 20 Ill. App. 3d 1068, 313 N.E.2d 663 (4 Dist. 1974).

—Validity

Aggravated kidnaping is a more serious offense than the lesser included offense of kidnaping; but where the sentencing for kidnaping elevated it to a more serious crime than aggravated kidnaping the result was an unconstitutionally disproportionate sentencing scheme. People v. Christy, 188 Ill. App. 3d 330, 135 Ill. Dec. 731, 544 N.E.2d 88 (3 Dist. 1989).

Sexual Assault

—Distinguished

Kidnaping is totally distinct from the crime of sexual assault since latter crime requires an act of sexual penetration by the use of force or threat of force. People v. Brown, 214 Ill. App. 3d 836, 158 Ill. Dec. 396, 574 N.E.2d 190 (1 Dist.), cert. denied, 141 Ill. 2d 547, 162 Ill. Dec. 495, 580 N.E.2d 121 (1991).

—Separate Offense

Where the record showed that a kidnapping was not merely incidental to a sexual assault, this did not support a reduction of defendant's sentence. People v. Lloyd, 277 Ill. App. 3d 154, 213 Ill. Dec. 786, 660 N.E.2d 43 (1 Dist. 1995).

Although defendant may have kidnapped his victims in order to facilitate the commission of sexual assaults and robberies, the aggravated kidnapping was a separate and distinct crime. People v. Muhammad, 257 Ill. App. 3d 359, 195 Ill. Dec. 798, 629 N.E.2d 106 (1 Dist. 1993).

The kidnaping committed by defendant was properly found to be a separate offense from the criminal sexual assault (720 ILCS 5/12-13). People v. Riley, 219 Ill. App. 3d 482, 162 Ill. Dec. 194, 579 N.E.2d 1008 (1 Dist. 1991).

Single Course of Action

—In General

Where defendant asserted that the imposition of concurrent sentences for aggravated kidnaping and armed robbery be reversed since they arose out of a single transaction in which the crime of rape was committed, the trial court found the armed robbery was complete prior to the kidnaping and rape, was independently motivated, and was committed in order to effect the rape. Consequently, the conviction for the charge for which the statute imposes the less severe penalty was set aside. People v. Sims, 20 Ill. App. 3d 1068, 313 N.E.2d 663 (4 Dist. 1974).

Single Course of Action (Cont'd)

—Armed Violence

Where the offense of armed violence (720 ILCS 5/33A-2) was incident to and motivated in effectuating the kidnaping, the conviction for armed violence had to be reversed. People v. Anthony, 38 Ill. App. 3d 190, 347 N.E.2d 179 (4 Dist. 1976).

—Not Shown

The kidnaping under this section was of such distance, duration and danger to the victim as to constitute a separate offense and was not merely incidental to the criminal sexual assault which later occurred. People v. Casiano, 212 Ill. App. 3d 680, 156 Ill. Dec. 762, 571 N.E.2d 742 (1 Dist.), cert. denied, 141 Ill. 2d 547, 162 Ill. Dec. 495, 580 N.E.2d 121 (1991).

Testimony

—Right to Confrontation

Defendant's convictions of aggravated criminal sexual assault, aggravated vehicular hijacking, armed robbery, and kidnapping, arising from an incident in which defendant and an accomplice robbed and raped a taxi driver, were reversed, because the trial court erred in admitting statements made by the victim, who was murdered prior to the beginning of the trial, to police officers and others, as the statements were testimonial in nature, and the admission violated defendant's right to confrontation under under Illinois Const., Art. I, § 8. People v. West, 2004 Ill. App. LEXIS 1536 (1 Dist. Dec. 22, 2004).

Unlawful Restraint

—Continuous Control

Where the complaining witness was in the defendant's continuous control, despite the fact that she was deceived prior to defendant's overt act, and both the confinement and the detainment were derived from this control, and both the confinement and the detainment were closely related acts, the conviction for kidnaping could stand, but the conviction for unlawful restraint should be vacated. People v. Kittle, 140 Ill. App. 3d 951, 95 Ill. Dec. 260, 489 N.E.2d 481 (2 Dist. 1986).

—Distinguished

One major distinction between kidnaping and unlawful restraint is that kidnaping involves a secret confinement, whereas unlawful restraint involves merely detaining another without legal authority. People v. Enoch, 122 Ill. 2d 176, 119 Ill. Dec. 265, 522 N.E.2d 1124, cert. denied, 488 U.S. 917, 109 S. Ct. 274, 102 L. Ed. 2d 263 (1988).

RESEARCH REFERENCES

Coercion, compulsion, or duress as defense to charge of kidnapping. 69 ALR4th 1005.

Child custody: When does state that issued previous custody determination have continuing jurisdiction under Uniform Child Custody Jurisdiction Act (UCCJA) or Parental Kidnapping Prevention Act (PKPA), 28 USCS § 1738A. 83 ALR4th 742.

Validity, construction, and application of "hold to service" provision of kidnapping statute. 28 ALR5th 754.

Seizure or detention for purpose of committing rape, robbery, or other offense as constituting separate crime of kidnapping. 39 ALR5th 283.

720 ILCS 5/10-2 Aggravated kidnaping

Sec. 10-2. *Aggravated kidnaping.* (a) A kidnaper within the definition of paragraph (a) of Section 10-1 [720 ILCS 5/10-1] is guilty of the offense of aggravated kidnaping when he:

(1) Kidnaps for the purpose of obtaining ransom from the person kidnaped or from any other person, or

(2) Takes as his victim a child under the age of 13 years, or a severely or profoundly mentally retarded person, or

(3) Inflicts great bodily harm, other than by the discharge of a firearm, or commits another felony upon his victim, or

(4) Wears a hood, robe or mask or conceals his identity, or

(5) Commits the offense of kidnaping while armed with a dangerous weapon, other than a firearm, as defined in Section 33A-1 of the "Criminal Code of 1961" [720 ILCS 5/33A-1], or

(6) Commits the offense of kidnaping while armed with a firearm, or

(7) During the commission of the offense of kidnaping, personally discharged a firearm, or

(8) During the commission of the offense of kidnaping, personally discharged a firearm that proximately caused great bodily harm, permanent disability, permanent disfigurement, or death to another person.

As used in this Section, "ransom" includes money, benefit or other valuable thing or concession.

(b) Sentence. Aggravated kidnaping in violation of paragraph (1), (2), (3), (4), or (5) of subsection (a) is a Class X felony. A violation of subsection (a)(6) is a Class X felony for which 15 years shall be added to the term of imprisonment imposed by the court. A violation of subsection (a)(7) is a Class X felony for which 20 years shall be added to the term of imprisonment imposed by the court. A violation of subsection (a)(8) is a Class X felony for which 25 years or up to a term of natural life shall be added to the term of imprisonment imposed by the court.

A person who is convicted of a second or subsequent offense of aggravated kidnaping shall be sentenced to a term of natural life imprisonment; provided, however, that a sentence of natural life imprisonment shall not be imposed under this Section unless the second or subsequent offense was committed after conviction on the first offense.

(Source: P.A. 85-1392; 89-707, § 15; 91-404, § 5; 92-434, § 5.)

Note.

This section was Ill.Rev.Stat., Ch. 38, para. 10-2.

Effect of Amendments.

The 1996 amendment by P.A. 89-707, effective June 1, 1997, in subsection (b), deleted the former subdivision (b)(1) designation preceding "Aggravated", in the first sentence deleted "for ransom" preceding "is a" and added the second sentence; and deleted subdivision (b)(2) which read "Aggravated kidnapping other than for ransom is a class 1 felony".

The 1999 amendment by P.A. 91-404, effective January 1, 2000, inserted "other than by the discharge of a firearm" following "bodily harm" in subsection (a)(3); inserted "other than a firearm" following "dangerous weapon" in subsection (a)(5); added subsections (a)(6) through (a)(8); and in the first paragraph of subsection (b) inserted "in violation of paragraph (1), (2), (3), (4), or (5) of subsection (a)" in the first sentence and added the last three sentences.

The 2001 amendment by P.A. 92-434, effective January 1, 2002, in subsection (a)(2) substituted "a" for "an institutionalized".

CASE NOTES

Analysis

Constitutionality
Accomplice Liability

—Conspiracy
—Multiple Defendants
—Shown
Another Felony
—Elements of Offense
Asportation
Child Abduction
—Elements of Offense
—Evidence Held Sufficient
Citizen's Arrest
Dangerous Weapon
—Aggravated Assault
—Elements of Offense
—Mace
—Shown
Elements of Offense
—Harm to Victim
—Kidnaping for Ransom
—Lack of Consent
—Ransom
—Secret Confinement
Escape
—Immaterial
Evidence Held Sufficient
Identification
—Held Sufficient
—Opportunity Sufficient
—When Sufficient
Illustrative Cases
Inconsistent Verdicts
Indictment
—Held Sufficient
Intent
—Voluntary Intoxication
Jurisdiction
Jury Instructions
—Lesser Included Offense
—Upheld
Kidnaping
—Distinguished
Lesser Included Offense
—Aggravated Assault
—Aggravated Battery
—Aggravated Sexual Assault
—Incidental Acts
—Kidnaping
—Rape Not Included
—Sexual Assault
—Unlawful Restraint
Mental State
—Appellate Review
—Knowledge
Multiple Convictions
—Constitutionality
—Not Inconsistent
—Predicate Felony
—Upheld
Multiple Offenses
—Evidence Held Insufficient
—Evidence Held Sufficient
—Merger
—Separate
Ransom
—In General
—Elements of Offense
—Not Required
—Release Immaterial
Robbery
—Distinguished
Secret Confinement
—Shown
Sentencing
—Constitutionality
—Appellate Review
—Disparity Upheld
—Double Enhancement
—Extended Term Held Improper
—Held Not Excessive
—Held Proper
—Maximum Extended Term
—Maximum Sentence
—Res Judicata
—Sentence Reduced
Separate Offenses
—Armed Robbery
—Battery
—Kidnaping
—Murder
—Not Shown
—Sexual Assault
Single Course of Action
—In General
—Aggravated Assault
—Armed Violence
—Continuous Control
—Evidence Held Sufficient
Lesser Included Offense
—Multiple Convictions Improper
—Not Shown
—Sexual Assault
Weapons
—Presence

Constitutionality

With regard 720 ILCS 5/10-2, the 15- and 20-year add-ons mandated by 1999 Ill. Laws 404 (codified at 720 ILCS 5/33A-1 violate the proportionate penalties clause of Ill. Const. art. I, § 11. People v. Moss, 206 Ill. 2d 503, 276 Ill. Dec. 855, 795 N.E.2d 208, 2003 Ill. LEXIS 1410 (2003).

Residential burglary is a crime, not less serious than aggravated kidnaping other than for ransom; therefore, the imposition of a mandatory minimum sentence for residential burglary and not for aggravated kidnaping does not violate the limitations of penalty provision of the Illinois Constitution. People v. Bales, 108 Ill. 2d 182, 91 Ill. Dec. 171, 483 N.E.2d 517 (1985).

Accomplice Liability

—Conspiracy

The fact that indictment did not set forth legal accountability as the basis for charging defendant with aggravated kidnapping as principal did not render the indictment defective, since the state could show that the kidnaping resulted from a conspiracy and the steps by which the conspirators effected the kidnaping, including every act of each conspirator in furtherance of the common purpose, without charging them with conspiracy. People v. Bolla, 114 Ill. App. 3d 442, 70 Ill. Dec. 118, 448 N.E.2d 996 (2 Dist. 1983).

—Multiple Defendants

In a prosecution for kidnaping carried out by several defendants pursuant to a common design, a defendant need not be actually present at the kidnaping if he is otherwise a party to the crime. People v. Bolla, 114 Ill. App. 3d 442, 70 Ill. Dec. 118, 448 N.E.2d 996 (2 Dist. 1983).

—Shown

Defendant could be proved guilty of aggravated kidnaping as an accomplice by proof that his conduct subsequent to the kidnaping and to the release raised a fair inference that he aided, agreed or attempted to aid others in the planning or commission of the offense. People v. Bolla, 114 Ill. App. 3d 442, 70 Ill. Dec. 118, 448 N.E.2d 996 (2 Dist. 1983).

Another Felony

—Elements of Offense

Where defendant's act of grabbing the complainant and throwing her against the wall was not sufficient in itself to sustain a charge of kidnaping, it was a prerequisite to aggravated kidnaping under subdivision (a)(3) of this section. People v. Young, 115 Ill. App. 3d 455, 71 Ill. Dec. 259, 450 N.E.2d 947 (2 Dist. 1983).

Factors to consider to determine if a kidnaping has occurred during the commission of another felony are (1) the duration of the detention or asportation, (2) whether the detention or asportation

Another Felony (Cont'd)

—Elements of Offense (Cont'd)
occurred during the commission of the separate offense, (3) whether the detention or asportation which occurred is inherent in the separate offense, and (4) whether the asportation or detention created a significant danger to the victim independent of that posed by the separate offense. People v. Smith, 91 Ill. App. 3d 523, 47 Ill. Dec. 1, 414 N.E.2d 1117 (1 Dist. 1980).

Asportation
Asportation was not essential to the offense of aggravated battery, since the aggravated battery occurred even before the victim was taken into the car, as defendant struck her in the face while she was in a parking area accessible to the public. Defendant was properly convicted of both aggravated battery and aggravated kidnaping. People v. Pugh, 162 Ill. App. 3d 1030, 114 Ill. Dec. 241, 516 N.E.2d 396 (1 Dist. 1987).

Child Abduction

—Elements of Offense
Lack of parental consent was not necessary to prove an aggravated kidnaping of a minor child under the age of 13 years under subdivision (a)(2) of this section. People v. Hutchinson, 26 Ill. App. 3d 368, 325 N.E.2d 115 (2 Dist. 1975).

—Evidence Held Sufficient
Evidence was held sufficient to sustain a defendant's conviction of aggravated kidnaping where the testimony of a nine year old victim was clear and convincing, and was corroborated by the testimony of the police officers and the admissions of the defendants that he was on the premises at the time in question. People v. Warmack, 44 Ill. App. 3d 243, 3 Ill. Dec. 76, 358 N.E.2d 76 (1 Dist. 1976).

Citizen's Arrest
Regardless of whether a defendant performed a valid citizen's arrest, his conduct went far beyond that necessary to effectuate it, and became aggravated kidnaping where defendant lured a victim home under false pretenses, disguised himself somewhat to avoid immediate detection, handcuffed the victim and bound his ankles, transported him to Chicago, and took steps to prevent anyone from rescuing the victim while defendant transported him. People v. Russell, 165 Ill. App. 3d 569, 116 Ill. Dec. 416, 519 N.E.2d 6 (5 Dist. 1987).

Dangerous Weapon

—Aggravated Assault
An individual can kidnap a victim while armed without necessarily putting the victim in reasonable apprehension of receiving a battery through the use of a deadly weapon; therefore, it is possible to commit the offense of aggravated kidnaping without committing aggravated assault, and the latter is, as a result, not a lesser included offense of the former. People v. Hobson, 77 Ill. App. 3d 22, 32 Ill. Dec. 940, 396 N.E.2d 53 (3 Dist. 1979).

—Elements of Offense
Aggravated kidnapping based on a sexual assault pursuant to subdivision (a)(3) of this section did not require proof of use of a deadly weapon. People v. Davis, 97 Ill. App. 3d 299, 52 Ill. Dec. 780, 422 N.E.2d 989 (1 Dist. 1981).

—Mace
A canister of mace is not a "dangerous weapon" as contemplated by the statute defining the offense of aggravated kidnaping. People v. Dressler, 317 Ill. App. 3d 379, 250 Ill. Dec. 867, 739 N.E.2d 630, 2000 Ill. App. LEXIS 892 (3 Dist. 2000).

—Shown
Where defendant allegedly used a knife for the purpose of threatening the life of kidnaping victim, and where the knife could have been deadly if used in the manner threatened, the knife was a deadly weapon even though the blade was not at least three inches long. People v. Samier, 129 Ill. App. 3d 966, 85 Ill. Dec. 233, 473 N.E.2d 601 (3 Dist. 1985).

Elements of Offense
A person guilty of kidnaping within the terms of 720 ILCS 5/10-1 is guilty of aggravated kidnaping when he knowingly inflicts great bodily harm or commits another felony upon his victim. People v. Masterson, 79 Ill. App. 2d 117, 223 N.E.2d 252 (3 Dist. 1967).

—Harm to Victim
The crime of aggravated kidnaping is complete when the kidnapper inflicts great bodily harm or commits another felony upon his victim. People v. Landis, 66 Ill. App. 2d 458, 214 N.E.2d 343 (1 Dist. 1966).

—Kidnaping for Ransom
Kidnaping for ransom (now aggravated kidnaping) contained three elements: (1) The unlawful seizure; (2) secreting; and (3) the extortion of ransom or other valuable thing or concession from such person so seized and secreted, or his parent, guardian, or legal custodian. Any one having to do with the perpetration of these three acts, or any of them, was guilty of the crime of kidnaping for ransom. People v. Petitti, 337 Ill. 625, 169 N.E. 749 (1929).

—Lack of Consent
The lack of consent to confinement is a necessary element to an aggravated kidnaping charge. People v. Ware, 11 Ill. App. 3d 697, 297 N.E.2d 289 (1 Dist. 1973).

—Ransom
If defendant attempted to collect ransom, he was equally guilty, with those who forcibly seized and secreted the victim, of kidnaping for ransom (now aggravated kidnaping). People v. Petitti, 337 Ill. 625, 169 N.E. 749 (1929).

—Secret Confinement
For purposes of the Illinois aggravated kidnapping statute, secret confinement may be shown by proof of either the secrecy of the confinement or the secrecy of the place of confinement; in this context, "secret" has been defined as concealed, hidden, or not made public, while "confinement," has been defined as the act of imprisoning or restraining someone. People v. Phelps, 211 Ill. 2d 1, 284 Ill. Dec. 268, 809 N.E.2d 1214, 2004 Ill. LEXIS 3 (2004).

Evidence that defendant enticed a child to briefly accompany him down an alley was sufficient to prove both secret confinement and asportation elements of aggravated kidnapping. People v. Banks, 344 Ill. App. 3d 590, 278 Ill. Dec. 785, 799 N.E.2d 503, 2003 Ill. App. LEXIS 1256 (1 Dist. 2003).

Evidence was sufficient to support a conviction for aggravated kidnaping where the defendant confined the complaining witness in a car while he drove through several alleys before finally parking in an alley next to a building where she could not open the passenger door. Such conduct constituted a secret confinement within the meaning of the statute. People v. Hamil, 20 Ill. App. 3d 901, 314 N.E.2d 251 (1 Dist. 1974).

Escape

—Immaterial
Evidence was sufficient to support defendant's conviction of felony murder based upon the underlying felony charge of aggravated kidnaping where the kidnaping was a continuing course of conduct despite defendant's attempt to show that the victim escaped. People v. Peters, 144 Ill. App. 3d 310, 98 Ill. Dec. 731, 494 N.E.2d 853 (2 Dist. 1986).

Evidence Held Sufficient
Where a witness recanted statements and testimony given at the witness' prior trial, the prior inconsistent statements were properly admitted as substantive evidence implicating defendant on charges of murder and aggravated kidnapping. The prior inconsistent statement was sufficient evidence, regardless of corroboration or other evidence, to support defendant's convictions for first-degree murder and aggravated kidnapping because the statement showed defendant's guilt beyond a reasonable doubt. Nevertheless, there was other evidence that supported defendant's convictions and testimony from other witnesses was consistent with the prior inconsistent statement. People v. Thomas, Ill. App. 3d , Ill. Dec. , N.E.2d , 2004 Ill. App. LEXIS 1486 (1 Dist. Dec. 13, 2004).

It was for the trier of fact to weigh the credibility of an acquitted fellow defendant's prior inconsistent statements identifying defendant as the perpetrator of a first-degree murder and aggravated

Evidence Held Sufficient (Cont'd)
kidnapping; since there was no reason for a reviewing court to substitute its credibility determination for that of the trier of fact, that prior statement evidence was sufficient to support convictions of both crimes. People v. Thomas, Ill. App. 3d , 290 Ill. Dec. 316, 821 N.E.2d 628, 2004 Ill. App. LEXIS 1021 (1 Dist. 2004).

Evidence that a victim was forced into a car that took her to defendant, that defendant brandished a gun, that the victim was forced to strip, that she was set on fire, that her clothing was then withheld, and that defendant conceded that he had inflicted great bodily harm, was sufficient to support defendant's conviction on a charge of aggravated kidnapping. People v. Phelps, 211 Ill. 2d 1, 284 Ill. Dec. 268, 809 N.E.2d 1214, 2004 Ill. LEXIS 3 (2004).

Evidence independent of defendant's confession corroborated the matters related in his confession and tended to show the occurrence of the offense of aggravated kidnapping, where witness who lived in the vicinity of where the abduction might have occurred heard a scream around the time when the victim would have been walking to meet her bus to go to work, victim's body was later found in building where defendant had been staying, victim had been strangled, and her body bore signs of other injuries. People v. Bounds, 171 Ill. 2d 1, 215 Ill. Dec. 28, 662 N.E.2d 1168 (1995), cert. denied, 519 U.S. 876, 117 S. Ct. 197, 136 L. Ed. 2d 133 (1996).

Sufficient evidence did exist whereby a rational trier of fact could have found the essential elements of aggravated kidnapping beyond a reasonable doubt. Enoch v. Gramley, 861 F. Supp. 718 (C.D. Ill. 1994), aff'd, 70 F.3d 1490 (7th Cir. 1995), cert. denied, 519 U.S. 829, 117 S. Ct. 95, 136 L. Ed. 2d 50 (1996).

Where each victim was detained both prior to and after being violated, significantly longer than the amount of time necessary to accomplish the defendant's sexual assault against her, this type of detention was not inherent in the sexual assault offense and indicated that the kidnaping of the victims was the result of independent criminal conduct, therefore, while the kidnaping was certainly related to the sexual assault, these charges were sufficiently dissimilar to warrant distinct criminal convictions. People v. Williams, 263 Ill. App. 3d 1098, 202 Ill. Dec. 561, 638 N.E.2d 207 (1 Dist.), appeal denied, 158 Ill. 2d 564, 206 Ill. Dec. 845, 645 N.E.2d 1367 (1994).

The victim's and other witnesses' testimony along with physical evidence was sufficient to sustain defendant's convictions for rape, deviate sexual assault, and aggravated kidnapping. People v. Eastland, 257 Ill. App. 3d 394, 195 Ill. Dec. 542, 628 N.E.2d 1006 (1 Dist. 1993), appeal denied, 155 Ill. 2d 568, 198 Ill. Dec. 547, 633 N.E.2d 9, 156 Ill. 2d 561, 202 Ill. Dec. 925, 638 N.E.2d 1119 (1994).

There was sufficient evidence supporting the trial court's decision that defendant was guilty of aggravated kidnaping beyond a reasonable doubt. People v. Hopkins, 247 Ill. App. 3d 951, 187 Ill. Dec. 688, 618 N.E.2d 279 (1 Dist. 1992), vacated in part, 151 Ill. 2d 570, 187 Ill. Dec. 669, 618 N.E.2d 260 (1993).

Evidence held sufficient to support convictions of murder, aggravated criminal sexual assault, armed robbery and aggravated kidnaping. People v. Ollins, 235 Ill. App. 3d 158, 176 Ill. Dec. 224, 601 N.E.2d 922 (1 Dist. 1992), appeal denied, 149 Ill. 2d 657, 183 Ill. Dec. 868, 612 N.E.2d 520 (1993).

Evidence was held to be sufficient to affirm defendant's aggravated kidnaping conviction. People v. Gonzales, 60 Ill. App. 3d 980, 17 Ill. Dec. 901, 377 N.E.2d 91 (1 Dist. 1978); People v. Graham, 60 Ill. App. 3d 1034, 18 Ill. Dec. 26, 377 N.E.2d 179 (1 Dist. 1978).

No reasonable doubt existed as to the guilt of the defendant of both aggravated kidnaping and intimidation (720 ILCS 5/12-6). People v. Turner, 35 Ill. App. 3d 550, 342 N.E.2d 158 (1 Dist. 1976).

Evidence that defendant supplied a shotgun, and traveled with the co-defendants to a location where the victims were abducted, was present when they were taken from the trunk of a car and was present when the victims were shot was sufficient to sustain verdict that the defendant was accountable for and guilty of the crime of aggravated kidnaping. People v. Gilliam, 16 Ill. App. 3d 659, 306 N.E.2d 352 (3 Dist. 1974).

Where defendants' presence in the immediate vicinity of where a kidnaping took place was clearly established, the car in which they were riding matched the description given by the kidnaping victim and an occurrence witness and was identified by them when observed at a later time, and the identification of the defendants in court by both the victim and the witness was heard by the trier of fact, all of these factors could not be said to be insufficient to support the verdict, despite the fact that the victim did not identify the defendant at lineup where testimony indicated that she did not identify anyone else or state that her attacker was not there, but rather she was simply unable to participate at all. People v. DeMorrow, 17 Ill. App. 3d 901, 308 N.E.2d 659 (4 Dist.), aff'd, 59 Ill. 2d 352, 320 N.E.2d 1 (1974).

Where a victim testified that she was abducted by defendant as she walked down the street near her home, defendant drove her to a secluded area where he forced her to perform several acts of oral copulation and raped her, defendant drove her back to the city and dropped her off in an alley on the southwest side of the city, and the victim testified that during the incident she was able to clearly look at defendant for substantial periods of time under adequate lighting conditions, and where, approximately six weeks after the incident, she attended a lineup, and positively identified defendant as the man who had abducted and attacked her, the complainant's testimony was clear, convincing and sufficient to support defendant's conviction for rape, deviate sexual assault, and aggravated kidnaping. People v. Barksdale, 24 Ill. App. 3d 489, 321 N.E.2d 489 (1 Dist. 1974), cert. denied, 506 U.S. 890, 113 S. Ct. 257, 121 L. Ed. 2d 189 (1992).

Where defendant was identified in court by four eyewitnesses, where victim positively identified defendant on the night of the occurrence after her arrival at the police station and again when he appeared in the line-up, where her testimony was corroborated by the testimony of the other complainants, and where other evidence also linked defendant to the crimes, including his arrest within hours of the crimes in possession of a car bearing the description and license number of the assailants' car, the evidence was sufficient to convict defendant. People v. Rosenborgh, 21 Ill. App. 3d 676, 315 N.E.2d 545 (1 Dist. 1974).

Evidence was sufficient to support the conviction of kidnaping, aggravated kidnaping, and armed robbery against defendant where the defendant with others disarmed troopers and kept them for approximately thirty minutes during daylight, notwithstanding the fact that there was a conflict in the testimony of the troopers as to whether defendant had glasses on and as to the defendant's weight. People v. Del Genio, 10 Ill. App. 3d 432, 294 N.E.2d 332 (2 Dist. 1973).

Evidence that the prosecutrix was driven some distance from her home and confined for a period of 45 minutes during which she was raped supported a conviction for aggravated kidnaping. People v. Canale, 52 Ill. 2d 107, 285 N.E.2d 133 (1972).

The totality of the evidence in the prosecution for aggravated kidnaping and rape did not discredit the accuracy of the identification testimony and was not insufficient to satisfy the prosecution's burden of proof. People v. Harden, 2 Ill. App. 3d 348, 276 N.E.2d 384 (1 Dist. 1971).

There was clear and convincing evidence of the guilt of defendant for both rape and aggravated kidnaping. People v. Smith, 95 Ill. App. 2d 235, 238 N.E.2d 186 (1 Dist. 1968).

Evidence was sufficient to sustain defendant's conviction of kidnaping for ransom. People v. Betson, 362 Ill. 502, 200 N.E. 594 (1936).

Identification

—Held Sufficient

Despite fact that the assistant State's attorney made prejudicial comments which violated defendant's right to due process, defendant's conviction was not reversed as there was overwhelming evidence of guilt, in that defendant was positively identified by the unimpeached testimony of two eyewitnesses, under circumstances establishing the credibility of that identification. People v. Guyon, 117 Ill. App. 3d 522, 73 Ill. Dec. 24, 453 N.E.2d 849 (1 Dist. 1983).

Where defendant was independently identified by the unimpeached testimony of both victims in a photo display, from a lineup, and again in court, the complainants viewed the accused under circumstances permitting a positive identification. People v. Guyon, 117 Ill. App. 3d 522, 73 Ill. Dec. 24, 453 N.E.2d 849 (1 Dist. 1983).

Eyewitness identification evidence was sufficient to sustain defendant's conviction of murder, armed robbery and attempted aggravated kidnaping. People v. Spencer, 107 Ill. App. 3d 835, 63 Ill. Dec. 672, 438 N.E.2d 603 (1 Dist. 1982).

Where victim positively identified defendant as her attacker at the hospital and in court after she had had ample opportunity to view him, where her testimony was corroborated by circumstantial

Identification (Cont'd)

—Held Sufficient (Cont'd)

evidence and several witnesses, and bloodstain where a found in defendant's shoe was the same type as that of the victim, the evidence was sufficient to convict defendant. People v. Hyche, 91 Ill. App. 3d 559, 47 Ill. Dec. 26, 414 N.E.2d 1142 (1 Dist. 1980).

The evidence regarding victim's identification of defendant as his assailant was sufficient to prove defendant's guilt beyond a reasonable doubt. People v. Sanders, 87 Ill. App. 3d 708, 43 Ill. Dec. 182, 410 N.E.2d 182 (1 Dist. 1980).

The victim's identification of both defendants who forced her and another victim into the trunk of an automobile was positive, convincing and sufficient to sustain their conviction for aggravated kidnaping. People v. Daniels, 67 Ill. App. 3d 663, 24 Ill. Dec. 65, 384 N.E.2d 932 (1 Dist. 1978).

Evidence of identification was sufficient to support convictions for rape (see now sexual assault), aggravated kidnaping, and armed robbery. People v. Henderson, 36 Ill. App. 3d 355, 344 N.E.2d 239 (1 Dist. 1976).

—Opportunity Sufficient

Where the state's evidence established that the victim was afforded a reasonable opportunity to make a positive identification of her assailant upon seeing his face briefly after she regained consciousness, the evidence was sufficient to sustain a conviction for rape and deviate sexual assault (see now criminal sexual assault), aggravated battery, aggravated kidnaping, burglary and armed violence. People v. Tate, 94 Ill. App. 3d 192, 50 Ill. Dec. 54, 418 N.E.2d 1048 (5 Dist. 1981).

—When Sufficient

Where the identification of the accused is at issue, the testimony of a single witness is sufficient to convict, even if the identification testimony is contradicted by the accused, provided that the witness is credible and the accused was viewed under circumstances which would permit a positive identification to be made. People v. Schroeder, 105 Ill. App. 3d 677, 61 Ill. Dec. 393, 434 N.E.2d 546 (2 Dist. 1982).

Illustrative Cases

Where the defendant forced the complainant to remain in his cab and transported her against her will to a building 20 minutes away, and took the victim to the rear of the building where he forced her to have sexual intercourse, the defendant committed aggravated kidnaping. People v. Dick, 153 Ill. App. 3d 670, 106 Ill. Dec. 366, 505 N.E.2d 1157 (1 Dist.), appeal denied, 110 Ill. Dec. 460, 511 N.E.2d 432 (1987).

The victim's testimony supported defendant's conviction for aggravated kidnaping where she testified that she was forced at knifepoint to leave her car and enter defendant's van, stated she was threatened at knifepoint throughout the ride in the van and confined against her will, and since confinement in an automobile satisfies the statutory requirement of secret confinement, defendant was proved guilty of kidnaping beyond a reasonable doubt. People v. Blake, 130 Ill. App. 3d 948, 85 Ill. Dec. 932, 474 N.E.2d 892 (2 Dist. 1985).

Complainant's testimony, the testimony of the other witnesses, and the physical evidence supported the finding that complainant was forcibly transported to a garage, secretly confined there, and raped, and that, therefore, the defendant committed aggravated kidnaping under subdivision (a)(3) of this section. People v. Watts, 139 Ill. App. 3d 837, 94 Ill. Dec. 200, 487 N.E.2d 1077 (1 Dist. 1985).

Pushing the complainant down a dark alley to a secluded yard area next to a garage demonstrated defendant's intent to secretly confine the complainant, furthermore, because a conviction of robbery was affirmed, the felony element of aggravated kidnaping was satisfied. People v. Kleba, 110 Ill. App. 3d 345, 66 Ill. Dec. 179, 442 N.E.2d 605 (1 Dist. 1982).

Where a defendant forced complainant into his car by pulling her by the hair, with a threat that she would never see her home again if she did not go quietly, where she was then forced into his family's home as he twisted her arm and again threatened her, where, when the only person indicated to have been in close proximity made his presence known, complainant's cry for help was stifled by defendant, and where, when that person had gone, defendant victimized her by the commission of a forcible felony upon her, such evidence was sufficient to establish defendant's guilt of aggravated kidnaping beyond a reasonable doubt. People v. McKnight, 72 Ill. App. 3d 136, 28 Ill. Dec. 212, 390 N.E.2d 379 (1 Dist. 1979).

An appellate court properly disregarded codefendants' where contention that their victims participated in the kidnaping since defendants offered no proof that victims concocted the kidnaping scheme, where the testimony of each victim was entirely consistent with and fully corroborated the testimony of the other, and where defendants, exercising their privilege not to take the stand, introduced no evidence to contradict the victims' testimony. People v. Ware, 11 Ill. App. 3d 697, 297 N.E.2d 289 (1 Dist. 1973).

Inconsistent Verdicts

Defendant's kidnaping conviction based on secret confinement (720 ILCS 5/10-1(a)(1)) was not legally inconsistent with the trial court's finding of not guilty of aggravated kidnaping. People v. Riley, 219 Ill. App. 3d 482, 162 Ill. Dec. 194, 579 N.E.2d 1008 (1 Dist. 1991).

Indictment

—Held Sufficient

Both the original and the amended informations as to aggravated kidnaping counts effectively charged a crime, and enabled the defendant to prepare a defense, where the charge referred to the appropriate sections of the Criminal Code; furthermore, the defendant was afforded liberal discovery, and failed to show any prejudice from the claimed defect. People v. Sanders, 80 Ill. App. 3d 809, 36 Ill. Dec. 48, 400 N.E.2d 468 (5 Dist. 1980).

Where count of the indictment charging aggravated kidnaping set forth all the elements and stated the name of the victim and the date and city where the offense occurred, defendant was apprised of the precise offense charged with sufficient specificity to prepare his defense and be able to use the conviction as a bar to future prosecution for the same conduct, even though the indictment failed to state that the confinement of the victim, a child under the age of 13, occurred without the consent of her parent or legal guardian. People v. Zboralski, 33 Ill. App. 3d 912, 338 N.E.2d 925 (3 Dist. 1975).

An indictment was sufficient which charged a defendant with having attempted to "knowingly and secretly confine" the victim, as the defendant was made aware of the specific acts constituting the charge against him and the date and the place the offense was alleged to have been committed, as it was obvious that a judicial determination of the defendant's guilt or innocence would act as a bar to subsequent prosecutions, and as there was no issue of the victim's parents' consent. People v. Williams, 131 Ill. App. 2d 280, 268 N.E.2d 730 (1 Dist. 1971), aff'd, 52 Ill. 2d 455, 288 N.E.2d 406 (1972).

Indictment which charged this offense in the language of the statute was held to be sufficient. People v. Bauer, 111 Ill. App. 2d 211, 249 N.E.2d 859 (2 Dist. 1969).

Intent

—Voluntary Intoxication

A defendant's voluntary drinking could not be characterized as the state of drunkenness which would negate proof of intent that he did not knowingly attempt to kidnap a girl under age 13 at gunpoint. People v. Marsh, 118 Ill. App. 2d 298, 255 N.E.2d 13 (1 Dist. 1969).

Jurisdiction

Where the initial abduction and sexual acts occurred in one state, the offender could not be tried in another state into which the defendant later transported the victim during the kidnapping. People v. Blanck, 263 Ill. App. 3d 224, 200 Ill. Dec. 773, 635 N.E.2d 1356 (2 Dist.), appeal denied, 157 Ill. 2d 507, 205 Ill. Dec. 170, 642 N.E.2d 1287 (1994).

Jury Instructions

—Lesser Included Offense

Defendant was not denied due process when the circuit court refused his instruction on the lesser included offense of unlawful restraint, holding that the jury could have believed part of his testimony and part of the victim's testimony and, therefore, could have rejected the greater offense of aggravated kidnaping and

Jury Instructions (Cont'd)

—Lesser Included Offense (Cont'd)

found that the lesser offense of unlawful restraint existed. People v. Frampton, 248 Ill. App. 3d 238, 187 Ill. Dec. 950, 618 N.E.2d 541 (1 Dist. 1993).

—Upheld

Where the indictment charging defendant under subdivision (a)(3) of this section, committing another felony upon his victim, alleged that he had committed both the felony of murder and the felony of aggravated criminal sexual assault, and the trial court only instructed the jury that one who kidnaps another commits aggravated kidnaping if he "inflicts great bodily harm" upon the victim, defendant's contention that he was unconstitutionally convicted of an offense different from the one for which he was indicted failed because the effect of the trial court's instruction was to narrow the charge, not to add a charge.

Kidnaping

—Distinguished

Aggravated kidnaping is a separate offense from simple kidnaping; it requires proof of the elements of simple kidnaping, but in addition, proof of one or more of the elements contained in subsection (a) of this section. People v. Davis, 105 Ill. App. 3d 549, 61 Ill. Dec. 48, 433 N.E.2d 1376 (4 Dist. 1982).

Lesser Included Offense

—Aggravated Assault

Aggravated assault under 720 ILCS 5/12-2(a)(1) is a lesser included offense of aggravated kidnaping as defined by subdivision (a)(5) of this section. People v. Roberts, 71 Ill. App. 3d 124, 27 Ill. Dec. 532, 389 N.E.2d 596 (5 Dist. 1979).

—Aggravated Battery

Where aggravated battery offense merged into the aggravated kidnaping offense, the sentence entered on the aggravated battery conviction was error. People v. Jolliff, 183 Ill. App. 3d 962, 132 Ill. Dec. 350, 539 N.E.2d 913 (4 Dist. 1989).

—Aggravated Sexual Assault

Where the aggravated kidnaping did not arise out of the same act as the aggravated criminal sexual assault, and neither offense was an included offense of the other, the conviction for aggravated kidnaping stood with the conviction for aggravated criminal sexual assault. People v. Hines, 165 Ill. App. 3d 289, 116 Ill. Dec. 382, 518 N.E.2d 1362 (4 Dist.), cert. denied, 121 Ill. 2d 577, 122 Ill. Dec. 442, 526 N.E.2d 835, cert. denied, 488 U.S. 895, 109 S. Ct. 236, 102 L. Ed. 2d 225 (1988).

—Incidental Acts

There is an inequity inherent in permitting kidnaping prosecutions of those who, in reality, committed lesser or different offenses, of which temporary seizure, asportation or detention played an incidental part. People v. Smith, 91 Ill. App. 3d 523, 47 Ill. Dec. 1, 414 N.E.2d 1117 (1 Dist. 1980).

—Kidnaping

Kidnaping, a class 2 felony, is a lesser included offense of aggravated kidnaping, a class 1 felony, since aggravated kidnaping requires the same elements as kidnaping plus proof of one of the five additional elements in subsection (a), such as being armed with a dangerous weapon. People v. Christy, 188 Ill. App. 3d 330, 135 Ill. Dec. 731, 544 N.E.2d 88 (3 Dist. 1989).

The offense of kidnaping is an included offense of any aggravated kidnaping of the victim. People v. Hines, 165 Ill. App. 3d 289, 116 Ill. Dec. 382, 518 N.E.2d 1362 (4 Dist.), cert. denied, 121 Ill. 2d 577, 122 Ill. Dec. 442, 526 N.E.2d 835, cert. denied, 488 U.S. 895, 109 S. Ct. 236, 102 L. Ed. 2d 225 (1988).

Where the offense of kidnaping, as a lesser included offense of aggravated kidnaping, arose from closely related acts, it was improper to convict defendant of both offenses. People v. Earl, 104 Ill. App. 3d 846, 60 Ill. Dec. 680, 433 N.E.2d 722 (2 Dist. 1982).

—Rape Not Included

The trial court did not err in entering judgments of conviction and sentences for rape and aggravated kidnaping, because rape and aggravated kidnaping are not lesser included offenses of each other. People v. Miller, 58 Ill. App. 3d 1019, 16 Ill. Dec. 343, 374 N.E.2d 1118 (4 Dist. 1978).

—Sexual Assault

The offense of deviate sexual assault (now criminal sexual assault) is not a lesser included offense of aggravated kidnaping. People v. Schultz, 73 Ill. App. 3d 379, 29 Ill. Dec. 765, 392 N.E.2d 322 (3 Dist. 1979).

Offenses of rape (now sexual assault) and aggravated kidnaping which arose from a series of closely related acts, were not lesser included offenses, and both convictions were affirmed. People v. Richardson, 50 Ill. App. 3d 550, 8 Ill. Dec. 365, 365 N.E.2d 603 (1 Dist. 1977).

No error was committed in convicting defendant for offenses of both aggravated kidnaping and rape (now sexual assault) since the confinement and transportation of the victim were incidental to the rape and not an offense arising from a single course of conduct. People v. Neal, 37 Ill. App. 3d 713, 346 N.E.2d 178 (3 Dist. 1976).

Kidnaping is not always an included offense in a case of rape (now sexual assault). People v. Henderson, 36 Ill. App. 3d 355, 344 N.E.2d 239 (1 Dist. 1976).

—Unlawful Restraint

Unlawful restraint is a lesser included offense of aggravated kidnaping, in that all of the elements of unlawful restraint are included in aggravated kidnaping. People v. Frampton, 248 Ill. App. 3d 238, 187 Ill. Dec. 950, 618 N.E.2d 541 (1 Dist. 1993).

Unlawful restraint is a lesser included offense of aggravated kidnaping. People v. Bell, 217 Ill. App. 3d 985, 160 Ill. Dec. 657, 577 N.E.2d 1228 (1 Dist.), cert. denied, 142 Ill. 2d 655, 164 Ill. Dec. 920, 584 N.E.2d 132 (1991).

Convictions for unlawful restraint and kidnaping from one continuing course of action could not stand because they are lesser included offenses of aggravated kidnaping. People v. Turner, 128 Ill. 2d 540, 132 Ill. Dec. 390, 539 N.E.2d 1196, cert. denied, 493 U.S. 939, 110 S. Ct. 337, 107 L. Ed. 2d 326 (1989).

Where the offense of unlawful restraint was an included offense of aggravated kidnaping, and defendant was convicted of aggravated kidnaping, the conviction for unlawful restraint was vacated. People v. Hines, 165 Ill. App. 3d 289, 116 Ill. Dec. 382, 518 N.E.2d 1362 (4 Dist.), cert. denied, 121 Ill. 2d 577, 122 Ill. Dec. 442, 526 N.E.2d 835, cert. denied, 488 U.S. 895, 109 S. Ct. 236, 102 L. Ed. 2d 225 (1988).

Unlawful restraint is a lesser included offense of aggravated kidnaping, because all of the elements of unlawful restraint are included within aggravated kidnaping. People v. Hopkins, 107 Ill. App. 3d 422, 63 Ill. Dec. 73, 437 N.E.2d 722 (1 Dist. 1982).

Where alleged offense of aggravated kidnaping arose from transaction as robbery offense, for which probable cause was found, and was added to the information, conviction of the lesser included offense of unlawful restraint was permissible, even though preliminary hearing judge had found no probable cause on such charge. People v. Nash, 90 Ill. App. 3d 612, 45 Ill. Dec. 683, 413 N.E.2d 16 (1 Dist. 1980).

While separate judgments of conviction may be entered where more than one offense arises from a series of incidental or closely related acts, separate judgments of conviction may not be entered for lesser included offenses; since the elements of unlawful restraint are necessarily present in aggravated kidnaping, defendant's conviction for unlawful restraint must be vacated. People v. Riley, 89 Ill. App. 3d 438, 44 Ill. Dec. 673, 411 N.E.2d 1039 (1 Dist. 1980).

Mental State

—Appellate Review

The inquiry of the appellate court concerning the requisite establishment of the mental element to support convictions of rape (now sexual assault), deviate sexual assault (now aggravated criminal sexual assault) and aggravated kidnaping is limited and court need only consider if there was evidence from which the jury could find that the defendant acted knowingly. People v. Utinans, 55 Ill. App. 3d 306, 13 Ill. Dec. 53, 370 N.E.2d 1080 (1 Dist. 1977).

—Knowledge

Kidnaping requires proof of knowledge, a particular form of

Mental State (Cont'd)

—Knowledge (Cont'd)
general intent. People v. Utinans, 55 Ill. App. 3d 306, 13 Ill. Dec. 53, 370 N.E.2d 1080 (1 Dist. 1977).

Multiple Convictions

—Constitutionality
Entering judgment on both aggravated kidnaping and aggravated battery does not violate the due process clause as double enhancement. People v. Pugh, 162 Ill. App. 3d 1030, 114 Ill. Dec. 241, 516 N.E.2d 396 (1 Dist. 1987).

—Not Inconsistent
Guilty verdicts for attempted murder, armed violence predicated on battery, aggravated battery, and aggravated kidnaping are not mutually inconsistent. People v. Moritz, 173 Ill. App. 3d 498, 123 Ill. Dec. 464, 527 N.E.2d 1102 (4 Dist. 1988).

—Predicate Felony
Under this section a defendant may be convicted of both the felony that is the predicate for the aggravated kidnaping charge and aggravated kidnaping itself. Nelson v. Thieret, 793 F.2d 146 (7th Cir.), cert. denied, 479 U.S. 938, 107 S. Ct. 418, 93 L. Ed. 2d 369 (1986).

—Upheld
Defendant's convictions for attempt rape (now sexual assault), robbery and aggravated kidnaping were based on separate physical acts, and, therefore, were upheld. People v. Kleba, 110 Ill. App. 3d 345, 66 Ill. Dec. 179, 442 N.E.2d 605 (1 Dist. 1982).

Multiple Offenses

—Evidence Held Insufficient
Evidence was held insufficient to sustain convictions for aggravated criminal sexual assault, aggravated kidnaping, and unlawful restraint. People v. Jackson, 178 Ill. App. 3d 785, 127 Ill. Dec. 914, 533 N.E.2d 996 (1 Dist. 1989).

—Evidence Held Sufficient
Evidence was sufficient to sustain defendant's convictions for rape (now sexual assault) and aggravated kidnaping. People v. McDonald, 125 Ill. 2d 182, 125 Ill. Dec. 781, 530 N.E.2d 1351 (1988).

The evidence was sufficient to support a finding of guilty of murder, armed robbery, and aggravated kidnaping beyond a reasonable doubt and to support the imposition of the death penalty. People v. Titone, 115 Ill. 2d 413, 105 Ill. Dec. 923, 505 N.E.2d 300 (1986), cert. denied, 484 U.S. 873, 108 S. Ct. 210, 98 L. Ed. 2d 161 (1987).

Where victim watched the defendant shoot and kill one person and saw him standing with a revolver in his hand beside the body of another, and where the defendant still had this revolver in his possession during the time he and the victim were in the motel room where the alleged rape occurred, evidence was sufficient to uphold the defendant's rape conviction, and his conviction for aggravated kidnaping, because resistance by the victim would have been futile and would have endangered her life. People v. Morgan, 112 Ill. 2d 111, 97 Ill. Dec. 430, 492 N.E.2d 1303 (1986), cert. denied, 479 U.S. 1101, 107 S. Ct. 1329, 94 L. Ed. 2d 180 (1987).

The evidence was sufficient to prove defendant guilty beyond a reasonable doubt of rape, deviate sexual assault (now aggravated criminal sexual assault), aggravated kidnaping and unlawful restraint. People v. Olesch, 143 Ill. App. 3d 577, 97 Ill. Dec. 508, 492 N.E.2d 1381 (1 Dist. 1986).

Evidence was held sufficient to sustain defendant's conviction of murder, aggravated kidnaping, deviate sexual assault (now aggravated criminal sexual assault), rape (now sexual assault) and attempted murder. People v. Johnson, 114 Ill. 2d 170, 102 Ill. Dec. 342, 499 N.E.2d 1355 (1986).

The evidence fully supported the jury's verdict of defendant's guilt of charge of rape (now sexual assault), armed robbery, and aggravated kidnaping. People v. Clark, 124 Ill. App. 3d 14, 79 Ill. Dec. 427, 463 N.E.2d 981 (1 Dist. 1984).

The circumstantial evidence was sufficient to prove the guilt of the defendants of the murders and kidnaping beyond a reasonable doubt. People v. Hobson, 117 Ill. App. 3d 191, 72 Ill. Dec. 518, 452 N.E.2d 771 (4 Dist. 1983).

Testimony as well as physical evidence overwhelmingly supported the verdicts of guilty for aggravated kidnaping and murder. People v. Kubat, 94 Ill. 2d 437, 69 Ill. Dec. 30, 447 N.E.2d 247 (1983), vacated on other grounds, 679 F. Supp. 788 (N.D. Ill. 1988), aff'd, 867 F.2d 351 (7th Cir. 1989).

Evidence was found sufficient to convict defendant of rape (now sexual assault), deviate sexual assault (now aggravated criminal sexual assault), armed robbery, and aggravated kidnaping. People v. Johnson, 109 Ill. App. 3d 511, 65 Ill. Dec. 137, 440 N.E.2d 992 (1 Dist. 1982).

Evidence held sufficient to sustain convictions for aggravated sexual assault and aggravated kidnaping where the complainant testified that she was grabbed from behind and forced into a car, she identified the defendant as the person who grabbed her, she was forced to accompany the defendant and his companion to the companion's apartment, and once inside, both defendants raped the victim, and where the victim subsequently led police to the defendant's home. People v. Davis, 97 Ill. App. 3d 299, 52 Ill. Dec. 780, 422 N.E.2d 989 (1 Dist. 1981).

The evidence was not so palpably contrary to the verdict or so unreasonable, improbable or unsatisfactory as to cause a reasonable doubt as to the guilt of defendant of aggravated kidnaping and deviate sexual assault (now aggravated criminal sexual assault). People v. Walsh, 80 Ill. App. 3d 754, 36 Ill. Dec. 167, 400 N.E.2d 587 (1 Dist. 1980).

The evidence was sufficient to sustain the defendant's convictions for deviate sexual assault (now aggravated criminal sexual assault), aggravated battery and aggravated kidnaping. People v. Leverson, 69 Ill. App. 3d 726, 26 Ill. Dec. 101, 387 N.E.2d 931 (1 Dist. 1979).

Considering the mutually supportive testimony of two witness and an accomplice, in addition to other evidence presented at trial, the evidence was clearly sufficient to justify the jury's verdict of guilty of aggravated kidnaping, murder, and attempted armed robbery. People v. Thomas, 72 Ill. App. 3d 28, 27 Ill. Dec. 908, 389 N.E.2d 1316 (1 Dist. 1979).

Evidence held sufficient to support defendants' convictions for murder, aggravated kidnaping and rape (now sexual assault). People v. Evans, 80 Ill. App. 3d 444, 35 Ill. Dec. 805, 399 N.E.2d 1333 (1 Dist. 1979).

Where the evidence was overwhelming, conclusive and was corroborated by defendant's admission to his brother-in-law, evidence was sufficient to support defendant's convictions of aggravated kidnaping and murder. People v. Fletcher, 59 Ill. App. 3d 310, 17 Ill. Dec. 49, 375 N.E.2d 1333 (1 Dist. 1978).

The evidence supported convictions for aggravated kidnaping and deviate sexual assault (now aggravated criminal sexual assault). People v. Utinans, 55 Ill. App. 3d 306, 13 Ill. Dec. 53, 370 N.E.2d 1080 (1 Dist. 1977).

Evidence was held sufficient to support convictions for charges of aggravated kidnaping, armed robbery, and burglary where a codefendant's testimony was corroborated by his wife, the money was found in the trunk of defendant's automobile, and a voice identification was made by one of the victims. People v. VanZile, 48 Ill. App. 3d 972, 6 Ill. Dec. 747, 363 N.E.2d 429 (4 Dist. 1977).

—Merger
Offenses of armed robbery, kidnaping and aggravated kidnaping did not merge into a single conviction of armed robbery despite fact that they all arose out of the same conduct, since the conviction and sentence for each offense must stand where more than one offense arises from a series of closely related acts, the crimes are clearly distinct, and require different elements of proof. People v. Boyce, 41 Ill. App. 3d 53, 353 N.E.2d 287 (1 Dist. 1976).

—Separate
The jury was justified in finding defendant guilty of both the offense of aggravated battery and the offense of aggravated kidnapping where the basis for the aggravated battery was the initial beating and choking of victim in a parking lot, and the separate conduct which gave rise to the aggravated kidnapping was a sexual assault and harm which occurred after the victim was dragged unconscious across the parking lot and 160 feet into a sorghum field. People v. Franzen, 251 Ill. App. 3d 813, 190 Ill. Dec. 847, 622

Multiple Offenses (Cont'd)

—Separate (Cont'd)
N.E.2d 877 (2 Dist. 1993), appeal denied, 154 Ill. 2d 564, 197 Ill. Dec. 490, 631 N.E.2d 712 (1994).

The offenses of aggravated kidnaping and rape were separate and distinct crimes and required different elements of proof; that the kidnaping would be aggravated due to the commission of the rape would not render them the same for prosecution. People v. Jones, 6 Ill. App. 3d 669, 286 N.E.2d 87 (5 Dist. 1972), aff'd, 60 Ill. 2d 300, 325 N.E.2d 601 (1975).

Ransom

—In General
Kidnaping for ransom is the unlawful seizure of a person, the secreting of that person, and the extortion of ransom or other valuable thing or concession from the person seized and secreted, or from his parent, guardian, or legal custodian; however, 720 ILCS 5/10-1(a)(1) does not require unlawful seizure if the secret confining is against the individual's will. People v. Long, 39 Ill. 2d 40, 233 N.E.2d 389 (1968).

If ransom is demanded the kidnaping is considered aggravated kidnaping. People v. Masterson, 79 Ill. App. 2d 117, 223 N.E.2d 252 (3 Dist. 1967).

—Elements of Offense
Collecting ransom may be sufficient evidence upon which to sustain a conviction of kidnaping for ransom. People v. Bolla, 114 Ill. App. 3d 442, 70 Ill. Dec. 118, 448 N.E.2d 996 (2 Dist. 1983).

—Not Required
A demand for ransom is not an essential element of the offense as described in this section. People v. Masterson, 79 Ill. App. 2d 117, 223 N.E.2d 252 (3 Dist. 1967).

—Release Immaterial
The fact that a victim may have been released and was free of detention before ransom was paid was immaterial where the offense as described in subdivision (a)(1) of this section had already been committed and was complete. People v. Bolla, 114 Ill. App. 3d 442, 70 Ill. Dec. 118, 448 N.E.2d 996 (2 Dist. 1983).

Robbery

—Distinguished
Where the victim was driven for a short distance, approximately 20 minutes from where he first encountered defendants and defendants took control of his car and personal property while threatening the use of force it was clear that there was a robbery and not kidnaping. People v. Smith, 91 Ill. App. 3d 523, 47 Ill. Dec. 1, 414 N.E.2d 1117 (1 Dist. 1980).

Secret Confinement

—Shown
Circumstantial evidence was sufficient to establish that the defendant secretly confined a 10 year old boy before killing him where the boy was last seen leaving a boat ramp at about the same time as the defendant and traveling in the same direction as the defendant, the boy was supposed to be riding home but never made it there, his body was found a week later in a shallow grave in another county, two hairs matching the boy's were found in the defendant's car, and the boy's blood was found in the defendant's car's trunk. People v. Buss, 187 Ill. 2d 144, 240 Ill. Dec. 520, 718 N.E.2d 1, 1999 Ill. LEXIS 663 (1999), cert. denied, 529 U.S. 1089, 120 S. Ct. 1723, 146 L. Ed. 2d 644 (2000).

Evidence was sufficient to show that defendant intended to secretly confine the victims where he approached two girls, nine and ten years old, in his car, offered them candy, told them he would take them wherever they wanted to go if they got in the car and, after being rebuffed, continued to prowl the neighborhood fleeing only when approached by the mother of one of the girls. People v. Williams, 295 Ill. App. 3d 663, 230 Ill. Dec. 369, 693 N.E.2d 498 (3 Dist. 1998).

Where the victim was dragged against her will from a well-lit parking lot to a place in a dark field, concealed from public view and not free to leave, secret confinement was proven. People v. Franzen, 251 Ill. App. 3d 813, 190 Ill. Dec. 847, 622 N.E.2d 877 (2 Dist. 1993), appeal denied, 154 Ill. 2d 564, 197 Ill. Dec. 490, 631 N.E.2d 712 (1994).

Sentencing

—Constitutionality
Fifteen-year enhancement for aggravated kidnapping violates the proportionate penalties clause of the Illinois Constitution and is unenforceable. People v. Baker, 341 Ill. App. 3d 1083, 276 Ill. Dec. 458, 794 N.E.2d 353, 2003 Ill. App. LEXIS 1077 (4 Dist. 2003).

The elements of the armed violence counts were not identical to the elements of the aggravated criminal sexual abuse counts or the aggravated kidnapping counts, therefore differences between sentences did not violate the proportionate penalties clause. People v. Koppa, 184 Ill. 2d 159, 234 Ill. Dec. 479, 703 N.E.2d 91 (1998).

The issue of constitutionality of the statutory penalties for aggravated kidnaping and armed violence is not waived by failing to raise it in the circuit court; as a general rule, a constitutional challenge to a statute can be raised at any time. People v. Christy, 139 Ill. 2d 172, 151 Ill. Dec. 315, 564 N.E.2d 770 (1990).

Aggravated kidnaping is a more serious offense than the lesser included offense of kidnaping; but where the sentencing for kidnaping elevated it to a more serious crime than aggravated kidnaping, the result was an unconstitutionally disproportionate sentencing scheme. People v. Christy, 188 Ill. App. 3d 330, 135 Ill. Dec. 731, 544 N.E.2d 88 (3 Dist. 1989).

—Appellate Review
Where at the first sentencing hearing, when the sentence of probation was entered on the aggravated kidnaping offense, the trial judge stated the aggravated battery conviction merged into the kidnaping offense; however, at the second sentencing hearing, after revocation, the trial judge entered a separate sentence on defendant's aggravated battery conviction to run concurrently with the sentence on aggravated kidnaping; defendant did not waive the issue and, it could be considered on appeal. People v. Jolliff, 183 Ill. App. 3d 962, 132 Ill. Dec. 350, 539 N.E.2d 913 (4 Dist. 1989).

Where defendant was improperly convicted and sentenced for both armed robbery and armed violence based on the same act it was necessary to remand cause to the trial court for resentencing on defendant's convictions for armed robbery and for aggravated kidnaping; although the sentence imposed for aggravated kidnaping by the trial court fell within the permissible range of sentences allowed by 730 ILCS 5/5-8-1, appellate court would not speculate as to how the trial court would have ruled had it not been mistaken as to number and severity of the offenses. People v. Jones, 89 Ill. App. 3d 1030, 45 Ill. Dec. 332, 412 N.E.2d 683 (1 Dist. 1980).

—Disparity Upheld
Where the chances of the two victims of getting killed had been greater at the hands of one defendant than they were at the hands of a codefendant, this was a valid distinction, and the defendant's sentence was proper. People v. VanZile, 48 Ill. App. 3d 972, 6 Ill. Dec. 747, 363 N.E.2d 429 (4 Dist. 1977).

—Double Enhancement
Predicated felony of aggravated kidnapping was enhanced from kidnapping by the aggravated factor of concealment of identity, and the weapon factor enhanced aggravated kidnapping to armed violence; therefore there was no improper double enhancement. People v. Koppa, 184 Ill. 2d 159, 234 Ill. Dec. 479, 703 N.E.2d 91 (1998).

—Extended Term Held Improper
Where the trial court found that defendant's crimes of attempted first degree murder (720 ILCS 5/9-1 et seq.), aggravated criminal sexual assault (720 ILCS 5/12-14), and aggravated kidnapping (720 ILCS 5/10-2) were committed in an exceptionally brutal and heinous manner and it imposed an extended term sentence pursuant to 730 ILCS 5/5-8-2(a)(2) on the attempted murder and sexual assault charges, those required reversal where the enhancing element had not been specified in the indictment nor proved beyond a reasonable doubt, as required by Apprendi; however, no reversal was required of the consecutive sentencing imposed pursuant to 730 ILCS 5/5-8-4(a) because Apprendi did not apply to consecutive sentencing. People v. Lucas, Ill. App. 3d , Ill. Dec. , N.E.2d , 2003 Ill. App. LEXIS 342 (1 Dist. Mar. 26, 2003).

Sentencing (Cont'd)

—Extended Term Held Improper (Cont'd)

Giving petitioner an extended term sentence on an aggravated kidnaping conviction, which was not within the most serious class of offenses for which he was convicted, was not permitted by the extended term sentencing statute (730 ILCS 5/5-8-2). People v. Perruquet, 181 Ill. App. 3d 660, 130 Ill. Dec. 284, 537 N.E.2d 351 (5 Dist. 1989).

—Held Not Excessive

Sentence held not excessive for conviction of aggravated kidnaping. People v. Carter, 107 Ill. App. 2d 474, 246 N.E.2d 320 (2 Dist. 1969), cert. denied, 397 U.S. 1008, 90 S. Ct. 1236, 25 L. Ed. 2d 421 (1970).

—Held Proper

Sentence of 10 to 25 years imposed upon defendant for the kidnaping and rape of 12 year old girl did not constitute cruel and unusual punishment. People v. Huff, 45 Ill. 2d 186, 258 N.E.2d 356 (1970).

—Maximum Extended Term

The defendant was improperly sentenced to an extended term of 60 years' imprisonment for aggravated kidnaping, since aggravated kidnapping is a Class need ordinary symbol for 1 felony for which the maximum extended term is not 60 years, but 30 years (see 730 ILCS 5/5-8-2). People v. Spreitzer, 123 Ill. 2d 1, 121 Ill. Dec. 224, 525 N.E.2d 30, cert. denied, 488 U.S. 917, 109 S. Ct. 274, 102 L. Ed. 2d 262 (1988).

Trial court erred in sentencing defendant to an extended term of 45 years for aggravated kidnaping, since aggravated kidnaping is a Class 1 felony for which an offender may be sentenced to no more than 30 years even under an extended term (see 730 ILCS 5/5-8-2). People v. Guyon, 117 Ill. App. 3d 522, 73 Ill. Dec. 24, 453 N.E.2d 849 (1 Dist. 1983).

—Maximum Sentence

Where the trial court imposed a sentence of 25 years for an aggravated kidnaping charge, and the sentence for a Class 1 felony is a maximum of 15 years, it was necessary to reduce defendant's sentence to 15 years. People v. Williams, 159 Ill. App. 3d 527, 111 Ill. Dec. 131, 512 N.E.2d 35 (1 Dist. 1987).

The trial court erred in sentencing defendant to an extended term of 30 years for the offense of aggravated kidnaping other than for ransom, the most serious offense for which defendant was convicted, and which carried a maximum sentence of 15 years. People v. Walsh, 101 Ill. App. 3d 1146, 57 Ill. Dec. 257, 428 N.E.2d 937 (1 Dist. 1981), overruled on other grounds, 111 Ill. App. 3d 814, 67 Ill. Dec. 448, 444 N.E.2d 684 (1982).

—Res Judicata

Where petitioner's extended term sentence for aggravated kidnaping was shown to be void, fundamental fairness required that petitioner be allowed to challenge that sentence again, the previous ruling on the matter notwithstanding. People v. Perruquet, 181 Ill. App. 3d 660, 130 Ill. Dec. 284, 537 N.E.2d 351 (5 Dist. 1989).

—Sentence Reduced

The nature of the crimes of rape and aggravated kidnaping of a 13 year old girl, and the fact that there was no evidence of defendant's being armed, although serious did not indicate that the best interests of society or of the defendants would be served by foreclosing them from the possibility of rehabilitation by being considered for parole before serving 20 years, less time for good behavior; thus, the sentences of each defendant was reduced. People v. Jones, 6 Ill. App. 3d 669, 286 N.E.2d 87 (5 Dist. 1972), aff'd, 60 Ill. 2d 300, 325 N.E.2d 601 (1975).

Separate Offenses

—Armed Robbery

Defendant's conviction of attempt armed robbery was not vacated as an included offense of his aggravated kidnaping conviction since armed robbery and aggravated kidnaping are separate and distinct offenses, despite fact that the kidnaping became aggravated because of the armed robbery. People v. Boyce, 41 Ill. App. 3d 53, 353 N.E.2d 287 (1 Dist. 1976).

—Battery

The commission of aggravated battery in the parking lot was sufficient to raise the offense of kidnaping to aggravated kidnaping. People v. Pugh, 162 Ill. App. 3d 1030, 114 Ill. Dec. 241, 516 N.E.2d 396 (1 Dist. 1987).

Defendant's actions indicated that it was his purpose to transport the victim and secretly to confine her where defendant forced the victim into the car very soon after initially accosting her, and held her down on the back seat so as to conceal her. Kidnapping was not incidental to the separate offense of battery. People v. Pugh, 162 Ill. App. 3d 1030, 114 Ill. Dec. 241, 516 N.E.2d 396 (1 Dist. 1987).

Each of defendant's convictions had a different factual basis and, therefore, both convictions would stand where defendant's action in striking the victim in the parking lot and in the car were separate acts from his transporting her with the intent to confine her. Where more than one offense arises from a series of incidental or closely related acts and the offenses are not, by definition, lesser included offenses, convictions with concurrent sentences can be entered. Defendant was properly convicted of both aggravated battery and aggravated kidnaping. People v. Pugh, 162 Ill. App. 3d 1030, 114 Ill. Dec. 241, 516 N.E.2d 396 (1 Dist. 1987).

—Kidnaping

Defendant's convictions for aggravated kidnaping while armed with a dangerous weapon, and aggravated kidnaping based upon a subsequent deviate sexual assault (now aggravated criminal sexual assault), were proper where the kidnaping of the victim with a dangerous weapon, and the subsequent deviate sexual assault upon her which gave rise to a second count of aggravated kidnaping, which occurred some time after the original abduction and at a different location, were not part of the same transaction, but were two distinct acts which justified multiple kidnaping convictions. People v. Schultz, 73 Ill. App. 3d 379, 29 Ill. Dec. 765, 392 N.E.2d 322 (3 Dist. 1979).

—Murder

Acts of taking victim to Illinois and confining her were not incidental to murder but rather supported an independent charge of kidnapping. People v. Moreland, 292 Ill. App. 3d 616, 226 Ill. Dec. 814, 686 N.E.2d 597 (1 Dist. 1997), appeal denied, 179 Ill. 2d 606, 235 Ill. Dec. 572, 705 N.E.2d 445 (1998).

—Not Shown

Where the separate, "ultimate" offense, such as robbery or rape, could not be committed in the form planned without the limited asportation inherent in the crime, a conviction for kidnaping in addition to the other crime was improper. People v. Pugh, 162 Ill. App. 3d 1030, 114 Ill. Dec. 241, 516 N.E.2d 396 (1 Dist. 1987).

—Sexual Assault

Where a rape (now sexual assault) was a separate offense from a kidnaping because a separate physical act formed the basis for each offense, the defendant's conviction and sentence for rape and aggravated kidnaping must stand. People v. Jones, 169 Ill. App. 3d 883, 120 Ill. Dec. 563, 524 N.E.2d 593 (1 Dist.), appeal denied, 122 Ill. 2d 588, 125 Ill. Dec. 230, 530 N.E.2d 258 (1988).

Although the offenses of rape (now sexual assault) and aggravated kidnaping arose from a series of closely related acts, these offenses were not lesser included offenses, defendant's conviction for rape and aggravated kidnaping were proper. People v. Jones, 53 Ill. App. 3d 197, 10 Ill. Dec. 857, 368 N.E.2d 452 (1 Dist. 1977).

While it is true that, as a general rule, in order for multiple convictions to be proper it must be possible to distinguish between those acts constituting one offense and those acts constituting another, an exception was made where a rape (now sexual assault) was itself the aggravating factor to kidnaping charge, and the rape was therefore an essential element of the crime of aggravated kidnaping, but convictions for both rape and aggravated kidnaping could stand. People v. Scott, 45 Ill. App. 3d 487, 4 Ill. Dec. 45, 359 N.E.2d 878 (1 Dist.), aff'd, 69 Ill. 2d 85, 12 Ill. Dec. 736, 370 N.E.2d 540 (1977).

Although the offenses were closely related, defendant could properly be convicted of deviate sexual assault (see now 720 ILCS 5/12-13) and aggravated kidnapping. People v. Rehbein, 54 Ill. App. 3d 93, 11 Ill. Dec. 736, 369 N.E.2d 190 (1 Dist. 1977), aff'd, 74 Ill. 2d 435, 24 Ill. Dec. 835, 386 N.E.2d 39 (1978).

Separate Offenses (Cont'd)

—Sexual Assault (Cont'd)

That a kidnaping would be aggravated due to the commission of a rape (now sexual assault) would not have rendered them the same act for prosecution. People v. Henderson, 36 Ill. App. 3d 355, 344 N.E.2d 239 (1 Dist. 1976).

Aggravated kidnaping and rape (now sexual assault), although committed as a series of acts against the same victim, are two separate and distinct offenses and a sentence might properly be imposed for each offense. People v. Whiteaker, 30 Ill. App. 3d 848, 334 N.E.2d 200 (2 Dist. 1975).

An aggravated kidnaping conviction can stand in addition to a rape (now sexual assault) conviction. People v. Long, 30 Ill. App. 3d 815, 333 N.E.2d 534 (2 Dist. 1975).

Single Course of Action

—In General

Where a defendant's objective, motive and purpose in committing an aggravated kidnaping was to effect a rape, the two offenses were not distinct and separate; the defendant's spiriting his victim to another part of the state was a change in purpose and conduct aimed at avoiding capture, and this established that his objective, motive and purpose had changed from his earlier behavior culminating in the rape. People v. Elliott, 46 Ill. App. 3d 887, 5 Ill. Dec. 529, 361 N.E.2d 852 (4 Dist. 1977).

—Aggravated Assault

The court erred in entering a judgment of guilty on the charge of aggravated assault, arising out of acts closely related to those that formed the basis for the conviction of aggravated kidnaping. People v. Roberts, 71 Ill. App. 3d 124, 27 Ill. Dec. 532, 389 N.E.2d 596 (5 Dist. 1979).

—Armed Violence

Defendant's multiple convictions for aggravated kidnaping and armed violence could not stand where both offenses were carved from a single physical act; accordingly, defendant's conviction on the charge of aggravated kidnaping was vacated and his conviction for the more serious offense of armed violence was sustained. People v. Viens, 109 Ill. App. 3d 1017, 65 Ill. Dec. 525, 441 N.E.2d 660 (2 Dist. 1982), cert. denied, 461 U.S. 917, 103 S. Ct. 1900, 77 L. Ed. 2d 287 (1983).

—Continuous Control

Where the detainment and confinement of the victim were derived from the defendant's continuous control over her, the aggravated kidnaping and unlawful restraint charges were carved from the same physical act, and since a defendant cannot be convicted of more than one offense arising from the same physical act, the trial court erred in sustaining the conviction for unlawful restraint. People v. Tate, 94 Ill. App. 3d 192, 50 Ill. Dec. 54, 418 N.E.2d 1048 (5 Dist. 1981).

—Evidence Held Sufficient

Evidence held sufficient that the severe beating of the victim and the later abduction resulted from a continuous state of mind so as to find defendant guilty of aggravated kidnaping. People v. Earl, 104 Ill. App. 3d 846, 60 Ill. Dec. 680, 433 N.E.2d 722 (2 Dist. 1982).

—Lesser Included Offense

Convictions for unlawful restraint and kidnaping from one continuing course of action could not stand because they were lesser included offenses of aggravated kidnaping. People v. Turner, 128 Ill. 2d 540, 132 Ill. Dec. 390, 539 N.E.2d 1196, cert. denied, 493 U.S. 939, 110 S. Ct. 337, 107 L. Ed. 2d 326 (1989).

—Multiple Convictions Improper

Multiple convictions based upon the same physical act cannot stand. Where defendant, while armed with a dangerous weapon, kidnaped the victim, robbed him, and then murdered him, such conduct involved three offenses: murder, armed robbery, and aggravated kidnaping, but this was not a situation where separate abductions occurred on the same victim at different intervals, or more than one victim was unlawfully confined; accordingly, the felony murder conviction and the second conviction for aggravated kidnaping were reversed. People v. Klinkhammer, 105 Ill. App. 3d 747, 61 Ill. Dec. 480, 434 N.E.2d 835 (3 Dist. 1982).

—Not Shown

Defendant's conduct could not be viewed as a single transaction intended to acquire property through the use of force where defendant knew his kidnaping scheme had been foiled prior to his attempt to force victim's husband into a car, and there was a considerable time lapse between the act of kidnaping the victim and the attempt to rob her husband; therefore, defendant's convictions for both aggravated kidnaping and attempt armed robbery stood. People v. Mulcahey, 50 Ill. App. 3d 421, 8 Ill. Dec. 627, 365 N.E.2d 1013 (4 Dist. 1977), aff'd, 72 Ill. 2d 282, 21 Ill. Dec. 176, 381 N.E.2d 254 (1978).

—Sexual Assault

Conviction for aggravated kidnaping could be based on the same conduct that formed the basis for an aggravated sexual assault conviction. People v. Charles, 217 Ill. App. 3d 509, 160 Ill. Dec. 404, 577 N.E.2d 534 (2 Dist. 1991).

A defendant could not stand convicted of both aggravated kidnaping and aggravated criminal sexual assault if the crimes arose from the same physical acts and required proof of identical elements; thus, his conviction for the less serious offense, aggravated kidnaping, would be vacated. People v. McDarrah, 175 Ill. App. 3d 284, 124 Ill. Dec. 827, 529 N.E.2d 808 (2 Dist. 1988).

Where offenses of aggravated kidnapping and deviate sexual assault arose from a series of incidental or closely related acts and the offenses were not lesser included offenses of each other, the convictions for both aggravated kidnaping and deviate sexual assault (now aggravated criminal sexual assault) were proper. People v. Drummond, 103 Ill. App. 3d 621, 59 Ill. Dec. 332, 431 N.E.2d 1089 (1 Dist. 1981).

Defendant was properly convicted of aggravated kidnaping based upon a deviate sexual assault, (now aggravated criminal sexual assault), notwithstanding the fact that the offenses arose from the same physical act. People v. Schultz, 73 Ill. App. 3d 379, 29 Ill. Dec. 765, 392 N.E.2d 322 (3 Dist. 1979).

A defendant's separate convictions for aggravated kidnaping and deviate sexual assault could not stand when it was clear that his objective, purpose and motive in kidnaping the victim was to commit deviate sexual assault. People v. Donaldson, 44 Ill. App. 3d 280, 3 Ill. Dec. 107, 358 N.E.2d 107 (4 Dist. 1976).

Where the kidnaping was motivated by and committed in order to achieve defendant's objective of perpetrating the rape (now sexual assault), the conviction for aggravated kidnaping (the charge for which the statute imposes the less severe penalty) had to be set aside. People v. Meredith, 37 Ill. App. 3d 895, 347 N.E.2d 55 (4 Dist. 1976).

Weapons

—Presence

Although victims were, for the most part, unaware of the presence of a gun after a defendant's initial threat to induce their entering an apartment, and there was no sufficient showing of force made, the mere knowledge that the gun was present in the apartment coupled with the early display of willingness to use it by the defendant was sufficient to instill fear in the two victims. People v. Ware, 11 Ill. App. 3d 697, 297 N.E.2d 289 (1 Dist. 1973).

LEGAL PERIODICALS

For article, "Survey of Illinois Law: Criminal Law and Procedure," see 21 S. Ill. U.L.J. 759 (1997).

RESEARCH REFERENCES

Validity, construction, and application of "hold to service" provision of kidnapping statute. 28 ALR5th 754.

720 ILCS 5/10-3 Unlawful restraint

Sec. 10-3. *Unlawful restraint.* (a) A person commits the offense of unlawful restraint when he knowingly without legal authority detains another.

(b) Sentence. Unlawful restraint is a Class 4 felony.
(Source: P.A. 79-840.)

Note.
This section was Ill.Rev.Stat., Ch. 38, para. 10-3.

Illinois Administrative Code.
See 59 Illinois Administrative Code, § 119.261, 77 Illinois Administrative Code, §§ 210.2250, 260.1750, 270.2250, 518.1610, 220.2800, 115.321, 250.435, 245.72, 350.681, 295.3040, 225.1050.

CASE NOTES

Analysis

Constitutionality
In General
Accomplice Liability
—Shown
Armed Robbery
—Distinguished
Construction
Detention Under Mental Health Code
Elements of Offense
—Weapon
Evidence Held Insufficient
Evidence Held Sufficient
Identification
—Held Sufficient
Illustrative Cases
Indictment
—Held Sufficient
Jury Instructions
Kidnaping
—Distinguished
Lesser Included Offense
—Aggravated Kidnaping
—Armed Robbery
—Home Invasion
—Kidnaping
—Sexual Assault
—Unlawful Restraint
Multiple Offenses
—Evidence Held Insufficient
—Evidence Held Sufficient
—Separate Acts
Necessity Defense
Probable Cause
—Lacking
Restraint
—Evidence Held Insufficient
—Physical Force Not Necessary
Sentencing
—Maximum Term
—Minimum Term
—Multiple Offenses
Separate Offenses
—In General
—Armed Robbery
—Contributing to Delinquency of Minor
—Murder
—Rape
—Sexual Assault
Single Course of Action
—Armed Violence
—Continuous Control
—Lesser Offenses
—Sexual Abuse
—Sexual Assault
—Time Lapse Insufficient
Verdicts

Constitutionality
Because the amendment to the Criminal Code of 1961, adding the offense of aggravated unlawful restraint (720 ILCS 5/10-3.1) made the underlying offenses of kidnaping and unlawful restraint proportional, the armed violence statute (720 ILCS 5/33A-1), as applied to unlawful restraint, is not unconstitutional. People v. Bloyer, 200 Ill. App. 3d 872, 146 Ill. Dec. 857, 558 N.E.2d 1056 (2 Dist. 1990).

To detain another is commonly understood to mean causing a restriction of another's freedom to move about, and this statute makes plain that only legal authority can justify the detention of another; the statutory language is not so vague that the ultimate decision as to its meaning rests on the opinions and whims of the trier of fact, and the fact that there may be a degree of uncertainty in some borderline case does not render the statute unconstitutional in all cases. People v. Wisslead, 108 Ill. 2d 389, 92 Ill. Dec. 226, 484 N.E.2d 1081 (1985).

It was not clearly irrational for the legislature to prescribe greater penalties for unlawful restraint than for aggravated assault, and the designation of unlawful restraint as a Class 4 felony was a valid exercise of the legislative power. People v. Wisslead, 108 Ill. 2d 389, 92 Ill. Dec. 226, 484 N.E.2d 1081 (1985).

The armed violence statute, as applied to the unlawful restraint statute, violates the constitutional assurances of due process and proportionate penalties. People v. McNeil, 125 Ill. App. 3d 876, 81 Ill. Dec. 256, 466 N.E.2d 1058 (1 Dist. 1984).

The policy underlying Ill. Const. (1970), Art. I, § 2, and Ill. Const. (1970), Art. I, § 11, would be violated if the penalty prescribed for an offense is greater than the penalty prescribed for a less serious offense; therefore, a sentence which could be imposed for the offense of armed violence based on unlawful restraint with a category I weapon, being greater than the sentence for the more serious offense of aggravated kidnaping based on similar facts, was constitutionally disproportionate. People v. Wisslead, 94 Ill. 2d 190, 68 Ill. Dec. 606, 446 N.E.2d 512 (1983).

In General
Detention must be wilful, against the victim's consent, and prevent movement from one place to another. People v. Bowen, 241 Ill. App. 3d 608, 182 Ill. Dec. 43, 609 N.E.2d 346 (4 Dist.), appeal denied, 151 Ill. 2d 568, 186 Ill. Dec. 386, 616 N.E.2d 339, cert. denied, 510 U.S. 946, 114 S. Ct. 387, 126 L. Ed. 2d 336 (1993).

The gist of unlawful restraint is the detention of a person by some conduct which prevents him from moving from one place to another. People v. Kittle, 140 Ill. App. 3d 951, 95 Ill. Dec. 260, 489 N.E.2d 481 (2 Dist. 1986).

False imprisonment (now unlawful restraint) in its legal meaning is an aggravated assault, and the gist of the offense is the actual and unlawful restraint or detention of one person against his will by another, by actual force or reasonably apprehended force, though actual force is not necessary. People v. Cohoon, 315 Ill. App. 259, 42 N.E.2d 969 (4 Dist. 1942).

Accomplice Liability

—Shown
Where the record proved defendant's guilt on each charge beyond a reasonable doubt as a willing participant in a criminal enterprise, there was no doubt that defendant was legally accountable for the conduct of his companions and, as such, shared equally in their guilt. People v. Ruiz, 94 Ill. 2d 245, 68 Ill. Dec. 890, 447 N.E.2d 148 (1982), cert. denied, 462 U.S. 1112, 103 S. Ct. 2465, 77 L. Ed. 2d 1341 (1983).

Armed Robbery

—Distinguished
The defendant's convictions for both armed robbery and armed violence were not improper where the armed violence charge arose out of the unlawful restraint which occurred when the offenders accosted the victim at gunpoint and pushed him into the car and the armed robbery charge arose from later conduct when the offenders took the victim's watch, wallet, briefcase, glasses and car. People v. McEwen, 104 Ill. App. 3d 410, 60 Ill. Dec. 144, 432 N.E.2d 1043 (1 Dist. 1982).

The offense of unlawful restraint does not merge into armed robbery, since the elements of these two crimes differ; knowing detention without legal authority is not an element of armed robbery and, therefore, unlawful restraint is not a lesser included offense of armed robbery. People v. Surges, 101 Ill. App. 3d 962, 57 Ill. Dec. 332, 428 N.E.2d 1012 (1 Dist. 1981).

Construction

Defendant's sentence was affirmed; the sentence enhancement under 18 U.S.C.S. § 924(e) and U.S. Sentencing Guidelines Manual § 4B1.4 (2003) was proper because the Illinois crime of unlawful restraint, 720 ILCS 5/10-3 was a "violent felony" for the purposes of the armed-career-criminal statute. United States v. Wallace, 326 F.3d 881, 2003 U.S. App. LEXIS 7145 (7th Cir. 2003), cert. denied, U.S. , 124 S. Ct. 265, 157 L. Ed. 2d 191 (2003).

Detention Under Mental Health Code

An initially authorized detention under the Mental Health Code (405 ILCS 5/1-101 et seq.) may be followed by a unlawful detention that is actionable as false imprisonment. Sassali v. DeFauw, 297 Ill. App. 3d 50, 231 Ill. Dec. 646, 696 N.E.2d 1217 (2 Dist. 1998).

A lawful detention pursuant to a provision of the Mental Health Code (405 ILCS 5/101 et seq.) cannot be the basis of a false imprisonment claim. Sassali v. DeFauw, 297 Ill. App. 3d 50, 231 Ill. Dec. 646, 696 N.E.2d 1217 (2 Dist. 1998).

Elements of Offense

—Weapon

The presence of a weapon is not an element of unlawful restraint. People v. Wisslead, 94 Ill. 2d 190, 68 Ill. Dec. 606, 446 N.E.2d 512 (1983).

Evidence Held Insufficient

Evidence was insufficient to find defendants guilty beyond a reasonable doubt of criminal sexual assault. People v. Yeargan, 229 Ill. App. 3d 219, 170 Ill. Dec. 810, 593 N.E.2d 699 (1 Dist.), cert. denied, 146 Ill. 2d 650, 176 Ill. Dec. 820, 602 N.E.2d 474 (1992).

Evidence that defendant committed act of restraint was insufficient to sustain unlawful restraint conviction. People v. Haybron, 153 Ill. App. 3d 906, 106 Ill. Dec. 662, 506 N.E.2d 369 (3 Dist. 1987).

Where one of the victims described her assailant as six inches taller than the defendant, and was unable to pick out defendant's mug shot, her identification of the defendant was insufficient to support a conclusion of guilt beyond a reasonable doubt as to armed robbery, home invasion and unlawful restraint. People v. Ash, 102 Ill. 2d 485, 82 Ill. Dec. 373, 468 N.E.2d 1153 (1984).

Evidence Held Sufficient

Evidence was sufficient to support conviction for unlawful restraint. People v. Daniel, 311 Ill. App. 3d 276, 243 Ill. Dec. 678, 723 N.E.2d 1279, 2000 Ill. App. LEXIS 59 (2 Dist. 2000).

Evidence was sufficient to find defendants guilty of criminal sexual assault and unlawful restraint, where victim testified that defendants grabbed her arms and held her facedown on the couch while they and the others had sex with her, and other witnesses gave corroborative testimony. People v. Hermosillo, 256 Ill. App. 3d 1020, 194 Ill. Dec. 916, 628 N.E.2d 413 (1 Dist. 1993), appeal denied, 154 Ill. 2d 564, 197 Ill. Dec. 491, 631 N.E.2d 713 (1994).

Evidence was sufficient to prove defendant guilty of criminal sexual assault, unlawful restraint, and intimidation, where defendant threatened a 16 year old minor with a mop and a bottle, hit her on the head with a belt, and then forced her to submit to two acts of vaginal intercourse. People v. Stevens, 255 Ill. App. 3d 812, 195 Ill. Dec. 933, 629 N.E.2d 518 (1 Dist. 1992).

The trial court did not err in holding the defendant guilty of unlawful restraint where the evidence showed the defendant's curious mode of entry, the spontaneous and continued violence towards his wife (the victim) and the previous history of violence and harassment. People v. Williams, 222 Ill. App. 3d 129, 164 Ill. Dec. 214, 582 N.E.2d 1158 (1 Dist. 1991), appeal denied, 144 Ill. 2d 642, 169 Ill. Dec. 150, 591 N.E.2d 30 (1992).

There was sufficient credible evidence to convict defendant where inconsistencies in the complainant's testimony could be considered to be minor. People v. Laughlin, 163 Ill. App. 3d 115, 114 Ill. Dec. 380, 516 N.E.2d 535 (1 Dist. 1987).

There was sufficient evidence presented to the jury to enable it to find defendant guilty beyond a reasonable doubt of unlawful restraint where the victim gave positive and detailed identification of defendant, whom she observed at close range under well-lighted conditions, and testimony placed defendant at the scene of the crime and showed that he had the opportunity to commit the crime during a crucial interval that corresponded to the time the incident occurred. People v. Plaintinga, 132 Ill. App. 3d 512, 87 Ill. Dec. 771, 477 N.E.2d 1299 (1 Dist. 1985).

The evidence presented provided an ample basis for the jury's determination that defendant was guilty of attempted rape, deviate sexual assault (now aggravated criminal sexual assault), attempted armed robbery, and unlawful restraint. People v. McDowell, 121 Ill. App. 3d 491, 76 Ill. Dec. 883, 459 N.E.2d 1018 (1 Dist. 1984).

Evidence was sufficient to sustain defendant's conviction of attempted murder, armed robbery, attempted armed robbery and unlawful restraint. People v. Vaughn, 100 Ill. App. 3d 1082, 56 Ill. Dec. 508, 427 N.E.2d 840 (1 Dist. 1981).

Evidence of defendant's guilt of attempt murder, aggravated battery and unlawful restraint was sufficient. People v. Childs, 95 Ill. App. 3d 606, 51 Ill. Dec. 99, 420 N.E.2d 513 (1 Dist. 1981).

Evidence was sufficient to establish defendant's guilt beyond a reasonable doubt. People v. Surges, 101 Ill. App. 3d 962, 57 Ill. Dec. 332, 428 N.E.2d 1012 (1 Dist. 1981); People v. Robinson, 102 Ill. App. 3d 884, 58 Ill. Dec. 23, 429 N.E.2d 1356 (1 Dist. 1981).

There was no need for corroboration of victim's testimony in light of his credible and positive testimony in prosecution of robbery and unlawful restraint; the evidence of unlawful restraint was sufficient. People v. Flores, 79 Ill. App. 3d 869, 35 Ill. Dec. 182, 398 N.E.2d 1132 (1 Dist. 1979).

Evidence of identification held sufficient to support convictions for armed robbery, theft, and unlawful restraint where not only did the victim's identification testimony connect defendants with the crimes, but so did the identification testimony of a police officer that he observed the defendants in the stolen car and the victim's black fur coat which the police recovered from one defendant. This other evidence of guilt more than overcame any deficiency in the identification testimony of the complaining witness who could only muster a general description of defendants. People v. Scott, 20 Ill. App. 3d 880, 314 N.E.2d 671 (1 Dist. 1974).

Evidence was sufficient for conviction of defendant for unlawful restraint, murder, and robbery. People v. Jennings, 11 Ill. App. 3d 132, 296 N.E.2d 19 (5 Dist. 1973).

Where all of the witnesses who identified defendant were in a good position to observe, and did observe defendant under conditions that lent veracity to their observations, where they identified defendant in a line-up and at trial, and they asserted their positiveness and remained unshaken on cross-examination, the guilt of the defendant was firmly grounded on sufficient evidence and defendant's guilt was proved beyond a reasonable doubt. People v. Jennings, 11 Ill. App. 3d 132, 296 N.E.2d 19 (5 Dist. 1973).

Evidence was sufficient to sustain defendant's conviction of murder, armed robbery, and unlawful restraint. People v. Hyde, 1 Ill. App. 3d 831, 275 N.E.2d 239 (5 Dist. 1971).

Identification

—Held Sufficient

Where a complainant viewed defendant's face under reasonably good light for 30 to 60 seconds as she and the assailant were face to face while he had one hand over her mouth, this was adequate opportunity to observe the defendant at the time of the crime, and where complainant gave an accurate description of her attacker and had always identified only the defendant as her attacker, a "show up" identification, even if suppressed, did not necessarily taint a later identification. People v. Davenport, 49 Ill. App. 3d 130, 7 Ill. Dec. 38, 363 N.E.2d 1200 (2 Dist. 1977).

Illustrative Cases

Defendant's detention of his son was unreasonable and without lawful authority where he threatened suicide and held his son hostage. People v. Walker, 130 Ill. App. 3d 58, 85 Ill. Dec. 396, 473 N.E.2d 995 (2 Dist. 1985).

Unlawful restraint occurred where defendant held onto the complainant, both by her arm and by her leg, impairing her freedom of locomotion, since she was not free to go or to stay as she desired. People v. Satterthwaite, 72 Ill. App. 3d 483, 29 Ill. Dec. 3, 391 N.E.2d 162 (4 Dist. 1979).

In suit arising out of detention of plaintiff by defendant merchant, where testimony of plaintiff and defendant showed substantial disparities, it was difficult, if not impossible, to see how all the testimony viewed in its aspect most favorable to the plaintiff could overwhelmingly favor the defendants on the issue of the plaintiff's wrongful detention, and the trial court erred in directing a verdict

Illustrative Cases (Cont'd)
for the defendant. Gaszak v. Zayre of Ill., Inc., 16 Ill. App. 3d 50, 305 N.E.2d 704 (1 Dist. 1973).

Indictment

—Held Sufficient

The information charging a defendant with unlawful restraint was sufficient to specify the nature of the offense charged because the offense of unlawful restraint did not involve specific statements or objects such as are involved in perjury or destruction of evidence, nor did the statutory language involved, "knowingly without legal authority detains another," leave room for wide speculation as to the nature of the conduct alleged. People v. Wisslead, 108 Ill. 2d 389, 92 Ill. Dec. 226, 484 N.E.2d 1081 (1985).

Jury Instructions

Where the evidence clearly showed that victim was more than merely detained without authority as her hands were bound tightly behind her back with a coat hanger, her presence inside her apartment was kept secret from boyfriend, there were blood stains throughout most of the apartment, a knife was used to inflict the wounds, and the many and various wounds inflicted upon victim by her assailant resulted in her death, it was reasonable in light of the evidence that attorney not tender an instruction on unlawful restraint and his failure to do so did not prejudice petitioner. Enoch v. Gramley, 861 F. Supp. 718 (C.D. Ill. 1994), aff'd, 70 F.3d 1490 (7th Cir. 1995), cert. denied, 519 U.S. 829, 117 S. Ct. 95, 136 L. Ed. 2d 50 (1996).

Kidnaping

—Distinguished

Although the evidence was ample to support a defendant's aggravated kidnaping conviction, the same acts could not be the basis for a conviction of unlawful restraint of a child. People v. Banks, 344 Ill. App. 3d 590, 278 Ill. Dec. 785, 799 N.E.2d 503, 2003 Ill. App. LEXIS 1256 (1 Dist. 2003).

One major distinction between kidnaping and unlawful restraint is that kidnaping involves a secret confinement, whereas unlawful restraint involves merely detaining another without legal authority. People v. Enoch, 122 Ill. 2d 176, 119 Ill. Dec. 265, 522 N.E.2d 1124, cert. denied, 488 U.S. 917, 109 S. Ct. 274, 102 L. Ed. 2d 263 (1988).

Lesser Included Offense

—Aggravated Kidnaping

Where the offense of unlawful restraint was an included offense of aggravated kidnaping, and defendant was convicted of aggravated kidnaping, the conviction for unlawful restraint was unlawful. People v. Hines, 165 Ill. App. 3d 289, 116 Ill. Dec. 382, 518 N.E.2d 1362 (4 Dist.), cert. denied, 121 Ill. 2d 577, 122 Ill. Dec. 442, 526 N.E.2d 835, cert. denied, 488 U.S. 895, 109 S. Ct. 236, 102 L. Ed. 2d 225 (1988).

Unlawful restraint is a lesser included offense of aggravated kidnaping, because all of the elements of unlawful restraint are included within aggravated kidnaping. People v. Hopkins, 107 Ill. App. 3d 422, 63 Ill. Dec. 73, 437 N.E.2d 722 (1 Dist. 1982).

While separate judgments of conviction may be entered where more than one offense arises from a series of incidental or closely related acts, separate judgments of conviction may not be entered for lesser included offenses; since the elements of unlawful restraint are necessarily present in aggravated kidnaping, defendant's conviction for unlawful restraint must be vacated. People v. Riley, 89 Ill. App. 3d 438, 44 Ill. Dec. 673, 411 N.E.2d 1039 (1 Dist. 1980).

—Armed Robbery

Unlawful restraint is not a lesser included offense of armed robbery, as the two crimes require proof of different elements. People v. Crespo, 118 Ill. App. 3d 815, 74 Ill. Dec. 425, 455 N.E.2d 854 (1 Dist. 1983).

—Home Invasion

Unlawful restraint cannot be an included offense of home invasion since the scienter requirement is quite different in the two offenses. People v. Kuykendall, 108 Ill. App. 3d 708, 64 Ill. Dec. 270, 439 N.E.2d 521 (4 Dist. 1982).

—Kidnaping

Convictions for unlawful restraint and kidnaping from one continuing course of action could not stand because they were lesser included offenses of aggravated kidnaping. People v. Turner, 128 Ill. 2d 540, 132 Ill. Dec. 390, 539 N.E.2d 1196, cert. denied, 493 U.S. 939, 110 S. Ct. 337, 107 L. Ed. 2d 326 (1989).

—Sexual Assault

Unlawful restraint is a lesser included offense of aggravated criminal sexual assault. People v. Allman, 180 Ill. App. 3d 396, 129 Ill. Dec. 332, 535 N.E.2d 1097 (1 Dist. 1989).

Unlawful restraint and indecent liberties with a child were lesser included offenses of rape (now sexual assault); therefore, defendant could not be convicted of all three charges arising from one act. People v. Alexander, 127 Ill. App. 3d 1007, 83 Ill. Dec. 651, 470 N.E.2d 1071 (1 Dist. 1984), cert. denied, 471 U.S. 1019, 105 S. Ct. 2027, 85 L. Ed. 2d 308 (1985).

All the elements of unlawful restraint are present in rape (now sexual assault). People v. Williams, 115 Ill. App. 3d 276, 71 Ill. Dec. 163, 450 N.E.2d 851 (1 Dist. 1983); People v. McCann, 76 Ill. App. 3d 184, 31 Ill. Dec. 737, 394 N.E.2d 1055 (2 Dist. 1979).

—Unlawful Restraint

Unlawful restraint is not necessarily a lesser included offense of criminal sexual assault. People v. Alvarado, 235 Ill. App. 3d 116, 175 Ill. Dec. 778, 600 N.E.2d 1236 (3 Dist. 1992).

Unlawful restraint is a lesser included offense of kidnaping. People v. Kittle, 140 Ill. App. 3d 951, 95 Ill. Dec. 260, 489 N.E.2d 481 (2 Dist. 1986).

Multiple Offenses

—Evidence Held Insufficient

Evidence was held insufficient to sustain convictions for aggravated criminal sexual assault, aggravated kidnaping, and unlawful restraint. People v. Jackson, 178 Ill. App. 3d 785, 127 Ill. Dec. 914, 533 N.E.2d 996 (1 Dist. 1989).

Evidence was held insufficient to find defendant guilty of rape, robbery and unlawful restraint. People v. Wright, 147 Ill. App. 3d 302, 100 Ill. Dec. 899, 497 N.E.2d 1261 (1 Dist. 1986).

—Evidence Held Sufficient

Convictions for aggravated criminal sexual assault and unlawful restraint were not subject to reversal where complainant's testimony was corroborated by her mother, the investigating officer and treating physician, and where defendant's arguments about the sufficiency question were at best attacks on the credibility of the state's witnesses or attempts to create conflicts or inconsistencies in their testimony. People v. Jackson, 203 Ill. App. 3d 1, 148 Ill. Dec. 422, 560 N.E.2d 1019 (1 Dist. 1990).

The evidence was sufficient to prove defendant guilty beyond a reasonable doubt of rape (now sexual assault), deviate sexual assault (now aggravated criminal sexual assault), aggravated kidnaping and unlawful restraint. People v. Olesch, 143 Ill. App. 3d 577, 97 Ill. Dec. 508, 492 N.E.2d 1381 (1 Dist. 1986).

Evidentiary rulings and assistance of counsel at trial were held sufficient to sustain defendant's conviction of murder, attempted murder, armed robbery and unlawful restraint. People v. Reese, 121 Ill. App. 3d 977, 77 Ill. Dec. 390, 460 N.E.2d 446 (1 Dist. 1984).

Where the state's evidence established that the testifying victim had several opportunities to view defendant, the testimony of a single witness, if positive and credible, was sufficient to convict even though contradicted by the accused, therefore the evidence was sufficient to sustain defendant's convictions for armed robbery, aggravated battery, and unlawful restraint. People v. Perez, 94 Ill. App. 3d 377, 49 Ill. Dec. 949, 418 N.E.2d 969 (1 Dist. 1981).

Testimony was sufficient to support the verdicts of robbery and unlawful restraint. People v. Flores, 79 Ill. App. 3d 869, 35 Ill. Dec. 182, 398 N.E.2d 1132 (1 Dist. 1979).

—Separate Acts

Defendant's convictions for criminal sexual assault (720 ILCS 5/12-13) and unlawful restraint were based on separate acts, the sexual assault arising from his penetration, and his unlawful restraint from detaining the victim as she struggled to get away and pleaded with defendant to let her leave his apartment. People v. Defyn, 222 Ill. App. 3d 504, 165 Ill. Dec. 41, 584 N.E.2d 220 (1

Multiple Offenses (Cont'd)

—Separate Acts (Cont'd)
Dist. 1991), cert. denied, 144 Ill. 2d 637, 169 Ill. Dec. 145, 591 N.E.2d 25 (1992).

The defendant's conviction of residential burglary and unlawful restraint was not improper where the evidence established that the defendant committed two separate criminal acts: (1) residential burglary when he entered the house with the intent to commit unlawful restraint, and (2) unlawful restraint when he forcibly detained his wife and would not allow her to leave. People v. Williams, 222 Ill. App. 3d 129, 164 Ill. Dec. 214, 582 N.E.2d 1158 (1 Dist. 1991), appeal denied, 144 Ill. 2d 642, 169 Ill. Dec. 150, 591 N.E.2d 30 (1992).

Necessity Defense

Evidence held sufficient to prove claim of unlawful restraint. People v. Bergin, 227 Ill. App. 3d 32, 169 Ill. Dec. 20, 590 N.E.2d 939 (2 Dist. 1992).

Where defendant stated that he entered victim's home solely to rescue victim and to protect her and her family, a defense of necessity did relate to defendant's convictions of intimidation and unlawful restraint because defendant's necessity defense related only to his entry into the victim's home and the defense of necessity in no way related to threatening the victim or holding a pillow to her face. People v. Bergin, 227 Ill. App. 3d 32, 169 Ill. Dec. 20, 590 N.E.2d 939 (2 Dist. 1992).

Probable Cause

—Lacking
Under this section, a merchant may detain a customer only when he has probable cause to believe that the person has wrongfully taken or has actual possession of and is about to wrongfully take merchandise, but not in a case where a customer was observed removing an item from her coat before entering a checkout line, as merchant did not have probable cause to believe she was still in wrongful possession of any merchandise. Gaszak v. Zayre of Ill., Inc., 16 Ill. App. 3d 50, 305 N.E.2d 704 (1 Dist. 1973).

Restraint

—Evidence Held Insufficient
Even if unlawful restraint were considered to be a lesser included offense of criminal sexual assault, the lesser offense was not established where the state failed to prove beyond a reasonable doubt that complainant was unable to give a knowing consent and that defendant knew she was not able to consent. People v. Hunt, 150 Ill. App. 3d 874, 104 Ill. Dec. 201, 502 N.E.2d 464 (2 Dist. 1986).

—Physical Force Not Necessary
Actual or physical force is not a necessary element of unlawful restraint as long as an individual's freedom of locomotion is impaired. People v. Bowen, 241 Ill. App. 3d 608, 182 Ill. Dec. 43, 609 N.E.2d 346 (4 Dist.), appeal denied, 151 Ill. 2d 568, 186 Ill. Dec. 386, 616 N.E.2d 339, cert. denied, 510 U.S. 946, 114 S. Ct. 387, 126 L. Ed. 2d 336 (1993).

Physical force is not necessary to accomplish restraint as long as the individual's freedom of locomotion is impaired. People v. Warner, 98 Ill. App. 3d 433, 53 Ill. Dec. 956, 424 N.E.2d 747 (4 Dist. 1981).

In order to constitute false imprisonment (now unlawful restraint), it is not necessary to show that the person guilty thereof used physical violence, laid hands on the person falsely imprisoned, or confined him in a jail or prison; but evidence will be sufficient if, at any place or time, he in any manner restrained such person of his liberty, detained him in any manner from going where he wished, or prevented him from doing what he desired. People v. Scalisi, 324 Ill. 131, 154 N.E. 715 (1926).

Sentencing

—Maximum Term
Sentences of not less than five years nor more than nine imposed for each offense of aggravated assault, a Class A misdemeanor, and unlawful restraint, a Class 4 felony, exceeded the maximum permissible terms as set forth in 730 ILCS 5/5-8-1. People v. Salvaggio, 38 Ill. App. 3d 482, 348 N.E.2d 243 (1 Dist. 1976).

—Minimum Term
A sentence of one year's imprisonment for unlawful restraint, the minimum sentence for a Class 4 felony, was proper where the court found that probation would deprecate the seriousness of the offense. People v. Paulick, 174 Ill. App. 3d 868, 124 Ill. Dec. 311, 529 N.E.2d 28 (2 Dist. 1988).

—Multiple Offenses
Where a defendant was convicted of armed robbery, armed violence, aggravated battery, and unlawful restraint, but sentenced only on armed robbery and unlawful restraint, he should have been sentenced on the conviction for armed violence based upon unlawful restraint. Since there was no authority for the appellate court to vacate the lesser offense and remand for sentencing on the greater, the convictions of aggravated battery and armed violence on which no sentence was entered were vacated. People v. Smith, 111 Ill. App. 3d 494, 67 Ill. Dec. 329, 444 N.E.2d 565 (1 Dist. 1982).

Separate Offenses

—In General
While the offense of unlawful restraint is often committed in conjunction with other offenses, it is punishable as a separate crime if the restraint is independent of the other offenses and arose out of separate acts. People v. Alvarado, 235 Ill. App. 3d 116, 175 Ill. Dec. 778, 600 N.E.2d 1236 (3 Dist. 1992).

—Armed Robbery
The offenses of unlawful restraint and armed robbery are based on separate acts, each requiring proof of a different element, thus, convictions and sentences for both offenses can be proper. People v. Boclair, 106 Ill. App. 3d 515, 62 Ill. Dec. 265, 435 N.E.2d 1237 (1 Dist. 1982).

—Contributing to Delinquency of Minor
Unlawful restraint and contributing to the dependency or neglect of a child have separate elements, thus preventing either offense from being an included offense of the other by definition, nor is one carved from the same act as the other; therefore, the offenses do not merge. People v. Warner, 98 Ill. App. 3d 433, 53 Ill. Dec. 956, 424 N.E.2d 747 (4 Dist. 1981).

—Murder
Where defendant forcibly took victim to abandoned building and came up from behind her as she was attempting to defend herself from another and pinned her arms against her body so as to prevent her movement and to allow another to place some type of rope or cord around her neck with which he then choked her, these acts were separate and distinct from those giving rise to the attempted murder charge and the trial court did not err in entering judgment on defendant's conviction for unlawful restraint. People v. McNutt, 146 Ill. App. 3d 357, 100 Ill. Dec. 24, 496 N.E.2d 1089 (1 Dist. 1986).

—Rape
Defendant's conviction for unlawful restraint was not invalid as a matter of law where it was incidental to the perpetrator's primary goal to commit rape. People v. Plaintinga, 132 Ill. App. 3d 512, 87 Ill. Dec. 771, 477 N.E.2d 1299 (1 Dist. 1985).

—Sexual Assault
When a defendant has been convicted of both unlawful restraint and criminal sexual assault, the conviction of unlawful restraint must be vacated. People v. Bowen, 241 Ill. App. 3d 608, 182 Ill. Dec. 43, 609 N.E.2d 346 (4 Dist.), appeal denied, 151 Ill. 2d 568, 186 Ill. Dec. 386, 616 N.E.2d 339, cert. denied, 510 U.S. 946, 114 S. Ct. 387, 126 L. Ed. 2d 336 (1993).

Defendant's argument that his unlawful restraint conviction must be vacated because it arose out of the same physical act as the aggravated criminal sexual assault conviction was without merit where the aggravated criminal sexual assault conviction arose from his sexual penetration of complainant, and the unlawful restraint conviction arose from his detention of her. People v. Jackson, 203 Ill. App. 3d 1, 148 Ill. Dec. 422, 560 N.E.2d 1019 (1 Dist. 1990).

Single Course of Action

—Armed Violence
A conviction for armed violence based on the underlying felony of

Single Course of Action (Cont'd)

—Armed Violence (Cont'd)
unlawful restraint is improper. People v. Faysom, 131 Ill. App. 3d 517, 86 Ill. Dec. 566, 475 N.E.2d 945 (1 Dist. 1985).

Convictions for both armed violence and the underlying felony of unlawful restraint cannot stand where a single physical act is the basis of both charges; in such a situation, judgment should be entered and sentence imposed only on the more serious offense. People v. Smith, 111 Ill. App. 3d 494, 67 Ill. Dec. 329, 444 N.E.2d 565 (1 Dist. 1982).

—Continuous Control
Where the evidence indicated that the complaining witness was in the defendant's continuous control, despite the fact that she was deceived prior to defendant's overt act, and both the confinement and the detention were derived from this control, and where the unlawful restraint was a lesser included offense of kidnaping and both the confinement and the detention were closely related acts, the conviction for kidnaping should stand, and the conviction for unlawful restraint should be vacated. People v. Kittle, 140 Ill. App. 3d 951, 95 Ill. Dec. 260, 489 N.E.2d 481 (2 Dist. 1986).

Where the detention and confinement of the victim were derived from the defendant's continuous control over her, the aggravated kidnaping and unlawful restraint charges were carved from the same physical act, and since a defendant cannot be convicted of more than one offense arising from the same physical act, the trial court erred in sustaining the conviction for unlawful restraint. People v. Tate, 94 Ill. App. 3d 192, 50 Ill. Dec. 54, 418 N.E.2d 1048 (5 Dist. 1981).

—Lesser Offenses
The convictions of armed violence and reckless conduct were vacated where these charges arose as a result of identical conduct from which arose more serious convictions of armed robbery and unlawful restraint. People v. Funches, 34 Ill. App. 3d 1015, 341 N.E.2d 195 (3 Dist. 1976).

—Sexual Abuse
Where an act that constituted the force required to prove sexual abuse was the same act that constituted unlawful restraint, convictions for both offenses could not stand. People v. Paulick, 174 Ill. App. 3d 868, 124 Ill. Dec. 311, 529 N.E.2d 28 (2 Dist. 1988).

—Sexual Assault
Where unlawful restraint offense out of the same physical act as a rape (now sexual assault) defendant's conviction for the lesser offense of unlawful restraint was vacated. People v. Wrice, 140 Ill. App. 3d 494, 94 Ill. Dec. 920, 488 N.E.2d 1313 (1 Dist. 1986).

Where defendant offered victim a ride, then carried her to a rural area and raped her, the trial court erred in entering convictions for both rape (now sexual assault) and unlawful restraint as there were not two acts committed which were sufficient to support convictions for both rape and unlawful restraint. People v. Bachman, 92 Ill. App. 3d 419, 47 Ill. Dec. 253, 414 N.E.2d 1369 (3 Dist. 1981).

—Time Lapse Insufficient
The short time lapse that occurred between the unlawful restraint and the subsequent rape (now sexual assault) failed to remove the offense from the same course of conduct, and thus, defendant's conviction for unlawful restraint was vacated. People v. Jung Oh Kim, 148 Ill. App. 3d 191, 101 Ill. Dec. 507, 498 N.E.2d 831 (1 Dist. 1986).

Verdicts
Where defendant asserted that his convictions of two counts of aggravated criminal sexual assault in violation of 720 ILCS 5/12-14 were legally inconsistent with his acquittal for unlawful restraint in violation of 720 ILCS 5/10-3, the court found criminal defendants were not permitted to challenge convictions on the basis that they were legally inconsistent with acquittals on other charges. People v. McCoy, 207 Ill. 2d 352, 278 Ill. Dec. 551, 799 N.E.2d 269, 2003 Ill. LEXIS 1496 (2003).

LEGAL PERIODICALS

For article, "Criminal Law: 1988-89 Illinois Law Survey," see 21 Loy. U. Chi. L.J. 307 (1989-90).

For article, "Criminal Law: 1985-86 Illinois Law Survey," see 18 Loy. U. Chi. L.J. 435 (1986-87).

720 ILCS 5/10-3.1 Aggravated Unlawful Restraint

Sec. 10-3.1. *Aggravated Unlawful Restraint.* (a) A person commits the offense of aggravated unlawful restraint when he knowingly without legal authority detains another while using a deadly weapon.

(b) Sentence. Aggravated unlawful restraint is a Class 3 felony.
(Source: P.A. 84-930.)

Note.
This section was Ill.Rev.Stat., Ch. 38, para. 10-3.1.

CASE NOTES

ANALYSIS

Constitutionality
Elements of Offense
—Intent
—Motive
Evidence
—Sufficient
Ineffective Assistance of Counsel
Mental State
—Intent
Separate Offenses
—Inconsistent Verdicts Upheld
—Same Act
Unlawful Restraint
—Evidence Held Sufficient

Constitutionality
The offense of armed violence predicated on unlawful restraint is unconstitutionally disproportionate to aggravated kidnapping under Ill. Const., (1970), Art. I, §§ 2, 11; therefore armed violence cannot be predicated on unlawful restraint. People v. Murphy, 261 Ill. App. 3d 1019, 200 Ill Dec. 9, 635 N.E.2d 110 (2 Dist. 1994).

Because of the amendment to the Criminal Code adding the offense of aggravated unlawful restraint, effective January 1, 1986, which made the underlying offenses of kidnaping and unlawful restraint proportional, the armed violence statute (720 ILCS 5/33A-1 et seq.), as applied to unlawful restraint, is not unconstitutional. People v. Bloyer, 200 Ill. App. 3d 872, 146 Ill. Dec. 857, 558 N.E.2d 1056 (2 Dist. 1990).

Elements of Offense

—Intent
A conviction for unlawful restraint requires proof of a separate intent to detain an individual. People v. Sperow, 170 Ill. App. 3d 800, 121 Ill. Dec. 417, 525 N.E.2d 223 (4 Dist.), appeal denied, 122 Ill. 2d 589, 125 Ill. Dec. 231, 530 N.E.2d 259 (1988).

—Motive
Motive is not an element of the offense of aggravated unlawful restraint. People v. Watkins, 238 Ill. App. 3d 253, 179 Ill. Dec. 422, 606 N.E.2d 254 (1 Dist. 1992).

Evidence

—Sufficient
Circumstantial evidence was sufficient to establish that the defendant detained a 10 year old boy before killing him by use of a deadly weapon where the boy was last seen leaving a boat ramp at about the same time as the defendant and traveling in the same direction as the defendant, the boy was supposed to be riding home but never made it there, his body was found a week later in a shallow grave in another county, two hairs matching the boy's were found in the defendant's car, the boy's blood was found in the defendant's car's trunk, and the boy was killed with a knife like one

Evidence (Cont'd)

—Sufficient (Cont'd)
owned by the defendant. People v. Buss, 187 Ill. 2d 144, 240 Ill. Dec. 520, 718 N.E.2d 1, 1999 Ill. LEXIS 663 (1999), cert. denied, 529 U.S. 1089, 120 S. Ct. 1723, 146 L. Ed. 2d 644 (2000).

Ineffective Assistance of Counsel
Although, the commutation of defendant's death sentence for violation of 720 ILCS 5/9-1(a), (b)(3), (b)(8), 10-3.1 rendered the Ill. Const. art VI, § 4(b) and Ill. Sup. Ct. R. 603, 609(a) sentencing issues moot, the trial court erroneously concluded that defendant's claim of ineffective assistance of trial counsel could be resolved by the appointment of different counsel on appeal. People v. Moore, 207 Ill. 2d 68, 278 Ill. Dec. 36, 797 N.E.2d 631, 2003 Ill. LEXIS 778 (2003).

Mental State

—Intent
Knowing intent to detain cannot be derived from or incidental to the intent to commit another criminal act. People v. Sperow, 170 Ill. App. 3d 800, 121 Ill. Dec. 417, 525 N.E.2d 223 (4 Dist.), appeal denied, 122 Ill. 2d 589, 125 Ill. Dec. 231, 530 N.E.2d 259 (1988).

Requirement of a separate intent to detain does not eliminate the possibility of a conviction of unlawful restraint as well as another offense and the evidence must show that the restraint was independent of the other offense and punishable as such. People v. Sperow, 170 Ill. App. 3d 800, 121 Ill. Dec. 417, 525 N.E.2d 223 (4 Dist.), appeal denied, 122 Ill. 2d 589, 125 Ill. Dec. 231, 530 N.E.2d 259 (1988).

Separate Offenses

—Inconsistent Verdicts Upheld
Conviction of aggravated assault was not inconsistent with acquittal of the more serious offense of unlawful restraint, even though the same act of pointing a gun at victim could have supported a guilty verdict as to the unlawful restraint offense, and aggravated assault and unlawful restraint are composed of different elements; jury's inconsistency in acquitting defendant of one crime but not of another, both of which could be supported by the same act, was at most a logical inconsistency rather than a legal inconsistency and did not present reversible error. People v. Lucien, 66 Ill. App. 3d 280, 22 Ill. Dec. 927, 383 N.E.2d 735 (5 Dist. 1978).

—Same Act
Where the state alleged two separate acts of aggravated assault and aggravated unlawful restraint, the court ruled both offenses were predicated on the same physical act and vacated the conviction of aggravated assault. People v. Murphy, 261 Ill. App. 3d 1019, 200 Ill Dec. 9, 635 N.E.2d 110 (2 Dist. 1994).

Unlawful Restraint

—Evidence Held Sufficient
Proof of defendant's seizure and detention of the victim with a gun and without legal authority was sufficient to establish guilt of aggravated unlawful restraint. People v. Watkins, 238 Ill. App. 3d 253, 179 Ill. Dec. 422, 606 N.E.2d 254 (1 Dist. 1992).

Proof of a defendant's seizure and detention of his daughter with his knife drawn was sufficient to establish his guilt of aggravated unlawful restraint beyond a reasonable doubt. People v. Algarin, 200 Ill. App. 3d 740, 146 Ill. Dec. 494, 558 N.E.2d 457 (1 Dist. 1990).

Evidence that showed defendant tackled the woman, slapped her and straddled her as co-defendant approached and fatally wounded the woman was sufficient to sustain a conviction for unlawful restraint. People v. Watts, 170 Ill. App. 3d 815, 121 Ill. Dec. 427, 525 N.E.2d 233 (4 Dist. 1988).

Evidence was sufficient to show that defendant intended to detain victim. People v. Sperow, 170 Ill. App. 3d 800, 121 Ill. Dec. 417, 525 N.E.2d 223 (4 Dist.), appeal denied, 122 Ill. 2d 589, 125 Ill. Dec. 231, 530 N.E.2d 259 (1988).

720 ILCS 5/10-4 Forcible Detention

Sec. 10-4. *Forcible Detention.* (a) A person commits the offense of forcible detention when he holds an individual hostage without lawful authority for the purpose of obtaining performance by a third person of demands made by the person holding the hostage, and

(1) the person holding the hostage is armed with a dangerous weapon as defined in Section 33A-1 of this Code [720 ILCS 5/33A-1], or

(2) the hostage is known to the person holding him to be a peace officer or a correctional employee engaged in the performance of his official duties.

(b) Forcible detention is a Class 2 felony.
(Source: P.A. 79-941.)

Note.
This section was Ill.Rev.Stat., Ch. 38, para. 10-4.

CASE NOTES

Elements of Offense

—Intent
Forcible detention requires that the offender be able to form the intent to obtain performance of his demands by a third person. Evans v. Meyer, 742 F.2d 371 (7th Cir. 1984).

720 ILCS 5/10-5 Child Abduction

Sec. 10-5. *Child Abduction.* (a) For purposes of this Section, the following terms shall have the following meanings:

(1) "Child" means a person under the age of 18 or a severely or profoundly mentally retarded person at the time the alleged violation occurred; and

(2) "Detains" means taking or retaining physical custody of a child, whether or not the child resists or objects; and

(3) "Lawful custodian" means a person or persons granted legal custody of a child or entitled to physical possession of a child pursuant to a court order. It is presumed that, when the parties have never been married to each other, the mother has legal custody of the child unless a valid court order states otherwise. If an adjudication of paternity has been completed and the father has been assigned support obligations or visitation rights, such a paternity order should, for the purposes of this Section be considered a valid court order granting custody to the mother.

(b) A person commits child abduction when he or she:

(1) Intentionally violates any terms of a valid court order granting sole or joint custody, care or possession to another, by concealing or detaining the child or removing the child from the jurisdiction of the court; or

(2) Intentionally violates a court order prohibiting the person from concealing or detaining the child or removing the child from the jurisdiction of the court; or

(3) Intentionally conceals, detains or removes the child without the consent of the mother or lawful custodian of the child if the person is a putative father and either: (A) the paternity of the child has not been legally established or (B) the paternity of

the child has been legally established but no orders relating to custody have been entered. However, notwithstanding the presumption created by paragraph (3) of subsection (a), a mother commits child abduction when she intentionally conceals or removes a child, whom she has abandoned or relinquished custody of, from an unadjudicated father who has provided sole ongoing care and custody of the child in her absence; or

(4) Intentionally conceals or removes the child from a parent after filing a petition or being served with process in an action affecting marriage or paternity but prior to the issuance of a temporary or final order determining custody; or

(5) At the expiration of visitation rights outside the State, intentionally fails or refuses to return or impedes the return of the child to the lawful custodian in Illinois; or

(6) Being a parent of the child, and where the parents of such child are or have been married and there has been no court order of custody, conceals the child for 15 days, and fails to make reasonable attempts within the 15 day period to notify the other parent as to the specific whereabouts of the child, including a means by which to contact such child, or to arrange reasonable visitation or contact with the child. It is not a violation of this Section for a person fleeing domestic violence to take the child with him or her to housing provided by a domestic violence program; or

(7) Being a parent of the child, and where the parents of the child are or have been married and there has been no court order of custody, conceals, detains, or removes the child with physical force or threat of physical force; or

(8) Conceals, detains, or removes the child for payment or promise of payment at the instruction of a person who has no legal right to custody; or

(9) Retains in this State for 30 days a child removed from another state without the consent of the lawful custodian or in violation of a valid court order of custody; or

(10) Intentionally lures or attempts to lure a child under the age of 16 into a motor vehicle, building, housetrailer, or dwelling place without the consent of the parent or lawful custodian of the child for other than a lawful purpose.

For the purposes of this subsection (b), paragraph (10), the luring or attempted luring of a child under the age of 16 into a motor vehicle, building, housetrailer, or dwelling place without the consent of the parent or lawful custodian of the child shall be prima facie evidence of other than a lawful purpose.

(c) It shall be an affirmative defense that:

(1) The person had custody of the child pursuant to a court order granting legal custody or visitation rights which existed at the time of the alleged violation; or

(2) The person had physical custody of the child pursuant to a court order granting legal custody or visitation rights and failed to return the child as a result of circumstances beyond his or her control, and the person notified and disclosed to the other parent or legal custodian the specific whereabouts of the child and a means by which such child can be contacted or made a reasonable attempt to notify the other parent or lawful custodian of the child of such circumstances and make such disclosure within 24 hours after the visitation period had expired and returned the child as soon as possible; or

(3) The person was fleeing an incidence or pattern of domestic violence; or

(4) The person lured or attempted to lure a child under the age of 16 into a motor vehicle, building, housetrailer, or dwelling place for a lawful purpose in prosecutions under subsection (b), paragraph (10).

(d) A person convicted of child abduction under this Section is guilty of a Class 4 felony. A person convicted of a second or subsequent violation of paragraph (10) of subsection (b) of this Section is guilty of a Class 3 felony. It shall be a factor in aggravation for which a court may impose a more severe sentence under Section 5-8-1 of the Unified Code of Corrections [730 ILCS 5/5-8-1], if upon sentencing the court finds evidence of any of the following aggravating factors:

(1) that the defendant abused or neglected the child following the concealment, detention or removal of the child; or

(2) that the defendant inflicted or threatened to inflict physical harm on a parent or lawful custodian of the child or on the child with intent to cause such parent or lawful custodian to discontinue criminal prosecution of the defendant under this Section; or

(3) that the defendant demanded payment in exchange for return of the child or demanded that he or she be relieved of the financial or legal obligation to support the child in exchange for return of the child; or

(4) that the defendant has previously been convicted of child abduction; or

(5) that the defendant committed the abduction while armed with a deadly weapon or the taking of the child resulted in serious bodily injury to another; or

(6) that the defendant committed the abduction while in a school, regardless of the time of day or time of year; in a playground; on any conveyance owned, leased, or contracted by a school to transport students to or from school or a school related activity; on the real property of a school; or on a public way within 1,000 feet of the real property comprising any school or playground. For purposes of this paragraph (6), "playground" means a piece of land owned or controlled by a unit of local government that is designated by the unit of local government for use solely or primarily for children's recreation; and "school" means a public or private elementary or secondary school, community college, college, or university.

(e) The court may order the child to be returned to the parent or lawful custodian from whom the child was concealed, detained or removed. In addition to any sentence imposed, the court may assess any reasonable expense incurred in searching for or returning the child against any person convicted of violating this Section.

(f) Nothing contained in this Section shall be construed to limit the court's contempt power.

(g) Every law enforcement officer investigating an alleged incident of child abduction shall make a written police report of any bona fide allegation and the disposition of such investigation. Every police report completed pursuant to this Section shall be compiled and recorded within the meaning of Section 5.1 of "An Act in relation to criminal identification and investigation", approved July 2, 1931, as now or hereafter amended [20 ILCS 2630/5.1].

(h) Whenever a law enforcement officer has reasons to believe a child abduction has occurred, he shall provide the lawful custodian a summary of her or his rights under this Act, including the procedures and relief available to her or him.

(i) If during the course of an investigation under this Section the child is found in the physical custody of the defendant or another, the law enforcement officer shall return the child to the parent or lawful custodian from whom the child was concealed, detained or removed, unless there is good cause for the law enforcement officer or the Department of Children and Family Services to retain temporary protective custody of the child pursuant to the Abused and Neglected Child Reporting Act, as now or hereafter amended [320 ILCS 5/1 et seq.].
(Source: P.A. 85-1440; 86-312; 90-494, § 2; 92-434, § 5.)

Note.

This section was Ill.Rev.Stat., Ch. 38, para. 10-5.

Cross References.

For provision authorizing the criminal courts to enforce an order of protection upon violation of this section, see 725 ILCS 5/112A-23.

Effect of Amendments.

The 1997 amendment by P.A. 90-494, effective January 1, 1998, in subsection (d), in the introductory language, added the second sentence; in subdivision (d)(5) substituted "or" for a period"; and added subdivision (d)(6).

The 2001 amendment by P.A. 92-434, effective January 1, 2002, in subsection (a)(1) substituted "a" for "an institutionalized".

CASE NOTES

ANALYSIS

Constitutionality
—In General
—As Applied
—Due Process
—Equal Protection
—Proportionality
—Standing
In General
Affirmative Defense
—Legal Custody
Affirmative Defenses
—Domestic Violence
—Joint Custody
—Necessity
—Paternity
Application
Burden of Proof
—Permissive Inference
Construction
—Concealing or Detaining
—Parental Distinction
Contempt
—Double Jeopardy
—Elements of Offense
Court Order Violation
—Elements of Offense
—Evidence
—Evidence Held Sufficient
Defenses
—Necessity Not Shown
Definitions
—Lawful Purpose
Domestic Violence
—Cumulative Evidence
Evidence Held Sufficient
HIV Testing
Indictment
—Lawful Purpose
Intent
—Age of Victim
—Evidence Held Sufficient
Jurisdiction
Jury Instructions
—Due Process
Legislative Intent
Lesser Included Offense
—Indirect Criminal Contempt
Luring a Child
—Elements of Offense
—Intent
—Language Spoken
—Lawful Purpose
—Prima Facie Evidence
—Waving Gesture
Purpose

Constitutionality

—In General

This section does not create a mandatory presumption or improperly shift the burden of proof to the defendant and is therefore not unconstitutional per se. People v. Joyce, 234 Ill. App. 3d 394, 174 Ill. Dec. 763, 599 N.E.2d 547 (2 Dist.), cert. denied, 210 Ill. App. 3d 1059, 155 Ill. Dec. 578, 606 N.E.2d 1231 (1992).

The child abduction statute does not violate the due process and equal protection clauses of the United States and Illinois Constitutions. People v. Morrison, 223 Ill. App. 3d 176, 165 Ill. Dec. 330, 584 N.E.2d 509 (3 Dist. 1991), cert. denied, 144 Ill. 2d 640, 169 Ill. Dec. 148, 591 N.E.2d 28 (1992).

Subdivision (b)(10) of this section is not unconstitutionally vague. People v. Williams, 133 Ill. 2d 449, 141 Ill. Dec. 444, 551 N.E.2d 631 (1990).

The legislature did not act unreasonably nor exercise its power too broadly when it defined child as a person under the age of 16 in subdivision (b)(10) of this section, and made it an offense to lure a child of that age into an automobile for an unlawful purpose. People v. Rogers, 133 Ill. 2d 1, 139 Ill. Dec. 714, 549 N.E.2d 226 (1989), cert. denied, 498 U.S. 827, 111 S. Ct. 84, 112 L. Ed. 2d 56 (1990).

This statute is not facially or as applied violative of the ex post facto provisions of U.S. Const., Art. I, § 9 or Ill. Const. (1970), Art. I, § 16. People v. Caruso, 152 Ill. App. 3d 1074, 105 Ill. Dec. 821, 504 N.E.2d 1339 (2 Dist.), aff'd, 119 Ill. 2d 376, 116 Ill. Dec. 548, 519 N.E.2d 440 (1987), cert. denied, 488 U.S. 829, 109 S. Ct. 83, 102 L. Ed. 2d 59 (1988).

—As Applied

In a prosecution of defendant for child abduction for an unlawful purpose, the trial court abused its discretion by denying defendant's motion for a bill of particulars specifying the nature of the alleged unlawful purpose, and by so doing the court rendered the criminal statute unconstitutionally vague in its application because, if

Constitutionality (Cont'd)

—As Applied (Cont'd)
defendant could not find out what the alleged wrongful acts—beyond private thoughts—were, it would not be possible to support the affrmative defense of lawful purpose, as provided for in the statute. People v. Woodrum, Ill. App. 3d , 290 Ill. Dec. 475, 821 N.E.2d 787, 2004 Ill. App. LEXIS 1535 (1 Dist. 2004).

Subdivision (b)(10) of this section was not unconstitutional as applied to a defendant who lured a child into an automobile for a criminal purpose, and enforcement of this section did not unduly interfere with defendant's freedoms of speech and association protected by U.S. Const., Amends. I and XIV. People v. Williams, 133 Ill. 2d 449, 141 Ill. Dec. 444, 551 N.E.2d 631 (1990).

—Due Process
Subdivision (b)(10) of this section is not in violation of the proportionate penalties or due process clauses of the Illinois Constitution. People v. Patten, 230 Ill. App. 3d 922, 172 Ill. Dec. 471, 595 N.E.2d 1141 (1 Dist.), cert. denied, 146 Ill. 2d 644, 176 Ill. Dec. 814, 602 N.E.2d 468 (1992).

A father's interest in the companionship, care, custody, and management of his illegitimate child, while cognizable and substantial, was subject to the state's countervailing interest in protecting the custodial right of one parent from the abductive abuses of the other; therefore, this section did not violate the father's substantive due process right in the continued care and custody of his child. People v. Morrison, 223 Ill. App. 3d 176, 165 Ill. Dec. 330, 584 N.E.2d 509 (3 Dist. 1991), cert. denied, 144 Ill. 2d 640, 169 Ill. Dec. 148, 591 N.E.2d 28 (1992).

—Equal Protection
This section does not violate the state's constitutional guarantee of equal protection regarding gender/neutrality. People v. Morrison, 223 Ill. App. 3d 176, 165 Ill. Dec. 330, 584 N.E.2d 509 (3 Dist. 1991), cert. denied, 144 Ill. 2d 640, 169 Ill. Dec. 148, 591 N.E.2d 28 (1992).

Where the natural father had resided with his illegitimate child from his birth and had provided uninterrupted financial and emotional support and exhibited all characteristics of responsibility toward his child that would be expected of a child's natural mother or a legally-adjudicated father, and the natural father and the mother lived together and shared family responsibilities with the child as if they were lawfully married to each other, the application of the child abduction statute under these facts deprived the natural father of equal protection of the law. People v. Morrison, 223 Ill. App. 3d 176, 165 Ill. Dec. 330, 584 N.E.2d 509 (3 Dist. 1991), cert. denied, 144 Ill. 2d 640, 169 Ill. Dec. 148, 591 N.E.2d 28 (1992).

—Proportionality
This section does not violate the proportionality clause of Ill. Const. (1970), Art. I, § 2 in that it does not create impermissible prosecutorial discretion, since the State could have chosen to prosecute defendant under 720 ILCS 5/8-4, in which case defendant would have been convicted of only a Class A misdemeanor. People v. Joyce, 234 Ill. App. 3d 394, 174 Ill. Dec. 763, 599 N.E.2d 547 (2 Dist.), cert. denied, 210 Ill. App. 3d 1059, 155 Ill. Dec. 578, 606 N.E.2d 1231 (1992).

—Standing
Defendant lacked standing to challenge this section on the ground that subdivision (b)(10) of this section is overbroad because it makes an "attempt to lure" punishable the same as a completed act, where the defendant was not charged with attempt but was charged with the completed act of luring a child. People v. Rogers, 133 Ill. 2d 1, 139 Ill. Dec. 714, 549 N.E.2d 226 (1989), cert. denied, 498 U.S. 827, 111 S. Ct. 84, 112 L. Ed. 2d 56 (1990).

Defendant could not challenge the constitutionality of the presumption that he engaged in other than a lawful purpose under subdivision (b)(10) of this section because, as construed and applied to him, the presumption was not applicable where the state proffered criminal sexual abuse as the actual unlawful purpose. People v. Rogers, 133 Ill. 2d 1, 139 Ill. Dec. 714, 549 N.E.2d 226 (1989), cert. denied, 498 U.S. 827, 111 S. Ct. 84, 112 L. Ed. 2d 56 (1990).

In General
Advancement of the state's interest in preventing child abduction by persons not having legal custody of the child was sufficiently important to withstand a natural father's claimed deprivation of a liberty interest in the care and custody of his child under this section. People v. Morrison, 223 Ill. App. 3d 176, 165 Ill. Dec. 330, 584 N.E.2d 509 (3 Dist. 1991), cert. denied, 144 Ill. 2d 640, 169 Ill. Dec. 148, 591 N.E.2d 28 (1992).

Since its enactment in 1979, this section has developed from legislation directed at the specific problem of the violation of a court order awarding custody, to the current legislation which covers a broad range of child abduction and child snatching problems. People v. Algarin, 200 Ill. App. 3d 740, 146 Ill. Dec. 494, 558 N.E.2d 457 (1 Dist. 1990).

Affirmative Defense

—Legal Custody
Trial court could not order a parent convicted of abducting her own children to turn over custody of the children to the other parent when the parent/offender had legal custody of the children at the time she committed the offense. People v. Olsewski, 257 Ill. App. 3d 1018, 196 Ill. Dec. 434, 630 N.E.2d 131 (2 Dist.), appeal denied, 156 Ill. 2d 564, 202 Ill. Dec. 928, 638 N.E.2d 1122 (1994).

Affirmative Defenses

—Domestic Violence
Defendant's attempt to offer the affirmative defense of subdivision (c)(3) that when he took the child he was fleeing an incidence of domestic violence was insufficient where the evidence of spanking and pinching by babysitter caring for the child was not found by the trial court to constitute domestic violence. People v. Welacha, 186 Ill. App. 3d 860, 134 Ill. Dec. 581, 542 N.E.2d 927 (1 Dist. 1989).

—Joint Custody
Joint custody is not an affirmative defense under this statute. People v. Harrison, 82 Ill. App. 3d 530, 37 Ill. Dec. 820, 402 N.E.2d 822 (4 Dist. 1980).

—Necessity
The defendant failed to establish the defense of necessity in his prosecution for child abduction where: (1) the defendant asserted that the Department of Child and Family Services did not want to relinquish custody of his son because it had dragged out the litigation process for over 2 ½ years, that his son had sustained a head injury that required stitches, an eye injury, various cuts and blisters, and that he had contracted pneumonia for which he was not medically treated; (2) the defendant also asserted he had undergone a series of tests required by the department and had taken a required parenting class but had still not been awarded custody of his son; and (3) the defendant stated that he took his son because he was trying to protect his child and his own constitutional rights to the care and custody of his son; but (4) the defendant did not identify and the record did not disclose an imminent danger to his son that was averted by the defendant's abduction; and (5) the defendant was well aware that abduction of his son was not the sole remedy available to gain custody. People v. Azizarab, 317 Ill. App. 3d 995, 251 Ill. Dec. 571, 740 N.E.2d 1142, 2000 Ill. App. LEXIS 934 (1 Dist. 2000).

—Paternity
When defendant removed child from her mother's home, defendant had neither established paternity nor was presumed by law to be the father of the child, and thus defendant could be convicted of child abduction; the court's finding of paternity, which came long after the actions at issue, could not provide a defense to the child abduction charge. People v. Shephard, 171 Ill. App. 3d 977, 121 Ill. Dec. 795, 525 N.E.2d 1102 (1 Dist. 1988).

Application
Although the detention of the children occurred both before and after the enactment of this section, this section did not apply to the continued detention of children after passage of the statute, or to other events occurring before the enactment of the statute. People v. Caruso, 152 Ill. App. 3d 1074, 105 Ill. Dec. 821, 504 N.E.2d 1339 (2 Dist.), aff'd, 119 Ill. 2d 376, 116 Ill. Dec. 548, 519 N.E.2d 440 (1987), cert. denied, 488 U.S. 829, 109 S. Ct. 83, 102 L. Ed. 2d 59 (1988).

Burden of Proof

—Permissive Inference
Subdivision (b)(10) raises only a permissive inference which

Burden of Proof (Cont'd)

—Permissive Inference (Cont'd)
allows, but does not require, the trier of fact to infer the elemental fact of intent from proof of nonconsent, placing no burden of any kind on the defendant. People v. Tirado, 254 Ill. App. 3d 497, 193 Ill. Dec. 563, 626 N.E.2d 1114 (1 Dist. 1993).

Construction

—Concealing or Detaining
Since this section distinguishes between two types of court orders, there was no support for the state's proposition that the order granting possession of husband's two minor children, which clearly fell within subdivision, implied that wife could not conceal or detain the child so as to also fall within subdivision (b)(2) of this section. Accordingly, because there was no court order which prohibited wife from concealing or detaining son, wife's conviction for violating this section was reversed. People v. Dworzanski, 220 Ill. App. 3d 185, 162 Ill. Dec. 884, 580 N.E.2d 1263 (1 Dist. 1991), cert. denied, 143 Ill. 2d 642, 167 Ill. Dec. 404, 587 N.E.2d 1019 (1992).

—Parental Distinction
Any distinction in this section between unwed mothers and fathers is sufficiently justified by the state's compelling interest in curbing abduction of illegitimate children from one unwed parent by the other. People v. Morrison, 223 Ill. App. 3d 176, 165 Ill. Dec. 330, 584 N.E.2d 509 (3 Dist. 1991), cert. denied, 144 Ill. 2d 640, 169 Ill. Dec. 148, 591 N.E.2d 28 (1992).

Contempt

—Double Jeopardy
Because defendant was charged with the felony of child abduction under subdivision (b)(1) of this section, and pleaded guilty, he could not be again prosecuted for the same conduct under the criminal contempt proceedings without being twice put in jeopardy, in violation of U.S. Const., Amend. V and Ill. Const. (1970), Art. I, § 10. In re D'Altomo, 211 Ill. App. 3d 914, 156 Ill. Dec. 320, 570 N.E.2d 796 (1 Dist. 1991).

Indirect criminal contempt and child abduction are the same offense for double jeopardy purposes. People v. Doherty, 165 Ill. App. 3d 630, 116 Ill. Dec. 323, 518 N.E.2d 1303 (2 Dist. 1988).

Where a contempt proceeding and the sanction were for civil contempt rather than criminal contempt, the prosecution of defendant for child abduction did not offend double jeopardy principles. People v. Doherty, 165 Ill. App. 3d 630, 116 Ill. Dec. 323, 518 N.E.2d 1303 (2 Dist. 1988).

Because it was apparent that child abduction by violating a court order, and indirect criminal contempt for failure to comply with a custody order, were virtually the same offense and each offense required proof that defendant intentionally violated a custody order, the state could not prosecute the offense of child abduction without placing defendant in double jeopardy. People v. Rodriguez, 162 Ill. App. 3d 149, 113 Ill. Dec. 121, 514 N.E.2d 1033 (2 Dist. 1987).

—Elements of Offense
The language of this section established that child abduction and indirect criminal contempt for failure to comply with a custody order are virtually the same offense and each requires proof that defendant intentionally violated a custody order. In re D'Altomo, 211 Ill. App. 3d 914, 156 Ill. Dec. 320, 570 N.E.2d 796 (1 Dist. 1991).

As a necessary element of child abduction, the state must prove defendant intentionally violated the terms of the court order of custody, a violation which subjects defendant to the court's contempt power of punishment. People v. Caruso, 119 Ill. 2d 376, 116 Ill. Dec. 548, 519 N.E.2d 440 (1987), cert. denied, 488 U.S. 829, 109 S. Ct. 83, 102 L. Ed. 2d 59 (1988).

Court Order Violation

—Elements of Offense
A defendant who fails to perform his affirmative duty to surrender custody of his children to their mother pursuant to a court order may be guilty of child abduction. People v. Caruso, 119 Ill. 2d 376, 116 Ill. Dec. 548, 519 N.E.2d 440 (1987), cert. denied, 488 U.S. 829, 109 S. Ct. 83, 102 L. Ed. 2d 59 (1988).

The state must show that defendant, by concealing, detaining or removing the child from the jurisdiction of the court, failed to comply with the terms of the court order requiring him to surrender custody of the children to the mother, and if the alleged detention of the children was not in violation of the custody order, defendant would not be guilty of child abduction under subdivision (b)(1). People v. Caruso, 119 Ill. 2d 376, 116 Ill. Dec. 548, 519 N.E.2d 440 (1987), cert. denied, 488 U.S. 829, 109 S. Ct. 83, 102 L. Ed. 2d 59 (1988).

—Evidence
Observations made by the trial court that defendant had sat in the juvenile court and was familiar with the proceedings there did not indicate that the judge based his finding that defendant violated subdivision (b)(2) of this section on matters outside the record. People v. Williams, 105 Ill. App. 3d 372, 61 Ill. Dec. 259, 434 N.E.2d 412 (1 Dist. 1982).

—Evidence Held Sufficient
Evidence would permit a jury to conclude that when defendant removed daughter from school on February 17, 1983, she intended to violate the order awarding custody to husband, where defendant admitted that husband told her about having custody in many telephone conversations, defendant admitted receiving the petition for habeas corpus wherein it was alleged that the order had been entered, and further, defendant had received documents in Washington that explained why daughter was going to Illinois to live with husband. People v. Rodriguez, 169 Ill. App. 3d 131, 119 Ill. Dec. 717, 523 N.E.2d 185 (2 Dist. 1988).

Defenses

—Necessity Not Shown
The court did not err in declining to give weight to defendant's necessity defense because even if she reasonably believed that husband was intoxicated, she failed to present any evidence that the son was in danger as a result of his father's condition. Moreover, because the trial court was entitled to find that defendant "concealed" son by telling police officer that she did not know where he was, it could reasonably have found that the state had overcome her necessity defense by proving that she had acted beyond the scope of what was reasonably necessary to protect son. People v. Dworzanski, 220 Ill. App. 3d 185, 162 Ill. Dec. 884, 580 N.E.2d 1263 (1 Dist. 1991), cert. denied, 143 Ill. 2d 642, 167 Ill. Dec. 404, 587 N.E.2d 1019 (1992).

Definitions

—Lawful Purpose
Just as the ordinary meaning of the phrase, "other than a lawful purpose," means any purpose which is unlawful, the ordinary meaning of the phrase, "for a lawful purpose," refers to any purpose that is lawful. People v. Joyce, 210 Ill. App. 3d 1059, 155 Ill. Dec. 578, 569 N.E.2d 1189 (2 Dist.), cert. denied, 141 Ill. 2d 552, 162 Ill. Dec. 500, 580 N.E.2d 126 (1991).

The phrase "other than a lawful purpose," as used in subdivision (b)(10) of this section does not fail to give adequate notice as to what action or conduct will subject one to criminal penalties nor is the phrase so obscure that people of common intelligence must necessarily guess at its meaning and differ as to its applicability. People v. Williams, 133 Ill. 2d 449, 141 Ill. Dec. 444, 551 N.E.2d 631 (1990).

"Other than a lawful purpose" implies actions which violate the Criminal Code, but cannot reasonably be said to involve violations of administrative regulations or city ordinances. People v. Williams, 133 Ill. 2d 449, 141 Ill. Dec. 444, 551 N.E.2d 631 (1990).

Domestic Violence

—Cumulative Evidence
Defendant's contention that she was denied a fair trial in prosecution for abducting her daughter from child's father because the trial court limited the evidence in support of her defense that she was fleeing an incidence or pattern of domestic violence, was meritless, for the testimony of repeated harassment, including specific incidents of harassment and abuse that ended more than a month before the abduction, could be deemed cumulative of other testimony or evidence. People v. Griffith, 249 Ill. App. 3d 1046, 189 Ill. Dec. 813, 620 N.E.2d 1130 (1 Dist. 1993).

Evidence Held Sufficient

Evidence was sufficient to support defendant's conviction of child abduction beyond a reasonable doubt where evidence showed that defendant left with defendant and mother's young child without giving notice to the mother, that the daughter was never at the residence of defendant's mother even though the mother learned that is where the daughter had been taken, and defendant was apprehended in the middle of the night crossing the Mexican border with the daughter into the United States 19 days after defendant and the daughter first disappeared. People v. Manning, 334 Ill. App. 3d 882, 268 Ill. Dec. 600, 778 N.E.2d 1222, 2002 Ill. App. LEXIS 968 (1 Dist. 2002), appeal denied, 202 Ill. 2d 686, 272 Ill. Dec. 363, 787 N.E.2d 178 (2003).

Ample evidence existed for the jury to convict defendant of child abduction where, absent defendant's denials, which the jury was free to accept or reject in light of the circumstances presented, all the evidence and testimony corroborated the testimony given by the victim regarding the events of March 12 and the identification of defendant, his appeal and the blue car he was driving. People v. Tirado, 254 Ill. App. 3d 497, 193 Ill. Dec. 563, 626 N.E.2d 1114 (1 Dist. 1993).

HIV Testing

In the absence of any evidence that defendant had any purpose to commit sexual penetration or other sexual conduct at the time of inviting neighborhood children into his parents' condominium, the trial court had no grounds for requiring that he be tested for HIV/AIDS. People v. Woodrum, Ill. App. 3d , 290 Ill. Dec. 475, 821 N.E.2d 787, 2004 Ill. App. LEXIS 1535 (1 Dist. 2004).

Indictment

—Lawful Purpose

Even though indictment did not specify any particular unlawful purpose harbored by the defendant at the time he allegedly attempted to lure the child into his car, the defendant was sufficiently apprised of both the nature and the elements of the offense. People v. Joyce, 210 Ill. App. 3d 1059, 155 Ill. Dec. 578, 569 N.E.2d 1189 (2 Dist.), cert. denied, 141 Ill. 2d 552, 162 Ill. Dec. 500, 580 N.E.2d 126 (1991).

Intent

—Age of Victim

The victim's age, while relevant to the specific crime which could be charged, has absolutely no bearing on defendant's intent. People v. Embry, 177 Ill. App. 3d 96, 126 Ill. Dec. 503, 531 N.E.2d 1130 (4 Dist. 1988).

—Evidence Held Sufficient

In a prosecution for child abduction, evidence was sufficient to establish that the defendant intentionally violated the law and intended to keep the child in Wisconsin in violation of the custody order in spite of defendant's contention that he lacked the requisite intent. People v. Welacha, 186 Ill. App. 3d 860, 134 Ill. Dec. 581, 542 N.E.2d 927 (1 Dist. 1989).

The evidence proved beyond reasonable doubt and to a moral certainty that defendant not only was aware of the order for custody but deliberately sought to evade it by taking the child from the school and keeping him in her custody for a number of days. People v. Williams, 105 Ill. App. 3d 372, 61 Ill. Dec. 259, 434 N.E.2d 412 (1 Dist. 1982).

Jurisdiction

The Illinois statute on criminal jurisdiction (720 ILCS 5/1-5) was broad enough to reach conduct of an accused in violation of this section occurring outside Illinois' territorial limits, because the offense as charged was based on defendant's failure to comply with a court order by detaining his children which, under the circumstances, was properly deemed to be an omission of a duty, in violation of 720 ILCS 5/1-5(c). People v. Caruso, 152 Ill. App. 3d 1074, 105 Ill. Dec. 821, 504 N.E.2d 1339 (2 Dist.), aff'd, 119 Ill. 2d 376, 116 Ill. Dec. 548, 519 N.E.2d 440 (1987), cert. denied, 488 U.S. 829, 109 S. Ct. 83, 102 L. Ed. 2d 59 (1988).

Jury Instructions

—Due Process

Nonpattern instruction, which stated that: "If you find that at the time the defendant lured or attempted to lure a child under the age of sixteen years old into a motor vehicle and he did so without the consent of a parent or lawful custodian of the child, you may infer it was for other than a lawful purpose" did not violate due process by creating a mandatory presumption which caused the jurors to assume that there was no choice but to make the instructed presumption, relieving them of their duty to find the ultimate facts of defendant's guilt beyond a reasonable doubt, based on evidence adduced by the State. People v. Patten, 230 Ill. App. 3d 922, 172 Ill. Dec. 471, 595 N.E.2d 1141 (1 Dist.), cert. denied, 146 Ill. 2d 644, 176 Ill. Dec. 814, 602 N.E.2d 468 (1992).

Legislative Intent

The legislative history of subdivision (b)(10) reveals the concern that attempted luring of a child is as serious a threat to the safety of a child as a successful abduction. People v. Patten, 230 Ill. App. 3d 922, 172 Ill. Dec. 471, 595 N.E.2d 1141 (1 Dist.), cert. denied, 146 Ill. 2d 644, 176 Ill. Dec. 814, 602 N.E.2d 468 (1992).

Implicit in this section is the legislature's recognition of the importance to children of a stable home environment and secure family relationships. People v. Morrison, 223 Ill. App. 3d 176, 165 Ill. Dec. 330, 584 N.E.2d 509 (3 Dist. 1991), cert. denied, 144 Ill. 2d 640, 169 Ill. Dec. 148, 591 N.E.2d 28 (1992).

There is no reason to pre-suppose that the legislature ever intended that the kidnaping statute encompass parental abductions as does this section. People v. Algarin, 200 Ill. App. 3d 740, 146 Ill. Dec. 494, 558 N.E.2d 457 (1 Dist. 1990).

Lesser Included Offense

—Indirect Criminal Contempt

The trial court was correct to refuse defendant's tendered lesser-included-offense instruction on indirect criminal contempt, since the underlying custody order was entered in a different county and indirect criminal contempt is not an offense under the code. People v. Logsdon, 271 Ill. App. 3d 276, 207 Ill. Dec. 624, 647 N.E.2d 1117 (5 Dist. 1995).

Indirect criminal contempt is a lesser included offense of child abduction by violating a court order, because a conviction for child abduction would necessarily establish all of the elements of an indirect criminal contempt. People v. Doherty, 165 Ill. App. 3d 630, 116 Ill. Dec. 323, 518 N.E.2d 1303 (2 Dist. 1988).

Luring a Child

—Elements of Offense

Subdivision (b)(10) of this section requires the state to prove that defendant: (1) intentionally lured or attempted to lure; (2) a child under the age of 16; (3) into a motor vehicle, building, housetrailer, or dwelling; and (4) without the consent of the parent or lawful custodian of the child. People v. Marcotte, 217 Ill. App. 3d 797, 160 Ill. Dec. 474, 577 N.E.2d 799 (5 Dist. 1991), cert. denied, 143 Ill. 2d 644, 167 Ill. Dec. 406, 587 N.E.2d 1021 (1992).

Not making the words "other than a lawful purpose" an element of the offense is consistent with the statute's legislative history; namely, that a child abduction under subdivision (b)(10) of this section is complete when one intentionally attempts to lure a child into a car. People v. Marcotte, 217 Ill. App. 3d 797, 160 Ill. Dec. 474, 577 N.E.2d 799 (5 Dist. 1991), cert. denied, 143 Ill. 2d 644, 167 Ill. Dec. 406, 587 N.E.2d 1021 (1992).

—Intent

Under this section, the State is obligated to prove defendant's intent to lure children for other than a lawful purpose. People v. Joyce, 234 Ill. App. 3d 394, 174 Ill. Dec. 763, 599 N.E.2d 547 (2 Dist.), cert. denied, 210 Ill. App. 3d 1059, 155 Ill. Dec. 578, 606 N.E.2d 1231 (1992).

Defendant did not demonstrate due process was denied where the court relied upon evidence, independent of that related to the statutory presumption of "other than a lawful purpose," to establish intent. People v. Embry, 177 Ill. App. 3d 96, 126 Ill. Dec. 503, 531 N.E.2d 1130 (4 Dist. 1988).

—Language Spoken

Defendant's fluency in English was an important issue for the jury to consider since subdivision (b)(10) of this section provides a defendant will be guilty of such crime where the defendant lures or attempts to lure a child; proof of such luring will include statements

Luring a Child (Cont'd)

—Language Spoken (Cont'd)

of communication from the defendant to his prey. People v. Tirado, 254 Ill. App. 3d 497, 193 Ill. Dec. 563, 626 N.E.2d 1114 (1 Dist. 1993).

—Lawful Purpose

The words "other than a lawful purpose" do not constitute an element of the child abduction offense which must be proved under subdivision (b)(10) of this section, but do provide an affirmative defense in accordance with subdivision (c)(4). People v. Marcotte, 217 Ill. App. 3d 797, 160 Ill. Dec. 474, 577 N.E.2d 799 (5 Dist. 1991), cert. denied, 143 Ill. 2d 644, 167 Ill. Dec. 406, 587 N.E.2d 1021 (1992).

Subdivision (b)(10) creates nothing more than a permissible inference of "other than a lawful purpose"; therefore, the validity of the permissive presumption rests on an evaluation of the presumption as applied to the particular defendant before the court. People v. Embry, 177 Ill. App. 3d 96, 126 Ill. Dec. 503, 531 N.E.2d 1130 (4 Dist. 1988).

—Prima Facie Evidence

By failing to instruct the jurors that prima facie evidence may be rebutted or contradicted, the trial court created a mandatory presumption of other than a lawful purpose, which denied the defendant his due process rights. People v. Joyce, 210 Ill. App. 3d 1059, 155 Ill. Dec. 578, 569 N.E.2d 1189 (2 Dist.), cert. denied, 141 Ill. 2d 552, 162 Ill. Dec. 500, 580 N.E.2d 126 (1991).

Although "lawful purpose" in prosecutions under subdivision (b)(10) of this section, is an affirmative defense under subdivision (c)(4), which must be raised by the defendant, where jury instructions created a mandatory presumption of other than a lawful purpose, the defendant was entitled to a new trial. People v. Marcotte, 217 Ill. App. 3d 797, 160 Ill. Dec. 474, 577 N.E.2d 799 (5 Dist. 1991), cert. denied, 143 Ill. 2d 644, 167 Ill. Dec. 406, 587 N.E.2d 1021 (1992).

—Waving Gesture

The state failed to prove two elements of the offense of child abduction, namely the elements of "unlawful intent" and "attempted entry" where defendant's alleged waving gesture to victim was insufficient to establish either a specific unlawful intent or that he was attempting to lure victim into his jeep. People v. Wenger, 258 Ill. App. 3d 561, 197 Ill. Dec. 274, 631 N.E.2d 277 (1 Dist.), appeal denied, 156 Ill. 2d 565, 202 Ill. Dec. 930, 638 N.E.2d 1124 (1994).

Purpose

Subsection (e) was not intended to be used as a tool for effecting a change in custody but rather as a means of reestablishing the status quo by giving the court the power to "return" the children to their lawful custodian. People v. Olsewski, 257 Ill. App. 3d 1018, 196 Ill. Dec. 434, 630 N.E.2d 131 (2 Dist.), appeal denied, 156 Ill. 2d 564, 202 Ill. Dec. 928, 638 N.E.2d 1122 (1994).

The remedial purpose of this section is to protect the welfare of children who are the sad detritus of a divorce proceeding, by attempting to establish a stable environment for them and to protect the rights of the custodial parent under a judgment. People v. Caruso, 152 Ill. App. 3d 1074, 105 Ill. Dec. 821, 504 N.E.2d 1339 (2 Dist.), aff'd, 119 Ill. 2d 376, 116 Ill. Dec. 548, 519 N.E.2d 440 (1987), cert. denied, 488 U.S. 829, 109 S. Ct. 83, 102 L. Ed. 2d 59 (1988).

LEGAL PERIODICALS

For comment, "Intentional Infliction of Emotional Distress: Recovery of Damages for Victims of Parental Kidnapping," see 1984 S. Ill. U.L.J. 145.

For article, "The Tort of Custodial Interference—Toward a More Complete Remedy to Parental Kidnappings," see 1983 U. Ill. Rev. 229 (1983).

RESEARCH REFERENCES

Kidnapping or related offense by taking or removing of child by or under authority of parent or one in loco parentis. 20 ALR4th 823.

Liability of legal or natural parent, or one who aids and abets, for damages resulting from abduction of own child. 49 ALR4th 7.

Pending proceeding in another state as ground for declining jurisdiction under § 6(a) of the Uniform Child Custody Jurisdiction Act (UCCJA) or the Parental Kidnapping Prevention Act (PKPA), 28 USCS § 1738A(g). 20 ALR5th 700.

Recognition and enforcement of out-of-state custody decree under § 13 of the Uniform Child Custody Jurisdiction Act (UCCJA) or the Parental Kidnapping Prevention Act (PKPA), 28 USCS § 1738A(a). 40 ALR5th 227.

720 ILCS 5/10-5.5 Unlawful visitation interference

Sec. 10-5.5. *Unlawful visitation interference.* (a) As used in this Section, the terms "child", "detain", and "lawful custodian" shall have the meanings ascribed to them in Section 10-5 of this Code [720 ILCS 5/10-5].

(b) Every person who, in violation of the visitation provisions of a court order relating to child custody, detains or conceals a child with the intent to deprive another person of his or her rights to visitation shall be guilty of unlawful visitation interference.

(c) A person committing unlawful visitation interference is guilty of a petty offense. However, any person violating this Section after 2 prior convictions of unlawful visitation interference is guilty of a Class A misdemeanor.

(d) Any law enforcement officer who has probable cause to believe that a person has committed or is committing an act in violation of this Section shall issue to that person a notice to appear.

(e) The notice shall:

(1) be in writing;

(2) state the name of the person and his address, if known;

(3) set forth the nature of the offense;

(4) be signed by the officer issuing the notice; and

(5) request the person to appear before a court at a certain time and place.

(f) Upon failure of the person to appear, a summons or warrant of arrest may be issued.

(g) It is an affirmative defense that:

(1) a person or lawful custodian committed the act to protect the child from imminent physical harm, provided that the defendant's belief that there was physical harm imminent was reasonable and that the defendant's conduct in withholding visitation rights was a reasonable response to the harm believed imminent;

(2) the act was committed with the mutual consent of all parties having a right to custody and visitation of the child; or

(3) the act was otherwise authorized by law.

(h) A person convicted of unlawful visitation interference shall not be subject to a civil contempt citation for the same conduct for violating visitation provisions of a court order issued under the Illinois Marriage and Dissolution of Marriage Act [750 ILCS 5/101 et seq.].

(Source: P.A. 88-96, § 5.)

Effective Date.
This section became effective January 1, 1994, pursuant to Ill. Const. (1970), Art. IV, § 10 and 5 ILCS 75/1.

CASE NOTES

ANALYSIS

Constitutionality
—Due Process
—Equal Protection
—Separation of Powers
—Vagueness
Affirmative Defenses
Probable Cause
Purpose

Constitutionality

—Due Process
A person of fair intelligence is given fair warning as to what conduct is proscribed and this section provides sufficient guidelines for its application. People v. Warren, 173 Ill. 2d 348, 219 Ill. Dec. 533, 671 N.E.2d 700 (1996).

—Equal Protection
Even though the detention and concealment under the interference statute may also constitute deprivation under the abuse statute (750 ILCS 5/607), thereby giving a noncustodial parent the option to proceed under either statute, the fact that particular conduct by a defendant presents a plaintiff with the opportunity to elect either a civil or criminal penalty does not in and of itself implicate equal protection. People v. Warren, 173 Ill. 2d 348, 219 Ill. Dec. 533, 671 N.E.2d 700 (1996).

The legislature is not restrained from remedying a particular problem merely because that problem exists for one group of individuals and not for another; given that a divorced custodial parent and divorced joint custodial parents are not similarly situated for purposes of the Act, equal protection is not offended by their different treatment. People v. Warren, 173 Ill. 2d 348, 219 Ill. Dec. 533, 671 N.E.2d 700 (1996).

The law is neutral on its face, including within its coverage any individual, including one who may be a stranger to the parent-child relationship. People v. Warren, 173 Ill. 2d 348, 219 Ill. Dec. 533, 671 N.E.2d 700 (1996).

—Separation of Powers
The provision in the statute which prohibits the court's imposition of civil contempt sanctions following a conviction for unlawful visitation interference is an undue infringement on the court's inherent powers; but, since the intent of the legislature may be given effect without the invalid civil contempt provision and the legislative debates indicate the legislature would have passed the bill without the unlawful provision, the invalid provision can be severed. People v. Warren, 173 Ill. 2d 348, 219 Ill. Dec. 533, 671 N.E.2d 700 (1996).

—Vagueness
The phrase "otherwise authorized by law" is not unconstitutionally vague; it means simply that conduct in detaining or concealing a child is, for reasons not expressly provided by the Act, permissible by law. People v. Warren, 173 Ill. 2d 348, 219 Ill. Dec. 533, 671 N.E.2d 700 (1996).

Affirmative Defenses
The manner in which the affirmative defense operates does not render the statute's language unconstitutionally vague; it is sufficient for purposes of due process that the parties understand that mutual consent is available as a defense to a charge of unlawful visitation interference. People v. Warren, 173 Ill. 2d 348, 219 Ill. Dec. 533, 671 N.E.2d 700 (1996).

Probable Cause
Law enforcement officials are not dependent, for application of the statute, on their private conceptions. People v. Warren, 173 Ill. 2d 348, 219 Ill. Dec. 533, 671 N.E.2d 700 (1996).

Mere unsupported allegations by a complainant are insufficient to support even the issuance of a notice to appear. People v. Warren, 173 Ill. 2d 348, 219 Ill. Dec. 533, 671 N.E.2d 700 (1996).

Purpose
The purpose of the statute is to provide a remedy for and to deter violations of interference by any person, including the child's custodial parent, with a noncustodial parent's right to visitation. People v. Warren, 173 Ill. 2d 348, 219 Ill. Dec. 533, 671 N.E.2d 700 (1996).

720 ILCS 5/10-6 Harboring a runaway

Sec. 10-6. *Harboring a runaway.* (a) Any person, other than an agency or association providing crisis intervention services as defined in Section 3-5 of the Juvenile Court Act of 1987 [705 ILCS 405/3-5], or an operator of a youth emergency shelter as defined in Section 2.21 of the Child Care Act of 1969 [225 ILCS 10/2.21], who, without the knowledge and consent of the minor's parent or guardian, knowingly gives shelter to a minor, other than a mature minor who has been emancipated under the Emancipation of Mature Minors Act [750 ILCS 30/1 et seq.], for more than 48 hours without the consent of the minor's parent or guardian, and without notifying the local law enforcement authorities of the minor's name and the fact that the minor is being provided shelter commits the offense of harboring a runaway.

(b) Any person who commits the offense of harboring a runaway is guilty of a Class A misdemeanor.
(Source: P.A. 86-278; 86-386.)

Note.
This section was Ill.Rev.Stat., Ch. 38, para. 10-6.

720 ILCS 5/10-7 Aiding and abetting child abduction

Sec. 10-7. *Aiding and abetting child abduction.* (a) A person violates this Section when:

(i) Before or during the commission of a child abduction as defined in Section 10-5 [720 ILCS 5/10-5] and with the intent to promote or facilitate such offense, he or she intentionally aids or abets another in the planning or commission of child abduction, unless before the commission of the offense he or she makes proper effort to prevent the commission of the offense; or

(ii) With the intent to prevent the apprehension of a person known to have committed the offense of child abduction, or with the intent to obstruct or prevent efforts to locate the child victim of a child abduction, he or she knowingly destroys, alters, conceals or disguises physical evidence or furnishes false information.

(b) Sentence. A person who violates this Section commits a Class 4 felony.
(Source: P.A. 84-1308.)

Note.
This section was Ill.Rev.Stat., Ch. 38, para. 10-7.

720 ILCS 5/10-8 Unlawful sale of a public conveyance travel ticket to a minor

Sec. 10-8. *Unlawful sale of a public conveyance travel ticket to a minor.* (a) A person commits the offense of unlawful sale of a public conveyance travel ticket to a minor when the person sells a ticket for travel on any public conveyance to an unemancipated minor under 17 years of age without the consent of the minor's parents or guardian for passage to a destination outside this state and knows the minor's age or fails to take reasonable measures to ascertain the minor's age.

(b) Evidence. The fact that the defendant demanded, was shown, and reasonably relied upon written evidence of a person's age in any transaction forbidden by this Section is competent evidence, and may be considered in any criminal prosecution for a violation of this Section.

(c) Definition. "Public Conveyance", includes an airplane, boat, bus, railroad, train, taxicab or other vehicle used for the transportation of passengers for hire.

(d) Sentence. Unlawful sale of a public conveyance travel ticket to a minor is a Class C misdemeanor.

(Source: P.A. 86-336.)

Note.

This section was Ill.Rev.Stat., Ch. 38, para. 10-8.

Article 12.

Bodily Harm

720 ILCS 5/12-3.2 Domestic Battery

Sec. 12-3.2. *Domestic Battery.* (a) A person commits domestic battery if he intentionally or knowingly without legal justification by any means:

(1) Causes bodily harm to any family or household member as defined in subsection (3) of Section 112A-3 of the Code of Criminal Procedure of 1963, as amended [725 ILCS 5/112A-3];

(2) Makes physical contact of an insulting or provoking nature with any family or household member as defined in subsection (3) of Section 112A-3 of the Code of Criminal Procedure of 1963, as amended [725 ILCS 5/112A-3].

(b) Sentence. Domestic battery is a Class A Misdemeanor. Domestic battery is a Class 4 felony if the defendant has any prior conviction under this Code for domestic battery (Section 12-3.2) [720 ILCS 5/12-3.2] or violation of an order of protection (Section 12-30) [720 ILCS 5/12-30], or any prior conviction under the law of another jurisdiction for an offense which is substantially similar. Domestic battery is a Class 4 felony if the defendant has any prior conviction under this Code for first degree murder (Section 9-1) [720 ILCS 5/9-1], attempt to commit first degree murder (Section 8-4) [720 ILCS 5/8-4], aggravated domestic battery (Section 12-3.3) [720 ILCS 5/12-3.3], aggravated battery (Section 12-4) [720 ILCS 5/12-4], heinous battery (Section 12-4.1) [720 ILCS 5/12-4.1], aggravated battery with a firearm (Section 12-4.2) [720 ILCS 5/12-4.2], aggravated battery of a child (Section 12-4.3) [720 ILCS 5/12-4.3], aggravated battery of an unborn child (Section 12-4.4) [720 ILCS 5/12-4.4], aggravated battery of a senior citizen (Section 12-4.6) [720 ILCS 5/12-4.6], stalking (Section 12-7.3) [720 ILCS 5/12-7.3], aggravated stalking (Section 12-7.4) [720 ILCS 5/12-7.4], criminal sexual assault (Section 12-13) [720 ILCS 5/12-13], aggravated criminal sexual assault (12-14) [720 ILCS 5/12-14], kidnapping (Section 10-1) [720 ILCS 5/10-1], aggravated kidnapping (Section 10-2) [720 ILCS 5/10-2], predatory criminal sexual assault of a child (Section 12-14.1) [720 ILCS 5/12-14.1], aggravated criminal sexual abuse (Section 12-16) [720 ILCS 5/12-16], unlawful restraint (Section 10-3) [720 ILCS 5/10-3], aggravated unlawful restraint (Section 10-3.1) [720 ILCS 5/10-3.1], aggravated arson (Section 20-1.1) [720 ILCS 5/20-1.1], or aggravated discharge of a firearm (Section 24-1.2) [720 ILCS 5/24-1.2], or any prior conviction under the law of another jurisdiction for any offense that is substantially similar to the offenses listed in this Section, when any of these offenses have been committed against a family or household member as defined in Section 112A-3 of the Code of Criminal Procedure of 1963 [725 ILCS 5/112A-3]. In addition to any other sentencing alternatives, for any second or subsequent conviction of violating this Section, the offender shall be mandatorily sentenced to a minimum of 72 consecutive hours of imprisonment. The imprisonment shall not be subject to suspension, nor shall the person be eligible for probation in order to reduce the sentence.

(c) Domestic battery committed in the presence of a child. In addition to any other sentencing alternatives, a defendant who commits, in the presence of a child, a felony domestic battery (enhanced under subsection (b)), aggravated domestic battery (Section 12-3.3 [720 ILCS 5/12-3.3]), aggravated battery (Section 12-4 [720 ILCS 5/12-4]), unlawful restraint (Section 10-3 [720 ILCS 5/10-3]), or aggravated unlawful restraint (Section 10-3.1 [720 ILCS 5/10-3.1]) against a family or household member, as defined in Section 112A-3 of the Code of Criminal Procedure of 1963 [725 ILCS 5/112A-3], shall be required to serve a mandatory minimum imprisonment of 10 days or perform 300 hours of community service, or both. The defendant shall further be liable for the cost of any counseling required for the child at the discretion of the court in accordance with subsection (b) of Section 5-5-6 of the Unified Code of Corrections [730 ILCS 5/5-5-6]. For purposes of this Section, "child" means a person under 16 years of age who is the defendant's or victim's child or step-child or who is a minor child residing within the household of the defendant or victim. For purposes of this Section, "in the presence of a child" means in the physical presence of a child or knowing or having reason to know that a child is present and may see or hear an act constituting one of the offenses listed in this subsection.

(Source: P.A. 86-979; 88-467, § 25; 90-734, § 5; 91-112, § 5; 91-262, § 5; 91-928, § 5; 92-16, § 88; 92-827, § 5; 93-336, § 5; 93-809, § 5.)

Note.

This section was Ill.Rev.Stat., Ch. 38, para. 12-3.2.

Section 996 of P.A. 92-16 contains a "no acceleration or delay" provision, and Section 997 contains a "no revival or extension" provision.

Effect of Amendments.

The 1993 amendment by P.A. 88-467, effective July 1, 1994, added the second sentence of subsection (b).

The 1998 amendment by P.A. 90-734, effective January 1, 1999, in subsection (b) substituted the second sentence for "A second and subsequent violation is a Class 4 felony."

The 1999 amendment by P.A. 91-112, effective October 1, 1999, inserted the second sentence in subsection (b).

The 1999 amendment by P.A. 91-262, effective January 1, 2000, added subsection (c).

The 2000 amendment by P.A. 91-928, effective June 1, 2001, combined the amendments by P.A. 91-112 and P.A. 91-262, and rewrote subsection (c), which formerly read: "For any conviction for domestic battery, if a person under 18 years of age who is the child of the offender or of the victim was present and witnessed the domestic battery of the victim, the defendant is liable for the cost of any counseling required for the child at the discretion of the court in accordance with subsection (b) of Section 5-5-6 of the Unified Code of Corrections."

The 2001 amendment by P.A. 92-16, effective June 28, 2001, amending the versions of the section before and after amendment by P.A. 91-928, combined the amendments by P.A. 91-112, P.A. 91-262 and P.A. 91-928.

The 2002 amendment by P.A. 92-827, effective August 22, 2002, in subsection (b) in the second sentence inserted the following: "first degree murder (Section 9-1), attempt to commit first degree murder (Section 8-4), aggravated domestic battery (Section 12-3.3)","heinous battery (Section 12-4.1), aggravated battery with a firearm (Section 12-4.2), aggravated battery of a child (Section 12-4.3), aggravated battery of an unborn child (Section 12-4.4), aggravated battery of a senior citizen (Section 12-4.6),", "criminal sexual assault (Section 12-13), aggravated criminal sexual assault (12-14), kidnapping (Section 10-1), aggravated kidnapping (Section 10-2), predatory criminal sexual assault of a child (Section 12-14.1), aggravated criminal sexual abuse (Section 12-16)"and "aggravated arson (Section 20-1.1), or aggravated discharge of a firearm (Section 24-1.2)" and made a related change.

The 2003 amendment by P.A. 93-336, effective January 1, 2004, inserted references to "or any prior conviction under the law of another jurisdiction for any offense that is substantially similar" twice in subsection (b).

The 2004 amendment by P.A. 93-809, effective January 1, 2005, in the fourth sentence of subsection (b) inserted "or subsequent", deleted "within 5 years of a previous conviction for violating this Section" after "violating this Section", and substituted "72" for "48".

CASE NOTES

ANALYSIS

Burden of Proof
Collateral Estoppel
Construction
Evidence
Lesser Included Offense
—Cruelty to a Child
—Home Invasion
Multiple Convictions
—Different Acts
Penalty
Physical Contact
Self-Defense
Sentence
Spanking
—Jury Instructions

Burden of Proof

Where the defendant convicted of a battery on his ten year old son admittedly beat the child, there was no need for the state to meet the unreasonable burden of proving that each mark on the child's body was made by the defendant or that the injuries could not have been caused by an other event. People v. Lee, 84 Ill. App. 3d 441, 39 Ill. Dec. 881, 405 N.E.2d 860 (3 Dist. 1980).

Collateral Estoppel

Notwithstanding the determination at an order for protection hearing that a husband did not physically abuse or harm his wife, the husband's conviction for domestic battery was upheld as it was unclear whether unfairness to the state would result from application of the collateral estoppel doctrine. People v. Wouk, 317 Ill. App. 3d 33, 250 Ill. Dec. 603, 739 N.E.2d 64, 2000 Ill. App. LEXIS 838 (1 Dist. 2000).

The State was not collaterally estopped from pursuing subsequent criminal prosecutions for domestic battery and violation of a protection order where it was not a party to the initial proceeding; in the initial proceeding the wife had filed a petition pro se and was represented by a private attorney. People v. Krstic, 292 Ill. App. 3d 720, 226 Ill. Dec. 909, 686 N.E.2d 692 (1 Dist. 1997).

Construction

District court did not err in construing defendant's prior felony conviction for domestic battery, 720 ILCS 5/12-3.2, as a crime of violence under U.S. Sentencing Guidelines Manual § 2L1.2(b)(1)(A)(ii) (2001) because it fell under the general definition of a crime of violence under § 2L1.2, cmt., application n. 1(B)(ii). United States v. Alvarenga-Silva, 324 F.3d 884, 2003 U.S. App. LEXIS 6345 (7th Cir. 2003), cert. denied, U.S. , 124 S. Ct. 246, 157 L. Ed. 2d 177 (2003).

Evidence

After the trial court declared a mistrial with regard to two charges of domestic battery against defendant, the State was precluded from retrying defendant on double jeopardy grounds, because the trial court was too hasty in declaring a mistrial when allegedly prejudicial testimony was elicited from the victim during cross-examination with regard to her making domestic battery charges against three other men; defendant was not given an opportunity to explain the gist of the cross-examination and otherwise object to the motion for mistrial. People v. Dahlberg, Ill. App. 3d , 291 Ill. Dec. 357, 823 N.E.2d 649, 2005 Ill. App. LEXIS 102 (2 Dist. 2005).

Where defendant was charged with committing the offense of domestic battery in violation of 720 ILCS 5/12-3.2(a)(2) and the statements of the victim, who was unavailable at trial, made to the police officer while the victim was visibly upset but after the victim had already spoken to a backup officer were admitted under the excited utterance exception to the hearsay rule, this violated defendant's rights under the Confrontation Clause, U.S. Const. Amend. VI. The victim's statements to the officer were testimonial, since they were out-of-court statements that were offered to establish an element of the offense charged, and the statements were, therefore, barred since defendant had no prior chance to cross-examine the victim. People v. Victors, 353 Ill. App. 3d 801, 289 Ill. Dec. 154, 819 N.E.2d 311, 2004 Ill. App. LEXIS 1373 (2 Dist. 2004).

Lesser Included Offense

—Cruelty to a Child

Defendant's conviction of battery was vacated where it arose from the same physical acts as the conviction for cruelty to a child; both convictions arose from defendant's act in striking the child with a switch, and under the circumstances presented, battery was a lesser included offense of the former crime of cruelty to a child. People v. Virgin, 60 Ill. App. 3d 964, 18 Ill. Dec. 361, 377 N.E.2d 846 (3 Dist. 1978).

—Home Invasion

Domestic battery was not a lesser included offense of home invasion. People v. Priest, 297 Ill. App. 3d 797, 232 Ill. Dec. 385, 698 N.E.2d 223 (4 Dist. 1998).

Multiple Convictions

—Different Acts

The defendant's conduct consisted of separate, multiple acts; the fact that the defendant entered his ex-wife's home was an overt or outward manifestation supporting the home invasion count and the separate act of causing ex-wife bodily harm supported the domestic battery act. People v. Priest, 297 Ill. App. 3d 797, 232 Ill. Dec. 385, 698 N.E.2d 223 (4 Dist. 1998).

Penalty

Defendant failed in his argument that the penalty for domestic

Penalty (Cont'd)
battery violates the proportionate penalties clause by permitting judges to grant supervision to defendants convicted of a Class A misdemeanor, such as simple battery, but denying judges that same discretion for those defendants convicted of domestic battery, which is also a Class A misdemeanor, because battery and domestic battery do not share identical elements, i.e., battery applies to any individual, and domestic battery applies to all family or household members. People v. Pickens, Ill. App. 3d , 290 Ill. Dec. 776, 822 N.E.2d 58, 2004 Ill. App. LEXIS 1543 (1 Dist. 2004).

Physical Contact
720 ILCS 5112-3.2(a)(2) provides a person of ordinary intelligence with a reasonable opportunity to distinguish between lawful and unlawful conduct so that he or she may act accordingly. More specifically, a person of ordinary intelligence can determine what constitutes insulting or provoking physical contact. People v. Taher, 329 Ill. App. 3d 1007, 264 Ill. Dec. 184, 769 N.E.2d 1021, 2002 Ill. App. LEXIS 326 (1 Dist. 2002).

Self-Defense
Evidence was sufficient to disprove self-defense in a prosecution for domestic battery arising from a fight between the defendant and his brother in which the brother's nose was broken where the only evidence suggesting that the defendant acted in self-defense came from a police officer, who testified that on the night of the incident, the defendant told him that he hit the victim because the victim grabbed him around the neck, but (1) the defendant's sister testified that the defendant jumped the victim after losing money in the card game, and (2) the victim testified that he could not recall how he was injured, but that he had no physical contact with the defendant before his nose was broken. People v. Grayson, 321 Ill. App. 3d 397, 254 Ill. Dec. 420, 747 N.E.2d 460, 2001 Ill. App. LEXIS 240 (4 Dist. 2001), appeal denied, 195 Ill. 2d 585, 258 Ill. Dec. 97, 755 N.E.2d 480 (2001).

Sentence
Under the 1996 version of this section, the use of the word "violation," instead of "conviction," showed that the legislature did not intend that a second conviction of domestic battery was required to enhance a defendant's charge. People v. Jones, 306 Ill. App. 3d 793, 239 Ill. Dec. 811, 715 N.E.2d 256, 1999 Ill. App. LEXIS 243 (2 Dist. 1999), appeal denied, 306 Ill. 2d 793, 239 Ill. Dec. 811, 723 N.E.2d 1166 (1999).

Spanking

—Jury Instructions
Trial court abused its discretion in refusing to add non-pattern language to an instruction on domestic battery to allow jurors to consider whether a parent accused of violence against an older teen-aged child was actually attempting to exercise reasonable discipline. People v. Roberts, 351 Ill. App. 3d 684, 286 Ill. Dec. 524, 814 N.E.2d 174, 2004 Ill. App. LEXIS 921 (4 Dist. 2004).

The trial court properly refused an instruction which read "Parents have a legal right to spank their children" because the other instructions given, taken as a whole, fully and fairly defined the applicable law, and the refused instruction was not impartial or free from argument. People v. Walters, 211 Ill. App. 3d 102, 155 Ill. Dec. 786, 570 N.E.2d 6 (4 Dist.), cert. denied, 139 Ill. 2d 603, 159 Ill. Dec. 115, 575 N.E.2d 922 (1991).

LEGAL PERIODICALS

For article, "Defending the Indefensible to Further a Later Case: Sanctioning Respondents in Illinois Domestic Violence Cases," see 23 N. Ill. U. L. Rev. 403 (2003).

For article, "Survey of Illinois Law: Criminal Procedure," see 26 S. Ill. U.L.J. 815 (2002).

For article, "Making a Federal Case Out of a Woman's Issue," see 6 Chi. B. Rec. 39 (1992).

RESEARCH REFERENCES

Admissibility of expert or opinion testimony on battered wife or battered woman syndrome. 18 ALR4th 1153.

Admissibility at criminal prosecution of expert testimony on battering parent syndrome. 43 ALR4th 1203.

720 ILCS 5/12-3.3 Aggravated domestic battery

Sec. 12-3.3. *Aggravated domestic battery.* (a) A person who, in committing a domestic battery, intentionally or knowingly causes great bodily harm, or permanent disability or disfigurement commits aggravated domestic battery.

(b) Sentence. Aggravated domestic battery is a Class 2 felony. Any order of probation or conditional discharge entered following a conviction for an offense under this Section must include, in addition to any other condition of probation or conditional discharge, a condition that the offender serve a mandatory term of imprisonment of not less than 60 consecutive days. A person convicted of a second or subsequent violation of this Section must be sentenced to a mandatory term of imprisonment of not less than 3 years and not more than 7 years or an extended term of imprisonment of not less than 7 years and not more than 14 years.
(Source: P.A. 91-445, § 5.)

Note.
P.A. 91-445, § 95, contains a "no acceleration or delay" provision.

Effective Date.
This section became effective January 1, 2000, pursuant to Ill. Const. (1970), Art. IV, § 10 and 5 ILCS 75/1.

CASE NOTES

Constitutionality
The definition of "family or household member," which included persons who "have or had a dating relationship," found in 725 Ill. Comp. Stat. Ann. 5/112A-3 (2000) and used in 720 Ill. Comp. Stat. 5/12-3.3, was not unconstitutionally vague as applied to defendant charged with aggravated domestic violence because both defendant and the victim of the aggravated domestic violence testified that they had been in a dating relationship for at least a year prior to the violence and that they intended to live together after defendant was released from incarceration. The relationship constituted a "dating relationship" and defendant was provided with a reasonable opportunity to determine that his conduct against the victim was prohibited by the domestic violence statute. People v. Johnson, 341 Ill. App. 3d 583, 276 Ill. Dec. 15, 793 N.E.2d 774, 2003 Ill. App. LEXIS 823 (1 Dist. 2003).

The activity that is the subject of 720 Ill. Comp. Stat. Ann. 5/12-3.3(a) (2000) is not an activity protected by the First Amendment, and thus, a defendant does not have standing to argue that the statute is vague on its face or as applied to someone other than himself. People v. Johnson, 341 Ill. App. 3d 583, 276 Ill. Dec. 15, 793 N.E.2d 774, 2003 Ill. App. LEXIS 823 (1 Dist. 2003).

LEGAL PERIODICALS

For article, "Defending the Indefensible to Further a Later Case: Sanctioning Respondents in Illinois Domestic Violence Cases," see 23 N. Ill. U. L. Rev. 403 (2003).

720 ILCS 5/12-4.10 (As enacted by P.A. 93-111) Endangering the life and health of an emergency service provider

Sec. 12-4.10. *Endangering the life and health of an emergency service provider.* (a) A person commits the offense of endangering the life and health of an emergency service provider if an emergency service provider experiences death, great bodily harm, disability, or disfigurement as a result of entering a structure containing a clandestine drug laboratory designed or intended to produce an unlawful controlled substance or designed or intended to produce ingredients used in the manufacture of an unlawful controlled substance.

(b) In this Section:

"Emergency service provider" means a peace officer, a firefighter, an emergency medical technician-ambulance, an emergency medical-technician-intermediate, an emergency medical technician-paramedic, an ambulance driver or other medical or first aid personnel.

"Structure" means any house, apartment building, shop, barn, warehouse, building, vessel, railroad car, cargo container, motor vehicle, housecar, trailer, trailer coach, camper, mine, floating home, watercraft, any structure capable of holding a clandestine laboratory or any real property.

(c) Sentence. Endangering the life and health of an emergency service provider is a Class X felony.
(Source: P.A. 93-111, § 5.)

Section Set Out Twice.
The section above is as enacted by P.A. 93-111. For the version of this section as enacted by P.A. 93-340, see the following section, also numbered 720 ILCS 5/12-4.10.

Effective Date.
Section 99 of P.A. 93-111 made this act effective upon becoming law. The Act was approved July 8, 2003.

720 ILCS 5/12-4.10 (As enacted by P.A. 93-340) Drug related child endangerment

Sec. 12-4.10. *Drug related child endangerment.* (a) A person commits the offense of drug related child endangerment when he or she endangers the life and health of a child by knowingly exposing the child to a clandestine drug laboratory environment by performing any of the following acts:

(1) producing, manufacturing, or preparing a controlled substance; or

(2) producing, manufacturing, or preparing an ingredient required to manufacture a controlled substance; or

(3) storing chemicals used in the controlled substance manufacturing process in a structure to which the child has access; or

(4) storing contaminated apparatus used in the controlled substance manufacturing process in a structure to which the child has access; or

(5) storing chemical waste and other by-products created during the controlled substance manufacturing process in a structure to which the child has access; or

(6) storing any device used for the ingestion of controlled substances in a structure to which the child has access.

(b) In this Section:

"Child" means a person under the age of 18 years.

"Structure" means any house, apartment building, shop, barn, warehouse, building, vessel, railroad car, cargo container, motor vehicle, house car, trailer, trailer coach, camper, mine, floating home, watercraft, any structure capable of holding a clandestine laboratory or any real property.

(c) Sentence. A person convicted of drug related child endangerment is guilty of a Class 2 felony.
(Source: P.A. 93-340, § 5.)

Section Set Out Twice.
The section above is as enacted by P.A. 93-340. For the version of this section as enacted by P.A. 93-111, see the preceding section, also numbered 720 ILCS 5/12-4.10.

Effective Date.
Section 99 of P.A. 93-340 made this section effective upon becoming law. The Act was approved July 24, 2003.

720 ILCS 5/12-4.11 Aggravated drug related child endangerment

Sec. 12-4.11. *Aggravated drug related child endangerment.* (a) A person commits the offense of aggravated drug related child endangerment when he or she:

(1) commits a violation of drug related child endangerment; and

(2) the child experiences death, great bodily harm, disability or disfigurement as a result of the drug related child endangerment.

(b) Sentence. Aggravated drug related child endangerment is a Class X felony.
(Source: P.A. 93-340, § 5.)

Effective Date.
Section 99 of P.A. 93-340 made this section effective upon becoming law. The Act was approved July 24, 2003.

OFFENSES AGAINST PERSONS

NEGLECTED CHILDREN OFFENSE ACT

720 ILCS 130/0.01 Short title

Sec. 0.01. *Short title.* This Act may be cited as the Neglected Children Offense Act.
(Source: P.A. 86-1324.)

Derivation.
Title: An Act to define and punish the crimes of contributing to the dependency and neglect of children and to the delinquency of children.
Cite: 720 ILCS 130/0.01 et seq.
Source: L. 1915, p. 368. Title amended by L. 1965, p. 2852.
Date: Approved June 23, 1915.

Note.
This section was Ill.Rev.Stat., Ch. 23, para. 2359.9.

CASE NOTES

Contempt

Court properly adjudicated defendant, whose children had been adjudicated wards of the court and placed under the guardianship of the Department of Children and Family Services (DCFS) of indirect criminal contempt, for wilfully violating a court order by failing to contact DCFS and failing to visit the children. In re B.J., 268 Ill. App. 3d 449, 206 Ill. Dec. 23, 644 N.E.2d 791 (4 Dist. 1994).

720 ILCS 130/1 [Dependent and neglected child defined]

Sec. 1. For the purposes of this Act a dependent and neglected child shall mean any child who while under the age of 18 years, for any reason is destitute, homeless or abandoned; or dependent upon the public for support; or has not proper parental care or guardianship; or habitually begs or receives alms; or is found living in any house of ill fame or with any vicious or disreputable person; or has a home which by reason of neglect, cruelty or depravity on the part of its parents, guardian or any other person in whose care it may be is an unfit place for such child; and any child who while under the age of 10 years is found begging, peddling or selling any articles or singing or playing any musical instrument for gain upon the street or giving any public entertainments or accompanies or is used in aid of any person so doing.
(Source: Laws 1955, p. 1411.)

Note.

This section was Ill.Rev.Stat., Ch. 23, para. 2360.

CASE NOTES

Right to Select School

Where the juvenile division of a circuit court declared three children to be dependent within the meaning of the former Act to Define and Punish the Crime of Contributing to Dependency (see now this section), and, with the father's consent, it was ordered that the children be committed to the care, custody and control of a charitable corporation, the children had the right to attend the public school of the district in which the charitable corporation was located. Dean v. Board of Educ., 386 Ill. 156, 53 N.E.2d 875 (1944).

720 ILCS 130/1a [Delinquent child defined]

Sec. 1a. For the purposes of this Act a delinquent child is any minor who prior to his 17th birthday has violated or attempted to violate, regardless of where the act occurred, any federal or State law or municipal ordinance.
(Source: P.A. 85-573.)

Note.

This section was Ill.Rev.Stat., Ch. 23, para. 2360a.

720 ILCS 130/2 [Contributing to dependency and neglect of children]

Sec. 2. Any parent, legal guardian or person having the custody of a child under the age of 18 years, who knowingly or wilfully causes, aids or encourages such person to be or to become a dependent and neglected child as defined in section 1 [720 ILCS 130/1], who knowingly or wilfully does acts which directly tend to render any such child so dependent and neglected, or who knowingly or wilfully fails to do that which will directly tend to prevent such state of dependency and neglect is guilty of the Class A misdemeanor of contributing to the dependency and neglect of children, except that a person who relinquishes a child in accordance with the Abandoned Newborn Infant Protection Act [325 ILCS 2/1 et seq.] is not guilty of that misdemeanor. Instead of imposing the punishment hereinbefore provided, the court may release the defendant from custody on probation for one year upon his or her entering into recognizance with or without surety in such sum as the court directs. The conditions of the recognizance shall be such that if the defendant appears personally in court whenever ordered to do so within the year and provides and cares for such neglected and dependent child in such manner as to prevent a continuance or repetition of such state of dependency and neglect or as otherwise may be directed by the court then the recognizance shall be void, otherwise it shall be of full force and effect. If the court is satisfied by information and due proof under oath that at any time during the year the defendant has violated the terms of such order it may forthwith revoke the order and sentence him or her under the original conviction. Unless so sentenced, the defendant shall at the end of the year be discharged. In case of forfeiture on the recognizance the sum recovered thereon may in the discretion of the court be paid in whole or in part to someone designated by the court for the support of such dependent and neglected child.
(Source: P.A. 77-2350; 92-408, § 96.5; 92-432, § 96.5.)

Note.

This section was Ill.Rev.Stat., Ch. 23, para. 2361.

Effect of Amendments.

The 2001 amendment by P.A. 92-408, effective August 17, 2001, inserted "except that a person who relinquishes a child in accordance with the Abandoned Newborn Infant Protection Act is not guilty of that misdemeanor" in the first sentence.

The 2001 amendment by P.A. 92-432, effective August 17, 2001, inserted "except that a person who relinquishes a child in accordance with the Abandoned Newborn Infant Protection Act is not guilty of that misdemeanor" in the first sentence.

Although the amendments made to this section by P.A. 92-408, § 96.5 and P.A. 92-432, § 96.5 did not take into account the amendments made by the other, the amendments have been combined into a single version by the publisher.

CASE NOTES

Analysis

Charging Document
—Held Sufficient
—Insufficient
Evidence Held Sufficient
In Loco Parentis
Information
—Insufficient

Intent
—Duty to Inquiry
—Essential Element
Knowing or Wilful Neglect
—Not Shown
Merger of Offenses
Multiple Convictions
Power of Court
Proof

Charging Document

—Held Sufficient

Complaint that charged defendant with endangering minor's health by failing to get medical attention for minor's injuries sufficiently set forth the elements of the child endangerment offense under former 720 ILCS 150/4 (see now this section). People v. Berg, 171 Ill. App. 3d 316, 121 Ill. Dec. 515, 525 N.E.2d 573 (3 Dist. 1988).

—Insufficient

Indictment filed pursuant to former similar provision which failed to allege that defendant committed violation "knowingly or wilfully" but instead stated that defendant performed act "unlawfully and without lawful excuse" was void for failure to properly charge defendant with violation. People v. Scholl, 339 Ill. App. 7, 88 N.E.2d 681 (3 Dist. 1949).

Evidence Held Sufficient

There was sufficient evidence to find defendants guilty of contributing to the dependency and neglect of a minor where officers could not find clean dry clothing for the children, the bulk of the limited food found in the apartment was either spoiled or infested with roaches and there was evidence of inadequate supervision. People v. Melton, 282 Ill. App. 3d 408, 217 Ill. Dec. 795, 667 N.E.2d 1371 (1 Dist. 1996).

In Loco Parentis

To be guilty of the offense of contributing to the dependency or neglect of a child, one must be a parent of that child or stand in loco parentis thereto. People v. Warner, 98 Ill. App. 3d 433, 53 Ill. Dec. 956, 424 N.E.2d 747 (4 Dist. 1981).

Information

—Insufficient

Information was insufficient to charge the crime of contributing to the dependency and neglect of defendant's seven minor children under former provision. People v. Standerfer, 339 Ill. App. 454, 90 N.E.2d 229 (4 Dist. 1950).

Where an information charged that defendant did "knowingly and wilfully fail to do that which did directly tend to prevent such state of dependency and neglect, to-wit: did eject said children from their home," the information was insufficient in that it did not allege that the two children were dependent and neglected children within the meaning of 720 ILCS 130/1. People v. Anderson, 295 Ill. App. 27, 14 N.E.2d 527 (1 Dist. 1938).

Intent

—Duty to Inquiry

Police officer's failure to make inquiries was not reasonable, where information could have been easily obtained and was necessary before concluding that parents had intentionally neglected their children. BeVier v. Hucal, 806 F.2d 123 (7th Cir. 1986).

—Essential Element

Information on a parent's intent is an essential element of child neglect. BeVier v. Hucal, 806 F.2d 123 (7th Cir. 1986).

Knowing or Wilful Neglect

—Not Shown

Facts known by defendant police officer weakly supported an inference that children were being neglected where the children were in direct sunlight on an extremely hot day; they were listless, filthy, and living near machinery and livestock; and one had severe blistering diaper rash for which he had been taken to the hospital; however, there was no evidence of knowing or wilful neglect because the defendant knew that the plaintiff had taken the blistered child to the hospital and had retained a new babysitter. BeVier v. Hucal, 806 F.2d 123 (7th Cir. 1986).

Merger of Offenses

Unlawful restraint and contributing to the dependency or neglect of a child have separate elements, preventing either offense from being an included offense of the other by definition, nor is one carved from the same act as the other; therefore, the offenses do not merge. People v. Warner, 98 Ill. App. 3d 433, 53 Ill. Dec. 956, 424 N.E.2d 747 (4 Dist. 1981).

Multiple Convictions

Endangerment conviction (720 ILCS 5/12-21.6) and neglect conviction were based on the same act and were thus violative of the one act one crime rule; not that one can never be guilty of both endangerment and neglect. People v. Melton, 282 Ill. App. 3d 408, 217 Ill. Dec. 795, 667 N.E.2d 1371 (1 Dist. 1996).

Power of Court

While the statutes do not specifically allow a court to require visitation by a parent with a child, such power is implied and exists. In re J.C., 248 Ill. App. 3d 905, 187 Ill. Dec. 657, 617 N.E.2d 1378 (4 Dist. 1993).

Proof

Under former Criminal Code (see now this section), in order to prove the offense of contributing to the delinquency of children it was not necessary that the child who was the subject of the crime should be a delinquent child, or should become a delinquent child, but the crime was complete when acts were committed which directly tended to render the child delinquent. People v. Klyczek, 307 Ill. 150, 138 N.E. 275 (1923).

LEGAL PERIODICALS

For article, "Crime or Punishment: The Parental Corporal Punishment Defense — Reasonable and Necessary, or Excused Abuse?", see 1998 U. Ill. L. Rev. 413.

RESEARCH REFERENCES

Parents' criminal liability for failure to provide medical attention to their children. 118 ALR5th 253.

720 ILCS 130/2a [Contributing to the delinquency of children; penalty]

Sec. 2a. Any person who knowingly or wilfully causes, aids or encourages any boy or girl to be or to become a delinquent child, or who knowingly or wilfully does acts which directly tend to render any such child so delinquent is guilty of the Class A misdemeanor of contributing to the delinquency of children. Instead of imposing such punishment the court may release the defendant from custody on probation for 1 year upon his or her entering into recognizance with or without surety in such sum as the court may direct.
(Source: P.A. 77-2350.)

Note.

This section was Ill.Rev.Stat., Ch. 23, para. 2361a.

CASE NOTES

Analysis

Applicability of Criminal Code
Evidence Held Insufficient
Penalty

—Due Process
—Standing to Contest

Applicability of Criminal Code

The probation conditions enumerated in former provisions of the Criminal Code (see now 730 ILCS 5/5-6-1) were not applicable to the crime of contributing to the delinquency of a minor, which contains a different procedure for probation. People v. Wethington, 76 Ill. App. 2d 110, 220 N.E.2d 870 (4 Dist. 1966).

Evidence Held Insufficient

The conduct of a "house parent" at a private home for children did not constitute contributing to the delinquency of boys where he allowed boys who threatened to run away from the children's home to stay at his apartment while he insisted that the boys return to the home. People v. Rauhauser, 6 Ill. App. 3d 927, 287 N.E.2d 78 (1 Dist. 1972).

Penalty

—Due Process

Defendant failed to meet his burden of proving that the difference between penalties for contributing to a child's delinquency and for the delinquent offense itself violated due process. People v. Rauh, 197 Ill. App. 3d 692, 143 Ill. Dec. 884, 554 N.E.2d 819 (3 Dist. 1990).

—Standing to Contest

Defendant had standing to contest a disproportionate penalty for contributing to the delinquency of a child even though he did not actually receive the allegedly disproportionate penalty. People v. Rauh, 197 Ill. App. 3d 692, 143 Ill. Dec. 884, 554 N.E.2d 819 (3 Dist. 1990).

720 ILCS 130/3 [Testimony by spouse]

Sec. 3. The husband or wife of the defendant shall be a competent witness to testify in any case brought under this Act and to any and all matters relevant thereto.
(Source: Laws 1915, p. 368.)

Note.

This section was Ill.Rev.Stat., Ch. 23, para. 2362.

WRONGS TO CHILDREN ACT

720 ILCS 150/0.01 Short title

Sec. 0.01. *Short title.* This Act may be cited as the Wrongs to Children Act.
(Source: P.A. 86-1324.)

Derivation.

Title: An Act to prevent and punish wrongs to children.
Cite: 720 ILCS 150/0.01 et seq.
Source: L. 1877, p. 90.
Date: Approved May 17, 1877.

Note.

This section was Ill.Rev.Stat., Ch. 23, para. 2350.

720 ILCS 150/1 [Using or employing a child for injurious, dangerous or immoral purposes prohibited]

Sec. 1. It shall be unlawful for any person having the care, custody or control of any child under the age of fourteen years, to exhibit, use or employ, or in any manner, or under any pretense, sell, apprentice, give away, let out, or otherwise dispose of any such child to any person in or for the vocation or occupation, service or purpose of singing, playing on musical instruments, rope or wire walking, dancing, begging, or peddling, or as a gymnast, contortionist, rider or acrobat in any place whatsoever, or for any obscene, indecent or immoral purpose, exhibition or practice whatsoever, or for, or in any business, exhibition or vocation injurious to the health or dangerous to the life or limb of such child, or cause, procure or encourage any such child to engage therein. Nothing in this section contained shall apply to or affect the employment or use of any such child as a singer or musician in any church, school or academy (or at any respectable entertainment), or the teaching or learning the science or practice of music.
(Source: Laws 1877, p. 90.)

Note.

This section was Ill.Rev.Stat., Ch. 23, para. 2351.

CASE NOTES

ANALYSIS

Constitutionality
—Due Process
Judicial Immunity

Constitutionality

—Due Process

This Law and the Registration Act (730 ILCS 152/101 et seq.) subject all sex offenders as defined by the Act to the registration and notification provisions, and law enforcement authorities have no discretion to determine which offenders would be exposed to public dissemination, therefore a hearing would serve no purpose and lack of one does not deprive a defendant of due process. People v. Logan, 302 Ill. App. 3d 319, 235 Ill. Dec. 539, 705 N.E.2d 152 (2 Dist. 1998).

Judicial Immunity

Where plaintiffs brought an action pursuant to 42 U.S.C. § 1983, challenging that a court order removing their son from their custody and appointing a guardian to consent to medical treatment and to the administration of blood transfusions to the child, and sued the judge who entered the order, the judge was protected by judicial immunity since his authority was based on, among other things, this Act. Staelens v. Yake, 432 F. Supp. 834 (N.D. Ill. 1977).

720 ILCS 150/2 [Taking or employment of a child prohibited]

Sec. 2. It shall also be unlawful for any person to take, receive, hire, employ, use, exhibit, or have in custody any child under the age and for the purposes prohibited in the first section of this act.
(Source: Laws 1877, p. 90.)

Note.

This section was Ill.Rev.Stat., Ch. 23, para. 2352.

720 ILCS 150/3 [Placing a child in the custody of the court]

Sec. 3. When upon examination before any court it appears that any child within the age previously mentioned in this Act was engaged or used for or in

any business, exhibition, vocation, or purpose prohibited in this Act; and when upon the conviction of any person of a criminal assault upon a child in his custody, the court before whom such conviction is had, shall deem it desirable for the welfare of such child, that the person so convicted should be deprived of its custody; thereafter such child shall be deemed to be in the custody of court, and such court may in its discretion, make such order as to the custody thereof as now is, or hereafter may be, provided by law in cases of vagrant, truant, disorderly, pauper, or destitute children.
(Source: P.A. 77-1274.)

Note.
This section was Ill.Rev.Stat., Ch. 23, para. 2353.

RESEARCH REFERENCES

Legal malpractice in defense of parents at proceedings to terminate parental rights over dependent or neglected children. 18 ALR5th 902.

720 ILCS 150/3.1 [Single parents of children under 6; employment]

Sec. 3.1. No agency of the State or unit of local government shall require a single parent or other person having the care, custody or control of any child under the age of 6 to accept employment that would unreasonably interfere with such responsibilities to the child. It is unlawful for any person acting under color of law to require or to attempt to require such employment of a parent or other person having the care, custody or control of such a child.
(Source: P.A. 80-860.)

Note.
This section was Ill.Rev.Stat., Ch. 23, para. 2353.1.

720 ILCS 150/4: Repealed by P.A. 88-479, § 30, effective September 9, 1993.

720 ILCS 150/4.1 [Abandonment of school bus by driver]

Sec. 4.1. It is unlawful for any school bus driver to wilfully abandon the school bus while it contains any children who are without other adult supervision, except in an emergency where the driver is seeking help or otherwise acting in the best interests of the children.
(Source: P.A. 87-526.)

Note.
This section was Ill.Rev.Stat., Ch. 23, para. 2354.1.

Illinois Administrative Code.
See 92 Illinois Administrative Code, § 1035.15.

720 ILCS 150/5 [Sentence]

Sec. 5. Any person convicted under the provisions of the preceding sections, shall for the first offense be guilty of a Class A misdemeanor; and for a second or any subsequent offense shall be guilty of a Class 4 felony.
(Source: P.A. 77-2346.)

Note.
This section was Ill.Rev.Stat., Ch. 23, para. 2355.

720 ILCS 150/5.1 Permitting sexual abuse of a child

Sec. 5.1. *Permitting sexual abuse of a child.* (a) A person responsible for a child's welfare commits the offense of permitting sexual abuse of a child if he or she has actual knowledge of and permits an act of sexual abuse upon the child, or permits the child to engage in prostitution as defined in Section 11-14 of the Criminal Code of 1961 [720 ILCS 5/11-14].

(b) In this Section:

"Child" means a minor under the age of 17 years.

"Person responsible for the child's welfare" means the child's parent, step-parent, legal guardian, or other person having custody of a child, who is responsible for the child's care at the time of the alleged sexual abuse.

"Sexual abuse" includes criminal sexual abuse or criminal sexual assault as defined in Section 12-13, 12-14, 12-14.1, 12-15, or 12-16 of the Criminal Code of 1961 [720 ILCS 5/12-13, 720 ILCS 5/12-14, 720 ILCS 5/12-14.1, 720 ILCS 5/12-15, or 720 ILCS 5/12-16].

"Prostitution" means prostitution as defined in Section 11-14 of the Criminal Code of 1961 [720 ILCS 5/11-14].

"Actual knowledge" includes credible allegations made by the child.

(c) This Section does not apply to a person responsible for the child's welfare who, having reason to believe that sexual abuse has occurred, makes timely and reasonable efforts to stop the sexual abuse by reporting the sexual abuse in conformance with the Abused and Neglected Child Reporting Act [325 ILCS 5/1 et seq.] or by reporting the sexual abuse, or causing a report to be made, to medical or law enforcement authorities or anyone who is a mandated reporter under Section 4 of the Abused and Neglected Child Reporting Act [325 ILCS 5/4].

(d) Whenever a law enforcement officer has reason to believe that the child or the person responsible for the child's welfare has been abused by a family or household member as defined by the Illinois Domestic Violence Act of 1986 [750 ILCS 60/101 et seq.], the officer shall immediately use all reasonable means to prevent further abuse under Section 112A-30 of the Code of Criminal Procedure of 1963 [725 ILCS 5/112A-30].

(e) An order of protection under Section 111-8 of the Code of Criminal Procedure of 1963 [725 ILCS 5/111-8] shall be sought in all cases where there is reason to believe that a child has been sexually abused by a family or household member. In considering appropriate available remedies, it shall be presumed that awarding physical care or custody to the abuser is not in the child's best interest.

(f) A person may not be charged with the offense of permitting sexual abuse of a child under this Section until the person who committed the offense is charged with criminal sexual assault, aggravated criminal sexual assault, predatory criminal sexual assault of a child, criminal sexual abuse, aggravated criminal sexual abuse, or prostitution.

(g) A person convicted of permitting the sexual abuse of a child is guilty of a Class 1 felony. As a condition of any sentence of supervision, probation, conditional discharge, or mandatory supervised release, any person convicted under this Section shall be ordered to undergo child sexual abuse, domestic violence, or other appropriate counseling for a specified duration with a qualified social or mental health worker.

(h) It is an affirmative defense to a charge of permitting sexual abuse of a child under this Section that the person responsible for the child's welfare had a reasonable apprehension that timely action to stop the abuse or prostitution would result in the imminent infliction of death, great bodily harm, permanent disfigurement, or permanent disability to that person or another in retaliation for reporting. (Source: P.A. 85-1433; 88-680, § 50-10; 89-428, § 265; 89-462, § 265; 91-696, § 50-10; 92-827, § 10.)

Note.

This section was Ill.Rev.Stat., Ch. 23, para. 2355.1.

P.A. 91-696, § 1, effective April 13, 2000, provides for the purpose of the Act, and is quoted in a note under 720 ILCS 5/32-4.

Section 990-1 of P.A. 91-696 contains a severability provision.

Effect of Amendments.

The 1994 amendment by P.A. 88-680, effective January 1, 1995, in subsection A, in the first sentence, substituted a comma for "or" preceding "step-parent", inserted "legal guardian, or other person having custody of a child" and inserted "or knowingly permits, induces, promotes, or arranges for the child to engage in prostitution as defined in Section 11-14 of the Criminal Code of 1961"; and in subsection B substituted "is" for "shall be" and substituted "1 felony" for "A misdemeanor".

The 1995 amendment by P.A. 89-428, effective December 13, 1995 and the 1996 amendment by P.A. 89-462, effective May 29, 1996, made identical amendments: they each in subsection A, in the first sentence, inserted "12-14.1".

The 2000 amendment by P.A. 91-696, effective April 13, 2000, reenacted this section with no additional changes.

The 2002 amendment by P.A. 92-827, effective August 22, 2002, rewrote the section to the extent that a detailed comparison would be impracticable.

CASE NOTES

Constitutionality

The statute is unconstitutionally vague as it is unclear what the "reasonable steps" are that a parent must take in order to comply with the statute. People v. Maness, 191 Ill. 2d 478, 247 Ill. Dec. 490, 732 N.E.2d 545, 2000 Ill. LEXIS 831 (2000).

Public Act 88-680, which amended this section, violates the single subject clause of the Illinois Constitution (Ill. Const. 1970, Art. IV, § 8). People v. Cervantes, 189 Ill. 2d 80, 243 Ill. Dec. 233, 723 N.E.2d 265 (1999).

Public Act 89-428 was enacted in violation of the single subject rule of the state constitution and is therefore invalid in its entirety. Johnson v. Edgar, 176 Ill. 2d 499, 224 Ill. Dec. 1, 680 N.E.2d 1372 (1997).

Public Act 88-680 violates the single subject rule and is unconstitutional in its entirety. People v. Dainty, 299 Ill. App. 3d 235, 233 Ill. Dec. 475, 701 N.E.2d 118 (3 Dist. 1998), appeal denied, 187 Ill. 2d 576, 244 Ill. Dec. 187, 724 N.E.2d 1271 (2000).

OFFENSES AGAINST THE PUBLIC

ILLINOIS ABORTION LAW OF 1975

720 ILCS 510/10 [Reports on abortions]

Sec. 10. A report of each abortion performed shall be made to the Department on forms prescribed by it. Such report forms shall not identify the patient by name, but by an individual number to be noted in the patient's permanent record in the possession of the physician, and shall include information concerning:

(1) Identification of the physician who performed the abortion and the facility where the abortion was performed and a patient identification number;

(2) State in which the patient resides;

(3) Patient's date of birth, race and marital status;

(4) Number of prior pregnancies;

(5) Date of last menstrual period;

(6) Type of abortion procedure performed;

(7) Complications and whether the abortion resulted in a live birth;

(8) The date the abortion was performed;

(9) Medical indications for any abortion performed when the fetus was viable;

(10) The information required by Sections 6(1)(b) and 6(4)(b) of this Act [720 ILCS 510/6], if applicable;

(11) Basis for any medical judgment that a medical emergency existed when required under Sections 6(2)(a) and 6(6) [720 ILCS 510/6] and when required to be reported in accordance with this Section by any provision of this Law; and

(12) The pathologist's test results pursuant to Section 12 of this Act [720 ILCS 510/12].

Such form shall be completed by the hospital or other licensed facility, signed by the physician who performed the abortion or pregnancy termination, and transmitted to the Department not later than 10 days following the end of the month in which the abortion was performed.

In the event that a complication of an abortion occurs or becomes known after submission of such form, a correction using the same patient identification number shall be submitted to the Department within 10 days of its becoming known.

The Department may prescribe rules and regulations regarding the administration of this Law and shall prescribe regulations to secure the confidentiality of the woman's identity in the information to be provided under the "Vital Records Act" [410 ILCS

535/1 et seq.]. All reports received by the Department shall be treated as confidential and the Department shall secure the woman's anonymity. Such reports shall be used only for statistical purposes.

Upon 30 days public notice, the Department is empowered to require reporting of any additional information which, in the sound discretion of the Department, is necessary to develop statistical data relating to the protection of maternal or fetal life or health, or is necessary to enforce the provisions of this Law, or is necessary to develop useful criteria for medical decisions. The Department shall annually report to the General Assembly all statistical data gathered under this Law and its recommendations to further the purpose of this Law.

The requirement for reporting to the General Assembly shall be satisfied by filing copies of the report with the Speaker, the Minority Leader and the Clerk of the House of Representatives and the President, the Minority Leader and the Secretary of the Senate and the Legislative Research Unit, as required by Section 3.1 of "An Act to revise the law in relation to the General Assembly", approved February 25, 1874, as amended [25 ILCS 5/3.1], and filing such additional copies with the State Government Report Distribution Center for the General Assembly as is required under paragraph (t) of Section 7 of the State Library Act [15 ILCS 320/7].
(Source: P.A. 84-1438.)

Note.
This section was Ill.Rev.Stat., Ch. 38, para. 81-30.

CASE NOTES

Applicability
Sections 10 and 11 of the Illinois Abortion Law (this section and 720 ILCS 510/11) relate to reports and records which are required to be filed with the Department of Health, and there is no indication that these statutory provisions are intended to apply to other matters, so as to extend the physician-patient privilege. People v. Florendo, 95 Ill. 2d 155, 69 Ill. Dec. 65, 447 N.E.2d 282 (1983).

720 ILCS 510/10.1 [Report of complications from abortion]

Sec. 10.1. Any physician who diagnoses a woman as having complications resulting from an abortion shall report, within a reasonable period of time, the diagnosis and a summary of her physical symptoms to the Illinois Department of Public Health in accordance with procedures and upon forms required by such Department. The Department of Public Health shall define the complications required to be reported by rule. The complications defined by rule shall be those which, according to contemporary medical standards, are manifested by symptoms with severity equal to or greater than hemorrhaging requiring transfusion, infection, incomplete abortion, or punctured organs. If the physician making the diagnosis of a complication knows the name or location of the facility where the abortion was performed, he shall report such information to the Department of Public Health.

Any physician who intentionally violates this Section shall be subject to revocation of his license pursuant to paragraph (22) of Section 22 of the Medical Practice Act of 1987 [225 ILCS 6/22].
(Source: P.A. 85-1209.)

Note.
This section was Ill.Rev.Stat., Ch. 38, para. 81-30.1.

720 ILCS 510/11 [Penalty for violations of Law]

Sec. 11. (1) Any person who intentionally violates any provision of this Law commits a Class A misdemeanor unless a specific penalty is otherwise provided. Any person who intentionally falsifies any writing required by this Law commits a Class A misdemeanor.

Intentional, knowing, reckless, or negligent violations of this Law shall constitute unprofessional conduct which causes public harm under Section 22 of the Medical Practice Act of 1987, as amended [225 ILCS 6/22]; Sections 10-45 and 15-50 of the Nursing and Advanced Practice Nursing Act [225 ILCS 65/10-45 and 225 ILCS 65/15-50], and Section 21 of the Physician Assistant Practice Act of 1987, as amended [225 ILCS 95/21].

Intentional, knowing, reckless or negligent violations of this Law will constitute grounds for refusal, denial, revocation, suspension, or withdrawal of license, certificate, or permit under Section 30 of the Pharmacy Practice Act of 1987, as amended [225 ILCS 85/30]; Section 7 of the Ambulatory Surgical Treatment Center Act, effective July 19, 1973, as amended [210 ILCS 5/7]; and Section 7 of the Hospital Licensing Act [210 ILCS 85/7].

(2) Any hospital or licensed facility which, or any physician who intentionally, knowingly, or recklessly fails to submit a complete report to the Department in accordance with the provisions of Section 10 of this Law [720 ILCS 510/10] and any person who intentionally, knowingly, recklessly or negligently fails to maintain the confidentiality of any reports required under this Law or reports required by Sections 10.1 or 12 of this Law [720 ILCS 510/10.1 or 720 ILCS 510/12] commits a Class B misdemeanor.

(3) Any person who sells any drug, medicine, instrument or other substance which he knows to be an abortifacient and which is in fact an abortifacient, unless upon prescription of a physician, is guilty of a Class B misdemeanor. Any person who prescribes or administers any instrument, medicine, drug or other substance or device, which he knows to be an abortifacient, and which is in fact an abortifacient, and intentionally, knowingly or recklessly fails to inform the person for whom it is prescribed or upon whom it is administered that it is an abortifacient commits a Class C misdemeanor.

(4) Any person who intentionally, knowingly or recklessly performs upon a woman what he represents to that woman to be an abortion when he knows or should know that she is not pregnant commits a Class 2 felony and shall be answerable in civil damages equal to 3 times the amount of proved damages.
(Source: P.A. 85-1209; 90-742, § 35.)

Note.
This section was Ill.Rev.Stat., Ch. 38, para. 81-31.

Effect of Amendments.
The 1998 amendment by P.A. 90-742, effective August 13, 1998, substituted "Section 10-45 and 15-50 of the Nursing and Advanced Practice Nursing Act" for "Section 25 of the Illinois Nursing Act of 1987, as amended" in the second paragraph of subsection (1); and deleted "approved July 1, 1953, as amended" from the end of the third paragraph of subsection (1).

CASE NOTES

Analysis

Applicability
Evidence Held Insufficient
Evidence Held Sufficient
Intent
—Implied
—Proof of Knowledge and Intent
Standing

Applicability
Sections 10 and 11 of the Illinois Abortion Law (720 ILCS 510/10 and this section) relate to reports and records which are required to be filed with the Department of Health, and there is no indication that these statutory provisions are intended to apply to other matters, so as to extend the physician-patient privilege. People v. Florendo, 95 Ill. 2d 155, 69 Ill. Dec. 65, 447 N.E.2d 282 (1983).

Evidence Held Insufficient
The evidence was insufficient to support a conviction for manslaughter by abortion. People v. Braune, 363 Ill. 551, 2 N.E.2d 839 (1936).

Evidence Held Sufficient
Under the former Criminal Abortion Statute (see now 720 ILCS 510/1 et seq.), where a medical expert testified that in his opinion an abortion was performed and it was impossible to induce a rubber tube into the vagina unless a speculum was used to open the vagina, and the prosecuting witness testified that after a doctor told her she was pregnant, she went to the defendant's drugstore where he closed the store, told her to go in the back room, inserted an orange tubing in her uterus, packed it with cotton and told her to remove the tubing the next day when the bleeding started, and she paid him the agreed price, a finding that the defendant used an instrument with intent to procure a miscarriage was clearly justified. People v. Fulton, 84 Ill. App. 2d 280, 228 N.E.2d 203 (1 Dist. 1967).

Evidence, despite denial of defendant, was held clearly sufficient to justify a finding that defendant used an instrument with the intent to procure a miscarriage in violation of the abortion statute. People v. Gomez, 29 Ill. 2d 432, 194 N.E.2d 299 (1963).

The evidence was sufficient to sustain a conviction for criminal abortion under former Ill.Rev.Stat., ch. 38, para 3 (see now this section). People v. Murawski, 2 Ill. 2d 143, 117 N.E.2d 88 (1954).

Intent

—Implied
Under a similar prior provision, an attempt to produce a miscarriage that was not necessary to preserve life, by forcing instruments into the womb of a pregnant woman, was such an unlawful act that the law implied therefrom a criminal intent. Scott v. People, 141 Ill. 195, 30 N.E. 329 (1892).

—Proof of Knowledge and Intent
Under a similar prior provision, acts of the defendant in a prosecution for illegal abortion, tending to show his knowledge of a woman's pregnancy and his intention to commit an abortion upon her, could be proved whether they were prior or subsequent to the particular act charged in the indictment. Scott v. People, 141 Ill. 195, 30 N.E. 329 (1892).

Standing
No plaintiff had standing to question a ban on sale of abortifacients except upon the prescription of a physician, since each plaintiff was either a physician or under a physician's care, so no plaintiff was directly affected by the ban. Wynn v. Scott, 449 F. Supp. 1302 (N.D. Ill. 1978), aff'd, 599 F.2d 193 (7th Cir. 1979).

LEGAL PERIODICALS

For note: "Fetal Tissue Transplants: A Proposal to Amend the Uniform Anatomical Gift Act," see U. Ill. L. Rev. 1095 (1989).

720 ILCS 510/11.1 [Referral fee prohibited]

Sec. 11.1. (a) The payment or receipt of a referral fee in connection with the performance of an abortion is a Class 4 felony.

(b) For purposes of this Section, "referral fee" means the transfer of anything of value between a doctor who performs an abortion or an operator or employee of a clinic at which an abortion is performed and the person who advised the woman receiving the abortion to use the services of that doctor or clinic.
(Source: P.A. 81-1119.)

Note.
This section was Ill.Rev.Stat., Ch. 38, para. 81-31.1.

720 ILCS 510/12 [Analysis of tissue removed]

Sec. 12. The dead fetus and all tissue removed at the time of abortion shall be submitted for a gross and microscopic analysis and tissue report to a board eligible or certified pathologist as a matter of record in all cases. The results of the analysis and report shall be given to the physician who performed the abortion within 7 days of the abortion and such physician shall report any complications relevant to the woman's medical condition to his patient within 48 hours of receiving a report if possible. Any evidence of live birth or of viability shall be reported within 7 days, if possible, to the Department by the pathologist. Intentional failure of the pathologist to report any evidence of live birth or of viability to the Department is a Class B misdemeanor.
(Source: P.A. 83-1128.)

Note.
This section was Ill.Rev.Stat., Ch. 38, para. 81-32.

CASE NOTES

Constitutionality

—Fetus Research
Sections concerning research and experimentation with fetuses

Constitutionality (Cont'd)

—Fetus Research (Cont'd)
and with aborted tissue held constitutional. Wynn v. Scott, 449 F. Supp. 1302 (N.D. Ill. 1978), aff'd, 599 F.2d 193 (7th Cir. 1979).

LEGAL PERIODICALS

For note: "Fetal Tissue Transplants: A Proposal to Amend the Uniform Anatomical Gift Act," see U. Ill. L. Rev. 1095 (1989).

720 ILCS 510/12.1 [Use of tissue from fetus or dead infant not obtained from abortion]

Sec. 12.1. Nothing in this Act shall prohibit the use of any tissues or cells obtained from a dead fetus or dead premature infant whose death did not result from an induced abortion, for therapeutic purposes or scientific, research, or laboratory experimentation, provided that the written consent to such use is obtained from one of the parents of such fetus or infant.
(Source: P.A. 81-884.)

Note.
This section was Ill.Rev.Stat., Ch. 38, para. 81-32.1.

LEGAL PERIODICALS

For note: "Fetal Tissue Transplants: A Proposal to Amend the Uniform Anatomical Gift Act," see U. Ill. L. Rev. 1095 (1989).

720 ILCS 510/13 [Refusal to participate in abortion]

Sec. 13. No physician, hospital, ambulatory surgical center, nor employee thereof, shall be required against his or its conscience declared in writing to perform, permit or participate in any abortion, and the failure or refusal to do so shall not be the basis for any civil, criminal, administrative or disciplinary action, proceeding, penalty or punishment. If any request for an abortion is denied, the patient shall be promptly notified.
(Source: P.A. 81-1078.)

Note.
This section was Ill.Rev.Stat., Ch. 38, para. 81-33.

720 ILCS 510/14 [Severability; regulations]

Sec. 14. (1) If any provision, word, phrase or clause of this Act or the application thereof to any person or circumstance shall be held invalid, such invalidity shall not affect the provisions, words, phrases, clauses or application of this Act which can be given effect without the invalid provision, word, phrase, clause, or application, and to this end the provisions, words, phrases, and clauses of this Act are declared to be severable.

(2) Within 60 days from the time this Section becomes law, the Department shall issue regulations pursuant to Section 10 [720 ILCS 510/10]. Insofar as Section 10 [720 ILCS 510/10] requires registration under the "Vital Records Act" [410 ILCS 535/1 et seq.], it shall not take effect until such regulations are issued. The Department shall make available the forms required under Section 10 [720 ILCS 510/10] within 30 days of the time this Section becomes law. No requirement that any person report information to the Department shall become effective until the Department has made available the forms required under Section 10 [720 ILCS 510/10]. All other provisions of this amended Law shall take effect immediately upon enactment.
(Source: P.A. 83-1128.)

Note.
This section was Ill.Rev.Stat., Ch. 38, para. 81-34.

CASE NOTES

Severability
Provisions of this Act found to be unconstitutional were held severable, consistent with the severability clause. Wynn v. Scott, 449 F. Supp. 1302 (N.D. Ill. 1978), aff'd, 599 F.2d 193 (7th Cir. 1979).

720 ILCS 510/15 [Short title]

Sec. 15. This Act shall be known and may be cited as the "Illinois Abortion Law of 1975".
(Source: P.A. 81-1078.)

Note.
This section was Ill.Rev.Stat., Ch. 38, para. 81-35.

Illinois Abortion Parental Consent Act of 1977

720 ILCS 515/1 through 720 ILCS 515/5: Repealed by P.A. 89-18, § 90, effective June 1, 1995.

Note.
For similar provisions, see the Parental Notice of Abortion Act of 1995 at 750 ILCS 70/1 et seq.

Parental Notice of Abortion Act of 1983

720 ILCS 520/1 through 720 ILCS 520/10: Repealed by P.A. 89-18, § 95, effective June 1, 1995.

Note.
For similar provisions see the Parental Notice of Abortion Act of 1995 at 750 ILCS 70/1 et seq.

Adoption Compensation Prohibition Act

720 ILCS 525/0.01 Short title

Sec. 0.01. *Short title.* This Act may be cited as the Adoption Compensation Prohibition Act.
(Source: P.A. 86-1324.)

Derivation.

Title: An Act to prevent the payment or receipt of compensation for placing out children for adoption or for the purpose of providing care.

Cite: 720 ILCS 525/0.01 et seq.

Source: L. 1955, p. 1881.

Date: Approved July 14, 1955.

Note.

This section was Ill.Rev.Stat., Ch. 40, para. 1700.

720 ILCS 525/1 [Receipt of compensation for placing child prohibited]

Sec. 1. No person and no agency, association, corporation, institution, society, or other organization, except a child welfare agency as defined by the Child Care Act of 1969, as now or hereafter amended [225 ILCS 10/1 et seq.], shall request, receive or accept any compensation or thing of value, directly or indirectly, for placing out of a child.
(Source: P.A. 86-820.)

Note.

This section was Ill.Rev.Stat., Ch. 40, para. 1701.

CASE NOTES

Analysis

Constitutionality
In General
Applicability
—Compensation
—Transfer of Unborn Children
Attorneys
Contract
—Consulting Service Agreement
—Enforceability
Fee Increase
Purpose

Constitutionality

The former Adoption Act (see now 720 ILCS 525/0.01 et seq.) was not unconstitutionally vague or overbroad. People v. Schwartz, 64 Ill. 2d 275, 1 Ill. Dec. 8, 356 N.E.2d 8 (1976).

In General

The former Adoption Act (see now 720 ILCS 525/0.01 et seq.) prevented circumvention of the legislative goal through informal placement agreements which did not contemplate formal adoption proceedings, but which had the same practical effect. People v. Schwartz, 64 Ill. 2d 275, 1 Ill. Dec. 8, 356 N.E.2d 8 (1976).

Applicability

—Compensation

The former Adoption Act (see now 720 ILCS 525/0.01 et seq.) did not simply prohibit the actual placement of children by an unlicensed person; rather, it prohibited the request or receipt of compensation for the placing out of a child. People v. Schwartz, 64 Ill. 2d 275, 1 Ill. Dec. 8, 356 N.E.2d 8 (1976).

—Transfer of Unborn Children

The former Adoption Act (see now 720 ILCS 525/0.01 et seq.) prohibited an agreement that a fee would be paid for the transfer of a yet unborn child as clearly as an arrangement for the compensated placement of a child in being. People v. Schwartz, 64 Ill. 2d 275, 1 Ill. Dec. 8, 356 N.E.2d 8 (1976).

Attorneys

Under the former Adoption Act (see now 750 ILCS 50/0.01 et seq.), an attorney could not act as a paid intermediary or placement agent for a party desiring to buy or sell a child; that Act treated an attorney in the same manner as any other individual who did not qualify for its exemption. People v. Schwartz, 64 Ill. 2d 275, 1 Ill. Dec. 8, 356 N.E.2d 8 (1976).

Contract

—Consulting Service Agreement

An agreement with a company that offered support and travel services for persons wishing to adopt children from China did not violate the Adoption Compensation Prohibition Act. Regensburger v. China Adoption Consultants, 138 F.3d 1201 (7th Cir. 1998).

—Enforceability

There was no enforceable contract between the individual couples and defendant, which set the placement fee, where the only document executed by these couples prior to the announced increase in fee was the agreement with respect to their willingness to abide by certain terms and conditions of the adoption process. Crismore v. Catholic Social Serv., 133 Ill. App. 3d 1088, 89 Ill. Dec. 211, 479 N.E.2d 1217 (3 Dist. 1985).

Fee Increase

The mere fact that there was a difference in bargaining power between agency and the individual couples was not sufficient, of itself, to support a conclusion that agency imposed an unconscionable contractual provision when it notified the individual couples of an increase in adoption fee. Crismore v. Catholic Social Serv., 133 Ill. App. 3d 1088, 89 Ill. Dec. 211, 479 N.E.2d 1217 (3 Dist. 1985).

Purpose

The purpose of former Ill.Rev.Stat., ch. 4, para. 12-1 et seq. (see now 720 ILCS 525/0.01 et seq.) was to prevent profiteering in the placement of children and to eliminate so called "baby markets" and "baby brokers." People v. Schwartz, 64 Ill. 2d 275, 1 Ill. Dec. 8, 356 N.E.2d 8 (1976).

LEGAL PERIODICALS

For comment, "Prohibiting Payments to Surrogate Mothers: Love's Labor Lost and the Constitutional Right of Privacy," see 20 J. Marshall L. Rev. 715 (1987).

For article, "Surrogate Parenthood: A Need for Legislative Direction," see 71 Ill. B. J. 412 (1983).

RESEARCH REFERENCES

Criminal liability of one arranging for adoption of child through other than licensed child placement agency ("baby broker acts"). 3 ALR4th 468.

720 ILCS 525/2 [Payment of compensation prohibited]

Sec. 2. No person shall pay or give any compensation or thing of value, directly or indirectly, for placing out of a child to any person or to any agency, association, corporation, institution, society, or other organization except a child welfare agency as defined by the Child Care Act of 1969, as now or hereafter amended [225 ILCS 10/1 et seq.].
(Source: P.A. 86-820.)

Note.

This section was Ill.Rev.Stat., Ch. 40, para. 1702.

720 ILCS 525/3 [Placing out defined]

Sec. 3. As used in this Act the term "placing out" means to arrange for the free care of a child in a family other than that of the child's parent, stepparent, grandparent, brother, sister, uncle or aunt or

legal guardian, for the purpose of adoption or for the purpose of providing care.
(Source: Laws 1955, p. 1881.)

Note.
This section was Ill.Rev.Stat., Ch. 40, para. 1703.

CASE NOTES

In General
The definition of "placing out" in former Ill.Rev.Stat., ch. 4, para. 12-1 (see now this section) was not vague. People v. Schwartz, 64 Ill. 2d 275, 1 Ill. Dec. 8, 356 N.E.2d 8 (1976).

720 ILCS 525/4 [Compensation of licensed child welfare agency permitted; medical expenses permitted]

Sec. 4. The provisions of this Act shall not be construed to prevent the payment of salaries or other compensation by a licensed child welfare agency, as that term is defined by the Child Care Act of 1969, as now or hereafter amended [225 ILCS 10/1 et seq.], to the officers or employees thereof; nor shall it be construed to prevent the payment by a person with whom a child has been placed out of reasonable and actual medical fees or hospital charges for services rendered in connection with the birth of such child, if such payment is made to the physician or hospital who or which rendered the services or to the natural mother of the child or to prevent the receipt of such payment by such physician, hospital, or mother.
(Source: P.A. 86-820.)

Note.
This section was Ill.Rev.Stat., Ch. 40, para. 1704.

CASE NOTES

Attorney Fees
Because former Ill.Rev.Stat., ch. 4, para. 12-4 (see now this section) exempted payment of medical and hospital charges in certain circumstances, where a lump sum was paid to an attorney in an adoption case, a certain amount could legitimately have represented attorney fees and expenses and costs which would be disbursed through the attorney, and the entire amount requested may not have represented compensation paid for the placing out of the child; it was, therefore, proper for a complaint to allege that some portion of the requested amount is in excess of the allowable legal and medical fees, for if the entire fee fell within the exempted categories, no violation of the statute would have existed. People v. Schwartz, 64 Ill. 2d 275, 1 Ill. Dec. 8, 356 N.E.2d 8 (1976).

LEGAL PERIODICALS

For article, "Surrogate Parenthood: A Need for Legislative Direction," see 71 Ill. B. J. 412 (1983).

720 ILCS 525/4.1 Payment of certain expenses

Sec. 4.1. *Payment of certain expenses.* (a) A person or persons who have filed or intend to file a petition to adopt a child under the Adoption Act [750 ILCS 50/0.01 et seq.] shall be permitted to pay the reasonable living expenses of the biological parents of the child sought to be adopted, in addition to those expenses set forth in Section 4 [720 ILCS 525/4], only in accordance with the provisions of this Section.

"Reasonable living expenses" means the reasonable costs of lodging, food, and clothing for the biological parents during the period of the biological mother's pregnancy and for no more than 30 days after the birth of the child. The term does not include expenses for lost wages, gifts, educational expenses, or other similar expenses of the biological parents.

(b) The petitioners may seek leave of the court to pay the reasonable living expenses of the biological parents. They shall be permitted to pay the reasonable living expenses of the biological parents only upon prior order of the circuit court where the petition for adoption will be filed, or if the petition for adoption has been filed in the circuit court where the petition is pending.

(c) Payments under this Section shall be permitted only in those circumstances where there is a demonstrated need for the payment of such expenses to protect the health of the biological parents or the health of the child sought to be adopted.

(d) Payment of their reasonable living expenses, as provided in this Section, shall not obligate the biological parents to place the child for adoption. In the event the biological parents choose not to place the child for adoption, the petitioners shall have no right to seek reimbursement of moneys paid to the biological parents pursuant to a court order under this Section.

(d-5) *(As enacted by P.A. 93-1063, effective June 1, 2005)* No person or entity shall offer, provide, or co-sign a loan or any other credit accommodation, directly or indirectly, with a biological parent or a relative of a biological parent based on the contingency of a surrender or placement of a child for adoption.

(e) Within 14 days after the completion of all payments for reasonable living expenses of the biological parents under this Section, the petitioners shall present a final accounting of all those expenses to the court. The accounting shall include vouchers for all moneys expended, copies of all checks written, and receipts for all cash payments. The accounting shall also include the verified statements of the petitioners, each attorney of record, and the biological parents or parents to whom or on whose behalf the payments were made attesting to the accuracy of the accounting.

(f) If the placement of a child for adoption is made in accordance with the Interstate Compact on the Placement of Children [45 ILCS 15/1 et seq.], and if the sending state permits the payment of any expenses of biological parents that are not permitted under this Act, then the payment of those expenses shall not be a violation of this Act. In that event, the petitioners shall file an accounting of all payments of the expenses of the biological parent or parents with the court in which the petition for adoption is filed or is to be filed. The accounting shall include a copy of the statutory provisions of the sending state that permit payments in addition to those permitted by this Act and a copy of all orders entered in the sending state that relate to expenses of the biological parents paid by the petitioners in the sending state.

(g) The petitioners shall be permitted to pay the reasonable attorney's fees of the biological parents' attorney in connection with proceedings under this Act or in connection with proceedings for the adoption of the child. The attorney's fees shall be paid only after a petition seeking leave to pay those fees is filed with the court in which the adoption proceeding is filed or to be filed. The court shall review the petition for leave to pay attorney's fees, and if the court determines that the fees requested are reasonable, the court shall permit the petitioners to pay them. If the court determines that the fees requested are not reasonable, the court shall determine and set the reasonable attorney's fees of the biological parents' attorney which may be paid by the petitioners.

(h) The court may appoint a guardian ad litem for an unborn child to represent the interests of the child in proceedings under this Section.

(Source: P.A. 87-1129, § 3; 88-148, § 5; 93-1063, § 10.)

Effective Date.

This section became effective January 1, 1993, pursuant to Ill. Const. (1970), Art. IV, § 10 and 5 ILCS 75/1.

Effect of Amendments.

The 1993 amendment by P.A. 88-148, effective January 1, 1994, added subsections (e) through (h).

The 2005 amendment by P.A. 93-1063, effective June 1, 2005, inserted subsection (d-5).

720 ILCS 525/5 [Penalty]

Sec. 5. Any person, agency, association, corporation, institution, society, or other organization violating the provisions of this Section shall be guilty of illegal placement of children and upon first conviction for an offense under this Act shall be guilty of a Class 4 felony; and upon conviction for any subsequent offense under this Act shall be guilty of a Class 3 felony.

(Source: P.A. 84-170.)

Note.

This section was Ill.Rev.Stat., Ch. 40, para. 1705.

CASE NOTES

Sufficiency of Complaint

Where the complaint informed defendant of the nature of the charges with sufficient specificity to withstand defendant's objections, and also informed defendant of the date and location of the alleged offense, the name of the complainant, and the acts which constituted the offense, charging the offense in the language of the statute adequately informed defendant of the conduct charged against him. People v. Schwartz, 64 Ill. 2d 275, 1 Ill. Dec. 8, 356 N.E.2d 8 (1976).

CHILD CURFEW ACT

720 ILCS 555/0.01 Short title

Sec. 0.01. *Short title.* This Act may be cited as the Child Curfew Act.

(Source: P.A. 86-1324.)

Derivation.

Title: An Act relating to a curfew for certain children.
Cite: 720 ILCS 555/0.01 et seq.
Source: L. 1963, p. 3323.
Date: Approved August 23, 1963.

Note.

This section was Ill.Rev.Stat., Ch. 23, para. 2370.9.

Cross References.

As to additional consequences for violating this Act, under the Illinois Vehicle Code, see 625 ILCS 5/6-110.

720 ILCS 555/1 Curfew

Sec. 1. *Curfew.* (a) Definitions. In this Section.

(1) "Curfew hours" means:

(A) Between 12:01 a.m. and 6:00 a.m. Saturday;

(B) Between 12:01 a.m. and 6:00 a.m. on Sunday; and

(C) Between 11:00 p.m. on Sunday to Thursday, inclusive, and 6:00 a.m. on the following day.

(2) "Emergency" means an unforeseen combination of circumstances or the resulting state that calls for immediate action. The term includes, but is not limited to a fire, a natural disaster, an automobile accident, or any situation requiring immediate action to prevent serious bodily injury or loss of life.

(3) "Establishment" means any privately-owned place of business operated for a profit to which the public is invited including but not limited to any place of amusement or entertainment.

(4) "Guardian" means:

(A) a person who, under court order, is the guardian of the person of a minor; or

(B) a public or private agency with whom a minor has been placed by a court.

(5) "Minor" means any person under 17 years of age.

(6) "Parent" means a person who is:

(A) a natural parent, adoptive parent, or step-parent of another person; or

(B) at least 18 years of age and authorized by a parent or guardian to have the care and custody of a minor.

(7) "Public Place" means any place to which the public or a substantial group of the public has access and includes but is not limited to streets, highways, and the common areas of schools, hospitals, apartment houses, office buildings, transport facilities, and shops.

(8) "Remain" means to:

(A) linger or stay; or

(B) fail to leave premises when requested to do so by a police officer or the owner, operator, or other person in control of the premises.

(9) "Serious bodily injury" means bodily injury that creates a substantial risk of death or that causes death, serious permanent disfigurement, or protracted loss or impairment of the function of any bodily member or organ.

(b) Offenses.

(1) A minor commits an offense if he or she remains in any public place or on the premises of any establishment during curfew hours.

(2) A parent or guardian of a minor or other person in custody or control of a minor commits an offense if he or she knowingly permits the minor to remain in any public place or on the premises of any establishment during curfew hours.

(c) Defenses. It is a defense to prosecution under subsection (b) that the minor was:

(A) accompanied by the minor's parent or guardian or other person in custody or control of the minor;

(B) on an errand at the direction of the minor's parent or guardian, without any detour or stop;

(C) in a motor vehicle involved in interstate travel;

(D) engaged in an employment activity or going to or returning home from an employment activity, without any detour or stop;

(E) involved in an emergency;

(F) on the sidewalk abutting the minor's residence or abutting the residence of a next-door neighbor if the neighbor did not complain to the police department about the minor's presence;

(G) attending an official school, religious, or other recreational activity supervised by adults and sponsored by a government or governmental agency, a civic organization, or another similar entity that takes responsibility for the minor, or going to or returning home from, without any detour or stop, an official school, religious, or other recreational activity supervised by adults and sponsored by a government or governmental agency, a civic organization, or another similar entity that takes responsibility for the minor;

(H) exercising First Amendment rights protected by the United States Constitution, such as the free exercise of religion, freedom of speech, and the right of assembly; or

(I) married or had been married or is an emancipated minor under the Emancipation of Minors Act.

(d) Enforcement. Before taking any enforcement action under this Section, a law enforcement officer shall ask the apparent offender's age and reason for being in the public place. The officer shall not issue a citation or make an arrest under this Section unless the officer reasonably believes that an offense has occurred and that, based on any response and other circumstances, no defense in subsection (c) is present.

(e) A person convicted of a violation of any provision of this Section shall be guilty of a petty offense and shall be fined not less than $10 nor more than $500, except that neither a person who has been made a ward of the court under the Juvenile Court Act of 1987 [705 ILCS 405/1-1 et seq.], nor that person's legal guardian, shall be subject to any fine. In addition to or instead of the fine imposed by this Section, the court may order a parent, legal guardian, or other person convicted of a violation of subsection (b) of this Section to perform community service as determined by the court, except that the legal guardian of a person who has been made a ward of the court under the Juvenile Court Act of 1987 [705 ILCS 405/1-1 et seq.] may not be ordered to perform community service. The dates and times established for the performance of community service by the parent, legal guardian, or other person convicted of a violation of subsection (b) of this Section shall not conflict with the dates and times that the person is employed in his or her regular occupation.

(Source: P.A. 79-159; 89-682, § 10; 93-1092, § 5.)

Note.

This section was Ill.Rev.Stat., Ch. 23, para. 2371.

Illinois Administrative Code.

See 17 Illinois Administrative Code, § 130.50, 92 Illinois Administrative Code, §§ 1040.25, 1040.29, 1040.36, 1040.37, 1040.40, 1040.41, 1040.46, 1040.25, 1040.29, 1040.36, 1040.37, 1040.40, 1040.41, 1040.46, 1040.107.

Effect of Amendments.

The 1996 amendment by P.A. 89-682, effective January 1, 1997, added the section catchline; in subsection (a), in the introductory language, inserted a comma after the first occurrence of "legal guardian"; in subsection (b) inserted a comma after "legal guardian" and inserted "or her"; and in subsection (c), in the first sentence, substituted "$500, except that neither a person who has been made a ward of the court under the Juvenile Court Act of 1987, nor that person's legal guardian, shall be subject to any fine" for "$100" and added the second and third sentences.

The 2005 amendment by P.A. 93-1092, effective March 29, 2005, rewrote the section.

CASE NOTES

Analysis

Constitutionality
Action In Criminal Court
Duty of Officer
Municipal Curfew
—No Conflict
Probation

Constitutionality

The primary interest advanced by the state to justify the restrictions of this section as to time, place and circumstance is the traditional right of the state to protect its children; the state is justified in acting upon this interest. People v. Chambers, 66 Ill. 2d 36, 4 Ill. Dec. 308, 360 N.E.2d 55 (1976).

This section does not sweep too broadly, even though it is not confined with particularity to geographical areas of the state in which the crime rate is extraordinarily high; the question of geographical scope is a matter for legislative, rather than judicial, determination. People v. Chambers, 66 Ill. 2d 36, 4 Ill. Dec. 308, 360 N.E.2d 55 (1976).

Action In Criminal Court

Curfew violation charges brought under the Illinois Criminal

Action In Criminal Court (Cont'd)
Code were properly dismissed as 720 ILCS 405/5-120, 5-125 required that such charges be brought through the juvenile system, not the criminal courts. People v. Bradley M., 352 Ill. App. 3d 291, 287 Ill. Dec. 406, 815 N.E.2d 1209, 2004 Ill. App. LEXIS 1061 (3 Dist. 2004).

Duty of Officer
Arresting officer who did not question the defendant as to his age but accepted information on drivers' license which indicated that defendant was over the age of 21 was not under a duty to seek information concerning consent or lack of consent as required by the curfew statute. People v. Coleman, 50 Ill. App. 3d 1053, 7 Ill. Dec. 581, 364 N.E.2d 742 (3 Dist. 1977).

Municipal Curfew

—No Conflict
A municipal curfew ordinance which applied to persons under age 18 was constitutional and was not in conflict with the state curfew statute where the state legislature had clearly expressed its intent to allow municipalities to adopt their own curfew ordinance and had specifically allowed municipalities to increase the requirements of their ordinances over those of the state statute, which only applied to persons under age 17. Village of Deerfield v. Greenberg, 193 Ill. App. 3d 215, 140 Ill. Dec. 530, 550 N.E.2d 12 (2 Dist. 1990).

Probation
Trial court's denial of petition to revoke probation for violation of curfew law was a judicial finding that the probation order had not been violated, and this being so, the court was without authority to expand the original probation order of probationer, who was not subject to curfew law, and without authority to impose a fine either under this section or otherwise. People v. McIntosh, 131 Ill. App. 2d 989, 267 N.E.2d 759 (4 Dist. 1971).

LEGAL PERIODICALS

For article, "Recent Developments in Nontraditional Alternatives in Juvenile Justice," see 28 Loy. U. Chi. L.J. 719 (1997).

720 ILCS 555/2 [More restrictive ordinances permitted]

Sec. 2. County, municipal and other local boards and bodies authorized to adopt local police laws and regulations under the constitution and laws of this State may exercise legislative or regulatory authority over this subject matter by ordinance or resolution incorporating the substance of this Act or increasing the requirements thereof or otherwise not in conflict with this Act.
(Source: Laws 1963, p. 3323.)

Note.
This section was Ill.Rev.Stat., Ch. 23, para. 2372.

CASE NOTES

Increase in Requirements
A municipal curfew ordinance which applied to persons under age 18 was constitutional and was not in conflict with the state curfew statute where the state legislature had clearly expressed its intent to allow municipalities to adopt their own curfew ordinance and had specifically allowed municipalities to increase the requirements of their ordinances over those of the state statute, which only applied to persons under age 17. Village of Deerfield v. Greenberg, 193 Ill. App. 3d 215, 140 Ill. Dec. 530, 550 N.E.2d 12 (2 Dist. 1990).

CHAPTER 725
CRIMINAL PROCEDURE

CODE OF CRIMINAL PROCEDURE OF 1963

TITLE IV.

PROCEEDINGS TO COMMENCE PROSECUTION

Article 112A.

Domestic Violence: Order of Protection

725 ILCS 5/112A-1 Construction
725 ILCS 5/112A-2 Commencement of Actions
725 ILCS 5/112A-3 Definitions
725 ILCS 5/112A-4 Persons protected by this article
725 ILCS 5/112A-5 Pleading; non-disclosure of address
725 ILCS 5/112A-6 Application of rules of civil procedure; criminal law
725 ILCS 5/112A-7 Trial by jury
725 ILCS 5/112A-8 Subject matter jurisdiction
725 ILCS 5/112A-9 Jurisdiction over persons
725 ILCS 5/112A-10 Process
725 ILCS 5/112A-11 Service of Notice of Hearings
725 ILCS 5/112A-12 Hearings
725 ILCS 5/112A-13 Continuances
725 ILCS 5/112A-14 Order of protection; remedies
725 ILCS 5/112A-15 Mutual orders of protection; correlative separate orders
725 ILCS 5/112A-16 Accountability for Actions of Others
725 ILCS 5/112A-17 Emergency order of protection
725 ILCS 5/112A-18 30-Day interim order of protection
725 ILCS 5/112A-19 Plenary Order of Protection
725 ILCS 5/112A-20 Duration and extension of orders
725 ILCS 5/112A-21 Contents of orders
725 ILCS 5/112A-22 Notice of orders
725 ILCS 5/112A-22.5 Filing of an order of protection issued in another state
725 ILCS 5/112A-22.10 Short form notification
725 ILCS 5/112A-23 Enforcement of orders of protection
725 ILCS 5/112A-24 Modification and re-opening of orders
725 ILCS 5/112A-25 Immunity from Prosecution
725 ILCS 5/112A-26 Arrest without warrant
725 ILCS 5/112A-27 Law enforcement policies
725 ILCS 5/112A-28 Data maintenance by law enforcement agencies
725 ILCS 5/112A-29 Reports by law enforcement officers
725 ILCS 5/112A-30 Assistance by law enforcement officers
725 ILCS 5/112A-31 Limited law enforcement liability

CODE OF CRIMINAL PROCEDURE OF 1963

TITLE IV.

PROCEEDINGS TO COMMENCE PROSECUTION

Article 112A.

Domestic Violence: Order of Protection

725 ILCS 5/112A-1 Construction

Sec. 112A-1. *Construction.* This Article shall be interpreted in accordance with the purposes and rules of construction set forth in Section 102 of the Illinois Domestic Violence Act of 1986 [750 ILCS 60/102]. Each of the provisions of the Illinois Domestic Violence Act of 1986 [750 ILCS 60/101 et seq.] which are included in this Article shall govern the issuance, recording and enforcement of orders of protection in criminal proceedings.
(Source: P.A. 84-1305.)

Note.
This section was Ill.Rev.Stat., Ch. 38, para. 112A-1.

Cross References.
As to the authority of a court to issue an order of protection in accordance with this section for persons arrested, see 725 ILCS 5/109-1.

CASE NOTES

Domestic Violence
The Illinois Domestic Violence Act (750 ILCS 60/101 et seq.) which is to be construed together with this Act, carves out an exception to the public duty doctrine and elevates the holder of an order of protection to a status above that of other members of the general public; it singles out those who are victims of domestic violence as persons in need of special protection by law enforcement officials. Calloway v. Kinkelaar, 261 Ill. App. 3d 63, 199 Ill. Dec. 389, 633 N.E.2d 1380 (5 Dist. 1994), aff'd, 168 Ill. 2d 312, 213 Ill. Dec. 675, 659 N.E.2d 1322 (1995).

LEGAL PERIODICALS

For article, "Orders of Protection and the Battered Woman Syndrome," see 23 Loy. U. Chi. L.J. 397 (1991-92).

725 ILCS 5/112A-2 Commencement of Actions

Sec. 112A-2. *Commencement of Actions.* (a) Actions for orders of protection are commenced in conjunction with a delinquency petition or a criminal prosecution by filing a petition for an order of protection, under the same case number as the delinquency petition or the criminal prosecution, to be granted during pre-trial release of a defendant, with any dispositional order issued under Section 5-710 of the Juvenile Court Act of 1987 [705 ILCS 405/5-710], or as a condition of release, supervision, conditional discharge, probation, periodic imprisonment, parole or mandatory supervised release, or in conjunction with imprisonment or a bond forfeiture warrant, provided that:

(i) the violation is alleged in an information, complaint, indictment or delinquency petition on file, and the alleged offender and victim are family or household members; and

(ii) the petition, which is filed by the State's Attorney, names a victim of the alleged crime as a petitioner.

(b) Withdrawal or dismissal of any petition for an order of protection prior to adjudication where the petitioner is represented by the state shall operate as a dismissal without prejudice.

(c) Voluntary dismissal or withdrawal of any delinquency petition or criminal prosecution or a finding of not guilty shall not require dismissal of the action for the order of protection; instead, in the

discretion of the State's Attorney, it may be treated as an independent action and, if necessary and appropriate, transferred to a different court or division. Dismissal of any delinquency petition or criminal prosecution shall not affect the validity of any previously issued order of protection, and thereafter subsection (b) of Section 112A-20 [725 ILCS 5/112A-20] shall be inapplicable to that order.
(Source: P.A. 86-1300; 87-443; 87-1186, § 1; 90-590, § 2001-25.)

Note.
This section was Ill.Rev.Stat., Ch. 38, para. 112A-2.

Effect of Amendments.
The 1998 amendment by P.A. 90-590, effective January 1, 1999, substituted "Section 5-710" for "Section 5-23" in subsection (a).

LEGAL PERIODICALS

For article, "Defending the Indefensible to Further a Later Case: Sanctioning Respondents in Illinois Domestic Violence Cases," see 23 N. Ill. U. L. Rev. 403 (2003).

725 ILCS 5/112A-3 Definitions

Sec. 112A-3. *Definitions.* For the purposes of this Article, the following terms shall have the following meanings:

(1) "Abuse" means physical abuse, harassment, intimidation of a dependent, interference with personal liberty or willful deprivation but does not include reasonable direction of a minor child by a parent or person in loco parentis.

(2) "Domestic violence" means abuse as described in paragraph (1).

(3) "Family or household members" include spouses, former spouses, parents, children, stepchildren and other persons related by blood or by present or prior marriage, persons who share or formerly shared a common dwelling, persons who have or allegedly have a child in common, persons who share or allegedly share a blood relationship through a child, persons who have or have had a dating or engagement relationship, persons with disabilities and their personal assistants, and caregivers as defined in paragraph (3) of subsection (b) of Section 12-21 of the Criminal Code of 1961 [720 ILCS 5/12-21]. For purposes of this paragraph, neither a casual acquaintanceship nor ordinary fraternization between 2 individuals in business or social contexts shall be deemed to constitute a dating relationship.

(4) "Harassment" means knowing conduct which is not necessary to accomplish a purpose which is reasonable under the circumstances; would cause a reasonable person emotional distress; and does cause emotional distress to the petitioner. Unless the presumption is rebutted by a preponderance of the evidence, the following types of conduct shall be presumed to cause emotional distress:

(i) creating a disturbance at petitioner's place of employment or school;

(ii) repeatedly telephoning petitioner's place of employment, home or residence;

(iii) repeatedly following petitioner about in a public place or places;

(iv) repeatedly keeping petitioner under surveillance by remaining present outside his or her home, school, place of employment, vehicle or other place occupied by petitioner or by peering in petitioner's windows;

(v) improperly concealing a minor child from petitioner, repeatedly threatening to improperly remove a minor child of petitioner's from the jurisdiction or from the physical care of petitioner, repeatedly threatening to conceal a minor child from petitioner, or making a single such threat following an actual or attempted improper removal or concealment, unless respondent was fleeing from an incident or pattern of domestic violence; or

(vi) threatening physical force, confinement or restraint on one or more occasions.

(5) "Interference with personal liberty" means committing or threatening physical abuse, harassment, intimidation or willful deprivation so as to compel another to engage in conduct from which she or he has a right to abstain or to refrain from conduct in which she or he has a right to engage.

(6) "Intimidation of a dependent" means subjecting a person who is dependent because of age, health or disability to participation in or the witnessing of: physical force against another or physical confinement or restraint of another which constitutes physical abuse as defined in this Article, regardless of whether the abused person is a family or household member.

(7) "Order of protection" means an emergency order, interim order or plenary order, granted pursuant to this Article, which includes any or all of the remedies authorized by Section 112A-14 of this Code [725 ILCS 5/112A-14].

(8) "Petitioner" may mean not only any named petitioner for the order of protection and any named victim of abuse on whose behalf the petition is brought, but also any other person protected by this Article.

(9) "Physical abuse" includes sexual abuse and means any of the following:

(i) knowing or reckless use of physical force, confinement or restraint;

(ii) knowing, repeated and unnecessary sleep deprivation; or

(iii) knowing or reckless conduct which creates an immediate risk of physical harm.

(9.5) "Stay away" means for the respondent to refrain from both physical presence and nonphysical contact with the petitioner whether direct, indirect (including, but not limited to, telephone calls, mail, email, faxes, and written notes), or through third parties who may or may not know about the order of protection.

(10) "Willful deprivation" means wilfully denying a person who because of age, health or disability

requires medication, medical care, shelter, accessible shelter or services, food, therapeutic device, or other physical assistance, and thereby exposing that person to the risk of physical, mental or emotional harm, except with regard to medical care and treatment when such dependent person has expressed the intent to forgo such medical care or treatment. This paragraph does not create any new affirmative duty to provide support to dependent persons.
(Source: P.A. 85-293; 87-1186, § 1; 92-253, § 5; 93-811, § 5.)

Note.
This section was Ill.Rev.Stat., Ch. 38, para. 112A-3.

Effect of Amendments.
The 2001 amendment by P.A. 92-253, effective January 1, 2002, inserted in subdivision (3) "and caregivers as defined in paragraph (3) of subsection (b) of Section 12-21 of the Criminal Code of 1961" in the first sentence and made a stylistic change.

The 2004 amendment by P.A. 93-811, effective January 1, 2005, inserted subdivision (9.5).

CASE NOTES

Analysis

In General
Family or Household Member

In General
The definition of "family or household member," which included persons who "have or had a dating relationship," found in 725 ILCS 5/112A-3, and used in 720 ILCS 5/12-3.3, was not unconstitutionally vague as applied to defendant charged with aggravated domestic violence because both defendant and the victim of the aggravated domestic violence testified that they had been in a dating relationship for at least a year prior to the violence and that they intended to live together after defendant was released from incarceration. The relationship constituted a "dating relationship" and defendant was provided with a reasonable opportunity to determine that his conduct against the victim was prohibited by the domestic violence statute. People v. Johnson, 341 Ill. App. 3d 583, 276 Ill. Dec. 15, 793 N.E.2d 774, 2003 Ill. App. LEXIS 823 (1 Dist. 2003).

Family or Household Member
Even though the indictment charging defendant with killing his seven-week-old son did not state that the victim was a family or household member and the jury instruction the trial court gave to the jury did not ask that the jury make a finding that the victim was a family or household member, the trial court's action in enhancing defendant's sentence based on its finding that the victim was a family or household member was not reversible error as defendant was informed about the possibility of an enhanced sentence based on that finding, overwhelming evidence supported a finding that the victim was a family or household member, defendant did not object at any time to the characterization of the victim as a family or household member and defendant could not show that he was prejudiced by the charging instrument or the jury instruction that the trial court gave to the jury. People v. Davis, 352 Ill. App. 3d 570, 287 Ill. Dec. 916, 816 N.E.2d 1127, 2004 Ill. App. LEXIS 1210 (2 Dist. 2004).

LEGAL PERIODICALS

For article, "Making a Federal Case Out of a Woman's Issue," see 6 Chi. B. Rec. 39 (1992).

RESEARCH REFERENCES

"Cohabitation" for purposes of domestic violence statutes. 71 ALR5th 285.

725 ILCS 5/112A-4 Persons protected by this article

Sec. 112A-4. *Persons protected by this article.* (a) The following persons are protected by this Article:
(i) any person abused by a family or household member;
(ii) any minor child or dependent adult in the care of such person; and
(iii) any person residing or employed at a private home or public shelter which is housing an abused family or household member.
(b) A petition for an order of protection may be filed only by a person who has been abused by a family or household member or by any person on behalf of a minor child or an adult who has been abused by a family or household member and who, because of age, health, disability, or inaccessibility, cannot file the petition. However, any petition properly filed under this Article may seek protection for any additional persons protected by this Article.
(Source: P.A. 84-1305; 87-1186, § 1.)

Note.
This section was Ill.Rev.Stat., Ch. 38, para. 112A-4.

725 ILCS 5/112A-5 Pleading; non-disclosure of address

Sec. 112A-5. *Pleading; non-disclosure of address.* (a) A petition for an order of protection shall be in writing and verified or accompanied by affidavit and shall allege that petitioner has been abused by respondent, who is a family or household member. The petition shall further set forth whether there is any other pending action between the parties. During the pendency of this proceeding, each party has a continuing duty to inform the court of any subsequent proceeding for an order of protection in this or any other state.
(b) If the petition states that disclosure of petitioner's address would risk abuse of petitioner or any member of petitioner's family or household or reveal the confidential address of a shelter for domestic violence victims, that address may be omitted from all documents filed with the court. If disclosure is necessary to determine jurisdiction or consider any venue issue, it shall be made orally and in camera. If petitioner has not disclosed an address under this subsection, petitioner shall designate an alternative address at which respondent may serve notice of any motions.
(Source: P.A. 84-1305; 87-1186, § 1.)

Note.
This section was Ill.Rev.Stat., Ch. 38, para. 112A-5.

725 ILCS 5/112A-6 Application of rules of civil procedure; criminal law

Sec. 112A-6. *Application of rules of civil procedure; criminal law.* (a) Any proceeding to obtain, modify, reopen or appeal an order of protection, whether commenced alone or in conjunction with a civil or criminal proceeding, shall be governed by the rules of civil procedure of this State. The standard of proof in such a proceeding is proof by a preponderance of the evidence, whether the proceeding is heard in criminal or civil court. The Code of Civil Procedure [735 ILCS 5/1-101 et seq.] and Supreme Court and local court rules applicable to civil proceedings, as now or hereafter amended, shall apply, except as otherwise provided by law. Civil law on venue, discovery, and on penalties for untrue statements shall not apply to order of protection proceedings heard under this Article 112A.

(b) Criminal law on discovery, venue, and on penalties for untrue statements apply to orders of protection proceedings heard under this Article 112A.

(Source: P.A. 84-1305; 87-1186, § 1; 90-235, § 5.)

Note.

This section was Ill.Rev.Stat., Ch. 38, para. 112A-6.

Effect of Amendments.

The 1997 amendment by P.A. 90-235, effective January 1, 1998, in the section catchline added at the end "criminal law"; in subsection (a), in the fourth sentence, inserted "discovery" and substituted "under this Article 112A" for "in Criminal Court"; and added subsection (b).

LEGAL PERIODICALS

For article, "Defending the Indefensible to Further a Later Case: Sanctioning Respondents in Illinois Domestic Violence Cases," see 23 N. Ill. U. L. Rev. 403 (2003).

725 ILCS 5/112A-7 Trial by jury

Sec. 112A-7. *Trial by jury.* There shall be no right to trial by jury in any proceeding to obtain, modify, vacate or extend any order of protection under this Article. However, nothing in this Section shall deny any existing right to trial by jury in a criminal proceeding.

(Source: P.A. 84-1305; 87-895, § 3-24; 87-1186, § 1; 88-45, § 2-57.5.)

725 ILCS 5/112A-8 Subject matter jurisdiction

Sec. 112A-8. *Subject matter jurisdiction.* Each of the circuit courts shall have the power to issue orders of protection.

(Source: P.A. 84-1305.)

Note.

This section was Ill.Rev.Stat., Ch. 38, para. 112A-8.

725 ILCS 5/112A-9 Jurisdiction over persons

Sec. 112A-9. *Jurisdiction over persons.* In child custody proceedings, the court's personal jurisdiction is determined by this State's Uniform Child-Custody Jurisdiction and Enforcement Act [750 ILCS 36/1 et seq.]. Otherwise, the courts of this State have jurisdiction to bind (i) State residents, and (ii) non-residents having minimum contacts with this State, to the extent permitted by the long-arm statute, Section 2-209 of the Code of Civil Procedure, as now or hereafter amended [735 ILCS 5/2-209].

(Source: P.A. 84-1305; 93-108, § 402.4.)

Note.

This section was Ill.Rev.Stat., Ch. 38, para. 112A-9.

Effect of Amendments.

The 2003 amendment by P.A. 93-108, effective January 1, 2004, in the first sentence, substituted "Uniform Child-Custody Jurisdiction and Enforcement Act" for "Uniform Child Custody Jurisdiction Act" and deleted 'as now or hereafter amended" at the end.

725 ILCS 5/112A-10 Process

Sec. 112A-10. *Process.* (a) Summons. Any action for an order of protection, whether commenced alone or in conjunction with another proceeding, is a distinct cause of action and requires that a separate summons be issued and served, except that in pending criminal cases, the summons may be delivered to respondent in open court. The summons shall be in the form prescribed by Supreme Court Rule 101(d), except that it shall require respondent to answer or appear within 7 days, and shall be accompanied by the petition for the order of protection, any supporting affidavits, if any, and any emergency order of protection that has been issued. The enforcement of an order of protection under Section 112A-23 [725 ILCS 5/112A-23] shall not be affected by the lack of service or delivery, provided the requirements of subsection (a) of that Section are otherwise met.

(b) Fees. No fee shall be charged for service of summons.

(c) Expedited service. The summons shall be served by the sheriff or other law enforcement officer at the earliest time and shall take precedence over other summonses except those of a similar emergency nature. Special process servers may be appointed at any time, and their designation shall not affect the responsibilities and authority of the sheriff or other official process servers. Process shall not be served in court.

(d) Remedies requiring actual notice. The counseling, payment of support, payment of shelter services, and payment of losses remedies provided by paragraphs 4, 12, 13, and 16 of subsection (b) of Section 112A-14 [725 ILCS 5/112A-14] may be granted only if respondent has been personally served with process, has answered or has made a general appearance.

(e) Remedies upon constructive notice. Service of process on a member of respondent's household or by publication, in accordance with Sections 2-203, 2-206 and 2-207 of the Code of Civil Procedure, as now or hereafter amended [735 ILCS 5/2-203, 735 ILCS 5/2-206 and 735 ILCS 5/2-207], shall be adequate for the remedies provided by paragraphs 1, 2, 3, 5, 6, 7, 8, 9, 10, 11, 14, 15, and 17 of subsection (b) of Section 112A-14 [725 ILCS 5/112A-14], but only if:

(i) petitioner has made all reasonable efforts to accomplish actual service of process personally upon respondent, but respondent cannot be found to effect such service; and (ii) petitioner files an affidavit or presents sworn testimony as to those efforts.

(f) Default. A plenary order of protection may be entered by default (1) for any of the remedies sought in the petition, if respondent has been served with documents in accordance with subsection (a) and if respondent then fails to appear on the specified return date or on any subsequent hearing date agreed to by the parties or set by the court; or (2) for any of the remedies provided under subsection (e), if the defendant fails to answer or appear in accordance with the date set in the publication notice or the return date indicated on the service of a household member.
(Source: P.A. 84-1305; 87-1186, § 1.)

Note.
This section was Ill.Rev.Stat., Ch. 38, para. 112A-10.

725 ILCS 5/112A-11 Service of Notice of Hearings

Sec. 112A-11. *Service of Notice of Hearings.* A party presenting a petition or motion to the court shall provide the other parties with written notice of the date, time and place of the hearing thereon, together with a copy of any petition, motion or accompanying affidavit not yet served upon that party, and shall file proof of that service, in accordance with Supreme Court Rules 11 and 12, unless notice is excused by Section 112A-17 of this Article [725 ILCS 5/112A-17], or by the Code of Civil Procedure, Supreme Court Rules or local rules.
(Source: P.A. 84-1305.)

Note.
This section was Ill.Rev.Stat., Ch. 38, para. 112A-11.

725 ILCS 5/112A-12 Hearings

Sec. 112A-12. *Hearings.* (a) A petition for an order of protection shall be treated as an expedited proceeding, and no court shall transfer or otherwise decline to decide all or part of such petition, except as otherwise provided herein. Nothing in this Section shall prevent the court from reserving issues when jurisdiction or notice requirements are not met.

(b) A criminal court may decline to decide contested issues of physical care, custody, visitation, or family support, unless a decision on one or more of those contested issues is necessary to avoid the risk of abuse, neglect, removal from the state or concealment within the state of the child or of separation of the child from the primary caretaker.

(c) The court shall transfer to the appropriate court or division any issue it has declined to decide. Any court may transfer any matter which must be tried by jury to a more appropriate calendar or division.

(d) If the court transfers or otherwise declines to decide any issue, judgment on that issue shall be expressly reserved and ruling on other issues shall not be delayed or declined.
(Source: P.A. 84-1305; 87-1186, § 1.)

Note.
This section was Ill.Rev.Stat., Ch. 38, para. 112A-12.

725 ILCS 5/112A-13 Continuances

Sec. 112A-13. *Continuances.* (a) Petitions for Emergency Orders. Petitions for emergency remedies shall be granted or denied in accordance with the standards of Section 217 of the Illinois Domestic Violence Act of 1986 [750 ILCS 60/217], regardless of respondent's presence in court or appearance.

(b) Petitions for Interim and Plenary Orders. Any action for an order of protection is an expedited proceeding. Continuances should be granted only for good cause shown and kept to the minimum reasonable duration, taking into account the reasons for the continuance. If the continuance is necessary for some, but not all, of the remedies requested, hearing on those other remedies shall not be delayed.
(Source: P.A. 84-1305; 91-357, § 243.)

Note.
This section was Ill.Rev.Stat., Ch. 38, para. 112A-13.

Effect of Amendments.
The 1999 amendment by P.A. 91-357, effective July 29, 1999, inserted "of the Illinois Domestic Violence Act of 1986" in subsection (a).

725 ILCS 5/112A-14 Order of protection; remedies

Sec. 112A-14. *Order of protection; remedies.* (a) Issuance of order. If the court finds that petitioner has been abused by a family or household member, as defined in this Article, an order of protection prohibiting such abuse shall issue; provided that petitioner must also satisfy the requirements of one of the following Sections, as appropriate: Section 112A-17 [725 ILCS 5/112A-17] on emergency orders, Section 112A-18 [725 ILCS 5/112A-18] on interim orders, or Section 112A-19 [725 ILCS 5/112A-19] on plenary orders. Petitioner shall not be denied an order of protection because petitioner or respondent is a minor. The court, when determining whether or not to issue an order of protection, shall not require physical manifestations of abuse on the person of the victim. Modification and extension of prior orders of protection shall be in accordance with this Article.

(b) Remedies and standards. The remedies to be included in an order of protection shall be determined in accordance with this Section and one of the following Sections, as appropriate: Section 112A-17 [725 ILCS 5/112A-17] on emergency orders, Section 112A-18 [725 ILCS 5/112A-18] on interim orders, and Section 112A-19 [725 ILCS 5/112A-19] on plenary orders. The remedies listed in this subsection shall be in addition to other civil or criminal remedies available to petitioner.

(1) Prohibition of abuse. Prohibit respondent's harassment, interference with personal liberty, intimidation of a dependent, physical abuse or willful deprivation, as defined in this Article, if such abuse has occurred or otherwise appears likely to occur if not prohibited.

(2) Grant of exclusive possession of residence. Prohibit respondent from entering or remaining in any residence or household of the petitioner, including one owned or leased by respondent, if petitioner has a right to occupancy thereof. The grant of exclusive possession of the residence shall not affect title to real property, nor shall the court be limited by the standard set forth in Section 701 of the Illinois Marriage and Dissolution of Marriage Act [750 ILCS 5/701].

(A) Right to occupancy. A party has a right to occupancy of a residence or household if it is solely or jointly owned or leased by that party, that party's spouse, a person with a legal duty to support that party or a minor child in that party's care, or by any person or entity other than the opposing party that authorizes that party's occupancy (e.g., a domestic violence shelter). Standards set forth in subparagraph (B) shall not preclude equitable relief.

(B) Presumption of hardships. If petitioner and respondent each has the right to occupancy of a residence or household, the court shall balance (i) the hardships to respondent and any minor child or dependent adult in respondent's care resulting from entry of this remedy with (ii) the hardships to petitioner and any minor child or dependent adult in petitioner's care resulting from continued exposure to the risk of abuse (should petitioner remain at the residence or household) or from loss of possession of the residence or household (should petitioner leave to avoid the risk of abuse). When determining the balance of hardships, the court shall also take into account the accessibility of the residence or household. Hardships need not be balanced if respondent does not have a right to occupancy.

The balance of hardships is presumed to favor possession by petitioner unless the presumption is rebutted by a preponderance of the evidence, showing that the hardships to respondent substantially outweigh the hardships to petitioner and any minor child or dependent adult in petitioner's care. The court, on the request of petitioner or on its own motion, may order respondent to provide suitable, accessible, alternate housing for petitioner instead of excluding respondent from a mutual residence or household.

(3) Stay away order and additional prohibitions. Order respondent to stay away from petitioner or any other person protected by the order of protection, or prohibit respondent from entering or remaining present at petitioner's school, place of employment, or other specified places at times when petitioner is present, or both, if reasonable, given the balance of hardships. Hardships need not be balanced for the court to enter a stay away order or prohibit entry if respondent has no right to enter the premises.

If an order of protection grants petitioner exclusive possession of the residence, or prohibits respondent from entering the residence, or orders respondent to stay away from petitioner or other protected persons, then the court may allow respondent access to the residence to remove items of clothing and personal adornment used exclusively by respondent, medications, and other items as the court directs. The right to access shall be exercised on only one occasion as the court directs and in the presence of an agreed-upon adult third party or law enforcement officer.

(4) Counseling. Require or recommend the respondent to undergo counseling for a specified duration with a social worker, psychologist, clinical psychologist, psychiatrist, family service agency, alcohol or substance abuse program, mental health center guidance counselor, agency providing services to elders, program designed for domestic violence abusers or any other guidance service the court deems appropriate.

(5) Physical care and possession of the minor child. In order to protect the minor child from abuse, neglect, or unwarranted separation from the person who has been the minor child's primary caretaker, or to otherwise protect the well-being of the minor child, the court may do either or both of the following: (i) grant petitioner physical care or possession of the minor child, or both, or (ii) order respondent to return a minor child to, or not remove a minor child from, the physical care of a parent or person in loco parentis.

If a court finds, after a hearing, that respondent has committed abuse (as defined in Section 112A-3 [725 ILCS 5/112A-3]) of a minor child, there shall be a rebuttable presumption that awarding physical care to respondent would not be in the minor child's best interest.

(6) Temporary legal custody. Award temporary legal custody to petitioner in accordance with this Section, the Illinois Marriage and Dissolution of Marriage Act [750 ILCS 5/601 et seq.], the Illinois Parentage Act of 1984 [750 ILCS 45/1 et seq.], and this State's Uniform Child-Custody Jurisdiction and Enforcement Act [750 ILCS 36/1 et seq.].

If a court finds, after a hearing, that respondent has committed abuse (as defined in Section 112A-3 [725 ILCS 5/112A-3]) of a minor child, there shall be a rebuttable presumption that awarding temporary legal custody to respondent would not be in the child's best interest.

(7) Visitation. Determine the visitation rights, if any, of respondent in any case in which the court awards physical care or temporary legal custody of a

minor child to petitioner. The court shall restrict or deny respondent's visitation with a minor child if the court finds that respondent has done or is likely to do any of the following: (i) abuse or endanger the minor child during visitation; (ii) use the visitation as an opportunity to abuse or harass petitioner or petitioner's family or household members; (iii) improperly conceal or detain the minor child; or (iv) otherwise act in a manner that is not in the best interests of the minor child. The court shall not be limited by the standards set forth in Section 607.1 of the Illinois Marriage and Dissolution of Marriage Act [750 ILCS 5/607.1]. If the court grants visitation, the order shall specify dates and times for the visitation to take place or other specific parameters or conditions that are appropriate. No order for visitation shall refer merely to the term "reasonable visitation".

Petitioner may deny respondent access to the minor child if, when respondent arrives for visitation, respondent is under the influence of drugs or alcohol and constitutes a threat to the safety and well-being of petitioner or petitioner's minor children or is behaving in a violent or abusive manner.

If necessary to protect any member of petitioner's family or household from future abuse, respondent shall be prohibited from coming to petitioner's residence to meet the minor child for visitation, and the parties shall submit to the court their recommendations for reasonable alternative arrangements for visitation. A person may be approved to supervise visitation only after filing an affidavit accepting that responsibility and acknowledging accountability to the court.

(8) Removal or concealment of minor child. Prohibit respondent from removing a minor child from the State or concealing the child within the State.

(9) Order to appear. Order the respondent to appear in court, alone or with a minor child, to prevent abuse, neglect, removal or concealment of the child, to return the child to the custody or care of the petitioner or to permit any court-ordered interview or examination of the child or the respondent.

(10) Possession of personal property. Grant petitioner exclusive possession of personal property and, if respondent has possession or control, direct respondent to promptly make it available to petitioner, if:

(i) petitioner, but not respondent, owns the property; or

(ii) the parties own the property jointly; sharing it would risk abuse of petitioner by respondent or is impracticable; and the balance of hardships favors temporary possession by petitioner.

If petitioner's sole claim to ownership of the property is that it is marital property, the court may award petitioner temporary possession thereof under the standards of subparagraph (ii) of this paragraph only if a proper proceeding has been filed under the Illinois Marriage and Dissolution of Marriage Act, as now or hereafter amended [750 ILCS 5/101 et seq.].

No order under this provision shall affect title to property.

(11) Protection of property. Forbid the respondent from taking, transferring, encumbering, concealing, damaging or otherwise disposing of any real or personal property, except as explicitly authorized by the court, if:

(i) petitioner, but not respondent, owns the property; or

(ii) the parties own the property jointly, and the balance of hardships favors granting this remedy.

If petitioner's sole claim to ownership of the property is that it is marital property, the court may grant petitioner relief under subparagraph (ii) of this paragraph only if a proper proceeding has been filed under the Illinois Marriage and Dissolution of Marriage Act, as now or hereafter amended [750 ILCS 5/101 et seq.].

The court may further prohibit respondent from improperly using the financial or other resources of an aged member of the family or household for the profit or advantage of respondent or of any other person.

(12) Order for payment of support. Order respondent to pay temporary support for the petitioner or any child in the petitioner's care or custody, when the respondent has a legal obligation to support that person, in accordance with the Illinois Marriage and Dissolution of Marriage Act [750 ILCS 5/101 et seq.], which shall govern, among other matters, the amount of support, payment through the clerk and withholding of income to secure payment. An order for child support may be granted to a petitioner with lawful physical care or custody of a child, or an order or agreement for physical care or custody, prior to entry of an order for legal custody. Such a support order shall expire upon entry of a valid order granting legal custody to another, unless otherwise provided in the custody order.

(13) Order for payment of losses. Order respondent to pay petitioner for losses suffered as a direct result of the abuse. Such losses shall include, but not be limited to, medical expenses, lost earnings or other support, repair or replacement of property damaged or taken, reasonable attorney's fees, court costs and moving or other travel expenses, including additional reasonable expenses for temporary shelter and restaurant meals.

(i) Losses affecting family needs. If a party is entitled to seek maintenance, child support or property distribution from the other party under the Illinois Marriage and Dissolution of Marriage Act, as now or hereafter amended [750 ILCS 5/101 et seq.], the court may order respondent to reimburse petitioner's actual losses, to the extent that such reimbursement would be "appropriate temporary relief", as authorized by subsection (a)(3) of Section 501 of that Act [750 ILCS 5/501].

(ii) Recovery of expenses. In the case of an improper concealment or removal of a minor child, the court may order respondent to pay the reasonable expenses incurred or to be incurred in the search for and recovery of the minor child, including but not limited to legal fees, court costs, private investigator fees, and travel costs.

(14) Prohibition of entry. Prohibit the respondent from entering or remaining in the residence or household while the respondent is under the influence of alcohol or drugs and constitutes a threat to the safety and well-being of the petitioner or the petitioner's children.

(14.5) Prohibition of firearm possession. (a) When a complaint is made under a request for an order of protection, that the respondent has threatened or is likely to use firearms illegally against the petitioner, and the respondent is present in court, or has failed to appear after receiving actual notice, the court shall examine on oath the petitioner, and any witnesses who may be produced. If the court is satisfied that there is any danger of the illegal use of firearms, it shall include in the order of protection the requirement that any firearms in the possession of the respondent, except as provided in subsection (b), be turned over to the local law enforcement agency for safekeeping. If the respondent fails to appear, or refuses or fails to surrender his or her firearms, the court shall issue a warrant for seizure of any firearm in the possession of the respondent. The period of safekeeping shall be for a stated period of time not to exceed 2 years. The firearm or firearms shall be returned to the respondent at the end of the stated period or at expiration of the order of protection, whichever is sooner.

(b) If the respondent is a peace officer as defined in Section 2-13 of the Criminal Code of 1961 [720 ILCS 5/2-13], the court shall order that any firearms used by the respondent in the performance of his or her duties as a peace officer be surrendered to the chief law enforcement executive of the agency in which the respondent is employed, who shall retain the firearms for safekeeping for the stated period not to exceed 2 years as set forth in the court order.

(15) Prohibition of access to records. If an order of protection prohibits respondent from having contact with the minor child, or if petitioner's address is omitted under subsection (b) of Section 112A-5 [725 ILCS 5/112A-5], or if necessary to prevent abuse or wrongful removal or concealment of a minor child, the order shall deny respondent access to, and prohibit respondent from inspecting, obtaining, or attempting to inspect or obtain, school or any other records of the minor child who is in the care of petitioner.

(16) Order for payment of shelter services. Order respondent to reimburse a shelter providing temporary housing and counseling services to the petitioner for the cost of the services, as certified by the shelter and deemed reasonable by the court.

(17) Order for injunctive relief. Enter injunctive relief necessary or appropriate to prevent further abuse of a family or household member or to effectuate one of the granted remedies, if supported by the balance of hardships. If the harm to be prevented by the injunction is abuse or any other harm that one of the remedies listed in paragraphs (1) through (16) of this subsection is designed to prevent, no further evidence is necessary to establish that the harm is an irreparable injury.

(c) Relevant factors; findings.

(1) In determining whether to grant a specific remedy, other than payment of support, the court shall consider relevant factors, including but not limited to the following:

(i) the nature, frequency, severity, pattern and consequences of the respondent's past abuse of the petitioner or any family or household member, including the concealment of his or her location in order to evade service of process or notice, and the likelihood of danger of future abuse to petitioner or any member of petitioner's or respondent's family or household; and

(ii) the danger that any minor child will be abused or neglected or improperly removed from the jurisdiction, improperly concealed within the State or improperly separated from the child's primary caretaker.

(2) In comparing relative hardships resulting to the parties from loss of possession of the family home, the court shall consider relevant factors, including but not limited to the following:

(i) availability, accessibility, cost, safety, adequacy, location and other characteristics of alternate housing for each party and any minor child or dependent adult in the party's care;

(ii) the effect on the party's employment; and

(iii) the effect on the relationship of the party, and any minor child or dependent adult in the party's care, to family, school, church and community.

(3) Subject to the exceptions set forth in paragraph (4) of this subsection, the court shall make its findings in an official record or in writing, and shall at a minimum set forth the following:

(i) That the court has considered the applicable relevant factors described in paragraphs (1) and (2) of this subsection.

(ii) Whether the conduct or actions of respondent, unless prohibited, will likely cause irreparable harm or continued abuse.

(iii) Whether it is necessary to grant the requested relief in order to protect petitioner or other alleged abused persons.

(4) For purposes of issuing an ex parte emergency order of protection, the court, as an alternative to or as a supplement to making the findings described in paragraphs (c)(3)(i) through (c)(3)(iii) of this subsection, may use the following procedure:

When a verified petition for an emergency order of protection in accordance with the requirements of Sections 112A-5 and 112A-17 [725 ILCS 5/112A-5 and 725 ILCS 5/112A-17] is presented to the court, the court shall examine petitioner on oath or affirmation. An emergency order of protection shall be issued by the court if it appears from the contents of the petition and the examination of petitioner that the averments are sufficient to indicate abuse by respondent and to support the granting of relief under the issuance of the emergency order of protection.

(5) Never married parties. No rights or responsibilities for a minor child born outside of marriage attach to a putative father until a father and child relationship has been established under the Illinois Parentage Act of 1984 [750 ILCS 45/1 et seq.]. Absent such an adjudication, no putative father shall be granted temporary custody of the minor child, visitation with the minor child, or physical care and possession of the minor child, nor shall an order of payment for support of the minor child be entered.

(d) Balance of hardships; findings. If the court finds that the balance of hardships does not support the granting of a remedy governed by paragraph (2), (3), (10), (11), or (16) of subsection (b) of this Section, which may require such balancing, the court's findings shall so indicate and shall include a finding as to whether granting the remedy will result in hardship to respondent that would substantially outweigh the hardship to petitioner from denial of the remedy. The findings shall be an official record or in writing.

(e) Denial of remedies. Denial of any remedy shall not be based, in whole or in part, on evidence that:

(1) Respondent has cause for any use of force, unless that cause satisfies the standards for justifiable use of force provided by Article VII of the Criminal Code of 1961 [720 ILCS 5/7-1 et seq.];

(2) Respondent was voluntarily intoxicated;

(3) Petitioner acted in self-defense or defense of another, provided that, if petitioner utilized force, such force was justifiable under Article VII of the Criminal Code of 1961 [720 ILCS 5/7-1 et seq.];

(4) Petitioner did not act in self-defense or defense of another;

(5) Petitioner left the residence or household to avoid further abuse by respondent;

(6) Petitioner did not leave the residence or household to avoid further abuse by respondent;

(7) Conduct by any family or household member excused the abuse by respondent, unless that same conduct would have excused such abuse if the parties had not been family or household members.

(Source: P.A. 87-743; 87-1186, § 1; 89-367, § 15; 93-108, § 402.4.)

Note.

This section was Ill.Rev.Stat., Ch. 38, para. 112A-14.

Effect of Amendments.

The 1995 amendment by P.A. 89-367, effective January 1, 1996, added subdivision (b)(14.5).

The 2003 amendment by P.A. 93-108, effective January 1, 2004, substituted "Uniform Child-Custody Jurisdiction and Enforcement Act" for "Uniform Child Custody Jurisdiction Act" in the first sentence of subsection (b)(6).

RESEARCH REFERENCES

Crimes against spouse within exception permitting testimony by one spouse against other in criminal prosecution—Modern state cases. 74 ALR4th 223.

725 ILCS 5/112A-15 Mutual orders of protection; correlative separate orders

Sec. 112A-15. *Mutual orders of protection; correlative separate orders.* Mutual orders of protection are prohibited. Correlative separate orders of protection undermine the purposes of this Article. If separate orders of protection in a criminal or delinquency case are sought, there must be compliance with Section 112A-2 [725 ILCS 5/112A-2]. Nothing in this Section prohibits a party from seeking a civil order of protection.

If correlative separate orders of protection result after being sought in separate criminal or delinquency actions in accordance with Section 112A-2 [725 ILCS 5/112A-2], that fact shall not be a sufficient basis to deny any remedy to either petitioner or to prove that the parties are equally at fault or equally endangered.

(Source: P.A. 84-1305; 87-1186, § 1.)

Note.

This section was Ill.Rev.Stat., Ch. 38, para. 112A-15.

725 ILCS 5/112A-16 Accountability for Actions of Others

Sec. 112A-16. *Accountability for Actions of Others.* For the purposes of issuing an order of protection, deciding what remedies should be included and enforcing the order, Article 5 of the Criminal Code of 1961 [720 ILCS 5/5-1 et seq.] shall govern whether respondent is legally accountable for the conduct of another person.

(Source: P.A. 84-1305.)

Note.

This section was Ill.Rev.Stat., Ch. 38, para. 112A-16.

725 ILCS 5/112A-17 Emergency order of protection

Sec. 112A-17. *Emergency order of protection.* (a) Prerequisites. An emergency order of protection shall issue if petitioner satisfies the requirements of this subsection for one or more of the requested remedies. For each remedy requested, petitioner shall establish that:

(1) The court has jurisdiction under Section 112A-9 [725 ILCS 5/112A-9];

(2) The requirements of Section 112A-14 [725 ILCS 5/112A-14] are satisfied; and

(3) There is good cause to grant the remedy, regardless of prior service of process or of notice upon the respondent, because:

(i) For the remedies of "prohibition of abuse" described in Section 112A-14(b)(1) [725 ILCS 5/112A-14], "stay away order and additional prohibitions" described in Section 112A-14(b)(3) [725 ILCS 5/112A-14], "removal or concealment of minor child" described in Section 112A-14(b)(8) [725 ILCS 5/112A-14], "order to appear" described in Section 112A-14(b)(9) [725 ILCS 5/112A-14], "physical care and possession of the minor child" described in Section 112A-14(b)(5) [725 ILCS 5/112A-14], "protection of property" described in Section 112A-14(b)(11) [725 ILCS 5/112A-14], "prohibition of entry" described in Section 112A-14(b)(14) [725 ILCS 5/112A-14], "prohibition of access to records" described in Section 112A-14(b)(15) [725 ILCS 5/112A-14], and "injunctive relief" described in Section 112A-14(b)(16) [725 ILCS 5/112A-14], the harm which that remedy is intended to prevent would be likely to occur if the respondent were given any prior notice, or greater notice than was actually given, of the petitioner's efforts to obtain judicial relief;

(ii) For the remedy of "grant of exclusive possession of residence" described in Section 112A-14(b)(2) [725 ILCS 5/112A-14], the immediate danger of further abuse of petitioner by respondent, if petitioner chooses or had chosen to remain in the residence or household while respondent was given any prior notice or greater notice than was actually given of petitioner's efforts to obtain judicial relief, outweighs the hardships to respondent of an emergency order granting petitioner exclusive possession of the residence or household. This remedy shall not be denied because petitioner has or could obtain temporary shelter elsewhere while prior notice is given to respondent, unless the hardships to respondent from exclusion from the home substantially outweigh those to petitioner.

(iii) For the remedy of "possession of personal property" described in Section 112A-14(b)(10) [725 ILCS 5/112A-14], improper disposition of the personal property would be likely to occur if respondent were given any prior notice, or greater notice than was actually given, of petitioner's efforts to obtain judicial relief, or petitioner has an immediate and pressing need for possession of that property.

An emergency order may not include the counseling, legal custody, payment of support or monetary compensation remedies.

(b) Appearance by respondent. If respondent appears in court for this hearing for an emergency order, he or she may elect to file a general appearance and testify. Any resulting order may be an emergency order, governed by this Section. Notwithstanding the requirements of this Section, if all requirements of Section 112A-18 [725 ILCS 5/112A-18] have been met, the Court may issue a 30-day interim order.

(c) Emergency orders: court holidays and evenings.

(1) Prerequisites. When the court is unavailable at the close of business, the petitioner may file a petition for a 21-day emergency order before any available circuit judge or associate judge who may grant relief under this Article. If the judge finds that there is an immediate and present danger of abuse to petitioner and that petitioner has satisfied the prerequisites set forth in subsection (a) of Section 112A-17, that judge may issue an emergency order of protection.

(1.5) Issuance of order. The chief judge of the circuit court may designate for each county in the circuit at least one judge to be reasonably available to issue orally, by telephone, by facsimile, or otherwise, an emergency order of protection at all times, whether or not the court is in session.

(2) Certification and transfer. Any order issued under this Section and any documentation in support thereof shall be certified on the next court day to the appropriate court. The clerk of that court shall immediately assign a case number, file the petition, order and other documents with the court and enter the order of record and file it with the sheriff for service, in accordance with Section 112A-22 [725 ILCS 5/112A-22]. Filing the petition shall commence proceedings for further relief, under Section 112A-2 [725 ILCS 5/112A-2]. Failure to comply with the requirements of this subsection shall not affect the validity of the order.

(Source: P.A. 84-1305; 87-1186, § 1; 90-392, § 5.)

Note.

This section was Ill.Rev.Stat., Ch. 38, para. 112A-17.

Effect of Amendments.

The 1997 amendment by P.A. 90-392, effective January 1, 1998, added subdivision (c)(1.5).

725 ILCS 5/112A-18 30-Day interim order of protection

Sec. 112A-18. *30-Day interim order of protection.* (a) Prerequisites. An interim order of protection shall issue if petitioner has served notice of the hearing for that order on respondent, in accordance with Section 112A-11 [725 ILCS 5/112A-11], and satisfies the requirements of this subsection for one or more of the requested remedies. For each remedy requested, petitioner shall establish that:

(1) The court has jurisdiction under Section 112A-9 [725 ILCS 5/112A-9];

(2) The requirements of Section 112A-14 [725 ILCS 5/112A-14] are satisfied; and

(3) A general appearance was made or filed by or for respondent; or process was served on respondent in the manner required by Section 112A-10 [725 ILCS 5/112A-10]; or the petitioner is diligently attempting to complete the required service of process.

An interim order may not include the counseling, payment of support or monetary compensation remedies, unless the respondent has filed a general appearance or has been personally served.

(b) Appearance by respondent. If respondent appears in court for this hearing for an interim order, he or she may elect to file a general appearance and testify. Any resulting order may be an interim order, governed by this Section. Notwithstanding the requirements of this Section, if all requirements of Section 112A-19 [725 ILCS 5/112A-19] have been met, the Court may issue a plenary order of protection.
(Source: P.A. 84-1305; 87-1186, § 1.)

Note.
This section was Ill.Rev.Stat., Ch. 38, para. 112A-18.

725 ILCS 5/112A-19 Plenary Order of Protection

Sec. 112A-19. *Plenary Order of Protection.* A plenary order of protection shall issue if petitioner has served notice of the hearing for that order on respondent, in accordance with Section 112A-11 [725 ILCS 5/112A-11], and satisfies the requirements of this Section for one or more of the requested remedies. For each remedy requested, petitioner must establish that:

(1) The court has jurisdiction under Section 112A-9 [725 ILCS 5/112A-9];

(2) The requirements of Section 112A-14 [725 ILCS 5/112A-14] are satisfied; and

(3) A general appearance was made or filed by or for respondent or process was served on respondent in the manner required by Section 112A-10 [725 ILCS 5/112A-10]; and

(4) Respondent has answered or is in default.
(Source: P.A. 84-1305.)

Note.
This section was Ill.Rev.Stat., Ch. 38, para. 112A-19.

725 ILCS 5/112A-20 Duration and extension of orders

Sec. 112A-20. *Duration and extension of orders.* (a) Duration of emergency and interim orders. Unless re-opened or extended or voided by entry of an order of greater duration:

(1) Emergency orders issued under Section 112A-17 [725 ILCS 5/112A-17] shall be effective for not less than 14 nor more than 21 days;

(2) Interim orders shall be effective for up to 30 days.

(b) Duration of plenary orders. Except as otherwise provided in this Section, a plenary order of protection shall be valid for a fixed period of time not to exceed 2 years. A plenary order of protection entered in conjunction with a criminal prosecution shall remain in effect as follows:

(1) if entered during pre-trial release, until disposition, withdrawal, or dismissal of the underlying charge; if, however, the case is continued as an independent cause of action, the order's duration may be for a fixed period of time not to exceed 2 years;

(2) if in effect in conjunction with a bond forfeiture warrant, until final disposition or an additional period of time not exceeding 2 years; no order of protection, however, shall be terminated by a dismissal that is accompanied by the issuance of a bond forfeiture warrant;

(3) until expiration of any supervision, conditional discharge, probation, periodic imprisonment, parole or mandatory supervised release and for an additional period of time thereafter not exceeding 2 years; or

(4) until the date set by the court for expiration of any sentence of imprisonment and subsequent parole or mandatory supervised release and for an additional period of time thereafter not exceeding 2 years.

(c) Computation of time. The duration of an order of protection shall not be reduced by the duration of any prior order of protection.

(d) Law enforcement records. When a plenary order of protection expires upon the occurrence of a specified event, rather than upon a specified date as provided in subsection (b), no expiration date shall be entered in Department of State Police records. To remove the plenary order from those records, either party shall request the clerk of the court to file a certified copy of an order stating that the specified event has occurred or that the plenary order has been vacated or modified with the sheriff, and the sheriff shall direct that law enforcement records shall be promptly corrected in accordance with the filed order.

(e) Extension of orders. Any emergency, interim or plenary order of protection may be extended one or more times, as required, provided that the requirements of Section 112A-17, 112A-18 or 112A-19 [725 ILCS 5/112A-17, 725 ILCS 5/112A-18 or 725 ILCS 5/112A-19], as appropriate, are satisfied. If the motion for extension is uncontested and petitioner seeks no modification of the order, the order may be extended on the basis of petitioner's motion or affidavit stating that there has been no material change in relevant circumstances since entry of the order and stating the reason for the requested extension. Extensions may be granted only in open court and not under the provisions of Section 112A-17(c) [725 ILCS 5/112A-17], which applies only when the court is unavailable at the close of business or on a court holiday.

(f) Termination date. Any order of protection which would expire on a court holiday shall instead expire at the close of the next court business day.

(g) Statement of purpose. The practice of dismissing or suspending a criminal prosecution in exchange for issuing an order of protection undermines the purposes of this Article. This Section shall not be construed as encouraging that practice.
(Source: P.A. 84-1305; 87-1186, § 1.)

Note.
This section was Ill.Rev.Stat., Ch. 38, para. 112A-20.

725 ILCS 5/112A-21 Contents of orders

Sec. 112A-21. *Contents of orders.* (a) Any order of protection shall describe, in reasonable detail and not by reference to any other document, the following:

(1) Each remedy granted by the court, in reasonable detail and not by reference to any other document, so that respondent may clearly understand what he or she must do or refrain from doing. Pre-printed form orders of protection shall include the definitions of the types of abuse, as provided in Section 112A-3 [725 ILCS 5/112A-3]. Remedies set forth in pre-printed form orders shall be numbered consistently with and corresponding to the numerical sequence of remedies listed in Section 112A-14 [725 ILCS 5/112A-14] (at least as of the date the form orders are printed).

(2) The reason for denial of petitioner's request for any remedy listed in Section 112A-14 [725 ILCS 5/112A-14].

(b) An order of protection shall further state the following:

(1) The name of each petitioner that the court finds was abused by respondent, and that respondent is a member of the family or household of each such petitioner, and the name of each other person protected by the order and that such person is protected by this Act.

(2) For any remedy requested by petitioner on which the court has declined to rule, that that remedy is reserved.

(3) The date and time the order of protection was issued, whether it is an emergency, interim or plenary order and the duration of the order.

(4) The date, time and place for any scheduled hearing for extension of that order of protection or for another order of greater duration or scope.

(5) For each remedy in an emergency order of protection, the reason for entering that remedy without prior notice to respondent or greater notice than was actually given.

(6) For emergency and interim orders of protection, that respondent may petition the court, in accordance with Section 112A-24 [725 ILCS 5/112A-24], to re-open that order if he or she did not receive actual prior notice of the hearing, in accordance with Section 112A-11 [725 ILCS 5/112A-11], and alleges that he or she had a meritorious defense to the order or that the order or any of its remedies was not authorized by this Article.

(c) Any order of protection shall include the following notice, printed in conspicuous type: "Any knowing violation of an order of protection forbidding physical abuse, harassment, intimidation, interference with personal liberty, willful deprivation, or entering or remaining present at specified places when the protected person is present, or granting exclusive possession of the residence or household, or granting a stay away order is a Class A misdemeanor. Grant of exclusive possession of the residence or household shall constitute notice forbidding trespass to land. Any knowing violation of an order awarding legal custody or physical care of a child or prohibiting removal or concealment of a child may be a Class 4 felony. Any willful violation of any order is contempt of court. Any violation may result in fine or imprisonment."

(d) An emergency order of protection shall state, "This Order of Protection is enforceable, even without registration, in all 50 states, the District of Columbia, tribal lands, and the U.S. territories pursuant to the Violence Against Women Act (18 U.S.C. 2265). Violating this Order of Protection may subject the respondent to federal charges and punishment (18 U.S.C. 2261-2262)."

(e) An interim or plenary order of protection shall state, "This Order of Protection is enforceable, even without registration, in all 50 states, the District of Columbia, tribal lands, and the U.S. territories pursuant to the Violence Against Women Act (18 U.S.C. 2265). Violating this Order of Protection may subject the respondent to federal charges and punishment (18 U.S.C. 2261-2262). The respondent may be subject to federal criminal penalties for possessing, transporting, shipping, or receiving any firearm or ammunition under the Gun Control Act (18 U.S.C. 922(g)(8) and (9))."

(Source: P.A. 84-1305; 86-1300; 87-1186, § 1; 93-944, § 5.)

Note.

This section was Ill.Rev.Stat., Ch. 38, para. 112A-21.

Effect of Amendments.

The 2004 amendment by P.A. 93-944, effective January 1, 2005, added subsections (d) and (e).

CASE NOTES

Construction with Other Laws

The notice requirements contained in subsection (c) of this section is not inconsistent with the sentencing scheme provided for in 720 ILCS 5/12-30; under these requirements, a respondent is accurately advised that a violation of an order of protection is a Class A misdemeanor and it is not necessary for a respondent to be informed of the possibility of enhanced penalties due to prior convictions. People v. Ramos, 316 Ill. App. 3d 18, 249 Ill. Dec. 269, 735 N.E.2d 1094, 2000 Ill. App. LEXIS 732 (2 Dist. 2000).

Compliance with the service requirements contained in this section and 725 ILCS 5/112A-22 is not required before a defendant may be charged with violating an order of protection pursuant to 720 ILCS 5/12-30. People v. Ramos, 316 Ill. App. 3d 18, 249 Ill. Dec. 269, 735 N.E.2d 1094, 2000 Ill. App. LEXIS 732 (2 Dist. 2000).

725 ILCS 5/112A-22 Notice of orders

Sec. 112A-22. *Notice of orders.* (a) Entry and issuance. Upon issuance of any order of protection, the clerk shall immediately, or on the next court day if an emergency order is issued in accordance with subsection (c) of Section 112A-17 [725 ILCS 5-112A/17], (i) enter the order on the record and file it in accordance with the circuit court procedures and (ii) provide a file stamped copy of the order to respondent, if present, and to petitioner.

(b) Filing with sheriff. The clerk of the issuing judge shall, or the petitioner may, on the same day that an order of protection is issued, file a copy of that order with the sheriff or other law enforcement officials charged with maintaining Department of State Police records or charged with serving the order upon respondent. If the order was issued in accordance with subsection (c) of Section 112A-17 [725 ILCS 5/112A-17], the clerk shall on the next court day, file a certified copy of the order with the Sheriff or other law enforcement officials charged with maintaining Department of State Police records.

(c) Service by sheriff. Unless respondent was present in court when the order was issued, the sheriff, other law enforcement official or special process server shall promptly serve that order upon respondent and file proof of such service, in the manner provided for service of process in civil proceedings. Instead of serving the order upon the respondent, however, the sheriff, other law enforcement official, or special process server may serve the respondent with a short form notification as provided in Section 112A-22.10 [725 ILCS 5/112A-22.10]. If process has not yet been served upon the respondent, it shall be served with the order or short form notification.

(c-5) If the person against whom the order of protection is issued is arrested and the written order is issued in accordance with subsection (c) of Section 112A-17 [725 ILCS 5/112A-17] and received by the custodial law enforcement agency before the respondent or arrestee is released from custody, the custodial law enforcement agent shall promptly serve the order upon the respondent or arrestee before the respondent or arrestee is released from custody. In no event shall detention of the respondent or arrestee be extended for hearing on the petition for order of protection or receipt of the order issued under Section 112A-17 of this Code [725 ILCS 5/112A-17].

(d) Extensions, modifications and revocations. Any order extending, modifying or revoking any order of protection shall be promptly recorded, issued and served as provided in this Section.

(Source: P.A. 84-1305; 87-1186, § 1; 90-392, § 5; 92-162, § 5.)

Note.

This section was Ill.Rev.Stat., Ch. 38, para. 112A-22.

Effect of Amendments.

The 1997 amendment by P.A. 90-392, effective January 1, 1998, in subsection (a) inserted "or on the next court day if an emergency order is issued in accordance with subsection (c) of Section 112A-7"; in subsection (b) added the second sentence; and added subsection (c-5).

The 2001 amendment by P.A. 92-162, effective January 1, 2002, in subsection (c) inserted the second sentence, and at the end of the third sentence added "or short form notification".

CASE NOTES

Construction with Other Laws

Compliance with the service requirements contained in 725 ILCS 5/112A-21 and this section is not required before a defendant may be charged with violating an order of protection pursuant to 720 ILCS 5/12-30. People v. Ramos, 316 Ill. App. 3d 18, 249 Ill. Dec. 269, 735 N.E.2d 1094, 2000 Ill. App. LEXIS 732 (2 Dist. 2000).

725 ILCS 5/112A-22.5 Filing of an order of protection issued in another state

Sec. 112A-22.5. *Filing of an order of protection issued in another state.* (a) A person entitled to protection under an order of protection issued by the court of another state, tribe, or United States territory may file a certified copy of the order of protection with the clerk of the court in a judicial circuit in which the person believes that enforcement may be necessary.

(b) The clerk shall:

(1) treat the foreign order of protection in the same manner as a judgment of the circuit court for any county of this State in accordance with the provisions of the Uniform Enforcement of Foreign Judgments Act [735 ILCS 5/12-650 et seq.], except that the clerk shall not mail notice of the filing of the foreign order to the respondent named in the order; and

(2) on the same day that a foreign order of protection is filed, file a certified copy of that order with the sheriff or other law enforcement officials charged with maintaining Department of State Police records as set forth in Section 112A-22 of this Act [725 ILCS 5/112A-22].

(c) Neither residence in this State nor filing of a foreign order of protection shall be required for enforcement of the order by this State. Failure to file the foreign order shall not be an impediment to its treatment in all respects as an Illinois order of protection.

(d) The clerk shall not charge a fee to file a foreign order of protection under this Section.

(e) The sheriff shall inform the Department of State Police as set forth in Section 112A-28 of this Act [725 ILCS 5/112A-28].

(Source: P.A. 91-903, § 5.)

Effective Date.

This section is effective January 1, 2001, pursuant to Ill. Const. (1970), Art. IV, § 10 and 5 ILCS 75/1.

725 ILCS 5/112A-22.10 Short form notification

Sec. 112A-22.10. *Short form notification.* (a) Instead of personal service of an order of protection under Section 112A-22 [750 ILCS 60/112A-22], a sheriff, other law enforcement official, or special process server may serve a respondent with a short form notification. The short form notification must include the following items:

(1) The respondent's name.

(2) The respondent's date of birth, if known.

(3) The petitioner's name.

(4) The names of other protected parties.

(5) The date and county in which the order of protection was filed.

(6) The court file number.

(7) The hearing date and time, if known.
(8) The conditions that apply to the respondent, either in checklist form or handwritten.
(9) The name of the judge who signed the order.
(b) The short form notification must contain the following notice in bold print:
"The order of protection is now enforceable. You must report to the office of the sheriff or the office of the circuit court in (name of county) County to obtain a copy of the order of protection. You are subject to arrest and may be charged with a misdemeanor or felony if you violate any of the terms of the order of protection."
(c) Upon verification of the identity of the respondent and the existence of an unserved order of protection against the respondent, a sheriff or other law enforcement official may detain the respondent for a reasonable time necessary to complete and serve the short form notification.
(d) When service is made by short form notification under this Section, it may be proved by the affidavit of the sheriff, other law enforcement official, or special process server making the service.
(e) The Attorney General shall provide adequate copies of the short form notification form to law enforcement agencies in this State.
(Source: P.A. 92-162, § 5.)

Effective Date.
This section is effective January 1, 2002 pursuant to Ill. Const. (1970), Art. IV, § 10 and 5 ILCS 75/1.

725 ILCS 5/112A-23 Enforcement of orders of protection

Sec. 112A-23. *Enforcement of orders of protection.* (a) When violation is crime. A violation of any order of protection, whether issued in a civil, quasi-criminal proceeding, shall be enforced by a criminal court when:
(1) The respondent commits the crime of violation of an order of protection pursuant to Section 12-30 of the Criminal Code of 1961 [720 ILCS 5/12-30], by having knowingly violated:
(i) remedies described in paragraphs (1), (2), (3), (14), or (14.5) of subsection (b) of Section 112A-14 [725 ILCS 5/112A-14],
(ii) a remedy, which is substantially similar to the remedies authorized under paragraphs (1), (2), (3), (14) or (14.5) of subsection (b) of Section 214 of the Illinois Domestic Violence Act of 1986 [750 ILCS 60/214], in a valid order of protection, which is authorized under the laws of another state, tribe or United States territory,
(iii) or any other remedy when the act constitutes a crime against the protected parties as defined by the Criminal Code of 1961 [720 ILCS 5/1-1 et seq.].
Prosecution for a violation of an order of protection shall not bar concurrent prosecution for any other crime, including any crime that may have been committed at the time of the violation of the order of protection; or
(2) The respondent commits the crime of child abduction pursuant to Section 10-5 of the Criminal Code of 1961 [720 ILCS 5/10-5], by having knowingly violated:
(i) remedies described in paragraphs (5), (6) or (8) of subsection (b) of Section 112A-14 [725 ILCS 5/112A-14], or
(ii) a remedy, which is substantially similar to the remedies authorized under paragraphs (1), (5), (6), or (8) of subsection (b) of Section 214 of the Illinois Domestic Violence Act of 1986 [750 ILCS 60/214], in a valid order of protection, which is authorized under the laws of another state, tribe or United States territory.
(b) When violation is contempt of court. A violation of any valid order of protection, whether issued in a civil or criminal proceeding, may be enforced through civil or criminal contempt procedures, as appropriate, by any court with jurisdiction, regardless where the act or acts which violated the order of protection were committed, to the extent consistent with the venue provisions of this Article. Nothing in this Article shall preclude any Illinois court from enforcing any valid order of protection issued in another state. Illinois courts may enforce orders of protection through both criminal prosecution and contempt proceedings, unless the action which is second in time is barred by collateral estoppel or the constitutional prohibition against double jeopardy.
(1) In a contempt proceeding where the petition for a rule to show cause sets forth facts evidencing an immediate danger that the respondent will flee the jurisdiction, conceal a child, or inflict physical abuse on the petitioner or minor children or on dependent adults in petitioner's care, the court may order the attachment of the respondent without prior service of the rule to show cause or the petition for a rule to show cause. Bond shall be set unless specifically denied in writing.
(2) A petition for a rule to show cause for violation of an order of protection shall be treated as an expedited proceeding.
(c) Violation of custody or support orders. A violation of remedies described in paragraphs (5), (6), (8), or (9) of subsection (b) of Section 112A-14 [725 ILCS 5/112A-14] may be enforced by any remedy provided by Section 611 of the Illinois Marriage and Dissolution of Marriage Act [750 ILCS 5/611]. The court may enforce any order for support issued under paragraph (12) of subsection (b) of Section 112A-14 [725 ILCS 5/112A-14] in the manner provided for under Articles V and VII of the Illinois Marriage and Dissolution of Marriage Act [750 ILCS 5/501 et seq. and 750 ILCS 5/701 et seq.].
(d) Actual knowledge. An order of protection may be enforced pursuant to this Section if the respondent violates the order after respondent has actual knowledge of its contents as shown through one of the following means:

(1) By service, delivery, or notice under Section 112A-10 [725 ILCS 5/112A-10].

(2) By notice under Section 112A-11 [725 ILCS 5/112A-11].

(3) By service of an order of protection under Section 112A-22 [725 ILCS 5/112A-22].

(4) By other means demonstrating actual knowledge of the contents of the order.

(e) The enforcement of an order of protection in civil or criminal court shall not be affected by either of the following:

(1) The existence of a separate, correlative order entered under Section 112A-15 [725 ILCS 5/112A-15].

(2) Any finding or order entered in a conjoined criminal proceeding.

(f) Circumstances. The court, when determining whether or not a violation of an order of protection has occurred, shall not require physical manifestations of abuse on the person of the victim.

(g) Penalties.

(1) Except as provided in paragraph (3) of this subsection, where the court finds the commission of a crime or contempt of court under subsections (a) or (b) of this Section, the penalty shall be the penalty that generally applies in such criminal or contempt proceedings, and may include one or more of the following: incarceration, payment of restitution, a fine, payment of attorneys' fees and costs, or community service.

(2) The court shall hear and take into account evidence of any factors in aggravation or mitigation before deciding an appropriate penalty under paragraph (1) of this subsection.

(3) To the extent permitted by law, the court is encouraged to:

(i) increase the penalty for the knowing violation of any order of protection over any penalty previously imposed by any court for respondent's violation of any order of protection or penal statute involving petitioner as victim and respondent as defendant;

(ii) impose a minimum penalty of 24 hours imprisonment for respondent's first violation of any order of protection; and

(iii) impose a minimum penalty of 48 hours imprisonment for respondent's second or subsequent violation of an order of protection unless the court explicitly finds that an increased penalty or that period of imprisonment would be manifestly unjust.

(4) In addition to any other penalties imposed for a violation of an order of protection, a criminal court may consider evidence of any violations of an order of protection:

(i) to increase, revoke or modify the bail bond on an underlying criminal charge pursuant to Section 110-6 [725 ILCS 5/110-6];

(ii) to revoke or modify an order of probation, conditional discharge or supervision, pursuant to Section 5-6-4 of the Unified Code of Corrections [730 ILCS 5/5-6-4];

(iii) to revoke or modify a sentence of periodic imprisonment, pursuant to Section 5-7-2 of the Unified Code of Corrections [730 ILCS 5/5-7-2].

(Source: P.A. 86-1300; 87-743; 87-1186, § 1; 90-732, § 10; 93-359, § 5.)

Note.

This section was Ill.Rev.Stat., Ch. 38, para. 112A-23.

Effect of Amendments.

The 1998 amendment by P.A. 90-732, effective August 11, 1998, added subsections (a)(1)(ii) and (a)(2)(ii), and the (a)(1)(i), (a)(1)(iii), and (a)(2)(i) designations; in subsection (a)(1)(i) substituted "paragraphs (1), (2), (3), (14), or (14.5)" for "paragraphs (1), (2), (3), or (14)"; and made minor stylistic changes.

The 2003 amendment by P.A. 93-359, effective January 1, 2004, substituted "shall" for "may" in the introductory language of subsection (a).

725 ILCS 5/112A-24 Modification and re-opening of orders

Sec. 112A-24. *Modification and re-opening of orders.* (a) Except as otherwise provided in this Section, upon motion by petitioner, the court may modify an emergency, interim, or plenary order of protection:

(1) If respondent has abused petitioner since the hearing for that order, by adding or altering one or more remedies, as authorized by Section 112A-14 [725 ILCS 5/112A-14]; and

(2) Otherwise, by adding any remedy authorized by Section 112A-14 [725 ILCS 5/112A-14] which was:

(i) reserved in that order of protection;

(ii) not requested for inclusion in that order of protection; or

(iii) denied on procedural grounds, but not on the merits.

(b) Upon motion by petitioner or respondent, the court may modify any prior order of protection's remedy for custody, visitation or payment of support in accordance with the relevant provisions of the Illinois Marriage and Dissolution of Marriage Act [750 ILCS 5/101 et seq.].

(c) After 30 days following the entry of a plenary order of protection, a court may modify that order only when changes in the applicable law or facts since that plenary order was entered warrant a modification of its terms.

(d) Upon 2 days notice to petitioner, in accordance with Section 112A-11 [725 ILCS 5/112A-11], or such shorter notice as the court may prescribe, a respondent subject to an emergency or interim order of protection issued under this Article may appear and petition the court to re-hear the original or amended petition. Any petition to re-hear shall be verified and shall allege the following:

(1) that respondent did not receive prior notice of the initial hearing in which the emergency or interim order was entered, in accordance with Sections 112A-11 and 112A-17 [725 ILCS 5/112A-11 and 725 ILCS 5/112A-17]; and

(2) that respondent had a meritorious defense to the order or any of its remedies or that the order or

any of its remedies was not authorized under this Article.

(e) If the emergency or interim order granted petitioner exclusive possession of the residence and the petition of respondent seeks to re-open or vacate that grant, the court shall set a date for hearing within 14 days on all issues relating to exclusive possession. Under no circumstances shall a court continue a hearing concerning exclusive possession beyond the 14th day except by agreement of the parties. Other issues raised by the pleadings may be consolidated for the hearing if neither party nor the court objects.

(f) This Section does not limit the means, otherwise available by law, for vacating or modifying orders of protection.

(Source: P.A. 85-293; 87-1186, § 1.)

Note.

This section was Ill.Rev.Stat., Ch. 38, para. 112A-24.

725 ILCS 5/112A-25 Immunity from Prosecution

Sec. 112A-25. *Immunity from Prosecution.* Any individual or organization acting in good faith to report the abuse of any person 60 years of age or older or to do any of the following in complying with the provisions of this Article shall not be subject to criminal prosecution or civil liability as a result of such action: providing any information to the appropriate law enforcement agency, providing that the giving of any information does not violate any privilege of confidentiality under law; assisting in any investigation; assisting in the preparation of any materials for distribution under this Article; or by providing services ordered under an order of protection.

(Source: P.A. 84-1305 incorporating 84-1232; 84-1438.)

Note.

This section was Ill.Rev.Stat., Ch. 38, para. 112A-25.

725 ILCS 5/112A-26 Arrest without warrant

Sec. 112A-26. *Arrest without warrant.* (a) Any law enforcement officer may make an arrest without warrant if the officer has probable cause to believe that the person has committed or is committing any crime, including but not limited to violation of an order of protection, under Section 12-30 of the Criminal Code of 1961 [720 ILCS 5/12-30], even if the crime was not committed in the presence of the officer.

(b) The law enforcement officer may verify the existence of an order of protection by telephone or radio communication with his or her law enforcement agency or by referring to the copy of the order provided by petitioner or respondent.

(Source: P.A. 87-1186, § 1.)

725 ILCS 5/112A-27 Law enforcement policies

Sec. 112A-27. *Law enforcement policies.* Every law enforcement agency shall develop, adopt, and implement written policies regarding arrest procedures for domestic violence incidents consistent with the provisions of this Article. In developing these policies, each law enforcement agency is encouraged to consult with community organizations and other law enforcement agencies with expertise in recognizing and handling domestic violence incidents.

(Source: P.A. 87-1186, § 1.)

725 ILCS 5/112A-28 Data maintenance by law enforcement agencies

Sec. 112A-28. *Data maintenance by law enforcement agencies.* (a) All sheriffs shall furnish to the Department of State Police, daily, in the form and detail the Department requires, copies of any recorded orders of protection issued by the court, and any foreign orders of protection filed by the clerk of the court, and transmitted to the sheriff by the clerk of the court pursuant to subsection (b) of Section 112A-22 of this Act [725 ILCS 5/112A-22]. Each order of protection shall be entered in the Law Enforcement Automated Data System on the same day it is issued by the court. If an emergency order of protection was issued in accordance with subsection (c) of Section 112A-17 [725 ILCS 5/112A-17], the order shall be entered in the Law Enforcement Automated Data System as soon as possible after receipt from the clerk.

(b) The Department of State Police shall maintain a complete and systematic record and index of all valid and recorded orders of protection issued or filed pursuant to this Act. The data shall be used to inform all dispatchers and law enforcement officers at the scene of an alleged incident of abuse or violation of an order of protection of any recorded prior incident of abuse involving the abused party and the effective dates and terms of any recorded order of protection.

(c) The data, records and transmittals required under this Section shall pertain to any valid emergency, interim or plenary order of protection, whether issued in a civil or criminal proceeding or authorized under the laws of another state, tribe, or United States territory.

(Source: P.A. 87-1186, § 1; 90-392, § 5; 91-903, § 5.)

Effect of Amendments.

The 1997 amendment by P.A. 90-392, effective January 1, 1998, in subsection (a) added the third sentence.

The 2000 amendment by P.A. 91-903, effective January 1, 2001, inserted "and any foreign orders of protection filed by the clerk of the court" in the first sentence of subsection (a); inserted "or filed" in the first sentence of subsection (b); and inserted "or authorized under the laws of another state, tribe, or United States territory" in subsection (c).

725 ILCS 5/112A-29 Reports by law enforcement officers

Sec. 112A-29. *Reports by law enforcement officers.* (a) Every law enforcement officer investigating an alleged incident of abuse between family or household members shall make a written police report of any bona fide allegation and the disposition of such investigation. The police report shall include the victim's statements as to the frequency and severity of prior incidents of abuse by the same family or household member and the number of prior calls for police assistance to prevent such further abuse.

(b) Every police report completed pursuant to this Section shall be recorded and compiled as a domestic crime within the meaning of Section 5.1 of the Criminal Identification Act [20 ILCS 2630/5.1].
(Source: P.A. 87-1186, § 1.)

725 ILCS 5/112A-30 Assistance by law enforcement officers

Sec. 112A-30. *Assistance by law enforcement officers.* (a) Whenever a law enforcement officer has reason to believe that a person has been abused by a family or household member, the officer shall immediately use all reasonable means to prevent further abuse, including:

(1) Arresting the abusing party, where appropriate;

(2) If there is probable cause to believe that particular weapons were used to commit the incident of abuse, subject to constitutional limitations, seizing and taking inventory of the weapons;

(3) Accompanying the victim of abuse to his or her place of residence for a reasonable period of time to remove necessary personal belongings and possessions;

(4) Offering the victim of abuse immediate and adequate information (written in a language appropriate for the victim or in Braille or communicated in appropriate sign language), which shall include a summary of the procedures and relief available to victims of abuse under subsection (c) of Section 112A-17 [725 ILCS 5/112A-17] and the officer's name and badge number;

(5) Providing the victim with one referral to an accessible service agency;

(6) Advising the victim of abuse about seeking medical attention and preserving evidence (specifically including photographs of injury or damage and damaged clothing or other property); and

(7) Providing or arranging accessible transportation for the victim of abuse (and, at the victim's request, any minors or dependents in the victim's care) to a medical facility for treatment of injuries or to a nearby place of shelter or safety; or, after the close of court business hours, providing or arranging for transportation for the victim (and, at the victim's request, any minors or dependents in the victim's care) to the nearest available circuit judge or associate judge so the victim may file a petition for an emergency order of protection under subsection (c) of Section 112A-17 [725 ILCS 5/112A-17]. When a victim of abuse chooses to leave the scene of the offense, it shall be presumed that it is in the best interests of any minors or dependents in the victim's care to remain with the victim or a person designated by the victim, rather than to remain with the abusing party.

(b) Whenever a law enforcement officer does not exercise arrest powers or otherwise initiate criminal proceedings, the officer shall:

(1) Make a police report of the investigation of any bona fide allegation of an incident of abuse and the disposition of the investigation, in accordance with subsection (a) of Section 112A-29 [725 ILCS 5/112A-29];

(2) Inform the victim of abuse of the victim's right to request that a criminal proceeding be initiated where appropriate, including specific times and places for meeting with the State's Attorney's office, a warrant officer, or other official in accordance with local procedure; and

(3) Advise the victim of the importance of seeking medical attention and preserving evidence (specifically including photographs of injury or damage and damaged clothing or other property).

(c) Except as provided by Section 24-6 of the Criminal Code of 1961 [720 ILCS 5/24-6] or under a court order, any weapon seized under subsection (a)(2) shall be returned forthwith to the person from whom it was seized when it is no longer needed for evidentiary purposes.
(Source: P.A. 87-1186, § 1; 88-498, § 5.)

725 ILCS 5/112A-31 Limited law enforcement liability

Sec. 112A-31. *Limited law enforcement liability.* Any act of omission or commission by any law enforcement officer acting in good faith in rendering emergency assistance or otherwise enforcing this Article shall not impose civil liability upon the law enforcement officer or his or her supervisor or employer, unless the act is a result of willful or wanton misconduct.
(Source: P.A. 87-1186, § 1.)

CHAPTER 735
CIVIL PROCEDURE

CODE OF CIVIL PROCEDURE

ARTICLE VIII.

EVIDENCE

Part 8.

Privileged Communications

735 ILCS 5/8-801 Husband and wife

Part 26.

Minors

735 ILCS 5/8-2601 [Out-of-court statement]

ARTICLE XI.

INJUNCTION

Part 1.

In General

735 ILCS 5/11-101 Temporary restraining order
735 ILCS 5/11-102 Preliminary injunction
735 ILCS 5/11-103 Bond
735 ILCS 5/11-104 Bond before court or clerk
735 ILCS 5/11-105 Filing of bond
735 ILCS 5/11-106 Injunctive relief on Saturday, Sunday or legal holiday
735 ILCS 5/11-107 Seeking wrong remedy not fatal
735 ILCS 5/11-107.1 Injunctive relief for the father of an unborn child in an abortion related decision by the mother
735 ILCS 5/11-108 Motion to dissolve
735 ILCS 5/11-109 Affidavits in support of motion to dissolve
735 ILCS 5/11-110 Assessing damages

ARTICLE XXI.

CHANGE OF NAME

735 ILCS 5/21-101 Proceedings; parties
735 ILCS 5/21-102 Petition
735 ILCS 5/21-103 Notice by publication
735 ILCS 5/21-104 Process and notice to persons outside this State

CODE OF CIVIL PROCEDURE

ARTICLE VIII.

EVIDENCE

Part 8.

Privileged Communications

735 ILCS 5/8-801 Husband and wife

Sec. 8-801. *Husband and wife.* In all actions, husband and wife may testify for or against each other, provided that neither may testify as to any communication or admission made by either of them to the other or as to any conversation between them during marriage, except in actions between such husband and wife, and in actions where the custody, support, health or welfare of their children or children in either spouse's care, custody or control is directly in issue, and as to matters in which either has acted as agent for the other.
(Source: P.A. 83-408.)

Note.

This section was Ill.Rev.Stat., Ch. 110, para. 8-801.

CASE NOTES

ANALYSIS

In General
Applicability
—Spouses of Incompetents
Competency
Disqualification
Grantees Rather than Heirs
Joint and Mutual Will
—Competency to Testify
Legislative Intent
—Preservation of Privacy
Notice to Employer
Purpose
Testimony
—Admissible
—Inadmissible
—Incompetent
—Widow

In General

This section should be invoked only at the time a specific occasion arises through a question or answer which invades the marital relationship intended to be protected by this section. People v. Butt, 76 Ill. App. 3d 587, 32 Ill. Dec. 54, 395 N.E.2d 1 (2 Dist. 1979).

Applicability

—Spouses of Incompetents

Marital privilege did not preclude first wife's attempts to discover antenuptial agreement between her former husband and his second wife, in support of her proceeding seeking increased child support, because the parties were not married when they made the agreement, and the plain language of the statute limits the privilege to communications between married people. Puterbaugh v. Puterbaugh, 327 Ill. App. 3d 792, 261 Ill. Dec. 967, 764 N.E.2d 582, 2002 Ill. App. LEXIS 110 (3 Dist. 2002).

This section applies to spouses of persons incompetent to testify. Babcock v. McDonnell, 105 Ill. 2d 267, 85 Ill. Dec. 511, 473 N.E.2d 1316 (1985).

Competency

The court erred in holding that plaintiff's wife was not a competent witness, and while defendant could, under the provisions of the predecessor to this section have secured a subpoena from the clerk of the court to produce plaintiff's wife as a witness in the court and formally offered her as such a witness, he was not required to do so where the matter was fully presented to the court, and the court definitely held that she was not a competent witness either for or against plaintiff. Zaremba v. Skurdialis, 395 Ill. 437, 70 N.E.2d 617 (1946).

Where a husband is disqualified by reason of interest, his wife is also incompetent, and such incompetency continues after the marriage relation is dissolved, either by death or divorce. Heineman v. Hermann, 385 Ill. 191, 52 N.E.2d 263 (1943).

Disqualification

Section 8 of the former Evidence Act (see now this section) clearly retained the common-law disqualification and rendered either husband or wife incompetent to attest the other's will. Kent v. Vollmer, 4 Ill. 2d 81, 122 N.E.2d 229 (1954).

Neither husband nor wife at common law could testify to communications and conversations occurring between them during coverture, and that incompetency continued after the marriage relation was severed, either by divorce or death; former

Disqualification (Cont'd)
Ill.Rev.Stat., ch. 52, para. 5 (see now this section) left the common law in force except in suits or causes between husband and wife. Zimmer v. Zimmer, 298 Ill. 586, 132 N.E. 216 (1921).

Grantees Rather than Heirs
Where the adverse parties were not suing as heirs but as grantees, the disability described in this section does not apply. Dunn v. Heasley, 375 Ill. 43, 30 N.E.2d 628 (1940).

Joint and Mutual Will

—Competency to Testify
Where some of the crucial averments contained in the affidavit of wife were matters which she could not competently testify to because of this section, but there was no denial of the execution of the joint and mutual will between the husband and the wife, the court could find that there was a contractual agreement between husband and wife relating to the disposition of their property by such joint and mutual will since the object and purpose of the agreement could be determined from a reading of the joint and mutual will itself. In re Estate of Willis, 33 Ill. App. 3d 279, 337 N.E.2d 35 (3 Dist. 1975).

Legislative Intent

—Preservation of Privacy
While the intention of former Ill.Rev.Stat., ch. 51, para. 5 (see now this section) is salutary, it is intended to preserve the privacy of personal communications between spouses and is not a blanket rule designed to prevent one spouse from testifying where the other spouse is a party to an action. People v. Butt, 76 Ill. App. 3d 587, 32 Ill. Dec. 54, 395 N.E.2d 1 (2 Dist. 1979).

Notice to Employer
Under prior similar law, a widow was not a competent witness to the conversation between her husband and his field boss as to her deceased husband giving his employer notice within 30 days of an accident under the Workers' Compensation Act (820 ILCS 305/1 et seq.). Ohio Oil Co. v. Industrial Comm'n, 293 Ill. 461, 127 N.E. 743 (1920).

Purpose
The purpose of the amendment to this section was to enable husband and wife to testify for or against each other in certain cases designated in the amendment as "all civil actions," this amendment does not purport to change any other provision of this Act. Heineman v. Hermann, 385 Ill. 191, 52 N.E.2d 263 (1943).

Testimony

—Admissible
Under former Ill.Rev.Stat., ch. 51, para. 5 (see now this section), trial court did not err in admitting the testimony of wife of one of the co-indictees, concerning a conversation she had with conspirator where co-indictee was not an trial; wife was called by the state as a witness in a criminal prosecution, and she did not testify either for or against her husband. People v. Barnett, 347 Ill. 127, 179 N.E. 450 (1931).

—Inadmissible
The trial court correctly excluded wife's testimony as to what the grantor said to her when he handed her the deed, because she was incompetent to testify as to any conversation between them during coverture, and by depositing the deed in grantor's trunk she was not acting as his agent. Dunn v. Heasley, 375 Ill. 43, 30 N.E.2d 628 (1940).

The interest of the witness' husband in the subject matter of the litigation rendered her incompetent to testify, regardless of her relation to the subject matter of the suit, and regardless of the fact he was not directly a party to the petition filed. Casper Nat'l Bank v. Jenner, 268 Ill. 142, 108 N.E. 998 (1915).

—Incompetent
Under similar prior law, where testator's widow was a party defendant and was called as a witness by complainant, the witness' statement that in her judgment the testator was not capable of transacting ordinary business was based largely on conversations between herself and the testator or between the testator and others, the court should not have admitted her testimony in reference to the mental condition of the testator or the conversation between the son and father's real estate. Donnan v. Donnan, 236 Ill. 341, 86 N.E. 279 (1908).

—Widow
In a wrongful death action, the plaintiff, a widow, was not competent to testify to any conversation with her late husband during the existence of the marriage relation. Neice v. Chicago & A. R.R., 254 Ill. 595, 98 N.E. 989 (1912).

LEGAL PERIODICALS

For article, "Reconciling Attorney-Client Privilege with the Rules of Professional Conduct," see 81 Ill. B.J. 410 (1993).

For note, "Making Form Follow Function: Considerations in Creating and Applying a Statutory Parent-Child Privilege," see U. Ill. L. Rev. 879 (1990).

For note, "The Psychiatrist-Patient Privilege in Illinois," see 10 Loy. U. Chi. L.J. 525 (1978-79).

RESEARCH REFERENCES

Spouse's betrayal or connivance as extending marital communications privilege to testimony of third person. 3 ALR4th 1104.

Communication between unmarried couple living together as privileged. 4 ALR4th 422.

Testimonial privilege for confidential communications between relatives other than husband and wife — state cases. 6 ALR4th 544.

Existence of spousal privilege where marriage was entered into for purpose of barring testimony. 13 ALR4th 1305.

Applicability of marital privilege to written communications between spouses inadvertently obtained by third person. 32 ALR4th 1177.

Communications between spouses as to joint participation in crime as within privilege of interspousal communications. 62 ALR4th 1134.

Crimes against spouse within exception permitting testimony by one spouse against other in criminal prosecution — modern state cases. 74 ALR4th 223.

Competency of one spouse to testify against other in prosecution for offense against third party as affected by fact that offense against spouse was involved in same transaction. 74 ALR4th 277.

Adverse presumption or inference based on party's failure to produce or examine spouse — modern cases. 79 ALR4th 694.

Testimonial privilege for confidential communications between relatives other than husband and wife — state cases. 62 ALR5th 629.

Competency of one spouse to testify against other in prosecution for offense against child of both or either or neither. 119 ALR5th 275.

Part 26.
Minors

735 ILCS 5/8-2601 [Out-of-court statement]

Sec. 8-2601. (a) An out-of-court statement made by a child under the age of 13 describing any act of child abuse or any conduct involving an unlawful sexual act performed in the presence of, with, by, or on the declarant child, or testimony by such of an out-of-court statement made by such child that he or she complained of such acts to another, is admissible in any civil proceeding, if: (1) the court conducts a hearing outside the presence of the jury and finds that the time, content, and circumstances of the statement provide sufficient safeguards of reliability; and (2) the child either: (i) testifies at the proceeding; or (ii) is unavailable as a witness and there is corroborative evidence of the act which is the subject of the statement.

(b) If a statement is admitted pursuant to this Section, the court shall instruct the jury that it is for the jury to determine the weight and credibility to be given to the statement and that, in making its determination, it shall consider the age and maturity of the child, the nature of the statement, the circumstances under which the statement was made, and any other relevant factors.

(c) The proponent of the statement shall give the adverse party reasonable notice of an intention to offer the statement and the particulars of the statement.

(Source: P.A. 85-1440.)

Note.

This section was Ill.Rev.Stat., Ch. 110, para. 8-2601.

CASE NOTES

ANALYSIS

Applicability
Construction with Other Laws
Determination of Reliability

Applicability

The hearsay exception provided by this section applied to a proceeding to adjudicate a person as a sexually dangerous person and to have him committed. People v. Dinwiddie, 306 Ill. App. 3d 294, 239 Ill. Dec. 893, 715 N.E.2d 647 (5 Dist. 1999), appeal denied, 185 Ill. 2d 640, 242 Ill. Dec. 143, 720 N.E.2d 1098 (1999).

Construction with Other Laws

When a mother filed a petition for an order of protection, under the Domestic Violence Act, 750 ILCS 60/101 et seq., seeking to restrict contact between her child's father and her child, in which she sought "physical care" of her child, rather than temporary legal custody, the admission of her child's hearsay statements of sexual abuse was governed by 735 ILCS 5/8-2601, and not by 750 ILCS 5/606(e) of the Marriage Act. In re Flannery, 328 Ill. App. 3d 602, 263 Ill. Dec. 274, 768 N.E.2d 34, 2002 Ill. App. LEXIS 238 (2 Dist. 2002), appeal denied, 201 Ill. 2d 565, 271 Ill. Dec. 924, 786 N.E.2d 182 (2002).

In a proceeding commenced by a mother for an order of protection on behalf of her minor child against the father of the child, the court properly applied 750 ILCS 5/606(e) to admit hearsay statements of the child that the father sexually abused during an overnight visit; although both that statute and this section concern the admission of hearsay statements by abused children in civil proceedings, the former statute addresses the admission of those statements when the alleged abuser is the parent and specifically mentions that it applies to hearings concerning visitation with the child. Daria W. v. Bradley W., 317 Ill. App. 3d 194, 250 Ill. Dec. 505, 738 N.E.2d 974, 2000 Ill. App. LEXIS 830 (3 Dist. 2000).

Determination of Reliability

Hearsay could not be used to corroborate a child's hearsay statement of sexual abuse, so the child's physical conduct accompanying her statements was not sufficient corroboration. In re Flannery, 328 Ill. App. 3d 602, 263 Ill. Dec. 274, 768 N.E.2d 34, 2002 Ill. App. LEXIS 238 (2 Dist. 2002), appeal denied, 201 Ill. 2d 565, 271 Ill. Dec. 924, 786 N.E.2d 182 (2002).

The declarant child's testimony is not required to demonstrate reliability under subdivision (a)(1). In re Rudd, 293 Ill. App. 3d 367, 227 Ill. Dec. 861, 688 N.E.2d 342 (4 Dist. 1997).

Trial court erroneously determined minor's statements were unreliable where it based its determination on who was testifying about the minor's statements rather than on time, content and circumstances of proffered statements. In re Rudd, 293 Ill. App. 3d 367, 227 Ill. Dec. 861, 688 N.E.2d 342 (4 Dist. 1997).

LEGAL PERIODICALS

For article, "Survey of Illinois Law [1988-89] — Evidence," see 14 S. Ill. U.L.J. 983 (1990).

ARTICLE XI.
INJUNCTION

Part 1.
In General

735 ILCS 5/11-101 Temporary restraining order

Sec. 11-101. *Temporary restraining order.* No temporary restraining order shall be granted without notice to the adverse party unless it clearly appears from specific facts shown by affidavit or by the verified complaint that immediate and irreparable injury, loss, or damage will result to the applicant before notice can be served and a hearing had thereon. Every temporary restraining order granted without notice shall be indorsed with the date and hour of signing; shall be filed forthwith in the clerk's office; shall define the injury and state why it is irreparable and why the order was granted without notice; and shall expire by its terms within such time after the signing of the order, not to exceed 10 days, as the court fixes, unless within the time so fixed the order, for good cause shown, is extended for a like period or unless the party against whom the order is directed consents that it may be extended for a longer period. The reasons for the granting of the extension shall be stated in the written order of the court. In case a temporary restraining order is granted without notice, the motion for a preliminary injunction shall be set for hearing at the earliest possible time and takes precedence over all matters except older matters of the same character; and when the motion comes on for hearing the party who obtained the temporary restraining order shall proceed with the application for a preliminary injunction and, if he or she does not do so, the court shall dissolve the temporary restraining order.

On 2 days' notice to the party who obtained the temporary restraining order without notice or on such shorter notice to that party as the court may prescribe, the adverse party may appear and move its dissolution or modification and in that event the court shall proceed to hear and determine such motion as expeditiously as the ends of justice require.

Every order granting an injunction and every restraining order shall set forth the reasons for its entry; shall be specific in terms; shall describe in reasonable detail, and not by reference to the complaint or other document, the act or acts sought to be restrained; and is binding only upon the parties to the action, their officers, agents, employees, and attorneys, and upon those persons in active concert

or participation with them who receive actual notice of the order by personal service or otherwise.
(Source: P.A. 84-554.)

Note.
This section was Ill.Rev.Stat., Ch. 110, para. 11-101.

CASE NOTES

Analysis

In General
Accounting of Damages
Agreed Order
—Not Subject to Review
Answer Not Filed
—Motion Properly Granted
—Order Warranted
Appealability
—In General
—As of Right
Applicability
—Environmental Protection Act
—Interlocutory Injunction
Bald Assertions
Basis of Order
Bond Requirement
Burden of Proof
—Petitioner
Complaint
—Requirements
—Sufficiency Not Shown
—Sufficiency Shown
Compliance
—Shown
Construction
—With Supreme Court Rule 307
Contempt
—In General
—Notice
Damages
De Facto Attachment
—Invalid
Delay of Hearing
—Improper
—Irreparable Damage
Discontinued Actions
—Injunctions Unnecessary
Discretion of Court
—In General
—Abuse of Discretion Shown
—Scope of Authority
Disobeying Order
—Not Permitted
Dissolution of Order
—Effect
—Factors
—Held Improper
Duration of Order
—Fairness
—Unlimited Duration
Error in Issuance
Evidentiary Hearing
—When Required
Ex Parte Hearing
—Illustrative Cases
—Justification
Exceptional Remedy
—In General
Extensions
—Effect
—Notice
—Repeated Extensions
Extent of Injunction
—In General
Factors
—In General
Failure to Obtain Preliminary Injunction
—Effect
Fair Question Not Raised
—Order Wrongfully Issued
Granting Injunction
—Care Required
Hearing
—Required
—Sufficient
—Time of Hearing
Immediate and Irreparable Harm
—Allegations Required
Improper Ex Parte Issuance
—Notice Not Provided
Improperly Broad and Imprecise Language
—Stricken
Injunction Improperly Denied
Injunction Improperly Granted
Injunction Properly Denied
Injunction Properly Granted
Injunction Stricken
—Prohibitions Overbroad
Injunction Sufficiently Precise
—Illustrative Cases
Injunction Without Notice
—Extreme Urgency Required
—No Presumption of Validity
Injunctions
—In General
—Defined
—Guidelines to Form
—Specific Performance
—Specificity
Irreparable Injury
—In General
Issuance of Injunction
—In General
—Discretion of Court
—Facts Required
—Held Improper
—Held Proper
—Insufficient Evidence
—Irreparable Harm
—Issues of Law vs. Fact
—Notice
—Success on the Merits
Issuance with Notice
—Likelihood of Success Required
Jurisdiction
—Effect of Appeal
—Personal Jurisdiction
—Petition Not Filed
—Prior Notice
Knowledge
Lack of Specificity
—Shown
Legislative Intent
Level of Restraint
—Reasonable Protection
Limitations
—Scope
Mandatory Temporary Injunction
—In General
—Inappropriate
—Judicial Discretion
—Requirements
Merits in Doubt
—Relief Granted
Modification
—Jurisdiction
Motion
—Sufficient Facts Shown
Motion for Dissolution
—Damage and Harm Lacking

Motion Properly Denied
—Illustrative Cases
Motion Properly Granted
Multiple Interpretations
—Illustrative Cases
Nature of Relief
—Illustrative Cases
—Preliminary Injunction
—Provisional
Need
—Not Shown
No Answer
—Hearing Not Required
Non Specific Injunction
—Held Valid
Notice
—In General
—Informal Notice
—Lack of Notice
—Local Rules
—Mandatory
—Not Given
—Not Required
—Relief Without Notice
—Requirements
—Sufficient
—Time Limit
—Verified Petition
—Waiver of Objection
Opportunity to Oppose Order
—Required
Oral Argument
—Not Proper Evidence
Order Sufficiently Specific
—Illustrative Cases
Parties Bound
—Relationship with Defendants
Pendente Lite
Petitioner
—Burden
Pleadings
—Held Sufficient
Precise Terms
—Purpose
Preliminary Injunction
—Essential Elements
Purpose
—In General
—Maintain Status Quo
Reduction of Fines
Remedy at Law
—In General
—Inadequate
—Shown
Requisite Showing
—Elements
—Fair Question
—Lawful Right
Review
—In General
—Based on Sufficiency of the Motion
—Requirements
—Standard of Review
Scope
—Injunctions Included
—Permanent Injunction
Scope of Protection
—Unlawful or Injurious Interference
Service upon Attorneys
Specific Facts
—Purpose
—Required
Status Quo
—In General
Subject of Injunction
—Funds
Success on Merits
—Elements
—Likelihood Must Be Shown
Temporary Injunction
—In General
—Abuse of Discretion
Temporary Restraining Order
—Held Improper
Undue Prejudice
—Failure to Give Reasons
Use of Transcript
—Supplements Order
Vacation of Order
—Proper
Violation
—Aiding and Abetting
—Effect
Without Notice and Hearing
—In General
—Appropriate Situations

In General

Critical inquiry into determining whether a temporary restraining order should be issued without notice to adverse party is whether during the period it takes to give such notice the opponent will take measures to destroy the substance of the litigation or obstruct the court in some way from dealing effectively with the issues and whether proper notice might have averted litigation by promptly testing the validity of injunctive relief. C.D. Peters Constr. Co. v. Tri-City Regional Port Dist., 281 Ill. App. 3d 41, 216 Ill. Dec. 876, 666 N.E.2d 44 (5 Dist. 1996), appeal denied, 168 Ill. 2d 584, 219 Ill. Dec. 560, 671 N.E.2d 727 (1996).

A preliminary injunction is merely provisional in nature, its office being only to preserve the status quo until a final hearing on the merits. People v. Van Tran Elec. Corp., 152 Ill. App. 3d 175, 105 Ill. Dec. 173, 503 N.E.2d 1179 (5 Dist. 1987).

A temporary restraining order is a drastic, emergency remedy which may issue only in exceptional circumstances and for a brief duration. Abulhafedh v. Secretary of State, 161 Ill. App. 3d 413, 112 Ill. Dec. 900, 514 N.E.2d 563 (2 Dist. 1987).

A preliminary injunction does not decide controverted facts or the merits of the cause; rather it only shows that sufficient cause has been made to authorize or require the court to preserve the rights in issue until a final hearing on the merits. People ex rel. Hartigan v. National Anti-Drug Coalition, 124 Ill. App. 3d 269, 79 Ill. Dec. 786, 464 N.E.2d 690 (1 Dist. 1984).

Whether a temporary restraining order is with or without notice, it is issued upon a summary showing of the necessity of the order to prevent immediate and irreparable harm. Peoples Gas Light & Coke Co. v. City of Chicago, 117 Ill. App. 3d 353, 72 Ill. Dec. 865, 453 N.E.2d 740 (1 Dist. 1983).

While a preliminary mandatory injunction should only be granted in cases where great necessity or extreme urgency is clearly established, where a condition of rest will inflict irreparable injury, it is proper that a preliminary mandatory injunction be issued. Board of Trustees v. Bakalis, 64 Ill. App. 3d 967, 21 Ill. Dec. 732, 382 N.E.2d 26 (1 Dist. 1978).

Ordinarily a temporary injunction is issued for the purpose of maintaining the status quo, and it may properly issue wherever questions of law or fact to be ultimately determined are grave and difficult and if the injury to the moving party will be immediate, certain and great if it is denied, while the loss or inconvenience to the opposing party will be comparatively small and insignificant if it is granted. Town of Cicero v. Weilander, 35 Ill. App. 2d 456, 183 N.E.2d 40 (1 Dist. 1962).

If it appears from the face of the complaint that there is no equity in it and no sufficient grounds are disclosed therein why the court should interfere, it is error to grant a temporary injunction. Biehn v. Tess, 340 Ill. App. 140, 91 N.E.2d 160 (1 Dist. 1950).

Accounting of Damages

Where an injunction was issued without notice and without bond restraining appellants from attempting to take possession of disputed property, appellants having been kept out of the use of the property, for which appellee had paid no rent, required an accounting of the damages sustained by reason of entry of the injunction

Accounting of Damages (Cont'd)
and retention of the property by appellee. Miovsky v. Georgeoff, 363 Ill. 60, 200 N.E. 855 (1936).

Agreed Order

—Not Subject to Review
An injunction order whose terms were agreed to by all parties involved is not a judicial determination of the parties' rights, and generally is not subject to appellate review. Moran v. Breiner, 99 Ill. App. 3d 306, 54 Ill. Dec. 790, 425 N.E.2d 1007 (1 Dist. 1981).

Answer Not Filed

—Motion Properly Granted
Where no answer has been filed, the motion for a temporary restraining order is properly granted on the uncontroverted facts of the verified complaint. Stanton v. City of Chicago, 177 Ill. App. 3d 519, 126 Ill. Dec. 779, 532 N.E.2d 464 (1 Dist. 1988).

—Order Warranted
In light of city's failure to file any responsive pleadings to plaintiff's complaint, plaintiff made a sufficient summary showing of irreparable harm and inadequate remedy at law to warrant imposition of a temporary restraining order. Stanton v. City of Chicago, 177 Ill. App. 3d 519, 126 Ill. Dec. 779, 532 N.E.2d 464 (1 Dist. 1988).

Appealability

—In General
A temporary restraining order is not appealable, while a preliminary injunction is appealable. Kengott v. County of Lake, 42 Ill. App. 3d 621, 1 Ill. Dec. 248, 356 N.E.2d 374 (2 Dist. 1976).

A temporary restraining order issued under former Ill.Rev.Stat., ch. 69, para. 3-1 (see now this section) was appealable under Rule 307, Supreme Court Rules. Kable Printing Co. v. Mount Morris Bookbinders Union Local 65-B, 63 Ill. 2d 514, 349 N.E.2d 36 (1976).

It makes no difference with respect to an appeal if the order in dispute was a temporary restraining order, or a temporary injunction. Buckingham Corp. v. Vesolowski, 17 Ill. App. 3d 58, 307 N.E.2d 703 (1 Dist. 1974).

The court agreed with the opinion expressed in Bohn Aluminum & Brass Co. v. Barker, 3 Ill. App. 3d 600, 278 N.E.2d 247; a temporary restraining order is not appealable. Kirchenberg v. Chicago Transit Auth., 13 Ill. App. 3d 184, 300 N.E.2d 482 (1 Dist. 1973).

A temporary restraining order under this section is not appealable while a preliminary injunction issued 735 ILCS 5/11-102 is appealable. Paddington Corp. v. Foremost Sales Promotions, Inc., 13 Ill. App. 3d 170, 300 N.E.2d 484 (1 Dist. 1973).

—As of Right
Rule 301, Supreme Court Rules, provides that every final judgment of a circuit court in a civil case is appealable as of right; however, only those interlocutory orders enumerated in Rule 307, Supreme Court Rules, are appealable as of right, and a trial court order denying the states motion for a temporary restraining order had the effect of determining substantial rights of the parties which were subject to irreparable harm if review were delayed, and such denial was not appealable as of right. People ex rel. Pollution Control Bd. v. Lloyd A. Fry Roofing Co., 4 Ill. App. 3d 675, 281 N.E.2d 757 (1 Dist. 1972).

Finality of judgment shall be determined by reference to the primary effect of an order rather than to its form; thus, where denial of a motion for a temporary restraining order had the effect of determining substantial rights of the parties which would be irreparably lost if review were delayed, such a denial was appealable as of right under Rule 301, Supreme Court Rules. People ex rel. Pollution Control Bd. v. Lloyd A. Fry Roofing Co., 4 Ill. App. 3d 675, 281 N.E.2d 757 (1 Dist. 1972).

Applicability

—Environmental Protection Act
This section does not apply to injunctive actions under the Environmental Protection Act (415 ILCS 5/1 et seq.). People v. Conrail Corp., 245 Ill. App. 3d 167, 184 Ill. Dec. 467, 613 N.E.2d 784 (5 Dist.), appeal denied, 152 Ill. 2d 566, 190 Ill. Dec. 897, 622 N.E.2d 1214 (1993).

—Interlocutory Injunction
Where the application was for a stay order, injunctive in nature, and its denial was in effect the denial of an interlocutory injunction, it did not matter that the application for stay order was heard in the pending proceeding rather than in a separate suit for injunctive relief. School Dist. No. 46 v. Del Bianco, 68 Ill. App. 2d 145, 215 N.E.2d 25 (2 Dist. 1966).

Bald Assertions
Plaintiff's emergency petition set out eight different ways in which it would be irreparably harmed if injunctive relief was not granted, however, these statements did not adequately show that the plaintiff would suffer irreparable harm if injunctive relief were not granted, because they were bald assertions. Diamond Sav. & Loan Co. v. Royal Glen Condominium Ass'n, 173 Ill. App. 3d 431, 122 Ill. Dec. 113, 526 N.E.2d 372 (2 Dist. 1988).

Basis of Order
Whether the temporary restraining order is with or without notice, it is based upon a summary showing of the necessity of the order to prevent immediate and irreparable injury. Jurco v. Stuart, 110 Ill. App. 3d 405, 66 Ill. Dec. 207, 442 N.E.2d 633 (1 Dist. 1982).

Bond Requirement
The requirement of bond for interlocutory relief is designed to protect defendants by underwriting their losses in the event the interlocutory injunction is dissolved and damages are assess against the plaintiff; courts should only issue preliminary injunctions, or temporary restraining orders, without bond with great caution. Hill v. Village of Pawnee, 16 Ill. App. 3d 208, 305 N.E.2d 740 (4 Dist. 1973).

Burden of Proof

—Petitioner
A party seeking an injunction must establish that it has a clear right which ought to be protected, that it is likely to succeed on the merits, that there is no adequate legal remedy, and that irreparable harm will occur if the injunction is not granted. Millard Maintenance Serv. Co. v. Bernero, 207 Ill. App. 3d 736, 152 Ill. Dec. 692, 566 N.E.2d 379 (1 Dist. 1990).

A party seeking a temporary restraining order need only show that he raises a fair question regarding the existence of his right and that the court should preserve the status quo until the case can be decided on the merits. Stanton v. City of Chicago, 177 Ill. App. 3d 519, 126 Ill. Dec. 779, 532 N.E.2d 464 (1 Dist. 1988).

To obtain a preliminary injunction under former ch. 69, para. 3-1 (see now this section), plaintiff must establish that (1) it possesses a protected right; (2) there will be irreparable injury if the injunctive relief is not granted; (3) the remedy at law is inadequate; and (4) there is a likelihood that plaintiff will succeed on the merits. Allstate Amusement Co. of Ill., Inc. v. Pasinato, 96 Ill. App. 3d 306, 51 Ill. Dec. 866, 421 N.E.2d 374 (1 Dist. 1981).

A preliminary injunction is an extraordinary remedy, and, thus, to warrant its issuance, a party must clearly show a need to preserve the status quo in that he will be susceptible to irreparable damage if the injunction does not issue, and that there is a probability of ultimate success on the merits of his claim. Spunar v. Clark Oil & Ref. Corp., 53 Ill. App. 3d 477, 11 Ill. Dec. 382, 368 N.E.2d 990 (1 Dist. 1977).

Complaint

—Requirements
A well-pleaded complaint for injunctive relief must contain on its face a clear right to relief and allege facts which establish the right to such relief in a positive, certain and precise manner. Nameoki Tp. v. Von Dee Cruse, 155 Ill. App. 3d 889, 108 Ill. Dec. 503, 508 N.E.2d 1080 (5 Dist. 1987).

A temporary injunction cannot be predicated solely upon the pleadings where the material factual issues are controverted and the answer raises a complete defense. Lipkin v. Burnstine, 18 Ill. App. 2d 509, 152 N.E.2d 745 (1 Dist. 1958).

—Sufficiency Not Shown
Complaint and affidavit which merely alleged that state aid and

Complaint (Cont'd)

—Sufficiency Not Shown (Cont'd)
student instructional time was being lost, that students were being demoralized by actions of defendants, and that pickets were hindering construction of a new school building did not allege facts sufficient to demonstrate immediate irreparable injury to plaintiff prior to the giving of notice to defendants. Board of Educ. v. Parlor, 81 Ill. App. 3d 667, 37 Ill. Dec. 498, 402 N.E.2d 388 (5 Dist. 1980), aff'd, 85 Ill. 2d 397, 54 Ill. Dec. 249, 424 N.E.2d 1152 (1981).

Where the motion for a temporary restraining order (TRO), was totally silent as to any specific facts indicating that immediate and irreparable injury would result before notice could be given to defendants, and the court's order granting the TRO did not define the injury or state why it was irreparable or why the order was granted without notice, the TRO should have been vacated. Bettendorf-Stanford Bakery Equip. Co. v. International Union of United Auto., Aerospace & Agric. Implement Workers, 49 Ill. App. 3d 20, 6 Ill. Dec. 920, 363 N.E.2d 867 (5 Dist. 1977).

Where defendants failed to attack the sufficiency of the complaint to justify the issuance without notice defendant could not attack the complaint on appeal from a finding of contempt. Board of Educ. of Kankakee Sch. v. Kankakee Fed'n of Teachers Local No. 886, 46 Ill. 2d 439, 264 N.E.2d 18 (1970).

A complaint which fails to distinguish between matters which were stated upon complaint's own knowledge and those which were stated on information and belief is defective and an injunction issued pursuant thereto is void. Christian Hosp. v. People ex rel. Murphy, 223 Ill. 244, 79 N.E. 72 (1906).

—Sufficiency Shown
Where wife's complaint demonstrated that injunctive relief was necessary to prevent loss of entire fund, wife alleged facts which indicated the inadequacy of any legal remedy available to her; thus, her motion was not defective in this regard. In re Grauer, 133 Ill. App. 3d 1019, 88 Ill. Dec. 962, 479 N.E.2d 982 (1 Dist. 1985).

Where wife properly maintained her right to claim the income from husband's legal practice as part of her marital property settlement, wife's motion did demonstrate an ascertainable and legally protectible right. In re Grauer, 133 Ill. App. 3d 1019, 88 Ill. Dec. 962, 479 N.E.2d 982 (1 Dist. 1985).

The numerous allegations in plaintiff's verified complaint seeking a temporary restraining order concerning enforcement of the city's "Winter Gas Termination and Reconnection Ordinance," were sufficient to show irreparable harm to plaintiff absent the issuance of a temporary restraining order. Peoples Gas Light & Coke Co. v. City of Chicago, 117 Ill. App. 3d 353, 72 Ill. Dec. 865, 453 N.E.2d 740 (1 Dist. 1983).

The verified complaint with accompanying affidavits set out sufficient facts to invoke the jurisdiction of the court over the subject matter and thereby warranted the issuance of the temporary restraining order without notice and hearing. County of Lake v. Spare Things, 27 Ill. App. 3d 179, 326 N.E.2d 186 (2 Dist. 1975).

Compliance

—Shown
Where court's injunction order it stated the reasons for the entry of the injunction, and it specified the acts to be enjoined, the order clearly met the requirements of this section. Tie Sys. v. Telecom Midwest, Inc., 203 Ill. App. 3d 142, 148 Ill. Dec. 483, 560 N.E.2d 1080 (1 Dist. 1990).

Construction

—With Supreme Court Rule 307
All matters pertaining to TROs should comport with the intent and purpose of Rule 307(d), Supreme Court Rules, which is to provide a process for a quick review of the granting or denial of a TRO. Harper v. Missouri Pac. R.R., 264 Ill. App. 3d 238, 201 Ill. Dec. 760, 636 N.E.2d 1192 (5 Dist.), appeal denied, 157 Ill. 2d 500, 205 Ill. Dec. 162, 642 N.E.2d 1279 (1994).

Contempt

—In General
Where a court of equity issues an injunction, with jurisdiction of the subject matter and the persons and upon pleadings properly invoking its action, the injunction must be obeyed however erroneous the action of the court may be, until it is reversed for error by orderly review, either by the court itself or a higher court; disobedience of such an injunction is contempt of the lawful authority of the court, and punishable as such. Board of Educ. of Kankakee Sch. v. Kankakee Fed'n of Teachers Local No. 886, 46 Ill. 2d 439, 264 N.E.2d 18 (1970).

The circuit court had the broad equitable jurisdiction to enter an injunction order; that being so, the defendant had no alternative, but to obey said order until it was stayed by the appellate court; since there was ample evidence in the record that the defendant violated the injunction, it was proper for the court to use its contempt powers. East Side Health Dist. v Village of Caseyville, 38 Ill. App. 2d 438, 187 N.E.2d 534 (4 Dist. 1963).

—Notice
Actual notice, by personal service of the order or otherwise, is all that is required to obtain personal jurisdiction over the defendant to hold him in contempt for violating a temporary restraining order. County of Lake v. Spare Things, 27 Ill. App. 3d 179, 326 N.E.2d 186 (2 Dist. 1975).

Damages
In all cases where an injunction is dissolved by any court in this state, the court, before final disposition of the suit and upon receiving written suggestions by the party claiming damages, shall hear evidence and assess such damages as the nature of the case may require; however, a court cannot dissolve something that does not exist if the controversy becomes moot. Buckingham Corp. v. Vesolowski, 17 Ill. App. 3d 58, 307 N.E.2d 703 (1 Dist. 1974).

De Facto Attachment

—Invalid
A motion for a preliminary injunction which does not specify one of the enumerated reasons in 735 ILCS 5/4-101 for issuing an attachment, but which is a de facto attachment, is invalid. Carriage Way Apts. v. Pojman, 172 Ill. App. 3d 827, 122 Ill. Dec. 717, 527 N.E.2d 89 (2 Dist. 1988).

Delay of Hearing

—Improper
A hearing on a preliminary injunction that was delayed for more than a short period of time, or a hearing scheduled for an unspecified date in the not immediately foreseeable future, did not comport with this section. Jurco v. Stuart, 110 Ill. App. 3d 405, 66 Ill. Dec. 207, 442 N.E.2d 633 (1 Dist. 1982).

—Irreparable Damage
Issuance of an ex parte temporary restraining order is permissible only if the delay caused by notice and a hearing will irreparably damage the applicant. Board of Trustees v. Cook County College Teachers Union Local 1600, 42 Ill. App. 3d 1056, 1 Ill. Dec. 807, 356 N.E.2d 1089 (1 Dist. 1976).

Discontinued Actions

—Injunctions Unnecessary
A court of equity will not grant an injunction to prevent in the future that which in good faith has been discontinued before the commencement of the action in the absence of evidence that the offense is likely to be repeated in the future. Eads Coal Co. v. UMW of Am., 27 Ill. App. 3d 692, 327 N.E.2d 115 (5 Dist. 1975).

Discretion of Court

—In General
The trial court is vested with the discretion to grant or deny injunctive relief, while the role of the reviewing court is to determine whether the trial court's findings are contrary to the manifest weight of the evidence; the reviewing court will not set aside an injunction unless defendant can show that the trial court abused its discretion and ruled against the manifest weight of the evidence. Millard Maintenance Serv. Co. v. Bernero, 207 Ill. App. 3d 736, 152 Ill. Dec. 692, 566 N.E.2d 379 (1 Dist. 1990).

While ordinarily the continuance or dissolution of a temporary injunction rests in the discretion of the court, and the court is vested with great discretion in deciding such matters, the court

Discretion of Court (Cont'd)

—In General (Cont'd)

must properly apply equitable rules and fairly weigh the facts in deciding whether the plaintiff is entitled to the extraordinary relief of an injunction. Eads Coal Co. v. UMW of Am., 27 Ill. App. 3d 692, 327 N.E.2d 115 (5 Dist. 1975).

—Abuse of Discretion Shown

Physician failed to raise a fair question about right to relief from an order summarily suspending hospital privileges, so that the trial court abused its discretion in issuing a temporary restraining order against the suspension; the hospital board, through the chief executive officer, had inherent power to act in an emergency to protect the quality of patient care, and, furthermore, a provision in the hospital bylaws requiring summary suspensions to be based on medical staff recommendations was satisfied in that the recommendations had arisen out of a peer review, not a lay executive decision. Lo v. Provena Covenant Med. Ctr., 342 Ill. App. 3d 975, 277 Ill. Dec. 521, 796 N.E.2d 607, 2003 Ill. App. LEXIS 1186 (4 Dist. 2003), appeal denied, Ill. 2d , 283 Ill. Dec. 135, 807 N.E.2d 976 (2004); Lo v. Provena Covenant Med. Ctr., 342 Ill. App. 3d 975, 277 Ill. Dec. 521, 796 N.E.2d 607, 2003 Ill. App. LEXIS 1186 (4 Dist. 2003), appeal denied, 207 Ill. 2d 605, 283 Ill. Dec. 135, 807 N.E.2d 976 (2004).

Where prospective commercial lessee failed to establish that he would suffer irreparable harm if a preliminary injunction was not issued, and where owner and developer would potentially suffer irreparable harm if the preliminary injunction was issued, the trial court abused its discretion in issuing the preliminary injunction in favor of commercial lessee. Handy Andy Home Imp. Ctrs. v. American Nat'l Bank & Trust Co., 177 Ill. App. 3d 647, 126 Ill. Dec. 852, 532 N.E.2d 537 (2 Dist. 1988).

Where commercial lessee would suffer irreparable harm if a preliminary injunction was not issued, and where it was extremely difficult to measure the lost revenues that commercial lessee would suffer as a result of the opening of a store, and where owner and developer would not suffer any irreparable harm as a result of a preliminary injunction in favor of commercial lessee and where commercial lessee was likely to succeed on the merits of a claim against owner and developer; the trial court abused its discretion in denying the preliminary injunction in favor of commercial lessee. Handy Andy Home Imp. Ctrs. v. American Nat'l Bank & Trust Co., 177 Ill. App. 3d 647, 126 Ill. Dec. 852, 532 N.E.2d 537 (2 Dist. 1988).

The court abused its discretion in granting the plaintiff's motion for a temporary restraining order when the plaintiff failed to show a likelihood of success on the merits and abused its discretion in extending the temporary restraining order for a period of 98 days. Abulhafedh v. Secretary of State, 161 Ill. App. 3d 413, 112 Ill. Dec. 900, 514 N.E.2d 563 (2 Dist. 1987).

Entry of a temporary restraining order was an abuse of discretion where the verified petitions failed to allege specific facts that immediate and irreparable injury, loss, or damage would result to the applicant before notice could be served and a hearing had thereon. In re Schmidt, 118 Ill. App. 3d 467, 74 Ill. Dec. 93, 455 N.E.2d 123 (1 Dist. 1983).

—Scope of Authority

Trial judge, on a petition for a preliminary injunction heard two days after the complaint was filed, may not issue a permanent injunction and then refuse to hold a hearing on the merits of the case. Kengott v. County of Lake, 42 Ill. App. 3d 621, 1 Ill. Dec. 248, 356 N.E.2d 374 (2 Dist. 1976).

On appeal, the sole question presented is whether the trial court abused its discretion in denying the plaintiff temporary injunctive relief, and unless there has been such abuse of discretion, the order of the trial court will not be disturbed. Rutledge v. St. Vincent Mem. Hosp., 67 Ill. App. 2d 156, 214 N.E.2d 131 (5 Dist. 1966).

Disobeying Order

—Not Permitted

The fact that a restraining order either interferes with a right constitutionally guaranteed or is so vague and overbroad that it may do so does not of itself permit the defendant to disobey the order. Cooper v. Rockford Newspapers, Inc., 50 Ill. App. 3d 250, 8 Ill. Dec. 508, 365 N.E.2d 746 (2 Dist. 1977).

Dissolution of Order

—Effect

The dismissal of a complaint for a permanent injunction, whether by a trial court or by a reviewing court upon appeal, does not constitute an adjudication that the issuance of a preliminary injunction was wrongful. Meyer v. Marshall, 62 Ill. 2d 435, 343 N.E.2d 479 (1976).

—Factors

An injunction may be dissolved as to its prospective effect where a court finds that equity no longer justified its continuance, but the party seeking dissolution must make the necessary showing that he is entitled to such relief. Eads Coal Co. v. UMW of Am., 27 Ill. App. 3d 692, 327 N.E.2d 115 (5 Dist. 1975).

—Held Improper

General statements that plaintiffs "are not able to furnish bond for the injunction prayed for herein, and if notice of their application for injunction were required to be given they would be unduly prejudiced and great and irreparable harm and injury will result to them" were mere conclusions and did not justify failure to give notice or to give proper bond, therefore it was error not to dissolve the temporary injunction. Clayton v. Hubbard, 33 Ill. App. 2d 439, 179 N.E.2d 845 (4 Dist. 1962).

Duration of Order

—Fairness

To allow a temporary restraining order of unlimited duration is to have a preliminary injunction without giving the one party a fair opportunity to oppose the application and to show, if he can, why an injunction should not issue. Jurco v. Stuart, 110 Ill. App. 3d 405, 66 Ill. Dec. 207, 442 N.E.2d 633 (1 Dist. 1982).

—Unlimited Duration

To allow a temporary restraining order of unlimited duration is to have a preliminary injunction without giving the one party a fair opportunity to oppose the application and to show, if he can, why an injunction should not issue. Jurco v. Stuart, 110 Ill. App. 3d 405, 66 Ill. Dec. 207, 442 N.E.2d 633 (1 Dist. 1982).

Error in Issuance

The rule is well established that when a court of equity issues an injunction with jurisdiction over the subject matter and the parties, such an injunction, however erroneous, must be obeyed until it is set aside. Board of Trustees v. Cook County College Teachers Union Local 1600, 42 Ill. App. 3d 1056, 1 Ill. Dec. 807, 356 N.E.2d 1089 (1 Dist. 1976).

Evidentiary Hearing

—When Required

An evidentiary hearing on an application for a preliminary injunction is normally required where a verified answer has been filed denying material allegations in the complaint. Peoples Gas Light & Coke Co. v. City of Chicago, 117 Ill. App. 3d 353, 72 Ill. Dec. 865, 453 N.E.2d 740 (1 Dist. 1983).

Ex Parte Hearing

—Illustrative Cases

Where the judge and the plaintiff, with knowledge of the fact the counsel was on his way to the courtroom, proceeded with the entry of a temporary restraining order without bothering to wait for him, the temporary restraining order was in effect an ex parte order. Board of Trustees v. Cook County College Teachers Union Local 1600, 42 Ill. App. 3d 1056, 1 Ill. Dec. 807, 356 N.E.2d 1089 (1 Dist. 1976).

—Justification

In determining whether on ex parte hearing was justified, the critical inquiry is whether, during the period it takes to give notice, the opponent will take such measures as to destroy the substance of the litigation or otherwise obstruct the court from dealing effectively with the issues, and whether proper notice might have averted litigation by immediately testing the validity of injunctive relief. Hirschauer v. Chicago Sun-Times, 192 Ill. App. 3d 193, 139 Ill. Dec. 245, 548 N.E.2d 630 (1 Dist. 1989).

Exceptional Remedy

—In General

A temporary restraining order is a drastic, emergency remedy which may issue only in exceptional circumstances and for a brief duration. Jurco v. Stuart, 110 Ill. App. 3d 405, 66 Ill. Dec. 207, 442 N.E.2d 633 (1 Dist. 1982).

Extensions

—Effect

A temporary restraining order that is extended indefinitely still maintains its status as a temporary restraining order until the requirements of the court have been satisfied. Diamond Sav. & Loan Co. v. Royal Glen Condominium Ass'n, 173 Ill. App. 3d 431, 122 Ill. Dec. 113, 526 N.E.2d 372 (2 Dist. 1988).

Where defendant's motion to dissolve the temporary restraining order alleged that a carbon monoxide leak had been remedied, but the defendant presented no other basis to support his motion, the restraining order should have been extended until the court heard evidence to determine whether the defendant's building was still dangerous to the health and safety of its tenants. City of Chicago v. Westphalen, 93 Ill. App. 3d 1110, 49 Ill. Dec. 419, 418 N.E.2d 63 (1 Dist. 1981), cert. denied and appeal dismissed, 455 U.S. 996, 102 S. Ct. 1625, 71 L. Ed. 2d 858 (1982).

—Notice

Where the initial issuance of the temporary restraining order was entered ex parte, but the defendant had notice with respect to the order extending the temporary restraining order, the 10 day time limit was not applicable. Abulhafedh v. Secretary of State, 161 Ill. App. 3d 413, 112 Ill. Dec. 900, 514 N.E.2d 563 (2 Dist. 1987).

—Repeated Extensions

An order, although labeled as a temporary restraining order, had the effect of a preliminary injunction where the court repeatedly extended the order for a total of 98 days and failed to set a date for a hearing so that the defendant could present evidence and legal argument. Abulhafedh v. Secretary of State, 161 Ill. App. 3d 413, 112 Ill. Dec. 900, 514 N.E.2d 563 (2 Dist. 1987).

Extent of Injunction

—In General

The restraint imposed by an injunction should not be more extensive than is reasonably required to protect the interests of the party in whose favor it is granted, and should not be so broad as to prevent defendant from exercising his rights. Streif v. Bovinette, 88 Ill. App. 3d 1079, 44 Ill. Dec. 372, 411 N.E.2d 341 (5 Dist. 1980).

Factors

—In General

For a preliminary injunction to be granted, movant must establish a protectable interest, a likelihood of success on the merits, an irreparable injury in the absence of injunctive relief, no adequate remedy at law, and the grant of the temporary relief should outweigh any possible injury which the defendant might suffer by its issuance. Wilson v. Wilson, 217 Ill. App. 3d 844, 160 Ill. Dec. 752, 577 N.E.2d 1323 (1 Dist. 1991).

Failure to Obtain Preliminary Injunction

—Effect

Failure to subsequently obtain a preliminary injunction does not retroactively invalidate a temporary restraining order. In re Betts, 200 Ill. App. 3d 26, 146 Ill. Dec. 441, 558 N.E.2d 404 (4 Dist. 1990), appeal denied, 136 Ill. 2d 541, 153 Ill. Dec. 370, 567 N.E.2d 328 (1991).

Fair Question Not Raised

—Order Wrongfully Issued

Although plaintiff distributor was not required to conclusively establish its right to relief before a temporary restraining order would properly issue, the pleadings did not raise even a "fair question" that an alleged oral contract, if it existed at all, was breached by the defendants' newspaper's termination notice; therefore, the temporary restraining order was wrongfully issued. Hirschauer v. Chicago Sun-Times, 192 Ill. App. 3d 193, 139 Ill. Dec. 245, 548 N.E.2d 630 (1 Dist. 1989).

Granting Injunction

—Care Required

As an extraordinary remedy, a preliminary injunction should be granted only pursuant to the utmost care. Spunar v. Clark Oil & Ref. Corp., 53 Ill. App. 3d 477, 11 Ill. Dec. 382, 368 N.E.2d 990 (1 Dist. 1977).

Hearing

—Required

While a temporary restraining order may be in effect beyond 10 days, a hearing must be set within a short time thereafter so as to prevent the potential significant consequences of allowing a summary proceeding to exist for more than a short period of time. Abulhafedh v. Secretary of State, 161 Ill. App. 3d 413, 112 Ill. Dec. 900, 514 N.E.2d 563 (2 Dist. 1987).

—Sufficient

Where husband was permitted to file a memorandum in opposition to the preliminary injunction as well as an itemized statement indicating his business and personal financial needs and was not denied his opportunity to speak at the hearing, the trial court granted him a full and adequate hearing prior to granting the preliminary injunction. In re Grauer, 133 Ill. App. 3d 1019, 88 Ill. Dec. 962, 479 N.E.2d 982 (1 Dist. 1985).

—Time of Hearing

Under former Ill.Rev.Stat., ch. 69, para. 3-1 (see now this section), a temporary restraining order with notice which was to exist beyond a 10 day period was a proper order where a hearing on the preliminary injunction would be scheduled immediately following the expiration of the 10 day order. Jurco v. Stuart, 110 Ill. App. 3d 405, 66 Ill. Dec. 207, 442 N.E.2d 633 (1 Dist. 1982).

Immediate and Irreparable Harm

—Allegations Required

The complaint did not contain sufficient factual allegations of immediate and irreparable harm to alleviate the need for notice. G&J Parking Co. v. City of Chicago, 168 Ill. App. 3d 382, 119 Ill. Dec. 112, 522 N.E.2d 774 (1 Dist. 1988).

Improper Ex Parte Issuance

—Notice Not Provided

Where nothing in the record indicated why a minimum of notice, such as a telephone call, could not have been provided to the defendant, or how plaintiff would have been irreparably harmed before notice could have been giving, and where notice to the defendant would not have jeopardized plaintiff's claim for injunctive relief, ex parte issuance of a temporary restraining order was wrongful. Hirschauer v. Chicago Sun-Times, 192 Ill. App. 3d 193, 139 Ill. Dec. 245, 548 N.E.2d 630 (1 Dist. 1989).

Improperly Broad and Imprecise Language

—Stricken

The portion of the first clause of the order which enjoined the defendant from "annoying or harassing the plaintiff in any manner as described in plaintiff's complaint" was stricken since the language used was improperly broad and imprecise. Streif v. Bovinette, 88 Ill. App. 3d 1079, 44 Ill. Dec. 372, 411 N.E.2d 341 (5 Dist. 1980).

Injunction Improperly Denied

The trial court erred in refusing to issue a mandatory injunction requiring the removal of a causeway and reconstruction of the bridge which had been in existence when plaintiff purchased an island for recreational purposes, where in destroying the bridge and constructing a causeway, defendants had materially altered the character of the easement and increased the burden on the servient tenement so that plaintiffs were unable to use and enjoy that portion of the lake or lakebed which was previously accessible under the bridge, but which now was covered by the causeway. Triplett v. Beuckman, 40 Ill. App. 3d 379, 352 N.E.2d 458 (5 Dist. 1976).

Injunction Improperly Denied (Cont'd)

A temporary restraining order or an extension of an existing temporary restraining order would have served the court's purposes, where the entry of such an order would have permitted the court to hear arguments on defendants' motion to dismiss and at that time to reconsider, if necessary, the issuance of a preliminary injunction. Seagram Distillers Co. v. Foremost Sales Promotions, Inc., 13 Ill. App. 3d 166, 300 N.E.2d 490 (1 Dist. 1973).

Pursuant to former Ill.Rev.Stat., ch. 69, para. 3-1 (see now this section) where at the time the state sought judicial enforcement of the Pollution Control Board's order directing defendant to cease operations until it could install effective pollution abatement equipment, by requesting a temporary restraining order, where the appellate court had not granted defendant a stay, it was an abuse of discretion for the trial court to deny plaintiff's motion for a temporary restraining order. People ex rel. Pollution Control Bd. v. Lloyd A. Fry Roofing Co., 4 Ill. App. 3d 675, 281 N.E.2d 757 (1 Dist. 1972).

Injunction Improperly Granted

Where plaintiff failed to show that it possessed a trade secret subject to misappropriation by defendants, the trial court erred in enjoining them from producing similar devices. Palin Mfg. Co. v. Water Tech., Inc., 103 Ill. App. 3d 926, 59 Ill. Dec. 553, 431 N.E.2d 1310 (1 Dist. 1982).

Where the need for the preliminary injunction entered was unclear, particularly in light of fact that plaintiff had not even requested it until the court invited her to do so, and the entry of the preliminary injunction served to alter the status quo by requiring defendant to close its stations or change its display practices, the preliminary injunction was erroneously granted. Spunar v. Clark Oil & Ref. Corp., 53 Ill. App. 3d 477, 11 Ill. Dec. 382, 368 N.E.2d 990 (1 Dist. 1977).

Injunction Properly Denied

Where the pleadings failed to show either that plaintiffs had no adequate alternative remedies or that injunctive relief was necessary to avoid irreparable harm, trial court's denial of injunctive relief, without an evidentiary hearing, was not an abuse of discretion. Allstate Amusement Co. of Ill., Inc. v. Pasinato, 96 Ill. App. 3d 306, 51 Ill. Dec. 866, 421 N.E.2d 374 (1 Dist. 1981).

Although the loss of staff privileges had caused plaintiff physician inconvenience, and probably, loss of income, this fact, of itself, did not require that the trial court enjoin the defendant hospital from refusing to reappoint plaintiff to the staff of the defendant hospital, in light of the fact that the hospital's by-laws provided that "final responsibility" for such action rested with the Governing Board, and the issuance of a temporary injunction would have, in effect, determined for the Governing Board the manner in which that responsibility was to be discharged. Rutledge v. St. Vincent Mem. Hosp., 67 Ill. App. 2d 156, 214 N.E.2d 131 (5 Dist. 1966).

Where defendants filed no answer, the propriety of the order denying the injunction sought by plaintiffs was to be determined from the amended complaint, without consideration of what purported to be averments of fact in defendants' motion to strike and dismiss, and the well pleaded allegations of fact in the amended complaint were required to be taken as true. Rutledge v. St. Vincent Mem. Hosp., 67 Ill. App. 2d 156, 214 N.E.2d 131 (5 Dist. 1966).

Injunction Properly Granted

Injunctions were properly ordered where real property used as security for a mortgage loan was part of the subject matter of the litigation, to maintain the status quo during pendency of the litigation to prevent immediate and irreparable injury, loss or damage. All Seasons Excavating Co. v. Bluthardt, 216 Ill. App. 3d 504, 159 Ill. Dec. 703, 576 N.E.2d 372 (1 Dist. 1991).

Entry of preliminary injunction against the disinterment of defendants' father on grounds that there was no strong and convincing evidence to show that there was a reason to disinter the body was upheld. Hough v. Weber, 202 Ill. App. 3d 674, 147 Ill. Dec. 857, 560 N.E.2d 5 (2 Dist. 1990).

Where plaintiff alleged that to prevent the closing of the district's community colleges, it was urgent that a sum claimed for reimbursement to the community college board be deposited with the clerk of the circuit court before September 30, 1977, the facts supported finding that the preliminary mandatory injunction prevented grave injury to plaintiff, imposed no undue hardship on defendants and was therefore properly within the trial court's discretion. Board of Trustees v. Bakalis, 64 Ill. App. 3d 967, 21 Ill. Dec. 732, 382 N.E.2d 26 (1 Dist. 1978).

Injunction Stricken

—Prohibitions Overbroad

To the extent an injunction was overbroad, portions of it would be vacated, though the balance of the injunction was affirmed. Binder Plumbing & Heating, Inc. v. Plumbers & Pipefitters Local Union 99, 253 Ill. App. 3d 972, 192 Ill. Dec. 779, 625 N.E.2d 934 (4 Dist. 1993).

It was necessary to strike an injunction which stated that defendant could not interfere in any way with plaintiffs' use and enjoyment of their property rights and business operations; these prohibitions are couched in the most general and expansive terms possible, without defining or particularizing the rights to be preserved or the mode in which they are to be prevented from being infringed. Streif v. Bovinette, 88 Ill. App. 3d 1079, 44 Ill. Dec. 372, 411 N.E.2d 341 (5 Dist. 1980).

Injunction Sufficiently Precise

—Illustrative Cases

The trial court's order was sufficiently precise to meet the standard of this section where the court's oral injunction order, from which the written order was drafted, clearly afforded trade secret protection only to plaintiff's schematics of its analog circuitry and of the circuitry which interfaces its analog circuitry to its digital circuitry and the order in no way purported to enjoin defendants from purchasing or using standard electric components. Televation Telecommunication Sys. v. Saindon, 169 Ill. App. 3d 8, 119 Ill. Dec. 500, 522 N.E.2d 1359 (2 Dist. 1988).

Injunction Without Notice

—Extreme Urgency Required

The granting of injunctive relief without notice is an extraordinary remedy and is appropriate only under the most extreme and urgent circumstances. Board of Educ. v. Parlor, 81 Ill. App. 3d 667, 37 Ill. Dec. 498, 402 N.E.2d 388 (5 Dist. 1980), aff'd, 85 Ill. 2d 397, 54 Ill. Dec. 249, 424 N.E.2d 1152 (1981).

—No Presumption of Validity

The granting of injunctive relief without notice is not favored because it is a drastic remedy appropriate only under the most extreme circumstances; therefore, although a presumption of validity ordinarily attaches to an order of a court, no such presumption is indulged in favor of injunctive relief granted in absence of notice. Geesbreght v. Geesbreght, 63 Ill. App. 3d 37, 19 Ill. Dec. 866, 379 N.E.2d 738 (1 Dist. 1978).

Injunctions

—In General

The practical effect of a temporary restraining order issued with notice is the same as a preliminary injunction issued with notice. A temporary restraining order issued and a preliminary injunction issued with notice, neither of limited duration, are the same type of relief and both require the showing of the likelihood of ultimate success on the merits. Kaplan v. Kaplan, 98 Ill. App. 3d 136, 53 Ill. Dec. 449, 423 N.E.2d 1253 (1 Dist. 1981).

—Defined

The word "injunction," as used in Rule 307, Supreme Court Rules, does not cover a temporary restraining order per this section. Kirchenberg v. Chicago Transit Auth., 13 Ill. App. 3d 184, 300 N.E.2d 482 (1 Dist. 1973).

—Guidelines to Form

The guidelines as to the form of an injunction order are not so inflexible as to preclude variation therefrom. Somerset Importers, Ltd. v. Gold Std. Liquors, Inc., 18 Ill. App. 3d 39, 309 N.E.2d 286 (1 Dist. 1974).

—Specific Performance

An action for injunction, seeking to restrain a breach of contract, being in substance a suit for specific performance, is governed by rules applicable to that remedy and such equitable enforcement of agreements will not be granted where the agreement is vague,

Injunctions (Cont'd)

—Specific Performance (Cont'd)
indefinite and uncertain. Tucker v. Carter Oil Co., 315 Ill.App. 264, 43 N.E.2d 99 (4 Dist. 1942).

—Specificity

Injunction order violated the requirements of this section by referring to another document instead of specifying in express terms what actions are to be enjoined; the proper remedy was to remand the order to the trial court with instructions to modify the order in compliance with the statutory requirements. Howard Johnson & Co. v. Feinstein, 241 Ill. App. 3d 828, 182 Ill. Dec. 396, 609 N.E.2d 930 (1 Dist. 1993).

Injunction order, by which liquor distributor sought to enjoin defendants from selling distributive products at prices below those stipulated in accordance with the Fair Trade Act, was sufficiently specific in its terms and described in reasonable detail the acts sought to be restrained within the requirements of former Ill.Rev.Stat., ch. 69, para. 3-1, (see now this section). Somerset Importers, Ltd. v. Gold Std. Liquors, Inc., 18 Ill. App. 3d 39, 309 N.E.2d 286 (1 Dist. 1974).

Irreparable Injury

—In General

An irreparable injury is one which cannot be adequately compensated in damages or be measured by any certain pecuniary standard. Diamond Sav. & Loan Co. v. Royal Glen Condominium Ass'n, 173 Ill. App. 3d 431, 122 Ill. Dec. 113, 526 N.E.2d 372 (2 Dist. 1988).

Issuance of Injunction

—In General

Preliminary injunctions or temporary restraining orders without notice and without bond, to say the least, should issue only under the most grave circumstances, and such interlocutory relief falls within a class separate and apart from interlocutory relief with notice and bond. Hill v. Village of Pawnee, 16 Ill. App. 3d 208, 305 N.E.2d 740 (4 Dist. 1973).

—Discretion of Court

The issuance of a preliminary injunction is within the sound discretion of the trial court upon a prima facie demonstration of necessity and a court of review will not set aside the injunction order unless there is a manifest abuse of discretion or an error of law. K.F.K. Corp. v. American Continental Homes, Inc., 31 Ill. App. 3d 1017, 335 N.E.2d 156 (2 Dist. 1975).

The granting of a temporary injunction is in the sound discretion of the trial court, and the appellate court will not interfere with the exercise of discretion unless the chancellor has patently violated some established rule of law or principle of equity. Moehling v. N. & J. Enters., Ltd., 15 Ill. App. 3d 987, 305 N.E.2d 183 (1 Dist. 1973).

The remedies of preliminary injunction and temporary restraining order are extraordinary in nature and should be granted only after serious consideration and due circumspection; however, the granting or denial of such relief rests in the sound discretion of the trial court. Hill v. Village of Pawnee, 16 Ill. App. 3d 208, 305 N.E.2d 740 (4 Dist. 1973).

Whether a petition for a temporary injunction should be granted or denied, rests largely in the discretion of the trial court. Rutledge v. St. Vincent Mem. Hosp., 67 Ill. App. 2d 156, 214 N.E.2d 131 (5 Dist. 1966).

—Facts Required

A mere statement of a conclusion substantially in the words of the statute is insufficient; facts upon which the conclusion may be inferred is a prerequisite before the injunction may issue without notice. Clayton v. Hubbard, 33 Ill. App. 2d 439, 179 N.E.2d 845 (4 Dist. 1962).

—Held Improper

Where the motion submitted by plaintiff indicated that he only sought monies allegedly due and owing him from defendants pursuant to an employment agreement, then plaintiff did not make a sufficient showing to entitle him to a temporary injunctive relief. Kaplan v. Kaplan, 98 Ill. App. 3d 136, 53 Ill. Dec. 449, 423 N.E.2d 1253 (1 Dist. 1981).

Where the injury plaintiff complained of, which was a breach of the employment contract, was capable of being measured and corrected by an award of money damages alone, then plaintiff was not entitled to injunctive relief. Kaplan v. Kaplan, 98 Ill. App. 3d 136, 53 Ill. Dec. 449, 423 N.E.2d 1253 (1 Dist. 1981).

Where money damages is an adequate remedy, injunctive relief is not proper. Allstate Amusement Co. of Ill., Inc. v. Pasinato, 96 Ill. App. 3d 306, 51 Ill. Dec. 866, 421 N.E.2d 374 (1 Dist. 1981).

Where plaintiffs waited three months from time defendants notified them of their intentions not to vacate the plaintiffs' premises, to file a complaint, there was no showing of "great necessity" or "extreme urgency" so as to justify the issuance of a temporary injunction. Moehling v. N. & J. Enters., Ltd., 15 Ill. App. 3d 987, 305 N.E.2d 183 (1 Dist. 1973).

The record did not sufficiently show plaintiff's right to possession of devised premises to justify the drastic action taken by way of the mandatory feature of the court's injunction order. National Bank v. River Forest State Bank, 3 Ill. App. 3d 209, 278 N.E.2d 501 (1 Dist. 1971).

Injunction order which restrained the husband from entering his marital home which did not set forth the reason for its issuance and was not specific in its terms did not comply with former Ill.Rev.Stat., ch. 69, para. 3-1 (see now this section). Hoda v. Hoda, 122 Ill. App. 2d 283, 258 N.E.2d 386 (2 Dist. 1970).

Where no facts were presented to indicate than an emergency existed or that irreparable harm would result if an injunction did not issue, all of the material allegations contained in the complaint were controverted by the answer filed by the defendants, and the affirmative defense filed by defendants alleged that the defendant would suffer irreparable harm if the injunction were to issue, the trial court, resolving the controversy upon the pleadings alone, erred in granting a temporary injunction because it was not the purpose of a temporary injunction to decide controverted facts or the merits of the case. Compton v. Paul K. Harding Realty Co., 87 Ill. App. 2d 219, 231 N.E.2d 267 (5 Dist. 1967).

Order for temporary injunction to prevent discontinuance of water services was improper where on the day complaint was filed, defendants restored water service pursuant to agreement made in open court to restore and continue the service unless due notice be given plaintiffs and the court and this agreement had been observed so that at the time of the injunctive order service had been furnished under the agreement for a period of six months. Peterson v. Domestic Util. Servs. Co., 33 Ill. App. 2d 374, 179 N.E.2d 444 (1 Dist. 1962).

Where the only basis alleged for termination of a partnership was the failure to account properly which was denied by defendant's sworn answer, and the chancellor in restraining defendant presumably anticipated the likelihood that plaintiff would prevail on the issue; but there was no allegation that plaintiff gave defendant the notice prescribed for termination and nothing in the pleadings to justify the anticipation of plaintiff's success, and the injunction granted plaintiff virtually the substantial remedies he sought, because defendant was restrained from writing bonds and was not limited to those written on plaintiff's security, which went beyond the rightful scope of the temporary injunctive remedy, and if the injunction had remained in effect the result would have been the deprivation of defendant of his means of livelihood, with the only apparent benefit to plaintiff, taking defendant's affirmative defense as true, coming from his own misconduct, the chancellor abused his discretion in granting the injunction. Perry v. Eson, 8 Ill. App. 2d 423, 132 N.E.2d 66 (1 Dist. 1956).

Where there was nothing to show, either in the bill of complaint or in the affidavit thereto attached, that the plaintiff would be unduly prejudiced if the injunction were not issued without notice, the injunction had to be reversed. Thulin v. National Ice & Fuel Corp., 293 Ill. App. 155, 11 N.E.2d 986 (1 Dist. 1937).

—Held Proper

City of Springfield (Illinois) had the power under 65 ILCS5/11-125-2 to prevent pollution of a lake it used for its public water system, and the appellate court directed the trial court to enjoin development of property that was part of a village unless the city approved the developers' subdivision plan. City of Springfield v. Hashman, 332 Ill. App. 3d 748, 266 Ill. Dec. 321, 774 N.E.2d 427, 2002 Ill. App. LEXIS 781 (4 Dist. 2002), appeal denied, 202 Ill. 2d 663, 272 Ill. Dec. 355, 787 N.E.2d 170 (2002).

Issuance of Injunction (Cont'd)

—Held Proper (Cont'd)

The totality of the prohibition was contained within the four corners of injunctive order; therefore, the defendants were clearly advised of the precise conduct enjoined and the injunction was valid under former Ill.Rev.Stat., ch. 69, para. 3-1 (see now this section). Buckingham Corp. v. Modern Liquors, Inc., 16 Ill. App. 3d 534, 306 N.E.2d 655 (1 Dist. 1973).

Defendants' refusal to preserve the substance of the controversy pending the court's determination, even preliminarily, of the issues could, in the court's discretion, have justified the issuance of a temporary restraining order under this section but not a preliminary injunction under Ill.Rev.Stat., ch. 110, para. 11-102 a preliminary injunction being more extensive relief than was required. Seagram Distillers Co. v. Foremost Sales Promotions, Inc., 13 Ill. App. 3d 166, 300 N.E.2d 490 (1 Dist. 1973).

Picketing, while a mode of communicating ideas, is not constitutionally protected speech and a temporary restraining order issued against unlawful picketing by a teachers' union was not a prior restraint violation of the First Amendment. Board of Educ. of Kankakee Sch. v. Kankakee Fed'n of Teachers Local No. 886, 46 Ill. 2d 439, 264 N.E.2d 18 (1970).

A temporary injunction was necessary to preserve the status quo and to prevent the defendants from proceeding to enlarge their building into two apartments, which might have weakened the structure, causing irreparable harm. Scholz v. Barbee, 344 Ill. App. 630, 101 N.E.2d 845 (2 Dist. 1951).

Under former similar provision concerning a motion was sufficient to warrant an injunction where the bill alleged that defendants threatened to remove a building which constituted a part of the mortgaged premises, and the removal of which would undoubtedly have diminished the value of such premises. Williams v. Chicago Exhibition Co., 188 Ill. 19, 58 N.E. 611 (1900).

—Insufficient Evidence

Where, if the injunction had not been granted, appellees would have run the risk of being prosecuted for operating their businesses without a license or if they closed then their investment, which was substantial, would have been destroyed and their customers would have been lost, those allegations did not authorize the issuance of the preliminary injunction without notice and certainly not without bond. Kessie v. Talcott, 305 Ill. App. 627, 27 N.E.2d 857 (2 Dist. 1940).

—Irreparable Harm

Because, absent injunctive relief, the union could continue to shut off access to work site, contractor would suffer irreparable harm without injunctive relief. Binder Plumbing & Heating, Inc. v. Plumbers & Pipefitters Local Union 99, 253 Ill. App. 3d 972, 192 Ill. Dec. 779, 625 N.E.2d 934 (4 Dist. 1993).

The application for a temporary injunction must allege that irreparable harm will result if the status quo is impaired. Compton v. Paul K. Harding Realty Co., 87 Ill. App. 2d 219, 231 N.E.2d 267 (5 Dist. 1967).

—Issues of Law vs. Fact

In determining the probability of ultimate success on the merits, before granting or denying a temporary injunction a distinction should be made between issues of law and issues of fact. Chicago Motor Coach Co. v. Budd, 346 Ill. App. 385, 105 N.E.2d 140 (1 Dist. 1952).

—Notice

The requirements for the issuance of temporary restraining orders without notice are substantially the same under both this section and 750 ILCS 5/101 et seq. Bashwiner v. Bashwiner, 126 Ill. App. 3d 365, 81 Ill. Dec. 359, 466 N.E.2d 1161 (1 Dist. 1984).

—Success on the Merits

The probability of ultimate success on the merits depends no only on the sufficiency of plaintiff's complaint but also on the defenses raised by the answer. Brooks v. La Salle Nat'l Bank, 11 Ill. App. 3d 791, 298 N.E.2d 262 (1 Dist. 1973).

The granting of a temporary injunction is not automatic; a showing must be made that there is a probability of ultimate success on the merits. Chicago Motor Coach Co. v. Budd, 346 Ill. App. 385, 105 N.E.2d 140 (1 Dist. 1952).

Issuance with Notice

—Likelihood of Success Required

A temporary restraining order issued with notice as well as a preliminary injunction issued with notice, neither of limited duration, are the same type of relief and require a showing of the likelihood of ultimate success on the merits of the case. Kable Printing Co. v. Mount Morris Bookbinders Union Local 65-B, 63 Ill. 2d 514, 349 N.E.2d 36 (1976).

Jurisdiction

—Effect of Appeal

Notice of appeal deprives a court of jurisdiction to allow amendments to modify pleadings, orders, or injunctions. Carriage Way Apts. v. Pojman, 172 Ill. App. 3d 827, 122 Ill. Dec. 717, 527 N.E.2d 89 (2 Dist. 1988).

—Personal Jurisdiction

Where defendant was timely and personally served with the writ of injunction, and the language of the writ explicitly set forth the acts sought to be restrained, there was sufficient compliance with former Ill.Rev.Stat., ch. 69, para. 3-1 (see now this section) to bind the defendant with the personal jurisdiction necessary for enforcement of the contempt order. County of Lake v. Spare Things, 27 Ill. App. 3d 179, 326 N.E.2d 186 (2 Dist. 1975).

—Petition Not Filed

The court lacked jurisdiction to issue the temporary restraining order and did not have jurisdiction to enter the contempt and modification orders where plaintiff did not file a verified petition or an affidavit or any documents requesting the issuance of a temporary restraining order. In re Kowalski, 186 Ill. App. 3d 269, 134 Ill. Dec. 176, 542 N.E.2d 176 (3 Dist. 1989).

—Prior Notice

Prior notice is not necessary for the court to obtain jurisdiction to issue a temporary restraining order. County of Lake v. Spare Things, 27 Ill. App. 3d 179, 326 N.E.2d 186 (2 Dist. 1975).

Knowledge

Evidence in contempt proceedings was ample to justify the conclusion that the respondent had actual knowledge of the injunction and its terms. People ex rel. Scott v. Master Barbers & Beauty Culturists Ass'n, 9 Ill. App. 3d 981, 293 N.E.2d 393 (1 Dist. 1973).

Lack of Specificity

—Shown

An injunction requiring several plaintiff's to deposit in escrow in one account or several accounts the aggregate sum of money without stating who was to contribute what amounts was invalid for lack of specificity. Carriage Way Apts. v. Pojman, 172 Ill. App. 3d 827, 122 Ill. Dec. 717, 527 N.E.2d 89 (2 Dist. 1988).

Legislative Intent

Had the legislature intended temporary restraining orders without notice to extend beyond 10 days, it could have expressly so provided. In re Pick, 119 Ill. App. 3d 1061, 75 Ill. Dec. 865, 458 N.E.2d 33 (2 Dist. 1983).

Level of Restraint

—Reasonable Protection

The restraint imposed by an injunction should not be more extensive than is reasonably required to protect the interests of the party in whose favor it is granted, and should not be so broad as to prevent defendant from exercising his rights. People ex rel. Traiteur v. Abbott, 27 Ill. App. 3d 277, 327 N.E.2d 130 (5 Dist. 1975).

Limitations

—Scope

Every temporary restraining order granted without notice shall expire by its terms in a period not to exceed ten days; however, since this section does not consider temporary restraining orders issued with notice, it does not apply to temporary restraining orders issued with notice and there is no such limitation. Lawter Int'l, Inc. v. Carroll, 107 Ill. App. 3d 938, 63 Ill. Dec. 659, 438 N.E.2d 590 (1 Dist. 1982).

Mandatory Temporary Injunction

—In General

The requirements are stringent for the issuance of a mandatory temporary injunction prior to final hearing, and is permissible only if the right of one party is clearly established and the infringement of that right by another is causing serious injury; this is particularly true if complete relief may be afforded after final hearing. National Bank v. River Forest State Bank, 3 Ill. App. 3d 209, 278 N.E.2d 501 (1 Dist. 1971).

—Inappropriate

Where complete relief may be afforded the complainant upon a final hearing, the plaintiffs are not entitled to a temporary injunction which is mandatory in nature. Moehling v. N. & J. Enters., Ltd., 15 Ill. App. 3d 987, 305 N.E.2d 183 (1 Dist. 1973).

—Judicial Discretion

A mandatory temporary injunction is not granted as a matter of right, but is a form of relief, extraordinary in nature, to be granted only in rare cases of great necessity or extreme urgency when sound judicial discretion requires the court to act. National Bank v. River Forest State Bank, 3 Ill. App. 3d 209, 278 N.E.2d 501 (1 Dist. 1971).

—Requirements

For a mandatory temporary injunction to issue prior to a final hearing, the right of one party must be clearly established and the infringement of that right by another must be causing serious injury, particularly if complete relief may be afforded after final hearing. Moehling v. N. & J. Enters., Ltd., 15 Ill. App. 3d 987, 305 N.E.2d 183 (1 Dist. 1973).

Merits in Doubt

—Relief Granted

Where wife's motion requested an order preserving the status quo between the parties and protecting property which would be lost or dissipated, injunctive relief could be granted even if the movant's ultimate success on the merits was in serious doubt. In re Grauer, 133 Ill. App. 3d 1019, 88 Ill. Dec. 962, 479 N.E.2d 982 (1 Dist. 1985).

Modification

—Jurisdiction

A trial court had jurisdiction to modify a preliminary injunction after notice of appeal from the order for that injunction had been filed where the modification implemented the appealed injunction. Sears, Roebuck & Co. v. Fair Emp. Practices Comm'n, 29 Ill. App. 3d 276, 330 N.E.2d 874 (4 Dist. 1975).

Motion

—Sufficient Facts Shown

Where wife's motion described husband's frequent attempts to hide or divert assets and the fact that he was, at that time, in arrears in support payments to wife, these facts alone provided a sufficient basis from which one could infer irreparable harm absent court protection. In re Grauer, 133 Ill. App. 3d 1019, 88 Ill. Dec. 962, 479 N.E.2d 982 (1 Dist. 1985).

Motion for Dissolution

—Damage and Harm Lacking

A motion to dissolve a temporary restraining order should be allowed where the record fails to show the irreparable damage and harm required by this section. Geesbreght v. Geesbreght, 63 Ill. App. 3d 37, 19 Ill. Dec. 866, 379 N.E.2d 738 (1 Dist. 1978).

Motion Properly Denied

—Illustrative Cases

The trial court did not abuse its discretion in denying plaintiff's motion for a temporary restraining order since the requirements that plaintiff be suffering irreparable harm and that no adequate remedy at law exist had not been met. Citizens Utils. Co. v. O'Connor, 116 Ill. App. 3d 369, 71 Ill. Dec. 792, 451 N.E.2d 946 (2 Dist. 1983).

Motion Properly Granted

Wife's motion for a temporary restraining order was presented and properly granted. In re Grauer, 133 Ill. App. 3d 1019, 88 Ill. Dec. 962, 479 N.E.2d 982 (1 Dist. 1985).

Multiple Interpretations

—Illustrative Cases

The injunction order was not so specific and clear as to be susceptible of only one interpretation where it enjoined the defendants from enforcing sections 9c and 18 of the Cigarette Tax Act (35 ILCS 130/9c and 35 ILCS 130/18) against individuals transporting cigarettes into Illinois. O'Leary v. Allphin, 64 Ill. 2d 500, 1 Ill. Dec. 363, 356 N.E.2d 551 (1976).

Nature of Relief

—Illustrative Cases

On balance, the order more closely resembled a preliminary injunction than a temporary restraining order in substance rather than from where the order stated that the matter came before the trial court on the petition for a temporary injunction and that telephonic notice was given to the defendants. Proulx ex rel. Proulx v. Illinois High Sch. Ass'n, 125 Ill. App. 3d 781, 81 Ill. Dec. 34, 466 N.E.2d 620 (4 Dist. 1984).

—Preliminary Injunction

Since notice was given and a hearing of legal argument was held prior to the grant of injunctive relief, the relief granted was a preliminary injunction. Spunar v. Clark Oil & Ref. Corp., 53 Ill. App. 3d 477, 11 Ill. Dec. 382, 368 N.E.2d 990 (1 Dist. 1977).

—Provisional

A preliminary injunction is merely provisional in nature and concludes no rights, its office being merely to preserve the status quo until final hearing on the merits, a preliminary injunction, therefore, is not proper where it tends to change the status quo of the parties rather than preserve it. Spunar v. Clark Oil & Ref. Corp., 53 Ill. App. 3d 477, 11 Ill. Dec. 382, 368 N.E.2d 990 (1 Dist. 1977).

Need

—Not Shown

Allegations of mere opinion, conclusion, or belief are not sufficient to show a need for injunctive relief. Allstate Amusement Co. of Ill., Inc. v. Pasinato, 96 Ill. App. 3d 306, 51 Ill. Dec. 866, 421 N.E.2d 374 (1 Dist. 1981).

No Answer

—Hearing Not Required

Where party filed no answer to a complaint for an injunction, an evidentiary hearing was not required. Carriage Way Apts. v. Pojman, 172 Ill. App. 3d 827, 122 Ill. Dec. 717, 527 N.E.2d 89 (2 Dist. 1988).

Non Specific Injunction

—Held Valid

Where the injunction order was prepared by plaintiffs' lawyers in anticipation that it would issue a hearing, where it did not set forth the reasons for its issuance, and where the acts were not described; instead, the injunction referred back to the complaint for details of locations and places where it should have application, the injunction was valid under former Ill.Rev.Stat., ch. 69, para. 3-1 (see now this section). Paschen Contractors, Inc. v. Burrell, 14 Ill. App. 3d 748, 303 N.E.2d 246 (1 Dist. 1973).

Notice

—In General

The temporary restraining order allows injunctive relief without notice upon a showing that immediate and irreparable injury, loss, or damage will result to the applicant before notice can be served and a hearing had thereon; this provision, aside from its 10 day limitation and certain procedural niceties, essentially duplicates the remedy still afforded by preliminary injunctions, which the legislature amended insubstantially in 1967. People ex rel. Pollution Control Bd. v. Lloyd A. Fry Roofing Co., 4 Ill. App. 3d 675, 281 N.E.2d 757 (1 Dist. 1972).

Notice (Cont'd)

—In General (Cont'd)

While the court has wide discretion as to whether a temporary injunction will issue, no presumptions are indulged in favor of action without notice, and such injunction should not be issued unless it clearly appears from verified facts that rights of the applicant will be unduly prejudiced unless the injunction be granted without notice. G. H. Sternberg & Co. v. Cellini, 16 Ill. App. 3d 1, 305 N.E.2d 317 (5 Dist. 1973).

—Informal Notice

Where notice was given by telephone to defendant's attorney 3 hours 58 minutes before a temporary restraining order was granted, the order was not issued without adequate notice. Northwest Sub. Congregation Beth Judea, Inc. v. Rosen, 103 Ill. App. 3d 1137, 59 Ill. Dec. 751, 432 N.E.2d 335 (2 Dist. 1982).

Informal notice has been recognized as sufficient notice for purposes of issuing a temporary restraining order. Northwest Sub. Congregation Beth Judea, Inc. v. Rosen, 103 Ill. App. 3d 1137, 59 Ill. Dec. 751, 432 N.E.2d 335 (2 Dist. 1982).

—Lack of Notice

The defendant municipality did not properly raise the validity of the court's order enjoining it from interfering with plaintiff's business merely by stating that it was issued without notice when in view of the wording of former Ill.Rev.Stat., ch. 69, para. 3 (see now this section) lack of notice did not necessarily render the order void. Walter v. City of W. Chicago, 39 Ill. App. 3d 297, 349 N.E.2d 437 (2 Dist. 1976).

—Local Rules

Circuit court rule that required 72 hours' notice of hearing on all motions was not in conflict with 735 ILCS 5/11-102, though if plaintiff had proceeded under this section for a temporary restraining order which may expressly be granted without notice under exigent circumstances, a conflict between the circuit court rule and the statute would exist. Sarah Bush Lincoln Health Ctr. v. Berlin, 268 Ill. App. 3d 184, 205 Ill. Dec. 325, 643 N.E.2d 276 (4 Dist. 1994).

—Mandatory

The statutory notice provisions are not mere technicalities; the law does not favor the granting of injunctive relief without notice, and such a drastic remedy is appropriate only under the most extreme circumstances. Hawthorne Bank of Wheaton v. Village of Glen Ellyn, 154 Ill. App. 3d 661, 107 Ill. Dec. 97, 506 N.E.2d 988 (2 Dist. 1987).

—Not Given

This section gives the defendant a right to file a motion to dissolve when a TRO is issued without notice. Harper v. Missouri Pac. R.R., 264 Ill. App. 3d 238, 201 Ill. Dec. 760, 636 N.E.2d 1192 (5 Dist.), appeal denied, 157 Ill. 2d 500, 205 Ill. Dec. 162, 642 N.E.2d 1279 (1994).

In failing to give defendants effective notice prior to entry of a temporary restraining order and to state why that order was issued without notice, the circuit court committed error and the extension of the temporary restraining order after it had expired by its terms and the failure to set a hearing on the motion for a preliminary injunction prior to the extension of the temporary restraining order were also improper however, these errors did not void either the temporary restraining order or its extension; neither did they invalidate the contempt proceedings based on these orders. Board of Trustees v. Cook County College Teachers Union Local 1600, 42 Ill. App. 3d 1056, 1 Ill. Dec. 807, 356 N.E.2d 1089 (1 Dist. 1976).

—Not Required

The court erred in granting the injunction without notice restraining wife from incurring certain debts where husband made no adequate showing that a delay of a few minutes or hours would harm him and wife was available as shown by the fact that she was served writs of summons and injunction on the day the complaint was filed. Berenson v. Berenson, 34 Ill. App. 2d 376, 181 N.E.2d 357 (1 Dist. 1962).

—Relief Without Notice

Injunctive relief without notice is an extraordinary remedy appropriate only under the most extreme and urgent circumstances. Hirschauer v. Chicago Sun-Times, 192 Ill. App. 3d 193, 139 Ill. Dec. 245, 548 N.E.2d 630 (1 Dist. 1989).

—Requirements

The trial judge may only issue injunctions without notice in situations where it definitely appears from facts set forth in the pleadings that immediate and irreparable injury would result if notice was required. Hill v. Village of Pawnee, 16 Ill. App. 3d 208, 305 N.E.2d 740 (4 Dist. 1973).

—Sufficient

Notice given to a defendant by telephone 30 minutes before the motion for a temporary restraining order was granted was sufficient where plaintiff was faced with an imminent disruption of its business operations. American Warehousing Servs., Inc. v. Weitzman, 169 Ill. App. 3d 708, 127 Ill.Dec. 494, 533 N.E.2d 366 (1 Dist., 1988).

—Time Limit

If a temporary restraining order is issued with notice, then the 10 day time limit does not apply. Abulhafedh v. Secretary of State, 161 Ill. App. 3d 413, 112 Ill. Dec. 900, 514 N.E.2d 563 (2 Dist. 1987).

—Verified Petition

A verified petition is a necessary requirement in order to permit the court to act without notice to a defendant and would have to be considered the statutory equivalent of notice. In re Kowalski, 186 Ill. App. 3d 269, 134 Ill. Dec. 176, 542 N.E.2d 176 (3 Dist. 1989).

—Waiver of Objection

The motion to dissolve an injunction issued without notice waives the point that no notice was given. Grossman v. Grossman, 304 Ill. App. 507, 26 N.E.2d 678 (1 Dist. 1940).

Opportunity to Oppose Order

—Required

Once the functional equivalence to a preliminary injunction is demonstrated, the party against whom such an order is entered must be given a fair opportunity to oppose the application and to show, if he can, why an injunction should not issue. Peoples Gas Light & Coke Co. v. City of Chicago, 117 Ill. App. 3d 353, 72 Ill. Dec. 865, 453 N.E.2d 740 (1 Dist. 1983).

Oral Argument

—Not Proper Evidence

Oral argument is not considered proper evidence for issuance of a preliminary injunction. Peoples Gas Light & Coke Co. v. City of Chicago, 117 Ill. App. 3d 353, 72 Ill. Dec. 865, 453 N.E.2d 740 (1 Dist. 1983).

Order Sufficiently Specific

—Illustrative Cases

A temporary restraining order which prohibited defendant from "providing mortgages or any other financing of whatever kind in Illinois" was not too vague and unclear to specifically give defendant notice as to what conduct was prohibited. People v. Evans, 165 Ill. App. 3d 942, 117 Ill. Dec. 513, 520 N.E.2d 864 (1 Dist. 1988).

Where the court specified how husband was to spend money designated for business and personal expenses, the order was not defective. In re Grauer, 133 Ill. App. 3d 1019, 88 Ill. Dec. 962, 479 N.E.2d 982 (1 Dist. 1985).

Parties Bound

—Relationship with Defendants

This section is a codification of the common law doctrine that a decree of injunction not only binds the defendants, but also those identified with them in interest, in privity with them, represented by them, or subject to their control. Stavros v. Karkomi, 28 Ill. App. 3d 996, 329 N.E.2d 563 (1 Dist. 1975).

Pendente Lite

An injunction pendente lite is a preliminary injunction, not a temporary injunction. Schwalm Elecs., Inc. v. Electrical Prods. Corp., 14 Ill. App. 3d 348, 302 N.E.2d 394 (1 Dist. 1973).

Petitioner

—Burden

In order to show likelihood of success on the merits, all that is necessary is that the petitioning party raise a fair question as to the existence of the right claimed. People ex rel. Hartigan v. National Anti-Drug Coalition, 124 Ill. App. 3d 269, 79 Ill. Dec. 786, 464 N.E.2d 690 (1 Dist. 1984).

Pleadings

—Held Sufficient

As to the question whether or not the complaint must state a cause of action before a temporary injunction may issue, it has been said that the question presented is not whether the complaint is not demurrable, but does it prima facie state a cause of action; if it does, then the court in its discretion to keep the matter in status quo may issue the temporary injunction. Scholz v. Barbee, 344 Ill. App. 630, 101 N.E.2d 845 (2 Dist. 1951).

Precise Terms

—Purpose

The terms of an injunction should be as definite, clear and precise as possible in order that there may be no excuse or reason for misunderstanding or disobeying it. People ex rel. Traiteur v. Abbott, 27 Ill. App. 3d 277, 327 N.E.2d 130 (5 Dist. 1975).

A proper injunction order must couch its directions or prohibitions in terms so definite, clear and precise as to demand obedience or to be capable of enforcement or execution. People ex rel. Traiteur v. Abbott, 27 Ill. App. 3d 277, 327 N.E.2d 130 (5 Dist. 1975).

Preliminary Injunction

The function of a preliminary injunction is to maintain the status quo until the case is disposed of on the merits. Peoples Gas Light & Coke Co. v. City of Chicago, 117 Ill. App. 3d 353, 72 Ill. Dec. 865, 453 N.E.2d 740 (1 Dist. 1983).

—Essential Elements

The existence of a protectable interest in the plaintiff which will suffer irreparable harm if the injunction is not issued and the likelihood of the plaintiff succeeding on the merits seem to be essential elements for the issuance of a preliminary injunction. Buzz Barton & Assocs. v. Giannone, 108 Ill. 2d 373, 91 Ill. Dec. 636, 483 N.E.2d 1271 (1985).

Purpose

—In General

The purpose of a temporary restraining order is to allow the trial court to preserve the status quo until it can hold a hearing to determine whether it should grant a preliminary injunction or until the court can consider the case on its merits; the plaintiff is not required to make out a case which would entitle him to judgment at trial; rather, he only needs to show that he raises a "fair question" about the existence of his right and that the court should preserve the status quo until the case can be decided on the merits. Citizens Utils. Co. v. O'Connor, 116 Ill. App. 3d 369, 71 Ill. Dec. 792, 451 N.E.2d 946 (2 Dist. 1983).

Temporary restraining orders and preliminary injunctions serve totally different purposes; a preliminary injunction is the primary means of obtaining injunctive relief prior to trial on the merits, which relief is exceptional in its own right where as a temporary restraining order is an emergency remedy of extremely brief duration which may issue only in exceptional circumstances and only until the trial court can hear arguments or evidence, as the circumstances require, on the subject matter of the controversy and otherwise determine what relief is appropriate. Paddington Corp. v. Foremost Sales Promotions, Inc., 13 Ill. App. 3d 170, 300 N.E.2d 484 (1 Dist. 1973).

The purpose of an injunction is to preserve the substance of the litigation from destruction until the court has had an opportunity to be advised of the facts and circumstances necessary to make a ruling. Chicago Motor Coach Co. v. Budd, 346 Ill. App. 385, 105 N.E.2d 140 (1 Dist. 1952).

—Maintain Status Quo

The purpose of a temporary restraining order is to allow the trial court to preserve the status quo until it can hold a hearing to determine whether it should grant a preliminary injunction. Hirschauer v. Chicago Sun-Times, 192 Ill. App. 3d 193, 139 Ill. Dec. 245, 548 N.E.2d 630 (1 Dist. 1989).

The purpose of a temporary restraining order is to maintain the status quo until a hearing can be had on an application for a preliminary injunction. Jurco v. Stuart, 110 Ill. App. 3d 405, 66 Ill. Dec. 207, 442 N.E.2d 633 (1 Dist. 1982); Peoples Gas Light & Coke Co. v. City of Chicago, 117 Ill. App. 3d 353, 72 Ill. Dec. 865, 453 N.E.2d 740 (1 Dist. 1983); In re Pick, 119 Ill. App. 3d 1061, 75 Ill. Dec. 865, 458 N.E.2d 33 (2 Dist. 1983); Abulhafedh v. Secretary of State, 161 Ill. App. 3d 413, 112 Ill. Dec. 900, 514 N.E.2d 563 (2 Dist. 1987).

The temporary restraining order and the preliminary injunction both serve the purpose of maintaining the status quo until the trial court can consider the case on the merits. Hill v. Village of Pawnee, 16 Ill. App. 3d 208, 305 N.E.2d 740 (4 Dist. 1973); Kaplan v. Kaplan, 98 Ill. App. 3d 136, 53 Ill. Dec. 449, 423 N.E.2d 1253 (1 Dist. 1981).

The purpose of a temporary injunction is to maintain the status quo until the case can be decided on its merits, the status quo to be preserved is the last, actual, uncontested status which preceded the pending controversy. Biehn v. Tess, 340 Ill. App. 140, 91 N.E.2d 160 (1 Dist. 1950); Rutledge v. St. Vincent Mem. Hosp., 67 Ill. App. 2d 156, 214 N.E.2d 131 (5 Dist. 1966).

Reduction of Fines

Fines imposed against union for violating initial temporary restraining order entered during a strike by faculty members against public junior colleges could be reduced by the appellate court pursuant to Rule 615(b)(4), Supreme Court Rules, in view of mitigating circumstances, including the failure to give adequate notice to defendants and the fact that three of the days covered by the temporary restraining order constituted the Labor Day weekend, when no classes would have been held even had the strike been called off. Board of Trustees v. Cook County College Teachers Union Local 1600, 42 Ill. App. 3d 1056, 1 Ill. Dec. 807, 356 N.E.2d 1089 (1 Dist. 1976).

Remedy at Law

—In General

A temporary restraining order will not be issued if there is an adequate remedy at law; a remedy at law is considered adequate if it is concise, complete, and would provide the same practical and efficient resolution as the equitable remedy would provide. Diamond Sav. & Loan Co. v. Royal Glen Condominium Ass'n, 173 Ill. App. 3d 431, 122 Ill. Dec. 113, 526 N.E.2d 372 (2 Dist. 1988).

Injunctive relief is not available when there is an adequate remedy at law. Oxequip Health Indus., Inc. v. Canalmar, Inc., 94 Ill. App. 3d 955, 50 Ill. Dec. 517, 419 N.E.2d 625 (1 Dist. 1981).

—Inadequate

The amount of money which a contractor would lose by improper shutting off of access to its work site would be difficult to calculate, making a suit for monetary damages an inadequate remedy, nor would any other remedy at law be adequate. Binder Plumbing & Heating, Inc. v. Plumbers & Pipefitters Local Union 99, 253 Ill. App. 3d 972, 192 Ill. Dec. 779, 625 N.E.2d 934 (4 Dist. 1993).

—Shown

Assuming that plaintiff was entitled to the rents for the period prior to a judicial sale, its remedy at law would be a suit to recover damages for every month it did not receive payments to which it was entitled, not an equitable remedy. Diamond Sav. & Loan Co. v. Royal Glen Condominium Ass'n, 173 Ill. App. 3d 431, 122 Ill. Dec. 113, 526 N.E.2d 372 (2 Dist. 1988).

Requisite Showing

—Elements

A proceeding seeking a temporary restraining order requires only a summary showing of irreparable harm and inadequate remedy at law. Stanton v. City of Chicago, 177 Ill. App. 3d 519, 126 Ill. Dec. 779, 532 N.E.2d 464 (1 Dist. 1988).

—Fair Question

A temporary restraining order should not be refused or dissolved merely because the court may not be absolutely certain the plaintiff has the right he claims; rather, the plaintiff need only show that he

Requisite Showing (Cont'd)

—Fair Question (Cont'd)

raises a "fair question" about the existence of his right and that the court should preserve the status quo until the case can be decided on the merits. Hirschauer v. Chicago Sun-Times, 192 Ill. App. 3d 193, 139 Ill. Dec. 245, 548 N.E.2d 630 (1 Dist. 1989).

—Lawful Right

Contractor's right of ingress and egress from its work site was a clearly ascertainable right needing protection, for purposes of granting a temporary restraining order. Binder Plumbing & Heating, Inc. v. Plumbers & Pipefitters Local Union 99, 253 Ill. App. 3d 972, 192 Ill. Dec. 779, 625 N.E.2d 934 (4 Dist. 1993).

In order that an injunction be granted, it should be clear that the plaintiff has a lawful right for which he seeks protection; his right must be certain and clearly ascertained. Schwalm Elecs., Inc. v. Electrical Prods. Corp., 14 Ill. App. 3d 348, 302 N.E.2d 394 (1 Dist. 1973).

Review

—In General

An appellate court reviewing an order of injunction will not consider issues not presented to the trial court and not appearing in the record. Board of Trustees v. Bakalis, 64 Ill. App. 3d 967, 21 Ill. Dec. 732, 382 N.E.2d 26 (1 Dist. 1978).

—Based on Sufficiency of the Motion

Where the injunctive relief, either a temporary restraining order or a preliminary injunction was issued before counsel for defendants responded to the motion, the review of the trial court's issuance of the relief granted rested solely on the sufficiency of the motion. Kaplan v. Kaplan, 98 Ill. App. 3d 136, 53 Ill. Dec. 449, 423 N.E.2d 1253 (1 Dist. 1981).

—Requirements

The reviewing court must examine the complaint and petition as a whole and reach a conclusion on the basis of all the proper and necessary allegations to determine what caused the lower court to issue the injunction. Mitchell v. Mitchell, 10 Ill. App. 2d 437, 135 N.E.2d 109 (1 Dist. 1956).

—Standard of Review

The granting or denial of a temporary restraining order is within the sound discretion of the circuit court and its determination should not be overturned on review unless there has been an abuse of discretion. Abulhafedh v. Secretary of State, 161 Ill. App. 3d 413, 112 Ill. Dec. 900, 514 N.E.2d 563 (2 Dist. 1987).

Scope

—Injunctions Included

The plain language of this section expressly encompasses injunctions, and not merely restraining orders. Stavros v. Karkomi, 28 Ill. App. 3d 996, 329 N.E.2d 563 (1 Dist. 1975).

—Permanent Injunction

A permanent injunction does not need to conform with this section. Rosenbaum v. Rosenbaum, 184 Ill. App. 3d 987, 133 Ill. Dec. 661, 541 N.E.2d 872 (1 Dist.), appeal denied, 136 Ill. Dec. 606, 545 N.E.2d 130 (1989), cert. denied, 494 U.S. 1004, 110 S. Ct. 1297, 108 L. Ed. 2d 474 (1990).

Scope of Protection

—Unlawful or Injurious Interference

A temporary injunction does not vest plaintiff with a permanent right, but merely protects the rights of plaintiff from unlawful or injurious interference; the plaintiff is not entitled to the same measure of protection at all times and under all circumstances. Eads Coal Co. v. UMW of Am., 27 Ill. App. 3d 692, 327 N.E.2d 115 (5 Dist. 1975).

Service upon Attorneys

Where summons against defendant was returned "not found," but written notice of the application for a temporary restraining order was given to defendant's attorney, such notice served as notice to defendant; service on each defendant was only required by former Ill.Rev.Stat., ch. 69, para. 3 of the Injunctions Act (see now this section) to the extent they could be conveniently served. Esperson v. Fox, 177 Ill. App. 141 (1 Dist. 1913).

Specific Facts

—Purpose

An injunction should be as definite, clear and precise in its terms as is possible so that there may be no excuse or reason for failing to comprehend or obey its prohibitions; the act enjoined or directions given must be delineated with the particularity requisite to command obedience, enable enforcement, and allow an understanding of exactly what is forbidden. Streif v. Bovinette, 88 Ill. App. 3d 1079, 44 Ill. Dec. 372, 411 N.E.2d 341 (5 Dist. 1980).

—Required

A temporary restraining order without notice and hearing should be granted only where the verified complaint or affidavit sets forth specific facts to sufficiently apprise the court that immediate harm and irreparable injury will result if notice is given and a hearing held. Geesbreght v. Geesbreght, 63 Ill. App. 3d 37, 19 Ill. Dec. 866, 379 N.E.2d 738 (1 Dist. 1978).

Trial court's failure to include the name of each product subject to injunction and its specific fair trade price rendered the injunction invalid for lack of specificity under former Ill.Rev.Stat., ch. 69, para. 3-1 (see now this section). Paddington Corp. v. Westville Beverage Mart, Inc., 12 Ill. App. 3d 555, 299 N.E.2d 554 (1 Dist. 1973).

Injunction must conform to standards of specificity, it should be so worded that the party enjoined may know from a reading of the order what he is restrained from doing, and it must be complete in the details of its prohibition or direction; it must be clear enough so that what the court intends is easily discernible. Paschen Contractors, Inc. v. Burrell, 14 Ill. App. 3d 748, 303 N.E.2d 246 (1 Dist. 1973).

Status Quo

—In General

The status quo to be preserved by a preliminary injunction is the last, actual, peaceable, uncontested status which preceded the pending controversy. Spunar v. Clark Oil & Ref. Corp., 53 Ill. App. 3d 477, 11 Ill. Dec. 382, 368 N.E.2d 990 (1 Dist. 1977).

The circumstances would have permitted the trial court to issue a temporary restraining order as the defense counsel specifically told the court that they would not maintain the status quo. Paddington Corp. v. Foremost Sales Promotions, Inc., 13 Ill. App. 3d 170, 300 N.E.2d 484 (1 Dist. 1973).

Subject of Injunction

—Funds

Where the funds which are the subject of the injunction are also the subject of the dispute, the use of an injunction restraining control is valid. Carriage Way Apts. v. Pojman, 172 Ill. App. 3d 827, 122 Ill. Dec. 717, 527 N.E.2d 89 (2 Dist. 1988).

Success on Merits

—Elements

To show a likelihood of success on the merits, a party must: (1) raise a fair question as to the existence of the right claimed, (2) lead the court to believe that he will probably be entitled to the relief prayed for if the proof sustains his allegations, and (3) make it appear advisable that the positions of the parties stay as they are until the court has an opportunity to consider the merits of the case. Abulhafedh v. Secretary of State, 161 Ill. App. 3d 413, 112 Ill. Dec. 900, 514 N.E.2d 563 (2 Dist. 1987).

—Likelihood Must Be Shown

Before a temporary restraining order with notice may be issued a party must show a likelihood of success on the merits of the case. Abulhafedh v. Secretary of State, 161 Ill. App. 3d 413, 112 Ill. Dec. 900, 514 N.E.2d 563 (2 Dist. 1987).

Temporary Injunction

—In General

A temporary injunction is merely provisional in its nature, and

Temporary Injunction (Cont'd)

—In General (Cont'd)
does not conclude a right. Klein's Restaurant Corp. v. McLain, 293 Ill. App. 54, 11 N.E.2d 644 (1 Dist. 1937).

—Abuse of Discretion
Where it did not allege in its pleadings that defendants were using knowledge available to them while in the employment of plaintiff in bidding against plaintiff, and plaintiff's complaint alleged only that it feared defendants "may" use such knowledge, the fact that a plaintiff apprehended that some wrong may be done was not sufficient to cause the issuance of temporary injunction, and the entry of an order granting a preliminary injunction, based upon the pleadings alone, was an abuse of the trial court's discretion. Summit Elec. Co. v. Mayrent, 17 Ill. App. 3d 545, 308 N.E.2d 313 (1 Dist. 1974).

Temporary Restraining Order

—Held Improper
Where the trial court meticulously followed the procedural requirements prescribed by former Ill.Rev.Stat., ch. 69, para. 3-1 (see now this section) except that no notice of the issuance of the temporary restraining order was given to the defendant prior to its issuance and no bond was required, and where irreparable damage and harm required as a condition precedent to the issuance of a temporary restraining order without notice and without bond was not shown in the record, it followed that the trial court should have allowed the defendant's motion to dissolve the temporary restraining injunction; accordingly, the order of the trial court issuing the temporary restraining order without notice and refusing to dissolve it was reversed, and cause was remanded to the trial court to consider issue of damages under former Ill.Rev.Stat., ch. 69, para. 12 (see now this section). Bohn Aluminum & Brass Co. v. Barker, 20 Ill. App. 3d 20, 312 N.E.2d 722 (4 Dist. 1974).

Undue Prejudice
The pleadings must contain an allegation of facts from which the court can infer the need for protecting the plaintiff from undue prejudice which would arise if notice to the adverse party were required. Clayton v. Hubbard, 33 Ill. App. 2d 439, 179 N.E.2d 845 (4 Dist. 1962).

It is the court, judge, or master to whom it must appear, from the facts stated in the bill or affidavit, that the rights of the complainant will be unduly prejudiced, and not the complainant himself. Christian Hosp. v. People ex rel. Murphy, 223 Ill. 244, 79 N.E. 72 (1906).

—Failure to Give Reasons
Although the order for injunction gave no reasons for its issuance, no reversible error resulted from the form of the order, since the defense did not seem to be prejudiced by lack of understanding of the court's reasons for ruling. Binder Plumbing & Heating, Inc. v. Plumbers & Pipefitters Local Union 99, 253 Ill. App. 3d 972, 192 Ill. Dec. 779, 625 N.E.2d 934 (4 Dist. 1993).

Use of Transcript

—Supplements Order
Where the trial transcript showed that the court clearly indicated its reasons for issuing injunctive relief, the order was not defective for failure to specify the irreparable harm or the reasons for its issuance. In re Grauer, 133 Ill. App. 3d 1019, 88 Ill. Dec. 962, 479 N.E.2d 982 (1 Dist. 1985).

Vacation of Order

—Proper
Where plaintiffs never moved for a preliminary injunction, vacation of the temporary restraining order, at the conclusion of the hearing, was proper. Krebs v. Mini, 53 Ill. App. 3d 787, 10 Ill. Dec. 673, 368 N.E.2d 159 (2 Dist. 1977).

Violation
Wife's petition for a rule to show cause why a securities company should not be held in contempt for allowing her husband to remove money from an individual retirement account (IRA), in violation of an order which the court issued under § 501(a)(2)(i) of the Illinois Marriage and Dissolution of Marriage Act, 750 ILCS 5/501(a)(2)(i) was dismissed, because the wife sought an order requiring the company to fund the husband's IRA at previous levels using its own money, and that relief was not available in a civil contempt proceeding. Blankshain v. Blankshain, 346 Ill. App. 3d 750, 282 Ill. Dec. 120, 805 N.E.2d 739, 2004 Ill. App. LEXIS 212 (1 Dist. 2004).

—Aiding and Abetting
Defendant could be found guilty of aiding and abetting parties in violating an injunction even though other parties had been acquitted or not prosecuted. People ex rel. Scott v. Master Barbers & Beauty Culturists Ass'n, 9 Ill. App. 3d 981, 293 N.E.2d 393 (1 Dist. 1973).

—Effect
As a general rule, where an injunction is granted and the decree operates in personam, an act done in violation of the injunction is not a nullity. Bezin v. Ginsburg, 59 Ill. App. 3d 429, 16 Ill. Dec. 595, 375 N.E.2d 468 (1 Dist. 1978).

Without Notice and Hearing

—In General
Power to grant a temporary restraining order without notice and hearing can be invoked only where the verified complaint or affidavit sets forth specific facts to sufficiently apprise the court that immediate and irreparable injury, loss or damage will result if notice and hearing are had. County of Lake v. Spare Things, 27 Ill. App. 3d 179, 326 N.E.2d 186 (2 Dist. 1975).

—Appropriate Situations
The issuance of a temporary restraining order without notice is not favored as it is a drastic remedy, which is only appropriate under the most extreme circumstances. In re Pick, 119 Ill. App. 3d 1061, 75 Ill. Dec. 865, 458 N.E.2d 33 (2 Dist. 1983).

LEGAL PERIODICALS

For article, "Some Preliminary Thoughts About Preliminary Injunctions," see 85 Ill. B.J. 12 (1997).

For article, "Interlocutory Injunctions," see 6 Chi. B. Rec. 12 (1992).

For article, "Keeping Clean: Avoiding Hazardous Waste Liability," see 1 CBA Rec. 17 (1987).

For article, "Citizen Remedies Against Errant Illinois Public Servants," see 11 S. Ill. U.L.J. 285 (1987).

For article, "Cases of First Impression: Prosecution and Defending Against Motions for Temp. Restraining Orders," see 70 Ill. B.J. 568 (1982).

For article, "Injunction Relief Pendente Lite: The Current State of the Law," see 70 Ill. B.J. 746 (1982).

RESEARCH REFERENCES

Lockup option defense to hostile corporate takeover. 66 ALR4th 180.

735 ILCS 5/11-102 Preliminary injunction

Sec. 11-102. *Preliminary injunction.* No court or judge shall grant a preliminary injunction without previous notice of the time and place of the application having been given the adverse party.
(Source: P.A. 84-282.)

Note.
This section was Ill.Rev.Stat., Ch. 110, para. 11-102.

CASE NOTES

ANALYSIS

In General
Adequate Remedy at Law

—In General
—Injunction Improperly Awarded
—Not Shown
Appellate Review
—Discretionary
—Scope of Review
—Standard of Review
Applicability
Balancing Test
Burden of Proof
—In General
—Entitlement to Relief
—Met
—Not Met
—Objections
Classification of Order
—Construction with Other Laws
Contempt
Dangerous Situation
Decision to Enjoin
—Factors
Defective Pleadings
Delay of Hearing
—Improper
Discontinued Actions
—Injunction Precluded
Discretion of Court
—In General
—Abuse Shown
—Caution Required
—Requirements
—Review
Dissolution of Order
—Properly Granted
Duty of Court
Emergency Injunction
Enjoining Secured Creditor
—Violation Required
Entitlement to Injunction
—Factors Considered
Evidentiary Hearing
Good Cause
Grounds to Dissolve
—Continuance Not Justified
—Delay in Prosecution
Injunction Improperly Denied
Injunction Inappropriate
Injunction Properly Denied
Injunction Upheld
Interlocutory Injunction
Irreparable Harm
—In General
—Not Shown
—Pleadings
—Shown
Issuance Factors
—In General
—Elements
—Inconvenience to Parties
—Notice
—Parties' Rights
Issuance of Injunction
Issuance of Temporary Injunction
—Improper
Level of Restraint
Likelihood of Success
—Must Be Shown
Money Damages
Motion for Preliminary Injunction
—Verified Pleadings
Necessary Party
—In General
Notice
—In General
—By Telephone
—Dissolution
—Duty of Court
—Exceptions
—Good Faith Notice
—Illustrative Cases
—Local Rules
—One Day's Notice
—Plaintiff's Duty
—Purpose
—Required
Opportunity to Oppose Order
—Required
Oral Argument
—Not Proper Evidence
Pleadings
—Held Insufficient
—Responsive Pleadings
Precise Terms
—Required
—Shown
Propriety
—Status Quo
Purpose
—In General
—Maintain Status Quo
—Preliminary Injunction
—Rights and Merits
Requirements
—Actual Loss Unnecessary
—With or Without Notice
Service of Summons
Standing
—Relief
Status Quo
Success on Merits
—Required Showing
Temporary Restraining Orders and Preliminary Injunctions
—Distinguished
Test
—Necessity of Injunction
Three-Tiered System
—In General
Unlimited Duration
—Unfair
Unnamed Party
—Bound by Injunction
—Illustrative Cases
Verification of Petition
—In General
Waiver of Notice
—Not Shown
—Shown

In General

A preliminary injunction is a provisional remedy which concludes no rights. Gannett Outdoor of Chicago v. Baise, 163 Ill. App. 3d 717, 114 Ill. Dec. 760, 516 N.E.2d 915 (1 Dist. 1987).

A preliminary injunction should be granted only when monetary damages cannot adequately compensate plaintiff for its injury or damages cannot be measured with reasonable certainty by pecuniary standards. Delcon Group, Inc. v. Northern Trust Corp., 159 Ill. App. 3d 275, 111 Ill. Dec. 262, 512 N.E.2d 378 (2 Dist. 1987).

An injunction is an exceptional remedy which is not granted as a matter of course, but only with great caution and only when plaintiff's right to such relief is clearly established. Delcon Group, Inc. v. Northern Trust Corp., 159 Ill. App. 3d 275, 111 Ill. Dec. 262, 512 N.E.2d 378 (2 Dist. 1987).

A preliminary injunction is an extraordinary remedy, the use of which is applicable only to situations where an extreme emergency exists and serious harm would result in the absence of the injunction. Buzz Barton & Assocs. v. Giannone, 108 Ill. 2d 373, 91 Ill. Dec. 636, 483 N.E.2d 1271 (1985).

When the proper circumstances are presented it, a court exercising traditional and inherent chancery powers may intervene in the administrative process by furnishing the provisional relief of a preliminary injunction which will serve to maintain the status quo pending the completion of the administrative agency. Kurtzworth v.

In General (Cont'd)
Illinois Racing Bd., 92 Ill. App. 3d 564, 48 Ill. Dec. 6, 415 N.E.2d 1290 (5 Dist. 1981).

A temporary injunction may be properly issued although the one who seeks it does not sustain his suit on the merits. Office Elecs., Inc. v. Grafic Forms, Inc., 72 Ill. App. 3d 456, 28 Ill. Dec. 594, 390 N.E.2d 953 (2 Dist. 1979).

A temporary injunction is an extraordinary remedy and extreme and urgent circumstances are necessary before it will be issued without notice. Sangamo Elec. Co. v. United Auto., 42 Ill. App. 3d 563, 1 Ill. Dec. 263, 356 N.E.2d 389 (4 Dist. 1976).

Preliminary injunctions, or temporary restraining orders, without notice and without bond, to say the least, should issue only under the most grave circumstances, and such interlocutory relief falls within a class separate and apart from interlocutory relief with notice and bond. Hill v. Village of Pawnee, 16 Ill. App. 3d 208, 305 N.E.2d 740 (4 Dist. 1973).

An injunction pendente lite is a preliminary injunction, not a temporary injunction. Schwalm Elecs., Inc. v. Electrical Prods. Corp., 14 Ill. App. 3d 348, 302 N.E.2d 394 (1 Dist. 1973).

A preliminary injunction is an extraordinary remedy and it is a prerequisite to the awarding of such relief that a party clearly show that he will be irreparably damaged if the injunction does not issue and that there is a probability of ultimate success on the merits. Western Leasing Co. v. Kirkpatrick, 4 Ill. App. 3d 704, 281 N.E.2d 444 (1 Dist. 1972); Schwalm Elecs., Inc. v. Electrical Prods. Corp., 14 Ill. App. 3d 348, 302 N.E.2d 394 (1 Dist. 1973); G. H. Sternberg & Co. v. Cellini, 16 Ill. App. 3d 1, 305 N.E.2d 317 (5 Dist. 1973).

Allegations verified on information and belief are insufficient to support an injunction. Phelan v. Wright, 54 Ill. App. 2d 178, 203 N.E.2d 587 (1 Dist. 1964).

It is indispensable to the right to temporary injunction that all material facts alleged be properly verified by affidavit. Phelan v. Wright, 54 Ill. App. 2d 178, 203 N.E.2d 587 (1 Dist. 1964).

Where a preliminary injunction is applied for on the face of the complaint, the complaint must be verified. Phelan v. Wright, 54 Ill. App. 2d 178, 203 N.E.2d 587 (1 Dist. 1964).

Where a preliminary injunction is based upon the face of the complaint, the facts relied upon to establish such right must be alleged positively and with certainty and precision. Phelan v. Wright, 54 Ill. App. 2d 178, 203 N.E.2d 587 (1 Dist. 1964).

The requirement of notice is mandatory, and the provision permitting dispensing with notice under certain circumstances is to be strictly construed. Schaefer v. Stephens-Adamson Mfg. Co., 36 Ill. App. 2d 310, 183 N.E.2d 575 (1 Dist. 1962).

Adequate Remedy at Law

—In General
Courts of equity will not interfere by injunction to prevent the enforcement of an ordinance on the ground that it is invalid when the defendant has an adequate remedy at law. Brown v. City of Sullivan, 350 Ill. App. 400, 113 N.E.2d 208 (3 Dist. 1953).

—Injunction Improperly Awarded
Where all of petitioner's causes of action were at law and sought monetary damages, awarding a preliminary injunction was an abuse of discretion since petitioner could find adequate relief through monetary damages. Delcon Group, Inc. v. Northern Trust Corp., 159 Ill. App. 3d 275, 111 Ill. Dec. 262, 512 N.E.2d 378 (2 Dist. 1987).

A temporary injunction should not have been entertained where the lessees had an adequate remedy at law in the municipal court where a forcible-entry proceeding was pending, and the validity of a proposed notice to exercise the option by the lessee could and should have been determined in the municipal court. Bernier v. Benson, 21 Ill. App. 2d 532, 159 N.E.2d 39 (1 Dist. 1959).

—Not Shown
Where the potential loss was difficult to calculate, and plaintiff proved defendants' calculations were flawed, plaintiff had no adequate remedy at law. Gannett Outdoor of Chicago v. Baise, 163 Ill. App. 3d 717, 114 Ill. Dec. 760, 516 N.E.2d 915 (1 Dist. 1987).

Appellate Review
In reviewing the discretion exercised by the trial court in ordering a preliminary injunction, an appellate court may decide only whether the petitioner has demonstrated a prima facie case, that there is a fair question as to the existence of the rights claimed, that the circumstances lead to a reasonable belief that they probably will be entitled to the relief sought, if the evidence sustains the allegations of the petition, and that matters should be kept in status quo until the case can be decided on its merits, or, in other words, whether there was a sufficient showing to sustain the order of the trial court. City of Chicago v. Airline Canteen Serv., 64 Ill. App. 3d 417, 20 Ill. Dec. 897, 380 N.E.2d 1106 (1 Dist. 1978).

A temporary restraining order pursuant to 735 ILCS 5/11-101 is non-appealable while a preliminary injunction is appealable. Paddington Corp. v. Foremost Sales Promotions, Inc., 13 Ill. App. 3d 170, 300 N.E.2d 484 (1 Dist. 1973).

—Discretionary
While the decision to grant or deny a preliminary injunction rests within the sound discretion of the trial court, review is afforded in order to determine whether plaintiff had abused its discretion unless it is found that the trial court had abused the exercise of this discretion, the order of preliminary injunction will not be set aside. Summit Elec. Co. v. Mayrent, 17 Ill. App. 3d 545, 308 N.E.2d 313 (1 Dist. 1974).

—Scope of Review
Where the injunctive relief, either a temporary restraining order under 735 ILCS 5/11-101 or a preliminary injunction of this section was issued before counsel for defendants responded to the motion, the review of the trial court's issuance of the relief granted rested solely on the sufficiency of the motion. Kaplan v. Kaplan, 98 Ill. App. 3d 136, 53 Ill. Dec. 449, 423 N.E.2d 1253 (1 Dist. 1981).

In ruling on a motion for a preliminary injunction, controverted facts or the merits of the case are not decided. City of Chicago v. Airline Canteen Serv., 64 Ill. App. 3d 417, 20 Ill. Dec. 897, 380 N.E.2d 1106 (1 Dist. 1978).

The reviewing court's role in reviewing the grant or denial of a preliminary injunction is strictly limited to determining whether the trial court correctly exercised its broad discretionary power. Dixon v. Village of Lombard, 50 Ill. App. 3d 590, 8 Ill. Dec. 745, 365 N.E.2d 1131 (2 Dist. 1977).

Former Ill.Rev.Stat., ch. 69, para. 3-1 (see now this section) was not relegated to negative injunctions, but encompassed factual scenarios wherein affirmative equitable relief was sought. Stavros v. Karkomi, 39 Ill. App. 3d 113, 349 N.E.2d 599 (1 Dist. 1976).

Inducing breach of contract is a tortious act for which damages may be recovered, and is a proper subject for injunctive relief. Norman v. Local 4, International Bhd. of Elec. Workers, 40 Ill. App. 2d 422, 189 N.E.2d 687 (4 Dist. 1963).

The disposition of an application for a temporary injunction does not, of course, preclude in any way an inquiry into the sufficiency of the complaint or counterclaim upon a motion to dismiss, or determine the case on the merits at all. O'Brien v. Matual, 14 Ill. App. 2d 173, 144 N.E.2d 446 (2 Dist. 1957).

—Standard of Review
A court of review should confine itself to a determination of whether the trial court has properly exercised its broad discretionary powers; each substantive issue should be considered only insofar as necessary to determine whether the trial court abused its discretion. A.B. Dick Co. v. American Pro-Tech, 159 Ill. App. 3d 786, 112 Ill. Dec. 649, 514 N.E.2d 45 (1 Dist. 1987).

A reviewing court will not disturb the findings of the trial court unless they are against the manifest weight of the evidence. A.B. Dick Co. v. American Pro-Tech, 159 Ill. App. 3d 786, 112 Ill. Dec. 649, 514 N.E.2d 45 (1 Dist. 1987).

The standard of review of an order granting a preliminary injunction is whether the trial court abused its discretion in issuing the injunction. Kirsner v. Johnson & Johnson Prods., Inc., 118 Ill. App. 3d 564, 74 Ill. Dec. 262, 455 N.E.2d 292 (1 Dist. 1983).

As it is not the purpose of the preliminary injunction to determine controverted rights or decide the merits of the case, a court of review looks to the sufficiency of the evidence only for the limited purpose of ascertaining whether the trial court's discretion has been abused. Baal v. McDonald's Corp., 97 Ill. App. 3d 495, 52 Ill. Dec. 957, 422 N.E.2d 1166 (1 Dist. 1981).

In reviewing the trial court's judgment denying or allowing a preliminary injunction, the reviewing court should not substitute its judgment for that of the lower court unless it is convinced that

Appellate Review (Cont'd)

—Standard of Review (Cont'd)

the lower court abused its discretion. Dixon v. Village of Lombard, 50 Ill. App. 3d 590, 8 Ill. Dec. 745, 365 N.E.2d 1131 (2 Dist. 1977).

Applicability

The use of a preliminary injunction is applicable only to situations where an extreme emergency exists and irreparable and serious injury result in the absence of the injunction. Dixon v. Village of Lombard, 50 Ill. App. 3d 590, 8 Ill. Dec. 745, 365 N.E.2d 1131 (2 Dist. 1977).

Balancing Test

The trial court must conclude that the need for temporary relief outweighs the possible detriment to the defendant. Donald McElroy, Inc. v. Delaney, 72 Ill. App. 3d 285, 27 Ill. Dec. 892, 389 N.E.2d 1300 (1 Dist. 1979).

Burden of Proof

—In General

Plaintiffs have the burden of proving that they are entitled to injunctive relief, and in order to meet this burden, plaintiffs must establish by a preponderance of the evidence that (1) they possess a certain and clearly ascertained right which needs protection; (2) they will suffer irreparable injury without the protection of the injunction; (3) there is no adequate remedy at law for the injury; and (4) they are likely to be successful on the merits. Baal v. McDonald's Corp., 97 Ill. App. 3d 495, 52 Ill. Dec. 957, 422 N.E.2d 1166 (1 Dist. 1981); Hoover v. Crippen, 151 Ill. App. 3d 864, 105 Ill. Dec. 8, 503 N.E.2d 848 (3 Dist. 1987); Delcon Group, Inc. v. Northern Trust Corp., 159 Ill. App. 3d 275, 111 Ill. Dec. 262, 512 N.E.2d 378 (2 Dist. 1987); Gannett Outdoor of Chicago v. Baise, 163 Ill. App. 3d 717, 114 Ill. Dec. 760, 516 N.E.2d 915 (1 Dist. 1987); A.B. Dick Co. v. American Pro-Tech, 159 Ill. App. 3d 786, 112 Ill. Dec. 649, 514 N.E.2d 45 (1 Dist. 1987); Service Sys. Corp. v. Van Bortel, 174 Ill. App. 3d 412, 123 Ill. Dec. 833, 528 N.E.2d 378 (1 Dist. 1988).

—Entitlement to Relief

Plaintiff must establish to the satisfaction of the trial court that he will probably be entitled to the relief requested if the proof should sustain his allegations. Donald McElroy, Inc. v. Delaney, 72 Ill. App. 3d 285, 27 Ill. Dec. 892, 389 N.E.2d 1300 (1 Dist. 1979).

The plaintiff or counterclaimant is not required upon application for a preliminary injunction to make out a case which would entitle him, at all events, to relief at the final hearing; he need only prima facie show for this purpose that he raises a fair question as to the existence of the right he claims, present circumstances which lead to a belief that he probably will be entitled to relief, if the proof sustains his allegations, and satisfy the court that matters should be preserved in their present state and status quo until the cause can be disposed of on its merits. O'Brien v. Matual, 14 Ill. App. 2d 173, 144 N.E.2d 446 (2 Dist. 1957).

—Met

Plaintiffs met their burden of proof where they showed by the preponderance of the evidence that they had a protectible interest in a franchise, that they would suffer irreparable injury by the loss of the franchise, that they had no adequate remedy at law, and that they were likely to be successful on the merits. Baal v. McDonald's Corp., 97 Ill. App. 3d 495, 52 Ill. Dec. 957, 422 N.E.2d 1166 (1 Dist. 1981).

—Not Met

Having found that plaintiffs failed to plead and/or prove how they would be irreparably injured unless the status quo was preserved, the order of the trial court denying plaintiffs' motion for a preliminary injunction was affirmed. Dixon v. Village of Lombard, 50 Ill. App. 3d 590, 8 Ill. Dec. 745, 365 N.E.2d 1131 (2 Dist. 1977).

—Objections

When the motion for preliminary injunction came on for hearing and the order for preliminary injunction was presented for entry by the court it was incumbent upon defendants to then specifically object to the order and to call the attention of the court to any alleged ground or statute upon which such objection was based. Somerset Importers, Ltd. v. Gold Std. Liquors, Inc., 18 Ill. App. 3d 39, 309 N.E.2d 286 (1 Dist. 1974).

Classification of Order

Where defendant municipality, in its answer filed three weeks after an order was issued enjoining it from interfering with plaintiff's business, did not in any way refer to the order as being a temporary restraining order or question its duration, it would have been unfair and arbitrary to render the order a nullity by designating it a temporary restraining order, long since expired; instead, the order in question was a preliminary injunction requiring notice except under exceptional circumstances, except that the question of notice was waived by the municipality and a motion to quash the injunction raised no determinative issue and was properly denied. Walter v. City of W. Chicago, 39 Ill. App. 3d 297, 349 N.E.2d 437 (2 Dist. 1976).

—Construction with Other Laws

The temporary restraining order and the preliminary injunction both serve the purpose of maintaining the status quo until the trial court can consider the case on the merits. Kaplan v. Kaplan, 98 Ill. App. 3d 136, 53 Ill. Dec. 449, 423 N.E.2d 1253 (1 Dist. 1981).

The practical effect of a temporary restraining order of 735 ILCS 5/11-101 issued with notice is the same as a preliminary injunction of this section issued with notice; a temporary restraining order issued with notice and a preliminary injunction issued with notice, neither of limited duration, are the same type of relief and both require the showing of the likelihood of ultimate success on the merits. Kaplan v. Kaplan, 98 Ill. App. 3d 136, 53 Ill. Dec. 449, 423 N.E.2d 1253 (1 Dist. 1981).

Contempt

Where defendants failed to attack the sufficiency of the complaint to justify the issuance without notice defendant cannot attack the complaint on appeal from a finding of contempt. Board of Educ. of Kankakee Sch. v. Kankakee Fed'n of Teachers Local No. 886, 46 Ill. 2d 439, 264 N.E.2d 18 (1970).

Where a court of equity issues an injunction, with jurisdiction of the subject matter and the persons and upon pleadings properly invoking its action, the injunction must be obeyed however erroneous the action of the court may be, until it is reversed for error by orderly review, either by the court itself or a higher court; disobedience of such an injunction is contempt of the lawful authority of the court, and punishable as such. Board of Educ. of Kankakee Sch. v. Kankakee Fed'n of Teachers Local No. 886, 46 Ill. 2d 439, 264 N.E.2d 18 (1970).

Dangerous Situation

Where a temporary injunction is sought to remedy an imminently dangerous situation, the equity court is not bound to wait for any specified period of time before it can require the defendant's appearance at a hearing to authorize a city to abate hazards which expose the public to risk of injury. City of Chicago v. Cicero, 133 Ill. App. 2d 446, 273 N.E.2d 529 (1 Dist. 1971).

Decision to Enjoin

—Factors

The decision whether to intervene by preliminary injunction lies within the sound discretion of the court and that discretion encompasses consideration of the peculiar facts of each case, the traditional powers of courts of chancery, precedent, matters of public policy and public concern, and statutes; matters of principal concern will generally involve the availability of adequate alternative relief, the necessity to prevent irreparable injury or irretrievable loss and the deprivation of some constitutional right without due process of law. Kurtzworth v. Illinois Racing Bd., 92 Ill. App. 3d 564, 48 Ill. Dec. 6, 415 N.E.2d 1290 (5 Dist. 1981).

Defective Pleadings

Complaint for injunctive relief was fatally defective since it failed to allege injuries to plaintiffs, thereby failing to establish irreparable harm. Mingare v. DeVito, 67 Ill. App. 3d 371, 24 Ill. Dec. 253, 385 N.E.2d 20 (1 Dist. 1978).

Trial court issued a defective preliminary injunction in a child custody dispute where the petition for citation nor the court's order granting the injunction averred that immediate and irreparable harm would result during the time it takes to provide the opposing

Defective Pleadings (Cont'd)
party with notice and an opportunity to be heard. Bullard v. Bullard, 66 Ill. App. 3d 132, 22 Ill. Dec. 876, 383 N.E.2d 684 (5 Dist. 1978).

Delay of Hearing

—Improper

A hearing on a preliminary injunction that was delayed for more than a short period of time or a hearing scheduled for an unspecified date in the not immediately foreseeable future, did not comport with the statutory scheme under former similar provisions of the Injunction Act (see now this section). Jurco v. Stuart, 110 Ill. App. 3d 405, 66 Ill. Dec. 207, 442 N.E.2d 633 (1 Dist. 1982).

Discontinued Actions

—Injunction Precluded

A court of equity will not grant an injunction to prevent in the future that which in good faith has been discontinued before the commencement of the action in the absence of evidence that the offense is likely to be repeated in the future. Eads Coal Co. v. UMW of Am., 27 Ill. App. 3d 692, 327 N.E.2d 115 (5 Dist. 1975).

Discretion of Court

—In General

The issuance or denial of a preliminary injunction is addressed to the trial court's sound discretion. A.B. Dick Co. v. American Pro-Tech, 159 Ill. App. 3d 786, 112 Ill. Dec. 649, 514 N.E.2d 45 (1 Dist. 1987).

Whether to grant a preliminary injunction is a matter within the discretion of the trial court. Delcon Group, Inc. v. Northern Trust Corp., 159 Ill. App. 3d 275, 111 Ill. Dec. 262, 512 N.E.2d 378 (2 Dist. 1987).

—Abuse Shown

Where enforcement of a restrictive covenant in an employment agreement would be an effort to prevent competition per se, issuance of a preliminary injunction to enforce the covenant was an abuse of discretion. Iroquois Indus. Corp. v. Popik, 91 Ill. App. 3d 505, 47 Ill. Dec. 279, 415 N.E.2d 4 (1 Dist. 1980).

A provision in an order for a preliminary injunction which enjoined the disclosure of portions of a company's affirmative action plan was improper where this information was on a form filed with the Fair Employment Practices Commission. Sears, Roebuck & Co. v. Fair Emp. Practices Comm'n, 29 Ill. App. 3d 276, 330 N.E.2d 874 (4 Dist. 1975).

—Caution Required

The issuance of a preliminary injunction is within the sound discretion of the trial judge and is to be used cautiously and in cases of great necessity only. Dixon v. Village of Lombard, 50 Ill. App. 3d 590, 8 Ill. Dec. 745, 365 N.E.2d 1131 (2 Dist. 1977).

The remedies of preliminary injunction as temporary restraining order are extraordinary in nature and should be granted only after serious consideration and due circumspection; however, the granting or denial of such relief rests in the sound discretion of the trial court. Hill v. Village of Pawnee, 16 Ill. App. 3d 208, 305 N.E.2d 740 (4 Dist. 1973).

—Requirements

The granting or refusing of a preliminary injunction rests largely in the discretion of the Chancellor to whom the application is made; the showing by the pleadings and evidence, if there be such, which must be made to obtain a temporary injunction or to resist a motion to dissolve such is less than what must be made to obtain a final and permanent injunction on the merits. O'Brien v. Matual, 14 Ill. App. 2d 173, 144 N.E.2d 446 (2 Dist. 1957).

—Review

The granting or denial of the preliminary injunction is largely in the sound discretion of the chancellor but review is afforded to determine if he has abused that discretion. Western Leasing Co. v. Kirkpatrick, 4 Ill. App. 3d 704, 281 N.E.2d 444 (1 Dist. 1972).

Dissolution of Order

—Properly Granted

Where it appears that an injunction is issued without notice, in a case where notice should have been given, or where the statute requires a bond to be given as a condition precedent to issuing a preliminary injunction and none is required, the motion to dissolve the injunction must be granted. Kessie v. Talcott, 305 Ill. App. 627, 27 N.E.2d 857 (2 Dist. 1940).

Duty of Court

The trial court must conclude that the need for temporary relief outweighs the possible detriment to the defendant. Donald McElroy, Inc. v. Delaney, 72 Ill. App. 3d 285, 27 Ill. Dec. 892, 389 N.E.2d 1300 (1 Dist. 1979).

While ordinarily the continuance or dissolution of a temporary injunction rests in the discretion of the court, and the court is vested with great discretion in deciding such matters, the court must properly apply equitable rules and fairly weigh the facts in deciding whether the plaintiff is entitled to the extraordinary relief of an injunction. Eads Coal Co. v. UMW of Am., 27 Ill. App. 3d 692, 327 N.E.2d 115 (5 Dist. 1975).

If it appears from the facts that the issuance of the temporary injunction without notice was not warranted, then it would be the duty of the appellate court to reverse the order overruling the motion to dissolve the injunction. American Dixie Shops, Inc. v. Springfield Lords, Inc., 8 Ill. App. 2d 129, 130 N.E.2d 532 (3 Dist. 1955).

Where a preliminary injunction was issued without notice, in a case where a notice should have been given, it was the duty of the appellate court, aside from any other question and without reference to the merits of the case as made by the averments of the complaint, to reverse the order denying the motion to dissolve the injunction upon that ground. Crown Bldg. Corp. v. Monroe Amusement Corp., 326 Ill. App. 430, 62 N.E.2d 32 (1 Dist. 1945).

Emergency Injunction

An injunction is an extraordinary remedy requiring urgent and extreme circumstances before it may be issued without notice. Board of Educ. v. Parlor, 85 Ill. 2d 397, 54 Ill. Dec. 249, 424 N.E.2d 1152 (1981).

The fact that the plaintiff filed his complaint on a Thursday, but did not present its motion for an emergency injunction until the following Monday, did not negate the allegation that an emergency existed and that it would be unduly prejudiced if the injunction would not be issued without notice, since the plaintiff presented the motion on the second court date following the filing of the complaint. Sunset Hills Homeowners Ass'n v. Karel, 39 Ill. App. 2d 477, 189 N.E.2d 41 (1 Dist. 1963).

Where the exigency is genuine and not feigned, the danger imminent and not remote, the injury real and not imaginary, an injunction may issue without notice. Streamwood Home Bldrs., Inc. v. Brolin, 25 Ill. App. 2d 39, 165 N.E.2d 531 (1 Dist. 1960).

Every case determining whether injunction without notice should issue must rest upon its own facts, and if the chancellor's discretion is reasonably exercised it will not be interfered with by a court of review. Streamwood Home Bldrs., Inc. v. Brolin, 25 Ill. App. 2d 39, 165 N.E.2d 531 (1 Dist. 1960).

In action by a partner against co-partner to vacate the temporary injunction, and to discharge the receiver, the partner had not made a sufficient showing to warrant issuance of a temporary injunction, or appointing a receiver without notice to the co-partner. Pearson v. Behrens, 350 Ill. App. 254, 112 N.E.2d 521 (2 Dist. 1953).

Enjoining Secured Creditor

—Violation Required

A secured party's right to collect its collateral should not be interfered with absent a showing that the secured party is violating the terms of the loan agreement. Delcon Group, Inc. v. Northern Trust Corp., 159 Ill. App. 3d 275, 111 Ill. Dec. 262, 512 N.E.2d 378 (2 Dist. 1987).

Entitlement to Injunction

—Factors Considered

In order to be entitled to a preliminary injunction, a plaintiff must show (1) a clear right or interest needing protection, (2) the absence of an adequate remedy at law, (3) irreparable harm if the injunction is not granted, and (4) a reasonable likelihood of success on the merits. Bartelstein v. Sorkin, 214 Ill. App. 3d 663, 158 Ill.

Entitlement to Injunction (Cont'd)

—Factors Considered (Cont'd)
Dec. 327, 574 N.E.2d 121 (1 Dist.), appeal denied, 141 Ill. 2d 536, 162 Ill. Dec. 482, 580 N.E.2d 108 (1991).

Evidentiary Hearing
An evidentiary hearing on an application for a preliminary injunction is normally required where a verified answer has been filed denying material allegations in the complaint. Peoples Gas Light & Coke Co. v. City of Chicago, 117 Ill. App. 3d 353, 72 Ill. Dec. 865, 453 N.E.2d 740 (1 Dist. 1983).

The nature of an evidentiary hearing depends on the status of the pleading; an evidentiary hearing is required where there is a question of material fact, thus, such a hearing is not required where no answer is filed. Kable Printing Co. v. Mount Morris Bookbinders Local 65-B, 27 Ill. App. 3d 500, 327 N.E.2d 46 (2 Dist. 1975), aff'd, 63 Ill. 2d 514, 349 N.E.2d 36 (1976).

If the trial court intended to enter a preliminary injunction it was necessary to hold an evidentiary hearing; where no hearing was held, the entry of this type of injunction was error. Paddington Corp. v. Foremost Sales Promotions, Inc., 13 Ill. App. 3d 170, 300 N.E.2d 484 (1 Dist. 1973).

Good Cause
If the subject of the injunction is property which may be destroyed, or if the plaintiff only seeks to maintain the status quo until the ultimate issue is decided, an injunction may properly be allowed without establishing probable success on the merits. Gannett Outdoor of Chicago v. Baise, 163 Ill. App. 3d 717, 114 Ill. Dec. 760, 516 N.E.2d 915 (1 Dist. 1987).

Although the issuance of an injunction without bond rests largely in the discretion of the court, the record must show "good cause" for the exercise of that discretion. Schaefer v. Stephens-Adamson Mfg. Co., 36 Ill. App. 2d 310, 183 N.E.2d 575 (1 Dist. 1962).

Grounds to Dissolve

—Continuance Not Justified
An injunction may be dissolved as to its prospective effect where a court finds that equity no longer justified its continuance, but the party seeking dissolution must make the necessary showing that he is entitled to such relief. Eads Coal Co. v. UMW of Am., 27 Ill. App. 3d 692, 327 N.E.2d 115 (5 Dist. 1975).

—Delay in Prosecution
A delay in prosecution may constitute a ground for a motion to dissolve an injunction unless a sufficient cause for the delay is presented. Eads Coal Co. v. UMW of Am., 27 Ill. App. 3d 692, 327 N.E.2d 115 (5 Dist. 1975).

Injunction Improperly Denied
Plaintiffs had a right to seek injunctive relief for breach of the lease provision granting the right of quiet and peaceful possession and enjoyment when the conduct of landlord substantially interfered with plaintiffs' use and enjoyment of the premises; therefore, refusal of the trial court to grant the preliminary injunction was error. Blue Cross Ass'n v. 666 N. Lake Shore Drive Assocs., 100 Ill. App. 3d 647, 56 Ill. Dec. 190, 427 N.E.2d 270 (1 Dist. 1981).

Injunction Inappropriate
The issuance of a preliminary injunction was inappropriate where the plaintiffs' claim was based on the Consumer Fraud and Deceptive Business Practices Act (815 ILCS 505/1 et seq.) because under that Act, injunctive relief is not available to private citizens. Martin v. Eggert, 174 Ill. App. 3d 71, 123 Ill. Dec. 841, 528 N.E.2d 386 (2 Dist. 1988).

Complaint which merely states as legal conclusions that defendant acted fraudulently and that, should the defendant exercise its legal remedies under contract, plaintiff would be irreparability harmed, is insufficient to support the issue of a preliminary injunction; rather, plaintiff must set forth those facts in detail and with particularity which reveal his right to injunctive relief. G. H. Sternberg & Co. v. Cellini, 16 Ill. App. 3d 1, 305 N.E.2d 317 (5 Dist. 1973).

It was an abuse of discretion to issue a temporary injunction on an unverified complaint, which was not supported by a verified petition or affidavit. Phelan v. Wright, 54 Ill. App. 2d 178, 203 N.E.2d 587 (1 Dist. 1964).

Injunction Properly Denied
A trial court's denial of preliminary injunctive relief was not an abuse of discretion where it was not against the manifest weight of the evidence to determine that a building restoration company was unlikely to succeed in showing that its formulas, method of supervising jobs, and method of servicing customers were unique, original or confidential or that its sources of equipment and supplies were confidential. Central Bldg. & Cleaning Co. v. Vodnansky, 84 Ill. App. 3d 586, 40 Ill. Dec. 331, 406 N.E.2d 32 (1 Dist. 1980).

Allegations made on information and belief that plaintiff believed that if notice of the application for injunction was given to the defendants, said money would be forthwith withdrawn and secreted before a hearing could be had did not support an injunction and were insufficient to warrant obviating the necessity of notice. Tri Square Realty Corp. v. Bressler, 17 Ill. App. 2d 336, 149 N.E.2d 798 (1 Dist. 1958).

Injunction Upheld
Trial court did not err in enjoining the employee from soliciting, selling to, or servicing customers the employee serviced while the employee was employed by the corporation because the corporation sufficiently established a protectable business interest where the corporation invested millions of dollars each year using the efforts of a team to acquire customers and cultivate extensive customer buying information over a long period of time in anticipation of developing business, and the corporation protected this information through a computer system accessible by password. Hanchett Paper Co. v. Melchiorre, 341 Ill. App. 3d 345, 275 Ill. Dec. 164, 792 N.E.2d 395, 2003 Ill. App. LEXIS 858 (2 Dist. 2003).

Entry of preliminary injunction preventing the disinterment of defendants' father on grounds that there was no strong and convincing evidence to show that there was a reason to disinter the body was upheld. Hough v. Weber, 202 Ill. App. 3d 674, 147 Ill. Dec. 857, 560 N.E.2d 5 (2 Dist. 1990).

Evidence held sufficient to uphold a preliminary injunction based upon the enforceability of the restrictive covenants in an employment contract. Lee/O'Keefe Ins. Agency, Inc. v. Ferega, 163 Ill. App. 3d 997, 114 Ill. Dec. 919, 516 N.E.2d 1313 (4 Dist. 1987).

The injunction ordered by the trial court against operation of a dog kennel as a public nuisance was not overbroad nor, under the evidence, too drastic where the county zoning board permitted up to three dogs at each residence. People ex rel. Traiteur v. Abbott, 27 Ill. App. 3d 277, 327 N.E.2d 130 (5 Dist. 1975).

Permanent injunctions may not be entered without a trial on the merits where defendant is not in default, since the judgment of the injunction quoted in the notice of appeal indicated a permanent injunction and since plaintiff requested immediate entry of such injunction, the court had to assume, where no other contrary indications existed, that the court entered a permanent injunction. James B. Beam Distilling Co. v. Foremost Sales Promotions, Inc., 13 Ill. App. 3d 176, 300 N.E.2d 488 (1 Dist. 1973).

Where allegations of fact in the unanswered verified complaint and the accompanying affidavit of appellees were factually sufficient to justify the issuance of the temporary injunction without notice and without bond, the Appellate court did not abuse its discretion in granting the injunction. Ortscheid v. Siegman, 331 Ill. App. 13, 72 N.E.2d 353 (2 Dist. 1947).

Interlocutory Injunction
An interlocutory injunction must stand or fall on the pleadings as they existed at the time the order was entered. Schaefer v. Stephens-Adamson Mfg. Co., 36 Ill. App. 2d 310, 183 N.E.2d 575 (1 Dist. 1962).

Irreparable Harm

—In General
The irreparable harm incurred would have been the removal of plaintiff's outdoor advertising sign because the removal of the sign would cause plaintiff to lose income and sales. Gannett Outdoor of Chicago v. Baise, 163 Ill. App. 3d 717, 114 Ill. Dec. 760, 516 N.E.2d 915 (1 Dist. 1987).

Where defendant acquired confidential information which could be used to undermine plaintiff's business, and he had called upon several customers with whom he had contact while employed by

Irreparable Harm (Cont'd)

—In General (Cont'd)

plaintiff, this was sufficient to establish a threat of irreparable harm for purposes of a preliminary injunction. Donald McElroy, Inc. v. Delaney, 72 Ill. App. 3d 285, 27 Ill. Dec. 892, 389 N.E.2d 1300 (1 Dist. 1979).

To justify injunctive relief by enforcement of a restrictive covenant of employment, it was necessary for plaintiff to prove that he would be irreparably damaged in his business if the injunction did not issue. Leavitt Co. v. Plattos, 27 Ill. App. 3d 598, 327 N.E.2d 356 (1 Dist. 1975).

—Not Shown

Plaintiffs failed to allege or establish any irreparable injury by their exclusion from a "unique" swim meet. Proulx ex rel. Proulx v. Illinois High Sch. Ass'n, 125 Ill. App. 3d 781, 81 Ill. Dec. 34, 466 N.E.2d 620 (4 Dist. 1984).

—Pleadings

The mere allegations of irreparable damage alone is nothing more than a statement of a conclusion, and hence, an insufficient basis for injunctive relief. G. H. Sternberg & Co. v. Cellini, 16 Ill. App. 3d 1, 305 N.E.2d 317 (5 Dist. 1973).

Reasons which the plaintiff set out in his complaint, wherein he stated he had no adequate remedy at law, sufficiently showed irreparable damage of the degree necessary to authorize the granting of preliminary relief; the landlord was required to restore plaintiff to possession of his apartment where plaintiff alleged that he had no place to live and did not have the use of any of his personal effects as a result of the landlord's conduct. Brooks v. La Salle Nat'l Bank, 11 Ill. App. 3d 791, 298 N.E.2d 262 (1 Dist. 1973).

The factual allegations of the complaint showed the necessity for an injunction; and no prayer for waiver of notice or any averment that the giving of notice would be prejudicial, were necessary since the court could conclude from the facts which were alleged, that the plaintiff would suffer irreparable and substantial injury if the injunction was delayed until notice could be given. Streamwood Home Bldrs., Inc. v. Brolin, 25 Ill. App. 2d 39, 165 N.E.2d 531 (1 Dist. 1960).

—Shown

An exception to the general rule precluding injunctive relief against arbitration of collective bargaining disputes existed, where maintenance of the status quo was necessary to protect the integrity of the arbitral process itself; the exception applied to a situation in which a public employee union was able to establish that if it were not granted preliminary injunctive relief against planned furloughs and layoffs occasioned by an Illinois budgetary crisis, the financial impact of any later arbitration award would have been so devastating that the State would have had to seek relief from it. AFSCME, Council 31 v. Schwartz, 343 Ill. App. 3d 553, 278 Ill. Dec. 169, 797 N.E.2d 1087, 2003 Ill. App. LEXIS 1221 (5 Dist. 2003), appeal denied sub nom. Am. Fedn. of State v. Schwartz, 207 Ill. 2d 597, 283 Ill. Dec. 132, 807 N.E.2d 973 (2004).

Where the evidence showed a legitimate threat to plaintiff's business interest, irreparable harm may have resulted if this interest was not protected by a preliminary injunction. Gannett Outdoor of Chicago v. Baise, 163 Ill. App. 3d 717, 114 Ill. Dec. 760, 516 N.E.2d 915 (1 Dist. 1987).

Issuance Factors

—In General

To obtain a preliminary injunction the moving party must show: (1) he possesses a right which needs protection; (2) he has a substantial likelihood of succeeding on the merits; (3) he has no adequate remedy at law; (4) he will suffer irreparable injury without the injunction; and (5), in the absence of preliminary relief, he will incur a greater injury than would be received by the objector if the relief was granted. Johnson v. Gene's Supermarket, Inc., 117 Ill. App. 3d 295, 72 Ill. Dec. 778, 453 N.E.2d 83 (4 Dist. 1983).

—Elements

Circuit court's preliminary injunction order lacked a legal and factual basis, and the prevailing highway commissioner did not submit a proper request for injunctive relief, as he did not file a complaint, counterclaim, or motion requesting injunctive relief, or establish that he was entitled to the extraordinary remedy by establishing that any of the elements for a preliminary existed. Bd. of Educ. v. Miller, 349 Ill. App. 3d 806, 285 Ill. Dec. 868, 812 N.E.2d 688, 2004 Ill. App. LEXIS 819 (1 Dist. 2004).

In order for a preliminary injunction to properly issue, the petitioner must establish a likelihood of ultimate success on the merits of the case, and that there is a need to preserve the status quo to prevent an irreparable injury for which there is no adequate remedy at law. Kirsner v. Johnson & Johnson Prods., Inc., 118 Ill. App. 3d 564, 74 Ill. Dec. 262, 455 N.E.2d 292 (1 Dist. 1983).

—Inconvenience to Parties

One important consideration upon an application for a preliminary injunction is the relative inconvenience to be caused the respective parties if the application be allowed or denied. O'Brien v. Matual, 14 Ill. App. 2d 173, 144 N.E.2d 446 (2 Dist. 1957).

—Notice

Although plaintiff does not have to give notice prior to instituting suit, the fact that such was not done certainly is a factor to be considered before issuance of an injunction without notice. Sangamo Elec. Co. v. United Auto., 42 Ill. App. 3d 563, 1 Ill. Dec. 263, 356 N.E.2d 389 (4 Dist. 1976).

Where no answer has been filed, a preliminary injunction may be issued solely on the sufficiency of the complaint, where an answer has been filed, both pleadings must be considered, and if the answer contains denials of material allegations, contained in the complaint, a hearing on those matters must be allowed before an injunction may issue. Summit Elec. Co. v. Mayrent, 17 Ill. App. 3d 545, 308 N.E.2d 313 (1 Dist. 1974).

The eventual right of a plaintiff to the issuance of a temporary injunction is not a factor in determining whether he is required to give notice to the defendant of his application therefor. American Dixie Shops, Inc. v. Springfield Lords, Inc., 8 Ill. App. 2d 129, 130 N.E.2d 532 (3 Dist. 1955).

Only in those cases where it appears from the complaint or affidavit accompanying the same that the rights of the plaintiff will be unduly prejudiced is a court warranted in granting an injunction without notice to the defendants of the application therefor. Brown v. City of Sullivan, 350 Ill. App. 400, 113 N.E.2d 208 (3 Dist. 1953); American Dixie Shops, Inc. v. Springfield Lords, Inc., 8 Ill. App. 2d 129, 130 N.E.2d 532 (3 Dist. 1955); Tri Square Realty Corp. v. Bressler, 17 Ill. App. 2d 336, 149 N.E.2d 798 (1 Dist. 1958); Streamwood Home Bldrs., Inc. v. Brolin, 25 Ill. App. 2d 39, 165 N.E.2d 531 (1 Dist. 1960); Berenson v. Berenson, 34 Ill. App. 2d 376, 181 N.E.2d 357 (1 Dist. 1962); G. H. Sternberg & Co. v. Cellini, 16 Ill. App. 3d 1, 305 N.E.2d 317 (5 Dist. 1973); Hill v. Village of Pawnee, 16 Ill. App. 3d 208, 305 N.E.2d 740 (4 Dist. 1973).

Issuance of injunction without notice was not an abuse of such discretion. Terminal R.R. Ass'n v. International Ass'n of Machinists, 333 Ill. App. 288, 77 N.E.2d 448 (4 Dist. 1948).

—Parties' Rights

A preliminary injunction should not be refused or dissolved merely because the court may not be absolutely certain the plaintiff or counterclaimant has the right he claims. O'Brien v. Matual, 14 Ill. App. 2d 173, 144 N.E.2d 446 (2 Dist. 1957).

Issuance of Injunction

The general rule seems to be that when a complaint is presented to a court praying for relief which the court has jurisdiction to grant upon a final hearing, and such complaint recites facts which give prima facie a right to such relief, the court may grant a temporary injunction where the effect will be to maintain the status quo of the matters involved. Brown v. City of Sullivan, 350 Ill. App. 400, 113 N.E.2d 208 (3 Dist. 1953).

Allowing the issuance of an injunction without requiring sound discretion of the court, a sufficient showing must be made on which to base the discretion. Grossman v. Grossman, 304 Ill. App. 507, 26 N.E.2d 678 (1 Dist. 1940).

Issuance of Temporary Injunction

In the absence of facts showing good cause for dispensing with notice, no temporary injunction should be issued without notice. Schaefer v. Stephens-Adamson Mfg. Co., 36 Ill. App. 2d 310, 183 N.E.2d 575 (1 Dist. 1962).

Issuance of Temporary Injunction (Cont'd)

—Improper

The issuance of the temporary injunction without notice and without bond was obviously improper and the motion to dismiss should have been allowed. East Side Health Dist. v. Village of Caseyville, 35 Ill. App. 2d 443, 183 N.E.2d 20 (4th Dist. 1962).

Level of Restraint

The restraint imposed by an injunction should not be more extensive than is reasonably required to protect the interests of the party in whose favor it is granted, and should not be so broad as to prevent defendant from exercising his rights. People ex rel. Traiteur v. Abbott, 27 Ill. App. 3d 277, 327 N.E.2d 130 (5 Dist. 1975).

Likelihood of Success

—Must Be Shown

A preliminary injunction is improper where it appears from the record, that plaintiff failed to show a likelihood of success on the merits. Rock Island Bank v. Paul, 48 Ill. App. 3d 874, 6 Ill. Dec. 180, 362 N.E.2d 815 (3 Dist. 1977).

A temporary restraining order issued with notice and a preliminary injunction issued with notice, neither of limited duration, are the same type of relief, and require a showing of the likelihood of ultimate success on the merits of the case. Kable Printing Co. v. Mount Morris Bookbinders Union Local 65-B, 63 Ill. 2d 514, 349 N.E.2d 36 (1976).

Money Damages

Where the motion submitted by plaintiff indicated that he only sought monies allegedly due and owing him from defendants pursuant to the employment agreement, then plaintiff did not make a sufficient showing to entitle him to a temporary injunctive relief. Kaplan v. Kaplan, 98 Ill. App. 3d 136, 53 Ill. Dec. 449, 423 N.E.2d 1253 (1 Dist. 1981).

Where the injury plaintiff complained of, which was a breach of the employment contract, was capable of being measured and corrected by an award of money damages alone, then plaintiff was not entitled to injunctive relief. Kaplan v. Kaplan, 98 Ill. App. 3d 136, 53 Ill. Dec. 449, 423 N.E.2d 1253 (1 Dist. 1981).

Motion for Preliminary Injunction

—Verified Pleadings

The fact that plaintiff did not verify its motion for a preliminary injunction was immaterial, since the motion was not a "subsequent pleading." Interstate Material Corp. v. City of Chicago, 150 Ill. App. 3d 944, 103 Ill. Dec. 593, 501 N.E.2d 910 (1 Dist. 1986).

Necessary Party

—In General

To be a necessary party, the individual or entity involved must have a present substantial interest, as opposed to a mere expectancy or future contingency, in the controverted matter such that the legal entanglement cannot be resolved without either (1) affecting that interest or (2) leaving the interest of those who are before the court in an embarrassing or inequitable position. Stavros v. Karkomi, 39 Ill. App. 3d 113, 349 N.E.2d 599 (1 Dist. 1976).

Notice

—In General

An injunction is an extraordinary remedy; one without notice is considered most drastic and should be granted only under extreme circumstances. Streamwood Home Bldrs., Inc. v. Brolin, 25 Ill. App. 2d 39, 165 N.E.2d 531 (1 Dist. 1960).

It is the general rule that an injunction should not be granted without notice and bond unless it clearly appears from the complaint that the plaintiffs bring themselves within some established exception which expressly prohibits the issuing of such injunctions without notice to the defendant and without bond. Brown v. City of Sullivan, 350 Ill. App. 400, 113 N.E.2d 208 (3 Dist. 1953).

—By Telephone

The practice of attorneys dealing with injunctions in labor disputes to accept a telephone call as notice when the opposing party intends to seek an injunction is not to be viewed as a satisfactory replacement for formal notice, but it is at least better than no notice at all, and does give opposing counsel the opportunity to appear when the petition is presented to the court. Board of Educ. v. Parlor, 85 Ill. 2d 397, 54 Ill. Dec. 249, 424 N.E.2d 1152 (1981).

—Dissolution

Where there was nothing in the complaint which would indicate that the rights of the plaintiff would be unduly prejudiced if notice had been given of plaintiff's application for the injunction, the injunction granted under the former Injunction Act (see now this section) should have been dissolved. Daskal v. Daskal, 71 Ill. App. 2d 471, 219 N.E.2d 4 (1 Dist. 1966).

—Duty of Court

Where it appears that a temporary injunction issued without notice in a case where a notice should have been given, it is the duty of the appellate court, without reference to the merits of the cause, to reverse the order denying the motion to dissolve the injunction on that ground. Brown v. City of Sullivan, 350 Ill. App. 400, 113 N.E.2d 208 (3 Dist. 1953).

—Exceptions

Verified complaint made a showing sufficient under former Ill.Rev.Stat., ch. 69, para. 3 (see now this section) that the rights of the plaintiff would have been unduly prejudiced if a restraining order were not to issue, immediately, without notice. American Device Mfg. Co. v. International Ass'n of Machinists, Local 673, 105 Ill. App. 2d 299, 244 N.E.2d 862 (5 Dist. 1969).

The circumstances countenanced by the courts for granting an injunction without notice have been in very restricted areas, such as where the facts of the case, or the history of the parties, disclosed that the giving of notice would result in accelerating the very act sought to be enjoined, or where the act to be enjoined was either taking place or would be undertaken or completed in the time required for notice. Streamwood Home Bldrs., Inc. v. Brolin, 25 Ill. App. 2d 39, 165 N.E.2d 531 (1 Dist. 1960).

The exceptions to the rule that notice is required before judicial authority is exercised, are rare; they embrace cases where by a stroke of the pen, a movement of the hand, or a tour de force executed overnight the defendant intends to and can destroy the substance of the litigation and thus defeat the power of the court to do justice. Skarpinski v. VFW of United States, 343 Ill. App. 271, 98 N.E.2d 858 (1 Dist. 1951).

—Good Faith Notice

Some notice is better than none, and if a complainant is unable to comply with the court rules in reference to giving notice and serving copies of the pertinent pleadings, he can show his good faith by giving some sort of notice to the opposite party. Streamwood Home Bldrs., Inc. v. Brolin, 25 Ill. App. 2d 39, 165 N.E.2d 531 (1 Dist. 1960).

—Illustrative Cases

Plaintiff's allegation, based on information of a contemplated sale or transfer of the beneficial interest, where plaintiffs were in open and notorious possession of a parcel of real estate, fell short of an allegation of facts "that the rights of the plaintiffs will be unduly prejudiced," which would obviate the notice requirement of this section. Schaefer v. Stephens-Adamson Mfg. Co., 36 Ill. App. 2d 310, 183 N.E.2d 575 (1 Dist. 1962).

—Local Rules

Circuit court rule that required 72 hours' notice of hearing on all motions was not in conflict with this section, though if plaintiff had proceeded under 735 ILCS 5/11-101 for a temporary restraining order which may expressly be granted without notice under exigent circumstances, a conflict between the circuit court rule and the statute would exist. Sarah Bush Lincoln Health Ctr. v. Berlin, 268 Ill. App. 3d 184, 205 Ill. Dec. 325, 643 N.E.2d 276 (4 Dist. 1994).

—One Day's Notice

There was no abuse of discretion in hearing a matter on only one day's notice where an injunction issued without notice was based on a petition which alleged only the conclusion that irreparable injury would result if notice was given and a hearing held. Geesbreght v. Geesbreght, 63 Ill. App. 3d 37, 19 Ill. Dec. 866, 379 N.E.2d 738 (1 Dist. 1978).

Notice (Cont'd)

—Plaintiff's Duty

The fact that plaintiff might eventually be entitled to an injunction is not involved in determining the issue as to whether notice should or should not have been given; the duty rests upon the plaintiff of making it clear to the court that the giving of notice might result in undue prejudice to its rights and this could only be accomplished by fact allegations demonstrating that the delay required by giving notice would result in defeating the purpose for which the injunction was sought. American Dixie Shops, Inc. v. Springfield Lords, Inc., 8 Ill. App. 2d 129, 130 N.E.2d 532 (3 Dist. 1955).

—Purpose

The apparent purpose of requiring a notice is to give defendants an opportunity to show that the injunction should not issue. Grossman v. Grossman, 304 Ill. App. 507, 26 N.E.2d 678 (1 Dist. 1940).

—Required

When an injunction is issued without notice in a case where notice should have been given, the appellate court will reverse the order upon that ground without regard to any other question. Skarpinski v. VFW of United States, 343 Ill. App. 271, 98 N.E.2d 858 (1 Dist. 1951); Schaefer v. Stephens-Adamson Mfg. Co., 36 Ill. App. 2d 310, 183 N.E.2d 575 (1 Dist. 1962).

Opportunity to Oppose Order

—Required

Once the functional equivalence to a preliminary injunction is demonstrated, the party against whom such an order is entered must be given a fair opportunity to oppose the application and to show, if he can, why an injunction should not issue. Peoples Gas Light & Coke Co. v. City of Chicago, 117 Ill. App. 3d 353, 72 Ill. Dec. 865, 453 N.E.2d 740 (1 Dist. 1983).

Oral Argument

—Not Proper Evidence

Oral argument is not considered proper evidence for issuance of a preliminary injunction. Peoples Gas Light & Coke Co. v. City of Chicago, 117 Ill. App. 3d 353, 72 Ill. Dec. 865, 453 N.E.2d 740 (1 Dist. 1983).

Pleadings

—Held Insufficient

Plaintiffs' complaint which only stated that they would "suffer immediate and irreparable injury" if the injunction was not granted, was merely a conclusion and did not support the issuance of a preliminary injunction without notice or bond, which requires the presentation of specific facts which demonstrate that immediate and irreparable harm are threatened. Hill v. Village of Pawnee, 16 Ill. App. 3d 208, 305 N.E.2d 740 (4 Dist. 1973).

—Responsive Pleadings

When no responsive pleadings were filed, the trial court was not precluded from issuing an injunction upon the previously undisputed facts alleged in the verified complaint which was incorporated by reference. Kable Printing Co. v. Mount Morris Bookbinders Local 65-B, 27 Ill. App. 3d 500, 327 N.E.2d 46 (2 Dist. 1975), aff'd, 63 Ill. 2d 514, 349 N.E.2d 36 (1976).

Where no responsive pleading has been filed, a preliminary injunction may be issued solely on the sufficiency of the complaint. Kable Printing Co. v. Mount Morris Bookbinders Local 65-B, 27 Ill. App. 3d 500, 327 N.E.2d 46 (2 Dist. 1975), aff'd, 63 Ill. 2d 514, 349 N.E.2d 36 (1976).

Precise Terms

—Required

A proper injunction order must couch its directions or prohibitions in terms so definite, clear and precise as to demand obedience or to be capable of enforcement or execution. People ex rel. Traiteur v. Abbott, 27 Ill. App. 3d 277, 327 N.E.2d 130 (5 Dist. 1975).

The terms of an injunction should be as definite, clear and precise as possible in order that there may be no excuse or reason for misunderstanding or disobeying it. People ex rel. Traiteur v. Abbott, 27 Ill. App. 3d 277, 327 N.E.2d 130 (5 Dist. 1975).

—Shown

Where the order was sufficiently definite to apprise the parties of its scope and to safeguard the interests of both plaintiff and defendants pending the outcome of the litigation, the order of preliminary injunction was proper. Donald McElroy, Inc. v. Delaney, 72 Ill. App. 3d 285, 27 Ill. Dec. 892, 389 N.E.2d 1300 (1 Dist. 1979).

Propriety

—Status Quo

A preliminary injunction is not proper where it tends to change the status quo of the parties rather than to preserve it. People v. Van Tran Elec. Corp., 152 Ill. App. 3d 175, 105 Ill. Dec. 173, 503 N.E.2d 1179 (5 Dist. 1987).

Purpose

—In General

The function of a preliminary injunction is to maintain the status quo until the case is disposed of on the merits. Peoples Gas Light & Coke Co. v. City of Chicago, 117 Ill. App. 3d 353, 72 Ill. Dec. 865, 453 N.E.2d 740 (1 Dist. 1983).

The purpose of a temporary or preliminary injunction is not to determine the merits but to maintain the status quo. Sangamo Elec. Co. v. United Auto., 42 Ill. App. 3d 563, 1 Ill. Dec. 263, 356 N.E.2d 389 (4 Dist. 1976).

The primary purpose of a preliminary injunction is to preserve matters in status quo until the court has had an opportunity to consider the cause upon its merits, or upon a motion to dismiss, i.e., to prevent such acts during the pendency of the action as would preclude the court from giving the plaintiff or counterclaimant his remedy at the end of the litigation if he be entitled to such. O'Brien v. Matual, 14 Ill. App. 2d 173, 144 N.E.2d 446 (2 Dist. 1957).

The primary purpose of issuing an injunction is to maintain a status which exists and to cause no change until a hearing can be had, but it is not usually permissible as a preliminary injunction to issue what is known as a mandatory injunction which changes the status. Alwar Forming Mach. Co. v. F. & W. Metal Forming Mach. Co., 301 Ill. App. 591, 23 N.E.2d 229 (1 Dist. 1939).

—Maintain Status Quo

A preliminary injunction or a temporary restraining order serves the purpose of preserving the status quo until the trial court can consider the case on its merits. Hill v. Village of Pawnee, 16 Ill. App. 3d 208, 305 N.E.2d 740 (4 Dist. 1973).

—Preliminary Injunction

The primary purpose of a preliminary injunction is to preserve the status quo until there can be a final hearing on the merits. Brooks v. La Salle Nat'l Bank, 11 Ill. App. 3d 791, 298 N.E.2d 262 (1 Dist. 1973).

—Rights and Merits

It is not the purpose of the preliminary injunction to determine controverted rights or decide the merits of the case. People v. Van Tran Elec. Corp., 152 Ill. App. 3d 175, 105 Ill. Dec. 173, 503 N.E.2d 1179 (5 Dist. 1987).

Requirements

—Actual Loss Unnecessary

Plaintiff need not show an actual loss of sales or profits before the trial court can grant a preliminary injunction. Gannett Outdoor of Chicago v. Baise, 163 Ill. App. 3d 717, 114 Ill. Dec. 760, 516 N.E.2d 915 (1 Dist. 1987).

—With or Without Notice

A preliminary injunction may be granted with or without notice, and if the latter, there must be a showing of immediate and irreparable injury; additionally, the movant must establish the likelihood of ultimate success on the merits of the case. Kable Printing Co. v. Mount Morris Bookbinders Union Local 65-B, 63 Ill. 2d 514, 349 N.E.2d 36 (1976).

Caution and circumspection must be the watchwords to guide the court's action, when notice has not been given in a interlocutory injunction, and any doubts as to the wisdom of issuance must be

Requirements (Cont'd)

—With or Without Notice (Cont'd)
resolved against the action. Schaefer v. Stephens-Adamson Mfg. Co., 36 Ill. App. 2d 310, 183 N.E.2d 575 (1 Dist. 1962).

Service of Summons
Defendant could not claim prejudice because she was, in fact, served four days prior to the day of appearance; if the defendant had been prejudiced by the mode of service, she should have appeared specially to quash the summons, and, not having done so, the objection was waived. City of Chicago v. Cicero, 133 Ill. App. 2d 446, 273 N.E.2d 529 (1 Dist. 1971).

Standing

—Relief
Merely because the plaintiff has standing to sue does not mean that recovery or injunctive relief can be based on actual or potential injury to a nonparty to the suit. Kirsner v. Johnson & Johnson Prods., Inc., 118 Ill. App. 3d 564, 74 Ill. Dec. 262, 455 N.E.2d 292 (1 Dist. 1983).

Status Quo
A preliminary injunction is not proper where it tends to change the status quo of the parties rather than preserving it. Rock Island Bank v. Paul, 48 Ill. App. 3d 874, 6 Ill. Dec. 180, 362 N.E.2d 815 (3 Dist. 1977).

The status quo which should be preserved by a preliminary injunction is the last, actual, peaceable, uncontested status which preceded the pending controversy, and the necessity of the preliminary injunction should be made apparent by appropriate allegations showing that a change in the status would cause irreparable injury. O'Brien v. Matual, 14 Ill. App. 2d 173, 144 N.E.2d 446 (2 Dist. 1957).

Success on Merits

—Required Showing
In order to show a likelihood of success on the merits, a party is not required to make out a case which in all events will warrant relief in the final hearing; all that is necessary is that the petitioning party raise a fair question as to the existence of the right claimed, lead the court to believe that he probably will be entitled to the relief prayed for if the proof should sustain his allegations, and make it appear advisable that the position of the parties should stay as they are until the court has had an opportunity to consider the case on the merits. Baal v. McDonald's Corp., 97 Ill. App. 3d 495, 52 Ill. Dec. 957, 422 N.E.2d 1166 (1 Dist. 1981).

The probability of ultimate success on the merits depends not only on the sufficiency of plaintiff's complaint but also on the defenses raised by the answer. Brooks v. La Salle Nat'l Bank, 11 Ill. App. 3d 791, 298 N.E.2d 262 (1 Dist. 1973).

Plaintiff was required to establish that he was probably entitled to succeed ultimately on the merits as a prerequisite to obtaining a preliminary injunction. Lipkin v. Burnstine, 18 Ill. App. 2d 509, 152 N.E.2d 745 (1 Dist. 1958).

Temporary Restraining Orders and Preliminary Injunctions

—Distinguished
Temporary restraining orders and preliminary injunctions serve totally different purposes; a preliminary injunction is the primary means of obtaining injunctive relief prior to trial on the merits, which relief is exceptional in its own right where as a temporary restraining order is an emergency remedy of extremely brief duration which may issue only in exceptional circumstances and only until the trial court can hear arguments or evidence, as the circumstances require, on the subject matter of the controversy and otherwise determine what relief is appropriate. Paddington Corp. v. Foremost Sales Promotions, Inc., 13 Ill. App. 3d 170, 300 N.E.2d 484 (1 Dist. 1973).

Test

—Necessity of Injunction
To test the necessity for issuance of an interlocutory injunction without notice, the court must ask whether, in the time required to procure the defendant's appearance, the defendant could and would do that which would seriously obstruct the power of the court to deal justly and effectively with the issue in dispute. Schaefer v. Stephens-Adamson Mfg. Co., 36 Ill. App. 2d 310, 183 N.E.2d 575 (1 Dist. 1962).

Three-Tiered System

—In General
The structure contemplated by this Article is the three-tiered system of injunctive relief similar to that practiced in the federal court, which consists of temporary restraining orders, preliminary injunctions and permanent injunctions. Jurco v. Stuart, 110 Ill. App. 3d 405, 66 Ill. Dec. 207, 442 N.E.2d 633 (1 Dist. 1982).

Unlimited Duration

—Unfair
To allow a temporary restraining order of unlimited duration is to have a preliminary injunction without giving the one party a fair opportunity to oppose the application and to show if he can why an injunction should not issue. Jurco v. Stuart, 110 Ill. App. 3d 405, 66 Ill. Dec. 207, 442 N.E.2d 633 (1 Dist. 1982).

Unnamed Party

—Bound by Injunction
One may be bound by an injunction although he is not a named party to such action provided that the requisite involvement and receipt of actual notice is established. Stavros v. Karkomi, 39 Ill. App. 3d 113, 349 N.E.2d 599 (1 Dist. 1976).

—Illustrative Cases
Even though a bank characterized itself as a mere naked land trustee of certain real estate in the controversy and did not take a position concerning resolution of the matter in dispute, such entity clearly was involved in the realty at issue and received actual notice of the pending ancillary enforcement proceedings so as to be bound by the order entered by the trial court requiring it to execute a quit claim deed to the property to the plaintiffs. Stavros v. Karkomi, 39 Ill. App. 3d 113, 349 N.E.2d 599 (1 Dist. 1976).

Verification of Petition

—In General
There is disagreement among Illinois appellate courts regarding whether a petition for a preliminary injunction must be verified. Hoover v. Crippen, 151 Ill. App. 3d 864, 105 Ill. Dec. 8, 503 N.E.2d 848 (3 Dist. 1987).

Waiver of Notice

—Not Shown
Failure to give notice of an application for a temporary injunction is not waived by the filing of a motion to dissolve or by urging other grounds therein. American Dixie Shops, Inc. v. Springfield Lords, Inc., 8 Ill. App. 2d 129, 130 N.E.2d 532 (3 Dist. 1955).

Where a motion to dissolve a preliminary injunction specifies as grounds for such motion, the failure to give notice and other grounds which go the to the merits, the failure to give notice is not waived. Wagner v. Okner, 306 Ill.App. 601, 29 N.E.2d 385 (1 Dist., 1940).

—Shown
Although an order of court may be void ab initio for lack of due process, such as notice, a defect can easily be waived, and it was waived where the defendant answered plaintiff's motion for a preliminary injunction on the merits and then filed a counter-complaint. Walter v. City of W. Chicago, 39 Ill. App. 3d 297, 349 N.E.2d 437 (2 Dist. 1976).

LEGAL PERIODICALS

For article, "Injunction Relief Pendente Lite: The Current State of the Law," see 70 Ill. B.J. 746 (1982).

735 ILCS 5/11-103 Bond

Sec. 11-103. *Bond.* The court in its discretion, may before entering a restraining order or a preliminary injunction, require the applicant to give bond in such sum, upon such condition and with such security as may be deemed proper by the court, for the payment of such costs and damages as may be incurred or suffered by any party who is found to have been wrongfully enjoined or restrained.

No such bond shall be required of any governmental office or agency.

A surety upon a bond or undertaking under Article XI of this Act [735 ILCS 5/11-101 et seq.] submits to the jurisdiction of the court and irrevocably appoints the clerk of the court as the surety's agent upon whom any papers affecting the surety's liability on the bond or undertaking may be served. Such liability may be enforced on motion without the necessity of an independent action. The motion and such notice of motion as the court prescribes may be served on the clerk of the court who shall forthwith mail copies to the persons giving the security if their addresses are known.

(Source: P.A. 83-707.)

Note.

This section was Ill.Rev.Stat., Ch. 110, para. 11-103.

CASE NOTES

ANALYSIS

In General
Applicability
—Preliminary Injunctions
—Stay of Judgment
Bond
—Court's Discretion
—Letters of Credit Insufficient
—Notice and Hearing
Bond Properly Denied
Contempt
—Elements
—Specificity of Injunction
Damages for Delay
—Precluded
Discretion of Court
—In General
—Bond Mandatory
—Good Cause
—Limited
Dissolution of Injunction
—Action on Bond
—Grounds
—Ruling Required
Error in Injunction Bond
—Harmless
—Order Not Voided
Failure to Require Bond
—Order Not Reversed
Injunction Without Bond
—In General
—Determination by Court
—Error
—Financial Interest
—Good Cause Not Shown
—Good Cause Shown
—Nonprofit Associations
—Prejudice to Defendant
—Public Interest
Lack of Bond
—Remedy
Minimizing Potential for Loss
—Escrow
Purpose
Purpose Not Satisfied
Waiver

In General

Sections 9 and 12 of the former Injunction Act (see now this section and 735 ILCS 5/11-110) were intended to be read together, with former section 9 granting to the court the authority to require a bond for damages and former section 12 prescribing the proper procedure to be followed in applying for a damage award. Stocker Hinge Mfg. Co. v. Darnel Indus., Inc., 94 Ill. 2d 535, 69 Ill. Dec. 71, 447 N.E.2d 288 (1983).

Applicability

—Preliminary Injunctions

Former Ill.Rev.Stat., Ch. 69, para. 8 (see now this section) was only applicable where preliminary injunctions were issued, and had no application to permanent injunctions entered upon a final hearing, where there could be no motion to dissolve. Chicago Title & Trust Co. v. De Lasaux, 336 Ill. 522, 168 N.E. 640 (1929).

—Stay of Judgment

Where an injunction to stay the enforcement of a judgment was sought, this was controlled by former section 8 of the Injunctions Act (see now this section), which made the giving of a bond mandatory, and a defendant was not permitted to recover damages when he was at fault in not calling the attention of the court to the statute, which, if it had been done, would have undoubtedly caused the court to refuse to order the issuance of the injunction without requiring a bond. Presbyterian Distrib. v. Chicago Nat'l Bank, 21 Ill. App. 2d 188, 157 N.E.2d 789 (1 Dist. 1959).

Bond

—Court's Discretion

Trial court abused its discretion when it conditioned issuance of a preliminary injunction against development of apartment houses on land adjoining natural prairie and savanna on a public interest group's provision of a bond in an amount that equaled a century's worth of income for the public interest group. Save the Prairie Soc'y v. Greene Dev. Group, Inc., 338 Ill. App. 3d 800, 273 Ill. Dec. 489, 789 N.E.2d 389, 2003 Ill. App. LEXIS 523 (1 Dist. 2003).

Temporary restraining order was not void even though the statutory requirement of a bond was neither met nor waived as question of whether to require a bond was one which rested in the sound discretion of the trial court and the refusal to require bond, even if erroneous, did not void the order. American Warehousing Servs., Inc. v. Weitzman, 169 Ill. App. 3d 708, 120 Ill. Dec. 171, 523 N.E.2d 1082 (1 Dist. 1988).

—Letters of Credit Insufficient

The plain language of this section states that applicants may be required to give bond; there are no decisions under this section which support the proposition that letters of credit may be given in lieu of a bond. Powell v. Home Run Inn, Inc., 202 Ill. App. 3d 94, 147 Ill. Dec. 463, 559 N.E.2d 803 (1 Dist. 1990).

—Notice and Hearing

When a preliminary injunction order is issued after notice and hearing, it is not error for the trial court to issue the injunction without bond. K.F.K. Corp. v. American Continental Homes, Inc., 31 Ill. App. 3d 1017, 335 N.E.2d 156 (2 Dist. 1975).

Bond Properly Denied

Where defendants offered no evidence at hearing to support the notion that a bond was required, but rather, conducted business with plaintiffs for approximately one year and during that period, plaintiffs never failed to pay for their purchases, the trial court properly exercised its discretion in denying bond. Falcon, Ltd. v. Corr's Natural Beverages, Inc., 165 Ill. App. 3d 815, 117 Ill. Dec. 480, 520 N.E.2d 831 (1 Dist. 1987).

Contempt

—Elements

Where an injunction has been issued and contempt proceedings follow, the only questions for determination are whether the court had jurisdiction to issue the order and if it did whether that order

Contempt (Cont'd)

—Elements (Cont'd)
has been violated. Farwell v. Horton, 301 Ill.App. 372, 22 N.E.2d 958 (2 Dist. 1939).

—Specificity of Injunction
In reviewing contempt conviction a pertinent factor which must be considered is the specificity of the injunction order. O'Leary v. Allphin, 64 Ill. 2d 500, 1 Ill. Dec. 363, 356 N.E.2d 551 (1976).

Damages for Delay

—Precluded
Where an injunction is dissolved on the ground of the insufficiency of the bond, and a new injunction is immediately requested, or if the original injunction is retained, and time is given in which to file a new bond, damages for the delay will not be allowed. American Warehousing Servs., Inc. v. Weitzman, 169 Ill. App. 3d 708, 127 Ill.Dec. 494, 533 N.E.2d 366 (1 Dist., 1988).

Discretion of Court

—In General
The question of whether to require a bond prior to issuance of a temporary restraining order or preliminary injunction is one which rests in the sound discretion of the trial court. Aurora Steel Prods. v. United Steelworkers, 94 Ill. App. 3d 97, 49 Ill. Dec. 638, 418 N.E.2d 492 (2 Dist. 1981).

Making a bond a prerequisite to the issuance of an injunction is a matter in the sound judicial discretion of the chancellor. Bowman Shoe Co. v. Bowman, 21 Ill. App. 2d 423, 158 N.E.2d 112 (2 Dist. 1959).

Former Ill.Rev.Stat., ch. 69, Sec. 9 (see now this section) recognized, and the opinions of the appellate court of the first district court reinforced, that making a bond a prerequisite to the issuance of an injunction is a matter in the sound discretion of the chancellor. Mitchell v. Mitchell, 10 Ill. App. 2d 437, 135 N.E.2d 109 (1 Dist. 1956).

—Bond Mandatory
Pursuant to former section 9 of the Injunction Act (see now this section) it was not within the sound discretion of the trial court to issue a restraining order or injunction for good cause shown without requiring the plaintiff to post bond. Hoffman v. City of Evanston, 101 Ill. App. 2d 440, 243 N.E.2d 478 (1 Dist. 1968).

—Good Cause
Although the issuance of an injunction without bond rests largely in the discretion of the court, the record must show good cause for the proper exercise of that discretion. Therefore, where the record in the case was silent as to the reason for not requiring the bond, the appellate court affirmed the restraining order and remanded the cause to the trial court for hearing on the bond. Seay & Thomas, Inc. v. Kerr's, Inc., 58 Ill. App. 2d 391, 208 N.E.2d 22 (1 Dist. 1965).

—Limited
A defendant shall not be deprived of the security of a bond except where a showing is made that complainant was unable to give bond or that he was capable of responding in damages or that no injury could result if the bond was excused. GE Co. v. Local 997 UAW of Am., 8 Ill. App. 2d 154, 130 N.E.2d 758 (3 Dist. 1955).

Dissolution of Injunction

—Action on Bond
Where union did not pursue its statutory remedy to appeal from wrongful issuance of temporary injunction and claim damages under the procedure prescribed by the statute, but brought an action on the bond itself, union was limited by the express provisions of the bond. United Mail Order, Whse. & Retail Employees Union v. Montgomery Ward & Co., 6 Ill. App. 2d 477, 128 N.E.2d 645 (1 Dist. 1955).

Upon the dissolution of an injunction there is an immediate cause of action upon the bond accruing to the party against whom the injunction was directed for the costs and damages sustained in and about the dissolution of such injunction, and the fact that the court has failed to assess damages or finally dispose of the case is no defense to such action. Shackleford v. Bennett, 237 Ill. 523, 86 N.E. 1073 (1908).

—Grounds
Where it appears that an injunction is issued without notice, in a case where notice should have been given, or where the statute requires a bond to be given as a condition precedent to issuing a preliminary injunction and none is required, the motion to dissolve the injunction must be granted. Kessie v. Talcott, 305 Ill. App. 627, 27 N.E.2d 857 (2 Dist. 1940).

—Ruling Required
The trial court erred in modifying injunction orders without first ruling on defendant's motions to dissolve or vacate the injunctions, where the motions urged that the injunctions were invalid because they were issued without notice, without bond and without any showing that there was good cause for waiver of the bond, as provided in former similar provision (see now this section). Byrne v. Byrne, 62 Ill. App. 2d 336, 211 N.E.2d 1 (1 Dist. 1965).

Error in Injunction Bond

—Harmless
Where a preliminary injunction was properly issued, any error in the setting of the injunction bond would not render the injunction void. Bonner v. Westbound Records, Inc., 49 Ill. App. 3d 543, 7 Ill. Dec. 409, 364 N.E.2d 570 (1 Dist. 1977).

—Order Not Voided
The trial court is vested with discretion; even if the trial court refuses to require bond and that refusal is erroneous, it does not void the order. Lums Restaurant Corp. v. Bloomington Restaurant Invs., Inc., 92 Ill. App. 3d 1143, 48 Ill. Dec. 478, 416 N.E.2d 751 (4 Dist. 1981).

Failure to Require Bond

—Order Not Reversed
Where a temporary restraining order or preliminary injunction has been properly issued, any error in failing in require a bond or in setting an inadequate bond does not injure the party against whom the order is allowed, and the order will not be reversed simply because of the absence or inadequacy of bond. American Warehousing Servs., Inc. v. Weitzman, 169 Ill. App. 3d 708, 127 Ill.Dec. 494, 533 N.E.2d 366 (1 Dist., 1988).

Injunction Without Bond

—In General
A bond for a temporary injunction may not be required where, for good cause shown, the court is of the opinion that the injunction ought to be granted without bond. Compton v. Paul K. Harding Realty Co., 87 Ill. App. 2d 219, 231 N.E.2d 267 (5 Dist. 1967).

It is necessary that the excuse of the bond for good cause be justified by facts evident in the record. Compton v. Paul K. Harding Realty Co., 87 Ill. App. 2d 219, 231 N.E.2d 267 (5 Dist. 1967).

A bond for the issuance of an injunction may not be required where, for good cause shown, the court is of the opinion that the injunction ought to be granted without bond; however, it is necessary that the excuse of the bond for good cause be justified by facts evident in the record. County of DuPage v. C. B. Robinette, 77 Ill. App. 2d 167, 221 N.E.2d 769 (2 Dist. 1966).

—Determination by Court
The propriety of an issuance of an injunction without bond or notice must be determined solely upon the pleadings before the court when it entered the order. Mitchell v. Mitchell, 10 Ill. App. 2d 437, 135 N.E.2d 109 (1 Dist. 1956).

—Error
Where order enjoining defendants from conducting a civil service examination, without there having first been compliance with the mandatory statutory requirement that plaintiff file a bond to cover payment of such costs and damages as might be suffered by any defendants, was found to have been wrongfully entered, the court was without authority to issue the injunction. Belpedio v. Civil Service Comm'n, 108 Ill. App. 2d 131, 246 N.E.2d 822 (1 Dist. 1969).

Where the order for temporary injunction under former Ill.Rev.Stat., ch. 69, para. 8 (see now this section) did not provide

Injunction Without Bond (Cont'd)

—Error (Cont'd)

for the issuance of a bond, it was error. Wise v. City of Chicago, 36 Ill. App. 2d 196, 183 N.E.2d 538 (1 Dist. 1962).

The issuance of the temporary injunction without notice and without bond was obviously improper and the motion to dismiss should have been allowed. East Side Health Dist. v. Village of Caseyville, 35 Ill. App. 2d 443, 183 N.E.2d 20 (4th Dist. 1962).

—Financial Interest

Chancellor did not abuse his discretion by not requiring plaintiff to post a bond because case was not one where a very highly valued interest in property was immobilized as a result of the imposition of temporary injunction to the extent that there was a serious financial matter. Brooks v. La Salle Nat'l Bank, 11 Ill. App. 3d 791, 298 N.E.2d 262 (1 Dist. 1973).

Where assets involved are of such a nature that defendant can destroy the substance of the litigation by a stroke of the pen, a movement of the hand, and where it appears from the pleadings that the plaintiff by reason of the past wrongful conduct of the party to be enjoined has good cause and reason to apprehend such action, the issuance of an injunction without bond or notice will be allowed. Mitchell v. Mitchell, 10 Ill. App. 2d 437, 135 N.E.2d 109 (1 Dist. 1956).

—Good Cause Not Shown

General statements that plaintiffs "are not able to furnish bond for the injunction prayed for herein, and if notice of their application for injunction were required to be given they would be unduly prejudiced and great and irreparable harm and injury will result to them" were mere conclusions and did not justify failure to give notice or to give proper bond; therefore it was error not to dissolve the temporary injunction. Clayton v. Hubbard, 33 Ill. App. 2d 439, 179 N.E.2d 845 (4 Dist. 1962).

Where there was no allegation that irreparable damage would be suffered in case the court refused to enter an order for a temporary injunction, nor was there anything in the hearing which would help sustain the court's order, and where the only witness who testified was one for the town, and he testified that a month before the filing of the suit he had inspected the camp and had found certain unsanitary conditions, but there was no showing that the conditions testified to by the witness were in existence at the time of the filing of the suit, the trial court improperly issued a temporary injunction against defendant without a bond from the plaintiff. Town of Cicero v. Weilander, 35 Ill. App. 2d 456, 183 N.E.2d 40 (1 Dist. 1962).

Where, if the injunction had not been granted, appellees would have run the risk of being prosecuted for operating their businesses without a license or if they closed, then their investment, which was substantial, would have been destroyed and their customers would have been lost, those allegations did not authorize the issuance of the preliminary injunction without notice and certainly not without bond. Kessie v. Talcott, 305 Ill. App. 627, 27 N.E.2d 857 (2 Dist. 1940).

—Good Cause Shown

It was not an abuse of discretion to issue an injunction without notice and without bond where the trial court had the right to consider allegations pertaining to the property of plaintiff in defendant's possession, where plaintiff had been deprived of the property by the fraud of the defendant, where plaintiff was seriously ill and under the care of a physician and incapable of gainful employment, where the only asset plaintiff had was the remainder of funds from loans on insurance policies, where the value of assets of plaintiff in the hands of defendant was substantial, where the amount of bond that would be required would be far in excess of the money that defendant had available, and where the ordering of a bond would therefore work an undue hardship on defendant. Mitchell v. Mitchell, 10 Ill. App. 2d 437, 135 N.E.2d 109 (1 Dist. 1956).

—Nonprofit Associations

Both the waiving of bond when granting an injunction to a nonprofit association, and the requiring of a bond after a hearing were, the exercise of sound discretion by the chancellor. Sunset Hills Homeowners Ass'n v. Karel, 39 Ill. App. 2d 477, 189 N.E.2d 41 (1 Dist. 1963).

—Prejudice to Defendant

Where the injunction order did not restrain the defendants from doing anything that they had a lawful right to do, it was evident that no injury could come to the defendants through the injunction, and consequently there was no abuse by the court in issuing the injunction without bond. GE Co. v. Local 997 UAW of Am., 8 Ill. App. 2d 154, 130 N.E.2d 758 (3 Dist. 1955).

—Public Interest

Whether the basis for the granting of an injunction without bond is that the "public interest" is involved or for any other reason, there must be a showing made, and a mere recital in the order issuing the injunction is not sufficient; there is no rule of law which says that in every case where a public interest is involved the court may, without any further showing, order the issuance of a temporary injunction without bond. Town of Cicero v. Weilander, 35 Ill. App. 2d 456, 183 N.E.2d 40 (1 Dist. 1962).

Lack of Bond

—Remedy

If a party is aggrieved by the lack of a bond or the inadequacy of the bond posted, his remedy is to petition in the trial or reviewing court to require a bond in an amount sufficient to cover his potential damages should the preliminary injunction or restraining order later be found to have been wrongfully issued. American Warehousing Servs., Inc. v. Weitzman, 169 Ill. App. 3d 708, 127 Ill.Dec. 494, 533 N.E.2d 366 (1 Dist., 1988); Powell v. Home Run Inn, Inc., 202 Ill. App. 3d 94, 147 Ill. Dec. 463, 559 N.E.2d 803 (1 Dist. 1990).

Minimizing Potential for Loss

—Escrow

Injunctions need not be dissolved if entered without bond, particularly when the funds in dispute are put into escrow, and thus, the potential for any loss is minimal. Carriage Way Apts. v. Pojman, 172 Ill. App. 3d 827, 122 Ill. Dec. 717, 527 N.E.2d 89 (2 Dist. 1988).

Purpose

The requirement of bond for interlocutory relief is designed to protect defendants by underwriting their losses in the event the interlocutory injunction is dissolved and damages are assess against the plaintiff; courts should only issue preliminary injunctions, or temporary restraining orders, without bond with great caution. Hill v. Village of Pawnee, 16 Ill. App. 3d 208, 305 N.E.2d 740 (4 Dist. 1973).

The purpose of the bond is to secure defendants for damages which may be assessed in the event the injunction is unlawfully issued. GE Co. v. Local 997 UAW of Am., 8 Ill. App. 2d 154, 130 N.E.2d 758 (3 Dist. 1955).

The purpose of requiring a bond is to assure to the defendant in the event of the preliminary injunction is later dissolved and damages for the unlawful suing out of the injunction are assessed against the plaintiff, that those damages will be paid. Atkinson Trust Sav. Bank v. De Roo, 332 Ill. App. 251, 75 N.E.2d 46 (2 Dist. 1947).

Purpose Not Satisfied

Where from the time condominium was purchased by defendant and the time defendant's mother commenced residing there, plaintiff never requested that defendant's mother pay rent, and it was not until the original temporary maintenance order was entered that plaintiff made his written demands for rent upon defendant's mother, the evidence did not satisfy the statutory purpose for posting bond, which is to protect the enjoined party from any damages or costs he may incur as a result of a wrongful injunction. In re Meyer, 146 Ill. App. 3d 83, 100 Ill. Dec. 128, 496 N.E.2d 1193 (1 Dist. 1986).

Waiver

Defendant waived the requirement of this section regarding a bond by failing to suggest or insist on the provision of this section, and he was therefore not in a position to urge that an interlocutory order be reversed. Russell v. Russell, 329 Ill. App. 580, 70 N.E.2d 70 (1 Dist. 1946).

RESEARCH REFERENCES

Recovery of damages resulting from wrongful issuance of injunction as limited to amount of bond. 30 ALR4th 273.

735 ILCS 5/11-104 Bond before court or clerk

Sec. 11-104. *Bond before court or clerk.* The bond may be entered into before the court granting or ordering the injunction, or before the clerk of the court, if the court has approved the security.
(Source: P.A. 82-280.)

Note.
This section was Ill.Rev.Stat., Ch. 110, para. 11-104.

735 ILCS 5/11-105 Filing of bond

Sec. 11-105. *Filing of bond.* All bonds required by Article XI of this Act [735 ILCS 5/11-101 et seq.] shall be filed with the clerk of the court who is to certify the injunctive order or judgment.
(Source: P.A. 83-707.)

Note.
This section was Ill.Rev.Stat., Ch. 110, para. 11-105.

RESEARCH REFERENCES

Effect of testamentary gift to child conditioned upon specified arrangements for parental control. 11 ALR4th 940.

735 ILCS 5/11-106 Injunctive relief on Saturday, Sunday or legal holiday

Sec. 11-106. *Injunctive relief on Saturday, Sunday or legal holiday.* When an application is made on a Saturday, Sunday, legal holiday or on a day when courts are not in session for injunctive relief and there is filed with the complaint an affidavit of the plaintiff, or his, her or their agent or attorney, stating that the benefits of injunctive relief will be lost or endangered, or irremediable damage occasioned unless such injunctive relief is immediately granted, and stating the bases for such alleged consequence, and if it appears to the court from such affidavit that the benefits of injunctive relief will be lost or endangered, or irremediable damage occasioned unless such injunctive relief is immediately granted, and if the plaintiff otherwise is entitled to such relief under the law, the court may grant injunctive relief on a Saturday, Sunday, legal holiday, or on a day when courts are not in session; and it shall be lawful for the clerk to certify, and for the sheriff or coroner to serve such order for injunctive relief on a Saturday, Sunday, legal holiday or on a day when courts are not in session as on any other day, and all affidavits and bonds made and proceedings had in such case shall have the same force and effect as if made or had on any other day.
(Source: P.A. 82-280.)

Note.
This section was Ill.Rev.Stat., Ch. 110, para. 11-106.

CASE NOTES

Emergency
The fact that the plaintiff filed his complaint on a Thursday, but did not present its motion for an emergency injunction until the following Monday, did not negate the allegations that an emergency existed and that it would be unduly prejudiced if the injunction would not be issued without notice, since the plaintiff presented the motion on the second court date following the filing of the complaint. Sunset Hills Homeowners Ass'n v. Karel, 39 Ill. App. 2d 477, 189 N.E.2d 41 (1 Dist. 1963).

735 ILCS 5/11-107 Seeking wrong remedy not fatal

Sec. 11-107. *Seeking wrong remedy not fatal.* Where relief is sought under Article XI of this Act [735 ILCS 5/11-101 et seq.], and the court determines, on motion directed to the pleadings, or on motion for summary judgment or upon trial, that the plaintiff has pleaded or established facts which entitle the plaintiff to relief but that the plaintiff has sought the wrong remedy, the court shall permit the pleadings to be amended, on just and reasonable terms, and the court shall grant the relief to which plaintiff is entitled on the amended pleadings or upon the evidence. In considering whether a proposed amendment is just and reasonable, the court shall consider the right of the defendant to assert additional defenses, to demand a trial by jury, to plead a counterclaim or third party complaint, and to order the plaintiff to take additional steps which were not required under the pleadings as previously filed.
(Source: P.A. 82-280.)

Note.
This section was Ill.Rev.Stat., Ch. 110, para. 11-107.

RESEARCH REFERENCES

Recovery of damages resulting from wrongful issuance of injunction as limited to amount of bond. 30 ALR4th 273.

735 ILCS 5/11-107.1 Injunctive relief for the father of an unborn child in an abortion related decision by the mother

Sec. 11-107.1. *Injunctive relief for the father of an unborn child in an abortion related decision by the mother.* In any case when a married woman wishes to have an abortion performed upon her, and her spouse, who is the father of the unborn child, is opposed to the performance of that abortion, a court may hear testimony from both parties and balance the rights and interests of those parties.

When the interests of the husband in preventing the abortion outweigh those of the wife in having an abortion performed after the unborn child is viable, the court may issue an injunction against the performance of the abortion but only where the court makes a finding that the mother's life or physical health are not in danger.
(Source: P.A. 84-1000.)

Note.
This section was Ill.Rev.Stat., Ch. 110, para. 11-107.1.

735 ILCS 5/11-108 Motion to dissolve

Sec. 11-108. *Motion to dissolve.* A motion to dissolve an injunction may be made at any time before or after answer is filed. Upon a motion to dissolve an injunction after answer is filed the court shall decide the motion upon the weight of the evidence.
(Source: P.A. 82-280.)

Note.
This section was Ill.Rev.Stat., Ch. 110, para. 11-108.

CASE NOTES

ANALYSIS

Appeal
—Order Not Final
Court's Duty
—In General
Dissolution
—Delay in Prosecution
—Factors
Injunction Binding
Raising Objections
—Timing

Appeal

—Order Not Final
An order allowing a motion to dissolve or partially dissolve a temporary injunction is interlocutory and is not appealable. Liberty Nat'l Bank v. City of Chicago, 342 Ill. App. 328, 96 N.E.2d 663 (1 Dist. 1950).

Court's Duty

—In General
A motion for dissolution of an injunction requires the court to engage in a specific analysis of new facts or changed conditions to determine whether the injunction should stand. Robert A. Besner & Co. v. Lit Am., Inc., 214 Ill. App. 3d 619, 158 Ill. Dec. 590, 574 N.E.2d 703 (1 Dist.), appeal denied, 141 Ill. 2d 560, 162 Ill. Dec. 508, 580 N.E.2d 134 (1991).

Dissolution

—Delay in Prosecution
A delay in prosecution may constitute a ground for a motion to dissolve an injunction unless a sufficient cause for the delay is presented. Eads Coal Co. v. UMW of Am., 27 Ill. App. 3d 692, 327 N.E.2d 115 (5 Dist. 1975).

—Factors
Preliminary injunction prohibiting plaintiff's competitor from comparing formulas for products made by both plaintiff and the competitor should have been dissolved after plaintiff disclosed the very information it sought to protect in a bid proposal to one of the competitor's customers; the comparison of the formulas ceased to be proprietary or protectable when plaintiff republished it. Carus Chem. Co. v. Calciquest, Inc., 341 Ill. App. 3d 897, 276 Ill. Dec. 172, 793 N.E.2d 931, 2003 Ill. App. LEXIS 884 (3 Dist. 2003).

An injunction may be dissolved as to its prospective effect where a court finds that equity no longer justified its continuance, but the party seeking dissolution must make the necessary showing that he is entitled to such relief. Eads Coal Co. v. UMW of Am., 27 Ill. App. 3d 692, 327 N.E.2d 115 (5 Dist. 1975).

Injunction Binding
The court had power to grant a writ of injunction, conferred by the filing of the complaint, and therefore had power to determine judicially the sufficiency of the complaint to authorize the injunction; even if the court erred in granting the writ or in not requiring notice, the writ was nevertheless binding upon the defendants until its dissolution or until the defendants appealed successfully to a higher court. Christian Hosp. v. People ex rel. Murphy, 223 Ill. 244, 79 N.E. 72 (1906).

Raising Objections

—Timing
While it would have been more efficient for city to raise its objections prior to issuance of the preliminary injunction, the city was not precluded from raising their objections in a motion to dissolve the preliminary injunction. International Ass'n of Firefighters Local 23 v. City of E. St. Louis, 206 Ill. App. 3d 580, 152 Ill. Dec. 22, 565 N.E.2d 264 (5 Dist. 1990).

735 ILCS 5/11-109 Affidavits in support of motion to dissolve

Sec. 11-109. *Affidavits in support of motion to dissolve.* The plaintiff may support the complaint and the defendant may support the answer by affidavits filed with the same, which may be read in evidence on the hearing of the motion to dissolve the injunction.
(Source: P.A. 82-280.)

Note.
This section was Ill.Rev.Stat., Ch. 110, para. 11-109.

CASE NOTES

Pleading
Affidavits were not to be received under former section 17 of the Injunction Act (see now this section) on motion to dissolve an injunction before there was an answer or other pleading to the bill. Crown Bldg. Corp. v. Monroe Amusement Corp., 326 Ill. App. 430, 62 N.E.2d 32 (1 Dist. 1945).

735 ILCS 5/11-110 Assessing damages

Sec. 11-110. *Assessing damages.* In all cases where a temporary restraining order or a preliminary injunction is dissolved by the circuit court or by the reviewing court, the circuit court, after the dissolution of the temporary restraining order or preliminary injunction, and before finally disposing of the action shall, upon the party claiming damages by reason of such temporary restraining order or preliminary injunction, filing a petition under oath setting forth the nature and amount of damages suffered, determine and enter judgment in favor of the party who was injured by such temporary restraining order or preliminary injunction for the damages which the party suffered as a result thereof, which judgment may be enforced as other judgments for the payment of money. However, a failure so to assess damages as hereinabove set out shall not operate as a bar to an action upon the injunction bond.
(Source: P.A. 82-280.)

Note.
This section was Ill.Rev.Stat., Ch. 110, para. 11-110.

CASE NOTES

ANALYSIS

In General
Amount of Damages

—Actual Damage
—Inseparability of Expenses
—Loss Not Shown
—Market Value
Applicability
—In General
—Amended Filings
—Dissolution Prior to Disposition
—Federal Courts
—Improper Temporary Restraining Order
—Insufficient Bond
—Receivership Expenses
—Temporary Restraining Order
Attorney Fees
—Defense on Merits
—Limited
—Partial Dissolution of Injunction
—Provided as Gratuity
—Recoverability
—Strict Construction
Availability
—Dissolution Before Disposition
Award Proper
—Illustrative Cases
Burden of Proof
—Claimant
Conditional Injunction
—Liability for Wrongful Issuance
Construction
—In General
—Strict
Court's Duty
—Determination of Damages
Damages Precluded
—Illustrative Cases
—No Wrongful Issuance Ruling
Denial of Motion
—Effect
Discretion of Court
—Award Properly Granted
Dissolution
—Denial of Motion
—Expiration Distinguished
—Merger with Permanent Injunction
—Not Dispositive
—Partial
—Temporary Restraining Order
Equal Protection
—Not Violated
Expenses
Expiration of Injunction
—Damages Hearing Precluded
Jurisdiction
—Interlocutory Appeal
Limitations
—Actual Damages
Malicious Prosecution Action
—Not Barred
Motion to Dissolve
—In General
—Question Preserved
Petitions for Damages
—By Counterclaim
Preliminary Assessment
Prerequisite
—Adjudication
Preservation of Damages
—Timely Filing Required
Purpose
Recovering Damages
—Retroactive
—Wrongful Injunction Required
Requirements
—Prior Adjudication
—Tortious Conduct
Scope
—Allowable Damages
—Attorney Fees
—Dissolution Costs
—Restraining Action
—Result of Injunction
—Wrongfully Issued Orders
Short Term Injunction
—Timely Expiration
Untimely Dissolution
—Claim Denied
Wrongfully Granted Injunction
—Liability

In General

The propriety of the issuance of the TRO becomes moot once the TRO is no longer in existence, except for the question of assessing damages for the wrongful issuance of such. Harper v. Missouri Pac. R.R., 264 Ill. App. 3d 238, 201 Ill. Dec. 760, 636 N.E.2d 1192 (5 Dist.), appeal denied, 157 Ill. 2d 500, 205 Ill. Dec. 162, 642 N.E.2d 1279 (1994).

Where petitioner had established his entitlement to damages pursuant to this section, an injunction was wrongfully issued. Boltz v. Estate of Bryant, 175 Ill. App. 3d 1056, 125 Ill. Dec. 576, 530 N.E.2d 985 (1 Dist. 1988).

This section is to be strictly construed and applied. Emerson Elec. Co. v. Sherman, 150 Ill. App. 3d 832, 104 Ill. Dec. 151, 502 N.E.2d 414 (1 Dist. 1986).

Amount of Damages

—Actual Damage

Upon the dissolution of an injunction the assessment of damages should rest upon equitable grounds and should not exceed the damages actually sustained. R. M. C. Corp. v. Genco, Inc., 330 Ill. App. 192, 71 N.E.2d 189 (1 Dist. 1946).

—Inseparability of Expenses

Under former Ill.Rev.Stat., ch. 69, para. 12 (see now this section), where the chancellor was unable to make a clear distinction and finding as to the services necessarily incurred in the partial dissolution of the temporary injunction, a strict construction and application of the statute required the disallowance of the fees sought. Cromwell Paper Co. v. Wellman, 23 Ill. App. 2d 263, 162 N.E.2d 500 (1 Dist. 1959).

—Loss Not Shown

Where the evidence tended to show that defendants were manufacturing at to full capacity before and after the injunction, defendants did not suffer any damage due to the injunction. R. M. C. Corp. v. Genco, Inc., 330 Ill. App. 192, 71 N.E.2d 189 (1 Dist. 1946).

—Market Value

The measure of damages is the difference between the fair cash reasonable market value of the items in controversy on the day the injunction was issued and such value on the day it was dissolved. Kolin v. Leitch, 351 Ill. App. 66, 113 N.E.2d 806 (1 Dist. 1953).

Applicability

—In General

This section applies only to preliminary injunctions and temporary restraining orders; it does not apply to permanent injunctions. Buzz Barton & Assocs. v. Giannone, 108 Ill. 2d 373, 91 Ill. Dec. 636, 483 N.E.2d 1271 (1985).

—Amended Filings

Where, after a motion to dissolve a temporary restraining order (TRO) was filed, the trial court continued the TRO under an amended complaint but never held a hearing on defendant's subsequent motion to dissolve the TRO based on the amended complaint, there was no order ruling that the TRO was properly issued which, if the defendant had failed to appeal, would be the law of the case barring the defendant from recovering statutory damages. Hirschauer v. Chicago Sun-Times, 192 Ill. App. 3d 193, 139 Ill. Dec. 245, 548 N.E.2d 630 (1 Dist. 1989).

A motion to dissolve an injunction should have been heard first, before any new or amended filings by the guardian were enter-

Applicability (Cont'd)

—Amended Filings (Cont'd)

tained. Boltz v. Estate of Bryant, 175 Ill. App. 3d 1056, 125 Ill. Dec. 576, 530 N.E.2d 985 (1 Dist. 1988).

—Dissolution Prior to Disposition

Preliminary injunctions or temporary restraining orders had to be dissolved prior to a determination of the case on the merits in order to fall within the purview of section 12 of the former Injunction Act (see now this section). Stocker Hinge Mfg. Co. v. Darnel Indus., Inc., 94 Ill. 2d 535, 69 Ill. Dec. 71, 447 N.E.2d 288 (1983).

Where no motion was ever made by defendants to dissolve the temporary injunction until after a holding on the merits, such motion came too late to allow for a damage award under this section. House of Vision, Inc. v. Hiyane, 42 Ill. 2d 45, 245 N.E.2d 468 (1969).

Trial court did not fail in assessing damages upon the dissolution of a temporary injunction in the court's final decree for the authorities have held that this is not the type of dissolution envisioned by the statute in that it was not dissolved "before finally disposing of the suit". Smith v. Smith, 5 Ill. App. 2d 383, 125 N.E.2d 693 (4 Dist. 1955).

The statute clearly applies only where the injunction "is dissolved" and "before finally disposing of the suit." Schien v. City of Virden, 5 Ill. 2d 494, 126 N.E.2d 201 (1955).

—Federal Courts

This statute cannot be applied in the federal courts because this provision was a remedial statute which governed procedure in the state courts and which could have no force or effect in federal courts. Progressive Steelworkers Union v. Int'l Harvester Corp., 70 F.R.D. 691 (N.D. Ill. 1976).

This is a remedial statute the terms of which govern the procedure in the state courts, and as such it can have no force and effect in the federal courts. Official Aviation Guide Co. v. American Aviation Assocs., 162 F.2d 541 (7th Cir. 1947).

—Improper Temporary Restraining Order

Prior adjudication that a temporary restraining order was wrongfully issued is a prerequisite to the recovery of statutory damages. C.D. Peters Constr. Co. v. Tri-City Regional Port Dist., 281 Ill. App. 3d 41, 216 Ill. Dec. 876, 666 N.E.2d 44 (5 Dist. 1996), appeal denied, 168 Ill. 2d 584, 219 Ill. Dec. 560, 671 N.E.2d 727 (1996).

Where the record indicates the possibility that a party subject to an improperly issued temporary restraining order would suffer compensable damages, the issue as to the order's propriety is not moot. Hawthorne Bank of Wheaton v. Village of Glen Ellyn, 154 Ill. App. 3d 661, 107 Ill. Dec. 97, 506 N.E.2d 988 (2 Dist. 1987).

—Insufficient Bond

Where an injunction is dissolved on the ground of the insufficiency of the bond, and a new injunction is immediately requested, or if the original injunction is retained, and time is given in which to file a new bond, damages for the delay will not be allowed. American Warehousing Servs., Inc. v. Weitzman, 169 Ill. App. 3d 708, 127 Ill.Dec. 494, 533 N.E.2d 366 (1 Dist., 1988).

—Receivership Expenses

The expense of a receivership may not be considered an element of damage flowing from the issuance of an injunction and a trial court abused its discretion when it taxed the costs of a receivership against a defendant. Compton v. Paul K. Harding Realty Co., 6 Ill. App. 3d 488, 285 N.E.2d 574 (5 Dist. 1972).

—Temporary Restraining Order

When a temporary restraining order is dissolved before a final determination of the case on its merits, damages may be assessed under the provisions of this section. Panduit Corp. v. All States Plastic Mfg. Co., 84 Ill. App. 3d 1144, 40 Ill. Dec. 224, 405 N.E.2d 1316 (1 Dist. 1980).

Attorney Fees

—Defense on Merits

Where the evidence showed that plaintiff's attorney fees and costs were necessary expenses in connection with the trial upon the merits rather than upon the motion to dissolve the preliminary injunction, fees and costs were not recoverable under former section 12 of the Injunction Act (see now this section). Lawrence Ave. Bldg. Corp. v. Van Heck, 317 Ill. App. 59, 45 N.E.2d 687 (1 Dist. 1942).

In a case where the sole relief asked was a permanent injunction with a preliminary injunction granted pendente lite, and a decree upon the merits was entered in favor of the defendants, the defendants under former Ill.Rev.Stat., ch. 69, para. 12 (see now this section) were not entitled to recover sums expended for solicitors' fees for services rendered in the defense of the case on the merits and in subsequent appeals. Nester Johnson Mfg. Co. v. Goldblatt, 297 Ill. App. 190, 17 N.E.2d 371 (1 Dist. 1938), aff'd, 371 Ill. 570, 21 N.E.2d 723 (1939).

—Limited

Counsel fees unnecessarily incurred to obtain dissolution of a preliminary injunction were not allowed under former Ill.Rev.Stat., ch. 69, para. 12 (see now this section). Cromwell Paper Co. v. Wellman, 23 Ill. App. 2d 263, 162 N.E.2d 500 (1 Dist. 1959).

—Partial Dissolution of Injunction

Reasonable attorney fees may be awarded upon the partial dissolution of a preliminary injunction; but no such damages may be awarded unless it is possible to isolate those attorney fees necessarily incurred in obtaining dissolution of the objectionable portions of the injunction from those incurred generally. American Warehousing Servs., Inc. v. Weitzman, 169 Ill. App. 3d 708, 127 Ill.Dec. 494, 533 N.E.2d 366 (1 Dist., 1988).

Where a motion is made to dissolve an injunction in its entirety, but only part of the injunction is determined to have been improperly entered, and it is not possible to isolate that portion of the movant's attorney fees incurred in obtaining dissolution, no fees are available to the movant. American Warehousing Servs., Inc. v. Weitzman, 169 Ill. App. 3d 708, 127 Ill.Dec. 494, 533 N.E.2d 366 (1 Dist., 1988).

—Provided as Gratuity

An individual is not entitled to recover for the value of services that he has obtained without expense, obligation, or liability; because a defendant's legal representation was provided as a gratuity, he could not recover the fees as damages. Label Printers v. Pflug, 246 Ill. App. 3d 435, 186 Ill. Dec. 516, 616 N.E.2d 706 (2 Dist.), appeal denied, 152 Ill. 2d 561, 190 Ill. Dec. 891, 622 N.E.2d 1208 (1993).

—Recoverability

Attorney fees reasonably incurred in obtaining dissolution of a temporary restraining order are recoverable damages. American Warehousing Servs., Inc. v. Weitzman, 169 Ill. App. 3d 708, 120 Ill. Dec. 171, 523 N.E.2d 1082 (1 Dist. 1988); American Warehousing Servs., Inc. v. Weitzman, 169 Ill. App. 3d 708, 127 Ill.Dec. 494, 533 N.E.2d 366 (1 Dist., 1988).

A defendant may recover as damages, upon the dissolution of a temporary injunction, the attorney fees and costs which he has paid for services rendered in obtaining a dissolution of an injunction, but not those rendered in the general defense of the suit. Compton v. Paul K. Harding Realty Co., 6 Ill. App. 3d 488, 285 N.E.2d 574 (5 Dist. 1972).

Pursuant to former section 12 of the Injunction Act, (see now this section) a defendant may recover as damages, on dissolution of an injunction, the solicitor's fees which he has paid or become obligated to pay for services rendered in obtaining the dissolution of the injunction, but not for those rendered in the general defense of the suit. Kolin v. Leitch, 351 Ill. App. 66, 113 N.E.2d 806 (1 Dist. 1953).

Where counsel fees are necessarily incurred in procuring the dissolution of an injunction, they may be allowed as damages; when, however, they are incurred in defeating the suit generally, they cannot be assessed as damages under this provision. Keith v. Henkleman, 173 Ill. 137, 50 N.E. 692 (1898).

—Strict Construction

Under former Ill.Rev.Stat., ch. 69, para. 12 (see now this section) counsel fees could be assessed as damages necessarily incurred in procuring the dissolution of a wrongfully issued temporary injunction, if it was dissolved before the cause was heard on the merits for final judgment; however, the statute was strictly construed and applied. Cromwell Paper Co. v. Wellman, 23 Ill. App. 2d 263, 162 N.E.2d 500 (1 Dist. 1959).

Availability

—Dissolution Before Disposition

The fact that a temporary restraining order or preliminary injunction is not dissolved before a hearing on the merits and merges into the permanent injunction when a plaintiff prevails, does not mean that a legal determination that it was wrongfully issued has been made. Furthermore, there can be no assessment of damages by the summary procedure created in this section. R.L. Polk & Co. v. Ryan, 296 Ill. App. 3d 132, 230 Ill. Dec. 749, 694 N.E.2d 1027 (4 Dist. 1998), appeal denied, 179 Ill. 2d 617, 235 Ill. Dec. 576, 705 N.E.2d 449 (1998).

Attorney fees and other damages may be recovered only if the preliminary injunction has been dissolved before the case is disposed of on the merits, and thus adjudicated to have been wrongfully issued. Emerson Elec. Co. v. Sherman, 150 Ill. App. 3d 832, 104 Ill. Dec. 151, 502 N.E.2d 414 (1 Dist. 1986).

Award Proper

—Illustrative Cases

The circuit court correctly awarded damages for wrongful issuance of temporary restraining order. Jefco Lab., Inc. v. Carroo, 136 Ill. App. 3d 826, 91 Ill. Dec. 518, 483 N.E.2d 1004 (1 Dist. 1985).

Burden of Proof

—Claimant

Where the trial court dissolves a temporary restraining order (TRO) or preliminary injunction prior to disposing of the merits of the case, the party who was enjoined is entitled to recover damages incurred as a result of the TRO or preliminary injunction; the party claiming damages, however, must establish that the TRO or preliminary injunction was wrongfully issued. Peisker v. King, 140 Ill. App. 3d 640, 94 Ill. Dec. 930, 488 N.E.2d 1323 (2 Dist. 1986).

A party may be entitled to damages if a temporary restraining order (TRO) is dissolved by the trial court or the appellate court, however, the party asserting injury as a result of a wrongfully issued TRO must demonstrate the possibility of damages to avoid a finding on appeal that the issues are moot. Keene v. Lane, 137 Ill. App. 3d 793, 92 Ill. Dec. 639, 485 N.E.2d 450 (2 Dist. 1985).

Conditional Injunction

—Liability for Wrongful Issuance

The granting of a preliminary injunction or temporary restraining order being conditioned upon the party who is granted preliminary injunction being held liable for damages if the issuance was wrongful does not violate due process. Buzz Barton & Assocs. v. Giannone, 108 Ill. 2d 373, 91 Ill. Dec. 636, 483 N.E.2d 1271 (1985).

Construction

—In General

Sections 9 and 12 of the former Injunction Act (see now 735 ILCS 5/11-103 and this section) were intended to be read together, with section 9 granting to the court the authority to require a bond for damages and section 12 prescribing the proper procedure to be followed in applying for a damage award. Stocker Hinge Mfg. Co. v. Darnel Indus., Inc., 94 Ill. 2d 535, 69 Ill. Dec. 71, 447 N.E.2d 288 (1983).

—Strict

This section is to be strictly construed and damages are to be awarded under it only if the preliminary injunction has been dissolved before the case is disposed of on the merits, and thus adjudicated to have been wrongfully issued. Hirschauer v. Chicago Sun-Times, 192 Ill. App. 3d 193, 139 Ill. Dec. 245, 548 N.E.2d 630 (1 Dist. 1989).

Section 12 of the former Injunction Act (see now this section), which provided a summary mode for assessing damages, was to be strictly construed and applied. Stocker Hinge Mfg. Co. v. Darnel Indus., Inc., 94 Ill. 2d 535, 69 Ill. Dec. 71, 447 N.E.2d 288 (1983).

Court's Duty

—Determination of Damages

After the dissolution of a temporary restraining order or preliminary injunction, but before final disposition of an action, the trial court is required, upon the petition of the party injured by the temporary restraining order of preliminary injunction, to determine and enter judgment for damages in favor of that party. Hirschauer v. Chicago Sun-Times, 192 Ill. App. 3d 193, 139 Ill. Dec. 245, 548 N.E.2d 630 (1 Dist. 1989).

Damages Precluded

—Illustrative Cases

Defendants were not entitled to recover damages where there was no determination that the temporary restraining order, which enjoined the construction of a barn, was wrongfully issued. Peisker v. King, 140 Ill. App. 3d 640, 94 Ill. Dec. 930, 488 N.E.2d 1323 (2 Dist. 1986).

—No Wrongful Issuance Ruling

Any claim for statutory damages resulting from the wrongful issuance of preliminary injunctive relief would be untimely because defendant obtained no ruling of wrongful issuance prior to an adjudication on the merits nor did defendant preserve the issue through a timely motion to dissolve the order of preliminary relief. Pasquinelli v. Village of Mundelein, 257 Ill. App. 3d 1057, 196 Ill. Dec. 416, 630 N.E.2d 113 (2 Dist. 1994).

Denial of Motion

—Effect

The denial of a motion to dissolve a temporary restraining order was not considered to be a denial of a motion to dissolve a preliminary injunction for damages purposes where no such motion was ever made. Emerson Elec. Co. v. Sherman, 150 Ill. App. 3d 832, 104 Ill. Dec. 151, 502 N.E.2d 414 (1 Dist. 1986).

Discretion of Court

—Award Properly Granted

The trial court did not abuse its discretion in awarding damages based on the wrongful issuance of a preliminary injunction. Knapp v. Palos Community Hosp., 176 Ill. App. 3d 1012, 126 Ill. Dec. 362, 531 N.E.2d 989 (1 Dist. 1988), cert. denied, 493 U.S. 847, 110 S. Ct. 141, 107 L. Ed. 2d 100 (1989).

Dissolution

—Denial of Motion

Where the trial court meticulously followed the procedural requirements prescribed by former Ill.Rev.Stat., ch. 69, para. 3-1 (see now 735 ILCS 5/11-101) except that no notice of the issuance of the temporary restraining order was given to the defendant prior to its issuance and no bond was required, and where irreparable damage and harm required as a condition precedent to the issuance of a temporary restraining order without notice and without bond was not shown in this record, it followed that the trial court should have allowed the defendant's motion to dissolve the temporary restraining injunction; accordingly, the order of the trial court issuing the temporary restraining order without notice and refusing to dissolve it was reversed, and cause was remanded to the trial court to consider issue of damages under former Ill.Rev.Stat., ch. 69, para. 12 (see now this section). Bohn Aluminum & Brass Co. v. Barker, 20 Ill. App. 3d 20, 312 N.E.2d 722 (4 Dist. 1974).

Where trial court denied defendant's motion to dissolve temporary injunction, that order was not appealed and therefore became a final judgment that the temporary injunction was properly issued; therefore, not having been wrongfully issued and not having been dissolved prior to the hearing on the merits of the case, damages were not assessable. Schien v. City of Virden, 5 Ill. 2d 494, 126 N.E.2d 201 (1955).

—Expiration Distinguished

Expiration of an injunction by its own terms is not equivalent to the dissolution of the injunction, and an injunction that has expired by its own terms can no longer be dissolved because a court cannot dissolve that which no longer exists. Panduit Corp. v. All States Plastic Mfg. Co., 84 Ill. App. 3d 1144, 40 Ill. Dec. 224, 405 N.E.2d 1316 (1 Dist. 1980); Emerson Elec. Co. v. Sherman, 150 Ill. App. 3d 832, 104 Ill. Dec. 151, 502 N.E.2d 414 (1 Dist. 1986).

—Merger with Permanent Injunction

Where temporary injunction was not dissolved before a determi-

Dissolution (Cont'd)

—Merger with Permanent Injunction (Cont'd)

nation on the merits, and since it merged with the permanent injunction issued by the trial court, damages were not assessable under this section. United Mail Order, Whse. & Retail Employees Union v. Montgomery Ward & Co., 9 Ill. 2d 101, 137 N.E.2d 47 (1956).

If a temporary injunction is not dissolved before the hearing on the merits, or if it is merged into the permanent injunction when plaintiff prevails, or if it becomes functus officio by reason of the complaint being dismissed, there has been no legal determination that it was wrongfully issued and there can be no assessment of damages. Schien v. City of Virden, 5 Ill. 2d 494, 126 N.E.2d 201 (1955).

Where a labor union's first petition for damages alleged the wrongful issuance of a temporary injunction, the order dismissing the union's claim for damages on a finding by the trial court that the temporary injunction had become functus officio by the issuance of the final, order by the granting of a permanent injunction and was a final appealable, order and as to the union operated as a bar to any subsequent action involving the same issues. Montgomery Ward & Co. v. United Retail, Whsle. & Dept. Store Employees, 348 Ill. App. 198, 108 N.E.2d 784 (1 Dist. 1952).

There was no evidence upon which an assessment of damages for services rendered in the matter of the temporary injunction could be based where the complaint had been dismissed on appeal after the temporary injunction had been made permanent, and thus the allowance of damages for counsel's fees must be disallowed in toto. R. M. C. Corp. v. Genco, Inc., 330 Ill. App. 192, 71 N.E.2d 189 (1 Dist. 1946).

—Not Dispositive

As a general rule, the mere dissolution of a temporary restraining order prior to a final determination on the merits does not by itself establish that it was wrongfully entered. Hirschauer v. Chicago Sun-Times, 192 Ill. App. 3d 193, 139 Ill. Dec. 245, 548 N.E.2d 630 (1 Dist. 1989).

Dissolution of a temporary restraining order (TRO) at the conclusion of hearing on a preliminary injunction did not operate as a determination that the TRO had been wrongfully entered. Stocker Hinge Mfg. Co. v. Darnel Indus., Inc., 94 Ill. 2d 535, 69 Ill. Dec. 71, 447 N.E.2d 288 (1983).

—Partial

Under former Ill.Rev.Stat., ch. 69, para. 12 (see now this section) damages for partial dissolution of an injunction were allowed on the same basis as upon full dissolution and if the assessment was made only for services performed exclusively on the motion to dissolve, and damages which are remote, speculative and incapable of ascertainment could not be allowed. Cromwell Paper Co. v. Wellman, 23 Ill. App. 2d 263, 162 N.E.2d 500 (1 Dist. 1959).

—Temporary Restraining Order

Dissolution of temporary restraining order at conclusion of hearing on a preliminary injunction does not constitute a determination that the temporary restraining order was wrongfully entered. C.D. Peters Constr. Co. v. Tri-City Regional Port Dist., 281 Ill. App. 3d 41, 216 Ill. Dec. 876, 666 N.E.2d 44 (5 Dist. 1996), appeal denied, 168 Ill. 2d 584, 219 Ill. Dec. 560, 671 N.E.2d 727 (1996).

Equal Protection

—Not Violated

Holding the party who was granted preliminary injunction liable for all damages properly proved to have been caused by the wrongful issuance of the preliminary injunction is justified and did not violate the right to equal protection. Buzz Barton & Assocs. v. Giannone, 108 Ill. 2d 373, 91 Ill. Dec. 636, 483 N.E.2d 1271 (1985).

Expenses

Reimbursement under this section must be confined to those expenses necessarily incurred in procuring the dissolution of the temporary injunction. House of Vision, Inc. v. Hiyane, 42 Ill. 2d 45, 245 N.E.2d 468 (1969).

Expiration of Injunction

—Damages Hearing Precluded

Where no motion to dissolve preliminary injunction had been made and it had expired of its own terms, the appellate court could not order a hearing for the assessment of damages. Emerson Elec. Co. v. Sherman, 150 Ill. App. 3d 832, 104 Ill. Dec. 151, 502 N.E.2d 414 (1 Dist. 1986).

Jurisdiction

—Interlocutory Appeal

Circuit court had jurisdiction to enter its judgment for damages for the wrongful issuance of a temporary restraining order, although an interlocutory appeal had been taken as to the court's dissolution of temporary restraining order. Jefco Lab., Inc. v. Carroo, 136 Ill. App. 3d 826, 91 Ill. Dec. 518, 483 N.E.2d 1004 (1 Dist. 1985).

Limitations

—Actual Damages

Damages recoverable under former Ill.Rev.Stat. ch. 69, para. 12 (see now this section) were limited to damages actually suffered during the life or pendency of the injunction. Bank of Lyons v. Schultz, 78 Ill. 2d 235, 35 Ill. Dec. 758, 399 N.E.2d 1286 (1980).

Malicious Prosecution Action

—Not Barred

An award of damages pursuant to this section did not bar an action for malicious prosecution. Schultz v. Bank of Lyons, 66 Ill. App. 3d 698, 23 Ill. Dec. 477, 384 N.E.2d 113 (1 Dist. 1978), aff'd, 78 Ill. 2d 235, 35 Ill. Dec. 758, 399 N.E.2d 1286 (1980).

Motion to Dissolve

—In General

A timely motion to dissolve preserves the question of damages under this section for the wrongful issuance of a temporary restraining order or preliminary injunction, even where the order expires by its own terms before it can be reviewed. American Warehousing Servs., Inc. v. Weitzman, 169 Ill. App. 3d 708, 127 Ill.Dec. 494, 533 N.E.2d 366 (1 Dist., 1988).

—Question Preserved

A timely motion to dissolve preserves the question of even where the order expired by its own terms before it could be reviewed. American Warehousing Servs., Inc. v. Weitzman, 169 Ill. App. 3d 708, 120 Ill. Dec. 171, 523 N.E.2d 1082 (1 Dist. 1988).

Petitions for Damages

—By Counterclaim

Defendant's claim for damages stemming from alleged wrongful preliminary injunction constituted a counterclaim and, therefore, the trial court exceeded its authority in granting the voluntary dismissal without his consent. Marion Metal & Roofing Co. v. Wood, 243 Ill. App. 3d 890, 184 Ill. Dec. 173, 612 N.E.2d 1049 (5 Dist. 1993).

Preliminary Assessment

Damages claimed under former section 12 of the Injunction Act (see now this section) had to be based on the wrongful issuance of the temporary injunction and could not be assessed until there had been a determination that the temporary injunction was wrongfully issued. Illinois Funeral Home Owners Ass'n v. Cemetery Workers, 19 Ill. App. 2d 375, 153 N.E.2d 865 (1 Dist. 1958).

Under former section 12 of the Injunction Act (see now this section), where a temporary injunction was dissolved, the defendant was entitled to suggest his damages and have them assessed, whether the case had been disposed of on the merits or not. Illinois Funeral Home Owners Ass'n v. Cemetery Workers, 19 Ill. App. 2d 375, 153 N.E.2d 865 (1 Dist. 1958).

Prerequisite

—Adjudication

A prior adjudication that the temporary restraining order was wrongfully issued is a prerequisite to recovery of statutory damages. Hirschauer v. Chicago Sun-Times, 192 Ill. App. 3d 193, 139 Ill. Dec. 245, 548 N.E.2d 630 (1 Dist. 1989).

Damages claimed under temporary injunction are based on the wrongful issuance of the temporary injunction, and cannot be

Prerequisite (Cont'd)

—Adjudication (Cont'd)

assessed until there has been a legal determination that the temporary injunction was wrongfully issued. Schien v. City of Virden, 5 Ill. 2d 494, 126 N.E.2d 201 (1955).

Preservation of Damages

—Timely Filing Required

The issue of damages under this section must be preserved by the timely filing in the trial court of a motion to dissolve the injunction. Hirschauer v. Chicago Sun-Times, 192 Ill. App. 3d 193, 139 Ill. Dec. 245, 548 N.E.2d 630 (1 Dist. 1989).

The fact that the expiration of an injunction by its own terms is not the equivalent of dissolution does not mean that damages under this section are never available in those cases, but the key to the preservation of the question of damages for short term preliminary injunctions lies in the timely filing in the trial court of a motion to dissolve the injunction. Emerson Elec. Co. v. Sherman, 150 Ill. App. 3d 832, 104 Ill. Dec. 151, 502 N.E.2d 414 (1 Dist. 1986).

Purpose

The purpose of this section is to provide a summary means of assessing damages for the wrongful issuance of a temporary injunction; it should be applied only to temporary, not permanent, injunctions. House of Vision, Inc. v. Hiyane, 42 Ill. 2d 45, 245 N.E.2d 468 (1969).

This section is intended to provide relief against the wrongful issuance of a temporary injunction and to provide a mode of assessing damages for the wrongful issuance of a temporary injunction which is dissolved before final judgment. L & R Ins. Agency, Inc. v. McPhail, 92 Ill. App. 2d 107, 235 N.E.2d 153 (5 Dist. 1968).

The purpose of this section was to provide a summary mode of assessing damages for the wrongful issuance of a temporary injunction upon its dissolution before final judgment, and the statute applies only to temporary injunctions. Schien v. City of Virden, 5 Ill. 2d 494, 126 N.E.2d 201 (1955).

The statute relating to injunctions was intended to provide relief for wrongful issuance of an injunction. Nestor Johnson Mfg. Co. v. Goldblatt, et al., 371 Ill. 570, 21 N.E.2d 723 (1939).

The purpose of former section 12 of the Injunction Act (see now this section) was to give to the party injured by the wrongful suing out of an injunction the right to have his damages assessed, and to a decree awarding the same to him, wholly irrespective of whether an injunction bond has been given or not, or of the amount of the penalty of the bond, if one had been given. Kohlsaat v. Crate, 144 Ill. 14, 32 N.E. 481 (1892).

Recovering Damages

—Retroactive

A litigant who is successful in obtaining a dissolution of a preliminary injunction should be able to recover damages from the time he was first improperly enjoined, assuming that he complies with the requirements of this section. In re Schmidt, 118 Ill. App. 3d 467, 74 Ill. Dec. 93, 455 N.E.2d 123 (1 Dist. 1983); Hawthorne Bank of Wheaton v. Village of Glen Ellyn, 154 Ill. App. 3d 661, 107 Ill. Dec. 97, 506 N.E.2d 988 (2 Dist. 1987).

—Wrongful Injunction Required

Damages could be recovered under former section 12 of the Injunction Act (see now this section) only if the preliminary injunction had been dissolved before the case was disposed of on the merits, and thus adjudicated to have been wrongfully issued. Office Elecs., Inc. v. Grafic Forms, Inc., 72 Ill. App. 3d 456, 28 Ill. Dec. 594, 390 N.E.2d 953 (2 Dist. 1979).

Requirements

—Prior Adjudication

A damages award under section 12 of the former Injunction Act (see now this section) required a prior adjudication that the temporary restraining order or preliminary injunction had, in fact, been wrongfully entered. Stocker Hinge Mfg. Co. v. Darnel Indus., Inc., 94 Ill. 2d 535, 69 Ill. Dec. 71, 447 N.E.2d 288 (1983).

—Tortious Conduct

In order to recover damages under former section 12 of the Injunction Act (see now this section), for wrongful issuance of an injunction it is not necessary for the plaintiff to prove that the obtaining of the injunction was a tortious act. Lawrence Ave. Bldg. Corp. v. Van Heck, 317 Ill. App. 59, 45 N.E.2d 687 (1 Dist. 1942).

Scope

—Allowable Damages

Damages could be awarded under section 12 of the former Injunction Act (see now this section) only in connection with preliminary injunctions or temporary restraining orders. Stocker Hinge Mfg. Co. v. Darnel Indus., Inc., 94 Ill. 2d 535, 69 Ill. Dec. 71, 447 N.E.2d 288 (1983).

—Attorney Fees

Damages under this section include attorney fees. Boltz v. Estate of Bryant, 175 Ill. App. 3d 1056, 125 Ill. Dec. 576, 530 N.E.2d 985 (1 Dist. 1988).

—Dissolution Costs

Damages awarded on the dissolution of an injunction were governed by equitable principles, and nothing would be allowed which was not the natural and proximate result of the wrong committed. Reed v. New York Nat'l Exch. Bank, 230 Ill. 50, 82 N.E. 341 (1907).

—Restraining Action

Where a court's restraining action does not constitute an injunction, no relief is available under this section. Bank of Aspen v. Fox Cartage, Inc., 126 Ill. 2d 307, 127 Ill. Dec. 952, 533 N.E.2d 1080 (1989).

—Result of Injunction

Damages recoverable for wrongful suing out of a writ of injunction must be such as naturally and proximately result therefrom, and remote speculative damages cannot be taken into consideration. Kolin v. Leitch, 351 Ill. App. 66, 113 N.E.2d 806 (1 Dist. 1953).

—Wrongfully Issued Orders

This section permits damage actions after dissolution of temporary restraining orders or preliminary injunctions, but is addressed only to situations where the TRO or preliminary injunction has been wrongfully issued; it does not apply where injunctive relief has been denied. In re Holem, 153 Ill. App. 3d 1095, 106 Ill. Dec. 939, 506 N.E.2d 739 (5 Dist. 1987).

Short Term Injunction

—Timely Expiration

Assessment of damages was available in those cases where a short term preliminary injunction expired by its own terms before an appellate court could consider whether the preliminary injunction was improperly issued, if a motion to dissolve the injunction was timely filed in the trial court. Panduit Corp. v. All States Plastic Mfg. Co., 84 Ill. App. 3d 1144, 40 Ill. Dec. 224, 405 N.E.2d 1316 (1 Dist. 1980).

Untimely Dissolution

—Claim Denied

Applicant for approval of a regional pollution control facility's claim for damages failed where at the trial court a temporary restraining order was entered but was not dissolved before the suit was disposed of. Concerned Boone Citizens, Inc. v. M.I.G. Invs., Inc., 144 Ill. App. 3d 334, 98 Ill. Dec. 253, 494 N.E.2d 180 (2 Dist. 1986).

Wrongfully Granted Injunction

—Liability

The party who is granted a preliminary injunction which is later dissolved as having been wrongfully issued is treated somewhat differently than a party whose judgment is reversed on appeal, as instead of merely restoring any benefit received from the erroneous judgment or decree, the party who is wrongfully issued a preliminary injunction is liable for all damages caused by the wrongful issuance. Buzz Barton & Assocs. v. Giannone, 108 Ill. 2d 373, 91 Ill. Dec. 636, 483 N.E.2d 1271 (1985).

LEGAL PERIODICALS

For article, "Civil Procedure: 1988-89 Illinois Law Survey," see 21 Loy. U. Chi. L.J. 241 (1989-90).

For article, "Civil Procedure: 1985-86 Illinois Law Survey," see 18 Loy. U. Chi. L.J. 317 (1986-87).

ARTICLE XXI.
CHANGE OF NAME

735 ILCS 5/21-101 Proceedings; parties

Sec. 21-101. *Proceedings; parties.* If any person who is a resident of this State and has resided in this State for 6 months desires to change his or her name and to assume another name by which to be afterwards called and known, the person may file a petition in the circuit court of the county wherein he or she resides praying for that relief. If it appears to the court that the conditions hereinafter mentioned have been complied with and that there is no reason why the prayer should not be granted, the court, by an order to be entered of record, may direct and provide that the name of that person be changed in accordance with the prayer in the petition. The filing of a petition in accordance with this Section shall be the sole and exclusive means by which any person committed under the laws of this State to a penal institution may change his or her name and assume another name. However, any person convicted of a felony, misdemeanor criminal sexual abuse when the victim of the offense at the time of its commission is under 18 years of age, misdemeanor sexual exploitation of a child, misdemeanor indecent solicitation of a child, or misdemeanor indecent solicitation of an adult in this State or any other state who has not been pardoned may not file a petition for a name change until 10 years have passed since completion and discharge from his or her sentence. A person who is required to register as a sex offender under the Sex Offender Registration Act [730 ILCS 150/1 et seq.] may not file a petition for a name change until the person is no longer under a duty to register under that Act. A petitioner may include his or her spouse and adult unmarried children, with their consent, and his or her minor children where it appears to the court that it is for their best interest, in the petition and prayer, and the court's order shall then include the spouse and children. Whenever any minor has resided in the family of any person for the space of 3 years and has been recognized and known as an adopted child in the family of that person, the application herein provided for may be made by the person having that minor in his or her family.

An order shall be entered as to a minor only if the court finds by clear and convincing evidence that the change is necessary to serve the best interest of the child. In determining the best interest of a minor child under this Section, the court shall consider all relevant factors, including:

(1) The wishes of the child's parents and any person acting as a parent who has physical custody of the child.

(2) The wishes of the child and the reasons for those wishes. The court may interview the child in chambers to ascertain the child's wishes with respect to the change of name. Counsel shall be present at the interview unless otherwise agreed upon by the parties. The court shall cause a court reporter to be present who shall make a complete record of the interview instantaneously to be part of the record in the case.

(3) The interaction and interrelationship of the child with his or her parents or persons acting as parents who have physical custody of the child, step-parents, siblings, step-siblings, or any other person who may significantly affect the child's best interest.

(4) The child's adjustment to his or her home, school, and community.

(Source: P.A. 87-409; 88-25, § 5; 89-192, § 5; 89-462, § 310.)

Note.

This section was Ill.Rev.Stat., Ch. 110, para. 21-101.

Effect of Amendments.

The 1993 amendment by P.A. 88-25, effective July 6, 1993, added the fourth sentence of the first paragraph.

The 1995 amendment by P.A. 89-192, effective January 1, 1996, in the first paragraph, in the fourth sentence, inserted "misdemeanor criminal sexual abuse when the victim of the offense at the time of its commission is under 18 years of age, misdemeanor sexual exploitation of a child, misdemeanor indecent solicitation of a child, or misdemeanor indecent solicitation of an adult".

The 1996 amendment by P.A. 89-462, effective May 29, 1996, in the first paragraph, in the fourth sentence, substituted "10" for "2" and added the fifth sentence.

CASE NOTES

Analysis

Constitutionality
In General
Abuse of Discretion
—Not Shown
Applicability
—Minors
Best Interests of Child
—Factors
—Illustrative Cases
—Use of Restraint
Burden of Proof
—Not Met
Evidence of Agreement
Jurisdiction
—Circumvention
—Shown
Standard of Review
—In General
Standing

Constitutionality

This statute does not violate equal protection by allowing only custodial parents the right to petition for a name change; the legislature could reasonably conclude that only parents with legal custody should be allowed such a right and would be in the best position to bring such a petition on behalf of the child. In re Charnogorsky, 302 Ill. App. 3d 649, 236 Ill. Dec. 234, 707 N.E.2d 79 (1 Dist. 1998).

In General

The Illinois statutory provisions with reference to court proceedings changing a name, under similar prior provision, are not exclusive but are merely permissive, and the common law is not abrogated. Solomon v. Solomon, 5 Ill. App. 2d 297, 125 N.E.2d 675 (1 Dist. 1955).

Paramount concern to a trial court when considering a name change of a minor is the child's best interests, but a noncustodial parent who is exercising his/her visitation rights and paying child support must be afforded actual notice and an opportunity to be heard before the trial court makes such a determination. Sanjuan-Moeller v. Moeller (In re Sanjuan-Moeller), 343 Ill. App. 3d 202, 277 Ill. Dec. 650, 796 N.E.2d 736, 2003 Ill. App. LEXIS 1115 (2 Dist. 2003).

Abuse of Discretion

—Not Shown

Under similar prior provision, where there was no evidence of coercion, no evidence of confusion or pressure, and a significant period of time elapsed between the divorce and subsequent desire for a name change, the trial court did not abuse its discretion in determining that the proposed name change was in the best interests of a child. Ahlden v. Craig, 164 Ill. App. 3d 1090, 115 Ill. Dec. 106, 518 N.E.2d 728 (4 Dist. 1987).

Under similar prior provision, the trial court did not abuse its discretion by granting the noncustodial father's petition to enjoin the custodial mother from changing the surname of their minor children. In re Schaefer, 161 Ill. App. 3d 841, 113 Ill. Dec. 725, 515 N.E.2d 710 (1 Dist. 1987).

Under similar prior provision, where former wife contesting former husband's parentage of child had child's name changed without notice to former husband and in violation of prior custody orders, there was no abuse of discretion in the order directing former wife to restore child's original name. Lawrence v. Lawrence, 86 Ill. App. 3d 810, 41 Ill. Dec. 908, 408 N.E.2d 330 (1 Dist. 1980).

Applicability

—Minors

Under similar prior provision, the change of name of a minor child is an incident to custody. In re Presson, 102 Ill. 2d 303, 80 Ill. Dec. 294, 465 N.E.2d 85 (1984).

Best Interests of Child

—Factors

Son was allowed to change his surname to his stepfather's surname where he articulated clear and plausible reasons, including the fact that: (1) he had lived with his mother and the stepfather for over seven years and considered them his "real family," (2) he had not seen his father in four years, had not heard from his father by telephone since moving to Illinois, and seldom received mail from his father, and (3) having a name different from the other members of his "real family," including his step-siblings, created difficulties for him in school and elsewhere. Howard ex rel Bailey v. Bailey, 343 Ill. App. 3d 1201, 279 Ill. Dec. 201, 799 N.E.2d 1004, 2003 Ill. App. LEXIS 1346 (2 Dist. 2003).

Under similar prior provision, the factors to consider in determining whether a name change would be in the best interest of a child are: (1) the wishes of the child and the parents; (2) stated reasons for the proposed name change; (3) the child's age and maturity; (4) the nature of the family situation; (5) the strength of the tie between the child and each parent; (6) any misconduct toward or neglect of the child by the parent opposing the change; and (7) the name by which the child had customarily been called. Dattilo v. Groth, 222 Ill. App. 3d 467, 165 Ill. Dec. 17, 584 N.E.2d 196 (1 Dist. 1991).

—Illustrative Cases

The trial court's finding that a name change was not in the best interests of a very young child at the time was not against the manifest weight of the evidence where the child's father sought to have his surname added to the child's name, but the child was too young to express her own wishes or to have any problem with adjustment to home, school, or community. Stockton v. Oldenburg, 305 Ill. App. 3d 897, 238 Ill. Dec. 1013, 713 N.E.2d 259 (4 Dist. 1999).

Under similar prior provision, the trial court properly may have found that to use petitioner's surname as the child's middle name was in the child's best interest; the middle name change would not be disruptive as a last name change might be and would affirm the child's relationship with his father, with whom he did not live. Dattilo v. Groth, 222 Ill. App. 3d 467, 165 Ill. Dec. 17, 584 N.E.2d 196 (1 Dist. 1991).

Under similar prior provision, the circuit court properly enjoined the custodial parent and minor from changing minor's name in any legal proceeding or using any other name in official records or membership applications or records; however, the court's order was overbroad in that it extended to name changes in informal situations within the family. In re Presson, 102 Ill. 2d 303, 80 Ill. Dec. 294, 465 N.E.2d 85 (1984).

Under similar prior provision, where father maintained an active interest in his daughter, loved her, continued to support her and had committed no wrong toward her, the granting of a name change to the daughter furthered no purpose other than that of a temporary, and superficial, expedient, the best interest of the child was served by denying the change of name, awaiting her maturity and leaving the decision whether to change her name to her at a time when she would be aided by her own desires and perceptions. In re Omelson, 112 Ill. App. 3d 725, 68 Ill. Dec. 307, 445 N.E.2d 951 (5 Dist. 1983).

—Use of Restraint

Under similar prior provision, in determining whether or not any restraint should have been put upon plaintiff's action in aiding minor child to change his name, the first and most important consideration before the trial court should be the welfare of the child. Solomon v. Solomon, 5 Ill. App. 2d 297, 125 N.E.2d 675 (1 Dist. 1955).

Burden of Proof

—Not Met

While the minor would undoubtedly feel some confusion and embarrassment whether or not her name is changed, testimony of three isolated instances was insufficient to demonstrate clearly that a change was in her best interests and where the father desired the name not be changed, the mother failed to meet the burden of proof. In re Mattson, 240 Ill. App. 3d 993, 181 Ill. Dec. 810, 608 N.E.2d 1284 (2 Dist. 1993).

Evidence of Agreement

While testimony indicated a divorced couple discussed potential names for child born after the divorce, it did not establish an agreement as to the child's last name. In re Charnogorsky, 302 Ill. App. 3d 649, 236 Ill. Dec. 234, 707 N.E.2d 79 (1 Dist. 1998).

Jurisdiction

—Circumvention

Under similar prior provision, where former wife petitioned in the chancery division for change of child's name, and assumedly with no notice to former husband and no notice to the court hearing the petition that the domestic relations division had retained jurisdiction, the trial court properly found that plaintiff circumvented the jurisdiction of the domestic relations division by securing the name change in a proceeding filed in the chancery division. Lawrence v. Lawrence, 86 Ill. App. 3d 810, 41 Ill. Dec. 908, 408 N.E.2d 330 (1 Dist. 1980).

—Shown

Under similar prior provision, where the matter of a change of name of a minor child of divorced parents was a matter incidental to the custody of the child, the court had the jurisdiction to entertain the motion and to enter the order involved in the appeal. Solomon v. Solomon, 5 Ill. App. 2d 297, 125 N.E.2d 675 (1 Dist. 1955).

Standard of Review

—In General

Under similar prior provision, the standard of review in determining whether a minor child's surname should be changed is the best interest of the child. In re Schaefer, 161 Ill. App. 3d 841, 113 Ill. Dec. 725, 515 N.E.2d 710 (1 Dist. 1987).

Standing

Noncustodial parent did not have standing to bring petition to change child's name. In re Charnogorsky, 302 Ill. App. 3d 649, 236 Ill. Dec. 234, 707 N.E.2d 79 (1 Dist. 1998).

LEGAL PERIODICALS

For article, "Survey of Illinois Law: Criminal Law and Procedure," see 21 S. Ill. U.L.J. 759 (1997).

735 ILCS 5/21-102 Petition

Sec. 21-102. *Petition.* The petition shall set forth the name then held, the name sought to be assumed, the residence of the petitioner, the length of time the petitioner has resided in this State, and the state or country of the petitioner's nativity or supposed nativity. The petition shall be signed by the person petitioning or, in case of minors, by the parent or guardian having the legal custody of the minor. The petition shall be verified by the affidavit of some credible person.
(Source: P.A. 87-409.)

Note.

This section was Ill.Rev.Stat., Ch. 110, para. 21-102.

735 ILCS 5/21-103 Notice by publication

Sec. 21-103. *Notice by publication.* (a) Previous notice shall be given of the intended application by publishing a notice thereof in some newspaper published in the municipality in which the person resides if the municipality is in a county with a population under 2,000,000, or if the person does not reside in a municipality in a county with a population under 2,000,000, or if no newspaper is published in the municipality or if the person resides in a county with a population of 2,000,000 or more, then in some newspaper published in the county where the person resides, or if no newspaper is published in that county, then in some convenient newspaper published in this State. The notice shall be inserted for 3 consecutive weeks, the first insertion to be at least 6 weeks before the return day upon which the petition is to be filed, and shall be signed by the petitioner or, in case of a minor, the minor's parent or guardian, and shall set forth the return day of court on which the petition is to be filed and the name sought to be assumed.

(b) The publication requirement of subsection (a) shall not be required in any application for a change of name involving a minor if, before making judgment under this Article, reasonable notice and opportunity to be heard is given to any parent whose parental rights have not been previously terminated and to any person who has physical custody of the child. If any of these persons are outside this State, notice and opportunity to be heard shall be given under Section 21-104 [735 ILCS 5/21-104].

(c) The Director of State Police or his or her designee may apply to the circuit court for an order directing that the notice and publication requirements of this Section be waived if the Director or his or her designee certifies that the name change being sought is intended to protect a witness during and following a criminal investigation or proceeding.
(Source: P.A. 87-409; 91-62, § 5.)

Note.

This section was Ill.Rev.Stat., Ch. 110, para. 21-103.

Effect of Amendments.

The 1999 amendment by P.A. 91-62, effective January 1, 2000, added subsection (c).

CASE NOTES

Constitutionality

735 ILCS 5/103(b) (1998) is unconstitutional to the extent that it allows a custodial parent to change the name of his or her child without actual notice to the noncustodial parent. Sanjuan-Moeller v. Moeller (In re Sanjuan-Moeller), 343 Ill. App. 3d 202, 277 Ill. Dec. 650, 796 N.E.2d 736, 2003 Ill. App. LEXIS 1115 (2 Dist. 2003).

735 ILCS 5/21-104 Process and notice to persons outside this State

Sec. 21-104. *Process and notice to persons outside this State.* (a) Process in change of name proceedings shall be governed by this Code.

(b) Notice in all change of name proceedings required for the exercise of jurisdiction over a person outside this State shall be given in a manner best calculated to give actual notice and shall be given in one of the following manners:

(1) By personal delivery outside this State in the manner prescribed for service of process within this State.

(2) In the manner prescribed by the law of the place in which the service is made for service of process in that place in an action in any of its courts of general jurisdiction.

(3) By any form of mail addressed to the person to be served and requesting a receipt.

(4) As directed by the court if other means of notification are ineffective.

(c) Notice under this Section shall be served, mailed, or delivered at least 10 days before any hearing in this State.

(d) Proof of service outside this State may be made by affidavit of the individual who made the service or in the manner prescribed by the law of this State, the order pursuant to which the service is made, or the law of the place in which the service is made. If service is made by mail, proof may be a receipt signed by the addressee or other evidence of delivery to the addressee.
(Source: P.A. 87-409.)

Note.

This section was Ill.Rev.Stat., Ch. 110, para. 21-104.

CHAPTER 740
CIVIL LIABILITIES

Breach of Promise Act

740 ILCS 15/0.01 Short title
740 ILCS 15/1 [Legislative declaration]
740 ILCS 15/2 [Limitation on damages]
740 ILCS 15/3 [Punitive, exemplary, vindictive or aggravated damages]
740 ILCS 15/4 [Notice]
740 ILCS 15/5 [Failure to give notice]
740 ILCS 15/6 [Commencement of action]
740 ILCS 15/7 [Application of act]
740 ILCS 15/8 [Effect on criminal laws]
740 ILCS 15/9 [Construction; severability]
740 ILCS 15/10 [Effective date]

Frauds Act

740 ILCS 80/1 [Writing and signature required]

Parental Responsibility Law

740 ILCS 115/1 [Short title]
740 ILCS 115/2 [Definitions]
740 ILCS 115/3 Liability
740 ILCS 115/4 [Enforcement of liability]
740 ILCS 115/5 Limitation on damages; damages allowable
740 ILCS 115/6 [Other causes of action]
740 ILCS 115/7 [Code of Civil Procedure]

Parental Right of Recovery Act

740 ILCS 120/1 [Short title]
740 ILCS 120/2 [Definitions]
740 ILCS 120/3 [Sale of illegal drug to minor]
740 ILCS 120/4 [Jointly and severally liable]

Right to Breastfeed Act

740 ILCS 137/1 Short title
740 ILCS 137/5 Purpose
740 ILCS 137/10 Breastfeeding Location
740 ILCS 137/15 Private right of action
740 ILCS 137/99 Effective date

Breach of Promise Act

740 ILCS 15/0.01 Short title

Sec. 0.01. *Short title.* This Act may be cited as the Breach of Promise Act.
(Source: P.A. 86-1324.)

Derivation.
Title: An Act relating to actions for breach of promise or agreement to marry.
Cite: 740 ILCS 15/0.01 et seq.
Source: L. 1947, p. 1181.
Date: Approved July 9, 1947.

Note.
This section was Ill.Rev.Stat., Ch. 40, para. 1800.

740 ILCS 15/1 [Legislative declaration]

Sec. 1. It is hereby declared, as a matter of legislative determination, that the remedy heretofore provided by law for the enforcement of actions based upon breaches of promises or agreements to marry has been subject to grave abuses and has been used as an instrument for blackmail by unscrupulous persons for their unjust enrichment, due to the indefiniteness of the damages recoverable in such actions and the consequent fear of persons threatened with such actions that exorbitant damages might be assessed against them. It is also hereby declared that the award of monetary damages in such actions is ineffective as a recompense for genuine mental or emotional distress. Accordingly, it is hereby declared as the public policy of the state that the best interests of the people of the state will be served by limiting the damages recoverable in such actions, and by leaving any punishments of wrongdoers guilty of seduction to proceedings under the criminal laws of the state, rather than to the imposition of punitive, exemplary, vindictive or aggravated damages in actions for breach of promise or agreement to marry. Consequently, in the public interest, the necessity for the enactment of this chapter is hereby declared as a matter of legislative determination.
(Source: Laws 1947, p. 1181.)

Note.
This section was Ill.Rev.Stat., Ch. 40, para. 1801.

CASE NOTES

Analysis

Constitutionality
Applicability
—Action for Return of Ring
Elements of Damage
Sexual Intercourse

Constitutionality
The Act of 1947 relating to actions for breach of promise or agreement to marry (see now this Act), did not prohibit an action, but merely limited the damages recoverable to actual damages; the legislature held as public policy that punitive damages could not be recovered under the action in question, and in denying such damages as a basis of recovery, the Act was not in contravention of Section 19 of Article II of the 1870 Illinois Constitution, (see now Ill. Const., (1970), Art. I, § 23). Smith v. Hill, 12 Ill. 2d 588, 147 N.E.2d 321 (1958).

The Act of 1947 relating to actions for breach of promise or agreement to marry (see now this Act), which affected all members of the same class, and being established as the public policy of the state on the question involved, and not being arbitrary or unreasonable, did not violate Section 22 of Article IV of the 1870 Illinois Constitution (see now Ill. Const. (1970), Art. IV, § 13). Smith v. Hill, 12 Ill. 2d 588, 147 N.E.2d 321 (1958).

The Act of 1947 relating to actions for breach of promise or agreement to marry (see now this Act), which restricted recovery to actual damages, which term included both general and special damages and encompassed compensatory damages because they were synonymous, did not invade any judicial functions of the courts and in barring punitive damages merely established a "public policy" that in the interest of society in the particular class of cases, such damages should not be awarded; since such damages were allowed in the interest of society, and not to recompense solely the individual, to deny them could not be said to have denied any constitutional right or to have encroached upon any judicial function, or to have violated any constitutional guaranty of separation of powers. Smith v. Hill, 12 Ill. 2d 588, 147 N.E.2d 321 (1958).

Applicability

—Action for Return of Ring
A replevin suit for the return of an engagement ring and other

Applicability (Cont'd)

—Action for Return of Ring (Cont'd)

gifts made on the condition of marriage is not an action for the breach of a promise to marry; therefore, the plaintiff's replevin action for the return of the engagement ring was not barred for any failure to comply with this Act, and the trial court did not err in denying the defendant's motion to dismiss. Vann v. Vehrs, 260 Ill. App. 3d 648, 198 Ill. Dec. 640, 633 N.E.2d 102 (2 Dist. 1994).

Elements of Damage

Seduction, pregnancy and childbirth may not be properly considered as elements of damage in an action for breach of promise to marry. White v. Prenzler, 19 Ill. App. 2d 231, 153 N.E.2d 477 (3 Dist. 1958).

Sexual Intercourse

Sexual intercourse between consenting adults is generally not tortious conduct. Hertel v. Sullivan, 261 Ill. App. 3d 156, 198 Ill. Dec. 574, 633 N.E.2d 36 (4 Dist.), appeal denied, 157 Ill. 2d 501, 205 Ill. Dec. 162, 642 N.E.2d 1279 (1994).

LEGAL PERIODICALS

For article, "The Case Against Caps," see 75 Ill. B. J. 164 (1986).

RESEARCH REFERENCES

Rights in respect of engagement and courtship presents when marriage does not ensue. 44 ALR5th 1.

740 ILCS 15/2 [Limitation on damages]

Sec. 2. The damages to be recovered in any action for breach of promise or agreement to marry shall be limited to the actual damages sustained as a result of the injury complained of.
(Source: Laws 1947, p. 1181.)

Note.

This section was Ill.Rev.Stat., Ch. 40, para. 1802.

CASE NOTES

ANALYSIS

Damages
—In General
Evidence
—Seduction

Damages

—In General

In a breach of promise action under a prior similar provision (see now this section and 740 ILCS 15/3), a plaintiff was entitled to a cause of action for damages actually sustained when he or she had suffered injury, and a vested right to punitive, exemplary, vindictive or aggravated damages arose only when such damages had been allowed by a judgment in the plaintiff's favor. This statute did not take away the cause of action for breach of promise or the right to the damages actually sustained by the aggrieved party; what the statute did deny was a right in the plaintiff to aggravated or exemplary damages for a seduction and pregnancy alleged to have been induced in consequence of the trust and confidence imposed in the defendant by reason of his previous agreement to marry, the legislature could properly restrict the allowance of such damages without denying a constitutional right to them. Smith v. Hill, 12 Ill. 2d 588, 147 N.E.2d 321 (1958).

Evidence

—Seduction

Under a prior similar provision (see now this section), seduction committed under a promise of marriage was admissible in a breach of promise action as evidence in aggravation of damages. Smith v. Hill, 12 Ill. 2d 588, 147 N.E.2d 321 (1958).

740 ILCS 15/3 [Punitive, exemplary, vindictive or aggravated damages]

Sec. 3. No punitive, exemplary, vindictive or aggravated damages shall be allowed in any action for breach of promise or agreement to marry.
(Source: Laws 1947, p. 1181.)

Note.

This section was Ill.Rev.Stat., Ch. 40, para. 1803.

CASE NOTES

Damages

—In General

In a breach of promise action under a prior similar provision (see now 740 ILCS 15/2 and this section), a plaintiff was entitled to a cause of action for damages actually sustained when he had suffered injury, and a vested right to punitive, exemplary, vindictive or aggravated damages arose only when such damages had been allowed by a judgment in the plaintiff's favor. This statute did not take away the cause of action for breach of promise or the right to the damages actually sustained by the aggrieved party; what the statute did deny was a right in the plaintiff to aggravated or exemplary damages for a seduction and pregnancy alleged to have been induced in consequence of the trust and confidence imposed in the defendant by reason of his previous agreement to marry, and the legislature could properly restrict the allowance of such damages without denying a constitutional right to them. Smith v. Hill, 12 Ill. 2d 588, 147 N.E.2d 321 (1958).

740 ILCS 15/4 [Notice]

Sec. 4. Within three months from the date that the breach of promise or agreement to marry occurred, unless such breach occurred prior to the effective date of the act, any person who is about to commence any civil action in any court for breach of promise or agreement to marry shall give to the person against whom said action is to be brought, or send in a sealed envelope with first class postage prepaid and deposited in the United States mail to such person at his or her last known address, notice in writing, signed by the person who is about to commence said action, giving the date upon which the promise or agreement to marry was made, and the date upon which the marriage ceremony was to have been performed, stating the damages suffered by the person signing said notice and stating whether the person signing said notice is or is not still willing to marry the person to whom the statement is given. If the breach occurred prior to the effective date of this act the notice herein required shall be served within three months after such effective date.
(Source: Laws 1947, p. 1181.)

Note.

This section was Ill.Rev.Stat., Ch. 40, para. 1804.

CASE NOTES

ANALYSIS

Choice of Law

Compliance
Notice
—Strict Construction

Choice of Law

In case involving a broken engagement, Illinois law clearly governed under the most significant contacts test; to the extent that the parties ironed out the details of the proposed marriage, they did so in Illinois (or on a plane back to Chicago), where woman lived and worked, man purchased woman's wedding ring in Chicago, and he got down on one knee and restated the marital promise there (it had been originally proposed in Florida), the parties eventually planned to be married in Chicago, and had begun searching for appropriate wedding locations in that area; these aspects of the agreement to marry were sufficient to convince court that Illinois law should govern the parties' transaction. Wildey v. Springs, 47 F.3d 1475 (7th Cir. 1995).

Compliance

Plaintiff substantially complied with notice requirements even though her notice did not specify the exact date on which the promise was made. Schwalb v. Wood, 288 Ill. App. 3d 498, 223 Ill. Dec. 823, 680 N.E.2d 773 (3 Dist. 1997).

Substantial compliance with the notice requirements of the Act is sufficient. Schwalb v. Wood, 288 Ill. App. 3d 498, 223 Ill. Dec. 823, 680 N.E.2d 773 (3 Dist. 1997).

Notice

—Strict Construction

The history behind actions for the breach of a promise to marry argues in favor of a strict construction; the strictures of this Act exist because these actions were unpopular and subject to abuse. Wildey v. Springs, 47 F.3d 1475 (7th Cir. 1995).

740 ILCS 15/5 [Failure to give notice]

Sec. 5. If the notice provided for by Section 4 [740 ILCS 15/4] is not given as provided in that section, any such civil action for breach of promise or agreement to marry shall be dismissed and the person to whom any such cause of action accrued shall be forever barred from further suing.
(Source: Laws 1947, p. 1181.)

Note.
This section was Ill.Rev.Stat., Ch. 40, para. 1805.

CASE NOTES

Compliance

Plaintiff substantially complied with notice requirements even though her notice did not specify the exact date on which the promise was made. Schwalb v. Wood, 288 Ill. App. 3d 498, 223 Ill. Dec. 823, 680 N.E.2d 773 (3 Dist. 1997).

Substantial compliance with the notice requirements of the Act is sufficient. Schwalb v. Wood, 288 Ill. App. 3d 498, 223 Ill. Dec. 823, 680 N.E.2d 773 (3 Dist. 1997).

740 ILCS 15/6 [Commencement of action]

Sec. 6. Actions on promises or agreements to marry shall be commenced within one year next after the cause of action accrued.
(Source: Laws 1947, p. 1181.)

Note.
This section was Ill.Rev.Stat., Ch. 40, para. 1806.

740 ILCS 15/7 [Application of act]

Sec. 7. This act shall apply to all actions for breach of promise or agreement to marry begun after the effective date of this act, even though the alleged breach of promise or agreement to marry on which the action is based occurred prior to such effective date.
(Source: Laws 1947, p. 1181.)

Note.
This section was Ill.Rev.Stat., Ch. 40, para. 1807.

740 ILCS 15/8 [Effect on criminal laws]

Sec. 8. Nothing herein contained shall be deemed to repeal or amend any provisions of the criminal laws of this state.
(Source: Laws 1947, p. 1181.)

Note.
This section was Ill.Rev.Stat., Ch. 40, para. 1808.

740 ILCS 15/9 [Construction; severability]

Sec. 9. This act shall be liberally construed to effectuate the objects and purposes thereof and the public policy as herein declared. If any section, clause, sentence, paragraph or part of this act shall for any reason be adjudged by any court of competent jurisdiction to be invalid, such judgment shall not affect, impair or invalidate the remainder thereof, but shall be confined in its operation to the section, clause, sentence, paragraph or part thereof directly involved in the controversy in which such judgment shall have been rendered. If the application of this act, or any part thereof, to any person or circumstance shall be adjudged by such court to be invalid or ineffectual for any reason, such judgment shall not affect the application of this act, or part thereof, to any other person or circumstance.
(Source: Laws 1947, p. 1181.)

Note.
This section was Ill.Rev.Stat., Ch. 40, para. 1809.

740 ILCS 15/10 [Effective date]

Sec. 10. This Act shall become effective on January 1, 1948.
(Source: Laws 1947, p. 1181.)

Note.
This section was Ill.Rev.Stat., Ch. 40, para. 1810.

FRAUDS ACT

740 ILCS 80/1 [Writing and signature required]

Sec. 1. That No action shall be brought, whereby to charge any executor or administrator upon any special promise to answer any debt or damages out of his own estate, or whereby to charge the defendant upon any special promise to answer for the debt, default or miscarriage of another person, or to charge any person upon any agreement made upon consideration of marriage, or upon any agreement that is not to be performed within the space of one year from the making thereof, unless the promise or agreement upon which such action shall be brought, or some memorandum or note thereof, shall be in writing, and signed by the party to be charged therewith, or some other person thereunto by him lawfully authorized.

(Source: R.S. 1874, p. 540.)

Note.

This section was Ill.Rev.Stat., Ch. 59, para. 1.

CASE NOTES

Analysis

In General
Antenuptial Agreement
—In General
—Conveyance of Property
—Statute Not Applicable
Applicability
—Adoption Contracts
—Bankruptcy
—Bond Purchase
—Boundary Disputes
—Child Support Agreement
—Co-Partnership Agreement
—Comity of State
—Debt of Another
—Depositions
—Easements
—Employment Contracts
—Endorsement
—Equitable Estoppel
—Estoppel
—Executory Contracts
—Fraud
—Fraudulent Conveyance
—Judicial Sale
—Lack of Signature
—Land Trusts
—Leases
—Liability of Promisor
—Loan Application
—Marriage
—One Year Rule
—Personal Services
—Sale of Business
—Strangers Precluded
—Test
—Trusts
—U.C.C.
—Wills
Authority of Agent
—In General
—Ratification by Principal
Bankruptcy
—Waiver
Binding Agreement Not Shown
Child Support Agreement
—Enforceable
Contracts
—In General
—Affect on Validity
—Connection of Documents
—Consideration
—Conveyances
—Detrimental Reliance
—Divorce Proceeding
—Employment
—Enforceable
—Executed
—Executed in Another State
—Forbearance
—Motion to Dismiss
—Not Illegal
—Notice
—One Year Rule
—Oral Extensions
—Oral Purchase Agreement
—Partly Oral
—Possession
—Preexisting Debt
—Presumptions
—Repudiation
—Sufficient Writing
—Tenant's Loss of Rights
Contributory Negligence
Damages
—Mitigation
Debt of Another
—Application
—Collateral Promise
—Enforcement
—Illustrative Cases
—Joint and Several Obligation
—Liability
—Not Enforceable
—Statute Not Applicable
Dedication
—Statute Not Applicable
Defense
—In General
—Burden of Proof
—Demurrers
—Denied
—Entitlement
—Illegality
—Not Applicable
—Not Waived
Employment Contracts
—In General
—Contingency Termination
—Definite Term
—Employee Handbook
—Enforceable
—Full Performance
—Illustrative Cases
—Lifetime
—No Violation
—Not Enforceable
—Oral Modification
—Part Performance
—Performance Within One Year
—Reliance
—Statute Not Applicable
—Writing Held Insufficient
Estoppel
—In General
—Allowed
—Not Shown
—Requirements
—Shown
Evidence
—Memoranda
—Motion for Summary Judgment
Executed Contracts
—Exception Not Allowed
Express Trust
Factual Question
Franchise Agreement
—Barred
Full Performance
—Defense Barred
—Defense Inapplicable
—Effect

—One Year Rule
—Test
Impression of Trust
Indefinite Duration Clause
—Not Enforceable
Interpretation
Investment Securities
—Not Applicable
Legislative Intent
License Agreement
—Barred
Multiple Documents
—Insufficiently Connected
—Requirements
One Year Rule
Option Contracts
—Enforceable
Oral Contracts
—In General
—Agency
—Burden of Proof
—Full Performance
—Nonperformance
—One Year Rule
—Partnership Agreement
—Part Performance
—Payment of Money
—Performance by One Party
—Real Estate
—Recognized in Another State
—Specific Performance
—Unjust Enrichment
—Void
—Wills
Oral Lease
—One Year Rule
—Partial Performance
Oral Promises
—Breach
—Consideration
—Enforceable
—Not Enforceable
—Permanent Employment
—Real Estate Conveyance
—Statute Not Applicable
—Wrongful Termination
Oral Trust
—Voidable
Original and Independent Promise
Parol Evidence
—Admissible to Correct Mistake
—Boundary Line Disputes
—Interpretation of Rental Agreement
—Not Admissible
—State Law
—Statements of Authorized Agent
Part Performance
—In General
—Acts of Preparation
—Application
—Character
—Enforcement
—Oral Contract
—Question of Fact
—Reliance
—Statute Not Applicable
—Sufficient
Past Performance
Payment by Check
—Insufficient Writing
Performance Within One Year
—In General
—Agreement Enforceable
—Application
—Test
Pleadings
—Amendments
—Motion to Amend
—Motion to Dismiss
—Waiver
Promissory Estoppel
Purchase Order
—Modification upon Completion
Purpose
Ratification
Securities
—Writings Sufficient
Settlements
Signature
Special Promise
Specific Performance
—In General
—Lifetime Care
—Not Granted
—Part Performance
—Specified Consideration Required
Statute as Bar
—Calculations
Statute Not a Bar
Substantial Performance
—Adoption
Sufficient Performance
Sufficient Writing
—Letters
—Not Shown
—Parties' Interest
—Price Terms Not Shown
—Signatures
—Terms of Sale
Surety Contracts
—Application
—Standing
Validity
—Parol Evidence
Waiver
—Not Shown
Written Memorandum

In General

This Act has a procedural effect that did not preclude the Secretary of Agriculture's reparation order or impair the remedies provided under the Perishable Agricultural Commodities Act (7 U.S.C. § 499a et seq.). United Potato Co. v. Burghard & Sons, 18 F. Supp. 2d 894 (N.D. Ill. 1998).

The Statute of Frauds is procedural in form and its main proximate goal is evidentiary; it is largely based on distrust of the ability of juries to determine the truth of testimony that there was or was not a contract. Monetti, S.P.A. v. Anchor Hocking Corp., 931 F.2d 1178 (7th Cir. 1991).

The Statute of Frauds is designed to make the contractual process cheaper and more certain by encouraging the parties to a contract to memorialize their agreement. Monetti, S.P.A. v. Anchor Hocking Corp., 931 F.2d 1178 (7th Cir. 1991).

Where the agreement is original and independent, it is not within the statute, but if it is a collateral agreement, it is within the Statute of Frauds; the agreement may be regarded as original, and not within the statute, although it directly involves the interests of or concerns a third party, or may relate to an act, or the performance thereof, by one not a party to the contract. Resseter v. Waterman, 151 Ill. 169, 37 N.E. 875 (1894).

The moral wrong alone of refusing to be bound by an agreement because it fails to comply with the Statute of Frauds does not suffice to estop a defendant from asserting the statute as a defense. Loeb v. Gendel, 23 Ill. 2d 502, 179 N.E.2d 7 (1961).

For a contract to come within the Statute of Frauds, its terms must affirmatively show that it is not to be performed within one year; the statute does not apply if it appears from a reasonable interpretation of the terms of the agreement that it is capable of being performed within a year. Hall v. Gruesen, 22 Ill. App. 2d 465, 161 N.E.2d 345 (1 Dist. 1959).

The Statute of Frauds may not be availed of for the purpose of accomplishing a fraud and where one seeks to invoke the statute, after having by acts, representations, or promises induced another

In General (Cont'd)

party to do or forbear the doing of any act, so that such acts or representations constitute a fraud on the other party, the Statute of Frauds may not in such case be utilized as a defense. Lowenberg v. Booth, 330 Ill. 548, 162 N.E. 191 (1928).

To satisfy the Statute of Frauds, the writing itself must contain on its face or by reference to other writings, the names of the vendor and of the vendee, a description of the property sufficiently definite to identify the same as the subject matter of the contract, the price, the terms and conditions of sale, and the signature of the party to be charged. Thompson v. Wiegand, 9 Ill. 2d 63, 136 N.E.2d 781 (1956).

The Illinois Statute of Frauds is substantive in nature, and not remedial. Oakes v. Chicago Fire Brick Co., 311 Ill. App. 111, 35 N.E.2d 522 (1 Dist. 1941), aff'd, 388 Ill. 474, 58 N.E.2d 460 (1944).

Antenuptial Agreement

—In General

Written instrument that was not executed until a considerable time after the parties' marriage was a sufficient memorandum of the parties' oral antenuptial agreement that neither party would claim any interest in the property of the other to remove the oral antenuptial agreement from the bar of the Statute of Frauds. Lee v. Central Nat'l Bank & Trust Co., 56 Ill. 2d 394, 308 N.E.2d 605 (1974).

A parol antenuptial agreement is void under the Statute of Frauds. Richardson v. Richardson, 148 Ill. 563, 36 N.E. 608 (1893).

Reducing a verbal antenuptial agreement to writing after marriage will not take it out of the Statute of Frauds. McAnnulty v. McAnnulty, 120 Ill. 26, 11 N.E. 397 (1887).

—Conveyance of Property

An alleged verbal antenuptial agreement clearly came into the provisions of the statute of frauds and was, therefore, void; thus, a conveyance of a deed from husband to wife (under the purported/void agreement) was a mere voluntary conveyance and void as against the husband's judgment creditors. Keady v. White, 168 Ill. 76, 48 N.E. 314 (1897).

—Statute Not Applicable

Where husband and wife in contemplation of marriage made oral promises to each other to convey and hold all of their respective property during their married life, in joint tenancy with rights of survivorship, and made each other beneficiaries of their respective insurance policies which were performed in full by husband and at least partially by wife, the promises were in addition to their promises of marriage and as an additional consideration for the contract; therefore, the Statute of Frauds was not applicable and the promises were enforceable. Sun Life Assurance Co. v. Hoy, 174 F. Supp. 859 (E.D. Ill. 1959).

Applicability

—Adoption Contracts

Where a child has fully performed its obligations under a contract to adopt and allowing the contract to remain unenforced would be inequitable, the child is entitled to a decree for specific performance, provided the contract be proven according to the standard of proof required; therefore, the Statute of Frauds does not apply to this adoption contract. Winkelmann v. Winkelmann, 345 Ill. 566, 178 N.E. 118 (1931).

—Bankruptcy

Debtor had no rights in leased premises on date when it filed Chapter 11 petition for relief, and the occupied premises were not property of the estate where debtor had no lease and was at best a month-to-month tenant, which tenancy was validly terminated before debtor filed bankruptcy petition; if the debtor wished to remain in possession of the premises, it had to negotiate and execute a written lease agreeable to the plaintiff. 308 W. Randolph Bldg. Venture v. Victory Pipe Craftsmen, Inc., 8 Bankr. 635 (Bankr. N.D. Ill. 1981).

—Bond Purchase

Where lawyer had advised plaintiff that bank had the right and power to enter into an agreement with plaintiff to repurchase the bonds which was based upon the opinion which he had received on the subject from the Comptroller of Currency of the United States, to the effect that the bank had such power, did not state a cause of action based upon the Statute of Frauds. Awotin v. Healy, 291 Ill. App. 193, 9 N.E.2d 640 (1 Dist. 1937).

Where defendant, a lawyer, had given the plaintiff an opinion to the effect that he, defendant, believed that bank had the right to enter into the contract with the defendant, for the repurchase of bank bonds, the alleged promise of defendant was collateral to the contract entered into with the bank, and although this contract was subsequently held to be ultra vires, contract was within the Statute of Frauds. Awotin v. Healy, 291 Ill. App. 193, 9 N.E.2d 640 (1 Dist. 1937).

—Boundary Disputes

Where there is a dispute between adjoining landowners as to the true boundary line between their respective lands or if the line between their respective lands is unascertained, the agreement to establish a line, when so in dispute or unascertained, may be implied from the unequivocal acts and declarations of the parties, either expressed or implied, and such an agreement may be enforced either in law or in equity, whether the period of limitation has run or not. Ginther v. Duginger, 6 Ill. 2d 474, 129 N.E.2d 147 (1955).

Title to real estate cannot be transferred by parol, but owners of adjoining tracts may, by a parol agreement, settle a disputed boundary between them. Skinner v. Francisco, 404 Ill. 356, 88 N.E.2d 867 (1949).

—Child Support Agreement

Oral agreement providing for child support was held unenforceable since it could not be performed within one year as the youngest child would not be of age for more than a dozen years thereafter. Opdahl v. Johnson, 306 Ill. App. 145, 28 N.E.2d 308 (1 Dist. 1940).

—Co-Partnership Agreement

Where two separate owners of real estate, purchased by their separate funds, enter into a co-partnership with reference to a sale thereof by a parol contract, such contract is within the Statute of Frauds. Goldstein v. Nathan, 158 Ill. 641, 42 N.E. 72 (1895).

—Comity of State

Where appellant failed to establish the intention of the parties that an agreement for employment was to be wholly performed in Illinois, and it being admitted that the contract was enforceable in Pennsylvania where made, the comity of states rule required its enforcement in Illinois. Oakes v. Chicago Fire Brick Co., 388 Ill. 474, 58 N.E.2d 460 (1944).

—Debt of Another

Under the statute of frauds, the promise to pay the debt of another, after the same is incurred, is void, unless made upon a consideration and reduced to writing; but where goods, money, or services are furnished to a third person, at the request and upon the credit of the promisor, the undertaking is clearly original, and in such case the Statute of Frauds does not apply. Raveret-Wever Printing Co. v. Wright, 301 Ill. App. 421, 23 N.E.2d 203 (1 Dist. 1939).

—Depositions

A deposition may qualify as a signed writing for Statute of Frauds purposes. Bower v. Jones, 978 F.2d 1004 (7th Cir. 1992).

—Easements

Although agreement was not executed in conformity with the Statute of Frauds, this fact did not necessarily preclude the existence of an easement. Peterson v. Corrubia, 21 Ill. 2d 525, 173 N.E.2d 499 (1961).

—Employment Contracts

The fact that plaintiff was employed as president of the bank for eight months of a purported three-year term, for a salary that was less than provided for in an unsigned contract, did not constitute partial performance sufficient to remove the bar of the Statute of Frauds. Prodromos v. Howard Sav. Bank, 295 Ill. App. 3d 470, 229 Ill. Dec. 718, 692 N.E.2d 707 (1 Dist. 1998).

The minutes from a directors' meeting were insufficient to remove the bar against unsigned employment contracts set forth in

Applicability (Cont'd)

—Employment Contracts (Cont'd)
the Statute of Frauds. Prodromos v. Howard Sav. Bank, 295 Ill. App. 3d 470, 229 Ill. Dec. 718, 692 N.E.2d 707 (1 Dist. 1998).

A court must examine the precise terms of an oral promise to determine whether the occurrence of a stated contingency would complete performance of the contract, in which case the promise would be outside the Statute of Frauds, or whether such occurrence would frustrate the performance of the contract, in which case the promise would be within the statute's one-year provision; oral promise of employment, cast in terms of lasting as long as the employee wants the job is capable of performance within one year and thus outside the Illinois Statute of Frauds. Taylor v. Canteen Corp., 69 F.3d 773 (7th Cir. 1995).

Plaintiff could not rely on his actual employment of over a month to render enforceable an employment contract that was otherwise unenforceable under the Statute of Frauds. Lessman v. Universal Spray Applications, Inc., 690 F. Supp. 679 (N.D. Ill. 1988).

While a letter from defendant employer was not signed, but confirmed the existence of an oral contract as well as some of its terms, it did not constitute a memorandum or note signed by the party to be charged that the contract was to last two years; even though the language clearly contemplated the possibility plaintiff would leave defendant's employ before the end of two years, just as clearly, it contained no express or implied promise of two years' employment, and as duration being an "essential term" of the alleged contract, which the writing clearly did not speak to "with reasonable certainty," the alleged contract was within the Statute of Frauds and unenforceable. Rubin v. Rudolf Wolff Commodity Brokers, Inc., 636 F. Supp. 258 (N.D. Ill. 1986).

The possibility of an employee's termination within one year does not necessarily remove an employment contract from the reach of the Statute of Frauds; similarly, the possibility that an employee may die or resign within the first year does not necessarily save the oral agreement from the bar of this section. Brudnicki v. GE Co., 535 F. Supp. 84 (N.D. Ill. 1982).

Whether the possibility of an employee's death or termination takes the employment agreement from the bar of the Statute of Frauds in a specific case depends in large part on the underlying purpose and specific terms of the agreement itself. Brudnicki v. GE Co., 535 F. Supp. 84 (N.D. Ill. 1982).

—Endorsement
Attempt on the part of party suing for specific performance to produce agreement in written form by making a typewritten endorsement was ineffectual in removing it from the prohibition of the Statute of Frauds. Whitelaw v. Brady, 3 Ill. 2d 583, 121 N.E.2d 785 (1954).

—Equitable Estoppel
The Statute of Frauds does not itself authorize the application of the doctrine of equitable estoppel for the breach of a promise which the law does not regard as binding and does not amount to fraud. Rosenstein v. Ida Prods. Co., 362 F. Supp. 642 (N.D. Ill. 1973).

—Estoppel
In certain instances, where fraud or material misrepresentation had occurred, the guilty party may be estopped to assert the Statute of Frauds as a defense. Sinclair v. Sullivan Chevrolet Co., 31 Ill. 2d 507, 202 N.E.2d 516 (1964).

Where hiring of a carpenter and laborer was from week to week, the contract might have been performed within a year, and the contract was fully performed by plaintiff, defendant was estopped from relying upon the Statute of Frauds. Warszawa v. White Eagle Brewing Co., 299 Ill. App. 509, 20 N.E.2d 343 (1 Dist. 1939).

—Executory Contracts
Where an alleged contract is purely executory, neither side having performed, application of the Statute of Frauds is justified by the attendant proof problems and the increased likelihood of perjury. Meyer v. Logue, 100 Ill. App. 3d 1039, 56 Ill. Dec. 707, 427 N.E.2d 1253 (1 Dist. 1981).

The Statute of Frauds may be invoked to avoid executory contracts, but not contracts that have been carried into execution. Pearce v. Pearce, 184 Ill. 289, 56 N.E. 311 (1900).

An executory contract for the sale of land, orally made, is within the provisions of the Statute of Frauds and may be avoided by the defendant when he relies upon the statute by demurrer, plea, or answer. Ropacki v. Ropacki, 354 Ill. 502, 188 N.E. 400 (1933).

—Fraud
Court declined to dismiss for failure to state a claim, Fed. R. Civ. P. 12(b)(6), based on the Illinois statute of frauds, 740 ILCS 80/1, a sales agent's breach of contract action against a corporation. Documents attached to the complaint that described the commission the sales agent could receive if the contract lasted three or even five years established that the contract could, but not that it must, last more than a year; thus, the sales agent had not pled himself out of court by pleading more than was required by Fed. R. Civ. P. 8. Hirtzer v. Avery Dennison Corp., 265 F. Supp. 2d 936, 2003 U.S. Dist. LEXIS 9205 (N.D. Ill. 2003).

No person shall be permitted to take advantage of his own wrong, thus no one may utilize the Statute of Frauds to work an injustice or fraud. Loeb v. Gendel, 23 Ill. 2d 502, 179 N.E.2d 7 (1961).

The Statute of Frauds cannot be availed of for the purpose of perpetrating a fraud. Vischer v. Dow Jones & Co., 339 Ill. App. 617, 91 N.E.2d 90 (1 Dist. 1950).

Courts will not permit the Statute of Frauds to be invoked where the effect will be to accomplish a fraud. Wood v. Armstrong, 401 Ill. 111, 81 N.E.2d 468 (1948).

—Fraudulent Conveyance
A judgment is not a lien upon property which has been conveyed in fraud to creditors, for the reason that such a conveyance is good between the parties, and the grantor retains no equitable title, so that an equitable lien can only be secured by a proceeding to set aside the fraudulent conveyance; that rule does not apply to a case where there is a secret trust and the grantor is still the real owner; neither is it true in the case of an attachment, since the Statute of Frauds and perjuries makes a conveyance with intent to disturb, delay, hinder, or defraud creditors void as against creditors. Pease v. Frank, 263 Ill. 500, 105 N.E. 299 (1914).

—Judicial Sale
A verbal agreement to extend the time for redemption from a judicial sale is valid and not affected by the Statute of Frauds. Doner v. Phoenix Joint Stock Land Bank, 381 Ill. 106, 45 N.E.2d 20 (1942).

—Lack of Signature
The lack of a signature does not constitute a "magic" bar to the enforcement of the terms of an agreement, even where the agreement is within the Statute of Frauds. Grauer v. Value & Primer Corp., 47 Ill. App. 3d 152, 5 Ill. Dec. 540, 361 N.E.2d 863 (2 Dist. 1977).

—Land Trusts
A trust predicated upon a promise to hold land for the use and benefit of the grantor is express and can be enforced only by a writing. Ramsay v. Ramsay, 10 Ill. App. 2d 459, 135 N.E.2d 172 (1 Dist. 1956).

A land trust created by parol is utterly void and of no effect. Murray v. Behrendt, 399 Ill. 22, 76 N.E.2d 431 (1947).

Where there was nothing more than an oral contract for the sale of land, executed as to the vendee and executory as to the vendor, wherein, after a period of years, the vendor was guilty of a simple breach of contract, the Statute of Frauds rendered the vendee's rights under the contract unenforceable. Murray v. Behrendt, 399 Ill. 22, 76 N.E.2d 431 (1947).

Statute of Frauds was intended to prevent persons holding the title to lands from creating a trust, appointing a trustee, declaring who should be the beneficiary and declaring the terms of the trust, in any other manner than in writing; it was not intended to prevent the holder of the legal title from agreeing with the holder of the equitable title upon other terms than those by which he was originally entitled to have a conveyance of the legal title. Worden v. Crist, 106 Ill. 326 (1883).

—Leases
Where oral lease ran for more than a year after its making, it was unenforceable under the Statute of Frauds. 308 W. Randolph Bldg. Venture v. Victory Pipe Craftsmen, Inc., 8 Bankr. 635 (Bankr. N.D. Ill. 1981).

The Statute of Frauds applies to an oral contract to execute a written lease. 308 W. Randolph Bldg. Venture v. Victory Pipe Craftsmen, Inc., 8 Bankr. 635 (Bankr. N.D. Ill. 1981).

Applicability (Cont'd)

—Leases (Cont'd)

Where an oral agreement for a tenancy is unenforceable because of the Statute of Frauds, the oral agreement results in a month-to-month tenancy. 308 W. Randolph Bldg. Venture v. Victory Pipe Craftsmen, Inc., 8 Bankr. 635 (Bankr. N.D. Ill. 1981).

Where a parol lease is made, fixing the amount of rent and the time of its payment, and fixing the term at a greater period than one year, it is clearly within the Statute of Frauds; and the tenant entering under such voidable contract and paying rent at the sum fixed by the contract, becomes a tenant from month to month. Kachigian v. Minn, 23 Ill. App. 3d 722, 320 N.E.2d 173 (1 Dist. 1974).

In an action to recover damages for defendant's alleged trespass on a 120 acre tract of farm land owned by plaintiffs, the defense of possession and part performance under an oral lease was not available to defendant. Scoville v. Dehart, 17 Ill. App. 2d 419, 150 N.E.2d 369 (3 Dist. 1958).

—Liability of Promisor

This section requires that the liability to which that of the promisor is supposed to be collateral should be one which can be enforced by proceedings at law or inequity and therefore, unless it appears that some person, other than the promisor, has incurred an actual liability with respect to the subject matter of the promise, the agreement is not within the Statute of Frauds, although the third person may be under an imperfect or merely moral obligation to respond. Resseter v. Waterman, 151 Ill. 169, 37 N.E. 875 (1894).

—Loan Application

Where the terms of the application for a loan, the contract for the making of the loan was not to be completed within one year from the time of the acceptance of the application or the making of the contract, it was necessary that the acceptance of the application, or some note or memorandum thereof, if it were accepted, to be valid, be in writing and signed by the party to be charged therewith, or some other person thereunto by him lawfully authorized. Snow v. Schulman, 352 Ill. 63, 185 N.E. 262 (1933).

—Marriage

Where husband made parol promise prior to marriage, that if wife would marry him, he would surrender fraternal organization certificate which he then held and would procure a new one naming her as beneficiary, the agreement was void under the Statute of Frauds since no action should be brought to charge any person on any agreement made in consideration of marriage, unless the agreement or some memorandum or note thereof should be in writing and signed by the party to be charged therewith or some person thereunto by him lawfully authorized. Anglemire v. Policemen's Benev., 301 Ill. App. 277, 22 N.E.2d 713 (2 Dist. 1939).

Agreement by one to bequeath money to another if the latter agreed not to marry one person and marry a second came within the Statute of Frauds. Austin v. Kuehn, 211 Ill. 113, 71 N.E. 841 (1904).

—One Year Rule

Auto dealership manager's oral at-will contract was completely performed as of his termination and, because all that remained for performance was the dealership's payment of money, enforcement was not barred by the statute of frauds. Lunn Partners Multiple Opportunities Portfolio, L.P. v. Brakulis, F. Supp. 2d , 2004 U.S. Dist. LEXIS 11968 (N.D. Ill. June 25, 2004).

Letter regarding the permanency of an employee's European work assignment did not satisfy the Statute of Frauds as the portion of the alleged contract that could not be performed within one year was not in writing and signed by the party to be charged; the letter made no mention of the permanent European residence agreement, and instead reaffirmed that the employee was an at-will employee. Czerska v. United Airlines, Inc., 292 F. Supp. 2d 1102, 2003 U.S. Dist. LEXIS 21696 (N.D. Ill. 2003).

Alleged oral contractual agreement to review adequacy of plaintiffs' insurance each year was incapable of being performed within a one year period and was therefore unenforceable under the Statute of Frauds. Furtak v. Moffett, 284 Ill. App. 3d 255, 219 Ill. Dec. 660, 671 N.E.2d 827 (1 Dist. 1996), appeal denied, 171 Ill. 2d 564, 222 Ill. Dec. 430, 677 N.E.2d 964 (1997).

An oral agreement specifying performance for a calendar year, and years beyond provided subsequent conditions are met could not be completed within one year of its creation, and was therefore barred by the Illinois Statute of Frauds. Hammond Group, Ltd. v. Spalding & Evenflo Cos., 69 F.3d 845 (7th Cir. 1995).

A contract which might have been performed within one year, as it could have been terminated at any time by either party or might have been terminated within the year by the death of the plaintiff, was not a contract that was to be performed within one year. Mead v. Chicago & N.W. Ry., 189 Ill. App. 323 (1 Dist. 1914).

Where the parties' oral contract could not be completed within a year and there was no claim of misrepresentation, promissory estoppel did not bar application of the Illinois Statute of Frauds, 740 ILCS 80/1; in addition, because a distributor failed to allege conduct directed at a third party, it could not recover for tortuous interference, the action was properly denied for failure to state a claim. Uncommon USA, Inc. v. Wing Enters., F. Supp. 2d , 2003 U.S. Dist. LEXIS 14249 (N.D. Ill. Aug. 14, 2003).

—Personal Services

Rendition of personal services, the value of which may be pecuniarily estimated, or which can be adequately compensated at law, will not remove an oral contract to devise land in exchange for such services from the operation of the Statute of Frauds. Fierke v. Elgin City Banking Co., 366 Ill. 66, 7 N.E.2d 875 (1937).

A decedent's oral agreement to compensate for personal services by will, where the decedent neither at the time of the promise nor at the time of his death had any real estate, was not within the statute of frauds and for breach of such an agreement recovery may be had against the decedent's estate. Moreen v. Estate of Carlson, 365 Ill. 482, 6 N.E.2d 871 (1937).

The mere expression of an intention to convey property, which does not culminate in a binding agreement with mutual obligations, is not a contract which can be specifically enforced; the performance of personal services which can be estimated in money and for which a recovery can be had at law will not take a contract out of the Statute of Frauds. Flannery v. Woolverton, 329 Ill. 424, 160 N.E. 762 (1928).

—Sale of Business

The transaction for the sale of a business involved one overarching agreement, although detailed in seven separate documents, and its primary purpose was not the sale of goods; thus, the U.C.C Statute of Frauds (810 ILCS 5/2-201) was not applicable. Midwest Mfg. Holding v. Donnelly Corp., 975 F. Supp. 1061 (N.D. Ill. 1997).

—Strangers Precluded

The Statute of Frauds can not be interposed by strangers to the agreement. Hartley v. Hartley, 290 Ill.App. 92, 7 N.E.2d 906 (2 Dist. 1937).

—Test

Test to determine if an agreement is subject to the one-year provision of the statute of frauds is whether, when it was made, the agreement was capable of full performance within one year, not whether full performance was likely; Illinois allows the use of equitable estoppel to bar an opponent's statute of frauds defense. R.R Donnelley & Sons Co. v. Jet Messenger Serv., F. Supp. 2d , 2003 U.S. Dist. LEXIS 25421 (N.D. Ill. May 24, 2003).

The test for determining whether an agreement is within this section is not whether it was performed within one year, but whether when the agreement was made, it could have been performed within a year, and if so, it does not come within the section. In re Strand, 86 Ill. App. 3d 827, 42 Ill. Dec. 37, 408 N.E.2d 415 (1 Dist. 1980).

—Trusts

Trusts created by construction, implication, or operation of law, need not be in writing, but may be proved by parol evidence; trusts ex maleficio are adjudged and enforced by the courts, and this section does not apply to them. Ropacki v. Ropacki, 354 Ill. 502, 188 N.E. 400 (1933).

The Statute of Frauds does not apply to a verbal trust in personal property. Maher v. Aldrich, 205 Ill. 242, 68 N.E. 810 (1903).

—U.C.C.

Where defendants were in the business of growing soybeans and

Applicability (Cont'd)

—U.C.C. (Cont'd)
other grains and selling their crops to grain companies, they were considered merchants with respect to such sales; since the defendants were merchants, 810 ILCS 5/2-201(2) operated to bar the defendants from asserting the defense of the Statute of Frauds. Campbell v. Yokel, 20 Ill. App. 3d 702, 313 N.E.2d 628 (5 Dist. 1974).

—Wills
Prior will of testatrix, executed prior to her marriage, together with a verbal ante-nuptial agreement reduced to writing after the marriage, did not constitute an equitable assignment and was outside the Statute of Frauds. Lee v. Central Nat'l Bank & Trust Co., 11 Ill. App. 3d 60, 296 N.E.2d 81 (2 Dist. 1973).

The requirements for the writing and signing of wills should follow the Statute of Frauds. Kolowski v. Fausz, 103 Ill. App. 528 (4 Dist. 1902).

Authority of Agent

—In General
An agent can only sign a contract for the sale of real estate containing such terms as his principal authorized him to execute, and such authority must be in writing signed by the principal in order to comply with the Statute of Frauds. Fieschko v. Herlich, 32 Ill. App. 2d 280, 177 N.E.2d 376 (2 Dist. 1961).

—Ratification by Principal
An agent's unauthorized act in entering into a purchase agreement for the sale of real estate may be ratified by the principal so as to avoid the application of this section. Fieschko v. Herlich, 32 Ill. App. 2d 280, 177 N.E.2d 376 (2 Dist. 1961).

Bankruptcy

—Waiver
Waiver of the Statute of Frauds prior to filing the petition in bankruptcy was binding upon the trustee in bankruptcy. In re German, 193 F. Supp. 948 (S.D. Ill. 1961).

Binding Agreement Not Shown
The informal writings between the parties did not constitute a binding settlement agreement as they did not manifest a desire by each party to be bound to the material terms of the proposed deal. Abbott Labs. v. Alpha Therapeutic Corp., 164 F.3d 385 (7th Cir. 1999).

Child Support Agreement

—Enforceable
Alleged agreement that father would pay child support of $50 per week until date of child's eighteenth birthday could have been performed in one year and, therefore, was not barred by the Statute of Frauds, even though child's eighteenth birthday was more than a year away at the time of the agreement. In re Strand, 86 Ill. App. 3d 827, 42 Ill. Dec. 37, 408 N.E.2d 415 (1 Dist. 1980).

Contracts

—In General
Even assuming the parties intended oral negotiations to be binding, an oral contract was unenforceable under the Statute of Frauds Act, 740 ILCS 80/1, due to its five year term; furthermore, the company's preparation of a mockup and sample of the bandage packaging and concept book and design of sales display ads were not sufficient to allege the partial performance exception to the Statute of Frauds. Jolly Group, Ltd. v. Medline Indus., F. Supp. 2d , 2004 U.S. Dist. LEXIS 10770 (N.D. Ill. Apr. 30, 2004).

Manufacturer, who was not a party to contracts between its predecessor and sales representatives, could not assert a statute of frauds defense to the contracts. Fararo v. Sink LLC, F. Supp. 2d , 2002 U.S. Dist. LEXIS 23022 (N.D. Ill. Nov. 25, 2002).

Lubricant manufacturer's motion for summary judgment on a distributor's claims of breach of an oral contract and an implied contract was granted where the parties had entered a written agreement that controlled their distributorship relationship and even if the written agreement had not barred the claims, the Illinois Statute of Frauds, 740 ILCS 80/1, rendered the alleged contract invalid, the alleged contract failed for lack of essential terms, and the alleged contract was terminable at will. Bell Fuels, Inc. v. Chevron U.S.A. Inc., F. Supp. 2d , 2000 U.S. Dist. LEXIS 22341 (N.D. Ill. Mar. 21, 2000).

The Statute of Frauds cannot be applied unless the court finds a valid, enforceable agreement as it operates only to make an otherwise valid contract voidable; therefore, whether a contract exists in the first place is a question of the intent of the parties. Paist v. Town & Country Corp., 772 F. Supp. 412 (N.D. Ill. 1991).

As to contracts generally, a party named in the contract may become bound by its provisions even though he has not signed it. Welsh v. Jakstas, 401 Ill. 288, 82 N.E.2d 53 (1948).

Where the parties did not agree on the construction to be given to the language employed in the context, and some of the terms were ambiguous or susceptible to more than one interpretation, the exhibits attached to the complaint substantially showed the agreement between the parties. Bertlee Co. v. Illinois Publishing & Printing Co., 320 Ill. App. 490, 52 N.E.2d 47 (1943).

To take a case out of the operation of the Statute of Frauds, the evidence should establish with reasonable certainty not only that an agreement was made, but also its terms, clearly and specifically. Nelson v. Nelson, 334 Ill. 43, 165 N.E. 159 (1929).

In order to take a case out of the operation of the Statute of Frauds, a contract to convey should be clear and certain in its terms, and established by testimony of an undoubted character, which is clear, definite, and unequivocal. Barrett v. Geisinger, 148 Ill. 98, 35 N.E. 354 (1893).

—Affect on Validity
The Statute of Frauds is substantive in nature and affects the validity of the contract. Oakes v. Chicago Fire Brick Co., 311 Ill. App. 111, 35 N.E.2d 522 (1 Dist. 1941), aff'd, 388 Ill. 474, 58 N.E.2d 460 (1944).

—Connection of Documents
Where a contract refers to another instrument or to a certain part thereof by specific designation, it is proper that the court know what such provision of the other instrument is. Bertlee Co. v. Illinois Publishing & Printing Co., 320 Ill. App. 490, 52 N.E.2d 47 (1943).

A complete contract, binding under the former Statute of Frauds, may be gathered from letters, writings, and telegrams between the parties relating to the subject matter of the contract and so connected with each other that they may be fairly said to constitute one paper relating to the contract, though only one of the writings may be signed by the party to be charged. Western Metals Co. v. Hartman Ingot Metal Co., 303 Ill. 479, 135 N.E. 744 (1922).

A paper signed by the party to be charged cannot be incorporated in a paper not signed by him by a reference in the latter; the signed paper must refer to the unsigned paper in clear and distinct terms. Western Metals Co. v. Hartman Ingot Metal Co., 303 Ill. 479, 135 N.E. 744 (1922).

After the several writings connect themselves together into one complete memorandum, parol proof is proper to show that the several writings apply to the subject matter of the suit, and not to some other sale; the signed writing or writings must refer expressly to the other writing, or the several writings must be so connected, either physically or otherwise, as to show by internal evidence that they relate to the same contract. Western Metals Co. v. Hartman Ingot Metal Co., 303 Ill. 479, 135 N.E. 744 (1922).

—Consideration
Plaintiff's forbearance of a civil action based on the 1992 agreements was new and valuable consideration that removed the 1995 contract from the statute of frauds. T.L. Swint Indus., Inc. v. Wright, 16 F. Supp. 2d 937 (N.D. Ill. 1998).

There is no requirement that the consideration for the promise shall be expressed in writing and may be furnished by oral testimony. Dunlap v. Hopkins, 95 F. 231 (7th Cir. 1899).

—Conveyances
Where deceased conveyed to his son a tract of land by deed which stated an agreement that the land was accepted by the son as his full and entire share of his father's estate, the agreement was not within the Statute of Frauds. Kershaw v. Kershaw, 102 Ill. 307 (1882).

Contracts (Cont'd)

—Detrimental Reliance

Performance or part performance must be founded upon, and referable to the specific terms of the agreement, and the performance relied upon must place the party who has performed in such a situation that it would be a fraud upon him if the agreement were not carried out. Nelson v. Nelson, 334 Ill. 43, 165 N.E. 159 (1929).

—Divorce Proceeding

Where the parties to a divorce proceeding contract in respect to alimony and property rights arising out of the marriage relationship, and the provisions agreed to are incorporated in the decree, the contract becomes merged in the decree, and the rights of the parties are thereafter based upon the decree, not the agreement, and the requirement of the Statute of Frauds that contracts concerning real estate be in writing has no application. Guyton v. Guyton, 17 Ill. 2d 439, 161 N.E.2d 832 (1959).

—Employment

Promise that employee could work for as long as he desired did not run afoul of the statute of frauds because employee could have decided to leave within a year. Strzelecki v. Schwarz Paper Co., 824 F. Supp. 821 (N.D. Ill. 1993).

—Enforceable

Statute of Frauds did not prohibit the enforcement of contract which, by the acceptance of the defendants, became a contract in writing, and a down payment was made upon the goods ordered. Calo, Inc. v. AMF Pinspotters, Inc., 31 Ill. App. 2d 2, 176 N.E.2d 1 (1 Dist. 1961).

—Executed

Executed contracts, as opposed to executory contracts, are never voided by the Statute of Frauds. Estate of Jesmer v. Rohlev, 241 Ill. App. 3d 798, 182 Ill. Dec. 282, 609 N.E.2d 816 (1 Dist. 1993).

—Executed in Another State

As a general rule, a contract valid in the state where it is executed may be enforced in another state; a contract executed in Kansas, which related to sale of property in that state, if valid in that state, although it may be prohibited by the Statute of Frauds, would be enforced by Illinois courts. Miller v. Wilson, 146 Ill. 523, 34 N.E. 1111 (1893).

—Forbearance

In an action for breach of a guaranty contract, there was a genuine issue of material fact precluding summary judgment; the consultant's forbearance of a civil action based on 1992 agreements might be considered new and valuable consideration that took the 1995 guaranty contract out of the statute of frauds. T.L. Swint Indus., Inc. v. Premier Sales Group, Inc., 983 F. Supp. 772 (N.D. Ill. 1997).

—Motion to Dismiss

Subcontractor's motion to dismiss was denied as to a management services company's claims arising from an alleged breach of a contract; the Statute of Frauds did not bar the assertion of the claims because: (1) it was not clear whether the company was asserting claims pursuant to a standard supplier contract, which could not be fully performed within one year, or under a separate agreement with the subcontractor, which could be fully performed within one year; and (2) even if the standard supplier contract was the only existing agreement between the parties, the company had alleged facts which, if proven, would establish a claim for equitable estoppel and would bar the subcontractor's Statute of Frauds defense. R.R Donnelley & Sons Co. v. Jet Messenger Serv., F. Supp. 2d , 2003 U.S. Dist. LEXIS 25421 (N.D. Ill. May 24, 2003).

A plaintiff in a suit on a contract within the Statute of Frauds should not be allowed to resist a motion to dismiss, backed by an affidavit that the defendant denies the contract was made, by arguing that his luck may improve in discovery. DF Activities Corp. v. Brown, 851 F.2d 920 (7th Cir. 1988).

Where in making the motion to dismiss, defendant thereby admitted the truth of the allegation that the memorandum in writing was made by him, whether the promise which was made was collateral or original was a matter of fact to be determined at the trial. Raveret-Wever Printing Co. v. Wright, 301 Ill. App. 421, 23 N.E.2d 203 (1 Dist. 1939).

—Not Illegal

Where a seller intended to sell merchandise at ceiling prices, the contract was not illegal because the amount of the ceiling price was uncertain at the time the contract was first made; a purchase order in the cotton goods business was meant to be at ceiling prices. This was further evidence of the intention of the parties to comply with rather than violate the Price Control Act. Charm Tred Mills, Inc. v. Erle P. Halliburton, Inc., 202 F.2d 294 (7th Cir. 1953).

—Notice

Notice, actual or constructive, of a contract which is void under the Statute of Frauds, will not prevent the person having notice from becoming a purchaser of the property from the original owner. Wright v. Raftree, 181 Ill. 464, 54 N.E. 998 (1899).

—One Year Rule

Because the parties agreed that the entertainment company and the motorcycle sports sanctioning body contemplated an promotion agreement that could not be performed within a year it fell within 740 ILCS 80/1; even though the entertainment company did not produce a document reflecting approval by that sanctioning body's board, it was not required to do so at the pleading stage; its pleadings sufficiently alleged that the promotion agreement's enforceability, as it attached a copy of the alleged agreement and letters from its attorneys confirming its own approval of the agreement. JamSports & Entm't, LLC v. Paradama Prods., Inc., F. Supp. 2d , 2003 U.S. Dist. LEXIS 6100 (N.D. Ill. Apr. 15, 2003).

Evidence of an oral contractual agreement as a school bus driver covering a period of less than one year would not be limited by this section; however, it would limit an action trying to establish a contractual agreement which would cover two or more school years. Foiles v. North Greene Unit Dist. No. 3, 261 Ill. App. 3d 186, 198 Ill. Dec. 562, 633 N.E.2d 24 (4 Dist. 1994).

Oral promise to pay plaintiff employee appreciated value of 15 shares of company stock did not meet the requirements of the Frauds Act because the agreement provided that plaintiff would be awarded the appreciated value of his "phantom stock" upon his retirement from the company and because plaintiff was in his early thirties when he entered into the agreement, and because, by his own account, he planned to work for many more years, the contract did not seem to have been performable within the span of a year; but since plaintiff fully performed his end of the bargain when he delivered the securities, he could seek full payment from defendant according to the terms of the oral agreement. Strzelecki v. Schwarz Paper Co., 824 F. Supp. 821 (N.D. Ill. 1993).

Where a contract extends to a point in time, be it death or some other circumstance, at which time the full service contemplated will have been rendered, and that point of time could occur within one year, the Statute of Frauds will not be a bar to the enforcement of the action. Estate of Jesmer v. Rohlev, 241 Ill. App. 3d 798, 182 Ill. Dec. 282, 609 N.E.2d 816 (1 Dist. 1993).

To be outside of the one-year provision of the Statute of Frauds, the contract must be capable of being fully performed within one year and not simply terminated by some contingency such as death or bankruptcy. Cohn v. Checker Motors Corp., 233 Ill. App. 3d 839, 175 Ill. Dec. 98, 599 N.E.2d 1112 (1 Dist. 1992).

Where plaintiff author sought to prove that she had a contract with defendant publisher based upon a pilot study, and plaintiff admitted that the pilot program was to run for more than one year and that the defendant promised to buy books over a three year period, the duration of the pilot study, the contract was unenforceable. Respect Inc. v. Committee on Status of Women, 781 F. Supp. 1358 (N.D. Ill. 1992).

An oral agreement to amend a written agreement was held not to be enforceable over a Statute of Frauds defense where the amendatory agreement was executory and subject to the Statute of Frauds. Central Information Fin. Servs., Ltd. v. First Nat'l Bank, 128 Ill. App. 3d 1052, 84 Ill. Dec. 226, 471 N.E.2d 992 (4 Dist. 1984).

A personal contract which might or might not have been performed according to the intention of the parties, but was intended that it extend for a period of more than one year, and which could have been performed at any time, and which called for an annual salary, could have been performed in one year and so, was not

Contracts (Cont'd)

—One Year Rule (Cont'd)
within the Statute of Frauds. Balstad v. Solem Mach. Co., 26 Ill. App. 2d 419, 168 N.E.2d 732 (2 Dist. 1960).

Courts have interpreted this section to provide that a contract is unenforceable only if it is impossible of performance in one year. Balstad v. Solem Mach. Co., 26 Ill. App. 2d 419, 168 N.E.2d 732 (2 Dist. 1960).

—Oral Extensions
Oral extensions of written contracts with extensions which cannot be performed within one year are not exempt. Dickens v. Quincy College Corp., 245 Ill. App. 3d 1055, 185 Ill. Dec. 822, 615 N.E.2d 381 (4 Dist. 1993).

—Oral Purchase Agreement
Enforcement of oral agreement whereby defendant cab companies agreed to give plaintiff the exclusive right to purchase all of their retired cabs was barred by the Statute of Frauds. Cohn v. Checker Motors Corp., 233 Ill. App. 3d 839, 175 Ill. Dec. 98, 599 N.E.2d 1112 (1 Dist. 1992).

Oral purchase agreement covering the 1956-57 garden season was capable of being performed in less than one year, and the contract did not fall with the statute. Hall v. Gruesen, 22 Ill. App. 2d 465, 161 N.E.2d 345 (1 Dist. 1959).

—Partly Oral
Where plaintiff alleged that it fully performed its part of the bargain for a period of fifteen years, the allegation of performance was sufficient to take the alleged oral contract out of the Statute of Frauds, and allowed the plaintiff to maintain his breach of contract claim. Skinner v. Shirley of Hollywood, 723 F. Supp. 50 (N.D. Ill. 1989).

A contract which is partly oral and partly written is considered oral for its legal effect. Koch v. Illinois Power Co., 175 Ill. App. 3d 248, 124 Ill. Dec. 461, 529 N.E.2d 281 (3 Dist. 1988).

—Possession
If performance and possession are relied upon to establish a contract and remove it from the application of the Statute of Frauds, the proof must be clear and convincing that the promisee went into possession under the contract and made valuable improvements upon the property with his own means and upon the faith of the promise and with the knowledge of the promisor. Pocius v. Fleck, 13 Ill. 2d 420, 150 N.E.2d 106 (1958).

—Preexisting Debt
There was a genuine issue of material fact as to whether defendant guarantor and defendant corporation owed significant sums of money to the consultant at the time a 1995 guaranty contract was executed and thus whether the guaranty contract fell within the statute of frauds, thus precluding summary judgment. T.L. Swint Indus., Inc. v. Premier Sales Group, Inc., 983 F. Supp. 772 (N.D. Ill. 1997).

—Presumptions
Where the bill alleged that defendant proposed to and promised and agreed with plaintiff and plaintiff agreed to and accepted the proposition to convey land and that defendant represented and stated to plaintiff and upon her statements, representations, and promises plaintiff agreed, it was nowhere stated that the promises and agreements were not in writing, therefore plaintiff was not required to do more than set out the contract in his bill, and compliance with the Statute of Frauds was presumed. Barker v. Hauberg, 325 Ill. 538, 156 N.E. 806 (1927).

—Repudiation
Where the owner may lawfully refuse to perform a contract, he may lawfully sell and convey to another, and, by so doing, repudiate the contract; a purchaser from him will not be affected by the prior sale, rendered void by the Statute of Frauds. Wright v. Raftree, 181 Ill. 464, 54 N.E. 998 (1899).

—Sufficient Writing
In an action for breach of contract, the defendant was not entitled to dismissal for failure to state a claim, notwithstanding the absence of a written contract between the parties, where the plaintiff alleged that there were several documents which when taken together were sufficient to satisfy the statute, including the defendant's signed request for proposals, the plaintiff's bid letter which proposed terms and conditions, duration, and pricing, the plaintiff's pricing schedules, the plaintiff's invoices to the defendant, the defendant's checks, and a termination letter sent by the defendant. Dedicated Transp., Inc. v. Volkswagen of Am., Inc., 201 F.R.D. 337, 2001 U.S. Dist. LEXIS 10051 (N.D. Ill. 2001).

The Statute of Frauds does not require that the contract itself be reduced to writing; it is sufficient if there be a memorandum or note of the contract in writing, signed by the party to be charged or by some one by him duly authorized. Kohlbrecher v. Guettermann, 329 Ill. 246, 160 N.E. 142 (1928).

It was not necessary, in order to take the contract of sale out of the former Statute of Frauds, that there be a formal written contract, nor was it necessary that the written memorandum by complete in one writing. Western Metals Co. v. Hartman Ingot Metal Co., 303 Ill. 479, 135 N.E. 744 (1922).

A writing, in order to meet the requirements under the Statute of Frauds, need not give all the details, but it must express the substance of the contract with reasonable certainty, either by its own terms or by reference to some other agreement or matter from which it can be ascertained with like reasonable certainty. Frazer v. Howe, 106 Ill. 563 (1883).

—Tenant's Loss of Rights
Claim that loss of rights as tenant under agreement would result in the loss of some future advantage dependent upon future performance of the agreement by both parties did not warrant the conclusion that to deny enforcement of the contract would result in fraud or injustice to plaintiff, so as to warrant the application of equitable considerations to the operation of Statute of Frauds. Conness v. Conness, 94 Ill. App. 2d 281, 236 N.E.2d 753 (3 Dist. 1968).

Contributory Negligence
The contributory negligence of the deceased's next of kin can eliminate any damage recovery by that person but it does not defeat the action. McDonnell v. McPartlin, 303 Ill. App. 3d 391, 236 Ill. Dec. 826, 708 N.E.2d 412 (1 Dist. 1999).

Damages

—Mitigation
Evidence that plaintiff refused to undergo a dangerous operation was inadmissible to prove failure to mitigate damages, but as this evidence affected only mitigation of damages, any error in admitting it became harmless when the jury found for the defendants on liability. McDonnell v. McPartlin, 303 Ill. App. 3d 391, 236 Ill. Dec. 826, 708 N.E.2d 412 (1 Dist. 1999).

Debt of Another

—Application
An action cannot lie on one's promise to answer for the debt of another unless such promise is in writing. Hartbarger v. SCA Servs. Inc., 200 Ill. App. 3d 1000, 146 Ill. Dec. 633, 558 N.E.2d 596 (5 Dist. 1990).

—Collateral Promise
Where the agent of an owner made an oral promise to see that a company furnishing brick to a contractor would be paid, this was a collateral promise to pay the debt of another, and was unenforceable under this section; however, a letter from the owner, signed by him, was a sufficient writing under this section. Bonner & Marshall Co. v. Hansell, 189 Ill. App. 474 (1 Dist. 1914).

—Enforcement
A promise to pay the debt of another which is not written and signed cannot be enforced either in law or in equity. Brown & Shinitzky Chartered v. Dentinger, 118 Ill. App. 3d 517, 74 Ill. Dec. 98, 455 N.E.2d 128 (1 Dist. 1983); Hartbarger v. SCA Servs. Inc., 200 Ill. App. 3d 1000, 146 Ill. Dec. 633, 558 N.E.2d 596 (5 Dist. 1990).

—Illustrative Cases
Husband's promise to repay loan of $100 from plaintiff to his wife held promise to repay debt of another and therefore within the Statute of Frauds. Laughlin v. Dalton, 200 Ill. App. 342 (2 Dist. 1916).

Debt of Another (Cont'd)

—Illustrative Cases (Cont'd)

Under the Statute of Frauds, a promise to pay the debt of another must be in writing but first there must be an existing debt; therefore, where defendant promised plaintiff to pay for goods which plaintiff would later deliver to a third person and which, at the time of the promise, had not been delivered, no debt existed from third person to the plaintiff so the promise of defendant to pay was an original undertaking, and not merely a promise to pay the debt of another. Lusk v. Throop, 189 Ill. 127, 59 N.E. 529 (1901).

—Joint and Several Obligation

If a party to a contract is held liable for all damages resulting from the breach of a joint and several contractual obligation, that party is not being held to answer for what is exclusively the debt of another, but is being held responsible for an obligation which is his directly because of the joint and several nature of the obligation; in such a situation, the requirement of a signed writing containing a special promise to answer for the debt, default or miscarriage of another person is inapplicable. Brokerage Resources, Inc. v. Jordan, 80 Ill. App. 3d 605, 35 Ill. Dec. 940, 400 N.E.2d 77 (1 Dist. 1980).

—Liability

In order that the promise to answer for the debt of another can be held to be within the statute, it is essential that there be a binding and subsisting obligation or liability to the promisee, to which the promise is collateral; in other words, the party for whom the promise has been made must be liable to the party to whom it is made. Resseter v. Waterman, 151 Ill. 169, 37 N.E. 875 (1894).

—Not Enforceable

Without proof of writing, defendant's alleged oral promise to assume her deceased husband's debt is unenforceable because it is in contravention of the Statute of Frauds. Swartzberg v. Dresner, 107 Ill. App. 3d 318, 63 Ill. Dec. 211, 437 N.E.2d 860 (1 Dist. 1982).

—Statute Not Applicable

Where plaintiff's appeal from a judgment in favor of defendant in action based on an account stated was predicated upon defendant's personal liability and not upon an undertaking by him to be responsible for another's debt or undertaking, by its terms, the Statute of Frauds was not applicable. Malkov Lumber Co. v. Wolf, 3 Ill. App. 3d 52, 278 N.E.2d 481 (1 Dist. 1971).

Dedication

—Statute Not Applicable

So far as an agreement to dedicate a street to the pubic was concerned, it was not affected by the Statute of Frauds, because a dedication may be by parol. Marlow v. Rich, 252 Ill. 442, 96 N.E. 921 (1911).

Defense

—In General

The Statute of Frauds may be availed of as a defense without specifically mentioning it if facts are stated sufficiently showing that the defendant seeks the protection of the statute. McCrystall v. Connor, 331 Ill. 107, 162 N.E. 375 (1928).

—Burden of Proof

Where the defense of the Statute of Frauds was raised by the appellant, the burden of proving facts justifying the application of the bar was upon appellant to show that the oral employment agreement was to be performed wholly within this state. Oakes v. Chicago Fire Brick Co., 388 Ill. 474, 58 N.E.2d 460 (1944).

—Demurrers

The benefit of the statute of frauds as a defense could be taken by demurrer where it did not affirmatively appear from the bill that the agreement relied on was not evidenced by a writing duly signed. Link v. Emrich, 336 Ill. 337, 168 N.E. 316 (1929).

—Denied

Where plaintiff's failure to have agreement put in writing was induced by defendant's intentionally misleading advice and promises, defendant was not allowed to interpose the Statute of Frauds to render the agreement void and unenforceable. Loeb v. Gendel, 23 Ill. 2d 502, 179 N.E.2d 7 (1961).

—Entitlement

Only the party being charged with a contract, lease or other obligation is entitled to invoke the Statute of Frauds. Nassau Terrace Condominium Ass'n v. Silverstein, 182 Ill. App. 3d 221, 130 Ill. Dec. 669, 537 N.E.2d 998 (1 Dist. 1989).

—Illegality

Under Rule 8(c), F.R.Civ.P., the defense of illegality in determining whether a valid enforceable contract existed should be set forth affirmatively. Charm Tred Mills, Inc. v. Erle P. Halliburton, Inc., 202 F.2d 294 (7th Cir. 1953).

—Not Applicable

The defense of the Statute of Frauds was without merit where the evidence sufficiently established the fact that there was an oral agreement by the deceased to devise his property to the complainants in consideration of the services to be rendered to him; plaintiff, at the request of the deceased, discontinued teaching school in order to care for him, and the evidence disclosed that such services were efficiently rendered to the time of the deceased's death, and that, in addition, plaintiff and her husband had expended their own money for his support. Fleming v. Dillon, 370 Ill. 325, 18 N.E.2d 910 (1938).

—Not Waived

Where there was no evidence that defendants broadcasting company and radio station explicitly acknowledged the existence and subject matter of a contract with plaintiff radio personality, and preliminary negotiations showed only that a contract did not yet exist, defendants had not waived the Illinois statute of frauds as a defense. Dumas v. Infinity Broad. Corp., F. Supp. 2d , 2003 U.S. Dist. LEXIS 22779 (N.D. Ill. Dec. 17, 2003).

Where purchasers sued for specific performance of a contract for the sale of real estate, and in their complaint, prayed that the court find and establish that a valid written contract was duly executed, vendor was not required to plead the Statute of Frauds, as the only issue in the case was whether there was a valid written contract. Young v. Kowske, 402 Ill. 114, 83 N.E.2d 500 (1948).

Employment Contracts

—In General

Employer's representations to the employee did not create a contract for permanent employment because oral contracts for lifetime employment were barred by the Illinois Statute of Frauds. Miller v. Ford Motor Co., 254 F. Supp. 2d 1024, 2003 U.S. Dist. LEXIS 5542 (N.D. Ill. 2003).

A contract having a duration of more than one year, such as a contract for permanent employment, should be in writing. Koch v. Illinois Power Co., 175 Ill. App. 3d 248, 124 Ill. Dec. 461, 529 N.E.2d 281 (3 Dist. 1988).

—Contingency Termination

Where an alleged contract for permanent employment could have ended due to plaintiff's death or cessation of business by the employer within one year, such situations would not be the equivalent of full performance within one year; termination due to a contingency, such as death of an employee, and full performance are distinct situations. Koch v. Illinois Power Co., 175 Ill. App. 3d 248, 124 Ill. Dec. 461, 529 N.E.2d 281 (3 Dist. 1988).

—Definite Term

In a proceeding for breach of contract by employee against employer, an oral contract which was not of indefinite duration but was allegedly for a term of 36 years and in which plaintiff would be employed until he reached age 62 when he would receive certain benefits, was unenforceable under the Statute of Frauds. Gilliland v. Allstate Ins. Co., 69 Ill. App. 3d 630, 26 Ill. Dec. 444, 388 N.E.2d 68 (1 Dist. 1979).

—Employee Handbook

Plaintiff's contention that an oral contract for employment was partially memorialized in defendants' manual of policies and procedures was without merit as the contract still fell within the Statute of Frauds. Gilliland v. Allstate Ins. Co., 69 Ill. App. 3d 630, 26 Ill. Dec. 444, 388 N.E.2d 68 (1 Dist. 1979).

Employment Contracts (Cont'd)

—Enforceable

Plaintiff's retirement from business pursuits or his voluntary departure from employment were contingencies that could have occurred within a year, in which case the contract would have been fully performed, and thus the Statute of Frauds was not a bar to enforcement. Martin v. Federal Life Ins. Co., 109 Ill. App. 3d 596, 65 Ill. Dec. 143, 440 N.E.2d 998 (1 Dist. 1982).

—Full Performance

An alleged oral agreement could not be enforced on the basis of the plaintiff's full performance where: (1) the plaintiff physician alleged an oral agreement pursuant to which he was to work for the defendant physicians for two years at a lower rate of pay and then be made a full partner; but (2) a written contract between the plaintiff and the defendant's corporation provided for a two year term of employment and that the corporation anticipated offering the plaintiff the opportunity to become a shareholder, but was under no obligation to do so, and that the plaintiff was under no obligation to buy shares in the event they were offered. Taimoorazy v. Bloomington Anesthesiology Serv., 122 F. Supp. 2d 967, 2000 U.S. Dist. LEXIS 17251 (N.D. Ill. 2000).

—Illustrative Cases

Where employer promises to employ employee as long as employee meets job requirements, statute of frauds applies to bar such contract unless a writing exists. Milazzo v. O'Connell, 925 F. Supp. 1331 (N.D. Ill. 1996), aff'd, 108 F.3d 129 (7th Cir. 1997).

Personal reference binder manual, supervisor's seminar personnel policy procedures and evidence of the good cause requirement for discharge, as well as the three warning policy, were sufficient writings to remove employment contract from the statute of fraud. Vajda v. Arthur Andersen & Co., 253 Ill. App. 3d 345, 191 Ill. Dec. 965, 624 N.E.2d 1343 (1 Dist. 1993).

Although oral employment agreement called for the payment of commissions as long as the customer reordered the same style number of fabric and those reorders could come in forever, it was just as possible that the reorders could cease before the expiration of one year; plaintiff could also have died before one year had passed from the time the agreement was made thus obviating the payment of reorder commissions; therefore, the agreement was not barred by the Statute of Frauds, despite the fact that performance actually exceeded one year. Stein v. Malden Mills, Inc., 9 Ill. App. 3d 266, 292 N.E.2d 52 (1 Dist. 1972).

—Lifetime

Where plaintiff was fully compensated for the work that he performed, part performance of lifetime employment contract did not take the case out of the statute of frauds. McInerney v. Charter Golf, Inc., 176 Ill. 2d 482, 223 Ill. Dec. 911, 680 N.E.2d 1347 (1997).

A lifetime employment contract is, in essence, a permanent employment contract, inherently anticipating a relationship of long duration certainly longer than a year; therefore, a writing is required for the fair enforcement of lifetime employment contracts. McInerney v. Charter Golf, Inc., 176 Ill. 2d 482, 223 Ill. Dec. 911, 680 N.E.2d 1347 (1997).

—No Violation

Where an oral employment contract would be completely executed in less than one year, it did not violate the Statute of Frauds. Office Elecs., Inc. v. Grafic Forms, Inc., 72 Ill. App. 3d 456, 28 Ill. Dec. 594, 390 N.E.2d 953 (2 Dist. 1979).

—Not Enforceable

Where plaintiff could not point to any written contract or provision promising a lifetime of reappointments after October 1990, merely accepting past offers of two year reappointments did not constitute partial performance and oral contract was not enforceable. Tabora v. Gottlieb Mem. Hosp., 279 Ill. App. 3d 108, 215 Ill. Dec. 870, 664 N.E.2d 267 (1 Dist. 1996).

—Oral Modification

While a contract containing a covenant not to compete for a period longer than a year does not run afoul of the Statute of Frauds, a contract containing a term of employment for such a period does; therefore, an employment contract, even with its oral modifications, was not unenforceable under the Statute of Frauds. Wyatt v. Dishong, 127 Ill. App. 3d 716, 83 Ill. Dec. 1, 469 N.E.2d 608 (5 Dist. 1984).

—Part Performance

Notwithstanding that the plaintiff performed his obligations without pay for nine months before the contract at issue was terminated, this partial performance did not take the oral agreement outside of the statute of frauds since, under the partial-performance exception to the statute of frauds, it must be impractical to compensate the performing party for only the value of the partial performance. Fischer v. First Chicago Capital Mkts., Inc., 195 F.3d 279 (7th Cir. 1999).

Normal employment contracts do not involve the kind of partial performance that bars application of the Statute of Frauds. Mariani v. School Dirs. of Dist. 40, 154 Ill. App. 3d 404, 107 Ill. Dec. 90, 506 N.E.2d 981 (3 Dist. 1987).

—Performance Within One Year

An alleged oral agreement which provided for an "ongoing consulting relationship" under which the plaintiff was to be paid an annual fee for the duration of certain bonds, which were to last up to 27 years, in exchange for continuing administrative services could not be completed within one year, notwithstanding that the plaintiff could have been paid the present value of what he would have earned over time in the first year, since the plaintiff still could not completely perform within one year. Fischer v. First Chicago Capital Mkts., Inc., 195 F.3d 279 (7th Cir. 1999).

Where employer's oral promises to employ employee for as long as employee wanted, promise was capable of being performed within one year and was not within the statute of frauds. Milazzo v. O'Connell, 925 F. Supp. 1331 (N.D. Ill. 1996), aff'd, 108 F.3d 129 (7th Cir. 1997).

The trial court erroneously applied the Statute of Frauds to bar a claim of breach of an employment contract where the plaintiff employee alleged that she had been promised that she would be immediately designated a permanent employee of defendant's and also appointed a member of their President's Council if she accepted the terms and conditions of the offer "then and there," which she did, and her part performance was a question of fact that could not be decided on a motion to dismiss her complaint. Davies v. Martel Lab. Servs., Inc., 189 Ill. App. 3d 694, 136 Ill. Dec. 951, 545 N.E.2d 475 (1 Dist. 1989).

—Reliance

In the context of an employment relationship, reasonable reliance is insufficient to bar the application of the statute of frauds. McInerney v. Charter Golf, Inc., 176 Ill. 2d 482, 223 Ill. Dec. 911, 680 N.E.2d 1347 (1997).

—Statute Not Applicable

The Statute of Frauds was not applicable where in an employment contract appellant agreed to pay plaintiff five percent of the renewal premiums received on all policies of insurance sold by him, and in force at the time he quit his employment, for a period of one year after such time as the employment might terminate, and at the time he resigned from the appellant's employ he was receiving from the appellant monthly checks of $115 each, which represented five percent of the amount of the renewal premiums paid on policies previously sold by him. Collins v. Addicks, 351 Ill. App. 266, 114 N.E.2d 801 (2 Dist. 1953).

The Statute of Frauds is for the purpose of preventing fraud and cannot be interposed as a defense in equity when it would have such effect; where the plaintiff had performed the terms of his employment, to deny him relief on the ground that the terms of the employment were not in writing and not to be performed within one year would be a fraud upon the plaintiff, and therefore the Statute of Frauds does not apply. Collins v. Addicks, 351 Ill. App. 266, 114 N.E.2d 801 (2 Dist. 1953).

—Writing Held Insufficient

Where the only statement contained in a writing which purported to evidence the existence of a multiyear contract was that the Board of School Directors voted to extend a three year contract to a superintendent, and where no statements were ever recorded which would evidence the substance of the contract itself, the writing was insufficient to satisfy the Statute of Frauds. Mariani v. School Dirs. of Dist. 40, 154 Ill. App. 3d 404, 107 Ill. Dec. 90, 506 N.E.2d 981 (3 Dist. 1987).

Employment Contracts (Cont'd)

—Writing Held Insufficient (Cont'd)

Where there was insufficient evidence of a writing to show that the defendant had intended to employ the plaintiff as city chemist and bacteriologist for a period of two years, plaintiff could not recover damages when the city fired her. Westgate v. City of Aurora, 229 Ill. App. 84 (2 Dist. 1923).

Estoppel

—In General

Where there is an express contract governing the relationship out of which an alleged promise emerged, such contract leaves no gap in the remedial system for an estoppel-like remedy to fill. Taimoorazy v. Bloomington Anesthesiology Serv., 122 F. Supp. 2d 967, 2000 U.S. Dist. LEXIS 17251 (N.D. Ill. 2000).

—Allowed

Illinois allows the use of equitable estoppel to bar an opponent's Statute of Frauds defense. Bower v. Jones, 978 F.2d 1004 (7th Cir. 1992).

—Not Shown

Plaintiff was not estopped from asserting the Statute of Frauds as a bar to an alleged 15 year oral agreement because with the absence of fraud or misrepresentation the defendant acted solely upon his own judgment and at his own risk. Ceres Ill., Inc. v. Illinois Scrap Processing, 114 Ill. 2d 133, 102 Ill. Dec. 379, 500 N.E.2d 1 (1986).

There was no basis for the trial court's holding that plaintiff was equitably estopped from asserting the Statute of Frauds as a defense where there was no misrepresentation or concealment of material facts and where both parties had access to the same information regarding contract negotiations. Ceres Ill., Inc. v. Illinois Scrap Processing, Inc., 130 Ill. App. 3d 798, 86 Ill. Dec. 48, 474 N.E.2d 1245 (1 Dist. 1984).

—Requirements

In order to assert equitable estoppel as a defense to a Statute of Frauds claim, the party must show, among other things, proof of an intentional misrepresentation or concealment of a material fact by the party to be estopped. Bower v. Jones, 978 F.2d 1004 (7th Cir. 1992).

In order to trump the Statute of Frauds, a party must invoke the doctrine of equitable estoppel, which differs from promissory estoppel in that the party asserting it must additionally allege words or conduct amounting to a misrepresentation or concealment of material facts. Cohn v. Checker Motors Corp., 233 Ill. App. 3d 839, 175 Ill. Dec. 98, 599 N.E.2d 1112 (1 Dist. 1992).

A party's decision to make expenditures and to change its position in reliance on an oral promise is an insufficient basis for equitable estoppel in the absence of fraud or misrepresentation. Ceres Ill., Inc. v. Illinois Scrap Processing, Inc., 130 Ill. App. 3d 798, 86 Ill. Dec. 48, 474 N.E.2d 1245 (1 Dist. 1984).

—Shown

The amended complaint sufficiently stated allegations that fell within the definition of estoppel, and the motion to dismiss was denied. Genin, Trudeau & Co. v. Integra Dev. Int'l, 845 F. Supp. 611 (N.D. Ill. 1994).

Evidence

—Memoranda

Writings consisting of correspondence, minutes, memoranda and illustrative and actual "Experience for Dividend" reports which the parties exchanged evidenced the existence and the terms of their agreement and satisfied the Statute of Frauds, and full performance by plaintiff of its obligations under the agreement removed it from the Statute of Frauds. American College of Surgeons v. Lumbermens Mut. Cas. Co., 142 Ill. App. 3d 680, 96 Ill. Dec. 719, 491 N.E.2d 1179 (1 Dist. 1986).

A letter corroborative of the testimony of witnesses in regard to the time when the promise was made was properly admitted as a memorandum made by the party at the time, and sworn to have been correctly made, in connection with the evidence of the plaintiff upon that question, however, the letter might not be evidence for any other purpose. Dunlap v. Hopkins, 95 F. 231 (7th Cir. 1899).

—Motion for Summary Judgment

Evidence was sufficient to grant appellee's motion for summary judgment based on the Statute of Frauds. Derby Meadows Util. Co. v. Inter-Continental Real Estate, 202 Ill. App. 3d 345, 147 Ill. Dec. 646, 559 N.E.2d 986 (1 Dist. 1990).

Executed Contracts

—Exception Not Allowed

While contract may have been "executed" with regard to claims for commissions for sales made prior to its termination, it was clearly "executory" with regard to sales subsequent to the termination of the contract, and the completed performance exception to the Statute of Frauds did not apply. Hammond Group, Ltd. v. Spalding & Evenflo Cos., 69 F.3d 845 (7th Cir. 1995).

Application of an exception for executed contracts to the surety provisions of the Statute of Frauds would render these provisions totally meaningless; a performing party in normal circumstances does not attempt to enforce a surety contract until after performance under the contract is complete and the primary debtor has failed to satisfy his obligation. Brown & Shinitzky Chartered v. Dentinger, 118 Ill. App. 3d 517, 74 Ill. Dec. 98, 455 N.E.2d 128 (1 Dist. 1983).

Executed contracts are never within the Statute of Frauds. Warszawa v. White Eagle Brewing Co., 299 Ill. App. 509, 20 N.E.2d 343 (1 Dist. 1939).

The Statute of Frauds cannot be invoked to avoid a contract which has been carried into execution. Hartley v. Hartley, 290 Ill.App. 92, 7 N.E.2d 906 (2 Dist. 1937).

Defendant was estopped from relying on this section where a contract had been fully performed by the plaintiff, since an executed contract could not come within the provisions of this section. Mead v. Chicago & N.W. Ry., 189 Ill. App. 323 (1 Dist. 1914).

Express Trust

In the absence of a writing, where a beneficiary sought to obtain real property which he had not owned since 1908, and attempted to span a half-century lapse of title by asserting that all who owned the realty after him were acting solely as his trustees, his allegations did not plead a constructive trust, but an express trust, because the "trusts" were based solely upon promises allegedly made successively to the beneficiary by his mother and wife to hold the land for his use and benefit, and neither conveyance was claimed to have been caused or provoked by reason of a fraud or an abuse of confidence and fiduciary relationship (the absolute prerequisites to a constructive trust); express trust was void for want of a writing. Ramsay v. Ramsay, 10 Ill. App. 2d 459, 135 N.E.2d 172 (1 Dist. 1956).

Factual Question

It was a factual question whether letter from bank to air conditioning installer constituted a commitment to pay for such installation, in case involving application of Statute of Frauds. Grand-Kahn Elec., Inc. v. Transportation Bldg. Corp., 15 Ill. App. 3d 580, 304 N.E.2d 743 (1 Dist. 1973).

Franchise Agreement

—Barred

A franchise agreement which contemplated a duration of several years and involved continuing obligations on the part of all parties was incapable of being performed within one year and was barred by the Statute of Frauds. Libby-Broadway Drive-In, Inc. v. McDonald's Sys., 72 Ill. App. 3d 806, 28 Ill. Dec. 802, 391 N.E.2d 1 (1 Dist. 1979).

Full Performance

—Defense Barred

Complete performance on the part of one of the parties to an oral agreement bars application of this Act. Noesges v. Servicemaster Co., 233 Ill. App. 3d 158, 174 Ill. Dec. 240, 598 N.E.2d 437 (2 Dist. 1992).

Where full performance was possible within one year, plaintiff's arguments that the Illinois Statute of Frauds provisions bars defendant's fraudulent inducement defense was without merit. FDIC v. Bruno, 777 F. Supp. 1432 (N.D. Ill. 1991).

Full Performance (Cont'd)

—Defense Barred (Cont'd)

Where plaintiff's divestiture of his interest in a rival company was the only obligation under the agreement which he promised to perform, performance of the promise barred a defense based on the Statute of Frauds. Adams v. Lockformer Co., 167 Ill. App. 3d 93, 117 Ill. Dec. 826, 520 N.E.2d 1177 (1 Dist. 1988).

Full and complete performance of a contract for years takes the case out of the Statute of Frauds because the statute was not intended to permit the perpetration of a fraud. Collins v. Addicks, 351 Ill. App. 266, 114 N.E.2d 801 (2 Dist. 1953).

—Defense Inapplicable

Attorneys' performance of their part of the agreement, representing defendant's adult son in legal matters, proved the existence of a contract with the defendant for payment of their services, and thus the statute of frauds was inapplicable. Greenberger, Krauss & Tenenbaum v. Catalfo, 293 Ill. App. 3d 88, 227 Ill. Dec. 230, 687 N.E.2d 153 (1 Dist. 1997).

—Effect

Where plaintiff, pursuant to an oral agreement, agreed to develop, beta test and make ready for distribution a computer software package, and he duly performed all obligations required of him under the contract, this Act did not prevent enforcement of the oral agreement as alleged, and defendant's motion to dismiss should have been denied. Noesges v. Servicemaster Co., 233 Ill. App. 3d 158, 174 Ill. Dec. 240, 598 N.E.2d 437 (2 Dist. 1992).

Full performance on the part of one of the parties to an oral agreement bars application of this Act, and there is no requirement that the full performance take place within one year. Noesges v. Servicemaster Co., 233 Ill. App. 3d 158, 174 Ill. Dec. 240, 598 N.E.2d 437 (2 Dist. 1992).

Where the parties orally agreed that plaintiff would provide insurance coverage for defendant's corporation and that defendant would pay the premiums, and, although plaintiff fully performed as promised, defendant failed to pay the premiums due and incurred a debt which was never paid, the plaintiff's full performance in reliance upon defendant's promise rendered the contract enforceable and not governed by the Statute of Frauds. Jakubik v. Rounis, 175 Ill. App. 3d 551, 125 Ill. Dec. 8, 529 N.E.2d 1084 (1 Dist. 1988).

Performance of a contract takes it out of the Statute of Frauds. Pearce v. Pearce, 184 Ill. 289, 56 N.E. 311 (1900).

It is axiomatic that complete performance on one side of an oral agreement bars application of the Illinois Statute of Frauds. Lucas v. Niehaus, 341 Ill. App. 454, 94 N.E.2d 525 (4 Dist. 1950); McIntosh v. Magna Sys., 539 F. Supp. 1185 (N.D. Ill. 1982); Skinner v. Shirley of Hollywood, 723 F. Supp. 50 (N.D. Ill. 1989).

—One Year Rule

When one party to a contract completes his performance, the one-year provision of this section does not prevent enforcement of the promises of the other party. Noesges v. Servicemaster Co., 233 Ill. App. 3d 158, 174 Ill. Dec. 240, 598 N.E.2d 437 (2 Dist. 1992).

—Test

The proper test to determine whether this section is applicable is whether a contract or agreement by its terms is capable of full performance within a year, not whether such occurrence is likely. FDIC v. Bruno, 777 F. Supp. 1432 (N.D. Ill. 1991).

Impression of Trust

To impress a trust on property by parol evidence it is essential, even though the Statute of Frauds is not pleaded, that the facts be established by clear and convincing proof, and unless the testimony is of that character the court must deny relief. Maley v. Burns, 6 Ill. 2d 11, 126 N.E.2d 695 (1955).

Indefinite Duration Clause

—Not Enforceable

Oral agreements for delivery of ice cream which were to remain in effect as long as a defendant distributor served the customers "acquainted" with a plaintiff broker were unenforceable under the Statute of Frauds as the duration clause was indefinite and, therefore, the agreements were required to be in writing to be enforceable. R.J. Corp. v. Connelly Food Prods., Inc., 175 Ill. App. 3d 655, 125 Ill. Dec. 108, 529 N.E.2d 1184 (1 Dist. 1988).

Interpretation

Where an ambiguity exists in a contract, the interpretation which the parties themselves have placed upon the agreement is used in determining its true meaning. Bertlee Co. v. Illinois Publishing & Printing Co., 320 Ill. App. 490, 52 N.E.2d 47 (1943).

Investment Securities

—Not Applicable

A case which deals with the allegedly fraudulent transfer of investment securities will be controlled by Article VIII of the Uniform Commercial Code (810 ILCS 5/8-101 et seq.), rather than by this Act. Crawford County State Bank v. Marine Am. Nat'l Bank, 199 Ill. App. 3d 236, 145 Ill. Dec. 224, 556 N.E.2d 842 (4 Dist. 1990).

Legislative Intent

It was not intended by the adoption of the Statute of Frauds to protect fraud and facilitate its perpetration, but to prevent it. Kulik v. Kapusta, 303 Ill. 208, 135 N.E. 402 (1922).

It was not intended by the adoption of the Statute of Frauds to facilitate the perpetuation of and to protect fraud, but to prevent it, and the courts have never lent themselves to assist or protect fraud and will not permit the statute to be used as an engine of fraud, as its purpose was its suppression. Union Mut. Life Ins. Co. v. White, 106 Ill. 67 (1883).

License Agreement

—Barred

A 15 year oral license agreement for the storage of scrap on plaintiff's property was barred by this section since it was not to be performed within the space of one year from its making. Ceres Ill., Inc. v. Illinois Scrap Processing, Inc., 130 Ill. App. 3d 798, 86 Ill. Dec. 48, 474 N.E.2d 1245 (1 Dist. 1984).

Multiple Documents

—Insufficiently Connected

Several writings admitted the existence of a contract of sale, but the question presented was whether there was a memorandum of this contract of sale, complete in all its terms, and signed by the defendant in error, and where there was no contention that a memorandum existed unless the letters signed by it were connected with the confirmation as to make the confirmation and the letters a memorandum sufficient to satisfy the requirements of the Statute of Frauds, there was nothing in the letters, or in any papers to which the letters referred that stated any of the terms of the contract. Western Metals Co. v. Hartman Ingot Metal Co., 303 Ill. 479, 135 N.E. 744 (1922).

—Requirements

When several documents are used, they need not all be signed under the Illinois Statute of Frauds, so long as the signed writing expressly refers to the unsigned writing or the documents are so connected, physically or otherwise, as to show that they relate to the same contract. Bower v. Jones, 978 F.2d 1004 (7th Cir. 1992).

It is possible to satisfy the Statute of Frauds from statements made in more than one document; however, the main document must specifically refer to any others, and the parties can not resort to parol proof to supply any missing elements or connecting links. Mariani v. School Dirs. of Dist. 40, 154 Ill. App. 3d 404, 107 Ill. Dec. 90, 506 N.E.2d 981 (3 Dist. 1987).

A "writing" sufficient to satisfy the Statute of Frauds may be made up of several documents, which may consist of various forms such as notes, papers, letters and telegrams, so long as, taken together, they contain on their face, or by reference to other writings, the names of the parties, an identification of the subject matter of the contract, and the terms and conditions of the contract. American College of Surgeons v. Lumbermens Mut. Cas. Co., 142 Ill. App. 3d 680, 96 Ill. Dec. 719, 491 N.E.2d 1179 (1 Dist. 1986).

One Year Rule

Where a seller sued a middleman for breach of an oral agreement regarding inserts for the sale of magazine subscriptions and merchandise that were included in a third party's credit card bills, the middleman failed to establish that the parties' oral agreement did

One Year Rule (Cont'd)
not create an enforceable contract under the Illinois Statute of Frauds, 740 ILCS 80/1 et seq., because although middleman argued that even though each discrete advertisement insert promotion lasted only four months, the requirements of the parties under the middleman's agreement with the third party lasted much longer, this did not establish that the agreement could not have been performed within one year. Newsub Magazine Servs. LLC v. Heartland Direct, Inc., F. Supp. 2d , 2004 U.S. Dist. LEXIS 4121 (N.D. Ill. Mar. 15, 2004).

Option Contracts

—Enforceable
Where notice exercising the option to buy a hotel was given in writing signed by the attorney for the appellees, and appellants, upon receipt of same, at once employed an attorney to draft a proposed sales contract in accordance with the provisions of the option, the option was specifically enforceable against the appellants. Welsh v. Jakstas, 401 Ill. 288, 82 N.E.2d 53 (1948).

Oral Contracts

—In General
When the contract was entered into, there appeared to have been no concealment or misrepresentation of fact but mere oral promises concerning future performances which the law did not regard as binding; therefore, the suit was barred as a matter of law. Sinclair v. Sullivan Chevrolet Co., 31 Ill. 2d 507, 202 N.E.2d 516 (1964).

A parol agreement which does not, by its terms, extend for any definite time, is not void under the Statute of Frauds; the test of enforceability under this section is directed to the time of performance and not to the time of the incurring of the obligation under which performance is to be made; if full performance such as the parties intended could possibly, at the time of the making of the contract, be completed within a year, no matter how unlikely or improbable that might be, the alleged contract was not within the statutory ban. Vischer v. Dow Jones & Co., 339 Ill. App. 617, 91 N.E.2d 90 (1 Dist. 1950).

When an alleged contract is oral, and the Statute of Frauds is pleaded, there must have been such performance as will take the contract out of the prohibition of such statute; but when a contract is proved, and it is founded upon a good and valuable consideration, and has been performed by one party, a court of equity will decree its specific performance at the suit of such party. Watson v. Hobson, 401 Ill. 191, 81 N.E.2d 885 (1948).

The Statute of Frauds does not vitiate the oral contract, but merely denies the right to compel its performance. Stein v. McKinney, 313 Ill. 84, 144 N.E. 795 (1924).

To take an oral contract out of the Statute of Frauds on account of performance all acts of such alleged performance must be clear and definite and referable exclusively to the contract. Lounsberry v. Deverman, 299 Ill. 493, 132 N.E. 485 (1921).

—Agency
An oral contract of agency to sell real estate does not authorize the agent to sign the name of his principal to a written contract of sale. People v. Gore, 322 Ill. 67, 152 N.E. 584 (1926).

—Burden of Proof
The burden is upon the party seeking the application of equitable principles not only to establish the terms and conditions of the parol agreement but also to show that enforcement of the parol agreement is required to prevent fraud or injustice. Conness v. Conness, 94 Ill. App. 2d 281, 236 N.E.2d 753 (3 Dist. 1968).

—Full Performance
Statutes which subject transactions to a Statute of Frauds provision, including contracts that cannot be performed within a year (see this section), contracts for the sale of an interest in land (740 ILCS 80/2), contracts for the sale of goods (810 ILCS 5/2-201), and contracts for the sale of securities (810 ILCS 5/8-319) do not explicitly provide that full performance by one party operates to take the oral contract out of the Statute of Frauds; however, case law fully supports this result. Meyer v. Logue, 100 Ill. App. 3d 1039, 56 Ill. Dec. 707, 427 N.E.2d 1253 (1 Dist. 1981).

An oral contract fully performed by one party takes it out of the Statute of Frauds. Maurer v. Loeb, 338 Ill. App. 644, 88 N.E.2d 494 (1 Dist. 1949).

A parol agreement which the Statute of Frauds requires to be in writing is, when performed, as good and valid as if it had been in writing. Hartley v. Hartley, 290 Ill.App. 92, 7 N.E.2d 906 (2 Dist. 1937).

—Nonperformance
When the vendor under an oral contract declines to perform and sets up the Statute of Frauds, an action at law will lie against him for any part of the purchase price which he has received. Nelson v. Fricke, 335 Ill. App. 273, 81 N.E.2d 763 (2 Dist. 1948).

—One Year Rule
The development and use of a version of the photograph could have been completed within one year, taking the agreement outside the provisions of the Statute of Frauds. Meyer v. Marilyn Miglin, Inc., 273 Ill. App. 3d 882, 210 Ill. Dec. 257, 652 N.E.2d 1233 (1 Dist. 1995), appeal denied, 164 Ill. 2d 566, 214 Ill. Dec. 322, 660 N.E.2d 1271 (1995).

Parol agreement was within the purview of this section of the Statute of Frauds since it was an oral agreement that could not be performed within the space of one year; the trial court was correct in holding the agreement unenforceable because it violated the prohibitions specifically delineated in this section of the Statute of Frauds; unless the terms of an oral lease agreement can be completely fulfilled within one year from the date of its making, it falls within the prohibition of this section of the Statute of Frauds. Kachigian v. Minn, 23 Ill. App. 3d 722, 320 N.E.2d 173 (1 Dist. 1974).

An oral contract which cannot be performed within the space of one year is unenforceable in law as violating the Statute of Frauds. Marvin Glass & Assocs. v. Gardel, 419 F.2d 1284 (7th Cir. 1970).

An oral employment agreement for one year, starting June 6, 1960, and made May 31, 1960, was unenforceable under the Statute of Frauds. Sinclair v. Sullivan Chevrolet Co., 45 Ill. App. 2d 10, 195 N.E.2d 250 (3 Dist.), aff'd, 31 Ill. 2d 507, 202 N.E.2d 516 (1964).

Oral agreement to bread shrimp which was to run concurrently with written contracts was contrary to the Illinois Statute of Frauds because the agreement would not be performed within the space of one year from the making. Refrigeradora Del Noroeste v. Appelbaum, 248 F.2d 858 (7th Cir. 1957), cert. denied, 356 U.S. 901, 78 S. Ct. 561, 2 L. Ed. 2d 580 (1958).

In order to bring a parol contract within the Statute of Frauds, it must appear affirmatively that the contract was not to be performed within the year; the statute applies only to contracts which, by their terms, are not to be performed within the year, and not to contracts which may not be performed within that time. Walker v. Johnson, 96 U.S. 424, 24 L. Ed. 834 (1877).

—Partnership Agreement
Defendants' motion to dismiss the corporation's complaint that alleged breach of a joint venture agreement, fraudulent inducement, tortious interference with contract, and unjust enrichment would be denied where the corporation sufficiently alleged a breach of a joint venture agreement that was not barred by the Illinois Statute of Frauds, 740 ILCS 80/1 et seq., because (1) while the performance by the corporation lasted for five years, there was no evidence to support or refute the possibility that at the time of the alleged agreement, the contract could not have been performed in one year since the agreement was to work together to market textiles that theoretically could have ended at any point, and (2) the corporation argued that the oral agreement was evidenced by many numerous writings. Associated Textile, Inc. v. Veeraraja, F. Supp. 2d , 2002 U.S. Dist. LEXIS 17088 (N.D. Ill. Sept. 11, 2002).

Mere fact that the subject matter upon which the partnership was to act may have involved the development and improvement of real estate did not bring the oral partnership agreement within the Statute of Frauds. Gardenhire v. Ray, 302 Ill. App. 268, 23 N.E.2d 927 (4 Dist. 1939).

—Part Performance
Statute of Frauds is designed to prevent false claims by requiring a writing to evidence the parties' contractual intent; when one party fully performs his part of the alleged oral contract, however, the courts recognize that this very performance strongly indicates the existence of a contract, and such performance tends to minimize the

Oral Contracts (Cont'd)

—Part Performance (Cont'd)

dangers that the Statute of Frauds was designed to prevent. Meyer v. Logue, 100 Ill. App. 3d 1039, 56 Ill. Dec. 707, 427 N.E.2d 1253 (1 Dist. 1981).

—Payment of Money

Where oral agreement extended the time for making one payment of purchase money required by written contract, and accelerated another, since this was not an oral contract of conveyance it was not required that it be proved that plaintiffs took possession under the oral contract in order to avoid the Statute of Frauds; to take an oral promise, not a contract to convey real estate, out of the Statute of Frauds, the evidence should establish with reasonable certainty not only that an agreement was made but also its terms clearly and specifically; the performance relied on must place the party who has performed in such a situation that it would be fraud upon him if the agreement were not carried out. Rose v. Dolejs, 1 Ill. 2d 280, 116 N.E.2d 402 (1953).

—Performance by One Party

An oral contract is not unenforceable under the Statute of Frauds if the contract has been performed completely by one party. Estate of Jesmer v. Rohlev, 241 Ill. App. 3d 798, 182 Ill. Dec. 282, 609 N.E.2d 816 (1 Dist. 1993).

—Real Estate

Where there was before the court a deed containing the names of the parties, a description of the land and a power of attorney, a check for $200, accepted by defendant, which represented the consideration, the essential elements of the oral contract appeared in the deed and check and constituted such a memorandum as rendered the Statute of Frauds inapplicable. Allen v. Meyer, 14 Ill. 2d 284, 152 N.E.2d 576 (1958).

Generally, oral agreements to establish liens on real estate are within the Statute of Frauds, and are therefore unenforceable. Watson v. Hobson, 401 Ill. 191, 81 N.E.2d 885 (1948).

Where an oral agreement of the sale of real estate is fully performed, and a valuable consideration paid and possession taken under the contract, the purchaser or grantee may in equity rely upon his equitable title for a defense, although a deed has not been delivered before a judgment is taken by a third person against the grantor. Doll v. Walter, 305 Ill. App. 188, 27 N.E.2d 231 (2 Dist. 1940).

An oral contract, of land, is not within the Statute of Frauds if it has been completely performed by one of the parties thereto. Fleming v. Dillon, 370 Ill. 325, 18 N.E.2d 910 (1938).

A deed executed in pursuance of an oral agreement, without any reference therein to the terms of the contract, is not a sufficient note or memorandum to take the transaction out of the terms of this Act. Holsz v. Stephen, 362 Ill. 527, 200 N.E. 601 (1936).

Where oral contracts for the sale of an interest in land have been executed by the delivery and acceptance of deeds, and nothing remains to be done but the payment of money, the Statute of Frauds does not apply, but if anything else is to be done the statute does apply. Rogan v. Arnold, 233 Ill. 19, 84 N.E. 58 (1908).

Oral contract to purchase land was within purview of Statute of Frauds where there was no consideration paid or to be paid and there was no clearness or satisfactoriness of proof which was required in order to enforce a verbal contract with respect to land under the theory of part performance. Ferbrache v. Ferbrache, 110 Ill. 210 (1884).

—Recognized in Another State

The Statute of Frauds was not a bar to a suit brought in this state on an oral contract, not to be performed within one year, made in another state and valid and enforceable in that state. Oakes v. Chicago Fire Brick Co., 388 Ill. 474, 58 N.E.2d 460 (1944).

—Specific Performance

Specific performance is not a matter of right, but rests in the sound discretion of the court, to be determined from all of the facts and circumstances; it is only on the principle that it is unjust and inequitable to permit a contract to remain unexecuted that a court of equity will grant relief, and where the promisee shows no substantial change for the worse in his position in consequence of the agreement, relief will be denied. Galapeaux v. Orviller, 4 Ill. 2d 442, 123 N.E.2d 321 (1954).

—Unjust Enrichment

If the defendants' efforts due as a result of an oral agreement produced royalties, they would be entitled to maintain an action under the equitable theory of unjust enrichment, even if the services were rendered after the date the express contract because unenforceable. Marvin Glass & Assocs. v. Gardel, 419 F.2d 1284 (7th Cir. 1970).

—Void

Oral agreement between son and his father, in the lifetime of the latter, by which father paid to his son $500 in consideration of son's agreement to release to his father all his father's interest in estate was void under the Statute of Frauds, as not being in writing. Gary v. Newton, 201 Ill. 170, 66 N.E. 267 (1903).

—Wills

Where a bill shows affirmatively that a contract or promise to make a will is not in writing, the defense of the Statute of Frauds may be raised by demurrer, and a contract to make a will devising real property is held to be a contract for the sale of real property. Wilke v. Miller, 171 Ill. 556, 49 N.E. 484 (1898).

Oral Lease

—One Year Rule

Where it was not disputed that an oral lease could not be performed within a year, it came within the Statute of Frauds. Scoville v. Dehart, 17 Ill. App. 2d 419, 150 N.E.2d 369 (3 Dist. 1958).

—Partial Performance

Where tenants made oral agreement with landlord for five year lease after expiration of one year written lease, extensive permanent improvements made by tenants and possession were sufficient to indicate partial performance and remove agreement from the Statute of Frauds. Mossison v. Herrick, 130 Ill. 631, 22 N.E. 537 (1889).

Oral Promises

—Breach

The mere breach of the grantee's oral promise did not constitute such fraud as to take the case out of the Statute of Frauds. Wood v. Armstrong, 401 Ill. 111, 81 N.E.2d 468 (1948).

—Consideration

A parol promise in consideration of which a deed of conveyance was made may be enforced in equity. Ropacki v. Ropacki, 354 Ill. 502, 188 N.E. 400 (1933).

—Enforceable

Where an oral promise made to pay unpaid tradesman was amply supported by the evidence, and the promisor received benefit upon the strength of such promise, the promise should be enforceable. Oscar H. Wilke, Inc. v. Vinci, 96 Ill. App. 2d 189, 237 N.E.2d 768 (1 Dist. 1968).

—Not Enforceable

Statute of frauds barred employer's alleged oral promise of employment from being enforceable under promissory estoppel theory. Milazzo v. O'Connell, 925 F. Supp. 1331 (N.D. Ill. 1996), aff'd, 108 F.3d 129 (7th Cir. 1997).

The asserted promise on the part of the defendant to pay his father's debt, not being in writing and duly signed, could not be enforced either at law or in equity by the father's creditors. Reisch v. Bowie, 367 Ill. 126, 10 N.E.2d 663 (1937).

—Permanent Employment

The trial court erred in dismissing former employee's allegation of a breach of an oral employment contract; allegations of fraud may estop a party from relying on the Statute of Frauds. Johnson v. George J. Ball, Inc., 248 Ill. App. 3d 859, 187 Ill. Dec. 634, 617 N.E.2d 1355 (2 Dist. 1993).

Employer's petition to the Federal Immigration and Naturalization Service representing its intention to employ plaintiff for three years did not constitute a promise on which plaintiff could reason-

Oral Promises (Cont'd)

—Permanent Employment (Cont'd)

ably rely, even though it could satisfy the Statute of Frauds. Geva v. Leo Burnett Co., 931 F.2d 1220 (7th Cir. 1991).

The promise of permanent employment is not enforceable under the one year provision of this section. Lamaster v. Chicago & N.E. Ill. Dist. Council of Carpenters Apprentice & Trainee Program, 766 F. Supp. 1497 (N.D. Ill. 1991).

—Real Estate Conveyance

When a donee by deed has received realty under an oral promise to hold it for the donor or another, and has, in reliance on the Statute of Frauds, refused to perform the promise and has retained the property for his own use, relief by way of a constructive trust is generally denied; a recognized exception to the rule prevails, however, where a confidential relationship exists between the grantor and grantee. Bremer v. Bremer, 411 Ill. 454, 104 N.E.2d 299 (1952).

An oral contract to transfer real estate or an interest in real estate is unenforceable under the Statute of Frauds, unless the performance and conduct of the parties, pursuant to such oral contract, is of such a nature as to make it enforceable in a court of equity. Ellison v. Ellison, 372 Ill. 323, 23 N.E.2d 718 (1939).

Before an oral promise to convey real estate is taken out of the operation of the Statute of Frauds, the partial performance must be of such character that it is impossible or impracticable to place the parties in status quo, to restore or compensate the party performing for what he has parted with, or the value of his performance. Ellison v. Ellison, 372 Ill. 323, 23 N.E.2d 718 (1939).

Where a father made an oral promise to convey a farm to his son so that he would have the title after the death of the father if the son would live upon it, improve it with lasting and permanent improvements, and pay the taxes, and the son took possession of the land and performed the contract on his part, equity would enforce a specific performance of the contract. Burgess v. Burgess, 306 Ill. 19, 137 N.E. 403 (1922).

—Statute Not Applicable

Where, before the delivery of building materials, the general contractor promised a materials supplier that he would pay for such materials, and upon the strength of this promise the materials were delivered to a subcontractor, the promise of the general contractor to pay for the materials was not a collateral one but an original one, and not merely a promise to pay the debt of another, so that the statute of frauds had no application. Granite City L. & C. Co. v. Board of Educ., 203 Ill. App. 134 (4 Dist. 1916).

—Wrongful Termination

An employee's action in which he alleged he was wrongfully terminated in violation of oral promises made by his employer was barred by the Statute of Frauds since the contract was incapable of being performed within one year and his agreement with his employer was never put into writing. Evans v. Fluor Distrib. Cos., 799 F.2d 364 (7th Cir. 1986).

Oral Trust

—Voidable

An oral trust in violation of the Statute of Frauds is voidable at the election of the trustee, but not void, and that defense may be waived by the failure to plead or assert the defense. In re German, 193 F. Supp. 948 (S.D. Ill. 1961).

A parol trust is obnoxious to the Statute of Frauds, but is not absolutely void; it is voidable only at the election of the trustee who may waive the benefit of the statute and acknowledge the trust. Klass v. Hallas, 16 Ill. 2d 161, 157 N.E.2d 261 (1959).

Original and Independent Promise

Factfinder was entitled to conclude that mother's agreement to pay attorney fees for her adult son was not mother's promise to pay the son's debt but a promise to pay a debt she had originally incurred, and thus was outside of the statute of frauds. Greenberger, Krauss & Tenenbaum v. Catalfo, 293 Ill. App. 3d 88, 227 Ill. Dec. 230, 687 N.E.2d 153 (1 Dist. 1997).

A bank's promise of indemnity was not a special promise within the purview of the Statute of Frauds, rather, the bank's promise of indemnity was an original and independent promise that was outside the Statute of Frauds. Villarreal v. Metropolitan Bank & Trust Co., 277 Ill. App. 3d 188, 213 Ill. Dec. 812, 660 N.E.2d 69 (1 Dist. 1995).

Parol Evidence

—Admissible to Correct Mistake

There is no doubt that parol evidence is admissible to show the real agreement between parties when a mistake has been made in the written contract and the evidence is for the purpose of making the contract conform to the original intent of the parties. Brosam v. Employer's Mut. Cas. Co., 61 Ill. App. 2d 183, 209 N.E.2d 350 (4 Dist. 1965).

—Boundary Line Disputes

Where a boundary line between two estates is indefinite or unascertained, the owners may, by parol agreement, establish a division line, and the line thus defined will afterwards control their deeds notwithstanding the Statute of Frauds. Nitterauer v. Pulley, 401 Ill. 494, 82 N.E.2d 643 (1948).

—Interpretation of Rental Agreement

Parol evidence was properly admitted to determine the interpretation of rental agreement. Claude S. Corp. v. Henry's Drive-In, Inc., 51 Ill. App. 2d 289, 201 N.E.2d 127 (1 Dist. 1964).

—Not Admissible

The use of oral evidence to get around the requirement of a writing would be bootstrapping, would sap the Statute of Frauds of most of its force, and is therefore forbidden. Monetti, S.P.A. v. Anchor Hocking Corp., 931 F.2d 1178 (7th Cir. 1991).

Oral evidence is inadmissible to connect the several papers or show that they relate to the same transaction; if it is necessary to use oral evidence to show that the papers are parts of one contract of sale, then the contract becomes partly oral and partly written, and the courts have then introduced all the mischiefs which the statute of frauds and perjuries was intended to prevent. Western Metals Co. v. Hartman Ingot Metal Co., 303 Ill. 479, 135 N.E. 744 (1922).

—State Law

The question of whether oral evidence is admissible to show that an ambiguous document satisfies the requirements of the Statute of Frauds is ultimately one of state law, as it is substantive rather than procedural for purposes of determining, in accordance with the Erie doctrine, whether state or federal law applies. Monetti, S.P.A. v. Anchor Hocking Corp., 931 F.2d 1178 (7th Cir. 1991).

—Statements of Authorized Agent

The Statute of Frauds did not preclude admission of oral statements made by an authorized agent which assured appellants that the account that appellants had with the agent was safe and would be taken care of by the officers of the corporation. Wright v. Farmers' Nat'l Grain Corp., 74 F.2d 425 (7th Cir. 1934).

Decedent's promise was outside the Statute of Frauds where the consideration for it was such that it made him the direct primary debtor of a bank. United States v. Mitchell, 74 F.2d 571 (7th Cir. 1934).

Part Performance

—In General

In actions at law, part performance of a contract which is within the Statute of Frauds does not take it out of the operation of the statute. Scoville v. Dehart, 17 Ill. App. 2d 419, 150 N.E.2d 369 (3 Dist. 1958).

To take a case out of the Statute of Frauds upon the ground of part performance, all acts done thereunder must be clear and definite and referable exclusively to the contract. Seitman v. Seitman, 204 Ill. 504, 68 N.E. 461 (1903).

Acts relied on to show part performance will not operate to defeat the Statute of Frauds unless they are done under the contract itself and for the purpose of performing it; if they might have been done with other views, they will take the case out of the statute, since they cannot properly be said to be done by way of part performance of the agreement; it must appear that the party entered into possession of the land under the contract itself, and in performance of it, and that he was allowed to make valuable and permanent

Part Performance (Cont'd)

—In General (Cont'd)
improvements under his contract of purchase, and not otherwise. Clark v. Clark, 122 Ill. 388, 13 N.E. 553 (1887).

—Acts of Preparation
Acts of preparation, no matter how extensive, are insufficient to support a claim for partial performance. Genin, Trudeau & Co. v. Integra Dev. Int'l, 845 F. Supp. 611 (N.D. Ill. 1994).

—Application
The Statute of Frauds has no application where there has been part performance by one of the contracting parties in reliance upon the agreement. Davies v. Martel Lab. Servs., Inc., 189 Ill. App. 3d 694, 136 Ill. Dec. 951, 545 N.E.2d 475 (1 Dist. 1989).

The Statute of Frauds is not available as a defense where there has been sufficient performance by one of the contracting parties in reliance on the agreement to answer for the debt of another. Payne v. Mill Race Inn, 152 Ill. App. 3d 269, 105 Ill. Dec. 324, 504 N.E.2d 193 (2 Dist. 1987).

Where a plaintiff had an adequate remedy at law for damages against a bank for an oral agreement by the bank to lend plaintiff's money and, for that reason, would not have been entitled to seek equitable relief, the doctrine of part performance had no application, and could not have operated to take the alleged oral agreement out of the Statute of Frauds. Gibbons v. Stillwell, 149 Ill. App. 3d 411, 102 Ill. Dec. 864, 500 N.E.2d 965 (5 Dist. 1986).

—Character
Before a contract is taken out of the Statute of Frauds, partial performance must be of such a character that it is impossible or impractical to place the parties in status quo or restore or compensate the party performing for what he has parted with, or the value of his performance must be so that refusal to complete the engagement would be a virtual fraud upon the party. Mariani v. School Dirs. of Dist. 40, 154 Ill. App. 3d 404, 107 Ill. Dec. 90, 506 N.E.2d 981 (3 Dist. 1987).

—Enforcement
Although it has been held that acts of part performance are sufficient, in a court of equity, to take an oral agreement out from under the operation of the Statute of Frauds, partial performance of an oral contract does not take an action of law from the operation of the Statute of Frauds. Gibbons v. Stillwell, 149 Ill. App. 3d 411, 102 Ill. Dec. 864, 500 N.E.2d 965 (5 Dist. 1986).

—Oral Contract
To take an oral promise which has been partly performed out of the Statute of Frauds, part of the performance must be such that a restoration of their previous condition is impracticable and a refusal to go on and complete the engagement would be a virtual fraud upon the parties. Holsz v. Stephen, 362 Ill. 527, 200 N.E. 601 (1936).

Where a purchaser of land under an oral contract has entered into possession under his contract, and has paid the purchase money, and made valuable and permanent improvements, so that a refusal to specifically perform the contract would operate as a fraud upon him, the vendor will be held to be estopped to avail himself of the provisions of the Statute of Frauds, and the contract will be specifically enforced. Barrett v. Geisinger, 148 Ill. 98, 35 N.E. 354 (1893).

Where a verbal contract has been made, and one party has knowingly aided or permitted the other to go on and do acts in part performance of the agreement, in full reliance upon such agreement as a valid and binding contract, and which would not have been done without the agreement, and are of such nature as to change the relations of the parties, and to prevent a restoration to their former condition, or an adequate compensation for the loss of a judgment at law for damages, then it would be a virtual fraud in the first party to interpose the Statute of Frauds as a bar to the completion of the contract, and thus secure for himself all the benefits of the acts already done in part performance, while the other party would not only lose all advantage from the bargain, but would be left without adequate remedy for its failure, or compensation for what he had done in pursuance of it. Barrett v. Geisinger, 148 Ill. 98, 35 N.E. 354 (1893).

Oral contact to erect church was not within Statute of Frauds since there was partial performance in payment of the purchase price, taking possession of the land and making improvements to it. Whitsitt v. Trustees of Preemption Presbyterian Church, 110 Ill. 125 (1884).

—Question of Fact
The plaintiff raised a genuine issue of material fact as to whether it entered into a letter of intent in reliance upon the defendant's alleged promises and conduct and, therefore, the doctrine of partial performance precluded the defendant from successfully asserting the statute of frauds on a motion for summary judgment. Trustmark Ins. Co. v. General Cologne Life, F. Supp. 2d , 2001 U.S. Dist. LEXIS 17212 (N.D. Ill. Oct. 15, 2001).

—Reliance
Where trial court found that a valid agreement to use lane had been created, that part performance by constructing and grading the lane had followed and that the defendant had stood by and watched the improvement of the lane and construction of a basement garage so as to make use of that lane without making any objection, it would have been fraud to permit the defendant to annul his agreement by invoking the Statute of Frauds. Mercer v. Sturm, 10 Ill. App. 3d 65, 293 N.E.2d 457 (3 Dist. 1973).

—Statute Not Applicable
The fact plaintiff sought money damages precluded him from raising the partial performance exception to the Statute of Frauds. Dickens v. Quincy College Corp., 245 Ill. App. 3d 1055, 185 Ill. Dec. 822, 615 N.E.2d 381 (4 Dist. 1993).

Where plaintiffs asserted that unless they had been granted an extension of the time for making the payment, they would never have begun the construction of a home on the property in question, and in complete reliance on that agreement plaintiffs expended the sum of $16,000 or $17,000 in construction a dwelling while vendors stood quietly by and never once repudiated the oral agreement to extend the time for making payment, or attempted a forfeiture, to assert the Statute of Frauds at this time would work an injustice and fraud upon plaintiffs by depriving them of the sums expended in reliance upon the oral promise and the first payment of purchase money; the erection of a home on the premises was certainly such part performance as would take this oral agreement out of the Statute of Frauds. Rose v. Dolejs, 1 Ill. 2d 280, 116 N.E.2d 402 (1953).

Parol contract, in which father and mother promised son that, if he would move on to certain farm and improve it at his own expense, pay the taxes, and pay his father $600 a year as long as he lived, and pay his brother $2,500, he would have the farm on the death of his father, was held not to violate Statute of Frauds since plaintiff made part performance. White v. White, 231 Ill. 298, 83 N.E. 234 (1907).

Where there has been a partial performance, the Statute of Frauds will not apply. Barrett v. Geisinger, 148 Ill. 98, 35 N.E. 354 (1893).

Parol agreement between father and son which provided that if son would move onto land and improve it as needed and pay taxes then property would become absolute property of son upon death of the father was not with purview of Statute of Frauds since son made part performance by moving onto the land and, until the death of the father, occupied, cultivated and made improvements upon the land. Smith v. Yocum, 110 Ill. 142 (1884).

—Sufficient
Where plaintiff alleged that she gave up her business location, terminated all aspects of the business relevant to that location, and allowed the physical removal of her inventory in reliance upon defendant's agreement to purchase plaintiff's business, and where plaintiff could have been restored to the pre-performance status quo only if her previous business location, or something in the immediate area, was available, plaintiff's allegations were sufficient to show that the detriment she had suffered by beginning to perform her contractual obligations was such that the Statute of Frauds defense would not have been available. Payne v. Mill Race Inn, 152 Ill. App. 3d 269, 105 Ill. Dec. 324, 504 N.E.2d 193 (2 Dist. 1987).

Past Performance
When past performance by one party changes the relation of the

Past Performance (Cont'd)
parties, and adequate compensation for the loss by a judgment for damages, or restoration to their former condition is impossible, the Statute of Frauds will not act as a bar to the completion of the contract; however, where a party does not claim that compensatory damages are unavailable to him, the statute is not available. Taylor v. Canteen Corp., 789 F. Supp. 279 (C.D. Ill. 1992), modified on other grounds, 69 F.3d 773 (7th Cir. 1995).

Payment by Check

—Insufficient Writing
A realtor's contention that the Statute of Frauds did not apply to an alleged oral agreement for his commission as a result of full performance by him was meritless, as he did not "perform" the act of renewal of a lease which made his commission due, rather, it was performed by another party, and he therefore had nothing to do with the renewal; nor were defendants estopped from asserting the defense of the Statute of Frauds because, at the time of the renewal, neither of them had any interest whatsoever in the lease or the property. Lighthart v. Lindstrom, 24 Ill. App. 3d 918, 322 N.E.2d 70 (2 Dist. 1975).

A check given in connection with the sale of lands which is in the ordinary form and contains no reference to the essential terms of the contract of sale, does not constitute a sufficient memorandum within the Statute of Frauds. Fieschko v. Herlich, 32 Ill. App. 2d 280, 177 N.E.2d 376 (2 Dist. 1961).

Performance Within One Year

—In General
An acceleration clause which rendered an agreement capable of being terminated but not fully performed within one year did not remove the bar of the Statute of Frauds where the agreement called for 25 monthly payments. Silvestros v. Silvestros, 206 Ill. App. 3d 84, 150 Ill. Dec. 957, 563 N.E.2d 1084 (1 Dist. 1990).

Under Illinois law, a contract is unenforceable only if it is impossible of performance within one year. Brudnicki v. GE Co., 535 F. Supp. 84 (N.D. Ill. 1982).

A contract that would be terminated by the parties is not within the Statute of Frauds, since it could have been performed within one year. George F. Mueller & Sons v. Northern Ill. Gas Co., 12 Ill. App. 3d 362, 299 N.E.2d 601 (1 Dist. 1973).

—Agreement Enforceable
An oral agreement was not rendered unenforceable by reason of the fact that a personal undertaking in the agreement not to compete extended for a period of ten years. Hubbard v. Logsdon, 56 Ill. App. 3d 366, 14 Ill. Dec. 296, 372 N.E.2d 101 (4 Dist. 1978).

—Application
An oral agreement made on October 13, 1987 for the lease of land from March 1988 until December 1988 was unenforceable under the Statute of Frauds, since full performance could not have been completed within one year from the date the agreement was made. Sherwin v. Ault, 219 Ill. App. 3d 213, 161 Ill. Dec. 877, 579 N.E.2d 425 (3 Dist. 1991).

A contract is unenforceable only if it is impossible to perform the contract within one year; if, however, it appears from a reasonable interpretation of the terms of the agreement that it is capable of performance within one year, the Statute of Frauds is inapplicable. Hartbarger v. SCA Servs. Inc., 200 Ill. App. 3d 1000, 146 Ill. Dec. 633, 558 N.E.2d 596 (5 Dist. 1990).

To be outside the Statute of Frauds, a contract must be capable of being fully performed within one year and not simply terminated by some contingency such as death or bankruptcy. Gilliland v. Allstate Ins. Co., 69 Ill. App. 3d 630, 26 Ill. Dec. 444, 388 N.E.2d 68 (1 Dist. 1979).

Where an oral agreement between the parties stated that plaintiff could begin making payments whenever plaintiff "got on his feet," so long as defendant received $12,000 by the end of ten years, it was apparent that plaintiff could have paid defendant the entire sum within the period specified of one year, and the payment provision did not render the agreement unenforceable. Hubbard v. Logsdon, 56 Ill. App. 3d 366, 14 Ill. Dec. 296, 372 N.E.2d 101 (4 Dist. 1978).

It is the date the agreement is made, rather than the date performance is started, that marks the beginning of the year within the Statute of Frauds; if the agreement is capable of performance within a year, the Statute of Frauds does not apply. Lund v. Etnyre, 103 Ill. App. 2d 158, 242 N.E.2d 611 (2 Dist. 1969).

Where defendant told plaintiff that if plaintiff would breed a mare with a particular stallion, and if the issue should be a mare colt, he would purchase the colt, but also that he would want plaintiff to keep the colt for four months, considering that the gestation period in mares is about 11 months, the parties contemplated the contract's fulfillment in about 15 months from the date on which the mare should be successfully bred; therefore, the verbal contract could not have been performed within a year from the time it was entered into and void under the Statute of Frauds. Butler v. Shehan, 61 Ill. App. 561 (2 Dist. 1895).

—Test
The test to determine if an agreement is subject to the one-year provision of the Statute of Frauds is whether, when it was made, it was capable of full performance within one year, not whether full performance was likely. Silvestros v. Silvestros, 206 Ill. App. 3d 84, 150 Ill. Dec. 957, 563 N.E.2d 1084 (1 Dist. 1990).

Pleadings

—Amendments
Proper pleading of an affirmative defense such as the Statute of Frauds is not restricted to an original answer; the pleadings can be amended to conform to the proofs. Mapes v. Kalva Corp., 68 Ill. App. 3d 362, 24 Ill. Dec. 944, 386 N.E.2d 148 (2 Dist. 1979).

—Motion to Amend
Motion to amend pleadings to conform to the proof was allowed where the record revealed some evidence regarding defendants' theory of the case which could be considered to raise the defense of the Statute of Frauds. Wolfenberger v. Madison, 43 Ill. App. 3d 813, 2 Ill. Dec. 489, 357 N.E.2d 656 (2 Dist. 1976).

—Motion to Dismiss
Defendants' assertion that plaintiff's action was barred by the Statute of Frauds did not attack the sufficiency of the pleadings and was not properly raised in a motion pursuant to Ill.Rev.Stat., ch. 110, para. 2-615. Payne v. Mill Race Inn, 152 Ill. App. 3d 269, 105 Ill. Dec. 324, 504 N.E.2d 193 (2 Dist. 1987).

—Waiver
The Statute of Frauds is waived if not properly pled. Sanford v. Davis, 181 Ill. 570, 54 N.E. 977 (1899); Mapes v. Kalva Corp., 68 Ill. App. 3d 362, 24 Ill. Dec. 944, 386 N.E.2d 148 (2 Dist. 1979); Gilliland v. Allstate Ins. Co., 69 Ill. App. 3d 630, 26 Ill. Dec. 444, 388 N.E.2d 68 (1 Dist. 1979).

Promissory Estoppel
Under Illinois law, the statute of frauds is applicable to a promise claimed to be enforceable by virtue of the doctrine of promissory estoppel. Fischer v. First Chicago Capital Mkts., Inc., 195 F.3d 279 (7th Cir. 1999).

Statute of frauds is applicable to a promise claimed to be enforceable by virtue of the doctrine of promissory estoppel. Carl A. Hass Auto. Imports, Inc. v. Lola Cars Ltd., 933 F. Supp. 1381 (N.D. Ill. 1996).

It is logical that, if the Statute of Frauds bars enforcement of an oral contract which cannot be performed within one year, it also bars the courts from using promissory estoppel to imply the existence of a contract which cannot be performed within one year. Dickens v. Quincy College Corp., 245 Ill. App. 3d 1055, 185 Ill. Dec. 822, 615 N.E.2d 381 (4 Dist. 1993).

Plaintiffs' actions taken in reliance upon defendants' oral promise were insufficient to take the case out of the Statute of Frauds, as the doctrine of promissory estoppel did not apply to enforce contracts which fell within the Statute. Libby-Broadway Drive-In, Inc. v. McDonald's Sys., 72 Ill. App. 3d 806, 28 Ill. Dec. 802, 391 N.E.2d 1 (1 Dist. 1979).

Where case does not involve the Statute of Frauds the doctrine of promissory estoppel can be applied where one has relied on a promise and reacted to his detriment; where, however, a case is clearly within the Statute of Frauds, promissory estoppel is inapplicable. Sinclair v. Sullivan Chevrolet Co., 45 Ill. App. 2d 10, 195 N.E.2d 250 (3 Dist.), aff'd, 31 Ill. 2d 507, 202 N.E.2d 516 (1964).

Purchase Order

—Modification upon Completion

Where agreement referenced an undefined period demonstrating the parties' ability to terminate the agreement at any time or rely on additional materials, the writings did not contain the agreement's essential terms; therefore, contract did not satisfy statute of frauds. Carl A. Hass Auto. Imports, Inc. v. Lola Cars Ltd., 933 F. Supp. 1381 (N.D. Ill. 1996).

Purpose

The purpose of the Statute of Frauds is to prevent false and fraudulent claims by requiring a writing which evidences a contract. Skinner v. Shirley of Hollywood, 723 F. Supp. 50 (N.D. Ill. 1989).

The Statute of Frauds, in requiring contracts to be in writing is for the purpose, among others, of preventing a numerical majority of witnesses from taking advantage of their numbers in transactions required by law to be in writing; the effect of the statute, therefore, is to make the contract the best evidence, and, for practical purposes, almost conclusive evidence of the agreement of the parties. Biskupski v. Jaroszewski, 398 Ill. 287, 76 N.E.2d 55 (1947).

The Statute of Frauds, the only purpose of which is to prevent fraud, may not successfully be interposed as a defense in equity where the effect would be to accomplish a fraud. Fleming v. Dillon, 370 Ill. 325, 18 N.E.2d 910 (1938).

Ratification

Ratification by principal of a memorandum of a contract signed by his agent was sufficient compliance with the Statute of Frauds, although the agent was not properly authorized to enter into the contract. Perry v. Nevin Hotel Co., 349 Ill. App. 22, 109 N.E.2d 810 (3 Dist. 1952).

Securities

—Writings Sufficient

The requirements of the Statute of Frauds were satisfied in an action by a bank to construe its rights in securities delivered to the bank by the defendant where their agreement was evidenced by a series of writings, including a hypothecation agreement signed when the stocks were delivered, the signed powers of attorney given to bank, admissions contained in a Federal Reserve form, and the guarantee agreement with the defendant's fellow shareholders. Yorkville Nat'l Bank v. Schaefer, 71 Ill. App. 3d 137, 27 Ill. Dec. 263, 388 N.E.2d 1312 (2 Dist. 1979).

Settlements

Oral settlement agreement that included terms that could not be performed within one year was nonetheless enforceable because it was reached in a court-mandated settlement conference, held in the trial court's chambers, and the terms of the settlement were presented to the trial court. Rose v. Mavrakis, 343 Ill. App. 3d 1086, 278 Ill. Dec. 751, 799 N.E.2d 469, 2003 Ill. App. LEXIS 1233 (1 Dist. 2003), appeal denied, 207 Ill. 2d 627, 283 Ill. Dec. 141, 807 N.E.2d 982 (2004).

If not within the Statute of Frauds, a settlement may be oral and binding so long as there is an offer and acceptance to compromise and there is a meeting of the minds as to the terms of the agreement. McCracken Contracting Co. v. R. L. DePrizio & Assocs., 122 Ill. App. 3d 680, 78 Ill. Dec. 563, 462 N.E.2d 682 (1 Dist. 1984).

Signature

Although letter attached to a complaint seeking enforcement of an oral employment contract was not signed, and the defendant did not produce a signed copy, for purposes of a motion to dismiss, the district court assumed that a signed copy existed and that the "signing" requirement of this section was satisfied. Rubin v. Rudolf Wolff Commodity Brokers, Inc., 636 F. Supp. 258 (N.D. Ill. 1986).

Special Promise

An original or independent promise is not a "special promise" within the meaning of this section. Ricci v. Reed, 169 Ill. App. 3d 1062, 120 Ill. Dec. 307, 523 N.E.2d 1218 (1 Dist. 1988).

When a promise to guarantee a loan to another is part of the consideration for the loan, the promise is "original" and does not fall within the purview of the Statute of Frauds. Ricci v. Reed, 169 Ill. App. 3d 1062, 120 Ill. Dec. 307, 523 N.E.2d 1218 (1 Dist. 1988).

In order to determine if a promise is a "special promise" within the Statute of Frauds, the court will consider whether the promisor is a stranger to the transaction, without interest in it, and if so, the obligations of the statute will be strictly upheld. However, if he has a personal, immediate and pecuniary interest in a transaction in which a third party is the original obligor, the courts will give effect to the promise. Ricci v. Reed, 169 Ill. App. 3d 1062, 120 Ill. Dec. 307, 523 N.E.2d 1218 (1 Dist. 1988).

Where a borrower's principal was the sole shareholder of a corporation, and the lender requested the principal's personal guarantee prior to lending money to the corporation, the principal signed an "IOU," and when the lender asked for his personal guarantee of the entire loan, it received the principal's personal check before signing the subordinated loan agreement; the promise to pay was original and not collateral, and was not subject to the Statute of Frauds as a "special promise." Ricci v. Reed, 169 Ill. App. 3d 1062, 120 Ill. Dec. 307, 523 N.E.2d 1218 (1 Dist. 1988).

Specific Performance

—In General

The cases allowing specific performance to enforce an oral contract to will or devise property to another, in consideration of services to be rendered, are universally those in which a gross fraud would be suffered by the promisee if specific performance were denied. Linder v. Potier, 409 Ill. 407, 100 N.E.2d 602 (1951).

To satisfy the Statute of Frauds and to enable a party to enforce specific performance, the contract, or some note or memorandum thereof, must be complete in itself and cannot rest partly in writing and partly in parol. Holsz v. Stephen, 362 Ill. 527, 200 N.E. 601 (1936).

Where the statute of limitations would bar a recovery of large amount of money due the promisee, or where the improvements made or the services performed are of such a character that adequate compensation cannot be made and failure to carry out the contract will amount to a fraud upon the promisee, specific performance will be allowed. Flannery v. Woolverton, 329 Ill. 424, 160 N.E. 762 (1928).

—Lifetime Care

A suit for specific performance based on consideration of lifetime care is premature when brought during the lifetime of the one making the alleged promise to convey; there cannot be such full and complete performance on the part of the party furnishing the support as to take the transaction out of the provisions of the Statute of Frauds until the death of the party to be supported. Watson v. Hobson, 401 Ill. 191, 81 N.E.2d 885 (1948).

—Not Granted

The circuit court properly refused plaintiff's prayer for specific performance of a verbal contract made by defendant telephone company to provide plaintiff with telephone service at a given rate, notwithstanding plaintiff's part performance on the contract, whereby he paid money and rendered services to defendant; such a contract is only excused from the Statute of Frauds, and thus rendered specifically enforceable, where there is no adequate remedy to restore parties to their original positions, unlike present case, in which plaintiff could be restored to his original position by monetary compensation. Quinn v. Stark County Tel. Co., 122 Ill. App. 133 (2 Dist. 1905).

—Part Performance

The equitable doctrine that specific performance of verbal agreements will be decreed on the ground that part performance takes them out of the operation of the Statute of Frauds, is applied to cases where there have been such acts of performance by the party seeking to enforce the contract that the parties cannot be restored to their original relative positions, and the situation is such that to permit the defendant to invoke the statute, intended to prevent fraud, would be in effect to make it an engine of fraud. Quinn v. Stark County Tel. Co., 122 Ill. App. 133 (2 Dist. 1905).

—Specified Consideration Required

Memorandum of contracts for the sale of land must specify the consideration agreed upon, to be enforceable by specific performance. Hanlon v. Hayes, 404 Ill. 362, 89 N.E.2d 51 (1949).

Statute as Bar

—Calculations

In calculating the period for which the Statute of Frauds acts as a bar, it is not the term of performance which is the determining factor but the date of information of the contract in relation to the completion of performance. Rosenstein v. Ida Prods. Co., 362 F. Supp. 642 (N.D. Ill. 1973).

Statute Not a Bar

Claim by partners was not barred by the Statute of Frauds where, during a four month period, they made between 400 and 500 first sales calls and approximately a thousand repeat calls on customers, considerable progress was made in laying the ground work for future sales orders, and they were assured that the relationship was based on mutual trust and would last forever. Burton v. Hitachi Am., Ltd., 504 F.2d 721 (7th Cir. 1974).

Substantial Performance

—Adoption

Where an oral contract to adopt the plaintiff was clearly established, plaintiff had fully performed, and to allow the contract to remain unenforced was unfair, unjust and inequitable, there was such substantial performance of the contract by plaintiff as would have taken it out from under the application of the Statute of Frauds. Monahan v. Monahan, 14 Ill. 2d 449, 153 N.E.2d 1 (1958).

Sufficient Performance

Where son filed claim against executor of father's estate alleging that mother and father had agreed upon a testamentary plan that each would leave all his property to the other, conditioned on survival, and failing survival, to their two children in equal parts, so that ultimately said children would each receive half of the total estate of mother and father, and it was further alleged that in pursuance of the agreement each had properly executed a will carrying the testamentary plan into effect, and that the will signed by mother had been in full force and effect at the time of her death, by its provisions it was alleged that mother had bequeathed all her property to father, who had acquired all of mother's property on her death by reason of said agreement, and claimant further alleged that he was unable to append a copy of the will for the reason that it was withheld and secreted by others if the allegations were true, mother's will was a written instrument, and the making of the will in accordance with the alleged agreement would be sufficient performance to take the matter from under the Statute of Frauds, since the statute is never available as a defense where there has been sufficient performance by one party in reliance upon the agreement. Amschl v. Linenthal, 104 Ill. App. 2d 40, 243 N.E.2d 547 (1 Dist. 1969).

Sufficient Writing

—Letters

Defendant's letters satisfied the technical and theoretical requirements of the statute of frauds in plaintiff's action for breach of a concession agreement, where counsel for defendant referred specifically and internally to the amended concession agreement in letter informing plaintiff defendant was terminating the agreement, and the trial counsel's letters amounted to admissions that the parties completed the amended concession agreement. Roboserve, Inc. v. Kato Kagaku Co., 873 F. Supp. 1124 (N.D. Ill. 1995), modified on other grounds, 78 F.3d 266 (7th Cir. 1996), cert. denied, 519 U.S. 928, 117 S. Ct. 297, 136 L. Ed. 2d 215 (1996).

—Not Shown

The writing requirement of the statute was not satisfied by a letter of intent, since the documents did not state the essential terms of the alleged agreement with reasonable certainty and were not connected to each other so that the court could find that they related to the alleged contract. Trustmark Ins. Co. v. General Cologne Life, F. Supp. 2d , 2001 U.S. Dist. LEXIS 17212 (N.D. Ill. Oct. 15, 2001).

Writing did not satisfy the requirements of this section; writing contained only a promise to protect plaintiff's hours, but did not contain either a promise to pay a debt, or an obligation owed by defendant, or the terms and conditions of the undertaking. Storm & Assocs. v. Cuculich, 298 Ill. App. 3d 1040, 233 Ill. Dec. 101, 700 N.E.2d 202 (1 Dist. 1998).

—Parties' Interest

No commission was due to broker for the sale of a cable television system where the only writing was simply a formal expression of interest of the parties in furthering negotiations in an attempt to reach a final binding agreement for sale. Kepper v. Morris CATV, Inc., 48 Ill. App. 3d 410, 6 Ill. Dec. 149, 362 N.E.2d 784 (3 Dist. 1977).

—Price Terms Not Shown

Pursuant to the Statute of Frauds, and former 810 ILCS 5/8-319 relating to contracts for the sale of securities, writing requirement for contract which obligated corporation to repurchase withdrawing shareholder's shares was not satisfied by letters between corporation and withdrawing shareholder where no definite price term was found in the letters. Cafcas v. DeHaan & Richter, 699 F. Supp. 679 (N.D. Ill. 1988).

—Signatures

An instrument signed by all the parties sought to be bound was a sufficient memorandum to comply with the requirements of the Statute of Frauds. Hall v. Humphrey-Lake Corp., 29 Ill. App. 3d 956, 331 N.E.2d 365 (1 Dist. 1975).

Although draft of an agreement sent to defendant was not signed, his return letter acknowledged a receipt of the agreement; under the authorities this letter, and its acceptance, was a sufficient signing to meet the requirements of the Statute of Frauds. Dyrenforth v. Palmer Pneumatic Tire Co., 240 Ill. 25, 88 N.E. 290 (1909).

—Terms of Sale

Where sale terms of interest in a farm written on hotel stationery with the seller's signature, date, price and manner of payment, writing met the requirements of the Statute of Frauds. Thompson v. Wiegand, 9 Ill. 2d 63, 136 N.E.2d 781 (1956).

Surety Contracts

—Application

A plaintiff could not avoid the application of the Statute of Frauds to a surety contract by arguing that the contract was executed as opposed to executory, as this exception applied only to land transfers and to contracts not to be performed within the space of a year. Brown & Shinitzky Chartered v. Dentinger, 118 Ill. App. 3d 517, 74 Ill. Dec. 98, 455 N.E.2d 128 (1 Dist. 1983).

—Standing

A surety can maintain no action against his principal until he pays the debt. Resseter v. Waterman, 151 Ill. 169, 37 N.E. 875 (1894).

Validity

—Parol Evidence

A writing sufficient to comply with the requirements of the Statute of Frauds is neither necessarily nor presumptively a valid contract, but only evidence of one; the instrument does not conclusively prove its own character and validity and in every case it is a question of fact whether the parties adopted a writing as their agreement and it may always be shown by parol that a writing, however complete on its face, was never executed or delivered as a contract. Hall v. Humphrey-Lake Corp., 29 Ill. App. 3d 956, 331 N.E.2d 365 (1 Dist. 1975).

Waiver

—Not Shown

Evidence was insufficient to establish waiver of the statute of frauds where the plaintiff failed to point to any specific evidence that the defendant explicitly admitted the existence and substance of the alleged joint venture. Trustmark Ins. Co. v. General Cologne Life, F. Supp. 2d , 2001 U.S. Dist. LEXIS 17212 (N.D. Ill. Oct. 15, 2001).

Written Memorandum

A written memorandum signed by the defendant can be used by

Written Memorandum (Cont'd)
the plaintiff to avoid a Statute of Frauds defense. Geva v. Leo Burnett Co., 931 F.2d 1220 (7th Cir. 1991).

A written memorandum signed by the party to be charged confirming the essential terms of the otherwise unwritten agreement might satisfy the Statute of Frauds, regardless of the memorandum's intended recipient or purpose. Geva v. Leo Burnett Co., 931 F.2d 1220 (7th Cir. 1991).

No particular form of language is necessary to constitute a memorandum requisite to satisfy the requirements of the statute. Western Metals Co. v. Hartman Ingot Metal Co., 303 Ill. 479, 135 N.E. 744 (1922).

LEGAL PERIODICALS

For note, "McInerney v. Charter Golf, Inc.: The Court Swings and Misses", see 29 Loy. U. Chi. L.J. 907 (1998).

For article, "Survey of Illinois Law [1988-89] — Contracts," see 14 S. Ill. U.L.J. 739 (1990).

For article, "Pour-Over Lives: Estate Planning for the Second Marriage," see 74 Ill. B.J. 92 (1985).

For article, "The Statute of Frauds and the One Year Rule - A Legal Illusion," see 68 Ill. B.J. 716 (1980).

RESEARCH REFERENCES

Check given in land transaction as sufficient writing to satisfy statute of frauds. 9 ALR4th 1009.

Promise by one other than principal to indemnify one agreeing to become surety or guarantor as within statute of frauds. 13 ALR4th 1153.

Enforceability, by landowner, of subdivision developer's oral promise to construct or improve roads. 41 ALR4th 573.

Applicability of statute of frauds to promise to pay for legal services furnished to another. 84 ALR4th 994.

PARENTAL RESPONSIBILITY LAW

740 ILCS 115/1 [Short title]

Sec. 1. This Act shall be known and may be cited as the Parental Responsibility Law.
(Source: P.A. 76-1679.)

Derivation.
Title: An Act to authorize recovery of damages from parents or legal guardians due to the wilful injury to person or property by minor children.
Cite: 740 ILCS 115/1 et seq.
Source: P.A. 76-1679.
Date: Approved October 6, 1969.

Note.
This section was Ill.Rev.Stat., Ch. 70, para. 51.

CASE NOTES

ANALYSIS

Constitutionality
Parental Authority
—Search of Child's Room
Purpose

Constitutionality
This Act was held constitutional as a valid exercise of the police power of the state. Van Thournout v. Burge, 69 Ill. App. 3d 193, 25 Ill. Dec. 685, 387 N.E.2d 341 (2 Dist. 1979).

Parental Authority

—Search of Child's Room
Implicit in the rights and duties imposed upon a parent is the right to exert parental authority and control over minor's surrounding; therefore, a minor's mother could give valid consent to a warrantless police search of minor's locked bedroom located in her home. People v. Salyer, 44 Ill. App. 3d 854, 3 Ill. Dec. 648, 358 N.E.2d 1333 (3 Dist. 1977).

Purpose
The legislative purpose of this Act is twofold: (1) to compensate innocent victims of juvenile misconduct that is willful or malicious; and, (2) to place upon the parents the obligation to control a minor child so as to prevent intentional harm to others. Van Thournout v. Burge, 69 Ill. App. 3d 193, 25 Ill. Dec. 685, 387 N.E.2d 341 (2 Dist. 1979); Robison v. First State Bank, 144 Ill. App. 3d 991, 99 Ill. Dec. 190, 495 N.E.2d 637 (3 Dist. 1986).

LEGAL PERIODICALS

For article, "Survey of Illinois Law [1988-89] — Insurance," see 14 S. Ill. U.L.J. 1057 (1990).

For note on constitutional law and parental responsibility discussing Van Thournout v. Burge, 69 Ill. App.3d 193, 387 N.E.2d 341 (1979), see 68 Ill. B.J. 474 (1980).

RESEARCH REFERENCES

Criminal responsibility of parent for acts of child. 12 ALR4th 673.

Liability of adult assailant's family to third party for physical assault. 25 ALR5th 1.

740 ILCS 115/2 [Definitions]

Sec. 2. As used in this Act, unless the context otherwise requires, the terms specified have the meanings ascribed to them:

(1) "Legal guardian" means a person appointed guardian, or given custody, of a minor by a circuit court of the State, but does not include a person appointed guardian, or given custody, of a minor under the Juvenile Court Act or the Juvenile Court Act of 1987 [705 ILCS 405/1-1 et seq.].

(2) "Minor" means a person who is above the age of 11 years, but not yet 19 years of age.
(Source: P.A. 85-1209.)

Note.
This section was Ill.Rev.Stat., Ch. 70, para. 52.
The Juvenile Court Act, referred to above, was repealed. See now 705 ILCS 405/1-1 et seq.

CASE NOTES

Unemancipated Minor
Where testimony showed that parents maintained a furnished bedroom for son which he frequently used during short time period before the shootings, parents provided him with a vehicle that he used daily, he continued to receive mail at his parent's address and worked on the family farm in exchange for other consideration, trial court properly found that a person of ordinary caution and prudence would entertain a strong suspicion that son was an unemancipated minor residing with his parents at the time of the shooting and trial court erred in denying motion to convert parents from respondents in discovery to defendants under 740 ILCS 115/3. McGee v. Heimburger, 287 Ill. App. 3d 242, 222 Ill. Dec. 752, 678 N.E.2d 364 (4 Dist. 1997).

RESEARCH REFERENCES

Modern trends as to tort liability of child of tender years. 27 ALR4th 15.

740 ILCS 115/3 Liability

Sec. 3. *Liability.* The parent or legal guardian of an unemancipated minor who resides with such parent or legal guardian is liable for actual damages for the wilful or malicious acts of such minor which cause injury to a person or property, including damages caused by a minor who has been adjudicated a delinquent for violating Section 21-1.3 of the Criminal Code of 1961 [720 ILCS 5/21-1.3]. Reasonable attorney's fees may be awarded to a plaintiff that is not a governmental unit in any action under this Act.
(Source: P.A. 76-1679; 88-406, § 5; 90-311, § 5.)

Note.

This section was Ill.Rev.Stat., Ch. 70, para. 53.

Effect of Amendments.

The 1993 amendment by P.A. 88-406, effective August 20, 1993, added at the end "including damages caused by a minor who has been adjudicated a delinquent for violating Section 21-1.3 of the Criminal Code of 1961".

The 1997 amendment by P.A. 90-311, effective January 1, 1998, added the section catchline; and added the second sentence.

CASE NOTES

Analysis

Adequacy of Complaint
—Failure to Read Basis of Liability
Directed Verdict
Emancipation
—Burden of Proof
—Not Shown
Liability
—Basis
—Insurer's Duty
—Not Shown

Adequacy of Complaint

—Failure to Read Basis of Liability

Complaint against minor and his legal guardian, setting forth the theft of plaintiff's auto and resulting damages from that theft, as a whole, was sufficient to inform the adult defendant that the claim was being made for the theft and damage of plaintiff's auto, and that his involvement arose out of his position as guardian over the minor, and the failure to specifically base liability in the complaint on this Act was not fatal. Murray v. Cockburn, 124 Ill. App. 3d 724, 79 Ill. Dec. 938, 464 N.E.2d 842 (3 Dist. 1984).

Directed Verdict

In suit against parents of 14 year old child for injuries resulting from child's taking of plaintiff's car and subsequently becoming involved in a collision, the appellate court reversed the judgment of the trial court which granted the plaintiff's motion for a directed verdict, which was based on the contention that the operation of a vehicle without a license was sufficiently connected with injuries resulting from the operation to be deemed the cause of the injury, and remanded the case for presentation of facts to the jury. Lawrence v. Jones, 52 Ill. App. 3d 704, 10 Ill. Dec. 402, 367 N.E.2d 1011 (2 Dist. 1977).

Emancipation

—Burden of Proof

Emancipation may not be presumed but must be expressly or impliedly proven. Conrad v. Dickerson, 31 Ill. App. 3d 1011, 335 N.E.2d 67 (2 Dist. 1975).

—Not Shown

Where testimony showed that parents maintained a furnished bedroom for son which he frequently used during short time period before the shootings, parents provided him with a vehicle that he used daily, he continued to receive mail at his parent's address and worked on the family farm in exchange for other consideration, trial court properly found that a person of ordinary caution and prudence would entertain a strong suspicion that son was an unemancipated minor residing with his parents at the time of the shooting and trial court erred in denying motion to convert parents from respondents in discovery to defendants under this section. McGee v. Heimburger, 287 Ill. App. 3d 242, 222 Ill. Dec. 752, 678 N.E.2d 364 (4 Dist. 1997).

Liability

—Basis

Parents are not liable for the torts of their children merely because of the parent-child relationship. Allstate Ins. Co. v. Pruitt ex rel. Pruitt, 177 Ill. App. 3d 407, 126 Ill. Dec. 716, 532 N.E.2d 401 (1 Dist. 1988).

—Insurer's Duty

Homeowner's insurer had no duty to cover homeowner's liability under the Parental Responsibility Act where the action was based on minor's negligent operation of a dirt bike and homeowner's policy specifically excluded from coverage accidents arising out of the use of motorized land vehicles when not on the insured premises. Allstate Ins. Co. v. Panzica, 162 Ill. App. 3d 589, 114 Ill. Dec. 28, 515 N.E.2d 1299 (3 Dist. 1987).

—Not Shown

Where no liability was found for assault and battery as against the son, no liability could inure to his parents. Sklan v. Smolla, 95 Ill. App. 3d 658, 51 Ill. Dec. 161, 420 N.E.2d 575 (1 Dist. 1981).

740 ILCS 115/4 [Enforcement of liability]

Sec. 4. Any municipal corporation, county, township, village or any other political subdivision or department of the State of Illinois, or the United States or any of its instrumentalities, or any person, partnership, corporation, association or any incorporated or unincorporated religious, educational or charitable organization is entitled to enforce the liability imposed by this Act.
(Source: P.A. 76-1679; 88-406, § 5.)

Note.

This section was Ill.Rev.Stat., Ch. 70, para. 54.

Effect of Amendments.

The 1993 amendment by P.A. 88-406, effective August 20, 1993, inserted "or the United States or any of its instrumentalities,".

740 ILCS 115/5 Limitation on damages; damages allowable

Sec. 5. *Limitation on damages; damages allowable.* No recovery under this Act may exceed $2,500 actual damages for each person, or legal entity as provided in Section 4 of this Act [740 ILCS 115/4], for each occurrence of such wilful or malicious acts by the minor causing injury, in addition to taxable court costs and attorney's fees. In determining the damages to be allowed in an action under this Act for personal injury, only medical, dental and hospital expenses and expenses for treatment by Christian Science practitioners and nursing care appropriate thereto may be considered.
(Source: P.A. 81-588; 90-311, § 5.)

Note.

This section was Ill.Rev.Stat., Ch. 70, para. 55.

Cross References.

As to restitution damages payable by parents for the damages caused by their unemancipated minor at a cemetery or related grounds, see 765 ILCS 835/1.

Concerning hate crimes, and their relationship to this section, see 720 ILCS 5/12-7.1.

Concerning educational intimidation, and its relationship to this section, see 720 ILCS 5/12-7.2.

As to civil liability for retail theft, and its relationship to this section, see 720 ILCS 5/16A-7.

As to institutional vandalism, and its relationship to this section, see 720 ILCS 5/21-1.2.

Effect of Amendments.

The 1997 amendment by P.A. 90-311, effective January 1, 1998, added the section catchline; and in the first sentence, substituted "$2,500" for "$1,000," and added "and attorney's fees" at the end.

CASE NOTES

Judgment

—Offset

Where plaintiff's unemancipated 17-year-old forged his name on a withdrawal slip and withdrew $1,200 from the bank, responsibility for the bank's loss rested on the plaintiff and the bank was authorized to limit its loss to the amount exceeding $1,000, i.e., $200; therefore, the trial court properly offset the plaintiff's $1,000 judgment. Robison v. First State Bank, 144 Ill. App. 3d 991, 99 Ill. Dec. 190, 495 N.E.2d 637 (3 Dist. 1986).

LEGAL PERIODICALS

For article, "New Laws Okay Jail and Work for Juveniles," see 68 Ill. B.J. 514 (1980).

740 ILCS 115/6 [Other causes of action]

Sec. 6. This Act shall not affect the recovery of damages in any other cause of action where the liability of the parent or legal guardian is predicated on a common law basis.
(Source: P.A. 76-1679.)

Note.

This section was Ill.Rev.Stat., Ch. 70, para. 56.

740 ILCS 115/7 [Code of Civil Procedure]

Sec. 7. Section 12-107 of the Code of Civil Procedure, as now or hereafter amended [735 ILCS 5/12-107], is not applicable to judgments obtained under this Act.
(Source: P.A. 82-783.)

Note.

This section was Ill.Rev.Stat., Ch. 70, para. 57.

Parental Right of Recovery Act

740 ILCS 120/1 [Short title]

Sec. 1. This Act shall be known and may be cited as the Parental Right of Recovery Act.
(Source: P.A. 84-1041.)

Derivation.

Title: An Act to provide for a parental right of recovery for damages resulting from sale of illegal drugs to minors, and to amend certain Acts in relation to criminal law and penal institutions.

Cite: 740 ILCS 120/1 et seq.

Source: P.A. 84-1041.

Date: Certified November 26, 1985.

Note.

This section was Ill.Rev.Stat., Ch. 70, para. 601.

740 ILCS 120/2 [Definitions]

Sec. 2. For the purpose of this Act, unless the context clearly requires otherwise:

(1) "Illegal drug" means (i) any substance as defined and included in the Schedules of Article II of the Illinois Controlled Substances Act [720 ILCS 570/201 et seq.], (ii) any cannabis as defined in Section 3 of the Cannabis Control Act [720 ILCS 550/3], or (iii) any drug as defined in paragraph (b) of Section 3 of the Pharmacy Practice Act of 1987 [225 ILCS 85/3] which is obtained without a prescription or otherwise in violation of the law.

(2) "Minor" means a person who has not attained age 18.

(3) "Legal guardian" means a person appointed guardian, or given custody, of a minor by a circuit court of this State, but does not include a person appointed guardian, or given custody, of a minor under the Juvenile Court Act or the Juvenile Court Act of 1987 [705 ILCS 405/1-1 et seq.].

(4) "Parent" means any natural or adoptive parent of a minor.

(5) "Person" means any natural person, corporation, association, partnership or other organization.

(6) "Prescription" means any order for drugs, written or verbal, by a physician, dentist, veterinarian or other person authorized to prescribe drugs within the limits of his license, containing the following: (1) Name of the patient; (2) date when prescription was given; (3) name and strength of drug prescribed; (4) quantity, directions for use, prescriber's name, address and signature, and the United States Drug Enforcement Agency number where required, for controlled substances.

(7) "Sale or transfer" means the actual or constructive transfer of possession of an illegal drug, with or without consideration, whether directly or through an agent.
(Source: P.A. 85-1209.)

Note.

This section was Ill.Rev.Stat., Ch. 70, para. 602.

The Juvenile Court Act, referred to above, was repealed. See now 705 ILCS 405/1-1 et seq.

LEGAL PERIODICALS

For note: "Legislation Without Representation: How Veterinary Medicine Has Slipped Through the Cracks of Tort Reform," see 1990 U. Ill. L. Rev. 953.

740 ILCS 120/3 [Sale of illegal drug to minor]

Sec. 3. Any person who (1) sells or transfers an illegal drug to a minor or (2) supplies to a seller or to any other person an illegal drug which ultimately is sold or transferred to a minor, under circumstances where it is reasonably foreseeable that such drug may eventually be sold or transferred to a minor, shall be liable to the parent or legal guardian of the minor to whom such illegal drug is sold or transferred for any damages proximately caused by such sale or transfer. The parent or legal guardian may recover actual damages suffered by the minor, including any costs associated with treatment or rehabilitation of the minor for drug dependency. The parent or legal guardian may also recover actual damages suffered by such parent or legal guardian resulting from the sale or transfer of the illegal drug to the minor, including pain and suffering. In addition, the parent or legal guardian who is awarded actual damages under this Act shall be entitled to punitive damages as determined by the court or the jury as well as attorneys' fees as determined by the court.
(Source: P.A. 84-1041.)

Note.
This section was Ill.Rev.Stat., Ch. 70, para. 603.

740 ILCS 120/4 [Jointly and severally liable]

Sec. 4. Persons subject to liability under Section 3 [740 ILCS 120/3] shall be jointly and severally liable.
(Source: P.A. 84-1041.)

Note.
This section was Ill.Rev.Stat., Ch. 70, para. 604.

RIGHT TO BREASTFEED ACT

740 ILCS 137/1 Short title

Sec. 1. *Short title.* This Act may be cited as the Right to Breastfeed Act.
(Source: P.A. 93-942, § 1.)

Effective Date.
Section 99 of P.A. 93-942 made this Act effective upon becoming law. The Act was approved August 16, 2004.

740 ILCS 137/5 Purpose

Sec. 5. *Purpose.* The General Assembly finds that breast milk offers better nutrition, immunity, and digestion, and may raise a baby's IQ, and that breastfeeding offers other benefits such as improved mother-baby bonding, and its encouragement has been established as a major goal of this decade by the World Health Organization and the United Nations Children's Fund. The General Assembly finds and declares that the Surgeon General of the United States recommends that babies be fed breastmilk, unless medically contraindicated, in order to attain an optimal healthy start.
(Source: P.A. 93-942, § 5.)

740 ILCS 137/10 Breastfeeding Location

Sec. 10. *Breastfeeding Location.* A mother may breastfeed her baby in any location, public or private, where the mother is otherwise authorized to be, irrespective of whether the nipple of the mother's breast is uncovered during or incidental to the breastfeeding; however, a mother considering whether to breastfeed her baby in a place of worship shall comport her behavior with the norms appropriate in that place of worship.
(Source: P.A. 93-942, § 10.)

740 ILCS 137/15 Private right of action

Sec. 15. *Private right of action.* A woman who has been denied the right to breastfeed by the owner or manager of a public or private location, other than a private residence or place of worship, may bring an action to enjoin future denials of the right to breastfeed. If the woman prevails in her suit, she shall be awarded reasonable attorney's fees and reasonable expenses of litigation.
(Source: P.A. 93-942, § 15.)

740 ILCS 137/99 Effective date

Sec. 99. *Effective date.* This Act takes effect upon becoming law.
(Source: P.A. 93-942, § 99.)

Note.
P.A. 93-942, which enacted this Act, was approved August 16, 2004.

CHAPTER 760

TRUSTS AND FIDUCIARIES

INSTRUMENTS REGARDING ADOPTED CHILDREN ACT
760 ILCS 30/0.01 Short title
760 ILCS 30/1 Property rights
TRUSTS AND DISSOLUTIONS OF MARRIAGE ACT
760 ILCS 35/0.01 Short title
760 ILCS 35/1 [Effect on former spouse]

INSTRUMENTS REGARDING ADOPTED CHILDREN ACT

760 ILCS 30/0.01 Short title

Sec. 0.01. *Short title.* This Act may be cited as the Instruments Regarding Adopted Children Act.
(Source: P.A. 86-1324.)

Derivation.
Title: An Act relating to the construction of written instruments with regard to adopted children and to repeal an Act therein named.
Cite: 760 ILCS 30/0.01 et seq.
Source: L. 1955, p. 316.
Date: Approved June 9, 1955.

Note.
This section was Ill.Rev.Stat., Ch. 40, para. 1651.9.

760 ILCS 30/1 Property rights

Sec. 1. *Property rights.* For the purpose of determining the property rights of any person under any nontestamentary instrument, an adopted child's relationship to his or her adopting and natural parents shall be governed by Section 2-4 of the Probate Act of 1975 [755 ILCS 5/2-4]. For the purpose of determining the property rights of any person under any nontestamentary instrument, the changes made by this amendatory Act of 1997 apply to all nontestamentary instruments executed on or after January 1, 1998.
(Source: P.A. 86-842; 90-237, § 10.)

Note.
This section was Ill.Rev.Stat., Ch. 40, para. 1652.

Effect of Amendments.
The 1997 amendment by P.A. 90-237, effective January 1, 1998, added the section catchline; and rewrote the section.

CASE NOTES

ANALYSIS

Clear and Convincing Evidence
—Lawful Descendants
Illustrative Cases
Inheritances
—Lineal or Collateral Kindred
Rebuttable Presumption

Clear and Convincing Evidence

—Lawful Descendants
Descendant failed to meet his burden of proving, by clear and convincing evidence as demonstrated by the terms of the instrument, that testator actually intended to exclude adopteds from taking under his will; the testator's use of the terms "lawful descendants" and "per stirpes" did not amount to clear and convincing evidence of such intent so as to rebut the new presumption that an adopted child is deemed a child born to the adopting parent. First Nat'l Bank v. King, 263 Ill. App. 3d 813, 200 Ill. Dec. 416, 635 N.E.2d 755 (1 Dist. 1994), aff'd, 165 Ill. 2d 533, 209 Ill. Dec. 199, 651 N.E.2d 127 (1995).

Illustrative Cases
The statutory amendment, which corrected the outdated presumption of exclusion of adopteds did not create or confer a substantive right on a testator's adopted great-grandson, and thus no new fact existed to prevent the application of the doctrines of res judicata and collateral estoppel after previous litigation concerning distribution of the estate. Schuttler v. Ruark, 225 Ill. App. 3d 678, 167 Ill. Dec. 837, 588 N.E.2d 478 (2 Dist.), appeal denied, 145 Ill. 2d 644, 173 Ill. Dec. 13, 596 N.E.2d 637 (1992).

Inheritances

—Lineal or Collateral Kindred
An adopted child did not qualify as testator's "lawful issue" in a will construction suit, nor could an adopted child inherit by right of representation from the lineal or collateral kindred of his adoptive parents, when property was expressly limited to the "body or bodies of the parents by adoption." Sennot v. Collet-Oser, 36 Ill. App. 3d 928, 344 N.E.2d 783 (1 Dist. 1976).

Rebuttable Presumption
The presumption that an adopted child is a natural child remains subject to rebuttal upon a showing of contrary intent of the testator by clear and convincing evidence. Schuttler v. Ruark, 225 Ill. App. 3d 678, 167 Ill. Dec. 837, 588 N.E.2d 478 (2 Dist.), appeal denied, 145 Ill. 2d 644, 173 Ill. Dec. 13, 596 N.E.2d 637 (1992).

LEGAL PERIODICALS

For article, "Wills and Trusts: Disqualifying Adopted Adult 'Children'," see 78 Ill. B.J. 612 (1990).
For comment, "The Illinois Probate Act: Dispositions Subject to Contrary Will Intent," see 11 J. Marshall J. Prac. & Proc. 154 (1977).

RESEARCH REFERENCES

Adopted child as within class named in testamentary gift. 36 ALR5th 395.
Adopted child as within class named in deed or inter vivos trust instrument. 37 ALR5th 237.

TRUSTS AND DISSOLUTIONS OF MARRIAGE ACT

760 ILCS 35/0.01 Short title

Sec. 0.01. *Short title.* This Act may be cited as the Trusts and Dissolutions of Marriage Act.
(Source: P.A. 86-1324.)

Derivation.
Title: An Act in relation to the effect of a judgment of judicial termination of marriage on provisions in a revocable trust pertaining to the settlor's former spouse.
Cite: 760 ILCS 35/0.01 et seq.
Source: P.A. 82-428.
Date: Approved September 4, 1981.

Note.
This section was Ill.Rev.Stat., Ch. 148, para. 300.

760 ILCS 35/1 [Effect on former spouse]

Sec. 1. (a) Unless the governing instrument or the judgment of judicial termination of marriage expressly provides otherwise, judicial termination of the marriage of the settlor of a trust revokes every provision which is revocable by the settlor pertaining to the settlor's former spouse in a trust instrument or amendment thereto executed by the settlor before the entry of the judgment of judicial termination of the settlor's marriage, and any such trust shall be administered and construed as if the settlor's former spouse had died upon entry of the judgment of judicial termination of the settlor's marriage.

(b) A trustee who has no actual knowledge of a judgment of judicial termination of the settlor's marriage, shall have no liability for any action taken or omitted in good faith on the assumption that the settlor is married. The preceding sentence is intended to affect only the liability of the trustee and shall not affect the disposition of beneficial interests in any trust.

(c) "Trust" means a trust created by a nontestamentary instrument executed after the effective date of this Act, except that, unless in the governing instrument the provisions of this Act are made applicable by specific reference, the provisions of this Act do not apply to any (a) land trust; (b) voting trust; (c) security instrument such as a trust deed or mortgage; (d) liquidation trust; (e) escrow; (f) instrument under which a nominee, custodian for property or paying or receiving agent is appointed; or (g) a trust created by a deposit arrangement in a bank or savings institution, commonly known as "Totten Trust".

(d) The phrase "provisions pertaining to the settlor's former spouse" includes, but is not limited to, every present or future gift or interest or power of appointment given to the settlor's former spouse or right of the settlor's former spouse to serve in a fiduciary capacity.

(e) A provision is revocable by the settlor if the settlor has the power at the time of the entry of the judgment of judicial termination of the settlor's marriage to revoke, modify or amend said provision, either alone or in conjunction with any other person or persons.

(f) "Judicial termination of marriage" includes, but is not limited to, divorce, dissolution, annulment or declaration of invalidity of marriage.

(Source: P.A. 82-428; 90-655, § 179.)

Note.

This section was Ill.Rev.Stat., Ch. 148, para. 301.

Effect of Amendments.

The 1998 amendment by P.A. 90-655, effective July 30, 1998, in subsection (e) substituted "alone" for "along".

CASE NOTES

ANALYSIS

Applicability
—Individual Retirement Account
—Trust Not Shown
Creation of Trust
—Not Shown
Revocation of Trust
—Shown
Totten Trust
—Creation

Applicability

—Individual Retirement Account

Individual Retirement Account trust account was held to be not a savings account. Waller v. Davis, 225 Ill. App. 3d 998, 168 Ill. Dec. 40, 589 N.E.2d 154 (2 Dist.), appeal denied, 145 Ill. 2d 634, 173 Ill. Dec. 5, 596 N.E.2d 629 (1992).

An Individual Retirement Account is a trust (or custodial account) created or organized for the exclusive benefit of an individual or his or her beneficiaries. Waller v. Davis, 225 Ill. App. 3d 998, 168 Ill. Dec. 40, 589 N.E.2d 154 (2 Dist.), appeal denied, 145 Ill. 2d 634, 173 Ill. Dec. 5, 596 N.E.2d 629 (1992).

In case involving redesignation of beneficiary of former husband's Individual Retirement trust account following dissolution of marriage, unless the trust agreement, as the governing instrument or the parties' property settlement agreement, expressly provided that this section would not apply, or unless former husband redesignated ex-wife after their divorce in a written beneficiary designation subsequent to the divorce as required by the terms of the trust agreement, the decedent's predissolution designation of former wife as the beneficiary of the retirement account was revoked by operation of this Act at the time the marriage was judicially terminated. Waller v. Davis, 225 Ill. App. 3d 998, 168 Ill. Dec. 40, 589 N.E.2d 154 (2 Dist.), appeal denied, 145 Ill. 2d 634, 173 Ill. Dec. 5, 596 N.E.2d 629 (1992).

—Trust Not Shown

Where there was no evidence in the record that the deceased ever intended to create a trust, neither the CD's nor the annuity could be construed as trusts and this section did not apply. Deida v. Murphy, 271 Ill. App. 3d 296, 207 Ill. Dec. 616, 647 N.E.2d 1109 (5 Dist. 1995).

Creation of Trust

—Not Shown

Husband's election to participate in optional contributory life insurance plan did not constitute the creation of a trust within the meaning of this section which would have precluded former wife from recovering any contributory life insurance proceeds. Allen v. Allen, 226 Ill. App. 3d 576, 168 Ill. Dec. 733, 589 N.E.2d 1133 (2 Dist.), cert. denied, 146 Ill. 2d 621, 176 Ill. Dec. 791, 602 N.E.2d 445 (1992).

Revocation of Trust

—Shown

Where neither trust agreement nor the parties' property settlement in divorce expressly provided that this Act would not apply and the decedent did not re-designate his ex-wife, after their divorce in a written beneficiary designation, as required by the trust agreement, the decedent's predissolution designation of his wife as beneficiary of the trust was revoked by operation of this Act at the time the marriage was judicially terminated. Waller v. Davis, 225 Ill. App. 3d 998, 168 Ill. Dec. 40, 589 N.E.2d 154 (2 Dist.), appeal denied, 145 Ill. 2d 634, 173 Ill. Dec. 5, 596 N.E.2d 629 (1992).

Totten Trust

—Creation

A Totten trust or savings bank trust is created when a deposit is made by a person of his or her own money in his or her own name as trustee for another. Waller v. Davis, 225 Ill. App. 3d 998, 168 Ill. Dec. 40, 589 N.E.2d 154 (2 Dist.), appeal denied, 145 Ill. 2d 634, 173 Ill. Dec. 5, 596 N.E.2d 629 (1992).

RESEARCH REFERENCES

Divorce decree or settlement agreement as affecting divorced spouse's right to recover as named beneficiary on former spouse's individual retirement account. 99 ALR5th 637.

ILLINOIS SUPREME COURT RULES

Effective January 1, 1967 with amendments received through April 1, 2005.

Expedited Child Support Rules

RULE
100.1. Implementation of Expedited Child Support System.
100.2. Appointment, Qualification and Compensation of Administrative Hearing Officers.
100.3. Actions Subject to Expedited Child Support Hearings.
100.4. Authority of Administrative Hearing Officers.
100.5. Blood Tests.
100.6. Scheduling of the Hearings.
100.7. Conduct of the Hearing.
100.8. Absence of Party at Hearing.
100.9. Transfers for Judicial Hearings.
100.10. Submission of Recommendations to the Court.
100.11. Authority Retained by the Court.
100.12. Judicial Hearings.
100.13. Definitions.

Article II

Rules on Civil Proceedings in the Trial Court

Part A

Process and Notice

RULE
101. Summons and Original Process — Form and Issuance.

Part J

Miscellaneous

RULE
296. Enforcement of Order for Support.

Article VI

Appeals in Criminal Cases, Post-Conviction Cases, and Juvenile Court Proceedings

RULE
660. Appeals in Cases Arising under the Juvenile Court Act.
661. Appeals as Poor Persons by Minors Found to Be Delinquent.
662. Adjudication of Wardship and Revocation of Probation or Conditional Discharge.
663. Adoption — Appointment of a Guardian with Power to Consent.

Expedited Child Support Rules

Rule 100.1. Implementation of Expedited Child Support System.

(a) *Applicability to Circuits.* An Expedited Child Support System may be established in those judicial circuits which, with the approval of the Supreme Court, elect to implement the System and in such other judicial circuits as may be directed by the Supreme Court.

(b) *Submission of a Plan.* The chief judge of a judicial circuit which elects to create a System must submit a Plan of Implementation. The Plan may establish a circuit-wide system, a system in each county within the circuit or a system in any county in the circuit. The chief judges of two or more contiguous judicial circuits may submit a Plan for the creation of a single system encompassing those judicial circuits or encompassing contiguous counties within the judicial circuits.

(c) *The Plan.* Each Plan must:

(1) describe how the Plan will ensure that support orders will be expedited, setting forth the time frames and the mechanism for expediting matters eligible for a hearing before an administrative hearing officer;

(2) describe how the System will comply with the Federal time frames established for the IV-D program in regulations promulgated by the United States Department of Health and Human Services Office of Child Support Enforcement (codified at 45 C.F.R. 303), for the disposition of parentage and child support cases, and how compliance information shall be provided with respect to IV-D and non-IV-D cases;

(3) indicate whether the System is to be made available to nonparticipants in the IV-D program as specified in subsection (d) below;

(4) indicate which of the actions eligible for a hearing under Rule 100.3 will be subject to a hearing before an administrative hearing officer;

(5) designate the number of administrative hearing officers to be employed, and whether they will be employed full-time or part-time;

(6) indicate the compensation to be paid to each administrative hearing officer;

(7) describe the personnel policies applicable to employees of the System;

(8) describe the facilities and security arrangements to be used for hearings, including the days and hours of availability;

(9) describe the procedures for training administrative hearing officers;

(10) describe the documentation and forms required for an expedited child support hearing in addition to those required by the Supreme Court;

(11) describe the procedure for transmittal to a judge of contested prehearing motions, other matters that require a court order, recommended orders, and any other matters that require transfer or should be referred to a judge;

(12) describe the procedure for transfer of matters from a judge to an administrative hearing officer; and

(13) describe the procedure for action by a judge on an administrative hearing officer's recommendations.

(d) *Availability of System to Non-IV-D Participants.* A Plan may provide that the System is available in cases where both parties are non-IV-D participants and request access to the System. If the System is available to non-IV-D participants, administrative expenses must be appropriated by the county board and a plan for cost-sharing must be approved as provided in subsection (g) below.

(e) *Establishment of Demonstration Programs.* The Illinois Department of Public Aid may notify the Supreme Court of its desire to establish a demonstration program in one or more circuits or counties. Any such program shall be available to IV-D participants. Upon receipt of such notification, the Supreme Court will notify the chief judge of each judicial circuit of the Department's desire to establish a demonstration program. Each chief judge may submit a demonstration Plan to the Supreme Court which, upon approval, will submit the Plan to the Department. The Department may select one or more circuits or counties to participate in the demonstration program after reviewing the submitted Plans. The Department shall notify the Supreme Court of its decision. The submitted demonstration Plan shall include each element listed in subsection (c) above. In addition, each demonstration Plan shall include a projected budget for operation of the System. The demonstration Plan shall specify whether it is available to non-IV-D participants, and if so, shall provide that the portion of the administrative costs attributable to use by non-IV-D participants has been appropriated by the demonstration county and meets the requirements of subsection (g) below.

(f) *Supreme Court Review and Approval.* The Supreme Court shall review and approve or request that the chief judge modify any submitted Plan or demonstration Plan for compliance with the Act, these rules and, to the extent Federal reimbursement is sought, the rules of the IV-D program. Upon Supreme Court approval of a Plan, any nondemonstration county, circuit, multicircuit area or multicounty area may establish a System. Approved demonstration Plans will be submitted to the Department of Public Aid for review based on Department standards.

(g) *Funding.* Before establishment of a System according to a Supreme Court approved Plan, each participating nondemonstration county board or boards must appropriate the administrative expenses incurred to establish and maintain the non-IV-D portion of the System and the IV-D portion that is not subject to Federal reimbursement. A Plan for cost-sharing must be submitted to the Department of Public Aid for approval. Each chief judge shall be responsible for documenting and recording the number of IV-D and non-IV-D cases pending and disposed of in the System each month, and the portion of administrative expenses eligible for Federal reimbursement under the IV-D program, in such a manner as to insure Federal reimbursement. Information necessary for Federal reimbursement shall be submitted to the Department of Public Aid 14 days after the end of each month. The chief judge shall also submit copies of such information to the Supreme Court. The Illinois Department of Public Aid shall forward all reimbursement to the county in which the Plan is approved. The Supreme Court shall remain a signatory to the contract and shall maintain general supervisory oversight.

(h) *Administration.* Pursuant to rule, the chief judge of each judicial circuit shall be responsible for administering the System on a day-to-day basis, shall employ and terminate administrative hearing officers and other necessary staff, and shall review and evaluate the performance of each administrative hearing officer. Reviews shall be conducted quarterly in the first year of employment, and annually thereafter.

(i) *Reporting of Data.* The chief judge shall file a report with the Supreme Court within 35 days of the end of each State fiscal year detailing the number of:

(1) matters initially assigned to an administrative hearing officer;

(2) matters transferred to an administrative hearing officer;

(3) matters returned to an administrative hearing officer from a judge;

(4) matters submitted to a judge from an administrative hearing officer with recommendation for a court order;

(5) recommended court orders entered by a judge;

(6) recommended court orders rejected by a judge;

(7) matters submitted by an administrative hearing officer to a judge for hearings;

(8) IV-D and non-IV-D matters pending and disposed of in the System; and

(9) matters which complied or failed to comply with Federal time frames. The above data shall be reported for each fiscal year with respect to each administrative hearing officer and for the System as a whole.

(j) *Local Rules.* Each judicial circuit may adopt rules for the conduct of expedited child support hearings which are consistent with these rules and may determine which matters within the general classification of eligible actions shall be heard by administrative hearing officers.

(k) *Applicability of Other Acts, the Code of Civil Procedure and Rules of the Supreme Court.* The provisions of the Illinois Marriage and Dissolution of Marriage Act [750 ILCS 5/101 et seq.], the Illinois Parentage Act of 1984 [750 ILCS 40/1 et seq.], the Illinois Public Aid Code [305 ILCS 5/1-1 et seq.], the Revised Uniform Reciprocal Enforcement of Support Act [750 ILCS 20/1 et seq.], the Nonsupport of Spouse and Children Act [750 ILCS 15/1 et seq.], the State Mandates Act [30 ILCS 805/1 et seq.], the Code of Civil Procedure [735 ILCS 5/1-101 et seq.] and the rules of the Supreme Court shall be applicable to expedited child support hearings except insofar as these rules otherwise provide.

(Adopted 4-1-92, eff. immediately; amended 3-19-97, eff. 4-15-97.)

COMMITTEE COMMENTS

Rule 100.1 provides for the creation of an Expedited Child Support System in judicial circuits. It specifies that each judicial circuit which elects to create such a System must submit a Plan of Implementation to the Supreme Court for approval, identifies the matters which must be set forth in the Plan, and provides for Supreme Court review and approval. The rule addresses the availability of the System to various classes of participants, the use of demonstration programs, and funding of Systems. The rule makes judicial circuits responsible for administration of the System and reporting of data relative to the System. The rule also provides for the establishment of local rules to accompany these rules and specifies those other rules, acts and codes which apply to the conduct of the System.

Rule 100.2. Appointment, Qualification and Compensation of Administrative Hearing Officers.

(a) *Appointment.* Administrative hearing officers shall be hired by the chief judge of each judicial circuit, after satisfying the qualifications set by the Supreme Court. Candidates for the position of administrative hearing officer must apply for appointment with the chief judge of each judicial circuit.

(b) *Qualifications.* Administrative hearing officers must be licensed to practice law in Illinois and must have been engaged in the active practice of law for a minimum of three years.

(c) *Disqualification.* A full-time administrative hearing officer shall not practice law before any court. A part-time administrative hearing officer shall not practice law in any domestic relations matter or other matter which would qualify for an expedited hearing before an administrative hearing officer without the written consent of both parties. Upon appointment to a case, an administrative hearing officer shall notify the judge and withdraw from the case if any grounds appear to exist for disqualification under Supreme Court Rules 61 through 67.

(d) *Oath of Office.* Each administrative hearing officer shall take an oath of office similar to a judicial oath.

(e) *Compensation.* Each administrative hearing officer shall be compensated as provided in the Plan.

(f) *Communications with Attorneys.* Disciplinary rules governing the conduct of attorneys before a court remain applicable in expedited child support hearings. Disciplinary rules governing communications between an attorney and a judge govern communications between attorneys and administrative hearing officers.

(Adopted 4-1-92, eff. immediately.)

COMMITTEE COMMENTS

Rule 100.2 provides for the appointment, qualification, disqualification and compensation of administrative hearing officers. The rule specifies that administrative hearing officers take an oath of office and conduct hearings according to applicable disciplinary rules.

Rule 100.3. Actions Subject to Expedited Child Support Hearings.

(a) *Eligible Actions.* The following actions, if so provided for in the Plan, are eligible to be heard by an administrative hearing officer:

(1) actions pursuant to the Illinois Public Aid Code, as amended [305 ILCS 5/1-1 et seq.], to establish temporary and final child support and medical support, and to enforce or modify existing orders of child support and medical support;

(2) actions pursuant to the Illinois Parentage Act of 1984, as amended [750 ILCS 45/1 et seq.], to establish a parent and child relationship; to establish child support and medical support after parentage has been acknowledged or established, whether or not these issues were reserved at the time judgment was entered; and to enforce or modify existing child support and medical support orders;

(3) actions pursuant to the Illinois Marriage and Dissolution of Marriage Act, as amended [750 ILCS 5/101 et seq.], to establish temporary and final child support and medical support, whether or not these issues were reserved or could not be ordered at the time judgment was entered because the court lacked personal jurisdiction over the obligor; and to enforce or modify existing orders of child support and medical support;

(4) actions pursuant to the Nonsupport of Spouse and Children Act [750 ILCS 15/1 et seq.] to establish temporary child support and to enforce and modify such orders;

(5) actions pursuant to the Revised Uniform Reciprocal Enforcement of Support Act [750 ILCS 20/1 et seq.] to establish temporary and final child support and medical support, whether or not these issues were reserved or could not be ordered at the time judgment was entered because the court lacked personal jurisdiction over the obligor; and to enforce and modify existing child support and medical support orders; and

(6) any other child support or medical support matter.

(b) *Other Eligible Prejudgment Proceedings.* If provided for in the Plan, the System may be available in prejudgment proceedings for dissolution of marriage, declaration of invalidity of marriage and legal separation.

(Adopted 4-1-92, eff. immediately.)

COMMITTEE COMMENTS

Rule 100.3 lists those actions which are eligible to be heard by an administrative hearing officer if so specified in the judicial circuit's Plan of Implementation.

Rule 100.4. Authority of Administrative Hearing Officers.

(a) *Powers of Administrative Hearing Officers.* Administrative hearing officers shall have the authority to conduct child support hearings, to administer oaths and affirmations, to take testimony under oath or affirmation, to determine the admissibility of evidence, to propose findings of fact and to recommend orders to the judge based on such evidence as prescribed by the Act.

(b) *Accept Voluntary Agreements of Parties.* Administrative hearing officers may accept stipulations of fact and voluntary agreements of the parties setting the amount of child support to be paid or medical support liability and to recommend to the judge the entry of orders incorporating such agreements.

(c) *Accept Voluntary Acknowledgments of Parentage.* Administrative hearing officers may accept voluntary orders of parentage and recommend to the judge the entry of orders based on such acknowledgments. Prior to accepting an acknowledgment of parentage, administrative hearing officers shall advise the putative father of his rights and obligations.

(d) *Discovery.* Administrative hearing officers shall manage all stages of discovery, including hearings on citations to discover assets and setting deadlines for the completion of discovery, and to direct the submission to tests pursuant to section 11 of the Illinois Parentage Act of 1984 [750 ILCS 45/11] and Rule 100.5 below. Administrative hearing officers may not enter orders with respect to disputed discovery matters though they may recommend the entry of such orders to a judge. Discovery shall be conducted in accordance with these rules and shall be completed prior to the expedited child support hearing. No discovery shall be permitted after the hearing, except upon leave of court and good cause shown.

(e) *Compelling Appearance of the Obligor.* The person designated in the Plan may recommend that the judge issue a notice requiring the obligor to appear before the administrative hearing officer or in court.

(f) *Recommend Default Orders.* Administrative hearing officers may recommend that the judge issue a default order to absent parties who fail to respond to a notice to appear before the administrative hearing officer or such other orders as are specified in Rule 100.11(d).

(g) *Authority over Unemployed Obligor.* Administrative hearing officers may recommend that an unemployed obligor who is not making child support payments or who is unable to provide support be ordered to seek employment and may recommend that the obligor be required to submit periodic reports as to such efforts. Administrative hearing officers may recommend that the obligor be ordered to report to the appropriate agency to participate in job search, training or work programs.

(h) *Foreign Support Matters.* Administrative hearing officers may recommend that foreign support judgments or orders be registered as Illinois judgments or orders.

(i) *Non-IV-D Obligees.* Administrative hearing officers shall inform non-IV-D obligees of the existence and services of the IV-D program and provide applications if requested. Administrative hearing officers shall also inform such obligees that payment may be requested through the clerk of the circuit court. Any such request that payment be made through the clerk shall be noted in the recommended order to the judge.

(Adopted 4-1-92, eff. immediately.)

COMMITTEE COMMENTS

Rule 100.4 specifies the powers of administrative hearing officers relative to the conduct of child support hearings, management of discovery, authority over parties, and resolution of matters.

Rule 100.5. Blood Tests.

(a) *Order to Submit to Tests.* Administrative hearing officers may recommend, upon the request of a party, that the judge order the mother, child and alleged father to submit to appropriate tests to determine inherited characteristics including, but not limited to, blood types and genetic markers such as those found by Human Leucocyte Antigen (HLA) tests. The judge shall determine the appropriate tests to be conducted and appoint an expert to determine the testing procedures and conduct the tests.

(Adopted 4-1-92, eff. immediately.)

Note.

This Rule was enacted without a subsection (b).

COMMITTEE COMMENTS

Rule 100.5 provides the administrative hearing officers with authority to recommend submission to blood tests. The rule provides for the admissibility of blood test results, a party's objections to matters involving blood tests, the evidentiary value of blood tests and the cost of blood tests in matters before an administrative hearing officer.

Rule 100.6. Scheduling of the Hearings.

(a) *Assignment of Hearing Date.* If an action or a motion filed by a IV-D participant qualifies as an action over which an administrative hearing officer has authority, the person designated in the Plan shall assign a hearing date before an administrative hearing officer. Non-IV-D participants may request that the clerk assign eligible actions a hearing date before an administrative hearing officer. The procedure for fixing the date, time and place of a hearing before an administrative hearing officer shall be prescribed by circuit rule provided that not less than seven days' notice in writing shall be given to the parties or their attorneys of record. In cases in which the court has previously acquired jurisdiction over the responding party, the hearing shall be held on the scheduled date and not less than 21 days or more than 35 days of the date of filing of the action, unless continued by the administrative hearing officer or court upon good cause shown. In cases in which the court has not previously acquired jurisdiction over the responding party, the hearing shall be held on the scheduled date and not less than 21 days or more than 45 days of the date of filing of the action, unless continued by the administrative hearing officer or court upon good cause shown. The hearing shall be held at a location provided or authorized by the chief judge of the circuit.

(b) *Providing Notice of Hearing Date.* The person designated in the Plan shall serve notice of the action and the hearing date on respondent by regular mail to his or her last known address, unless the action is one over which no court has previously acquired personal jurisdiction, in which case service will be in the same manner as summonses are served in other civil proceedings. If service is made by mail, the person serving notice shall prepare a certificate of mailing to be included in the file.

(c) *Subpoenas.* The clerk of the circuit court may issue subpoenas upon, or prior to, the filing of a petition if the court has previously acquired jurisdiction over the subject matter of the underlying action.

(d) *Affidavit of Income and Expenses.* A form affidavit of income and expenses, in such form as the Supreme Court shall prescribe, may be served on the respondent with the petition initiating the proceedings before the administrative hearing officer. Each party should be requested to complete the form prior to the first appearance before the administrative hearing officer.

(Adopted 4-1-92, eff. immediately.)

COMMITTEE COMMENTS

Rule 100.6 sets forth the procedure for assignment of a hearing date before an administrative hearing officer, the time period in which a hearing must be held, and the procedure for providing notice to the responding party.

Rule 100.7. Conduct of the Hearing.

(a) *Established Rules of Evidence Apply.* Except as provided by this rule, the rules of evidence shall be liberally construed in all expedited child support hearings.

(b) *Documents Presumptively Admissible.* A party may offer in evidence, without foundation or other proof:

(1) the obligor's pay stubs or other employer-provided statement of gross income, deductions and net income or other records prepared by the employer in the usual course of business;

(2) documents provided by the obligor's insurance company which describe the dependent care coverage available to the obligor; and

(3) records kept by the clerk of the circuit court as to payment of child support.

If at least seven days written notice of the intention to offer the following documents in evidence is given to every other party, accompanied by a copy of the document, or if at the expedited child support hearing the other party does not object, a party may offer in evidence without foundation or other proof:

(1) the deposition of a witness, the statement of a witness which the witness would be allowed to express if testifying in person, if the statement is made by affidavit or by certification as provided in section 1-109 of the Code of Civil Procedure [735 ILCS 5/1-109];

(2) computer-generated documents and records, unless objected to by a party; and

(3) any other document not specifically covered by any of the foregoing provisions, and which is otherwise admissible under the rules of evidence.

(c) *Opinions of Expert Witnesses.* Notwithstanding the provisions of Rule 220, a party who proposes to use a written opinion of an expert witness or the testimony of an expert witness at the hearing may do so provided a written notice of such intention is given to every other party not less than seven days prior to the date of hearing, accompanied by a statement containing the identity of the expert, his qualifications, the subject matter, the basis of his conclusions, and his opinion.

(d) *Right to Subpoena Maker of a Document.* Any other party may subpoena the author or maker of a document admissible under this rule, at that party's expense, and examine the author or maker as if under cross-examination. The provisions of the Code of Civil Procedure relative to subpoenas, section 2-1101 [735 ILCS 5/2-1101], shall be applicable to expedited child support hearings and it shall be the duty of the party requesting the subpoena to modify the form to show that the appearance is set before an administrative hearing officer and to give the time and place set for the hearing.

(e) *Adverse Examination of Parties or Agents.* The provisions of the Code of Civil Procedure relative to the adverse examination of parties or agents, section 2-1102 [735 ILCS 5/2-1102], shall be applicable to expedited child support hearings as upon the trial of a case.

(f) *Compelling Appearance of Witness at Hearing.* The provisions of Supreme Court Rule 237 shall be equally applicable to expedited child support hearings as they are to trials.

(Adopted 4-1-92, eff. immediately.)

COMMITTEE COMMENTS

Rule 100.7 governs the conduct of expedited child support hearings and specifies that the rules of evidence apply to such hearings. The rule prescribes the circumstances under which certain specified documents are presumptively admissible in evidence. The rule sets forth the procedure for offering expert testimony and a party's right to subpoena the maker of admissible documents and to cross-examine parties and their agents. The rule also provides for compelling the appearance of a witness at an expedited child support hearing.

Rule 100.8. Absence of Party at Hearing.

(a) *Failure to be Present at Hearing.* The expedited child support hearing may proceed in the absence of the responding party if service has been made and the petitioning party and/or his or her attorney is present. Based upon the testimony of the petitioning party and any other evidence that may have been presented, the administrative hearing officer shall recommend that the judge enter an appropriate order. If the petitioning party does not agree to the recommended order, the administrative hearing officer shall immediately schedule a judicial hearing, record the date, time and place of the hearing upon a notice and provide such notice to the petitioning party at the expedited hearing. Such notice shall be sent to the nonappearing party by regular mail. If the petitioning party agrees to and signs the order, a copy of the signed order and a notification of the right to object to the order shall be served upon the nonappearing party as directed in subsection (b) below. If the petitioning party is not present, either in person or through an attorney, the administrative hearing officer may continue the matter or may strike the matter with leave to reinstate. Notification of such action shall be served upon the petitioning party by regular mail.

(b) *Service of Recommended Order and Notice.* If service to commence the hearing before the administrative hearing officer was made by regular mail, the notice and recommended order shall be served in the same manner as summonses are served in other civil proceedings or by certified mail, return receipt requested, mailed to the nonappearing party's last known address. If service to commence the hearing was as provided in the Code of Civil Procedure [735 ILCS 5/1-101 et seq.], the notice and recommended order shall be served by regular mail to the nonappearing party's last known address.

(c) *Objections.* The nonappearing party may file with the judge a written objection to the entry of the recommended order within 14 days after the order was mailed. If no objection is filed within 14 days, the nonappearing party is deemed to have accepted the recommended order. The judge may then enter the order, refer the case back to the administrative hearing officer for further proceedings, or conduct a judicial hearing. If a timely objection is filed, the judge must hold a judicial hearing and shall enter an appropriate order.
(Adopted 4-1-92, eff. immediately.)

COMMITTEE COMMENTS

Rule 100.8 governs the conduct of the expedited child support hearing in the absence of a party, the service of the recommended order and notice upon an absent party, and the filing of objections by an absent party.

Rule 100.9. Transfers for Judicial Hearings.

(a) *Domestic Relations Matters Other than Child Support and Parentage.* Any domestic relations matter other than child support and parentage, including but not limited to petitions for visitation, custody, distribution of property, petitions pursuant to section 513 of the Illinois Marriage and Dissolution of Marriage Act [750 ILCS 5/513], and spousal maintenance shall be transferred according to the judicial circuit's Plan to a judge for a judicial hearing. The administrative hearing officer shall proceed as scheduled with matters relative to child support or parentage. In actions to establish parentage where the putative father voluntarily acknowledges paternity, the recommended order shall include provisions for custody of the child in the mother and reasonable visitation for the father if both parties agree. If either party wishes to contest custody or visitation, the recommended order will be silent on those issues, but the contest will not delay the entry of the order establishing parentage and child support.

(b) *Prehearing Motions and Other Matters that Require a Court Order.* All prehearing motions and other matters that require a court order or judicial hearing, as defined in the Act and in these rules, shall be transferred to a judge for resolution in an expeditious manner. However, if the parties are in agreement as to the prehearing motion or other such matters, the administrative hearing officer shall transmit a recommended order, signed by both parties to a judge.

(c) *Matters Requiring Judicial Hearing.* All other matters requiring a judicial hearing, as provided for in the Act and in these rules, shall be immediately transferred according to the judicial circuit's Plan to a judge for a judicial hearing.

(d) *Service of Orders of Withholding Pending Judicial Hearing.* Whenever the parties disagree with part of the administrative hearing officer's recommendations, but do agree as to the existing obligation and no order for withholding was previously served upon the obligor's employer, the order for withholding shall be served upon the obligor's employer as to the existing support obligation pending judicial hearing on the contested matter.
(Adopted 4-1-92, eff. immediately.)

COMMITTEE COMMENTS

Rule 100.9 lists those matters which must be transferred to a judge for a judicial hearing or court order.

Rule 100.10. Submission of Recommendations to the Court.

(a) *Notice to Parties.* The administrative hearing officer shall present each party with a copy of the recommended order to be submitted to a judge. The administrative hearing officer shall also present each party with a written notice informing the parties of their right to request a judicial hearing and the procedures for so doing. The recommended order and notice shall be presented to each party at the conclusion of the hearing. If either party is not present at the conclusion of the hearing, either in person or through an attorney, the recommendation and order shall be mailed by regular mail to the party's last known address.

(b) *Acceptance of Recommended Order.* If both parties are present at the hearing and agree to the recommended order, they shall sign the recommended order. The administrative hearing officer shall transmit the signed recommended order to a judge as provided for in the Plan of Implementation.

(c) *Rejection of Recommended Order.* If either party does not agree to the recommended order or any part thereof, the administrative hearing officer shall immediately request a judicial hearing to resolve the contested matter. The administrative hearing officer shall record the date, time and place of such judicial hearing on a notice which shall be presented to the parties at the conclusion of the hearing. Notice shall be sent to nonappearing parties by regular mail. The administrative hearing officer shall transmit to a judge a written statement indicating those issues to which the parties agree and disagree, all documentary evidence and all schedules presented at the expedited child support hearing.

(d) *Administrative Hearing Officer May Not Testify.* An administrative hearing officer may not be called or compelled to testify as to what transpired before the administrative hearing officer with respect to contested matters.

(Adopted 4-1-92, eff. immediately.)

COMMITTEE COMMENTS

Rule 100.10 sets forth the procedure for submission of recommendations to a judge upon acceptance of a recommended order by both parties, and the presentation of the recommended order and of a written notice of the right to a judicial hearing to each party. The rule sets forth the procedure for scheduling a judicial hearing upon rejection of the recommended order by either party, notice to the parties of such hearing, and transmittal to the judge of a written statement indicating the issues to which the parties agree and those to which they disagree and of all documentary evidence presented at the expedited child support hearing.

Rule 100.11. Authority Retained by the Court.

(a) *Review Recommendations of Administrative Hearing Officers.* The judge shall review all recommended orders of an administrative hearing officer upon which parties agree and enter such orders as are appropriate as to all or part of the matters indicated on the recommended order.

(b) *Conduct Judicial Hearings.* The judge shall conduct judicial hearings on all prehearing motions the parties disagree with, the recommended order of the administrative hearing officer on any domestic relations matters other than uncontested child support and parentage matters, on objections to the entry of orders as provided for in Rule 100.6 and section 10 of the Act [750 ILCS 25/10], and on any other matters properly before the court.

(c) *Hear Contested Parentage Matters.* Only the judge may conduct trials in contested parentage cases.

(d) *Issue Special Orders.* Only the judge may issue body attachment orders, rules to show cause, or conduct contempt proceedings. The judge shall impose sanctions or relief in such cases as are appropriate.

(e) *Impose Sanctions.* Only the judge may impose sanctions pursuant to Supreme Court Rule 137.

(Adopted 4-1-92, eff. immediately.)

COMMITTEE COMMENTS

Rule 100.11 sets forth the judge's authority to review recommendations of administrative hearing officers, to conduct judicial hearings, to hear contested parentage actions, to issue special orders and to impose sanctions.

Rule 100.12. Judicial Hearings.

(a) *Recommended Orders Agreed Upon by the Parties.* The judge shall review the recommended orders of administrative hearing officers in a timely fashion. The judge (1) may enter an order consistent with the recommended order, (2) may reject all or part of the recommended order and refer the matter to the administrative hearing officer for further proceedings, or (3) may conduct judicial hearings as are necessary. The judge shall provide the administrative hearing officer with a copy of the entered order and may inform the administrative hearing officer if a recommended order was not accepted by the judge and the reasons for the changes or rejection. If the judge enters an order consistent with a recommended order, the effective date of the order shall be (1) the date on which the recommended order was signed by both parties, or (2) if the respondent party failed to appear and failed to file a timely objection to the recommended order pursuant to Rule 100.8(c), the date the recommended order was signed by the petitioning party. The order may specify the date payments of support are to begin, which may be different from the effective date of the order.

(b) *Recommended Orders Rejected by the Parties.* Upon receipt of a statement from the administrative hearing officer that the parties do not agree to all or part of a recommended order, the judge shall promptly conduct a judicial hearing to resolve any contested matters and shall enter an appropriate order.

(c) *Presentation of Order to the Parties.* The clerk of the circuit court shall mail a copy of all orders to the parties within five days of entry. If the parties are present in court at the time the order is entered, a copy shall be given to both parties in open court. If an order sets forth an amount for support, an immediate withholding order shall be specially certified and mailed to the obligee or his or her attorney for service.

(Adopted 4-1-92, eff. immediately.)

COMMITTEE COMMENTS

Rule 100.12 governs the procedure whereby a judge reviews recommended orders and enters judicial orders based thereon. The rule sets forth the conduct of further judicial hearings and the resolution of contested matters. The rule also provides for the presentation of orders to the parties.

Rule 100.13. Definitions.

For purposes of these rules, the following terms shall have the following meanings:

(a) "Act" shall mean the Expedited Child Support Act of 1990 [750 ILCS 25/1 et seq.].

(b) "Administrative hearing officer" shall mean the person employed by the chief judge of the circuit court of each circuit, county, multicounty area or multicircuit area establishing an expedited child support system for the purpose of hearing child support and parentage matters and recommending orders.

(c) "Expedited child support hearing" shall mean a hearing before an administrative hearing officer pursuant to the Act and these rules.

(d) "Plan" shall mean the plan submitted by the chief judge of a judicial circuit to the Supreme Court for the creation of an expedited child support system in such circuit pursuant to the Act and these rules.

(e) "System" shall mean the procedures and personnel created by the Act and these rules for the expedited establishment, modification, and enforcement of child support orders, and for the expedited establishment of parentage.

(f) "IV-D program" shall mean the Child Support Enforcement Program established pursuant to Title IV, Part D, of the Social Security Act (42 U.S.C. § 651 *et seq.*) as administered by the Illinois Department of Public Aid.

(Adopted 4-1-92, eff. immediately.)

COMMITTEE COMMENTS

Rule 100.13 defines certain terms, in accordance with the Expedited Child Support Act, as used throughout the Expedited Child Support Rules.

ARTICLE II

RULES ON CIVIL PROCEEDINGS IN THE TRIAL COURT

Part A

Process and Notice

Rule 101. Summons and Original Process — Form and Issuance.

(a) *General.* The summons shall be issued under the seal of the court, tested in the name of the clerk, and signed with his name. It shall be dated on the date it is issued, shall be directed to each defendant, and shall bear the address and telephone number of the plaintiff or his attorney, and if service or notices of motions or filings by facsimile transmission will be accepted, the telephone number of the facsimile machine of the plaintiff or his attorney.

(b) *Summons Requiring Appearance on Specified Day.*

(1) In an action for money not in excess of $50,000, exclusive of interest and costs, or in any action subject to mandatory arbitration where local rule prescribes a specific date for appearance, the summons shall require each defendant to appear on a day specified in the summons not less than 21 or more than 40 days after the issuance of the summons (see Rule 181(b)), and shall be in substantially the following form:

"In the Circuit Court of the ____________ Judicial Circuit, ____________ County, Illinois.

(Or, In the Circuit Court of Cook County, Illinois.)

"A.B., C.D., etc. (naming all plaintiffs) Plaintiffs v. "H.J., K.L., etc. (naming all defendants) Defendants	No. ____ Amount Claimed____

"SUMMONS

"To each defendant:

"You are hereby summoned and required to appear before this court at ____ at ____ o'clock ____M., on ____19____, to answer the complaint in this case, a copy of which is hereto attached. If you fail to do so, a judgment by default may be entered against you for the relief asked in the complaint.

"To the officer:

"This summons must be returned by the officer or other person to whom it was given for service, with indorsement of service and fees, if any, immediately after service and not less than three days before the day for appearance. If service cannot be made, this summons shall be returned so indorsed.

"This summons may not be served later than 3 days before the day for appearance.

Witness ____________, 19____

"(Seal of Court) ____________________

Clerk of Court

"Plaintiff's Attorney (or plaintiff, if he is not represented by attorney)

____

"Address ____________________

"Telephone No. ____________
Facsimile Telephone No.
____
(If service by facsimile transmission will be accepted, the telephone number of the plaintiff or plaintiff's attorney's facsimile machine is additionally required.)

"Date of service ____, 19____ (to be inserted by officer on copy left with defendant or other person).

"NOTICE TO DEFENDANTS

"(Here simple and specific instructions, conforming to local practice, shall be set out outlining procedure for appearance and trial of the type of case covered by the summons.)"

(2) In any action for forcible detainer or for recovery of possession of tangible personal property, the summons shall be in the same form, but shall require each defendant to appear on a day specified in the summons not less than seven or more than 40 days after the issuance of summons.

(3) If service is to be made under section 2-208 of the Code of Civil Procedure [735 ILCS 5/2-208] the return day shall be not less than 40 days or more than 60 days after the issuance of summons, and no default shall be taken until the expiration of 30 days after service.

(c) *Summons in Certain Other Cases in Which Specific Date for Appearance Is Required.* In all proceedings in which the form of process is not otherwise prescribed and in which a specific date for appearance is required by statute or by rules of court, the form of summons shall conform as nearly as may be to the form set forth in paragraph (b) hereof.

(d) *Summons Requiring Appearance Within 30 Days After Service.* In all other cases the summons shall require each defendant to file his answer or otherwise file his appearance within 30 days after service, exclusive of the day of service (see Rule 181(a)), and shall be in substantially the following form:

"In the Circuit Court of the ____ Judicial Circuit, ____ County, Illinois.

(Or, In the Circuit Court of Cook County, Illinois.)

"A.B., C.D., etc. (naming all plaintiffs) Plaintiffs v. "H.J., K.L., etc. (naming all defendants) Defendants	}	No. ____________

"SUMMONS

"To each defendant:

"You are summoned and required to file an answer to the complaint in this case, a copy of which is hereto attached, or otherwise file your appearance, in the office of the clerk of this court within 30 days after service of this summons, not counting the day of service. If you fail to do so, a judgment by default may be entered against you for the relief asked in the complaint.

"To the officer:

"This summons must be returned by the officer or other person to whom it was given for service, with indorsement of service and fees, if any, immediately after service. If service cannot be made, this summons shall be returned so indorsed.

"This summons may not be served later than 30 days after its date.

Witness ____________, 19____

"(Seal of Court) ____________________
Clerk of Court

"Plaintiff's Attorney (or plaintiff, if he is not represented by attorney)
____
"Address ____________________
"Telephone No. ____________________
"Facsimile Telephone No. ____________
(If service by facsimile transmission will be accepted, the telephone number of the plaintiff or plaintiff's attorney's facsimile machine is additionally required.)

"Date of service ____, 19____ (to be inserted by officer on copy left with defendant or other person)."

(e) *Summons in Cases under the Illinois Marriage and Dissolution of Marriage Act.* In all proceedings under the Illinois Marriage and Dissolution of Marriage Act, the summons shall include a notice on its reverse side referring to a dissolution action stay being in effect on service of summons, and shall state that any person who fails to obey a dissolution action stay may be subject to punishment for contempt, and shall include language:

(1) restraining both parties from physically abusing, harassing, intimidating, striking, or interfering with the personal liberty of the other party or the minor children of either party; and

(2) restraining both parties from removing any minor child of either party from the State of Illinois or from concealing any such child from the other party, without the consent of the other party or an order of the court.

(f) *Use of Wrong Form of Summons.* The use of the wrong form of summons shall not affect the jurisdiction of the court.

(Amended, eff. 8-3-70, 7-1-71, and 9-1-74; amended 5-28-82, eff. 7-1-82; amended 10-30-92, eff. 11-15-92; amended, eff. 1-20-93; amended 12-30-93, eff. 1-1-94; amended, eff. 2-1-96.)

COMMITTEE COMMENTS

(Revised September 1, 1974)

As adopted in 1967, Rule 101 was derived from former Rule 2, with changes in paragraph (b). Paragraph (b) was inserted in former Rule 2, effective January 1, 1964, to provide, for relatively small cases, the form of summons that had been in use in the Municipal Court of Chicago prior to that date. In cases up to $10,000.00, the time was changed to not less than 21 or more than 40 days. Effective August 3, 1970, the $10,000.00 limit was changed to $15,000.00. The appearance day in small claims is covered by Rule 283.

The appearance day in forcible entry and detainer cases was left at not less than seven or more than 40 days. To conform the practice to the requirements of notice in actions seeking restoration of property wrongfully detained, set forth by the Supreme Court of the United States in Fuentes v. Shevin (1972), 407 U.S. 67, subparagraph (b)(2) of the rule was amended in 1974 to provide for a summons in such cases returnable on a day specified in the summons, not less than seven or more than 40 days from issuance, as in forcible entry and detainer cases. Under the rule as amended, independent of the statutory remedy of replevin, a party seeking return of personal property may proceed in an action in the nature of an action in detinue at common law, and serve process in the manner provided.

Subparagraph (b)(3), added to former Rule 2 in 1964 and carried forward into Rule 101 in 1967, set 40 days as the return day on service made under section 16 of the Civil Practice Act [735 ILCS 5/2-208]. Effective July 1, 1971, this provision was amended to substitute for "40 days" the somewhat more flexible provision "not less than 40 days or more than 60 days."

The provision of paragraph (b) of this rule permitting specific instructions under the heading "Notice to Defendant" has probably not been adequately implemented by the judges of the trial courts. It is the Committee's view that the summons should give as much specific information to the defendant as possible. For instance, the particular court room number and place of holding court ought to be given. Instructions regarding the method of entering an appearance and a statement whether an answer must be filed with the appearance, or the date for filing an answer after an appearance, can be stated in the "Notice to Defendant." Rule 181, relating to appearance, expressly recognizes that the "Notice to Defendant" under Rule 101(b) is controlling.

In 1974, paragraph (d) was amended to insert in the specimen summons reference to the fact that a copy of the complaint is attached, thus conforming the language of the summons under paragraph (d) in this respect to the language in the summons under paragraph (b).

CASE NOTES

ANALYSIS

Effect on Jurisdiction
—In General
Failure to Issue
Fees
Invalid Summons
—Effect
—Shown
Local Rules
Purpose
Requirements
—Seal
—Time for Default
Return Day
—Factual Knowledge Sufficient
—Prejudice
Service
—Ministerial Act
—Sunday Service
Sufficient Notice
Timeliness
Waiver
—Filing
Wrong Form
—Incomplete
—Name of Party
—Notice Sufficient
—Substantial Compliance

Effect on Jurisdiction

—In General

Proper service of summons is a necessary prerequisite for in personam jurisdiction, absent a defendant's general appearance before the court; if a defendant has not been served properly and has not appeared to defend the cause, an order entered against her in the proceeding is void ab initio regardless of whether she had actual knowledge of the proceeding. Charter Bank & Trust v. Novak, 218 Ill. App. 3d 548, 161 Ill. Dec. 271, 578 N.E.2d 629 (2 Dist. 1991).

Failure to Issue

Where no summons was ever issued for any individual defendant, there was never any waiver of the issuance of summons, there was no entry of appearance for any individual defendant, except special appearance for the sole purpose of questioning the jurisdiction of the court, the clerk did not sign the summons, and there was not any direction for the summoning of any person except the attorney in fact, the trial court was without jurisdiction to enter default judgments against the defendants. Ohio Millers Mut. Ins. Co. v. Inter-Insurance Exch., 367 Ill. 44, 10 N.E.2d 393 (1937).

Fees

The circuit court does not have authority to fix a fee for a private process server and tax that fee as costs. Creditors Disct. & Audit, Inc. v. Zook, 130 Ill. App. 3d 402, 85 Ill. Dec. 689, 474 N.E.2d 417 (4 Dist. 1985).

Invalid Summons

—Effect

A judgment rendered after service of an invalid summons is void. Schorsch v. Fireside Chrysler-Plymouth, Mazda, Inc., 172 Ill. App. 3d 993, 123 Ill. Dec. 230, 527 N.E.2d 693 (2 Dist.), appeal denied, 123 Ill. 2d 567, 128 Ill. Dec. 900, 535 N.E.2d 411 (1988).

—Shown

A summons prepared by plaintiff's attorney, which was neither issued by the clerk nor signed or dated by the clerk, and was sent by plaintiff's attorney directly to the sheriff's office, was not a summons issued in conformance with subsection (a) of 735 ILCS 5/2-201 and subsection (a) of this Rule and was therefore invalid. Schorsch v. Fireside Chrysler-Plymouth, Mazda, Inc., 172 Ill. App. 3d 993, 123 Ill. Dec. 230, 527 N.E.2d 693 (2 Dist.), appeal denied, 123 Ill. 2d 567, 128 Ill. Dec. 900, 535 N.E.2d 411 (1988).

Local Rules

Local county rule additional two-day requirement for service imposed a greater burden on plaintiffs than that required by this Rule and promoted inconsistency in the State concerning the time frame for proper service, violating Rules 21(a), Supreme Court Rules, and the local rule was therefore invalid. Phalen v. Groeteke, 293 Ill. App. 3d 469, 228 Ill. Dec. 95, 688 N.E.2d 793 (3 Dist. 1997).

Purpose

The objectives of service of process are to notify the defendant of pending litigation and enable him to appear and defend, and to vest jurisdiction in the trying court. Charter Bank & Trust v. Novak, 218 Ill. App. 3d 548, 161 Ill. Dec. 271, 578 N.E.2d 629 (2 Dist. 1991).

Requirements

—Seal

Under former similar provision, all process had to be sealed with the seal of the court, and an execution not under the seal of the court was void; an execution which was void for such reason could not be amended after sale of land was complete. Weaver v. Peasley & Co., 163 Ill. 251, 45 N.E. 119 (1896).

—Time for Default

Where summons issued to defendant designated the time for default, the summons complied with subsection (b). Piasa Motor Fuels, Inc. v. Department of Revenue, 138 Ill. App. 3d 422, 93 Ill. Dec. 278, 486 N.E.2d 379 (5 Dist. 1985).

Return Day

—Factual Knowledge Sufficient

Where summons for two cases were issued on the respective

Return Day (Cont'd)

—Factual Knowledge Sufficient (Cont'd)
dates the cases were filed, both summons were returnable, both summons were served, but the sheriff did not return the same until the date of return, and the cases were continued for a week, when the defendants did not appear, then, although subsection (b) of this Rule provides for a return date in an unduly short period of time, factually the knowledge of the default judgment was a matter easily ascertainable by defense counsel, thus, defendants were properly served. Brown-Strauss Corp. v. Larson, 22 Ill. App. 3d 905, 317 N.E.2d 303 (2 Dist. 1974).

—Prejudice
Where summons was issued with a return day ten days later, and a defendant was actually served before the return day, the defendant could not claim prejudice because she was served four days prior to the day of appearance; if she had been prejudiced she should have appeared specially to quash the summons. City of Chicago v. Cicero, 133 Ill. App. 2d 446, 273 N.E.2d 529 (1 Dist. 1971).

Service

—Ministerial Act
Service of summons is a ministerial act and not a judicial act. Pedersen v. Logan Square State & Sav. Bank, 377 Ill. 408, 36 N.E.2d 732 (1941).

—Sunday Service
No exception was made to prohibit a summons in a civil case from being served on a Sunday under former Ill.Rev.Stat., ch. 110, para. 259.4 (see now this Rule); it was presumed that the legislature and courts were aware of the distinction between what constituted judicial acts, which could not be performed on Sunday, and ministerial acts, which could be performed on Sunday, per former Ill.Rev.Stat., ch. 38, para. 549, (repealed). The language of the former Civil Practice Act (see now 735 ILCS 5/1-101 et seq.), and the Rule adopted in pursuance thereof, cannot have read into them an exception not contained in the statute and not recognized at common law. Pedersen v. Logan Square State & Sav. Bank, 377 Ill. 408, 36 N.E.2d 732 (1941).

Sufficient Notice
Summons that the public housing authority served on the tenant did not comply with Ill. Sup. Ct. R. 101 which required that a summons contain a "NOTICE TO DEFENDANTS," setting out simple and specific instructions outlining the procedure for an appearance, and, thus, the trial court should have exercised its discretion and vacated the default judgment entered against the tenant in the public housing authority's forcible entry and detainer action. Rockford Hous. Auth. v. Donahue, 337 Ill. App. 3d 571, 271 Ill. Dec. 969, 786 N.E.2d 227, 2003 Ill. App. LEXIS 269 (2 Dist. 2003).

Timeliness
Where there was unexplained failure to obtain service on a party until months after the statute of limitations had run, it could hardly have been reasonable diligence to obtain service, so the court had authority to dismiss. Kohlhaas v. Morse, 36 Ill. App. 2d 158, 183 N.E.2d 16 (4 Dist. 1962).

If a plaintiff files a complaint near the end of the statutory time limit and then delays service of summons for an indefinite period, the time limit which was adopted as protection to the defendant against stale claims, is virtually nullified, thus frustrating the intent of this Rule. Kohlhaas v. Morse, 36 Ill. App. 2d 158, 183 N.E.2d 16 (4 Dist. 1962).

Waiver

—Filing
By filing a general appearance, the defendant waived all objections she may have had to jurisdiction. City of Chicago v. Cicero, 133 Ill. App. 2d 446, 273 N.E.2d 529 (1 Dist. 1971).

Wrong Form

—Incomplete
The use of a form without complete date and time information was no barrier to personal jurisdiction over the defendant. Charter Bank & Trust v. Novak, 218 Ill. App. 3d 548, 161 Ill. Dec. 271, 578 N.E.2d 629 (2 Dist. 1991).

—Name of Party
A summons which does not name a party on its face nor notify that party to appear is no summons at all, insofar as the unnamed person is concerned; when a defendant is not properly served, any order entered against that defendant is void ab initio, regardless of whether he had knowledge of the proceedings. Theodorakakis v. Kogut, 194 Ill. App. 3d 586, 141 Ill. Dec. 268, 551 N.E.2d 261 (1 Dist. 1990).

Where a summons named trust number 44289, while the proper trust number was 4289, the trial court was correct in finding that the summons did not bear the name of the defendant trust, and accordingly, the summons was invalid, even though the complaint which was attached to the summons designated the correct trust number. Theodorakakis v. Kogut, 194 Ill. App. 3d 586, 141 Ill. Dec. 268, 551 N.E.2d 261 (1 Dist. 1990).

—Notice Sufficient
Where a defendant was informed by the summons that she had been named in an identified pending litigation, pursuant to the summons' information, she called the clerk of the court and learned the date, time, and courtroom where she should appear, and according to her affidavit, on the correct date for the first hearing the defendant came both to the correct courtroom and to the court clerk's office, then the absence of the date, time, and courtroom number on her summons was not a sufficient basis to quash the summons; the summons fulfilled its objective of notifying the defendant of pending litigation so that she was enabled to appear and defend. Charter Bank & Trust v. Novak, 218 Ill. App. 3d 548, 161 Ill. Dec. 271, 578 N.E.2d 629 (2 Dist. 1991).

—Substantial Compliance
Under section 3-103 of the Administrative Review Law (735 ILCS 5/3-103), the form of the summons is to be according to the Supreme Court Rules, and as such, a use of the wrong form of summons will not defeat the jurisdiction of the court per subsection (e) of this Rule; since plaintiffs substantially complied with Rule 291, Supreme Court Rules, proceedings under the Administrative Review Law (735 ILCS 5/3-101 et seq.), the error of a third party, not in control of the aggrieved party, was not permitted to defeat that party's right to administrative review, especially where the aggrieved party acted with due diligence. Wilson v. Regional Bd. of Sch. Trustees, 179 Ill. App. 3d 485, 128 Ill. Dec. 508, 534 N.E.2d 690 (5 Dist. 1989).

Part J
Miscellaneous

Rule 296. Enforcement of Order for Support.

(a) *Scope of Rule.* This rule applies to any proceeding in which a temporary, final, or modified order of support is entered as provided by law. No provision of this rule affects the enforcement provisions of Section 706.1 of the Marriage and Dissolution of Marriage Act (Ill.Rev.Stat. 1987, ch. 40, para. 706.1) [750 ILCS 5/706.1].

(b) *Definitions.* For the purposes of this rule:

(1) "Order for Support" means any order of the court which provides for the periodic payment of funds for the support of a child, maintenance of a spouse, or combination thereof, whether temporary, final, or modified;

(2) "Obligor" means the individual who owes a duty to make payments under an order for support;

(3) "Obligee" means the individual to whom a duty of support is owed or the individual's legal representative.

(4) "Payor" means any payor of income to an obligor.

(c) *Payments to the Clerk.* All payments required under all orders for support must be made to the clerk of the circuit court in the county in which the Order for Support was entered, or the clerk of the circuit court of any other county to which the payment obligation may be transferred, as provided by law. This requirement may not be waived by the court or parties.

(d) *Order for Support.* Whenever an order for support is to be entered or modified, the court, in addition to any other requirements of law, shall forthwith enter an Order for Support in quadruplicate, in substantially the form set forth in subparagraph (o). The prevailing party must complete the form Order and present it to the court for the judge's signature.

(e) *Notice of Financial Aid.* The parties and counsel in any proceeding involving support must advise the court at the time of entry or modification of the order whether either the obligor or obligee or their children are receiving a grant of financial aid or support services under Articles III through VII, or section 10-1, of the Illinois Public Aid Code, as amended (Ill.Rev.Stat. 1987, ch. 23, para. 3-1 et seq., or par. 10-1) [305 ILCS 5/3-1 et seq., 305 ILCS 5/7-1 et seq., or 305 ILCS 5/10-1], and the court must enter its findings of record.

(f) *Petition for Abatement.* Upon written petition of the obligor, and after due notice to obligee (and the Department of Public Aid, if the obligee is receiving public aid), and upon hearing by the court, the court may temporarily reduce or totally abate the payments of support subject to the understanding that those payments will continue to accrue as they come due, to be paid at a later time. The reduction or abatement may not exceed a period of six months except that, upon further written petition of the obligor, notice to the obligee, and hearing, the reduction or abatement may be continued for an additional period not to exceed six months.

(g) *Clerk's Fund, Records and Disbursements.* The clerks of the circuit courts receiving payments pursuant to orders for support under paragraph (c) of this rule shall maintain records of:

(1) all such monies received and disbursed, and

(2) any delinquencies on such payments as required by law and by administrative order of the Supreme Court of Illinois.

Such records are admissible as evidence of payments received and disbursed. After receiving a payment pursuant to an order for support, the clerk shall promptly deposit that payment and issue a check drawn on an account of the circuit clerk to the obligee or other person or agency entitled thereto under the terms of the Order for Support. All payments shall be disbursed within 7 days after receipt thereof by the clerk of the circuit court.

(h) *Method of Payment to the Clerk of the Circuit Court.* When local circuit court rules allow payment of Orders for Support by personal check and the obligor submits a personal check which is not honored by the institution upon which it is drawn, the clerk of the circuit court may direct that all future payments be made by certified check, money order, United States currency, or credit card (with statutory fee), unless otherwise ordered by the court, and the court may order obligor to pay $50 to defray the cost of processing the dishonored check, to be paid within a time period to be determined by the court. Notice of future nonacceptance of personal checks shall be sent by the clerk of the circuit court to the obligor or payor by regular mail at the obligor's or payor's last known mailing address. The clerk's proof of mailing shall be spread of record. If a personal check used in payment of an Order for Support is not honored at the institution upon which it is drawn, the clerk of the circuit court shall forthwith notify the State's Attorney of the county, the Attorney General, if that office has the duty of enforcing the Order for Support on which the check was written, or the attorney appointed pursuant to section (k) of this rule.

(i) *Clerk's Notice of Delinquency.* Whenever an obligor is 14 days delinquent in payments pursuant to an Order for Support, the clerk of the circuit court shall, within 72 hours thereof, transmit a notice of delinquency directed to the obligor at the obligor's last known mailing address, by regular U.S. mail, postage prepaid, specifying that the delinquency will be referred for enforcement unless the payments due and owing, together with all subsequently accruing payments, are paid within 7 days thereafter. The court may waive this notice requirement on a case by case basis, and direct that immediate enforcement commence against the obligor.

(j) *Referral for Enforcement.* If the delinquency and all subsequent accrued obligations are not paid within the time period as specified in paragraph (i) of this rule, the clerk of the circuit court shall promptly refer to the matter for enforcement by reporting the delinquency to the State's Attorney of the county, the Title IV-D enforcement attorney, or the attorney appointed by the court pursuant to paragraph (k) of this rule. The clerk of the circuit court shall complete, sign, and verify the petition for contempt and appropriate notices, under the supervision of the enforcement counsel, but is not required to provide investigative services unless otherwise required by local circuit court rules.

(k) *Enforcement Counsel.*

(1) Enforcement counsel for those receiving a grant of financial aid under Article IV of the Illinois Public Aid Code [305 ILCS 5/4-1 et seq.] and parties who apply and qualify for support services pursuant to section 10-1 of such Code [305 ILCS 5/10-1] shall be as designated by an agreement made between the State of Illinois and

United States Government under 42 U.S.C. Title IV, Part D.

(2) The State's Attorney of each county may prosecute any criminal contempt or civil contempt brought for the enforcement of Orders for Support if not in conflict with the agreement described above between the State of Illinois and the United States Government.

(3) When the Presiding Judge of the county or of the Domestic Relations Division receives a letter from the State's Attorney of the county declining enforcement of Orders for Support under this rule, the Presiding Judge shall appoint counsel, to be known as support enforcement counsel, on a contract basis. The fees and expenses of the support enforcement counsel shall be paid by the county. The court may assess attorneys' fees against an obligor found in contempt.

(4) If the counsel responsible for enforcement under the Illinois Department of Public Aid or the State's Attorney of a county does not commence enforcement within 30 days after referral by the clerk of the circuit court, the court shall refer the matter to the support enforcement counsel of the county for further proceedings.

(5) Representation by counsel under this rule shall be limited to enforcement of Orders for Support and shall not include matters of visitation, custody, or property.

(6) A person entitled to monies under an Order for Support may institute independent enforcement proceedings. However, if enforcement proceedings under paragraph (k) of this rule are pending, then independent enforcement proceedings may be brought only by leave of court.

(*l*) *Contempt Proceedings for Enforcement of Orders for Support.* A failure to comply with payment obligations under an Order for Support may be enforced by contempt in the following manner:

(1) *Petition for Adjudication of Contempt.* The proceeding shall be initiated by the filing of a petition for adjudication of contempt in an action where an order for support was entered or as otherwise provided by law. The petition shall be verified pursuant to section 1-109 of the Code of Civil Procedure, as amended (Ill.Rev.Stat. 1987, ch. 110, par. 1-109) [735 ILCS 5/1-109] and specify in both its caption and body whether the relief sought is for indirect criminal contempt, indirect civil contempt, or both. The petition shall identify the relevant terms of the order for support being enforced, the court, and date of its entry, the last payment made under its provisions, the delinquency, and an allegation that the respondent obligor's failure to comply with the provisions of the order of support constitutes wilful indirect civil contempt, indirect criminal contempt, or both. A petition for adjudication of indirect civil contempt and indirect criminal contempt shall be filed in the same cause of action out of which the contempt arose.

(2) *Notice of Hearing.* A petition for adjudication of civil contempt may be presented *ex parte* to the court which, if satisfied that *prima facie* evidence of civil contempt exists, may order the respondent to show cause why he should not be held in contempt, or may instead set the petition itself for hearing and order that notice be given to the respondent. Notice of hearing on a petition for indirect civil contempt may be served by regular mail, postage prepaid, to the respondent's last known mailing address, or by any method provided in Rule 105(b)(1) or (2) (Ill.Rev.Stat. 1987, ch. 110A, par. 105(b)(1)(2)), as the court may direct. Notice by personal service shall be served not less than 7 days prior to hearing, and notice by mail not less than 10 days prior to hearing. Upon petition for adjudication of indirect criminal contempt being presented to the court, the court shall set the matter for arraignment and order summons to issue for respondent.

(A) *Body Attachment.* If a respondent fails to appear after receiving notice, or if the petition for adjudication of contempt alleges facts to show that the respondent will not respond to a notice, will flee the jurisdiction of the court, or will attempt to conceal himself from service, the court may issue a body attachment on the respondent, addressed to all law enforcement officers in the state or, in proceedings for indirect criminal contempt, for the arrest of the respondent.

(B) *Bond.* The court may fix bond on the body attachment order or warrant of arrest, as the case may be.

(3) *Contempt Hearing.* If the petition prays that respondent be held in indirect criminal contempt, or both indirect criminal contempt and indirect civil contempt, the hearing shall be conducted according to the applicable rules of the criminal law. However, if the court at the time of respondent's first appearance notifies the respondent that, if found to be in indirect criminal contempt, he will not be incarcerated for more than 6 months, fined a sum up to $500, or both, then respondent will not be entitled to a trial by jury. At the contempt hearing, a certified copy of the records of the clerk of the circuit court shall be received in evidence to show the amounts paid to the clerk, the dates of such payments, and the dates and amounts of disbursals. In indirect civil contempt cases the respondent has the burden of proving that such failure to pay was not wilful and that he does not have the present means to comply with any purge order the court may impose. The burden of proof shall be by a preponderance of the evidence in a civil contempt proceeding and beyond a reasonable doubt in a criminal contempt proceeding. After hearing, the court may:

(A) find in favor of the respondent and dismiss the petition or discharge the rule, as the case may be;

(B) continue the hearing under such terms as the court deems appropriate, including an order to seek work, if unemployed;

(C) find in favor of the petitioner and impose sanctions specifically including, but not limited to, the following;

(i) a direction to seek employment, if unemployed, and to participate in job search, training and work programs as provided by law;

(ii) keep a detailed accounting of all income and expenditures and submit same to the court until further order;

(iii) impose a sentence of imprisonment or periodic imprisonment with an appropriate purge order;

(iv) assess a fine;

(v) assess attorney's fees and costs;

(vi) initiate immediate wage withholding; or

(vii) such other sanctions as the court deems appropriate.

(m) *Supervision by the Administrative Office of Illinois Courts.* The Administrative Office of the Illinois Courts shall exercise supervision over the operation of this rule and shall submit an annual report to the Supreme Court together with its recommendation for any modification or amendment thereto. Oversight shall include, but not be limited to, promulgation of forms necessary to carry out the intent and purpose of this rule, initiating administrative procedures and standards for the effective operation of the rule, providing liaison between the various agencies of state and federal government concerning enforcement of orders for support and between the various branches of state government, and such other duties as may be directed by the Supreme Court from time to time hereafter.

(n) *Effective Date.* The Supreme Court will authorize experimental sites to operate pursuant to this Rule, in counties in which both the Chief Circuit Judge and the clerk of the circuit court have agreed to undertake the experimental use of the procedures contained herein, and have jointly sought the Court's permission to do so, by filing a petition with the Administrative Director.

(o) *Order for Support Form.* The Order for Support shall be in substantially the following form:

ORDER FOR SUPPORT FORM

In The Circuit Court of the ________ Judicial Circuit

________________ County, Illinois

In Re the Marriage of

Petitioner

and

Respondent

CASE NO. ________________

SUPPORT ACCOUNT NO.

____

File Stamp Here

UNIFORM ORDER FOR SUPPORT

IT IS HEREBY ORDERED that the Obligor make support payments in the gross sum of $ ____________ commencing on ______________ and a like sum payable [ ] weekly, [ ] bi-weekly, [ ] monthly, [ ] semi-monthly, or [ ] annually thereafter until further order of the court and transmit such payments to the clerk of the circuit court at the following address:

The clerk of the circuit court is directed to deposit all payments received and forward payment to the Obligee or Agency within 7 days.

*Note: If an Order of Protection prohibits disclosure of the address and telephone number of an Obligee, the information must be kept separate from the Order for Support.

OBLIGOR

FIRST NAME	M.I.	LAST NAME		
RESIDENCE	APT. NO.	CITY	STATE	ZIP
BIRTHDATE	SOCIAL SECURITY #	HOME TELEPHONE NUMBER	DRIVER'S LICENSE NUMBER	
PLACE OF EMPLOYMENT (PAYOR)	ADDRESS		PHONE NUMBER	

OBLIGEE

FIRST NAME*	M.I.	LAST NAME		
RESIDENCE	APT. NO.	CITY	STATE	ZIP
BIRTHDATE	SOCIAL SECURITY #	HOME TELEPHONE NUMBER		
PLACE OF EMPLOYMENT	ADDRESS		PHONE NUMBER	

PAYMENT

COMPLETE THIS SECTION ONLY IF PAYMENTS ARE TO BE MADE TO A PARTY OTHER THAN THE OBLIGEE

NAME			
ADDRESS	CITY	STATE	ZIP
IDENTIFICATION NO. (If Any)			

ENFORCEMENT AUTHORITY

☐ Attorney General of Illinois ☐ Illinois Department of Public Aid

☐ State's Attorney ________________ County

☐ Private Attorney: ________________

☐ Other: ________________

____

Reviewed and approved as to form

____

Clerk's Support Division

DATE: ________________

Page 2 - Order for Support Form

Support Account Number: ______________ Case Number: ______________

DEFINITIONS: "FREQUENCY" "Weekly" means every week on the same day (52 or 53 times per year); "Bi-weekly" means every other week on the same day (26 times a year); "Semi-monthly" means two different days of the month 15 days apart (24 times a year); "Monthly" means once each month on the same day (12 times a year); "Annually" means once each year on the same date (1 time a year). "UNALLOCATED SUPPORT" means a total amount for maintenance and child support and not a specific amount for either item. "OBLIGOR" means the party who has the obligation to pay the support or maintenance. "OBLIGEE" means the party who receives the support or maintenance. "PAYOR" means the employer (or bank, trust, etc.) of the Obligor who pays a salary or other monies to the Obligor.

			Amount	Start Date	End Date
☐ UNALLOCATED SUPPORT Whether support is allocated or unallocated, you must complete the shaded areas			Amount	Start Date	End Date
CHILDREN	First Name	Birth Date	Amount	Start Date	End Date
	First Name	Birth Date	Amount	Start Date	End Date
	First Name	Birth Date	Amount	Start Date	End Date
	First Name	Birth Date	Amount	Start Date	End Date
	First Name	Birth Date	Amount	Start Date	End Date

It is further ordered that the Obligor shall:

1) Obey this Order for Support until further order of the court or until modified in writing by the court;

2) Make all payments in the amounts and at the times specified herein;

3) Make all payments to the clerk of the circuit court at the address noted herein. Payments made to any other person may be regarded as a gift and not credited against the amounts due under the Order for Support;

4) Pay the clerk of the circuit court by certified check, personal check, money order, United States currency, or credit card (with statutory fee), unless otherwise ordered by the court. U.S. currency should not be sent through the mail.

5) Notify the clerk of the circuit court in writing of any change of name, address, employment status or daytime telephone number within 2 weeks of such change.

FAILURE TO OBEY ANY OF THE PROVISIONS OF THIS ORDER FOR SUPPORT, OR MAKING A PAYMENT BY PERSONAL CHECK WHICH IS NOT HONORED BY THE INSTITUTION ON WHICH IT IS WRITTEN, MAY SUBJECT OBLIGOR TO CONTEMPT OF COURT AND A POSSIBLE JAIL SENTENCE.

NOTICE TO OBLIGEE: You are directed to notify the circuit court in writing of any change of name or address within 2 weeks thereof.

NOTICE TO OBLIGOR: If there is a major change of conditions and you are unable to make a payment in the amount and time required, you may petition the court for modification of this order for support or you may petition the court for temporary abatement of the payments, setting forth the reasons in the petition. The petition will be set for hearing and you and the obligee will be given notice by mail. If the support payments are temporarily abated, the amount will continue to accrue and you will be required to repay those amounts at some future date.

ENTER: ______________ Date ______________ Judge

Clerk's Certificate of Mailing/Delivery

I, the clerk of the circuit court, certify that I: mailed a copy of this Order for Support to [ ] Obligor, [ ] Obligee [ ] Illinois Department of Public Aid by enclosing the same in an envelope addressed to said addressees with postage prepaid and deposited said envelope in a U.S. Postal Service Mail Box on the ______ (date) day of ______ (month), 19 ____ (year)

or I hand delivered a true copy to [ ] Obligor on the ______ day of ______, 19____.
and/or I delivered a true copy to [ ] Obligee on the ______ day of ______, 19____.

______________ Clerk

(Adopted 2-1-89, eff. immediately.)

COMMITTEE COMMENTS

Paragraph (a)

In addition to the Supreme Court's inherent rulemaking authority, section 802 of the Illinois Marriage and Dissolution of Marriage Act provides: "The Supreme Court and, subject to the Rules of the Supreme Court, the respective circuit courts, may adopt such rules as they deem necessary and expedient to carry out the provisions of this Act" (Ill.Rev.Stat. 1987, ch. 40, par. 802) [750 ILCS 5/802].

The Study Committee on Enforcement of Support Orders in its Reports of March 29, 1978, and the Ad Hoc Committee on Child Support Enforcement recommended that child support orders, maintenance orders, or a combination thereof, be included in any proposed Supreme Court rule.

This rule applies to any order of support entered pursuant to the Illinois Marriage and Dissolution of Marriage Act (Ill.Rev.Stat. 1987, ch. 40, para. 101 et seq.) [750 ILCS 5/101 et seq.], the Juvenile Court Act of 1987 (Ill.Rev.Stat. 1987, ch. 37, par. 806-9) [705 ILCS 405/1-1 et seq.], the Non-Support of Spouse and Children Act (Ill.Rev.Stat. 1987, ch. 40, para. 1101 et seq.) [750 ILCS 15/1 et seq.], the Illinois Domestic Violence Act of 1986 (Ill.Rev.Stat. 1987, ch. 40, par. 2311-1 et seq.) [750 ILCS 60/101 et seq.], the Revised Uniform Reciprocal Enforcement of Support Act (Ill.Rev.Stat. 1987, ch. 40, par. 1201 et seq.) [750 ILCS 20/1 et seq.], the Illinois Parentage Act of 1984 (Ill.Rev.Stat. 1987, ch. 40, par. 2501 et seq.) [750 ILCS 40/1 et seq.], the Illinois Public Aid Code (Ill.Rev.Stat. 1987, ch. 23, par. 1-1 et seq.) [350 ILCS 5/1-1 et seq.] and any other present or future acts involving the payment of child or spousal support.

Enforcement proceedings under section 706.1 of the Illinois Marriage and Dissolution of Marriage Act (Ill.Rev.Stat. 1987, ch. 40, par. 706.1) [750 ILCS 5/706.1] providing for immediate wage withholding may proceed in conjunction with this rule.

Paragraph (b)

These definitions were taken from section 706.1 of the Illinois Marriage and Dissolution of Marriage Act [750 ILCS 5/706.1]. The provisions of this rule are coordinated with existing law whenever possible. Any deviation from statutory or case law is noted in the commentary.

Paragraph (c)

Both the Study Committee on Enforcement of Child Support Orders and the Ad Hoc Committee on Child Support Enforcement rejected giving the court or parties discretion to make orders for support payable directly from the obligor to the obligee. If the purpose of this rule is to be achieved, mandatory and uniform procedures for payment of orders for support must be established and enforced.

Paragraph (d)

Presentation to the court by the prevailing party of a draft Order for Support is mandated so that the court's time will not be taken up collecting necessary data and filling in forms. Four copies are required so that the court, both parties, and the Department of Public Aid will have copies of the Order for Support. The draft Order for Support should be submitted promptly to the court after the hearing in which the issues of support are decided. The trial court must make a specific finding as to whether the obligee is receiving public aid. If, at the time of the entry of the original Order for Support or at any time thereafter, the obligee is placed on public aid, the Department of Public Aid is to have a copy of the order so that funds sent to the Department by the clerk of the circuit court may be properly credited. The individual counties are given discretion to decide whether they will accept payment by personal check as opposed to other forms of payment. The parties must notify the clerk of the circuit court of any change of address or other circumstances that may affect the administration of the Order for Support. This requirement of notification is in conformance with section 706.1(b) of the Illinois Marriage and Dissolution of Marriage Act [750 ILCS 5/706.1].

Paragraph (e)

It is the duty of the parties and counsel to advise the court if the obligee or child[ren] is receiving public aid at the time an Order for Support is either originally entered or modified. The court must enter its finding of record, and if the parties do not bring this issue before the court, the court must inquire.

Paragraph (f)

This paragraph applies only to the short-term inability of the obligor to pay support due to a temporary layoff from employment or other factors. It recognizes that obligors often become temporarily unemployed, rendering them unable to meet their support obligations. This provision is short of a written modification of the Order for Support. It allows the obligor to petition the court, prior to the filing of a petition for adjudication of contempt, for an opportunity to repay those amounts in small increments after employment is regained.

This rule is contrary to the holding of the appellate court in *Coons v. Wilder* (1981), 93 Ill. App. 3d 127, in which the court stated, "We find no statutory or case authority for the trial court to temporarily abate that portion of a support order the supporting parent is without means to presently pay ***." 93 Ill. App. 3d at 135.

The obligor has the option of filing for a modification of the Order for Support under section 510 of the Illinois Marriage and Dissolution of Marriage Act (Ill. Rev. Stat. 1987, ch. 40, par. 510) [750 ILCS 5/510]. If a court may modify an Order for Support under section 510 of the Act, it follows that it may also temporarily abate the Order for Support, subject to accrual, during a period of temporary unemployment of the obligor.

Paragraph (g)

The purpose of this paragraph is to make clear that under no circumstances may the clerk of the circuit court merely endorse over the check and mail it to the obligee. The clerk's doing so would create a serious recordkeeping problem if the obligee returned the check because it was not honored by the institution upon which it was written. Each payment must be deposited in an account of the clerk of the circuit court, who must then write a check and mail it to the obligee or agency within seven days of receipt.

The records of the clerk of the circuit court are admissible as evidence of payments received and disbursements made under Orders for Support. The clerk of the circuit court is also expected to maintain a record of the address to which each check is disbursed.

Paragraph (h)

Local court rules shall determine whether the clerk may accept personal checks in payment of Orders for Support. If the obligor or payor gives a personal check which is not honored by the institution upon which it is written, it is expected that prompt action will be taken by the office responsible for enforcing an Order for Support either through the filing of a criminal information or a contempt petition. This paragraph authorizes a $50 assessment against the obligor or payor for transmitting a check which is not honored by the institution upon which it is written.

Section 27.3b of "An Act to revise the law in relation to clerks of courts" (Ill. Rev. Stat. 1987, ch. 25, par. 27.3b) [705 ILCS 105/27.3b] provides: "The clerk of court may accept payment of fines and costs by credit card from an offender who has been convicted of a traffic offense, petty offense or misdemeanor." The section also states that the clerk is entitled to a service fee equal to $3 or the amount charged to the clerk for use of its services by the credit card issuer, whichever is greater. If criminal defendants are entitled to use credit cards to pay fines and costs, there is no reason why obligors should not be entitled to the same opportunity under Orders for Support.

It should be noted that the clerk of the circuit court may need a "buffer fund" to cover any possible NSF checks until they may be collected.

Paragraph (i)

This paragraph provides that the clerk of the circuit court will automatically send notice to any obligor who is 14 days delinquent in his or her payments under the Order for Support. The obligor then has seven days to correct the delinquency prior to enforcement proceedings being commenced. The last known mailing address of the obligor is sufficient for adequate notice since the obligor has a duty under the Order for Support to maintain a current address with the clerk of the court. If the obligor is consistently delinquent in making payments under the Order for Support, as shown by the clerk's records, the court may waive the notice requirement and allow enforcement proceedings to commence *instanter*.

Paragraph (j)

This paragraph provides that an attorney must be involved in the enforcement proceedings. Federal law provides for the designation of counsel when enforcement is pursuant to Title IV-D of the Social Security Act (42 U.S.C. § 651 et seq. (1982)). The clerk of the circuit court may complete the petition for adjudication of contempt under the supervision of the enforcement attorney, but the clerk is not required to locate an obligor unless local rules so direct.

Paragraph (k)

Under Federal law, the designation of counsel for enforcement purposes for one receiving support services under Title IV-D is pursuant to an agreement between the Illinois Department of Public Aid and the Federal government. Currently, that agreement designates the Attorney General of Illinois or the State's Attorney of a county under contract with the Illinois Department of Public Aid. In some instances such representation has worked well and in others it has not. In counties with an aggressive enforcement program, an attorney is needed in the courtroom practically every day. In small counties where the Attorney General is the designated counsel, it is difficult, if not impossible, to have an assistant Attorney General in that county on a daily basis.

Since prosecutorial discretion allows a State's Attorney to decline prosecution (*Marcisz v. Marcisz* (1976), 65 Ill. 2d 206), the court must have some means to appoint counsel to represent the petitioner (who is the clerk of the circuit court) upon the filing of a petition for adjudication of contempt. The court must not be forced to be the inquisitor during a contempt proceeding.

If the State's Attorney does not wish to prosecute, then the county is expected to pay the costs and expenses of a contract counsel, subject to being reimbursed by the obligor. It is best for each county to negotiate the terms and conditions of such contract counsel.

An obligee may initiate an enforcement proceeding under this rule, but if contempt proceedings have already been commenced, such intervention may occur only by leave of court, with the exception of immediate wage withholding under section 706.1 of the Illinois Marriage and Dissolution of Marriage Act [750 ILCS 5/706.1].

There is no statutory provision for the appointment of counsel for indigent respondents charged with indirect civil contempt. A respondent charged with indirect criminal contempt has the right to court-appointed counsel.

Although there are some Federal decisions which indicate that an indigent respondent in a civil contempt proceeding is entitled to court-appointed counsel (*Walker v. McLain* (10th Cir. 1985), 768 F.2d 118; *Sevier v. Turner* (6th Cir. 1984), 742 F.2d 262; *Ridgeway v. Baker* (5th Cir. 1983), 720 F.2d 1409), there are no United States Supreme Court or Illinois reviewing court cases that have yet so held. "Fundamental fairness does not require that counsel be appointed for post-conviction petitions. (*Rodriquez v. United States* (1969), 395 U.S. 327, 23 L. Ed. 2d 340, 89 S. Ct. 1715; *Johnson v. Avery* (1969), 393 U.S. 483, 21 L. Ed. 2d 718, 89 S. Ct. 747.)" *People v. Porter* (1988), 122 Ill. 2d 64, 74-75.

The Public Defender Act provides that:

"The public defender, as directed by the court, shall act as attorney, without fee, before any court within any county for all persons who are held in custody or who are charged with the commission of any criminal offense, and who the court finds are unable to employ counsel." Ill. Rev. Stat. 1987, ch. 34, par. 5604.

The court has no authority to extend the duties of the public defender and cannot appoint the public defender in civil contempt cases. The chief judge of a circuit has no authority to enter an administrative order directing judges to appoint the public defender to represent indigent respondents in civil contempt cases, even though the respondent may be incarcerated for refusing to obey the court's order. See *Maloney v. Bower* (1986), 113 Ill. 2d 473.

Paragraph (*l*)

Designating the petition as a "Petition for Adjudication of Civil (or Criminal) Contempt" and requiring that the nature of the contempt be stated in both the caption and body of the petition assures that the respondent will be informed of the specific nature of the contempt charged against him. (*People v. Waldron* (1986), 114 Ill. 2d 295.) It also informs the court of the specific sanctions sought by the petitioner. Furthermore, in a criminal contempt action, a petition entitled "Petition for Adjudication of Indirect Criminal Contempt" is less likely to cause confusion than one entitled "Petition for Rule to Show Cause," since the respondent is not required to "show cause" at all; rather, it is the petitioner who must prove the criminal contempt beyond a reasonable doubt.

The petitioner may request a preliminary hearing prior to filing the petition to determine whether civil or criminal contempt is the more appropriate cause of action. *Kay v. Kay* (1974), 22 Ill. App. 3d 530; *People v. Marcisz* (1975), 32 Ill. App. 3d 467, *affirmed in part and reversed in part* (1976), 65 Ill. 2d 206.

Both the petition for adjudication of indirect criminal and civil contempt may be filed in the same case out of which the contempt arose.

Notice in a civil contempt proceeding need not be by personal service or restricted mailing. A proceeding for indirect civil contempt is considered part of the main cause of action, therefore additional personal service is not required. (See *Leman v. Krentler-Arnold Hinge Last Co.* (1932), 284 U.S. 448, 76 L. Ed. 389, 52 S. Ct. 238.) In the *Leman* case, petitioner instituted a civil contempt action for violation of an injunctive order. The notice on the rule to show cause was sent by regular U.S. mail to respondent in another State. A motion to dismiss due to lack of personal service was denied. "As the proceeding for civil contempt for violation of [an] injunction should be treated as a part of the main cause, it follows that service of process for the purpose of bringing the respondent within the jurisdiction of the [court] was not necessary. The respondent was already subject to the jurisdiction of the court for purpose of all proceedings that were part of the equity suit ***. *** In this view nothing more was required in the present case than appropriate notice of the contempt proceeding, and that notice the respondent received." 284 U.S. at 454-55, 76 L. Ed. at 395, 52 S. Ct. at 240-41.

It is noted that Circuit Court of Cook County Rule 6.1(a) and section 713 of the Illinois Marriage and Dissolution of Marriage Act [750 ILCS 5/713] require notice to the obligor to be by certified mail, delivery restricted to obligor, or by personal service on the obligor before a body attachment may issue.

If notice by certified mail with restricted delivery is required, many times the obligor will not accept delivery, well knowing what awaits him should he accept delivery. If personal service is required, it may delay the enforcement process by weeks or months. The obligor can, therefore, by his own actions delay or even stop the enforcement proceedings by evading process. If the obligor is finally served and again fails to appear pursuant to the notice, a body attachment may issue, but may again take a substantial amount of time before it is served.

In light of the *Leman* case, the fact that the obligor knows he is delinquent, that many times the obligor seeks to avoid personal service or restricted mailing of notice, and that it is the duty of the obligor to maintain an accurate address with the clerk of the court, personal service or restrictive mailing ought not be required prior to the issuance of a body attachment.

If a respondent is unemployed, the court may direct him to seek employment without necessarily finding him in contempt. The court, in *In re Marriage of Page* (1987), 162 Ill. App. 3d 515, held that the Illinois Marriage and Dissolution of Marriage Act [750 ILCS 5/101 et seq.] "clearly does not authorize the trial court to order a person to seek or find employment, except as may be permitted upon a finding of contempt and as a condition of probation if imposed pursuant to section 505(b)(1)." (162 Ill. App. 3d at 519.) The court now has this authority pursuant to new section 505.1 of the Illinois Marriage and Dissolution of Marriage Act (Pub. Act 85-1155, effective January 1, 1989).

Paragraph (m)

A specific governmental body should exercise administrative control over the operation of a rule that affects a vase number of cases heard each day throughout the State. The Administrative Office of the Illinois Courts is best able to perform this function and can easily operate as liaison between the various brances [sic] of State government and between the State and Federal governments.

Paragraph (n)

In those counties in which the chief judges and the clerks of the circuit courts agree to participate in an experimental installation, and petition the Administrative Office for leave to implement it at this time, the rule would allow the Supreme Court to authorize a county to operate under the new rule.

Paragraph (o)

The Order for Support should be in substantially the form contained in the rule. This form follows the general format of the rule contained in the Civil Procedures Manual published by the Administrative Office of the Illinois Courts.

CASE NOTES

ANALYSIS

Burden of Proof
Construction with Statutes
Counties Not Adopting Rule
Due Process
Petition for Abatement
Petition for Modification

Burden of Proof

When a trial court issues a rule to show cause, the burden shifts to the respondent to show cause why he should not be held in contempt. Hall v. Clark (In re Keon C.), 344 Ill. App. 3d 1137, 279 Ill. Dec. 674, 800 N.E.2d 1257, 2003 Ill. App. LEXIS 1498 (4 Dist. 2003), appeal denied sub nom. In re Keon C., 208 Ill. 2d 538, 284 Ill. Dec. 340, 809 N.E.2d 1286 (2004).

Construction with Statutes

This Rule does not authorize the court to ignore 750 ILCS 5/505 and 750 ILCS 5/510, but merely provides an additional tool for the the court to use in fairly resolving child-support disputes. In re Fink, 275 Ill. App. 3d 960, 212 Ill. Dec. 297, 656 N.E.2d 1131 (4 Dist. 1995).

Counties Not Adopting Rule

The existence of this Rule provides authority for a court in a county which has not adopted this Rule to abate support payments subject to accrual of the abated amount in appropriate circumstances, and a party seeking modification of a support obligation is not denied equal protection of the laws by virtue of the fact that he resides in a county which has adopted the Rule. In re Fink, 275 Ill. App. 3d 960, 212 Ill. Dec. 297, 656 N.E.2d 1131 (4 Dist. 1995).

Due Process

In an indirect civil contempt hearing, a respondent is only entitled to minimal due process, which consists of notice and an opportunity to be heard. Hall v. Clark (In re Keon C.), 344 Ill. App. 3d 1137, 279 Ill. Dec. 674, 800 N.E.2d 1257, 2003 Ill. App. LEXIS 1498 (4 Dist. 2003), appeal denied sub nom. In re Keon C., 208 Ill. 2d 538, 284 Ill. Dec. 340, 809 N.E.2d 1286 (2004).

Petition for Abatement

Although there was no statutory or case authority to temporarily abate a portion of a support order the supporting parent was without present means to pay, there are limits to that general rule; if a payor of child support sacrifices $10,000 of income this year in exchange for receiving $20,000 of income in future years, the court should not allow him to impose the burden of child support on the custodian based on his current sacrifice and ignore his future benefit (which may not be reachable for child support at the time it is received). The rejection of abatement is no longer applicable to situations which, by their very nature, are inherently temporary. In re Horn, 272 Ill. App. 3d 472, 209 Ill. Dec. 130, 650 N.E.2d 1103 (4 Dist. 1995).

Petition for Modification

A trial court could properly grant a temporary abatement of support, subject to accrual, even though the obligor sought only modification of the support obligation. In re Fink, 275 Ill. App. 3d 960, 212 Ill. Dec. 297, 656 N.E.2d 1131 (4 Dist. 1995).

ARTICLE VI

APPEALS IN CRIMINAL CASES, POST-CONVICTION CASES, AND JUVENILE COURT PROCEEDINGS

Rule 660. Appeals in Cases Arising under the Juvenile Court Act.

(a) *Delinquent Minors.* Appeals from final judgments in delinquent minor proceedings, except as otherwise specifically provided, shall be governed by the rules applicable to criminal cases.

(b) *Other Proceedings.* In all other proceedings under the Juvenile Court Act, appeals from final judgments shall be governed by the rules applicable to civil cases.

(c) *All Proceedings.* In all appeals filed from proceedings under the Juvenile Court Act, the minor(s) shall be identified by first name and last initial or by initials only. The preferred method is first name and last initial. The alternative method of initials only is to be used when, due to an unusual first name or spelling, the preferred method would create a substantial risk of revealing a minor's identity. The name(s) of the involved minor(s) shall not appear on any documents filed with the Appellate Court or any subsequent court.

(Adopted 9-8-75, eff. 10-1-75; amended 7-1-85, eff. 8-1-85; amended 10-1-01, eff. immediately.)

Note.

The Juvenile Court Act, referred to above, was repealed. See now the Juvenile Court Act of 1987, 705 ILCS 405/1-1 et seq.

COMMITTEE COMMENTS

Rule 660 was added in 1975 to clarify the procedure in appeals from determinations under the Juvenile Court Act [see now 705 ILCS 405/1-1]. It provides simply that appeals from determinations in delinquency proceedings are governed by the rules applicable to appeals in criminal cases, and all other appeals under the Act are governed by the rules governing appeals in civil cases.

Paragraph (b) was amended in 1985 to delete references to "minors in need of supervision," "neglected minors" and "dependent minors," because of various additions, deletions and changes in the labels which are now applied to minors who may be adjudicated wards in proceedings before the circuit court.

COMMITTEE COMMENTS TO 2001 AMENDMENTS

Paragraph (c) was added effective October 1, 2001, to help protect the identities of minors. The amendment requires that their first name and last initial, or their initials only, appear on documents filed with the Appellate Court or any subsequent court. The requirement covers the parties' briefs, motions, and other similar papers. The amendment does not require deletion of names from the trial court record in preparing the record on appeal, nor does it address the means by which the Appellate Court or a subsequent court maintains the confidentiality of documents appearing in the record.

CASE NOTES

ANALYSIS

Applicability
—Delinquency Proceedings
—Retroactive
Authority of Appellate Judge
—Failure to Appeal
Authority of Trial Judge
—Excusal
Construction
Delinquency Proceedings
—Appeal by State
—Procedural Rules
—Right of Review
—Waiver
Finality
Need of Supervision
—Appeals
Neglect Proceeding
—Appeal Untimely
—Civil Rules
New Trial
Relation to Other Law
—Interlocutory Order
Relation to Other Rules
—Admonishment
—Interlocutory Appeals
—Stays
—Withdrawal of Counsel
Wardship
—Adjudication
—Dispositional Order
—Grounds to Appeal
—Timeliness

Applicability

—Delinquency Proceedings

By the use of the term "rules", subsection (a) incorporates the other Supreme Court Rules into delinquency appeals. In re R.C.K., 285 Ill. App. 3d 310, 220 Ill. Dec. 951, 674 N.E.2d 494 (2 Dist. 1996).

—Retroactive

This Rule may be applied retroactively, as it clarifies rather than changes, the procedure in appeals from determinations under the former Juvenile Court Act (see now 705 ILCS 405/1-1 et seq.). People v. Kerwood, 44 Ill. App. 3d 1040, 3 Ill. Dec. 773, 359 N.E.2d 183 (1 Dist. 1976).

Authority of Appellate Judge

—Failure to Appeal

An appellate court lacks jurisdiction to consider alleged errors in the original conviction of a minor as a delinquent, when the minor defendant does not file a notice of appeal from the order placing him on probation. People v. Tucker, 45 Ill. App. 3d 728, 4 Ill. Dec. 115, 359 N.E.2d 1067 (3 Dist. 1976).

Authority of Trial Judge

—Excusal

A trial judge does not have the authority to excuse compliance with the filing requirements of the Supreme Court Rules governing appeals. People v. Smith, 80 Ill. App. 3d 380, 35 Ill. Dec. 635, 399 N.E.2d 701 (4 Dist. 1980).

Construction

Subsection (a), by the use of the term "rules" simply refers to the other Supreme Court Rules; thus, it does not incorporate wholesale the general rules of criminal practice or the Code of Criminal Procedure, including 725 ILCS 5/116-1(b). In re W.C., 167 Ill. 2d 307, 212 Ill. Dec. 563, 657 N.E.2d 908 (1995).

Delinquency Proceedings

—Appeal by State

The state has a right to appeal a trial court's order dismissing a delinquency petition. People v. R.L.K., 67 Ill. App. 3d 451, 23 Ill. Dec. 737, 384 N.E.2d 531 (4 Dist. 1978).

—Procedural Rules

The term "rules" as used in subsection (a) of this Rule means simply the "Supreme Court Rules" applicable to criminal appeals, not rules codified in the Code of Criminal Procedure (720 ILCS 5/1-1 et seq.) or general rules of criminal trial practice. People v. C.L., 180 Ill. App. 3d 173, 128 Ill. Dec. 725, 534 N.E.2d 1330 (1 Dist. 1989).

Delinquency proceedings are not fully criminal in nature, and rules of procedure designed for criminal cases are not necessarily applicable. People v. Hershberger, 132 Ill. App. 3d 332, 87 Ill. Dec. 479, 477 N.E.2d 80 (4 Dist. 1985).

—Right of Review

While the rules permit interlocutory appeals from certain orders, under the former Juvenile Court Act (see now 705 ILCS 405/1-1 et seq.), the minor's right of review of delinquency proceedings is otherwise limited to final judgments, in accordance with rules governing criminal cases. People v. A.M., 94 Ill. App. 3d 86, 49 Ill. Dec. 630, 418 N.E.2d 484 (2 Dist. 1981).

—Waiver

There is a split among the appellate districts regarding whether waiver applies to juvenile proceedings; the fourth district has held that waiver principles apply equally in juvenile cases and criminal cases and the first district has held that waiver does not apply to appeals from delinquency proceedings. In re W.C., 261 Ill. App. 3d 508, 199 Ill. Dec. 160, 633 N.E.2d 956 (1 Dist. 1994), aff'd, 167 Ill. 2d 307, 212 Ill. Dec. 563, 657 N.E.2d 908 (1995).

Waiver does apply to appeals from delinquency findings and defendant waived his challenge of waiver of Miranda rights by failing to include it in his post-trial motion. In re W.C., 261 Ill. App. 3d 508, 199 Ill. Dec. 160, 633 N.E.2d 956 (1 Dist. 1994), aff'd, 167 Ill. 2d 307, 212 Ill. Dec. 563, 657 N.E.2d 908 (1995).

An appeal from an adjudication of delinquency is indistinguishable from criminal convictions, with respect to the rule that if the respondent failed to raise an issue in the trial court, it was waived and could not be considered on appeal, except pursuant to the plain error doctrine. People v. T.D., 81 Ill. App. 3d 369, 36 Ill. Dec. 594, 401 N.E.2d 275 (2 Dist. 1980).

Finality

The court had jurisdiction over an appeal in which the respondent asserted that the trial court erred in releasing the respondent's juvenile court records to the owner of an apartment complex, which was engaged in a civil action arising from the respondent's murder of a five year old child in a vacant apartment at the complex, since no matters remained pending before the trial court at the time of the appeal. People v. J.R., 307 Ill. App. 3d 175, 240 Ill. Dec. 375, 717 N.E.2d 468 (1 Dist. 1999).

Need of Supervision

—Appeals

Appeals in proceedings in which a minor is found to be in need of supervision are governed by the rules applicable to civil cases. Accordingly such appeals must be filed within 30 days after entry of the final judgment from which the appeal is taken, and the failure to do so would ordinarily deprive the reviewing court of jurisdiction and would require dismissal of the appeal. People v. Charles S., 83 Ill. App. 3d 515, 39 Ill. Dec. 51, 404 N.E.2d 435 (1 Dist. 1980).

Neglect Proceeding

Trial court's order finding that parents were unfit but that it was not in the best interests of their children to terminate the parents' parental rights was not a final order because it did not fix the parties' rights or finally resolve the issue of whether the parents' parental rights should be terminated, and the appellate court's judgment dismissing the State's appeal because the trial court's order was not a final judgment was upheld by the state supreme court. People v. Tracy H. (In re A.H.), 207 Ill. 2d 590, 280 Ill. Dec. 290, 802 N.E.2d 215, 2003 Ill. LEXIS 2274 (2003).

—Appeal Untimely

The appellate court lacked jurisdiction over parents' appeal of adjudicatory and dispositional orders that was filed more than one

Neglect Proceeding (Cont'd)

—Appeal Untimely (Cont'd)
year beyond the limit set by Rule 303, Supreme Court Rules, and this Rule. In re C.S., 294 Ill. App. 3d 780, 229 Ill. Dec. 225, 691 N.E.2d 161 (4 Dist. 1998).

Where a neglect finding was entered against father at an adjudicatory hearing, and following the dispositional hearing, a final appealable order was entered which awarded child into the custody of the Illinois Department of Children and Family Services, but child's notice of appeal was not filed until the 30 day time period provided by subsection (a) of Rule 303, Supreme Court Rules, the failure of the child to file a timely notice of appeal deprived the appellate court of jurisdiction. People v. Wheat, 68 Ill. App. 3d 471, 25 Ill. Dec. 7, 386 N.E.2d 278 (1 Dist. 1979).

—Civil Rules
Child neglect proceedings are to be considered civil in nature and are governed by civil appellate rules. People v. Robinson, 69 Ill. App. 3d 565, 26 Ill. Dec. 93, 387 N.E.2d 923 (1 Dist. 1979).

New Trial
Neither the provisions of the Juvenile Court Act (705 ILCS 405/1-1 et seq.) nor subsection (a) incorporates within delinquency procedures the requirement of a motion for a new trial under 725 ILCS 5/116-1. In re W.C., 167 Ill. 2d 307, 212 Ill. Dec. 563, 657 N.E.2d 908 (1995).

Relation to Other Law

—Interlocutory Order
An order dismissing a petition filed under the former Juvenile Court Act (see now 705 ILCS 405/1-1 et seq.) and ordering the institution of criminal proceedings is interlocutory and not appealable. People v. Hershberger, 132 Ill. App. 3d 332, 87 Ill. Dec. 479, 477 N.E.2d 80 (4 Dist. 1985).

Relation to Other Rules

—Admonishment
Where a court failed to admonish minors pursuant to Rule 605(b), Supreme Court Rules, which is made applicable to appeals by juveniles by subsection (a) of this Rule, then such failure excuses the minors' failure to comply with Rule 604(d), Supreme Court Rules, and allows the appellate court to reach the merits of the appeal. People v. F.D., 89 Ill. App. 3d 223, 44 Ill. Dec. 834, 411 N.E.2d 1200 (2 Dist. 1980).

—Interlocutory Appeals
Rule 308, Supreme Court Rules, is not applicable to interlocutory appeals from orders entered in delinquency proceedings under the former Juvenile Court Act (see now 705 ILCS 405/1-1). People v. Hershberger, 132 Ill. App. 3d 332, 87 Ill. Dec. 479, 477 N.E.2d 80 (4 Dist. 1985).

—Stays
It was error for trial court and appellate court to deny the motion for bond pending appeal on the ground of lack of jurisdiction, after a finding of juvenile delinquency and commitment to a correctional facility, since there was no statutory provision or rule providing that Rule 609, Supreme Court Rules, stays, does not apply in juvenile delinquency cases. Pulido v. People, 69 Ill. 2d 393, 14 Ill. Dec. 543, 372 N.E.2d 822 (1978).

—Withdrawal of Counsel
Petitions for change of custody under former section 705-8(3) of the Juvenile Court Act (see now subsection (3) of 705 ILCS 405/5-30) or for termination of wardship under former section 705-11(2) (see now subsection (2) of 705 ILCS 405/5-34), related to all categories of minors covered by the Juvenile Court Act, and not just to those adjudged to be delinquent, and could not be analogized to ancillary criminal proceedings simply because these sections also were applicable to the change of custody or termination of wardship of a ward of the court who happened to have been a delinquent; therefore, the appellate court should have granted the state defender's motion to withdraw as counsel for the minor in the appellate court. Kirwan v. Karns, 119 Ill. 2d 431, 116 Ill. Dec. 573, 519 N.E.2d 465 (1988).

Wardship

—Adjudication
A mere adjudication of wardship is not a final appealable order. People v. Lee, 73 Ill. App. 3d 449, 29 Ill. Dec. 747, 392 N.E.2d 304 (1 Dist. 1979).

—Dispositional Order
An adjudication of wardship coupled with a dispositional order is appealable. People v. Charles S., 83 Ill. App. 3d 515, 39 Ill. Dec. 51, 404 N.E.2d 435 (1 Dist. 1980).

In juvenile cases, an adjudication of wardship is generally not a final appealable order, it is the dispositional order from which an appeal lies, where the dispositional order has not been entered within 90 days of the adjudication of wardship, an appeal may be taken from the adjudicatory order. People v. Smith, 80 Ill. App. 3d 380, 35 Ill. Dec. 635, 399 N.E.2d 701 (4 Dist. 1980).

—Grounds to Appeal
A dispositional order committing a minor is predicated upon an adjudication of wardship and is a final judgment from which an appeal may be taken under the Juvenile Court Act (see now 705 ILCS 405/1-1) et seq.; if the minor was committed by a court which did not have jurisdiction to do so because it did not explicitly adjudge him a ward of the court, then he may appeal from the judgment of commitment upon that ground. People v. Davis, 44 Ill. App. 3d 970, 3 Ill. Dec. 548, 358 N.E.2d 1233 (1 Dist. 1976).

—Timeliness
Where more than 90 days passed between the adjudication of wardship and the entry of a dispositional order, Rule 662, Supreme Court Rules was triggered, and the notice of appeal from the adjudicatory order had to have been filed within 30 days of the expiration of the 90 day period, i.e., within 30 days before the entry of the dispositional order. People v. Smith, 80 Ill. App. 3d 380, 35 Ill. Dec. 635, 399 N.E.2d 701 (4 Dist. 1980).

Where a respondent mother filed a notice of appeal 12 days after the finding of neglect and adjudication of wardship but substantially before the trial court was to consider a dispositional order, the respondent's filing of a notice of appeal was premature, and the appellate court had no jurisdiction to consider the matter. People v. Lee, 73 Ill. App. 3d 449, 29 Ill. Dec. 747, 392 N.E.2d 304 (1 Dist. 1979).

Rule 661. Appeals as Poor Persons by Minors Found to Be Delinquent.

Upon the filing of a notice of appeal in any proceeding in which a minor has been found to be delinquent, or in which probation or conditional discharge imposed in such a proceeding has been revoked, appointment of counsel and the provision of a transcript of the adjudicatory and dispositional hearings without cost to the minors shall be governed by Rule 607.

(Adopted eff. 5-29-68; amended 9-8-75, eff. 10-1-75.)

COMMITTEE COMMENTS

(October 1, 1975)

Prior to 1975, Rule 661 set forth the procedure for obtaining counsel and a free transcript of the proceedings below in cases in which an appeal is taken from a delinquency proceeding in the juvenile court. This procedure was the same as that provided in Rule 607 in the case of appeals from judgments in criminal cases. In 1975, Rule 660 was added, making the rules dealing with appeals in criminal cases generally applicable to delinquency proceedings. It was thus unnecessary to repeat the substance of Rule 607 in Rule 661. Because Rule 607, by its terms, applies only to appeals from certain types of criminal cases, it was necessary to retain Rule 661 to make it plain that Rule 607 applies.

Rule 662. Adjudication of Wardship and Revocation of Probation or Conditional Discharge.

(a) *Adjudication of Wardship.* An appeal may be taken to the Appellate Court from an adjudication of wardship in the event that an order of disposition has not been entered within 90 days of the adjudication of wardship.

(b) *Revocation of Probation or Conditional Discharge.* An appeal may be taken to the Appellate Court from an order revoking probation or conditional discharge in the event that an order of disposition has not been entered within 90 days from the revocation of probation or conditional discharge.

(c) *Procedure.* The notice of appeal in appeals under this rule shall be filed within 30 days after the expiration of the 90 days specified in this rule and not thereafter.

(Adopted 9-8-75, eff. 10-1-75.)

COMMITTEE COMMENTS

(October 1, 1975)

In juvenile court proceedings, there is a two-step procedure. First a hearing is held to adjudicate the subject juvenile a ward of the court; then there is a separate hearing resulting in a disposition. If the dispositional hearing and order follow closely the adjudicatory hearing and order, judicial efficiency dictates that an appeal should be taken after disposition. If there is a long delay in disposing of the case, however, Rule 662 provides that an appeal may be taken from the first order. The period set is 90 days to account for normal delay caused by administrative problems. After that period, if the dispositional hearing has not been held, the juvenile may appeal. In such a case he must file his notice of appeal within 30 days of the expiration of the period, and not after. Thus the 6 months' period for application for leave to appeal provided in Rule 605(c) has no application. For similar reasons, the same provisions are applied to appeals from orders revoking probation or conditional discharge in juvenile cases.

CASE NOTES

Analysis

Appeal
—Dismissal Prior to Adjudication
—Premature
—Timeliness
Applicability
—Neglect Proceedings
Authority of Trial Judge
—Excusal
Construction
Delinquency Proceedings
—Right to Review
Limitations Period
Normal Delay
Wardship
—Adjudication
—Dispositional Order
—Interlocutory Appeals

Appeal

—Dismissal Prior to Adjudication

Where the petition for adjudication of wardship was dismissed prior to the adjudication, Ill. Sup. Ct. R. 662 did not give the appellate court jurisdiction over the appeal from the dismissal, as Ill. Sup. Ct. R. 662 only applied where there was an adjudication, and no order of adjudication was entered in the instant case. People ex rel. Devine v. Tiara W. (In re Tiona W.), 341 Ill. App. 3d 615, 275 Ill. Dec. 625, 793 N.E.2d 105, 2003 Ill. App. LEXIS 781 (1 Dist. 2003).

—Premature

Since respondent did not contend there had been an adjudication of wardship, the 90 day period of this Rule had not run and therefore respondent's appeal pursuant to this Rule was premature. In re A.P., 285 Ill. App. 3d 897, 221 Ill. Dec. 565, 675 N.E.2d 989 (2 Dist. 1997).

—Timeliness

This Rule is properly invoked where parents contest a determination that their son was a minor in need of supervision and the adjudication of wardship; however, where respondent failed to comply with this Rule since 90 days had not elapsed since the adjudicatory order, than there was no delay in entering the order, the appellate court had no authority to review the case. In re J.M., 151 Ill. App. 3d 1037, 105 Ill. Dec. 161, 503 N.E.2d 1167 (2 Dist. 1987).

This Rule makes an adjudication of wardship in a delinquency proceeding appealable after 90 days if no order of disposition has been entered, but a notice of appeal filed prior to the entry of the order from which appeal is taken, is a nullity. In re Winks, 150 Ill. App. 3d 657, 103 Ill. Dec. 888, 502 N.E.2d 35 (4 Dist. 1986).

Where parents, but not their minor son, were contesting the adjudication of wardship and the determination that their son was a minor in need of supervision, and an order of disposition had not been entered within 90 days of the adjudication of wardship, the parents properly invoked this Rule to appeal to the Supreme Court. In re Polovchak, 97 Ill. 2d 212, 73 Ill. Dec. 398, 454 N.E.2d 258 (1983), cert. denied, 465 U.S. 1065, 104 S. Ct. 1413, 79 L. Ed. 2d 740 (1984).

Applicability

—Neglect Proceedings

The language of subsection (a) of this Rule, which generally states that an appeal may be taken after 90 days from an adjudication of wardship if no dispositional order is entered, does not exclude neglect proceedings from its purview, and the rule is designed to allow an appeal, if there is a long delay in disposing of the case. People v. Lee, 73 Ill. App. 3d 449, 29 Ill. Dec. 747, 392 N.E.2d 304 (1 Dist. 1979).

Authority of Trial Judge

—Excusal

A trial judge does not have the authority to excuse compliance with the filing requirements of the Supreme Court Rules governing appeals. People v. Smith, 80 Ill. App. 3d 380, 35 Ill. Dec. 635, 399 N.E.2d 701 (4 Dist. 1980).

Construction

Under 705 ILCS 405/5-22 there may be a substantial lapse between an adjudication of wardship and an order of disposition and therefore this Rule cannot be read to insert "adjudication of delinquency" for "adjudication of wardship". In re A.P., 285 Ill. App. 3d 897, 221 Ill. Dec. 565, 675 N.E.2d 989 (2 Dist. 1997).

Delinquency Proceedings

—Right to Review

While the rules permit interlocutory appeal from certain orders under the Juvenile Court Act (see now 705 ILCS 405/1-1 et seq.), the minor's right of review of delinquency proceedings is otherwise limited to final judgments, in accordance with rules governing criminal cases. People v. A.M., 94 Ill. App. 3d 86, 49 Ill. Dec. 630, 418 N.E.2d 484 (2 Dist. 1981).

Limitations Period

Even if the 90 day period of this Rule had started to run when respondent was found guilty, the period would have been tolled by the State's appeal of transfer order and/or stay of the proceedings in juvenile court. In re A.P., 285 Ill. App. 3d 897, 221 Ill. Dec. 565, 675 N.E.2d 989 (2 Dist. 1997).

Normal Delay

A normal delay caused by administrative problems refers to situations such as where the juvenile court has jurisdiction to enter

Normal Delay (Cont'd)
an order of disposition but does not do so because the court is waiting for information from an administrative agency; normal delay does not refer to an interlocutory appeal. In re A.P., 285 Ill. App. 3d 897, 221 Ill. Dec. 565, 675 N.E.2d 989 (2 Dist. 1997).

Wardship

—Adjudication
An adjudication of wardship is not a final order for purposes of appeal, although subsection (a) of this Rule allows an appeal from an adjudication of wardship in the event that an order of disposition has not been entered within 90 days of the adjudication of wardship. People v. Belton, 102 Ill. App. 3d 1005, 58 Ill. Dec. 31, 429 N.E.2d 1364 (1 Dist. 1981).

—Dispositional Order
In juvenile cases, an adjudication of wardship is generally not a final appealable order, it is the dispositional order from which an appeal lies, where the dispositional order has not been entered within 90 days of the adjudication of wardship, an appeal may be taken from the adjudicatory order. People v. Smith, 80 Ill. App. 3d 380, 35 Ill. Dec. 635, 399 N.E.2d 701 (4 Dist. 1980).

A dispositional order revoking probation and ordering commitment to the Department of Corrections is a final appealable order. People v. Shannon, 45 Ill. App. 3d 876, 4 Ill. Dec. 497, 360 N.E.2d 433 (1 Dist. 1977).

—Interlocutory Appeals
In view of the fact that a court's order finding neglect and adjudicating wardship was not a final order, a motion under former section 72 of chapter 110 (see now 735 ILCS 5/2-1401), was an improper vehicle to challenge it; however, as an interlocutory order may be vacated or modified at any time before final judgment, and as the trial court denied the motion on the merits, the appellate court could reach the merits of the denial of the motion, despite its label. People v. Belton, 102 Ill. App. 3d 1005, 58 Ill. Dec. 31, 429 N.E.2d 1364 (1 Dist. 1981).

Rule 663. Adoption — Appointment of a Guardian with Power to Consent.

(a) An appeal may be taken to the Appellate Court from an order of the court empowering the guardian of the person of a minor to consent to the adoption of such a minor.

(b) The caption on an appeal taken from an order of the court empowering the guardian of the person of a minor to consent to the adoption of such a minor shall not include the name of the minor. Rather, the minor shall be identified by first name and last initial or by initials only. The preferred method is by first name and last initial. The alternative method of initials only is to be used when, due to an unusual first name or spelling, the preferred method would create a substantial risk of revealing the minor's identity.
(Adopted 9-8-75, eff. 10-1-75; amended 10-1-01, eff. immediately.)

COMMITTEE COMMENTS

Rule 663, added in 1975, makes an order empowering a guardian of the person of a minor to consent to the minor's adoption appealable. See Rule 307(a)(6).

COMMITTEE COMMENTS TO 2001 AMENDMENTS

Paragraph (b) was added October 1, 2001, to help protect the identities of minors. The amendment requires that their first name and last initial, or their initials only, appear in the caption.

User's Guide to the Index

This index contains treatment of the laws compiled in the *Illinois Domestic Relations and Related Laws Annotated, 2005 Edition.* Statutory provisions from the Illinois Compiled Statutes Annotated are referred to in the index by section number (e.g., 750: 5/302).

The index is a combination of two approaches to indexing, topical and descriptive word. The topical approach follows the organization of the Code, and the descriptive word approach uses nonlegal terms and popular names to describe legal terminology. LexisNexis® undertakes this dual approach to ensure main headings are derived from the statutory language of the Code, common legal jargon used by courts and lawyers, popular nonlegal terms, and customer contact suggestions. The result is a user-friendly index for both the lawyer and non-lawyer user.

We solicit your help in keeping this index as useful as possible and ask that you inform us of any popular names that may have eluded us and tell us of any errors we have made or improvements you think we should make. LexisNexis® maintains a **toll-free Index hotline (1-800-897-7922)** for use by those needing immediate help in locating a particular section or by those desiring to make comments or suggestions. Additionally, you may reach the Indexers by **fax (1-434-972-7686),** or by **Internet E-mail (lng-cho-indexing@lexisnexis.com).** For non-index questions and comments or to place orders, Customer Service may be reached by **toll-free telephone number (1-800-833-9844),** or by **toll-free fax (1-800-828-8341).**

A few basic suggestions for using this index are:

(1) *Begin your search with DEFINED TERMS.* DEFINED TERMS is a collection of entries for terms defined in the Illinois Domestic Relations and Related Laws Annotated. Starting a search in this heading exposes the index user to a diverse sampling of statutory terminology which could suggest to the user other headings to consult.

(2) *Cross references.* Pay close attention to and make full use of the index cross references. Cross references serve to keep indexes to a manageable size by reducing the amount of repetition of treatment under different headings. An index cross reference directs the index user to go to another part of the index to find treatment. For example, "ANTENUPTIAL AGREEMENTS, See PREMARITAL AGREEMENTS" directs the index user from the main heading ANTENUPTIAL AGREEMENTS to the main heading PREMARITAL AGREEMENTS. For another example, under the main heading SUPPORT AND MAINTENANCE, "Uniform interstate family support. See within this heading, 'Interstate family support'" directs the index user from the subheading, "Uniform interstate family support" to the subheading, "Interstate family support" within the same main heading.

(3) *Use descriptive words or phrases to aid in your search, including commonly used phrases or terms of art.* Examples would be CRIMINAL NEGLECT OF CHILDREN, DISSOLUTION OF MARRIAGE, and RUNAWAY AND HOMELESS YOUTHS.

Index

A

ABANDONED NEWBORN PROTECTION ACT, 325: 2/1 to 2/999.
Anonymity of relinquishing person, 325: 2/30.
Biological parent.
Presumption person relinquishing is, 325: 2/15.
Child-placing agency.
Contacting, 325: 2/40.
Duties, 325: 2/40.
Construction of act, 325: 2/70.
Definitions, 325: 2/10.
Department's duties, 325: 2/60.
Effective date of act, 325: 2/999.
Emergency medical facilities' duties, 325: 2/20.
Evaluation of program generally, 325: 2/65.
Fire stations' duties, 325: 2/20.
Hospitals' duties, 325: 2/20.
Immunities.
Personnel of facility accepting infant, 325: 2/27.
Relinquishing person, 325: 2/25.
Information packet to relinquishing person, 325: 2/35.
Intent to relinquish.
Presumption, 325: 2/15.
Medical assistance eligibility of infant, 325: 2/45.
Police stations.
Defined, 325: 2/10.
Duties, 325: 2/20.
Immunities, 325: 2/27.
Presumptions, 325: 2/15.
Public policy, 325: 2/5.
Repealer provision, 325: 2/75.
Report of acceptance of newborn infant, 325: 2/40.
Return of custody to parent, 325: 2/55.
Termination of parental rights.
Presumption by relinquishing, 325: 2/15.
Title of act, 325: 2/1.

ABANDONED SPOUSE.
Control over property.
Contracts, sales or encumbrances, 750: 65/12.

ABANDONMENT OF SCHOOL BUS BY DRIVER, 720: 150/4.1.

ABATEMENT OF ACTIONS.
Declaration of invalidity of marriage.
Death of party, 750: 5/302.
Dissolution of marriage.
Death of party subsequent to judgment not to abate action, 750: 5/401.

ABATEMENT OF SUPPORT PAYMENTS.
Petition, Sup. Ct. Rule 296.

ABDUCTION.
Child abduction, 720: 5/10-5.
Aiding and abetting, 720: 5/10-7.

ABORTIFACIENT.
Nonprescription sales, 720: 510/11.

ABORTION.
Abortifacient.
Nonprescription sales unlawful, 720: 510/11.
Physician notification requirements, 720: 510/11.
Alleged abortion performed upon nonpregnant woman, 720: 510/11.
Citation of title, 720: 510/15.
Complications, reports, 720: 510/10.1.

ABORTION —Cont'd
Conscious refusal to perform abortion, 720: 510/13.
Construction of act.
Severability, 720: 510/14.
Criminal acts.
Complications resulting from an abortion.
Failure to maintain confidentiality of reports, 720: 510/11.
Dead fetus pathological report of live birth or viability evidence, 720: 510/12.
Nonprescription abortifacient, 720: 510/11.
Physician reporting requirements.
Dead fetus pathological analysis, 720: 510/12.
Dead premature infant.
Therapeutic research on miscarried fetuses, 720: 510/12.1.
Disciplinary actions.
Reporting complications resulting from an abortion, 720: 510/10.1.
Willful violations of law, 720: 510/11.
Expenses of minor child, liability of parent, 750: 65/15.
Expenses of spouse, liability of other spouse, 750: 65/15.
Experimentation upon fetus.
Miscarried fetuses, 720: 510/12.1.
Father's injunctive relief.
Unborn child, 735: 5/11-107.1.
Fetus.
Therapeutic research on miscarried fetuses, 720: 510/12.1.
Fraud.
Alleged abortion performed upon nonpregnant woman, 720: 510/11.
Injunctive relief.
Father of unborn child, 735: 5/11-107.1.
Medical care right of conscience, 720: 510/13.
Minor's expenses, liability of parent, 750: 65/15.
Mother's decision relating to abortion.
Injunctive relief for father of unborn child, 735: 5/11-107.1.
Parental notice act, 750: 70/1 to 70/99.
See ABORTION, PARENTAL NOTICE.
Physician reporting requirements.
Complications resulting from an abortion, 720: 510/10.1.
Failure to maintain confidentiality of reports, 720: 510/11.
Contents of departmental reports, 720: 510/10.
Correcting prior submitted reports, 720: 510/10.
Department of public health, 720: 510/10.
Viability of fetus.
Pathologist's test results, 720: 510/10.
Physician unprofessional conduct.
Willful violations of law, 720: 510/11.
Punitive damages.
Fraud, 720: 510/11.
Referral fees prohibited, 720: 510/11.1.
Refusal to perform, 720: 510/13.
Right of conscience in medical care, 720: 510/13.
Rulemaking authority, 720: 510/10.
Registration under vital records act, 720: 510/14.
Severability of act, 720: 510/14.
Short title, 720: 510/15.
Spousal expenses, liability of other spouse, 750: 65/15.
Statistical data.
Filing reports with legislature, 720: 510/10.
Title of act, 720: 510/15.

ABORTION —Cont'd
Viability of fetus.
Dead fetus pathological analysis, 720: 510/12.

ABORTION, PARENTAL NOTICE.
Definitions, 750: 70/10.
Effective date of article, 750: 70/99.
Immunity.
Physicians and surgeons, 750: 70/45.
Legislative findings, 750: 70/5.
Minor's consent to abortion, 750: 70/30.
Notice to adult family member, 750: 70/15.
Exceptions, 750: 70/20.
Judicial waiver of notice.
Procedure, 750: 70/25.
Penalties, 750: 70/40.
Purpose of act, 750: 70/5.
Reports, 750: 70/35.
Severability of provisions, 750: 70/50.
Short title, 750: 70/1.
Waiver of notice, 750: 70/25.

ABSENTEE VOTING.
Domestic violence victims, participation in address confidentiality program, 750: 61/30.

ABUSE AND NEGLECT OF ELDERLY.
Generally, 320: 20/1 to 20/13.5.
See ELDER ABUSE AND NEGLECT.

ABUSE, CHILD SEXUAL ABUSE, 325: 15/0.01 to 15/7.

ABUSED, NEGLECTED OR DEPENDENT CHILDREN.
Abandoned newborn infant protection act, 325: 2/1 to 2/999.
See ABANDONED NEWBORN PROTECTION ACT.
Child sexual abuse, 325: 15/0.01 to 15/7.
Reporting child abuse and neglect generally, 325: 5/1 to 5/11.7.
See CHILD ABUSE, NEGLECT OR DEPENDENCY.

ABUSE OF FAMILY OR HOUSEHOLD MEMBER.
Domestic violence generally, 750: 60/101 to 60/401.
See DOMESTIC VIOLENCE.
Protective orders, 725: 5/112A-1 to 5/112A-31.
See PROTECTIVE ORDERS AGAINST DOMESTIC VIOLENCE.

ACCIDENT AND HEALTH INSURANCE.
Child support orders.
Beneficiary designation, 750: 5/505.2.
Child support payments.
Factor in support order, 750: 5/505.
Court ordered beneficiary designation, 750: 5/505.2.
Maintenance orders.
Beneficiary designation, 750: 5/505.2.

ACKNOWLEDGMENT OF PARENTAGE.
Establishing of parent and child relationship by consent, 750: 45/6.
Voluntary acknowledgment, 750: 45/6.

ACKNOWLEDGMENTS.
Adoption.
Forms of consent and surrender, 750: 50/10.

ACROBATS.
Child labor, 720: 150/1, 150/2.

ACTIONS.
Annulments.
Commencement, 750: 5/306.

ACTIONS —Cont'd
Breastfeeding.
Right to breastfeed act.
Private right of action for denial of right, 740: 137/15.
Child support.
Expedited support, 750: 25/1 to 25/13.
Dissolution of marriage.
Commencement, 750: 5/411.
Husband deserting family.
Wife defending in name of husband, 750: 65/3.
Invalidity of marriage, declarations of.
Commencement, 750: 5/306.
Maintenance.
During separation, 750: 5/402.
Married person's right to sue and be sued, 750: 65/1.
Defending in name of spouse, 750: 65/3.
Defending in own right or for others, 750: 65/2.
Parentage proceedings, 750: 40/1 to 45/27.
See PARENTAGE PROCEEDINGS.
Paternity.
Parties who may bring action, 750: 45/7.
Protection orders.
Domestic violence, 750: 60/201 to 60/227.1.
See DOMESTIC VIOLENCE.
Spousal support during separation, 750: 5/402.
Support.
Responsibility of relatives of public aid recipients.
Generally, 305: 5/10-1 to 5/10-27.
See PUBLIC AID.
Vexatious litigation.
Child custody orders.
Modification, 750: 5/610.

ADDRESS CONFIDENTIALITY.
Domestic violence victims, 750: 61/1 to 61/45.

ADMISSIONS.
Dissolution of marriage or legal separation or declaration of invalidity of marriage.
Respondent's admission as evidence, 750: 5/407.
Husband and wife, 735: 5/8-801.

ADOPTION, 750: 50/0.01 to 50/24.
Acknowledgments.
Forms of consent and surrender, 750: 50/10.
Adoption registry and medical information exchange, 750: 50/18.04 to 50/18.07.
Advisory council, 750: 50/18.07.
Definitions, 750: 50/18.06.
Fund, 750: 50/18.7.
Generally, 750: 50/18.07.
Identifying information disclosure, 750: 50/18.1 to 50/18.8.
Legislative intent, 750: 50/18.04.
Affidavits.
Consent or surrender.
Identification of father, 750: 50/11.
Costs, expenses, etc., 750: 50/14.
Appeals.
Appointment of a guardian with power to consent, Sup. Ct. Rule 663.
Judgment order for adoption, 750: 50/20b.
Attorneys' fees.
Biological parents.
Payment of expenses, 720: 525/4.1.
Availability of person for adoption, 750: 50/1.
Best interest of child, 750: 50/15, 50/15.1, 50/20a.
Biological parent registry, 750: 50/18.1 to 50/18.6.
Confidential intermediary, 750: 50/18.3a.
Establishment, 750: 50/18.1.
Fees, 750: 50/18.6.
Forms, 750: 50/18.2.
Identifying information to adoptive parents, 750: 50/18.4.
Immunity, 750: 50/18.5.
Notification requirements, 750: 50/18.3.
Sharing of identifying information, 750: 50/18.3.
Signed written statement required of biological parents, 750: 50/18.3.

ADOPTION —Cont'd
Biological parents.
Payment of living expenses, 720: 525/4.1.
Birth certificate.
Registration of new birth certificate, 750: 50/19.
Bonds, surety.
Foreign-born children, 750: 50/4.1.
"Born out of wedlock."
Word usage prohibited, 750: 50/18.
Child care act of 1969.
Compliance as placement under adoption act, 750: 50/4.1.
Child deemed born to adopting parents for property right determination purposes.
Instruments regarding adopted children, 760: 30/0.01, 30/1.
Citation of title, 750: 50/0.01.
Compensation for placement of child, 750: 50/21.
Compensation prohibition, 720: 525/1 to 525/5.
Child welfare exception, 720: 525/1.
Construction of act, 720: 525/4.
Penalty, 720: 525/5.
"Placing out" defined, 720: 525/3.
Prohibited conduct, 720: 525/2.
Short title, 720: 525/0.01.
Confidential intermediary, 750: 50/18.3a.
Biological parent registry, 750: 50/18.3a.
Confidentiality.
Records confidentiality, 750: 50/18.
Consent.
Adult consent, 750: 50/12.
Child consent, 750: 50/12.
Determination of validity, 750: 50/13.
Execution prior to effective date of act, 750: 50/23.
Forms of consent, 750: 50/10.
Foster family homes.
Guardian's consent, 750: 50/15.1.
Guardian with power, appeal of appointment, Sup. Ct. Rule 663.
Irrevocability, 750: 50/11.
Time limitation, 750: 50/9.
Limitation of actions, 750: 55/0.01, 55/1.
Requirements, 750: 50/8.
Construction of act, 750: 50/2.1.
Applicability of civil practice law, 750: 50/20.
Best interests and welfare of child, 750: 50/20a.
Effective date, 750: 50/24.
Partial invalidity, 750: 50/22.
Repeal of prior act.
Saving provisions, 750: 50/23.
Contests.
Notice requirement, 750: 55/1.
Short title of act, 750: 55/0.01.
Controlled substance found in child at birth.
Presumption parent unfit, 750: 50/1.
Criminal background check.
Fingerprint based criminal background check.
Investigation to include, 750: 50/6.
Death of biological parent.
Confidential intermediary.
Notification requirements, 750: 50/18.3a.
Death of child.
Prior to final judgment, 750: 50/14a.
Death of intended adoptive parent prior to entry of judgment, 750: 50/14b.
Decedents' estates.
Death of child before final judgment, 750: 50/14a.
Declaration of invalidity of marriage.
Legitimacy of child adopted of marriage declared invalid, 750: 5/303.
Declaration of paternity.
Notice to putative father, 750: 50/12a.
Definitions, 750: 50/1.
Depraved parent, presumption, 750: 50/1.
Disclaimer of paternity.
Notice to putative father, 750: 50/12a.
Effective date of act, 750: 50/24.
Emancipation of mature minors, 750: 30/1 to 30/11.

ADOPTION —Cont'd
Executions.
Consent or surrender prior to effective date of act, 750: 50/23.
Forms of consent and surrender, 750: 50/10.
Fees.
Appointment of confidential intermediary, 750: 50/18.3a.
Attorneys' fees.
Biological parents.
Payment of expenses, 720: 525/4.1.
Biological parent registry, 750: 50/18.6.
Compensation for placement of child, 750: 50/21.
Fingerprint based criminal background check.
Investigation to include, 750: 50/6.
Foreign-born child.
Interim order, 750: 50/13.
Investigation of petition, 750: 50/6.
Placement under act, 750: 50/4.1.
Forms.
Adoptee registration identification, 750: 50/18.2.
Biological parent identification, 750: 50/18.2.
Consent and surrender, 750: 50/10.
Affidavit of identification of father, 750: 50/11.
Declaration of paternity, 750: 50/12a.
Denial of identification exchange, 750: 50/18.2.
Information exchange authorization, 750: 50/18.2.
Notice to putative father of adoption, 750: 50/12a.
Surrendered child registration identification, 750: 50/18.2.
Foster care time limit.
Parent presumed unfit when child in foster care for certain time period, 750: 50/1.
Foster family homes.
Preference in adoption, 750: 50/15.1.
Guardian ad litem.
Inspection of confidential records.
Criteria, 750: 50/18.
State's attorney as child's counsel, 750: 50/13.
Guardian with power to consent.
Appeal, Sup. Ct. Rule 663.
Guidelines.
Best interests of child, 750: 50/15, 50/15.1.
Construction of act, 750: 50/20a.
Guardian's consent.
Foster family homes, 750: 50/15.1.
Welfare of child, 750: 50/15, 50/15.1.
Construction of act, 750: 50/20a.
Identifying information disclosure, 750: 50/18.1 to 50/18.8.
Adoption registry application, 750: 50/18.1b.
Effective date of registration, 750: 50/18.1c.
Mutually consenting registered parties, release of information to, 750: 50/18.1a.
"Illegitimate."
Word usage prohibited, 750: 50/18.
Illinois adoption registry and medical information exchange, 750: 50/18.04 to 50/18.07.
Immunity.
Biological parent registry, 750: 50/18.5.
Instruments regarding adopted children.
Child deemed born to adopting parents for property right determination purposes, 760: 30/0.01, 30/1.
Interim order, 750: 50/13.
Interstate compact on placement of children.
Compliance as placement under adoption act, 750: 50/4.1.
Invalidity of marriage, declaration of.
Legitimacy of child adopted of marriage declared invalid, 750: 5/303.
Investigations.
Filing of petition, 750: 50/6.
Judgments.
Affidavit of costs, expenses, etc., 750: 50/14.
Death of child before final judgment, 750: 50/14a.
Death of intended adoptive parent prior to judgment, 750: 50/14b.

ADOPTION —Cont'd
Judgments —Cont'd
Effect of judgment of adoption, 750: 50/17.
Entry of judgment, 750: 50/16.
Interim order, 750: 50/13.
Statute of limitations for attacking validity, 750: 55/0.01, 55/1.
Termination of parental rights, 750: 50/17.
Jurisdiction, 750: 50/4.
Legitimacy of child adopted of marriage declared invalid, 750: 5/303.
Limitation of actions.
Consent to adoption, 750: 55/0.01, 55/1.
Relief from final judgment or order, 750: 50/20b.
Living expenses, payment, 720: 525/4.1.
Loan or other credit accommodation.
Offering, providing or co-signing based on contingency of surrender or placement of child, 720: 525/4.1.
Medical histories of child, 750: 50/18.4a.
Medical information exchange between adoptive parents and birth parents.
Illinois adoption registry and medical information exchange, 750: 50/18.04 to 50/18.07.
Mental health histories of child, 750: 50/18.4a.
Names.
Changes, 735: 5/21-101.
Identity of parties by initials or pseudonyms, 750: 50/18.
New birth certificate registration, 750: 50/19.
Notice.
Biological parent or sibling information, 750: 50/18.4.
By publication, 750: 50/7.
Medical and mental health histories of child, 750: 50/18.4a.
Putative father, 750: 50/12a.
Oaths.
Confidential intermediary, 750: 50/18.3a.
Parentage proceedings.
Establishment as adoptive parent, 750: 45/4.
Generally, 750: 40/1 to 45/27.
Parties defendant, 750: 50/7.
Person available for adoption, 750: 50/1.
Petitions, 750: 50/5.
Appointment of confidential intermediary, 750: 50/18.3a.
Interim order, 750: 50/13.
Investigation, 750: 50/6.
Post-placement investigation, 750: 50/6.
Presumption of unfitness, 750: 50/1.
Property rights of adopted children.
Instruments regarding, child deemed born to adopting parents, 760: 30/0.01, 30/1.
Public records.
Confidentiality, 750: 50/18.
Putative father.
Affidavit of identification, 750: 50/11.
Declaration of paternity, 750: 50/12a.
Defined, 750: 50/1.
Disclaimer of paternity, 750: 50/12a.
Notice of adoption, 750: 50/12a.
Putative father registry, 750: 50/12.1.
Qualifications.
Who may adopt a child, 750: 50/2.
Who may be adopted, 750: 50/3.
Race or ethnic heritage of child.
Child placement by department of children and family services, 20: 505/7.
Religion.
Consideration in placement, 20: 505/7, 750: 50/15.
Reports.
Investigation, 750: 50/6.
Residence requirement, persons adopting child, 750: 50/2.
Rulemaking authority, 750: 50/4.1.
Sanctions.
Confidential intermediary, 750: 50/18.3a.
Sealing of records, 750: 50/18.
Service of process.
Notice to putative father, 750: 50/12a.
Short title, 750: 50/0.01.

ADOPTION —Cont'd
Standby adoption.
Consent given by parent, 750: 50/9.
Consent form, 750: 50/10.
Judgment, time for applying, 750: 50/13.1.
Entry, 750: 50/14.
Order, 750: 50/13.1.
State's attorney.
Appointment as guardian ad litem, 750: 50/13.
Statute of limitations.
Consent to adoption, 750: 55/0.01, 55/1.
Relief from final judgment or order, 750: 50/20b.
Summons or process, 750: 50/7.
Notice to putative father, 750: 50/12a.
Surrender, 750: 50/8.
Execution prior to effective date of act, 750: 50/23.
Forms of surrender, 750: 50/10.
Irrevocability, 750: 50/11.
Time limitation, 750: 50/9.
Temporary custodial care.
Determination of availability, 750: 50/13.
Termination of parental rights.
Effect of entry of judgment, 750: 50/17.
Title of act, 750: 50/0.01.
Unborn child.
Forms of consent and surrender, 750: 50/10.
Unfit persons.
Defined, 750: 50/1.
Requirements for finding, 750: 50/8.
Validity.
Attack upon or proceedings contesting, 750: 55/0.01, 55/1.
Venue, 750: 50/4.
Vital records.
New certificate of birth.
Registration, 750: 50/19.
Who may adopt a child, 750: 50/2.
Who may be adopted, 750: 50/3.

ADOPTION COMPENSATION, 720: 525/0.01 to 525/5.
Biological parents.
Payment of living expenses, 720: 525/4.1.
Child welfare agency exception, 720: 525/1.
Construction of act, 720: 525/4.
Guardians ad litem.
Payment of expenses, appointment for unborn child, 720: 525/4.1.
Living expenses, payment, 720: 525/4.1.
Loan or other credit accommodation.
Offering, providing or co-signing based on contingency of surrender or placement of child, 720: 525/4.1.
Penalty, 720: 525/5.
"Placing out" defined, 720: 525/3.
Prohibited, 720: 525/2.
Short title, 720: 525/0.01.

ADOPTION REGISTRY AND MEDICAL INFORMATION EXCHANGE, 750: 50/18.04 to 50/18.07.
Advisory council, 750: 50/18.07.
Fund, 750: 50/18.7.
Generally, 750: 50/18.05.
Legislative intent, 750: 50/18.04.

ADULTERY.
Grounds for dissolution of marriage, 750: 5/401.

AFFIDAVITS.
Adoption.
Consent or surrender.
Identification of father, 750: 50/11.
Costs, expenses, etc., 750: 50/14.
Child custody.
Temporary custody awarded on basis of affidavit, 750: 5/603.
Uniform child custody jurisdiction and enforcement.
Contents of pleadings, 750: 36/209.
Child marriages.
Consent of one parent, 750: 5/203.
Dissolution of marriage.
Simplified dissolution procedure, 750: 5/454.

AFFIDAVITS —Cont'd
Injunctions.
Dissolution of injunction.
Supporting of complaint and answer, 735: 5/11-109.
Relief on Saturday, Sunday or legal holiday, 735: 5/11-106.
Marriage dissolution proceedings.
Temporary relief filings, 750: 5/501.
Marriages of children.
Consent of one parent, 750: 5/203.
Parentage proceedings.
Blood and tissue test reports, 750: 45/11.
Non-existence of parent and child relationship, initiation of proceeding by filing, 750: 45/7.
Protection orders.
Domestic violence, 750: 60/203.
Temporary maintenance or support, 750: 5/501.

AGGRAVATED DOMESTIC BATTERY, 720: 5/12-3.3.

AGGRAVATED KIDNAPPING, 720: 5/10-2.

AGGRAVATED UNLAWFUL RESTRAINT, 720: 5/10-3.1.

AGGRAVATING CIRCUMSTANCES.
Child abduction, 720: 5/10-5.

AGING, DEPARTMENT ON.
Family caregivers, 320: 65/1 to 65/99.
See FAMILY CAREGIVERS.
Older adult services, 320: 42/1 to 42/99.
See OLDER ADULT SERVICES.
Partnership for long-term care act.
Responsibility for generally, 320: 35/1 to 35/60.
Respite program, 320: 10/1 to 10/12.
See RESPITE PROGRAM.
Senior citizens' child care support act.
Coordination and development, 320: 45/15.
Senior health assistance program, 320: 50/20.
Senior pharmaceutical assistance act, 320: 50/1 to 50/99.

AIDING AND ABETTING.
Child abduction, 720: 5/10-7.

AIDS.
Child abuse, neglect or dependency.
Temporary caretaker provided results of tests, 325: 5/5.

AID TO AGED, BLIND OR DISABLED.
Support responsibility of relatives, determination and enforcement, 305: 5/10-1 to 5/10-27.
See PUBLIC AID.

AID TO FAMILIES WITH DEPENDENT CHILDREN.
Support responsibility of relatives, determination and enforcement, 305: 5/10-1 to 5/10-27.
See PUBLIC AID.

AIRLINES.
Ticket sales to minors.
Unlawful sale of travel ticket, 720: 5/10-8.

ALCOHOLISM AND SUBSTANCE ABUSE.
Child abuse and neglect reporting.
Required reports by treatment personnel, 325: 5/4.
Substance abuse services for women with children, 325: 5/7.3c.
Invalidity of marriage, declaration of.
Incapacity to consent because of dependency, 750: 5/301.

ALIENS.
Adoption of foreign-born child.
Investigation of petition, 750: 50/6.
Preadoption requirements, 750: 50/4.1.
Support orders, withholding of income to secure payment, 750: 5/706.1.

ALL-INCLUSIVE CARE FOR THE ELDERLY, 320: 40/1 to 40/30.

ALTERNATIVE DISPUTE RESOLUTION.
Dissolution of marriage.
Conciliation and mediation, 750: 5/404.
Joint custody award, mediation, 750: 5/602.1.
Joint parenting agreement to specify procedure, 750: 5/602.1.

ANNULMENT OF MARRIAGE, 750: 5/301 to 5/306.

ANSWERS.
Filing.
Summons requiring appearance within 30 days after service, Sup. Ct. Rule 101.
Injunctions.
Dissolution.
Supporting of answer by affidavit, 735: 5/11-109.

ANTENUPTIAL AGREEMENTS, 750: 10/1 to 10/11.
See PREMARITAL AGREEMENTS.

APPEALS.
Adoption.
Appointment of a guardian with power to consent, Sup. Ct. Rule 663.
Judgment order for adoption, 750: 50/20b.
Records confidentiality continued, 750: 50/18.
Child custody.
Uniform child custody jurisdiction and enforcement, 750: 36/314.
Criminal appeals.
Conditional discharges, Sup. Ct. Rule 662.
Probation revocation, Sup. Ct. Rule 662.
Dependent children, Sup. Ct. Rule 660.
Emancipation of mature minors.
Judgments or orders, 750: 30/11.
Guardianships.
Adjudication of wardship, Sup. Ct. Rule 662.
Adoption proceedings.
Appointment of a guardian with power to consent, Sup. Ct. Rule 663.
Indigent persons.
Juvenile delinquents, Sup. Ct. Rule 661.
Juvenile delinquency, Sup. Ct. Rule 660.
Indigent minors, Sup. Ct. Rule 661.
Marriage dissolution judgments, 750: 5/413.
Parentage proceedings.
Free transcript, 750: 45/18.
Pendency of appeal.
Maintenance granted and enforced during pendency, 750: 5/504.
Probation.
Revocation of probation, Sup. Ct. Rule 662.
Wardship adjudications, Sup. Ct. Rule 662.

APPEARANCES.
Child custody.
Uniform child custody jurisdiction and enforcement.
Immunity for personal jurisdiction for other proceedings, 750: 36/109.
Order to appear, 750: 36/210.
Expedited enforcement, 750: 36/308.
Child support.
Expedited support proceedings.
Failure to appear at administrative hearing, 750: 25/10; Sup. Ct. Rule 100.8.
Domestic violence protection orders.
Emergency order, appearance by respondent, 750: 60/217.
Thirty-day interim order, 750: 60/218.

ARREST.
Protective orders against domestic violence.
Abusing, neglecting or exploiting party, 750: 60/304.
Law enforcement policies regarding procedures, 725: 5/112A-27.
Warrantless arrests, 725: 5/112A-26, 750: 60/301.
Warrants.
Protection order violations, 750: 60/301.

ARTIFICIAL INSEMINATION.
Children born as a result.
Status, 750: 40/2.

ARTIFICIAL INSEMINATION —Cont'd
Donor not husband.
Status of donor as father, 750: 40/3.

ATTACHMENT.
Married persons, enforcement by or against, 750: 65/1.
Persons.
Support enforcement proceedings.
Failure of obligor to appear, 750: 5/713.

ATTORNEY DISCIPLINE AND PROFESSIONAL CONDUCT.
Vexatious litigation.
Child custody orders.
Modification, 750: 5/610.

ATTORNEY GENERAL.
Domestic violence victims' address confidentiality, 750: 61/1 to 61/45.
Interstate family support.
Duties, 750: 22/308.
Parentage proceedings.
Limitation on legal representation, 750: 45/18.

ATTORNEYS.
Appointment of counsel.
Dissolution of marriage.
Representation of interest of minor or dependent child, 750: 5/506.
Child custody, support or visitation.
Representation of interest of minor or dependent child, 750: 5/506.
Dissolution of marriage.
Appointment to represent interest of minor or dependent child, 750: 5/506.
Parentage proceedings.
Right to counsel, 750: 45/18.
Pro se representation.
Protection orders.
Commencement of action, 750: 60/202.
Support and maintenance.
Interstate family support.
Private counsel, 750: 22/309.

ATTORNEYS' FEES.
Adoption.
Biological parents.
Payment of expenses, 720: 525/4.1.
Child custody orders.
Modification, 750: 5/610.
Child custody, support or visitation.
Appointment to represent interest of minor or dependent child, 750: 5/506.
Uniform child custody jurisdiction and enforcement, 750: 36/312.
Dissolution of marriage, 750: 5/508.
Domestic violence protection orders.
Order for payment of losses, 750: 60/214.
Untrue statements, 750: 60/226.
Parentage proceedings, 750: 45/17.
Support and maintenance.
Interstate family support, 750: 22/313.
Visitation enforcement action vexatious and harassing, 750: 5/607.1.
Visitation order violations, 750: 5/607.1.

AUDITOR GENERAL.
Early intervention services.
Evaluation of system established, 325: 20/15.

B

BABY DROP-OFF LAW.
Abandoned newborn infant protection act, 325: 2/1 to 2/999.
See ABANDONED NEWBORN PROTECTION ACT.

BABY RICH ACT.
Adoption.
Best interest of child, 750: 50/15, 50/15.1, 50/20a.

BACKGROUND INVESTIGATIONS.
Child placed with relatives.
Department of children and family services, 20: 505/7.

BACKGROUND INVESTIGATIONS —Cont'd
Department of children and family services.
Placing child with relatives, 20: 505/7.

BADGES.
Domestic violence.
Assistance by law enforcement officers, 750: 60/304.

BAIL AND RECOGNIZANCE.
Increasing amount of bail.
Protective order violation, 725: 5/112A-23.
Modifying bail.
Protective order violation, 725: 5/112A-23.
Revocation of release.
Protective order violation, 725: 5/112A-23.

BANKS.
Support responsibility of relatives of public aid recipients.
Data match system designed and implemented by department of public aid, 305: 5/10-24 to 5/10-24.50.

BATTERED WIVES.
Protective orders, 725: 5/112A-1 to 5/112A-31.
See PROTECTIVE ORDERS AGAINST DOMESTIC VIOLENCE.

BATTERY.
Domestic battery, 720: 5/12-3.2.
Aggravated domestic battery, 720: 5/12-3.3.

BEGGING.
Neglected children, 720: 130/1.
Wrongs to children, 720: 150/1, 150/2.

BEHAVIOR DISORDERED CHILDREN.
Interagency board for hearing impaired/behavior disordered children, 325: 35/1 to 35/12.

BEST INTEREST OF CHILD.
Adoption guidelines, 750: 50/15, 50/15.1, 50/20a.
Change of name, 735: 5/21-101.
Child custody standards, 750: 5/602.
Dissolution of marriage or legal separation proceeding dismissed.
Custody judgment required, 750: 5/603.
Hearings, 750: 5/606.
Joint custody, 750: 5/602.1.
Modification of custody judgment, 750: 5/610.
Child visitation standards, 750: 5/607.
Parentage act.
Pre-trial recommendations, 750: 45/12.

BIGAMY.
Dissolution of marriage.
Ground, respondent having husband or wife living at time of marriage, 750: 5/401.
Invalidity declaration commencement, 750: 5/302.
Maintenance, 750: 5/702.
Prohibited, 750: 5/212.

BIOLOGICAL PARENT IDENTIFICATION FORM, 750: 50/18.2.

BIOLOGICAL PARENT REGISTRY, 750: 50/18.1.
Form of biological parent registration identification, 750: 50/18.2.
Registration fee, 750: 50/18.6.
Sharing of identifying information, 750: 50/18.3.

BIRTH CERTIFICATES.
Missing children.
Duty of local law enforcement agencies to investigate request, 325: 55/6.
Providing copies in response to inquiry, 325: 50/4, 55/4.

BIRTH CONTROL.
Services to minors, 325: 10/0.01, 10/1.

BLIND OR VISUALLY IMPAIRED.
Early intervention services, 325: 20/1 to 20/20.

BLOOD TESTS.
Child support proceedings.
Order to submit to test, Sup. Ct. Rule 100.5.
Parentage proceedings, 750: 45/11.

BOARDS.
Interagency board for hearing impaired/behavior disordered children, 325: 35/1 to 35/12.

BOATS AND OTHER WATERCRAFT.
Ticket sales.
Minors.
Unlawful sale of travel ticket, 720: 5/10-8.

BONDS, SURETY.
Adoption.
Foreign-born children, 750: 50/4.1.
Child support payment guarantees, 750: 5/706.2.
Injunctions, 735: 5/11-103 to 5/11-105.
Dissolution of TRO or preliminary injunction.
Failure to assess damages.
Bar to action on bonds, 735: 5/11-110.
Relief on Saturday, Sunday or legal holiday, 735: 5/11-106.
Maintenance payment guarantee, 750: 5/706.2.
Preliminary injunctions, 735: 5/11-103.
Restraining orders, 735: 5/11-103.
Spousal support payment guarantees, 750: 5/706.2.
Support payments, 750: 5/706.2.

BREACH OF PROMISE TO MARRY, 740: 15/0.01 to 15/10.

BREASTFEEDING.
Right to breastfeed act, 740: 137/1 to 137/99.
Actions.
Private right of action for denial of right, 740: 137/15.
Effective date of act, 740: 137/99.
Legislative declaration, 740: 137/5.
Locations for breastfeeding, 740: 137/10.
Short title of act, 740: 137/1.

BURDEN OF PROOF.
Adoption consent, 750: 50/8.
Child abuse and neglect reports.
Amendment, expungement or removal, 325: 5/7.16.
Child custody.
Leave to remove children, 750: 5/609.
Modification of orders, 750: 5/610.
Domestic violence protection orders, 750: 60/205.
Disclosure of privileged information, 750: 60/227.1.
Paternity.
Rebutting presumption, 750: 45/5.
Support and maintenance.
Interstate family support.
Registration of orders.
Defenses contesting validity or enforcement, 750: 22/607.

BUSES.
Minors.
Ticket sales.
Unlawful sale of travel ticket, 720: 5/10-8.

C

CANNABIS.
Sale to minors.
Parental right of recovery for damages, 740: 120/1 to 120/4.

CAPACITY TO MARRY.
Invalidity of marriage, declaration of.
Ground, lack of capacity to consent, 750: 5/301.

CAREER DEVELOPMENT, HIGH RISK YOUTH, 325: 25/0.01, 25/1.

CAREGIVERS.
Family caregivers, 320: 65/1 to 65/99.
See FAMILY CAREGIVERS.

CARETAKERS.
Protective orders, 725: 5/112A-14, 750: 60/212, 60/214.

CARETAKERS —Cont'd
Temporary protective custody of children, 325: 5/5.

CATASTROPHIC ILLNESSES.
Partnership for long-term care act generally, 320: 35/1 to 35/60.

CENTRAL MANAGEMENT SERVICES, DEPARTMENT OF.
Senior citizens and disabled persons prescription drug discount program.
Administration of program, 320: 55/25.
Limitation on state's obligation for cost of, 320: 55/47.
Report on, 320: 55/50.
General provisions, 320: 55/1 to 55/99.
Rulemaking, 320: 55/45.

CENTRAL REGISTER, CHILD ABUSE AND NEGLECT REPORTING.
Additional information contained, 325: 5/7.15.
Child protective service.
Determinations concerning report, 325: 5/7.12.
Classification of reports in, 325: 5/7.14.
Copy of information contained upon request, 325: 5/7.19.
Education and training program concerning, 325: 5/11.5.
Generally, 325: 5/7.7.
Requests for information from.
Entry of certain information concerning, 325: 5/7.8.
Telephone reports to, 325: 5/7.
Transmittal of copy to by child protective service unit, 325: 5/7.10.

CHAIN OF CUSTODY.
Parentage proceedings blood tests, 750: 45/11.

CHANGE OF NAME, 735: 5/21-101 to 5/21-104.
Notice to persons outside state, 735: 5/21-104.
Parentage proceedings, 750: 45/14.
Parties, 735: 5/21-101.
Petitions, 735: 5/21-102.
Service by publication, 735: 5/21-103.
Service outside state, 735: 5/21-104.

CHILD ABANDONMENT.
School bus driver, 720: 150/4.1, 150/5.

CHILD ABDUCTION, 720: 5/10-5.
Aiding and abetting, 720: 5/10-7.

CHILD ABUSE, NEGLECT OR DEPENDENCY.
Abandoned newborn infant protection act.
General provisions, 325: 2/1 to 2/999.
See ABANDONED NEWBORN PROTECTION ACT.
AIDS.
Temporary caretaker provided results, 325: 5/5.
Child custody hearings.
Previous statements of child as evidence, 750: 5/606.
Child sexual abuse, 325: 15/0.01 to 15/7.
Contributing to the delinquency of children, 720: 130/2a.
Contributing to the dependency and neglect of children, 720: 130/2.
Coroners.
Death of minor as result of abuse or neglect.
Investigation of suspected death, 325: 5/4.1.
Criminal neglect of children.
Competency of parent witnesses, 720: 130/3.
Contributing to the delinquency of children, 720: 130/2a.
Contributing to the dependency and neglect of children, 720: 130/2.
"Delinquent child" defined, 720: 130/1a.
"Dependent and neglected child" defined, 720: 130/1.
Short title, 720: 130/0.01.
Death of child.
Departmental report, 325: 5/4.2.

CHILD ABUSE, NEGLECT OR DEPENDENCY —Cont'd
Death of minor as result of abuse or neglect.
Investigation by coroner or medical examiner, 325: 5/4.1.
Delinquent child.
Defined, 720: 130/1a.
Dependent and neglected child.
Defined, 720: 130/1.
Disappearance of child.
Departmental report, 325: 5/4.3.
Domestic violence.
Generally, 750: 60/101 to 60/401.
See DOMESTIC VIOLENCE.
Evidence.
Child custody hearings.
Previous statements by child, 750: 5/606.
Immunity.
Reporting abuse or neglect, 325: 5/5, 5/9, 725: 5/112A-25.
Medical examiners.
Death of minor as result of abuse or neglect.
Investigations, 325: 5/4.1.
Protective orders, 725: 5/112A-1 to 5/112A-31.
See PROTECTIVE ORDERS AGAINST DOMESTIC VIOLENCE.
Reporting abuse and neglect, 325: 5/1 to 5/11.7.
Abused and neglected child reporting act.
Title of act, 325: 5/1.
Access to records, 325: 5/11.1.
Misdemeanor for making public identifying information, 325: 5/11.3.
Additional information, 325: 5/7.13.
Administrative decision.
Judicial review, 325: 5/11.6.
Agency responsible for receiving and investigating reports.
Department of children and family services, 325: 5/7.3.
Alcoholism or substance abuse services.
Referrals to when perpetrator addict or alcoholic, 325: 5/8.2.
Amendment of records, 325: 5/7.15.
Child protective service unit, 325: 5/7.18.
Notice, 325: 5/7.17.
Request by subject of report, 325: 5/7.16.
Assistance to circuit courts during stages of proceedings, 325: 5/8.3.
Burden of proof.
Amendment, expungement or removal of records upon request, 325: 5/7.16.
Capability of department for receiving reports, 325: 5/7.4.
Central register, 325: 5/7.7.
Additional information contained, 325: 5/7.15.
Child protective service.
Determinations concerning reports, 325: 5/7.12.
Classification of reports in, 325: 5/7.14.
Copy of information upon request, 325: 5/7.19.
Education and training program, 325: 5/11.5.
Requests for information from.
Entry of certain information concerning, 325: 5/7.8.
Telephone reports to, 325: 5/7.
Transmittal of copy to by child protective service unit, 325: 5/7.10.
Child left with relatives.
Child not considered neglected, 325: 5/3.
Child protective investigators.
Copies of autopsy reports in death cases, 325: 5/4.1.
Child protective service unit.
Amendment of records, 325: 5/7.18.
Denial of reasonable access to child by parents, 325: 5/7.5.
Determination whether report indicated or unfounded, 325: 5/7.12.
Establishment by department, 325: 5/7.2.
Forms for reporting distributed to, 325: 5/7.9.
Functions, 325: 5/7.2.

CHILD ABUSE, NEGLECT OR DEPENDENCY —Cont'd
Reporting abuse and neglect —Cont'd
Child protective service unit —Cont'd
Information about findings and actions taken to persons making report, 325: 5/11.2.
Local child abuse and neglect index maintained by, 325: 5/8.5.
Preliminary reports, 325: 5/7.10.
Procedures followed in investigations, 325: 5/7.4.
Reports transmitted to upon receipt, 325: 5/7.6, 5/7.8.
Training, 325: 5/7.2.
Transmittal of copy to state central register, 325: 5/7.10.
Circuit court assistance by department during stages of proceedings, 325: 5/8.3.
Classification of reports, 325: 5/7.14.
Communicable diseases test.
Results provided temporary caretakers, 325: 5/5.
Confidentiality as to persons seeking assistance under act, 325: 5/2.1.
Confidentiality of information received by temporary caretakers, 325: 5/5.
Confidentiality of records generally, 325: 5/11.
Continuing education on reporting, 325: 5/11.5.
Cooperation with other agencies, 325: 5/7.1.
Copy of information contained in report upon request, 325: 5/7.19.
Coroners.
Investigation of suspected death as result of abuse or neglect, 325: 5/4.1.
Report to coroner of suspected death as result of abuse, 325: 5/4.1.
Court and criminal justice system records not affected by act, 325: 5/11.4.
Court order prohibiting release of information, 325: 5/7.19.
Court orders to examine and interview child.
Child protective service unit denied reasonable access, 325: 5/7.5.
Criminal history record information, 325: 5/7.4.
Death as result of abuse or neglect.
Report to medical examiner or coroner, 325: 5/4.1.
Death of child, 325: 5/4.2.
Definitions, 325: 5/3.
Delegating investigative duties to department of state police, 325: 5/7.3.
Demonstrations of multidisciplinary teams, 325: 5/7.1.
Department of children and family services.
Duties upon receiving reports, 325: 5/2.
Determination of whether report indicated or unfounded, 325: 5/7.12.
Disappearance of child, 325: 5/4.3.
Disclosure of information, 325: 5/11.1a.
Disorderly conduct.
Transmitting false reports, 325: 5/4.
Emergency medical treatment to minor in temporary protective custody, 325: 5/5.
Employer discrimination against employee making reports, 325: 5/9.1.
Expungement of records, 325: 5/7.15.
Notice, 325: 5/7.17.
Request by subject of report, 325: 5/7.16.
Extended family members, 325: 5/11.2a.
Failure to report, 325: 5/4.02.
False reports, 325: 5/4.
Notice of penalty for making, 325: 5/7, 5/7.6.
Families seeking assistance in meeting child care responsibilities.
Use of services and facilities established by act, 325: 5/2.1.
Family preservation services, 325: 5/8.2.
Family's voluntary acceptance or refusal of services.
Report deemed founded, 325: 5/8.2.
Report deemed unfounded, 325: 5/8.1.
Felony for transmitting false reports, 325: 5/4.

CHILD ABUSE, NEGLECT OR DEPENDENCY —Cont'd
Reporting abuse and neglect —Cont'd
Forms for reporting.
Distribution to child protective service unit, 325: 5/7.9.
Guardianship administrator.
HIV tests, child's legally authorized representative for purposes of consenting to, 325: 5/5.
Hearings.
Refusal to amend, expunge or remove records upon request of subject, 325: 5/7.16.
HIV tests.
Results provided temporary caretakers, 325: 5/5.
Homemakers, 325: 5/8.2.
Immunity from liability, 325: 5/5, 5/9, 725: 5/112A-25.
Index.
Local index, 325: 5/8.5.
Indicated, 325: 5/7.14.
Individuals required to report, 325: 5/4.
Infant mortality reduction network service provider.
Assistance to pregnant addicts, 325: 5/7.3b.
Information about findings and actions taken by child protective service unit, 325: 5/11.2.
Initial written reports.
Content requirements, 325: 5/7.9.
Inter-agency agreements for information, 325: 5/7.20.
Intergovernmental missing child recovery act.
Access to records, 325: 5/11.1.
Intervention of local law enforcement agency.
Child protective service unit denied access to child, 325: 5/7.5.
Investigations.
Procedures followed, 325: 5/7.4.
Judicial review of administrative decisions, 325: 5/11.6.
Law enforcement agency taking temporary protective custody, 325: 5/5.
Listing of unfounded reports, 325: 5/7.7.
Local child abuse and neglect index, 325: 5/8.5.
Medical examiners.
Investigation of suspected death as result of abuse or neglect, 325: 5/4.1.
Report to examiner of suspected death as result of abuse, 325: 5/4.1.
Misdemeanor for failing to report or transmitting false reports, 325: 5/4.
Misdemeanor for making public identifying information, 325: 5/11.3.
Misdemeanor for unauthorized release of information, 325: 5/11.
Misdemeanor for willfully failing to report, 325: 5/4.02.
Monitoring rehabilitative services, 325: 5/8.4.
Multidisciplinary review committee, 325: 5/7.21.
Newborn or infant medical neglect.
Perinatal coordinator to review reports, 325: 5/7.3a.
Notice of amendment, expungement or removal, 325: 5/7.17.
Notice of hearing.
Amendment, expungement or removal of records upon request of subject, 325: 5/7.16.
Notice of penalty for making false reports, 325: 5/7, 5/7.6.
Notice of taking into temporary protective custody, 325: 5/5.
Notice upon receiving truancy reports, 325: 5/7.4.
Perinatal coordinator, 325: 5/7.3a.
Duties, 325: 5/7.3a.
Persons required to report, 325: 5/4.
Failure to report, 325: 5/4.02.
Photographs of physical environment in which abuse or neglect took place, 325: 5/6.
Physicians' assistants.
Persons required to report, 325: 5/4.

CHILD ABUSE, NEGLECT OR DEPENDENCY —Cont'd
Reporting abuse and neglect —Cont'd
Physicians taking temporary protective custody of child, 325: 5/5.
Physicians willfully failing to report.
Referral to medical disciplinary board for action, 325: 5/4.02.
Policies concerning status of court and criminal justice records.
Act not to affect, 325: 5/11.4.
Prayer for treatment or care of disease or remedial care.
Child not considered neglected or abused, 325: 5/3.
Pregnant addicts.
Referral to department of public health, 325: 5/7.3b.
Preliminary reports from child protective service unit, 325: 5/7.10.
Presumption of good faith, 325: 5/9.
Privileged communications.
Evidence not excluded by reason of, 325: 5/10.
Procedure for making reports, 325: 5/4.
Reports by telephone to central register, 325: 5/7.
Procedures followed in investigations, 325: 5/7.4.
Protective custody.
Temporary protective custody, 325: 5/5.
Public or private residential agencies or institutions.
Reporting and investigating abuse and neglect, 325: 5/2.
Records accessed, 325: 5/11.1.
Making public identifying information, 325: 5/11.3.
Rehabilitative services.
Monitoring by department, 325: 5/8.4.
Release of information harmful to subject of report.
Court order prohibiting, 325: 5/7.19.
Release of information to persons authorized, 325: 5/7.8.
Removal of records, 325: 5/7.15.
Notice, 325: 5/7.17.
Request by subject of report, 325: 5/7.16.
Requiring additional information, 325: 5/7.13.
School employees suspected of abuse or neglect.
Procedures for investigating reports, 325: 5/7.4.
School non-attendance.
Child not considered neglected or abused, 325: 5/4.
School of child, reports to, 325: 5/8.6.
Spiritual means through prayer for treatment or cure of disease, 325: 5/4.
State's attorneys authorized to receive unfounded reports, 325: 5/7.8.
Statewide citizen's committee on child abuse and neglect, 325: 5/11.7.
Substance abuse services for women with children, 325: 5/7.3c.
Teachers suspected of abuse or neglect.
Procedures for investigations, 325: 5/7.4.
Telephone reports.
Central register, 325: 5/7.
Statewide toll-free telephone number, 325: 5/7.6.
Temporary protective custody, 325: 5/5.
Testimony by persons making reports, 325: 5/10.
Toll-free telephone number, 325: 5/7.
Statewide number, 325: 5/7.6.
Training programs on reporting, 325: 5/11.5.
Truancy reports.
Notification to superintendent or school district, 325: 5/7.4.
Undetermined classification of reports as, 325: 5/7.14.
Unfounded reports, 325: 5/7.14.
Listing, 325: 5/7.7.
Persons authorized to receive, 325: 5/7.8.
Reports deemed, 325: 5/8.1.

CHILD ABUSE, NEGLECT OR DEPENDENCY —Cont'd
Reporting abuse and neglect —Cont'd
Voluntary agency protective services.
Utilization by department of children and family services, 325: 5/2.
X-rays by person required to investigate cases, 325: 5/6.
Uniform child custody jurisdiction and enforcement.
Emergency jurisdiction, 750: 36/204.
Warrant for physical custody of child, 750: 36/311.
Witnesses.
Criminal neglect of children.
Competency of parent witnesses, 720: 130/3.

CHILD AND SPOUSE SUPPORT UNIT.
Support responsibility of relatives of public aid recipients.
Generally, 305: 5/10-1 to 5/10-27.
See PUBLIC AID.

CHILD BORN OUT OF WEDLOCK.
Adoption consents.
Father of child, 750: 50/8.
Legitimacy of children born of marriage declared invalid, 750: 5/303.
Legitimacy of children born of prohibited or common law marriage, 750: 5/212.
Marriage license issuance.
Woman prior to application gives birth to illegitimate child, 750: 5/205.
Parentage proceedings generally, 750: 40/1 to 45/27.
See PARENTAGE PROCEEDINGS.

CHILD CARE.
Senior citizens' child care support.
Generally, 320: 45/1 to 45/25.

CHILD CARE FACILITIES.
Child abuse and neglect reporting.
Required reports by director or staff assistants, 325: 5/4.

CHILD CARE WORKERS.
Child abuse and neglect reporting.
Required reports, 325: 5/4.

CHILD CURFEW.
Curfew hours, 720: 555/1.
Ordinances.
Stricter requirements permissible, 720: 555/2.
Short title, 720: 555/0.01.

CHILD CUSTODY.
Agreements to dissolve marriage.
Provisions for, 750: 5/502.
Attorney appointment to represent interest of minor or dependent child, 750: 5/506.
Best interest of child, 750: 5/604.5.
Best interest standard.
Award determination, 750: 5/602.
Child abduction, 720: 5/10-5.
Aiding and abetting, 720: 5/10-7.
Commencement of proceeding, 750: 5/601.
Confidentiality of hearing records.
Order sealing records, 750: 5/606.
Dissolution of marriage agreements.
Provisions for, 750: 5/502.
Dissolution of marriage award standard, 750: 5/602.
Domestic violence.
Protection orders.
Enforcement of child custody violations, 750: 60/223.
Granting physical care and possession of minor child, 750: 60/214.
Modification, 750: 60/224.
Emancipation of mature minors, 750: 30/1 to 30/11.
Enforcement of orders, 750: 5/611.
Evidence as to abuse or neglect.
Previous statements made by child, 750: 5/606.
Exchange of custody for purposes of visitation.
Neutral site custody exchange act, 55: 82/1 to 82/99.

CHILD CUSTODY —Cont'd
Failure of party to comply with dissolution judgment, order or injunction.
Obligation of other party not suspended, 750: 5/509.
Gestational surrogacy generally, 750: 47/1 to 47/75.
See GESTATIONAL SURROGACY.
Guardian ad litem, appointment of attorney, 750: 5/506.
Hearings, 750: 5/606.
Husband-parent's testimony, 735: 5/8-801.
Interstate proceedings.
Uniform child custody jurisdiction and enforcement, 750: 36/101 to 36/405.
Interviews of children by court, 750: 5/604.
Investigations ordered by court, 750: 5/605.
Joint custody, 750: 5/602.1.
No presumption in favor or against, 750: 5/602.
Termination and modification, 750: 5/610.
Joint parenting agreement, 750: 5/602.1.
Joint parenting order, 750: 5/602.1.
Judgment enforcement or modification, procedure, 750: 5/511.
Judicial supervision, 750: 5/608.
Jurisdiction, 750: 5/601, 5/609, 60/208.
Uniform child custody jurisdiction and enforcement, 750: 36/101 to 36/405.
Leave to remove children, 750: 5/609.
Mediation, award of joint custody, 750: 5/602.1.
Missing children recovery.
Inquiry prior to granting or modifying child custody judgment, 325: 40/7.1.
Modification of orders, 750: 5/610.
Commencement of proceedings, 750: 5/601.
Neutral sites for parents to exchange custody for purposes of visitation, 55: 82/1 to 82/99.
Definitions, 55: 82/10.
Effective date, 55: 82/99.
Fee collected in civil cases to fund, 55: 82/15.
Fund, 55: 82/15.
Grant disbursement from fund, 55: 82/20.
Legislative findings, 55: 82/5.
Neutral site custody exchange act.
Act cited as, 55: 82/1.
Rules as to operation and standards, 55: 82/25.
Notice of proceeding, 750: 5/601.
Out-of-state parties, proceedings involving.
Registry of out-of-state judgments to be consulted, 750: 5/601.
Parentage proceedings.
Continuing jurisdiction of court to modify, 750: 45/16.
Judgments to contain provisions specifically concerning, 750: 45/14.
Presumption to be with mother.
Judgment containing no explicit award of custody, 750: 45/14.
Parental rights and responsibilities, 750: 5/602.1.
Parent's testimony, 735: 5/8-801.
Persons who may commence proceeding, 750: 5/601.
Post-judgment venue, 750: 5/512.
Presumptions, 750: 5/602.
Protective orders against domestic violence, 725: 5/112A-14.
Violation of order, 725: 5/112A-23.
Registry of out-of-state judgments consulted in proceeding involving out-of-state parties, 750: 5/601.
Removal from state, leave to remove, 750: 5/609.
Removal of child from homestead without consent of spouse, 750: 65/16.
Removal of child from jurisdiction of court.
Orders prohibiting, 750: 5/611.
Stepparent commencing proceeding, 750: 5/601.
Best interest of child that natural parent have custody, presumption, 750: 5/601.
Visitation rights, 750: 5/607.
Temporary custody orders, 750: 5/603.

CHILD CUSTODY —Cont'd
Temporary removal from state, 750: 5/609.
Uniform child custody jurisdiction and enforcement, 750: 36/101 to 36/405.
Appeals, 750: 36/314.
Appearance of parties.
Expedited enforcement, 750: 36/308.
Immunity for personal jurisdiction for other proceedings, 750: 36/109.
Order to appear, 750: 36/210.
Applicability of provisions.
Indian tribes, 750: 36/104.
International application, 750: 36/105.
Proceedings governed by other law, 750: 36/103.
Authority to make initial determinations, 750: 36/201.
Commencement of proceeding in other state.
Enforcement proceedings, 750: 36/307.
Stays, 750: 36/206.
Communications between courts, 750: 36/110.
Emergency jurisdiction, 750: 36/204.
Conclusiveness of determinations, 750: 36/106.
Conduct as cause to decline jurisdiction, 750: 36/208.
Construction of provisions.
Uniformity of interpretation, 750: 36/401.
Contest of determination, 750: 36/305.
Cooperation between courts, 750: 36/112.
Court costs, 750: 36/312.
Public officials, 750: 36/317.
Definitions, 750: 36/102.
Duty to enforce, 750: 36/303.
Effective date of act, 750: 36/403.
Effect of determinations, 750: 36/106.
Emergency jurisdiction, 750: 36/204.
Enforcement of registered determination, 750: 36/306.
Exclusive continuing jurisdiction, 750: 36/202.
Expedited enforcement, 750: 36/308.
Forum non conveniens, 750: 36/207.
Full faith and credit, out of state orders, 750: 36/313.
Grandfather provision, 750: 36/405.
Hague convention applicability.
Order for return of child, 750: 36/302.
Role of state's attorney, 750: 36/315.
Hearing, 750: 36/310.
Immunity for personal jurisdiction for other proceedings, 750: 36/109.
Inconvenient forum, 750: 36/207.
Indian tribes.
Applicability, 750: 36/104.
Information to be contained in pleadings, 750: 36/209.
Initial determinations.
Exclusive continuing jurisdiction, 750: 36/202.
Jurisdiction, 750: 36/201.
Modification of determination, 750: 36/203.
International application, 750: 36/105.
Joinder of parties, 750: 36/205.
Law enforcement officers, duties, 750: 36/316.
Modification of determination, 750: 36/203.
Notice.
Opportunity to be heard, 750: 36/205.
Persons outside state, 750: 36/108.
Registration of determination, 750: 36/305.
Order for return of child under Hague convention, 750: 36/302.
Order to appear, 750: 36/210.
Expedited enforcement, 750: 36/308.
Petitioner defined, 750: 36/301.
Petitions for expedited enforcement, 750: 36/308.
Physical custody of child taken by court, 750: 36/310.
Warrant issuance, 750: 36/311.
Pleadings.
Contents, 750: 36/209.
Priority given to certain issues, 750: 36/107.
Proceedings governed by other law, 750: 36/103.
Recognition of orders from outside state, 750: 36/313.
Records.
Preservation of records, 750: 36/112.

CHILD CUSTODY —Cont'd
Uniform child custody jurisdiction and enforcement —Cont'd
Registration of determination, 750: 36/305.
Enforcement of registered determination, 750: 36/306.
Remedies available for enforcement, 750: 36/303.
Requests of other courts, 750: 36/112.
Respondent defined, 750: 36/301.
Service of process.
Persons outside state, 750: 36/108.
Petition and order, 750: 36/309.
Severability of provisions, 750: 36/402.
Short title, 750: 36/101.
Simultaneous proceedings, 750: 36/206.
Enforcement proceedings, 750: 36/307.
Spousal privilege prohibited, 750: 36/310.
State's attorney, duties, 750: 36/315.
Stays pending appeal prohibited, 750: 36/314.
Temporary emergency jurisdiction, 750: 36/204.
Temporary visitation orders, 750: 36/304.
Testimony of witnesses outside state, 750: 36/111.
Transitional provision, 750: 36/405.
Uniformity of interpretation, 750: 36/401.
Unjustifiable conduct as cause to decline jurisdiction, 750: 36/208.
Visitation orders, 750: 36/304.
Vacation of temporary order, 750: 5/603.
Visitation, 750: 5/607.
Abuse.
Expedited procedures, 750: 5/607.1.
Agreements upon dissolution of marriage, 750: 5/502.
Attorney appointment to represent interest of minor or dependent child, 750: 5/506.
Domestic violence protection orders.
Determining rights, 750: 60/214.
Enforcement of visitation in cases of visitation abuse, 750: 5/607.1.
Exchange of custody for purposes of visitation.
Neutral site custody exchange act, 55: 82/1 to 82/99.
Failure of party to comply with dissolution judgment, order or injunction.
Obligation of other party not suspended, 750: 5/509.
First degree murder conviction of person with visitation rights.
Revocation of visitation rights previously granted, 750: 5/607.
Guardian ad litem for child, 750: 5/506.
Interviews by court of children, 750: 5/604.
Neutral site custody exchange act, 55: 82/1 to 82/99.
Orders.
Enforcement and modifications, 750: 5/607.1.
Parentage proceedings.
Continuing jurisdiction to modify order, 750: 45/16.
Judgments to contain provisions concerning, 750: 45/14.
Revocation, 750: 5/607.
Sex offenders convicted of offense upon victim less than 18 years of age, 750: 5/607.
Unlawful interference, 720: 5/10-5.5.
Wife-parent's testimony, 735: 5/8-801.

CHILD ENDANGERMENT.
Drug related child endangerment, 720: 5/12-4.10.
Aggravated drug related child endangerment, 720: 5/12-4.11.
Wrongs to children act, 720: 150/4.1, 150/5.

CHILD EXPLOITATION.
Commercial exploitation of children.
Penalty, 720: 150/5.
Prohibited conduct, 720: 150/1, 150/2.
Termination of custody rights, 720: 150/3.

CHILDHOOD DEVELOPMENT, EARLY INTERVENTION, 325: 20/1 to 20/20.

CHILD LABOR.
Commercial exploitation of children.
Penalty, 720: 150/5.
Prohibited conduct, 720: 150/1, 150/2.

CHILD LABOR —Cont'd
Commercial exploitation of children —Cont'd
Termination of custody rights, 720: 150/3.

CHILDNAPPING, 720: 5/10-5.
Aiding and abetting, 720: 5/10-7.

CHILD PLACEMENT.
Abandoned newborn protection act.
Child-placing agency, duties, 325: 2/50.
Adoption generally.
See ADOPTION.
Children and family services, department of.
Placement plan, 20: 505/7.3.
Considerations.
Department of children and family services, 20: 505/7.
Department of children and family services.
Considerations when placing child, 20: 505/7.
Multiple placements, limit on, 20: 505/7.7.
One church one child advisory board, 20: 505/7.1.
Siblings, 20: 505/7.4.
Individual needs of child considered, 20: 505/7.
Relatives.
Considerations by department of children and family services when placing child, 20: 505/7.
Siblings.
Placement by department, 20: 505/7.4.

CHILDREN AND FAMILY SERVICES, DEPARTMENT OF.
Abused, neglected or dependent children.
Reporting child abuse and neglect generally, 325: 5/1 to 5/11.7.
See CHILD ABUSE, NEGLECT OR DEPENDENCY.
Child custody supervision, 750: 5/608.
Child placement.
Placement plan, 20: 505/7.3.
Child placement services.
Considerations in placing child, 20: 505/7.
Multiple placements, limit on, 20: 505/7.7.
One church one child advisory board, 20: 505/7.1.
Siblings, 20: 505/7.4.
Criminal history record information, 20: 510/510-100.
Definition, 20: 510/510-5.
Early intervention services role, 325: 20/9.
Escaped inmates.
Exercise of powers assigned department concerning damages caused by, 20: 510/510-30.
Family support centers.
Demonstration project, 325: 30/1 to 30/9.
Guardianship administrator.
Abused and neglected child temporary protective custody.
Authorized representative for purposes of consenting to HIV tests, 325: 5/5.
High risk youth career development, 325: 25/0.01, 25/1.
Injunctions.
Power to initiate, 20: 510/510-25.
Missing children.
I SEARCH programs.
Contact with department, 325: 40/3.5.
Police and security force, 20: 510/510-200.
Powers.
Administering children and family services act, 20: 510/510-15.
Generally, 20: 510/510-10.
Juvenile court act, 20: 510/510-20.
Senior citizens' child care support act.
Training program development, 320: 45/15 to 45/25.
Short title of article, 20: 510/510-1.
State agency employees child care services act, 20: 510/510-35.
Statutory responsibilities pertaining to children, 20: 510/510-95.

CHILDREN AND MINORS.
Abandoned newborn infant protection act, 325: 2/1 to 2/999.
See ABANDONED NEWBORN PROTECTION ACT.
Abandonment.
School bus drivers, 720: 150/4.1, 150/5.
Abduction, 720: 5/10-5, 5/10-7.
Abortion law.
Parental notice of abortion requirements, 750: 70/1 to 70/99.
See ABORTION, PARENTAL NOTICE.
Abused, neglected or dependent children.
Child sexual abuse, 325: 15/0.01 to 15/7.
Reporting child abuse and neglect generally, 325: 5/1 to 5/11.7.
See CHILD ABUSE, NEGLECT OR DEPENDENCY.
Adoption, 750: 50/0.01 to 55/1.
See ADOPTION.
Aggravated kidnapping.
Child under 13 years, 720: 5/10-2.
Artificial insemination, status of child conceived by, 750: 40/2.
Birth control services to, 325: 10/0.01, 10/1.
Cannabis.
Sales to minors.
Parental right of recovery for damages, 740: 120/1 to 120/4.
Child endangerment.
Drug related child endangerment, 720: 5/12-4.10.
Aggravated drug related child endangerment, 720: 5/12-4.11.
Contracts.
Emancipated mature minors, rights and responsibilities, 750: 30/5.
Controlled substances.
Sales to minors.
Parental right of recovery for damages, 740: 120/1 to 120/4.
Criminal neglect, 720: 130/0.01 to 130/3.
Curfew hours, 720: 555/1.
Short title, 720: 555/0.01.
Stricter local ordinances, 720: 555/2.
Custody jurisdiction.
Uniform child custody jurisdiction and enforcement, 750: 36/101 to 36/405.
Custody of children generally.
See CHILD CUSTODY.
Domestic violence, 750: 60/101 to 60/401.
See DOMESTIC VIOLENCE.
Early intervention services, 325: 20/1 to 20/20.
Emancipation of mature minors, 750: 30/1 to 30/11.
Endangerment.
Wrongs to children, 720: 150/4.1, 150/5.
Exploitation.
Commercial exploitation, 720: 150/1 to 150/5.1.
Family purpose doctrine, 740: 115/1 to 115/7.
Family support centers.
Demonstration project, 325: 30/1 to 30/9.
Fingerprint cards for minors, 325: 45/1 to 45/3.
Harboring a runaway, 720: 5/10-6.
Hearing impaired and behavior disordered children.
Interagency board, 325: 35/1 to 35/12.
High risk youth career development, 325: 25/0.01, 25/1.
Identification cards.
Fingerprint cards for minors, 325: 45/1 to 45/3.
Interagency board for hearing impaired/behavior disordered children, 325: 35/1 to 35/12.
Invalidity of marriage, declaration of.
Underage marriages, 750: 5/301.
Kidnapping.
Aggravated kidnapping.
Child under 13 years, 720: 5/10-2.
Marriage.
Court ordered licenses, 750: 5/208.
Invalidity commencement, 750: 5/302.
Invalidity grounds, 750: 5/301.
License age requirements, 750: 5/203.

CHILDREN AND MINORS —Cont'd
Missing children.
Generally, 325: 40/1 to 55/7.
Name changes, 735: 5/21-101.
Parentage proceedings.
Generally, 750: 40/1 to 45/27.
See PARENTAGE PROCEEDINGS.
Parental notice of abortion, 750: 70/1 to 70/99.
See ABORTION, PARENTAL NOTICE.
Parental responsibility law, 740: 115/1 to 115/7.
Privacy.
Children's privacy protection and parental empowerment act, 325: 17/1 to 17/20.
Removal of child from homestead by spouse, 750: 65/16.
Sexual abuse, 325: 15/0.01 to 15/7.
Support.
See CHILD SUPPORT.
Surgical institute for children, 325: 60/0.01 to 60/12.
Ticket sales.
Public conveyance travel tickets.
Unlawful sale to minor, 720: 5/10-8.
Underage marriages.
Invalidity of marriage, declaration of, 750: 5/301.
Visitation interference, 720: 5/10-5.5.
Witnesses.
Child abuse cases, 735: 5/8-2601.
Sexual conduct performed in presence of minor, 735: 5/8-2601.
Wrongs to children.
Child endangerment, 720: 150/4.1.
Commercial exploitation, 720: 150/1 to 150/3.
Parent permitting child sexual abuse, 720: 150/5.1.
Penalty, 720: 150/5.
Short title, 720: 150/0.01.
Single parent employment restrictions, 720: 150/3.1.

CHILDREN'S PRIVACY PROTECTION AND PARENTAL EMPOWERMENT ACT, 325: 17/1 to 17/20.

CHILDREN WITH BEHAVIORAL DISORDERS.
Interagency board for hearing impaired/behavior disordered children, 325: 35/1 to 35/12.

CHILDREN WITH DISABILITIES.
Early intervention services, 325: 20/1 to 20/20.
Hearing impaired or behavior disordered children.
Interagency board for hearing impaired/behavior disordered children, 325: 35/1 to 35/12.

CHILDREN WITH HEARING IMPAIRMENTS.
Interagency board for hearing impaired/behavior disordered children, 325: 35/1 to 35/12.

CHILD SEXUAL ABUSE, 325: 15/0.01 to 15/7.
Child sexual abuse prevention act.
Short title, 325: 15/0.01.
Confidentiality of information.
Law enforcement and court records, 325: 15/5.
Cook county.
Child sexual abuse crisis intervention demonstration center, 325: 15/4.
Crisis intervention centers, 325: 15/4.
Receipt of funds from federal, voluntary, philanthropic or other sources, 325: 15/6.
Findings of general assembly, 325: 15/1.
Functions and goals of programs to be developed, 325: 15/3.
Funding for crisis intervention centers, 325: 15/6.
Grant programs, 325: 15/4.
Parent permitting sexual abuse, 720: 150/5.1.
Prevention programs and services.
Department of children and family services to develop, 325: 15/2.

CHILD SEXUAL ABUSE —Cont'd
Prevention programs and services —Cont'd
Functions and goals of programs to be developed, 325: 15/3.
Purposes of act, 325: 15/1.
Reports.
Department of children and family services to submit annual reports, 325: 15/7.
Treatment and counseling of sexually abused children and families.
Department of children and family services to provide, 325: 15/2.

CHILD SUPPORT.
Abatement of payments, Sup. Ct. Rule 296.
Agents receiving and disbursing payments, 750: 5/705.
Agreements of parties.
Expedited support.
Acceptance by administrative hearing officers, 750: 25/6; Sup. Ct. Rule 100.4.
Agreements to dissolve marriage, 750: 5/502.
Aid to families with dependent children.
Enforcement of obligation, 305: 5/4-1.7.
Appearance.
Expedited support.
Failure of party to appear, 750: 25/10; Sup. Ct. Rule 100.8.
Attachment of the body, 750: 5/713.
Attorney appointment to represent interest of minor or dependent child, 750: 5/506.
Automatic continuance of obligation.
Unpaid arrearage or delinquency on termination date, 750: 5/505, 45/13.1.
Blood tests.
Expedited support.
Order to submit to test, Sup. Ct. Rule 100.5.
Bonds to secure payment, 750: 5/706.2.
Calculation guidelines, 750: 5/505.
Change of circumstances.
Modification or termination.
Factors considered, 750: 5/510.
Circuit judge or associate judges.
Expedited support.
Authority retained by court, 750: 25/8.
Consumer reporting agency.
Obligor owing arrearage or delinquent in payment, information to agency, 750: 5/706.3.
Contempt.
Enforcement of support order, Sup. Ct. Rule 296.
Nonpayment, 750: 5/505.
Court authority to order, 750: 5/505.
Court ordered payments, 750: 5/513.
Data match system, financial institutions.
Support responsibility of relatives of public aid recipients, 305: 5/10-24 to 5/10-24.50.
Date of termination, 750: 5/505.
Debit authorization, 305: 5/10-16.7.
Default.
Net income not determined because of.
Amount ordered by court, 750: 5/505.
Definitions.
Expedited support, 750: 25/3; Sup. Ct. Rule 100.13.
Delinquencies, Sup. Ct. Rule 296.
Automatic continuance of obligation.
Unpaid arrearage or delinquency on termination date, 750: 5/505, 45/13.1.
Delinquency in payment, enforcement proceedings, 750: 5/710.
Driving privilege suspended, 750: 5/505.
Discovery.
Expedited child support.
Hearing officer to manage stages, 750: 25/6.
Dissolution of marriage.
Agreements, 750: 5/502.
Domestic violence.
Protection orders.
Enforcement of support order violations, 750: 60/223.
Modification, 750: 60/224.
Order for payment of support, 750: 60/214.
Drivers' licenses.
Family financial responsibility driving permit.
Issuance when driving privilege suspended for delinquency, 750: 5/505.

CHILD SUPPORT —Cont'd
Drivers' licenses —Cont'd
Suspension for nonpayment of child support, 750: 5/505.
Educational expenses.
Court ordered payments, 750: 5/513.
Support to include, 750: 5/505.
Termination, 750: 5/510.
Emancipation of mature minors, 750: 30/1 to 30/11.
Employment of obligor or termination from employment.
Report to obligee and clerk of court, 750: 5/505.
Employment search orders, 750: 5/505.1.
Enforcement, Sup. Ct. Rule 296.
Debit authorization, 305: 5/10-16.7.
Enforcement program, 750: 5/710.
Fees to reimburse covered counties, 750: 5/711.
Rules for certification, 750: 5/712.
Supervision, 750: 5/712.
Evidence.
Expedited support.
Administrative hearings, 750: 25/7; Sup. Ct. Rule 100.7.
Recommendations of administrative hearing officers based on, 750: 25/6.
Expedited support, 750: 25/1 to 25/13; Sup. Ct. Rules 100.1 to 100.13.
Actions eligible to be heard by an administrative hearing officer, 750: 25/5; Sup. Ct. Rule 100.3.
Act takes effect upon becoming law, 750: 25/13.
Administrative hearing officers.
Action heard by, 750: 25/5; Sup. Ct. Rule 100.3.
Appointment, Sup. Ct. Rule 100.2.
Authority, 750: 25/6.
Communicating with attorneys, Sup. Ct. Rule 100.2.
Compensation, Sup. Ct. Rule 100.2.
Conflicts of interest, Sup. Ct. Rule 100.2.
Disqualification, Sup. Ct. Rule 100.2.
Oath of office, Sup. Ct. Rule 100.2.
Qualifications, Sup. Ct. Rule 100.2.
Testimony as to contested matters, Sup. Ct. Rule 100.10.
Agreements of parties.
Acceptance by administrative hearing officers, 750: 25/6; Sup. Ct. Rule 100.4.
Appearance.
Failure of party to appear, 750: 25/10; Sup. Ct. Rule 100.8.
Authority of hearing officers, 750: 25/6.
Blood tests.
Order to submit to test, Sup. Ct. Rule 100.5.
Circuit judge or associate judges.
Authority retained by court, 750: 25/8.
Definitions, 750: 25/3; Sup. Ct. Rule 100.13.
Discovery.
Hearing officer to manage stages, 750: 25/6.
Effective date of act, 750: 25/13.
Establishment of system, 750: 25/4; Sup. Ct. Rule 100.1.
Evidence.
Administrative hearings, 750: 25/7; Sup. Ct. Rule 100.7.
Recommendations of administrative hearing officers based on, 750: 25/6.
Expedited child support act.
Short title, 750: 25/1.
Hearings.
Administrative hearings, 750: 25/6; Sup. Ct. Rules 100.6 to 100.8.
Judicial hearings, 750: 25/9; Sup. Ct. Rules 100.9 to 100.12.
Scheduling, 750: 25/7.
Motions, pre-hearing motions, 750: 25/7.
Non-IV-D obligees.
Information to be supplied by administrative hearing officers, 750: 25/6; Sup. Ct. Rule 100.4.
Notice of hearing, 750: 25/7; Sup. Ct. Rule 100.6.

CHILD SUPPORT —Cont'd
Expedited support —Cont'd
Notice of recommended order, 750: 25/7; Sup. Ct. Rule 100.10.
Service, 750: 25/10; Sup. Ct. Rule 100.8.
Orders for support.
Acceptance or rejection by court of recommended order, Sup. Ct. Rule 100.10.
Judicial orders, Sup. Ct. Rule 100.12.
Recommended orders.
Acceptance or rejection by court, Sup. Ct. Rule 100.10.
Review by court, Sup. Ct. Rule 100.11.
Orders agreed upon by parties, Sup. Ct. Rule 100.12.
Orders rejected by parties, Sup. Ct. Rule 100.12.
Parentage acknowledgments.
Acceptance by administrative hearing officers, 750: 25/6; Sup. Ct. Rule 100.4.
Public policy, 750: 25/2.
Purposes, 750: 25/2.
Service of notice to commence action, 750: 25/7.
Service of recommended order, 750: 25/10; Sup. Ct. Rule 100.8.
System established, 750: 25/4.
Transfers for judicial hearings.
Administrative hearings, 750: 25/7.
Unemployed obligors.
Recommendations of administrative hearing officers, 750: 25/6; Sup. Ct. Rule 100.4.
Witnesses.
Administrative hearing officer as witness in contested matters, Sup. Ct. Rule 100.10.
Failure of party to comply with dissolution judgment, order or injunction.
Obligation of other party to make payments not suspended, 750: 5/509.
Failure to make payments, contempt, penalties, 750: 5/505.
Family financial responsibility law.
Suspension of driver's license for nonpayment, 750: 5/505.
Fees to reimburse covered county for maintenance of child support enforcement program, 750: 5/711.
Financial institution data match system.
Support responsibility of relatives of public aid recipients, 305: 5/10-24 to 5/10-24.50.
Forms.
Order for enforcement, Sup. Ct. Rule 296.
Gestational surrogacy.
Duty to support child, 750: 47/30.
Guardian ad litem for child, appointment of attorney, 750: 5/506.
Guidelines for determining minimum amount, 750: 5/505.
Health insurance orders.
Child as beneficiary, 750: 5/505.2.
Hearings.
Contempt proceedings to enforce support orders, Sup. Ct. Rule 296.
Expedited support.
Administrative hearings, 750: 25/6; Sup. Ct. Rules 100.6 to 100.8.
Judicial hearings, 750: 25/9; Sup. Ct. Rules 100.9 to 100.12.
Scheduling, 750: 25/7.
Husband-parent's testimony, 735: 5/8-801.
Income withholding to secure payment.
Generally, 750: 28/1 to 28/999.
Intergovernmental agreement.
Unified child support services program, 750: 24/1 to 24/35.
Interstate family support.
General provisions, 750: 22/101 to 22/999.
See SUPPORT AND MAINTENANCE.
Judgment against person obligated to pay support.
New or existing orders entered by court deemed, 750: 5/505.
Judgment enforcement or modification, procedure, 750: 5/511.

CHILD SUPPORT —Cont'd
Jurisdiction.
Interstate family support.
Generally, 750: 22/201 to 22/209.
See SUPPORT AND MAINTENANCE.
Lien by operation of law, 750: 5/505.
Limitation of actions.
Court ordered withdrawals from decedents' estates, 750: 5/510.
Location of putative father and noncustodial parents.
Provision of information, 750: 5/714, 16/33, 45/14.5.
Mandatory payments to clerk, 750: 5/709.
Marital property.
Portion of estate set aside for support, maintenance, etc., 750: 5/503.
Marital property transfers, 750: 65/11.
Marital status of parents, support obligation not dependent on, 750: 45/3.
Marriage and dissolution of marriage act.
Application, 750: 5/801.
Modification of orders, 750: 5/510.
Motions, pre-hearing motions.
Expedited support, 750: 25/7.
New or existing support order deemed series of judgments against person obligated to pay, 750: 5/505.
Non-minor children, 750: 5/513.
Nonsupport.
Drivers' licenses, family financial responsibility law.
Suspension for nonpayment of child support, 750: 5/505.
Generally, 750: 16/1 to 16/999.
See NONSUPPORT OF CHILD OR SPOUSE.
Notice of delinquency, Sup. Ct. Rule 296.
Notice of hearing.
Contempt proceedings to enforce support orders, Sup. Ct. Rule 296.
Expedited support proceedings.
Administrative hearings, 750: 25/7; Sup. Ct. Rule 100.6.
Notice of proceedings to hold respondent in contempt, service, 750: 5/505.
Notice of recommended order.
Expedited support, 750: 25/7; Sup. Ct. Rule 100.10.
Obligation not dependent on marriage, 750: 45/3.
One-time charge upon amount of past-due support, 750: 5/505.
Orders for support.
Expedited support.
Acceptance or rejection by court of recommended order, Sup. Ct. Rule 100.10.
Judicial orders, Sup. Ct. Rule 100.12.
Recommended orders.
Acceptance or rejection by court, Sup. Ct. Rule 100.10.
Review by court, Sup. Ct. Rule 100.11.
Orders agreed upon by parties, Sup. Ct. Rule 100.12.
Orders rejected by parties, Sup. Ct. Rule 100.12.
Parentage acknowledgments.
Expedited support.
Acceptance by administrative hearing officers, 750: 25/6; Sup. Ct. Rule 100.4.
Voluntary acknowledgment of parentage, basis for seeking, 750: 45/6.
Parentage proceedings.
Automatic continuance of obligation.
Unpaid arrearage or delinquency on termination of obligation, 750: 45/13.1, 45/14.
Continuing jurisdiction of court to modify order, 750: 45/16.
Enforcement of judgment or order, 750: 45/15.
Financial information concerning ability to provide support.
Evidence, information obtained by subpoena, 750: 45/14.

CHILD SUPPORT —Cont'd
Parentage proceedings —Cont'd
Generally, 750: 40/1 to 45/27.
See PARENTAGE PROCEEDINGS.
Guidelines for determining award, 750: 45/14.
Interest on obligation due and unpaid, 750: 45/20.7.
Judgments to contain provisions concerning, 750: 45/14.
Payments to state disbursement unit, 750: 45/21.1.
Report by obligor of employment or termination from employment, 750: 45/14.
State case registry, information on entry of order, 750: 45/14.1.
Temporary order for child support, 750: 45/13.1.
Unemployed obligors, court's powers, 750: 45/15.1.
Unpaid arrearage or delinquency on termination of obligation.
Automatic continuance of obligation, 750: 45/13.1, 45/14.
Withholding of income to secure payment of support, 750: 45/20.
Procedures to avoid income withholding, 750: 45/20.
Parents' testimony, 735: 5/8-801.
Past due child support.
One time charge, 750: 5/505.
Payment pursuant to order, Sup. Ct. Rule 296.
Payments to court, 750: 5/507.
Payments to state disbursement unit, 750: 5/507.1.
Petitions.
Contempt proceedings to enforce support orders, Sup. Ct. Rule 296.
Post-judgment procedure, 750: 5/511.
Property disposition upon dissolution of marriage.
Use for, 750: 5/503.
Protective orders against domestic violence.
Order for payment, 725: 5/112A-14.
Violation of order, 725: 5/112A-23.
Public aid collection fee.
Imposition, 750: 5/516.
Public aid recipients.
Administrative orders, 305: 5/10-11.
Court enforcement, 305: 5/10-10.
Mandatory payments to clerk, 750: 5/709.
Payments, 750: 5/704.
Wage deduction orders, 750: 5/706.1.
Publication in newspaper of obligor's name when obligor owes arrearage or delinquent, 750: 5/706.3.
Receiving and disbursing agent, 750: 5/705.
Relief temporarily during proceedings, 750: 5/501.
Reports.
Report by obligor of new employment or termination from employment, 750: 5/505, 45/14.
Separate fund or trust upon dissolution of marriage, 750: 5/503.
Series of judgments against person obligated to pay, 750: 5/505.
Service of notice of contempt proceedings, 750: 5/505.
Service of notice to commence action.
Expedited support, 750: 25/7.
Service of process or provision of notice at last known address, 750: 5/505.
Severability of marriage and dissolution of marriage act, 750: 5/801.
State case registry.
Furnishing information on entry or modification of order, 750: 5/505.3.
Support and maintenance generally.
See SUPPORT AND MAINTENANCE.
Temporary orders.
Parentage proceedings, 750: 45/13.1.
Temporary relief during proceedings, 750: 5/501.
Termination date, 750: 5/505.

CHILD SUPPORT —Cont'd
Termination of support conditions, 750: 5/510.
Transfers for judicial hearings.
Expedited support.
Administrative hearings, 750: 25/7.
Unemployed obligors.
Employment search ordered by court, 750: 5/505.1.
Expedited support.
Recommendations of administrative hearing officers, 750: 25/6; Sup. Ct. Rule 100.4.
Unified child support services program, 750: 24/1 to 24/35.
Definitions, 750: 24/5.
Plan.
Components, 750: 24/15.
Subcontracts, 750: 24/20.
Submission to department, approval or rejection, management, restrictions, 750: 24/10.
Unified child support services act.
Act cited as, 750: 24/1.
Wage deduction orders, 750: 5/706.1.
Parentage proceedings, 750: 45/20.
Wife-parent's testimony, 735: 5/8-801.
Withholding of income to secure, 750: 5/706.1, 28/1 to 28/999, 45/20.
Automatic continuance of obligation.
Unpaid arrearage or delinquency on termination date of obligation, 750: 28/32.
Information concerning obligors, 305: 5/10-16.4.
Interstate family support, 750: 22/501 to 22/507.
National medical support notice.
Use to enforce health insurance coverage, 750: 28/22.
Witnesses.
Expedited support proceedings.
Contested matters.
Administrative hearing officer's testimony, Sup. Ct. Rule 100.10.
Husband and wife, 735: 5/8-801.

CHILD SUPPORT ENFORCEMENT PROGRAM, 750: 5/709 to 5/712.

CHILD SUPPORT GUIDELINES.
Determining minimum amount, 750: 5/505.

CHILD VISITATION, 750: 5/607.
Abuse.
Expedited procedures, 750: 5/607.1.
Agreement upon dissolution of marriage, 750: 5/502.
Attorney appointment to represent interest of minor or dependent child, 750: 5/506.
Child custody.
Uniform child custody jurisdiction and enforcement.
Temporary visitation orders, 750: 36/304.
Domestic violence protection orders.
Determining rights, 750: 60/214.
Modification, 750: 60/224.
Enforcement of visitation in cases of visitation abuse, 750: 5/607.1.
Exchange of custody for purposes of visitation.
Neutral site custody exchange act, 55: 82/1 to 82/99.
Failure of party to comply with dissolution judgment, order or injunction.
Obligation of other party not suspended, 750: 5/509.
First degree murder conviction of person with visitation rights.
Revocation of visitation rights previously granted, 750: 5/607.
Guardian ad litem for child, 750: 5/506.
Interviews of child by court, 750: 5/604.
Neutral site custody exchange act, 55: 82/1 to 82/99.
Orders.
Modifications and enforcement, 750: 5/607.1.
Parentage proceedings.
Continuing jurisdiction of court to modify order, 750: 45/16.

CHILD VISITATION —Cont'd
Parentage proceedings —Cont'd
Judgments to contain provisions concerning, 750: 45/14.
Revocation of privilege, 750: 5/607.
Sex offenders convicted of offense upon victim less than 18 years of age, 750: 5/607.
Stepparents, 750: 5/607.
Unlawful interference, 720: 5/10-5.5.

CHIROPRACTORS.
Child abuse and neglect reporting.
Required reports, 325: 5/4.
Elder abuse and neglect.
Failure to report, 320: 20/4.

CHRISTIAN SCIENCE PRACTITIONERS.
Elder abuse and neglect.
Failure to report, 320: 20/4.

CIRCUIT COURT CLERKS.
Adoptions.
Birth certificate issuance, 750: 50/19.
Confidentiality of records, 750: 50/18.
Disclaimer of paternity, 750: 50/12a.
Process service affidavit, 750: 50/7.
Putative father's notice, 750: 50/12a.
Attachment of the body orders, 750: 5/713.
Child support enforcement program, 750: 5/709 to 5/712.
Child support orders, state case registry, furnishing information, 750: 5/505.3.
Child support payments, mandatory payments to clerk, 750: 5/709.
Credit reporting agencies.
Parentage proceedings.
Child support arrearage or delinquent payments, 750: 45/20.5.
Disclaimer of paternity, 750: 50/12a.
Parentage proceedings.
Credit reporting agencies.
Child support arrearage or delinquent payments, 750: 45/20.5.
Payments of child support made to, 750: 45/21.
Public aid collection fees.
Collection duty, 750: 5/516.
Wage deduction orders.
Paternity proceedings, 750: 45/20.
Securing support payments, 750: 5/706.1.

CIRCUIT COURTS.
Adoptions.
Jurisdiction, 750: 50/4.
Paternity disclaimers, 750: 50/12a.
Child abuse and neglect reporting.
Assistance to circuit court, 325: 5/8.3.
Disclaimers of paternity, 750: 50/12a.
Emancipation of mature minors.
Jurisdiction, 750: 30/4.
Maintenance actions, 750: 5/402.
Marriage and dissolution of marriage rules.
Adoption power, 750: 5/802.
Marriage licenses.
Effective date, 750: 5/207.
Exception waivers, 750: 5/205.
Orders for those underage, 750: 5/208.
Paternity action jurisdiction, 750: 45/9.
Paternity disclaimers, 750: 50/12a.
Protection orders.
Domestic violence.
Jurisdiction, 750: 60/207.

CITIZEN'S COMMITTEE ON CHILD ABUSE AND NEGLECT, 325: 5/11.7.

CIVIL PROCEDURE CODE.
Marriage dissolution actions.
Applicability, 750: 5/410.
Name changes, 735: 5/21-101 to 5/21-104.
Protection orders.
Domestic violence.
Application of rules, 750: 60/205.

CIVIL PROCEDURE RULES.
Support orders.
Enforcement, Sup. Ct. Rule 296.

CLEAR AND CONVINCING EVIDENCE.
Adoption consent, 750: 50/8.

CLEAR AND CONVINCING EVIDENCE —Cont'd
Domestic violence protection orders.
Disclosure of privileged information, 750: 60/227.1.
Paternity presumption, 750: 45/5.

CLERKS OF COURT.
Child support payments, mandatory payments to clerk, 750: 5/709.
Credit reporting agencies.
Parentage proceedings.
Child support arrearage or delinquent payments, 750: 45/20.5.
Parentage proceedings.
Credit reporting agencies.
Child support arrearage or delinquent payments, 750: 45/20.5.
Payments of child support made to, 750: 45/21.

CLINICAL PSYCHOLOGISTS.
Child abuse and neglect reporting, 325: 5/4.
Early intervention services, 325: 20/1 to 20/20.
Elder abuse and neglect.
Failure to report, 320: 20/4.

COGNITIVE DEVELOPMENT.
Early intervention services, 325: 20/1 to 20/20.

COHABITATION.
Dissolution of marriage.
Effect of certain periods of cohabitation, 750: 5/401.
Living separate and apart.
Cohabitation period included, 750: 5/401.
Foreign marriage proved by, 750: 5/409.
Maintenance obligation terminated if party receiving cohabits with another, 750: 5/510.
Prohibited marriages.
Effect of cohabitation after removal of impediment, 750: 5/212.
Putative spouse, 750: 5/305.

COLLEGES AND UNIVERSITIES.
Dissolution of marriage.
Support for non-minor children and educational expenses, 750: 5/513.

COLLUSION.
Dissolution of marriage, 750: 5/408.

COMMENCEMENT OF ACTIONS.
Adoption proceedings, 750: 50/5.
Breach of promise to marry, 740: 15/6.
Child custody proceedings, 750: 5/601.
Declaration of invalidity of marriage, 750: 5/306.
Time of commencement, 750: 5/302.
Dissolution of marriage or legal separation, 750: 5/411.
Protective orders against domestic violence, 725: 5/112A-2.

COMMERCE AND COMMUNITY AFFAIRS, DEPARTMENT OF.
High risk youth career development, 325: 25/0.01, 25/1.

COMMERCIAL EXPLOITATION OF CHILDREN.
Penalty, 720: 150/5.
Prohibited conduct, 720: 150/1, 150/2.
Termination of custody rights, 720: 150/3.

COMMINGLED MARITAL AND NON-MARITAL PROPERTY.
Disposition upon marriage dissolution or invalidity, 750: 5/503.

COMMITTEES.
Child abuse and neglect, citizens committee on, 325: 5/11.7.
Senior pharmaceutical assistance review committee, 320: 50/15.

COMMON LAW MARRIAGES, 750: 5/214.
Legitimacy of children, 750: 5/212.

COMMUNICABLE OR INFECTIOUS DISEASES.
Child abuse and neglect.
Temporary caretaker provided results of test, 325: 5/5.

COMMUNICABLE OR INFECTIOUS DISEASES —Cont'd
Dissolution of marriage.
Grounds for, infection with communicable venereal disease, 750: 5/401.

COMMUNITY SENIOR SERVICES AND RESOURCE CENTERS, 320: 60/1 to 60/99.
Advisory committee, 320: 60/35.
Awareness campaign.
Department to design, 320: 60/32.
Bequests and gifts, 320: 60/32.
Definitions, 320: 60/15.
Duties of department, 320: 60/20.
Effective date of act, 320: 60/99.
Fund, 320: 60/40.
Funding and waivers, 320: 60/30.
Grants, 320: 60/25.
Legislative findings, 320: 60/5.
Legislative intent, 320: 60/10.
Title of act, 320: 60/1.

COMMUNITY SERVICE.
Nonsupport of spouse and children act conviction, 750: 5/505.

COMPLAINTS.
Injunctions.
Dissolution.
Supporting complaint by affidavit, 735: 5/11-109.
Parentage proceedings.
Determination of father and child relationship or non-existence of relationship, 750: 45/7.

COMPREHENSIVE HEALTH INSURANCE PLAN.
Board.
Senior pharmaceutical assistance act.
Study of catastrophic pharmaceutical assistance coverage, 320: 50/25.

COMPROMISE AND SETTLEMENT.
Marriage dissolution settlement agreements, 750: 5/502.
Parentage proceedings.
Settlement offers, 750: 45/12.1.

CONCILIATION.
Dissolution of marriage conference, 750: 5/404.

CONDOMS.
Service to minors, 325: 10/0.01, 10/1.

CONDONATION.
Dissolution of marriage.
Defenses, 750: 5/403.

CONFIDENTIAL INTERMEDIARY.
Appointment to obtain adoptee information, 750: 50/18.3a.

CONFIDENTIALITY.
Adoption records, 750: 50/18.
Adoption registry information, 750: 50/18.1.
Child abuse and neglect reporting.
Disclosure of information, 325: 5/11.1a.
Information received by temporary caretakers, 325: 5/5.
Persons seeking use of services and facilities established under act, 325: 5/2.1.
Records generated as result of reports or referrals, 325: 5/11.
Child custody hearing records.
Order sealing record, 750: 5/606.
Child sexual abuse.
Records or reports, 325: 15/5.
Domestic violence counselors and victims.
Privileged communications, 750: 60/227.
Domestic violence victim's address, 750: 61/1 to 61/45.
Early intervention services.
Personally identifiable information, 325: 20/12.
Health insurance orders.
Beneficiary designation, 750: 5/505.2.
Marital dissolution.
Address of residents, 750: 5/708.
Protection orders.
Domestic violence petitioner's address, 750: 60/203.

CONFIDENTIALITY —Cont'd
Registry for adoption information, 750: 50/18.1.
Senior citizens and disabled persons property tax relief and pharmaceutical assistance, 320: 25/8a.
Support and maintenance.
Interstate family support.
Nondisclosure of information in exceptional circumstances, 750: 22/312.

CONFLICT OF LAWS.
Marriage validity, 750: 5/213.
Nonresidents, 750: 5/217.
Prohibited marriages, 750: 5/216.
Paternity act of 1984, 750: 45/25.
Support, reciprocal enforcement, 750: 22/910.
Application of law of this state, 750: 22/303.
Registration of orders for enforcement.
Choice of law, 750: 22/604.

CONSCIENCE CLAUSE.
Abortions, 720: 510/13.

CONSENT TO ADOPTION, 750: 50/8.
Child or adult, 750: 50/12.
Forms of consent and surrender, 750: 50/10.
Foster family homes, guardian's consent, 750: 50/15.1.
Guardian with power, appeal of appointment, Sup. Ct. Rule 663.
Irrevocability, 750: 50/11.
Time for taking consent or surrender, 750: 50/9.

CONSENT TO ESTABLISHMENT OF PARENT-CHILD RELATIONSHIP, 750: 45/6.

CONSENT TO MARRIAGE.
Invalidity, declaration of.
Ground, lack of capacity to consent, 750: 5/301.

CONSIDERATION.
Premarital agreements.
Formalities, 750: 10/3.

CONSOLIDATION OF ACTIONS.
Domestic violence protection orders, 750: 60/202.

CONSTRUCTIVE NOTICE.
Protective orders against domestic violence, 725: 5/112A-10.

CONSUMER FRAUD AND DECEPTIVE BUSINESS PRACTICES.
Children's privacy protection and parental empowerment act.
Violation of act to constitute, 325: 17/20.

CONSUMMATION OF MARRIAGE.
Invalidity, declaration of.
Ground, lack of capacity to consummate, 750: 5/301.

CONTEMPT.
Child support.
Enforcement of support order, Sup. Ct. Rule 296.
Child support payments.
Imposition for nonsupport, 750: 5/505.
Domestic violence.
Protection orders.
Enforcement of violations, 750: 60/223.
Parentage proceedings.
Failure to comply with order of court, 750: 45/15.
Protective orders against domestic violence, 725: 5/112A-21, 5/112A-23, 750: 60/223.
Spousal support.
Enforcement of support order, Sup. Ct. Rule 296.
Support orders, withholding of income to secure payment.
Obligee falsely initiating proceedings, 750: 5/706.1.
Visitation order violations, 750: 5/607.1.

CONTINUANCES.
Protective orders against domestic violence, 725: 5/112A-13, 750: 60/213.

CONTINUING EDUCATION.
Child abuse and neglect reporting, 325: 5/11.5.

CONTORTIONISTS.
Using or employing child, 720: 150/1, 150/2.

CONTRACEPTIVES.
Service to minors, 325: 10/0.01, 10/1.

CONTRACTS.
Abandoned spouses control over property, 750: 65/12.
Adoption, instruments regarding property rights.
Child deemed born to adopting parents, 760: 30/0.01, 30/1.
Agreements to dissolve marriage.
Enforceability, 750: 5/502.
Antenuptial agreements, 750: 10/1 to 10/11.
Dissolution of marriage agreements.
Enforceability, 750: 5/502.
Emancipation of mature minors.
Rights and responsibilities, 750: 30/5.
Gestational surrogacy generally, 750: 47/1 to 47/75.
See GESTATIONAL SURROGACY.
Married persons rights.
Abandoned spouses control over property, 750: 65/12.
Power and liability, 750: 65/6.
Minors.
Emancipated mature minors, rights and responsibilities, 750: 30/5.
Premarital agreements, 750: 10/1 to 10/11.
State disbursement unit.
Public aid, 305: 5/10-26.2.
Unconscionability.
Premarital agreements, 750: 10/7.

CONTRIBUTING TO THE DELINQUENCY OF A MINOR, 720: 130/2a.
Criminal neglect of children, 720: 130/2a.

CONTRIBUTING TO THE DEPENDENCY AND NEGLECT OF CHILDREN, 720: 130/2.

CONTROLLED SUBSTANCES.
Drug related child endangerment, 720: 5/12-4.10.
Laboratories.
Drug related child endangerment.
Exposing child to clandestine drug laboratory environment, 720: 5/12-4.10, 5/12-4.11.
Sales to minors.
Parental right of recovery for damages, 740: 120/1 to 120/4.

CONVEYANCES.
Marital property, 750: 5/503.
Married persons rights.
Spouse under legal disability, 750: 65/17 to 65/21.

COOK COUNTY.
Child sexual abuse crisis intervention demonstration center, 325: 15/4.

CORONERS.
Child abuse and neglect reporting.
Access to records, 325: 5/11.1.
Investigation of reports of death resulting from abuse or neglect, 325: 5/4.1.
Required reports, 325: 5/4.

CORPORAL PUNISHMENT.
Excessive corporal punishment.
Definition of abused child or minor, 325: 5/3, 750: 50/1.

CORRECTIONS, DEPARTMENT OF.
Child abuse and neglect reporting.
Required reports, 325: 5/4.
Employees.
Forcible detention, holding employee hostage, 720: 5/10-4.

COUNCILS.
Interagency council on early intervention, 325: 20/4.
Local early intervention councils, 325: 20/6.

COUNSELORS.
Child abuse and neglect reporting.
Required reports, 325: 5/4.

COUNTY CLERKS.
Fetal alcohol syndrome pamphlet distribution, 750: 5/203.
Inherited metabolic disease pamphlets.
Distribution, 750: 5/204.
Maintenance payments, 750: 5/504.
Marriage certificates.
Filing, 750: 5/209.
Registration, 750: 5/210.
Reporting of numbers, 750: 5/211.
Marriage licenses.
Court ordered issuance, 750: 5/208.
Exceptions, 750: 5/205.
Fetal alcohol syndrome pamphlets.
Distribution, 750: 5/203.
Foreign jurisdiction laws, 750: 5/218.
Health certificate retention, 750: 5/206.
Inherited metabolic disease pamphlets.
Distribution, 750: 5/204.
Issuance when presented with accompaniments, 750: 5/203.
Recording of numbers, 750: 5/211.
Sexually transmitted disease pamphlets.
Distribution, 750: 5/204.
Unauthorized issuance.
Penalty, 750: 5/219.
Marriage solemnization, 750: 5/209.
Missing children.
Duties, 325: 50/4, 55/4.
Sexually transmitted disease pamphlets.
Distribution, 750: 5/204.

COURT COSTS AND FEES.
Child custody.
Uniform child custody jurisdiction and enforcement, 750: 36/312.
Public officials, 750: 36/317.
Child custody hearings, 750: 5/606.
Child custody orders.
Modification, 750: 5/610.
Child support enforcement program, 750: 5/711.
Parentage proceedings, 750: 45/17.
Notice to presumed father, 750: 45/9.1.
Public aid collection fee, 750: 45/22.
Protection orders.
Domestic violence.
Order for payment of losses, 750: 60/214.
Untrue statements, 750: 60/226.
Public aid collection fee.
Support of child or spouse obligation, collection in marriage dissolution proceedings, 750: 5/516.
Support and maintenance.
Interstate family support, 750: 22/313.
Visitation enforcement action vexatious and harassing, 750: 5/607.1.
Visitation order violations, 750: 5/607.1.

COUSINS.
Child placed with relatives.
Department of children and family services, 20: 505/7.

CREDITORS.
Married persons rights.
Creditor's rights, 750: 65/15.

CREDIT REPORTING AGENCIES.
Parentage proceedings.
Child support arrearage or delinquent payments.
Reporting information, 750: 45/20.5.

CREDIT UNIONS.
Support responsibility of relatives of public aid recipients.
Data match system designed and implemented by department of public aid, 305: 5/10-24 to 5/10-24.50.

CRIME VICTIMS.
Domestic violence victims.
Assistance by law enforcement officers, 750: 60/304.
Providing information or services to, 750: 60/401.

CRIMINAL ABDUCTION.
Aiding and abetting, 720: 5/10-7.

CRIMINAL HISTORY RECORDS.
Child placed with relatives.
Department of children and family services, 20: 505/7.

CRIMINAL LIABILITY.
Parties to crime.
Aiding and abetting child abduction, 720: 5/10-7.

CRIMINAL NEGLECT OF CHILDREN, 720: 130/0.01 to 130/3.
Competency of parent witnesses, 720: 130/3.
Contributing to the delinquency of children, 720: 130/2a.
Contributing to the dependency and neglect of children, 720: 130/2.
Delinquent child.
Defined, 720: 130/1a.
Dependent and neglected child.
Defined, 720: 130/1.
Short title.
Neglected children offense act, 720: 130/0.01.

CRIMINAL OFFENSES.
Abortion law generally.
See ABORTION.
Abused and neglected children reporting.
Failure to report or false reports, 325: 5/4, 5/4.02.
Adoption compensation.
Child welfare agency exception, 720: 525/1.
Construction of act, 720: 525/4.
Penalty, 720: 525/5.
"Placing out" defined, 720: 525/3.
Prohibited, 720: 525/2.
Short title, 720: 525/0.01.
Adoption registry information.
Disclosure, 750: 50/18.1.
Aggravated kidnapping, 720: 5/10-2.
Aggravated unlawful restraint, 720: 5/10-3.1.
Battery.
Domestic battery, 720: 5/12-3.2.
Aggravated domestic battery, 720: 5/12-3.3.
Child abandonment.
School bus driver, 720: 150/4.1, 150/5.
Child abduction, 720: 5/10-5.
Affirmative defense, 720: 5/10-5.
Aiding and abetting, 720: 5/10-7.
Child abuse and neglect.
Competency of parent witnesses, 720: 130/3.
Contributing to the delinquency of children, 720: 130/2a.
Contributing to the dependency and neglect of children, 720: 130/2.
Definitions, 720: 130/1, 130/1a.
Short title, 720: 130/0.01.
Child abuse and neglect reporting.
Making public identifying information, 325: 5/11.3.
Unauthorized release of information, 325: 5/11.
Child curfew, 720: 555/0.01 to 555/2.
Child endangerment, 720: 150/4.1, 150/5.
Drug related child endangerment, 720: 5/12-4.10.
Aggravated drug related child endangerment, 720: 5/12-4.11.
Childnapping, 720: 5/10-5.
Aiding and abetting, 720: 5/10-7.
Children wrongs.
Abandonment of children on school bus, 720: 150/4.1.
Child endangerment, 720: 150/4.1.
Commercial exploitation, 720: 150/1 to 150/3.
Parent permitting child sexual abuse, 720: 150/5.1.
Penalty, 720: 150/5.
Short title, 720: 150/0.01.

CRIMINAL OFFENSES —Cont'd
Children wrongs —Cont'd
Single parent employment restrictions, 720: 150/3.1.
Child sexual abuse.
Parent permitting sexual abuse, 720: 150/5.1.
Records or reports.
Unauthorized release, 325: 15/5.
Child support.
Nonpayment, 750: 5/505.
Defenses.
Child abduction, 720: 5/10-5.
Unlawful visitation interference, 720: 5/10-5.5.
Detention without lawful authority, 720: 5/10-3.1.
Domestic violence.
See DOMESTIC VIOLENCE.
Elder abuse and neglect.
Failure to report, 320: 20/4.
Failure to report or false reports, 325: 5/4, 5/4.02.
Forcible detention, 720: 5/10-4.
Harboring a runaway, 720: 5/10-6.
Kidnapping, 720: 5/10-1.
Aggravated kidnapping, 720: 5/10-2.
Child abduction, 720: 5/10-5.
Marriage code violations, 750: 5/215.
Protection orders.
Domestic violence, 750: 60/223.
Notice in order, 750: 60/221.
Violation of court orders, 725: 5/112A-21.
Runaway children.
Aiding and abetting child abduction, 720: 5/10-7.
Harboring a runaway, 720: 5/10-6.
Sex offenses.
Child sexual abuse.
Parent permitting sexual abuse, 720: 150/5.1.
Ticket sales to minors.
Unlawful sale of travel ticket, 720: 5/10-8.
Unlawful restraint, 720: 5/10-3, 5/10-3.1.
Unlawful visitation interference, 720: 5/10-5.5.

CRIMINAL PROCEDURE.
Commencement of prosecutions.
Protective orders against domestic violence, 725: 5/112A-2.
Domestic violence protection orders.
Enforcement of order when violation crime, 750: 60/223.
Proceedings.
Commencement in conjunction with criminal prosecution, 750: 60/202.
Nonsupport, prosecution and punishment, 750: 16/1 to 16/999.
See NONSUPPORT OF CHILD OR SPOUSE.

CRIPPLED CHILDREN.
University of Illinois.
Division of services for crippled children.
Early intervention services role, 325: 20/9.

CRISIS LINE OR HOTLINE PERSONNEL.
Child abuse and neglect reporting.
Required reports, 325: 5/4.

CRUELTY TO CHILDREN.
Generally.
See CHILD ABUSE, NEGLECT OR DEPENDENCY.

CRUELTY TO SPOUSE.
Dissolution of marriage grounds, 750: 5/401.

CURFEW FOR JUVENILES.
Curfew hours, 720: 555/1.
Short title, 720: 555/0.01.
Stricter local ordinances, 720: 555/2.

D

DAMAGES.
Adoption.
Identity disclosure of biological parents, 750: 50/18.1, 50/18.3a.
Breach of promise to marry, 740: 15/2, 15/3.

DAMAGES —Cont'd
Domestic violence protection orders.
Order for payment of losses, 750: 60/214.
Family purpose doctrine, 740: 115/3 to 115/5.
Gestational surrogacy, 750: 47/55.
Injunctions.
Dissolution of TRO or preliminary injunction, 735: 5/11-110.
Limitation of damages.
Breach of promise to marry, 740: 15/2.
Parental responsibility law, 740: 115/5.
Married person's right to recover, 750: 65/4.
Parental responsibility law, 740: 115/3 to 115/5.
Prisoners.
Escaped inmates of state-controlled institutions, 20: 510/510-30.

DANCERS.
Using or employing child, 720: 150/1, 150/2.

DANGEROUS WEAPONS OFFENSES.
Aggravated kidnapping, 720: 5/10-2.
Forcible detention, 720: 5/10-4.

DATA MATCH SYSTEM.
Support responsibility of relatives of public aid recipients.
Financial institution data match system, 305: 5/10-24 to 5/10-24.50.

DAYCARE CENTERS.
Child abuse and neglect reporting.
Required reports, 325: 5/4.

DEAF AND HEARING IMPAIRED.
Interagency board for hearing impaired/behavior disordered children, 325: 35/1 to 35/12.

DEATH.
Adoption proceedings, 750: 50/14a.
Child support or educational expenses.
Death of party obligated to pay, 750: 5/510.
Maintenance obligation terminated upon death of either party, 750: 5/510.

DEBTORS AND CREDITORS.
Married persons.
Creditor's rights, 750: 65/15.
Responsibility for liabilities of spouse, 750: 65/5.

DECEDENTS' ESTATES.
Adoption proceedings terminated by death.
Adoptive parent's interest in estate, 750: 50/14a.
Death of child before final judgment, 750: 50/14a.
Child support payments.
Court ordered withdrawals from estate, 750: 5/510.

DECLARATION OF INVALIDITY OF MARRIAGE, 750: 5/301 to 5/306.

DEEDS.
Adoption, instruments regarding property rights.
Child deemed born to adopting parents, 760: 30/0.01, 30/1.
Legal disability of spouse, 750: 65/17 to 65/21.
Married persons rights.
Spouse under legal disability, 750: 65/17 to 65/21.
Spouse under legal disability.
Conveyance of real estate, 750: 65/17 to 65/21.

DEFAULT JUDGMENTS.
Parentage proceedings, 750: 45/14.
Protective orders.
Domestic violence, 725: 5/112A-10.
Default, plenary order of protection, 750: 60/210.
Notice in conjunction with pending civil case, 750: 60/210.1.

DEFENSES.
Child abduction.
Affirmative defense, 720: 5/10-5.
Condonation.
Marriage dissolution, 750: 5/403.

DEFENSES —Cont'd
Recrimination.
Marriage dissolution, 750: 5/403.
Support and maintenance.
Interstate family support.
Nonparentage as defense, 750: 22/315.

DEFINED TERMS.
Abandon.
Abandoned newborn protection act, 325: 2/10.
Abandoned.
Uniform child custody jurisdiction and enforcement, 750: 36/102.
Abuse.
Criminal procedure, 725: 5/112A-3.
Domestic violence, 750: 60/103.
Elder abuse and neglect, 320: 20/2.
Abused and neglected child reporting, 325: 5/3.
Abused child.
Abandoned newborn protection act, 325: 2/10.
Adoption, 750: 50/1.
Reporting, 325: 5/3.
Abuser.
Elder abuse and neglect, 320: 20/2.
Address.
Address confidentiality for victim of domestic violence act, 750: 61/10.
Administrative expenses.
Expedited child support, 750: 25/3.
Administrative hearing officer.
Expedited child support, 750: 25/3.
Adoption disruption, 750: 50/1.
Adult with disabilities.
Domestic violence, 750: 60/103.
Advisory committee.
Community senior services and resources, 320: 60/15.
Older adult services act, 320: 42/10.
Agency.
Adoption, 750: 50/1.
An indicated report.
Abused and neglected child reporting, 325: 5/3.
An undetermined report.
Abused and neglected child reporting, 325: 5/3.
An unfounded report.
Abused and neglected child reporting, 325: 5/3.
Arrearage.
Expedited child support, 750: 25/3.
Parentage, 750: 45/20.
Support information concerning obligor, 750: 5/706.3.
Support orders, 750: 5/706.1.
At risk of having substantial developmental delay.
Early intervention services system, 325: 20/3.
Authorized pharmacy.
Relief and pharmaceutical assistance, 320: 25/3.17.
Senior citizens and disabled persons prescription drug discount program, 320: 55/15.
Availability of person for adoption, 750: 50/1.
Average wholesale price.
Senior citizens and disabled persons prescription drug discount program, 320: 55/15.
AWP.
Senior citizens and disabled persons prescription drug discount program, 320: 55/15.
Caregiver.
Elder abuse and neglect, 320: 20/2.
Family caregivers, 320: 65/15.
Respite program, 320: 10/2.
Cash assistance.
Relief and pharmaceutical assistance, 320: 25/4.
Center.
Community senior services and resources, 320: 60/15.
Certified nursing home.
Older adult services act, 320: 42/10.
Child-custody determination.
Uniform child custody jurisdiction and enforcement, 750: 36/102.

DEFINED TERMS —Cont'd
Child-custody proceeding.
Uniform child custody jurisdiction and enforcement, 750: 36/102.
Child find.
Early intervention services system, 325: 20/3.
Child or children.
Adoption, 750: 50/1.
Child abduction, 720: 5/10-5.
Child abuse, 720: 150/5.1.
Children's privacy protection and parental empowerment act, 325: 17/5.
Drug related child endangerment, 720: 5/12-4.10.
Family caregivers, 320: 65/15.
Interstate family support, 750: 22/101.
Missing child recovery, 325: 40/2.
Uniform child custody jurisdiction and enforcement, 750: 36/102.
Child-placing agency.
Abandoned newborn protection act, 325: 2/10.
Child protective service unit.
Abused and neglected child reporting, 325: 5/3.
Child support order.
Interstate family support, 750: 22/101.
Child support payment.
Mandatory child support payment to clerk, 750: 5/709.
Child support services.
Unified child support services program, 750: 24/5.
Child support specialist.
Unified child support services program, 750: 24/5.
Claimant.
Relief and pharmaceutical assistance, 320: 25/3.01.
Collector.
Senior citizens real estate tax deferral, 320: 30/2.
Commencement.
Uniform child custody jurisdiction and enforcement, 750: 36/102.
Community-integrated living arrangement.
Elder abuse and neglect, 320: 20/2.
Community living facility.
Elder abuse and neglect, 320: 20/2.
Community residential alternatives.
Elder abuse and neglect, 320: 20/2.
Compensation.
Gestational surrogacy act, 750: 47/10.
Comprehensive case management.
Older adult services act, 320: 42/10.
Confidential communication.
Domestic violence, 750: 60/227.
Consumer-directed.
Older adult services act, 320: 42/10.
Consumer reporting agency.
Support information concerning obligor, 750: 5/706.3.
Coordinated point of entry.
Older adult services act, 320: 42/10.
Counseling.
Child abuse and neglect, 325: 5/8.2.
Court.
Uniform child custody jurisdiction and enforcement, 750: 36/102.
Covered prescription drug.
Relief and pharmaceutical assistance, 320: 25/3.15.
Current child support case.
Unified child support services program, 750: 24/5.
Custodian.
Missing children records, 325: 50/1.
Missing children registration, 325: 55/1.
Custody exchange.
Neutral site custody exchange act, 55: 82/10.
Day care.
Child abuse and neglect, 325: 5/8.2.
DCFS.
Abandoned newborn protection act, 325: 2/10.
Delinquency.
Parentage, 750: 45/20.
Support information concerning obligor, 750: 5/706.3.
Support payments, 750: 5/706.1.

DEFINED TERMS —Cont'd
Detains.
Child abduction, 720: 5/10-5.
Developmental delay.
Early intervention services system, 325: 20/3.
Disabled person.
Relief and pharmaceutical assistance, 320: 25/3.14.
Senior citizens and disabled persons prescription drug discount program, 320: 55/15.
Domestic living situation.
Elder abuse and neglect, 320: 20/2.
Domestic violence, 725: 5/112A-3, 750: 60/103.
Address confidentiality for victim of domestic violence act, 750: 61/10.
Privileged communications, 750: 60/227.
Domestic violence counselor.
Privileged communications, 750: 60/227.
Domestic violence program.
Privileged communications, 750: 60/227.
Domestic violence victim.
Privileged communications, 750: 60/227.
Donor.
Gestational surrogacy act, 750: 47/10.
Drug manufacturer.
Senior citizens and disabled persons prescription drug discount program, 320: 55/15.
Duty of support.
Interstate family support, 750: 22/101.
Early intervention services, 325: 20/3.
Elder adult with disabilities.
Domestic violence, 750: 60/103.
Eligible adult.
Elder abuse and neglect, 320: 20/2.
Eligible infants and toddlers.
Early intervention services system, 325: 20/3.
Eligible participant.
Family caregivers, 320: 65/15.
Eligible senior.
Senior citizens and disabled persons prescription drug discount program, 320: 55/15.
Emergency.
Elder abuse and neglect, 320: 20/2.
Emergency assistance and advocacy.
Child abuse and neglect, 325: 5/8.2.
Emergency medical facility.
Abandoned newborn protection act, 325: 2/10.
Emergency medical professional.
Abandoned newborn protection act, 325: 2/10.
Emergency respite care, 320: 10/2.
Equity interest.
Senior citizens real estate tax deferral, 320: 30/2.
Excessive use of addictive drugs.
Marriage dissolution, 750: 5/401.
Expedited child support hearing, 750: 25/3.
Exploitation.
Domestic violence, 750: 60/103.
Missing child recovery, 325: 40/2.
Family.
Family support demonstration project, 325: 30/3.
Family caregiver, 320: 65/15.
Older adult services act, 320: 42/10.
Family caregiver support services, 320: 65/15.
Family or household member.
Criminal procedure, 725: 5/112A-3.
Domestic violence, 750: 60/103.
Family preservation services.
Child abuse and neglect, 325: 5/8.2.
Federal time frames.
Expedited child support, 750: 25/3.
Fingerprints.
Minor identification, 325: 45/2.
Fire station.
Abandoned newborn protection act, 325: 2/10.
Foreign placing agency.
Adoption, 750: 50/1.
IV-D child support program.
Unified child support services program, 750: 24/5.
IV-D program.
Expedited child support, 750: 25/3.

DEFINED TERMS —Cont'd
Frail individual.
Family caregivers, 320: 65/15.
Frail or disabled elderly adult.
Respite program, 320: 10/2.
Gamete.
Gestational surrogacy act, 750: 47/10.
Gestational surrogacy, 750: 47/10.
Parentage, 750: 45/2.5.
Gestational surrogacy contract, 750: 47/10.
Gestational surrogate, 750: 47/10.
Parentage, 750: 45/2.5.
Grandparent or older individual who is a relative caregiver.
Family caregivers, 320: 65/15.
Gross rent.
Relief and pharmaceutical assistance, 320: 25/3.04.
Guardian.
Emancipation of mature minors, 750: 30/3-4.
Harassment.
Criminal procedure, 725: 5/112A-3.
Domestic violence, 750: 60/103.
Health care provider.
Gestational surrogacy act, 750: 47/10.
Health services.
Older adult services act, 320: 42/10.
Hearing impaired/behavior disordered children, 325: 35/3.
High risk.
Youth career development, 325: 25/1.
High-risk adult with disabilities.
Domestic violence, 750: 60/103.
Homeless minor.
Emancipated minors, 750: 30/3-2.5.
Homemaker.
Child abuse and neglect, 325: 5/8.2.
Home or community based services.
Community senior services and resources, 320: 60/15.
Home state.
Interstate family support, 750: 22/101.
Uniform child custody jurisdiction and enforcement, 750: 36/102.
Homestead.
Senior citizens real estate tax deferral, 320: 30/2.
Hospital.
Abandoned newborn protection act, 325: 2/10.
Household.
Relief and pharmaceutical assistance, 320: 25/3.05.
Household income.
Relief and pharmaceutical assistance, 320: 25/3.06.
Senior citizens real estate tax deferral, 320: 30/2.
Illinois state enforcement agencies to recover children unit, 325: 40/2.
Immediate relatives.
Adoption, 750: 50/1.
Income.
Interstate family support, 750: 22/101.
Parentage, 750: 45/20.
Relief and pharmaceutical assistance, 320: 25/3.07.
Support payments, 750: 5/706.1.
Income-withholding order.
Interstate family support, 750: 22/101.
Individualized family service plan.
Early intervention services system, 325: 20/3.
Informal provider.
Family caregivers, 320: 65/15.
In-home respite care.
Respite program, 320: 10/2.
Initial determination.
Uniform child custody jurisdiction and enforcement, 750: 36/102.
Initiating state.
Interstate family support, 750: 22/101.
Initiating tribunal.
Interstate family support, 750: 22/101.
Intended parent.
Gestational surrogacy act, 750: 47/10.
Parentage, 750: 45/2.5.
Intercountry adoption, 750: 50/1.

DEFINED TERMS —Cont'd
Intercountry adoption coordinator, 750: 50/1.
Interference with personal liberty.
Criminal procedure, 725: 5/112A-3.
Domestic violence, 750: 60/103.
Internal revenue code.
Relief and pharmaceutical assistance, 320: 25/3.08.
Interstate compact on the placement of children, 750: 50/1.
Intimidation of a dependent.
Criminal procedure, 725: 5/112A-3.
Domestic violence, 750: 60/103.
In vitro fertilization.
Gestational surrogacy act, 750: 47/10.
I SEARCH unit.
Missing child recovery, 325: 40/2.
Issuing court.
Uniform child custody jurisdiction and enforcement, 750: 36/102.
Issuing state.
Interstate family support, 750: 22/101.
Uniform child custody jurisdiction and enforcement, 750: 36/102.
Issuing tribunal.
Interstate family support, 750: 22/101.
Joint custody, 750: 5/602.1.
KIDS.
Unified child support services program, 750: 24/5.
Lawful custodian.
Child abduction, 720: 5/10-5.
LEADS terminal.
Missing child recovery, 325: 40/2.
Legal custody.
Abandoned newborn protection act, 325: 2/10.
Legal guardian.
Parental responsibility, 740: 115/2.
Life care facility.
Elder abuse and neglect, 320: 20/2.
Local interagency agreement.
Early intervention services system, 325: 20/3.
Local law enforcement agency.
Child abuse reporting, 325: 5/3.
Minor identification and protection, 325: 45/2.
Location information.
Child support, 750: 5/714, 16/33.
Mandated reporter.
Elder abuse and neglect, 320: 20/2.
Manufacturer.
Senior pharmaceutical assistance act, 320: 50/10.
Marital property.
Disposition upon dissolution, 750: 5/503.
Mature minor.
Emancipation, 750: 30/3-2.
Medicaid.
Unified child support services program, 750: 24/5.
Medical evaluation.
Gestational surrogacy act, 750: 47/10.
Medical support.
Expedited child support, 750: 25/3.
Mental health evaluation.
Gestational surrogacy act, 750: 47/10.
Minor.
Emancipation of mature minors, 750: 30/3-1.
Identification and protection, 325: 45/2.
Parental responsibility, 740: 115/2.
Missing child.
Interagency recovery, 325: 40/2.
Registration, 325: 55/1.
Missing person.
Missing children records, 325: 50/1.
Modification.
Uniform child custody jurisdiction and enforcement, 750: 36/102.
Neglect.
Domestic violence, 750: 60/103.
Elder abuse and neglect, 320: 20/2.
Neglected child.
Abandoned newborn protection act, 325: 2/10.
Adoption, 750: 50/1.
Reporting, 325: 5/3.
Net income.
Child support payments, 750: 5/505.

DEFINED TERMS —Cont'd
Neutral site.
Neutral site custody exchange act, 55: 82/10.
Newborn infant.
Abandoned newborn protection act, 325: 2/10.
Non-compact state.
Adoption, 750: 50/1.
Notice date.
Instruments regarding adopted children, 760: 30/1.
Obligee.
Enforcement of order for support, Sup. Ct. Rule 296.
Expedited child support, 750: 25/3.
Health insurance, 750: 5/505.2.
Interstate family support, 750: 22/101.
Parentage, 750: 45/20.
Support payments, 750: 5/706.1.
Unified child support services program, 750: 24/5.
Obligor.
Attachment of the body, 750: 5/713.
Enforcement of order for support, Sup. Ct. Rule 296.
Expedited child support, 750: 25/3.
Health insurance, 750: 5/505.2.
Interstate family support, 750: 22/101.
Parentage, 750: 45/20.
Support information concerning obligor, 750: 5/706.3.
Support payments, 750: 5/706.1.
Unified child support services program, 750: 24/5.
Older adult.
Older adult services act, 320: 42/10.
Older individual.
Family caregivers, 320: 65/15.
Order for support.
Enforcement of order for support, Sup. Ct. Rule 296.
Income withholding to secure payment, 750: 5/706.1.
Information concerning obligor, 750: 5/706.3.
Parentage, 750: 45/20.
Order of protection.
Criminal procedure, 725: 5/112A-3.
Domestic violence, 750: 60/103.
Parent.
Adoption, 750: 50/1.
Children's privacy protection and parental empowerment act, 325: 17/5.
Emancipation of mature minors, 750: 30/3-3.
Minor identification and protection, 325: 45/2.
Rights to recover, 740: 120/2.
Parent and child relationship.
Parentage, 750: 45/2.
Payment.
Mandatory child support payments to clerk, 750: 5/709.
Payor.
Enforcement of order for support, Sup. Ct. Rule 296.
Parentage, 750: 45/20.
Support payments, 750: 5/706.1.
Perpetrator.
Abused and neglected child reporting, 325: 5/3.
Person.
Parental right of recovery, 740: 120/2.
Uniform child custody jurisdiction and enforcement, 750: 36/102.
Person acting as parent.
Uniform child custody jurisdiction and enforcement, 750: 36/102.
Personal information.
Children's privacy protection and parental empowerment act, 325: 17/5.
Person available for adoption, 750: 50/1.
Person-centered.
Older adult services act, 320: 42/10.
Person responsible for child's welfare.
Abused and neglected child reporting, 325: 5/3.
Petition.
Emancipation of mature minors, 750: 30/3-5.
Petitioner.
Criminal procedure, 725: 5/112A-3.
Domestic violence, 750: 60/103.

DEFINED TERMS —Cont'd
Petitioner —Cont'd
Uniform child custody jurisdiction and enforcement, 750: 36/301.
Physical abuse.
Criminal procedure, 725: 5/112A-3.
Domestic violence, 750: 60/103.
Physical custody.
Uniform child custody jurisdiction and enforcement, 750: 36/102.
Physical or mental condition which has a high probability of resulting in developmental delay.
Early intervention services system, 325: 20/3.
Physician.
Gestational surrogacy act, 750: 47/10.
Pilot program.
Partnership for long-term care, 320: 35/10.
Placing out.
Adoption compensation, 720: 525/3.
Plan.
Early intervention services system, 325: 20/3.
Expedited child support, 750: 25/3.
Unified child support services program, 750: 24/5.
Police station.
Abandoned newborn infant protection act, 325: 2/10.
Preadoption requirements, 750: 50/1.
Pre-embryo.
Gestational surrogacy act, 750: 47/10.
Pre-embryo transfer.
Gestational surrogacy act, 750: 47/10.
Pre-hearing motions.
Expedited child support, 750: 25/3.
Premarital agreement, 750: 10/2.
Premium.
Parentage, 750: 45/20.
Support payments, 750: 5/706.1.
Prescription.
Parental right of recovery, 740: 120/2.
Prescription drug.
Senior citizens and disabled persons prescription drug discount program, 320: 55/15.
Senior pharmaceutical assistance act, 320: 50/10.
Primary contact agency.
Missing child recovery, 325: 40/2.
Priority service area.
Older adult services act, 320: 42/10.
Priority service plan.
Older adult services act, 320: 42/10.
Program.
Unified child support services program, 750: 24/5.
Program administrator.
Senior citizens and disabled persons prescription drug discount program, 320: 55/15.
Program participant.
Address confidentiality for victim of domestic violence act, 750: 61/10.
Project.
Family support center, 325: 30/3.
Property.
Premarital agreements, 750: 10/2.
Property taxes accrued.
Relief and pharmaceutical assistance, 320: 25/3.09.
Provider.
Older adult services act, 320: 42/10.
Provider agency.
Elder abuse and neglect, 320: 20/2.
Provisions pertaining to the settlor's former spouse.
Trusts and fiduciaries.
Marriage dissolution, 760: 35/1.
Public conveyance.
Child abduction, 720: 5/10-8.
Public office.
Health insurance, 750: 5/505.2.
Parentage, 750: 45/20.
Support payments, 750: 5/706.1.
Putative father.
Adoption, 750: 50/1.

DEFINED TERMS —Cont'd
Qualifying property.
Senior citizens real estate tax deferral, 320: 30/2.
Ransom.
Kidnapping, 720: 5/10-2.
Real estate taxes.
Senior citizens real estate tax deferral, 320: 30/2.
Reasonable cost.
Relief and pharmaceutical assistance, 320: 25/3.16.
Recommendations.
Expedited child support, 750: 25/3.
Record.
Uniform child custody jurisdiction and enforcement, 750: 36/110.
Referral fee.
Abortion, 720: 510/11.1.
Regional administrative agency.
Elder abuse and neglect, 320: 20/2.
Register.
Interstate family support, 750: 22/101.
Registering tribunal.
Interstate family support, 750: 22/101.
Registrar.
Missing children records, 325: 50/1.
Missing children registration, 325: 55/1.
Regulation.
Relief and pharmaceutical assistance, 320: 25/3.10.
Related child.
Adoption, 750: 50/1.
Relative.
Placement of child with relative.
Department of children and family services, 20: 505/7.
Relinquish.
Abandoned newborn protection act, 325: 2/10.
Rent constituting property taxes accrued.
Relief and pharmaceutical assistance, 320: 25/3.11.
Residence.
Relief and pharmaceutical assistance, 320: 25/3.12.
Residential setting.
Older adult services act, 320: 42/10.
Resource and referral system.
Senior citizens child care support, 320: 45/10.
Respite care, 320: 10/2.
Family caregivers, 320: 65/15.
Respondent.
Uniform child custody jurisdiction and enforcement, 750: 36/301.
Responding state.
Interstate family support, 750: 22/101.
Responding tribunal.
Interstate family support, 750: 22/101.
Restructuring.
Older adult services act, 320: 42/10.
Rules.
Senior citizens and disabled persons prescription drug discount program, 320: 55/15.
Sale.
Parental right of recovery, 740: 120/2.
Senior.
Community senior services and resources, 320: 60/15.
Senior citizen.
Senior citizens child care support, 320: 45/10.
Senior pharmaceutical assistance act, 320: 50/10.
Service area.
Senior citizens child care support, 320: 45/10.
Services.
Older adult services act, 320: 42/10.
Special efforts.
Department of children and family services.
Child placement, 20: 505/7.
Spousal-support order.
Interstate family support, 750: 22/101.
Standby adoption, 750: 50/1.
State.
Interstate family support, 750: 22/101.
Uniform child custody jurisdiction and enforcement, 750: 36/102.

DEFINED TERMS —Cont'd
State disbursement unit.
Unified child support services program, 750: 24/5.
State's attorney.
Unified child support services program, 750: 24/5.
Stay away.
Domestic violence, 750: 60/103.
Order of protection, 725: 5/112A-3.
Structure.
Drug related child endangerment, 720: 5/12-4.10.
Subject of report.
Abused and neglected child reporting, 325: 5/3.
Substantiated case.
Elder abuse and neglect, 320: 20/2.
Support enforcement agency.
Interstate family support, 750: 22/101.
Supportive services.
Older adult services act, 320: 42/10.
Support order.
Interstate family support, 750: 22/101.
System.
Expedited child support, 750: 25/3.
Taxable year.
Relief and pharmaceutical assistance, 320: 25/3.13.
Tax deferred property.
Senior citizens real estate tax deferral, 320: 30/2.
Taxpayer.
Senior citizens real estate tax deferral, 320: 30/2.
Temporary assistance for needy families.
Unified child support services program, 750: 24/5.
Temporary protective custody.
Abandoned newborn protection act, 325: 2/10.
Abused and neglected child reporting, 325: 5/3.
Transfer.
Parental right of recovery, 740: 120/2.
Tribe.
Uniform child custody jurisdiction and enforcement, 750: 36/102.
Tribunal.
Interstate family support, 750: 22/101.
Trust.
Marriage dissolution, 760: 35/1.
Unfit person.
Adoption, 750: 50/1.
Unit of local government.
Missing child recovery, 325: 40/2.
Visitation abuse, 750: 5/607.1.
Warrant.
Uniform child custody jurisdiction and enforcement, 750: 36/102.
Willful deprivation.
Criminal procedure, 725: 5/112A-3.
Domestic violence, 750: 60/103.
Youth transitional housing program.
Emancipated minors, 750: 30/3-2.10.

DELINQUENT MINORS.
Appeals, Sup. Ct. Rule 660.
Indigent minors, Sup. Ct. Rule 661.
Contributing to delinquency of a minor, 720: 130/2a.
Criminal neglect of children, 720: 130/2a.
Criminal neglect of children.
"Delinquent child" defined, 720: 130/1a.
Definitions, 720: 130/1a.
Domestic violence protection orders.
Commencement in conjunction with delinquency petition, 725: 5/112A-2, 750: 60/202.

DENTISTS.
Child abuse and neglect reporting.
Required reports, 325: 5/4.
Elder abuse and neglect.
Failure to report, 320: 20/4.

DEOXYRIBONUCLEIC ACID (DNA) TESTS.
Parentage proceedings, 750: 45/11.

DEPENDENT CHILDREN.
Appeals, Sup. Ct. Rule 660.

DEPOSITIONS.
Child custody.
Uniform child custody jurisdiction and enforcement.
Testimony of witnesses outside state, 750: 36/111.

DEPRAVED PARENT.
Unfit person defined, presumption, 750: 50/1.

DESERTION.
Abandoned spouses control over property, 750: 65/11 to 65/13.
Ground for dissolution of marriage, 750: 5/401.
Married persons right to defend in name of deserting spouse, 750: 65/3.

DETENTION, FORCIBLE, 720: 5/10-4.

DETENTION WITHOUT LAWFUL AUTHORITY, 720: 5/10-3.1.

DEVELOPMENTAL DISABILITIES.
Early intervention services, 325: 20/1 to 20/20.

DISABLED OR HANDICAPPED.
Child support for non-minor children, 750: 5/513.
Disabled persons' property tax relief.
General provisions, 320: 25/1 to 25/13.
High risk youth career development, 325: 25/0.01, 25/1.
Marriage.
Invalidity grounds, 750: 5/301.
Prescription drugs.
Senior citizens and disabled persons prescription drug discount program, 320: 55/1 to 55/99.
Surgical institute for children, 325: 60/0.01 to 60/12.

DISCOVERY.
Support and maintenance.
Interstate family support.
Assistance with discovery, 750: 22/318.

DISCRIMINATION.
Child placement by department of children and family services.
Department not to discriminate against child or prospective adoptive or foster parents on basis of race, 20: 505/7.
Elder abuse and neglect reports by employee.
Employer discrimination, 320: 20/4.1.

DISMISSAL OF ACTIONS.
Domestic violence.
Protection orders, 750: 60/202.

DISORDERLY CONDUCT.
Child abuse or neglect reporting.
False reports, 325: 5/4.

DISPOSITION OF PROPERTY ON DISSOLUTION OF MARRIAGE, 750: 5/503.
Partition of real estate, 750: 5/514, 5/515.

DISPUTE RESOLUTION.
Dissolution of marriage.
Conciliation or mediation, 750: 5/404.
Joint custody award, mediation, 750: 5/602.1.
Joint parenting agreement to specify procedure, 750: 5/602.1.

DISSOLUTION OF MARRIAGE, 750: 5/401 to 5/802.
Action commencement, 750: 5/411.
Address disclosure, 750: 5/708.
Administrative aides employment, 750: 5/106.
Admission of respondent, 750: 5/407.
Agreements, 750: 5/502.
Annulment, 750: 5/301 to 5/306.
See INVALIDITY OF MARRIAGE, DECLARATION OF.

DISSOLUTION OF MARRIAGE —Cont'd
Antenuptial agreements, 750: 10/1 to 10/11.
See PREMARITAL AGREEMENTS.
Application of act, 750: 5/801.
Attorney appointment to represent interest of minor or dependent child, 750: 5/506.
Attorneys' fees, 750: 5/508.
Bifurcated basis of contested trials, 750: 5/403.
Certificate of dissolution.
Filing, 750: 5/707.
Child counseling.
Court ordered, 750: 5/404.1.
Child custody.
Awards standard, 750: 5/602.
Commencement of proceedings, 750: 5/601.
Generally.
See CHILD CUSTODY.
Joint custody consideration, 750: 5/602.1.
Temporary custody orders, 750: 5/603.
Uniform child custody jurisdiction and enforcement, 750: 36/101 to 36/405.
Child order modifications, 750: 5/510.
Children's educational expenses.
Court ordered support, 750: 5/513.
Support to include, 750: 5/505.
Termination of support, 750: 5/510.
Children's representation, 750: 5/506.
Child support payments, 750: 5/505.
Child support termination conditions, 750: 5/510.
Civil practice law applications, 750: 5/105.
Civil procedure, 750: 5/410.
Collusion, 750: 5/408.
Commencement of actions, 750: 5/411.
Commingled marital and non-marital property.
Disposition, 750: 5/503.
Conciliation conference and counseling, 750: 5/404.
Conciliation potential, 750: 5/404.
Condonation, 750: 5/403.
Conduct of petitioner.
Action bar, 750: 5/406.
Confidentiality of information.
Residential address, 750: 5/708.
Declaration of invalidity of marriage, 750: 5/301 to 5/306.
See INVALIDITY OF MARRIAGE, DECLARATION OF.
Default hearings, 750: 5/405.
Disposition of property, 750: 5/503.
Agreements, 750: 5/502.
Marital residence, 750: 5/701.
Real estate partition, 750: 5/514.
Filing of actions, 750: 5/515.
Domestic violence, 750: 60/101 to 60/401.
See DOMESTIC VIOLENCE.
Educational sessions for children.
Court ordered, 750: 5/404.1.
Employment search ordered by court, 750: 5/505.1.
Enforcement of judgment procedures, 750: 5/511.
Evidence.
Conciliation conference facts or report, 750: 5/404.
Extraordinary expenditure or transaction.
Notice of, 750: 5/501.1.
Fault of petitioner.
Action bar, 750: 5/406.
Foreign marriage proof, 750: 5/409.
Grounds, 750: 5/401.
Guidelines for determining minimum amount of child support, 750: 5/505.
Health insurance orders, 750: 5/505.2.
Hearings on default, 750: 5/405.
Independence of provisions, 750: 5/509.
Interpretation and construction, 750: 5/102.
Interview of child as to wishes on custody and visitation, 750: 5/604.
Invalidity of marriage, declaration of, 750: 5/301 to 5/306.
See INVALIDITY OF MARRIAGE, DECLARATION OF.
Joinder of additional parties, 750: 5/403.

DISSOLUTION OF MARRIAGE —Cont'd
Judgments, 750: 5/413.
Enforcement or modification procedure, 750: 5/511.
Independence of provisions, 750: 5/509.
Jurisdiction to decide child custody matters, 750: 5/601.
Jury trial, 750: 5/103.
Legislative declaration, 750: 5/102.
Liens to satisfy maintenance orders, 750: 5/703.
Maintenance award factors, 750: 5/504.
Maintenance during imprisonment, 750: 5/504.
Maintenance in the case of bigamy, 750: 5/702.
Maintenance liens, 750: 5/703.
Maintenance of spouse.
See SPOUSAL SUPPORT.
Maintenance order modifications, 750: 5/510.
Maintenance, payments to court, 750: 5/507.
Maintenance, termination upon cohabitation, 750: 5/510.
Maintenance, termination upon death, 750: 5/510.
Maintenance, termination upon remarriage, 750: 5/510.
Marital property, disposition, 750: 5/503.
Mediation, 750: 5/404.
Modification of judgment procedure, 750: 5/511.
Modification of orders, 750: 5/510.
Non-marital property, disposition, 750: 5/503.
Non-minor children support, 750: 5/513.
Parentage, 750: 40/1 to 45/27.
See PARENTAGE PROCEEDINGS.
Parental rights and responsibilities, 750: 5/602.1.
Partition of real estate, 750: 5/514.
Filing of actions, 750: 5/515.
Permanent maintenance, 750: 5/504.
Petition elements, 750: 5/403.
Petitioners' conduct.
Action bar, 750: 5/406.
Post-judgment proceedings, 750: 5/511.
Post-judgment venue, 750: 5/512.
Praecipe for summons.
Commencement of actions, 750: 5/411.
Stay action effected, 750: 5/501.1.
Premarital agreements, 750: 10/1 to 10/11.
See PREMARITAL AGREEMENTS.
Procedure for judgment enforcement or modification, 750: 5/511.
Process, 750: 5/410.
Proof of existence of grounds required, 750: 5/403.
Proof of foreign marriage, 750: 5/409.
Property disposition, 750: 5/503.
Marital residence, 750: 5/701.
Modification of orders, 750: 5/510.
Real estate partition, 750: 5/514.
Filing, 750: 5/515.
Protection orders, 750: 5/107.
Public aid collection fee, 750: 5/516.
Public aid recipients.
Payments, 750: 5/704.
Real estate partition, 750: 5/514.
Filing of actions, 750: 5/515.
Reconciliation potential, 750: 5/404.
Records, 410: 530/0.01 to 530/3.1.
Recrimination, 750: 5/403.
Relief temporarily, 750: 5/501.
Representation of children, 750: 5/506.
Residence possession, 750: 5/701.
Residency requirements, 750: 5/401.
Respondents' admissions, 750: 5/407.
Restraint of parties' actions.
Dissolution action stay, 750: 5/501.1.
Rules adoption by supreme court, 750: 5/802.
Sales to satisfy maintenance orders, 750: 5/703.
Service of process, 750: 5/410.
Petition filing, 750: 5/412.
Stay action effected, 750: 5/501.1.

DISSOLUTION OF MARRIAGE —Cont'd
Settlement agreements, 750: 5/502.
Severability of act, 750: 5/801.
Short title of act, 750: 5/101.
Simplified dissolution procedure, 750: 5/451 to 5/457.
Affidavit, 750: 5/454.
Applicability, 750: 5/451.
Brochure to describe proceedings, 750: 5/457.
Forms, 750: 5/453, 5/456.
Judgment, 750: 5/453.
Copies, 750: 5/455.
Petition, 750: 5/452.
Procedure, 750: 5/453.
Spousal support.
See SPOUSAL SUPPORT.
Spousal support order modifications, 750: 5/510.
Stays.
Dissolution action stay, 750: 5/501.1.
Support bonds, 750: 5/706.2.
Support for non-minor children, 750: 5/513.
Support for spouse.
See SPOUSAL SUPPORT.
Support order modifications, 750: 5/510.
Support payment agents, 750: 5/705.
Support payments to court, 750: 5/507.
Support payments to state disbursement unit, 750: 5/507.1.
Temporary custody order, 750: 5/603.
Temporary maintenance, 750: 5/504.
Temporary relief, 750: 5/501.
Trials by jury, 750: 5/103.
Trustees.
Assumption settlor married, no actual knowledge of termination of marriage.
Liability for action taken or omitted in good faith, 760: 35/0.01, 35/1.
Trusts.
Revocation of provisions revocable by settlor, 760: 35/0.01, 35/1.
Unemployed obligor, employment search ordered by court, 750: 5/505.1.
Venue, 750: 5/104.
Venue in post-judgment proceedings, 750: 5/512.
Wage deduction orders, 750: 5/706.1.

DISSOLUTION OF PROPERTY.
Trust or separate fund for support, maintenance, etc., of minors, 750: 5/503.

DIVORCE.
Dissolution of marriage, 750: 5/401 to 5/802.
See DISSOLUTION OF MARRIAGE.

DNA.
Parentage proceedings, 750: 45/11.

DOMESTIC ABUSE PROTECTION ADVOCATES, 750: 60/205.

DOMESTIC BATTERY, 720: 5/12-3.2.

DOMESTIC RELATIONS.
Abandoned newborn protection act, 325: 2/1 to 2/999.
Child custody jurisdiction.
Uniform child custody jurisdiction and enforcement, 750: 36/101 to 36/405.

DOMESTIC VIOLENCE.
Address of victim, confidentiality, 750: 61/1 to 61/45.
Absentee voting by participant, 750: 61/30.
Address confidentiality for victim of domestic violence act, 750: 61/1.
Application to have designated address serve as victim's address, 750: 61/15.
Assistance to persons applying, 750: 61/40.
Attorney general to administer program, 750: 61/11.
Cancellation of participant's certification, 750: 61/20.
Certification of applicant as program participant, 750: 61/15.
Change in residential address, cancellation of certification, 750: 61/20.
Definitions, 750: 61/10.

DOMESTIC VIOLENCE —Cont'd
Address of victim, confidentiality —Cont'd
Disclosure of address, circumstances, 750: 61/35.
False statements in application, criminal penalty, 750: 61/15.
Cancellation of certification, 750: 61/20.
Legislative findings, 750: 61/5.
Mail, forwarding to participant, 750: 61/25.
Mail returned as nondeliverable, cancellation of certification, 750: 61/20.
Name change, loss of certification, 750: 61/20.
Rules, 750: 61/45.
Use of designated address by agencies, 750: 61/25.
Voter registration records, address not available to public, 750: 61/30.
Voting by participant, 750: 61/30.
Arrest of abusing, neglecting or exploiting party, 750: 60/304.
Arrest without warrant, 750: 60/301.
Assistance by law enforcement officers, 750: 60/304.
Battery, 720: 5/12-3.2.
Aggravated domestic battery, 720: 5/12-3.3.
Child abuse and neglect reporting.
Generally, 325: 5/1 to 5/11.7.
See CHILD ABUSE, NEGLECT OR DEPENDENCY.
Required reports by program personnel, 325: 5/4.
Commencement of actions, 750: 60/202.
Confidentiality of victim's address. See within this heading, "Address of victim, confidentiality."
Contempt.
Protection orders.
Enforcement of violations, 750: 60/223.
Counselor-victim privilege, 750: 60/227.
Data maintenance by law enforcement agencies, 750: 60/302.
Definitions, 750: 60/103.
Dissolution of marriage.
Ground.
Physical or mental cruelty, 750: 5/401.
Enforcement policies by law enforcement agencies.
Development and implementation, 750: 60/301.1.
Exclusive possession of residence.
Venue for request, 750: 60/209.
Guardians.
Temporary substitute guardian.
High-risk adult with disabilities, 750: 60/213.3.
Health care counseling, 750: 60/401.
Immunity from prosecution.
Persons reporting abuse, 725: 5/112A-25.
Reporters of abuse, 725: 5/112A-25.
Independent counsel.
High-risk adults with disabilities, 750: 60/213.3.
Information or services provided to victims, 750: 60/401.
Interpretation and construction, 750: 60/102.
Law enforcement agency data maintenance, 750: 60/302.
Law enforcement limited liability, 750: 60/305.
Law enforcement officer reports, 750: 60/303.
Law enforcement policies development, 750: 60/301.1.
Law enforcement responsibility, 750: 60/301 to 60/305.
Legislative declaration, 750: 60/102.
New address established by victim.
Confidentiality, 750: 61/1 to 61/45.
Persons protected by act, 750: 60/201.
Protection orders, 725: 5/112A-1 to 5/112A-31, 750: 60/201 to 60/227.1.
Accountability for actions of others, 750: 60/216.
Burden of proof, 750: 60/205.
Consolidation, 750: 60/202.

DOMESTIC VIOLENCE —Cont'd
Protection orders —Cont'd
Contempt.
Enforcement of violations, 750: 60/223.
Contents, 750: 60/221.
Correlative separate orders, 750: 60/215.
Counselor-victim privilege, 750: 60/227.
Criminal courts.
Enforcement of violations, 750: 60/223.
Default, plenary order of protection, 750: 60/210.
Notice in conjunction with pending civil case, 750: 60/210.1.
Dismissal, 750: 60/202.
Domestic abuse advocates, 750: 60/205.
Duration, 750: 60/220.
Emergency order, 750: 60/217.
Duration and extension, 750: 60/220.
Modification or reopening, 750: 60/224.
Enforcement, 750: 60/223.
Extension, 750: 60/220.
False statements, 750: 60/226.
Filing and service fees, 750: 60/202.
Hearings, 725: 5/112A-12, 750: 60/212.
Hearsay evidence, 750: 60/213.1.
High-risk adult, access of, 750: 60/201.1.
Identity of domestic violence advocate or counselor, disclosure, 750: 60/227.1.
Immunity from prosecution, 750: 60/225.
Interim order, thirty-days, 750: 60/218.
Duration and extension, 750: 60/220.
Modification or reopening, 750: 60/224.
Issuance of order, 750: 60/214.
Jury trial, 750: 60/206.
Location of domestic violence program, disclosure, 750: 60/227.1.
Modification, 750: 60/224.
Mutual orders, 750: 60/215.
Non-disclosure of address, 750: 60/203.
Notice, 750: 60/222.
Remedies requiring actual or constructive notice, 750: 60/210.
Short form notification, 750: 60/222.10.
Notice of hearings, service, 750: 60/211.
Order of protection status, 750: 60/223.1.
Penalties for violations, 750: 60/223.
Pending civil cases.
Service of notice in conjunction with, 750: 60/210.1.
Personal jurisdiction, 750: 60/208.
Persons protected by act, 750: 60/201.
Petition, commencement of action, 750: 60/202.
Petition for rule to show cause, 750: 60/223.
Petition requirements, 750: 60/203.
Petitions, who may file, 750: 60/201.
Plenary order, 750: 60/219.
Duration and extension, 750: 60/220.
Modification, 750: 60/224.
Privileged communications between domestic violence counselors and victims, 750: 60/227.
Privileged information, other information privileged, 750: 60/227.1.
Privilege waiver, 750: 60/213.2.
Pro se petitions, 750: 60/202.
Remedies, 750: 60/214.
Constructive or actual notice required, 750: 60/210.
Reopening, 750: 60/224.
Rules of civil procedure, applicability, 750: 60/205.
Service by sheriff, 750: 60/222.
Short form notification, 750: 60/222.10.
Service of notice in conjunction with pending civil case, 750: 60/210.1.
Service of notice of hearings, 750: 60/211.
Service of process, 750: 60/210.
Standard of proof, 750: 60/205.
Subject matter jurisdiction, 750: 60/207.
Subsequent proceeding, continuing duty to inform court of, 750: 60/203.
Thirty day interim orders, 750: 60/218.
Duration and extension, 750: 60/220.
Untrue statements, 750: 60/226.
Venue, 750: 60/209.
Purposes, 750: 60/102.

DOMESTIC VIOLENCE —Cont'd
Reports.
Immunity of reporter from prosecution, 725: 5/112A-25.
Reports by law enforcement officers, 750: 60/303.
Service of process, 750: 60/210.
Notice in conjunction with pending civil case, 750: 60/210.1.
Notice of hearings, 750: 60/211.
Shelters, 20: 1310/0.01 to 1310/3.2.
Short title of act, 750: 60/101.
State police, department of.
Domestic violence.
Data maintenance, 750: 60/302.

DRIVERS' LICENSES.
Children's privacy protection and parental empowerment act.
Personal information.
Defined as including driver's license number, 325: 17/5.
Sale or purchase, 325: 17/10, 17/15.
Child support.
Family financial responsibility driving permit.
Issuance when driving privilege suspended for delinquency, 750: 5/505.
Suspension of driving privilege for delinquency, 750: 5/505.

DRUG DEPENDENCY.
Dissolution of marriage.
Ground, 750: 5/401.
Invalidity of marriage, declaration of.
Ground, lack of capacity to consent, 750: 5/301.

DRUGS.
Disabled or handicapped.
Prescription drugs.
Senior citizens and disabled persons prescription drug discount program, 320: 55/1 to 55/99.
Senior citizens.
Prescription drugs.
Senior citizens and disabled persons prescription drug discount program, 320: 55/1 to 55/99.

DRUNKENNESS.
Dissolution of marriage.
Ground, habitual drunkenness, 750: 5/401.
Invalidity of marriage, declaration of.
Ground, lack of capacity to consent, 750: 5/301.

DURESS.
Adoption consent.
Revocation restrictions, 750: 50/11.
Invalidity of marriage, declaration of, 750: 5/301.

E

EARLY CHILDHOOD INTERVENTION OMBUDSMAN, 325: 20/9.

EARLY INTERVENTION SERVICES.
Act takes effect upon becoming law, 325: 20/16.
Administrative rules, 325: 20/8.
Auditor general to conduct evaluation of system, 325: 20/15.
Components of statewide service system, 325: 20/7.
Confidentiality of personally identifiable information, 325: 20/12.
Contracting out responsibilities, 325: 20/13.32.
Definitions, 325: 20/3.
Early intervention services system act, 325: 20/1.
Effective date of act, 325: 20/16.
Establishment and implementation of program and personnel standards, 325: 20/10.
Family service plans, 325: 20/11.
Other programs, participation and eligibility, 325: 20/13.5.

EARLY INTERVENTION SERVICES —Cont'd
Fiscal responsibility, 325: 20/13.
Funding, 325: 20/13.
Revolving fund, 325: 20/20.
Individualized family service plans, 325: 20/11.
Other programs, participation and eligibility, 325: 20/13.5.
Insured families, 325: 20/13.10.
Exemption restricting use of insurance, 325: 20/13.25.
Expenses for covered families, 325: 20/13.20.
Insurance carrier, billing of, 325: 20/13.15.
Interagency council on early intervention, 325: 20/4.
Lead agency, 325: 20/5.
Legislative advisory committee, 325: 20/13.50.
Legislative findings, 325: 20/2.
Local interagency councils, 325: 20/6.
Local service areas, 325: 20/6.
Notice safeguard, 325: 20/12.
Ombudsman, 325: 20/9.
Other programs, participation and eligibility, 325: 20/13.5.
Personnel training, 325: 20/13.30.
Policy of state, 325: 20/2.
Private health insurance coverage, 325: 20/13.10.
Exemption restricting use of insurance, 325: 20/13.25.
Expenses for covered families, 325: 20/13.20.
Insurance carrier, billing of, 325: 20/13.15.
Procedural safeguards, 325: 20/12.
Role of other state entities, 325: 20/9.
Rules and regulations, 325: 20/8.
Standards, 325: 20/10.
Statewide service system components, 325: 20/7.
Training of personnel, 325: 20/13.30.

EDUCATION.
Child abuse and neglect reporting.
Report to child's school, 325: 5/8.6.
Child support for educational expenses, 750: 5/513.

ELDER ABUSE AND NEGLECT.
Access to eligible adults, 320: 20/13.
Annual reports to general assembly, 320: 20/11.
Authority to consent to services, 320: 20/9.
Coordination of efforts, department responsibilities, 320: 20/3.5.
Crimes against eligible adult.
Referral to law enforcement agency, 320: 20/5.
Department on aging records.
Access, 320: 20/8.
Department on aging responsibilities.
General provisions, 320: 20/3 to 20/13.
Discrimination against employee for making good faith report, 320: 20/4.1.
Face-to-face assessment upon receipt of report, 320: 20/5.
Failure to report, sanctions for, 320: 20/4.
Identity of person making report, disclosure, consent required, 320: 20/4.
Immunity from liability for making report, 320: 20/4.
Mandated reporters.
Procedure for making reports, 320: 20/4.
Testimony, 320: 20/4.2.
Prevention, department responsibilities, 320: 20/3.5.
Privileged communication between person required to report and client or patient, 320: 20/4.
Provider agencies.
Procedure upon receiving report, 320: 20/5.
Reports of abuse and neglect, 320: 20/4.
Retaliation by employer against employee making report, 320: 20/4.1.
Service care plan.
Developments by provider agency upon determination case substantiated, 320: 20/5.

ELDER ABUSE AND NEGLECT —Cont'd
Testimony by mandated reporter or person investigating report, 320: 20/4.2.
Training, department responsibilities, 320: 20/3.5.
Whistleblowers, 320: 20/4.
Discrimination or retaliation by employer prohibited, 320: 20/4.1.

ELECTIONS.
Absentee voting.
Domestic violence victims, participation in address confidentiality program, 750: 61/30.

EMANCIPATED MINORS.
Maintenance obligation terminated upon emancipation, 750: 5/510.
Mature minors, 750: 30/1 to 30/11.
Appeal, 750: 30/11.
Continuing jurisdiction over proceedings, 750: 30/6.
Definitions, 750: 30/3 to 30/3-5.
Emancipation of mature minors act, 750: 30/1.
Hearing, 750: 30/9.
Joinder, 750: 30/10.
Jurisdiction, 750: 30/4.
Modification, 750: 30/6.
Notice, 750: 30/8.
Petition, 750: 30/7.
Policy, 750: 30/2.
Purposes, 750: 30/2.
Rights and responsibilities, 750: 30/5.
Termination, 750: 30/6.
Support for non-minor children and educational expenses, 750: 5/513.

EMERGENCIES.
Child custody.
Uniform child custody jurisdiction and enforcement.
Emergency jurisdiction, 750: 36/204.
Warrant for physical custody of child, 750: 36/311.
Domestic violence.
Protection orders, 750: 60/217.
Duration, 750: 60/220.
Reopening of order, 750: 60/221.

EMERGENCY MEDICAL SERVICES.
Child abuse and neglect reporting.
Required reports by emergency medical technicians, 325: 5/4.

EMERGENCY RELIEF.
Domestic violence.
Protection orders, 750: 60/217.
Duration, 750: 60/220.
Reopening of order, 750: 60/221.

EMPLOYMENT.
Child abuse and neglect reporting.
Discrimination against employee making good faith report, 325: 5/9.1.
Child support.
Location of putative father and noncustodial parents.
Duty to provide information, 750: 5/714, 16/33, 45/14.5.
Obligor obtaining employment or termination from employment.
Report to obligee and clerk of court, 750: 5/505, 45/14.
Unemployed obligor, employment search ordered by court, 750: 5/505.1.
High risk youth career development, 325: 25/0.01, 25/1.
Income withholding orders, support enforcement.
Interstate family support.
Administrative enforcement, 750: 22/507.
Contest by obligor, 750: 22/506.
Employer of obligor.
Sending order to employer without filing petition, 750: 22/501.
Immunity of employer, 750: 22/504.
Penalties for noncompliance, 750: 22/505.
Parentage proceedings.
Unemployed obligors, court's powers, 750: 45/15.1.

EMPLOYMENT —Cont'd
Parentage proceedings —Cont'd
Withholding of income to secure payment of support, 750: 45/20.
Procedures to avoid income withholding, 750: 45/20.
Single parent employment restrictions.
Wrongs to children act, 720: 150/3, 150/3.1, 150/5.
Spousal support.
Unemployed obligor, employment search ordered by court, 750: 5/505.1.
Support and maintenance.
Unemployed obligor, employment search ordered by court, 750: 5/505.1.
Withholding of income to secure payment, 750: 5/706.1.
Support orders.
Income-withholding.
Interstate family support.
Administrative enforcement, 750: 22/507.
Contest by obligor, 750: 22/506.
Employer of obligor.
Sending order to employer without filing petition, 750: 22/501.
Immunity of employer, 750: 22/504.
Multiple orders, compliance, 750: 22/503.
Penalties for noncompliance, 750: 22/505.
Wage deduction orders.
Paternity proceedings, 750: 45/20.
Support payments, 750: 5/706.1.
Withholding of income notice.
Interstate family support, 750: 22/501 to 22/507.
Wrongs to children act.
Single parent employment restrictions, 720: 150/3, 150/3.1, 150/5.

EMPLOYMENT DISCRIMINATION.
Child abuse and neglect reporting.
Discrimination against employee making good faith report, 325: 5/9.1.

EMPLOYMENT SECURITY, DEPARTMENT OF.
High risk youth career development, 325: 25/0.01, 25/1.

ENDANGERMENT.
Child endangerment.
Wrongs to children act, 720: 150/4.1, 150/5.

ENDORSEMENTS.
Temporary restraining orders, 735: 5/11-101.

ENTRY OF JUDGMENT.
Adoption, 750: 50/16.
Dissolution of marriage or legal separation or declaration of invalidity of marriage, 750: 5/413.

ESCAPE.
Damages caused by inmates.
Department of children and family services.
Powers and duties concerning, 20: 510/510-30.

ESCROW ACCOUNTS.
Attachment of the body orders.
Account establishment, 750: 5/713.
Support enforcement through attachment orders.
Account establishment, 750: 5/713.

EVICTION.
Dissolution of marriage.
Marital residence possession, 750: 5/701.

EVIDENCE.
Child abuse, neglect or dependency.
Child custody hearings.
Previous statements by child, 750: 5/606.
Child custody.
Uniform child custody jurisdiction and enforcement.
Testimony of witnesses outside state, 750: 36/111.
Child custody hearings.
Abuse or neglect, previous statements by child, 750: 5/606.

EVIDENCE —Cont'd
Child custody orders.
Modification standard, 750: 5/610.
Child support.
Expedited support.
Administrative hearings, 750: 25/7; Sup. Ct. Rule 100.7.
Clear and convincing evidence.
Adoption consent, 750: 50/8.
Domestic violence protection orders.
Disclosure or privileged information, 750: 60/227.1.
Paternity presumption, 750: 45/5.
Dissolution of marriage.
Conciliation conference.
Facts or report, 750: 5/404.
Elder abuse and neglect.
Testimony by mandated reporter or person investigating report, 320: 20/4.2.
Foreign marriage, 750: 5/409.
Marriage dissolution proceedings.
Admission of respondent, 750: 5/407.
Parentage proceedings.
Blood and tissue test reports, 750: 45/11.
Support and maintenance.
Interstate family support.
Discovery.
Assistance with discovery, 750: 22/318.
Special rules of evidence and procedure, 750: 22/316.
Tickets on public conveyance unlawfully sold to minor, 720: 5/10-8.

EXECUTION OF JUDGMENTS.
Adoption.
Consent or surrender prior to effective date of act, 750: 50/23.
Forms of consent and surrender, 750: 50/10.

EXPEDITED CHILD SUPPORT, 750: 25/1 to 25/13; Sup. Ct. Rules 100.1 to 100.13.
See CHILD SUPPORT.

EXPERIMENTATION UPON FETUS.
Miscarried fetus, 720: 510/12.1.

EXPERT WITNESSES.
Parentage proceedings.
Blood test results, 750: 45/11.
Fees, 750: 45/17.

EXPLOITATION OF CHILDREN.
Commercial exploitation.
Penalty, 720: 150/5.
Prohibited conduct, 720: 150/1, 150/2.
Termination of custody rights, 720: 150/3.

EXPUNGEMENT OF RECORDS.
Child abuse and neglect reporting, 325: 5/7.15 to 5/7.18.
Domestic violence protection orders.
Expiration of plenary order of protection, 750: 60/220.

EXTORTION.
Child abduction, 720: 5/10-5.
Forcible detention, holding hostages, 720: 5/10-4.

F

FAILURE TO SUPPORT CHILD OR SPOUSE.
Non-support punishment act generally, 750: 16/1 to 16/999.
See NONSUPPORT OF CHILD OR SPOUSE.

FAITH HEALING.
Child abuse and neglect, 325: 5/4.

FALSE IMPRISONMENT.
Aggravated unlawful restraint, 720: 5/10-3.1.
Unlawful restraint, 720: 5/10-3.

FAMILY CAREGIVERS, 320: 65/1 to 65/99.
Definitions, 320: 65/15.
Department on aging.
Powers and duties, 320: 65/20.
Funding, 320: 65/40.
Legislative findings, 320: 65/5.

FAMILY CAREGIVERS —Cont'd
Legislative intent, 320: 65/10.
Services.
Respite and supplemental services.
Eligibility, 320: 65/30.
Support services, provision of, 320: 65/25.
Short title of act, 320: 65/1.
Training and support demonstration project, 320: 65/16.

FAMILY FINANCIAL RESPONSIBILITY DRIVING PERMIT.
Issuance when driving privilege suspended for child support delinquency, 750: 5/505.

FAMILY LAW.
Abuse of family members.
Protective orders, 725: 5/112A-1 to 5/112A-31.
See PROTECTIVE ORDERS AGAINST DOMESTIC VIOLENCE.
Adoption, 750: 50/0.01 to 55/1.
See ADOPTION.
Annulment of marriage, 750: 5/301 to 5/306.
See INVALIDITY OF MARRIAGE, DECLARATION OF.
Antenuptial agreements, 750: 10/1 to 10/11.
See PREMARITAL AGREEMENTS.
Child custody jurisdiction.
Uniform child custody jurisdiction and enforcement, 750: 36/101 to 36/405.
Child sexual abuse, 325: 15/0.01 to 15/7.
See CHILD SEXUAL ABUSE.
Declaration of invalidity of marriage, 750: 5/301 to 5/306.
See INVALIDITY OF MARRIAGE, DECLARATION OF.
Dissolution of marriage, 750: 5/401 to 5/802.
See DISSOLUTION OF MARRIAGE.
Divorce proceedings.
Dissolution of marriage, 750: 5/401 to 5/802.
See DISSOLUTION OF MARRIAGE.
Domestic violence, 750: 60/101 to 60/401.
See DOMESTIC VIOLENCE.
Emancipation of mature minors, 750: 30/1 to 30/11.
Interstate family support, 750: 22/101 to 22/999.
See SUPPORT AND MAINTENANCE.
Invalidity of marriage, declaration of, 750: 5/301 to 5/306.
See INVALIDITY OF MARRIAGE, DECLARATION OF.
Legal separation, 750: 5/402.
Marriage, 750: 5/201 to 5/219.
See MARRIAGE.
Marriage dissolution, 750: 5/401 to 5/802.
See DISSOLUTION OF MARRIAGE.
Married persons' rights, 750: 65/0.01 to 65/22.
Parentage, 750: 40/1 to 45/27.
See PARENTAGE PROCEEDINGS.
Premarital agreements, 750: 10/1 to 10/11.
See PREMARITAL AGREEMENTS.
Protective orders.
Abuse of family members, 725: 5/112A-1 to 5/112A-31.
See PROTECTIVE ORDERS AGAINST DOMESTIC VIOLENCE.
Spousal support.
Generally.
See SPOUSAL SUPPORT.
Visitation.
See VISITATION.

FAMILY PURPOSE DOCTRINE, 740: 115/1 to 115/7.

FAMILY SUPPORT CENTERS, 325: 30/7.
Demonstration project, 325: 30/1 to 30/9.

FATHERS.
Abortion.
Injunctive relief.
Father of unborn child, 735: 5/11-107.1.
Adoption.
Notice to putative father.
See ADOPTION.
Parentage proceedings generally.
See PARENTAGE PROCEEDINGS.

FEDERAL AID.
Respite program.
Funding, 320: 10/8.

FEES.
Abortion.
Referral fee, 720: 510/11.1.
Adoption.
Appointment of confidential intermediary, 750: 50/18.3a.
Biological parent registry, 750: 50/18.6.
Birth certificate issuance, 750: 50/19.
Compensation for placement of child, 750: 50/21.
Notice to putative fathers, 750: 50/12a.
Attachment of the body orders.
Escrow account exemptions, 750: 5/713.
Domestic violence.
Protection orders, 750: 60/202.
Service of summons, 750: 60/210.
Marriage licenses.
Required, 750: 5/203.
Public aid collection fee.
Imposition, 750: 5/516.
Wage deduction orders to secure support payments, 750: 5/706.1.

FETAL ALCOHOL SYNDROME.
Pamphlets on fetal alcohol syndrome.
Distribution of information, 750: 5/203.

FETUS.
Abortion generally.
See ABORTION.

FIDUCIARIES.
Adoption, instruments regarding property rights of adopted children.
Child deemed born to adopting parents.
Obligation of fiduciary to determine whether child taker under instrument, 760: 30/1.

FINANCIAL INSTITUTION DATA MATCH SYSTEM.
Support responsibility of relatives of public aid recipients, 305: 5/10-24 to 5/10-24.50.

FINES.
Child curfew violations, 720: 555/1.
Child support.
Location of putative father and noncustodial parents.
Failure to provide requested information, 750: 5/714, 16/33.
Domestic violence.
Protection orders.
Enforcement, 750: 60/223.
Notice in order, 750: 60/221.
Parentage proceedings.
Withholding of income to secure payment of support.
Payor violations, 750: 45/20.
Support orders, withholding of income to secure payment.
Payor violations, 750: 5/706.1.

FINGERPRINTS.
Minor identification, 325: 45/1 to 45/3.

FIREARMS.
Prohibition of firearms protection.
Protective orders against domestic violence.
Remedies, 725: 5/112A-14, 750: 60/214.

FORCE, MARRIAGE BY.
Invalidity of marriage, declaration of, 750: 5/301.

FORCIBLE DETENTION, 720: 5/10-4.

FORCIBLE ENTRY AND DETAINER, 720: 5/10-4.

FOREIGN-BORN CHILD.
Adoption, investigations, 750: 50/6.
Adoption, preadoption requirements, 750: 50/4.1.

FOREIGN MARRIAGE.
Proof of, 750: 5/409.

FORMS.
Adoption.
Adoptee registration identification, 750: 50/18.2.

FORMS —Cont'd
Adoption —Cont'd
Biological parent identification, 750: 50/18.2.
Consent and surrender, 750: 50/10.
Affidavit of identification of father, 750: 50/11.
Declaration of paternity, 750: 50/12a.
Denial of identification exchange, 750: 50/18.2.
Disclaimer of paternity, 750: 50/12a.
Information exchange authorization, 750: 50/18.2.
Notice to putative father, 750: 50/12a.
Surrendered child registration identification, 750: 50/18.2.
Adoption notice, 750: 50/7.
Child support.
Order for enforcement, Sup. Ct. Rule 296.
Expedited child support hearing, 750: 25/7.
Parentage proceedings.
Notice to presumed father, 750: 45/9.1.
Spousal support.
Order for enforcement, Sup. Ct. Rule 296.
Summons, Sup. Ct. Rule 101.
Support orders.
Enforcement, Sup. Ct. Rule 296.

FORUM NON CONVENIENS.
Protection orders.
Domestic violence, 750: 60/209.

FOSTER CARE.
Adoption by foster parents, 750: 50/15.1.

FOSTER PARENTS.
Adoption of foster children, 750: 50/15.1.
Child abuse and neglect reporting.
Required reports, 325: 5/4.

FRAUD.
Abortion.
Alleged abortion performed upon nonpregnant woman, 720: 510/11.
Adoption consent.
Revocation restrictions, 750: 50/11.

FRAUDS, STATUTE OF.
Writing and signature required, 740: 80/1.

FULL FAITH AND CREDIT.
Child custody.
Uniform child custody jurisdiction and enforcement.
Out of state orders, 750: 36/313.

G

GENERAL ASSEMBLY.
Elder abuse and neglect.
Annual reports to, 320: 20/11.
Senior citizens on state boards and commissions.
Purpose of legislation, 320: 5/1.

GESTATIONAL SURROGACY, 750: 47/1 to 47/75.
Actions to invalidate, 750: 47/70.
Applicability of act, 750: 47/75.
Contracts.
Breach, 750: 47/45.
Requirements, 750: 47/25.
Damages, 750: 47/55.
Definitions, 750: 47/10.
Eligibility, 750: 47/20.
Immunity, 750: 47/40.
Irrevocability, 750: 47/70.
Noncompliance, 750: 47/45.
Effect, 750: 47/50.
Parentage rights, 750: 47/15.
Parent-child relationship, establishment of, 750: 47/35.
Purpose of act, 750: 47/5.
Rulemaking, 750: 47/60.
Severability of provisions, 750: 47/65.
Short title of act, 750: 47/1.
Support of child, 750: 47/30.

GOVERNOR.
Early intervention services lead agency designation, 325: 20/5.

GRAND JURIES.
Child abuse and neglect reporting.
Access to records, 325: 5/11.1.

GRANDPARENTS.
Child placed with relatives.
Department of children and family services, 20: 505/7.
Visitation.
Court power to grant, 750: 5/607.
Facilitating contact between child and child's non-custodial parent, 750: 5/607.
Revocation of privilege, 750: 5/607.

GRANTS.
Child sexual abuse crisis intervention demonstration center, 325: 15/4.
Missing children recovery.
I SEARCH programs, 325: 40/4, 40/5.
Senior citizens' and disabled persons' property tax relief grants, 320: 25/4.

GREAT-GRANDPARENTS.
Child placed with relatives.
Department of children and family services, 20: 505/7.
Visitation.
Court power to grant, 750: 5/607.
Facilitating contact between child and child's non-custodial parent, 750: 5/607.
Revocation of privilege, 750: 5/607.

GUARDIANS AD LITEM.
Adoption compensation.
Payment of expenses, appointment for unborn child, 720: 525/4.1.
Adoptions.
Appointment, 750: 50/13.
Inspection of confidential records.
Criteria, 750: 50/18.
State's attorney as child's counsel, 750: 50/13.
Child custody proceedings.
Appointment by court, 750: 5/601.
Marriage dissolution.
Child custody proceedings.
Appointment by court, 750: 5/601.
Court ordered appointment for children, 750: 5/506.
Parentage proceedings.
Determination of father and child relationship or non-existence of relationship.
Representation by, 750: 45/7.

GUARDIANSHIPS.
Administrator.
Abused and neglected child temporary protective custody.
Authorized representative for purposes of consenting to HIV tests, 325: 5/5.
Adoption proceedings.
Appointment of a guardian with power to consent.
Appeals, Sup. Ct. Rule 663.
Appeals.
Adjudication of wardship, Sup. Ct. Rule 662.
Adoption proceedings.
Appointment of a guardian with power to consent, Sup. Ct. Rule 663.
Consent, power to consent to adoption.
Appeals, Sup. Ct. Rule 663.
Emancipation of mature minors.
Filing of petition by guardian, 750: 30/4.
Guardian defined, 750: 30/3-4.
Marriage.
Court ordered licenses, 750: 5/208.
Invalidity declaration.
Commencement, 750: 5/302.
Parentage proceedings.
Determination of father and child relationship or non-existence of relationship.
Representation of minor by general guardian, 750: 45/7.
Power to consent to adoption.
Appeals, Sup. Ct. Rule 663.

GUIDELINES FOR CHILD SUPPORT.
Determining minimum amount, 750: 5/505.

GYMNASTS.
Using or employing child, 720: 150/1, 150/2.

H

HABITUAL DRUNKENNESS.
Ground for dissolution of marriage, 750: 5/401.

HABITUAL OFFENDERS.
Adoption compensation.
Sentencing, 720: 525/5.

HARASSMENT.
Child custody orders.
Modification, 750: 5/610.

HARBORING A RUNAWAY, 720: 5/10-6.

HEALTH CARE FACILITIES.
Surgical institute for children, 325: 60/0.01 to 60/12.

HEALTH CARE INSURANCE.
Partnership for long-term care act.
General provisions, 320: 35/1 to 35/60.

HEALTH CARE PROFESSIONALS.
Domestic violence victims.
Counseling, 750: 60/401.
Elder abuse and neglect.
Failure to report, 320: 20/4.

HEARINGS.
Adoptions.
Counsel appointment, 750: 50/13.
Interim orders, 750: 50/13.
Attachment of the body orders, 750: 5/713.
Child abuse and neglect reporting.
Refusal to amend, expunge or remove, 325: 5/7.16.
Child custody, 750: 5/606.
Child support.
Contempt proceedings to enforce support orders, Sup. Ct. Rule 296.
Expedited support.
Administrative hearings, 750: 25/7.
Judicial hearings, 750: 25/9.
Scheduling, 750: 25/7.
Contempt.
Support orders.
Proceedings to enforce, Sup. Ct. Rule 296.
Domestic violence.
Protective orders, 725: 5/112A-12, 750: 60/212.
Rehearings, 750: 60/224.
Service of notice of hearings, 750: 60/211.
Emancipation of mature minors, 750: 30/9.
Expedited child support hearing, 750: 25/7.
Marriage dissolution.
Respondent in default, 750: 5/405.
Parentage proceedings.
Blood test objections, 750: 45/11.
Preliminary injunctions, 735: 5/11-101.
Spousal support.
Contempt proceedings to enforce support orders, Sup. Ct. Rule 296.
Support enforcement through attachment of the body, 750: 5/713.

HEARSAY EVIDENCE.
Domestic violence.
Protection orders.
Exception to rule, 750: 60/213.1.
Protective orders against domestic violence, 750: 60/213.1.

HIGH RISK YOUTH CAREER DEVELOPMENT, 325: 25/0.01, 25/1.

HOLIDAYS.
Domestic violence protection orders.
Emergency orders, 750: 60/217.
Injunctions, 735: 5/11-106.

HOMELESS PERSONS.
High risk youth career development, 325: 25/0.01, 25/1.

HOME RULE UNITS.
Missing children.
Preemption of jurisdiction, 325: 55/7.

HOMESTEADS.
Married person's rights.
Displacement, 750: 65/16.

HOMESTEADS —Cont'd
Married person's rights —Cont'd
Petitions to execute a deed or mortgage, 750: 65/17.
Court orders, 750: 65/19.
Filing requirements, 750: 65/18.
Security, 750: 65/20.
Tenancies by the entirety, 750: 65/22.
Validity, 750: 65/21.

HOODS.
Kidnapping.
Aggravated kidnapping.
Wearing hood to conceal identity, 720: 5/10-2.

HOSPITALS.
Child abuse and neglect reporting.
Required reports, 325: 5/4.
Surgical institute for children, 325: 60/0.01 to 60/12.

HOSTAGE HOLDING.
Forcible detention, 720: 5/10-4.

HOTLINE PERSONNEL.
Child abuse, neglect or dependency.
Reporting of child abuse and neglect.
Persons required to report, 325: 5/4.

HOUSEHOLD MEMBERS.
Domestic battery, 720: 5/12-3.2.
Domestic violence generally, 750: 60/101 to 60/401.
See DOMESTIC VIOLENCE.

HUMAN RIGHTS, DEPARTMENT OF.
Child abuse and neglect reporting.
Required reports, 325: 5/4.

HUSBAND AND WIFE.
Abandoned spouse, control over property, 750: 65/11.
Action against husband and wife together.
Defending in own right or for another, 750: 65/2.
Action by or against married person without joining spouse, 750: 65/1.
Adoption, 750: 50/0.01 to 55/1.
See ADOPTION.
Annulment of marriage, 750: 5/301 to 5/306.
See INVALIDITY OF MARRIAGE, DECLARATION OF.
Antenuptial agreements, 750: 10/1 to 10/11.
See PREMARITAL AGREEMENTS.
Artificially inseminated wife, status of husband, 750: 40/3.
Attachment, enforcement by married person, 750: 65/1.
Child custody.
Uniform child custody jurisdiction and enforcement, 750: 36/101 to 36/405.
Contracts made and liabilities incurred by married person, 750: 65/6.
Contracts, sales or encumbrances made by spouse, 750: 65/12.
Conveyances, spouse under legal disability.
Petition to convey real estate, 750: 65/17 to 65/20.
Creditors' rights, 750: 65/15.
Criminal neglect of children.
Competency as witness, 720: 130/3.
Damage recovered from spouse committing civil injury, 750: 65/4.
Debts or liabilities incurred before marriage, liability of spouse for, 750: 65/5.
Declaration of invalidity of marriage, 750: 5/301 to 5/306.
See INVALIDITY OF MARRIAGE, DECLARATION OF.
Deeds or mortgages.
Validity, 750: 65/21.
Defending action in own right or for other, 750: 65/2.
Defense by wife in name of deserting husband, 750: 65/3.
Dissolution of marriage, 750: 5/401 to 5/802.
See DISSOLUTION OF MARRIAGE.

HUSBAND AND WIFE —Cont'd
Divorce.
Dissolution of marriage, 750: 5/401 to 5/802.
See DISSOLUTION OF MARRIAGE.
Domestic violence.
Generally, 750: 60/101 to 60/401.
See DOMESTIC VIOLENCE.
Protective orders against abuse, 725: 5/112A-1 to 5/112A-31.
See PROTECTIVE ORDERS AGAINST DOMESTIC VIOLENCE.
Earnings, receiving, use and possessing by married person, 750: 65/7.
Emancipation of mature minors, 750: 30/1 to 30/11.
Interstate family support.
General provisions, 750: 22/101 to 22/999.
See SUPPORT AND MAINTENANCE.
Invalidity of marriage, declaration of, 750: 5/201 to 5/219.
See INVALIDITY OF MARRIAGE, DECLARATION OF.
Judgments, enforcement by married person, 750: 65/1.
Judgments, setting aside, 750: 65/13.
Legal disability, spouse under.
Petition to convey real estate, 750: 65/17 to 65/20.
Marriage, 750: 5/201 to 5/219.
See MARRIAGE.
Marriage dissolution, 750: 5/401 to 5/802.
See DISSOLUTION OF MARRIAGE.
Married persons' rights, 750: 65/0.01 to 65/22.
Mature minors' emancipation, 750: 30/1 to 30/11.
Name changes, 735: 5/21-101.
Parentage, 750: 40/1 to 45/27.
See PARENTAGE PROCEEDINGS.
Power of attorney.
Rights of married persons, 750: 65/14.
Premarital agreements, 750: 10/1 to 10/11.
See PREMARITAL AGREEMENTS.
Privileged communications, 735: 5/8-801.
Interstate family support.
Privilege not to apply, 750: 22/316.
Uniform child custody jurisdiction and enforcement.
Prohibition from invoking, 750: 36/310.
Property ownership by married person, 750: 65/9.
Property unlawfully possessed by married person, 750: 65/10.
Protective orders against domestic violence, 725: 5/112A-1 to 5/112A-31.
See PROTECTIVE ORDERS AGAINST DOMESTIC VIOLENCE.
Removal of child from homestead, 750: 65/16.
Spousal abuse.
Protective orders, 725: 5/112A-1 to 5/112A-31.
See PROTECTIVE ORDERS AGAINST DOMESTIC VIOLENCE.
Spousal support.
Generally.
See SPOUSAL SUPPORT.
Tenancy by the entirety, 750: 65/22.
Torts committed during marriage.
Suit by husband or wife, 750: 65/1.

HUSBAND-WIFE PRIVILEGE.
Uniform child custody jurisdiction and enforcement.
Prohibition from invoking, 750: 36/310.

I

IDENTIFICATION CARDS.
Fingerprint cards for minors, 325: 45/1 to 45/3.

ILLEGITIMACY.
Children of marriage declared invalid, 750: 5/303.
Children of prohibited marriage, 750: 5/212.
Marriage licenses.
Granting exception, 750: 5/205.
Parentage proceedings.
Generally, 750: 40/1 to 45/27.
See PARENTAGE PROCEEDINGS.

ILLINOIS ADOPTION REGISTRY AND MEDICAL INFORMATION EXCHANGE, 750: 50/18.04 to 50/18.07.

ILLITERATES.
High risk youth career development, 325: 25/0.01, 25/1.

IMMUNITY.
Abandoned newborn protection act.
Personnel of facility accepting infant, 325: 2/27.
Relinquishing person, 325: 2/25.
Adoption.
Biological parent registry, 750: 50/18.5.
Child abuse and neglect reporting.
Persons participating in good faith in making of report or referral, 325: 5/9.
Persons taking child into temporary protective custody, 325: 5/5.
Child custody.
Uniform child custody jurisdiction and enforcement.
Immunity for personal jurisdiction for other proceedings, 750: 36/109.
Domestic violence.
Law enforcement limited liability, 750: 60/305.
Persons reporting, 725: 5/112A-25.
Protection orders.
Reports of elder abuse, 750: 60/225.
Providing information or services to victims, 750: 60/401.
Elder abuse and neglect reports, 320: 20/4.
Employer's compliance with income-withholding order.
Interstate family support act, 750: 22/504.
Gestational surrogacy, 750: 47/40.
High-risk adult abuse.
Reporting immunities, 750: 60/225.
Law enforcement limited liability.
Domestic violence, 750: 60/305.
Protection orders.
Domestic violence.
Reports of elder abuse, 750: 60/225.
Support and maintenance.
Interstate family support.
Husband-wife and parent-child immunities not to apply, 750: 22/316.
Limited immunity of petitioner, 750: 22/314.

IMPOTENCY.
Dissolution of marriage.
Grounds, 750: 5/401.
Invalidity of marriage, declaration of.
Ground, lack of capacity to consummate, 750: 5/301.

IN CAMERA HEARINGS.
Domestic violence protection orders.
Disclosure of privileged information, 750: 60/227.1.

INCESTUOUS MARRIAGES, 750: 5/212.

INCOME WITHHOLDING.
Support and maintenance.
Automatic continuance of child support obligation.
Unpaid arrearage or delinquency on termination date of obligation, 750: 28/32.
Employer of obligor.
Sending order to employer without filing petition, 750: 22/501.
Income withholding for support act, 750: 28/1.
Interstate family support.
Administrative enforcement, 750: 22/507.
Contest by obligor, 750: 22/506.
Immunity of employer for complying, 750: 22/504.
Multiple orders, compliance, 750: 22/503.
Penalties for noncompliance, 750: 22/505.
National medical support notice.
Use to enforce health insurance coverage, 750: 28/22.

INCOME WITHHOLDING —Cont'd
Support and maintenance —Cont'd
Securing payment of support, 750: 5/706.1.
Parentage proceedings, 750: 45/20.

INCONVENIENT FORUM.
Child custody jurisdiction.
Uniform child custody jurisdiction and enforcement, 750: 36/207.
Domestic violence protection orders, 750: 60/209.

INDEXES.
Child abuse and neglect index.
Child protective service unit to maintain, 325: 5/8.5.

INDIANS.
Child custody.
Uniform child custody jurisdiction and enforcement.
Applicability, 750: 36/104.
Marriage, 750: 5/209.

INDIGENTS.
Adoption hearings.
Counsel appointment, 750: 50/13.
Appeals.
Juvenile delinquents, Sup. Ct. Rule 661.
Juvenile delinquents.
Appeals, Sup. Ct. Rule 661.
Surgical institute for children, 325: 60/0.01 to 60/12.

INFANTS.
Children generally.
See CHILDREN AND MINORS.

INFERENCES.
Child custody.
Uniform child custody jurisdiction and enforcement.
Self-incrimination privilege invoked, 750: 36/310.

INHERITED CHARACTERISTICS TESTS.
Parentage proceedings, 750: 45/11.

INHERITED METABOLIC DISEASE PAMPHLETS.
Distribution, 750: 5/204.

INJUNCTIONS, 735: 5/11-101 to 5/11-110.
Abortion related decisions by mother.
Relief for father of unborn child, 735: 5/11-107.1.
Affidavits.
Dissolution of injunction.
Supporting of complaint and answer, 735: 5/11-109.
Relief on Saturday, Sunday or legal holiday, 735: 5/11-106.
Amendment of pleadings.
Seeing wrong remedy, 735: 5/11-107.
Bonds, surety, 735: 5/11-103 to 5/11-105.
Dissolution of TRO or preliminary injunction.
Failure to assess damages.
Bar to action on bonds, 735: 5/11-110.
Relief on Saturday, Sunday or legal holiday, 735: 5/11-106.
Child custody.
Uniform child custody jurisdiction and enforcement.
Simultaneous proceedings, 750: 36/206.
Children and family services, department of.
Power to initiate, 20: 510/510-25.
Damages.
Dissolution of TRO or preliminary injunction, 735: 5/11-110.
Dissolution, 735: 5/11-108, 5/11-109.
Assessment of damages in cases where TRO's or preliminary injunctions are dissolved, 735: 5/11-110.
Dissolution of marriage.
Marital residence possession, 750: 5/701.
Domestic violence.
Protection orders.
Order for injunctive relief, 725: 5/112A-14.
Remedy, 750: 60/214.
Holidays, 735: 5/11-106.

INJUNCTIONS —Cont'd
Marriage dissolution.
Independence of provisions, 750: 5/509.
Residence possession, 750: 5/701.
Temporary relief, 750: 5/501.
Motion to dissolve, 735: 5/11-108, 5/11-109.
Protection orders.
Domestic violence.
Order for injunctive relief, 725: 5/112A-14.
Remedy, 750: 60/214.
Reasons for its entry, 735: 5/11-101.
Saturdays, 735: 5/11-106.
Seeking wrong remedy.
Amendment of pleadings, 735: 5/11-107.
Sundays, 735: 5/11-106.

INSURANCE.
Long-term care.
General provisions, 320: 35/1 to 35/60.

INTEREST.
Nonsupport of child or spouse.
Due and unpaid support obligations, 750: 16/20.
Support obligations due and unpaid, 750: 16/23.
Nonsupport of child or spouse, 750: 16/20.
Parentage proceedings, 750: 45/20.7.

INTERGOVERNMENTAL COOPERATION.
Child support.
Unified child support services program, 750: 24/1 to 24/35.

INTERSTATE CHILD CUSTODY PROCEEDINGS.
See CHILD CUSTODY.

INTERSTATE FAMILY SUPPORT ACT.
General provisions, 750: 22/101 to 22/999.
See SUPPORT AND MAINTENANCE.

INTESTINAL DISORDERS.
Inherited metabolic disease pamphlets.
Distribution, 750: 5/204.

INTOXICATION.
Dissolution of marriage.
Ground, habitual drunkenness, 750: 5/401.
Invalidity of marriage, declaration of.
Ground, lack of capacity to consent, 750: 5/301.

INVALIDITY OF MARRIAGE, DECLARATION OF, 750: 5/301 to 5/306.
Action commencement, 750: 5/306.
Administrative aides employment, 750: 5/105.
Admission of respondent, 750: 5/407.
Certificate of invalidity, filing with department of public health, 750: 5/707.
Child support payment orders, 750: 5/505.
Child support payments to clerk of court, 750: 5/709.
Civil practice law application, 750: 5/105.
Collusion, 750: 5/408.
Commencement time, 750: 5/302.
Commingled marital and non-marital property.
Disposition, 750: 5/503.
Default, respondent in, 750: 5/405.
Disposition of property, 750: 5/503.
Dissolution of marriage by divorce, 750: 5/401 to 5/802.
See DISSOLUTION OF MARRIAGE.
Fault or conduct of petitioner not bar to proceedings, 750: 5/406.
Filing of petition, cases requiring service by publication, 750: 5/412.
Grounds, 750: 5/301.
Guidelines for determining minimum amount of child support, 750: 5/505.
Interpretation and construction, 750: 5/102.
Judgments, 750: 5/413.
Enforcement or modification, procedure, 750: 5/511.
Jurisdiction to decide child custody matters, 750: 5/601.
Jury trials, 750: 5/103.
Legislative declaration, 750: 5/102.
Legitimacy of children, 750: 5/303.

INVALIDITY OF MARRIAGE, DECLARATION OF —Cont'd
Maintenance, 750: 5/504.
Marital property, disposition, 750: 5/503.
Non-marital property, disposition, 750: 5/503.
Parental rights and responsibilities, 750: 5/602.1.
Property disposition, 750: 5/503.
Protection order status, 750: 5/107.
Putative spouse, 750: 5/305.
Records, 410: 530/0.01 to 530/3.1.
Retroactivity, 750: 5/304.
Short title of act, 750: 5/101.
Temporary custody orders, 750: 5/603.
Trials by jury, 750: 5/103.
Trust or separate fund for support, maintenance, etc., of minors, 750: 5/503.
Venue, 750: 5/104.

INVESTIGATIONS.
Adoption, 750: 50/6.
Filing of petition, 750: 50/6.
Child abduction.
Law enforcement officers, 720: 5/10-5.
Law enforcement officers.
Child abduction, 720: 5/10-5.

IN VITRO FERTILIZATION.
Gestational surrogacy generally, 750: 47/1 to 47/75.
See GESTATIONAL SURROGACY.

IRRECONCILABLE DIFFERENCES.
Dissolution of marriage, 750: 5/401.
Grounds, 750: 5/401.

IRRETRIEVABLE BREAKDOWN OF MARRIAGE.
Dissolution of marriage, 750: 5/401.

J

JOB TRAINING.
Parentage proceedings.
Unemployed obligors.
Order to make application with jobs training partnership act provider, 750: 45/15.1.

JOINDER OF ACTIONS.
Domestic violence.
Protection orders, 750: 60/202.
Emancipation of minors, 750: 30/10.

JOINDER OF PARTIES.
Child custody.
Uniform child custody jurisdiction and enforcement, 750: 36/205.
Dissolution of marriage, 750: 5/403.
Married persons rights to defend in own right or for others, 750: 65/2.

JOINT AND SEVERAL LIABILITY.
Sale of illegal drugs to minors.
Parental right of recovery, 740: 120/4.

JOINT CUSTODY, 750: 5/602.1.
No presumption in favor of or against, 750: 5/602.
Termination and modification, 750: 5/610.

JOINT PARENTING AGREEMENT, 750: 5/602.1.

JOINT SIMPLIFIED DISSOLUTION PROCEDURE, 750: 5/451 to 5/457.

JUDGES.
Solemnization of marriages, 750: 5/209.

JUDGMENTS.
Abandoned spouses control over property.
Setting aside, 750: 65/13.
Adoptions, 750: 50/14.
Affidavit of costs, expenses, etc., 750: 50/14.
Death of child before final judgment, 750: 50/14a.
Effect of judgment of adoption, 750: 50/17.
Entry of judgment, 750: 50/16.
Interim order, 750: 50/13.

JUDGMENTS —Cont'd
Adoptions —Cont'd
Natural parents' rights after termination order, 750: 50/17.
Statute of limitations for attacking validity, 750: 55/0.01, 55/1.
Termination of parental rights, 750: 50/17.
Child support.
New or existing support order entered deemed series of judgments against obligor, 750: 5/505.
Default judgments.
Domestic violence protection orders, 725: 5/112A-10.
Plenary order of protection, 750: 60/210.
Notice in conjunction with pending civil case, 750: 60/210.1.
Parentage proceedings, 750: 45/14.
Dissolution of marriage, etc.
Joint simplified dissolution procedure, 750: 5/453.
Enforcement.
Preliminary injunctions.
Damages assessed on dissolution, 735: 5/11-110.
Entry.
Adoption, 750: 50/16.
Dissolution of marriage, etc., 750: 5/413.
Marital dissolution, 750: 5/413.
Enforcement procedure, 750: 5/511.
Independence of provisions, 750: 5/509.
Modification procedure, 750: 5/511.
Married persons.
Enforcement by or against, 750: 65/1.
Parentage proceedings, 750: 45/14.
Enforcement, 750: 45/15.
Modification, 750: 45/16.
Relief from judgments.
Abandoned spouse's control over property, setting aside, 750: 65/13.

JURISDICTION.
Adoption proceedings, 750: 50/4.
Child custody, 750: 5/601, 60/208.
Child support.
Interstate family support.
Generally, 750: 22/201 to 22/209.
See SUPPORT AND MAINTENANCE.
Domestic violence protection orders.
Declining to decide certain issues or remedies, 725: 5/112A-12.
Personal jurisdiction, 725: 5/112A-9, 750: 60/208.
Subject matter jurisdiction, 725: 5/112A-8, 750: 60/207.
Emancipation of mature minors, 750: 30/4.
Continuing jurisdiction over proceedings, 750: 30/6.
Marital dissolution.
Judgment enforcement or modification procedure, 750: 5/511.
Residency requirements, 750: 5/401.
Parentage proceedings, 750: 45/9.
Continuing jurisdiction, 750: 45/16.
Support and maintenance.
During separation actions, 750: 5/402.
Interstate family support, 750: 22/201 to 22/209.
See SUPPORT AND MAINTENANCE.

JURY AND JURY TRIAL.
Dissolution of marriage, 750: 5/103.
Domestic violence.
Protection orders, 750: 60/206.
Marriage dissolutions, 750: 5/103.
Parentage proceedings.
Demand for jury trial, 750: 45/13.
Protection orders.
Domestic violence, 750: 60/206.
Right to jury trial, 725: 5/112A-7.

JUVENILE COURTS AND PROCEEDINGS.
Appeals, Sup. Ct. Rules 660, 661.
Emancipation of mature minors, 750: 30/10.
Joinder with juvenile court proceedings, 750: 30/10.
Joinder.
Emancipation of mature minors, 750: 30/10.

JUVENILE DELINQUENCY, CONTRIBUTING TO.
Criminal neglect of minor, 720: 130/2a.

K

KIDNAPPING, 720: 5/10-1.
Aggravated kidnapping, 720: 5/10-2.
Child abduction, 720: 5/10-5.
Aiding and abetting, 720: 5/10-7.

KINSHIP.
Marriage prohibitions, 750: 5/212.

L

LAW ENFORCEMENT OFFICERS OR AGENCIES.
Child custody.
Uniform child custody jurisdiction and enforcement.
Duties, 750: 36/316.
Domestic violence protection orders.
See PROTECTIVE ORDERS AGAINST DOMESTIC VIOLENCE.
Elder abuse and neglect.
Failure to report, 320: 20/4.
Hostage.
Forcible detention of officer, 720: 5/10-4.
Immunity, domestic violence limited immunity, 750: 60/305.
Reports.
Child abduction, 720: 5/10-5.
Child abuse and neglect reporting, 325: 5/4.
Domestic violence.
Protection orders, 750: 60/303.
Visitation order violations.
Records of contempt orders, 750: 5/607.1.

LEGAL SEPARATIONS.
Admission of respondent, 750: 5/407.
Child custody generally.
See CHILD CUSTODY.
Child support payment orders, 750: 5/505.
Child support payments.
Mandatory payments to clerk, 750: 5/709.
Collusion, 750: 5/408.
Commencement of actions, 750: 5/411.
Default.
Respondent in default, 750: 5/405.
Fault or conduct of petitioner.
Not bar to proceedings, 750: 5/406.
Filing of petition.
Cases requiring service by publication, 750: 5/412.
Guidelines for determining minimum amount of child support, 750: 5/505.
Judgment, 750: 5/413.
Judgment enforcement or modification.
Procedure, 750: 5/511.
Maintenance, 750: 5/504.
Parental rights and responsibilities not diminished, 750: 5/602.1.
Petition for, 750: 5/403.
Support during separation, 750: 5/402.
Temporary custody orders, 750: 5/603.

LEGITIMATION OF CHILDREN.
See PARENTAGE PROCEEDINGS.

LICENSES.
Marriage licenses.
Accompaniments, 750: 5/203.
Age requirements, 750: 5/203.
Court orders for those underage, 750: 5/208.
Effective date, 750: 5/207.
Exceptions, 750: 5/205.
Foreign jurisdiction laws, 750: 5/218.
Formality requirement, 750: 5/201.
Form content, 750: 5/202.
Health certificate retention, 750: 5/206.
Unauthorized issuance.
Penalty, 750: 5/219.

LIENS.
Child support, 750: 5/505.
Maintenance orders, 750: 5/703.

LIENS —Cont'd
Marital dissolution.
Maintenance orders, 750: 5/703.

LIMITATION OF ACTIONS.
Adoption.
Consent to adoption, 750: 55/0.01, 55/1.
Relief from final judgment or order, 750: 50/20b.
Adoption contests.
Notice failure, 750: 55/1.
Antenuptial agreements, 750: 10/9.
Breach of promise to marry, 740: 15/6.
Child support.
Court ordered withdrawals from decedents' estates, 750: 5/510.
Declaration of invalidity of marriage.
Time of commencement, 750: 5/302.
Invalidity of marriage, declaration of.
Time of commencement of action, 750: 5/302.
Non-existence of parent and child relationship.
Action to declare, 750: 45/8.
Paternity actions, 750: 45/8.
Prenuptial agreements, 750: 10/9.

LIMITATION OF DAMAGES.
Breach of promise to marry, 740: 15/2.
Parental responsibility law, 740: 115/5.

LIVING SEPARATE AND APART.
Dissolution of marriage, 750: 5/401.

LONG-ARM JURISDICTION.
Child custody.
Uniform child custody jurisdiction and enforcement.
Appearance immunity for personal jurisdiction for other proceedings, 750: 36/109.
Domestic violence protection orders.
Jurisdiction over persons, 750: 60/208.

LONG-TERM CARE INSURANCE.
Partnership for long-term care, 320: 35/1 to 35/60.

LURING OF CHILD INTO MOTOR VEHICLE, BUILDING, ETC., 720: 5/10-5.

M

MAINTENANCE AND SUPPORT.
Child support.
See CHILD SUPPORT.
Generally.
See SUPPORT AND MAINTENANCE.

MARIJUANA.
Sale of illegal drug to minor.
Parental right to recovery, 740: 120/1 to 120/4.

MARITAL PRIVILEGE, 735: 5/8-801.

MARITAL PROPERTY.
Child support, 750: 65/11.
Disposition upon dissolution or invalidity of marriage, 750: 5/503.

MARRIAGE, 750: 5/201 to 5/219.
Administrative aides employment, 750: 5/106.
Adoption, 750: 50/0.01 to 55/1.
See ADOPTION.
Antenuptial agreements, 750: 10/1 to 10/11.
See PREMARITAL AGREEMENTS.
Breach of promise to marry, 740: 15/0.01 to 15/10.
Certificate completion, 750: 5/209.
Civil law application, 750: 5/105.
Common law marriages, 750: 5/214.
Contracts.
Writing and signature required, 740: 80/1.
Declaration of invalidity of marriage, 750: 5/301 to 5/306.
See INVALIDITY OF MARRIAGE, DECLARATION OF.
Dissolution of marriage.
Generally, 750: 5/401 to 5/802.
See DISSOLUTION OF MARRIAGE.

MARRIAGE —Cont'd
Domestic violence, 750: 60/101 to 60/401.
See DOMESTIC VIOLENCE.
Fetal alcohol syndrome pamphlets.
Distribution, 750: 5/203.
Foreign marriage, proof of, 750: 5/409.
Formalities, 750: 5/201.
Health certificate retention, 750: 5/206.
Inherited metabolic diseases.
Distribution of pamphlets, 750: 5/204.
Interpretation and construction of act, 750: 5/102.
Invalidity.
Person solemnizing not legally qualified, 750: 5/209.
Invalidity of marriage, declaration of, 750: 5/301 to 5/306.
See INVALIDITY OF MARRIAGE, DECLARATION OF.
Jury trials, 750: 5/103.
Legislative declaration, 750: 5/102.
Licenses.
Accompaniments, 750: 5/203.
Age requirements, 750: 5/203.
Court orders for those underage, 750: 5/208.
Effective date, 750: 5/207.
Exceptions, 750: 5/205.
Foreign jurisdiction, 750: 5/218.
Formality requirement, 750: 5/201.
Form content, 750: 5/202.
Unauthorized issuance, 750: 5/219.
Married persons' rights, 750: 65/0.01 to 65/22.
Minors.
Court ordered licenses, 750: 5/208.
Emancipation of mature minors, 750: 30/1 to 30/11.
Invalidity of marriage.
Commencement, 750: 5/302.
Grounds, 750: 5/301.
License age requirements, 750: 5/203.
Parentage proceedings.
Generally, 750: 40/1 to 45/27.
See PARENTAGE PROCEEDINGS.
Relationship and support not dependent on, 750: 45/3.
Parent and child relationship not dependent on marital status of parents, 750: 45/3.
Premarital agreements, 750: 10/1 to 10/11.
See PREMARITAL AGREEMENTS.
Prohibitions, 750: 5/212.
Marriages contracted out of state, 750: 5/216.
Protection order status, 750: 5/107.
Provision violations.
Penalties, 750: 5/215.
Records, 410: 530/0.01 to 530/3.1.
Marriage license.
Health certificate retention, 750: 5/206.
Registration of certificate, 750: 5/210.
Sexually transmitted diseases.
Distribution of pamphlets, 750: 5/204.
Short title of act, 750: 5/101.
Solemnization, 750: 5/209.
Validity, 750: 5/213.
Nonresidents, 750: 5/217.
Person solemnizing not legally qualified, 750: 5/209.
Prohibited marriages contracted in another state, 750: 5/216.

MARRIED PERSONS' RIGHTS, 750: 65/0.01 to 65/22.
Abandoned spouse's control over property, 750: 65/11.
Actions.
Right to sue and be sued, 750: 65/1.
Children, removal from homestead, 750: 65/16.
Contracts, 750: 65/6.
Contracts made by spouse, 750: 65/12.
Conveyance of real estate, spouse under legal disability, 750: 65/18 to 65/21.
Creditor's rights, 750: 65/15.
Damages, recovery, 750: 65/4.
Defending in name of spouse, 750: 65/3.
Defending in own right or for other, 750: 65/2.
Earnings, 750: 65/7.

MARRIED PERSONS' RIGHTS —Cont'd
Encumbrance made by spouse, 750: 65/12.
Homestead, removal of children from, 750: 65/16.
Judgments, setting aside, 750: 65/13.
Legal disability, spouse under, 750: 65/17.
Liabilities of spouse, responsibility for, 750: 65/5.
Petition to convey real estate, spouse under legal disability, 750: 65/18 to 65/20.
Power of attorney, 750: 65/14.
Property, 750: 65/9.
Control over by abandoned spouse, 750: 65/11.
Conveyance of real estate when spouse under legal disability, 750: 65/18 to 65/21.
Unlawful possession by spouse, 750: 65/10.
Rights of married persons act.
Short title, 750: 65/0.01.
Sales made by spouse, 750: 65/12.
Tenancy by the entirety, 750: 65/22.
Unlawful possession of property by spouse, 750: 65/10.

MATURE MINORS.
Emancipation, 750: 30/1 to 30/11.

MEDIATION.
Dissolution of marriage, 750: 5/404.
Joint custody award, 750: 5/602.1.
Joint parenting agreement.
Agreement to specify procedure, 750: 5/602.1.

MEDICAID.
Long-term care insurance.
General provisions, 320: 35/20 to 35/45.
Support responsibility of relatives, determination and enforcement, 305: 5/10-1 to 5/10-27.
See PUBLIC AID.

MEDICAL EXAMINERS.
Child abuse and neglect reporting.
Access to records, 325: 5/11.1.
Investigation of reports of death resulting from abuse or neglect, 325: 5/4.1.
Required reports, 325: 5/4.

MEDICAL INFORMATION EXCHANGE.
Adoptive parents and birth parents.
Illinois adoption registry and medical information exchange, 750: 50/18.04 to 50/18.07.

MEDICAL RECORDS.
Adopted children.
History of child and biological parent, 750: 50/18.4a.

MENTAL ANGUISH.
Marriage dissolution grants, 750: 5/401.

MENTAL CRUELTY.
Ground for dissolution of marriage, 750: 5/401.

MENTAL HEALTH AND DEVELOPMENTAL DISABILITIES.
Aggravated kidnapping.
Mentally retarded person, 720: 5/10-2.
Child support for non-minor children, 750: 5/513.
Department.
Early intervention services role, 325: 20/9.
Early intervention services, 325: 20/1 to 20/20.
Kidnapping.
Aggravated kidnapping.
Mentally retarded person, 720: 5/10-2.

METABOLIC DISEASE PAMPHLETS.
Distribution, 750: 5/204.

MINOR IDENTIFICATION, 325: 45/1 to 45/3.

MINORITIES.
High risk youth career development, 325: 25/0.01, 25/1.

MINORS.
Abortion, parental notice, 750: 70/1 to 70/99.
See ABORTION, PARENTAL NOTICE.

MINORS —Cont'd
Abuse.
See CHILD ABUSE, NEGLECT OR DEPENDENCY.
Custody.
See CHILD CUSTODY.
Custody jurisdiction.
Uniform child custody jurisdiction and enforcement, 750: 36/101 to 36/405.
Dependency.
See CHILD ABUSE, NEGLECT OR DEPENDENCY.
Generally.
See CHILDREN AND MINORS.
Neglect.
See CHILD ABUSE, NEGLECT OR DEPENDENCY.
Parentage proceedings.
Generally, 750: 40/1 to 45/27.
See PARENTAGE PROCEEDINGS.
Sexual abuse, 325: 15/0.01 to 15/7.
Support.
See CHILD SUPPORT.

MISCARRIAGE.
Induced miscarriage.
Abortion generally.
See ABORTION.

MISSING CHILDREN, 325: 40/1 to 55/7.
Automated data exchange system.
Implementation, 325: 40/6.
Birth certificates.
Custodians providing copies upon request, 325: 50/4, 55/4.
Central automated data repository.
Reports of missing persons kept in, 325: 40/7.
Child custody proceedings.
Inquiry prior to granting or modifying custody judgment, 325: 40/7.1.
County clerks.
Custodian duties, 325: 50/4, 55/4.
Custodian duties, 325: 50/4, 55/4.
Definitions, 325: 40/2, 50/1, 55/1.
Duties of department of state police, 325: 40/6, 50/2, 55/2.
Duties of registrar of vital records, 325: 50/3, 55/3.
Grants to I SEARCH programs, 325: 40/4, 40/5.
Home rule units.
Preemption of jurisdiction, 325: 55/7.
Intergovernmental missing child recovery act of 1984.
Title of act, 325: 40/1.
I SEARCH programs.
Department of children and family services.
Contact with, 325: 40/3.5.
Grants, 325: 40/4, 40/5.
Reports, 325: 40/8.
State grants, 325: 40/4, 40/5.
I SEARCH units.
Activities, 325: 40/3.
Establishment, 325: 40/3.
Monitoring, 325: 40/5.
Purposes, 325: 40/3.
Reports, 325: 40/8.
Law enforcement agencies data system (LEADS).
Entering reports by law enforcement agencies and policing bodies, 325: 40/7.
Establishment, 325: 40/6.
Law enforcement agency duties, 325: 40/7.
Local law enforcement duties, 325: 55/6.
Local registrars of vital records.
Custodian duties, 325: 50/4, 55/4.
Missing children records act.
Title of act, 325: 50/0.01.
Missing children registration law.
Title of act, 325: 50/0.01.
Notice by department of state police upon entry of report, 325: 50/2.
Registrar of vital records.
Custodian duties, 325: 50/4, 55/4.
Duties, 325: 50/3, 55/3.
Notice by department of state police upon receipt of report, 325: 50/2.

MISSING CHILDREN —Cont'd
Reports to governor and general assembly, 325: 40/8.
School duties, 325: 50/5, 55/5.
Title of act.
Intergovernmental missing child recovery act of 1984, 325: 40/1.
Missing children records act, 325: 50/0.01.
Missing children registration law, 325: 55/0.01.

MORTGAGES.
Legal disability of spouse, 750: 65/17 to 65/21.
Married persons rights.
Spouse under legal disability, 750: 65/17 to 65/21.
Spouse under legal disability, 750: 65/17 to 65/21.

MOTIONS.
Child support.
Expedited support.
Pre-hearing motions, 750: 25/7.
Domestic violence protection orders, modification and reopening, 750: 60/224.
Injunctions.
Dissolution, 735: 5/11-108, 5/11-109.
Preliminary injunctions, 735: 5/11-101.
Preliminary injunctions, 735: 5/11-101.

MUSICIANS.
Using or employing child, 720: 150/1, 150/2.

N

NAME CHANGES.
Change of name.
Marriage dissolution.
Restoration of name, 750: 5/413.
Notice by publication, 735: 5/21-103.
Notice to persons outside state, 735: 5/21-104.
Parties, 735: 5/21-101.
Petitions, 735: 5/21-102.
Process, 735: 5/21-103, 5/21-104.
Service by publication, 735: 5/21-103.
Service outside state, 735: 5/21-104.

NAMES.
Adoption.
Identity of parties by initials or pseudonyms, 750: 50/18.
Marriage dissolution.
Restoration of name, 750: 5/413.

NATIVE AMERICANS.
Marriage solemnization, 750: 5/209.

NEPHEWS.
Child placed with relatives.
Department of children and family services, 20: 505/7.

NEWBORNS.
Medical neglect reports.
Perinatal coordinator to review, 325: 5/7.3a.
Reports of suspected medical neglect involving, 325: 5/7.3a.

NEWSPAPERS.
Support obligor owing arrearage or delinquency, publication of name, 750: 5/706.3.

NEXT FRIEND.
Emancipation of mature minors.
Filing of petition, 750: 30/4.

NIECES.
Child placed with relatives.
Department of children and family services, 20: 505/7.

NO FAULT DIVORCE, 750: 5/401.

NON-MARITAL PROPERTY.
Disposition upon dissolution or invalidity of marriage, 750: 5/503.

NONRESIDENTS.
Support and maintenance.
Interstate family support.
Jurisdiction over nonresidents, 750: 22/201, 22/202.

NONSUPPORT ACTIONS.
Prosecution under act, sentence, 750: 5/505.

NONSUPPORT OF CHILD OR SPOUSE, 750: 16/1 to 16/999.
Attorney general to prosecute.
Cases referred to department of public aid, 750: 16/7.
Automatic continuance of obligation.
Unpaid arrearage or delinquency on date of termination of obligation, 750: 16/20.
Change in residence, notice, 750: 16/20.
Community service, offender ordered to perform, 750: 16/50.
Competency of husband or wife as witnesses, 750: 16/45.
Contempt, violation of support order, 750: 16/20.
Continuing offense, violations construed as, 750: 16/55.
Criminal contempt, failure to report new employment, 750: 16/20.
Default orders.
Proceedings against person whose order for support entered by default, 750: 16/10.
Domestic violence allegations, order of protection, 750: 16/65.
Driving privileges, suspension, 750: 16/50.
Earnfare program, certification of first offenders eligible for program, 750: 16/15.
Effective date, 750: 16/999.
Employment, unemployed offender ordered to seek, 750: 16/60.
Entry of support order before trial or after guilty plea or conviction, 750: 16/20.
Evidence to prove marriage or parents of child, 750: 16/40.
Execution, enforcement of recognizance, violation of support order, 750: 16/35.
Expungement of conviction.
First offender certified to earnfare program, 750: 16/15.
Failure to support, offense, 750: 16/15.
Family financial responsibility driving permit, issuance to offender, 750: 16/50.
Financial information concerning ability to provide support.
Evidence, information obtained by subpoena, 750: 16/20.
Fine, failure to support, 750: 16/15.
Payment, 750: 16/35.
Forfeiture of recognizance, violation of support order, 750: 16/35.
Guidelines and standards, entry of order, 750: 16/20.
Husband and wife as competent witnesses, 750: 16/45.
Income withholding for support act.
Orders subject to, 750: 16/22.
Indictment or information, proceedings by, 750: 16/10.
Interest on support obligations, 750: 16/23.
Due and unpaid obligations, 750: 16/20.
Job search services, unemployed offender ordered to use, 750: 16/60.
Jobs training partnership act providers.
Unemployed offender to make application with, 750: 16/60.
Judgments, order for support deemed series of judgments, 750: 16/20.
Lien, overdue support installments, 750: 16/20.
Non-support punishment act, 750: 16/1.
Order of protection, domestic violence allegations, 750: 16/65.
Pendente lite order before trial, 750: 16/20.
Presumption of ability to support, 750: 16/15.
Prior law, actions determined under, 750: 16/995.

NONSUPPORT OF CHILD OR SPOUSE —Cont'd
Professional license of offender, certification of violation, 750: 16/50.
Recognizance, probation on entry, 750: 16/35.
Restitution, 750: 16/15.
Sentence for failure to support, 750: 16/15.
Community service, work alternative program, 750: 16/50.
Service of process on obligor, 750: 16/20.
Severability of provisions, 750: 16/70.
State case registry, information to, entry or modification of order, 750: 16/30.
State disbursement unit, payment of support to, 750: 16/25.
State's attorneys to prosecute.
Proceedings instituted by person filing complaint, 750: 16/5.
Temporary support order before trial or after guilty plea or conviction, 750: 16/20.
Termination date on support obligation, 750: 16/20.
Unemployed obligors, order to seek employment, job search services, 750: 16/60.
Unpaid arrearage or delinquency on date of termination of obligation.
Automatic continuance of obligation, 750: 16/20.
Violation of support order, proceeding to trial, 750: 16/35.
Work alternative program, sentencing offender to, 750: 16/50.

NOTICE.
Abandoned spouses control over property, 750: 65/11.
Setting aside judgment, 750: 65/13.
Abortion, parental notice, 750: 70/1 to 70/99.
See ABORTION, PARENTAL NOTICE.
Adoption.
Biological parent or sibling information, 750: 50/18.4.
Medical and mental health histories of child, 750: 50/18.4a.
Parties defendant, 750: 50/7.
Putative father's notice, 750: 50/12a.
Adoption contests, 750: 55/1.
Breach of promise to marry actions, 740: 15/4, 15/5.
Child abuse, neglect or dependency.
Reporting abuse and neglect.
Amendment, expunction or removal of records, 325: 5/7.17.
Penalty for transmitting false reports, 325: 5/7, 5/7.6.
Taking into temporary custody, 325: 5/5.
Truancy report receipt, 325: 5/7.4.
Child custody.
Enforcement of orders, 750: 5/611.
Leave to remove children, 750: 5/609.
Modification of orders, 750: 5/610.
Proceedings generally, 750: 5/601.
Uniform child custody jurisdiction and enforcement.
Opportunity to be heard, 750: 36/205.
Persons outside state, 750: 36/108.
Registration of determination, 750: 36/305.
Child support.
Delinquencies in payment, Sup. Ct. Rule 296.
Expedited support.
Recommended orders, 750: 25/7, 25/10.
Health insurance orders, 750: 5/505.2.
Domestic violence.
Protection orders.
Consequences of violations of order, 750: 60/221.
Issuance, 750: 60/222.
Modification and reopening, 750: 60/224.
Notice of orders, 725: 5/112A-22.
Plenary orders of protection, 750: 60/219.
Service of notice of hearings, 750: 60/211.
Service of process, 750: 60/210.
Short form notification, 725: 5/112A-22.10, 750: 60/222.10.

NOTICE —Cont'd
Domestic violence —Cont'd
Protection orders —Cont'd
30-day interim order of protection, 750: 60/218.
Early intervention services, 325: 20/12.
Interstate family support act.
Contest by obligor of income-withholding orders, 750: 22/506.
Modification of child support order issued by another state, 750: 22/614.
Marital property transfers upon abandonment, 750: 65/11.
Marriage dissolution.
Clerk duty, 750: 5/413.
Extraordinary expenditures during action, 750: 5/501.1.
Temporary restraining orders, 750: 5/501.
Parentage proceedings.
Payment received by department of public aid for recording, 750: 45/23.
Withholding of income to secure payment of support, 750: 45/20.
Procedures to avoid income withholding, 750: 45/20.
Parental notice of abortion, 750: 70/1 to 70/99.
See ABORTION, PARENTAL NOTICE.
Paternity actions.
Presumed father, 750: 45/9.1.
Preliminary injunctions, 735: 5/11-102.
Protection orders.
Domestic violence.
Consequences of violations of order, 750: 60/221.
Issuance, 750: 60/222.
Modification and reopening, 750: 60/224.
Notice of orders, 725: 5/112A-22.
Plenary orders of protection, 750: 60/219.
Service of notice of hearings, 750: 60/211.
Service of process, 750: 60/210.
Short form notification, 725: 5/112A-22.10, 750: 60/222.10.
30-day interim order of protection, 750: 60/218.
Real estate partition actions, 750: 5/515.
Spousal support.
Delinquencies in payments, Sup. Ct. Rule 296.
Support orders.
Spousal support.
Delinquencies in payment, Sup. Ct. Rule 296.
Withholding of income to secure payments, 750: 5/706.1.
Temporary restraining orders, 735: 5/11-101.
Visitation orders.
Enforcement and modification, 750: 5/607.1.
Wage deduction orders to secure support payments, 750: 5/706.1.
Paternity proceedings, 750: 45/20.
Procedures to avoid income withholding, 750: 45/20.

NOTICE BY PUBLICATION.
Adoption, 750: 50/7.
Change of name, 735: 5/21-103.
Domestic violence.
Protective orders, 725: 5/112A-10.
Name changes, 735: 5/21-103.
Protective orders.
Domestic violence, 725: 5/112A-10.
Support obligor owing arrearage or delinquent in payment, 750: 5/706.3.

NOTICE OF HEARING.
Child support.
Contempt proceedings to enforce support orders, Sup. Ct. Rule 296.
Expedited support proceedings, 750: 25/7.
Contempt.
Support orders.
Proceedings to enforce, Sup. Ct. Rule 296.
Domestic violence.
Protection orders, 750: 60/211.
Emancipation of mature minors, 750: 30/8.
Expedited child support hearing, 750: 25/7.

NOTICE OF HEARING —Cont'd
Marriage dissolution.
Hearings when respondent in default, 750: 5/405.
Protective orders against domestic violence, 725: 5/112A-11.
Spousal support.
Contempt proceedings to enforce support orders, Sup. Ct. Rule 296.

NURSERY SCHOOLS.
Child abuse and neglect reporting.
Required reports by director or staff assistants, 325: 5/4.

NURSES.
Child abuse and neglect reporting.
Required reports, 325: 5/4.
Early intervention services, 325: 20/1 to 20/20.
Elder abuse and neglect.
Failure to report, 320: 20/4.

NURSING HOME ADMINISTRATORS.
Elder abuse and neglect.
Failure to report, 320: 20/4.

NURSING HOMES.
Older adult services act, 320: 42/1 to 42/99.
See OLDER ADULT SERVICES.

O

OATHS OR AFFIRMATIONS.
Adoption.
Confidential intermediary, 750: 50/18.3a.
Child support.
Expedited support.
Administrative hearing officer, Sup. Ct. Rule 100.2.

OCCUPATIONAL THERAPISTS.
Early intervention services, 325: 20/1 to 20/20.
Elder abuse and neglect.
Failure to report, 320: 20/4.

OLDER ADULT SERVICES, 320: 42/1 to 42/99.
Advisory committee, 320: 42/35.
Definitions, 320: 42/10.
Expansion of services, 320: 42/20.
Lead agency, designation of, 320: 42/15.
Nursing home conversion program, 320: 42/30.
Priority service areas, 320: 42/20.
Defined, 320: 42/10.
Purpose, 320: 42/5.
Reporting requirements, 320: 42/15.
Restructuring of services delivery system, 320: 42/25.
Short title of act, 320: 42/1.

OMBUDSMAN.
Early childhood intervention ombudsman, 325: 20/9.

ONE CHURCH ONE CHILD ADVISORY BOARD, 20: 505/7.1.

OPTOMETRISTS.
Early intervention services, 325: 20/1 to 20/20.
Elder abuse and neglect.
Failure to report, 320: 20/4.

ORDINANCES.
Child curfew.
Stricter requirements permissible, 720: 555/2.

OSTEOPATHS.
Child abuse and neglect reporting.
Required reports, 325: 5/4.
Elder abuse and neglect.
Failure to report, 320: 20/4.

P

PACE PROGRAM.
All-inclusive care for the elderly act.
General provisions, 320: 40/1 to 40/30.

PAMPHLETS.
Marriage licenses.
Fetal alcohol syndrome pamphlets.
Distribution, 750: 5/203.
Inherited metabolic disease pamphlets.
Distribution, 750: 5/204.
Sexually transmitted disease pamphlets.
Distribution, 750: 5/204.

PARENTAGE PROCEEDINGS, 750: 40/1 to 45/27.
Acknowledgment of parentage.
Voluntary acknowledgment, 750: 45/6.
Action as civil action, 750: 45/13.
Administrative determination of paternity, 750: 45/4.1.
Adoptions.
Adoptive parent, establishment of relationship, 750: 45/4.
Notice to putative fathers, 750: 50/12a.
Appeals.
Free transcript, 750: 45/18.
Artificial insemination.
Children born as a result.
Status, 750: 40/2.
Donor not husband.
Donor's status as father, 750: 40/3.
Attorney general.
Limitation on legal representation, 750: 45/18.
Blood tests, 750: 45/11.
Child custody.
Judgments, 750: 45/14.
Child's representative, appointment, capacity, 750: 45/14.1.
Child support.
Automatic continuance of obligation.
Unpaid arrearage or delinquency on termination of obligation, 750: 45/13.1, 45/14.
Financial information concerning ability to provide support.
Evidence, information obtained by subpoena, 750: 45/14.
Guidelines for determining award, 750: 45/14.
Interest on support obligation due and unpaid, 750: 45/20.7.
Judgments, 750: 45/14.
Payments to state disbursement unit, 750: 45/21.1.
Report by obligor of employment or termination from employment, 750: 45/14.
State case registry, information on entry of order, 750: 45/14.1.
Unpaid arrearage or delinquency on termination of obligation.
Automatic continuance of obligation, 750: 45/13.1, 45/14.
Voluntary acknowledgment of parentage, basis for seeking, 750: 45/6.
Code of civil procedure, provisions governing actions, 750: 45/13.
Complaint to determine father and child relationship or non-existence of relationship, 750: 45/7.
Consent of parties, establishment of relationship, 750: 45/6.
Contempt for failure to comply with order, 750: 45/15.
Costs, 750: 45/17.
DNA tests to determine inherited characteristics, 750: 45/11.
Employment of obligor or termination from employment.
Report to obligee and clerk of court, 750: 45/14.
Establishing order for support by consent.
Petition after voluntary acknowledgment of parentage, 750: 45/6.
Evidence.
Blood and tissue test reports, 750: 45/11.
Expedited child support system.
Generally, 750: 25/1 to 25/13.
Father and child relationship, determination, 750: 45/7.
Full faith and credit.
Foreign out-of-state paternity determinations, 750: 45/27.

PARENTAGE PROCEEDINGS —Cont'd
Gestational surrogacy generally, 750: 47/1 to 47/75.
See GESTATIONAL SURROGACY.
Illinois parentage act.
Short title, 750: 40/1.
Illinois parentage act of 1984.
Short title, 750: 45/1.
Interest on support obligation due and unpaid, 750: 45/20.7.
Interstate family support, 750: 22/701.
Nonparentage as defense, 750: 22/315.
Joinder of actions with other civil actions, 750: 45/9.
Judgment, 750: 45/14.
Enforcement, 750: 45/15.
Modification, 750: 45/16.
Jurisdiction, 750: 45/9.
Continuing jurisdiction of court, 750: 45/16.
Jury trials, 750: 45/13.
Limitation of actions, 750: 45/8.
Marriage.
Relationship and support not dependent on, 750: 45/3.
Minor parents duty to support, 750: 45/3.1.
Mother and child relationship, action to declare, 750: 45/19.
Natural father, establishment of relationship, 750: 45/4.
Natural father, presumption, 750: 45/5.
Natural mother, establishment of relationship, 750: 45/4.
Non-existence of mother and child relationship, action to declare, 750: 45/19.
Non-existence of parent and child relationship.
Determination, 750: 45/7.
Statute of limitations, 750: 45/8.
Notice to presumed father, 750: 45/9.1.
Other states' paternity determinations, 750: 45/27.
Out-of-state determinations.
Full faith and credit, 750: 45/27.
Parent and child relationship defined, 750: 45/2.
Parent and child relationship established, 750: 45/4.
Consent of parties, 750: 45/6.
Parent and child relationship not dependent on marriage, 750: 45/3.
Parties, determination of father and child relationship or non-existence of relationship, 750: 45/7.
Payment to clerk of circuit court, 750: 45/21.
Payment to department of public aid, 750: 45/21.
Collection fee, 750: 45/22.
Notice to clerk of payment received for recording, 750: 45/23.
Petition for establishment of parent and child relationship, 750: 45/6.
Presumption of custody with mother.
Judgment containing no explicit award of custody, 750: 45/14.
Presumption of paternity, 750: 45/5.
Pre-trial proceedings, 750: 45/10.
Pre-trial recommendations, 750: 45/12.
Protection orders.
Determination if order previously entered, 750: 45/15.2.
Provisions of judgments, 750: 45/14.
Public defenders.
Appointment to represent indigent defendant, 750: 45/18.
Public policy, 750: 45/1.1.
Repeal of paternity act, effect, 750: 45/25.
Report by obligor of employment or termination from employment, 750: 45/14.
Right to counsel, 750: 45/18.
Service of notice to presumed father, 750: 45/9.1.
Settlement offers, 750: 45/12.1.
Severability, 750: 45/26.

PARENTAGE PROCEEDINGS —Cont'd
State's attorneys.
Representation of mother or child upon request, 750: 45/18.
Statute of limitations, 750: 45/8.
Summons, required language, 750: 45/9.
Support obligations, interest on, 750: 45/20.7.
Surrogacy, establishing parent-child relationship, 750: 45/6.
Temporary child support order, 750: 45/13.1.
Transcripts.
Free transcript on appeal, 750: 45/18.
Unemployed obligors, court's powers, 750: 45/15.1.
Venue, 750: 45/9.
Visitation, custody or guardianship.
Petition to establish order for support by consent after voluntary acknowledgment of parentage, 750: 45/6.
Voluntary acknowledgment of parentage, 750: 45/6.
Withholding of income to secure payment of support, 750: 45/20.
Procedures to avoid income withholding, 750: 45/20.

PARENTAL NOTICE OF ABORTION, 750: 70/1 to 70/99.
See ABORTION, PARENTAL NOTICE.

PARENTAL RESPONSIBILITY LAW, 740: 115/1 to 115/7.

PARENTAL RIGHT OF RECOVERY.
Cannabis or controlled substance sales to minors, 740: 120/1 to 120/4.

PARENTAL RIGHTS, TERMINATION OF.
Wrongs to child act.
Court-ordered disposition, 720: 150/3.

PARENTS.
Adoption, 750: 50/0.01 to 55/1.
See ADOPTION.
Child custody generally.
See CHILD CUSTODY.
Child custody jurisdiction.
Uniform child custody jurisdiction and enforcement, 750: 36/101 to 36/405.
Children's privacy protection and parental empowerment act, 325: 17/1 to 17/20.
Child sexual abuse.
Parent permitting sexual abuse, 720: 150/5.1.
Child support.
Generally.
See CHILD SUPPORT.
Criminal neglect of children.
Competency as witnesses, 720: 130/3.
Emancipation of mature minors, 750: 30/1 to 30/11.
Gestational surrogacy generally, 750: 47/1 to 47/75.
See GESTATIONAL SURROGACY.
Interstate family support.
General provisions, 750: 22/101 to 22/999.
See SUPPORT AND MAINTENANCE.
Marriage of children.
Court ordered licenses, 750: 5/208.
Invalidity commencement, 750: 5/302.
Invalidity grounds, 750: 5/301.
License consent, 750: 5/203.
Parent depraved.
Presumption, unfit person defined, 750: 50/1.
Visitation rights of parent not granted custody of child, 750: 5/607.

PARENTS LIVING SEPARATE AND APART.
Parental rights and responsibilities not diminished, 750: 5/602.1.

PARTIES.
Adoption, parties defendant, 750: 50/7.
Change of name, 735: 5/21-101.
Name changes, 735: 5/21-101.
Protective orders against domestic violence.
Persons who may seek relief, 725: 5/112A-4.

PARTITION PROCEEDINGS.
Realty in marital dissolution proceedings, 750: 5/514.
Filing of actions, 750: 5/515.

PARTNERSHIP FOR LONG-TERM CARE ACT.
General provisions, 320: 35/1 to 35/60.

PATERNITY.
See PARENTAGE PROCEEDINGS.

PATHOLOGISTS.
Speech-language pathologists and audiologists.
Early intervention services, 325: 20/1 to 20/20.

PEACE OFFICERS.
Child custody.
Uniform child custody jurisdiction and enforcement.
Duties, 750: 36/316.
Hostage, forcible detention, 720: 5/10-4.

PEDDLERS.
Using or employing child, 720: 150/1, 150/2.

PENALTIES.
Child support.
Nonpayment, 750: 5/505.
Domestic violence.
Protection orders, 750: 60/223.
Marriage code violations, 750: 5/215.
Parentage proceedings.
Withholding of income to secure payment of support.
Payor violations, 750: 45/20.
Protection orders.
Domestic violence, 750: 60/223.
Violation of order, 725: 5/112A-23.
Support orders, withholding of income to secure payment.
Payor violations, 750: 5/706.1.
Wage deduction orders.
Paternity proceedings, 750: 45/20.
Securing support payments, 750: 5/706.1.

PENDENCY OF PROCEEDINGS.
Domestic violence protection orders.
Service of notice in conjunction with pending civil case, 750: 60/210.1.
Setting forth in petition, 725: 5/112A-5.

PENDENTE LITE.
Support order before trial for failure to support, 750: 16/20.

PERINATAL COORDINATOR.
Reports of suspected medical neglect involving newborns, 325: 5/7.3a.

PERSONAL PROPERTY.
Abandoned spouses control over, 750: 65/11 to 65/13.
Domestic violence.
Protective orders.
Possession of personalty, 725: 5/112A-14.
Married persons rights, 750: 65/9.
Unlawful possession by spouse, 750: 65/10.
Protective orders.
Domestic violence.
Possession of personalty, 725: 5/112A-14.

PETITIONS.
Abandoned spouses control over property, 750: 65/11.
Setting aside judgment, 750: 65/13.
Adoption.
See ADOPTION.
Change of name, 735: 5/21-102.
Child custody.
Uniform child custody jurisdiction and enforcement.
Expedited enforcement, 750: 36/308.
Service, 750: 36/309.
Child custody proceedings, 750: 5/601.
Child support.
Contempt proceedings to enforce support orders, Sup. Ct. Rule 296.
Surcharge imposition, 750: 5/505.
Contempt.
Support orders.
Proceedings to enforce, Sup. Ct. Rule 296.
Emancipation of mature minors, 750: 30/3-5.
Contents, 750: 30/7.
Filing, 750: 30/4.
Legal separation, 750: 5/403.

PETITIONS —Cont'd
Marital dissolution.
Elements, 750: 5/403.
Extraordinary expenditure notice, 750: 5/501.1.
Judgment modification or enforcement procedures, 750: 5/511.
Post-judgment proceedings, 750: 5/511.
Service of publication requirements, 750: 5/412.
Simplified dissolution procedure, 750: 5/452.
Name changes, 735: 5/21-102.
Parentage proceedings.
Withholding of income to secure payment of support, 750: 45/20.
Procedures to avoid income withholding, 750: 45/20.
Preliminary injunctions.
Assessment of damages on dissolution, 735: 5/11-110.
Protection orders.
Address of petitioner.
Non-disclosure, 725: 5/112A-5.
Contents, 725: 5/112A-5.
Domestic violence, 725: 5/112A-4.
Commencement of actions, 750: 60/202.
Pro se, 750: 60/202.
Requirements, 750: 60/203.
Rule to show cause, 750: 60/223.
Who may file, 750: 60/201.
Formal requisites, 725: 5/112A-5.
Real estate partitions, 750: 5/515.
Spousal support.
Contempt proceedings to enforce support orders, Sup. Ct. Rule 296.
Spouse under legal disability.
Conveyance of real estate, 750: 65/18 to 65/20.
Support payments.
Abatement, Sup. Ct. Rule 296.
Withholding of income to secure payment, 750: 5/706.1.
Visitation, 750: 5/607.
Visitation abuse, 750: 5/607.1.
Wage deduction orders.
Paternity proceedings, 750: 45/20.
Procedures to avoid income withholding, 750: 45/20.
Wage deduction orders to secure support payments, 750: 5/706.1.

PHARMACIES AND PHARMACISTS.
Pharmaceutical assistance act.
General provisions, 320: 25/1 to 25/13.
Senior citizens and disabled persons prescription drug discount program, 320: 55/1 to 55/99.
Eligible pharmacies, 320: 55/40.

PHYSICAL CRUELTY.
Grounds for dissolution of marriage, 750: 5/401.

PHYSICAL THERAPISTS.
Early intervention services, 325: 20/1 to 20/20.
Elder abuse and neglect.
Failure to report, 320: 20/4.

PHYSICIANS.
Abortion, parental notice, 750: 70/1 to 70/99.
See ABORTION, PARENTAL NOTICE.
Abused and neglected children reporting.
Access to records, 325: 5/11.1.
Failing to report, 325: 5/4.02.
Required to report, 325: 5/4.
Temporary protective custody of child, 325: 5/5.
Birth control services to minors, 325: 10/0.01, 10/1.
Child abuse and neglect reporting.
Access to records, 325: 5/11.1.
Failing to report, 325: 5/4.02.
Required reports, 325: 5/4.
Temporary protective custody of child, 325: 5/5.
Disciplinary actions.
Reporting complications resulting from an abortion, 720: 510/10.1.

PHYSICIANS —Cont'd
Disciplinary actions —Cont'd
Violation of abortion law as grounds, 720: 510/11.
Early intervention services, 325: 20/1 to 20/20.
Elder abuse and neglect.
Failure to report, 320: 20/4.
Unprofessional conduct.
Violation of abortion law, 720: 510/11.

PHYSICIANS' ASSISTANTS.
Child abuse, neglect or dependency.
Reporting abuse and neglect.
Persons required to report, 325: 5/4.

PLEADINGS.
Amendment.
Injunctive relief.
Seeking wrong remedy, 735: 5/11-107.
Child custody.
Uniform child custody jurisdiction and enforcement.
Contents, 750: 36/209.
Support and maintenance.
Interstate family support, 750: 22/311.

PODIATRISTS.
Child abuse and neglect reporting.
Required reports, 325: 5/4.
Elder abuse and neglect.
Failure to report, 320: 20/4.

POLICE.
Child abuse and neglect reporting.
Required reports, 325: 5/4.
Child custody.
Uniform child custody jurisdiction and enforcement.
Duties, 750: 36/316.
Domestic violence.
Protection orders.
Arrest without warrant, 750: 60/301.
Assistance, 750: 60/304.
Data maintenance, 750: 60/302.
Liability, 750: 60/305.
Reports, 750: 60/303.
Service of process, 750: 60/210.
Elder abuse and neglect.
Failure to report, 320: 20/4.
Hostage, forcible detention, 720: 5/10-4.
Protection orders.
Domestic violence.
Arrest without warrant, 750: 60/301.
Assistance, 750: 60/304.
Data maintenance, 750: 60/302.
Liability, 750: 60/305.
Reports, 750: 60/303.
Reports.
Child abduction, 720: 5/10-5.

POLICE STATIONS.
Abandoned newborn protection act.
Defined, 325: 2/10.
Duties, 325: 2/20.
Immunities, 325: 2/27.

POWER OF ATTORNEY.
Married person's rights, 750: 65/14.

PRAECIPES.
Dissolution of marriage or legal separation.
Commencement of actions, 750: 5/411.

PRAYER, TREATMENT OR CURE OF DISEASE.
Child abuse and neglect reporting.
Child not considered neglected or abused, 325: 5/3.

PREGNANCY.
Abortion.
See ABORTION.
Abortion fraud.
Alleged abortion performed on nonpregnant woman, 720: 510/11.
Birth control services to minors, 325: 10/0.01, 10/1.
Child abuse and neglect reporting.
Referral of pregnant addicts, 325: 5/7.3b.

PREGNANCY —Cont'd
Gestational surrogacy act, 750: 47/1 to 47/75.
See GESTATIONAL SURROGACY.

PRELIMINARY INJUNCTIONS.
Bond of applicant, 735: 5/11-103.
Dissolution.
Assessment of damages, 735: 5/11-110.
Injunctions in general, 735: 5/11-108, 5/11-109.
Hearings, 735: 5/11-101.
Marriage dissolution proceedings.
Independence of provisions, 750: 5/509.
Temporary relief, 750: 5/501.
Motion for hearing, 735: 5/11-101.
Notice, 735: 5/11-102.

PREMARITAL AGREEMENTS.
Amendment, 750: 10/4.
Content, 750: 10/4.
Definitions, 750: 10/2.
Effective date, 750: 10/11.
Enforcement, 750: 10/7.
Void marriages, 750: 10/8.
Formalities, 750: 10/3.
Interpretation and construction, 750: 10/10.
Limitation of actions, 750: 10/9.
Marriage effect, 750: 10/5.
Revocation, 750: 10/6.
Short title, 750: 10/1.

PREPONDERANCE OF EVIDENCE.
Domestic violence protection orders, 750: 60/205.

PRESCRIPTION MEDICINES.
Disabled or handicapped.
Senior citizens and disabled persons prescription drug discount program, 320: 55/1 to 55/99.
Senior citizens.
Senior citizens and disabled persons prescription drug discount program, 320: 55/1 to 55/99.
Senior pharmaceutical assistance act, 320: 50/1 to 50/99.

PRESUMPTIONS.
Abandoned newborn protection act, 325: 2/15.
Adoption.
Unfitness of person, 750: 50/1.
Best interest of child, maximum involvement of both parents.
Child custody proceedings, 750: 5/602.
Child abduction.
Mother's legal custody, parties not married, 720: 5/10-5.
Child abuse and neglect reporting.
Good faith of person required to report or refer, 325: 5/9.
Children's privacy protection and parental empowerment act.
Presumption of consent, 325: 17/15.
Custody of child with mother.
Parentage proceedings.
Judgment not containing explicit award of custody, 750: 45/14.
Domestic violence protective orders.
Grant of possession of residence, hardship presumption, 750: 60/214.
Joint custody.
No presumption in favor of or against, 750: 5/602.
Marital property, 750: 5/503.
Parentage proceedings.
Gestational surrogacy, 750: 47/15.
Judgment containing no explicit award of custody, 750: 45/14.
Parent depraved, 750: 50/1.
Paternity, 750: 45/5.
Rebuttable presumptions.
Child abuse.
Custody and visitation, 725: 5/112A-14, 750: 60/214.
Unfit parent, 750: 50/1.

PRETRIAL CONFERENCES.
Parentage proceedings, 750: 45/10.
Pre-trial recommendations, 750: 45/12.

PRINTOUTS.
Marriage, dissolution and invalidity records, 410: 530/2, 530/3.

PRISONERS.
Abandoned spouses control over property, 750: 65/11 to 65/13.
Escape.
Damages caused by escapees, 20: 510/510-30.
Name changes, 735: 5/21-101.

PRIVATE SCHOOLS.
Domestic violence protection orders.
Disclosure by, 750: 60/222.

PRIVILEGED COMMUNICATIONS.
Child abuse or neglect reporting.
Inapplicability, 325: 5/10.
Domestic violence.
Counselors and victims.
Communications, 750: 60/227.
Other privileged information, 750: 60/227.1.
Protection orders.
Waiver, 750: 60/213.2.
Elder abuse and neglect reports.
Communications between person required to report and client or patient, 320: 20/4.
Husband-wife privilege, 735: 5/8-801.
Interstate family support.
Privilege not to apply, 750: 22/316.
Uniform child custody jurisdiction and enforcement.
Prohibition from invoking, 750: 36/310.
Protective orders against domestic violence.
Domestic violence counselors and victims, 750: 60/227.
Other privileged information, 750: 60/227.1.
Waiver, 750: 60/213.2.

PROBATION AND CONDITIONAL DISCHARGE.
Appeals.
Revocation of probation, Sup. Ct. Rule 662.
Modification.
Protective order violation, 725: 5/112A-23.
Parentage proceedings.
Failure to comply with court order, 750: 45/15.
Revocation.
Appeals, Sup. Ct. Rule 662.
Protective order violation, 725: 5/112A-23.

PROBATION OFFICERS.
Child abuse and neglect reporting.
Required reports, 325: 5/4.

PROFESSIONAL COUNSELORS.
Child abuse and neglect reporting.
Individuals required to report, 325: 5/4.

PROFESSIONAL REGULATION, DEPARTMENT OF.
Child abuse and neglect reporting.
Access to records, 325: 5/11.1.

PROPERTY.
Abandoned spouses control over, 750: 65/11 to 65/13.
Domestic violence.
Protective orders.
Protection of property, 725: 5/112A-14.
Marriage dissolution.
Disposition, 750: 5/503.
Married person's rights, 750: 65/9, 65/10.
Protective orders.
Domestic violence.
Protection of property, 725: 5/112A-14.

PRO SE LITIGANTS.
Domestic violence.
Protection orders, 750: 60/202.

PROTECTIVE CUSTODY.
Child abuse and neglect reporting.
Temporary protective custody, 325: 5/5.

PROTECTIVE ORDERS.
Domestic violence, 725: 5/112A-1 to 5/112A-31.
See PROTECTIVE ORDERS AGAINST DOMESTIC VIOLENCE.

PROTECTIVE ORDERS —Cont'd
Parentage proceedings.
Determination if order previously entered, 750: 45/15.2.

PROTECTIVE ORDERS AGAINST DOMESTIC VIOLENCE, 725: 5/112A-1 to 5/112A-31, 750: 60/201 to 60/227.1.
Accountability for actions of others, 750: 60/216.
Remedies and standards, 725: 5/112A-16.
Address, non-disclosure, 750: 60/203.
Arrest.
Law enforcement policies regarding procedures, 725: 5/112A-27.
Warrantless arrest for violations, 725: 5/112A-26.
Balance of hardship, 725: 5/112A-14.
Burden of proof, 750: 60/205.
Child custody, 725: 5/112A-14.
Order of payment, 725: 5/112A-23.
Child support.
Payment of support, 725: 5/112A-14.
Violation of order, 725: 5/112A-23.
Civil procedural rules.
Application of rules, 725: 5/112A-6.
Commencement of actions, 725: 5/112A-2, 750: 60/202.
Consolidation with other civil proceedings, 750: 60/202.
Construction of provisions, 725: 5/112A-1.
Constructive notice, 725: 5/112A-10.
Contempt.
Enforcement of orders, 725: 5/112A-23.
Enforcement of violations, 750: 60/223.
Willful violation of order, 725: 5/112A-21.
Contents, 725: 5/112A-21, 750: 60/221.
Continuances, 725: 5/112A-13, 750: 60/213.
Correlative protective orders, 750: 60/215.
Correlative separate orders, 725: 5/112A-15.
Criminal courts.
Enforcement of violations, 750: 60/223.
Criminal procedure.
Enforcement of orders, 725: 5/112A-23.
Default orders, 725: 5/112A-10.
Default, plenary order of protection, 750: 60/210.
Notice in conjunction with pending civil case, 750: 60/210.1.
Definitions, 725: 5/112A-3.
Dismissal, 750: 60/202.
Domestic abuse advocates, 750: 60/205.
Domestic violence counselor-victim privilege, 750: 60/227.
Domestic violence generally, 750: 60/101 to 60/401.
See DOMESTIC VIOLENCE.
Duration, 725: 5/112A-20, 750: 60/220.
Emergency order, 750: 60/217.
Duration and extension, 725: 5/112A-17, 5/112A-20, 750: 60/220.
Modification or reopening, 725: 5/112A-24, 750: 60/224.
Enforcement, 725: 5/112A-23, 750: 60/223.
Limited law enforcement liability, 725: 5/112A-31.
Exclusive possession of residence.
Venue for request, 750: 60/209.
Extension, 725: 5/112A-20, 5/112A-22, 750: 60/220.
False statements, 750: 60/226.
Findings of court, 725: 5/112A-14.
Fourteen day emergency order, 725: 5/112A-17.
Duration and extension, 725: 5/112A-20.
Hearings, 725: 5/112A-12, 750: 60/212.
Hearsay evidence, 750: 60/213.1.
High-risk adult, access of, 750: 60/201.1.
Immunity from prosecution, 750: 60/225.
Incarceration for violation of order, 725: 5/112A-23.
Injunctive relief, 725: 5/112A-14.
Interim order of thirty days, 750: 60/218.
Duration and extension, 725: 5/112A-18, 5/112A-20, 750: 60/220.
Modification or reopening, 725: 5/112A-24, 750: 60/224.
Interpretation of provisions, 725: 5/112A-1.

PROTECTIVE ORDERS AGAINST DOMESTIC VIOLENCE —Cont'd
Issuance of orders, 725: 5/112A-14, 750: 60/214.
Jurisdiction.
Declining to decide certain issues or remedies, 725: 5/112A-12.
Personal jurisdiction, 725: 5/112A-9, 750: 60/208.
Subject matter jurisdiction, 725: 5/112A-8, 750: 60/207.
Jury and jury trial, 725: 5/112A-7, 750: 60/206.
Law enforcement agencies.
Data maintenance, 725: 5/112A-28, 750: 60/302.
Policies regarding arrest procedures, 725: 5/112A-27, 750: 60/301.1.
Law enforcement officers.
Arrest without warrant for violations, 725: 5/112A-26, 750: 60/301.
Assistance by, 725: 5/112A-30, 750: 60/304.
Limited liability for enforcement, 725: 5/112A-31, 750: 60/305.
Reports, 725: 5/112A-29, 5/112A-30, 750: 60/303.
Losses suffered as a direct result of abuse.
Order for payment, 725: 5/112A-14.
Modification, 725: 5/112A-22, 5/112A-24, 750: 60/224.
Mutual orders, 725: 5/112A-15, 750: 60/215.
Non-disclosure of address, 750: 60/203.
Notice.
Remedies requiring actual or constructive notice, 750: 60/210.
Notice by publication, 725: 5/112A-10.
Notice of hearing, 725: 5/112A-11.
Notice of orders, 725: 5/112A-22.
Short form notification, 725: 5/112A-22.10.
Order of protection status, 750: 60/223.1.
Parties.
Persons who may seek relief, 725: 5/112A-4.
Penalties.
Violation of order, 725: 5/112A-23.
Pendency of proceedings.
Service of notice.
Notice in conjunction with pending civil case, 750: 60/210.1.
Setting forth in petition, 725: 5/112A-5.
Personal property possession, 725: 5/112A-14.
Persons protected, 725: 5/112A-4, 750: 60/201.
Petitions, 725: 5/112A-4.
Address of petitioner.
Non-disclosure, 725: 5/112A-5.
Contents, 725: 5/112A-5.
Formal requisites, 725: 5/112A-5.
Pro se, 750: 60/202.
Requirements, 750: 60/203.
Who may file, 750: 60/201.
Plenary orders, 725: 5/112A-19, 750: 60/219.
Duration and extension, 725: 5/112A-20, 750: 60/220.
Modification, 725: 5/112A-24.
Preliminary orders.
Modification, 750: 60/224.
Privileged communications.
Domestic violence counselors and victims, 750: 60/227.
Other privileged information, 750: 60/227.1.
Privilege waiver, 750: 60/213.2.
Protection of property, 725: 5/112A-14.
Remedies and standards, 725: 5/112A-14, 750: 60/214.
Accountability for actions of others, 725: 5/112A-16.
Detailed description, 725: 5/112A-21.
Plenary orders, 725: 5/112A-19.
Requiring constructive or actual notice, 750: 60/210.
Re-openings, 725: 5/112A-24, 750: 60/224.
Reports.
Law enforcement officers, 725: 5/112A-29, 5/112A-30.
Revocation, 725: 5/112A-22.
Rules of civil procedure, applicability, 750: 60/205.

PROTECTIVE ORDERS AGAINST DOMESTIC VIOLENCE —Cont'd
Rules of court.
Application of rules, 725: 5/112A-6.
Separate orders.
Correlative separate orders, 725: 5/112A-15.
Service of process, 725: 5/112A-10, 5/112A-22, 750: 60/210.
By sheriff, 750: 60/222.
Short form notification, 750: 60/222.10.
Notice in conjunction with pending civil case, 750: 60/210.1.
Notice of hearings, 725: 5/112A-11, 750: 60/211.
Spousal support.
Order of payment, 725: 5/112A-14.
Violation of order, 725: 5/112A-23.
Standard of proof, 750: 60/205.
Subsequent proceeding, continuing duty to inform court, 750: 60/203.
Summons, 725: 5/112A-10, 750: 60/210.
Supreme court rules.
Application of rules, 725: 5/112A-6.
Thirty day interim order, 750: 60/218.
Duration and extension, 750: 60/220.
Transfers of cases or issues in cases, 725: 5/112A-12.
Trials, 725: 5/112A-7.
Untrue statements, 750: 60/226.
Venue, 750: 60/209.

PSYCHOLOGISTS.
Child abuse and neglect reporting.
Required reports, 325: 5/4.
Early intervention services, 325: 20/1 to 20/20.

PUBLIC AID.
Child support.
Collection fees, 750: 5/516.
Court enforcement, 305: 5/10-10.
Mandatory payments to clerk, 750: 5/709.
Payments, 750: 5/704.
Wage deduction orders, 750: 5/706.1.
Contracts with state disbursement unit, 305: 5/10-26.2.
Single parent employment restrictions.
Wrongs to children act, 720: 150/3, 150/3.1, 150/5.
Spousal support.
Court enforcement, 305: 5/10-10.
Support responsibility of relatives, 305: 5/10-1 to 5/10-27.
Ability to support, standards and regulations, 305: 5/10-3.
Actions brought on behalf of person in need of support from responsible relative, 305: 5/10-10.
Actions for judicial enforcement of support liability, 305: 5/10-10.
Action to enforce administrative order, 305: 5/10-15.
Administrative determination of paternity, 305: 5/10-17.7.
Administrative enforcement unit defined, 305: 5/10-3.
Administrative liens and levies on personal property, 305: 5/10-25.5.
Administrative liens and levies on real property, 305: 5/10-25.
Administrative order for income withholding, 305: 5/10-17.2.
Administrative order requiring responsible relative to comply with support, 305: 5/10-3.1, 5/10-11.
Enforcement, costs and fees, 305: 5/10-15.
Modification or release, petition, 305: 5/10-12 to 5/10-13.
Registration, 305: 5/10-17.1.
Relief from order, petition, 305: 5/10-14.1.
Administrative orders.
Issuance by child and spouse support unit, 305: 5/10-11.
Adverse rating from credit reporting agency.
Delayed payment from disbursement unit causing, 305: 5/10-26.5.
Alternative actions to enforce support, 305: 5/10-9.

PUBLIC AID —Cont'd
Support responsibility of relatives —Cont'd
Appeal of administrative order to comply.
Petition for modification or release, 305: 5/10-12 to 5/10-13.
Assignment of rights, title and interest in support obligation.
Acceptance of financial aid, 305: 5/10-1.
Automatic continuance of obligation.
Unpaid arrearage or delinquency on termination date, 305: 5/10-8.1, 5/10-10, 5/10-11.
Birth certificates.
Administrative determination of paternity.
New certificate, 305: 5/10-17.8.
Bond, security or guarantee to secure payment, 305: 5/10-16.3.
Child and spouse support unit, 305: 5/10-3.1.
Administrative orders.
Issuance by, 305: 5/10-11.
Child born out of wedlock.
Term child includes, 305: 5/10-2.
Child living with parent or parents.
When considered, 305: 5/10-2.
Child support payments to clerk of circuit court, 305: 5/10-10.3.
Collection of money owing because of failure of support.
Power of child and spouse support unit, 305: 5/10-3.1.
Compelling attendance of witnesses, 305: 5/10-13.8.
Conference request concerning termination of services or failure to provide services, 305: 5/10-3.1.
Copies as proof of records, 305: 5/10-13.4.
Court enforcement, 305: 5/10-10.
Date support obligation terminates included in order, 305: 5/10-8.1.
Debit authorization, 305: 5/10-16.7.
Declaration by responsible relative, 305: 5/10-5.
Declaration of public policy, 305: 5/10-1.
Deductibility of direct relatives' support payments.
Actions of recovery of financial aid, 305: 5/10-18.
Department of revenue.
Past due support information to, 305: 5/10-17.9.
Depositions, 305: 5/10-13.10.
Deposit of payments ordered under other laws, 305: 5/10-19.
Disclosure of information by responsible relative, 305: 5/10-3.1.
Discovery of financial information, request for.
Failure to comply, evidence allowed, 305: 5/10-10.
Electronic funds transfer committee, 305: 5/10-16.6.
Eligibility for support services, 305: 5/10-1.
Employers' obligations, 305: 5/10-23.
Employers providing information, 305: 5/10-3.1.
Evidence concerning ability to provide support.
Failure to comply with discovery request, 305: 5/10-10.
Evidentiary rules, hearings not subject to, 305: 5/10-13.2.
Examination of records to determine ability to support, 305: 5/10-13.1.
Extent of liability, 305: 5/10-2.
Failure to appear and testify or produce records and papers, 305: 5/10-13.9.
Federal income tax refund intercept, 305: 5/10-17.3.
Financial institutions data matches, 305: 5/10-24.5.
Charges on accounts by financial institutions, 305: 5/10-24.40.
Confidentiality of information provided, 305: 5/10-24.45.
Definitions, 305: 5/10-24.
Hardship imposed on financial institution.
Department to accommodate, 305: 5/10-24.35.

PUBLIC AID —Cont'd
Support responsibility of relatives —Cont'd
Financial institutions data matches —Cont'd
Immunity from liability, 305: 5/10-24.50.
Types of accounts to be reported, 305: 5/10-24.30.
Full support, support payments, 305: 5/10-8.
Health care expenses for child.
Duties of employer when coverage available to parent through employer, 305: 5/10-23.
Hearings not subject to technical rules of evidence or procedure, 305: 5/10-13.2.
Hearing to review department decisions, 305: 5/10-14.
Husband's liability, 305: 5/10-2.
Income withholding to secure payment.
Administrative order, 305: 5/10-17.2.
Income withholding for support act generally, 750: 28/1 to 28/999.
Orders subject to income withholding for support act, 305: 5/10-16.2.
Information to locate support obligor and others, 305: 5/10-3.3, 5/10-3.4.
Intercept of tax refunds.
Federal income tax, 305: 5/10-17.3.
State income tax refund and other payment intercept, 305: 5/10-17.5.
Interest on obligations due and unpaid, 305: 5/10-16.5.
Investigation and enforcement powers.
Powers of child and spouse support unit, 305: 5/10-3.1.
Investigations and determination of support obligation, 305: 5/10-6.
Job search, training or work programs.
Unemployed responsible relative ordered to participate in, 305: 5/10-11.1.
Judgments, new or existing support orders, 305: 5/10-8.1.
Judicial enforcement of court and administrative orders, 305: 5/10-16.
Licensing agencies.
Past due support information to, 305: 5/10-17.6.
Lien for overdue support, 305: 5/10-8.1.
Liens and levies on personal property, 305: 5/10-25.5.
Liens and levies on real property, 305: 5/10-25.
Location information concerning putative fathers and noncustodial parents, 305: 5/10-3.3.
Obtaining location information, 305: 5/10-3.4.
Modification or release of administrative order to comply, 305: 5/10-12 to 5/10-13.
Necessitous circumstances.
Proof of, 305: 5/10-13.5.
Notice of obligation, 305: 5/10-4.
Notice of support due, 305: 5/10-7.
Oaths.
Authority to administer, 305: 5/10-13.3.
Obtaining location information, 305: 5/10-3.4.
Office of the administrator.
Conduct of conferences as to services, 305: 5/10-3.1.
Other actions and remedies, 305: 5/10-17.
Other states.
Requests for administrative enforcement, 305: 5/10-17.11.
Parent locator service, 305: 5/10-3.2.
Parents' liability, 305: 5/10-2.
Partial support, support payments, 305: 5/10-8.
Paternity.
Administrative determination, 305: 5/10-17.7.
New birth certificate, 305: 5/10-17.8.
Payment of support to state disbursement unit, 305: 5/10-10.4.
Payment received.
Notice to clerk of circuit court, 305: 5/10-10.2.
Payment, security, bond or guarantee to secure, 305: 5/10-16.3, 5/10-17.4.
Payments of support generally, 305: 5/10-8.

PUBLIC AID —Cont'd
Support responsibility of relatives —Cont'd
Payments ordered under other laws.
Where deposited, 305: 5/10-19.
Payments to clerk of circuit court.
Child support payments, 305: 5/10-10.3.
Notice to obligor, 305: 5/10-10.4.
Penalty for failure to provide locator information, 305: 5/10-3.3.
Petition for modification of or release from administrative order.
By person receiving support, 305: 5/10-12.1.
By responsible relative, 305: 5/10-12.
Hearing, 305: 5/10-13.
Petition for relief from administrative order to comply, 305: 5/10-14.1.
Production of records, 305: 5/10-13.8.
Proof of records, 305: 5/10-13.4.
Public aid collection fee, 305: 5/10-10.1.
Purposes of provisions, 305: 5/10-1.
Receipt of payment.
Notice to clerk of circuit court, 305: 5/10-10.2.
Referrals to attorney general or units of local government.
Powers of child and spouse support unit, 305: 5/10-3.1.
Refund of taxes.
Federal income tax refund intercept, 305: 5/10-17.3.
State income tax refund and other payment intercept, 305: 5/10-17.5.
Registration of administrative order for support, 305: 5/10-17.1.
Reinvestigations and redeterminations of financial ability of responsible relatives, 305: 5/10-6.
Release from administrative order to comply, 305: 5/10-12 to 5/10-13.
Relief from administrative order, petition, 305: 5/10-14.1.
Requests to other states for administrative enforcement, 305: 5/10-17.11.
Review of department decisions, 305: 5/10-14.
Review of forms or questionnaires returned by responsible relative, 305: 5/10-6.
Review of orders for support.
Powers of child and spouse support unit, 305: 5/10-3.1.
Service of process or provision of notice.
Last known address of noncustodial parent, 305: 5/10-8.1.
Several liability of parents, 305: 5/10-2.
Social security numbers.
Requiring responsible relative to disclose, 305: 5/10-3.1.
Standards and regulations for determining ability to support, 305: 5/10-3.
State case registry, 305: 5/10-27.
Information to, entry or modification of order, 305: 5/10-10.5.
Administrative orders, 305: 5/10-11.2.
State disbursement unit, 305: 5/10-26.
Payments to, 305: 5/10-10.4, 750: 5/507.1, 15/2.2, 45/21.1.
State disbursement unit revolving fund, 305: 5/12-8.1.
State income tax refund and other payment intercept, 305: 5/10-17.5.
Subpoenas, 305: 5/10-13.6.
Child and spouse support unit, 305: 5/10-6.
Compelling attendance of witnesses and production of records, 305: 5/10-13.8.
Noncompliance, 305: 5/10-13.9.
Temporary order for child support, 305: 5/10-8.1.
Termination date included in order for support, 305: 5/10-8.1.
Time for filing petition.
Release from or modification of administrative order, 305: 5/10-12, 5/10-12.1.
Unemployed responsible relatives.
Participation in job search, training or work programs, 305: 5/10-11.1.

PUBLIC AID —Cont'd
Support responsibility of relatives —Cont'd
Unpaid arrearage or delinquency on termination date.
Automatic continuance of obligation, 305: 5/10-8.1, 5/10-10, 5/10-11.
Visitation of minor by person or persons providing support.
Orders of court entered for support providing, 305: 5/10-10.
Wife's liability, 305: 5/10-2.
Withholding income to secure payment.
Administrative order, 305: 5/10-17.2.
Income withholding for support act generally, 750: 28/1 to 28/999.
Orders subject to income withholding for support act, 305: 5/10-16.2.
Witnesses, compelling attendance, 305: 5/10-13.8.
Witness fees, 305: 5/10-13.7.
Wrongs to children act.
Single parent employment restrictions, 720: 150/3, 150/3.1, 150/5.

PUBLIC AID, DEPARTMENT OF.
All-inclusive care for the elderly act.
Administration generally, 320: 40/1 to 40/30.
Child support.
Payments to public aid recipients, 750: 5/704.
Child support enforcement program.
Supervision, 750: 5/712.
Child support, mandatory payments to clerk.
Payments to department, 750: 5/709.
Early intervention services role, 325: 20/9.
High risk youth career development, 325: 25/0.01, 25/1.
Interstate family support.
General provisions, 750: 22/101 to 22/999.
See SUPPORT AND MAINTENANCE.
Maintenance payments to public aid recipients, 750: 5/704.
Parentage proceedings.
Administrative paternity determinations, 750: 45/4.1.
Payment of child support to department, 750: 45/21.
Collection fee, 750: 45/22.
Notice to clerk of payment received for recording, 750: 45/23.
Partnership for long-term care.
General provisions, 320: 35/1 to 35/60.
Support, interstate.
Duties, 750: 22/310.

PUBLIC DEFENDERS.
Parentage proceedings.
Appointment to represent indigent defendant, 750: 45/18.

PUBLIC FUNDS.
Community senior services and resources fund, 320: 60/40.
Early intervention services revolving fund, 325: 20/20.

PUBLIC HEALTH, DEPARTMENT OF.
Abused and neglected children reporting.
Access to records, 325: 5/11.1.
Required reports, 325: 5/4.
Adoption registrants.
Fee levying, 750: 50/18.6.
Certificate of marital dissolution or invalidity.
Filing, 750: 5/707.
Child abuse and neglect reporting.
Access to records, 325: 5/11.1.
Required reports of field personnel, 325: 5/4.
Early intervention services role, 325: 20/9.
Invalidity of marriage certificate.
Filing, 750: 5/707.
Marital dissolution certificate.
Filing, 750: 5/707.
Marital invalidity declaration.
Certificate filing, 750: 5/707.
Marriage, dissolution and invalidity records, 410: 530/0.01 to 530/3.1.
Registry of adoption information.
Establishment, 750: 50/18.1.

PUBLIC UTILITIES.
Child support.
Location of putative father and noncustodial parents.
Provision of information, 750: 5/714, 16/33, 45/14.5.

PUNITIVE DAMAGES.
Abortion fraud, 720: 510/11.
Breach of promise to marry, 740: 15/3.

PUTATIVE FATHERS.
Adoption notice, 750: 50/12a.
Child abduction, 720: 5/10-5.
Child support.
Location.
Information provided, 750: 5/714, 16/33, 45/14.5.
Registry.
Adoption, 750: 50/12.1.
Visitation, petition by grandparents of putative father, 750: 5/607.

PUTATIVE SPOUSE.
Declaration of invalidity of marriage, 750: 5/305.

R

RAILROADS.
Ticket sales.
Unlawful sales to minors, 720: 5/10-8.

RANSOM.
Aggravated kidnapping.
Ransom defined, 720: 5/10-2.

REAL PROPERTY.
Abandoned spouses control over, 750: 65/11 to 65/13.
Marital dissolution.
Partitioning of real estate, 750: 5/514.
Filing of actions, 750: 5/515.
Married person's rights, 750: 65/9.
Unlawful possession by spouse, 750: 65/10.
Senior citizens' real estate tax deferral act.
General provisions, 320: 30/1 to 30/8.

REBATES.
Senior citizens and disabled persons prescription drug discount program.
Manufacturer rebate agreements, 320: 55/30.

RECONCILIATION.
Dissolution of marriage.
Conciliation conference, 750: 5/404.

RECORDATION.
Parentage proceedings.
Support payment received by department of public aid, 750: 45/23.

RECORDS.
Adoption proceedings.
Confidentiality, 750: 50/18.
Child custody.
Uniform child custody jurisdiction and enforcement.
Preservation of records, 750: 36/112.
Child support payments to court, 750: 5/507.
Maintenance support paid to court, 750: 5/507.
Marriage, dissolution and invalidity records, 410: 530/0.01 to 530/3.1.
Marriage licenses.
Health certificate retention, 750: 5/206.
Spousal support payments to court, 750: 5/507.

RECRIMINATION.
Marriage dissolution defense, 750: 5/403.

REFERRAL FEES.
Abortion, 720: 510/11.1.

REGISTRATION.
Child custody.
Uniform child custody jurisdiction and enforcement.
Enforcement of registered determination, 750: 36/306.

REGISTRATION —Cont'd
Child custody —Cont'd
Uniform child custody jurisdiction and enforcement —Cont'd
Registration of determination, 750: 36/305.

REGISTRY, BIOLOGICAL PARENT, 750: 50/18.1.
Form of biological parent registration identification, 750: 50/18.2.
Registration fee, 750: 50/18.6.
Sharing of identifying information, 750: 50/18.3.

REHABILITATION SERVICES, DEPARTMENT OF.
Child abuse and neglect reporting.
Access to records, 325: 5/11.1.
Early intervention services role, 325: 20/9.

RELATIVES.
Child placement by department of children and family services, 20: 505/7.

RELIGION.
Adoption.
Consideration in placement, 750: 50/15.
Child placement.
One church one child advisory board, 20: 505/7.1.

REMAND OF CASES.
Marital property disposition, 750: 5/503.

REMARRIAGE.
Maintenance obligation terminated, 750: 5/510.

REPORTS.
Abandoned newborn protection act.
Evaluation of program generally, 325: 2/65.
Report of acceptance of newborn infant, 325: 2/40.
Abortion.
Complications resulting from an abortion, 720: 510/10.1.
Confidentiality of reports, 720: 510/11.
Department of public health, 720: 510/10.
Failure to report live birth or viability evidence, 720: 510/12.
Statistical data, 720: 510/10.
Abuse and neglect of children, 325: 5/1 to 5/11.7.
See CHILD ABUSE, NEGLECT OR DEPENDENCY.
Adoption investigations, 750: 50/6.
Child abduction.
Law enforcement officers, 720: 5/10-5.
Child custody arrangements, 750: 5/605.
Child sexual abuse.
Department of children and family services to submit annual reports, 325: 15/7.
Child support.
Obligor obtaining employment or termination from employment, 750: 5/505, 45/14.
County clerks.
Marriage certificate numbers, 750: 5/211.
Domestic violence.
Immunity of reporter from prosecution, 725: 5/112A-25.
Protection orders.
Law enforcement officers' duty, 750: 60/303.
Elder abuse and neglect.
Good faith reporters immune from criminal or civil liability, 320: 20/4.
Expedited child support plan.
Federal rules compliance, 750: 25/4.
Interagency board for hearing impaired/behavior disordered children, 325: 35/11.
Law enforcement officers.
Child abduction, 720: 5/10-5.
Child abuse and neglect, 325: 5/4.
Domestic violence, protective orders, 750: 60/303.
Missing children recovery.
I SEARCH programs and I SEARCH units, 325: 40/8.
Newborns, suspected medical neglect involving, 325: 5/7.3a.

REPORTS —Cont'd
Protective orders.
Domestic violence.
Law enforcement officer's duty, 725: 5/112A-29, 5/112A-30, 750: 60/303.
Respite program.
Annual report, 320: 10/12.

RESIDENCE.
Marriage dissolution requirements, 750: 5/401.

RESPITE PROGRAM, 320: 10/1 to 10/12.
Administration, 320: 10/3.
Citation of act.
Short title, 320: 10/1.
Definitions, 320: 10/2.
Eligibility, 320: 10/5.
Family caregivers.
Eligibility for respite services, 320: 65/30.
Funding, 320: 10/8.
Legislative declaration, 320: 10/1.5.
No limit to care, 320: 10/4.
Purpose of act, 320: 10/1.5.
Reports, 320: 10/12.
Responsibilities, 320: 10/6.
Title of act.
Short title, 320: 10/1.
Worker training, 320: 10/11.

RESTITUTION.
Parentage proceedings.
Withholding of income to secure payment of support.
Payor violations, 750: 45/20.
Support orders, withholding of income to secure payment.
Payor violations, 750: 5/706.1.

RETALIATORY CONDUCT.
Child abuse and neglect reporting.
Discrimination against employee making good faith or report, 325: 5/9.1.

RETALIATORY DISCHARGE.
Parentage proceedings.
Withholding of income to secure payment of support.
Payor discharge of obligor, 750: 45/20.
Support orders, withholding of income to secure payment.
Discharge of obligor by payor, 750: 5/706.1.

REVENUE, DEPARTMENT OF.
Senior citizens' and disabled persons' property tax relief and pharmaceutical assistance.
Qualified persons list, 320: 25/13.

RIGHTS OF MARRIED PERSONS, 750: 65/0.01 to 65/22.

RIGHT TO BREASTFEED ACT, 740: 137/1 to 137/99.
See BREASTFEEDING.

RULE TO SHOW CAUSE.
Domestic violence protection orders.
Enforcement, 725: 5/112A-23.
Violations as contempt, 750: 60/223.

RUNAWAY AND HOMELESS YOUTHS.
Aiding and abetting child abduction, 720: 5/10-7.
Harboring a runaway, 720: 5/10-6.
Missing children.
Generally, 325: 40/1 to 55/7.
See MISSING CHILDREN.

S

SAFE HAVEN FOR INFANTS.
Abandoned newborn infant protection act, 325: 2/1 to 2/999.
See ABANDONED NEWBORN PROTECTION ACT.

SALES.
Abandoned spouses control over property, 750: 65/12.
Maintenance orders, 750: 5/703.

SALES —Cont'd
Marital dissolution.
Maintenance orders, 750: 5/703.

SALTIEL LAW.
Inherited metabolic disease pamphlets.
Distribution, 750: 5/204.

SAME-SEX MARRIAGES, 750: 5/212, 5/213.1.

SATURDAYS.
Injunctions, 735: 5/11-106.

SCHOOL BOARDS.
State board of education.
Child abuse and neglect reports, access to records, 325: 5/11.1.
Early intervention services role, 325: 20/9.
High risk youth career development, 325: 25/0.01, 25/1.

SCHOOL BUSES.
Child abandonment.
School bus driver, 720: 150/4.1, 150/5.
Drivers.
Child abandonment, 720: 150/4.1, 150/5.

SCHOOL DROPOUTS.
High risk youth career development, 325: 25/0.01, 25/1.

SCHOOLS.
Child abuse and neglect reporting.
Noncompliance with attendance law, 325: 5/4.
Report to child's school, 325: 5/8.6.
Required reports, 325: 5/4.
School employees suspected of abuse or neglect, 325: 5/7.4.
Domestic violence.
Protection orders.
Copy filing, 750: 60/222.
Early intervention services, 325: 20/1 to 20/20.
Missing children.
Duties, 325: 50/5, 55/5.
Protective orders.
Domestic violence.
Copy filing, 750: 60/222.

SELF-INCRIMINATION.
Child custody.
Uniform child custody jurisdiction and enforcement.
Inference from refusal to testify, 750: 36/310.
Support and maintenance.
Interstate family support.
Special rules of evidence, 750: 22/316.

SELF-REPRESENTATION.
Protection orders.
Commencement of action, 750: 60/202.

SENIOR CITIZENS.
Abuse reports.
Immunity from prosecution, 750: 60/225.
All-inclusive care for the elderly act.
General provisions, 320: 40/1 to 40/30.
Child care support, 320: 45/1 to 45/25.
Community senior services and resources, 320: 60/1 to 60/99.
Domestic violence.
Protection orders.
Reporting of abuse immunity, 750: 60/225.
Older adult services act, 320: 42/1 to 42/99.
See OLDER ADULT SERVICES.
Partnership for long-term care, 320: 35/1 to 35/60.
General provisions, 320: 35/1 to 35/60.
Prescription medicine.
Senior citizens and disabled persons prescription drug discount program, 320: 55/1 to 55/99.
Senior pharmaceutical assistance act, 320: 50/1 to 50/99.
Property tax relief and pharmaceutical assistance, 320: 25/1 to 25/13.
Protection orders.
Domestic violence.
Reporting of abuse immunity, 750: 60/225.
Real estate tax deferral, 320: 30/1 to 30/8.

SENIOR CITIZENS —Cont'd
Respite program, 320: 10/1 to 10/12.
See RESPITE PROGRAM.
Senior citizens' child care support, 320: 45/1 to 45/25.
Senior citizens on state boards and commissions, 320: 5/0.01, 5/1.
Senior citizens' property tax relief, 320: 25/1 to 25/13.
Senior citizens' real estate tax deferral, 320: 30/1 to 30/8.
Senior pharmaceutical assistance act, 320: 50/1 to 50/99.
State boards and commissions.
Senior citizens on state boards and commissions act, 320: 5/0.01, 5/1.

SENIOR CITIZENS AND DISABLED PERSONS PRESCRIPTION DRUG DISCOUNT PROGRAM ACT, 320: 55/1 to 55/99.

SENIOR HEALTH ASSISTANCE PROGRAM, 320: 50/20.

SENIOR PHARMACEUTICAL ASSISTANCE ACT, 320: 50/1 to 50/99.
Catastrophic pharmaceutical assistance coverage.
Study, 320: 50/25.
Citation of act, 320: 50/1.
Definitions, 320: 50/10.
Effective date of act, 320: 50/99.
Legislative findings, 320: 50/5.
Review committee, 320: 50/15.
Senior health assistance program, 320: 50/20.
Title of act, 320: 50/1.

SENTENCING.
Adoption compensation.
Habitual offenders, 720: 525/5.
Domestic violence.
Violation of protective order.
Revocation or modification of sentence of periodic imprisonment, 725: 5/112A-23.
Habitual offenders.
Adoption compensation, 720: 525/5.
Parentage proceedings.
Failure to comply with court order, 750: 45/15.
Protective orders.
Domestic violence.
Violation of order.
Revocation or modification of sentence of periodic imprisonment, 725: 5/112A-23.

SEPARATION OF SPOUSES.
Child custody generally.
See CHILD CUSTODY.
Spousal support, 750: 5/402.

SERVICE BY PUBLICATION.
Adoption notice, 750: 50/7.
Marriage dissolution proceedings, 750: 5/410.
Petition filing requirements, 750: 5/412.

SERVICE OF PROCESS.
Adoption.
Notice to putative father, 750: 50/12a.
Adoption notice, 750: 50/7.
Child custody.
Uniform child custody jurisdiction and enforcement.
Persons outside state, 750: 36/108.
Petition and order, 750: 36/309.
Child support.
At last known address of non-custodial parent, 750: 5/505.
Contempt proceedings for failure to make payments, 750: 5/505.
Expedited support.
Administrative hearings, 750: 25/7.
Recommended order, 750: 25/10.
Dissolution of marriage, 750: 5/410.
Domestic violence.
Notice in conjunction with pending civil case, 750: 60/210.1.
Notice of hearings, 750: 60/211.

SERVICE OF PROCESS —Cont'd
Domestic violence —Cont'd
Protection orders, 750: 60/210, 60/222.
Short form notification, 750: 60/222.10.
Emancipation of mature minors.
Hearing notice, 750: 30/8.
Marriage dissolution proceedings, 750: 5/104.
Time requirements, 750: 5/411.
Name changes, 735: 5/21-103, 5/21-104.
Parentage proceedings.
Blood and tissue test reports, 750: 45/11.
Notice to presumed father, 750: 45/9.1.
Withholding of income to secure payment of support, 750: 45/20.
Protective orders against domestic violence, 725: 5/112A-10, 5/112A-22, 750: 60/210.
By sheriff, 750: 60/222.
Short form notification, 750: 60/222.10.
Notice in conjunction with pending civil case, 750: 60/210.1.
Notice of hearings, 750: 60/211.
Support orders, withholding of income to secure payment, 750: 5/706.1.

SETTLEMENT.
Marriage dissolution settlement agreements, 750: 5/502.
Parentage proceedings.
Settlement offers, 750: 45/12.1.

SEX OFFENSES.
Child sexual abuse.
Parent permitting sexual abuse, 720: 150/5.1.
Child visitation privileges of offender convicted of offense upon victim less than 18 years of age, 750: 5/607.

SEXUAL ABUSE.
Child sexual abuse, 325: 15/0.01 to 15/7, 720: 150/5.1.

SHELTER CARE.
Domestic violence protection orders.
Order for payment of services, 750: 60/214.

SHERIFFS.
Domestic violence protection orders.
See PROTECTIVE ORDERS AGAINST DOMESTIC VIOLENCE.
Support enforcement orders.
Attachment of the body, 750: 5/713.

SHOTGUN MARRIAGES.
Invalidity of marriage, declaration of.
Ground, 750: 5/301.

SIBLING VISITATION.
Court power to grant, 750: 5/607.

SINGING.
Using or employing child, 720: 150/1, 150/2.

SINGLE PARENTS.
Employment, child under 6, 720: 150/3.1.

SOCIAL SECURITY NUMBERS.
Children's privacy protection and parental empowerment act.
Personal information.
Defined as including social security number, 325: 17/5.
Sale or purchase, 325: 17/10, 17/15.

SOCIAL SERVICES.
Single parent employment restrictions.
Wrongs to children act, 720: 150/3, 150/3.1, 150/5.
Support responsibility of relatives.
Determination and enforceability generally, 305: 5/10-1 to 5/10-27.
See PUBLIC AID.
Wrongs to children act.
Single parent employment restrictions, 720: 150/3, 150/3.1, 150/5.

SOCIAL WORKERS.
Child abuse and neglect reporting.
Required reports, 325: 5/4.
Early intervention services, 325: 20/1 to 20/20.

SOCIAL WORKERS —Cont'd
Elder abuse and neglect.
Failure to report, 320: 20/4.

SOLEMNIZATION OF MARRIAGE, 750: 5/209.

SPECIAL EDUCATION.
Interagency board for hearing impaired/behavior disordered children, 325: 35/1 to 35/12.

SPECIFIC PERFORMANCE.
Gestational surrogacy contracts.
Remedy unavailable for breach, 750: 47/50.

SPEECH IMPAIRED.
Early intervention services, 325: 20/1 to 20/20.

SPEECH-LANGUAGE PATHOLOGISTS AND AUDIOLOGISTS.
Early intervention services, 325: 20/1 to 20/20.

SPIRITUAL HEALING.
Child abuse and neglect, 325: 5/4.
Child abuse and neglect reporting.
Child not deemed neglected or abused, 325: 5/3.

SPOUSAL ABUSE.
Generally, 750: 60/101 to 60/401.
See DOMESTIC VIOLENCE.
Protective orders against domestic violence, 725: 5/112A-1 to 5/112A-31.
See PROTECTIVE ORDERS AGAINST DOMESTIC VIOLENCE.

SPOUSAL PRIVILEGE, 735: 5/8-801.
Child custody.
Uniform child custody jurisdiction and enforcement.
Prohibition from invoking, 750: 36/310.
Interstate family support.
Privilege not to apply, 750: 22/316.

SPOUSAL SUPPORT.
Abatement of payments, Sup. Ct. Rule 296.
Agents for receiving and disbursing payments, 750: 5/705.
Agreements to dissolve marriage, 750: 5/502.
Attachment of the body, 750: 5/713.
Failure of obligor to appear in enforcement proceedings, 750: 5/713.
Bonds to secure payment, 750: 5/706.2.
Change of circumstances.
Modification or termination.
Factors considered, 750: 5/510.
Consumer reporting agencies.
Obligor owing arrearage or delinquent, information to agency, 750: 5/706.3.
Contempt.
Enforcement of support order, Sup. Ct. Rule 296.
Delinquencies, Sup. Ct. Rule 296.
Dissolution of marriage agreements, 750: 5/502.
Domestic violence protection orders.
Enforcement of support order violation, 750: 60/223.
Modification, 750: 60/224.
Order for payment of support, 750: 60/214.
Employment search ordered by court, unemployed obligor, 750: 5/505.1.
Enforcement, Sup. Ct. Rule 296.
Failure of party to comply with dissolution judgment, order or injunction.
Obligation of other party to make payments not suspended, 750: 5/509.
Forms.
Order for enforcement, Sup. Ct. Rule 296.
Hearings.
Contempt proceedings to enforce support orders, Sup. Ct. Rule 296.
Interest charges for past due amounts.
Parentage proceedings, 750: 45/20.7.
Interstate family support.
General provisions, 750: 22/101 to 22/999.
See SUPPORT AND MAINTENANCE.

SPOUSAL SUPPORT —Cont'd
Judgment enforcement or modification procedure, 750: 5/511.
Maintenance during separation, 750: 5/402.
Marital property transfers, 750: 65/11.
Marriage and dissolution of marriage act.
Application, 750: 5/801.
Marriage dissolution agreements, 750: 5/502.
Modification of orders, 750: 5/510.
Nonsupport.
Generally, 750: 16/1 to 16/999.
See NONSUPPORT OF CHILD OR SPOUSE.
Notice of delinquency, Sup. Ct. Rule 296.
Notice of hearing.
Contempt proceedings to enforce support orders, Sup. Ct. Rule 296.
Payment pursuant to orders, Sup. Ct. Rule 296.
Payments to court, 750: 5/507.
Payments to state disbursement unit, 750: 5/507.1.
Parentage proceedings, 750: 45/21.1.
Petitions.
Contempt proceedings to enforce support orders, Sup. Ct. Rule 296.
Post-judgment procedure, 750: 5/511.
Post-judgment venue, 750: 5/512.
Protective orders against domestic violence.
Order for payment, 725: 5/112A-14.
Violation of order, 725: 5/112A-23.
Public aid collection fee.
Imposition, 750: 5/516.
Public aid recipients.
Administrative orders, 305: 5/10-11.
Support responsibility of relatives.
Determination and enforcement, 305: 5/10-1 to 5/10-27.
See PUBLIC AID.
Publication of obligor's name when obligor owes arrearage or delinquent, 750: 5/706.3.
Receiving and disbursing agent, 750: 5/705.
Relief temporarily during proceedings, 750: 5/501.
Separation support and maintenance, 750: 5/402.
Severability of marriage and dissolution of marriage act, 750: 5/801.
Support actions during separation, 750: 5/402.
Support and maintenance generally.
See SUPPORT AND MAINTENANCE.
Temporary relief during proceedings, 750: 5/501.
Termination, 750: 5/510.
Wage deduction orders, 750: 5/706.1.
Withholding of income to secure, 750: 5/706.1, 28/1 to 28/999.
Information concerning obligors, 305: 5/10-16.4.
Interstate family support, 750: 22/501 to 22/507.

SPOUSES.
Abandoned spouse, control over property, 750: 65/11.
Abuse.
Protective orders, 725: 5/112A-1 to 5/112A-31.
See PROTECTIVE ORDERS AGAINST DOMESTIC VIOLENCE.
Action against husband or wife sued together.
Defending in own right or for another, 750: 65/2.
Action by or against married person without joining spouse, 750: 65/1.
Action by wife in name of deserting husband, 750: 65/3.
Adoption, 750: 50/0.01 to 55/1.
See ADOPTION.
Annulment of marriage, 750: 5/301 to 5/306.
See INVALIDITY OF MARRIAGE, DECLARATION OF.
Antenuptial agreements, 750: 10/1 to 10/11.
See PREMARITAL AGREEMENTS.

SPOUSES —Cont'd
Artificially inseminated wife, status of husband, 750: 40/3.
Attachment, enforcement by married person, 750: 65/1.
Child custody.
Uniform child custody jurisdiction and enforcement, 750: 36/101 to 36/405.
Contracts made and liabilities incurred by married person, 750: 65/6.
Contracts, sales or encumbrances made by spouse, 750: 65/12.
Conveyances, spouse under legal disability.
Petition to convey real estate, 750: 65/17 to 65/20.
Creditors' rights, 750: 65/15.
Criminal neglect of children.
Competency as witness, 720: 130/3.
Damage recovered from spouse committing civil injury, 750: 65/4.
Debts or liabilities incurred before marriage, liability of spouse for, 750: 65/5.
Declaration of invalidity of marriage, 750: 5/301 to 5/306.
See INVALIDITY OF MARRIAGE, DECLARATION OF.
Deeds or mortgages, validity, 750: 65/21.
Defending action in own right or for other, 750: 65/2.
Defense of action by wife in name of deserting husband, 750: 65/3.
Divorce.
Dissolution of marriage, 750: 5/401 to 5/802.
See DISSOLUTION OF MARRIAGE.
Domestic abuse.
Protective orders against abuse, 725: 5/112A-1 to 5/112A-31.
See PROTECTIVE ORDERS AGAINST DOMESTIC VIOLENCE.
Earnings, receiving, using and possessing by married person, 750: 65/7.
Emancipation of mature minors, 750: 30/1 to 30/11.
Husband-wife privilege, 735: 5/8-801.
Interstate family support.
General provisions, 750: 22/101 to 22/999.
See SUPPORT AND MAINTENANCE.
Invalidity of marriage, declaration of, 750: 5/301 to 5/306.
See INVALIDITY OF MARRIAGE, DECLARATION OF.
Judgments, enforcement by married person, 750: 65/1.
Judgments, setting aside, 750: 65/13.
Legal disability, spouse under.
Petition to convey real estate, 750: 65/17 to 65/20.
Marriage, 750: 5/201 to 5/219.
See MARRIAGE.
Marriage dissolution, 750: 5/401 to 5/802.
See DISSOLUTION OF MARRIAGE.
Married persons' rights, 750: 65/0.01 to 65/22.
Mature minors' emancipation, 750: 30/1 to 30/11.
Parentage, 750: 40/1 to 45/27.
See PARENTAGE PROCEEDINGS.
Power of attorney, 750: 65/14.
Premarital agreements, 750: 10/1 to 10/11.
See PREMARITAL AGREEMENTS.
Property ownership by married person, 750: 65/9.
Property unlawfully possessed by married person, 750: 65/10.
Protective orders against domestic violence, 725: 5/112A-1 to 5/112A-31.
See PROTECTIVE ORDERS AGAINST DOMESTIC VIOLENCE.
Removal of children from homestead, 750: 65/16.
Spousal support.
Generally.
See SPOUSAL SUPPORT.
Tenancy by the entirety, 750: 65/22.
Torts committed during marriage, suit by husband or wife for, 750: 65/1.

STANDBY ADOPTIONS.
Consent given by parent, 750: 50/9.
Consent form, 750: 50/10.
Judgment, time for applying for, 750: 50/13.1.
Entry of judgment, 750: 50/14.
Order, 750: 50/13.1.

STATE CASE REGISTRY.
Child support orders.
Furnishing information on entry or modification of order, 750: 5/505.3.
Entry of order in parentage proceedings, 750: 45/14.1.

STATE DISBURSEMENT UNIT.
Collection and disbursement of support obligations.
Payments to, 750: 22/320.
Contracts with, 305: 5/10-26.2.

STATE POLICE.
Hostage, forcible detention, 720: 5/10-4.
Visitation order violations.
Record of contempt orders, 750: 5/607.1.

STATE POLICE, DEPARTMENT OF.
Child abuse and neglect reporting.
Access to records, 325: 5/11.1.
Missing children records, 325: 50/0.01 to 50/5.
Missing children recovery, 325: 40/1 to 40/8.
Missing children registration, 325: 55/0.01 to 55/7.

STATE'S ATTORNEYS.
Adoptions.
Appointment as guardian ad litem, 750: 50/13.
Annulments.
Commencement, 750: 5/302.
Child custody.
Uniform child custody jurisdiction and enforcement.
Duties, 750: 36/315.
Child support.
Unified child support services program, 750: 24/1 to 24/35.
Child support delinquency enforcement proceedings, 750: 5/710.
Marriage.
Invalidity declaration commencement, 750: 5/302.
Parentage proceedings.
Representation of mother or child upon request, 750: 45/18.

STATUTE OF FRAUDS.
Premarital agreements, writing required, 750: 10/3.
Amendment or revocation, 750: 10/6.
Writing and signature required generally, 740: 80/1.

STATUTE OF LIMITATIONS.
Adoption.
Consent to adoption, 750: 55/0.01, 55/1.
Relief from final judgment or order, 750: 50/20b.
Antenuptial agreements, 750: 10/9.
Breach of promise to marry, 740: 15/6.
Child support.
Court ordered withdrawals from decedents' estates, 750: 5/510.
Invalidity of marriage, declaration of.
Time of commencement, 750: 5/302.
Non-existence of parent and child relationship, action to declare, 750: 45/8.
Paternity actions, 750: 45/8.
Prenuptial agreements, 750: 10/9.

STAY AWAY ORDERS.
Domestic violence protection orders, 750: 60/214.

STAYS.
Child custody.
Uniform child custody jurisdiction and enforcement.
Simultaneous proceedings commenced, 750: 36/206.

STAYS —Cont'd
Child custody —Cont'd
Uniform child custody jurisdiction and enforcement —Cont'd
Stays pending appeal prohibited, 750: 36/314.
Dissolution of marriage.
Dissolution action stay, 750: 5/501.1.
Parentage proceedings.
Withholding of income to secure payment of support, petition to stay service, 750: 45/20.
Support orders, withholding of income to secure payment.
Petition to stay service of order, 750: 5/706.1.

STEP-BROTHER OR SISTER.
Child placed with relatives.
Department of children and family services, 20: 505/7.

STEPPARENTS.
Child custody proceeding, commencing, 750: 5/601.
Best interest of child that natural parent have custody, presumption, 750: 5/601.
Child placed with relatives.
Department of children and family services, 20: 505/7.
Visitation rights as child, 750: 5/607.

STOMACH DISORDERS.
Inherited metabolic disease pamphlets.
Distribution, 750: 5/204.

SUMMONS OR PROCESS.
Adoption, 750: 50/7.
Notice to putative father, 750: 50/12a.
Dating, Sup. Ct. Rule 101.
Domestic violence protection orders, 750: 60/210.
Formal requisites, Sup. Ct. Rule 101.
Form of summons, Sup. Ct. Rule 101.
Issuance of summons, Sup. Ct. Rule 101.
Marriage dissolution proceedings.
Action stay effected upon service, 750: 5/501.1.
Judgment enforcement or modification procedure, 750: 5/511.
Paternity actions.
Required language, 750: 45/9.
Praecipe for summons.
Marriage dissolution proceedings.
Commencement, 750: 5/411.
Protective orders against domestic violence, 725: 5/112A-10, 750: 60/210.
Seal of court, Sup. Ct. Rule 101.
Signatures, Sup. Ct. Rule 101.

SUNDAYS.
Injunctions, 735: 5/11-106.

SUPPORT AND MAINTENANCE.
Abatement of payments.
Petition, Sup. Ct. Rule 296.
Actions for maintenance during separation, 750: 5/402.
Agents for receiving and disbursing payments, 750: 5/705.
Agreements to dissolve marriage, 750: 5/502.
Attachment of the body, 750: 5/713.
Failure of obligor to appear in enforcement proceedings, 750: 5/713.
Attorney appointment to represent interest of minor or dependent child, 750: 5/506.
Attorney general.
Interstate family support.
Duties, 750: 22/308.
Award amount determination.
Factors in setting, 750: 5/504.
Bigamy.
Maintenance in case of, 750: 5/702.
Bond or guarantee, posting to secure payment, 750: 5/706.2.
Change of circumstances.
Modification or termination only upon showing.
Factors considered, 750: 5/510.
Child support.
General provisions.
See CHILD SUPPORT.

SUPPORT AND MAINTENANCE —Cont'd
Child support —Cont'd
Interstate family support, 750: 22/100 to 22/999. See within this heading, "Interstate family support."
Consumer reporting agencies.
Obligor owing arrearage or delinquent, information to agency, 750: 5/706.3.
Contempt proceedings to enforce support order, Sup. Ct. Rule 296.
Delinquencies, Sup. Ct. Rule 296.
Dissolution of marriage agreements, 750: 5/502.
Domestic violence protection orders.
Enforcement of support order violations, 750: 60/223.
Modification, 750: 60/224.
Order for payment of support, 750: 60/214.
Employment of obligor or termination from employment.
Report to obligee and clerk of court, 750: 5/505.
Employment search ordered by court, 750: 5/505.1.
Enforcement, Sup. Ct. Rule 296.
Failure of party to comply with dissolution judgment, order or injunction.
Obligation of other party to make payments not suspended, 750: 5/509.
Guardian ad litem for child, 750: 5/506.
Health insurance orders.
Beneficiary designation, 750: 5/505.2.
Imprisonment effect upon payments, 750: 5/504.
Interest on obligation due and unpaid.
Parentage proceedings, 750: 45/20.7.
Interstate family support, 750: 22/101 to 22/999.
Applicability of act.
Proceedings to which act applies, 750: 22/301.
Uniformity of application, 750: 22/901.
Applicability of law of this state, 750: 22/303.
Attorney general.
Duties, 750: 22/308.
Attorneys.
Private counsel, 750: 22/309.
Attorneys' fees, 750: 22/313.
Child custody or visitation.
State tribunal without jurisdiction to issue judgment under act, 750: 22/104.
Circuit court.
Tribunal of state, 750: 22/103.
Citation of act.
Short title, 750: 22/101.
Communications between tribunals, 750: 22/317.
Confidentiality.
Nondisclosure of information in exceptional circumstances, 750: 22/312.
Conflict of laws, 750: 22/910.
Applicability of law of this state, 750: 22/303.
Registration of orders for enforcement.
Choice of law, 750: 22/604.
Controlling child-support order.
Determination, recognition, 750: 22/207.
Filing determination request separately or with registration request, 750: 22/602.
Copies, evidence of facts, admissibility, 750: 22/316.
Costs, 750: 22/313.
Credit for payments, 750: 22/209.
Cumulative nature of remedies, 750: 22/103.
Defenses.
Nonparentage as defense, 750: 22/315.
Definitions, 750: 22/101.
Department of public aid.
Duties, 750: 22/310.
Responding tribunal, 750: 22/103.
Deposition or testimony by telephone, audiovisual or other electronic means, 750: 22/316.
Discovery.
Assistance with discovery, 750: 22/318.
Effective date, 750: 22/903, 22/904, 22/999.

SUPPORT AND MAINTENANCE —Cont'd
Interstate family support —Cont'd
Enforcement of child-support order.
Continuing jurisdiction, 750: 22/206.
Two or more orders with regard to same obligor, 750: 22/208.
Evidence.
Discovery.
Assistance with discovery, 750: 22/318.
Special rules of evidence and procedure, 750: 22/316.
Fax, telecopier or other means.
Documentary evidence transmitted by, admissibility, 750: 22/316.
Health, safety or liberty jeopardized.
Identifying information, nondisclosure, 750: 22/312.
Hearsay exception, 750: 22/316.
Home state.
Defined, 750: 22/101.
Identifying information.
Nondisclosure, exceptional circumstances, 750: 22/312.
Immunity.
Husband-wife or parent-child immunities not to apply, 750: 22/316.
Limited immunity of petitioner, 750: 22/314.
Inappropriate tribunal, 750: 22/306.
Income-withholding orders.
Administrative enforcement, 750: 22/502.
Administrative enforcement of orders, 750: 22/507.
Contest by obligor, 750: 22/506.
Defined, 750: 22/101.
Employer of obligor.
Sending order to employer without filing petition, 750: 22/501.
Immunity of employer, 750: 22/504.
Notice of contest.
Obligor to give, 750: 22/506.
Penalties for noncompliance, 750: 22/505.
Recognition of income-withholding order of another state, 750: 22/501.
Registration of orders, 750: 22/601 to 22/612. See within this subheading, "Registration of orders."
Initiating proceedings, 750: 22/301.
Initiating state.
Defined, 750: 22/101.
Initiating tribunal.
Defined, 750: 22/101.
Duties, 750: 22/304.
Interpretation and construction.
Cumulative nature of remedies, 750: 22/103.
Severability of provisions, 750: 22/903.
Uniformity, 750: 22/901.
Interstate rendition.
Conditions, 750: 22/802.
Grounds, 750: 22/801.
Issuance of support order.
State responding tribunal, 750: 22/401.
Jurisdiction.
Continuing jurisdiction.
Enforcement of child-support order, 750: 22/206.
Modification of child-support order, 750: 22/205.
Modification of spousal-support order, 750: 22/211.
Extended personal jurisdiction.
Bases for jurisdiction over nonresident, 750: 22/201.
Procedure when exercising jurisdiction over nonresident, 750: 22/202.
Modification of child-support order of foreign country or political subdivision, 750: 22/615.
Proceedings involving two or more states.
Continuing jurisdiction, 750: 22/205.
Enforcement and modification of support order by tribunal having, 750: 22/206.
Exclusive jurisdiction, 750: 22/205.
Initiating and responding tribunal of this state, 750: 22/203.
Simultaneous proceedings in another state, 750: 22/204.

SUPPORT AND MAINTENANCE —Cont'd
Interstate family support —Cont'd
Jurisdiction —Cont'd
Reconciliation with orders of other states.
Credit for payments, 750: 22/209.
Multiple child support orders for two or more obligees, 750: 22/208.
Recognition of child support orders, 750: 22/207.
Minor parent or guardian.
Actions by, 750: 22/302.
Modification of child support order issued by state tribunal.
Continuing jurisdiction, 750: 22/205.
Modification of child support order issued in another state.
Jurisdiction to modify order of foreign country or political subdivision, 750: 22/615.
Modification of child support order of another state.
Jurisdiction to modify order when individual parties reside in Illinois, 750: 22/613.
Notice to issuing tribunal, 750: 22/614.
Modification of spousal-support order issued by state tribunal.
Continuing jurisdiction, 750: 22/211.
Nonresident subject to personal jurisdiction under act or other state law.
Procedural and substantive law of state.
Applicability to, exceptions, 750: 22/210.
Obligee.
Defined, 750: 22/101.
Obligor.
Defined, 750: 22/101.
Parentage determination, 750: 22/701.
Nonparentage as defense, 750: 22/315.
Paternity, voluntary acknowledgment, admissibility, 750: 22/316.
Petition or comparable pleading.
Filing, initiating proceedings, 750: 22/301.
Filing with request for registration, 750: 22/602.
Requirements, 750: 22/311.
Pleadings and accompanying documents, 750: 22/311.
Presence of nonresident party.
Not required, 750: 22/316.
Proceedings to which act applies, 750: 22/301.
Recognition of child-support orders.
Controlling orders, 750: 22/207.
Registration of orders, 750: 22/601 to 22/615.
Authorized, 750: 22/601.
Choice of law, 750: 22/604.
Contest of validity or enforcement.
Burden of establishing defense, 750: 22/607.
Confirmed order, 750: 22/608.
Notice of registration of order, 750: 22/605.
Procedure, 750: 22/606.
Effect, 750: 22/603.
Modification of child support order of another state, 750: 22/611.
Effect of registration for modification, 750: 22/610.
Jurisdiction to modify order when individual parties reside in Illinois, 750: 22/613.
Notice to issuing tribunal, 750: 22/614.
Procedure to register for, 750: 22/609.
Recognition of order modified in another state, 750: 22/612.
Notice, 750: 22/605.
Procedure, 750: 22/602.
Two or more orders effected, 750: 22/602.
Notice of order, 750: 22/605.
Rendition.
Conditions, 750: 22/802.
Grounds, 750: 22/801.
Responding state.
Defined, 750: 22/101.
Responding tribunal.
Defined, 750: 22/101.
Duties, 750: 22/305.
Powers, 750: 22/305.

SUPPORT AND MAINTENANCE —Cont'd
Interstate family support —Cont'd
Self-incrimination.
Special rules of evidence, 750: 22/316.
Severability of provisions, 750: 22/903.
Short title of act, 750: 22/902.
State disbursement unit, payments of support to, 750: 22/320.
Support enforcement agency.
Defined, 750: 22/101.
Duties, 750: 22/307.
Receipt and disbursement of payments, 750: 22/319.
Support orders.
Administrative enforcement, 750: 22/502.
Child support order.
Defined, 750: 22/101.
Multiple child support orders for two or more obligees, 750: 22/208.
Recognition of child support orders, 750: 22/207.
Defined, 750: 22/101.
Establishment of order.
Petition to establish, 750: 22/401.
Jurisdiction.
Reconciliation with orders of other states, 750: 22/207 to 22/209.
Petition to establish order, 750: 22/401.
Registration of orders, 750: 22/601 to 22/612. See within this subheading, "Registration of orders."
Spousal-support order.
Defined, 750: 22/101.
Temporary child-support order.
State responding tribunal issuing, 750: 22/401.
Title of act.
Short title, 750: 22/101.
Tribunal.
Defined, 750: 22/101.
Inappropriate tribunal, 750: 22/306.
Initiating tribunal.
Defined, 750: 22/101.
Issuing tribunal.
Defined, 750: 22/101.
Receipt and disbursement of payments, 750: 22/319.
Responding tribunal.
Defined, 750: 22/101.
Tribunals of this state, 750: 22/102.
Two or more orders with regard to same obligor.
Enforcement of child-support order, 750: 22/208.
Judgment enforcement or modification procedure, 750: 5/511.
Jurisdiction.
Interstate family support, 750: 22/201 to 22/209. See within this heading, "Interstate family support."
Support separation actions, 750: 5/402.
Lien on real estate, 750: 5/703.
Marital property transfers, 750: 65/11.
Marriage and dissolution of marriage act applicability, 750: 5/801.
Marriage dissolution agreements, 750: 5/502.
Modification of provisions, 750: 5/510.
Non-minor children and educational expenses, 750: 5/513.
Nonresidents.
Interstate family support.
Jurisdiction over nonresidents, 750: 22/201, 22/202.
Nonsupport.
Generally, 750: 16/1 to 16/999.
See NONSUPPORT OF CHILD OR SPOUSE.
Notice of delinquency, Sup. Ct. Rule 296.
Parentage proceedings.
Generally, 750: 40/1 to 45/27.
See PARENTAGE PROCEEDINGS.
Interstate family support, 750: 22/701.
Payment pursuant to order, Sup. Ct. Rule 296.

SUPPORT AND MAINTENANCE —Cont'd
Payments to state disbursement unit.
Interstate family support, 750: 22/320.
Parentage proceedings, 750: 45/21.1.
Payment to court, 750: 5/507.
Payment to state disbursement unit, 750: 5/507.1.
Post-judgment procedure, 750: 5/511.
Post-judgment venue, 750: 5/512.
Public aid collection fee, 750: 5/516.
Public aid provisions, 750: 5/704.
Public aid recipients.
Administrative orders, 305: 5/10-11.
Court enforcement, 305: 5/10-10.
Publication in newspaper of obligor's name when obligor owes arrearage or delinquent, 750: 5/706.3.
Receiving and disbursing agent, 750: 5/705.
Reciprocal enforcement of support.
Repeal of revised uniform act, 750: 22/905.
Relief temporarily during proceedings, 750: 5/501.
Separate fund or trust for minor upon dissolution of marriage, 750: 5/503.
Separation support actions, 750: 5/402.
Severability of marriage and dissolution of marriage act, 750: 5/801.
Spousal support.
Interstate family support, 750: 22/100 to 22/999. See within this heading, "Interstate family support."
Temporary relief during proceedings, 750: 5/501.
Termination upon death, remarriage or cohabitation with another person, 750: 5/510.
Unemployed obligor, employment search ordered by court, 750: 5/505.1.
Uniform interstate family support act, 750: 22/100 to 22/999. See within this heading, "Interstate family support."
Wage deduction orders, 750: 5/706.1.
Withholding of income to secure payment, 750: 5/706.1, 28/1 to 28/999.
Automatic continuance of child support obligation.
Unpaid arrearage or delinquency on date of termination of obligation, 750: 28/32.
Information concerning obligors, 305: 5/10-16.4.
Interstate family support, 750: 22/501 to 22/507.

SUPREME COURT.
Child support.
Expedited child support plan review, 750: 25/4.
Expedited child support plan.
Review, 750: 25/4.
Marriage and dissolution of marriage act.
Rules adoption, 750: 5/802.

SUPREME COURT RULES.
Appeals.
Adoption proceedings.
Appointment of a guardian with power to consent, Sup. Ct. Rule 663.
Conditional discharges, Sup. Ct. Rule 662.
Juvenile proceedings, Sup. Ct. Rules 660, 661.
Probation revocation, Sup. Ct. Rule 662.
Wardship adjudications, Sup. Ct. Rule 662.
Child support.
Expedited support.
General provisions, Sup. Ct. Rules 100.1 to 100.13.
See CHILD SUPPORT.
Juvenile court proceedings.
Appeals, Sup. Ct. Rules 660 to 663.
Protective orders against domestic violence.
Application of rules, 725: 5/112A-6.

SURGICAL INSTITUTE FOR CHILDREN, 325: 60/0.01 to 60/12.

SURRENDER FOR ADOPTION, 750: 50/8.
Forms, 750: 50/10.
Irrevocability, 750: 50/11.

SURRENDER FOR ADOPTION —Cont'd
Time for taking, 750: 50/9.

SURROGATE PARENTS.
Establishing parent-child relationship, 750: 45/6.
Gestational surrogacy act, 750: 47/1 to 47/75.
See GESTATIONAL SURROGACY.

T

TAXES.
Senior citizens' real estate tax deferral act.
General provisions, 320: 30/1 to 30/8.

TAX EXEMPTIONS.
Disabled persons' property tax relief.
General provisions, 320: 25/1 to 25/13.
Senior citizens' and disabled persons' property tax relief.
General provisions, 320: 25/1 to 25/13.

TAXICABS.
Minors.
Ticket sales.
Unlawful sale of travel ticket, 720: 5/10-8.
Ticket sales.
Minors.
Unlawful sale of travel ticket, 720: 5/10-8.

TEACHERS.
Child abuse and neglect reporting.
Teacher suspected of abuse and neglect, 325: 5/7.4.

TEMPORARY ASSISTANCE FOR NEEDY FAMILIES.
Support responsibility of relatives, determination and enforcement, 305: 5/10-1 to 5/10-27.
See PUBLIC AID.

TEMPORARY CUSTODY ORDERS, 750: 5/603.

TEMPORARY MAINTENANCE OR TEMPORARY SUPPORT, 750: 5/501.

TEMPORARY RESTRAINING ORDERS, 735: 5/11-101.
Bond of applicant, 735: 5/11-103.
Dissolution.
Assessment of damages, 735: 5/11-110.
Injunctions in general, 735: 5/11-108, 5/11-109.
Marriage dissolution.
Independence of provisions, 750: 5/509.
Marriage dissolution proceedings.
Temporary relief, 750: 5/501.

TENANCIES BY THE ENTIRETY.
Married person's rights, 750: 65/22.

TERMINATION OF PARENTAL RIGHTS.
Abandoned newborn protection act.
Child-placing agency, duties, 325: 2/50.
Adoption.
Effect of entry of judgment, 750: 50/17.
Wrongs to child act.
Court-ordered disposition, 720: 150/3.

TICKETS.
Minors.
Public conveyance travel tickets.
Unlawful sale to minor, 720: 5/10-8.

TIME FOR FILING PLEADINGS AND OTHER PAPERS.
Answer.
Summons requiring appearance within 30 days after service, Sup. Ct. Rule 101.
Appearance.
Summons requiring appearance within 30 days after service, Sup. Ct. Rule 101.
Marriage dissolution temporary relief.
Response, 750: 5/501.
Notice of appeal.
Adjudication of wardship and revocation of probation or conditional discharge, Sup. Ct. Rule 662.

TOLL-FREE TELEPHONE NUMBERS.
Child abuse and neglect reporting, 325: 5/7.6.

TORTS.
Breach of promise to marry, 740: 15/0.01 to 15/10.
Cannabis tort claims.
Sales to minors.
Parental right of recovery for damages, 740: 120/1 to 120/4.
Controlled substances tort claims.
Sales to minors.
Parental right to recovery for damages, 740: 120/1 to 120/4.
Family purpose doctrine, 740: 115/1 to 115/7.
Husband or wife suit for tort committed during marriage, 750: 65/1.

TRAINING.
Child abuse and neglect reporting, 325: 5/11.5.
Senior citizens' child care support act.
Volunteer training program, 320: 45/15, 45/25.

TRANSCRIPTS.
Parentage proceedings.
Free transcript on appeal, 750: 45/18.

TRIAL.
Protective orders against domestic violence, 725: 5/112A-7.

TRIBES.
Solemnization and registration of marriage, 750: 5/209.

TRO'S, 735: 5/11-101.

TRUANCY.
Child abuse and neglect reporting.
Required reports, 325: 5/4.
Superintendent notification of truancy reports, 325: 5/7.4.

TRUSTEES.
Dissolution of marriage.
Assumption settlor married, no actual knowledge of termination of marriage.
Liability for action taken or omitted in good faith, 760: 35/0.01, 35/1.

TRUSTS.
Adoption, instruments regarding property rights.
Child deemed born to adopting parents, 760: 30/0.01, 30/1.
Dissolution of marriage.
Revocation of provisions by settlor, 760: 35/0.01, 35/1.

TUITION.
Child support for educational expenses, 750: 5/513.

U

UNBORN CHILD.
Abortion.
See ABORTION.

UNCLES.
Child placed with relatives.
Department of children and family services, 20: 505/7.

UNCONSCIONABILITY.
Premarital agreements.
Enforcement, 750: 10/7.

UNDERAGE MARRIAGES.
Invalidity of marriage, declaration of, 750: 5/301.
Judicial approval, 750: 5/208.
Minors generally.
See CHILDREN AND MINORS.

UNIFIED CHILD SUPPORT SERVICES PROGRAM, 750: 24/1 to 24/35.

UNIFORM LAWS.
Child custody jurisdiction and enforcement, 750: 36/101 to 36/405.
Support and maintenance.
Uniform interstate family support act, 750: 22/101 to 22/999.
See SUPPORT AND MAINTENANCE.

UNIFORM RECIPROCAL ENFORCEMENT OF SUPPORT ACT.
Repeal of revised act, 750: 22/905.

UNIVERSITY OF ILLINOIS.
Board of trustees.
Surgical institute for children, 325: 60/0.01 to 60/12.
Division of services for crippled children.
Early intervention services role, 325: 20/9.
Surgical institute for children.
Management and control vested in board of trustees, 325: 60/4.

UNLAWFUL RESTRAINT, 720: 5/10-3.
Aggravated unlawful restraint, 720: 5/10-3.1.

V

VENUE.
Adoption, 750: 50/4.
Dissolution of marriage, 750: 5/104.
Conciliation conference and counseling, 750: 5/404.
Judgment enforcement or modification procedure, 750: 5/511.
Partition of real estate, 750: 5/515.
Post-judgment proceedings, 750: 5/512.
Emancipation of mature minors, 750: 30/4.
Forum non conveniens.
Domestic violence protection orders, 750: 60/209.
Inconvenient forum.
Domestic violence protection orders, 750: 60/209.
Legal separation, 750: 5/402.
Maintenance actions, 750: 5/402.
Marital dissolution proceedings, 750: 5/104.
Judgment enforcement or modification procedure, 750: 5/511.
Post-judgment proceedings, 750: 5/512.
Partition proceedings.
Dissolution of marriage, 750: 5/515.
Paternity actions, 750: 45/9.
Protection orders against domestic violence, 750: 60/209.
Support during separation actions, 750: 5/402.

VERIFICATION.
Adoption petitions, 750: 50/5.
Domestic violence protection orders, 750: 60/203.
Emancipation of mature minors, petition, 750: 30/7.

VICTIMS OF DOMESTIC VIOLENCE.
Domestic violence generally.
See DOMESTIC VIOLENCE.

VISITATION.
See CHILD VISITATION.

VITAL RECORDS.
Adoption.
Birth certificate issuance, 750: 50/19.
Registering new birth certificate, 750: 50/19.
Birth certificates.
Adoption.
Issuance upon adoption, 750: 50/19.
Local registrars.
Missing children.
Duties, 325: 50/4, 55/4.
Paternity actions.
Birth certificate changes, 750: 45/14.
Registrar of vital records.
Missing children.
Duties, 325: 50/3, 50/4, 55/3, 55/4.

VOLUNTARY ACKNOWLEDGMENT OF PARENTAGE, 750: 45/6.

VOTER REGISTRATION.
Domestic violence victims, participation in address confidentiality program, 750: 61/30.

W

WAGE DEDUCTION ORDERS.
Child support, 750: 5/706.1.
Maintenance payments, 750: 5/706.1.

WAGE DEDUCTION ORDERS —Cont'd
Paternity proceedings, 750: 45/20.
Spousal support payments, 750: 5/706.1.
Support, interstate family support.
Income-withholding orders.
Administrative enforcement, 750: 22/502.
Defined, 750: 22/101.
Recognition of order of another state, 750: 22/501.
Registration, 750: 22/601 to 22/615.
Support orders.
Interstate family support.
Administrative enforcement, 750: 22/507.
Compliance with multiple orders, 750: 22/503.
Contest by obligor, 750: 22/506.
Employer of obligor.
Sending order to employer without filing petition, 750: 22/501.
Immunity of employer, 750: 22/504.
Penalties for noncompliance, 750: 22/505.

WAGES AND HOURS.
Married person's rights to earnings, 750: 65/7.

WARRANTS.
Child custody.
Uniform child custody jurisdiction and enforcement.
Physical custody of child taken by court, 750: 36/311.

WEDLOCK.
Premarital agreements, 750: 10/1 to 10/11.

WELFARE.
Single parent employment restrictions.
Wrongs to children act, 720: 150/3, 150/3.1, 150/5.
Support responsibility of relatives.
Determination and enforceability generally, 305: 5/10-1 to 5/10-27.
See PUBLIC AID.
Wrongs to children act.
Single parent employment restrictions, 720: 150/3, 150/3.1, 150/5.

WHISTLEBLOWER PROTECTION.
Elder abuse and neglect.
Discrimination or retaliation by employer prohibited, 320: 20/4.1.
Reports of abuse or neglect, 320: 20/4.

WILLS.
Adoption, instruments regarding property rights.
Child deemed born to adopting parents, 760: 30/0.01, 30/1.

WITHHOLDING OF INCOME.
Parentage proceedings.
Securing payment of support, 750: 45/20.
Support payments, 750: 28/1 to 28/999.
Automatic continuance of child support obligation.
Unpaid arrearage or delinquency on date of termination of obligation, 750: 28/32.
Interstate family support.
Administrative enforcement, 750: 22/507.
Contest by obligor, 750: 22/506.
Employer of obligor.
Sending order to employer without filing petition, 750: 22/501.
Immunity of employer, 750: 22/504.
Multiple orders, compliance, 750: 22/503.
Penalties for noncompliance, 750: 22/505.
Securing payment, 750: 5/706.1.

WITNESSES.
Child abuse and neglect.
Criminal neglect of children.
Competency of parent witnesses, 720: 130/3.
Child custody.
Husband and wife, 735: 5/8-801.

WITNESSES —Cont'd
Child custody —Cont'd
Uniform child custody jurisdiction and enforcement.
Testimony of witnesses outside state, 750: 36/111.
Child support.
Expedited support proceedings.
Contested matters.
Administrative hearing officer's testimony, Sup. Ct. Rule 100.10.
Husband and wife, 735: 5/8-801.
Child witnesses.
Abuse cases, 735: 5/8-2601.

WITNESSES —Cont'd
Child witnesses —Cont'd
Sexual conduct performed in presence of child, 735: 5/8-2601.
Elder abuse and neglect proceedings.
Testimony by mandated reporter or person investigating report, 320: 20/4.2.
Husband-wife privilege.
Uniform child custody jurisdiction and enforcement.
Prohibition from invoking, 750: 36/310.

WORK ALTERNATIVE PROGRAM.
Nonsupport of spouse and children act conviction, 750: 5/505.

X

X-RAYS.
Child abuse and neglect reporting.
Persons required to investigate cases, 325: 5/6.

Y

YOUTH CAREER DEVELOPMENT.
High risk youth, 325: 25/0.01, 25/1.

YOUTHS, DOMESTIC VIOLENCE.
Generally, 750: 60/101 to 60/401.
See DOMESTIC VIOLENCE.

Notes

Notes

Notes

Notes